U.S. Presidential Candidates and the Elections

U.S. Presidential Candidates and the Elections

A Biographical and Historical Guide

James T. Havel

VOLUME 1
THE CANDIDATES

MACMILLAN LIBRARY REFERENCE USA
Simon & Schuster Macmillan
NEW YORK

Prentice Hall International
LONDON MEXICO CITY NEW DELHI SINGAPORE SYDNEY TORONTO

To Roberta,
Who brings grace and delight to my life, and to Julie, Emily, Jay, and Lianna, who together represent the best legacy I have to offer the future. They are the sum of my joy, a part of my tears, most of my hopes, none of my fears—but always the source and recipients of all of my love.

Macmillan Library Reference USA
Simon & Schuster Macmillan
1633 Broadway
New York, NY 10019

Library of Congress Catalog Card Number: 96–12074

Printed in the United States of America

Printing Number

1 2 3 4 5 6 7 8 9 10

Library of Congress Cataloging-in-Publication Data

Havel, James T.
U.S. presidential elections and the candidates : a biographical and historical guide / James T. Havel.
2 v.
Contents: v. 1. The candidates --v. 2. The elections, 1789-1992.
ISBN 0–02–864622–1 (v. 1)--ISBN 0–02–864623–1 (v. 2)
1. Elections--United States --History. 2. Presidential candidates--United States --Biography. 3. Presidents --Unites States --Election.
I. Title.
JK528.H38 1996
324.6'3'0973 --dc20

This paper meets the requirements of ANSI/NISO Z39.48–1992 (Permanence of Paper).

CONTENTS

PREFACE

U.S. Presidential Candidates and the Elections: A Biographical and Historical Guide is the culmination of more than 30 years of work identifying and gathering data on the vast array of men and women who have sought to hold the highest office in the land. The guide grew out of the author's lifelong fascination with American presidential elections and particularly the role of third parties in our nation's electoral history.

As students of electoral politics know, there is a dearth of coverage of third-party and less famous candidates in historical reference works, while biographical information on major contenders for the presidency abounds. Yet, third parties and their leaders often altered the political landscape significantly, out of all proportion to the number of votes they garnered. For example, the Prohibition Party was the first to suggest the direct election of United States Senators. Victoria Claflin Woodhull, the first woman to seek the presidency, ran on an obscure Equal Rights Party platform in 1872. And many of the innovations of the New Deal were articulated first in the platforms of the Socialist and Socialist Labor parties.

Quite apart from the substantive contributions of minor party candidates, the relatively unknown presidential contenders often added color, zest, and humor to our national election contests. People such as Lar Daly, in his unforgettable Uncle Sam suit; George Francis Train and his egocentric oratory; and Henry Krajewski, who strolled the campaign trail with a pig on a leash—all added to the quadrennial celebration of presidential election campaigns and our enjoyment of this unique theater of history. With the exception of a line or two in some election histories, however, these people and events are mere footnotes that have passed into oblivion.

The guide is divided into two volumes: *The Candidates* and *The Elections*. *Volume 1: The Candidates* is an alphabetically arranged biographical directory whose purpose is to preserve basic information on the lives of the great, the infamous, and the ludicrous who have sought to become president or vice president, without passing judgment on their aspirations or achievements. The casual reader or ardent scholar can find here a simple, unvarnished recitation of biographical details—often supplied by the candidates themselves through biographical questionnaires, but frequently obtained through consulting myriad resources and archival materials.

Volume 2 of this work, *The Elections, 1789-1992*, provides a brief but detailed summary of each presidential election, including information on the parties and their platforms, conventions, and primary and election results. A bibliography of key works consulted in the preparation of this work concludes this volume.

ACKNOWLEDGMENTS

In compiling the essential information about candidates and elections for this work, the author relied upon the kind assistance of candidates and their families, librarians, election officials, newspaper staff, and numerous other individuals. It would be an egregious error to fail to acknowledge with gratitude the time and energy they devoted to bringing this project to fruition. Similarly, the suggestions of the editors at Macmillan—particularly Catherine Carter, Sabrina Bowers, and Andy Ambraziejus, who assisted in the final preparation of the manuscript — helped improve the format of this work. Their valuable support is sincerely appreciated.

INTRODUCTION

In the attempt to be comprehensive, *U.S. Presidential Candidates and the Elections* uses a liberal definition of a *candidate*. Unlike *2 United States Code 431*, which defines a *candidate* as "an individual who seeks nomination for election, or election, to Federal office. . . . " and then ties its definition to the solicitation of funds in excess of $5,000, there is no monetary requirement to qualify for inclusion in *Volume 1: The Candidates*, nor is a specific threshold of votes necessary. Rather, any individual who meets any one of the following three criteria is considered a candidate:

1. One who seeks nomination or election (including self-declared independent candidates with no discernible following)
2. One who is offered for consideration for nomination or election, as president or vice president
3. One who receives convention, popular, or electoral votes for either office—even if the individual declined the honor or was uninformed of its bestowal

Thus, a person who is considered for a party nomination, but never actually placed into active consideration, is likely to be found on these pages as a "candidate for nomination." So, too, is a person who received votes in a party convention, even though he or she never sought either office. Similarly, anyone appearing on a ballot or receiving a party nomination, will be listed herein as an official "candidate for president" or "candidate for vice president," notwithstanding the fact that he or she may have served as a surrogate candidate or have dropped off a ticket after nomination.

Nonetheless, a work of this magnitude is bound to overlook persons who rightfully belong within its scope of coverage. It was obvious as the research for *Volume 1: The Candidates* progressed that references to candidates are so scattered and ephemeral that a truly comprehensive guide would be unattainable. Prior to the creation of the Federal Election Commission (FEC) in 1975, candidates for president were not required to register in any single place. Today, despite the laws governing registration, many lesser-known candidates still do not file with the FEC. And it is equally apparent that some deceased candidates left only the barest traces of their candidacy on the public record, while others, still living, for whatever reasons, have not provided the author with information sufficient to create a full biographical account in this work. These unavoidable gaps may be partially filled by alert readers who note mistakes or who possess additional data that can improve future editions of this work. Such readers are encouraged to contribute their suggestions to the author.

It is important to note that the biographical listing, despite its broad definition of *candidate*, does not include fantasy candidates who never existed (e.g., Huckleberry Hound), commercial candidates intended to promote certain products (e.g., Vippy Bunny), or satire efforts (e.g., Archie Bunker, Vanna Lite). There are some exceptions, however. For example, Yetta Bronstein and Eric Sebastian are included, even through subsequent events revealed that these "real" candidates did not exist. They are, to be sure, historical aberrations, but they are interesting ones and are retained for that reason.

STRUCTURE OF THE ENTRIES

In a given entry, only those categories for which there are data are included. For example, if a candidate has no performing credits, such as motion picture or radio, the category is not listed in the entry. The only exception is children; if the candidate had no children, this fact is indicated. Within each category information is given in chronological order when possible. The miscellaneous category contains any significant information that does not fit into the other categories. The following sample illustrates the structure of each entry.

> **GERARD, JAMES WATSON** b. Aug 25, 1867, Geneseo, NY; d. Sep 6, 1951, Southhampton, NY; par. James Watson and Jennie Jones (Angel) Gerard; m. Mary A. Daly, Jun 1901; c. none. **EDUC.:** A.B., Columbia U., 1890, A.M., 1891; LL.B., NY Law School, 1892. **POLIT. & GOV.:** elected assoc. justice, Supreme Court of NY, 1908–13; appointed special U.S. envoy to Mexico, 1910; appointed U.S. ambassador to Germany, 1913–17; Democratic candidate for U.S. Senate (NY), 1914; treas., Dem. Nat'l. Cmte., to 1932; ***candidate for Democratic nomination to presidency of the U.S., 1920, 1924;*** delegate, Dem. Nat'l. Conv., 1924, 1928, 1944; ***candidate for Democratic nomination to vice presidency of the U.S., 1924;*** chm., Finance Cmte., Dem. Nat'l. Cmte., 1934; appointed special U.S. ambassador to coronation of King George VI, 1936; appointed member, Advisory Board, Point Four Program, 1950. **BUS. & PROF.:** atty.; admitted to NY bar, 1892; assoc., Bowers and Sands (law firm), New York, NY, 18922–99, partner, 1899; partner, Laughlin, Gerard, Bowers and Halpin (law firm), New York, 1917–44; pres., Lawyers' Advertising Co.; owner, mining interests, MT; farmer, MT; pres., Traho Metallic Joint Corp.; pres., Schloetter Process Corp. **MIL.:** pvt., 2d lt., maj., 7th Regt., NY National Guard, 1890–1900. **MEM.:** ABA; NY Bar Assn.; Assn. of the Bar of the City of New York; New York Dispensary (dir.; pres.); Mexican C. of C. of the U.S., Inc. (dir.); NY State Economic Council (dir.); Comm. for the Relief of Belgium (chm.); Council of Ex-ambassadors; Union Club; Tuxedo Club; University Club; Riding Club; Fencers Club; SAR. **AWARDS:** Legion of Honor (France). **HON. DEG.:** LL.D., Columbia U., 1930. **WRITINGS:** *My Four Years in Germany* (1917); *Face to Face with Kaiserism* (1918); *My First Eighty Three Years in America* (1951). **REL.:** Episc. **RES:** New York, NY.

KEY

b.	date and location of birth
d.	date and location of death
par.	parents
m.	spouse(s)
c.	children
Educ.	education, including degrees, institutions, and dates
Polit. & Gov.	political and governmental service and activities
Bus. & Prof.	business and professional activities, with general information given before and known specifics, such as • Motion Picture credits • Radio credits • TV credits • recordings
Mil.	military service and awards
Mem.	memberships in organizations
Awards	nonmilitary awards
Hon. Deg.	honorary degrees
Writings	books, poems, plays, speeches, songs (the formats of non-books are indicated after the title of each work)

Rel.	religion
Misc.	miscellaneous
Res./Mailing Address	primary residence for deceased candidates; mailing address for living candidates

Information in *U.S. Presidential Candidates and the Elections: A Biographical and Historical Guide* is current through 1995. It should be noted, however, that information regarding the 1996 election has been excluded, even though the Prohibition Party had selected its 1996 nominees prior to the publication deadline, Colin Powell had decided not to run, and a host of candidates had already filed with the Federal Election Commission. Rather than relate an incomplete story of that forthcoming election, it was deemed more appropriate to restrict the work to elections held from 1789 through 1992.

ABBREVIATIONS FOR VOLUME 1

A.A.	Associate of Arts
A.A.A.	Agricultural Adjustment Administration
A.A.C.	Army Air Corps
A.A.F.	Army Air Force
A&M	Agricultural and Mechanical
A & P	Atlantic and Pacific
AAAS	American Association for the Advancement of Science
AAUP	American Association of University Professors
AAUW	American Association of University Women
A.B.	Bachelor of Arts
ABA	American Bar Association
acad.	academy
A.C.L.U.	American Civil Liberties Union
adj. gen.	adjutant general
adm.	admiral
AEF	American Expeditionary Forces
AFL	American Federation of Labor
A.F.T.R.A.	American Federation of Television and Radio Artists
A.I.A.	American Institute of Architects
A.I.E.E.	American Institute of Electrical Engineers
aka	also known as
A.M.	Master of Arts
A.M.E.	African Methodist Episcopal
APSA	American Political Science Association
Apt.	Apartment
A.S.C.A.P.	American Society of Composers, Authors and Publishers
A.S.C.E.	American Society of Civil Engineers
A.S.M.E.	American Society of Mechanical Engineers
Assn.	Association
assoc.	associate
asst.	assistant
atty.	attorney
atty. gen.	attorney general
AUS	Army of the United States
Ave.	Avenue
b.	born
B.A.	Bachelor of Arts
Bapt.	Baptist
B.B.A.	Bachelor of Business Administration
B.C.E.	Bachelor of Civil Engineering
B.C.L.	Bachelor of Civil Law
B.D.	Bachelor of Divinity
B.E.	Bachelor of Education
B.E.E.	Bachelor of Electrical Engineering
B.F.A.	Bachelor of Fine Arts
B.L.	Bachelor of Laws
Blvd.	Boulevard
brev.	brevetted
B.S.	Bachelor of Science
BSA	Boy Scouts of America
B.S.A.	Bachelor of Agricultural Science
B.S.D.	Bachelor of Didactic Science
B.S.Ed.	Bachelor of Science in Education
B.S.T.	Bachelor of Sacred Theology
B.Th.	Bachelor of Theology
Bus. & Prof.	business and professional career
c.	children; circa
capt.	captain
CBS	Columbia Broadcasting System
chm.	chairman
CIA	Central Intelligence Agency
CIO	Congress of Industrial Organizations
C.L.U.	Chartered Life Underwriter
cmte.	committee
c/o	in care of
co.	company
C. of C.	Chamber of Commerce
col.	colonel
Coll.	College
comm.	commission
corp.	corporation; corporal
C.P.A.	Certified Public Accountant
C.S.A.	Confederate States Army
cty.	county
d.	died; daughter of
D.	Doctor
D.Ag.	Doctor of Agriculture
DAR	Daughters of the American Revolution
DC	District of Columbia
D.C.L.	Doctor of Civil Law
D.D.	Doctor of Divinity
D.D.S.	Doctor of Dental Surgery
D.E.	Doctor of Engineering; Doctor of Education
D.Eng.	Doctor of Engineering
dept.	department
D.F.A.	Doctor of Fine Arts

D. H. L.	Doctor of Hebrew Literature
dir.	director
div.	division
D.Litt.	Doctor of Literature
D.M.D.	Doctor of Dental Medicine
D.M.S.	Doctor of Medical Science
D.O.	Doctor of Osteopathy
D.P.A.	Doctor of Public Administration
D.P.H.	Diploma in Public Health; Doctor of Public Health; Doctor of Public Hygiene
D.Pub.	Doctor of Public Service
Dr.	Doctor; Drive
D.S.	Doctor of Science
D.Sc.	Doctor of Science
D.Sc.O.	Doctor of Science in Oratory
D.S.T.	Doctor of Sacred Theology
D.V.M.	Doctor of Veterinary Medicine
D.V.S.	Doctor of Veterinary Surgery
E.	East
ed.	editor
E.D.	Doctor of Engineering
Ed.B.	Bachelor of Education
Ed.D.	Doctor of Education
Ed.M.	Master of Education
Educ.	educational career
E.E.	Electrical Engineer
Episc.	Episcopalian
ETO	European Theater of Operations
exec.	executive
F.A.	Field Artillery
F.A.C.S.	Fellow, American College of Surgeons
FBI	Federal Bureau of Investigation
G.A.O.	General Accounting Office
GAR	Grand Army of the Republic
gen.	general
gov.	governorship
gov. gen.	governor general
grad.	graduate
GSA	Girl Scouts of America
G.S.A.	General Services Administration
H.H.D.	Doctor of Humanities
hist.	historical
hon.	honorary
H.S.	high school
IAEA	International Atomic Energy Agency
IBM	International Business Machines
I.E.E.E.	Institute of Electrical and Electronics Engineers
Inc.	Incorporated
Inst.	institute
I.R.E.	Institute of Radio Engineers
JAGD	Judge Advocate General's Department
JCS	Joint Chiefs of Staff
J.D.	Doctor of Jurisprudence
jg	junior grade
J.O.U.A.M.	Junior Order of United American Mechanics
Jr.	junior
J.S.D.	Doctor of Juristic Science
Jud.	Judicature
L.H.D.	Doctor of Humane Letters
Litt.D.	Doctor of Letters
LL.B.	Bachelor of Laws
LL.D.	Doctor of Laws
LL.M.	Master of Laws
lt.	lieutenant
lt. col.	lieutenant colonel
Ltd.	Limited
lt. gen.	lieutenant general
lt. gov.	lieutenant governorship
m.	married
m. 2d	second marriage
m. 3d	third marriage
m. 4th	fourth marriage
m. 5th	fifth marriage
M.A.	Master of Arts
M.Agr.	Master of Agriculture
maj.	major
maj. gen.	major general
M.B.	Bachelor of Medicine
M.B.A.	Master of Business Administration
M.C.E.	Master of Civil Engineering
M.D.	Doctor of Medicine
M.D.V.	Doctor of Veterinary Medicine
M.E.	Mechanical Engineer
M.Ed.	Master of Education
M.E.E.	Master of Electrical Engineering
Mem.	member of
M.F.A.	Master of Fine Arts
Mil.	Military career
M.L.	Master of Laws
M.Litt.	Master of Literature
M.M.E.	Master of Mechanical Engineering
M.P.H.	Master of Public Health
Mr.	Mister
M.R.E.	Master in Religious Education
Mrs.	Mistress
M.S.	Master of Science
M.Sc.	Master of Science
M.S.T.	Master of Sacred Theology
M.S.W.	Master of Social Work
Mt.	Mount
Mus.B.	Bachelor of Music
Mus.D.	Doctor of Music
Mus.M.	Master of Music

N.	North
NAACP	National Association for the Advancement of Colored People
NAM	National Association of Manufacturers
NBC	National Broadcasting Company
N.E.	Northeast
NEA	National Education Association
NRA	National Recovery Administration; National Rifle Association
N.S.P.E.	National Society of Professional Engineers
N.W.	Northwest
Obit.	obituary
O.D.	Doctor of Optometry
OPA	Office of Price Administration
ORC	Officer Reserve Corps
OSS	Office of Strategic Services
O.U.A.M.	Order of United American Mechanics
OWI	Office of War Information
p.	page
par.	parents
P.W.O.	professional women's organization
pfc	private first class
Pharm.D.	Doctor of Pharmacy
Pharm.M.	Master of Pharmacy
Ph.B.	Bachelor of Philosophy
Ph.D.	Doctor of Philosophy
Phil. Soc.	Philosophical Society
P.O.	Post Office
Polit. & Gov.	political and governmental career
pp.	pages
pres.	president (but *not* when assistant or advisor etc. to the president)
Presb.	Presbyterian
prof.	professor
psych.	psychological
PTO	Pacific Theater of Operations
pvt.	private
Q.M.C.	Quartermaster Corps
q.v.	quod vide (i.e., "which see")
R.C.	Roman Catholic
RCA	Radio Corporation of America
Rd.	road
R.D.	Rural Delivery
REA	Rural Electrification Administration
Ref.	references consulted
Regt.	Regiment
Rel.	religion
Res.	residence
Rev.	Reverend
R.F.D.	Rural Free Delivery
RFC	Reconstruction Finance Corporation
R.N.	Registered Nurse
ROTC	Reserve Officers Training Corps
R.R.	Railroad
s.	son of
S.	South
S.A.M.E.	Society of American Military Engineers
SAR	Sons of the American Revolution
SCVCW or SCV	Sons of Confederate Veterans, Civil War
S.E.	Southeast
S.E.C.	Securities Exchange Commission
sgt.	sergeant
S.J.D.	Doctor of Juristic Science
soc.	society
Sp.	Specialist
Sr.	senior
St.	Street
S.T.B.	Bachelor of Sacred Theology
S.T.D.	Doctor of Sacred Theology
SUVCW or SUV	Sons of Union Veterans, Civil War
S.W.	Southwest
Th.L.	Licentiate in Theology
T.P.A.	Travelers Protective Agency
U.	University
U.A.W.	United Automobile Workers
U.C.T.	United Commercial Travelers
U.D.C.	United Daughters of the Confederacy
U.E. & M.W.	United Electrical and Machine Workers
U.M.W. of A.	United Mine Workers of America
U.N.	United Nations
UNESCO	U.N. Educational, Scientific, and Cultural Organization
UNRRA	United Nations Relief and Rehabilitation Administration
U.S.	United States
U.S.A.R.	United States Army Reserve
U.S.C.G.	United States Coast Guard
U.S.M.C.	United States Marine Corps
U.S.N.R.	United States Naval Reserve
U.S.O.	United Service Organizations
USS	United States Ship
U.S.V.	United States Volunteers
VA	Veterans Administration
VFW	Veterans of Foreign Wars
W.	West
W.A.A.	War Assets Administration
WAC	Women's Army Corps
WAVES	Women's Reserve, U. S. Naval Reserve
W.C.T.U.	Women's Christian Temperance Union
WPA	Works Progress Administration

WPB	War Production Board
WSB	Wage Stabilization Board
WSCS	Women's Society for Christian Service
WWI	World War I
WWII	World War II
YMCA	Young Men's Christian Association
YMHA	Young Men's Hebrew Association
YWCA	Young Women's Christian Association
YWHA	Young Women's Hebrew Association

The Candidates

ABBOTT, CONRAD MILO. d. Prior to 1983. POLIT. & GOV.: ***candidate for Democratic nomination to presidency of the U.S., 1976.*** RES.: Sunderland, MA.

ABBOTT, JOHN HANCOCK. POLIT. & GOV.: ***candidate for Democratic nomination to presidency of the U.S., 1988, 1992.*** MAILING ADDRESS: P.O. Box 134, Santa Clara, CA 95052.

ABBOTT, JOSEPH CARTER. b. Jul 15, 1825, Concord, NH; d. Oct 8, 1881, Wilmington, NC; par. Aaron and Nancy (Badget) Abbott; m. 3d, Ellen C. Tasker; c. none. EDUC.: grad., Phillips Acad., Andover, NH, 1846; studied law under L.D. Stevens, David Cross, and Asa Fowler. POLIT. & GOV.: member, NH State Council, Native American Party; delegate, NH State Whig Convention, 1852 (chm., Resolutions Cmte.); member, NH State Whig Central Cmte.; appointed adj. gen. of NH, 1856–61; delegate, NC State Constitutional Convention, 1868; appointed U.S. commissioner to settle boundary dispute between New Hampshire and Canada; elected as a Republican to the NC State Legislature, 1868; elected as a Republican to U.S. Senate (NC), 1868–71; ***candidate for Republican nomination to vice presidency of the U.S., 1872***; appointed collector, Port of Wilmington, 1874–76; appointed inspector of posts, southern coasts, 1876; special agent, U.S. Dept. of the Treasury. BUS. & PROF.: journalist; atty.; admitted to NH Bar, 1852; lumber manufacturer; owner, ed., *Manchester (NH) Daily American*, 1851, 1852–57; ed., *New Hampshire Statesman*, Concord, 1851–52; ed., *Boston (MA) Atlas and Bee*, 1859–61; ed., *Wilmington Post*, 1871–81; owner, Cape Fear Building Co. MIL.: lt. col., Seventh Regt., New Hampshire Volunteers, 1861, col., 1863, brev. brig. gen., 1865. MEM.: Fremont Club; NH Hist. Soc. WRITINGS: *The Military Movement of Governor Holden* (1871); *Considerations* (187?). REL.: Presb. MISC.: founded Abbottsburg, NC. RES.: Wilmington, NC.

ABEL, JEANNE CLAIRE ALLGEIER b. Feb 14, 1937, Cincinnati, OH; par. Mark and Mildred (Feige) Allgeier; m. Alan Irwin Abel, Sep 11, 1959; c. Jennifer. EDUC.: U. of Cincinnati, 1955–58. POLIT. & GOV.: created ficitional candidate Yetta Bronstein (q.v.)—***Best Party candidate for presidency of the U.S., 1964, 1968.*** BUS. & PROF.: actress, Cincinnati Playhouse, Cincinnati, 1956–59; dir. of plays, Gates Theatre, Sausalito, CA, 1962–63; author; stage and television performer; partner, Abel-Child Productions; star of television commercials, educational and industrial films. CREDITS (PLAYS): *Shadow and Substance*; *Sabrina*; *Jenny Kissed Me*; *Visit to a Small Planet*; *Holiday for Lovers*; *White Sheep of the Family*; *Desk Set*; *Witness for the Prosecution*; *The Seven Year Itch*; *Tobacco Road*; *Picnic*; *Sweet Bird of Youth*; *Sweeney Agonistes*; *Doris*; *Comedy Improvisations*; *Is There Sex After Death?* (writer, producer, dir.). WRITINGS: *The Button Book* (1967); *Is There Sex After Death*; *The Last Man*. REL.: agnostic. MAILING ADDRESS: Crow Hollow Lane, Westport, CT 06880.

ABIZAID, JOSEPH R. POLIT. & GOV.: ***independent candidate for presidency of the U.S., 1976.*** MAILING ADDRESS: 31 Firth Rd., Roslindale, Boston, MA 02131.

ABOLAFIA, LOUIS. b. Feb 23, 1943, New York, NY. d. Oct. 30, 1995, San Francisco, CA. EDUC.: grad., H.S. of Music and Art; School of Visual Arts; City Coll. of New York; Art Students' League; National Acad. POLIT. & GOV.: independent candidate for gov. of NY, 1966; ***Cosmic Love Party candidate for presidency of the U.S., 1968; Aesthetic Awareness Party candidate for presidency of the U.S., 1972; Bicentennial Baby Party candidate for presidency of the U.S., 1976; Nudist Party candidate for presidency of the U.S., 1980.*** BUS. & PROF.: artist; operator, Home for Runaways, New York, NY. MEM.: Bust Out (Bureau Underscoring the Social Tradition of Uncovered Tops). MISC.: self-styled "hippie" and "egomaniac." RES.: San Francisco, CA.

ABRAM IV, ALFRED. b. Nov 24, 19??, Lake Charles, LA; par. Alfred and Lauretta (Thompson) Abram; m. Janice Marie Abram; c. none. EDUC.: B.A., Texas Southern U., 1972. POLIT. & GOV.: ***candidate for Democratic nomination to presidency of the U.S., 1988***. BUS. & PROF.: sailor; chm. of the board, NBC. MIL.: PN3, U.S. Navy, 1957. MEM.: NAACP. REL.: R.C. MAILING ADDRESS: 4814 Beechaven, Houston, TX 77053.

ABRAMCZYK, THOMAS JEFFREY. POLIT. & GOV.: ***Capitalist Party candidate for presidency of the U.S., 1988***. MAILING ADDRESS: 1875 Westfield, Trenton, MI 48183.

ACHLEY, TEDDY M. POLIT. & GOV.: ***independent candidate for presidency of the U.S., 1980***. MAILING ADDRESS: Box 24, Chugwater, WY 82210.

ADAMS, ALVA BLANCHARD. b. Oct 29, 1875, Del Norte, CO; d. Dec 1, 1941, Washington, DC; par. Alva and Ella (Nye) Adams; m. Elizabeth L. Matty, Oct 25, 1909; c. Ella (Mrs. Joseph A. Uhl); Elizabeth (Mrs. James W. Booth); Alva Blanchard, Jr.; William H. EDUC.: Ph.B., Yale U., 1896; LL.B., Columbia U., 1899. POLIT. & GOV.: elected cty. atty., Pueblo Cty., CO, 1909–11; member, Pueblo (CO) City Charter Convention, 1911; elected city atty., Pueblo, 1911–15; chm., Pueblo Cty. Council of Defense, 1917–18; appointed and subsequently elected as a Democrat to U.S. Senate (CO), 1923–41; ***candidate for Democratic nomination to vice presidency of the U.S., 1940***. BUS. & PROF.: atty.; admitted to CO Bar, 1899; partner, Adams and Gast (law firm), Pueblo, 1908–10; pres., Pueblo Savings and Trust Co.; vice pres., dir., Western National Bank; dir., Standard Fire Brick Co. MIL.: maj., JAGD, U.S. Army, 1918–19. MEM.: Masons (33°); ABA; Pueblo Bar Assn.; Shriners; CO Bar Assn.; Chevy Chase Club; University Club; Minnoqua Club; Elks; Colorado State U. (Regent, 1911–12). RES.: Pueblo, CO.

ADAMS, ANNETTE ABBOTT. b. Mar 12, 1877, Prattville, CA; d. Oct 26, 1956, Sacramento, CA; par. Hiram Brown and Annette Frances (Stubbs) Abbott; m. Martin H. Adams, Aug 12, 1906; c. none. EDUC.: grad., Chico State Normal School, 1897; B.L., U. of CA, 1904, J.D., 1912. POLIT. & GOV.: appointed asst. U.S. atty., Northern District of CA, 1914–18; appointed U.S. atty., Northern District of CA, 1918–20; appointed asst. atty. gen. of the U.S., 1920–21; ***candidate for Democratic nomination to presidency of the U.S., 1920***; chm., Women Lawyers for Roosevelt, 1932; appointed asst. special counsel for the U.S. in oil litigation cases, 1935–41; appointed special asst. to the atty. gen. of the U.S., 1940–41; appointed and subsequently elected presiding justice, District Court of Appeals, Third District of CA, 1942–52. BUS. & PROF.: atty.; principal, Modoc Cty. (CA) H.S., 1907–10; admitted to CA Bar, 1912; partner, Adams and Ogden (law firm), San Francisco, CA, 1913–14; law practice, San Francisco, 1921. MEM.: AAUW; League of Women Voters; American Women's Assn. (hon. member); California Club; American Law Inst. (charter member); ABA; CA Bar Assn.; San Francisco Bar Assn.; Native Daughters of the Golden West; California Civic League; Delta Delta Delta. HON. DEG.: LL.D., Mills Coll., 1950. RES.: San Francisco, CA.

ADAMS, CEIL BROWNE (See CEIL BROWNE).

ADAMS, CHARLES A. POLIT. & GOV.: ***independent candidate for presidency of the U.S., 1988***. MAILING ADDRESS: 200 Cloud Springs Rd., Apt. 8-D, Fort Oglethorpe, GA 30742.

ADAMS, CHARLES FRANCIS. b. Aug 18, 1807, Boston, MA; d. Nov 21, 1886, Boston; par. John Quincy (q.v.) and Louisa Catherine (Johnson) Adams; m. Abigail Brown Brooks, Sep 5, 1829; c. Henry Brooks; Charles Francis, Jr.; John Quincy II (q.v.); Louisa (Mrs. Charles Kuhn); Brooks; Arthur; Mary (Mrs. H. P. Quincy). EDUC.: Boston Latin School; A.B., Harvard U., 1825; studied law under Daniel Webster (q.v), Boston. POLIT. & GOV.: elected as a Whig to the MA State House, 1840–43; elected as a Whig to the MA State Senate, 1843–45; chm., Free Soil Party National Convention, 1848; ***Free Soil Party candidate for vice presidency of the U.S., 1848***; Free Soil Party candidate for U.S. House (MA), 1852; elected as a Republican to U.S. House (MA), 1859–61; appointed U.S. minister to Great Britain, 1861–68; ***candidate for Democratic nomination to presidency of the U.S., 1868***; appointed U.S. arbitrator at Geneva Tribunal to Settle Alabama Claims, 1871–72; ***Republican candidate for vice presidency of the U.S., 1872 (declined); Anti-Masonic Party candidate for presidency of the U.S., 1872; candidate for Liberal Republican Party nomination to presidency of the U.S., 1872***; candidate for Republican nomination to gov. of MA, 1875; ***candidate for Republican nomination to presidency of the U.S., 1876; candidate for American National Party nomination to presidency of the U.S., 1876 (declined)***; Democratic candidate for gov. of MA, 1876. BUS. & PROF.: atty.; admitted to MA Bar, 1829; partner with Daniel Webster in law firm, Boston, 1828; contributor, *North America Review*, 1829–43; founder, *The Boston Whig*, 1846; author. MEM.: Masons (Concorta Lodge, Royal Arch, 1852); Harvard U. (overseer, 1869–81; declined presidency, 1869). HON. DEG.: LL.D., Harvard U., 1864. WRITINGS: *Minnesota as Seen by Travelers* (1827); *An Appeal from the New to the Old Whigs, by a Whig of the Old School* (1835); *Reflections Upon the Present State of the Currency of the United States* (1837); *Further Reflections* (1837); *Texas and the Massachusetts Resolutions* (1844); *How to Settle the Texas Question* (1845); *Letters to Mrs. Adams* (1848); *Works of John Adams* (ed., 1850–56); *What Makes Slavery a Question of National Concern* (1855); *Address on the Occasion of Opening the New Town Hall in Braintree, July 29, 1858*; *Conservation and Reform* (1860);

The Republican Party a Necessity (1860); *The Union and the Southern Rebellion: Farewell Address to His Constituents* (1861); *Struggle for Neutrality in America* (1871); *The Life of John Adams* (1871); *Address on Life, Character, and Services of William H. Seward* (1873); *Address Before the Phi Beta Kappa* (1873); *Memoir of John Quincy Adams* (1874–77); *Lincoln and Seward* (1874); *Address at Amherst College Before the Social Union* (1875); *Address Before the Literary Societies of Colby University* (1875); *The Progress of Liberty* (1876); *Notes on Railroad Accidents* (1879); *Three Papers on Educational Topics* (1879). REL.: Unitarian. RES.: Boston, MA.

ADAMS, JOHN. b. Oct 30, 1735 (Oct 19, 1734 O.S.), Braintree, MA; d. Jul 4, 1826, Quincy, MA; par. John and Susanna (Boylston) Adams; m. Abigail Smith, Oct 25, 1764; c. Abigail; John Quincy (q.v.); Susanna; Charles; Thomas Boylston. EDUC.: B.A., Harvard Coll., 1755. POLIT. & GOV.: elected surveyor of highways, Braintree, 1761; elected selectman and overseer of the poor, Braintree, 1764–68; appointed advocate gen., Admiralty Court, 1768 (declined); elected to MA State House, 1773; delegate, Continental Congress, 1774, 1775, 1788; elected chief justice, MA Superior Court, 1775; member, Cmte. to Draft Declaration of Independence, 1776; appointed chm., Board of War and Ordnance; signed Declaration of Independence, Aug 2, 1776; appointed U.S. minister to France, 1778–79; elected delegate, MA State Constitutional Convention, 1779, 1820; appointed minister plenipotentiary to negotiate peace treaties with Great Britain, 1779; appointed interim congressional representative to the Netherlands, 1780; appointed minister plenipotentiary to the Netherlands, 1780; appointed minister plenipotentiary to Great Britain, 1785; ***Federalist candidate for presidency of the U.S., 1789, 1792, 1800; elected as a Federalist to vice presidency of the U.S., 1789–97; elected as a Federalist to presidency of the U.S., 1797–1801***. BUS. & PROF.: atty.; schoolteacher, Worcester, MA, 1755; admitted to MA Bar, 1758; law practice, Boston, MA; farmer; author. HON. DEG.: LL.D., Harvard Coll., 1781; LL.D., Yale U., 1788. WRITINGS: *A Dissertation on Canon and Feudal Law* (1765); *Thoughts on Government* (1776); *History of the Dispute with America from Its Origins in 1754* (1784); *Defence of the Constitutions of Government of the United States of America* (1787–88); *Discourses on Davila* (1805); *Correspondence of the Late President Adams* (1810); *Novanglus and Massachusetts* (1819); *Correspondence Between the Hon. John Adams and the late William Cunningham, Esq.* (1823). REL.: Unitarian. RES.: Quincy, MA.

ADAMS, JOHN QUINCY. b. Jul 11, 1767, Braintree, MA; d. Feb 23, 1848, Washington, DC; par. John (q.v.) and Abigail (Smith) Adams; m. Louisa Catherine Johnson, Jul 26, 1797; c. George Washington; John; Charles Francis (q.v.); Louisa Catherine. EDUC.: B.A., Harvard U., 1787; U. of Leyden; studied law under Theophilus Parsons. POLIT. & GOV.: appointed private secretary, U.S. minister to Russia, 1781; appointed sec., U.S. minister to Great Britain, 1785; appointed U.S. minister to the Netherlands, 1794–96; appointed U.S. minister plenipotentiary to Portugal, 1796; appointed U.S. minister plenipotentiary to Prussia, 1797; commissioned to draft commercial treaty with Sweden, 1798; appointed as a Federalist to MA State Senate, 1802; Federalist candidate for U.S. House (MA), 1802, 1808 (declined); elected as a Federalist to U.S. Senate (MA), 1803–08; appointed U.S. minister to Russia, 1809–14; appointed assoc. justice, Supreme Court of the U.S., 1811 (declined); appointed U.S. representative to negotiate peace treaty with Great Britain, 1814; appointed U.S. minister to Great Britain, 1815–17; appointed U.S. sec. of state, 1817–25; ***independent candidate for presidency of the U.S., 1820; elected as a Whig to presidency of the U.S., 1825–29 (in a contest decided by U.S. House of Reps.); National Republican candidate for presidency of the U.S., 1828***; elected as a Whig (Anti-Mason) to U.S. House (MA), 1831–48; Anti-Masonic Party candidate for gov. of MA, 1834; Democratic candidate for U.S. Senate (MA), 1836. BUS. & PROF.: atty.; admitted to MA Bar, 1791; law practice, Boston, MA; author; prof. of rhetoric and belles lettres, Harvard U., 1806–09. MEM.: Phi Beta Kappa; American Phil. Soc.; Harvard U. (overseer, 1830–48); American Acad. (pres.); MA Hist. Soc. WRITINGS: *Jubilee of the Constitution* (1789); *An Answer to Paine's Rights of Man* (1793); *Letters on Silesia* (1804); *Letter to Hon. Harrison Gray Otis* (1808); *Lecture of Rhetoric and Oratory* (1810); *Duplicate Letters, the Fisheries and the Mississippi*; *Documents Relating to Transactions at the Negotiation of Ghent* (1822); *Eulogy on the Life and Character of James Monroe* (1831); *Dermot MacMorrough, or the Conquest of Ireland* (1834); *Oration on the Life and Character of Gilbert Motier de La Fayette* (1835); *Eulogy on the Life and Character of James Madison* (1836); *Letters from John Quincy Adams to His Constituents of the Twelfth Congressional District in Massachusetts* (1837); *Oration Before the Inhabitants of Newburyport* (1837); *Discourse on Education* (1840); *Social Compact* (1842); *New England Confederacy of 1648* (1843); *Life of General Lafayette* (1847); *Version of the Psalms*. REL.: Unitarian. RES.: Quincy, MA.

ADAMS II, JOHN QUINCY. b. Sep 22, 1833, Boston, MA; d. Aug 14, 1894, Quincy, MA; par. Charles Francis (q.v.) and Abigail Brown (Brooks) Adams; m. Fanny Cadwallader Crowninshield, Apr 29, 1861; c. John Quincy III; George Caspar; Charles Francis III; Fannie Cadwallader; Arthur; Abigail (Mrs. Robert Homans). EDUC.: Boston Latin School; A.B., Harvard U., 1853. POLIT. & GOV.: trial judge, Quincy, 1859; appointed col., staff of Gov. John A. Andrew (MA), 1861–66; elected as a Republican to MA State House, 1865; Democratic candidate for gov. of MA, 1866, 1867, 1868, 1869, 1870, 1871, 1879; Democratic candidate for MA State House, 1867, 1868; ***candidate for Democratic nomination to presidency of the U.S., 1868***; elected as a Democrat to MA State House, 1869, 1871, 1874; ***candidate for Straight-Out (Taproot) Democratic Party nomination to presidency of the U.S., 1872; Straight-Out (Taproot) Democratic Party candidate for vice presidency of the U.S., 1872***; Democratic candidate for lt. gov. of MA, 1873; elected town moderator, Quincy, 20 years; appointed U.S. sec. of the navy by President Grover Cleveland (q.v.), (declined); appointed member, Metropolitan Sewer Comm., Boston, MA, 1887; appointed member, Rapid Transit Comm., Boston, 1891. BUS. & PROF.: atty.; admitted to Boston (MA) Bar, 1855; farmer, Quincy; dir., various corporations. MEM.: Harvard U. (overseer, 1877–94). WRITINGS: *Massachusetts and South Carolina* (1868); *An Appeal to the Mechanics and Laboring Men of New England* (1870). REL.: Unitarian. RES.: Quincy, MA.

ADAMS, JOSEPH COCKRELL, JR. par. Joseph Cockrell Adams. POLIT. & GOV.: ***independent candidate for presidency of the U.S., 1976, 1988***. MAILING ADDRESS: 2011 Richard Jones Green Hills, Nashville, TN 37215.

ADAMS, R. JERRY. POLIT. & GOV.: ***independent candidate for presidency of the U.S., 1988***. MAILING ADDRESS: OR.

ADAMS, SAMUEL. b. Sep 27, 1722, Boston, MA; d. Oct 2, 1803, Boston; par. Samuel and Mary (Fifield) Adams; m. Elizabeth Wells, Dec 6, 1764; c. Samuel (infant); Samuel; Joseph; Mary; Hannah. EDUC.: B.A., Harvard U., 1740, M.A., 1743. POLIT. & GOV.: member, Cmte. to Visit Schools, Boston, 1753; tax collector, Boston, 1756–64; drafted Boston Instructions to Delegates, Stamp Act Congress, 1764; leader, Boston Tea Party; elected member, General Court of MA, 1765–74; elected member, Continental Congress, 1774–82; signer of Declaration of Independence, 1776; delegate, MA State Constitutional Convention, 1779, 1788; pres., MA State Senate, 1781; Federalist candidate for U.S. House (MA), 1788; elected as a Federalist to lt. gov. of MA, 1789–94; elected as a Federalist to gov. of MA, 1794–97; ***Federalist candidate for presidency of the U.S., 1796***. BUS. & PROF.: merchant, Counting House of Thomas Cushing, Boston; partner (with his father, Samuel Adams), Malt House, Boston; author. MEM.: Whipping Post Club; Caucus Club; Sons of Liberty (founder). WRITINGS: *Writings of Samuel Adams* (1804–08). REL.: Congregationalist. MISC.: wrote under names "Vindex" and "Valerius Poplicola"; known as the "Father of the American Revolution." RES.: Boston, MA.

ADAMS, SAMUEL ED. b. May 13, 1876, Westfield, MA; d. Jan 3, 1927, Albuquerque, NM; par. Sherman and Frances Ellen (Selley) Adams; m. Mary Lee Campbell, Dec 2, 1903. EDUC.: FL State Coll., 1892–94; George Washington U., 1907–08. POLIT. & GOV.: ***candidate for Republican nomination to vice presidency of the U.S., 1920***. BUS. & PROF.: fruit grower; business and promotion mgr., daily newspapers; ed., *Fruit Grower and Farmer*, 1910–27; ed., *Public Affairs*, Washington, DC, to 1926; assoc. ed., *American Fruit Grower Magazine*, Chicago, IL. MEM.: National Federation of Uncle Sam's Voters (dir. gen.); American Agricultural Editors' Assn. (pres.); Republican Dry League (founder); American Pomological Assn.; American Farm Bureau Federation; National Farmers Union; Grange; Farmers National Council; National Apple Growers Assn.; Assn. of Agricultural Engineers; VA Hist. Soc.; Masons; Rotary Club; Hamilton Club; Advertising Club; National Press Club; City Club. REL.: Episc. RES.: Greenwood, VA.

ADASKIN, DAVID RANDALL. b. Feb 11, 1963, Rochester, NY; par. Murray Alan and Joyce Arlene (Popp) Adaskin; single. EDUC.: B.S., Rensselaer Polytechnic Inst., 1985. POLIT. & GOV.: ***independent candidate for presidency of the U.S., 1984***. BUS. & PROF.: electrical engineer. MAILING ADDRESS: 21 Church 6, RPI, Troy, NY 12181.

ADDAMS, JANE. b. Sep 6, 1860, Cedarville, IL; d. May 21, 1935, Chicago, IL; par. John Huy and Sarah (Weber) Addams; single. EDUC.: A.B., Rockford Coll., 1881; Women's Medical Coll. of PA. POLIT. & GOV.: vice pres., Progressive Party National Cmte., 1914; ***candidate for Farmer-Labor Party nomination to presidency of the U.S., 1920 (withdrew); independent candidate for presidency of the U.S., 1924 (declined); National Progressive Party candidate for vice presidency of the U.S., 1928 (declined)***. BUS. & PROF.: settlement worker; lecturer; author; cofounder (with Ellen Gates Starr), Hull House, Chicago, 1889 (head resident). MEM.: National Conference of Charities and Corrections (pres., 1909); Women's International League for Peace (pres.); Women's Peace Party (chm., 1915); International Congress of Women (pres.); DAR (expelled, 1917); National American Women Suffrage Assn. (vice pres., 1911–14); Illinois Equal Suffrage Assn. (vice pres.); Rockford Coll. (trustee); Chicago Women's Club; Woman's City Club; Twentieth Century Club; Fortnightly Club. Awards.: Nobel Peace Prize (with Nicholas Murray Butler, q.v.), 1931; Gold Medal of Military Merit (Greece); Bryn Mawr Achievement Award, 1931. HON. DEG.: LL.D., U. of WI, 1904; LL.D., Smith Coll., 1910; A.M., Yale U., 1910; LL.D., Tufts U., 1923; LL.D., Northwestern U., 1929; LL.D., U. of Chicago, 1930. WRITINGS: *Democracy and Social Ethics* (1902); *Newer Ideals of Peace* (1907); *The Spirit of Youth and the City Streets* (1909); *Twenty Years at Hull House* (1910); *A New Conscience and an Ancient Evil* (1911); *The Long Road of Women's Memory* (1916); *Peace and Bread in Time of War* (1922); *The Second Twenty Years at Hull House* (1930); *The Excellent Becomes the Permanent* (1932); *My Friend, Julia Lathrop* (1935). REL.: Presb. RES.: Chicago, IL.

ADKINS, GORDON HALLMAN. b. Oct 29, 1936, Little Rock, AR; par. Gordon Elmo and Hazel Louise (Hallman) Adkins; m. Janie Lee Wilson, Jan 23, 1960; c. Gordon Hallman, Jr.; Harry Wilson "Buddy"; John David. EDUC.: Castle Heights Military Acad., Lebanon, TN; Tulsa U. POLIT. & GOV.: ***People's Party candidate for presidency of the U.S., 1980, 1988***. BUS. & PROF.: real estate investor; consultant in sales and marketing. MEM.: North Dallas Full Gospel Business Men's Fellowship International (vice pres., 1979). REL.: Bapt. MISC.: convicted of mail fraud, OK, 1967; arrested for failure to pay bills, 1980. MAILING ADDRESS: 914 North Tillery Ave., Dallas, TX 75211.

AGNEW, SPIRO THEODORE. b. Nov 9, 1918, Baltimore, MD; par. Theodore Spiro and Margaret (Akers) Agnew; m. Elinor Isabel Judenfind, May 27, 1942; c. James Rand; Pamela Lee; Susan Scott; Elinor Kimberly. EDUC.: Johns Hopkins U.; LL.B., U. of Baltimore, 1947. POLIT. & GOV.: member, Baltimore Cty. (MD) Board of Appeals, 1957–61 (chm.); candidate for judge, Third Judicial Circuit Court, Baltimore Cty., 1960; elected as a Republican, county executive, Baltimore Cty., 1962–66; elected as a Republican to gov. of MD, 1967–69; ***elected as a Republican to vice presidency of the U.S., 1969–73 (resigned); candidate for Republican nomination to presidency of the U.S., 1972, 1976 (satire effort)***. BUS. & PROF.: instructor, U. of Baltimore, 1959–66; claims adjuster, Lumbermen's Mutual Casualty Co.; personnel dir., Schreibers Food Stores; atty.; admitted to MD Bar, 1947; assoc., Karl F. Steinman (law firm); consultant, Pathlite, Inc., Crofton, MD; international trade consultant; dir., Chesapeake National Bank; developer, Virgin Islands. MIL.: capt., U.S. Army, 1941–45, 1951; Bronze Star; four Battle Stars; Combat Infantry Badge. MEM.: Loch Raven Kiwanis; Loch Raven Inter-Communications Council; American Legion; MD Bar Assn.; Baltimore Cty. Bar Assn.; ABA; Ahepa; Phi Alpha Delta; VFW; National Assn. of Counties (dir., 1963); National Governors' Conference (executive committee); Republican Governors Assn.; Republican Coordinating Cmte.; Advisory Comm. on Intergovernmental Relations, 1969. HON. DEG.: LL.D., Drexel U.; LL.D., Loyola Coll.; LL.D., Morgan State Coll.; LL.D., OH State U.; LL.D., U. of MD. WRITINGS: *The Canfield Decision* (1976); *Go Quietly . . . or Else* (1980). REL.: Episc. MAILING ADDRESS: 78 Columbia Dr., Rancho Mirage, CA 92270.

AGNOLI, BRUNO. b. Jan 6, 1911, New York, NY; par. Anthony and Victoria Anna (Gatti) Agnoli; m. Nellie Giberso Taylor, 1938; c. Brenda (Perlstein); Tonia (Greger); Marena Lia; Diana (Binns); Elissa (Monprode); Annetta (Pepper); Gina. EDUC.: grad., Toms River (NJ) H.S. POLIT. & GOV.: Democratic county committeeman, NJ, 30 years; special investigator, Irregular Voting, 1932–42; Democratic candidate for sheriff of Ocean Cty., NJ, 1950; member, Ocean Cty. Democratic Exec. Cmte.; chm., Ocean Cty. Electric Board, 1959–60; pres., Regular Democratic Organization of Ocean Cty., 1960–; Democratic candidate for Ocean Cty. Board of Freeholders, 1960, 1973; municipal chm., Ocean Cty. Democratic Party, 1964; delegate, Dem. Nat'l. Conv., 1964, 1968, 1972; member, NJ State Democratic Cmte., 1969–78; pres., Cty. Seat Democratic Club; commissioner of registration, Ocean Cty., 1969–74; ***candidate for Democratic nomination to vice presidency of the U.S., 1972***. BUS. & PROF.: policeman, Dover Township, NJ, 1932–38; special sheriff's deputy, constable, Ocean Cty., 1935–45; construction contractor. MEM.: Taxpayers Assn. REL.: R.C. MAILING ADDRESS: 113 James St., Toms River, NJ 08753.

AGRAN, LAWRENCE A. (LARRY) b. 1945; par. Reuben and Selma Agran; m. Phyllis; c. Ken. EDUC.: grad., North Hollywood (CA) H.S.; B.A., U. of CA (Berkeley), 1966; J.D., Harvard Law School, 1969. POLIT. & GOV.: legal counsel, CA State Senate Cmte. on Health and Welfare, 1971–74; appointed as a Democrat to Irvine (CA) City Council, 1978–84; elected as a Democrat, mayor of Irvine, CA, 1984–90; Democratic candidate for mayor of Irvine, 1990; ***candidate for Democratic nomination to presidency of the U.S., 1992***. BUS. & PROF.: atty.; exec. dir., Center for Innovative Diplomacy, Irvine. MIL.: U.S.A.R., 1962–70. MEM.: Phi Beta Kappa. WRITINGS: *The Cancer Connection*. REL.: Jewish. MAILING ADDRESS: 17931-F Sky Park Circle, Irvine, CA 92714.

AHERN, FRANK JOSEPH. b. Jun 25, 1925, New Orleans, LA; par. James William and Ethel A. (Kleyle) Ahern; m. Joan DeLuzain (divorced, 1958); c. Kenneth Michael; Patrick Michael; Cathlyn Ann; Terry Lynn. EDUC.: Jesuit H.S.; S. J. Peters H.S., 1943; B.B.A., Tulane U., 1949, M.B.A., 1956; IBM Systems Research Inst. POLIT. & GOV.: candidate for Democratic nomination to gov. of LA, 1967; candidate for LA state superintendent of public education, 1972; ***candidate for Democratic nomination to presidency of the U.S., 1976, 1980, 1988, 1992; independent candidate for presidency of the U.S., 1992***. BUS. & PROF.: systems engineer, IBM Corp., programming systems representative, product marketing representative; sales representative, General Electric Co.; pres., Computer Investment Corp.; chm. of the board, Computer Associates, Inc., 1965–. MIL.: pvt., U.S.C.G., 1943–46, corp., 2d lt. (Reserves), 1947–52, capt. (Reserves), 1952–63; two Purple Hearts with Star; Bronze Star; three Presidential Unit Citations; Navy Commendation Medal; Good Conduct Medal; United Nations Medal; Korean Presidential Unit Citation (4 Battle Stars); Asiatic-Pacific Medal (4 Stars). MEM.: Young Men's Business Club of New Orleans; Marine Corps League; VFW (vice commander); Marine Corps Reserve Officers Assn.; Data Processing Management Assn.; Disabled American Veterans (vice commander); American Legion. WRITINGS: *The Other Presidents*; *The Other IBM*; *John*; *A Herd of Pelicans*; *The Eye*; *A Herd of Eagles*; *Shame America*; *My View*. REL.: R.C. MAILING ADDRESS: 2110 Royal St., #417, New Orleans, LA 70116.

AIKEN, JOHN WILLIAM. b. Aug 12, 1896, Saugus, MA; d. Dec 14, 1968, Bridgeport, CT; par. John Thomas and Alice (Smyth) Aiken; m. Florence Messier, May 1922; c. Mildred; Richard; Edith Cheeseman; Elaine Benton; John R.; one other. EDUC.: Northeastern Evening H.S., 1914–17. POLIT. & GOV.: Socialist Labor Party candidate for MA state auditor, 1922; Socialist Labor Party candidate for gov. of MA, 1930, 1934; member, National Exec. Cmte., Socialist Labor Party, 1930–68; ***Socialist Labor Party candidate for vice presidency of the U.S., 1932; Socialist Labor Party candidate for presidency of the U.S., 1936, 1940***; Socialist

Labor Party candidate for U.S. Senate (CT), 1946. BUS. & PROF.: furniture finisher; contributor, *Weekly People*. MIL.: sgt., Motor Transport Corps, U.S. Army, WWI. RES.: East Hartford, CT.

ALBAUGH, ARLA ALLEN. b. Mar 7, 1906, Dennison, OH; m. daughter of Mr. Silverberg, Aug 13, 1926; c. one son. EDUC.: grad., Dennison H.S., 1925; Ohio School of Commercial Art; John Huntingdon School of Polytechnics; Cleveland School of Art; U. of Cincinnati. POLIT. & GOV.: Socialist Labor Party candidate for gov. of OH, 1944 (withdrew), 1946, 1950, 1954, 1956, and one other time; ***Socialist Labor Party candidate for vice presidency of the U.S., 1944; Socialist Labor Party candidate for presidency of the U.S., 1944***; delegate, Socialist Labor Party National Convention, 1948, 1956; Socialist Labor Party candidate for state treasurer of PA; Socialist Labor Party candidate for U.S. Senate (PA), 1962, 1964; FL representative, Socialist Labor Party. BUS. & PROF.: photograph engraver and lithographic artist; employee, National Service Engraving Co., Washington, DC; leader, "Albaugh's Hi-Seven" band; owner, flower shop, Cleveland, OH; machinist, Thompson Valve Co.; employee, Zimmerman Picture Molding Co.; commercial artist, *The Shopping News*. MEM.: Photo Engravers Union; Photo Lithographers Union. MAILING ADDRESS: 1501 South 22nd Court, Hollywood, FL 33020.

ALBERT, CARL. b. May 10, 1908, McAlester, OK; par. Ernest Homer and Leona Ann (Scott) Albert; m. Mary Sue Greene Harmon, Aug 20, 1942; c. Mary Frances; David Ernest. EDUC.: A.B., U. of OK, 1931; B.A., Oxford U., 1933, B.C.L., 1934; LL.D., Oklahoma City U. POLIT. & GOV.: elected delegate, OK State Democratic Convention, 1948; elected as a Democrat to U.S. House (OK), 1947–77; Democratic whip, 1955–61; majority leader, 1961–71; Speaker, 1971–77; delegate, Dem. Nat'l. Conv., 1952, 1956, 1964, 1968 (permanent chm.), 1972, 1976; delegate, Democratic Mid-Term Conference, 1974; ***candidate for Democratic nomination to vice presidency of the U.S., 1976***. BUS. & PROF.: atty.; admitted to OK Bar, 1936; law clerk, Federal Housing Administration, 1935–37; law practice, Oklahoma City, 1937; atty., Sayre Oil Co., 1937–38; law practice, Mattoon, IL, 1938–39; atty., Ohio Oil Co., 1939–40; law practice, McAlester, 1946–47. MIL.: lt. col., U.S. Army, 1941–46; Bronze Star; MEM.: Southern Methodist U. (trustee); Rhodes Scholar; Elks; Masons; Lions; Kappa Alpha; OK Bar Assn.; Phi Beta Kappa; Isaac Walton League; American Legion; VFW. AWARDS: Heart of the Year Award, American Heart Assn., 1971; Old St. George's Award, United Methodist Church, 1971; Minute Man of the Year Award, Reserve Officers Assn., 1972; Henry B. Bennett Distinguished Service Award, OK State U., 1971; named to Oklahoma Hall of Fame. WRITINGS: *Little Giant* (1990). REL.: Methodist. MAILING ADDRESS: 21 East Washington St., McAlester, OK.

ALBRIGHT, GRADY. POLIT. & GOV.: ***candidate for Democratic nomination to vice presidency of the U.S., 1972***. MAILING ADDRESS: FL.

ALCORN, JAMES LUSK. b. Nov 14, 1816, Golconda, IL; d. Dec 20, 1894, Coahoma Cty., MS; par. James and Hannah Louisa (Lusk) Alcorn; m. Mary Catherine Stewart, 1839; m. 2d, Amelia Walton Glover, Dec 19, 1850; c. Catherine Mary; Glover; James; Justina; Milton Stewart; Rosebud; Henry Lusk; Gertrude; Angeline. EDUC.: public schools, Livingston Cty., KY; grad., Cumberland Coll.; studied law. POLIT. & GOV.: deputy sheriff, Livingston Cty., 1839–44; elected as a Whig to KY State House, 1843–44; elected as a Whig to MS State House, 1846–47, 1856–57, 1865; elected as a Whig to MS State Senate, 1848–56; delegate, MS State Constitutional Convention, 1851, 1861, 1868, 1890; presidential elector, Whig Party, 1852; Whig candidate for U.S. House (MS), 1856; Whig candidate for gov. of MS, 1857 (declined); pres., MS Levee Board, 1858; elected as a Republican to U.S. Senate (MS), 1865 (not seated); elected as a Republican to gov. of MS, 1869–71; elected as a Republican to U.S. Senate (MS), 1871–77; ***candidate for Republican nomination to vice presidency of the U.S., 1872, 1880***; independent candidate for gov. of MS, 1873; candidate for Republican nomination to gov. of MS, 1881 (declined); People's-Greenback Party candidate for gov. of MS, 1881 (declined). BUS. & PROF.: schoolteacher, Jackson, AR; atty.; admitted to KY Bar, 1843; law practice, Delta, MS, 1844–73; law practice, Friar Point, MS, 1873–94. MIL.: brig. gen., MS State Militia, 1861–62. WRITINGS: *Address to the People of Coahoma County . . . on the Subject of Levees* (1858); *Views . . . on the Political Situation in Mississippi* (1867); *Letter . . . Relative to Overflowed Lands of the Mississippi River* (1870); *The Case of Mississippi Stated* (1871); *Extension of Ku Klux Klan Act* (1872); *Mississippi River Levees* (1873); *Civil Rights* (1874). RES.: Coahoma Cty., MS.

ALDEA, STEVEN (STUART) GEORGE. POLIT. & GOV.: candidate for U.S. House (NY), 1976; ***Democratic Bipublican Party candidate for presidency of the U.S., 1976***. MAILING ADDRESS: 40 Greenway Circle, Syosset, NY 11791.

ALGER, FERRIS. POLIT. & GOV.: ***Big Deal Party candidate for vice presidency of the U.S., 1984***. MAILING ADDRESS: Rt. 3, Old York Rd., New Hope, PA 18938.

ALGER, RUSSELL ALEXANDER. b. Feb 27, 1836, Lafayette Township, OH; d. Jan 24, 1907, Washington, DC; par. Russell and Caroline (Moulton) Alger; m. Annette H. Henry, Apr 2, 1861; c. Caroline (Mrs. Henry D. Shelden); Fay (Mrs. William E. Bailey); Francis A.; Russell Alger, Jr.; Frederick M.; four others. EDUC.: Richfield (OH) Acad.; studied law in offices of Wolcott and Upson, Akron, OH, 1857. POLIT. & GOV.: delegate, Rep. Nat'l. Conv., 1884; elected as a Republican to gov. of MI, 1885–87; ***candidate for Republican nomination to presidency of the U.S., 1888, 1892***; presidential elector, Republican Party, 1888; appointed U.S. sec. of war, 1897–99; appointed and subsequently elected as a Republican to U.S. Senate (MI), 1902–07. BUS. & PROF.: lumberman; farmer; schoolteacher, 1856–57; atty.; admitted to OH Bar, 1859; assoc., Otis and Coffinbury (law firm), Cleveland, OH, 1859–60; pres., Moore, Alger and Co. (lumber) 1866–81 (subsequently, R. A. Alger and Co.); pres., Alger, Smith and Co. (lumber), 1881–1907; pres., Manistique Lumbering Co.; owner, Volunteer Iron Mine; dir., Detroit National Bank; dir., State Savings Bank; dir., United States Express Co. MIL.: pvt., capt., Second Regt., Michigan Volunteer Cavalry, 1861, maj., 1862; lt. col., Sixth Regt., Michigan Volunteer Cavalry, 1862; col., Fifth Regt., Michigan Volunteer Cavalry, 1863; brev. brig. gen., U.S. Volunteers, 1864; brev. maj. gen., U.S. Volunteers, 1865. MEM.: Grand Army of the Republic (commander in chief, 1889); Loyal Legion; Union League; Ohio Soc. of New York. WRITINGS: *The Spanish-American War* (1901). RES.: Detroit, MI.

ALIOTO, TOM. POLIT. & GOV.: ***independent candidate for presidency of the U.S., 1980***. MAILING ADDRESS: P.O. Box 99449, San Francisco, CA 94109.

ALLEN, GRACE ETHEL CECILE ROSALIE (GRACIE). b. Jul 26, 1906, San Francisco, CA; d. Aug 27, 1964, Hollywood, CA; par. George W. and Margaret (Darragh) Allen; m. George Burns, Jan 7, 1926; c. Sandra Jean (adopted); Ronald John (adopted). EDUC.: Star of the Sea Convent School, San Francisco, CA. POLIT. & GOV.: ***Surprise Party candidate for presidency of the U.S., 1940***. BUS. & PROF.: comedienne; player, Vaudeville with George Burns, 1923; actress. MOTION PICTURE CREDITS: *The Big Broadcast* (1932); *International House* (1933); *College Humor* (1933); *Many Happy Returns* (1934); *Six of a Kind* (1934); *Two Girls and a Sailor*; *We're Not Dressing* (1934); *Here Comes Cookie* (1935); *Love in Bloom* (1936); *Big Broadcast of 1936* (1936); *College Holiday* (1936); *Damsel in Distress* (1937); *College Swing* (1938); *Gracie Allen Murder Case* (1939); *Mr. and Mrs. North* (1942). WRITINGS: *How to Become President* (1940). RADIO CREDITS: appeared on *Eddie Cantor Show*, 1930; star, *George Burns and Gracie Allen Show*, 1930–50. TELEVISON CREDITS: star, *George Burns and Gracie Allen Show*, 1950–58. RES.: Beverly Hills, CA.

ALLEN, HARLAN C. b. Oct 22, 1891, Morgan Cty., KY; d. Aug 15, 1966 Charleston, WV; par. David V. and Sarah Jane (Easterling) Allen; m. Mary A. Edwards, Oct 14, 1913; c. Mrs. G. L. Terhune; Mrs. D. L. Thompson. EDUC.: Kentucky Normal School; Columbia Law School; Louisville Law School; Atlanta Law School; M.A. (Theology), LL.D., Clarksburg School of Theology, 1957. POLIT. & GOV.: candidate for Democratic nomination to gov. of WV, 1936; ***candidate for Democratic nomination to presidency of the U.S., 1940***. BUS. & PROF.: teacher; atty., Charleston, 1920; agent, Western and Southern Life Insurance Co., 1920; gen. mgr., Industrial Loan Co., 1920; contributor, *Carter County (KY) Herald*; contributor, *N. E. A. Service*; contributor, *Herald Post*. MIL.: U.S. Army, WWI. MEM.: Odd Fellows; J.O.U.A.M. WRITINGS: *An Appeal to Parents* (1920); *Americanism in Showers of Fire and Brimstone* (1923); *Murmurings in Rhyme* (1928); *A Guest of Dr. Garratt of the Hill Country* (1930). REL.: Bapt. MISC.: established world's first domestic relations clinic, 1928. RES.: Charleston, WV.

ALLEN, HENRY JUSTIN. b. Sep 11, 1868, Pittsfield, PA; d. Jan 17, 1950, Wichita, KS; par. John and Rebecca Elizabeth (Goodin) Allen; m. Elsie Jane Nuzman, Oct 19, 1893; c. Frederick; Kathrine; Justin; Henrietta. EDUC.: grad., Baker U., 1890. POLIT. & GOV.: sec. to Gov. William E. Stanley (KS), 1899–1903; Progressive Party candidate for gov. of KS, 1914; elected as a Republican to gov. of KS, 1919–23; ***candidate for Republican nomination to presidency of the U.S., 1920; candidate for Republican nomination to vice presidency of the U.S. 1920***; appointed special adviser on St. Lawrence Seaway, U.S. State Dept.; appointed special commissioner for Near East Relief, 1924; publicity dir., Republican National Campaign, 1928, 1932; appointed as a Republican to U.S. Senate (KS), 1929–30; Republican candidate for U.S. Senate (KS), 1930; appointed asst. to the president, RFC, 1932; pres., KS State Board of Charities. BUS. & PROF.: journalist; ed., *Manhattan (KS) Nationalist*, 1894; war correspondent, 1898–99; reporter, chief editorial writer, advertising mgr., *Salina (KS) Daily Republican*, partner, 1903–05; partner (with Joseph L. Bristow), *Ottawa (KS) Herald*, 1895–1905, owner, 1905–07; owner, *Wichita (KS) Beacon*, 1907–28, Washington correspondent, 1914–16; chm. of the board, *Wichita Daily Beacon* Publishing Co.; pres., Beacon Building Co.; chm., Journalism Dept., The University Afloat, 1926–27; ed., *Topeka (KS) State Journal*, 1935–59. MEM.: Great Lakes–St. Lawrence Tidewater Assn. (pres.); American Red Cross (relief worker, France, 1917–18); Baker U. (trustee); Delta Tau Delta; Wichita Club; KS Club; Kiwanis; Cosmo Club; British Children's Aid; Save the Children Federation (chm., 1941–42). HON. DEG.: A.M., Baker U.; Kansas Wesleyan U.; LL.D., U. of Denver; LL.D., Washburn Coll. WRITINGS: *The Party of the Third Part* (1922); *Treatise on the Kansas Industrial Court Act*. REL.: Methodist. RES.: Wichita, KS.

ALLEN, HENRY TUREMAN. b. Apr 13, 1859, Sharpsburg, KY; d. Aug 30, 1930, Buena Vista Spring, PA; par. Sanford and Susan (Shumate) Allen; m. Dora Johnston, Jul 12, 1887; c. Jeannette; Daria; Henry Tureman, Jr. EDUC.: Peekskill Military Acad.; A.M., Georgetown Coll., 1898; grad., U.S. Military Acad., 1882; LL.D., Lincoln Memorial U., 1915; LL.D., Georgetown U., 1922. POLIT. & GOV.: ***candidate for Democratic nomination to presidency of the U.S., 1924; candidate for Democratic nomination to vice presidency of the U.S.,***

1928. BUS. & PROF.: soldier. MIL.: commissioned 2d lt., Second Cavalry, U.S. Army, 1882; promoted through grades to lt. col., 1901, brig. gen., 1917, maj. gen., 1917, retired, 1923; instructor, U.S. Military Acad., 1888–90; military attache, Russia, 1890–95; military attache, Germany, 1897–98; military gov.of Leyte, 1901; appointed commander, Armed Forces in Germany, 1919; Distinguished Service Medal; Croix de Guerre with Palm; Legion of Honor (commander); Order of Leopold (commander); Order of Prince Danilo; Medal de la Solidaridad (Panama); Grand Cordon of Order of the Crown (Italy); Croix de Guerre with Palm (Belgium). WRITINGS: *Reconnaissance of Copper, Tannana and Kuyukuk Rivers* (1886); *Military System of Sweden* (1895); *My Rhineland Journal* (1923); *The Rhineland Occupation* (1926). RES.: Washington, DC.

ALLEN, JAMES BROWNING. b. Dec 28, 1912, Gadsden, AL; d. Jun 1, 1978, Gulf Shores, AL; par. George Columbus and Mary Ethel (Browning) Allen; m. Marjorie J. (Pittman) Stephens, Mar 16, 1940; m. 2d, Maryon Pittman Mullins, Aug 7, 1964; c. Mary Rebecca; James Browning, Jr.; Debbie Allen; J. Sanford III (stepson); John Pittman (stepson); Maryon Foster (stepdaughter). EDUC.: U. of AL, 1928–33. POLIT. & GOV.: elected as a Democrat to AL State House, 1939–43; elected as a Democrat to AL State Senate, 1947–51; elected as a Democrat to lt. gov. of AL, 1951–55, 1963–67; delegate, Dem. Nat'l. Conv., 1952; candidate for Democratic nomination to gov. of AL, 1954; presidential elector, Democratic Party, 1964; elected as a Democrat to U.S. Senate (AL), 1969–78; ***candidate for Republican nomination for vice presidency of the U.S., 1976***. BUS. & PROF.: atty.; admitted to AL Bar, 1935; law practice, Gadsden, AL, 1935–78. MIL.: lt. (jg), U.S.N.R., 1943–46; Dwight David Eisenhower Distinguished Service Medal, VFW, 1978. MEM.: ABA; AL Bar Assn.; Etowah Bar Assn.; American Legion; VFW; U. of AL Alumni Club; 1925 F Street Club; Alpha Sigma Phi. AWARDS: Heacock Gold Medal, Alabama TB Assn., 1965; Gold Medal, Southern TB Assn., 1972; Two Gold Gavels, U.S. Senate. HON. DEG.: LL.D., Troy State U., 1975. REL.: Church of Christ. RES.: Gadsden, AL.

ALLEN, SEYMOUR E. POLIT. & GOV.: Republican candidate for MA State House, 1930; Republican candidate for Springfield (MA) City Council; ***National (Greenback) Party candidate for presidency of the U.S., 1932 (withdrew)***. RES.: East Springfield, MA.

ALLEN, STANLEY FRANKLIN. b. 1952; married; children. POLIT. & GOV.: ***independent candidate for presidency of the U.S., 1992***. MAILING ADDRESS: 3175 South Hoover St., Suite 631, Los Angeles, CA 90007.

ALLEN, WILLIAM. b. Dec 27, 1803, Edenton, NC; d. Jul 11, 1879, Chillicothe, OH; par. Nathaniel and Sarah "Fanny" (Colburn or Coulston) Allen; m. Effie McArthur Coones, 1842; c. Effie (Mrs. David H. Scott). EDUC.: Chillicothe (OH) Acad.; studied law under Judge Scott; studied law under Col. Edward King. POLIT. & GOV.: elected as a Democrat to U.S. House (OH), 1833–35; Democratic candidate for U.S. House (OH), 1834, 1836, 1858, 1860; elected as a Democrat to U.S. Senate (OH), 1837–49; Democratic candidate for U.S. Senate (OH), 1849; elected as a Democrat to gov. of OH, 1874–76; Democratic candidate for gov. of OH, 1875; ***candidate for Democratic nomination to presidency of the U.S., 1876; candidate for National Independent (Greenback) Party nomination to presidency of the U.S., 1876***. BUS. & PROF.: atty.; admitted to OH Bar, 1827; partner (with Col. Edward King), law firm, Chillicothe, 1827–79; farmer; stock breeder. MISC.: known as "Earthquake" Allen; originated slogan "Fifty-Four Forty or Fight," 1844. RES.: Chillicothe, OH.

ALLEN, WILLIAM DEAN, SR. POLIT. & GOV.: ***candidate for Republican nomination to presidency of the U.S., 1988***. BUS. & PROF.: national dir., Constitutional Rights Foundation; lobbyist, Mainland Cmte. to Support Your Local Police. MAILING ADDRESS: P.O. Box 920952, Houston, TX 77292-0952.

ALLEN, WILLIAM VINCENT. b. Jan 28, 1847, Midway, OH; d. Jan 12, 1924, Los Angeles, CA; par. Reverend Samuel and Phoebe (Pugh) Allen; m. Blanche Mott, May 2, 1870; c. three daughters; one son. EDUC.: Upper IN U.; studied law under L. L. Ainsworth, West Union, IA. POLIT. & GOV.: Democratic candidate for U.S. House (IA), 1878; elected as a Populist, judge, Ninth Judicial District of NE, 1891–93, 1917–21; permanent chm., NE People's Party State Convention, 1892, 1894, 1896; elected as a Populist to U.S. Senate (NE), 1893–99; chm., People's Party National Convention, 1896; ***candidate for People's Party nomination to presidency of the U.S., 1896***; People's Party candidate for U.S. Senate (NE), 1899; appointed and subsequently elected as a Populist, judge, Ninth Judicial District of NE, 1899; appointed as a Populist to U.S. Senate (NE), 1899–1901; member, People's (Fusion) Party National Cmte., 1901; ***candidate for Allied People's Party nomination to presidency of the U.S., 1904***. BUS. & PROF.: atty.; admitted to IA Bar, 1869; law practice, West Union, IA, 1869–84; law practice, Madison, NE, 1901–17. MIL.: pvt., Co. G, 32d IA Volunteer Infantry, 1863–65. MEM.: Farmers' Alliance. RES.: Madison, NE.

ALLEN, WILLIS. EDUC.: U. of Southern CA. POLIT. & GOV.: ***candidate for Democratic nomination to presidency of the U.S., 1940***. BUS. & PROF.: salesman; partner (with Lawrence Allen), Cinema Advertising Agency, Hollywood, CA. MEM.: California Retirement Life Payment Assn. (campaign mgr.); Payroll Guarantee Assn. MISC.: "Ham and Eggs" pension plan advocate; known as "the greatest yell leader ever developed at the University of Southern California." MAILING ADDRESS: 634 Cherokee Ave., Los Angeles, CA.

ALLENSWORTH, DON. POLIT. & GOV.: ***independent candidate for presidency of the U.S., 1992.***

ALLIS, EDWARD PHELPS. b. May 12, 1824, Cazenovia, NY; d. Apr 1, 1889, Milwaukee, WI; par. Jere and Mary (White) Allis; m. Margaret Maria Watson, 1848; c. Edward Phelps, Jr.; William W.; Charles; Ernst; Margie; John; Gilbert; Louis; Maud; Frank; one other daughter. EDUC.: grad., Union Coll., 1845. POLIT. & GOV.: Greenback Party candidate for gov. of WI, 1877, 1881; ***candidate for Greenback Party nomination to presidency of the U.S., 1880, 1884.*** BUS. & PROF.: manufacturer; owner, Allis and Allen (tannery), Two Rivers, WI, 1846–54; banker and realtor, 1854–61; partner (with John P. McGregor), real estate firm, 1854; owner, Edward P. Allis Co. (machinery manufacturing); owner, Reliance Iron Works, Milwaukee, 1861–89; producer of flour mill roller equipment and Corliss Engine. MEM.: Milwaukee Advancement Assn. REL.: Unitarian. RES.: Milwaukee, WI.

ALLISON, WILLIAM BOYD. b. Mar 2, 1829, Perry, OH; d. Aug 4, 1908, Dubuque, IA; par. John and Margaret (Williams) Allison; m. Anna Carter, Feb, 1854; m. 2d, Mary Nealley, Jun, 1873; c. none. EDUC.: Wooster (OH) Acad.; Allegheny Coll.; grad., Western Reserve Coll., 1849; studied law. POLIT. & GOV.: candidate for district atty., Ashland, OH, 1856; delegate, IA State Republican Convention, 1859; delegate, Rep. Nat'l. Conv., 1860; appointed to staff of the gov. of IA, 1861; elected as a Republican to U.S. House (IA), 1863–71; candidate for Republican nomination to U.S. Senate (IA), 1869, 1870; elected as a Republican to U.S. Senate (IA), 1873–1908 (majority leader, 1897, 1904–06, 1907–08); ***candidate for Republican nomination to presidency of the U.S., 1888, 1896***; chm., Brussels Monetary Conference, 1892; ***candidate for Republican nomination to vice presidency of the U.S., 1896, 1900.*** BUS. & PROF.: atty.; admitted to OH Bar, 1852; law practice, Dubuque, IA, 1857–1908; partner, Samuel and Allison (law firm), Dubuque, IA. MIL.: lt. col., Iowa Volunteers, 1861. RES.: Dubuque, IA.

ALLOTT, GORDON LLEWELLYN. b. Jan 3, 1907, Pueblo, CO; d. Jan 17, 1989, Englewood, CO; par. Leonard John and Betha Louise (Reese) Allott; m. Welda Olive Hall, May 15, 1934; c. Roger Hall; Gordon Llewellyn, Jr. EDUC.: B.A., U. of CO, 1927, LL.B., 1929. POLIT. & GOV.: elected as a Republican, cty. atty., Prowers Cty., CO, 1934, 1940–46; chm., Young Republican League of CO, 1935–38; city atty., Lamar, CO, 1937–39; member, National Cmte., Young Republicans, 1938–40, chm., 1941–46; dir., Young Republican Activities, Rep. Nat'l. Cmte., 1940; elected district atty., Fifteenth Judicial District of CO, 1946–48; delegate, Rep. Nat'l. Conv., 1948, 1952, 1956, 1960, 1964, 1968, 1972; elected as a Republican to lt. gov. of CO, 1950–54; vice chm., CO State Board of Parole, 1951–55; elected as a Republican to U.S. Senate (CO), 1955–73; appointed U.S. representative to the U.N., 1962; appointed U.S. delegate, Interparliamentary Union; appointed member, National Monument Comm.; ***candidate for Republican nomination to presidency of the U.S., 1964***; Republican candidate for U.S. Senate (CO), 1972; appointed gen. counsel, Interstate Commerce Comm., 1973; candidate for delegate, Rep. Nat'l. Conv., 1976. BUS. & PROF.: atty.; admitted to CO Bar, 1929; law practice, Pueblo, CO, 1929–30; law practice, Lamar, CO 1930–89; dir., First Federal Savings and Loan Assn., Lamar, 1934–60. MIL.: maj., U.S.A.A.C., 1942–46; col., U.S.A.R.; South Pacific Theater Medal with seven Battle Stars. MEM.: Masons; CO Bar Assn. (pres., 1942); CO State Board of Bar Examiners (1948–50); ABA; Republican Club of CO; Phi Gamma Delta; U.S. Senate Republican Policy Cmte. (chm., 1969–72); Southeast CO Livestock Assn. (sec., 1933–35); American Legion; VFW; Rotary Club; Delta Sigma Pi; Airplane Owners and Pilots Assn.; Flying Farmers of America. Awards.: Alumni Achievement Award, U. of CO, 1965; Legislative Cmte. Distinguished Service Award, NEA, 1968; named to Colorado Club Athletic Hall of Fame, 1969. HON. DEG.: D.E., CO School of Mines, 1967; LL.D., U. of CO, 1969; LL.D., CO Coll., 1964; LL.D., CO State U., 1968. REL.: Episc. RES.: Denver, CO.

ALPERT, RICHARD (See BABA RAM DASS).

ALT, DOTTIE KAY HINKLE. b. Aug 15, 1943, Harrisonburg, VA; par. Daniel Carl and Leafy Ethel (Pitsenbarger) Hinkle; m. Lowell E. Alt, Jr.; c. Sally Kay; Gregory Lowell. EDUC.: grad., Petersburg (WV) H.S., 1961; A.B., WV U., 1968; Lehigh Cty. (PA) Community Coll.; PA State U.; Lehigh U. POLIT. & GOV.: ***Recess Party candidate for presidency of the U.S., 1980.*** BUS. & PROF.: research asst., WV U., 1966– 68; obtained WV teaching certificate. MEM.: Kappa Delta Pi; Mortar Board; Chimes; Li-Toon-Awa; student government, WV U. (vice pres., 1964); Gamma Phi Beta; AAUW; Imperial Gardens Social Group; Lehigh Valley Bicycle Safety Cmte. REL.: Lutheran. MAILING ADDRESS: 1051 North Tenth St., Whitehall, PA 18052.

ALTGELD, JOHN PETER. b. Dec 30, 1847, Niader Selters, Nassau, Germany; d. Mar 12, 1902, Joliet, IL; par. John Peter and Mary (Lanehart) Altgeld; m. Emma Ford, Nov 21, 1877; c. infant son. EDUC.: public schools, Mansfield, OH; studied law. POLIT. & GOV.: city atty., Savannah, MO; elected as a Democrat, state's atty., Andrew Cty., MO, 1874–75; Democratic candidate for U.S. House (IL), 1884; elected as a Democrat, judge, Superior Court of Cook Cty., IL, 1886–91 (chief justice); elected as a Democrat to gov. of IL, 1893–97; Democratic candidate for gov. of IL, 1896; ***candidate for Democratic nomination to presidency of the U.S., 1896; candidate for People's Party nomination to presidency of the U.S., 1896***; delegate, Dem. Nat'l. Conv., 1896; independent candidate for mayor of Chicago, IL, 1899. BUS. & PROF.: schoolteacher, MO; atty.;

admitted to MO Bar, 1869; law practice, Chicago, IL, 1878–86, 1897–1902. MIL.: pvt., 164th Ohio Infantry, U.S. Army, 1863–65. MEM.: Germania Club; Sunset Club; North Shore Club. WRITINGS: *Our Penal Machinery and Its Victims* (1884); *Live Questions* (1899); *The Cost of Something for Nothing* (1904). REL.: R.C. MISC.: advocate of free coinage of silver. RES.: Chicago IL.

ALTIZER, TYLER. POLIT. & GOV.: ***candidate for Democratic nomination to presidency of the U.S., 1988***. MAILING ADDRESS: 10434 West 44th Ave., #38, Wheatridge, CO 80033.

ALVORD, GENE P. POLIT. & GOV.: ***candidate for Democratic nomination to presidency of the U.S., 1988***. MAILING ADDRESS: 4902 North McBride, Tacoma, WA 98407.

AMERICA, GEORGE WASHINGTON (aka HASSAN M. M. ROMIEH). b. Aug 29, 1942, Washington, DC; par. Betty Naulty (adopted); m. Cathy Elizabeth Reynolds, May 10, 1980 (divorced, 1984); m. 2d, Sherry Guinn. EDUC.: high school, 1955–58; B.A., Journalism Coll., Cologne, West Germany, 1964; M.E., Engineering Coll., Cologne, West Germany. POLIT. & GOV.: ***independent candidate for presidency of the U.S., 1988, 1992***. BUS. & PROF.: publisher; freelance writer, reporter, publisher, 1957–75; owner, International Freedom Organization, publishers, 1975–; informer, FBI, 1979–; owner, Americana Publishing and Media Co., New York, NY. WRITINGS: *Strength For Peace* (1980). REL.: Presb. MAILING ADDRESS: 142 West 112th St., Suite B-45, New York, NY 10026-3703.

AMES, ALBERT ALONZO. b. Jan 18, 1842, Garden Prairie, IL; d. Nov 16, 1911, Minneapolis, MN; par. Alfred Elisha and Martha Ames; m. Sarah Strout, 1862; m. 2d, name unknown; c. Maureen; Frank E.; Charles C.; John W.; Edie F. (Mrs. W. E. Rockford). EDUC.: grad., Central H.S., Minneapolis, 1857; studied medicine under Alfred Elisha Ames, M.D.; M.D., Rush Medical Coll., 1862. POLIT. & GOV.: elected as a Republican to MN State House, 1867–69; elected as a Republican to Minneapolis (MN) City Council, 1875; elected as a Republican to mayor of Minneapolis, 1877–79, 1883–85 (Democrat), 1887–89 (Democrat), 1901–02 (Republican; resigned); appointed health officer, Minneapolis, 1877; Democratic candidate for lt. gov. of MN, 1879; Democratic candidate for U.S. House (MN), 1882, 1896, 1900 (withdrew); Democratic candidate for gov. of MN, 1886 (took oath of office in contested proceeding); Democratic candidate for Minneapolis Park Board, 1888; ***candidate for Democratic nomination to vice presidency of the U.S., 1888***; Independent (People's Party) candidate for gov. of MN, 1896; independent candidate for mayor of Minneapolis, 1898; Republican candidate for mayor of Minneapolis, MN, 1902. BUS. & PROF.: printer, *Northwestern Democrat*, Minneapolis; physician; medical practice, Minneapolis, 1862, 1865–68, 1874–1911; managing ed., *Alta (CA) Californian*, 1868–74; surgeon, Soldiers' Home, Minneapolis; ed., *The News Letter*. MIL.: pvt., sgt., Company B, Ninth Minnesota Volunteer Infantry, 1862; 1st lt., asst. surgeon, Seventh Minnesota Volunteer Infantry, 1862–64, surgeon, 1864–65. MEM.: Masons (master; high priest); Knights Templar (eminent commander; grand generalissimo); Knights of Pythias (chancellor commander); Elks (exalted ruler); Grand Army of the Republic. MISC.: indicted for graft, but released, 1903. RES.: Minneapolis, MN.

AMOS, ISAIAH H. b. Jun 8, 1844, Mt. Savage, MD; d. Dec 24, 1915, Portland, OR; par. William and Rachel (Whitehouse) Amos; m. Lilian Jane Sadler, Apr 15, 1868; c. William Frederick; Lilian Edna; Grace Mildred. EDUC.: public schools. POLIT. & GOV.: sec., Cuyahoga Cty. (OH) Prohibition Party Central Cmte.; Prohibition Party candidate for OH State House, 1872; member, OR Prohibition Party State Central Cmte., 1888–1915 (chm., 1896–1908); member, Prohibition Party National Cmte., 1892–1900; Prohibition Party candidate for OR State Senate; Prohibition Party candidate for mayor of Portland, OR; ***candidate for Prohibition Party nomination to vice presidency of the U.S., 1904***; Prohibition Party candidate for gov. of OR, 1906; Prohibition Party candidate for U.S. Senate (OR), 1908; Prohibition Party candidate for Multnomah Cty. (OR) Comm., 1914. BUS. & PROF.: partner, Lockwood, Van Dorn and Taylor (Hardware Store), Cleveland, OH, 1865–87; representative, Metal Lines, 1893–1915. MEM.: OR Sunday School Assn. (sec.); International Sunday School Assn.; World's Temperance Congress (organizer, 1905); Auld Lang Syne Soc.; YMCA (dir.); OR Civic League. REL.: Episc. (superintendent, All Saints Episcopal Sunday School, Cleveland, OH; superintendent, Trinity Sunday School, Portland, OR; vestryman). MISC.: promoted first OR initiative campaign for local option, 1914. RES.: Portland, OR.

AMSDEN, DIANA AVERY. b. Jan 28, 1934, Los Angeles, CA; par. Theodore Price and Winifred Marguerite (Stahly) Amsden; single. EDUC.: B.A., U. of NM, 1953, Ph.D. candidate, 1972; M.A., Harvard U.; M.A., U. of Denver. POLIT. & GOV.: ***candidate for Libertarian Party nomination to vice presidency of the U.S., 1972***; national sec., Libertarian Party, 1972–; ***candidate for Libertarian Party nomination to presidency of the U.S., 1976***. BUS. & PROF.: anthropologist. REL.: atheist. MAILING ADDRESS: 3707 Mesa Verde, N.E., Albuquerque, NM.

ANDERSEN, LEONARD MORGENSEN. b. Nov 16, 1944, Yonkers, NY; par. James P. and Ethel A. (Visinger) Andersen; single. EDUC.: A.A.Sc., Westchester Community Coll., 1965; B.S., U. of AZ, 1972. POLIT. & GOV.: New Workers Party candidate for mayor of New York,

NY, 1973; ***New Workers Party candidate for presidency of the U.S., 1976***; independent candidate for U.S. Senate (NY), 1980. BUS. & PROF.: chemical engineer; deep sea diver; inventor; chemical technician, RSA Corp., Ardsley, NY, 1965; chemical technician, Stauffer Chemical Co., Dobbs Ferry, NY, 1968–69; chemical engineer, Engelhard Industries, East Newark, NJ, 1973–74; self-employed chemical engineer, 1975. MIL.: U.S. Army, 1966–68. MEM.: American Inst. of Chemical Engineering. REL.: R.C. MAILING ADDRESS: 46 Alexander Ave., Yonkers, NY 10704.

ANDERSON, CLINTON PRESBA. b. Oct 23, 1895, Centerville, SD; d. Nov 11, 1975, Albuquerque, NM; par. Andrew Jay and Hattie Belle (Presba) Anderson; m. Henrietta E. McCartney, Jun 22, 1921; c. Sherburne Presba; Nancy (Mrs. Ben Roberts). EDUC.: Dakota Wesleyan U., 1913–15; U. of MI, 1915–16. POLIT. & GOV.: chm., NM State Democratic Central Cmte., 1928–39; elected as a Democrat, state treasurer of NM, 1933–34; appointed county and state administrator, Emergency Relief Administration, 1935– 36; appointed chm., Unemployment Compensation Comm. of NM, 1936–38; delegate, Dem. Nat'l. Conv., 1936, 1944, 1948, 1952, 1956, 1968; dir., U.S. Coronado Exposition, 1939–40; elected as a Democrat to U.S. House (NM), 1941–45; appointed U.S. sec. of agriculture, 1945–48; elected as a Democrat to U.S. Senate (NM), 1949–73; ***candidate for Democratic nomination to vice presidency of the U.S., 1956***. BUS. & PROF.: reporter, Albuquerque, 1918–22; mgr., Insurance Dept., New Mexico Loan and Mortgage Co., 1921–24; owner, insurance agency, Albuquerque, 1925–75; pres., Mountain State Mutual Casualty Co., Albuquerque; dairy farmer. MEM.: Delta Theta Phi; Masons; Elks; Rotary Club (pres., Rotary International, 1932–33); Pi Kappa Delta; Sears-Roebuck Foundation. HON. DEG.: L.H.D., Dakota Wesleyan U., 1933; D.Ag., NM Coll. of Agriculture and Mechanic Arts, 1946; LL.D., St. Lawrence U., 1946; LL.D., U. of MI, 1946; LL.D., Missouri Valley Coll., 1949; LL.D., U. of AK, 1965. REL.: Presb. MISC.: appeared in the film "The Quiet American" as an extra. RES.: Albuquerque, NM.

ANDERSON, DENNIS McCARTY. b. Oct 28, 1934, Delaware, OH; par. Ira D. and Virginia (McCarty) Anderson; m. Doris Suzanne Konopka; c. Suzanne Elizabeth. EDUC.: B.A., Oberlin Coll., 1957; M.A., Northwestern U., 1964, Ph.D., 1970. POLIT. & GOV.: war chm. and member, Evanston (IL) Regular Democratic Organization, 1962–64, 1966–67; Foundation Fellowship staff member, office of IA Gov. Harold E. Hughes (q.v.), 1965; candidate for delegate-at-large (OH), Dem. Nat'l. Conv., 1972; member, Wood Cty. (OH) Democratic Central Cmte., 1974; member, McCarthy '76 State Coordinating Cmte. of Ohio, 1976; independent presidential elector, OH, 1976; ***independent (Cmte. for a Constitutional Presidency) candidate for vice presidency of the U.S., 1976***. BUS. & PROF.: asst. prof. of political science, Bowling Green State U. MEM.: APSA REL.: Presb. MAILING ADDRESS: 425 Clough St., Bowling Green, OH 43402.

ANDERSON, GORDON LEE. b. Jan 28, 1930, Tacoma, WA; par. Anton O. and Helen A. (Hamilton) Anderson; single. EDUC.: B.A., U. of WA, 1954, M.F.A., 1958. POLIT. & GOV.: ***independent candidate for presidency of the U.S., 1988, 1992***. BUS. & PROF.: art teacher, 1958–72; cartoonist; poet; sculptor; instructor, Memphis (TN) Coll. of Art; instructor, Seattle (WA) U.; instructor, Seattle Creative Activities Center; instructor, Cornish School of Allied Arts; instructor, Kirkland Seven Arts School. MIL.: commissioned 1st lt., U.S. Air Force. MEM.: Delta Tau Delta; Delta Psi Delta; Northwest Inst. of Sculptors; U. of WA Art Fraternity. REL.: none. AWARDS: received prizes from juried art shows; Art on Pine Street Award; Bellevue Annual Festival Selection for Travel Show; Washington State Liturgical Art Award; Washington State Sculpture Award; Huntington Hartford Resident Fellowship. MISC.: noted rare car collector. MAILING ADDRESS: 8642 Island Dr. South, Seattle, WA 98118.

ANDERSON, HENRY WATKINS. b. Dec 20, 1870, Dinwiddie Cty., VA; d. Jan 7, 1954, Richmond, VA; par. William W. and Laura (Marks) Anderson; single. EDUC.: studied law in offices of Staples and Munford, Richmond, VA; LL.B., Washington and Lee U., 1898. POLIT. & GOV.: ***candidate for Republican nomination to presidency of the U.S., 1920; candidate for Republican nomination to vice presidency of the U.S., 1920***; Republican candidate for gov. of VA, 1921; appointed special asst. atty. gen. of the U.S., 1921–23; appointed U.S. agent for Mexican claims, 1924; appointed member, National Law Enforcement Comm., 1929. BUS. & PROF.: clerk, Richmond and Danville R.R. Co.; sec., Roanoke Board of Trade; insurance agent; atty.; admitted to VA Bar, 1898; partner, Munford and Anderson (law firm), Richmond, 1898–1901; partner, Munford, Hunton, Williams and Anderson (law firm), Richmond, 1901–32; partner, Hunton, Williams, Anderson, Gay and Moore (law firm), Richmond, 1932–54; vice pres., Virginia Passenger and Power Co.; vice pres., Norfolk and Portsmouth Traction Co.; gen. counsel, International and Great Northern R.R., 1912–14; vice pres., Atlantic Life Insurance Co.; dir., Planters National Bank; special counsel, Baltimore and Ohio R.R. MEM.: Westmoreland Club; Commonwealth Club of Richmond; Metropolitan Club; New York Club; Virginia War Relief Assn. (pres., 1915–17); American National Red Cross (state dir., 1917); Roumanian Comm. (lt. col.; chm., 1917–18; commissioner to Balkan States, 1918– 19). Awards.: Star of Roumania (grand officer); Order of the Crown (Roumania); Order of Regina Maria (Roumania); Grand Cross of the Grand Commander (Serbia); Order of Saint Sava (Serbia); Serbian Red Cross; Royal Order of the Saviour (Greece); Order of Prince Danilo I (Montenegro); Order of Saint Anne (Russia); War Cross (Czecho-Slovakia); War Medal (Italy); War Medal (France). HON. DEG.: LL.D., Washington and Lee U., 1916. RES.: Richmond, VA.

ANDERSON, JOHN BAYARD. b. Feb 15, 1922, Rockford, IL; par. E. Albin and Mabel Edna (Ring) Anderson; m. Keke Machakos, Jan 4, 1953; c. John Bayard, Jr.; Diane; Karen Beth; Eleanora; Susan Kimberly. EDUC.: A.B., U. of IL, 1942, J.D., 1946; LL.M., Harvard U., 1949. POLIT. & GOV.: staff, U.S. high commissioner in Germany; member, Career Diplomatic Service, U.S. Dept. of State, 1952–55; elected as a Republican, state's atty., Winnebago Cty., IL, 1956–60; elected as a Republican to U.S. House (IL), 1961–81; delegate, Rep. Nat'l. Conv., 1972; ***candidate for Republican nomination to presidency of the U.S., 1980; independent (National Unity Party; National Independent Party) candidate for presidency of the U.S., 1980, 1984 (withdrew); National Unity Party of KY candidate for presidency of the U.S., 1984***. BUS. & PROF.: atty.; admitted to IL Bar, 1946; instructor, Northeastern U. School of Law; law practice, Rockford, IL, 1946–52, 1955; political commentator, WLS-TV, Chicago, IL, 1981–. MIL.: field artillery, U.S. Army, 1943–45; four Battle Stars. MEM.: American Legion; University Club of Rockford; Winnebago Cty. Bar Assn.; U. of IL Alumni Assn.; Trinity Coll. (member, Board of Education); Youth for Christ (dir.); Volunteers of America (dir.); Phi Beta Kappa. HON. DEG.: LL.D., Wheaton Coll., 1970; LL.D., Shimer Coll., 1971; LL.D., Biola Coll., 1971; LL.D., North Park College and Theological Seminary, 1972; LL.D., Geneva Coll., 1972; LL.D., Houghton Coll., 1972. WRITINGS: *We Propose: A Modern Congress and Republican Papers* (contributor, 1968); *Between Two Worlds: A Congressman's Choice* (1970); *Congress and Conscience* (ed., 1970); *Vision and Betrayal in America* (1975); *The American Economy We Need* (1984). REL.: Evangelical Free Church (trustee). MISC.: named "Layman of the Year," National Assn. of Evangelicals, 1964. MAILING ADDRESS: 2711 Highcrest Rd., Rockford, IL 61107.

ANDERSON, MARLEE. POLIT. & GOV.: ***independent candidate for vice presidency of the U.S., 1992***. MAILING ADDRESS: IL.

ANDERSON, RANDALL LOUIS. b. Jun 2, 1964, Blue Earth, MN; par. Warren Eugene and Violet Idell (Egger) Anderson; single. EDUC.: Blue Earth H.S. POLIT. & GOV.: ***Wage-Earner Party of America candidate for presidency of the U.S., 1980, 1984***. BUS. & PROF.: commercial artist, newspaper, Blue Earth. REL.: Methodist. MAILING ADDRESS: 1020 East Second St., Blue Earth, MN 56013.

ANDERSON, ROBERT E. POLIT. & GOV.: ***independent candidate for vice presidency of the U.S., 1988***. MAILING ADDRESS: 27 East Pentagon St., Altadena, CA 91001.

ANDERSON, ROBERT EARL "BOB." POLIT. & GOV.: ***P. S. Party candidate for presidency of the U.S., 1988***. MAILING ADDRESS: c/o Jeanne Rich Anderson, 7515 Golden Rod Ave., Magna, UT 84044.

ANDERSON, SHARON SCARRELLA. POLIT. & GOV.: ***candidate for Republican nomination to presidency of the U.S., 1992***. MAILING ADDRESS: 1058 Summitt Ave., St. Paul, MN.

ANDERSON, THOMAS JEFFERSON. b. Nov 7, 1910, Nashville, TN; par. William Joseph and Nancy Lucas (Joseph) Anderson; m. Carolyn Montague Jennings, Dec 24, 1936; c. Carol (Mrs. Sam M. Porter, Jr.). EDUC.: Baylor Military School, 1930; B.A., Vanderbilt U., 1934. POLIT. & GOV.: ***Conservative Party of VA candidate for vice presidency of the U.S., 1960 (declined); candidate for American Party nomination to presidency of the U.S., 1972; American Party candidate for vice presidency of the U.S., 1972***; national chm., American Party, 1972–78; ***American Party candidate for presidency of the U.S., 1976***; independent candidate for U.S. Senate (TN), 1978; independent candidate for gov. of TN, 1978. BUS. & PROF.: securities salesman, Gray-Shillinglaw and Co., Nashville, 1934–36; salesman, Nunn-Schweb Securities Co., 1936–39; southern sales mgr., *Southern Agriculturist*, Nashville, 1943–47; farmer; rancher; pres., Southern Farm Publishers, 1948–71; publisher, *Florida Growers and Ranchers*; publisher, *Farm and Ranch*, 1953–63; newspaper columnist, "Straight Talk," 1958–; pres., American Way Features, 1965–. MIL.: lt., U.S. Navy, 1943–46. MEM.: John Birch Soc. (National Council 1959–76); American Agricultural Editors Assn. (pres., 1953–54); Phi Delta Theta (province pres., 1936–39); We-The-People (national chm., 1966–72); Union League; Rotary Club. Awards.: Liberty Award, Congress of Freedom, 1964; Public Address Award, Freedoms Foundation of Valley Forge, 1959; "Man of the Year" Award, God and Country Rally, 1966. HON. DEG.: LL.D., Bob Jones U., 1968. WRITINGS: *Straight Talk* (1967); *Silence Is Not Golden, It's Yellow* (1973). REL.: Southern Methodist. MAILING ADDRESS: Norton Creek Club, Route 4, Gatlinburg, TN 37738.

ANDERSON, WENDELL RICHARD. b. Feb 1, 1933, St. Paul, MN; par. Theodore M. and Gladys (Nord) Anderson; m. Mary Christine McKee, Aug 11, 1963; c. Amy; Elizabeth; Brett. EDUC.: B.A., U. of MN, 1954, LL.B., 1960. POLIT. & GOV.: elected as a Democrat-Farmer Laborite to MN State House, 1959–63; elected as a Democrat-Farmer Laborite to MN State Senate, 1963–71; chm., MN Humphrey for President Cmte., 1968; elected as a Democrat-Farmer Laborite to gov. of MN, 1971–77; ***candidate for Democratic nomination to vice presidency of the U.S., 1972, 1976***; chm., Democratic Governors' Conference, 1974; member, exec. cmte., Dem. Nat'l. Cmte., 1974; temporary chm., Dem. Nat'l. Conv., 1976; appointed as a Democrat to U.S. Senate (MN) 1977–79; Democratic candidate for U.S. Senate (MN) 1978; candidate for Democratic nomination to U.S. Senate (MN), 1984. BUS. & PROF.: atty.; admitted to MN Bar, 1960; dir., St. Paul Sister City Corp. MIL.: 2d lt., U.S. Army, 1956–57. MEM.: MN Bar Assn.; Ramsey Cty. Bar Assn.; U.S. Olympians; MN Alumni Club; Phi

Delta Phi. REL.: Protestant. MISC.: member of U.S. Olympic Hockey Team, 1956; U.S. Amateur Hockey Team, 1955, 1957; named one of two "Outstanding Minnesota Legislators," Eagleton Inst., 1967. MAILING ADDRESS: 1006 Summit Ave., St. Paul, MN 55102.

ANDERSON, WILLIAM ROBERT. b. Jun 17, 1921, Bakerville, TN; par. David Hensely and Mary (McKelvey) Anderson; m. Yvonne Etzel, Jun 10, 1943 (divorced); m. 2d, Patricia Walters, Dec 26, 1980; c. Michael David; William Roberts. EDUC.: grad., Columbia Military Acad., 1939; B.S., U.S. Naval Acad., 1942. POLIT. & GOV.: consultant to President John F. Kennedy (q.v.), 1962–63; elected as a Democrat to U.S. House (TN), 1965–73; ***candidate for Democratic nomination to presidency of the U.S., 1972***. BUS. & PROF.: naval officer; executive, Computer Corp., 1973–. MIL.: commissioned ensign, U.S. Navy, 1942, capt., 1960–62; instructor of naval tactics, U. of ID, 1951; commander, USS *Wahoo*, Pearl Harbor, HI, 1953–55; head, Tactical Dept., Submarine School, 1955–56; staff, Naval Reactor Branch, Atomic Energy Comm., Washington, DC, 1956– 57; commander, USS *Nautilus*, 1957–59; Bronze Star. MEM.: American Legion; Amvets; NY Explorer Club; VFW; National Soc. for Crippled Children and Adults (sponsor). AWARDS: Legion of Merit; Stephen Decatur Prize, Navy League of the United States; Distinguished Service Award, City of New York; Christopher Columbus International Communications Award; Bronze Plaque, Advertising Club of New York, 1958; Elisha Kent Kane Medalist, Geographical Soc. of Philadelphia, 1959; Patron's Medal, Royal Geographical Soc., 1959; award, Boys Clubs of America, 1959; Leadership Award, Freedoms Foundation, 1960. HON. DEG.: D.Sc. (hon.), Defiance Coll., 1959. WRITINGS: *Nautilus 90 North* (1959); *First Under the North Pole* (1959); *The Useful Atom* (1966). MISC.: commander of USS *Nautilus* during first transpolar voyage under ice, 1959. MAILING ADDRESS: Waverly, TN.

ANDREWS, JOAN. POLIT. & GOV.: ***Right to Life Party candidate for vice presidency of the U.S., 1988***. MAILING ADDRESS: 71 Swarthmore, Newark, DE 19711.

ANDREWS, MATT. b. c. 1910; married. POLIT. & GOV.: ***candidate for Democratic nomination to vice presidency of the U.S., 1980***. Bus. & Prof.: restaurant owner, Kintnerville, NJ. MAILING ADDRESS: Kintnerville, NJ.

ANDREWS, THOMAS COLEMAN. b. Feb 19, 1899, Richmond, VA; d. Apr 19, 1989; par. Cheatham William and Dora Lee (Pittman) Andrews; m. Rae Wilson Reams, Oct 18, 1919; c. Thomas Coleman, Jr.; Wilson Pittman. EDUC.: D.C.S., Pace Coll., 1954. POLIT. & GOV.: VA state auditor of public accounts, 1931–33; appointed member, VA Public Utilities Rate Study Comm., 1933; comptroller, dir. of finance, dir. of utilities, executive sec. to Sinking Fund Comm., Richmond, 1938–40; dir. of corporate audits, Government Accounting Office, 1945–47; appointed chm., Accounting and Auditing Study Group, Hoover Comm., 1948; appointed U.S. commissioner of internal revenue, 1953–55; ***States' Rights (Constitution; American Constitution; Conservative; American; and Independent) Party candidate for presidency of the U.S., 1956***; independent candidate for U.S. House (VA), 1960; ***independent candidate for presidency of the U.S., 1960***. BUS. & PROF.: accountant; chief accountant, F. W. Lafrentz and Co., Richmond, 1918–22; founder, T. Coleman Andrews Co. (C.P.A.s), 1922; dir., Hardi-Gardens, Inc., 1931–33; employee, Fiscal Division, U.S. Dept. of War, 1941; employee, contract negotiation officer, U.S. Dept. of the Navy, 1942; cofounder, Bowles, Andrews and Towne (actuaries), 1948; pres., chm. of the board, American Fidelity and Casualty Co., Inc., 1955–63; pres., chm. of the board, Fidelity Banker Life Insurance Co., 1955–63, chm. of the board, 1963–65; chm. of the board, National Liberty Life Insurance Co. 1965–67; chm., Service Enterprises, Inc., 1967–. MIL.: officer, U.S.C.G., 1943–45; Bronze Star. MEM.: Richmond C. of C. (pres., 1958); American Inst. of Certified Public Accountants (pres., 1950–51); Virginia Soc. of Certified Public Accountants; American Accounting Assn.; Federal Government Accountants' Assn.; Masons (32°); Shriners (knight commander, Court of Honor); Commonwealth Club of Richmond; Bohemia Club of San Francisco; U. of Richmond School of Business Administration (adviser); Rotunda Club; Shenandoah Club; Municipal Finance Officers' Assn.; National Assn. of Cost Accountants; Richmond Memorial Hospital (dir.); Beta Alpha Psi; Beta Gamma Sigma; Omicron Delta Kappa; Pi Kappa Alpha. AWARDS: Alexander Hamilton Award, U.S. Dept. of the Treasury, 1955; First Award, Tax Exec. Inst., 1955; Award for Public Service, Virginians of Maryland; Award for Outstanding Service, American Inst. of Certified Public Accountants, 1947; named to Accounting Hall of Fame, OH State U. HON. DEG.: LL.D., U. of MI, 1955; Sc.D., U. of Richmond, 1955; LL.D., Grove City Coll., 1963. REL.: Episc. RES.: Richmond, VA.

ANGEL, DREW MORRIS. POLIT. & GOV.: ***candidate for Republican nomination to presidency of the U.S., 1988, 1992***. MAILING ADDRESS: P.O. Box 60823, Sunnyvale, CA 94088.

ANTON, VICTORIA. m. John Jacob Anton. POLIT. & GOV.: ***independent candidate for presidency of the U.S., 1976***. MISC.: known as "Saint Ms. Victoria Anton, M. J." MAILING ADDRESS: 1370 66th St., Brooklyn, NY 11219.

APODACA, JERRY. b. Oct 3, 1934, Las Cruces, NM; par. Raymond and Elisa (Alvarez) Apodaca; m. Clara Melendres, Aug 18, 1956; c. Cynthia Kay; Carolyn Rae; Gerald Craig; Jeffrey Don; Judith Marie. EDUC.: B.S., U. of NM, 1957. POLIT. &

GOV.: elected as a Democrat to NM State Senate, 1967–75; delegate, Dem. Nat'l. Conv., 1968, 1976 (co-chm.); chm., NM State Democratic Central Cmte., 1969–70; member, National Democratic Policy Council, 1969–; elected as a Democrat to gov. of NM, 1975–79; ***candidate for Democratic nomination to vice presidency of the U.S., 1976***. BUS. & PROF.: teacher, Valley H.S., Albuquerque, NM, 1957–60; owner, Jerry Apodaca Insurance Agency, Las Cruces, NM; owner, Jerry Apodaca Realty, Las Cruces, NM; pres., Family Shoe Center of NM. MIL.: U.S.C.G. MEM.: Dona Ana Cty. March of Dimes (dir., 1962); Las Cruces C. of C.; Phi Delta Theta. REL.: R.C. MAILING ADDRESS: 2410 Acoma, Las Cruces, NM 88001.

APOLLO, MICH ZAGER. POLIT. & GOV.: ***independent candidate for presidency of the U.S., 1988***. MAILING ADDRESS: 1434 Emerson Ave., McLean, VA 22101.

APPLEGATE, DOUGLAS. b. Mar 27, 1928, Steubenville, OH; par. Earl Douglas and Mary Margaret (Longacre) Applegate; m. Betty Jean Engstrom, 1950; c. Kirk Douglas; David Allen. EDUC.: grad., Steubenville H.S., 1947; Aetna Inst., 1951. POLIT. & GOV.: elected as a Democrat to OH State House, 1961–69; delegate-at-large, Dem. Nat'l. Conv., 1964; pres., Jefferson Cty. (OH) Young Democratic Club, 1966–67; appointed member, OH State Comm. of Interstate Cooperation; delegate, National River and Harbor Congress, 1969; elected as a Democrat to OH State Senate, 1969–77; appointed Member, OH State Constitutional Revision Comm.; elected as a Democrat to U.S. House (OH), 1977–95; ***candidate for Democratic nomination to presidency of the U.S., 1988***. BUS. & PROF.: salesman, Earl D. Applegate (realtors), Steubenville, 1950–57; real estate broker, realtor, 1957–77. MEM.: Steubenville Board of Realtors; OH Assn. of Real Estate Boards; National Assn. of Real Estate Boards; Elks; Eagles; Steubenville Community Club; Catholic Community Center; Polish National Alliance. AWARDS: named "Outstanding Young Man of America," U.S. Junior C. of C., 1965; nominated for "John F. Kennedy Young Democrat of the Year" Award, 1967; named "Outstanding Ohio Legislator," Disabled American Veterans, 1975. REL.: Presb. MAILING ADDRESS: Berkeley Place-Lover's Lane, Steubenville, OH 43952.

ARABULA THE DIVINE GUEST (aka "SIX WITH ADDED SIX"). POLIT. & GOV.: ***American Party candidate for presidency of the U.S., 1920***. MISC.: mysterious candidate who used "Arabula the Divine Guest" as a pseudonym, promising to later reveal identity; reportedly had six letters in first name and six letters in second name, with no middle name. RES.: Montclair, NJ.

ARBIT, STEVEN MARK. POLIT. & GOV.: ***independent candidate for presidency of the U.S., 1984***. MAILING ADDRESS: 27590 Bradford Lane, Southfield, MI 48076.

ARD, E. M. POLIT. & GOV.: ***independent candidate for presidency of the U.S., 1976***. MAILING ADDRESS: Box 1306, Decatur, AL 35601.

ARMSTRONG, ANNE LEGENDRE. b. Dec 27, 1927, New Orleans, LA; par. Armant and Oliver (Martindale) Legendre; m. Tobin Armstrong, Apr 12, 1950; c. John Barclay II; Katharine Armant; Sarita Storey; Tobin Jr.; James Legendre. EDUC.: B.A., Vassar Coll., 1949. POLIT. & GOV.: vice chm., chm., Kenedy Cty. (TX) Republican Exec. Cmte., 1958–61; member, TX Republican State Convention Cmte., 1960; member, Rep. Nat'l. Cmte., 1968–73; member, TX Republican State Central Cmte., 1961–66; delegate, Rep. Nat'l. Conv., 1964, 1968, 1972 (sec.); chm., Texas Turn Out Our Vote, 1964; Member, Texas Candidate Cmte., 1964–65; deputy state vice chm., TX Republican State Central Cmte., 1965–66, state vice chm., 1966–68; member, Steering Cmte., Women for Nixon, 1968; elected to Kenedy Cty. School Board, 1968–74; member, exec. cmte., Rep. Nat'l. Cmte., 1969–73, co-chm., 1971–73; appointed member, Defense Advisory Cmte. of Women in the Service, 1971–74; appointed member, Cost of Living Council, 1973–74; appointed member, Federal Property Council, 1973–74; appointed counselor to the president, 1973–74; appointed member, Wage-Price Council, 1974–75; appointed U.S. ambassador and minister plenipotentiary to Great Britain, 1975–77; ***candidate for Republican nomination to vice presidency of the U.S., 1976, 1980***; appointed member, Advisory Council, U.S. Bicentennial Administration; appointed member, Policy Board, National Security and International Affairs Council, 1978–81; ***candidate for Republican nomination to presidency of the U.S., 1980***; chm., Victory '80; co-chm., Reagan-Bush Campaign, 1980; chair, Foreign Intelligence Advisory Board, 1987. BUS. & PROF.: dir., Stratford Hall, 1971–77; dir., American Express Co.; dir., Union Carbide Corp.; dir., First City Bancorp of Texas; dir., Braniff International Co.; dir., General Motors Corp.; dir., General Foods Corp.; lecturer, Georgetown U., 1977–; dir., Boise Cascade Corp.; dir., International Harvester Corp. MEM.: Costal Bend Tuberculosis and Respiratory Disease Assn. (dir.); Tulane U. (member, President's Council 1977–80); Atlantic Council (dir. 1977–); Congressional Award Board (1980–); Bob Hope USO Center Campaign (co-chm., 1979–); John F. Kennedy School, Harvard U. (visitor 1978); Hoover Institution (overseer 1978); Smithsonian Institution (regent 1978–); Guggenheim Foundation (trustee 1980–); English Speaking Union (chm., 1977–80); Economic Club of NY; Southern Methodist U. (trustee 1977–); Phi Beta Kappa; Council of Foreign Relations; Center for Strategic and International Studies (vice chm., Exec. Cmte., 1977–). AWARDS: Gold Medal, National Inst. of Social Sciences, 1977; Republican Woman of the Year, 1979; Texan of the Year, 1981; Presidential Medal of Freedom, 1987. HON. DEG.: LL.D., U. of Bristol, 1976; LL.D., Washington and Lee U., 1976; LL.D., Williams Coll., 1977; LL.D., St. Mary's Coll., 1978; LL.D., Tulane U., 1978. REL.: Episc. MAILING ADDRESS: Armstrong Ranch, Armstrong, TX 78338.

ARMSTRONG, BRUCE F. POLIT. & GOV.: ***Reformed Conservative Republican Party candidate for presidency of the U.S., 1980***; chm., Reformed Conservative Republican Party National Cmte. MAILING ADDRESS: 440 Darsby St., Vista, CA 92083.

ARMSTRONG, JAMES. b. Aug 29, 1748, Carlisle, PA; d. May 6, 1828, Carlisle;, par. Gen. John and Rebecca (Lyon) Armstrong; m. Mary Stevenson; c. John. EDUC.: Nassau Hall, NJ; Philadelphia (PA) Acad.; Coll. of NJ; Dr. John Morgan's School; M.D., U. of PA, 1769; medical studies, London, England, 1785–88. POLIT. & GOV.: ***Federalist candidate for presidency of the U.S., 1789***; appointed assoc. judge, Cumberland Cty., PA, 1791, 1808–28; elected as a Federalist to U.S. House (PA), 1793–95. BUS. & PROF.: physician; medical practice, Winchester, VA; medical practice, Mifflin Cty., PA. MIL.: medical officer, Revolutionary War. MEM.: Dickinson Coll. (trustee, 1796–1826; pres., Board of Trustees, 1808–24). REL.: Presb. (trustee). RES.: Carlisle, PA.

ARMSTRONG, THOMAS A. b. Aug 15, 1840, Steubenville, OH; d. Oct 1, 1887, Allegheny, PA; par. John Armstrong; single. EDUC.: public schools. POLIT. & GOV.: Greenback Party candidate for lt. gov. of NY, 1876; National Greenback-Labor Party candidate for gov. of PA, 1882, 1886 (declined); ***candidate for National Greenback Party nomination to presidency of the U.S., 1884***. BUS. & PROF.: printer, Pittsburgh, PA, 1857–87; asst. foreman, *Pittsburgh Chronicle*, 1857–62; senior ed., *The Labor Tribune*, Pittsburgh, 1877–87. MIL.: sgt., Company I, 139th PA Volunteers, 1862–65; wounded at Flint's Hill, Sep 21, 1864; wounded at Cedar Creek, VA, Oct 19, 1864. MEM.: Knights of Labor; Pittsburgh Trade Assembly (pres.); Typographical Union #7; Grand Army of the Republic; Industrial League (organizer, 1865); Press Club (dir.); Union Veteran Legion. REL.: Methodist. RES.: Pittsburgh, PA.

ARNALL, ELLIS GIBBS. b. Mar 20, 1907, Newnan, GA; par. Joe Gibbs and Bessie Lena (Ellis) Arnall; m. Mildred DeLaney Slemons, Apr 6, 1935; m. 2d, Ruby Hamilton McCord, Jul 15, 1981; c. Alva Slemons; Alice Slemons (Mrs. Harty). EDUC.: Mercer U., 1924; A.B., U. of the South, 1928; LL.B., U. of GA, 1931. POLIT. & GOV.: elected as a Democrat to GA State House, 1933–37 (Speaker pro tempore, 1933–37); elected as a Democrat, atty. gen. of GA, 1939–43; elected as a Democrat to gov. of GA, 1943–47; ***candidate for Democratic nomination to presidency of the U.S., 1944; candidate for Democratic nomination to vice presidency of the U.S., 1948***; appointed dir., U.S. Office of Price Stabilization, 1952. BUS. & PROF.: atty.; admitted to GA Bar, 1931; pres., Columbus National Life Insurance Co., Newnan, 1946–; pres., Independent Film Producer Export Corp., Beverly Hills, CA, 1948–60; chm. of the board, Coastal State Life Insurance Co., Atlanta, GA, 1956–; partner, Arnall, Golden and Gregory (law firm), Atlanta, GA; dir., Atlanta American Motor Hotel Corp.; dir., Sun Life Group, Inc.; dir., First National Bank of Newnan; dir., Alterma Foods Inc.; dir., Midland Capitol Corp.; dir., Reishton Co.; dir., Simmons Plating Works. MEM.: Soc. of Motion Picture Arts and Sciences; International Inst. of Arts and Sciences (fellow); Franklin D. Roosevelt Memorial Comm. (dir., 1977–); Mercer U. (trustee); American Jud. Soc.; National Assn. of Life Insurance Companies (chm. of the board, 1955–); ABA; Federal Bar Assn.; GA Bar Assn.; Atlanta Lawyers Club; National Comm. for UNESCO (1947–51, 1963–; delegate, Fifth Conference, Paris, France, 1949); Anglo-American Film Conference (delegate, 1950, 1953–56); Sphinx Club; Gridiron Club; Phi Beta Kappa; Phi Delta Phi; Kappa Alpha; U. of the South (trustee, 1946–60); Masons; J.O.U.A.M.; GA Junior C. of C.; Young Democratic Club (chm., Fourth GA Congressional District); Modern Woodmen of the World; Phi Kappa Phi. AWARDS: Distinguished Service Award, GA Junior C. of C., 1934; Transportation Hall of Fame, 1977. HON. DEG.: LL.D., Atlanta Law School, 1942; LL.D., Piedmont Coll., 1943; D.C.L., U. of the South, 1947; LL.D., Bryan Coll., 1948. WRITINGS: *The Sales Tax is an Additional Tax*; *The Shore Dimly Seen* (1946); *What the People Want* (1947). REL.: Bapt. MAILING ADDRESS: 213 Jackson St., Newnan, GA 30263.

ARNDT, RUSSELL LEE. b. Aug 24, 1946, Vandalia, IL; par. Carl McKinley and Violet (Elam) Arndt; m. Alice Lobrigo Marsengill, Nov 26, 1982; c. none. EDUC.: IL Central Coll. POLIT. & GOV.: ***candidate for Democratic nomination to presidency of the U.S., 1984***. BUS. & PROF.: inspector, Caterpillar Tractor Co., 1964–. MIL.: Sp/4, U.S. Army, 7 years; staff sgt., Air National Guard, 7 years. MEM.: United Automobile, Aerospace and Agricultural Implement Workers of America (steward, Local 974). REL.: Southern Bapt. MAILING ADDRESS: 815 Spring Bay Rd., Box 55, East Peoria, IL 61611.

ARNEY, JOUETT EDGAR. b. Sep 8, 1932, Lilly Dale, TN; par. Stanley Goble and Bertha Claudine (Melton) Arney; m. Willie Mae Maynard (divorced); m. 2d, Rose Arney; c. Kathy Jean; Eddie Dean; Robyn; Annette. EDUC.: Livingston Acad.; Emaus Bible Coll.; Moody Bible Coll.; A.A., United Christian Bible School, 1974; Kansas City (KS) Community Coll. POLIT. & GOV.: candidate for Democratic nomination to U.S. House (KS), 1978; ***Freedom of Choice Party candidate for presidency of the U.S., 1988, 1992***. BUS. & PROF.: gauge, tool and die maker; co-owner, furniture-appliance store; salesman, automotive industry; securities investor; writer; ordained minister, United Christian Church and Ministerial Assn., 1973. MIL.: corp., acting sgt., U.S. Air Force (Honor and Color Guards), 1950–54. MEM.: VFW; American Legion; Little League (organizer). WRITINGS: "Judas Judges" (unpublished). REL.: All Faith Pentecostal (minister). MISC.: convicted of murder, two counts of kidnapping, and aggravated battery. MAILING ADDRESS: P.O. Box 2, Lansing, KS 66043.

ARNOLD, GARY RICHARD. b. 1941. POLIT. & GOV.: Republican candidate for U.S. House (CA), 1982, 1983; ***candidate for Republican nomination to presidency of the U.S., 1984***; candidate for Republican nomination to U.S. House (CA), 1986. BUS. & PROF.: businessman. MAILING ADDRESS: 2-1645 East Cliff Dr., Santa Cruz, CA 95062.

ARNOLD, LAVERN ROMMAL. POLIT. & GOV.: ***independent candidate for presidency of the U.S., 1984***. MAILING ADDRESS: 10456 President Dr., Blaine, MN 55434.

ARNOLD, STANLEY NORMAN. b. May 26, 1915, Cleveland, OH; par. Morris L. and Mildred (Stearn) Arnold; m. Barbara Anne Laing, Aug 31, 1946; c. Jennifer Laing. EDUC.: B.S., U. of PA, 1937. POLIT. & GOV.: appointed chm., White House Library Fund Raising Cmte., 1961–63; founding member, National Businessmen for Humphrey, 1968; founding member, National Citizens for Humphrey, 1968; ***candidate for Democratic nomination to vice presidency of the U.S., 1972; candidate for Democratic nomination to presidency of the U.S., 1976***. BUS. & PROF.: cofounder, vice pres., Pick & Pay Supermarkets, Inc., Cleveland, OH, 1937–51 (vice pres., 1953–55); vice pres., dir., Cottage Creamery Co., Cleveland, OH, 1937–51; merchandising executive, William H. Weintaub Advertising Agency, New York, NY, 1951; merchandising executive, Young and Rubicam Agency, New York, 1952–55, head, Sales Promotion Division, 1955–58; owner, Stanley Arnold and Associates, Inc. (consulting firm), New York, 1958–. MEM.: Les Amis D'Escoffier; Lotos Club; National Arthritic Foundation (governor); Independent School Fund (pres.); Dutch Treat Club; Fifth Ave. Club. WRITINGS: *Tale of the Blue Horse and Other Million Dollar Adventures* (1968); *I Ran Against Jimmy Carter* (1979). MAILING ADDRESS: 605 Park Ave., New York, NY 10022.

ARNOLD, STEVE C. b. Mar 29, 1884, Moundridge, KS; d. Mar 22, 1961, Oceanside, CA; m. Laura Witt; c. Benjamin R. EDUC.: B.A., McPherson Coll.; M.A., Pharm.D., Valparaiso U. POLIT. & GOV.: delegate, Rep. Nat'l. Conv., 1908, 1948; elected as a Republican to MT State House, 1927–33; Republican candidate for lt. gov. of MT, 1932; appointed nonvoting member, MT State House, 1933–35; elected as a Republican to MT State Senate, 1935–55; appointed sec. of state of MT, 1955–57; ***candidate for Republican nomination to presidency of the U.S., 1956***. BUS. & PROF.: pharmacist; teacher, Chicago (IL) Business Coll.; owner, drug store, Hudson, KS; rancher, Stillwater Cty., MT, 1915–50; rancher, Finley Point, Flathead Lake, MT, 1950–61. MIL.: KS National Guard, 4 years. MEM.: Masons (Scottish Rite); Shriners. REL.: Lutheran Evangelical Church. Address: Polson, MT.

ARTHUR, CHESTER ALAN. b. Oct 5, 1830, Fairfield, VT; d. Nov 18, 1886, New York, NY; par. Reverend William and Malvina (Stone) Arthur; m. Ellen Herndon, Oct 29, 1859; c. Chester Alan, Jr.; Ellen; William Lewis Herndon. EDUC.: B.A., Union Coll., 1848, M.A., 1851; studied law, Ballston Springs, NY. POLIT. & GOV.: delegate, NY State Republican Convention, 1856, 1876 (chm.); appointed member, New York City Republican Exec. Cmte., 1867; chm., Central Grant Club of NY, 1868; chm., exec. cmte., NY State Republican Cmte., 1868; appointed collector, Port of New York, 1871–78; delegate, Rep. Nat'l. Conv., 1876, 1880; ***elected as a Republican to vice presidency of the U.S., 1880–81; succeeded to office of presidency of the U.S. upon death of President James A. Garfield (q.v.), September 2, 1881, and served until March 3, 1885; candidate for Republican nomination to presidency of the U.S., 1884***. BUS. & PROF.: schoolteacher, Schaghticoke, NY, 1846–48; principal, North Pownal (VT) Acad., 1851–53; atty.; admitted to NY Bar, 1854; partner, Culver, Parker and Arthur (law firm), New York, 1854–56; partner (with Henry D. Gardiner), law firm, New York, 1856–61; counsel, New York Tax Comm., 1869–70; partner, Arthur, Phelps, Knevels, and Ransom (law firm), New York, 1878–81; law practice, New York, 1885–86; pres., NY Railway Co., New York, 1885. MIL.: judge advocate gen., NY Militia, 1857; engineer-in-chief, inspector gen., quartermaster gen., brig. gen., NY Militia, 1861–63. MEM.: Phi Beta Kappa; Psi Upsilon. REL.: Episc. RES.: New York, NY.

ARTMAN, SAMUEL RALEIGH. b. May 5, 1866, New Augusta, IN; d. Jun 1930; m. Adelia Cobb, May 1, 1889. EDUC.: public schools, New Augusta, IN; IN State Normal Coll. POLIT. & GOV.: elected judge, IN Circuit Court, c. 1907; elected member, IN Legislature; member, IN State Industrial Board; member, IN State Public Service Comm.; ***candidate for Prohibition Party nomination to presidency of the U.S., 1908***. BUS. & PROF.: atty.; schoolteacher; admitted to Boone Cty. (IN) Bar; law practice, Lebanon, IN; law practice, Indianapolis, IN, to 1929. WRITINGS: *Indiana Circuit Court Decision Relative to Liquor Licenses: Decision in Full of Judge Samuel R. Artman, of the Circuit Court of Indiana*; *The Legalized Outlaw* (1908); *Within the Length of the Cable Tow* (1918); Indiana Workmen's Compensation Manual . . . (1924). MISC.: Noted for decision in *Soltau v. Young*, Circuit Court of Boone Cty., holding that IN's saloon license law was unconstitutional and that common law prohibition prevailed, 1907. RES.: Lebanon, IN.

ASCHENBACH, JOHN. POLIT. & GOV.: ***independent candidate for vice presidency of the U.S., 1992***. MAILING ADDRESS: IL.

ASHBROOK, JOHN MILAN. b. Sep 21, 1929, Johnstown, OH; d. Apr 24, 1982, Newark, OH; par. William Albert and Marie (Swank) Ashbrook; m. Joan Eilene Needels, Jul 3, 1948 (divorced, 1971); m. 2d, Jean Spencer; c. Barbara (Mrs. Joseph Robertson); Laura (Mrs. John Susko); Madeline. EDUC.: grad., Johnstown H.S., 1946; B.S. (cum laude), Harvard

U., 1952; J.D., OH State U., 1955. POLIT. & GOV.: precinct committeeman, Johnstown Republican Party, 1954–82; appointed special counsel to the atty. gen. of OH, 1955–57; chm., OH League of Young Republicans, 1955; chm., Licking Cty. (OH) Republican Central Cmte., 1956–60; chm., Young Republican National Federation, 1957–59; delegate, Rep. Nat'l. Conv., 1956 (alternate), 1960, 1964, 1968, 1980; elected as a Republican to OH State House, 1957–61; elected as a Republican to U.S. House (OH), 1961–82; ***candidate for Republican nomination to presidency of the U.S., 1968, 1972; candidate for Republican nomination to vice presidency of the U.S., 1980***; candidate for Republican nomination to U.S. Senate (OH), 1982. BUS. & PROF.: atty.; admitted to OH Bar, 1955; law practice, Johnstown, OH, 1955–82; publisher, *Johnstown Independent*, 1953–82; publisher, *Granville (OH) Sentinel*; publisher, *Centerburg (OH) Gazette*. MIL.: U.S. Navy, 1946–48. MEM.: Sigma Delta Chi; Delta Theta Phi; Masons (32°); Kiwanis; Knights of Pythias; Elks; Lions; Young Americans for Freedom (adviser); Conservative Book Club (adviser); Conservative Victory Fund (chm.); American Conservative Union (chm., 1966–71); Cmte. of One Million Against the Admission of Red China to the United Nations; Asian People's Anti-Communist League; Ashland Coll. (dir.); Mental Health Assn. (dir.); Atlantic Youth Congress (delegate, 1958); United Appeal of Licking Cty.; Johnstown Little League (cofounder). Awards.: named one of 15 "Outstanding Young Men in Politics," by Sen. Paul Douglas (q.v.), *Esquire Magazine*, 1958; received Freedom Award, Order of Lafayette, 1970. HON. DEG.: LL.D., Ashland Coll., 1963. REL.: Bapt. MISC.: member of Byrd Antarctic Expedition, 1946–47. RES.: Johnstown, OH.

ASHMAN, MARY JANE. b. May 21, 1911, Chicago, IL; par. Lewis Bichorn and Mary Louise (Hutton) Ashman; m. Robert Clinton Murray (divorced); c. none. EDUC.: B.A. (cum laude), Carleton Coll.; Northwestern U. POLIT. & GOV.: ***Space Ticket candidate for presidency of the U.S., 1976***. BUS. & PROF.: author; script writer; lecturer; radio commentator, "Yankee Farm Journal," WWII; radio host, "Food for Thought." MEM.: Writers Guild of America, West, Inc.; Soc. of Children's Book Writers; Torrey Pines Assn.; APRO UFOs; NICAP UFOs. WRITINGS: *Crazy* (under pseud. of Jane Doe); *Our Friends from Outer Space* (unpublished); "Junior UFOs" (unpublished); "M• Pet" (unpublished); television programs—"Let's Go Out of This World"; "Inside Television"; "The Diamond Lens"; "Secret of the Incas"; "The Woman at Seven Brothers"; radio programs—"Women in the Making of America"; "Gallant American Women"; "Americans All-Immigrants All" (Gold Microphone Award; American Legion Plaque); "Men of Destiny"; "Titans of Science"; "From the Ends of the Earth"; "America Sings"; "Consumer Time"; "Living"; "Make It Yourself"; movies—"Hell Casts No Shadows"; "The Bible Speaks"; "American Political Conventions"; "Young Love"; "Trailing the Saucers" (newspaper series). REL.: Christian Scientist. MISC.: received playwriting fellowship, National Theatre Conference. MAILING ADDRESS: 7451 Herschel Ave., Apt. D, San Diego, CA 92037.

ASK, MIHRAN NICHOLAS. b. Mar 22, 1886, Shabin Karahisar, Sivar Province, Western Armenia, Ottoman Empire; d. Feb 6, 1979, Morgan Hill, CA; par. Nicholas and Zanazan (Arakelian) Ask; married; c. four sons; three daughters. EDUC.: B.A., Union Coll., Lincoln, NE, 1916; U. of NE, 1916–17; Union Theological Seminary, 1918. POLIT. & GOV.: candidate for city clerk, Hollister, CA, 1946; ***candidate for Republican nomination to presidency of the U.S., 1960, 1964; Peace Party candidate for presidency of the U.S., 1960, 1964; independent candidate for presidency of the U.S., 1972***; Survival Party candidate for gov. of CA, 1966. Bus. & Prof.: journalist; minister; author; publisher; printer; lecturer; historian; chronologist (specializing in prophecy and doctrinal fundamentals); reporter, *College View (NE) Gazette*, 1916; owner, M. N. Ask and Co. (printers), New York, NY, 1918; founder, *The Jubilee*, 1918; founder, *The Central News*, New York, 1920; founder, *Neighborly Talks*, New York, 1921; editor-in-chief, *Forest Hills (NY) News*, 1923; ed., *Purpose*; ed., *Inspirational Series;* pres., treasurer, Journalism Publishing Co., Inc., 1926; founder, owner, ed., *Newspaper and Magazine Writing*, 1927; assoc. ed., *Circulation Builder*, 1927; founder, pastor, The Remnant Church, Gilroy, CA; ed., publisher, *Prophecy Magazine*; dietitian; naturopath; family relations counselor. MEM.: American Tract Soc.; American Bible Soc.; Union Coll. Alumni Assn.; Bible Sabbath Assn.; National Travel Club; United Clergymen's International; U.N. Tenth Anniversary Commemorative Meetings; Remnant Movement. WRITINGS: *Armenian Pocket Diary* (1918); *Outline of World Peace*; *Call for Pauls* (1922); *Who's Who in Journalism* (ed., 1925–27); *Askian Loan Plan; An Open Letter Addressed to the delegates at the S. F. World Conference; The Remnant Movement; One Free World; How to End the War Within Six Months; The Turkish Question and Its Relation to World Wars II & III ; The Challenge to World Democracies; How to Prevent World War III; Reply to Willkie's "One World"; Shem Ham Japheth; World Union; Prophetic World Map; Prophecy and History; What the Prophets of God Can Do; Prophecy and Victory; Peace or War: Which Shall We Have?; The Remnant Church; Action Cooperative Industries; The Four Gospels in One; Reference Bible; The Underscored Bible; The Bible Interpreted; How to Read, Study and Understand the Bible; Roll Call of World Conditions; Prophetic Guidelines for World Peace* (1970). REL.: Remnant Church (founder; pastor; elder). MISC.: received first prize, *True Story Magazine*, 1924. RES.: Gilroy, CA.

ASKEW, REUBIN O'DONOVAN. b. Sep 11, 1928, Muskogee, OK; par. Leo Goldberg and Alberta (O'Donovan) Askew; m. Donna Lou Harper, Aug 11, 1956; c. Angela Adair; Kevin O'Donovan. EDUC.: B.S., FL State U., 1951; U. of Denver; LL.B., U. of FL, 1956. POLIT. & GOV.: appointed asst. county solicitor, Escambia Cty., FL, 1956–58; elected as a Democrat to FL State House, 1959–63; elected as a Democrat to FL State Senate, 1963–71 (president pro tempore); elected as a Democrat to gov. of FL, 1971–79; ***candidate for Democratic nomination to vice presidency of the U.S., 1972, 1984***; vice chm., Southern Governors' Conference, 1973–74, chm., 1974–75; delegate, Dem. Nat'l. Conv., 1972 (keynoter),

1976; ***candidate for Democratic nomination to presidency of the U.S., 1976, 1984***; appointed chm., Presidential Advisory Board on Ambassadorial Appointments, 1972–79; appointed special U.S. representative for trade negotiations, 1979–81; appointed chm., Select Cmte. on Immigration and Refugee Policy, 1979; candidate for Democratic nomination to U.S. Senate (FL), 1988 (withdrew). BUS. & PROF.: atty.; admitted to FL Bar, 1956; partner, Levin, Askew, Warfield, Graff and Mabie (law firm), Pensacola, FL, 1956–70; partner, Greenberg, Traurig, Askew, Hoffman, Lipoff, Quentel, and Wolff, P. A. (law firm), Miami, FL, 1981–. MIL.: paratrooper, U.S. Army, 1946–47; capt., U.S. Air Force, 1951–53. MEM.: ABA; FL Bar Assn.; Dade Cty. Bar Assn.; Masons; Rotary Club; American Legion; Florida Tuberculosis and Health Assn. (exec. cmte., 1960–65); Children's Home Soc.; American Jud. Soc. (dir., 1979–); Education Comm. of the States (chm., 1973–); Shriners; Alpha Phi Omega; Order of the Coif; Phi Alpha Delta; Delta Tau Delta; Ancient Arabic Order of the Nobles of the Mystic Shrine. AWARDS: received "Profile in Courage" Award, John F. Kennedy Lodge of B'nai B'rith, 1972; Special Award, National Wildlife Federation, 1972; "Conservationist of the Year" Award, FL Audubon Soc., 1973; National William Booth Award, Salvation Army, 1973; Herbert H. Lehman Ethics Award, 1973; JFK Award, National Council of Jewish Women, 1973; Theodore Roosevelt Award, International Platform Assn., 1975; Hubert Harley Award, American Jud. Soc., 1975; Human Relations Award, National Conference of Christians and Jews, 1976; Leadership Honor Award, American Inst. for Planning, 1978; Medal, FL Bar Foundation, 1979; Distinguished Community Service Award, Brandeis U., 1979; Champion of Higher Independent Education in Florida Award, 1979; Ethics in Government Award, Common Cause, 1980. Hon Deg.: LL.D., Notre Dame U., 1973; LL.D., U. of Miami, 1975; LL.D., U. of West FL, 1978; LL.D., Barry Coll., 1979; L.H.D., Stetson U., 1973; D.P.A., Rollins Coll., 1972; LL.D., FL Southern Coll., 1972; L.H.D., Eckerd Coll., 1973; L.H.D., Bethune-Cookman Coll., 1975; L.H.D., St. Leo Coll., 1975. REL.: Presb. (elder, 1960–). MAILING ADDRESS: 1401 Brickell Ave., PH-1, Miami, FL 33131.

ASPIN, LESLIE. b. Jul 21, 1938, Milwaukee, WI; d. May 21, 1995, Washington, DC; par. Leslie and Marie (Orth) Aspin; m. Maureen Shea, Jan 11, 1969 (divorced). EDUC.: B.A. (summa cum laude), Yale U., 1960; M.A., Oxford U., 1962; Ph.D., Massachusetts Inst. of Technology, 1965. POLIT. & GOV.: staff, U.S. Sen. William Proxmire (q.v.), 1960–63; staff asst., Council of Economic Advisors, 1964; campaign dir., Proxmire for U.S. Senate Campaign, 1964; chm., First District (WI) Democratic Party, 1969–70; elected as a Democrat to U.S. House (WI), 1971–93; ***candidate for Democratic nomination to vice presidency of the U.S., 1980***; appointed U.S. sec. of defense, 1993 (resigned, 1994). BUS. & PROF.: asst. prof. of economics, Marquette U., 1969–71. MIL.: capt., U.S. Army, 1966–68; Distinguished Service Award. MEM.: Junior C. of C.; American Legion; Phi Beta Kappa; Urban Observatory. WRITINGS: *How Much Defense Spending is Enough?* (with Jack Kemp, q.v., 1976); *Foreign Intelligence* (1980). REL.: Episc. RES.: East Troy, WI.

ATCHISON, DAVID RICE. b. Aug 11, 1807, Frogtown, KY; d. Jan 26, 1886, Gower, MO; par. William and Catherine (Allen) Atchison; single. EDUC.: grad., Transylvania U., 1828; studied law under Charles Humphreys. POLIT. & GOV.: elected as a Democrat to MO State House, 1835–37, 1839–41; Democratic candidate for MO State House, 1840; appointed judge, Platte Cty. (MO) Circuit Court, 1841–43; appointed and subsequently elected as a Democrat to U.S. Senate (MO), 1843–55 (president pro tempore, 1846–49, 1852–54); *succeeded to the office of presidency of the U.S., March 4, 1849, by virtue of his position as president pro tempore of the Senate, pending inauguration of president-elect, and served for one day*; ***candidate for Democratic nomination to vice presidency of the U.S., 1852***; Democratic candidate for U.S. Senate (MO), 1855. BUS. & PROF.: atty.; admitted to KY Bar, 1830; law practice, Liberty, MO, 1830; farmer. MIL.: capt., maj. gen., MO Militia. REL.: Presb. MISC.: cities of Atchison, KS, and Atchison Cty., MO, named after him; active with "Border Ruffians," 1855–56. RES.: Liberty, MO.

ATCHLEY, TEDDY MACK. b. Dec 10, 1965, San Jose, CA; par. Ted M. and Carol (Matz) Atchley; single. EDUC.: Chugwater (WY) H.S. POLIT. & GOV.: ***Crazily Independent candidate for presidency of the U.S., 1980, 1984***. BUS. & PROF.: humor columnist, *Chugwater High School Paper*; elected class pres., Chugwater H.S. REL.: Christian. MAILING ADDRESS: Box 24, Chugwater, WY 82210.

ATKINSON, FREDERICK WAYNE. POLIT. & GOV.: ***candidate for Democratic nomination to presidency of the U.S., 1980***. MAILING ADDRESS: 10818 Gold Flat Rd., NV City, CA.

AUGUSTINE, CAESAR SERRATO. b. Apr 2, 1949, San Antonio, TX; par. Caesar Augusto Serrato and Carmen Johnson Martinez; single. EDUC.: San Jacinto H.S., Houston, TX. POLIT. & GOV.: ***candidate for Republican nomination to presidency of the U.S., 1984, 1988; candidate for Democratic nomination to presidency of the U.S., 1984, 1988***; independent candidate for U.S. Senate (CA), 1986. BUS. & PROF.: inventor; naval architect; musician. MEM.: National Federation of Organized Politicians; Presidential Republican Task Force (Medal of Merit). REL.: supporter of nine major world religions. MISC.: inventor of bottomless oil supertanker. MAILING ADDRESS: 21500 Califa, #120, Woodland Hills, CA 91367.

AUGUSTITUS, ALBERT ANTHONY. POLIT. & GOV.: ***candidate for Democratic nomination to presidency of the U.S., 1980***. MAILING ADDRESS: 585 Cleveland St., Hazleton, PA 18201.

AUSTIN, WARREN ROBINSON. b. Nov 12, 1877, High Gate, VT; d. Dec 25, 1962, Burlington, VT; par.

Chauncey Goodrich and Anne Mathilda (Robinson) Austin; m. Mildred Mary Lucas, Jun 26, 1901; c. Warren Robinson; Edward Lucas. EDUC.: Ph.B., U. of VT, 1899; studied law under C. G. Austin and Sons, St. Albans, VT, 1899–1902. POLIT. & GOV.: state's atty., Franklin Cty., VT, 1904–06; appointed U.S. commissioner, 1907–15; chm., VT Republican State Convention, 1908; elected as a Republican, mayor of St. Albans, VT, 1909; appointed delegate, Congress of the Mint, 1912; appointed member, U.S. Court for China, 1917; delegate, Rep. Nat'l. Conv., 1928, 1940, 1944; elected as a Republican to U.S. Senate (VT), 1931–46; ***candidate for Republican nomination to presidency of the U.S., 1940***; appointed special U.S. ambassador to the U.N., 1946; appointed ambassador of the U.S. to the U.N., 1947–53. BUS. & PROF.: atty.; admitted to VT Bar, 1902; partner, C. G. Austin and Sons (law firm), St. Albans, VT, 1902–16; admitted to practice before the Bar of the Supreme Court of the U.S., 1914; atty., American International Corp. in China, 1916–17; atty., Seims-Carey Railway and Canal Co.; law practice, Burlington, VT, 1917–31; vice pres., Dy-O-La Dye Co.; vice pres., Johnson-Richardson, Ltd.; vice pres., Queen City Realty Co. MEM.: School for Advanced International Studies and Foreign Training Center, Lafayette Coll. (trustee); U. of VT (trustee, 1914–41); Harry S. Truman Library (hon. vice chm., Board of Trustees); Masons (33°); Odd Fellows; Elks (exalted ruler); Bennington Club; Ethan Allen Club; Alfalfa Club (mgr.); Alibi Club; India House Club; (pres., 1923); ABA; VT Bar Assn. (pres., 1923); Far Eastern Bar Assn.; Ahepan; SAR; China Soc. of America; Rotary Club (pres.); Military Order of the Loyal Legion; Kappa Sigma; St. Bernard Club; Farm Bureau; Future Farmers of America; Soc. of the Cincinnati; One Hundred Per Cent Club, IBM; Phi Beta Kappa; American Jud. Soc.; National Tulip Soc.; Bittersweet Club; Washington Monument Soc.; VT Hist. Soc.; Vermont Council for World Affairs. AWARDS: Received Order of Carlos Manuel de Cespedes (Cuba); Theodore Roosevelt Distinguished Service Medal; First Annual Award, American Assn. for the U.N., 1947; Gold Medal, International Benjamin Franklin Soc.; "Man of the Year" Award, Kappa Sigma; Gold Medal, National Inst. of Social Science; Churchman Award, Council for Social Action, Congregational Christian Church; Award for Outstanding Citizenship, Disabled American Veterans of New York; Yale Political Union Award; Distinguished Achievement Award, New York Grand Masonic Lodge. HON. DEG.: LL.D., U. of VT, 1932; LL.D., Columbia U., 1944; LL.D., Norwich U., 1944; LL.D., Dartmouth Coll., 1946; LL.D., U. of the State of NY, 1946; LL.D., Bates Coll., 1947; LL.D., Boston U., 1947; LL.D., Lafayette Coll., 1947; LL.D., Princeton U., 1947; D.C.L., U. of VT, 1947; LL.D., American U., 1948; LL.D., Middlebury Coll., 1949; LL.D., Georgetown U., 1951; LL.D., Harvard U., 1951; LL.D., Syracuse U., 1951; LL.D., Tulane U., 1951; LL.D., U. of Santo Domingo, 1959. REL.: Congregationalist. RES.: Burlington, VT.

AUTENRIETH, JOSEPH LEE. POLIT. & GOV.: MO state chm., Prohibition Party; treasurer, exec. cmte., National Prohibition Party; ***candidate for Prohibition Party nomination to presidency of the U.S., 1972***. BUS. & PROF.: minister, Christian Fundamental Church, St. Louis, MO; pres., St. Louis (MO) Christian Geriatric Assn. MISC.: Charged with fraud by MO Division of Securities in connection with bond sales for construction of nursing home, 1977; filed bankruptcy, 1980; convicted of 14 counts of mail fraud, 1982. MAILING ADDRESS: 3424 Longfellow Blvd., St. Louis, MO 63104.

AVERICK, NATHAN J. POLIT. & GOV.: ***candidate for Democratic nomination to presidency of the U.S., 1992***. MAILING ADDRESS: 2737 Fargo, Chicago, IL 60645.

AVERILL, CHARLES NORTON. b. Sep 22, 1938, Washington, DC; par. Wilbur Norton and Barbara Hortense (Giles) Averhill; m. Dorothy Garnette Winstead; m. 2d, Nancy Jo Joseph (separated); c. Gregory Patrick; Shari Estelle. EDUC.: Bladensburg H.S.; Columbia Technical School. POLIT. & GOV.: ***American Peoples Freedom Party candidate for presidency of the U.S., 1976***. BUS. & PROF.: architectural and structural designer; painter; roofer; carpenter; gardener. REL.: Christian. MAILING ADDRESS: 9245 All Saints Rd., Laurel, MD 20810.

AVERY, CHARLES ROBERT "CHUCK." b. Apr 29, 1944, Indianapolis, IN; par. William E. and Mildred L. (Jacobs) Avery; single. EDUC.: grad., Ben Davis H.S., Indianapolis, 1962; El Camino Community Coll., Torrance, CA. POLIT. & GOV.: coordinator, Peace and Freedom Party, Indianapolis; national executive sec., People's Party, 1971–; ***candidate for People's Party nomination to vice presidency of the U.S., 1972***. BUS. & PROF.: factory worker; political activist. MEM.: Gay Liberation Front (coordinator, Los Angeles, CA and Indianapolis); antiwar movement. REL.: none. MAILING ADDRESS: 1404 M St., N.W., Washington, DC 20005.

AXELROD, DANIEL M. POLIT. & GOV.: ***independent candidate for presidency of the U.S., 1980***. MAILING ADDRESS: 132 Ascot Court, Downingtown, PA 19335.

AYCOCK, CHARLES BRANTLEY. b. Nov 1, 1859, Fremont, NC; d. Apr 4, 1912, Raleigh, NC; par. Benjamin and Serena (Hooks) Aycock; m. Varina D. Woodard, May 20, 1881; m. 2d, Cora L. Woodard, Jan 17, 1891; c. Ernest; Charles Brantley; Alice; William Benjamin; Mary Lily; Connor Woodard; John Lee; Louise Rountree; Frank Daniels; Brantley. EDUC.: Wilson Collegiate Inst., 1872–75; Kingston Collegiate Inst., 1876; Ph.B., U. of NC, 1880; read law. POLIT. & GOV.: appointed county superintendent of schools, Wayne Cty., NC, 1880–82; presidential elector, Democratic Party, 1888, 1892; candidate for Democratic nomination to U.S. House (NC), 1890; appointed U.S. district atty. for NC, 1893–98; elected as a Democrat to gov. of NC, 1901–05; ***candidate for Democratic nomination to vice presidency of the U.S., 1904***; chm., NC Democratic State Convention, 1906; candidate for Democratic nomination to U.S. Senate (NC), 1911. BUS. & PROF.: schoolteacher, Fremont, NC; atty.; admitted to NC Bar, 1881; law practice, Goldsboro, NC, 1881–1901, 1906–09; dir., Negro Normal School; cofounder, *Daily Argus*, Goldsboro, NC, 1885; law practice, Raleigh, NC, 1909–12. HON. DEG.: LL.D., U. of ME, 1905; LL.D., U. of NC, 1907. MEM.: U. of NC (trustee). REL.: Bapt. RES.: Goldsboro, NC.

AYRES, WILLIAM AUGUSTUS. b. Apr 19, 1867, Elizabethtown, IL; d. Feb 17, 1952, Washington, DC; par. William Warren and Katherine (Drumm) Ayres; m. Aldula Pease, Dec 30, 1896; c. Margaret Eleanor (Mrs. William Frederick Weigester); Kathryn Elizabeth (Mrs. Henry Janney Nichols, Jr.); Pauline Williams (Mrs. Harold Nordmark Williams). EDUC.: Garfield U., 1888–90. POLIT. & GOV.: appointed clerk, KS State Court of Appeals, 1897–1901; elected as a Democrat, prosecuting atty., Sedgwick Cty., KS, 1907–11; elected as a Democrat to U.S. House (KS), 1915–21, 1923–34; Democratic candidate for U.S. House (KS), 1920; delegate, Dem. Nat'l. Conv., 1924; ***candidate for Democratic nomination to presidency of the U.S., 1928***; appointed member, Federal Trade Comm., 1934–54. BUS. & PROF.: atty.; admitted to KS Bar, 1893; partner, Blake and Ayres (law firm), Wichita, KS, 1893; partner, Noble, Ayres, McCorkle and Fair (law firm), Wichita, to 1934; dir., Fourth National Bank of Wichita. MEM.: Masons (33°); Shriners; ABA; Federal Bar Assn.; KS Bar Assn.; Commercial Law League; Knights of Pythias; Odd Fellows; Elks; Wichita C. of C.; Wichita Club. HON. DEG.: LL.D., Friends' U., 1942. REL.: Christian Church. RES.: Wichita, KS.

AZULAY, NAOMI L. POLIT. & GOV.: New Alliance Party candidate for NY State Assembly, 1982; ***Independent Alliance Party candidate for vice presidency of the U.S., 1984***. BUS. & PROF.: regional staff writer, *The National Alliance*, Denver, CO, 1984–. MISC.: first openly gay candidate to run for office in New York City. MAILING ADDRESS: P.O. Box 18987, Denver, CO 80218.

B

BABBITT, BRUCE EDWARD. b. Jun 27, 1938, Los Angeles, CA; par. Paul J. and Frances Babbitt; m. Harriet Coons, 1969; c. Christopher; Thomas Jeffrey. EDUC.: B.A. (magna cum laude), Notre Dame U., 1960; M.S., U. of Newcastle (England), 1963; J.D., Harvard U., 1965. POLIT. & GOV.: appointed special asst. to dir., VISTA, Washington, DC, 1965–67; elected as a Democrat, atty. gen. of AZ, 1975–78; elected as a Democrat to gov. of AZ, 1978–87; delegate, Dem. Nat'l. Conv., 1980; appointed member, Presidential Comm. to Investigate Three Mile Island; ***candidate for Democratic nomination to presidency of the U.S., 1988***; appointed U.S. sec. of the interior, 1993–. BUS. & PROF.: atty.; admitted to AZ Bar, 1965; partner, Brown and Bain (law firm), Phoenix, AZ, 1967–74. MEM.: Phoenix LEAP Comm.; AZ Bar Assn.; Dougherty Foundation (trustee); Verde Valley School (trustee); National Assn. of Attorneys General. AWARDS: Outstanding Young Man, Jaycees, 1974; Don Bolles Award, 1976; National Thomas Jefferson Award. WRITINGS: *Color and Light: The Southwest Canvasses of Louis Akin* (1973); *Grand Canyon: An Anthology* (1978). REL.: R.C. MAILING ADDRESS: 2095 East Camelback Rd., Phoenix, AZ 85016.

BABCOCK, EDWARD VOSE. b. Jan 31, 1864, Fulton, NY; d. Sep 2, 1948, Pittsburgh, PA; par. Leaman B. and Harriet (Vose) Babcock; m. 2d, Mary Dundore Arnold, Jun 2, 1902; c. Dorothy Arnold; Edward Vose; Fred Courtney. EDUC.: public schools, Oswego Cty., NY. POLIT. & GOV.: appointed and subsequently elected as a Republican to Pittsburgh City Council, 1911–12; elected as a Republican, mayor of Pittsburgh, 1918–22; ***candidate for Republican nomination to presidency of the U.S., 1920***; appointed and subsequently elected as a Republican, judge, Allegheny Cty. (PA) Comm., 1925–31. BUS. & PROF.: teacher, Poughkeepsie (NY) Business Coll.; lumberman, Detroit, MI; founder, pres., E. V. Babcock and Co. (lumber), Pittsburgh, 1885; pres., Babcock Coal and Coke Co., 1912; dir., Cambria Steel Co. REL.: Presb. RES.: Pittsburgh, PA.

BABSON, ROGER WARD. b. Jul 6, 1875, Gloucester, MA; d. Mar 5, 1967, Lake Wales, FL; par. Nathaniel and Ellen (Stearns) Babson; m. Grace Margaret Knight, Mar 29, 1900; m. 2d, Nono O'Dougherty, Jun 1, 1959; c. Edith Low Webber Mustard. EDUC.: B.S., MA Inst. of Technology, 1898; LL.D., U. of FL, 1927. POLIT. & GOV.: appointed asst. U.S. sec. of labor, 1917–20; ***Prohibition Party candidate for presidency of the U.S., 1940; candidate for Prohibition Party nomination to presidency of the U.S., 1944 (declined)***. BUS. & PROF.: electrical contractor; financial statistician; founder, Babson's Reports, Inc.; founder, Babson Inst.; founder, Babson Educational Inst.; founder, Utopia Coll. (later Midwest Inst.), 1947; co-founder, Webber Coll.; financial lecturer; vice pres., Newton Trust Co.; vice pres., Boston, Worcester and New York R.R. Co.; dir., MS River Power Co.; dir., Sierra Pacific Electric Co.; dir., Truckee River Power Co.; dir., NM and AZ Land Co.; dir., Hudson-Mohawk Power Co.; dir., Home Insurance Co.; chm., Gravity Research Foundation, 1948–67. MEM.: Royal Statistical Soc. (fellow); University Club of Boston. HON. DEG.: LL.D., Elon Coll., 1937; LL.D., Hendrix Coll., 1938; LL.D., American Theological Seminary 1939; LL.D., Lebanon Valley Coll., 1940; LL.D., Stetson U., 1940. WRITINGS: *Business Barometers* (1909); *Selected Investments* (1911); *Commercial Paper* (with Ralph May, 1912); *Bonds and Stocks* (1912); *The Future of the Working Classes* (1913); *The Future Method of Investing Money* (1914); *The Future of the Nations* (1915); *The Future of World Peace* (1915); *The Future of South America; The Future of the Railroads; W. B. Wilson and the Department of Labor* (1919); *Cox the Man* (1920); *The Future of the Churches* (1921); *The Fundamentals of Prosperity* (1920); *Business Fundamentals; Enduring Investments* (1921); *Making Good in Business* (1921); *New Tasks for Old Churches* (1922); *What is Success?* (1923); *Recent Labor Progress* (1924); *Religion and Business; Instincts and Emotions* (1927); *A Business Man's Creed* (1928); *Easy Street* (1930); *New Ways to Make Money; Storing Up Triple Reserves* (1929); *Investment Fundamentals* (1930); *Washington and the Depression* (1932); *Cheer Up* (1932); *Fighting Business Depressions* (1932); *Finding a Job; Washington and the Revolutionists; The New Dilemma* (1934); *What*

About God? (1935); *Actions and Reactions—Autobiography of Roger W. Babson* (1935); *A Revival is Coming* (1936); *How to Increase Church Attendance* (with others, 1936); *Cape Ann—A Tourist Guide* (with Foster H. Saville, 1936); *If Inflation Comes* (1937); *The Sea Made Men* (1937); *Washington and Inflation* (1937); *Coalition or Chaos?; Consumer Protection; The Folly of Installment Buying; Twenty Ways to Save Money; Business and Investing Fundamentals; Our Campaign for the Presidency; Looking Ahead Fifty Years; Better Living for Less Money; Before Making Important Decisions; Can These Dry Bones Live?; Business Barometers and Investment; Gravity—Our Enemy Number One; Gravity and Ventilation; Gravity and Sitting.* REL.: Congregationalist (moderator, national council, 1936–38). MISC.: predicted 1929 stock market crash. RES.: Wellesley Hills, MA.

BACON, AUGUSTUS OCTAVIUS. b. Oct 20, 1839, Bryan Cty., GA; d. Feb 14, 1914, Washington, DC; par. Rev. Augustus Octavius and Mary Louisa (Jones) Bacon; m. Virginia Lamar, Apr 19, 1864; c. Augustus Octavius; Mary Louisa; Augusta; Lamar. EDUC.: A.B., U. of GA, 1859, LL.B., 1860. POLIT. & GOV.: presidential elector, Democratic Party, 1868; elected as a Democrat to GA State House of Reps., 1870–80 (Speaker, 1873–75, 1877–82; Speaker pro tempore, 1875–76), 1892–93; delegate, GA State Democratic Convention, 1880 (pres.); candidate for Democratic nomination to gov. of GA, 1882, 1883, 1886; delegate, Dem. Nat'l. Conv., 1884; elected as a Democrat to U.S. Senate (GA), 1895–1914; ***candidate for Democratic nomination to presidency of the U.S., 1908***. BUS. & PROF.: atty.; admitted to GA Bar, 1866; law practice, Macon, GA, 1866–1914; adj., 9th GA Regt., C.S.A., 1861, capt., 1865. MEM.: U. of GA (trustee); Smithsonian Institution (regent). HON. DEG.: LL.D., U. of GA, 1909. REL.: Bapt. RES.: Macon, GA.

BACON, LEONARD WOOLSEY. b. Jan 1, 1830, New Haven, CT; d. May 12, 1907, Assonet, MA; par. Leonard and Lucy (Johnson) Bacon; m. Susan Bacon, Oct 7, 1857; m. 2d, Letitia Wilson Jordan, Jun 26, 1890; c. Leonard Woolsey, Jr. EDUC.: Andover Acad.; grad., Yale U., 1850, M.D., 1856; grad., Yale Divinity School, 1857. POLIT. & GOV.: ***Independent candidate for presidency of the U.S., 1900***. BUS. & PROF.: ordained minister, Congregational Church, 1856; pastor, Congregational Church, Litchfield, CT, 1857–60; state missionary, Congregational General Assn. of CT; pastor, Congregational Church, Stamford, CT; pastor, Congregational Church, Brooklyn, NY; pastor, Congregational Church, Baltimore, MD; pastor, American Church, Geneva, Switzerland, 1872–77; pastor, Park Congregational Church, Norwich, CT, 1878; pastor, Woodland Presbyterian Church, Philadelphia, PA; pastor, Second Congregational Church, Norwich, 1887–92; pastor, Ancient Independent Presbyterian Church, Savannah, GA; pastor, Assonet, MA, 1902–06; author. WRITINGS: *Congregational Hymn and Tune Book* (1858); *Fair Answers to Fair Questions* (1868); *The Life, Speeches and Discourses of Father Hyacinthe* (1870); *An Inside View of the Vatican Council* (1872); *The Abbe Tigrane* (1875); *Church Music Papers* (1876); *Church Papers* (1877); *A Life Worth Living—Life of Emily Bliss Gould* (1878); *Crimes Against Society; Sunday Observance and Sunday Law* (1881); *The Sabbath Question* (coauthor with G. B. Bacon, 1882); *The Church Book: Hymns and Tunes* (1883); *Hymns of Martin Luther* (1883); *The Simplicity That is Christ* (coauthor, 1885); *Norwich, The Rose of New England* (1896); *History of American Christianity* (1897); *Irenics and Polemics* (1898); *Young People's Societies* (1900); *Anti-Slavery Before Garrison* (coauthor, 1903); *Story of the Congregationalists* (1904). REL.: Congregationalist. RES.: Assonet, MA.

BADGLEY, DONALD. b. Oct 27, 1918, Poughkeepsie, NY; par. George Corliss and Agnes (Goerke) Badgley; m. Marjorie Jaminet, Jun 3, 1950 (d. Oct 4, 1956); m. 2d, Margaret Patterson, Apr 27, 1957; c. David Jaminet; Paul Nimon; George Patterson. EDUC.: grad., Oakwood School, 1937; Guilford Coll., 1939–40. POLIT. & GOV.: candidate for road superintendent, La Grange, NY, 1948; candidate for town supervisor, La Grange, 1957; elected as a Republican to NC State House, 1963–65; candidate for Republican nomination to gov. of NC, 1964; candidate for Conservative Party nomination to U.S. House (NY), 1976; ***candidate for Republican nomination to presidency of the U.S., 1980, 1984***. BUS. & PROF.: farmer; land developer; life insurance salesman; real estate agent. MIL.: staff sgt., U.S. Air Force, 1942–46. MEM.: C. of C.; Masons; Community Chest; Civitans; Oakwood School Alumni Assn. (treas.); Family Service Assn.; American Red Cross (chapter chm.); BSA (chapter chm.); United Way. WRITINGS: *Thus Says Rabboni* (1976); *The Perfect Calendar* (1980); *Disciple of the Word* (1983). REL.: Soc. of Friends. MISC.: Received Certificate of Appreciation, NY State Dept. of Corrections, 1984. MAILING ADDRESS: P.O. Box 167, Poughkeepsie, NY 12602.

BADILLO, HERMAN. b. Aug 21, 1929, Caguas, Puerto Rico; par. Francisco and Carmen (Rivera) Badillo; m. Norma Lit, 1949 (divorced); m. 2d, Irma Deutsch Leibling, May 7, 1961; c. Loren; Mark; David Alan. EDUC.: B.B.A. (magna cum laude), City Coll. of New York, 1951; LL.B. (cum laude), Brooklyn Law School, 1954, J.D., (cum laude), 1967. POLIT. & GOV.: appointed NY State deputy commissioner of real estate, 1962; appointed commissioner, Dept. of Relocation, New York, NY, 1963–66; elected as a Democrat, pres., Borough of Bronx, NY, 1966–70; delegate, NY State Constitutional Convention, 1967; delegate, Dem. Nat'l. Conv., 1968, 1972, 1976, 1980; candidate for Democratic nomination to mayor of New York, 1969, 1973; elected as a Democrat to U.S. House (NY), 1971–78; ***candidate for Democratic nomination to vice presidency of the U.S., 1972***; delegate, Democratic Mid-Term Conference, 1974, 1978; appointed deputy mayor of New York, 1978–79. BUS. & PROF.: C.P.A., 1956–; employee, Ferro, Berdon and Co. (C.P.A.s), 1951–55; atty.; admitted to NY Bar, 1955; partner,

Permut and Badillo (law firm), New York, 1955–62; partner, Stroock and Stroock and Lavan, New York, 1970–73; partner, Cohn, Glickstein, Lurie, Ostrin, Lubell and Lubell, New York, 1979–; adjunct prof., Fordham U., 1970–. MEM.: Beta Gamma Sigma; Alpha Beta Psi; National Conference of Christians and Jews; New York U. (trustee, 1970–); John F. Kennedy Democratic Club (founder, 1960); Mt. Sinai Hospital (dir.); Sigma Alpha. HON. DEG.: LL.D., City Coll. of New York, 1972. WRITINGS: *A Bill of No Rights: Attica and the American Prison System* (1972). REL.: Bapt. MAILING ADDRESS: 405 West 259th St., Bronx, NY 10471.

BAGLEY, HUGH GARLAND. b. Aug 13, 1931, La Grange, GA; par. E. J. and Erin Mary (Matthews) Bagley; m. Barbara Jane Bagley, Feb 25, 1952; c. Patrick; Debra; Mitzi; Gina; Crystal; Darryl. EDUC.: 6th grade, Linwood School, Columbus, GA. POLIT. & GOV.: candidate for Democratic nomination to sheriff, Monterey Cty., CA, 1960; candidate for mayor of Seaside, CA, 1968, 1970; candidate for mayor of Phenix City, AL, 1975; candidate for Democratic nomination to gov. of CA, 1982, 1986; ***candidate for Democratic nomination to presidency of the U.S., 1984***. BUS. & PROF.: laborer, Pacific Grove, CA, 6 years; self-employed businessman, CA, 20 years; owner, flea market, Keyes, CA. REL.: Bapt. MISC.: Advocate of annexation of Mexico to the U.S. MAILING ADDRESS: 5440 Frontage Rd., Keyes, CA 95328.

BAILEY, PEARL MAE. b. Mar 29, 1918, Newport News, VA; d. Aug 17, 1990, Philadelphia, PA; par. Joseph James and Ella Mae Bailey; m. (divorced); m. 2d, John Randolph Pinkett, Jr., Aug 31, 1948 (divorced, Mar 1952); m. 3d, Louis Bellson, Jr., Nov 19, 1952; c. Tony (adopted); Dee Dee (adopted). EDUC.: Joseph Singerly School, Philadelphia; William Penn H.S., Philadelphia. POLIT. & GOV.: appointed special representative, U.S. delegation to the U.N., 1975; ***candidate for Republican nomination to presidency of the U.S., 1976; candidate for Democratic nomination to presidency of the U.S., 1976***. BUS. & PROF.: singer, 1933–; actress; contract artist, Coral Records, Columbia Records, Decca Records; nightclub performer, 1950– . FILM CREDITS: *St. Louis Woman* (1946); *Variety Girl* (1947); *Isn't It Romantic?* (1948); *Amos and the Girl* (1950); *Bless You All* (1950); *House of Flowers* (1954); *Carmen Jones* (1954); *That Certain Feeling* (1956); *St. Louis Blues* (1958); *Porgy and Bess* (1959); *All the Fine Young Cannibals* (1960); *Call Me Madame* (1967); *Hello Dolly* (1967–68); *The Pearl Bailey Show* (1970–71). MEM.: American Guild of Variety Artists; Screen Actors Guild; A.F.T.R.A.; American Guild of Musical Artists; Actors' Equity Assn. AWARDS: Donaldson Award, 1956; Tony Award, 1967–68; "Entertainer of the Year," *Cue Magazine*, 1967; March of Dimes Award, 1968; U.S.O. Woman of the Year Award, 1969; citation from Mayor John V. Lindsay (q.v.), New York, NY. WRITINGS: *Raw Pearl* (1969); *Talking to Myself* (1971); *Pearl's Kitchen* (1973); *Duey's Tale* (1975); *Hurry Up, America and Spit* (1976). REL.: Humanitarian. RES.: Northridge, CA 91324.

BAILEY, THOMAS WILLIAM. b. Aug 7, 1930, Nanticoke, PA; par. Thomas C. and Grace (Samuel) Bailey; m. Evelyn Shepperson; c. Thomas William, Jr.; Susan Carol; Beth Anne. EDUC.: grad., Danville (PA) H.S.; B.A., Gettysburg Coll. POLIT. & GOV.: ***American People's Party candidate for presidency of the U.S., 1976, 1992***; chm., American People's Party, 1976–. BUS. & PROF.: accounting supervisor, Mobil Oil Corp.; estate planner, Prudential Insurance Co.; employee, U.S. Price Comm.; employee, U.S. Dept. of Labor; employee, U.S. Dept. of Health, Education, and Welfare. MIL.: U.S. Army, Korean War. MEM.: Big Brothers; Pi Lamda Sigma. REL.: Christian. MAILING ADDRESS: 247 Wyoming St., Wilkes-Barre, PA 18705.

BAIN, GEORGE WASHINGTON. b. Sep 24, 1840, Lexington, KY; d. May 28, 1927, Lexington; par. George Washington and Jane (West) Bain; m. Anne M. Johnson, Aug 30, 1860; c. George; John. EDUC.: County Acad., KY, 1848–58. POLIT. & GOV.: ***candidate for Prohibition Party nomination to vice presidency of the U.S., 1888 (declined); candidate for Prohibition Party nomination to presidency of the U.S., 1892***; member, Prohibition National Cmte., 1896–1900; Socialist Party candidate for U.S. House (KY), 1908. BUS. & PROF.: temperance advocate; Chautauqua and Lyceum Lecturer, 1880–1927; ed., *Good Templar's Advocate*; ed., *Riverside Weekly*, 1873–77. MIL.: col., U.S. Army. MEM.: Independent Order of Good Templars (grand councilor, 1871; grand worthy chief Templar of KY, 1872–79). REL.: Methodist (Sunday school superintendent; steward; trustee). MISC.: known as the "Silver-Tongued Orator of Temperance." RES.: Lexington, KY.

BAKER, ANDREW JACKSON. b. Sep 4, 1842, Grenada, MS; d. Jun 21, 1912, Los Angeles, CA; par. Jesse R. and Martha (Talbert) Baker; m. Elizabeth Newsome; c. Rhode Semmes; Mrs. Grantland S. Long; Andrew Jackson, Jr.; Mrs. Alexander T. Wingfield; William P.; Mrs. J. E. Henderson. EDUC.: U. of MS, c. 1861; studied law, 1865. POLIT. & GOV.: elected as a Democrat to MS State House, 1877–79 (Montgomery Cty.), 1883–84 (Lafayette Cty.); elected as a Democrat to TX State House, 1891–93; appointed and subsequently elected as a Democrat, TX state land commissioner, 1894–99; ***candidate for Democratic nomination to vice presidency of the U.S., 1912***. BUS. & PROF.: merchant, Montgomery Cty., MS, 1865; atty.; admitted to MS Bar, 1865; law practice, Oxford, MS, 1865–84; moved to TX, 1884; hardware business, Tom Greene Cty., TX; merchant, banker, San Angelo, TX, 1884–1912. MIL.: col., Co. A, 11th MS Volunteer Infantry, C.S.A., 1861–65; wounded at Antietam; wounded and captured at Gettysburg; prisoner-of-war, Fort Delaware. RES.: San Angelo, TX.

BAKER, DE VERE FRANKLIN. b. Dec 14, 1915, Tremonton, UT; par. Clarence Henry and Bertha May (Jensen) Baker; m. Nola Ines Hawks; c. Jacquetta Joan; Tamara Dee. EDUC.: grad., Davis H.S. POLIT. & GOV.: ***Candidate for Democratic nomination to presidency of the U.S., 1980***. BUS. & PROF.: oceanographer; explorer; shipbuilder, San Francisco, CA; filmmaker; author; producer, "I Search for Adventure" television series. MIL.: capt., U.S. Navy, 1934. WRITINGS: *The Raft Lehi* (1959); four other books. REL.: Church of Jesus Christ of Latter-Day Saints. MISC.: noted for Lehi raft expeditions in 1950s and 1960s. MAILING ADDRESS: 1133 20th, San Pedro, CA 90731.

BAKER, GERALD LEO "JERRY." b. Aug 8, 1932, Cresco, IA; par. Leo Jacob and Emma Agnes (Smith) Baker; single. EDUC.: B.S., Iowa State U., 1955. POLIT. & GOV.: candidate for Democratic nomination to U.S. Senate (IA), 1978; independent candidate to U.S. Senate (IA), 1978; ***candidate for Democratic nomination to presidency of the U.S., 1980; Big Deal Party candidate for presidency of the U.S., 1984***. BUS. & PROF.: computer programmer, Lincoln Laboratory, MA Inst. of Technology; mathematician, Chamberlain Co.; teacher of mathematics, German, chemistry, and physics; typewriter salesman, Cedar Falls, IA. MEM.: Mensa; Intertel. WRITINGS: *Design of High Explosive Plastic Shell* (1961). REL.: Christian (nee R.C.). MAILING ADDRESS: 2119 College St., Cedar Falls, IA 50613.

BAKER, HAROLD JAMES, JR. par. Harold James Baker, Sr. POLIT. & GOV.: ***independent candidate for presidency of the U.S., 1992***. MAILING ADDRESS: Virginia Domiciliary, Section 1, White City, OR 97503.

BAKER, HOWARD HENRY, JR. b. Nov 15, 1925, Huntsville, TN; par. Howard Henry and Dora (Ladd) Baker; m. Joy Dirksen, Dec 22, 1951; c. Darek Dirksen; Cynthia. EDUC.: grad., The McCallie School, 1943; Tulane U.; U. of the South; LL.B., J.D., U. of TN, 1949; LL.D., Tusculum Coll.; D.C.L., Southwestern U. of Memphis. POLIT. & GOV.: presidential elector, Republican Party, 1956; Republican candidate for U.S. Senate (TN), 1964; elected as a Republican to U.S. Senate (TN), 1967–80 (minority leader, 1977–81; majority leader, 1981–85); delegate, Rep. Nat'l. Conv., 1968, 1972, 1976 (keynoter); ***candidate for Republican nomination to presidency of the U.S., 1976, 1980, 1988; candidate for Republican nomination to vice presidency of the U.S., 1976, 1980***; appointed chief of staff to the president of the U.S., 1987–89. BUS. & PROF.: atty.; admitted to TN Bar, 1949; partner, Baker, Worthington, Barnett and Crossley (law firm); chm. of the board, First National Bank, Oneida, TN; pres., Colonial Natural Gas Co., Wytheville, VA, to 1967. MIL.: lt. (jg), U.S. Navy, 1943–46. MEM.: U.S.N.R.; ABA; TN Bar Assn.; Knoxville Bar Assn.; Scott Cty. Bar Assn.; Scarabbean Soc.; Phi Delta Phi; Pi Kappa Phi. REL.: Presb. MAILING ADDRESS: P.O. Box 2702, Washington, DC 20013.

BAKER, JEFFERSON TASWELL, JR. b. Mar 25, 1900, Cedar Hill, TX; par. Jefferson Taswell and Georgia Thalle (Strauss) Baker; m. Doris Mae Upton, Oct 10, 1921; m. 2d, Claribel Victoria Vinas, Oct 15, 1941; c. Reginald Gordon; Charlotte Diane (Mrs. Nathan Camards); Jefferson Taswell, III. EDUC.: North TX Agricultural Coll., 1925–26; Southwest TX Teachers Coll., 1926–27; Jefferson U. Law School, 1928–30; U. of Houston, 1940–41; J.D., Dixie U., 1932; B.S., Northwestern U., 1945. POLIT. & GOV.: member, City Charter Comm., Pasadena, TX, 1952; ***independent candidate for presidency of the U.S., 1976***. BUS. & PROF.: atty.; admitted to AR Bar, 1933; real estate broker; teacher, 1932–44; law practice, Texarkana, AR, 1933; real estate and mortgage loan broker, Baker Real Estate and Mortgage Co., Pasadena, TX, 1933–; instructor, U.S. Navy Radio School, Northwestern U., 1944–45; chm. of the board, Alcanus, Inc., 1959–; chm. of the board, McSalb, Inc., 1959–. MIL.: capt., U.S. Army, 1933–34; adm., TX Navy, 1972. MEM.: International Acad. of Forensic Psychology (fellow); Alpha Beta Sigma (charter member; chancellor, 1928–; pres., 1968–); Sports Car Club of America (competition driver, 1958–71). REL.: R.C. MISC.: named Kentucky Colonel (honorary). MAILING ADDRESS: 713 Armor Ave., Pasadena, TX 77502.

BAKER, LARRY LEE. POLIT. & GOV.: ***Candidate for Democratic nomination to presidency of the U.S., 1980, 1984, 1992***. MAILING ADDRESS: 1010 South Main St., Colfax, WA 99111.

BAKER, NEWTON DIEHL. b. Dec 3, 1871, Martinsburg, WV; d. Dec 25 1937, Shaker Heights, OH; par. Newton Diehl and Margaret (Dukehart) Baker; m. Elizabeth Leopold, Jul 5, 1902; c. Elizabeth; Newton Diehl; Margaret. EDUC.: B.A., Johns Hopkins U., 1892; LL.B., Washington and Lee U., 1894. POLIT. & GOV.: appointed private sec., postmaster gen. of the U.S., 1896–97; appointed and subsequently elected city solicitor, Cleveland, OH, 1902–12; elected mayor, Cleveland, OH, 1912–16; appointed U.S. sec. of the interior, 1913 (declined); ***candidate for Democratic nomination to vice presidency of the U.S., 1916, 1924, 1932***; appointed U.S. sec. of war, 1916–21; delegate, Dem. Nat'l. Conv., 1924, 1928; ***candidate for Democratic nomination to presidency of the U.S., 1924, 1928, 1932, 1936***; appointed judge, Permanent Court of Arbitration, 1928; appointed member, Law Enforcement Comm., 1929; ***candidate for coalition nomination to vice presidency of the U.S., 1936 (declined)***. BUS. & PROF.: atty.; law practice, Martinsburg, WV, 1897; partner, Baker, Hostetler, Sidlo and Patterson (law firm), Cleveland; dir., Cleveland Trust Co.; dir., Baltimore and Ohio R.R. Co.; dir., RCA; dir., Goodyear Tire and Rubber Co. MEM.: American Jud. Soc. (pres.); Woodrow Wilson Foundation (pres.); National Economy League (member, Advisory Council); Officers' Reserve Corps (col., 1921); Cosmos Club; Soc. of the Cincinnati; Phi Gamma Delta; Union Club; University Club; City Club; Cleveland C. of C.; Army and Navy Club. AWARDS: Distinguished Service Medal, 1929 United States; medal, National Inst. for Social Sciences, 1933. WRITINGS: *Why We Went to War* (1936). REL.: Episc. RES.: Cleveland, OH.

BAKER, PHILIP VERNON. b. Apr 6, 1917, Sanders, KY; par. Fred and Mattie Belle (Harsin) Baker; m. Ida Mae Harmon; c. Stephanie Verna, Apr 30 1949. EDUC.: U. of HI; U. of Louisville; UT State Agricultural Coll.; Kansas City (MO) Junior Coll.; Boseman Agricultural Coll. POLIT. & GOV.: candidate for Democratic nomination to U.S. House (KY), 1964, 1966, 1968, 1970, 1972, 1974, 1976, 1978; ***candidate for Democratic nomination to presidency of the U.S., 1976, 1984***. BUS. & PROF.: owner, Phil's Aircraft Sales and Service, Shively, KY; owner, Phil's Flight School; owner, Louisville School of Aviation Technology; co-owner, Phil and Ida's Bookstore; owner, Phil's Auto Sales; owner, Baker's Garage; farmer; rancher. MIL.: U.S. Air Force. MEM.: Common Cause; A.C.L.U.; KY Civil Liberties Union; American Inst. of Aeronautics and Astronautics; The Cmte. of the Future; The Federation of American Scientists; American Chemical Soc.; NRA; Business Aircraft Assn.; National Pilots Assn.; Airplane Owners and Pilots Assn.; AARP; KY Christian Leadership Conference; Disabled American Veterans (life member); American Legion; Smithsonian Institution; Public Citizen. WRITINGS: *Why I Want to Be Your President in 1976* (1976). REL.: Bapt. MAILING ADDRESS: 4136 Hillview Ave., Shively, KY 40216.

BAKER, SAMUEL AARON. b. Nov 7, 1874, Patterson, MO; d. Sep 16, 1933, Jefferson City, MO; par. Samuel Aaron and Mary Amanda (McGhee) Baker; m. Nell R. Tuckley, Jun 1, 1904; c. Mary Elizabeth. EDUC.: B.S.D., Cape Girardeau State Teachers Coll., 1897; A.B., MO Wesleyan Coll.; U. of MO; LL.D., MO Valley Coll., 1922. POLIT. & GOV.: elected as a Republican, MO state superintendent of schools, 1919–23; Republican candidate for MO state superintendent of schools, 1922; elected as a Republican to gov. of MO, 1925–29; ***candidate for Republican nomination to vice presidency of the U.S., 1928 (declined)***. BUS. & PROF.: instructor, Wayne Cty. (MO) Inst.; teacher, Bethel, MO, 1895; principal, Mill Spring, MO, 1896; appointed superintendent of schools, Piedmont, MO, 1897–99; principal, Jefferson City (MO) H.S., 1899–1905; principal, Joplin (MO) H.S., 1905–10; appointed superintendent of schools, Richmond, MO, 1910–13; appointed superintendent of schools, Jefferson City, 1913–19. MEM.: Masons; Knights of Pythias (grand vice chancellor, 1920); NEA; Southwest Pedagogical Soc. (pres., 1905–07); MO State Teachers Assn. (pres., 1920); Wayne Cty. Teachers Assn. (pres., 1897–99); MO State Assn. of City School Superintendents (pres., 1913). REL.: Presb. RES.: Jefferson City, MO.

BAKER, THOMAS J. POLIT. & GOV.: ***independent candidate for presidency of the U.S., 1984.*** MAILING ADDRESS: 427 54th St., Brooklyn, NY 11220.

BAKER, WILLIAM W. "BILL." b. Cincinnati, OH; m. Virginia; c. Julie; Tricia. POLIT. & GOV.: ***candidate for Populist Party nomination to presidency of the U.S., 1984***; national chm., Populist Party National Cmte., 1984–. BUS. & PROF.: archaeologist; author; radio talk show host; college prof.; scholar, biblical history. MIL.: U.S.C.G. WRITINGS: *Theft of a Nation*. REL.: Christian. MISC.: fluent in Hebrew and Arabic. MAILING ADDRESS: P.O. Box 11134, Las Vegas, NV 89111.

BAKKER, TAMMY FAYE LA VALLEY. b. International Falls, MN; d. ——— (Fairchild) La Valley and Fred Grover (stepfather); m. Jimmy Bakker (divorced); m. 2d, Roe Messner; c. Tammy Sue; Jamie Charles. POLIT. & GOV.: ***candidate for Democratic nomination to vice presidency of the U.S., 1988***. BUS. & PROF.: religious entertainer; television personality "PTL Club," Christian Broadcasting Network; cosmetics manufacturer. WRITINGS: *I Gotta Be Me* (1978). REL.: Christian. MISC.: candidacy sponsored by Ray Rollinson (q.v.). MAILING ADDRESS: c/o New Covenant Church, 1900 Central Florida Parkway, Orlando, FL 32869-0788.

BALCSIK, EDWARD MATTHEW. POLIT. & GOV.: ***Nouveau-Century Party candidate for presidency of the U.S., 1988***. MAILING ADDRESS: Mapes 204, Ripon Coll., Ripon, WI 54971.

BALDING, OWEN FRANK. b. Jul 17, 1917, Decatur, IL; par. Frank and Ada (Newberry) Balding; m. Rene C. Gianetta; c. none. EDUC.: IL State U., 1935–39; Millikin U., 1958–60 (summers). POLIT. & GOV.: ***Vote for Yourself Party candidate for presidency of the U.S., 1980, 1984***. BUS. & PROF.: schoolteacher, Decatur, IL; accountant, Illinois Power Co., 1948–53. REL.: Protestant. MAILING ADDRESS: 566 Carolina Ave., Decatur, IL 62522.

BALDWIN, RAYMOND EARL. b. Aug 31, 1893, Rye, NY; d. Oct 4, 1986, Fairfield, CT; par. Lucian Earl and Sarah Emily (Tyler) Baldwin; m. Edith Lindholm, Jun 29, 1922; c. Lucian Earl III; Raymond Earl, Jr.; Tyler. EDUC.: B.A., Wesleyan U., 1916; LL.B., Yale Law School, 1921. POLIT. & GOV.: chm., Republican Town Cmte., Stratford, CT; prosecutor, Stratford Town Court, 1927–30; judge of Town Court, Stratford, CT, 1930–33; elected as a Republican to CT State House, 1930–30 (majority leader, 1933–35); elected as a Republican, town chm., Stratford, 1930–37; delegate, CT Republican State Convention, 1938, 1940, 1942, 1944, 1946, 1948; elected as a Republican to gov. of CT, 1939–40, 1943–46; delegate, Rep. Nat'l. Conv., 1940, 1944, 1948; ***candidate for Republican nomination to presidency of the U.S., 1940, 1944, 1948;*** Republican (Union Party) candidate for gov. of CT, 1940; elected as a Republican to U.S. Senate (CT), 1946–49; appointed assoc. justice, CT Supreme Court of Errors, 1949–63 (chief justice, 1959–63); chm., CT State Constitutional

Convention, 1965; appointed state trial referee, 1963–86. BUS. & PROF.: atty.; admitted to CT Bar, 1921; assoc., McKinstry, Taylor and Paterson (law firm), New York, NY, 1921; law practice (with Phillip Pond), New Haven, CT, 1920–24; partner, Pullman and Comley (law firm), Bridgeport, CT, 1928–38, 1940–43, 1947–; dir., Russell Manufacturing Co.; dir., Middlesex Mutual Assurance Co.; dir., Bridgeport Hospital; dir., Connecticut Mutual Life Insurance Co.; dir., Hartford Fire Insurance Co.; dir., Hartford Accident and Indemnity Co.; dir., Bridgeport Brass Co.; dir., First National Bank and Trust Co. MIL.: ensign, U.S. Navy, 1917–18, lt. (jg), 1918–19. MEM.: Phi Delta Phi; Hartford Club; Cupheag Club; Masons (32°); Shriners; Delta Tau Delta; Elks; Loyal Order of Moose; Eagles; Redmen; Grange; American Legion; VFW; Forty and Eight; ABA; CT Bar Assn.; Bridgeport Bar Assn.; American Jud. Soc.; Graduates' Club of New Haven; University Club of Bridgeport; Yale Club of NY; Wesleyan U. (trustee); Kent School (trustee); Wilbraham Acad. (trustee). HON. DEG.: LL.D., Wesleyan U., 1939; LL.D., Trinity Coll., 1940; LL.D., Bloomfield Coll. and Seminary, 1946; L.H.D., Lincoln Memorial U., 1948. REL.: Episc. (chancellor, Episcopal Diocese of CT). RES.: Stratford, CT.

BALDWIN, SIMEON EBEN. b. Feb 5, 1840, New Haven, CT; d. Jan 20, 1927, New Haven, CT; par. Roger Sherman and Emily (Perkins) Baldwin; m. Susan Winchester, Oct 19, 1865; C. Florence Winchester; Roger Sherman; Helen Harriet (Mrs. Warren Randall Gilman). EDUC.: Hopkins Grammar School, New Haven, CT; A.B., Yale U., 1861, A.M., 1864. POLIT. & GOV.: member, New Haven (CT) Public Parks Comm.; elected member, New Haven (CT) Common Council; Republican candidate for CT State Senate, 1867; appointed member, CT Statute Revision Comm., 1873; appointed member, CT Comm. on Legal Procedures, 1879; appointed member, CT Tax Reform Comm., 1885; appointed assoc. justice, CT Supreme Court of Errors, 1893–1907, chief justice, 1907–10; appointed U.S. delegate, International Prison Congress, 1900, 1900 (vice pres.); appointed U.S. delegate, Universal Congress of Lawyers and Jurists, 1904 (vice pres.); elected as a Democrat to gov. of CT, 1911–15; ***candidate for Democratic nomination to presidency of the U.S., 1912***; Democratic candidate for U.S. Senate (CT), 1914; appointed chm., CT Tax Revision Comm., 1915–17. BUS. & PROF.: atty.; admitted to CT Bar, 1863; instructor in law, Yale U., 1869–72, prof. of law, 1872–1919, prof. emeritus, 1919–27; author. MEM.: ABA (founder; pres., 1890); Missionary Soc. of CT (dir.); New Haven Hospital (dir.); Assn. of American Law Schools (pres., 1902); Phi Beta Kappa; International Law Assn. (pres., 1899–1901); CT Democratic Club (pres., 1889); New Haven Congregational Club (pres.); YMCA (pres.); American Social Science Assn. (pres., 1897); New Haven Colony Hist. Soc. (pres., 1884–96); CT Archaeological Soc. (pres., 1899); American Hist. Soc. (pres., 1905); Hopkins Grammar School (pres., board of trustees); APSA (pres., 1910); American Soc. for Judicial Settlement of International Disputes (pres., 1911); CT Acad. of Arts and Sciences (pres.); L'Institut de Droit Compare; Colonial Soc. of MA; MA Hist. Soc.; American Antiquarian Soc.; AAAS (fellow; vice pres., 1903); American Phil. Soc.; National Inst. of Arts and Sciences; National Inst. of Arts and Letters; General Hospital Soc. of CT (dir.); Inst. of International Law; Archaeological Inst. of America (vice pres., 1898; pres., CT Soc., 1914). HON. DEG.: LL.D., Harvard U., 1891; LL.D., Columbia U., 1911; LL.D., Wesleyan U., 1912; LL.D., Yale U., 1916. WRITINGS: *Baldwin's Connecticut Digest* (1871, 1882); *Baldwin's Cases on Railroad Law* (1896); *Modern Political Institutions* (1898); *Two Centuries' Growth of American Law* (coauthor, 1901); *American Railroad Law* (1904); *American Judiciary* (1905); *The Relation of Education to Citizenship* (1912); *Life and Letters of Simeon Baldwin* (1919); *The Young Man and the Law* (1919); *Osborn's History of Connecticut* (coauthor, 1925). REL.: Congregationalist (moderator, General Conference). RES.: New Haven, CT.

BALLARD, CLAUDE THOMAS. POLIT. & GOV.: ***independent candidate for presidency of the U.S., 1976***. MAILING ADDRESS: 520 Gentleman Rd., San Antonio, TX 78201.

BALLARD, GEORGE H., III. POLIT. & GOV.: ***candidate for Democratic nomination to presidency of the U.S., 1992***. MAILING ADDRESS: 1001 East Sedgwick St., Philadelphia, PA 19150.

BANE, BERNARD MAURICE. b. Nov 23, 1924, Salem, MA; par. Julius and Rhoda (Trop) Bane; single. EDUC.: Northeastern U., 1945–48. POLIT. & GOV.: independent candidate for U.S. Senate (MA), 1970 (withdrew); Republican candidate for MA State House, 1970; ***candidate for Democratic nomination to presidency of the U.S., 1972***; independent candidate for MA State House, 1976. BUS. & PROF.: sales and merchandising, 1949–55; with Ivy League Enterprise, Boston, MA, 1955–65; author; publisher, proprietor, BMB Publishing Co., Boston, MA, 1965–. MEM.: American Trial Lawyers Assn.; Local Miss America Pageant (chm., 1961); American Soc. of Notaries. WRITINGS: *The Bane in Kennedy's Existence; Controlled Brinksmanship; Is President John F. Kennedy Alive . . . and Well?* (1973); *Breaking Through* (1984); *On the Impact of Morality in Our Times* (1985). REL.: Jewish. MAILING ADDRESS: 430 Broadway, Cambridge, MA 02138.

BANGERTER, BRUCE RUDOLPH. b. Nov 1, 1937, Salt Lake Cty., UT; par. Herman Rudolph and Laura Andrea (Lund) Bangerter; m. Billie Roeen Aebischer, Jan 20, 1967 (divorced, Mar 5, 1980); c. Brent; Bennett; Bryce; Bradley. EDUC.: Brigham Young U., 1960–64. POLIT. & GOV.: American Independent Party candidate for U.S. House (UT), 1972; American Party candidate for U.S. Senate (UT), 1974; American Party candidate for UT State Senate, 1976; ***candidate for American Party nomination to vice presidency of the U.S., 1976***; independent candidate for U.S. House (UT), 1978; independent candidate for U.S. Senate (UT), 1980. BUS. &

PROF.: subcontractor, Murray, UT; shipping clerk; systems programmer, BMA Data Processing, 1977–; computer consultant. MIL.: sgt. E/4, U.S.C.G., 1956–60. REL.: Church of Jesus Christ of Latter Day Saints. MAILING ADDRESS: 777 West 5900 South, Murray, UT 84107.

BANKHEAD, JOHN HOLLIS. b. Jul 8, 1872, Moscow, AL; d. Jun 12, 1946, Bethesda, MD; par. John Hollis and Tallulah James (Brockman) Bankhead; m. Musa Harkins, Dec 26, 1894; c. Marion (Mrs. Charles B. Crow); Walter Will; Louise (Mrs. H. M. Davis). EDUC.: A.B., U. of AL, 1891, LL.D.; LL.B., Georgetown U., 1893; LL.D., AL Polytechnic Inst. POLIT. & GOV.: elected as a Democrat to AL State House, 1903–05; candidate for Democratic nomination to U.S. Senate (AL), 1926; elected as a Democrat to U.S. Senate (AL), 1931–46; delegate, Dem. Nat'l. Conv., 1936, 1940; ***candidate for Democratic nomination to vice presidency of the U.S., 1944***. BUS. & PROF.: atty.; admitted to AL Bar, 1893; law practice, Jasper, AL, 1893–1946; Partner, Bankhead and Bankhead (law firm), Jasper and Birmingham, AL, 1904; pres., Bankhead Coal Co., 1911–25. MIL.: maj., AL National Guard, 1901–03. MEM.: Red Cross (chm., Walker Cty., AL, WWI); AL State Dept. of Archives and History (dir.); U. of AL (trustee); Sigma Alpha Epsilon; Phi Beta Kappa; Southern Club. AWARDS: Distinguished Service Award, American Farm Bureau Federation, 1941. REL.: Methodist. MISC.: brother of William Brockman Bankhead (q.v.). RES.: Jasper, AL.

BANKHEAD, WILLIAM BROCKMAN. b. Apr 12, 1874, Moscow, AL; d. Sep 15, 1940, Bethesda, MD; par. John Hollis and Tallulah James (Brockman) Bankhead; m. Adalaide Eugene Sledge, Jan 31, 1900; m. 2d, Florence McGuire, Jan 16, 1915; c. Evelyn Eugenia; Tallulah. EDUC.: A.B., U. of AL, 1893, A.M., 1896; LL.B., Georgetown U., 1895. POLIT. & GOV.: city atty., Huntsville, AL, 1898–1902; elected as a Democrat to AL State House, 1900–01; solicitor, Fourteenth State Judicial Circuit of AL, 1910–14; candidate for Democratic nomination to U.S. House (AL), 1914; elected as a Democrat to U.S. House (AL), 1917–40 (majority leader, 1934–36; Speaker, 1936–40); delegate, Dem. Nat'l. Conv., 1940 (keynoter); ***candidate for Democratic nomination to vice presidency of the U.S., 1940***. BUS. & PROF.: atty.; admitted to AL Bar, 1895; law practice, Huntsville, AL, 1895. MEM.: Tammany Hall; Phi Beta Kappa; Anawanda Club. Misc.: brother of John Hollis Bankhead (q.v.). RES.: Jasper, AL.

BANKS, NATHANIEL SARTLE PRENTICE. b. Jan 30, 1816, Waltham, MA; d. Sep 1, 1894, Waltham; par. Nathaniel Prentice and Rebecca (Greenwood) Banks; m. Mary Theodosia Palmer, Mar 1847; c. Maude; Harry; Mary (Mrs. Paul Sterling); Joseph Fremont. EDUC.: public schools. POLIT. & GOV.: Democratic candidate for MA State House, 1844, 1845, 1846, 1847; elected as a Democrat to MA State House, 1849–50 (Speaker, 1851–52); pres., MA State Constitutional Convention, 1853; elected as a Coalition Democrat to U.S. House (MA), 1853–55; elected as an American Party candidate to U.S. House (MA), 1855–57 (Speaker); ***North American Party candidate for presidency of the U.S., 1856; candidate for Republican nomination to presidency of the U.S., 1856; candidate for Republican nomination to vice presidency of the U.S., 1856, 1860***; elected as a Republican to U.S. House (MA) 1857, 1865–70 (Union Republican), 1875–79 (Liberal Republican), 1889–91; elected as a Republican to gov. of MA, 1858–61; Liberal-Republican candidate for U.S. House (MA), 1872; ***received 1 electoral vote for vice presidency of the U.S., 1872***; elected as a Liberal-Republican (Democrat-Labor Reformer) to MA State Senate, 1874; candidate for Republican nomination to U.S. House (MA), 1878, 1890; appointed U.S. marshal for MA, 1879–88. BUS. & PROF.: atty.; admitted to Suffolk Cty. (MA) Bar, 1839; ed., *Lowell (MA) Democrat*, 1840–41; proprietor, ed., *Middlesex (MA) Reporter*, 1841–42; clerk, Boston Customhouse, Boston, MA, 1843–49; pres., Illinois Central R.R., 1861; investor, Darien Canal Co., 1869; chief mgr., Commonwealth Fund Co., 1871. MIL.: maj. gen. of volunteers, U.S. Army, 1861–65. MEM.: Waltham Dramatic Soc.; Total Abstinence Soc.; Boston Club (pres.); Council 20, American Protective Assn. WRITINGS: *An Oration . . . Before the Neptune and Boyden Fire Companies* (1842); *A Statement of the Claims of Massachusetts and Maine* (1852); *Pursuits of Industry in Large and Crowded Cities* (1857); *An Address to . . . the Legislature of Massachusetts* (1858, 1859, 1860, 1861); *An Address Delivered . . . at the Custom House* (1865); *Emancipated Labor in Louisiana* (1865); *The Reconstruction of States* (1865); *Sutro Tunnel* (1873); *Revision of the Tariff* (1878). REL.: Protestant. MISC.: known as "Bobbin Boy." RES.: Waltham, MA.

BANKS, ROBERT CHARLES. b. Nov 4, 1949, Newport News, VA; par. Robert Charles and Evelyn (King) Banks; m. Matilda G. Banks; c. Charles Pulliam; Raymond Pulliam. EDUC.: grad., Carver H.S., Newport News. POLIT. & GOV.: ***independent candidate for presidency of the U.S., 1984***. BUS. & PROF.: janitor, shipyard, Newport News; minister. REL.: Holy. MAILING ADDRESS: 624 30th St., Newport News, VA 23607.

BARBOUR, PHILIP PENDLETON. b. May 25, 1783, Gordonsville, VA; d. Feb 25, 1841, Washington, DC; par. Thomas and Mary (Thomas) Barbour; m. Frances Todd Johnson, 1804; c. seven. EDUC.: grad., Coll. of William and Mary, 1799. POLIT. & GOV.: elected as a Democrat to VA State House of Delegates, 1813–14; elected as a Democrat to U.S. House (VA), 1814–25 (Speaker, 1821–23), 1827–30; appointed judge, General Court of VA, 1825–27; elected member, VA State Constitutional Convention, 1829–30 (president pro tempore; pres.); appointed judge, U.S. District Court of Eastern VA, 1830–36; pres., Philadelphia Free Trade Convention, 1831; ***candidate for Democratic nomination to vice presidency of the***

U.S., 1832; appointed assoc. justice, Supreme Court of the U.S., 1836–41; refused nominations for chancellor, atty. gen., judge of court of appeals, gov., U.S. Senate (VA). BUS. & PROF.: atty.; admitted to VA Bar, 1800; law practice, Bardstown, KY; law practice, Gordonsville, VA, 1801–12. RES.: Gordonsville, VA.

BARBOUR, WILLIAM WARREN. b. Jul 31, 1888, Monmouth Beach, NJ; d. Nov 22, 1943, Washington, DC; par. William and J. Adelaide (Sprague) Barbour; m. Elysabeth Cochran Carrere, Dec 1, 1921; c. Elysabeth Cochran (Mrs. James Henry Higgins); Warren; Sharon. EDUC.: grad., Browning School, 1906; Princeton U. POLIT. & GOV.: elected as a Republican to Rumson (NJ) Borough council, 1922; elected as a Republican, mayor of Rumson, NJ, 1923–28; appointed and subsequently elected as a Republican to U.S. Senate (NJ), 1931–37, 1938–43; Republican candidate for U.S. Senate (NJ), 1936; appointed member, NJ Unemployment Compensation Comm., 1937; ***candidate for Republican nomination to presidency of the U.S., 1940***. BUS. & PROF.: industrialist; asst. treas., Linen Thread Co., 1908, pres., 1917–31; dir., United Shoe Machinery Co.; dir., Central Hanover Bank and Trust Co. MIL.: 1st lt., capt., NY National Guard, 10 years. MEM.: Union League; Soc. of Mayflower Descendants; Soc. of Colonial Wars; SAR; Soc. of the Cincinnati; Masons; Metropolitan Club; National Training School for Boys (trustee); Textile Alliance; American Tariff League (pres., 1923); Monmouth Cty. Organization for Social Service (dir.); Monmouth Memorial Hospital (dir.); BSA (regional dir.). REL.: Presb. MISC.: amateur heavyweight boxing champion of the U.S. and Canada, 1910–11. RES.: Locust, NJ.

BARELA, FRANK, III. b. Mar 22, 1955, Los Angeles, CA; par. Frank, Jr. and Baca Barela; single; c. daughter. EDUC.: Ph.D. (Business Administration). POLIT. & GOV.: candidate for mayor of Phoenix, AZ; candidate for Republican nomination to gov. of AZ; ***candidate for Republican nomination to presidency of the U.S., 1992***. BUS. & PROF.: officer, CIA; foreign service officer, U.S. Dept. of State. MIL.: U.S. Army, 1972; Good Conduct Medal. MEM.: People's Revolutionary Continental Army; American Southwest Gunfighters Assn. REL.: R.C. MISC.: claims to be "master spy," "five-star general," and "hired gun." MAILING ADDRESS: 1712-C East Villa St., #316, Phoenix, AZ 85006.

BARKER, WHARTON. b. May 1, 1846, Philadelphia, PA; d. Apr 8, 1921, Philadelphia; par. Abraham and Sarah (Wharton) Barker; m. Margaret Corlies Baker, Oct 16, 1867; c. Samuel Haydock; Rodman; Folger. EDUC.: Short's Latin School; A.B., U. of PA, 1866, A.M., 1869. POLIT. & GOV.: chief organizer, Anti-Third Term Campaign against President U.S. Grant (q.v.), 1876; mgr., James A. Garfield (q.v.) for President Pre-Nomination Campaign, 1880; mgr., Benjamin Harrison (q.v.) for President Campaign, 1884, 1888; ***People's Party candidate for presidency of the U.S., 1900; advocate of Commonweal Party, 1902***. BUS. & PROF.: financier; publicist; partner, Barker Brothers and Co. (banking firm), Philadelphia, 1866–1921; founder, The Investment Co., Philadelphia; founder, The Finance Co., Philadelphia; adviser to Russian government on coal and iron mining, 1876–1917; appointed special financial agent in the U.S. for Russian government, 1878; adviser to Chinese government; publisher, *Penn Monthly*, 1869–80; ed., publisher, *The American* (incorporating *Penn Monthly*), 1880–91, 1894–1900. MIL.: organizer, Third U.S. Colored Troops, 1863. MEM.: Penn Club of Philadelphia (pres.); Union League; Art Club; Manufacturers' Club; Acad. of Natural Sciences; Acad. of Political Science; U. of PA (trustee, 1880–1921); Order of Knights of St. Stanislaus (Russia, 1879); Hist. Soc. of PA; American Phil. Soc. WRITINGS: *The Great Issues* (1902). MISC.: noted authority on Far Eastern affairs. RES.: Philadelphia, PA.

BARKER, WINTON EVERETT. b. Aug 22, 1929, Chicago, IL; par. John Carson and Esther (Westring) Barker; m. Audrey Alicia Marion Young, Sep 29, 1959; c. Ruth; Arlene; Allan; Ronald. EDUC.: grad., Steinmetz H.S., Chicago; certificate, LaSalle Extension U.; grad., St. Paul Bible Coll.; certificate, U. of MN. POLIT. & GOV.: ***Independent Republican candidate for presidency of the U.S., 1976, 1980***. BUS. & PROF.: accounting clerk; taxi driver; cashier, Clow Corp., Oak Brook, IL; accountant, Jaidinger Manufacturing Co., Chicago, IL; driver, St. Paul Yellow Cab Co.; owner-driver, Town Taxi. WRITINGS: *Straights Against Deviants* (1970); *Financial Status Certainty* (1970). REL.: Protestant Christian (Moody Church, Chicago, IL, 1935–54; Christian and Missionary Alliance, 1954–78; Baptist General Conference, 1963–68). MAILING ADDRESS: 228 Aurora Lane, Circle Pines, MN 55014.

BARKLEY, ALBEN WILLIAM. b. Nov 24, 1877, Graves Cty., KY; d. Apr 30, 1956, Lexington, VA; par. John Wilson and Electra A. (Smith) Barkley; m. Dorothy Brower, Jun 23, 1903; m. 2d, Mrs. Carleton S. Hadley, Nov 18, 1949; c. David Murrell; Marion Frances (Mrs. Max O. Truitt); Laura Louise (Mrs. Douglas MacArthur III). EDUC.: A.B., Marvin Coll., 1897; Emory Coll., 1897–98; U. of VA Law School, 1902. POLIT. & GOV.: elected prosecuting atty., McCracken Cty., KY, 1905–09; elected judge, McCracken Cty. (KY) Court, 1909–13; elected as a Democrat to U.S. House (KY), 1913–27; chm., KY State Democratic Convention, 1919, 1924; delegate, Dem. Nat'l. Conv., 1920, 1924, 1928, 1930 (temporary chm.), 1936 (temporary chm.), 1940 (permanent chm.), 1948 (temporary chm.; keynoter); elected as a Democrat to U.S. Senate (KY), 1927–49 (majority leader, 1937–47; minority leader, 1947–49), 1955–56; ***candidate for Democratic nomination to vice presidency of the U.S., 1928, 1932, 1940, 1944, 1952; candidate for Democratic nomination to presidency of the U.S., 1948, 1952; elected as a Democrat to vice presidency of the U.S., 1949–53***. BUS. & PROF.: atty.; admitted to KY Bar, 1901; law practice, Paducah, KY. MEM.: Phi Beta Kappa; Interparliamentary Union (pres., American Group); Delta Tau Delta; Phi Alpha

Delta; Loyal Order of Moose; Loyal Order of Red Men; Elks; Rotary Club; Lions Club; Alfalfa Club. AWARDS: Collier Award, 1947; "KY Outstanding Citizen" Award, KY Press Assn., 1948; Franklin Delano Roosevelt Four Freedoms' Award, 1949; Algernon Sidney Sullivan Award, 1949; Congressional Gold Medal, 1949; Award, Junior C. of C., 1953; Citation, Transylvania Coll., 1954. HON. DEG.: LL.D., U. of Louisville; LL.D., U. of KY; LL.D., Center Coll.; LL.D., MI State U.; LL.D., DePaul U.; LL.D., Westminster Coll.; LL.D., Rider Coll.; D.H.L., U. of FL; D.H.L., Dropsie Coll.; M.S., Bryant Coll. WRITINGS: *That Reminds Me* (1954). REL.: Methodist. MISC.: known as "The Veep." RES.: Paducah, KY.

BARLOW, JOSEPH LORENZO. b. Oct 27, 1818, Kent, CT; d. Oct 24, 1896, Bemus Heights, NY; par. Herman Barlow; m. Rosina Hurlburd, Aug 31, 1841; m. 2d, Mrs. Putnam, Dec 16, 1845; c. Mrs. Simeon Rowley; son (d. 1846). POLIT. & GOV.: ***Anti-Masonic Party candidate for vice presidency of the U.S., 1872***; chm., American Prohibition Party National Convention, 1884. BUS. & PROF.: printer, *Danbury (CT) Gazette*; publisher, *Bridgeport (CT) Standard*; ed., *Western New Yorker*; ed., *Sussex County Home Journal*, Deckertown, NJ, 1850; ed., *Mirror of Temperance*, Port Jervis, NY; lay preacher, Baptist Church; ordained minister, Baptist Church, 1853; pastor, Baptist Church, Seymour, CT, 1853–54; pastor, Baptist Church, Sandisfield, MA; pastor, First Baptist Church, Greenfield Center, NY; pastor, First Baptist Church, Stillwater, NY; pastor, John Street Baptist Church, Lansingburgh, NY, 1862; pastor, Baptist Church, Broadalbin, NY, 1863–68; pastor, Baptist Church, Ridgetown, CT; pastor, Baptist Church, Dundee, IL; pastor, Baptist Church, Bloomingdale, IL; pastor, First Baptist Church, Menomonee, WI, 1880–81; pastor, Grundy Centre Baptist Church, Grundy Centre, IA, 1888; pastor, Baptist Church, Hagadorn's Mills, NY, 1896. MIL.: chaplain, 125th Regt., NY Volunteers, 1862–63; captured by Confederate Army at Harper's Ferry, 1862. MEM.: National Christian Assn. (lecturer; vice pres., 1882). WRITINGS: *Endless Being*; "Moses" (poem). REL.: Bapt. RES.: Bloomingdale, IL.

BARNES, JOHN A. "JACK." b. 1941. POLIT. & GOV.: ***candidate for Democratic nomination to presidency of the U.S., 1992***. MAILING ADDRESS: RR #1, Caney, KS 67335.

BARNES, JOHN MAHLON. b. Jun 22, 1866, Lancaster, PA; d. Feb 22, 1934, Washington, DC; m. Mabel H. King; c. Myrle. EDUC.: Soldiers Orphan School, Mt. Joy, PA, 1875–82; Chautauqua correspondence courses, 1883–85. POLIT. & GOV.: sec., Philadelphia (PA) Local, Socialist Labor Party, 1892–99; Socialist Labor Party candidate for U.S. House (PA), 1892; PA state sec., Socialist Labor Party, 1893–99; ***candidate for Socialist Labor Party nomination to presidency of the U.S., 1896 (withdrew)***; Socialist Labor Party candidate for auditor gen. of PA, 1897; Socialist Labor Party candidate for gov. of PA, 1898; founder, Socialist Party, 1899; sec., Philadelphia (PA) Socialist Party, 1899–1904; national sec., Socialist Party, 1905–11; Socialist Party candidate for U.S. House (IL), 1908; national campaign mgr., Socialist Party, 1908, 1912, 1924; sec., Allegheny Cty. (PA) Socialist Party, 1918–19; sec., Cook Cty. (IL) Socialist Party, 1921–22. BUS. & PROF.: cigar-maker, Philadelphia, PA, 1882–1905; mgr., Cooperative Cigar Factories, Philadelphia, PA, and Chicago, IL; business mgr., *The New Day*, 1920–21. MEM.: International Cigarmakers Union of America (sec., Local 100, Philadelphia, PA, 1891–93, 1896–99; sec., Local 165, 1901–04; delegate, International Conventions); AFL (delegate, National Convention, 27 times, 1892–1921); Knights of Labor (1884–87); American Freedom Foundation (dir., 1919); Workingmen's Sick and Death Benefit Fund. REL.: Humanist. RES.: Chicago, IL.

BARNETT, JOHN THOMAS. b. Jun 22, 1869, Potsdam, NY; d. Feb 1, 1942, Denver, CO; par. John and Catharine (Kennedy) Barnett; m. Sue Sayre Nash, Jan 24, 1906; m. 2d, Emily Louise Schlesiner, Mar 7, 1917; m. 3d, Maybelle Fuller, Feb 3, 1932; c. Frank Fuller (stepson); Dana Fuller (stepson). EDUC.: grad., State Normal and Training School, Potsdam, NY, 1891; LL.B., Chicago Coll. of Law, 1896. POLIT. & GOV.: appointed asst. city atty., Chicago, IL, c. 1896 (declined); sec., CO State Democratic Central Cmte., 1896–1908, 1912–16; Democratic candidate for CO State Senate, 1898; appointed cty. atty., Ouray Cty., CO, 1899–1910; candidate for Democratic nomination to atty. gen. of CO, 1902; elected as a Democrat, atty. gen. of CO, 1909–11; member, Dem. Nat'l. Cmte. (CO), 1913–28; ***candidate for Democratic nomination to presidency of the U.S., 1924***; candidate for Democratic nomination to U.S. Senate (CO), 1932; pres., CO State Planning Comm. BUS. & PROF.: principal, Silverton (CO) Public Schools, 1891–93; owner, ed., *Silverton (CO) Miner*, 1891–94; atty.; admitted to IL Bar, 1896; assoc., Moran, Kraus and Mayer (law firm), Chicago, IL, 1896; partner (with James H. Teller), law firm, Denver, CO, 1911–13; partner (with John Campbell), law firm, Denver, 1913–20; pres., Mountain Producers Corp. (oil production), 1920–42; dir., Standard Oil of Indiana; dir., First National Bank of Denver; chief counsel, Arkansas Valley Irrigation Co. MEM.: University Club; Denver Club; Cherry Hills Club; Elks; Knights of Pythias; Modern Woodmen of America. REL.: R.C. RES.: Denver, CO.

BARNETT, ROSS ROBERT. b. Jan 22, 1898, Standing Pine, MS; d. Nov 6, 1987, Jackson, MS; par. John William and Virginia and (Chadwick) Barnett; m. Mary Pearl Crawford, Aug 22, 1929; c. Quida (Mrs. Atkins); Ross Robert, Jr.; Virginia (Mrs. Branum). EDUC.: B.S., MS Coll., 1922; Vanderbilt U.; LL.B. (cum laude), U. of MS, 1926, LL.D. POLIT. & GOV.: candidate for Democratic nomination to gov. of MS, 1951, 1955, 1967; elected as a Democrat to gov. of MS, 1960–64; ***candidate for Democratic nomination to presidency of the U.S., 1960***; delegate, Dem. Nat'l.

Conv., 1976. BUS. & PROF.: teacher, Pontoto (MS) H.S., 1922–24; farmer, Madison Cty., MS; atty.; admitted to MS Bar, 1926; partner, Barnett, Montgomery, McClintock and Cunningham (law firm), Jackson, MS. MIL.: pvt., U.S. Army, 1918–19. MEM.: MS Bar Assn. (pres., 1943–44); Jackson and Hinds Cty. Bar Assn. (pres.); ABA; National Exchange Club; MS Farm Assn.; Kappa Alpha (hon. member); Jackson Selective Service Board (award for service as counsel); Citizens Council; Leake Cty. Band; Baptist Young People's Union (pres.); MS Coll. Literary Soc. (pres.); MS Heart Assn. (chm.; dir.); MS Coll. State Alumni Assn. (pres.); U. of MS Alumni Assn. of Hinds Cty. (pres.); Shriners; Jackson Travelers Club; MS Travelers Assn.; U.T.C. Assn.; Woodmen of the World; American Legion; Loyal Order of Moose; Elks. REL.: Bapt. (deacon). RES.: Jackson, MS.

BARNHART, RAYMOND ANDERSON. b. Jan 12, 1928, Elgin, IL; par. O. E. and Alice (Anderson) Barnhart; m. Jacqueline Price; c. Whitney Allison Williams; Mallory Ann (Mrs. Mark Rousselot). EDUC.: B.A., Marietta Coll., 1950; M.A., U. of Houston, 1951. POLIT. & GOV.: elected as a Republican to Pasadena (TX) City Council, 1965–69; Republican candidate for mayor of Pasadena, TX, 1969; elected as a Republican to TX State House, 1973–75; Republican candidate for TX State House, 1974; co-chm., TX Citizens for Reagan, 1976; delegate, Rep. Nat'l. Conv., 1976, 1980; ***candidate for Republican nomination to vice presidency of the U.S., 1976***; precinct chm., Republican Party, Pasadena, TX; chm., Senatorial District Cmte., Republican Party, Pasadena, TX; chm., Harris Cty. (TX) Republican Central Cmte., 1975–77; chm., Republican Party State Central Cmte., 1977–79; appointed commissioner, TX State Dept. of Highways and Public Transportation, 1979–81; dir., TX Turnpike Authority, 1979–81; appointed federal highway administrator, 1981–89. BUS. & PROF.: college instructor, 4 years; construction contractor, 20 years; pres., Barney Insurance Agency, Pasadena, TX, 1956–78; salesman, Barmore Insurance Agency, Pasadena, TX, 1978–81. MIL.: U.S. Army, 1946–47. MEM.: Rotary Club. AWARDS: "Outstanding Male Citizen," TX Junior C. of C., 1974; "Outstanding Representative," TX Conservative Union, 1977; Torch of Freedom Award, Young Americans for Freedom, 1978. REL.: Methodist. MAILING ADDRESS: 1005 Dusky Rose, Pasadena, TX 77502.

BARNUM, PHINEAS TAYLOR. b. Jul 5, 1810, Bethel, CT; d. Apr 7, 1891, Bridgeport, CT; par. Philo F. and Irena (Taylor) Barnum; m. Charity Hallet, Nov 8, 1829; m. 2d, Nancy Fish, Sep 16, 1874; c. Caroline (Mrs. David W. Thompson); Helen (Mrs. Samuel H. Hurd); Frances; Pauline T. (Mrs. Nathan Seeley); Phineas Taylor (illegitimate). EDUC.: public schools. POLIT. & GOV.: Democratic candidate for gov. of CT, 1852 (declined); elected as a Republican to CT State House, 1865–67, 1877–78; Republican candidate for U.S. House (CT), 1867; elected as a Republican, mayor of Bridgeport, 1875; ***candidate for Prohibition Party nomination to presidency of the U.S., 1888 (declined); candidate for Republican nomination to presidency of the U.S., 1888***. BUS. & PROF.: showman; storekeeper, Bethel; ed., *The Herald of Freedom*, Bethel, 1831–35; promoter, Joice Heth (reputedly George Washington's nurse), 1835; owner, Barnum's American Museum, 1841–65; owner, *New York (NY) Illustrated News*, 1853; owner, P. T. Barnum's "Greatest Show on Earth" (circus), 1871–81; founder, Barnum and Bailey's Circus, 1881; brought Jenny Lind to U.S. for concert tour, 1850; popularized "freak shows"; patron of Gen. and Mrs. Tom Thumb (entertainers). MEM.: Fairfield Cty. Agricultural Soc. (pres.); Assn. for the Exhibition of the Industry of All Nations (pres., 1854). WRITINGS: *Barnum's New Year's Address* (1851); *Life of P. T. Barnum, Written by Himself*, (1855); *Humbugs of the World* (1865); *Struggles and Triumphs* (1869); *Lion Jack* (1876); *Jack in the Jungle* (1880); *The Art of Money Getting* (1883); *How I Made Millions* (1888); *Dick Broadhead* (1888); *The Wild Beasts, Birds, and Reptiles of the World: The Story of Their Capture* (1888); *Funny Stories* (1890); *Dollars and Sense, or How to Get On* (1890); *The Will of P. T. Barnum* (1891); *Why I Am a Universalist* (1895). REL.: Universalist. MISC.: arrested several times for various writings and schemes. RES.: Bridgeport, CT.

BARNUM, RICHARD CLARENCE. b. Sep 6, 1879, Ennis, TX; d. Aug 27, 1961, Cleveland, OH; par. Frank E. and Minnie (Church) Barnum; m. Mary E. Fair, Dec 16, 1911; c. none. EDUC.: grad., Garretsville (OH) H.S.; Hiram Coll., 1 year. POLIT. & GOV.: ***Single Tax Party candidate for vice presidency of the U.S., 1920***. BUS. & PROF.: publisher; book agent, gen. agent, F. B. Dickerson Co., Cleveland, OH, 1901–10; pres., dir., The R. C. Barnum Co. (publishers), Cleveland, OH, 1910–35; purchased the F. B. Dickerson Co., 1915, H. L. Baldwin Co., 1917, The Pioneer Press, 1918; mgr., Barnum Service Co., Cleveland, OH. MEM.: Subscription Book Publishers Assn. (pres., 1915). WRITINGS: *The People's Home Library*, (1926); *The "Federal" List of Current Publications* (1932); *Federal Lifetime Revision Service* (1932). RES.: Cleveland, OH.

BARNUM, WILLIAM HENRY. b. Sep 17, 1818, Boston Corner, NY; d. Apr 30, 1889, Lime Rock, CT. EDUC.: public schools. POLIT. & GOV.: elected as a Democrat to CT State House, 1851–52; delegate, National Union Convention, 1866; elected as a Democrat to U.S. House (CT), 1867–76; delegate, Dem. Nat'l. Conv., 1868, 1872, 1876, 1880, 1884, 1888; elected as a Democrat to U.S. Senate (CT), 1876–79; chm., Dem. Nat'l. Cmte., 1876–89; ***candidate for Democratic nomination to presidency of the U.S., 1880***. BUS. & PROF.: partner, iron business, Lime Rock. RES.: Lime Rock, CT.

BARRETT, MARLENE K. POLIT. & GOV.: ***independent (Cmte. for a Constitutional Presidency) candidate for vice presidency of the U.S., 1976***. MAILING ADDRESS: 18 Princeton Place, St. Louis, MO 63130.

BARRETT, PAT. POLIT. & GOV.: ***candidate for Democratic nomination to vice presidency of the U.S., 1972***. MAILING ADDRESS: IL.

BARRETT, PRINCE. b. Mar 8, 1929, Gassaway, TN; par. Pete and Ella (Spurlock) Barrett; m. (divorced); c. six. EDUC.: Dupont H.S., TN; Barber Coll.; Middle TN State U. POLIT. & GOV.: candidate for Republican nomination to mayor of Portland, TN, 1970s; ***candidate for Republican nomination to presidency of the U.S., 1980***. BUS. & PROF.: barber. MIL.: U.S.C.G.; various awards from U.S.C.G. REL.: Bapt. MAILING ADDRESS: 533 Melrose Dr., Lebanon, TN 37087.

BARRON, ELIZABETH CERVANTES. m. Robert C. Barron; c. three. POLIT. & GOV.: chairperson, Santa Clara Cty. (CA) Peace and Freedom Party; presidential elector, Peace and Freedom Party, 1976; Peace and Freedom Party candidate for CA state controller, 1978; ***Peace and Freedom Party candidate for vice presidency of the U.S., 1980***. MAILING ADDRESS: 1574 Albatross Dr., #2, Sunnyvale, CA 94586.

BARRY, DAVE. b. Armonk, NY; m. Elizabeth Barry; c. Robert. EDUC.: grad., Haverford Coll., 1969. POLIT. & GOV.: ***independent candidate for presidency of the U.S., 1992***. BUS. & PROF.: reporter, ed., *Daily Local News*, West Chester, PA, 1971–75; with Associated Press, instructor in business writing, Philadelphia, PA, 1975–83; columnist, *The Miami (FL) Herald*, 1983–; humorist. AWARDS: Distinguished Writing Award, Soc. of Newspaper Editors, 1987; Pulitzer Prize for Commentary, 1988. WRITINGS: *Taming of the Screw: Several Million Homeowners' Problems Sidestepped* (1983); *Babies and Other Hazards of Sex* (1984); *Bad Habits: A One Hundred Precent Fact Free Book* (1985); *Stay Fit and Healthy Until You're Dead* (1985); *Dave Barry's Guide to Marriage and/or Sex* (1987); *Claw Your Way to the Top* (1987); *Dave Barry's Greatest Hits* (1988); *Dave Barry Slept Here* (1989); *Dave Barry Turns 40*. MAILING ADDRESS: c/o Miami Herald, 1 Herald Plaza, Miami, FL 33101.

BARTLETT, DEWEY FOLLETT. b. Mar 28, 1919, Marietta, OH; d. Mar 1, 1979, Tulsa, OK; par. David A. and Jessie (Follett) Bartlett; m. Ann C. Smith, Apr 2, 1945; c. Dewey Follett, Jr.; Joan Chilton; Michael Hopkins. EDUC.: grad., Lawrenceville (NJ) H.S., 1938; B.S., Princeton U., 1942; LL.D., Marietta Coll. POLIT. & GOV.: elected as a Republican to OK State Senate, 1963–67; elected as a Republican to gov. of OK, 1967–71; delegate, Rep. Nat'l. Conv., 1968; ***candidate for Republican nomination to presidency of the U.S., 1968***; member, exec. cmte., Republican Governors Conference, 1969; Republican candidate for gov. of OK, 1970; elected as a Republican to U.S. Senate (OK), 1973–79. BUS. & PROF.: partner, Keener Oil Co., Tulsa, OK, 1951–71; pres., Dewey Supply Co., 1953–56; rancher, Wagner Cty., OK, 1958–64, Tulsa Cty., OK, 1958–79, Delaware Cty., OK, 1968–79. MIL.: capt., U.S.C.G., 1942–45; Air Medal. MEM.: Interstate Oil Compact Comm. (chm., 1970); Tulsa C. of C.; Salvation Army (dir.); American Red Cross (Tulsa Chapter dir.); Independent Petroleum Assn. of America (dir.); OK Independent Producers Assn. (dir.); Ozark Regional Comm. (co-chm.); OK Cattlemens Assn.; American Riflemen's Assn. REL.: R.C. RES.: Oklahoma City, OK.

BARTLETT, ROLLIE JAMES. b. Sep 25, 1916, Paducah, KY; par. William Webster and Lula (Schmitt) Bartlett; m. Laurine Wood (d. 1969); m. 2d, Velda Marie Robertson; c. Rollie Brent. EDUC.: grad., Reedland H.S., 1934; U. of KY, 1941; U. of Louisville, 1942; Purdue U., 1967; J. Stuart Writing School; Paducah Community Coll., 1976. POLIT. & GOV.: ***independent (Cmte. for a Constitutional Presidency) candidate for vice presidency of the U.S., 1976***. BUS. & PROF.: sanitary engineer; meter repairman, Paducah Water Works, 1934, superintendent of distribution, 1942–73; owner, Tri-State Meter Repair and Supply Co., Paducah, KY. MIL.: U.S. Army Corps of Engineers, 1943–46; two Bronze Stars. MEM.: American Water Works Assn.; Lions; Dukes of Paducah; Admiral of Natural Waterways. REL.: Bapt. MAILING ADDRESS: 125 Birch St., Paducah, KY 42001.

BARTON, JAMES WILLIAM. c. William James Barton (q.v.). POLIT. & GOV.: ***Commulist Party candidate for vice presidency of the U.S., 1980***. MAILING ADDRESS: 4500 College Ave., Alton, IL 62002.

BARTON, OTHO RICHARD. POLIT. & GOV.: ***American Party candidate for presidency of the U.S., 1976***. MISC.: known as "Otho the Lamb, the Lion of God, Alfla Omega," and "Otho Richard Barton Jesus Christ Super Star One of the True Church of God." MAILING ADDRESS: CA.

BARTON, WILLIAM JAMES COMMODORE. par. James William Barton (q.v.). POLIT. & GOV.: ***Commulist Party candidate for presidency of the U.S., 1980; candidate for Republican nomination to presidency of the U.S., 1984***. MAILING ADDRESS: 4500 College Ave., Alton, IL 62002.

BASCOM, HENRY CLAY. b. Sep 3, 1844, Crown Point Center, NY; d. Dec 22, 1896, Ocala, FL; par. Daniel W. Bascom; m. daughter of R. J. Saxe, 1874; m. 2d, Ellen L. Forbes, 1886. EDUC.: Fort Edward Collegiate Inst.; studied law under Daniel W. Bascom. POLIT. & GOV.: Republican candidate for school commissioner, c. 1870; member, Prohibition Party National Cmte., 1880–96; Prohibition Party candidate for gov. of NY, 1882, 1885; delegate, NY State Prohibition Convention; delegate, Prohibition Party National Convention, 1884, 1888; member, NY State Prohibition Party Exec. Cmte., to 1896 (treas.); ***candidate for Prohibition Party nomination to presidency of the U.S., 1892***; presidential elector, Prohibition Party, 1892; Prohibition Party candidate for NY State Constitutional Convention, 1894. BUS. & PROF.: author; accountant; correspondent; partner, Yedder Pattern Works, Troy, NY, 1879–84, proprietor, 1884–96; lecturer; temperance advocate. WRITINGS: "Requited, or a Knight in Livery" (poem). REL.: Methodist (Sunday school superintendent). RES.: Troy, NY.

BASS, CHARLOTTA A. SPEARS. b. Oct 1880, Sumter, SC; d. Apr 12, 1969, Los Angeles, CA; par. Hiram and Kate Spears; m. Joseph Bass, 1912. EDUC.: Brown U.; Columbia U.; U. of CA, Los Angeles. POLIT. & GOV.: delegate, Pan-African Conference, 1919; western regional dir., Willkie for President, 1940; People's candidate for Los Angeles (CA) City Council, 1945; founder, Progressive Party, 1948; co-chm., Women for Wallace, 1948; delegate, Progressive Party National Convention, 1948; Progressive Party candidate for U.S. House (CA), 1950; ***Progressive Party candidate for vice presidency of the U.S., 1952***. BUS. & PROF.: advertising solicitor, Providence, RI, 1900–1910; salesman, *The California Eagle*, Los Angeles, CA, 1910–12, managing ed., 1912–34, ed., 1934–54, publisher; co-chm., Southern CA Cmte., People's World, (west coast organ of the Communist Party), 1957–69. MEM.: United Negro Improvement Assn. (pres., Los Angeles Branch, 1920s); Los Angeles Cmte. for the Defense of the Bill of Rights; Cmte. for the Protection of the Foreign Born; World Student Congress (delegate, 1950); Peace Cmte. of the World Congress (delegate, 1950); Home Protective Assn. (founder); Industrial Business Council (founder, 1930); Progressive Educational Assn. WRITINGS: *Forty Years: Memoirs from the Pages of a Newspaper* (1960). MISC.: first negro member of a grand jury in Los Angeles Cty. Court, 1943. RES.: Los Angeles, CA.

BASS, WILLIE ISAAC. b. Nov 3, 1895, Harnett Cty., NC; d. Nov 3, 1966, Fayetteville, NC; par. Isaac and Adeline (Johnson) Bass; m. Annie Jones; c. Willie Irene; Annie Myron; Pat (adopted). EDUC.: night school. POLIT. & GOV.: ***Church of God Party candidate for vice presidency of the U.S., 1952***. BUS. & PROF.: laborer, 1905–07; mill operator, 1907–11; farmer; hog rancher; employee, Phillips Motor Co.; mechanic, Buick Co.; employee, Stage Co.; mechanic and sales mgr., Robertson Oil Co.; mgr., Ford dealership; Oldsmobile dealer; owner, automobile repair shop; owner, bus line, jitney business; operator, gasoline service station; owner, trailer court and trailer sales business, 1947–53; revivalist; preacher; bishop, Church of God (gen. overseer, SC and FL, 1948, NC, 1949–66). MIL.: machinist mate, second class, U.S. Navy, WWI. MEM.: Knights of the Ku Klux Klan; American Legion; Woodmen of the World. WRITINGS: *Two Roads—Defeat or Success* (1953). REL.: Church of God. RES.: Fayetteville, NC.

BASSFORD, ABRAHAM, IV. b. Oct 16, 1936, New York, NY; par. Abraham III and Flora Elizabeth (Dexter) Bassford; single. EDUC.: grad., Stuyvesant H.S., New York, 1954; Wagner Coll., 1955–65; A.B., NY Theological Seminary, 1968. POLIT. & GOV.: member, NY State Democratic Central Cmte., 1972; national sec., Socialist Party, U.S.A., 1973–75; ***candidate for Socialist Party nomination to presidency of the U.S., 1976***; delegate, Socialist Party National Convention, 1987. BUS. & PROF.: social worker; teacher; psychotherapist; reporter; supervisor of instruction, Echo Writers Workshop. MEM.: Student Peace Union (organizer); Public Enterprise Cmte.; World Federalist Assn.; Bay Ridge Independent Democrats; Bay Ridge-Sunset Park Mental Health Cmte. REL.: United Methodist. MAILING ADDRESS: 2727 West State St., Milwaukee, WI 53208.

BATCHELOR, GEORGE MERL. b. Nov 25, 1904, Ogden, UT; married. EDUC.: UT State U., 1942; international correspondence courses. POLIT. & GOV.: cty. chm., Weber Cty. (UT) American Party Central Cmte., 2 years; American Party candidate for U.S. Senate (UT), 1976, 1978, 1980; ***candidate for American Party nomination to presidency of the U.S., 1984***. BUS. & PROF.: businessman, 1969–; electrical contractor. MEM.: Five Points Lions Club (pres.); Plasterers Union; Electrical Union. REL.: Church of Jesus Christ of Latter Day Saints. MAILING ADDRESS: 505 Seventh St., Ogden, UT 84404.

BATES, EDWARD. b. Sep 4, 1793, Belmont, VA; d. Mar 25, 1869, St. Louis, MO; par. Thomas Fleming and Caroline Matilda (Woodson) Bates; m. Julia Davenport Coalter, May 29, 1823; c. Joshua Barton; John Coalter; Barton; Fleming; Holmes Conrad; Nancy; Fanny Means; Julian; Richard; Matilda; Woodson; six others. EDUC.: private tutors; Charlotte Hall Acad., St. Mary's Cty., MD; studied law under Rufus Easton, St. Louis, 1814–16; LL.D., Harvard U., 1858. POLIT. & GOV.: appointed prosecuting atty., St. Louis Circuit, MO Territory, 1816; appointed atty. gen. of MO, 1820–22; delegate, MO State Constitutional Convention, 1820; appointed U.S. district atty. (MO), 1821–26; elected as a Whig to MO State House, 1822–24, 1834–36; elected as a Whig to U.S. House (MO), 1827–29; Whig Party candidate for U.S. House (MO), 1828; elected as a Whig to MO State Senate, 1830–34; appointed U.S. sec. of war, 1850 (declined); ***candidate for Whig Party nomination to presidency of the U.S., 1852***; appointed judge, St. Louis Land Court, 1853; presidency, Whig Party National Convention, 1856; *candidate for Republican nomination to presidency of the U.S., 1860*; appointed atty. gen. of the U.S., 1861–64. BUS. & PROF.: atty.; admitted to MO Bar, 1816; partner (with Joshua Barton), law firm, St. Louis, 1816–23. MIL.: VA Militia, 1813. MEM.: River and Harbor Improvement Convention (pres., 1847). REL.: Soc. of Friends. RES.: St. Louis, MO.

BATES, GEORGE. POLIT. & GOV.: ***independent candidate for presidency of the U.S., 1864***. MISC.: fictitious candidate promoted by Edward Bates (q.v.).

BATTLE, GEORGE GORDON. b. Oct 26, 1868, Cool Spring Plantation, Edgecomb Cty., NC; d. Apr 29, 1949, Fredericksburg, VA; par. Turner Westray and Lavinia Bassett (Daniel) Battle; m. Martha Bagby, Apr 12, 1898; c. none. EDUC.: U. of NC, 1882–83; M.A., U. of VA, 1889; studied law under Jacob Battle, Rocky Mount, NC; Columbia Law School. POLIT. & GOV.: appointed asst. district atty., New York Cty., NY, 1892–97; Democratic candidate for district atty., New York Cty., 1909; delegate, Dem. Nat'l. Conv., 1920, 1928; ***candidate for Democratic nomination to presidency of the U.S., 1924***. BUS. & PROF.: atty.; admitted to NY Bar, 1891; law practice, New York; partner, Battle and Marshall (law firm), New York, 1901–11; partner, O'Gorman, Battle and Marshall (law firm), New York; partner, Levy, Fowler and Neaman (law firm), New York; partner, Battle, Fowler, Stokes and Kheel (law firm), New York. MIL.: member, Seventh Regt., National Guard of NY, 1891–96. MEM.: Soc. for the Encouragement of Labor Legislation; People's Forum (vice pres.); ABA; NY Bar Assn.; Assn. of the Bar of the City of New York; New York Southern Soc.; American Acad. of Political and Social Science; North Carolina Soc. of New York (pres.); Girls Service League of America; Tammany Hall (Grand Sachem); The Virginians; Downtown Club; Metropolitan Club; Manhattan Club; Cmte. on Educational Publicity in the Interests of World Peace; Salvation Army; Sweet Briar Coll. (patron); Masons; St. Nicholas Club; Calumet Club; Parks and Playgrounds Assn. (pres.); Church Club; National Democratic Club; Seneca Club. REL.: Episc. RES.: New York, NY.

BATTLE, JOHN STEWART. b. Jul 11, 1890, New Bern, NC; d. Apr 9, 1972, Charlottesville, VA; par. Rev. Henry Wilson and Margaret (Stewart) Battle; m. Mary Jane Lipscomb, Jun 12, 1918; c. John Stewart, Jr.; William Cullen. EDUC.: Wake Forest Coll., LL.D.; LL.B., U. of VA, 1913. POLIT. & GOV.: elected as a Democrat to VA State House of Delegates, 1929–33; elected as a Democrat to VA State Senate, 1933–49; elected as a Democrat to gov. of VA, 1950–54; delegate, Dem. Nat'l. Conv., 1952, 1956; ***candidate for Democratic nomination to presidency of the U.S., 1952, 1956***; appointed member, U.S. Comm. on Civil Rights, 1957–59. BUS. & PROF.: atty.; admitted to VA Bar, 1913; law practice, Charlottesville, VA; partner (with Lemuel F. Smith), law practice, Charlottesville, 1917–21; partner, Perkins, Battle and Minor (law firm), Charlottesville, 1921–49; partner, McGuire, Woods and Battle (law firm), Charlottesville, 1954–69; dir., American Gas and Electric Co.; dir., Virginia-Carolina Chemical Co.; dir., Fredericksburg and Potomac R.R. Co.; dir., National Bank and Trust Co. MIL.: pvt., U.S. Army, WWI. MEM.: Masons; Phi Beta Kappa; VA Bar Assn. (pres., 1940–41); Alpha Tau Omega; Alumni Assn. of the U. of VA (pres.); American Legion; Shriners; Omicron Delta Kappa; Elks; Kiwanis (pres., Charlottesville Chapter); Richmond Commonwealth Club. HON. DEG.: LL.D., Hampden-Sydney Coll., 1950; LL.D., U. of Richmond, 1952; LL.D., William and Mary Coll. REL.: Bapt. RES.: Charlottesville, VA.

BAUDER, GARY LEE. b. Nov 28, 1949, Sturgis, MI; par. Ray Orlo, Jr., and Grace Marguerite (Haney) Bauder; single. EDUC.: A.A., Glen Oaks Community Coll., 1970; certificate in junior accounting, MI State Technical Inst. and Rehabilitation Center, 1974. POLIT. & GOV.: treas., St. Joseph Cty. (MI) Young Democrats, 1968–70; precinct delegate, St. Joseph Cty. Democratic Party, 1970; ***independent candidate for presidency of the U.S., 1980, 1984***. BUS. & PROF.: sec.-treas., Glen Oaks Community Coll. Circle K, 1968–70; mgr., B. & F. Tax and Accounting Service Corp., Sturgis, 1974–76, pres., dir., 1976–; dir., B. & F. Tax Training Inst., Sturgis, MI; teacher, Sturgis Public Schools; notary public. MEM.: Distributive Education Clubs of America; Glen Oaks Community Coll. Alumni Assn.; Sturgis C. of C.; Sturgis Jaycees; American Management Assn.; National Small Business Assn.; St. Joseph Cty. Wheelchair Sports Boosters Assn.; International Platform Assn.; National Audubon Soc.; Smithsonian Institution. AWARDS: "Outstanding Service Award," MI Assn. of Distributive Education Clubs of America, 1970; "Outstanding Service Award," Glen Oaks Community Coll. Boosters, 1970; named "Officer of the Year," Distributive Education Clubs of America, 1970–71. REL.: Methodist. MAILING ADDRESS: 221 Susan Ave., Sturgis, MI 49091.

BAUER, NYLES. POLIT. & GOV.: ***independent candidate for presidency of the U.S., 1988***. MAILING ADDRESS: 1425 East Linden, Tucson, AZ 85719.

BAUMAN, ROBERT EDMUND. b. Apr 4, 1937, Bryn Mawr, PA; par. John Carl and Florence (House) Bauman; m. Carol Gene Dawson, 1960 (divorced); c. Edward Carroll; Eugenie Marie; Victoria Anne; James Shields. EDUC.: B.S., Georgetown U., 1959, J.D., 1964. POLIT. & GOV.: appointed page, U.S. House, 1953–55; appointed page, U.S. Senate, 1954; staff, Judiciary Cmte., U.S. House, 1955–59; pres., Georgetown U. Young Republican Club, 1959–60; national chm., Youth for Nixon, 1960; delegate, Rep. Nat'l. Conv., 1964, 1972 (alternate), 1976, 1980; member, exec. cmte., Young Republican National Federation, 1965–67; exec. dir., MD Citizens for Nixon-Agnew, 1968; elected as a Republican to MD State Senate, 1971–73; elected as a Republican to U.S. House (MD), 1973–81; member, Federal Hospital Council; ***candidate for Republican nomination to vice presidency of the U.S., 1976***. BUS. & PROF.: atty.; admitted to MD Bar, 1959; law practice, 1968–. Received "Outstanding Young American" Award, 1970. MEM.: Young Americans for Freedom (founder; chm., 1962–65); American Conservative Union (founder; dir.; sec.); ABA; MD Bar Assn.; Talbot Cty. Bar Assn.; DC Bar Assn.; MD Farm Bureau; Isaac Walton League; Elks; Easton Jaycees; Talbot Cty. Humane Soc.; Capitol Hill Club. WRITINGS: articles in *National Review*; *Human Events*; *Washingtonian*; and *New Guard*; *The Gentleman from Maryland: The Conscience of a Gay Conservative*. REL.: R.C. MISC.: arrested in homosexual incident and subsequently became an advocate for gay rights. MAILING ADDRESS: Glebe House, R-5, Easton, MD 21601.

BAUMGARTNER, DONALD M. Polit. & Gov.: ***candidate for Democratic nomination to presidency of the U.S., 1992***. Mailing Address: 1600 Cooly, #3, Missoula, MT 59802.

BAYARD, JAMES ASHETON. b. Nov 15, 1799, Wilmington, DE; d. Jun 13, 1880, Wilmington, DE; par. James Asheton and Ann (Bassett) Bayard; m. Ann Francis, Jul 8, 1823; c. Thomas Francis (q.v.). Educ.: Princeton U.; grad., Union Coll., 1818. Polit. & Gov.: Democratic candidate for U.S. House (DE), 1827, 1828, 1832, 1834; appointed dir., Bank of the U.S., 1834; appointed U.S. district atty. for DE, 1837–41; Democratic candidate for U.S. Senate (DE), 1838; elected as a Democrat to U.S. Senate (DE), 1851–63 (resigned); delegate, DE State Constitutional Convention, 1852– 53; delegate, Dem. Nat'l. Conv., 1856; ***candidate for Democratic nomination to vice presidency of the U.S., 1856***; appointed as a Democrat to U.S. Senate (DE), 1867–69. Bus. & Prof.: atty.; admitted to DE Bar, 1822; law practice, Wilmington. Res.: Wilmington, DE.

BAYARD, THOMAS FRANCIS. b. Oct 29, 1828, Wilmington, DE; d. Sep 28, 1898, Dedham, MA; par. James Asheton (q.v.) and Ann (Francis) Bayard; m. Louisa Sewell Lee, Oct 28, 1856; m. 2d, Mary Willing Clymer, Nov 7, 1889; c. Thomas Francis, Jr.; Florence (Mrs. William S. Hilles); Mabel (Mrs. Samuel Dennis Warren); James Asheton; Philip; Ellen (Mrs. Reinhold A. Lewenhaupt); William Shippen; Willing Francis; Katherine Lee; Mary; Ann Francis; Louisa Lee (Mrs. Frank Angell). Educ.: Francis L. Hawks School, Flushing, NY; studied law. Polit. & Gov.: appointed U.S. district atty. for DE, 1853–54; elected as a Democrat to DE State House, 1869; elected as a Democrat to U.S. Senate (DE), 1869–85 (president pro tempore, 1881); ***candidate for Democratic nomination to presidency of the U.S., 1872, 1876, 1880, 1884***; delegate, Dem. Nat'l. Conv., 1876; member, Electoral Comm., 1877; appointed U.S. sec. of state, 1885–89; appointed U.S. ambassador to Great Britain, 1893–97. Bus. & Prof.: atty.; admitted to DE Bar, 1851; law practice, Wilmington, 1851–53; partner (with William Shippen, Jr.), law practice, Philadelphia, PA, 1854–58; law practice, Wilmington, 1858–69. Mil.: 1st lt., DE Guard, 1861. Hon. Deg.: LL.D., Harvard U., 1877; LL.D., U. of MI, 1891; D.C.L., Cambridge U., 1896; D.C.L., Oxford U., 1896. Writings: *White and Black Children in Public Schools* (1872); *Use of the Army in Louisiana* (1875); *Civil Rights* (1875); *Unwritten Law* (1877); *The True Relation of Agriculture to Industry* (1878); *Hard Times and Their Remedy* (1878); *Daniel Webster and the Spoils System* (1882); *Mecklenburg's Declaration of Independence* (1882); *Oration on Webster Commemoration Day* (1882); *Oration* (1885); *Address Before the Literary Societies of the University of Kansas* (1886); *Oration to Caesar Rodney* (1889); *Disinterested Public Service* (1891); *Individual Freedom* (1895). Res.: Wilmington, DE.

BAYH, BIRCH EVANS, JR. b. Jan 22, 1928, Vigo Cty., IN; par. Birch Evans and Leah Ward (Hollingsworth) Bayh; m. Marvella Hern, Aug 24, 1952; m. 2d, Katherine Halpin, 1981; c. Birch Evans III. Educ.: grad., Fayette Township (IN) H.S., 1945; B.S., Purdue U., 1951; IN State U., 1952–53; J.D., IN U., 1960. Polit. & Gov.: elected as a Democrat to IN State House, 1955–63 (minority leader, 1957, 1961; Speaker, 1959); elected as a Democrat to U.S. Senate (IN), 1963–81; national chm., Young Citizens for Johnson, 1964; delegate, Dem. Nat'l. Conv., 1968, 1976; ***candidate for Democratic nomination to presidency of the U.S., 1972, 1976; candidate for Democratic nomination to vice presidency of the U.S., 1972***; Democratic candidate for U.S. Senate (IN), 1980. Bus. & Prof.: farmer, Terre Haute, IN, 1952–57; atty.; admitted to IN Bar, 1961; law practice, Terre Haute, IN, 1961–; partner, Marshall, Batman and Day (law firm), Terre Haute, IN, 1961–; senior partner, Bayh, Tabbert and Capehart (law firm), Indianapolis, IN and Washington, DC, 1981–. Mil.: U.S. Army, 1946–48. Mem.: Ceres; Alpha Zeta; Gimlet; *Indiana Law Journal,* (board of editors); Order of the Coif; Alpha Tau Omega; U.S. Merchant Marine Acad. (board of visitors); Purdue U. Alumni Assn.; Isaac Walton League; Junior C. of C.; Farm Bureau; Farmers Union; Wabash Valley Assn.; Red Cross; Volunteers of America; Elks; Masons; Wabash Valley Fair Board; Indiana Soc. of Washington; Indiana Easter Seals (chm., 1965–67); ABA; IN Bar Assn.; Vigo City Bar Assn.; IN U. Alumni Assn. Awards.: "Outstanding Young Man in Indiana," Indiana Junior C. of C., 1959; one of ten "Outstanding Young Men in America," U.S. Junior C. of C., 1963; "Outstanding member of Indiana General Assembly," 1961. Hon. Deg.: LL.D., Anderson Coll.; LL.D., Purdue U.; L.H.D., Salem Coll. Writings: *The Making of an Amendment* (1966); *One Heartbeat Away* (1968); articles in *Indiana Law Journal*. Rel.: Methodist (Centenary Methodist Church, Terre Haute, IN). Misc.: lightweight boxing champion, varsity baseball team, senior class pres., Purdue U. Mailing Address: 1575 I St., N.W., Suite 1025, Washington, DC 20005.

BEACH, DAVID SHERMAN. b. Feb 26, 1861, Bridgeport, CT; d. Mar 22, 1948, Bridgeport, CT; m. Mary J. Meeker (d. 1919); c. John H.; David F.; Harlan P. Polit. & Gov.: ***People's National Independent (Looking Glass) Party candidate for presidency of the U.S., 1920, 1924, 1928, 1932, 1936, 1940, 1944, 1948***. Bus. & Prof.: inventor; statistician. Misc.: self-styled "Financial Giant of the U.S."; "World Actuary"; and "The Most Progressive Man in the World"; discovered method of extracting rubber from osage oranges; popularized "backyard plantations"; invented solid rubber automobile wheel made from osage oranges. Rel.: United Church of Bridgeport. Res.: Bridgeport, CT.

BEAGLE, DONALD RAY. b. Dec 28, 1921, Ben's Run, WV. Polit. & Gov.: candidate for Democratic nomination to gov. of TX, 1978; candidate for cty. judge, TX; ***Independent***

Patriotic candidate for presidency of the U.S., 1980. BUS. & PROF.: welder. MIL.: U.S.C.G. MAILING ADDRESS: 612 South Twin City Highway, Nederland, TX 77627.

BEAL, DANA. POLIT. & GOV.: *Grassroots Party candidate for vice presidency of the U.S., 1988*. MAILING ADDRESS: c/o Oliver Steinberg, 1503 Branston, St. Paul, MN 55108.

BEAMGARD, DONALD INNES. b. Jun 9, 1922, Atwood, KS; par. Clarence William and Gladys M. (Innes) Beamgard; m. Vala June Argabright, Aug, 1946; c. Richard Stuart; Kent Douglas. EDUC.: B.S., Fort Hays (KS) State U.; OH State U. POLIT. & GOV.: elected as a Non-Partisan to School Board, Atwood, KS; elected as a Non-Partisan to Atwood City Council; elected Atwood Township trustee; elected Atwood Township treas.; elected as a Non-Partisan, mayor of Atwood, KS; appointed member, Governor's Board of Disabilities; appointed member, Governor's Board for State Hospital Efficiency; *candidate for Democratic nomination to presidency of the U.S., 1992*. BUS. & PROF.: motel owner; postmaster. MIL.: pvt., 14th Armored Div., 25th Tank, U.S. Army, 1942–46; Purple Heart. MEM.: Masons; Odd Fellows; American Legion (life member); VFW; Disabled American Veterans; C. of C.; Rotary; Camp Lakeside Board; Retarded Children Assn. AWARDS: Rawlings Cty. (KS) "Man of the Year" Award, 2 times. REL.: Methodist. MAILING ADDRESS: R.R. 1, Box 16B, Atwood, KS 67730.

BEARD, EDWARD PETER. b. Jan 20, 1940, Providence, RI; par. Thomas James and Anna (Fitzpatrick) Beard; m. Marsha Louise Pelosi, Oct 12, 1963; c. Edward Peter, Jr.; Diane. EDUC.: Hope H.S., Providence. POLIT. & GOV.: elected as a Democrat to RI State House, 1973–75; member, RI State Democratic Central Cmte., 1973–75; chm., 28th District Democratic Cmte., RI, 1973–75; appointed chm., Governor's Task Force on Nursing Home Inspections (RI); elected as a Democrat to U.S. House (RI), 1975–81; *candidate for Democratic nomination to presidency of the U.S., 1980 (withdrew)*; Democratic candidate for U.S. House (RI), 1980. MIL.: Sp/5, RI National Guard, 1960–66. MEM.: Painters' Union 195, AFL-CIO; St. Vincent De Paul Soc.; RI Assn. for Retarded Children; RI Medical Center Organization of Family and Friends; National Council of Senior Citizens (hon. member); Elks. AWARDS: "Liberty Under Law" Award, Eagles, 1975; Joe Kappler Senior Citizen Hall of Fame Award, 1976; named "Man of the Year," *Rhode Islander Magazine*, 1974; "Man of the Year," Cranston Democratic Women's Club, 1976. REL.: R.C. MAILING ADDRESS: 200 Bay View Ave., Cranston, RI 02905.

BEASLEY, JAMES MERCER. POLIT. & GOV.: *independent candidate for presidency of the U.S., 1988*. MAILING ADDRESS: 9360 Lavell St., La Mesa, CA 92041.

BEATTY, WARREN (nee WARREN BEATY). b. Mar 30, 1938, Richmond, VA; par. Ira O. and Kathlyn (MacLean) Beaty; single. EDUC.: grad., Washington and Lee H.S., Arlington, VA; School of Speech and Drama, Northwestern U., 1955–56; Stella Adler Theatre Studio, 1956–57. POLIT. & GOV.: *candidate for Democratic nomination to presidency of the U.S., 1976*. BUS. & PROF.: actor; summer stock, Gateway Theatre, Long Island, NY; dir. Television: lead, "The Curly Headed Kid," NBC. Plays: "The Curly Headed Kid"; "A Hatful of Rain"; "The Happiest Millionaire"; "Visit to a Small Planet"; "The Boy Friend"; "Compulsion"; "A Loss of Roses." Movies: "Splendor in the Grass" (1961); "The Roman Spring of Mrs. Stone" (1961); "All Fall Down" (1962); "Lilith" (1963); "Mickey One" (1965); "Promise Her Anything" (1965); "Kaleidoscope" (1966); "Bonnie and Clyde" (1967); "The Only Game in Town" (1969); "McCabe and Mrs. Miller" (1971); "Dollars" (1971); "The Parallax View" (1974); "The Fortune" (1975); "Shampoo" (1975); "Heaven Can Wait" (1978); "Reds" (Producer, dir., 1981); "Dick Tracy" (1990?). MAILING ADDRESS: c/o John Springer Associates, 667 Madison Ave., NY, NY 10021.

BEAUBIEN, ROBERT LEE. POLIT. & GOV.: *independent candidate for presidency of the U.S., 1980*. MAILING ADDRESS: Rural Route/Seventh St., Chugwater, WY 82210.

BECKHAM, JOHN CREPPS WICKLIFFE. b. Aug 5, 1865, Bardstown, KY; d. Jan 9, 1940, Louisville, KY; par. William Netherton and Julia Tevis (Wickliffe) Beckham; m. Jean Raphael Fuqua, Nov 21, 1900; c. Eleanor Raphael; John Crepps Wickliffe, Jr. EDUC.: Roseland Acad.; Central U., 1884–86. POLIT. & GOV.: page, KY State House, 1881–82; pres., Young Democrats of Nelson Cty., KY, 1890s; elected as a Democrat to KY State House, 1894–98 (Speaker, 1898); Democratic candidate for lt. gov. of KY, 1899 (lost, but was declared elected by KY Legislature); succeeded and subsequently elected as a Democrat to gov. of KY upon assassination of Gov. William Goebel, 1900–1907; delegate, Dem. Nat'l. Conv., 1900, 1904, 1908, 1912, 1916, 1920; *candidate for Democratic nomination to vice presidency of the U.S., 1904*; Democratic candidate for U.S. Senate (KY), 1906, 1920; elected as a Democrat to U.S. Senate (KY), 1915–21; Democratic candidate for gov. of KY, 1927; appointed member, KY Public Service Comm., 1936; appointed commissioner, KY State Dept. of Business Regulation, 1936; appointed chm., KY State Government Reorganization Comm., 1936; candidate for Democratic nomination to U.S. Senate (KY), 1936. BUS. & PROF.: atty.; admitted to KY Bar, 1889; principal, Bardstown (KY) Public School, 1888–93; law practice, Bardstown, KY, 1893; senior partner, Beckham, Hamilton and Beckham (law firm), Louisville, KY. HON. DEG.: LL.D., U. of KY, 1902. REL.: Presb. RES.: Louisville, KY.

BECKMAN, MARTIN JAMES "RED." b. 1940, Minneapolis, MN; m. Earlene. EDUC.: grad., Coll. of St. Thomas, 1962. POLIT. & GOV.: ***candidate for Democratic nomination to presidency of the U.S., 1984***; candidate for Democratic nomination to gov. of MT, 1992. BUS. & PROF.: vice pres. for finance, dir., treas., Hauenstein and Burmeister, Inc. MEM.: National Assn. of Accountants; American Inst. of Certified Public Accountants. WRITINGS: *The Law That Never Was* (coauthor, 1985). MAILING ADDRESS: 2711 North Lockwood Frontage Rd., Route 5, Billings, MT 59101.

BECKWITH, FRANK ROSCOE. b. Dec 11, 1904, Indianapolis, IN; d. Aug 24, 1965, Indianapolis, IN; par. Frank and Aletha (Grubbs) Beckwith; single. EDUC.: grad., Arsenal Technical H.S., 1921; studied law under Sumner A. Clancy, assoc. dean, Benjamin Harrison Law School, 1930–31. POLIT. & GOV.: delegate, IN State Republican Convention, 1926; candidate for Republican nomination to IN State House; field organizer, IN State Republican Cmte., 1928; dir. of industrial safety, IN Industrial Board, 1929–33; public defender, Marion Cty. (IN) Criminal Court, 1951–58; Republican candidate for Indianapolis (IN) City Council, 1951; urban coordinator, Eisenhower-Nixon Campaign, 1956; appointed member, IN State Comm. on Aging and the Aged, 1957–61; ***candidate for Republican nomination to presidency of the U.S., 1960, 1964***; candidate for Republican nomination to U.S. House (IN), 1962. BUS. & PROF.: founder, operator, City Market Shopping and Delivery Service, Indianapolis, 1921–28; publisher, *Indianapolis Tribune;* atty.; admitted to IN Bar, 1931; admitted to practice before the bar of the Supreme Court of the U.S., 1943; law practice, Indianapolis, IN, 1933–65; gen. counsel, George P. Stewart Publishing Co., Indianpolis, IN, 1947–65. MEM.: Yankee Doodle Civic Foundation, Inc. (pres., 1949–61); NAACP (legal redress chm., Indianapolis); Northwest Indianapolis Civic League; Third Ward Civic League; Indianapolis Church Federation (finance committee); Marion Cty. Tuberculosis Assn. (speakers' bureau); Hoosier Republican League, Inc.; Marion Cty. Republican League; Citizens War Bond Cmte. (exec. sec., WWI); National Bar Assn.; Marion Cty. Bar Assn.; Federation of Associated Clubs (legislative committee); Thursday Coterie Club; Elks; Indianapolis Camp of American Woodmen; Crispus Attucks Scholarship Fund; Grace Matthews Scholarship Fund; Indianapolis Recorder Charities, Inc. WRITINGS: *The Negro Lawyer and the War* (1943). AWARDS: Richard Allen Award, A.M.E. Church, 1954; Humanitarian Award, Alpha Chi Pi Omega, 1955; Civic Award, 1960; Human Rights Award, Bethel Men's Club, 1958. REL.: A.M.E. Church. RES.: Indianapolis, IN.

BECTOR, MARTIN REUBEN. POLIT. & GOV.: ***Artisian Party candidate for presidency of the U.S., 1988***. MAILING ADDRESS: 2321 Santa Rita, Las Vegas, NV 89104.

BEDELL, EDWARD JOHN. b. Sep 8, 1894, Jackson Cty., IN; par. Isaiah and Cynthia Ann (Smith) Bedell; m. Edna Hazel Laughlin, Jan 13, 1932. EDUC.: 11th grade, public high school; correspondence courses. POLIT. & GOV.: cty. chm., IN Greenback Party; IN State chm., Greenback Party; national treas., national chm., Greenback Party; ***Greenback Party candidate for vice presidency of the U.S., 1952***. BUS. & PROF.: contractor; builder and designer, 1924–; author; songwriter. MIL.: corp., U.S.C.G. Artillery Corps, WWI; security guard, WWII. MEM.: Lions Club. WRITINGS: *The Girl of the Pines; Dream Gold*; "The G.I.'s Dream Girl" (song); "Now You Want to Say Goodbye" (song). REL.: Bapt. RES.: Englewood, FL 33533.

BEECKMAN, ROBERT LIVINGSTON. b. Apr 15, 1866, New York, NY; d. Jan 21, 1935, Santa Barbara, CA; par. Gilbert Livingston and Margaret Atherton (Foster) Beeckman; m. Eleanor Thomas, Oct 8, 1902; m. 2d, Edna Marston Burke, Sep 1, 1923; c. none. EDUC.: public and private schools. POLIT. & GOV.: elected as a Republican to RI State House, 1909–11; elected as a Republican to RI State Senate, 1913–15; elected as a Republican to gov. of RI, 1915–21; delegate, Rep. Nat'l. Conv., 1920; ***candidate for Republican nomination to vice presidency of the U.S., 1920***; Republican candidate for U.S. Senate (RI), 1922. BUS. & PROF.: member, NY Stock Exchange, 1887–1906; partner, Lapsley, Beeckman and Co., New York, NY, 1887–1906; dir., Newport Industrial Trust Co.; dir., International Silver Co. MEM.: Knickerbocker Club; Brook Club; Metropolitan Club. REL.: Episc. RES.: Newport, RI.

BEEMONT, JACK J. H. b. 1917. POLIT. & GOV.: ***candidate for Republican nomination to presidency of the U.S., 1992***. MAILING ADDRESS: 3818 Ruby Ave., Kansas City, KS 66106.

BEGIN, LESTER DALE. EDUC.: grad., Stanford U. POLIT. & GOV.: ***independent candidate for presidency of the U.S., 1992***. BUS. & PROF.: engineer; designer; inventor. MEM.: Taxpayers of America. MISC.: invented laptop computer, flat television screen, blood purification laster extractor. MAILING ADDRESS: 5324 West Bradbury Rd., Turlock, CA 95380.

BEHRMAN, MARTIN. b. Oct 14, 1864, New York, NY; d. Jan 12, 1926, New Orleans, LA; par. Henry and Frederica Behrman; m. Julia Collins, 1887; c. Isabella; Nellie (Mrs. Nat W. Bond); Stanley; eight others. EDUC.: German-American School; St. Philip's Public School. POLIT. & GOV.: elected assessor, New Orleans, LA, 1888; elected member, New Orleans School Board, 1892–1906; clerk, City Council, New Orleans, LA, 1892–96; appointed pres., LA State Board of Assessors; delegate, LA State Constitutional Convention, 1898, 1921; elected as a Democrat, state auditor of LA, 1904–05; elected as a Democrat, mayor of New Orleans, LA, 1905–21, 1925–26; Democratic candidate for mayor of New Orleans, LA, 1920; delegate, Dem. Nat'l.

Conv., 1924; ***candidate for Democratic nomination to presidency of the U.S., 1924***. BUS. & PROF.: solicitor, Edison Electric Co., to 1896; dir., American Bank and Trust Co. MEM.: League of American Municipalities (pres., 1917–18); Choctaw Club; French Opera Club; Lake Shore Club; Alhambra Club. REL.: R.C. RES.: New Orleans, LA.

BELL, JOHN. b. Feb 15, 1796, Nashville, TN; d. Sep 10, 1869, Stewart Cty., TN; par. Samuel and Margaret (Edmiston) Bell; m. Sally Dickinson, Dec 10, 1818; m. 2d, Jane Erwin Yeatman, 1835; c. Mary (Mrs. David Manley); John, Jr.; David Dickinson; Fanny (Mrs. Thomas Maney); Sally (Mrs. Edwin A. Keeble); Jane "Jennie" Erwin; Ann "Nannie" Lorraine. EDUC.: grad., U. of Nashville, 1814. POLIT. & GOV.: elected as a Democrat to TN State Senate, 1817–19; elected as a Democrat to U.S. House (TN), 1827–41 (Speaker, 1834); founder, Whig Party, 1834; appointed U.S. sec. of war, 1841; elected as a Whig to TN State Senate, 1847; elected as a Whig to U.S. Senate (TN), 1847–59; ***candidate for American (Know-Nothing) Party nomination to presidency of the U.S., 1856; candidate for Republican nomination to presidency of the U.S., 1860; Constitutional Union Party candidate for presidency of the U.S., 1860***. BUS. & PROF.: atty.; admitted to TN Bar, 1816; law practice, Nashville, TN, 1816–26; law practice, Franklin, TN. RES.: Nashville, TN.

BELLAMY, CAROL. b. 1942, Plainfield, NJ. EDUC.: B.A. (cum laude), Gettysburg Coll., 1963; J.D., NY U., 1963. POLIT. & GOV.: appointed asst. commissioner, Dept. of Mental Health and Mental Retardation Services, New York, NY, 1971–72; elected as a Democrat to NY State Senate, 1972; elected as a Democrat, pres., New York City Council, 1978–; dir., NY Metropolitan Transportation Authority; delegate, Dem. Nat'l. Conv., 1980; ***candidate for Democratic nomination to presidency of the U.S., 1980 (declined)***; Liberal Party candidate for mayor of New York, 1985; director, Peace Corps, 1993–. BUS. & PROF.: atty.; assoc., Cravath, Swaine and Moore (law firm), New York, 1968–71; volunteer, Peace Corps, Guatemala, 1964–65. MEM.: National League of Cities (chm., Human Development Cmte.). MAILING ADDRESS: 305 Henry St., Brooklyn, NY 11201.

BELLIZZI, ANTHONY T. b. 1955, Bridgeport, CT; married. POLIT. & GOV.: ***independent candidate for presidency of the U.S., 1992***. BUS. & PROF.: youth dir., St. Gregory's Bellerose and Our Lady of Lourdes, Queens Village, NY. MAILING ADDRESS: 90-21 Springfield Blvd., Queens Village, NY 11428.

BELLUSO, NICK M. "NICK-REAGAN." b. 1922; m. Virginia Belluso; c. eight. POLIT. & GOV.: ***independent candidate for presidency of the U.S., 1960***; Anti-Abortion candidate for Democratic nomination to U.S. House (GA), 1974; candidate for Democratic nomination to gov. of GA, 1978; Independent Republican candidate for gov. of GA, 1978; ***Independent Republican candidate for presidency of the U.S., 1980***; candidate for Republican nomination to U.S. Senate (GA), 1980; Republican candidate for GA sec. of state, 1982. BUS. & PROF.: investment counselor; owner, Nick Belluso Associates (tax service), Atlanta, GA. MISC.: organized first Presidential Kookie Candidate Convention, 1979; noted for attempting to hypnotize voters through television advertising during 1978 gubernatorial campaign. MAILING ADDRESS: 2719 Wesley Chapel Rd., Decatur, GA 30034.

BENDER, RILEY ALVIN. b. Jul 8, 1890, Crescent City, IL; d. Mar 6, 1973, Chicago, IL; par. Edward C. and Rachel Josephine (Davis) Bender; m. Margaret Grady; c. Lorraine Xavier (Mrs. Joseph T. Page). EDUC.: public schools; U. of IL. POLIT. & GOV.: Democratic candidate for IL State Senate, 1938; Democratic ward committeeman, Chicago, IL, 1940; member, IL State Democratic Central Cmte.; member, IL State Democratic Senate Cmte.; ***candidate for Republican nomination to presidency of the U.S., 1944, 1948, 1952***. BUS. & PROF.: hotel mgr.; operator, music store; prize fighter; wrestler; plumber; grass seed wholesaler; scout for Theodore Roosevelt (q.v.). MEM.: IL Soc. for the Prevention of Automobile Accidents (founder; pres.); Southtown Recreation Cmte. (chm.); West Lawn Improvement Assn. (pres.); Veteran Boxer Assn. (sec.). MISC.: self-styled "New Guard Republican"; won 1948 IL Republican presidential primary. REL.: Methodist. RES.: Chicago, IL.

BENEDICT, LORD ROBERT. POLIT. & GOV.: ***The First Party candidate for presidency of the U.S., 1980***. MAILING ADDRESS: P.O. Box 522, Dinuba, CA 93618.

BENKERT, WILLIAM RUDOLPH. b. 1852, Philadelphia, PA; d. Sep 11, 1936, Davenport, IA; par. George and Catherine Benkert; m. Catherine M. "Kitty" Robinson, Apr 9, 1882. EDUC.: Western Coll., Cedar Rapids, IA. POLIT. & GOV.: national chm., United Christian Party, 1897–36; member, IA Exec. Cmte., United Christian Party, 1898–1900; ***United Christian Party candidate for presidency of the U.S., 1900 (declined)***; presidential elector, United Christian Party, 1908. BUS. & PROF.: insurance agent; minister, Church of God; ed., *The United Christian*, Davenport, IA. REL.: Church of God. RES.: Davenport, IA.

BENNET, JAMES HENRY ARLINGTON. b. 1825, Ireland; d. after 1855. EDUC.: LL.D., A.M., M.D. POLIT. & GOV.: ***candidate for independent nomination to vice presidency of the U.S., 1844 (declined; replaced by Sidney Rigdon, q.v.)***; independent candidate for gov. of IL, 1846. BUS. & PROF.: atty.; accountant; prof., Inst. of Accountants, New York, NY; physician; proprietor, principal, Arlington House School, Long Island, NY; author. MEM.: Accountants Soc. of

PA (prof.); Accountants Soc. of NY (pres.); Medico-Chirurgical Soc. of U. of the State of NY. WRITINGS: *The American System of Practical Book-Keeping* (1820); *The Art of Swimming* (1846); *A System of Book-Keeping by Single Entry* (1846); *Hell Demolished, Heaven Gained, Science Triumphant—Moses, the Old Jew, on His Back, and the Almighty Vindicated . . .* (1855); *A New Revelation of Mankind* (1855). REL.: Church of Jesus Christ of Latter-Day Saints (nee Protestant Episcopal Church). RES.: New York, NY.

BENNET, WILLIAM STILES. b. Nov 9, 1870, Port Jervis, NY; d. Dec 1, 1962, Central Valley, NY; par. James and Alice Leonora (Stiles) Bennet; m. Gertrude Witschief, Jun 30, 1896; c. Augustus Witschief; Sarah Alice (Mrs. W. G. McKeldin); Mary Florence (Mrs. Allin Hugh Pierce); Edna Grace (Mrs. John Nuveen, Jr.). EDUC.: grad., Port Jervis Acad., 1889; LL.B., Albany Law School, 1892; LL.D., Ursinus Coll., 1910. POLIT. & GOV.: official reporter, Board of Supervisors, Orange Cty., NY, 1892–93; elected as a Republican to NY State Assembly, 1901–03; justice, Municipal Court, New York, NY, 1903; elected as a Republican to U.S. House (NY), 1905–11; appointed judge, U.S. District Court, 1906 (declined); appointed member, U.S. Immigration Comm., 1907–10; delegate, Rep. Nat'l. Conv., 1908, 1916 (parliamentarian); Republican candidate for U.S. House (NY), 1910, 1916, 1936, 1944; appointed asst. treas. of the U.S., 1911 (declined); candidate for Republican nomination to gov. of NY, 1912; appointed appraiser, Port of NY, 1912 (declined); appointed asst. atty. gen. of the U.S., 1929 (declined); ***candidate for Republican nomination to vice presidency of the U.S., 1936***; appointed member, Program Cmte., Rep. Nat'l. Conv., 1937; elected delegate, NY State Constitutional Convention, 1938; appointed member, National Comm. on Prisons and Prison Labor (pres.). BUS. & PROF.: atty.; admitted to the Bar of NY, 1892; law practice, New York, 1892–1920; vice pres., gen. counsel, Edward Hines Associated Lumber Interests, Chicago, IL, 1920–23; law practice, New York, 1933–62; lecturer, Columbia U., 1939–42; partner, Bennet, House and Courts (law firm), New York. MEM.: Masons (32°); Elks; Moose; Delta Chi; 17th International Congress Against Alcoholism (delegate, 1923); ABA; NY Bar Assn.; New York Cty. Lawyers Assn.; Empire State Soc.; SAR (pres., 1942–45; chancellor gen., 1946); National Republican Club (first vice pres., 1935); Union League (vice pres., 1940–43); NAACP (founding patron). AWARDS: Minute Man Award, SAR, 1954. REL.: Presb. RES.: New York, NY.

BENNEY, JACK. b. c. 1936, Lancaster, PA. POLIT. & GOV.: independent candidate for U.S. House (MS), 1974, 1976; ***independent candidate for presidency of the U.S., 1976***. BUS. & PROF.: pres., Pollution and Consumers Foundation; radio commentator, WJLJ, Tupelo, MS. MEM.: NAACP; Southern Media Coalition; National Black Media Coalition; National Citizens Cmte. for Broadcasting; Wilderness Soc.; National Parks and Conservation Assn.; Wildlife Federation; NRA; Fishing Club of America; AARP; National Retired Teachers Assn.; American Legion; Smithsonian Institution; National Geographic Soc.; American Chemical Soc.; Common Cause. MAILING ADDRESS: 1608 Patterson Dr., Tupelo, MS 38801.

BENNINGTON, WESLEY HENRY. b. May 15, 1861, North Robinson, OH; d. Oct 30, 1928, Cleveland, OH; par. Thomas and Harriet (Lininger) Bennington; m. Elizabeth Bear, Dec 24, 1889; c. Earl Thomas; David Era; Wesley Henry, Jr.; Paul Wayland; Fern Elizabeth (Mrs. William Jackson Sutton). EDUC.: LL.B., OH Northern U., 1886. POLIT. & GOV.: elected prosecuting atty., Shawnee Cty., KS, 1895; People's Party candidate for lt. gov. of KS, 1898; ***National Independent (Greenback) Party candidate for vice presidency of the U.S., 1928***. BUS. & PROF.: atty.; inventor; admitted to KS Bar, 1886; partner, Bennington and Clemens (law firm), Kansas City, KS; law practice, Topeka, KS; pres., Bennington Typewriter Co. MEM.: Kansas League for the Initiative and Referendum (pres., 1892). REL.: Free Thinker. MISC.: invented word-printing typewriter, dehydrator (1915), pressure cooker (1918), fruit press (1924); advocate of single tax, women's suffrage, and peace movements. RES.: Cleveland, OH.

BENNS, GEORGE WILLIAM. b. May 8, 1911, New York, NY; married; c. none. EDUC.: grad., high school. POLIT. & GOV.: candidate for Democratic nomination to U.S. House (MD), 1976, 1978, 1986, 1988, 1990; candidate for Republican nomination to U.S. House (MD), 1980, 1981; candidate for Democratic nomination to U.S. Senate (MD), 1990; ***candidate for Democratic nomination to presidency of the U.S., 1992***. BUS. & PROF.: musician; machinist; carpenter. MEM.: Carpenters' Union; AARP; Common Cause; Czecho-Slovak American Club; Machinists' Union; Union of Musicians. AWARDS: Award, United Communities Against Poverty. WRITINGS: *Primer for a Peaceful Revolution—As Guaranteed by the Constitution* (1970, 1977). REL.: R.C. MAILING ADDRESS: 8715 Leonard Dr., Silver Spring, MD 20910.

BENO, JOHN RICHARDSON. b. Nov 13, 1931, Council Bluffs, IA; par. George Schendele and Fern (Richardson) Beno; single. EDUC.: State U. of IA, 1950–51; B.A., Loras Coll., 1955; St. Thomas Seminary, 1955–59; Creighton U.; M.R.E., Loyola U., 1970. POLIT. & GOV.: chm., Tri-County War on Poverty, La Junta, CO, 1965–66; member, Board of Directors, CO Migrant Council, 1965–66; ***candidate for Democratic nomination to presidency of the U.S., 1972***; chm., Pueblo Cty. (CO) Democratic Central Cmte., 1975–78; elected as a Democrat to CO State Senate, 1979–. BUS. & PROF.: priest; assoc. pastor, Diocese of Pueblo, CO, 1959–66; dir., religious education/liturgy, Diocese of Pueblo, 1966–70; exec. dir., Federation of Diocesan Liturgical Commissions, 1970–73; dir., Ministry of Christian Service, Mission Office and Priests' Council, Diocese of Pueblo, 1973–. MEM.: Chicano Democratic Caucus; Women's Career Development Center (dir.); A.C.L.U.;

League of Women Voters; Pueblo C. of C.; Common Cause. REL.: R.C. MAILING ADDRESS: 2701 East 12th St., Pueblo, CO 81001.

BENOIT, GARY EDWARD. b. Jul 28, 1953, Northampton, MA; par. Richard Austin and Catherine J. (Keiran) Benoit; m. Laura Ann Jones, 1978; c. Joseph Edward; Margaret Mary. EDUC.: B.S. (magna cum laude), U. of Lowell, 1976. POLIT. & GOV.: delegate, Dem. Nat'l. Conv., 1976, 1980; ***candidate for Democratic nomination to vice presidency of the U.S., 1976***. BUS. & PROF.: temporary technical aide, Wiscasset Atomic Power Plant, 1975; eastern mgr., American Opinion Speakers' Bureau, Belmont, MA, 1977–82; national dir., Tax Reform Immediately, 1982–. MEM.: Sigma Pi Sigma; John Birch Soc. (chapter leader); Tax Reform Immediately. REL.: R.C. MAILING ADDRESS: 161 South St., Northampton, MA 01060.

BENOIT, JOSAPHET T. b. Mar 3, 1900, St. Madeline, Quebec, Canada; d. May 9, 1976, Manchester, NH; par. Ulric and Olevine Benoit; m. Germaine Mathieu, 1943; c. Jean; Francoise (Mrs. Joseph Lozier). EDUC.: B.A., U. of Montreal, 1921, Ph.D., 1927; Litt.D.; Ph.D., Sorbonne U., 1935. POLIT. & GOV.: chm., NH State Democratic Central Cmte., 1944–45; delegate, Dem. Nat'l. Conv., 1944; presidential elector, Democratic Party, 1944; elected as a Democrat (non-partisan), mayor of Manchester, NH, 1944–62; chm., Manchester School Board, 1944–c. 1955; Democratic candidate for U.S. House (NH), 1946; ***candidate for Democratic nomination to presidency of the U.S., 1952***; keynoter, NH State Democratic Convention, 1958; appointed NH state dir., Small Business Administration, 1962–73. BUS. & PROF.: author; ed., French language newspaper, Fitchburg, MA; ed., French language newspaper, Pawtucket, RI; ed., French language newspaper, Woonsocket, RI; asst. sec., Fraternal Soc., Woonsocket, RI, 1935–37; ed., French language newspaper, Sudbury, Canada; editor-in-chief, *L'Avenir National*, Manchester, 1937–43. MIL.: C.O.T.C. training, 1914–18. MEM.: Knights of Columbus; Societe des Gens de Lettres (assoc., 1935); French Acad. (officer, 1937); Knights of St. Gregory. AWARDS: Richelius Medal, French Acad., 1936; Grand Medal, Diploma, L'Alliance Francaise, 1945; Brotherhood Award, National Conference of Christians and Jews, 1962; Manchester Citizen of the Year, 1962. WRITINGS: *Rois ou Esclaves* (1931); *L'Ame Franco-Americaine* (1935); *Catechisme d'Histoire Franco-Americaine* (1940). HON. DEG.: LL.D., St. Anselms Coll. REL.: R.C. RES.: Manchester, NH.

BENSON, ALLAN LOUIS. b. Nov 6, 1871, Plainwell, MI; d. Aug 19, 1940, Yonkers, NY; par. Adelbert L. and Rose (Morris) Benson; m. Mary Hugh, Nov 19, 1899; c. Mary (Mrs. Charles Lloyd Jackson); Welton Harris; Allan Louis, Jr.; James Adelbert. EDUC.: public schools. POLIT. & GOV.: Socialist Party candidate for U.S. House (NY), 1912, 1914; ***Socialist Party candidate for presidency of the U.S., 1916***; resigned from Socialist Party over war issue, 1918. BUS. & PROF.: author; reporter, 1890–97; asst. managing ed., *Detroit (MI) Journal*, 1897–1901; managing ed., *Detroit Times*, 1901–06; managing ed., *Washington (DC) Times*, 1906–07; writer, *Pearson's Magazine*, 1908–16; editorialist, *Appeal to Reason*, 1914–16; founder, *Reconstruction Magazine*, 1918–20; ed., *The Gold Book Magazine*, 1919–20. MEM.: National Arts Club. WRITINGS: *Socialism Made Plain* (1904); *Confessions of Capitalism* (1904); *What Help Can Any Workingman Expect from Taft or Bryan?* (1908); *The Usurped Power of the Courts* (1911); *The Growing Grocery Bill* (1912); *The Truth About Socialism* (1913); *Our Dishonest Constitution* (1914); *The Bombshell That Henry Ford Fired* (1914); *Socialism: The Lone Foe of War* (1914); *If Not Socialism—What?* (1914); *A Way to Prevent War* (1915); *Inviting War to America* (1916); *The New Henry Ford* (1923); *The Story of Geology* (1927); *Daniel Webster: A Biography* (1929). REL.: agnostic. RES.: Yonkers, NY.

BENSON, EZRA TAFT. b. Aug 4, 1899, Whitney, ID; d. May 30, 1994, Salt Lake City, UT; par. George Taft and Sarah S. (Dunkley) Benson; m. Flora Smith Amussen, Sep 10, 1926; c. Reed; Mark; Barbara; Beverly; Bonnie; Flora Beth. EDUC.: Oneida Stake Acad., Preston, ID; UT State Agricultural Coll., 1918–21; B.S., Brigham Young U., 1926, M.S.; ID State Coll., 1927; U. of CA, 1937–38. POLIT. & GOV.: appointed U.S. sec. of agriculture, 1953–61; ***1976 Cmte. candidate for presidency of the U.S., 1968; candidate for American Independent Party nomination to vice presidency of the U.S., 1968; candidate for American Party nomination to presidency of the U.S., 1976***. BUS. & PROF.: missionary, Church of Jesus Christ of Latter-Day Saints, Great Britain and Europe, 1921–23; apostle, Quorum of Twelve, 1943–85, prophet, 1985–94; farm operator, 1923–30; cty. agricultural agent, U. of ID Extension Service, 1929–30, extension economist and marketing specialist, 1930–38; organizer, sec., ID Cooperative Council, 1933–38; exec. sec., National Council of Farmer Cooperatives, 1939–41; dir., Olson Brothers, Inc.; author. MEM.: American Inst. of Cooperatives (vice chm., 1942–49; chm., 1952); Farm Foundation (dir., 1946–50); National Agricultural Advisory Cmte. (WWII); National Farm Credit Comm., 1940–43; First International Conference on Farm Organizations (U.S. delegate, 1946); American Marketing Assn.; Farm Economics Assn.; Delta Nu; Alpha Zeta; BSA (national exec. board, 1948–66); Brigham Young U. (trustee). AWARDS: Silver Antelope Award, BSA, 1951, Silver Buffalo Award, 1954; Gamma Sigma Delta Scholarship; U. of CA Fellowship; Distinguished Service Award, U. of WI, 1952. HON. DEG.: H.H.D., Coll. of Osteopathic Physicians and Surgeons, 1951; LL.D., U. of UT, 1953; D.Agr., ID State Coll., 1953; D.Agr., MI State U., 1955; D.Pub.Service, Brigham Young U., 1955; LL.D., Bowdoin Coll., 1955; LL.D., U. of ME, 1956; D.Sc., Rutgers U., 1955. WRITINGS: *Farmers at the Crossroads; The Red Carpet; Title of Liberty; So Shall Ye Reap; The American Heritage of Freedom—A Plan of God* (series); *Stand Up for Freedom; The Threat to Our Freedom; The Internal Threat to the American*

Way of Life; Conspiracy + Complacency = Disaster; New Horizons in Farming; The Threat of Communism; Cross Fire. REL.: Church of Jesus Christ of Latter-Day Saints (prophet, 1985–94). RES.: Salt Lake City, UT.

BENSON, LUCY PETERS WILSON. b. Aug 25, 1927, New York, NY; par. Willard Oliver and Helen (Peters) Wilson; m. Bruce Buzzell Benson, Mar 30, 1950; c. none. EDUC.: B.A., Smith Coll., 1949, M.A., 1955. POLIT. & GOV.: appointed member, Governor's Special Comm. to Revise Sunday Closing Laws (MA), 1961; appointed member, Special Legislative Comm. to Study Budgetary Powers of Trustees of the U. of MA, 1961–62; appointed member, Governor's Comm. to Revise State Salaries (MA), 1963; appointed member, MA Advisory Board on Higher Educational Policy, 1962–65; appointed member, MA Educational Advisory Comm. on Racial Imbalance and Education, 1964–65; appointed member, MA Advisory Comm., U.S. Comm. on Civil Rights, 1964–73; appointed vice chm., MA Advisory Council on Education, 1965–68; appointed member, MA Comm. on Children and Youth, 1967; appointed member, Public Advisory Cmte. on U.S. Trade Policy, 1968; appointed sec. of human services, MA State Dept. of Human Services, 1975–77; ***League of Women Voters draft choice for candidate for presidency of the U.S., 1976 (declined)***; appointed member, Special Comm. on Administrative Revision, U.S. House, 1976–77; appointed undersec. of state for security assistance, science and technology, U.S. Dept. of State, 1977–81. BUS. & PROF.: pres., Benson and Associates, Arlington, VA, 1977–80; trustee, Northeast Utilities; dir., Continental Can Co.; dir., Continental Group, Inc.; dir., Dreyfus Fund, Inc.; dir., Dreyfus Liquid Asset, Inc.; dir., Dreyfus Special Income Fund, Inc.; dir., Federal Dept. Stores; dir., Mitre Corp.; dir., Grumman Corp.; dir., Science Applications Inc. MEM.: League of Women Voters (pres., Amherst, MA, 1957–61; dir., MA, 1957–61; MA state pres., 1961–65; member, National Board of Directors, 1965–66; second vice pres., 1966–68; national pres., 1968–74); Dreyfus Third Century Fund (dir.); Urban Coalition (steering committee, 1968; exec. cmte., 1970–75, 1980–; co-chm., 1973–75); Common Cause (exec. committee, 1970–75); Amherst Town Meeting, 1957–; Educational Development Center (trustee, 1967–72); National Urban League (trustee); A.C. L.U.; United Nations Assn.; NAACP; Amherst Human Relations Council; Assn. of American Indian Affairs; East African Wildlife Soc.; Boston Human Rights Council; Wildlife Preservation Trust for Channel Islands; Women's Equity Action League; John F. Kennedy School of Government, Harvard U. (member, Board of Visitors); National Acad. for Public Administration; Council on Foreign Relations; National News Council (chairperson); Alfred P. Sloan Foundation (trustee, 1975–77); Smith Coll. (trustee, 1975–80); Brookings Institution (trustee, 1974–77); Trilateral Comm. AWARDS: Achievement Award, Bureau of Government Research, U. of MA, 1963; Distinguished Service Award, Boston Coll., 1965; Distinguished Civic Leadership Award, Tufts U., 1965; Radcliffe Fellow, Radcliffe Inst., 1965–67; Smith College Medal, 1969; Distinguished Service Award, Northfield Mt. Hermon School, 1976; Medallion, American Defense Preparedness Assn., 1980. HON. DEG.: L.H.D., Wheaton Coll., 1965; LL.D., U. of MA, 1969; LL.D., U. of MD, 1972; H.H.D., Bucknell U., 1972; L.H.D., Carleton Coll., 1973; LL.D., Amherst Coll., 1974; LL.D., Clark U., 1975; H.H.D., Springfield Coll., 1981; H.H.D., Bates Coll., 1982. WRITINGS: *Turning the Supertanker* (1979); *World Trade and Investment Freedom.* MAILING ADDRESS: 46 Sunset Ave., Amherst, MA 01002.

BENTLEY, CHARLES EUGENE. b. Apr 30, 1841, Warner, NY; d. Feb 4, 1905, Los Angeles, CA; m. Persis Freeman, Oct 7, 1863; c. Isaac Madison; Lucy; two other daughters; two other sons. EDUC.: Monroe Inst.; Oneida Conference Seminary, Oneida, NY. POLIT. & GOV.: chm., NE Prohibition Party State Convention, 1884; Prohibition Party candidate for NE State House, 1884; Prohibition Party candidate for U.S. House (NE), 1886; state chm., NE Prohibition Party, 1890–94; Prohibition Party candidate for gov. of NE, 1892; member, Prohibition Party National Cmte., 1892–96; Prohibition Party candidate for U.S. Senate (NE), 1894; ***National (Liberty; Free Silver Prohibition) Party candidate for presidency of the U.S., 1896***; chm., NE Liberty Party. BUS. & PROF.: farmer; ordained minister, Baptist Church, 1880–1905; pastor, Bethesda Baptist Church, Surprise, NE, 1880–1905. REL.: Baptist. MISC.: died in Los Angeles hotel under "mysterious" circumstances. RES.: Surprise, NE.

BENTLEY, THOMAS. POLIT. & GOV.: ***independent candidate for presidency of the U.S., 1980, 1984***. MEM.: American Freedom League. MAILING ADDRESS: Free Lance Ltd., 90 Park St., Arcade, NY 14009.

BENTON, SHIRLEY ROENA. POLIT. & GOV.: ***candidate for Republican nomination to presidency of the U.S., 1984***. MAILING ADDRESS: 770 Fulton St., Brooklyn, NY 11238.

BENTON, THOMAS HART. b. Mar 14, 1782, Hillsboro, NC; d. Apr 10, 1858, Washington, DC; par. Jesse and Ann (Gooch) Benton; m. Elizabeth McDowell, 1821; c. Elizabeth (Mrs. William Carey Jones); Jessie Ann (Mrs. John C. Fremont); Sarah (Mrs. Richard Taylor Jacob); Susan (Mrs. Gauldree de Boileau); James McDowell; John Randolph; McDowell. EDUC.: Chapel Hill Coll.; Coll. of William and Mary. POLIT. & GOV.: elected as a Democrat to TN State Senate, 1809–11; candidate for trustee, St. Louis, MO, 1819; elected trustee, St. Louis, MO, 1820; elected as a Democrat to U.S. Senate (MO), 1821–51; ***candidate for Democratic nomination to presidency of the U.S., 1836 (declined)***; Democratic candidate for U.S. Senate (MO), 1850; elected as a Democrat to U.S. House (MO), 1853–55; Democratic candidate for gov. of MO, 1856. BUS. & PROF.: atty.; admitted to Nashville (TN) Bar, 1806; law practice, Franklin, TN, 1806; ed., *Missouri Enquirer,* St. Louis, MO,

1818–20. MIL.: col., TN Volunteers, 1812–13; lt. col., 39th U.S. Infantry, 1813–15. MEM.: American Acad. of Languages and Belles Letters. WRITINGS: *Thirty Years View* (1854–56); *An Examination of the Dred Scott Case; History of the Workings of Congress, 1820–50; Abridgement of the Debates of Congress, 1789-1856.* REL.: Methodist. RES.: St. Louis, MO.

BENTSEN, LLOYD MILLARD, JR. b. Feb 11, 1921, Mission, TX; par. Lloyd Millard and Edna Ruth (Colbath) Bentsen; m. Beryl Ann Longino, Nov 27, 1943; c. Lloyd Millard III; Lan Chase; Tina Ann (Mrs. Eric Maedgen). EDUC.: LL.B., U. of TX, 1942. POLIT. & GOV.: elected as a Democrat, cty. judge, Hidalgo Cty., TX, 1946–48; elected as a Democrat to U.S. House (TX), 1948–55; delegate, Dem. Nat'l. Conv., 1956, 1980; elected as a Democrat to U.S. Senate (TX), 1971–93; ***candidate for Democratic nomination to presidency of the U.S., 1976, 1988, 1992; candidate for Democratic nomination to vice presidency of the U.S., 1984; Democratic candidate for vice presidency of the U.S., 1988***; appointed U.S. sec. of the treasury, 1993–94. BUS. & PROF.: atty.; admitted to TX Bar, 1942; law practice, McAllen, TX, 1945–48; founder, Consolidated American Life Insurance Co.; pres., Lincoln Consolidated Life Insurance Co., Houston, TX, 1955–70; dir., Lockheed Aircraft Corp.; dir., Continental Oil Co.; dir., Panhandle Eastern Pipeline; dir., Trunkline Gas; dir., Bank of the Southwest. MIL.: pvt., maj., U.S.A.A.F., 1942–45; Distinguished Flying Cross; Air Medal with Three Oak Clusters. MEM.: Sigma Nu; U.S. Air Force Reserves (col.); TX Bar Assn.; Texas Presbyterian Foundation (trustee); United Fund (dir.); Houston Soc. for the Performing Arts (dir.); Houston C. of C. (dir.); BSA (member, Sam Houston Council); U. of TX Development Board. REL.: Presb. MAILING ADDRESS: 711 Polk St., Houston, TX 77002.

BERGER, META SCHLICHTING. b. Feb 23, 1873, Milwaukee, WI; d. Jun 16, 1944, Thiensville, WI; par. Bernard and Matilda (Kraik) Schlichting; m. Victor L. Berger, Dec 4, 1897; c. Dorothea "Doris" A. Welles (Hursley); Dr. Elisa R. Edelman. EDUC.: Milwaukee (WI) Normal School. POLIT. & GOV.: elected as a Socialist (Non-Partisan) to Milwaukee (WI) Board of Education, 1909–39; sec., Congressional Women's Cmte., Washington, DC, 1911–12; member, Women's Cmte., Socialist Party, 1913; member, WI State Board of Education, 1917–19; regent, Milwaukee (WI) Normal School, 1927–28; member, Board of Regents, U. of WI, 1928– 34; ***candidate for Socialist Party nomination to vice presidency of the U.S., 1928 (declined), 1932 (declined)***; member, exec. cmte., Socialist Party, 1929–36; ***candidate for Socialist Party nomination to presidency of the U.S., 1932 (declined)***; left Socialist Party, 1936. BUS. & PROF.: teacher, Milwaukee, WI, to 1897. MEM.: Women's International League for Peace and Freedom (national publicity chm.); Berger National Foundation; Milwaukee Maternity Hospital and Free Dispensary Assn. (dir.); WI Women Suffrage Assn.; Woman's School Alliance. RES.: Thiensville, WI.

BERGLAND, DAVID PETER. b. Jun 5, 1935, Mapleton, IA; par. Cedores P. and Gwendolyn (McCalman) Bergland; m. Carol Diane Gilbert, Nov 1957; m. 2d, Nicole Dionne Jones Norman, Feb 1975; c. Jona Joy; Brenda; Tani. EDUC.: grad., high school, Long Beach, CA, 1952; Long Beach (CA) City Coll., 1955–57; B.A., U. of CA at Los Angeles, 1966; LL.B., U. of Southern CA, 1969. POLIT. & GOV.: regional treas., Libertarian Party, 1973; elected regional chm., Libertarian Party, 1974; Libertarian Party candidate for atty. gen. of CA, 1974; ***Libertarian Party candidate for vice presidency of the U.S., 1976***; national chm., Libertarian Party, 1978; Libertarian Party candidate for U.S. Senate (CA), 1980; ***Libertarian Party candidate for presidency of the U.S., 1984***. BUS. & PROF.: ed., *Southern California Law Review*; atty.; admitted to CA Bar, 1969; staff atty., O'Melveny and Myers (law firm), Los Angeles, CA, 1969–72; prof., Western State U. Coll. of Law, 1970–; assoc., Rutan and Tucker (law firm), Santa Ana, CA, 1972–74; partner, Bergland, Martin and McLaughlin (law firm), Newport Beach, CA, 1974–; contributor, *Western State Law Review*; contributor, *Reason*. MIL.: U.S. Army, 1953–55. MEM.: Order of the Coif. MAILING ADDRESS: Bergland, Martin and McLaughlin, Suite 300, 369 San Miguel Dr., Newport Beach, CA 92660.

BERGLAND, ROBERT SELMER "BOB." b. Jul 22, 1928, Roseau, MN; par. Selmer Bennett and Mabel (Evans) Bergland; m. Helen Elaine Grahn, Jun 24, 1950; c. Dianne; Linda; Stevan; Jon; Allan; Billy; Franklyn. EDUC.: U. of MN, 2 years. POLIT. & GOV.: sec., Roseau Cty. (MN) Democratic-Farmer-Labor Party Central Cmte., 1951–52, chm., 1953–54; appointed chm., MN State Agricultural Stabilization and Conservation Service Cmte., U.S. Dept. of Agriculture, 1961–62; appointed dir., Midwest Agricultural Stabilization and Conservation Service, 1963–68; Democratic-Farmer-Labor Party candidate for U.S. House (MN), 1968; elected as a Democratic-Farmer-Laborite to U.S. House (MN), 1971–77; ***candidate for Democratic nomination to vice presidency of the U.S., 1972***; appointed U.S. sec. of agriculture, 1977–81. BUS. & PROF.: field representative, MN Farmers Union, 1948–50; farmer, Roseau, MN, 1950–; pres., Farmland-Eaton World Trade, Arlington, TX, 1981–. MEM.: Masons; Lions; Eagles; Sons of Norway; MN Farmers Union; National Farmers Organization; U. of MN (Gold Letter Award; Sears-Roebuck Scholarship). REL.: Lutheran. MAILING ADDRESS: Route 3, Roseau, MN 56751.

BERGONZI, EDWARD. POLIT. & GOV.: ***Workers' League candidate for vice presidency of the U.S., 1984***. MAILING ADDRESS: MN.

BERISH, GEORGE L. POLIT. & GOV.: ***American Political Party candidate for presidency of the U.S., 1992***. MAILING ADDRESS: 60 North Beretania St., #3502, Honolulu, HI 96817.

BERMAN, ARTHUR JAY. POLIT. & GOV.: ***independent candidate for presidency of the U.S., 1984***. MAILING ADDRESS: 37 Glenwood Rd., West Hartford, CT 06107.

BERRIGAN, DANIEL J. b. May 9, 1921, Virginia, MN; par. Thomas William and Freda (Fromhart) Berrigan; single. EDUC.: B.A., St. Andrew-on-Hudson Coll., 1946; M.A., Woodstock Coll., 1952; West Coll.; Th.L., Gregorian U. of Rome. POLIT. & GOV.: ***candidate for Democratic nomination to vice presidency of the U.S., 1972***. BUS. & PROF.: joined Soc. of Jesus, 1939; ordained priest, Roman Catholic Church, 1952; teacher, St. Peter's Preparatory School, Jersey City, NJ, 1945–49; ministerial work, Europe, 1953–54; teacher of French and philosophy, Brooklyn Preparatory School, 1954–57; prof., LeMoyne Coll., 1957–63; on sabbatical in Europe, 1962–63; ed., *Jesuit Missions*, New York, NY, 1963–65; Office of Economic Opportunity, 1967; dir., United Religious Work, Cornell U., 1966–69; prof. of theology, Woodstock Coll., 1972–; visiting lecturer, U. of Manitoba, 1973; author; poet; lecturer. MIL.: auxiliary military chaplain, U.S. Army, 1954. MEM.: Walter Farrell Guild (religious dir., 1954–57); Catholic Peace Fellowship (founder). AWARDS: Lamont Poetry Award, 1957; Frederick G. Melcher Book Award, Unitarian-Universalist Assn., 1970; National Book Award nomination, 1957, 1970; Thomas More Award, 1971. WRITINGS: *Time Without Number* (1957); *The Bridge; Essays in the Church* (1959); *Encounters* (1960); *The Bow in the Clouds: Man's Covenant with God* (1961); *World for Wedding Ring* (1962); *No One Walks Waters* (1966); *False Gods, Real Men* (1966); *They Call Us Dead Men: Reflections on Life and Conscience* (1966); *Consequences: Truth and 1967* (1967); *Go From Here: A Prison Journal; Love, Love at the End* (1968); *Night Flight to Hanoi* (1968); *The Trial of the Catonsville Nine* (1970); *Trial Poems* (with Thomas Lewis, 1970); *No Bars to Manhood* (1970); *Dark Night of Resistance* (1971); *America is Hard to Find* (1972); *Encounters: Poetry; Absurd Convictions, Modest Hopes* (with Lee Lockwood, 1972); *Geography of Faith* (with Robert Coles); *Conversations after Prison* (1972); *Jesus Christ* (1973); *Prison Poems* (1973); *Selected and New Poems; Lights on in the House of the Dead* (1974); *The Raft is Not the Shore* (with Thich Nhat-Hahn, 1975); *A Book of Parables* (1977); *The Uncommon Book of Prayer* (1977); *A Book of Psalms; Beside the Sea of Glass; The Song of the Lamb; The Words Our Savior Taught Us; Portraits; Of Those I Love; The Prayer of the Lamb* (1977); *The Discipline of the Mountain* (1979); *We Die Before We Live; Conversations with the Very Ill* (1980); *Ten Commandments for the Long Haul* (1981); *The Nightmare of God; Steadfastness of the Saints; The Mission; May All Creatures Live; Block Island; To Dwell in Peace: An Autobiography* (1986). REL.: R.C. MISC.: active in anti-Vietnam War movement; convicted in case of conspiracy and destruction of draft files, Catonsville, MD, 1968; paroled, 1972; brother of Philip Francis Berrigan (q.v.). MAILING ADDRESS: 99 Claremont Ave., New York, NY 10027.

BERRIGAN, PHILIP FRANCIS. b. Oct 5, 1923, Two Harbors, MN; par. Thomas William and Freda (Fromhart) Berrigan; m. Elizabeth McAllister, 1969; c. Frida; one other. EDUC.: A.B., Holy Cross Coll., 1950; B.S., Loyola U. of the South, 1959; M.A., Xavier U., 1961. POLIT. & GOV.: ***candidate for Democratic nomination to vice presidency of the U.S., 1972***. BUS. & PROF.: ordained priest, Roman Catholic Church, 1950; asst. pastor, Archdiocese of Washington, DC, 1955–56; prof. of English, student counselor, St. Augustine H.S., New Orleans, LA, 1956–63; dir. of promotion, St. Joseph's Soc. of the Sacred Heart, New York, NY, 1963–64; instructor in English, Epiphany Coll., 1964; asst. pastor, St. Peter Claver Church, Baltimore, MD; lecturer on race, peace, and poverty; author. MIL.: 2d lt., U.S. Army, 1943–46. MEM.: Southern Christian Leadership Conference; NAACP; Congress on Racial Equality; Student Non-Violent Coordinating Cmte.; Fellowship of Reconciliation; Catholic Peace Fellowship (co-chm.); Baltimore Interfaith Peace Mission. WRITINGS: *No More Strangers* (1965); *Punishment for Peace* (1969); *Prison Journals of a Priest Revolutionary* (1970); *Widen on the Prison Gates* (1974); *Of Beasts and Beastly Images* (1979). REL.: R.C. MISC.: active in anti-Vietnam War movement; convicted in two cases of destruction of draft files; acquitted of conspiracy charges. MAILING ADDRESS: 1933 Park Ave., Baltimore, MD 21217.

BERRY, GALE BERNELL, SR. c. Gale Bernell, Jr. POLIT. & GOV.: ***candidate for Democratic nomination to presidency of the U.S., 1988***. MAILING ADDRESS: Concord, CA.

BERRY, GEORGE LEONARD. b. Sep 12, 1882, Lee Valley, TN; d. Dec 4, 1948, Pressman's Home, TN; par. Thomas Jefferson and Cornelia (Trent) Berry; m. Marie Margaret Cehres, Aug 7, 1907; c. none. EDUC.: self-taught. POLIT. & GOV.: candidate for Democratic nomination to gov. of TN, 1914, 1936 (declined), 1938 (declined); candidate for Democratic nomination to U.S. Senate (TN), 1916, 1938; labor adviser, American Comm. to Negotiate Peace, 1919; alternate delegate, Dem. Nat'l. Conv., 1920; ***candidate for Democratic nomination to presidency of the U.S., 1924; candidate for Democratic nomination to vice presidency of the U.S., 1924, 1928***; chm., Labor Division, Democratic National Campaign, 1928; appointed member, Labor Advisory Board, Cotton Textile Industry, National Recovery Administration; appointed member, Mediation Board, Steel and Coal Industries, National Labor Board, National Recovery Administration, 1933; appointed divisional administrator, National Recovery Administration; appointed coordinator for industrial cooperation, 1935–37; appointed as a Democrat to U.S. Senate (TN), 1937–38. BUS. & PROF.: union official; employee, *Jackson (MS) Evening News*, 1891; employee, various printing plants in St. Louis, MO, Omaha, NE, Denver, CO, and San Francisco, CA, 1891–1907; farmer; banker. MIL.: pvt., U.S. Army, 1898; maj., U.S. Army, 1918–19; citations from Maj. Gen. Black, Army Corps of Engineers, and President Woodrow Wilson (q.v.); Legion of Honor; Victory Medal. MEM.: Allied Printing Trades Council (sec.,

1905); Labor Council (sec., 1906); International Pressmen and Assistants' Union of North America (pres., 1907–48); AFL (vice pres.); International Allied Printing Trades Assn. (pres.); British Trade Union Congress (AFL delegate, 1912); International Economic Congress (delegate, 1912); International Printers' Congress (delegate, 1912); National Soc. of Operative Printers and Assistants of England (hon. member); American Soc. of Military Engineers; American Legion (founder; national vice commander); Printing Machine Managers Soc. of Great Britain (hon. member); Masons (32°; Knights Templar; Shriners); St. Bride's Masonic Lodge of England (hon. member); Printing Trades Council Masonic Assn.; Elks; Moose; Eagles; NY Club; Labor's Non-Partisan League (founder, 1936); Odd Fellows; Rotary International; Press Club of Seattle; Oldtime Baseball Players Assn.; National Geographic Soc.; Lambs Club. WRITINGS: *Labor Conditions Abroad* (1912); various pamphlets. REL.: Bapt. MISC.: convicted of income tax evasion, 1948. RES.: Pressmen's Home, TN.

BERRY, MICHAEL T. POLIT. & GOV.: sec., Socialist Labor Party, Haverhill, MA; sec., MA State Socialist Labor Party General Cmte., 1904; Socialist Labor Party candidate for gov. of MA, 1900, 1902, 1904; delegate, Socialist Labor Party National Convention, 1904; ***candidate for Socialist Labor Party nomination to presidency of the U.S., 1904***. BUS. & PROF.: Shoemaker. RES.: Haverhill, MA.

BERRY, WILLIAM HARVEY. b. Sep 9, 1852, Edwardsville, IL; d. Jun 19, 1928, Chester, PA; par. Benjamin D. and Mary F. Berry; m. Sue Schofield, Oct 1, 1879. EDUC.: Mechanic's Inst., Buffalo, NY. POLIT. & GOV.: elected as a Democrat, mayor of Chester, Pennsylvania, 1905–06; elected as a Democrat, state treas. of Pennsylvania, 1907–09; ***candidate for Democratic nomination to vice presidency of the U.S., 1908***; candidate for Democratic nomination to gov. of PA, 1910; Keystone Party candidate for gov. of PA, 1910; Democratic candidate for state treas. of PA, 1912; delegate, Dem. Nat'l. Conv., 1920; Democratic candidate for mayor of Chester, PA, 1923. BUS. & PROF.: inventor; consulting engineer; pres., Berry Engineering Co.; author; minister. WRITINGS: *Supply and Demand the Only Source of Value* (1898); *Restricted Industry* (1900); *Address on the Occasion of a Complimentary Banquet* (1908); *Our Economic Troubles and the Way Out* (1912); *De Leon-Berry Debate* (1915); *Preparedness for Peace* (1916). REL.: Methodist. MISC.: invented high pressure, superheating boiler. RES.: Chester, PA.

BERTASAVAGE, NORMAN WALTER. b. Nov 14, 1937, Branch Township, PA; par. Anthony H. and Juel (Dronick) Bertasavage; m. Noreen Delong; c. June; Jeffrey; Jon. EDUC.: grad., Minersville (PA) H.S., 1954; Bloomsburg (PA) U., 1977–78. POLIT. & GOV.: member, Republican Cty. Central Cmte., PA, 1977–; candidate for Republican nomination to U.S. House (PA), 1978, 1986; candidate for Republican nomination to U.S. Senate (PA), 1980; chm., EDCNP Recycling Advisory Cmte., 1985–89; ***candidate for Republican nomination to presidency of the U.S., 1992***; cty. chm., Solid Waste Advisory Cmte. BUS. & PROF.: self-employed salesman. MIL.: master sgt., U.S. Air Force, 1954–74. REL.: R.C. MAILING ADDRESS: RD #4, Box 4104, Branch Township, Pottsville, PA 17901.

BERTRAND, LEWIS (nee ISIDORE LOUIS BIERMAN). b. May 27, 1896, New York, NY; d. Sep 29, 1974, Paris, France; par. Adolph and Regina Rifka (Berkowitz) Bierman; single. EDUC.: DeWitt Clinton H.S., New York; City Coll. of New York; Columbia U.; Hunter Coll.; New School; Universidad de San Carlos (Guatemala); Ecole d'Interpretes (Geneva); Dolmetscher-Institut (Germany). POLIT. & GOV.: ***Mankind's Assembly candidate for presidency of the U.S., 1960***. BUS. & PROF.: translator; linguist; language instructor; writer; teacher, schools of business administration in Copenhagen and Malmo; teacher, schools of journalism in Sao Paulo and Santander, Spain; chm., language dept., Instituto Pedagogico-Barquisimeto, Venezuela; instructor, NY U., 1963–65; operator, Language Service Center-Brazilian Book Center, New York, 1936–45; owner, Bertrand Languages, Inc., New York, 1955–74; commentator, "Bertrand's Belfry Tower," radio program, 1969–70; dir., Bertrand Studio; contributing ed., *Quinto Lingo*. MIL.: pvt., U.S. Army, 1918–19. MEM.: American Translators Assn.; Mankind's Assembly (founder; sec.-gen.). AWARDS: "Mr. Translator" citation, American Translators Assn., 1962; Alexander Gode Medal, 1971. WRITINGS: *Dictionaries Ahoy!* (series); "New York—A Spanish Language Outpost" (essay, 1956); *Selected Writings of Simon Bolivar* (translator, 1951); *Life in the Spanish Colonies* (1955); *Hablemos* (contributor). REL.: Vedanta Soc. (nee Jewish). RES.: New York, NY.

BEST, FRANK ELLISON. b. Feb 21, 1883, Marengo, IL; d. Jul 2, 1966, Indianapolis, IN; par. Edward Charles and Rebecca Ann (Wheelon) Best; m. Emilia Augusta Harm, Dec 28, 1915; c. Kenneth Harm; Donald Marshall; Walter Edwin. EDUC.: grad., NY State Teachers Coll., 1904; registered engineer, WA, 1936, IN, 1938. POLIT. & GOV.: ***candidate for Democratic nomination to presidency of the U.S., 1948***. BUS. & PROF.: high school teacher, Jamestown, NY, 1905; teacher, industrial arts dept., Queen Anne H.S., Seattle, WA, 1905–12, chm., 1912–20; instructor, U. of WA School of Engineering; inventor; mechanical engineer; pres., Frank E. Best, Inc., Seattle, 1920–23; pres., chm. of the board, Best Universal Lock Co., Inc., Seattle, 1923–28, Wilmington, DE, 1928–31, Indianapolis, IN, 1938– 66; pres., Best Motors, Inc., DE, 1931. MEM.: Vigilance, Inc. (founder, 1951); C. of C. AWARDS: Ph.Eng. (hon.) WRITINGS: *The Structure of the Physical Universe* (1934); *The Periodic System* (1934); *Immortality* (1937); *The U.S. in Biblical Prophecy* (1946); *God's Plan of Redemption* (1948). REL.: Methodist (teacher, Felt Bible Class). MISC.: holder of over 100 patents for locks, plastic airplanes, oil-less roller bearings, navigation devices, aircraft compasses and stabilizers, and airplane wings. RES.: Indianapolis, IN.

BEVEL, JAMES LUTHER. b. Oct 19, 1936, Ittabena, MS; m. Diane Judith Nash; c. Sherrillyn Jill; Douglas John. EDUC.: B.A., American Baptist Theological Seminary, 1961. POLIT. & GOV.: ***Freedom for LaRouche (Economic Recovery) Party candidate for vice presidency of the U.S., 1992***. BUS. & PROF.: ordained minister, Baptist Church, 1959; pastor, Baptist Church, Dixon, TN, 1959–61; organizer, Mississippi Free Press, 1961; composer; civil rights activist. MIL.: U.S.N.R., 1954–55. MEM.: Nashville Student Movement (chm., 1960–61); Student Non-Violent Coordinating Cmte. (cofounder, 1961); Southern Christian Leadership Conference (organizer; dir., Birmingham Movement, 1963; project dir., 1965); Council of Federated Organizations in MS (sponsor, 1962–64); Spring Mobilization to End the War in Vietnam (chm., 1967); Poor People's Campaign (dir., Nonviolence Workshop, 1968); Students of Education and Economic Development (founder, 1984). AWARDS: Peace Award, War Resisters League, 1963; Rosa Parks Award, Southern Christian Leadership Conference, 1965. WRITINGS: "Dod-Dog" (song, 1954); "I Know We'll Meet Again" (song, 1969); "Why Was a Darkly Born" (song, 1961). REL.: Bapt. MISC.: participated in sit-in demonstrations; Selma march, 1965. MAILING ADDRESS: 6705 S. Merrill St., #1B, Chicago, IL 60649.

BEVERIDGE, ALBERT JEREMIAH. b. Oct 6, 1862, Sugar Tree Ridge, OH; d. Apr 27, 1927, Indianapolis, IN; par. Thomas H. and Frances E. (Parkinson) Beveridge; m. Katherine Langsdale, Nov 24, 1887; m. 2d, Catherine Eddy, Aug 7, 1907; c. Albert Jeremiah, Jr.; Abby Spencer. EDUC.: Ph.B., De Pauw U., 1885, A.M., 1888, LL.D., 1902; studied law in office of Sen. Joseph Ewing McDonald (q.v.). POLIT. & GOV.: elected as a Republican to U.S. Senate (IN), 1889–1911; delegate, Rep. Nat'l. Conv., 1908, 1920; Republican candidate for U.S. Senate (IN), 1910, 1914 (Progressive), 1922; Progressive Party candidate for gov. of IN, 1912; ***candidate for Republican nomination to vice presidency of the U.S., 1912, 1924***; chm., Progressive Party National Convention, 1912. BUS. & PROF.: atty.; admitted to IN Bar, 1887; assoc., McDonald and Butler (law firm), Indianapolis, IN, 1887; author. MEM.: American Acad. of Arts and Letters; National Inst. of Arts and Letters. AWARDS: Pulitzer Prize for American Biography, 1920. HON. DEG.: LL.D., U. of PA, 1920; LL.D., Lafayette Coll., 1921; LL.D., Brown U., 1921. WRITINGS: *The Russian Advance* (1903); *The Young Man and the World* (1905); *The Bible as Good Reading* (1906); *The Meaning of the Times* (1907); *Americans of Today and Tomorrow* (1908); *Work and Habits* (1908); *Pass Prosperity Around* (1912); *The Invisible Government* (1912); *What is Back of the War* (1915); *Life of John Marshall* (2 Vols., 1916–19); *The State and the Nation* (1924); *The Art of Public Speaking* (1924); *Abraham Lincoln, 1809–1858* (1928). RES.: Indianapolis, IN.

BIAGGI, MARIO. b. Oct 26, 1917, New York, NY; par. Salvatore and Mary (Campari) Biaggi; m. Marie Wassil, Apr 20, 1941; c. Jacqueline; Barbara; Richard; Mario II. EDUC.: LL.B., NY Law School, 1963. POLIT. & GOV.: appointed asst. sec. of state of NY, 1966; elected as a Democrat to U.S. House (NY), 1969–88 (resigned); delegate, Dem. Nat'l. Conv., 1972, 1976, 1980; first vice chm., NY State Democratic Congressional Delegation; appointed U.S. delegate, Enthronement of Pope John Paul I, 1978; ***candidate for Democratic nomination to vice presidency of the U.S., 1980***. BUS. & PROF.: detective lt., New York Police Dept., 1942–65; community relations specialist, NY State Division of Housing, 1961–63; atty.; admitted to NY Bar, 1963; senior partner, Biaggi, Ehrlich and Long (law firm), New York, 1966–. MEM.: Patrolmen's Benevolent Assn. (first vice pres.; acting pres., 1947–51); Police Widows' Relief Fund (dir.); Police Recreation Center (dir.); Police Pension Fund (dir.); Municipal Credit Union (dir.); ABA; Bronx Cty. Bar Assn.; Trial Lawyers Assn.; NAACP (life member); Navy League; Columbia Associations in Civil Service (pres., National Council); National Police Officers Assn. of America (pres., 1967); Knights of Columbus; Elks; Civil Air Patrol; American Acad. for Professional Law Enforcement; American Jud. Soc.; Bronx Soc. of Arts and Letters; Order of Ahepa; Columbian Lawyers Assn.; American Soc. of Italian Legions of Merit. AWARDS: Medal of Valor, National Police Officers Assn., 1961; Order of Cyprus; National Front Gold Medal (Bulgaria); Star of Solidarity (Italy), 1961; National Police Hall of Fame, 1961; Public Service Award, Greek Orthodox Archdiocese of North and South America; Cavaliere, Order of Merit, 1965; Medal of Honor, New York Police Dept., 1967; Italian-American Hall of Fame, 1976 REL.: R.C. MISC.: convicted of bribery, extortion, racketeering, 1988; resigned from Congress as result of conviction in Wedtech Scandal. MAILING ADDRESS: 100 East Mosholu Parkway, Bronx, NY 10458.

BICKLE, TRAVIS. POLIT. & GOV.: ***independent candidate for presidency of the U.S., 1988***. MAILING ADDRESS: 1006 Linwood Ave., Valparaiso, IN 46383.

BIDEN, JOSEPH ROBINETTE. b. Nov 20, 1942, Scranton, PA; par. Joseph Robinette and Jean (Finnegan) Biden; m. Neilia Hunter; m. 2d, Jill Tracy Jacobs, Jun 17, 1977; c. Joseph Robinette III: Robert Hunter; Naomi Christina; Ashley Blazer. EDUC.: Archmere Acad.; B.A., U. of DE, 1965; J.D., Syracuse U., 1968. POLIT. & GOV.: elected as a Democrat to New Castle Cty. (DE) Council, 1971–73; elected as a Democrat to U.S. Senate (DE), 1973–; delegate, Democratic Mid-Term Conference, 1974; member, Dem. Nat'l. Cmte., 1975–; ***candidate for Democratic nomination to presidency of the U.S., 1984, 1988 (withdrew)***. BUS. & PROF.: atty.; admitted to DE Bar, 1968; senior partner, Biden and Walsh (law firm), Wilmington, DE, 1968–72. MEM.: Leukemia Soc.; Big Brothers; Century Club; New Castle Cty. Bar Assn.; DE Bar Assn.; ABA; American Trial Lawyers Assn. HON. DEG.: L.H.D., American International Coll., 1973; LL.D., U. of Scranton, 1976; LL.D., Marshall U., 1979; D.P.A., Villanova U., 1978; D.H., King's Coll., 1979. REL.: R.C. MAILING ADDRESS: 6 Montchan Dr., Wilmington, DE 19807.

BIDWELL, JOHN. b. Aug 5, 1819, Ripley Hills, Chautauqua Cty., NY; d. Apr 4, 1900, Chico, CA; par. Abram and Clarissa (Griggs) Bidwell; m. Annie Ellicott Kennedy, Apr 16, 1868. EDUC.: Kingsville Acad. POLIT. & GOV.: member, Cmte. to Formulate CA Proclamation of Independence, 1846; delegate, CA Constitutional Convention, 1849; elected member, CA Senate, 1849; census supervisor, State of CA, 1850, 1860; delegate, CA State Democratic Convention, 1851, 1854 (vice pres.), 1860 (vice pres.); delegate, Dem. Nat'l. Conv., 1860; delegate, Rep. Nat'l. Conv., 1864; elected as a Unionist to U.S. House (CA), 1865–67; delegate, Philadelphia Convention, 1866; candidate for Union Party nomination to gov. of CA, 1867; AntiMonopoly Party candidate for gov. of CA, 1875; delegate, Anti-Chinese Convention, Sacramento, CA, 1886; chm., CA State Prohibition Party Convention, 1888, 1890; delegate, Prohibition Party National Convention, 1888; presidential elector, Prohibition Party, 1888; Prohibition Party candidate for gov. of CA, 1890; American Party candidate for gov. of CA, 1890; ***Prohibition Party candidate for presidency of the U.S., 1892; National School House Party candidate for presidency of the U.S., 1892***. BUS. & PROF.: principal, Kingsville Acad., 1836–38; miner; business mgr., bookkeeper, John A. Sutter Enterprises; winemaker; farmer; owner, Rancho Chico. MIL.: maj., U.S. Army, Mexican War; brig. gen., Fifth Brigade, CA Militia, 1863. MEM.: U. of CA (regent). WRITINGS: *John Bidwell's Trip to California, 1841* (1842); *Echoes of the Past* (1900). REL.: Presb. MISC.: member, first immigrant train to CA from MO, 1841; discovered gold during CA Gold Rush, 1849. RES.: Chico, CA.

BIENIEK, LINDA STREICHER. POLIT. & GOV.: ***candidate for Republican nomination to presidency of the U.S., 1988***. MAILING ADDRESS: 3164 N. W. 43rd St., Fort Lauderdale, FL 33309.

BIGELOW, HERBERT SEELY. b. Jan 4, 1870, Elkhart, IN; d. Nov 11, 1951, Clifton, OH; par. Edwin and Anna (Pratt) Bigelow; m. Helen Niebling; c. none. EDUC.: Oberlin Coll., 1886–91; A.B., Western Reserve U., 1894; Lane Theological Seminary, 1895. POLIT. & GOV.: Democratic candidate for sec. of state of OH, 1902; pres., OH State Constitutional Convention, 1912; elected as a Democrat to OH State House, 1913–15; ***candidate for Farmer-Labor Party nomination to presidency of the U.S., 1920***; sec., OH Conference for Progressive Political Action, 1924; Democratic candidate for OH State House, 1927; Democratic candidate for U.S. House (OH), 1934, 1938; elected as an independent to Cincinnati (OH) City Council, 1935–37, 1939–41; elected as a Democrat to U.S. House (OH), 1937–39. BUS. & PROF.: ordained minister, Congregational Church, 1895; pastor, Vine St. (People's) Congregational Church, Cincinnati, 1895–1951; lecturer, Brookwood Labor Coll., 1932. MEM.: Americans for Democratic Action; Land and Liberty League; A.C.L.U.; Federal Council of Churches; American Assn. for Old Age Security (vice pres.); Berger National Foundation (member, National Council). WRITINGS: *Religion of Revolution* (1916). REL.: Congregationalist. RES.: Cincinnati, OH.

BIGENHO, MERLE P. m. Marcella Bigenho. POLIT. & GOV.: delegate, Socialist Party National Convention, 1976; ***candidate for Socialist Party nomination to vice presidency of the U.S., 1976 (declined)***; Socialist Party candidate for U.S. House (FL), 1988. MAILING ADDRESS: 2729 N. E. 20th Court, Ft. Lauderdale, FL 33305.

BILAL, JOHN (nee JOHN W. VANN). c. one son; two daughters. POLIT. & GOV.: ***candidate for Democratic nomination to presidency of the U.S., 1980***. MAILING ADDRESS: 800 Cronin Dr., Vallejo, CA 94590.

BILBO, THEODORE GILMORE. b. Oct 13, 1877, Juniper Grove, MS; d. Aug 21, 1947, New Orleans, LA; par. James Oliver and Beedy (Wallace) Bilbo; m. Lillian S. Herrington, May 25, 1898; m. 2d, Linda R. Gaddy, Jan 27, 1903; c. Jessie Forrest (Mrs. C. Lamar Smith); Lt. Col. Theodore Gilmore. EDUC.: U. of Nashville, 1897–1900; Vanderbilt U., 1905–07; U. of MI, 1908. POLIT. & GOV.: candidate for circuit clerk, Pearl River Cty., MS, 1903; elected as a Democrat to MS State Senate, 1908–12; elected as a Democrat to lt. gov. of MS, 1912–16; elected as a Democrat to gov. of MS, 1916–20, 1928–32; candidate for Democratic nomination to U.S. House (MS), 1920; candidate for Democratic nomination to gov. of MS, 1923; ***candidate for Democratic nomination to presidency of the U.S., 1928***; delegate, Dem. Nat'l. Conv., 1928; elected as a Democrat to U.S. Senate (MS), 1935–47. BUS. & PROF.: teacher, MS, 6 years; licensed minister, Bobolochitto Baptist Assn.; owner, girls' boarding school, Wiggins, MS; atty.; admitted to MS Bar, 1908; partner, Bilbo and Shipman (law firm), Poplarville, MS, 1913–16; farmer; owner, *Free Lance*, Jackson, MS, 1923–; employee, A.A.A., Washington, DC, 1932. MEM.: Masons (32°). REL.: Bapt. MISC.: indicted several times for bribery, acquitted, 1914. Address: Poplarville, MS.

BILLINGS, THEODORE CONRAD. b. May 6, 1906, Whitehouse, OH; par. Conrad and Mary Ann (Struder) Billings; m. Phyllis Hines; c. Merry Ann; Kathy Sue. EDUC.: Whitehouse (OH) Public Schools; Acad. of Aeronautics, Long Island, NY, 1942; U. of Lawsonomy, IA, 1946–47. POLIT. & GOV.: ***Constitution Party candidate for vice presidency of the U.S., 1964***; national chm., Constitution Party, 1968–70. BUS. & PROF.: owner, Lifeguard Foods (health foods), Denver, CO; publisher, *National Constitution Newsletter*. MIL.: U.S. Air Force, WWII. MEM.: Honest Dollar Cmte. (national chm.); John Adams Cmte. WRITINGS: writings on natural economics, health, politics. REL.: Christian. MAILING ADDRESS: Lifeguard Foods, 1121 East 9th Ave., Denver, CO.

BILLS, V. ALEX. POLIT. & GOV.: ***Independent candidate for presidency of the U.S., 1980***. MAILING ADDRESS: 5824 N. W. 64, Oklahoma City, OK 73132.

BILSBARROW, WILLIAM. POLIT. & GOV.: delegate, Socialist Labor Party National Convention, 1900, 1904; ***candidate for Socialist Labor Party nomination to presidency of the U.S., 1904***. RES.: St. Louis, MO.

BINGHAM, HIRAM. b. Nov 19, 1875, Honolulu, HI; d. Jun 6, 1956, Washington, DC; par. Rev. Hiram and Minerva Clarissa (Brewster) Bingham; m. Alfreda Mitchell, Nov 20, 1900; m. 2d, Suzanne Carroll Hill, Jun 28, 1937; c. Woodbridge; Hiram; Alfred Mitchell; Charles Tiffany; Brewster; Mitchell; Jonathan Brewster. EDUC.: A.B., Yale U., 1898; M.A., U. of CA, 1900; M.A., Harvard U., 1901, Ph.D., 1905; Litt.D., U. of Curzco, 1912. POLIT. & GOV.: U.S. delegate, First Pan-American Scientific Congress, 1908; delegate, Rep. Nat'l. Conv., 1916 (alternate), 1920 (alternate), 1924, 1928, 1932, 1936; presidential elector, Republican Party, 1916; elected as a Republican to lt. gov. of CT, 1923–25; elected as a Republican to gov. of CT, 1925 (resigned); member, Aircraft Board, 1925; elected as a Republican to U.S. Senate (CT), 1924–33; appointed chm., American Samoan Comm., 1930; ***candidate for Republican nomination to vice presidency of the U.S., 1932***; Republican candidate for U.S. Senate (CT), 1932; appointed chm., Loyalty Review Board, U.S. Civil Service Comm., 1951–53. BUS. & PROF.: Austin Teaching Fellow, Harvard U., 1901–02, 1904–05; preceptor in history and politics, Princeton U., 1905–06; explored Bolivar's route across Venezuela and Colombia, 1906–07; lecturer on South American geography and history, Yale U., 1907–09, asst. prof., 1909–15, prof., 1915–24; Albert Shaw Lecturer, Johns Hopkins U., 1910; explored Spanish trade route, Buenos Aires to Lima, 1908–09; dir., Yale Peruvian Expedition, 1911; explored ruins of Machu Picchu; located Vitcos, last Inca capital; dir., Peruvian expeditions, 1912, 1914–15; adviser, Yale U. Library; lecturer, South Sea Islands, Naval Training Schools, 1942–43; dir., Washington Loan and Trust Co.; vice pres., Colmena Oil Co. MIL.: capt., Tenth F.A., CT National Guard, 1916; commissioned lt. col., U.S.A.A.C., 1917; commanding officer, Aviation Instruction Center, Issodoun, France, 1918; Officier de l'Ordre de l'Etoile Noire (France); Gran Official de la Orden del Liberador (Venezuela). MEM.: Royal Geographic Soc. (fellow); National Geographic Soc. (hon. life member); Hispanic Soc. of America; American Antiquarian Soc.; National Acad. of History (hon. member); Lima Geographic Soc. (corresponding member); National Acad. of History (Venezuela); Sigma Psi; Elizabethan Club; National Aeronautics Assn. (pres., 1928–31); Masons; Graduate Club of New Haven; Century Club; Metropolitan Club; Chevy Chase Club. WRITINGS: *Journal of an Expedition Across Venezuela and Colombia* (1909); *Across South America* (1911); *Vitcos, the Last Inca Capital* (1912); *In the Wonderland of Peru* (1913); *The Monroe Doctrine, An Obsolete Shibboleth* (1913); *The Future of the Monroe Doctrine* (1920); *An Explorer in the Air Service* (1920); *Inca Land* (1922); *Freedom Under the Constitution* (1924); *Machu Picchu* (1930); *Elihu Yale, Governor, Collector, and Benefactor* (1938); *Elihu Yale—The American Nabob of Queen Square* (1939); *Lost City* (1948). REL.: Congregationalist. RES.: Washington, DC.

BINKLEY, MARDELLE R. POLIT. & GOV.: ***Boobs Up Party candidate for presidency of the U.S., 1980***. BUS. & PROF.: student. MAILING ADDRESS: 364th E., Roy, WA 98580.

BINKLEY, ROBERT B. POLIT. & GOV.: ***independent candidate for presidency of the U.S., 1984***. MAILING ADDRESS: 16150 Keith Harrow, #1808, Houston, TX 77084.

BIRD, MARTHA SCARBOROUGH. POLIT. & GOV.: ***candidate for Democratic nomination to vice presidency of the U.S., 1924***.

BIRNBERG, ROBERT MICHAEL. b. May 27, 1948, New York, NY; par. Alexander and Harriet (Fox) Birnberg; m. Caprice Dea Franklin, 1980; c. Samantha; Matthew. EDUC.: Public School 22, Yonkers, NY, 1954–60; Walt Whitman Junior H.S., Yonkers, 1960–62; Longfellow Junior H.S., Yonkers, 1962–63; grad., Roosevelt H.S., Yonkers, 1966; B.A., U. of Denver, 1970, M.A., 1972. POLIT. & GOV.: elected precinct committeeman, Democratic Party, Boulder, CO, 1976; delegate, Boulder Cty. (CO) Democratic Conventions; delegate, CO Democratic State Conventions; ***independent candidate for presidency of the U.S., 1988***. BUS. & PROF.: social studies teacher, Boulder Valley (CO) Public Schools, 1970–; curriculum dir. for social studies, Broomfield Heights Middle School, Broomfield, CO; guidance counselor. MEM.: National Middle School Assn.; National Council of Social Studies; Boulder Valley Federation of Teachers (pres., 1974–76); CO Federation of Teachers (vice pres., 1975–77). AWARDS: winner, Dental Oratorical Contest, Yonkers, NY, 1963. REL.: Jewish. MAILING ADDRESS: c/o Caprice Dea Birnberg, 4424 South Xenia St., Denver, CO 80237.

BIRNEY, JAMES GILLESPIE. b. Feb 4, 1792, Danville, KY; d. Nov 25, 1857, Eagleswood, NJ; par. James and Martha (Reed) Birney; m. Agatha McDowell, Feb 1, 1816; m. 2d, Elizabeth Fitzhugh, Mar 25, 1841; c. Dion; David Bell; Fitzhugh; James; William; Arthur Hopkins; Martha; George; Florence. EDUC.: grad., Coll. of NJ, 1810; studied law under Alexander J. Dallas, Philadelphia, PA. POLIT. & GOV.: elected to Danville (KY) Town Council, 1814; elected to KY State House, 1816–18; elected to AL State House, 1819; elected solicitor, Fifth AL District; elected alderman, Huntsville, AL, 1828; presidential elector, Democratic Party, 1828; elected mayor of Huntsville, AL, 1829; ***Liberty Party candidate for presidency of the U.S., 1840, 1844***; Liberty Party candidate for gov. of MI, 1843, 1845;

Democratic candidate for MI State House, 1844; chm., Free Soil Party National Convention, 1848. BUS. & PROF.: atty.; admitted to KY Bar, 1814; law practice, Danville, KY; southwest agent, American Colonization Soc., 1832; planter, AL; publisher, *The Philanthropist*, Cincinnati, OH, 1836–37. MEM.: KY Anti-Slavery Soc. (Founder, 1835); American Colonization Soc.; American Bible Soc.; American Anti-Slavery Soc. (exec. sec., 1837); World Anti-Slavery Convention (vice pres., 1840); Centre Coll. (trustee); U. of AL (trustee). WRITINGS: *Letter on Colonization* (1834); articles in *Q.A.S. Magazine* and *Emancipator* (1837–44); *Letter to the Presbyterian Church* (1834); *Addresses and Speeches* (1835); *Vindication of the Abolitionists* (1835); *Letter to Colonel Stone* (1836); *Address to Slaveholders* (1837); *Argument on Fugitive Slave Case* (1837); *Letter to F. H. Elmore* (1838); *Political Obligations of Abolitionists* (1839); *Report on the Duty of Political Action* (1839); *The American Churches: The Bulwark of American Slavery* (1840); *Examination of the Decision of the U.S. Supreme Court* (1850). REL.: Presb. MISC.: advocate of abolition, free public schools, temperance. RES.: Cincinnati, OH.

BISHOP, JOHN EDWARD. POLIT. & GOV.: ***candidate for Republican nomination to presidency of the U.S., 1984***; candidate for Republican nomination to U.S. Senate (CA), 1986. MAILING ADDRESS: 13409 Granada, #A, Houston, TX 77015.

BISHOP, MICHAEL L. b. 1964. POLIT. & GOV.: ***independent candidate for presidency of the U.S., 1980***. MAILING ADDRESS: 8658 Blackhaw Court, Jacksonville, FL 32210.

BISHOP, RICHARD MOORE. b. Nov 4, 1812, Fleming Cty., KY; d. Mar 2, 1893, Jacksonville, FL; m. Mary Threkeld, 1833; c. James A.; R. H.; W. T.; three daughters. EDUC.: frontier schools. POLIT. & GOV.: elected on Citizens' Ticket to Cincinnati (OH) City Council, 1857–59 (pres.); elected as a Democrat to mayor of Cincinnati, 1859–61; delegate, OH State Constitutional Convention, 1873; elected as a Democrat to gov. of OH, 1878–80; ***candidate for Democratic nomination to vice presidency of the U.S., 1880 (withdrew)***. BUS. & PROF.: grocer, Cincinnati, 1848–93; pres., Wells and Co. (wholesale grocery), Cincinnati; pres., R. M. Bishop and Co. (wholesale grocery), Cincinnati, 1848. REL.: Campbellite Baptist Church (pres., General Christian Missionary Convention). RES.: Cincinnati, OH.

BIXLER, WILFORD B. b. 1905, Stow, OH; d. May 9, 1973, Akron, OH; par. Perry A. and Elizabeth (Beckley) Bixler; m. Helen Van Berg, 1931. EDUC.: grad., Hiram Coll.; LL.B., Western Reserve Law School. POLIT. & GOV.: city prosecutor, Akron, OH, 1936–37; elected as a Democrat to OH State House, 1939–42; Democratic candidate for mayor of Akron, OH, 1939; ***candidate for Democratic nomination to presidency of the U.S., 1948***; delegate, Dem. Nat'l. Conv., 1948; candidate for Democratic nomination to OH State Senate, 1958. BUS. & PROF.: atty.; partner (with Harry Van Berg and W. J. Laub), law practice, Akron, OH; treas., *Summit County (OH) Democrat*, 1956; treas., Greater Akron Publishing Co., 1956. MIL.: harbor patrol officer, lt., U.S. Navy, WWII. MEM.: Akron City Club; Stan Hywet Hall Foundation; Stow Hist. Soc. RES.: Akron, OH.

BLACK, EARL EDWARD. b. Jul 31, 1933, Caney, KS; par. James Cleo and Clara Jane (Mills) Black; single. EDUC.: eighth grade, Caney and Wayside, KS; Bartlesville (OK) Business Coll., 14 months. POLIT. & GOV.: ***independent candidate for presidency of the U.S., 1980, 1984***. BUS. & PROF.: employee, Salsman Oil Co. (service station), Caney, KS. MIL.: corp., U.S. Army, 5 years. MEM.: American Legion; VFW. REL.: Protestant. MAILING ADDRESS: Bos 19X1, 211 South High, Overland Park, KS 66201.

BLACK, GUY TEMPLETON. b. 1947. POLIT. & GOV.: ***independent candidate for presidency of the U.S., 1988, 1992***. BUS. & PROF.: owner, Quest, Inc. (dog guide hearing support), Cleveland, OH; notary public; author; photographer. MAILING ADDRESS: 753 Brayton Ave., Cleveland, OH 44113.

BLACK, HENRY. b. 1900; d. c. 1970. POLIT. & GOV.: ***candidate for Republican nomination to presidency of the U.S., 1944, 1948; candidate for Republican nomination to vice presidency of the U.S., 1944***; candidate for delegate, Rep. Nat'l. Conv., 1944; ***candidate for Democratic nomination to presidency of the U.S., 1944; Equal Rights Party candidate for presidency of the U.S., 1944, 1948; Equal Rights Party candidate for vice presidency of the U.S., 1944***; candidate for Republican nomination to U.S. Senate (OR), 1944. BUS. & PROF.: owner, Henry Black and Co. (painters), Portland, OR, 1926–70; owner, Henry Apts., Portland; owner, Pan American Wallpaper Co., Portland, 1960; ed., *Political Advertiser and Soldiers' Gazette*. RES.: Portland, OR.

BLACK, JAMES. b. Sep 23, 1823, Lewisburg, PA; d. Dec 16, 1893, Lancaster, PA; par. John and Jane (Egbert) Black; m. Eliza Murray, Mar 27, 1845; c. William Murray; Mary (Mrs. E. Lane Schofield); four others. EDUC.: Lewisburg Acad., 1840–43; studied law under James F. Linn and Col. William B. Fordney, 1844–46. POLIT. & GOV.: founder, Lancaster Prohibition Party, 1852; member, PA Prohibition Party State Central Cmte., 1853–56; delegate, PA State Republican Convention, 1856; delegate, Rep. Nat'l. Conv., 1856; founder, National Prohibition Party, 1869; delegate, Prohibition Party National Convention, 1869 (chm.), 1872, 1876, 1880, 1884, 1888, 1892; ***candidate for Prohibition Party nomination to vice presidency of the U.S., 1872; Prohibition Party candidate for presidency of the U.S., 1872***; member, Prohibition Party National Cmte., 1869–76,

1880–82, 1884–88; chm., Prohibition Party National Cmte., 1876–80; ***candidate for Prohibition Party nomination to presidency of the U.S., 1884***; Prohibition Party candidate for supreme judge, PA State Supreme Court, 1888; Prohibition Party candidate for U.S. House (Pennsylvania); Prohibition Party candidate for district atty., Lancaster Cty., PA. BUS. & PROF.: member, Engineer Corps, 1839; financial agent, Atlantic and St. Lawrence R.R., 1850–52; agent, Mutual Life Insurance Co., 1869–83; farmer; atty.; admitted to Lancaster (PA) Bar, 1846; law practice, Lancaster, 1846–93. MEM.: National Temperance Soc. (founder, 1865); Publication House (founder); Ocean Grove (NJ) Camp Meeting Assn. (founder, 1869); Washington Temperance Soc., 1840; Lancaster Lodge, Independent Order of Good Templars (right grand worthy councilor, 1864; grand worthy councilor, 1860, 1863; grand chief templar of PA, 1858–62); Conestoga Division, Sons of Temperance, 1846; Odd Fellows (trustee, Monterey Lodge); Lancaster Cty. Agricultural Soc. WRITINGS: *Cider Tract* (1864); *Is There a Necessity for a Prohibition Party?* (1876); *The National Prohibition Party* (1880); *A Brief History of the Prohibition Reform Party* (1880); *The Prohibition Party* (1885); *History of the National Prohibition Party* (1893). REL.: Methodist Episcopal Church (trustee, 1846–73; Sunday school superintendent, 30 years; founder, East King Street Mission; member, Board of Stewarts, Philadelphia Conference). MISC.: owned most extensive temperance library in the world. RES.: Lancaster, PA.

BLACK, JEREMIAH SULLIVAN. b. Jan 10, 1810, Stony Creek, PA; d. Aug 19, 1883, York, PA; par. Henry and Mary (Sullivan) Black; m. Mary Forward, Mar 23, 1836; c. Rebecca; Anna; Henry; Chauncey Forward; Mrs. Mary Clayton. EDUC.: Acad., Bridgeport, PA; studied law under Chauncey Forward. POLIT. & GOV.: appointed deputy atty. gen., Somerset Cty., PA, 1830; Democratic candidate for U.S. House (PA), 1841 (withdrew); appointed presiding judge, PA State Court of Common Pleas, 1842; elected chief justice, PA Supreme Court, 1851–57; appointed atty. gen. of the U.S., 1857–60; appointed U.S. sec. of state, 1860–61; appointed assoc. justice, Supreme Court of the U.S., but not confirmed, 1861; reporter, Supreme Court of the U.S., 1861; ***candidate for Democratic nomination to presidency of the U.S., 1868, 1872, 1876, 1880***; delegate, PA State Constitutional Convention, 1872; Democratic candidate for U.S. Senate (PA), 1874. BUS. & PROF.: atty.; admitted to PA Bar, 1831; law practice (with James F. Shunk); law practice (with Ward H. Lamson), Washington, DC; counsel for President Andrew Johnson (q.v.) during impeachment trial, 1867; counsel for Samuel J. Tilden (q.v.) during election contest, 1876; farmer; contributor, *Galaxy*; contributor, *North American Review*. WRITINGS: *Eulogy to Andrew Jackson* (1845); *Address Before Agricultural Society* (1854); *Religious Liberty* (1856); *Observations on Senator Douglas's Views* (1859); *Observations on Territorial Sovereignty* (1860); *Letter to the Secretary of War* (1862); *Speech at Democratic Mass Convention* (1863); *The Doctrine of the Democratic and Abolition Parties Contrasted* (1864); *Federal Jurisdiction in the Territories* (1883); *Railroad Monopoly* (1883); *Essays and Speeches* (1886). REL.: Disciples of Christ (Campbellite). RES.: York, PA.

BLACK, JOHN CHARLES. b. Jan 27, 1839, Lexington, MS; d. Aug 17, 1915, Chicago, IL; par. Rev. John C. and Josephine Louisa (Culbertson) Black; m. Adaline L. Griggs, Sep 28, 1867; c. Mrs. Grace Vrooman; John Donald; Josephine L.; Mrs. Helen Elizabeth Abbot. EDUC.: Wabash Coll.; A.M., Knox Coll., LL.D.; studied law, Chicago, IL. POLIT. & GOV.: Democratic-Liberal Republican candidate for lt. gov. of IL, 1872; Democratic candidate for U.S. House (IL), 1876, 1884; Democratic candidate for U.S. Senate (IL), 1879; Democratic candidate for gov. of IL, 1884 (declined); delegate, Dem. Nat'l. Conv., 1884; ***candidate for Democratic nomination to vice presidency of the U.S., 1884 (withdrew), 1888; candidate for American Prohibition Party nomination to presidency of the U.S., 1884***; appointed U.S. commissioner of pensions, 1885–89; elected as a Democrat to U.S. House (IL), 1893–95; appointed U.S. atty. for northern IL, 1895–99; Gold Standard Democratic Party candidate for gov. of IL, 1896; appointed member, U.S. Civil Service Comm., 1903–13 (pres., 1904–13). BUS. & PROF.: soldier; atty.; admitted to IL Bar, 1867; law practice, Danville, IL, 1867–1915. MIL.: pvt., 11th Indiana Infantry, 1861; maj., 37th Illinois Infantry, 1861, lt. col., 1862, col., 1862, brev. brig. gen., 1865, resigned, 1865. MEM.: Grand Army of the Republic (IL dept. commander, 1898, 1903–04; commander in chief, 1903–04); Military Order of the Loyal Legion (IL dept. commander, 1895–97). AWARDS: Medal of Honor, 1893. HON. DEG.: LL.D., Dickinson Coll. REL.: Presb. RES.: Chicago, IL.

BLACK, SHIRLEY JANE TEMPLE. b. Apr 23, 1928, Santa Monica, CA; par. George Francis and Gertrude (Cregier) Temple; m. John Agar, Jr., Sep 19, 1945; m. 2d, Charles A. Black, Dec 16, 1950; c. Linda Susan Agar Falaschi; Charles Alden; Lori Alden. EDUC.: grad., Westlake School for Girls, 1945; . POLIT. & GOV.: candidate for Republican nomination to U.S. House (CA), 1967; member, Women's Advisory Cmte. for Nixon/Agnew, 1968; member, CA State Republican Central Cmte., 1968–; appointed member, CA State Council on Criminal Justice, 1969; appointed member, CA State Advisory Hospital Council, 1969; appointed member, U.S. Delegation to the U.N., 1969–70; appointed U.S. delegate, U.N. Conference on Human Environment, 1970–72; appointed special asst. to the chm., President's Council on Environmental Quality, 1972–74; appointed delegate, U.S.S.R.-U.S. Conference on the Treaty on Environment, 1972; appointed member, U.S. Comm. to UNESCO, 1973–74; appointed U.S. Ambassador to Ghana, 1974–76; appointed White House Chief of Protocol, 1976–77; ***candidate for Republican nomination to vice presidency of the U.S., 1980***; appointed U.S. delegate, U.N. Conference on African Refugee Problems, 1981; appointed U.S. Ambassador to Czechoslovakia, 1989–93. BUS. & PROF.: actress; narrator, "Shirley Temple Storybook," NBC-TV series, 1958; hostess, "Shirley Temple Show," NBC-TV series, 1960; dir., Bank of CA;

dir., BANCAL Tri-State Corp.; dir., Firemen's Fund Insurance Co.; dir., Del Monte Corp. Motion picture credits: *Stand Up and Cheer* (1934); *Little Miss Marker* (1934); *Change of Heart* (1934); *Now I'll Tell* (1934); *Baby Take a Bow* (1934); *Now and Forever* (1934); *Bright Eyes* (1934); *Our Little Girl* (1935); *The Little Colonel* (1935); *Curly Top* (1935); *The Littlest Rebel* (1935); *Captain January* (1936); *Poor Little Rich Girl* (1936); *Dimples* (1936); *Stowaway* (1936); *Wee Willie Winkie* (1937); *Heidi* (1937); *Rebecca of Sunnybrook Farm* (1938); *Little Miss Broadway* (1938); *Just Around the Corner* (1938); *The Little Princess* (1939); *Susannah of the Mounties* (1939); *Young People* (1940); *The Blue Bird* (1940); *Kathleen* (1941); *Miss Annie Rooney* (1942); *Since You Went Away* (1944); *I'll Be Seeing You* (1944); *Kiss and Tell* (1945); *War Party* (1946); *The Bachelor and the Bobby-Soxer* (1946); *That Hagen Girl* (1947); *Honeymoon* (1947); *Fort Apache* (1948); *Mr. Belvedere Goes to College* (1949); *Adventure in Baltimore* (1949); *The Story of Seabiscuit* (1950); *Kiss for Corliss*. WRITINGS: *My Young Life* (1945); *Child Star* (1988). MEM.: League of Women Voters; San Francisco Symphony Assn.; Asia Foundation; Acad. of Motion Picture Arts and Sciences; Acad. of Television Arts and Sciences (hon. gov.); Bay Area Educational Television Assn.; San Francisco Light Opera Assn.; Sierra Club; U.S. Citizens Space Task Force; Inst. for the Study of Economic Systems; Commonwealth Club of CA; National Cmte. on U.S./China Relations; National Wildlife Federation (dir.); International Federation of Multiple Sclerosis Societies (dir.); Multiple Sclerosis Soc. (dir.); American Soc. for International Law; World Affairs Council (dir.); U.N. Assn. of the U.S. (dir.); Council on Foreign Relations; San Francisco Health Facilities Planning Assn. AWARDS: Dame, Knights of Malta, 1968; fellow, U. of Notre Dame, 1972; hon. ID colonel, 1935; col., Hawaiian National Guard; col., 108th Regt., IL National Guard; hon. colonel-in-chief, CA National Guard; American Exemplar Medal, 1979; Ceres Medal, Food and Agricultural Organization, 1975; Kiwanis Award, 1967; John Swett Award, CA Teachers Assn.; Annual Layman's Award, Alameda Education Assn. REL.: Episc. MAILING ADDRESS: 115 Lakeview Dr., Woodside, CA 94062.

BLACKBURN, JOSEPH CLAY STYLES. b. Oct 1, 1838, Spring Station, KY; d. Sep 12, 1918, Washington, DC; par. Edward M. and Lavinia S. Blackburn; m. Therese Graham, Feb 10, 1858; m. 2d, Mrs. Mary E. Blackburn, Dec 11, 1901; c. Mrs. W. P. Hall; Mrs. Thomas Gale. EDUC.: Sayres Inst.; A.B., Centre Coll., 1857, LL.D.; studied law under George E. Kincaid. POLIT. & GOV.: elected as a Democrat to KY State House, 1871–75; elected as a Democrat to U.S. House (KY), 1875–85; elected as a Democrat to U.S. Senate (KY), 1885–97, 1901–07 (minority leader, 1906–07); delegate, Dem. Nat'l. Conv., 1896, 1900, 1904; ***candidate for Democratic nomination to presidency of the U.S., 1896; candidate for Democratic nomination to vice presidency of the U.S., 1896***; Democratic candidate for U.S. Senate (KY), 1897, 1907; appointed member, Isthmian Canal Comm., gov. of Canal Zone, 1907–09; appointed resident commissioner, Lincoln Memorial, Washington, DC, 1914–18. BUS. & PROF.: atty.; admitted to KY Bar, 1858; law practice, Chicago, IL, 1858–60; law practice, Desha Cty., AR, 1865–68; planter, Desha Cty., AR, 1865–68; law practice, Versailles, KY, 1868–19??. MIL.: pvt., C.S.A., 1861, lt. col., 1865. RES.: Versailles, KY.

BLACKMER, JOHN. b. Jul 18, 1828, Plymouth, MA; d. Apr 15, 1895, Springfield, MA; par. John and Esther (Bartlett) Blackmer; m. Ellen S. Dearborn, Oct 22, 1863; c. Helen (Mrs. George F. Poole); John Allen. EDUC.: Phillips Acad., Andover, MA; grad., Brown U.; M.D., Harvard U., 1854. POLIT. & GOV.: member, School Board, Sandwich, NH; founder, NH Prohibition Party, 1867; state chm., NH Prohibition Party; ***candidate for Prohibition Party nomination to vice presidency of the U.S., 1872***; Prohibition Party candidate for gov. of NH, 1872, 1873, 1874; member, MA Prohibition Party State Cmte., 1875–95; Prohibition Party candidate for lt. gov. of MA, 1881, 1882, 1883, 1886, 1887, 1888; Prohibition Party candidate for gov. of MA, 1889, 1890; Prohibition Party candidate for mayor of Springfield, MA, 1892, 1893; Prohibition Party candidate for MA State Senate; Prohibition Party candidate for U.S. House (MA); chm., MA State Prohibition Party, 1894. BUS. & PROF.: physician, Effingham, NH, 1854–59; asst. physician, Hospital for the Insane, Augusta, ME; asst. asylum physician, Concord, NH, 1865–66; physician, Sandwich, NH; physician, Provincetown, MA, 1874–77; physician, Springfield, MA, 1877–94; asst. physician, McLean Asylum, Somerville, MA. ed., *The Prohibition Herald*, Lancaster, NH, 1871–72; ed., *The Domestic Journal;* ed., *Weekly Evangelist*, Springfield, MA; contributor, *Homestead*. MIL.: asst. surgeon, 41st MA Regt., U.S. Army, 1860, surgeon, 1862; appointed asst. surgeon, U.S. Navy, 1863–65. MEM.: Carroll Cty. (NH) Medical Soc.; NH Medical Soc.; Grand Army of the Republic; Cmte. to Obtain Submission of the Norwegian Mode to the People (chm.). WRITINGS: *Prescribing Alcoholics* (1880). REL.: Congregationalist (Sunday school superintendent). RES.: Springfield, MA.

BLAINE, JAMES GILLESPIE. b. Jan 31, 1830, West Brownsville, PA; d. Jan 27, 1893, Washington, DC; par. Elphraim Lyon and Maria Louise (Gillespie) Blaine; m. Harriet Stanwood, Jun 30, 1850; c. Walker; Emmons; James Gillespie, Jr.; Alice (Mrs. John J. Coppinger); Margaret (Mrs. Walter Damrosch); Harriet S. (Mrs. Beale); Stanwood. EDUC.: grad., Washington Coll., 1847. POLIT. & GOV.: founder, ME Republican Party, 1854; appointed state printer of ME, 1855; delegate, Rep. Nat'l. Conv., 1856; elected as a Republican to ME State House, 1858–62 (Speaker, 1860–62); chm., ME State Republican Central Cmte., 1859–81; elected as a Republican to U.S. House (ME), 1863–76 (Speaker, 1869–75); ***candidate for Republican nomination to vice presidency of the U.S., 1872***; leader, "Half-Breed" Republicans; appointed and subsequently elected as a Republican to U.S. Senate (ME), 1875–81; ***candidate for Republican nomination to presidency of the U.S., 1876, 1880, 1888, 1892***; appointed U.S. sec. of state, 1881, 1889–92; ***Republican candidate for presidency of the U.S., 1884***; pres., Pan American Congress, 1889. BUS. & PROF.: teacher, Western Military Inst.,

Blue Lick Springs, KY, 1847–50; teacher, PA Institution for the Blind, 1852–54; editorial staff, *Portland (ME) Advertiser*, 1857–60; ed., *Kennebec (ME) Journal*, 1854–60. WRITINGS: *Journal of the Pennsylvania Institution for the Instruction of the Blind, From Its Foundation* (1854); *Memoir of Luther Severance* (1856); *Report on Systems of Disbursements, Labor and Discipline in the Maine State Prison* (1859); *Eulogy of Garfield* (1882); *Foreign Policy of the Garfield Administration* (1882); *Twenty Years in Congress* (2 Vols., 1884–86); *Political Discussions: Legislative, Diplomatic and Popular* (1887); *Progress and Development of the Western World* (1892); *Columbus and Columbia* (1892); *Condensed History of American Tariff Acts* (1896). REL.: Congregationalist (nee Presb.). MISC.: known as "The Plumed Knight" and "The Continental Liar from the State of Maine." RES.: Augusta, ME.

BLAINE, JOHN JAMES. b. May 4, 1875, Wingville Township, WI; d. Apr 16, 1934, Boscobel, WI; par. James Ferguson and Elizabeth (Johnson-Brunstad) Blaine; m. Anna C. McSpaden, Aug 23, 1904; c. Helen (adopted). EDUC.: grad., Montford H.S.; LL.B., Valparaiso U., 1896. POLIT. & GOV.: elected as a Republican to mayor of Boscobel, WI, 1901–04, 1906–07; elected member, Grant Cty. (WI) Board of Supervisors, 1901–04; delegate, WI Republican State Convention, 1902, 1904; candidate for Republican nomination to U.S. House (WI), 1904; elected as a Republican to WI State Senate, 1909–13; delegate, Rep. Nat'l. Conv., 1912, 1916, 1920, 1924; Independent Progressive Republican candidate for gov. of WI, 1914; elected as a Republican to atty. gen. of WI, 1919–21; elected as a Republican to gov. of WI, 1921–27; elected as a Republican to U.S. Senate (WI), 1927–33; ***candidate for Republican nomination to presidency of the U.S., 1932***; candidate for Republican nomination to U.S. Senate (WI), 1932; appointed member, RFC, 1933–34. BUS. & PROF.: atty.; admitted to WI Bar, 1896; law practice, Montford, WI, 1896–97; law practice, Boscobel, WI, 1897–1934; partner, Austin-Blaine Farm Co. MEM.: Wilson National Progressive Republican League (vice pres., 1912). REL.: Lutheran. RES.: Boscobel, WI.

BLAIR, FRANCIS PRESTON, JR. b. Feb 19, 1821, Lexington, KY; d. Jul 8, 1875, St. Louis, MO; par. Francis Preston and Eliza Violet (Gist) Blair; m. Appolene Alexander, Sep 8, 1847; c. Andrew Alexander. EDUC.: U. of NC; grad., Princeton U., 1841; Transylvania U. POLIT. & GOV.: appointed atty. gen. of NM Territory; elected as a Democrat to MO State House, 1852–56; elected as a Free Soiler to U.S. House (MO), 1857–59 (resigned), 1861–62, 1863–64 (resigned); Republican candidate for U.S. House (MO), 1860; chm., Comm. on Military Defense, 1861; appointed collector of internal revenue, St. Louis, MO, 1866 (rejected by Senate); appointed U.S. minister to Austria (rejected by Senate); ***candidate for Democratic nomination to presidency of the U.S., 1868; Democratic candidate for vice presidency of the U.S., 1868***; elected as a Democrat to U.S. Senate (MO), 1871–73; Democratic candidate for U.S. Senate (MO), 1873; appointed MO state superintendent of life insurance, 1874–75. BUS. & PROF.: atty.; admitted to KY Bar, 1843; law practice, St. Louis, MO, 1843–45; ed., *Missouri Democrat;* appointed commissioner of Pacific R.R. MIL.: pvt., U.S. Army, 1846; col., U.S. Volunteers, 1861, brig. gen., 1861, maj. gen., 1862. WRITINGS: *The Life and Public Services of General William O. Butler* (1848). RES.: St. Louis, MO.

BLAIR, HENRY WILLIAM. b. Dec 6, 1834, Campton, NH; d. Mar 14, 1920, Washington, DC; par. William Henry and Lois (Baker) Blair; m. Eliza Ann Nelson, Dec 20, 1859; c. Henry P. EDUC.: Holme's Plymouth Acad.; Tilton Acad.; studied law in office of William Leverett, Plymouth, NH, 1856. POLIT. & GOV.: appointed solicitor, Grafton Cty., NH, 1860–65; elected as a Republican to NH State House, 1866; elected as a Republican to NH State Senate, 1867–68; elected as a Republican to U.S. House (NH), 1875–79, 1903–05; elected as a Republican to U.S. Senate (NH), 1879–91; ***candidate for Republican nomination to presidency of the U.S., 1884 (declined), 1892; candidate for American Party nomination to presidency of the U.S., 1884 (declined)***; appointed judge, U.S. District Court, 1891 (declined); candidate for Republican nomination to U.S. Senate (NH), 1891; appointed U.S. minister to China, 1891. BUS. & PROF.: atty.; admitted to NH Bar, 1859; law practice, Plymouth, NH, 1859; law practice, Washington, DC. MIL.: capt., lt. col., 15th NH Volunteers, Civil War; wounded twice during Civil War. AWARDS: A.M. (hon.), Dartmouth Coll., 1873. WRITINGS: *The Temperance Movement—Or the Conflict of Man with Alcohol* (1888); *The Future of the Temperance Reform* (1895). MISC.: resigned as U.S. minister to China when Chinese government objected to his opposition to Chinese immigration; authored Sunday Rest Bill, bill creating U.S. Dept. of Labor, soldiers' pension bills. RES.: Manchester, NH.

BLAKE, MORGAN. b. 1889, Fayetteville, TN; d. Jul 26, 1953, Atlanta, GA; m. Corrie Hoffmann; c. William. EDUC.: LL.B., Vanderbilt U., 1911. POLIT. & GOV.: ***independent candidate for presidency of the U.S., 1948***. BUS. & PROF.: reporter, *Nashville (TN) Tennessean*, 1911–13; reporter, *Nashville Banner*, 1913–15; sports ed., *The Atlanta Journal*, 1916–40, editorial columnist, 1940–53. MEM.: Agoga Men's Bible Class; Atlanta Optimist Club; Masons (33°; Scottish Rite); Shriners; GA Citizens Council; Fulton-DeKalb Hospital Authority. WRITINGS: *Sports Editor Finds Christ* (1952). REL.: Bapt. (radio Sunday school teacher). MISC.: noted for halting riot at Atlanta Federal Penitentiary, Dec 1944. RES.: Atlanta, GA.

BLAKEY, JAMES WHITAKER. b. Jun 25, 1965, Philadelphia, PA; par. Churchill Lyon and Gretchen Elizabeth (Whitaker) Blakey; single. EDUC.: Mullica Hill Friends Private School, 1972–80. POLIT. & GOV.: Save the U.S. Party candidate for gov. of NJ, 1977; Save the U.S. Party candidate for mayor of Wenonah, NJ, 1978; Save the U.S. Party candidate for freeholder, Gloucester Cty., NJ, 1979; ***Save the U.S. Party candidate***

for presidency of the U.S., 1980. BUS. & PROF.: custodian. MEM.: Youth for South Jersey Statehood; Eastern PA Sports Collectors Assn. REL.: Conventional Atheist. MAILING ADDRESS: 100 South West Ave., Wenonah, NJ 08090.

BLANCATO, DOROTHY MUNS. b. Jan 6, 1926, Chicago, IL; par. George and Florence (Leedy) Muns; m. Salvatore Blancato, May 15, 1953; c. Nancy Armen; Maria Carmella; Ann Clare; Samuel Francis; Thomas Muns. EDUC.: A.A., Stephens Coll., 1945; Pittsburgh Art Inst., 1947–48. POLIT. & GOV.: ***Independent Alliance candidate for vice presidency of the U.S., 1984 (withdrew)***. BUS. & PROF.: display designer, Bonwit Teller Co., Philadelphia, PA, 1945–47; interior display designer, Kaufman's, Pittsburgh, PA, 1948–49; owner, Blancato Interiors, Beaver, PA, 1955–. MEM.: American Inst. of Interior Designers. MAILING ADDRESS: 680 Dutch Ridge Rd., Beaver, PA 15009.

BLANCHARD, CHARLES ALBERT. b. Nov 8, 1848, Galesburg, IL; d. Dec 20, 1925, Wheaton, IL; par. Jonathan (q.v.) and Mary Avery (Bent) Blanchard; m. Margaret Ellen Milligan, Oct 16, 1873; m. 2d, Jennie Carothers, Jun 30, 1886; m. 3d, Dr. Frances Carothers, Feb 19, 1896; c. Mary Belle (Mrs. Joseph Weaver); Julia Eleanor; Rachel Geraldine (Mrs. Harold Mackensie); Clara Lovancia (Mrs. Leonard Bushnell King); Jane Caroline (Mrs. John Flint Blanchard); Mildred Nora (Mrs. Glenn Byron Ogden). EDUC.: A.B., Wheaton Coll., 1870; D.D., Monmouth Coll., 1896. POLIT. & GOV.: ***candidate for American Prohibition Party nomination to presidency of the U.S., 1884***. BUS. & PROF.: agent, lecturer, National Christian Assn., 1870–72; principal, preparatory school, Wheaton, IL, 1872–74; prof. of English language and literature, Wheaton Coll., 1874–78, vice pres., 1878–82, pres., prof. of philosophy, 1882–1925; ordained minister, Congregational Church, 1878; preacher, First Presbyterian Church, Paxton, IL; preacher, Independent Cumberland Presbyterian Church, Streator, IL; pastor, College Church of Christ, Wheaton, 1878–83; pastor, Chicago Ave. Church, Chicago, IL, 1883–85. MEM.: National Fundamentalist Assn. (vice pres.); Chicago Tract Soc. (dir.); Africa-Inland Mission (dir.); Christian and Missionary Alliance (vice pres.); Sabbath Assn. of IL (pres.); IL State Teachers' Assn. (pres., College Section); National Christian Assn. (pres., 1903–04). WRITINGS: *Educational Papers* (1883); *Modern Secret Societies* (1903); *Light on the Last Days* (1913); *An Old Testament Gospel: An Analysis of the Book of Jonah* (1913–25); *Getting Things from God* (1915); *Visions and Voices* (1916). REL.: Congregationalist. MISC.: noted as leader of "fundamentalist" Christianity. RES.: Wheaton, IL.

BLANCHARD, JONATHAN. b. Jan 19, 1811, Rockingham, VT; d. May 14, 1892, Wheaton, IL; par. Jonathan and Mary (Lovel) Blanchard; m. Mary Avery Bent, 1838; c. Charles Albert (q.v.); four other sons; seven daughters. EDUC.: grad., Middlebury Coll., 1832; Andover Acad.; D.D., Lane Theological Seminary, 1838. POLIT. & GOV.: delegate, American National Party National Convention, 1875; ***candidate for American National Party nomination to presidency of the U.S., 1876 (withdrew); candidate for American Prohibition Party nomination to presidency of the U.S., 1884; American Party candidate for presidency of the U.S., 1884 (withdrew)***. BUS. & PROF.: teacher, 1825; teacher, Plattsburg Acad., 1832–34; ordained minister, Presbyterian Church, 1838; pastor, Sixth Presbyterian Church, Cincinnati, OH, 1838–47; founder, ed., *Herald and Presbyter*; pres., Knox Coll., Galesburg, IL, 1845–57; minister, First Church, Galesburg, 1850–60; founder, ed., *Christian Era*, Galesburg, 1858; pres., Wheaton (IL) Coll., 1860–82, pres. emeritus, 1882–92; ed., *Christian Cynosure*, 1879. MEM.: Anti-Secret Society Assn.; National Christian Assn.; World Anti-Slavery Convention (delegate, London, England, 1843). WRITINGS: *A Debate on Slavery* (1846); *Free Masonry Illustrated* (1879). REL.: Presb. RES.: Wheaton, IL.

BLAND, RICHARD PARKS. b. Aug 10, 1835, Hartford, KY; d. Jun 15, 1899, Lebanon, MO; par. Stoughton Edward and Margaret Parks (Nall) Bland; m. Virginia Elizabeth "Virdie" Mitchell, Dec 17, 1873; c. Virgie; Fanny; Theo; Ewing Charles; George Vest; Hattie; Margaret Nall; John Lilburn; Virginia M. EDUC.: Hartford (KY) Acad.; studied law. POLIT. & GOV.: appointed cty. treas., Carson Cty., Territory of UT, 1860–64; elected as a Democrat to U.S. House (MO), 1873–95, 1897–99; Democratic candidate for U.S. House (MO), 1894; ***candidate for Democratic nomination to presidency of the U.S., 1896; candidate for Democratic nomination to vice presidency of the U.S., 1896***. BUS. & PROF.: schoolteacher; miner, CA and NV, 1855–65; atty.; law practice, Virginia City, Territory of UT, 1861–65; law practice (with C. C. Bland), Rolla, MO, 1865–69; law practice, Lebanon, MO, 1869–72. MIL.: member, Col. Jack Hayes' Expedition against Paiute Indians, 1860. MEM.: Masons. MISC.: noted as a leader of the Free Silver Movement. RES.: Lebanon, MO.

BLAUVELT, KAREN-LEE. POLIT. & GOV.: ***independent candidate for presidency of the U.S., 1988***. MAILING ADDRESS: 1 Edgewood Rd., Billerica, MA 01821.

BLESSITT, ARTHUR OWEN. b. Oct 27, 1940, Greenville, MS; par. Arthur Owen N. and Mary Virginia (Campbell) Blessitt; m. Sherry Anne Simmons; c. Gina; Joel; Joy; Joshua; Joseph. EDUC.: grad., Linn H.S.; MS Coll., Clinton, MS; Golden Gate Theological Seminary, Mill Valley, CA. POLIT. & GOV.: ***candidate for Democratic nomination to presidency of the U.S., 1976***. BUS. & PROF.: evangelist; ordained minister, Baptist Church, Oct 26, 1960; operator, Jesus Nightclub, Hollywood, CA. WRITINGS: *Turned On to Jesus; Tell the World; 40 Days at the Cross; Adventures in Faith; Simon; Life's Greatest Trip;* "The Jesus Witness" (recording); "Soul Sermon" (recording); "Give Me a 'J'" (movie); "Go-Go-Arthur" (movie). REL.: Bapt. MISC.: known as the "Minister of Sunset Strip"; carried religious cross 11,000 miles across U.S., Europe and Africa. MAILING ADDRESS: 9143 South West 77th Ave., Miami, FL 93156.

BLISS, CORNELIUS NEWTON. b. Jan 26, 1833, Fall River, MA; d. Oct 9, 1911, New York, NY; par. Asahel Newton and Irene Borden (Luther) Bliss; m. Elizabeth Mary Plumer, Mar 30, 1859; c. Cornelius Newton, Jr.; Lizzie Plumer. EDUC.: public schools, Fall River, MA; Fisher's Acad. POLIT. & GOV.: candidate for Republican nomination to gov. of NY, 1885 (declined), 1891 (declined); chm., NY State Republican Central Cmte., 1887–88; delegate, Pan-American Conference, 1889–90; treas., Rep. Nat'l. Cmte., 1892–1908; appointed U.S. sec. of the interior, 1897–99; ***candidate for Republican nomination to vice presidency of the U.S., 1900 (declined)***. BUS. & PROF.: partner, John J. and Eben Wright and Co. (dry goods), Boston, MA, 1866–81; partner, Bliss, Fabyan and Co. (dry goods), New York, 1881–1911; trustee, American Surety Co.; trustee, Central Trust Co.; dir., Home Insurance Co.; dir., pres., Fourth National Bank; dir., American Cotton Co.; dir., Equitable Life Assurance Co. MEM.: American Protective Tariff League (pres.); Players Club; Riding Club; Merchants Club; NY Hospital (pres.); New England Soc.; C. of C. (vice pres.); National Civic Federation (exec. cmte.); Union Club; Century Club; Union League; Metropolitan Club; Broadway Tabernacle (trustee); Jekyl Island Club. REL.: Congregationalist. RES.: New York, NY.

BLOCK, SUSAN MARILYN. b. Jun 10, 1955, Philadelphia, PA; par. Morris and Myrtle (Gardner) Block; m. Maximillian Lobkowicz. EDUC.: B.A., Yale U.; M.A., Pacific Western U., Ph.D. POLIT. & GOV.: ***The Block Party candidate for presidency of the U.S., 1992***. BUS. & PROF.: author; publisher; radio and television star; talk show host, radiophone; sex therapist. WRITINGS: *Dr. Susan Block's Journal* (1991, 1992). REL.: Jewish. MAILING ADDRESS: 8306 Wilshire Blvd., #1047, Beverly Hills, CA 90211.

BLOCK, WALTER EDWARD. b. Aug 21, 1941, New York, NY; par. Abraham and Ruth (Peps) Block; m. Mary Beth Zimmer; c. Mathew. EDUC.: B.A., Brooklyn Coll., 1965; Ph.D., Columbia U., 1972. POLIT. & GOV.: Free Libertarian Party candidate for NY State Assembly, 1972; ***candidate for Libertarian Party nomination to vice presidency of the U.S., 1976***. BUS. & PROF.: research asst., National Bureau of Economic Research, 1967; instructor, Bronx Community Coll., 1967–68; instructor, State U. of NY, Stony Brook, NY, 1967–68; instructor, NY U., 1969; asst. prof., Rutgers U., 1968–71; asst. prof. of economics, Baruch Coll., 1971–74; publisher, *Outlook*; asst. ed., *Business Week*, 1974–75; freelance writer, 1975–; author. MEM.: Center for Libertarian Studies (treas.); American Economic Assn.; Earhart Foundation (fellow, 1966–67). WRITINGS: *Defending the Undefendable: Pimps, Prostitutes, Libelers, Slanderers, Blackmailers and Other Heroes in the Rogues Gallery of American Society* (1975). REL.: none. MAILING ADDRESS: c/o Dept. of Economics, Baruch Coll., 17 Lexington Ave., NY, NY 10010.

BLOMBERG, IVAR RUEBEN. b. Jul 9, 1906, La Grange, IL; par. Joseph and Emilie (Elmblade) Blomberg; m. Vivian E. Carlson; c. Kristin; Caryn; Donna. EDUC.: Albion Coll. POLIT. & GOV.: ***Commandments Party candidate for presidency of the U.S., 1976***. BUS. & PROF.: publisher; lapidary; author. WRITINGS: *Discombobulated Ostriches*. REL.: The Ten Commandments. MAILING ADDRESS: Burt Lake, MI 49717.

BLOMEN, CONSTANCE ZIMMERMAN. b. Jun 25, 1929, Minneapolis, MN; d. Carle C. and Madeleine (Andrist) Zimmerman; m. Henning Albert Blomen (q.v.), Feb 17, 1969 (divorced); m. 2d, ? Furdeck; c. Colee. EDUC.: grad., Boston Museum of Fine Arts School; B.S.Ed., Tufts U., 1954. POLIT. & GOV.: New England field worker, Socialist Labor Party, 1976–; ***Socialist Labor Party candidate for vice presidency of the U.S., 1976***. BUS. & PROF.: political organizer, Socialist Labor Party; teacher and art supervisor, Manchester (MA) Public Schools; district sales mgr., World Book Encyclopedia Co. MAILING ADDRESS: 25 County St., Ipswich, MA 01938.

BLOMEN, HENNING ALBERT. b. Sep 28, 1910, New Bedford, MA; par. Gustav A. and Clara E. (Magnuson) Blomen; m. Apr 27, 1945 (divorced); m. 2d, Constance Zimmerman (q.v.), Feb 17, 1969 (divorced); c. Frances (Mrs. Tripp); Colee. EDUC.: grad., Somerville (MA) H.S., 1928. POLIT. & GOV.: state organizer, PA Socialist Labor Party; member, exec. cmte., Socialist Labor Party National Cmte.; Socialist Labor Party candidate for MA State Senate; Socialist Labor Party candidate for MA State Auditor; Socialist Labor Party candidate for gov. of MA, 1938, 1940, 1942, 1944, 1956, 1958, 1960, 1962, 1964, 1966, 1970, 1972, 1974; delegate, Socialist Labor Party National Convention, 1964 (Platform Cmte.), 1968 (Platform Cmte.); ***Socialist Labor Party candidate for vice presidency of the U.S., 1964; Socialist Labor Party candidate for presidency of the U.S., 1968;*** Socialist Labor Party candidate for U.S. Senate (MA), 1976. BUS. & PROF.: employee, Dewey and Almy Chemical Co., Division of W. R. Grace, Inc., 1938–69. REL.: Brotherhood of Man. MAILING ADDRESS: 25 County St., Ipswich, MA 01938.

BLOOD, JAMES HARVEY (aka DR. J. H. HARVEY). b. Dec 29, 1833, Dudley, MA; d. Dec 29, 1885, British Gold Coast, Africa; par. Nathaniel and Clarinda Blood.; m. (divorced, 1866); m. 2d, Victoria Claflin Woodhull (q.v.), 1866 (divorced, 1868), 1869 (divorced, 1876); m. 3d, Mrs. Nathan Fogg; c. two. POLIT. & GOV.: claimed to have been elected city auditor, St. Louis, MO, 1865; delegate, Equal Rights (Cosmic, Free Love, People's) Party National Convention, 1872;

candidate for Equal Rights (Cosmic, Free Love, People's) Party nomination to vice presidency of the U.S., 1872; corresponding sec., Central National Cmte., Equal Rights (Cosmic, Free Love, People's) Party, 1872; delegate, Greenback Party National Convention, 1880. BUS. & PROF.: reporter, *St. Louis (MO) Times*; medicine showman; ed., *Woodhull & Claflin's Weekly*; ed., *Greenback Labor Chronicle*, Auburn, ME, 1878–79; clerk, Governor's Island, NY; baker; hypnotist; lecturer; spiritualist. MIL.: col., Sixth MO Regt., U.S. Army, 1861. MEM.: Soc. of Spiritualists of St. Louis (pres.). REL.: Spiritualist. MISC.: advocate of free love and vegetarianism. RES.: St. Louis, MO.

BLOW, HENRY TAYLOR. b. Jul 15, 1817, Southampton, VA; d. Sep 11, 1875, Saratoga, NY; par. Peter and Elizabeth (Taylor) Blow; m. Minerva Grimsley; c. twelve. EDUC.: grad. (cum laude), St. Louis U., 1835. POLIT. & GOV.: elected as a Free Soil-Whig to MO State Senate, 1854–58; delegate, Rep. Nat'l. Conv., 1860; appointed U.S. minister to Venezuela, 1861–62; elected as a Republican to U.S. House (MO), 1863–67; appointed U.S. minister to Brazil, 1869–71; appointed member, Board of Commissioners, District of Columbia, 1874–75; ***candidate for Republican nomination to presidency of the U.S., 1876 (deceased)***. BUS. & PROF.: lead miner, Southwestern MO; pres., Iron Mountain R.R. RES.: St. Louis, MO.

BOCOCK, THOMAS STANLEY. b. May 18, 1815, Buckingham Cty., VA; d. Aug 5, 1891, Appomattox Cty., VA; par. John Thomas and Mary (Flood) Bocock; m. Sarah P. Flood, 1846; m. 2d, Annie Faulkner; c. one son; four daughters. EDUC.: B.A., Hampden-Sidney Coll., 1838; studied law under Willis Bocock. POLIT. & GOV.: elected as a Democrat to VA State House of Delegates, 1842–45, 1869–70, 1877–78; elected prosecuting atty., Appomattox Cty., VA, 1845–46; delegate, Dem. Nat'l. Conv., 1856, 1868, 1876, 1880; elected as a Democrat to U.S. House (VA), 1847–61; ***candidate for Democratic nomination to presidency of the U.S., 1860***; elected to Confederate House of Reps., 1861–62 (Speaker, 1862). BUS. & PROF.: atty.; law practice, Buckingham Cty., VA; counsel, Atlantic, Mississippi and Ohio R.R.; counsel, Richmond and Allegheny R.R. MEM.: VA Bar Assn.; Hampden-Sidney Coll. (dir., 1880s). REL.: Presb. RES.: Appomattox Cty., VA.

BODDIE, RICHARD BENJAMIN. b. Oct 19, 1938, Elmira, NY; par. Rev. Charles Emerson and Mary Lavinia (Johnson) Boddie; m. Ann Lynette Snellings, Jul 27, 1963; c. Jordana Lynette; Roxanne Marie; Erica Lynn. EDUC.: Baldwin-Wallace Coll., Bera, OH, 1956–57; A.B., Bucknell U., 1961; J.D., Syracuse U., 1970. POLIT. & GOV.: fund raiser, Bergland for President Campaign, 1984; ***candidate for Libertarian Party nomination to presidency of the U.S., 1992; candidate for Libertarian Party nomination to vice presidency of the U.S., 1992***; Libertarian Party candidate for U.S. Senate (CA), 1992. BUS. & PROF.: motivator; trainer; bank mgr., Chase Lincoln-First Bank, Rochester, NY, 1962–67; host, video ombudsman, "Citizen Advocate" (television program), WCNY-TV, 1969–70; assoc., Denson and Kurtzman (law firm), Rochester, NY, 1971–76; host, "Black to White" (radio program), WAXC-AM, 1971–77; columnist, *About Time Magazine*, 1977–76; deputy dir., American Arbitration Assn., Rochester, NY, 1973–77; micrographic sales representative, Eastman Kodak, 1977–78; field life underwriter, NY Life, Long Beach, CA, 1978–80; Amway Distributor; law clerk, investigator, Giles, Callahan, McCune, Willis and Edwards (law firm), Tustin, CA, 1980–81; exec. dir., Conflict Resolution Services, Huntington Beach, CA, 1980–; business development officer, Wells Fargo Bank, Newport Beach, CA, 1981–83; dir. of marketing, house counsel, R. W. McCarthy and Associates, Irvine, CA; investment sales and financial planner, First Meridian Financial, Newport Beach, CA, 1981–83; pres. and founder, The Motivators, Huntington Beach, CA, 1983–; accounts receivable administrator, Xerox Corp., Santa Ana, CA, 1987–89; adjunct prof., U. of La Verne, School of Continuing Education, Orange Cty., CA, 1989–. MEM.: BSA (Eagle Scout); Advocates for Self-Government; Alpha Phi Alpha; American Center for Conflict Resolution (dir.); Delta Upsilon; Foundation for Economic Education; Huntington Beach Community Clinic (dir.); National Assn. of Self-Employed; National Speakers Assn.; American Arbitration Assn.; ABA; American Red Cross; Black Media Assn.; Colgate Rochester Divinity School (trustee); National Bar Assn.; National Center for Dispute Settlement; St. Simons Episcopal Church (vestryman). AWARDS: one of the "Outstanding Young Men in America," Junior C. of C., 1970; Bertha Schwartz Memorial Award for Outstanding Community Service, 1970; received Urban League Award, 1976. REL.: Judeo-Christian Zen Episcopal Pantheist Religious Science Existentialist. MISC.: Niagara District A.A.U. Decathlon Championship, 1959, 1960; "Most Valuable Player," Bucknell Track and Field, 1960, 1961; student body pres., Syracuse Law School, 1969–70; Rochester Track Club Hall of Fame, 1972. MAILING ADDRESS: 8855 Atlanta Ave., #301, Huntington Beach, CA 92646.

BOGNUDA, ABRAHAM WASHINGTON. POLIT. & GOV.: ***Whig candidate for presidency of the U.S., 1992***. MAILING ADDRESS: c/o S. Jon Gudmonds, 1701 West Stowell Rd., Santa Maria, CA 93474.

BOGUE, ALAN. b. Nov 15, 1867, Arlington, WI; d. Sep 17, 1953, Sioux Falls, SD; par. Alan and Ellen (Stevenson) Bogue; m. Jane Allison Dunlop, Jun 7, 1898; c. Everett Alan; Robert William; Beatrice (Mrs. Jewell Paulson). EDUC.: Poynette Presbyterian Coll.; LL.B., U. of WI, 1894. POLIT. & GOV.: delegate, Rep. Nat'l. Conv., 1912; elected as a Republican to SD State Senate, 1923–27; ***candidate for Republican nomination to presidency of the U.S., 1932***. BUS. & PROF.: atty.; law practice, Centerville, SD, 1894–1944; partner (with Everett A. Bogue), law practice, Parker, SD; law practice, Sioux Falls, 1944–53; farmer. MEM.: SD Bar Assn. REL.: Presb. RES.: Vermilion, SD.

BOIES, HORACE. b. Dec 7, 1827, Aurora, NY; d. Apr 4, 1923, Long Beach, CA; par. Heber and Esther "Hattie" (Henshaw) Boies; m. Adella King, May 10, 1848; m. 2d, Versalia M. Barbar, 1857; c. E. Louis; Herbert B.; Jessica "Jessie" B.; Nellie (Mrs. John Carson). EDUC.: public schools, Erie Cty., NY; studied law under S. S. Clark, Erie Cty., NY. POLIT. & GOV.: elected as a Republican to NY State Assembly, 1859–61; Republican candidate for NY State Assembly, 1860; elected as a Democrat to gov. of IA, 1890–94; ***candidate for Democratic nomination to presidency of the U.S., 1892, 1896, 1900; candidate for Democratic nomination to vice presidency of the U.S., 1892, 1896, 1900***; appointed U.S. sec. of agriculture, 1892 (declined); Democratic candidate for gov. of IA, 1893; Democratic candidate for U.S. House (IA), 1902. BUS. & PROF.: atty.; farmer; law practice, Buffalo, NY, 1849–67; law practice, Waterloo, IA, 1867–1923; partner, Boies and Allen (law firm), Waterloo, IA, 1867; partner, Boies and Couch (law firm; subsequently Boies, Couch and Boies), Waterloo, IA; partner, Boies and Boies (law firm), Waterloo, IA. MEM.: NY Bar Assn.; Independent Order of Good Templars. REL.: unaffiliated Christian. RES.: Waterloo, IA.

BONA, FRANK JOSEPH. b. Jul 31, 1921, Buffalo, NY; par. Russell and Sarah (Pollizzotto) Bona; m. Nancy J. Janas (Janaziewicz); c. Frank; John; Rosanne; Bonita; Nancy. EDUC.: grad., Grover Cleveland H.S., Buffalo, NY; Canisius Coll.; LL.B., Cornell U., 1946. POLIT. & GOV.: ***candidate for Democratic nomination to presidency of the U.S., 1972, 1976, 1980, 1992***. BUS. & PROF.: atty.; law practice, Buffalo, NY, 1949–; adjudicator, VA, 1946–49. MIL.: U.S. Air Force, 1942–44. MEM.: NY Bar Assn. REL.: R.C. MAILING ADDRESS: 135 Delaware Ave., Buffalo, NY 14202.

BOND, CHRISTOPHER SAMUEL. b. Mar 6, 1939, St. Louis, MO; par. Arthur Doerr and Elizabeth (Green) Bond; m. Carolyn Ann Reid, May 13, 1967. EDUC.: B.A. (cum laude), Princeton U., 1960; LL.B., U. of VA, 1963; LL.D., Westminster Coll., 1973; LL.D., William Jewell Coll., 1973; D.Litt., Drury Coll., 1976. POLIT. & GOV.: law clerk to chief justice, U.S. Court of Appeals for the Fifth Circuit, 1963–64; Republican candidate for U.S. House (MO), 1968; appointed asst. atty. gen. of MO, 1969–70; elected as a Republican to state auditor of MO, 1971–73; elected as a Republican to gov. of MO, 1973–77, 1981–85; ***candidate for Republican nomination to vice presidency of the U.S., 1976***; Republican candidate for gov. of MO, 1976; elected as a Republican to U.S. Senate (MO), 1987–. BUS. & PROF.: atty.; admitted to the Bar of the Supreme Court of the U.S., 1967; assoc., Covington and Burling (law firm), Washington, DC, 1965–67; law practice, Mexico, MO, 1968–. MEM.: Optimists; Junior C. of C.; MO Bar Assn.; VA Bar Assn.; School of the Ozarks (trustee); Republican Governors' Assn. (chm., 1974); Omicron Delta Kappa; Cottage Club; Order of the Coif; Great Plains Legal Foundation (pres., 1977–); National Governors' Conference (exec. cmte., 1974–75). AWARDS: Outstanding Graduating Student, U. of VA Law School, 1963; one of ten "Outstanding Young Men in America," U.S. Junior C. of C., 1974. REL.: Presb. MAILING ADDRESS: 14 South Jefferson Rd., Mexico, MO 65265.

BOND, HORACE JULIAN. b. Jan 14, 1940, Nashville, TN; par. Horace Mann and Julia Agnes (Washington) Bond; m. Alice Louise Clopton, Jul 28, 1961; m. 2d, Pamela S. Horowitz, Mar 1990; c. Horace Mann II; Phyllis Jane; Michael Julian; Jeffrey Alvin; Julia Louise. EDUC.: B.A., Morehouse Coll., 1971. POLIT. & GOV.: elected as a Democrat to GA State House, 1965–75 (twice barred from seat, 1966); ***candidate for Democratic nomination to vice presidency of the U.S., 1968, 1972***; elected as a Democrat to GA State Senate, 1975–; ***candidate for Democratic nomination to presidency of the U.S., 1976 (withdrew); candidate for Independent (Cmte. for a Constitutional President) nomination to vice presidency of the U.S., 1976; Independent Freedom Party candidate for presidency of the U.S., 1976 (declined); The Black Assembly candidate for presidency of the U.S., 1976 (declined)***; member, exec. cmte., GA State Democratic Central Cmte.; candidate for Democratic nomination to U.S. House (GA), 1986. BUS. & PROF.: dir., Student Voice, Inc.; dir., Southern Educational and Research Assn.; reporter, *Atlanta (GA) Inquirer*, 1960–61, managing ed., 1963; author; poet; lecturer; community organizer. MEM.: New Democratic Coalition (dir.); Voter Education Project (dir.); NAACP; Delta Ministry Project (dir.); National Sharecroppers' Fund (dir.); Highlander Research and Educational Center (dir.); Student Non-Violent Coordinating Council (founder, 1960; communications dir., 1961–66); Southern Regional Council (dir.); Southern Conference Educational Fund, Inc. (dir.); Robert F. Kennedy Memorial Fund (dir.); Martin Luther King, Jr. Memorial Center for Social Change (dir.); Cmte. for Appeal for Human Rights (founder, 1960; exec. sec., 1961); African-American Inst. (dir.); Southern Poverty Law Center (dir.); Southern Elections Fund (pres.); Center for Community Change (dir.); Southern Correspondents Reporting Racial Equality Wars; Phi Kappan (hon. member); A.C.L.U. (adviser); Inst. of Applied Politics (trustee); National Council of Churches (dir.). HON. DEG.: LL.D., Dalhousie U., 1969; LL.D., U. of Bridgeport, 1969; LL.D., Wesleyan U., 1969; LL.D., U. of OR, 1969; D.C.L., Lincoln U., 1970; LL.D., U. of Syracuse, 1970; LL.D., Harvard U., 1971; LL.D., Morgan State Teachers Coll., 1971; LL.D., Wilberforce Coll., 1971; LL.D., Tuskegee Inst., 1971; LL.D., Eastern MI U., 1971; LL.D., Bard Coll.; LL.D., U. of CT; LL.D., Howard U., 1971; LL.D., Detroit Inst. of Technology, 1973; LL.D., NH Coll., 1973. WRITINGS: *A Time to Speak, a Time to Act* (1972). MAILING ADDRESS: 794 Juniper St., N.E., Atlanta, GA 30308.

BONGIOVANNI, JOSEPH THOMAS. b. 1911; m. Virginia Bongiovanni; c. fifteen. POLIT. & GOV.: candidate for Democratic nomination to U.S. House (FL), 1974; ***candidate for Democratic nomination to presidency of the***

U.S., 1980. BUS. & PROF.: aluminum window manufacturer. WRITINGS: *Christian Capitalism* (1959). MAILING ADDRESS: 1401 N.W. 194th St., Miami, FL 33169.

BONNELL, KENNETH MYRON. b. Feb 22, 1928, Haverhill, MA; par. John Robert and Grace (Hartford) Bonnell; m. Joyce Lefebvre; m. 2d, Elizabeth Correro; c. Kenneth Mark; Linda Anne; Debra Elizabeth; stepchildren: Veronica Berry; Denise Hancock. EDUC.: grad., Haverhill (MA) H.S., 1945. POLIT. & GOV.: ***independent candidate for presidency of the U.S., 1980, 1984, 1988***. BUS. & PROF.: radio news dir.; technical writer; salesman, dental laboratories; salesman, industrial cleaners; placement counselor, employment office; newspaper columnist, *Delta (MS) Democrat-Times*, Greenville, MS; dir. of public relations and marketing, Delta Medical Center, Greenville, MS, 1976–84; pres., trophy and plaque shop, Greenville, MS, 1985–. MIL.: RMCS, E-8, U.S. Navy, 1945–67. MEM.: Kiwanis; CT Little League (sec.-treas.); CT Hist. Soc.; Private Library (pres., board of trustees). WRITINGS: *Our Navy* (1960s); *This Day* (1960s). REL.: R.C. (nee Presb.). MAILING ADDRESS: 3532 South Woodlawn Dr., Greenville, MS 38701.

BONNETTE, EDMOND J. c. Melanie; Desiree. POLIT. & GOV.: ***candidate for Democratic nomination to vice presidency of the U.S., 1972***. MEM.: Let Us Vote (chm.). MISC.: advocate of 18-year-old voting. MAILING ADDRESS: 1812 Sicklerville Rd., Sicklerville, NJ 08081.

BONNIWELL, EUGENE CLEOPHAS. b. Sep 25, 1872, Philadelphia, PA; d. Jun 3, 1964, Philadelphia, PA; par. James Evander Berry and Elizabeth (O'Doherty) Bonniwell; m. Madeleine Helene Curry, Aug 28, 1934; c. Eugene Cahill; Robert Budd; John Green; Bernard Leonard; Madeleine Helen (Mrs. William Bodo); Alfred Eugene; Eleanor Mary (Mrs. John J. Hosey). EDUC.: Broad Street Acad.; LL.B., U. of PA, 1893. POLIT. & GOV.: solicitor, Dept. of Collections, Philadelphia, PA; Democratic (Key Party) candidate for U.S. House (PA), 1910, 1912; elected judge, Municipal Court, Philadelphia, PA, 1913–53; Democratic-Fair Play Party candidate for gov. of PA, 1918, 1926; ***candidate for Democratic nomination to presidency of the U.S., 1920***; appointed clerk and librarian, Municipal Court, Philadelphia, PA, 1953-1963; appointed trial commissioner, Municipal Court, Philadelphia, PA, 1954-1964. BUS. & PROF.: atty.; employee, law office of Edwin Megargee; partner, Green and Bonniwell (law firm), Philadelphia, PA, 1893–1913. MEM.: SAR (pres., Philadelphia Chapter, 1917–19, 1943–44; chancellor gen., 1920–22; national trustee, 1943–45); ABA; PA Bar Assn.; Bar Assn. of Philadelphia; Order of Washington; Order of Lafayette; Soc. of the War of 1812; Sons of Union Veterans; Soc. of Saint George; Friendly Sons of Saint Patrick; Elks; Moose; Eagles; One Hundred Club; Valley Green Canoe Club; Reciprocity Club; Middle Atlantic Amateur Athletic Union (pres., 1938–48); Amateur Athletic Union of the U.S. (vice pres., 1949); PA Firemen's Assn. (pres., 1915–21); Knights of Columbus. Awards.: commander, Order of the Crown of Italy, 1924; chevalier, Order of Polonia Restituta, 1931; commander, Order of Danilio I of Montenegro, 1919. WRITINGS: "Quo Vadis?" *Dickinson Law Review* (1954). RES.: Philadelphia, PA.

BOOTH, NEWTON. b. Dec 25, 1825, Salem, IN; d. Jul 14, 1892, Sacramento, CA; par. Beebe and Hannah (Pitts) Booth; m. Mrs. J. T. Glover, Feb 29, 1892; c. none. EDUC.: grad., DePauw U., 1846. POLIT. & GOV.: elected as a Republican to CA State Senate, 1863; elected as a Republican to gov. of CA, 1871–75; elected as an Anti-Monopolist to U.S. Senate (CA), 1875–81; ***candidate for National Independent (Greenback) Party nomination to presidency of the U.S., 1876 (withdrew); National Independent (Greenback) Party candidate for vice presidency of the U.S., 1876 (declined)***. BUS. & PROF.: atty.; wholesale grocer, Sacramento, CA, 1850–57; law practice, Terre Haute, IN, 1850, 1857–60; merchant, Sacramento, CA, 1860–92; law practice, Sacramento, CA, 1860–92; contributor, *Sacramento Union*. MEM.: IN Bar Assn. WRITINGS: *Spiritual: A Lecture Delivered in . . . Sacramento, October 28, 1863* (1865); *Newton Booth of California: His Speeches and Addresses* (1894). REL.: Protestant. RES.: Sacramento, CA.

BOOTH, ROBERT ASBURY. b. May 15, 1858, Yamhill Cty., OR; d. Apr 28, 1944, Eugene, OR; par. Robert and Mary (Minor) Booth; m. Clintona A. La Raut, May 15, 1881; c. Echo Vivian; Robert Roy; Floyd Wilson; Barbara Wenzori. EDUC.: grad., Umpqua Acad., 1875; grad., Healds Business Coll., San Francisco, CA, 1879. POLIT. & GOV.: delegate, Rep. Nat'l. Conv., 1896; delegate, OR Republican State Convention, 20 years; elected as a Republican to OR State Senate, 1901–09; Republican candidate for U.S. Senate (OR), 1914; appointed member, OR State Board of Highway Commissioners, 5 years (chm., 3 years); appointed member, OR State Park Comm.; ***candidate for Republican nomination to vice presidency of the U.S., 1932***. BUS. & PROF.: merchant, 1880–85; publisher, *Drain (OR) Echo*; principal, OR State Normal School, 1886–87; bookkeeper, Sugar Pine Door and Lumber Co., 1888, sec., 1889, mgr., 1895, owner, 1899–1944; founder, First National Bank, Grants Pass, OR, 1889, cashier, pres., 1889–1905; vice pres., Grants Pass Banking and Trust Co., 2 years; pres., Douglas National Bank, Roseburg, OR, 5 years; pres., Umpqua Hotel Co.; founder, dir., mgr., vice pres., Booth-Kelly Lumber Co., 1897–1944; founder, pres., OR Land and Live Stock Co., 1906–44; founder, Ochoco Timber Co., 1923–44. MEM.: Rotary Club; Commercial Club of Portland; Commercial Club of Eugene; Willamette U. (trustee, 35 years); OR Tuberculosis Soc. (dir.). HON. DEG.: LL.D., Coll. of the Puget Sound, 1922; LL.D., Willamette U., 1923; M.A. (hon.), U. of OR, 1929. REL.: Methodist. MISC.: presented state of OR with heroic bronze equestrian statue; founded student loan programs at U. of OR, OR Agricultural Coll., Reed Coll., Willamette U., and Pacific Coll. RES.: Eugene, OR.

BOOZER, MELVIN. b. 1946, Washington, DC; d. Mar 6, 1987, Washington, DC; par. Mrs. Lossie M. Brown; single (partner: Robert Lee). EDUC.: grad., Dunbar H.S., Washington, DC, 1963; grad., Dartmouth Coll., 1967; Oberlin Coll.; M.A., Yale U. POLIT. & GOV.: alternate delegate, Dem. Nat'l. Conv., 1980; ***candidate for Democratic nomination to vice presidency of the U.S., 1980***; member, Steering Cmte., Jesse Jackson for President Campaign, 1984. BUS. & PROF.: Peace Corps worker, Brazil, 1967–70; prof. of sociology, U. of MD; Washington dir., National Gay and Lesbian Task Force, Washington, DC, 1981–83; Public Information Coordinator, District of Columbia Assn. for Retarded Citizens, 1983–87. MEM.: District of Columbia Gay Activists Alliance (pres., 1979–81); Langston Hughes-Eleanor Roosevelt Democratic Club (co-chm., 1983–84); Americans for Democratic Action (dir.); Dunbar Cadet Corps (col.); Lesbian and Gay Democratic Caucus. AWARDS: "Outstanding Teen-Ager," Junior C. of C., Washington, DC, 1963. MISC.: noted as gay rights activist. RES.: Washington, DC.

BORAH, WILLIAM EDGAR. b. Jun 29, 1865, Fairfield, IL; d. Jan 19, 1940, Washington, DC; par. William Nathan and Elizabeth (West) Borah; m. Mamie McConnell, Apr 21, 1895; c. none. EDUC.: Southern IL Acad.; grad., U. of KS, 1889; read law. POLIT. & GOV.: Silver Republican candidate for U.S. House (ID), 1896; Republican candidate for U.S. Senate (ID), 1903; elected as a Republican to U.S. Senate (ID), 1907–40 (chm., Foreign Relations Cmte., 1924–40); member, Rep. Nat'l. Cmte., 1908–12; delegate, Rep. Nat'l. Conv., 1912, 1920; ***candidate for Republican nomination to presidency of the U.S., 1912, 1916, 1920, 1928, 1936; candidate for Republican nomination to vice presidency of the U.S., 1912, 1916; Prohibition Party candidate for presidency of the U.S., 1932 (declined)***. BUS. & PROF.: atty.; law practice, Lyons, KS, 1890–91; law practice, Boise, ID, 1891–1940. MEM.: KS Bar Assn. REL.: Presb. MISC.: opponent of World Court; strict isolationist; prohibition advocate; reform advocate of direct election of public officials; opponent of League of Nations. RES.: Boise, ID.

BORDEN, JAMES GEORGE. b. Oct 30, 1949, New Bedford, MA; par. Walter Crapo and Mary (Smakis) Borden; m. Gail Ann Pauline; m. 2d, Rebecca Wei Xiu Cai; c. James George, Jr.; Jason Richard; Misty Lee. EDUC.: grad., New Bedford H.S., 1967; Southeastern MA U., 1974–75. POLIT. & GOV.: independent candidate for MA State Senate, 1974; independent candidate for Wareham Board of Selectmen, 1978; ***independent candidate for presidency of the U.S., 1992***. BUS. & PROF.: drug counselor, Aid Center, New Bedford, MA, 1974–80; special education teacher, New Bedford (MA) School Dept., 1980–84; teacher, counselor, HI School Dept., Hilo, HI, 1985–; counselor, Child and Family Serive, State of HI, 1986–91; counselor, Salvation Army, 1992–. MEM.: Amnesty International; Center for Defense Information. REL.: none. MAILING ADDRESS: 50A Maile St., Apt. 21, Hilo, HI 96720.

BOREN, DAVID LYLE. b. Apr 21, 1941, Washington, DC; par. Lyle H. (q.v.) and Christine (McKown) Boren; m. Janna Lou Little, Sep 7, 1968 (divorced, 1976); m. 2d, Molly Shi, Dec 1977; c. David Daniel; Carrie Christine. EDUC.: B.A. (summa cum laude), Yale U., 1963; M.A., Oxford U., 1965; J.D., U. of OK, 1968. POLIT. & GOV.: asst. to dir. of liaison, Office of Civil and Defense Mobilization, Washington, DC, 1960-1962; propaganda analyst in Soviet affairs, U.S. Information Agency, Washington, DC, 1962–63; member, Speakers Bureau, Embassy of the U.S., London, England, 1963–65; elected as a Democrat to OK State House, 1966–74; delegate, Dem. Nat'l. Conv., 1968; elected as a Democrat to gov. of OK, 1975–79; elected as a Democrat to U.S. Senate (OK), 1979–95; ***candidate for Democratic nomination to presidency of the U.S., 1988 (declined); candidate for Democratic nomination to vice presidency of the U.S., 1988***. BUS. & PROF.: member, residential counseling staff, U. of OK, 1965–66; atty.; law practice, Seminole, OK, 1968–74; chm., government dept., OK Baptist U., 1969–74; pres. U. of OK, 1995–. MEM.: OK Bar Assn.; Assn. of U.S. Rhodes Scholars; Order of the Coif; Phi Beta Kappa; Sigma Delta Rho; Phi Delta Phi; Yale Club of Western OK. AWARDS: Rhodes Scholar; Bledsoe Memorial Prize in Law, U. of OK, 1968; "Outstanding Military Graduate," U.S. Army ROTC; one of ten "Outstanding Young Men in the U.S.," U.S. Junior C. of C., 1967. REL.: Methodist. MAILING ADDRESS: Seminole, OK 74868.

BOREN, JAMES HARLAN. b. Dec 10, 1925, Wheatland, OK; par. James Basil and Una Lee (Hamilton) Boren; m. Irene Cheek, Aug 16, 1946; m. 2d, Alice Irene Peters, Oct 23, 1977; c. Richard Vincent; James Stanley. EDUC.: Hardin Coll., 1943–46; B.A., U. of TX, 1948, grad. study, 1952–54, Ph.D., 1969; A.B., CA State Coll. at Long Beach, 1950; A. M., U. of Southern CA, 1950. POLIT. & GOV.: pres., U. of TX Young Democrats, 1952; chief accountant, TX State Dept. of Agriculture, 1952–54; chm., Precinct 100, Tarrant Cty. (TX) Democratic Central Cmte., 1956; campaign mgr., Ralph Yarborough for Governor of Texas, 1956; campaign mgr., Ralph Yarborough for U.S. Senate, 1957; appointed administrative asst., U.S. Sen. Ralph Yarborough, 1957–61; appointed deputy dir., U.S. Operations Mission to Peru, 1961; appointed deputy dir., U.S. Agency for International Development, Mission to Peru, 1961–63; appointed dir., Partners of the Alliance for Progress, 1963–70; appointed special asst. to U.S. coordinator, Alliance for Progress, 1963–70; ***Bureaucratic Party candidate for presidency of the U.S., 1972; Bureaucratic Party candidate for vice presidency of the U.S., 1980, 1984***; Democratic candidate for U.S. House (VA), 1986; ***candidate for Democratic nomination to presidency of the U.S., 1992; Apathy Party candidate for presidency of the U.S., 1992***. BUS. & PROF.: author; lecturer; humorist; chm., World Tapes for Education; prof. of education and chm., education dept., Arlington State Coll., Arlington, TX, 1954–56; pres., Boren Oil and Gas Corp., 1956–57; dir., Development Services International, 1970–76; pres., James H. Boren and Associates; pres., Mumbles, Ltd., 1976–. MIL.: U.S.A.R.; U.S.N.R., 1943–46. MEM.: Phi Delta

Kappa; National Assn. of Professional Bureaucrats (founder; pres., 1968–); APSA; American Foreign Service Assn.; U.S. Senate Administrative Assistants Assn.; Burro Club of the U.S. (pres., 1960); Order of Artus; North Austin Exchange Club (charter member; sec.); Direct Relief Foundation (member, International Advisory Board, 1970–); Educational Communications Assn. (chm. of the board); National Press Club; National Press Assn.; Omicron Delta Gamma; Authors Guild; American Freedom from Hunger Foundation (dir.); IBOB. AWARDS: Outstanding Alumnus Award, Long Beach State Coll., 1961; Meritorious Service Award, Agency for International Development, 1964; Communication Through Humor Award, Toastmasters International, 1977. HON. DEG.: L.H.D., Nathaniel Hawthorne Coll., 1967. WRITINGS: *When in Doubt, Mumble: A Bureaucrat's Handbook* (1972); *Have Your Way with Bureaucrats* (1974); *The Bureaucrat's Zoo* (1976); *Mumblepeg* (newsletter). REL.: Methodist. MISC.: won North American Cow Chip Throwing Championship, 1972. MAILING ADDRESS: James H. Boren and Associates, 908 National Press Building, Washington, DC 20004.

BOREN, LYLE HAGLER. b. May 11, 1909, Wexahachie, TX; d. Jul 2, 1992, OK City, OK; par. Mark Latimer and Nanie Mae (Weatherall) Boren; m. Christine McKown, Dec 26, 1936; c. David Lyle (q.v.); Susan Hope Dorman. EDUC.: B.A., East Central State Coll., 1928; M.A., OK State U., 1936. POLIT. & GOV.: pres., OK Democratic Fraternity, 1934–36; elected as a Democrat to U.S. House (OK), 1937–47; candidate for Democratic nomination to U.S. House (OK), 1946; ***candidate for Democratic nomination to presidency of the U.S., 1964***; appointed deputy procurement officer, U.S. Dept. of the Treasury; appointed asst. insurance commissioner, State of OK, 1970–73. BUS. & PROF.: farmer; author; schoolteacher, Wolf, OK, 1930–35; asst. to the president, U.S. Freight and Universal Car Loading Co.; pres., OK Cattle Co., 1946–55; pres., Seminole Petroleum Co., 1948–57; pres., Boren and Malone Co.; Washington representative, Assn. of Western Railways, 1953–70; pres., Bodrain Co., 1965–. MIL.: lt. commander, U.S.N.R., 1936–55. MEM.: OK Cattlemen's Assn. (founder; pres.); Elks; Odd Fellows; Rotary Club; American Legion; Pi Kappa Delta; Eugene Field Soc. of Authors and Writers; Knights of Pythias; BSA (Silver Beaver Award). WRITINGS: *Who is Who in Oklahoma* (1935); *Fables in Labels* (1940); "History of the Santa Fe Trail," *East Central Journal* (1935); *Evening Bells*. REL.: Church of Christ. RES.: Oklahoma City, OK.

BORGLUM, JOHN GUTZON DE LA MOTHE. b. Mar 25, 1871, Bear Lake, ID; d. Mar 6, 1941, Chicago, IL; par. Dr. James de la Mothe and Cristine (Michelson) Borglum; m. Mrs. Elizabeth Putnam, 1889 (divorced, 1908); m. 2d, Mary Williams Montgomery, May 19, 1909; c. James Lincoln; Mary Ellis (Mrs. David Vhay); infant son. EDUC.: St. Mary's Acad.; Julian Acad., Paris, France; Ecole des Beaux Arts, Paris, France. POLIT. & GOV.: appointed member, NY State Boxing Comm. ; ***National Service Party candidate for vice presidency of the U.S., 1920***. BUS. & PROF.: sculptor; painter; author; aerodynamic engineer. AWARDS: M.A. (hon.), Princeton U.; Gold Medal, Louisiana Purchase Exposition; Knight, Order of Danneborg (Denmark), 1931; Knight, Order of Polonia Restituta, 1931. MEM.: Masons (32°); Ku Klux Klan (1923); NY Parks Assn.; Assn. of American Painters and Sculptors; Aero Club of America; Salmagundi Club; Architectural League of NY; Non-Partisan League; International Sporting Club (pres., 1921); Royal Soc. of British Artists; Societe Nationale des Beaux Arts of Paris; Metropolitan Club; Players Club; Fencers Club. REL.: raised R.C. (nee Church of Jesus Christ of Latter Day Saints). HON. DEG.: LL.D., Oglethorpe U.; Dr. of Letters, Dakota Wesleyan U., 1939. MISC.: noted for national memorial at Mt. Rushmore, SD; marble head of Lincoln in U.S. Capitol Rotunda; Sheridan Equestrian, Washington, DC. RES.: Stamford, CT.

BORKENHAGEN, DAVID MARSHALL. POLIT. & GOV.: ***independent candidate for presidency of the U.S., 1992***. MAILING ADDRESS: OR.

BORTZMEYER, OSCAR C. b. Jun 23, 1875, Cleveland, OH; d. Nov 27, 1953, Portland, OR; m. Lelia G. Stearns, 1905; c. none. EDUC.: Cleveland public schools; business college, Cleveland, OH. POLIT. & GOV.: appointed sec., Municipal Civil Service Comm., Portland, OR; ***candidate for Republican nomination to presidency of the U.S., 1916***; appointed sec., OR State Civil Service Comm., 1917; public service commissioner of OR, 1929–31; chief probation officer, counselor, Juvenile Division, Multnomah Cty. (OR) Court of Domestic Relations, 1931–53. BUS. & PROF.: banker; civil servant. MEM.: Masons; Elks; Goodwill Industries (financial campaign mgr.); Salvation Army (chm., Advisory Board, 1920–38); Royal Rosarians; Portland Methodist City Church Extension Soc. (pres.). REL.: Methodist (trustee, Rose City Church). RES.: Portland, OR.

BOSA, RICHARD P. POLIT. & GOV.: ***candidate for Republican nomination to presidency of the U.S., 1992***. MAILING ADDRESS: Berlin, NH.

BOST, ERNEST WILLIAM. POLIT. & GOV.: ***candidate for Republican nomination to presidency of the U.S., 1980, 1984***. MAILING ADDRESS: 1505 East McDowell Rd., Phoenix, AZ 85036.

BOSWELL, CLINTON VIRGINIA. POLIT. & GOV.: ***candidate for Democratic nomination to presidency of the U.S., 1964***. MAILING ADDRESS: Decatur, GA.

BOTHWELL, SHIRLEY MARIE OAKES. b. Apr 8, 1936, Lenoir, NC; par. Delbert P. and Esalee Anna

Oakes; m. Lt. Col. James H. Bothwell; c. Jamie Helene. EDUC.: Ph.D. in Teacher Education and Nursing, Mars Hill Baptist Coll. POLIT. & GOV.: ***Independent Nuclear Navy Party candidate for presidency of the U.S., 1976, 1980***. BUS. & PROF.: U.S. Navy (retired). MEM.: Parent-Teachers' Assn. REL.: Methodist. MAILING ADDRESS: 8065 Milton Ave., Baltimore, MD 21207.

BOTTS, JOHN MINOR. b. Sep 16, 1802, Dumfries, VA; d. Jan 7, 1869, Culpepper, VA; par. Benjamin A. and Jane (Tyler) Botts; m. Mary Whiting Blair. EDUC.: public schools; studied law. POLIT. & GOV.: elected as a Whig to VA State House of Delegates, 1833–39; delegate, Whig Party National Convention, 1839, 1852; elected as a Whig to U.S. House (VA), 1839–43, 1847–49; Whig candidate for U.S. House (VA), 1842, 1848, 1850; delegate, VA State Constitutional Convention, 1850; American Party candidate for U.S. House (VA), 1854; ***candidate for American Party nomination to presidency of the U.S., 1860; candidate for Constitutional Union Party nomination to presidency of the U.S., 1860***; candidate for delegate, VA Secession Convention, 1860; appointed to U.S. Senate (VA), 1864 (declined); delegate, Southern Loyalist Convention, 1866. BUS. & PROF.: atty.; law practice, Richmond, VA, 1820–26, 1852–61; farmer, Henrico Cty., VA. MEM.: VA Bar Assn. WRITINGS: *The Great Rebellion: Its Secret History, Rise, Progress and Disastrous Failure* (1866). MISC.: imprisoned during Civil War for Union sympathies, 1862. RES.: Richmond, VA.

BOTTUM, JOSEPH HENRY. b. Aug 7, 1903, Faulkton, SD; d. Jul 4, 1984, Rapid City, SD; par. Joseph Henry and Sylvia Grace (Smith) Bottum; m. Nellie Bergita Bang, Aug 20, 1929; c. Mary Jo Bruce. EDUC.: Yankton Coll., 1920; LL.B., U. of MI, 1923; grad., U. of SD, 1927. POLIT. & GOV.: state's atty., Faulkton, SD, 1932–36; chm., SD Young Republican League, 1934–42; appointed dir. of Taxation, State of SD, 1937–43; candidate for Republican nomination to gov. of SD, 1942; ***candidate for Republican nomination to presidency of the U.S., 1944***; chm., SD State Republican Central Cmte., 1946–48; candidate for Republican nomination to U.S. House (SD), 1950; elected as a Republican to lt. gov. of SD, 1960–62; appointed as a Republican to U.S. Senate (SD), 1962–63; Republican candidate for U.S. Senate (SD), 1962; appointed judge, Seventh Judicial District, 1969–78. BUS. & PROF.: atty.; law practice, St. Paul, MN, 1928–30; partner, Jacobs and Bottum (law firm), Faulkton, SD, 1930–36; partner, Bottum and Beal (law firm), Rapid City, SD, 1955-. MEM.: Lamda Chi Alpha; Elks; Masons (33°); Scottish Rite (chapter commandery; Red Cross of Constantine); Shriners (potentate); Odd Fellows; Rapid City C. of C. (pres., 1945); BSA (pres., Black Hills Council); Rapid City Community Chest (pres.); Phi Delta Phi; SD Bar Assn.; ABA; American Jud. Soc.; Pennington Cty. Bar Assn.; Lions; Royal Order of Jesters; Capitol Hill Club; National Sojourners. REL.: Congregationalist. RES.: Rapid City, SD.

BOUCK, WILLIAM MORLEY. b. Sep 5, 1868, Independence, IA; d. Nov 3, 1945, Sedro Woolley, WA; married; c. two sons, three daughters. EDUC.: Princeton (MN) H.S. POLIT. & GOV.: WA state chm., Farmer-Labor Party; Farmer-Labor Party candidate for U.S. House (WA), 1920, 1930; delegate, Farmer-Labor Party National Convention, 1924; ***Farmer-Labor Party candidate for vice presidency of the U.S., 1924 (withdrew)***; Farmer-Labor (Communist) Party candidate for gov. of WA, 1936; chm., Cooperative Commonwealth Party. BUS. & PROF.: prospector, miner, 1892–1902; farmer, Skagit Cty., WA, 1902–45; officer, Commonwealth Coll. MEM.: People's Legislative Service; International Labor Defense Cmte. (member, National Cmte., 1928); National Grange (WA state master, 1917–21; expelled for secessionist activities, 1921); Western Progressive Farmers (pres., 1921); various farmers' movements. RES.: Sedro Woolley, WA.

BOUSQUET, NORMAN J. (aka JESUS CHRIST II). POLIT. & GOV.: ***independent candidate for presidency of the U.S., 1984***. MAILING ADDRESS: Worcester, MA.

BOUTELLE, PAUL BENJAMIN (aka KWAME MONTSHO AJAMU SOMBURU). b. Oct 13, 1934, New York, NY; par. Anton Charles and Anna May (Benjamin) Boutelle; m. (divorced); m. 2d, Zakiya NT Sheffield; c. Daryl; Boutelle; Khalid; Mauri Sumbru. EDUC.: Junior H.S. 120, New York, 3 1/2 years; Eastern School of Real Estate, 1958; Laney Community Coll.; CA State U., Hayward. POLIT. & GOV.: Freedom Now Party candidate for NY State Senate, 1964; Socialist Workers Party candidate for pres., Borough of Manhattan, NY, 1965; Socialist Workers Party candidate for atty. gen. of NY, 1966; ***Socialist Workers Party candidate for vice presidency of the U.S., 1968***; Socialist Workers Party candidate for mayor of New York, 1969; Socialist Workers Party candidate for U.S. House (NY), 1970; Socialist Workers Party candidate for U.S. House (CA), 1974, 1976; Socialist Workers Party candidate for mayor of Oakland, CA, 1977; member, Party Development and Newsletter Cmtes., National Black Independent Political Party, 1981–. BUS. & PROF.: salesman, Mar-Rahman Real Estate Brokers, 1958; representative, Field Enterprises Educational Corp., 1959–61; dir., Pan-African Book Distributors, 1961–63; sales representative, The Negro Book Club, 1961–63; sales representative, Encyclopedia Britannica, 1963–64, 1966, 1969; lecturer, Africa Information Service, New York, 1972–; salesman, Pathfinder Press; columnist, *The Militant*, 1967. MEM.: Young Socialist Alliance, 1960–61; Fair Play for Cuba Cmte., 1961–63; Cmte. to Aid Monroe Defendants, 1962–63; Organization of Afro-American Unity, 1964; Afro-Americans Against the War in Vietnam (founder; chairperson, 1965); Black United Action Front of Harlem (sec., 1966–67); Cmte. of Black Americans for the Truth About the Middle East (chm., 1970); Cmte. for Caribbean Freedom. WRITINGS: *Case for a Black Party* (ed., 1967); *Black Uprisings* (ed., 1968); *Murder in*

Memphis (1968). REL.: atheist. MAILING ADDRESS: 3938 Altamont Ave., Oakland, CA 94605.

BOWLER, WILLIAM HARRISON "BILL." EDUC.: D.D. POLIT. & GOV.: candidate for Republican nomination to U.S. House (AZ), 1968; ***candidate for American Party nomination to presidency of the U.S., 1976; candidate for American Party nomination to vice presidency of the U.S., 1976***. BUS. & PROF.: minister; pastor, Shadow Mountain Baptist Temple, Tucson, AZ. REL.: Bapt. MAILING ADDRESS: Shadow Mountain Baptist Temple, 6900 West Oracle Rd., Tucson, AZ.

BOWLES, CHESTER BLISS. b. Apr 5, 1901, Springfield, MA; d. May 25, 1986, Essex, CT; par. Charles Allen and Nellie (Harris) Bowles; m. Julie Mayo Fisk; m. 2d, Dorothy Stebbins, Feb 22, 1934; c. Barbara; Chester Bliss, Jr.; Cynthia; Sarah; Samuel. EDUC.: grad., Choate School, 1919; B.S., Yale U., 1924. POLIT. & GOV.: delegate, Dem. Nat'l. Conv., 1940, 1944, 1948, 1956, 1960 (chm., Platform Cmte.); presidential elector, Democratic Party, 1940; appointed CT state rationing administrator, 1942; appointed CT state dir., OPA, 1942–43; appointed gen. mgr., OPA, 1943, dir., 1943–46; appointed member, WPB, 1943–46; appointed member, Petroleum Council for War, 1943–46; appointed dir., Office of Economic Stabilization, 1946; appointed chm., Economic Stabilization Board, 1946; American delegate, UNESCO Conference, 1946; member, National Comm. for UNESCO, 1946–47; appointed special asst. to the sec. gen., U.N., 1947–48; elected as a Democrat to gov. of CT, 1949–51; Democratic candidate for gov. of CT, 1950; appointed U.S. ambassador to India, 1951–53, 1963–69; appointed U.S. ambassador to Nepal, 1951–53; ***candidate for Democratic nomination to presidency of the U.S., 1952, 1960***; elected as a Democrat to U.S. House (CT), 1959–61; appointed undersec., U.S. Dept. of State, 1961; appointed president's special representative for Asian, African and Latin American affairs, 1961–63; ***candidate for Democratic nomination to vice presidency of the U.S., 1972***. BUS. & PROF.: employee, *Springfield (MA) Republican*, 1924–25; employee, George Batten Co., 1925–29; founder, Benton and Bowles, Inc., New York, NY, 1929–36, chm. of the board, 1936–41; Shaw Lecturer, Bryn Mawr Coll., 1953–54; Berkeley Lecturer, U. of CA, 1956; Godkin Lecturer, Harvard U., 1956; Chubb Lecturer, Yale U., 1957; author. MEM.: Woodrow Wilson Foundation (trustee); Asia Soc.; U.S.C.G. Acad. (visitor); Fletcher School of Law and Diplomacy (adviser); CT State Grange; Fund for Peaceful Atomic Development (dir.); Cruising Club of America; Inst. for International Education (dir.); American Council of Learned Societies (dir.); Franklin D. Roosevelt Foundation (dir.); Eleanor Roosevelt Memorial Foundation (trustee); Rockefeller Foundation (trustee); Inst. of African-American Relations (trustee). AWARDS: FDR Award, 1950; Roosevelt College Award, 1953. HON. DEG.: LL.D., American U., 1946; LL.D., Howard U., 1954; LL.D., Oberlin Coll., 1957; LL.D., Bard Coll., 1957; LL.D., RI U., 1958; LL.D., U. of MI, 1961; LL.D., Yale U., 1968; LL.D., Davidson Coll., 1972; D.Sc., The New School for Social Research. WRITINGS: *Tomorrow Without Fear* (1946); *Ambassador's Report* (1954); *The New Dimensions of Peace* (1955); *American Politics in a Revolutionary World* (1956); *Africa's Challenge to America* (1956); *Ideas, People, and Peace* (1958); *The Coming Political Breakthrough* (1959); *The Conscience of a Liberal* (1962); *The Makings of a Just Society* (1963); *View From New Delhi* (1969); *Promises to Keep* (1971); *Mission to India* (1974). REL.: Unitarian. RES.: Essex, CT.

BOYD, J. L. R. POLIT. & GOV.: candidate for gov. of GA, 1938, 1940; ***candidate for Prohibition Party nomination to vice presidency of the U.S., 1944***. BUS. & PROF.: atty.; law practice, GA; pres., Building and Loan Assn., GA. WRITINGS: *The Evasion of the Small Loan Laws of Georgia as Practiced by Certain Licensed Salary-Buyers in the State of Georgia* (1928). MAILING ADDRESS: GA.

BOYD, LINN. b. Nov 22, 1800, Nashville, TN; d. Dec 17, 1859, Paducah, KY; par. Abraham Boyd; m. Alice C. Bennett, Oct 20, 1832; m. 2d, Mrs. Anna L. (Rhey) Dixon, Apr 15, 1850; c. Rhey. EDUC.: self-taught. POLIT. & GOV.: elected as a Democrat to KY State House, 1827–32; Democratic candidate for U.S. House (KY), 1833, 1837; elected as a Democrat to U.S. House (KY), 1835–37, 1839–55 (Speaker, 1851–55); ***candidate for Democratic nomination to presidency of the U.S., 1852; candidate for Democratic nomination to vice presidency of the U.S., 1856***; candidate for Democratic nomination to gov. of KY, 1859; elected as a Democrat to lt. gov. of KY, 1859 (died before assuming office). BUS. & PROF.: farmer, Calloway Cty., KY. MISC.: noted for securing Jackson Purchase from Chickasaw Indians, 1819. RES.: Paducah, KY.

BOYDSTON, JOHN EDWIN. POLIT. & GOV.: ***independent candidate for presidency of the U.S., 1988***. BUS. & PROF.: priest. MAILING ADDRESS: 200 Strong St., Bowie, TX 76230.

BRADFORD, CHADWICK LYNN. POLIT. & GOV.: ***independent candidate for presidency of the U.S., 1992***. MAILING ADDRESS: 1134 West Loyola Ave., Box 1842, Chicago, IL 60626.

BRADFORD, DREW. POLIT. & GOV.: ***independent candidate for presidency of the U.S., 1992***. MAILING ADDRESS: 267 Griggs Dr., Princeton, NJ 08540.

BRADFORD, ROBERT WAYNE. EDUC.: college. POLIT. & GOV.: ***independent candidate for presidency of the U.S., 1984, 1988***. BUS. & PROF.: investment banker,

Memphis, TN. MISC.: inmate, Maxwell Federal Prison Camp, Montgomery, AL, 1978–79; incarcerated at U.S. Medical Center for Federal Prisoners, Springfield, MO, for illegal sale of securities, 1983–; incarcerated at Federal Correctional Institution, Memphis, TN, 1987. MAILING ADDRESS: 1900 West Sunshine St., Springfield, MO 65802.

BRADLEY, THOMAS. b. Dec 29, 1917, Calvert, TX; par. Lee Thomas and Crenner (Hawkins) Bradley; m. Ethel Mae Arnold, May 4, 1941; c. Lorraine; Phyllis. EDUC.: LL.B., Southwest U., 1956; U. of CA at Los Angeles. POLIT. & GOV.: member, CA State Democratic Central Cmte.; elected as a Democrat to Los Angeles (CA) City Council, 1963–73; candidate for mayor of Los Angeles, CA, 1969; elected as a Democrat to mayor of Los Angeles, CA, 1973–93; appointed member, National Energy Advisory Council; appointed member, National Comm. on Productivity and Work Quality; appointed member, Peace Corps Advisory Council; appointed member, Advisory Council on Intergovernmental Relations; appointed member, Joint Comm. on Mental Health of Children; delegate, Democratic Mid-Term Conference, 1974; co-chairperson, Dem. Nat'l. Conv., 1976; ***candidate for Democratic nomination to vice presidency of the U.S., 1976***; Democratic candidate for gov. of CA, 1982, 1986. BUS. & PROF.: officer, Los Angeles (CA) Police Dept., 1940–62; atty.; dir., Bank of Finance; law practice, Los Angeles, CA, 1962–63. MEM.: Los Angeles Urban League; NAACP; Southern CA Conference on Community Relations; Los Angeles Cty. Conference of Negro Elected Officials; Langston Law Club; ABA; CA Bar Assn.; Los Angeles Cty. Bar Assn.; U.N. Assn. of Los Angeles (dir.); World Affairs Council; Social Order of Blue Shield; Town Hall; National Urban Fellows; National Urban Coalition; San Fernando Valley State Coll. (Community Advisory Board); Educational Opportunity Scholarship Fund; National League of Cities (pres., 1974); League of CA Cities (Los Angeles pres., 1968–69); Southern CA Assn. of Governments (pres., 1968–69); National Assn. of Regional Councils (pres., 1969–71); U. of Southern CA Medical Center Auxiliary (Los Angeles City Advisory Council); Kappa Alpha Psi; Grand Polemarch; U. Religious Conference (Student Board). AWARDS: "Man of the Year, A.M.E. Church, 1974; "Newsmaker of the Year," National Assn. of Media Women, 1974; Los Amigos de la Humanidad Award, U. of Southern CA, 1974; Alumnus of the Year Award, U. of CA, 1974; Thurgood Marshall Award, NAACP, 1975; Sword of the Haganah (Israel), 1974; David Ben Gurion Award, 1974; numerous additional awards. HON. DEG.: LL.D., Loyola Marymount Coll.; LL.D., CA Lutheran Coll.; LL.D., Brandeis U. REL.: A.M.E. Church (trustee). MISC.: Letterman, Track Team, U. of CA at Los Angeles; All City Champion, 440 yards; Southern CA Champion, 440 yards, Polytech H.S. MAILING ADDRESS: 3807 Welland Ave., Los Angeles, CA 90008.

BRADLEY, THOMAS JOSEPH, JR. POLIT. & GOV.: ***candidate for Democratic nomination to presidency of the U.S., 1992***. MAILING ADDRESS: 225 Hollywood Rd., Fairview, NC 28730.

BRADLEY, WILLIAM O'CONNELL. b. Mar 18, 1847, Lancaster, KY; d. May 23, 1914, Washington, DC; par. Robert McAfee and Nancy Ellen (Totten) Bradley; m. Margaret Robertson Duncan, Jul 11, 1867; c. George Robertson; Christine South. EDUC.: private school, Somerset, KY. POLIT. & GOV.: appointed page, KY State House, 1861; elected as a Republican, prosecuting atty., Garrard Cty., KY, 1870; presidential elector, Liberal Republican Party, 1872; Republican candidate for U.S. House (KY), 1872, 1876; Republican candidate for U.S. Senate (KY), five times; delegate, Rep. Nat'l. Conv., 1880, 1884, 1888, 1892, 1900, 1904, 1908; Republican candidate for gov. of KY, 1887, 1891; ***candidate for Republican nomination to vice presidency of the U.S., 1888, 1896, 1900***; appointed U.S. minister to Korea (Chosen), 1889 (declined); member, Rep. Nat'l. Cmte., 1890–96; elected as a Republican to gov. of KY, 1895–99; ***candidate for Republican nomination to presidency of the U.S., 1896***; elected as a Republican to U.S. Senate (KY), 1909–14. BUS. & PROF.: atty.; law practice, Louisville, KY. MIL.: pvt., U.S. Volunteers, Civil War. MEM.: KY Bar Assn. REL.: Presb. (nee Bapt.). Address: Louisville, KY.

BRADLEY, WILLIAM WARREN "BILL." b. Jul 28, 1943, Crystal City, MO; par. Warren W. and Susan (Crowe) Bradley; m. Ernestine Schlant, Jan 14, 1974; c. Theresa Anne. EDUC.: B.A., Princeton U., 1965; M.A. (cum laude; Rhodes Scholar), Oxford U., 1968; D., St. Peter's Coll., 1974; D., Marist Coll., 1977. POLIT. & GOV.: campaign worker, William Scranton (q.v.) for President Campaign, 1964; elected as a Democrat to U.S. Senate (NJ), 1979–; ***candidate for Democratic nomination to presidency of the U.S., 1984, 1988; candidate for Democratic nomination to vice presidency of the U.S., 1992***. BUS. & PROF.: player, NY Knickerbockers professional basketball team, 1967–77; public official. Mil: 1st lt., U.S. Air Force Reserves, 1967–78. MEM.: Fellowship of Christian Athletes; Cottage Club; National Conference of Christians and Jews; Princeton U. Dept. of Political Affairs (adviser). AWARDS: one of 200 Young American Leaders, *Time Magazine*, 1975; one of 10 "Outstanding Young Men in America," U.S. Junior C. of C., 1977. WRITINGS: *Life on the Run* (1976); *The Fair* (1984). REL.: Presb. MISC.: known as "Dollar Bill." MAILING ADDRESS: 1605 Vauxhall Rd., Union, NJ 07083.

BRADSHAW, NOAH THOMAS. b. May 15, 1945, Crisfield, MD; par. Coulbourne Hollis Bradshaw; m. Carolyn Jo Ramsey; c. Mark Thomas; Scott Alan; Tammy Renee. EDUC.: grad., Crisfield H.S., 1963; grad. (exec. automation), American Inst., 1963; grad., Learning Labs, Breany Coll., 1984. POLIT. & GOV.: ***candidate for Republican nomination to presidency of the U.S., 1984; independent candidate for presi-***

dency of the U.S., 1984. BUS. & PROF.: regional sales mgr., computer software distributorship, Marietta, GA; received various professional sales awards. MIL.: E-5, U.S. Army, 1966–67. MEM.: Marietta C. of C.; Marietta Junior C. of C. REL.: Methodist. MAILING ADDRESS: 2192 Tully Wren, Marietta, GA 30066.

BRAGG, EDWARD STUYVESANT. b. Feb 20, 1827, Unadilla, NY; d. Jun 20, 1912, Fond du Lac, WI; par. Joel and Margaretha (Kohl) Bragg; m. Cornelia Colman, Jan 2, 1854. EDUC.: Geneva (later Hobart) Coll.; LL.D., 1898. POLIT. & GOV.: elected district atty., Fond du Lac Cty., WI, 1854–56; delegate, Dem. Nat'l. Conv., 1860, 1872, 1880, 1884, 1892, 1896; Democratic candidate for U.S. House (WI), 1862; delegate, Union Convention, 1866; appointed postmaster, Fond du Lac, WI, 1866; elected as a Democrat to WI State Senate, 1868–69; Democratic candidate for U.S. Senate (WI), 1874; elected as a Democrat to U.S. House (WI), 1877–83, 1885–87; appointed envoy extraordinary and minister plenipotentiary to Mexico, 1888–89; ***candidate for National (Gold) Democratic Party nomination to presidency of the U.S., 1896***; appointed U.S. consul gen., Havana, Cuba, 1902; appointed U.S. consul gen., Hong Kong, China, 1902–06. BUS. & PROF.: atty.; law practice, Unadilla, NY, 1848–50; law practice, Fond du Lac, WI, 1850–1906. MIL.: capt., Sixth WI Infantry, 1861, maj., 1861, lt. col., 1862, col., 1863, brig. gen. of volunteers, 1865. MEM.: NY Bar Assn. HON. DEG.: LL.D., Appleton Coll., 1902. RES.: Fond du Lac, WI.

BRAMLETTE, THOMAS ELLIOTT. b. Jan 3, 1817, Cumberland Cty., KY; d. Jan 12, 1875, Louisville, KY; par. Col. Ambrose Bramlette; m. Sallie Travis, Sep 1837; m. 2d, Mrs. Mary E. (Graham) Adams, June 3, 1874; c. Thomas T.; Collanne; Eugene; five others. EDUC.: public schools; studied law. POLIT. & GOV.: elected as a Whig to KY State House, 1841–43; appointed state's atty. for KY, 1849–51; Whig candidate for U.S. House (KY), 1853; elected judge, Sixth Judicial Circuit of KY, 1856–62; appointed U.S. district atty. for KY, 1862; elected as a Union Democrat to gov. of KY, 1863–67; candidate for Union Party nomination to U.S. Senate (KY), 1863 (declined); delegate, Dem. Nat'l. Conv., 1864; ***candidate for Democratic nomination to vice presidency of the U.S., 1864 (declined)***; Democratic candidate for U.S. Senate (KY), 1867; ***received 3 electoral votes for vice presidency of the U.S., 1872***. BUS. & PROF.: atty.; law practice, Columbia, KY, 1852–56; law practice, Louisville, KY, 1867–75. MIL.: col., Third KY Infantry, U.S. Army, 1861–63, maj. gen., 1863. MEM.: KY Bar Assn. RES.: Louisville, KY.

BRANCH, EMMANUEL L. POLIT. & GOV.: ***candidate for Republican nomination to presidency of the U.S., 1992***. MAILING ADDRESS: 3940 Evans Quarry Rd., Dodgeville, WI 53533.

BRANDBORG, CHARLES W. b. Aug 13, 1847, Hallund, Sweden; d. Mar 28, 1916, Henning, MN; m. Betsy Nelson, 1875; c. Harris A.; Lloyd N.; Carl W.; Ellen B.; Ralph V.; Jennie T.; Otto F.; Sten S.; Emmett T. POLIT. & GOV.: ***Socialist Labor Party of MN candidate for presidency of the U.S., 1900***; presidential elector, Socialist Labor Party, 1900; delegate, Socialist Labor Party National Convention, 1904; Socialist Industrial Party candidate for gov. of MN, 1910. BUS. & PROF.: farmer, Henderson, MN, 1873–81, Vining, MN, Henning, MN. RES.: Henning, MN.

BRANDEIS, LOUIS DEMBITZ. b. Nov 13, 1856, Louisville, KY; d. Oct 5, 1941, Washington, DC; par. Adolph and Fredericka (Dembitz) Brandeis; m. Alice Goldmark, Mar 23, 1891; c. Susan (Mrs. Jacob H. Gilbert); Elizabeth (Mrs. Paul A. Raushenbush). EDUC.: Annen Realschule, Dresden, Germany, 1873–75; LL.B. (summa cum laude), Harvard U., 1877. POLIT. & GOV.: appointed assoc. justice, Supreme Court of the U.S., 1916–39; ***candidate for Democratic nomination to presidency of the U.S., 1920; candidate for Progressive Party nomination to vice presidency of the U.S., 1924***. BUS. & PROF.: atty.; law practice, Boston, MA, 1879–1916; partner, Warren and Brandeis (law firm), Boston, 1879–97; partner, Brandeis, Dunbar and Nutter (law firm), Boston, 1897–1916. MEM.: Federation of American Zionists; American Jewish Congress (pres.); Palestine Economic Corp. (dir.); International Zionist Conference (pres., 1920); Public Franchise League; Civic Federation of New England (vice pres.); Provisional Cmte. for General Zionist Affairs (chm., 1914–16); MO Bar Assn.; Civil Service Reform Assn.; American Citizenship Cmte. of Boston; New England Free Trade League; Harvard Law School Assn.; Phi Beta Kappa. AWARDS: A.M. (hon.), Harvard U., 1891. WRITINGS: *Other People's Money* (1914); *Business: A Profession* (1914); *The Curse of Bigness*. REL.: Jewish. RES.: Washington, DC.

BRANIGAN, ROGER DOUGLAS. b. Jul 26, 1902, Franklin, IN; d. Nov 19, 1975, Lafayette, IN; par. Elba L. and Zula (Francis) Branigan; m. Josephine Mardis, Nov 2, 1929; c. Roger Douglas, Jr.; Robert M. EDUC.: A.B., Franklin Coll., 1923; LL.B., Harvard U., 1926. POLIT. & GOV.: appointed prosecuting atty., Franklin, IN, 1926–29; appointed gen. counsel, Federal Land Bank, Louisville, KY, 1930–38; appointed gen. counsel, Farm Credit Administration, Louisville, KY, 1933–38; chm., Tippecanoe Cty. (IN) Democratic Central Cmte., 1938–56; permanent chm., IN State Democratic Convention, 1948; appointed chm., IN State Conservation Comm., 1948–50; elected as a Democrat to gov. of IN, 1965–69; delegate, Dem. Nat'l. Conv., 1968; ***candidate for Democratic nomination to presidency of the U.S., 1968***; appointed chm., IN Revolutionary War Bicentennial Comm., 1971–75. BUS. & PROF.: atty.; partner, Stuart, Branigan, Ricks and Schilling (law firm), Lafayette, IN, 1969–75; dir., Lafayette Life Insurance Co.; dir., Lafayette National Bank, 1958–75; dir., General Telephone Co. of IN, 1958–75; dir., National Home Corp., 1966–75; dir., Duncan

Electric Co.; dir., Erie, Lackawana Railway Co. MIL.: capt., U.S. Army, 1942–46, lt. col., 1946; Legion of Merit; Army Commendation Medal. MEM.: American College of Trial Lawyers; American Law Inst.; American College of Probate Counselors; American Jud. Soc. (dir.); IN Bar Assn.; ABA; Phi Delta Phi; Theta Alpha Phi; Alpha Pi Omega; Phi Delta Theta; IN Hist. Soc. (trustee); Franklin Coll. (trustee, 1937–75); Purdue U. (trustee, 1950–55); BSA (pres., Harrison Trails Council); Associated Colleges of IN; Lilly Endowment (dir.); Newcomen Soc.; Conner Prairie Farms, Inc. (dir.); Elks; Masons; Harvard Law School Assn.; American Legion (pres., 1951–52); C. of C. (pres.); IN Soc. of Chicago (vice pres.); American Counsel Assn.; Sagamore of the Wabash; Chicago Legal Club; Indianapolis Press Club; Town and Gown Club; U. of MI Lawyers Club; Indianapolis Literary Club. HON. DEG.: LL.D., Franklin Coll., 1956; LL.D., Butler U., 1965; LL.D., IN U., 1969; LL.D., Vincennes U., 1970; LL.D., IN State U., 1972. REL.: Bapt. RES.: Lafayette, IN.

BRANNING, JON S. POLIT. & GOV.: ***candidate for Democratic nomination to presidency of the U.S., 1984***; candidate for Democratic nomination to U.S. Senate (NY), 1990. MAILING ADDRESS: 102-35 67th Rd., Forest Hills, NY 11375.

BRANTING, VIVIAN de MILT. d. Before 1986; married. POLIT. & GOV.: ***independent candidate for presidency of the U.S., 1980***. RES.: Colonial Heights, VA.

BREATHITT, EDWARD THOMPSON, JR. b. Nov 26, 1924, Hopkinsville, KY; par. Edward Thompson and Mary Jo (Wallace) Breathitt; m. Frances Holleman, Dec 20, 1948; c. Mary Fran; Linda Kay; Susan Holleman; Edward Thompson III. EDUC.: B.A., U. of KY, 1948, J.D., 1950, LL.D. POLIT. & GOV.: member, Campaign Staff, Alben Barkley (q.v.) for U.S. Senate Campaign; member, State Speakers' Bureau, Adlai Stevenson (q.v.) Presidential Campaign, 1952; pres., Young Democratic Clubs of KY, 1952; elected as a Democrat to KY State House, 1953–59; appointed member, KY Governor's Comm. on Mental Health, 1955–59; appointed KY state personnel commissioner, 1959–60; appointed KY state public service commissioner, 1961–62; elected as a Democrat to gov. of KY, 1963–67; member, Dem. Nat'l. Cmte., 1967–72; delegate, Dem. Nat'l. Conv., 1972, 1976, 1980; ***candidate for Democratic nomination to vice presidency of the U.S., 1972***. BUS. & PROF.: atty.; partner, Tremble, Soyars and Breathitt (law firm), Hopkinsville, KY, 1952–72; vice pres., Southern Railway Systems, Washington, DC MIL.: aviation cadet, U.S.A.A.C., 1943–45. MEM.: Junior C. of C.; Kiwanis; Elks; Hopkinsville C. of C.; Pendennis Club; Phi Alpha Delta; Lamp and Cross (pres.); Omicron Delta Kappa; Sigma Alpha Epsilon; Beta Gamma Sigma; KY Farm Bureau; American Legion; Shriners; Masons; KY Bar Assn.; Christian Cty. Bar Assn.; International Club. AWARDS: Lincoln Key Award for Civil Rights Leadership, 1966; "Sportsman of the Year," KY League of Sportsmen, 1966; "Conservationist of the Year," *Outdoor Life*, 1967; Distinguished Service Award, U.S. Dept. of the Interior, 1968; "Outstanding Citizen Award," Hopkinsville C. of C., 1977. HON. DEG.: LL.D., Marshall Coll.; LL.D., KY Wesleyan Coll. REL.: Methodist. MAILING ADDRESS: 1720 South VA St., Hopkinsville, KY 42240.

BRECK, DEANNA DIVERS. b. Nov 16, 1937, Roanoke, VA; par. Maurice Edie and Henrietta Divers Benard (Davis) Wirt; m. William G. Breck, Aug 3, 1956; c. Michael Douglas; William C. E.; Stephen K.J.L.; David M.M.A.F.; Nancy Leigh; Robert Barrett; Henrietta "Wendy" Divers; Jan-Christian. EDUC.: A.A. (with honors in business), AZ Western Coll., 1976. POLIT. & GOV.: ***independent candidate for presidency of the U.S., 1980***. BUS. & PROF.: administrative asst., YMCA, Alexandria, VA; office mgr., Hawthorne Cabinets; office mgr., insurance office, Yuma, AZ. MEM.: Mothers March of Dimes (chm., Yuma, AZ chapter, 3 years); Rape Crisis Center (volunteer). AWARDS: Scouting awards; Civic Award for Volunteers, American Legion; Award, March of Dimes. REL.: Church of Jesus Christ of Latter-Day Saints. MAILING ADDRESS: 6473 Coybrook Dr., West Jordan, UT 84084.

BRECKINRIDGE, HENRY SKILLMAN. b. May 25, 1886, Chicago, IL; d. May 2, 1960, New York, NY; par. Maj. Gen. Joseph Cabell and Louise Ludlow (Dudley) Breckinridge; m. Ruth Bradley Woodman, Jul 7, 1910; m. 2d, Aida de Acosta Root, Aug 5, 1927; m. 3d, Margaret Lucy Smith, Mar 27, 1947; c. Elizabeth Foster; Louise Dudley; Madeline Houston. EDUC.: A.B., Princeton U., 1907; LL.B., Harvard U., 1910. POLIT. & GOV.: appointed member, Board of Park Commissioners, Lexington, KY, 1911–13; appointed asst. U.S. sec. of war, 1913–16; appointed chm., Comm. for the Relief of American Citizens in Europe, 1914; delegate, Dem. Nat'l. Conv., 1932; appointed counsel, U.S. Senate Cmte. to Investigate Dirigible Disasters, 1933; Constitutional Party candidate for U.S. Senate (NY), 1934; ***candidate for Democratic nomination to presidency of the U.S., 1936***; appointed member, Citizens Cmte. on Control of Crime (NY); incorporator, NY World's Fair, 1939. BUS. & PROF.: atty.; law practice, Lexington, KY, 1910–13; first vice pres., Pacific Hardware and Steel Co., San Francisco, CA, 1916–17; law practice, New York, NY, 1922–60. MIL.: maj., Officers Reserve Corps, 1917 (active service), lt. col., 1919. MEM.: SAR; William Holland Wilmer Foundation (sec.-treas.); Navy League of the U.S. (pres., 1919–21; organized first Navy Day); American Olympic Fencing Team, 1920, 1928 (capt.); American International Fencing Team, 1921, 1923, 1926; Assn. for the Defense of the Constitution; Amateur Fencers League of America (pres., 1925–30); National Amateur Athletic Federation of America (pres.); ABA; KY Bar Assn.; NY Bar Assn.; Assn. of the Bar of the City of New York; American Law Inst.; Military Order of the World War; American Legion; Loyal Legion; Air Law Inst. of Northwestern U. (adviser); Inst. of the Aeronautical Sciences, Inc.; Metropolitan Club; Army and Navy

Club; Princeton Club; University Club; Lawyers' Club; Fencers' Club. Hon.Deg.: LL.D., U. of KY, 1915; LL.D., Tusculum Coll., 1935; D.C.L., Bishop's Coll., 1940; M. Phys.Ed., International YMCA Coll. WRITINGS: . . . *Shall Not Perish*. REL.: Presb. RES.: New York, NY.

BRECKINRIDGE, JOHN. b. Dec 2, 1760, Staunton, VA; d. Dec 14, 1806, Lexington, KY; par. Robert and Letitia (Preston) Breckinridge; m. Mary Cabell, 1785; c. nine. EDUC.: Coll. of William and Mary, 1778–80; studied law. POLIT. & GOV.: elected to VA House of Burgesses, 1780 (not seated, due to age); atty. gen. of KY, 1795–97; elected as a Democratic-Republican to KY State House, 1797–1801 (Speaker, 1799–1801); elected as a Democratic-Republican to U.S. Senate (KY), 1801–05; ***candidate for Democratic-Republican nomination to vice presidency of the U.S., 1804***; appointed atty. gen. of the U.S., 1805–06. BUS. & PROF.: atty. MEM.: VA Bar Assn. RES.: Lexington, KY.

BRECKINRIDGE, JOHN CABELL. b. Jan 21, 1821, Lexington, KY; d. May 17, 1875, Lexington, KY; par. Joseph Cabell and Mary Clay (Smith) Breckinridge; m. Mary Cyrene Burch, Dec 1843; c. Joseph Cabell; Clifton Rodes. EDUC.: grad., Centre Coll., 1839; Coll. of NJ; Transylvania U. POLIT. & GOV.: elected as a Democrat to KY State House, 1849–51; elected as a Democrat to U.S. House (KY), 1851–55; appointed U.S. minister to Spain, 1855 (declined); delegate, Dem. Nat'l. Conv., 1856; ***elected as a Democrat to vice presidency of the U.S., 1857–61; candidate for Democratic nomination to presidency of the U.S., 1860; candidate for Democratic nomination to vice presidency of the U.S., 1860; Southern Democratic Party candidate for presidency of the U.S., 1860***; elected as a Democrat to U.S. Senate (KY), 1861 (expelled); appointed sec. of war, Confederate States of America, 1865. BUS. & PROF.: atty.; law practice, Lexington, KY, 1845–47, 1869–74; vice pres., Elizabethtown, Lexington and Big Sandy R.R. MIL.: maj., Third KY Volunteers, 1847–48; brig. gen., C.S.A., 1861, maj. gen., 1862–65. MEM.: KY Bar Assn. REL.: Presb. MISC.: fled to Europe following Civil War; returned to U.S., 1869. RES.: Lexington, KY.

BREED, CHARLES AYARS. b. Jan 31, 1927, Paw Paw, MI. EDUC.: B.S., Western MI U.; M.A., U. of WI. POLIT. & GOV.: ***independent candidate for presidency of the U.S., 1984***. BUS. & PROF.: artist; dir. of art, National Music Acad., 1958–62; assoc. prof. of art and dept. chm., Delta Coll., 1962–. Commissioned Works: twelve stations of the cross, Indian River Catholic Church, 1955; cross, Memorial Presbyterian Church, Midland, MI, 1957; window panels, William Dixon Home, Midland, MI, 1960; eternal flame, Temple Beth El, Spring Valley, NY, 1966; icon screen, Hellenic Orthodox Church, Bloomfield Hills, MI, 1968. MEM.: NEA (life member); MI Art Education Assn. (treas., 1955; pres., 1956); American Craftsmen Council; MI Council of Art; Awareness, Inc. (dir., 1962–64); Midland Art Council (dir., 1965–68); Midland Center for the Arts (dir., 1967–72); Lansing Council of Arts (member, 1971–72). WRITINGS: "Plastic as a New Art Form," *House Beautiful*, Feb 1962; "Plastic—The Visual Arts in Crafts," *Crafts & Craftsmen*, 1967. AWARDS: Research Fellow, Dow Foundation, 1961; National Merit Award, Music Contemporary Crafts, NY, 1966; "Outstanding Teacher of the Year," Bergstein Foundation, 1967. MISC.: noted for work in plastics. MAILING ADDRESS: 4202 Sherwood Court, Midland, MI 48640.

BREHM, MARIE CAROLINE. b. Jun 30, 1859, Sandusky, OH; d. Jan 21, 1926, Long Beach, CA; par. William Henry and Elizabeth R. (Rhode) Brehm; single. EDUC.: public schools, Sandusky, OH, 1866–77; studied languages and civics under private tutors. POLIT. & GOV.: Prohibition Party candidate for U. of IL Board of trustees, 1902, 1904, 1908; appointed delegate, 12th International Congress on Alcoholism, London, England, 1909; appointed U.S. representative, 14th International Congress Against Alcoholism, 1913; member, Prohibition Party National Cmte., 1916–24 (vice chm., 1919); ***candidate for Prohibition Party nomination to vice presidency of the U.S., 1916***; delegate, Cmte. of 48 National Convention, 1920; chm., Prohibition Party National Convention, 1920; ***Prohibition Party candidate for vice presidency of the U.S., 1920 (declined), 1924***; delegate, Prohibition Party National Convention, 1924. BUS. & PROF.: lecturer, W.C.T.U., 1891–1926; superintendent, Franchise Dept., National W.C.T.U., 1896. MEM.: IL W.C.T.U. (1891; district pres., 1892–97; state recording sec., 1895; state superintendent of institutes, 1896; pres., 1901–06); International Conference of Reformers (delegate, 1889, 1900, 1901); Equal Suffrage Assn. (IL State pres.); Inter-Church Temperance Federation (delegate, 13th World's Congress on Alcoholism, The Hague, Holland, 1911); CA State Women's Legislative Council (first vice pres., 1921–26); Christian Endeavor Soc.; Scientific Soc. of Mt. Carmel; Chicago Political Equality League; Scientific Temperance Federation, U.S.A.; Irish Bible Temperance Soc.; Loyal Temperance Legion; Chautauqua Women's Club. REL.: Presb. (deacon, 1924–25; member, General Assembly Permanent Cmte. on Temperance, Board of Temperance and Moral Welfare, 1906). RES.: Wheaton, IL.

BREIDENTHAL, JOHN WILLIAM. b. Jun 22, 1857, Sibley Cty., MN; d. Jan 15, 1910, Kansas City, KS; par. Matthew and Henrietta E. Breidenthal; m. Julia Slaughter, Sep 26, 1882; c. Nellie B. (Mrs. Charles L. Davies); Willard J.; Herbert M.; Maurice L. EDUC.: public schools, Terre Haute, IN. POLIT. & GOV.: delegate, National (Greenback) Party National Convention, 1876; National (Greenback) Party candidate for lt. gov. of KS, 1884; founder, Union Labor Party, 1887; state chm., KS State Union Labor Party, 1887; People's Party candidate for U.S. Senate (KS), 1891, 1897; state chm., KS State People's Party Central Cmte., 1892–96; appointed KS state banking commissioner, 1893–1901; Democratic (Free Silver; People's) Party candidate for gov. of KS, 1900; ***candidate for People's Party nomination to vice presidency of the U.S., 1900***; member, People's (Fusion) Party National Cmte., 1901. BUS. & PROF.: farmer, KS, 1877–1910; clerk, real estate office, Chetopa, KS, 1882; owner, Neosho Valley Investment Co., 1884, sec.; promoter, Cooperative Colonization Project, Topolobampa, Mexico, 1890; founder, pres., People's National Bank of Kansas City; vice pres., mgr., The Banking Trust Co. of Kansas, Kansas City, 1901–08; founder, Riverview State Bank; founder, Anchor Life Insurance Co. MEM.: Masons. WRITINGS: *Banking and Trust Laws of Kansas*. RES.: Topeka, KS.

BRENNAN, JOHN. POLIT. & GOV.: ***candidate for Republican nomination to presidency of the U.S., 1976***. MAILING ADDRESS: Vin-Home, Perrymonte Rd., Pittsburgh, PA 15237.

BRENNEMAN, BEN HOWARD. POLIT. & GOV.: ***independent candidate for presidency of the U.S., 1988***. MEM.: Psychotics for a Better America. MAILING ADDRESS: Route 1, Box 656, North Garden, VA 72959.

BRESLAU, V. F. b. 1929, IL. POLIT. & GOV.: ***independent candidate for presidency of the U.S., 1968, 1980***. MISC.: self-styled "Itinerant candidate." MAILING ADDRESS: Chicago, IL.

BREWER, A. CLARKE. POLIT. & GOV.: elected as a Democrat to AR State House, 1879–81; presidential elector, Democratic Party, 1880 (resigned); ***Independent Democratic Party candidate for presidency of the U.S., 1880***. BUS. & PROF.: farmer; plantation owner, Crittenden Cty., AR. MIL.: pvt., 19th TN Volunteers, C.S.A., 1861–65. RES.: Crittenden Cty., AR.

BREWSTER, DANIEL BAUGH. b. Nov 23, 1923, Baltimore, MD; par. Daniel Baugh and Ottolie Young (Wickes) Brewster; m. Anne Bullitt, Apr 29, 1967; c. Daniel Baugh III; Gerry Leiper. EDUC.: Gilman School; St. Paul's Acad., Concord, NH, 1942; Princeton U., 1942; Johns Hopkins U., 1946; LL.B., U. of MD, 1949. POLIT. & GOV.: appointed member, Veterans Advisory Comm., 1947; appointed member, Comm. to Study MD Unemployment Compensation Law, 1951; elected as a Democrat to MD State House of Delegates, 1951–59; appointed member, Burke Comm. to Study the Judiciary of MD, 1952; appointed Baltimore city representative, Port of Baltimore Comm., 1954–55; appointed vice chm., Comm. to Review the State Roads Comm. Program, 1957; elected as a Democrat to U.S. House (MD), 1959–63; elected as a Democrat to U.S. Senate (MD), 1963–69; delegate, Dem. Nat'l. Conv., 1964, 1968; ***candidate for Democratic nomination to presidency of the U.S., 1964***; Democratic candidate for U.S. Senate (MD), 1968. BUS. & PROF.: atty.; law practice, Towson, MD; owner, grain and cattle farm, Glyndon, MD. MIL.: pvt., troop commander, 2d lt., U.S.C.G., 1942–46; U.S.C.G. Reserves (lt. col.); Purple Heart; Gold Star; Bronze Star. MEM.: ABA; MD State Bar Assn.; Baltimore Cty. Bar Assn.; MD State Fair and Agricultural Soc. (pres.); VFW; Disabled American Veterans. REL.: Episc. MISC.: indicted for bribery, 1969; convicted and sentenced, 1972; case retried, 1974; entered plea of "No Contest," 1975. MAILING ADDRESS: Golf Course Rd., West, Owings Mills, MD 21117.

BREWSTER, ROBERT L. b. c. 1931; married; c. Gregg; Cynthia. EDUC.: B.S., IN State U. POLIT. & GOV.: candidate for Democratic nomination to U.S. Senate (FL), 1974, 1984; ***candidate for Democratic nomination to presidency of the U.S., 1976, 1980, 1984***. BUS. & PROF.: management officer, G.S.A., Chicago, IL; contract specialist, Wright Patterson Air Force Base, Dayton, OH; contract specialist, Ammunition Procurement and Supply Agency, Joliet, IL; contract specialist, National Aeronautics and Space Administration, John F. Kennedy Space Center, Cape Canaveral, FL. MEM.: Christian (Non-Lawyer) Cmte. MAILING ADDRESS: 2100 Howell Branch, Apt. 36E, Maitland, FL 32751.

BRICKER, JOHN WILLIAM. b. Sep 6, 1893, Mt. Sterling, OH; d. Mar 22, 1986, Columbus, OH; par. Lemuel Spencer and Laura (King) Bricker; m. Harriet Day, Sep 4, 1920; c. John Day. EDUC.: Mt. Sterling H.S.; A.B., OH State U., 1916, LL.B., 1920. POLIT. & GOV.: solicitor, village of Grandview Heights, OH, 1920–28; pres., Buckeye Republican Club, 1923–34; appointed asst. atty. gen. of OH, 1923–27; appointed member, OH State Utilities Comm., 1929–33; elected as a Republican, atty. gen. of OH, 1933–37; delegate, Rep. Nat'l. Conv., 1936, 1940, 1948, 1952, 1956, 1960, 1964, 1968, 1972, 1976; Republican candidate for gov. of OH, 1936; elected as a Republican to gov. of OH, 1939–45; ***candidate for Republican nomination to presidency of the U.S., 1940, 1944, 1948; Republican candidate for vice presidency of the U.S., 1944; America First Party candidate for vice presidency of the U.S., 1944 (declined);*** elected as a Republican to U.S. Senate (OH), 1947–59; ***candidate for Republican nomination to vice presidency of the U.S., 1948***; Republican candidate for U.S. Senate (OH), 1958; member, exec. cmte., Rep. Nat'l. Cmte. BUS. & PROF.: atty.; atty., Postlewaite and Bricker; partner, Bricker, Marburger, Evatt and Barton (law firm), Columbus, 1945–86; partner, Bricker and Eckler (law firm), Columbus; dir., Republic Steel Corp., 1959–86; dir., Buckeye Savings and Loan Co., 1960–86; dir., Buckeye Steel Castings Co., 1961–86; pres., Mayflower Insurance Co.; dir., Reynolds Spring Co. MIL.: 1st lt., chaplain, U.S. Army, 1917–18. MEM.: Delta Chi; Order of the Coif; Columbus Bar Assn. (pres., 1936–37); OH Bar Assn.; ABA; University Club; Rotary Club; OH State Faculty Torch Club; American Legion; Eagles; Optimist Club; Veterans Republican Club; Buckeye Republican Club; Crichton Club; Masons (33°; Knights Templar; Scottish

Rite; Shriners; Supreme Council); OH State U. (trustee, 1947–86); American Jud. Soc.; Delta Sigma Rho; Kit Kat Club; Defiance Coll. (trustee); Denison U. (trustee); Franklin U. (trustee). HON. DEG.: LL.D., OH State U., 1939; LL.D., Boston U., 1944. REL.: Congregationalist. RES.: Columbus, OH.

BRIDGES, HENRY STYLES. b. Sep 9, 1898, West Pembroke, ME; d. Nov 26, 1961, East Concord, NH; par. Earl Leopold and Alina Roxana (Fisher) Bridges; m. (divorced); m. 2d, Sally Clement, Jun 30, 1928; m. 3d, Doloris Thauwald, Feb 11, 1944; c. Henry Styles, Jr.; David Clement; John Fisher. EDUC.: grad., U. of ME, 1918. POLIT. & GOV.: appointed member, NH State Public Service Comm., 1930–35; vice chm., dir. of speakers bureau, NH State Republican Central Cmte.; member, Board of Arbitration, New England Milk Marketing Plan; elected as a Republican to gov. of NH, 1935–37; delegate, Rep. Nat'l. Conv., 1936, 1940, 1956; ***candidate for Republican nomination to vice presidency of the U.S., 1936, 1940***; elected as a Republican to U.S. Senate (NH), 1937–61 (minority leader, 1952; president pro tempore, 1953–54; chm., Cmte. on Appropriations, 1947–48, 1953–54); appointed member, National Forest Reservation Comm.; ***candidate for Republican nomination to presidency of the U.S., 1940; candidate for Democratic nomination to presidency of the U.S., 1952***; appointed member, Hoover Comm. on Governmental Reorganization, 1954–55; chm., Republican Policy Cmte., 1955–60. BUS. & PROF.: instructor, Sanderson Acad., 1918–19; cty. agricultural agent and extension specialist, U. of NH, 1921–22; sec., NH Farm Bureau Federation, 1922–24; ed., *Granite Monthly*, 1924–26; dir., NH Investment Co., 1924– 29; pres., trustee, NH Savings Bank; dir., Rumford Printing Co.; dir., sec.-treas., Farm Bureau Mutual Automobile Insurance Co. MIL.: lt., Quartermaster Reserve Corps, U.S.A.R., 1925–37. MEM.: Concord Public Library (trustee); Masons; Shriners; U. of ME Alumni Assn. of Southern NH (pres., 1933–34); Elks; Odd Fellows; Kiwanis (trustee; vice pres.); Reserve Officers Assn. of the U.S (pres., Concord Chapter). HON. DEG.: LL.D., U. of ME, 1935; M.A., Dartmouth U., 1935; LL.D., U. of NH, 1935; LL.D., Northeastern U., 1938; LL.D., IA Wesleyan Coll.; LL.D., Alma Coll.; LL.D., Villanova U.; LL.D., Portia Law School; LL.D., Rider Coll.; D.C.L., Carroll Coll.; D.C.L., New England Coll.; D.Litt., FL State Coll.; D.S., Norwich U.; D.P.A., Suffolk U. REL.: Congregationalist (nee Methodist). RES.: East Concord, NH.

BRIDGES, JAMES ROBERT. POLIT. & GOV.: ***candidate for Democratic nomination to presidency of the U.S., 1992***. MAILING ADDRESS: 5445 Willis Ave., Dallas, TX 75206.

BRIEN, WILLIAM GIVEN. b. Apr 27, 1831, Alexandria, TN; d. Nov 23, 1913, Nashville, TN; par. John Smith and Sarah Ann (Ashworth) Brien; m. Susan E. Johnson, May 3, 1853; c. William Given, Jr.; Mrs. John J. Norton. EDUC.: grad., Cumberland Coll.; M.D., Nashville Medical Coll., 1877. POLIT. & GOV.: independent candidate for U.S. House (TN), 1872; member, Cumberland (TN) Free Bridge Board of Commissioners, 1872; member, National Exec. Cmte., Labor Reform Party, 1872; delegate, Labor Reform Party National Convention, 1872; ***candidate for Labor Reform Party nomination to vice presidency of the U.S., 1872***; appointed special judge in TN Circuit and Criminal Courts. BUS. & PROF.: schoolteacher, Wilson Cty., TN; atty.; partner (with Judge E. H. East), law practice, Nashville; partner (with Thomas A. Kercheval), law practice, Nashville; partner (with Judge Abraham DeMoss), law practice, Nashville; prof. of medical jurisprudence, Nashville Medical Coll. (subsequently part of the U. of TN), 1877–94. MIL.: appointed brig. gen., TN National Guard, c. 1875. MEM.: Odd Fellows; Temple of Honor; Independent Order of Good Templars; Sons of Temperance. HON. DEG.: LL.D., U. of TN. REL.: R.C. (nee Bapt.). RES.: Nashville, TN.

BRIGGS, AMOS. b. Jan 22, 1825, Penn's Manor, PA; d. Sep 1, 1902, Tullytown, PA. EDUC.: public schools; studied law, Philadelphia, PA. POLIT. & GOV.: Republican candidate for judge, Philadelphia (PA) District Court, 1861 (declined); elected as a Republican to Philadelphia (PA) Common Council, 1863; appointed and subsequently elected as a Republican, judge, Philadelphia (PA) District Court, 1872–83; Republican candidate for judge, Philadelphia (PA) District Court, 1882, 1886; Prohibition Party candidate for judge, Supreme Court of PA, 1892; ***candidate for Prohibition Party nomination to presidency of the U.S., 1892***. BUS. & PROF.: teacher; atty.; law practice, Philadelphia, PA, 1848–72. MEM.: PA Bar Assn. RES.: Philadelphia, PA.

BRIGGS, JOHN CHERRY "JACK." b. Nov 15, 1917, Colquitt, GA; par. William Thomas Carlyle and Minnie Maud (Holder) Briggs; m. 2d, Edmy Bertha Rayna; c. Gary Owen; Timothy Allen. EDUC.: B.A., U. of OR, 1967. POLIT. & GOV.: public information officer, AK State Dept. of Health and Welfare; candidate for Juneau (AK) City Council, 1968; ***Crusade for Logic candidate for presidency of the U.S., 1976; Alaskan Homesteader candidate for presidency of the U.S., 1980***. BUS. & PROF.: Alaskan homesteader; environmental activist. MIL.: pvt., U.S. Army; advanced through grades to major. MEM.: NRA; VFW; American Legion; Colfax Cty. Wildlife and Conservation Assn. (NM); Trout Unlimited; Reserve Officers Assn. REL.: Bapt. MAILING ADDRESS: Box 481, Raton, NM 87740.

BRIGGS, WILLIAM. m. Mae. POLIT. & GOV.: delegate, Socialist Party National Convention, 1975 (chairperson); ***candidate for Socialist Party nomination to presidency of the U.S., 1976 (declined)***. MAILING ADDRESS: 2610 East Main St., Ventura, CA 93003.

BRINKHOFF, ANDREA SUE. b. Sep 25, 1963, Lamar, MO; par. E. J. and Anna (Stolting) Brinkhoff; single. EDUC.: high school, Jasper, MO. POLIT. & GOV.: ***independent candidate for presidency of the U.S., 1980***. BUS. & PROF.: student; farm laborer, Jasper, MO; saleswoman, Avon Products. REL.: Methodist. MAILING ADDRESS: Route 1, Jasper, MO 64755.

BRINKLEY, DAVID McCLURE. b. Jul 10, 1920, Wilmington, NC; par. William Graham and Mary McDonald (West) Brinkley; m. Ann Fischer, Oct 11, 1946; m. 2d, Susan Adolph, Jun 10, 1972; c. Alan; Joel; John. EDUC.: U. of NC, 1938–40; Vanderbilt U. POLIT. & GOV.: ***candidate for Republican nomination to vice presidency of the U.S., 1972***. BUS. & PROF.: news commentator; reporter, *Wilmington Star-News*, 1938–40; reporter, bureau mgr., United Press Assns., 1941–43; news writer, broadcaster, NBC radio and NBC-TV, Washington, DC, 1943–81; Washington correspondent, News Caravan Program, 1951; anchorman, "This Week," ABC-TV, 1981–. MIL.: sgt., U.S. Army, 1940–41. MEM.: Cosmos Club; National Press Club; Sigma Delta Chi. AWARDS: School Bell Award, 1957; Emmy, 1958, 1959, 1960; du Pont Award, 1958; Sylvania Award, 1958; Peabody Award, 1959. REL.: Presb. MAILING ADDRESS: 5515 Uppingham St., Chevy Chase 15, MD 20815.

BRISBEN, JOHN QUINN. b. Sep 6, 1934, Enid, OK; par. John and Olive (Quinn) Brisben; m. Andrea Rosagen, 1955; c. Rebecca; Michael. EDUC.: A.B., U. of OK, 1955; U. of WI, 1955–58. POLIT. & GOV.: Socialist Party candidate for mayor of Chicago, IL, 1975; state chm., IL Socialist Party Central Cmte., 1975–; ***candidate for Socialist Party nomination to presidency of the U.S., 1976 (declined); Socialist Party candidate for vice presidency of the U.S., 1976***; alternate delegate, Socialist Party National Convention, 1987; ***Socialist Party candidate for presidency of the U.S., 1992***. BUS. & PROF.: schoolteacher, Chicago (IL) public schools, 1962–90; teacher, Harlan H.S., Chicago, 1965–90. MEM.: Chicago Teachers Union (member, House of Delegates, 1967–); Teachers for Integrated Schools (board member, 1963–67); Congress on Racial Equality; United Farm Workers (boycott captain); Southern Christian Leadership Conference. AWARDS: "Teacher of the Year," Teachers for Integrated Schools, 1964; Superintendent's Incentive Award, 1982; Award of Appreciation, Southwest Cmte. on Peaceful Equality, 1983. REL.: atheist. MAILING ADDRESS: 784 East 100th Place, Chicago, IL 60628.

BRISTOW, BENJAMIN HELM. b. Jun 20, 1832, Elkton, KY; d. Jun 22, 1896, New York, NY; par. Francis M. and Emily E. (Helm) Bristow; m. Abbie S. Briscoe, Nov 21, 1854; c. William A.; Mrs. Eben Draper. EDUC.: grad., Jefferson Coll., 1851. POLIT. & GOV.: elected as a Republican to KY State Senate, 1863–65; appointed U.S. atty. for KY, 1867–70; appointed U.S. solicitor gen., 1870–72; appointed atty. gen. of the U.S., 1874 (withdrawn); appointed U.S. sec. of the treasury, 1874–76; ***candidate for Republican nomination to presidency of the U.S., 1876***. BUS. & PROF.: atty.; partner (with Francis M. Bristow), law firm, 1853–57; partner (with Judge R. L. Pease), law firm, Hopkinsville, KY, 1857–61; law practice, Louisville, KY, 1865–67; partner (with John M. Harlan, q.v.), law firm, 1870; partner, Bristow, Peet, Burnett and Opdyke (law firm; subsequently Bristow, Opdyke and Willcox), New York, NY, 1874–96. MIL.: lt. col., 25th KY Infantry, U.S. Volunteers, 1861; col., 8th KY Cavalry, U.S. Volunteers, 1863; brev. maj. gen. of Volunteers, 1863 (declined). MEM.: ABA (pres., 1879); KY Bar Assn.; Bar Assn. of the City of NY (vice pres.); Civil Service Reform Assn. (vice pres.); Metropolitan Club; Union Club (gov.); Union League; Soc. of the Army of the Cumberland. MISC.: noted for exposure of Whiskey Ring, 1875. RES.: New York, NY.

BRITT, GEORGE GITTION, JR. b. May 19, 1949, Brooklyn, NY; par. George Gittion and Mary Jane (Pattilo) (q.v.) Britt; m. Yvonne Oles, Nov 24, 1974; c. none. EDUC.: B.A., Cheyney State Coll., 1972; U. of CO; U. of MI, 1974. POLIT. & GOV.: member, exec. cmte., Philadelphia (PA) Democratic Central Cmte., 1970–76; candidate for Democratic nomination to PA State House, 1970, 1972; member, Council for Equal Job Opportunity, 1970–(chair, 1981); appointed chm., PA State Dept. of Commerce, 1972–74; candidate for Democratic nomination to U.S. House (PA), 1974, 1978, 1986; candidate for Democratic nomination to mayor of Philadelphia, PA, 1975, 1979; ***candidate for Democratic nomination to presidency of the U.S., 1976, 1984, 1988***; candidate for Democratic nomination to city controller, Philadelphia, PA, 1981. BUS. & PROF.: asst., U. of PA Hospital, 1968–70; chief exec. officer, Britt, Morales, Patterson, McGhee Corp., Philadelphia, PA, 1978–; public relations counselor, United Minority Enterprise Assn.; community organizer; activist. MEM.: National Assn. of Puerto Rican Youth (chm. of the board, 1974–); Comm. for the Delivery of Effective Public Service; National League of Cities; U.S. Conference of Mayors; Urban League; NAACP; Cobbs Creek Community Assn.; Philadelphia Community Development Program (chm., 1970–72); American Soc. for Public Administration; International City Management Assn.; Community Programs, Inc.; Assn. of Government Accountants; National Service League; NY City Club; Faculty Club of the U. of PA; Hilltop Club. AWARDS: named Honorary Citizen of TX, 1972; Honorary Citizen of Minneapolis, MN, 1972; Honorary Citizen of AR, 1978; Honorary Citizen of AL, 1978; Honorary Citizen of MN, 1978; Honorary Citizen of WV, 1978. REL.: Bapt. MAILING ADDRESS: 906 South 60th St., Philadelphia, PA 19143.

BRITT, MARY JANE. b. Oct 5, 1920, Norlina, NC; par. Charles and Cornelia (Thomas) Pattilo; m. George Britt; c. Kevin; Andre; Anthony; George, Jr. (q.v.); Wilhelmina. EDUC.: Booker T. Washington H.S., Norfolk, VA. POLIT. & GOV.: Board of Education; Democratic committeewoman; Democratic mayoralty inspector; candidate for city controller, Philadelphia,

PA, 1973; ***candidate for Democratic nomination to presidency of the U.S., 1976***. BUS. & PROF.: housewife. MEM.: National Assn. of Puerto Rican Youth (dir.); Inst. for Advancement of Puerto Rican Public Affairs; Pittsburgh Youth Corp.; Community Civic Assn.; Lidwater Youth Assn. REL.: Bapt. MAILING ADDRESS: 906 South 60th St., Philadelphia, PA 19143.

BRITTON, HARRY ROBERT. b. Dec 2, 1925, Erie, PA; par. Harry R. and Carolyn (Marquadt) Britton; m. Lillian Almeda (separated); c. Robert; Philip; Elaine. EDUC.: Harborcreek H.S. POLIT. & GOV.: ***Independent Husband Liberation Party candidate for presidency of the U.S., 1972***. BUS. & PROF.: industrial engineer, General Electric Co., Erie, PA, to 1966. MEM.: Harborcreek Bible Church. REL.: nondenominational Christian. MISC.: involved in planning, methods, and time studies; committed to Warren (PA) State Hospital, 1967; escaped, 1970; captured and returned to Bellevue Hospital, New York, NY. MAILING ADDRESS: Gospel Mission, 810 Fifth St., N.W., Washington, DC 20001.

BROADHEAD, JAMES OVERTON. b. May 29, 1819, Charlottesville, VA; d. Aug 7, 1898, St. Louis, MO; par. Achilles and Mary Winston (Carr) Broadhead; m. Mary S. Dorsey, May 13, 1847; c. Mrs. W. M. Horton; Mary B.; Charles S. EDUC.: high school, Albemarle Cty., VA; U. of VA, 1835–36; studied law under Edward Bates (q.v.), St. Louis. POLIT. & GOV.: delegate, MO State Constitutional Convention, 1845, 1861, 1863, 1875; elected as a Whig to MO State House, 1846–47; elected as a Whig to MO State Senate, 1850–53; organizer, Cmte. of Safety (to resist pro-Southern forces, Civil War); appointed U.S. atty. for Eastern MO, 1861; appointed provost-marshal gen., 1863; delegate, Dem. Nat'l. Conv., 1868, 1872; delegate, Railroad Convention, 1875; appointed special U.S. atty., Whiskey Ring Cases, 1876; ***candidate for Democratic nomination to presidency of the U.S., 1876***; elected as a Democrat to U.S. House (MO), 1883–85; appointed special U.S. commissioner to France to investigate spoilation claims, 1885; appointed U.S. minister to Switzerland, 1893–97. BUS. & PROF.: tutor, Edward Bates Family, St. Louis, MO, 1837; atty.; admitted to MO Bar, 1842; law practice, Bowling Green, MO, 1842–59; partner (with Fidelio C. Sharp), law practice, St. Louis, MO, 1859–76; partner, Broadhead, Slayback and Haeussler (law firm), St. Louis, MO, 1876–98. MIL.: lt. col., U.S.V., 1863. MEM.: ABA (pres., 1878). RES.: St. Louis, MO.

BROCK, WILLIAM EMERSON, III. b. Nov 23, 1930, Chattanooga, TN; par. William Emerson and Myra (Kruesi) Brock; m. Laura Handly, Jan 11, 1957; c. William Emerson IV; Oscar Handly; Laura Hutcheson; John Kruesi. EDUC.: B.S., Washington and Lee U., 1953. POLIT. & GOV.: chm., Hamilton Cty. (TN) Republican Central Cmte.; national committeeman, TN Young Republicans, 1961–; elected as a Republican to U.S. House (TN), 1963–71; delegate, Rep. Nat'l. Conv., 1964, 1968, 1972, 1976; elected as a Republican to U.S. Senate (TN), 1971–77; ***candidate for Republican nomination to vice presidency of the U.S., 1976***; Republican candidate for U.S. Senate (TN), 1976; chm., Rep. Nat'l. Cmte., 1977–81; appointed U.S. special trade representative (with cabinet rank), 1981–85; appointed U.S. sec. of labor, 1985–87; Republican candidate for U.S. Senate (MD), 1994. BUS. & PROF.: production asst., Brock Candy Co., 1956–63, vice pres. of marketing, 1963–. MIL.: lt. (jg), U.S. Navy, 1953–56; lt., U.S.N.R.; Korean War Ribbon; U.N. Ribbon. MEM.: C. of C.; Junior C. of C.; American Legion; Chowder and Marching Soc.; Area Literacy Movement; Sigma Alpha Epsilon; Trilateral Comm.; Brookings Institution; Freedoms Foundation (trustee); Big Sisters/Big Brothers (dir.); 70001, Inc. (dir.). AWARDS: "Outstanding Young Man of the Year," TN Junior C. of C., 1965; Distinguished Service Award, Chattanooga Junior C. of C., 1966; Outstanding Service Award, Teen-Age Republican, 1967; Outstanding Service Award, Young Republican National Federation; Distinguished Legislator, Young Americans Inaugural Cmte., 1969. REL.: Presb. MAILING ADDRESS: c/o Brock Group, 1130 Connecticut Ave., N.W., #305, Washington, DC 20036.

BRONSTEIN, YETTA. b. Feb 14, early twentieth century; m. Horace Bronstein; c. Marvin. EDUC.: audited courses in NY colleges. POLIT. & GOV.: ***Best Party candidate for presidency of the U.S., 1964, 1968***; Best Party candidate for mayor of New York, NY, 1965; Best Party candidate for gov. of AL, 1966; Best Party candidate for member of Parliament, Great Britain. BUS. & PROF.: housewife. AWARDS: awarded "Best Citizen of Bruckner Boulevard" Trophy, 1965; First Prize, Big Apple Contest; U.S.O. Plaque; Cherry Sister's Award, 1967. WRITINGS: *The President I Almost Was* (1966). REL.: Jewish. MISC.: fictional character created by Jeanne Abel (q.v.) as a satire on American politics; offered to withdraw from presidential campaign if President Lyndon B. Johnson (q.v.) would select her as his running mate, 1964. MAILING ADDRESS: 507 Fifth Ave., New York, NY.

BROODY, GEORGE S., JR. par. George S. Broody, Sr. POLIT. & GOV.: ***candidate for Democratic nomination to vice presidency of the U.S., 1980***. MAILING ADDRESS: PA.

BROOKE, EDWARD WILLIAM. b. Oct 26, 1919, Washington, DC; par. Edward W. and Helen (Seldon) Brooke; m. Remigia Ferrari-Scacco, Jun 7, 1947; m. 2d, Anne Fleming, 1979; c. Remi Coyle; Edwina Helene; Edward William IV. EDUC.: B.S., Howard U., 1940; LL.B., Boston U., 1948, LL.M., 1949. POLIT. & GOV.: Republican candidate for sec. of the Commonwealth of MA, 1960; appointed chm., Boston (MA) Finance Cmte., 1961–62; elected as a Republican, atty. gen. of MA, 1963–67; delegate, Rep. Nat'l. Conv., 1964, 1968; elected as a Republican to U.S. Senate (MA), 1967–79; appointed member, President's Comm. on Housing; appointed member, Comm.

on Wartime Relocation; appointed member, President's Comm. on Civil Rights Under Law; ***candidate for Republican nomination to vice presidency of the U.S., 1968, 1976***; Republican candidate for U.S. Senate (MA), 1978. BUS. & PROF.: atty.; admitted to MA Bar, 1948; ed., *Boston University Law Review*, 1948; partner, O'Connor and Hannan (law firm), Washington, DC; limited partner, Bear Stearns and Co., New York, NY. MIL.: 2d lt., capt., U.S. Army, 1942–45; Bronze Star; Combat Infantryman's Badge. MEM.: ABA (fellow); Boston Bar Assn.; MA Bar Assn.; American Acad. of Arts and Sciences; Boston Opera Co. (dir.); BSA (National Council); Boys Clubs of America (dir.); Amvets (MA commander, 1954–55; national judge advocate, 1955–75); National Low Income Housing Coalition (chm., 1979–); Old North Church (chancellor); Boston U. (trustee); Boston Council for International Visitors (dir.); New England Hospital (dir.); Republican Club of MA; National Assn. of Attorneys General. AWARDS: Distinguished Service Award, Amvets, 1952; Charles Evans Hughes Award, National Conference of Christians and Jews, 1967; Spingarn Medal, MA Chapter, NAACP, 1967; Grand Cross of Merit, 1976. HON. DEG.: J.D., Portia Law School, 1963; D.P.A., Northeastern U., 1964; D.Sc., Worcester Polytechnical Inst., 1965; LL.D., American International Coll., 1965; LL.D., Emerson Coll., 1965; D.Sc., Lowell Technological Inst., 1967; LL.D., George Washington U., 1967; LL.D., Howard U., 1967; LL.D., Boston U., 1968; LL.D., Johns Hopkins U., 1968; LL.D., Hampton Inst., 1968; LL.D., Morehouse Coll., 1968; LL.D., Catholic U. of America, 1968; D.P.A., Suffolk U., 1969; LL.D., Bowdoin Coll., 1969; LL.D., North Adams State Coll., 1969; LL.D., Skidmore Coll., 1969; L.H.D., Framingham State Coll., 1970; LL.D., U. of MA, 1971; LL.D., Boston State Coll., 1971; LL.D., U. of NH, 1971; LL.D., Xavier U., 1971; LL.D., Amherst Coll., 1972. WRITINGS: *The Challenge of Change* (1966). REL.: Episc. MAILING ADDRESS: 535 Beacon St., Newton Center, MA 02159.

BROOKHART, SMITH WILDMAN. b. Feb 2, 1869, Scotland Cty., MO; d. Nov 15, 1944, Whipple, AZ; par. Abram Colar and Cynthia (Wildman) Brookhart; m. Jennie Hearne, Jun 22, 1897; c. Samuel Colar; Charles Edward; John Robert; Smith Wildman; Florence Hearn; Edith Alma; Joseph Warren. EDUC.: grad., Southern IA Normal School, 1889; studied law in offices of Payne and Sowers and Wherry and Walker, 1889–92. POLIT. & GOV.: appointed cty. atty., Washington Cty., IA, 1895–1901; chm., IA Republican State Convention, 1912; candidate for Republican nomination to U.S. Senate (IA), 1920, 1932, 1936; elected as a Republican to U.S. Senate (IA), 1922–26, 1927–33; ***candidate for Republican nomination to vice presidency of the U.S., 1924***; appointed special adviser, A.A.A., U.S. Dept. of Agriculture, 1933–35. BUS. & PROF.: teacher, 5 years; farmer; atty.; admitted to IA Bar, 1892; law practice, Washington, IA; partner, S. W. and J. L. Brookhart (farmers). MIL.: member, IA National Guard, 1894–1919, 2d lt., 1898, lt. col., 1917. MEM.: Farmers Union; Farm Bureau; American Legion; Spanish-American War Veterans; NRA; Knights of Pythias; Commercial Club; People's Legislative Service; Public Ownership League of America; American Palma Rifle Team, 1912 (World Champions). WRITINGS: *Rifle Training in War* (1918, 1920). RES.: Washington, IA.

BROOKS, DAVID V. POLIT. & GOV.: ***candidate for Democratic nomination to presidency of the U.S., 1976***. MAILING ADDRESS: Box 829, Raleigh, NC 27602.

BROOKS, ERASTUS. b. Jan 13, 1815, Portland, ME; d. Nov 25, 1886, West New Brighton, NY; par. James and Elizabeth (Folsom) Brooks; m. Margaret Dawes; c. Bertha; one other daughter; one son. EDUC.: Brown U.; LL.D., Cornell U. POLIT. & GOV.: elected as an American (Know-Nothing) to NY State Senate, 1853–55; American (Know-Nothing) Party candidate for gov. of NY, 1856; delegate, American (Know-Nothing) Party National Convention, 1856; ***candidate for American (Know-Nothing) Party nomination to presidency of the U.S., 1856***; delegate, Constitutional Union Party National Convention, 1860; elected delegate, NY State Constitutional Convention, 1866–67, 1872–73; delegate, Dem. Nat'l. Conv., 1868; elected as a Democrat to NY State Assembly, 1878–85; appointed member, NY State Board of Health, 1880. BUS. & PROF.: journalist; founder, Yankee, Wiscasset, ME; schoolteacher, Haverhill, MA; ed., *Haverhill (MA) Gazette*; reporter, *Portland (ME) Advertiser*, ed., 1840; foreign correspondent, 1843; ed., *New York (NY) Express*, 1836–77; founder, Associated Press. MEM.: NY Inst. for the Instruction of the Deaf and Dumb (trustee); Nursery and Childs Hospital (trustee); Cornell U. (trustee). WRITINGS: *Controversy on Church Property*. REL.: Episc. RES.: West New Brighton, NY.

BROOKS, GERRY. POLIT. & GOV.: ***candidate for Democratic nomination to presidency of the U.S., 1984***. MAILING ADDRESS: 2056 Calvert St., Detroit, MI 48206.

BROOKS, JOHN ANDERSON. b. Jun 3, 1836, Germantown, KY; d. Feb 3, 1897, Memphis, TN; par. John T. and Elizabeth B. (Anderson) Brooks; m. Sue E. Osborn, Oct 14, 1857; m. 2d, Sue E. Robertson, 1859; c. John T.; Lida; Bessie; Susie; infant. EDUC.: grad., Bethany Coll., 1856, D.D. POLIT. & GOV.: Prohibition Party candidate for gov. of MO, 1884; state chm., MO Prohibition Party State Central Cmte., 1887; ***Prohibition Party candidate for vice presidency of the U.S., 1888***; member, Prohibition Party National Cmte., 1892–96. BUS. & PROF.: atty.; minister; pres., Flemingsburg (KY) Coll., 1856–58, 1861–63; pastor, Christian Church, Flemingsburg; pastor, Christian Church, Eminence, KY; pastor, Christian Church, Winchester, KY, 1865–70; pastor, First Christian Church, St. Louis, MO, 1870; pastor, Christian Church, Mexico, MO; pastor, Christian Church, Warrensburg, MO; pastor, Christian Church, Belton, MO; pastor, Independence Avenue Christian Church, Kansas City, MO. MEM.: MO Prohibition Alliance (pres., 1880); Sons of Temperance; Ancient Order of United Workmen (grand foreman, 1879; grand master workman, 1880; supreme master workman, 1886); Francis Murphy Movement; Independent Order of Good Templars; National Prohibition Bureau (southwestern district agent, 1886). HON. DEG.: A.M., Bethany Coll. REL.: Disciples of Christ (pres., MO General Conference, 3 years). RES.: Kansas City, MO.

BROOKWATER, LOUIS. POLIT. & GOV.: ***independent candidate for presidency of the U.S., 1876***. RES.: IA.

BROOM, JACOB. b. Jul 25, 1808, Baltimore, MD; d. Nov 28, 1864, Washington, DC; par. James Madison Broom. EDUC.: classical. POLIT. & GOV.: appointed deputy PA state auditor, 1840–48; clerk, Philadelphia (PA) Orphan's Court, 1848–52; chm., Native American Party National Convention, 1852; ***Native American Party candidate for presidency of the U.S., 1852***; elected as an American Whig to U.S. House (PA), 1855–57; candidate for American Whig Party nomination to U.S. House (PA), 1856, 1858. BUS. & PROF.: atty.; admitted to PA Bar, 1832; law practice, Philadelphia, PA. RES.: Philadelphia, PA.

BROUGHTON, CHARLES ELMER. b. Oct 22, 1873, Lamartine, WI; d. Oct 31, 1956, Sheboygan, WI; par. John and Emma (Cortleyou) Broughton; m. Emma Born, Jun 23, 1898; c. Charles Elmer. EDUC.: night school. POLIT. & GOV.: member, Dem. Nat'l. Cmte., 1932–41 (vice chm., 1936); delegate, Dem. Nat'l. Conv., 1932; appointed chm., Federal Home Loan Bank of Chicago, 1938–51; ***candidate for Democratic nomination to presidency of the U.S., 1952***. BUS. & PROF.: ed.; publisher; freelance writer, city ed., *Fond du Lac (WI) Journal*, 1884–1903; ed., *Campbellsport (WI) News*, 1903–07; ed., publisher, *Sheboygan (WI) Press*, 1907–52; pres., WHBL radio, 1952–56; pres., Press Publishing Co.; dir., North Shore Land Co.; dir., Kingsberry Brewing Co. MEM.: WI Defense Savings Cmte. (state chm., 1941); colonel, WI Governor's Staff, 1933; Masons; Odd Fellows; Knights of Pythias; Elks (state pres., 1929; grand esteemed leading knight; chm. of the board of grand trustees, 1945; grand exalted ruler, 1946–47); Elks National Foundation (hon. founder, 1929); Sigma Delta Chi; Milwaukee Press Club; Milwaukee Athletic Club; National Press Club; Union League; State Hist. Soc. of WI (curator). AWARDS: Distinguished Service Medal, Salvation Army, 1942. RES.: Sheboygan, WI.

BROUGHTON, JOSEPH MELVILLE. b. Nov 17, 1888, Raleigh, NC; d. Mar 6, 1949, Washington, DC; par. Joseph Melville and Sallie (Harris) Broughton; m. Alice Harper Willson, Dec 14, 1916; c. Alice Willson; Joseph Melville, III; Robert Bain; Woodson Harris. EDUC.: grad., Hugh Morson Acad., 1906; A.B., Wake Forest Coll., 1910; LL.B., Harvard U., 1913; Duke U., 1913. POLIT. & GOV.: member, Raleigh (NC) School Board; acting superintendent of public instruction, Wake Cty., NC, 1914; elected as a Democrat to NC State Senate, 1927–31; delegate, NC State Democratic Convention, 1936 (keynoter; temporary chm.); presidential elector, Democratic Party, 1936; elected as a Democrat to gov. of NC, 1941–45; ***candidate for Democratic nomination to vice presidency of the U.S., 1944***; elected as a Democrat to U.S. Senate (NC), 1949. BUS. & PROF.: teacher, principal, high school, Bunn, NC, 1910–12; reporter, *Winston-Salem (NC) Journal*, 1912; atty.; admitted to NC Bar, 1914; law practice, Raleigh, NC. MEM.: Raleigh C. of C. (pres.); Raleigh Community Chest (pres.); Wake Forest Coll. (trustee); Olivia Raney Public Library (trustee); U. of NC (trustee); Shaw U. (trustee); Raleigh School Comm.; NC Bar Assn. (pres., 1936); Wake Cty. Bar Assn.; ABA; Masons; Junior Order, Modern Woodmen of the World; Watauga Club. HON. DEG.: LL.D., Wake Forest Coll., 1941; LL.D., U. of NC, 1942. WRITINGS: *The Legal Status of Women in NC; The Language of the Law* (1936); *Social and Economic Aspects of Trusts* (1937). REL.: Bapt. (Sunday school superintendent; teacher, men's Bible class). RES.: Raleigh, NC.

BROWDER, EARL RUSSELL. b. May 20, 1891, Wichita, KS; d. Jun 27, 1973, Princeton, NJ; par. William and Martha (Hankins) Browder; m. (divorced); m. 2d, Raissa Irene Berkman, Moscow, U.S.S.R., 1926; c. Felix Earl; Andrew; William. EDUC.: left school at age 10; LL.B., Lincoln-Jefferson Coll., 1912. POLIT. & GOV.: charter member, United Communist Party, 1921; delegate, Congress of the Red International of Labor Unions, 1921 (alternate, Exec. Bureau); member, Central Exec. Cmte., Workers Party, 1921; member, Control Cmte., Communist International, 1924; gen. sec., Communist Party, 1930–44; ***Communist Party candidate for presidency of the U.S., 1936, 1940***; Communist Party candidate for U.S. House (NY), 1940; expelled from the Communist Party, 1946. BUS. & PROF.: accountant; ed.; author; lecturer; revolutionary; assoc. ed., *Toiler*, 1914; organized Office Service Associates; employee, Trade Union Educational League; ed., *The Workers World*, 1919; ed., *The Workers Monthly*; mgr., Farmers' Cooperative Store, Olathe, KS; managing ed., *Labor Herald*, 1924; ed., *Political Affairs*; editor-in-chief, *Daily Worker*, 1944; American representative, Soviet Government Publishing House, 1946–49; contributing ed., *New Masses*. MEM.: League for Democratic Control (founder); AFL Bookkeepers, Stenographers and Accountants Union (local pres., 1913–17); The Cooperative League of America (member, Technical Advisory Board); International Workers Order; Syndicalist League of North America; Workers Educational League (1912); Pan-Pacific Trade Union Secretariat (sec., 1927–28); Communist Political Assn. (pres., 1944–45); Trade Union Educational League (National Cmte., 1921); Office Workers Union 12755; Student Congress Against War (1932); League for the Struggle for Negro Rights; Friends of the Soviet Union (National Cmte.). WRITINGS: *A System of Accounts for a Small Consumers' Cooperative; Communism in the U.S.* (1935); *What is Communism?* (1936); *U.S.A. and U.S.S.R.: Their Relative Strength; How to Halt Crisis and War; War, Peace and Socialism; The Coming Economic Crisis; Chinese Lessons for American Marxists; Decline of the Left Wing of American Labor;*

The "Miracle" of November 2nd; In Defense of Communism Against W. Z. Foster's "New Route to Socialism"; The People's Front (1938); *Fighting for Peace* (1939); *War or Peace with Russia* (1939); *The Second Imperialist War* (1940); *The Way Out* (1941); *Victory and After* (1942); *Teheran—Our Path in War and Peace* (1944); *American Marxists and the War* (1945); *Marx and America; World Communism and U.S. Foreign Policy* (1948). MISC.: served 16 months in federal penitentiary for antidraft conspiracy, 1919–20 (pardoned, 1933); served 1 year for violation of passport laws, 1941–42. RES.: Yonkers, NY.

BROWN, AARON VENABLE. b. Aug 15, 1795, Brunswick Cty., VA; d. Mar 8, 1859, Washington, DC; par. Rev. Aaron and Elizabeth (Melton) Brown; m. Sarah Woodford Burruss; m. 2d, Mrs. Cynthia (Pillow) Saunders; c. Charles J.; Laura Louise; Myra M.; Walter; Aaron; Gideon Pillow. EDUC.: grad., Westrayville Acad.; grad., U. of NC, 1814 (valedictorian); studied law under Judge Trimble, Nashville, TN, 1815–17. POLIT. & GOV.: elected as a Democrat to TN State Senate, 1821–25; elected as a Democrat to TN State House, 1831–33; elected as a Democrat to U.S. House (TN), 1839–45; Democratic candidate for gov. of TN, 1843; elected as a Democrat to gov. of TN, 1845–47; delegate, TN Convention, 1850; delegate, Dem. Nat'l. Conv., 1852; ***candidate for Democratic nomination to vice presidency of the U.S., 1856***; appointed postmaster gen. of the U.S., 1857–59. BUS. & PROF.: atty.; admitted to TN Bar, 1817; partner (with James Knox Polk, q.v.), law practice, Giles Cty., TN, 1818. RES.: Columbia, TN.

BROWN, ADDISON. m. Ann V. Brown. POLIT. & GOV.: ***independent (Flying Saucer; Outer Space) candidate for vice presidency of the U.S., 1960***. BUS. & PROF.: instructor, Mt. Hood Community Coll., Portland, OR, 1972–74; author; philosopher. WRITINGS: *A Bridge from the Spirit to Reality* (1973); *A Business System That Solves These Problems* (1973); *Living as an Art Form* (1973); *The Articles; The Believer Plan for World Peace*. MAILING ADDRESS: 2409 North East Killingsworth, Portland, OR 97211.

BROWN, AVO LOYCE LOWE. b. Apr 9, 1926, Hollis, OK; par. Felix Clabe and Sarah Isabelle (Hardin) Lowe; m. Robert Bruce Brown; c. three. EDUC.: B.S., M.A.; doctoral student; OK Baptist U.; West TX State Coll.; South West Baptist Theological Seminary. POLIT. & GOV.: ***Theo-Dem Party candidate for presidency of the U.S., 1976***. BUS. & PROF.: teacher; author; housewife. MEM.: church organizations. WRITINGS: *Consider My Name* (1976). REL.: Christian. MAILING ADDRESS: c/o General Delivery, Mobeetie, TX 79061.

BROWN, BENJAMIN GRATZ. b. May 28, 1826, Lexington, KY; d. Dec 13, 1885, Kirkwood, MO; par. Mason and Judith A. (Bledsoe) Brown; m. Mary Hansome Gunn, Aug 12, 1858; c. Lillian Mason; Van Wyck; Gratz Knox; Mary G. (Mrs. Presley Carr Lane); Violet Gratz; Margaretta Mason; Eloise Elsie; Judith B. (Mrs. Leslie Dana); Robert Bruce. EDUC.: Transylvania U., 1845; grad., Yale U., 1847; Louisville (KY) Law School. POLIT. & GOV.: elected as a Democrat to MO State House, 1852–59; delegate, Dem. Nat'l. Conv., 1856; founder, Republican Party, 1856; Free Soil Party candidate for gov. of MO, 1857; delegate, Rep. Nat'l. Conv., 1860; delegate, MO Radical Emancipation and Union Convention, 1863; elected as a Republican to U.S. Senate (MO), 1863–67; elected as a Republican to gov. of MO, 1871–73; ***candidate for Liberal Republican Party nomination to presidency of the U.S., 1872; Liberal Republican Party candidate for vice presidency of the U.S., 1872; candidate for Labor Reform Party nomination to presidency of the U.S., 1872; Liberal Republican Party of Colored Men candidate for vice presidency of the U.S., 1872; Democratic Party candidate for vice presidency of the U.S., 1872***; appointed master in chancery, U.S. Circuit Court of MO, 1885. BUS. & PROF.: atty.; admitted to KY Bar, 1849; law practice, St. Louis, MO; chief ed., *Missouri Democrat*, 1854–59; owner, Citizens Railway Co., St. Louis, MO, 1859; partner, Ironton Granite Co. MIL.: col., Fourth Regt., MO Volunteers, 1861, brig. gen. MEM.: MO General Emancipation Soc. (1862). WRITINGS: *Speech on Gradual Emancipation* (1857); *Address: Slavery in Its National Aspects as Related to Peace and War* (1862); *Freedom for Missouri* (1862); *Freedom as Related to Our National and State Administrations* (1863); *Freedom and Franchise Inseparable* (1864); *Immediate Abolition of Slavery by Act of Congress* (1864); *Universal Suffrage* (1865); *Oration* (1866); *Arithmetic: Its Logical and Historical Development* (1877); *Geometry, Old and New: Its Problems and Principles* (1879). REL.: Episc. (nee Presb.). RES.: Kirkwood, MO.

BROWN, DANIEL RUSSELL. b. Mar 28, 1848, Bolton, CT; d. Feb 28, 1919, Providence, RI; par. Araba Harrison and Harriet Marilla (Dart) Brown; m. Isabel Barrows, Oct 14, 1874; c. Milton Barrows; Isabel; Hope Caroline. EDUC.: Manchester Acad. POLIT. & GOV.: elected as a Republican to Providence (RI) Common Council, 1880–84; Republican candidate for mayor of Providence, RI, 1886 (declined); presidential elector, Republican Party, 1888; elected as a Republican to gov. of RI, 1892–95; ***candidate for Republican nomination to vice presidency of the U.S., 1896***. BUS. & PROF.: head salesman, Francis and Co. (hardware), Rockville and Hartford, CT; partner, Butler, Brown and Co., Providence, RI, 1870–77; partner, Brown Brothers Co., Providence, RI, 1877–1919; publisher, *The Evening News*, Providence. MEM.: YMCA. REL.: Congregationalist. RES.: Providence, RI.

BROWN, EDMUND GERALD "PAT" BROWN. b. Apr 21, 1905, San Francisco, CA; par. Edmund Joseph and Ida (Schuckman) Brown; m. Bernice Layne, Oct 30, 1930; c. Barbara (Mrs. Philip Corwin; Mrs. Charles Edward Casey); Cynthia (Mrs. Steven Goldberg; Mrs. Joseph Kelly); Edmund Gerald, Jr. (q.v.); Kathleen (Mrs. George Rice). EDUC.: U. of CA Extension; LL.B., San Francisco Law School, 1927. POLIT. & GOV.: member, Democratic Cty. Central Cmte., 1934–36; delegate, Dem. Nat'l. Conv., 1940, 1944, 1948, 1952,

1956, 1960, 1964, 1976; chm., Speakers' Bureau, Roosevelt for President, 1940, 1944; appointed dir., Golden Gate Bridge Comm., 1942; dir., CA Code Comm.; elected as a Democrat, district atty., City and Cty. of San Francisco, CA, 1943–51; appointed chm., San Francisco (CA) Coordinating Council, 1947; chm., Jackson Day Dinner, 1948; permanent chm., CA State Democratic Convention, 1948; elected as a Democrat, atty. gen. of CA, 1951–59; ***candidate for Democratic nomination to presidency of the U.S., 1952, 1960, 1964; candidate for Democratic nomination to vice presidency of the U.S., 1956, 1960***; elected as a Democrat to gov. of CA, 1959–67; Democratic candidate for gov. of CA, 1966; appointed chm., National Comm. on the Reform of Federal Criminal Laws, 1966; appointed member, Franklin Delano Roosevelt Memorial Comm.; appointed chm., CA Council on Environment and Economic Balance. BUS. & PROF.: atty.; admitted to CA Bar, 1927; law practice, San Francisco, CA, 1927–43; partner, Ball, Hunt, Hart and Brown (law firm), Beverly Hills, CA. MEM.: Elks; Olympic Club; Native Sons of the Golden West; St. Thomas More Soc. (Appeal Agent, WWII); American Coll. of Trial Lawyers (Fellow); District Attorneys' Assn. of CA (pres., 1950–51); Western Assn. of Attorneys General (pres.); National Assn. of Attorneys General (member, exec. board); San Francisco Bar Assn.; ABA; CA State Bar Assn.; Beverly Hills Bar Assn.; NY Board of Trade (vice pres.); Commonwealth Commercial Club; Jonathan Club. HON. DEG.: LL.D., U. of San Francisco, 1959; LL.D., U. of San Diego, 1961; LL.D., U. of Santa Clara, 1961; D.C.L., CA Coll. of Medicine, 1964; L.H.D., U. of Judaism, 1965. WRITINGS: *Youth—Don't Be a Chump*; *Public Justice; Private Mercy*; *Reagan and Reality*. REL.: R.C. MAILING ADDRESS: 460 Magellan Ave., San Francisco, CA.

BROWN, EDMUND GERALD "JERRY," JR. b. Apr 7, 1938, San Francisco, CA; par. Edmund Gerald (q.v.) and Bernice (Layne) Brown; single. EDUC.: U. of Santa Clara, 1955–56; Sacred Heart Novitiate, Los Gatos, CA, 1956–60; B.A., U. of CA at Berkeley, 1961; J.D., Yale U., 1964. POLIT. & GOV.: law clerk, Justice Matthew O. Tobriner, CA Supreme Court, 1964–65; appointed member, CA State Narcotics Rehabilitation Advisory Council, 1966–68; alternate delegate, Dem. Nat'l. Conv., 1968; vice chairperson, Southern California McCarthy for President Campaign, 1968; member, CA State Democratic Central Cmte., 1968– (chm., 1989–); appointed member, Los Angeles Cty. (CA) Crime Comm., 1969–70; elected trustee, Los Angeles (CA) Community Colleges, 1969–70; elected as a Democrat, sec. of state of CA, 1971–75; elected as a Democrat to gov. of CA, 1975–83; ***candidate for Democratic nomination to presidency of the U.S., 1976, 1980, 1992; NM American Independent Party candidate for vice presidency of the U.S., 1976 (declined); Eagle Party candidate for vice presidency of the U.S., 1976; candidate for Democratic nomination to vice presidency of the U.S., 1980***; Democratic candidate for U.S. Senate (CA), 1982. BUS. & PROF.: atty.; admitted to CA Bar, 1965; staff atty., Tuttle and Tuttle (law firm), Los Angeles, CA, 1966–69. MEM.: CA Bar Assn.; Los Angeles Cty. Bar Assn.; California Democratic Council (1967). REL.: R.C. MISC.: known to opponents as "Governor Moonbeam." MAILING ADDRESS: 3022 Washington St., San Francisco, CA 94115.

BROWN, ELBRIDGE GERRY. b. Apr 15, 1850, Boston, MA; d. Aug 30, 1928, Brockton, MA; m. Anna W. Brown; c. Alice (Mrs. F. H. Scott); Jennie (Mrs. Chester H. Eames); Elbridge Gerry, Jr. EDUC.: grad., English H.S., Boston, MA, 1866. POLIT. & GOV.: elected as a Republican to Boston City Council, 1884; People's Party candidate for U.S. House (MA), 1892, 1894; member, People's Party National Cmte., 1892–1905; People's Party candidate for gov. of MA, 1895; delegate, People's Party National Convention, 1896, 1900; Democratic candidate for mayor of Brockton, MA, 1898; ***candidate for People's Party nomination to vice presidency of the U.S., 1900***; Democratic candidate for MA state auditor, 1899, 1900; Democratic (Social Democratic) candidate for lt. gov. of MA, 1906; Independence League candidate for lt. gov. of MA, 1907; appointed MA state supervisor of small loans, 1911–15 (removed); elected as a Democrat to MA State House, 1915. BUS. & PROF.: printer; publisher, *The Volunteer*, English H.S., Boston; apprentice, Prentiss and Deland (printers), Boston; reporter, *Boston Post*; co-owner, ed., *Bunker Hill (MA) Times*; reporter, *East Boston Advocate*, 1871; city and night ed., *Saturday Evening Gazette*, Boston, 1872; ed., *Boston Journal of Commerce*; ed., *Spiritualist Scientist*; ed., *Brockton Diamond*; reformer. MEM.: Typographical Union; Onset Bay Spiritualist Assn.; Masons; Central Labor Union. REL.: Spiritualist. RES.: Brockton, MA.

BROWN, FRED HERBERT. b. Apr 12, 1879, Ossipee, NH; d. Feb 3, 1955, Somersworth, NH; par. Dana J. and Nellie (Allen) Brown; m. Edna C. McHarg, May 16, 1925. EDUC.: Dartmouth Coll., 1899–1900; studied law under James A. Edgerly; Boston U. School of Law, 1904–06. POLIT. & GOV.: elected city solicitor, Somersworth, NH, 1910–14; elected delegate, NH State Constitutional Convention, 1912; presidential elector, Democratic Party, 1912; elected as a Democrat to mayor of Somersworth, NH, 1914–23; appointed U.S. district atty. for NH, 1914–23; elected as a Democrat to gov. of NH, 1923–25; Democratic candidate for gov. of NH, 1924; ***candidate for Democratic nomination to presidency of the U.S., 1924***; appointed member, NH State Public Service Comm., 1925–33; elected as a Democrat to U.S. Senate (NH), 1933–39; Democratic candidate for U.S. Senate (NH), 1938; appointed comptroller gen. of the U.S., 1939–40; appointed member, U.S. Tariff Comm., 1940–41. BUS. & PROF.: baseball player; catcher, Boston Braves, National League; atty.; admitted to NH Bar, 1907; law practice, Somersworth, NH, 1907–08. MEM.: NH Bar Assn.; Masons; Knights of Pythias; Knights Templar. RES.: Somersworth, NH.

BROWN, GEORGE SCRATCHLEY. b. Aug 17, 1918, Montclair, NJ; d. Dec 5, 1978, Washington, DC; par.

Thoburn Kay and Frances Katherine (Scratchley) Brown; m. Alice Norvell Warwick Colhoun, May 19, 1942; c. Dudley K.; Daniel W.; Susanah B. EDUC.: U. of MO, 1936–37; B.S., U.S. Military Acad., 1941; grad., National War Coll., 1957. POLIT. & GOV.: appointed asst. to U.S. sec. of defense, 1959–61; ***Ku Klux Klan candidate for presidency of the U.S., 1976***. BUS. & PROF.: soldier. MIL.: commissioned 2d lt., U.S.A.A.F., 1941; promoted through ranks to col., 1944, brig. gen., 1957, maj. gen., 1964, lt. gen., 1966, gen., 1968; commander, 662d Troop Carrier Group, 1950–51; commander, 56th Fighter Interceptor Wing, Air Defense Command, 1951–52; dir. of operations, Fifth Air Force, Korea, 1952–53; commander, 3525th Pilot Training Wing, AZ, 1953–56; exec. to chief of staff, U.S. Air Force, 1957–59; commander, Eastern Transport Air Service, McGuire Air Force Base, NJ, 1963–64; commander, Joint Task Force 2, Sandia Base, NM, 1964–66; asst. to the chm., JCS, 1966–68; gen., Seventh Air Force, 1968–70; commander, Air Force Systems Command, 1970–73; chief of staff, U.S. Air Force, 1973–74; chm., JCS, 1974–78; Presidential Unit Citation with Oak Leaf Cluster; Defense Distinguished Service Medal; Distinguished Service Cross; Silver Star; Legion of Merit with Two Oak Leaf Clusters; Bronze Star; Air Medal with Three Oak Leaf Clusters; Croix de Guerre with Palm; Distinguished Flying Cross with Oak Leaf Cluster; Indonesian Military Service Star, First Class; Distinguished Flying Cross (England); American Defense Service Medal; Grand Cross, Order of Merit, Second Class (Germany); Gallantry Cross with Palm (Vietnam); Silver Star, Order of Military Merit Ulchi (Korea). MEM.: Order of National Security Merit Tong II: Order of Aeronautical Merit (Brazil); National Order of Vietnam; Air Force Distinguished Service Order, First Class; Order of Daedalians; Alfalfa Club; Adirondack Club; Legion of Honor (France). REL.: Episc. RES.: Ft. Myer, VA.

BROWN, JOE E. b. 1938. POLIT. & GOV.: ***independent candidate for vice presidency of the U.S., 1980***. BUS. & PROF.: actor in western movies, Hollywood, CA; evangelist; pastor, First Alliance Church, Tampa, FL. REL.: Christian. MISC.: self-styled former devil worshipper. MAILING ADDRESS: First Alliance Church, 10114 North Newport Ave., Tampa, FL.

BROWN, ORVILLE HARRIS. b. May 26, 1923, Louisville, KY; par. Earl and Goldie (Wells) Brown; m. Mary Alice Stamps; m. 2d, Mary Jo Brown; m. 3d, Sue Fugio; c. Orville Harris, Jr.; Joseph Carl; Linda J.; Peggy M.; Dana G.; Deana K. EDUC.: grad., high school, 1941. POLIT. & GOV.: ***candidate for Democratic nomination to presidency of the U.S., 1980***. BUS. & PROF.: retail salesman; retail mgr.; employee, Ford Motor Co. MEM.: Parent-Teachers' Assn. (pres., local school). REL.: Lutheran. MAILING ADDRESS: 142 Stoll Ave., Louisville, KY 40206.

BROWN, PRENTISS MARSH. b. Jun 18, 1889, St. Ignace, MI; d. Dec 19, 1973, St. Ignace, MI; par. James John and Minnie (Gagnon) Brown; m. Marion E. Walker, Jun 16, 1916; c. Mariana Frances Rudolph; Ruth Margaret Evanshevski; James John; Barbara Jean Laing; Patricia Jane Watson; Prentiss Marsh, Jr.; Paul W. EDUC.: A.B., Albion Coll., 1911, LL.D., 1937. POLIT. & GOV.: city atty., St. Ignace, MI, 1914–33; prosecuting atty., Cheboygan Cty., MI; prosecuting atty., Mackinac Cty., MI, 1914–26; chm., MI State Democratic Convention, 1924, 1932, 1934, 1936, 1938, 1940; Democratic candidate for U.S. House (MI), 1924; Democratic candidate for judge, MI Supreme Court, 1928; appointed member, MI State Board of Law Examiners, 1930–41; pres., St. Ignace (MI) School Board; elected as a Democrat to U.S. House (MI), 1933–37; appointed and subsequently elected as a Democrat to U.S. Senate (MI), 1936–43; ***candidate for Democratic nomination to vice presidency of the U.S., 1936, 1940***; Democratic candidate for U.S. Senate (MI), 1942; appointed administrator, OPA, 1943–44; appointed member, MI State Hist. Comm., 1948–65; appointed chm., Mackinac Bridge authority, 1952–73; delegate, Dem. Nat'l. Conv., 1952. BUS. & PROF.: sec., dean of Graduate School, U. of IL, 1912–14; atty.; admitted to MI Bar, 1914; law practice, St. Ignace, MI; pres., First National Bank of St. Ignace, 1933–65; partner, Brown, Lund and Fitzgerald (law firm), Washington, DC, 1943–73; chm. of the board, Detroit Edison Co., 1944–54; dir., National Bank of Detroit, 1948–66; pres., Arnold Transit Co.; chm. of the board, Federal Reserve Bank of Chicago (Detroit Branch); member, exec. cmte., Assn. of Edison Illuminating Companies; dir., Parke, Davis and Co., 1955–63; incorporator, Atomic Reactor Development Co.; pres., Essex Light and Power Co., Ltd.; pres., dir., Peninsular Electric Light Co.; pres., dir., Washtenaw Light and Power Co.; vice pres., dir., Edison Illuminating Co. of Detroit; vice pres., dir., St. Clair Edison Co.; vice pres., Union Terminal Piers; dir., Great Lakes Sugar Co.; adviser, Brown, Fenlon, Lund and Babcock (law firm). MEM.: Detroit Hist. Soc. (trustee); BSA (pres., Detroit Council); Delta Tau Delta; Delta Sigma Rho; Phi Beta Kappa; Albion Coll. (trustee); Masons (33°); Knights of Pythias; Recess Club; Detroit Club. HON. DEG.: LL.B., U. of IL, 1937; J.D., Detroit Coll. of Law, 1942; D.A., Wayne U.; LL.D., U. of MI, 1952. REL.: Methodist. MISC.: named "Ablest Democrat in Senate," Senate Press Gallery, 1942. RES.: St. Ignace, MI.

BROWN, REED VANCE. par. Doris S. Brown. POLIT. & GOV.: candidate for Democratic nomination to U.S. House (FL), 1988; Democratic nomination to U.S. Senate (NM), 1988; ***candidate for Democratic nomination to presidency of the U.S., 1988***. MAILING ADDRESS: 21133 South West 85th Ave., Studio #209, Saga Bay, FL 35157.

BROWN-GERDINE, KAREN E. POLIT. & GOV.: ***independent candidate for presidency of the U.S., 1992***. MAILING ADDRESS: 714 East 18th Ave., Suite 202, Denver, CO 80203.

BROWNE, CEIL EVAN. m. John Adams; c. two. EDUC.: PA State U. POLIT. & GOV.: founder, Christian Moralist Party, 1963; founder, World Christian and Moralist Party, 1972; ***Worldcamp Party candidate for presidency of the U.S., 1972; Christian Party candidate for presidency of the U.S., 1976***. BUS. & PROF.: radical cancer therapist; freelance writer; owner, Adams Import-Export Co., Hollywood, FL; lecturer in England and America. MEM.: Cushing International Foundation for Freedom from Cancer (officer; formerly known as Hope of Cancer Foundation of Jamaica). REL.: R.C. MISC.: advocate of vegetable juice diet; liver injections; coffee enemas in cancer treatment. MAILING ADDRESS: 10411 Northwest 18th Place, Pembroke Lakes, FL 33024.

BROWNELL, MARK. POLIT. & GOV.: ***candidate for Universal Party nomination to presidency of the U.S., 1972***. BUS. & PROF.: pres., Understanding, Elsinore, CA. MAILING ADDRESS: Elsinore, CA.

BROWNLEE, TRAVES VIRGIL. b. Apr 24, 1945, Keokuk, IA; par. Traves LeRoy and Cececile (LaVone) Brownlee; m. Arletta Faye Brownlee, Aug 1, 1964; c. Tamara Jayne; Traves, Jr.; James LeRoy; Rodney Wayne; Penny LaVone. EDUC.: IL Baptist Inst., Washington, IL, 3 years. POLIT. & GOV.: American Party candidate for atty. gen. of DE, 1982; ***American Party candidate for vice presidency of the U.S., 1984***. BUS. & PROF.: ordained minister, Baptist Church, 1970; pastor, Baptist Church, Frederica, DE; co-owner, home improvement business, to 1976; salesman; lecturer. MIL.: U.S. Air Force, 1962–64. MEM.: Americans for Constitutional Taxation (founder). REL.: Reformed Bapt. (Hist.). MISC.: noted tax protestor; arrested, Feb 1981. MAILING ADDRESS: P.O. Box 288, Frederica, DE 19946.

BRUCE, BLANCHE KELSO. b. Mar 1, 1841, Farmville, VA; d. Mar 17, 1898, Washington, DC; par. unknown white father and Polly Bruce; m. Josephine B. Wilson, Jun 24, 1878; c. Roscoe Conkling. EDUC.: Oberlin Coll., 1866–68; LL.D., Howard U., 1893. POLIT. & GOV.: delegate, Rep. Nat'l. Conv., 1868, 1872, 1876, 1880, 1884, 1888, 1892, 1896; appointed supervisor of elections, Tallahatchie Cty., MS, 1869; appointed sergeant-at-arms, MS State Senate, 1870; appointed assessor, Bolivar Cty., MS, 1871; appointed Sheriff, Bolivar Cty., MS, 1871–74; appointed member, Board of Levee Commissioners of the MS River, 1872; appointed superintendent of education, Bolivar Cty., MS, 1872–73; member, Floreyville (MS) Board of Aldermen; elected as a Republican to U.S. Senate (MS), 1875–81; appointed register, U.S. Dept. of the Treasury, 1881–85, 1895–98; ***candidate for Republican nomination to vice presidency of the U.S., 1880, 1888***; appointed recorder of deeds, Washington, DC, 1889–95, 1897. BUS. & PROF.: slave to 1861; tobacco field hand; factory worker; escaped to Lawrence, KS, 1861; principal, negro school, Lawrence, KS, 1861–65; schoolteacher, Hannibal, MO, 1865; printer's apprentice, Hannibal, MO, 1865; porter, "Columbia" steamboat, MS River; public official. MEM.: Howard U. (trustee, 1894–98). RES.: Floreyville.

BRUCH, CHERYL ANDREA (See WILLIAM LYLE KNAUS).

BRUMBAUGH, MARTIN GROVE. b. Apr 14, 1862, Huntingdon Cty., PA; d. Mar 14, 1930, Pinehurst, NC; par. George Boyer and Martha (Peightal) Brumbaugh; m. Anna Konigmacher, Jul 30, 1884; m. 2d, Flora Belle Parks, Jan 29, 1916; c. two. EDUC.: B.E., Juniata Coll., 1881, M.E., 1883, B.S., 1885, M.S., 1887; A.M., U. of PA, 1894, Ph.D., 1895; U. of Jena (Germany), 1895. POLIT. & GOV.: cty. superintendent of schools, Huntingdon Cty., PA, 1884–90; appointed commissioner of education, Puerto Rico, 1900–1902; superintendent of public schools, Philadelphia, PA, 1906–15; appointed member, PA State Board of Education, 1911–17; elected as a Republican to gov. of PA, 1915–19; ***candidate for Republican nomination to presidency of the U.S., 1916***. BUS. & PROF.: prof., PA State Normal School, 1882–83; minister, Church of the Brethren; state conductor of teacher institutes (LA), 1886–91; prof. of pedagogy, U. of PA, 1895–1900, 1902–06; pres., Juniata Coll., 1895–1906, 1924–30. MEM.: Union League; PA State Teachers Assn. (pres., 1898); PA State Hist. Soc.; Pennsylvania German Soc.; PA Huguenot Soc.; Five O'Clock Club; Colonial Club; Philadelphia Schoolmen's Club. HON. DEG.: LL.D., Mt. Morris Coll., 1901; LL.D., Franklin and Marshall Coll., 1902; LL.D., PA Coll., 1911; LL.D., U. of Pittsburgh, 1916; LL.D., U. of ME, 1919; Litt.D., Lafayette Coll., 1915; L.H.D., Susquehanna Coll., 1917. WRITINGS: *Juniata Bible Lectures* (1890); *Stories of Pennsylvania* (with J. S. Walton, 1893); *Liberty Bell Leaflets* (with J. S. Walton, 1894); *Lectures* in the *Book of Ruth* (1895); *History of the Church of the German Baptist Brethren* (1895); *Standard Readers* (1896–98); *The Making of a Teacher* (1905); *Life and Teachings of Christopher Dock* (1906); *Story of Roosevelt* (1922); *Lippincott Educational Series* (ed.). REL.: Church of the Brethren (Dunkers). RES.: Huntingdon, PA.

BRUST, JEAN T. m. William Z. Brust. POLIT. & GOV.: Workers' Party candidate for U.S. House (MN), 1976, 1978; ***Workers' League candidate for vice presidency of the U.S., 1984***. MAILING ADDRESS: 260 Westview Dr., Apt. 302, West St. Paul, MN 55118.

BRYAN, CHARLES WAYLAND. b. Feb 10, 1867, Salem, IL; d. Mar 4, 1945, Lincoln, NE; par. Judge Silas Lillard and Mariah Elizabeth (Jennings) Bryan; m. Mary "Bessie" Louise Brokaw, Nov 29, 1892; c. Silas Millard; Virginia; Mary Louise (Mrs. Harnsberger). EDUC.: U. of Chicago, 1885; IL Coll. POLIT. & GOV.: political sec. and business agent for William Jennings Bryan (q.v.), 1897–1925; col., staff of the governor of NE, 1897–1902; elected as a Democrat to mayor of Lincoln, NE, 1915–17, 1935–37; candidate for Democratic nomination to gov. of NE, 1916, 1918; chm., Lincoln Park Board; elected city commissioner, Lincoln, 1921–22; superintendent of streets and public improvements, Lincoln, 1921–23; elected as a Democrat to gov. of NE, 1923–25, 1931–35; ***candidate for Democratic nomination to presidency of the U.S., 1924; Democratic candidate for vice presidency of the U.S., 1924***; Democratic candidate for gov. of NE, 1926, 1928, 1942; candidate for Democratic nomination to U.S. Senate (NE), 1934; independent candidate for gov. of NE, 1938; candidate for Democratic nomination to U.S. House (NE), 1940. BUS. & PROF.: salesman, sec., Purity Extract Co., Lincoln, 1891; broker, Omaha, NE; publisher, assoc. ed., *The Commoner,* Lincoln, 1901–23; owner, ed., *American Homestead,* 5 years; farmer; wholesale coal business; owner, State Coal Co. MEM.: Independent Order of Odd Fellows; Woodmen of the World; Elks; Lincoln C. of C.; NE Dry Federation (pres.); Kiwanis; University Club; Municipal Ownership League. REL.: Fundamentalist Bapt. RES.: Lincoln, NE.

BRYAN, JAMES GERALD.

b. Dec 22, 1931, Williston, ND; par. Jack F. and Dorothy K. (Caim) Bryan; m. Evelyne M. McCollum; c. Robert J.; Dorothy Wynn; Kristina M.; Kelly D.; Shannon E.; Patrick J.; Sami J. EDUC.: B.S., U. of OR, 1959, postgrad. courses. POLIT. & GOV.: member, exec. cmte., Libertarian Party, 1972; ***candidate for Libertarian Party nomination to presidency of the U.S., 1972***. BUS. & PROF.: teacher; coach; securities dealer; management consultant. REL.: atheist. MAILING ADDRESS: 6250 South West Oleson Rd., Portland, OR 97223.

BRYAN, WILLIAM JENNINGS.

b. Mar 18, 1860, Salem, IL; d. Jul 26, 1925, Dayton, TN; par. Silas Lillard and Mariah Elizabeth (Jennings) Bryan; m. Mary Elizabeth Baird, Oct 1, 1884; c. Ruth (Mrs. Reginald A. Owen); William Jennings, Jr.; Grace (Mrs. Richard L. Hargreaves). EDUC.: Whipple Acad.; A.B. (summa cum laude; valedictorian), IL Coll., 1881, A.M., 1884; LL.B., Union Coll. of Law, 1883. POLIT. & GOV.: delegate, NE State Democratic Convention, 1888; elected as a Democrat to U.S. House (NE), 1891–95; Democratic candidate for U.S. Senate (NE), 1894; delegate, Dem. Nat'l. Conv., 1896, 1904, 1920, 1924; ***Democratic candidate for presidency of the U.S., 1896, 1900, 1908; People's Party candidate for presidency of the U.S., 1896, 1900; Silver Party candidate for presidency of the U.S., 1896; Silver Republican Party candidate for presidency of the U.S., 1900; candidate for Democratic nomination to presidency of the U.S., 1904, 1912, 1920, 1924***; appointed U.S. sec. of state, 1913–15; candidate for delegate, Dem. Nat'l. Conv., 1916; ***Prohibition Party candidate for presidency of the U.S., 1920 (declined); candidate for Democratic nomination to vice presidency of the U.S., 1924 (declined)***. BUS. & PROF.: atty.; admitted to IL Bar, 1883; law practice, Jacksonville, IL, 1883–87; law practice, Lincoln, NE, 1888–1921; ed., *Omaha (NE) World-Herald,* 1894–96; lecturer on bimetallism, 1897–98; publisher, *The Commoner,* Lincoln, 1901–13; newspaper columnist. MIL.: col., Third Regt., NE Volunteer Infantry, 1898. MEM.: National Dry Federation (pres., 1918). HON. DEG.: LL.D., U. of NE; LL.D., U. of MD; LL.D., U. of AZ. WRITINGS: *The First Battle* (1897); *Republic or Empire?* (1899); *Under Other Flags* (1904); *Letter to a Chinese Official* (1906); *British Rule in India* (1906); *The Old World and Its Ways* (1907); *Speeches* (1909); *Heart to Heart Appeals* (1917); *The Menace of Darwinism* (1921); *The Bible and Its Enemies* (1921); *In His Image* (1922); *Shall Christianity Remain Christian?* (1924); *Memoirs of William Jennings Bryan* (1925). REL.: Presb. (vice moderator, gen. assembly, 1925). MISC.: noted for "Cross of Gold" speech before 1896 Dem. Nat'l. Conv. and participation for prosecution in Scopes Trial as a defender of literal truth of biblical version of creation; known as "The Great Commoner." RES.: Lincoln, NE.

BRYANT, CECIL FARRIS.

b. Jul 26, 1914, Ocala, FL; par. Charles Cecil and Lela (Farris) Bryant; m. Julia Burnett, Sep 18, 1940; c. Julia Lovett; Cecilia Ann; Allison Adair. EDUC.: Emory U., 1931–32; B.S., U. of FL, 1935; J.D., Harvard U., 1938. POLIT. & GOV.: elected as a Democrat to FL State House, 1942, 1947–57 (Speaker, 1953–55); delegate, Dem. Nat'l. Conv., 1952, 1960 (alternate), 1964 (chm., FL Delegation), 1968; elected as a Democrat to gov. of FL, 1961–65; appointed dir., Office of Emergency Planning, Executive Office of the President, 1966–67; chm., Advisory Comm. on Intergovernmental Relations, 1966–69; member, National Security Council, 1966–67; ***candidate for Democratic nomination to presidency of the U.S., 1968***; candidate for Democratic nomination to U.S. Senate (FL), 1970. BUS. & PROF.: atty.; admitted to FL Bar, 1938; law practice, Ocala, FL, 1940–60; partner, Green and Bryant (law firm); pres., Voyager Life Insurance Co., 1965–; pres., National Life of Florida Corp., 1968–; partner, Bryant, Dickens, Rumph, Franson and Miller (law firm), Jacksonville, FL, 1970–; dir., American Bank of FL; dir., American National Bank; dir., Fidelity Federal Savings and Loan; chm. of the board, Channel 12-TV, Jacksonville, FL, 1972–; chm. of the board, Worth Avenue National Bank; dir., Air Florida System, Inc.; partner, Bryant, Miller and Olive (law firm), Tallahassee, FL; trustee, Walter Realty Investors, Inc.; dir., Insurance Exchange of the Americas; pres., For Profit, Inc.; chief exec. officer, First Protection Life Insurance Co.; chief exec. officer, Voyager Property and Casualty Co.; chief exec. officer, Voyager Investors Life Insurance Co.; chief exec. officer, Voyager Warranty Corp.; pres., Voyager Service Agreements Inc.; chief exec. officer, United Heritage Services Corp.; chief exec. officer, Voyager Life and Health Insurance Co.; chief exec. officer, Voyager Insurance Services Inc.; pres., Voyager Reinsurance Co.; pres., Economy Life Insurance Co.; pres., Voyager Division; chief exec. officer, Voyager Guaranty Insurance Co.; chief exec. officer, Voyager Indemnity Insurance Co. MIL.: lt., U.S. Navy, 1942–46. MEM.: Blue Key; Gold Key; FL Southern Coll. (trustee); Jacksonville U. (trustee); ABA; FL Bar Assn.; Marion Cty. C. of C. (pres., 1950); FL Junior C. of C. (vice pres., 1948); Phi Delta Phi; Kappa Delta

Phi; Masons; Shriners; Elks (exalted ruler, 1948); Ocala Rotary Club (pres., 1948); American Legion; VFW; Young Democrats Club; Alpha Tau Omega; Alpha Kappa Psi; BSA (district chm.); FL C. of C. (dir.); FL Council of 100; Alpha Phi Omega. AWARDS: one of five "Outstanding Young Men in Florida," FL Junior C. of C., 1948; "Most Promising First Termer," Crocker Politics Commentator, 1947; "Outstanding Legislator," 1949, 1951, 1953; received Top Management Award, Sales and Marketing Executives Assn., 1976. HON. DEG.: LL.D., Rollins Coll.; LL.D., FL State U.; LL.D., FL Atlantic U.; LL.D., FL Southern Coll. WRITINGS: *Government and Politics of Florida* (co-author). REL.: Methodist (district lay chm., board of stewards). MAILING ADDRESS: 1016 East Palm St., Ocala, FL.

BRYANT, THOMAS CHESTER. b. Mar 22, 1912, Decatur, AL; par. Thomas Asberry and Georgia Ann (Rayborn) Bryant; single. EDUC.: Morgan Cty., 1929; U. of TN, 1936–37. POLIT. & GOV.: ***Innovative candidate for presidency of the U.S., 1976***. BUS. & PROF.: inventor; writer; mgr., grocery store, 1929–36; salesman, Fuller Brush Co., 1939; owner, grocery store, Knoxville, TN, 1938–39; life insurance salesman, Home Beneficial Life Insurance Co., Inc., 1940–55; real estate salesman, 1942–55. MIL.: U.S. Army. MEM.: American Legion; Disabled American Veterans. WRITINGS: *The United States of America and World-Wide Satellite Mail Service* (1965); *My Theory About the Mystery of the Bermuda Triangle* (1975). REL.: Methodist. MISC.: originated "Yours for Victory" slogan in WWII; invented banana-flavored peanut butter; developed concept of satellite transmission of mail; developed concept of computerized shopping and banking. MAILING ADDRESS: 207 Burns St., Knoxville, TN 37914.

BRYANT, WILLIAM CULLEN. b. Nov 3, 1794, Cummington, MA; d. Jun 12, 1878, New York, NY; par. Peter and Sarah (Snell) Bryant; m. Frances Fairchild, Jun 11, 1821; c. Julia Sands; Frances (Mrs. Parke Godwin). EDUC.: district schools; Williams Coll., 1810; studied law under Mr. Howe, 1811–14, and William Baylies, 1814. POLIT. & GOV.: ***candidate for Independent Liberal Republican Party nomination to presidency of the U.S., 1872 (declined)***. BUS. & PROF.: poet; hymnist; journalist; atty.; admitted to MA Bar, 1815; law practice, Plainfield, MA, 1815; partner (with George A. Ives), law firm, Great Barrington, MA, 1815–25; contributor, *United States Literary Gazette*, 1824–25; co-editor, *New York Review*, 1825–25; co-editor, *Athenaeum Magazine*, 1825–26; asst. ed., *Evening Post*, New York, 1826–29, ed., 1829–78. MEM.: Philotechnian Literary Soc.; Loyal National League; Loyal Publication Assn.; American Free Trade League (pres., 1863–67); NY Homeopathic Soc. (pres., 1841); Associative Movement; Sketch Club; Century Club; Cmte. on National Affairs; National Freedman's Relief Assn.; National Acad. of the Arts of Design (prof. of mythology and antiquities); NY Lyceum (lecturer). WRITINGS: *The Embargo* (1808); *Poems* (1821); *Tales of the Glauber Spa* (ed., 1832); *Poems* (1832); *The Fountain, and Other Poems* (1842); *The White-Footed Doe, and Other Poems* (1844); Look From "Thy Sphere of Endless Days" (hymn); *Letters of a Traveller* (1850); *Letters from the East* (1869); *The Illiad* (translator, 1870); *The Odyssey* (translator, 1871); *Poems* (1876); *Poetical Works* (1883); *Complete Prose* (1884). REL.: Unitarian. RES.: New York, NY.

BRYK, WILLIAM MICHAEL. POLIT. & GOV.: ***independent candidate for presidency of the U.S., 1992***. MAILING ADDRESS: 335 East 58th St., #5R, New York, NY 10022.

BUBAR, BENJAMIN CALVIN, JR. b. Jun 17, 1917, Blaine, ME; d. May 15, 1995, Waterville, ME; par. Benjamin Calvin and Mary Louise (Heal) Bubar; m. Virginia A. Ireland, Feb 14, 1946; c. Benjamin Calvin III; Mark Ireland. EDUC.: Ricker Coll., Houlton, ME; Colby Coll., Waterville, ME; Howard Coll.; Yale U. POLIT. & GOV.: campaign worker, Bubar for Governor Campaign (ME), 1936; elected as a Republican to ME State House, 1939–45; elected municipal selectman, town mgr., Weston, ME, 1940–43; town mgr., Blaine, ME, 1948; legislative agent, Protestant Churches of ME, 1953–1995; ***candidate for Prohibition Party nomination to presidency of the U.S., 1968; candidate for Prohibition Party nomination to vice presidency of the U.S., 1968, 1984 (declined)***; delegate, President's National Conference on Crime; ***Prohibition Party candidate for presidency of the U.S., 1976; National Statesman (Prohibition) Party candidate for presidency of the U.S., 1980***; member, Populist Party National Cmte., 1984. BUS. & PROF.: ordained minister, Baptist Church, 1950; pastor, various Baptist churches, ME; superintendent, ME Christian Civic League, 1952–; owner, ed., *Mars Hill (ME) View*, 1947–51; ed., *Civic League Record*, 1952–. MEM.: Lord's Day Alliance of the U.S. (dir.); American Council on Alcohol Problems (dir.); Christian Schools, Inc. (dir.); Glen Cove Bible Coll. (dir.); North American Assn. of Alcohol Problems; Assn. for the Advancement of Instruction About Alcohol. REL.: Bapt. RES.: Waterville, ME.

BUCHANAN, JAMES. b. Apr 23, 1791, Stony Batter, PA; d. Jun 1, 1868, Lancaster, PA; par. James and Elizabeth (Speer) Buchanan; single. EDUC.: B.A., Dickinson Coll., 1809; studied law under James Hopkins, 1809. POLIT. & GOV.: appointed asst. prosecutor, Lebanon Cty., PA, 1813–14; elected as a Federalist to PA State House, 1814–15; Federalist candidate for U.S. House (PA), 1816; elected as a Federalist to U.S. House (PA), 1821–31; appointed U.S. minister to Russia, 1831–34; elected as a Democrat to U.S. Senate (PA), 1834–45; appointed atty. gen. of the U.S., 1839 (declined); appointed assoc. justice of the Supreme Court of the U.S., 1844 (declined); ***candidate for Democratic nomination to presidency of the U.S., 1844, 1848, 1852***; appointed U.S. sec. of state, 1845–49; appointed U.S. minister to Great Britain, 1853–56; ***elected as a Democrat to presidency of the U.S., 1857–61***. BUS. & PROF.: atty.; admitted to PA Bar, 1812; author; law practice, Lancaster, PA,

1812–14, 1816–20; member, Shippen's Co., Lancaster, PA, 1814; partner (with Molton C. Rogers), law firm, Lancaster, PA. MIL.: volunteer, War of 1812. MEM.: Masons (master, 1817); Franklin and Marshall Coll. (pres., board of trustees, 1853). WRITINGS: *Mr. Buchanan's Administration on the Eve of the Rebellion* (1866). REL.: Presb. RES.: Lancaster, PA.

BUCHANAN, JAMES. b. Oct 14, 1847, Waveland, IN; par. Alexander and ____ (Rice) Buchanan; m. Ann Cordelia Wilson, Dec 25, 1862. EDUC.: grad. (summa cum laude), Waveland Acad., 1858; read law under Isaac A. Rice. POLIT. & GOV.: chm., Greenback (National) Party National Convention, 1874; Greenback (National) Party candidate for U.S. House (IN), 1876; ***candidate for Greenback (National) Party nomination to presidency of the U.S., 1876***; chm., IN State National Greenback Labor Party Convention, 1878; delegate, Greenback (National) Party National Convention, 1879; Greenback Party candidate for U.S. Senate (IN), 1879. BUS. & PROF.: atty.; admitted to IN Bar, 1861; law practice, Attica, IN, 1861–70; law practice, Indianapolis, IN, 1870–; partner, Buchanan, Williams and Whitehead (law firm), Indianapolis. REL.: Presb. RES.: Indianapolis, IN.

BUCHANAN, PATRICK JOSEPH. b. Nov 2, 1938, Washington, DC; par. William Baldwin and Catherine E. (Crum) Buchanan; m. Shelley Ann Scarney, May 8, 1971. EDUC.: A.B. (cum laude), Georgetown U., 1961; M.S., Columbia U., 1962. POLIT. & GOV.: appointed exec. asst. to President Richard M. Nixon (q.v.), 1966–69; member, President's Comm. on White House Fellowships, 1969–73; appointed special asst. to the president, 1969–73; consultant to Presidents Richard M. Nixon and Gerald R. Ford (q.v.), 1973–74; speechwriter for President Ronald W. Reagan, 1986–; ***candidate for Republican nomination to presidency of the U.S., 1988 (withdrew), 1992***. BUS. & PROF.: columnist; editorial writer, *St. Louis (MO) Globe-Democrat*, 1962–64, asst. editorial writer, 1964–66; syndicated columnist, *New York (NY) Times*, 1975–78; syndicated columnist, *Chicago (IL) Tribune-New York (NY) News*, 1978–86; commentator, NBC Radio Network, 1978–; author. MEM.: University Club; American Council of Young Political Leaders (vice pres., 1974–75, 1976–79). WRITINGS: *The New Majority* (1973); *Conservative Votes, Liberal Victories* (1975). REL.: R.C. MAILING ADDRESS: 1017 Savile Lane, McLean, VA 22101.

BUCHANAN, WALTER RALPH "BUCK." b. Feb 2, 1909, St. Louis, MO; par. Frank Leslie and Mary Jane (Keeter) Buchanan; m. Leah Mae Lyon; c. Barbara Lee; Dorothy Louise; Walter Ralph, Jr.; Robert Bruce; Darlene Linda. EDUC.: Loyola U., 1928–32; certificate in drivers' education, U. of CA at Los Angeles; U. of Southern CA; Southwestern U.; D.D. (doctor of divinity). POLIT. & GOV.: candidate for Democratic nomination to U.S. House (CA), 1934, 1962, 1972; candidate for Los Angeles (CA) School Board, 1963; candidate for Democratic nomination to U.S. Senate (CA), 1964, 1968, 1976; ***candidate for Democratic nomination to presidency of the U.S., 1964, 1972, 1976, 1984, 1988***; candidate for Democratic nomination to gov. of CA, 1970; candidate for Democratic nomination to mayor of Los Angeles, CA, 1973. BUS. & PROF.: real estate broker; contractor; playground dir., Los Angeles, CA; dir. of recreation, Los Angeles Cty. (CA) Juvenile Hall, 1929–34; owner, dir., Circle "B" Boys Ranch; owner, Buchanan's International News Press; owner, Buchanan's International Driving School, Los Angeles, CA; driving instructor, Los Angeles (CA) Board of Education; officer, Los Angeles (CA) Police Dept.; minister, Buchanan's Universal Life and Missionary Church, Los Angeles, CA. MIL.: 2d lt., U.S.M.C.; corp., CA National Guard. MEM.: Al Malakah Shrine; Santa Monica Young Democrats Club; Young Democratic Club; Malibu Democratic Club; Fernwood Democratic Club (pres.); Democrats of America, Inc.; International Pentathalon Games, Inc.; Common Cause; League of Women Voters; Nader's Raiders; Los Angeles Junior C. of C. (assoc. member). WRITINGS: *Buchanan's Auto Driving Guide*. REL.: Universal Life Missionary Church (nee Presb.). MAILING ADDRESS: c/o Buchanan's International Driving School, 11467 West WA Blvd., Los Angeles, CA 90066.

BUCK, CLAYTON DOUGLASS. b. Mar 21, 1890, Buena Vista, DE; d. Jan 28, 1965, Buena Vista, DE; par. Francis N. and Margaret (Douglass) Buck; m. Alice du Pont Wilson, May 5, 1921; c. Clayton Douglass, Jr.; Dorcas Van Dyke (Mrs. Donald K. Farquhar); Paul E. Wilson (stepson); Mrs. William E. Haible (stepdaughter). EDUC.: Friends' School, Wilmington, DE; U. of PA. POLIT. & GOV.: chief engineer, DE State Highway Dept., 1920–29; elected as a Republican to gov. of DE, 1929–37; member, Rep. Nat'l. Cmte., 1930–37; ***candidate for Republican nomination to presidency of the U.S., 1936***; elected as a Republican to U.S. Senate (DE), 1943–49; Republican candidate for U.S. Senate (DE), 1948; appointed DE state tax commissioner, 1953–57. BUS. & PROF.: highway engineer; pres., Equitable Trust Co., Wilmington, DE, 1931–41, chm. of the board, 1941–65. MIL.: pvt., U.S. Army, 1917–19. MEM.: Union League; Wilmington Club. HON. DEG.: LL.D., U. of DE, 1936. REL.: Episc. RES.: Buena Vista, DE.

BUCK, G. P. POLIT. & GOV.: ***independent candidate for presidency of the U.S., 1992***. MAILING ADDRESS: 1006 Old Greylord Rd., Newark, NJ.

BUCKINGHAM, EDWARD TAYLOR. b. May 12, 1874, Metuchen, NJ; d. after 1943; par. Walter Taylor and Helen Emeline (Tolles) Buckingham; m. Bessie Louise Russell Budau, Jun 3, 1903; c. Russell Budau; Edward Taylor, Jr. EDUC.: A.B., Yale U., 1895, LL.B., 1897. POLIT. & GOV.: elected justice of the peace, 1898, 1900, 1904; city clerk, Bridgeport, CT, 1901–09; elected as a Democrat to mayor of Bridgeport, CT, 1909–11, 1929–33; appointed CT state commissioner of workmen's compensation, 1913–28, 1933–43; member, Board of Recreation, 1921–29; elected member, Bridgeport (CT) Board of Education, 1928–31; ***candidate for Democratic nomination to vice presidency of the U.S., c. 1932***. BUS. & PROF.: atty.; admitted to CT Bar, 1897; law practice, Bridgeport, CT, 1898; partner, Buckingham and Bent (law firm), Bridgeport, CT. MEM.: Bridgeport Bar Assn. (pres.); Fairfield Cty. Bar Assn.; Yale Alumni Assn. of Fairfield Cty.; CT Recreation Assn. (pres.); Bridgeport C. of C.; VFW (hon. member); Disabled American Veterans; National Naval Veterans of the U.S.; CT Motor Club (vice pres.); Bridgeport Kiwanis (pres.); Odd Fellows; Knights of Pythias; Arions Club; Germania Club; Masons; Elks; Improved Order of Red Men; Bridgeport Sportsmen's Club (pres.). REL.: Congregationalist. MISC.: received several tennis cups, Bridgeport; member, Yale Law School Baseball Team, 1897. RES.: Bridgeport, CT.

BUCKLEY, JAMES LANE. b. Mar 9, 1923, New York, NY; par. William Frank and Aloise (Steiner) Buckley; m. Ann Frances Cooley, May 22, 1953; c. Peter Pierce; James Frederick Wiggin; Priscilla Langford; William Frank; David Lane; Andrew Thurston. EDUC.: B.A., Yale U., 1943, LL.B., 1949. POLIT. & GOV.: campaign mgr., William F. Buckley (q.v.) for mayor of New York, 1965; Conservative Party candidate for U.S. Senate (NY), 1968; elected as a Conservative to U.S. Senate (NY), 1971–77; ***candidate for Republican nomination to presidency of the U.S., 1976; candidate for Republican nomination to vice presidency of the U.S., 1976***; Republican candidate for U.S. Senate (NY), 1976; Republican candidate for U.S. Senate (CT), 1980; appointed U.S. undersec. of state for security assistance, science and technology, 1981–82; appointed judge, U.S. Court of Appeals, 1985–. BUS. & PROF.: atty.; admitted to CT Bar, 1949; assoc., Wiggin and Dana (law firm), New Haven, CT, 1949–53; vice pres., dir., Catawba Corp., 1953–70; dir., Donaldson, Lufken and Jenrette, 1977–81; pres., Borealis Exploration Ltd.; pres., Radio Free Europe-Radio Liberty, 1982–85. MIL.: lt. (jg), U.S. Navy, 1943–46. MEM.: National Audubon Soc.; International Oceanographic Foundation; National Wildlife Federation; Wilderness Soc.; Explorers Club. WRITINGS: *If Men Were Angels* (1975). HON. DEG.: LL.D., St. John's U.; LL.D., Sacred Heart U. REL.: R.C. MAILING ADDRESS: 4980 Quebec, N. W., Washington, DC 20016.

BUCKLEY, WILLIAM FRANK, JR. b. Nov 24, 1925, New York, NY; par. William Frank and Aloise (Steiner) Buckley; m. Patricia Taylor, Jul 6, 1950; c. Christopher T. EDUC.: U. of Mexico, 1943; B.A. (cum laude), Yale U., 1950. POLIT. & GOV.: Conservative Party candidate for mayor of New York, 1965; appointed member, Advisory Cmte., U.S. Information Agency, 1969–72; appointed member, U.S. Delegation to the U.N., 1973; ***candidate for Republican nomination to vice presidency of the U.S., 1976***. BUS. & PROF.: author; asst. instructor in Spanish, Yale U., 1947–51; ed., Yale *Daily News;* assoc. ed., *American Mercury*, 1952; founder, editor-in-chief, *National Review*, 1955–; syndicated columnist, "On the Right," 1962–; host, *Firing Line* (television program), 1966; chm. of the board, Starr Broadcasting Group, Inc., 1966–; lecturer in municipal government, New School of Social Research, 1967–68; commentator on national conventions, ABC-TV, 1968. MIL.: 2d lt., U.S. Army, 1944–46. MEM.: Torch Honor Soc.; Elizabethan Club; Fence Club; Skull and Bones; Council on Foreign Relations; Mont Pelerin Soc.; National Press Club; Century Club; Bohemian Club. AWARDS: Class Day Orator Award; George Sokolsky Award, American Jewish League Against Communism, 1966; Distinguished Journalism Achievement Award, U. of Southern CA, 1968; Emmy Award, 1969; Liberty Bell Award, New Haven Cty. Bar Assn., 1969; Man of the Year Award, Young Americans for Freedom, 1970. HON. DEG.: L.H.D., Seton Hall U., 1966; L.H.D., Niagara U., 1967; L.H.D., Mt. St. Mary's Coll., 1969; LL.D., Syracuse U., 1969; LL.D., Ursinus Coll., 1969; LL.D., Lehigh U., 1970; D.Sc.O., Curry Coll., 1970; Litt.D., St. Vincent Coll., 1971; LL.D., Lafayette Coll., 1972; LL.D., St. Anselm's Coll., 1973; Litt.D., Fairleigh Dickinson U., 1973; Litt.D., Alfred U., 1974; LL.D., St. Bonaventure U., 1974; LL.D., St. Peter's Coll. WRITINGS: *God and Man at Yale* (1951); *McCarthy and His Enemies* (with L. Brent Bozell, 1954); *Up From Liberalism* (1959); *Racing at Sea* (contributor, 1959); *The Intellectual* (contributor, 1960); *Rumbles Right and Left* (1963); *What is Conservatism?* (contributor, 1964); *Dialogues in Americanism* (contributor, 1964); *The Unmaking of a Mayor* (1966); *The Jeweler's Eye* (1968); *Violence in the Streets* (contributor, 1968); *The Beatles Book* (contributor, 1968); *Spectrum of Catholic Attitudes* (contributor, 1969); *Great Ideas Today Annual* (contributor, 1970); *The Cmte. and Its Critics* (1962); *Odyssey of a Friend* (1970); *The Governor Listeth* (1970); *Cruising Speed* (1971); *& Inveighing We Will Go* (1972); *American Conservative Thought in the 20th Century* (ed., 1970); *Four Reforms* (1973); *United Nations Journal* (1974); *Execution Eve* (1975); *Saving the Queen* (1976); *Essay on Hayek* (1976); *Airborne, Stained Glass* (1978); *A Hymnal* (1978); *Who's on First* (1980); *Marco Polo, If You Can* (1982); *Atlantic High* (1982). REL.: R.C. MAILING ADDRESS: Wallacks' Point, Stamford, CT.

BUCKNER, SIMON BOLIVAR. b. Apr 1, 1823, Hart Cty., KY; d. Jan 8, 1914, Munfordville, KY; par. Aylett Hartswell and Elizabeth Ann (Morehead) Buckner; m. Mary Jane Kingsbury, May 2, 1850; m. 2d, Delia Hayes Claiborne, Jun 10, 1885; c. Lily (Mrs. Morris b. Belknap); Simon Bolivar, Jr. EDUC.: B.S., U.S. Military Acad., 1844. POLIT. & GOV.: inspector gen. of KY, 1860–61; elected as a Democrat to gov. of KY, 1887–91; elected as a Democrat, delegate, KY State Constitutional Convention, 1891; ***National (Gold Democratic) Party candidate for presidency of the U.S., 1896***. BUS. & PROF.: soldier; land speculator; superintendent of construction, Chicago (IL) Customs House; newspaperman; pres., insurance company, New Orleans, LA, 1866–68; ed., *Louisville (KY) Courier*, 1868–87; farmer. MIL.: brev. 2d lt., U.S. Army Infantry, 1844; advanced through grades to capt., 1847; asst. instructor in ethics, U.S. Military Acad., 1845–46, asst. instructor in infantry tactics,

1848–50; resigned from U.S. Army, 1855; col., IL Volunteers; offered commission as brig. gen., U.S. Army, 1861 (refused); brig. gen., C.S.A., 1861, prisoner-of-war, 1862, maj. gen., 1863, lt. gen., 1864. MEM.: Knights of the Golden Circle. WRITINGS: article, *Putnam's Magazine*, Apr 1853. REL.: Episc. RES.: Munfordville, KY.

BUCOLO, FRANK ANTONY. POLIT. & GOV.: ***independent candidate for presidency of the U.S., 1980***. MAILING ADDRESS: 375 New Dover Rd., Colonia, NJ 07067.

BUFFINGTON, LARRY JOE. POLIT. & GOV.: ***candidate for Democratic nomination to presidency of the U.S., 1988***. REL.: Christian. MAILING ADDRESS: 1314 Summit Rd., Benton, AR 72015.

BULKELEY, MORGAN GARDNER. b. Dec 26, 1837, East Haddam, CT; d. Nov 6, 1922, Hartford, CT; par. Eliphalet Adams and Lydia S. (Morgan) Bulkeley; m. Fannie Briggs Houghton, Feb 11, 1885; c. Morgan Gardner, Jr.; Elinor Houghton; Houghton. EDUC.: grad., high school, Hartford. POLIT. & GOV.: member, Republican General Cmte., Kings Cty., NY; elected as a Republican to Hartford City Council, 1874; elected as a Republican to Board of Aldermen, Hartford, 1875–76; elected as a Republican to mayor of Hartford, 1880–88; Republican candidate for gov. of CT, 1882; delegate, Rep. Nat'l. Conv., 1888, 1892, 1896; elected as a Republican (by the State Legislature) to gov. of CT, 1889–93; Republican candidate for U.S. Senate (CT), 1893, 1910; ***candidate for Republican nomination to vice presidency of the U.S., 1896***; elected as a Republican to U.S. Senate (CT), 1905–11; pres., Comm. on Improvements of the State Capitol of CT. BUS. & PROF.: merchant, Brooklyn, NY, 1852–72; partner, H. P. Morgan and Co., New York, NY, 1858–72; pres., U.S. Bank of Hartford, 1872–79; pres., National League of Professional Baseball Clubs, 1876; pres., Aetna Life Insurance Co., 1879–1922. MIL.: member, 13th Regt., NY National Guard, Civil War. MEM.: GAR (CT department commander, 1903); Hartford Club; National Trotting Assn. AWARDS: Baseball Hall of Fame. HON. DEG.: A.M., Yale U., 1889; LL.D., Trinity Coll., 1917. REL.: Congregationalist. RES.: Hartford, CT.

BULKLEY, ROBERT JOHNS. b. Oct 8, 1880, Cleveland, OH; d. Jul 21, 1965, Bratenahl, OH; par. Charles Henry and Roberta (Johns) Bulkley; m. Katharine Pope, Feb 17, 1909; m. 2d, Mrs. Helen Graham Robbins, Mar 31, 1934; c. Robert Johns; William Pope; Katharine (Mrs. John Fross Paton; Mrs. Louis A. Cherry); Rebecca Johns (Mrs. Preston Howard Saunders). EDUC.: A.B., Harvard U., 1902, A.M., 1906. POLIT. & GOV.: elected as a Democrat to U.S. House (OH), 1911–15; chm., Legal Cmte., General Munitions Board, Council of National Defense, 1917; chm., War Industries Board; reorganized Legal Dept., U.S. Shipping Board, Emergency Fleet Corp.; elected as a Democrat to U.S. Senate (OH), 1930–39; Democratic candidate for U.S. Senate (OH), 1938; appointed member, U.S. Board of Appeals on Visa Cases, 1941–45; delegate, Dem. Nat'l. Conv., 1952; ***candidate for Democratic nomination to presidency of the U.S., 1952***. BUS. & PROF.: atty.; ed., *Harvard Crimson*, 1902; partner, Bulkley, Butler and Pillen (law firm), Cleveland; chm. of the board, Bank of Ohio of Cleveland; pres., Bulkley Building Co., Cleveland, 1920–65; dir., Chesapeake and Ohio Railway Co., 1946–65. MEM.: U. School of Cleveland (trustee); OH Northern Opera Assn. (pres.); Cosmos Club; Hermit Club; City Club; Rowfant Club. RES.: Cleveland, OH.

BULOW, WILLIAM JOHN. b. Jan 13, 1869, Moscow, OH; d. Feb 26, 1960, Washington, DC; par. Joseph and Elizabeth (Ebendorf) Bulow; m. Katherine Reedy, Nov 25, 1899; m. 2d, Sarah Johnson Farrand, Oct 15, 1922; c. Maurine; Kathleen Chloe (Mrs. Benedict A. Plotnicki); William John. EDUC.: LL.B., U. of MI, 1893. POLIT. & GOV.: elected as a Democrat to SD State Senate, 1899–1901; elected as a Democrat, city atty., Beresford, SD, 1902–12, 1913–27; elected as a Democrat to mayor of Beresford, SD, 1912–13; appointed temporary judge, Union Cty., SD, 1918; Democratic candidate for gov. of SD, 1924; elected as a Democrat to gov. of SD, 1927–31; delegate, SD Democratic State Conventions; delegate, Dem. Nat'l. Conv., 1928; ***candidate for Democratic nomination to vice presidency of the U.S., 1928***; elected as a Democrat to U.S. Senate (SD), 1931–43; candidate for Democratic nomination to U.S. Senate (SD), 1942. BUS. & PROF.: atty.; admitted to SD Bar, 1893; law practice, Beresford, SD, 1894–1927; law practice, Washington, DC, 1943–60. REL.: Lutheran. RES.: Beresford, SD.

BUMPERS, DALE LEON. b. Aug 12, 1925, Charleston, AR; par. William Rufus and Lattie (Jones) Bumpers; m. Betty Lou Flanagan, Sep 4, 1949; c. Dale Brent; William Mark; Margaret Brooke. EDUC.: U. of AR, 1943, 1946–48; LL.B., Northwestern U., 1951, J.D., 1965. POLIT. & GOV.: city atty., Charleston, 1952–70; elected member, Franklin Cty. (AR) Board of Education, 1952–70; elected member, Charleston School Board, 1957–70 (pres., 1969–70); appointed special justice, Supreme Court of AR; elected as a Democrat to gov. of AR, 1971–75; delegate, Dem. Nat'l. Conv., 1972; member, Dem. Nat'l. Cmte.; elected as a Democrat to U.S. Senate (AR), 1975–; ***candidate for Democratic nomination to presidency of the U.S., 1980, 1984, 1988 (declined); candidate for Democratic nomination to vice presidency of the U.S., 1984***. BUS. & PROF.: pres., Charleston Hardware and Furniture Co., Charleston, 1951–66; atty.; admitted to AR Bar, 1952; law practice, Charleston, 1952–70; operator, Angus Cattle Farm, 1966–70. MIL.: pvt., U.S.M.C., 1943–46. MEM.: Charleston C. of C. (pres.); Charleston Industrial Development Corp.; United Fund (chm.); Boy Scout Fund (chm.); Cancer Fund Drive (chm.). REL.: Methodist. MAILING ADDRESS: P.O. Box 98, Charleston, AR 72933.

BURCH, JAMES HARRY. b. Dec 17, 1942, Washington, DC; par. James B. and Pearl (Schulze) Burch; m. Julia E. Tucker (divorced); c. Nathan; Jeffrey. EDUC.: St. Joseph's Coll., Rensselaer, IN, 2 years; B.A., U. of Dayton; Catholic U.; American U. POLIT. & GOV.: candidate for Democratic nomination to VA State House of Delegates, 1971; candidate for Democratic nomination to U.S. House (VA), 1972; ***Ownership candidate for Democratic nomination to presidency of the U.S., 1980***. BUS. & PROF.: builder; real estate developer; log exporter; owner, video business (depositions and legal services); management consultant; political consultant. MEM.: Fairfax Cty. Cancer Soc.; United Givers' Fund; The Inst. for the Study of Economic Systems; VA Citizens' Consumer Council; The Potential Research Foundation of Phoenix; Food and Energy Foundation (dir.). REL.: R.C. MISC.: studied for priesthood; worked for 5 years on War on Poverty, Hunger,and Malnutrition projects. MAILING ADDRESS: 7916 Wellington Rd., Alexandria, VA 22308.

BURDELL, J. W. b. Jul 25, 1925, Holiday, TX; par. Theodore and Gladys Burdell; m. Tony Burdell; c. none. EDUC.: sixth grade, public schools, Westbrook, TX. POLIT. & GOV.: ***Unity Party candidate for presidency of the U.S., 1976***. BUS. & PROF.: farmer, Sherman, TX; fitter and rigger; oilfield roughneck; welder, 1963–; truck driver. MIL.: seaman first class, U.S. Navy, 1942–46. MEM.: Amvets; VFW; American Legion. REL.: Christian. MAILING ADDRESS: 1025 East Houston, Sherman, TX 74090.

BURDETTE, NATHAN. POLIT. & GOV.: ***The Power Party candidate for presidency of the U.S., 1984***. BUS. & PROF.: rancher, Rio Bravo, TX; businessman, Rio Bravo; owner, Burdette's Saloon, Rio Bravo. MAILING ADDRESS: Rio Bravo, TX.

BURKE, JOHN. b. Feb 25, 1859, Sigourney, IA; d. May 14, 1937, Rochester, MN; par. John and Mary (Ryan) Burke; m. Mary E. Kane, Aug 22, 1891; c. Elizabeth; Thomas J.; Marian. EDUC.: LL.B., U. of IA, 1886. POLIT. & GOV.: elected as a Democrat to ND State House, 1891–93; elected as a Democrat to ND State Senate, 1893–95; Democratic candidate for atty. gen. of ND, 1894; judge, Cty. Court, Rolette Cty., ND, 1896–1906; Democratic candidate for U.S. House (ND), 1896; elected as a Democrat to gov. of ND, 1907–13; ***candidate for Democratic nomination to presidency of the U.S., 1912; candidate for Democratic nomination to vice presidency of the U.S., 1912***; appointed treas. of the U.S., 1913–21; Democratic candidate for U.S. Senate (ND), 1916; delegate, Dem. Nat'l. Conv., 1924; elected assoc. justice, ND State Supreme Court, 1925–35, chief justice, 1935–37. BUS. & PROF.: atty.; admitted to IA Bar, 1886; partner, Burke and Burke (law firm), Des Moines, IA, 1886–88; law practice, Devils Lake, ND; assoc., Brokerage Firm, New York, NY, 1921–22. MEM.: Masons; Elks. REL.: Unitarian (nee R.C.). MISC.: known as "Honest John" Burke. RES.: Bismarck, ND.

BURKE, STEPHEN. POLIT. & GOV.: elected as a Democrat, selectman, Macomb, NY; ***candidate for Democratic nomination to presidency of the U.S., 1992***. MAILING ADDRESS: Route 1, Box 242 (Heuvelton) Bishop Rd., Macomb, NY 13654.

BURKE, WYNONIA BREWINGTON. b. 1950, Sampson Cty., NC. POLIT. & GOV.: New Alliance Party candidate for AZ State House, 1988; ***New Alliance Party candidate for vice presidency of the U.S., 1988***. MEM.: Coharie Indian Nation (NC); Cmte. for Fair Elections (AZ State Chair, 1988); Business and Professional Women's Organization. MAILING ADDRESS: Tucson, AZ.

BURKETT, ELMER JACOB. b. Dec 1, 1867, Glenwood, IA; d. May 23, 1935, Lincoln, NE; par. Henry W. and Catharine (Kearney) Burkett; m. Fannie Fern Wright, Sep 1, 1891; c. Mrs. R. C. Van Kirk; Mrs. Raymond Farquahar; Mrs. M. M. Meyers. EDUC.: B.S., Tabor Coll., 1890; LL.B., U. of NE, 1893, LL.M., 1895. POLIT. & GOV.: elected as a Republican to NE State House, 1897–99; elected as a Republican to U.S. House (NE), 1899–1905; elected as a Republican to U.S. Senate (NE), 1905–11; delegate, Rep. Nat'l. Conv., 1908, 1912; Republican candidate for U.S. Senate (NE), 1910; Republican candidate for gov. of NE, 1912 (declined); ***candidate for Republican nomination to vice presidency of the U.S., 1916;*** Republican candidate for U.S. House (NE), 1928. BUS. & PROF.: principal, Leigh (NE) Public Schools, 1890–92; atty.; admitted to NE Bar, 1893; law practice, Lincoln, NE, 1893–95; partner, Tingley and Burkett (law firm), 1893–98; partner, Burkett and Greenlee (law firm), 1898–1906; partner, Burkett, Wilson, Brown and Wilson (law firm), 1906–35; dir., First National Bank; dir., First Trust Co.; partner, Burkett, Wilson, Brown and Van Kirk (law firm), Lincoln, NE. MEM.: Tabor Coll. (trustee, 1895–1905); Masons (33⁻); Ancient Order of United Workmen; Modern Woodmen of America; Royal Highlanders; Mystic Shrine; National Geographic Soc.; Innocents; ABA; NE State Bar Assn.; C. of C.; University Club; W. O. W. REL.: Methodist (trustee). RES.: Lincoln, NE.

BURKITT, FRANK. b. Jul 5, 1843, Lawrenceburg, TN; d. Nov 18, 1914, Okolona, MS; m. Mattie Schrimsher, Dec 30, 1866; m. 2d, Mary Elizabeth Mitchell, Dec 30, 1906; c. Ed Russell; Mary (Mrs. King); Mrs. Cecil Dossett; Mrs. Howard Gaskin. EDUC.: Professor Henry's School, VA; studied law. POLIT. & GOV.: elected as a Democrat to MS State House, 1887–91, 1983–1897, 1907–11; elected as a Democrat, delegate, MS State Constitutional Convention, 1890 (refused to sign constitution); presidential elector, Democratic Party, 1892 (resigned); People's Party candidate for U.S. House (MS), 1892; People's Party candidate for U.S. Senate (MS), 1894; People's Party candidate for gov. of MS, 1895; ***candidate for People's Party nomination to vice presidency of the U.S., 1896; candidate for People's (Anti-Fusionist) Party nomination to presidency of the U.S., 1900***; member, People's Party National Cmte., 1901; elected as a Democrat to MS State Senate, 1911–14. BUS. & PROF.: real estate investor; publisher; teacher, AL and MS, 1865–72; atty.; admitted to MS Bar, 1872; law practice, Houston, MS, 1872; ed., *Houston Messenger*, 1872–76; ed., *Chickasaw Messenger;* ed., *People's Messenger*, Okolona, 1876–1914. MIL.: pvt., Ninth TN Cavalry, C.S.A., 1861–63, lt., 1863–65, capt., 1865. MEM.: MS farmers' Alliance; Masons (grand master, 1879); Knights Templar (grand commandery, 1904); Okolona C. of C.; Odd Fellows; National Farmers' Alliance and Industrial Union (delegate, National Convention, 1890); Grange (officer, 1874); Knights of Labor; Industrial Legion (vice commander in chief); Knights of Pythias. RES.: Okolona, MS.

BURNER, JAMES ALLEN. b. May 24, 1935, Winchester, VA; par. James William and Mary Susan (Copenhaver) Burner; single. EDUC.: high school, Charleston, WV; Albany Bible Inst., Albany, NY. POLIT. & GOV.: candidate for justice of the peace, Kabletown District, WV, 1956; ***candidate for Democratic nomination to presidency of the U.S., 1976, 1980, 1984, 1988***. BUS. & PROF.: employee, U.S. G.S.A., Washington, DC; minister, Salvation Army. MIL.: U.S. Army, 1952. MEM.: Disabled American Veterans; American Legion. REL.: Salvation Army (nee Methodist). MAILING ADDRESS: P.O. Box 116, Summit Point, WV 25446.

BURNETT, ULYSSES. POLIT. & GOV.: ***candidate for Democratic nomination to presidency of the U.S., 1992***. MAILING ADDRESS: c/o Operation America Cares, Ann Miller, 1200 Washington St., Apt. 504, Gary, IN 46407.

BURNHAM, GEORGE F. POLIT. & GOV.: ***candidate for People's Party nomination to vice presidency of the U.S., 1904***. RES.: MA.

BURNING WOOD, CHIEF. (See AUSTIN MARION BURTON).

BURNS, ACCOUNTABILITY EINSTEIN BELCHER (aka GEORGE C. BURNS). b. Dec 25, 1926, Tulsa, OK; single; c. Stephanie. EDUC.: 276 college semester hours; claims several "secret" Ph.D. degrees. POLIT. & GOV.: candidate for Democratic nomination to U.S. House (OH), 1964; candidate for sheriff, Tulsa Cty., OK; candidate for School Board, Tulsa, OK, 1973; candidate for Democratic nomination to mayor of Tulsa, OK, 1974, 1980; candidate for Democratic nomination to gov. of OK, 1974; candidate for Democratic nomination to U.S. Senate (OK), 1974; candidate for Democratic nomination to Tulsa Cty. (OK) commissioner, 1976; ***candidate for Democratic nomination to presidency of the U.S., 1976; National Independence Party candidate for presidency of the U.S., 1976***. BUS. & PROF.: mathematician; management consultant; auditor; teacher; prof.; employee, aerospace industry; master planner; environmental auditor; inventor. MIL.: U.S. Navy, 1945–46. REL.: Universalist. MISC.: inventor, MARS-HEARS Project; calls himself MARSian No. 1. MAILING ADDRESS: 928 South Erie, Tulsa, OK 74112.

BURNS, EUGENE MORLEY. b. Dec 3, 1940, New Brunswick, NJ; par. Gladys Burns. EDUC.: Rutgers U. POLIT. & GOV.: ***candidate for Libertarian Party nomination to presidency of the U.S., 1984 (withdrew)***. BUS. & PROF.: news commentator, news dir., WWHG radio, Hornell, NY, 1961; radio news commentator in Boston, MA, Philadelphia, PA, and York, PA; news commentator, operations mgr., and talk show host, WKIS radio, Orlando, FL, 1967–. AWARDS: first place awards, FL Bar Assn.; Award, Greater Orlando Press Club. WRITINGS: "Crisis of Conscience: Liberal Democrat to Libertarian," *The Financial Security Digest*, Aug/Sep 1983, pp. 60–63. MAILING ADDRESS: 1617 East Livingstone St., Orlando, FL 32803.

BURNS, MARY BOYLE. POLIT. & GOV.: ***candidate for Democratic nomination to presidency of the U.S., 1948***; delegate, Dem. Nat'l. Conv., 1956. MAILING ADDRESS: 230 Western Ave., Toledo, OH.

BURNS, ROBIN REX. b. Jul 17, 1957, Santa Monica, CA; par. Walter and Margaret (Kepler) Burns; single. EDUC.: Narbonne H.S., Harbor City, CA; San Francisco State U. POLIT. & GOV.: ***ACE-ELI Party candidate for presidency of the U.S., 1976***. BUS. & PROF.: student, San Francisco State U. MEM.: Philadelphia Eagles Fan Club (pres.); Verducci 7 Crime Club. REL.: all. MAILING ADDRESS: 770 Lake Merced Blvd., San Francisco, CA 94132.

BURNSIDE, AMBROSE EVERETT. b. May 23, 1824, Liberty, IN; d. Sep 13, 1881, Bristol, RI; par. Edghill and Pamelia (Brown) Burnside; m. Mary Bishop, Apr 27, 1852; c. none. EDUC.: Beech Grove Acad.; grad., U.S. Military Acad., 1847. POLIT. & GOV.: Democratic candidate for U.S. House (RI), 1857; ***candidate for Republican nomination to vice presidency of the U.S., 1864***; elected as a Republican to gov. of RI, 1866–69; elected as a Republican to U.S. Senate (RI), 1875–81. BUS. & PROF.: soldier; inventor; partner, Myers and Burnside (merchant tailors), Liberty, IN; treas., Illinois Central R.R., 1857–64, dir., 1864–81; pres., Cincinnati and Martinville R.R., 1865; pres., Rhode Island Locomotive Works, 1866; pres., Indianapolis and Vincennes R.R. Co., 1867; dir., Narragansett Steamship Co., 1867. MIL.: commissioned 2d lt., Third Artillery, U.S. Army, 1847–52; maj. gen., RI Militia; organized First RI Regt., U.S.V., 1861; commissioned brig. gen., 1861, maj. gen., 1862; named commander of the Army of the Potomac, U.S. Army; relieved of command for failure of Fredericksburg Campaign; forced to resign from U.S. Army upon Court of Inquiry assertion of blame for failure in Petersburg Campaign, 1865. MEM.: GAR (commander in chief, 1871–72). WRITINGS: *The Burnside Expedition* (1882). MISC.: invented Burnside Breechloader Rifle, 1852. RES.: Bristol, RI.

BURR, AARON. b. Feb 6, 1756, Newark, NJ; d. Sep 14, 1836, Port Richmond, NY; par. Aaron and Esther (Edwards) Burr; m. Mrs. Theodosia (Bartow) Prevost, Jul 1782; m. 2d, Mrs. Stephen Jumel, Jul 1833; c. Theodosia; Frederick Prevost (stepson); Bartow Prevost (stepson). EDUC.: grad., Coll. of NJ, 1772; studied theology, Litchfield, CT, 1733. POLIT. & GOV.: elected as an Anti-Federalist to NY State Assembly, 1784–85, 1798–99; atty. gen. of NY, 1789–90; commissioner of revolutionary claims, 1791; elected as an Anti-Federalist to U.S. Senate (NY), 1791–97; ***Anti-Federalist candidate for presidency of the U.S., 1792***; Democratic candidate for U.S. Senate (NY), 1796; ***Democratic-Republican candidate for presidency of the U.S., 1796, 1800; elected as a Democratic-Republican to vice presidency of the U.S., 1801–05***; pres., NY State Constitutional Convention, 1801; Democratic-Republican candidate for gov. of NY, 1804. BUS. & PROF.: atty.; admitted to NY Bar, 1782; law practice, Albany, NY, 1782–83; law practice, New York, NY, 1783–89, 1812–36. MIL.: lt. col., Continental Army, 1775–79. MEM.: Tammany Soc. REL.: agnostic (nee Presb.). MISC.: received same number of electoral votes for pres. as Thomas Jefferson (q.v.), who was intended to be the presidential candidate, contest resolved in House of Reps.; killed Alexander Hamilton (q.v.) in duel, 1804; tried for treason for attempting to create a republic in southwestern U.S., acquitted, 1807. RES.: Port Richmond, NY.

BURRITT, ELIHU. b. Dec 8, 1810, New Britain, CT; d. Mar 6, 1879, New Britain, CT; par. Elihu and Elizabeth (Hinsdale) Burritt; single. EDUC.: public schools, to 1825. POLIT. & GOV.: ***Liberty League candidate for vice presidency of the U.S., 1848 (declined)***; appointed U.S. consul, Birmingham, England, 1863–70. BUS. & PROF.: blacksmith, Worcester, MA, 1828–39; teacher; reformer; publisher, *The Literary Gemini*, Worcester, 1839–40; publisher, *Christian Citizen*, Worcester, 1844–51; ed., *Peace Advocate*, Worcester, 1849–51; publisher, *Bond of Brotherhood;* ed., *Citizen of the World*, Philadelphia, PA, 1852; lecturer; farmer, New Britain, CT. MEM.: League of Universal Brotherhood (founder, 1846); Brussels Peace Congress (organizer, 1848); Frankfort Peace Congress (delegate, 1850); London Peace Conference (delegate, 1851); Manchester Peace Conference (delegate, 1852); Edinburgh Peace Conference (delegate, 1853); National Compensated Emancipation Co. (organizer, 1856). WRITINGS: *Sparks from the Anvil* (1848); *Miscellaneous Writings* (1850); *Olive Leaves* (1853); *Thoughts of Things at Home and Abroad* (1854); *Handbook of the Nations* (1856); *Walk from John O'Groats to Land's End* (1864); *Walk from London to Land's End and Back* (1864); *The Mission of Great Sufferings* (1867); *Walks in the Black Country* (1868); *Lectures and Speeches* (1869); *Ten Minute Talks* (1873); *Chips from Many Blocks* (1878). REL.: Congregationalist. MISC.: known as the "Learned Blacksmith." RES.: Worcester, MA.

BURRITT, SCOTT ALLAN. b. May 31, 1952, Elmhurst, IL; par. Silvius and Marcella (Hakanson) Burritt; m. Anita Priggie; c. Steven; Thomas. EDUC.: B.S., Northern IL U. POLIT. & GOV.: treas., Village of Itasca, IL, 1984–85; capital improvements commissioner, Village of Bloomingdale, IL; ***independent candidate for presidency of the U.S., 1992***. BUS. & PROF.: C.P.A.; partner, regional accountancy business, 6 years; private practice, 1985–. MIL.: U.S. Army, 1971–73. REL.: Lutheran. MAILING ADDRESS: 29 South Webster St., Suite 350, Naperville, IL 60540.

BURROWS, JULIUS CAESAR. b. Jan 9, 1837, Northeast, PA; d. Nov 16, 1915, Kalamazoo, MI; par. William and Maria Burrows; m. Jennie S. Hibbard, Jan 29, 1856; m. 2d, Frances S. Peck, Dec 25, 1867; c. Mrs. George McNeir. EDUC.: Kingsville Acad.; Grand River Inst.; studied law in offices of Cadwell and Simonds. POLIT. & GOV.: elected circuit court commissioner, 1864; elected prosecuting atty., Kalamazoo Cty., MI, 1866–70; appointed supervisor of internal revenue for MI and WI, 1868 (declined); elected as a Republican to U.S. House (MI), 1873–75, 1879–83, 1885–95 (Speaker Pro Tempore); Republican candidate for U.S. House (MI), 1874, 1882; delegate, Rep. Nat'l. Conv., 1884, 1908 (temporary chm.); appointed solicitor of U.S. Treasury, 1884 (declined); elected as a Republican to U.S. Senate (MI), 1895–1911; ***candidate for Republican nomination to vice presidency of the U.S., 1908***; candidate for Republican nomination to U.S. Senate (MI), 1910; appointed vice chm., National Monetary Comm., 1908–12. BUS. & PROF.: schoolteacher, 1853–54; atty.; admitted to OH Bar, 1859; principal, Madison School, Lake Cty., OH, 1856–57; principal, Union School, Jefferson, OH, 1858–59; principal, Richland Seminary, Kalamazoo, MI, 1860–61; law practice, Kalamazoo, 1861–1915; partner (with A. A. Knappen), law firm, Kalamazoo, 1861; partner (with Henry F. Stevens), law firm, Kalamazoo, 1867–68. MIL.: capt., 17th Regt., MI Volunteer Infantry, 1862–63. HON. DEG.: LL.D., Kalamazoo Coll. RES.: Kalamazoo, MI.

BURTON, AUSTIN MARION (aka CHIEF BURNING WOOD). b. Mar 17, 1918, Wenatchee, WA; par. John F. and Mary Vera (Maguire) Burton; m. Mary Burton. EDUC.: B.A., U. of WA, 1943. POLIT. & GOV.: ***candidate (as Chief Burning Wood) for Republican nomination to presidency of the U.S., 1968, 1976; candidate for Republican nomination to vice presidency of the U.S., 1968, 1972, 1976***;

Puritan Party candidate for U.S. House (NH), 1972. BUS. & PROF.: public information officer, U.S.C.G. Auxiliary; account exec., advertising agency; wholesale button business, Greenwich Village, NY. MIL.: lt. (jg), U.S.N.R. MEM.: Free and Accepted Masons. REL.: Episc. MISC.: Oneida Indian; won 1968 NH Republican vice presidential primary. MAILING ADDRESS: Gourmet Dining Club, Wampum Savers Teepee, P.O. Box 1951, Louisville, KY 40201.

BURTON, PHILLIP. b. Jun 1, 1926, Cincinnati, OH; d. Apr 10, 1983, San Francisco, CA; m. Sala Galant, 1953; c. Joy. EDUC.: grad., George Washington H.S., San Francisco, CA, 1944; A.B., U. of Southern CA, 1947; LL.B., Golden Gate Law School, 1952. POLIT. & GOV.: national officer, Young Democrats; elected as a Democrat to CA State Assembly, 1957–65; delegate, Atlantic Treaty Assn., 1959; elected as a Democrat to U.S. House (CA), 1965–83; founder, CA Democratic Council; delegate, Dem. Nat'l. Conv., 1968, 1972; ***candidate for Democratic nomination to vice presidency of the U.S., 1972***; chm., Democratic Study Group, 1971–73; delegate, Democratic Mid-Term Conference, 1974. BUS. & PROF.: atty.; admitted to CA Bar, 1952; admitted to practice before the Bar of the Supreme Court of the U.S., 1956; law practice, San Francisco, CA. MIL.: U.S. Army, WWII and Korean War. MEM.: Blue Key (pres., U. of Southern CA); George Washington H.S. Alumni Assn.; 88th Congress Democratic Club (sec.). RES.: San Francisco, CA.

BURTON, THEODORE ELIJAH. b. Dec 20, 1851, Jefferson, OH; d. Oct 28, 1929, Washington, DC; par. Rev. William and Elizabeth (Grant) Burton; single. EDUC.: Grand River Inst.; IA Coll.; A.B., Oberlin Coll., 1872, A.M., 1875. POLIT. & GOV.: elected as a Republican to U.S. House (OH), 1889–91, 1895–1909, 1921–28; Republican candidate for U.S. House (OH), 1890, 1908; delegate, Rep. Nat'l. Conv., 1904, 1908, 1912, 1924 (temporary chm.); delegate, Interparliamentary Union (Exec. Council, 1904–14, 1921–29); Republican candidate for mayor of Cleveland, OH, 1907; appointed chm., Inland Waterways Comm., 1907–09; member, National Monetary Comm., 1908–12; elected as a Republican to U.S. Senate (OH), 1909–15, 1928–29; chm., National Waterways Comm., 1909–12; ***candidate for Republican nomination to presidency of the U.S., 1916; candidate for Republican nomination to vice presidency of the U.S., 1916, 1924***; member, Foreign Debt Comm., 1922–27; chm., U.S. Delegation, Conference on Control of Traffic in Arms, 1925. BUS. & PROF.: atty.; admitted to OH Bar, 1875; law practice, Cleveland, OH; pres., Merchants National Bank, New York, NY, 1917–19; Stafford Little lecturer, Princeton U., 1919; Cutler lecturer, Rochester U., 1922. MEM.: American Peace Soc. (pres., 1911–15, 1925–29); Grant Family Assn. of the U.S. (pres.); Union Club; Rowfant Club; Metropolitan Club. HON. DEG.: LL.D., Oberlin Coll., 1900; LL.D., Dartmouth Coll., 1907; LL.D., OH U., 1907; LL.D., St. John's Coll., 1913; LL.D., NY U., 1919. WRITINGS: *Financial Crises and Periods of Industrial and Commercial Depression* (1902); *Life of John Sherman* (1906); *Corporations and the State* (1911); *Some Political Tendencies of the Time and the Effect of the War Thereon* (1919); *The Constitution: Its Origin and Distinctive Features* (1923). RES.: Cleveland, OH.

BUSH, CAROLYN DOROTHY. single. POLIT. & GOV.: ***candidate for Democratic nomination to presidency of the U.S., 1984***. MAILING ADDRESS: 906 Dunbar St., Richmond, VA 23226.

BUSH, GEORGE HERBERT WALKER. b. Jun 12, 1924, Milton, MA; par. Prescott Sheldon and Dorothy (Walker) Bush; m. Barbara Pierce, Jan 6, 1945; c. George W.; John E.; Neil M.; Marvin P.; Dorothy W. EDUC.: grad., Phillips Acad., Andover, MA, 1942; B.A., Yale U., 1948. POLIT. & GOV.: chm., Harris Cty. (TX) Republican Central Cmte., 1963–64; delegate, Rep. Nat'l. Conv., 1964, 1968; Republican candidate for U.S. Senate (TX), 1964, 1970; elected as a Republican to U.S. House (TX), 1967–71; appointed U.S. ambassador to the U.N., 1971–73; chm., Rep. Nat'l. Cmte., 1973–74; appointed chief, U.S. Liaison Office to People's Republic of China, 1974–75; appointed dir., CIA, 1975–77; ***candidate for Republican nomination to vice presidency of the U.S., 1976; candidate for Republican nomination to presidency of the U.S., 1980; elected as a Republican to vice presidency of the U.S., 1981–89; elected as a Republican to presidency of the U.S., 1989–93; Republican candidate for presidency of the U.S., 1992***. BUS. & PROF.: founder, Bush-Overbey Oil Development, Inc., Midland, TX, 1953; co-founder, dir., Zapata Petroleum Corp., Midland, TX, 1953–59; pres., Zapata Off Shore Co., Houston, TX, 1956–64, chm. of the board, 1964–66; member, exec. cmte., First International Bank of Houston, 1977; dir., Eli Lilly Co.; dir., Texasgulf Inc.; dir., First International Bancshares; adjunct prof., Rice U. MIL.: ensign, U.S.N.R., 1942–45, lt. (jg), 1945; Distinguished Flying Cross with three Air Medals; National Security Medal; National Intelligence Distinguished Service Medal; shot down in combat over Boin Island, Sep 1944. MEM.: TX Heart Fund (chm.); Phi Beta Kappa; Holly Hall (trustee); Delta Kappa Epsilon; Hedgecroft Hospital (trustee); Phillips Acad. (trustee); Episcopal Church Foundation (adviser). HON. DEG.: LL.D., Adelphi U., 1972; LL.D., Beaver Coll., 1972; LL.D., Northern MI U., 1973; H.H.D., Austin Coll., 1973; LL.D., Franklin Pierce Coll.; LL.D., Allegheny Coll. WRITINGS: *Looking Forward* (1987). REL.: Episc. MAILING ADDRESS: Houston, TX.

BUSHFIELD, HARLAN JOHN. b. Aug 6, 1882, Atlantic, IA; d. Sep 27, 1948, Miller, SD; par. John Andrew and Cora E. (Pearson) Bushfield; m. Vera Cahalan, Apr 15, 1912; c. John Pearson; Mary Janith (Mrs. John Work); Harlan John, Jr. EDUC.: Dakota Wesleyan U., 1899–1901, LL.D., 1939; LL.B., U. of MN, 1904. POLIT. & GOV.: elected state's atty., Hand Cty., SD, 1907–11; chm., SD State Republican Central Cmte., 1936;

elected as a Republican to gov. of SD, 1939–43; ***candidate for Republican nomination to presidency of the U.S., 1940; candidate for Republican nomination to vice presidency of the U.S., 1940***; elected as a Republican to U.S. Senate (SD), 1943–48. BUS. & PROF.: atty.; admitted to SD Bar, 1904; law practice, Miller, SD; farmer. MEM.: Masons; Shriners; Knights Templar; Knights of Pythias; ABA; SD Bar Assn.; National Grange; Independent Order of Odd Fellows. REL.: Presb. RES.: Miller, SD.

BUTLER, BENJAMIN FRANKLIN. b. Nov 5, 1818, Deerfield, NH; d. Jan 11, 1893, Washington, DC; par. John and Charlotte (Ellison) Butler; m. Sarah Hildreth, May 16, 1844; c. Paul (d. 1850); Paul; Blanche (Mrs. Adelbert Ames); Benjamin Israel. EDUC.: Phillips Exeter Acad.; Lowell (MA) H.S., 1832–34; grad., Waterbury (ME) Coll. (now Colby U.), 1838; studied law under William Smith. POLIT. & GOV.: delegate, Dem. Nat'l. Conv., 1844, 1856, 1860, 1880, 1884; appointed U.S. sec. of war, 1845 (declined); Democratic candidate for MA State House, 1848; Democratic candidate for U.S. House (MA), 1852, 1856, 1858; elected as a Democrat to MA State House, 1853; ***candidate for Democratic nomination to vice presidency of the U.S., 1852, 1856***; Democratic candidate for MA State Senate, 1857; elected as a Democrat to MA State Senate, 1858; candidate for Democratic nomination to gov. of MA, 1858, 1859; Democratic candidate for gov. of MA, 1860, 1871, 1873, 1879; appointed military gov. of New Orleans, LA, 1862; ***candidate for Republican nomination to presidency of the U.S., 1864, 1884; candidate for Republican nomination to vice presidency of the U.S., 1864 (declined)***; elected as a Republican to U.S. House (MA), 1867–75; elected as a Greenbacker to U.S. House (MA), 1877–79; candidate for Republican nomination to gov. of MA, 1871, 1872; ***candidate for Prohibition Party nomination to presidency of the U.S., 1872***; Republican candidate for U.S. House (MA), 1874; Greenback Party candidate for gov. of MA, 1878; National Labor Party candidate for gov. of MA, 1879; ***candidate for Greenback Party nomination to presidency of the U.S., 1880***; elected as a Greenback-Democrat to gov. of MA, 1883–84; Greenback-Democratic candidate for gov. of MA, 1883; ***candidate for Democratic nomination to presidency of the U.S., 1884; Greenback Labor (National) Party candidate for presidency of the U.S., 1884; Anti-Monopoly Party candidate for presidency of the U.S., 1884***. BUS. & PROF.: schoolteacher, Waterbury, ME, 1836–38; atty.; admitted to MA Bar, 1840; law practice, Lowell, MA, 1840–61. MIL.: pvt., Lowell (MA) City Guard, 1840, col., 1850; brig. gen., U.S. Army, 1861, maj. gen., 1861, resigned commission, 1865. MEM.: Hunkers; Masons; Men's Soc. for Diffusing Missionary Knowledge; Erosophian Adelphi; Albany Temperance Soc. (vice pres., 1832); Congressional Temperance Soc. HON. DEG.: LL.D., Dartmouth Coll., 1888. WRITINGS: *Butler's Book* (1892). REL.: Bapt. MISC.: commanding gen. in capture of New Orleans; alleged atrocities earned him nickname of "Beast" Butler; dispatched to NY to maintain order during 1864 elections; one of House mgr.s during impeachment proceedings against President Andrew Johnson (q.v.). RES.: Gloucester, MA.

BUTLER, MARION. b. May 20, 1863, Sampson Cty., NC; d. Jun 3, 1938, Takoma Park, MD; par. Wiley and Romelia (Ferrell) Butler; m. Florence Faison, Aug 31, 1893; c. Pocahontas; Marion; Edward F.; Florence F.; Wiley. EDUC.: Salem (NC) H.S.; A.B., U. of NC, 1885. POLIT. & GOV.: elected as a Democrat to NC State Senate, 1890; founder, People's Party, 1892; chm., NC People's Party State Convention, 1892; chm., NC People's Party Central Cmte., 1892; presidential elector, People's Party, 1892; chm., People's Party National Exec. Cmte., 1896–1904; elected as a Populist (People's Party) to U.S. Senate (NC), 1896–1901; ***candidate for People's Party nomination to presidency of the U.S., 1896 (declined); candidate for People's Party nomination to vice presidency of the U.S., 1896 (declined)***; People's Party candidate for U.S. Senate (NC), 1901; delegate, Rep. Nat'l. Conv., 1912, 1916, 1920, 1924, 1928, 1932. BUS. & PROF.: principal, Salem (NC) Acad., 1885–88; owner, *Clinton (NC) Caucasian*, 1888–94; owner, *Raleigh (NC) Caucasian*, 1894; atty.; admitted to NC Bar, 1899; law practice, Raleigh, NC; law practice, Washington, DC; partner, various mining interests. MEM.: North Carolina Farmers Alliance (local pres., 1888; pres., 1891–92); National Farmers Alliance and Industrial Union (first vice pres., 1891; delegate, St. Louis and Memphis Conventions, 1892; pres., 1894); U. of NC (trustee, 1891–99); Cotton and Tobacco Cooperative Marketing Assn. of the South. RES.: Raleigh, NC.

BUTLER, NICHOLAS MURRAY. b. Apr 2, 1862, Elizabeth, NJ; d. Dec 7, 1947, New York, NY; par. Henry L. and Mary J. (Murray) Butler; m. Susanna Edwards Schuyler, Feb 8, 1887; m. 2d, Kate La Montagne, Mar 5, 1907; c. Sarah Schuyler (Mrs. Neville Lawrence). EDUC.: A.B., Columbia U., 1882, A.M., 1883, Ph.D., 1884, University Fellow in Philosophy, 1882–85; student in Berlin and Paris, 1884–85. POLIT. & GOV.: member, NJ State Board of Education, 1887–95; delegate, Rep. Nat'l. Conv., 1888, 1908, 1920, 1924, and 5 other times; appointed NJ commissioner, Paris Exposition, 1889; pres., NJ Council of Education, 1891; member, College Council of NY State, 1892–96; pres., Paterson (NJ) Board of Education, 1892–93; chm., NY State Republican Convention, 1912; ***Republican candidate for vice presidency of the U.S., 1912; candidate for Republican nomination to presidency of the U.S., 1920***; appointed member, NY Comm. on Reorganization of Government, 1925–26; appointed vice chm., NY Mayor's Cmte. on Planning and Development, 1926–27. BUS. & PROF.: asst. in philosophy, Columbia U., 1885–86, tutor, 1886–89, prof., 1889–90, dean, 1890–01, pres., 1901–45, pres. emeritus, 1945–47; pres., Barnard Coll. and Teachers Coll., 1901–45; pres., Coll. of Pharmacy, 1904–45; pres., Bard Coll., 1928–44; pres., NY Post-Graduate Medical School, 1931–45; pres., NY Coll. for Training of Teachers, 1886–91; founder, College Entrance Examining Board, 1893, chm., 1901–04; Watson Professor of American History, 1923; dir., NY Life Insurance Co. MEM.: International Congress of Arts and Sciences; St. Louis Exposition (chm., Administrative Board, 1904); Lake Mohonk Conference on International Arbitration (chm., 1907, 1909, 1910, 1911, 1912); National Cmte.

on Reconstruction of the U. of Louvain, 1915–25; American Branch, Conciliation Internationale (pres., 1907; ed., Paris Branch, 1906–37); Rogers Memorial Library (pres., 1932–47); Carnegie Foundation (trustee, 1905–47); Carnegie Endowment for International Peace (pres., 1925–45, pres. emeritus, 1945–47); Carnegie Corp. (trustee, 1925–45, chm., 1937–45); Cathedral of St. John the Divine (trustee, 1914–47); American-Slav Inst. (pres., 1924–47); Barnard Coll. (trustee); Teachers Coll. (trustee); Columbia U. Press (trustee); College Assn. of the Middle States and MD (pres., 1895); Soc. for Psychical Research; NY Acad. of Sciences; Congress of the Royal Inst. for Public Health (vice pres., 1920); Citizens Budget Cmte. of NY (pres., 1936–46); Membre de l'Institut de France (1923–47); American Acad. of Arts and Letters (1911–47; Chancellor, 1924–28; pres., 1928–41); The Pilgrims (vice pres., 1913–28; pres., 1928–46); American Phil. Soc.; American Psych. Assn.; NEA (pres., 1895; trustee, 1896–98); American Hist. Assn.; NY Hist. Soc.; Germanistic Soc. (pres., 1906–07; dir., 1908–17; hon. vice pres., 1930–47); American Scandinavian Soc. (pres., 1908–11); American Acad. in Rome; Universal Settlement Soc. (pres., 1905–14); France-America Soc. (pres., 1914–24); American Red Cross; NY C. of C.; Lycee Francaise de NY; American Hellenic Soc. (pres., 1917–47); Italy-America Soc. (pres., Board of trustees, 1929–35); American Soc. of the French Legion of Honor, Inc. (hon. pres.); Bricklayers, Masons and Plasterers International Union of America; Phil. Soc.; National Inst. of Social Science; NY Acad. of Public Education; Psi Upsilon; Phi Beta Kappa; Amigos Mexicanos del Pueblo de Norte-America; Associazione Internazionale per gli Studi Mediterranei; Stresemann Memorial Friedens-Stiftung (vice pres.); Pan-American Soc. of Santiago, Cuba (hon. pres.); Pan American Trade Cmte. (gov.); International Benjamin Franklin Soc. (hon. vice pres.); Institut des Hautes Etudes Internationales; German-American Writers Assn.; Inst. of Journalists; Instituto de Investigaciones Historicas; NY Genealogical and Biographical Soc. (Fellow); Union Club; Century Club; Metropolitan Club; University Club; Round Table Club; Columbia University Club; Lawyers Club; Lotos Club (pres., 1923–24); Bohemian Club; Athenaeum; Reform Club; Southampton Club; Beach of Southampton Club; American Club of Paris; British Schools and University Club; Authors Club; Players Club; City Club. AWARDS: Nobel Peace Prize, 1931; Mark Twain Medal, 1936; Union Federale des Combattants Medal (France), 1936; Insignia of the Order of Merit (Dominican Republic), 1937; Erasmus Medal, 1937; Honorary Citizen of Trujillo City, 1937; Grand Cross of the Legion of Honor, 1937; Grand White Cordon, Order of Jae (China), 1938; Medal, NY Acad. of Public Education, 1938; Diploma of Honor, La Academia Mexicana Correspondiente de la Espanola, 1939; National Historical Order of Merit of "Carlos Manuel de Cespedes" (Cuba), 1940; Alexander Hamilton Medal, 1947; numerous other decorations. WRITINGS: *Columbia University Contributions to Philosophy and Education* (1888–1902); *Educational Review* (ed., 1889–1920); *The Great Educator Series* (1892–1901); *The Teachers Professional Library* (1894–1929); *International Padagogische Bibliothek* (co-editor); *The Meaning of Education* (1898, 1915); *True and False Democracy* (1907); *The American as He Is* (1908); *Education in the United States* (1910); *Philosophy* (1911); *Why Should We Change Our Form of Government?* (1912); *Bibliothek d. Amerikanischen Kulturgeschichte* (1912); *The International Mind* (1913); *World in Ferment* (1918); *Is America Worth Saving?* (1920); *Scholarship and Service* (1921); *Building the American Nation* (1923); *The Faith of a Liberal* (1924); *The Path to Peace* (1930); *Looking Forward* (1932); *Between Two Worlds* (1934); *The Family of Nations* (1938); *Across the Busy Years* (1939); *Why War?* (1940); *Liberty, Equality, Fraternity* (1942); *The World Today* (1946). REL.: Episc. RES.: New York, NY.

BUTLER, WILLIAM ORLANDO. b. Apr 19, 1791, Jessamine Cty., KY; d. Aug 6, 1880, Carrollton, KY; par. Percival and Mildred (Hawkins) Butler. EDUC.: grad., Transylvania U., 1812; studied law under Robert Wickliffe. POLIT. & GOV.: elected as a Democrat to KY State House, 1817–19; elected as a Democrat to U.S. House (KY), 1839–43; Democratic candidate for gov. of KY, 1844; ***candidate for Democratic nomination to presidency of the U.S., 1848, 1852; Democratic candidate for vice presidency of the U.S., 1848***; Democratic candidate for U.S. Senate (KY), 1851; ***candidate for Democratic nomination to vice presidency of the U.S., 1852, 1856***; appointed to gov. of Nebraska Territory, 1855 (declined); delegate, Peace Convention, 1861. BUS. & PROF.: farmer; atty.; admitted to KY Bar, 1817; law practice, Carrollton, KY, 1817. MIL.: capt., U.S. Army, 1813, brev. maj., 1816; maj. gen., U.S. Army, 1846; Sword of Gratitude from U.S. Congress for Gallantry in Battle of Monterey, Mexico. WRITINGS: *The Boatman's Horn and Other Poems*. RES.: Carrollton, KY.

BUTZ, EARL LAUER. b. Jul 3, 1909, Albion, IN; par. Herman Lee and Ada Tillie (Lower) Butz; m. Mary Emma Powell, Dec 22, 1937; c. William Powell; Thomas Earl. EDUC.: B.S.A., Purdue U., 1932, Ph.D., 1937; U. of Chicago, 1936. POLIT. & GOV.: appointed asst. U.S. sec. of agriculture, 1954–57; appointed chm., U.S. Delegation, Food and Agricultural Organization, 1955, 1957; member, IN Republican State Central Cmte., 1958–62; member, White House Task Force on Foreign Economic Development, 1969–70; appointed U.S. sec. of agriculture, 1971–76; appointed counselor to the president on natural resources; delegate, Rep. Nat'l. Conv., 1976; ***candidate for Republican nomination to presidency of the U.S., 1976***. BUS. & PROF.: farmer, Noble Cty., IN, 1933; research asst., Purdue U., 1934–35, instructor, 1937–39, asst. prof., 1939–43, assoc. prof., 1943–46, prof., 1946–54, 1971–, dean of agriculture, 1957–67, dean of continuing education, 1968–71; vice pres., Purdue Research Foundation, 1968–71; research economist, Federal Land Bank, Louisville, KY, 1935–36; research economist, Brookings Institution, 1944, 1951; research staff, National Bureau of Economic Research, 1944–45; lecturer, U. of WI, 1946–65; lecturer, Rutgers U., 1950–58; dir., Standard Life Insurance Co. of IN, 1951–71; chm. of the board, Commodity Credit Corp., 1954–57; dir., Ralston Purina Co., 1958–71; dir., J. I. Case

Co.; dir., International Minerals and Chemical Corp., 1960–71; dir., Stokely-Van Camp Co., 1969–71; dir., Investment Seminar Farm Foundation, Chicago, IL; dir., Foundation for American Agriculture, Washington, DC. MEM.: Farm Foundation (dir., 1960–70); Foundation for American Agriculture (dir., 1957–71); Nutrition Foundation (trustee, 1967–71); American Farm Economics Assn. (vice pres., 1948; sec.-treas., 1953–54); American Acad. of Farm Managers and Rural Appraisers (vice pres., 1951); IN Acad. of Social Sciences (vice pres., 1948); Canadian-American Cmte.; International Conference of Agricultural Economists; Sigma Xi; Alpha Gamma Rho (national pres., 1948–50); Sigma Delta Chi; Tau Kappa Alpha; Alpha Zeta; Scabbard and Blade; Skull and Crescent; Kiwanis; Capitol Hill Club; National Planning Assn.; AAUP; Columbia Club. AWARDS: "Outstanding Communicator of the Year," Toastmasters International, 1972; Commendation, 106th Annual Session, Grange, 1972; Distinguished Service Award, Meritorious Service Award, American Farm Bureau Federation, 1972. WRITINGS: *The Production Credit System for Farmers* (1944); *Price Fixing for Food Stuffs* (1952). MAILING ADDRESS: 311 Jefferson Dr., West Lafayette, IN 47906.

BYERLEY, LESTER FRANCIS, JR. b. 1944; par. Lester F. Byerley. POLIT. & GOV.: ***United National Independence Party candidate for presidency of the U.S., 1980, 1984; candidate for Democratic nomination to presidency of the U.S., 1984 (withdrew), 1992***. BUS. & PROF.: house painter. MAILING ADDRESS: 51 Division St., Manahawkin, NJ 08050.

BYERS, BRUCE EDWARD. POLIT. & GOV.: ***independent candidate for presidency of the U.S., 1988***. MAILING ADDRESS: 9999 Kempwood Dr., #331, Houston, TX 77080.

BYNUM, PAUL. b. Jan 8, 1914, Hana, OK; par. Jasper Tally and Mary Elizabeth (McElhany) Bynum,; m. Georgia Nemo, 1935; m. 2d, Mary Lucille Bratcher, 1939; m. 3d, Doris Opal Bloom, 1950; c. Paul Richard; Patricia L. Hamilton; Doris Dyan Hummel. EDUC.: grad., Chandler (AZ) H.S., 1931. POLIT. & GOV.: ***candidate for Democratic nomination to presidency of the U.S., 1980 (withdrew)***. BUS. & PROF.: farm laborer; box factory worker; construction laborer; shipyard welder; journeyman carpenter, 25 years. MEM.: Toastmasters (pres., Chapter 64, 1955–56). REL.: agnostic (acknowledging unknown supreme intelligence). MAILING ADDRESS: 1838 Sandalwood Dr., Santa Maria, CA 93454.

BYRD, HARRY FLOOD. b. Jun 10, 1887, Martinsburg, WV; d. Oct 20, 1966, Berryville, VA; s. Richard Evelyn and Eleanor Bolling (Flood) Byrd; m. Ann Douglas Beverly, Oct 7, 1913; c. Harry Flood, Jr.; Westwood; Beverly; Richard Evelyn. EDUC.: Shenandoah Valley Acad., Winchester, VA. POLIT. & GOV.: elected as a Democrat to VA State Senate, 1915–25; appointed VA state fuel commissioner, 1918; chm., VA State Democratic Central Cmte., 1922–25; delegate, Dem. Nat'l. Conv., 1924, 1928, 1952, 1956; elected as a Democrat to gov. of VA, 1926–30; member, Dem. Nat'l. Cmte., 1928–40; ***candidate for Democratic nomination to presidency of the U.S., 1932, 1940, 1944***; appointed and subsequently elected as a Democrat to U.S. Senate (VA), 1933–65; ***candidate for Democratic nomination to vice presidency of the U.S., 1936; candidate for Republican nomination to presidency of the U.S., 1944; American First Party candidate for vice presidency of the U.S., 1952; Constitution Party candidate for vice presidency of the U.S., 1952; States Rights Party of KY candidate for presidency of the U.S., 1956; SC for Independent Electors candidate for presidency of the U.S., 1956; Conservative Party of VA candidate for presidency of the U.S., 1960 (declined); received 15 electoral votes for presidency of the U.S., 1960***. BUS. & PROF.: farmer, Berryville, VA; journalist; publisher, *Winchester (VA) Star*, 1903–66; publisher, *Harrisonburg (VA) Daily News Record*, 1923–66; pres., Valley Turnpike Co., 1908–18; pres., Winchester Cold Storage Co.; apple and peach orchardist, 1906–66. MEM.: Masons; Elks; Moose; Phi Beta Kappa. AWARDS: award, American Good Government Soc., 1953. HON. DEG.: LL.D., Coll. of William and Mary, 1926. REL.: Episc. RES.: Berryville, VA.

BYRD, ROBERT CARLYLE (nee CORNELIUS CALVIN SALE, JR.). b. Nov 20, 1917, North Wilkesboro, NC; par. Cornelius Calvin and Ada (Kirby) Sale (foster parents: Titus Dalton and Vlurma Sale Byrd); m. Erma Ora James, May 29, 1937; c. Mona Carole; Marjorie Ellen. EDUC.: grad., Mark Twain H.S., 1934; Beckley Coll.; Concord Coll.; Morris Harvey Coll., 1950–51; Marshall U., 1951–52; George Washington U.; J.D., American U., 1963. POLIT. & GOV.: elected as a Democrat to WV State House of Delegates, 1947–51; elected as a Democrat to WV State Senate, 1951–53; elected as a Democrat to U.S. House (WV), 1953–59; elected as a Democrat to U.S. Senate (WV), 1959– (majority whip, 1971–77; majority leader, 1977–81, 1987–88; minority leader, 1981–87); delegate, Dem. Nat'l. Conv., 1960; ***candidate for Democratic nomination to presidency of the U.S., 1976, 1980***. BUS. & PROF.: clerk; butcher; public official. MEM.: Masons; Odd Fellows; Ku Klux Klan (Kleagle, 1942; resigned); Moose; Elks; Knights of Pythias; Lions; Democratic Conference (sec., 1967–71). REL.: Bapt. MISC.: noted fiddler. MAILING ADDRESS: Sophia, WV 25929.

BYRER, SAMUEL WOODS. b. After 1903; par. Harry Hopkins and May (Griffin) Byrer. POLIT. & GOV.: ***candidate for Republican nomination to presidency of the U.S., 1948***. REL.: Methodist Episc. MAILING ADDRESS: Martinsburg, WV.

BYRNES, JAMES FRANCIS. b. May 2, 1879, Charleston, SC; d. Apr 9, 1972, Columbia, SC; par. James Francis and Elizabeth E. (McSweeney) Byrnes.; m. Maude Fusch Perkins, May 2, 1906; c. none. EDUC.: public schools. POLIT. & GOV.: official court reporter, Second Circuit Court of SC, 1900–1908; elected solicitor, Second Circuit Court of SC, 1908–10; elected as a Democrat to U.S. House (SC), 1911–25; delegate, Dem. Nat'l. Conv., 1920, 1932, 1936, 1940, 1952; candidate for Democratic nomination to U.S. Senate (SC), 1924; elected as a Democrat to U.S. Senate (SC), 1931–41; ***candidate for Democratic nomination to presidency of the U.S., 1940; candidate for Democratic nomination to vice presidency of the U.S., 1940***; appointed assoc. justice, Supreme Court of the U.S., 1941–42; appointed dir., Office of Economic Stabilization, 1942; appointed dir., Office of War Mobilization, 1943–45; appointed U.S. sec. of state, 1945–47; elected as a Democrat to gov. of SC, 1951–55. BUS. & PROF.: atty.; admitted to SC Bar, 1903; ed., *Journal and Review*, Aiken, SC, 1903–07; partner, Nichols, Wyche and Byrnes (law firm), Spartanburg, SC, 1925–31. MEM.: Masons; Shriners; Knights of Pythias. AWARDS: Distinguished Service Medal, from President Truman. HON. DEG.: LL.D., John Marshall Coll.; LL.D., U. of SC; LL.D., U. of PA; LL.D., Columbia U.; LL.D., Yale U.; LL.D., Washington and Lee U. WRITINGS: *Speaking Frankly* (1947); *All in One Lifetime* (1958). REL.: Episc. (nee R.C.). RES.: Columbia, SC.

BYRNES, JOHN WILLIAM. b. Jun 12, 1913, Green Bay, WI; d. Jan 12, 1985, Marshfield, WI; par. Charles W. and Harriet (Schumacher) Byrnes; m. Barbara Preston, Feb 15, 1947; c. John Robert; Michael Preston; Bonnie Jean; Charles Kirby; Barbara Harriet; Elizabeth Alice. EDUC.: B.A., U. of WI, 1936, LL.B., 1938. POLIT. & GOV.: appointed special deputy commissioner of banking of WI, 1938–40; elected as a Republican to WI State Senate, 1941–45 (majority leader, 1943); elected as a Republican to U.S. House (WI), 1945–73; keynoter, Young Republican Federation National Convention, 1947; keynoter, WI State Republican Convention, 1948; delegate, Rep. Nat'l. Conv., 1956, 1960, 1964 (chm., WI Delegation), 1968; member, Civil Service Claims Comm.; member, War Claims Comm.; ***candidate for Republican nomination to presidency of the U.S., 1964***. BUS. & PROF.: atty.; admitted to WI Bar, 1939; admitted to the Bar of DC, 1972; partner, Foley, Lardner, Hollabaugh and Jacobs (law firm), Washington, DC, 1973. MEM.: Elks; WI Bar Assn.; DC Bar Assn.; Junior C. of C.; Chowder and Marching Soc. AWARDS: George Washington Award, American Good Government Soc., 1962; Distinguished Public Service Award, The Tax Foundation, 1963. HON. DEG.: LL.D., Lawrence U., 1962. REL.: R.C. MAILING ADDRESS: 201 Main St., Green Bay, WI.

CADWELL, JACK S. POLIT. & GOV.: ***independent candidate for presidency of the U.S., 1976***. MAILING ADDRESS: Hastings Pond Rd., Warwick Star Route, Orange, MA 01364.

CAEN, HERB EUGENE. b. Apr 3, 1916, Sacramento, CA; par. Lucien and Augusta (Gross) Caen; m. Sally Gilbert, Feb 15, 1952 (divorced, 1959); m. 3d, Maria Theresa Shaw, Mar 9, 1963; c. Christopher; Deborah (stepdaughter). EDUC.: Sacramento (CA) Junior Coll., 1934. POLIT. & GOV.: ***candidate for Democratic nomination to presidency of the U.S., 1984***. BUS. & PROF.: journalist; reporter, *Sacramento Union*, 1932–36; daily columnist, *San Francisco (CA) Chronicle*, 1936–50, 1958–; columnist, *San Francisco Examiner*, 1950–58; author. MIL.: pvt., capt., U.S.A.A.F., 1942–45; Medaille de la Liberation (France, 1949). MEM.: San Francisco Press Club. WRITINGS: *The San Francisco Book* (1948); *Baghdad-by-the-Bay* (1949); *Baghdad* (1950); *Don't Call It Frisco* (1953); *Caen's Guide to San Francisco* (1957); *Only in San Francisco* (1960, with Don Kingman); *City on Golden Hills* (1968); *The Cable Car and the Dragon* (1972); *One Man's San Francisco* (1976). MAILING ADDRESS: 1054 Chestnut St., San Francisco, CA 94109.

CAFFERY, DONELSON. b. Sep 10, 1835, Franklin, LA; d. Dec 30, 1906, New Orleans, LA; par. Donelson and Lydia (Murphy) Caffery; m. Bethia Celestine Richardson, 1869; c. Edward; Ralph Earl; Charles; six others. EDUC.: St. Mary's Coll., Baltimore, MD; LA U.; studied law in office of Joseph W. Walker, Franklin, LA. POLIT. & GOV.: court clerk, 1866; delegate, LA State Constitutional Convention, 1879; elected as a Democrat to LA State Senate, 1892; appointed and subsequently elected as a Democrat to U.S. Senate (LA), 1892–1901; permanent chm., National (Gold Democratic) Party National Convention, 1896; ***National (Gold Democratic) Party candidate for presidency of the U.S., 1900 (declined)***; Fusion Party candidate for gov. of LA, 1900. BUS. & PROF.: atty.; admitted to LA Bar, 1867; law practice, Franklin, LA, 1867–1906; sugar planter. MIL.: lt., 13th LA Regt., C.S.A., 1862–65. WRITINGS: *Aldredge on Free Coinage of Silver* (1896). REL.: Presb. RES.: Franklin, LA.

CAGGIANO-RUBIN, ZACOE PATRICIA ANN MARY. par. Mr. Caggiano; m. Lann Rubin, II; c. Kephre; Heru Ru. POLIT. & GOV.: ***independent candidate for presidency of the U.S., 1988; independent candidate for vice presidency of the U.S., 1988***. BUS. & PROF.: foundress, "papess," high priestess, Our Lady of Liberty Church. MEM.: Positive Action for Mothers and Children (exec. dir.). REL.: Our Lady of Liberty Church. MAILING ADDRESS: 36 South Main, Liberty, NY 12754.

CAHILL, JOHN PATRICK. POLIT. & GOV.: ***candidate for Democratic nomination to presidency of the U.S., 1992***. MAILING ADDRESS: Brooklyn, NY.

CAIN, DARYL O. POLIT. & GOV.: ***Microbe candidate for Democratic nomination to presidency of the U.S., 1980***. BUS. & PROF.: minister; founder, pres., International Green Olive Tree Orphanage Foundation, Inc.; inventor. REL.: Fundamentalist Christian. MISC.: inventor of a key unit, single pedal brake accelerator. MAILING ADDRESS: 641 Clair St., San Diego, CA 92154.

CAIN, PERRY JOSEPH. b. Sep 20, 1960, Liberal, KS; par. Donald L. and Kay (Fugger) Cain; single. EDUC.: grad., Union H.S., Tulsa, OK; Oral Roberts U., 1979–. POLIT. & GOV.: ***Conservative College Christian Party candidate for presidency of the U.S., 1980***. BUS. & PROF.: employee, Dillons Food Stores, Great Bend, KS; employee, McCartney's Foods, Tulsa, OK; student, Oral Roberts U. MEM.: Young Americans for Freedom; College Republican Club; National Forensics League;

Great Bend (KS) Student Council (pres., 1978). AWARDS: various forensics awards. REL.: R.C. MAILING ADDRESS: 2504 West Broadway, Broken Arrow, OK 74102.

CALDER, WILLIAM MUSGRAVE. b. Mar 3, 1869, Brooklyn, NY; d. Mar 3, 1945, Brooklyn, NY; par. Alexander Grant and Susan Musgrave (Ryan) Calder; m. Katherine Edna Harloe, Feb 14, 1893; c. Elsie Frances (Mrs. Robert Corwin Lee); William Musgrave, Jr. EDUC.: Cooper Inst. POLIT. & GOV.: appointed building commissioner, Brooklyn, NY, 1902–03; elected as a Republican to U.S. House (NY), 1905–15; delegate, Rep. Nat'l. Conv., 1908, 1912, 1916, 1920, 1924, 1928, 1932, 1936, 1940; ***candidate for Republican nomination to vice presidency of the U.S., 1912, 1928***; elected as a Republican to U.S. Senate (NY), 1917–23; Republican candidate for U.S. Senate (NY), 1922; presidential elector, Republican Party, 1929. BUS. & PROF.: carpenter's apprentice, Brooklyn; owner, pres., William M. Calder Co. (construction), NY, 1907–43; dir., Lawyers Title and Trust Co.; dir., Lumber Mutual Casualty Insurance Co.; dir., Prudence Realization Corp.; dir., Brooklyn National Life Insurance Co. MEM.: National Republican Club (pres., 1924–27); Masons; Elks; Brooklyn C. of C.; NY C. of C.; Chevy Chase Club; Crescent Club; Mantauk Club; Brooklyn Sunday School Assn. HON. DEG.: LL.D., George Washington U., 1920; LL.D., Syracuse U., 1921; LL.D., Fordham U., 1922; LL.D., Gonzales Coll., 1922. REL.: Dutch Reformed Church. MISC.: author of first national daylight savings law, 1918. RES.: Brooklyn, NY.

CALDERWOOD, WILLIS GREENLEAF. b. Jul 25, 1866, Fox Lake, WI; d. May 22, 1956, Minneapolis, MN; par. John and Emily Bethiah (Greenleaf) Calderwood; m. Alice M. Cox, Jun 9, 1892. EDUC.: grad., Wesleyan Methodist Seminary, 1886; grad., American Correspondence U., 1890. POLIT. & GOV.: sec., Hennepin Cty. (MN) Prohibition Cmte., 1893; exec. cmte., MN State Prohibition Cmte., 1897–1910, chm., 1911–14, 1916–18; member, Prohibition Party National Cmte., 1904–24 (sec., 1905–12; exec. cmte., 1912–16; vice chm., 1916–20); Prohibition Party candidate for MN State House, 1904, 1906; Prohibition Party candidate for U.S. House (At-Large, MN), 1912; Prohibition Party candidate for gov. of MN, 1914; Prohibition Party candidate for U.S. Senate (MN), 1916, 1918; ***candidate for Prohibition Party nomination to presidency of the U.S., 1916***; member, exec. cmte., National Party, 1919; campaign worker, U.S. Rep. Charles Randall (q.v.); ***candidate for Prohibition Party nomination to vice presidency of the U.S., 1920 (withdrew)***. BUS. & PROF.: schoolteacher, Dakota Territory, 1886–89; teacher, Commercial Coll., Minneapolis, MN, 1889–94; agent, Northwestern Life Insurance Co., 1894–98; prohibition worker, Australia, 1921–23; dir., National Prohibition Facts Service, 1926–; author; syndicated columnist; treas., Sterling Engineers, Inc. MEM.: Ministers' Life and Casualty Union (founder; treas.); Pi Gamma Mu; Commonwealth Club; Saturday Lunch Club; Non-Partisan Prohibition League (chm., 1888); MN Civic Reform Assn. (pres.). WRITINGS: "Prohibition as a Present Political Platform," *Annals of the American Academy of Social Sciences*, Vol. 32, No. 2; "The Objections to Cty. Option," *Vindicator*, Feb 3, 1912; "Not Good Men But Good Party," *National Prohibitionist*, Jul 16, 1908; *The Faith of the Fathers* (1912); *Manual of Politics; Do It Right First—An Analysis of Cty. Option*. REL.: Methodist. RES.: Minneapolis, MN.

CALDWELL, HENRY CLAY. b. Sep 4, 1832, Marshall Cty., VA (now WV); d. Feb 15, 1915, Los Angeles, CA; par. Van and Susan M. Caldwell; m. Harriet Benton, Mar 25, 1857. EDUC.: public schools; studied law in the office of Wright and Knapp, Keosauqua, IA, 1852. POLIT. & GOV.: elected prosecuting atty., Keosauqua, IA, 1856–58; elected as a Republican to IA State House, 1858–61; delegate, Rep. Nat'l. Conv., 1860; appointed judge, U.S. District Court for AR, 1864–90; appointed judge, U.S. Circuit Court, 8th Judicial Circuit, 1890–1903; appointed chief justice, Supreme Court of the U.S., 1888 (declined); ***candidate for People's Party nomination to presidency of the U.S., 1896; candidate for Republican nomination to presidency of the U.S., 1896; candidate for Coalition (People's-Democratic-Republican) nomination to vice presidency of the U.S., 1896; candidate for Democratic nomination to vice presidency of the U.S., 1900 (declined)***. BUS. & PROF.: atty.; admitted to IA Bar, 1852; assoc., partner, Wright and Knapp (law firm), Keosauqua, IA, 1852. MIL.: maj., Third IA Cavalry, U.S. Army, 1861, col., 1864. MEM.: AR Bar Assn. HON. DEG.: LL.D., Little Rock U. REL.: Methodist. RES.: Little Rock, AR.

CALHOUN, JOHN CALDWELL. b. Mar 18, 1782, Abbeville, SC; d. Mar 31, 1850, Washington, DC; par. Patrick and Martha (Caldwell) Calhoun; m. Floride Bonneau Calhoun (cousin), Jan 1811; c. Anna Marie (Mrs. Thomas Clemson); Andrew Pickens; Cornelia; Elizabeth; Floride; James Edward; John B.; Patrick; William Lowndes. EDUC.: B.A., Yale U., 1804, LL.D., 1822; studied law under Tapping Reeve, Litchfield, CT, 1805–06. POLIT. & GOV.: elected as a Democrat to SC State House, 1808–09; elected as a Democrat to U.S. House (SC), 1811–17; appointed U.S. sec. of war, 1817–25; ***candidate for Democratic nomination to presidency of the U.S., 1824, 1844, 1848; elected as a Democrat to vice presidency of the U.S., 1825–32 (resigned)***; elected as a Democrat to U.S. Senate (SC), 1832–44, 1845–50; appointed U.S. sec. of state, 1844–45. BUS. & PROF.: atty.; admitted to SC Bar, 1807; law practice, Abbeville, SC. MEM.: Phi Beta Kappa; South Western Convention (delegate). HON. DEG.: LL.D., Hamilton Coll., 1821; LL.D., Columbia U., 1825. WRITINGS: *A Disquisition on Government; A Discourse on the Constitution and Government of the U.S.; SC Exposition* (1828); *The Works* (1851–55). REL.: Presb. RES.: Fort Hill, SC.

CALLAHAN, JOHN FRANCIS. b. Dec 31, 1940, Meriden, CT; m. Susan E. Kirschner, 1970; c. one. EDUC.:

B.A., U. of CT, 1963; M.A., U. of IL, 1964, Ph.D., 1970. POLIT. & GOV.: candidate for Democratic nomination to U.S. House (OR), 1970; ***independent (Cmte. for a Constitutional Presidency) candidate for vice presidency of the U.S., 1976***; independent presidential elector, 1976, 1980. BUS. & PROF.: instructor in English, Lewis and Clark Coll., 1967–68; asst. prof., 1968–73, assoc. prof., 1973–; visiting assoc. prof., CA State U. at Hayward, 1970. MEM.: Modern Language Assn.; Northwest American Studies Assn. AWARDS: Younger Humanist Fellow, National Endowment for Humanities, 1973–74. WRITINGS: *The Illusions of a Nation: Myth And History in the Novels of F. Scott Fitzgerald* (1972). MAILING ADDRESS: 5207 S.W. Pomona St., Portland, OR.

CALLAHAN, JOHN M. b. Dec 16, 1865, Goldens Bridge, NY; d. May 10, 1956, Madison, WI; par. M. J. and Johanna (Walsh) Callahan; m. Minnie A. Powers, Sep 12, 1889; c. Gertrude Leona; Alice Beatrice (Mrs. H. S. Roswell); Julia Tormey. EDUC.: grad., high school, Prescott, WI; private tutors; received Unlimited State Certificate (WI), 1894. POLIT. & GOV.: superintendent of schools, Menasha, WI, 1901–18; appointed WI state dir. of vocational education, 1918–21; elected WI state superintendent of schools, 1921–29; delegate, Dem. Nat'l. Conv., 1924; ***candidate for Democratic nomination to presidency of the U.S., 1924***; Democratic candidate for U.S. Senate (WI), 1934. BUS. & PROF.: bricklayer; teacher, Spring Valley, WI, 1885–89; ward principal, Crookston (MN) Public Schools, 1889–90; supervising principal, public schools, Glenwood City, WI, 1890–98; supervising principal, public schools, New Richmond, WI, 1898–1901. MEM.: NEA; National Superintendents Assn.; National Soc. for Vocational Education; Madison Club; Rotary Club; Milwaukee City Club; WI Anti-Tuberculosis Assn. (pres., 1938–45); WI Education Assn.; American Vocational Assn.; WI Assn. of School Administrators; Elks. HON. DEG.: LL.D., U. of WI, 1950. REL.: R.C. RES.: Madison, WI.

CAMEJO, PETER MIGUEL. b. Dec 31, 1939, New York, NY; par. Daniel Camejo Octavio and Elvia Guanche Revenga; single. EDUC.: grad., Great Neck (NY) North Senior H.S., 1958; MA Inst. of Technology, 1958–61; U. of CA, Berkeley, CA, 1967–69. POLIT. & GOV.: National Committeeman, Socialist Workers Party, 1963–; Socialist Workers Party candidate for mayor of Berkeley, CA, 1967; elected to U. of CA Student Senate, c. 1968; Socialist Workers Party candidate for U.S. Senate (CA), 1968; Socialist Workers Party candidate for U.S. Senate (MA), 1970; ***Socialist Workers Party candidate for presidency of the U.S., 1976***; field organizer, Socialist Workers Party, Southwest, 1977–. BUS. & PROF.: organizer, Socialist Workers Party, 1967–; unskilled laborer; computer operator. MEM.: Young Socialist Alliance (national sec., 1962); NAACP; Fair Play for Cuba Cmte. (New England dir., 1960–61); Anti-War Student Mobilization Cmte. (member, National Coordinating Cmte.). WRITINGS: *How to Make a Revolution in the U.S.* (1969); *Why Guevara's Guerrilla Strategy Has No Future* (1972); *Who Killed Jim Crow?* (1975); *The Racist Offensive Against Busing; Racism, Revolution, Reaction: 1861–1877—The Rise and Fall of Radical Reconstruction* (1976); *Liberalism, Ultraleftism or Mass Action; The Lesser Evil? The Left Debates the Democratic Party and Social Change* (1978); *The Nicaraguan Revolution* (ed., 1979). REL.: atheist. MISC.: arrested several times for student and antiwar activism. MAILING ADDRESS: 1250 Wilshire Blvd., Los Angeles, CA 90017.

CAMERON, ANGUS. b. Jul 4, 1826, Caledonia, NY; d. Mar 30, 1897, La Crosse, WI; par. Duncan Angus and Sarah (McCall) Cameron; m. Mary Baker, Feb 21, 1856. EDUC.: Genesee Wesleyan Seminary; Geneseo Acad.; studied law in offices of Wadsworth and Cameron, Buffalo, NY, 1850; grad., National Law School, 1853. POLIT. & GOV.: elected as a Republican to WI State Senate, 1863–64, 1871–72; delegate, Rep. Nat'l. Conv., 1864; elected as a Republican to WI State House, 1866–67 (Speaker); elected as a Republican to U.S. Senate (WI), 1875–81, 1881–85; ***candidate for Republican nomination to vice presidency of the U.S., 1876***. BUS. & PROF.: schoolteacher; atty.; admitted to NY Bar, 1853; partner, Wadsworth and Cameron (law firm), Buffalo, NY, 1853–56; Banker, Cameron and Wing Banking House, Buffalo, NY, 1857; law practice, La Crosse, WI, 1857–97. MEM.: U. of WI (Regent, 1866–75). RES.: La Crosse, WI.

CAMERON, BRUCE J. POLIT. & GOV.: ***candidate for Libertarian Party nomination to presidency of the U.S., 1980***. MAILING ADDRESS: P.O. Box 32326, Phoenix, AZ 85064.

CAMERON, JAMES DONALD. b. May 14, 1833, Middletown, PA; d. Aug 30, 1918, Donegal Springs, PA; par. Simon (q.v.) and Margaret (Brua) Cameron; m. Mary McCormick, May 20, 1856; m. 2d, Elizabeth Sherman, May 9, 1879; c. Eliza (Mrs. Alexander Rogers); James McCormick; Mary; Margaretta (Mrs. John William Clark); Rachel (Mrs. Chandler Hale); Martha (Mrs. Ronald Lindsey). EDUC.: A.B., Coll. of NJ (now Princeton U.), 1852, A.M., 1855. POLIT. & GOV.: delegate, Rep. Nat'l. Conv., 1868, 1876, 1880; appointed U.S. sec. of war, 1876–77; elected as a Republican to U.S. Senate (PA), 1877–97; chm., Rep. Nat'l. Cmte., 1880–84; ***candidate for Republican nomination to presidency of the U.S., 1896***. BUS. & PROF.: clerk, cashier, pres., National Bank of Middletown, 1832–1918; pres., Northern Central R.R. Co. of PA, 1863–74; farmer. MEM.: NY Club. RES.: Harrisburg, PA.

CAMERON, SIMON. b. Mar 8, 1799, Lancaster, PA; d. Jun 26, 1889, Lancaster, PA; par. Charles and Martha (Pfoutz) Cameron; m. Margaretta Brua, Oct 16, 1822; c. James Donald (q.v.); William Brua; John Colin; Ann Eliza; Mary; James Buchanan; Simon; Rachel (Mrs. James Burnside); Virginia

Rolette (Mrs. Wade MacVeagh); Margaretta (Mrs. Richard S. Haldeman). POLIT. & GOV.: appointed state printer of PA, 1825–27; appointed adj. gen. of PA, 1826; appointed commissioner for Winnebago Indian claims, 1838; Democratic candidate for U.S. House (PA), 1838; elected as a Democrat to U.S. Senate (PA), 1845–49, as a Republican, 1857–61, 1867–77; candidate for Democratic nomination to U.S. Senate (PA), 1849, 1851; ***candidate for Republican nomination to vice presidency of the U.S., 1856, 1860***; leader, Republican Party of PA, 1857–77; ***candidate for Republican nomination to presidency of the U.S., 1860***; appointed U.S. sec. of war, 1861–62; appointed U.S. minister to Russia, 1862; Republican candidate for U.S. Senate (PA), 1863; delegate, Rep. Nat'l. Conv., 1864; delegate, Loyalist Convention, 1866. BUS. & PROF.: printer's apprentice; ed., *Bucks Cty. (PA) Messenger*, 1821; ed., Bucks Cty. Democrat, 1821; mgr., *Pennsylvania Intelligencer*, Harrisburg, PA, 1821; employee, Gales and Stratton (printing house), Washington, DC, 1822; owner, *Harrisburg Republican*, 1824; builder, North Central R.R.; founder, cashier, Bank of Middletown, 1832; iron manufacturer; insurance broker. WRITINGS: *The Political Issues and Duties of the Presidential Campaign Summed Up in a Few Words* (1860); *Speeches of Messrs. Cameron and Seward on the Tariff* (1860). REL.: Presb. RES.: Lancaster, PA.

CAMPBELL, ALEXANDER. b. Oct 4, 1814, Concord, PA; d. Aug 8, 1898, La Salle, IL. EDUC.: public schools. POLIT. & GOV.: elected as a Whig to mayor of La Salle, IL, 1852–58; elected as a Republican to IL State House, 1858–59; elected as a Unionist, delegate, IL State Constitutional Convention, 1862; independent candidate for U.S. House (IL), 1870; elected as an independent to U.S. House (IL), 1875–77; National Democratic candidate for U.S. House (IL), 1876, 1878; Greenback Party candidate for U.S. Senate (IL), 1879; ***candidate for Greenback Party nomination to presidency of the U.S., 1876, 1880, 1884***; presidential elector, Greenback Party, 1880. BUS. & PROF.: clerk, Lyon, Short and Co. (iron works), 1834–40; superintendent, Juniata Forge (iron works), PA, 1840–44; mgr., Mill Creek Furnace, PA, 1844–46; mgr., Potomac Furnace, Loudon Cty., VA, 1846; mgr., Greenup Furnace, KY, 1846–48; superintendent, Madison Iron and Milling Co., Pilot Knob, MO, 1848–49; superintendent, Stella Iron Works, Maramac, MO, 1850; owner, General Land Agency, La Salle, IL, 1851–98; coal prospector. WRITINGS: *Address to Congress* (1861); *The True American System of Finance* (1864); *The True Greenback* (1868). MISC.: known as "The Father of the Greenback Party." RES.: La Salle, IL.

CAMPBELL, GILBERT. b. Nov 23, 1947, Los Alamos, NM; par. Gilbert L. and Lollie Griffin (Watrous) Campbell; m. Carmen Aida Yurrita; c. none. EDUC.: Fort Lewis Coll.; B.S., U. of CO, 1972. POLIT. & GOV.: ***Everybody for President candidate for presidency of the U.S., 1984***. BUS. & PROF.: journalist; educational consultant; youth counselor; photographer; printer; author; political activist. WRITINGS: *Sex is the Root of All Evil* (1964); *I'll Never Forget Whats-Her-Name* (1965); *Everybody for President* (1984). MISC.: candidate for Student Senate, Fort Lewis Coll., 1966. MAILING ADDRESS: 2034 Pearl St., Boulder, CO 80302.

CAMPBELL, JAMES EDWIN. b. Jul 7, 1843, Middletown, OH; d. Dec 18, 1924, Columbus, OH; par. Dr. Andrew and Laura P. (Reynolds) Campbell; m. Elizabeth Owens, Jan 4, 1870; c. four. EDUC.: Miami U., Oxford, OH; studied law. POLIT. & GOV.: appointed deputy collector of internal revenue for OH, 1863; elected as a Democrat, prosecuting atty., Butler Cty., OH, 1876–80; Democratic candidate for U.S. House (OH), 1882, 1906; elected as a Democrat to U.S. House (OH), 1884–89; elected as a Democrat to gov. of OH, 1890–92; delegate, Dem. Nat'l. Conv., 1892, 1920, 1924; Democratic candidate for gov. of OH, 1891, 1895; ***candidate for Democratic nomination to presidency of the U.S., 1892, 1986, 1916, 1920, 1924***; appointed member, Comm. to Codify the Laws of OH, 1908–11. BUS. & PROF.: atty.; admitted to OH Bar, 1865; law practice, Hamilton, OH, 1867; law practice, Columbus, OH. MIL.: U.S. Army, 1863; master's mate, MS Squadron, U.S. Navy, 1863–64. REL.: Presb. RES.: Columbus, OH.

CAMPBELL, LEWIS DAVIS. b. Aug 9, 1811, Franklin, OH; d. Nov 26, 1882, Hamilton, OH; par. Samuel and Mary (Small) Campbell; m. Jane H. Reily; c. three daughters. POLIT. & GOV.: Whig candidate for U.S. House (OH), 1840, 1842, 1844, 1858; elected as a Whig to U.S. House (OH), 1849–58; ***candidate for American (Know-Nothing) Party nomination to presidency of the U.S., 1856***; delegate, Union Convention, 1866; delegate, Soldiers' Convention, 1866; appointed U.S. minister to Mexico, 1866–67; elected as a Democrat to OH State Senate, 1869–70; elected as a Democrat to U.S. House (OH), 1871–73; pres., OH State Constitutional Convention, 1873. BUS. & PROF.: apprentice printer, *Cincinnati (OH) Gazette*, 1828–31; publisher, *Hamilton (OH) Intelligencer*, 1831–35; atty.; admitted to OH Bar, 1835; law practice, Hamilton, OH, 1835–50. MIL.: col., 69th Regt., OH Volunteers, 1861–62. RES.: Hamilton, OH.

CAMPS, WILLIAM ALLEN. b. 1945; c. Cira J. Camps. POLIT. & GOV.: ***Pan-American Party candidate for presidency of the U.S., 1984***. BUS. & PROF.: real estate investor. MAILING ADDRESS: 219 East Craig, San Antonio, TX 78212.

CANNON, JOSEPH GURNEY. b. May 7, 1836, Guilford, NC; d. Nov 12, 1926, Danville, IL; par. Dr. Horace Franklin and Gulielma (Hollingsworth) Cannon; m. Mary Pamela Reed, Jan 1862; c. Mabel (Mrs. Ernest X. LeSuere); Helen; infant son. EDUC.: studied law under John P. Usher, Terre Haute, IN; Cincinnati Law School. POLIT. & GOV.: elected state's atty., 27th Judicial District of IL, 1861–68; Republican candidate for U.S. House (IL), 1870, 1890, 1912; elected as a Republican to U.S. House (IL), 1873–91, 1893–1913 (Speaker, 1903–11), 1915–23; ***candidate for Republican nomination to vice presidency of the U.S., 1896***; chm., Rep. Nat'l. Conv., 1904; ***candidate for Republican nomination to presidency of the U.S., 1908***. BUS. & PROF.: atty.; admitted to IL Bar, 1858; law practice, Terre Haute, IN, 1858; law practice, Tuscola, IL, 1859–78; law practice, Danville, IL, 1878–1926; founder, dir., Second National Bank of Danville. HON. DEG.: LL.D., U. of IL, 1903. MISC.: known as "Uncle Joe" Cannon. REL.: Methodist Episcopal Church (nee Soc. of Friends). RES.: Danville, IL.

CAPLETTE, RAYMOND JOSEPH. b. Oct 30, 1932, Webster, MA; par. Joseph Henry Rudolph and Laura (Morris) Caplette; m. Alene Marie Sanders (divorced, 1954, 1972); c. Raelene; Kim; Michelle; Joseph; Sherri; Jaqi. EDUC.: A.A., L.A. Pierce Coll.; diploma in hypnotherapy; Northridge Coll., 1953. POLIT. & GOV.: candidate for Democratic nomination to U.S. Senate (CA), 1982; ***candidate for Democratic nomination to presidency of the U.S., 1984, 1992***. BUS. & PROF.: machinist. MIL.: sgt., U.S.M.C., 1949–53. MEM.: Your Heritage Assn.; Viet Nam Original Kung Fu International Assn. REL.: R.C. MAILING ADDRESS: 8000 Owensmouth Ave., Canoga Park, CA 91304.

CAPPELLA-PETERS, CLARISSA. POLIT. & GOV.: ***independent candidate for presidency of the U.S., 1980; candidate for Republican nomination to presidency of the U.S., 1988***. MAILING ADDRESS: 116-36 St., Nederland, TX 77627.

CAPPER, ARTHUR. b. Jul 14, 1865, Garnett, KS; d. Dec 19, 1951, Topeka, KS; par. Herbert and Isabelle (McGrew) Capper; m. Florence Crawford, Dec 1, 1892; c. none. EDUC.: grad., high school, Garnett, KS, 1884. POLIT. & GOV.: delegate, Rep. Nat'l. Conv., 1908; pres., Board of Regents, KS Agricultural Coll., 1910–13; candidate for Republican nomination to gov. of KS, 1912; elected as a Republican to gov. of KS, 1915–19; elected as a Republican to U.S. Senate (KS), 1919–49; ***candidate for Republican nomination to presidency of the U.S., 1924, 1940***. BUS. & PROF.: publisher; owner, WIBW (radio station), Topeka, KS; owner, KCKN (radio station), Kansas City, KS; compositor, *Topeka Daily Capitol*, 1884, publisher and owner, 1892–1951; publisher, owner, *Capper's Weekly*; publisher, owner, *Kansas Farmer*; publisher, owner, *Household Magazine;* publisher, owner, *Capper's Farmer;* publisher, owner, *Missouri Ruralist*; publisher, owner, *Ohio Farmer;* publisher, owner, *Pennsylvania Farmer*; publisher, owner, *Michigan Farmer;* publisher, owner, *Kansas City Kansan*; publisher, owner, *Poultry Culture;* publisher, owner, *Rural Trade;* dir., Farmers National Bank of Topeka. MEM.: International Farmers Congress (pres., 1919); Red Cross (member, National Board); 4-H Clubs (dir.); BSA (National Council); Masons; Shriners; Moose; Independent Order of Odd Fellows; Elks; Workmen; Topeka Club; National Press Club; Capper Foundation for Crippled Children (founder); Goodfellows Club of Topeka (founder); Topeka Provident Assn. (dir.); YMCA (dir.); National Municipal League; National Soc. for Crippled Children; NY Advertising Club; Modern Woodmen of America; Knights of Pythias; Sigma Delta Chi; World's Christian Endeavor Union; American Bible Soc.; American Businessmen's Research Foundation; KS Editorial Assn. (pres., 1913); Royal Neighbors; Rotary Club. REL.: Christian. RES.: Topeka, KS.

CARDENAS, TOM. POLIT. & GOV.: ***candidate for Democratic nomination to presidency of the U.S., 1984***. MAILING ADDRESS: 2809 Whitley Ave., Corcoran, CA 93212.

CAREY, DENNIS BARKER. POLIT. & GOV.: ***independent candidate for presidency of the U.S., 1992***. BUS. & PROF.: skilled tradesman; political analyst; soldier. MISC.: self-styled member of African American Evolutionary Army. MAILING ADDRESS: 2601 Harding, Detroit, MI 48214.

CAREY, HENRY CHARLES. b. Dec 15, 1793, Philadelphia, PA; d. Oct 13, 1879, Philadelphia, PA; par. Matthew Carey; m. sister of C. R. Leslie. POLIT. & GOV.: ***candidate for Republican nomination to vice presidency of the U.S., 1856***; delegate, PA State Constitutional Convention, 1872. BUS. & PROF.: economist; publisher; partner, Carey, Lea, and Carey (publishing house), Philadelphia, PA, 1817–21, pres., 1821–35. WRITINGS: *The Rates of Wages* (1835); *Principles of Political Economy* (1837–40); *The Credit System in France, Great Britain and the U.S.* (1838); *Commercial Associations in France and England* (1845); *Past, Present and Future* (1848); *Harmony of Interests: Manufacturing and Commercial* (1851); *Slave Trade, Domestic and Foreign* (1853); *Letters to the President* (1858); *The Principles of Social Science* (1858–59); *Miscellaneous Works* (1869); *French and American Tariffs; Unity of Law* (1872). REL.: R.C. MISC.: leader of American Nationalist School of Economics; converted to protectionist doctrines, 1844. RES.: Philadelphia, PA.

CAREY, HUGH LEO. b. Apr 11, 1919, Brooklyn, NY; par. Dennis J. and Margaret (Collins) Carey; m. Helen Owen, Feb 27, 1947; m. 2d, Evangeline Gouletas, Apr 11, 1981; c. Alexandria; Christopher; Susan; Peter; Hugh Leo, Jr.; Michael; Donald; Marianne; Nancy; Helen; Bryan; Paul; Kevin; Thomas. EDUC.: LL.B., St. John's Coll., 1951. POLIT. & GOV.: elected as a Democrat to U.S. House (NY), 1960–75; delegate, Interparliamentary Union Conference, 1961; elected as a Democrat to gov. of NY, 1975–83; delegate, Democratic Mid-Term Conference, 1974; ***candidate for Democratic nomination to presidency of the U.S., 1976, 1980***. BUS. & PROF.: atty.; admitted to NY Bar, 1951; admitted to the Bar of the Supreme Court of the U.S., 1963; law practice, Brooklyn, NY; vice pres., Peerless Oil and Chemical Corp.; dir., Peerless Chemical of Puerto Rico. MIL.: maj., U.S. Army, WWII; lt. col., U.S.A.R.; Bronze Star; Combat Infantry Award; Croix De Guerre with Silver Star;

Knight of the Order of the Holy Sepulchre of Jerusalem. MEM.: BSA (Finance Council); VFW; American Legion; Catholic War Veterans; Knights of Columbus; Emerald Assn. (dir.); Phi Delta Phi; Cathedral Club (dir.); Boys League School; Gallaudet Coll. for the Deaf (dir.); National Democratic Club (gov.); Young Democrats of NY (chm., 1946); U.S. Merchant Marine Acad. (member, Board of Visitors); Friendly Sons of St. Patrick; Ancient Order of Hibernians; Sales Executive Club; Galway Men's Assn. (hon.); National Conference of Christians and Jews; Marymount Coll. (dir.); St. Vincent's Home for Boys (dir.); Salesman's Assn. of the American Chemical Industry. AWARDS: Man of the Year Award, NY State Federation of Citizens for Educational Freedom, 1964. HON. DEG.: LL.D., St. John's Coll., 1967; LL.D., Canisius Coll.; LL.D., Yeshiva U.; LL.D., Long Island U.; LL.D., Villanova U.; LL.D., Polytechnical Inst. of NY. REL.: R.C. MAILING ADDRESS: 61 Prospect Park West, Brooklyn, NY 11215.

CAREY, JAMES F. b. Aug 19, 1867, Haverhill, MA; d. Jul 1914; m. Clara Louise Stevens. EDUC.: public schools. POLIT. & GOV.: pres., Labor Party Convention, Haverhill, 1892; People's Party candidate for local office, Haverhill, 1894; delegate, Socialist Labor Party National Convention, 1896; Socialist Labor Party candidate for mayor of Haverhill, 1896, 1897; elected as a Socialist Labor Party member, pres., Haverhill Common Council, 1897; founder, Social Democratic Party, 1898; elected as a Social Democrat to MA State House, 1898–1903; Social Democratic Party candidate for MA State House, 1903; Socialist Party candidate for U.S. House (MA), 1904, 1910; national organizer, Socialist Party; Socialist Party candidate for gov. of MA, 1905, 1906, 1908, 1911, 1912 (declined); member, Socialist Party National Cmte., 1908–11; ***candidate for Socialist Party nomination to presidency of the U.S., 1908 (withdrew)***; presidential elector, Socialist Party (MA), 1912; MA state sec., Socialist Party, 1912; chm., Socialist Party National Convention, 1912; Socialist Party candidate for Haverhill City Council, 1912; appointed MA state commissioner of the unemployed (not confirmed by State Senate); Workers Party candidate for U.S. Senate (PA), 1926. BUS. & PROF.: shoemaker; labor organizer. MEM.: Nationalist Club; AFL (delegate, National Convention, 1898); National Boot and Shoemakers' Union (founder; chm., National Convention, 1895, at which three shoemakers' organizations merged); International Boot and Shoemakers' Union. WRITINGS: *Society's Right to Land and Capital* (1899); *Child Labor* (1899); *Debate on Socialism Held at Faneuil Hall* (with Frederick J. Stimson, 1903); "Socialism: The Creed of Despair" (debate with George B. Hugo, 1909); "The Menace of Socialism" (debate with Thomas I. Gasson, 1911). REL.: Unitarian. MISC.: one of three leaders of unemployment agitation on Boston Common, 1894. RES.: Haverhill, MA.

CAREY, VINCENT J. POLIT. & GOV.: Right to Life Party candidate for U.S. House (NY), 1970; ***Right to Life Party candidate for presidency of the U.S., 1976***. MAILING ADDRESS: 1123 Little Neck Ave., North Bellmore, NY 11710.

CARLISLE, JOHN GRIFFIN. b. Sep 5, 1835, Campbell Cty., KY; d. Jul 31, 1910, New York, NY; par. L. H. and Mary A. (Reynolds) Carlisle; m. Mary Jane Goodson, Jan 15, 1857; c. John Griffin, Jr.; William Kinkead; Libbon Logan. EDUC.: public schools; studied law under J. W. Stevenson and W. B. Kinkead. POLIT. & GOV.: elected as a Democrat to KY State House, 1859–61; presidential elector, Democratic Party, 1864 (declined), 1876 (alternate); Democratic candidate for KY State Senate, 1865; elected as a Democrat to KY State Senate, 1867–71; delegate, Dem. Nat'l. Conv., 1868; elected as a Democrat to lt. gov. of KY, 1871–75; elected as a Democrat to U.S. House (KY), 1877–90 (Speaker, 1883–89); ***candidate for Democratic nomination to presidency of the U.S., 1884, 1892, 1896***; elected as a Democrat to U.S. Senate (KY), 1890–93; appointed U.S. sec. of the treasury, 1893–97. BUS. & PROF.: schoolteacher, Covington, KY; atty.; admitted to KY Bar, 1858; law practice, Covington, KY, 1858–97; ed., *Louisville (KY) Daily Ledger*, 1872; law practice, New York, NY, 1897–1910. MEM.: Anti-Imperialist League of Boston (vice pres.); Southern Soc.; Manhattan Club. RES.: Covington, KY.

CARLSON, ERNEST JOEL. b. Jan 8, 1908, Aspen, CO; par. Charley and Edla (Huren) Carlson; m. Ellen Duncan (divorced); c. two sons. EDUC.: grad., Kansas City Coll. of Osteopathic Medicine, 1932; intern, Stone Memorial Hospital, Carthage, MO; intern, East Town Hospital, Dallas, TX. POLIT. & GOV.: candidate for Republican nomination to CO State House, 1976; candidate for Republican nomination to gov. of CO, 1978; ***candidate for Republican nomination to presidency of the U.S., 1980***. BUS. & PROF.: osteopathic physician; cty. physician, Park Cty., CO, 1959–62; clinical medical practice, Fairplay, CO; lobbyist, Constitutional Government Associates, 1975. MEM.: Lincoln Club of CO; National Osteopathic Assn.; CO State Osteopathic Assn. WRITINGS: *Healing Power of God: The Synthesis of Medical Methods* (1966). REL.: Protestant. MAILING ADDRESS: Auditorium Hotel, #231, 1406 Stout St., Denver, CO 80202.

CARLSON, FRANK. b. Jan 23, 1893, Concordia, KS; d. May 30, 1987, Concordia, KS; par. Charles E. and Anna (Johnson) Carlson; m. Alice Fredrickson, Aug 26, 1919; c. Millard E. Ross (foster son); Eunice Marie (Mrs. Ed Rolfs). EDUC.: Concordia Normal and Business Coll.; KS State Coll. POLIT. & GOV.: elected as a Republican to KS State House, 1929–33; chm., KS State Republican Cmte., 1932–34; elected as a Republican to U.S. House (KS), 1935–47; elected as a Republican to gov. of KS, 1947–50; appointed member, Hoover Comm. on the Reorganization of Government; chm., Interstate Oil Compact Comm., 1949; vice chm., President's National Safety Conference, 1950; elected as a Republican to U.S. Senate (KS),

1950–69; appointed U.S. delegate to the U.N.; ***candidate for Republican nomination to presidency of the U.S., 1968***. BUS. & PROF.: farmer, Concordia; stockman, 1914–87. MIL.: pvt., U.S. Army, 1918–19. MEM.: American Legion; Masons (33°); Farm Bureau; National Governors' Conference (chm., 1949); Council of State Governments (chm., 1950); International Council of Christian Leadership; Menninger Foundation; Inst. of Logopedics. AWARDS: elected to Agricultural Hall of Fame, 1964. HON. DEG.: LL.D., Bob Jones U., 1951; LL.D., Springfield Coll., 1953; LL.D., William Jewell Coll., 1955; LL.D., St. Benedict's Coll., 1961; LL.D., KS State U., 1962; LL.D., Baker U.; LL.D., Southwestern U.; LL.D., Ottawa U. REL.: Bapt. RES.: Concordia, KS.

CARLSON, GRACE MARIE HOLMES. b. Nov 13, 1906, St. Paul, MN; d. Jul 7, 1992, Madison, WI; par. James A. and Mary J. (Nuebel) Holmes; m. Gilbert E. Carlson, Jul 28, 1934; c. none. EDUC.: B.A., Coll. of St. Catherine, St. Paul, 1929; M.A., U. of MN, 1930, Ph.D., 1933. POLIT. & GOV.: charter member, Socialist Workers Party, 1938; Socialist Workers Party candidate for U.S. Senate (MN), 1940 (Trotskyite Anti-War), 1942, 1946; Socialist Workers Party candidate for mayor of St. Paul, MN, 1942; ***Socialist Workers Party candidate for vice presidency of the U.S., 1948***; Socialist Workers Party candidate for U.S. House (MN), 1950. BUS. & PROF.: teaching asst., lecturer in psychology, U. of MN, 1930–35; vocational rehabilitation counselor, MN State Dept. of Education, 1935–40; organizer, lecturer, Socialist Workers Party, 1940–52; personal sec., St. Mary's Hospital, Minneapolis, MN, 1952–55; instructor in psychology and communications, St. Mary's School of Nursing, Minneapolis, MN, 1955–64; prof., St. Mary's Junior Coll., 1964–79. MEM.: Sigma Xi; Pi Lamda Theta; American Psych. Assn. (assoc., 1932; member, 1958); AAUP; Common Cause; MN Psych. Assn.; Acad. of Religion and Mental Health. REL.: R.C. MISC.: only woman among 18 members of the Socialist Workers Party imprisoned for violating the Smith Act, 1943–45. RES.: Minneapolis, MN.

CARLSON, WILLIAM EDWARD. b. 1938; m. Donna Carlson; c. two. EDUC.: grad., high school. POLIT. & GOV.: candidate for Sebring (FL) City Council, 1973; ***candidate for Republican nomination to presidency of the U.S., 1980***. BUS. & PROF.: owner, White's Auto and Home Supply Store #695, Sebring, FL; employee, Trailways. MAILING ADDRESS: 624 Tases-Chee, Sebring, FL 33870.

CARMACK, EDWARD WARD. b. Nov 5, 1858, Castilian Springs, TN; d. Nov 9, 1908, Nashville, TN; par. F. M. and Catherine Carmack; m. Elizabeth Cobey Dunnington, Apr 1890. EDUC.: Webb School, Culleska, TN; Jacinto Acad.; studied law. POLIT. & GOV.: city atty., Columbia, TN, 1881; elected as a Democrat to TN State House, 1884; delegate, Dem. Nat'l. Conv., 1896, 1900, 1904; elected as a Democrat to U.S. House (TN), 1897–1901; elected as a Democrat to U.S. Senate (TN), 1901–07; ***candidate for Democratic nomination to vice presidency of the U.S., 1904***; Democratic candidate for U.S. Senate (TN), 1906; candidate for Democratic nomination to gov. of TN, 1908. BUS. & PROF.: ed., *Columbia Herald;* atty.; admitted to TN Bar, 1879; law practice, Columbia; editorial staff, editor-in-chief, *Nashville American*, 1886–88; founder, *Nashville Democrat*, 1888; ed., *Memphis (TN) Commercial-Appeal*, 1892–96. REL.: Christian (Campbellite). MISC.: murdered by Duncan B. and Robin Cooper, Nov 9, 1908. RES.: Memphis, TN.

CARMODY, STEPHEN. POLIT. & GOV.: ***candidate for Democratic nomination to presidency of the U.S., 1980***. MAILING ADDRESS: Apt. 2A, 880 Grove St., Haddonfield, NJ 08031.

CARNEY, CHARLES JOSEPH. b. Apr 17, 1913, Youngstown, OH; d. Oct. 7, 1987, Youngstown, OH; par. Michael G. and Florence Grogan (Grimm) Carney; m. Mary Lucille Manning, Nov 12, 1938; c. Mary Ellen (Mrs. John Leshinsky); Ann (Mrs. James Murphy). EDUC.: grad., Memorial H.S., Campbell, OH; Youngstown State U., 3 years. POLIT. & GOV.: elected as a Democrat to OH State Senate, 1950–70 (minority leader, 1969–70); elected as a Democrat to U.S. House (OH), 1971–79; ***candidate for Democratic nomination to presidency of the U.S., 1976***; Democratic candidate for U.S. House (OH), 1978. BUS. & PROF.: labor leader. MEM.: United Rubber Workers Union (pres., Local 102; pres., District Council 1, 1940–43; staff representative and district dir., 1942–50); United Steelworkers of America (staff representative, 1950–68); Knights of Columbus; Mahonning Cty. CIO Industrial Council; Farm Grange; Elks; Moose; Eagles; Youngstown Catholic Service League; Mahonning Cty. CIO (trustee). HON. DEG.: H.H.D., Central State U. of OH, 1959; LL.D., Coll. of Osteopathic Medicine and Surgery, 1972. REL.: R.C. RES.: Youngstown, OH.

CARPENTER-SWAIN, FAY TURNER (aka FIFI CARPENTER-SWAIN; PRINCESS RUNNING WATERS RED LEGS SAINT SWANEE; H.R.H. FIFI C. T. ROCKEFELLER; PRINCESS FIFI 3 TAFT $ (CASH) (p) PICKWILDLIFE RUNNING WATERS ROCKEFELLER). b. Nov 26, 1915, IL; m. 2d, John R. Walters Clay; m. 3d, Guy W. Rockefeller (q.v.); c. six. POLIT. & GOV.: ***candidate for Democratic nomination to presidency of the U.S., 1956, 1960, 1964, 1968, 1972, 1976, 1980; candidate for Democratic nomination to vice presidency of the U.S., 1964, 1976***; candidate for Democratic nomination to U.S. House (KY), 1974; candidate for Democratic nomination to gov. of IN, 1978; candidate for Democratic nomination to gov. of KY, 1983. BUS. & PROF.: leader, artist colony, Denison, IL; self-styled

Indian "Native American" princess. REL.: Bapt. MAILING ADDRESS: Flannery Hotel, 405 Garrard St., Covington, KY 41011.

CARR, BILLIE J. b. Jun 1, 1928, Houston, TX; d. William Brooks and Irene (Martin) McClain; m. Mr. Carr (divorced); c. David Brooks; Billy Brooks; Michael Lloyd; Marshal Bokie; Debra (Mrs. La Croix). EDUC.: U. of Houston, 1946–48, 1971. POLIT. & GOV.: member, Harris Cty. (TX) Democratic Central Cmte., 1954–72 (political organizer, 1954–); member, TX State Democratic Central Cmte., 1964–66, 1972–; cochairperson, McGovern-Shriver Campaign, 1972; member, Dem. Nat'l. Cmte., 1972–; delegate, Dem. Nat'l. Conv., 1976; ***candidate for Democratic nomination to presidency of the U.S., 1984***. BUS. & PROF.: political activist; pres., Billie Carr and Associates, Inc., Houston, TX. MEM.: National Forensic League (life member); National Women's Political Caucus; A.C.L.U.; Common Cause; Americans for Democratic Action; National New Democratic Coalition (cochair, 1975–). WRITINGS: *How to Do It or Organizing a Precinct Can Be Fun* (1969); *Billie Carr's 1983 Harris Cty. Political Directory* (1983). MAILING ADDRESS: 2418 Travis, Suite 3, Houston, TX 77006.

CARR, JULIAN SHAKESPEARE. b. Oct 12, 1845, Chapel Hill, NC; d. Apr 29, 1924, Chicago, IL; par. John Wesley and Eliza Pannel (Bullock) Carr; m. Nannie Graham Parrish, Feb 17, 1873; c. Eliza Morehead (Mrs. Henry Corwin Flower); Lala Ruth (Mrs. William F. Patton); Julian Shakespeare, Jr.; Albert Marvin; Claiborn McDowell; Austin Heaton. EDUC.: grad., U. of NC. POLIT. & GOV.: pres. of the board, Durham (NC) Public Library; elected as a Democrat to NC State House; delegate, Dem. Nat'l. Conv., 1920 and 13 other times; candidate for Democratic nomination to gov. of NC, 1896 (withdrew); ***candidate for Democratic nomination to vice presidency of the U.S., 1900***; volunteer aide, federal food administrator, 1917–19. BUS. & PROF.: manufacturer; pres., Blackwell Durham Tobacco Co., to 1904; pres., First National Bank of Durham; pres., Ormond Mining Co.; vice pres., NC Joint Stock Bank; pres., dir., Durham Hosiery Mills; vice pres., Southern Immigration Land and Title Co.; pres., Southern Manganese Co.; vice pres., Durham Fertilizer Co.; pres., Golden Belt Manufacturing Co.; owner, Occoneechee Farm; pres., NC Bessemer Co.; pres., Durham and Roxboro R.R. Co.; pres., Durham and Charlotte R.R. Co.; pres., Durham Electric Light Co.; pres., Commonwealth Cotton Factory; vice pres., Durham Cotton Manufacturing Co.; vice pres., Greensboro Blast Furnace Co. MIL.: pvt., Barringer's Brigade, Hampton's Corps, Company K, Third NC Cavalry, C.S.A., Civil War. MEM.: NC Children's Home (trustee); Methodist Orphanage (trustee); Greensboro Woman's Coll. (trustee); Training School for Colored People (trustee); U. of NC (trustee); Trinity Coll. (trustee); NC Colored Normal School (dir.); Oxford Orphan Asylum (dir.); Battle Abbey (pres.); Masons; Zeta Psi; American U. (trustee); Old Ladies' Home (trustee); Confederate Home for Women (trustee); Coll. for Colored People, Augusta, GA (trustee); Methodist Chautauqua, Junaluska, NC (trustee); Confederate Soldiers' Home (pres.); United Confederate Veterans (maj. gen., NC Div.; commander in chief; lt. gen., Army of Northern VA; hon. commander in chief for life). REL.: Methodist (delegate, Ecumenical Methodist Conference, London, England, 1881; delegate, Robert Raikes Sunday School Centennial, 1878). RES.: Durham, NC.

CARRIER, FLOYD C. d. after 1945, CA. EDUC.: Yale U., 1943. POLIT. & GOV.: ***Prohibition Party candidate for vice presidency of the U.S., 1944 (declined)***. BUS. & PROF.: physician; minister, Seventh-Day Adventist Church; temperance advocate; gen. sec., American Temperance Soc., Seventh-Day Adventist Church, Washington, DC, 1942–45; divested of ministerial credentials, Seventh-Day Adventist Church, 1945. REL.: Seventh-Day Adventist (member, exec. cmte., IN Conference, 1937; minister, Pacific Union Conference, to 1942; delegate, Education and Missionary Volunteer Council, Boulder, CO, 1943; member, Coll. of Medical Evangelists, CA, 1944; member, Central CA Conference, 1944–45; member, General Conference, 1942–45). MAILING ADDRESS: Arlington, CA.

CARRIS, ALVIN GLEN. b. Oct 12, 1907, Sterling, KS; m. Eunice Carris, Aug 19, 1948; c. Alvin Glen, Jr.; six others. POLIT. & GOV.: ***candidate for Republican nomination to presidency of the U.S., 1980, 1984***. BUS. & PROF.: notary public; pilot, 1932–; refrigerator repairman; farmer, Baca Cty., CO; employee, Beech Aircraft, Wichita, KS; mechanic, Indian Motorcycle Shop, Wichita; employee, Stearman Aircraft, Wichita; employee, Boeing Aircraft, Wichita; aircraft inspector, Cessna Aircraft, Wichita; hearing aid salesman; farmer, MO, 1949; grocer, Alden, KS; insurance agent; securities dealer; grocer, Pawnee Rock, KS. MIL.: flying instructor, U.S.A.A.C., 1942–44. MEM.: OX5 Aviation Pioneer Club of America; NRA; American Legion. MAILING ADDRESS: Box 278, Pawnee Rock, KS 67567.

CARROLL, GEORGE WASHINGTON. b. Apr 11, 1855, Mansfield, LA; d. Dec 14, 1935, Beaumont, TX; par. Frank L. and Sarah (Long) Carroll; m. Underhill Mixon, 1877; c. George Washington, Jr.; Charles; Lee; infant. EDUC.: private schools, Pleasant Hill, LA. POLIT. & GOV.: elected alderman, Beaumont, TX, 10 years (pres.); Prohibition Party candidate for gov. of TX, 1902; ***Prohibition Party candidate for vice presidency of the U.S., 1904***; chm., Beaumont (TX) Democratic Central Cmte., 1935. BUS. & PROF.: capitalist; clerk, gen. mgr., vice pres., Long and Co. (subsequently Beaumont Lumber Co.), Beaumont, TX, 1874–1902; pres., Yellow Pine Oil Co.; pres., dir., Gladys City Oil, Gas and Manufacturing Co., 1892; pres., Atlantic Rice Mills Co.; dir., Beaumont, Sour Lake and Western R.R.; vice pres., Park Bank and Trust Co.; dir., Nona Mills Co.; dir., Beaumont National Bank; vice pres., dir., Commercial National Bank; owner, *Baptist Standard;* philanthropist. MEM.: Hoo Hoo Club; Anti-Saloon League (TX exec. board);

YMCA (pres., 1893; dir., to 1922; life dir., pres. emeritus, 1927). REL.: Bapt. (deacon). MISC.: made substantial donations to YMCA, Baptist Church, and Baylor U. RES.: Beaumont, TX.

CARROLL, JAMES MICHAEL "MIKE." POLIT. & GOV.: ***independent candidate for presidency of the U.S., 1992***. MAILING ADDRESS: P.O. Box 518, Madison, MS 39130.

CARROLL, JERRY LEON. m. Anita Rae Carroll. POLIT. & GOV.: ***independent candidate for presidency of the U.S., 1980, 1984, 1988, 1992***. MAILING ADDRESS: 3568 East Mariposa Rd., #5, Stockton, CA 95205.

CARROLL, PAUL A. b. 1902. EDUC.: D.D.S., Cincinnati Coll. of Dental Surgery, 1927. POLIT. & GOV.: ***candidate for Populist Party nomination to vice presidency of the U.S., 1984; Populist Party of OH candidate for presidency of the U.S., 1984***. BUS. & PROF.: dentist, general practice, Cincinnati, OH. MEM.: American Dental Assn. (life member). MAILING ADDRESS: 2808 Erie Ave., Cincinnati, OH 45208.

CARSKADON, THOMAS ROSABAUM. b. May 17, 1837, Sheetz's Mill, VA (now Headsville, WV); d. Jan 21, 1905, Keyser, WV; m. Sarah J. Babb, 1858; c. Thomas Reynolds. POLIT. & GOV.: appointed U.S. assessor, Second WV District, 1861–66; delegate, WV State Constitutional Convention, 1862; presidential elector, Republican Party, 1868, 1872, 1876; member, WV Republican State Central Cmte., 1885; Prohibition Party candidate for gov. of WV, 1888, 1900; member, Prohibition Party National Cmte., 1892–1905 (exec. cmte.); ***candidate for Prohibition Party nomination to vice presidency of the U.S., 1892, 1900***. BUS. & PROF.: farmer, Keyser, 1858–1905; orator; abolitionist; author; temperance advocate. MEM.: Prohibition National Bureau; National Farmers' Alliance and Industrial Union (delegate, National Convention, 1890). WRITINGS: *Silos and Ensilage*. REL.: Methodist Episcopal Church (delegate, General Conference, 1876). MISC.: known as "The Lincoln of WV." RES.: Keyser, WV.

CARTER, JAMES EARL "JIMMY," JR. b. Oct 1, 1924, Archery, GA; par. James Earl and Lillie (Gordy) Carter; m. Rosalyn Smith, Jul 7, 1946; c. John William; James Earl III; Donnel Jeffrey; Amy Lynn. EDUC.: GA Southwestern U., 1941–42; GA Inst. of Technology, 1942–43; B.S., U.S. Naval Acad., 1947; Union Coll., 1952. POLIT. & GOV.: elected to Sumpter Cty. (GA) School Board, 1955–62 (chm., 1960–62); appointed member, Americus and Sumpter Cty. (GA) Hospital authority, 1956–70; appointed member, Sumpter Cty. (GA) Library Board, 1961; elected as a Democrat to GA State Senate, 1963–67; pres., West Central GA Area Planning and Development Comm., 1964; candidate for Democratic nomination to gov. of GA, 1966; elected as a Democrat to gov. of GA, 1971–75; ***candidate for Democratic nomination to vice presidency of the U.S., 1972; elected as a Democrat to presidency of the U.S., 1977–81; Democratic candidate for presidency of the U.S., 1980***. BUS. & PROF.: farmer, Plains, GA; owner, peanut farm and warehouse, Plains, 1953–; pres., Plains Development Corp., 1963; lobbyist, GA Milk Producers, Inc., 1975. MIL.: lt., U.S. Navy, 1947–53. MEM.: Lions (district gov., 1968–69); GA Crop Improvement Assn. (dir., 1957–63; pres., 1961); GA Planning Assn. (pres., 1968); March of Dimes (state chm., 1968–70). AWARDS: Gold Medal, International Inst. for Human Rights, 1979; International Mediation Medal, American Arbitration Assn., 1979; Martin Luther King Jr. Non-Violent Peace Prize, 1979. HON. DEG.: LL.D., Morris Brown Coll., 1972; LL.D., Morehouse Coll., 1972; LL.D., U. of Notre Dame, 1977; LL.D., Emory U., 1979; LL.D., Kwansei Gakuin U., Japan, 1981; LL.D., GA Southwestern Coll., 1981; D.E., GA Inst. of Tech., 1979; Ph.D. (hon.), Weizmann Inst. of Science, 1980; Ph.D. (hon.), Tel Aviv U., 1983; numerous others. WRITINGS: *Why Not the Best?* (1975); *A Government as Good as Its People* (1977); *Keeping Faith: Memoirs of a President* (1982); *The Blood of Abraham: Insights into the Middle East; Everything to Gain* (coauthor, 1987); *Turning Point: A Candidate, A State, and A Nation Coming of Age* (1992). REL.: Bapt. (deacon). MAILING ADDRESS: 1 Woodland Dr., Plains, GA 31780.

CARTER, OLGA RINE. m. LeRoy Thomas, Jr. POLIT. & GOV.: ***candidate for Democratic nomination to presidency of the U.S., 1984***. MAILING ADDRESS: unknown.

CARTER, REGINALD. b. May 6, 1906, Kimball, McDowell Cty., WV; par. Jesse and Hannah (Waller) Carter; m. Grace Coleman, 1948; c. Regina; Ivanne; Jacqueline; Susan; Debra; Jaunice; Froe; Reginald, Jr. EDUC.: Bluefield (VA) State Coll., 1925–26; certificate, Bodee Dental Inst., New York, NY, 1928; certificate, L. L. Cook School of Electricity, Chicago, IL, 1930. POLIT. & GOV.: ***Independent Afro-American Unity Party candidate for vice presidency of the U.S., 1960***; member, Action Team for Nixon-Agnew, 1968. BUS. & PROF.: asst. to publisher, *Independent Observer*, Beckley, WV, 1930–33; artist, CC & B Coal Co., Glendale, WV, 1934–36; founder, Carter Printing Co., Bluefield, 1939; artist, advertising department, NEHI Bottling Co., Bluefield, 1940–59; artist, safety department, Koppers Coal Co., Keystone, WV, 1942–45; publisher, *Los Angeles News*, Inglewood, CA, 1959–; dir., *Tabloid Teen Post;* exec. vice pres., Human Economics for Liberation of Poverty, Inc., Los Angeles, CA; owner, Carter Printing Co., Los Angeles; publisher, *Negro Reporter International*; ed., *The Banner*. MEM.: Kiwanis International (coordinator of communications, Division Nineteen; life member; division lt. gov., 1977–78; special asst. to the gov., CA-NV-HI District, 1978–79; district chm. for graphics, 1979–80); Masons; Black Press Bureau; Press Photographers Club; Phi Beta Sigma (life member). AWARDS: Outstanding Service Award, Los Angeles Police Dept., 1970. REL.:

Methodist. MAILING ADDRESS: 1538 West Florence Ave., Los Angeles, CA 90047.

CARTER, S. P. POLIT. & GOV.: ***United Christian Party candidate for vice presidency of the U.S., 1908 (declined)***. RES.: unknown.

CARTER, WILLIAM HODDING, III. b. Apr 7, 1935, New Orleans, LA; par. William Hodding, Jr., and Betty (Werlein) Carter; m. Margaret Ainsworth Wolfe, Jun 21, 1957 (divorced, 1978); m. 2d, Patricia Derian, 1978; c. Catherine Ainsworth; Elizabeth Fearn; William Hodding IV; Margaret Lorraine. EDUC.: grad., Greenville (MS) H.S.; B.A., Princeton U., 1957; Nieman Fellow, Harvard U., 1965–66. POLIT. & GOV.: co-chm., MS Young Democrats, 1965–68; delegate, Dem. Nat'l. Conv., 1968, 1972; member, O'Hara Rules Reform Comm., Dem. Nat'l. Cmte., 1969–72; ***candidate for Democratic nomination to vice presidency of the U.S., 1972***; delegate, Democratic Mid-Term Conference, 1974; member, exec. cmte., MS Democratic Party, 1976–; appointed asst. U.S. sec. of state of public affairs, 1977–81. BUS. & PROF.: reporter, *Delta Democrat-Times*, Greenville, 1959–62, managing ed., 1962–65, ed., 1965–77; vice pres., Time Publishing Co., Greenville; vice pres., Industrial Supply Co. MIL.: lt., U.S.M.C., 1957–59. MEM.: Atlantic Assn. of Young Political Leaders (exec. cmte.); American Council of Young Political Leaders (dir.); Atlantic Council (dir.); Robert F. Kennedy Memorial (dir.); Common Cause; Southern Regional Council (exec. cmte.); Twentieth Century Fund (dir.); A.C.L.U.; Inst. of Politics; MS Action for Progress; Greenville Day Care Center; MS Press Assn. (dir.); Sigma Delta Chi; Pulitzer Prize Jury, 1971; MS Democratic Conference; L.Q.C. Lamar Soc.; Mary Holmes Coll.; MS Council on Human Relations; Cmte. for Public Justice, MS Advisory Cmte., U.S. Civil Rights Comm.; Loyal Democrats of MS (founder); South African Leader Exchange Program; Soc. of Professional Journalists; Quadrangle Club. AWARDS: Sigma Delta Chi Award (editorial writing), 1961; Urban Service Award, Office of Economic Opportunity, 1967; Lawrence Appley Youth Leadership Award, American Management Assn., 1968; Silver Em Award, U. of MS, 1968; Robert F. Kennedy Award, MS Council on Human Relations, 1970; Distinguished Achievement Award, U. of CA School of Journalism, 1972. WRITINGS: *The South Strikes Back* (1950); *We Dissent* (contributor, 1963); *Race and News Media* (contributor, 1967). REL.: Episc. MAILING ADDRESS: 2201 C St., N.W., Washington, DC 20520.

CARTER, WILLIE FELIX. b. Jun 15, 1943, Fort Worth, TX; par. Hughert and Willie Fair (Howard) Carter; m. Evelyn Baker (divorced); m. 2d, Lisa Marie Smith, Jul 31, 1986; c. Dwayne; Elaine; Terry; Rickie; Richie; Camila; Curtis; Shirley. EDUC.: grad., I. M. Terrell H.S., 1961; Tarrant Cty. (TX) Junior Coll., 2 years. POLIT. & GOV.: delegate, TX State Democratic Convention, 1984; ***candidate for Democratic nomination to presidency of the U.S., 1988, 1992; independent candidate for presidency of the U.S., 1992***. BUS. & PROF.: junior flight mechanic, Bell Helicopter, 1960s; owner, Carter's Radio and Television, Fort Worth, 1964–. MIL.: U.S. Air Force, 4 years; senior master sgt., U.S. Air Force Reserves. MEM.: TX Electronics Assn.; U.S. C. of C.; Tarrant Cty. Democratic Club; Aviation Fellowship. REL.: Pentecostal Church of God in Christ. MAILING ADDRESS: 4623 Miller Ave., Fort Worth, TX 76119.

CARY, "JACKPINE" BOB. b. Oct 20, 1921, Joliet, IL; par. Rex L. and Cornelia (Heun) Cary; m. Lillian Kluge, Feb 1, 1948; c. Marjory Lynn Kaveney; Barbara Kay Hall. EDUC.: A.A., Joliet Community Coll., 1941; Chicago Acad. of Fine Arts, 1946–47. POLIT. & GOV.: ***Independent Fishermen's Party candidate for presidency of the U.S., 1980***. BUS. & PROF.: author; artist; photographer; outdoor ed., *Joliet Herald News*, 1950–56; reporter, *Joliet Spectator*, 1956–57, managing ed., 1965–66; outdoor broadcaster, WJOL radio, Chicago, IL, 1957; outdoor ed., *Chicago Daily News*, 1958–66; fishing guide, owner, Canadian Border Outfitters, Ely, MN, 1966–74; managing ed., *Ely Echo*, 1974–; columnist, "A View from the North Country," *Ely Echo*; columnist, "Birdshot and Backlashes, *Ely Echo*. MIL.: sgt., U.S.M.C., 1942–45. MEM.: Assn. of Great Lakes Outdoor Writers; Forensic and Walleye Soc. WRITINGS: *Winter Camping* (1978); *Big Wilderness Canoe Manual* (1978). MAILING ADDRESS: Ely Echo, 2 East Sheridan, Ely, MN 55731.

CARY, SAMUEL FENTON. b. Feb 18, 1814, Cincinnati, OH; d. Sep 29, 1900, Cincinnati, OH; par. William and Rebecca (Fenton) Cary; m. Maria Louisa Allen, 1836; m. 2d, Lida S. Stillwell, 1847; c. Mrs. E.W. Sayre; Samuel Fenton, Jr.; Jessie. EDUC.: grad., Miami U., Oxford, OH, 1835, LL.D.; grad., Cincinnati Law School, 1837. POLIT. & GOV.: elected judge, Supreme Court of OH, 1835 (declined); delegate, Rep. Nat'l. Conv., 1864; appointed collector of internal revenue, First District of OH, 1865; elected as a Republican to U.S. House (OH), 1867–69; Republican candidate for U.S. House (OH), 1868; Democratic candidate for U.S. House (OH), 1870; candidate for lt. gov. of OH, 1875; ***Greenback (Independent National) Party candidate for vice presidency of the U.S., 1876***. BUS. & PROF.: atty.; admitted to OH Bar, 1837; law practice (with William B. Caldwell), Cincinnati, 1837–45; temperance advocate; lecturer; writer; farmer; ed., *Ohio Temperance Organ*, 1852–53; ed., *Crusader*, 1856–57. MIL.: paymaster gen., OH Troops, 1844–48; asst. provost marshall, Cincinnati, Civil War. MEM.: Sons of Temperance (grand worthy of OH; most worthy patriarch, 1848–50); Miami U. (trustee). WRITINGS: *Cary Memorials; General Cary on the Aims of the Independent Greenback Party*. REL.: Presb. (founder, College Hill Presbyterian Church). MISC.: known as "General Cary." RES.: Cincinnati, OH.

CASAD, ROLAND CORTEZ. b. c. 1876, KS; d. Jan 14, 1951, Los Angeles, CA. POLIT. & GOV.: candidate for U.S. Senate (CA); candidate for U.S. House (CA); ***candidate***

for Prohibition Party nomination to presidency of the U.S., 1936. BUS. & PROF.: rancher. MISC.: advocate of short hours; elimination of taxes; depreciating dollar; monetary reform. RES.: Los Angeles, CA.

CASE, CLIFFORD PHILIP. b. Apr 16, 1904, Franklin Park, NJ; d. Mar 5, 1982, Washington, DC; par. Clifford Philip and Jeannette (Benedict) Case; m. Ruth Miriam Smith, Jul 13, 1928; c. Mary Jane (Mrs. William M. Weaver); Ann (Mrs. John C. Holt); Clifford Philip III. EDUC.: A.B., Rutgers Coll., 1925; LL.B., Columbia U., 1928. POLIT. & GOV.: elected to Rahway (NJ) Common Council, 1938–42; elected as a Republican to NJ State House of Assembly, 1943–44; elected as a Republican to U.S. House (NJ), 1945–53; elected as a Republican to U.S. Senate (NJ), 1955–79; delegate, Rep. Nat'l. Conv., 1956, 1964, 1968, 1972, 1976; ***candidate for Republican nomination to presidency of the U.S., 1968***; member, U.N. Cmte. on Peaceful Uses of the Seabed, 1971; candidate for Republican nomination to U.S. Senate (NJ), 1978. BUS. & PROF.: atty.; admitted to NJ Bar, 1928; law practice, New York, NY; assoc., Simpson, Thacher and Bartlett (law firm), 1928–29, partner, 1939–53; counsel, Wallet-Prevost, Colt and Wosle (law firm), 1979–82; visiting prof., Rutgers U., 1979. MEM.: ABA; NY State Bar Assn.; Assn. of the Bar of the City of New York; New York Cty. Bar Assn.; Delta Upsilon; Phi Beta Kappa; Elks; Downtown Assn.; Metropolitan Club; Ilderan Outing Club; Rutgers U. (trustee); Fund for the Republic (pres., 1953–54); Phi Delta Phi; Essex Club; Federal City Club; Century Assn.; Council on Foreign Relations; Columbia Law Journal of Law and Social Problems (dir.); Freedom House (chm. of the board, 1979–82). HON. DEG.: LL.D., Rutgers Coll., 1955; LL.D., Middlebury Coll., 1956; LL.D., Rollins Coll., 1957; LL.D., Rider Coll., 1959; LL.D., Bloomfield Coll., 1962; LL.D., Columbia U., 1967; LL.D., Princeton U., 1967; LL.D., Upsala Coll., 1969; D.P.S., Seton Hall U., 1971; LL.D., Yeshiva U., 1976; LL.D., Fairleigh Dickinson U., 1979; LL.D., Kean Coll., 1979; LL.D., Ramapo Coll., 1979. REL.: Presb. (nee Reformed Church in America; member, Board of Foreign Missions). RES.: Rahway, NJ.

CASEY, ROBERT P. b. Jan 9, 1932, Jackson Heights, NY; par. Alphonsus L. and Marie (Cummings) Casey; m. Ellen Theresa Harding; c. eight. EDUC.: grad. (cum laude), Holy Cross Coll.; A.B., LL.B., George Washington U. POLIT. & GOV.: elected as a Democrat to PA State Senate, 1963–67; alternate delegate, Dem. Nat'l. Conv., 1964; first vice pres., PA State Constitutional Convention, 1967–68; delegate, Dem. Nat'l. Conv., 1968; elected as a Democrat, auditor gen. of PA, 1969–77; delegate, Democratic Mid-Term Conference, 1978; elected as a Democrat to gov. of PA, 1987–1995; ***candidate for Democratic nomination to presidency of the U.S., 1992***. BUS. & PROF.: atty.; admitted to Lackawanna Cty. (PA) Courts, Supreme and Superior Courts of PA, DC Court, Federal Court, and Middle District of PA Court. MEM.: Order of the Coif; Cancer Drive; Lackawanna United Fund Drive; Coalition of Northeastern Governors (chm.) WRITINGS: "Counter Claims Against the U.S.," *George Washington Law Review*, Jan 1957. REL.: R.C. MAILING ADDRESS: Governor's Office, State Capitol, Harrisburg, PA.

CASS, GEORGE WASHINGTON. b. Mar 12, 1810, Dresden, Muskingum Cty., OH; d. Mar 21, 1888, New York, NY; par. George W. and Sophia (Lord) Cass. EDUC.: Detroit Acad.; grad. (with special honors), U.S. Military Acad., 1832. POLIT. & GOV.: Democratic candidate for gov. of PA, 1863, 1868; ***candidate for Democratic nomination to vice presidency of the U.S., 1864***. BUS. & PROF.: engineer; railroad exec.; asst. superintendent of construction, Cumberland Road, U.S. Army Corps of Engineers, 1832–36; merchant, Brownsville, PA, 1840; founder, Adams Express Co., 1849, pres., 1856–62; pres., Boston, St. Louis and Richmond R.R., 1855; pres., Ohio and Pennsylvania R.R. Co. (later consolidated as Pittsburgh, Fort Wayne and Chicago R.R.), 1856–81, dir., 1881–88; pres., Continental Improvement Co., 1869–74; pres., Grand Rapids and Indiana R.R. Co., 1869–74; pres., Southern Railway Security Co., 1870–73; pres., Northern Pacific R.R. Co., 1872–75. MIL.: appointed brev. 2d lt., Seventh Infantry, U.S. Army, 1st lt., 1836; brig. gen., PA Volunteers. MEM.: U.S. Military Acad. (visitor, 1859). MISC.: erected first cast-iron tubular-arch bridge built in the U.S., 1837. RES.: PA.

CASS, LEWIS. b. Oct 9, 1782, Exeter, NH; d. Jun 17, 1866, Detroit, MI; par. Jonathan and Mary (Gilman) Cass; m. Elizabeth Spencer, 1806; c. Eliza; Lewis, Jr.; Mary Sophia (Mrs. Augustus Canfield); Matilda (Mrs. Henry Ledyard); Isabella "Belle" (Baroness von Limburg). EDUC.: Exeter Acad.; studied law under Gov. R. J. Meigs. POLIT. & GOV.: elected as a Democrat to OH State House, 1806; appointed U.S. marshall, OH, 1807–12; appointed gov. of MI Territory, 1813–31; appointed U.S. sec. of war, 1831–36; appointed U.S. minister to France, 1836; elected as a Democrat to U.S. Senate (MI), 1845–48, 1849–57; ***candidate for Democratic nomination to presidency of the U.S., 1844, 1852, 1856; candidate for Democratic nomination to vice presidency of the U.S., 1844; Democratic candidate for presidency of the U.S., 1848; candidate for American (Know-Nothing) Party nomination to presidency of the U.S., 1856***; appointed U.S. sec. of state, 1857–60. BUS. & PROF.: schoolteacher, Wilmington, DE; farmer, Zanesville, OH; atty.; admitted to OH Bar, 1802; law practice, OH, 1802. MIL.: col., Third OH Regt., 1812–13, brig. gen., 1813–14. MEM.: American Hist. Assn. (pres.); Masons. WRITINGS: *History, Traditions, Languages, &c. of the Indians Living in the U.S.* (1823); *Historical and Scientific Sketches of Michigan* (coauthor); *France: Its King, Court and Government* (1840). RES.: Detroit, MI.

CASSADORE, PHILIP. b. May 28, 1933, Peridot, AZ; par. Alfred (Chief Broken Arrow) and Maude (Hinton) Cassadore; m. Marcine Sisto; c. Eddie; Jonell; Jennifer. EDUC.: grad., Globe H.S., Globe, AZ; Brigham Young U., 1954; Phoenix (AZ)

Coll., 1960–63. POLIT. & GOV.: representative, San Carlos Apache Tribal Council; ***Geronimo Party candidate for presidency of the U.S., 1972 (withdrew)***. BUS. & PROF.: exec. dir., San Carlos Apache Community Action Program; radio commentator; singer; music scholar; lecturer; consultant on Apache history. REL.: Indigenous Apache Religion. MAILING ADDRESS: P.O. Box 5, Peridot, AZ 85542.

CASTRO, ALBERT C., JR. b. Jan 26, 1928, Milwaukee, WI; par. Albert and Aurora (Cardenas) Castro; m. Patricia Louise Rutzen, 1954; c. Jeffrey; Lisa Marie; David. EDUC.: grad., Boys Technical H.S., 1945; TX Coll. of Mines. POLIT. & GOV.: chm., Greenfield, Greendale, Hales Corners Democratic Unit, 1969–71; member, Milwaukee Cty. (WI) Democratic Party, 1969–73 (chm., 1976; chm., Southwest Suburban Cmte.); member, Administrative Cmte., WI Democratic Party, 1971–; chm., WI McGovern for President Campaign, 1972; delegate, Dem. Nat'l. Conv., 1972, 1976; chm., WI Udall for President Campaign, 1976; ***candidate for Democratic nomination to vice presidency of the U.S., 1976***. BUS. & PROF.: sheetmetal worker. MIL.: pfc, U.S. Army, 1945–47. MEM.: Cmte. on Political Education, AFL-CIO (Milwaukee Cty. chm., 1969–71); AFL-CIO Building Trades Union (Local 24); Holy Name Soc.; Southside Scholarship Foundation; Catholic War Veterans. REL.: R.C. MAILING ADDRESS: 4471 South 83rd St., Greenfield, WI 53220.

CATES, NORMAN FRANKLIN. b. Nov 28, 1927, Durham, NC; par. Eugene Cameron and Josephine (Wright) Cates; m. Eloise Schuller; c. Franklin E.; Douglas K.; Anne Marie; Christopher A. EDUC.: grad., High Point (NC) H.S., 1946; B.S., Embry-Riddle Aeronautical U., 1973. POLIT. & GOV.: ***independent candidate for presidency of the U.S., 1976***; appointed member, Public Safety Comm., Ocala, FL, 1976–80; independent candidate for Ocala City (FL City Council, 1982; appointed member, Airport Advisory Board, Ocala, FL, 1982–. BUS. & PROF.: dir. of personnel and safety, Ocala Lumber Sales Co., Ocala, FL, 1976–83; insurance agent, Ocala, FL, 1984–. MIL.: U.S. Navy, 1945–48; U.S. Army, 1949–56, 1963–75; Bronze Star; Distinguished Flying Cross; Air Medal; Army Commendation Medal; Vietnamese Cross of Gallantry with Silver Palm. MEM.: Retired Officers Assn.; Lions Club. WRITINGS: "Eternal Vigilance," *Aviation Digest*, 1971; "The Thrill Addict and You," *Aviation Digest*, 1972. REL.: Christian and Missionary Alliance. MAILING ADDRESS: 1532 North East 17th Court, Ocala, FL 32670.

CATON, JOHN DEAN. b. Mar 19, 1812, Monroe, NY; d. Jul 30, 1895, Chicago, IL; par. Robert and Hannah (Dean) Caton; m. Laura Adelaide Sherill, Jul 1835. EDUC.: Utica Acad., 1829; Grosvenor H.S., Rome, NY, 1831; studied law, LL.D., Hamilton Coll., 1866. POLIT. & GOV.: sec., First IL Political Convention, 1834; elected justice of the peace, Ottawa, IL; appointed and subsequently elected assoc. justice, Supreme Court of IL, 1842–43, 1843–64 (chief justice, 1855, 1857–64); candidate for assoc. justice, Supreme Court of IL, 1843; ***candidate for Democratic nomination to vice presidency of the U.S., 1864***. BUS. & PROF.: atty.; admitted to IL Bar, 1835; law practice, Ottawa, IL; pres., IL and MS Telegraph Co., 1852–67. WRITINGS: *Matter and a Supreme Intelligence* (1864); *A Summer in Norway* (1875); *The Last of the Illinois and a Sketch of the Pottawatomies* (1876); *Order of the Prairies* (1876); *The Antelope and Deer of America* (1877); *Miscellanies* (1880); *The Early Bench and Bar of Illinois* (1893). RES.: Ottawa, IL.

CATT, CARRIE CLINTON LANE CHAPMAN. b. Jan 9, 1859, Ripon, WI; d. Mar 9, 1947, New Rochelle, NY; par. Lucius and Maria (Clinton) Lane; m. Leo Chapman, Feb 12, 1885; m. 2d, George William Catt, Jun 10, 1890; c. none. EDUC.: B.S., IA State Coll., 1880. POLIT. & GOV.: superintendent of schools, Mason City, IA, 1883–85; member, Women's Comm., Council on National Defense, WWI; ***candidate for National American Woman's Suffrage Association nomination to presidency of the U.S., 1920 (declined)***. BUS. & PROF.: ed., *Mason City Republican*, 1885–86; suffrage advocate, 1887; schoolteacher; pres., Women Citizen Corp., 1918–31. MEM.: National American Woman Suffrage Assn. (pres., 1900–1904, 1915–20); IA Woman Suffrage Assn. (lecturer; organizer, 1887–90); International Woman Suffrage Alliance (pres., 1904–23); National League of Women Voters (founder, 1920; hon. pres.); National Cmte. on the Cause and Cure of War (founder, 1925; chm., 1925–32; hon. chm., 1932–47); Women's Action Cmte. for Victory and a Lasting Peace (hon. chm., 1943–47); Inst. for Pacific Relations; League of Nations Assn. (vice pres., 1923); American Assn. for the U.N. AWARDS: Order of the White Rose (Finland, 1942); Pictorial Review Prize, 1930; Hebrew Medal, 1933; Turkish Government Stamp, 1935; award, American Women's Assn., 1940; award, General Federation of Women's Clubs, 1940; award, National Inst. of Social Sciences, 1941; award, Chi Omega, 1941; Presidential Citation of Honor, 1936; award, New York City Federation of Women's Clubs, 1930. HON. DEG.: LL.D., Smith Coll.; LL.D., U. of WY; LL.D., IA State Coll.; LL.D., Moravian Coll. for Women, 1940. RES.: New Rochelle, NY.

CATTANACH, JAMES SCOTT. POLIT. & GOV.: ***independent candidate for presidency of the U.S., 1980***. MAILING ADDRESS: 137 North Union Ave., Los Angeles, CA 90026.

CAUSSEY, CHARLES. POLIT. & GOV.: ***candidate for Democratic nomination to presidency of the U.S., 1992***. MAILING ADDRESS: UT.

CELESTE, RICHARD F. b. Nov 11, 1937, Cleveland, OH; par. Frank P. and Margaret (Lewis) Celeste; m. Dagmar

Ingrid Braun, 1962 (divorced, 1995); c. Eric; Christopher; Gabriella; Noelle; Natalie; Stephen. EDUC.: B.A. (magna cum laude), Yale U., 1959; Ph.B. in politics, Oxford U., 1962. POLIT. & GOV.: staff liaison officer, Peace Corps, 1963, dir., Washington, DC, 1979– 81; special asst. to U.S. ambassador to India, 1963–67; elected as a Democrat to OH State House, 1970–74 (majority whip, 1972–74); member, exec. cmte., OH State Democratic Central Cmte.; elected as a Democrat to lt. gov. of OH, 1974–79; Democratic candidate for gov. of OH, 1978; elected as a Democrat to gov. of OH, 1983–91; ***candidate for Democratic nomination to presidency of the U.S., 1988***; coordinator, Campaign for National Healthcare Reform, Democratic Party, 1993. BUS. & PROF.: public relations. MEM.: American Soc. of Public Administration; Americans for Democratic Action; Italian Sons and Daughters of America. AWARDS: Rhodes Scholar, Oxford U., 1962. WRITINGS: *It's Not Just Politics, America* (1976); *Pioneering a Hunger Free World* (1977). REL.: Methodist. MAILING ADDRESS: Columbus, OH 43215.

CENTANNI, KEVIN P. POLIT. & GOV.: ***independent candidate for presidency of the U.S., 1988***. MAILING ADDRESS: 4733 Loveland St., Metairie, LA 70006.

CHADBOURNE, MARGARET. POLIT. & GOV.: ***candidate for Democratic nomination to vice presidency of the U.S., 1924***. RES.: New York, NY.

CHAFIN, EUGENE WILDER. b. Nov 1, 1852, East Troy, WI; d. Nov 30, 1920, Long Beach, CA; par. Samuel Evans and Betsy A. (Pollard) Chafin; m. Carrie A. Hunkins, Nov 24, 1881; c. Desdemona. EDUC.: LL. B., U. of WI, 1875. POLIT. & GOV.: elected justice of the peace, Waukesha, WI; elected police magistrate, Waukesha, WI; elected member, Waukesha Board of Education; member, public library board, Waukesha; Prohibition Party candidate for district atty., Waukesha Cty., 1881; Prohibition Party candidate for U.S. House (WI), 1882; delegate, Prohibition Party National Convention, 1884, 1888, 1892, 1896, 1900, 1904, 1908, 1912, 1916, 1920; member, Prohibition Party National Cmte., 1888–96, 1912–20; Prohibition Party candidate for atty. gen. of WI, 1886, 1900, 1904; Prohibition Party candidate for gov. of WI, 1898, 1908; Prohibition Party candidate for U.S. House (IL), 1902; Prohibition Party candidate for atty. gen. of IL, 1904; ***Prohibition Party candidate for presidency of the U.S., 1908, 1912***; Prohibition Party candidate for U.S. Senate (AZ), 1914. BUS. & PROF.: atty.; admitted to WI Bar, 1875; law practice, Waukesha, 1876–1900; superintendent, Washingtonian Home, Chicago, IL, 1901–04; temperance advocate; admitted to practice before the Bar of the Supreme Court of the U.S., 1909. MEM.: Waukesha Cty. Agricultural Soc. (pres.); Independent Order of Good Templars (district chief templar; grand counselor, 1885; grand chief templar, 1886–90; grand electoral superintendent, 1893–1901); International Supreme Lodge of Good Templars (WI delegate); Epworth League (pres.). WRITINGS: *The Voter's Handbook* (1876); *Lives of the Presidents* (1896); *Lincoln: The Man of Sorrow* (1908); *Washington as a Statesman* (1909); *Government by Political Parties* (1910); *One Standard of Morals* (1911); *Government by Administration* (1912); *The Master Method of the Great Reform* (1913). REL.: Methodist Episcopal Church. RES.: Waukesha, WI.

CHALFANT, EARL R. POLIT. & GOV.: ***candidate for Prohibition Party nomination to presidency of the U.S., 1944***. MISC.: nominated himself at convention. RES.: CA.

CHALFANT, MATTHEW C. b. Sep 3, 1963, New Albany, IN; par. Joseph Shaw and Harriet V. (Strange) Chalfant; single. EDUC.: New Albany (IN) H.S. POLIT. & GOV.: ***candidate for Republican nomination to presidency of the U.S., 1980***. BUS. & PROF.: self-employed; owner, Leatherstuff, Ltd., New Albany; owner, Sno-Go (landscaping and snow removal), New Albany. MEM.: Junior Classical League. WRITINGS: *The Effects of Trichloromethane on the Phantom Leaf Effect, as Seen Through Kirlian Photography*. MAILING ADDRESS: 6 Trimingham Rd., New Albany, IN 47150.

CHAMBERLAIN, GEORGE EARLE. b. Jan 1, 1854, Natchez, MS; d. Jul 9, 1928, Washington, DC; par. Charles Thomson and Pamelia A. (Archer) Chamberlain; m. Sarah Newman Welch, May 21, 1879; c. Charles Thomson; Mrs. Lucie Blair; Mrs. Marguerite Gaither; Mrs. Carrie Lee Wood; George Earle, Jr.; Mrs. Fannie Tevis. EDUC.: A.B., B.L., Washington and Lee U., 1876. POLIT. & GOV.: deputy cty. clerk, Linn Cty., OR, 1877–79; elected as a Democrat to OR State House, 1880–82; district atty., Third OR Judicial District, 1884–86; chm., Linn Cty. Democratic Central Cmte., 1890; appointed and subsequently elected as a Democrat to atty. gen. of OR, 1891–95; district atty., Fourth OR Judicial District, 1900–1903; elected as a Democrat to gov. of OR, 1903–09; elected as a Democrat to U.S. Senate (OR), 1909–21; ***candidate for Democratic nomination to vice presidency of the U.S., 1912***; Democratic candidate for U.S. Senate (OR), 1920; appointed member, U.S. Shipping Board, 1921–23. BUS. & PROF.: atty.; admitted to OR Bar, 1879; law practice, Albany, OR; ed., *Albany States Rights Democrat*, 1882; law practice, Portland, OR; law practice, Washington, DC. MEM.: Albany Temperance Soc. REL.: Presb. RES.: Albany, OR.

CHAMBERLIN, EDWIN MARTIN. b. Nov 7, 1835, West Cambridge, MA; d. Feb 23, 1893, Cambridge, MA; par. Daniel and Maria M. (Martin) Chamberlain; m. Emma Frances Lurvey, 1868; c. Edwin Martin, Jr.; Frances Maria (Mrs. Frank Irving Whittemore); Florence Augusta; Bertha Martin (Mrs. Robert Hastings Treadwell); Charlotte Abby (Mrs. Charles Edward Stratton). EDUC.: Yale Coll.; Harvard Law School. POLIT. & GOV.: chm., MA Labor Reform Cmte., 1869–74;

Labor Reform Party candidate for gov. of MA, 1869, 1871; chm., Labor Reform Party National Convention, 1872; ***candidate for Labor Reform Party nomination to vice presidency of the U.S., 1872***; vice pres., Independent National (Greenback) Party National Cmte.; delegate, Independent National (Greenback) Party National Convention, 1876. BUS. & PROF.: atty.; law practice, Chicago, IL, 1858–59; journalist; ed., owner, *The Echo*; steward, Adams House, Boston, MA. MIL.: 2d lt., 12th Battery, MA Volunteer Light Artillery, 1862, 1st lt., 1862–65. MEM.: GAR (commander, Post 7); Union Boat Club (pres.; captain); Knights of St. Crispin; Sovereigns of Industry; Industrial Order of the People (1866); Workingmen's Inst. WRITINGS: *Free Trade* (1868); *Speech at Faneuil Hall* (1871); *The Sovereigns of Industry* (1875); *Eight Hours and the Margins of Profits* (1888); *Reply to Edward Atkinson on the Margin of Profits*. REL.: Congregationalist. MISC.: advocate of women's suffrage, temperance reform, and improved labor conditions. RES.: Boston, MA.

CHAMBERS, BARZILLAI J. "BENJAMIN." b. Dec 5, 1817, Montgomery Cty., KY; d. Sep 16, 1895; par. Walker and Talitha Cumi (Mothershead) Chambers; m. Susan Wood, 1852; m. 2d, Emma Montgomery, 1854; m. 3d, Harriet A. Killough, 1861; c. one son; two daughters; one other infant. EDUC.: public schools. POLIT. & GOV.: elected district surveyor, Robertson Land District, TX, 1847; elected alderman, Cleburne, TX; Democratic candidate for TX State House, 1876; National (Greenback) Party candidate for TX State House, 1878; delegate, National (Greenback) Party National Convention, 1879; member, exec. cmte., National (Greenback) Party National Cmte., 1879–84; ***Union Greenback Labor Party candidate for vice presidency of the U.S., 1880; National (Greenback) Party candidate for vice presidency of the U.S., 1880***. BUS. & PROF.: surveyor; farmer, Navarro Cty., TX, 1855; farmer, Johnson Cty., TX; land speculator, Navarro Cty.; atty.; admitted to TX Bar, 1860; merchant, Cleburne, TX, 1867–71; partner (with J. W. Brown), Bank and Exchange House, 1871–75; incorporator, Narrow-Gauge R.R. from Dallas to Cleburne, c. 1875; publisher, *The Chronicle* (Greenback newspaper), Cleburne, 1876. MIL.: capt., KY Volunteers, aide-de-camp in TX, 1837–38; member, TX State Troops, 1864. MEM.: Masons. WRITINGS: *The Great War of Monarchy Versus Republicanism* (1888); *Sacred Coin Contracts*; *Open Letter to President Cleveland*. REL.: Christian Church. MISC.: noted as ardent secessionist; donated land for establishment of Cleburne as cty. seat of Johnson Cty., TX; opposed ratification of TX State Constitution of 1876 because of homestead exemption provision. RES.: Cleburne, TX.

CHANDLER, ALBERT BENJAMIN "HAPPY." b. Jul 14, 1898, Corydon, KY; d. Jun 15, 1991, Versailles, KY; par. Joseph and Callie (Saunders) Chandler; m. Mildred Watkins, Nov 12, 1925; c. Marcella (Mrs. John P. Gregg; Mrs. Thomas D. Miller); Mildred (Mrs. John K. Cabell; Mrs. Mimi C. Lewis); Albert Benjamin, Jr.; Joseph Daniel. EDUC.: A.B., Transylvania Coll., 1921, LL.D., 1936; Harvard U., 1921–22; LL.B., U. of KY, 1924, LL.D., 1937. POLIT. & GOV.: appointed master commissioner of circuit court, Woodford Cty., KY, 1928; elected as a Democrat to KY State Senate, 1929–31; elected as a Democrat to lt. gov. of KY, 1931–35; chm., Woodford Cty. (KY) Democratic Exec. Cmte., 1932–44; elected as a Democrat to gov. of KY, 1935–39, 1955–59; appointed and subsequently elected as a Democrat to U.S. Senate (KY), 1939–45; member, Dem. Nat'l. Cmte.; delegate, Dem. Nat'l. Conv., 1956; ***candidate for Democratic nomination to presidency of the U.S., 1956, 1960***; candidate for Democratic nomination to gov. of KY, 1963, 1967, 1973; ***candidate for American Independent Party nomination to vice presidency of the U.S., 1968 (declined)***; independent candidate for gov. of KY, 1971. BUS. & PROF.: atty.; admitted to KY Bar, 1924; law practice, Versailles, KY, 1924; receiver, Inter-Southern Life Insurance Co., 1932; founder, KY Home Life Insurance Co., 1932; counsel, American Life and Accident Insurance Co., 1933; tobacco grower; elected high commissioner of baseball, 1945–51; dir., Coastal State Life Insurance Co.; vice pres., dir., First Flight Golf Co.; chm. of the board, Daniel Boone Fried Chicken, Inc.; commissioner, Continental Football League, 1965–. MIL.: capt., U.S. Army, 1918–19. MEM.: American Legion; Forty and Eight; Pi Kappa Alpha; Masons (32°; Shriner; Knight Templar); International Baseball Congress (pres.); Ty Cobb Foundation (trustee); U. of KY (trustee); Transylvania Coll. (trustee); KY Mountain Club (hon.). AWARDS: Kentuckian of the Year, KY Press Assn.; elected member, KY Sports Hall of Fame; received Cross of Military Service, U.D.C., 1959; Bishop's Medal, Episcopal Church, 1959; Jefferson Davis Medal, 1975; elected member, National Baseball Hall of Fame, 1982; Award, National Conference of Christians and Jews, 1983. WRITINGS: *Heroes, Plain Folks, and Skunks* (1989). REL.: Episc. RES.: Versailles, KY.

CHANDLER, BARTON EUGENE. b. 1938; m. Joyce L. C. POLIT. & GOV.: ***independent candidate for presidency of the U.S., 1980***; candidate for Republican nomination to gov. of NE, 1982; candidate for Democratic nomination to gov. of NE, 1986. BUS. & PROF.: warehouseman, Ace Hardware, Lincoln, NE; bus driver. MAILING ADDRESS: 2856 Garfield St., Lincoln, NE 68502.

CHANG, EYAN V. POLIT. & GOV.: ***independent candidate for presidency of the U.S., 1992***. MAILING ADDRESS: 1328 Wawona, San Francisco, CA 94116.

CHANLER, LEWIS STUYVESANT. b. Sep 24, 1869, Newport, RI; d. Feb 28, 1942, New York, NY; par. John Winthrop and Margaret Astor (Ward) Chanler; m. Alice Chamberlain, Oct 24, 1890; m. 2d, Julia Lynch Olin Benkard, May 22, 1921; c. Lewis Stuyvesant; Alida (Mrs. William Christian Bohn); William Chamberlain. EDUC.: Cambridge U.; LL.B., Columbia U., 1899. POLIT. & GOV.: delegate, NY State Democratic Convention, 1896; elected as a Democrat to Dutchess Cty.

(NY) Board of Supervisors, 1903–07; elected as a Democrat (Independence League) to lt. gov. of NY, 1907–09; Democratic candidate for gov. of NY, 1908; ***candidate for Democratic nomination to presidency of the U.S., 1908; candidate for Democratic nomination to vice presidency of the U.S., 1908***; elected as a Democrat to NY State Assembly, 1909–11; appointed member, NY State Canal Board. BUS. & PROF.: atty.; admitted to NY Bar, 1899; law practice, New York, NY, 1899–25; horse breeder. MEM.: Princess Club; White Club; Rockaway Hunt Club; Chanler Democratic Club (founder, 1891); House of Refuge (mgr.); Hudson River State Hospital (mgr.); Assn. of the Bar of the City of New York; Masons; St. Nicholas Soc.; Pilgrim Club; Knickerbocker Club; Lawyers Club; Manhattan Club; Church Club. MISC.: advocate of Irish independence. RES.: Tuxedo Park, NY.

CHAPIN, ALFRED CLARK. b. Mar 8, 1848, South Hadley, MA; d. Oct 2, 1936, Montreal, Canada; par. Ephraim and Josephine (Clark) Chapin; m. Grace Stebbins, Feb 24, 1884; c. Grace. EDUC.: A.B., Williams Coll., 1869, LL.D., 1909; LL.B., Harvard U., 1871. POLIT. & GOV.: elected as a Democrat to NY State Assembly, 1882–83 (Speaker, 1883); elected as a Democrat, state comptroller of NY, 1884–87; elected as a Democrat, mayor of Brooklyn, NY, 1888–91; ***candidate for Democratic nomination to presidency of the U.S., 1888 (declined)***; elected as a Democrat to U.S. House (NY), 1891–93; appointed NY State railroad commissioner, 1893–1997. BUS. & PROF.: atty.; admitted to NY Bar, 1872; law practice, New York, NY. MEM.: Young Men's Democratic Club of Brooklyn (pres.); Union Club; Metropolitan Club; Alpha Delta Phi; Whist Club. RES.: Brooklyn, NY.

CHAPLIN, CHARLES SPENCER "CHARLIE." b. Apr 16, 1889, London, England; d. Dec 25, 1977, Vevey, Switzerland; par. Charles Spencer and Hannah Chaplin; m. Mildred Harris; m. 2d, Lita Grey; m. 3d, Paulette Goddard (divorced, 1942); m. 4th, Oona O'Neill, Jun 16, 1943; c. Charles Spencer; Sydney; Geraldine; Michael; Josephine; Victoria; Jane; Eugene O'Neill; Annette-Emilie; one other son. EDUC.: public schools, London, England. POLIT. & GOV.: ***candidate for Democratic nomination to presidency of the U.S., 1924***. BUS. & PROF.: actor; writer; composer; employed in Vaudeville, 1896; first appearance as Billy in "Sherlock Holmes"; made screen debut, Keystone Film Co., 1914; with Essanay Co., 1915; Mutual Film Corp., 1916; signed with First National Exhibitors Circuit to make eight two-reel pictures for $1,000,000, 1917; producer, owner, Motion Picture Studio, Hollywood, CA; founding member, United Artists Corp. MOTION PICTURE CREDITS: *Making a Living* (1914); *Kid Auto Races at Venice* (1914); *Mabel's Strange Predicament* (1914); *Between Showers* (1914); *A Film Johnnie* (1914); *Tango Tangle* (1914); *His Favorite Pastime* (1914); *Cruel, Cruel Love* (1914); *The Star Border* (1914); *Mabel at the Wheel* (1914); *Twenty Minutes of Love* (1914); *The Knock-out* (1914); *Tillie's Punctured Romance* (1914); *Caught in a Cabaret* (1914); *Caught in the Rain* (1914); *A Busy Day* (1914); *The Fatal Mallet* (1914); *Her Friend the Bandit* (1914); *Mabel's Busy Day* (1914); *Mabel's Married Life* (1914); *Laughing Gas* (1914); *The Property Man* (1914); *The Face on the Barroom Floor* (1914); *Recreation* (1914); *The Masquerader* (1914); *His New Profession* (1914); *The Rounders* (1914); *The New Janitor* (1914); *These Love Pangs* (1914); *Dough and Dynamite* (1914); *Gentlemen of Nerve* (1914); *His Musical Career* (1914); *His Trysting Place* (1914); *Getting Acquainted* (1914); *His Prehistoric Past* (1914); *His New Job* (1915); *A Night Out* (1915); *The Champion* (1915); *In the Park* (1915); *A Jitney Elopement* (1915); *The Tramp* (1915); *By the Sea* (1915); *Work* (1915); *A Woman* (1915); *The Bank* (1915); *Shanghaied* (1915); *A Night in the Show* (1915); *Carmen* (1916); *Police* (1916); *The Floorwalker* (1916); *The Fireman* (1916); *The Vagabond* (1916); *One a.m.* (1916); *The Count* (1916); *The Pawnshop* (1916); *Behind the Screen* (1916); *The Rink* (1916); *Easy Street* (1917); *The Cure* (1917); *The Immigrant* (1917); *The Adventurer* (1917); *Triple Trouble* (1918); *A Dog's Life* (1918); *The Bond* (1918); *Shoulder Arms* (1918); *Sunnyside* (1919); *A Day's Pleasure* (1919); *The Kid* (1920); *The Idle Class* (1921); *Pay Day* (1922); *The Pilgrim* (1923); *A Woman of Paris* (dir., 1923); *The Gold Rush* (1924); *The Circus* (1928); *City Lights* (1931); *Modern Times* (1936); *Great Dictator* (1940); *The Gold Rush* (remake, 1942); *Monsieur Verdoux* (1947); *Limelight* (1952); *A King in New York* (1957); *A Countess from Hong Kong* (1967). MEM.: Legion of Honor (Chevalier, France); Societe des Beaux Arts, Paris, France; A.S.C.A.P.; Lambs Club; Tuna Club (Catalina). AWARDS: World Peace Prize, World Peace Council, 1953; K.B.E., 1975; Special Acad. Award for Film Achievements, 1977. WRITINGS: *My Trip Abroad* (1922); *My Wonderful Visit* (1930); *Charles Chaplin: My Autobiography* (1964); *My Life in Pictures* (1974). MISC.: known as "The Little Tramp"; left U.S. as result of paternity scandal, 1944. RES.: Vevey, Switzerland.

CHAPMAN, CHARLES CLARKE. b. Jul 2, 1853, Macomb, IL; d. Apr 5, 1944, Fullerton, CA; par. Sidney S. and Rebecca Jane (Clarke) Chapman; m. Lizzie Pearson, Oct 23, 1884; m. 2d, Clara Irvin, Sep 3, 1898; c. Ethel Marguerite (Mrs. William Harold Wickett); Charles Stanley; Irvin Clarke. EDUC.: public schools. POLIT. & GOV.: elected mayor of Fullerton, CA, 1904; member, CA Republican State Central Cmte.; Republican candidate for CA State Senate, 1912; delegate, Rep. Nat'l. Conv., 1916, 1924; ***candidate for Republican nomination to presidency of the U.S., 1924***; appointed member, CA State Immigration and Housing Comm. BUS. & PROF.: bricklayer; superintendent for erection of buildings, Chicago, IL, 1871–73; merchant, 1873–76; founder, publishing business, Galesburg, IL, 1878; pres., partner, Chapman Brothers Co., Chicago, IL, 1880–94; orange grower, Fullerton, CA, 1894–1944; rancher; chm. of the board, Bank of America, Fullerton, CA; pres., Charles C. and S. J. Chapman Co.; pres., Chapman Orchards Co.; pres., Southern Meat Co.; pres., Fullerton Community Hotel Co.; pres., Placentia Orchard Co.; pres., Commercial National Bank of Los Angeles; vice pres., Farmers and Merchants Bank of Fullerton; pres., Fullerton Improvement Co.;

dir., Bank of America of San Francisco; chm. of the board, Bank of Italy. MEM.: Christian Board of Publication (dir.); CA Christian Coll. (trustee); CA Christian Mission Soc. (pres., 1901–09); Masons (32°; Knights Templar; Shriners); Pomona Coll. (trustee, 1907–15); Chapman Coll. (founder); American Acad. of Political and Social Sciences; Chicago Hist. Soc.; Los Angeles City Club; San Diego State Normal School (trustee, 1913); Pacific Coast Club. REL.: Disciples of Christ (pastor, First Christian Church, Fullerton, CA). MISC.: built hospital in Nantungchow, China; known as the "Father of the Valencia Orange Industry." RES.: Fullerton, CA.

CHAPMAN, THOMAS L. POLIT. & GOV.: ***independent candidate for presidency of the U.S., 1992***. BUS. & PROF.: minister. MAILING ADDRESS: 3705 Glenoak Dr., South, Lakeland, FL 33809.

CHAPPELL, WILLIAM VENROE, JR. b. Feb 3, 1922, Kendrick, FL; d. Mar 30, 1989, Bethesda, MD; par. William Venroe and Laura (Kemp) Chappell; m. Marguerite Gutshall, Mar 25, 1944; c. Judith Jane (Mrs. Edward Taylor; Mrs. Gadd); Deborah Kay (Mrs. Thomas Bond); William Venroe III; Christopher Clyde. EDUC.: B.A., U. of FL, 1947, LL.B., 1949, J.D., 1967. POLIT. & GOV.: elected prosecuting atty., Marion Cty., FL, 1950–54; elected as a Democrat to FL State House, 1955–65 (Speaker, 1961–63), 1967–69; alternate delegate, Dem. Nat'l. Conv., 1960; elected as a Democrat to U.S. House (FL), 1969–89; ***candidate for Democratic nomination to vice presidency of the U.S., 1972***; delegate, Democratic Mid-Term Conference, 1974. BUS. & PROF.: atty.; admitted to FL Bar, 1949; partner, Chappell and Rowland (law firm), Ocala, FL, 1949; partner, Sturgis and Chappell (law firm), Ocala; owner, J. & J. Electric Co.; owner, Ellzey Plumbing, Inc.; dir., Bank of Belleview. MIL.: lt. (jg), U.S. Navy, 1942–46; capt., U.S.N.R., 1946–78. MEM.: Phi Alpha Delta; Tau Kappa Alpha; Inter-American Bar Assn.; ABA; FL Bar Assn.; Marion Cty. Bar Assn.; American Trial Lawyers Assn.; Acad. of Florida Trial Lawyers; American Legion; VFW; AMVETS; Masons (York Rite; Shriner); Elks; Moose; Young Democrats (pres.); Ocala Jaycees (pres.); Ocala Lions (pres.). AWARDS: Allen Morris Awards for Most Valuable Member and Most Effective Debater, FL State House, 1967; "Watchdog of the Treasury" Award, National Associated Businessmen, 1971–72. HON. DEG.: LL.D., Emby-Riddle Aeronaut U., 1977; LL.D., Flagler Coll., 1978. REL.: Methodist. RES.: Ocala, FL.

CHAPPLE, JOHN BOWMAN. b. Nov 20, 1899, Ashland, WI; par. John Crockett and Myrta (Bowman) Chapple; m. Irene Mary McDonnell, Jun 22, 1922; c. Alice Myrta; Jeanne Irene; John Donnell. EDUC.: U. of WI, 1917–18, 1935; Ph.B., Yale U., 1924; American Inst. of Banking, 1929–30. POLIT. & GOV.: Republican candidate for U.S. Senate (WI), 1932, 1934; Republican candidate for gov. of WI, 1936, 1938; Independent Republican (Townsend Plan) candidate for U.S. Senate (WI), 1938; chm., WI State Council of Defense, 1944; appointed member, WI State Comm. on Human Rights, 1949–; ***candidate for Republican nomination to presidency of the U.S., 1956***; Independent Democratic candidate for U.S. House (WI), 1960. BUS. & PROF.: ed.; author; composer; reporter, *Ashland Daily Press*, 1915–25, ed., 1925–; reporter, *Milwaukee (WI) Journal*; reporter, *Milwaukee Sentinel*; reporter, *Janesville (WI) Gazette*; editorial writer, *National Magazine*, Boston, MA, to 1924. MIL.: 2d lt., U.S. Army, 1918–19. MEM.: Zeta Psi; Fighters for MacArthur (founder; pres.). WRITINGS: *LaFollette Socialism* (1931); *Private Ownership and American Progress* (1931); *Is Gag Rule to Be Tolerated in Wisconsin?* (1931); *U. off the Track* (1931); *LaFollette Road to Communism* (1936); *The Stories Behind America's Patriotic Songs* (1942); *The Wisconsin Islands* (1945); *The Squibber Book* (1945); *A Small Town Editor's View of Life* (1948); *Challenge to the Republican Party* (1951); *An Editor Fights to Save America* (1951); *Victory of Christian Prayer Over Communism* (1954); *The Power of Going Direct to the Lord and His Son, Jesus Christ* (1955); *Catholic Beginnings in Wisconsin* (1961); *The Catholic Foundation* (1972); *The Catholic Foundation of Wisconsin* (1975); "We'll Sing Sing Sing to Victory!" (song); "Breathing for Jesus" (song, 1971); other songs. REL.: R.C. (nee Presb.). MAILING ADDRESS: 1209 Ellis Ave., Ashland, WI 54806.

CHASE, JUNE. POLIT. & GOV.: ***independent candidate for presidency of the U.S., 1984***. MAILING ADDRESS: P.O. Box 813, Creswell, OR 97426.

CHASE, SALMON PORTLAND. b. Jan 13, 1808, Cornish, NH; d. May 7, 1873, New York, NY; par. Ithamar and Janette (Ralston) Chase; m. Katherine Jane Garniss, Mar 4, 1834; m. 2d, Eliza Ann Smith, Sep 26, 1839; m. 3d, Sarah Bella Dunlop Ludlow, Nov 6, 1846; c. Catherine Jane "Kate" (Mrs. William Sprague); Amelia Janette; Janette Ralston "Nettie" (Mrs. William S. Hoyt); Josephine Ludlow; Lizzie (d. 1842); Lizzie (d. 1844). EDUC.: Mr. Dunham's School, Windsor, VT; Cincinnati (OH) Coll., 1821; Royalton Acad.; grad., Dartmouth Coll., 1826; studied law under William Wirt (q.v.), Washington, DC. POLIT. & GOV.: delegate, National Rep. Nat'l. Conv., 1832; candidate for Whig Party nomination to OH State Senate, 1840; elected as a Whig to Cincinnati (OH) City Council, 1840; delegate, Liberty Party National Convention, 1843, 1847; ***Liberty Party candidate for vice presidency of the U.S., 1848 (declined)***; delegate, Free Soil Party National Convention, 1848; elected as a Free Soil-Democrat to U.S. Senate (OH), 1849–55; founder, Independent Democratic Party, 1852; elected as a Free Soil-Democrat to gov. of OH, 1855–57; ***Spirit Medium Party candidate for presidency of the U.S., c. 1856***; elected as a Republican to gov. of OH, 1857–60; ***candidate for Republican nomination to presidency of the U.S., 1856, 1860, 1864, 1868***; elected as a Republican to U.S. Senate (OH), 1860–61; appointed U.S. sec. of the treasury, 1861–64; delegate, National Peace Convention, 1861, 1868; appointed chief justice, Supreme

Court of the U.S., 1864–73; ***candidate for Democratic nomination to presidency of the U.S., 1868 (declined), 1872; candidate for Liberal Republican Party nomination to presidency of the U.S., 1872; candidate for Prohibition Party nomination to presidency of the U.S., 1872***. BUS. & PROF.: atty.; admitted to OH Bar, 1829; schoolteacher; law practice, Cincinnati, OH, 1830; partner, Chase and Eels (law firm), Cincinnati, to 1838; partner, Chase and Bell (law firm), Cincinnati, 1838–48; partner, Chase, Ball and Wells (law firm), 1848–49; partner, Chase, Ball and Hoadly (law firm), 1849; solicitor, Bank of the U.S., 1834; dir., Lafayette Bank of Cincinnati. MEM.: Cincinnati Lyceum (founder, 1830; lecturer). WRITINGS: *Statutes of Ohio* (1833–35). REL.: Protestant Episcopal Church. MISC.: known as "attorney general" for runaway slaves; presided over impeachment trial of President Andrew Johnson (q.v.). RES.: Cincinnati, OH.

CHASE, SIMEON BREWSTER. b. Apr 18, 1828, Gibson, PA; d. Jan 9, 1909, Hallstead, PA; par. Amasa and Sarah (Guile) Chase; m. Fanny Du Bois, May 1, 1851; c. N. Du Bois; Emmet C.; George Amasa. EDUC.: grad., Hamilton Coll., 1851; studied law, Montrose, PA. POLIT. & GOV.: delegate, Rep. Nat'l. Conv., 1856; elected as a Republican to PA State House, 1856–58 (acting Speaker, 1857); chm., PA State Republican Convention, 1857, 1858; candidate for Republican nomination to gov. of PA, 1857; permanent chm., Prohibition Party National Convention, 1872; ***candidate for Prohibition Party nomination to presidency of the U.S., 1872***; Prohibition Party candidate for gov. of PA, 1872 and one other time; chm., Prohibition Party National Cmte., 1872–76; Prohibition Party candidate for justice, PA State Supreme Court, 1887; Prohibition Party candidate for U.S. House (PA), 1878, 1880, 1892. BUS. & PROF.: teacher, 1842; atty.; law practice, Easton, PA; co-owner (with E. B. Chase), *Montrose Democrat*, 1851. MEM.: Sons of Temperance; Independent Order of Good Templars (right worthy grand templar, 1858–63; grand chief templar of PA, 7 years). WRITINGS: *A Digest of the Laws, Rules, and Usages of the Independent Order of Good Templars; Digest and Treatise on Parliamentary Law; An Exposition of the Order of Good Templars* (1864); *The Good of the Order* (1870); *Manual or Exposition of the Independent Order of Good Templars* (1872); *History of Good Templars*. REL.: Presb. (commissioner, General Assembly; ruling elder, First Presbyterian Church of Great Bend, 51 years). RES.: Montrose, PA.

CHASE, SOLON. b. Jan 14, 1822, Chase's Mills, ME; d. Nov 24, 1909, Chase's Mills, ME; par. Isaac and Eunice Chase; married; c. Carroll; James J.; Isaac. EDUC.: Gorham Seminary; U.S. Military Acad. (rejected for physical reasons). POLIT. & GOV.: elected as a Republican to ME State House, 1861–62; appointed collector of internal revenue (ME), by President Andrew Johnson (q.v.), not confirmed; delegate, Independent National (Greenback) Party National Convention, 1876 (vice pres.); campaigner, Greenback Party, 1876–84; pres., ME Greenback Party State Convention, 1878; Greenback Party candidate for U.S. House (ME), 1878; postmaster, Chase's Mills, ME, 1879; ***candidate for Independent National (Greenback) Party nomination to presidency of the U.S., 1880, 1884***; National (Greenback) Party candidate for gov. of ME, 1880 (declined), 1882; National (Greenback) Party candidate for U.S. Senate (ME), 1880; ***candidate for Anti-Monopoly Party nomination to presidency of the U.S., 1884***. BUS. & PROF.: publisher, *Chase's Mills Chronicle*, 1875–79; publisher, *Greenback Labor Chronicle*, Portland, ME, 1880; publisher, *Chase's Enquirer*, 1880–81; publisher, *Them Steers*, Auburn, ME, 1882–83; lecturer; farmer, Chase's Mills. MISC.: known as "Uncle Solon"; addressed Cooper's Union, New York, NY, Sep 17, 1879. RES.: Chase's Mills, ME.

CHASSEE, LEO JEANNOT. b. 1892, Menominee, MI; deceased; par. David Chassee. EDUC.: grad., U. of WI; Milwaukee State Teachers Coll.; Northwestern U.; Ph.D.; LL.D. POLIT. & GOV.: candidate for Democratic nomination to gov. of WI, 1930; ***candidate for Democratic nomination to presidency of the U.S., 1932; candidate for Socialist Party nomination to presidency of the U.S., 1932***; candidate for Republican nomination to gov. of WI, 1934, 1938; ***candidate for Republican nomination to presidency of the U.S., 1936***; member, Milwaukee Cty. (WI) Republican Central Cmte. (removed, 1938). BUS. & PROF.: schoolteacher, Marinette; instructor, City Coll. of NY; instructor, Columbia U.; atty., Milwaukee, WI; prof. of political science, St. Norbert's Coll., West De Pere, WI; author. MIL.: U.S. Army, WWI. WRITINGS: *A Study of Student Loans and Their Relation to Higher Educational Finance* (1925); *Management of Personal Income* (1927). RES.: Milwaukee, WI.

CHAVEZ, ANTHONY SOLOMON. b. Jul 10, 1931, El Paso, TX; par. Jose Refugio Ramos II and Marciana (Estrada) Chavez; single. EDUC.: A.A., San Bernardino Valley Coll.; B.A., CA Polytechnic State U. POLIT. & GOV.: ***candidate for Democratic nomination to presidency of the U.S., 1980, 1984***. BUS. & PROF.: soldier. MIL.: U.S. Army, 11 years. REL.: R.C. MAILING ADDRESS: 2121 Monterey St., San Luis Obispo, CA 93401.

CHAVEZ, CESAR ESTRADA. b. Mar 31, 1927, Yuma, AZ; d. Apr 23, 1993, San Luis, AZ; par. Librado and Juana (Estrada) Chavez; m. Helen Fabela, Oct 22, 1948; c. Fernando; Sylvia; Linda; Anna; Eloise; Anthony "Birdie"; Paul; Elizabeth. EDUC.: seventh grade, Brawley Elementary School. POLIT. & GOV.: ***candidate for Democratic nomination to vice presidency of the U.S., 1972; candidate for Democratic nomination to presidency of the U.S., 1976***. BUS. & PROF.: farm worker; labor organizer; organizer, community service organization, 1952–58, gen. dir., 1958–62; founder, National Farm Workers Assn., 1962 (merged with Agricultural Workers Organizing Cmte., AFL-CIO, to form United Farm Workers Organizing Cmte., 1966); pres., United Farm Workers Organizing Cmte.,

1966–72; pres., United Farm Workers of America, 1973–. MIL.: U.S.N.R., 1944–45. MEM.: National Agricultural Workers Union; United Farm Workers Organizing Cmte., AFL-CIO (pres., 1966–72). AWARDS: Presidential Medal of Freedom, 1994. REL.: R.C. RES.: Delano, CA.

CHAVEZ, VENTURA. m. Crusita Chavez. POLIT. & GOV.: ***People's Constitutional Party candidate for presidency of the U.S., 1968***. BUS. & PROF.: aircraft painter. MEM.: Alianza Federal De Mercedes. MAILING ADDRESS: 5430 Evans Rd., S.W., Albuquerque, NM.

CHENAULT, W. L. POLIT. & GOV.: Republican candidate for U.S. House (AL), 1920; ***candidate for Republican nomination to presidency of the U.S., 1924***. RES.: Russellville, AL.

CHICK, JOHN MARTIN. b. Apr 14, 1942, Patchogue, NY; par. James Edward and Alice Marie (Trembley) Chick; m. Anna Morgan; m. 2d, Mildred Morgan (divorced); c. Edward; Roxeanne. EDUC.: 11th Grade, Moravia Central School. POLIT. & GOV.: elected as a Democrat, town supervisor, Throop, NY, 1968; elected as a Democrat, town justice, Throop, 1976; chief of fire department, Throop; ***candidate for Democratic nomination to presidency of the U.S., 1980***. BUS. & PROF.: asst. maintenance engineer, Mercy Hospital, Auburn, NY; service technician, Agway Petroleum, Auburn, NY. MEM.: Elks; Northern Central NY Firemen's Assn. (exec. dir., legislative representative); Cayuga Cty. Burn Chapter (pres.); Chief's Assn. of Cayuga Cty. (pres.); Firemen's Assn. of the State of NY; NY State Fire Chief's Assn.; Cayuga Cty. Fire Advisory Board. AWARDS: "Man of the Year" Award, Throop Fire Dept.; "Outstanding First Field Days" Award, Throop Fire Dept. REL.: R.C. MAILING ADDRESS: R.D. #5, State St. Rd., Auburn, NY 13021.

CHILDERS, PEGGY ANN. POLIT. & GOV.: candidate for Democratic nomination to U.S. House (GA), 1983, 1984; ***candidate for Democratic nomination to presidency of the U.S., 1984, 1988***. MAILING ADDRESS: #6, 646 Roswell St., N.E., Marietta, GA 30061.

CHILDRESS, MICHAEL OWEN. POLIT. & GOV.: ***independent candidate for vice presidency of the U.S., 1988***. MEM.: Psychotics for a Better America. MAILING ADDRESS: P.O. Box 36, North Garden, VA 22959.

CHILDS, BARRY WAYNE. b. Jan 9, 1952, Battle Creek, MI; par. Kenneth Wentworth and Theresa (Morrel) Childs; single. EDUC.: Eau Gallie H.S., Melbourne, FL; Dale Carnegie courses. POLIT. & GOV.: ***independent candidate for presidency of the U.S., 1988, 1992***. BUS. & PROF.: marketing. REL.: Christian. MAILING ADDRESS: 6702 Magnolia Lane, #24, New Orleans, LA 70127.

CHILDS, GEORGE WILLIAM. b. May 12, 1829, Baltimore, MD; d. Feb 3, 1894, Philadelphia, PA; m. Emma Bouvier Peterson. EDUC.: M.A., Princeton U. POLIT. & GOV.: ***candidate for Republican nomination to presidency of the U.S., 1888 (declined)***. BUS. & PROF.: owner, George W. Childs and Co. (confectionery business), 1848; assoc., R. E. Peterson and Co. (book sellers), 1849–54; partner, Childs and Peterson (book sellers), 1854–60; assoc., J. B. Lippincott and Co., 1860–61; founder, *American Publishers Circular and Literary Gazette*, 1863–70; owner, publisher, *Philadelphia Public Ledger*, 1864–94; philanthropist. MIL.: apprentice, U.S. Navy, 1842–43. MEM.: U.S. Military Acad. (visitor). WRITINGS: *Recollections of General Grant* (1885); *Recollections by George W. Childs* (1890). REL.: Protestant Episcopal Church. RES.: Bryn Mawr, PA.

CHILES, LAWTON MAINOR, JR. b. Apr 30, 1930, Lakeland, FL; par. Lawton Mainor and Margaret (Patterson) Chiles; m. Rhea May Grafton, Jan 27, 1951; c. Tandy M.; Lawton Mainor III; Edward G.; Rhea Gay. EDUC.: B.S., B.A., U. of FL, 1952, LL.B., 1955. POLIT. & GOV.: elected as a Democrat to FL State House, 1959–67; elected as a Democrat to FL State Senate, 1967–71; elected as a Democrat to U.S. Senate (FL), 1971–89; ***candidate for Democratic nomination to vice presidency of the U.S., 1972***; delegate, Democratic Mid-Term Conference, 1974; member, Dem. Nat'l. Cmte. (FL); elected as a Democrat to gov. of FL, 1991–. BUS. & PROF.: atty.; admitted to FL Bar, 1955; law practice, Lakeland, FL, 1955–. MIL.: 1st lt., U.S. Army, 1953–54. MEM.: Alpha Tau Omega; Phi Delta Phi; Florida Blue Key; U. of FL Hall of Fame; FL Bar Assn.; Kiwanis; Lakeland Quarterback Club; March of Dimes (Lakeland chm., 1964); C. of C.; U. of FL Law Center (trustee, 1968–); United Fund of Greater Lakeland (chm., 1967); Polk Cty. Cancer Crusade (chm., 1968); YMCA Century Club; FL Southern Coll. (trustee, 1971–); Eckerd Coll. (trustee, 1971). AWARDS: Distinguished Service Award, FL Assn. for Retarded Children, 1968; Governor's Award for Conservation, 1968; Wildlife Conservation Award, National Wildlife Federation, 1968; Commendation Award, FL Agriculture Council; Meritorious Public Service Award, Legislative Poll; Award of Special Merit, United Fund; "Outstanding Young Man Award," Junior C. of C.; Victory Crusade Award, American Cancer Soc. HON. DEG.: LL.D., FL Southern Coll., 1971; LL.D., Jacksonville U., 1971. REL.: Presb. MAILING ADDRESS: 940 Lake Hollingsworth Dr., Lakeland, FL 33803.

CHIMENTO, CARMEN CHRISTOPHER. b. 1931; m. Susan M. Chimento. POLIT. & GOV.: candidate for Democratic nomination to U.S. Senate (NH), 1974; American Party candidate for U.S. Senate (NH), 1974, 1975; ***candidate for Republican nomination to presidency of the U.S., 1976; candidate for Democratic nomination to presidency of the U.S., 1976; candidate for American Party nomination to presidency of the U.S., 1976***; candidate for Democratic nomination to gov. of NH, 1972, 1976; candidate for Republican nomination to gov. of NH, 1976; candidate for Republican nomination to U.S. Senate (NH), 1976, 1978, 1980; candidate for Democratic nomination to U.S. House (NH), 1984. BUS. & PROF.: electronics technician; software writing consultant. MAILING ADDRESS: 166 Mudjekeewis Trail, Medford Lake, NJ 08055.

CHISHOLM, SHIRLEY ANITA ST. HILL.

b. Nov 30, 1924, Brooklyn, NY; par. Charles Christopher and Ruby (Seale) St. Hill; m. Conrad Q. Chisholm, Oct 8, 1949 (divorced, 1977); m. 2d, Arthur Hardwick, Jr., Nov 26, 1977. EDUC.: B.A. (cum laude), Brooklyn Coll., 1946; M.A., Columbia U., 1952. POLIT. & GOV.: elected as a Democrat to NY State Assembly, 1965–69; elected as a Democrat to U.S. House (NY), 1969–83; member, Dem. Nat'l. Cmte. (NY), 1968–; ***candidate for Democratic nomination to presidency of the U.S., 1972; candidate for Democratic nomination to vice presidency of the U.S., 1972, 1980***; delegate, Dem. Nat'l. Conv., 1972, 1976; delegate, Democratic Mid-Term Conference, 1974. BUS. & PROF.: nursery schoolteacher, Mt. Calvary Child Care Center, 1946–52; dir., Friend in Need Nursery, 1952–53; dir., Hamilton-Madison Child Care Center, 1953–59; educational consultant, New York (NY) Division of Day Care, 1959–64; Purington Chair, Mt. Holyoke Coll., South Hadley, MA, 1983–. MEM.: Central Brooklyn Coordinating Council (consultant); Bethune Memorial Cmte., National Council of Negro Women; Inst. for Studies in Education (Advisory Council); Advisory Cmte., Black Enterprise Magazine; Americans for Democratic Action (dir.); NY Young Democrats (adviser); Advisory Board on Migrant Studies, State U. Coll.; Salvation Army (adviser); Cosmopolitan Young People's Symphony Orchestra (dir.); Southern Elections Fund (trustee); Women's Equity Action League (adviser); Brooklyn Museum (adviser); Adelphi U. Octet Associates (adviser); Long Island U. (trustee); Brooklyn Coll. Alumni Assn.; League of Women Voters; Democratic Women's Workshop; NAACP; Brooklyn Home for Aged People; National Assn. of College Women; Bedford-Stuyvesant Political League; Key Women, Inc.; National Organization of Women. AWARDS: Achievement Award, Yeshiva U.; Alumna of the Year Award, Brooklyn Coll. Alumni Bulletin, 1957; Award for Outstanding Work in the Field of Child Welfare, Brooklyn Women's Council, 1957; Key Woman of the Year Award, 1963; Cmte. of Friends Plaque, 1965; Citation for Outstanding Service, Sisterhood of Concord Baptist Church, 1965; Human Relations Award, Central Nassau Club of Business and Professional Women, 1965; Outstanding Service in Good Government Award, Christian Women's Retreat, 1965; Certificate of Honor, Junior H.S. 271, Brooklyn, NY, 1965; Woman of Achievement, Key Women, Inc., 1965; Humanitarian Award, Y.I.A. Community Corp.; Citizen of the Year Award, United Factory Workers; Deborah Gannett Award, National Media Women; 12th Annual Achievement Award, New York City Police Dept.; Dr. Martin Luther King Award, Bottle and Cork Sales Club; Golden Doughnut Award, The Salvation Army; Sojourner Truth Award, Assn. for the Study of Negro Life and History, 1969; Russwurm Award, Newspaper Publishers Assn., 1969. HON. DEG.: LL.D., Talladega Coll., 1967; LL.D., Wilmington Coll., 1969; L.H.D., Hampton Inst., 1970; L.H.D., Coppin State Coll., 1971; LL.D., William Patterson Coll., 1971; LL.D., La Salle Coll., 1971; LL.D., U. of ME, 1971; LL.D., Portland U., 1971; LL.D., Capital U., 1971; D.H.L., Pratt Inst., 1969 (declined), 1972; LL.D., Kenyon Coll., 1973; LL.D., U. of Cincinnati; LL.D., Smith Coll.; LL.D., Aquinas Coll.; LL.D., Reed Coll. WRITINGS: *Unbought and Unbossed* (1970); *Rather Be Black Than Female* (1970); *The Good Fight* (1973). REL.: Methodist. MAILING ADDRESS: 1028 St. Johns Place, Brooklyn, NY 11213.

CHISHOLM, TERRY.

POLIT. & GOV.: ***candidate for Democratic nomination to vice presidency of the U.S., 1980***. MAILING ADDRESS: CA?

CHRISTENSEN, JAN PETER.

b. Oct 13, 1947, New York, NY; par. Conrad Lincoln and Eleanor (Ingalls) Christensen; m. Alice Spencer; m. 2d, Marilyn Hebert Kneeter; c. Eric Hebert (stepson). EDUC.: Hope Coll.; Ulster Cty. Community Coll.; A.A., Hudson Valley Community Coll.; B.A., State U. of NY at Albany, 1975, M.S., 1976. POLIT. & GOV.: ***National Sea Song Party candidate for presidency of the U.S., 1992 (withdrew); Independent Party candidate for vice presidency of the U.S., 1992***. BUS. & PROF.: ed., *Engineering Society*; songwriter; folk musician; singer; environmentalist. MIL.: U.S.N.R., 1965–72 (active duty, Hospital Corps, 1969–71). MEM.: Hudson River Sloop Clearwater, Inc.; Hudson River Sloop Singers; volunteer, NY Public Library. REL.: none. MAILING ADDRESS: 2765 West 5th St., #17B, Brooklyn, NY 11224.

CHRISTENSEN, PARLEY PARKER.

b. Jul 19, 1869, Weston, ID; d. Feb 10, 1954, Los Angeles, CA; par. Peter and Sophia M. Christensen; single. EDUC.: A.B., U. of UT, 1890; LL.B., Cornell U., 1897. POLIT. & GOV.: chm., Cornell U. Republican Club; superintendent of schools, Toole Cty., UT, 1892–95; sec., UT State Constitutional Convention, 1895; elected as a Republican, prosecuting atty., Salt Lake Cty., UT, 1901–06; elected as a Republican to UT State House, 1910–12; Republican candidate for U.S. House (UT), two times; organizer, UT Labor Party; permanent chm., Cmte. of 48 National Convention, 1920; delegate, Labor Party National Convention, 1920; chm., Farmer-Labor Party National Convention, 1920; ***Farmer-Labor Party candidate for presidency of the U.S., 1920***; member, exec. cmte., Conference for Progressive Political Action, 1924; elected member, IL State Legislature; Progressive

Party candidate for U.S. Senate (IL), 1926; elected member, City Council, Los Angeles, CA, 10 years. BUS. & PROF.: schoolteacher, principal, Murray and Grantsville, UT, Schools, 1890–95; Teamster; railroad worker; atty.; law practice, UT, 1897–1921; law practice, Chicago, IL, 1921. MEM.: Universala Esperanto Asocio; Elks (grand esquire); Odd Fellows (grand representative of UT); Chicago Federation of Labor (delegate); News Writers Union. REL.: Unitarian. RES.: Salt Lake City, UT.

CHRISTMAS, RICHARD E. b. 1942; par. Dorothea Christmas. POLIT. & GOV.: ***candidate for Democratic nomination to presidency of the U.S., 1980***. BUS. & PROF.: gas station attendant, 1962–74; unemployed. MAILING ADDRESS: 1735 Boston Blvd., Lansing, MI 48910.

CHRISTOPHERSON, CHARLES ANDREW. b. Jul 23, 1871, Amherst, MN; d. Nov 2, 1951, Sioux Falls, SD; par. Knudt and Julia (Nelson) Christopherson; m. Abbie M. Deyoe, Nov 30, 1897; c. Charles Andrew, Jr. EDUC.: Sioux Falls Business College and Normal School. POLIT. & GOV.: elected member, Board of Education, Sioux Falls, SD, 1908–18 (pres., 1911–15); elected as a Republican to SD State House, 1913–17 (Speaker, 1915–17); elected as a Republican to U.S. House (SD), 1919–33; Republican candidate for U.S. House (SD), 1932, 1934; delegate, SD Republican State Convention, 1938, 1940, 1942; appointed state administrator of war savings (SD), 1941–43; delegate, Rep. Nat'l. Conv., 1944; ***candidate for Republican nomination to presidency of the U.S., 1944***; exec. mgr., SD State War Finance Council. BUS. & PROF.: atty.; admitted to SD Bar, 1893; law practice, Sioux Falls, SD, 1894–1951; pres., chm. of the board, Union Savings Bank. MEM.: Sons of Norway; Masons (grand commander; potentate; Ancient Arabic Order of the Nobles of the Mystic Shrine, AAONMS); Elks (exalted ruler); Independent Order of Odd Fellows (noble grand); Moose; Knights of Pythias; Minnehaha Club. REL.: Congregationalist. RES.: Sioux Falls, SD.

CHURCH, FRANK FORRESTER, JR. b. Jul 25, 1924, Boise, ID; d. Apr 7, 1984, Bethesda, MD; par. Frank Forrester and Laura (Bilderback) Church; m. Jean Bethine Clark, Jun 21, 1947; c. Frank Forrester III; Chase Clark. EDUC.: B.A., Stanford U., 1947, LL.B., 1950; Harvard U., 1948. POLIT. & GOV.: state chm., ID Young Democrats, 1952–54; Democratic candidate for ID State House, 1952; ID State Democratic Convention (keynoter), 1952; elected as a Democrat to U.S. Senate (ID), 1957–81; delegate, Dem. Nat'l. Conv., 1960 (keynoter), 1972; delegate, U.S. Mission to the U.N., 1966; delegate, U.S.-Canada Interparliamentary Conference, 1969, 1970, 1971; ***candidate for Democratic nomination to vice presidency of the U.S., 1972, 1976; candidate for Democratic nomination to presidency of the U.S., 1976***; Democratic candidate for U.S. Senate (ID), 1980. BUS. & PROF.: atty.; admitted to ID Bar, 1950; law practice, Boise, ID, 1950–56; partner, Whitman and Ransom (law firm), Washington, DC, 1981–84. MIL.: pvt., U.S. Army, 1942–44, 1st lt., 1944–46; Bronze Star. MEM.: Crusade for Freedom (ID chm., 1954–55); ABA; ID Bar Assn.; American Legion; VFW; Soc. of Mayflower Descendants; Phi Beta Kappa. AWARDS: National Award, American Legion Oratorical Contest, 1941; Joffre Debate Medal, Stanford U., 1947; one of ten "Outstanding Young Men in America," National Junior C. of C., 1957; "Conservationist of the Year," National Wildlife Federation, 1965. REL.: Presb. RES.: Boise, ID.

CHURCH, SANFORD ELIAS. b. Apr 18, 1815, Milford, NY; d. May 14, 1880, Albion, NY; par. Ozias and Permelia (Sanford) Church; m. Ann Wild, 1840; c. Sanford; one other. EDUC.: Henrietta Acad.; studied law under Josiah A. Eastman, Scottsville, NY. POLIT. & GOV.: employee, cty. clerk, South Barre, NY, 1834; elected as a Democrat to NY State Assembly, 1841–43; Democratic candidate for U.S. House (NY), 1846, 1862; appointed and subsequently elected district atty., South Barre, NY, 1846–50; elected as a Democrat to lt. gov. of NY, 1850–55; elected as a Democrat, state comptroller of NY, 1857–59; Democratic candidate for state comptroller of NY, 1863; delegate, NY State Constitutional Convention, 1867; ***candidate for Democratic nomination to presidency of the U.S., 1868***; elected chief justice, NY Court of Appeals, 1870–80. BUS. & PROF.: schoolteacher; atty.; admitted to NY Bar, 1835; admitted to the Bar of the Supreme Court of the U.S., 1841; partner (with Judge Bessac), law firm, South Barre, NY, 1841–44; partner (with Noah Davis), law firm, 1844–58; partner (with John G. Sawyer), law firm, 1858–65; partner, Church, Munger and Cook (law firm), Rochester, NY, 1865. RES.: South Barre, NY.

CISNEROS, HENRY GABRIEL. b. Jun 11, 1947, San Antonio, TX; par. J. George and Elvira (Munguia) Cisneros; m. Mary Alice Perez, 1969; c. Teresa Angelica; Mercedes Christina. EDUC.: B.A., TX A&M U., 1968, M. of Urban and Regional Planning, 1970; White House Fellow, 1971–72; M.P.A., Harvard U., 1973; D. Public Administration, George Washington U., 1975. POLIT. & GOV.: appointed administrative asst. to the city mgr., San Antonio, TX, 1968; appointed administrative asst. to the city mgr., Bryan, TX, 1968; appointed asst. dir., Dept. of Model Cities, San Antonio, TX, 1969–70; appointed asst. to the U.S. sec. of health, education and welfare, 1971–72; elected as a Democrat to the San Antonio (TX) City Council, 1975–81; elected as a Democrat, mayor of San Antonio, TX, 1981–89; trustee, San Antonio City Public Service Board; trustee, San Antonio City Water Board; chm., San Antonio Fire and Police Pension Fund; member, Strategy Council, Dem. Nat'l. Cmte.; appointed member, President's Federalism Council; appointed member, National Bipartisan Comm. on Central America; ***candidate for Democratic nomination to vice presidency of the U.S., 1984***; appointed U.S. sec. of housing and urban development, 1993–. BUS. & PROF.: asst. to the exec. vice pres., National League of Cities, Washington, DC, 1970–71; teaching asst., Dept. of Urban Studies and Planning,

MA Inst. of Technology, 1972; asst. prof., Division of Environmental Studies, U. of TX, San Antonio, 1974–93. MIL.: capt., U.S. Army, 1968. MEM.: Twentieth Century Fund Educational Task Force; Eisenhower Foundation; TX A&M U. (Cmte. on Visual Arts); Trinity U. (Business Advisory Cmte.); United San Antonio (tri-chairperson); San Antonio Symphony Soc. (dir., 1974–75); Police Foundation; U.S. Conference of Mayors (pres., 1986); Council on Foreign Relations; National Council for Urban Economic Development. AWARDS: Jefferson Award, American Inst. for Public Service, 1982; Torch of Liberty Award, Anti-Defamation League of B'nai B'rith, 1982. REL.: R.C. MAILING ADDRESS: 2002 West Houston, San Antonio, TX 78207.

CLAPP, MOSES EDWIN. b. May 21, 1851, Delphi, IN; d. Mar 6, 1929, Accotink, VA; par. Harvey Spaulding and Abbie Jane (Vandercook) Clapp; m. Hattie Allen, Dec 20, 1874; c. one son; two daughters. EDUC.: LL.B., U. of WI, 1873. POLIT. & GOV.: elected cty. atty., St. Croix Cty., WI, 1878–80; elected as a Republican, atty. gen. of MN, 1887–93; candidate for Republican nomination to gov. of MN, 1896; elected as a Republican to U.S. Senate (MN), 1901–17; ***candidate for Republican nomination to presidency of the U.S., 1912***; candidate for Republican nomination to U.S. Senate (MN), 1916. BUS. & PROF.: atty.; admitted to WI Bar, 1873; law practice, Hudson, WI, 1873–81; law practice, Fergus Falls, MN, 1881–91; law practice, St. Paul, MN, 1891–1901; law practice, Washington, DC, 1918–29; partner, Clapp and Fertich (law firm), Washington, DC; vice pres., gen. counsel, American Development Corp., Washington, DC, 1923. RES.: Accotink, VA.

CLARK, EDWARD EMERSON. b. May 4, 1930, Middleboro, MA; par. Fletcher, Jr. and Marguarite (Swift) Clark; m. Alicia Garcia Cobos, 1970; c. Edward Emerson, Jr. EDUC.: grad., Tabor Acad., 1948; A.B., Dartmouth Coll., 1952; LL.B., J.D., Harvard U., 1957. POLIT. & GOV.: member, Libertarian Party National Cmte., 1972–79; chm., Free Libertarian Party of NY, 1972; chm., Libertarian Party of CA, 1973–74; member, Los Angeles (CA) Health Systems Agency, 1977; independent (Libertarian) candidate for gov. of CA, 1978; ***Libertarian Party candidate for presidency of the U.S., 1980***. BUS. & PROF.: atty.; admitted to NY Bar, 1957; assoc., Donovan, Leisure, Newton and Irvine (law firm), New York, NY, 1957–64; law practice, Sausalito, CA, 1964–67; counsel, Atlantic Richfield Corp., Los Angeles, CA, 1967–. MIL.: ensign, U.S.N.R., 1952, lt. (jg), 1954. MEM.: Sigma Chi; CA Bar Assn.; NY Bar Assn.; Balance the Budget Drive, National Taxpayers' Union (co-chm.). WRITINGS: *New Beginning* (1980). MAILING ADDRESS: 3445 Monterey Rd., San Marino, CA 91108.

CLARK, EDWARD THORNE. b. 1856, Halifax Cty., NC; d. Apr 7, 1932, Northampton Cty., NC; par. David and Anna M. (Thorne) Clark; m. Margaret Lillington; m. 2d, Eloise Bradley; c. A. L.; David; Mrs. F. W. Graves. POLIT. & GOV.: elected as a Populist to NC State Senate, 1897–99; ***independent candidate for presidency of the U.S., 1908***. BUS. & PROF.: atty.; law practice, Weldon, NC. REL.: Episc. MISC.: brother of Walter A. Clark (q.v.). RES.: Weldon, NC.

CLARK, HERBERT PORTER, JR. par. Herbert Porter Clark, Sr. POLIT. & GOV.: ***candidate for Republican nomination to vice presidency of the U.S., 1992***. BUS. & PROF.: unemployed. MISC.: disabled. MAILING ADDRESS: Concord, NH.

CLARK, JAMES BEAUCHAMP "CHAMP." b. Mar 7, 1850, Lawrenceburg, KY; d. Mar 2, 1921, Washington, DC; par. John Hampton and Aletha Jane (Beauchamp) Clark; m. Genevieve Bennett, Dec 14, 1881; c. Joel Bennett (q.v.). EDUC.: KY U.; grad., Bethany Coll., 1873, LL.D., 1914; grad., Cincinnati Law School, 1875. POLIT. & GOV.: city atty., LA, MO, 1878–81; city atty., Bowling Green, MO, 1878–81; presidential elector, Democratic Party, 1880; elected prosecuting atty., Pike Cty., MO, 1885–89; elected as a Democrat to MO State House, 1889–91; delegate, Trans-Mississippi Congress, 1891; elected as a Democrat to U.S. House of Reps. (MO), 1893–95, 1897–1921 (minority leader, 1907–11, 1919–21; Speaker, 1911–19); Democratic candidate for U.S. House (MO), 1894, 1920; chm., Dem. Nat'l. Conv., 1904; ***candidate for Democratic nomination to presidency of the U.S., 1912, 1916, 1920***. BUS. & PROF.: atty.; admitted to MO Bar, 1875; pres., Marshall Coll., WV, 1873–74; ed., *Daily News*, Louisiana, MO, 1876–80; ed., *Riverside, (MO) Press*, c. 1880; law practice, Bowling Green, MO, 1880–1921. MEM.: Trans-Mississippi Congress (vice pres., 1891). RES.: Bowling Green, MO.

CLARK, JOEL BENNETT "CHAMP." b. Jan 8, 1890, Bowling Green, MO; d. Jul 13, 1954, Gloucester, MA; par. James Beauchamp (q.v.) and Genevieve (Bennett) Clark; m. Mariam Marsh, Oct 2, 1922; m. 2d, Violet Heming, Oct 6, 1945; c. Champ; Wilbur Marsh; Kimball. EDUC.: A.B., U. of MO, 1913, LL.D.; LL.B., George Washington U., 1914. POLIT. & GOV.: parliamentarian, U.S. House, 1913–17; delegate, Dem. Nat'l. Conv., 1916 (parliamentarian), 1920, 1928, 1936, 1940; ***candidate for Democratic nomination to vice presidency of the U.S., 1924***; elected as a Democrat to U.S. Senate (MO), 1933–45; ***candidate for Democratic nomination to presidency of the U.S., 1940***; candidate for Democratic nomination to U.S. Senate (MO), 1944; appointed assoc. justice, U.S. Court of Appeals, DC, 1945–54. BUS. & PROF.: atty.; admitted to MO Bar, 1914; law practice, St. Louis, MO, 1919–54; author. MIL.: capt., U.S.A.R., 1917; lt. col., U.S. Army, 1917–18, col., 1919. MEM.: American Legion (national commander); 35th Div. Veterans Assn. (commander); National Guard Assn. of the U.S. (pres.); Order of the Coif; Phi Beta Kappa; Delta Tau Delta; Phi Delta Phi; Delta Sigma Rho; Masons; Odd Fellows; Chevy

Chase Club; Smithsonian Institution (regent, 1940–44); Noonday Club. HON. DEG.: LL.D., Marshall Coll.; LL.D., Bethany Coll.; LL.D., Washington and Lee U. WRITINGS: *John Quincy Adams: "Old Man Eloquent"* (1932); *Constitution, Manual and Digest of Practice of the U.S. House of Representatives* (1913–16); *Social Studies* (coauthor, 1934). REL.: Presb. RES.: St. Louis, MO.

CLARK, MORTON. POLIT. & GOV.: ***candidate for Democratic nomination to vice presidency of the U.S., 1924***. RES.: unknown.

CLARK, THOMAS OGLE. b. 1870. POLIT. & GOV.: ***independent candidate for presidency of the U.S., 1904***. WRITINGS: *At the Gate and Other Poems* (1904). RES.: MD.

CLARK, WALTER A. b. Aug 19, 1846, Halifax Cty., NC; d. May 19, 1924, Raleigh, NC; par. David and Anna M. (Thorne) Clark; m. Susan Washington Graham, Jan 28, 1874; c. Mrs. J. Ernest Erwin; Mrs. John A. McLean; David; Walter; William A. Graham; John W.; Thorne. EDUC.: Captain Tew's Military Acad., 1860–61; A.B., U. of NC, 1864, A.M., 1867, LL.D., 1888; LL.B., Columbia Law School, 1867. POLIT. & GOV.: appointed and subsequently elected judge, Superior Court of NC, 1885–89; candidate for Democratic nomination to gov. of NC, 1888 (declined), 1896 (declined); appointed and subsequently elected judge, Supreme Court of NC, 1889–1924 (chief justice, 1903–24); ***candidate for Democratic nomination to vice presidency of the U.S., 1896***; candidate for Democratic nomination to U.S. Senate (NC), 1912; appointed member, National War and Labor Board, 1918–19. BUS. & PROF.: atty.; admitted to NC Bar, 1868; law practice, Scotland Neck, NC; law practice, Raleigh; railroad counsel; ed., *Raleigh (NC) News*; . MIL.: drill master, C.S.A., 1861; adj., 35th NC Regt., C.S.A., 1863, maj.; lt. col., col., 70th NC Regt., C.S.A., 1864–65. MEM.: Masons. WRITINGS: *Methodism in North Carolina* (1880); *Mudcut Circular* (1880); *State Records* (ed., 1895–1901); *Histories of North Carolina Regiments* (ed., 1901); *Annotated Code of Civil Procedure; Constant's Memoirs of Napoleon*, (translator, 1895). REL.: Methodist (delegate, General Conference). MISC.: brother of Edward Thorne Clark (q.v.). RES.: Raleigh, NC.

CLARK, WILLIAM LLOYD. b. Jan 29, 1869, Mt. Sterling, IL; par. Thomas A. and Laura Alice (Briggs) Clark; married; c. Virgil; Wendell H.; Maynard. EDUC.: Chaddock Coll., Quincy, IL, 1889. POLIT. & GOV.: Prohibition Party candidate for U.S. House (IL), 1908, 1916; ***candidate for Prohibition Party nomination to vice presidency of the U.S., 1916 (withdrew)***. BUS. & PROF.: author; publisher, ed., *The Rail Splitter*, Milan, IL, 1902–; ed., *Opinion*, Quincy; ed., *One True Friend*; lecturer on Anti-Catholic themes. MEM.: American Protective Assn. (lecturer); Guardians of Liberty; Knights of Luther; Pathfinders; Masons; Ku Klux Klan. WRITINGS: *The Church Supper and the Lodge; The Devil's Theology* (1895); *Hell at Midnight in Davenport* (1908); *Hell at Midnight in Springfield* (1910); *The Devil's Prayer Book* (1912); *Reminiscences of a Reformer's Life, or, Twenty Five Years on the Skirmish Line Against Political Romanism* (1913); *Washington in the Grasp of Rome* (1914); *The Story of a Stormy Life: An Autobiography* (1924); *Popery Unmasked* (1924); *The House of the Good Shepherd* (1928); *The Devil in a Bath Tub; Three Keys to Hell, or, Rum, Romanism and Ruin; Small Gun Spiked* (1929); *The Story of My Battle with the Scarlet Beast* (1932); *From Belshazzar to Roosevelt* (1935); *The Decay of a Nation; Open Letter to the President of the United States; Woman's Heroism; The Knights of Columbus Unmasked; The Fight for a Nation's Life; Messages of Love and Hate; Al Smith and the White House; The Menace of Al Smith; Foxe's Book of Martyrs; Politics and Politicians; Behind Convent Bars; Words of Wisdom; The Taxation of Church Property; The Harlotry of the Silver Screen; Roman Oaths and Papal Curses; An Open Letter to Cardinal Mundelein; Private Diary of an Anti-Papal Propagandist; Billy Sunday Unmasked; Crimes of Priests; Our Sunday Visitor Unmasked; From Roman Dungeon to Civil Liberty; The White Slave Girls of America; The Anti-Catholic Joke Book; Pat's Grip on the Government; The School Plot Unmasked; Peoria by Gaslight; Prison Poems of Andy Lockhart*. REL.: Methodist. RES.: Rock Island, IL.

CLARK, WILLIAM RAMSEY. b. Dec 18, 1927, Dallas, TX; par. Tom C. and Mary (Ramsey) Clark; m. Georgia Welch, Apr 16, 1949; c. Ronda Kathleen; Thomas Campbell. EDUC.: B.A., U. of TX, 1949; A.M., J.D., U. of Chicago, 1950. POLIT. & GOV.: appointed asst. atty. gen. of the U.S., 1965–66; appointed acting atty. gen. of the U.S., 1966–67; appointed atty. gen. of the U.S., 1967–69; ***candidate for Democratic nomination to presidency of the U.S., 1972; candidate for Democratic nomination to vice presidency of the U.S., 1972***; candidate for Democratic nomination to U.S. Senate (NY), 1974, 1976; delegate, Dem. Nat'l. Conv., 1976. BUS. & PROF.: atty.; admitted to TX Bar, 1951; admitted to the Bar of the Supreme Court of the U.S., 1956; admitted to DC Bar, 1969; admitted to NY Bar, 1970; partner, Clark, Reed and Clark (law firm), Dallas, 1951–61; partner, Paul, Weiss, Goldberg, Rifkind, Wharton and Garrison (law firm), New York, NY, 1969–70; partner, Clark, Wulf, Levine and Peratis (law firm), New York, 1970–; adjunct prof., Howard U., 1969–72; adjunct prof., Brooklyn Law School, 1973–. MIL.: corp., U.S.M.C. Reserves, 1945–46. MEM.: ABA; Federal Bar Assn.; Dallas Bar Assn.; State Bar of TX; American Jud. Soc.; Southwestern Legal Foundation. WRITINGS: *Crime in America* (1967). MAILING ADDRESS: 6393 Lakeview Dr., Falls Church, VA.

CLARK-DAVIS, GAVIN. POLIT. & GOV.: ***candidate for Republican nomination to presidency of the U.S., 1992***. MAILING ADDRESS: 1898 Troy St., Long Beach, CA 90815.

CLARKE, JOHN HESSIN. b. Sep 18, 1857, Lisbon, OH; d. Mar 22, 1945, San Diego, CA; par. John and Melissa

(Hessin) Clarke; single. EDUC.: A.B., Western Reserve U., 1877, A.M., 1888, LL.D. POLIT. & GOV.: Democratic candidate for U.S. Senate (OH), 1903; candidate for Democratic nomination to U.S. Senate (OH), 1914 (withdrew); appointed judge, U.S. District Court for Northern District of OH, 1914–16; appointed assoc. justice, Supreme Court of the U.S., 1916–22; ***candidate for Democratic nomination to presidency of the U.S., 1924***. BUS. & PROF.: atty.; admitted to OH Bar, 1878; law practice, Lisbon, OH, 1878–80; law practice, Youngstown, OH, 1880–97; law practice, Cleveland, OH, 1897–1914; gen. counsel, New York, Chicago, and St. Louis R.R., 13 years; gen. counsel, Nickel Plate R.R.; regional counsel, Erie R.R.; regional counsel, The Pullman Co.; partner, *Youngstown Vindicator*. MEM.: League of Nations Non-Partisan Assn. of the U.S. (pres., 1922–30); World Peace Foundation (trustee, 1923–31); Youngstown Public Library (hon. life trustee); Cleveland Public Library (trustee, 1903–06); Phi Beta Kappa; Cleveland City Club; Cuyamaca Club; San Diego University Club. HON. DEG.: 1916; LL.D., Brown U., 1924. REL.: Unitarian. MISC.: peace advocate. RES.: Youngstown, OH.

CLARKSON, BRIAN "AARON." b. Mar 1, 1973, Chicago, IL; par. Helen Clarkson; single. EDUC.: grad. (with honors), Lone Oak H.S., Paducah, KY, 1992; Westminster Coll., 1992–. POLIT. & GOV.: ***candidate for Democratic nomination to presidency of the U.S., 1992***. BUS. & PROF.: student. MEM.: Future Business Leaders of America (treas.; reporter); Key Club; Beta Club; Future Young Democrat. AWARDS: Governor's Scholar; nominated for Who's Who. REL.: Southern Bapt. MAILING ADDRESS: 6650 Old Mayfield Rd., Paducah, KY 42003.

CLAUSON, JAMES R. POLIT. & GOV.: ***independent candidate for presidency of the U.S., 1984***. MAILING ADDRESS: Route 2, Box 521H, Cleveland, OH 37311.

CLAWSON, MARGARET LOIS. b. Nov 22, 1911, Marion, IN; d. Oliver Douglas and Elizabeth Idella (Akers) Clawson; m. Dr. J. R. Stewart (divorced, 1947); c. Alice Jane (Mrs. Keith G. Pailthorp). EDUC.: A.B., DePauw U., 1933; Ball State Teacher's Coll., 1941; Marion Coll., 1957; IN U., 1957; Butler U., 1957. POLIT. & GOV.: ***Independent Non-Partisan candidate for presidency of the U.S., 1980***. BUS. & PROF.: teacher of Latin and social science, Marion, IN, 1934–36; stationery and wedding style consultant, L. S. Ayers Dept. Store, 1936–38; employee, Wolf and Dessaurs Dept. Store, Fort Wayne, IN; night desk clerk, YWCA, 1942; employee, Methodist Hospital Laboratory, Indianapolis, IN, 1957; psychiatric researcher, 1975–80; author. MEM.: Mortar Board; Kappa Kappa Gamma; Kappa Kappa Kappa; AAUW; YWCA Travel Club. WRITINGS: *Fairness: Psychiatric Study* (1975; Revised, 1977); *Wisdom, Wit and Poetry* (1979). REL.: Christian Science (nee Methodist). MAILING ADDRESS: 315 South Gallatin St., Apt. 306, Marion, IN 46952.

CLAY, CASSIUS MARCELLUS. b. Oct 19, 1810, Madison Cty., KY; d. Jul 22, 1903, White Hall, KY; par. Green and Sally (Lewis) Clay; m. Mary Jane Warfield, Feb 26, 1832 (divorced, 1878); m. 2d, Dora Richardson, Nov 9, 1894 (divorced, 1898); c. Brutus J.; Green; Mary Barr; Frank; Cassius Marcellus, Jr. (deceased); Cassius Marcellus, Jr.; Laura (q.v.); Annie; Sally Lewis; Flora; Launey (adopted). EDUC.: Richmond Acad.; Coll. of St. Joseph, 1827–28; Transylvania U., 1829–31, LL.D.; B.A., Yale U., 1832; Transylvania Law School. POLIT. & GOV.: elected as a Whig to KY State House, 1835, 1837, 1840; Whig candidate for KY State House, 1836, 1841; delegate, Whig Party National Convention, 1840; Anti-Slavery candidate for gov. of KY, 1850; ***candidate for Republican nomination to vice presidency of the U.S., 1856, 1860; candidate for Republican nomination to presidency of the U.S., 1860***; appointed U.S. minister to Spain, 1861 (declined); appointed U.S. minister to Russia, 1861–69; joined Democratic Party, 1871; *candidate for Liberal Republican Party nomination to vice presidency of the U.S., 1872*. BUS. & PROF.: atty.; admitted to bar, 1797; law practice, Lexington, KY; publisher, *The True American*, 1845–48; publisher, *Examiner*, Louisville, KY, 1849; owner, Cassius M. Clay and Co. (banking house), 1854. MIL.: capt., U.S. Volunteer Infantry, 1846 (prisoner-of-war, 1847); founded Clay Battalion, 1861; maj. gen., U.S.V., 1862. MEM.: KY Hist. Soc. WRITINGS: *Life, Memoirs, Writings and Speeches of Cassius M. Clay* (1886). REL.: Deist (nee Bapt.). MISC.: abolitionist; founder, Berea Coll. RES.: White Hall, KY.

CLAY, PRINCESS FIFI 3 TAFT $ PICK-WILDLIFE-RUNNINGWATERS (See FAY T. CARPENTER-SWAIN).

CLAY, GUY WALTERS (aka GUY W. ROCKEFELLER TAFT and GUY-TAFT CLAY WALTERS). POLIT. & GOV.: ***candidate for Democratic nomination to presidency of the U.S., 1976***. MAILING ADDRESS: 405 Garrard St., Suite 268, Flannery Hotel, Covington, KY 41011.

CLAY, HENRY. b. Apr 12, 1777, Hanover Cty., VA; d. Jun 29, 1852, Washington, DC; par. John and Elizabeth (Hudson) Clay; m. Lucretia Hart, Apr 11, 1799; c. Thomas Hart; James Brown; John Morrison; Henry, Jr.; Laura; Eliza; Theodore Wythe; Anne (Mrs. Henry Erwin); Susan Hart (Mrs. Martin Duralde); Henrietta; Lucretia. EDUC.: studied law under George Wythe. POLIT. & GOV.: copyist, clerk of High Court of Chancery; commonwealth's atty.; elected to KY State House, 1803–06, 1808–10 (Speaker, 1810); elected to U.S. Senate (KY), 1806–07, 1810–11, 1831–42, 1849–52; elected to U.S. House (KY), 1811–14, 1815–20, 1823–25 (Speaker, 1811–14, 1815–20, 1823–25); appointed commissioner, Ghent Peace Conference, 1814; ***Democratic-Republican candidate for presidency of the U.S., 1824; independent candidate for vice presidency of the***

U.S., 1824; appointed U.S. sec. of state, 1825–29; National Republican candidate for presidency of the U.S., 1832; candidate for Whig Party nomination to presidency of the U.S., 1840, 1848; Whig Party candidate for presidency of the U.S., 1844; Clay Whig Party candidate for presidency of the U.S., 1848. BUS. & PROF.: atty.; law practice, Lexington, KY; prof. of law, Transylvania U.; plantation owner, KY. MEM.: Masons (junior warden). REL.: Bapt. MISC.: known as the "Great Pacificator"; developed American System of Internal Improvements; authored MO Compromise of 1820 and Compromise of 1850. RES.: Lexington, KY.

CLAY, JOHN ERNEST. b. Nov 27, 1921, Kansas City, MO; par. Ernest Worman and Gertrude (Turfler) Clay; adopted son of Charles Clay; m. Theodora Summerfield Buchman, Mar 11, 1944 (divorced, Aug 1973); m. 2d, Mary A. Dailey, Oct 20, 1973; c. Peter Worman; Robert Scott. EDUC.: B.A., Carleton Coll., 1943; J.D., Harvard U., 1948. POLIT. & GOV.: member, Draft Adlai Stevenson for President Cmte., 1952; chm., 13th Congressional District Cmte. for Adlai Stevenson III for State Treasurer; co-chm., 13th Congressional District Sidney Yates for Senator; chm., Glencoe (IL) Board of Education, 1966–68; co-chm., 13th Congressional District Citizens for McCarthy, 1968; organizer, IL Republicans and Independents for McCarthy, 1968; co-chairperson, IL McCarthy Cmte., 1976; ***independent (Cmte. for a Constitutional Presidency) candidate for vice presidency of the U.S., 1976***. BUS. & PROF.: atty.; admitted to IL Bar, 1948; assoc., Taylor, Miller, Busch and Magner (law firm), Chicago, IL, 1948–51; partner, Mayer, Brown and Platt (law firm), Chicago, 1951–. MIL.: 2d lt., U.S. Army, 1945–46. MEM.: Phi Beta Kappa; Glencoe Democratic Club (founder; pres.); Democratic Federation of IL; Cmte. on IL Government; Independent Voters of IL (Board member); Chicago Bar Assn. (chm., Cmte. on Civil Rights; chm., Corp. Law Cmte.; Cmte. on Securities Laws); Chicago Council of Lawyers; Lawyers Action Cmte. to End the War in Vietnam (organizer; co-chm.); Friends of the Glencoe Library (treas.); Dearborn Parkway Playground Assn. (pres.); Associates of the Inst. for Psychoanalysis (pres.); American Veterans Cmte. (IL state chm., National Planning Cmte.); Men for ERA; First National Conference on Optimum Population and Environment (treas., 1970); Law Club; Monroe Club. REL.: no preference. MAILING ADDRESS: 231 South La Salle St., Chicago, IL 60604.

CLAY, LAURA. b. Feb 9, 1849, White Hall, KY; d. Jun 29, 1941, Lexington, KY; par. Cassius Marcellus (q.v.) and Mary Jane (Warfield) Clay; single. EDUC.: grad., Sayre Inst., 1865; Mrs. Sara Hoffman's Finishing School; U. of MI, 1880; State Coll. of KY, 1885–86. POLIT. & GOV.: delegate, Dem. Nat'l. Conv., 1920; ***candidate for Democratic nomination to presidency of the U.S., 1920***; Democratic candidate for KY State Senate, 1923; delegate, KY State Repeal Convention, 1933. BUS. & PROF.: women's suffrage advocate. MEM.: KY Woman Suffrage Assn. (pres., 1881–88); KY Equal Rights Assn. (pres., 1888–1912); National American Woman Suffrage Assn. (auditor, 1895; Board of Directors, 1895–1911); Woman's Club of Central KY; Woman's Peace Party (1915–17); Southern States Woman Suffrage Conference (vice pres., 1913); W.C.T.U. REL.: Episc. MISC.: first woman to receive votes for presidency of the U.S. in major party nominating convention; received one vote for pres. on 34th ballot, Dem. Nat'l. Conv., 1920. RES.: Lexington, KY.

CLAY, LUCIUS DUBIGNON. b. Apr 23, 1897, Marietta, GA; d. Apr 17, 1978, Cape Cod, MA; par. Alexander Stephen and Sarah Francis (White) Clay; m. Marjorie McKeown, Sep 21, 1918; c. Lucius Dubignon, Jr.; Frank Butner. EDUC.: B.S., U.S. Military Acad., 1918. POLIT. & GOV.: appointed page, U.S. Senate, c. 1910; delegate, International Congress on Navigation, 1934; appointed U.S. ambassador and personal representative of the pres. to the Federal Republic of Germany, 1961–62; appointed chm., Foreign Aid Study Comm., 1963; ***candidate for Republican nomination to presidency of the U.S., 1964***; chm., Republican National Finance Cmte., 1965–68; appointed chm., Federal National Mortgage Assn., 1970–73. BUS. & PROF.: soldier; businessman; chm. of the board, Continental Can Co., Inc., 1950–62; senior partner, Lehman Brothers, Inc., 1963–73; trustee, Central Savings Bank; dir., General Motors Corp.; dir., U.S. Lines; dir., Chase Manhattan Bank; dir., Marine Midland Trust Corp.; dir., Newmount Mining Corp.; dir., Metropolitan Life Insurance Co.; dir., Lehman Corp. MIL.: commissioned 2d lt., U.S. Army, 1918, 1st lt., 1918, capt. (temporary), 1918; instructor, Officers' Training Camp, 1918–19; asst. prof. of military science and tactics, AL Polytechnical Inst., 1920–21; construction quartermaster and post engineer, Fort Belvoir, VA, 1921–24; instructor in civil engineering, U.S. Military Acad., 1924–27; with Field Mapping, 11th Engineers, Canal Zone, 1927–30; asst. to district engineer, Pittsburgh, PA, 1930–33; asst. to chief of engineers, River and Harbor Section, 1933–37; consultant on Water Resource Development, National Power Corp., Commonwealth of the Philippines, 1937–38; superintendent of construction, Denison Dam, 1938–40; asst. to the administrator, Civil Aeronautics Administration, 1940–41; brig. gen. (temporary), dir. of material, Army Services Forces, 1942–44; commander, Normandy Base, 1944; dept. dir., War Mobilization and Reconversion, 1945; appointed deputy military gov. of Germany, 1945–47; brig. gen. (permanent), commander in chief of European Command, and Military Gov. of Germany, 1947–49; gen. (temporary), 1947; maj. gen. (permanent), 1948; retired with rank of gen. (permanent), 1948; Distinguished Service Medal with Two Oak Leaf Clusters, 1945; Bronze Star. MEM.: Columbia Presbyterian Hospital (trustee; vice pres.); Army and Navy Club; University Club; Links Club; Bohemian Club; Blind Brook Club; National Foundation for Medical Education (trustee); Alfred P. Sloan Foundation (trustee); Eisenhower Exchange Fellowships (trustee); Crusade for Freedom (chm.); A.S.C.E.; S.A.M.E. AWARDS: Gold Medal, National Inst. of Social Sciences, 1962; National Brotherhood Award, National Conference of Christians and Jews, 1962; Legion of Merit; Knight Commander, Order of the British Empire; Order of Kutuzov, First Class (U.S.S.R.); Honorary Citizen of Berlin (1962). WRITINGS: *Decision in Germany* (1950); *Germany and the Fight for Freedom* (1950). REL.: Methodist. RES.: New York, NY.

CLAYTON, JOHN MIDDLETON. b. Jul 24, 1796, Dagsborough, DE; d. Nov 9, 1856, Dover, DE; par. James and Sarah (Middleton) Clayton; m. Sarah Ann Fisher, 1822. EDUC.: grad. (with highest honors), Yale U., 1815; Litchfield Law School. POLIT. & GOV.: elected as a Whig to DE State House of Delegates, 1824; sec. of state of DE, 1826–28; elected as a National Republican to U.S. Senate (DE), 1829–36, as a Whig, 1845–49, 1853–56; delegate, DE State Constitutional Convention, 1831; chief justice, Supreme Court of DE, 1837–39; ***candidate for Whig Party nomination to presidency of the U.S., 1844, 1848; candidate for Whig Party nomination to vice presidency of the U.S., 1844 (withdrew)***; appointed U.S. sec. of state, 1849–50; ***candidate for American (Know-Nothing) Party nomination to presidency of the U.S., 1856***. BUS. & PROF.: atty.; admitted to DE Bar, 1819; law practice, Dover, DE, 1819; farmer, New Castle, DE. REL.: Presb. MISC.: negotiated Clayton-Bulwer Treaty, 1850. RES.: Dover, DE.

CLEAVER, HENRY PAUL, JR. b. Jul 17, 1923, Wilmington, DE; par. Henry Paul and Hannah (Varn) Cleaver; m. Christine Frederica Mayhoffer; c. none. EDUC.: Baker U., 1950, 1954; Washburn U. Law School. POLIT. & GOV.: candidate for Republican nomination to U.S. Senate (KS), 1960; ***candidate for Republican nomination to presidency of the U.S., 1976, 1984***. BUS. & PROF.: soldier. MIL.: corp., U.S. Army, 1943–45. MEM.: Independent Student Assn. (1950–54). REL.: Christian. MAILING ADDRESS: P.O. Box 225, Niverville, NY 12130-0228.

CLEAVER, LEROY ELDRIDGE. b. Aug 31, 1935, Wabbaseka, AR; par. Leroy and Thelma Hedy (Robinson) Cleaver; m. Kathleen Neal, Dec 27, 1967; c. Antonio Maceo; Joju. EDUC.: public school, Los Angeles, CA; high school diploma, San Quentin State Prison. POLIT. & GOV.: ***Peace and Freedom (New Politics) Party candidate for presidency of the U.S., 1968***; Independent Conservative candidate for U.S. House (CA), 1984; Conservative candidate for Berkeley (CA) City Council, 1984; candidate for Republican nomination to U.S. Senate (CA), 1986; nonpartisan candidate for Bay Area Rapid Transit Board, San Francisco, CA, 1992. BUS. & PROF.: marijuana salesman; chm., Black House Council; minister of defense, Black Panther Party for Self-Defense, to 1971; founder, Revolutionary People's Communications Network, 1971; staff writer, *Ramparts Magazine;* contributor, *Esquire*; contributor, *Black Dialogue*; contributor, *Liberator;* contributor, *Mademoiselle;* author; lecturer; fashion designer; boutique owner, Hollywood, CA; founder, Eldridge Cleaver Crusades; operator, Recycling Pickup Service, San Francisco, CA. MEM.: Foundation of Christian Ministry; Eldridge Cleaver Crusades; Black Panther Party for Self-Defense. WRITINGS: *Soul on Ice* (1968); *Post-Prison Writings and Speeches* (1969); *Eldridge Cleaver's Black Papers* (1969); *Soul on Fire* (1978). REL.: born-again Christian (nee Nation of Islam). MISC.: imprisoned in Soledad Prison (1954, possession of marijuana); imprisoned in San Quentin State Prison (parole violation and assault); imprisoned in Folsom State Prison (1957–66); self-styled "full-time revolutionary"; instructor, Social Analysis 139X , U. of CA, Berkeley, CA; fled U.S. in Nov 1968 to avoid return to prison due to reversal of court decision; in Cuba, 1969; in Algeria, 1970–75; returned to Alameda Cty. (CA) Jail, 1976; converted to evangelical Christianity; convicted of Nov 1987 theft of table and desk from building undergoing renovation, Oakland, CA; sentenced to 3 years probation, Jun 28, 1988; charged with possession of cocaine, Jun 1992. MAILING ADDRESS: 2616 Asby Ave., "B," Berkeley, CA 94705.

CLEGG, BILLY JOE. b. Apr 25, 1928, Tulsa, OK; par. Ruby Roselyn Chipman (foster parents: Mr. and Mrs. Thomas Clegg); m. Betty Shirley Green; c. Joe Darrell; Carmen Ruth. EDUC.: OK City (OK) U. POLIT. & GOV.: founder, Loyal US Party, Nov 1970; *Loyal U.S.A.* ***Party candidate for Democratic nomination to presidency of the U.S., 1972, 1976, 1988, 1992; Loyal U.S.A. Party candidate for presidency of the U.S., 1972; Loyal American Party candidate for presidency of the U.S., 1976***; independent candidate for gov. of OK, 1978; candidate for Republican nomination to U.S. Senate (OK), 1980; candidate for Democratic nomination to gov. of OK, 1986; ***Save America Progressive Party candidate for presidency of the U.S., 1992; candidate for Republican nomination to presidency of the U.S., 1992***. BUS. & PROF.: mailbag advertising dir., Independent Postal System of America, 1968–70; ordained minister, Baptist Church. MIL.: sgt., U.S. Air Force, 1946–68. REL.: Bapt. MISC.: sponsored Col. Oliver North (q.v.) for Republican presidential nomination, 1988. MAILING ADDRESS: 251 Eisenhower Dr., Suite 177, Biloxi, MS 39531.

CLEMENS, SAMUEL LANGHORNE (aka MARK TWAIN and THOMAS JEFFERSON SNODGRASS). b. Nov 30, 1835, Florida, MO; d. Apr 21, 1910, Redding, CT; par. John Marshall and Jane (Lampton) Clemens; m. Olivia L. Langdon. EDUC.: public schools, Hannibal, MO. POLIT. & GOV.: appointed private sec. to gov., Territory of NV; ***Anti-Doughnut Party candidate for presidency of the U.S., 1880***. BUS. & PROF.: author; humorist; apprentice printer, 1847; itinerant typesetter, 1852; river pilot; city ed., *Virginia City, (NV) Enterprise*, 1862; miner; lecturer; founder, C. L. Webster and Co. (publishing house), 1884. MEM.: American Acad. of Arts and Letters. HON. DEG.: M.A., Yale U., 1888, Litt.D., 1901; LL.D., U. of MO, 1902; Litt.D., Oxford U., 1907. WRITINGS: *The Jumping Frog* (1867); *The Innocents Abroad* (1869); *Autobiography and First Romance* (1871); *Roughing*

It (1872); *Sketches Old and New* (1873); *The Gilded Age* (with Charles Dudley Warner, 1873); *Adventures of Tom Sawyer* (1876); *Punch Brothers Punch* (1878); *Tramp Abroad* (1880); *The Prince and the Pauper* (1882); *The Stolen White Elephant* (1882); *Life on the Mississippi* (1883); *The Adventures of Huckleberry Finn* (1885); *Connecticut Yankee in King Arthur's Court* (1889); *The American Claimant* (1892); *Merry Tales* (1892); *The £1,000,000 Bank Note* (1893); *Pudd'n Head Wilson* (1894); *Tom Sawyer Abroad* (1894); *Joan of Arc* (1896); *Following the Equator* (1898); *The Man That Corrupted Hadleyburg* (1900); *Double-Barreled Detective Story* (1902); *Articles on Christian Science* (1903); *Dog's Tale* (1903); *Eve's Diary* (1905); *Horse's Tale* (1906); *The $30,000 Bequest* (1908); *Christian Science* (1907); *Autobiography of Mark Twain; Captain Stormfield's Visit to Heaven* (1908). RES.: Redding, CT.

CLEMENT, FRANK GOAD. b. Jun 2, 1920, Dickson, TN; d. Nov 4, 1969, Nashville, TN; par. Robert Samuel and Maybelle (Goad) Clement; m. Lucille Christianson, Jan 6, 1940; c. Robert Nelson; Frank Goad, Jr.; James Gary. EDUC.: Cumberland U., 1939; LL.B., Vanderbilt U., 1942. POLIT. & GOV.: chief counsel, TN State Utilities Comm., 1946–50; elected as a Democrat to gov. of TN, 1953–59, 1963–67; temporary chm., Dem. Nat'l. Conv., 1956 (keynoter); ***candidate for Democratic nomination to vice presidency of the U.S., 1956***; Democratic candidate for U.S. Senate (TN), 1966. BUS. & PROF.: atty.; admitted to Tennessee bar, 1941; agent, FBI, 1941–43; law practice, Nashville and Dickson, TN, 1946–52, 1959–62; law practice, Nashville, TN, 1967–69. MIL.: 1st lt., U.S. Army, 1943–46, 1950. MEM.: American Legion (state commander, 1948–49); Dickson Cty. Junior C. of C.; Sigma Alpha Epsilon; Phi Delta Phi; Masons (32°; Shriner); Young Democratic Clubs of Tennessee (pres., 1946–48); TN Bar Assn.; Omicron Delta Kappa; Red Cross; Kiwanis; March of Dimes (state chm.); Southern Governors Conference (chm.); Southern Regional Education Board (chm.); Cordell Hull Foundation for International Education (chm., 1955–59). AWARDS: "Outstanding Young Man," TN Junior C. of C., 1948; one of ten "Outstanding Young Men in America," U.S. Junior C. of C., 1953; Special Service Award, Southern Psychiatric Assn., 1958; Special Award, National Assn. for Mental Health, 1958. HON. DEG.: LL.D., Vanderbilt U.; LL.D., Baylor U.; LL.D., Bob Jones U. REL.: Methodist (lay preacher). RES.: Dickson, TN.

CLEMENTS, WILLIAM PERRY, JR. b. Apr 13, 1917, Dallas, TX; par. William Perry and Evelyn (Cammack) Clements; m. 2d, Rita Crocker, Mar 8, 1975; c. b. Gill; Nancy Seay. EDUC.: grad., Southern Methodist U., D.H.L., 1974. POLIT. & GOV.: appointed deputy sec., U.S. Dept. of Defense, 1973–77; elected as a Republican to gov. of TX, 1979–83, 1987–91; ***candidate for Republican nomination to presidency of the U.S., 1980 (declined)***. BUS. & PROF.: roughneck, oil fields, TX; oil driller; founder, chm. of the board, SEDCO, Inc., 1947–73, 1977. MEM.: Southern Methodist U. (trustee; gov.); BSA (National Exec. Board); American Assn. of Oil Well Drilling Contractors (pres.); Independent Petroleum Assn. of America; TX Mid Continent Oil and Gas Assn.; TX State Hist. Assn.; International Assn. of Drilling Contractors; Southern Governors Assn.; National Governors Assn.; Garden of the Gods Club; Houston Petroleum Club; Dallas Petroleum Club; Chaparral Club; Chevy Chase Club; Koon Kreek Club. AWARDS: Distinguished Public Service Award, U.S. Dept. of Defense, 1975; Bronze Palm, President Gerald R. Ford, 1976. REL.: Episc. MAILING ADDRESS: 1901 N. Akard, Dallas, TX 75201.

CLENDENAN, ROY JAMES. POLIT. & GOV.: ***candidate for Democratic nomination to presidency of the U.S., 1984, 1988, 1992***; candidate for Democratic nomination to U.S. House (OH), 1986. MAILING ADDRESS: 15111 Clifton, #3, Lakewood, OH 44107.

CLEVELAND, STEPHEN GROVER. b. Mar 18, 1837, Caldwell, NJ; d. Jun 24, 1908, Princeton, NJ; par. Rev. Richard Falley and Ann (Neal) Cleveland; m. Frances Folsom, Jun 2, 1886; c. Ruth; Esther C.; Marion; Richard Folsom; Francis Grover. EDUC.: public schools; LL.D., Princeton U., 1897. POLIT. & GOV.: elected ward supervisor, Buffalo, NY, 1862; appointed asst. district atty., Erie Cty., NY, 1863–66; Democratic candidate for district atty., Erie Cty., NY, 1865; elected as a Democrat, sheriff of Erie Cty., NY, 1870–73; elected as a Democrat, mayor of Buffalo, NY, 1881–82; elected as a Democrat to gov. of NY, 1883–85; ***elected as a Democrat to presidency of the U.S., 1885–89, 1893–97; Democratic candidate for presidency of the U.S., 1888; candidate for Democratic nomination to presidency of the U.S., 1904***. BUS. & PROF.: clerk, teacher, Inst. for the Blind, New York, NY, 1853; clerk, Bowen and Rogers (law firm), Buffalo, NY, 1855–59; partner, Vanderpoel and Cleveland (law firm), Buffalo, 1866–69; partner, Laning, Cleveland and Folsom (law firm), Buffalo, 1869–70; partner, Cleveland and Bissell (law firm), 1873–81; law practice, New York, 1889–92; trustee, Equitable Life Assurance Soc. of the U.S. MEM.: Assn. of Life Insurance Presidents (chm., 1907–08); National Civic Federation (member, exec. cmte.); Princeton U. (trustee, 1901–08). WRITINGS: *Presidential Problems* (1904); *Writings and Speeches of Grover Cleveland* (George F. Parker, ed.); *Principles and Purposes of Our Form of Government, as Set Forth in Public Papers of Grover Cleveland* (Francis Gottsberger, compiler). REL.: Presb. RES.: Buffalo, NY.

CLINTON, DeWITT. b. Mar 2, 1769, Little Britain, NY; d. Feb 11, 1828, Albany, NY; par. James and Mary (DeWitt) Clinton; m. Maria Franklin, Feb 13, 1796; m. 2d, Catherine Jones, May 8, 1819; c. James Henry; Mary; Walter; Charles; Henry; DeWitt, Jr.; George Washington; Franklin; Julia Catherine; Juliana. EDUC.: A.B., Columbia U., 1786. POLIT. & GOV.: private sec. to Gov. George Clinton (q.v.), NY, 1790–95;

sec., Board of Regents, State U. of NY; sec., Board of Commissioners of NY State Fortifications; elected as a Democrat to NY State Assembly, 1797; elected as a Democrat to NY State Senate, 1798–1802, 1806–11; member, NY State Council of Appointment, 1801–03, 1806–07; delegate, NY State Constitutional Convention, 1801; elected as a Democrat to U.S. Senate (NY), 1802–03; leader, NY State Democratic-Republican Party, 1803; elected as a Democrat to mayor of New York, NY, 1803–07, 1809–15; NY State Canal Commissioner, 1810–24; elected as a Democrat to lt. gov. of NY, 1811–13; ***Peace Party candidate for presidency of the U.S., 1812***; elected as a Democrat to gov. of NY, 1817–21, 1825–28; ***candidate for Democratic-Republican nomination to presidency of the U.S., 1824, 1828***; appointed U.S. minister to England, 1825 (declined). BUS. & PROF.: atty.; admitted to NY Bar, 1789; law practice, New York, NY; naturalist. MEM.: Public School Soc. of NY (pres., 1805); NY Orphan Asylum (patron); NY City Hospital (patron); NY Hist. Soc. (pres., 1817); Literary and Phil. Soc. (founder, 1816); American Acad. of Art (second pres.); American Bible Soc. (vice pres.); Columbia U. (regent); NY U. (regent, 1808–25). HON. DEG.: LL.D., Rutgers U., 1812; LL.D., Columbia U., 1826; LL.D., U. of OH, 1825. WRITINGS: *Introductory Discourse* (1814); *Memoir of the Antiquities of the Western Parts of the State of NY* (1820). REL.: Presb. (Education Soc.). MISC.: noted for construction of Erie Canal; discovered native American wheat and a new fish, *Salma otsego*. RES.: New York, NY.

CLINTON, GEORGE. b. Jul 26, 1739, Little Britain, NY; d. Apr 20, 1812, Washington, DC; par. Charles and Elizabeth (Denniston) Clinton; m. Cornelia Tappan, Feb 7, 1770; c. George Washington; Cornelia (Mrs. Edmond Genet); four other daughters. POLIT. & GOV.: clerk, NY Court of Common Pleas, 1759; district atty. (NY), 1765; surveyor, New Windsor, NY, 1765; elected to NY Colonial Assembly, 1768; member, NY Cmte. of Correspondence, 1774; delegate, Second Continental Congress, 1775–76; elected as a Democratic-Republican to gov. of NY, 1777–95, 1801–04; elected as a Democratic-Republican to lt. gov. of NY, 1777 (declined); pres., NY State Ratification Convention, 1789; ***Anti-Federalist (Democratic-Republican) candidate for vice presidency of the U.S., 1789, 1792, 1796***; elected as an Anti-Federalist to NY State Assembly, 1800–1801; elected as a Democratic-Republican to vice presidency of the U.S., 1805–12; candidate for Democratic-Republican nomination to presidency of the U.S., 1808. BUS. & PROF.: atty.; admitted to NY Bar, 1755; law practice, New Britain, NY. MIL.: lt., NY Rangers, 1758; brig. gen., Continental Army, 1775–77. WRITINGS: *Cato Letters* (1787). REL.: Presb. RES.: New York, NY.

CLINTON, WILLIAM JEFFERSON "BILL" (nee WILLIAM JEFFERSON BLYTHE IV). b. Aug 1946, Hope, AR; par. William Jefferson Blythe III and Virginia (Dwire) Blythe; adopted by Roger and Virginia (Dwire) Clinton; m. Hillary Rodham, 1975; c. Chelsea. EDUC.: B.S. in International Affairs, Georgetown U., 1968; U. Coll., Oxford U., 1968–70; J.D., Yale U., 1973. POLIT. & GOV.: TX state coordinator, McGovern for President Campaign, 1972; staff atty., U.S. House Cmte. on the Judiciary, 1974; Democratic candidate for U.S. House (AR), 1974; elected as a Democrat, atty. gen. of AR, 1977–79; chm. of the board, AR State Housing Development Corp.; chm., State and Local Election Division, Dem. Nat'l. Cmte.; elected as a Democrat to gov. of AR, 1979–81, 1983–93; Democratic candidate for gov. of AR, 1980; ***candidate for Democratic nomination to presidency of the U.S., 1988; candidate for Democratic nomination to vice presidency of the U.S., 1988; elected as a Democrat to presidency of the U.S., 1993–***. BUS. & PROF.: atty.; prof. of law, U. of AR, Fayetteville, AR; law practice, 1973–76; counsel, Wright, Lindsey and Jennings (law firm), Little Rock, AR, 1981–82. MEM.: ABA; AR Bar Assn.; National Assn. of Attorneys General; Democratic Leadership Council (chm., 1990–91); Education Comm. of the States (chm., 1986–87); National Governors' Assn. (chm., 1986–87; chm., Task Force on Health Care, 1990–91); Southern Growth Policy Board (chm., 1985–86); National Assn. for Gifted Children (adviser, 1991–). REL.: Bapt. MISC.: changed name to William Jefferson Clinton at age 15. MAILING ADDRESS: White House, 1600 Pennsylvania Ave., Washington, DC.

CLOGHER, ROBERT ALEXANDER. b. Apr 22, 1917, New York, NY; par. Alexander Clarke and Louise (Coogan) Clogher; m. 2d, Evelyn Jane Kennett; c. David; Susan; Mary; Billy; Ultimothy. EDUC.: grad., Hackley School, 1934; Hamilton Coll., 1934–36; B.S., Columbia U., 1940; M.A., New School for Social Research, 1950. POLIT. & GOV.: ***Nudist Party candidate for presidency of the U.S., 1968***; chm., Nudist National Cmte. BUS. & PROF.: surveyor, CA Division of Highways, 1937–68; land mgr., 1968–; ed., *National Pornographic Magazine*. MEM.: National Pornographic Soc. (exec. sec.). REL.: Perfect Christian Divine Way. MAILING ADDRESS: 10 Cascade St., Brookdale, CA 95007.

CLOUGH, FRANK A. POLIT. & GOV.: ***independent candidate for presidency of the U.S., 1992***. MAILING ADDRESS: MO?

CLOUTIER, JOSEPH ANDREW RDH. POLIT. & GOV.: ***independent candidate for presidency of the U.S., 1980 (declined)***. MAILING ADDRESS: 603 West Ocean Blvd., Long Beach, CA 90802.

COATES, A. U. POLIT. & GOV.: Prohibition Party candidate for gov. of IA, 1901; member,]Prohibition Party National Cmte., 1904–08; ***candidate for Prohibition Party nomination to vice presidency of the U.S., 1904 (withdrew)***. RES.: IA.

COATES, REYNELL. b. Dec 10, 1802, Philadelphia, PA; d. Apr 28, 1886, Camden, NJ; par. Samuel and Amy (Hornor) Coates; m. Margaretta Abbott, 1828; c. two infants. EDUC.: M.D., U. of PA, 1823; medical training, PA Hospital. POLIT. & GOV.: ***Native American Party candidate for vice presidency of the U.S., 1852***. BUS. & PROF.: surgeon; resident physician, PA Hospital, 1824; prof. of natural science, Alleghany Coll., 1829–30; cofounder, Philadelphia Medical Acad.; medical practice, Bristol, England, 1830–32; member, Scientific Corps, South-Seas Expedition, 1835; scientist; naturalist; pedagogue; poet; lecturer; essayist; statesman; contributor, *North American Medical and Surgical Journal*; contributor, *Surgical Journal*; contributor, *American Journal of Medicine and Physical Science*; contributor, *Journal of the Academy of Natural Sciences*; ed., *Graham's Magazine*. MEM.: Patriotic Order of the United Sons of America (founder). WRITINGS: *Hope; The Gambler's Wife; Address of the Native Americans to the Native and Naturalized Citizens of the U.S.; Remarks on the Floating Apparatus and Other Peculiarities of the Genus Zanthina* (1825); *Christian Charity; Cyclopedia of Practical Medicine and Surgery* (1826–40); *Reminiscences of a Voyage to India* (1833); *Oration on the Defects of the Present System of Medical Instruction* (1835); *Popular Medicine* (1838); *Address . . . on History of Organic Development and Means of Improving the Mental and Physical Faculties* (1839); *Syllabus of a Course of Popular Lectures on Physiology* (1840); *Physiology for Schools* (1840); *Natural Philosophy for Schools* (1845); *Native American National Address* (1845); *Leaflets of Memory* (1845–46); *First Lines of Physiology* (1846); *First Lines of Natural Philosophy* (1846); *The Boudoir Annual* (ed., 1847); *An Examination of Silver's Marine Governor* (1858); *To the Americans of West New Jersey in the Congressional Canvass in the First District* (1858); *Introductory Lecture to the Class of the Female Medical College of Pennsylvania* (1861). REL.: Soc. of Friends. MISC.: noted for eccentricity in impaling entomological specimens on clothing. RES.: Camden, NJ.

COBB, HOWELL. b. Sep 7, 1815, Cherry Hill, Jefferson Cty., GA; d. Oct 9, 1868, New York, NY; par. John A. and Sarah (Rootes) Cobb; m. Mary Ann Lamar, May 29, 1835; c. John Addison; Lamar; Howell, Jr.; Andrew Jackson; Mary Ann Lamar; Sarah Mildred; Lizzie Craig; five infants. EDUC.: grad. (with honors), U. of GA, 1834; studied law under General Harden. POLIT. & GOV.: presidential elector, Democratic Party (GA), 1836; elected by the legislature, state solicitor gen., Western Circuit of GA, 1837–41; elected as a Democrat to U.S. House (GA), 1843–51 (Speaker, 1849–51), 1855–57; elected as a Democrat to gov. of GA, 1851–53; ***candidate for Democratic nomination to vice presidency of the U.S., 1852***; Democratic candidate for U.S. Senate (GA), 1854; appointed U.S. sec. of the treasury, 1857–60; chm., Constitutional Convention, Confederate States of America, 1861; ***candidate for president, Confederate States of America, 1861***. BUS. & PROF.: atty.; admitted to GA Bar, 1836; law practice, Athens, GA; partner (with James Jackson), law firm, Macon, GA, 1865. MIL.: brig. gen., C.S.A., 1862, maj. gen., 1863–64. REL.: nonaffiliated. RES.: Athens, GA.

COBB, IRVIN SHREWSBURY. b. Jun 23, 1876, Paducah, KY; d. Mar 10, 1944, New York, NY; par. Joshua Clark and Manie (Saunders) Cobb; m. Laura Spencer Baker, Jun 12, 1900; c. Elizabeth (Mrs. Rogers). EDUC.: LL.D., U. of GA, 1918; LL.D., Dartmouth Coll., 1919; LL.D., U. of KY, 1942. POLIT. & GOV.: staff, office of the gov. of KY, 1918–21; ***candidate for Democratic nomination to presidency of the U.S., 1920***. BUS. & PROF.: author; shorthand reporter; ed., *Paducah Daily News*, 1895; writer, "Sour Mash" (column), *Louisville (KY) Evening Post*, 1898–1901; managing ed., *Paducah News Democrat*, 1901–04; ed., humor section, *New York Evening Sun*, 1904–05; humor writer, *New York Evening World* and *Sunday World*, 1905–11; contributor, *Saturday Evening Post*, 1911–22; war correspondent, 1914–15, 1917–18; contributor, *Cosmopolitan Magazine*, 1922–32; lecturer; radio guest, 1930–36; actor, various motion pictures, 1934–36; screen playwright, 1932–42. MIL.: maj., U.S.A.R., 1922. MEM.: United Confederate Veterans (col.); Legion of Honor (chevalier); Southern Soc. of NY; The Kentuckians; National SCV; Elks; Lambs Club; Bohemian Club; Family Club. AWARDS: O. Henry Award for Best Short Story, 1922. MOTION PICTURE CREDITS: *Steamboat Round the Bend; Pepper; Hawaii Calls; The Young in Heart*. WRITINGS: *Funabashi* (1907); *Mr. Busybody* (1908); *Back Home* (1912); *Cobb's Anatomy* (1912); *The Escape of Mr. Trimm* (1913); *Cobb's Bill of Fare* (1913); *Sergeant Bagby* (with Bozeman Bulger, 1913); *Roughing It De Luxe* (1914); *Europe Revisited* (1914); *Paths to Glory* (1915); *Guilty as Charged* (with Harry Burke, 1915); *Back Home* (with Bayard Veiller, 1915); *Old Judge Priest* (1915); *Under Sentence* (with Roi Cooper Megrue, 1916); *Fibble, D.D.* (1916); *Speaking of Operations* (1916); *Local Color* (1916); *Speaking of Prussians* (1917); *Those Times and These* (1917); *The Glory of the Coming* (1918); *The Thunders of Silence* (1918); *The Life of the Party* (1919); *From Place to Place* (1919); *Oh, Well, You Know How Women Are!* (1919); *The Abandoned Farmers* (1920); *A Plea for Old Cap Collier* (1921); *Jeff Poindexter* (1922); *One Third Off* (1921); *Sunday Accounts* (1922); *Stickfuls, Snake Doctor, A Laugh a Day* (1923); *Goin' on Fourteen* (1924); *Alias Ben Alibi* (1924); *Here Comes the Bride* (1925); *More Laughs for More Days* (1925); *On An Island That Cost Twenty-Four Dollars* (1926); *Some United States* (1927); *Prose and Cons* (1926); *Chivalry Peak* (1927); *Ladies and Gentlemen* (1927); *All Aboard* (1928); *Happy New Year* (1928); *This Man's World* (1929); *Irvin Cobb at His Best* (1929); *Red Likker* (1929); *To Be Taken Before Sailing* (1930); *Both Sides of the Street* (1930); *Incredible Truth* (1931); *Down Yonder* (1932); *One Way to Stop A Panic* (1933); *Murder Day by Day* (1933); *Faith, Hope and Charity* (1934); *Judge Priest Turns Detective* (1936); *Azam* (1937); *Four Useful Pups* (1939); *Exit Laughing* (1941); *Glory, Glory, Hallelujah* (1941); *Roll Call* (1942); *Curtain Call* (1944); *New York Through Funny Glasses* (series); *The Hotel Clerk* (series); *Live Talks with Dead Ones; Making Peace at Portsmouth; The Belled Buzzard; Twixt the Bluff and the Sound; Shakespeare's Seven Ages and Mine; The Island of Adventure*. RES.: New York, NY.

COCHRANE, JOHN. b. Aug 27, 1813, Palatine, NY; d. Feb 7, 1898, New York, NY; par. Walter Livingston and

Cornelia Wynchie (Smith) Cochrane. EDUC.: Union Coll.; grad., Hamilton Coll., 1831; studied law. POLIT. & GOV.: appointed surveyor, Port of New York, 1852–57; elected as a States Rights Democrat to U.S. House (NY), 1857–61; States Rights Democratic candidate for U.S. House (NY), 1860; delegate, Dem. Nat'l. Conv., 1860; elected as a Republican-Unionist, atty. gen. of NY, 1863–65; chm., Independent Republican Party National Convention, 1864; ***Independent Republican Party candidate for vice presidency of the U.S., 1864 (withdrew)***; appointed U.S. collector of internal revenue, 1869; appointed U.S. minister to Uruguay and Paraguay, 1869 (declined); elected pres., New York (NY) Common Council, 1872; delegate, Liberal Republican Party National Convention, 1872 (chm., NY Delegation); elected as a Democrat to New York Board of Aldermen, 1883; appointed police justice, New York, 1889. BUS. & PROF.: atty.; admitted to NY Bar, 1834; law practice, Palatine, NY, 1834; law practice, Oswego, NY; law practice, Schenectady, NY; law practice, New York, NY, 1846–98. MIL.: col., 65th NY Infantry, U.S.V., 1861, brig. gen., 1862–63. MEM.: Soc. of the Cincinnati (pres., to 1898); Tammany Hall (sachem, 1889); NY C. of C.; St. Nicholas Soc.; NY Hist. Soc.; Loyal Legion (pres., NY Commandery); Army of the Potomac; SAR; GAR. RES.: New York, NY.

COCKBURN, CHARLES D. m. Diana Cockburn. POLIT. & GOV.: ***candidate for Democratic nomination to presidency of the U.S., 1976***. BUS. & PROF.: retired. MAILING ADDRESS: 287 Cleveland Ave., Uniontown, PA 15401.

COCKRAN, WILLIAM BOURKE. b. Feb 28, 1854, Cty. Sligo, Ireland; d. Mar 1, 1923, Washington, DC; par. Martin and Harriet (Knight) Cockran; m. Mary Elizabeth Jackson, Jul 15, 1879; m. 2d, Rhoda Elizabeth Mack, Jun 18, 1888; m. 3d, Anne Louise Ide, Nov 5, 1906; c. infant. EDUC.: Marist Brothers School, Lille, France; studied law under Judge Abram R. Tappan, Mt. Vernon, NY. POLIT. & GOV.: delegate, NY State Democratic Convention, 1881; appointed counsel to sheriff, NY Cty., NY, 1883; delegate, Dem. Nat'l. Conv., 1884, 1892, 1904, 1920; elected as a Democrat to U.S. House (NY), 1887–89, 1891–95, 1904–09, 1921–23; appointed member, Comm. to Revise Judicial Article of the NY State Constitution, 1890; ***candidate for Democratic nomination to vice presidency of the U.S., 1892***; Progressive Party candidate for U.S. House (NY), 1912. BUS. & PROF.: schoolteacher, private academy; principal, teacher, public school, Westchester Cty., NY; atty.; admitted to NY Bar, 1876; law practice, Mt. Vernon, NY, 1876–78; law practice, New York, NY, 1878–1923. MEM.: Irving Hall Democracy (spokesman, 1881); Tammany Hall (grand sachem, 1905–08); Metropolitan Club; Meadow Brook Manhattan Club; The Brook Club; Lambs Club; Riding Club; National Arts Club; Lotos Club. AWARDS: Knight Commander of the Order of St. Gregory the Great, 1916; Laetare Medal, U. of Notre Dame, 1901. HON. DEG.: LL.D., St. Francis Xavier Coll., 1887; LL.D., Georgetown Coll., 1900; LL.D., Manhattan Coll., 1902. REL.: R.C. RES.: Long Island, NY.

COCKRELL, FRANCIS MARION. b. Oct 1, 1834, Warrensburg, MO; d. Dec 13, 1915, Washington, DC; par. Joseph and Nancy (Ellis) Cockrell; m. Arethusa Dorcas Stapp, Jul 21, 1853; m. 2d, Anna Eliza Mann, Apr 26, 1866; m. 3d, Anna Ewing, Jul 24, 1873; c. John Joseph; William Suddath; Ewing; Marion (Mrs. Edson Fessenden Gallaudet); Francis Marion; Ephraim Brevard; Allen Vardaman; Ann Ewing (Mrs. Lambros A. Coromilas; Mrs. Camillo Casati); Henry Ewing. EDUC.: grad., Chapel Hill Coll., 1853; studied law. POLIT. & GOV.: candidate for Democratic nomination to gov. of MO, 1872; elected as a Democrat to U.S. Senate (MO), 1875–1905 (minority leader, 1903–05); delegate, Dem. Nat'l. Conv., 1896, 1904; ***candidate for Democratic nomination to presidency of the U.S., 1900, 1904***; appointed member, Interstate Commerce Comm., 1905–10; appointed U.S. commissioner to reestablish boundary between TX and NM, 1911–15; appointed member, U.S. Board of Ordnance and Fortifications, 1913–15. BUS. & PROF.: atty.; admitted to MO Bar, 1855; law practice, Warrensburg, MO. MIL.: pvt., capt., C.S.A., 1861–63, brig. gen., 1863–65. MEM.: Columbia Inst. for the Deaf and Dumb (dir.). REL.: Presb. RES.: Warrensburg, MO.

CODY, JACK. POLIT. & GOV.: ***independent candidate for presidency of the U.S., 1980, 1984***. MAILING ADDRESS: 321 North Ewing, Apt. 205, Dallas, TX.

COFFIN, LORENZO SWEET. b. Apr 9, 1823, Alton, NH; d. Jan 17, 1915, Fort Dodge, IA; par. Rev. Stephen and Deborah (Philbrook) Coffin; m. Cynthia T. Curtis, 1848; m. 2d, Mary C. Chase, Feb 1857. EDUC.: Wolfboro Acad., Wolfboro, NH; Oberlin Coll., 18 months. POLIT. & GOV.: elected superintendent of schools, Fort Dodge, IA, 1863; appointed member, IA State Board of Railroad Commissioners, 1883–88; Prohibition Party candidate for gov. of IA, 1906; ***United Christian Party candidate for vice presidency of the U.S., 1908***. BUS. & PROF.: teacher, Geauga Seminary, Chester, OH; landowner; livestock breeder; ordained minister, Free Will Baptist Church; preacher; philanthropist. MIL.: quartermaster, sgt., chaplain, 32d IA Infantry, U.S. Army, 1862–63. MEM.: White Button Movement (founder, 1893); Hope Hall (founder; Farm for Discharged Convicts); Home for Aged and Disabled Railroad Men (founder; dir.); IA State Anti-Saloon League (pres.); Railroad Temperance Assn. (founder; pres., 1893); Farmers' Congress (delegate, 1889). REL.: Free Will Bapt. RES.: Fort Dodge, IA.

COHEN, HARRY. b. Mar 10, 1919, Philadelphia, PA; par. Samuel and Clara (Kohen) Cohen; single. EDUC.: B.A., Temple U., 1940, M.A., 1956; M.B.Sci., NY U., 1961; M.D., Second Army Headquarters Medical School, 1944. POLIT. & GOV.: candidate for Democratic nomination to gov. of GA, 1940; candidate for Democratic nomination to U.S. Senate (NJ), 1951; candidate for Democratic nomination to mayor of Chicago, IL, 1955; chm., Democratic Party of the U.S.A., 1957–;

candidate for Democratic nomination to presidency of the U.S., 1972. BUS. & PROF.: physician; politician. MIL.: U.S. Army, 1940–43, claims rank of gen., 1943–50 (unverified). MEM.: VFW; Disabled American Veterans; American Legion; Lions; Rotary Club; Kiwanis; Moose; Elks; Masons; Phi Beta Kappa; Temple U. Alumni Assn.; NY U. Alumni Assn. REL.: Presb. MISC.: claims to hold the Medal of Honor and sundry military decorations, various records in golfing and running; claims to have been offered the position of atty. gen. of the U.S. by President Lyndon B. Johnson (q.v.); self-styled "Greatest Man in the World." MAILING ADDRESS: 244 Milton St., Camden, NJ 08101.

COHEN, NAOMI. b. Nov 13, 1927, New York, NY; m. 1948; c. two. POLIT. & GOV.: ***Workers World Party candidate for vice presidency of the U.S., 1980, 1988***. BUS. & PROF.: folk singer; ed., *Fighting Back*. WRITINGS: "Songs of Struggle" (I and II; tape cassette; 45 rpm recording). REL.: Jewish. MAILING ADDRESS: c/o *Fighting Back*, 19 West 21st St., Room 703B, New York, NY 10010.

COINER, CLAIBORNE BENTON. b. Jun 11, 1912, Fort Defiance, VA; d. Oct 3, 1963, Waynesboro, VA; par. Claiborne Benton and Lula (Watts) Coiner; m. Agnes McClung (Mrs. W. D. Messimer); c. Mrs. Charles Patton; Claiborne McClung. EDUC.: Auga Military Acad. POLIT. & GOV.: appointed chm., VA Cmte. on Constitutional Government; ***Conservative Party of VA candidate for presidency of the U.S. (as stand-in for Harry Flood Byrd, q.v.), 1960***; candidate for Democratic nomination to member, Augusta Cty. (VA) Board of Supervisors, 1963. BUS. & PROF.: pres., Coiner Flying Service, Waynesboro, VA; owner, Waynesboro Airport; farmer; assoc., Coiner Parts, Inc. MIL.: flight instructor, War Training Service Program, WWII. MEM.: Shenandoah Valley, Inc.; C. of C. (dir.); United Community Fund (dir.); Kiwanis; Congress of Conservative Cmtes.; First Presbyterian Church Men's Bible Class (pres.); Civil Air Patrol (wing commander, WWII). REL.: Presb. (deacon). MISC.: committed suicide. RES.: Waynesboro, VA.

COLBY, ANTHONY OWEN. POLIT. & GOV.: ***independent (Cmte. for a Constitutional Presidency) candidate for vice presidency of the U.S., 1976***. MAILING ADDRESS: IA.

COLBY, BAINBRIDGE. b. Dec 22, 1869 St. Louis, MO; d. Apr 11, 1950, Bemus Point, NY; par. John Peck and Frances (Bainbridge) Colby; m. Nathalia Sedgwick, Jun 22, 1895; m. 2d, Anne Ahlstrand Ely, Nov 1, 1929; c. Katherine Sedgwick (Mrs. Frederick Prime Delafield); Nathalie Sedgwick; Frances Bainbridge (Mrs. Robert Cameron Rogers). EDUC.: A.B., Williams Coll., 1890; Columbia U.; LL.B., NY U., 1892. POLIT. & GOV.: elected as a Republican (Fusionist) to NY State Assembly, 1901–03; founder, Progressive Party, 1912; delegate, Progressive Party National Convention, 1912; Progressive Party candidate for U.S. Senate (NY), 1914, 1916; appointed commissioner, U.S. Shipping Board, 1917–19; appointed member, U.S. Shipping Board Emergency Fleet Corp., 1917–19; delegate, American Mission to Inter-Allied Conference, 1917; appointed U.S. sec. of state, 1920–21; ***candidate for Democratic nomination to presidency of the U.S., 1920***; delegate, Dem. Nat'l. Conv., 1924. BUS. & PROF.: atty.; admitted to NY Bar, 1892; law practice, New York, NY, 1892–1921; partner, Wilson and Colby (law firm), Washington, DC, 1921–23; law practice, Washington, DC, 1923–36. MEM.: Colby Coll. (trustee); ABA; Assn. of the Bar of the City of New York; Civil Service Reform Assn.; Missouri Soc. of New York (pres.); Phi Beta Kappa; Alpha Delta Phi; Lawyers Club; Rockaway Hunting Club; University Club; Metropolitan Club; Manhattan Club; Squadron A Veterans Club; Washington Metropolitan Club; Chautauqua Cty. Hist. Soc.; Authors League of America; American Liberty League (founder, 1934). HON. DEG.: LL.D., OH Northern U., 1914; LL.D., Moores Hill Coll., 1914; LL.D., Lincoln Memorial U., 1917; LL.D., Colby Coll., 1933. WRITINGS: *The Close of Woodrow Wilson's Administration and the Final Years*. REL.: Episc. RES.: New York, NY.

COLE, JOHN. POLIT. & GOV.: chm., American Mandate Party; ***American Mandate Party candidate for presidency of the U.S., 1976***. BUS. & PROF.: freelance writer. MAILING ADDRESS: 3508 L St., Vancouver, WA.

COLE, MARIANNE ADAMS. POLIT. & GOV.: ***God and American USA Party candidate for presidency of the U.S., 1984***. MAILING ADDRESS: Rural Route #1, 22850 23 Mile Rd., Olivet, MI 49076.

COLEMAN, RUTH. POLIT. & GOV.: *candidate for* ***Democratic nomination to presidency of the U.S., 1992***. BUS. & PROF.: minister. MISC.: known as "Dr. Reverend Ruth Coleman." MAILING ADDRESS: 8652 38th Ave. South, Seattle, WA 98118.

COLER, BIRD SIM. b. Oct 9, 1867, Champaign IL; d. Jun 12, 1941, Brooklyn, NY; par. William N. Coler; m. Emily Moore, Oct 18, 1886; c. Eugene Bird. EDUC.: grad., Polytechnic Inst.; Philips Acad. POLIT. & GOV.: Democratic candidate for alderman-at-large, Brooklyn, NY, 1892; delegate, Dem. Nat'l. Conv., 1896; elected as a Democrat, controller of New York, NY, 1897–1901; candidate for Democratic nomination to gov. of NY, 1900; Democratic candidate for gov. of NY, 1902; ***candidate for Democratic nomination to presidency of the U.S., 1904***; elected as an independent, pres., Borough of Brooklyn, NY, 1906–09; ***candidate for Democratic nomination to vice presidency of the U.S., 1908***; appointed commissioner of charities, New York, NY, 1917–27; Fusion Party candidate for pres., Board of Aldermen, New York, NY, 1929. BUS. & PROF.: banker; partner, W. N. Coler and Co. (banking house); vice pres., Greensboro Public Service Corp.; pres., Guardian Trust Co. MEM.: Bushwick Club; Merchants Club; National Democratic Club; Grolier Club; Lawyers Club; Manhattan Club; Lotos Club; NY Stock Exchange; 23rd Ward Democratic Club (1891). WRITINGS: *Municipal Government, as Illustrated by the Charter, Finances and Public Charities of New York* (1900); *The Financial Effects of Consolidation; Municipal Government and Tunnels and Bridges*. RES.: New York, NY.

COLFAX, SCHUYLER. b. Mar 23, 1823, New York, NY; d. Jan 13, 1885, Mankato, MN; par. Schuyler and Hannah (Stryker) Colfax; m. Evelyn E. Clark, Oct 10, 1844; m. 2d, Ellen W. Wade, Nov 18, 1868; c. Schuyler III. EDUC.: public schools. POLIT. & GOV.: appointed deputy auditor, South Bend, IN, 1841–49; asst. enrolling clerk, IN Senate, 1842–44; candidate for clerk, IN House of Reps., 1847; sec., Chicago River and Harbors Convention, 1847; delegate, Whig Party National Convention, 1848, 1852; elected as a Whig, delegate, IN State Constitutional Convention, 1850; Whig candidate for U.S. House (IN), 1851; delegate, National Native American Party Council, 1855; elected as a Republican to U.S. House (IN), 1855–69 (Speaker, 1863–69); candidate for Republican nomination to gov. of IN, 1856 (declined), 1860 (declined); ***candidate for Republican nomination to presidency of the U.S., 1860, 1868, 1872, 1876; candidate for Republican nomination to vice presidency of the U.S., 1864, 1872; elected as a Republican to vice presidency of the U.S., 1869–73***; offered position as U.S. sec. of state, 1871 (declined); *candidate for Liberal Republican Party nomination to presidency of the U.S., 1872*; Greenback Party candidate for U.S. House (IN), 1878 (declined), 1882. BUS. & PROF.: correspondent, *Indiana State Journal*, 1842–43; ed., *South Bend Free Press*, 1843–45; owner, ed., *St. Joseph Valley Register*, 1845; offered editorship, *New York Tribune* (declined); lecturer. MEM.: Independent Order of Odd Fellows. HON. DEG.: LL.D., IN U., 1869; LL.D., Otterbein Coll., 1873. WRITINGS: *The "Laws of Kansas"* (1856); *Free Sugar* (1857); *Kansas—The Lecompton Constitution* (1858); *Fremont's Hundred Days in Missouri* (1862); *Life and Principles of Abraham Lincoln* (1865); *Education of the Heart* (1868); *The Mormon Question* (1870); *Life and Services of General U.S. Grant; Example and Effort* (1872); *The Northern Pacific Railroad* (187?); *Landmarks of Life to Be Found on a New Year's Day Journey* (1883). REL.: Dutch Reformed Church. MISC.: involved in Credit Mobilier scandals, but exonerated, 1873. RES.: South Bend, IN.

COLL, EDWARD THOMAS "NED." b. 1940. POLIT. & GOV.: Public Party candidate for U.S. House (CT), 1970; ***candidate for Democratic nomination to presidency of the U.S., 1972; independent candidate for presidency of the U.S., 1972***. BUS. & PROF.: founder, dir., The Revitalization Corps, Hartford, CT, 1964–; social worker; exec., insurance agency, to 1964. AWARDS: one of ten "Outstanding Young Men in America," National Junior C. of C., 1971. MAILING ADDRESS: 38 White St., Hartford, CT 06114.

COLLAMER, JACOB. b. Jan 8, 1791, Troy, NY; d. Nov 9, 1865, Woodstock, VT; par. Samuel and Elizabeth (Van Ornum) Collamer; m. Mary N. Stone, Jul 15, 1817. EDUC.: grad., U. of VT, 1810, LL.D., 1850; studied law under Mr. Longworthy and Benjamin Swift. POLIT. & GOV.: elected as a Whig to VT State House, 1821–22, 1827–28; state's atty., Windsor Cty., VT, 1822–24; assoc. judge, VT Supreme Court, 1833–42; delegate, VT State Constitutional Convention, 1836; elected as a Whig to U.S. House (VT), 1843–49; appointed postmaster gen. of the U.S., 1849–50; elected judge, VT Circuit Court, 1850–54; elected as a Republican to U.S. Senate (VT), 1855–65; ***candidate for Republican nomination to vice presidency of the U.S., 1856; candidate for Republican nomination to presidency of the U.S., 1860***. BUS. & PROF.: atty.; admitted to VT Bar, 1813; law practice, Randolph Center, VT, 1813–16; law practice, Royalton, VT, 1816–36; law practice, Woodstock, VT, 1836–55; prof. of medical jurisprudence, VT Medical Coll., 1843–49, pres., 1855–62. MIL.: lt. of artillery, VT State Militia, 1812. HON. DEG.: LL.D., Dartmouth Coll., 1855. RES.: Woodstock, VT.

COLLINS, EDWARD HICOK. b. Apr 13, 1936, Bayside, NY; par. John Hicok and Hedvig Martha Klara (Lehnert) Collins. EDUC.: A.B., Yale U., 1958; Nassau Community Coll., 1968–72. POLIT. & GOV.: ***Nude Run Party candidate for presidency of the U.S., 1976***. BUS. & PROF.: poet; instructor, Wilbraham Acad., Wilbraham, MA, 1958–59; medical researcher, Columbia Presbyterian Medical Center, New York, NY, 1959–60; teacher, Baldwin (NY) H.S., 1959–61; policeman, Long Island State Parkway Police, 1961–72; teacher, Westbury H.S., 1962–63; headmaster, Escuela de Eduardo Merida, Yucatán, Mexico, 1967; advertising salesman, *Citizen Shopper*, DeKalb, IL; freelance journalist; trackman, Chicago and Northwestern R.R. REL.: atheist. MISC.: jailed for streaking, DeKalb Cty., IL; self-styled "Son of God." MAILING ADDRESS: 1115 Pleasant St., DeKalb, IL 60115.

COLLINS, FREDERICK WILLIAM. b. Jan 18, 1873, Paterson, NJ; d. Dec 24, 1948, Newark, NJ; par. Henry Alderton and Margaret (Stretch) Collins; m. Mary Washburn, Jun 15, 1893; m. 2d, Flora Bell Brooks, Oct 12, 1905; m. 3d, Ethel Nora Brooks, Jun 23, 1910; c. Edward William; Charles Orville; Gladys Elizabeth; Frederick Alderton. EDUC.: American Conservatory of Music; grad., Philadelphia Coll. of Anatomy, 1897; M.D., PA Medical Coll., 1902; grad., American Coll. of Naturopathy, 1907; grad., NJ Coll. of Osteopathy, 1910; grad., Palmer School of Chiropractic, 1911. POLIT. & GOV.: ***Constitutional Liberty League candidate for presidency of the U.S., 1920***. BUS. & PROF.: fireman, brakeman, freight handler, Erie R.R. Co., 14 years; operator, dairy store; operator, music store; contractor; naturopathic physician; owner, Modern School of Music, Hoboken, NJ, 1896; dean, First National U. of Naturopathy, Newark, NJ, 1905–48; founder, NJ Coll. of Chiropractic, Newark, NJ, 1910–32; author. MEM.: American Acad. of Chiropractic Research; NJ Chiropractors Assn.; Hudson Cty. Osteopathic Assn.; NJ Assn. of Spondylotherapists; American Naturopathic Soc.; NJ Naturopathic Soc.; NJ State Osteopathic Soc.; NJ Anti-Vivisection Soc.; National League for Medical Freedom; Masons (32°); Improved Order of Red Men; Knights of Malta; Elks; One Hundred Year Club. HON. DEG.: D.Naturopathy, American Coll. of Naturopathy, 1915. WRITINGS: *Volume No. 1 Iridiagnosis* (1919); *Reductions of Dislocations Without Anesthesia* (1924); *Collins' Pedopractic* (1932); *Bunk or Fact of Astrology* (1934); *Heart Disease* (1947); *The Common Cold* (1947). REL.: Episc. RES.: Newark, NJ.

COLLINS, MARTHA LAYNE. b. Dec 7, 1936, Bagdad, KY; par. Everett Larkin and Mary Lorena (Taylor) Hall; m. Bill Louis Collins, Jul 3, 1959; c. Stephen Louis; Marla Ann. EDUC.: Lindenwood Coll., 1955–56; B.S., U. of KY, 1959. POLIT. & GOV.: member, Woodford Cty. (KY) Democratic Exec. Cmte., 1963; state coordinator for women's activities, Democratic Party of KY, 1971–72; delegate, Dem. Nat'l. Conv., 1972, 1980, 1984 (temporary chm.); member, Dem. Nat'l. Cmte., 1972–76; delegate, Democratic National Mid-Term Conference, 1974; sec., KY State Democratic Central Cmte., 1974–79; elected clerk, KY State Court of Appeals, 1975; clerk, KY State Supreme Court, 1975–79; chairwoman, 51.3 Percent Cmte. for Carter-Mondale (KY), 1976; appointed member, KY Comm. on Women; elected as a Democrat to lt. gov. of KY, 1979–83; elected as a Democrat to gov. of KY, 1983–87; ***candidate for Democratic nomination to vice presidency of the U.S., 1984***. BUS. & PROF.: teacher, public schools, KY, 1959–63, 1967–71; teacher, Fairdale H.S., Louisville, KY; teacher, Seneca H.S., Louisville; teacher, Woodford Cty. Junior H.S., Versailles, KY; exec. dir., Friendship Force, 1977–. MEM.: Chi Omega; Panhellenic Board; Student Women's Advisory Board; National Conference of Appellate Court Clerks; Business and Professional Women's Club; Eastern Star; Democratic Women's Club; U. of KY Alumni Assn.; Psi Omega; Jaycee-ettes (pres., Woodford Cty., KY Chapter); Women's Missionary Union (pres.). AWARDS: Woman of Achievement, Woodford Cty. (KY) Business and Professional Women's Club, 1976. REL.: Bapt. MAILING ADDRESS: Route 4, Nicholasville Pike, Versailles, KY 40383.

COLLINS, RICHARD CHANDLER. b. Oct 21, 1922, Norfolk, VA; par. Chiles Chandler and Naomi Grace (Hoy) Collins; m. Nancy Jean McConnell; c. Douglas Whitney; Neil Edward; Kevin Richard. EDUC.: ninth grade, Twentynine Palms H.S., Twentynine Palms, CA, 1938. POLIT. & GOV.: ***independent candidate for presidency of the U.S., 1976***. BUS. & PROF.: employee, U.S. Postal Service; mail carrier. REL.: Protestant. MAILING ADDRESS: P.O. Box 234, San Ramon, CA 94583.

COLLINS, THOMAS LEROY. b. Mar 10, 1909, Tallahassee, FL; d. Mar 12, 1991, Tallahassee, FL; par. Marvin H. and Mattie (Brandon) Collins; m. Mary Call Darby, Jun 29, 1932; c. Leroy; Jane; Mary Call; Darby. EDUC.: Eastman Coll.; LL.B., Cumberland U., 1931. POLIT. & GOV.: elected as a Democrat to FL State House, 1935–41; elected as a Democrat to FL State Senate, 1941–55; elected as a Democrat to gov. of FL, 1955–61; delegate, Dem. Nat'l. Conv., 1956, 1960 (chm.); ***candidate for Democratic nomination to vice presidency of the U.S., 1956***; chm., Southern Regional Education Board, 1955–57; member, National Advisory Council, Peace Corps; chm., National Public Advisory Cmte. on Area Development, U.S. Dept. of Commerce; appointed dir., Community Relations Service, U.S. Dept. of Commerce, 1964–65; appointed undersec., U.S. Dept. of Commerce, 1965–66; Democratic candidate for U.S. Senate (FL), 1968; member, FL State Constitutional Revision Comm., 1977–78; Southern legal counsel, 1977–; member, Tallahassee Research and Development authority, 1978–. BUS. & PROF.: grocery clerk; bank teller, 1928–29; atty.; admitted to FL Bar, 1931; admitted to AR Bar, 1931; admitted to TN Bar, 1931; pres., National Assn. of Broadcasters, 1961–64; law practice, Tampa, FL, 1966–68; counsel, Ervin, Varn, Jacobs, Odom and Kitchen (law firm), Tallahassee, FL, 1970–91. MIL.: lt., U.S. Navy, WWII. MEM.: Sigma Alpha Epsilon; National Conference of Christians and Jews (Honor Corps); ABA; International Radio and Television Soc.; National Municipal League; U.S. International C. of C.; National Governors Conference (chm.); Southern Governors Conference (chm.); Cmte. on Goals for Higher Education in the South (chm., 1961–62); Randolph Macon Women's Coll. (trustee); National Cathedral School (gov.); March of Dimes (FL state chm., 1951); Community Chest; American Red Cross; FL C. of C. (dir.); Tallahassee Junior C. of C. (pres., 1935); Elks; Masons; Odd Fellows; Woodmen of the World; Exchange Club of Tallahassee (member, Board of Control, 1936; pres.). AWARDS: Nelson Paynter Award, A.C.L.U., 1978. HON. DEG.: LL.D., Rollins Coll., 1955; LL.D., FL Southern U., 1955; LL.D., FL State U., 1956. REL.: Episc. (nee Methodist). RES.: Tallahassee, FL.

COLQUITT, ALFRED HOLT. b. Apr 20, 1824, Monroe, GA; d. Mar 26, 1894, Washington, DC; par. Walter Terry and Nancy H. (Lane) Colquitt; m. Dorothy Tarver, May 1848; m. 2d, Sarah Tarver, 1856; c. Welborn; Hugh; Hattie; Laura; Dorothy; Walter Terry II; daughter. EDUC.: grad., Princeton U., 1844. POLIT. & GOV.: asst. sec., GA State Senate, 1849; elected as a Democrat to U.S. House (GA), 1853–55; delegate, Dem. Nat'l. Conv., 1856, 1860, 1868; candidate for Democratic nomination to gov. of GA, 1857; elected as a Democrat to GA State House, 1858; presidential elector, Constitutional Union Party (GA), 1860; delegate, GA Secession Convention, 1861; pres., GA State Democratic Convention, 1870, 1872; ***received 5 electoral votes for vice presidency of the U.S., 1872***; elected as a Democrat to gov. of GA, 1876–82; appointed and subsequently elected as a Democrat to U.S. Senate (GA), 1883–94. BUS. & PROF.: ordained minister, Methodist

Church; farmer; atty.; admitted to GA Bar, 1845; law practice, Monroe, GA; law practice, Macon, GA, 1848. MIL.: maj., U.S. Army, 1846–48; brig. gen., Sixth GA Regt., C.S.A., 1862, maj. gen. MEM.: GA Agricultural Soc. (pres., 1870–76); International Sunday School Assn. (pres., 1878–82); Cotton Exposition (pres., Board of Management, 1881); Macon Cty. (GA) Bar Assn.; National Temperance Soc.; Congressional Temperance Soc. REL.: Methodist. MISC.: known as the "Hero of Olustee." RES.: Macon, GA.

COLTER, J. PAUL. POLIT. & GOV.: ***independent candidate for presidency of the U.S., 1976***. MAILING ADDRESS: 172 Elm St., Geneva, OH 44041.

COLVIN, DAVID LEIGH. b. Jan 28, 1880, South Charleston, OH; d. Sep 7, 1959, Yonkers, NY; par. David Taylor and Maria (Larkin) Colvin; m. Mamie White (q.v.), Sep 19, 1906; c. Virginia Leigh (Mrs. Robert A. Pierson). EDUC.: American Temperance U., Harriman, TN; A.B., OH Wesleyan U., 1900; U. of CA; U. of Chicago; Ph.D., Columbia U., 1913. POLIT. & GOV.: Prohibition Party candidate for U.S. House (NY), 1914, 1922; Prohibition Party candidate for U.S. Senate (NY), 1916; Prohibition Party candidate for mayor of New York, NY, 1917; *Prohibition Party candidate for vice presidency of the U.S., 1920*; member, Prohibition Party National Cmte., to 1959 (exec. sec., National Campaign Cmte., 1916; national chm., 1925–32); Law Preservation Party candidate for U.S. Senate (NY), 1932; ***Prohibition Party candidate for presidency of the U.S., 1936; candidate for Prohibition Party nomination to presidency of the U.S., 1948 (withdrew)***. BUS. & PROF.: realtor; lecturer, to 1955; Washington ed., *National Enquirer*, Indianapolis, IN, 1923–24. MIL.: capt., U.S. Army, 1918. MEM.: Intercollegiate Prohibition Assn. (pres., 1899–1908, 1912–20); World Prohibition Federation (vice pres., 1918–34; treas., 1934–48; pres., 1948; hon. pres.); International Reform Federation (pres., 1937–59); National Temperance Council (vice pres., 1913–23); NY Civic League (vice pres.); Cmte. of 60 on National Prohibition (sec., 1916–20); National Legislative Conference (sec., 1917–25); United Cmte. on War Temperance Activities in the Army and Navy (treas., 1917–20); Flying Squadron Foundation (national legislative superintendent, 1923–24); United Cmte. for Prohibition Enforcement (sec., 1924–25); Alpha Tau Omega; National Conference of Organizations Supporting the 18th Amendment (vice pres.); Prohibition Board of Strategy; National Prohibition Emergency Cmte. (treas.); New Crusade for National Prohibition. WRITINGS: *The Bicameral Principle in the New York Legislature* (1913); *Prohibition in the United States* (1926). REL.: Methodist. RES.: New York, NY.

COLVIN, JOHN A. POLIT. & GOV.: ***Industrial Reform Party candidate for vice presidency of the U.S., 1888***. RES.: KS.

COLVIN, MAMIE WHITE. b. Jun 12, 1883, Westview, OH; d. Oct 30, 1955, Clearwater, FL; par. Rev. Levi and Mary Belle (Audelson) White; m. David Leigh Colvin (q.v.), Sep 19, 1906; c. Virginia Leigh (Mrs. Robert A. Pierson). EDUC.: A.B., Wheaton Coll., 1905; Columbia U., 1906–07, 1909–10; D.A. in Oratory, Staley Coll. of the Spoken Word, 1937; Yale School of Alcohol Studies, 1944. POLIT. & GOV.: delegate, Prohibition Party National Convention, 1908, 1912, 1920, 1940, 1948; Prohibition Party candidate for U.S. House (NY), 1918, 1922; Prohibition Party candidate for lt. gov. of NY, 1918; Prohibition Party candidate for NY State Assembly, 1923; member, Prohibition Party National Cmte., 1920–28; ***candidate for Prohibition Party nomination to vice presidency of the U.S., 1948 (declined)***. BUS. & PROF.: temperance advocate; reformer; editor-in-chief, *Union Signal;* editor-in-chief, *Woman's Temperance Work*, 1926–43; editor-in-chief, *Young Crusaders;* author. MEM.: W.C.T.U. (pres., NY Cty., 1916–21; state vice pres., 1921–26; state pres., 1926–44; national vice pres., 1933–44; national pres., 1944–55); World W.C.T.U. (first vice pres.); Prohibition Trust Fund Assn. (pres., 1932–55); National Temperance and Prohibition Council (first vice pres., 1949–51); DAR; League of Women Voters; Wheaton Coll. Scholastic Honor Soc. (1932); National Council of Women (dir.; vice pres.); Business and Professional Women's Club; Women's Advisory Cmte., U.S. Army; Intercollegiate Prohibition Assn.; Women's National Radio Cmte. AWARDS: winner of Silver, Gold, Grand Gold, Diamond, and Grand Diamond Medals in national oratorical contests; winner of college, state, interstate, and national intercollegiate oratorical contests, Intercollegiate Prohibition Assn., 1904. HON. DEG.: LL.D., Houghton Coll., 1946; LL.D., Wheaton Coll., 1947; L.H.D., Southwestern U., 1948. REL.: Methodist Episcopal Church (delegate, General Conference, 1936, 1948). RES.: New York, NY.

COMMONER, BARRY. b. May 28, 1917, Brooklyn, NY; par. Isidore and Goldie (Yarmolinsky) Commoner; m. Gloria C. Gordon, Dec 1, 1946; m. 2d, Lisa Feiner, Aug 26, 1980; c. Lucy Allison; Frederic Gordon. EDUC.: A.B. (cum laude), Columbia U., 1937; M.A., Harvard U., 1938, Ph.D., 1941. POLIT. & GOV.: appointed chm., Special Consulting Group on the Sonic Boom, U.S. Dept. of the Interior, 1967–68; appointed member, Advisory Council on Environmental Education, Office of Education, U.S. Dept. of Health, Education, and Welfare, 1971; appointed member, Secretary's Advisory Council, U.S. Dept. of Commerce, 1976; ***Citizens Party candidate for presidency of the U.S., 1980***. BUS. & PROF.: biologist; asst. in biology, Harvard U., 1938–40; instructor in biology, Queens Coll., 1940–42; assoc. ed., *Science Illustrated*, 1946–47; assoc. prof. in plant physiology, Washington U., St. Louis, MO, 1947–53, prof., 1953–76, university prof. of environmental science, 1976– (chm., Dept. of Botany, 1965–69; dir., Center for the Biology of Natural Systems, 1965–); Editorial Board, *Review of Cytology*, 1957–65; Editorial Board, *Theoretical Biology*, 1960–64; Editorial Board, *World Book Encyclopedia*, 1968–; member, Advisory Board, *Science Year*, 1967–72; Editorial Advisory Board, *Journal* *of Human Ecology,* 1970–. MIL.: lt., U.S.N.R., 1942–46. MEM.: St. Louis Cmte. for Nuclear Information (pres., 1965–66; dir., 1966–); National TB Cmte. on Air Conservation, 1966–68; Scientists' Inst. for Public Information (dir., 1963–; co-chm., 1967–69; chm., 1969–78); Chaim Weizmann Centenary Celebration (sponsor, 1974–75); Coalition of Health Communities (adviser, 1975); Rachel Carson Trust for the Living Environment (Board of Consulting Experts, 1967–); Universities National Anti-War Fund (dir.); National Soc. of Naturalists; Soil Assn. of England; American Inst. of Biological Sciences; In These Times (sponsor, 1976–); Hon. Chemosphere (1972–); AAAS (fellow; chm., Cmte. on Science in Promotion of Human Welfare, 1958–65, dir., 1967–74; chm., Cmte. on Environmental Alterations, 1969–74); American School Health Assn. (hon. member); Soc. of Biological Chemists; Soc. of General Physiologists; American Soc. of Plant Physiologists; Sierra Club; National Parks Assn. (trustee, 1968–70); American Chemical Soc.; American Soc. of Biological Chemists; Federation of American Scientists; Ecology Soc. of America; Inst. of Environmental Education (trustee); Phi Beta Kappa; Sigma Xi. AWARDS: Newcomb Cleveland Prize, AAAS, 1953; First Humanist Award, International Humanist and Ethical Union, 1970; Phi Beta Kappa Award, 1972; International Prize, City of Cervia, Italy, 1973; Order of Merit (commander; Italy, 1977); Premio Iglesias, Sardinia, Italy, 1978. HON. DEG.: D.Sc., Hahnemann Medical Coll. and Hospital, 1963; D.Sc., Grinnell Coll., 1968; D.Sc., Lehigh U., 1969; D.Sc., Williams Coll., 1970; D.Sc., Ripon Coll., 1971; D.Sc., Colgate U., 1972; LL.D., U. of CA, 1967; LL.D., Clark U., 1974. WRITINGS: *Science and Survival* (1966); *The Closing Circle* (1972); *La Technologia del Profitto* (1973); *The Poverty of Power* (1976); *Ecologia e Lotte Sociali* (1976); *The Politics of Energy* (1979). REL.: Jewish. MAILING ADDRESS: 25 Crestwood Dr., Clayton, MO 63105.

COMPTON, CHARLES C. "CHARLIE" b. Jan 17, 1914, Nashville, TN; m. (divorced; remarried, 1945); c. Faith; Hope; Charity; Abraham; Daniel. EDUC.: eighth grade, public schools, Nashville, TN. POLIT. & GOV.: ***candidate for Democratic nomination to presidency of the U.S., 1952, 1968, 1972, 1976, 1980***; candidate for Republican nomination to gov. of FL, 1954; ***candidate for Republican nomination to presidency of the U.S., 1972, 1980; candidate for American Independent Party nomination to presidency of the U.S., 1972; candidate for Peace and Freedom Party nomination to presidency of the U.S., 1972, 1980***. BUS. & PROF.: horseman; jockey, 1929–49; breeder of thoroughbred horses. MAILING ADDRESS: P.O. Box 513, Sierra Madre, CA 91024.

CONANT, JOHN ASHBEL. b. Aug 16, 1829, Chaffeeville, CT; par. Lucius and Marietta (Eaton) Conant; m. Caroline A. Chapman, May 11, 1852; m. 2d, Mrs. Marietta (French) Brown, Nov 18, 1864; c. John Winslow; Henry Wilbur; George Andrew; Julius Deloraine. EDUC.: District School, Gurleyville, CT; Furnace District School, Tolland, CT. POLIT. & GOV.: ***American Prohibition Party candidate for vice presidency of the U.S., 1884***; Prohibition Party candidate for CT state treas., 1906. BUS. & PROF.: assoc. (with D. P. Conant), silk mill, Mansfield, CT; employee, Gurleyville Silk Mill, 1844; employee, O. S. Chaffee Silk Mill, 1845–47; farmer; employee, George R. Hanks Silk Mill, 1847; employee, Atwood and Russ Silk Mill, Atwoodville, CT, 1847–49; jack spinner, American Mill, Rockville, CT, 1851; overseer, James Royce Silk Mill, Gurleyville, 1852–54; employee, Cheney Brothers Silk Mill, Mansfield Hollow, CT, 1854–56; overseer, Watertown (CT) Manufacturing Co., 1857–59; overseer, Hoopskirt Factory, Watertown, 1859; employee, Holmes, Booth and Haydens, Waterbury, CT, 1859–61; employee, J. H. Holland Silk Co., Willimantic, CT, 1864–1907. MEM.: New England Christian Assn. (pres.). REL.: Congregationalist (nee Methodist). RES.: Willimantic, CT.

CONDIT, BRYANT SEARS. POLIT. & GOV.: ***independent candidate for presidency of the U.S., 1992***. MAILING ADDRESS: 1818 Evans Ave., Apt. 111, Cheyenne, WY 82001.

CONDIT, TOM. POLIT. & GOV.: ***candidate for Peace and Freedom Party nomination to presidency of the U.S., 1984***; Peace and Freedom Party candidate for U.S. House (CA), 1988. MAILING ADDRESS: CA.

CONDE, CARMEN A. b. Mar 10, 1945, Wilmington, DE; m. divorced, 1965; c. none. EDUC.: high school; San Luis Obispo Community Coll. POLIT. & GOV.: ***independent candidate for presidency of the U.S., 1980***. BUS. & PROF.: laborer, various jobs. MEM.: chess club. REL.: R.C. MAILING ADDRESS: 1341 Osos St., Apt. 16, San Luis Obispo, CA 93401.

CONE, FREDERICK PRESTON. b. Sep 28, 1871, Benton, FL; d. Jul 28, 1948, Lake City, FL; par. William Henry and Sarah Emily (Branch) Cone; m. Ruby Scarborough, Jan 30, 1901; m. 2d, Mildred Thompson, Aug 24, 1929; c. Jessie Francis (Mrs. Mark Byron III; Mrs. Carl W. Brimmer). EDUC.: FL Agricultural Coll.; Jasper Normal Coll.; read law under Bascom H. Palmer, Lake City, FL. POLIT. & GOV.: elected as a Democrat to mayor of Lake City, 1902–07; elected as a Democrat to FL State Senate, 1907–13 (pres., 1911); delegate, Dem. Nat'l. Conv., 1912, 1924, 1932; elected as a Democrat to gov. of FL, 1937–41; ***candidate for Democratic nomination to presidency of the U.S., 1940***. BUS. & PROF.: teacher, rural school, FL; atty.; admitted to FL Bar, 1892; partner, Cone and Chapman (law firm), Lake City, FL; pres., Columbia Cty. Bank, 1910–48. MEM.: Masons (Shriner); Elks; Lake City Club; Rotary Club; FL Bar Assn.; Columbia Cty. Bar Assn. REL.: Bapt. RES.: Lake City, FL.

CONGDON, ROBERT ADGATE "BOB." EDUC.: college grad. POLIT. & GOV.: ***The Planet Party candidate for presidency of the U.S., 1992***. MAILING ADDRESS: 807 Lonsdale Building, Duluth, MN 55802.

CONGRESS, RICHARD H. POLIT. & GOV.: ***Socialist Workers Party candidate for presidency of the U.S., 1980***. MAILING ADDRESS: 14 Charles Lane, New York, NY 10014.

CONKLING, ROSCOE. b. Oct 30, 1829, Albany, NY; d. Apr 18, 1888, New York, NY; par. Alfred and Eliza (Cockburn) Conkling; m. Julia Seymour, Jun 25, 1855. EDUC.: Mt. Washington Collegiate Inst., New York, NY, 1842–46; studied law in office of Spencer and Kurnan, 1846. POLIT. & GOV.: appointed district atty., Oneida Cty., NY, 1850; elected mayor of Utica, NY, 1858–59; elected as a Republican to U.S. House (NY), 1859–63, 1865–67; Republican candidate for U.S. House (NY), 1862; elected as a Union Republican to U.S. Senate (NY), 1867–81 (resigned); tendered appointment as chief justice, Supreme Court of the U.S., 1873 (declined); ***candidate for Republican nomination to presidency of the U.S., 1876, 1880***; Republican candidate for U.S. Senate (NY), 1881; appointed assoc. justice, Supreme Court of the U.S., 1882 (declined). BUS. & PROF.: atty.; admitted to NY Bar, 1850; assoc., Spencer and Kurnan (law firm), Utica, 1850–81; law practice, New York, NY, 1881–88. MISC.: known as a machine politician and opponent of civil service reform; resigned from U.S. Senate in protest of President Garfield's policies, 1881. RES.: New York, NY.

CONLAN, JOHN BERTRAND, JR. b. Sep 17, 1930, Oak Park, IL; par. John Bertrand and Ruth S. (Anderson) Conlan; m. Irene Seville Danielson, Sep 13, 1968; c. Christopher Douglas; Kevin Matthew. EDUC.: B.S., Northwestern U., 1951; LL.B., Harvard U., 1954; U. of Cologne, 1954–55; Hague Acad. of International Law, 1958. POLIT. & GOV.: appointed asst. corporation counsel, Chicago, IL, 1955–56; member, AZ Republican State Central Cmte., 1962–; elected as a Republican to AZ State Senate, 1965–73; appointed member, Governor's Crime Comm. (AZ), 1967–70; member, Council on Organization of AZ State Government, 1967–70; elected as a Republican to U.S. House (AZ), 1973–77; candidate for Republican nomination to U.S. Senate AZ), 1976; ***candidate for American Party nomination to presidency of the U.S., 1976***; candidate for Republican nomination to U.S. House (AZ), 1986. BUS. & PROF.: atty.; admitted to IL Bar, 1954; admitted to AZ Bar, 1966; admitted to DC Bar, 1977; instructor, U. of MD, 1958–59; instructor, AZ State U., 1962; partner, Hughes, Hughes and Conlan (law firm), Phoenix, AZ, 1966–; chm. of the board, General Automation, Inc., Anaheim, CA, 1979–; dir., Telmark Inc. MIL.: capt., U.S. Army, 1956–61. MEM.: ABA; AZ Bar Assn.; DC Bar Assn.; IL Bar Assn.; Fulbright Scholars (1954–55); Delta Upsilon; Capitol Hill Club; Elks; Moose. AWARDS: "Outstanding Young Men in America," U.S. Junior C. of C., 1965; George Washington Honor Medal, Freedoms Foundation of Valley Forge, 1957, 1973; Leader in Government Award, Religious Heritage of America, 1975. REL.: Christian. MAILING ADDRESS: 5937 Cheney St., Paradise Valley, AZ 85253.

CONLEY, PAUL BEECHER. m. Irene Conley. POLIT. & GOV.: ***candidate for Republican nomination to presidency of the U.S., 1988, 1992***. MAILING ADDRESS: RD #1, Box 252, Schenevus, NY 12155.

CONNALLY, JOHN BOWDEN. b. Feb 27, 1917, Floresville, TX; d. Jun 15, 1993, Houston, TX; par. John Bowden and Lela (Wright) Connally; m. Idanell Brill, Dec 21, 1940; c. John Bowden III: Sharon; Mark. EDUC.: LL.B., U. of TX, 1941. POLIT. & GOV.: sec. to U.S. Rep. Lyndon B. Johnson (q.v.), 1939; administrative asst. to U.S. Sen. Lyndon B. Johnson, 1949; appointed U.S. sec. of the navy, 1961–63; elected as a Democrat to gov. of TX, 1963–69; delegate, Dem. Nat'l. Conv., 1956, 1960, 1964, 1968; member, U.S. Advisory Council on Executive Organization, 1969–70; appointed U.S. sec. of the treasury, 1971–72; ***candidate for Republican nomination to vice presidency of the U.S., 1972, 1976***; appointed special adviser to the president of the U.S., 1973; member, President's Foreign Intelligence Advisory Board; member, Advisory Comm. on the Reform of the International Monetary System; ***candidate for Republican nomination to presidency of the U.S., 1976, 1980***. BUS. & PROF.: atty.; admitted to TX Bar, 1941; pres., gen. mgr., KVET radio, Austin, TX, 1946–49; assoc., Powell, Wirtz and Rahaut (law firm), Austin, TX, 1949–52; counsel, Sid W. Richardson and Perry R. Bass, Fort Worth, TX, 1952–61; partner, Vinson, Elkins, Searls, Connally and Smith (law firm), Houston, TX, 1969–71, 1972–; dir., Falconbridge Nickel Mines, Ltd., Canada, 1973–; dir., Justin Industries; dir., First City Bancorp of TX; dir., First National Bank of Floresville; dir., Continental Airlines, Inc.; dir., Dr. Pepper Co.; dir., Chapman Energy, Inc.; dir., Signal Companies, Inc.; dir., American Physicians Service Group, Inc.; gen. counsel, American General Companies; dir., Primefax, Inc.; dir., Surgicare, Inc. MIL.: lt. commander, U.S. Navy, 1941–46; Legion of Merit; Bronze Star. MEM.: Andrew W. Mellon Foundation (trustee, 1973–); Conference Board of NY; Santa Gertrudis Breeders International (dir., 1973–); Houston C. of C. (vice chm., 1975–); Pin Oaks Horse Show Assn. (dir., 1973–); U. of TX Ex-Students Assn.; Foundation for Business, Politics and Economics (dir.); American Trauma Soc. (dir.); Methodist Hospital (dir.); Southwestern Legal Foundation (dir.); Houston Metropolitan Racquet Club (dir.). AWARDS: Distinguished Alumnus Award, U. of TX Ex-Students Assn., 1961. REL.: Methodist. MISC.: wounded during assassination of President John F. Kennedy (q.v.), Dallas, TX, Nov 22, 1963; forced into bankruptcy, 1988. RES.: Houston, TX.

CONNORS, TERRENCE RUSSELL. POLIT. & GOV.: ***candidate for Republican nomination to presidency***

of the U.S., 1988. MAILING ADDRESS: Route 3, Box 213-3, MacClenny, FL 32063.

CONOVER, JAMES MILTON. b. Aug 16, 1890, Swedesboro, NJ; d. May 6, 1972, Mullica Hill, NJ; par. Samuel Shull and Atlantic Dean (Moore) Conover; single. EDUC.: Montpelier Seminary; Ph.B., Dickinson Coll., 1913, Sc.D., 1933; M.A., U. of MN, 1916; M.A., Harvard U., 1934; grad. study, Oxford U., U. of Munich, and U. of Paris (Inst. of Urbanism); LL.B., Vanderbilt U., 1955, J.D., 1969. POLIT. & GOV.: Independent Republican candidate for U.S. Senate (CT), 1932; ***candidate for Prohibition Party nomination to presidency of the U.S., 1964; candidate for Prohibition Party nomination to vice presidency of the U.S., 1964 (declined)***. BUS. & PROF.: correspondent, *Boston (MA) Herald*, 1908–09; teacher, public schools, Swedesboro, 1909–10; teacher, St. Matthew's Episcopal School, Burlingame, CA, 1913–15; atty.; admitted to IN Bar, 1916; bill drafter, IN Legislature, 1917; fellow in political science, IN U., 1916–17; instructor in government, U. of PA and Camden YMCA, 1919–20; researcher, Brookings Institution, 1921–22, assoc., 1922–32; instructor, NY U., 1922–24, 1946–47; faculty, Yale U., 1924–30, assoc. prof., 1930–35; investigated Indian and French communities in Canada, 1941–42; resident researcher, Catholic U. of America, 1942–43; researcher, Middle American Research Inst., 1943–44; law practice, Chicago, IL, 1944–45; law adjudicator, U.S. VA, 1946–48; seminarian, Columbia U., 1948–53; lecturer, Rutgers U., 1949; assoc. prof., Seton Hall U., 1947–60, prof., 1960–68, prof. emeritus, 1968–72; contributor, various journals. MIL.: pvt. 3d Class, NJ Infantry, 1917; corp., 104th Engineers, 29th Div., U.S. Army, 1917; commissioned 2d lt., 42d Div., U.S. Army, WWI; diplomatic courier, American Comm. to Negotiate Peace, Paris, 1919. MEM.: NJ Assn. of Private Colleges and Universities (exec. sec., 1958–60); American Legion (founder, 1919); American Immigrant Inst. of CT (pres., 1934–35); Royal Soc. of Teachers; Holland Soc. of NY; Huguenot Soc. of NJ; Swedish Colonial Soc.; Soc. of Colonial Wars; ABA; Federal Bar Assn.; Inter-American Bar Assn.; Order of Founders and Patriots of America; Assn. of Princeton Graduate Alumni; SAR; Delta Theta Phi; Phi Kappa Psi; Pi Gamma Mu; Grange (7°); Harvard Club; Oxford Soc.; Van Kouwenhoven–Conover Family Assn. WRITINGS: *The General Land Office* (1923); *The Federal Power Commission* (1923); *The Office of Experiment Stations* (1924); *Working Manual of Original Sources in American Government* (1924); *Working Manual of Civics* (1925); *Political Theory* (co-author, 1959). AWARDS: Bernard J. McQuald Distinguished Service Medal, Seton Hall U., 1969. RES.: Newark, NJ.

CONRAD, WILLIAM G. b. Aug 3, 1848, Warren Cty., VA; d. Mar 6, 1914, Winchester, VA; par. James W. Conrad. POLIT. & GOV.: elected as a Democrat to mayor of Benton, MT; elected as a Democrat to MT Territorial Senate, 1879–80; Democratic candidate for U.S. Senate (MT), 1898, one other time; ***candidate for Democratic nomination to presidency of the U.S., 1908; candidate for Democratic nomination to vice presidency of the U.S., 1908***. BUS. & PROF.: clerk, partner, I. G. Baker and Co., Fort Benton, MT, c. 1860; rancher, MT; land speculator. MISC.: known as the "Cattle King of Montana." RES.: Benton, MT.

CONWAY, TERESA ANN. POLIT. & GOV.: ***independent candidate for presidency of the U.S., 1992***. MAILING ADDRESS: 1600 South Joyce St., B-1404, Arlington, VA 22202.

CONYERS, JOHN JAMES, JR. b. May 16, 1929, Detroit, MI; par. John James and Lucille Janice (Simpson) Conyers; m. Monica Ann Esters, Jun 4, 1990. EDUC.: B.A., Wayne State U., 1957, J.D., 1958; LL.D., Wilberforce U., 1969. POLIT. & GOV.: sec., 15th Congressional District Democratic Cmte.; legal asst. to U.S. Rep. John Dingell, 1958–61; referee, MI State Workmen's Compensation Dept., 1961–63; elected as a Democrat to U.S. House (MI), 1965–; ***candidate for The Black Assembly nomination to presidency of the U.S., 1976 (declined)***; delegate, Dem. Nat'l. Conv., 1968, 1972, 1976; candidate for Democratic nomination to mayor of Detroit, MI, 1989. BUS. & PROF.: atty.; admitted to MI Bar, 1959; partner, Conyers, Bell and Townsend (law firm), Detroit, MI, 1959–61; gen. counsel, three labor locals, Detroit, MI, 1959–64. MIL.: 2d lt., Corps of Engineers, U.S. Army, 1950–54; Combat Citation, U.S. Army; Merit Citation, U.S. Army. MEM.: NAACP (member, Detroit Exec. Board, 1963–); Kappa Alpha Psi; Wolverine Bar Assn.; MI Liberties Union (adviser); A.C.L.U. (member, Detroit Exec. Cmte., 1964–); Members of Congress for Peace Through Law; Detroit Trade Union Leadership Council; U.A.W. (education dir.); Martin Luther King Memorial Center (trustee); Southern Election Fund (trustee, 1970–); Americans for Democratic Action (vice chm., 1970); Council on Foreign Relations; Multi-Cultural Inst.; Joint Action for Community Service (dir., 1968–); Cmte. on Human Rights; Cotillon Club; African American Inst. (dir.); Cmte. on Racial Justice (dir.); Detroit Inst. of Arts (dir.); National Alliance Against Racist and Political Repression (dir.); National League of Cities (dir.). AWARDS: Rosa Parks Award, Southern Christian Leadership Conference. WRITINGS: "To Change the Course of History," *Many Shades of Black* (coauthor, 1969); "Politics and the Black Revolution," *Ebony* (1961); *American Militarism* (contributor, 1970); *War Crimes and the American Conscience* (contributor, 1970); *Anatomy of an Undeclared War* (contributor, 1972). REL.: Bapt. MAILING ADDRESS: 19970 Canterbury Rd., Detroit, MI 48221.

COOK, AUGUST "GEMINI." b. 1942, CA; single. POLIT. & GOV.: ***candidate for Democratic nomination to presidency of the U.S., 1976; Oregon Good Times Party candidate for presidency of the U.S., 1976***; Oregon Good Times Party candidate for gov. of OR, 1978. BUS. & PROF.: experimental farmer; yogi; philosopher; "Universal

People Perceptor"; author; inventor; environmentalist; ed., *Joyous Cosmology—Daybook Changes*; owner, Creative Crazyness, Inc. MAILING ADDRESS: Kellogg Rt. Box 48B, Oakland, OR 97462.

COOK, LEON FREDERICK. b. Jul 30, 1939, Red Lake, MN; m. Dana Lee Johnson, Oct 20, 1962; c. Kristin Lee; Thomas Lee; Trisha Lee. EDUC.: B.S., St. John's U., 1963; M.S.W., U. of MN, 1966. POLIT. & GOV.: delegate, Dem. Nat'l. Conv., 1972; ***candidate for Democratic nomination to vice presidency of the U.S., 1972***; elected representative, Red Lake Band of Chippewa Indians Tribal Council, 1974–78; Democratic-Farmer-Labor Party candidate for Minneapolis (MN) City Council, 1975. BUS. & PROF.: social worker; dir., Edward F. Waite Neighborhood House, Indian Services Program, Minneapolis, 1963–66; consultant, administrative asst. to director, Minneapolis Community Action Agency, 1966–67; project review officer, manpower specialist, equal employment officer, Indian programs officer, Economic Development Administration, U.S. Dept. of Commerce, Duluth, MN, 1967–68; field coordinator/senior economic development specialist, Economic Development Administration, U.S. Dept. of Commerce, Phoenix, AZ, 1968–70; dir., Office of Economic Development, U.S. Bureau of Indian Affairs, U.S. Dept. of the Interior, Washington, DC, 1970–71; dir., Dept. of Indian Education, Minneapolis Public Schools, 1971–73; dir., MN Indian Resource Development, 1973–74; freelance consultant, 1974–76; dir., Demonstration Project on the Treatment and Prevention of Child Abuse and Child Neglect, U.S. Dept. of Health, Education and Welfare, 1976; senior consultant, Control Data Corp., 1976–78; dir., American Indian Management Consortium, 1978–. MEM.: United Way of Greater Minneapolis (vice pres.); Minneapolis Foundation (trustee); St. John's Preparatory School (Alumni Board of Directors); Catholic Welfare Services (dir.); Campaign for Human Development (dir.); National Congress of American Indians (pres., 1971–73); MN Press Council (1973–77); MN Blue Cross and Blue Shield (trustee, 1973–77); Hennepin Cty. Bar Ethics Cmte. (1976–77); Minneapolis Urban Coalition (treas., 1973–75); MN Higher Education Coordinating Cmte. (1973–76); Pillsbury-Waite Neighborhood Services (dir., 1975–77); Economic Development Advisory Council, MN State Dept. of Economic Development (1972–75); MN State Mental Health Advisory Council; St. John's U. Advisory Council (1974–76). WRITINGS: *Economic Development in Indian Country* (1970); *Indians of Today* (1971); *Indian Country's Power Structure* (1973). REL.: R.C. (member, Pastoral Council, Archdiocese of St. Paul and Minneapolis). MAILING ADDRESS: 5016 13th Ave., South, Minneapolis, MN 55417.

COOK, SILAS W. b. Dec 5, 1844, Amsterdam, NY; d. Jun 7, 1935, Guernsey, WY; m. Ada Fair, 1883; c. Mrs. Cora Wildy; Orin; Mrs. Helen Polk. POLIT. & GOV.: elected mayor of Guernsey, WY; elected justice of the peace, Guernsey; ***independent candidate for presidency of the U.S., 1900***. BUS. & PROF.: oil industry, PA; rig builder. MIL.: U.S. Army, Civil War. RES.: Guernsey, WY.

COOLEY, MARVIN LAMAR. b. Dec 30, 1926, Gilbert, AZ; par. Freeman and Pearl Wallrade (Whipple) Cooley. POLIT. & GOV.: ***candidate for American Party nomination to presidency of the U.S., 1976; candidate for American Party nomination to vice presidency of the U.S., 1976***. MISC.: sentenced to three years in Florence (AZ) State Prison for income tax evasion. MAILING ADDRESS: Mesa, AZ.

COOLIDGE, GRACE ANNA GOODHUE. b. Jan 3, 1879, Burlington, VT; d. Jul 8, 1957, Northampton, MA; par. Andrew Issachar and Lemira (Barrett) Goodhue; m. John Calvin Coolidge (q.v.), Oct 4, 1905; c. John; Calvin. EDUC.: Ph.B., U. of VT, 1902, LL.D., 1929. POLIT. & GOV.: member, Hoover-Curtis Eastern Campaign Cmte., 1932; ***candidate for Republican nomination to presidency of the U.S., 1936***. BUS. & PROF.: teacher, Clarke School for the Deaf, Northampton, MA, 1902–05. MEM.: Mercersburg Acad. (trustee, to 1945); Motion Picture Research Council (hon. vice pres.); Clarke School for the Deaf (chm., Board of Corp.). HON. DEG.: LL.D., Boston U., 1924; LL.D., George Washington U., 1929; LL.D., Smith Coll., 1929. REL.: Congregationalist. RES.: Northampton, MA.

COOLIDGE, JOHN CALVIN. b. Jul 4, 1872, Plymouth, VT; d. Jan 5, 1933, Northampton, MA; par. John Calvin and Victoria J. (Moor) Coolidge; m. Grace Anna Goodhue (q.v.) Coolidge, Oct 4, 1905; c. John; Calvin. EDUC.: Black River Acad.; St. Johnsbury Acad.; A.B., Amherst Coll., 1895; studied law in office of Hammond and Field, Northampton, MA. POLIT. & GOV.: elected member, Northampton City Council, 1899; city solicitor, Northampton, 1900–1901; clerk of cty. courts, MA, 1904; elected as a Republican to MA State House, 1907–08; elected as a Republican to mayor of Northampton, MA, 1910–11; elected as a Republican to MA State Senate, 1912–15 (pres., 1914–15); elected as a Republican to lt. gov. of MA, 1916–18; elected as a Republican to gov. of MA, 1919–20; ***candidate for Republican nomination to presidency of the U.S., 1920, 1928, 1932; elected as a Republican to vice presidency of the U.S., 1921–23; succeeded to the presidency of the U.S. upon death of Warren G. Harding (q.v.), August 3, 1923; subsequently elected as a Republican to presidency of the U.S., 1923–29; candidate for Democratic nomination to presidency of the U.S., 1924***; chm., Nonpartisan Railroad Comm. BUS. & PROF.: atty.; admitted to MA Bar, 1897; law practice, Northampton, MA; dir., New York Life Insurance Co. MEM.: Phi Beta Kappa; Foundation of the Blind (hon. pres.). HON. DEG.: LL.D., Amherst Coll., 1919; LL.D., Tufts U.; LL.D., Williams Coll.; LL.D., Bates Coll.; LL.D., Wesleyan U.; LL.D., U. of VT. WRITINGS: *The Autobiography of Calvin Coolidge* (1929). REL.: Congregationalist (hon. moderator, National

Council of Congregational Churches, 1923–33). MISC.: known as "Silent Cal." RES.: Northampton, MA.

COOLIDGE, MARCUS ALLEN. b. Oct 6, 1865, Westminster, MA; d. Jan 23, 1947, Miami Beach, FL; par. Frederick Spaulding and Ellen Drusilla (Allen) Coolidge; m. Ethel Louise Warren, Oct 1, 1898; c. Louise (Mrs. Donald Fell Carpenter); Judith (Mrs. Gordon Hughes); Helen (Mrs. Harry H. Woodring, q.v.). EDUC.: public schools; Bryant and Stratton Commercial Coll. POLIT. & GOV.: chm., treas., Wilson Advisory Cmte., 1916; elected as a Democrat to mayor of Fitchburg, MA, 1916; appointed special U.S. envoy to Poland, 1919; chm., MA Democratic State Convention, 1920; delegate, Dem. Nat'l. Conv., 1920, 1924; ***candidate for Democratic nomination to presidency of the U.S., 1924***; member, treas., MA State Democratic Central Cmte.; presidential elector, Democratic Party (MA), 1928; elected as a Democrat to U.S. Senate (MA), 1931–37. BUS. & PROF.: employee, Chair and Rattan Business; gen. contractor, 1883–05; pres., Fitchburg Machine Works, 1905; pres., Seneca Falls (NY) Machine Co.; dir., Safety Fund National Bank; dir., Cooperative Bank of Fitchburg. MEM.: Cushing Acad. (trustee; pres.). REL.: Universalist. RES.: Fitchburg, MA.

COOMBS, CHARLES F. b. c. 1924. EDUC.: 11th grade. POLIT. & GOV.: ***independent candidate for presidency of the U.S., 1976***. BUS. & PROF.: barber, Mattcawan State Hospital, Beacon, NY. MAILING ADDRESS: P.O. Box 506, Beacon, NY 12508.

COOPER, EDWIN M. b. 1885; d. Feb 26, 1971, Montebello, CA; married; c. Colin E.; Carol Faye. EDUC.: A.B., U. of Southern CA, LL.B., 1910. POLIT. & GOV.: Prohibition Party candidate for atty. gen. of CA, 1954, 1958; ***Prohibition Party candidate for vice presidency of the U.S., 1956***; member, treas., CA State Prohibition Party Central Cmte.; member, Los Angeles Cty. (CA) Prohibition Party Central Cmte. BUS. & PROF.: professional staff, YMCA, New York, NY; staff, United Services Organization, New York; atty.; admitted to CA Bar, 1910; partner, Cooper and Cooper (law firm), Montebello, CA. MEM.: YMCA; United Service Organization. REL.: Methodist (assoc. lay leader, District Conference). RES.: Montebello, CA.

COOPER, JACK. b. Nov 30, 1876, MO; d. Apr 1, 1953, La Center, OR; m. Elizabeth Cooper; c. Mrs. Jack Garnett; Mrs. Thelma Garnett; Harry; Bob. POLIT. & GOV.: ***candidate for Democratic nomination to presidency of the U.S., 1912***. BUS. & PROF.: engineer, Meier and Frank Co., Portland, OR. RES.: La Center, OR.

COOPER, JAMES ROBERT. POLIT. & GOV.: ***candidate for Democratic nomination to presidency of the U.S., 1992***. MAILING ADDRESS: 1503 Kings Highway, Dallas, TX 75208.

COOPER, PETER. b. Feb 12, 1791, New York, NY; d. Apr 4, 1883, New York, NY; par. John and Margaret (Campbell) Cooper; m. Sarah Bedell, Dec 22, 1813; c. Sarah Amanda; Peter William; John Campbell; Benjamin Bedell; Edward; Sarah Amelia (Mrs. Abram Stevens Hewitt). EDUC.: public schools, Peekskill, NY, for 3 quarters. POLIT. & GOV.: elected as a Democrat, asst. alderman, New York Common Council, 1828–31; elected as a Democrat, alderman, New York Common Council, 1840–42; candidate for Democratic nomination to mayor of New York, 1845; appointed controller of New York, 1855 (declined); ***candidate for Labor Reform Party nomination to presidency of the U.S., 1872 (declined); National Independent (Greenback) Party candidate for presidency of the U.S., 1876***; National Independent (Greenback) Party candidate for U.S. Senate (NY), 1879. BUS. & PROF.: apprentice coachmaker, 1808–11; coachmaker; grocer, Bedell and Cooper, New York, 1818; glue manufacturer, New York, 1821; partner, Canton Iron Works, Baltimore, MD, 1828–32; built Baltimore and Ohio R.R., 1830; promoter, Atlantic cable; pres., NY, Newfoundland and London Telegraph Co.; pres., North American Telegraph Co., 1855; factory owner; philanthropist. MEM.: Public School Soc.; Citizens Assn. of NY (pres.); Cooper Union Coll. (founder, 1857); Tammany Soc.; Demilt Milk Dispensary (trustee); NY Juvenile Asylum (vice pres., 1882); NY Gallery of Fine Arts (trustee); NY Sanitary Assn.; Emigrant Protective Soc.; American Emigrant Co.; Soc. for the Prevention of Cruelty to Animals; Home for Old Men and Aged Couples; NY Indian Peace Comm. AWARDS: Bessemer Gold Medal Award, Iron and Steel Inst. of Great Britain, 1870. HON. DEG.: LL.D., U. of NY, 1879; WRITINGS: *Political and Financial Ideas of Peter Cooper with an Autobiography* (1877); *Autobiography of Peter Cooper; Ideas for a Science of Good Government* (1883). REL.: Unitarian. MISC.: rolled first structural iron for fireproof buildings, Trenton, NJ, 1845; first U.S. iron manufacturer to use Bessemer process, 1856; inventor of washing machine, self-rocking cradle, and other devices to reduce manual labor. RES.: New York, NY.

COOPER, WILLIAM PRENTICE. b. Sep 28, 1895, Shelbyville, TN; d. May 18, 1969, Rochester, MN; par. William Prentice and Argentine (Shofner) Cooper; m. Hortense Hayes Powell, Apr 22, 1950; c. William Prentice III; James Hayes Shofner; John Norman Powell. EDUC.: Vanderbilt U., 1914–15; A.B., Princeton U., 1917; LL.B., Harvard U., 1921. POLIT. & GOV.: elected as a Democrat to TN State House, 1923–25; appointed atty. gen., Eighth Judicial Circuit of TN, 1925–26; city atty., Shelbyville, TN; city atty., Lewisburg, TN; elected as a Democrat to TN State Senate, 1937–39; elected as a Democrat to gov. of TN, 1939–45; member, TN State Hist. Comm., 1941–69; delegate, Dem. Nat'l. Conv., 1944; ***candidate for Democratic nomination to vice presidency of the U.S., 1944***; appointed U.S. ambassador to Peru, 1946–48; elected delegate, TN State

Constitutional Convention, 1953 (pres.). BUS. & PROF.: atty.; admitted to TN Bar, 1922; law practice, Shelbyville, TN; law practice, Lewisburg, TN; organizer, Duck River Electric Membership Corp.; dir., People's National Bank; farmer. MIL.: pvt., gun master, Battery E, 307th F.A., U.S. Army, 1918, 2d lt., 1918; Baron de Kubertine Medal. MEM.: American Legion (State Commander of TN; Postwar Planning Comm.); TN Bar Assn.; Phi Delta Theta; University Club; Lions Club (charter member); Assn. of Army, Navy and Air Force Veterans of Canada (life member); Freolac Club; Rotary Club; Webb School (trustee, 1952–66); Southern Governors Freight Rate Equalization Cmte. (chm., 1939–43); Southern Governors Conference (chm., 1943–45); Victory Garden Program (chm., 1941–45); Acad. of Political Science; Cumberland Club. HON. DEG.: LL.D., Lincoln Memorial U., 1940; LL.D., Muhlenberg Coll., 1942; LL.D., Hartwick Coll., 1943. WRITINGS: *The Christ of Land, Sea and Air* (1955). REL.: Lutheran (member, exec. cmte.). RES.: Shelbyville, TN.

COORS, WILLIAM K. b. 1916, Golden, CO. EDUC.: grad., Princeton U., 1938. POLIT. & GOV.: ***Whig Party candidate for vice presidency of the U.S., 1976 (declined)***. BUS. & PROF.: brewmaster; chm., chief exec. officer, Adolf Coors Co., Golden, CO; dir., Denver and Rio Grande Western R.R. MAILING ADDRESS: 130 Vine St., Denver, CO 80206.

COPE, GILBERT. b. Feb 16, 1917, West Chester, PA; par. Joseph and Ellen (Fussell) Cope; single. EDUC.: grad., Friends Boarding School, Barnesville, OH, 1935. POLIT. & GOV.: Constitution Party candidate for U.S. House (PA), 1970; ***candidate for Democratic nomination to presidency of the U.S., 1976, 1984***. BUS. & PROF.: retired. REL.: none (nee Religious Soc. of Friends). MAILING ADDRESS: 1021 South Concord Rd., West Chester, PA 19380.

COPELAND, ROYAL SAMUEL. b. Nov 7, 1868, Dexter, MI; d. Jun 17, 1938, Washington, DC; par. Roscoe Pulaski and Frances Jane (Holmes) Copeland; m. Frances Spalding, Jul 15, 1908; c. Royal Spalding; Alice. EDUC.: MI State Normal Coll.; M.D., U. of MI, 1889; postgrad. study in medicine, England, France, Germany, Switzerland, and Belgium. POLIT. & GOV.: elected mayor of Ann Arbor, MI, 1901–03; pres., Ann Arbor Park Board, 1905–06; pres., Ann Arbor Board of Education, 1907–08; appointed member, U.S. Pension Examining Board, 1917; commissioner of health, pres., New York (NY) Board of Health, 1918–23; elected as a Democrat to U.S. Senate (NY), 1923–38; delegate, Dem. Nat'l. Conv., 1924; ***candidate for Democratic nomination to presidency of the U.S., 1924***; candidate for Democratic nomination to mayor of New York, 1937; candidate for Republican nomination to mayor of New York, 1937. BUS. & PROF.: ophthalmologist; medical practice, Bay City, MI, 1890–95; house surgeon, U. Hospital, Ann Arbor, MI, 1889–90; asst. prof. of ophthalmology and otology, U. of MI, Ann Arbor, MI, 1889–90, prof., 1895–1908; dean, NY Flower Hospital and Medical Coll., 1908–18. MEM.: American Coll. of Surgeons (fellow); Epworth League (treas.); National Council of Defense (member, NY State Cmte., Medical Section, 1917); MI State Tuberculosis Assn. (trustee, 1900–1908); American Ophthalmological and Otological Assn. (pres., 1904–05). HON. DEG.: A.M., Lawrence U., 1897; A.M., Hahnemann Coll., 1921; LL.D., Syracuse U., 1923; LL.D., Oglethorpe U., 1927; D.Sc., Temple U., 1934. WRITINGS: *Refraction* (with A. E. Ibershoff, 1899–1905); *The Health Book* (1924); *Dr. Copeland's Home Medical Book* (1935). REL.: Methodist (delegate, Ecumenical Conference, London, England, 1900). RES.: Suffern, NY.

COPELAND, SOLOMON. d. 1845?; m. Mary Copeland; c. Thomas; John; Mary Ann. POLIT. & GOV.: appointed administrator of estates, Henry Cty., TN; member, Henry Cty. Court Comm.; elected Henry Cty. surveyor, 1839–41; elected as a Democrat to TN State House, 1841–43; ***independent candidate for vice presidency of the U.S., 1844 (declined)***. BUS. & PROF.: soldier; surveyor. MIL.: col. REL.: Church of Jesus Christ of Latter-Day Saints. RES.: Paris, TN.

CORNWALL, KERNEY DUANE. b. Dec 3, 1936, Ellensburg, WA; par. Herbert Alexander and Thelma Esther (Reynolds) Cornwall; m. Andrea F. Johnson (divorced); c. Alexander Duane; Capt. James Forrest; Kelly Ann; Anthony Brett. EDUC.: Edmonds (WA) H.S.; Edmonds Community Coll., 1967–68. POLIT. & GOV.: ***Left Handers of America candidate for presidency of the U.S., 1988***. BUS. & PROF.: wholesale meat cutter, 32 years. MIL.: U.S. Air Force, 1954–55. MEM.: NRA (life member); Parents-Teachers Assn.; Woodridge BSA; Order of the Arrow. AWARDS: Golden Arrow Award; District Award of Merit, BSA, 1982. WRITINGS: *Cornwall Family History* (1989). REL.: Lutheran. MAILING ADDRESS: 6909 South 123rd, Apt. 149, Seattle, WA 98178.

CORREGAN, CHARLES HUNTER. b. Dec 11, 1860, Oswego, NY; d. Jun 19, 1946, Syracuse, NY; par. William H. and Susannah (Gilmore) Corregan; m. Margaret Watson, May 3, 1890; c. Donald; Jeanne; Charles Ronald; Neil; Kenneth. EDUC.: grad., Oswego H.S., 1879; studied law, 1879–81. POLIT. & GOV.: Socialist Labor Party candidate for U.S. House (NY), 1896; Socialist Labor Party candidate for Syracuse City School Board, 1897; Socialist Labor Party candidate for gov. of NY, 1898, 1900, 1928; ***Socialist Labor Party candidate for presidency of the U.S., 1904***; delegate, Socialist Labor Party National Convention, 1904, 1924. BUS. & PROF.: printer; reporter, *Owego Times*, 1881–84; foreman, *Auburn (NY) Dispatch*, 1887–88; foreman, *Syracuse Standard*, 1889–92; mgr., NY Labor News Co., 1902–04; foreman, *New York (NY) Daily People*, 1904; staff, *Syracuse Journal*. MEM.: International Typographical Union; Central Trades and Labor Assembly of Syracuse (pres.,

1893); State Federation of Labor of NY (vice pres., 1903). REL.: Episc. RES.: Syracuse, NY.

CORTELYOU, GEORGE BRUCE. b. Jul 26, 1862, New York, NY; d. Oct 23, 1940, Huntington, NY; par. Peter Collins and Rose (Seary) Cortelyou; m. Lily Morris, Sep 15, 1888; c. George Bruce, Jr.; William Winthrop; Grace; Helen; Peter Collins. EDUC.: grad., Hempstead (Long Island) Inst., 1879; grad., MA State Normal School, 1882; LL.B., Georgetown U., 1895; LL.M., Columbian (George Washington) U., 1896. POLIT. & GOV.: private sec. to government officials, 1889–95; stenographer to president of the U.S., 1895, exec. clerk, 1896–98, asst. sec. to the president, 1898–1900, sec., 1900–1903; appointed U.S. sec. of commerce and labor, 1903–04; chm., Rep. Nat'l. Cmte., 1904–07; appointed postmaster gen. of the U.S., 1905–07; appointed U.S. sec. of the treasury, 1907–09; ***candidate for Republican nomination to presidency of the U.S., 1908; candidate for Republican nomination to vice presidency of the U.S., 1908***. BUS. & PROF.: stenographer; atty.; general law and verbatim reporter, NY, 1883–85; principal, preparatory schools, NY, 1885–89; pres., Consolidated Gas Co. of NY, 1909–35; dir., NY Life Insurance Co.; dir., D. Appleton-Century Co. MEM.: McKinley National Memorial Assn. (hon. pres.); Miriam Osborn Memorial Home Assn. (pres.); National Electric Light Assn. (pres.); Edison Electric Inst. (pres.). HON. DEG.: LL.D., Georgetown U., 1903; LL.D., KY Wesleyan U., 1905; LL.D., U. of IL, 1905; LL.D., Columbian (George Washington) U., 1932. RES.: Long Island, NY.

CORWIN, THOMAS. b. Jul 29, 1794, Bourbon Cty., KY; d. Dec 18, 1865, Washington, DC; par. Matthias and Patience (Halleck) Corwin; m. Sarah Ross, 1822; c. five. POLIT. & GOV.: elected prosecuting atty., Warren Cty., OH, 1818–28; elected as a Whig to OH State Senate, 1922–23, 1929; elected as a Whig to U.S. House (OH), 1831–41, as a Republican, 1859–61; elected as a Whig to gov. of OH, 1840–42; Whig Party candidate for gov. of OH, 1842; pres., OH Whig Party State Convention, 1844; presidential elector, Whig Party (OH), 1844; elected as a Whig to U.S. Senate (OH), 1845–50; ***candidate for Whig Party nomination to presidency of the U.S., 1848; candidate for Whig Party nomination to vice presidency of the U.S., 1848***; appointed U.S. sec. of the treasury, 1850–53; appointed U.S. minister to Mexico, 1861–64. BUS. & PROF.: atty.; admitted to OH Bar, 1817; law practice, Lebanon, OH; law practice, Washington, DC, 1864–65. REL.: Bapt. RES.: Lebanon, OH.

COSBY, BILL. b. Jul 12, 1937, Philadelphia, PA; par. William Henry and Anna Cosby; m. Camille Hanks, Jan 25, 1964; c. Erika Ranee; Erinn Charlene; Ennis William; Ensa Camille; Evin Harrah. EDUC.: Temple U.; Ph.D. (education), U. of MA. POLIT. & GOV.: ***candidate for Democratic nomination to presidency of the U.S., 1988***. BUS. & PROF.: actor; entertainer; comedian; appeared in numerous nightclubs (including The Gaslight, New York, NY; Hungry I, San Francisco, CA; Shoreham Hotel, Washington, DC; Basin St. East, New York, NY; Hilton, Las Vegas, NV; Harrah's, Lake Tahoe, NV). TELEVISION CREDITS: guest appearances on numerous TV programs (including *The Electric Company*, 1972); costar, *I Spy*, 1966–68; star, *The Bill Cosby Show*, 1969, 1972–73; star, *Fat Albert and the Cosby Kids*, 1972; star, *Cos*, 1976. MOTION PICTURE CREDITS: *To All My Friends on Shore* (television, 1971); *Hickey and Boggs* (1972); *Man and Boy* (1972); *Uptown Saturday Night* (1974); *Let's Do It Again* (1975); *Mother, Jugs and Speed* (1976); *A Piece of the Action* (1977); *Top Secret* (television, 1978); *California Suite* (1978); *Devil and Max Devlin* (1979). Recordings: "Revenge"; "To Russell, My Broth, With Whom I Slept"; "200 M.P.H."; "Why Is There Air"; "Wonderfulness"; "It's True, It's True, Bill Cosby is a Very Funny Fellow—Right, I Started Out as a Child"; "8:15"; "12:15." MIL.: U.S.N.R., 1956–60. MEM.: Rhythm and Blues Hall of Fame (pres., 1968–). WRITINGS: *The Wit and Wisdom of Fat Albert* (1973); *Fatherhood* (1986); *Bill Cosby's Personal Guide to Power Tennis*. AWARDS: eight Grammy Awards, National Acad. of Performing Arts and Sciences; four Emmy Awards, Academy of Television Arts and Sciences, 1966, 1967, 1968, 1969; named "Number One in Comedy Field," Top Artists on Campus Poll, 1968. MAILING ADDRESS: c/o SAH Enterprises, Inc., 1900 Avenue of the Americas, Suite 1900, Century City, CA 90067.

COSTA, FRANCES H. POLIT. & GOV.: ***Independent Alliance Party candidate for vice presidency of the U.S., 1984***. MAILING ADDRESS: ME.

COTNER, ROBERT EUGENE. b. Mar 19, 1946, Broken Arrow, OK; par. Ed James and Ruth Rosemary (Weldon) Cotner; m. Helen Forrest, 1965; m. 2d, Sandi Franklin, 1970; m. 3d, Judy Sutton; m. 4th, Edie singleton, 1982 (divorced); c. none. EDUC.: CIA schools; U.S. Army schools. POLIT. & GOV.: ***candidate for Democratic nomination to presidency of the U.S., 1980, 1984, 1988***. BUS. & PROF.: paralegal; businessman; employee, CIA, 1962–72; licensed private investigator, 1967–79; minister. MIL.: U.S. Army, 1963–64; OK National Guard, 1964–65. MEM.: Junior C. of C.; American Legion; NRA; Constitutional Bill of Rights Cmte. REL.: nondenominational Christian (minister). MISC.: campaigned as way of advertising for a wife; former prison inmate. MAILING ADDRESS: Box 129, Bixby, OK 74008.

COUGHLIN, CHARLES EDWARD. b. Oct 25, 1891, Hamilton, Canada; d. Oct 27, 1979, Bloomfield Hills, MI; par. Thomas J. and Amelia (Mahoney) Coughlin; single. EDUC.: honor grad., U. of Toronto, 1911; LL.D., Notre Dame U., 1933. POLIT. & GOV.: ***candidate for Democratic nomination to presidency of the U.S., 1936***; founder, Union Party, 1936. BUS. & PROF.: radio commentator; author; ordained priest, Roman Catholic Church, 1916; teacher of philosophy, Assumption Coll., Western U., 1916–22; pastor, Shrine of the Little Flower, Royal Oak, MI, 1926–79; publisher, *Social Justice;* owner, Social Justice, Inc. MEM.: National Union for Social Justice (founder); Radio League of the Little Flower (founder); Social Justice Poor Soc. (founder). WRITINGS: *Christ or the Red Serpent* (1930); *By the Sweat of Thy Brow* (1931); *Father Coughlin's Radio Sermons* (1931); *The New Deal in Money* (1933); *A Series of Lectures on Social Justice* (1935); *Money—Questions and Answers* (1936); *A Series of Lectures on Social Justice* (1936); *Am I an Anti-Semite?* (1939); *Why Leave Our Own?* (1939). REL.: R.C. RES.: Royal Oak, MI.

COULTER, JOHN LEE. b. Apr 16, 1881, Mallory, MN; d. Apr 16, 1959, Washington, DC; par. John and Catherine (McVeety) Coulter; m. Phoebe Everett Frost, Sep 23, 1911; c. John Lee; Kirkley Schley; David Creswell. EDUC.: A.B., U. of ND, 1904, A.M., 1905; studied law, 1904–05; Ph.D., U. of WI, 1908; U. of MN; IA State Coll. POLIT. & GOV.: special agent, MN State Board of Health, 1909–10; expert special agent, U.S. Census Bureau, 1910–12, in charge of Agricultural Division, 1912–14; member, WV Council of Defense, 1917–18; expert, National Exports Council, 1917; expert, War Industries Board, 1918; ***candidate for Republican nomination to vice presidency of the U.S., 1924***; chief economist, chm. of the advisory board, U.S. Tariff Comm., 1929, member, 1930–34; appointed member, U.S. Comm. for Reciprocity Information, 1934–35; member, U.S. Rural Credit Comm. BUS. & PROF.: economist; statistician; instructor, IA State Coll., 1907; instructor, U. of WI, 1907–08; instructor, U. of MN, 1908–09, asst. prof. of economics, 1909–10; prof. of rural economics, Knapp School of Country Life, 1914–15; dean, WV Coll. of Agriculture, 1915–21; dir., Agricultural Experiment Station, WV Coll. of Agriculture, 1915–21; pres., ND A&M Coll., 1921–29; lecturer, George Washington U., 1910–13; lecturer, Summer School of the South, 1910–11; ed., *Quarterly Journal of the American Statistical Association;* ed., *American Economic Review.* MIL.: maj., U.S. Army Signal Corps, 1918–19; staff, U.S. Army Overseas Educational Comm., 1918–19; Chevalier, Legion of Honor (France). MEM.: Masons; American Statistical Assn. (fellow); American Economic Assn.; APSA; American Assn. for Labor Legislation; American Assn. of Agricultural Colleges and Experiment Stations (vice pres., 1917, 1927); Farm Economics Assn.; National Economics League; Phi Beta Kappa; Greater ND Soc.; Cosmos Club. HON. DEG.: LL.D., U. of ND 1922; D.Sc., ND State Agricultural Coll., 1950. WRITINGS: *Economic History of the Red River Valley of the North* (1910); *Cooperation Among Farmers* (1911); *The Problem of Rural Credit* (1913); *Postwar Fiscal Problems and Policies* (1945); *The Potawatomie Treaty of July 29, 1829* (1955). REL.: Presb. RES.: Fargo, ND.

COUNTRYMAN, CARL CHAPIN. b. 1874; deceased. POLIT. & GOV.: ***candidate for Republican nomination to presidency of the U.S., 1944, 1948***. BUS. & PROF.: cook on liberty ship; teacher. WRITINGS: *Three Senses . . . A Few Poems* (1898); *When the Task is Done* (1915); *I Am and I Aspire* (1944). MISC.: walked across U.S., 1908; filed suit against America First Cmte. for plagiarism, 1941. RES.: New York, NY.

COURTNEY, GREGORY ALLEN. POLIT. & GOV.: ***candidate for Democratic nomination to presidency of the U.S., 1988***. MAILING ADDRESS: 8041 Venetian Dr., Clayton, MO 63105.

COURTNEY, KENT H. b. Oct 23, 1918, St. Paul, MN; par. Joseph Frank and Zella Edana (Smith) Courtney; m. Phoebe Greene; c. Kent H., Jr. EDUC.: Fortier H.S., New Orleans, LA; B.B.A., Tulane U. POLIT. & GOV.: candidate for New Orleans City Council, 1954; States Rights Party candidate for gov. of LA, 1960; ***Conservative Party of NJ candidate for vice presidency of the U.S., 1960***; Conservative Party candidate for U.S. Senate (LA), 1962; press aide, Lester Maddox (q.v.) for President Campaign, 1968; member, American Party National Cmte., 1969–70; independent candidate for U.S. House (LA), 1976. BUS. & PROF.: publisher, 1954–; publisher, *Free Men Speak;* ed., *The Independent American,* New Orleans, 1954–; lecturer; commentator, "The Radio Edition of *The Independent American*"; publisher, Associated Pelican Printing Co.; commercial officer, British consulate, New Orleans, LA; pilot, Pan American World Airways; instructor in economics, Tulane U.; market research analyst; asst. to the president, banana import firm. MIL.: pilot, U.S. Navy, WWII. MEM.: Hoover Comm. on Government Economy (alternate member); Liberty Amendment Cmte. (LA state chm.); American Legion (chapter countersubversion chm.); Conservative Soc. of America (founder; national chm., 1961–70); Ten Million Americans Mobilizing for Justice (chm., New Orleans Branch, 1954); John Birch Soc. (chapter leader); New Orleans C. of C. (membership dir.). WRITINGS: *The C.S.A. Political Action Handbook for Anti-Communists; The Rockefeller Candidacy, A C.S.A. White Paper; Fantastic Foreign Aid; How the U.S. is Being Communized; The Black Panthers; Follow the North Star; Who is a Conservative; McGovern, The Superdove Who Would Be President; Philip A. Hart—Does This Senator Represent You?; G.O.P. Now Under Liberal Control; What Moderate Republicanism Really Means; America Needs an Anti-Communist Party; Beware of Lindsay; How Did Your Senators Vote on Aid to Communism; Meet Senator John Sparkman; Impeach Abe Fortas; Hubert Humphrey's Public Record; George Wallace, The People's Choice; A New Horizon for America; The Open Housing Laws Must be Repealed; Preserving Patriotism for Posterity; Civil Rights Myths and Communist Realities* (with Medford Evans); *The Case of General Edwin A. Walker* (with Phoebe Courtney, 1961); *America's Un-elected Rulers* (with Phoebe Courtney); *Disarmament—A Blue Print for Surrender* (with Phoebe Courtney); *Tax-Fax; The Silencers.* REL.: R.C. MAILING ADDRESS: The Conservative Party of America, P.O. Box 4254, New Orleans 18, LA.

COURTON, CLARENCE LAVERN. b. Apr 22, 1924, Westville, OK; par. Clarence and Izora (Woodall) Courton; m. (divorced); c. Charles; Stephen; Edward. EDUC.: B.S.M.E., Dartmouth Coll., 1947. POLIT. & GOV.: ***candidate for Republican nomination to presidency of the U.S., 1976, 1984***. BUS. & PROF.: spooler, Tidewater Oil Refinery, 1956; senior field engineer, Bechtel, 1956–62; general design engineer, 1962–64; engineer, Lehigh Design, 1964; lead mechanical and piping engineer, Universal Design, 1964–66; hydraulic engineer, Page Communications Antenna Division, 1966; superintendent of mechanical maintenance, Continental/Marathon/Amerada Oil, 1966–68; employee, CDI, 1968–69; employee, TAD, 1969; unit engineer, ARDE, 1969–71; structural engineer and HVAC designer, ARDE, 1971; construction supervisor, Harrah's Lake Tahoe Operations, 1971–73; designer, Air Products, 1973; project engineer, CF Industries, Inc., 1973–75; engineer, Davy Powergas Engineering and Construction, 1975; construction mgr., CF Industries, Inc., 1975–. Mil: U.S. Navy. MEM.: Diplomatic Courier Assn. REL.: Muslim. MAILING ADDRESS: Route 14, Box 1890, Lakeland, FL 33802.

COUSINS, NORMAN. b. Jun 24, 1915, Union Hill, NJ; d. Nov 30, 1990, Los Angeles, CA; par. Samuel and Sara Barry (Miller) Cousins; m. Ellen Kopf, Jun 23, 1939; c. Andrea; Amy Loveman; Candis Hitzig; Sara Kit; Shikego Sasamori (adopted). EDUC.: Columbia U., 1936. POLIT. & GOV.: appointed member, Mayor's Task Force on Air Pollution, New York, NY, 1966–; ***candidate for Democratic nomination to presidency of the U.S., 1976***. BUS. & PROF.: ed.; journalist; educational writer, *New York Post*, 1934–35; literary ed., *Current History*, 1935–40; exec. ed., *Saturday Review*, 1940–42, ed., 1942–71, 1973–77; ed., *World Magazine*, 1972–73; ed., *Saturday Review/World*, 1973–74; dir., Saturday Review/World, Inc.; ed., *U.S.A.*; U.S. government lecturer in India, Pakistan, Ceylon, 1951; Japan-American exchange lecturer, 1953; adjunct prof., Dept. of Psychiatry and Behavioral Sciences, U. of CA, Los Angeles, CA, 1970s; author. MEM.: National Educational Television (chm., Board of Directors, 1969–70); National Programming Council for Public TV (chm., 1970–); Overseas Bureau, OWI (editorial board, WWII); CT Fact-Finding Comm. on Education (chm., 1948–52); Citizens Cmte. for a Nuclear Test Ban Treaty (co-chm.); Comm. to Study the Organization of Peace; United World Federalists (hon. pres.); Cmte. for Culture and Intellectual Exchange, International Cooperation Year (chm., 1965); Hiroshima Peace Center Assn.; Charles F. Kettering Foundation (trustee); Teachers Coll., Columbia U. (trustee); Samuel H. Kress Foundation (dir.); Educational Broadcasting Corp.; World Assn. of World Federalists (pres.); P. E. N.; U.N. Assn. (dir., U.S.); Council on Foreign Relations; Coffee House Club; National Press Club; Overseas Press Club; Century Club. AWARDS: Thomas Jefferson Award for Advancement of Democracy in Journalism, 1948; Tuition Plan Award, 1951; Benjamin Franklin Citation, 1956; Wayne U. Award, 1956; Lane Bryant Citation, 1958; John Dewey Award, 1958; NY State Citizens Educational Comm. Award, 1959; Publius Award, NY United World Federalists, 1964; Eleanor Roosevelt Peace Award, 1963; Overseas Press Club Award, 1965; Distinguished Citizen Award, CT Bar Assn., 1965; NY Acad. of Public Education Award, 1966; Family of Man Award, 1968; Aquinas Coll. Annual Award, 1968; National Magazine Award, Assn. of Deans of Journalism Schools, 1969; Peace Medal, U.N., 1971; Carr Van Anda Award, 1971; Gold Medal, National Arts Club, 1972; Journalism Honor Award, U. of MO, 1972; Irita Van Doren Book Award, 1972; Henry Johnson Fisher Award, Magazine Publishers Assn., 1977; Human Resources Award, 1978; Convocation Medal, American Coll. of Cardiology; Albert Schweitzer Prize for Humanitarianism, 1990. HON. DEG.: Litt.D., American U., 1948; L.H.D., Boston U., 1953; L.H.D., Colby Coll., 1953; L.H.D., Denison U., 1954; LL.D., Washington and Jefferson Coll., 1956; LL.D., Syracuse U., 1956; LL.D., Albright Coll., 1957; Litt.D., Elmira Coll., 1957; Litt.D., Ripon Coll., 1957; Litt.D., Wilmington Coll., 1957; Litt.D., U. of VT, 1957; L.H.D., Colgate U., 1958; LL.D., Temple U., 1958; Ed.D., RI Coll. of Education, 1958; Litt.D., Newark State Coll., 1958; LL.D., Dusquesne U., 1964; LL.D., U. of RI, 1965; Litt.D., U. of Bridgeport, 1965; LL.D., Chapman Coll., 1965; D.H.L., Lafayette Coll., 1965; Litt.D., U. of AZ, 1965; Litt.D., Brandeis U., 1965; Litt.D., U. of Notre Dame, 1965; Litt.D., MI State U., 1967; D.L., U. of NC, 1969; D.L., U. of Denver, 1971; Litt.D., Maryville Coll., 1975; Litt.D., U. of AL, 1975. WRITINGS: *The Good Inheritance; The Democratic Chance* (1942); *Modern Man is Obsolete* (1945); *Talks with Nehru* (1951); *Who Speaks for Man?* (1952); *In God We Trust: The Religious Beliefs of the Founding Fathers* (1958); *A Treasury of Democracy* (ed., 1941); *Anthology of the Poetry of Freedom* (ed., 1943); *Writing for Love or Money* (ed., 1949); *Doctor Schweitzer of Lambarene* (ed., 1960); *In Place of Folly* (ed., 1961); *Present Tense: An American Editor's Odyssey* (ed., 1967); *The Improbable Triumvirate* (ed., 1972); *The Celebration of Life* (1975); *Anatomy of an Illness as Perceived by the Patient* (1979); *Head First: The Biology of Hope; The Healing Heart; Great American Essays* (ed.); *March's Dictionary-Thesaurus* (editorial supervisor, 1958). RES.: Wayne, NJ.

COUTERMARSH, JOSEPH ALPHONSO. b. 1874, Lebanon, NH; d. Aug 17, 1939, Troy, NY. EDUC.: D.D.S., Dartmouth Coll. POLIT. & GOV.: candidate for selectman, Lebanon, NH; candidate for road agent, NH; candidate for U.S. House (NH); delegate, Dem. Nat'l. Conv., 1932; ***candidate for Democratic nomination to presidency of the U.S., 1936***. BUS. & PROF.: dentist; storekeeper. MISC.: opponent of capital punishment. RES.: Lebanon, NH.

COUZENS, JAMES JOSEPH, JR. b. Aug 26, 1872, Chatham, Ontario, Canada; d. Oct 22, 1936, Detroit, MI; par. James Joseph and Emma (Clift) Couzens; m. Margaret Ann Manning, Aug 31, 1898; c. Frank; Madeleine (Mrs. William R. Yaw); Margot (Mrs. William Jeffries Chewning, Jr.; Mrs. J. C. Herbert Bryant); Edith Valerie; James; Homer. EDUC.: public schools; Chatham Business Coll., Chatham, Ontario, Canada. POLIT. & GOV.: appointed commissioner of street railways,

Detroit, MI, 1913–15; appointed commissioner of police, Detroit, MI, 1916–18; appointed member, U.S. Fuel Administration (Wayne Cty., MI, chm.), 1917; elected as a Republican to mayor of Detroit, MI, 1919–22; appointed and subsequently elected as a Republican to U.S. Senate (MI), 1922–36; ***candidate for Republican nomination to vice presidency of the U.S., 1932***; candidate for Republican nomination to U.S. Senate (MI), 1936. BUS. & PROF.: railroad car checker, Michigan Central R.R., 1890–97; clerk, Malcomson Fuel Co., Detroit, MI, 1897–1903; employee, Ford Motor Co., 1903–05, dir., 1905–19, business mgr., treas., to 1915, vice pres., 1915; pres., Highland Park State Bank, 1909; pres., Bank of Detroit, 1916–23; vice pres., Ford Motor Co. of Canada, Ltd.; dir., Ford Motor Co. of England, Ltd.; dir., Detroit Trust Co.; founder, First National Bank of Birmingham (MI), 1933; founder, Wabeek State Bank, Detroit, MI; pres., Rogers Shoe Co.; dir., Old Detroit National Bank. MEM.: U.S. C. of C. (dir.); Children's Fund of MI (founder, 1929); Detroit Board of Commerce (pres.); Detroit City Club; Detroit Automobile Club; Detroit Boat Club; Congressional Club; Chevy Chase Club; Burning Tree Club. REL.: Presb. RES.: Pontiac, MI.

COVELLO, PHILIP JOSEPH. b. Sep 19, 1954, Brooklyn, NY; par. Croce E. and Rosaria (Prestigacamo) Covello; m. Fran Carpentier, Oct 16, 1977; c. none. EDUC.: B.A., Brooklyn Coll. POLIT. & GOV.: ***candidate for Democratic nomination to presidency of the U.S., 1984***. BUS. & PROF.: officer, Independence Savings Bank, Brooklyn, NY. MEM.: Kiwanis. REL.: R.C. Address: 1528 West Tenth St., Brooklyn, NY 11204.

COWDREY, ROBERT HALL. b. Oct 1, 1852, Lafayette, IN; par. James Smith and Frances E. (Waldo) Cowdrey; m. Ella Louise Hitchcock, Dec 15, 1875; c. Frederic Manning; Walter; Alice Louise; Robert. EDUC.: grad. (with honors), Chicago (IL) Coll. of Pharmacy, 1875. POLIT. & GOV.: delegate, Union Labor Party National Convention, 1888; ***United Labor Party candidate for presidency of the U.S., 1888***. BUS. & PROF.: ed., *Pharmacist and Chemist*, Chicago Coll. of Pharmacy, Chicago, IL, 1875–82; druggist, Chicago, IL; ed., *Druggists' Journal;* owner, Cowdrey, Clark and Co. (printing firm), Chicago, IL, 1882–87; sec., Chicago Condensing Co., Chicago, IL, 1887. MEM.: Chicago Land and Labor Club (pres., 1887); Chicago Single Tax Club. WRITINGS: *Foiled, By a Lawyer* (1885); *A Tramp in Society* (1891). RES.: Chicago, IL.

COX, BLANCHE MARIE. b. Jul 14, 1940, Ashland, KY. POLIT. & GOV.: ***independent candidate for presidency of the U.S., 1992***. BUS. & PROF.: owner, gas station and fast food restaurant. MEM.: Eight is Enough Term Limitation Cmte. MAILING ADDRESS: Box 548, Highway 98 and Marine St., Carrabelle, FL 32322.

COX, JACOB DOLSON. b. Oct 27, 1828, Montreal, Canada; d. Aug 4, 1900, Magnolia, MA; par. Jacob Dolson and Thedia Redelia (Kenyon) Cox; m. Helen C. Finney, Nov 29, 1849; c. Helen Finney; Jacob Dolson; Kenyon; Charles Norton; Brewster; Dennison; Charlotte Hope. EDUC.: studied law, 1842–44; grad., Oberlin Coll., 1851, A.M., 1854. POLIT. & GOV.: superintendent of schools, Warren, OH, 1851–53; delegate, OH State Republican Convention, 1855; elected as a Republican to OH State Senate, 1859–61; elected as a Republican to gov. of OH, 1866–68; chm., Rep. Nat'l. Conv., 1868; appointed commissioner of internal revenue, 1868 (declined); appointed U.S. sec. of the interior, 1869–70; ***candidate for Prohibition Party nomination to presidency of the U.S., 1872; candidate for Liberal Republican Party nomination to presidency of the U.S., 1872; candidate for Liberal Republican Party nomination to vice presidency of the U.S., 1872***; elected as a Republican to U.S. House (OH), 1877–79; appointed railroad commissioner, New York, NY (declined); appointed U.S. minister to Spain, 1897 (declined). BUS. & PROF.: schoolteacher; employee, banking and brokerage firm; atty.; admitted to OH Bar, 1853; law practice, 1853–1900; law practice, Warren, OH, 1853; law practice, Cincinnati, OH, 1870; pres., Toledo, Wabash and Western Railway, 1873–78; dean, Cincinnati Law School, 1881–97; pres., U. of Cincinnati, 1885–89; military book critic, *Nation*, 1874–1900. MIL.: brig. gen., OH Militia; brig. gen., U.S.V., 1861, maj. gen., 1862 (recommissioned, 1864), resigned, 1866. MEM.: Royal Microscopial Soc. of London; American Microscopical Soc. (pres.); AAAS (fellow); American Phil. Soc. (hon. member); Belgium Microscopical Soc. (corresponding member). AWARDS: Gold Medal, Antwerp Exposition, 1891. HON. DEG.: LL.D., Dennison U., 1866; LL.D., U. of NC, 1867; LL.D., Yale U., 1877. WRITINGS: *Atlanta* (1882); *The March to the Sea: Franklin and Nashville* (1882); *The Second Battle of Bull Run as Connected with the Fitz-John Porter Case* (1882); *The Battle of Franklin, Tennessee, November 30, 1864* (1897); *Life of General Sherman* (contributor, 1899); *Military Reminiscences of the Civil War* (1900). REL.: Presb. RES.: Oberlin, OH.

COX, JAMES C. POLIT. & GOV.: ***independent candidate for presidency of the U.S., 1992***. MAILING ADDRESS: 429 Caroline St., #4, P.O. Box 764, Key West, FL 33041.

COX, JAMES MIDDLETON. b. Mar 31, 1870, Jacksonburg, OH; d. Jul 15, 1957, Dayton, OH; par. Gilbert and Eliza (Andrews) Cox; m. Mayme L. Harding, May 25, 1893 (divorced, 1910); m. 2d, Margaretta Parker Blair, Sep 15, 1917; c. Helen (Mrs. Daniel J. Mahoney); James Middleton, Jr.; John; Anne (Mrs. Robert Chambers); Barbara (Mrs. Garner Anthony). EDUC.: Amanda (OH) H.S. POLIT. & GOV.: sec., U.S. Rep. Paul Sorg (OH), 1894–97; elected as a Democrat to U.S. House (OH), 1909–13; elected as a Democrat to gov. of OH, 1913–15, 1917–21; ***Democratic candidate for presidency of the U.S., 1920; candidate for Democratic nomination to presidency of the U.S., 1924, 1932***; vice chm., American Delegation, World Monetary and Economic Conference, 1933; appointed as a Democrat to U.S. Senate (OH), 1946 (declined). BUS. & PROF.:

publisher; schoolteacher, 1886; reporter, *Middleton Signal;* reporter, *Cincinnati (OH) Enquirer,* 1892–94; owner, publisher, *Dayton (OH) Daily News,* 1898–1957; owner, publisher, *Springfield (OH) Press-Republic,* 1905–57; organizer, The News League of OH; owner, publisher, *Miami (FL) Metropolis,* 1923–57; owner, publisher, *Canton (OH) News,* 1923–30; owner, publisher, *Springfield Sun,* 1928–57; owner, WHIO radio, Dayton, 1934; owner, WIOD radio, Miami, 1936; owner, WSB radio, Atlanta, GA, 1939; owner, publisher, *Atlanta Journal,* 1939–57; owner, publisher, *Dayton Journal-Herald,* 1948–57; owner, publisher, *Atlanta Constitution,* 1950–57. MEM.: U. of Miami (founder, 1925). AWARDS: Red Cross Medal of Merit, 1913. HON. DEG.: LL.D., OH State U., 1946. WRITINGS: *Journey Through My Years* (1946). REL.: Episc. (nee United Brethren Church). RES.: Dayton, OH.

COX, JAMES RENSHAW. b. Mar 7, 1886, Pittsburgh, PA; d. Mar 20, 1951, Pittsburgh, PA; single. EDUC.: public schools, Lawrenceville, PA; St. Mary's Parochial School, Pittsburgh, PA; A.B., Duquesne U., 1907; St. Vincent's Archabbey and Seminary, 1908–11; M.A. (economics), U. of Pittsburgh, 1923; Ph.D., St. Francis Coll., Loretto, PA, 1926. POLIT. & GOV.: organizer, Liberty Jobless Party (with William Hope Harvey, q.v.), 1932; ***Jobless Party candidate for presidency of the U.S., 1932 (withdrew)***; appointed member, PA Comm. for the Unemployed; appointed member, PA Recovery Board, National Recovery Administration. BUS. & PROF.: newsboy; mgr., taxicab company, Pittsburgh, PA; ordained priest, Roman Catholic Church, 1911; asst. rector, Epiphany Church, Pittsburgh; superintendent, Pittsburgh Lyceum; principal, night school; chaplain, cty. jail; military chaplain, Base Hospital 27, U. of Pittsburgh Unit, 1917–19; chaplain, Mercy Hospital; pastor, Old Saint Patrick's Church, Pittsburgh. MEM.: A.C.L.U.; National Religion and Labor Foundation (1933). REL.: R.C. MISC.: known as the "Mayor of Shantytown" and the "Pastor of the Poor" for his charitable work; organized "Blue Shirts" and led orderly hunger march of jobless men on Washington, DC, Jan 5, 1932, petitioning Congress and the president for "Bread and Jobs, Bonus, Beer." RES.: Pittsburgh, PA.

COX, JAMES WESLEY. b. Sep 10, 1935, Knoxville, IA; par. Commodore Dewey and Lola Luela (Godfrey) Cox; m. Sandra Mae Potter; c. none. EDUC.: G.E.D., 1963; Peninsula Junior Coll., Port Angeles, WA. POLIT. & GOV.: ***Independent Democratic candidate for presidency of the U.S., 1980***. BUS. & PROF.: farm laborer; construction worker; commercial fisherman; high lead logger (chokerman); painter. MIL.: U.S. Air Force, 1952–56; U.S. Army, 1956–57. REL.: Church of God. MAILING ADDRESS: P.O. Box 1022, Port Angeles, WA 98362.

COX, WILLIAM J. b. 1941. EDUC.: J.D., Southwestern U. School of Law, 1973. POLIT. & GOV.: appointed deputy district atty., Los Angeles Cty., CA; ***National Policy Referendum Party candidate for presidency of the U.S., 1980***. BUS. & PROF.: policeman, Los Angeles, CA; atty.; admitted to CA Bar, 1973; practice, Long Beach, CA. MAILING ADDRESS: 1227 East Ocean Blvd., Long Beach, CA.

COX, WILLIAM WESLEY. b. Feb 5, 1864, Effingham Cty., IL; d. Oct 28, 1948, St. Louis, MO; par. Nelson and Susan R. (Hall) Cox; m. Margaret Brennan, 1885; c. Mabel Anney; Lillie Scherer; Ruth Dausch; Genevieve; Carl; Florence Kellerhaus. EDUC.: public schools. POLIT. & GOV.: Socialist Labor Party candidate for U.S. House (IL), 1898, 1902, 1904 (withdrew); Socialist Labor Party candidate for lt. gov. of IL, 1900; delegate, Socialist Labor Party National Convention, 1904, 1920; ***Socialist Labor Party candidate for vice presidency of the U.S., 1904***; Socialist Labor Party candidate for U.S. House (MO), 1914; ***Socialist Labor Party candidate for presidency of the U.S., 1920***; Socialist Labor Party candidate for U.S. Senate (MO), 1922, 1926, 1928, 1934, 1944; Socialist Labor Party candidate for gov. of MO, 1924, 1932, 1936, 1940; Socialist Labor Party candidate for mayor of St. Louis, MO, 2 times; member, exec. cmte., Socialist Labor Party, 1937–42; Socialist Labor Party candidate for various municipal and township offices. BUS. & PROF.: farmhand; coal miner; brickmaker; preacher, Methodist Episcopal Church, Church of God, and Christian Church, 1894–97; paper hanger; interior decorator. MEM.: Workers' International Industrial Union (organizer). REL.: Materialist. RES.: St. Louis, MO.

COXEY, JACOB SECHLER. b. Apr 16, 1854, Selinsgrove, PA; d. May 18, 1951, Massillon, OH; par. Thomas and Mary (Sechler) Coxey; m. Caroline Ammerman, Oct 1874 (divorced, 1888); m. 2d, Henrietta Sophia Jones, Sep 8, 1890; c. Jesse A.; Horace L.; Albert H.; Legal Tender; Ruth Patricia; Mary; David N.; Jacob Sechler, Jr. EDUC.: public schools, Danville, PA. POLIT. & GOV.: People's Party candidate for U.S. House (OH), 1894; People's (Prohibition) Party candidate for gov. of OH, 1895, 1897; ***candidate for People's Party nomination to presidency of the U.S., 1896***; independent candidate for U.S. Senate (OH), 1916; ***candidate for Progressive Party nomination to presidency of the U.S., 1924***; delegate, Progressive Party National Convention, 1924 (not seated); Progressive Party candidate for U.S. House (OH), 1924; candidate for Republican nomination to U.S. House (OH), 1928, 1930; ***candidate for Republican nomination to presidency of the U.S., 1932; Farmer-Labor Party candidate for vice presidency of the U.S., 1932 (withdrew); Farmer-Labor Party candidate for presidency of the U.S., 1932, 1936 (withdrew)***; elected as a Republican, mayor of Massillon, OH, 1931–33; Republican candidate for mayor of Massillon, 1933; candidate for Republican nomination to U.S. Senate (OH), 1934; Union Party candidate for U.S. House (OH), 1936; candidate for Democratic nomination to U.S. House (OH), 1942; Democratic candidate for mayor of Massillon, 1943. BUS. & PROF.: stationary engineer, rolling mills; scrap iron business; quarried for silica and sandstone, Massillon, 1881–1929; publisher, ed., *The Human Vs. Gold Standard;* publisher, ed., *The Truth About Money Weights and Measures;* stock farmer, KY. MEM.: Commonweal of Christ; Good Roads Assn. (founder; pres.). WRITINGS: *Coxey's Own Story* (1914). REL.: Theosophist (nee Episc.). MISC.: led "Coxey's Army," in 1894 and 1914, to demand relief for unemployed workers and migratory workers; hence, known as "General Coxey"; imprisoned for 20 days for walking on Capitol grass during march. RES.: Massillon, OH.

COY, ELMER WILLIAM. b. Nov 6, 1906, Dayton, OH; par. Harley and Estella (Benke) Coy; m. Bernetta Gallagher; c. Lauretta Anne; Catherine Coy Glenn. EDUC.: grad., Fairmont H.S., 1924; Miami U., Oxford, OH; B.S., OH State U., 1928. POLIT. & GOV.: ***candidate for Republican nomination to presidency of the U.S., 1968***. BUS. & PROF.: insurance agent, All American Insurance Agency, Inc. MEM.: college fraternity. REL.: R.C. MISC.: led successful campaign to defeat payroll tax increase in referendum, Toledo, OH, 1961. MAILING ADDRESS: 3110 Cambridge Ave., Toledo, OH 43610.

COYLE, BETTY JEAN. b. 1935; m. (divorced); c. five. POLIT. & GOV.: *independent candidate for presidency of the U.S., 1980*. BUS. & PROF.: exec. sec., 18 years. MAILING ADDRESS: Rowlett, TX; 618 Thornwood, Dallas, TX.

COYLE, RHONDA LEE. b. 1951, Hagerstown, MD; c. two. EDUC.: A.S. in Electronics Technology. POLIT. & GOV.: *independent candidate for presidency of the U.S., 1992*. MIL.: U.S. Air Force, 1970–73. MAILING ADDRESS: 3540-244 S.W. Archer Rd., Gainesville, FL 32608.

COYNE, WILLIAM. b. Jul 14, 1866, Calumet, IN; d. Oct 30, 1933, Wilmington, DE; married; c. William Carroll; Philip. POLIT. & GOV.: delegate, Dem. Nat'l. Conv., 1920; ***candidate for Democratic nomination to presidency of the U.S., 1924***; appointed member, Regional Planning Comm.; appointed member, DE Boxing Comm.; appointed member, Mayor's Relief Cmte., Wilmington, DE. BUS. & PROF.: employee, Traffic Dept., Consolidated Lake Superior Co., Sault Ste. Marie, Canada, to 1904; dir., vice pres. of sales, E. I. du Pont de Nemours and Co., Wilmington, DE, 1904–33; dir., Canadian Industries, Ltd.; dir., Dunlop Tire and Rubber Goods, Ltd.; dir., Farmers Bank of DE. MEM.: Wilmington Club; Knights of Columbus; Wilmington C. of C. REL.: R.C. MISC.: received one vote for pres. on 86th ballot, Dem. Nat'l. Conv., 1924. RES.: Wilmington, DE.

COYNE-CARNAC, SHEILA (See SHEILA DOYLE COYNE-CARNAC O'DAY).

COZZINI, GEORGIA PURVIS. b. Feb 14, 1915, Springfield, MO; d. Oct 10, 1983, Milwaukee, WI; par. William Joseph and Mary (Pryor) Purvis; m. Artemio Cozzini, 1936; c. Gina Cozzini Harrington; Bruce. EDUC.: grad. (with honors), West Allis H.S., Milwaukee, WI; WI State Teachers' Coll., one year. POLIT. & GOV.: delegate, Socialist Labor Party National Convention, 1940, 1944, 1948, 1952 (Platform Cmte.), 1956, 1960 (Platform Cmte.), 1964 (Platform Cmte.), 1968, 1972, 1976, 1980; Socialist Labor Party candidate for gov. of WI, 1942, 1944, 1948, 1970, 1974; Socialist Labor Party candidate for U.S. Senate (WI), 1946, 1952, 1957, 1958, 1962; organizer, Section Milwaukee, Socialist Labor Party, 1948–83; ***Socialist Labor Party candidate for vice presidency of the U.S., 1956, 1960***; member, Socialist Labor Party National Exec. Cmte., 1959–83. BUS. & PROF.: housewife; cashier; clerk; receptionist; press-clipping reader. REL.: none. RES.: Milwaukee, WI.

CRAFT, ROGER EARL. b. Dec 17, 1946, Sutton, WV; par. James Fletcher and Leerie D. (Walker) Craft; divorced; c. Andrea; Gina; Lisa; Roger Charles; Ashley. EDUC.: grad., Sutton (WV) H.S., 1964; Whiting Business School, Cleveland, OH, 1964; Cuyahoga Community Coll., 1964–65; Austin Peay State U., 1966–67; Pasadena Playhouse Coll., 1969; course work, Insurance Education Assn. POLIT. & GOV.: ***independent candidate for presidency of the U.S.**, 1988*. BUS. & PROF.: personal lines underwriter, Yosemite/Great Falls Insurance Companies, Los Angeles, CA, 1971–74; vice pres., mgr., Welch and Co., Fountain Valley and Los Angeles, CA, 1974–86; owner, R. E. Craft Insurance Services, Pacific Palisades, CA, 1987–. MIL.: Sp/5 legal clerk/court recorder, U.S. Army, 1968. WRITINGS: *None as Known to Party*. REL.: Methodist. MAILING ADDRESS: 17250 Sunset Blvd., Suite #213, Pacific Palisades, CA 90272.

CRAMER, LINDA JOAN CARTER. b. Jun 11, 1942, Wenatchee, WA; par. Oliver James and Arlene May (Hoyle) Carter; m. Joseph B. Cramer IV (divorced); c. daughter. EDUC.: grad., Pomona (CA) H.S.; I-CAN Program, Pasadena, CA. POLIT. & GOV.: ***independent candidate for presidency of the U.S., 1992***. BUS. & PROF.: bookbinder, Spokane, WA; waitress, Greyhound Depot, Santa Barbara, CA; recipient, Supplemental Security Income, 1960–. REL.: Bapt. MAILING ADDRESS: 735 Santa Barbara, Pasadena, CA 91101.

CRANE, PHILIP MILLER. b. Nov 3, 1930, Chicago, IL; par. George Washington and Cora (Miller) Crane; m. Arlene Catherine Johnson, Feb 14, 1959; c. Catherine Anne; Susanna Marie; Jennifer Elizabeth; Rebekah Caroline; George Washington V; Rachel Ellen; Sarah Emma; Carrie Esther. EDUC.: DePauw U., 1948–50; B.A., Hillsdale Coll., 1952; U. of MI, 1952–54; U. of Vienna, 1953–56; M.A., U. of IN, 1961, Ph.D., 1963. POLIT. & GOV.: public relations dir., Vigo Cty. (IN) Republican Cmte., 1962; dir. of research, Goldwater for

President Campaign, 1964; public relations adviser to Richard M. Nixon (q.v.); elected as a Republican to U.S. House (IL), 1969–; ***candidate for Republican nomination to vice presidency of the U.S., 1976, 1980***; delegate, Rep. Nat'l. Conv., 1980; ***candidate for Republican nomination to presidency of the U.S., 1980***. BUS. & PROF.: advertising mgr., Hopkins Syndicate, Inc., Chicago, IL, 1956–58; teaching asst., IN U., 1959–62; asst. prof., Bradley U., 1963–67; dir. of schools, Westminster Acad., 1967–68. MIL.: Sp/3, U.S. Army, 1954–56. MEM.: University Professors for Academic Order; Young Americans for Freedom (adviser, 1965–); American Conservative Union (dir.; chm., 1977–79); Intercollegiate Studies Inst. (dir.); Hillsdale Coll. (trustee); American Hist. Assn.; Organization of American Historians; American Acad. of Political and Social Sciences; Acad. of Political Science; Philadelphia Soc.; A.S.C.A.P.; Phi Alpha Theta; Pi Gamma Mu; IN Hist. Soc.; International Platform Assn.; U.S. Capitol Hist. Soc. AWARDS: Distinguished Alumnus Award, Hillsdale Coll., 1968; Independence Award, 1974; William McGovern Award, Chicago Soc., 1969; Freedoms Foundation Award, 1973. HON. DEG.: LL.D., Grove City Coll., 1975. WRITINGS: *Democrat's Dilemma* (1964); *Continuity in Crisis* (contributor, 1974); *Crisis in Confidence* (contributor, 1974); *Sum of Good Government* (1976); *Surrender in Panama* (1978). REL.: Methodist. MAILING ADDRESS: 307 Man Awa Trail, Mt. Prospect, IL 60056.

CRANE, WINTHROP MURRAY. b. Apr 23, 1853, Dalton, MA; d. Oct 2, 1920, Dalton, MA; par. Zenas Marshall and Louise (Laflin) Crane; m. Mary Benner, Feb 5, 1880; m. 2d, Josephine Porter Boardman, 1906; c. Winthrop Murray, Jr. EDUC.: Wilbraham Acad.; Williston Seminary. POLIT. & GOV.: delegate, Rep. Nat'l. Conv., 1892, 1896, 1904, 1908, 1916, 1920; member, Rep. Nat'l. Cmte., 1892–96, 1904, 1908; elected as a Republican to lt. gov. of MA, 1897–99; elected as a Republican to gov. of MA, 1900–1902; appointed U.S. sec. of the treasury, 1902 (declined); appointed and subsequently elected as a Republican to U.S. Senate (MA), 1904–13; ***candidate for Republican nomination to vice presidency of the U.S., 1908***. BUS. & PROF.: employee, proprietor, Crane and Co. (paper manufacturers), Dalton, MA, 1870–1920; proprietor, Old Berkshire Mill; proprietor, Pioneer Mill; proprietor, Bay State Mill, Dalton, MA; proprietor, Government Mill. HON. DEG.: A.M., Williams Coll., 1897; LL.D., Harvard U., 1903. REL.: Congregationalist. RES.: Dalton, MA.

CRANFILL, JAMES BRITTON. b. Sep 12, 1858, Parker Cty., TX; d. Dec 28, 1942, Dallas, TX; par. Eaton and Martha Jane (Galloway) Cranfill; m. Ollie Allen, Sep 1, 1878. EDUC.: public schools; M.D., TX Medical Board, 1879. POLIT. & GOV.: delegate, TX State Democratic Convention, 1884; state chm., TX Prohibition Party, 1887; member, Prohibition Party National Cmte., 1888–1900, 1904–12 (exec. cmte.); ***Prohibition Party candidate for vice presidency of the U.S., 1892; candidate for Prohibition Party nomination to presidency of the U.S., 1908***. BUS. & PROF.: cowboy; teacher, Crawford, TX; physician; medical practice, Turnersville, TX, 1879–82; ed., *Turnersville Effort*, 1881–82; ed., *Gatesville (TX) Advance*, 1882–86; ed., *Waco (TX) Advance*, 1886–88; financial sec., Baylor U., 1888–89; superintendent, TX Baptist Missions, 1889–92; ordained minister, Baptist Church, 1890; pastor, First Baptist Church, Waco; founder, ed., *Texas Baptist Standard*, 1892–1904; ed., *Baptist Tribune*, 1905–07; editorial writer, *Associated Prohibition Press;* ed., *Baptist Bookman*, 1917–18; co-editor, *The Pilot*, 1925; ed., *The Advance*, 1928–42; pres., Dallas Real Estate Exchange; literary ed., *Texas Christian Advocate;* lecturer, Southwest Baptist Theological Seminary, 1921. MEM.: Baptist Young People's Union (vice pres., 1891–93); TX Eclectic Medical Assn. (hon. member); Ministers' Relief Board, Southern Baptist Convention; Bishop Coll. (trustee); Southwest Baptist Theological Seminary (trustee); Philomathesian Soc. of Baylor U. (hon. member); American Sociological Assn.; TX Poetry Soc.; TX Press Assn. (sec.); Trinity River Navigation Cmte. (chm.); Old Trail Drivers' Assn.; Dallas C. of C.; Dallas Automobile Club; Dallas Town and Gown Club. HON. DEG.: LL.D., Simmons Coll., 1900; LL.D., Baylor U., 1920. WRITINGS: *Caroll's Sermons* (ed., 1895); *Courage and Comfort* (1899); *Cranfill's Heart Talks* (1906); *Riley's History of Texas Baptists* (1907); *R. C. Buckner's Life of Faith and Works* (coauthor, 1914); *We Would See Jesus* (ed.; authored by George W. Truett, 1915); *Dr. J. B. Cranfill's Chronicles* (1916); *The River of Life* (ed.); *Dr. J. B. Cranfill's Joke Book* (1917); *Golden Years—An Autobiography of Mrs. W. L. Williams* (ed., 1921); *Carroll's History of Texas Baptists* (ed., 1923); *From Nature to Grace* (1925); *From Memory* (1937); *Baptists and Their Doctrines* (ed.); *Evangelistic Sermons by B. H. Carroll* (ed.); *B. H. Carroll's Interpretation of the English Bible* (ed., 13 vols.); *A Quest for Souls* (ed.); *God's Call to America* (ed.). REL.: Southern Bapt. (superintendent of missions, 1889; vice pres., TX General Convention, 1928–29, 1936–37). RES.: Dallas, TX.

CRANSTON, ALAN MacGREGOR. b. Jun 19, 1914, Palo Alto, CA; par. William MacGregor and Carol (Dixon) Cranston; m. Geneva McMath, Nov 6, 1940; m. 2d, Norma Weintraub, May 19, 1978 (divorced); m. 3d, Cathy Lee Pattiz, Dec 24, 1989; c. Robin MacGregor; Kim MacGregor. EDUC.: Pomona Coll., 1932–33; U. of Mexico, 1933; A.B., Stanford U., 1936. POLIT. & GOV.: chief, Foreign Language Division, OWI, Washington, DC, 1942–44; pres., CA Democratic Council, 1953–57; member, exec. cmte., CA Democratic State Central Cmte., 1954–67; delegate, Dem. Nat'l. Conv., 1956; elected as a Democrat, CA State Controller, 1959–67; candidate for Democratic nomination to U.S. Senate (CA), 1964; Democratic candidate for CA state controller, 1966; elected as a Democrat to U.S. Senate (CA), 1969–93 (majority whip, 1977–81; minority whip, 1981–87); ***candidate for Democratic nomination to presidency of the U.S., 1976, 1984; candidate for Democratic nomination to vice presidency of the U.S., 1984***. BUS. & PROF.: foreign correspondent, International News Service, 1936–38; Washington representative, Common Council for American Unity, 1940–41; exec. sec.,

Council for American-Italian Affairs, Inc., Washington, DC, 1945–46; partner, Ames-Cranston Co. (construction; real estate), Palo Alto, CA, 1947–58; pres., Homes for a Better America, Inc., 1967–68; vice pres., Carlsberg Financial Corp., Los Angeles, CA, 1968. MIL.: pvt., sgt., U.S. Army, 1944–45. MEM.: Trilateral Comm.; United World Federalists (pres., 1949–52); Overseas Press Club; Sigma Nu; Los Angeles Press Club; Moose; Elks. WRITINGS: *Mein Kampf* (Anti-Hitler version, 1939); *The Big Story* (1940); *The Killing of Peace* (1945). REL.: Protestant. MISC.: involved in savings and loan scandal, 1989; reprimanded by U.S. Senate, 1991. MAILING ADDRESS: 10697 Somma Way, Los Angeles, CA 90024.

CRAWFORD, SAMUEL JOHNSON. b. Apr 15, 1835, Lawrence Cty., IN; d. Oct 21, 1913, Topeka, KS; par. William and Jane (Morrow) Crawford; m. Isabel Marshall Chase, Nov 27, 1866; c. Florence C. (Mrs. Arthur Capper); George Marshall. EDUC.: read law under S.W. Short, Bedford, IN; LL.B., Cincinnati Law School, 1858. POLIT. & GOV.: delegate, KS State Republican Convention, 1859; elected as a Republican to KS State House, 1861; elected as a Republican to gov. of KS, 1865–69; ***independent candidate for presidency of the U.S., 1868***; Republican candidate for U.S. Senate (KS), 1871; pres., KS State Liberal Republican Convention, 1872; Independent Greenback Party candidate for U.S. House (KS), 1876; appointed KS claims agent, Washington, DC, 1877–91; independent candidate for U.S. House (KS), 1878. BUS. & PROF.: atty.; admitted to IN Bar, 1859; law practice, Topeka, KS, 1868, 1876; law practice, Emporia, KS, 1969–76; law practice, Washington, DC, 1876–1911; farmer, KS, 1869–1913. MIL.: capt., Troop A, Second KS Cavalry, 1861; col., 83d U.S. Colored Troops, 1863–64; brev. brig. gen., U.S.V., 1865; col., 19th KS Cavalry, 1868. MEM.: Kansas State Hist. Soc. (vice pres.); Loyal Legion; Kansas Authors Club (pres.); GAR; Masons (Scottish Rite). WRITINGS: *Kansas in the Sixties* (1911). RES.: Topeka, KS.

CRAWFORD, WILLIAM HARRIS. b. Feb 24, 1772, Nelson Cty., VA; d. Sep 15, 1834, Elberton, Oglethorpe Cty., GA; par. Joel and Fannie (Harris) Crawford; m. Susanna Girardin, 1804; c. Nathaniel Macon; John; William Harris, Jr.; Robert; William W. "Bibb"; Caroline (Mrs. George Mortimer Dudley); Eliza Ann; Susan. EDUC.: Richmond Acad., Augusta, GA, 1796–98; studied law. POLIT. & GOV.: elected as a Democratic-Republican to GA State Senate, 1803–07; elected as a Democratic-Republican to U.S. Senate (GA), 1807–13 (pres. pro tempore, 1812); appointed U.S. sec. of war, 1813 (declined); appointed U.S. minister to France, 1813–15; appointed agent for sale of land donated to U.S. by Lafayette, 1815; appointed U.S. sec. of war, 1815–16; ***candidate for Democratic-Republican nomination to presidency of the U.S., 1816***; appointed U.S. sec. of the treasury, 1816–25; ***Democratic-Republican candidate for presidency of the U.S., 1824***; appointed judge, U.S. circuit court for Northern GA, 1827–34; ***candidate for Democratic nomination to vice presidency of the U.S., 1828***. BUS. & PROF.: schoolteacher, Richmond Acad., Auga, GA, rector, 1796–99; atty.; admitted to GA Bar, 1799; law practice, Lexington, GA, 1799. MEM.: American Bible Soc.; American Colonization Soc. (vice pres.). WRITINGS: *Georgia Laws* (compiler, 1799). RES.: Crawford, GA.

CREGAN, DONALD. POLIT. & GOV.: ***independent candidate for presidency of the U.S., 1976***. MAILING ADDRESS: 203 Inaqua St., Hollywood, FL 33021.

CRESWELL, JOHN ANGEL JAMES. b. Nov 18, 1828, Port Deposit, MD; d. Dec 23, 1891, Elkton, MD; par. John G. and Rebecca E. (Webb) Creswell; m. Hannah J. Richardson; c. none. EDUC.: grad. (with honors), Dickinson Coll., 1848. POLIT. & GOV.: Whig candidate for delegate, MD Reform State Convention, 1850; delegate, Dem. Nat'l. Conv., 1852, 1856; elected as a Republican to MD State House of Delegates, 1862; appointed adj. gen. of MD, 1862–63; elected as a Republican to U.S. House (MD), 1863–65; Republican candidate for U.S. House (MD), 1864; elected as a Republican to U.S. Senate (MD), 1865–67; delegate, Rep. Nat'l. Conv., 1864, 1868; delegate, Loyalist Convention, 1866; delegate, Border States Convention, 1867; elected sec. of the U.S. Senate, 1868 (declined); ***candidate for Republican nomination to vice presidency of the U.S., 1868***; appointed postmaster gen. of the U.S., 1869–74; counsel, AL Claims, U.S. Court Commissioners, 1874–76. BUS. & PROF.: atty.; admitted to MD Bar, 1850; law practice, Elkton, MD; vice pres., National Bank of Elkton; pres., two banks. REL.: Presb. MISC.: introduced one-cent postcard. RES.: Elkton, MD.

CRITTENDEN, JOHN JORDAN. b. Sep 10, 1787, Versailles, KY; d. Jul 26, 1863, Frankfort, KY; par. John and Judith (Harris) Crittenden; m. Sarah O. "Sally" Lee, May 27, 1811; m. 2d, Maria Todd Innes, Nov 13, 1826; m. 3d, Mrs. Elizabeth Ashley, Feb 27, 1853; c. George Bibb; Thomas Leonidas; Robert; Eugenia; Ann Mary Coleman; Cornelia Young; Sarah Lee Watson; John Jordan, Jr.; Eugene. EDUC.: Pisgah Acad.; WA Coll.; grad., Coll. of William and Mary, 1806. POLIT. & GOV.: appointed atty. gen. of IL Territory, 1809–10; elected to KY State House, 1811–17 (Speaker, 1815–16), 1825, 1829–32 (Speaker); elected as a Unionist to U.S. Senate (KY), 1817–19, 1835–41, 1842–48, 1855–61; appointed U.S. district atty. for KY, 1827–29; appointed assoc. justice, Supreme Court of the U.S., 1828 (not confirmed); appointed sec. of the commonwealth of KY, 1834; appointed atty. gen. of the U.S., 1841, 1850–53; ***candidate for Whig Party nomination to presidency of the U.S., 1848 (declined)***; elected as a Unionist to gov. of KY, 1849; ***candidate for Constitutional Union Party nomination to presidency of the U.S., 1860***; elected as a Unionist to U.S. House (KY), 1861–63. BUS. & PROF.: atty.; admitted to KY Bar, 1806; law practice, Woodford Cty., KY, 1806; law practice, Russellville, KY, 1814. MIL.: aide-de-camp to Gen. Sam Hopkins, 1812;

aide-decamp, First KY Militia, 1813; aide-de-camp to Gov. Isaac Shelby, 1813. REL.: Presb. MISC.: noted as author of the "Crittenden Compromise." RES.: Frankfort, KY.

CROMMELIN, JOHN GERAERDT. b. Oct 2, 1902, Montgomery, AL; d. 1969, Wetumpka, AL; par. John Geraerdt and Katherine Vasser (Gunter) Crommelin; m. Lillian Eoff, Dec 1, 1930; c. Katharine; Jill; John. EDUC.: U. of VA, 1917; U.S. Naval Acad., 1919, grad., 1923. POLIT. & GOV.: candidate for Democratic nomination to U.S. Senate (AL), 1950, 1954, 1956, 1960, 1962, 1966, 1968; independent candidate for U.S. Senate (AL), 1950; candidate for Democratic nomination to gov. of AL, 1958; candidate for Democratic nomination to mayor of Montgomery, AL, 1959; ***National States Rights Party candidate for vice presidency of the U.S., 1960***; candidate for Democratic nomination to U.S. House (AL), 1964; *candidate for Democratic nomination to presidency of the U.S., 1968*. BUS. & PROF.: naval officer; ed., *The New Patriot*. MIL.: midshipman, U.S. Navy; advanced through grades to rear adm., 1919–50; member of "Blue Angels" stunt-flying squadron, U.S. Navy; served on USS *Enterprise* and *Liscomb Bay* (chief of staff). MEM.: Christian Defense League (eastern regional dir.); Americans for American Action. REL.: Episc. RES.: Wetumpka, AL.

CROSS, WILBUR LUCIUS. b. Apr 10, 1862, Mansfield, CT; d. Oct 5, 1948, New Haven, CT; par. Samuel and Harriet Maria (Gurley) Cross; m. Helen Baldwin Avery, Jul 17, 1889; c. Wilbur Lucius, Jr.; Samuel Avery; Elizabeth Baldwin; Arthur William. EDUC.: A.B., Yale U., 1885, Ph.D., 1889. POLIT. & GOV.: elected as a Democrat to gov. of CT, 1931–39; ***candidate for Democratic nomination to vice presidency of the U.S., 1932***; Democratic candidate for gov. of CT, 1938. BUS. & PROF.: teacher; instructor, Shadyside Acad., Pittsburgh, PA, 1889–94; instructor, Sheffield Scientific School, Yale U., 1894–97, asst. prof., 1897–1902, prof. of English, 1902–21; dean, Graduate School, Yale U., 1916–30, Sterling Professor of English, 1921–30, acting provost, 1922–23; ed., *Yale Review;* lecturer, Columbia U., 1903; author. MEM.: CT Coll. for Women (trustee); American Acad. of Arts and Letters (chancellor); Soc. of Mayflower Descendants (hon. member); Graduate Club (pres., 1922–26); Elizabethan Club (pres., 1927–29); National Inst. of Arts and Letters (pres.); American Phil. Soc.; Soc. of the Cincinnati; Soc. of Colonial Wars; Soc. of Colonial Governors; SAR; Phi Beta Kappa; Psi Upsilon; Authors Club of NY. AWARDS: Chevalier, Legion of Honor (France). HON. DEG.: Litt.D., Yale U.; Litt.D., U. of SC; Litt.D., Columbia U.; Litt.D., U. of MI; Litt.D., Brown U. WRITINGS: *Development of the English Novel* (1899); *Macbeth* (ed., 1900); *Ivanhoe* (ed., 1903); *Silas Marner* (ed., 1903); *New International Encyclopedia* (ed., English Literature, 1903); *Works of Laurence Sterne and Fitzgerald's Life of Sterne* (ed., 1904); *Stevenson's Inland Voyage and Travels with a Donkey* (ed., 1909); *Life and Times of Laurence Sterne* (1909); *Defoe's Robinson Crusoe* (ed., 1911); *Sterne's Political Romance* (ed., 1914); *History of Henry Fielding* (1918); *An Outline of Biography* (1924); *Lounsbury's Life and Times of Tennyson* (ed., 1925); *Sentimental Journey* (ed., 1926); *Modern English Novel* (1929); *Four Contemporary Novelists* (1930). REL.: Episc. RES.: New Haven, CT.

CROWLEY, JEREMIAH D. POLIT. & GOV.: Socialist Labor Party candidate for gov. of NY, 1916, 1922, 1926, 1930; ***Socialist Labor Party candidate for vice presidency of the U.S., 1928***; Socialist Labor Party candidate for U.S. Senate (NY), 1932; Socialist Labor Party candidate for U.S. House (NY), 1934; Industrial Government Party candidate for U.S. House (NY), 1938. RES.: Syracuse, NY.

CRUZ, ROBERT F. POLIT. & GOV.: ***candidate for Democratic nomination to presidency of the U.S., 1984***. BUS. & PROF.: rancher, Uvalde, TX. MAILING ADDRESS: Kincaid Hotel, 103 North St., Uvalde, TX 78801.

CRYTS, PHILLIP WAYNE. par. William Cryts, Sr.; m. Sandra Cryts. POLIT. & GOV.: ***candidate for Populist Party nomination to presidency of the U.S., 1984***; Democratic candidate for U.S. House (MO), 1986, 1988. BUS. & PROF.: soybean farmer, Puxico, MO. MISC.: arraigned for leading raid on bankrupt grain elevator at New Madrid, MO; grand jury refused to indict; acquitted, 1983; fined, 1985. MAILING ADDRESS: Route 2, Box 327, Puxico, MO 63690.

CUDE, JIMMY H. POLIT. & GOV.: ***independent candidate for presidency of the U.S., 1976***. MAILING ADDRESS: 10442 Lockyer St., Apt. 6, Dallas, TX.

CULBERSON, CHARLES ALLEN. b. Jun 10, 1855, Dadeville, AL; d. Mar 19, 1925, Washington, DC; par. David Browning and Eugenia (Kimbal) Culberson; m. Sallie Harrison, Dec 7, 1882; c. Mary. EDUC.: grad., VA Military Inst., 1874; U. of VA, 1876–77. POLIT. & GOV.: delegate, TX State Democratic Convention, 1890; elected cty. atty., Marion Cty., TX; atty. gen. of TX, 1890–94; elected as a Democrat to gov. of TX, 1894–98; delegate, Dem. Nat'l. Conv., 1896, 1900, 1904, 1908, 1912, 1916; elected as a Democrat to U.S. Senate (TX), 1899–1923 (minority leader, 1907–09); ***candidate for Democratic nomination to presidency of the U.S., 1908***; candidate for Democratic nomination to U.S. Senate (TX), 1922. BUS. & PROF.: atty.; admitted to TX Bar, 1877; law practice, Jefferson, TX; law practice, Dallas, TX 1887–1925; partner, Brookout and Culberson (law firm), Dallas, TX. REL.: Bapt. RES.: Dallas, TX.

CULLEN, EDGAR MONTGOMERY. b. Dec 4, 1843, Brooklyn, NY; d. May 23, 1922, Brooklyn, NY; par. Dr. Henry James and Eliza (McCue) Cullen; single. EDUC.: Kinderhook Coll.; A.B., Columbia U., 1860, A.M., 1863; Troy Polytechnic Inst. POLIT. & GOV.: appointed asst. district atty., Brooklyn, NY, 1872–75; appointed brig. gen., engineer-in-chief, staff of Gov. Samuel J. Tilden (q.v.), 1875; elected as a Democrat, justice of the Supreme Court of NY, 1880–1900; appointed and subsequently elected as a Democrat-Republican, assoc. justice of the NY State Court of Appeals, 1900–13 (chief justice, 1904–13); ***candidate for Democratic nomination to presidency of the U.S., 1908***. BUS. & PROF.: atty.; admitted to NY Bar, 1867; partner, McCue, Hall and Cullen (law firm), Brooklyn, 1867–70; partner, Hall and Cullen (law firm), Brooklyn, 1870; partner, Cullen and Dykman (law firm), Brooklyn, 1914–22. MIL.: 2d lt., Second U.S. Infantry, U.S. Army, 1862, 1st lt., 1863; col., 96th NY Infantry, 1862–65. HON. DEG.: LL.D., Columbia U., 1892; LL.D., Union Coll., 1905; LL.D., Harvard U., 1915. REL.: Episc. RES.: Brooklyn, NY.

CULLOM, SHELBY MOORE. b. Nov 22, 1829, Monticello, KY; d. Jan 28, 1914, Washington, DC; par. Richard Northcraft and Elizabeth (Coffey) Cullom; m. Hannah M. Fisher, Dec 12, 1855; m. 2d, Julia Fisher, May 5, 1863; c. Ella; Carrie. EDUC.: Rock River (IL) Seminary; studied law in offices of Stuart and Edwards, Springfield, IL. POLIT. & GOV.: presidential elector, Whig Party, 1852, 1856; elected city atty., Springfield, IL, 1855; elected as a Republican to IL State House, 1856, 1860 (Speaker), 1861, 1873–74 (Speaker); elected as a Republican to U.S. House (IL), 1865–71; delegate, Rep. Nat'l. Conv., 1868, 1872, 1884, 1892, 1908; elected as a Republican to gov. of IL, 1877–83; elected as a Republican to U.S. Senate (IL), 1883–1913 (majority leader, 1910–11, 1912–13); ***candidate for Republican nomination to presidency of the U.S., 1888, 1892, 1896; candidate for Republican nomination to vice presidency of the U.S., 1892***; candidate for Republican nomination to U.S. Senate (IL), 1912; appointed chm., Lincoln Memorial Comm., 1913–14; appointed member, Hawaiian Islands Code Comm. BUS. & PROF.: atty.; admitted to IL Bar, 1855; law practice, Springfield, IL. MEM.: Smithsonian Institution (regent, 1885–1913). WRITINGS: *Fifty Years of Public Service* (1911). REL.: Methodist. RES.: Springfield, IL.

CULVER, JOHN CHESTER. b. Aug 8, 1932, Rochester, MN; par. William C. and Mary (Miller) Culver; m. Ann T. Cooper, Jun 15, 1958; c. Christina; Rebecca; Catherine; Chester John. EDUC.: grad., Franklin H.S., Cedar Rapids, IA, 1950; A.B. (cum laude), Harvard U., 1954, LL.B., 1962; Lionel de Jersey Harvard Scholar, Emmanuel Coll., Cambridge U. POLIT. & GOV.: legislative asst. to U.S. Sen. Edward Moore Kennedy (q.v.), 1962–63; elected as a Democrat to U.S. House (IA), 1965–75; delegate, Dem. Nat'l. Conv., 1968; elected as a Democrat to U.S. Senate (IA), 1975–81; ***candidate for Democratic nomination to presidency of the U.S., 1980***; Democratic candidate for U.S. Senate (IA), 1980; chm., Democratic Study Group. BUS. & PROF.: business mgr., Culver Rent-a-Car, 1959; dean of men, Harvard U. Summer School, 1960; atty.; admitted to IA Bar, 1963; partner, McGuire, Bernau and Culver (law firm), Cedar Rapids, 1963–65; partner, Arent, Fox, Kintner, Plotkin and Kahn (law firm), Washington, DC, 1981–. MIL.: capt., U.S.M.C., 1955–58; maj., U.S.M.C. Reserves, 1959. MEM.: IA Bar Assn.; Federal Bar Assn.; Linn Cty. Bar Assn.; Harvard U. (overseer, 1975–). REL.: Presb. MAILING ADDRESS: 1050 Connecticut Ave., N.W., Washington, DC 20036.

CUMMINGS, HOMER STILLE. b. Apr 30, 1870, Chicago, IL; d. Sep 10, 1956, Washington, DC; par. Uriah C. and Audie (Schuyler Stille) Cummings; m. Helen Woodruff Smith, Jun 27, 1897 (divorced, 1907); m. 2d, Marguerite T. Owings, 1909 (divorced, 1928); m. 3d, Mary Cecilia Waterbury, Apr 2, 1929; m. 4th, Julia M. Alter, Jul 13, 1942; c. Dickinson Schuyler. EDUC.: Ph.B., Yale U., 1891, LL.B., 1893. POLIT. & GOV.: Democratic candidate for CT state sec. of state, 1896; delegate, Dem. Nat'l. Conv., 1900, 1904, 1920 (temporary chm.), 1924, 1932, 1936, 1940, 1944, 1948; member, Dem. Nat'l. Cmte., 1900–1925 (vice chm., 1913–19; chm., 1919–20); elected as a Democrat to mayor of Stamford, CT, 1900–1902, 1904–06; Democratic candidate for U.S. House (CT), 1902; corporation counsel, Stamford, 1908–12; appointed state's atty., Fairfield Cty., CT, 1914–24; Democratic candidate for U.S. Senate (CT), 1916; appointed member, CT State Council of Defense, 1917; ***candidate for Democratic nomination to presidency of the U.S., 1920, 1924***; appointed chm., CT State Comm. on Prison Conditions, 1930; appointed gov. gen. of the Philippine Islands, 1933 (declined); appointed atty. gen. of the U.S., 1933–39; arbitrator, Beagle Channel Islands Case between Argentina and Chile, 1938; presidential elector, Democratic Party, 1940, 1944; elected member, Greenwick (CT) Town Cmte., to 1951. BUS. & PROF.: atty.; admitted to CT Bar, 1893; law practice, Stamford, 1893–1933, 1939–56; counsel, Cummings and Lockwood (law firm), Stamford, 1909–33; partner, Cummings, Stanley, Truitt and Cross (law firm), Washington, DC; admitted to practice before the Bar of the Supreme Court of the U.S.; dir., First Stamford National Bank; dir., sec., Cummings Cement Co.; dir., Chickamauga Cement Co.; pres., Varuna Spring Water Co. MEM.: Mayors' Assn. of CT (pres., 1902–03); Stamford Board of Trade (pres., 1903–09); Inst. of Judicial Administration (fellow); ABA; NY Bar Assn.; DC Bar; American Jud. Soc. (vice pres.); American Law Inst.; American Soc. of International Law; Masons (Royal Arcanum; Knights of Pythias); Odd Fellows; Knights of the Maccabees; Elks; Fraternal Order of Eagles; National Democratic Club; Metropolitan Club; National Press Club; Burning Tree Club. HON. DEG.: LL.D., Lake Forest U., 1934; LL.D., Rollins Coll., 1934; LL.D., Oglethorpe U., 1934; D.H.L., Lincoln Memorial U., 1935; LL.D., John Marshall Coll., 1935; LL.D., PA Military Coll., 1938. WRITINGS: *Liberty Under Law and Administration* (1934); *Federal Justice* (with Carl McFarland, 1937); *We Can Prevent Crime* (1937); *The Tired Sea* (1939). REL.: Congregationalist. RES.: Washington, DC.

CUMMINS, ALBERT BAIRD. b. Feb 15, 1850, Carmichael, PA; d. Jul 30, 1926, Des Moines, IA; par. Thomas

Layton and Sarah (Baird) Cummins; m. Ida L. Gallery, Jun 24, 1874; c. Kate. EDUC.: Waynesburg (PA) Coll., 3 years; studied law in offices of McClellan and Hodges, Chicago, IL. POLIT. & GOV.: delegate, Rep. Nat'l. Conv., 1880, 1884, 1888, 1892, 1896, 1900, 1904, 1908, 1912, 1916, 1920, 1924; elected as a Republican to IA State House, 1888–90; presidential elector, Republican Party, 1892; chm., IA State Republican Convention, 1892, 1896; Republican candidate for U.S. Senate (IA), 1894, 1900, 1908; member, Rep. Nat'l. Cmte., 1896–1900; elected as a Republican to gov. of IA, 1902–08; ***candidate for Republican nomination to vice presidency of the U.S., 1908***; elected as a Republican to U.S. Senate (IA), 1908–27 (pres. pro tempore, 1919–25); ***candidate for Republican nomination to presidency of the U.S., 1912, 1916***; candidate for Republican nomination to U.S. Senate (IA), 1926. BUS. & PROF.: carpenter; clerk, recorder's office, Clayton Cty., IA; surveyor; asst. chief engineer, Cincinnati, Richmond and Fort Wayne R.R.; atty.; admitted to IL Bar, 1875; law practice, Chicago, IL, 1875–78; law practice, Des Moines, IA, 1878–1926. HON. DEG.: LL.D., Waynesburg (PA) 1903; LL.D., Cornell Coll., 1904. REL.: Congregationalist. RES.: Des Moines, IA.

CUNNINGHAM, BOB. POLIT. & GOV.: ***candidate for Democratic nomination to presidency of the U.S., 1992***. MAILING ADDRESS: P.O. Box 588, Pawleys Island, SC 29585.

CUNNINGHAM, CHARLES EDWARD. b. Jul 1, 1823, Frederick Cty., MD; d. Apr 2, 1895, Little Rock, AR; par. James and Catherine (Campbell) Cunningham; m. Elizabeth A. Jones, 1849; c. Charles F.; Kate C.; Nannie R. (Mrs. S. W. Sparks); Mollie; James M.; Bessie (Mrs. John J. Cockrell); George E.; Nettie (Mrs. J. E. Clark). EDUC.: classical studies, MD and VA. POLIT. & GOV.: elected member, Little Rock (AR) School Board; delegate, Independent National (Greenback) Party National Convention, 1876, 1884; Greenback-Labor Party candidate for Pulaski Cty. (AR) cty. clerk, 1877; Greenback-Labor Party candidate for AR state sec. of state, 1878; Greenback-Labor Party candidate for AR state auditor, 1880; Greenback Party candidate for U.S. House (AR), 1882; delegate, Anti-Monopoly Party National Convention, 1884; member, Greenback Party National Cmte., 1884; Agricultural Wheeler Party candidate for gov. of AR, 1886; ***Union Labor Party candidate for vice presidency of the U.S., 1888***. BUS. & PROF.: miner; freightman; farmer, Johnson Cty., MO, 1854–62; owner, saw and planing mill, Little Rock, 1865–95; farmer, Little Rock, 1865–95. MEM.: Irish Land League. RES.: Little Rock, AR.

CUNNINGHAM, CLAUDE CARNOT "DOC." b. 1873, Calloway Cty., MO; d. Dec 5, 1953, Houston, TX; m. Sarah F. Cunningham. POLIT. & GOV.: ***candidate for Democratic nomination to presidency of the U.S., 1948, one other time***. BUS. & PROF.: mgr., Majestic Theatre, Houston, TX, 1903; entertainer. REL.: R.C. RES.: Houston, TX.

CUNNINGHAM, KATHLEEN "KATE" RICHARDS O'HARE. b. Mar 26, 1877, Ada, KS; d. Jan 10, 1948, Benicia, CA; par. Andrew and Lucy (Thompson) Richards; m. Francis Patrick O'Hare, Jan 1, 1902 (divorced, 1928); m. 2d, Charles C. Cunningham, Nov 28, 1928; c. Francis Richards; Kathleen; Eugene Robert; Victor Edwin. EDUC.: Normal School, NE; International School of Social Economy. POLIT. & GOV.: Socialist Party candidate for U.S. House (KS), 1902, 1910; member, National Women's Cmte., Socialist Party, 1910–12, international sec., 1912–18; member, National Exec. Cmte., Socialist Party, 1912–16; Socialist Party candidate for OK state commissioner of charities and corrections, 1907; Socialist Party delegate, Second International, 1913; ***candidate for Socialist Party nomination to vice presidency of the U.S., 1916, 1920***; staff, U.S. Rep. Thomas R. Amlie, 1937–38; appointed asst. dir., CA State Dept. of Penology, 1939. BUS. & PROF.: teacher; social worker; machinist apprentice, 1894; temperance advocate; penal reformer; socialist organizer; lecturer; ed., *National Ripsaw*, 1912–18; ed., *Social Revolution*, 1918; ed., *American Vanguard*, 1920–23; instructor, dean of women, Commonwealth Coll., 1923–24, 1926–28; field dir., Campaign Against Convict Labor, 1923. MEM.: Industrial Workers of the World; International Order of Machinists; Teachers' Union; Llano Co-Operative Colony, 1922–24; Commonwealth Coll. (founder, 1923; trustee); End Poverty in CA. WRITINGS: *What Happened to Dan* (1904); *The Sorrows of Cupid* (1910); *Law and the White Slaves* (1911); *Common Sense and the Liquor Question* (1911); *Church and Social Problems* (1911); *World Peace* (1918); *Kate O'Hare's Prison Letters* (1919); *Americanism and Bolshevism* (1919); *In Prison* (1920). REL.: Materialist (nee Disciples of Christ). MISC.: sentenced to MO State Penitentiary for violation of Espionage Act; served from 1917–20; sentence commuted by President Woodrow Wilson (q.v.); full pardon granted by President Calvin Coolidge (q.v.); led Children's Crusade for Amnesty for Political Prisoners, 1922. RES.: St. Louis, MO.

CUNNINGHAM, MATTHEW J. POLIT. & GOV.: ***candidate for Republican nomination to presidency of the U.S., 1980, 1988***. MAILING ADDRESS: 10911 Meads Ave., Orange, CA 92669.

CUNNINGHAM, PAUL EDWARD. b. Dec 19, 1931, Franklin Cty., PA; par. Lawrence and Anna (Mills) Cunningham; m. Beulah Welsh; c. Susan Ann; Paul Edward II. EDUC.: eighth grade. POLIT. & GOV.: ***candidate for Constitutional Party nomination to presidency of the U.S., 1976***. BUS. & PROF.: grocer; meat salesman; restaurant owner, Chambersburg, PA; pastor, Independent Baptist Church. MIL.: U.S. Army, Korean War. REL.: Independent Bapt. MAILING ADDRESS: 1240 South Fourth St., Chambersburg, PA 17201.

CUNNINGHAM, SIS. POLIT. & GOV.: ***candidate for independent nomination to vice presidency of the U.S., 1992 (declined)***. MAILING ADDRESS: unknown.

CUOMO, MARIO MATTHEW. b. Jun 15, 1932, Queens Cty., NY; par. Andreas and Immaculata (Giordano) Cuomo; m. Matilda N. Raffa, Jun 1954; c. Margaret I. (Mrs. Peter Perpignano); Andrew M.; Maria C.; Madeline C.; Christopher C. EDUC.: B.A. (summa cum laude), St. John's Coll., 1953, LL.B. (cum laude), 1956. POLIT. & GOV.: confidential asst. to Judge Adrian P. Burke, NY State Court of Appeals, 1956–58; candidate for Democratic nomination to mayor of New York, NY, 1973 (withdrew), 1977; candidate for Democratic nomination to lt. gov. of NY, 1974; appointed sec. of state of NY, 1975–79; elected as a Democrat to lt. gov. of NY, 1979–83; elected as a Democrat to gov. of NY, 1983–95; temporary chm., keynoter, Dem. Nat'l. Conv., 1984; ***candidate for Democratic nomination to presidency of the U.S., 1984, 1988 (withdrew), 1992; candidate for Democratic nomination to vice presidency of the U.S., 1984, 1992***. BUS. & PROF.: atty.; admitted to NY Bar, 1956; admitted to the Bar of the Supreme Court of the U.S., 1960; assoc., Corner, Weisbrod, Froeb and Charles (law firm), Brooklyn, NY, 1958–63, partner, 1963–75; faculty member, St. John's Coll. Law School, 1963–75. MEM.: Big Brothers of America (regional dir.); Federation of Italian-American Democratic Organizations; Columbia Lawyers Assn.; ABA; NY State Bar Assn.; Brooklyn Bar Assn.; Nassau Cty. Bar Assn.; Queens Cty. Bar Assn.; Assn. of the Bar of the City of New York; American Jud. Soc.; St. John's U. Alumni Federation (chm., 1970–72); Catholic Lawyers Guild of Queens Cty. (pres., 1966–67); Skull and Circle; First Ecumenical Comm. of Christians and Jews (charter member); Pi Alpha Sigma; Delta Theta Phi. AWARDS: Pietas Medal, St. John's U., 1972; Man of the Year Award, Glendal Chapter, UNICO National, 1974; Humanitarian Award, Long Beach Lodge, B'nai B'rith, 1975; Rapallo Award, Columbia Lawyers Assn., 1976; Dante Medal, Italian Government-American Assn. of Teachers of Italian, 1976; Silver Medallion, Columbia Coalition, 1976; Public Administration Award, C. W. Post Coll., 1977. WRITINGS: "Appellate Advocacy," *New York Law Journal Revista*, Oct 11, 1963; *New York City Secondary School System* (1966); *Forest Hills Diary: The Crisis of Low-Income Housing* (1974); *Diaries of Mario M. Cuomo: The Campaign for Governor* (1984). REL.: R.C. MAILING ADDRESS: Office of the Governor, State Capitol, Albany, NY 12224.

CURLEY, JAMES MICHAEL. b. Nov 20, 1874, Boston, MA; d. Nov 12, 1958, Boston, MA; par. Michael and Sarah (Clancy) Curley; m. Mary Emily Herlihy, Jun 27, 1906; m. 2d, Mrs. Gertrude M. Casey Dennis, Jan 7, 1937; c. James Michael, Jr.; Mary; Paul; Leo; George; Francis; Dorothea. EDUC.: Boston Evening H.S. POLIT. & GOV.: Democratic candidate for Boston Common Council, 1898; elected as a Democrat to Boston Common Council, 1900–1901; elected as a Democrat to MA State House, 1902–03; elected as a Democrat to Boston Board of Aldermen, 1904–09; elected as a Democrat to Boston City Council, 1910–11; elected as a Democrat to U.S. House (MA), 1911–14, 1943–45; elected as a Democrat to mayor of Boston, MA, 1914–18, 1922–26, 1930–34, 1945–49; Democratic candidate for mayor of Boston, MA, 1917, 1939, 1941, 1949, 1951, 1955; Democratic candidate for U.S. House (MA), 1918; elected as a Democrat to gov. of MA, 1936–37; Democratic candidate for U.S. Senate (MA), 1936; ***candidate for Democratic nomination to vice presidency of the U.S., 1936***; Democratic candidate for gov. of MA, 1938; member, Dem. Nat'l. Cmte. (MA), 1941–42; appointed member, MA State Labor Comm., 1957–58. BUS. & PROF.: salesman, Logan, Johnston and Co., Boston; real estate investor; insurance agent, Boston, 1902–58; partner, Curley Brothers; trustee, Hibernia Savings Bank, pres., 1919–38; dir., Curley Luck Gold Mining Co.; pres., Engineers Group, Inc., 1941. MEM.: Boston C. of C.; Ancient and Honorable Artillery Co.; Elks; Knights of Columbus; Catholic Club of NY; MA Mayors' Assn.; Mayors' Assn. of the U.S.; University Club; Roxbury Tammany Club (founder, 1902). AWARDS: Order of the Rising Sun (Japan); Order of St. Sophia (Serbia); Order of the Commander of the Crown of Italy; Medal of Gratitude (France). HON. DEG.: LL.D., Suffolk Law School, 1935. WRITINGS: *I'd Do It Again* (1957). REL.: R.C. MISC.: convicted of corruption in office, 1937, 1941; jailed for five months, 1947. RES.: Boston, MA.

CURRAN, THOMAS. POLIT. & GOV.: ***candidate for Socialist Labor Party nomination to presidency of the U.S., 1900***; sec., Board of Appeal, Socialist Labor Party, 1900; officer, Socialist Labor Party National Convention, 1900. RES.: Providence, RI.

CURRY, CHARLES EWING. b. Sep 8, 1918, Kansas City, MO; par. Charles F. and Janet (Boone) Curry; m. Susanne Shutz, 1960; c. Laura; Janet; Charles; Maxine; Pauline (Mrs. Robert Knox). EDUC.: A.B., U. of KS, 1940. POLIT. & GOV.: elected as a Democrat, judge, Jackson Cty. (MO) Court (presiding judge), 1963–70; appointed chm., Carter Transition Cmte., 1976–77; member, Dem. Nat'l. Cmte., 1976–81 (chm., Midwestern Caucus, 1976–80; treas., 1981–); ***candidate for Democratic nomination to presidency of the U.S., 1984 (withdrew)***. BUS. & PROF.: chm., Charles F. Curry and Co., Kansas City, MO; chm., dir., Home Savings Assn., Kansas City, MO, 1947–83; dir., First National Charter Corp., Kansas City, MO, 1972–82; chm., Kansas City Corp. for Industrial Development, Kansas City, MO, 1978–80. MIL.: ensign, lt., U.S. Navy, 1942–45. MEM.: Phi Beta Kappa; Phi Delta Theta; Kansas City C. of C. (pres., 1974–75); William Jewell Coll. (dir., 1960–76); Stephens Coll. (dir., 1967–74); U.S. League of Savings Associations; Kansas City Neighborhood Alliance (chm., 1980–81); Harry S. Truman Good Neighbor Foundation; Civic Council of Greater Kansas City (dir., 1977–81). AWARDS: "Mister Kansas City" Award, Kansas City C. of C., 1977; Civic Service Award,

Hyman Brand Hebrew Acad., 1978; award, National Conference of Christians and Jews, 1980; "Friends of Freedom" Award, Coalition for a Democratic Majority, 1981. HON. DEG.: LL.D., William Jewell Coll., 1981. REL.: Bapt. MAILING ADDRESS: 20 West Ninth St., Kansas City, MO 64105.

CURTIN, ANDREW GREGG. b. Apr 22, 1817, Bellefonte, PA; d. Oct 7, 1894, Bellefonte, PA; par. Roland and Jean (Gregg) Curtin; m. Catherine Irvine Wilson, May 29, 1844; c. Mary Wilson (Mrs. George F. Harris); Jane Gregg (Mrs. William H. Sage); Martha (Mrs. Kidder Randolph Breese); William Wilson; Katharine (Mrs. Moses DeWitt Burnet); Myron Stanley; Bessie Elliot. EDUC.: Mr. Brown's School, Bellefonte, PA; Harrisburg (PA) Acad.; Milton Acad.; grad., Dickinson Coll., 1837; studied law under W. W. Potter and Judge John Reed. POLIT. & GOV.: presidential elector, Whig Party, 1848, 1852; Whig Party candidate for gov. of PA, 1854 (declined); appointed sec. of the commonwealth of PA, 1855–58; ex-officio superintendent of public schools of PA; elected as a Republican (People's Party) to gov. of PA, 1861–67; Republican candidate for U.S. Senate (PA), 1867; ***candidate for Republican nomination to vice presidency of the U.S., 1868***; appointed U.S. minister to Russia, 1869–72; ***candidate for Liberal Republican Party nomination to presidency of the U.S., 1872***; elected delegate, PA State Constitutional Convention, 1872; ***candidate for Independent National (Greenback) Party nomination to presidency of the U.S., 1876; candidate for Independent National (Greenback) Party nomination to vice presidency of the U.S., 1876***; candidate for Democratic nomination to U.S. Senate (PA), 1877; Democratic candidate for U.S. House (PA), 1878; elected as a Democrat to U.S. House (PA), 1881–87. BUS. & PROF.: atty.; admitted to PA Bar, 1839; partner (with John Blanchard), law firm, Bellefonte, PA. MEM.: Farmers' H.S. (subsequently Agricultural Coll. of PA and PA State U.; trustee). WRITINGS: *Contested Election Papers* (1879); *Fitz-John Porter* (1886). REL.: Presb. RES.: Bellefonte, PA.

CURTIS, CHARLES. b. Jan 25, 1860, Topeka, KS; d. Feb 8, 1936, Washington, DC; par. Orren Arms and Helene (Pappan) Curtis; m. Annie Elizabeth Baird, Nov 27, 1884; c. Permelia (Mrs. Charles Peasly George); Harry King; Leona (Mrs. Webster Knight II). EDUC.: public schools; studied law under Alfred H. Cass. POLIT. & GOV.: elected as a Republican, cty. atty., Shawnee Cty., KS, 1884–88; elected as a Republican to U.S. House (KS), 1893–1909; elected as a Republican to U.S. Senate (KS), 1907–13, 1915–29 (pres. pro tempore, 1911; asst. minority leader, 1915–24; Republican floor leader, 1924–29); delegate, Rep. Nat'l. Conv., 1908; delegate, KS State Republican Conventions; candidate for Republican nomination to U.S. Senate (KS), 1912; ***candidate for Republican nomination to vice presidency of the U.S., 1924; candidate for Republican nomination to presidency of the U.S., 1928; elected as a Republican to vice presidency of the U.S., 1929–33; Republican candidate for vice presidency of the U.S., 1932***. BUS. & PROF.: fruit salesman; jockey; hack driver; atty.; admitted to KS Bar, 1881; law practice, Topeka, KS; law practice, Washington, DC, 1933–36. REL.: Bapt. MISC.: of Native American ancestry. RES.: Topeka, KS.

CURTIS, DEAN ADAMS. b. 1956, Bethesda, MD; par. Charles and Joanne Curtis; single. POLIT. & GOV.: ***candidate for Democratic nomination to presidency of the U.S., 1992***. BUS. & PROF.: computer expert; ed., filmmaker, El Segundo, CA. MISC.: advocate of "Employee Democracy"; led employee buyout of Hughes Aircraft Corp. MAILING ADDRESS: 23 30th Ave., #3, Venice, CA 90291.

CURTIS, JAMES LANGDON. b. Feb 19, 1808, Stratford, CT; d. Nov 10, 1903, Stratford, CT; par. Daniel and Maria (Fairweather) Curtis; m. Clarissa Racey; c. Clara J.; Adelaide (Mrs. Eastbur Hastings); Laura (Mrs. George Hastings); Julia (Mrs. James G. Munson). POLIT. & GOV.: Greenback Party candidate for U.S. House (NY); Greenback-Labor Party candidate for gov. of CT, 1884; ***American Party candidate for presidency of the U.S., 1888***. BUS. & PROF.: merchant; real estate investor, TX; partner, Franklinite Steel and Zinc Co. MIL.: col., 9th Regt., NY Volunteers, 1835; gen., Civil War. RES.: Stratford, CT.

CURTIS, MERRITT BARTON. b. Aug 31, 1892, San Bernardino, CA; d. May 16, 1966, Winston-Salem, NC; par. Israel Hamilton and Lida Allen (Mee) Curtis; m. Frances Claire Bracewell, Apr 23, 1917; c. Elizabeth Holman (Mrs. Raymond F. Hesch); Ann Hamilton (Mrs. Henry T. Holsapple). EDUC.: A.B., U. of CA (Berkeley), 1916; LL.B., George Washington U., 1927. POLIT. & GOV.: ***Constitution Party candidate for presidency of the U.S., 1960; Constitution Party of TX candidate for vice presidency of the U.S., 1960***. BUS. & PROF.: soldier; atty.; admitted to CA Bar ; admitted to Bar of DC; admitted to Bar of the U.S. Court of Claims; admitted to Bar of the U.S. Court of Military Appeals; pres., United Services Life Insurance Co., 1941–46; agent, Military Services Insurance Underwriters, 1953–66; sec., Commissioned Officers Underwriters, Inc.; vice pres., sec., treas., General Services Life Insurance Co., 1958–59. MIL.: commissioned 2d lt., U.S.M.C., 1917; advanced through grades to brig. gen., 1944; retired, 1949; Navy Commendation with Ribbon. MEM.: Retired Officers Assn. (dir. of public relations, 1955–58); National Sojourners (pres., 1948–49; sec.-treas., ed., 1949–53); Defenders of the American Constitution (sec.; gen. counsel); American Coalition of Patriotic Societies (vice pres.); Friends of the Pusan Children's Charity Hospital (sec.); American Council for Friendship with the Arab World (pres.; treas.); Military Order of the World Wars (commander); Military Order of the Carabao (vice commander); Military Order of Foreign Wars; CA Soc. of the Sons of the Revolution; U.S. Navy League; Naval Order of the U.S.; Marine Corps Assn.; Soc. of the Globe and Anchor; American Legion; CA Alumni Assn.;

General Alumni Assn. and Law Assn., George Washington U.; International Lodge, Ancient Free and Accepted Masons (life member, Peking, China); Chung Te Consistory (life member); Almas Temple, Ancient Arabic Order of Nobles of the Mystic Shrine (life member, Shriners Hospitals for Crippled Children); Heroes of '76 (national commander); National Defense Masonic Club (dir.); Army and Navy Club; National Press Club; Sphinx Club; Phi Gamma Delta; Phi Alpha Delta. REL.: Protestant Episcopal Church. RES.: Washington, DC.

CURTIS, THOMAS BRADFORD. b. May 14, 1911, St. Louis, MO; d. Jan 10, 1992, St. Louis, MO; par. Edward Glion and Isabel (Wallace) Curtis; m. Susan Ross Chivvis; c. Elizabeth (Mrs. Thomas Allen); Leland; Allan Glasgow; Charles Miller; Jonathan Bradford. EDUC.: A.B., Dartmouth Coll., 1932; LL.B., Washington U., 1935. POLIT. & GOV.: appointed member, Board of Election Commissioners, St. Louis Cty., MO, 1942; member, St. Louis Cty. (MO) Republican Central Cmte., 1946–50; appointed member, MO State Board of Law Examiners, 1948–50; elected as a Republican to U.S. House (MO), 1951–69; ***candidate for Republican nomination to vice presidency of the U.S., 1960***; delegate, Rep. Nat'l. Conv., 1964, 1976, 1980; Republican candidate for U.S. Senate (MO), 1968, 1974; appointed member, President's Comm. on an All-Volunteer Armed Forces, 1969–70; appointed chm., Ozark Natural Scenic Riverways Advisory Comm., 1969–72; appointed member, President's Task Force on International Development, 1970–71; appointed member, Task Force on Financing Congressional Campaigns; appointed member, U.S. Territorial Expansion Memorial Comm.; appointed member, U.S. Advisory Comm. on International Education and Cultural Affairs, 1971–75; appointed chm., Rent Advisory Board, 1971; dir., Corp. for Public Broadcasting, 1972, chm., 1971–73; appointed chm., Federal Election Comm., 1975–76; member, MO State Republican Central Cmte., 1981. BUS. & PROF.: atty.; admitted to MO Bar, 1934; law practice, St. Louis, MO, 1934–92; vice pres., gen. counsel, *Encyclopedia Britannica*; vice pres., *Encyclopedia Britannica* Educational Corp., 1969–73; dir., Public Media Inc.; dir., Library Resources Inc.; dir., Lincoln Foundation; chm. of the board, Lafayette Federal Savings and Loan Assn., 1974; partner, Curtis, Crossen, Hensley and Allen (law firm). MIL.: lt. commander, U.S. Navy, 1942–45. MEM.: Dartmouth Coll. (trustee); William Woods Coll. (trustee); Twentieth Century Foundation (chm., 1971); Special Cmte. on Real Estate Taxation and Education Financing; U.S. C. of C.; National Coll. of Education (trustee); YMCA Community Coll. (trustee, 1970–73); Lincoln Inst. (trustee); Webster Coll. (trustee); Center for Inter-Strategic Studies (trustee); ABA; MO State Bar Assn.; St. Louis City Bar Assn.; St. Louis Cty. Bar Assn.; Phi Sigma Kappa; Phi Delta Phi. AWARDS: Ellis Forshee Award, MO Federation for the Blind, 1958; Alumni Citation, Washington U., 1960; Newel Perry Award, National Federation for the Blind, 1961; Congressional Distinguished Service Award, APSA, 1963; Silver Beaver Award, BSA, 1972. HON. DEG.: M.A., Dartmouth Coll., 1951; LL.D., Westminster Coll., 1962; J.D., Washington U., 1964, LL.D., Washington U., 1969. WRITINGS: *87 Million Jobs* (1962); *The Kennedy Round* (1970). REL.: Unitarian. RES.: Webster Groves, MO.

CUSHING, VOLNEY BYRON. b. Jan 31, 1856, Frankfort, ME; deceased; par. Theophilus Peter and Eunice Colby (Dorr) Cushing; m. Nellie M. Pearson, Jan 19, 1886; c. Max Pearson. EDUC.: public schools, Bangor, ME. POLIT. & GOV.: Prohibition Party candidate for gov. of ME, 1888; presidential elector, Prohibition Party, 1888; Prohibition Party candidate for U.S. House (ME), 1890, 1904, 1914; ***candidate for Prohibition Party nomination to presidency of the U.S., 1892***; member, Prohibition Party National Cmte., 1892–1900, 1904–08; state chm., ME Prohibition Party, 1892–96; Prohibition Party candidate for U.S. House (NY), 1916. BUS. & PROF.: hatter, Bangor, ME; hatter, Boston, MA; minister, Unitarian Church, IA, 1878–85; temperance advocate; lecturer, ME, 1885–. REL.: Unitarian. RES.: Bangor, ME.

CUTTEN, GEORGE BARTON. b. Apr 11, 1874, Amherst, Nova Scotia, Canada; d. Nov 2, 1962, Northampton, MA; par. William Freeman and Abbie Ann (Trefry) Cutten; m. Minnie Warren Brown, 1898; c. Margarita Joy; Muriel Grace; Claire; William Francis. EDUC.: B.A., Acadia U., 1896, M.A., 1897, LL.D., 1914; B.D., Yale U., 1897, Ph.D., 1902, B.D., 1903; D.D., Colgate U., 1911; D.D., McMaster Coll., 1920. POLIT. & GOV.: dir. of rehabilitation, Halifax Relief Comm., Halifax, Nova Scotia; ***candidate for Prohibition Party nomination to presidency of the U.S., 1944***. BUS. & PROF.: Ordained Baptist minister, 1897; pastor, Montowese, CT, 1897–99; pastor, Howard Avenue Church, New Haven, CT, 1899–1904; pastor, First Church, Corning, NY, 1904–07; pastor, First Church, Columbus, OH, 1907–10; pres., Acadia U., Wolfville, Nova Scotia, 1910–12; pres., Colgate U., 1922–42; acting pres., Colgate-Rochester Division School, 1943–44. MIL.: capt., maj., U.S. Army, 1916–17. MEM.: International Assn. of Torch Clubs (pres., 1931); YMCA (pres., National Council, 1931); Phi Beta Kappa. HON. DEG.: Ph.D., NY State Coll. for Teachers, 1932; L.H.D., Muhlenburg Coll., 1935; D.Sc., Alfred U., 1942. WRITINGS: *The Case of John Kinsel* (1902); *Christian Life in a Baptist Church* (1906); *The Psychology of Alcoholism* (1907); *The Psychological Phenomenon of Christianity* (1908); *Three Thousand Years of Mental Healing* (1911); *Mind: Its Origin and Goal* (1925); *The Threat of Leisure* (1926); *Speaking With Tongues: Historically and Psychologically Considered* (1927); *Silversmiths of Utica* (1936); *Silversmiths of the State of New York* (1939); *Instincts and Religion* (1940); *Should Prohibition Return?* (1944); *The Silversmiths of North Carolina* (1948); *The Silversmiths of Virginia* (1951); *The Silversmiths of Georgia* (1958). REL.: Bapt. RES.: Chapel Hill, NC.

DABBS, HENRY HERBERT. b. 1894; d. Jan 11, 1972, Herrin, IL; m. Minnie Wright; c. Margaret Melton; Naomi Bradshaw; Claudine Robinson. POLIT. & GOV.: ***candidate for Prohibition Party nomination to vice presidency of the U.S., 1964***. BUS. & PROF.: minister, First Church of God, Herrin, IL; minister, Nazarene Churches in IL; coal miner. MEM.: Local 1776, U.M.W. of A. REL.: Church of the Nazarene. RES.: Herrin, IL.

DABBS, VERNON MATTHEW (aka JOSPHY EDGAR HOOVER, JR.). b. Apr 9, 1928, French Morocco, Africa. EDUC.: Durham Cty. (NC) Schools; New York City (NY) schools; U.S. Military Acad., West Point, NY; Military Acad. of Communism; England Military Acad.; The Citadel; Valley Forge Military Acad.; U.S. Naval Acad.; other military academies. POLIT. & GOV.: ***candidate for Democratic nomination to presidency of the U.S., 1976***. BUS. & PROF.: soldier. MIL.: U.S. Army; U.S.M.C. MAILING ADDRESS: Route #2, Lakeview Rd. and Birch Dr., Durham, NC.

DAGUMAN, WILLIAM M. b. Dec 27, 1926, Pearl Harbor, HI; par. Marcelino M. and Sophia (Marteliano) Daguman; m. Rosalino S. Soler, Mar 1954 (divorced); c. Shirley; Edith; William, Jr.; Dwight; Daniel; Jacquelino; Valentino; David. EDUC.: FL State U. POLIT. & GOV.: ***candidate for Republican nomination to vice presidency of the U.S., 1988***. BUS. & PROF.: accountant; criminologist. MIL.: lt. col., Filipino Scouts, 1941–45, col.; rear adm., U.S. Navy, 1946–65; lt. gen., White House Military Advisor, 1977; hon. gen., U.S. Army, 1982; Good Conduct Medal; World War II Medal; Korean Conflict Medal; Congressional Recognition Certificate as Central American Freedom Fighter; Secretary of Defense Certificate. MEM.: Republican Presidential Task Force; U.S. Defense Cmte.; National Congressional Cmte.; Democratic Study Group. REL.: R.C. MAILING ADDRESS: 282 Raymond St., San Francisco, CA 94134.

DAKIN, SUSANNA BIXBY. b. May 6, 1932, Los Angeles, CA; par. Richard Young and Susanna Patterson (Bryant) Dakin; m. Halton C. Arp, Sep 13, 1962 (divorced); c. Kristana Marta Arp; Alissa Jan Arp; Andrice Susanna Arp. EDUC.: B.A., Scripps Coll., 1954; M.F.A., Los Angeles Cty. (CA) Art Inst., 1959. POLIT. & GOV.: ***candidate for Democratic nomination to presidency of the U.S., 1984***. BUS. & PROF.: self-employed artist, 1954–84; writer; educator; publisher, *Pasadena (CA) Eagle*, 1972–73; publisher, *Astro Artz*, 1978–84. MEM.: League of Women Voters; Common Cause; People for the American Way; Environmental Action; National Organization for Women; Congress on Racial Equality; A.C.L.U.; Pacific Oaks Coll. Children's School (dir., 1969–78); Pacific Futures, Inc. (dir., 1977–84); Hear Hight School (dir., 1982–84); SANE; Fine Arts Soc. MAILING ADDRESS: c/o Allan Kaprow, 228 Main St., #2, Venice, CA 90291.

DALEY, RICHARD JOSEPH. b. May 15, 1902, Chicago, IL; d. Dec 20, 1976, Chicago, IL; par. Michael and Lillian (Dunne) Daley; m. Eleanor Guilfoyle, Jun 23, 1936; c. Patricia (Mrs. William F. Thompson); Mary Carol (Mrs. Robert Vanecko); Eleanor; Richard Joseph, Jr.; Michael; John; William. EDUC.: B.A., DePaul U., LL.B., 1933. POLIT. & GOV.: elected as a Democrat to IL State House, 1936–38; elected as a Democrat to IL State Senate, 1938–46 (minority leader, 1941–46); chm., 11th Ward Democratic Cmte., 1948; appointed dir. of revenue (IL), 1948–50; elected as a Democrat, Cook Cty. (IL) clerk, 1950–55; delegate, Dem. Nat'l. Conv., 1952, 1956; elected as a Democrat to mayor of Chicago, IL, 1955–76; chm., Cook Cty. (IL) Democratic Central Cmte.; ***candidate for Democratic nomination to presidency of the U.S., 1968, 1972; candidate for Democratic nomination to vice presidency of the U.S., 1968, 1972***. BUS. & PROF.: atty.; admitted to IL Bar, 1933. MEM.: ABA; IL Bar Assn.; Chicago Bar Assn.; Valentine Boys Club (dir.); St. Joseph Home of the Friendless (dir.); Fellowship House (dir.); U.S. Conference of Mayors (pres., 1959);

Knights of Columbus; Elks; Moose; Bridgeport Area BSA (chm.). REL.: R.C. RES.: Chicago, IL.

DALL, CURTIS BEAN. b. Oct 24, 1896, New York, NY; d. Jun 28, 1991, Alexandria, VA; par. Charles Austin and Mary (Bean) Dall; m. Anna Eleanor Roosevelt, Jun 5, 1926 (divorced, 1934); m. 2d, Katharine Miller Leas, Dec 15, 1938; c. Anna Eleanor Seagraves; Curtis Roosevelt; Katharine Gurr (Mrs. Earle Boulton III); Stephen Austin; James Humphrey; Mary Bean (Mrs. C. Dary Durham, Jr.). EDUC.: grad., Mercersberg Acad., 1916; B.A., Princeton U., 1920. POLIT. & GOV.: national chm., Constitution Party, 1960–64; ***candidate for Republican nomination to presidency of the U.S., 1968 (withdrew); candidate for American Party nomination to presidency of the U.S., 1976***. BUS. & PROF.: stockbroker; investment counselor; partner, Goodbody and Co. (investments), 1930–32; organizer, Tennessee Gas and Transmission Co., 1940; promoter of natural gas and oil exploration, San Antonio, TX, 1945–51, Philadelphia, PA, 1951; dir., Distillers and Brewers Corp. of America, 1933–; partner, Fenner, Beane and Ungerleiden; owner, Curtis B. Dall Corp., 1939–; partner, Tex-Mo Drilling Co., 1950; patriotic organization exec., 1960–82. MIL.: ensign, U.S. Navy, 1918–19; NY National Guard, 1920–23; col., U.S. Air Force, 1942–45. MEM.: Chicago Board of Trade (gov., 1933–34); NY Stock Exchange (1930–); Assn. of Stock Exchange Firms (gov., 1933–40); Liberty Lobby (1960–91; chm. of the board, 1969–82; chm. emeritus); Military Order of the World Wars; SAR; SCV; VFW; Nassau Club; Princeton Cap and Gown Club; Army-Navy Club. AWARDS: Patrick Henry Award, VA Conservative Party, 1969; Citation, Polish Freedom Fighters in the U.S., 1971; Freedom Award; Order of Lafayette, 1971; Certificate of Appreciation, Military Order of World Wars, 1973. WRITINGS: *FDR, My Exploited Father-in-Law* (1964); *The War Lords of Washington* (1972). REL.: Episc. RES.: Alexandria, VA.

DALLAS, GEORGE MIFFLIN. b. Jul 10, 1792, Philadelphia, PA; d. Dec 31, 1864, Philadelphia, PA; par. Alexander James and Arabella Maria (Smith) Dallas; m. Sophia Nicklin, May 23, 1813; c. Philip Nicklin. EDUC.: A.B., Coll. of NJ, 1810. POLIT. & GOV.: sec., U.S. Mission to Russia, 1813; appointed solicitor, U.S. Bank, 1815–17; appointed deputy atty. gen. of Philadelphia, PA, 1817; elected as a Democrat to mayor of Philadelphia, 1828; appointed U.S. district atty. for Eastern PA, 1829–31; elected as a Democrat to U.S. Senate (PA), 1831–33; appointed atty. gen. of PA, 1833–35; appointed U.S. minister to Russia, 1837–39; ***elected as a Democrat to vice presidency of the U.S., 1845–49; candidate for Democratic nomination to presidency of the U.S., 1848***; appointed U.S. minister to Great Britain, 1856–61. BUS. & PROF.: atty.; admitted to PA Bar, 1813; law practice, New York, NY, 1815–17; law practice, Philadelphia, 1839–44. MIL.: enlisted in U.S. Army, 1812. HON. DEG.: LL.D., Coll. of NJ, 1854. REL.: Presb. RES.: Philadelphia, PA.

DALY, LAWRENCE JOSEPH SARSFIELD (aka LAR "AMERICA FIRST" DALY). b. Jan 22, 1912, Gary, IN; d. Apr 18, 1978, Evergreen Park, IL; par. Lawrence and Winifred (Glavey) Daly; m. Estelle Dorothy Martin, 1938 (divorced); m. 2d, Alice Ainley Brennan, Feb 10, 1948; c. Carol Patricia; Lawrence Joseph, Jr.; Christopher John; Christina Alice (Mrs. Cooper); Colleen Marie; Winifred Ann. EDUC.: Carmelite Sisters Orphan Home, Hammond, IN; Holy Cross Catholic Parochial School; De LaSalle Inst., Chicago, IL (one year of high school). POLIT. & GOV.: chm., MacArthur for President Cmte., 1936; candidate for Democratic nomination to Cook Cty. (IL) superintendent of schools, 1938; candidate for Chicago School Board, 2 times; candidate for Democratic nomination to U.S. Senate (IL), 1942 (under name of Sarsfield), 1962, 1970; ***candidate for Republican nomination to presidency of the U.S., 1948, 1956, 1960, 1968, 1976***; candidate for Republican nomination to U.S. Senate (IL), 1950, 1954, 1960, 1966, 1970, 1974, 1978; candidate for Republican nomination to mayor of Chicago, 1955, 1959, 1967; candidate for Republican nomination to gov. of IL, 1956, 1964; candidate for Republican nomination to U.S. House (IL), 1957, 1969, 1973; candidate for Republican nomination to IL state superintendent of public instruction, 1958; candidate for Democratic nomination to mayor of Chicago, 1959, 1963, 1971; *candidate for Democratic nomination to presidency of the U.S., 1960, 1964, 1968, 1972, 1976; America First (Tax Cut) Party candidate for presidency of the U.S., 1960, 1968*; chm., America First Party; *independent write-in candidate for presidency of the U.S., 1968, 1972*; independent write-in candidate for U.S. Senate (IL), 1970, 1972; candidate for Democratic nomination to clerk of circuit court, Cook Cty., 1971; independent write-in candidate for gov. of IL, 1972. BUS. & PROF.: fruit and vegetable peddler, Chicago, 1928–36; owner, Daly Brothers Moving and Storage Business, Chicago, 1936–40; owner, jobber, American Stool and Chair Co., Chicago, 1940–78; tavern singer; violinist; furniture manufacturer; composer. MEM.: Christ-One (founder). WRITINGS: *Appeal to the Christian World* (1942); *The Platform of the Christian Action Party* (1944); "There's a Star-Spangled Banner Waving Somewhere" (song, 1974). REL.: R.C. RES.: Chicago, IL.

DALY, ROBERT T. "BOB." b. Aug 12, 1928. EDUC.: B.A., U. of CA, Santa Barbara, 1952; grad. work in school psychology. POLIT. & GOV.: Democratic candidate for OR State House, 1968; candidate for Portland (OR) City Council; candidate for Portland School Board; elected member, Multnomah Cty. (OR) Democratic Central Cmte., 1969–73; ***candidate for Democratic nomination to presidency of the U.S., 1972***; candidate for Democratic nomination to U.S. Senate (OR), 1974. BUS. & PROF.: mathematics teacher; educational administrator and counselor, Fort Lewis, WA; employment counselor, OR; researcher, Inst. of Urban Affairs; school psychologist, Shelton School District; coach; aviation electronics technician; accountant; writer; salesman. MIL.: U.S. Navy, WWII. MEM.: AFL-CIO; Vice Presidential Project (dir.). MISC.: won suit against Shelton School District for dismissal as a school psychologist, 1965, reinstated, 1973; won first racial discrimination suit by a white person in OR, May 10, 1971. MAILING ADDRESS: 2209 Northwest Everett, #15, Portland, OR 97210.

DANA, CHARLES ANDERSON. b. Aug 8, 1819, Hinsdale, NH; d. Oct 17, 1897, West Island, NY; par. Anderson and Ann (Denison) Dana; m. Eunice MacDaniel, Mar 2, 1846; c. Ruth; Paul; Zoe; Eunice. POLIT. & GOV.: appointed asst. U.S. sec. of war, 1863–64; ***candidate for Democratic nomination to presidency of the U.S., 1884***. BUS. & PROF.: journalist; teacher, managing trustee, Brook Farm, 1841–46; asst. ed., *Boston (MA) Daily Chronotype*, 1846–47; city ed., managing ed., *New York (NY) Tribune*, 1847–62; ed., *Chicago (IL) Republican*, 1865; owner, ed., *New York (NY) Sun*, 1868–97. MIL.: served as field observer, Union Army, 1863–64. MEM.: Buffalo Coffee Club; SAR (vice pres. gen.); New England Soc. HON. DEG.: A.B., Harvard U., 1861. WRITINGS: *The Black Ant* (1848); *New American Encyclopedia* (with George Ripley, 1858–63); *Household Book of Poetry* (1857); *Life of Ulysses S. Grant* (1868); *The Art of Newspaper Making* (1895); *Fifty Perfect Poems* (co-editor); *Recollections of Civil War* (1898); *Eastern Journeys* (1898). MISC.: noted for "human interest" variety of journalism; fought Tweed Ring, Grant administration. RES.: New York, NY.

DANE, ROBERT. POLIT. & GOV.: ***candidate for Republican nomination to presidency of the U.S., 1976***. MAILING ADDRESS: P.O. Box 1284, St. Joseph, MO 64502.

DANFORTH, ELLIOTT. b. Mar 6, 1850, Middleburgh, NY; d. Jan 7, 1906, New York, NY; par. Judge Peter S. Danforth; m. Ida Prince, 1874; c. Edward; Mrs. Edward L. Knight. EDUC.: Schoharie Acad.; studied law under Peter S. Danforth. POLIT. & GOV.: elected as a Democrat to president of the village of Bainbridge, NY, 3 times; delegate, Dem. Nat'l. Conv., 1880, 1884, 1888, 1892, 1896, 1900; Democratic candidate for U.S. House (NY), 1884 (declined); candidate for Democratic nomination to NY state treas., 1884; appointed deputy state treas. of NY, 1884–89; elected as a Democrat, NY state treas., 1889–94; member, NY State Democratic Central Cmte., 1896–1906 (chm., 1896–98; chm., exec. cmte., 1899); Democratic candidate for lt. gov. of NY, 1898; ***candidate for Democratic nomination to vice presidency of the U.S., 1900***. BUS. & PROF.: atty.; admitted to NY Bar, 1871; law practice, Middleburgh, NY, 1871–74; law practice, Bainbridge, NY, 1874–94; partner (with G. H. Windsor), law firm, Bainbridge, NY, 1878–80; law practice, New York, NY, 1894–1906; pres., First National Bank of Bainbridge. MEM.: Independent Order of Odd Fellows; Canton Nemo of Albany; Elks; Masons; Ancient Order of United Workmen; ABA; Soc. of American Authors. WRITINGS: *Address . . . at the 230* (1891); *Old Schoharie* (1892); *The Indians of New York* (1894); *An Address . . . before the Green Bay Cty. Agricultural Society* (1895); *The Extraordinary Collection of Autograph Letters Belonging to the late Hon. Elliott Danforth* (1912). REL.: Presb. RES.: New York, NY.

DANIEL, JOHN WARWICK. b. Sep 5, 1842, Lynchburg, VA; d. Jun 29, 1910, Lynchburg, VA; par. Judge William, Jr., and Sarah Anne (Warwick) Daniel; m. Julia E. Munnell, 1869. EDUC.: Lynchburg Coll.; Dr. Gessner Harrison's University School; U. of VA, 1865–66. POLIT. & GOV.: elected as a Democrat to VA State House of Delegates, 1869–72; elected as a Democrat to VA State Senate, 1875–81; presidential elector, Democratic Party, 1876; candidate for Democratic nomination to gov. of VA, 1877; delegate, Dem. Nat'l. Conv., 1880, 1888, 1892, 1896, 1900; Democratic candidate for gov. of VA, 1881; elected as a Democrat to U.S. House (VA), 1885–87; elected as a Democrat to U.S. Senate (VA), 1887–1910; ***candidate for Democratic nomination to presidency of the U.S., 1896, 1908; candidate for Democratic nomination to vice presidency of the U.S., 1896***. BUS. & PROF.: atty.; admitted to VA Bar, 1866; law practice, Lynchburg. MIL.: 2d lt., 1st lt., adj. gen., Company A, 11th VA Infantry, C.S.A., 1861, capt., 1862, maj., 1864. HON. DEG.: LL.D., Washington and Lee U., 1883; LL.D., U. of MI, 1887. WRITINGS: *Attachments Under the Code of Virginia* (1869); *Negotiable Instruments* (1876). RES.: Lynchburg, VA.

DANIEL, WILLIAM. b. Jan 24, 1826, Deals Island, MD; d. Oct 12, 1897, Mt. Washington, MD; par. Travers Daniel; m. Ellen Young, 1860. EDUC.: grad., Dickinson Coll., 1848; studied law under William O. Waters. POLIT. & GOV.: elected as a member of the American Party to MD State House of Delegates, 1853–57; elected to MD State Senate, 1857–58 (resigned); elected delegate, MD State Constitutional Convention, 1864; candidate for judge, Circuit Court of MD; delegate, Prohibition Party National Convention, 1884 (temporary chm.); ***Prohibition Home Protection Party candidate for vice presidency of the U.S., 1884***; state chm., MD Prohibition Party, 1887–89; member, Prohibition Party National Cmte., 1888–92. BUS. & PROF.: atty.; admitted to MD Bar, 1851; law practice, Somerset Cty., MD, 1851–58; law practice, Baltimore, MD, 1858–97. MEM.: Kelso Home for Orphans (trustee); Glyndon Park Camp Grounds (founder, 1889); MD State Temperance Alliance (founder; pres., 1872–84); Male Free School (sec.-treas.); Colvin Inst. (sec.-treas.); Centennial Biblical Inst. (trustee); Baltimore Preachers' Aid Soc. (mgr.); Dickinson Coll. (trustee); Baltimore Assn. for the Moral and Educational Improvement of the Colored People (founder); National Prohibition Bureau. REL.: Methodist Episcopal Church (trustee, Mt. Vernon Methodist Episcopal Church; trustee and treas., Educational Fund, Baltimore Annual Conference). MISC.: known as the "Little Giant." RES.: Baltimore, MD.

DANIELS, JOSEPHUS. b. May 18, 1862, Washington, DC; d. Jan 15, 1948, Raleigh, NC; par. Josephus and Mary

Cleaves (Seabrook) Daniels; m. Addie Worth Bagley, May 2, 1888; c. Adelaide; Josephus; Worth Bagley; Jonathan Worth; Frank Arthur. EDUC.: Wilson Collegiate Inst. POLIT. & GOV.: state printer of NC, 1887–93; chief clerk, U.S. Dept. of the Interior, 1893–95; member, Dem. Nat'l. Cmte., 1896–1916; appointed U.S. sec. of the navy, 1913–21; ***candidate for Democratic nomination to presidency of the U.S., 1920, 1924***; delegate, Dem. Nat'l. Conv., 1924; appointed U.S. ambassador to Mexico, 1933–42. BUS. & PROF.: ed., *Wilson (NC) Advance*, 1880; atty.; admitted to NC Bar, 1885; ed., *Raleigh (NC) State Chronicle*, 1885–94; ed., *Raleigh News and Observer*, 1894–1948. MEM.: North Carolina Press Assn. (pres., 1884); U. of NC (trustee); U. of NC Alumni Assn. (sec.); National Editorial Assn.; Wilson Foundation (trustee); Jefferson Memorial Comm.; Woodrow Wilson Foundation; Franklin D. Roosevelt Foundation. HON. DEG.: LL.D., U. of NC; LL.D., OH Wesleyan U.; LL.D., Wake Forest Coll.; LL.D., Davidson U.; LL.D., U. of MD; LL.D., Dickinson U.; Litt.D., Washington and Lee U. WRITINGS: *Life of Worth Bagley* (1898); *The Navy and the Nation* (1919); *Our Navy at War* (1922); *Life of Woodrow Wilson* (1924); *Tar Heel Editor* (1939); *In Politics* (ed., 1940); *The Wilson Era: Peace, 1913–1917* (1944); *The Wilson Era: War, 1917–1923* (1945); *Shirt Sleeve Diplomat* (1947). REL.: Methodist. RES.: Raleigh, NC.

DANIELS, RON. b. 1942, Beckly, WV. EDUC.: B.A., M.A., Rockefeller U.; M.A., State U. of NY. POLIT. & GOV.: pres., National Black Political Assembly, 1974–80; national cochair, National Black Independent Political Party, 1980–85; southern regional coordinator, deputy dir., Jesse Jackson for President Campaign, 1988; ***candidate for Democratic nomination to presidency of the U.S., 1992; independent candidate for presidency of the U.S., 1992***. BUS. & PROF.: author; lecturer; prof.; syndicated columnist; social activist. MEM.: Campaign for a New Tomorrow; National Rainbow Coalition (exec. dir., 1987). MISC.: endorsed by International Green Party. MAILING ADDRESS: Box 27798, McPherson Square Station, Washington, DC 20038-7798.

DARLING, LOWELL. b. 1942, Rock Island, IL; m. Kathy Darling (divorced, 1974). EDUC.: U. of IL. POLIT. & GOV.: independent candidate for gov. of CA, 1978; ***independent candidate for presidency of the U.S., 1984***. BUS. & PROF.: artist; anthro-apologist; prankster. HON. DEG.: Ph.D., National Coll. of Naturopathic Medicine. WRITINGS: *One Hand Shaking* (1980). MISC.: known as a "conceptual artist." MAILING ADDRESS: 849 1/2 North Seward St., Hollywood, CA 90038.

DARNELL, SAMUEL DALE. b. Oct 26, 1973, Elizabeth City, NC; par. James Earl and Carolyn Louise (Dail) Darnell; single. EDUC.: Perquimans Union School. POLIT. & GOV.: ***independent candidate for vice presidency of the U.S., 1988***. BUS. & PROF.: student. REL.: Methodist. MAILING ADDRESS: P.O. Box 48, Durante Neck, NC 27930.

DARRIN, DAVID. POLIT. & GOV.: ***candidate for Republican nomination to presidency of the U.S., 1944; candidate for Democratic nomination to presidency of the U.S., 1944***. MAILING ADDRESS: Washington, DC.

DASCHLE, THOMAS ANDREW. b. Dec 9, 1947, Aberdeen, SD; m. Laurie Susan Klinkel; m. 2d, Linda Hall, 1984; c. Kelly; Nathan. EDUC.: B.A., SD State U., 1969. POLIT. & GOV.: chief legislative aide, field coordinator, U.S. Sen. James Abourezk, 1973–77; elected as a Democrat to U.S. House (SD), 1979–87; ***candidate for Democratic nomination to vice presidency of the U.S., 1980***; elected as a Democrat to U.S. Senate (SD), 1987–; minority leader, 1995–. BUS. & PROF.: representative, financial investment firm. MIL.: 1st lt., U.S. Air Force, 1969–72. AWARDS: one of ten "Outstanding Young Men in America," U.S. Junior C. of C., 1982; National Commander's Award, Disabled American Veterans, 1980; named "Friend of Education," SD, 1982. REL.: R.C. MAILING ADDRESS: Aberdeen, SD.

DASS, BABA RAM (nee RICHARD ALPERT). b. Apr 6, 1931, Boston, MA; par. George and Gertrude (Levin) Alpert; single. EDUC.: A.B., Tufts U., 1952; M.A., Wesleyan U., 1954; Ph.D., Stanford U., 1957. POLIT. & GOV.: ***independent candidate for presidency of the U.S., 1976***. BUS. & PROF.: instructor, Stanford U.; visiting fellow, U. of CA, 1960–61; staff, Center for Research in Personality, Harvard U., 1959; asst. prof., Harvard U., 1958–63; writer; lecturer; yogi; psychotherapist; instructor, Naropa Inst., Boulder, CO; guru; lecturer, Esalen Inst. MEM.: Castalia Foundation (founder); International Foundation for Internal Freedom (founder). WRITINGS: *Identification and Child Rearing* (coauthor, 1960); *The Psychedelic Experience* (with Timothy Leary and Ralph Metzner, 1964); *LSD: The Inside Story* (with Sidney Cohen, 1966); *Remember, Be Here Now* (1971); *The Only Dance There Is* (coauthor, 1974); *Grist for the Mill* (1977); *Journey of Awakening* (1978); *Miracle of Love* (1979). REL.: all. MISC.: noted for early experiments on psychedelic drugs (with Timothy Leary). MAILING ADDRESS: P.O. Box 928, Soquel, CA 95073.

DATTNER, JOYCE. POLIT. & GOV.: Poor and Working People's Party candidate for NY State Assembly, 1976; founding member, New Alliance Party, 1979; ***New Alliance Party candidate for vice presidency of the U.S., 1988***. MEM.: New York City Unemployed and Welfare Council (founder; pres.). REL.: Jewish. MAILING ADDRESS: 1470 West Winnemac, Chicago, IL 60640.

DAUGHERTY, PAUL CHARLES. b. Apr 30, 1956, St. Mary's, OH; par. John Pierce and Anne Marie (Morlath) Daugherty; m. Carol Lynn Wade; c. Casey Daniel; Ryan Andrew. EDUC.: State U. of NY; B.S., PA State U., 1986; U.S. Navy Nuclear Power School; U.S. Navy Electronics School. POLIT. & GOV.: ***candidate for Republican nomination to presidency of the U.S., 1992; Bull Moose Party candidate for presidency of the U.S., 1992***. BUS. & PROF.: engineer; Navy Underwater Systems Corp. contractor, 1986–88; subcontractor, GA Power Plant Tootle Project, 1988; contractor, Omaha Public Power District, 1988–90; augmentation engineer and subcontractor, engineering department, Savannah River Site, Westinghouse Power, 1990–92. MIL.: ET 1, U.S. Navy, 1976–82; Good Conduct Award; Sea Service Ribbon. MEM.: Rotary Club; Inst. of Electrical and Electronic Engineers (1985–); PA State U. Alumni Assn. REL.: R.C. MAILING ADDRESS: 16 Converse Dr. Aiken, SC 29803.

DAVIDSON, THOMAS J. POLIT. & GOV.: ***independent candidate for presidency of the U.S., 1980***. MAILING ADDRESS: 1732 Circle Rd., Severn, MD 21144.

DAVIS, ANGELA YVONNE. b. Jan 26, 1944, Birmingham, AL; par. B. Frank and Sallye E. Davis; m. Hilton Braithwaite, Jul 6, 1980; c. none. EDUC.: grad., Elizabeth Irwin H.S., New York, NY, 1961; B.A. (magna cum laude), Brandeis U., 1965; U. of Paris; Johann Wolfgang von Goethe U., 1965–67; M.A., U. of CA, 1968, doctoral studies, 1968–. POLIT. & GOV.: lecturer, Communist Party, U.S.A.; ***independent candidate for presidency of the U.S., 1972; Communist Party, U.S.A. candidate for vice presidency of the U.S., 1980, 1984***. BUS. & PROF.: asst. prof., U. of CA, Los Angeles, CA, 1969–70 (dismissed for radical activities; reinstated). MEM.: Black Students Council; San Diego Black Conference; Student Non-Violent Coordinating Council; Black Panthers; Soledad Brothers Defense Cmte. AWARDS: Lenin Peace Prize. HON. DEG.: Ph.D., Lenin U. WRITINGS: *If They Come in the Morning: Voices of Resistance* (1971); *Angela Davis: An Autobiography* (1979). REL.: Congregationalist. MISC.: indicted for illegal purchase of arms; friend of George Jackson, an inmate in Soledad Prison; fled CA following death of Jackson in attempted escape using weapon belonging to Davis; named to FBI. "Ten Most Wanted" list; arrested and confined without bail; finally released following public controversy, 1972; acquitted Jun 4, 1972. MAILING ADDRESS: 10463 Royal Oak, Oakland, CA 94605.

DAVIS, BILLY M. b. 1938, Bay Springs, MS; married; children. EDUC.: LL.B., Jackson School of Law, 1966; B.S., MS State U., 1967. POLIT. & GOV.: candidate for Democratic nomination to gov. of MS, 1983; ***Independent Party candidate for vice presidency of the U.S., 1984***. BUS. & PROF.: government teacher, junior high school, MS; atty.; partner, Davis and Sims (law firm), Biloxi, MS; farmer and cattle rancher, Biloxi, MS. MIL.: 3d Div., U.S.M.C., 1950s; active reserve, 1960s. MEM.: ABA; MS State Future Farmers Assn. (officer); MS Education Students Assn. (pres.); American Agriculture Assn. (delegate, 1978); National Democratic Policy Cmte.; Club of Life; Schiller Inst. MAILING ADDRESS: Route 7, Box 455, Laurel, MS 39440.

DAVIS, CUSHMAN KELLOGG. b. Jun 16, 1838, Henderson, NY; d. Nov 27, 1900, St. Paul, MN; par. Horatio N. and Clarissa S. (Cushman) Davis; m. Laura Bowman, 1864; m. 2d, Anna Malcolm Agnew, 1880; c. none. EDUC.: Carroll Coll.; grad., U. of MI, 1857; studied law under Alexander W. Randall, Waukesha, WI. POLIT. & GOV.: elected as a Republican to MN State House, 1867; appointed U.S. atty. for MN, 1868–73; elected as a Republican to gov. of MN, 1874–75; Republican candidate for U.S. Senate (MN), 1875, 1881; elected as a Republican to U.S. Senate (MN), 1887–1900; ***candidate for Republican nomination to presidency of the U.S., 1896 (withdrew); candidate for Republican nomination to vice presidency of the U.S., 1896***; U.S. delegate to Paris Peace Conference, 1898. BUS. & PROF.: atty.; admitted to WI Bar, 1859; law practice, Waukesha, WI; partner, Gorman and Davis (law firm), St. Paul, MN, 1865; partner, Davis, Kellogg and Severance (law firm), St. Paul. MIL.: lt., asst. adj. gen., Company B, 28th WI Volunteer Infantry, 1861–64. HON. DEG.: LL.D., U. of MI, 1886. WRITINGS: *Modern Feudalism* (1870); *The Law in Shakespeare* (1884); *Treatise on International Law, Including American Diplomacy* (1901). REL.: Episc. RES.: St. Paul, MN.

DAVIS, DAVID. b. Mar 9, 1815, Cecil Cty., IN; d. Jun 26, 1886, Bloomington, IL; par. Dr. David and Ann (Mercer) Davis; m. Sarah Woodruff, Oct 30, 1838; m. 2d, Adeline Burr, Mar 14, 1883; c. George Perrin; Lucy; Mercer. EDUC.: grad., Kenyon Coll., 1832; studied law under Judge Henry W. Bishop, Lenox, MA; LL.B., Yale U., 1835. POLIT. & GOV.: Whig Party candidate for IL State Senate, 1840; elected as a Whig to IL State House, 1844; delegate, IL State Constitutional Convention, 1847; elected presiding judge, 8th Judicial Circuit of IL, 1848–62; delegate, Rep. Nat'l. Conv., 1860; appointed member, Comm. on Investigation of Claims in Western Dept. of the U.S., 1861 appointed assoc. justice, Supreme Court of the U.S., 1862–77; ***candidate for Democratic nomination to presidency of the U.S., 1868, 1880; Labor Reform Party candidate for presidency of the U.S., 1872 (declined); candidate for Liberal Republican Party nomination to presidency of the U.S., 1872; candidate for Prohibition Party nomination to presidency of the U.S., 1872; received one electoral vote for presidency of the U.S., 1872***; member, U.S. Electoral Comm., 1876; elected as an Independent-Democrat to U.S. Senate (IL), 1877–83 (pres. pro tempore, 1881–83); ***candidate for Greenback Party nomination to presidency of the U.S., 1876, 1880, 1884; candidate for Democratic nomination to vice presidency of the U.S., 1880 (declined)***. BUS. & PROF.: atty.; admitted to IL Bar, 1835; law practice, Pekin, IL, 1835; law practice, Bloomington, IL, 1836. MEM.: IL State Bar Assn. (pres., 1884). HON. DEG.: LL.D., Beloit (WI) Coll., 1863; LL.D., IL Wesleyan U., 1865; LL.D., Williams Coll., 1873; LL.D., St. John's Coll., 1874. REL.: Protestant Episcopal Church. RES.: Bloomington, IL.

DAVIS, EDMUND JACKSON. b. Oct 2, 1827, St. Augustine, FL; d. Feb 7, 1883, Austin, TX; par. William Goodwin and Mary Ann (Channer) Davis; m. Ann Britton, 1858. EDUC.: cadet, U.S. Military Acad.; studied law, Corpus Christi, TX. POLIT. & GOV.: clerk, post office, Galveston, TX, 1849; deputy collector of customs on Rio Grande, 1850–52; elected district atty., Webb Cty., TX, 1853–55; judge, District Court, Austin, TX, 1855–61; candidate for delegate, TX Secession Convention, 1860; appointed chief justice, TX Supreme Court, 1865 (declined); delegate, TX State Constitutional Convention, 1866, 1868–69 (pres.); elected as a Republican to gov. of TX, 1870–74; Republican candidate for gov. of TX, 1873, 1880; ***candidate for Republican nomination to vice presidency of the U.S., 1872, 1880; candidate for Republican nomination to presidency of the U.S., 1880***; Republican candidate for U.S. House (TX), 1882. BUS. & PROF.: atty.; law practice, Laredo, TX; law practice, Corpus Christi, TX; law practice, Brownsville, TX; law practice, Austin, TX. MIL.: col., First TX Cavalry, U.S. Army, 1861, brig. gen., 1864. MEM.: Ancient Free and Accepted Masons (Rio Grande Lodge No. 81); TX Hist. Soc. RES.: Austin, TX.

DAVIS, GARRETT. b. Sep 10, 1801, Mt. Sterling, KY; d. Sep 22, 1872, Paris, KY; par. Jeremiah Davis; m. Miss Trimble, 1852; m. 2d, Mrs. Elliot, 1846. POLIT. & GOV.: elected as a Whig to KY State House, 1833–35; elected as a Henry Clay Whig to U.S. House (KY), 1839–47; Whig Party candidate for lt. gov. of KY, 1848 (declined); delegate, KY State Constitutional Convention, 1849; American (Know-Nothing) Party candidate for gov. of KY, 1855 (declined); ***candidate for American (Know-Nothing) Party nomination to presidency of the U.S., 1856 (declined)***; elected as a Whig to U.S. Senate (KY), 1861–67, as a Democrat, 1867–72. BUS. & PROF.: clerk; atty.; admitted to KY Bar, 1823; law practice, Paris, KY. MEM.: Smithsonian Institution (regent, 1864). RES.: Paris, KY.

DAVIS, GARRY (See DAVIS, SOL GARETH "GARRY").

DAVIS, HARRY SIMEON. b. Oct 18, 1962, Jersey City, NJ; par. Sidney Joseph and Lucy (Raab) Davis; single. EDUC.: Colonia Senior H.S., Avenel, NJ. POLIT. & GOV.: ***Conservative Students Party candidate for presidency of the U.S., 1980***. BUS. & PROF.: crew chief, Woodbridge Township (NJ) Main Public Library; page; employee, McDonald's Corp.; intern, Congressman Edward Patton, 1980. MEM.: Young Americans for Freedom; The Conservative Caucus; Woodbridge Township Young Democrats. REL.: Jewish. MAILING ADDRESS: 515 Murray St., Avenel, NJ 07001.

DAVIS, HENRY GASSAWAY. b. Nov 16, 1823, Baltimore, MD; d. Mar 11, 1916, Washington, DC; par. Caleb and Louisa Warfield (Brown) Davis; m. Kate Anne Bantz, Feb 22, 1853; c. Hallie D. (Mrs. Stephen B. Elkins, q.v.); Kate B. (Mrs. R. M. G. Brown); Grace T.; Henry Gassaway, Jr.; John T. EDUC.: cty. schools. POLIT. & GOV.: elected as a Union Conservative to WV State House of Delegates, 1865; elected as a Democrat to WV State Senate, 1868–71; elected as a Democrat to U.S. Senate (WV), 1871–83; delegate, Dem. Nat'l. Conv., 1868, 1872; appointed delegate, Pan-American Congress, 1889, 1901; appointed member, Intercontinental Railway Survey Comm., 1890–94; appointed member, U.S. Permanent Pan-American R.R. Comm., 1901–16; ***Democratic candidate for vice presidency of the U.S., 1904***. BUS. & PROF.: plantation superintendent, to 1843; brakeman, conductor, agent, Baltimore and Ohio R.R., 1843–58; lumberman; pres., Piedmont National Bank, Piedmont, WV, 1858; merchant; pres., West Virginia Central and Pittsburgh R.R., 1882–1902; pres., Coal and Coke R.R. of WV, 1906–12; pres., Davis Trust Co., Elkins, WV. WRITINGS: *National and State Policies . . .* (1874); *Alternatives, Changes, and Discrepancies in the Official Finance Reports . . . Speeches . . . on . . . Resolution to Appoint a Special Cmte. of the Senate . . .* (1876); *Treasury Reports and Bookkeeping* (1877); *The Pan-American Railway . . .* (1906). RES.: Elkins, WV.

DAVIS, HENRY WINTER. b. Aug 16, 1817, Annapolis, MD; d. Dec 30, 1865, Baltimore, MD; par. Rev. Henry Lyon and Jane (Brown) Davis; m. Constance T. Gardiner, Oct 30, 1845; m. 2d, Nancy Morris, Jan 26, 1857; c. two daughters. EDUC.: grad., Kenyon Coll., 1837; studied law at U. of VA, 1839. POLIT. & GOV.: elected as an American (Know-Nothing) to U.S. House (MD), 1855–61, 1863–65; ***candidate for Republican nomination to vice presidency of the U.S., 1860***; organizer, Constitutional Union Party, 1860. BUS. & PROF.: atty.; law practice, Alexandria, VA, to 1850; law practice, Baltimore, MD, 1850–65; leader of Radical Republicans in U.S. House. MEM.: Smithsonian Institution (regent). WRITINGS: *The War of Ormuzd and Ahriman in the Nineteenth Century*; *Speeches and Addresses in Congress*. REL.: Protestant Episcopal Church. RES.: Baltimore, MD.

DAVIS, JAMES CURRAN. b. May 17, 1895, Franklin, GA; d. Dec 28, 1981, Atlanta, GA; par. Thomas Benjamin and Lura Viola (Mooty) Davis; m. Mary Lou Martin, Dec 26, 1932; c. Mary Martin (Mrs. Edward G. Bowen). EDUC.: Reinhardt Coll., 1909–10; Emory Coll., 1910–12; read law in offices of Bryan and Middlebrooks, Atlanta, GA. POLIT. & GOV.: elected as a Democrat to GA State House, 1925–28; atty., GA State Dept. of Industrial Relations, 1928–31; atty., DeKalb Cty., GA, 1931–34; judge, Superior Court, Stone Mountain Judicial Circuit, GA, 1934–47; reemployment committeeman, Selective Service Board, DeKalb Cty., GA, 1941–81; elected as a Democrat to U.S. House (GA), 1947–63; delegate, Dem. Nat'l. Conv., 1948, 1952; ***candidate for Democratic nomination to presidency of the U.S., 1952, 1956***; member, GA State Democratic Exec. Cmte.; candidate for Democratic nomination to U.S.

House (GA), 1962. BUS. & PROF.: atty.; admitted to GA Bar, 1919; law practice, Atlanta, GA, 1919–34; dir., DeKalb Cty. Federal Savings and Loan Assn.; publisher, *Atlanta Times*, 1964–65. MIL.: 1st lt., capt., U.S.M.C., 1917–19. MEM.: Sigma Alpha Epsilon; Masons; Ku Klux Klan; American Legion; Lions; Lawyers Club of Atlanta (pres., 1924–25); Odd Fellows (pres.); J.O.U.A.M.; ABA (chm., District Americanization Cmte., 1925); President's Club of Atlanta; Atlanta Bar Assn.; GA Motor Club (dir.). REL.: Methodist. RES.: Stone Mountain, GA.

DAVIS, JAMES HARVEY. b. Dec 24, 1853, Walhalla, SC; d. Jan 31, 1940, Kaufman, TX; par. W. B. and Salina (Moore) Davis; m. Belle Barton, Dec 25, 1878. EDUC.: public schools. POLIT. & GOV.: elected judge, Franklin Cty., TX, 1878–82; national organizer, People's Party, 1891–1900; member, People's Party National Cmte., 1892–1900; People's Party candidate for atty. gen. of TX, 1892; People's Party candidate for U.S. House (TX), 1894, 1896; ***candidate for People's Party nomination to presidency of the U.S., 1896; candidate for People's Party nomination to vice presidency of the U.S., 1900***; appointed superintendent of agriculture for the Philippines, 1914 (declined); elected as a Democrat to U.S. House (TX), 1915–17; candidate for Democratic nomination to U.S. House (TX), 1916. BUS. & PROF.: schoolteacher, Winnsboro, TX, 1875–78; atty.; admitted to TX Bar, 1882; law practice, Mt. Vernon, TX, 1882–1900; ed., *Franklin Cty. (TX) Herald*; ed., *Greenville (TX) Herald*; ed., *Alliance Vindicator*; lecturer, Farmers' Alliance; farmer, Sulphur Springs, TX; temperance advocate. MEM.: National Cmte. for an Income Tax; TX Anti-Saloon League (dir.); National Abstainers' Union (Advisory Cmte.); TX Press Assn. (pres., 1886–88). REL.: Church of Christ. RES.: Sulphur Springs, TX.

DAVIS, JEFFERSON FINIS. b. Jun 3, 1808, Christian Cty., KY; d. Dec 6, 1889, New Orleans, LA; par. Samuel Emory and Jane (Cook) Davis; m. Sarah Knox Taylor, Jun 30, 1835; m. 2d, Varina Howell, Feb 26, 1845; c. Samuel Emory; Margaret Howell; Jefferson; Joseph Evan. EDUC.: St. Thomas' Coll., 1821; Transylvania U., 1821; grad. (cum laude), U.S. Military Acad., 1828. POLIT. & GOV.: delegate, MS State Democratic Convention, 1844; presidential elector, Democratic Party, 1844; elected as a Democrat to U.S. House (MS), 1845–46; appointed and subsequently elected as a Democrat to U.S. Senate (MS), 1847–51, 1857–61; ***candidate for Democratic nomination to presidency of the U.S., 1848, 1860; candidate for Democratic nomination to vice presidency of the U.S., 1848, 1852***; Democratic candidate for gov. of MS, 1851; ***Spirit Medium Party candidate for vice presidency of the U.S., c. 1852***; appointed U.S. sec. of war, 1853–57; ***elected president, Confederate States of America, 1861–65***. BUS. & PROF.: soldier; cotton planter, 1835–45. MIL.: commissioned 2d lt., U.S. Army, 1828, 1st lt., 1833, resigned, 1835; col., First Regt., MS Volunteers, 1846–47; commissioned maj. gen., MS Militia, 1861; captured by Union forces, Irwinville, GA, May 10, 1865; imprisoned at Fortress Monroe, VA, 1865–67; indicted for treason but released on bond, May 14, 1867. WRITINGS: *The Rise and Fall of the Confederate Government* (1878–81). REL.: Episc. RES.: Biloxi, MS.

DAVIS, JOHN. b. Jan 13, 1787, Northboro, MA; d. Apr 19, 1854, Worcester, MA; par. Isaac and Anna (Brigham) Davis; m. Eliza Bancroft, Mar 29, 1822; c. John Chandler Bancroft; George Henry; Horace; Hasbrouck; Andrew McFarland. EDUC.: Leicester Acad.; grad. (with honors), Yale U., 1812; studied law under Francis Blake, Worcester, MA. POLIT. & GOV.: elected as a National Republican to U.S. House (MA), 1824–34; elected as a Whig to gov. of MA, 1834–35, 1841–43; elected as a Whig to U.S. Senate (MA), 1835–41, 1845–53; ***candidate for Whig Party nomination to vice presidency of the U.S., 1844***. BUS. & PROF.: atty.; admitted to MA Bar, 1815; law practice, Worcester, MA, 1815. MEM.: American Antiquarian Soc. (pres.). RES.: Worcester, MA.

DAVIS, JOHN WILLIAM. b. Apr 13, 1873, Clarksburg, WV; d. Mar 24, 1955, Charleston, SC; par. John James and Anna (Kennedy) Davis; m. Julia T. McDonald, Jun 20, 1899; m. 2d, Ellen Graham Bassel, Jan 2, 1912; c. Julia McDonald (Mrs. William McMillan Adams; Mrs. Paul West; Mrs. Charles Pratt Healy). EDUC.: A.B., Washington and Lee U., 1892, LL.B., 1895. POLIT. & GOV.: elected as a Democrat to WV State House of Delegates, 1899; presidential elector, Democratic Party, 1900; delegate, Dem. Nat'l. Conv., 1904, 1908, 1912, 1916, 1920, 1924, 1928, 1932; appointed member, WV State Comm. on Uniform State Laws, 1909; elected as a Democrat to U.S. House (WV), 1911–13; appointed solicitor gen. of the U.S., 1913–18; appointed U.S. ambassador to Great Britain, 1918–21; member, American Delegation for Conference with Germans on Treatment and Exchange of Prisoners of War, 1918; ***candidate for Democratic nomination to presidency of the U.S., 1920; Democratic candidate for presidency of the U.S., 1924***. BUS. & PROF.: atty.; admitted to WV Bar, 1895; asst. prof. of law, Washington and Lee U., 1896–97; law practice, Clarksburg, WV, 1897–1913; partner, Davis, Polk, Wardell, Gardiner and Reed (law firm; later Davis, Polk, Wardell, Gardiner, Sunderland and Kiendl), New York, NY, 1921–55. MEM.: American Red Cross (counselor, 1913–18); Middle Temple (Hon. Bencher); ABA (pres., 1922); WV Bar Assn. (pres., 1906); Assn. of the Bar of the City of New York (pres., 1931–32); Phi Kappa Psi; Phi Beta Kappa; Masons (32°); Metropolitan Club; National Press Club; Lawyers Club; Century Club; University Club; Recess Club; Down Town Club; Piping Rock Creek Club; The Links. HON. DEG.: LL.D., Washington and Lee U., 1915; LL.D., U. of WV, 1919; LL.D., U. of Birmingham, England, 1919; LL.D., U. of Glasgow, 1920; LL.D., Union U., 1921; LL.D., Yale U., 1921; LL.D., Dartmouth Coll., 1923; LL.D., Brown U., 1923; LL.D., Princeton U., 1924; LL.D., Oberlin Coll., 1947; LL.D., NY U., 1951; D.C.L., Oxford U., 1950; D.C.L., Columbia U., 1953; D.C.L., Hofstra Coll., 1953. WRITINGS: *The Treaty-Making Power of the United States* (1920); *Party Government in the United States* (1929). REL.: Presb. RES.: Locust Valley, Long Island, NY.

DAVIS, JONATHAN McMILLAN. b. Apr 26, 1871, Franklin Township, Bourbon Cty., KS; d. Jun 27, 1943, Fort Scott, KS; par. Jonathan McMillan and Eve (Holeman) Davis; m. Mollie Purdon, Sep 26, 1894; m. 2d, Mary E. (Winston) Raymond, Dec 16, 1931; c. Russell; Mary McCormick; Lola Becker. EDUC.: U. of KS, 1888–91; U. of NE, 1892–93. POLIT. & GOV.: member, Bourbon Cty. (KS) Democratic Central Cmte., 1893–1900; chm., Democratic Congressional Cmte., Second Congressional District, KS, 1898; alternate-at-large, Dem. Nat'l. Cmte., 1900; elected as a Democrat to KS State House, 1901–03, 1907–13; Democratic candidate for KS State House, 1904; elected as a Democrat to KS State Senate, 1913–17; Democratic candidate for KS State Senate, 1916; Democratic candidate for gov. of KS, 1920, 1924, 1926; elected as a Democrat to gov. of KS, 1923–25; delegate, Dem. Nat'l. Conv., 1924; ***candidate for Democratic nomination to presidency of the U.S., 1924; candidate for Democratic nomination to vice presidency of the U.S., 1924***; Democratic candidate for U.S. Senate (KS), 1930; candidate for Democratic nomination to gov. of KS, 1936; independent candidate for gov. of KS, 1938. BUS. & PROF.: farmer, Bronson, KS. MEM.: Independent Order of Odd Fellows; Masons; Eagles; Elks; Moose; Kiwanis; Knights of Pythias. REL.: Methodist. MISC.: arrested day after expiration of term as gov., indicted twice for bribery; acquitted both times. RES.: Bronson, KS.

DAVIS, MITCHELL JAY. POLIT. & GOV.: ***independent candidate for presidency of the U.S., 1988***. MAILING ADDRESS: 88 Central Park West, New York, NY 10023.

DAVIS, RAYMOND M. b. 1882, Ritchie Cty., WV. EDUC.: rural schools. POLIT. & GOV.: ***candidate for Republican nomination to presidency of the U.S., 1940***; official observer, U.N. Conference, 1945; candidate for delegate, Rep. Nat'l. Conv., 1948. BUS. & PROF.: laborer, oil fields; railroad telegrapher; street car conductor, Los Angeles, CA; author; pres., Davis-Wilson Coal Co., Morgantown, WV; partner, Lucas, Davis Co. (merchandise brokers), Morgantown; sec.-treas., R. M. Davis Coal Co., Morgantown. WRITINGS: *Proposed New International Order* (1942); *The World Begins to Live* (1946). MISC.: pacifist; proponent of U.S. Dept. of Peace; drafted U.N. for Peace Charter, 1945. RES.: Morgantown, WV.

DAVIS, ROGER T. b. Apr 18, 1935, IL; par. Gladys (Morley) Davis. POLIT. & GOV.: ***American Political Party candidate for presidency of the U.S., 1984, 1988, 1992***; American Political Party candidate for gov. of IL, 1986. BUS. & PROF.: wood chopper. MAILING ADDRESS: Route 1, Barry, IL 62312.

DAVIS, SOL GARETH "GARRY." b. Jul 28, 1921, Bar Harbor, ME; par. Meyer and Hilda (Emery) Davis; m. Esther Audrey Peters, Apr 13, 1950 (divorced); m. 2d, Gloria Sandler, Sep 18, 1954; c. three sons; one daughter. EDUC.: Carnegie Inst. of Technology, 1940–41; M.A., Gurukula Inst., Bangalore, India, 1960. POLIT. & GOV.: founder, World Citizen Party, 1954; ***World Citizen Party candidate for presidency of the U.S., 1972, 1976, 1984, 1988***; World Citizen Party candidate for mayor of Washington, DC, 1986; ***New World Order Party candidate for presidency of the U.S., 1992***. BUS. & PROF.: actor; understudy to Danny Kaye; appeared on Broadway in "Let's Face It!" (1940–41), "Three To Make Ready" (1946), "Bless You All" (1951), "Stalag 17" (1953–54); toolmaker; employee, travel agency, New York, NY, 1960; employee, Culligan Industrial Water Service, France, 1971; author. MIL.: bomber pilot, U.S.A.A.F., 1941–45; shot down over Peenemunde, Germany, 1944; interned in Sweden; escaped. MEM.: United World Federalists (resigned); Assn. for the International Registry of World Citizens and People's Assembly (founder); World Service Authority (founder, 1971). WRITINGS: *The World Is My Country* (1961); *World Government, Ready or Not!* (1985). REL.: Unitarian. MISC.: renounced U.S. citizenship to become "World Citizen No. 1," May 26, 1948; arrested at least 27 times; has experienced repeated legal difficulties due to lack of national citizenship. MAILING ADDRESS: 300 Maple St., Burlington, VT 05401.

DAVIS, STERLING P., JR. b. 1932; m. Zula G. Davis. POLIT. & GOV.: elected as a Democrat to MS State Legislature, 1956–60; judge, Fifth District, DeKalb Cty., MS; independent candidate for U.S. Senate (MS), 1982; ***candidate for Democratic nomination to presidency of the U.S., 1984***. MAILING ADDRESS: Route 2, DeKalb, MS 39328.

DAVISON, HENRY POMEROY. b. Jun 13, 1867, Troy, PA; d. May 6, 1922, Locust Valley, Long Island, NY; par. George B. and Henrietta (Pomeroy) Davison; m. Kate Trubee, Apr 13, 1893; c. Henry Pomeroy, Jr.; Frederick Trubee; Alice (Mrs. Artemus L. Gates); Frances. EDUC.: grad., Graylock Inst., 1886; NY Law School; LL.D., U. of PA, 1913. POLIT. & GOV.: ***candidate for Republican nomination to presidency of the U.S., 1920***. BUS. & PROF.: banker; employee, Pomeroy Brothers (banking house), Bridgeport, CT, 1886–91; teller, Astor Place National Bank, New York, NY, 1891–94; asst. cashier, Liberty National Bank, New York, 1894–95, cashier, 1895–98, vice pres., 1898–99, pres., 1899–1902; vice pres., First National Bank, 1902; partner, J. P. Morgan and Co., New York, 1909; dir., chm., exec. cmte., Bankers Trust Co.; dir., First Security Co.; dir., American Foreign Securities Co.; dir., New Jersey and New York R.R. Co.; dir., Guaranty Safe Deposit Co. MEM.: American Red Cross (chm., War Council, 1917–19; maj. gen.; chm., World League of Red Cross Societies, 1919); American Museum of Natural History (trustee; treas.); National Inst. of Social Sciences (treas.); Century Club; Metropolitan Club; Union League Club; University Club; Jekyl Island Club; Piping Rock Club; The Links; National Golf Links of America. AWARDS: Distinguished Service Medal;

named commander, Legion of Honor (France); Knight of the Order of the Crown of Italy. HON. DEG.: LL.D., Yale U.; LL.D., Harvard U.; LL.D., Columbia U.; LL.D., Princeton U.; LL.D., Williams Coll.; LL.D., Bowdoin Coll.; LL.D., NY U. WRITINGS: *The American Red Cross in the Great War* (1920). RES.: New York, NY.

DAWES, CHARLES GATES. b. Aug 27, 1865, Marietta, OH; d. Apr 23, 1951, Evanston, IL; par. Rufus R. and Mary Beman (Gates) Dawes; m. Caro D. Blymer, Jan 24, 1889; c. Rufus Fearing; Carolyn Ericson; Dana McCutcheon; Virginia (Mrs. Richard T. Cragg). EDUC.: A.B., Marietta Coll., 1884, A.M., 1887; LL.B., Cincinnati Law School, 1886. POLIT. & GOV.: member, exec. cmte., Rep. Nat'l. Conv., 1896; appointed comptroller of the currency, 1897–1901; appointed first dir., U.S. Bureau of the Budget, 1921; ***candidate for Republican nomination to presidency of the U.S., 1924, 1928, 1932; elected as a Republican to vice presidency of the U.S., 1925–29; candidate for Republican nomination to vice presidency of the U.S., 1928, 1932***; appointed U.S. ambassador to Great Britain, 1929–32; appointed pres., RFC, 1932–33. BUS. & PROF.: atty.; banker; admitted to NE Bar, 1886; law practice, Lincoln, NE, 1886–94; pres., Central Trust Co., 1902–21, chm., 1921–25, hon. chm., 1930–31; hon. chm. of the board, Central Republic Bank and Trust Co., 1931–32; chm. of the board, City National Bank and Trust Co., 1932–51. MIL.: brig. gen., U.S. Army Corps of Engineers, 1917–19. MEM.: Chicago World's Fair (Finance Cmte., 1933); Chicago Club; Onwentsia Club; Commercial Club; Union League; University Club; Glenview Club. AWARDS: Nobel Peace Prize, 1926; Distinguished Service Medal; Companion of the Bath; commander, Order of St. Maurice and St. Lazarus (Italy); Order of Leopold (Belgium); Legion of Honor (France, 1919). WRITINGS: *Banking System of the United States* (1892); *Essays and Speeches* (1915); *Journal of the Great War* (1921); *First Year of the Budget of the United States* (1923); *Notes as Vice President* (1935); *How Long Prosperity* (1937); *A Journal of Reparations* (1939); *Journal as Ambassador to Great Britain* (1939); *A Journal of the McKinley Years* (1950). REL.: Congregationalist. RES.: Evanston, IL.

DAWSON, MAUREEN GAYLE. POLIT. & GOV.: ***independent candidate for presidency of the U.S., 1992***. MAILING ADDRESS: Box 817, Banff, Alberta, Canada.

DAY, HORACE H. b. Jul 10, 1813, Great Barrington, MA; d. Aug 23, 1878, Manchester, NH; par. William and Mary (Pixley) Day; m. Sarah Wyckoff, Apr 25, 1838 (divorced, 1844); m. 2d, Catherine Alice Day, Sep 14, 1844; c. Sarah (Mrs. Richard W. Bicknell); Nicholas Wyckoff; Horace Waldron; Edward Maynard. POLIT. & GOV.: delegate, Labor Reform Party National Convention, 1872; member, exec. cmte., National Labor Reform Party, 1872; delegate, Equal Rights (Cosmic, Free Love, People's) Party National Convention, 1872; ***candidate for Labor Reform Party nomination to presidency of the U.S., 1872; candidate for Greenback Party nomination to presidency of the U.S., 1876***. BUS. & PROF.: manufacturer; rubber producer, New Brunswick, NJ, 1828–52; owner, Niagara Water Power Co.; manufacturer, Car Springs, 1848; built Power Canal, Niagara Falls, NY, 1860. MEM.: National Labor Union (first vice pres., 1872); Industrial Brotherhood; National Industrial Congress (delegate, 1874); New England Labor Reform Soc. (vice pres., 1871). WRITINGS: *To the Public* (1851); *The Financial System Unmasked and Dissected* (1872). MISC.: involved in protracted litigation with Charles Goodyear over production rights; upon court victory by Goodyear in 1852, Day's rubber business collapsed. RES.: New Brunswick, NJ.

DAY, STEPHEN ALBION. b. Jul 13, 1882, Canton, OH; d. Jan 5, 1950, Evanston, IL; par. William Rufus and Mary Elizabeth (Shaefer) Day; m. Mary Thayer, Nov 14, 1905; m. 2d, Shirley Spoerer; c. Mary Elizabeth; Helen; Stephanie; Stephen Albion, Jr.; Robert L. EDUC.: A.B., U. of MI, 1905; George Washington U. POLIT. & GOV.: sec. to Chief Justice Melville W. Fuller (q.v.), 1905–07; appointed counsel, U.S. Dept. of the Treasury, 1926–28; ***candidate for Republican nomination to presidency of the U.S., 1936***; elected as a Republican to U.S. House (IL), 1941–45; Republican candidate for U.S. House (IL), 1944. BUS. & PROF.: atty.; admitted to OH Bar, 1907; author; partner, Solders, Thayer, Mansfield and Day (law firm), Cleveland, OH, 1907; partner, Pam, Hurd and Day (law firm), Chicago, IL, 1908–12; law practice, Evanston, IL, 1945–50; counsel, Dawes Brothers, Inc. MEM.: ABA; IL Bar Assn.; Chicago Bar Assn.; Chicago Law Inst.; Psi Upsilon; National Industrial Peace League (pres., 1917); Union League; Hamilton Club. WRITINGS: *Federal Appellate Jurisdiction* (revised, 1917); *The Constitutionalists* (1936); *We Must Save the Republic* (1941). REL.: Christian Church. RES.: Evanston, IL.

DAYLONG, BLYTH WILLIAM. POLIT. & GOV.: ***candidate for Democratic nomination to presidency of the U.S., 1988***. MAILING ADDRESS: 915 Main St., Neenah, WI 54956.

DAYTON, WILLIAM LEWIS. b. Feb 17, 1807, Baskingridge, NJ; d. Dec 1, 1864, Paris, France; par. Joel and Nancy (Lewis) Dayton; m. Margaret Elmendorf Van Der Veer, May 22, 1833; c. William Lewis, Jr.; four other sons; two daughters. EDUC.: grad., Princeton U., 1825; studied law, Litchfield, CT; read law under Peter D. Vroom, Somerville, NJ. POLIT. & GOV.: elected as a Whig to NJ State Legislative Council, 1837; assoc. judge, Supreme Court of NJ, 1838–42; appointed and subsequently elected as a Whig to U.S. Senate (NJ), 1842–51; Whig candidate for U.S. Senate (NJ), 1850; ***candidate for Republican nomination to presidency of the U.S., 1856, 1860; Republican candidate for vice presidency of the U.S., 1856***; appointed atty. gen. of NJ, 1857–61; ***candidate for Republican nomination to***

vice presidency of the U.S., 1860; appointed U.S. minister to France, 1861–64. BUS. & PROF.: atty.; admitted to NJ Bar, 1830; law practice, Freehold, NJ; law practice, Trenton, NJ, 1841–42, 1851. MEM.: Smithsonian Institution (regent). HON. DEG.: LL.D., Princeton U., 1857. RES.: Trenton, NJ.

DEAN, DOIL ESKINE. POLIT. & GOV.: ***candidate for Republican nomination to presidency of the U.S., 1992***. MAILING ADDRESS: 7160 Dodge, Romulus, MI 48174.

DEAN, THADDEUS J. married; c. Thaddeus M.; Edwin L.; Luella M. POLIT. & GOV.: sec., Socialist Labor Party, Seattle, WA, 1900; ***candidate for Socialist Labor Party nomination to vice presidency of the U.S., 1900***. BUS. & PROF.: physician. RES.: Seattle, WA.

DEANGLIS, KATHERINE A. POLIT. & GOV.: ***candidate for Republican nomination to vice presidency of the U.S., 1976; independent candidate for vice presidency of the U.S., 1976; candidate for Democratic nomination to presidency of the U.S., 1980***. MAILING ADDRESS: 9117 Pinewood Dr., Loveland, Cincinnati, OH 45140.

DEARBORN, HENRY ALEXANDER SCAMMELL. b. Mar 3, 1783, Exeter, NH; d. Jul 29, 1851, Portland, ME; par. Gen. Henry and Dorcas Osgood (Marble) Dearborn; m. Hannah Swet, May 3, 1807; c. Henry George Raleigh; William; Julia Margaretta (Mrs. Clapp). EDUC.: grad., Coll. of William and Mary, 1803; studied law under William Wirt (q.v.). POLIT. & GOV.: appointed superintendent of fortifications, Portsmouth, NH, 1806; appointed collector, Boston Custom House, 1812–29; Jeffersonian Republican candidate for gov. of MA, 1817; elected as a Jeffersonian Republican to MA State House, 1829–30; member, Governor's Council, MA, 1830; delegate, MA State Constitutional Convention, 1830; elected as an independent to MA State Senate, 1830; elected as an independent to U.S. House (MA), 1831–33; independent candidate for U.S. House (MA), 1832; appointed adj. gen. of MA, 1835–43; elected mayor of Roxbury, MA, 1847–51; ***Native American (Know-Nothing) Party candidate for vice presidency of the U.S., 1848***. BUS. & PROF.: atty.; admitted to MA Bar, 1805; law practice, Salem, MA; author. MIL.: brig. gen., MA Militia, 1812; capt., Ancient and Honorable Artillery Co., 1816. MEM.: American Acad.; Massachusetts Horticultural Soc. (pres.). HON. DEG.: LL.D., Harvard U., 1831. WRITINGS: *Address Before the Berkshire Agricultural Society; Memories of Mount Auburn; History of Navigation and Naval Architecture; Centennial Address on the Settlement of Roxbury; Memoir on the Commerce and Navigation of the Black Sea and the Trade and Maritime Geography of Turkey and Egypt* (1819); *Defense of General Henry Dearborn Against the Attack of General William Hull* (1824); *Monography of the Genius Camelia* (translator, 1838); *Life of Jesus Christ; Life of Com. Bainbridge; Life of W. R. Lee, U.S.A.; Letters on Internal Improvements and Commerce of the West* (1839); *A Sketch of the Life of the Apostle Eliot* (1850); *Grecian Architecture*. RES.: Roxbury, MA.

DeBATES, ESTELLE. b. 1960, Sioux Falls, SD. EDUC.: U. of MN. POLIT. & GOV.: organizer, Socialist Workers Party, Chicago, IL; Socialist Workers Party candidate for city clerk, Chicago, IL, 1991; ***Socialist Workers Party candidate for vice presidency of the U.S., 1992***. BUS. & PROF.: machinist; garment worker; staff writer, *The Militant*, New York, NY. MEM.: Second International Youth Conference for the Reunification of Korea (delegate, 1992); International Assn. of Machinists; Young Socialist Alliance (1982–). MAILING ADDRESS: 191 7th Ave., New York, NY 10011.

DEBERRY, CLIFTON. b. 1925, Holly Springs, MS; m. Carol Elinor Dobbs. EDUC.: grad., Wendell Phillips H.S., Chicago, IL. POLIT. & GOV.: Socialist Workers Party candidate for councilman-at-large, Brooklyn, NY, 1963; ***Socialist Workers Party candidate for presidency of the U.S., 1964, 1980 (as proxy for Andrew Pulley, q.v.)***; Socialist Workers Party candidate for mayor of New York, NY, 1965, 1969; Socialist Workers Party candidate for gov. of NY, 1970; ***Socialist Workers Party candidate for vice presidency of the U.S., 1972 (as proxy for Andrew Pulley, q.v.)***; NY organizer, Socialist Workers Party. BUS. & PROF.: trade union official; house painter; lecturer; political activist. MEM.: Farm Equipment Union; Negro Labor Congress (founder, 1950); Station Wagons-to-Montgomery (organizer, 1956); Negro American Labor Council (founder, 1960). MISC.: first African-American candidate for president to appear on a general election ballot; son-in-law of Farrell Dobbs (q.v.). MAILING ADDRESS: c/o Socialist Workers Party, 2864 Telegraph Ave., Oakland, CA 94609.

DEBS, EUGENE VICTOR. b. Nov 5, 1855, Terre Haute, IN; d. Oct 20, 1926, Elmhurst, IL; par. Jean Daniel and Marguerite Marie (Betterich) Debs; m. Katherine Metzel, Jun 9, 1885; c. none. EDUC.: public schools. POLIT. & GOV.: elected city clerk, Terre Haute, IN, 1879–83; elected as a Democrat to IN State House, 1885–87; ***candidate for People's Party nomination to presidency of the U.S., 1896***; founder, Social Democratic Party, 1897 (member, exec. cmte.); ***Social Democratic Party candidate for presidency of the U.S., 1900; Socialist Party candidate for presidency of the U.S., 1904, 1908, 1912, 1920***; Socialist Party candidate for U.S. House (IN), 1916; ***candidate for Farmer-Labor Party nomination to presidency of the U.S., 1920; candidate for Socialist Party nomination to presidency of the U.S., 1924***; national chm., Socialist Party, 1924–26. BUS. & PROF.: lecturer; labor organizer; locomotive fireman, Terre Haute and Indianapolis R.R., 1871–74; employee, Hulman and Co. (wholesale groceries), 1875–79; ed., *Firemen's Magazine*, 1878–94; assoc. ed., *Appeal to Reason*, 1904–10; ed., *Rip-Saw*; ed., *American Appeal*, 1925–26. MEM.: Brotherhood of Locomotive Firemen (grand sec. and treas.,

1880–93); Brotherhood of Railway Brakemen (organizer, 1884); Switchmen's Mutual Aid Assn. (founder, 1885); American Railway Union (pres., 1893–97); United Mine Workers (organizer, 1897); Western Federation of Miners (organizer, 1897); National Council for Social Democracy (chm., 1897–98); Industrial Workers of the World (founder, 1905); People's Council; Brotherhood of Railway Carmen. WRITINGS: *Law, Labor and Liberty* (1896); *Winning a World* (1900); *The Federal Government and the Chicago Strike* (1904); *Unionism and Socialism* (1904); *The Socialist Party or the Working Class* (1904); *The American Movement* (1904); *Industrial Unionism* (1905); *Class Unionism* (1909); *Craft Unionism* (1909); *Revolutionary Unionism* (1909); *The Growth of Socialism; Liberty; You Railroad Men; Danger Ahead for the Socialist Party in Playing the Game of Politics* (1912); *Labor and Freedom* (1916); *Eugene V. Debs' Canton Speech; Economics, Labor and Capital; Walls and Bars* (1927); *Speeches of Eugene V. Debs* (1929). MISC.: charged with conspiracy in Western Roads Strike, acquitted, 1894; spent six months in jail for contempt of court during Pullman Strike, 1894; convicted of violation of espionage laws and sentenced to 10 years in prison, 1919; released by order of President Warren G. Harding (q.v.), 1921. RES.: Terre Haute, IN.

DECARLO, JOHN PAUL. b. Jun 2, 1928, Alabama City, AL; par. Paul Sebastian and Mary Josephine (Damico) DeCarlo; m. Elizabeth Collins, Jun 19, 1950; c. Mary Elise. EDUC.: Howard Coll., 1952; LL.B., Birmingham Law School, 1959; J.D., Cumberland School of Law, 1965. POLIT. & GOV.: deputy district atty., Birmingham, AL, 1965–72; national campaign coordinator, George C. Wallace (q.v.) for President Campaign, 1968; appointed asst. dir. of banking, AL; appointed assoc. judge, AL Court of Criminal Appeals, 1972–; campaign adviser, George Wallace Campaign, 1972; ***candidate for Democratic nomination to vice presidency of the U.S., 1972***. BUS. & PROF.: atty.; admitted to AL Bar. MIL.: U.S. Army. MEM.: ABA; AL Bar Assn.; Birmingham Bar Assn.; American Jud. Soc.; American Trial Lawyers Assn.; Sigma Delta Kappa. REL.: R.C. MAILING ADDRESS: 3236 Norwood Blvd., Birmingham, AL 35234.

DECHERT, ALAN. POLIT. & GOV.: ***candidate for Democratic nomination to presidency of the U.S., 1988***. MAILING ADDRESS: c/o Cmte. for a Sustainable Soc., Florence Wallack, 1442A Walnut St., #180, Berkeley, CA 94709.

DECKER, RUTHERFORD LOSEY. b. May 27, 1904, Wellsburg, NY; d. Sep 21, 1972, Liberty, MO; m. Gladys Decker; c. two daughters; James D. EDUC.: Elmira Free Acad.; Colgate U.; Colgate Theological Seminary. POLIT. & GOV.: ***Prohibition Party candidate for presidency of the U.S., 1960; candidate for Prohibition Party nomination to presidency of the U.S., 1964 (declined)***; presidential elector, American Party, 1968. BUS. & PROF.: minister; missionary, American Baptist Home Mission Soc., La Veta, CO, 1923; pastor, Berkeley Baptist Church, Denver, CO; served pastorates in Fort Morgan, CO, and Laramie, WY; founder, Denver (CO) Rescue Mission; founder, CO School of the Bible; pastor, Temple Baptist Church, Kansas City, MO, 1943–72. MEM.: Rocky Mountain Bible Conference (pres.); KS-MO Baptist Welfare Assn. (pres.); Temple Foundation (founder); National Assn. of Evangelicals (founder; vice pres., 1943; pres., 1946–47; exec. sec., 1948–52). HON. DEG.: D.D., John Brown U., 1945; LL.D., Houghton Coll., 1946. REL.: Bapt. (pres., CO Convention). RES.: Kansas City, MO.

DEFELICE, GERALD THOMAS. b. May 8, 1949, New Haven, CT; par. Frank Carl and Laura (Mastiangelo) Defelice; single. EDUC.: B.A., Providence Coll., 1971; Southern CT State Coll., 1971–72; Northeastern U., 1975–76. POLIT. & GOV.: candidate for Republican nomination to gov. of CT, 1978; ***candidate for Republican nomination to presidency of the U.S., 1980, 1984, 1988; independent candidate for presidency of the U.S., 1992***. BUS. & PROF.: employee, fashion and trend design, textile industry; employee, petroleum allocation and sales; employee, automotive sales and service; employee, import and export business. MEM.: Providence Coll. Alumni Assn. (pres., Boston Chapter, 1976). REL.: R.C. MAILING ADDRESS: 1320 Cromwell Hills Dr., Cromwell, CT 06416.

DEFOSSE, DANIEL G. POLIT. & GOV.: ***candidate for Democratic nomination to presidency of the U.S., 1984***. MAILING ADDRESS: 142 Timberlane, Antioch, IL 60002.

DEHART, FRANK. POLIT. & GOV.: ***candidate for Republican nomination to presidency of the U.S., 1988***. MAILING ADDRESS: P.O. Box 1105, Des Moines, IA 50311.

DEHERRERA, PRIMERO HENRY. POLIT. & GOV.: ***independent candidate for presidency of the U.S., 1992***. MAILING ADDRESS: 1472 Knox Court, Denver, CO 80204.

DEJOHN, ROBERT. POLIT. & GOV.: ***independent candidate for presidency of the U.S., 1980***. MAILING ADDRESS: 318 South Fairview Ave., Upper Darby, PA 19082.

DE LA MATYR, GILBERT. b. Jul 8, 1825, Pharsalia, NY; d. May 17, 1892, Akron, OH. EDUC.: grad., Methodist Episcopal Theological Course, 1854. POLIT. & GOV.: elected as a Nationalist-Democrat to U.S. House (IN), 1879–81; Prohibition Party candidate for U.S. Senate (IN), 1881; Union Labor Party candidate for gov. of CO, 1888; ***candidate for Union Labor Party nomination to presidency of the U.S., 1888; candidate for Prohibition Party nomination to vice presidency of the U.S., 1892***. BUS. & PROF.: minister; itinerant elder, Methodist Episcopal Church, 1868 (presiding elder, one term); pastor, Methodist Episcopal Church, Indianapolis, IN; pastor, Methodist Episcopal Church, Denver, CO, 1881; pastor, First

Methodist Episcopal Church, Akron, OH, 1889–92. MIL.: chaplain, Eighth Regt., NY Heavy Artillery, U.S. Army, 1862–65. REL.: Methodist Episcopal Church. RES.: Akron, OH.

DE LEON, DANIEL. b. Dec 14, 1852, Curaçao, West Indies; d. May 11, 1914, New York, NY; par. Solomon and Sarah (Jesurum) DeLeon; m. Sara Lobo, Aug 2, 1882; m. 2d, Betha Canary, Jun 10, 1892; c. Grover Cleveland; Solon; two infant sons. EDUC.: A.M., Ph.B., U. of Leyden; LL.B., Columbia U., 1878. POLIT. & GOV.: Socialist Labor Party candidate for gov. of NY, 1891, 1902, 1904; Socialist Labor Party candidate for NY State Assembly, 1892, 1898, 1899; Socialist Labor Party candidate for NY state sec. of state, 1893; Socialist Labor Party candidate for U.S. House (NY), 1894, 1896, 1908; delegate, Socialist Labor Party National Convention, 1896, 1900, 1904, 1912 (chm.); ***candidate for Socialist Labor Party nomination to presidency of the U.S., 1896 (declined)***. BUS. & PROF.: assoc. ed., Spanish newspaper, New York, NY; atty.; law practice, TX; ed., *Weekly People*, 1892–1914; ed., *Daily People*, 1900–1914; Prize lecturer on Latin American diplomacy, Columbia U., 1886–91. MEM.: Knights of Labor (1885); Socialist Trade and Labor Alliance (founder, 1895); Industrial Workers of the World (founder, 1905; ousted, 1908); Workers' International Industrial Union (founder, 1908). WRITINGS: *What Means This Strike?* (1898); *Two Pages from Roman History* (1903); *Socialist Reconstruction of Society* (1905); *Abolition of Poverty* (1911); *Capitalism Means War; Capitalism vs. Socialism; A Decadent Jeffersonian on the Socialist Gridiron; Socialism vs. "Individualism"; Ten Canons of the Proletarian Revolution; Anti-Semitism: Its Cause and Cure; As to Politics; Berger's Hit and Misses; Burning Question of Trades Unionism; De Leon-Berry Debate; De Leon-Carmody Debate; De Leon-Harriman Debate; Father Gassoniana; Fifteen Questions; Flashlights of the Amsterdam Congress; Industrial Unionism; James Madison and Karl Marx; Marx on Mallock; Money; Reform or Revolution; Russia in Revolution; Socialism vs. Anarchism; The Trusts; Ultra-montanism; The Eighteenth Brumaire of Louis Napoleon* (translator); *The Mysteries of the People* (translator); *Unity; Vulgar Economy; Watson on the Gridiron; Woman's Suffrage*. MISC.: active in Nationalist Movement; chief theoretician of Socialist Labor Party. RES.: Pleasantville, NY.

DELLUMS, RONALD VERNIE. b. Nov 24, 1935, Oakland, CA; par. Vernie and Willa Dellums; m. (divorced); m. 2d, Leola Roscoe Higgs; c. Machael; Pamela; Piper; Erick; Brandy. EDUC.: A.B., Oakland City Coll., 1958; B.A., San Francisco State Coll., 1960; M.S.W., U. of CA, 1962. POLIT. & GOV.: elected as a Democrat to Berkeley (CA) City Council, 1967–71; elected as a Democrat to U.S. House (CA), 1971–; ***candidate for Democratic nomination to vice presidency of the U.S., 1972, 1976 (declined)***; delegate, Dem. Nat'l. Conv., 1976; ***The Black Assembly candidate for presidency of the U.S., 1976 (declined); candidate for Democratic nomination to presidency of the U.S., 1980***. BUS. & PROF.: psychiatric social worker, CA State Dept. of Mental Hygiene, 1962–64; program dir., Bayview Community Center, San Francisco, CA, 1964–66; dir., Hunters Point Youth Opportunity Center, 1965– 66; planning consultant, Bay Area Social Planning Council, 1966–67; dir., Concentrated Employment Program, San Francisco Economic Opportunity Council, 1967–68; senior consultant, Social Dynamics, Inc., 1968–70; lecturer, San Francisco State Coll.; lecturer, U. of CA at Berkeley. MIL.: U.S.M.C. Reserves, 1954–56. MEM.: Black Caucus; Congressional Cmte. to Preserve Religious Freedom; Congress for Peace Through Law; Democratic Study Group; A.C.L.U.; NAACP (life member). AWARDS: "Man of the Year," *Sun Reporter*; "Outstanding Politician of the Year," Oakland Black Caucus; one of 100 "Most Influential Blacks," *Ebony Magazine*; one of "America's Top 200 Young Leaders," *Time Magazine*, 1974. HON. DEG.: LL.D., Wilberforce U., 1975. MAILING ADDRESS: 1039 Amito Dr., Berkeley, CA 94705.

DEL SESTO, CHRISTOPHER. b. Mar 10, 1907, Providence, RI; d. Dec 27, 1973; par. Eraclio and Rose (Geremia) Del Sesto; m. Lola Elda Faraone, Oct 12, 1933; c. Christopher T.; Ronald W.; Gregory T. EDUC.: B.B.A. (cum laude), Boston U., 1928; LL.B. (cum laude), Georgetown U., 1939; NY U.; U. of Miami; Practicing Law Inst. of NY. POLIT. & GOV.: chief accountant, state treasurer's office, RI; member, RI State Unemployment Relief Comm.; member, RI State Retirement Board; member, RI State Emergency Public Works Comm.; budget dir., State of RI, 1933; dir. of finance, State of RI, 1935; staff, chief accountant of S.E.C.; special asst. to atty. gen. of the U.S., Anti-Trust Division, Dept. of Justice, 1937–40; RI state dir., OPA, WWII; Republican candidate for mayor of Providence, RI, 1952; Republican candidate for gov. of RI, 1956, 1960; elected as a Republican to gov. of RI, 1959–61; ***candidate for Republican nomination to vice presidency of the U.S., 1960 (declined)***; assoc. justice, RI Superior Court, 1966–73. BUS. & PROF.: C.P.A.; atty.; admitted to DC Bar, 1937; admitted to RI Bar, 1940; admitted to practice before U.S. Dept. of the Treasury, Tax Court of the U.S., and the Supreme Court of the U.S.; partner, Del Sesto and Biener (law firm), Providence, RI; instructor, Taunton (MA) H.S., Boston U., Northeastern U. MEM.: ABA; RI Bar Assn.; RI Soc. of Certified Public Accountants; RI State Coll. (trustee); American Inst. of Accountants; St. Liberato Catholic Soc.; National Assn. of Cost Accountants; Dunes Club; Italo-American Club of RI. AWARDS: citation for Civilian Contribution to War Effort, *Providence Journal*, 1944. RES.: RI.

DELUCA, RONALD D. b. 1949. EDUC.: D.D.S., U. of Detroit, 1974. POLIT. & GOV.: ***Christian Conservative Coalition Party candidate for presidency of the U.S., 1988***. BUS. & PROF.: dentist; dental practice, Detroit, MI; dental practice, Garden City, MI. MAILING ADDRESS: 7110 Venoy, Garden City, MI 48135.

DELZINGARO, CHRISTINA. POLIT. & GOV.: ***candidate for Democratic nomination to presidency of the U.S.,***

1984. MAILING ADDRESS: 1266 Prince Ave., #1, Athens, GA 30606.

DE MAINTENON, RALPH. POLIT. & GOV.: ***independent candidate for presidency of the U.S., 1988***. MAILING ADDRESS: P.O. Box 20041, Lowry Air Force Base, Denver, CO 80230.

DEMAREE, THOMAS BASCOM. b. Oct 25, 1844, Harrodsburg, KY; d. Sep 16, 1916. EDUC.: public schools, Mackville, KY. POLIT. & GOV.: delegate, Prohibition National Convention, 1876; member, Prohibition Party National Cmte., 1876–84, 1900–1916; Prohibition Party candidate for U.S. House (KY), 1894, 1906; Prohibition Party candidate for gov. of KY, 1895, 1903; state chm., KY State Prohibition Party, 1899–1916; ***candidate for Prohibition Party nomination to vice presidency of the U.S., 1908***. BUS. & PROF.: schoolteacher, Mercer City, KY; lecturer, Independent Order of Good Templars. MIL.: pvt., Company C, 11th KY Cavalry, Civil War; prisoner-of-war, 1863–64. MEM.: Independent Order of Good Templars. RES.: Union Mills, KY.

DEMARIS, GEORGE. POLIT. & GOV.: ***Save the U.S. Party candidate for vice presidency of the U.S., 1980***. MAILING ADDRESS: Box 118, Harrisonville, NJ 08039.

DEMKO, JOHN FRANK. b. Oct 14, 1931, Bridgeport, CT; par. John S. and Julia R. Demko; m. Beverly L. Voight; c. none. EDUC.: Congress H.S., Bridgeport, CT, 1946–47. POLIT. & GOV.: Social Democrat candidate for town clerk, Bridgeport, CT, 1970; ***Independent Democratic candidate for presidency of the U.S., 1976***. BUS. & PROF.: gen. machine operator, Portor Box Machine Co., Bridgeport, CT, 1949–52; employee, Avco-Lycoming, Stratford, CT; employee, CT Fair Assn.; importer-exporter; owner, JFD Writers and Talent Club, Bridgeport, CT; notary public, 1960–; restricted radio-telephone operator's permit, Federal Communications Comm. MIL.: pvt., U.S. Army, 1952–54; U.S. Army Honor Guard, Fort Myers, VA, 1953; Korean Service Medal with Bronze Star; U.N. Service Medal; National Defense Service Medal; Presidential Unit Citation; Purple Heart; Combat Infantry Badge. MEM.: VFW; National Veterans Fraternity, Inc. MAILING ADDRESS: P.O. Box 264, Bridgeport, CT 06601.

DEMOREST, WILLIAM JENNINGS. b. Jun 10, 1822, New York, NY; d. Apr 9, 1895, New York, NY; m. Margaret W. Poole, 1845 (d. 1857); m. 2d, Ellen Louise Curtis; c. William Curtis; Vienna W. (Mrs. J. M. Gano); Henry C.; Evelyn L. (Mrs. Alexander G. Rea). EDUC.: public schools. POLIT. & GOV.: Prohibition Party candidate for lt. gov. of NY, 1885, 1888; presidential elector, Prohibition Party, 1888; Prohibition Party candidate for mayor of New York, NY, 1890; ***candidate for Prohibition Party nomination to presidency of the U.S., 1892***. BUS. & PROF.: employee, mercantile business; journalist; publisher, *Mirror of Fashion;* publisher, *New York Illustrated News*, 1859; publisher, *Phunniest Phun;* publisher, *Demorest's Monthly Magazine;* publisher, *Young America;* publisher, *The Constitution;* partner, J. J. Little and Co. (printing firm); temperance advocate; abolitionist. MEM.: National Anti-Nuisance League (pres.); Washingtonians; Sons of Temperance; National Prohibition Bureau (treas.); National Constitutional League. WRITINGS: *The Purpose and Policy of Prohibition* (co-author). REL.: Reformed Church. RES.: New York, NY.

DENBY, EDWIN. b. Feb 18, 1870, Evansville, IN; d. Feb 8, 1929, Detroit, MI; par. Charles and Martha (Fitch) Denby; m. Marion Bartlett Thurber, Mar 18, 1911; c. Edwin, Jr.; Marion. EDUC.: grad., Evansville (IN) H.S.; LL.B., U. of MI, 1896. POLIT. & GOV.: elected as a Republican to MI State House, 1903–05; elected as a Republican to U.S. House (MI), 1905–11; Republican candidate for U.S. House (MI), 1910; pres., Detroit (MI) Charter Comm., 1913–14; appointed chief probation officer, Recorder's Court, Detroit, MI, 1920; appointed U.S. sec. of the navy, 1921–24; ***candidate for Republican nomination to presidency of the U.S., 1924***. BUS. & PROF.: Chinese Imperial Maritime Customs Service, 1887–94; atty.; admitted to MI Bar, 1896; law practice, Detroit, MI; partner, Denby, Kennedy and O'Brien (law firm), Detroit, MI, 1924–29; founder, Hupp Motor Co.; incorporator, Federal Motor Truck Co.; incorporator, Detroit Motor Bus Co.; dir., National Bank of Commerce, Detroit, MI; dir., Denby Motor Truck Co. MIL.: gunner's mate, USS *Yosemite*, 1898; pvt., U.S.M.C., 1917, maj. (reserves), 1919. MEM.: Detroit Board of Commerce (pres., 1916–17); Detroit Club; University Club. REL.: Episc. MISC.: noted football player at U. of MI; implicated in Teapot Dome Scandal, 1924; exonerated by U.S. Supreme Court, 1927. RES.: Detroit, MI.

DENISON, JOHN GREENE. b. May 25, 1947, Los Angeles, CA; par. Frank Greene, Jr. and Ruth Jane (Petit) Denison; m. claims 31 common law marriages; c. Lafayette Greene. EDUC.: U. of PA, 1965–67; U. of OR, 1975. POLIT. & GOV.: ***candidate for Republican nomination to presidency of the U.S., 1988***. BUS. & PROF.: artist; writer, 1969–; asst. foreman, city dump, Palo Alto, CA, 1973–74; volunteer minister, Church of Scientology, Flag Land Base, Clearwater, FL, 1976–; contributor, *Canadian Forum*, Toronto, Canada, 1971; contributor, *Denver Quarterly*, 1978; contributor, *Kansas Quarterly*, 1980; contributor, *New York Times Book Review*, 1987. MEM.: National Organization for Women (founding member, 1972). REL.: Christian Science; Church of Scientology. MISC.: received Sharpshooter Award, NRA, 1959. MAILING ADDRESS: 447 Irvine Ave., Newport Beach, CA 92663.

DENNERIL, NORBERT GEORGE, JR. b. 1929. POLIT. & GOV.: candidate for Democratic nomination to U.S. Senate (OH), 1982; ***candidate for Democratic nomination to presidency of the U.S., 1988***. MAILING ADDRESS: 23441 Sprague Rd., Columbia Township, OH 44028.

DENNIS, DELMAR DANIEL. b. May 9, 1940, Scott Cty., MS; par. William Benjamin and Carrie Anna Spier; m. Joyce E. Caldwell, Jun 1, 1957 (divorced, 1967); m. 2d, Nancy Stradley, May 26, 1968; c. Rebekah Joyce; Delma Suellen; Delmar Andrew; Stephen Stradley; Melanie Jane. EDUC.: grad., Harperville (MS) H.S.; Clarke Memorial Ministerial Coll., Newton, MS. POLIT. & GOV.: public relations dir., American Party; ***American Party candidate for presidency of the U.S., 1984, 1988***. BUS. & PROF.: Baptist preacher, 1954–58; ordained minister, Baptist Church, 1958–68; undercover agent, FBI, 3 years; staff, John Birch Soc., 1969–74; publisher, *Mountain Trails*, Pigeon Forge, TN; publisher, *Good News*, Pigeon Forge, TN. MEM.: White Christian Protective and Legal Defense Fund; Rotary Club (pres.); Masons (32°); Shriners; Knights Templar. REL.: Southern Bapt. MISC.: noted as paid informer in cases against the Ku Klux Klan. MAILING ADDRESS: Route 3, Walnut Grove Rd., Sevierville, TN 37862.

DENNISON, WILLIAM. b. Nov 23, 1815, Cincinnati, OH; d. Jun 15, 1882, Columbus, OH; par. William and Mary (Carter) Dennison; m. Anna E. Neil, c. 1840; c. Neil; Herman; Alan; Lizzie (Mrs. Forsyth); Anna (Mrs. Herbert R. Smith); Lucy (Mrs. Rufus Clarke); Jennie. EDUC.: grad., Miami U., Oxford, OH, 1835; read law in office of Nathaniel G. Pendleton. POLIT. & GOV.: elected member, Columbus (OH) City Council; elected as a Whig to OH State Senate, 1848–50; presidential elector, Whig Party, 1852; delegate, Rep. Nat'l. Conv., 1856, 1860, 1864 (chm.), 1868, 1872, 1876, 1880; elected as a Republican to gov. of OH, 1861–63; candidate for Republican nomination to U.S. Senate (OH), 1861, 1880; appointed postmaster gen. of the U.S., 1864–66; ***candidate for Republican nomination to vice presidency of the U.S., 1872, 1880***; appointed commissioner, DC, 1874–78. BUS. & PROF.: atty.; admitted to OH Bar, 1840; law practice, Columbus, OH, 1840–48; pres., Exchange Bank; promoter, Hocking Valley R.R.; pres., Columbus and Xenia R.R.; founder, Columbus Rolling Mills. MEM.: Franklin Cty. Agricultural Soc. HON. DEG.: LL.D., Marietta Coll., 1860. RES.: Columbus, OH.

DENOMA, MICHAEL BERNARD. POLIT. & GOV.: ***candidate for Republican nomination to presidency of the U.S., 1980***. MAILING ADDRESS: 8217 Ackley St., Alexandria, VA 22309.

DEPEW, CHAUNCEY MITCHELL. b. Apr 23, 1834, Peekskill, NY; d. Apr 5, 1928, New York, NY; par. Isaac and Martha (Mitchell) Depew; m. Elise A. Hegeman, Nov 9, 1871; m. 2d, May Palmer, Dec 27, 1901; c. Chauncey Mitchell, Jr. EDUC.: Mrs. Westbrook's Acad.; grad., Peekskill Military Acad., 1852; A.B., Yale U., 1856, LL.D., 1887. POLIT. & GOV.: delegate, NY State Republican Convention, 1858; elected as a Republican to NY State Assembly, 1861–63; elected as a Republican, NY state sec. of state, 1863–65; appointed U.S. minister to Japan, 1865 (declined); appointed cty. clerk, Westchester Cty., NY, 1867; elected NY state immigration commissioner, 1870 (declined); Liberal Republican Party candidate for lt. gov. of NY, 1872; appointed member, NY State Capitol Comm., 1874; appointed NY state boundary commissioner, 1875; Republican candidate for U.S. Senate (NY), 1881, 1910; elected as a Republican to U.S. Senate (NY), 1885 (declined), 1899–1911; ***candidate for Republican nomination to presidency of the U.S., 1888***; delegate, Rep. Nat'l. Conv., 1888, 1892, 1896, 1900, 1904, 1908, 1912, 1916, 1920, 1924; appointed U.S. sec. of state, 1892 (declined); ***candidate for Republican nomination to vice presidency of the U.S., 1896***. BUS. & PROF.: orator; atty.; admitted to NY Bar, 1858; counsel, dir., New York and Harlem R.R., 1866–69; counsel, New York Central and Hudson River R.R., 1869, gen. counsel, 1875, second vice pres., 1882–85, pres., 1885–98, chm. of the board, 1899; dir., Chicago and Northwestern R.R., 1877; pres., West Shore R.R., to 1898; chm. of the board, New York Central R.R., 1898–1928; dir., Western Union Telegraph Co.; dir., Chicago, St. Paul, Minneapolis and Omaha R.R. Co.; dir., Cleveland, Cincinnati, Chicago and St. Louis Railway Co.; dir., Canada Southern Railway Co.; dir., The Wagner Palace Car Co.; dir., Union Trust Co.; dir., Equitable Life Assurance Soc.; dir., Western Transit Co.; dir., West Shore and International Bridge Co.; dir., Morris Run Coal Mining Co.; dir., Clearfield Bituminous Coal Corp.; dir., Hudson River Bridge Co.; dir., The Canadian Southern Bridge Co.; dir., Niagara River Bridge Co.; dir., Brooklyn Storage and Warehouse Co.; dir., NY Mutual Gas Light Co.; trustee, American Safe Deposit Co.; dir., Niagara Grand Island Bridge Co.; dir., Tonawanda Island Bridge Co.; dir., Beech Creek R.R. Co.; dir., Buffalo Erie Basin R.R. Co.; dir., Buffalo, Thousand Islands and Portland R.R. Co.; dir., Carthage and Adirondack Railway; dir., Carthage, Watertown and Sackets Harbor R.R. Co.; dir., Central Dock and Terminal Railway; dir., Chesapeake and Ohio Railway Co.; dir., Clearwater and Raquette Lake R.R. Co.; trustee, American Surety Co.; dir., Columbus, Hope and Greensburg R.R. Co.; dir., Delaware and Hudson Co.; dir., Detroit River Tunnel Co.; dir., Dunkirk, Allegheny Valley and Pittsburgh R.R. Co.; dir., Fulton Chain R.R. Co.; dir., Fulton Navigation Co.; dir., Gouveneur and Oswegatchie R.R. Co.; dir., Jersey City and Bayonne R.R. Co.; dir., Lake Erie, Alliance and Wheeling R.R. Co.; chm. of the board, Lake Shore and Michigan Southern Railway Co.; dir., Mahoning Coal R.R. Co.; dir., Mercantile Trust Co.; dir., Merchants Dispatch Transportation Co.; dir., MI Central R.R. Co.; dir., Michigan, Midland and Canada R.R. Co.; dir., Mohawk and Malone Railway Co.; dir., New Jersey Junction R.R. Co.; dir., New Jersey Shore Line R.R. Co.; dir., New York and Ottawa Railway Co.; dir., New York and Putnam R.R. Co.; dir., New York, Chicago and St. Louis R.R. Co.; dir., NY State Realty and Terminal Co.; dir., Niagara Falls Branch R.R. Co.; dir., Oswego and Rome R.R. Co.; dir., Pine Creek Railway Co.; dir., Raquette Lake Railway Co.; dir., Rome, Watertown and Ogdensburg R.R. Co.; dir., Rutland R.R. Co.; dir., St. Lawrence and Adirondack Railway Co.; dir., Spuyten Duyvil and Port Morris R.R. Co.; dir., Standard Trust Co.; dir., Syracuse, Geneva and Corning Railway Co.; dir., Terminal Railway of Buffalo; dir., Tivoli Hollow R.R. Co.; dir., Toledo, Canada Southern and Detroit Railway Co.; dir., Toluca Electric Light and Power Co.; dir., Utica and Black River R.R. Co.; dir., Wallkill Valley R.R. Co. MIL.: col., judge advocate, 5th Div., NY National Guard, 1873–81. MEM.: Soc. of the Cincinnati; Yale Corp. (fellow); NY U. (regent, 1874–1904); Union League Club (pres.); Yale Alumni Assn. (pres.); Lotus Club; Montauk Club; SAR (NY pres.); Metropolitan Club; University Club; Century Club; Lawyers Club; Tuxedo Club; Republican Club; Press Club; Players' Club; Quaint Club. WRITINGS: *My Memories of Eighty Years* (1922). RES.: New York, NY.

DERN, GEORGE HENRY. b. Sep 8, 1872, Scribner, NE; d. Aug 27, 1936, Washington, DC; par. John and Elizabeth (Dern) Dern; m. Lottie Brown, Jun 7, 1899; c. Mary Joanna (Mrs. Harry Baxter); John; Louise; William Brown; Margaret; Elizabeth Ida; James George. EDUC.: grad., Fremont (NE) Normal Coll., 1888; U. of NE, 1893–94. POLIT. & GOV.: elected as a Democrat-Progressive to UT State Senate, 1915–23; member, UT State Council of Defense; elected as a Democrat to gov. of UT, 1925–33; ***candidate for Democratic nomination to vice presidency of the U.S., 1932***; appointed U.S. sec. of war, 1933–36. BUS. & PROF.: miner, UT, 1894; treas., Mercur Gold Mining and Milling Co., 1894–1900; gen. mgr., Consolidated Mercur Gold Mines Co., 1900–1913; gen. mgr., Tintic Mining Co., Silver City, UT, 1915–19; mgr., various other mining interests; vice pres., mgr., Holt-Christensen Process Co., 1913; dir., Security National Bank; dir., First Security Trust Co.; dir., First National Bank; dir., Mutual Creamery Co.; joint inventor (with Theodore P. Holt), Holt-Dern Ore Roaster. MEM.: American Inst. of Mining and Metallurgical Engineers; Masons (33°; Knights Templar; Shriners; Grand Master of UT, 1913); National Governors' Conference (chm., 1929–30); Delta Tau Delta; American Mining Congress (dir.); Commercial Club; University Club; Alta Club; Rotary Club. REL.: Congregationalist. RES.: Salt Lake City, UT.

DER SARKISIAN, ROSA. b. Jul 26, 1930, Lowell, MA. POLIT. & GOV.: ***Kosmokracy candidate for presidency of the U.S., 1976***. MISC.: known as "Messiah God Rosa the Rose"; "Goddess, Dictator, Messiah God Rosa the Rose . . . Boss, President, Dictator, God, Messiah, Commander-in-Chief, Spiritual Leader, Political Advisor, Legal-Judicial Chief"; "Mother-Boss, Dictator-President, Teacher-Ruler"; founder of Kosmokracy. MAILING ADDRESS: P.O. Box 25829, Los Angeles, CA 90025.

DE SHON, CHARLES WESLEY. b. Feb 21, 1925, Clarksdale, MO; par. Everett and Maggie (Johynson) De Shon; m. Joann Whetston (divorced); c. Pamela Ann; Wesley Dean; Terrence Charles; Brian Wayne; Mitchell Joel. EDUC.: Union Star H.S. POLIT. & GOV.: candidate for Democratic nomination to mayor of St. Joseph, MO, 1966, 1978; ***Whig Party candidate for presidency of the U.S., 1976, 1980***. BUS. & PROF.: carpenter; plumber; farmer; electrician; packing house worker; railroad employee; owner, gasoline station, St. Joseph, MO; dairyman; brewery employee. MIL.: meteorologist, U.S. Navy, WWII. WRITINGS: *I Found Heaven on the Road to Hell*. REL.: Christian. MAILING ADDRESS: 2811 South 36th St., St. Joseph, MO 64503.

DESMOND, JOHN J., JR. par. John J. Desmond, Sr. POLIT. & GOV.: ***independent candidate for presidency of the U.S., 1976***. MISC.: inmate, McNeil Island Federal Penitentiary, Steilacoom, WA. MAILING ADDRESS: Box 1000, Steilacoom, WA 98388.

DETWEILER, RAYMOND FREED. POLIT. & GOV.: ***independent candidate for presidency of the U.S., 1992***. BUS. & PROF.: carpenter. MAILING ADDRESS: 27 Franklin Ave., Souderton, PA 18964.

DEUKMEJIAN, GEORGE. b. Jun 6, 1928, Albany, NY; par. George and Alice (Gairdan) Deukmejain; m. Gloria M. Saatjian, 1957; c. Leslie Ann; George Krikor; Andrea Diane. EDUC.: B.A., Siena Coll.; J.D., St. John's U. POLIT. & GOV.: elected as a Republican to CA State Assembly, 1963–67; elected as a Republican to CA State Senate, 1967–79; elected as a Republican to atty. gen. of CA, 1979–83; elected as a Republican to gov. of CA, 1983–91; ***candidate for Republican nomination to presidency of the U.S., 1988; candidate for Republican nomination to vice presidency of the U.S., 1988***. BUS. & PROF.: atty., 1952–. MIL.: pvt., corp., U.S. Army, 1953–55. MEM.: Lions; Elks; C. of C. REL.: Episc. MAILING ADDRESS: 5366 East Broadway, Long Beach, CA 90903.

DEUTSCH, BARRY J. POLIT. & GOV.: ***candidate for Democratic nomination to presidency of the U.S., 1992***. MAILING ADDRESS: New York, NY.

DEVER, PAUL ANDREW. b. Jan 15, 1903, Boston, MA; d. Apr 11, 1958, Cambridge, MA; par. Joseph Patrick and Anna Amelia (McAlevy) Dever; single. EDUC.: grad., Boston Latin School, 1919; Pace Inst.; Northeastern U.; LL.B. (cum laude), Boston U., 1926. POLIT. & GOV.: elected as a Democrat to MA State House, 1929–35; elected as a Democrat to atty. gen. of MA, 1935–41; Democratic candidate for gov. of MA, 1940, 1952; Democratic candidate for lt. gov. of MA, 1946; elected as a Democrat to gov. of MA, 1949–53; ***candidate for Democratic nomination to presidency of the U.S., 1952***; delegate, Dem. Nat'l. Conv., 1952 (keynoter), 1956. BUS. & PROF.: atty.; admitted to MA Bar, 1926; law practice, MA, 1926–58; lecturer, Boston U. School of Law, 1941–42. MIL.: lt. commander, U.S.N.R., 1942–45. MEM.: American Legion; VFW; Elks; Phi Delta Phi; Boston Bar Assn.; Cambridge Bar Assn.; ABA; Woolsack Soc.; Knights of Columbus (grand knight); Ancient and Honorable Artillery Co. (chm., Boston Chapter). REL.: R.C. RES.: Boston, MA.

DEVER, WILLIAM EMMETT. b. Mar 13, 1862, Woburn, MA; d. Sep 3, 1929, Chicago, IL; par. Patrick James and Mary A. (Lynch) Dever; m. Katherine E. Conway, Jan 5, 1885; c. Daniel R.; George A. EDUC.: LL.B., Chicago Coll. of Law, 1890. POLIT. & GOV.: member, Cook Cty. (IL) Democratic Central Cmte.; member, Chicago (IL) Planning Comm.; elected as a Democrat, alderman, 17th Ward, Chicago, 1902–10; judge, Superior Court of Cook Cty., 1910–16; justice, IL State Court of Appeals, 1916–23; elected as a Democrat to mayor of Chicago, 1923–27; delegate, Dem. Nat'l. Conv., 1924; ***candidate for Democratic nomination to presidency of the U.S., 1924***; Democratic candidate for mayor of Chicago, 1926. BUS. & PROF.: leather manufacturer, Woburn, MA, 1881–84; employee, White and Co., 1884–86; employee, Grey, Clark and Engle, Chicago, 1886–89; atty.; admitted to IL Bar, 1890; law practice, Chicago; vice pres., Trust Officer, Bank of America, 1927–29. HON. DEG.: LL.D., Chicago Coll. of Law, 1924; LL.D., Northwestern U., 1923; LL.D., St. Bonaventure's Coll., 1925. RES.: Chicago, IL.

DEVERS, ANDREW SAMUEL. b. Apr 22, 1968, Ankara, Turkey; par. Martin Saul and Alice (Hammerstrom) Devers; single. EDUC.: grad., York (PA) H.S., 1986. POLIT. & GOV.: ***candidate for Democratic nomination to presidency of the U.S., 1988***. BUS. & PROF.: student; artist; writer; publisher, *Small Press Comix*. MAILING ADDRESS: 661 Colonial Ave., York, PA 17403.

DEVOS, RICHARD MARVIN. b. Mar 4, 1926, Grand Rapids, MI; par. Simon C. and Ethel R. (Dekker) DeVos; m. Helen J. Van Wesep, Feb 7, 1953; c. Richard Marvin, Jr.; Daniel George; Suzanne Cheryl; Douglas Lee. EDUC.: Calvin Coll., 1946. POLIT. & GOV.: ***candidate for American Party nomination to presidency of the U.S., 1976; candidate for Republican nomination to presidency of the U.S., 1980***. BUS. & PROF.: partner, Wolverine Air Service, 1946–49; pres., Ja-Ri Corp., 1949; pres., Amway Corp., 1959–; pres., Amway of Canada, Ltd., 1964–; pres., Amway of Australia, 1970–; pres., Amway Mutual Fund; pres., Amway Global, Inc.; pres., Amway GmbH. (West Germany); pres., Amway Management Co.; pres., Amway Ltd. of Hong Kong; pres., Amway International Inc.; pres., Amway Ltd. (United Kingdom); pres., Amway Intercontinental Inc.; pres., Amway Ltd. of Ireland; pres., Amway Ltd. of Japan; pres., Amway Sdn. Bhd. of Malaysia; dir., sec., Amway Distributors Assn. of the U.S.; co-chm., MBS, Inc.; co-chm., Amway Communications Corp.; chm., Reference Map International; pres., Mutual Sports, Inc.; pres., Ada Report, Inc.; pres., Statitrol, Inc.; pres., Nutrilite Products, Inc., Buena Park, CA; dir., Old Kent Bank and Trust, Grand Rapids, MI; co-chm., Mutual Broadcasting System, Inc.; pres., Amway Stock Transfer Co.; pres., Amway Hotel Corp.; pres., Amway Ltd. (Netherlands); dir., Gospel Films, Muskegon, MI. MIL.: U.S.A.A.F., 1944–46. MEM.: Kent Cty. Tuberculosis and Emphysema Soc. (pres.); Grand Rapids Junior Achievement (pres., 1966–67); Rockford Coll. (trustee); St. Mary's Hospital (adviser); Freedoms Foundation; Grand Rapids Sales and Marketing Executives; Direct Selling Assn. (vice pres.); Christian Freedom Foundation; Grand Valley State Coll. (member, Board of Control); Kent Cty. United Way (dir.); Robert Schuller Ministries; National Association of Manufacturers; New Grand Rapids Cmte. (chm.); Economic Club; Rotary Club; Roundtable; National Congressional Leadership Council (chm.); International Year of the Disabled Person (dir.). AWARDS: Alexander Hamilton Award, Freedoms Foundation; Distinguished Salesman of the Year Award, Grand Rapids Sales and Marketing Executives; Business Leader of the Year Award, Religious Heritage of America; Hall of Fame Award, Direct Selling Assn.; Industry Week "Excellence in Management" Award; Thomas Jefferson Freedom of Speech Award, Kiwanis International; MI Week Volunteer Leadership Award; Distinguished Service Award, Rotary Club; Marketing Man of the Year Award, West MI Chapter, American Marketing Assn.; American Enterprise Executive Award, National Management Assn.; Free Enterprise Award, Americanism Educational League. HON. DEG.: LL.D., Oral Roberts U., 1976; LL.D., Grove City (PA) Coll., 1976; LL.D., Northwood Inst., 1977; LL.D., Dickinson Law School, 1980; LL.D., Pepperdine Coll., 1980. WRITINGS: *Believe!* (1975). REL.: Christian Reformed Church (elder; member, Board of Missions; pres., Missionary Soc.; chm., Finance Cmte.). MAILING ADDRESS: 7154 Windy Hill Rd., Grand Rapids, MI 49506.

DEWEY, GEORGE. b. Dec 26, 1837, Montpelier, VT; d. Jan 16, 1917, Washington, DC; par. Dr. Julius Yeamans and Mary (Perrin) Dewey; m. Susan Boardman Goodwin, Oct 24, 1867 (d. 1872); m. 2d, Mrs. Mildred (McLean) Hazen, Nov 9, 1899; c. George Goodwin. EDUC.: M.M.S., Norwich U., 1854; grad. (cum laude), U.S. Naval Acad., 1858. POLIT. & GOV.: appointed member, U.S. Philippine Comm., 1899; ***candidate for Democratic nomination to presidency of the U.S., 1900; candidate for Democratic nomination to vice presidency of the U.S., 1900; candidate for Republican nomination to presidency of the U.S., 1900; candidate for Republican nomination to vice presidency of the U.S., 1900***. BUS. & PROF.: naval officer. MIL.: commissioned lt., U.S. Navy, 1861; lt. commander, 1865; instructor, U.S. Naval Acad., 1868–70; commander, 1872; capt., 1884; lighthouse inspector, 1876–77; chief, Bureau of Equipment, 1889–95; pres., Board of Inspection and Survey, 1895–97; commodore, 1896; rear adm., 1898; adm. of the navy, 1899; pres., General Board of the Navy, 1900–1917; commanded squadron; participated in Battle of Manila, which annihilated Spanish Asiatic Squadron; thanked by Resolution of U.S. Congress for achievements in Spanish-American War. HON. DEG.: LL.D., U. of PA, 1898; LL.D., Princeton U., 1898. RES.: Washington, DC.

DEWEY, THOMAS EDMUND. b. Mar 24, 1902, Owosso, MI; d. Mar 16, 1971, Bar Harbor, ME; par. George Martin and Annie (Thomas) Dewey; m. Frances E. Hutt, Jun 16, 1928; c. Thomas Edmund, Jr.; John Martin. EDUC.: A.B., U. of MI, 1923; LL.B., Columbia U., 1925. POLIT. & GOV.: district capt., Tenth Assembly District Republican Cmte., 1926–31; chm., Board of Governors, NY Young Republican Club, 1930–31; chief asst. U.S. atty., Southern District of NY, 1931–33; appointed U.S. atty., Southern District of NY, 1933; appointed special prosecutor of organized crime, New York Cty., NY, 1935–37; elected as a Republican to district atty., New York Cty., 1937; Republican candidate for gov. of NY, 1938; ***candidate for Republican nomination to presidency of the U.S., 1940***; elected as a Republican to gov. of NY, 1943–55; ***Republican candidate for presidency of the U.S., 1944, 1948***. BUS. & PROF.: atty.; admitted to NY Bar, 1926; assoc., Larkin, Rathbone and Perry (law firm), 1925–26; assoc., McNamara and Seymour (law firm), New York, 1927–31; partner, Dewey, Ballantine, Bushby, Palmer and Wood (law firm), New York, 1955. MEM.: Phi Delta Phi; Phi Mu Alpha; SAR; NY City Mission Soc.; U. of MI Club of NY; NY Heart Assn. (trustee); YMCA (trustee); Roosevelt Hospital (trustee); American College of Trial Lawyers (fellow); ABA; NY Bar Assn.; Assn. of the Bar of the City of New York; New York Cty. Lawyers' Assn.; Council on Foreign Relations; New York Young Republican Club (chm., Board of Governors); Columbia University Club; Bankers Club; Tuxedo Club; Pilgrims Club; Masons (33°); Links Club; Blindbrook Club; Recess Club; Downtown Club; Hill Club; City Midday Club; Indian Creek Club; Augusta National Club. AWARDS: Medal of Excellence, Columbia U., 1936; Cardinal Newman Distinguished Service Award, U. of IL, 1939. HON. DEG.: LL.M., U. of MI, 1937; LL.D., Tufts Coll., 1937; LL.D., Brown U., 1938; LL.D., Dartmouth Coll., 1939; LL.D., St. Lawrence U., 1941; LL.D., NY U., 1942; LL.D., Union Coll., 1943; LL.D., Alfred U., 1945; LL.D., Fordham U., 1946; LL.D., Columbia U., 1947; LL.D., Colgate U., 1947; LL.D., Hamilton Coll., 1947; LL.D., Williams Coll., 1949; LL.D., St. Bonaventure Coll., 1950; LL.D., Yeshiva U., 1951; LL.D., U. of Rochester, 1957. WRITINGS: *The Case Against the New Deal*; *Journey to the Far Pacific* (1952); *Thomas E. Dewey on the Two Party System* (1966). REL.: Episc. RES.: New York, NY.

DIAMOND, GEORGE ROBERT. POLIT. & GOV.: ***candidate for Democratic nomination to presidency of the U.S., 1988***. MAILING ADDRESS: 16271 Fourth St., Guerneville, CA 95446.

DIAMOND, JEROME J. POLIT. & GOV.: ***independent candidate for presidency of the U.S., 1984***. MAILING ADDRESS: NJ.

DICK, ROBERT JAMES. POLIT. & GOV.: ***independent candidate for presidency of the U.S., 1984***. MAILING ADDRESS: 9309 Garfield St., Riverside, CA 92503.

DICKERMAN, RICHARD A. b. 1954; par. Roy P. Dickerman. POLIT. & GOV.: ***independent candidate for presidency of the U.S., 1976***. BUS. & PROF.: student. MAILING ADDRESS: 2045 Telegraph Rd., Lemay, St. Louis, MO 63125.

DICKEY, MAURICE. POLIT. & GOV.: ***candidate for Democratic nomination to presidency of the U.S., 1988***. MAILING ADDRESS: RFD 2, Rockwood, PA 15557.

DICKINSON, DANIEL STEVENS. b. Sep 11, 1800, Goshen, CT; d. Apr 12, 1866, New York, NY; par. Daniel T. and Mary (Caulkins) Dickinson; m. Lydia Knapp, 1822. EDUC.: public schools; studied law in offices of Clark and Clapp, Norwich, CT. POLIT. & GOV.: appointed postmaster, Guilford, NY, 1827–32; elected first pres., Town of Binghamton, NY, 1834; delegate, Dem. Nat'l. Conv., 1835, 1844, 1848, 1852; elected as a Democrat to NY State Senate, 1837–41 (Democratic leader); Democratic candidate for lt. gov. of NY, 1840; elected as a Democrat to lt. gov. of NY, 1842–44; appointed and subsequently elected as a Democrat to U.S. Senate (NY), 1844–51; presidential elector, Democratic Party, 1844; Democratic candidate for U.S. Senate (NY), 1850; ***candidate for Democratic nomination to presidency of the U.S., 1852, 1860***; appointed collector, Port of New York, 1853 (declined); elected as a Unionist to atty. gen. of NY, 1861–63; appointed member, North West Boundary Comm., 1864; delegate, Union Convention, 1864; ***candidate for Republican nomination to vice presidency of the U.S., 1864***; appointed U.S. district atty. for southern NY, 1865–66. BUS. & PROF.: apprentice clothier, NY; schoolteacher, NY; land surveyor; atty.; admitted to NY Bar, 1828; law practice, Guilford, NY. RES.: Guilford, NY.

DICKINSON, LESTER JESSE. b. Oct 29, 1873, Derby, IA; d. Jun 4, 1968, Des Moines, IA; par. Levi D. and Willamine (Morton) Dickinson; m. Myrtle Call, Aug 21, 1901; c. Levi Call; Ruth Alice. EDUC.: B.S., Cornell Coll., 1898; LL.B., U. of IA, 1899. POLIT. & GOV.: city clerk, Algona, IA, 1900–1904; prosecuting atty., Kossuth Cty., IA, 1909–13; member, IA State Republican Central Cmte., 1914–18; elected as a Republican to U.S. House (IA), 1919–31; elected as a Republican to U.S. Senate (IA), 1931–37; temporary chm., Rep. Nat'l. Conv., 1932; Republican candidate for U.S. Senate (IA), 1936, 1938; ***candidate for Republican nomination to presidency of the U.S., 1936***. BUS. & PROF.: atty.; admitted to IA Bar, 1899; partner (with T. P. Harrington), law firm, Algona, IA, 1899–1934; partner, Dickinson and Dickinson (law firm), Des Moines, IA; partner, Dickinson, Throckmorton, Parker, Mannheimer and Raife (law firm), Des Moines, IA. MIL.: 2d lt., 52d Infantry, IA National Guard, 1900–1902. MEM.: Cornell Coll. (trustee); Phi Delta Phi. HON. DEG.: LL.D., Cornell Coll., 1936. REL.: Congregationalist. RES.: Des Moines, IA.

DiDONATO, FLORENZO. b. 1936. POLIT. & GOV.: ***candidate for Democratic nomination to presidency of the U.S., 1988***. MAILING ADDRESS: Arlington, MA.

DIERLAM, JESSE HOWELL. b. Sep 14, 1934, Seadrift, TX; par. Jesse Howell and Effie Ileana Dierlam; m. Jacqueline Dierlam, Oct 1, 1955; m. 2d, Genevieve Jacobson, Sep 14, 1978; c. Linda; Matthew; Douglass. EDUC.: A.A. (electrical engineering), Vallejo Junior Coll., 1961. POLIT. & GOV.: ***candidate for Democratic nomination to presidency of the U.S., 1984***. BUS. & PROF.: electrical engineer; real estate salesman; insurance salesman. MIL.: apprentice electrician, U.S. Navy, More Island Naval Shipyard, Vallejo, CA, journeyman, 1961; production ship planner (electrician), production controller, U.S. Army, 1950; National Guard; U.S. Air Force, 1951–56. MEM.: Masons. REL.: Christian. MAILING ADDRESS: 2467 McKenzie Ave., Anchorage, AK 99503.

DIES, MARTIN. b. Nov 5, 1900, Colorado, TX; d. Nov 4, 1972, Lufkin, TX; par. Martin and Olive M. (Cline) Dies; m. Myrtle McAdams, Jun 3, 1920; c. Martin; Robert M.; Jack. EDUC.: Wesley Coll.; Cluster Springs Acad.; B.A., U. of TX at Austin, 1919; LL.B., National U., 1920. POLIT. & GOV.: elected district judge, TX; elected as a Democrat to U.S. House (TX), 1931–45, 1953–59 (chm. of the House Cmte. on Un-American Activities); ***candidate for Democratic nomination to presidency of the U.S., 1940, 1944***; candidate for Democratic nomination to U.S. Senate (TX), 1941, 1957; delegate, TX State Constitutional Convention, 1944. BUS. & PROF.: atty.; admitted to TX Bar, 1920; law practice, Marshall, TX, 1920–22; law practice, Orange, TX, 1922; rancher; farmer, Jasper, TX; instructor, East TX Law School, Beaumont, TX, 1930; partner, Dies, Stephenson and Dies (law firm), Orange, TX. WRITINGS: *The Trojan Horse of America* (1940). REL.: Christian (Disciples) Church. RES.: Jasper, TX.

DIETERLE, CHARLES. b. Feb 20, 1950, Weld Cty., CO; par. foster parents; single. EDUC.: CO Orphans' Home, Denver, CO, 1950–53; CO State Home and Training School, Grand Junction, CO, 1963–70. POLIT. & GOV.: nonpartisan candidate for City Council, Boulder, CO, 1981; ***candidate for Democratic nomination to presidency of the U.S., 1984***. BUS. & PROF.: custodian; advocate for handicapped. MEM.: People First of CO (pres.); National Representative for the Handicapped, Inc. (pres.). REL.: Presb. MISC.: first acknowledged mentally retarded person to seek presidency. MAILING ADDRESS: 1155 Marine, Apt. 112, Boulder, CO 80302.

DIETRICH, DON WILLIAM. POLIT. & GOV.: ***independent candidate for presidency of the U.S., 1988***. MAILING ADDRESS: P.O. Box 94211, Atlanta, GA 30318.

DILLAYE, STEPHEN DEVALSON. b. 1820, Plymouth, NY; d. 1884; married; c. Blanche. EDUC.: LL.B., Harvard U., 1845. POLIT. & GOV.: ***Greenback (Radical Faction) Party candidate for presidency of the U.S., 1880 (declined); candidate for Greenback Party nomination to presidency of the U.S., 1880***. BUS. & PROF.: author; atty. WRITINGS: *Letter to the Hon. Howell Cobb* (1858); *A Brief History of the Pittsburgh Forgery Case* (1860); *Address Before the Cty. Convention at Syracuse, March 18, 1869, in Favor of Female Suffrage* (1869); *Assignats and Mandats* (1877); *The Money and Finances of the French Revolution in 1789* (1877); *The Empire of Money* (1879); *The Life and Public Services of Gen. James B. Weaver* (1880); *Our Presidential Candidates and Political Compendium* (1880); *Monopolies: Their Origin, Growth and Development* (1882). RES.: NY.

DILWORTH, MARCUS RAY, JR. b. Mar 18, 1968, Jackson, MS; par. Marcus Ray and Velma Christine (Thompson) Dilworth; single. EDUC.: Yazoo City (MS) H.S. POLIT. & GOV.: ***candidate for Democratic nomination to presidency of the U.S., 1984***. REL.: Bapt. MAILING ADDRESS: 813 Prentiss Ave., Yazoo City, MS 39194.

DINSMORE, MARVIN A. POLIT. & GOV.: ***candidate for Democratic nomination to presidency of the U.S., 1924***. BUS. & PROF.: atty.; admitted to AL Bar; law practice, Birmingham, AL. MEM.: Ku Klux Klan. RES.: Birmingham, AL.

DIORIO, RUSSELL. POLIT. & GOV.: ***candidate for Democratic nomination to presidency of the U.S., 1980***. MAILING ADDRESS: 1126 Hartford Ave., Johnston, RI 02919.

DIRKSEN, EVERETT McKINLEY. b. Jan 4, 1896, Pekin, IL; d. Sep 7, 1969, Washington, DC; par. Johann Frederick and Antje (Conrady) Dirksen; m. Louella Carver, Dec 24, 1927; c. Danice Joy (Mrs. Howard H. Baker, Jr., q.v.). EDUC.: LL.B., U. of MN, 1917. POLIT. & GOV.: elected commissioner of finance, City Comm., Pekin, IL, 1927–31; candidate for Republican nomination to U.S. House (IL), 1930; elected as a Republican to U.S. House (IL), 1933–49; vice chm., Republican National Congressional Cmte., 1938–46; delegate, Rep. Nat'l. Conv., 1940, 1944, 1948, 1952, 1956; ***candidate for Republican nomination to presidency of the U.S., 1944, 1948, 1968***; elected as a Republican to U.S. Senate (IL), 1951–69 (minority whip, 1957–59; minority leader, 1959–69); chm., Republican National Senate Campaign Cmte., 1952–56. BUS. & PROF.: gen. mgr., Cook Dredging Co., 1922–25; co-owner, wholesale bakery, Pekin, IL, to 1933; atty.; admitted to DC Bar, 1936; admitted to IL Bar, 1937; law practice, Pekin, IL; partner, Baer, Witherall and Davis (law firm), Pekin, IL, 1949. MIL.: 2d lt., Balloon Co., F.A., U.S. Army, 1918–19. MEM.: American Legion; VFW; Elks; Moose; Masons (33°; O.E.S.; Shriners); IL Bar Assn.; DC Bar Assn.; Eagles; Independent Order of Odd

Fellows; Isaac Walton League. HON. DEG.: LL.D., Hope Coll., 1949; LL.D., Bradley U., 1949; LL.D., Lincoln Memorial U., 1951; LL.D., De Paul U., 1951; LL.D., Hanover Coll., 1965; LL.D., Lewis Coll., 1966; LL.D., St. Louis U., 1967; LL.D., Knox Coll., 1968. REL.: Reformed Church. MISC.: appeared in *The Monitors* (film, 1969). RES.: Pekin, IL.

DISALLE, MICHAEL VINCENT. b. Jan 6, 1908, New York, NY; d. Sep 15, 1981, Pescara, Italy; par. Anthony C. and Assunta (D'Arcangelo) Disalle; m. Myrtle Eugene England, Dec 19, 1929; c. Diana; Antoinette; Barbara; Constance; Michael E. EDUC.: J.D., Georgetown U., 1931. POLIT. & GOV.: appointed asst. district counsel, Home Owners' Loan Corp., 1933–36; member, Cty. Democratic Central Cmte., 1936–40; elected as a Democrat to OH State House, 1937–39; Democratic candidate for OH State Senate, 1938; appointed asst. city law dir., Toledo, OH, 1939–41; elected as a Democrat to Toledo (OH) City Council, 1941–43, vice mayor, 1944–47; delegate, Dem. Nat'l. Conv., 1944 (alternate), 1948, 1956; Democratic candidate for U.S. House (OH), 1946; elected as a Democrat to mayor of Toledo, OH, 1948–50; member, OH State Democratic Exec. Cmte., 1948–49; candidate for Democratic nomination to U.S. Senate (OH), 1950; appointed dir., Office of Price Stabilization, 1950–52; appointed dir., Office of Economic Stabilization, 1952; Democratic candidate for U.S. Senate (OH), 1952; Democratic candidate for gov. of OH, 1956, 1962; elected as a Democrat to gov. of OH, 1959–63; ***candidate for Democratic nomination to presidency of the U.S., 1960***; appointed member, Advisory Comm. on Intergovernmental Relations, 1961–63. BUS. & PROF.: atty.; admitted to OH Bar, 1931; law practice, Toledo, OH, 1931; partner, DiSalle, Green and Haddad (law firm); counsel, Chapman, Duff and Lenzini (law firm), Washington, DC, 1971–; distinguished prof., U. of MA. MIL.: National Guard, WWII. MEM.: International Centre for Settlement of Investment Disputes (member, Panel of Arbitrators, 1967–74); Phi Sigma Alpha; Toledo Labor-Management Citizens Comm. (chm.); OH Assn. of Municipalities (founder; pres., 1949); U.S. Conference of Mayors (chm., Advisory Board, 1949); ABA; Federal Bar Assn.; OH Bar Assn.; Columbus Bar Assn.; Toledo Bar Assn.; Bar Assn. of DC; Delta Theta Phi. AWARDS: "Outstanding Man of the Year," Junior C. of C., 1944; Speaker of the Year, Tau Kappa Alpha, 1951; Outstanding Alumnus, Georgetown Student Bar Assn., 1962; Interfaith Movement Award, 1962. HON. DEG.: LL.D., Notre Dame U., 1949; M.S., U. of Bridgeport, 1951; LL.D., Miami U., 1959; LL.D., Bowling Green State U., 1960; LL.D., U. of Toledo, 1960; LL.D., Kent State U., 1960; LL.D., U. of Akron, 1960; D.H.L., U. of OH, 1963. WRITINGS: *Second Choice* (with Lawrence G. Blochman). REL.: R.C. RES.: Toledo, OH.

DITMAN, JOSEPH G. POLIT. & GOV.: ***candidate for American Party nomination to presidency of the U.S., 1888***. BUS. & PROF.: businessman. WRITINGS: *From the Atlantic to the Pacific: A Lecture Delivered at Hermon Presbyterian Church, Frankford, November 11, 1886, for the Benefit of the Church Fund* (1886). RES.: Philadelphia, PA.

DIX, CARL. POLIT. & GOV.: founding member, Revolutionary Communist Party, U.S.A.; ***Anticandidate for presidency of the U.S., 1984, 1988***. BUS. & PROF.: lecturer; author; activist; organizer, Biko Lives Festival, 1985–88. MIL.: U.S. Army, 1970. WRITINGS: *Draw the Line* (coauthor, 1985); *Revolution, Not Elections, Is the Way Out of This Madness* (1988). MEM.: Vietnam Veterans Against the War; Mass Proletarian War Crimes Tribunal (panel moderator, 1981); Revolutionary Internationalist Movement (founder, 1984); Black Workers Congress; African Liberation Support Cmte.; Fort Lewis 6. MISC.: sentenced to two years in Leavenworth (KS) Military Prison for resistance to Vietnam War, 1970. MAILING ADDRESS: c/o Revolutionary Communist Party, 3449 North Sheffield, Chicago, IL 60657.

DIX, JOHN ALDEN. b. Dec 25, 1860, Glens Falls, NY; d. Apr 9, 1928, New York, NY; par. James Lawton and Laura (Stevens) Dix; m. Gertrude Thomson, Apr 24, 1889; c. John W. EDUC.: grad., Glens Falls Acad., 1879; A.B., Cornell U., 1883. POLIT. & GOV.: delegate, Dem. Nat'l. Conv., 1904; chm., Washington Cty. (NY) Democratic Central Cmte., 1906; Democratic candidate for lt. gov. of NY, 1908; chm., NY State Democratic Central Cmte., 1910; elected as a Democrat to gov. of NY, 1911–13; ***candidate for Democratic nomination to presidency of the U.S., 1912; candidate for Democratic nomination to vice presidency of the U.S., 1912***. BUS. & PROF.: partner, Reynolds and Dix (black marble), Glens Falls, NY, 1882–87; partner, Thomson and Dix (lumber), Albany, NY, 1887–97; pres., Iroquois Pulp and Paper Co.; pres., Moose River Lumber Co., McKeever, NY; vice pres., Blandy Paper Co., Greenwich, NY; treas., American Wood Board Paper Co., Thomson, NY; dir., Standard Wall Paper Co., Hudson Falls, NY; vice pres., First National Bank of Albany; dir., Albany Trust Co.; dir., Glens Falls Trust Co.; dir., National Bank of Schuylersville; dir., Hudson Falls and Adirondack Trust Co.; partner, Dix and Bangs (stock brokers), New York, NY. MEM.: Theta Delta Chi; Masons; Cornell U. (trustee). HON. DEG.: LL.D., Hamilton Coll., 1912. REL.: Episc. RES.: New York, NY.

DIXON, JOSEPH MOORE. b. Jul 31, 1867, Snow Camp, NC; d. May 22, 1934, Missoula, MT; par. Hugh W. and Flora (Murchison) Dixon; m. Caroline M. Worden, Mar 12, 1896; c. Virginia Dean; Florence Leach; Dorothy Allen; Mary Jo Hills; Betty Stearns; Frank; Peggy. EDUC.: Earlham Coll.; A.B., Guilford Coll., 1889. POLIT. & GOV.: appointed asst. prosecuting atty., Missoula Cty., MT, 1893–95; elected as a Republican to prosecuting atty., Missoula Cty., MT, 1895–97; elected as a Republican to MT State House, 1901–03; elected as a Republican to U.S. House (MT), 1903–07; delegate, Rep. Nat'l. Conv., 1904, 1916; elected as a Republican to U.S. Senate (MT),

1907–13; chm., Progressive Party National Convention, 1912; chm., Roosevelt Progressive National Campaign Cmte., 1912; Progressive Party candidate for U.S. Senate (MT), 1912; elected as a Republican to gov. of MT, 1921–25; ***candidate for Republican nomination to vice presidency of the U.S., 1924***; Republican candidate for gov. of MT, 1924; Republican candidate for U.S. Senate (MT), 1928; appointed first asst. sec. of the interior, 1929–33. BUS. & PROF.: atty.; admitted to MT Bar, 1892; law practice, Missoula, MT; publisher, ed., newspaper, Missoula, MT; dairy farmer, Flathead Valley, MT. RES.: Missoula, MT.

DOAN, W. S. POLIT. & GOV.: ***candidate for Prohibition Party nomination to vice presidency of the U.S., 1904.*** RES.: unknown.

DOBBIN, JAMES COCHRAN. b. Jan 17, 1814, Fayetteville, NC; d. Aug 4, 1857, Fayetteville, NC; par. John Moore and Anness (Cochran) Dobbin; m. Louisa Holmes, 1838; c. Mary Louisa Anderson; James Cochran, Jr.; John Holmes. EDUC.: Fayette (NC) Acad.; William Bingham School; grad., U. of NC, 1832; studied law. POLIT. & GOV.: elected as a Democrat to U.S. House (NC), 1845–47; elected as a Democrat to NC State House of Commons, 1848–52 (Speaker, 1850); delegate, Dem. Nat'l. Conv., 1852; Democratic candidate for U.S. Senate (NC), 1852; appointed U.S. sec. of the navy, 1853–57; ***candidate for Democratic nomination to vice presidency of the U.S., 1856***. BUS. & PROF.: atty.; admitted to NC Bar, 1835; law practice, Fayetteville, NC. RES.: Fayetteville, NC.

DOBBS, FARRELL. b. Jul 25, 1907, Queen City, MO; d. Nov 2, 1983, Pinole, CA; par. Isaac T. and Ora L. (Smith) Dobbs; m. Marvel S. Scholl, Apr 23, 1927; c. Carol Elinor (Mrs. Clifton DeBerry, q.v.); Mary Lou (Mrs. Paul Montauk); Sharon Lee (Mrs. Eli Finer; Mrs. Buch). EDUC.: North H.S., Minneapolis, MN. POLIT. & GOV.: national labor sec., Socialist Workers Party, 1940–48, national chm., 1949–53, national sec., 1953–74; Socialist Workers Party candidate for mayor of New York, NY, 1945; Socialist Workers Party candidate for gov. of NY, 1946; ***Socialist Workers Party candidate for presidency of the U.S., 1948, 1952, 1956, 1960***. BUS. & PROF.: dyer, Strutwear Knitting Co., Minneapolis, MN, 1925; reaper and thresher, ND, 1926; telephone equipment installer, Western Electric Co., MN, IA, and NE, 1926–29, foreman, 1930–31, planning engineer, 1931–32; yardman, Pittsburgh Coal Co., Minneapolis, MN, 1933–34; sec.-treas., General Drivers Local 544, Minneapolis, MN, 1934–38; general organizer, International Brotherhood of Teamsters, 1934–39; political organizer; employee, Monad Press, New York, NY; ed., *The Militant*, 1943–48. WRITINGS: *Trade Union Problems; The Voice of Socialism; Teamster Rebellion* (1972); *Teamster Power* (1973); *Teamster Politics* (1975); *Teamster Bureaucracy* (1977); *Revolutionary Continuity: The Early Years, 1848–1917; Revolutionary Continuity: Birth of the Communist Movement, 1918–1922; Counter-Mobilization: A Strategy to Fight Racist and Fascist Attacks; The Structure and Organizational Principles of the Party*. REL.: none. MISC.: organized Minneapolis Teamster Strike, 1934; imprisoned for 16 months for Smith Act violation, Sandstone Federal Prison, MN, 1941–42. RES.: Brooklyn, NY.

DOCKERY, ALEXANDER MONROE. b. Feb 11, 1845, Gallatin, MO; d. Dec 26, 1926, Gallatin, MO; par. Willis E. and Sarah Ellen (McHaney) Dockery; m. Mary E. Bird, Apr 14, 1869; c. eight. EDUC.: Macon Acad.; M.D., St. Louis (MO) Medical Coll., 1865; Bellevue Coll., 1865–66; Jefferson Medical Coll., 1865–66. POLIT. & GOV.: elected pres., Board of Education, Chillicothe, MO, 1871–73; cty. physician, Livingston Cty., MO, 1870–74; chm., Congressional Cmte.; elected member, City Council, Gallatin, MO, 1878–81, mayor, 1881–83; chm., MO State Democratic Convention, 1886, 1901; elected as a Democrat to U.S. House (MO), 1883–99; elected as a Democrat to gov. of MO, 1901–05; ***candidate for Democratic nomination to vice presidency of the U.S., 1904***; delegate, Dem. Nat'l. Conv., 1904; elected pres., Board of Education, Gallatin, MO, 1906–12; treas., MO State Democratic Central Cmte., 1912; appointed third asst. postmaster gen. of the U.S., 1913–21. BUS. & PROF.: physician; medical practice, Linneus, MO, 1865; medical practice, Chillicothe, MO, 1866–73; founder, cashier, Farmers' Exchange Bank, Gallatin, MO, 1874–82. MEM.: U. of MO at Columbia (curator, 1872–82); Gallatin Commercial Club (founder, 1907); Gallatin Chautauqua Assn. (pres., 1911); St. Louis Masonic Home (dir.); Odd Fellows (grand master); MO State Odd Fellows Home (pres.); Masons (eminent commander, 1880; grand master of MO, 1881–82; grand high priest, 1883–84). HON. DEG.: LL.D., U. of MO, 1906. REL.: Methodist Episcopal Church. RES.: Gallatin, MO.

DOCKING, GEORGE. b. Feb 23, 1904, Clay Center, KS; d. Jan 20, 1964, Washington, DC; par. William and Meda (Donley) Docking; m. Virginia Blackwell, Jan 24, 1925; c. Robert Blackwell (q.v.); George R. EDUC.: Western Military Acad.; A.B., U. of KS at Wichita, 1925. POLIT. & GOV.: Democratic candidate for gov. of KS, 1954, 1960; elected as a Democrat to gov. of KS, 1957–61; chm., Interstate Oil Compact Comm.; ***candidate for Democratic nomination to presidency of the U.S., 1960***; appointed dir., Export-Import Bank, 1961–64. BUS. & PROF.: banker; cashier, KS Reserve State Bank, Topeka, KS, 1929–31; vice pres., Kaw River Fertilizer Co.; cashier, First National Bank, Lawrence, KS, 1931–37, vice pres., 1937–42, pres., 1942–59; treas., KS Public Service Co., Lawrence, KS, 1939–64; chm. of the board, Union State Bank, Arkansas City, KS, 1959–64. MEM.: Delta Tau Delta; Beta Gamma Sigma; De Molay Legion of Honor; Elks; Eagles; Moose; Kansas City Club; University Club of Washington; KS State Hist. Soc.; Douglas Cty. Assn. for the Prevention of Infantile Paralysis; Lawrence Knife and Fork Club; U. of KS Student Housing Assn. (treas.). HON. DEG.: LL.D., St. Benedict's Coll., 1960. REL.: Presb. RES.: Lawrence, KS.

DOCKING, ROBERT BLACKWELL. b. Oct 9, 1925, Kansas City, MO; d. Oct 8, 1983, Arkansas City, KS; par. George (q.v.) and Mary Virginia (Blackwell) Docking; m. Meredith Martha Gear, 1950; c. William Russell; Thomas Robert. EDUC.: B.S. (cum laude), U. of KS, 1948; grad., Graduate School of Banking, U. of WI. POLIT. & GOV.: chm., Douglas Cty. (KS) Democratic Central Cmte., 1954–56; vice pres., KS Democratic Veterans, 1957; treas., Fifth District Democratic Cmte.; elected as a Democrat to Arkansas (KS) City Comm., 1963–66; elected as as Democrat to mayor of Arkansas City, 1963–66; chm., Joint City Commissions, Arkansas City–Winfield, KS, 1963–66; appointed member, Small Business Administration Advisory Board; elected as a Democrat to gov. of KS, 1967–75; delegate, Dem. Nat'l. Conv., 1968, 1972, 1976; chm., Interstate Oil Compact Comm.; ***candidate for Democratic nomination to presidency of the U.S., 1972***; delegate, Democratic Mid-Term Conference, 1974. BUS. & PROF.: banker; credit analyst, William Volker Co., 1948–50; cashier, asst. trust officer, First National Bank, 1950–56; employee, Union State Bank, Arkansas City, 1956–59, pres., 1959–83; owner, Docking Insurance Agency; asst. treas., dir., KS Public Service Co.; pres., Local Government Research Corp.; pres., City National Bank, Guymon, OK, 1978–83; owner, Docking Development Co.; dir., Fourth National Bank and Trust Co.; dir., First KS Life Insurance Co.; dir., Cimarron Investment Co.; dir., Cimarron Insurance Co.; dir., Cimarron Life Insurance Co.; dir., Plains Insurance Co.; dir., Cimarron Finance Co. MIL.: corp., U.S.A.A.F., 1943–46; U.S. Air Force Reserves (1st lt., 1946–51). MEM.: Community Chest (pres.); United Fund (pres.); American Red Cross (chapter chm.); Arkansas City C. of C. (pres.); American Legion (commander, Arkansas City); Cowley Cty. Bankers Assn.; American Assn. of Criminology; Beta Theta Pi; Beta Gamma Sigma; Delta Sigma Pi; Masons (32°; Shriners); Elks; Eagles; Rotary Club; KS League of Municipalities; Arkansas Basin Development Assn.; United Service Organization; Independent Oil and Gas Assn.; KS Livestock Assn.; U. of KS Alumni Assn.; International Platform Assn.; American Assn. for the U.N.; American G.I. Forum; Moose; Cowley Cty. Sportsmen's Club; KS Bank Management Comm. AWARDS: Young Man of the Year, KS Junior C. of C., 1959; received Key to Oil Patch Award, KS Independent Oil and Gas Assn., 1973; Conservation Award, KS Wildlife Assn., 1973; Citizenship Award, National Convention of A.M.E. United Churches, 1974; Distinguished Kansan Award, 1981. REL.: Presb. RES.: Arkansas City, KS.

DODGE, AUGUSTUS CAESAR. b. Jan 2, 1812, St. Genevieve, MO; d. Nov 20, 1883, Burlington, IA; par. Henry (q.v.) and Christina (McDonald) Dodge; m. Clara Ann Hertich, Mar 19, 1837. EDUC.: self-taught. POLIT. & GOV.: appointed registrar, Public Land Office, Burlington, IA, 1838–41; elected as a Democrat, territorial delegate, U.S. House (IA), 1840–46; presidential elector, Democratic Party, 1848; elected as a Democrat to U.S. Senate (IA), 1848–55; appointed U.S. minister to Spain, 1855–59; Democratic candidate for gov. of IA, 1859; Democratic candidate for U.S. Senate (IA), 1860; delegate, Dem. Nat'l. Conv., 1864; ***candidate for Democratic nomination to vice presidency of the U.S., 1864, 1868***; elected as an independent to mayor of Burlington, IA, 1874–75. BUS. & PROF.: lead miner, Galena, IL; lecturer. MIL.: lt., U.S.V., Indian Wars, 1832; appointed brig. gen., 2d Brigade, 1st Div., IA Militia, 1839. RES.: Burlington, IA.

DODGE, EARL FARWELL. b. Dec 24, 1932, Malden, MA; par. Earl Farwell and Dorothy (Harris) Dodge; m. Barbara Viola Regan, Jul 20, 1951; c. Earl Farwell III; Barbara F. Pittman; Allen C.; Faith D.; Calvin G.; Karen J.; Michael R. EDUC.: public schools, Malden, MA; night school, Malden, MA; grad., Inst. on Alcohol and Other Narcotics, Evanston, IL, 1969. POLIT. & GOV.: exec. sec., MA State Prohibition Party, 1953–56; Prohibition Party candidate for Governor's Council of MA, 1954; Prohibition Party candidate for MA state sec. of the commonwealth, 1956; exec. sec., national chm., Prohibition Party National Cmte., 1957–63; state chm., IN State Prohibition Party, 1958–61; Prohibition Party candidate for cty. commissioner, IN, 1958; Prohibition Party candidate for Town Council, IN, 1959; Prohibition Party candidate for U.S. House (IN), 1960; Prohibition Party candidate for U.S. Senate (KS), 1966; exec. sec., Prohibition Party National Cmte., 1967–87, chm., c. 1987–; state chm., MI Prohibition Party, 1967–71; appointed member, Community Relations Board, Kalamazoo, MI, 1967–70; Prohibition Party candidate for Kalamazoo (MI) City Comm., 1969; state chm., CO Prohibition Party, 1974; Prohibition Party candidate for gov. of CO, 1974, 1982; member, CO State Elections Advisory Board, 1974; ***Prohibition Party candidate for vice presidency of the U.S., 1976***; National Statesman (Prohibition) Party candidate for gov. of CO, 1978; temporary chm., National Statesman (Prohibition) Party National Convention, 1979; ***National Statesman (Prohibition) Party candidate for vice presidency of the U.S., 1980***; temporary chm., Prohibition Party National Convention, 1983, 1991 (temporary and permanent chm.); ***Prohibition Party candidate for presidency of the U.S., 1984, 1988, 1992***; Prohibition Party candidate for U.S. Senate (CO), 1986. BUS. & PROF.: ed., *The National Statesman;* ed., *Civic Forum,* 1975–79; life insurance agent, CO, 1974–; prohibition advocate. MEM.: National Christian Citizens Cmte. (sec.-treas., 1963–65; pres., 1966–70); National Prohibition Foundation, Inc. (trustee, 1959–; sec.-treas., 1974–); National Temperance and Prohibition Council (pres., 1972–74; sec., 1974–); CO Alcohol and Drug Education, Inc. (sec., 1973–); National Civic League, Inc. (sec.-treas., 1975–); American Political Item Collectors; CO Political Item Collectors; BSA; CO Right to Life Cmte. (pres., 1976–); Good Government Assn. of Kalamazoo (pres., 1968–70); Partisan Prohibition Hist. Soc. (pres., 1983–). AWARDS: Good Government Award, Kalamazoo, MI, 1971, 1978. REL.: Bapt. (chm., Beth Eden Baptist Church School Board; Sunday school superintendent; deacon). MAILING ADDRESS: 10105 West 17th Place, Lakewood, CO 80215.

DODGE, HENRY. b. Oct 12, 1782, Vincennes, IN; d. Jun 19, 1867, Burlington, IA; par. Israel and Nancy Ann

(Hunter) Dodge; m. Christina McDonald, 1800; c. Augustus Caesar (q.v.); eight others. EDUC.: limited. POLIT. & GOV.: sheriff, St. Genevieve, MO, 1805–21; appointed marshall, territory of MO, 1813; appointed gov., territory of WI, 1836–41, 1845–48; elected as a Democrat, territorial delegate, U.S. House (WI), 1841–45; elected as a Democrat to U.S. Senate (WI), 1848–57; ***candidate for Democratic nomination to presidency of the U.S., 1852***; appointed gov. of WA territory, 1857 (declined). BUS. & PROF.: lead miner, Galena, IL; soldier. MIL.: maj. gen., MO Militia, 1814; col., MI Volunteers, 1832; maj., Mounted U.S. Rangers, Upper Mississippi Valley, 1832–33; col., First U.S. Dragoons, 1836. RES.: Burlington, IA.

DOERSCHUCK, GANA H. POLIT. & GOV.: ***candidate for Republican nomination to presidency of the U.S., 1992***. BUS. & PROF.: real estate broker. MAILING ADDRESS: Palm Beach, FL.

DOHENY, EDWARD LAURENCE. b. Aug 10, 1856, Fond Du Lac, WI; d. Sep 8, 1935, Beverly Hills, CA; par. Patrick and Eleanor Elizabeth (Quigley) Doheny; m. Carrie Estelle Betzold, Aug 22, 1900; c. Edward Laurence. EDUC.: grad., Fond Du Lac (WI) H.S., 1872. POLIT. & GOV.: delegate, Dem. Nat'l. Conv., 1920; ***candidate for Democratic nomination to vice presidency of the U.S., 1920 (withdrew); candidate for Democratic nomination to presidency of the U.S., 1924***. BUS. & PROF.: petroleum producer; gold and silver prospector, 20 years; petroleum prospecting and production, 1892–1935; chm. of the board, Mexican Petroleum Co., Ltd., 1907; chm. of the board, Pan-American Petroleum and Transport Co., 1916; chm. of the board, Petroleum Securities Co.; pres., Doheny-Stone Drill Co.; pres., Los Nietos Producing and Refining Co., Ltd. MEM.: Council on National Defense (Oil Subcommittee, 1917); CA Club; Jonathan Club; Bohemian Club; Union League Club. REL.: R.C. MISC.: indicted but acquitted of bribery in Teapot Dome scandals, 1925. RES.: Los Angeles, CA.

DOHONEY, EBENEZER LAFAYETTE. b. Oct 13, 1832, Adair Cty., KY; m. Mary Susan Johnson, 1862. EDUC.: Columbia Coll.; LL.B., U. of Louisville, 1857. POLIT. & GOV.: appointed district atty., Eighth Judicial District, TX, 1865–66; elected as a Democrat to TX State Senate, 1869–73; elected as a Democrat, delegate, TX Constitutional Convention, 1875; Greenback Party candidate for U.S. House (TX), 1882; member, Prohibition Party National Cmte., 1882–92; delegate, Prohibition Party National Convention, 1884; Prohibition Party candidate for gov. of TX, 1886; ***candidate for Prohibition Party nomination to vice presidency of the U.S., 1888***; organizer, People's Party, 1891; People's Party candidate for chief justice, TX Criminal Court of Appeals, 1892, 1894; independent candidate for district judge, TX, 1896. BUS. & PROF.: atty. MIL.: capt., Ninth TX Cavalry, Civil War. WRITINGS: *The Origin and Destiny of Man; Man: His Origin, Nature, and Destiny* (1885); *The Providence of God in the Affairs of Men and Nations; The Progress of Philosophy; The Liquor Traffic; Prison Reform; The Constitution of Man in the Physical, Psychical and Spiritual Worlds*. RES.: Paris, TX.

DOLE, ROBERT JOSEPH. b. Jul 22, 1923, Russell, KS; par. Doran Ray and Bina (Talbott) Dole; m. Phyllis Holden, Jun 12, 1948 (divorced, 1972); m. 2d, Mary Elizabeth Hanford, 1975; c. Robin. EDUC.: U. of AZ; U. of KS; A.B., Washburn U., 1949, LL.B. (magna cum laude), 1952. POLIT. & GOV.: elected as a Republican to KS State House, 1951–53; elected as a Republican, cty. atty., Russell Cty., KS, 1953–61; elected as a Republican to U.S. House (KS), 1961–69; elected as a Republican to U.S. Senate (KS), 1969– (majority leader, 1985–87, 1995; minority leader, 1987–95); delegate, Mexico-U.S. Interparliamentary Group; appointed chm., Rep. Nat'l. Cmte., 1971–73; member, U.S. UNESCO Comm., 1969–; ***Republican candidate for vice presidency of the U.S., 1976; candidate for Republican nomination to presidency of the U.S., 1980, 1988***. BUS. & PROF.: atty. MIL.: capt., U.S. Army, 1943–48; Bronze Star with Oak Leaf Cluster; Combat Infantry Badge; Purple Heart with Oak Leaf Cluster. MEM.: Kiwanis (lt. gov.); Masons; 4-H Fair Assn.; Elks; BSA; GSA; Isis Shriners; U.S. C. of C.; VFW; Disabled American Veterans; American Legion; American Medical Center, Denver, CO (supervisor); William Allen White Foundation (trustee); Kappa Sigma; ABA; KS Bar Assn.; Russell Cty. Bar Assn.; Kansas Cty. Attorneys Assn.; Washburn Alumni Assn. AWARDS: Distinguished Service Award, Americans for Constitutional Action; National Easter Seal Award; Outstanding Kansan to Overcome Handicap, Disabled American Veterans. HON. DEG.: LL.D., Washburn U., 1969. REL.: Methodist. MAILING ADDRESS: 1326 Lincoln St., Russell, KS 67665.

DOLLIVER, JONATHAN PRENTISS. b. Feb 6, 1858, Kingwood, VA (now WV); d. Oct 15, 1910, Fort Dodge, IA; par. Rev. James J. and Elizabeth "Eliza" J. (Brown) Dolliver; m. Louise Pearsons, Nov 20, 1895; c. Margaret Eliza; Frances Pearsons; Jonathan Prentiss. EDUC.: A.B., WV U., 1876. POLIT. & GOV.: delegate, Rep. Nat'l. Conv., 1876; city solicitor, Fort Dodge, IA, 1880–87; elected as a Republican to U.S. House (IA), 1889–1900; ***candidate for Republican nomination to vice presidency of the U.S., 1900 (withdrew), 1908***; appointed and subsequently elected as a Republican to U.S. Senate (IA), 1900–1910. BUS. & PROF.: schoolteacher, Sandwich, IL; atty.; admitted to IA Bar, 1878; law practice, Fort Dodge, IA. HON. DEG.: LL.D., Bethany Coll., 1900; LL.D., Cornell Coll., 1902; LL.D., Miami U., 1905. REL.: Methodist. RES.: Fort Dodge, IA.

DOMENICI, PETER "PETE" VICHI. b. May 7, 1932, Albuquerque, NM; par. Cherubino and Alda (Vichi) Domenici; m. Nancy L. Burk, Jan 15, 1958; c. Lisa; Peter; Nella;

Clare; David; Nannette; Helen; Paula. EDUC.: U. of Albuquerque, 1952–54; B.S., U. of NM, 1954; J.D., U. of Denver, 1958. POLIT. & GOV.: elected as a Republican to Albuquerque (NM) City Comm., 1966–69 (chm., 1967–69); appointed member, Governor's Policy Board for Law Enforcement, 1967–68; chm., Model Cities Joint Advisory Cmte., 1967–68; elected as a Republican to U.S. Senate (NM), 1973–; ***candidate for Republican nomination to vice presidency of the U.S., 1976, 1988***. BUS. & PROF.: atty.; teacher, public schools, Albuquerque, NM, 1954–55; admitted to NM Bar, 1958; partner, Domenici and Bonham (law firm), Albuquerque, NM, 1958–72. MEM.: National League of Cities; Middle Rio Grande Council of Governments; National Alliance for the Mentally Ill. AWARDS: "Outstanding Young Man of Albuquerque," Albuquerque Junior C. of C., 1967. HON. DEG.: LL.D., U. of NM; LL.D., Georgetown U. School of Medicine; H.H.D., NM State U. REL.: R.C. MAILING ADDRESS: 402 15th St., S.W., Albuquerque, NM 87104.

DONAHEY, ALVIN VICTOR. b. Jul 7, 1873, Cadwallader, OH; d. Apr 8, 1946, Columbus, OH; par. John C. and Catherine (Chaney) Donahey; m. Mary Edith Harvey, Jan 5, 1897; c. at least 10. EDUC.: public schools. POLIT. & GOV.: clerk of Goshen Township, Tuscarawas Cty., OH, 1898–1903; cty. auditor, Tuscarawas Cty., OH, 1905–09; elected member, Board of Education, New Philadelphia, OH, 1909–11; elected delegate, OH State Constitutional Convention, 1912; elected as a Democrat, state auditor of OH, 1913–21; Democratic candidate for gov. of OH, 1920; elected as a Democrat to gov. of OH, 1923–29; ***candidate for Democratic nomination to presidency of the U.S., 1928, 1940; candidate for Democratic nomination to vice presidency of the U.S., 1928, 1940***; elected as a Democrat to U.S. Senate (OH), 1935–41. BUS. & PROF.: learned printer's trade; pres., Donahey Clay Products Co.; pres., Motorists Mutual Insurance Co.; dir., OH National Bank. WRITINGS: *The Beak and Claws of America* (1931). RES.: Huntsville, OH.

DONAHEY, GERTRUDE WALTON. b. Aug 4, 1908, Tuscarawas Cty., OH; par. George Sebastian and Mary Ann (Thomas) Walton; m. John W. Donahey, 1930; c. John William, Jr. EDUC.: business college. POLIT. & GOV.: field aide to U.S. Sen. Stephen M. Young, 1963–69, exec. asst., 1964; member-at-large, Platform Cmte., OH Democratic Party, 1964, 1968; delegate, Dem. Nat'l. Conv., 1964, 1968; elected as a Democrat, state treas. of OH, 1971–; ***candidate for Democratic nomination to presidency of the U.S., 1976, 1980***. BUS. & PROF.: private sec., 1930; community volunteer, 1930–; politician. MEM.: Business and Professional Women's Club of OH; National Assn. of Auditors, Comptrollers and Treasurers; Municipal Finance Officers Assn.; Mental Health Assn. of OH; Central OH Rose Soc.; Delta Kappa Gamma; OH Extension Homemakers Council. AWARDS: "Outstanding Woman Award," OH Extension Homemakers Council. HON. DEG.: D.P.S., Rio Grande Coll., 1974. REL.: Episc. MAILING ADDRESS: 2838 Sherwood Rd., Columbus, OH 43209.

DONATO, ROBERT PATRICK. POLIT. & GOV.: ***independent candidate for presidency of the U.S., 1980***. MAILING ADDRESS: 6640 Miramar Parkway, Miramar, FL 33023.

DONELSON, ANDREW JACKSON. b. Aug 25, 1799, Nashville, TN; d. Jun 26, 1871, Memphis, TN; par. Samuel and Mary (Smith) Donelson; m. Emily Donelson, 1824; m. 2d, Mrs. Elizabeth Randolph, 1841. EDUC.: U. of Nashville; grad., U.S. Military Acad., 1819; Transylvania U. POLIT. & GOV.: sec. to President Andrew Jackson (q.v.), 1828–37; appointed U.S. chargé d'affaires to Republic of TX, 1844; appointed U.S. minister to Prussia, 1846–48; appointed U.S. minister to Germany, 1848–49; ***candidate for American (Know-Nothing) Party nomination to presidency of the U.S., 1856; American (Know-Nothing) Party candidate for vice presidency of the U.S., 1856***. BUS. & PROF.: atty.; admitted to TN Bar, 1823; cotton plantation owner, Bolivar Cty., MS; ed., *Washington Union*, 1851–52; law practice, Memphis, TN; soldier. MIL.: commissioned 2d lt. of engineers, U.S. Army, 1819–22; aide-de-camp to Gen. Andrew Jackson, Seminole War. WRITINGS: *Reports of Explorations* (1855). RES.: Memphis, TN.

DONNELLY, EDWIN. POLIT. & GOV.: ***independent candidate for presidency of the U.S., 1992***. MAILING ADDRESS: 215 Piedmont Ave., Apt. #3, Cincinnati, OH 45219.

DONNELLY, IGNATIUS. b. Nov 3, 1831, Philadelphia, PA; d. Jan 1, 1901, Minneapolis, MN; par. Dr. Philip Carroll and Catharine Frances (Gavin) Donnelly; m. Katharine McCaffrey, Sep 10, 1855; m. 2d, Marian Hanson, Feb 22, 1898. EDUC.: Central H.S., Philadelphia, PA, 1849; studied law in office of Benjamin Harris Brewster. POLIT. & GOV.: Democratic candidate for U.S. House (PA), 1855 (declined); Republican candidate for MN State Senate, 1857; elected as a Republican to lt. gov. of MN, 1859–63; elected as a Republican to U.S. House (MN), 1863–69; Republican candidate for U.S. House (MN), 1868, 1870 (Free Trade Party); chm., National Anti-Monopoly Convention, 1872; elected to MN State Senate, 1874–78; Greenback-Democratic candidate for U.S. House (MN), 1878; Democratic candidate for U.S. House (MN), 1884; elected to MN State Legislature, 1887–1901; Farmer-Labor Party candidate for gov. of MN, 1888 (withdrew); People's Party candidate for gov. of MN, 1892; member, People's Party National Cmte., 1892–94; ***candidate for People's Party nomination to presidency of the U.S., 1892, 1896, 1900; People's (Anti-Fusionist) Party candidate for vice presidency of the U.S., 1900***. BUS. & PROF.: atty.; admitted to PA Bar, 1852; law practice, Philadelphia, PA, 1852–57; farmer; ed.; author; lecturer; land speculator, Nininger, MN, 1856–57; publisher, *Dakota Cty. (MN) Sentinel*, 1859; publisher, *The Anti-Monoplist*, 1874–79; law practice, MN, 1878–1901; ed., *The Representative*, St. Paul, MN, 1893–1900. MEM.: State Farmers' Alliance of MN (pres.); Dakota Cty. Agricultural Soc. (founder). WRITINGS: *Atlantis: The Ante-Diluvian World* (1882); *Ragnarok: The Age of Fire and Gravel* (1883); *The Great Cryptogram* (1888); *Caesar's Column* (1891); *Doctor Huguet; The Golden Bottle; The American People's Money*. REL.: Spiritualist (nee R.C.). RES.: Hastings, MN.

DONNELLY, LEO CHARLES. b. Dec 25, 1889, Cadillac, MI; d. May 30, 1958, Dansville, MI; par. William Charles and Emma (Barker) Donnelly; m. Emma Keightley (d. 1928); m. 2d, Viola Filatrault; c. Martha Jane Mueller; Anne Elizabeth. EDUC.: M.D., Detroit Coll. of Medicine, 1911. POLIT. & GOV.: founder, Social Credit Party, 1935; candidate for Democratic nomination to U.S. House (MI) 1936, 1956, 1958; ***Greenback Party candidate for presidency of the U.S., 1944***; candidate for Republican nomination to MI State House, 1948; candidate for Republican nomination to U.S. House (MI), 1955; candidate for Democratic nomination to U.S. House (MI), 1956. BUS. & PROF.: city physician, Detroit, MI, 1910–11; physician (specializing in bloodless surgery); staff, Pontiac State Hospital, 2 years; house surgeon, Harper Hospital; staff, St. Mary's Hospital; pastor, Westminster Community Church, Detroit, MI, 1942–58; staff, Lapeer State Home and Training School, 1947; publisher, *Health Advocate*; patent medicine and cancer cure salesman. MIL.: capt., U.S. Army, WWI; orthopedic surgeon, Base Hospital, Seine-Inferieure, France, 1916. MEM.: American Physio-Therapy Inst. REL.: Protestant. MISC.: expelled from Wayne Cty. (MI) Medical Soc., 1926; medical license revoked, 1938 (restored, 1947); tried for insanity, 1958; charged with cancer cure fraud, but case dismissed due to death of defendant, 1958. RES.: Detroit, MI.

DOOLITTLE, JAMES ROOD. b. Jan 3, 1815, Washington Cty., NY; d. Jul 27, 1897, Edgewood, RI; par. Reuben and Sarah (Rood) Doolittle; m. Mary L. Cutting, Jul 27, 1837; c. four sons; two daughters. EDUC.: Middlebury (VT) Acad.; grad., Hobart Coll., 1834, A.M., 1837. POLIT. & GOV.: founding member, Free Soil Party, 1847; district atty., Wyoming Cty., NY, 1847–50; elected judge, First Judicial Circuit of WI, 1853–56; elected as a Republican to U.S. Senate (WI), 1857–69; chm., Union National Convention, 1866; ***candidate for Democratic nomination to presidency of the U.S., 1868***; Democratic candidate for gov. of WI, 1871; chm., Dem. Nat'l. Conv., 1872; Democratic candidate for U.S. House (IL), 1878. BUS. & PROF.: atty.; admitted to NY Bar, 1837; law practice, Rochester, NY, 1837–41; law practice, Warsaw, NY, 1841–51; law practice, Chicago, IL, 1871; acting pres., trustee, and prof., U. of Chicago Law School. HON. DEG.: LL.D., Hobart Coll., 1854; LL.D., Racine Coll., 1887. WRITINGS: *United States in the Light of Prophecy*. RES.: Racine, WI.

DORRELL, JAMES CARTER. b. Jan 12, 1953, Poughkeepsie, NY; par. Carter Eaton and Nancy (Hill) Dorrell; m. (divorced); c. Gabreal; Jason; Julia. EDUC.: G.E.D.; college art courses. POLIT. & GOV.: ***independent candidate for presidency of the U.S., 1988***. BUS. & PROF.: dishwasher; stocker, K-Mart; cook, Kentucky Fried Chicken; sanitation engineer; custodian, elementary school; busboy; waiter; apartment painter and maintenance man; heating and air conditioning technician. MEM.: BSA; McKinney Bible Church. AWARDS: Third Place Award for Acrylics, McKinney Art Club Show. REL.: Non-Denominational Christian (McKinney Bible Church). MISC.: conscientious objector. MAILING ADDRESS: Route 1, Box 133, Princeton, TX 75077.

DORSEY, JACK. POLIT. & GOV.: candidate for Democratic nomination to U.S. Senate (GA), 1972, 1978; ***candidate for Democratic nomination to presidency of the U.S., 1976; One Party candidate for vice presidency of the U.S., 1976***. MAILING ADDRESS: 3605 Lawrenceville Rd., Tucker, GA 30084.

DORSEY, STEPHEN WALLACE. b. Feb 28, 1842, Benson, VT; d. Mar 20, 1916, Los Angeles, CA; par. John W. and Marie H. Dorsey; m. Helen Mary Wack, Nov 20, 1865; m. 2d, Laura Bigelow; c. Clayton Chauncey; two others. EDUC.: academic. POLIT. & GOV.: member, Rep. Nat'l. Cmte., 1868–80 (chm., exec. cmte., 1876–80); delegate, Rep. Nat'l. Conv., 1872, 1876, 1880; elected as a Republican to U.S. Senate (AR), 1873–79; ***independent candidate for presidency of the U.S., 1880***. BUS. & PROF.: pres., Sandusky Tool Co.; pres., AR Central Railway Co.; cattle rancher; mine owner, NM and CO, to 1892. MIL.: pvt., col., First OH Light Artillery, U.S. Army, 1861–65. MISC.: indicted for conspiring to defraud U.S. government, acquitted, 1881. Residence: Los Angeles, CA.

DORSHEIMER, WILLIAM EDWARD. b. Feb 5, 1832, Lyons, NY; d. Mar 26, 1888, Savannah, GA; par. Philip and Sarah Dorsheimer; m. Isabella Patchen. EDUC.: Phillips Andover Acad.; Harvard Coll., 1849–51; studied law, Buffalo, NY. POLIT. & GOV.: appointed U.S. district atty., Northern District of NY, 1867–71, Southern District of NY, 1885–86; member, Board of Park Commissioners, Buffalo, NY; delegate, Liberal Republican Party National Convention, 1872; elected as a Democrat to lt. gov. of NY, 1874–80; appointed commissioner of NY State Survey, 1876–83 (pres., 1883); delegate, Dem. Nat'l. Conv., 1876; Democratic candidate for U.S. Senate (NY), 1879; appointed commissioner of state reservation at Niagara, NY, 1883; elected as a Democrat to U.S. House (NY), 1883–85; ***candidate for Democratic nomination to presidency of the U.S., 1884***. BUS. & PROF.: atty.; admitted to NY Bar, 1854; law practice, Buffalo, NY, 1854; owner, ed., *New York (NY) Star*, 1886; law practice, New York, NY, 1879–85. MIL.: maj., U.S. Army, 1861. MEM.: Buffalo Hist. Soc. (founder); Buffalo

Fine Arts Acad. (founder). HON. DEG.: A.M., Harvard Coll., 1859. RES.: Buffalo, NY.

DOTY, CHARLES RICHARD. b. Jan 26, 1924, Webb City, OK; par. Charles Frederick and Bertha Olive (Pringle) Doty; m. Lila Marie Speakman; c. Charles Richard, Jr.; Rebeccah Ann; Vickie Lynn. EDUC.: grad., Webb City (OK) H.S., 1942; B.S., OK State U., 1954. POLIT. & GOV.: ***candidate for Democratic nomination to presidency of the U.S., 1984, 1988; candidate for Republican nomination to presidency of the U.S., 1992***. BUS. & PROF.: accounting and sales in fields of petroleum, aircraft, and food; administrative asst., National Guard; notary public; precinct inspector; real estate investor, Tulsa, OK; pres. and pastor gen., Universal Church of God. MIL.: A/S, S2/C, U.S. Navy, 1942–45. MEM.: War Veterans Against Nuclear Weapons; NRA; VFW; American Legion; AARP. REL.: Protestant (Universal Church of God). MAILING ADDRESS: 1366 East 52nd St., North, Tulsa, OK 74126.

DOUGLAS, LEWIS WILLIAMS. b. Jul 2, 1894, Bisbee, AZ; d. Mar 7, 1974; par. James Stuart and Josephine Leah (Williams) Douglas; m. Peggy Zinsser, Jun 19, 1921; c. James Stuart; Lewis W.; Sharman. EDUC.: B.A., Amherst Coll., 1916, LL.D., 1933; MA Inst. of Technology, 1916–17. POLIT. & GOV.: elected as a Democrat to AZ State House, 1923–25; elected as a Democrat to U.S. House (AZ), 1927–33 (resigned); appointed dir., U.S. Bureau of the Budget, 1933–34; ***candidate for Republican nomination to presidency of the U.S., 1936; candidate for Republican nomination to vice presidency of the U.S., 1936***; appointed shipping administrator, U.S. Dept. of War, 1942–44; appointed special adviser to Gen. Lucius Clay (q.v.), German Control Council, 1945; appointed U.S. ambassador to Great Britain, 1947–50; chm., National Policy Board. BUS. & PROF.: instructor, Amherst Coll., 1920; vice pres., dir., American Cyanamid Co., 1934–38; principal, vice chancellor, McGill U., Montreal, Canada, 1938–39; pres., Mutual Life Insurance Co. of NY, 1940–47, chm. of the board, 1947–59, chm., exec. cmte., Board of Directors, 1959–; hon. chm., Southern AZ Bank and Trust Co.; hon. chm., Douglas Investment Co.; dir., Technical Studies, Inc.; dir., Western Bancorp; dir., International Nickel Co.; dir., Newmont Mining Corp.; dir., Union Corp., Ltd.; dir., Nichols Engineering and Research Corp.; chm., U.S. Investment Cmte., Northern Assurance Co.; chm., Employer's Liability Assurance Co. MIL.: 2d lt., 347th Regt., U.S. Army; 1st lt., 91st Div., U.S. Army, WWI; citation from Gen. John J. Pershing (q.v.); Croix de Guerre; Grand Croix de la Legion d'Honneur; Grand Croix de l'Order de la Couronne (Belgium); Honorary Knight of the Grand Cross, Order of the British Empire. MEM.: American Assembly (pres.; chm.); Alfred P. Sloan Foundation (pres.); American Museum of Natural History; Amherst Coll. (trustee); Acad. of Political Science (pres.; trustee); American Shakespeare Festival and Acad. (national chm.); National Soc. for the Prevention of Blindness (hon. pres.); Memorial Hospital (Advisory Board); English-Speaking Union (hon. chm.); National Inst. for Social Sciences (vice pres.); Alpha Delta Phi; American Legion; American Phil. Soc. (trustee). AWARDS: one of twelve "Outstanding Young Men," America's Young Men, 1934. HON. DEG.: LL.D., Harvard U., 1933; LL.D., Queens Coll., 1938; LL.D., Princeton U., 1938; LL.D., Brown U., 1938; LL.D., NY U., 1938; LL.D., Wesleyan U., 1938; LL.D., U. of AZ, 1940; LL.D., Leeds U., 1948; LL.D., U. of Bristol, 1949; LL.D., U. of St. Andrews, 1949; LL.D., U. of London, 1949; LL.D., U. of Edinburgh, 1950; LL.D., U. of Birmingham (England), 1950; LL.D., U. of Glasgow, 1950; LL.D., U. of CA, 1951; LL.D., McGill U., 1951; LL.D., Columbia U., 1951; LL.D., Dalhousie U., 1951; D.C.L., Oxford U., 1948. REL.: Episc. RES.: Sonoita, AZ.

DOUGLAS, PAUL HOWARD. b. Mar 26, 1892, Salem, MA; d. Sep 24, 1976, Washington, DC; par. James Howard and Annie (Smith) Douglas; m. Dorothy S. Wolff, 1915 (divorced, 1930); m. 2d, Emily Taft, 1931; c. Helen Schaeffer (Mrs. Paul Klein); John Woolman; Dorothea Carol (Mrs. Robert John); Paul Wolfe; Jean (Mrs. Ned Bandler). EDUC.: A.B., Bowdoin Coll., 1913; A.M., Columbia U., 1915, Ph.D., 1921; Harvard U., 1915–16. POLIT. & GOV.: appointed sec., PA Comm. on Unemployment, 1930; adviser, NY Comm. on Unemployment, 1930; appointed member, IL Housing Comm., 1931–33; member, Consumers' Advisory Board, National Recovery Administration, 1933–35; Fusion candidate for mayor of Chicago, IL, 1935 (withdrew); social security adviser, 1938–39; elected as a Democrat, alderman, Chicago, IL, 1939–42; candidate for Democratic nomination to U.S. Senate (IL), 1942; delegate, Dem. Nat'l. Conv., 1948, 1952, 1956, 1964, 1968; elected as a Democrat to U.S. Senate (IL), 1949–67; ***candidate for Democratic nomination to presidency of the U.S., 1952***; Democratic candidate for U.S. Senate (IL), 1966; appointed chm., President's Comm. on Urban Affairs, 1967–68; appointed chm., Cmte. on Tax Reform, 1969. BUS. & PROF.: instructor in economics, U. of IL, 1916–17; asst. prof. of economics, Reed Coll., 1917–18; industrial relations work with Emergency Fleet Corp., 1918–19; assoc. prof. of economics, U. of WA, 1919–20; asst. prof., U. of Chicago, 1920–23, assoc. prof., 1923–25, prof., 1925–29; visiting prof., Amherst Coll., 1924–27; faculty, New School of Social Research, 1966–69. MIL.: pvt., lt. col., U.S.M.C., 1942–45; Bronze Star. MEM.: American Commonwealth Political Fund (chm., 1935); Columbia U. Intercollegiate Socialist Soc. (pres., 1915); Intercollegiate Socialist Soc. (exec. cmte., 1915–16); Freedom House (trustee, 1967–69); Econometric Soc. (fellow); American Acad. of Arts and Sciences; American Economic Assn. (pres., 1947); American Statistical Assn.; Proportional Representation League; Royal Economics Assn.; American Phil. Soc.; Phi Beta Kappa; Delta Upsilon; Federal City Club; Chicago Literary Club; Chicago City Club; Quadrangle Club; Elks; American Legion; VFW. AWARDS: Guggenheim Fellow, 1931; received Sidney Hillman Award, 1957; John F. Kennedy Award, Catholic Inter-racial Council, 1970. HON. DEG.: LL.D., Bowdoin Coll.; LL.D., MacMurray Coll.; LL.D., Bates Coll.; LL.D., DePauw Coll.; LL.D., St. Ambrose Coll.; LL.D., Lake Forest Coll.; LL.D., William and Mary U.; LL.D., Oberlin Coll.; LL.D., New School for Social Research; LL.D., U.

of Rochester; LL.D., Knox Coll.; LL.D., Bryant Coll.; LL.D., Bucknell U.; LL.D., Amherst Coll.; Litt.D., Rollins Coll.; L.H.D., U. of Southern IL; L.H.D., Lincoln Coll.; L.H.D., U. of IL. WRITINGS: *American Apprenticeship and Industrial Education* (1921); *Worker in Modern Economic Society* (1923); *Wages of the Family* (1925); *Soviet Russia in the Second Decade* (coauthor, 1928); *Adam Smith, 1776–1926* (1928); *Real Wages in the United States, 1890–1926* (1930); *The Coming of a New Party* (1930); *Movement of Real Wages* (coauthor, 1930); *The Problem of Unemployment* (coauthor, 1931); *Standards of Unemployment Insurance* (1933); *The Theory of Wages* (1934); *Controlling Depressions* (1935); *Social Security in the United States* (1936); *Ethics in Government* (1952); *Economy in the National Government* (1952); *America in the Marketplace* (1966); *In Our Time* (1968); *In the Fullness of Time* (1972). REL.: Unitarian (nee Soc. of Friends). RES.: Chicago, IL.

DOUGLAS, STEPHEN ARNOLD.

b. Apr 23, 1813, Brandon, VT; d. Jun 3, 1861, Chicago, IL; par. Dr. Stephen A. and Sarah (Fisk) Douglass; m. Martha Martin, Apr 7, 1847; m. 2d, Adele Cutts, 1856. EDUC.: Brandon Acad.; Canadaigua (NY) Acad. POLIT. & GOV.: state's atty., First Judicial District of IL, 1834–35; founder, IL Democratic Party; elected as a Democrat to IL State House of Reps., 1836–37; registrar, U.S. Land Office, Springfield, IL, 1837–39; sec. of state of IL, 1840; judge, IL Supreme Court, 1841–42; elected as a Democrat to U.S. House (IL), 1843–47; elected as a Democrat to U.S. Senate (IL), 1847–61; ***candidate for Democratic nomination to presidency of the U.S., 1852, 1856; Democratic candidate for presidency of the U.S., 1860***. BUS. & PROF.: atty.; admitted to IL Bar, 1834. MISC.: noted for "Lincoln-Douglas" debates during 1858 IL senatorial campaign, which brought Abraham Lincoln (q.v.) to national attention despite his defeat by Douglas; known as the "Little Giant." RES.: Chicago, IL.

DOUGLAS, SYLVESTER M.

b. Jan 24, 1833, Leyden, NY; par. Lester and Sarah (Potter) Douglas; m. Louisa Smith, Nov 8, 1854; c. Janet. POLIT. & GOV.: delegate, American Party National Convention, 1888; ***National School House Party candidate for vice presidency of the U.S., 1892***; Democratic candidate for OR state dairy and food commissioner, 1904. BUS. & PROF.: temperance lecturer. MEM.: British-American Assn. RES.: Rochester, NY.

DOUGLAS, WILLIAM ORVILLE.

b. Oct 16, 1898, Maine, MN; d. Jan 19, 1980, Washington, DC; par. William and Julia Bickford (Fiske) Douglas; m. Mildred M. Riddle, Aug 16, 1923; m. 2d, Mercedes Hester, Dec 14, 1954 (divorced, 1963); m. 3d, Joan Martin, Aug 1963 (divorced); m. 4th, Cathleen Heffernan, Jul 1966; c. Mildred Riddle (Mrs. Norman T. Read); William Orville. EDUC.: A.B., Whitman Coll., 1920; LL.B., Columbia U., 1925. POLIT. & GOV.: special adviser to William J. Donovan, bankruptcy investigation, New York, NY, 1929–32; sec. to Comm. on the Study of the Business of Federal Courts, 1930–32; dir., Protective Comm. Study, Securities and Exchange Comm., 1934–36; appointed commissioner, Securities and Exchange Comm., 1936–39 (chm., 1937); appointed assoc. justice, Supreme Court of the U.S., 1939–75; ***candidate for Democratic nomination to presidency of the U.S., 1940, 1952; candidate for Democratic nomination to vice presidency of the U.S., 1940, 1944, 1948, 1952***. BUS. & PROF.: atty.; admitted to NY Bar, 1926; law practice, New York, NY, 1925–27; law faculty, Columbia U., 1925–28; law faculty, Yale U., 1928–34. MIL.: pvt., U.S. Army, 1918. MEM.: Yale Club; University Club; Phi Alpha Delta; Delta Sigma Rho; Beta Theta Pi; Masons; ABA; NY Bar Assn.; Columbia University Club; Graduates Club; Phi Beta Kappa; Masons; Royal Geographic Soc.; Himalayan Club; Overseas Press Club. HON. DEG.: A.M., Yale U., 1932; LL.D., Whitman Coll., 1938; LL.D., Wesleyan U., 1940; LL.D., Washington and Jefferson Coll., 1942; LL.D., William and Mary Coll., 1943; LL.D., Rollins Coll., 1947; LL.D., National U., 1949; LL.D., New School for Social Research, 1952; LL.D., U. of Toledo, 1956; LL.D., Bucknell U., 1958; LL.D., Dalhousie U., 1958; LL.D., Colby Coll., 1961. WRITINGS: *Democracy and Finance* (1940); *Being An American* (1948); *Of Men and Mountains* (1950); *Strange Lands and Friendly People* (1951); *Beyond the High Himalayas* (1952); *North From Malaya* (1953); *An Almanac of Liberty* (1954); *We the Judges* (1955); *Russian Journey* (1956); *The Right of the People* (1958); *Exploring the Himalaya* (1958); *West of the Indus* (1958); *My Wilderness—East to Katahdin* (1960); *My Wilderness—The Pacific West* (1961); *A Living Bill of Rights* (1961); *Democracy's Manifesto* (1962); *The Anatomy of Liberty* (1963); *Mr. Lincoln and the Negroes* (1963); *Freedom of the Mind* (1963); *A Wilderness Bill of Rights* (1965); *The Bible and the Schools* (1966); *Farewell to Texas* (1967); *Towards a Global Federalism* (1968); *Points of Rebellion* (1969); *International Dissent* (1970); *Holocaust or Hemispheric Cooperation* (1970); *The Three Hundred Years War* (1972); *Go East Young Man* (1974). REL.: Presb. RES.: Goose Prairie, WA.

DOUGLASS, FREDERICK AUGUSTUS (nee FREDERICK AUGUSTUS WASHINGTON BAILEY).

b. Feb 1817, Tuckahoe, MD; d. Feb 20, 1895, Washington, DC; par. unknown white father and Harriet Bailey; m. Anna Murray, Sep 14, 1838; m. 2d, Helen Pitts, Jan 1884; c. Charles Remond; Annie; Rosetta (Mrs. Nathan Sprague); Lewis Henry; Frederick, Jr. EDUC.: self-educated. POLIT. & GOV.: ***candidate for Liberty League nomination to presidency of the U.S., 1848; Abolitionist (Liberty) Party candidate for vice presidency of the U.S., 1856***; delegate, Loyalist Convention, 1866; appointed sec., Santo Domingo Comm., 1871; ***Equal Rights (Cosmic, Free Love, People's) Party candidate for vice presidency of the U.S., 1872 (declined)***; presidential elector, Republican Party, 1872; appointed U.S. marshal, DC, 1877–81; recorder of deeds, DC, 1881–86; ***candidate for Republican nomination to presidency of the U.S., 1888***; appointed U.S. minister to Haiti, 1889–91. BUS. & PROF.: slave to Capt. Aaron Anthony, 1817–38; escaped to Baltimore, MD, 1838; house servant; common laborer; abolitionist; publisher, *North Star,* Rochester, NY, 1847–50; ed., *Frederick Douglass's Paper,* 1850–60; ed., *Frederick Douglass's Monthly,* Rochester, NY, 1858–64; ed., *The New National Era,* Washington, DC, 1869–72; adviser to John Brown; journalist; lecturer. MEM.: MA Anti-Slavery Soc. (lecturer, 1841); East Baltimore Mental Improvement Soc.; American Anti-Slavery Soc.; Freeman's Savings and Trust Co. (pres., 1874); New England Anti-Slavery Soc. HON. DEG.: LL.D., Howard U., 1872. WRITINGS: *Narrative of the Life of Frederick Douglass* (1845); *Vie de Frederic Douglass Traduite nar S. K. Parkes* (1848); *Letter to Thomas Auld* (1848); *Lectures on American Slavery* (1851); *The Claims of the Negro, Ethnologically Considered* (1854); *My Bondage and My Freedom* (1855); *The Anti-Slavery Movement* (1855); *Two Speeches* (1857); *Eulogy of the Late Hon. Wm. Jay* (1859); *Sklaverei und Freiheit* (1860); *The Slave's Appeal to Great Britain* (1862); *Men of Color to Arms* (1863); *Speech Before the American Anti-Slavery Society* (1864); *Life and Times of Frederick Douglass* (1882); *Speech on the Seventy-Ninth Anniversary of the Birth of Lincoln* (1888); *The Nation's Problem* (1889); *Lecture on Haiti* (1893). REL.: Methodist. MISC.: advocate of women's suffrage; raised 54th and 55th MA Colored Regiments, Civil War. RES.: Washington, DC.

DOUGLASS, JOHN JOSEPH. b. Feb 9, 1873, East Boston, MA; d. Apr 5, 1939, West Roxbury, MA; par. John and Elizabeth (McLaughlin) Douglass; m. Marion G. Cummings, Nov 25, 1925; c. Paul. EDUC.: grad., East Boston (MA) H.S., 1889; A.B., Boston Coll., 1893, A.M., 1896; LL.B., Georgetown U., 1896. POLIT. & GOV.: elected as a Democrat to MA State House, 1899–1903, 1907–09, 1913–15; ***candidate for Democratic nomination to presidency of the U.S., 1908***; delegate, MA State Constitutional Convention, 1917–18; elected as a Democrat to U.S. House (MA), 1925–35; delegate, Dem. Nat'l. Conv., 1928, 1932; candidate for Democratic nomination to U.S. House (MA), 1934; appointed commissioner of Penal Institutions, Boston, MA, 1939. BUS. & PROF.: atty.; admitted to MA Bar, 1897; law practice, Boston, MA; author; playwright. RES.: West Roxbury, MA.

DOUGLASS, WILLIAM CAMPBELL. b. Nov 17, 1852, Pleasant Hill, GA; d. Apr 19, 1928, Raleigh, NC; par. Dr. John C. and Sarah Isabelle (Birch) Douglass; m. Josie Tysor, 1874; c. Rev. John J.; Walter; Clarence; Mrs. William Hayes; William Birch; Dr. S.E.; Mrs. Theodore Richards, Jr.; Clyde A.; Joseph C.; Mrs. L. T. Buchanan, Jr. EDUC.: Collingsworth Inst., Talbottom, GA; read law under Marmaduke S. Robins, Asheboro, NC. POLIT. & GOV.: appointed solicitor, Eighth Judicial District of NC, 1895; ***Independent Democratic candidate for presidency of the U.S., 1896***; elected as a Democrat to NC State House, 1907–09. BUS. & PROF.: schoolteacher, 3 years; businessman, Asheboro, NC, 1877; atty.; admitted to NC Bar, 1880; law practice, Troy, NC, 1880–88; partner (with Thomas J. Shaw), law firm, Carthage, NC, 1888–95; partner (with Union L. Spence), law firm, Carthage, 1895–96; partner (with J. Newton Holding), law firm, Raleigh, NC, 1896–97; partner (with Robert W. Simms), law firm, Raleigh; turpentine manufacturer, 1905–08; partner (with Winfield H. Lyon), law firm, Raleigh, 1908–11; partner (with Clyde A. Douglass), law firm, Raleigh, 1911–28. MEM.: Wake Cty. Bar Assn. (pres., 1926–27); NC Bar Assn.; ABA; Odd Fellows (grand master); Masons. REL.: Bapt. MISC.: noted Negro politician. RES.: Raleigh, NC.

DOW, NEAL. b. Mar 20, 1804, Portland, ME; d. Oct 2, 1897, Portland, ME; par. Josiah and Dorcas (Allen) Dow; m. Maria Cornelia Durant Maynard, Jan 20, 1830; c. Louisa Dwight; Edward; Emma Maynard; Frederick N.; Cornelia Maria; Henry; Josiah; Russell Congdon; Frank Allen. EDUC.: Master Hall's School, Portland, ME; Master Taylor's School, Portland; Friend's Acad., New Bedford, MA; Portland Acad. POLIT. & GOV.: appointed colonel, staff of Gov. Edward Kent (ME), 1840; charter member, Republican Party, 1852; elected mayor of Portland, 1850–51, 1855–56; candidate for mayor of Portland, ME, 1852; elected as a Republican to ME State House, 1859–61; ***candidate for Prohibition Party nomination to presidency of the U.S., 1872; Prohibition Party candidate for presidency of the U.S., 1880***; presidential elector, Prohibition Party, 1888. BUS. & PROF.: partner, Josiah Dow and Son (tannery), 1820–74; member, Portland Fire Dept., 1822–47 (chief engineer, 1837–47); temperance advocate; clerk, Deluge Engine Co.; trustee, Manufacturers and Traders Bank; pres., Portland Gaslight Co.; dir., Maine Central R.R. Co.; dir., Androscoggin and Kennebec R.R. Co. MIL.: col., 13th Regt., ME Volunteers, 1861; brig. gen., U.S.V., 1862; prisoner-of-war, 1864; exchanged for Gen. Fitzhugh Lee. MEM.: ME Temperance Soc. (founder, 1834); New England Sabbath Protective League (vice pres.); Portland Atheneum (sec.); ME Charitable Mechanics' Assn.; ME Temperance Union (founder, 1837); Young Men's Temperance Soc. (delegate; sec., Portland Branch, 1833); World Temperance Convention (pres., 1853). WRITINGS: *The Prohibition of the Liquor Traffic; On the American War* (1862); *The Results of Twenty-Five Years of Prohibition in Maine; The Maine Law: Its Complete Vindication* (1877); *The Liquor Question* (1887); *A Letter from Neal Dow; A History of Prohibition in Maine* (1898); *The Reminiscences of Neal Dow: Recollections of Eighty Years* (1898). REL.: Soc. of Friends. MISC.: known as "Father of the Maine Law." RES.: Portland, ME.

DOWD, DOUGLAS FITZGERALD. b. Dec 7, 1919, San Francisco, CA; par. Mervyn and Sybil E. (Seid) Dowd; m. Kathryn M. "Kay" (Hayes) Dowd; c. Jeffrey; Jennifer. EDUC.: A.B., U. of CA, Berkeley, 1948, Ph.D., 1951. POLIT. & GOV.: ***Peace and Freedom Party candidate for vice presidency of the U.S., 1968 (withdrew)***. BUS. & PROF.: economist; lecturer in economics and business administration, U. of CA, 1950–53; asst. prof., prof. of economics, Cornell U., 1953–71; prof. of economics, Antioch Coll./West, San Francisco, CA,

1972–. MIL.: capt., U.S. Air Force, 1942–46. MEM.: Young Progressive Citizens of America (campus chm., 1948); Mobilization to End the War in Vietnam (old, 1966–69; new, 1969–70; American Economic History Assn.; British Economic History Assn.; Students for a Democratic Society (campus sponsor). WRITINGS: *Modern Economic Problems in Historical Perspective; Thorstein Veblen* (1966). MAILING ADDRESS: 1145 Filbert St., San Francisco, CA.

DOWDY, GEORGE A. POLIT. & GOV.: delegate, Dem. Nat'l. Conv., 1972; ***candidate for Democratic nomination to vice presidency of the U.S., 1972***. MAILING ADDRESS: 808 Baltimore St., Memphis, TN.

DOWLER, ARTHUR F. POLIT. & GOV.: Socialist Labor Party candidate for gov. of TX, 1906; member, Socialist Labor Party National Cmte., 1908–11; ***candidate for Socialist Labor Party nomination to vice presidency of the U.S., 1908***; Socialist Labor Party candidate for gov. of IA, 1916; Socialist Party candidate for U.S. Senate (IA), 1920. RES.: El Paso, TX.

DOWNEY, MAGDALENE RUTH. b. 1913, OH; m. Keith Downey (divorced). EDUC.: B.A., OH Wesleyan U. POLIT. & GOV.: campaign aide, McCarthy for pres., 1968; ***independent (Cmte. for a Constitutional Presidency) candidate for vice presidency of the U.S., 1976***. BUS. & PROF.: sec., WPA, Washington, DC; sec., OSS, Washington, DC; staff, Continuing Education Program, U. of WI Extension Service. MAILING ADDRESS: 2632 Trojan Dr., Green Bay, WI 54301.

DOWNEY, ROBERT JACK. POLIT. & GOV.: ***independent candidate for presidency of the U.S., 1992***. MAILING ADDRESS: 125 Grand Ave., Suite 28, Pacific Grove, CA 93950.

DOWNEY, SEAN MORTON, JR. (aka **CALVIN FINCH).** b. Dec 9, 1933, New York, NY; par. Sean Morton and Barbara (Bennett) Downey; m. 1954 (divorced); m. 2d, Joan Tyrrell, 1962 (divorced); m. 3d, Kim Cotton, 1977; c. Melissa; Tracey; Kelli; EDUC.: B.S., NY U., 1955; LL.B., La Salle U., 1962; Ph.D., Valley Christian U., Fresno, CA. POLIT. & GOV.: member, Dem. Nat'l. Cmte., 1972–76; finance chm., Carter for President, 1976; ***candidate for Democratic nomination to presidency of the U.S., 1980; candidate for American Independent Party nomination to presidency of the U.S., 1980***. BUS. & PROF.: nightclub singer, Mapes Hotel and Sahara Hotel, Reno, NV; disc jockey; composer; performer; businessman; radio exec.; first league sec., American Basketball Assn.; founder, World Team Boxing Assn., 1976; pres., Silverstate Broadcasting Corp., Sparks, NV; lobbyist, National Right to Life Cmte., Orlando, FL; radio talk show host, WDBO, Orlando, FL; radio talk show host, KFBK, Sacramento, CA, to 1984; radio talk show host, WMAQ, Chicago, IL; talk show host, "The Morton Downey, Jr. Show," WWOR-TV, Secaucus, NJ. MEM.: Life Amendment Political Action Cmte. (chm.); National Right to Life Cmte. Awards.: Vatican Medal for Humanitarian Work. WRITINGS: Songs: "Please Don't Mention My Name"; "Treasure of Love"; "Ballad of Billy Brown"; "I Believe America"; "Last Day on Earth"; "Teach Me How to Pray"; "Colorado Rain"; "Ten Years of Hard Labor"; "Gotta Right to Live"; "Sounds of Yesterday"; "Because We're Young"; "Franklin Delano Roosevelt"; "Harry S. Truman"; "American History"; "Red Neck American Heroes"; "John Fitzgerald Kennedy"; "Roaring 20's"; "Those Were the 50's"; "You Cheated"; "Boulevard of Broken Dreams"; Lyrics: "Little Rose"; Instrumentals: "South Swell"; "You Alone." REL.: R.C. MISC.: served 61 days in jail for bouncing a check, Mira Loma, CA; accosted by "skinheads" in airport and branded with swastika, ridiculed, and forced to quit television, 1989. MAILING ADDRESS: 2155 Howard, Sparks, NV 89431.

DOWNEY, SHERIDAN. b. Mar 9, 1884, Laramie, WY; d. Oct 25, 1961, San Francisco, CA; par. Stephen Wheeler and Evangeline Victoria (Owen) Downey; m. Helen Symons, Nov 15, 1910; c. Margaret Emily Dinsmore; Sheridan; Helen Jane Wilcox; Richard Symons; Patricia June. EDUC.: U. of WY; LL.B., U. of MI, 1907. POLIT. & GOV.: elected district atty., Albany Cty., WY, 1909–12; Democratic candidate for lt. gov. of CA, 1934; Democratic candidate for U.S. House (CA), 1936; elected as a Democrat to U.S. Senate (CA), 1938–50 (resigned); ***candidate for Democratic nomination to vice presidency of the U.S., 1940***. BUS. & PROF.: atty.; admitted to WY Bar, 1907; law practice, Laramie, WY; partner (with S. W. Downey, Jr.), law firm, Sacramento, CA, 1912. WRITINGS: *Onward America* (1933); *Why I Believe in the Townsend Plan* (1936); *Pensions or Penury?* (1939); *Highways to Prosperity* (1940); *They Would Rule the Valley* (1948); *Truth About the Tidelands*. MISC.: pension advocate; follower of End Poverty in CA (EPIC), Townsend Plan, and Ham and Eggs movements. RES.: San Francisco, CA.

DOWNS, ED. POLIT. & GOV.: chm., Aberdeen Cty. (SD) Democratic Central Cmte., 1949; chm., SD State Democratic Central Cmte.; ***candidate for Democratic nomination to presidency of the U.S., 1952***. MAILING ADDRESS: Aberdeen, SD.

DOWNS, SOLOMON WEATHERSBEE. b. 1801, Montgomery Cty., TN; d. Aug 14, 1854, Crab Orchard Springs, KY. EDUC.: grad., Transylvania U., 1823; studied law. POLIT. & GOV.: U.S. district atty. for LA, 1845–47; member, LA State Constitutional Convention; elected as a Democrat to U.S. Senate (LA), 1847–53; ***candidate for Democratic nomination to vice presidency of the U.S., 1852***; appointed collector, Port of New Orleans, 1853. BUS. & PROF.: atty.; admitted to LA Bar, 1826; law practice, Bayou Sara, West Feliciana Parish,

LA; law practice, New Orleans, LA, 1845–53. RES.: New Orleans, LA.

DOYLE, JAMES GEORGE. b. Mar 20, 1949, Fresno, CA; par. Charles Dennis and Elinore Freida (Vagim) Doyle; m. Dortha Ann Brock; c. Thomas James Lewis (stepson). EDUC.: G.E.D. POLIT. & GOV.: independent candidate for Fresno (CA) City Council, 1973, 1975, 1977; independent candidate for mayor of Fresno, CA, 1985; ***independent candidate for presidency of the U.S., 1988***. BUS. & PROF.: employee, Pacific Bell, 1974–. MIL.: Sp/4, U.S. Army, 1968–70; Purple Heart; Combat Infantry Badge; Air Medal; Vietnam Service Medal; Vietnam Campaign Ribbon; National Defense Service Medal. MEM.: Vietnam Veterans of America, Inc. (pres., Chapter 247). REL.: nonbeliever. MAILING ADDRESS: 134 West Yale, Fresno, CA 93705.

DREW. POLIT. & GOV.: ***New World Council candidate for presidency of the U.S., 1988***. MAILING ADDRESS: 325 Pennsylvania Ave., S.E., Suite 310, Washington, DC 20003.

DREW, SIMON P. W. POLIT. & GOV.: ***Independent Political Party Lincoln Republican candidate for vice presidency of the U.S., 1928***. BUS. & PROF.: minister; pastor, St. Stephen's Colored Baptist Church, Astoria, NY, 1901; pastor, Baptist Church, Philadelphia, PA, 1928; pastor, Baptist Church, Boston, MA, 1930. MISC.: known as "Dr. Drew"; indicted for mail fraud, convicted, and received suspended sentence, 1930. RES.: Astoria, NY.

DREWS, ROBIN ARTHUR. b. May 6, 1913, Coos Bay, OR; m. 1974; c. one. EDUC.: B.A., U. of OR, 1938; M.A., U. of MI, 1947, Ph.D., 1952. POLIT. & GOV.: ***New Party of Oregon candidate for vice presidency of the U.S., 1968***. BUS. & PROF.: prof. of social sciences, U. of the Ryukyus, 1952–53; asst. prof., assoc. prof., MI State U., 1953–56; prof. of anthropology, Lewis and Clark Coll., 1965–. MEM.: American Anthropological Assn.; Assn. for Asian Studies; American Inst. for Pacific Relations. MAILING ADDRESS: c/o Dept. of Anthropology, Lewis and Clark Coll., 0615 S.W. Palatine Hill, Portland, OR 97219.

DRINAN, ROBERT FREDERICK. b. Nov 15, 1920, Boston, MA; par. James Joseph and Ann M. (Flanagan) Drinan; single. EDUC.: A.B., Boston Coll., 1942, M.A., 1947; LL.B., Georgetown U., 1949, LL.M., 1950; Doctor of Theology, Gregorian U., 1954; S.TL., Weston Coll., 1954; studied, Florence, Italy, 1954–55. POLIT. & GOV.: elected as a Democrat to U.S. House (MA), 1971–81; delegate, Dem. Nat'l. Conv., 1972; ***candidate for Democratic nomination to vice presidency of the U.S., 1972***. BUS. & PROF.: priest; ordained, Soc. of Jesus, Roman Catholic Church, 1953; dean, Boston Coll. Law School, 1956–70; corresponding ed., America, 1958–70; editor-in-chief, *Family Law Quarterly*, 1967–70; prof. of law, Georgetown U., 1981–. MEM.: American Jud. Soc.; American Bar Foundation (fellow); Assn. of American Law Schools; American Law Inst.; American Acad. of Arts and Sciences (fellow, 1966); MA Bar Assn.; Boston Bar Assn. (council, 1959–62); Americans for Democratic Action (pres.); A.C.L.U. (adviser); Newton Cultural Affairs (trustee); National Conference of Christians and Jews (trustee); National Interreligious Task Force on Soviet Jewry (founder); U.S. Comm. on Civil Rights (member, MA Advisory Comm., 1962–70); Democratic Study Group; Members of Congress for Peace Through Law. AWARDS: Gold Medal Award, MA Bar Assn., 1966. Hon. Deg: LL.D., Long Island U.; LL.D., Worcester State Coll.; LL.D., Kenyon Coll.; LL.D., Loyola U.; LL.D., U. of Chicago; LL.D., U. of Lowell; LL.D., U. of Bridgeport; LL.D., Gonzaga U.; LL.D., U. of Santa Clara; LL.D., RI Coll.; LL.D., Framingham State Coll.; LL.D., Villanova U.; LL.D., Syracuse U.; LL.D., St. Joseph's U.; LL.D., Long Island U.; LL.D., Worcester State Coll.; LL.D., Hebrew Union Coll. WRITINGS: *Religion, the Courts, and Public Policy* (1963); *Democracy, Dissent and Disorder* (1969); *Vietnam and Armageddon* (1970); *Honor the Promise: America's Commitment to Israel* (1977); *The Right to Be Educated* (ed., 1968); *Beyond the Nuclear Freeze* (ed., 1983). REL.: R.C. MAILING ADDRESS: c/o Georgetown U. Law Center, 600 New Jersey Ave., N.W., Washington, DC.

DRISCOLL, ALFRED EASTLACK. b. Oct 25, 1902, Pittsburgh, PA; d. Mar 9, 1975, Haddonfield, NJ; par. Alfred Robie and Mattie (Eastlack) Driscoll; m. Antoinette Ware Tatem, May 1932; c. Patricia Ware; Alfred Tatem; Peter Eastlack. EDUC.: A.B., Williams Coll., 1925; LL.B., Harvard U., 1928. POLIT. & GOV.: elected member, Haddonfield (NJ) Board of Education, 1929–37; member, Haddonfield (NJ) Borough Comm.; dir., Haddonfield (NJ) Borough Dept. of Revenue and Finance, 1937–47; member, Princeton Survey Comm.; elected as a Republican to NJ State Senate, 1938–43 (majority leader, 1940); member, NJ Civilian Defense Council; member, NJ Comm. on State Administrative Reorganization, 1945; commissioner, NJ State Dept. of Alcoholic Beverage Control, 1941–47; elected as a Republican to gov. of NJ, 1947–55; ***candidate for Republican nomination to presidency of the U.S., 1948***; vice chm., President's Comm. on Intergovernmental Relations, 1954–55; member, NJ State Tax Policy Comm., 1969–75; member, NJ State Hist. Comm., 1971–75. BUS. & PROF.: atty.; admitted to NJ Bar, 1929; partner, Starr, Summerill and Lloyd (law firm), 1929–47; dir., West Title Co.; member, Advisory Board, Camden Trust Co.; member, exec. cmte., Warner-Lambert Co., 1954–71, pres., 1954–67, chm. of the board, 1967, hon. chm. of the board, dir., 1967–71; dir., Chemical Fund. MEM.: NJ Bar Assn.; National Assn. of State Liquor Administrators (chm.); YMCA (trustee); Haddonfield Hist. Soc.; Haddonfield Civic Assn.; Psi Upsilon; Williams Coll. Club; Downtown Club; National Municipal League (pres., 1963–67); Williams Coll. (trustee); Samuel H. Kress Foundation (trustee); Harvard Law School

Council (dir.); Friends of NJ Public Broadcasting; NJ Audubon Soc.; NJ Hist. Soc.; Taconic Country Club; Metropolitan Club. HON. DEG.: LL.D., Williams Coll.; LL.D., Princeton U.; LL.D., Rutgers U.; LL.D., Beaver U.; LL.D., Rider Coll.; LL.D., John Marshall Coll.; LL.D., Lafayette U. REL.: Presb. (trustee). MISC.: known as the "Father of the NJ Turnpike." RES.: Haddonfield, NJ.

DRISCOLL, CARROLL. b. 1936. POLIT. & GOV.: ***Right to Life Party candidate for vice presidency of the U.S., 1980***. BUS. & PROF.: housewife; teacher. MAILING ADDRESS: NJ.

DRUCKER, ROBERT. b. 1925. POLIT. & GOV.: ***candidate for Republican nomination to presidency of the U.S., 1988***. BUS. & PROF.: retired; investment broker. MAILING ADDRESS: Plantation, FL.

DRUFENBROCK, DIANE JOYCE. b. Oct 7, 1929, Evansville, IN; par. George Lehning and Bessie Julia (Litmer) Drufenbrock; single. EDUC.: grad., Memorial H.S., Evansville, IN, 1948; B.A., Alverno Coll., 1953; M.S. Marquette U., 1959; Ph.D., U. of IL, 1961; Bodwin Coll., 1965. POLIT. & GOV.: elected member, Area Council, Social Development Comm. of Milwaukee Cty., WI, 1977–79, commissioner, 1979–; national treas., Socialist Party, 1977–; delegate, Socialist International, 1978; ***Socialist Party candidate for vice presidency of the U.S., 1980***; delegate-at-large, Socialist Party National Convention, 1987. BUS. & PROF.: joined religious order of School Sisters of St. Francis, 1952; teacher, St. Matthias School, Milwaukee, WI, 1952–53; teacher, Sacred Heart School, Lombard, IL, 1953–57; teacher, St. Joseph H.S., Kenosha, WI, 1957–59; instructor, prof. of mathematics, Alverno Coll., 1961–74; cofounder, writer, distributor, *South Side Urban News*, Milwaukee, WI; teacher, St. Joan Antida H.S., Milwaukee, WI, 1979–80; coordinator, computer-assisted instruction, St. Adelbert Elementary School, Milwaukee, WI, 1970–80; lecturer in mathematics, U. of WI, Parkside, WI, 1980–. MEM.: Mathematical Assn. of America (state chairperson, 1966); National Council of Teachers of Mathematics; AAUP; Pi Mu Epsilon; Craft Raft (co-organizer; charter member); Parent Advocates (chief organizer; dir. of training); Milwaukee Catholic Symphony; Commonwealth Bank (corporator; trustee, 1973–79); Project Equality (dir., 1975–79); Outpost Natural Foods Cooperative; Milwaukee Tenants Union. AWARDS: Cooperative Fellowship, National Science Foundation, 1960–61. WRITINGS: "On the Groups of Order 32," *Illinois Journal of Mathematics* (1962); *Short Course for Elementary Teachers: A Listening Guide and Audio Tapes* (1962); "The Problem of Arithmetic," *Education Bulletin of the School Sisters of St. Francis* (1962); "Attitudes and Appreciations in Present Day Mathematics," *Chicago Archdiocesan Newsletter*, spring, 1962; "Teachers Study UICSM," *Wisconsin Mathematics Teacher*, Feb 1963; "Teaching Directed Numbers in the Middle Grades," *Wisconsin Mathematics Teacher*, 1964. REL.: R.C. MAILING ADDRESS: 2522A West Grant St., Milwaukee, WI 53215.

DRUMMER, JOHN NEAL, JR. par. John Neal Drummer. POLIT. & GOV.: ***independent candidate for presidency of the U.S., 1988***. MAILING ADDRESS: V-10, Wedgefield Plantation, Georgetown, SC 29440.

DUBOSE, NORRIS JAMES, JR. par. Norris James Dubose. POLIT. & GOV.: ***candidate for Democratic nomination to vice presidency of the U.S., 1988; candidate for Democratic nomination to presidency of the U.S., 1992***. MAILING ADDRESS: 9918 LaDuke St., Kensington, MD 20008.

DUFF, JAMES HENDERSON. b. Jan 21, 1883, Mansfield, PA; d. Dec 20, 1969, Washington, DC; par. Joseph Miller and Margaret (Morgan) Duff; m. Jean Taylor, Oct 26, 1909; c. none. EDUC.: A.B., Princeton U., 1904; U. of PA Law School, 1904–06; LL.B., U. of Pittsburgh, 1907. POLIT. & GOV.: presidential elector, Progressive Party, 1912; city solicitor, Carnegie, PA; delegate, Rep. Nat'l. Conv., 1932, 1936, 1940, 1948, 1952; appointed atty. gen. of PA, 1943–46; elected as a Republican to gov. of PA, 1947–51; member, PA Pardon Board; ***candidate for Republican nomination to presidency of the U.S., 1948***; elected as a Republican to U.S. Senate (PA), 1951–57; Republican candidate for U.S. Senate (PA), 1956. BUS. & PROF.: atty.; admitted to PA Bar, 1907; partner, Duff, Scott and Smith (law firm), Pittsburgh, PA, 1907–43; partner, Davis, Richberg, Tydings, Landa and Duff (law firm), Washington, DC; pres., Virginia Manor Co. MEM.: Masons; Elks; Moose; Eagles; Rotary Club; Carnegie Library (life trustee); Allegheny Cty. Bar Assn. HON. DEG.: LL.D., U. of Pittsburgh; LL.D., U. of PA Law School, 1947; LL.D., Duquesne U., 1947; LL.D., Albright Coll., 1947; LL.D., PA Military Coll., 1947; LL.D., Lafayette Coll., 1947; LL.D., Franklin and Marshall Coll., 1947; LL.D., Washington and Jefferson Coll., 1947; LL.D., Temple U., 1947; LL.D., St. Francis Coll., 1947; LL.D., Geneva Coll.; LL.D., Lincoln U.; L.H.D., Villanova Coll., 1948; LL.D., Jefferson Medical Coll.; LL.D., Elizabethtown Coll.; LL.D., Lebanon Valley Coll.; LL.D., Drexel Inst.; LL.D., Lehigh U.; LL.D., Rollins Coll.; D.C.L., Hahnemann Medical Coll. and Hospital; Litt.D., Waynesburg Coll.; D.Sc., Philadelphia Coll. of Osteopathy. REL.: Presb. RES.: Harrisburg, PA.

DUKAKIS, MICHAEL STANLEY. b. Nov 3, 1933, Boston, MA; par. Panos and Euterpe (Boukis) Dukakis; m. Katharine Dickson, Jun 20, 1963; c. John; Andrea; Kara. EDUC.: B.A., Swarthmore Coll., 1955; LL.B., Harvard U., 1960. POLIT. & GOV.: member, Town Meeting, Brookline, MA, 1959; chm., Town Cmte., Brookline, MA, 1960–62; elected as a Democrat to MA State House, 1963–71; alternate delegate, Dem. Nat'l. Conv., 1968, delegate, 1980; Democratic candidate for lt. gov. of

MA, 1970; elected as a Democrat to gov. of MA, 1975–79, 1983–91; candidate for Democratic nomination to gov. of MA, 1978; ***Democratic candidate for presidency of the U.S., 1988***. BUS. & PROF.: atty.; admitted to MA Bar, 1960; partner, Hill and Barlow (law firm), Boston, MA, 1960–74; lecturer, dir. of intergovernmental studies, John F. Kennedy School of Government, Harvard U., 1979–82; moderator, "The Advocates," WGBH-TV. MIL.: U.S. Army, 1955–57. MEM.: New England Regional Comm. (co-chair); Students for Democratic Action (campus chm.); Phi Beta Kappa. REL.: Greek Orthodox. MAILING ADDRESS: 85 Perry St., Brookline, MA 02146.

DUKE, DAVID ERNEST. b. Jul 1, 1950, Tulsa, OK; par. David H. and Mamie (Crick) Duke; m. Chloe D. (divorced); c. Erika; Kristine. EDUC.: military school, GA; B.A., LA State U., 1974. POLIT. & GOV.: candidate for Democratic nomination to LA State Senate, 1974, 1978; ***candidate for Democratic nomination to presidency of the U.S., 1980, 1988; won NH Democratic vice presidential primary, 1988; candidate for Democratic nomination to vice presidency of the U.S., 1988; Populist Party candidate for presidency of the U.S., 1988***; elected as a Republican to LA State House, 1989–; candidate for Republican nomination to U.S. Senate (LA), 1990; Republican candidate for gov. of LA, 1991; ***candidate for Republican nomination to presidency of the U.S., 1992***. BUS. & PROF.: Kirby Vacuum Cleaner salesman; teacher, Agency for International Development, Vientiane, Laos, 1971; ed., *Ku Klux Klan Newspaper*; owner, Patriot (National) Advertising Agency. MEM.: Knights of the Ku Klux Klan (member, 1966; grand dragon of LA; National Information Officer, 1973; national dir.; grand wizard; exec. dir.); National Party; White Youth Alliance (founder, 1969); National Assn. for the Advancement of White People (pres.); Red Cross. AWARDS: received Highest Honors, Basic R.O.T.C., LA State U.; Declaration of Freedom Award; named hon. col., AL Militia, 1972. WRITINGS: *Finders-Keepers* (pseud. James Konrad). REL.: Methodist. MAILING ADDRESS: P.O. Box 624, Metairie, LA 70181.

DUKE, WILLIE GEORGE. b. Apr 13, 1934, Campbell, OH; d. Oct 14, 1985, Pittsburgh, PA; par. Willie Daniel and Odessa (Perkins) Duke; m. Edna Smith, Aug 21, 1954; m. 2d, Kathryn Jane Landahl, Oct 24, 1970; c. Arnetta; Loreatha Hawkins; Linda Cook; Audrey Tillis; Willie Samuel. EDUC.: grad., East H.S., Youngstown, OH, 1953; grad., Evangelical Church Alliance, 1964; real estate course, Youngstown State U., 1 year. POLIT. & GOV.: ***candidate for Democratic nomination to presidency of the U.S., 1984; Independent Democratic candidate for presidency of the U.S., 1984***. BUS. & PROF.: minister; employee, Sharon Steel Corp., 3 years; founder, pastor, Truth Chapel, Inc., Youngstown, OH, 1969–85; dir., Mt. Hope Park Cemetery; pres., Duke Enterprises. MEM.: Fairflight Archery Club; Mt. Mariah House of Prayer. WRITINGS: religious tracts. REL.: Pentecostal. MISC.: originator of Team Rally; Truth Chapel Hotline; Truth Chapel Revival Crusade. RES.: Youngstown, OH.

DUKES, MILTON J. POLIT. & GOV.: candidate for Democratic nomination to gov. of SC, 1962, 1974; candidate for Democratic nomination to U.S. House (SC), 1972, 1976; ***candidate for Democratic nomination to presidency of the U.S., 1976***. BUS. & PROF.: businessman, Charleston, SC. MAILING ADDRESS: 110 Colekett St., Summerville, SC.

DULLES, JOHN FOSTER. b. Feb 25, 1888, Washington, DC; d. May 24, 1959, Washington, DC; par. Rev. Allen Macy and Edith (Foster) Dulles; m. Janet Pomeroy Avery, Jun 26, 1912; c. John Watson Foster; Lillias Pomeroy (Mrs. Robert Hinshaw); Avery. EDUC.: B.A., Princeton U., 1908; Sorbonne, Paris, France, 1908–09; LL.B., George Washington U., 1911. POLIT. & GOV.: appointed sec. to the Hague Peace Conference, 1907; appointed member, Second Pan-American Scientific Congress, 1917; appointed asst. to the chm., War Trade Board, 1918; counsel, American Comm. to Negotiate Peace, 1918–19; appointed member, Reparations Comm. and Supreme Economic Council, 1919; legal adviser, Polish Plan of Financial Stabilization, 1927; appointed U.S. representative, Berlin Debt Conference, 1933; appointed member, NY State Banking Board, 1943–46, 1949–52 (chm.); delegate, Rep. Nat'l. Conv., 1944; appointed U.S. delegate, U.N. Organizing Conference, 1945; appointed U.S. delegate, U.N. General Assembly, 1946–48, 1950; appointed as a Republican to U.S. Senate (NY), 1949; Republican candidate for U.S. Senate (NY), 1949; appointed consultant to U.S. sec. of state, 1950; appointed U.S. ambassador to Japanese Peace Negotiations, 1951; appointed U.S. sec. of state, 1953–59; ***candidate for Republican nomination to presidency of the U.S., 1956 (declined)***. BUS. & PROF.: atty.; admitted to NY Bar, 1911; partner, Sullivan and Cromwell (law firm), New York, NY, 1911–49; trustee, Bank of NY; dir., Fifth Avenue Bank; dir., American Bank Note Co.; dir., International Nickel Co. of Canada, Ltd.; dir., American Agricultural Chemical Co.; dir., Babcock and Wilcox Corp.; dir., Gold Dust Corp.; dir., Overseas Security Corp.; dir., Shenandoah Corp.; dir., United Cigar Stores; dir., American Cotton Oil Co.; dir., United Railways of St. Louis; dir., European Textile Corp. MEM.: American Geographic Soc.; Carnegie Endowment for International Peace (trustee); Union Theological Seminary (trustee); NY Public Library (trustee); Rockefeller Foundation (trustee); Assn. of the Bar of the City of New York; Phi Beta Kappa; Phi Delta Phi; University Club; Down Town Assn.; Century Club of NY; Washington Metropolitan Club; Piping Rock Club; General Education Board. AWARDS: award, Freedoms Foundation, 1949; St. Francis of Assisi Peace Medal, 1951; AMVETS Peace Award, 1952; Grand St. Post Award, American Legion, 1952; Meritorious Service Award, Military Chaplain Assn., 1952; Brotherhood Award, National Conference of Christians and Jews, 1952; award, NY Board of Trade, 1952; award, Roosevelt Memorial Assn., 1952;

Gold Certificate of Merit, VFW, 1954; H. H. Arnold Award, Air Force Assn., 1954; Man of the Year Award, *Time Magazine*, 1955; Man of the Year Award, Advertising Club of NY, 1955; Baronial Order of the Magna Charta (England), 1955; U.S. Medal of Freedom, 1959. HON. DEG.: LL.D., Tufts U., 1939; LL.D., Princeton U., 1946; LL.D., Wagner Coll., 1947; LL.D., Northwestern U., 1947; LL.D., Union Coll., 1948; LL.D., U. of PA, 1949; LL.D., Lafayette Coll., 1949; LL.D., Amherst U., 1950; LL.D., Seoul National U., 1950; LL.D., U. of AZ, 1951; LL.D., St. Joseph's Coll., 1951; LL.D., St. Lawrence U., 1952; LL.D., Johns Hopkins U., 1952; LL.D., Fordham U., 1952; LL.D., Harvard U., 1952; LL.D., Columbia U., 1954; LL.D., Georgetown U., 1954; LL.D., U. of SC, 1955; LL.D., IN U., 1955; LL.D., IA State U., 1956. WRITINGS: *War, Peace and Change* (1939); *War or Peace* (1950); *Spiritual Legacy* (1960). REL.: Presb. RES.: New York, NY.

DuMONT, DONALD HALLECK. b. Jul 19, 1903, Brooklyn, NY; d. Sep 16, 1976, Chicago, IL; par. William H. B. and Lillian Felton (Balcom) DuMont; m. Esther Viola Nystrom (d. 1966); m. 2d, Helen Olivia Ekblad, Oct 1967; c. James K.; Donna Rae Burns; Bruce B.; Walter (stepson). EDUC.: Montclair (NJ) H.S.; M.E., Rensselaer Polytechnic Inst., 1924. POLIT. & GOV.: candidate for chm., Rep. Nat'l. Cmte., 1949; ***candidate for Republican nomination to presidency of the U.S., 1952, 1968, 1972, 1976***; candidate for 35th Ward alderman, Chicago, IL, 1955; candidate for Republican nomination to U.S. Senate (IL), 1966; candidate for Republican nomination to mayor of Chicago, IL, 1967, 1971, 1975; candidate for delegate, IL State Constitutional Convention, 1969; *independent candidate for presidency of the U.S., 1972*. BUS. & PROF.: production engineer, Public Service Production Co., Newark, NJ, 1924–26; fire protection engineer, Walter Kidde and Co., Bloomfield, NJ, 1926–46; operator, owner, DuMont Marine Service, Inc., New London, CT, 1930–49; employee, Logan Square Post Office, Chicago, IL, 1950–; employee, Good Humor Corp., Chicago, IL, 1952–70; employee, Laminators Unlimited, Chicago, IL. MEM.: Liberty Amendment Cmte.; Theta Xi; International Platform Assn. (board of directors, 1969); Rensselaer Alumni Assn.; Republimericans Promoting Integration of Christ into National Affairs (founder, 1949); God's Own People (founder). WRITINGS: *The Republimerican Retort* (newsletter). REL.: Evangelical Free Church of America. RES.: Chicago, IL.

DUNN, WILLIAM J. POLIT. & GOV.: ***candidate for Republican nomination to presidency of the U.S., 1980***. MAILING ADDRESS: Box 77, Narberth, PA 19072.

DUNNING, EARL. POLIT. & GOV.: ***People's National Independent (Look Glass) Party candidate for vice presidency of the U.S., 1948***. BUS. & PROF.: railroad conductor; pensioner. RES.: Saginaw, MI.

DU PONT, PIERRE SAMUEL "PETE," IV. b. Jan 22, 1935, Wilmington, DE; par. Pierre Samuel and Jane (Holcomb) du Pont; m. Elise Ravenel Wood, 1957; c. Elise; Pierre; Benjamin; Eleuthere. EDUC.: grad., Phillips Exeter Acad., 1952; B.S.M.E., Princeton U., 1956; LL.B., Harvard U., 1963. POLIT. & GOV.: elected as a Republican to DE State House, 1969–71; elected as a Republican to U.S. House (DE), 1971–77; elected as a Republican to gov. of DE, 1977–85; ***candidate for Republican nomination to presidency of the U.S., 1988***. BUS. & PROF.: atty.; admitted to DE Bar, 1964; staff, photo department, E. I. du Pont Co. MIL.: U.S.N.R., 1957–60. MAILING ADDRESS: P.O. Box 1988, Rockland, DE 19732.

DU PONT, THOMAS COLEMAN. b. Dec 11, 1863, Louisville, KY; d. Nov 11, 1930, Wilmington, DE; par. Antoine Bidermann and Ellen Susan (Coleman) du Pont; m. Alice du Pont, Jan 17, 1889; c. Ellen Coleman; Alice Hounsfield; Francis Victor; Renee de Pellepont; Eleuthere Irene. EDUC.: Urbana U.; Chauncy Hall School; MA Inst. of Technology. POLIT. & GOV.: member, Rep. Nat'l. Cmte., 1908–30; alternate delegate, Rep. Nat'l. Conv., 1908; ***candidate for Republican nomination to presidency of the U.S., 1916, 1920***; chm., DE Republican State Cmte.; appointed to U.S. Senate (DE), 1921–22; Republican candidate for U.S. Senate (DE), 1922 (long and short terms); ***candidate for Republican nomination to vice presidency of the U.S., 1924***; elected as a Republican to U.S. Senate (DE), 1925–28. BUS. & PROF.: surveyor, Louisville and Southern Exposition; engineer, Central Coal and Iron Co., 1883, pres.; engaged in coal and iron mining in KY, 1883–1930; gen. mgr., Johnson Co., Johnstown, PA, 1893; steel manufacturer; engaged in construction industry and management of street railway systems; pres., E. I. du Pont de Nemours Powder Co., 1902–15; pres., McHenry Coal Co.; pres., Main Jellico Mountain Coal Co.; pres., Wilmington Trust Co. MEM.: A.S.M.E.; Engineering Assn. of the South; American Acad. of Political and Social Science; Engineers and Architects Club; American Soc. of Mining Engineers; Southern Club of Philadelphia; Metropolitan Club; Lawyers' Club; Manhattan Club; Wilmington Club; Rittenhouse Club. RES.: Wilmington, DE.

DUPONT, WILLIAM JOSEPH. b. May 28; par. William Joseph and ____ Rose Dupont; married, 1953; c. son. POLIT. & GOV.: ***candidate for Democratic nomination to presidency of the U.S., 1988***. BUS. & PROF.: soldier. MIL.: armed forces, PTO, WWII. REL.: R.C. MAILING ADDRESS: Rural Route 1, Dwight, IL 60420.

DURAND, C. HOMER. POLIT. & GOV.: candidate for Republican nomination to gov. of OH, 1922; ***candidate for Republican nomination to presidency of the U.S., 1924***. BUS. & PROF.: advocate of repeal of Prohibition. MEM.: Personal Liberty League (orator). RES.: Cashocton, OH.

DURANTE, JAMES FRANCIS "JIMMY." b. Feb 10, 1893, New York, NY; d. Jan 29, 1980, Santa Monica, CA; par. Barthelmeo and Rosa Durante; m. Jeanne Olsen, 1916; m. 2d, Margie Little, Dec 14, 1960; c. CeCe Alicia. EDUC.: public schools, New York, NY. POLIT. & GOV.: ***independent candidate for presidency of the U.S., c. 1952***. BUS. & PROF.: entertainer; comedian; actor; singer; employee, barbershop; piano player, Tony's Saloon, Coney Island, NY; band leader; partner, Club Durante; Broadway debut, 1927; partner, Clayton, Jackson and Durante (comedy team), 1930; radio performer, 1943–50; television performer, 1950–80. CREDITS: Films: *The Passionate Plumber*; *Student Tour*; *George White's Scandals*; *Land Without Music*; *Carnival*; *Start Cheering*; *Sally, Irene and Mary*; *Music for Millions*; *On An Island with You*; *Jumbo* (1936). Plays: *Show Girl* (1928); *The New Yorkers* (1930); *Get Rich Quick Wallingford*; *The Cuban*; *Her Cardboard Lover*; *Strike Me Pink* (1934); *Red, Hot and Blue* (1937). MEM.: Actors Equity Assn.; Screen Actors Guild; A.F.T.R.A.; American Guild of Variety Artists; A.S.C.A.P. AWARDS: Peabody Award, 1951. WRITINGS: *Schnozzle Durante's Song Book*. REL.: R.C. MISC.: known as "The Schnozz." RES.: Beverly Hills, CA.

DUREN, B. KWAKU. b. Apr 14, 1943, Beckley, WV; par. William and Willie Wade (Bennett) Duren; m. separated; c. three. EDUC.: CA State U. at Long Beach; Peoples Coll. of Law. POLIT. & GOV.: Southern CA chair, Black Panther Party; member, National Black Independent Political Party; Peace and Freedom Party candidate for Long Beach (CA) School Board, 1974; Peace and Freedom Party candidate for Los Angeles (CA) School Board, 1978; Peace and Freedom Party candidate for U.S. House (CA), 1986, 1988; Chair, CA State Peace and Freedom Party, 1988; ***New Alliance Party candidate for vice presidency of the U.S., 1988***. BUS. & PROF.: labor organizer; community economic development specialist; community organizer. MEM.: Los Angeles Coalition Against Police Brutality (founder); CA Community Economic Development Assn. (board member); Lawyers Referral Service (board member); Union of Legal Service Workers of Los Angeles (pres.). WRITINGS: *Profiles In Black* (1977). REL.: none. MAILING ADDRESS: 7427 South Crenshaw Blvd., Los Angeles, CA 90043.

DURKEE, CHARLES. b. Dec 10, 1805, Royalton, VT; d. Jan 14, 1870, Omaha, NE; par. Harvey and Patta (Robinson) Durkee; m. Catherine P. Dana, c. 1830; m. 2d, Caroline Lake, Jan 1840. EDUC.: Burlington (VT) Acad. POLIT. & GOV.: member, WI Territorial Legislature, 1836–38, 1847–48; member, Liberty Party; independent candidate for gov. of WI, 1848; elected as a Free Soiler to U.S. House (WI), 1849–53; Free Soil-Liberty Party candidate for U.S. House (WI), 1852; ***Liberty Party candidate for vice presidency of the U.S., 1852***; elected as a Republican to U.S. Senate (WI), 1855–61; appointed gov. of UT Territory, 1865–69. BUS. & PROF.: merchant; farmer; lumberman. MEM.: World's Peace Convention (delegate, 1861). REL.: Methodist. MISC.: founder of Southport (now Kenosha), WI. RES.: Omaha, NE.

DURKIN, JOHN ANTHONY. b. Mar 29, 1936, Brookfield, MA; par. Joseph and Charlotte (Dailey) Durkin; m. Patricia Moses, 1965; c. Andrea E.; John E.; Sheilagh J. EDUC.: B.A., Holy Cross Coll., 1959; LL.B., J.D., Georgetown U., 1965. POLIT. & GOV.: town moderator, Brookfield, MA, 1959; appointed asst. to the U.S. controller of currency, Washington, DC, 1963–66; appointed asst. to the asst. atty. gen. of NH, 1966–67; appointed asst. atty. gen. of NH, 1967–68; insurance commissioner of NH, 1968–73; Democratic candidate for U.S. Senate (NH), 1974 (election contested and seat declared vacant), 1980; elected as a Democrat to U.S. Senate (NH), 1975–81; delegate, Dem. Nat'l. Conv.; ***candidate for Democratic nomination to presidency of the U.S., 1980***. BUS. & PROF.: atty.; admitted to NH Bar, 1966; admitted to MA Bar, 1966; partner, Perito, Duerk, Carlson and Pinco (law firm), Washington, DC, 1981–. MIL.: lt. commander, U.S. Navy, 1959–61. MEM.: Common Cause; Council for Better Schools; Navy League; Federal Bar Assn.; NH Bar Assn.; MA Bar Assn.; Elks; National Assn. of Insurance Commissioners (dir., 1970–73). REL.: R.C. MAILING ADDRESS: Perito, Duerk, Carlson and Pinco, 1001 Connecticut Ave., N.W., Washington, DC 20008.

DURRETT, ROGER. POLIT. & GOV.: ***candidate for Republican nomination to presidency of the U.S., 1992***. BUS. & PROF.: actor. MAILING ADDRESS: Charlotte, NC.

DYKE, WILLIAM DANIEL. b. Apr 25, 1930, Princeton, IL; par. Alfred D. and Vinnie P. (Thompson) Dyke; m. Joan Piper, 1953; c. Wade; Sarah; Kathryn. EDUC.: Bradley U., 1949–50; B.A., De Pauw U., 1952; LL.B., U. of WI, 1955. POLIT. & GOV.: elected city atty., Jefferson, WI, 1961; asst. to the lt. gov. of WI, 1963–64; elected as a Republican to mayor of Madison, WI, 1969–74; Republican candidate for gov. of WI, 1974; appointed member, Urban Transportation Advisory Council, U.S. Dept. of Transportation; adviser, U.S. Dept. of Housing and Urban Development; adviser, U.S. Dept. of State; ***American Independent Party candidate for vice presidency of the U.S., 1976***. BUS. & PROF.: radio and television announcer, 1956–59; atty.; law practice, Madison, WI, 1960–; instructor, Madison Vocational, Technical, and Adult School, 1964–68; breeder of Appaloosa horses; building subcontractor. MIL.: pvt., U.S. Army, 1952–55. MEM.: ABA; American Jud. Soc.; WI Bar Assn.; Dane Cty. Bar Assn.; WI Reserve Officers Assn.; National League of Cities (dir.); Alpha Tau Omega; WI League of Municipalities (dir.); WI Alliance of Cities (vice pres., dir.). AWARDS: Man of the Year, WI Reserve Officers Assn., 1971. WRITINGS: *The Horse Business* (1975). REL.: Christian. MAILING ADDRESS: 512 Green St., Mt. Horeb, WI 53572.

EAGLES, MIKE. POLIT. & GOV.: ***candidate for Republican nomination to presidency of the U.S., 1984; candidate for Democratic nomination to presidency of the U.S., 1984.*** MAILING ADDRESS: 479 East Belmont Ave., Fresno, CA 93701.

EAGLETON, THOMAS FRANCIS. b. Sep 4, 1929, St. Louis, MO; par. Mark David and Zitta Louis (Swanson) Eagleton; m. Barbara Ann Smith, Jan 21, 1956; c. Terence Francis; Christin. EDUC.: A.B. (cum laude), Amherst Coll., 1950; LL.B. (cum laude) Harvard U., 1953. POLIT. & GOV.: elected circuit atty., St. Louis, MO, 1957–61; elected as a Democrat to atty. gen. of MO, 1961–65; elected as a Democrat to lt. gov. of MO, 1965–69; elected as a Democrat to U.S. Senate (MO), 1969–87; delegate, Dem. Nat'l. Conv., 1972; ***Democratic candidate for vice presidency of the U.S., 1972 (resigned); candidate for Democratic nomination to presidency of the U.S., 1984.*** BUS. & PROF.: atty.; admitted to MO Bar, 1953; law practice, St. Louis, MO, 1953–56. MIL.: U.S.N.R., 1948–49. MEM.: St. Louis Bar Assn.; Lawyers Assn.; Delta Kappa Epsilon; National Assn. of Attorneys General (dir., 1963); MO State Prosecuting Attorneys Assn. (pres., 1959); National District Attorneys Assn.; St. Louis Civil Liberties Cmte.; St. Louis Junior C. of C.; Clayton Junior C. of C.; Alpha Kappa Psi. AWARDS: "Furtherance of Justice Award," National District Attorneys Assn., 1957; Civil Liberties Award, St. Louis Civil Liberties Cmte., 1960; Distinguished Service Award, St. Louis Junior C. of C.; Distinguished Service Award, Clayton Junior C. of C., 1962; Civic Award, Alpha Kappa Psi; Bicentennial Award, St. Louis Bar Assn., 1964; named one of top 100 Young Leaders in the U.S., *Life Magazine*. HON. DEG.: J.D., Suffolk U., 1958; J.D., Park Coll., 1969; J.D., Amherst Coll., 1970; J.D., Rockhurst Coll., 1970; J.D., St. Louis U., 1973. MAILING ADDRESS: 5313 Cardinal Court, N.W., Washington, DC 20016.

EAKMAN, MARVIN A. POLIT. & GOV.: ***candidate for Democratic nomination to presidency of the U.S., 1984.*** BUS. & PROF.: salesman, Outlook Publications, Minneapolis, MN. MAILING ADDRESS: 3323 Sheridan Ave., North, Minneapolis, MN 55412.

EAQUINTA, JAMES. POLIT. & GOV.: ***candidate for Republican nomination to presidency of the U.S., 1992.*** MAILING ADDRESS: 1145 Willow Lane, Fairfield, CA 94533.

EARLE, THOMAS. b. Apr 21, 1796, Leicester, MA; d. Jul 14, 1849, Philadelphia, PA; par. Pliny and Patience (Buffum) Earle; m. Mary Hussey, Jul 1820; c. Caroline (Mrs. Richard P. White); Phebe H. (Mrs. Joseph Gibbons); George H.; Henry; one other. EDUC.: Leicester Acad.; studied law under John Sergeant (q.v.), 1824. POLIT. & GOV.: delegate, PA State Constitutional Convention, 1837; ***Liberty (Abolition) Party candidate for vice presidency of the U.S., 1840 (declined); candidate for Liberty Party nomination to vice presidency of the U.S., 1844.*** BUS. & PROF.: clerk, Earle and Chase Co., Worcester, MA, 1816; partner, Earle and Barker (merchants), Philadelphia, PA; atty.; admitted to PA Bar, 1825; law practice, Philadelphia, PA; ed., *Columbian Observer;* ed., *The Standard;* ed., *The Mechanic's Free Press and Reform Advocate;* ed., *The Pennsylvanian;* abolitionist. MEM.: PA Soc. for Promoting the Abolition of Slavery (counsel, 1826–49); American Anti-Slavery Soc. WRITINGS: *Essay on the Rights of States to Alter and Annul Their Charters* (1823); *Essay on Penal Law in Pennsylavania* (1827); *Treatise on Railroad and Internal Communications* (1830); *The Systematic Speller* (1844); *The Life, Travels and Opinions of Benjamin Lundy* (1847); *Sismondi's Italian Republics* (translator); *Grammatical Dictionary of the French and English Languages*. REL.: Soc. of Friends. MISC.: leading proponent of PA constitutional reform, 1837. RES.: Philadelphia, PA.

EARLY, STEPHEN TYREE. b. Aug 27, 1889, Crozet, VA; d. Aug 11, 1951, Washington, DC; par. Thomas Joseph and Ida Virginia (Wood) Early; m. Helen Wrenn, Sep 17,

1921; c. Stephen Tyree; Helen Virginia (Mrs. William Niles Elam, Jr.); Thomas Augustus. EDUC.: public and private schools. POLIT. & GOV.: advance representative, Franklin D. Roosevelt (q.v.) for Vice President Campaign, 1920; appointed asst. to the president, 1933–37; appointed press sec. to the president, 1937–45; ***candidate for Democratic nomination to vice presidency of the U.S., 1944***; appointed undersec. of defense, 1949; appointed first deputy sec., U.S. Dept. of Defense, 1949–50. BUS. & PROF.: Washington staff, United Press, 1908–13; Washington staff, Associated Press, 1913–17, 1920–27; press relations officer, U.S. C. of C., 1919–20; Washington representative, Paramount News and Paramount Publix Corp., 1927–33; vice pres., Pullman, Inc., Chicago, IL, 1945–48; vice pres., Pullman Standard Car Manufacturing Co., Chicago, IL, 1948–51. MIL.: 2d lt., U.S. Army, 1917, capt., 1919; staff, *The Stars and Stripes*; lt. col., U.S.A.R., 1919–51; Silver Star Citation; Distinguished Service Medal, 1945. MEM.: MD State Fair, Inc. (dir.); Police Boys Club of Washington (dir.); American National Red Cross (dir.); Metropolitan Club; National Press Club; Columbia Century Club; Burning Tree Club; Alfalfa Club; Chicago Club. REL.: Bapt. RES.: Washington, DC.

EASON, JAMES HENRY. POLIT. & GOV.: ***independent candidate for presidency of the U.S., 1976***. MAILING ADDRESS: 277 Golden Gate Ave., San Francisco, CA 94102.

EAST, EDWARD HAZZARD. b. Oct 1, 1830, Davidson Cty., TN; d. Nov 12, 1904, Nashville, TN; par. Edward Hyde and Cecelia (Buchanan) East; m. Mrs. Ida T. Ward, 1868; c. Edine H.; Bessie Cecelia. EDUC.: grad., Washington Inst., 1850; B.L., Lebanon U., 1854. POLIT. & GOV.: elected as a Whig to TN State House, 1859–60; appointed TN state sec. of state, 1862–65; appointed U.S. district atty. for Middle District of TN, 1865 (declined); elected chancellor, Davidson Cty., TN, 1865–74; elected as a Greenbacker to TN State House, 1875–77; National (Greenback) Party candidate for gov. of TN, 1878; ***candidate for Prohibition Party nomination to presidency of the U.S., 1892***; Prohibition Party candidate for gov. of TN, 1892. BUS. & PROF.: atty.; admitted to TN Bar, 1850; law practice, Nashville, TN; counsel, Nashville, Chattanooga and St. Louis Railway Co., 1874–1904. MEM.: Tennessee Hospital for the Insane (pres., Board of Directors); Vanderbilt U. (trustee); POLIT. & GOV.: Nashville (trustee); TN School for the Blind (pres., Board of Trustees); TN State Normal School (Board of Managers); Peabody School for Teachers (trustee). HON. DEG.: LL.D., U. of Nashville, 1880. REL.: Methodist Episcopal Church, South (steward; lay delegate, General Conference, 1881; Sunday school teacher). MISC.: known as "Judge East." RES.: Nashville, TN.

EASTER, ANDREW J. b. 1897, Baltimore, MD; m. twice; c. three daughters. EDUC.: Baltimore Polytechnic Inst.; grad. (with honors), MD Inst. of Fine Arts, 1917; PA Acad. of Fine Arts, 1917–18; U. of MD Law School. POLIT. & GOV.: candidate for Democratic nomination to U.S. Senate (MD), 1956, 1958, 1962; ***candidate for Democratic nomination to presidency of the U.S., 1960, 1964***; candidate for Democratic nomination to gov. of MD, 1966. BUS. & PROF.: designer; draftsman; naval architect, U.S. Dept. of the Navy; architect, Hydrofoil Corp., Annapolis, MD; artist. MAILING ADDRESS: 6420 Belair Rd., Baltimore 6, MD.

EASTMAN, BARBARA S. POLIT. & GOV.: ***independent candidate for presidency of the U.S., 1992***. MAILING ADDRESS: 29255 Fox Run Lane, Valley Center, CA 92082.

EATON, CHARLES FREDERICK FRANCIS, SR. b. Feb 11, 1908, Kent, OH; par. Porter Roy and Grace Rose (Adams) Eaton; m. Mary Elizabeth; c. Virginia; Charles Frederick, Jr.; Mary Jane; Susan; Thomas. EDUC.: eighth grade, public schools; commercial business and technical trade courses. POLIT. & GOV.: ***candidate for Democratic nomination to presidency of the U.S., 1976***. BUS. & PROF.: pres., plumbing, heating and insulation firm, Mansfield, OH. MEM.: Elks; Knights of Columbus; American Caucus; American Cause; American Security Council; Friends of the FBI. REL.: R.C. MAILING ADDRESS: 620 West Cook Rd., Mansfield, OH 44907.

EATON, EPHRAIM LLEWELLYN. b. Mar 27, 1846, Hebron, WI; par. Almon Ransom and Orissa (Haskin) Eaton; m. Mary E. Miner, 1868; m. 2d, Louise Bates, Oct 13, 1891; c. Starr S.; Howard; Helen; Dorothy. EDUC.: Milton (WI) Acad.; B.A., Garrett Bible Inst., 1877, B.D., 1884; D.D., Lawrence U., 1890. POLIT. & GOV.: Prohibition Party candidate for U.S. House (WI), 1892; Prohibition Party candidate for gov. of IA, 1897 (withdrew); delegate, Prohibition Party National Convention; ***candidate for Prohibition Party nomination to vice presidency of the U.S., 1900***; Prohibition Party candidate for U.S. House (PA), 1902; Prohibition Party candidate for gov. of WI, 1906. BUS. & PROF.: school teacher, 1866–76; ordained minister, Methodist Episcopal Church, 1871; pastor, Methodist Episcopal Church, Beloit, WI, 1871; pastor, Methodist Episcopal Church, Madison, WI; pastor, Methodist Episcopal Church, La Crosse, WI; pastor, Methodist Episcopal Church, Janesville, WI; pastor, Methodist Episcopal Church, Milwaukee, WI; pastor, Methodist Episcopal Church, Racine, WI; pastor, Methodist Episcopal Church, Des Moines, IA, 1896; pastor, North Avenue Methodist Episcopal Church, Alleghany, PA, 1900–1918; Chautauqua lecturer; temperance advocate. MEM.: Independent Order of Good Templars (1864). WRITINGS: *The Millennial Dawn Heresy* (1911); *Winning the Fight Against Drink* (1912); *Our Spirit Nature; The Science of Mental Healing* (1918); *Beyond This Life; Why Are We Wet?* (1931).

REL.: Methodist Episcopal Church (presiding elder, Madison, WI District, 1883–87; member, General Conference, 1888, 1896, 1900). RES.: Madison, WI.

EBRIGHT, DON HAROLD. b. 1902, Columbus, OH; par. Rollie C. and Blanche (Hoskins) Ebright; m. Martha Miller; c. James Newton; one other. EDUC.: Coll. of Commerce; OH State U. POLIT. & GOV.: appointed dir. of finance, Akron, OH, 1936–39; elected as a Republican to state treas. of OH, 1939–51; ***candidate for Republican nomination to presidency of the U.S., 1948***. BUS. & PROF.: OH National Bank, Columbus, OH; First National Bank, Akron, OH. MAILING ADDRESS: 2416 Southway Dr., Columbus, OH.

EDDY, ROY NATHAN. b. Apr 23, 1913, Lawrence, KS; par. Dick Leander and Gertrude Russ (Swickard) Eddy; m. Alma M. Morgan; c. R. Gerald; Lawrence N. EDUC.: military schools; grad., Command and General Staff College, Fort Leavenworth, KS. POLIT. & GOV.: ***Restoration Party candidate for vice presidency of the U.S., 1976***. BUS. & PROF.: asst. dir. of training, chief of detectives, commanding officer of research and development, police dept., Miami, FL; real estate broker. MIL.: member, FL National Guard; col., U.S. Army (administrative officer; post auditor; fuel conservation officer; provost marshall; trial judge advocate; battalion exec. officer; district rail transportation officer; special courts investigation officer; troubleshooter, Military Government of Germany; troop transport commander). MEM.: Fraternal Order of Police; International Assn. of Chiefs of Police; City of Miami Supervisors Council (life member); National Assn. of Fee Appraisers; various real estate associations. REL.: nondenominational Christian (nee Methodist). MAILING ADDRESS: Route 1, Box 724B, St. Cloud, FL 32769.

EDGE, GARY LEE. POLIT. & GOV.: ***independent candidate for presidency of the U.S., 1988***. MAILING ADDRESS: 75N Oak St., Apt. 309, Platteville, WI 53818.

EDGE, WALTER EVANS. b. Nov 20, 1873, Philadelphia, PA; d. Oct 29, 1956, New York, NY; par. William and Mary (Evans) Edge; m. Lady Lee Phillips, Jun 10, 1907; m. 2d, Camilla Loyall Ashe Sewall, Dec 9, 1922; c. Camilla; Mary Esther; Loyall; Howard; Walter Evans, Jr. EDUC.: public schools. POLIT. & GOV.: journal clerk, NJ State Senate, 1897–99; sec., NJ State Senate, 1901–04; presidential elector, Republican Party, 1904, 1908; delegate, Rep. Nat'l. Conv., 1908 (alternate), 1920, 1924, 1928, 1932, 1936, 1940, 1944, 1952, 1956; elected as a Republican to NJ State House, 1910 (majority leader); elected as a Republican to NJ State Senate, 1911–17 (majority leader; pres., 1915); elected as a Republican to gov. of NJ, 1917–19 (resigned), 1943–47; elected as a Republican to U.S. Senate (NJ), 1919–29 (resigned); ***candidate for Republican nomination to vice presidency of the U.S., 1920, 1936; candidate for Republican nomination to presidency of the U.S., 1928***; appointed U.S. ambassador to France, 1929–33. BUS. & PROF.: printer's devil, *Atlantic City (NJ) Review*, 1890–94; employee, Dorland Advertising Agency, Atlantic City; owner, publisher, *Atlantic City Guest*; publisher, *Atlantic City Daily Press*; publisher, *Atlantic City Evening Union*. MIL.: 2d lt., Company F, Fourth U.S.V., 1899; capt., Company L, Third Regt., NJ National Guard, lt. col. MEM.: Union League Club of Philadelphia; Union League Club of NY; The Brook Club; NY Club; Metropolitan Club; Alibi Club; Washington (DC) Club; Traveleer Club; Paris Club. HON. DEG.: LL.D., Rutgers U., 1918; LL.D., Nancy U. (France), 1937; LL.D., Gettysburg Coll., 1944; LL.D., Gill Coll., 1945; LL.D., Drexel U., 1945; LL.D., Princeton U., 1946. WRITINGS: *A Jerseyman's Journal*. REL.: Episc. RES.: Ventnor City, NJ.

EDGERTON, ALFRED PECK. b. Jan 11, 1813, Plattsburg, NY; d. May 14, 1897, Hicksville, OH; par. Bela and Phebe (Ketchum) Edgerton; m. Charlotte Dixon, Feb 9, 1841; c. Frances Delord (Mrs. Alwyn A. Alvord); Charlotte Elizabeth (Mrs. Satterlee Swartwout); Anna Eliza (Mrs. George Manierre); Henry H.; Alfred Peck, Jr.; Dixon. EDUC.: Plattsburg Acad. POLIT. & GOV.: elected as a Democrat to OH State Senate, 1845–47; delegate, Dem. Nat'l. Conv., 1848, 1856 (chm., Cmte. on Organization), 1864; elected as a Democrat to U.S. House (OH), 1851–55; appointed financial agent for OH, New York, NY, 1853–56; Democratic candidate for lt. gov. of IN, 1868; ***candidate for Straight-Out (Taproot) Democratic Party nomination to vice presidency of the U.S., 1872***; Straight-Out (Taproot) Democratic Party candidate for gov. of IN, 1872 (declined); appointed member, U.S. Civil Service Comm., 1885–89 (pres.); pres., Board of Education, Fort Wayne, IN. BUS. & PROF.: ed., Plattsburg, NY, 1833; clerk, mercantile house, New York, NY, 1833–37; agent, American Land Co., Hicksville, OH, 1837–51; partner, Hicks Land Co.; gen. mgr., Wabash and Erie Canal, 1859–68. MEM.: Purdue U. (trustee). WRITINGS: *Finances and Taxation* (1868); *Address . . . at Annual Meeting of the . . . Old Settlers Association* (1878); *Address . . . to the Graduating Class of the Central Grammar School* (1879); *Address Before the Northwestern Ohio and North-Eastern Indiana District Fair Association* (1879); *Address . . . President of the Board of School Trustees, to the Graduating Class of the Fort Wayne Grammar School* (1882); *Address . . . at the Ceremony of Unveiling the Soldiers' Monument* (1882); *A Spicy Letter* (1884); *Remarks . . . at Annual Meeting of the Old Settlers Association . . .* (1884); *Address . . . to the Veterans of the 21st Regiment of the OH Volunteers* (1884); *Letter* (1886); *Letter of A. P. Edgerton on His Removal from the Civil Service Commission* (1889); *Civil Service Affairs* (1890); *Old Settlers' Speech* (1895). REL.: Episc. RES.: Hicksville, OH.

EDGERTON, JAMES ARTHUR. b. Jan 30, 1869, Plantsville, OH; d. Dec 3, 1938, Beverly Hills, VA; par. Richard and Tamar (Vernon) Edgerton; m. Blanche Mae

Edgerton (2d cousin), Mar 21, 1895; c. James Clark; Joseph Selby; Esther; John Eldon; Justin Lincoln; Elizabeth. EDUC.: Bartlett (OH) Acad.; B.A., National Normal U., Lebanon, OH, 1887, M.A., 1895; Marietta (OH) Coll. POLIT. & GOV.: sec., NE State People's Party, 1895; appointed chief clerk, NE State Labor Bureau, 1895–99; chm., NE People's Party State Cmte., 1895–96; delegate, People's Party National Convention, 1896, 1903; sec., People's Party National Cmte., 1896–1904; People's Party candidate for clerk, U.S. House, 1897; member, People's Party National Exec. Cmte., 1904–08; organized People's Democratic Party of NJ; appointed member, War Industries Board, 1917–19; appointed Federal Prohibition dir. for NJ, 1920; ***Prohibition Party candidate for vice presidency of the U.S., 1928***; Prohibition Party candidate for gov. of VA, 1937. BUS. & PROF.: managing ed., *Evening Herald*, Kalamazoo, MI; ed., *Marietta (OH) Register;* author; ed., *Lincoln (NE) Independent*, 1890–91; ed., *Standard*, Kearney, NE, 1891–93; legislative correspondent, NE; ed., *Lincoln Herald;* editorial staff, *Rocky Mountain News*, Denver, CO, 1899–1903; editorial staff, American Press Assn., 1904, 1908–13; editorial staff, *Watson's Magazine*, 1905; editorial writer, *New York (NY) American*, 1907; purchasing agent, U.S. Post Office Dept., 1913–20; manufacturer's agent, Washington, DC; dean, instructor in Christian philosophy, Galahad Coll., Asheville, NC, 1932. MEM.: Independence League (gen. organizer, 1906); National New Thought Alliance (pres., 1909–14); International New Thought Alliance (pres., 1914–24, 1934–38); NE Reform Press Assn. (pres., 1892); Knights of Pythias; American Acad. of Political and Social Science; Jefferson-Lincoln League (pres., 1928); American Press Humorists' Assn.; Industrial Legion (adj.-gen.). WRITINGS: *Poems* (1889); *A Better Day* (1890); *Populist Handbook for 1894; Populist Handbook for NE* (1895); *Voices of the Morning* (1898); *Songs of the People* (1902); *Glimpses of the Real* (1903); *In the Gardens of the God* (1904); "Old Fashioned Philosophy," *Primary Education*, Volume XIII (1905); *New Thought: the Coming Religion* (1919); *The Philosophy of Jesus* (1928); *Invading the Invisible* (1930). REL.: New Thought. RES.: Alexandria, VA.

EDISON, CHARLES. b. Aug 3, 1890, Llewellyn Park, West Orange, NJ; d. Jul 31, 1969, New York, NY; par. Thomas Alva and Mina (Miller) Edison; m. Carolyn Hawkins, Mar 27, 1918; c. none. EDUC.: Carteret Acad.; Hotchkiss School; MA Inst. of Technology, 1909–13. POLIT. & GOV.: asst., Naval Consulting Board, 1917–19; appointed NJ state dir., National Recovery Administration, 1933; appointed member, National Emergency Council, 1934–36; appointed regional dir., Federal Housing Administration, 1934–36; appointed member, National Recovery Board, 1935; appointed asst. U.S. sec. of the navy, 1937–39; appointed U.S. sec. of the navy, 1939–40; elected as a Democrat to gov. of NJ, 1941–45; ***National Citizens' Independent League candidate for presidency of the U.S., 1944***; appointed member, NJ Welfare Council; member, exec. cmte., NY Conservative Party. BUS. & PROF.: asst., Thomas Alva Edison, Inc., West Orange, NJ, 1914–26, pres., dir., 1926–50; chm. of the board, McGraw-Edison Co., 1957–61; pres., dir., Edison Storage Battery Co.; pres., dir., Edison Wood Products, Inc.; pres., dir., Edison Cement Corp.; pres., dir., Thomas A. Edison, Ltd. (Great Britain); pres., dir., Thomas A. Edison, Ltd. (Canada); pres., dir., Edison-Splitdorf Corp.; pres., dir., Edison Botanic Research Corp.; pres., dir., City View Storage Co.; pres., dir., Metropolitan Cement Corp.; pres., dir., E. K. Medical Gas Laboratories, Inc.; dir., Howe Folding Furniture, Inc.; dir., Terminal and Transit Corp.; dir., Jones and Laughlin Steel Corp.; dir., International Telephone and Telegraph Corp.; dir., U.S. Life Insurance Co. MEM.: Canadian Club; Marco Polo Club; The Brook Club (trustee); 1925 F Street Club; St. Anthony Club; Lake Placid Club; West Orange Liberty Loan Organization (chm.); Newark Museum (trustee); United Service to China, Inc. (hon. national chm.; hon. dir.); Town Hall, Inc. (chm., Board of Trustees, 1944–47); National Municipal League (pres., 1947–50); North American Wildlife Foundation (trustee); Stevens Inst. of Technology (trustee); Navy League of the U.S. (life member); SAR; MA Inst. of Technology Alumni Assn.; National Geographic Soc.; Newcomen Soc.; NJ Hist. Soc.; John Ericson Soc.; Delta Psi; China Inst. in America (vice president; trustee); Cmte. for the Monroe Doctrine; Citizens Cmte. for the Hoover Comm. Reports; Cmte. of One Million (founder; member, Steering Cmte.); Americans for Constitutional Action (founder; trustee); Essex Cty. Council; National Inst. of Social Sciences; National Council for Historic Sites and Buildings; Naval Order of the U.S.; American Bureau for Medical Aid to China (dir.); Army and Air National Guard Assn.; Radio Liberty (trustee); National Patrol Torpedo Veterans Assn.; Thomas Alva Edison Foundation (hon. president; trustee); Phi Beta Kappa (hon. member); Federal Hall Memorial Assn., Inc.; Edison Birthplace Assn., Inc. (trustee); Omicron Delta Alpha; Junior Achievement (dir.); Metropolitan Museum of Art; Hotchkiss School (trustee); American Emergency Cmte. for Tibetan Refugees, Inc. (dir.); Deafness Research Foundation (dir.); American Afro-Asian Education Exchange, Inc. (dir.); Young Americans for Freedom (member, National Advisory Cmte.); Citizens Foreign Relations Cmte. (member, exec. cmte.); Armstrong Memorial Research Foundation, Inc. (member, exec. cmte.); American-Russian C. of C. (dir.). HON. DEG.: LL.D., John Marshall Coll., 1940; LL.D., Newark U., 1941; LL.D., Rutgers U., 1941; LL.D., Upsala Coll., 1943; LL.D., Hobart Coll., 1944; LL.D., William Smith Coll., 1944; LL.D., Lafayette Coll., 1945; D.Eng., Stevens Inst. of Technology, 1949; D.C.S., NY U., 1950; H.H.D., IN Technical Coll., 1956. WRITINGS: *Flotsam and Jetsam* (poems, 1967). REL.: Methodist. RES.: Orange, NJ.

EDMUNDS, GEORGE FRANKLIN. b. Feb 1, 1828, Richmond, VT; d. Feb 27, 1919, Pasadena, CA; par. Ebenezer and Naomi (Briggs) Edmunds; m. Susan Marsh Lyman, Aug 1852; c. one daughter. EDUC.: public schools; studied law; A.M., U. of VT, 1855, LL.D., 1879. POLIT. & GOV.: elected as a Republican to VT State House, 1854–59 (Speaker, 1856–59); elected as a Republican to VT State Senate, 1861–62 (pres. pro tempore); appointed and subsequently elected as a Republican to U.S. Senate (VT), 1866–91 (pres. pro tempore, 1883–85); delegate, Loyalist Convention, 1866; ***candidate for Republican nomination to presidency of the U.S., 1880, 1884***; chm., Monetary Comm., Indianapolis Monetary Conference, 1897. BUS. & PROF.: atty.; admitted to VT Bar, 1849; law practice (with A. B. Maynard), Richmond, VT, 1849–51; law practice, Burlington, VT, 1851–91; law practice, Philadelphia, PA, 1891–1919. HON. DEG.: LL.D., Middlebury Coll., 1869; LL.D., Trinity Coll., 1887; LL.D., Dartmouth Coll., 1890. REL.: Soc. of Friends. RES.: Burlington, VT.

EDWARDS, EDWARD IRVING. b. Dec 1, 1863, Jersey City, NJ; d. Jan 26, 1931, Jersey City, NJ; par. William W. and Emma J. (Nation) Edwards; m. Jule Blanche Smith, Nov 14, 1888; c. Edward Irving, Jr.; Elizabeth Jule (Mrs. Jerome La Due). EDUC.: NY U., 1880–82; studied law under William D. Edwards, 1882. POLIT. & GOV.: member, Hudson Cty. (NJ) Democratic Cmte., 1911; elected as a Democrat, NJ state comptroller, 1911–17; elected as a Democrat to NJ State Senate, 1918–20; delegate, Dem. Nat'l. Conv., 1920, 1924, 1928; ***candidate for Democratic nomination to presidency of the U.S., 1920, 1924***; elected as a Democrat to gov. of NJ, 1920–23; elected as a Democrat to U.S. Senate (NJ), 1923–29; Democratic candidate for U.S. Senate (NJ), 1928. BUS. & PROF.: messenger boy, First National Bank, Jersey City, NJ, 1882, asst. to the president, 1903–11, cashier, 1911–16, pres., 1916–25, chm. of the board, 1925–31; vice pres., Merchants' National Bank; dir., National Paper and Type Co.; dir., Raritan River R.R. Co.; dir., Standard Motor Construction Co. MEM.: Masons. REL.: Episc. MISC.: committed suicide. RES.: Jersey City, NJ.

EDWARDS, EDWIN WASHINGTON. b. Aug 7, 1927, Marksville, LA; par. Clarence W. and Agnes (Brouillette) Edwards; m. Elaine Schwartzenburg, Apr 5, 1949; c. Anna Laure (Mrs. John Edmond); Victoria Elaine (Mrs. Danny Arledge); Stephen Randolph; David Edwin. EDUC.: public schools; LL.B., LA State U., 1949. POLIT. & GOV.: elected to Crowley (LA) City Council, 1954–62; elected as a Democrat to LA State Senate, 1964–65; elected as a Democrat to U.S. House (LA), 1965–72; delegate, Dem. Nat'l. Conv., 1972; elected as a Democrat to gov. of LA, 1972–80, 1984–90, 1992–; chm., Interstate Oil Compact Comm., 1975–; ***candidate for Democratic nomination to presidency of the U.S., 1980***. BUS. & PROF.: atty.; admitted to LA Bar, 1949; law practice, Crowley; senior partner, Edwards, Edwards and Broadhurst (law firm), Crowley. MIL.: U.S. Naval Air Corps, 1945–46. MEM.: National Governors' Conference (host, 1976); Lions (pres.); International Rice Festival (pres.); Greater Crowley C. of C.; American Legion (adj.); Crowley Industrial Foundation. AWARDS: National Thomas Jefferson Award, 1974. HON. DEG.: J.D., LA State U., 1969. REL.: R.C. MAILING ADDRESS: Crowley, LA 70526; 15919 Highland Rd., Baton Rouge, LA 70810.

EDWARDS, INDIA MOFFETT. b. Jun 16, 1895, Nashville, TN; d. Jan 14, 1990, Sebastopol, CA; par. John Archibald and India H. (Thomas) Walker; m. Daniel Sharp, Dec 22, 1917; m. 2d, John F. Moffett, Mar 6, 1920 (divorced); m. 3d, Herbert Threlkeld Edwards, Jun 19, 1942; c. John Holbrook Moffett; India "Cissy" (Mrs. John Letcher Williams). EDUC.: grad., Central H.S., St. Louis, MO. POLIT. & GOV.: volunteer, Women's Division, Dem. Nat'l. Cmte., 1944, exec. sec., 1945–47, assoc. dir., 1947–48, exec. dir., 1948–50; vice chm., Dem. Nat'l. Cmte., 1950–56; appointed U.S. delegate, World Health Conference, 1951; ***candidate for Democratic nomination to vice presidency of the U.S., 1952 (withdrew)***; dir., Washington Office, NY State Dept. of Commerce, 1957–59; appointed official, Office of Emergency Planning, Washington, DC, c. 1964. BUS. & PROF.: development consultant; society ed., *Chicago (IL) Tribune*, 1918–36, woman's page ed., 1936–42. MEM.: Girls Club of America (pres.); Women's National Democratic Club; Women's National Press Club; District of Columbia Health and Welfare Council; Friendship House (board member). WRITINGS: *Pulling No Punches* (1977). REL.: Presb. RES.: Harwood, MD.

EDWARDS, JAMES BURROWS. b. Jun 24, 1927, Hawthorne, FL; par. O. Morton and Bertie Ray (Hieronymus) Edwards; m. Ann Norris Darlington, Aug 1951; c. James Burrows, Jr.; Catharine Darlington. EDUC.: B.S., Coll. of Charleston, 1950; D.M.D. (with honors), U. of Louisville, 1955; U. of PA Medical School, 1957–58; oral surgery residency, Henry Ford Hospital, Detroit, MI, 1958–60; diplomat, American Board of Oral Surgery, 1963. POLIT. & GOV.: fund-raiser, Goldwater for President Campaign, 1964; chm., Charleston (SC) Republican Party, 1964–69; delegate, Rep. Nat'l. Conv., 1968, 1972, 1976, 1980, 1984; SC Dental Assn. representative, Governor's Statewide Cmte. for Comprehensive Health Care Planning, 1968–72; appointed member, Federal Hospital Council, 1969–73; chm., First Congressional District (SC) Republican Party, 1970–71; Republican candidate for U.S. House (SC), 1971, 1974; member, Cmte. for the Re-Election of the President, 1972; member, SC Republican Steering Cmte.; chm., Charleston Cty. (SC) Republican Steering Cmte.; elected as a Republican to SC State Senate, 1973–74; elected as a Republican to gov. of SC, 1975–79; ***candidate for Republican nomination to vice presidency of the U.S., 1976***; appointed U.S. sec. of energy, 1981–82. BUS. & PROF.: deck officer, Alcoa Steamship Co., 1950–51; lecturer in oral surgery, Royal Soc. of Oral Surgeons; dentist; dental intern and resident, Henry Ford Hospital, Detroit, MI, 1957–60; clinical assoc., Coll. of Dental Medicine, U. of SC, 1970–77, asst. professor, 1977–82, professor, 1982–; pres., Medical U. of SC, 1982–. MIL.: U.S. Maritime Service, 1944–47; lt. commander, U.S.N.R., 1955–57. MEM.: American Dental Assn.; American Soc. of Oral Maxillfacial Surgeons; American Board of Oral Surgery; International Dental Federation; American Coll. of Dentistry (fellow); American Soc. of Oral Surgeons; Omicron Delta Kappa; Phi Delta; Pi Kappa Phi; AHEPA;

Coastal Carolina Council; BSA (dir.); Charleston Cty. Hospital (trustee); Greater Charleston YMCA (trustee); Baker Hospital (trustee); Coll. Preparatory School (trustee); SC Dental Assn.; Charleston Dental Assn. (pres., 1974); Coastal District Dental Soc. (pres.); Chalmers J. Lyons Acad. of Oral Surgery; British Assn. of Oral Surgeons; Southeastern Soc. of Oral Surgeons; Oral Surgery Political Action Cmte. (chm., 1971–73); Delta Sigma Delta; Masons; International Soc. of Oral Surgeons; SC Soc. of Oral Surgeons (pres.); Navy League of the U.S. (Charleston Council). AWARDS: Thomas P. Hinman Medal, 1977; James B. Edwards School, 1981; Humanitarian Award, La Societe Francaise de Bienfraisance, 1984; Founders' Medal, Coll. of Charleston, 1985. HON. DEG.: Litt.D., Coll. of Charleston, 1975; H.H.D., Francis Marion Coll., 1978; LL.D., U. of SC, 1975; LL.D., Bob Jones U., 1976; LL.D., The Citadel, 1977; D.Soc.Sci., U. of Louisville, 1982; D.Sc., Erskine Coll., 1982; D.Sc., Georgetown U., 1982. REL.: Methodist (Administrative Board, Hibben United Methodist Church). MISC.: class pres., U. of Louisville. MAILING ADDRESS: 1 Darlington Lane, Mt. Pleasant, SC 29464.

EDWARDS, JOHN HOLLOWAY. POLIT. & GOV.: ***independent candidate for president of the U.S., 1976***. MAILING ADDRESS: 110 County Line Rd., Massapequa, NY 11758.

EDWARDS, WILLIAM DAVIS. b. Feb 25, 1920, Moss Point, MS; d. Aug 5, 1992, San Francisco, CA; par. Charles Henry and Georgia Ann (Davis) Edwards; m. Shellia Zuber, 1941; m. 2d, Lisa Edwards, 1960 (divorced, 1977); m. 3d, Rani D.; c. Lawrence; Diana; Davis; Maureen; Raman; Rogen. EDUC.: San Francisco City Coll., 1939–40. POLIT. & GOV.: member, Communist Party, 1930s; charter member, New Democratic Party of Canada; delegate, Socialist Party National Convention, 1976; member, Socialist Party National Cmte., c. 1976; ***candidate for Socialist Party nomination to vice presidency of the U.S., 1976 (declined); Socialist Party candidate for vice presidency of the U.S., 1992***. BUS. & PROF.: employee, Golden Gate Park, San Francisco, CA; pile driver, 12 years; sailor, 30 years; sea cook; member, Merchant Marine; union official; owner, 4 Yellow taxicabs, San Francisco, CA. MIL.: second cook, chief cook, chief steward, U.S. Navy, 1942. MEM.: Young Communist League; Black social groups; Black civic groups; Cooks' and Dishwashers' Union (Local 101); Marine Cooks and Stewards Union (dispatcher; business mgr.); Pile Drivers Union. REL.: Methodist. MISC.: Golden Gloves boxer. RES.: San Francisco, CA.

EFAW, FRITZ WILLIAM. b. Dec 10, 1946, Stillwater, OK; par. Forrest Clark and Leanah (Damme) Efaw; single. EDUC.: B.S., MA Inst. of Technology, 1969; London School of Economics, 1974–75; A.A., Architect Assn., London, England, 1975. POLIT. & GOV.: member, General Management Cmte., Southwark-Bermondsey Labour Party, 1974–76; delegate, Dem. Nat'l. Conv., 1976; ***candidate for Democratic nomination to vice presidency of the U.S., 1976***; represented Democrats Abroad at Dem. Nat'l. Conv., 1976. BUS. & PROF.: computer programmer, U. of London, 1969–73; urban planner, London, England, 1975; author. MEM.: Theta Xi; Union of American Exiles in Britain (pres., 1971–77); National Amnesty Council (program coordinator, 1976–77); Assn. of Scientific, Technological, and Managerial Staffs (shop steward, 1971–73); Concerned Americans Abroad; Britain-Vietnam Assn. AWARDS: grad. studies grant, Social Science Research Council, United Kingdom, 1973. WRITINGS: various book reviews and political commentary in *New Statesman*, *Tribune*, *Race Today*, *UK*, and *Nation*. MISC.: indicted for draft evasion. MAILING ADDRESS: 3364 Navaho Trail, Smynra, GA 30080.

EHINGER, CALVIN CARL. b. Jul 14, 1936; m. Dolly Ehinger, 1959; c. Tracy; Derek; Brian; Bart; Kirk; Felicia. POLIT. & GOV.: elected as a Non-Partisan to Lawndale (CA) City Council, 1972–; elected mayor of Lawndale, 1976–; ***Independent Christian candidate for presidency of the U.S., 1976***. BUS. & PROF.: bricklayer; construction worker; owner, CKBD Ehinger Co., Lawndale. REL.: Lutheran. MAILING ADDRESS: 16123 Grevillea Ave., Lawndale, CA 90260.

EHLERS, DELBERT L. b. 1953. POLIT. & GOV.: ***independent candidate for presidency of the U.S., 1992***. BUS. & PROF.: farmer, Dunlap, IA; fence builder, Ute, IA. MAILING ADDRESS: Box 237, 428 Monona Ave., Ute, IA 51060.

EHRENREICH, RON. b. 1950, Philadelphia, PA; m. Sondra; c. Hannah; Samuel. EDUC.: grad., Temple U., 1972; M.A., Maxwell School of Public Affairs, Syracuse U., 1977. POLIT. & GOV.: ed., New York State Socialist Party Newsletter; member, Socialist Party National Cmte., 1983– (vice chair; co-chair, 1987–); delegate, Socialist Party National Convention, 1987; ***Socialist Party candidate for vice presidency of the U.S., 1988***. BUS. & PROF.: teacher, Syracuse, NY; instructor in social sciences, State U. of NY Coll. of Technology; community activist. MEM.: Temple U. Student Body (pres.); Syracuse Real Food Co-Op; National Student Assn. (vice president); Syracuse Co-operative Federal Credit Union (founder, 1981; treas.; loan officer); New Jewish Agenda; Industrial Cooperative Assn.; National Center for Employee Ownership; Assn. for Union Democracy; Industrial Workers of the World; American Sociological Assn. (Marxist Section); Mobilization for Survival; Greenpeace; Syracuse Peace Council. WRITINGS: "Consumers and Organizational Democracy," *Organizational Democracy and Political Processes* (1983). MAILING ADDRESS: Syracuse, NY.

EIFORD, MAURICE. POLIT. & GOV.: ***independent candidate for presidency of the U.S., 1980***. MAILING ADDRESS: 280 Cinema Dr., Johnstown, PA 15905.

EISENHOWER, DWIGHT DAVID "IKE." b. Oct 14, 1890, Denison, TX; d. Mar 28, 1969, Washington, DC; par. David Jacob and Ida Elizabeth (Stover) Eisenhower; m. Mamie Geneva Doud, Jul 1, 1916; c. Doud Dwight; John Sheldon Doud. EDUC.: B.S., U.S. Military Acad., 1915; grad., Infantry Tank School, 1920; grad., Command and General Staff School, 1926; grad., Army War Coll., 1928; grad., Army Industrial Coll., 1933. POLIT. & GOV.: exec. asst., U.S. sec. of war, 1929–33; ***candidate for Republican nomination to presidency of the U.S., 1944, 1948 (declined); candidate for Democratic nomination to presidency of the U.S., 1944, 1948 (declined); elected as a Republican to presidency of the U.S., 1953–61***. BUS. & PROF.: army officer; appointed pres., Columbia U., 1948–52. MIL.: commissioned 2d lt., U.S. Army, 1915, capt., 1917, lt. col., 1918, maj., 1920, brig. gen., 1941, maj. gen., 1942, lt. gen., 1942, gen., 1943; supreme commander, AEF in Europe, 1943–45; gen. of the army, U.S. Army, 1944, chief of staff, 1945–48; commander, NATO Forces in Europe, 1950–52; U.S. Distinguished Service Medal with 4 Oak Leaf Clusters; Legion of Merit; Distinguished Service Medal (U.S. Navy); Cross of Liberation (France); Grand Cross of Legion of Honor; Croix de Guerre with 2 Palms; Grand Cordon of the Order of Leopold with Palm; Cross de Guerre of 1940 with Palm (Belgium); Grand Cross of the Order of George I (Greece); Royal Order of the Savior (Greece); Knight, Grand Cross of the Military Order of Italy; Chevalier of the Order of Polonia Restituta (Poland); Order of Malta; Order of the Aztec Eagle, First Class (Mexico); Supreme Order of the Chrysanthemum (Japan); Order of the Lion (Netherlands); Order of the Holy Sepulcher; Order of Bath; Order of Merit (Great Britain); Order of Victory (U.S.S.R.); Order of Suvarov (U.S.S.R.). MEM.: English-Speaking Union of the U.S. (chm.). AWARDS: General Sylvanus Thayer Patriot's Medal, Freedom's Foundation, 1961; Bronze Award, Freedom House; Medal of Honor, Roosevelt Memorial Assn.; Churchman Award; Army and Navy Union Medal; Poor Richard Club Medal; Gold Medal, PA Soc. of NY; Certificate of Merit, Catholic War Veterans; American Hebrew Medal, 1945; Freedoms Foundation Award; George F. Peabody Radio Award; Certificate of Merit, VFW; Bernard Baruch Distinguished Service Medal, VFW; Civil Rights Award of Honor, National Negro Council; America's Democratic Legacy Silver Medallion, Anti-Defamation League of B'nai B'rith; Golden Anniversary Award, Boys Clubs of America; Gold Medal, National Conference of Christians and Jews; World Peace Award, Amvets, 1958; Universal Brotherhood Award, Jewish Theological Seminary, 1959; Army and Navy Legion of Valor Award; Big Brother of the Year Award, 1960; Hoover Medal; Horatio Alger Award; American Patriots Medal; George Catlett Marshall Award; Atoms for Peace Award. HON. DEG.: LL.D., Coll. of William and Mary; LL.D., Williams Coll.; LL.D., Yale U.; LL.D., American U.; LL.D., Bard Coll.; LL.D., U. of Rochester; LL.D., Rutgers U.; LL.D., U. of Santo Domingo; LL.D., Baylor U.; LL.D., Boston U.; LL.D., U. of CA at Los Angeles; LL.D., Temple U.; LL.D., TX A&M U.; LL.D., U. of Toronto; LL.D., Cambridge U.; LL.D., Catholic U. of America; LL.D., Washburn U.; LL.D., Washington Coll.; LL.D., U. of WV; LL.D., The Citadel; LL.D., Military Coll. of SC; LL.D., Columbia U.; LL.D., Dartmouth Coll.; LL.D., U. of Delhi; LL.D., U. of Denver; LL.D., U. of Edinburgh; LL.D., Franklin and Marshall Coll.; LL.D., Georgetown U.; LL.D., Gettysburg Coll.; LL.D., Grinnell Coll.; LL.D., Harvard U.; LL.D., U. of HI; LL.D., Johns Hopkins U.; LL.D., KS State U.; LL.D., Lafayette Coll.; LL.D., Messiah Coll.; LL.D., Mt. St. Mary's Coll.; LL.D., NY U.; LL.D., Nihon U.; LL.D., Northwestern U.; LL.D., U. of Notre Dame; LL.D., PA State U.; LL.D., U. of PA; LL.D., U. of the Philippines; LL.D., Princeton U.; LL.D., Queens U. of Ireland; LL.D., U. of Richmond; LL.D., U. of Ankara; LL.D., U. of Athens; LL.D., U. of Brazil; LL.D., U. of Caen, France; LL.D., Corpus Christi Coll.; LL.D., Jewish Theological Seminary; LL.D., George Washington U.; LL.D., Hofstra Coll.; LL.D., Trinity Coll.; LL.D., U. of Pittsburgh; LL.D., Norwich U.; LL.D., U. of Louvain; LL.D., U.S. Air Force Acad. WRITINGS: *Crusade in Europe* (1948); *Mandate for Change* (1963); *Waging Peace* (1965); *At Ease* (1967). REL.: Presb. MISC.: brother of Milton Stover Eisenhower (q.v.). RES.: Gettysburg, PA.

EISENHOWER, MILTON STOVER. b. Sep 15, 1899, Abilene, KS; d. May 2, 1985, Baltimore, MD; par. David Jacob and Ida Elizabeth (Stover) Eisenhower; m. Helen Elsie Eakin, Oct 12, 1927; c. Milton Stover, Jr.; Ruth Eakin (Mrs. Snider). EDUC.: B.S., KS State U., 1924. POLIT. & GOV.: appointed vice consul, U.S. consulate, Edinburgh, Scotland, 1924–26; appointed asst. to the U.S. sec. of agriculture, 1926–28; appointed dir. of information, U.S. Dept. of Agriculture, 1928–41, coordinator of land use programs, 1937–42; appointed dir., War Relocation Authority, 1942; appointed assoc. dir., OWI, 1942–43; appointed member, Famine Emergency Relief Comm., 1946; appointed member, Exec. Board, UNESCO, 1946; chm., U.S. National Comm. for UNESCO, 1946–48; delegate, UNESCO Conference, 1946, 1947, 1948, 1949; appointed member, President's Comm. on Government Reorganization, 1953–60; appointed special ambassador for Latin America, 1953, 1956, 1957–60, 1968–69; appointed gov., New York Stock Exchange, 1962–65; appointed chm., President's Comm. on the Causes and Prevention of Violence, 1968–69; appointed member, President's Comm. on Atlantic-Pacific Interoceanic Canal Study, 1965–70; appointed member, President's Comm. on International Radio Broadcasting, 1972–73; ***independent (National Unity Party) candidate for vice presidency of the U.S., 1980***. BUS. & PROF.: reporter, acting city ed., *Abilene (KS) Daily Reflector*, 1917–18, city ed., 1920–21; asst. professor of journalism, KS State U., 1921–24, pres., 1943–50; pres., PA State U., 1950–56; pres., Johns Hopkins U., 1956–67, 1971–72, president emeritus, 1967–71, 1972–85; dir., Chessie System, Inc.; dir., Baltimore and Ohio R.R.; dir., Cincinnati and Ohio Railway. MEM.: National Soc. of Pershing Rifles; Rotary Club; Church Soc. for College Work (dir.); Enoch Pratt Free Library (trustee); Inst. for International Education (trustee, 1951–53); National Soc. for Crippled Children (trustee, 1950–53); Soc. for the Advancement of Management (vice pres., 1944–45); Johns Hopkins Hospital (dir.); Greater Baltimore Medical Center (dir.); Washington Coll. (gov.); National Cmte. for Economic Development (trustee,

1947–51); Freedoms Foundation (dir., 1951; chm., Awards Jury, 1950); Geisinger Memorial Hospital (dir., 1952–67); American-Korean Foundation (chm., 1952–53); U.S. Naval Acad. (visitor, 1958–61); AAAS (fellow); APSA (hon. member); KS Acad. of Science; MD Acad. of Science; Phi Kappa Phi; Phi Beta Kappa; Sigma Alpha Epsilon; Sigma Delta Chi; Alpha Zeta; Omicron Delta Kappa; Delta Sigma Pi; Fund for Adult Education (dir., 1953–61); American Council on Education; Assn. of Land Grant Colleges and State Universities (pres., 1951–52); National Planning Assn.; Manhattan Country Club. AWARDS: Horatio Alger Award, American Schools and Colleges Assn., 1952; Thomas F. Cunningham Award, International House, 1954; Order of Boyaca (Colombia, 1954); Great Cross, Order of the Condor of the Andes (Bolivia); Order of the Liberator in the Class of Grand Cordon (Venezuela); Republic of Korea Award, 1956; Order Nacional Al Merito en el Grado de Gran Cruz (Ecuador, 1959); Professor Extraordinary, National U. of Mexico, 1957. HON. DEG.: LL.D., Wichita U., 1944; D.Sc., Colorado State Coll., 1945; H.L.D., U. of NE, 1949; LL.D., Lafayette Coll., 1950; LL.D., Temple U., 1950; Litt.D., Jefferson Medical Coll., 1951; LL.D., U. of Pittsburgh, 1951; Litt.D., Westminster Coll., 1951; H.H.D., Bucknell U., 1952; LL.D., Johns Hopkins U., 1952; LL.D., U. of ME, 1952; LL.D., Beaver Coll., 1953; Dr. Pol. Sci., Central U. of Venezuela, 1953; LL.D., Elizabethtown Coll., 1953; Dr. Pol. Sci., U. of the Andes, 1953; LL.D., U. of Pennsylvania, 1953; LL.D., U. of San Marcos (Peru), 1953; LL.D., Lincoln U., 1954; LL.D., U. of Rhode Island, 1954; LL.D., Western MI State Coll., 1954; LL.D., Boston U., 1956; LL.D., Pennsylvania Military Coll., 1956; LL.D., Morgan State Coll., 1957; LL.D., Syracuse U., 1957; LL.D., Franklin and Marshall Coll., 1958; LL.D., U. of Maryland, 1958. WRITINGS: *The U.S. Department of Agriculture: Its Structure and Functions* (coauthor, 1930); *The Wine is Bitter* (1963); *The President is Calling* (1974). REL.: Episc. RES.: Baltimore, MD.

EISENMAN, ABRAM.

b. Feb 4, 1914, Savannah, GA; d. Jun 24, 1981, Savannah, GA; par. David and Fannie (Rabinowitz) Eisenman; m. Georgia Russell, Mar 26, 1939; c. Russell; Robert E. EDUC.: grad., Savannah (GA) H.S., 1929; U. of GA, 1931. POLIT. & GOV.: candidate for Savannah City Council, 1958; candidate for Democratic nomination to GA State Senate, 1966; ***People's Peace candidate for Democratic nomination to presidency of the U.S., 1968, 1972, 1976***. BUS. & PROF.: employee, radiator specialty company, Charlotte, NC, 1938; radio announcer, WSAV, Savannah; radio announcer, WCOS, Columbia, SC; radio announcer, WAAT, Newark, NJ; radio announcer, WPAT, Paterson, NJ; radio announcer, WJZ, New York, NY; radio announcer, WJIV (now WEAS), Savannah, 1950–60; gen. mgr., WSOK, Savannah, GA, 1960–70; ship-fitter, Savannah Shipyards; ed., *The Savannah Sun*, 1953–63; radio business, 1939–81. MEM.: Americans for Democratic Action. WRITINGS: *It's Your World; Why I Should Be President* (2 vols., 1963, 1969); "Israel's Greatest Victory" (poem); "Tribute to F. D. R." (poem); "To the Memory of J. F. K." (poem); "How to Make History" (poem); "The Modern Crusaders" (poem); "Cool It, Man" (poem); "Tell It Like It Is" (poem); "Oh, Have I Got Problems" (poem). REL.: Jewish. MISC.: Senior Men's Tennis Champion, Savannah, 1970. RES.: Savannah, GA.

EISENMAN, WILLIAM JOHN.

b. Feb 4, 1944, Hazleton, PA; par. Edgar Eugene and Dorothy Martha Eisenman; single. EDUC.: grad., Arts H.S., Newark, NJ; Professional Business School, 1967; Newspaper Inst. of America, 1979–. POLIT. & GOV.: ***Constitutional Values Party candidate for presidency of the U.S., 1980***. BUS. & PROF.: insurance clerk; real estate salesman; fiction writer; pantographer. MEM.: League of United Handicapped Workers (sec.-treas.); United Citizens Assn. Against Censorship (public relations supervisor). WRITINGS: fiction (in press, 1972, 1975, 1975, 1976). REL.: Protestant (nonpracticing). MAILING ADDRESS: 116 Elm St., Lodi, NJ 07644.

EKERN, HERMAN LEWIS.

b. Dec 27, 1872, Pigeon Falls, Trempealeau Cty., WI; d. Dec 4, 1954, Madison, WI; par. Even and Elizabeth (Grimsrud) Ekern; m. Lily C. Anderson, Aug 16, 1899; c. Elsie (Mrs. William G. Fisher); Lila (Mrs. Horace H. Ratcliff); John; George; Irene (Mrs. Winfield V. Alexander); Dorothy. EDUC.: LL.B., U. of Wisconsin, 1894. POLIT. & GOV.: elected district atty., Trempealeau Cty., WI, 1895–99; elected as a Republican to WI State Assembly, 1903–09 (Speaker, 1907–09); appointed deputy commissioner of insurance of WI, 1909–10; commissioner of insurance of WI, 1911–15; alternate delegate, Rep. Nat'l. Conv., 1920; elected as a Republican to atty. gen. of WI, 1923–27; delegate, Rep. Nat'l. Conv., 1924; dir. of finance, Progressive Party, 1926; candidate for Republican nomination to lt. gov. of WI, 1926; ***candidate for Republican nomination to vice presidency of the U.S., 1928***; chm., WI State Republican Central Cmte., 1929–32; chm., WI State Unemployment Comm., 1931; appointed as a Republican to lt. gov. of WI, 1938; Progressive Party candidate for U.S. Senate (WI), 1938; appointed chm., WI Deep Waterway Comm. BUS. & PROF.: atty.; admitted to WI Bar, 1894; law practice, Whitehall, WI, 1894–1911; law practice, Madison, WI, 1915–54; partner, Ekern and Meyers (law firm); partner, Ekern, Meyers and Matthias (law firm); partner, Ekern, Naujoks and Ekern (law firm), Chicago, IL, 1951–54. MEM.: U. of Wisconsin (regent, 1939–43); U. of Wisconsin Foundation (dir.); Lutheran Brotherhood (pres.); Foreign Bondholders Protective Council (dir.); National Multiple Sclerosis Soc. (dir.); ABA; WI Bar Assn.; IL Bar Assn.; Chicago Bar Assn.; American-Scandinavian Foundation; Acad. of Political Science; Newcomen Soc.; Masons; Kiwanis; Sons of Norway; Ygdrasil. HON. DEG.: LL.D., Capital Coll., 1935; LL.D., Thiel Coll., 1939; LL.D., U. of Wisconsin, 1944. REL.: Lutheran. RES.: Madison, WI.

ELEY, DAVID CORNELIUS (See PROPHET OF THE INCARNATION).

ELIJAH, PROPHET (nee CHARLES EDWARD STEWART). b. Oct 19, 1943, Beckley, WV; par. Robert O. and Elsie Mae (Persinger) Stewart; single. EDUC.: Long Island U., 1977; Columbia U. POLIT. & GOV.: ***independent candidate for presidency of the U.S., 1980, 1984, 1988***; independent candidate for U.S. House (DC), 1990. BUS. & PROF.: quality inspector, Western Electric Co., Whitestone, NY, 1964–; dir., The Church of Jesus, Inc., 1976–. MIL.: U.S. Army, 1961–64. WRITINGS: *The Time of the End*. REL.: Christian. MAILING ADDRESS: 326 Columbus Ave., Apt. 5F, New York, NY 10023.

ELKINS, STEPHEN BENTON. b. Sep 26, 1841, Perry Cty., OH; d. Jan 4, 1911, Washington, DC; par. Col. Philip Duncan and Sarah Pickett (Withers) Elkins; m. Sallie Jacobs, Jun 10, 1866; m. 2d, Hallie L. Davis, Apr 14, 1875; c. Davis; Katherine H.; Stephen Benton; Richard; Blaine; one other daughter; one other child. EDUC.: A.B., U. of Missouri, 1860, A.M., 1868. POLIT. & GOV.: member, NM Territorial Legislature, 1864–65; district atty., Territory of NM, 1866–67; appointed atty. gen. of NM Territory, 1867–68; appointed U.S. district atty., Territory of NM, 1868–72; elected territorial delegate, U.S. House (NM), 1873–77; member, Rep. Nat'l. Cmte., 1875 (chm., 1884); appointed U.S. sec. of war, 1891–93; Republican candidate for U.S. Senate (WV), 1892; elected as a Republican to U.S. Senate (WV), 1895–1911; ***candidate for Republican nomination to vice presidency of the U.S., 1900***. BUS. & PROF.: school teacher, Cass Cty., MO; atty.; admitted to MO Bar, 1864; law practice, Messilia, NM, 1864; vice pres., West Virginia Central and Pittsburgh Railway Co.; vice pres., Piedmont and Cumberland Railway Co.; pres., Santa Fe First National Bank, 1869–79; owner, Morgantown and Kingwood R.R., 1902–07; shareholder, Coal and Coke Railway; pres., Davis Coal and Coke Co.; shareholder, coal mining interests, WV. MIL.: capt., 77th MO Infantry, U.S. Army, 1861. MEM.: Union League; Republican Club; Ohio Soc.; United Service Club; Metropolitan Club; Manhattan Athletic Club; Southern Soc.; American Geographical Soc.; Metropolitan Museum of Art (patron); American Museum of Natural History (patron); Army and Navy Club; Chevy Chase Club. MISC.: founded town of Elkins, WV. RES.: Elkins, WV.

ELLIS, SETH HOCKETT. b. Jan 3, 1830, Martinsville, OH; d. Jun 23, 1904, Waynesville, OH; par. Robert and Anna Hockett (Moon) Ellis; m. Rebecca J. Tressler, Aug 21, 1851; c. Charles; Mrs. Foster; others. EDUC.: public schools, Clinton and Warren counties, OH. POLIT. & GOV.: Prohibition Party candidate for lt. gov. of OH, 1893; Prohibition Party candidate for U.S. House (OH), 1894; Prohibition Party candidate for gov. of OH, 1895; Union Reform (Silver Republican, Liberty, People's and Negro Protective) Party candidate for OH State Food and Dairy Commissioner, 1898; Union Reform Party candidate for gov. of OH, 1899; ***Union Reform Party candidate for presidency of the U.S., 1900***. BUS. & PROF.: farmer, Waynesville, OH; vice pres., Farmers' Cooperative Harvesting Machine Co., Springfield, OH. MEM.: Grange (Ohio state master, 1873–79, 1888–92, 1896–1900; chm., OH State Exec. Cmte., 1879–88, 1892–96, 1900–04; national chaplain; member, National Exec. Cmte.); OH State U. (trustee, 1879–87); OH Agricultural Experiment Station (member, Board of Control, 1887). WRITINGS: articles in the *Ohio Farmer*, 1900–04; "The Union Reform Party," *Independent*, Oct 11, 1900. REL.: Orthodox Soc. of Friends. MISC.: reputed to be first person ever placed in nomination to president by direct vote of party members. RES.: Waynesville, OH.

ELLMAKER, AMOS. b. Feb 2, 1787, Lancaster Cty., PA; d. Nov 28, 1851, Lancaster, PA; m. Mary R. Elder, Jun 13, 1816. EDUC.: grad., Princeton Coll.; studied law under Judge Reeve, Litchfield, CT; studied law under Thomas Elder, Harrisburg, PA. POLIT. & GOV.: deputy atty. gen. of Dauphin Cty., PA, 1809–12; elected as an Anti-Mason to PA State House, 1812–14; appointed president judge, Twelfth Judicial District of PA, 1815–16; elected as an Anti-Mason to U.S. House (PA), 1815; appointed atty. gen. of PA, 1816–19, 1828–29; appointed U.S. sec. of war, 1820 (declined); ***Anti-Masonic Party candidate for vice presidency of the U.S., 1832***; Anti-Masonic Party candidate for U.S. Senate (PA), 1833. BUS. & PROF.: atty.; admitted to PA Bar, 1808; law practice, Harrisburg, PA; law practice, Lancaster, PA, 1821–51. MIL.: aide to General Forster, 1814. REL.: Episc. RES.: Harrisburg, PA.

ELLSWORTH, BARRY ALAN. b. Feb 27, 1954, Tooele, UT; par. Cecil Dean and Barbara Marie (Paulick) Ellsworth; single. EDUC.: U. of Utah; B.A., Brigham Young U. POLIT. & GOV.: ***candidate for Democratic nomination to presidency of the U.S., 1992; New Paradigm Party candidate for presidency of the U.S., 1992***. BUS. & PROF.: stock broker; chief exec. officer, pres., management consulting firm; author; lecturer. WRITINGS: *Living in Love With Yourself* (1988); *. . . And You Wonder Why Your Life Isn't Working?* (1990); *The Tale of Princess Charming* (1992). REL.: none. MAILING ADDRESS: 6337 South Highland Dr., B-120, Salt Lake City, UT 84121.

ELLSWORTH, OLIVER. b. Apr 29, 1745, Windsor, CT; d. Nov 26, 1807, Windsor, CT; par. Col. David and Jemima (Leavitt) Ellsworth; m. Abigail Wolcott, 1772; c. William Wolcott; Oliver, Jr.; Henry Leavitt; daughter; possibly others. EDUC.: B.A. (magna cum laude), Princeton U., 1766; studied theology under Rev. John Smalley. POLIT. & GOV.: elected as a Whig to CT Colonial House of Reps., 1775; member, CT Cmte. of the Pay Table, 1776; state's atty., Hartford Cty., CT, 1777; delegate, Continental Congress, 1777–83; member, CT Council of Safety, 1779; member, Governor's Council, State of CT, 1780–84, 1801–07; appointed U.S. commissioner of the treasury, 1784 (declined); judge, Superior Court of CT, 1784–89;

delegate, U.S. Constitutional Convention, 1787; elected as a Federalist to U.S. Senate (CT), 1789–96; ***Federalist Party candidate for vice presidency of the U.S., 1796***; appointed chief justice, Supreme Court of the U.S., 1796–99; appointed U.S. minister to France, 1799; appointed chief justice, Supreme Court of CT, 1807 (declined). BUS. & PROF.: farmer; wood chopper; atty.; admitted to CT Bar, 1771; law practice, Windsor, CT, 1771–75; law practice, Hartford, CT, 1775. MEM.: Cliosophic Soc. (founder). HON. DEG.: LL.D., Yale U., 1790; LL.D., Dartmouth Coll., 1797; LL.D., Princeton U., 1797. REL.: Congregationalist. RES.: Windsor, CT.

ELLSWORTH, WILLIAM LEDYARD. married; c. son. POLIT. & GOV.: ***American Political Alliance candidate for presidency of the U.S., 1880, 1884***. BUS. & PROF.: inventor. MIL.: appointed capt., asst. quartermaster, New York Volunteers, Feb 19, 1863, mustered out, Aug 14, 1863. WRITINGS: *The Life and Personal History of Captain Ellsworth, Candidate of the American Alliance for President of the United States*. MISC.: invented smokeless gunpowder, rights to which were purchased by the German government; sued by wife for nonsupport, 1890, after philandering with a woman in a hotel room; wife's petition withdrawn after Ellsworth fled penniless to undisclosed location. RES.: New Haven, CT.

ELY, JOSEPH BUELL. b. Feb 22, 1881, Westfield, MA; d. Jun 13, 1956, Westfield, MA; par. Henry Wilson and Sarah N. (Buell) Ely; m. Harriet Z. Dyson, May 1, 1906; c. Richard. EDUC.: A.B., Williams Coll., 1902; LL.B., Harvard U., 1905. POLIT. & GOV.: appointed and subsequently elected district atty., Berkshire and Hampden Counties, MA, 1915–16; delegate, Dem. Nat'l. Conv., 1924, 1928; elected as a Democrat to gov. of MA, 1931–35; ***candidate for Republican nomination to vice presidency of the U.S., 1936; candidate for Democratic nomination to presidency of the U.S., 1940, 1944***. BUS. & PROF.: atty.; admitted to MA Bar, 1905; law practice, Westfield, MA, 1905; senior partner, Ely, Bradford, Bartlett, Thompson and Brown (law firm), Westfield, 1935–56; partner, Ely, King, Kingsbury and Corcoran (law firm), Springfield, MA; pres., dir., American Woolen Co.; dir., Hampden National Bank and Trust Co.; dir., International Hydro-Electric Systems; dir., New England Power Assn.; dir., New England Electric Systems; dir., Torrington Co.; dir., Eastern Racing Assn. MEM.: Phi Delta Theta; Elks; Colony Club; Union Club; City Club of Boston. HON. DEG.: LL.D., Williams Coll., 1931; LL.D., Holy Cross Coll.; LL.D., Wesleyan U. REL.: Congregationalist. RES.: Boston, MA.

EMERSON, EDWARD WALDO. b. Jul 10, 1844, Concord, MA; d. Jan 27, 1930, Concord, MA; par. Ralph Waldo and Lydia (Jackson) Emerson; m. Annie Shephard Keyes, Sep 19, 1874; c. William; Charles Lowell; John; Ellen Tucker (Mrs. Charles Milton Davenport); Florence (Mrs. Gerrit Forbes); William Forbes; Raymond Emerson. EDUC.: A.B., Harvard U., 1866, M.D., 1874; studied art under Frederick Crowinshield; Museum of Fine Arts, Boston, MA, 1882–85. POLIT. & GOV.: ***National Party candidate for presidency of the U.S., 1900***. BUS. & PROF.: clerk, Burlington and Missouri R.R., Burlington, IA; physician; medical practice, Concord, MA, 1874–80; instructor in art anatomy, Museum of Fine Arts, Boston, MA, 1885–1905; author. MEM.: American Acad. of Arts and Sciences (fellow); MA Hist. Soc.; Social Circle of Concord; Saturday Club of Boston. WRITINGS: *Emerson in Concord* (1888); *Correspondence of John Sterling and Ralph Waldo Emerson* (ed., 1897); *Centenary Edition of Works of Ralph Waldo Emerson* (ed., 1903); *Life and Letters of General Charles Russell* (ed., 1907); *Emerson's Journals* (co-editor, with W. E. Forbes, 1909); *Life of Ebenezer Rockwood Hoar* (with M. Storey, 1911); *Henry Thoreau, As Remembered by a Young Friend* (1917); *Early History of the Saturday Club of Boston* (1918); *Essays, Addresses and Poems* (1930). RES.: Concord, MA.

EMERSON, F. W. POLIT. & GOV.: Prohibition Party candidate for gov. of KS, 1902; state chm., NE Prohibition Party, 1906; Prohibition Party candidate for U.S. House (IL), 1908; Prohibition Party candidate for U.S. House (ME), 1910, 1914; ***candidate for Prohibition Party nomination to presidency of the U.S., 1912 (withdrew); candidate for Prohibition Party nomination to vice presidency of the U.S., 1912 (withdrew)***; member, exec. cmte., Prohibition Party, 1912–16; Prohibition Party candidate for gov. of WI, 1914, 1926 (?). RES.: San Francisco, CA.

EMERSON, ROBERT C. POLIT. & GOV.: ***candidate for Democratic nomination to presidency of the U.S., 1992***. MAILING ADDRESS: Route 2, Box 369, Wedowee, AL 36278.

EMERY, STEPHEN. b. Aug 20, 1908, Passaic, NJ; par. Albert and Anna (Urban) Emery; m. Emma Wisnewski; c. Joan; Arleen; Lee Ann; Susan. EDUC.: Boys' H.S. of Brooklyn; Hunter Coll. POLIT. & GOV.: member, NY Socialist Labor Party State Cmte., 1942; ***Socialist Labor Party candidate for vice presidency of the U.S., 1948, 1952***; Socialist Labor Party candidate for U.S. Senate (NY), 1950, 1958, 1962; delegate, Socialist Labor Party National Convention, 1952, 1956 (member, Platform Cmte.), 1960 (member, Platform Cmte.); Socialist Labor Party candidate for president, New York (NY) City Council, 1953, 1957, 1961; Socialist Labor Party candidate for lt. gov. of NY, 1954; Socialist Labor Party candidate for controller of New York, 1969; Socialist Labor Party candidate for gov. of NY, 1970; Industrial Party candidate for U.S. House (OH), 1976, 1978. BUS. & PROF.: subway dispatcher, New York City Transit System, 1937–70; salesman; bank clerk; machinist; recreation teacher. MEM.: French Inst. of NY. REL.: none. MAILING ADDRESS: 80-05 171st St., Jamaica, Long Island, NY.

ENGLEFIELD, RICHARD HASTINGS. POLIT. & GOV.: ***candidate for Republican nomination to presidency of the U.S., 1976***. BUS. & PROF.: publisher; exec. MAILING ADDRESS: c/o F. William Englefield, Hankinson Rd., Granville, OH.

ENGLERIUS, MAXIMUS T. POLIT. & GOV.: ***American Tradition Party candidate for presidency of the U.S., 1980 (withdrew), 1984, 1988***. BUS. & PROF.: Blue Eagle Services. MAILING ADDRESS: 2319 First Ave., South, Seattle, WA 98144.

ENGLISH, CHARLES P. POLIT. & GOV.: ***candidate for Republican nomination to presidency of the U.S., 1984***. MAILING ADDRESS: 1820 S.W. 62nd Ave., Miami, FL 33158.

ENGLISH, ERNEST E., JR. par. Ernest English, Sr. POLIT. & GOV.: ***candidate for Democratic nomination to presidency of the U.S., 1992***. MAILING ADDRESS: 121 Cady St., Rochester, NY 14608.

ENGLISH, JAMES EDWARD. b. Mar 13, 1812, New Haven, CT; d. Mar 2, 1890, New Haven, CT; par. James and Nancy (Griswold) English; m. Caroline Augusta Fowler, Jan 25, 1837; m. 2d, Anna Robinson Morris, Oct 7, 1885; c. Henry Fowler; three others. EDUC.: public schools. POLIT. & GOV.: elected as a Democrat to New Haven (CT) Board of Selectmen, 1847–61; elected member, New Haven Common Council, 1848–49; elected as a Democrat to CT State House, 1855, 1872; elected as a Democrat to CT State Senate, 1856–58; Democratic candidate for lt. gov. of CT, 1860; elected as a Democrat to U.S. House (CT), 1861–65; delegate, Union Convention, 1866; Democratic candidate for gov. of CT, 1866, 1869, 1871, 1880; elected as a Democrat to gov. of CT, 1867–68, 1870; ***candidate for Democratic nomination to presidency of the U.S., 1868, 1880***; presidential elector, Democratic Party, 1868, 1876, 1884; Democratic candidate for U.S. House (CT), 1872; appointed as a Democrat to U.S. Senate (CT), 1875–76; Democratic candidate for U.S. Senate (CT), 1876. BUS. & PROF.: apprentice carpenter and joiner; master builder; building contractor; owner, English and Welch Lumber Co., New Haven, 1835; owner, New Haven Clock Co., 1855; pres., Goodyear Metallic Rubber Shoe Co., 1855–90; pres., Connecticut Savings Bank, 1857–90; dir., Plainville Manufacturing Co.; dir., Bristol Brass Co. MEM.: Yale Corp. (fellow); Sheffield Scientific School (councilor). HON. DEG.: M.A., Yale U., 1873. REL.: Episc. RES.: New Haven, CT.

ENGLISH, WILLIAM HAYDEN. b. Aug 27, 1822, Lexington, IN; d. Feb 7, 1896, Indianapolis, IN; par. Elisha G. and Mahala (Eastin) English; m. Emma Mardulia Jackson, Nov 17, 1847; c. William Eastin; Rosalind (Mrs. Willoughby Walling). EDUC.: Hanover Coll., 3 years; studied law. POLIT. & GOV.: delegate, IN State Democratic Convention, 1840; appointed postmaster, Lexington, IN, 1841; principal clerk, IN State House, 1843; clerk, U.S. Dept. of the Treasury, 1844–48; delegate, Dem. Nat'l. Conv., 1848; clerk, U.S. Senate, 1850; sec., IN State Constitutional Convention, 1851; elected as a Democrat to IN State House, 1851–52 (Speaker); elected as a Democrat to U.S. House (IN), 1853–61; chm., IN State Democratic Central Cmte., 1879; appointed member, IN Soldiers and Sailors Monument Comm.; ***Democratic candidate for vice presidency of the U.S., 1880***. BUS. & PROF.: atty.; admitted to IN Bar, 1840; law practice, Lexington, IN, 1840–61; admitted to practice before the Bar of the Supreme Court of the U.S.; pres., Indianapolis First National Bank, 1863–77; author. MEM.: IN Hist. Soc. (pres.); Indianapolis Clearinghouse Assn. (pres.); Smithsonian Institution (Regent, 1853–61); IN Banking Assn. (pres.); SAR; Masons. WRITINGS: *History of Indiana* (1887); *Conquest of the Northwest* (1896); *Life of George Rogers Clark* (1896). RES.: Indianapolis, IN.

ENGVALSON, PAUL WILLARD. b. Sep 29, 1941, Los Angeles, CA; married; c. John. POLIT. & GOV.: ***Holy Spirit Party candidate for presidency of the U.S., 1976***. MAILING ADDRESS: 736 Gould Ave., Hermosa Beach, CA 90254.

ENNIS, ROBERT ELLSWORTH. b. 1901, Washington, DC; par. Robert B. Ennis; m. Blanche Lurene Taylor, 1934; c. Robert Taylor; one daughter. EDUC.: LL.B., Columbia U. (now merged with Catholic U. of America), 1930; LL.B., National U. POLIT. & GOV.: sec., Prince Georges (MD) Republican Club, 1924–36; appointed justice of the peace, MD; Republican candidate for MD State House of Delegates; Republican candidate for MD state's atty.; Republican candidate for U.S. House (MD), 1952, 1954, 1958; candidate for Republican nomination to U.S. House (MD), 1960, 1962; ***candidate for Republican nomination to presidency of the U.S., 1964***. BUS. & PROF.: atty. MIL.: U.S. Navy, 1918–23, and during WWII. MEM.: American Legion (founder, Capitol Heights Post, 1936). MAILING ADDRESS: 411 Capitol Heights Blvd., Capitol Heights, MD 20027.

ENRIGHT, RICHARD EDWARD. b. Aug 30, 1871, Campbell, NY; d. Sep 4, 1953, East Meadow, NY; par. Michael H. and Jett (Bennett) Enright; m. Jeane Paterson Smith, Nov 27, 1918. EDUC.: Elmira Business Coll. POLIT. & GOV.: appointed commissioner of police, New York, NY, 1918–25; ***candidate for Democratic nomination to vice presidency of the U.S., 1924***. BUS. & PROF.: telegrapher, Elmira, NY; telegrapher, Queens, NY; lt., New York City Police Dept., 1898–1918; publisher, *Pulp Magazine*; dir., United Service Detective Bureau; promoter, burglar alarms; pres., Richard E. Enright, Inc.; vice pres., Gainsborough Art Galleries. MIL.: col., U.S.A.R.; commander, Order of Vasa (Sweden); Order of Dannebrog (Denmark); Order of St. Olaf (Norway); Crown of Italy (Italy); Order of Isabella the Catholic (Spain); Order of Leopold III (Belgium); Order of the Golden Cross (Austria); Order of St. Sava (Serbia); officer, Order of Ferdinand I (Rumania); Order of the Redeemer (Greece); Victorian Order (Great Britain); Order of the Sun (Peru); chevalier, Legion of Honor (France). MEM.: Police Lieutenants' Benevolent Assn. (pres.); Police Relief Fund (founder; trustee; vice president); International Police Conference (pres.); Elks. WRITINGS: *Address . . . Before the Motor Truck Association* (1920); *Address . . . at the Dinner of the Mayor's Public Welfare Cmte.* (1920); *Address . . . Delivered at the Dinner of the Casualty and Surety Club of New York* (1920); *Address . . . to Kings County Grand Jurors* (1921); *Vultures of the Dark* (1924); *Enright Proposes Civic Center for City* (1924); *The Borrowed Shield* (1925); *Nakts vanaji: kriminalromans* (1928). REL.: R.C. RES.: New York, NY.

ERHARDT, KENNETH ANDREW. b. Mar 7, 1949, Newark, NJ; par. Andrew and Rose Erhardt; single. EDUC.: B.A., William Paterson Coll. of New Jersey, 1973; J.D., Western State U., 1978. POLIT. & GOV.: ***independent candidate for presidency of the U.S., 1980 (withdrew)***. BUS. & PROF.: atty.; admitted to NJ Bar, 1978. MEM.: Delta Theta Phi; Legal Action on Smoking and Health; Consumer Rights Advocacy (Advisory Board). REL.: R.C. MAILING ADDRESS: 6010 Mt. Aguilar Dr., San Diego, CA 92111.

ERICKSON, LESLIE. POLIT. & GOV.: ***Farmer-Labor Party candidate for vice presidency of the U.S., 1936***. MISC.: described as a "newcomer" to politics. RES.: Minneapolis, MN.

ERICKSON, OSCAR ADOLPH "ERIK," JR. b. Nov 26, 1942, Crookston, MN; par. Oscar Adolph, Sr. and Edith Grace (Baird) Erickson; m. (divorced); c. none. EDUC.: Southern CA Coll., 2½ years; certificate, Navave School of Health Sciences, 1 year; certificate, Hospital of the Good Samaratan, Los Angeles, CA, 1 year; Santa Barbara (CA) City Coll., 1 year; Acad. Pacific Business and Travel Coll., Los Angeles, CA. POLIT. & GOV.: ***candidate for Republican nomination to presidency of the U.S., 1992***. BUS. & PROF.: certified surgical technologist; certified clinical perfusionist; physician's asst.; inventor; received 2 U.S. patents; 1 United Kingdom patent. Mil. : hospital corpsman, operating room technician, hospitalman 3d class, U.S. Navy, 1964–68. WRITINGS: "Automated Safety Valve for the Decompression of Cardiotomy Reservoirs" (article, 1983). MEM.: Delta Kappa; Assn. of Surgical Technologists; American Soc. of Extracorporeal Technology. REL.: Assembly of God/Presb. MAILING ADDRESS: 7080 Hollywood Blvd., Suite 616, Los Angeles, CA 90028.

ERVIN, SAMUEL JAMES "SAM," JR. b. Sep 27, 1896, Morganton, NC; d. Apr 23, 1985, Winston-Salem, NC; par. Samuel James and Laura Theresa (Powe) Ervin; m. Margaret Bruce Bell, Jun 18, 1924; c. Samuel James III; Margaret Leslie (Mrs. Gerald M. Hansler); Laura Powe (Mrs. William E. Smith). EDUC.: A.B., U. of NC, 1917; LL.B., Harvard U., 1922. POLIT. & GOV.: elected as a Democrat to NC State House, 1923–27, 1931–33; chm., Burke Cty. (NC) Democratic Exec. Cmte., 1924; trustee, Morganton (NC) Graded Schools, 1929–30; member, NC State Democratic Exec. Cmte., 1930–37; judge, Burke Cty. Criminal Court, 1935–37; judge, NC Superior Court, 1937–43; appointed member, NC State Board of Law Examiners, 1944–46; elected as a Democrat to U.S. House (NC), 1946–47; chm., NC Comm. for Improvement of the Administration of Justice, 1947–49; assoc. justice, NC State Supreme Court, 1948–54; elected as a Democrat to U.S. Senate (NC), 1955–75; delegate, Dem. Nat'l. Conv., 1956, 1960, 1964, 1968; delegate, Democratic Mid-Term Conference, 1974; ***candidate for Democratic nomination to presidency of the U.S., 1976***. BUS. & PROF.: atty.; admitted to NC Bar, 1919; law practice, Morganton, NC, 1922–. MIL.: Company I, 28th Infantry, 1st Div., U.S. Army, WWI; National Guard; French Fourragere; Purple Heart with Oak Leaf Clusters; Silver Star; Distinguished Service Cross. MEM.: U. of NC (trustee, 1932–35, 1945–46); American Legion; VFW; Disabled American Veterans; Soc. of the 1st Div.; Army and Navy Legion of Valor; Morganton C. of C.; NC Literary and Hist. Assn.; Southern History Assn.; Soc. of Mayflower Descendants (NC gov., 1950–52); General Alumni Assn. of the U. of NC (pres., 1947–48); Soc. of the Cincinnati; SAR; Sigma Upsilon; Phi Delta Phi; Masons (33°; Knights Templar); Moose; Kiwanis; Kip; Davidson Coll. (trustee, 1948–58); ABA; NC Bar Assn.; American Jud. Soc.; NC State Bar; Newcomen Soc. AWARDS: Cross of Military Service, U.D.C.; Good Citizenship Medal, SAR; Distinguished Citizenship Certificate, NC Citizens Assn.; Patriotic Service Medal, American Coalition of Patriotic Societies; grand orator, Grand Lodge of Masons of NC, 1963. HON. DEG.: LL.D., U. of NC, 1951; LL.D., Western Carolina Coll., 1955; D.P.A., Suffolk U., 1957; LL.D., Wake Forest U., 1971; LL.D., Davidson Coll., 1972; LL.D., George Washington U., 1972; LL.D., St. Andrews Presbyterian Coll., 1972; LL.D., Boston U., 1973; L.H.D., Wilkes Coll., 1973; D.Con.L., Appalachian U., 1974; Litt.D., Catawba Coll., 1974; LL.D., Colgate U., 1974; LL.D., Drexel U., 1974; LL.D., U. of Cincinnati, 1974; LL.D., U. of NC at Charlotte, 1974; LL.D., Belmont Abbey Coll., 1975; J.D., New England School of Law, 1975; LL.D., Warner Pacific Coll., 1975; LL.D., Anderson Coll., 1976. WRITINGS: *A Colonial History of Rowan County, North Carolina* (1917); *Role of the Supreme Court—Policymaker or Adjudicator?* (with Ramsey Clark, q.v.; 1970); *Ervins of Williamsburg County* (1972); *Senator Sam Ervin's Best Stories* (with Thad Stem, Jr. and Alan Butler, 1973); *Quotations from Chairman Sam: Wit and Wisdom of Senator Sam Ervin* (1973); *The Whole Truth: The Watergate Conspiracy* (1981); *Humor of a Country Lawyer* (1983); *Preserving the Constitution: Autobiography of Senator Sam J. Ervin, Jr.* (1984). REL.: Presb. (elder, Morganton Presbyterian Church). MISC.: chair of U.S. Senate Select Cmte. on Presidential Campaign Activities during Watergate Scandal, 1973–74. RES.: Morganton, NC.

ERWIN, ANDREW C. par. Judge Alexander Smith Erwin; m. Camilla McWhorter; c. Sarah (Mrs. Leon Milton Leathers). POLIT. & GOV.: campaign mgr., William G. McAdoo (q.v.) for President, Clarke Cty., GA, 1924; elected as a Democrat to mayor of Athens, GA, 1918–21; delegate, Dem. Nat'l. Conv., 1924, 1928; ***candidate for Democratic nomination to vice presidency of the U.S., 1924***. BUS. & PROF.: journalist; ed., *Athens Banner-Herald*. MIL.: U.S. Army, WWI. REL.: Presb. MISC.: noted for anti–Ku Klux Klan speech at 1924 Dem. Nat'l. Conv.. RES.: Athens, GA.

ESSEX, CLINTON GEORGE. b. Dec 20, 1932, Ferndale, MI; par. Joseph Clinton and Grace Alice (Prowse) Essex; m. Margart Loraine Essex, Sep 8, 1958 (divorced); c. none. EDUC.: Flint (MI) Junior Coll.; A.A., Belleville Area Coll., 1971; B.A., Webster U., 1974, M.A., 1976. POLIT. & GOV.: ***Neo-International Scientific Socialist Party candidate for presidency of the U.S., 1976, 1980, 1984***. BUS. & PROF.: employee, *Fenton (MI) Independent*; computer operator; civil service technician, 1969–76. MIL.: staff sgt., U.S. Air Force, 1951–55, sgt., 1958–67; Air Medal; Korean Service Medal; U.N. Service Medal. MEM.: AAAS (1976–78); World Future Soc. (1976–78); Greater St. Louis Federal Business Assn. (1975–76). REL.: Neo-International Scientific Socialism (N.I.S.S.) Naturalism. MAILING ADDRESS: P.O. Box 672, Fenton, MI 48430-0672.

ESTABROOK, HENRY DODGE. b. Oct 23, 1854, Alden, NY; d. Dec 22, 1917, Tarrytown, NY; par. Experience and Caroline Augusta (Maxwell) Estabrook; m. Clara Campbell, Oct 23, 1879; c. Blanche Deuel (Mrs. Karl G. Roebling). EDUC.: Omaha (NE) public schools; LL.B., Washington U., 1875. POLIT. & GOV.: elected regent, U. of NE, 1894–97; ***candidate for Republican nomination to presidency of the U.S., 1916***. BUS. & PROF.: reporter; atty.; admitted to NE Bar, 1875; law practice, Omaha, 1875–96; partner, Lowden, Estabrook and Davis (law firm), Chicago, IL, 1896–1902; counsel, Western Union Telegraph Co., solicitor, 1902; orator; partner, Noble, Estabrook and McHarg (law firm). MEM.: ABA; NY State Bar Assn.; Union League; Saddle and Bicycle Club; Marquette Club; Law Club; Twentieth Century Club; The Forty Clubs of Chicago; Lawyers' Club; Players' Club; Lotos Club; Metropolitan Club; Magnetic Club; Automobile Club of America. RES.: Tarrytown, NY.

ESTOCIN, MICHAEL J. b. Apr 27, 1931, Turtle Creek, PA; missing in action, Vietnam, Apr 26, 1967; par. Michael J. Estocin, Sr.; m. Marie; c. three daughters. EDUC.: grad., Slippery Rock State Coll., 1953. POLIT. & GOV.: ***independent candidate for presidency of the U.S., 1976***. BUS. & PROF.: naval pilot. MIL.: commander, U.S. Navy, 1953–67. MISC.: reported missing in action over Vietnam, Apr 26, 1967; parents conducted campaign to dramatize problems facing families of prisoners-of-war and persons missing-in-action. RES.: Turtle Creek, PA.

ETTL, JOSEPH GEORGE. b. Apr 23, 1913, South Bend, IN; par. Michael and Elizabeth (Bruck) Ettl; m. Madeline Graf; c. Frederick; Joseph Graf; Barbara L.; Gregory M. EDUC.: A.B., IN U., 1936, LL.B., 1939, J.D., 1967. POLIT. & GOV.: Republican candidate for IN State House, 1940; candidate for Republican nomination to prosecutor, St. Joseph Cty., IN, 1946; candidate for Republican nomination to IN State Senate, 1948; Republican candidate for judge, Superior Court, St. Joseph Cty., 1950; Republican candidate for cty. commissioner, St. Joseph Cty., 1954; ***candidate for Republican nomination to presidency of the U.S., 1964***; cty. atty., St. Joseph Cty., 1970; atty., Board of Zoning Appeals and Plan Comm.; atty., Green and Portage Townships, IN; member, St. Joseph Cty. Election Board; member, St. Joseph Cty. Sheriff's Merit Board. BUS. & PROF.: atty.; admitted to IN Bar, 1939; partner, Ettl and Ettl (law firm), South Bend, IN. MEM.: Elks; Masons (Scottish Rite; Orak Shrine; Avalon Grotto); American Legion; VFW; St. Joseph Cty. Bar Assn.; IN Bar Assn.; ABA; South Bend Junior C. of C. (pres.). REL.: United Methodist. MAILING ADDRESS: 23007 State Rd. 23, South Bend, IN.

EVANS, CHARLES RAY. b. Nov 2, 1941, Parkersburg, WV; par. Pauline Evans; m. Treva Jean Van Atten, 1964 (divorced, 1983); c. Betty Ann. EDUC.: B.S. (magna cum laude), MI State U., 1963; M.S., MA Inst. of Technology, 1965; Ph.D., Polytechnic Inst. of Brooklyn, 1971. POLIT. & GOV.: ***candidate for Republican nomination to presidency of the U.S., 1988***. BUS. & PROF.: clerk, law library, Office of Education, U.S. Dept. of Health, Education and Welfare, Washington, DC, 1960; engineering aide, U.S. Navy Bureau of Ships, Washington, DC, 1961; student trainee, Diamond Ordnance Fuze Labs, Washington, DC, 1962; engineer, Raytheon Manufacturing Co., Wayland, MA, 1963–66; lecturer, U. of Singapore, Singapore, 1970–72; lecturer, U. of Adelaide, South Australia, 1972–78; study leave, U.N., Geneva, Switzerland, 1977–78; contractor, Resource Sciences Arabia, Ltd., Dhahran, Saudi Arabia, 1983–84; contractor, Compass: Data Directions, Inc., Columbus, OH, 1984. AWARDS: Danforth Foundation Book Award; Bausch and Lomb Science Award; Harvard Book Award; MI State U. Scholarship; NASA Traineeship, Polytechnic Inst. of Brooklyn; New York State Regents Fellowship. WRITINGS: various technical engineering papers; "Evolution of Pulses in Parametric Wave Interactions Utilized in the Initial-Value Mode," *Journal of Applied Physics* (with E. S. Cassedy), Nov 1972; "UNCTAD: Should Group B Remain Group B," *Journal of World Trade Law*, May 1978; *Another Vision* (1987). MAILING ADDRESS: P.O. Box 7070, Des Moines, IA 50309.

EVANS, CLYDE. b. Dec 8, 1944, Columbus, OH; par. Lewis and Mary Ann (McNally) Evans; single. POLIT. & GOV.: ***Precedent Party candidate for presidency of the U.S., 1976, 1980***. BUS. & PROF.: musician; waiter; restauranteur; bar owner; comedian. MEM.: Demolay; American Federation of Musicians (Local 103); International Order of Old Bastards;

Clyde Evans International Fan Club. REL.: atheist. MAILING ADDRESS: 251 East Roosevelt St., Baton Rouge, LA 70802.

EVANS, DANIEL JACKSON. b. Oct 16, 1925, Seattle, WA; par. Daniel Lester and Irma (Ide) Evans; m. Nancy Ann Bell, Jun 6, 1959; c. Daniel Jackson; Mark L.; Bruce M. EDUC.: B.S., U. of WA, 1948, M.S., 1949. POLIT. & GOV.: elected as a Republican to WA State House, 1956–65 (Republican floor leader, 1961–65); elected as a Republican to gov. of WA, 1965–77; chm., Campaign Cmte., National Republican Governors, 1965–66, member, Policy Cmte., 1967–68, 1972; member, Steering Cmte., Education Comm. of the States, 1967–68; member, National Republican Coordinating Comm., 1967–68; delegate, Rep. Nat'l. Conv., 1968 (keynoter), 1972; member, Republican Governors' Advisory Cmte. to the President, 1969; appointed member, Advisory Comm. on Intergovernmental Relations, 1972–77; appointed member, Federal Advisory Comm., Project Independence, 1974; appointed member, National Comm. on Productivity and Work Quality, 1975; appointed member, President's Vietnamese Refugee Advisory Cmte., 1975; ***candidate for Republican nomination to vice presidency of the U.S., 1976***; chm., Pacific Northwest Electric Power and Conservation Planning Council, 1981–83; appointed and subsequently elected as a Republican to U.S. Senate (WA), 1983–89. BUS. & PROF.: asst. mgr., Mountain-Pacific Chapter, Assn. of General Contractors, 1953–59; civil engineer; partner, Gray and Evans (civil engineers), Seattle, WA, 1959–65; pres., Evergreen State Coll., Olympia, WA, 1977–83. MIL.: lt., U.S.N.R., 1943–46, 1951–53. MEM.: BSA; Urban Coalition (member, Steering Cmte., 1969); Trilateral Comm.; Urban Inst.; Carnegie Council on Policy Studies in Higher Education; Carnegie Foundation for the Advancement of Teaching (trustee); National Governors Conference (chm., 1973–74); Western Governors Conference (chm., 1968–69); Comm. of Cities in the 70's; Republican Governors' Assn. (chm., Policy Cmte., 1970–71); Nature Conservancy (trustee); Twentieth Century Fund (trustee); Council of State Governments (pres., 1972). AWARDS: Key Man Award, Seattle Junior C. of C., 1955; Outstanding Freshman Legislator Award, 1957; Human Rights Award, Pacific Northwest Chapter, National Assn. of Intergroup Relations Officials, 1968; Scales of Justice Award, National Council on Crime and Delinquency, 1968; Award for Service to Profession, Consulting Engineers Council, 1969; Silver Beaver Award, BSA, 1970, Silver Antelope Award, 1970; Public Official of the Year Award, WA Environmental Council, 1970; Distinguished Eagle Award, BSA; Distinguished Citizen Award, National Municipal League, 1977. REL.: Congregationalist. MAILING ADDRESS: Evergreen State Coll. of Education, Overhulse Rd., Olympia, WA 98505.

EVANS, DOROTHY ANN. c. three. POLIT. & GOV.: ***independent candidate for vice presidency of the U.S., 1980***. MAILING ADDRESS: Phoenix, AZ.

EVANS, EDWARD D. b. 1870. POLIT. & GOV.: candidate for Republican nomination to gov. of OK, 1926; ***independent candidate for presidency of the U.S., 1928***; independent candidate for U.S. Senate (OK), 1930. BUS. & PROF.: farmer, Mooreland, OK. RES.: Mooreland, OK.

EVANS, GEORGE. b. Jan 12, 1797, Hallowell, ME; d. Apr 5, 1867, Portland, ME; par. Daniel and Joanna (Hains) Evans; m. Ann Dearborn, Oct 1820; c. three. EDUC.: Hallowell Acad.; Monmouth Acad.; grad., Bowdoin Coll., 1815, A.M., 1818, LL.D., 1847; studied law under Frederick Allen. POLIT. & GOV.: elected as a National Republican to ME State House, 1825–29 (Speaker, 1829); elected as a Whig to U.S. House (ME), 1829–41; elected as a Whig to U.S. Senate (ME), 1841–47; ***Whig Party candidate for vice presidency of the U.S., 1844 (declined)***; Whig Party candidate for U.S. Senate (ME), 1846; ***candidate for Whig Party nomination to presidency of the U.S., 1848; candidate for Whig Party nomination to vice presidency of the U.S., 1848***; chm., Comm. on Mexican Claims, 1849–50; elected atty. gen. of ME, 1853–55, 1856. BUS. & PROF.: atty.; admitted to ME Bar, 1818; law practice, Gardiner, ME, 1818–47, 1851–54; law practice, Hallowell, ME; law practice, Portland, ME, 1854–67; pres., Kennebec and Portland R.R. MEM.: Bowdoin Coll. (overseer, 1827– 45; trustee, 1845–67); ME Hist. Soc. HON. DEG.: LL.D., Washington Coll., 1846. RES.: Portland, ME.

EVANS, HENRY CLAY. b. Jun 18, 1843, Juniata Cty., PA; d. Dec 12, 1921, Chattanooga, TN; par. Jesse Bateman and Anna (single) Evans; m. Adelaide Durand, Feb 18, 1869; c. Henry Clay; Anita Clay (Mrs. David Foote Sellers); Nell (Mrs. Joseph Wilson Johnson). EDUC.: grad., business school, Chicago, IL, 1861. POLIT. & GOV.: agent, U.S. Dept. of War, 1864–65; elected as a Republican to mayor of Chattanooga, TN, 1881–85; chm., Board of Education, Chattanooga; elected as a Republican to U.S. House (TN), 1889–91; Republican candidate for U.S. House (TN), 1890, 1892; appointed asst. U.S. postmaster gen., 1893; Republican candidate for gov. of TN, 1894 (lost in recount), 1906; delegate, Rep. Nat'l. Conv., 1892, 1896, 1900, 1904, 1908, 1912; ***candidate for Republican nomination to vice presidency of the U.S., 1896***; appointed U.S. commissioner of pensions, 1897–1902; appointed U.S. consul gen., London, England, 1902–05; elected as a Non-Partisan, commissioner of health and education, Chattanooga, 1911; Republican candidate for U.S. Senate (TN), 1918. BUS. & PROF.: manufacturer; employee, Wasson Car Works, Chattanooga, 1870–72; employee, Chattanooga Car and Foundry Co., 1872–74, pres., 1885–1917; superintendent, sec., treas., vice pres., gen. mgr., Roane Iron Co., 1884–94; cashier, First National Bank, Chattanooga, 1884–85. MIL.: corp., Company A, 41st Regt., WI Volunteer Infantry, 1864. MEM.: U. of TN (trustee); U. of Chattanooga (trustee). HON. DEG.: LL.D., U. of Chattanooga, 1913. REL.: Presb. RES.: Chattanooga, TN.

EVANS, JAMES LEROY MODRELL. b. Feb 27, 1914, Freewater, OR; par. Jesse James and Loretta Anne (Modrell) Evans; m. Lily Osterback (divorced); c. Lea Lily; Ilene Ann; Julie Mae; Connie Madeline. EDUC.: grad., Crawford Navigation School. POLIT. & GOV.: ***Hevan on Earth Party candidate for presidency of the U.S., 1976***. BUS. & PROF.: deep sea fisherman; songwriter; ice cream vendor; organizer, South Pacific Engineering Corp., 1949; miner; prospector; ed., *Forward Cooperation;* ed., *Aware and Awake*. MEM.: The Forward Club (founder, 1950); Hevan on Earth Foundation; Sons and Daughters of Noah. WRITINGS: "A Friend" (song); "Texas" (song); "Forward" (song). REL.: Theist. MISC.: known as "Captain Jim" and "The Reincarnation of Noah"; claims to have contact with ancestors from outer space; claims to possess stigmata from crucifixion; imprisoned for teaching self-healing, 1955. MAILING ADDRESS: 4404 13th St., Bacliff, TX 77518.

EVANS, RONALD WAYNE. b. Mar 23, 1927, Beaverton, MI; par. Allison Campbell Pennington and Edna Esther (Walke) Evans; m. Mabel Jane Longstreth, 1944; c. Wayne; Robert James; Sandra Kaye Calhoun; David Lee; Larry Dennis; Thomas Raymond; Timothy. EDUC.: grad., Beaverton (MI) H.S., 1945; Central MI U.; U. of MI; MI State U. POLIT. & GOV.: member, Gladwin Cty. (MI) Democratic Party Platform Cmte.; elected as a Democrat to Beaverton Board of Aldermen, 1964–68; U.S. Labor Party candidate for lt. gov. of MI, 1974; ***U.S. Labor Party candidate for vice presidency of the U.S., 1976***. BUS. & PROF.: laborer, Beaverton, 1946–47; laborer, concrete tile and block factory; wood and tree surgeon, 1947–48; assembly line and spot welder, Flint, MI, 1948–51; senior technician, Dow Chemical Co., Midland, MI, 1951–76; chemist, Kentile Floors, 1977–79, scheduler, 1981–84, resident engineer, 1984–; superintendent, PMR Printing, 1979–84; contributor, *Executive Intelligence Review*, 1977–78; contributing ed., *Fusion Magazine*. MIL.: seaman first class, U.S. Navy, 1944–46; American Area Ribbon. MEM.: Fusion Energy Fund; Beaverton Sports Boosters; National Caucus of Labor Cmtes.; United Steelworkers Union (shop steward, 15 years; candidate for union local president, 1971); U.A.W.; U.M.W. of A. REL.: Cartesian Amborsean Christian Humanist (nee Evangelical Church). MAILING ADDRESS: 212 Seeley St., Beaverton, MI 48612.

EVANS, SAMUEL. POLIT. & GOV.: elected as a Democrat to TX State Senate, 1873; Union Labor Party candidate for U.S. House (TX), 1888; ***Union Labor Party candidate for vice presidency of the U.S., 1888 (declined)***. BUS. & PROF.: land speculator; developer. MIL.: capt., col. RES.: Tarrant Cty., TX.

EVANS, WILLIAM WADSWORTH, JR. b. May 6, 1921, Paterson, NJ; par. William Wadsworth and Isabel V. (Blouvelt) Evans; m. Marie Archbold; c. William Wadsworth III; Roy; Douglas; Deborah; Clifford. EDUC.: U. of VA; LL.B., U. of Miami, 1950. POLIT. & GOV.: elected as a Republican to mayor of Wyckoff, NJ, 1958–59; elected as a Republican to NJ State House, 1960–61; chm., NJ Citizens for Goldwater, 1964; ***candidate for Republican nomination to presidency of the U.S., 1968***. BUS. & PROF.: atty.; admitted to FL Bar, 1950; admitted to NJ Bar, 1951; partner, Evans, Hand, Allabough and Amoresano, (law firm), Paterson, NJ. MIL.: U.S.M.C., WWII. MEM.: FL Bar Assn.; Passaic Cty. Bar Assn.; NJ State Bar Assn.; ABA; Rotary Club; Hamilton Club; Delta Theta Phi. MAILING ADDRESS: 474 Caldwell Dr., Wyckoff, NJ.

EVELYN, EVYLIN MARTHA (HEMPLE) EICHELBERGER (aka EVYLIN #501-14-7038). b. Feb 12, 1920, Fargo, ND; par. Sixten Christian Algot and Martha Magdolena (White) Hemple; m. George Clarence Eichelberger (Drake); c. Georgie Anne; Stephen John; Joseph Christian; Lynne Mary; Richard Clair. EDUC.: grad., high school, Fargo, ND; ND State Agricultural Coll., 1941–42, 1968. POLIT. & GOV.: appointed judge of elections, Verona, ND, 1942 (declined); Non-Partisan candidate for gov. of CA, 1970, 1974; ***Non-Partisan candidate for presidency of the U.S., 1972, 1976***; Non-Partisan candidate for U.S. Senate (ND), 1974. BUS. & PROF.: bookkeeper, auditor, Powers Hotel Co., Fargo, ND, 1942–45; farm owner, ND; homemaker. MEM.: Parent-Teachers Assn. of Fargo; YMCA and YWCA. REL.: Lutheran (MO Synod). MAILING ADDRESS: 936 Mission, San Francisco, CA 94103.

EVERETT, EDWARD. b. Apr 11, 1794, Dorchester, MA; d. Jan 15, 1865, Boston, MA; par. Rev. Oliver and Lucy (Hill) Everett; m. Charlotte Gray Brooks, May 8, 1822; c. Edward Brooks; Anne Gorham; Grace Fletcher; Sydney; William. EDUC.: grad. (summa cum laude), Harvard U., 1811, M.A., 1814; Ph.D., U. of Gîttingen, 1817. POLIT. & GOV.: elected as a National Republican to U.S. House (MA), 1825–35; elected as a Whig (Anti-Mason) to gov. of MA, 1836–1940; Whig Party candidate for gov. of MA, 1839; appointed U.S. minister to Great Britain, 1841–45; appointed U.S. sec. of state, 1852–53; elected as a Whig to U.S. Senate (MA), 1853–54; ***Constitutional Union Party candidate for vice presidency of the U.S., 1860***; presidential elector, Republican Party, 1864. BUS. & PROF.: ed., *Harvard Lyceum*, 1814; tutor; poet; ordained minister, Unitarian Church, 1814; pastor, Brattle Street Unitarian Church, Boston, MA, 1814–15; Elios professor of Greek, Harvard U., 1815–26, pres., 1846–49; ed., *North American Review*, 1820; contributor, *New York Ledger*, 1858–59. MEM.: Harvard U. (overseer, 1827–46, 1849–54, 1862–65); Union Club. HON. DEG.: LL.D., Cambridge U., 1840; LL.D., Dublin U., 1840; D.C.L., Oxford U., 1840. WRITINGS: *Orations and Speeches on Various Occasions* (1853–68). REL.: Unitarian. RES.: Boston, MA.

EVERMAN, MICHAEL EARL. b. Oct 18, 1957, Chanute, KS; par. H. E. and Marilyn (Edmondson) Everman; m. Cheryl Hammans Smith (divorced); m. 2d, Caroly Graap; c. Annie

Mae. EDUC.: grad., Chanute H.S., 1976; grad., U.S. Army Finance and Accounting School, Defense and Intelligence Inst., 1976; U. of CO; National Coll. of Business; Neosho Cty. (KS) Community Coll., 1979. POLIT. & GOV.: ***American Freedom Party candidate for presidency of the U.S., 1980***. BUS. & PROF.: pres., Autofind, Inc.; pres., Starfire Productions, Inc.; pres., Starfire Racing, Ltd. MIL.: U.S. Army, 1976– 78; honor soldier; named "Outstanding Soldier," 1977; "Soldier of the Quarter," 1977. MEM.: Assn. of American College Students (pres.); Wheelers and Dealers, Inc. (pres.); Chanute Auto Club (pres.); Phoenix CB Club (sec.-treas.); Red Cross; Babe Ruth Baseball; Men's Softball; National Street Rod Assn.; Midwest Auto Club (pres.). REL.: Protestant. MISC.: elected student senator, Neosho Cty. Community Coll. MAILING ADDRESS: 107 North Grant, #2, Chanute, KS 66720.

EVERT, MARTHA M. b. Aug 1922; m. Bernard H. Evert; c. two daughters. POLIT. & GOV.: candidate for school dir.; ***candidate for Democratic nomination to presidency of the U.S., 1968, 1976; Anti-Socialist American Party candidate for presidency of the U.S., 1976***. BUS. & PROF.: R.N. MAILING ADDRESS: 29 Highland Dr., Camp Hill, PA 17011.

EWING, CHARLES WESLEY. POLIT. & GOV.: Prohibition Party candidate for lt. gov. of MI, 1966; ***candidate for Prohibition Party nomination to presidency of the U.S., 1972***; national chm., Prohibition Party, 1971–79; national chm., National Statesman (Prohibition) Party, 1979–83; permanent chm., National Statesman (Prohibition) Party National Convention, 1979; parliamentarian, Prohibition Party National Convention, 1983. BUS. & PROF.: minister; pastor, Royal Oak, MI. MEM.: Illinois Anti-Saloon League (asst. state dir.); National Prohibition Foundation (vice pres., 1983). WRITINGS: "I'm a Fanatic" (series, in *National Statesman*); *The Bible and Its Wines*. MAILING ADDRESS: 321 West Harrison Ave., Royal Oak, MI 48067.

EWING, OSCAR ROSS. b. Mar 8, 1889, Greensburg, IN; d. Jan 8, 1980, Chapel Hill, NC; par. George McClellan and Nettie Moore (Ross) Ewing; m. Helen E. Dennis, Nov 4, 1915; m. 2d, Mary Whiting MacKay (Thomas), Oct 12, 1955; c. James Dennis; George McClellan. EDUC.: A.B., IN U., 1910; LL.B., Harvard U., 1913. POLIT. & GOV.: appointed delegate, International Conference for Limitation on the Manufacture of Narcotics, 1931; asst. chm., Dem. Nat'l. Cmte., 1940–42; appointed vice chm., Dem. Nat'l. Cmte., 1942; appointed special asst., U.S. Dept. of Justice, 1947; appointed administrator, Federal Security Agency, 1947–52; ***candidate for Democratic nomination to presidency of the U.S., 1952***. BUS. & PROF.: atty.; instructor, U. of IA Law School, 1913–14; partner, Weyl, Jewett and Ewing (law firm), Indianapolis, IN, 1915–16; asst. counsel, Vandalia R.R. Co., St. Louis, MO, 1916; asst. to gen. counsel, Pennsylvania Lines West of Pittsburgh, 1917; partner, Hughes, Schurman and Dwighs (law firm), New York, NY, 1920–37; partner, Hughes, Hubbard and Ewing (law firm), 1937–47. MIL.: commissioned 1st lt., U.S. Army Signal Corps, 1918; capt., U.S. Army Air Service, 1918. MEM.: Research Triangle Foundation (dir.); Research Triangle Regional Planning Comm. (chm.); New York Cty. Bar Assn.; Assn. of the Bar of the City of New York; ABA; NY State Bar Assn.; Beta Theta Pi; University Club; Down Town Club; Davison Club of Duke U. Medical Center (charter member); Medical Foundation of the U. of NC Medical Center (charter member); Torch Clubs International. HON. DEG.: LL.D., U. of NC, 1967; LL.D., IN U., 1970. REL.: Episc. RES.: Chapel Hill, NC.

EWING, THOMAS, JR. b. Aug 7, 1829, Lancaster, OH; d. Jan 21, 1896, New York, NY; par. Thomas and Maria Wills (Boyle) Ewing; m. Ellen Ewing Cox, Jan 18, 1856; c. William Cox; Thomas; Hampton Denman; Beall; Mrs. Edwin M. Martin. EDUC.: grad., Brown U., 1854; Cincinnati Law School, 1855. POLIT. & GOV.: private sec. to President Zachary Taylor (q.v.), 1849–50; delegate, KS Constitutional Convention, 1858; Leader, Anti-Lecompton Constitution Campaign, KS; delegate, Peace Convention, 1861; chief justice, KS Supreme Court, 1861–62; offered positions of U.S. sec. of war and U.S. atty. gen. by President Andrew Johnson (q.v.) (declined); ***candidate for Democratic nomination to vice presidency of the U.S., 1868 (withdrew); candidate for Labor Reform Party nomination to presidency of the U.S., 1872 (declined); candidate for Labor Reform Party nomination to vice presidency of the U.S., 1872***; delegate, OH State Constitutional Convention, 1873–74; elected as a Democrat to U.S. House (OH), 1877–81; Democratic candidate for U.S. Senate (OH), 1878; Democratic candidate for gov. of OH, 1879; ***candidate for Democratic nomination to presidency of the U.S., 1880***. BUS. & PROF.: atty.; admitted to OH Bar, 1855; law practice, Cincinnati, OH, 1855–56; partner, Ewing, Sherman and McCook (law firm), Leavenworth, KS, 1856–61; law practice, Washington, DC, 1865–71; acting vice pres., Cincinnati Law Coll., 1881; law practice, New York, NY, 1881–96; partner (with Milton L. Southard), law firm, New York; partner, Ewing, Whitman and Ewing (law firm), New York, 1893. MIL.: commanding col., 11th Kansas Volunteers, 1862, brig. gen., 1863, brev. maj. gen., 1865. MEM.: Ohio Soc. of New York (founder and pres., 1886–89); U. of OH (trustee, 1878–83). HON. DEG.: A.M., Brown U.; LL.D., Georgetown Coll., 1870. WRITINGS: *Argument in the Case of Dr. Samuel Mudd* (1865); *Speech at Cooper Institute* (1868); *Joint Discussions on the Finance Question* (1876); *There is a Faith Due to the People* (1877); *Address at Marietta Centennial Celebration* (1888); *Address Before the Sons of the American Revolution* (189?). REL.: Christian (nee R.C.). RES.: Cincinnati, OH.

EYRING, KENNETH J. POLIT. & GOV.: ***independent candidate for presidency of the U.S., 1980***. MAILING ADDRESS: 104 Mar-Kan Dr., Northport, NY.

EZELL, RAY. POLIT. & GOV.: ***independent candidate for presidency of the U.S., 1988***. MAILING ADDRESS: 1441 Purcell Rd., Lawrenceville, GA 30245.

FABISH, THOMAS STANLEY. b. Oct 1, 1932, Chicago, IL; par. Edward and Frances (Suchalski) Fabish; single. EDUC.: diplomat in court reporting, Chicago Coll. of Commerce, 1967. POLIT. & GOV.: member, Kane Cty. (IL) Republican Central Cmte.; candidate for Republican nomination to Kane Cty. (IL) treas., 1984; ***candidate for Republican nomination to presidency of the U.S., 1988, 1992***. BUS. & PROF.: freelance court reporter, Chicago, IL. MIL.: communications specialist, U.S. Air Force, 1952–55; Korean Service Medal; National Defense Service Medal; Good Conduct Medal; U.N. Service Medal. REL.: independent. MAILING ADDRESS: 66 Grove St., Elgin, IL 60121.

FACKLER, JOHN D. b. Jan 18, 1878, Adrian, OH; d. Oct 19, 1953, Cleveland, OH; par. Mathies C. and Mary (Boyce) Fackler; m. Alice May Hankinson, Aug 12, 1902; c. Margaret Elizabeth (Mrs. Wendell Herrick); Ruth Marjorie (Mrs. James R. Hinchlifee, Jr.; Mrs. Richard Whitney Taylor); Mary Alice (Mrs. James Rick III). EDUC.: Savannah Acad.; B.A., Coll. of Wooster, 1900; Harvard U.; Western Reserve U. POLIT. & GOV.: elected as a Republican to Glenville (OH) Town Council, 1905–08; delegate, OH State Constitutional Convention, 1911; chm., Cuyahoga Cty. Bull Moose Party, 1912; appointed deputy state commissioner, 1914–16; ***candidate for Republican nomination to presidency of the U.S., 1924***. BUS. & PROF.: school teacher, Clear Creek Township, OH; financial sec., Coll. of Wooster, 1901–02; atty.; admitted to OH Bar, 1905; partner, Fackler, Wilcox and Morris (law firm), Cleveland, OH, 1905; partner, Fackler and Dye (law firm), Cleveland, OH; pres., Realty Corp. of Cleveland; pres., Perkins Building Co., Cleveland, OH; dir., Reliance Electric and Engineering Co., Cleveland, OH; dir., Central National Bank, Cleveland, OH. MEM.: Coll. of Wooster (trustee); ABA; OH State Bar Assn.; Cleveland Bar Assn.; SAR; Masons; Phi Beta Kappa; Phi Delta Phi; Delta Sigma Rho; Canterbury Club; City Club of Cleveland; The Mid-Day Club; Union Club of Cleveland; American Rose Assn. REL.: Presb. RES.: Cleveland, OH.

FAIRBANKS, CHARLES WARREN. b. May 11, 1852, Unionville Center, OH; d. Jun 4, 1918, Indianapolis, IN; par. Loriston Monroe and Mary Adelaide (Smith) Fairbanks; m. Cornelia Cole, Oct 6, 1874; c. Adelaide (Mrs. John W. Timmons; Mrs. L. D. Causey); Warren Charles; Frederick Cole; Richard Monroe; Robert. EDUC.: A.B., OH Wesleyan U., 1872, A.M., 1875; Cleveland Law School. POLIT. & GOV.: campaign mgr., Walter Q. Gresham (q.v.) for President, 1888; delegate, Rep. Nat'l. Conv., 1888, 1896 (temporary chm.), 1900, 1904, 1912; chm., IN State Republican Convention, 1892, 1898, 1914; Republican candidate for U.S. Senate (IN), 1893; elected as a Republican to U.S. Senate (IN), 1897–1905; member, Joint British-American High Comm. on Adjustment of Canadian Question, 1898; ***candidate for Republican nomination to vice presidency of the U.S., 1900, 1908; elected as a Republican to vice presidency of the U.S., 1905–09; candidate for Republican nomination to presidency of the U.S., 1908, 1916***; appointed U.S. representative to Quebec Terentenary Celebration, 1908; ***Republican candidate for vice presidency of the U.S., 1916***. BUS. & PROF.: Associated Press representative, Pittsburgh, PA, and Cleveland, OH, 1872–74; atty.; admitted to OH Bar, 1874; law practice, Indianapolis, IN, 1874–1918. MEM.: OH Wesleyan U. (trustee, 1885); American U. (trustee); De Pauw U. (trustee); Smithsonian Institution (regent); IN Forestry Assn.; Methodist Hospital of IN (pres.). HON. DEG.: LL.D., OH Wesleyan U., 1901; LL.D., Baker U., 1903; LL.D., IA State U., 1903; LL.D., Northwestern U., 1907. WRITINGS: *Life and Speeches of Hon. Charles Warren Fairbanks* (edited by William Henry Smith, 1904). REL.: Methodist. RES.: Indianapolis, IN.

FAIRCHILD, CLINTON L. POLIT. & GOV.: ***independent candidate for presidency of the U.S., 1988***. MAILING ADDRESS: P.O. Box 3016, Laurel, MS 39442.

FAIRCHILD, LUCIUS. b. Dec 27, 1831, Kent, OH; d. May 23, 1896, Madison, WI; par. Jairus Cassius and Sally

(Blair) Fairchild; m. Frances Bull, Apr 27, 1864; c. Mary; Caryl Frances; Sally. EDUC.: Carroll Coll.; LL.D., U. of WI, 1864. POLIT. & GOV.: delegate, CA Gubernatorial Nominating Convention, c. 1854; elected as a Democrat, clerk, Dane Cty. (WI) Circuit Court, 1858; elected as a Republican to sec. of state of WI, 1863–66; elected as a Republican to gov. of WI, 1866–72; appointed U.S. consul, Liverpool, England, 1872–78; appointed U.S. consul, Paris, France, 1878–80; appointed U.S. minister to Spain, 1880–82; ***candidate for Republican nomination to presidency of the U.S., 1884; candidate for Republican nomination to vice presidency of the U.S., 1884***; Republican candidate for U.S. Senate (WI), 1885; appointed federal commissioner for Cherokee Indian affairs (OK), 1885. BUS. & PROF.: joined "Forty-Niners" in CA gold rush, 1849; prospector; miner; atty.; admitted to WI Bar, 1860. MIL.: joined First Wisconsin Volunteer Regt., 1861; lt. col., Second Wisconsin Volunteer Regt., 1862, col., 1862; brig. gen., U.S.V., 1863. MEM.: GAR (senior commander in chief, 1868–70; WI state commander, 1886; national commander in chief, 1886); Military Order of the Loyal Legion (national commander in chief, 1893–95); National Soldiers' and Sailors' Convention (pres., 1868); International Exposition of Railway Appliances (pres., 1883). REL.: Episc. RES.: Madison, WI.

FAIRFIELD, JOHN. b. Jan 20, 1797, Saco, ME; d. Dec 24, 1847, Washington, DC; par. Ichabod and Sarah (Nason) Scamman Fairfield; m. Anna Paine Thornton, Sep 25, 1825; c. nine. EDUC.: Limerick Acad.; Thornton Acad.; Bowdoin Coll.; studied law under Judge Shelpley. POLIT. & GOV.: reporter, Supreme Court of ME, 1832–35; elected as a Democrat to U.S. House (ME), 1835–38; elected as a Democrat to gov. of ME, 1838–39, 1841–43; Democratic candidate for gov. of ME, 1840; elected as a Democrat to U.S. Senate (ME), 1843–47; ***candidate for Democratic nomination to vice presidency of the U.S., 1844***. BUS. & PROF.: atty.; admitted to ME Bar, 1826; law practice, Biddleford and Saco, ME; partner (with George Thacher), law firm. MIL.: privateer, War of 1812. MEM.: Thornton Acad. (trustee, 1826; pres., Board of Trustees, 1845–47). WRITINGS: *Supreme Court Reports* (1835–37). REL.: Congregationalist. RES.: Saco, ME.

FALCONE, STEPHEN M. POLIT. & GOV.: ***independent candidate for presidency of the U.S., 1992***. MAILING ADDRESS: ID?

FALKE, LEE CHARLES. b. Jun 21, 1930, Dayton, OH; par. Lee J. and Elizabeth (Schwieterman) Falke; m. Patricia Sheerer; c. Joseph; Mary Elizabeth; Lee Charles, Jr. EDUC.: U. of Dayton, 1948–51; B.A., OH State U., 1952, LL.B., 1955. POLIT. & GOV.: asst. prosecuting atty., Montgomery Cty., OH, 1957–60; elected as a Democrat, prosecuting atty., Montgomery Cty., OH, 1965–; member, Montgomery Cty. (OH) Democratic Exec. Cmte.; appointed member, Governor's Advisory Panel on Rehabilitation and Corrections, 1974; candidate for delegate, Dem. Nat'l. Conv. (OH), 1976; ***candidate for Democratic nomination to presidency of the U.S., 1976***. BUS. & PROF.: atty.; admitted to OH Bar, 1955; assoc., Estabrook, Finn and McKee (law firm), 1955–57; partner, Young, Pryor, Lynn, Falke and Jerardi (law firm), Dayton, OH, 1958–. MEM.: Young Democratic Club of Montgomery Cty. (pres., 1964); Gem City Democratic Club (asst.treas., 1970–); OH Citizens' Council on Crime and Delinquency (Cmte. on Corrections); U. of Dayton Law School (dir.); Dangerous Offender Project, OH State U. (Advisory Cmte.); National District Attorneys Assn. (vice president); ABA; OH Bar Assn.; Dayton Bar Assn.; Montgomery Cty. Law Enforcement Officers Assn. (pres., 1966–68); Ohio Prosecuting Attorneys' Assn. (pres., 1971); American Trial Lawyers Assn.; American Jud. Soc.; Dayton Lawyers' Club; Phi Delta Theta; Phi Delta Phi (pres., 1954); Knights of Columbus (dir., 500 Council, 1961–). AWARDS: Outstanding Achievement Award, U. of Dayton, 1968; Outstanding Prosecutor of the Year Award, Ohio Prosecuting Attorneys' Assn., 1971; Excellent Service Award, OH Supreme Court, 1972. REL.: R.C. MAILING ADDRESS: 2230 Patterson Blvd., Dayton, OH 45419.

FARENTHOLD, FRANCES TARLTON "SISSY." b. Oct 2, 1926, Corpus Christi, TX; par. Benjamin Dudley and Catherine (Bluntzer) Tarlton; m. George E. Farenthold, Oct 6, 1950; c. Dudley Tarlton; George E., Jr.; Emilie; James Dougherty; Vincent Bluntzer. EDUC.: A.B., Vassar U., 1946; LL.B., U. of TX, 1949. POLIT. & GOV.: appointed member, Corpus Christi Human Relations Comm.; appointed member, TX Human Relations Cmte., 1963–68; appointed member, TX Advisory Cmte. to U.S. Comm. on Civil Rights, 1968; elected as a Democrat to TX State House, 1969–73; candidate for Democratic nomination to gov. of TX, 1972; ***candidate for Democratic nomination to vice presidency of the U.S., 1972***; national co-chm., Citizens to Elect McGovern-Shriver, 1972. BUS. & PROF.: atty.; admitted to TX Bar, 1949; law practice, 1949–65, 1967–76; asst. professor of law, TX Southern U., Houston, TX; dir. of legal aid, Nueces Cty., TX, 1965–67; pres., Wells Coll., Aurora, NY, 1976–80. MEM.: ABA; TX Bar Assn.; Nueces Cty. Bar Assn.; Corpus Christi Bar Foundation; Goodwill Industries; Corpus Christi Deanery, National Council of Catholic Women; ACLU (member, National Advisory Council); Pan American Round Table; Junior League; Citizens Cmte. for Community Improvement; Organization for the Preservation of an Unblemished Shoreline (1964–); National Women's Political Caucus (chairperson, 1973–75); Vassar Coll. (trustee); Mental Health Law Project (dir.). AWARDS: Lyndon B. Johnson Woman of the Year Award, 1973. HON. DEG.: LL.D., Hood Coll., 1973; LL.D., Boston U., 1973; LL.D., Regis Coll., 1976. REL.: R.C. MAILING ADDRESS: Wells Coll., Aurora, NY 13026; Taylor House, Aurora, NY 13026.

FARIS, HERMAN PRESTON. b. Dec 25, 1858, Bellefontaine, OH; d. Mar 20, 1936, Deepwater, MO; par.

Samuel Davies and Sarah Plumer (Preston) Faris; m. Adda Winters, Apr 26, 1880; m. 2d, Mrs. Sallie A. (Kelly) Lewis, Feb 6, 1911; c. Sarah Olivia (Mrs. Paul McGeehan); Florence Julia (Mrs. G. C. Lingle); Adda Winters (Mrs. H. F. Finks). EDUC.: public schools. POLIT. & GOV.: acting deputy clerk, District Court, Trinidad, CO, 1878; Prohibition Party candidate for Constable, Clinton, MO; Prohibition Party candidate for MO state sec. of state, 1888; sec., MO Prohibition Party State Cmte.; delegate, Prohibition Party National Convention, 1888, 1892, 1896, 1900, 1904, 1908, 1912, 1916, 1920, 1924; Prohibition Party candidate for gov. of MO, 1896, 1908, 1920; member, Prohibition Party National Cmte., 1900–1928 (treas.); ***candidate for Prohibition Party nomination to vice presidency of the U.S., 1920; Prohibition Party candidate for presidency of the U.S., 1924***; Prohibition Party candidate for U.S. Senate (MO), 1926, 1932. BUS. & PROF.: printer's devil, *The Southwest Missouri Enterprize*, Clinton, MO, 1871; office boy, Brinkerhoff and Smith, Clinton, MO; pres., treas., mgr., Brinkerhoff-Faris Trust and Savings Co., Clinton, MO, 1887–1936; vice pres., Clinton Realty Co.; vice pres., Benton Land Co. MEM.: Anti-Saloon Army (1893); Independent Order of Good Templars; MO Dry Federation (founder); Clinton YMCA (pres.); Modern Woodmen of the World. REL.: Presb. (delegate, General Assembly, 1898, 1903, 1922; ruling elder). MISC.: died in automobile accident. RES.: Clinton, MO.

FARLEY, JAMES ALOYSIUS. b. May 30, 1888, Grassy Point, NY; d. Jun 9, 1976, New York, NY; par. James and Ellen (Goldrick) Farley; m. Elizabeth A. Finnegan, Apr 28, 1920; c. Elizabeth; (Mrs. Glenn D. Montgomery); Ann (Mrs. Edward J. Hickey, III); James Aloysius, Jr. EDUC.: grad., Packard Commercial School, 1906. POLIT. & GOV.: elected as a Democrat, town clerk, Stony Point, NY, 1912–19; port warden, Port of NY, 1918–19; chm., Rockland Cty. (NY) Democratic Cmte., 1919–29; elected as a Democrat, supervisor, Rockland Cty., NY, 1920–23; appointed member, NY State Athletic Comm., 1923–33 (chm., 1925–33); elected as a Democrat to NY State Assembly, 1923; delegate, Dem. Nat'l. Conv., 1924, 1928, 1932, 1936, 1940, 1944, 1948, 1952, 1956; sec., NY State Democratic Central Cmte., 1928–30, chm., 1930–44; chm., Dem. Nat'l. Cmte., 1932–40; appointed postmaster gen. of the U.S., 1933–40; ***candidate for Democratic nomination to presidency of the U.S., 1940, 1944, 1952; candidate for Democratic nomination to vice presidency of the U.S., 1940***; appointed member, Comm. on the Reorganization of the Executive Branch, 1953; appointed member, NY State Banking Board, 1955. BUS. & PROF.: bookkeeper, Merlin Heilholtz Paper Co., New York, NY, 1906; sales mgr., Universal Gypsum Co., 1906–26; pres., James A. Farley and Co. (building materials), 1926–29; pres., dir., General Builders Supply Corp., 1929–33, 1949; chm. of the board, Coca-Cola Export Corp., 1940; chm. of the board, dir., Coca-Cola Co. of Canada, Ltd.; pres., dir., Coca-Cola International; dir., Compania Embotelladora Coca-Cola, S.A.; dir., Coca-Cola Co. MEM.: National Press Club; Catholic Club of NY; Economic Club; National Democratic Club of NY (vice pres., 1930); Ancient Order of Hibernians; Sales Executive Club; Friendly Sons of St. Patrick; Empire State Foundation and Liberal Arts Coll. (dir.); Circumnavigators Club; Alfred E. Smith Memorial Foundation (trustee); Cordell Hull Foundation (trustee); American Soc.; Cmte. for Economic Development (trustee); American Acad. of Political and Social Science; Albany Soc. of NY; Knights of Columbus; Rockland Cty. Soc. of NY; Order of Red Men; Elks (NY State pres., 1924–25); Tompkins Cove Social Club; Stony Point Social Club; Congressional Country Club; Eagles; Manhattan Club; NY State Hist. Assn.; NY Cuban C. of C.; Export Managers Club of NY, Inc.; Mexican C. of C. in the U.S., Inc.; Pan-American Soc., Inc.; Wing Club; Latin American Section of the NY Board of Trade. AWARDS: Order of Francisco de Miranda (Venezuela); Captain Robert Dollar Memorial Award for Distinguished Contributions to the Advancement of American Foreign Trade; award, Freedoms Foundation, 1953; Cardinal Newman Award, 1956; award, American Irish Hist. Soc., 1956; Cross of Isabel la Catolica (Spain). HON. DEG.: D.C.L., U. of the South, 1933; LL.D., Canisius Coll., 1934; LL.D., Manhattan Coll., 1934; LL.D., John Marshall Coll. of Law, 1934; LL.D., Niagara U., 1935; D.C.L., Lincoln Memorial U., 1935; LL.D., Hendrix Coll., 1939; LL.D., Oglethorpe U., 1940; D.C.L., St. Ambrose Coll., 1941; D.C.L., Villanova Coll., 1942; LL.D., Seattle U., 1950; LL.D., Ithaca Coll., 1951; LL.D., Loras Coll., 1951; LL.D., St. Anselm's Coll., 1951; LL.D., St. Joseph's Coll., 1955; LL.D., Long Island U., 1957; D.S.C., NY U., 1950; D.S.C., Suffolk U., 1956; LL.D., Citation U., 1950; D.S.C., U. of FL, 1950; D.S.S., Duquesne U., 1953. WRITINGS: *Behind the Ballots* (1938); *Jim Farley's Story* (1948). REL.: R.C. RES.: New York, NY.

FARLEY, WILLIAM. b. 1942. POLIT. & GOV.: ***candidate for Democratic nomination to presidency of the U.S., 1988 (declined)***. BUS. & PROF.: pres., Farley Industries; pres., Fruit of the Loom Underwear Co. MAILING ADDRESS: 6300 Sears Tower, Chicago, IL 60606.

FARNER, DAVID PAUL. b. Dec 24, 1963, Newport News, VA; par. Richard L. and Barbara A. (Nick) Farner; single. EDUC.: W. T. Woodson H.S., Fairfax, VA, 1978–. POLIT. & GOV.: ***independent candidate for presidency of the U.S., 1980***. BUS. & PROF.: student. REL.: Presb. MAILING ADDRESS: 9610 Jomar Dr., Fairfax, VA 22032.

FARQUHAR, ARTHUR BRIGGS. b. Sep 28, 1838, Sandy Spring, MD; d. Mar 5, 1925, York, PA; par. William Henry and Margaret (Briggs) Farquhar; m. Elizabeth Jessop, Sep 26, 1860; c. William E.; Percival; Frances. EDUC.: Hollowell's School for Boys, Alexandria, VA. POLIT. & GOV.: appointed PA commissioner, World's Columbian Exposition, 1892–93; delegate, Coast Defense Convention, 1897; ***National Party candidate for presidency of the U.S., 1900 (declined)***; delegate, National Conservation Congress, 1909; appointed chm., York

(PA) City Planning Comm.; appointed chm., York Tree Comm.; delegate, American Industrial Comm. to France, 1916; appointed member, PA Defense Organizations, 1917. BUS. & PROF.: managed father's farm, 1 year; machinist, York, 1856; partner, machinist firm, York, 1858–62, sole proprietor, 1862; pres., A. B. Farquhar Co., Ltd. (agricultural machinery), 1889; owner, *York Gazette;* landowner; author; political economist. MEM.: York Hospital (pres.); York Municipal League (pres.); York Oratorio Soc. (pres.); National Assn. of Executive Commissioners (pres., 1897); National Conservation Assn. (dir.); PA Conservation Assn. (pres.); U.S. C. of C. (vice president; dir.); PA State Housing and Town Planning Assn. (pres.). HON. DEG.: LL.D., Kenyon Coll., 1902. WRITINGS: *Economic and Industrial Delusions* (1891). REL.: Episc. RES.: York, PA.

FARRELL, JOHN J. b. 1869, Hudson, OH; d. Jul 28, 1946, Lake Mille Lacs, MN; par. Daniel and Mary Farrell; m. Mabel L. Sanborn, 1902; c. John, Jr.; Robert; Elizabeth. EDUC.: grad., U. of MN. POLIT. & GOV.: appointed MN state dairy and food commissioner, 1915–18; Democratic candidate for U.S. House (MN), 1918; delegate, Dem. Nat'l. Conv., 1920 (Credentials Cmte.), 1924, 1928; Democratic candidate for U.S. Senate (MN), 1924; ***candidate for Democratic nomination to vice presidency of the U.S., 1924***; chm., MN State Democratic Central Cmte., 1931; appointed U.S. marshall for MN, 1935–46. BUS. & PROF.: employee, Crescent Creamery Co., St. Paul, MN, 1887–97; owner, creamery, Scott, Carver and Sibley counties, MN, 1897–1915. MEM.: National Dairy Products Comm. (sec., 1918–22); American Dairy, Food and Drug Officials Assn. (pres., 1916); MN Dairy Food Products Assn. (sec., 1922); National Creamery Buttermakers Assn. (pres., 1906–20); Dairy Products Assn. of the North West (sec.); Carver Cty. Agricultural Soc. (pres., 1898); American Agricultural Comm. (1918–19); National Dairy Show (charter member; dir.); National Dairy Council (dir.); MN State Agricultural Soc. RES.: St. Paul, MN.

FASSETT, JACOB SLOAT. b. Nov 13, 1853, Elmira, NY; d. Apr 21, 1924, Vancouver, British Columbia, Canada; par. Newton Pomeroy and Martha Ellen (Sloat) Fassett; m. Jennie Louise Crocker, Feb 13, 1879; c. Bryant Sloat; Newton Crocker; Margaret (Mrs. Frederick Grady Hodgson); Carol; Truman Edmund; Mary; Jacob Sloat; Jennie (Mrs. Paul Nevin). EDUC.: A.B., U. of Rochester, 1875, A.M.; studied law in offices of Smith, Robertson and Fassett, Elmira, NY; U. of Heidelberg, 1880–81. POLIT. & GOV.: elected district atty., Chemung Cty., NY, 1878–80; delegate, Rep. Nat'l. Conv., 1880, 1888, 1892 (temporary chm.), 1908, 1916; elected as a Republican to NY State Senate, 1884–91 (pres. pro tempore, 1889–91); sec., Rep. Nat'l. Cmte., 1888–92; Republican candidate for gov. of NY, 1891; appointed U.S. collector of customs, Port of New York, 1891; ***candidate for Republican nomination to vice presidency of the U.S., 1896, 1908***; delegate, NY State Constitutional Convention, 1904; elected as a Republican to U.S. House (NY), 1905–11; Republican candidate for U.S. House (NY), 1910; chm., NY State Republican Advisory Convention, 1918. BUS. & PROF.: atty.; admitted to NY Bar, 1878; law practice, Elmira, NY, 1878–96; proprietor, *Elmira Daily Advertiser,* 1879–96; vice pres., Second National Bank, Elmira; vice pres., Commercial State Bank, Sioux City, IA; lumberman; owner, mining interests, Korea. MEM.: SAR; Masons (32°); Elks; Elmira C. of C.; Alpha Delta Phi; Union League; University Club; Fellowcraft Club; Century Club; City Club of Elmira; Rotary Club. HON. DEG.: LL.D., Colgate U., 1901. REL.: Bapt. RES.: Elmira, NY.

FAUBUS, ORVAL EUGENE. b. Jan 7, 1910, Combs, AR; d. Dec 14, 1994, Conway, AR; par. John Samuel and Addie (Joslin) Faubus; m. Alta Mozell Haskins, Nov 21, 1931 (divorced, 1969); m. 2d, Elizabeth Drake Thompson-Westmoreland, Mar 21, 1969 (murdered, 1983); m. 3d, Jan Wittenburg, Nov 23, 1986; c. Farrell Eugene; Frederick King; Kim Elizabeth (stepdaughter); Ricci Westmoreland (stepdaughter). EDUC.: Huntsville Vocational School, 1934; U. of AR Extension. POLIT. & GOV.: circuit clerk and cty. recorder, Madison Cty., AR, 1939–42; appointed acting postmaster, Huntsville, AR, 1946–47, postmaster, 1953–54; appointed AR highway commissioner, asst. to the governor, and dir. of highways, 1949–53; elected as a Democrat to gov. of AR, 1955–67; delegate, Dem. Nat'l. Conv., 1956; ***candidate for Democratic nomination to presidency of the U.S., 1960; National States Rights Party candidate for presidency of the U.S., 1960***; candidate for Democratic nomination to gov. of AR, 1970. BUS. & PROF.: school teacher, 1928–38; owner, ed., *Madison County (AR) Record,* 1947–69; owner, *Arkansas Statesman,* 1960–69; publisher, ed., *The Spectator,* 1968–69; pres., Recreational Enterprises, Inc. (operators of Dogpatch, U.S.A., in Ozarks), 1969–70; with Aegis Service Corp., 1970–; bank teller. MIL.: maj., U.S. Army, 1942–46; Combat Infantry Badge; Bronze Star; six Battle Stars. MEM.: Southern Governors' Conference (chm., 1962–63); National Governors' Conference (exec. cmte., 1960); 35th Infantry Div. Assn. (pres., 1954–55); Alpha Kappa Lamda; BSA (rural scout commissioner, Northwest AR, 1924–38); Madison Cty. C. of C. (pres., 1953–54); American Legion; VFW; Disabled American Veterans; SCV; Elks; Masons (32°); Lions (sec.-treas., Huntsville, AR, 1939); Lone Scouts; Future Farmers of America; Combs 4-H Club (pres., 1927); Ozark Playground Assn. (Madison Cty. dir., 1940). AWARDS: "Man of the Year," American Legion, 1957; one of 10 "Most Admired Men," 1958; "Municipal Man of the Year," 1965; "Conservationist of the Year," 1966. WRITINGS: *In This Faraway Land; Down From the Hills* (2 vols., 1985). REL.: Bapt. RES.: Houston, TX 77079.

FAUNTROY, WALTER EDWARD. b. Feb 6, 1933, Washington, DC; par. William T. and Ethel (Vine) Fauntroy; m. Dorothy Simms, Aug 3, 1957; c. Marvin Keith. EDUC.: B.A. (cum laude), VA Union U., 1955, D.D., 1968; B.D., Yale U., 1969. POLIT. & GOV.: vice chm., White House Conference to Fulfill These Rights, 1966; chm., Washington Metropolitan Area Transit authority, 1967; vice chm., District of Columbia City Council, 1967–69; elected as a Democrat, delegate, U.S. House (DC), 1971–91; delegate, National Black Political Caucus, 1972; delegate, Dem. Nat'l. Conv., 1972, 1976; ***candidate for Democratic nomination to presidency of the U.S., 1972***; candidate for Democratic nomination to mayor of Washington, DC, 1990. BUS. & PROF.: ordained minister, Baptist Church, 1958; pastor, New Bethel Baptist Church, Washington, DC, 1958–; founder, dir., Model Inner City Community Organization, Inc., Washington, DC. MEM.: Southern Christian Leadership Conference (dir.); Inter-Religious Cmte. on Race Relations (dir.); March on Washington for Jobs and Freedom (coordinator, 1963); DC Coalition of Conscience (chm., 1965); Selma to Montgomery March (coordinator, 1965); Poor People's Campaign (national coordinator, 1969); Leadership Conference on Civil Rights; Yale U. Council (1969–74); Martin Luther King, Jr., Center for Social Change (chm., board of directors, 1969–). HON. DEG.: LL.D., Muskingum Coll., 1971. REL.: Bapt. MAILING ADDRESS: 4105 17th St., N.W., Washington, DC 20011.

FAZZARI, CLARITA "CHI CHI." b. 1936; m. (divorced). POLIT. & GOV.: ***independent candidate for presidency of the U.S., 1988, 1992***. BUS. & PROF.: mambo dancer, 1950s; real estate investor; owner, kiwi farm; owner, Bobbie's Buckeye Bar and Brothel, Pahrump, NV. MISC.: known as the "Cuban Fireball"; received $800,000 divorce settlement, invested it, and became a millionaire. MAILING ADDRESS: c/o Shirley Quaill, 750 Powell St., San Francisco, CA 94108.

FEATHER, RAYFORD G. POLIT. & GOV.: sec., Prohibition Party National Convention, 1983; sec., Prohibition Party National Cmte., 1983–; ***candidate for Prohibition Party nomination to vice presidency of the U.S., 1984 (declined)***. MEM.: National Prohibition Foundation (trustee). MAILING ADDRESS: 8 Dogwood Dr., Lewisburg, PA 17837.

FEELEY, GEORGE THOMAS, JR. par. George Thomas Feeley, Sr. POLIT. & GOV.: ***independent candidate for presidency of the U.S., 1980***. MAILING ADDRESS: 665 N.E. 85th St., Miami, FL 33138.

FEENEY, KENNETH DUANE. POLIT. & GOV.: ***independent candidate for presidency of the U.S., 1988***. MAILING ADDRESS: 6363 West Camp Wisdom Rd., #1235, Dallas, TX 75236.

FEIFFER, JULES RALPH. b. Jan 26, 1929, New York, NY; par. David and Rhode (Davis) Feiffer; m. Judith Sheftel, Sep 17, 1961; c. Kate. EDUC.: Art Students League, New York, NY, 1946; Pratt Inst., 1947–51. POLIT. & GOV.: ***independent candidate for presidency of the U.S., 1968***. BUS. & PROF.: asst. to Will Eisner (syndicated cartoonist), 1946–51; cartoonist, "Clifford" (syndicated Sunday page); engaged in various art jobs, 1953–56; contributing cartoonist, *Village Voice*, 1956–; contributing cartoonist, *London (England) Observer*, 1958–66; contributing cartoonist, *London Sunday Telegraph*, 1966–; contributing cartoonist, *Playboy*, 1959–; syndicated cartoonist, 1959–. MIL.: U.S. Army, 1951–53. MEM.: National Cmte. for a Sane Nuclear Policy (sponsor); Authors Guild; Dramatists Guild; P. E. N. AWARDS: Acad. Award for Cartoons, 1961; George Polk Memorial Award, 1962; Outer Circle Drama Critics Award, 1969, 1970. WRITINGS: *Sick, Sick, Sick* (1959); *Passionella and Other Stories* (1960); *The Explainers* (1961); *Crawling Arnold* (1961); *Boy, Girl, Boy, Girl* (1962); *Hold Me* (1962; musical review, 1961); *Harry, The Rat With Women* (1963); *Feiffer's Album* (1963); *The Unexpurgated Memoirs of Bernard Mergendeiler* (1965); *The Great Comic Book Heroes* (1965); *Feiffer's Marriage Manual* (1967); *Little Murders* (play; voted "Best Play of Year" by London critics; Obie Award; Outer Circle Drama Critics Award, 1967); *Feiffer on Civil Rights* (1967); *God Bless* (play, 1968); *The White House Murder Case* (1970); *Little Murders* (screen play, 1971); *Carnal Knowledge* (screen play, 1971); *Pictures at a Prosecution* (1971); *Feiffer on Nixon: The Cartoon Presidency* (1974); *Knock, Knock* (play, 1976); *Hold Me* (1977); *Ackroyd* (1977); *Tantrum* (1979). REL.: Jewish. MAILING ADDRESS: 11 Montague Terrace, Brooklyn, NY.

FEIMER, DORIS. POLIT. & GOV.: ***American Party candidate for vice presidency of the U.S., 1992***. MAILING ADDRESS: ND; c/o American Party, P.O. Box 597, Provo, UT 84603.

FEINSTEIN, DIANNE GOLDMAN. b. Jun 22, 1933, San Francisco, CA; par. Leon and Betty (Rosenburg) Goldman; m. Jack Derman (divorced); m. 2d, Bertram Feinstein, Nov 11, 1962; m. 3d, Richard Blum, Jan 20, 1980; c. Katherine Anne. EDUC.: B.S., Stanford U., 1955. POLIT. & GOV.: appointed asst. to CA Industrial Welfare Comm., Los Angeles, CA, 1956–57; appointed member, vice chairperson, CA Women's Board of Terms and Parole, Los Angeles, CA, 1962–66; appointed member, Mayor's Comm. on Crime, San Francisco, CA, 1967–69; appointed chairperson, San Francisco City and Cty. Advisory Comm. for Adult Detention, 1967–69; elected as a Democrat, supervisor, City and Cty. of San Francisco, CA, 1970–78 (pres., Board of Supervisors, 1970–72, 1974–76, 1978); delegate, General Assembly, Assn. of Bay Area Governments, 1970– (exec. cmte.); Democratic candidate for mayor of San Francisco, CA, 1971, 1975; appointed member, Bay Conservation and Development Comm., 1973–78; delegate, Dem. Nat'l. Conv., 1976, 1980; appointed chairperson, Environmental Management Task Force, Assn. of Bay Area Governments, 1976–78; succeeded to the office of mayor and subsequently elected as a Democrat, mayor of San Francisco, CA, 1978–88; ***candidate for Democratic nomination to vice presidency of the U.S., 1984***; Democratic candidate for gov. of CA, 1990; elected as a

Democrat to U.S. Senate (CA), 1993–. BUS. & PROF.: intern, Coro Foundation, San Francisco, CA, 1955–56; public official. MEM.: Lone Mountain Coll. (chm., Board of Regents, 1972–75); Multi-Culture Inst. (dir.); CA Tomorrow; Bay Area Urban League; Planning and Conservation League; Friends of the Earth; Chinese Culture Foundation; North Central Coast Regional Comm.; Sierra Club; Propeller Club; Commonwealth Club; March of Dimes (dir., 1978–); League of Women Voters; CA Elected Women's Assn.; NAACP. AWARDS: Women of Achievement Award, Business and Professional Women's Clubs of San Francisco, 1970; Distinguished Woman Award, *San Francisco Examiner*, 1970; Coro Award, 1979; SCOPUS Award, 1981. HON. DEG.: LL.D., Golden Gate U., 1977; D.P.A., U. of Manila, 1981; H.H.D., Philippine Women's U., 1981. REL.: Raised R.C./Jewish. MAILING ADDRESS: 2030 Lyon St., San Francisco, CA 94115.

FELLOWS, LYNN. b. Feb 5, 1894, Plankinton, SD; d. 1971. EDUC.: LL.B., U. of SD, 1927. POLIT. & GOV.: Plankinton (SD) city atty., 1927–42, 1950–60; elected as a Democrat to SD State House, 1931–35; Aurora Cty. (SD) state's atty., 1936–42, 1959–61; Democratic candidate for gov. of SD, 1944; chm., SD State Democratic Central Cmte.; ***candidate for Democratic nomination to presidency of the U.S., 1948 (stand-in for President Harry S. Truman (q.v.) in SD presidential primary).*** BUS. & PROF.: atty.; admitted to SD Bar, 1927; law practice, Plankinton, SD. MEM.: Phi Delta Phi; Fourth Judicial Circuit Bar Assn.; SD Bar. RES.: Plankinton, SD.

FELLURE, LOWELL JACKSON "JACK." b. 1932. POLIT. & GOV.: ***candidate for Republican nomination to presidency of the U.S., 1988, 1992***. BUS. & PROF.: pres., Unique International (national/international marketing), Hurricane, WV; preacher. REL.: Bapt.; became "Born-Again" fundamentalist Christian, 1951. MISC.: opponent of communism, socialism, homosexuality. MAILING ADDRESS: P.O. Box 507, Hurricane, WV 25526.

FENTON, REUBEN EATON. b. Jul 4, 1819, Carroll, NY; d. Aug 25, 1885, Jamestown, NY; par. George W. and Elsie (Owen) Fenton; m. Jane Frew, 1838; m. 2d, Elizabeth Scudder, Jun 14, 1844; c. Josephine (Mrs. Frank Edward Gifford); Jeannette (Mrs. Albert Gilbert, Jr.); Reuben Eaton, Jr. EDUC.: Fredonia Acad.; Cary's Acad.; studied law in offices of Waite Brothers, Jamestown, NY. POLIT. & GOV.: elected supervisor, Town of Carroll, NY, 1843–51; elected as a Democrat to NY State Assembly, 1849; elected as a Democrat to U.S. House (NY), 1853–55; founding member, Republican Party of NY; Republican candidate for U.S. House (NY), 1854; pres., NY State Republican Convention, 1855; elected as a Republican to U.S. House (NY), 1857–64; candidate for Republican nomination to gov. of NY, 1862 (declined); elected as a Republican to gov. of NY, 1864–69; ***candidate for Republican nomination to presidency of the U.S., 1864, 1872; candidate for Republican nomination to vice presidency of the U.S., 1864, 1868***; elected as a Republican to U.S. Senate (NY), 1869–75; appointed chm., U.S. Comm. to International Monetary Conference, Paris, France, 1878; Republican candidate for U.S. Senate (NY), 1881. BUS. & PROF.: merchant; lumberman; pres., First National Bank, Jamestown, NY. MIL.: col., 162d Regt., NY State Militia. RES.: Jamestown, NY.

FERENCY, ZOLTON A. b. Jun 30, 1922, Detroit, MI; par. John and Mary (Jankovics) Ferency; m. Ellen Jane Dwyer, Jun 14, 1947; c. Michael John; Mark Dwyer. EDUC.: B.A., MI State U., 1946; J.D., Detroit Coll. of Law, 1952; Wayne State U., 1952–55. POLIT. & GOV.: personnel technician, Detroit, MI, 1946–48; relocation dir., Detroit Slum Clearance Program, 1948–53; vice chm., 14th District Democratic Cmte., Detroit, MI, 1956–62; appointed chm., MI Liquor Control Comm., 1957–58; appointed dir., MI Workmen's Compensation Dept., 1958–60; exec. sec. to governor of MI, 1961–62; chm., MI State Democratic Central Cmte., 1963–68; Democratic candidate for gov. of MI, 1966; delegate, Dem. Nat'l. Conv., 1968; candidate for Democratic nomination to gov. of MI, 1970, 1978; founder, Human Rights Party, 1970; Human Rights Party candidate for gov. of MI, 1974; ***candidate for People's Party nomination to vice presidency of the U.S., 1976***; Non-Partisan candidate (sponsored by Human Rights Party) for MI State Supreme Court, 1972, 1976. BUS. & PROF.: atty.; admitted to MI Bar, 1953; lecturer, MI State Bar Inst.; lecturer, Inst. on Continuing Legal Education; partner, Ferency, Sweeney and Markus (law firm), Detroit, MI, 1953–55; partner, Marston, Ganos and Ferency (law firm), 1960–61; partner, Hardy, Starr and Ferency (law firm), Lansing, MI, 1966–; professor of labor relations, MI State U. MIL.: master sgt., U.S. Army, 1942–45; ETO Ribbon with 3 Battle Stars. MEM.: MI State Bar; Hungarian-American Democratic Club; U.A.W. (Local 212); AFL-CIO; NAACP; Catholic War Veterans; Polish-Hungarian Federation (dir.); VFW. WRITINGS: *Workmen's Compensation Practices* (1964). REL.: R.C. MAILING ADDRESS: 120 Maplewood, East Lansing, MI 48910.

FERGUSON, CLINTON. b. Apr 16, 1918, Kansas City, MO; par. Russell Bernard and Eula (Ogle) Ferguson; single. EDUC.: grad., Baton Rouge (LA) H.S.; LA State U., 4½ years. POLIT. & GOV.: ***candidate for Democratic nomination to presidency of the U.S., 1988, 1992***. BUS. & PROF.: pricer, drug store, 3½ years; employee, *Gulfport (MS) Star*. MIL.: corp., U.S. Army, 3½ years. MEM.: American Legion. REL.: Soc. of Friends. MAILING ADDRESS: Dom 2, VAMC Biloxi, Biloxi, MS 39531.

FERGUSON, GLORIA JEAN SANDRA. b. Feb 13, 1950, Philipsburg, PA; par. Joseph Paul and Helen June (Josephson) Gomola; m. John Lester Gaylyn Ferguson (divorced); c. Lori Ann; John Joseph; eight foster children. EDUC.: grad., Bald Eagle H.S., 1968; PA State U. POLIT. & GOV.: ***candidate for Democratic nomination to presidency of the U.S., 1988, 1992***. BUS. & PROF.: employee, U.S. Postal Service; real estate agent; model; flight instructor; private investigator; owner, State Aerial Farms Statistics, Inc., Poleto, OH; narcotics officer, PA State Police. MEM.: GSA; Cub Scouts of America (den mother); Ladies Aid (treas.). AWARDS: foster program awards; award, Cub Scouts of America; Softball awards; National Driving Award, U.S. Postal Service; "Best Shot" Award, Handgun Competition; named "Best Neighbor of the Year," 1982. WRITINGS: "Loving Relationships" (unpublished). REL.: R.C. MAILING ADDRESS: 212 West High St., Apt. 4, Bellefonte, PA 16823.

FERGUSON, JAMES EDWARD. b. Aug 31, 1871, Bell Cty., TX; d. Sep 21, 1944, Austin, TX; par. James Edward and Fannie (Fitzpatrick) Ferguson; m. Mariam Amanda Wallace (q.v.), Dec 31, 1899; c. Ouida Wallace (Mrs. George S. Nalle); Ruby Dorrace (Mrs. Stuart Watt). EDUC.: public school; studied law. POLIT. & GOV.: elected as a Democrat to gov. of TX, 1915–17; candidate for Democratic nomination to gov. of TX, 1918; ***American Party candidate for presidency of the U.S., 1920***; American Party candidate for U.S. Senate (TX), 1922. BUS. & PROF.: laborer; bellhop; grape picker; roustabout; teamster; miner; foreman, bridge-building crews, TX; farmer, Bell Cty., TX; atty.; admitted to TX Bar, 1897; law practice, Belton, TX; law practice, Temple, TX; founder, Temple State Bank, Temple, TX; landowner. MEM.: Masons; Elks; Modern Woodmen of the World; Knights of Pythias; Odd Fellows. REL.: Bapt. MISC.: known as "Farmer Jim" Ferguson; impeached and removed from gov., Aug 25, 1917. RES.: Temple, TX.

FERGUSON, JOSEPH TERRENCE "JUMPING JOE." b. May 12, 1892, Shawnee, OH; d. Oct 22, 1979, Columbus, OH; par. Terrence and Amanda (Palmer) Ferguson; m. Clara M. Kost, Nov 17, 1921; c. Theresa Voldness; Joan Gotherman; Clara Littleboy; Anna Hohenbrink; Helen Voldness; James; Terrence; Jerome; Thomas. EDUC.: St. Mary's Commercial H.S., Shawnee, OH. POLIT. & GOV.: appointed state examiner, OH State Industrial Comm., 1914–16; appointed state examiner, office of the OH state auditor, 1916–28; candidate for Democratic nomination to OH state auditor, 1928; Democratic candidate for OH state auditor, 1930, 1932, 1934, 1952, 1956; elected as a Democrat, OH state auditor, 1937–53, 1971–75; candidate for Democratic nomination to gov. of OH, 1942; ***candidate for Democratic nomination to presidency of the U.S., 1944***; Democratic candidate for U.S. Senate (OH), 1950; Democratic candidate for OH state treas., 1954; Democratic candidate for city auditor, Columbus, OH, 1957; elected as a Democrat, OH state treas., 1959–63; delegate, Dem. Nat'l. Conv., 1972. BUS. & PROF.: newsboy; paymaster, Peabody Coal Co., pre-1914; employee, Pittsburgh Coal Co.; employee, Colonial Finance Co., Barberton, OH; auditor, financial institutions. MEM.: Knights of Columbus (life member); Grange; Elks; Eagles; Moose; Holy Name Soc.; National Assn. of State Auditors, Comptrollers, and Treasurers (pres.). AWARDS: "Mr. Democrat of OH," 1962; "Auditor Emeritus of OH," 1977. WRITINGS: *A Short History of Ohio Land Grants* (1939). REL.: R.C. RES.: Upper Arlington, OH.

FERGUSON, MIRIAM AMANDA WALLACE "MA." b. Jun 13, 1875, Bell Cty., TX; d. Jun 25, 1961, Austin, TX; par. Joseph Lapsley and Eliza (Garrison) Wallace; m. James Edward Ferguson (q.v.), Dec 31, 1899; c. Ouida Wallace (Mrs. George S. Nalle); Ruby Dorrace (Mrs. Stuart Watt). EDUC.: Salado Coll.; Baylor Coll. for Women, Belton, TX. POLIT. & GOV.: ***candidate for Prohibition Party nomination to presidency of the U.S., 1916***; elected as a Democrat to gov. of TX, 1925–27, 1933–35; candidate for Democratic nomination to gov. of TX, 1926, 1930, 1940. BUS. & PROF.: housewife; public official. REL.: Episc. RES.: Belton, TX.

FERGUSON, WILLIAM PORTER FRISBEE. b. Dec 13, 1861, Delhi, NY; d. Jun 24, 1929, Franklin, PA; par. P. Rice and Electa A. (Frisbee) Ferguson; m. Lena Grace Hathaway, Apr 5, 1887; c. Horace Porter Frisbee; Josiah Deming; Dorothy Hilda. EDUC.: Walton (NY) Acad., 1884; B.D., Drew Theological Seminary, 1887; A.B., TX Wesleyan U., 1889 (declined LL.D. on grounds that university owned saloon property). POLIT. & GOV.: Prohibition Party candidate for U.S. House (NY), 1898; Prohibition Party candidate for U.S. House (PA), 1914; ***candidate for Prohibition Party nomination to presidency of the U.S., 1916***; Prohibition Party candidate for PA State House, 1918. BUS. & PROF.: served in Methodist Episcopal Foreign Mission to Mexico, 1887–89; pastor, Bangall, NY, 1889–90; principal, Mohawk Inst., Utica, NY, 1891–92; pastor, Presbyterian Chaurch, Whitesboro, NY, 1892–96; ed., *Voice*, 1897–99; ed., *New Voice*, 1899–1902; pastor, Universalist Church, Harriman, TN, 1904–05; ed., *Citizen*, Harriman, 1904–05; pastor, Third Universalist Church, Brooklyn, NY, 1905–07; ed., *Defender*, 1905–07; ed., *National Prohibitionist*, Chicago, IL, 1907–11; ed., *Venango Daily Herald*, Franklin, PA, 1912–19; ed., *Vindicator*, Franklin, 1911–16; ed., *News-Herald*, Franklin, 1919–29; lecturer on prohibition; explorer and lecturer on American archeology; discovered prehistoric city on Isle Royale in Lake Superior. WRITINGS: *The Canteen in the United States* (1900); *Prohibition in the United States* (1902); *History of the Prohibition Party* (1910); "When the Tide Comes In," *National Prohibitionist*, Jul 28, 1910; "Bring Up the Regiment," *Vindicator*, Oct 31, 1913. REL.: Universalist. RES.: Franklin, PA.

FERNANDEZ, BENJAMIN. b. Feb 25, 1925, Kansas City, KS; m. Jackie Fernandez. EDUC.: Washington H.S., East Chicago, IN; B.A., U. of the Redlands; M.B.A., NY U., 1952. POLIT. & GOV.: national chm., Republican

National Hispanic Assembly, 1975–78; member, financial section, Cmte. for the Re-Election of the President, 1972; ***candidate for Republican nomination to presidency of the U.S., 1980, 1984, 1988***. BUS. & PROF.: migrant farmworker; marketing analyst, General Electric Corp., 1951; national dir. of marketing research, O. A. Sutton Corp., 1955–60; owner, consultant firm (bank and savings and loan association consulting), Los Angeles, CA, 1960–. MISC.: born in freight car in Kansas City, KS. MAILING ADDRESS: 4321 Matilija Ave., #5, Sherman Oaks, CA 91423.

FERRARI-SOLDO, JOHN JOSEPH DANIEL DAVI (See SOLDO, JOHN JOSEPH DANIEL).

FERRARO, GERALDINE ANNE. b. Aug 26, 1935, Newburgh, NY; par. Dominick and Antonetta L. (Corrieri) Ferraro; m. John Zaccaro, 1960; c. Donna; John; Laura. EDUC.: B.A., Marymount Coll., 1956; J.D., Fordham U., 1960; NY U. Law School, 1978. POLIT. & GOV.: appointed asst. district atty., Queens Cty., NY, 1974–78; chief, Special Victims Bureau, 1974–78; appointed member, Advisory Council for Housing, New York City (NY) Civil Court, 1978–; elected as a Democrat to U.S. House (NY), 1979–85; sec., U.S. House Democratic Caucus, 1980–85; delegate, Dem. Nat'l. Conv., 1980, 1984 (chairperson, Platform Cmte.); ***Democratic candidate for vice presidency of the U.S., 1984***; candidate for Democratic nomination to U.S. Senate (NY), 1992. BUS. & PROF.: teacher, public school, New York, NY, 1956–61; atty.; admitted to NY Bar, 1961; admitted to practice before the Bar of the Supreme Court of the U.S., 1978; law practice, New York, 1961–74. MEM.: District Attorneys Assn. (dir.); Catholic Lawyers' Guild (dir.); Queens Cty. Bar Assn.; Queens Cty. Women's Bar Assn. (pres.); NY Bar Assn.; 31st Assembly Regular Democratic Club; Columbian Lawyers' Assn. (pres.). WRITINGS: *Ferraro*. REL.: R.C. MISC.: first woman nominated for the vice presidency of the U.S. by a major political party. MAILING ADDRESS: 22 Deepene Rd., Forest Hills, NY 11375.

FERRE, MAURICE ANTONIO. b. Jun 23, 1935, Ponce, Puerto Rico; par. Jose Antonio and Florence (Salichs) Ferre; m. Maria Mercedes Malaussena, Aug 25, 1955; c. Mary Isabel; Jose Luis; Carlos Maurice; Maurice Raimundo; Francisco; Florence. EDUC.: grad., Lawrenceville (NJ) School, 1953; B.S.A.E., U. of Miami, 1957. POLIT. & GOV.: elected as a Democrat to FL State House, 1966–67; elected as a Democrat to Miami (FL) City Comm., 1967–70; interim mayor of Miami, 1973; elected as a Democrat to mayor of Miami, 1974–78; ***candidate for Democratic nomination to vice presidency of the U.S., 1976***; Democratic candidate for mayor of Miami, 1987. BUS. & PROF.: vice pres., Ferre Florida Corp. (real estate), Miami, 1960–64, pres., 1964–; senior vice pres., Maule Industries, Inc. (building materials), Miami, 1961–63, pres., 1963–. MEM.: U. of Miami (dir.); Barry Coll. (dir.); Lawrenceville School (dir.); United Way (trustee); Greater Miami Philharmonic Soc. (gov.); Council for International Visitors (pres.); BSA (Southern FL Council); 1973 Cerebral Palsy Walkathon (chm.); March of Dimes (exec. cmte.); Miami Heart Inst. (dir.); Miami-Dade Cty. C. of C. (dir.); Cmte. of 21 (first vice president); FL Council of 100; Community Television Foundation of South FL (dir.); Inter-American Center Authority (vice chm.); Economic Soc. of South FL; Young Presidents' Organization; Museum of Science and Space Transit Planetarium (board member); Young Democratic Club of FL; National Conference of Christians and Jews. AWARDS: "Man of the Year," Miami Junior C. of C., 1968; Silver Medallion Award, National Conference of Christians and Jews, 1968; "Democrat of the Year," Young Democratic Club of FL, 1969; "Outstanding Young Man of Miami," 1970; Columbus Soc. Award, 1975; National Humanitarian Award, B'nai B'rith, 1975. MAILING ADDRESS: 1643 Brickell Ave., Miami, FL 33129.

FERRIS, WOODBRIDGE NATHAN. b. Jan 6, 1853, Spencer, NY; d. Mar 23, 1928, Washington, DC; par. John, Jr. and Estella (Reed) Ferris; m. Helen Frances Gillespie, Dec 1875; m. 2d, Mary Ethel McCloud, Aug 14, 1921; c. Carleton G.; Phelps; one other son. EDUC.: Spencer Union Acad.; Candon Union Acad.; Oswego Acad.; Oswego Normal and Training School, 1870–73; U. of MI Medical School, 1873–74. POLIT. & GOV.: superintendent of schools, Pittsfield, IL, 1879–84; Democratic candidate for U.S. House (MI), 1892; Democratic candidate for MI state superintendent of public instruction, 189?; Democratic candidate for gov. of MI, 1904, 1920; elected as a Democrat to gov. of MI, 1913–16; elected as a Democrat to U.S. Senate (MI), 1923–28; delegate, Dem. Nat'l. Conv., 1924; ***candidate for Democratic nomination to presidency of the U.S., 1924***. BUS. & PROF.: principal, Spencer Acad., 1874–75; principal, Business College and Acad., Freeport, IL, 1875–76; professor, Rock River U., Dixon, IL, 1876–77; principal, Dixon (IL) Business College and Acad., 1878–79; pres., Ferris Inst., Big Rapids, MI, 1884–1928; pres., Big Rapids (MI) Savings Bank. MEM.: Knights of Pythias; Masons; Modern Woodmen of the World; Big Rapids Board of Trade. HON. DEG.: LL.D., U. of MI Medical School; Master of Pedagogy, MI State Normal Coll.; LL.D., Olivet Coll. RES.: Big Rapids, MI.

FETIAK, JEROME P. POLIT. & GOV.: ***candidate for Democratic nomination to presidency of the U.S., 1992; independent candidate for presidency of the U.S., 1992***. MAILING ADDRESS: 12 Valley Rd., Port Washington, NY 11050.

FEUER, ISRAEL. POLIT. & GOV.: Peace and Freedom Party candidate for CA state sec. of state, 1970; ***candidate for Peace and Freedom Party nomination to presidency of the U.S., 1980***. BUS. & PROF.: community organizer. MAILING ADDRESS: P.O. Box 24858, Los Angeles, CA 90024.

FEY, SUSAN CAROLE. b. Oct 9, 1942, Chicago, IL; par. Edgar and Helen (Kwaltkowski) Fey; m. (divorced); m. 2d, (divorced); c. three. EDUC.: B.A., Northwestern U., 1964; M.A., U. of Santa Monica, 1991. POLIT. & GOV.: ***candidate for Democratic nomination to presidency of the U.S., 1992***. BUS. & PROF.: occupational therapist; high school teacher; founder, Childrens' Treatment Center; social worker; retail business mgr., Benedeck and Fey, Berwyn, IL; administrator; author; founder, Early Intervention Program. MEM.: Taos Mental Health Assn. (dir.); Taos Valley School (dir.). REL.: Movement of Spiritual Inner Awareness. MAILING ADDRESS: 1710 Fletcher St., Chicago, IL 60657.

FIELD, JAMES GAVIN. b. Feb 24, 1826, Walnut, VA; d. Oct 12, 1901, Gordonsville, VA; par. Judge Lewis Yancy and Maria (Duncan) Field; m. Miss Cowherd, 1854; m. 2d, Miss Logwood, 1882. EDUC.: classical studies; studied law under Judge Richard H. Field. POLIT. & GOV.: sec., CA Constitutional Convention, 1850; commonwealth's atty., Culpepper Cty., VA, 1859–65; atty. gen. of VA, 1877–82; ***People's Party candidate for vice presidency of the U.S., 1892***; member, People's (Fusion) Party National Cmte., 1901. BUS. & PROF.: merchant, Fairfax, VA; atty.; admitted to VA Bar, 1852; farmer, Gordonsville, VA. MIL.: employee, pay dept., U.S. Army, 1848; maj., C.S.A., 1861–65; lost leg in Battle of Slaughter's Mountain. REL.: Bapt. RES.: Gordonsville, VA.

FIELD, MOSES WHEELOCK. b. Feb 10, 1828, Watertown, NY; d. Mar 14, 1889, Detroit, MI; par. William and Rebecca (Wheelock) Field; m. Mary Kercheval, Feb 2, 1858; c. Alice (Mrs. Francis Woodbridge); Edythe (Mrs. George Shaffer Young); Vincent; Mary (Mrs. H. J. Maxwell Grylls); Alfred; Egbert; Rebecca; Freeman; Mable (Mrs. Eugene Ramino Grasselli); Agnes (Mrs. William Frederick Grote). EDUC.: grad., Victor Acad., Victor, NY. POLIT. & GOV.: elected alderman, City Council, Detroit, MI, 1863–65; chm., Board of School Inspectors, Detroit, MI; member, MI State Republican Central Cmte.; elected as a Republican to U.S. House (MI), 1873–75; Republican candidate for U.S. House (MI), 1874; organizer, National Independent (Greenback) Party, 1876; chm., MI Independent (Greenback) Party Central Cmte.; chm., National Independent (Greenback) Party National Convention, 1876; ***candidate for National Independent (Greenback) Party nomination to vice presidency of the U.S., 1876; National Independent (Greenback) Party candidate for vice presidency of the U.S., 1876***. BUS. & PROF.: farmer, Detroit, MI; merchant, Stephens and Field Co., Detroit, MI, 1844–89; traveling salesman, wholesale grocery, Detroit, MI, 1844, subsequently proprietor; owner, bonded warehouse; real estate investor. MEM.: U. of MI (regent, 1888); MI Insane Asylum (trustee); Masons. REL.: Swedenborgian. MISC.: donated 50 acres for Linden Park, Detroit, MI, 1875. RES.: Hamtramck Township, MI.

FIELD, STEPHEN JOHNSON. b. Nov 4, 1816, Haddam, CT; d. Apr 9, 1899, Washington, DC; par. David Dudley and Submit (Dickinson) Field; m. Virginia Swearingen, Jun 2, 1859; c. none. EDUC.: grad. (summa cum laude; valedictorian), Williams Coll., 1837; studied law with John Van Buren, New York, NY, 1838–40. POLIT. & GOV.: elected alcalde, Marysville District, CA, 1850; elected to CA Assembly, 1850–51; elected justice, CA Supreme Court, 1857–63 (chief justice, 1859–63); appointed assoc. justice, Supreme Court of the U.S., 1863–97; ***candidate for Democratic nomination to presidency of the U.S., 1868, 1880, 1884***; appointed member, Comm. to Review California's Code of Laws, 1873. BUS. & PROF.: instructor, Albany Female Acad.; atty.; admitted to NY Bar, 1841; partner (with brother, David Dudley Field), law firm, New York, NY, 1841–48; law practice, Marysville, CA, 1848–57; professor of law, U. of CA, 1869–99. HON. DEG.: LL.D., Williams Coll., 1866. WRITINGS: *Reminiscences of Early Days in California* (1877). RES.: Washington, DC.

FIELDS, WILLIAM CLAUDE (nee WILLIAM CLAUDE DUKENFIELD). b. Apr 9, 1879, Philadelphia, PA; d. Dec 25, 1946, Pasadena, CA; par. James and Kate (Felton) Dukenfield; m. Harriet Veronica Hughes, Apr 8, 1900; c. William Claude, Jr. POLIT. & GOV.: ***Bull Moose Party candidate for presidency of the U.S., 1940***. BUS. & PROF.: comedian; in Vaudeville; appeared in Broadway productions of Ziegfield Follies and Earl Carroll's Vanities; movie actor; appeared on the Chase and Sanborn *Radio Hour*, 1937. Motion picture credits: *So's Your Old Man*; *It's the Old Army Game*; *The Potters*; *Six of a Kind*; *One in a Million*; *It's a Gift*; *David Copperfield*; *Mississippi*; *The Man on the Flying Trapeze*; *Poppy*; *The Big Broadcast of 1938*; *The Bank Dick*; *Never Give a Sucker an Even Break*; *My Little Chickadee*. WRITINGS: *Fields for President* (1939). REL.: agnostic. RES.: Hollywood, CA.

FIELDS, WILLIAM JASON. b. Dec 29, 1874, Willard, KY; d. Oct 21, 1954, Grayson, KY; par. Christopher C. and Alice (Rucker) Fields; m. Dora McDavid, Oct 28, 1893; c. Forrest G.; Robert Forde; Everett E.; Frank C.; William Earl; Elizabeth. EDUC.: public schools; U. of KY; studied law. POLIT. & GOV.: elected as a Democrat to U.S. House (KY), 1911–23; elected as a Democrat to gov. of KY, 1923–27; delegate, Dem. Nat'l. Conv., 1924; ***candidate for Democratic nomination to vice presidency of the U.S., 1924***; commonwealth atty., 37th Judicial District of KY, 1932–35; appointed member, KY State Workmen's Compensation Board, 1936–44. BUS. & PROF.: farmer, Olive Hill, KY; real estate business, Olive Hill, KY; traveling salesman, grocery and dry goods business, 1899–1910; atty.; admitted to KY Bar, 1927; co-owner, insurance agency, 1940–45. MEM.: Masons. RES.: Olive Hill, KY.

FIELDS, WILLIAM LAWRENCE. POLIT. & GOV.: ***Flying Tiger Party candidate for vice presidency of***

the U.S., 1972; treas., Flying Tiger Party. MAILING ADDRESS: P.O. Box 1094, Manila, Philippines.

FIGUEROA, FERNANDO RIVERA. b. Aug 18, 1963, Brooklyn, NY. POLIT. & GOV.: ***candidate for Democratic nomination to presidency of the U.S., 1992***. BUS. & PROF.: community activist. MISC.: fought drug abuse in Hanover Acres Project, Allentown, PA. MAILING ADDRESS: 16 South Sixth St., Allentown, PA 18102.

FIKES, HOMER. POLIT. & GOV.: ***candidate for American Party nomination to vice presidency of the U.S., 1972 (withdrew)***. MAILING ADDRESS: TX.

FILENE, EDWARD ALBERT. b. 1860, Salem, MA; d. Sep 26, 1937, Paris, France; par. William and Clara (Ballin) Filene; single. EDUC.: grad., high school; Harvard U. POLIT. & GOV.: ***American Home Progressive Party candidate for vice presidency of the U.S., 1928***; appointed chm., MA State Recovery Board, 1933–34; appointed chm., Metropolitan Planning Comm., Boston, MA. BUS. & PROF.: merchant; treas., gen. mgr., William Filene's Sons Co., Boston, MA, 1903–08, pres., 1908–37; pres., Consumer Distribution Corp., 1935. MEM.: Credit Union National Extension Bureau (founder, 1921); Boston C. of C. (dir., 1909–10); C. of C. of the U.S. (founder; chm., War Shipping Cmte.; member, Cmte. on Financing War); International C. of C. (vice pres., Sixth Congress, 1912); Twentieth Century Fund (founder; president); Credit Union National Assn. (pres., 1934); American Assn. for Labor Legislation (vice president); Public Franchise League of Boston (pres.); League to Enforce Peace (vice chm.); American Statistical Assn.; America-Italy Soc.; Taylor Soc.; National Economic League; American Acad. of Political and Social Science; National Inst. of Public Affairs; Netherland-America Foundation (patron); Austro-American Inst. of Education (life member); America-Austria Soc.; English Speaking Union; American Soc. of the French Legion of Honor; National Municipal League; Soc. for the Advancement of Management; Business Hist. Soc.; Stable Money Assn. (hon. vice president); Finance Cmte. for the Relief of Americans in Paris; Good Will Fund, Inc. (founder); Cleveland C. of C.; American C. of C. (London); American-Russian C. of C.; MA Credit Union Assn. (founder, 1917); National Cmte. on People's Banks; Credit Union National Extension Bureau (pres., 1921–35); Associated Merchandising Corp.; Co-Operative League (founder, 1921); East Asiatic Soc.; Asiatic Soc. of Japan; Council of Foreign Relations; Foreign Policy Assn.; National Inst. of Social Sciences; American Civic Assn.; American Economic Assn.; Filene Cooperative Assn.; National Child Labor Cmte.; Women's Trade Union League; American Assn. for Labor Legislation (vice president); History of Science Soc.; American Club; Cercle Artistique et Litteraire; Union Interalliee of Paris; Beacon Hill Assn.; Ford Hall Forum; Advertising Club; Badminton Club; Economic Club; Twentieth Century Club; National Arts Club; The Town Hall; Cosmos Club. AWARDS: Order of the Crown (Italy); Order of the White Lion (Czechoslovakia); Great Gold Cross of Merit (Austria); officer, Legion of Honor (France, 1937). HON. DEG.: LL.D., Lehigh U., 1931; LL.D., Rollins Coll., 1932; LL.D., Tulane U., 1935. WRITINGS: *The Way Out* (1924); *More Profits from Merchandising* (1925); *The Model Stock Plan* (1930); *Successful Living in This Machine Age* (1931); *Speaking of Change* (1939). RES.: Boston, MA.

FILLMORE, MILLARD. b. Jan 7, 1800, Locke, NY; d. Mar 8, 1874, Buffalo, NY; par. Nathaniel and Phoebe (Millard) Fillmore; m. Abigail Powers, Feb 5, 1826; m. 2d, Caroline Carmichael McIntosh, Feb 10, 1858; c. Millard Powers; Mary Abigail. EDUC.: studied law, Montville and Moravia, NY, 1819–21; studied law, Buffalo, NY, 1822. POLIT. & GOV.: elected as an Anti-Mason to NY State Assembly, 1829–31; elected as a Whig to U.S. House (NY), 1833–35, 1837–43; ***candidate for Whig Party nomination to vice presidency of the U.S., 1844***; Whig Party candidate for gov. of NY, 1844; elected as a Whig, state comptroller of NY, 1847–49; ***candidate for Whig Party nomination to presidency of the U.S., 1848, 1852; elected as a Whig to vice presidency of the U.S., 1849–50; succeeded to the presidency of the U.S., 1850–53; American (Know-Nothing) Party candidate for presidency of the U.S., 1856; Whig Party candidate for presidency of the U.S., 1856***; elected chm., Buffalo (NY) Cmte. of Public Defense, 1862; pres., Commercial Convention, Louisville, KY, 1869. BUS. & PROF.: apprentice wood carver, 1814–18; school teacher, Scott, NY, 1818–19; atty.; admitted to Erie Cty. (NY) Bar, 1823; law practice, Aurora, NY, 1823; admitted to NY Bar, 1827; partner, Fillmore, Hall and Haven (law firm), Buffalo, NY, 1835; appointed chancellor, U. of Buffalo, 1846–67. MIL.: commander, Home Guard, 1846. MEM.: Buffalo Hist. Soc. (pres., 1862–67); Buffalo Club (pres., 1867); Buffalo General Hospital (pres., 1870). HON. DEG.: D.C.L., Oxford U., 1855 (declined). WRITINGS: *Is It Right to Require Any Religious Test as a Qualification to Be a Witness in a Court of Justice?* (1832); *Early Life of Hon. Millard Fillmore* (1880). REL.: Unitarian. MISC.: wrote under name of "Juridicus." RES.: Buffalo, NY.

FINCH, CHARLES CLIFTON. b. Apr 4, 1927, Pope, MS; d. Apr 22, 1986, Batesville, MS; par. Carl Bedford and Ruth Christine (McMinn) Finch; m. Zelma Lois Smith, Nov 20, 1952; c. Janet Herrington; Virginia Anne; Charles Clifton, II; Stephen Nicholas. EDUC.: B.A., U. of MS, 1956, LL.B., 1958. POLIT. & GOV.: elected as a Democrat to MS State House, 1959–64; elected district atty., 17th Judicial Circuit of MS, 1964–72; candidate for Democratic nomination to lt. gov. of MS, 1971; elected as a Democrat to gov. of MS, 1976–80; candidate for Democratic nomination to U.S. Senate (MS), 1978; ***candidate for Democratic nomination to presidency of the U.S., 1980; candidate for American Independent Party nomination to presidency of the U.S., 1980 (withdrew)***. BUS. & PROF.:

atty.; admitted to MS Bar, 1958; law practice, Batesville, MS. MIL.: U.S. Army, 1945–47. MEM.: ABA; MS Bar Assn.; Panola Cty. Bar Assn. (pres.); American Trial Lawyers Assn. (assoc. ed., *Journal of the American Trial Lawyers Association*); MS Trial Lawyers Assn. (pres., 1969); Farm Bureau; American Legion; VFW; Masons (32°; Shriners); Lions; Civitan Club; Moose; Odd Fellows. REL.: Bapt. RES.: Jackson, MS.

FINERTY, JOSEPH M. POLIT. & GOV.: ***independent candidate for presidency of the U.S., 1984***. MAILING ADDRESS: 4508 Dartmoor Lane, Alexandria, VA 22310.

FINLEY, EBENEZER BYRON. b. Jul 31, 1833, Orrville, OH; d. Aug 22, 1916, Bucyrus, OH. EDUC.: public schools; studied law, Bucyrus, OH, 1859–61. POLIT. & GOV.: elected as a Democrat to U.S. House (OH), 1877–81; appointed adj. gen. of OH, 1884; appointed circuit judge, Third Judicial Circuit of OH; ***candidate for People's Party nomination to vice presidency of the U.S., 1896 (declined)***. BUS. & PROF.: atty.; admitted to OH Bar, 1862; law practice, Bucyrus, OH. MIL.: 1st lt., Company K, 24th OH Volunteer Infantry, 1861–62. MISC.: was advanced as possible replacement for Thomas Watson (q.v.), during speculation that Watson would resign from People's Party ticket in 1896. RES.: Bucyrus, OH.

FIOLA, NELL K. b. 1919; married; c. Patricia Mikelson; one other daughter. POLIT. & GOV.: ***Independent Republican candidate for presidency of the U.S., 1956, 1976, 1980, 1984, 1988***. BUS. & PROF.: saleswoman; bank teller; advertising saleswoman; pensioner; prophetess. MEM.: New Millennium Cmte. MAILING ADDRESS: 1008 West Burnsville Parkway, Apt. 225, Crosstown, Burnsville, MN 55337.

FISH, HAMILTON. b. Aug 3, 1808, New York, NY; d. Sep 6, 1893, Garrison-on-Hudson, NY; par. Nicholas and Elizabeth (Stuyvesant) Fish; m. Julia Kean, Dec 15, 1836; c. Stuyvesant; Nicholas; Hamilton; five daughters. EDUC.: Dr. Bancels French School; grad. (summa cum laude), Columbia U., 1827; studied law under Peter A. Jay. POLIT. & GOV.: New York City and Cty. (NY) Commissioner of Deeds, 1832–33; Whig Party candidate for NY State Assembly, 1834; elected as a Whig to U.S. House (NY), 1843–45; Whig Party candidate for U.S. House (NY), 1844; Whig Party candidate for lt. gov. of NY, 1846; ***candidate for Whig Party nomination to presidency of the U.S., 1848; candidate for Whig Party nomination to vice presidency of the U.S., 1848, 1852***; elected as a Whig to lt. gov. of NY, 1848–49; elected as a Whig to gov. of NY, 1849–50; elected as a Whig to U.S. Senate (NY), 1851–53; appointed U.S. commissioner for relief of prisoners, Civil War; appointed U.S. sec. of state, 1869–77; Republican candidate for U.S. Senate (NY), 1881. BUS. & PROF.: atty.; admitted to NY Bar, 1830; law practice, New York, NY. MEM.: Union Defense Cmte.; Soc. of the Cincinnati (pres.-gen., 1854–93); Columbia U. (trustee; chm. of the Board of Trustees); Astor Library (trustee); Union League Club (pres.); NY Hist. Soc. (pres., 1867–69). REL.: Episc. RES.: Garrison-on-Hudson, NY.

FISH, HAMILTON, JR. b. Dec 7, 1888, Garrison-on-Hudson, NY; d. Jan 18, 1991, Cold Spring, NY; par. Hamilton and Emily M. (Mann) Fish; m. Grace Chapin, Sep 24, 1921; m. 2d., Marie Blackton, 1966; m. 3d, Alice Desmond, 1976 (divorced); m. 4th, Lydia Ambrogio; c. Hamilton, Jr.; Elizabeth Pyne. EDUC.: grad., St. Mark's School; B.A. (cum laude), Harvard U., 1910; grad., Army and General Staff Coll., AEF. POLIT. & GOV.: elected as a Progressive Republican to NY State Assembly, 1914–16; elected as a Republican to U.S. House (NY), 1920–45; ***candidate for Republican nomination to vice presidency of the U.S., 1928, 1936***; delegate, Rep. Nat'l. Conv., 1928, 1932; ***candidate for Republican nomination to presidency of the U.S., 1936, 1940***; Republican candidate for U.S. House (NY), 1944. BUS. & PROF.: author; oil developer; vice pres., John C. Paige and Co. (general insurance), New York, NY. MIL.: capt., Company K, 15th NY National Guard (colored), 1917; maj., 369th Infantry, U.S. Army, 1919; col., Officers Reserve Corps; Croix de Guerre; Silver Star. MEM.: American Legion (founder); National Comm. to Keep America Out of Foreign Wars (1939); VFW; Soc. of the Cincinnati; National Grange. AWARDS: All American Tackle, Harvard U. MISC.: noted as an "isolationist." RES.: New York, NY.

FISH, HENRY. b. Feb 14, 1824, Montreal, Canada; d. May 26, 1876, Port Huron, MI; m. Frances S. Peets, Oct 19, 1846; c. Gertrude. POLIT. & GOV.: delegate, Prohibition Party National Convention, 1867, 1872 (temporary chm.); Prohibition Party candidate for gov. of MI, 1870, 1872; ***candidate for Prohibition Party nomination to vice presidency of the U.S., 1872***; Prohibition Party candidate for U.S. House (MI), 1873; member, Board of Education, Port Huron, MI. BUS. & PROF.: farmer, Mt. Clemens, MI, to 1848; teacher; publisher, *Enterprise*, Utica, MI, 1838; partner, A. and H. Fish (mercantile and lumber business), Port Huron, MI, 1848–76; temperance advocate. MEM.: Albion Coll. (trustee). REL.: Methodist Episcopal Church (pres., State Convention, 1871; delegate, General Conference, 1872). RES.: Port Huron, MI.

FISHER, LOUIS. b. Mar 20, 1913, Baltimore, MD; par. Abraham and Gussie (Lorber) Fisher; m. Anne Grill; m. 2d, (separated); c. Nina; Jack. EDUC.: high school. POLIT. & GOV.: Socialist Labor Party candidate for U.S. Senate (WI); Socialist Labor Party candidate for gov. of WI, 1940; state sec., IL Socialist Labor Party; Socialist Labor Party candidate for IL state sec. of state, 1944; Socialist Labor Party candidate for gov. of IL, 1948, 1952; Socialist Labor Party candidate for U.S. Senate (IL), 1956, 1960, 1968, 1970, 1974; delegate, Socialist Labor Party National Convention, 1956, 1960, 1964, 1968; ***Socialist Labor Party candidate for presidency of the U.S., 1972***. BUS. & PROF.: silk spotter, dry cleaning industry. MAILING ADDRESS: 1209 Sherwin Ave., Apt. 809, Chicago, IL 60626.

FISHER, PAUL CARY. b. Oct 10, 1913, Lebanon, KS; par. Carey Albert and Alice (Bales) Fisher; m. Monique Deschamps; c. Terry; Caroleen; Pomm; Marteen; Paul, Jr.; Morgan; Scott. EDUC.: grad., high school, 1931; KS Wesleyan U., 1931–34; B.S., KS State U., 1939. POLIT. & GOV.: ***candidate for Democratic nomination to presidency of the U.S., 1960, 1968, 1992***; candidate for Democratic nomination to U.S. House (NV), 1986. BUS. & PROF.: industrialist; author; economist; public accountant; practical engineer; inventor; pres., Fisher-Armour Manufacturing Co., 1950; pres., Fisher Pen Co., 1950–. MEM.: Phi Kappa Phi. WRITINGS: *Road to Freedom* (1960); *Tax Reform—America at the Brink* (1968). MAILING ADDRESS: 14226 Greenleaf St., Sherman Oaks, CA 91403.

FISHER, ROLLAND ERNEST. b. Jun 3, 1900, Newport, NE; par. Prentice E. and Anna (Cline) Fisher; m. Esther Postlewait; c. Edith Joy; Lois Joan Rogers; George Allan; Robert Parkhurst. EDUC.: public schools, Amelia, Chambers, and Newport, NE; A.A., Central Coll., McPherson, KS, 1920; Greenville (IL) Coll., 1924; A.B., U. of KS, 1928. POLIT. & GOV.: Prohibition Party candidate for KS State Senate, 1948; exec. sec., KS State Prohibition Party, 1948–50, state chm., 1962–68; Prohibition Party candidate for KS state sec. of state, 1950; member, exec. cmte., Prohibition Party National Cmte., vice chm., 1963–67; Prohibition Party candidate for KS state treas., 1958; Prohibition Party candidate for KS state auditor, 1958, 1960, 1962, 1964; Prohibition Party candidate for gov. of KS, 1966, 1972; ***candidate for Prohibition Party nomination to presidency of the U.S., 1968; Prohibition Party candidate for vice presidency of the U.S., 1968***. BUS. & PROF.: ordained minister, Free Methodist Church; pastor, Free Methodist Churches, 1928–47, 1950–64; evangelist, 1947–48, 1964–; ed., *The News Letter*, 1944–47, 1950–54; ed., *Kansas Statesman*, 1949–50; pastor, Coe Memorial Free Methodist Church, Kansas City, KS, 1953–60; pastor, Topeka Free Methodist Church, Topeka, KS, 1960–. MIL.: corp., U.S.M.C., 1920–23. MEM.: Topeka Ministers Alliance; National Holiness Assn.; Topeka Rescue Mission (dir.); National Assn. of Evangelicals; KS Free Methodist ministers Conference; Topeka Evangelical Ministers Fellowship; KS United Dry Forces; KS Free Methodist Loan Board (treas., 1954–). REL.: Free Methodist (sec., KS Conference, 1947–64). MAILING ADDRESS: 1132 Polk, Topeka, KS 66612.

FISK, CLINTON BOWEN. b. Dec 8, 1828, Griggsville, NY; d. Jul 9, 1890, New York, NY; par. Benjamin Bigford and Lydia (Aldrich) Fisk; m. Jeanette A. Crippen, Feb 20, 1850; c. Mary (Mrs. Park); one other. EDUC.: Albion Seminary, 1843; MI Central Coll., 1844; U. of ME. POLIT. & GOV.: Law candidate for justice of the peace, Coldwater, MI, 1855; appointed asst. commissioner of Bureau of Refugees, Freedmen and Abandoned Lands (KY and TN), Freedmen's Bureau, 1865; appointed member, Board of Indian Commissioners, 1874–90 (pres., 1881–90); *candidate for American Prohibition Party nomination to presidency of the U.S., 1884; candidate for Prohibition Party nomination to presidency of the U.S., 1884; candidate for Prohibition Party nomination to vice presidency of the U.S., 1884*; appointed member, MO State Comm. for Southwest-Pacific R.R.; Prohibition Party candidate for gov. of NJ, 1886; *Prohibition Party candidate for presidency of the U.S., 1888*. BUS. & PROF.: farmhand; teacher, to 1846; clerk, John Keyes Store, Manchester, MI, 1847; clerk, M. Hannahs and Son, Albion, MI, 1848; partner, Crippen and Kellogg, Coldwater, MI, 1848; partner, Crippen and Fisk (exchange bank); partner, Crippen Exchange Bank, Coldwater, MI, 1850; farmer, Coldwater, MI; western financial agent, Aetna Insurance Co., St. Louis, MO, 1858; vice pres., South Pacific R.R., 1867–77; banker; member, Board of Governors, Methodist Book Concern, 1876–90; pres., East TN Land Co.; treas., Missouri and Pacific R.R. Co. MIL.: officer, MO Home Guards; col., 33d MO Volunteers, 1862; brig. gen., U.S.V., 1862, maj. gen., 1864. MEM.: National Prohibition Bureau (pres.); National Temperance Soc.; Fisk U. (trustee); Dickinson Coll. (trustee); Pennington Seminary (trustee); Albion Coll. (trustee); Drew Theological Seminary (trustee); NY City Church Extension and Missionary Soc. (vice president). WRITINGS: *Plain counsel for Freedmen; Rules for Government of the Freedman's Court*. REL.: Methodist Episcopal Church (delegate, General Conference, 1874; delegate, Ecumenical Conference, 1881; Missionary Board). MISC.: founder, Fisk U., 1866. RES.: Seabright Station, NJ.

FITHIAN, EDWIN J. EDUC.: Doctor. POLIT. & GOV.: ***candidate for Prohibition Party nomination to vice presidency of the U.S., 1920***. RES.: Grove City, PA.

FITHIAN, GEORGE WASHINGTON. b. Jul 4, 1854, Willow Hill, IL; d. Jan 21, 1921, Memphis, TN. EDUC.: public schools; studied law. POLIT. & GOV.: elected prosecuting atty., Jasper Cty., IL, 1876–84; elected as a Democrat to U.S. House (IL), 1889–95; Democratic candidate for U.S. House (IL), 1894; ***candidate for Democratic nomination to vice presidency of the U.S., 1896***; appointed railroad and warehouse commissioner of IL, 1895–97; delegate, Dem. Nat'l. Conv., 1920. BUS. & PROF.: printer's apprentice, Mt. Carmel, IL; atty.; admitted to IL Bar, 1875; law practice, Newton, IL; farmer; stock raiser, Newton, IL; owner, cotton plantation, Falcon, MS. RES.: Newton, IL.

FITLER, EDWIN HENRY. b. Dec 2, 1825, Philadelphia, PA; d. May 31, 1896, Philadelphia, PA; par. William and Elizabeth (Wonderly) Fitler; m. Josephine R. Baker, 1950; c. Edwin Henry, Jr.; William W. EDUC.: studied law under Charles E. Lex. POLIT. & GOV.: appointed member, Board of Finance, Centennial Exposition, 1875–76; elected as a Republican mayor of Philadelphia, PA, 1887; ***candidate for Republican nomination to presidency of the U.S., 1888***. BUS. & PROF.: partner, George J. Weaver and Co., Philadelphia, 1848 (subsequently known as Weaver, Fitler and Co.; Philadelphia Cordage Works; Edwin H. Fitler and Co., 1870); pres., dir., National Bank of Northern Liberties; dir., North Pennsylvania R.R. MEM.: American Cordage Manufacturers Assn. (pres.); Union League (pres., 1890–93); Jefferson Medical Coll. (pres., Board of trustees, 1892); Philadelphia Art Club (founder). RES.: Philadelphia, PA.

FITTS, NANCY. POLIT. & GOV.: ***National Unity Party candidate for vice presidency of the U.S., 1980 (withdrew)***. Possibly same person identified as Nancy B. Flint (q.v.). MAILING ADDRESS: unknown.

FITZPATRICK, BENJAMIN. b. Jun 30, 1802, Greens Cty., GA; d. Nov 21, 1869, Wetumpka, AL; par. William and Anne (Phillips) Fitzpatrick; m. Sarah Terry Elmore, Jul 19, 1827; m. 2d, Aurelia Blassingame, Nov 29, 1846; c. Elmore Joseph; Phillips; Morris Martin; James Madison; Thomas Sumpter; John Archer; Aurelia; Benjamin. EDUC.: public schools; studied law under Nimrod E. Benson. POLIT. & GOV.: appointed deputy sheriff, Autauga Cty., AL; solicitor, Montgomery (AL) Judicial Circuit, 1822–23; presidential elector, Democratic Party, 1840; elected as a Democrat to gov. of AL, 1841–45; appointed and subsequently elected as a Democrat to U.S. Senate (AL), 1848–49, 1853–61 (pres. pro tempore, 1857–60); ***candidate for Democratic nomination to vice presidency of the U.S., 1856; candidate for Democratic nomination to presidency of the U.S., 1860; Democratic candidate for vice presidency of the U.S., 1860 (declined)***; elected pres., AL State Constitutional Convention, 1865. BUS. & PROF.: atty.; admitted to AL Bar, 1823; partner (with Henry Goldthwaite), law firm, Montgomery, AL, 1823–27; plantation owner, AL, 1827–69. RES.: Montgomery, AL.

FLAGMAN, GALE. POLIT. & GOV.: ***candidate for Farmer-Labor Party nomination to presidency of the U.S., 1928***. MAILING ADDRESS: Mason City, IA.

FLAHERTY, PETER F. b. Jun 24, 1925, Pittsburgh, PA; par. Pete and Anne (O'Toole) Flaherty; m. Nancy Houlihan, Aug 29, 1958; c. Shawn; Pete; Brian; Maggie; Greg. EDUC.: Mt. Mercy Coll.; WV U.; LL.B., U. of Notre Dame, 1951; M.P.A., U. of Pittsburgh, 1967. POLIT. & GOV.: Republican candidate for Mt. Lebanon (PA) School Board, 1952; appointed asst. atty., Allegheny Cty., PA, 1957–64; elected as a Democrat to Pittsburgh (PA) City Council, 1966–69; elected as a Democrat to mayor of Pittsburgh, 1970–77; Democratic candidate for U.S. Senate (PA), 1974, 1980; candidate for Democratic nomination to U.S. Senate (PA), 1976 (withdrew), 1988 (withdrew); delegate, Dem. Nat'l. Conv., 1976; ***candidate for Democratic nomination to vice presidency of the U.S., 1976***; appointed deputy atty. gen. of the U.S., 1977–78; Democratic candidate for gov. of PA, 1978; elected as a Democrat to Allegheny Cty. (PA) Comm., 198?–. BUS. & PROF.: timekeeper, Old Armstrong Cork Co.; atty.; admitted to FL Bar, 1966. MIL.: capt., U.S.A.A.C., 1942–46; Distinguished Unit Citation; Air Medal; two Battle Stars. MEM.: ABA; PA Bar Assn.; PA League of Cities (pres., 1972–73); National League of Cities (dir.). AWARDS: "Man of the Year," Pittsburgh Junior C. of C. REL.: R.C. MAILING ADDRESS: 5033 Castleman St., Pittsburgh, PA 15232.

FLEENOR, ROGER ALLEN "JOLLY ROGER." POLIT. & GOV.: ***candidate for American Independent Party nomination to presidency of the U.S., 1984; candidate for Libertarian Party nomination to presidency of the U.S., 1984; candidate for Peace and Freedom Party nomination to presidency of the U.S., 1984; candidate for Democratic nomination to presidency of the U.S., 1984; candidate for Republican nomination to presidency of the U.S., 1984; independent candidate for presidency of the U.S., 1984***. MAILING ADDRESS: unknown.

FLEMING, DAVID JAMES. POLIT. & GOV.: ***Visionary Constitutional Party candidate for presidency of the U.S., 1984***. MAILING ADDRESS: 1380 Garnel Ave., Suite E294, Pacific Beach, CA 92109.

FLETCHER, DUNCAN UPSHAW. b. Jan 6, 1859, Sumter Cty., GA; d. Jun 17, 1936, Washington, DC; par. Capt. Thomas Jefferson and Rebecca Ellen (McCowen) Fletcher; m. Anna Louise Paine, Jun 20, 1883; c. Ellen Abey (Mrs. Lionel Smith-Gordon); Louise Chapin (Mrs. Thomas Junior Kemp). EDUC.: Gordon Inst.; B.S., Vanderbilt U., 1880, studied law. POLIT. & GOV.: elected to Jacksonville (FL) City Council, 1887; elected as a Democrat to FL State House, 1893; elected as a Democrat to mayor of Jacksonville, 1893–95, 1901–03; chm., Board of Public Instruction, Duval Cty., FL, 1900–1906; chm., FL Democratic State Central Cmte., 1905–08; appointed and subsequently elected as a Democrat to U.S. Senate (FL), 1909–36; ***candidate for Democratic nomination to presidency of the U.S., 1928***; appointed member, U.S. Section, International High Comm.; appointed chm., U.S. Comm. on Rural Credits. BUS. & PROF.: atty.; admitted to FL Bar, 1881; partner, Fletcher and Wurts (law firm), Jacksonville, 1881. MEM.: John B. Stetson U. (trustee); St. Luke's Hospital Assn. (trustee); Children's Home Soc. of FL (vice pres.); Southern Commercial Congress (hon. pres., 1912–18); ABA; FL State Bar Assn.; Florida Soc. (pres.); Seminole Club; University Club; Gulf Coast Inland Waterways Assn. (pres., 1908); Mississippi to Atlantic Waterway Assn. (pres.); National Rivers and Harbors Congress; Jacksonville Public Library (trustee); Masons; Odd Fellows; Phi Delta Theta. HON. DEG.: LL.D., John B. Stetson U., 1921; LL.D., U.

of FL, 1933. REL.: Unitarian (vice pres., American Unitarian Assn.). RES.: Jacksonville, FL.

FLINT, NANCY B. POLIT. & GOV.: ***National Unity Party candidate for vice presidency of the U.S., 1980***. Possibly same person identified as Nancy Fitts (q.v.). MAILING ADDRESS: unknown.

FLOWER, ROSWELL PETTIBONE. b. Aug 7, 1835, Theresa, NY; d. May 12, 1899, Eastport, Long Island, NY; par. Nathan Monroe and Mary Ann (Boyle) Flower; m. Sarah M. Woodruff, December 26, 1859; c. Emma (Mrs. John B. Taylor). EDUC.: grad., Theresa (NY) H.S., 1851. POLIT. & GOV.: appointed asst. postmaster, Watertown, NY, 1854–60; chm., Jefferson Cty. (NY) Democratic Party; chm., NY State Democratic Party, 1877; elected as a Democrat to U.S. House (NY), 1881–83, 1889–91; candidate for Democratic nomination to gov. of NY, 1882; ***candidate for Democratic nomination to presidency of the U.S., 1884, 1888, 1896***; appointed pres., New York Subway Comm., 1886; Democratic candidate for lt. gov. of NY, 1888 (declined); elected as a Democrat to gov. of NY, 1893–95; chm. pro tempore, National (Gold Democratic) Party National Convention, 1896. BUS. & PROF.: bricklayer; teacher; dry goods merchant, Philadelphia, PA; employee, hardware store, Watertown, NY; jewelry; partner (with F. C. Benedict), brokerage firm, New York, NY; owner, Roswell P. Flower and Co. (banking and brokerage), New York, 1869; dir., Duluth and Iron Range R.R.; dir., Chicago, Rock Island and Pacific R.R.; dir., Minnesota Iron Co.; dir., New York Security and Trust Co.; dir., H. H. Babcock Co.; dir., Municipal Gas Co. of Albany; manufacturer. MEM.: New York Stock Exchange (1873); Manhattan Club; Democratic Club; Press Club; United Service Club; New England Soc. HON. DEG.: LL.D., Lawrence U., 1893. REL.: Presb. RES.: Watertown, NY.

FLOYD, JOHN. b. Apr 24, 1783, Floyd Station, KY; d. Aug 16, 1837, Sweetsprings, VA; par. John and Jane (Buchanan) Floyd; m. Letita Preston, May 1804; c. John Buchanan; eight others. EDUC.: Dickinson Coll.; M.D., U. of PA, 1806. POLIT. & GOV.: appointed justice of the peace, VA, 1807; elected as a Democrat to VA State House of Delegates, 1814–15; elected as a Democrat to U.S. House (VA), 1817–29; elected as a Democrat to gov. of VA, 1830–34; ***independent candidate for presidency of the U.S., 1832***. BUS. & PROF.: surgeon; medical practice, Christiansburg, VA. MIL.: maj., VA Militia, 1807–12, surgeon, 1812, brig. gen., 1812. REL.: R.C. (Convert). MISC.: received Virginia's 11 electoral votes for presidency of the U.S., 1832. RES.: Sweetsprings, VA.

FLYNN, RICHARD E. "BUD." POLIT. & GOV.: ***candidate for Democratic nomination to presidency of the U.S., 1976.*** MAILING ADDRESS: 11133 Burin Ave., Inglewood, CA 90304.

FLYNN, RICHARD FRANCIS. c. daughter. POLIT. & GOV.: ***candidate for Democratic nomination to presidency of the U.S., 1992***. BUS. & PROF.: author; counselor. MAILING ADDRESS: #194 Richmond Terrace, St. George, Staten Island, NY 10301.

FLYNN, WILLIAM SMITH. b. Aug 14, 1885, Providence, RI; d. Apr 13, 1966, Boston, MA; par. James A. and Elizabeth J. (Kelley) Flynn; m. Virginia M. Goodwin, Sep 22, 1931; c. none. EDUC.: A.B., Holy Cross Coll., 1907; LL.B., Georgetown U., 1910. POLIT. & GOV.: elected as a Democrat to RI State House, 1912–14, 1917–22 (Democratic minority leader, 1919–22); elected as a Democrat to gov. of RI, 1923–25; delegate, Dem. Nat'l. Conv., 1924, 1928, 1932, 1936, 1940; ***candidate for Democratic nomination to vice presidency of the U.S., 1924***; Democratic candidate for U.S. Senate (RI), 1924; appointed chm., RI Federal Advisory Board, Public Works Administration, 1933–34; member, Providence (RI) Charter Revision Comm., 1939; presidential elector, Democratic Party, 1940; div. dir., Providence Civilian Defense Council, 1942–43. BUS. & PROF.: purser, ticket agent, Providence Steamship Co.; atty.; admitted to RI Bar, 1911; admitted to Federal Bar, 1913; law practice, Providence, RI; sec., dir., United Transit Co. MEM.: Rhode Island Hospital (trustee); St. Joseph's Hospital (trustee); Butler Hospital (trustee); ABA; RI Bar Assn.; American Irish Hist. Soc.; Soc. of the Friendly Sons of St. Patrick; Sons of Irish Kings; Rhode Island Hist. Soc.; Elks; Eagles; Knights of Columbus; Pen and Pencil Club; Pomham Club. HON. DEG.: LL.D., Holy Cross Coll., 1923; LL.D., Georgetown U., 1924. REL.: R.C. RES.: Providence, RI.

FLYNT, LARRY CLAXTON. b. Nov 1, 1942, Magoffin Cty., KY; par. Larry Claxton and Edith (Arnett) Flynt; m. Althea Leasure, Aug 21, 1976; c. Tonya; Lisa; Teresa; Larry Claxton III. EDUC.: public schools, Saylersville, KY. POLIT. & GOV.: ***candidate for Republican nomination to presidency of the U.S., 1984***. BUS. & PROF.: factory worker, General Motors Corp., Dayton, OH, 1958, 1964–65; owner, operator, Hustler Clubs, Dayton, Columbus, Toledo, Akron, and Cleveland, OH, 1970–74; owner, publisher, *Hustler Magazine*, Los Angeles, CA, 1974–; owner, publisher, *Chic Magazine*, Los Angeles, CA, 1974–; publisher, *Gentleman's Companion*; owner, Flynt Distributing Co., Los Angeles, CA, 1976. MIL.: U.S. Army, 1958; U.S. Navy, 1959–64. REL.: Born-Again Christian. MISC.: noted as publisher of pornographic magazines; became "Born-Again Christian" under instruction of Ruth Carter Stapleton; obtained controversial sex tapes involving associates of Ronald Reagan (q.v.); obtained video tapes of John DeLorean in notorious drug scandal. MAILING ADDRESS: 2029 Century Park East, Suite 3800, Los Angeles, CA 90067.

FOGGYBOTTOM, MRS. (aka JOAN CUSHING). POLIT. & GOV.: ***Cocktail Party candidate for presi-***

dency of the U.S., 1988 (satire effort). BUS. & PROF.: character in musical presented at OMNI-Shoreham Hotel Marquee Cabaret Lounge, Washington, DC: played by Joan Cushing. MAILING ADDRESS: 1275 K St., N.W., Suite 800, Washington, DC 20005.

FOLK, JOSEPH WINGATE. b. Oct 28, 1869, Brownsville, TN; d. May 28, 1923, New York, NY; par. Henry Bate and Martha Cornelia (Estes) Folk; m. Gertrude Glass, Nov 10, 1896; c. none. EDUC.: LL.B., Vanderbilt U., 1890. POLIT. & GOV.: elected as a Democrat, circuit atty., St. Louis, MO, 1900–1904; elected as a Democrat to gov. of MO, 1905–09; candidate for Democratic nomination to U.S. Senate (MO), 1908; ***candidate for Democratic nomination to vice presidency of the U.S., 1908; candidate for Democratic nomination to presidency of the U.S., 1912***; appointed solicitor, U.S. Dept. of State, 1913; appointed chief counsel, Interstate Commerce Comm., 1914–18; Democratic candidate for U.S. Senate (MO), 1918. BUS. & PROF.: atty.; admitted to TN Bar, 1890; partner (with Henry Bate Folk), law firm, Brownsville, TN, 1890–94; partner (with J. W. E. Moore), law firm, St. Louis, MO, 1894–97; partner (with Frank M. Estes), law firm, St. Louis; lecturer, 1909–10; law practice, Washington, DC. MEM.: Jefferson Club (founder; pres., 1898–99); Lincoln Farm Assn. (pres., 1909–16); ABA; DC Bar Assn.; American Soc. of International Law; National Press Assn.; St. Louis C. of C.; Washington C. of C.; SAR; Masons; Knights of Pythias; Kappa Alpha; Mercantile Club. HON. DEG.: LL.D., U. of MO, 1905; LL.D., William Jewell Coll., 1906; LL.D., Drury Coll., 1907; LL.D., Westminster Coll., 1907; LL.D., Southwestern Baptist U., 1908; LL.D., Baylor U., 1919. REL.: Bapt. RES.: St. Louis, MO.

FOLSOM, JAMES ELISHA. b. Oct 9, 1908, Farmers Acad., Coffee Cty., AL; d. Nov 21, 1987, Cullman, AL; par. Joshua M. and Eulala (Dunnavant) Folsom; m. Sara Carnley; m. 2d, Jamelle Dorothy Moore, May 6, 1948; c. Rachael; Melissa; James Elisha, Jr.; Joshua; five others. EDUC.: U. of AL; Howard Coll.; WA U. POLIT. & GOV.: Northern AL Administrator, WPA, 1933–36; candidate for Democratic nomination to U.S. House (AL), 1936, 1938; candidate for Democratic nomination to gov. of AL, 1942, 1962, 1966, 1970, 1974, 1978, 1982; delegate, Dem. Nat'l. Conv., 1944; elected as a Democrat to gov. of AL, 1947–51, 1955–59; ***candidate for Democratic nomination to presidency of the U.S., 1948 (withdrew)***; candidate for Democratic nomination to U.S. Senate (AL), 1958. BUS. & PROF.: insurance exec., 1937–46. MIL.: U.S. Army, 1943; U.S. Merchant Marine, 1944. MISC.: known as "Big Jim" Folsom (6 feet, 8 inches tall). RES.: Montgomery, AL.

FONG, HIRAM LEONG. b. Oct 1, 1907, Honolulu, HI; par. Lum and Chai Ha Shee Lum Fong; m. Ellyn Lo, Jun 25, 1938; c. Hiram Leong; Rodney; Merie Ellen; Marvin Allan. EDUC.: St. Louis Coll.; B.A. (cum laude), U. of HI, 1930; LL.B., Harvard U., 1935. POLIT. & GOV.: deputy atty., City and Cty. of Honolulu, HI, 1935–38; elected as a Republican to HI Territorial House, 1938–54 (Vice Speaker, 1944–48; Speaker, 1948–54); vice pres., HI State Constitutional Convention, 1950; delegate, Rep. Nat'l. Conv., 1952, 1956, 1960, 1968, 1972; elected as a Republican to U.S. Senate (HI), 1959–77; U.S. delegate, Argentine Independence Celebration, 1960; U.S. delegate, Canadian-U.S. Interparliamentary Convention, 1961, 1965, 1967, 1968; ***candidate for Republican nomination to presidency of the U.S., 1964, 1968***; U.S. delegate, Interparliamentary Union Convention, 1966, 1974; U.S. delegate, Mexican- U.S. Interparliamentary Conference, 1968; appointed member, Comm. on Revision of the Federal Court Appellate System, 1975–. BUS. & PROF.: clerk, supply dept., U.S. Navy Yard, Pearl Harbor, HI, 1924–27; chief clerk, suburban water system, City and Cty. of Honolulu, HI, 1930–32; atty.; admitted to HI Bar, 1935; partner, Fong, Miho, Choy and Robinson (law firm), Honolulu, HI, 1935–; pres., Ocean View Cemetery Ltd., 1938; pres., chm. of the board, Market City Ltd., 1945; pres., chm. of the board, Finance Factors, 1952; pres., chm. of the board, Finance Realty Co., 1953; pres., chm. of the board, Grand Pacific Life Insurance Co., 1957; pres., chm. of the board, Finance Investment Co., 1957; pres., chm. of the board, Finance Factors Building Ltd., 1957; pres., chm. of the board, Finance Home Builders Ltd., 1958; pres., chm. of the board, Finance Factors Foundation Ltd., 1958; chm. of the board, Highway Construction Co. Ltd.; banana farmer; rancher. MIL.: 1st lt., maj., U.S.A.A.F., 1942–44; col., U.S. Air Force Reserves. MEM.: BSA; Kalihi Community Improvement Club; Downtown Improvement Club; YMCA; Palolo Chinese Old Men's Home (trustee); Chinese Students' Alliance (Building Fund); Hall of Fame of Great Americans (elector, 1959–); Bar Assn. of HI; Harvard Law School Assn.; Phi Beta Kappa; Tu Chiang Sheh; U. of HI Alumni Assn.; McKinley Alumni Assn.; American Legion; VFW; Warriors of the Pacific; Hawaiian Chinese Civic Assn.; Chinese C. of C.; Chinese American Club; Harvard Club of HI; Commercial Associates; Honolulu C. of C.; U.S. Military Acad. (Board of Visitors, 1971–); U.S. Naval Acad. (Board of Visitors, 1974–). AWARDS: Award for Outstanding Service to Brotherhood, National Conference of Christians and Jews, 1960; Meritorious Service Citation, National Assn. of Retired Civil Employees, 1963; Horatio Alger Award, 1970; Outstanding Service Award, Japanese American Citizens League, 1970; Golden Plate Award, American Acad. of Achievement, 1971; Outstanding Service Award, Organization of Chinese Americans, 1973; award, National Soc. of Daughters of the Founders and Patriots of America, 1974; Certificate, Pacific Asian World, 1974. HON. DEG.: LL.D., U. of HI, 1953; LL.D., Tufts Coll., 1960; LL.D., Lafayette Coll., 1960; LL.D., Lynchburg Coll., 1970; LL.D., Lincoln U., 1971; LL.D., U. of Guam, 1975; LL.D., St. Johns U., 1976; LL.D., CA-Western School of Law, 1976; L.H.D., Long Island U., 1968. REL.: Congregationalist. MAILING ADDRESS: 1102 Alewa Dr., Honolulu, HI 96817.

FOOTE, CHARLES C. b. Mar 30, 1811, Olean, NY; d. May 3, 1891, Detroit, MI; m. Clarissa C. Clark, Sep 10, 1840;

m. 2d, Hannah E. Merritt, Aug 3, 1858; c. Charles A.; Gertrude H. (Mrs. George R. Milton); James C. EDUC.: grad., Oberlin Coll., 1840; Fairfield Medical School. POLIT. & GOV.: ***candidate for National Liberty Party nomination to presidency of the U.S., 1848; National Liberty Party candidate for vice presidency of the U.S., 1848***; American Party candidate for gov. of MI, 1882; active in Prohibition Party. BUS. & PROF.: minister; ordained, 1840; pastor, Maume, OH; pastor, Bergen, NY; pastor, Mt. Clemens, MI; pastor, White Lake, MI; agent, Refuge Home Soc., Detorit, MI, 1854; agent, Freedman's Aid Soc., c. 1866; chaplain, Detroit (MI) House of Correction, 1869–73; chaplain, Seaman's Bethel. WRITINGS: *American Women Responsible for the Existence of American Slavery* (1846). RES.: White Lake, MI.

FORAKER, JOSEPH BENSON. b. Jul 5, 1846, Rainsboro, OH; d. May 10, 1917, Cincinnati, OH; par. Thomas S. and Margaret (Reece) Foraker; m. Julia Bundy, Oct 4, 1870; c. Arthur; Joseph Benson, Jr.; Florence Louise; Julia B.; one other. EDUC.: Salem Acad.; OH Wesleyan U.; B.A., Cornell U., 1869; studied law. POLIT. & GOV.: auditor, Highland Cty., OH; elected judge, Superior Court, Cincinnati, OH, 1879–82; Republican candidate for gov. of OH, 1883, 1889; delegate, Rep. Nat'l. Conv., 1884, 1888, 1892, 1896, 1900, 1904; ***candidate for Republican nomination to vice presidency of the U.S., 1884***; elected as a Republican to gov. of OH, 1885–89; chm., OH State Republican Convention, 1886, 1890, 1896, 1900; ***candidate for Republican nomination to presidency of the U.S., 1888, 1908***; elected as a Republican to U.S. Senate (OH), 1897–1909; ***Lincoln Party candidate for presidency of the U.S., 1908 (declined)***; Republican candidate for U.S. Senate (OH), 1909; candidate for Republican nomination to U.S. Senate (OH), 1914. BUS. & PROF.: atty.; admitted to OH Bar, 1869; law practice, Cincinnati, OH, 1869–1917. MIL.: pvt., sgt., 1st lt., brev. capt., 89th OH Infantry, U.S.V., 1862–65. WRITINGS: *Notes of a Busy Life* (1916). REL.: Methodist Episc. RES.: Cincinnati, OH.

FORBES, RALPH. married; c. daughter. POLIT. & GOV.: candidate for Republican nomination to lt. gov. of AR, 1986; state chm., Arkansas Populist Party, 1987; ***candidate for Populist Party nomination to presidency of the U.S., 1988; candidate for Populist Party nomination to vice presidency of the U.S., 1988***. MAILING ADDRESS: AR.

FORD, GERALD RUDOLPH "JERRY," JR. (nee LESLIE LYNCH KING, JR.). b. Jul 14, 1913, Omaha, NE; par. Leslie Lynch and Dorothy Ayer (Gardner) King (raised by mother and stepfather, Gerald Rudolff Ford); m. Elizabeth "Betty" Bloomer, Oct 15, 1948; c. Michael Gerald; John Gardner; Steven Meigs; Susan Elizabeth. EDUC.: B.A., U. of MI, 1935; LL.B., Yale U., 1941. POLIT. & GOV.: delegate, Kent Cty. (MI) Republican Convention, 1946, 1948; delegate, MI State Republican Convention, 1946, 1948; elected as a Republican to U.S. House (MI), 1948–73 (minority leader, 1965–73); U.S. delegate, Interparliamentary Union, 1959, 1961; ***candidate for Republican nomination to vice presidency of the U.S., 1960***; delegate, Rep. Nat'l. Conv., 1964, 1968 (permanent chm.), 1972 (permanent chm.); member, Rep. Nat'l. Cmte., 1972–73; ***appointed as a Republican to vice presidency of the U.S., 1973–74; succeeded to the presidency of the U.S., 1974–77; Republican candidate for presidency of the U.S., 1976; candidate for Republican nomination to presidency of the U.S., 1980 (declined)***. BUS. & PROF.: atty.; admitted to MI Bar, 1941; partner, Buchen and Ford (law firm), Grand Rapids, MI, 1941–49. MIL.: lt. commander, U.S. Navy, 1942–46. MEM.: ABA; MI Bar Assn.; Grand Rapids Bar Assn.; Delta Kappa Epsilon; Phi Delta Phi; Masons; University Club; Peninsular Club; Bilderberg Group Conference, 1962; VFW; American Legion; Army-Navy Club. AWARDS: Distinguished Service Award, Grand Rapids Junior C. of C., 1948; one of ten "Outstanding Young Men in the U.S.," National Junior C. of C., 1950; Silver Anniversary All-American, *Sports Illustrated*, 1959; Distinguished Congressional Service Award, APSA, 1961; George Washington Award, American Good Government Soc., 1966; National Football Foundation and Hall of Fame Award, 1972. HON. DEG.: LL.D., MI State U., 1965; LL.D., Albion Coll., 1965; LL.D., Spring Arbor Coll., 1965; LL.D., Western MI U., 1973; LL.D., Grand Valley State Coll., 1973; LL.D., Buena Vista Coll.; LL.D., Grove City Coll.; LL.D., Parsons Coll.; LL.D., American International Coll. WRITINGS: *A Time to Heal* (1979). REL.: Episc. MAILING ADDRESS: P.O. Box 927, Rancho Mirage, CA 92270.

FORD, HENRY. b. Jul 30, 1863, Dearborn, MI; d. Apr 7, 1947, Dearborn, MI; par. William and Mary (Litogot) Ford; m. Clara Jane Bryant, Apr 11, 1888; c. Edsel Bryant. EDUC.: public schools, to 1878. POLIT. & GOV.: ***candidate for Prohibition Party nomination to presidency of the U.S., 1916, 1920; candidate for Democratic nomination to presidency of the U.S., 1916, 1924; candidate for Republican nomination to presidency of the U.S., 1916, 1936***; appointed member, Wage Umpire Board, 1918; Democratic candidate for U.S. Senate (MI), 1918; ***candidate for Farmer-Labor Party nomination to presidency of the U.S., 1920; candidate for Prohibition Party nomination to vice presidency of the U.S., 1920 (withdrew); Independent Progressive Party candidate for presidency of the U.S., 1924; American Home Progressive Party candidate for presidency of the U.S., 1928 (declined); George Washington Party candidate for presidency of the U.S., 1940 (declined)***. BUS. & PROF.: industrialist; machine-shop apprentice, James Flower Brothers and Co., Detroit, MI; machine-shop apprentice, Detroit Dry Dock Co., Detroit, MI, 1879–84; operator, sawmill; chief engineer, Edison Illuminating Co., 1887; founder, chief engineer, Detroit Automobile Co., 1899–1901; founder, Henry Ford Co.; founder, vice pres., Ford Motor Co., 1903–06, pres., 1906–19, 1943–47. MEM.: Ford Foundation (cofounder, 1936); Soc. of Automotive Engineers; Detroit Board of Commerce; Detroit Club; Automobile Club of America; Ford Hospital (founder). AWARDS: Gold Medal, Grand Order of the Great Eagle (Germany, 1938); James Watt International Medal, 1938; Mark Twain Medal, 1942; citation, Kosciusko Foundation; citation, Copernican Quadricentennial National Cmte., 1943; Distinguished Service Medal, American Legion, 1944; Gold Medal, American Petroleum Inst., 1946. HON. DEG.: D.E., Rensselaer Polytechnic Inst., 1925; D.Eng., U. of MI, 1926; LL.D., Colgate U., 1935; D.Eng., MI State Coll., 1936; LL.D., National U. of Ireland, 1927. WRITINGS: *My Life and Work* (1925); *Today and Tomorrow* (1926); *Edison as I Knew Him* (1930); *Moving Forward* (1931). MISC.: pioneered development of assembly line production techniques, profit-sharing plans, and other industrial innovations; chartered Oskar II (known as the "Ford Peace Ship") to sail to Europe to halt World War I by neutral arbitration. RES.: Dearborn, MI.

FORD, JAMES WILLIAM. b. December 22, 1893, Pratt City, AL; d. Jun 21, 1957, New York, NY; m. 2d, Reva Ford; c. three sons. EDUC.: grad., Fisk U. POLIT. & GOV.: delegate, World Congress of the Communist Internationale, 1928; ***Communist Party candidate for vice presidency of the U.S., 1932, 1936, 1940***; Communist Party candidate for U.S. House (NY), 1934. BUS. & PROF.: coal miner; blacksmith; furnace laborer; railroad worker; employee, U.S. Post Office, Chicago, IL (dismissed, 1928). MIL.: U.S. Army, 1917; denied entrance into U.S. Army Radio School; joined French forces; served with distinction, WWI. MEM.: National Negro Congress; National Cmte. to Defend Negro Leadership in Brooklyn (exec. dir.); American Negro Labor Congress (founder, 1925); Trade Union Unity League (chm., Negro Dept.); League for Struggle for Negro Rights; International Labor Union Congress (delegate, 1928); International Trade Union Congress of Negro Workers (first sec.); U.S. Congress Against War Cmte.; Negro Labor Victory Cmte. (organizer). MISC.: arrested in NY for demonstrating against U.S. intervention in Haiti, 1929. RES.: New York, NY.

FORD, JOEL JUDSON. POLIT. & GOV.: ***independent candidate for presidency of the U.S., 1988***. MAILING ADDRESS: 1003 State Line Rd., Ringgold, GA 37412.

FORD, RAYMOND. POLIT. & GOV.: ***candidate for Populist Party nomination to presidency of the U.S., 1984***. BUS. & PROF.: labor organizer, NV. MAILING ADDRESS: NV.

FORD, THOMAS H. POLIT. & GOV.: delegate, American (Know-Nothing) Party National Convention, 1855; elected as a Republican to lt. gov. of OH; ***candidate for Republican nomination to vice presidency of the U.S., 1856***. RES.: OH.

FORD, WILLIAM CLAY. b. Mar 14, 1925, Detroit, MI; par. Edsel Bryant and Eleanor (Clay) Ford; m. Martha Firestone; c. Martha (Mrs. Peter Morse); Sheila; William Clay, Jr.; Elizabeth. EDUC.: Detroit U. School, Grosse Pointe, MI; Hotchkiss School, Lakeville, CT; B.S., Yale U., 1949. POLIT. & GOV.: ***independent (Committee for a Constitutional Presidency) candidate for vice presidency of the U.S., 1976 (withdrew)***. BUS. & PROF.: dir., vice pres. for product design, Ford Motor Co.; owner, pres., Detroit Lions, Inc.; dir., Manufacturers National Bank of Detroit. MIL.: U.S. Navy, 1943–45. MEM.: Masons (Knights Templar); Edison Inst. (chm.); Hotchkiss School (trustee); Henry Ford Hospital (sec.-treas.); Edsel B. Ford Inst. for Medical Research (pres.); Michigan Heart Assn.; Eisenhower Medical Center (trustee); National Tennis Hall of Fame (dir.); United Foundation of Detroit (dir.). REL.: Protestant Episc. MAILING ADDRESS: Ford Motor Co., P.O. Box 2110, Dearborn, MI 48123.

FOSDICK, RAYMOND BLAINE. b. Jun 9, 1883, Buffalo, NY; d. Jul 18, 1972, Newton, CT; par. Frank Sheldon and Annie Inez (Weaver) Fosdick; m. Winifred Finlay, December 2, 1910; m. 2d, Elizabeth Richardson Miner, Apr 21, 1936; c. Susan; Raymond Blaine, Jr. EDUC.: Colgate U., 1901–03; A.B., A.M., Princeton U., 1905; LL.B., NY Law School, 1908. POLIT. & GOV.: appointed first asst. to New York (NY) Commissioner of Accounts, 1907–09; appointed asst. corporation counsel, New York, 1909–10; New York commissioner of accounts, 1910–12; appointed comptroller, auditor, Dem. Nat'l. Cmte., 1912; elected member, New York Board of Education, 1915–16; appointed personal representative of U.S. sec. of war to Mexican border, 1916; appointed chm., U.S. Comm. on Training Camp Activities; appointed undersec. gen., League of Nations, 1919–20; ***candidate for Democratic nomination to vice presidency of the U.S., 1924***. BUS. & PROF.: law clerk, office of Richard Welling; mathematics teacher, Harrison, NY; atty.; admitted to NY Bar, 1908; assoc. ed., *American Journal of Criminal Law and Criminology*, 1914; civilian aide to Gen. John J. Pershing (q.v.), 1919; founder, League of Nations Press Bureau, 1920; partner, Curtis, Fosdick and Belknap (law firm), New York, 1920–36; pres., Rockefeller Foundation, 1936–48; pres., General Education Board, 1936–48. MEM.: American Phil. Soc.; Rockefeller Inst. for Medical Research; Rockefeller Foundation; Laura Spelman Rockefeller Memorial; International Education Board (dir.); China Medical Board (dir.); Spelman Fund (dir.); League of Nations Non-Partisan Assn. (founder, 1923); President's Birthday Ball Comm. for Infantile Paralysis; Danbury Hospital (trustee); Cyrenius H. Booth Library (trustee); Newtown Forest Assn. (trustee); Princeton U. (trustee); American Museum for Political and Social Science; American Inst. of International Law; National Inst. of Social Sciences; ABA; Phi Beta Kappa; Delta Upsilon; Coffee House Club; Whitehall Club; City Club; Century Club; American Club of London; Authors Club of London; Union Interalliee; Boudinot Fellow. AWARDS: Distinguished Service Medal, 1918; Legion of Honor (France, 1949); Woodrow Wilson Award, Woodrow Wilson Foundation, 1962. HON. DEG.: LL.D., Colgate U., 1925; LL.D., CO Coll., 1925; LL.D., Princeton U., 1948; LL.D., Amherst U., 1948; LL.D.,

Columbia U., 1949; LL.D., Wesleyan U., 1949; LL.D., U. of Edinburgh, 1949; LL.D., Swarthmore Coll., 1950; LL.D., Dartmouth Coll., 1951. WRITINGS: *Princeton Verses* (ed., 1904); *European Police Systems* (1914); *American Police Systems* (1920); *Keeping Our Fighters Fit* (1918); *The Old Savage in the New Civilization* (1928); *Toward Liquor Control* (coauthor, 1934); *The Story of the Rockefeller Foundation* (1952); *Within Our Power* (1952); *Annals of the Fosdick Family* (1953); *John D. Rockefeller, Jr.: A Portrait* (1956); *Chronicle of a Generation* (1958); *Adventure in Giving: The Story of the General Education Board* (1962); *Letters on the League of Nations* (1966); *The League and the United Nations After Fifty Years* (1972). RES.: Newtown, CT.

FOSS, EUGENE NOBLE. b. Sep 24, 1858, West Berkshire, VT; d. Sep 13, 1939, Jamaica Plain, MA; par. George Edmund and Marcia Cordelia (Noble) Foss; m. Lilla R. Sturtevant, Jun 12, 1884; c. Noble; Benjamin Sturtevant; Esther (Mrs. George Gordon Moore); Helen (Mrs. William W. Hobbs). EDUC.: Franklin County Acad.; U. of VT, 1877–79, A.B., 1901. POLIT. & GOV.: Republican candidate for U.S. House (MA), 1902; delegate, Rep. Nat'l. Conv., 1904; Democratic candidate for lt. gov. of MA, 1909; elected as a Democrat to U.S. House (MA), 1910–11; elected as a Democrat to gov. of MA, 1911–13; independent candidate for gov. of MA, 1912; ***candidate for Democratic nomination to presidency of the U.S., 1912***; candidate for Republican nomination to gov. of MA, 1915; ***candidate for Prohibition Party nomination to presidency of the U.S., 1916***; Democratic candidate for gov. of MA, 1919, 1922; candidate for Democratic nomination to U.S. Senate (MA), 1930. BUS. & PROF.: traveling salesman, St. Albans Manufacturing Co.; mgr., B. F. Sturtevant Co. (iron and steel manufacturers), Boston, MA, 1882–84, treas., gen. mgr., 1884; pres., Becker-Brainerd Milling Machine Co., 1901–39; dir., Massachusetts Electric Co.; dir., Mexican Central Railway Co.; dir., U.S. Smelting, Refining and Mining Co.; pres., Burgess Mills; dir., First National Bank; dir., Manhattan Railway Co.; dir., Chicago Junction R.R.; dir., Union Stock Yards Co.; dir., Hyde Park National Bank; pres., Maverick Mills; vice pres., Real Estate Exchange of MA; dir., Boston Land Co.; dir., American Loan and Trust Co.; dir., American Pneumatic Service Co.; dir., Bridgewater Water Co.; dir., Brooklyn Heights R.R. Co.; dir., Brooklyn Rapid Transit Co.; dir., pres., Mead-Morrisson Manufacturing Co. MEM.: U. of VT (trustee); Beacon Soc. (dir.); New Algonquin Club; Boston Merchants Assn. (dir.); Newton Theological Institution (trustee); Boston C. of C. (dir.); Colby Coll. (trustee); Hebron Acad. (trustee); VT Acad. (trustee); Boston Baptist Hospital (trustee); Moody School (trustee); Boston YMCA (trustee); Robert B. Brigham Hospital (dir.); Boston City Club; Eliot Club; New England Shoe and Leather Assn. (dir.); Boston Art Club; Exchange Club; Jamaica Club; Highland Club. HON. DEG.: LL.D., U. of VT, 1912. REL.: Bapt. RES.: Jamaica Plain, MA.

FOSS, JOSEPH JACOB "JOE." b. Apr 17, 1915, Sioux Falls, SD; par. Frank Ole and Mary Esther (Lacey) Foss; m. June Esther Shakstad, Aug 9, 1942; m. 2d, Donna Wild Hall; c. Cheryl June; Joseph Jacob, Jr.; Mary Jo; Joseph Frank. EDUC.: Sioux Falls Coll., 1934–35; Augustana Coll., 1936–37; B.A., U. of SD, 1940. POLIT. & GOV.: elected as a Republican to SD State House, 1948–53; candidate for Republican nomination to gov. of SD, 1950; elected as a Republican to gov. of SD, 1955–59; ***candidate for Republican nomination to presidency of the U.S., 1956***; Republican candidate for U.S. House (SD), 1958; appointed member, American Battle Monuments Comm. BUS. & PROF.: co-owner, Foss Flying Service, Sioux Falls, SD, 1945–53; co-owner, Foss Motor Co., Sioux Falls, SD, 1953–55; appointed commissioner, American Football League, 1960–66; dir., KLM Royal Dutch Airlines. MIL.: 2d lt., maj., U.S.M.C., 1940–45; col., U.S. Air Force, Korean War; lt. col., brig. gen., SD Air National Guard; Silver Star; Bronze Star; Purple Heart; Medal of Honor, 1943; shot down 26 enemy aircraft during World War II. MEM.: National Assn. for Crippled Children and Adults (dir.); American Legion (vice chm., Comm. on Aeronautics); South Dakota Crippled Children and Adults Assn. (dir.; pres.); Easter Seal Campaign (national chm., 1956); Air Force Assn. (national dir.); National Governors' Conference (dir., 1956-957); VFW; Elks; Masons (Shriner); Kiwanis; Sioux Falls Club; U.S. Air Force Acad. (dir.); Sigma Alpha Epsilon; Outdoor Writers Assn.; NRA (pres.). AWARDS: Beaver Award, BSA. REL.: Methodist (steward). MAILING ADDRESS: P.O. Box 566, Scottsdale, AZ 85252.

FOSTER, GARY STEVEN. POLIT. & GOV.: independent candidate for U.S. House (IL), 1988; ***independent candidate for presidency of the U.S., 1988***. MAILING ADDRESS: 185 North Wabash Ave., Suite 1212, Chicago, IL 60601.

FOSTER, WILLIAM EDWARD (aka WILLIAM ZEBULON FOSTER). b. Feb 25, 1881, Taunton, MA; d. Sep 1, 1961, Moscow, U.S.S.R.; par. James and Elizabeth (McLaughlin) Foster; m. Esther Abramovich, Mar 23, 1918; c. Sylvia Kolko (stepdaughter); David (stepson). EDUC.: public schools, Philadelphia, PA, to 1891. POLIT. & GOV.: ***Communist (Workers) Party candidate for presidency of the U.S., 1924, 1928, 1932***; chm., Workers Party, 1924; gen. sec., Communist Party, c. 1930; Communist Party candidate for gov. of NY, 1930; national chm., Communist Party, 1932–57, chm. emeritus, 1957–61. BUS. & PROF.: sculptor's apprentice, 1892; employee, American Type Founders Co., 1895–98; employee, fertilizer industry, 1898–1900; logger; lumberjack; dockworker; farmhand; trolley car conductor; metal worker; merchant seaman; hobo; shepherd; railroad worker; canvasman; author; union organizer, AFL, 1916–21; organized packinghouse workers, 1917–18; organized steel strike, 1919; union organizer, U.M.W. of A., 1926–28. MEM.: Syndicalist League of America (founder, 1912–14); Friends of the Soviet Union (National Cmte.); League to Struggle for Negro Rights; Workers School of New York; U.S. Congress Against War; Workers Cultural Federation (dir.); A.C.L.U. (member, National Cmte., to 1930); Garland Fund (dir.); Trade Union Unity League (national sec.); All America Anti-Imperialist League (National Cmte., 1928); International Trade Union Educational League (founder, 1916); Trade Union Educational League (founder; national sec., 1920); AFL Railway Carmen's Union; Industrial Workers of the World (1909; delegate, Trade Unions Secretariat, 1910, not seated). WRITINGS: *Trade Unionism the Road to Freedom; The Revolutionary Crisis, 1918–1920; The Railroaders Next Step—Amalgamation; The Bankruptcy of the American Labor Movement; The Great Steel Strike and Its Lessons* (1920); *The Russian Revolution* (1921); *Misleaders of Labor* (1927); *Towards Soviet America* (1932); *From Bryan to Stalin* (1937); *Syndicalism* (with Earl Ford); *Pages from a Worker's Life* (1939); *Your Questions Answered* (1939); *Outline History of the Americas* (1951); *History of the Communist Party, U.S.A.* (1952); *The Negro People in American History* (1954); *History of the Three Internationals* (1955); *Outline History of the World Trade Union Movement* (1956); numerous pamphlets and articles. REL.: none (nee R.C.). MISC.: indicted for criminal syndicalism in 1922, but not convicted; spent six months in jail in NY, 1930, for illegal demonstration; indicted for violation of Smith Act, 1948, but released for reasons of health. RES.: Chicago, IL.

FOUTCH, MARSHA AILEEN MARY ELIZABETH LANNAN. b. Aug 23, 1946, Moline, IL; par. Joseph Murl McCracken and Vera (Kovalchuck) Lannan; m. Timothy Gene Dopler Foutch (divorced); c. Nicolette Corrinne (Mrs. Jason Hartman Lemon). EDUC.: Alleman Catholic H.S., Rock Island, IL, 1960–64; St. Anthony's Hospital School of Nursing, Rock Island, IL, 1973–74, 1991; Black Hawk Coll., Moline IL; Marycrest Coll., Davenport, IA, 1973–74; R.N. POLIT. & GOV.: ***candidate for Democratic nomination to presidency of the U.S., 1988, 1992***. BUS. & PROF.: psychiatric nurse; nurse, Hammond Henry District Hospital, Geneseo, IL; nurse, Illini Hospital, Silvis, IL; nurse, East Moline State Hospital, East Moline, IL; visiting nurse, Moline, IL; visiting nurse, Oak Glen Nursing Home, Coal Valley, IL; home health professional, Davenport, IA, and Phoenix, AZ; nurse, Scottsdale (AZ) Camelback Hospital; nurse, Phoenix (AZ) Health Care Center. MEM.: Anthonettes (pres., 1963); Illinois Nurses Assn. (Public Relations, 5th District, 1973); Quad City League of Native Americans; National Organization for Women; Viet Nam Veterans of America; American Legion Auxiliary; VFW; Quad City Music Guild; National Depressive and Manic Depressive Assn.; Alcoholics Anonymous. REL.: R.C. MISC.: diagnosed manic-depressive; noted for harassment and publicly professing infatuation with U.S. Rep. Lane Evans. MAILING ADDRESS: 1215 15th St., Apt. 203, Moline, IL 61265.

FOUTS, SENECA FOOTE. b. Aug 26, 1876, Big Rapids, MI; d. May 18, 1945, Portland, OR; par. Philetus F. and Eugenia (Stafford) Fouts; m. Marjorie E. Baker, Jan 4, 1907; c. Seneca, Jr. EDUC.: LL.B., U. of OR, 1905. POLIT. & GOV.: elected as a Republican to OR State House, 1911–13; member, OR Draft Board, WWII; ***candidate for Republican nomination to vice presidency of the U.S., 1932***; Republican candidate for OR State House, 1936; appointed member, Battleship Oregon Comm., 1944. BUS. & PROF.: atty.; admitted to OR Bar, 1905; partner (with A. J. Derby), law practice, Hood River, OR, 1905–06; law practice, Portland, OR, 1906–09; partner (with Alexander Sweek), law practice, Portland, 1909–45. MIL.: 2d Oregon Infantry, U.S. Army, Spanish-American War. MEM.: Townsend Club; United Spanish American War Veterans (dept. commander; U.S. liaison officer); Phi Delta Phi; Military Order of the Serpent; American Legion; Forty and Eight; Eagles; Elks. RES.: Portland, OR.

FOWLER, JERRY LEE. b. 1950; m. Rebecca C. Fowler; c. Dixie Crystal Sugar; Wendy Carol. EDUC.: A.A., Greenville Technical Coll. POLIT. & GOV.: ***candidate for Democratic nomination to presidency of the U.S., 1984***. BUS. & PROF.: construction worker; owner, Fowler's Building and Remodeling Co., Greer, SC. MAILING ADDRESS: Greer, SC.

FOX, CHRISTOPHER C. POLIT. & GOV.: ***independent candidate for presidency of the U.S., 1992***. MAILING ADDRESS: 3307 Mordecai St., Apt. A, Durham, NC 27705.

FOX, JEROME FRANCIS. b. Mar 26, 1904, Chilton, WI; d. Sep 13, 1957, Chilton, WI; par. Leo P. and Pauline A. (Hanert) Fox; m. Rosemary E. Bachhuber; c. Jerome L.; Kathleen; Thomas; Michael; John; Rosemary; Terence. EDUC.: B.S., Notre Dame U., 1924; Marquette U., 1926–28; LL.B., U. of WI, 1930. POLIT. & GOV.: elected as a Democrat to Calumet Cty. (WI) Board of Supervisors, 1930–31; city atty., Chilton, WI, 1930–32; elected as a Democrat to WI State Assembly, 1930–34 (Democratic floor leader); candidate for Democratic nomination to gov. of WI, 1938; chm., WI Democratic State Central Cmte., 1948–52; delegate, Dem. Nat'l. Conv., 1948, 1952, 1956; elected as a Democrat to mayor of Chilton, WI, 1948; ***candidate for Democratic nomination to presidency of the U.S., 1952***. BUS. & PROF.: instructor in chemistry, Trinity Coll. (IA), 1924–26; atty.; admitted to WI Bar, 1930; partner (with Leo J. Fox), law firm, Chilton, WI, 1930–57; state counsel, Homeowners Loan Corp., 1934–35; lobbyist, Wisconsin Natural Gas. MIL.: lt., Aviation Branch, U.S.N.R., WWII. MEM.: Calumet Bar Assn. (vice pres.); Third Judicial District Bar Assn. (pres.); WI Bar Assn.; Catholic Order of Foresters; Phi Alpha Delta; Crown and Anchor (hon.); Alpha Chi; Knights of Columbus; C. of C. REL.: R.C. RES.: Chilton, WI.

FRANCE, JOSEPH IRWIN. b. Oct 11, 1873, Cameron, MO; d. Jan 26, 1939, Port Deposit, MD; par. Joseph Henry and Hannah Fletcher (James) France; m. Evalyn S. (Nesbitt) Tome, Jun 24, 1903; m. 2d, Tatiana Vladimirovna Dechtereva, Jul 13, 1927 (divorced, 1938). EDUC.: Canandaigua Acad.; A.B., Hamilton Coll., 1895; U. of Leipzig; grad.,

Medical Dept., Clark U., 1897; M.D., Coll. of Physicians and Surgeons, 1903. POLIT. & GOV.: member, MD State Planning Comm.; appointed member, MD State Board of Health; elected as a Republican to MD State Senate, 1905–09; delegate, Rep. Nat'l. Conv., 1908; elected as a Republican to U.S. Senate (MD), 1917–23; ***candidate for Republican nomination to presidency of the U.S., 1920, 1932***; Republican candidate for U.S. Senate (MD), 1922, 1934. BUS. & PROF.: physician; chm., Dept. of Natural Science, Jacob Tome Inst., Port Deposit, MD, 1897; medical practice, Baltimore, MD, 1903–23; engaged in finance and international trade, 1908–39; sec., Medical and Chirurgical Faculty of MD, 1916–17; medical practice, Port Deposit, MD, 1923–39; pres., Republic International Corp. MEM.: Jacob Tome Inst. (vice pres., board of trustees); Hamilton Coll. (trustee); Masons. REL.: Presb. MISC.: awarded Elihu Root Fellowship to study at U. of Leipzig; studied Russian economic conditions, 1921. RES.: Port Deposit, MD.

FRANCIS, DAVID ROWLAND. b. Oct 1, 1850, Richmond, KY; d. Jan 15, 1927, St. Louis, MO; par. John Broaddus and Eliza Caldwell (Rowland) Francis; m. Jane Perry, Jan 20, 1876; c. John D.; David Rowland, Jr.; Charles Broaddus; Talton Turner; Thomas; Sidney R. EDUC.: A.B., Washington U., 1870. POLIT. & GOV.: delegate, Dem. Nat'l. Conv., 1884; elected as a Democrat to mayor of St. Louis, MO, 1885–89; elected as a Democrat to gov. of MO, 1889–93; appointed U.S. sec. of the interior, 1896–97; appointed pres., Louisiana Purchase Centennial Exposition, 1904; ***candidate for Democratic nomination to vice presidency of the U.S., 1908 (declined), 1920 (withdrew)***; candidate for Democratic nomination to U.S. Senate (MO), 1910; appointed U.S. ambassador extraordinary and minister plenipotentiary to Russia, 1916–18. BUS. & PROF.: clerk, partner, Shryock and Rowland (commission house), 1870–77; pres., D. R. Francis and Brothers (commission house), 1877; grain merchant; vice pres., Merchants-Laclede National Bank; pres., Madison Cty. Ferry Co.; trustee, New York Life Insurance Co.; dir., Mississippi Life Insurance Co.; owner, *St. Louis Republic;* pres., Covenant Mutual Life Insurance Co.; vice pres., Mississippi Valley Trust Co.; vice pres., Union Casualty and Surety Co.; dir., Brazoria Land and Cattle Co.; dir., Merchants Bridge Co.; dir., Laclede Building Co.; dir., Covenant Life Insurance Co.; dir., Rialto Building Co.; dir., Festus Realty Co.; dir., Columbia Realty Co.; dir., St. Louis Trust Co. MEM.: Merchants Exchange (pres., 1884); U. of MO (pres., Board of Curators); Hospital Saturday and Sunday Assn. (pres.); MO Hist. Soc.; St. Louis Art Museum (dir.); Western Commercial Congress (pres., 1891); Knights Templar; St. Louis Club; Noonday Club; Kinloch Club; Round Table Club; Cuivre Club; Reform Club. HON. DEG.: LL.D., U. of MO, 1892; LL.D., Shurtleff Coll., 1903; LL.D., St. Louis U., 1904; LL.D., Washington U., 1905. WRITINGS: *A Tour of Europe in Nineteen Days* (1903); *The Universal Exposition of 1904* (1913). RES.: St. Louis, MO.

FRANCIS, ENNIS. b. 1917; married. POLIT. & GOV.: chairlady, Harlem/East Harlem Model Cities Policy Cmte.; female district leader, 70th NY Assembly District, Part B; ***Ownership candidate for Democratic nomination to vice presidency of the U.S., 1980***. BUS. & PROF.: urban planner; community leader; founder, Community Corp. MEM.: Harlem Youth Activities Unlumited (resigned, 1972); Poor People's Campaign; Southern Christian Leadership Conference (member, Clearing House Cmte., Resurrection City). AWARDS: honored in dedication of Ennis Francis Dormitory, Ebenezer H.S., Ebenezer, Nigeria, 1962; Frederick Douglass Award, New York Urban League, 1971; New York City Citation of Merit; Award for Outstanding Services to Our Community, Model Cities Staff of Parent Leadership Program, 1972; award, Youth Scholarship Program, Staff of Model Cities, 1973; Lady of the Year Award, Canaan Baptist Church, 1973. REL.: Bapt. MISC.: advocate of employee ownership of businesses. MAILING ADDRESS: 315 North 115th St., New York, NY 10026.

FRANCIS, JOHN M. POLIT. & GOV.: Socialist Labor Party candidate for IL state treas., 1906; Socialist Labor Party candidate for IL state auditor, 1908; Socialist Labor Party candidate for U.S. Senate (IL), 1910, 1914; Socialist Labor Party candidate for gov. of IL, 1912, 1916, 1920; ***candidate for Socialist Labor Party nomination to presidency of the U.S., 1912***; member, Socialist Labor Party National Cmte., 1916–19 (exec. cmte.); expelled from Socialist Labor Party, 1920. BUS. & PROF.: coal miner, Du Quoin, IL. MEM.: Industrial Workers of the World (delegate, National Convention, 1906). RES.: Du Quoin, IL.

FRANKLIN, CRAIG. POLIT. & GOV.: ***candidate for Libertarian Party nomination to vice presidency of the U.S., 1992***. MAILING ADDRESS: unknown.

FRANKLIN, DAVID. b. 1925. EDUC.: A.B. (cum laude), Harvard U., 1949. POLIT. & GOV.: ***candidate for Democratic nomination to presidency of the U.S., 1968***. BUS. & PROF.: translator, scientific tracts. MISC.: had 458 letters to the editor published in various newspapers between 1950 and 1965; advertised social views in *New York Times* from Sep 20, 1959. MAILING ADDRESS: 1601 56th St., Brooklyn, NY 11204.

FRAZIER, LYNN JOSEPH. b. December 21, 1874, Medford, MN; d. Jan 11, 1947, Riverdale, MD; par. Thomas and Lois Brackett Hoar (Nile) Frazier; m. Lottie Jane Stafford, Nov 26, 1903; m. 2d, Mrs. Catherine (Behrens) W. Paulson, Sep 7, 1937; c. Unie Mae (Mrs. Emerson Clifford Church); Versie Fae (Mrs. Stanley Harry Gaines); Vernon; Willis; Lucille (Mrs. Vernon Lutz Derrickson). EDUC.: grad., Mayville State Normal School, 1895; B.A., U. of ND, 1901. POLIT. & GOV.: elected as a Republican to gov. of ND, 1917–21 (recalled); ***candidate for Farmer-Labor Party nomination to presidency of the U.S., 1920***; elected as a Republican to

U.S. Senate (ND), 1923–41; candidate for Republican nomination to U.S. Senate (ND), 1940. BUS. & PROF.: farmer, Hoople, ND. MEM.: Modern Woodmen of America; Non-Partisan League. REL.: Methodist. RES.: Hoople, ND.

FREDERICHS, MICHAEL JAMES. b. Apr 20, 1967, Des Plaines, IL; par. Glenn William and Joy Ann (Heideman) Frederichs; single. EDUC.: John Hersey H.S., Arlington Heights, IL. POLIT. & GOV.: ***By Invitation Only Party candidate for president of the United States, 1984***. BUS. & PROF.: student; part-time jobs. MEM.: Dr. Who Fan Club of America. REL.: Methodist. MAILING ADDRESS: 420 Hillcrest Dr., Prospect Heights, IL 60070.

FREDERICKSON, CHARLES RICHARD. b. Oct 3, 1875, Lawrence, KS; d. Jun 26, 1955, Coshocton, OH; par. Anthony and Anna Louise (Larson) Frederickson; m. Elizabeth Brent, Apr 18, 1899; m. 2d, Mrs. Phoebe Nixon Williams, December 1, 1936; c. Mary Flemings (Mrs. Arthur Oudry Davis); Phebe Brent (Mrs. John Alfred Wright); Charles Richard, Jr.; Elizabeth Brent (Mrs. Stuart Holness Lane). EDUC.: grad., Lawrence Business U., 1892. POLIT. & GOV.: presidential elector, Republican Party, 1920; delegate, Rep. Nat'l. Conv., 1928, 1932, 1936, 1940; appointed to U.S. Senate (OH), 1928 (declined); campaign mgr., Myers Y. Cooper for Governor of OH Campaign, 1928; chm., OH State Republican Cmte.; ***candidate for Republican nomination to presidency of the U.S., 1936***. BUS. & PROF.: printer's apprentice, *Sports Afield*, 1892; organizer, Frederickson Co., Chicago, IL, 1908; pres., American Art Works, Inc., 1911–55, treas., 1914–55; vice pres., treas., chm. of the board, American Colortype Co., Clifton, NJ, 1944–52. MEM.: Ohio Manufacturers' Assn. (pres., 1924–25); OH C. of C. (vice pres., 1929–32); Regency Club. AWARDS: Silver Beaver Award, BSA; Silver Antelope Award, BSA. RES.: Coshocton, OH.

FREDETTE, PHILLIP ARTHUR. b. Aug 15, 1926, Springfield, MA; par. Joseph Edmund and Melora (Hammel) Fredette; m. Jean Marie DuChamp; c. Ann; Dorothy Jean; Robert; Joseph; William; Nancy. EDUC.: sixth grade, St. Aloysius Catholic School, Indian Orchard, MA; M.A., Secret Science. POLIT. & GOV.: ***candidate for Republican nomination to presidency of the U.S., 1976***. BUS. & PROF.: self-employed; composer; woodsman. MIL.: U.S. Army, 1944. WRITINGS: "Time Alone" (song). REL.: R.C. MAILING ADDRESS: 1104 Worthington St., Springfield, MA.

FREEMAN, CARL FLOYD. b. Apr 4, 1919, Red Oak, GA; par. John David and Mary Lucy (Ogletree) Freeman; m. Keron Dale Blissitt; c. none. EDUC.: eleventh grade, North Clayton H.S., 1940; diploma in communications. POLIT. & GOV.: ***candidate for Democratic nomination to presidency of the U.S., 1976, 1980***. BUS. & PROF.: operator, radio and television repair business, Decatur, GA. REL.: Christian. MAILING ADDRESS: 3157 Robin Rd., Decatur, GA 30032.

FREEMAN, DEBRA HANANIA. EDUC.: D.P.H. POLIT. & GOV.: U.S. Labor Party candidate for U.S. House (MD), 1978; candidate for Democratic nomination to U.S. House (MD), 1982, 1984; candidate for pres., Baltimore (MD) City Council, 1983; candidate for Democratic nomination to U.S. Senate (MD), 1986; chair, Lyndon H. LaRouche for President Democratic Nomination Campaign, 1988; ***independent (Economic Recovery Party) candidate for vice presidency of the U.S., 1988, 1992***. BUS. & PROF.: public health official; dir., LaRouche AIDS Program, Baltimore, MD. MAILING ADDRESS: 12 Helms Pick Court, Catonsville, MD.

FREGOE, KENNETH. POLIT. & GOV.: ***candidate for Democratic nomination to presidency of the U.S., 1976, 1980***. MAILING ADDRESS: P.O. Box 153, Unity Acres, Orwell, NY 13426.

FREI, MICHAEL JOSEPH. b. Jan 8, 1948, Caro, MI; par. William Charles and Vernetta (Hinton) Frei; m. Mary Margaret Jimenez; c. Eric; Roland; Heidi; Cheryl; Ingrid; Kurt. EDUC.: B.A., MI State U., 1972; Officer Training School, U.S. Air Force, San Antonio, TX, 1973; Undergraduate Navigator Training School, U.S. Air Force, Sacramento, CA, 1973–74; Squadron Officer School, U.S. Air Force Extension Course Inst., 1974; Air Command and Staff Coll., U.S. Air Force Extension Course Inst., 1975–76. POLIT. & GOV.: ***independent candidate for presidency of the U.S., 1988***. BUS. & PROF.: laborer, Linwood Concrete Pipe Co., Linwood, MI, 1971; crane operator, Munich, Germany, 1972; lifeguard, Stadtwerke Muenchen, Munich, Germany, 1972; sales representative, ZEP Manufacturing Co., Roseville, MI, 1977–79. MIL.: officer, 463d Tactical Airlift Wing, U.S. Air Force, 1973–77; capt., U.S. Air Force, 1979–86; Combat Readiness Award; Small Arms Marksmanship Medal; National Defense Medal. MEM.: Officers' Club. MISC.: noted for campaign against homosexual officers in U.S. Air Force (who were allegedly responsible for his discharge); campaigned as a "Real Man" against gay rights. MAILING ADDRESS: 4040 River Rd., Oscoda, MI 48750.

FREIBERG, WARREN. POLIT. & GOV.: ***candidate for Populist Party nomination to presidency of the U.S., 1984***. BUS. & PROF.: radio broadcaster. MAILING ADDRESS: unknown.

FREIFIELD, BARRY M. POLIT. & GOV.: ***independent candidate for presidency of the U.S., 1980***. MAILING ADDRESS: Athenian Cmte., c/o Cindy Freifeld, 3 Lindron Ave., Smithtown, NY 11787.

FRELIGH, DAVID. POLIT. & GOV.: ***independent candidate for presidency of the U.S., 1988***. MAILING ADDRESS: 6512 Don Julio, Long Beach, CA 90815.

FRELINGHUYSEN, FREDERICK THEODORE. b. Aug 4, 1817, Millstone, NJ; d. May 20, 1885, Newark, NJ; par. Frederick and Jane (Dumont) Frelinghuysen; adopted son of Theodore (q.v.) and Charlotte (Mercer) Frelinghuysen; m. Matilde Elizabeth Griswold, Jan 25, 1842; c. Theodore; Matilde Griswold (Mrs. Henry Winthrop Gray); Charlotte Louise; Frederick; George Griswold; Sarah Helen (Mrs. John Davis; Mrs. Charles Laurie McCawley). EDUC.: grad., Rutgers U., 1836; studied law under Theodore Frelinghuysen. POLIT. & GOV.: appointed city atty., Newark, NJ, 1849–54; elected to Newark (NJ) City Council, 1850; delegate, Peace Convention, 1861; appointed atty. gen. of NJ, 1861–66; appointed and subsequently elected as a Republican to U.S. Senate (NJ), 1866–69, 1871–77; Republican candidate for U.S. Senate (NJ), 1868, 1876; appointed U.S. minister to Great Britain, 1870 (declined); ***candidate for Republican nomination to vice presidency of the U.S., 1876***; member, Electoral Comm., 1876–77; appointed U.S. sec. of state, 1881–85. BUS. & PROF.: atty.; admitted to NJ Bar, 1839; law practice, Newark, NJ, 1839–85; counsel, Central R.R. of New Jersey; counsel, Morris Canal and Banking Co. MEM.: Rutgers U. (trustee, 1851–55); American Bible Soc. (pres., 1884–85). HON. DEG.: LL.D., Rutgers U., 1864. REL.: Dutch Reformed Church. MISC.: known as a "Stalwart" Republican. RES.: Newark, NJ.

FRELINGHUYSEN, THEODORE. b. Mar 28, 1787, Millstone, NJ; d. Apr 12, 1862, New Brunswick, NJ; par. Gen. Frederick and Gertrude (Schenck) Frelinghuysen; m. Charlotte Mercer, 1809; m. 2d, Harriet Pumpelly, Oct 14, 1857; c. Frederick Theodore (adopted, q.v.). EDUC.: grad. (magna cum laude), Princeton U., 1804; read law under Richard Stockton. POLIT. & GOV.: elected as a Whig to atty. gen. of NJ, 1817–27; elected justice, Supreme Court of NJ, 1826 (declined); Adams Democratic candidate for U.S. Senate (NJ), 1826; elected as an Adams Democrat to U.S. Senate (NJ), 1829–35; elected as a Whig to mayor of Newark, NJ, 1836–39; ***Whig Party candidate for vice presidency of the U.S., 1844***. BUS. & PROF.: farmer; atty.; admitted to NJ Bar, 1808; sergeant at law, 1817; law practice, Newark, NJ; chancellor, U. of the City of New York, 1838–50; pres., Rutgers Coll., 1850–62. MIL.: capt., Volunteer Militia, 1812. MEM.: American Board for Foreign Missions (pres., 1841–57); American Tract Soc. (pres., 1842–48); American Bible Soc. (pres., 1846–62); American Sunday School Union (vice pres., 1826–60); American Colonization Soc.; American Temperance Union. REL.: Reformed Church. RES.: New Brunswick, NJ.

FREMONT, JOHN CHARLES. b. Jan 21, 1813, Savannah, GA; d. Jul 13, 1890, New York, NY; par. Jean Charles and Ann Beverly Whiting (Pryor) Fremont; m. Jessie Benton, Oct 19, 1841; c. Elizabeth. EDUC.: Charleston Coll., 1829–31 (expelled). POLIT. & GOV.: appointed civil gov. of CA, 1847; member, U.S.-Mexico Boundary Comm., 1849; elected as a Free Soil-Democrat to U.S. Senate (CA), 1850–51; ***Republican candidate for presidency of the U.S., 1856; National American (Know-Nothing) Party candidate for presidency of the U.S., 1856; candidate for Republican nomination to presidency of the U.S., 1860; Radical Republican Party candidate for presidency of the U.S., 1864 (withdrew)***; appointed gov., territory of Arizona, 1878–83. BUS. & PROF.: soldier; explorer; quartz miner, Mariposa, CA; investor, Kansas Pacific R.R.; investor, Memphis and Little Rock R.R.; pres., Memphis and El Paso R.R., 1865–73. MIL.: instructor in mathematics, Natchez, U.S. Navy, 1833–35; commissioned 2d lt., Topographical Corps, U.S. Army, 1838; maj., CA Volunteers, 1846; lt. col., U.S. Mounted Rifles, 1846, resigned, 1848; arrested in Stockton-Kearney dispute for mutiny; court martialed, Washington, DC, 1847–48; convicted, but penalty remitted by President Polk; maj. gen., U.S. Army, 1861, removed, 1861; reappointed, 1862–64; rank restored, 1890. AWARDS: Prussian Gold Medal, 1852; The Founder's Medal, Royal Geographical Soc. (England), 1854. WRITINGS: *Report of the Exploring Expedition of the Rocky Mountains* (1843); *Memoirs*. REL.: Christian (married in Roman Catholic Church). MISC.: participated in exploration of Des Moines River; Carolina Mountains; Upper Mississippi and Missouri rivers, 1838; Iowa Territory, 1840; Wind River; Rocky Mountains; Oregon, California, and New Mexico; Great Salt Lake Basin, 1843; Sierra Nevadas; participated in conquest of California; helped capture Los Angeles from Mexico, 1846; lost fortune in railroad ventures, 1870; known as the "Pathfinder." RES.: Mariposa, CA.

FRENCH, JASON EDWARD. POLIT. & GOV.: ***independent candidate for presidency of the U.S., 1980***. MAILING ADDRESS: 16600 Sylvester Rd., Reno, NV 89511.

FREY, EDWARD FRANK. b. Los Angeles, CA. POLIT. & GOV.: ***independent candidate for presidency of the U.S., 1976***. MEM.: Masons (40 years). MISC.: self-styled "Almighty God." MAILING ADDRESS: 1750 Colorado Blvd., Eagle Rock, CA.

FREY, LOUIS, JR. b. Jan 11, 1934, Rutherford, NJ; par. Louis and Mildred (Engel) Frey; m. Marcia Turner, Nov 1956; c. Julia; Lynn; Louis III; Lauren; Chris. EDUC.: B.A. (cum laude), Colgate U., 1955; J.D. (with honors), U. of MI, 1961. POLIT. & GOV.: appointed asst. cty. solicitor, Orlando, FL, 1961–63; acting gen. counsel, FL State Turnpike Authority, 1966–67; member, FL Republican State Exec. Cmte. (treas.); elected as a Republican to U.S. House (FL), 1969–79; member, Peace Corps Advisory Board; member, ACTION Agency Advisory Board; delegate, Rep. Nat'l. Conv., 1972; member, Republican Task Force on Campus Unrest; chm., Republican Task Force on Drug

Abuse; ***candidate for Republican nomination to vice presidency of the U.S., 1976***; candidate for Republican nomination to gov. of FL, 1978, 1986. BUS. & PROF.: asst. ed., *University of Michigan Law Review*; atty.; admitted to FL Bar, 1961; partner, Gurney, Skolfield and Frey (law firm), Winter Park, FL, 1963–67; partner, Mateer, Frey, Young and Harbert (law firm), Orlando, FL, 1967–71. MIL.: lt. (jg), U.S. Navy, 1955–58. MEM.: Florida Federation of Young Republicans (chm.); Order of the Coif; RETRO, Inc. (organized); Phi Gamma Delta; Phi Delta Phi; U.S.N.R. (commander); 91st Club (pres.); Winter Park Youth Center (dir.); American Cancer Soc. (dir.); Florida Symphony (assoc.); Orange Cty. Bar Assn.; FL Bar Assn.; ABA. REL.: Lutheran. MAILING ADDRESS: 139 Genius Dr., Winter Park, FL 32789.

FRIEDMAN, J. J. POLIT. & GOV.: ***National Unity Party candidate for vice presidency of the U.S., 1980***. MAILING ADDRESS: unknown.

FRIEDMAN, JONATHAN MALCOLM. b. Jul 31, 1959, Bronx, NY; par. Herbert Irwin and Elaine (Barosin) Friedman; single. EDUC.: North Miami Beach (FL) Senior H.S., 1976–80. POLIT. & GOV.: member, Elmwood Park (NJ) Youth Week Planning Board, 1974; elected as an Independent Democratic Progressivist to Elmwood Park (NJ) Municipal Council, 1976; ***Independent Democratic Progressivist candidate for presidency of the U.S., 1976***. BUS. & PROF.: shipping clerk, Joshua-Meier Div., W. R. Grace Co., North Bergen, NJ. REL.: Jewish. MAILING ADDRESS: 698 Blvd., Elmwood Park, NJ 07407.

FRIEDMAN, LOUIS JOSEPH. b. 1916. EDUC.: D.D.S., U. of Southern CA, 1942. POLIT. & GOV.: ***candidate for Democratic nomination to presidency of the U.S., 1976, 1988***. BUS. & PROF.: dentist; dental practice, Sherman Oaks, CA. MEM.: American Dental Assn. MAILING ADDRESS: 475 Calle El Segunda, Suite 2, Palm Springs, CA 92263.

FRIEDMAN, MOSHE. POLIT. & GOV.: ***candidate for Democratic nomination to presidency of the U.S., 1992***. MAILING ADDRESS: Kollel Chaverim for Moshe Friedman, Avrahum Yahov Feinstein, 452 Bradford Ave., Staten Island, NY 10309.

FRIEDMAN, SAMUEL HERMAN. b. Feb 20, 1897, Denver, CO; d. Mar 17, 1990, Bronx, NY; m. Isabelle B. Friedman; m. 2d, Mary. EDUC.: New York (NY) public schools; A.B., City Coll. of New York, 1917; M.A., Columbia U., 1940; Ph.D. candidate, NY U., 1970s. POLIT. & GOV.: Socialist Party candidate for U.S. House (NY), 1934; Socialist Party candidate for NY State Senate, 1940s; Socialist Party candidate for city controller, New York, twice, 1940s; Socialist Party candidate for lt. gov. of NY, 1940s; Socialist Party candidate for pres., City Council, New York, NY, 1940s; ***Socialist Party candidate for vice presidency of the U.S., 1952, 1956***; chm., New York Socialist Party, 1949; member, vice chm., National Exec. Cmte., Socialist Party; member, National Cmte., Social Democrats, U.S.A. BUS. & PROF.: social science teacher, high school; ed., *The College Mercury*, City Coll. of New York, 1917; public relations consultant; ed., labor papers, 1919–60; asst. news ed., copy chief, *Women's Wear Daily;* asst. news ed., copy ed., *Daily News Record;* founder, dir., ed., *New Leader;* ed., *Socialist Call;* publicity staff, fund raiser, United Jewish Appeal of Greater New York; founder, exec. dir., Rebel Arts. MEM.: American Federation of Teachers; United Federation of Teachers; Community and Social Agency Employees Union, CIO (pres., charter member, Local 1707); Government and Civic Employees Organizing Cmte., CIO (pres.); New York Labor History Assn. (dir.); United Jewish Appeal/Federation of Coop Village (chm.); Cooperative Inst. Assn. (pres., New York chapter); Workers Defense League (vice pres.); Rebel Arts (founder); Grand Street Consumers Cooperative; The Reunion of Old Timers (vice pres.); Cooperative Village (educational dir.); League for Industrial Democracy (pres., NY Chapter; dir., 1953–); Intercollegiate Socialist Soc. WRITINGS: *Rebel Song Book: Eighty-Seven Socialist and Labor Songs for Voice and Piano* (1935). REL.: Jewish. MISC.: suspended as editor of college newspaper for defending pacifism, 1917; arrested for disorderly conduct, 1949; jailed in 1964 for civil rights sit-in. RES.: New York, NY.

FRIEDMAN, SEYMOUR. POLIT. & GOV.: candidate for Democratic nomination to U.S. House (NY), 1962, 1972; ***National Civil Rights Party candidate for vice presidency of the U.S., 1964***. BUS. & PROF.: atty. MAILING ADDRESS: 19 Court St., Brooklyn, NY; Flushing, NY.

FRIETAS, DONALD L. b. 1939. EDUC.: A.B., U. of CA; J.D., U. of CA at Davis, 1971. POLIT. & GOV.: ***independent candidate for presidency of the U.S., 1976; independent candidate for vice presidency of the U.S., 1976***. BUS. & PROF.: atty.; admitted to CA Bar, 1971; atty., legal dept., Pacific Gas and Electric Co., San Francisco, CA. MAILING ADDRESS: 2587 Le Conte Ave., Berkeley, CA 94709.

FRITZ, JOHN PAUL. b. Dec 18, 1926, Independence, KS; par. George Louis and Lillian May (Dreher) Fritz; m. Mariko Nabeshima; c. Mary Nabeshima. EDUC.: grad., high school, Independence, KS, 1943; U. of CA at Los Angeles, 1950–53. POLIT. & GOV.: ***World Government candidate for presidency of the U.S., 1964, 1976; World Government candidate for president of the World, 1964, 1976, 1980***; candidate for Republican nomination to HI State House, 1974; ***World Citizens Party candidate for presidency of the U.S., 1980;*** candidate for Democratic nomination to U.S. Senate (HI), 1980. BUS. & PROF.: consultant, Tokyo Technology Science; U.S. Liaison Office, Australia; inventor; ed., *World Citizen Friendship Magazine*. MIL.: U.S. Maritime Service; U.S.C.G.; U.S. Army

Corps of Engineers. MEM.: World Citizen Planetary Federalists; We, The People; Common Cause; A.C.L.U.; International Pen Friend Soc.; Lighter Than Air Soc. REL.: Universal Life Church. MAILING ADDRESS: 889 Hei Kera, Kochi City, Japan 78301.

FROST, DAVID. b. Dec 19, 1925, Brooklyn, NY; par. Charles and Regina (Sad) Frost; m. Ruthann Steinberg; c. Michael Joseph; Jane Alice. EDUC.: B.S., City Coll. of New York 1946, M.S. (education), 1949; M.S., NY U., 1952, Ph.D., 1960. POLIT. & GOV.: candidate for Democratic nomination to U.S. Senate (NJ), 1966; chm., New Jersey Peace and Freedom Alternative; ***New Jersey Peace and Freedom Alternative candidate for vice presidency of the U.S., 1968***. BUS. & PROF.: tutor in biology, City Coll. of New York, 1946–49; instructor, private school, 1949–52; lecturer, asst. prof., science dept., U. Coll., Rutgers U., 1952–59, adjunct prof., 1953–; mgr., scientific editorial section, Squibb Inst. for Medical Research, Princeton, NJ, 1959–. MEM.: Plainfield Joint Defense Cmte. (co-chm.); S.A.N.E.; Rutgers U. Coll. Teachers' Assn. (pres.); AAAS; American Soc. of Pharmacology and Experimental Therapeutics; New York Acad. of Science; Council of Biology Educators (sec.). REL.: Unitarian. MAILING ADDRESS: 1229 East Seventh St., Plainfield, NJ 07062.

FRY, DANIEL WILLIAM. b. Jul 19, 1908, Verdon, MN; par. Fred Nelson and Clara Jane (Baehr) Fry; m. Elma Alice Donnelly, Aug 6, 1934; m. 2d, Tahahlita B. Mantzurani Turley, Mar 3, 1965; m. 3d, Florence Durkee, Feb 21, 1975; c. William Daniel; Joan Louise (Mrs. Richard Allen Woolfe); Julene Marie. EDUC.: U. of CA at Los Angeles, 3 years; Ph.D., St. Andrews U., London, England, 1960. POLIT. & GOV.: ***Universal Party candidate for vice presidency of the U.S., 1972***. BUS. & PROF.: employee, Aero-Jet, White Sands, NM; engineer, Crescent Engineering and Research Co., 1940– (vice pres., 1956–), El Monte, CA; dir., Astrolab Testing Corp., 1958–60; pres., Merlin Development Co., Inc., 1964–; author; missile engineer, White Sands Missile Range, 1951; UFO expert; ed., *Understanding Magazine*, 1956–. MEM.: Understanding, Inc. (international pres.); Josephine Cty. Hist. Soc. (life member); Engineers Soc.; Palm Springs Ranch Club; Wisdom Hall of Fame (1970); Smithsonian Institution; International Platform Assn.; National Hist. Soc. WRITINGS: *The White Sands Incident* (1954); *To Men of Earth* (1955); *Steps to the Stars* (1956); *Atoms, Galaxies and Understanding* (1960); *The Curve of Development* (1965). MISC.: claims to have had contact with extraterrestrial beings, White Sands Proving Grounds, NM, 1950. MAILING ADDRESS: 560 Pleasant Valley Rd., Merlin, OR 97532.

FRY, FIELDING L., II. POLIT. & GOV.: ***candidate for Democratic nomination to presidency of the U.S., 1976; independent candidate for presidency of the U.S., 1976***. MAILING ADDRESS: Catch-Up Cmte., 11401 Democracy Lane, Potomac, MD.

FRY, STEPHEN. POLIT. & GOV.: ***candidate for Farmer-Labor Party nomination to presidency of the U.S., 1924 (nominated himself from the galleries of the convention)***. RES.: unknown.

FUBAR (aka FUTURISTIC URANIUM BIO ATOMIC ROBOT). POLIT. & GOV.: ***Thank God It's FUBAR (T.G.I.F.) Party candidate for presidency of the U.S., 1980 (satire effort)***. BUS. & PROF.: robot; entertainer. MAILING ADDRESS: Beverly Hills, CA.

FULANI, LENORA B. b. Apr 25, 1950, Chester, PA; m. (divorced); c. Ainka; Amani. EDUC.: B.A., Hofstra U., 1971; M.A., Columbia U., 1972; Ph.D., City U. of NY, 1984. POLIT. & GOV.: New Alliance Party candidate for lt. gov. of NY, 1982; New Alliance Party candidate for mayor of New York, NY, 1985, 1989; named "independent mayor of Harlem," New York, NY, 1985; appointed member, AIDS Advisory Board, National Inst. of Mental Health, 1986; New Alliance Party candidate for gov. of NY, 1986; member, Exec. Board, New Alliance Party (coordinator, Women of Color Caucus); ***Peace and Freedom Party candidate for presidency of the U.S., 1988; Independent (New Alliance) Party candidate for presidency of the U.S., 1988, 1992; candidate for Democratic nomination to presidency of the U.S., 1992; Liberty Union Party candidate for presidency of the U.S., 1992***. BUS. & PROF.: psychologist; instructor, Bank Street Coll., Medgar Evers Coll., Coll. of New Rochelle, and Empire State Coll., 1979–83; research assoc., Family Day Care Project, La Guardia Community Coll., 1979–80; research evaluator, Special Education, New York Board of Education, 1980–81; research psychologist, Bank Street Coll., 1981–82; instructor, Inst. for Social Therapy and Research, New York, 1982–83, education dir., 1983–84, dir., 1984–86, dir. of community clinics, 1986–; faculty, East Side Inst. for Short Term Psychotherapy, 1984–; consultant, Barbara Taylor School, New York, 1985–. MEM.: American Orthopsychiatric Assn. (co-chair, Women's Inst., 1986); National Congress of Political Black Women; American Psych. Assn.; Women of Color Caucus, New Alliance Party (national chairperson); War Resisters League; Assn. for the Development of Social Therapy; Campaign for Fair Elections and Democracy; Assn. of Black Psychologists. AWARDS: Chester Coll. Scholarship Award, 1968; University Scholarship, City U. of NY, 1974; Pamela Galiber Memorial Award, City U. of NY, 1977; Sloan Minority Fellowship, 1979; research fellowship, U. of CA at La Jolla, 1980; fellowship in doctoral research, Black Analysis Inc., 1980; Community Service Award, American Red Cross of Greater NY, 1986; Community Service Award, Alpha Kappa Alpha, 1986; Community Service Award, Girl's Club of New York, 1987; Award for Upgrading Medical Services in Harlem, Charles Drew Soc., 1987; named finalist in KOOL Achievers Award Competition, 1987. REL.: Bapt. MAILING ADDRESS: 884 West End Ave., #75, New York, NY 10025.

FULBRIGHT, JAMES WILLIAM. b. Apr 9, 1905, Sumner, MO; d. Feb. 9, 1995, Washington, DC; par. Jay and Roberta (Waugh) Fulbright; m. Elizabeth Kremer Williams, Jun 15, 1932; c. Elizabeth Williams (Mrs. John Winnacker); Roberta Waugh (Mrs. Edward Thaddeus Foote II). EDUC.: A.B., U. of AR, 1925; B.A., Oxford U., 1928, M.A., 1931; LL.B. (with distinction), George Washington U., 1934. POLIT. & GOV.: special atty., Anti-Trust Division, U.S. Dept. of Justice, Washington, DC, 1934–35; elected as a Democrat to U.S. House (AR), 1943–45; delegate, International Conference on Education, 1944; elected as a Democrat to U.S. Senate (AR), 1945–75; delegate, Dem. Nat'l. Conv., 1948, 1952, 1956, 1960, 1964; ***candidate for Democratic nomination to presidency of the U.S., 1952***; delegate, Ninth General Assembly, U.N., 1954; ***candidate for Democratic nomination to vice presidency of the U.S., 1968***. BUS. & PROF.: atty.; admitted to Bar of DC, 1934; instructor in law, George Washington U., 1935–36; newspaper publisher; farmer; lumberman; banker; lecturer in law, U. of AR, 1936–39, pres., 1939–41; counsel, Hogan and Hartson (law firm), Washington, DC, 1975–; counsel, United Arab Emirates, 1976–. MEM.: Sigma Chi; Rotary; Phi Delta Phi; Phi Beta Kappa; Order of the Coif. AWARDS: Rhodes Scholarship, 1928; Japan Foundation Award, 1974; Honorary Knight of the British Empire, 1975; Benjamin Franklin Medal, 1977. HON. DEG.: LL.D., Oxford U., 1953. WRITINGS: *Old Myths and New Realities* (1964); *Prospects for the West* (1965); *The Arrogance of Power* (1967); *The Pentagon Propaganda Machine* (1970); *The Crippled Giant* (1972). REL.: Disciples of Christ. MISC.: member of college football and soccer teams. RES.: Washington, DC.

FULLER, ALVAN TUFTS. b. Feb 27, 1878, Boston, MA; d. Apr 30, 1958, Boston, MA; par. Alvan Bond and Flora A. (Tufts) Fuller; m. Viola Davenport, Jul 12, 1910; c. Lydia (Mrs. George T. Bottomly); Mary (Mrs. Robert L. Henderson); Alvan Tufts, Jr.; Peter Davenport. EDUC.: public schools. POLIT. & GOV.: elected as a Republican to MA State House, 1915–17; delegate, Rep. Nat'l. Conv., 1916; elected as a Republican to U.S. House (MA), 1917–21; elected as a Republican to lt. gov. of MA, 1921–24; elected as a Republican to gov. of MA, 1925–29; ***candidate for Republican nomination to presidency of the U.S., 1928; candidate for Republican nomination to vice presidency of the U.S., 1928 (declined), 1932, 1936***. BUS. & PROF.: bicycle business, 1896; founder, owner, Packard Motor Car Co., Boston, MA; chm. of the board, Cadillac-Oldsmobile Co., Boston, MA. MEM.: Boston Museum of Fine Arts (trustee); Boston U. (trustee); Newton Theological Institution (trustee); New England Conservatory of Music (trustee); Boston Symphony Orchestra (trustee); Odd Fellows; Masons (33°); Elks; Knights of Pythias; Algonquin Club. HON. DEG.: LL.D., Boston U.; LL.D., Tufts Coll.; LL.D., Boston Coll.; LL.D., Bates Coll.; LL.D., Holy Cross Coll. REL.: Bapt. RES.: Boston, MA.

FULLER, MELVILLE WESTON. b. Feb 11, 1833, Augusta, ME; d. Jul 4, 1910, Sorrento, ME; par. Frederick Augustus and Catherine Martin (Weston) Fuller; m. Calista Ophelia Reynolds, Jun 28, 1858; m. 2d, Mary Ellen Coolbaugh, May 30, 1866; c. Grace Weston (Mrs. Archibald Brown); Maud (Mrs. William H. Delius); Mary Coolbaugh (Mrs. Colin Clarke Manning; Mrs. William H. White); Mildred Louise (Mrs. Hugh Campbell Wallace); Pauline Coney (Mrs. J. Matt Aubrey; Mrs. Samuel Marcus Moore); Catherine Martin (Mrs. Theodore S. Beecher); Jane Brown (Mrs. Nathaniel L. Francis); Fanny Louise (Mrs. Robert F. Mason); Weston. EDUC.: Harvard U., 1854–55; A.B., Bowdoin Coll., 1853, A. M., 1856; studied law under George Melville Weston. POLIT. & GOV.: elected pres., Augusta (ME) Common Council, 1856; city solicitor, Augusta, 1856; elected delegate, IL State Constitutional Convention, 1862; elected as a Democrat to IL State House, 1863–65; delegate, Dem. Nat'l. Conv., 1864, 1872, 1876, 1880; appointed chief justice, Supreme Court of the U.S., 1888–1910; appointed arbitrator, Venezuelan-British Boundary Dispute, 1899; member, Permanent Court of Arbitration, Hague, Netherlands, 1900–1910; ***candidate for Democratic nomination to presidency of the U.S., 1908***. BUS. & PROF.: atty.; admitted to ME Bar, 1855; law practice, Augusta, 1855–56; assoc. ed., *The Age*, Augusta, 1855–56; law practice, Chicago, IL, 1856–88; partner (with S. K. Dow), law firm, Chicago, 1856–60; partner, Fuller and Ham (law firm), Chicago, 1862–64; partner, Fuller, Ham and Shepard (law firm), Chicago, 1864–66; partner, Fuller and Shepard (law firm), Chicago, 1866–68; partner, Fuller and Smith (law firm), Chicago, 1869–77. MEM.: Smithsonian Institution (chancellor); Peabody Education Fund (chm., board of trustees, 1901–10); Bowdoin Coll. (overseer, 1875–79; trustee, 1894–1901); American Acad. of Arts and Sciences; John F. Slater Fund (vice pres.); Phi Beta Kappa; American Soc. of International Law (vice pres.; exec. counsellor). HON. DEG.: LL.D., Bowdoin Coll., 1888; LL.D., Northwestern U., 1888; LL.D., Harvard U., 1891; LL.D., Yale U., 1901; LL.D., Dartmouth U., 1901. REL.: Episc. (vestryman). RES.: Chicago, IL.

FULTON, CHARLES WILLIAM. b. Aug 24, 1853, Lima, OH; d. Jan 27, 1918, Portland, OR; par. Jacob and Eliza A. (McAlister) Fulton; m. Ada M. Hobson, Sep 5, 1878; c. Frederick C. EDUC.: read law under A. H. Babcock, Pawnee City, NE. POLIT. & GOV.: elected as a Republican to OR State Senate, 1879–81, 1891–93, 1899–1901, 1903–05 (pres., 1893, 1901); presidential elector, Republican Party, 1888; city atty., Astoria, OR, 1880–82; elected as a Republican to U.S. Senate (OR), 1903–09; Republican candidate for U.S. Senate (OR), 1908; appointed U.S. minister to China, 1909 (declined); ***candidate for Republican nomination to presidency of the U.S., 1912***. BUS. & PROF.: schoolteacher, Pawnee City, NE, 1873–74; schoolteacher, Waterloo, OR, 1875; atty.; admitted to OR Bar, 1875; partner (with J. W. Robb), law firm, Astoria, OR, 1877. RES.: Astoria, OR.

FURDECK, CONSTANCE ZIMMERMAN BLOMEN **(See BLOMEN, CONSTANCE ZIMMERMAN).**

GABOR, PATRICK WILLIAM. b. Sep 10, 1942, Lackawanna, NY; par. Joseph John and Ann Marie (Mongraw) Gabor; m. (divorced); c. none. EDUC.: grad., Frontier Central H.S., Hamburg, NY, 1962; East Carolina Coll.; Columbus Coll., Columbus, GA; law school, Newport News, RI; administration school, Cherry Point, NC; gemology student. POLIT. & GOV.: ***Oppressed Party candidate for presidency of the U.S., 1976***. BUS. & PROF.: salesman and asst. advertising mgr., Sears; employee, clerk, typist, insurance analyst, National Rural Electric Cooperative Assn., 1966–67; vice pres., La Contesa Jewelers, Bowie, MD; vice pres., Toltec Distributors, Bowie, MD. MIL.: administrative chief, legal asst., U.S.M.C., 1962–66; pvt., U.S. Army, sgt., 1966; Meritorious Service Medal; Vietnam Service Medal; National Defense Service Medal; Good Conduct Medal. MAILING ADDRESS: 314 Duke St., Alexandria, VA 22314.

GABRIEL THE ARCHANGEL. POLIT. & GOV.: ***candidate for Democratic nomination to presidency of the U.S., 1984***. MAILING ADDRESS: Mira Loma, CA.

GAHRES, BILL. b. Nov 5, 1913, Mt. Carmel, PA; par. Arthur and Annette (Stitzer) Gahres; m. Marie Rompolski; c. Bill, Jr. EDUC.: grad., high school. POLIT. & GOV.: member, sec., Municipal Board, PA; township auditor, PA; candidate for NJ State Assembly; candidate for U.S. House (NJ); candidate for Republican nomination to U.S. House (NJ), 1970; Right to Die candidate for gov. of NJ, 1977, 1981; candidate for Ocean Cty. (NJ) freeholder, 1978, 1980; Down with Lawyers Party candidate for U.S. Senate (NJ), 1978; ***Down with Lawyers Party candidate for presidency of the U.S., 1980***; Down with Lawyers Party candidate for gov. of NJ, 1981. BUS. & PROF.: electrical contractor; elevator contractor; self-employed, 1945–; columnist, "Specifically Speaking," *The Statesman*. MEM.: Elks. REL.: Protestant. MAILING ADDRESS: 361 North Main St., Barnegat, NJ 08005.

GALIFIANAKIS, NICK. b. Jul 22, 1928, Durham, NC; par. Mike and Sophia (Kastrinakis) Galifianakis; m. Louise Cheatham Ruggles, Apr 5, 1963; c. Stephanie; Katherine; Jon Mark. EDUC.: A.B., Duke U., 1951, LL.B., 1953. POLIT. & GOV.: member, NC Cmte. on Mental Institutions, 1961–64, chm., 1965–; elected as a Republican to NC State House, 1961–67; member, NC Board of Science and Technology, 1965–; elected as a Republican to U.S. House (NC), 1966–73; Democratic candidate for U.S. Senate (NC), 1972; ***candidate for Democratic nomination to vice presidency of the U.S., 1972***. BUS. & PROF.: atty.; admitted to NC Bar, 1956; partner, Upchurch and Galifianakis (law firm), Durham, NC, 1956–; staff instructor, legal aid clinic, Duke U., 1956–59, asst. prof. of business law, 1960–67. MIL.: U.S.M.C., 1953–56; lt. col., U.S.M.C. Reserves, commanding officer, 41st Rifle Company, 1960–63; lt. col., Civil Air Patrol. MEM.: Delta Theta Phi; ABA; NC State Bar Assn.; Durham Cty. Bar Assn.; 15th Judicial District Bar Assn.; Junior C. of C.; Kiwanis; Young Democrats; March of Dimes (dir.); American Cancer Soc. (dir.); United Fund (dir.); Durham C. of C.; Hellenic Coll. (trustee); Cerebral Palsy (dir.); Durham Cty. Mental Health Assn. (dir.); AAUP; American Hellenic Educational Progressive Assn.; Durham Young Lawyers Club (pres.). AWARDS: Outstanding Young Man of the Year, NC Junior C. of C., 1963; Distinguished Service Award, NC Junior C. of C., 1963; one of ten Outstanding Young Men in America, 1964; Scarborough Award for Outstanding Public Service, 1971. REL.: Greek Orthodox Church (trustee, St. Barbara's Church, Durham, NC). MAILING ADDRESS: 2648 University Dr., Durham, NC 27707.

GALLAGHER, FRANCIS J. POLIT. & GOV.: ***Universal Peace Union candidate for vice presidency of the U.S., 1896 (withdrew)***. MEM.: Rhode Island Peace Soc.; Universal Peace Union. WRITINGS: *In Memoriam—Jonathan Goff Parkhurst, 1821–1907* (1907). RES.: Providence, RI.

GALLATIN, ABRAHAM ALFONSE ALBERT. b. Jan 29, 1761, Geneva, Switzerland; d. Aug 12, 1849, Astoria, NY; par. Jean and Sophie Albertine (Rolaz) Gallatin; m. Sophie Allegre, May 1789; m. 2d, Hannah Nicholson, Nov 11, 1793; c. James; Albert Rolaz; Frances. EDUC.: grad., Geneva Acad., 1779. POLIT. & GOV.: member, Harrisburg Conference to Revise U.S. Constitution, 1788; delegate, PA State Constitutional Convention, 1789; elected as a Democrat to PA State House, 1790–93, 1794 (declined); elected as a Democrat to U.S. Senate (PA), 1794 (not seated; election voided due to failure to meet citizenship requirement); elected as a Democrat to U.S. House (PA), 1795–1801 (Democratic minority leader); appointed U.S. sec. of the treasury, 1801–14; appointed U.S. negotiator, Treaty of Ghent, 1814; appointed U.S. minister to France, 1815–23; ***National Democratic candidate for vice presidency of the U.S., 1824 (withdrew)***; appointed U.S. minister to England, 1826–27. BUS. & PROF.: banker; came to U.S., 1780; tutor in French, Harvard U., 1781–83; pres., National (later Gallatin) Bank of New York City, 1831–39. MEM.: U. of the City of New York (founder; pres., 1831); American Ethnological Soc. (founder, 1842); NY Hist. Soc. (pres., 1843). HON. DEG.: LL.D., Columbia U., 1841. WRITINGS: *Considerations on the Currency and Banking System of the U.S.* (1831); *Memorial of the Committee Appointed by the "Free Trade" Convention Held in Philadelphia in . . . 1831* (1832); *Synopsis of the Indian Tribes Within the United States East of the Rocky Mountains and in the British and Russian Possessions in North America* (1836); *Notes on the Semi-Civilized Nations of Mexico, Yucatan and Central America. . . .* (1845). MISC.: instrumental in quelling Whiskey Rebellion, 1794. RES.: New Geneva, PA.

GANNETT, FRANK ERNEST. b. Sep 15, 1876, Bristol, NY; d. Dec 3, 1957, Rochester, NY; par. Joseph Charles and Maria (Brooks) Gannett; m. Caroline Werner, Mar 25, 1920; c. Sara Maria (Mrs. Charles Vincent McAdam); Dixon. EDUC.: B.A., Cornell U., 1898. POLIT. & GOV.: appointed sec., Philippine Comm., 1899; ***candidate for Republican nomination to presidency of the U.S., 1936, 1940; candidate for Republican nomination to vice presidency of the U.S., 1936***; vice chm., Rep. Nat'l. Cmte., 1942; appointed member, Finger Lakes Park Comm. BUS. & PROF.: journalist; editorial staff, *Cornell Sun*; mgr., *Cornell Magazine*; Cornell correspondent, *Ithaca (NY) Journal*; ed., *Cornell (NY) News*, 1900; city ed., *Ithaca Daily News*, 1900–1905, managing ed., business mgr.; ed., *Pittsburgh (PA) Index*, 1905–06; co-owner, *Elmira (NY) Gazette*, 1906; owner, *Elmira Star-Gazette*; owner, *Ithaca Journal*, 1912; owner, *Ithaca Journal-News*, 1919; owner, *Rochester (NY) Union and Advertiser*, 1918; owner, *Rochester Evening News*; owner, ed., *Rochester Times-Union*, 1918–48; owner, *Utica (NY) Observer-Dispatch*, 1921; owner, *Elmira Advertiser*, 1923; owner, *Elmira Telegram*, 1923; owner, *Newburgh News*, 1925; owner, *Plainfield (NJ) Courier News*, 1927; owner, *Beacon (NY) Journal and Herald*, 1927; owner, *Olean (NY) Herald*, 1927; owner, *Hartford (CT) Times*, 1928; owner, *Ogdensburg (NY) Republican Journal*, 1928; owner, *Rochester Republican Journal*, 1928; owner, *Rochester Democrat and Chronicle*, 1928; owner, *Albany (NY) Knickerbocker Press and Evening News*, 1928; owner, *Brooklyn (NY) Daily Eagle*, 1929; owner, *Malone (NY) Evening Telegram*, 1929; owner, *Danville Commercial News*, 1934; owner, *Saratoga Springs (NY) Saratogian*, 1934; owner, *Utica Daily Press*, 1934; owner, *Massena (NY) Observer*, 1937; owner, *Niagara Falls (NY) Gazette*, 1954; owner, radio and television stations; pres., Gannett Co., Inc.; dir., Teletypesetter Corp.; dir., Associated Press, 1935–40. MEM.: Advertising Club; University Club of New York; Frank E. Gannett Newspaper Foundation (founder, 1935); NY State Publishers Assn. (founder, 1919; pres.); NY Associated Dailies (pres., 1916–17); NY State Press Assn. (pres., 1917–18); SAR; National Cmte. to Uphold Constitutional Government (chm., 1937); Rochester Inst. of Technology (dir.); Soc. of the Genesee (pres.); Keuka Coll. (trustee); Masons (Shriner; Knights Templar); Cornell U. (trustee); Elks; Phi Beta Kappa (hon.); Rotary Club; City Club; Cornellian Council (pres., 1925–26); Cmte. of 100. AWARDS: Gold Citizenship Medal, VFW, 1940; Fairbanks Award, American Coll. Public Relations Assn., 1951; Citizen Award, SAR, 1951; Founders Award, Rochester Inst. of Technology, 1952; Award of Merit, hon. fellow, George Washington Carver Memorial Inst., 1952; Chevalier, Legion of Honor (France); Civic Medal, Rochester Museum of Arts and Sciences, 1955. HON. DEG.: M.A., Wesleyan U., 1929; Litt.D., Keuka Coll., 1939; LL.D., Alfred U., 1935; LL.D., Hobart Coll., 1937; LL.D., Oglethorpe U., 1939; LL.D., Hartwick Coll., 1941; LL.D., St. Bonaventure Coll., 1947; LL.D., U. of New Brunswick, 1951; LL.D., Syracuse U., 1953; Dr. of Journalism, Bradley U., 1955. WRITINGS: *Friars and Filipinos* (translator, 1900); *Britain Sees It Through* (1944); *The Fuse Sputters in Europe* (1946); *Winging Around the World* (1947). REL.: Unitarian. RES.: Rochester, NY.

GARCIA, JOSE M. POLIT. & GOV.: ***candidate for Republican nomination to presidency of the U.S., 1980***. MAILING ADDRESS: 1528 Sevilla Ave., Coral Gables, FL 33134.

GARCIA, THOMAS NIEL. POLIT. & GOV.: ***candidate for Democratic nomination to presidency of the U.S., 1984***. MEM.: National Organization of Voting Americans. MAILING ADDRESS: 340 Moss St., Apt. 813, Chula Vista, CA 92011.

GARDNER, EARL S. POLIT. & GOV.: ***candidate for Liberty Union nomination to presidency of the U.S., 1980***; Liberty Union candidate for U.S. Senate (VT), 1980. MAILING ADDRESS: Newfane, VT.

GARDNER, FREDERICK DOZIER. b. Nov 6, 1869, Hickman, KY; d. Dec 18, 1933, St. Louis, MO; par.

William Henry and Mary Ellen (Dozier) Gardner; m. Jeannette Vosburgh, Oct 10, 1894; c. William King; Dozier Lee; Janet (Mrs. Robert N. Hawes; Mrs. MacLean Hoggson). EDUC.: public schools, KY and TN. POLIT. & GOV.: elected as a Democrat to Board of Freeholders, St. Louis, MO, 1913–15; elected as a Democrat to gov. of MO, 1917–21; delegate, Dem. Nat'l. Conv., 1920, 1924, 1928; ***candidate for Democratic nomination to vice presidency of the U.S., 1924***. BUS. & PROF.: office boy, bookkeeper, sec., St. Louis Coffin Co., 1893, owner, c. 1900–1933; chm. of the board, Memphis Coffin Co., 1898; stock breeder, MO; lumberman, AR; dir., MS Valley Trust Co. Mem. Masons (Shriner); Elks; Knights of Pythias; Bogey Club. REL.: Methodist (trustee, Grace Methodist Church). RES.: St. Louis, MO.

GARDNER, HENRY JOSEPH. b. Jun 14, 1818, Dorchester, MA; d. Jul 21, 1892, Milton, MA; par. Dr. Henry and Clarissa (Holbrook) Gardner; m. Helen Elizabeth Cobb, Nov 21, 1843; c. four sons; three daughters. EDUC.: grad., Phillips Acad., 1834; grad., Bowdoin Coll., 1838. POLIT. & GOV.: elected member, Common Council, Boston, MA, 1850–54 (pres., 1852–53); elected as an American (Know-Nothing) to MA State House, 1851–52; delegate, MA State Constitutional Convention, 1853; elected as an American (Know-Nothing) to gov. of MA, 1854–58; ***candidate for American (Know-Nothing) Party nomination to vice presidency of the U.S., 1856***; American (Know-Nothing) Party candidate for gov. of MA, 1857. BUS. & PROF.: merchant; partner, Denney, Rice and Gardner (dry goods); partner, Read, Gardner and Co. (dry goods), 1860 (subsequently Gardner, Dexter and Co.); owner, Henry J. Gardner and Co. (dry goods), to 1876; resident agent, Massachusetts Life Insurance Co., 1876–92. HON. DEG.: A.M., Bowdoin Coll.; LL.D., Harvard U., 1855. RES.: Boston, MA.

GARDNER, JOHN WILLIAM. b. Oct 8, 1912, Los Angeles, CA; par. William and Marie (Flora) Gardner; m. Aida Morroquin, Aug 18, 1934; c. Stephanie Trimble; Francesca (Mrs. John R. Reese). EDUC.: A.B., Stanford U., 1934, A.M., 1936; Ph.D., U. of CA, 1938; fellow, John F. Kennedy Inst. of Politics, Harvard U. POLIT. & GOV.: appointed head, Latin American Section, Federal Communications Comm., 1942–43; appointed member, President's Task Force on Education, 1960, 1964 (chm.); appointed chm., U.S. Advisory Comm. on International Education and Cultural Affairs, 1962–64; appointed chm., White House Conference on Education, 1965; appointed U.S. sec. of health, education and welfare, 1965–68; ***candidate for Democratic nomination to presidency of the U.S., 1972***; appointed member, President's Comm. on White House Fellows, 1977. BUS. & PROF.: teaching asst., U. of CA, 1936–38; instructor in psychology, CT Coll., 1938–40; asst. prof., Mt. Holyoke Coll., 1940–42; staff, Carnegie Corp., 1946–47, exec. assoc., 1947–49, vice pres., 1949–55, pres., 1955–65, consultant, 1968–; pres., Carnegie Foundation for the Advancement of Teaching, 1955–65; visiting prof., MA Inst. of Technology, 1968–69. MIL.: capt., U.S.M.C., 1943–46; U.S. Air Force Exceptional Service Award, 1956. MEM.: Urban Coalition (chm., 1968–70); Common Cause (founder; pres., 1970–77); Aspen Inst. for Humanistic Studies (adviser, 1977–79); United Way of America (consultant, 1977); NY School of Social Work (trustee, 1949–55); Metropolitan Museum of Art (trustee, 1957–65); Stanford U. (trustee, 1968–); Rockefeller Brothers Fund (trustee, 1968–77); American Acad. of Arts and Sciences (fellow); National Acad. of Education (fellow); AAAS (dir.); Bohemian Club; Century Club; Coffee House Club; Cosmos Club; Federal City Club; Woodrow Wilson Foundation (dir., 1960–63). AWARDS: Presidential Medal of Freedom, 1964; Public Welfare Medal, National Acad. of Science, 1966; Social Justice Award, U.A.W., 1968; Democratic Legacy Award, Anti-Defamation League, 1968; Murray Green Medal, AFL-CIO, 1970; Christopher Award, 1971; Distinguished Service Award, American Inst. of Public Service, 1973. HON. DEG.: fellow, Stanford U., 1959; LL.D., U. of CA, 1959; numerous others. WRITINGS: *Excellence* (1961); *Self-Renewal* (1963); *No Easy Victories* (1968); *Recovery of Confidence* (1970); *In Common Cause* (1972); *Know or Listen to Those Who Know* (1975); *Morale* (1978); *To Turn the Tide* (ed.). MAILING ADDRESS: 2030 M St., N.W., Suite 603, Washington, DC 20036.

GARFIELD, JAMES ABRAM. b. Nov 19, 1831, Orange, OH; d. Sep 19, 1881, Elberon, NJ; par. Abram and Eliza (Ballou) Garfield; m. Lucretia Rudolph, Nov 11, 1858; c. James Rudolph (q.v.); Harry Augustus; Irving McDowell; Abram; Mary (Mrs. Joseph Stanley-Brown); Eliza Arabella (infant); Edward (infant). EDUC.: Geauga Seminary, 1849; Western Reserve Eclectic Inst., 1851–54; grad., Williams Coll., 1856. POLIT. & GOV.: elected as a Republican to OH State Senate, 1859; elected as a Republican to U.S. House (OH), 1863–80; member, Electoral Comm., 1877; elected as a Republican to U.S. Senate (OH), 1880 (declined); delegate, Rep. Nat'l. Conv., 1880 (OH Delegation chm.); ***elected as a Republican to presidency of the U.S., 1881***. BUS. & PROF.: driver and helmsman, Ohio Canal; schoolteacher, 1849; carpenter, 1850; minister, Disciples of Christ, 1856–61; atty.; admitted to OH Bar, 1860; prof. of Latin and Greek, Hiram Coll., 1856–71, pres., 1856–61. MIL.: lt. col., col., 42d OH Volunteer Infantry Regt., 1861; brig. gen., U.S.V., 1862; chief of staff, Army of the Cumberland, 1863; maj. gen., U.S.V., 1863. MEM.: Phi Beta Kappa; Masons (Master). WRITINGS: articles in *North American Review* and *Atlantic Monthly*. REL.: Disciples of Christ. MISC.: shot by Charles J. Guiteau, Jul 2, 1881, resulting in his death on Sep 19, 1881. RES.: Mentor, OH.

GARFIELD, JAMES RUDOLPH. b. Oct 17, 1865, Hiram, OH; d. Mar 24, 1950, Cleveland, OH; par. President James Abram (q.v.) and Lucretia (Rudolph) Garfield; m. Helen Newell, Dec 30, 1890; c. John Newell; James Abram; Newell; Rudolph Hills. EDUC.: St. Paul's School, Concord, NH; B.A., Williams Coll., 1885; Columbia U.; studied law in offices of Bangs and Stetson, New York, NY. POLIT. & GOV.: elected as a Republican to OH State Senate, 1896–99; appointed member, U.S. Civil Service Comm., 1902–03; appointed commissioner of corporations, U.S. Dept. of Commerce, 1903–07; appointed U.S. sec. of the interior, 1907–09; Progressive Party candidate for gov. of OH, 1914; member, Cleveland (OH) War Council, 1917; ***candidate for Republican nomination to presidency of the U.S., 1920***; appointed member, Emergency Board to Investigate Railroad Disputes, 1926; ***candidate for Republican nomination to vice presidency of the U.S., 1928***; appointed chm., U.S. Public Land Comm., 1929. BUS. & PROF.: atty.; admitted to OH Bar, 1888; partner, Garfield and Garfield (law firm), Cleveland, OH, 1888; partner, Garfield, MacGregor and Baldwin (law firm), Cleveland, OH, 1909–27; partner, Garfield and Rhoades (law firm), Mexico City, Mexico, 1917–30; partner, Garfield, Cross, MacGregor, Daoust and Baldwin (law firm), Cleveland, OH, 1927–44; partner, Garfield, Baldwin, Jamison, Hope and Ulrich (law firm), Cleveland, OH, 1944–50. MEM.: Theodore Roosevelt Assn. (founder, 1919; pres.); Williams Coll. (trustee); Western Reserve Hist. Soc. (trustee); Lake Erie Coll. (pres., Board of Trustees); Cleveland Foundation (counsel, 1914–44); Cleveland Welfare Federation (pres., 1917–30); Cleveland Community Fund (founder; trustee); Cleveland Humane Soc. (trustee); Lakeview Cemetery Assn. (trustee); Cleveland Hearing and Speech Center (trustee, 1938–50; pres., 1938–45); American Soc. of International Law; ABA; OH State Bar Assn.; Cleveland Bar Assn.; Alpha Delta Phi; Union Club of Cleveland; University Club of Cleveland; Williams Coll. Club of New York; University Club of New York. HON. DEG.: LL.D., U. of Pittsburgh, 1909; LL.D., Howard U., 1909; LL.D., Williams Coll., 1936. REL.: Episc. RES.: Mentor, OH.

GARFORD, ARTHUR L. b. Aug 4, 1858, Elyria, OH; d. Jan 23, 1933, Elyria, OH; par. George and Hannah (Lovett) Garford; m. Mary Nelson, Dec 14, 1881. EDUC.: Elyria (OH) H.S. POLIT. & GOV.: delegate, Rep. Nat'l. Conv., 1896, 1908, 1912, 1916, 1924, 1928, 1932; Progressive Party candidate for gov. of OH, 1912; Progressive Party candidate for U.S. Senate (OH), 1914; ***candidate for Republican nomination to presidency of the U.S., 1924***. BUS. & PROF.: cashier, Rice and Burnett (china imports), Cleveland, OH, 1877–80; bookkeeper, Savings Deposit Bank and Trust Co., Elyria, OH, 1880–90, cashier, chm. of the board; pres., Worthington Manufacturing Co.; pres., American Lace Manufacturing Co.; pres., Garford Co.; pres., Cleveland (OH) Automatic Machine Co.; dir., Standard Trust Bank, Cleveland, OH; pres., Electric Alloys Co.; dir., Perry Fay Co., Elyria, OH. MEM.: Elyria C. of C. (pres.); YMCA (patron); Union Club. REL.: Congregationalist. MISC.: invented bicycle saddle. RES.: Elyria, OH.

GARLAND, RAYMOND L. POLIT. & GOV.: Republican candidate for U.S. Senate (VA), 1970; ***United Sovereign Citizens Party candidate for vice presidency of the U.S., 1984***. MAILING ADDRESS: VA.

GARNER, JOHN NANCE. b. Nov 22, 1868, Detroit, TX; d. Nov 7, 1967, Uvalde, TX; par. John Nance and Sara (Guest) Garner; m. Ettie Rheiner, Nov 25, 1895; c. Tully. EDUC.: studied law, Clarksville, TX. POLIT. & GOV.: judge, Uvalde Cty., TX, 1893–96; elected as a Democrat to TX State House, 1898–1902; delegate, Dem. Nat'l. Conv., 1900, 1904, 1916, 1924; elected as a Democrat to U.S. House (TX), 1903–33 (Speaker, 1931–33); ***candidate for Democratic nomination to presidency of the U.S., 1932, 1936, 1940; elected as a Democrat to vice presidency of the U.S., 1933–41; candidate for Democratic nomination to vice presidency of the U.S., 1940***. BUS. & PROF.: atty.; admitted to TX Bar, 1890; law practice, Uvalde, TX; farmer, Uvalde Cty., TX. HON. DEG.: LL.D., John Marshall Coll. of Law, 1936; LL.D., Baylor U., 1936. REL.: Methodist. RES.: Uvalde, TX.

GARRY, KATHERINE M. POLIT. & GOV.: ***independent candidate for vice presidency of the U.S., 1984***. MAILING ADDRESS: 109 Broadway, Rockville Centre, NY 11570.

GARSON, BARBARA. b. Jul 7, 1941, Brooklyn, NY; d. Harry and Frances Garson; single; c. Juliet. EDUC.: Brooklyn Coll.; B.A., U. of CA, Berkeley, 1964. POLIT. & GOV.: founding member, Peace and Freedom Party; ***Socialist Party candidate for vice presidency of the U.S., 1992; Liberty Union Party candidate for vice presidency of the U.S., 1992***. BUS. & PROF.: ed., *Free Speech Movement Newsletter*, 1964–65; playwright; journalist; antiwar activist. AWARDS: Guggenheim Fellowship; National Endowment for the Arts Fellowship; OBIE Award. WRITINGS: *MacBird* (c. 1964); *The Department; The Dinosaur Door; All the Livelong Day: The Meaning and Demeaning of Routine Work* (1977); *The Electronic Sweatshop—How Computers are Transforming the Office of the Future to the Factory of the Past* (1989); *Security*. REL.: none. MAILING ADDRESS: 463 West St., #1108A, New York, NY 10014.

GARVIN, FLORENCE. b. Feb 27, 1876, Lonsdale, RI; d. Jul 10, 1968, Pasadena, CA; par. Lucius F. C. and Lucy W. (Southmayd) Garvin; single. EDUC.: Providence Girls' H.S.; Pembroke Coll., 1895–96, 1899–1900. POLIT. & GOV.: Progressive Party candidate for U.S. House (DE), 1924; first vice pres., Exec. Cmte., National Party, 1931; ***National Independent (Greenback) Party candidate for vice presidency of the U.S., 1936***. BUS. & PROF.: librarian, art-music dept., Providence Public Library; businesswoman. MEM.: Suffragist Cmte. of RI. MISC.: father was Democratic gov. of RI, 1903–05. RES.: Blackstone, Lonsdale, RI.

GARY, ELBERT HENRY. b. Oct 8, 1846, Wheaton, IL; d. Aug 15, 1927, New York, NY; par. Erastus and Susan A. (Vallette) Gary; m. Julia E. Graves, Jun 23, 1869; m.

2d, Emma T. Scott Townsend, Dec 2, 1905; c. Gertrude (Mrs. Harry W. Sutcliffe); Bertha (Mrs. Robert W. Campbell). EDUC.: Wheaton Coll.; studied law under Vallette and Cody (law firm), Naperville, IL; LL.B., U. of Chicago, 1867. POLIT. & GOV.: elected town pres., Wheaton, IL, 1872–73; elected cty. judge, DuPage Cty., IL, 1882–90; elected mayor, Wheaton, 1892; ***candidate for Republican nomination to presidency of the U.S., 1916, 1920***; appointed member, International High Comm. (U.S. Section), 1917. BUS. & PROF.: atty.; admitted to IL Bar, 1867; admitted to the Bar of the Supreme Court of the U.S., 1882; partner (with Noah E. Gary), law practice, Chicago, IL, 1873–79; partner, Gary, Cody and Gary (law firm), Chicago, 1879–92; gen. counsel, Northwestern Elevated R.R. Co.; gen. counsel, American Steel and Wire Co.; gen. counsel, Illinois Steel Co.; pres., Gary-Wheaton Bank, 1873–98; pres., Federal Steel Co.; chm. of the board, chief exec. officer, U.S. Steel Corp.; dir., Merchants Loan and Trust Co.; dir., New York Trust Co.; dir., Phoenix National Bank of New York; dir., Newburgh and South Shore Railway Co.; dir., New York and Jersey R.R. Co.; dir., Pittsburgh, Bessemer and Lake Erie R.R. Co.; dir., Pittsburgh Steamship Co.; dir., American Trust and Savings Bank; dir., Commercial National Bank; dir., Masontown and New Salem R.R. Co.; dir., Hudson and Manhattan R.R. Co.; dir., Joliet and Eastern Railway Co.; dir., Allis-Chalmers Co.; dir., American Bridge Co.; dir., American Land Co.; dir., American Mining Co.; dir., American Sheet and Tin Plate Co.; dir., American Steel Foundries Co.; dir., Carnegie Steel Co.; dir., Empire Bridge Co.; dir., H. C. Frick Coke Co.; dir., Huron Water Co.; dir., International Harvester Co.; dir., Lake Superior Consolidated Iron Mines; dir., Minnesota Iron Co.; dir., National Tube Co.; dir., Oliver Iron Mining Co.; dir., Shelby Steel Tube Co.; dir., Union Steel Co.; dir., U.S. Coal and Coke Co.; dir., U.S. Natural Gas Co.; dir., U.S. Steel Products Export Co.; dir., Duluth and Iron Range R.R. Co. MEM.: American Iron and Steel Inst. (pres., 1909–27); New York Ordnance District (chm., Advisory Board); Northwestern U. (trustee); Syracuse U. (trustee); NY C. of C.; Automobile Club of Ireland; Automobile Club of France; Automobile Club of Germany; Automobile Club of America; Automobile Club of Great Britain; Chicago Bar Assn. (pres., 1893–94); Metropolitan Club; Lawyer Club; Union League; Chicago Club. AWARDS: Order of the Sacred Treasure, Second Class (Japan, 1918); Order of Ouissan Alaouite Cherifien, Grand Officer (Morocco, 1920); Legion of Honor (France, 1920); Golden Cross of the Commandership of the Royal Battalion of George I (Greece, 1921); Grand Cross of the Knights of the Crown of Italy (1922). HON. DEG.: LL.D., McKendree Coll., 1906; LL.D., Lafayette Coll., 1915; Sc.D., U. of Pittsburgh, 1915; LL.D., Lincoln Memorial U., 1919; LL.D., Trinity Coll., 1919; LL.D., Syracuse U., 1921; LL.D., Northwestern U., 1922; D.C.S., NY U., 1925. REL.: Methodist Episc. (Sunday school teacher). RES.: New York, NY.

GASKING, LEVI MARTIN LUTHER, III. POLIT. & GOV.: ***candidate for Republican nomination to presidency of the U.S., 1988***. BUS. & PROF.: minister. MAILING ADDRESS: c/o Leon Clifford Gasking, 3105 Ave. A, Bay City, TX 77414.

GASTON, LUCY PAGE. b. May 19, 1860, Delaware, OH; d. Aug 20, 1924, Hinsdale, IL; par. Alexander Hugh and Henrietta (Page) Gaston; single. EDUC.: grad., high school, Lacon, IL; State Normal School, Normal, IL. POLIT. & GOV.: Prohibition Party candidate for Board of Trustees, U. of IL, 1896, 1920; ***candidate for Republican nomination to presidency of the U.S., 1920; candidate for Democratic nomination to presidency of the U.S., 1924***. BUS. & PROF.: schoolteacher; reformer; ed., *The Christian Citizen*, Harvey, IL, 1897; ed., *The Boy Magazine*; superintendent, Anti-Cigarette League, 1901–24; ed., *Anti-Cigarette Herald*. MEM.: W.C.T.U. (National Superintendent of Christian Citizenship); Anti-Cigarette League of America (founder; superintendent, 1901–24); Marshall Cty. Sunday School Assn. (pres.); Chicago Woman's City Club; Political Equality Club; Social Economics Club; National Christian Citizenship League. REL.: Congregationalist. RES.: Chicago, IL.

GASTON, WILLIAM ALEXANDER. b. May 1, 1859, Roxbury, MA; d. Jul 17, 1927, Barre, MA; par. William and Louisa Augusta (Beecher) Gaston; m. May Davidson Lockwood, Apr 9, 1892; c. William; John; Ruth (Mrs. Laurence Foster); Hope (Mrs. Cornelius Conway Felton). EDUC.: A.B., Harvard U., 1880, Harvard Law School, 1881–82. POLIT. & GOV.: col., staff of Gov. William E. Russell (q.v.), MA, 1890–1902; Democratic candidate for gov. of MA, 1902, 1903, 1926; Democratic candidate for U.S. Senate (MA), 1905, 1922; member, Dem. Nat'l. Cmte.; member, MA State Democratic Central Cmte.; chm., MA Comm. on War Efficiency, Cmte. on Public Safety, 1917–19; dir., U.S. Public Service Reserve; delegate, Dem. Nat'l. Conv., 1924; ***candidate for Democratic nomination to presidency of the U.S., 1924; candidate for Democratic nomination to vice presidency of the U.S., 1924***. BUS. & PROF.: atty.; admitted to Suffolk Cty. (MA) Bar, 1883; partner, Gaston and Whitney (law firm); partner, Gaston, Snow, Saltonstall and Hunt (law firm); member, Exec. Cmte., National Shawmut Bank, pres., 1907–20, chm. of the board, 1920–25; pres., Boylston Market Associates; pres., Killingly Trust Co.; dir., Second National Bank, Barre, MA; dir., Windham Cty. National Bank, Danielson, CT; dir., Gillette Safety Razor Co.; pres., Boston Elevated Railway Co., 1897–1902; farmer; dir., National Rockland Bank of Boston; dir., Big Sandy Coal Co.; dir., American Telephone and Telegraph; dir., Dodge Brothers, Inc.; dir., Elkhorn Coal and Coke Co.; dir., Columbian National Life Insurance Co.; dir., Kansas City Stock Yards; dir., E. Howard Clock Co.; dir., B. F. Sturtevant Co.; dir., Dudley Cooperative Bank; dir., Massachusetts Bonding and Insurance Co.; dir., Joseph Burnett Co.; trustee, Institution of Savings; owner, Forest Hill Cemetery; owner, Andrews Real Estate Trust; owner, Central Building Trust; owner, City Associates; owner, Congress Building Trust; owner, Minot Building Trust; owner, Petersham Associates. MEM.: YMCA; Liberty Loan Drive; Salvation Army Drive;

Worcester West Agricultural Assn. (pres.); Soc. for the Prevention of Cruelty to Animals; Free Hospital for Women; Florence Crittenden Home; Boston Elevated Mutual Aid Soc.; Civic Federation of New England; Boston Public Library (trustee); International Peace Forum; American Civic Assn. REL.: Episc. RES.: Boston, MA.

GAVIN, JAMES MAURICE. b. Mar 22, 1907, New York, NY; d. Feb 23, 1990, Baltimore, MD; par. Martin Thomas and Mary (Terrel) Gavin; m. Irma Margaret Baulsir, Sep 5, 1929 (divorced); m. 2d, Jean Emert Duncan, Jul 31, 1948; c. Caroline (Mrs. Richard K. O'Neill); Patricia; Aileen Lewis; Chloe Beatty; Barbara Margaret Fauntleroy. EDUC.: B.S., U.S. Military Acad., 1929; Infantry School, 1933; Command and General Staff School; Parachute School. POLIT. & GOV.: appointed U.S. ambassador to France, 1961–63; ***candidate for Republican nomination to presidency of the U.S., 1968***; appointed member, American Battle Monuments Comm. BUS. & PROF.: army officer; business exec.; exec. vice pres., Arthur D. Little, Inc., 1958–60, pres., 1960–61, chm. of the board, chief exec. officer, 1964–77, consultant, dir., 1977–79, consultant, 1979–; dir., John Hancock Mutual Life Insurance Co.; dir., American Electric Power Co. MIL.: enlisted as a pvt., U.S. Army, 1924; commissioned 2d lt., U.S. Army, 1929; advanced through grades to brig. gen., 1943, lt. gen., 1955; deputy chief of staff, U.S. Army; retired from U.S. Army, 1958; Croix de Guerre with Palm; Legion of Honor (grand officer); Distinguished Service Cross with Oak Leaf Cluster; Purple Heart; two Silver Stars; Distinguished Service Order (Great Britain). MEM.: Council on Foreign Relations; Tufts U. (life trustee); Center for International Affairs, Harvard U. (fellow). WRITINGS: *Airborne Warfare* (1947); *War and Peace in the Space Age* (1958); *France and the Civil War in America* (1962); *Crisis Now* (1968); *On to Berlin* (1978). MISC.: known as "Jumpin' Jim" and "Slim Jim." RES.: Cambridge, MA.

GAY, JAMES BRYANT, JR. POLIT. & GOV.: ***candidate for Democratic nomination to presidency of the U.S., 1992***. MAILING ADDRESS: Austin, TX.

GAYDOSH, FRANK WASIL. b. Mar 21, 1909, Berwick, PA; par. Wasil and Polly (Yedinak) Gaydosh; m. Leona Geneva Roach; c. Dorothy; Audry; Joyce; Lonny. EDUC.: Berwick (PA) H.S.; personality and sales courses. POLIT. & GOV.: Constitutional Party candidate for U.S. Senate (PA), 1968, 1970; ***candidate for American (Constitutional) Party nomination to presidency of the U.S., 1972; Restoration Party candidate for vice presidency of the U.S., 1976***. BUS. & PROF.: chm. of the board, Big Chief Markets; dir., Pioneer Dime Bank; gen. mgr., Carbondale Wholesale Coins; pres., Greater Forest City Industries. MEM.: American Patriots; Forest City Lions Club (pres.); Carbondale C. of C. (pres.); Christian Businessmen's Cmte. of Scranton (chm.). WRITINGS: *A Rock Foundation—Honest Money*. REL.: Fundamental Christian (Varden Bible Church). MAILING ADDRESS: 52 North Main St., Carbondale, PA 18407.

GAYNOR, WILLIAM JAY. b. Feb 23, 1849, Whitestown, NY; d. Sep 10, 1913, on board *Baltic*, about 600 miles off coast of Ireland; par. Keiron K. and Elizabeth (Handwright) Gaynor; m. Augusta Cole Mayer, Jan 27, 1887; c. Rufus William; Norman Joseph; Gertrude Emily (Mrs. William Seward Webb, Jr.); Edith Augusta (Mrs. Henry K. Vingut); Helen Deborah (Mrs. E. T. Bedford, II); Marion (Mrs. Ralph Heyward Isham); Ruth Merritt. EDUC.: Assumption Acad.; Whitestown Seminary; studied law, Utica, NY. POLIT. & GOV.: elected judge, Supreme Court of NY, 1893–1909; Democratic candidate for gov. of NY, 1894 (declined), 1912 (declined); Democratic candidate for judge, NY Court of Appeals, 1894 (declined); Democratic candidate for mayor of Brooklyn, NY, 1896 (declined); ***candidate for Democratic nomination to presidency of the U.S., 1908, 1912***; elected as a Democrat (independent) to mayor of New York, NY, 1909–13. BUS. & PROF.: teacher, Boston, MA; employee, Argus, New York, 1873; atty.; admitted to NY Bar, 1875; author of legal works. MIL.: judge advocate, 2d Brigade, NY National Guard, 1890. MISC.: shot in attempted assassination, Aug 9, 1909. RES.: Brooklyn, NY.

GEARY, JOHN WHITE. b. Dec 30, 1819, Mt. Pleasant, PA; d. Feb 8, 1873, Harrisburg, PA; par. Richard and Margaret (White) Geary; m. Margaret Ann Logan, 1843; m. 2d, Mary Church Henderson, 1858; c. Edward R.; John White, Jr.; William L. EDUC.: Jefferson Coll. POLIT. & GOV.: elected first alcalde, San Francisco, CA, 1848; appointed first postmaster, San Francisco, 1848; independent candidate for gov. of CA, 1849; first mayor of San Francisco, 1850; judge of first instance, San Francisco, 1850; chm., California Democratic Territorial Cmte.; appointed gov. of Utah Territory, 1855 (declined); appointed gov. of Kansas Territory, 1856–57 (resigned); elected as a Republican to gov. of PA, 1867–73; ***candidate for Labor Reform Party nomination to presidency of the U.S., 1872***. BUS. & PROF.: schoolteacher; clerk, Pittsburgh, PA; land speculator; civil engineer; atty.; admitted to PA Bar; surveyor; agent, State and Green River R.R. Co.; asst. superintendent and engineer, Allegheny and Portage R.R. MIL.: lt., PA Militia, 1835; lt. col., Second PA Regt., U.S. Army, 1846, col., 1848; col., 28th PA Volunteers, 1861, brig. gen., 1862; military gov. of Savannah, GA, after capture of city in Civil War; brev. maj. gen., 1865. REL.: Presb. RES.: Harrisburg, PA.

GEE, HOOVER MARK. POLIT. & GOV.: ***candidate for Republican nomination to presidency of the U.S., 1996***. MAILING ADDRESS: 507 Bush St., #206, San Francisco, CA 94108.

GEHRING, GEORGE JOSEPH, JR. b. 1931; par. George Joseph Gehring. EDUC.: D.D.S., Marquette U.,

1955. POLIT. & GOV.: ***independent candidate for presidency of the U.S., 1988, 1992***. BUS. & PROF.: dentist, Long Beach, CA. MEM.: American Dental Assn. MAILING ADDRESS: 532 East 29th St., Long Beach, CA 90806.

GENTRY, EDWARD EARL. b. Jan 30, 1904, Baxter, TN; par. John Byrd and Agnes Lee (Jernigan) Gentry; m. Mary Atla Spillman; c. Edward Earl, Jr.; Atla Maie; Lucy Lee; Robert Roy; Eunice Evelyn. EDUC.: self-taught. POLIT. & GOV.: ***Independent Republican candidate for presidency of the U.S., 1976***. BUS. & PROF.: operator, E. E. Gentry News Service. WRITINGS: "Consequences of Babylon" (unpublished). REL.: none. MAILING ADDRESS: Route 1, Box 139, Marthaville, LA 71450.

GEORGE, MALCOMBE. b. Nov 29, 1939, Fresno, CA. single. EDUC.: Fresno (CA) H.S.; Fresno U. POLIT. & GOV.: candidate for Fresno City Council, 1975; ***independent candidate for presidency of the U.S., 1976; candidate for Republican nomination to presidency of the U.S., 1980***. BUS. & PROF.: parapsychologist. REL.: Judaic-Christian. MAILING ADDRESS: 840 North Safford, Fresno, CA 93728.

GEORGE, WALTER FRANKLIN. b. Jan 29, 1878, Preston, GA; d. Aug 4, 1957, Vienna, GA; par. Robert Theodoric and Sarah (Stapleton) George; m. Lucy Heard, Jul 9, 1903; c. Heard Joseph; Joseph Marcus. EDUC.: B.S., Mercer U., 1900, B.L., 1901. POLIT. & GOV.: elected solicitor, Vienna (GA) City Court, 1906; elected solicitor gen., Cordele Judicial Circuit, GA, 1907–12; judge, Superior Court of GA, 1912–17; judge, GA State Court of Appeals, 1917; elected assoc. justice, Supreme Court of GA, 1917–22; elected as a Democrat to U.S. Senate (GA), 1922–57 (pres. pro tempore, 1955–57); delegate, Dem. Nat'l. Conv., 1928, 1952; ***candidate for Democratic nomination to presidency of the U.S., 1928, 1932***; appointed special U.S. ambassador to the North Atlantic Treaty Organization, 1957. BUS. & PROF.: atty.; admitted to GA Bar, 1901; law practice, Vienna, GA, 1901. HON. DEG.: LL.D., Mercer U., 1920. RES.: Vienna, GA.

GEPHARDT, RICHARD ANDREW. b. Jan 31, 1941, St. Louis, MO; par. Louis Andrew and Loreen Estelle (Cassell) Gephardt; m. Jane Ann Byrnes, Aug 13, 1966; c. Matthew; Christine; Katherine. EDUC.: grad., Southwest H.S., 1958; B.S., Northwestern U., 1962; J.D., U. of MI, 1965. POLIT. & GOV.: elected member, St. Louis (MO) Democratic Central Cmte., 1971–77; elected as a Democrat to U.S. House (MO), 1977– (majority leader, 1989–95; minority leader, 1995–); ***candidate for Democratic nomination to presidency of the U.S., 1988, 1992; candidate for Democratic nomination to vice presidency of the U.S., 1988***. BUS. & PROF.: atty.; admitted to MO Bar, 1965; partner, Thompson and Mitchell (law firm), St. Louis, 1965–77. MIL.: airman, MO Air National Guard, 1965–71, capt., 1971–77. MEM.: Bar Assn. of Metropolitan St. Louis (chair, Young Lawyer's Section, 1971–73); MO Bar Assn.; ABA; Kiwanis; BSA; Children's United Research Effort; Mid-Town Club; Young Lawyers' Soc. (chm., 1972–73); American Legion; DERU; Beta Theta Pi. AWARDS: American Spirit Honor Medal; Better Downtown Award, St. Louis, MO, 1973; Distinguished Service Award, St. Louis Jaycees, 1974. REL.: Bapt. MAILING ADDRESS: 4121 Fairview St., St. Louis, MO 63116.

GERARD, JAMES WATSON. b. Aug 25, 1867, Geneseo, NY; d. Sep 6, 1951, Southampton, NY; par. James Watson and Jennie Jones (Angel) Gerard; m. Mary A. Daly, Jun 1901; c. none. EDUC.: A.B., Columbia U., 1890, A.M., 1891; LL.B., NY Law School, 1892. POLIT. & GOV.: elected assoc. justice, Supreme Court of NY, 1908–13; appointed special U.S. envoy to Mexico, 1910; appointed U.S. ambassador to Germany, 1913–17; Democratic candidate for U.S. Senate (NY), 1914; treas., Dem. Nat'l. Cmte., to 1932; ***candidate for Democratic nomination to presidency of the U.S., 1920, 1924***; delegate, Dem. Nat'l. Conv., 1924, 1928, 1944; ***candidate for Democratic nomination to vice presidency of the U.S., 1924***; chm., Finance Cmte., Dem. Nat'l. Cmte., 1934; appointed special U.S. ambassador to coronation of King George VI, 1936; appointed member, Advisory Board, Point Four Program, 1950. BUS. & PROF.: atty.; admitted to NY Bar, 1892; assoc., Bowers and Sands (law firm), New York, NY, 1892–99, partner, 1899; partner, Laughlin, Gerard, Bowers and Halpin (law firm), New York, 1917–44; pres., Lawyers' Advertising Co.; owner, mining interests, MT; farmer, MT; pres., Traho Metallic Joint Corp.; pres., Schloetter Process Corp. MIL.: pvt., 2d lt., maj., 7th Regt., NY National Guard, 1890–1900. MEM.: ABA; NY Bar Assn.; Assn. of the Bar of the City of New York; New York Dispensary (dir.; pres.); Mexican C. of C. of the U.S., Inc. (dir.); NY State Economic Council (dir.); Comm. for the Relief of Belgium (chm.); Council of Ex-ambassadors; Union Club; Tuxedo Club; University Club; Riding Club; Fencers Club; SAR. AWARDS: Legion of Honor (France). HON. DEG.: LL.D., Columbia U., 1930. WRITINGS: *My Four Years in Germany* (1917); *Face to Face with Kaiserism* (1918); *My First Eighty Three Years in America* (1951). REL.: Episc. RES.: New York, NY.

GERBIG, GERALD M. POLIT. & GOV.: ***candidate for Democratic nomination to presidency of the U.S., 1984***. MAILING ADDRESS: Box 17, Ramsay, MI 49959.

GERHARDT, JOHN MARTIN. b. Jan 9, 1895, Raymond, SD; par. Wilbert (Sky) and Susanna Agnes (Masterson) Gerhardt; m. Myra O'Kelly; c. Joseph W.; Mary Ann St. Clair. EDUC.: high school. POLIT. & GOV.: elected as a Democrat to Board of Supervisors, Coles Cty., IL, 1963–67; nonpartisan candidate for mayor of Charleston, IL, 1965; ***candidate for***

Democratic nomination to presidency of the U.S., 1972. BUS. & PROF.: employee, Anton Langland Painting Firm, Turton, SD, 1911; machinist; owner, Gerhardt Painting and Decorating Co., 1930–70. MIL.: military service, WWI. MEM.: BSA; Old Grand-Dad Club. REL.: R.C. MAILING ADDRESS: 1435 Ninth St., Charleston, IL 61920.

GERMANI, PAUL KING. b. Jan 17, 1939, Boston, MA; par. George and Mary Teresa (King) Germani; single. EDUC.: B.S., U. of PA, 1961. POLIT. & GOV.: *candidate for Democratic nomination to presidency of the U.S., 1980*. BUS. & PROF.: mgr.; public relations consultant; high schoolteacher of French and Spanish. MIL.: capt., U.S. Army. MEM.: French National Honor Soc.; Kappa Sigma. REL.: R.C. MAILING ADDRESS: 114 First Ave., Osterville, MA 02655.

GERRY, ELBRIDGE. b. Jul 17, 1744, Marblehead, MA; d. Nov 23, 1814, Washington, DC; par. Thomas and Elizabeth (Greenleaf) Gerry; m. Ann Thompson, Jan 12, 1786; c. Elbridge, Jr.; Thomas Russell; one other son; four daughters. EDUC.: grad., Harvard Coll., 1762. POLIT. & GOV.: elected to MA Colonial House, 1772–75; member, Cmte. of Correspondence, 1773; member, Cmte. on Public Safety, 1775; member, Continental Congress, 1776–85; signer of Declaration of Independence, 1776; signer of Articles of Confederation; pres., Treasury Board, 1776–89; delegate, New Haven Convention, 1778; elected member, MA House, 1786; delegate, Federal Constitutional Convention, 1787 (refused to sign constitution); elected as an Anti-Federalist to U.S. House (MA), 1789–93; presidential elector, Democratic-Republican Party, 1797, 1804; appointed U.S. commissioner to France, 1797; Democratic-Republican candidate for gov. of MA, 1800, 1801, 1802, 1803, 1812; elected as a Democratic-Republican to gov. of MA, 1810–11; *elected as a Democratic-Republican to vice presidency of the U.S., 1813–14*. BUS. & PROF.: shipping tradesman; privateer. WRITINGS: *Observations on the New Constitution and On the Federal and State Conventions by a Columbian Patriot* (1788). REL.: Episc. RES.: MA.

GESS, MICHELE ANN. POLIT. & GOV.: *candidate for Republican nomination to presidency of the U.S., 1988, 1992*. MAILING ADDRESS: 918 17th Ave., Grafton, WI 53024.

GEYER, PAUL MARTIN. b. Feb 7, 1945, Jersey City, NJ; par. Robert Fulton and Agnes Catherine (Burgess) Geyer; single. EDUC.: B.A., Jersey City State Coll., 1963; M.A., OH Christian Coll., 1972. POLIT. & GOV.: elected member, Board of Education, Rahway, NJ, 1975–; American Party candidate for U.S. House (NJ), 1976; *independent candidate for presidency of the U.S., 1976*. BUS. & PROF.: employee, NASA-Grumman, 1967–70; teacher, junior high school, Rahway, NJ, 1970–72; member, fire dept., Rahway, NJ, 1972–. MEM.: Elks; Air Force Assn.; Disabled American Veterans. REL.: R.C. MAILING ADDRESS: 230 East Grand Ave., Rahway, NJ 07065.

GIAN-CURSIO, CHRISTOPHER. m. Jenne. POLIT. & GOV.: *American Vegetarian Party candidate for vice presidency of the U.S., 1960*. BUS. & PROF.: natural hygienist; nutrition counselor. MEM.: American Health Soc. (pres.). AWARDS: NY Natural Hygiene Soc. Award for Distinguished Service, 1952. MISC.: convicted of practicing medicine unlawfully, 1947; MAILING ADDRESS: 5455 Alton Rd., Miami Beach, FL 33140.

GIBNEY, JAYNE. married. POLIT. & GOV.: *candidate for Democratic nomination to presidency of the U.S., 1976*. MAILING ADDRESS: P.O. Box 2386, Brookings, OR 97415.

GIDDINGS, JOSHUA REED. b. Oct 6, 1795, Tioga Point, PA; d. May 27, 1864, Montreal, Canada; par. Joshua and Elizabeth (Pease) Giddings; m. Laura Waters, Sep 24, 1819; c. Laura (Mrs. George Washington Julian, q.v.); possibly others. EDUC.: studied law under Elisha Whittlesey, Canfield, OH. POLIT. & GOV.: elected as a Whig to OH State House, 1826–28; elected as a Whig to U.S. House (OH), 1839–42 (censured and resigned), 1842–59; delegate, Rep. Nat'l. Conv., 1856, 1860; *candidate for Republican nomination to vice presidency of the U.S., 1856*; appointed U.S. consul gen. to Canada, 1861–64. BUS. & PROF.: schoolteacher, Ashtabula, OH, 1812; farmer; atty.; admitted to OH Bar, 1821; law practice, Jefferson, OH, 1821–38; abolitionist. MIL.: served in War of 1812. WRITINGS: *The Exiles of Florida* (1858); *The History of the Rebellion* (1864). RES.: Jefferson, OH.

GILBERT, JEFERY S. POLIT. & GOV.: *independent candidate for presidency of the U.S., 1980*. MAILING ADDRESS: 1212 30th St., #1, Des Moines, IA 50311.

GILBRETH, GREGORY LEE. POLIT. & GOV.: *independent candidate for vice presidency of the U.S., 1980*. MAILING ADDRESS: 30575 Higuera, San Luis Obispo, CA.

GILL, FRANK. b. Canada. POLIT. & GOV.: *candidate for Prohibition Party nomination to presidency of the U.S., 1904*. RES.: PA.

GILL, RUSSELL BRYAN. POLIT. & GOV.: *independent candidate for presidency of the U.S., 1992*. MAILING ADDRESS: 819 Poplar St., Fort Wayne, IN 46802.

GILLETTE, HOWARD FRANK. b. Apr 9, 1873, Chicago, IL; d. Oct 23, 1943, Chicago, IL; par. James Frank and Jennie (Parker) Gillette; m. Cornelia Forbes Brookmire, Sep 11, 1911; c. Howard Frank, Jr. EDUC.: Harvard U., 1893–94; LL.B., Northwestern U., 1896. POLIT. & GOV.: ***candidate for Republican nomination to vice presidency of the U.S., 1912***. BUS. & PROF.: atty.; admitted to IL Bar, 1896; assoc., Hoyne, Follansbee and O'Connor (law firm), Chicago, IL; mgr., Western Office, W. O. Gay and Co. (commercial paper), Chicago; pres., Merrill, Cox and Co., Chicago, 1903–14; banker; partner, Richard Robinson and Co.; mgr., Park National Bank (merged with Chase Manhattan Bank), 1916–39. MEM.: Sea Scouts of America (founder, 1919; commodore, 1919–39; hon. commodore, 1939–43); BSA (member, National Board; pres., Chicago Council, 1922–29); Harvard Club (pres.); Chicago Club; University Club; Onwentsia Club; Casino Club; Tavern Club. AWARDS: Silver Buffalo Award, BSA 1929. REL.: Bapt. RES.: Chicago, IL.

GILHAUS, AUGUST. d. 1936. POLIT. & GOV.: Socialist Labor Party candidate for NY State Assembly, 1902; delegate, Socialist Labor Party National Convention, 1904, 1912 (chm.), 1924 (sergeant-at-arms); Socialist Labor Party candidate for U.S. House (NY), 1904; Socialist Labor Party candidate for NY state controller, 1905; member, Socialist Labor Party National Cmte., 1905; ***Socialist Labor Party candidate for presidency of the U.S., 1908; Socialist Labor Party candidate for vice presidency of the U.S., 1912, 1920***; Socialist Labor Party candidate for U.S. Senate (NY), 1916. BUS. & PROF.: bricklayer. RES.: Brooklyn, NY.

GILLIGAN, JOHN JOYCE. b. Mar 22, 1921, Cincinnati, OH; par. Harry Joseph and Blanche (Joyce) Gilligan; m. Mary Kathryn Dixon, Jun 28, 1945; c. John; Ellen; Kathleen; Donald. EDUC.: grad., St. Francis Xavier H.S., 1939; U. of Notre Dame, 1943; U. of Cincinnati, 1947. POLIT. & GOV.: elected member, Cincinnati (OH) City Council, 1953–64, 1967–68; candidate for Democratic nomination to U.S. House (OH), 1962; elected as a Democrat to U.S. House (OH), 1965–67; Democratic candidate for U.S. House (OH), 1966; Democratic candidate for U.S. Senate (OH), 1968; delegate, Dem. Nat'l. Conv., 1968; elected as a Democrat to gov. of OH, 1971–75; ***candidate for Democratic nomination to presidency of the U.S., 1972***; member, Dem. Nat'l. Cmte.; appointed administrator, Agency for International Development, 1977–81. BUS. & PROF.: instructor in literature, Xavier U., Cincinnati, 1948–53; partner, insurance agent, Gilligan and Sauter Associates (insurance agency); Distinguished Woodrow Wilson Fellow, International Center for Scholars, Smithsonian Institution, 1975; partner, John J. Gilligan consultants, 1975; faculty, U. of Notre Dame Law School. MIL.: lt. (jg), U.S.N.R., 1942–45; three Area Campaign Ribbons; five Battle Stars; two Naval Unit Citations; Silver Star. MEM.: Catholic Inter-Racial Council of Cincinnati (pres., 1961); Central Psychiatric Clinic (dir.); Playhouse-in-the-Park (dir.); Babies Milk Fund (dir.); Better Housing League (adviser); American Legion. AWARDS: fellow, John F. Kennedy Inst. of Politics, Harvard U., 1969; fellow, Adlai E. Stevenson Inst. of International Studies, U. of Chicago, 1969. HON. DEG.: LL.D., U. of Akron; LL.D., Wilberforce U.; LL.D., Miami U.; LL.D., Xavier U.; LL.D., U. of Toledo; LL.D., U. of Dayton. REL.: R.C. MAILING ADDRESS: c/o U. of Notre Dame Law School, Notre Dame, IN 46556.

GINSBERG, HERBERT R. POLIT. & GOV.: ***independent candidate for presidency of the U.S., 1976***. MAILING ADDRESS: Suite 500, Forrest Towers, Hattiesburg, MS 39401.

GISTARO, EDWARD M. POLIT. & GOV.: ***independent candidate for presidency of the U.S., 1980***. MAILING ADDRESS: 204 Fawn Dr., San Antonio, TX 78231.

GITLOW, BENJAMIN. b. Dec 22, 1891, Elizabethport, NJ; d. Jul 19, 1965, Crompond, NY; par. Louis A. and Katherine Gitlow; m. Badana Zeitlin, Dec 11, 1924; c. Benjamin. EDUC.: law school. POLIT. & GOV.: member, Socialist Party, 1907–19; delegate, NY State Socialist Party Convention, 1908, 1910; elected as a Socialist to NY State Assembly, 1917–18 (removed); founder, Communist Labor Party, 1919 (member, Labor Cmte.); ***Communist (Workers) Party candidate for vice presidency of the U.S., 1924, 1928***; Workers Party candidate for gov. of NY, 1926; ***independent candidate for presidency of the U.S., 1928***; member, Political Cmte. and Secretariat, Communist Party, sec., 1929 (expelled, 1929). BUS. & PROF.: clerk, department store, Newark, NJ; clothing cutter; ed., business mgr., *Revolutionary Age*; business mgr., *The Voice of Labor*, 1919; ed., *Freiheit*; sec.-treas., Industrial Lacquer and Chemical Corp.; anti-Communist lecturer; government witness. MEM.: National Left Wing Council (1919); Communist International (member, exec. cmte.); Red Trade Union International (member, exec. cmte.); Retail Clerks Union (pres.); Garland Fund (dir., 1926–33); Amalgamated Clothing Workers of America; Industrial Workers of the World; American Jewish League Against Communism, Inc. (dir.; adviser); Jewish National Workers Alliance; U.S.S.R. Soviet (hon. member, 1920). WRITINGS: "Left Wing Manifesto"; *America for the People* (1932); *Communist Unity* (1931); *I Confess: The Truth About American Communism* (1939); *The Whole of Their Lives* (1948). REL.: Jewish. MISC.: spent three years in Sing-Sing Penitentiary for violation of criminal syndicalist law, 1920s; known as "Tom Paine" and "John Pierce." RES.: New York, NY.

GIULIANI, RUDOLPH W. b. May 28, 1944, New York, NY. POLIT. & GOV.: appointed U.S. atty., New York, NY, to 1989; ***candidate for Republican nomination to vice presidency of the U.S., 1988***; Liberal Party candidate for mayor of New York, 1989; candidate for Republican nomination to mayor of New York, 1989; elected as a Republican to mayor of New York, 1994–. BUS. & PROF.: atty. MISC.: prosecutor of Rep. Mario Biaggi (q.v.) for bribery in Wedtech scandal. MAILING ADDRESS: Gracie Mansion, New York, NY.

GLASS, GEORGE CARTER. b. Jan 4, 1858, Lynchburg, VA; d. May 28, 1946, Washington, DC; par. Robert Henry and Augusta (Christian) Glass; m. Aurelia McDearmon Caldwell, Jan 12, 1886; m. 2d, Mrs. Mary Scott Meade, Jun 22, 1940; c. Paulus Powell; Carter; Mary Archer ;(Mrs. John Gherrant Boatright); Augusta Christian (Mrs. Robert McClanahan Allen; Mrs. Isaac Wallington Digges). EDUC.: public and private schools, Lynchburg, VA. POLIT. & GOV.: clerk, Lynchburg City Council, 1881–1901; delegate, Dem. Nat'l. Conv., 1892, 1896, 1900, 1904, 1908, 1912, 1916, 1920, 1924, 1928, 1932, 1936, 1940; delegate, VA State Democratic Convention, 1897; elected as a Democrat to VA State Senate, 1899–1903; delegate, VA State Constitutional Convention, 1901; elected as a Democrat to U.S. House (VA), 1902–19; member, Dem. Nat'l. Cmte., 1916–28; appointed U.S. sec. of the treasury, 1918–20; appointed and subsequently elected as a Democrat to U.S. Senate (VA), 1920–46 (pres. pro tempore, 1941–46); ***candidate for Democratic nomination to presidency of the U.S., 1920, 1924***; appointed U.S. sec. of the treasury, 1933 (declined). BUS. & PROF.: apprentice printer, *Lynchburg Daily Republican*; reporter, *Lynchburg Daily News*, 1880–88, ed., 1888; owner, *The Virginian*, 1896; employee, *Petersburg (VA) Post*; clerk, Atlantic, Mississippi and Ohio R.R.; owner, *Lynchburg Daily Advance*, 1896–1946. MEM.: U. of VA (member, Board of Visitors, 1898–1906); Phi Beta Kappa; Fight for Freedom Cmte. (hon. chm.); Masons; Elks; SCV; Oakwood Country Club. AWARDS: Roosevelt Medal, 1938. HON. DEG.: LL.D., Lafayette Coll., 1919; LL.D., U. of NC, 1921; LL.D., Washington and Lee U., 1921; LL.D., Wesleyan U., 1935; LL.D., Tufts U., 1935; LL.D., William and Mary Coll., 1935; LL.D., Yale U., 1935; LL.D., Princeton U., 1935; LL.D., Columbia U., 1941; LL.D., Dartmouth Coll., 1941; LL.D., Hamilton Coll., 1941; LL.D., U. of NY, 1941; LL.D., Lynchburg Coll., 1941. REL.: Methodist. RES.: Lynchburg, VA.

GLENN, CHARLES R. POLIT. & GOV.: ***candidate for American Independent Party nomination to presidency of the U.S., 1984; candidate for Populist Party nomination to presidency of the U.S., 1984***. MAILING ADDRESS: PA.

GLENN, FRANK S. b. Aug 24, 1932, Tyler, TX; married. EDUC.: B.S., TX A&M U., 1960; B.S., Tyler State Coll., 1975; M.S., TX Eastern U., 1976. POLIT. & GOV.: Republican candidate for U.S. House (TX), 1976, 1978; member, Smith Cty. (TX) Republican Exec. Cmte.; ***candidate for Republican nomination to vice presidency of the U.S., 1976***. BUS. & PROF.: pres., owner, East Texas Reprographics, Inc. MIL.: U.S.M.C., Korean War. MEM.: National Republican Congressional Council; National Small Business Assn.; East Texas Farm and Ranch Club. REL.: Bapt. MAILING ADDRESS: 2127 South Broadway, Tyler, TX 75701.

GLENN, HARRY. b. 1921. POLIT. & GOV.: ***candidate for Libertarian Party nomination to presidency of the U.S., 1988***. BUS. & PROF.: welder. MAILING ADDRESS: IN.

GLENN, JOHN HERSCHEL, JR. b. Jul 18, 1921, Cambridge, OH; par. John Herschel and Clara (Sproat) Glenn; m. Anna Margaret Castor, Apr 1943; c. Carolyn Ann; John David. EDUC.: B.S., Muskingum Coll., 1939; Navy Aviation Cadet, U. of IA, 1942; grad., Naval Air Training Center, 1943; grad., Navy Test Pilot Training School, 1954. POLIT. & GOV.: candidate for Democratic nomination to U.S. Senate (OH), 1964 (withdrew), 1970; elected as a Democrat to U.S. Senate (OH), 1975–; keynoter, Dem. Nat'l. Conv., 1976; ***candidate for Democratic nomination to presidency of the U.S., 1976, 1984, 1988; candidate for Democratic nomination to vice presidency of the U.S., 1976, 1984, 1988***. BUS. & PROF.: astronaut; businessman; vice pres., Royal Crown Cola Co., 1962–74 (pres., International Division, 1967–69); dir., Questor Corp., 1970–74. MIL.: commissioned 2d lt., U.S.M.C., 1943; advanced through grades to lt. col.; flight instructor, Advanced Flight Training, Corpus Christi, TX, 1949–51; asst. G-2/G-3, Amphibious Warfare School, Quantico, VA, 1951; project officer, Navy Bureau of Aeronautics, Washington, DC, 1956–69; participated in nonstop supersonic transcontinental flight, Jul 16, 1957; astronaut, Project Mercury, NASA, 1959–64; pilot, first American manned orbital flight, Feb 1962; five Distinguished Flying Crosses; 18 Air Medals; Astronaut Medal; Navy Unit Citation; Korean Presidential Unit Citation. MEM.: Soc. of Experimental Test Pilots; International Acad. of Astronautics (hon.); Aviation Hall of Fame. AWARDS: Distinguished Merit Award, Muskingum Coll.; Medal of Honor, New York City. HON. DEG.: D.Sc., Muskingum Coll., 1961. WRITINGS: *We Seven* (coauthor, 1962); *P.S. I Listened to Your Heartbeat*. REL.: Presb. (elder). MAILING ADDRESS: 1000 Urlin Ave., Columbus, OH 43215.

GLENN, ROBERT BRODNAX. b. Aug 11, 1854, Rockingham Cty., NC; d. May 16, 1920, Winnipeg, Canada; par. Chalmers L. and Annie S. (Dodge) Glenn; m. Nina Deaderick, Jan 8, 1878; c. Louise; Chalmers; Rebecca. EDUC.: Davidson Coll.; U. of VA; Pearson's Law School. POLIT. & GOV.: elected as a Democrat to NC State House, 1881; presidential elector, Democratic Party, 1884, 1892; appointed solicitor, NC District, 1886; candidate for solicitor, NC District, 1886; appointed U.S. district atty., Western District, NC, 1893–97; elected as a Democrat to NC State Senate, 1898–1905; elected as a Democrat to gov. of NC, 1905–09; ***candidate for Democratic nomination to presidency of the U.S., 1912***; appointed member, International Boundary Comm., 1920. BUS. & PROF.: atty.;

admitted to NC Bar, 1877; law practice, Danbury, NC, 1878; partner (with W. B. Glenn), law practice, 1886–91; partner, Manly and Hendren (law firm), 1891; asst. division counsel, Southern Railway; counsel, Western Union Telegraph Co. MIL.: capt., maj., NC State Guard, 1890–93. HON. DEG.: LL.D., U. of NC, 1907. REL.: Presb. RES.: Winston-Salem, NC.

GLICK, GEORGE WASHINGTON. b. Jul 4, 1827, Fairfield Cty., OH; d. Apr 13, 1911, Atchison, KS; par. Isaac and Mary Vickers (Sanders) Glick; m. Elizabeth Ryder, Sep 17, 1857; c. Jennie (Mrs. James W. Orr); Frederick H. EDUC.: Central Coll.; studied law under Ralph P. Buckland and Rutherford B. Hayes (q.v.). POLIT. & GOV.: delegate, Dem. Nat'l. Conv., 1856, 1868, 1884, 1892; Democratic candidate for OH State Senate, 1864; elected as a Democrat to KS State House, 1863–66, 1868, 1882–83; Democratic candidate for gov. of KS, 1868, 1884, 1886; elected as a Democrat to KS State Senate, 1873–77 (pres. pro tempore, 1877); appointed commissioner, Centennial Exposition, 1876; judge, Second Judicial District of KS, 1877–81; elected as a Democrat to gov. of KS, 1883–85; ***candidate for Democratic nomination to vice presidency of the U.S., 1884 (withdrew)***; appointed U.S. Pension Agent, Topeka, KS, 1885–92; member, KS State Board of Agriculture, 32 years (pres., 1902–03); appointed commissioner, Chicago Exposition, 1893; appointed commissioner, Trans-Mississippi and International Exposition, 1898; appointed commissioner, St. Louis Exposition; Democratic (People's Party) candidate for U.S. House (KS), 1900. BUS. & PROF.: atty.; admitted to OH Bar, 1850; law practice, Fremont, OH, 1850–59; partner, Otis and Glick (law firm), Atchison, KS, 1859–73; counsel, Central Branch, Union Pacific R.R., 1867–74; farmer, stockman, 1874–1903; owner, orange grove, FL. MIL.: col., judge advocate gen., 17th Regt., OH Militia, 1857; enlisted, 2d KS Regt., U.S. Army, 1864. MEM.: KS State Hist. Soc.; Masons (Knights Templar). REL.: Lutheran. RES.: Atchison, KS.

GLIDDEN, WILLIAM G. POLIT. & GOV.: ***independent candidate for presidency of the U.S., 1964***. MAILING ADDRESS: Cleveland, OH.

GLOVER, JAMES IRVIN. POLIT. & GOV.: ***independent candidate for presidency of the U.S., 1976, 1980, 1988; candidate for Democratic nomination to presidency of the U.S., 1980, 1984, 1988***. WRITINGS: *Boulder in the Sun* (1979). MAILING ADDRESS: 120 Pierre Ave., Garfield, NJ 07026.

GLOVER, JIM RONALD. b. Sep 5, 1942, Cleveland, OH; par. Hugh C. and Frieda (Cohen) Glover. EDUC.: grad., Collinwood H.S., Cleveland, OH; OH State U., 1½ years. POLIT. & GOV.: ***independent candidate for presidency of the U.S., 1992***. BUS. & PROF.: musician; writer; recording artist; welder, 1977–80. MIL.: U.S. Army R.O.T.C., OH State U., 1960–61. MEM.: Friends of Florida Folk; Anti-War Movement; Civil Rights Movement. WRITINGS: "Let's Talk Peace" (song); *Letter to Reagan and Andropov* (1983). REL.: no organized preference. MAILING ADDRESS: 3411 Maze Lane, Brandon, FL 33511.

GLOVER, MILDRED WILLIAMS. b. Nov 29, 1934, Savannah, GA; par. Tommy and Laura (Dutton) Williams; m. Rowland Glover, Jr.; m. 2d, William Hopkins, Jr., Dec 31, 1978; c. Kenneth; Roslynn. EDUC.: B.A., Savannah State Coll., 1958; M.A., NY U., 1963; Ph.D., U. of GA, 1970. POLIT. & GOV.: elected as a Democrat to GA State House, 1975–83; ***candidate for Democratic nomination to presidency of the U.S., 1984, 1988***; candidate for Democratic nomination to U.S. House (GA), 1986. BUS. & PROF.: asst. prof., Savannah State Coll., Savannah, GA, 1963–68; prof., Elizabeth City State U., NC, 1970–71; assoc. prof., Atlanta U., 1971–82. MEM.: Atlanta Business League; League of Women Voters; Atlanta Assn. of International Business; Black Women's Coalition; GA Voters' League; Atlanta Women's Network; GA Education Assn.; NEA. AWARDS: "Outstanding Educator in America" Award, GA Education Assn., 1974; Legislative Award, GA Assn. of Cty. Commissioners, 1978; Ford Foundation Fellowship, 1969; various civic awards. WRITINGS: dissertation on accounting; articles on business, accounting, and international business. REL.: Bapt. MAILING ADDRESS: 735 Lawton St., S.W., Atlanta, GA 30310.

GLOVER, WILLIAM ROY. b. Nov 13, 1935, Little Rock, AR; par. William Roy and Jacqueline (Evans) Glover; m. Janice Glover; c. Ronald Lee; Gigi Suzanne; William Roy III; James Robert; Richard Kendall. EDUC.: B.A. (cum laude), Vanderbilt U., 1957; M.B.A. (cum laude), Harvard Graduate School of Business Administration, 1961. POLIT. & GOV.: ***candidate for Democratic nomination to presidency of the U.S., 1980, 1984***. BUS. & PROF.: corporate controller, Alcon Laboratories, Inc., Fort Worth, TX, 1961–72; evening instructor in statistics, TX Christian U., 1961–62; owner, William R. Glover, CPA (financial consultants), Fort Worth, 1972–77; owner, dir., Abacus Business Systems, Naalehu, HI, 1977–. MIL.: lt. (jg), U.S. Navy, 1957–59. MEM.: American Assn. of Economists; American Statistical Assn.; American Inst. of Certified Public Accountants; American Management Assn.; Pharmaceutical Manufacturers Assn.; Cosmopolitan Club; American Independence Movement. MAILING ADDRESS: 4151 South West Loop, Fort Worth, TX 76132.

GOELLER, JEWELIE. POLIT. & GOV.: ***Natural People's League candidate for vice presidency of the U.S., 1980***. MAILING ADDRESS: ND.

GOFF, GUY DESPARD. b. Sep 13, 1866, Clarksburg, WV; d. Jan 7, 1933, Thomasville, GA; par. Nathan and

Laura E. (Despard) Goff; m. Louise Van Nortwick, Jun 14, 1897; m. 2d, Anita F. Baker, Sep 8, 1906; c. Louise (Mrs. Brazilla Carroll Reece, q.v.). EDUC.: A.B., Kenyon Military Acad., 1888; LL.B., Harvard U., 1891, A.M. POLIT. & GOV.: elected prosecuting atty., Milwaukee Cty., WI, 1895–99; appointed U.S. district atty., Eastern District of WI, 1911–15; appointed special asst., asst. to the atty. gen. of the U.S., 1917, 1920–23; appointed gen. counsel, member, U.S. Shipping Board, 1920–21; elected as a Republican to U.S. Senate (WV), 1925–31; ***candidate for Republican nomination to presidency of the U.S., 1928; candidate for Republican nomination to vice presidency of the U.S., 1928***. BUS. & PROF.: atty.; admitted to MA Bar, 1891; law practice, Boston, MA, 1891–93; law practice, Milwaukee, WI, 1893. MIL.: col., JAGD, U.S. Army, 1918–19. MEM.: Psi Upsilon. REL.: Episc. RES.: Clarksburg, WV.

GOFFIN, WILLIAM LEFTWICH. b. May 31, 1807, Bunker Hill, VA; d. Jan 3, 1870, Liberty, VA. EDUC.: Tucker's Law School. POLIT. & GOV.: elected as a Whig to VA State House of Delegates, 1836–37; elected as a Whig to U.S. House (VA), 1839–43, 1844–45, 1847–49; Whig Party candidate for U.S. House (VA), 1842; Whig (American) Party candidate for gov. of VA, 1859; ***candidate for Constitutional Union Party nomination to presidency of the U.S., 1860***; delegate, VA State Constitutional Convention, 1861. BUS. & PROF.: atty.; admitted to VA Bar, 1828; law practice, Liberty, VA; farmer. MIL.: capt., Home Guards, C.S.A., Civil War. RES.: Liberty, VA.

GOLDBERG, LAWRENCE W. POLIT. & GOV.: ***candidate for Democratic nomination to presidency of the U.S., 1980***. MAILING ADDRESS: 30 East Jefferson St., A 308, Media, PA 19063.

GOLDEN, RALPH G. POLIT. & GOV.: ***independent candidate for presidency of the U.S., 1980***. MAILING ADDRESS: 1002 Brice Rd., Rockville, MD 20852.

GOLDENGHOST, SHENANDOAH. POLIT. & GOV.: ***independent candidate for presidency of the U.S., 1976***. MAILING ADDRESS: P.O. Box 1723, Bisbee, AZ 85603; Eugene, OR.

GOLDWATER, BARRY MORRIS. b. Jan 1, 1909, Phoenix, AZ; par. Baron and Josephine (Williams) Goldwater; m. Margaret Johnson, Sep 22, 1934; m. 2d, Susan Wechsler, Feb 9, 1992; c. Joanne (Mrs. Thomas H. Ross); Barry Morris, Jr.; Michael; Margaret (Mrs. Richard Holt). EDUC.: Staunton Military Acad.; U. of AZ, 1928. POLIT. & GOV.: appointed member, Advisory Cmte. on Indian Affairs, U.S. Dept. of the Interior, 1948–50; elected as a Republican to Phoenix (AZ) City Council, 1949–53; elected as a Republican to U.S. Senate (AZ), 1953–65, 1969–87; ***Conservative Party of VA candidate for vice presidency of the U.S., 1960 (declined); candidate for Republican nomination to presidency of the U.S., 1960; candidate for Republican nomination to vice presidency of the U.S., 1960; Republican candidate for presidency of the U.S., 1964***. BUS. & PROF.: employee, Goldwater's, Inc., Phoenix, 1929–37, pres., 1937–53, chm. of the board, 1953–; partner, Rainbow Lodge and Trading Post, Navajo Indian Reservation. MIL.: 2d lt., U.S. Army, 1930; lt. col., U.S.A.A.C., 1941–45; organized AZ National Guard, chief of staff, 1946–52; Air Medal; China-Burma-India Campaign Star. MEM.: U.S. Air Force Reserve (brig. gen., 1959; maj. gen., 1962; retired, 1967); Heard Museum (dir.); Museum of Northern AZ (dir.); St. Joseph's Hospital (dir.); Royal Photographic Soc.; American Assn. of Indian Affairs (dir.); American Legion; VFW; Municipal League (vice pres.); American Inst. of Foreign Trade (dir.); Eta Mu Pi; Sigma Chi; Masons (32°; Shriners); Elks; Moose; Eastern Star; Alianza; Modern Woodmen of the World; Smokis. AWARDS: U.S. Junior C. of C. Award, 1937; Man of the Year Award, Phoenix, AZ, 1949. HON. DEG.: LL.D., U. of AZ, 1969. WRITINGS: *Arizona Portraits* (2 vols., 1940); *Journey Down the River of Canyons* (1940); *Speeches of Henry Ashurst; The Conscience of a Conservative* (1960); *Why Not Victory?* (1962); *Let's Try Freedom; Where I Stand* (1964); *The Face of Arizona* (1964); *People and Places* (1967); *Conscience of the Majority* (1970); *Delightful Journey* (1971); *The Coming Breakpoint* (1976); *Barry Goldwater and the Southwest* (1976); *With No Apologies* (1979). REL.: Episc. MAILING ADDRESS: 6250 North Hogan Dr., Scottsdale, AZ 85253.

GOMEZ, FERNANDO. b. Aug 4, 1931, Bogotá, Colombia; par. Arturo and Luz (Heredice) Gomez; m. Martha Porras; c. Rebecca Gomez Porras. EDUC.: A.A., Los Angeles Trade Technical Inst., 1969; B.S. (equivalent), Acad. of Computer Technology, 1970. POLIT. & GOV.: member, Worcester (MA) Election Comm., 1985–89; ***independent candidate for presidency of the U.S., 1992***. BUS. & PROF.: bilingual employment counselor, Worcester; Spanish teacher, Ware Cty. School System. MEM.: Worcester C. of C.; Main South Neighborhood Center (Exec. Board); Latin Assn. for Progress (Exec. Board); Family Health Center (Exec. Board); United Way (Leadership Training Program). REL.: Christian. MAILING ADDRESS: 4700 Westgrove Dr., #221, Raleigh, NC 27606.

GONAS, JOHN SAMUEL. b. May 14, 1907, Cross Park, PA; par. Samuel and Hazel (Stranka) Gonas; m. Theodosia Bonder, Sep 25, 1937; c. John Samuel, Jr.; Roy B. EDUC.: St. Thomas Coll.; U. of PA; B.S., Tri-State U.; Chicago Law School; John Marshall Law School; U. of Notre Dame; LL.B., LL.M. POLIT. & GOV.: asst. prosecuting atty., 1931; justice of the peace, 1935; elected as a Democrat to IN State House, 1937–39; member, IN State Budget Cmte., 1940; elected as a Democrat to IN State Senate, 1941–49; Democratic candidate for U.S. House (IN), 1946; judge, IN Juvenile Court, 1949–59; judge, IN State Appellate Court, 1959–63 (chief justice); ***candidate for Demo-***

cratic nomination to vice presidency of the U.S., 1960; candidate for Democratic nomination to presidency of the U.S., 1976, 1984; delegate, U.N. Conference on Crime and Juvenile Delinquency; delegate, International Congress of Juvenile Court Judges; candidate for Democratic nomination to U.S. House (IN), 1986; independent candidate for U.S. House (IN), 1986. BUS. & PROF.: atty.; admitted to IN Bar, 1929; legislator; judge. MEM.: ABA; IN State Bar Assn.; American Trial Lawyers Assn.; Juvenile Court Foundation (life member); American Ethnic Foundation (pres.); Juvenile Court Inst.; South Bend Optimist Club; Phi Kappa Theta; Benevolent and Protective Order of Elks; Indiana Fraternal Congress (pres.); Engineering Soc.; Chickasaw Nation (hon. chief); Sagamores of the Wabash (chieftain); Kentucky Colonel; Alabama Colonel; Oklahoma Colonel; Admiral of the Great Navy of Nebraska. AWARDS: Certificate of Award, Juvenile Court Inst.; Man of the Year, South Bend Optimist Club; Alumni Distinguished Service Award. WRITINGS: *Delinquency: There Is An Answer* (1968); *Trial Handbook for Indiana Lawyers* (1968). REL.: R.C. MAILING ADDRESS: 3120 Rue Renoir, Number 203, South Bend, IN 46615.

GONER, NORA E. b. 1868; married. POLIT. & GOV.: ***candidate for Republican nomination to presidency of the U.S., 1944***. BUS. & PROF.: domestic worker. RES.: Los Angeles, CA.

GONZALES, RUDOLFO "CORKY." b. Jun 18, 1928, Denver, CO; m. Geraldine Romero; c. eight. POLIT. & GOV.: district capt., Denver Democratic Party, 1957; CO coordinator, Viva Kennedy Campaign, 1960; chm., Denver Anti-Poverty Program, 1960 (Steering Cmte., 1967); dir., Neighborhood Youth Corp of Denver, 1964; chm. of the board, War on Poverty, 1966; ***Peace and Freedom Party candidate for vice presidency of the U.S., 1968***. BUS. & PROF.: professional boxer; packing house worker; lumberjack; businessman; owner, "Corky's Corner" bar, Denver, CO, 1952–; bail bondsman; owner, Viva, Denver, CO, 1959–; gen. agent, Summit Fidelity and Surety Co. of CO; farm worker; pres., dir., Crusade for Justice (Mexican-American civil rights organization), Denver, CO; poet; playwright; lecturer; political activist; community organizer; ed., *El Gallo*, Denver, CO; founder, Tlatelolco Free School. MEM.: Jobs for Progress (dir.); Crusade for Justice (founder, 1965; pres.); National Citizens Cmte. for Community Relations (pres., 1967); Job Opportunity Center of Denver (member, Community Board); Los Voluntarios (founder, 1963). WRITINGS: *The Revolutionary* (play); *A Cross for Maclovio* (play); "I Am Joaquin" (epic poem). MISC.: National A.A.U. Boxing Champion; third ranking featherweight boxing contender, National Boxing Assn. MAILING ADDRESS: c/o Crusade for Justice, 1567 Downing St., Denver, CO.

GONZALEZ, ANDREA. b. 1952, Brooklyn, NY; c. one daughter. EDUC.: B.A., Brooklyn Coll., 1972. POLIT. & GOV.: member, Puerto Rican Socialist Party; member, Puerto Rican Independence Party; member, Young Lords Party; member, Socialist Workers Party National Cmte., 1981–; ***Socialist Workers Party candidate for vice presidency of the U.S., 1984***. BUS. & PROF.: structural mechanic, McDonnell Aircraft Corp., Long Beach, CA; laborer, U.S. Steel Corp., Houston, TX; laborer, Area Metropolitan Transit Authority, Washington, DC; member, editorial board, *Perspectiva Mundial;* staff, Conference Against Registration and the Draft, 1981; member, editorial board, *Young Socialist*. MEM.: U.A.W.; United Steel Workers; National Organization for Women; Amalgamated Transit Union; Coalition of Labor Union Women; National Network in Solidarity with the People of Nicaragua (founder); Cmte. in Solidarity with the People of El Salvador (founder); Women's Coalition Against U.S. Intervention in Central America and the Caribbean (founder); Brooklyn Coll. Puerto Rican Alliance; Young Socialist Alliance (national sec.). REL.: raised R.C. MAILING ADDRESS: Jersey City, NJ.

GONZALEZ, OSCAR. POLIT. & GOV.: ***independent candidate for presidency of the U.S., 1980***. MAILING ADDRESS: 13 Cora St., River Rouge, MI.

GOODE, WILLIE WILSON. b. Aug 19, 1938, NC; m. Velma Williams; c. Muriel; W. Wilson, Jr.; Natashu. EDUC.: A.B., Morgan State U., 1961; M.G.A., U. of PA, 1968. POLIT. & GOV.: elected as a Democrat to mayor of Philadelphia, PA, 1983–91; ***candidate for Democratic nomination to vice presidency of the U.S., 1984***. BUS. & PROF.: exec. asst., operations mgr., Clarkies, Inc., 1963–65; claims adjuster, All State Insurance Co., 1965–66; organization official. MIL.: capt., U.S. Army; Army Commendation Medal, 1963. MEM.: Philadelphia Council for Community Advancement (pres., 1969–; dir., Housing and Employment, 1966–68); Community Leadership Seminar Program (chm., Steering Cmte.); Fellowship Comm.; Greater Philadelphia Partnership; Housing Assn. of Delaware Valley (pres.; dir.); Black Political Forum (pres.); Morgan State U. Alumni Assn. (pres.); World Affairs Council (dir.); Cmte. of Seventy (dir.); Philadelphia Tribune Charities (first vice pres.). AWARDS: Young Man of the Year Award, Jaycees of Philadelphia Community, 1972; Community Service Award, Philadelphia O.I.C., 1973. MAILING ADDRESS: 1601 Walnut St., Suite 310, Philadelphia, PA 19102.

GOODELL, WILLIAM. b. Oct 25, 1792, Coventry, NY; d. Feb 14, 1878, Janesville, WI; par. Frederic and Rhoda (Guernsey) Goodell; m. Clarissa C. Cady, Jul 4, 1823; c. Rhoda Livinia; one other daughter. POLIT. & GOV.: founder, Liberty Party, 1840; founder, Liberty League, 1847; ***Liberty Party candidate for presidency of the U.S., 1852***; founder, National Prohibition Party, 1869. BUS. & PROF.: clerk, mercantile firm, Providence, RI; reformer; promoter, Mercantile Library Assn., dir., 1827; ed., *Investigator and General Intelligencer*, Providence,

1827; publisher, *Genius of Temperance*, New York, NY, 1830; publisher, *Female Advocate*, New York, 1830; publisher, *Youth's Temperance Lecturer*, New York, 1830–36; publisher, *Emancipator*, 1833; ed., *Friend of Man*, Utica and Whitesboro, NY, 1836–42; publisher, *Anti-Slavery Lecturer;* founder, *Christian Investigator*, Utica, 1842; founder, Honeoye Church, Honeoye, NY, 1843; minister; ed., *American Jubilee*, New York, 1854; publisher, *Radical Abolitionist*, New York, 1854; publisher, *Principia*. MEM.: American Anti-Slavery Soc. (founder, 1833); Liberty League (founder, 1847). WRITINGS: *Views on American Constitutional Law, in Its Bearings Upon American Slavery* (1844); *The Democracy of Christianity* (1849); *Slavery and Anti-Slavery: A History of the Great Struggle in Both Hemispheres* (1852); *The American Slave Code, in Theory and Practice* (1853). REL.: Christian. RES.: New York, NY.

GOODIN, DYKE. POLIT. & GOV.: ***candidate for Democratic nomination to presidency of the U.S., 1984***. BUS. & PROF.: physician. MAILING ADDRESS: 2830 Henderson Mill Rd., Chamblee, GA 30341.

GOODLOE, THOMAS M., JR. par. Thomas M. Goddloe; m. Marie A. E. Goodloe. POLIT. & GOV.: elected as an American Independent to Board of County Commissioners, El Dorado Cty., CA, 1969–73; American Independent Party candidate for CA state sec. of state, 1970; American Independent Party candidate for CA state treas., 1974; chm., CA State American Independent Party Central Cmte., 1976–80; ***candidate for American Independent Party nomination to presidency of the U.S., 1976***; presidential elector, American Independent Party, 1976; chm., American Independent Party National Cmte., 1980–. MAILING ADDRESS: Newtown Rd., P.O. Box 864, Placerville, CA 95667.

GOODLUCK, JAMES R. POLIT. & GOV.: ***Tuition Cut Ticket candidate for presidency of the U.S., 1972; Tuition Cut Ticket candidate for vice presidency of the U.S., 1976***. MAILING ADDRESS: P.O. Box 5964, Cleveland, OH 44101.

GOODMAN, WILLIE ODELL. POLIT. & GOV.: ***candidate for Democratic nomination to presidency of the U.S., 1988***. MAILING ADDRESS: Route 1, Box 428, Dover, NC 28526.

GOODRICH, GLENN A. b. Feb 22, 1925, Orson, IA; par. Walter H. and Susie (Gillette) Goodrich; m. Gaynelle Tusha, 1950; c. D'Arcy; Christopher; Gregory. EDUC.: B.S., Creighton U., 1949. POLIT. & GOV.: elected as a Democrat to NE State Senate, 1971–79; ***candidate for Democratic nomination to vice presidency of the U.S., 1972***. BUS. & PROF.: soldier. MIL.: pvt., sgt., U.S. Army, 1943–46. MEM.: Rho Epsilon; Masons. REL.: Lutheran. MAILING ADDRESS: 4408 Walnut St., Omaha, NE 68105.

GOODRICH, JAMES PUTNAM. b. Feb 18, 1864, Winchester, IN; d. Aug 15, 1940, Winchester, IN; par. John Baldwin and Elizabeth Putnam (Edgar) Goodrich; m. Cora Frist, Mar 8, 1888; c. Pierre Frist. EDUC.: DePauw U.; studied law in offices of Watson and Engle, Winchester, IN, 1885. POLIT. & GOV.: chm., Randolph Cty. (IN) Republican Cmte.; chm., IN State Republican Central Cmte., 1901–10; delegate, Rep. Nat'l. Conv., 1908, 1920; member, exec. cmte., Rep. Nat'l. Cmte., 1912–16; elected as a Republican to gov. of IN, 1917–21; appointed member, National Conservation Comm.; ***candidate for Republican nomination to presidency of the U.S., 1920, 1924***; appointed chm., Indiana–St. Lawrence Waterways Comm., 1923; appointed trustee, American Relief Administration, 1922; appointed member, International St. Lawrence Waterways Comm., 1924; appointed member, Russian Relief Comm. BUS. & PROF.: teacher; atty.; admitted to IN Bar, 1886; partner, Watson, Macy and Goodrich (law firm), Winchester, IN, 1886–1910; partner, Monks, Robbins, Starr and Goodrich (law firm), Indianapolis, IN, 1910–14; receiver, Chicago, Cincinnati and Louisville R.R.; counsel, Goodrich and Emison (law firm), Indianapolis, 1921; pres., Peoples Loan and Trust Co., 1897–1940; owner, pres., Aetna Trust and Savings Bank, Indianapolis, 1921–23; pres., Union Heat, Light and Power Co.; pres., Patoka Coal Co.; vice pres., Goodrich Brothers Co.; vice pres., Railway Service and Supply Co.; vice pres., B. F. Goodrich Co.; vice pres., Engineers Inc.; sec.-treas., Winona Railway Co.; treas., Union Reduction Co.; dir., Indiana-Ohio Public Service Co.; dir., Eastern Indiana Telephone Co.; dir., Interstate Telephone and Telegraph Corp.; dir., Citizens Heat, Light and Power Co.; dir., Red River Refining Co.; dir., Investors Telephone Co.; dir., Indiana Telephone Corp.; dir., Jeffersonville Water Co.; dir., Washington Water and Gas Co. MEM.: Great Lakes–St. Lawrence Tide Water Assn. (member, exec. cmte.); Roosevelt Memorial Comm. (trustee); American Child Welfare Assn.; Civil Legion of America (vice pres.; member, exec. cmte.); Wabash Coll. (pres., Board of trustees); Presbyterian Theological Seminary (trustee); Masons; American-Russian C. of C. (1928); IN State Bar Assn.; Marion Cty. Bar Assn.; Randolph Cty. Bar Assn.; Indiana Bankers Assn.; SAR; Knights of Pythias; Phi Kappa Psi; Rotary International; Columbia Club; Tau Kappa Alpha (hon. member). HON. DEG.: M.A., Wabash Coll., 1915, LL.D., 1917; LL.D., U. of Notre Dame, 1917; LL.D., Hanover Coll., 1938. REL.: Presb. (Bible teacher; member, National Service Comm., 1917–18; member, Judicial Comm., 1919–22). RES.: Winchester, IN.

GOODWIN, GREGORY IIAMS. b. Aug 7, 1950, Portland, OR; par. Paul Jackson and Doris Dean (Beard) Goodwin; m. Connie Beth Parker; m. 2d, Denise Hawkins; c. Aaron McGregor; Jiiamah Helen. EDUC.: U.S.C.G. Acad., 1968–69; B.S., Baylor U., 1973. POLIT. & GOV.: independent candidate for lt. gov. of TX, 1978; independent candidate for U.S. Senate (OR), 1980; independent candidate for gov. of OR, 1982; ***independent candidate for presidency of the U.S., 1984, 1988***; independent candidate for Kauai (HI) Cty. Councilman, 1986. BUS. & PROF.: oil field laborer; roughneck; chemistry laboratory instructor; land surveyor; maintenance and groundskeeper; medical research asst.; cook; carpenter. MIL.: U.S.C.G. cadet, 1968–69. REL.: none. MAILING ADDRESS: c/o G. I. Goodwin for President for Life Reclamation Cmte., Nolan Miles Goodwin, treas., P.O. Box 1222, Hanalei, HI 96714.

GORDON, JACOB JOHN. b. 1921. POLIT. & GOV.: ***candidate for Democratic nomination to presidency of the U.S., 1968; New National Government candidate for presidency of the U.S., 1972; candidate for Republican nomination to presidency of the U.S., 1976, 1980, 1984; Anti-Shyster Legion candidate for presidency of the U.S., 1976***; candidate for Republican nomination to U.S. Senate (MA), 1978; ***independent candidate for presidency of the U.S., 1980, 1984.*** BUS. & PROF.: pres., International Funding and Insurance Assn. MIL.: sgt., U.S. Army, WWII; Bronze Star; Silver Star; Purple Heart. MEM.: Anti-Shyster Legion. MAILING ADDRESS: 8 Creswell Rd., Worcester, MA 01602.

GORDON, LAURA DE FORCE. b. Aug 17, 1838, North East, Erie Cty., PA; d. Apr 6, 1907, Lodi, CA; par. Abram and Catherine Doolittle (Allen) De Force; m. Dr. Charles H. Gordon, 1862 (divorced, 1880); c. none. EDUC.: Hastings Law Coll., 1878–79; read law. POLIT. & GOV.: Independent Party candidate for CA State Senate, 1871; ***candidate for Equal Rights (Cosmic, Free Love, People's) Party nomination to vice presidency of the U.S., 1872***. BUS. & PROF.: lecturer on spiritualism; atty.; admitted to CA Bar, 1879; admitted to the Bar of the Supreme Court of the U.S., 1887; journalist; joined wagon train to White Plains, NV, 1865–67; ed., women's column, *Narrow Gauge*, Stockton, CA, 1873; publisher, *Stockton Weekly Leader*, 1873; publisher, *Stockton Daily Leader*, 1874–75; correspondent, *Sacramento (CA) Bee*, 1877–78; correspondent, *Oakland (CA) Democrat*, 1977–78; law practice, San Francisco, CA, 1879–84; law practice, Stockton, 1884–1905; lobbyist; equal rights advocate. MEM.: Pacific Coast Press Assn.; CA Woman's Suffrage Soc. (pres., 1877, 1884–94); National Woman's Suffrage Assn. (CA delegate). WRITINGS: *The Great Geysers of California and How to Reach Them* (1877). REL.: Christian Spiritualist. MISC.: one of first women enrolled in a CA state university; one of first two women admitted to CA Bar; one of first two women admitted to practice before the Supreme Court of the U.S. RES.: Stockton, CA.

GORE, ALBERT ARNOLD. b. Dec 26, 1907, Granville, TN; par. Allen and Margie (Denny) Gore; m. Pauline La Fon, Apr 17, 1937; c. Nancy La Fon; Albert Arnold, Jr. (q.v.). EDUC.: B.S., State Teachers' Coll., Murfreesboro, TN, 1932; U. of TN; LL.B., Nashville YMCA Night Law School, 1936. POLIT. & GOV.: superintendent of schools, Smith Cty., TN, 1932–36; chm., TN Democratic Speakers' Bureau, 1934–36; TN commissioner of labor, 1936–37; elected as a Democrat to U.S. House (TN), 1939–44, 1945–53; elected as a Democrat to U.S. Senate (TN), 1953–71; delegate, Dem. Nat'l. Conv., 1956, 1968; ***candidate for Democratic nomination to vice presidency of the U.S., 1956, 1960***; Democratic candidate for U.S. Senate (TN), 1970; appointed U.S. delegate, General Assembly, U.N. BUS. & PROF.: schoolteacher, Overton Cty., TN; schoolteacher, Smith Cty., TN, 1926–30; atty.; admitted to TN Bar, 1936; law practice, Carthage, TN; instructor in law, Vanderbilt U., 1970–72; chm. of the board, Island Creek Coal Co., 1972–; dir., Occidental Petroleum Co.; owner, Cumberland Feed Mills, Carthage, TN; farmer. MIL.: U.S. Army, 1944. MEM.: TN Young Democrats (organizer, 1932); TN Education Assn. REL.: Bapt. MAILING ADDRESS: Carthage, TN 37030.

GORE, ALBERT ARNOLD, JR. b. Mar 31, 1948, Washington, DC; par. Albert Arnold (q.v.) and Pauline (La Fon) Gore; m. Mary Elizabeth "Tipper" Aitcheson, May 19, 1970; c. Karenna; Kristin; Sarah; Albert Arnold III. EDUC.: B.A. (cum laude), Harvard U., 1969; Graduate School of Religion, Vanderbilt U., 1971–72, law school, 1974–76. POLIT. & GOV.: elected as a Democrat to U.S. House (TN), 1977–85; elected as a Democrat to U.S. Senate (TN), 1985–1993; ***candidate for Democratic nomination to presidency of the U.S., 1988, 1992 (withdrew); candidate for Democratic nomination to vice presidency of the U.S., 1988; elected as a Democrat to vice presidency of the U.S., 1993–***. BUS. & PROF.: investigative reporter, editorial writer, *The Tennessean*, 1971–76; homebuilder; land developer; owner, Tanglewood Home Builders Co., 1971–76; livestock and tobacco farmer, 1973–. MIL.: U.S. Army, 1969–71. MEM.: Farm Bureau; Tennessee Jaycees; American Legion; VFW. AWARDS: University Scholar, Harvard U. WRITINGS: *Earth in the Balance* (1992). REL.: Bapt. MAILING ADDRESS: Route 2, Carthage, TN 37030.

GORGAS, WILLIAM CRAWFORD. b. Oct 3, 1854, Mobile, AL; d. Jul 4, 1920, London, England; par. Gen. Josiah and Amelia (Gayle) Gorgas; m. Marie Cook Coughty, Sep 15, 1885; c. Aileen (Mrs. William Daughterty Wrightson). EDUC.: A.B., U. of the South, 1875; M.D., Bellevue Hospital Medical Coll., 1879. POLIT. & GOV.: appointed member, Isthmian Canal Comm., 1907–20; ***candidate for Single Tax Party nomination to presidency of the U.S., 1920***. BUS. & PROF.: surgeon; soldier; intern, Bellevue Hospital, Bellevue, NY, 1878–80; dir., International Health Board, Rockefeller Foundation; dir., Yellow Fever Research, Rockefeller Foundation. MIL.: appointed surgeon, U.S. Army, 1880; capt., 1885; maj., Brigade of Surgeon Volunteers, 1898; major surgeon, 1898; chief sanitary officer, Havana, Cuba, 1898–1902; col., asst. surgeon gen., 1903; appointed chief sanitation officer, Panama Canal, 1904; surgeon gen. of U.S. Army, brig. gen., 1914; maj. gen., 1915; retired,

1918; U.S. Distinguished Service Medal, 1918. MEM.: First Pan-American Scientific Congress (delegate, 1908); Walter Reed Memorial Assn. (mgr., 1908–09); Congress of American Physicians and Surgeons (pres., 1913); International Hygiene Congress (delegate, 1920); AAAS (fellow); Army and Navy Club; Chevy Chase Club; Cosmos Club; American Coll. of Surgeons; Soc. of Tropical Medicine and Hygiene; Royal Sanitary Inst.; Royal Soc. of Edinburgh; NY Acad. of Medicine; Philadelphia Coll. of Physicians; American Medical Assn. (pres., 1909–10); American Public Health Assn.; American Social Hygiene Assn.; American Surgical Soc.; National Inst. for Social Science; Assn. of Military Engineers; American Soc. of Tropical Medicine (pres., 1909–10); National Assn. for the Study of Tuberculosis; Soc. of Sanitary and Moral Prophylaxis; American Phil. Soc.; National Geographic Soc.; National Conservation Assn.; French Soc. of Tropical Medicine and Hygiene; Cambridge Phil. Soc.; Washington Acad. of Science; National Acad. of Medicine (Venezuela); Philadelphia Acad. of Natural Sciences; Southern Soc. of Washington (pres., 1915); SCV; Round Table Club. AWARDS: Dawson Gold Medal, 1871; Cairo Congress of Medicine Medal, 1902; Mary Kingsley Medal, Liverpool School of Tropical Medicine, 1907; Gold Medal, U. of the South, 1912; Sir George Buchanan Gold Medal, Royal Sanitary Inst. of London, 1912; Public Welfare Medal, National Acad. of Science, 1914; Louis Livingstone Seaman Gold Medal, American Museum of Safety, 1914, Bronze Medal, 1916; Medallion, American Medical Assn., 1914; Gold Medal, Geographical Soc. of Chicago, 1916; Gold Medal, National Inst. of Social Science, 1917; Harben Gold Medal, Royal Inst. of Public Health, 1920; commander, Legion of Honor (France), 1919; grand officer, Order of the Crown of Italy, 1918; knight commander, Order of St. Michael and St. George (Great Britain). HON. DEG.: Sc.D., U. of PA, 1903; Sc.D., U. of the South, 1904; Sc.D., Harvard U., 1908; Sc.D., Brown U., 1909; Sc.D., Jefferson Medical Coll., 1909; LL.D., U. of AL, 1910; LL.D., Tulane U., 1911; LL.D., Johns Hopkins U., 1912; Sc.D., Columbia U., 1913; Sc.D., Oxford U., 1914; Sc.D., Princeton U., 1914; LL.D., Yale U., 1914; LL.D., Georgetown U., 1915; LL.D., U. of WA, 1915; LL.D., NY U., 1918; Sc.D., U. of Pittsburgh, 1920. RES.: Philadelphia, PA.

GORMAN, ARTHUR PUE. b. Mar 11, 1839, Woodstock, MD; d. Jun 4, 1906, Washington, DC; par. Peter and Elizabeth A. (Brown) Gorman; m. Hannah Donagan Schwartz; c. Arthur Pue, Jr.; five others. EDUC.: public schools. POLIT. & GOV.: appointed page, U.S. House, 1852; appointed page, postmaster, U.S. Senate, 1852–66; appointed U.S. collector of internal revenue, District of MD, 1866–69; elected as a Democrat to MD State House of Delegates, 1869–75 (Speaker, 1873–75); elected as a Democrat to MD State Senate, 1875–81; chm., MD State Democratic Central Cmte., 1877; elected as a Democrat to U.S. Senate (MD), 1881–99, 1903–06 (minority leader, 1889–93, 1895–98, 1903–06; majority leader, 1893–95); chm., Dem. Nat'l. Cmte., 1884; ***candidate for Democratic nomination to presidency of the U.S., 1892, 1900, 1904***; Democratic candidate for U.S. Senate (MD), 1899. BUS. & PROF.: dir., Chesapeake and Ohio Canal Co., 1869–72, pres., 1872–1906; state dir., Washington Branch, Baltimore and Ohio R.R. RES.: Laurel, MD.

GORMAN, MARTHA M. b. Jun 20, 1953, Geneva, NY; par. William Arthur and Nancy Ellen (Berg) Gorman; m. José Azate Zulvaga, Mar 16, 1974 (divorced, 1981); c. none. EDUC.: B.S./B.A., State U. of NY at Buffalo, 1983, M.L.S. POLIT. & GOV.: ***Everybody for President candidate for presidency of the U.S., 1984***. BUS. & PROF.: librarian; freelance writer; dir., U. of Los Andes Library, Bogotá, Colombia; dir., National Technical Information Services, Bogotá, Colombia; project administrator, Continental Telephone Co., Atlanta, GA. MEM.: Junior Achievement (dir.); American Translators Assn.; National Head Injury Foundation. WRITINGS: *Everybody for President* (1984). MAILING ADDRESS: 4282 Eldorado Springs Dr., Boulder, CO 80303.

GOULD, SYMON. b. 1893, New York, NY; d. Nov 24, 1963, Yonkers, NY; m. Eve Jacoby; c. Raphael Lawrence. EDUC.: Townsend Harris H.S., New York, NY. POLIT. & GOV.: founder, American Vegetarian Party, 1948; ***American Vegetarian Party candidate for vice presidency of the U.S., 1948, 1952, 1956; American Vegetarian Party candidate for presidency of the U.S., 1960***. BUS. & PROF.: publisher; debater; motion picture distributor; rare book dealer; poet, *The Call*; founder, American Library Service, 1922; mgr., New York movie house, 1930–40; founder, Eighth Street Playhouse, Greenwich Village, NY; ed., *The American Vegetarian*. MEM.: Soc. of Motion Picture Engineers; Health Club (founder); League for Public Discussion (dir., 1926); Film Arts Guild (founder, 1930). REL.: Ethical Culture Soc. MISC.: self-styled Bohemian. RES.: New York, NY.

GOUTHEY, ALDOPH PHILIP. POLIT. & GOV.: ***candidate for Prohibition Party nomination to presidency of the U.S., 1924; Prohibition Party candidate for vice presidency of the U.S., 1924 (declined)***. BUS. & PROF.: minister. WRITINGS: *The Tongue of Fire* (1921); *David* (1934). MISC.: known as "Doctor" Gouthey. RES.: Seattle, WA.

GRADY, JOHN LOUELLEAN. b. Nov 24, 1930, IA; m. Carol; c. Alice Marie; James John; Joseph Robert. EDUC.: M.D., Creighton U., Omaha, NE, 1960. POLIT. & GOV.: medical examiner for FL state atty.; elected city commissioner, Belle Glade, FL, four terms; elected mayor of Belle Glade, FL, three terms; American Party candidate for U.S. Senate (FL), 1974; ***candidate for American Party nomination to presidency of the U.S., 1976; candidate for Republican nomination to vice presidency of the U.S., 1976***; Republican candidate for U.S. Senate (FL), 1976. BUS. & PROF.: physician; chief of staff, Glades General Hospital; gen. practice, Belle Glade, FL; commentator, "An American Speaks." MIL.: U.S. Navy, 1951–55.

MEM.: Assn. of American Physicians and Surgeons (state pres.); FL Legislative and Research Cmte. (pres.); FL Citizens for Law and Decency (pres.); Belle Glade C. of C. (pres.); U.S. Junior C. of C.; Congress of Freedom; Americans for the Right-to-Life (national chm.); FL Right-to-Life Cmte. (founder); American Heart Assn. (dir.); American Cancer Soc. (dir.); NRA (life member); American Legion; Elks; Knights of Columbus; American Freedom Cmte.; John Birch Soc. (National Council). AWARDS: Distinguished Service Award, U.S. Junior C. of C., 1971; Liberty Award, Congress of Freedom, 1973, 1974; Florida Man of the Year, Knights of Columbus, 1970; Man of the Year, Women for Constitutional Government, 1973. WRITINGS: *Regional Government—A Blueprint for Tyranny; American Patriots in a Time of Crisis*. REL.: Christian. MAILING ADDRESS: 800 South Main St., Belle Glade, FL 33430.

GRAHAM, CHESTER ARTHUR. b. Mar 31, 1892, Mercer, PA; par. Arthur W. and Malinda (Taylor) Graham; m. Margaret Rutledge, 1921; m. 2d, Viola Jo Kreiner, 1944; c. James; Frank; Martha Hampton; Lois Wade; Donald; Margaret Rutledge; Laurie Wilson; Jean; Jere. EDUC.: B.A., Oberlin Coll., 1917; M.A., U. of IL, 1926, postgrad. study in international law; U. of Akron. POLIT. & GOV.: Socialist Party candidate for MI state treas., 1932; ***candidate for Socialist Party nomination to vice presidency of the U.S., 1948, 1976***. BUS. & PROF.: farmer; Americanization sec., YMCA, Akron, OH, 1919; dir. of Americanization, Akron (OH) Public Schools, 1920–25; assoc. dir., Pocono People's Coll., Henryville, PA, 1926–27; resident dir., Ashland Folk School, Grant, MI, 1928–38; minister, Grant Community Church, Grant, MI, 1928–38; state supervisor, Workers' Education, WI WPA, 1938–40; dir. of education, Consumer Cooperatives, Madison, WI, 1940–41; field worker, Education Dept., National Farmers Union, 1942; dir. of organization, Mid-Southern Farmers Union, 1943; exec. dir., Victory Food Cmte. of MI, 1944; gen. mgr., Kent County Farmers Union Cooperative, Belmont, MI, 1945–46; field worker, Friends Cmte. on National Legislation, 1947; ed., *Monthly Action Bulletin-North Dakota Farmers Union Daily*, 1948–55; commentator, ND Farmers Union radio series, 1948–55; field representative, American Labor Education Service, 1956–58; taught in summer labor schools; exec. sec., Illinois-Wisconsin Friends Cmte. on Legislation, 1959–61; lobbyist; activist. MEM.: Phi Delta Kappa; Pilgrim Foundation (asst. to dir., 1927–28); Cosmopolitan Club; Social Worker's Club (pres., 1922–25); Akron Federation of Churches (education chm., 1919–24); NEA; American Legion (commander, Akron, OH Post, 1922–23); Community Church Workers of North America (member, Board of Directors, 1937–39); League for Independent Political Action (state chm.); American Monetary Reform Assn. (vice chm.); MI Rural Electrification Assn. (treas.); National Council for Prevention of War (vice chm.); MI Farmers Union (sec.-treas.); Central States Cooperative League (dir.); Wolverine Cooperative Exchange (dir.); National Farmers Union; Cooperative Recreation Service (dir.); Madison (WI) Cooperative Dairy (dir.); ND Mental Health Assn. (pres., 1954); Northwest Education Cmte. of Farmers and Workers (chm., 1948–55); Community Chest; Mayor's Cmte. for United Nations Week, Columbus, OH (chm., 1956); Fellowship of Reconciliation (local chm.); Wayland Foundation, U. of WI (dir.); Cooperative Credit Union, Madison, WI (pres., 1956–66); WI Cmte. to End the Draft (chm., 1961–66); Madison Citizens for Peace in Vietnam (chm., 1965); Menominee Indian Tribe (lobbyist, 1958–59); WI Cmte. for Migrant Workers; United Nations Assn. (chm., Madison, WI Branch, 1961); Dane Cty. Cmte. for UNICEF (chm., 1963–66); Madison World Affairs Center (coordinator); IL Cmte. to Abolish Capital Punishment (sec., 1959–61); A.C.L.U. (dir., Western MI Chapter); Muskegon Priorities Council; American Friends Service Cmte.; National Planning Assn. (National Council). AWARDS: Spade Oration Citation, 1917; Croce di Guerra (Italy, 1918); Recognition and Appreciation Citation, Christian Rural Overseas Program, 1950; Page One Award, 1966; Public Citizen of the Year, 1974; Civil Libertarian Award, 1974; Award for Distinguished Services to United Nations, 1974; Meritorious Service Award, National Farmers Union, 1975. REL.: Soc. of Friends (Sunday school teacher; presiding clerk, IL Yearly Meeting, 1964–65; presiding clerk, Green Pastures Quarterly Meeting, 1973). RES.: Muskegon, MI.

GRAHAM, DANIEL ROBERT "BOB." b. Nov 9, 1936, Coral Gables, FL; par. Ernest R. and Hilda (Simmons) Graham; m. Adele Khoury, 1959; c. Gwendolyn Patricia; Glynn Adele; Arva Suzanne; Kendall Elizabeth. EDUC.: B.A., U. of FL, 1959; LL.B., Harvard U., 1962. POLIT. & GOV.: elected as a Democrat to FL State House, 1967–71; elected as a Democrat to FL State Senate, 1971–79; elected as a Democrat to gov. of FL, 1979–87; appointed member, National Comm. on Reform of Secondary Education; ***candidate for Democratic nomination to vice presidency of the U.S., 1984, 1988***; elected as a Democrat to U.S. Senate (FL), 1987–. BUS. & PROF.: atty.; admitted to FL Bar, 1962; cattle and dairy farmer; real estate developer; vice pres., Graham Co.; vice pres., sec., Sengra Development Corp., Miami Lakes, FL. MEM.: Phi Beta Kappa; ABA; FL Bar Assn.; Dade Cty. Bar Assn.; Urban Land Inst.; Florida Blue Key; Chancellor of the Honor Court; Sigma Nu; Southern Regional Education Board; National Foundation for the Improvement of Education; Builders Assn. of Southern Florida; YMCA; 4-H Youth Foundation; National Comm. for Citizens in Education; Senior Centers of Dade Cty.; Greater Miami C. of C.; Hialeah & Miami Springs C. of C. AWARDS: one of five Outstanding Young Men in Florida, Florida Junior C. of C., 1971; Outstanding First Term Member of the Senate, Allen Morris, 1971; Most Valuable Legislator, *St. Petersburg (FL) Times*, 1972; Lawmaker-Newsmaker of the Year, *Tallahassee (FL) Democrat*, 1972; Conservation Award, Sierra Club, 1972; Conservation Award, FL Wildlife Federation, 1972; Conservation Award, Save Our Bays Assn., 1972; Conservation Award, Audubon Soc., 1974. REL.: United Church of Christ. MAILING ADDRESS: 16141 Aberdeen Way, Miami Lakes, FL 33014.

GRAHAM, GEORGE SCOTT. b. Sep 13, 1850, Philadelphia, PA; d. Jul 4, 1931, Islip, NY; m. Emma Ellis, Dec 14, 1870; m. 2d, Pauline M. Wall, Jun 1898; c. Adele; George Ellis; Ethel Scott (Mrs. C. F. Wentz); Blanche (Mrs. Erskine Bains); Marion Hollister (Mrs. Graham Williams). EDUC.: LL.B., U. of PA, 1870; studied law under John Roberts, Philadelphia, PA. POLIT. & GOV.: elected as a Republican to Philadelphia (PA) Select Council, 1877–80; Republican candidate for district atty., Philadelphia Cty., PA, 1877; elected as a Republican-Democrat, district atty., Philadelphia Cty., 1880–99; delegate, Rep. Nat'l. Conv., 1892, 1924; elected as a Republican to U.S. House (PA), 1913–31; ***candidate for Republican nomination to vice presidency of the U.S., 1924***. BUS. & PROF.: atty.; admitted to PA Bar, 1971; law practice, Philadelphia, 1899–1931; partner, Graham and Gilfillan (law firm), Philadelphia; partner, Graham and L'Amoreaux (law firm), New York, NY; prof. of criminal law, U. of PA, 1887–98. MEM.: Knights Templar (grand commander of PA); Union League; Five O'Clock Club. HON. DEG.: LL.D., Lafayette Coll., 1889. RES.: Philadelphia, PA.

GRAHAM, JOHN MILTON. b. 1920. POLIT. & GOV.: ***Little People's Party candidate for presidency of the U.S., 1980***. BUS. & PROF.: owner, cook, Friendship Restaurant, Fort Smith, AR. MAILING ADDRESS: 3717 Wirsing Ave., Fort Smith, AR 72904.

GRAHAM, JOSEPH McDERMOTT, JR. par. Joseph McDermott Graham. POLIT. & GOV.: ***independent candidate for presidency of the U.S., 1980***. MAILING ADDRESS: 2503 Appleby Dr., Wanamassa, NJ 07712.

GRAHAM, TOM "CUZ." POLIT. & GOV.: ***independent candidate for presidency of the U.S., 1988***. BUS. & PROF.: cowboy; songwriter. MAILING ADDRESS: Mineola, TX.

GRAHAM, WILLIAM ALEXANDER. b. Sep 5, 1804, Vesuvius Furnace, NC; d. Aug 11, 1875, Saratoga Springs, NY; par. Gen. Joseph and Isabella (Davidson) Graham; m. Susannah Sarah Washington, Jun 8, 1836; c. Joseph; John Washington; William Alexander, Jr.; James Augustus; Robert Davidson; George Washington; Augustus Washington; Susan Washington; Alfred Octavius; Eugene. EDUC.: grad. (magna cum laude), U. of NC, 1824; studied law under Thomas Ruffin, Hillsboro, NC. POLIT. & GOV.: elected as a Whig to NC State House of Commons, 1833–40 (Speaker, 1838–40); elected as a Whig to U.S. Senate (NC), 1840–43, 1866 (not qualified due to prior service with Confederate States of America); elected as a Whig to gov. of NC, 1845–49; appointed U.S. ambassador to Spain, 1849 (declined); appointed U.S. ambassador to Russia, 1849 (declined); appointed U.S. sec. of the navy, 1850–52; ***Whig Party candidate for vice presidency of the U.S., 1852***; elected as an Anti-Secessionist to NC State Senate, 1854, 1862, 1865; ***Union Conservative Party candidate for presidency of the U.S., 1860; candidate for Constitutional Union Party nomination to presidency of the U.S., 1860***; pres. pro tempore, NC State Secession Convention, 1861–62; elected member, Confederate Senate (NC), 1864–65; appointed VA arbitrator, Virginia-Maryland Boundary Dispute, 1873–75. BUS. & PROF.: atty.; admitted to NC Bar, 1826; law practice, Hillsboro, NC. MEM.: Peabody Fund (trustee, 1867–75). REL.: Presb. RES.: Hillsboro, NC.

GRAHAM, WILLIAM FRANKLIN "BILLY." b. Nov 7, 1918, Charlotte, NC; par. William Franklin and Morrow (Coffey) Graham; m. Ruth McCue Bell, Aug 13, 1943; c. Virginia Leftwich; Anne Morrow; Ruth Bell; William Franklin; Nelson Edman. EDUC.: Bob Jones U., 1936; Th.B., FL Bible Seminary, 1940; A.B., Wheaton Coll., 1943. POLIT. & GOV.: ***candidate for Republican nomination to presidency of the U.S., 1968; Loyal USA Party candidate for vice presidency of the U.S., 1972***. BUS. & PROF.: ordained minister, Baptist Church; minister, First Church, Western Springs, IL; radio personality, "Songs in the Night," WCFL, Chicago, IL, 1943–45; first vice pres., Youth for Christ International, 1945–48; pres., Northwestern Coll., Minneapolis, MN, 1947–52; chm. of the board, World Wide Pictures, Inc.; conducted nationwide evangelistic crusades, 1949–; leader, "Hour of Decision" (weekly radio program), 1950–; founder, pres., Billy Graham Evangelistic Assn.; editor-in-chief, *Decision Magazine*. MEM.: United Bible Societies (1963–); Royal Literary Soc.; Royal Geographic Soc. (Fellow); Suburban Professional Mens Club (founder, 1943). AWARDS: Bernard Baruch Award, 1955; Humane Order of African Redemption, 1960; Gold Award, George Washington Carver Memorial Inst., 1963; Horatio Alger Award, 1965; International Brotherhood Award, National Conference of Christians and Jews, 1971; Sylvanus Thayer Award, Assn. of Graduates of the U.S. Military Acad., 1972; Franciscan International Award, 1972; Man of the South Award, 1974; Liberty Bell Award, 1975. HON. DEG.: D.D., Kings Coll., 1948; D.Humanities, Bob Jones U., 1948; LL.D., Houghton Coll., 1950; LL.D., Baylor U., 1950; D.D., William Jewell Coll.; LL.D., The Citadel; other hon. degrees. WRITINGS: *Calling Youth to Christ* (1947); *Revival in Our Times* (1950); *America's Hour of Decision* (1951); *Korean Diary* (1953); *Peace With God* (1953); *The Secret to Happiness* (1955); *My Answer* (1960); *World Aflame* (1965); *The Jesus Generation* (1971); *Angels: God's Secret Agents* (1975); *How to be Born Again* (1977); *The Holy Spirit* (1978). MAILING ADDRESS: 1300 Harmon Place, Minneapolis, MN 55403.

GRANGER, FRANCIS. b. Dec 1, 1792, Suffield, CT; d. Aug 31, 1868, Canandaigua, NY; par. Gideon and Mindwell (Pease) Granger; m. Cornelia Ruston Van Rensselaer, 1817; c. two. EDUC.: grad., Yale U., 1811; studied law. POLIT.

& GOV.: elected as a National Republican to NY State Assembly, 1826–28, 1830–32; Anti-Masonic Party candidate for gov. of NY, 1828 (declined); National Republican candidate for lt. gov. of NY, 1828; National Republican (Anti-Masonic) candidate for gov. of NY, 1830, 1832; delegate, Anti-Masonic Party National Convention, 1830; elected as a Whig to U.S. House (NY), 1835–37, 1839–41, 1841–43; Whig Party candidate for U.S. House (NY), 1836; ***Whig (Anti-Masonic) Party candidate for vice presidency of the U.S., 1836***; appointed postmaster gen. of the U.S., 1841; chm., NY Whig Party State Convention, 1850; delegate, Washington Peace Convention, 1861. BUS. & PROF.: atty.; admitted to New York Bar, 1816; law practice, Canandaigua, NY. RES.: Canandaigua, NY.

GRANT, FREDERICK DENT. b. May 30, 1850, St. Louis, MO; d. Apr 11, 1912, New York, NY; par. President Ulysses Simpson (q.v.) and Julia (Dent) Grant; m. Ida M. Honors, Oct 20, 1874; c. Julia (Princess Cantacuzene of Russia); Ulysses Simpson, III. EDUC.: grad., U.S. Military Acad., 1871. POLIT. & GOV.: ***candidate for Republican nomination to presidency of the U.S., 1888***; appointed U.S. minister to Austria, 1889–93; police commissioner, New York, NY, 1894–98; ***candidate for Republican nomination to vice presidency of the U.S., 1896***. BUS. & PROF.: soldier; engineer, Union Pacific and Colorado Railroads, 1871. MIL.: 2d lt., Fourth Cavalry, U.S. Army, 1871, 1st lt., 1876, lt. col., 1873, served on frontier, 1873–81, resigned, 1881; appointed col., 14th NY Infantry, 1898, brig. gen. of volunteers, 1898, discharged, 1899; appointed brig. gen. of volunteers, 1899, brig. gen., U.S. Army, 1901, maj. gen., 1906. MEM.: Military Order of the Loyal Legion; Soc. of Colonial Wars; Sons of the Revolution; Soc. of Foreign Wars; Union League; Badminton Club; Army and Navy Club. RES.: New York, NY.

GRANT, HIRAM ULYSSES (aka ULYSSES SIMPSON GRANT). b. Apr 27, 1822, Point Pleasant, OH; d. Jul 23, 1885, Mt. McGregor, NY; par. Jesse Root and Hannah (Green) Grant; m. Julia Boggs Dent, Aug 22, 1848; c. Frederick Dent (q.v.); Jesse Root (q.v.); Ulysses Simpson, Jr.; Ellen "Nellie" Wrenshall (Mrs. Algernon Charles Frederick Sartoris; Mrs. Franklin Hatch Jones). EDUC.: grad., U.S. Military Acad., 1843. POLIT. & GOV.: ***candidate for Republican nomination to presidency of the U.S., 1864, 1880***; appointed U.S. sec. of war ad interim, 1867–68; ***elected as a Republican to presidency of the U.S., 1869–77; National Workingmen's Party candidate for presidency of the U.S., 1872; American Political Alliance candidate for presidency of the U.S., 1880 (declined)***. BUS. & PROF.: army officer; farmer, St. Louis, MO, 1854–59; real estate salesman; employee, customs office; clerk, Jesse Root's Store (leather business), 1860–61; banker; partner, Grant and Ward (investment house), until 1884; author. MIL.: commissioned 2d lt., Fourth Infantry, U.S. Army, 1843, brev. capt., 1848, capt., 1853, resigned, 1854; commissioned col., 21st IL Volunteers, 1861, brig. gen., 1861, maj. gen. of volunteers, 1862; given command of U.S. Army in the West, 1863; lt. gen., commander in chief, U.S. Army, 1864, gen. of the army, 1866. MEM.: Loyal Legion (commander, NY commandery). WRITINGS: *Personal Memoirs* (1885). REL.: Methodist. MISC.: administration as president marked by scandal and corruption; known as "Unconditional Surrender" Grant. RES.: Mt. McGregor, NY.

GRANT, JESSE ROOT. b. Feb 6, 1858, St. Louis, MO; d. Jun 8, 1934, Los Altos, CA; par. President Ulysses Simpson (q.v.) and Julia (Dent) Grant; m. Elizabeth Chapman, Sep 21, 1880; m. 2d, Mrs. Lillian Burns Wilkins, Aug 26, 1918; c. Nellie (Mrs. William P. Cronan); Chapman. EDUC.: Cornell U.; Columbia U. School of Law, 1879. POLIT. & GOV.: ***candidate for Republican nomination to presidency of the U.S., 1908, 1912***. BUS. & PROF.: freelance civil engineer. MEM.: NY Democratic Club. WRITINGS: *In the Days of My Father, General Grant* (1925). RES.: Sausalito, CA.

GRASSO, ELLA TAMBUSSI. b. May 10, 1919, Windsor Locks, CT; d. Feb 5, 1981, Hartford, CT; par. James and Maria (Oliva) Tambussi; m. Thomas A. Grasso, Aug 31, 1942; c. Susane; James. EDUC.: B.A. (magna cum laude), Mt. Holyoke Coll., 1940, M.A., 1942. POLIT. & GOV.: appointed asst. state dir. of research, War Manpower Comm., 1943–46; elected as a Democrat to CT State House, 1953–57 (floor Leader, 1955); appointed member, Long Lane Farm Study Comm.; appointed member, Highway Finance Advisory Comm.; chm., CT Democratic Platform Cmte., 1956; elected as a Democrat to sec. of state of CT, 1959–71; delegate, Dem. Nat'l. Conv., 1960, 1964, 1968, 1976; appointed member, Board of Foreign Scholarships, 1961–66; chm., Comm. to Prepare for CT State Constitutional Convention; delegate, CT State Constitutional Convention, 1965; appointed chm., Planning Cmte., Governor's Comm. on the Status of Women; vice chm., exec. cmte., Human Rights and Opportunities, 1967; elected as a Democrat to U.S. House (CT), 1971–75; delegate, Democratic Mid-Term Conference, 1974; elected as a Democrat to gov. of CT, 1975–80 (resigned); member, Dem. Nat'l. Cmte., 1956–58; ***candidate for Democratic nomination to vice presidency of the U.S., 1976***. BUS. & PROF.: teaching asst., dept. of economics and sociology, Mt. Holyoke Coll., 1942; public official. MEM.: AAUW; CT Council of Catholic Women (dir.); Order of the Sons of Italy; CT Assn. for Children with Perceptual Learning Disabilities; League of Women Voters; Phi Beta Kappa; CT Coll. (trustee); Kappa Delta Pi; Alpha Delta Kappa; Mt. Holyoke Club; Greater Hartford Urban League (hon. dir.); American Council on Italian Migration (member, Hartford Advisory Board); Windsor Locks Public Library (dir.); Cmte. of 100, U. of Hartford Library (dir.); Project Cause, Office of Mental Retardation, CT Dept. of Health (dir.). AWARDS: Merit Award, Dept. of CT, Italian-American War Veterans of the U.S.; Woman of the Year Award, Greater Hartford Chapter and New Britain Chapter, American Cmte. on Italian Migration; Outstanding Service Award, CT Cystic Fibrosis Assn.; Citation, Order of the Sons of Italy; Leadership Citation, Loomis Inst.; Amita Award as "Outstanding Woman of Italian Parentage," 1959; American Heritage Award, 1961; Americanism Award, B'nai B'rith, 1963; Italian-American Gold Medal, Sons of Italy, 1963; Woman of the Year Award, Hartford Business and Professional Women's Club, 1964; Woman of the Year Award, Ladies Auxiliary, VFW, 1971; Silver Apple Award, CT Education Assn.; Most Distinguished Service Citation, American Legion; Knight in Order of Merit, Republic of Italy; Marconi Award, Sons of Italy in America and Canada; First Humanitarian Award, Knights of Khorassan. HON. DEG.: LL.D., Mt. Holyoke Coll., 1972; LL.D., Sacred Heart U. WRITINGS: "Canal Fever," *Hartford (CT) Courant*, May, 1969. REL.: R.C. (member, Church Council, St. Mary's Church, Windsor Locks, CT). RES.: Windsor Locks, CT.

GRATTO-IRWIN, KAREN LEE. b. Jul 25, 1949, Niagara Falls, NY; par. Edward Charles, Jr., and Alice Elizabeth (Robillard) Gratto; single; c. Paula Marie Irwin; Brandy Lee Irwin; Alwin Eugene Irwin, Jr.; Mark Allen Adona; Robert Jay Denny, Jr.; Richard Allyn Denny. EDUC.: college grad. POLIT. & GOV.: ***candidate for Democratic nomination to presidency of the U.S., 1992***. BUS. & PROF.: corporate dir., chief exec. officer, chief financial officer, Monarchy of the United States of America; exec., Technical Consultants, Inc. AWARDS: professional, Olympic, and service awards. MAILING ADDRESS: 12551 Nutwood Ave., #7, Garden Grove, CA 92640.

GRAVEL, MAURICE ROBERT "MIKE." b. May 13, 1930, Springfield, MA; par. Alphonse and Maria (Bourassa) Gravel; m. Rita Jeanette Martin, Aug 25, 1959; c. Martin Anthony; Lynn Denise. EDUC.: Assumption Coll., Worcester, MA, 1949–50; American International Coll., Springfield, MA, 1950–51; B.S., Columbia U., 1956. POLIT. & GOV.: elected as a Democrat to AK State House, 1962–68 (Speaker, 1964–66); candidate for Democratic nomination to U.S. House (AK), 1966; elected as a Democrat to U.S. Senate (AK), 1969–81; ***candidate for Democratic nomination to vice presidency of the U.S., 1972; candidate for People's Party nomination to presidency of the U.S., 1972 (declined)***; delegate, Dem. Nat'l. Conv., 1976; candidate for Democratic nomination to U.S. Senate (AK), 1980. BUS. & PROF.: owner, real estate company, Anchorage, AK, 1958–. MIL.: 2d lt., U.S. Army, 1951–54. MEM.: Anchorage Theater Assn. (pres.); Anchorage Tuberculosis Assn. (pres.); Assumption Coll. (trustee). HON. DEG.: LL.D., Assumption Coll.; LL.D., Western New England Coll. WRITINGS: *Jobs and More Jobs* (1968); *Citizen Power; The Senator Gravel Edition of the Pentagon Papers* (1971). REL.: Unitarian. MAILING ADDRESS: P.O. Box 2283, Anchorage, AK.

GRAVES, JOHN TEMPLE. b. Nov 9, 1856, Willington Church, SC; d. Aug 8, 1925, Washington, DC; par. Gen. James Porterfield and Katherine Floride (Calhoun) Townes Graves; m. Mattie Gardner Simpson, Apr 17, 1878; m. 2d, Annie E. Cothran, Dec 30, 1890; c. John Temple II. EDUC.: U. of GA, 1875. POLIT. & GOV.: presidential elector, Democratic Party, 1884 (FL), 1888 (GA); candidate for Democratic nomination to U.S. House (GA), 1886; candidate for Democratic nomination to U.S. Senate (GA), 1905 (withdrew due to poor health); ***candidate for National Independence League Party nomination to presidency of the U.S., 1908; National Independence League Party candidate for vice presidency of the U.S., 1908***; appointed col., staff of Gov. William J. Northen (GA). BUS. & PROF.: pres., Langrange Military Acad.; journalist; lecturer; ed., *Daily Florida Union*, 1881–83; ed., *Atlanta (GA) Daily Journal*, 1887–88; *Tribune of Rome* (GA), 1888–90; gen. mgr., Colleton Land Co., 1890; ed., *Jacksonville (FL) Herald*; ed., *Atlanta News*, 1902–07; editor-in-chief, proprietor, *Atlanta Daily Georgian*, 1905–07; editor-in-chief, *New York (NY) American*, 1907–15; editorial representative, Hearst newspaper chain, 1915–25. MEM.: NY Press Club (pres.). WRITINGS: *History of Florida Today; History of Colleton, South Carolina; Twelve Standard Lectures; Platform of Today; Speeches and Selections for Schools; The Negro; The Winter Resorts of Florida* (1883); *Eloquent Sons of the South* (coeditor, 1909). REL.: Presb. (elder). RES.: Washington, DC.

GRAVES, SAMUEL LEE. b. Aug 18, 1938, Greensboro, NC; married; c. Solomon; Patricia; Matthew; Mary. EDUC.: D.D. POLIT. & GOV.: ***candidate for Democratic nomination to presidency of the U.S., 1984, 1988***. BUS. & PROF.: minister, Church of God; pastor, Church of God, Greensboro, NC; costume jewelry salesman. REL.: Church of God. MISC.: convicted of disorderly conduct, impeding traffic, and carrying dangerous weapons, NJ, 1984; sentenced to NJ Adult Correctional Center. MAILING ADDRESS: 218 York St., Greensboro, NC 27401.

GRAVES, STEPHEN CAREY. POLIT. & GOV.: ***U.S. Taxpayers Party of WY candidate for vice presidency of the U.S., 1992***. BUS. & PROF.: physician. MAILING ADDRESS: 11006 Rye Hills Rd., South, Fort Smith, AR 72901.

GRAY, GEORGE. b. May 4, 1840, New Castle, DE; d. Aug 7, 1925, Wilmington, DE; par. Andrew Caldwell and Elizabeth Maria (Schofield) Gray; m. Harriet L. Black, Jun 2, 1870; m. 2d, Margaret Janiver Black, Aug 8, 1882; c. Andrew Caldwell; Anne Black; Emily Scofield (Mrs. Henry Thouron); Charles Black; George, Jr. EDUC.: A.B., Princeton U., 1859, A.M., 1863; Harvard U. POLIT. & GOV.: delegate, Dem. Nat'l. Conv., 1876, 1880, 1884, 1892, 1896; appointed atty. gen. of DE, 1879–85; elected as a Democrat to U.S. Senate (DE), 1885–99; ***candidate for Democratic nomination to presidency of the U.S., 1892, 1904, 1908***; member, Paris Peace Comm., 1898; member, Joint British-American High Comm., 1898; Democratic candidate for U.S. Senate (DE), 1899; appointed judge, U.S. Circuit Court of Appeals, 1899–1914; appointed judge, International Permanent Court of Arbitration, 1900–1925; appointed chm., Anthracite Coal Strike Comm., 1902; appointed umpire, U.S.–San Domingo Arbitration, 1903; appointed member, Tribunal, North American Coast Fisheries Arbitration, 1910; appointed member, British-American Comm. to Promote Peace, 1915; chm., U.S. Delegation, Pan-American Scientific Congress, 1915; appointed member, American-Mexican Comm., 1916. BUS. & PROF.: atty.; admitted to DE Bar, 1863; law practice, New Castle, DE, 1863–69; law practice, Wilmington, DE. MEM.: Smithsonian Institution (regent; chm., exec. cmte.); Carnegie Endowment for International Peace (trustee; vice pres.); Soc. of International Law (founder; vice pres.); American Red Cross (founder; dir.); American Phil. Soc.; English Speaking Union. HON. DEG.: LL.D., Princeton U., 1889; LL.D., Yale U., 1903. REL.: Presb. RES.: Wilmington, DE.

GRAY, HOSANNA JESSE O. POLIT. & GOV.: ***candidate for Democratic nomination to presidency of the U.S., 1988***. MAILING ADDRESS: c/o Major M. King, P.O. Box 1000, Battle Creek, MI 49017.

GRAY, ISAAC PUSEY. b. Oct 18, 1828, Chester Cty., PA; d. Feb 14, 1895, Mexico City, Mexico; par. John and Hannah (Worthington) Gray; m. Eliza Jaqua, Sep 8, 1850; c. Pierre; Bayard; Lyman (infant); Warren (infant). POLIT. & GOV.: Republican candidate for U.S. House (IN), 1866; elected as a Democrat to IN State Senate, 1868–72 (pres. pro tempore); delegate, Liberal Rep. Nat'l. Conv., 1872; member, Liberal Rep. Nat'l. Cmte., 1872; Democratic candidate for atty. gen. of IN, 1874 (declined); elected as a Democrat to lt. gov. of IN, 1876–80; succeeded to gov. of IN, 1880–81; Democratic candidate for U.S. Senate (IN), 1881; elected as a Democrat to gov. of IN, 1885–89; elected as a Democrat to U.S. Senate (IN), 1887 (declined); ***candidate for Democratic nomination to vice presidency of the U.S., 1888, 1892***; appointed U.S. minister to Mexico, 1893–95. BUS. & PROF.: clerk, New Madison, OH, 1846; atty.; admitted to IN Bar, 1850; law practice, Indianapolis, IN. MIL.: col., Fourth IN Cavalry, U.S. Army, 1862–63; col., 106th Regt. ("Minute Men"), IN Infantry, 1863; commissioned capt., Union City Guards, Randolph Battalion, IN Legion, 1863. REL.: Soc. of Friends. MISC.: credited with Indiana's ratification of Fifteenth Amendment to the Constitution of the U.S. RES.: Indianapolis, IN.

GRAY, JAMES HARRISON. b. 1916, Westfield, MA; d. Sep 19, 1986, Boston, MA; married; c. James H., Jr.; Geoffrey; Constance. EDUC.: Dartmouth Coll., 1937; U. of Heidelberg, 1938. POLIT. & GOV.: delegate, Dem. Nat'l. Conv., 1952; temporary chm., GA Democratic State Convention, 1958; chm., GA State Exec. Cmte., 1960, 1962–70; candidate for Democratic nomination to gov. of GA, 1966; ***candidate for Democratic nomination to presidency of the U.S., 1968***; elected as a Democrat to mayor of Albany, GA, 1976–86. BUS. & PROF.: editorial and feature writer, *Hartford (CT) Courant*; editorial and feature writer, *New York (NY) Herald-Tribune*; chm. of the board, pres., *Albany Herald*, 1946–86; chm. of the board, pres., Gray Communications Systems, Inc.; chm. of the board, WALB-TV, Inc.; chm. of the board, WJHG-TV, Inc.; chm. of the board, KTVE, Inc.; chm. of the board, Gray Transportation Co., Inc. MIL.: 2d lt., U.S. Army, 1942, maj., 1946. MEM.: Phi Beta Kappa; Rotary Club; C. of C. AWARDS: "Citizen of the Year," GA County Commissioners' Assn., 1959. REL.: Episc. MISC.: noted as staunch segregationist. RES.: Albany, GA.

GRAY, JESSE. b. May 14, 1923, Tunica, LA; m. Rosa Lee Brown, 1947; c. Jesse, Jr.; one other. EDUC.: Xavier Coll.; Southern U. POLIT. & GOV.: campaign mgr., Benjamin Davis for NY State Assembly, 1952, 1958; Democratic candidate for New York (NY) City Council, 1961, 1969; keynoter, Federation for Independent Political Action Convention, 1964; ***candidate for Democratic nomination to presidency of the U.S., 1968, 1976***; candidate for Democratic nomination to U.S. House (NY), 1970; elected as a Democrat to NY State Assembly, 1973–75; candidate for Democratic nomination to mayor of New York, 1973. BUS. & PROF.: tailor; rent strike leader; Black Power advocate; consultant, Mobilization for Youth, 1966; consultant, Harlem Backstreet Youth, Office of Economic Opportunity, 1967. MEM.: Harlem Tenants Council (1952); Lower Harlem Tenants Council (founder, 1956); Student Mobilization Cmte. to End the War in Viet Nam; Monroe Defense Cmte.; World Peace Congress (delegate, 1951); United May Day Cmte. (vice chm., 1952); Organization for Black Power (chm., 1963); Revolutionary Action Movement; Community Council for Housing; National Tenants Assn. (dir.); ACT (founder, 1964). MAILING ADDRESS: 270 Covent Ave., New York, NY.

GRAY, MICHELLE KATHLEEN. POLIT. & GOV.: ***candidate for Democratic nomination to vice presidency of the U.S., 1980***. MAILING ADDRESS: c/o Dorothy Gray, 762 Edgewood Lane, Los Altos, CA 94022.

GRAY, VERNON J. POLIT. & GOV.: ***independent candidate for presidency of the U.S., 1984***. MAILING ADDRESS: R.D. #1, Box 138 F, Dover-Foxcroft, ME 04426.

GRAYSON, RICHARD. b. Jun 4, 1951, New York, NY; par. Daniel and Marilyn (Sarrett) Grayson; single. EDUC.: B.A., Brooklyn Coll., 1973, M.F.A., 1976; M.A., Coll. of Staten Island, 1975. POLIT. & GOV.: ***candidate for Democratic nomination to vice presidency of the U.S., 1980***; nonpartisan candidate for Davie (FL) Town Council; ***candidate for Democratic nomination to presidency of the U.S., 1984, 1988***. BUS. & PROF.: prof. of English, Long Island U., 1975–78; prof. of English, City U. of New York, 1978–81; prof. of English, Broward

Community Coll., Davie, FL, 1981–; publisher, *Sylvia Ginsberg Newsletter*, Davie, FL; humorist; writer. MEM.: Cmte. for Immediate Nuclear War (treas.); Future Fetuses of America (founder). AWARDS: FL Arts Council Fellowship, 1981–82. WRITINGS: *With Hitler in New York*; *Lincoln's Doctor's Dog* (1982); *I Brake for Delmore Schwartz* (1983). REL.: none. MAILING ADDRESS: 2732 South University Dr., #8A, Davie, FL 33328.

GREAVES, PERCY LAURIE, JR. b. Aug 24, 1906, Brooklyn, NY; par. Percy Laurie and Grace I. (Dodge) Greaves; m. Edith Leslye Platt, Aug 23, 1930; m. 2d, Bettina Herbert Bien, Jun 26, 1971; c. Richard L.; Muriel A.; Charles Flint. EDUC.: B.S. (magna cum laude), Syracuse U., 1929; Columbia U., 1933–34; NY U., 1950–69. POLIT. & GOV.: assoc. research dir., Rep. Nat'l. Cmte., 1943–45; appointed chief minority staff, Joint Congressional Cmte. on Investigation of Pearl Harbor Attack, 1945–46; Free Libertarian Party candidate for U.S. Senate (NY), 1974; ***candidate for American Party nomination to presidency of the U.S., 1976***; member, Exec. Board, American Party, 1976–; ***candidate for American Independent Party nomination to presidency of the U.S., 1980; American Party candidate for presidency of the U.S., 1980***. BUS. & PROF.: economist; bookkeeper, American Trading Co., 1923–24; asst. advertising mgr., Gillette Safety Razor Co., 1929–32; advertising mgr., Batten, Barton, Durstine and Osborn (advertising agency), 1930; instructor in economics and foreign trade, Y.M.H.A., 1933–34; financial ed., *U.S. News*, 1934–36; advertising mgr., Pet and Carnation Milk Companies, 1936–38; public relations exec., Metropolitan Life Insurance Co., 1938–43; exec. dir., Foundation for Freedom, Inc., 1946–48; economic consultant, 1948–; author; lecturer; economic adviser, Christian Freedom Foundation, 1950–58; lecturer, Freedom School, Inc., 1957–61; Armstrong prof. of economics, U. of Plano, 1965–71; pres., Free Market Books, 1974–. MEM.: Foundation for Economic Education (1961–67); Foundation for Freedom, Inc. (exec. dir., 1946–48); American Economic Assn.; American Military Inst.; Naval Hist. Foundation; U.S. Naval Inst.; American Hist. Assn.; Beta Gamma Sigma; Phi Kappa Phi. WRITINGS: *Operation Immigration* (1947); *Perpetual War for Perpetual Peace* (contributor, 1952); *On Freedom and Free Enterprise* (contributor, 1956); glossary of Mises' *Human Action* (1967); *Toward Liberty* (contributor, 1971); *Understanding the Dollar Crisis* (contributor, 1973); *Mises Made Easier* (1974); *Free Market Economics: A Reader* (contributor, 1975). REL.: Episc. MAILING ADDRESS: 19 Pine Lane, Irvington-on-Hudson, NY 10533.

GREELEY, HORACE. b. Feb 3, 1811, Amherst, NY; d. Nov 29, 1872, Pleasantville, NY; par. Zaccheus and Mary (Woodburn) Greeley; m. Mary Young Cheney, Jul 5, 1836; c. Gabrielle; Ida; Arthur Young; Mary Inez; Raphael Uhland; Dotty; infant. EDUC.: public schools. POLIT. & GOV.: elected as a Whig to U.S. House (NY), 1848–49; Whig Party candidate for U.S. House (NY), 1850; Whig Party candidate for lt. gov. of NY, 1854; joined Republican Party, 1856; delegate, Rep. Nat'l. Conv., 1860; candidate for Republican nomination to U.S. Senate (NY), 1861, 1863; presidential elector, Republican Party, 1864; appointed U.S. minister to Austria, 1867 (declined); delegate, NY State Constitutional Convention, 1867; Republican candidate for U.S. House (NY), 1868, 1870; Republican candidate for NY state controller, 1869; ***candidate for Prohibition Party nomination to presidency of the U.S., 1872; candidate for Labor Reform Party nomination to presidency of the U.S., 1872 (withdrew); Liberal Republican Party candidate for presidency of the U.S., 1872; Liberal Republican Party of Colored Men candidate for presidency of the U.S., 1872; Democratic candidate for presidency of the U.S., 1872***. BUS. & PROF.: printer's apprentice, *Northern Spectator*, East Poultney, VT, 1826–30; journeyman printer, Erie, PA, and New York, NY, 1831; partner (with Francis Story), job printing business, 1833; partner (with Jonas Winchester), job printing business, 1833–34; publisher, *Morning Post*, 1833; publisher, *New Yorker*, 1834–41; ed., *The Jeffersonian*, 1838; contributor, *Daily Whig*; ed., *Log Cabin*, 1840; founder, ed., *New York Tribune*, 1841–72; chm. of the jury, World's Fair, London, England, 1851; commissioner, Paris Exposition, 1855; reformer; advocate of labor unions, cooperative shops, protective tariffs, temperance, women's rights, abolition, communal living, western expansion, and universal amnesty following Civil War. MEM.: NY Typographical Union (pres., 1850). WRITINGS: *Why I Am a Whig*; *Association Discussed* (1847); *Hints Toward Reform* (1850); *History of the Struggle for Slavery Extension or Restrictions in the United States* (1850); *Glances at Europe* (1851); *The Crystal Palace and Its Lessons* (1852); *An Overland Journey from New York to San Francisco in Summer of 1859* (1860); *The American Conflict* (1865–67); *Recollections of a Busy Life* (1868); *Essays Designed to Elucidate the Science of Political Economy* (1870); *The Formation of Character*; *What I Know of Farming* (1871); *Autobiography* (1872). REL.: Universalist. RES.: New York, NY.

GREEN, BERIAH. b. Mar 24, 1795, Preston, CT; d. May 4, 1874, Whitestown, NY; par. Beriah and Elizabeth (Smith) Green; m. Marcia Deming, Jan 21, 1821; m. 2d, Daraxa Foote, Aug 30, 1826; c. S.W.; 8 others. EDUC.: grad. (valedictorian), Middlebury Coll., 1819; Andover Seminary, 1820. POLIT. & GOV.: ***candidate for National Liberty Party nomination to presidency of the U.S., 1848***. BUS. & PROF.: teacher, Phillips Acad., 1820; ordained minister, Congregational Church, 1823; pastor, Congregational Church, Brandon, VT, 1823; pastor, Congregational Church, Kennebunk, ME, 1829; prof. of sacred literature, Western Reserve Coll., 1830–33; pres., Oneida Inst., 1833–43; pastor, Congregational Church, Whitesboro, NY, 1843–67; reformer; antislavery advocate. MEM.: American Anti-Slavery Soc. (founder; delegate, National Anti-Slavery Convention, 1833; pres., 1833). WRITINGS: *The Martyr* (1838); *The Miscellaneous Writings of Beriah Green* (1841); *History of the Quakers*; *Sketches of the Life and Writings of James Gillespie Birney* (1844); *Sermons and Discourses with a Few Essays and Addresses* (1860). REL.: Congregational Church. RES.: Whitestown, NY.

GREEN, DWIGHT HERBERT. b. Jan 9, 1897, Ligonier, IN; d. Feb 20, 1958, Chicago, IL; par. Harry and Minnie (Gerber) Green; m. Mabel Victoria Kingston, Jun 29, 1926; c. Nancy Kingston (Mrs. James Burnett Gilbert); Gloria K. (Mrs. Warren Gordon McPherson). EDUC.: Wabash Coll., 1915–17; Stanford U., 1919; Ph.B., U. of Chicago, 1920, J.D., 1922. POLIT. & GOV.: appointed special atty., Bureau of Internal Revenue, Washington, DC, 1926, Chicago, IL, 1927–32; appointed special asst. to U.S. atty., Northern District of IL; appointed U.S. district atty., Northern District of IL, 1932–41; elected as a Republican to gov. of IL, 1941–49; chm., IL War Council, 1941–45; chm., Midwest Postwar Planning Conference, 1943; delegate, Rep. Nat'l. Conv., 1948 (temporary chm.; keynoter), 1952, 1956; ***candidate for Republican nomination to presidency of the U.S., 1948***. BUS. & PROF.: reporter, *Chicago American;* atty.; admitted to IL Bar, 1922; law practice, Chicago, 1922–26, 1949; chm. of the board, Elmwood Park Bank, 1953–56. MIL.: 2d lt., U.S.A.A.C., 1917–19. MEM.: Research Foundation (dir.); John Harvard Assn.; Wabash Coll. (trustee); ABA; Federal Bar Assn.; IL Bar Assn.; Chicago Bar Assn.; Union League; Indiana Soc. of Chicago (pres., 1950–51, 1954–55); Military Order of World Wars; Legal Club of Chicago; United Cerebral Palsy Assn. of Chicago (pres., 1956–58; chm. of the board, 1957); Kappa Sigma; Phi Alpha Delta (supreme justice, 1936–38); American Legion; Forty and Eight; Masons (33°; Shriners; Knight Templar); Law Club; Tavern Club; Executives Club; Mid-Day Club; Chicago Athletic Assn.; Saddle and Cycle Club; Economic Club. HON. DEG.: LL.D., MacMurray Coll., 1941; LL.D., Blackburn Coll., 1941; LL.D., Northwestern U., 1942; LL.D., Knox Coll., 1945; LL.D., Monmouth Coll., 1947; LL.D., Lake Forest Coll., 1947; D.C.L., IL Wesleyan U., 1942. REL.: Episc. (nee Presb.). MISC.: conducted prosecutions of Al Capone and other notorious gangsters, c. 1931. RES.: Chicago, IL.

GREEN, ERNEST. POLIT. & GOV.: ***independent candidate for presidency of the U.S., 1976***. BUS. & PROF.: dishwasher, Temple Hotel, Pendleton, OR. MAILING ADDRESS: 626 South East Second St., Pendleton, OR 97801.

GREEN, GABRIEL. b. Nov 11, 1924, Whittier, CA; par. Seth Wellington and Alice Mae (Stebbins) Green; m. Helen Isabel Sibert (d. May 6, 1970); c. none. EDUC.: grad., Whittier Union H.S., 1942; Woodbury Business Coll., 1942; Art Center School of Photography, 1943; Los Angeles City Coll., 1946–48. POLIT. & GOV.: ***independent (Flying Saucer; Outer Space) candidate for presidency of the U.S., 1960 (withdrew)***; candidate for Democratic nomination to U.S. Senate (CA), 1962; ***Universal Party candidate for presidency of the U.S., 1972***. BUS. & PROF.: owner, operator, studio of modern photography, Los Angeles, 1947–50; photographer, *Los Angeles (CA) Board of Education,* 1956–59; founder, pres., Los Angeles Interplanetary Study Groups, 1956–59; founder, pres., Amalgamated Flying Saucer Clubs of America, 1959–; ed., *AFSCA World Report;* ed., *Flying Saucers International;* space-age economist. MIL.: photographer's mate/second class, U.S. Navy, 1943–46. WRITINGS: *Let's Face the Facts About Flying Saucers* (coauthor, 1967); *The United World—A Theocratic Democracy.* REL.: Universalist–New Age. MISC.: noted as advocate of "Universalism" and "Universal Economics"; claims over 100 sightings of flying saucers and direct contact with extraterrestrials. MAILING ADDRESS: 2004 North Hoover St., Los Angeles, CA 90027.

GREEN, JASON RALPH. b. Jan 20, 1966, Sheffield, England; par. Ralph and Ann (Mitchell) Green; single. EDUC.: grad., Berlin H.S.; U. of WI-Oshkosh, 1984–. POLIT. & GOV.: ***Liberal Socialist candidate for presidency of the U.S., 1988***. BUS. & PROF.: raised pheasants; roofer; research analyst, Anston Construction. MEM.: Eagle Scouts (Britain); Assn. to Defeat Lyndon LaRouche; various antinuclear and anti-NRA organizations. WRITINGS: *A Barrel of Dead Monkeys; The Problem of Chronic Industrial Pollution; Siberian Snowstorm: The Threat of Soviet Drug Running.* REL.: Church of England. MAILING ADDRESS: Route 1, Box 77, Green Lake, WI 54941.

GREEN, JOHN WILLIAM. b. Jun 24, 1930, Lockport, NY; par. William Ivan and Rachel (Furlong) Green; single. EDUC.: B.S., Canisius Coll., 1963; Niagara U.; Purdue U.; Bryant and Stratton Business Inst. POLIT. & GOV.: candidate for Republican nomination to U.S. Senate (NY), 1982; ***candidate for Republican nomination to presidency of the U.S., 1984; candidate for Right-to-Life Party nomination to presidency of the U.S., 1984; candidate for Conservative Party of NY nomination to presidency of the U.S., 1984***. BUS. & PROF.: insurance agent; owner, John W. Green Insurance and Tax Services, Lockport, NY; owner, Green Development, Lockport, NY. MIL.: sgt., U.S. Army, 1951–53; Army of Occupation Medal. MEM.: American Legion; VFW; Lockport Overseas Veterans Club; Fraternal Order of Redmen; Eagles; Moose; Knights of Columbus; Holy Name Soc.; Stolls Turtle Club. AWARDS: All Star Team Award, YMCA Basketball Tournament, 1948. REL.: R.C. MAILING ADDRESS: 225 Lock St., Lockport, NY 14094.

GREEN, JOSEPH J. POLIT. & GOV.: ***independent candidate for presidency of the U.S., 1980***. MAILING ADDRESS: 2360 Wilton Dr., Wilton Manors, FL 33305.

GREEN, RAY FERRILL. POLIT. & GOV.: ***independent candidate for presidency of the U.S., 1988, 1992***. MAILING ADDRESS: 1979 Columbus Ave., Roxbury, MA 02119.

GREEN, WARREN EVERETT. b. Mar 10, 1870, Jackson Cty., WI; d. Apr 27, 1945, Watertown, SD; par.

Chester and Mary Jane (Crawley) Green; m. Elizabeth Jane Parliament, Jan 17, 1899; c. Maxwell Eldon; George Chester; Mildred Grace; Edson Richard. EDUC.: public schools, Castlewood, SD, and Watertown, SD. POLIT. & GOV.: elected pres., Watertown School Board, 15 years; elected as a Republican to SD State Senate, 1907–09, 1923–27; appointed member, SD State Board of Charities and Corrections, 1913–19; elected as a Republican to gov. of SD, 1931–33; Republican candidate for gov. of SD, 1932; delegate, Rep. Nat'l. Conv., 1932 (chm., SD Delegation), 1936; ***candidate for Republican nomination to presidency of the U.S., 1936***. BUS. & PROF.: farmer; rancher, Hazel, SD, 1895–1945. MEM.: Masons; Kiwanis. REL.: Methodist. RES.: Hazel, SD.

GREEN, WAYNE SANGER, II. b. Sep 3, 1922, Littleton, NH; par. Wayne Sanger and Cleo (Willson) Green; m. Lin Haire; m. 2d, Sherry Smythe; c. Tully; Sage. EDUC.: B.S., Rensselaer Polytechnic Inst., 1948. POLIT. & GOV.: ***candidate for Republican nomination to vice presidency of the U.S., 1964***. BUS. & PROF.: publisher, *73* (amateur radio magazine); TV dir., WXEL, Cleveland, OH, 1951–52; pres., Karlson Associates, Brooklyn, NY, 1952–55; ed., *CQ Magazine*, New York, NY, 1955–60; publisher, *BYTE Magazine*, 1975–; ed., *Kiloband Microcomputing Magazine*, Peterborough, NH, 1976–; publisher, *Instant Software*, 1978–; author. MIL.: U.S.N.R., 1942–46. MEM.: Mensa (founder); Inst. of Amateur Radio. REL.: nonsectarian. MAILING ADDRESS: c/o 73 Magazine, Peterborough, NH 03458.

GREENBERG, SAMUEL. POLIT. & GOV.: ***independent candidate for presidency of the U.S., 1988 (withdrew)***. MAILING ADDRESS: 6403 Washington Blvd., Arlington, VA 22205.

GREENE, FRANCIS VINTON. b. Jun 27, 1850, Providence, RI; d. May 15, 1921, New York, NY; par. George Sears and Martha (Dana) Greene; m. Belle Eugenie Chevallie, Feb 25, 1879. EDUC.: grad., U.S. Military Acad., 1870. POLIT. & GOV.: appointed chm., Comm. on Canals, State of NY, 1899; delegate, Rep. Nat'l. Conv., 1900; pres., New York Cty. (NY) Republican Cmte., 1900; ***candidate for Republican nomination to vice presidency of the U.S., 1904***; appointed commissioner of police, New York, 1903–04. BUS. & PROF.: soldier; vice pres., pres., Barber-Asphalt Paving Co.; pres., Niagara-Lockport and Ontario Power Co. MIL.: 2d lt., 4th Artillery Service, U.S. Army, 1870; transferred to Corps of Engineers, 1872; 1st lt., 1874; military attache to U.S. legation to Russia, 1877–79; capt., 1883; instructor, U.S. Military Acad., 1885, resigned; maj., NY National Guard, 1889, col., 71st Regt., 1892, brig. gen., 1898, maj. gen., 1898; Order of St. Vladimir; Order of St. Anne; Star of Roumania; Roumanian Cross. MEM.: Century Club; University Club; Metropolitan Club; Lawyers Club; Buffalo Club; Metropolitan Club of Washington. WRITINGS: *The Russian Army and Its Campaigns in Turkey* (two vols., 1879); *Army Life in Russia* (1881); *The Mississippi Campaigns of the Civil War* (1882); *Biography of Nathaniel Greene, Major General in the Army of the Revolution* (1893); *The Revolutionary War and the Military Policy of the United States* (1911); *The Present Military Situation in the United States* (1915); *Our First Year in the Great War* (1918). RES.: Buffalo, NY.

GREENFIELD, ALBERT S. POLIT. & GOV.: ***candidate for Democratic nomination to vice presidency of the U.S., 1940***. RES.: unknown.

GREENLEE, JAMES S. b. MS. POLIT. & GOV.: ***candidate for Democratic nomination to presidency of the U.S., 1948, 1952, 1956, 1960, 1964, 1968, 1972***. BUS. & PROF.: factory worker, 1945; evangelist; revival and reformation leader; songwriter; singer. WRITINGS: songs—"Vote for Greenlee"; "Hurry Hurry Ye Freedom-Loving Americans"; "With Thy Love, We Will Press Forward"; "Let's Bring Back Prohibition, Real Soon"; "I'd Rather Praise God, For His Goodness." MISC.: self-styled as "God's Watchman for Our Nation and Hemisphere." MAILING ADDRESS: 1539 West 8th St., Room Twelve, Los Angeles, CA 90017.

GREENSPAN, ELLIOTT. POLIT. & GOV.: ***Economic Recovery Party candidate for vice presidency of the U.S., 1992***. MAILING ADDRESS: unknown.

GREENWAY, ISABELLA SELMES FERGUSON. b. Mar 22, 1886, Boone Cty., KY; d. Dec 18, 1953, Tucson, AZ; m. John Campbell Greenway (q.v.), Nov 4, 1923; m. 2d, Harry Orland King; c. John Selmes. EDUC.: public schools; Miss Chapin's School, New York, NY. POLIT. & GOV.: ***candidate for Democratic nomination to vice presidency of the U.S., 1932***; member, Dem. Nat'l. Cmte.; elected as a Democrat to U.S. House (AZ), 1933–37; appointed member, Mt. Rushmore National Memorial Comm., 1939. BUS. & PROF.: homesteader, Tyrone, NM, 1910; cattle rancher; resort operator, AZ; operator, Gilpin Air Lines, Los Angeles, CA, 1929–34; owner, operator, Arizona Inn, Tucson, AZ, 1929. MEM.: Women's Land Army (chm., 1918). RES.: Ajo, AZ.

GREENWAY, JOHN CAMPBELL. b. Jul 6, 1872, Huntsville, AL; d. Jan 19, 1926, New York, NY; par. Dr. Gilbert Christian and Alice (White) Greenway; m. Isabella (Selmes) Ferguson (q.v.), Nov 4, 1923; c. John Selmes. EDUC.: U. of VA, 1890–91; Phillips Acad., 1891–92; Ph.B., Yale U., 1895. POLIT. & GOV.: member, Board of Regents, U. of AZ; alternate delegate, Dem. Nat'l. Conv., 1924; ***candidate for Democratic nomination to vice presidency of the U.S., 1924***. BUS. & PROF.: machinist's helper, Carnegie Steel Corp., 1895; mining engineer; assoc., J. L. D. Speer and Co. (brokerage company), 1898–1901; asst. superintendent of mines, U.S. Steel

Corp., Ishpeming, MI, 1901–06; gen. superintendent, Oliver Mining Co., Mesaba Range, MN, 1906–10; gen. mgr., Calumet and Arizona Mining Co., 1910–26; gen. mgr., New Cornelia Copper Co.; vice pres., Tucson, Cornelia and Gila Bend R.R.; pres., Warren Co.; pres., Warren-Bisbee Street Railway Co.; dir., The 85 Mining Co.; dir., Gadsden Copper Co.; dir., Superior and Pittsburgh Copper Co.; managing dir., vice pres., Ahumeda Lead Co. (Mexico). MIL.: pvt., U.S. Volunteer Cavalry, 1898, 2d lt., lt., brev. capt.; maj., U.S. Army, 1917, lt. col., 101st U.S. Infantry, 26th Div., U.S. Army, WWI; member, "Rough Riders"; Distinguished Service Cross; Croix de Guerre with Two Palms; Order of the Legion of Honor; Croix de l'Etoile Noire. MEM.: AZ Council of Defense (chm., Defense Cmte.); Phi Kappa Psi; Yale Athletic Assn.; American Inst. of Mining and Metallurgical Engineers; Yale Engineering Soc.; Book and Snake Soc. (Yale U.); Yale Club of AZ (pres.); Officer Reserve Corps (col.; brig. gen., 1922). HON. DEG.: LL.D., U. of AZ. REL.: Episc. MISC.: noted All-American athlete, Yale U. RES.: Ajo, AZ.

GREENWOOD, WILLIAM BRUCE, JR. par. William Bruce Greenwood, Sr. POLIT. & GOV.: ***candidate for Republican nomination to presidency of the U.S., 1992; independent candidate for presidency of the U.S., 1992***. MAILING ADDRESS: 6096 St. Augustine Dr., Riverside, CA 92506.

GREER, JAMES M. b. c. 1848, Holly Springs, MS; m. Bettie Allen, 1877; c. three sons. EDUC.: VA Military Inst., 1864; read law. POLIT. & GOV.: elected judge of Criminal Court, Memphis, TN, 1883–84; cty. atty., Shelby Cty., TN; ***American Party candidate for vice presidency of the U.S., 1888 (declined)***. BUS. & PROF.: atty.; admitted to VA Bar; law practice, Memphis, TN, 1872; author. MIL.: cadet, Company A, VA Military Inst., 1864. RES.: Memphis, TN.

GREER, L. ALLEN. b. Mar 29, 1928, Elkhart, IN; par. Olander Allen and Teresa F. (Broehl) Greer; m. Doris B. Baird; c. Melinda C.; Allen D. EDUC.: grad., high school, Elkhart, IN; Lincoln Coll., Lincoln, IL, 1 year. POLIT. & GOV.: state treas., American Party of FL; vice chm., chm., American Party of FL; delegate, American Party National Convention, 1972; ***candidate for American Party nomination to presidency of the U.S., 1972; candidate for American Party nomination to vice presidency of the U.S., 1972 (withdrew)***. BUS. & PROF.: chm., pres., TransFlorida Bankshares, Inc.; gen. mgr., Remco, Inc., Chicago, IL; pres., Building Accessories, Inc., Sarasota, FL; pres., Permabilt Manufacturing, Inc. MIL.: U.S. Air Force, 1950–54. MEM.: Lincoln Christian Coll. (trustee). REL.: New Testament Fundamentalist. MAILING ADDRESS: 2538 Colorado St., Sarasota, FL 33577.

GREGORY, RICHARD CLAXTON "DICK." b. Oct 12, 1932, St. Louis, MO; m. Lillian Smith, 1959; c. Michele; Lynne; Pamela Inte; Paula Gration; Stephanie; Gregory; Christian; Ayanna; Miss; Yohance. EDUC.: Sumner H.S., 1954; Southern IL U., 1951–53, 1955–56. POLIT. & GOV.: chm., National Conference for New Politics, 1967; co-chm., New Party, 1969–; ***Peace and Freedom (Peace and Freedom Alternative; Freedom and Peace; New Politics; New) Party candidate for presidency of the U.S., 1968***; independent candidate for mayor of Chicago, IL, 1967; ***candidate for The Black Assembly nomination to presidency of the U.S., 1976***; co-chm., People's Party, 1969. BUS. & PROF.: mail clerk, U.S. Post Office; civil rights activist; comedian; nightclub performer, 1958–73; social satirist; author; lecturer; nutritionist; salesman, "Dick Gregory's Slim Safe Bahamian Diet"; assoc., Correction Connection, Inc. (diet marketing), Philadelphia, PA. MIL.: U.S. Army Special Services, 1953–55. AWARDS: "Outstanding Athlete," Southern IL U., 1953; Ebony-Topaz Heritage and Freedom Award, 1978. WRITINGS: *From the Back of the Bus* (1962); *Nigger* (1964); *What's Happening* (1965); *The Shadow That Scares Me* (1968); *Write Me In!* (1968); *No More Lies* (1971); *Dick Gregory's Bible Talks* (1971); *Dick Gregory's Political Primer* (1971); *Dick Gregory's Natural Diet for Folks Who Eat; Cookin' With Mother Nature* (1973); *Dick Gregory's Bible Talks with Commentary* (1974); *Up From Nigger* (1976); *Code Name Zorro: The Murder of Martin Luther King, Jr.* (1977). Recording: *The Light Side—The Dark Side*. MISC.: winner, MO Mile Championship, 1951, 1952; noted for hunger strike protests; advocate of Bahamian Diet as answer to obesity. MAILING ADDRESS: 1451 East 55th St., Chicago, IL 60615.

GRESHAM, WALTER QUINTIN. b. Mar 17, 1832, Lanesville, IN; d. May 28, 1895, Washington, DC; par. William and Sarah (Davis) Gresham; m. Matilda McGrain, Feb 11, 1858; c. Kate (Mrs. William H. Andrews); Otto. EDUC.: Corydon Seminary; IN U.; studied law under Judge William A. Porter. POLIT. & GOV.: Anti-Nebraska candidate for prosecuting atty., IN, 1854; American (Know Nothing) Party candidate for cty. clerk, IN, 1855; elected as a Republican to IN State House, 1861–63; Union Party candidate for U.S. House (IN), 1866, 1868; elected IN state debt agent, 1867; delegate, Rep. Nat'l. Conv., 1868; appointed collector, Port of New Orleans, 1869 (declined); appointed U.S. district atty., IN, 1869 (declined); appointed U.S. district judge for IN, 1869–82; Republican candidate for U.S. Senate (IN), 1880 (withdrew); appointed postmaster gen. of the U.S., 1882–84; ***candidate for Republican nomination to presidency of the U.S., 1884, 1888; candidate for Republican nomination to vice presidency of the U.S., 1884***; appointed U.S. sec. of the treasury, 1884; appointed judge, Seventh U.S. Judicial Circuit, 1884; ***People's Party candidate for presidency of the U.S., 1892 (declined)***; appointed U.S. sec. of state, 1893–95. BUS. & PROF.: atty.; admitted to IN Bar, 1854; partner (with Thomas C. Slaughter), law firm, IN, 1854; partner (with Judge John Butler), law firm, New Albany, IN, 1865. MIL.: division commander, U.S. Army, 1861, brig. gen., 1863, brev. maj. gen., 1865. RES.: Washington, DC.

GRIB, PETER G. POLIT. & GOV.: ***independent candidate for presidency of the U.S., 1980***. MAILING ADDRESS: 2 Lindron Ave., Smithtown, NY 11787.

GRIFFIN, GENE AUTRY. POLIT. & GOV.: ***candidate for Democratic nomination to presidency of the U.S., 1988***. MAILING ADDRESS: 115 Abram Ford Dr., Jackson, MS 39213.

GRIFFIN, GEORGE. POLIT. & GOV.: ***independent candidate for presidency of the U.S., 1980***. MAILING ADDRESS: GA.

GRIFFIN, JAMES C. "JIM." b. 1938, TN; m. Rhea Griffin, 1961; c. three. POLIT. & GOV.: appointed member, CA State Dept. of Motor Vehicles Panel; appointed member, CA Assemblyman Bruce Young's Advisory Panel; American Independent Party candidate for U.S. Senate (CA), 1980; American Independent Party candidate for gov. of CA, 1982; ***American Independent Party candidate for presidency of the U.S., 1988***. BUS. & PROF.: trucker. MEM.: CA Trucking Assn.; Norwalk Citizens Action Council (chm.); Moose; Elks; Norwalk Rod and Gun Club; Teamsters Union (Local 208); C. of C. AWARDS: nominated for Norwalk (CA) Citizen of the Year Award, 1975, 1976, 1977; CA Trucking Assn. Driving Champion, 1981. MAILING ADDRESS: c/o American Independent Party, 2069 Dacian Dr., Walnut, CA 91873.

GRIFFIN, SAMUEL MARVIN. b. Sep 4, 1907, Bainbridge, GA; d. Jun 13, 1982, Tallahassee, FL; par. Ernest Howard and Josephine "Josie" (Baker) Griffin; m. Mary Elisabeth Smith, Jul 11, 1931; c. Samuel Marvin, Jr.; Patsy. EDUC.: grad., Bainbridge (GA) H.S., 1925; A.B., The Citadel, 1929. POLIT. & GOV.: elected as a Democrat to GA State House, 1935–37; appointed exec. sec. to governor of GA, 1940; appointed adj. gen. of GA, 1944–47; candidate for Democratic nomination to lt. gov. of GA, 1946; elected as a Democrat to lt. gov. of GA, 1949–55; delegate, Dem. Nat'l. Conv., 1952, 1956; elected as a Democrat to gov. of GA, 1955–59; ***American Independent Party candidate for vice presidency of the U.S., 1968 (withdrew)***. BUS. & PROF.: teacher, Randolph-Macon Acad., Front Royal, VA, 1929; owner, ed., *Post Searchlight*, Bainbridge, GA, 1933–82; pres., radio station WMGR, Bainbridge, GA. MIL.: lt. col., U.S. Army, 1940–44; Unit Citation. MEM.: Masons; Shriners; GA Press Assn. (vice pres., 1946); Lions Club (pres.); Bainbridge C. of C. (pres.); Elks; Loyal Order of Moose; Junior Order of American Mechanics; American Legion; Sigma Delta Chi; VFW; Farm Bureau; State Rights Council of GA, Inc. (founder, 1955); Eagles; Modern Woodmen of the World; Gridiron Club; SAR; Ahepa. AWARDS: named "Man of the Year," Lions Club. REL.: Presb. (deacon). RES.: Bainbridge, GA.

GRIFFITH, MICHAEL LEE. b. Dec 5, 1944, Colorado Springs, CO; par. Henry Dale and Avanelle Marie (Schlemeyer) Griffith; m. Charlotte Marie Gaither, 1965; c. Selma Lee Adair. EDUC.: grad., Topeka (KS) H.S., 1963; AZ State U., 1964; Brevard Junior Coll., Cocoa, FL, 1965; U. of KS, 1966; B.A., Washburn U., 1970, J.D., 1975. POLIT. & GOV.: member, Shawnee Cty. (KS) Democratic Central Cmte.; ***candidate for Democratic nomination to presidency of the U.S., 1984***. BUS. & PROF.: reporter, *Topeka Daily Capital*, 1963–64; real estate broker, The Gaither Agency, Topeka, 1969–75; atty.; admitted to KS Bar, 1975; law practice, Topeka, 1975–78; real estate expert, G.S.A., 1979; realtor assoc., Topeka, 1983–84. AWARDS: Life Master, American Contract Bridge League. REL.: Non-Denominational Protestant. MISC.: All-State American Legion Baseball Team, 1960–63. MAILING ADDRESS: 1921 Sims St., Topeka, KS 66604.

GRIFFITHS, MARTHA WRIGHT. b. Jan 29, 1912, Pierce City, MO; par. Charles Elbridge and Nell (Sullinger) Wright; m. Hicks G. Griffiths. EDUC.: B.A., U. of MO, 1934; LL.B., U. of MI, 1940. POLIT. & GOV.: candidate for Democratic nomination to MI State House, 1946; member, MI State Democratic Central Cmte., 1947–48; elected as a Democrat to MI State House, 1949–53; Democratic candidate for U.S. House (MI), 1952; appointed and subsequently elected recorder, judge, Recorder's Court, Detroit, MI, 1953–55; elected as a Democrat to U.S. House (MI), 1955–75; delegate, Dem. Nat'l. Conv., 1956, 1968; ***candidate for Democratic nomination to vice presidency of the U.S., 1972, 1984***; elected as a Democrat to lt. gov. of MI, 1983–91. BUS. & PROF.: ed., *Michigan Law Review*; atty.; admitted to MI Bar, 1941; counsel, American Automobile Insurance Co., 1941–42; contract negotiator, Detroit Ordnance District, 1942–46; law practice, Detroit, MI, 1946; partner, Griffiths, Williams and Griffiths (law firm), Detroit, MI, 1947; dir., Chrysler Corp.; dir., Burroughs Corp.; dir., National Detroit Corp.; dir., American Automobile Club; dir., Consumers Power; dir., K-Mart; dir., Greyhound Corp. MEM.: MI Business and Professional Women's Clubs; Eastern Star; MI Humane Soc.; MI Bar Assn.; Detroit Bar Assn.; Detroit Hist. Soc. AWARDS: one of ten Best Michigan Legislators, Capitol Press Corps, 1951; one of twelve Women of Achievement, Detroit City Council, 1953. REL.: Presb. MISC.: noted advocate for Equal Rights Amendment to the U.S. Constitution. MAILING ADDRESS: 77940 McFadden Rd., Romeo, MI 48065.

GRIMMER, DERRICK P. POLIT. & GOV.: ***Grassroots Party candidate for vice presidency of the U.S., 1992***. MAILING ADDRESS: P.O. Box 8011, St. Paul, MN 55104.

GRISER, ROBERT KENNEDY. b. Jun 2, 1943, Allegheny, PA; par. Arthur and Irene J. (Seotte) Griser; m.

Wilma F. Griser; c. Marylynn; Donna M.; April. EDUC.: Venango Cty. (PA) Schools, 1950–63. POLIT. & GOV.: ***candidate for Democratic nomination to presidency of the U.S., 1984***. BUS. & PROF.: employee, Hyde Movers, 1964–67; employee, Pittsburgh Housing Authority, 1967–74; maintenance man, air tool and parts service company, Lawrenceville, PA, to 1981. MIL.: U.S. Army, 1964. REL.: Presb. MAILING ADDRESS: 4032 Willow St., Pittsburgh, PA 15201.

GRISWOLD, DEIRDRE. b. 1937, Arden, DE; m. 1960s (divorced, 1970s); c. one daughter. EDUC.: U. of Buffalo. POLIT. & GOV.: member, Socialist Workers Party, pre-1959; founder, Workers World Party, 1959; member, National Cmte., Workers World Party; delegate, 26th of July Celebration, Republic of Cuba, 1972; delegate, World Conference in Support of Korean Reunification, 1977; ***candidate for Peace and Freedom Party nomination to presidency of the U.S., 1980; Workers World Party candidate for presidency of the U.S., 1980***. BUS. & PROF.: supermarket packer; hospital laboratory technician; waitress; typist; typesetter; copy ed.; sec., Warehouse Workers Union, Buffalo, NY, 1958–61; employee, International War Crimes Tribunal, 1967; ed., *Workers World*, 1971–; antiwar activist. MEM.: trade unions; Molina Defense Cmte. (organizer; sec.); Youth Against War and Fascism (founder, 1962); Fifth Avenue Parade (organizer); Nixon Counter-Inaugural (organizer); Chelsea Childrens Center (dir.). WRITINGS: *Eyewitness Ethiopia: The Continuing Revolution; Indonesia: The Second Greatest Crime of the Century*. MISC.: arrested several times for antiwar activities; listed as one of 65 "Dangerous Radicals" by U.S. House Cmte. on Un-American Activities, 1970. MAILING ADDRESS: 422 Adams St., Hoboken, NJ.

GRISWOLD, DWIGHT PALMER. b. Nov 27, 1893, Harrison, NE; d. Apr 12, 1954, Bethesda, MD; par. Dwight H. and Clarissa (Palmer) Griswold; m. Erma Elliott, Sep 25, 1919; c. Dorothy Helen (Mrs. John H. Gayer); Dwight. EDUC.: grad., Kearney Military Acad., 1910; NE Wesleyan U., 1910–12; A.B., U. of NE, 1914. POLIT. & GOV.: elected as a Republican to NE State House, 1921–23; elected as a Republican to NE State Senate, 1925–29; Republican candidate for gov. of NE, 1932, 1934, 1936; elected as a Republican to gov. of NE, 1941–47; ***candidate for Republican nomination to presidency of the U.S., 1944***; candidate for Republican nomination to U.S. Senate (NE), 1946; appointed chief, U.S. Mission for Aid to Greece, 1947–48; elected as a Republican to U.S. Senate (NE), 1952–54. BUS. & PROF.: bank clerk, First National Bank, Gordon, NE, 1914–19, asst. cashier, cashier, dir., 1919–54; publisher, *Gordon (NE) Journal*, 1922–40; pres., Gering (NE) National Bank, 1951–54. MIL.: sgt., Fourth NE Infantry, U.S. Army, 1916–17; 1st lt., capt., 127th F.A., U.S. Army, 1917–18; staff, military government of Germany, 1947. MEM.: NE Press Assn. (pres., 1931); American Legion (state commander, 1930); Alpha Tau Omega; Masons (Shriner; worshipful master); U. of NE (regent, 1950–54). REL.: Presb. RES.: Scotts Bluff, NE.

GRITZ, JAMES GORDON "BO." b. Jan 18, 1939, Enid, OK; m. Claudia Jean King; c. James; Jay; Michell; Melody. EDUC.: B.S., U. of NE; M.A., American U.; M.Mil.Sci., U.S. Army Coll. and General Staff Coll. POLIT. & GOV.: ***Populist Party candidate for vice presidency of the U.S., 1988 (declined); candidate for American Independent Party nomination to presidency of the U.S., 1988***; candidate for Republican nomination to U.S. House (NV), 1988; ***Populist (American First) Party candidate for presidency of the U.S., 1992***. BUS. & PROF.: author; lecturer; commercial pilot; flight instructor; certified hypnotherapist; soldier. MIL.: lt. col., Green Berets, U.S. Army, 1957–79; intelligence officer and reconnaissance chief, Delta Force; commander, U.S. Army Special Forces, Latin America; 62 decorations including three Silver Stars, eight Bronze Stars, two Purple Hearts, Viet-Nam Medal of Honor, U.S. Presidential Citation. MEM.: NRA (life member); Disabled American Veterans; VFW; Military Order of the Purple Heart; American Legion; Special Operations Assn.; Special Forces Assn.; Kiwanis; AMVETS; Vietnam Veterans of America; Aircraft Owners and Pilots Assn.; Kentucky Colonels; Retired Officers' Assn.; National Intelligence/Counter Intelligence Assn.; BSA (scout master). AWARDS: George Washington Honor Medal, Freedom Foundation; Patrick Henry Patriotism Medal, Military Order of World Wars. WRITINGS: *A Nation Betrayed; Called to Serve*. MISC.: active in movement to obtain release of Americans who are missing in action or prisoners of war in Vietnam, 1982; trained Afghan Mujahideen; model for movies *Rambo*, *Uncommon Valor*, and *Mission MIA*; negotiated surrender of a white supremacist in ID, Aug 1992; sixth degree blackbelt in karate. MAILING ADDRESS: Box 472 HCR 31, Sandy Valley, NV 89019.

GROESBECK, WILLIAM SLOCUM. b. Jul 24, 1815, Schenectady, NY; d. Jul 7, 1897, Cincinnati, OH; par. John H. and Mary (Slocum) Groesbeck; m. Elizabeth Burnet, Nov 12, 1837; c. Telford; Herman J.; Robert Ludlow; Mrs. Keneim T. Digby; Julia; Mrs. Robert Ludlow Fowler; Rebekah B. (Mrs. Robert Hale Ives Goddard); three others. EDUC.: Augusta (KY) Coll.; grad., Miami U., Oxford, OH, 1834; studied law under Vachel Worthington. POLIT. & GOV.: appointed commissioner to codify laws of OH, 1852; elected as a Democrat, delegate, OH State Constitutional Convention, 1852; Democratic candidate for U.S. House (OH), 1854, 1858; appointed judge, Superior Court, Cincinnati, OH, 1854 (declined); elected as a Democrat to U.S. House (OH), 1857–59; candidate for Union Party nomination to U.S. Senate (OH), 1857; appointed member, Washington Peace Convention, 1861; elected as a Union-Democrat to OH State Senate, 1862–64; candidate for Union Party nomination to gov. of OH, 186?; delegate, Union National Convention, 1866; ***candidate for Democratic nomination to presidency of the U.S., 1872; candidate for Democratic nomination to vice presidency of the U.S., 1872; candidate for Liberal Republican Party nomination to vice presidency of the U.S., 1872; Independent Liberal Republican (Revenue Reform) Party candidate for presidency of the***

U.S., 1872; received 1 electoral vote for vice presidency of the U.S., 1872; independent candidate for gov. of OH, 1873 (declined); delegate, International Monetary Conference, Paris, France, 1878; member, Board of Trustees, OH State Sinking Fund. BUS. & PROF.: atty.; admitted to OH Bar, 1836; law practice, Cincinnati, OH, 1836–97; partner (with Charles Telford), law firm, Cincinnati, OH; partner (with Samuel J. Thomson), law firm, Cincinnati, OH, to 1857; prof., Cincinnati Law School, 1847–48; philanthropist; counsel for President Andrew Johnson (q.v.) during impeachment trial, 1868. MEM.: Cincinnati Museum Assn.; YMCA; Home Missionary Soc. WRITINGS: *Gold and Silver* (1877). REL.: Presb. RES.: Cincinnati, OH.

GRONNA, ASLE JORGENSON. b. Dec 10, 1858, Elkader, IA; d. May 4, 1922, Lakota, ND; m. Bertha Marie Ostby, Aug 31, 1884; c. Arthur Jackson. EDUC.: Caledonia Acad. POLIT. & GOV.: elected member, ND Territorial House, 1889; pres., Lakota (ND) Board of trustees; pres., Lakota Board of Education; chm., Nelson Cty. (ND) Republican Central Cmte., 1902–06; appointed member, Board of Regents, U. of ND, 1902; elected as a Republican to U.S. House (ND), 1905–11; elected as a Republican to U.S. Senate (ND), 1911–21; ***candidate for Republican nomination to vice presidency of the U.S., 1920***; Republican candidate for U.S. Senate (ND), 1920. BUS. & PROF.: schoolteacher, Wilmington, MN; farmer, Lakota, ND; banker. RES.: Lakota, ND.

GROSSMAN, JODIE. POLIT. & GOV.: ***independent candidate for presidency of the U.S., 1976***. MAILING ADDRESS: Rochester, NY.

GRUENING, ERNEST HENRY. b. Feb 6, 1887, New York, NY; d. Jun 16, 1974, Washington, DC; par. Emil and Phebe (Fridenberg) Gruening; m. Dorothy Elizabeth Smith, Nov 19, 1914; c. Ernest; Huntington Sanders; Peter Brown. EDUC.: grad., Hotchkiss School, 1903; A.B., Harvard U., 1907, M.D., 1912. POLIT. & GOV.: national publicity dir., LaFollette for President Campaign, 1924; dir., Division of Territorial and Island Possessions, U.S. Dept. of the Interior, 1934–39; appointed administrator, Puerto Rico Reconstruction Administration, 1935–37; administrator, Federal Emergency Relief Administration, Puerto Rico, 1935–36; gen. adviser, U.S. Delegation, 7th Pan American Conference, 1933; appointed member, AK International Highway Comm., 1938–42; appointed to gov. of AK Territory, 1939–53; delegate, Dem. Nat'l. Conv., 1952, 1956, 1960; keynoter, AK State Constitutional Convention, 1955; elected as a Democrat, provisional U.S. senator, pending admission of AK to the U.S., 1956–58; elected as a Democrat to U.S. Senate (AK), 1958–69; candidate for Democratic nomination to U.S. Senate (AK), 1968; ***candidate for Democratic nomination to vice presidency of the U.S., 1972***. BUS. & PROF.: physician; reporter, *Boston (MA) American*, 1911–12; asst. ed., *Boston Herald*, 1913–14; managing ed., *Boston Traveler*, 1914–16; managing ed., *Boston Journal*, 1916; managing ed., *New York (NY) Tribune*, 1917; pres., Prensa Printing Corp., 1919; gen. mgr., *La Prensa*, 1919; managing ed., *The Nation*, 1920–23, ed., 1933–34; founder, *Portland (ME) Evening News*, 1927, ed., 1927–32, contributing ed., 1932–37; ed., *New York Evening Post*, 1934; legislative consultant; pres., investment company. MIL.: enlisted in U.S. Army, 1918. MEM.: American Acad. of Political and Social Sciences; Council on Foreign Relations; St. Botolph Club; Foreign Policy Assn. (member, Cuban Comm., 1934; dir., 1932–36); Phi Beta Kappa; Harvard Club; Cosmos Club; Rotary Club. AWARDS: Hadassah Award; George W. Norris Award; Herbert H. Lehman Award; Margaret Sawyer Award; Order of the Aztec Eagle (Mexico). HON. DEG.: LL.D., U. of Alberta, 1950; LL.D., U. of AK, 1955; LL.D., Brandeis U., 1958; L.H.D., Wilmington Coll. WRITINGS: *These United States* (ed.); *Mexico and Its Heritage* (1928); *The Public Pays* (1931); *The State of Alaska* (1954); *An Alaskan Reader* (1967); *The Battle for Statehood* (1967). RES.: Washington, DC.

GRUHN, KARL. POLIT. & GOV.: ***independent (Committee for a Constitutional Presidency) candidate for vice presidency of the U.S., 1976***. BUS. & PROF.: owner, Tonka Mills, Inc., St. Bonifacius, MN. MAILING ADDRESS: Rt. 2, Box 506, Mound, MN 55364.

GUENTHER, IRVIN JAMES. b. Aug 26, 1926, Louisville, KY; par. Albert Tomas and Wilhelmia Frederica Caroline Christina (Combs) Guenther; m. Martha Ann Kinslow, 1978; m. 2d, Rose Roth; c. four stepchildren. EDUC.: eighth grade, St. Elizabeth's School, Louisville, KY. POLIT. & GOV.: ***candidate for Democratic nomination to presidency of the U.S., 1984, 1988, 1992; independent candidate for presidency of the U.S., 1992***. BUS. & PROF.: singer; actor; ventriloquist; appeared under television and radio stage names of "Jimmy Luv" and "Jimmy Costello"; voice of puppet "Maxie Guenther" (q.v.). MIL.: seaman first class, U.S. Navy; seaman first class, Merchant Marine. MEM.: A.F.T.R.A. REL.: R.C. MAILING ADDRESS: 3605 Chateau Lane, Louisville, KY 48219.

GUENTHER, MAXIE. POLIT. & GOV.: ***candidate for Democratic nomination to presidency of the U.S., 1980 (satire effort)***. BUS. & PROF.: puppet; invented by Irvin James Guenther (q.v.). MISC.: candidacy was effort to determine if Federal Election Comm. checked authenticity of registrants. MAILING ADDRESS: 3605 Chateau Lane, Louisville, KY 40219.

GUILD, CURTIS. b. Feb 2, 1860, Boston, MA; d. Apr 6, 1915, Boston, MA; par. Curtis and Sarah Crocker (Cobb) Guild; m. Charlotte Howe Johnson, Jun 1, 1892. EDUC.: A.B. (summa cum laude), Harvard U., 1881. POLIT. & GOV.: pres., MA State Republican Convention, 1895; delegate, Rep. Nat'l.

Conv., 1896; appointed asst. postmaster gen. of the U.S. (declined); appointed chm., U.S. Civil Service Comm. (declined); elected as a Republican to lt. gov. of MA, 1902–05; elected as a Republican to gov. of MA, 1906–09; ***candidate for Republican nomination to vice presidency of the U.S., 1908***; appointed special U.S. ambassador to Mexico, 1910; appointed U.S. ambassador to Russia, 1911–13. BUS. & PROF.: ed., *Harvard Crimson;* ed., *Harvard Lampoon;* bill collector; ed., *Commercial Bulletin,* Boston, 1881–1902, owner, 1902–15; pres., Anchor Linotype Printing Co. MIL.: 2d lt., Troop A, MA Volunteer Militia, 1895, brig. gen., 1898; inspector gen., Seventh U.S. Army Corps; Grand Officership, Order of the Crown of Italy, 1908; Grand Cordon, Order of St. Alexander Nevski (Russia). MEM.: Boston C. of C.; MA Republican Club (founder; pres., 1901); MA Hist. Soc.; Soc. of Colonial Wars; Order of Foreign Wars; SAR; Masons (33°); Press Club; Tavern Club. HON. DEG.: LL.D., Holy Cross Coll., 1906; LL.D., Williams Coll., 1908; S.T.D., U. of Geneva, 1909. REL.: Unitarian. RES.: Boston, MA.

GULLETTE, JOHN DEWAYNE. POLIT. & GOV.: ***candidate for Democratic nomination to presidency of the U.S., 1984***. MAILING ADDRESS: 7232 Cedar Lane, Brooksville, FL 33512.

GUNDERSON, GENEVIEVE. b. May 31, 1921, Kimball, MN; single. EDUC.: high school. POLIT. & GOV.: Socialist Labor Party candidate for mayor of Minneapolis, MN, 1969; ***Socialist Labor Party candidate for vice presidency of the U.S., 1972***; Industrial Government Party candidate for gov. of MN, 1974. BUS. & PROF.: dispatcher, Minneapolis Fire Dept. MAILING ADDRESS: 501 East 14th St., Minneapolis, MN 55404.

GURNEY, DANIEL SEXTON. b. Apr 13, 1931, Port Jefferson, Manhasset, NY; par. John R. and Roma (Sexton) Gurney; m. Arleo Bodie, 1955; m. 2d, Evi B., Jul 7, 1970; c. Justin B.; Alexander R.; John; Lyndee; Danny; Jimmy. EDUC.: Riverside (CA) Junior Coll.; grad., Melo Junior Coll., 1951. POLIT. & GOV.: ***Car and Driver Party candidate for presidency of the U.S., 1964***. BUS. & PROF.: professional auto racer, 1955–70; designer, Eagle Racing Cars; owner, All American Racers, Inc., Santa Ana, CA; commentator, CBS Sports. MIL.: 8th Anti-Aircraft Div., U.S. Army, 1952–54. MEM.: Screen Actors Guild; U.S. Auto Club; Sports Car Club of America; U.S. C. of C.; Championship Auto Racing Teams, Inc.; Soc. of Automotive Engineers; Federation Internationale de L'Automobile; International Motor Sports Assn.; Balboa Bay Club; Eagles; A.F.T.R.A.; Automobile Competition Cmte. for U.S.A. MISC.: winner, French Grand Prix, 1962; namesake of "Dan Gurney 200" auto race. MAILING ADDRESS: 2442 Littleton Place, Costa Mesa, CA.

GUTHRIE, JAMES. b. Dec 5, 1792, Bardstown, KY; d. Mar 13, 1869, Louisville, KY; par. Gen. Adam and Hannah (Polk) Guthrie; m. Eliza C. Prather, May 13, 1821; c. three daughters. EDUC.: McAllister's Acad., Bardstown, KY; studied law under Judge Rowan. POLIT. & GOV.: Democratic candidate for KY State House, twice; appointed commonwealth atty., KY, 1820; elected as a Democrat to KY State House, 1827–29; elected as a Democrat to KY State Senate, 1831–40 (Speaker pro tempore, twice); member, Louisville (KY) City Council; Democratic candidate for U.S. Senate (KY), 1835; pres., KY State Constitutional Convention, 1849; appointed U.S. sec. of the treasury, 1853–57; ***candidate for Democratic nomination to presidency of the U.S., 1860; candidate for Northern Democratic Party nomination to presidency of the U.S., 1860***; delegate, Peace Convention, 1861; delegate, Dem. Nat'l. Conv., 1864; ***candidate for Democratic nomination to vice presidency of the U.S., 1864***; elected as a Democrat (Conservative) to the U.S. Senate (KY), 1865–68; delegate, National Union Convention, 1866. BUS. & PROF.: transport business, KY to New Orleans, 1812; atty.; admitted to KY Bar, 1817; law practice, Bardstown, KY; law practice, Louisville, KY, 1820; pres., U. of Louisville; vice pres., pres., Louisville and Nashville R.R. Co., 1860–68; pres., Louisville and Portland Canal Co. RES.: Louisville, KY.

GUTIERREZ, DOLORES YOLANDA. POLIT. & GOV.: ***candidate for Democratic nomination to presidency of the U.S., 1988***. MAILING ADDRESS: 1008 East El Camino, #44, Sunnyvale, CA 94087.

GUY, WILLIAM LEWIS. b. Sep 30, 1919, Devils Lake, ND; par. William Lewis and Mable (Leet) Guy; m. Elizabeth Jean Mason, Jan 30, 1943; c. William Lewis III; James Mason; Deborah Jean; Holly Elice; Nancy Jo. EDUC.: B.S., ND Agricultural Coll., 1941; M.A., U. of MN, 1946. POLIT. & GOV.: elected member, Ameria (ND) School Board; member, ND State Democratic Central Cmte., 1950–60; elected as a Democrat to ND State House, 1959–61 (asst. minority leader, 1959); elected as a Democrat to gov. of ND, 1961–73; chm., Missouri River States Comm., 1961–62; appointed presidential election observer, South Vietnam, 1967; appointed member, President's Comm. on Health Facilities, 1968; delegate, Dem. Nat'l. Conv., 1968; ***candidate for Democratic nomination to vice presidency of the U.S., 1972***; Democratic candidate for U.S. Senate (ND), 1974; staff dir., Western Governors' Regional Energy Policy Office, Denver, CO, 1975–76. BUS. & PROF.: salesman, Balthouser-Moyer Livestock Agents, West Fargo, ND, 1946; asst. cty. agent, Cass Cty., ND, 1947; proprietor, Guy-Bean Farm Store, West Fargo, ND, 1947–50; instructor in agricultural economics, ND Agricultural Coll., 1952–58; instructor in political science, Concordia Coll., 1973–; farmer; dir., Fargo Insurance Agency, Fargo, 1973–. MIL.: lt. (senior grade), U.S.N.R., 1942–45. MEM.: Midwest Governors' Conference (chm.,

1962–63); National Governors' Conference (chm., 1967–68); Council of State Governments (chm., 1967); ND Community Federation (exec. dir., 1977); ND U. Alumni Assn. (pres., 1948); Gate City Toastmaster; Elks; American Legion. AWARDS: National 4-H Alumni Award, 1963; Silver Antelope Award, BSA, 1967; Outstanding Alumni Award, ND State U., 1964; ND National Leadership Award, 1971; Sioux Award, U. of ND, 1972. HON. DEG.: LL.D., Concordia Coll., 1971; LL.D., ND State U., 1973. REL.: Presb. MAILING ADDRESS: Casselton, ND 58102.

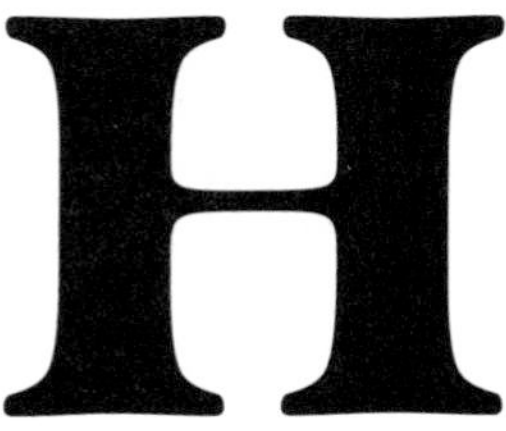

HAAG, JOHN RICHARD. b. 1931. POLIT. & GOV.: Peace and Freedom Party candidate for lt. gov. of CA, 1970; national organizer, Peace and Freedom Party, 1972; delegate, Peace and Freedom Party National Convention, 1972; Peace and Freedom Party candidate for U.S. House (CA), 1972; ***candidate for Peace and Freedom Party nomination to presidency of the U.S., 1980***; Peace and Freedom Party candidate for CA state sec. of state, 1986. BUS. & PROF.: peace activist; political organizer. MAILING ADDRESS: 1323 Lincoln Blvd., Santa Monica, CA 90401.

HAALAND, JASPER, JR. b. Oct 4, 1888, Yellow Medicine Cty., MN; par. Jasper Haaland Sr. POLIT. & GOV.: elected as a Non-Partisan Leaguer to MT State House, 1919–21; elected as a Non-Partisan Leaguer to MT State Senate, 1921–25; delegate, Farmer-Labor Party National Convention, 1924; member, Workers Party, 1924; independent (Communist) candidate for U.S. House (ND), 1934, 1936; chm., Communist Party of ND, 1936–; independent (Communist) candidate for U.S. Senate (ND), 1940; ***independent (Communist) candidate for vice presidency of the U.S., 1940***. BUS. & PROF.: homesteader, Hill Cty., MT, 1913; moved to Grandin, ND, 1926; farmer, Grandin, ND, 1926–. MEM.: Non-Partisan League; National Cmte. for Action; Equity Co-Operative Assn. WRITINGS: *Farmers and the War* (1940). RES.: Grandin, ND.

HACKETT, DONALD W., JR. POLIT. & GOV.: ***independent candidate for presidency of the U.S., 1988***. MAILING ADDRESS: 444 South Harbor Dr., Indian Rocks Beach, FL 34635.

HACKWORTHE, JOHNNIE MAE. b. Nov 16, 1904, Brenham, TX; par. Victor Wasson and Gertrude (Ralston) Hackett; m. Edwin Henry Shaufler, 1937; m. 3d, Herschel A. Watson (deceased 1957); c. Herschel A. Watson, Jr.; John Brooks Watson. EDUC.: high school (three years). POLIT. & GOV.: calendar clerk, TX State House, 1935–36; candidate for chief clerk, TX State House, 1937; candidate for Democratic nomination to U.S. House (TX), 1946; candidate for Democratic nomination to U.S. Senate (TX), 1961; candidate for Democratic nomination to gov. of TX, 1964, 1966, 1968, 1970; independent candidate for gov. of TX, 1970; ***candidate for Democratic nomination to presidency of the U.S., 1968, 1972, 1976; independent candidate for presidency of the U.S., 1968, 1972, 1976***. BUS. & PROF.: minister; pastor, Globe Church, Houston, TX; seer; prophetess; pres., American Bible Coll., Brenham, TX. MEM.: Fellowship House (founder); New Jerusalem Fellowship (chm.). REL.: Pentecostal. MISC.: confined to mental institutions for sanity hearings following threats against the lives of presidents Dwight D. Eisenhower (1955, 1960) and Lyndon B. Johnson (1964); declared sane by jury, 1955. MAILING ADDRESS: 6107 Tyne, Houston, TX.

HADLEY, ARTHUR TWINING. b. Apr 23, 1856, New Haven, CT; d. Mar 5, 1930, Kobe, Japan; par. James H. and Anne Loring (Twining) Hadley; m. Helen Harrison Morris, Jun 30, 1891; c. Morris; Hamilton; Laura Beaumont (Mrs. Nicholas Moseley). EDUC.: A.B. (summa cum laude), Yale U., 1876, student, 1876–77, A.M., 1887; U. of Berlin, 1878–79. POLIT. & GOV.: appointed commissioner of labor statistics, CT, 1885–87; appointed chm., Railroad Securities Comm., 1910; appointed chm., Comm. to Investigate the Condition of Railroads, 1911; ***candidate for Republican nomination to presidency of the U.S., 1920; candidate for Democratic nomination to presidency of the U.S., 1920***; Democratic candidate for U.S. Senate (CT), 1926 (declined due to affiliation with Republican Party). BUS. & PROF.: scholar; tutor, Yale U., 1879–83, lecturer, 1883–86, prof. of political science, 1886–91, prof. of political economy, 1891–99, pres., 1899–1921; assoc. ed., *Railroad Gazette*, 1887–89; Roosevelt prof., U. of Berlin, 1907–08; lecturer, Oxford U., 1914; dir., New York, New Haven and Hartford R.R.; dir., New York, Westchester and Boston R.R.; dir., Atchison, Topeka and Santa Fe R.R.; dir., Rutland R.R. of Vermont;

dir., Engineers Public Service Co., Boston, MA; dir., First National Bank of New Haven; dir., The Connecticut Co.; American ed., *Encyclopedia Britannica* (10th ed.). MEM.: Inst. for Government Research (trustee); Inst. of Economics (trustee); Brookings Institution (trustee, 1927–29); Carnegie Foundation for the Advancement of Teaching (trustee, 1905–21; chm., 1917–20); Hall of Fame of Great Americans (elector, 1900–1930); Political Economy Club of London; Advisory Council of International Education; World Court Cmte. of New Haven; Soc. of Civil Engineers; Phi Beta Kappa; Delta Kappa; Alpha Sigma Phi; Delta Kappa Epsilon; New Haven C. of C.; Yale Graduate Club Assn.; Quinnipiac Club; Yale Club of NY; Century Club; Royal Inst. of Public Health (hon. vice pres., 1920); British Acad.; American Economics Assn. (pres., 1898–1900); American Acad. of Arts and Letters; National Inst. of Arts and Letters (pres., 1925–27); International Inst. of Statistics; British Assn. for the Advancement of Science; American Phil. Soc.; American Hist. Assn.; American Acad. of Arts and Sciences; National Civil Service Reform League. HON. DEG.: LL.D., Harvard U., 1899; LL.D., Wesleyan U., 1899; LL.D., Yale U., 1899; LL.D., Columbia U., 1900; LL.D., Western Reserve U., 1900; LL.D., Johns Hopkins U., 1902; LL.D., Williams Coll., 1908; LL.D., Dartmouth Coll., 1909; LL.D., U. of CA, 1910; Ph.D., M.L.A., U. of Berlin, 1910; LL.D., Brown U., 1914. WRITINGS: *Railroad Transportation, Its History and Its Laws* (1885); *Connecticut Labor Reports* (1885–86); *Economics—An Account of the Relations Between Private Property and Public Welfare* (1896); *The Education of the American Citizen* (1901); *Freedom and Responsibility* (1903); *Standards of Public Morality* (1907); *Some Influences in Modern Philosophic Thought* (1913); *Undercurrents in American Politics* (1915); *Truth, a Civic Virtue* (1916); *The Moral Basis of Democracy* (1919); *Economic Problems of Democracy* (1923); *The Conflict Between Liberty and Equality* (1925); *Report on the System of Weekly Payments*. REL.: Church of Christ. RES.: New Haven, CT.

HADLEY, HERBERT SPENCER. b. Feb 20, 1872, Olathe, KS; d. Dec 1, 1927, St. Louis, MO; par. Maj. John Milton and Harriett (Beach) Hadley; m. Agnes Lee, Oct 8, 1901; c. John Milton; Henrietta; Herbert Spencer, Jr. EDUC.: grad., Olathe (KS) H.S.; A.B., U. of KS, 1892; LL.B. (first honors), Northwestern U., 1894. POLIT. & GOV.: first asst. city counselor, Kansas City, MO, 1898–1901; elected prosecuting atty., Jackson Cty., MO, 1901–03; candidate for prosecuting atty., Jackson Cty., 1902; elected as a Republican to atty. gen. of MO, 1905–09; delegate, Rep. Nat'l. Conv., 1908, 1912, 1916; elected as a Republican to gov. of MO, 1909–13; ***candidate for Republican nomination to vice presidency of the U.S., 1912***. BUS. & PROF.: atty.; founder, *Northwestern Law Review*; law practice, Kansas City, 1894–98, 1913–17; partner (with R. D. Brown), law firm, Kansas City, 1894; special counsel to railroads, 1913–16; prof. of law, U. of CO, 1917–23; counsel, State Railroad Comm. of CO, 1919–21; chancellor, Washington U., St. Louis, MO, 1923–27. MEM.: American Law Inst.; Rockefeller Foundation (trustee); Knife and Fork Club; Young Republican Club of MO; National Assn. of Attorneys General (founder). AWARDS: Order of Saints Maurizio e Lazzaro (Italy). HON. DEG.: LL.D., Northwestern U., 1909; LL.D., U. of MO, 1910; LL.D., Missouri Valley Coll., 1911; LL.D., Harvard U., 1925. WRITINGS: *The Missouri Crime Survey* (coauthor, 1926); *Standard Oil Trust; What the Railroads Owe the People; Rome and the World Today*. REL.: Soc. of Friends. RES.: St. Louis, MO.

HAGELIN, JOHN. b. Jun 9, 1954, Pittsburgh, PA; m. Margaret Cowhig. EDUC.: Ph.D., Harvard U., 1981. POLIT. & GOV.: ***Natural Law Party candidate for presidency of the U.S., 1992***. BUS. & PROF.: physicist, European Laboratory for Particle Physics, 1981–83; physicist, Stanford Linear Accelerator; prof. of physics, dir. of doctoral program in physics, Maharishi International U., 1983–. AWARDS: Kilby Young Innovator Science Award, 1992. WRITINGS: scientific articles. REL.: follower of Maharishi Mahesh Yogi. MISC.: noted authority on unified quantum field theories. MAILING ADDRESS: 1800 University Court, Fairfield, IA 52556.

HAIG, ALEXANDER MEIGS, JR. b. Dec 2, 1924, Bala Cynwyd, PA; par. Alexander Meigs and Regina Anne (Murphy) Haig; m. Patricia Antoinette Fox, May 24, 1950; c. Alexander P.; Brian F.; Barbara E. EDUC.: grad., Lower Merion H.S., Ardmore, PA, 1942; U. of Notre Dame, 1943; B.S., U.S. Military Acad., 1947; grad., Naval War Coll., 1960; M.A., Georgetown U., 1961; grad., Army War Coll., 1966. POLIT. & GOV.: appointed deputy special asst. to the sec. and deputy sec., U.S. Dept. of Defense, 1964–65; appointed military asst. to the asst. to the president for national security affairs, 1969–70; appointed deputy asst. to the president for national security affairs, 1970–73; appointed asst. to the president, chief of White House staff, 1973–74; ***candidate for Republican nomination to presidency of the U.S., 1980, 1984, 1988; candidate for Republican nomination to vice presidency of the U.S., 1980, 1988***; appointed U.S. sec. of state, 1981–82. BUS. & PROF.: soldier. MIL.: commissioned 2d lt., U.S. Army, 1947; advanced through grades to brig. gen., 1969, maj. gen., 1972, gen., 1973; chief of staff for operations, U.S. Dept. of the Army, 1962–64; military asst. to U.S. sec. of the army, 1964; battalion and bde. commander, 1st Infantry Div., U.S. Army, Vietnam, 1966–67; regimental commander, deputy commandant, U.S. Military Acad., 1967–69; appointed vice chief of staff, U.S. Army, 1973; retired, 1973; recalled to duty, 1974; commander in chief, U.S. European Command, 1974–79; supreme allied commander in Europe, SHAPE, 1974–79; Distinguished Service Cross; Silver Star with Oak Leaf Cluster; Legion of Merit with Two Oak Leaf Clusters; Bronze Star with Oak Leaf Cluster; Air Medal with 23 Oak Leaf Clusters; Army Commendation Medal; Purple Heart; National Order of Vietnam, 5th Class (grand officer); Gallantry Cross with Palm; Civil Actions Honor Medal, First Class; Medal of King Abdel-Aziz (Saudi Arabia); Distinguished Service Medal, U.S. Dept. of Defense. MEM.: Loyola Coll. (trustee); Soc. of the First Division (vice pres.). HON. DEG.: LL.D., Niagara U.; LL.D., U. of UT.

REL.: R.C. WRITINGS: *Caveat; Inner Circle.* MAILING ADDRESS: 4622 North 38th St., Arlington, VA 22207.

HAIG, ROBERT WAVERLY (See ROBERT WAVERLY HOPSON).

HAILE, FRANK LITTLE JOHN. POLIT. & GOV.: independent candidate for U.S. House (TN), 1964; ***independent candidate for presidency of the U.S., 1976***. MAILING ADDRESS: 302 West Clinch, Knoxville, TN.

HALE, JEFFREY L. b. 1940; m. Sandy H. EDUC.: John H. Patterson Co-Operative School. POLIT. & GOV.: ***People's Progressive (American) Party candidate for presidency of the U.S., 1980***. BUS. & PROF.: employee, Universal Tool Co., Dayton, OH, to 1979. MAILING ADDRESS: 1916 Pershing Blvd., Dayton, OH 45420.

HALE, JOHN PARKER. b. Mar 31, 1806, Rochester, NH; d. Nov 19, 1873, Dover, NH; par. John Parker and Lydia (O'Brien) Hale; m. Lucy C. Lambert; c. Lucy Lambert (Mrs. William Eaton Chandler). EDUC.: Phillips Exeter Acad.; grad., Bowdoin Coll., 1827. POLIT. & GOV.: elected as a Democrat to NH State House, 1832–34; appointed U.S. district atty. for NH, 1834–41; elected as a Democrat to U.S. House (NH), 1843–45; elected as a Free-Soiler to U.S. Senate (NH), 1847–53, 1855–65; ***Liberty Party candidate for presidency of the U.S., 1848 (withdrew); candidate for Free Soil (Free Democracy) Party nomination to presidency of the U.S., 1848; Free Soil (Free Democracy) Party candidate for presidency of the U.S., 1852***; candidate for Republican nomination to U.S. Senate (NH), 1864; appointed U.S. minister to Spain, 1865–69. BUS. & PROF.: atty.; admitted to NH Bar, 1830; law practice, Dover, NH; law practice, New York, NY. RES.: Dover, NH.

HALL, GUS (aka ARVO KUSTA HALBERG). b. Oct 8, 1910, Iron Range, MN; par. Matt and Susan Halberg; m. Elizabeth Turner, Sep 13, 1934; c. two. EDUC.: Lenin School, Moscow, U.S.S.R. POLIT. & GOV.: member, National Cmte., Young Communist League, 1926–33; member, County Farmer-Labor Party Cmte., MN, 1928; Communist Party candidate for Youngstown (OH) City Council, c. 1920s; member, Communist Party, U.S.A. National Cmte., 1934–, national sec., 1948–59, gen. sec., 1959–; gen. sec., Communist Party of OH, 1947–52; ***Communist Party, U.S.A. candidate for presidency of the U.S., 1972, 1976, 1980, 1984; candidate for Peace and Freedom Party nomination to presidency of the U.S., 1980***. BUS. & PROF.: lumberjack; steelworker; construction worker; political activist; ed., *Politic Affairs*. MIL.: machinist mate, first class, U.S. Navy, 1942–46. MEM.: United Steel Workers of America (founder, 1936); Steel Workers' Organizing Cmte. (OH); International Union of Hod Carriers and Common Laborers; Iron Workers Union. WRITINGS: *Communism: Mankind's Bright Horizon* (1965); *For a Radical Change—The Communist View* (1966); *Toward a Peace Ticket in 1968* (1967); *Imperialist Rivalries and the World Struggle for Peace* (1967); *For a Meaningful Alternative* (1967); *The Path to Revolution: The Communist Program* (1968); *On Course—The Revolutionary Process* (1969); *Working Class Approach to Women's Liberation; Toward Unity Against World Imperialism* (1969); *The Fight Against the Nixon-Agnew Road to Disaster* (1970); *Our Country in Crisis—The People Must Act!* (1970); *Hard Hats and Hard Facts* (1970); *The Erosion of U.S. Capitalism in the '70s* (1970); *The House of Imperialism is Crumbling* (1971); *Out of Indo-China . . . Our Goals for 1971 and How to Win them* (1971); *Racism: The Nation's Most Dangerous Pollutant; The Crisis of U.S. Capitalism and the Fight Back* (1975); *The Energy Rip-Off; Ecology—Can We Survive Under Capitalism?; Imperialism Today—An Evaluation of Major Issues and Events of Our Time; Imperialism Today—The Revolutionary Process; Labor Up-Front* (1979); *The Working Class Answer to the Deepening Crisis* (1980). MISC.: served jail sentence for participation in Minneapolis antiwar demonstrations, 1928; served six months in prison for participation in Minneapolis Teamsters Strike, 1932; led Little Steel Strike, 1937; served an eight-year term in federal penitentiary, Leavenworth, KS, for violation of Smith Act, 1950–58. MAILING ADDRESS: 230 Van Cortland Park Ave., Yonkers, NY 10705.

HALL, JOHN HICKLIN. b. Jul 17, 1855, Multnomah Cty., OR; par. Benjamin F. and Emily M. (Hicklin) Hall; m. Jessie E. Belcher, Dec 25, 1895; c. John H. EDUC.: Lafayette Acad.; Portland (OR) H.S. POLIT. & GOV.: elected as a Republican to OR State House, 1891–93; ***candidate for Republican nomination to vice presidency of the U.S., 1928***. BUS. & PROF.: atty.; admitted to OR Bar, 1887. MEM.: Commercial Club. RES.: Portland, OR.

HALL, LEE H. POLIT. & GOV.: ***independent candidate for presidency of the U.S., 1980***. MAILING ADDRESS: 6906 Moon Lake, San Antonio, TX 78244.

HALL, TRACY ALLEN "HOLLYWOOD." POLIT. & GOV.: ***independent candidate for presidency of the U.S., 1992***. MAILING ADDRESS: 4817 Manheim Ave., Beltsville, MD 20705.

HALLINAN, VINCENT WILLIAM. b. Dec 16, 1896, San Francisco, CA; d. Oct 2, 1992, San Francisco, CA; par. Patrick and Elizabeth (Sheehan) Hallinan; m. Vivian Moore; c. Patrick Sarsfield; Terence Tyrone; Michael de Valera; Conn Malachi; Matthew Brennis; Daniel Barry. EDUC.: St. Vincent's Acad., Pataluma, CA; A.B., LL.B., St. Ignatius Coll. (now U. of San Francisco), 1921. POLIT. & GOV.: ***Progressive Party candidate for presidency of the U.S., 1952***; candidate for judge, Superior Court of CA, 1972. Bus. & Prof.: clerk, law offices of Daniel A. Ryan; atty.; partner, Hallinan, Shapiro and Hallinan (law firm), San Francisco, CA. Mil.: U.S. Navy, WWI. Writings: *A Lion in Court* (1963). Rel.: none (nee R.C.). Misc.: served 18 months in McNeil Island Prison for income tax evasion; defended Harry Bridges, 1952. Res.: San Francisco, CA.

HALSTEAD, FREDRICK WOLF. b. Apr 21, 1927, Los Angeles, CA; d. Jun 2, 1988, Los Angeles, CA; par. Frank Harrison and Bloomah (Buckholtz) Halstead; m. Virginia Graza, May 20, 1957; c. Laura Ellen; Celia Maria; Frank William. Educ.: Hollywood H.S.; U. of CA, Los Angeles, 1946–48. Polit. & Gov.: member, National Cmte., Socialist Workers Party, 1962–; antiwar dir., Socialist Workers Party, 1965–; Socialist Workers Party candidate for comptroller, New York, NY, 1962; ***Socialist Workers Party candidate for presidency of the U.S., 1968***; Socialist Workers Party candidate for U.S. Senate (IL), 1972; Socialist Workers Party candidate for gov. of CA, 1978. Bus. & Prof.: merchant seaman, 1946–48; garment cutter, 1950–66; upholstery cutter, auto industry, Detroit, MI, 1953; staff writer, *The Militant*, 1955–66; political activist. Mil.: motor machinist mate, third class, Seventh Fleet, U.S. Navy, 1945–46. Mem.: National Farm Union (organizer, 1949); Square D Strike (organizer, 1954); International Ladies' Garment Workers Union; Fifth Avenue Vietnam Peace Parade Cmte. (organizer, 1966–68); chief marshall, Nov 13–15, 1969, and Apr 24, 1971, antiwar demonstrations, Washington, DC; National Peace Action Coalition; U.A.W. of America; G.I. Civil Liberties Defense Cmte.; New Mobilization to End the War in Vietnam (steering committee); Veterans for Peace. Writings: *Why Can't Everybody Have a Job?* (1961); *Harlem Stirs* (1966); *If This Be Revolution* (1967); *An Open Letter to GI's* (1968); *GIs Speak Out* (ed., 1968); *Interviews With Anti-War GIs* (1969); *Out Now: A Participant's Account of the American Movement Against the Vietnam War* (1978); *What Working People Should Know About the Dangers of Nuclear Power* (1979); *The 1985–86 Hormel Meat-Packers Strike in Austin, MN* (1986). Rel.: none. Res.: Chicago, IL.

HALUSKA, JOHN W. Polit. & Gov.: ***World Peace Nations candidate for presidency of the U.S., 1964***. Mem.: World Peace Nations Movement (founder). Mailing Address: 2427 N.E. California, Minneapolis, MN.

HALYARD, HELEN BETTY. b. Nov 24, 1950, Brooklyn, NY; par. Otis and Ruby Halyard; single. Educ.: Franklin D. Roosevelt H.S., Brooklyn, NY. Polit. & Gov.: organizer, Workers League, 1972–; Workers Party candidate for U.S. House (NY), 1976; ***Workers League candidate for vice presidency of the U.S., 1984***; Workers League candidate for mayor of Detroit, MI, 1985, 1989; asst. national sec., Workers League; ***Workers League candidate for presidency of the U.S., 1992***. Mem.: Young Socialists (national sec., 1974–76); Cmte. to Fight School Closures (chairperson, 1990). Rel.: none. Mailing Address: 9407 Charest, Hamtramck, MI 48212.

HAMBLEN, CARL STUART. b. Oct 20, 1908, Kellyville, TX; d. Mar 8, 1989, Santa Monica, CA; par. Rev. J. W. Hamblen; m. Suzy H., Apr 24, 1933; c. Veeva Obee Pressnel; Lisa Jaserie; Kim. Educ.: A.B., MacMurray State Teachers Coll., Abilene, TX. Polit. & Gov.: Democratic candidate for U.S. House (CA), 1938; ***Prohibition Party candidate for presidency of the U.S., 1952***. Bus. & Prof.: country and western singer; composer; recording artist; member, Billy Graham Crusade; radio singer, KFI, Los Angeles, CA; radio singer, KTWM, Hollywood, CA; broadcaster, KFWB, Los Angeles; actor, western movies; television host, *The Cowboy Church*, Los Angeles; owner, Hamblen Music Co.; partner, Voss Co. Songs: "This Old House"; "It is No Secret What God Can Do"; "Open Up Your Heart (And Let the Sunshine In)"; "But I'll Be Chasin' Women" (1949); "(Remember Me) I'm the One Who Loves You" (1950); "Mainliner" (1955); "The Lord is Counting on You"; "Golden River"; "May Mary"; "Little Old Rag Doll"; "Known Only to Him." Recordings—"Lonesome Cowboy"; "Be My Shepard"; "Beyond the Sunset"; "When the Lord Picks Up the Phone"; "A Few Things to Remember"; "Friends I Know"; "Go So Many Million Years"; "Desert Sunrise"; "Whistler's Dream"; "Sunnyside of the Mountain"; "Oh, How I Cried"; "I'll Be Gone"; "Hell Train"; "That'll Be The Day"; "This Book, My Brother"; "Old Pappy's New Banjo"; "You Must Be Born Again"; Albums—"Remember Me" (Coral, 1959); "Spell of the Yukon" (Columbia, 1961); "Grand Old Hymns" (RCA); "It Is No Secret" (RCA); "Beyond the Sun" (Camden, 1960); "Of God I Sing" (Columbia, 1962); "All Night Sing"; "Best Loved Sacred Songs"; "Pick of the Country"; "Sing for You"; "This Ole House"; "Visit With Stuart Hamblen"; "In the Garden." Mem.: Youth for Christ (Speaker). Rel.: Presb. Res.: Los Angeles, CA.

HAMBURG, ALBERT. b. Feb 17, 1932, Gering, NE; par. Conrad and Margaret (Hamburg) Hamburg; m. Wanda June Sanders (divorced); m. 2d, (divorced); m. 3d, (divorced); c. Michael Lee (q.v.); four other sons; one daughter; three other children. Polit. & Gov.: candidate for Democratic nomination to U.S. House (WY), 1972, 1974, 1976, 1978, 1980, 1982, 1984, 1986. 1988, 1990; candidate for Democratic nomination to U.S. Senate (WY), 1984; ***candidate for Democratic nomination to presidency of the U.S., 1984, 1988***; candidate for Democratic nomination to gov. of WY, 1986; ***candidate for Peace and Freedom Party nomination to presidency of the U.S., 1988***; New Alliance Party candidate for U.S. House (WY), 1988; ***independent candidate for presidency of the U.S., 1992***. Bus. & Prof.: writer; steeplejack; painting contractor; operator, trading post, Hell, WY; salvage operator; scavenger. Mil.: pvt., 4th Infantry Div., U.S. Army, WWII; 3d Infantry Div., Korean War, 1951–54; 4th Infantry Div., Vietnam War, 1967; Silver Star, Korean War. Mem.: War Veterans Against Nuclear Weapons.

REL.: none. MAILING ADDRESS: Route 2, Box A 15, Torrington, WY 82240.

HAMBURG, MICHAEL LEE. b. Aug 19, 1970, Torrington, WY; par. Albert (q.v.) and Wanda June (Sanders) Hamburg; single. EDUC.: Southeast H.S.; Torrington (WY) H.S. POLIT. & GOV.: ***candidate for Democratic nomination to presidency of the U.S., 1988***. BUS. & PROF.: busboy, Best Western Kings Inn; busboy, Little Moon Lake Supper Club; busboy, Taco Johns; busboy, Chicken Hut, Torrington, WY. REL.: none. MAILING ADDRESS: Box 37, Hawk Springs, WY 82217.

HAMBY, DAVID G. POLIT. & GOV.: ***Anti-Federalist Democratic-Republican candidate for presidency of the U.S., 1976***. MAILING ADDRESS: Elmhurst, IL.

HAMILTON, CHARLES GRANVILLE. b. Jul 18, 1905, Homestead, PA; par. Augustus William and Mary Catherine (Frey) Hamilton; m. Mary Elizabeth Casey, May 23, 1939. EDUC.: A.B., Berea Acad. and Coll., 1925; B.D., Columbia U., 1928; D.D., Ministerial Coll., 1941; M.A., U. of MI, 1947; Ph.D., Vanderbilt U., 1958; Union Theological Seminary; Princeton U.; SC U.; MS State U.; Furman U.; WI U.; Duke U.; Butler U.; Temple U.; Emory U.;PA State U.; Peabody Coll.; U. of IN; Tulane U. POLIT. & GOV.: elected as a Democrat to MS State House, 1940– 44 (floor leader, 1942); delegate, Dem. Nat'l. Conv., 1940, 1948, 1952 (credentials committee), 1956, 1960, 1964, 1968; chm., MS Volunteers for Stevenson, 1952, 1956; member, White House Traffic Safety Comm.; member, TN Constitutional Revision Comm.; ***candidate for Democratic nomination to vice presidency of the U.S., 1972***. BUS. & PROF.: ordained minister, Episcopal Church, 1932; rector, Mid-South Field, Episcopal Church, 1933–; chaplain, prof. of religious education, Okolona Coll., 1933–40; prof. of political science at Wood, Furman, Memphis State, Vanderbilt, and Southwestern universities, 1942–; columnist, *Aberdeen (MS) Examiner,* 1933–47; ed., *Journal of Mississippi History*, 1941–52; ed., *Crossroads*, 1958–; ed., *Christian Outlook*, 1960–; ed., *Churchman*, 1961–. MIL.: chaplain, U.S. Army, 1940–42. MEM.: MS Council for Christian Social Action (Quiet Hour Radio Broadcast, 1942); Rural Workers Fellowship (vice pres.; dir., 1955–); National Christian Mission (1940–41); American Hist. Soc.; Southern Hist. Soc.; MS Hist. Soc.; Eugene Field Soc.; Soc. of Sacred Songwriters; Pi Sigma Alpha; Phi Kappa Phi; Family Protection League (dir.); American Legion; SCV. AWARDS: "Mississippi Minister of the Year," 1953; Danforth Fellowship, 1955–60; research award, Acad. of Science, 1955; fellowship, St. Augustine's, Canterbury, England, 1961; fellow, Truman Library, 1963; Bell Telephone Fellow, 1964; hon. Kentucky Colonel. WRITINGS: *Hymns We Love* (1944); *Revolution* (1945); *The Prophet in Wartime* (1948); *Negro Education in Mississippi* (1952); *Lincoln and the Know Nothings* (1954); *48 in 48* (1955); *English Speaking Travellers in Brazil*; *Preaching is Flame*; *Scarlet of the Hills* (1968); *Singing Spirit* (ed., 1962); *Moments of Meditation* (ed., 1963); *Music of Eternity* (ed.); *Thunder in the Wilderness* (ed., 1965); *Grass on the Mountains* (ed., 1966); *Life's Benediction* (ed., 1972); *Poems of Justice* (contributor); *A Draught Outpoured* (contributor); *Poems for Life* (contributor). REL.: Episc. (delegate, Synod of Sewanee, 1935–39, 1953–54). MAILING ADDRESS: 115 Highland St., Aberdeen, MS 39730.

HAMILTON, DANIEL. POLIT. & GOV.: ***candidate for Republican nomination to vice presidency of the U.S., 1988***. MAILING ADDRESS: 774 Glen Meadow Dr., Sparks, NV 89431.

HAMILTON, LEE HERBERT. b. Apr 20, 1931, Daytona Beach, FL; par. Frank A. and Mayra (Jones) Hamilton; m. Nancy Ann Nelson, 1954; c. Tracy Lynn; Deborah Lee; Douglas Nelson. EDUC.: A.B. (cum laude), DePauw U., 1952, LL.D., 1971; Goethe U., 1952–53; J.D., IN U., 1956. POLIT. & GOV.: treas., Bartholomew Cty. (IN) Young Democrats, 1960–63, pres., 1963–64; chm., Citizens for Kennedy Cmte., 1960; chm., Citizens for Bayh for Senate Cmte., 1962; elected as a Democrat to U.S. House (IN), 1965–; delegate, Dem. Nat'l. Conv., 1968; delegate, Democratic Mid-Term Conference, 1974; ***candidate for Democratic nomination to vice presidency of the U.S., 1988, 1992; candidate for Democratic nomination to presidency of the U.S., 1992***. BUS. & PROF.: atty.; assoc., Wilkins, Witwer and Moran (law firm), Chicago, IL, 1956–58; partner, Sharpnack and Bigley (law firm), Columbus, IN, 1958–64; instructor, American Banking Inst., 1960–61. MEM.: IN Bar Assn.; Rotary Club; DePauw U. National Bequests Cmte.; C. of C.; Junior C. of C. AWARDS: Gold Key Award; college basketball and tennis awards, 1965. REL.: Methodist. MAILING ADDRESS: Columbus, IN.

HAMILTON, HUGH. POLIT. & GOV.: ***candidate for Republican nomination to presidency of the U.S., 1984; candidate for Democratic nomination to presidency of the U.S., 1984***. MAILING ADDRESS: CA?

HAMLIN, HANNIBAL. b. Aug 27, 1809, Paris Hill, ME; d. Jul 4, 1891, Bangor, ME; par. Cyrus and Anna (Livermore) Hamlin; m. Sarah Jane Emery, Dec 10, 1833; m. 2d, Ellen Vesta Emery, Sep 25, 1856; c. George; Charles; Cyrus; Sarah Jane; Hannibal Emery; Frank. EDUC.: Hebron Acad.; studied law in offices of Fessenden and Deblois, Portland, ME. POLIT. & GOV.: elected as a Democrat to ME State House, 1836–40 (Speaker, 1837, 1839–40), 1847; Democratic candidate for U.S. House (ME), 1840; elected as a Democrat to U.S. House (ME), 1843–47; elected as a Democrat to U.S. Senate (ME), 1848–57, as a Republican, 1857–61, 1869–81; elected as a Republican to gov. of ME, 1857; ***elected as a Republican to vice presidency of the U.S., 1861–65; candidate for Republican nomination to vice presidency of the U.S., 1864, 1868***; appointed collector, Port of Boston, 1865; ***candidate for Republican nomination to presidency of the U.S., 1868***; appointed U.S. minister to Spain, 1881–82. BUS. & PROF.: atty.; admitted to ME Bar, 1833; law practice, Hamden, ME, 1833; co-owner, *Oxford Jeffersonian*. REL.: Unitarian. RES.: Bangor, ME.

HAMLIN, THURMAN JEROME. b. Apr 30, 1924, Harlan, KY; par. John English La Fayette and Callie Belle (Slusher) Hamlin; m. Zola Lewis (divorced); c. April Dawn; Autumn Eve; John Franklin. EDUC.: B.S., U. of KY, 1947; Eastern Kentucky U., 1957; MI State U., 1963; U. of Detroit, 1965–66; Union Coll.; Berea Coll.; U.S. Naval Midshipmen's Coll. POLIT. & GOV.: candidate for Republican nomination to lt. gov. of KY, 1951; candidate for mayor of Jackson, MI, 1953; candidate for Republican nomination to gov. of KY, 1955, 1959, 1963, 1967, 1971, 1983, 1986; candidate for Republican nomination to MI State House, 1958, 1964; candidate for Republican nomination to KY State House, 1958; candidate for Board of Education; candidate for Republican nomination to U.S. House (KY), 1958, 1964, 1966, 1976, 1982; candidate for Republican nomination to U.S. Senate (KY), 1960, 1962, 1966, 1968, 1972, 1974, 1978, 1984, 1986; ***Hamlin President Party candidate for presidency of the U.S., 1960, 1964, 1968, 1972, 1976***. BUS. & PROF.: principal, teacher, coach, Harlan, KY, and Jackson, MI; educator, elementary schools. MEM.: VFW; YMCA REL.: Bapt. (Sunday school teacher). MISC.: claims to be world champion athlete and spelling champion. MAILING ADDRESS: The White House, 405 Hamlin Heaven Rd., Route 6, Box 405, London, KY 40741.

HAMMOND, JOHN HAYS. b. Mar 31, 1855, San Francisco, CA; d. Jun 8, 1936, Gloucester, MA; par. Richard Pindell and Sarah Elizabeth (Hays) Hammond; m. Natalie Harris, Jan 1, 1881; c. Harris; John Hays, Jr.; Richard Pindell; Natalie Hays. EDUC.: Ph.B., Sheffield Scientific School, Yale U., 1876, A.M., 1898; Royal School of Mines (Saxony). POLIT. & GOV.: consulting engineer, CA State Mining Bureau, 1888–92; ***candidate for Republican nomination to vice presidency of the U.S., 1908***; appointed special U.S. ambassador and representative of the president to the coronation of King George V, 1911; pres., Panama-Pacific Exposition Comm. to Europe, 1912; chm., World Court Congress, 1914–15; appointed chm., U.S. Coal Comm., 1922–23. BUS. & PROF.: mining engineer; special expert, U.S. Geological Survey, 1880; consulting engineer, Union Iron Works, San Francisco, CA, 1880–88; consulting engineer, Central Pacific R.R.; consulting engineer, Southern Pacific R.R.; mgr., Empire and North Star mines, Grass Valley, CA; pres., consulting engineer, Bunker Hill and Sullivan Mining and Concentrating Co.; consulting engineer, Cecil Rhodes; consulting engineer, Consolidated Gold Fields of South Africa; consulting engineer, British South Africa Co.; consulting engineer, Randfontein Estates Gold Mining Co.; consulting engineer, Barnato Brothers, 1893; consulting engineer, Guggenheim Exploration Co., 1903–07; consulting engineer, Tonopah Mining Co.; lecturer at Harvard U., Yale U., Columbia U., and Johns Hopkins U.; prof. of mining, Yale U., 1902–03; dir., Mount Whitney Power Co.; dir., Guanajuato Power Co. MEM.: Harvard Mining and Metallurgical Dept. (visitor); National League of Republican Clubs (pres.); AAAS (fellow); Metropolitan Club; Century Club; Engineers Club; Explorers Club; University Club; Chevy Chase Club; Cosmos Club; Metropolitan Club of WA; Union Club; International Congress of Mining and Metallurgy (pres., 1904); American Inst. of Mining and Metallurgical Engineers (pres., 1907–08); Institution of Mining and Metallurgy (Great Britain); A.S.M.E.; Archaeological Inst. of America; Royal Scottish Geographical Soc.; North American Civic League for Immigrants (chm., 1905); National Civic Federation; American Soc. for the Judicial Settlement of International Disputes (pres., 1910). AWARDS: William Lawrence Saunders Gold Medal, Inst. of Mining and Metallurgical Engineers, 1929. HON. DEG.: M.E., Colorado School of Mines, 1906; D.E., Stevens Inst. of Technology, 1906; LL.D., St. John's Coll., 1907; LL.D., Yale U., 1925; D.Eng., U. of PA, 1928; LL.D., Colby Coll., 1936. WRITINGS: *The Engineer* (1921); *The Truth of the Jameson Raid* (1918); *The Autobiography of John Hays Hammond* (1935). REL.: Episc. MISC.: leader of reform movement in Transvaal, 1895–96; arrested and sentenced to death; sentence commuted to 15 years; released on payment of $125,000 fine. RES.: Gloucester, MA.

HAMMOND, WILLARD B. b. Oct 1864, ME; d. Jan 18, 1919, Minneapolis, MN; m. 2d, Nellie T. Barber, 1898; c. Lester; infant. POLIT. & GOV.: Socialist Labor Party candidate for gov. of MN, 1896, 1898; Socialist Labor Party candidate for mayor of St. Paul, MN, 1898; recording sec., MN Socialist Labor Party, 1900; candidate for Socialist Labor Party nomination to gov. of MN, 1900; ***candidate for Socialist Labor Party nomination to presidency of the U.S., 1900; candidate for Socialist Labor Party nomination to vice presidency of the U.S., 1900***. BUS. & PROF.: jeweler; watchmaker, Minneapolis, MN, 1891–1919; employee, Eustis Brothers, Minneapolis, MN; compositor; employee, S. Jacobs and Co., Minneapolis, MN. MEM.: Typographical Union; Socialist Trade and Labor Alliance. RES.: Minneapolis, MN.

HAMON, JACOB L. "JAKE." b. 1875, KS; d. 1920; m. Georgia Perkins, 1898; c. two. EDUC.: U. of KS Law School. POLIT. & GOV.: chm., OK Republican Territorial Central Cmte., 1906; chm., OK State Republican Central Cmte., 1907; campaign mgr., Oklahoma Wood for President Campaign, 1920 (removed); campaign mgr., Oklahoma Lowden for President Campaign, 1920; ***candidate for Republican nomination to presidency of the U.S., 1920***; member, Rep. Nat'l. Cmte. (OK), 1920. BUS. & PROF.: atty.; law practice, Lawton, OK, 1901; real estate speculator; oil producer, Healdton Field, Ardmore, OK, 1911; dir., Oklahoma, New Mexico and Pacific R.R., 1913. MISC.: multimillionaire noted for "purchasing" nomination of Warren G. Harding (q.v.) as Republican presidential nominee, 1920. RES.: Ardmore, OK.

HAMPTON, JACK. b. Jul 4, 1911, New York, NY; par. Nathan and Rosa (Meyer) Hampton; m. JoAnne M. Pratt. EDUC.: U. of WI; U. of Southern CA; B.A., U. of CA, Los Angeles, 1950; U. of West Los Angeles School of Law. POLIT. & GOV.: founder, Peace and Freedom Party; Peace and Freedom Party candidate for CA state treas., 1970; Peace and Freedom Party candidate for city council, Santa Monica, CA, 1971; Peace and Freedom Party candidate for U.S. House (CA), 1972; delegate, Peace and Freedom Party National Convention, 1972; ***candidate for People's (Peace and Freedom; New) Party nomination to presidency of the U.S., 1972***. BUS. & PROF.: radio announcer; musician; orchestra leader; theatrical agent; music publisher; poet; classical guitarist; owner, Jack Hampton Theatrical Agency; founder, Paragon Music Publications; founder, Los Angeles Jazz Concert Hall, 1958. MIL.: U.S. Army, 1941–46. MEM.: active in numerous civil rights and antiwar organizations; NAACP; National Lawyers Guild; Trade Unionists for Peace; American Federation of Musicians; International Platform Assn. MAILING ADDRESS: 1819 Eleventh St., Santa Monica, CA 90404.

HAMPTON, TRENTON O. POLIT. & GOV.: ***independent candidate for presidency of the U.S., 1980***. MAILING ADDRESS: P.O. Box 115, Tabor, IA 51653.

HAMPTON, WADE. b. Mar 28, 1818, Charleston, SC; d. Apr 11, 1902, Columbia, SC; par. Col. Wade and Ann (FitzSimons) Hampton; m. Margaret Preston; m. 2d, Mary Singleton McDuffie; c. Wade, Jr. EDUC.: A.B., U. of SC, 1836; studied law. POLIT. & GOV.: elected as a Democrat to SC State House, 1853–57; elected as a Democrat to SC State Senate, 1857–61; Democratic candidate for gov. of SC, 1865; elected as a Democrat to gov. of SC, 1877–79; elected as a Democrat to U.S. Senate (SC), 1879–91; ***candidate for American Party nomination to presidency of the U.S., 1888 (declined)***; Democratic candidate for U.S. Senate (SC), 1890; appointed U.S. commissioner of Pacific railroads, 1893–99. BUS. & PROF.: plantation owner; dir., South Carolina R.R.; dir., Louisville, Cincinnati and Charleston R.R. MIL.: pvt., C.S.A., 1861; commander, Hampton's Legion; brig. gen., C.S.A., 1862, maj. gen., 1863, lt. gen., 1864; wounded several times during Civil War. MEM.: SC Coll. (trustee, 1861–69, 1877–79); Medical Coll. of SC (trustee, 1875). REL.: Episc. MISC.: advocate of gold standard. RES.: Columbia, SC.

HAMRE, FREDERICK CHARLES. POLIT. & GOV.: ***candidate for Democratic nomination to presidency of the U.S., 1984***. MAILING ADDRESS: P.O. Box 1234, Springfield, MA 01101.

HANCE, KENT RAYMOND. b. Nov 14, 1942, Dimmitt, TX; par. Raymond L. and Beral (Cole) Hance; m. Carol Hays, 1964; c. Ron; Susan. EDUC.: B.B.A., TX Technical U., 1965; LL.B., U. of TX, 1968. POLIT. & GOV.: elected as a Democrat to TX State Senate, 1975–79; elected as a Democrat to U.S. House (TX), 1979–85; ***candidate for Democratic nomination to presidency of the U.S., 1980***; candidate for Democratic nomination to U.S. Senate (TX), 1984; joined Republican Party, 1985; candidate for Republican nomination to gov. of TX, 1986. BUS. & PROF.: atty.; admitted to TX Bar, 1968; law practice, Lubbock, TX; instructor, TX Technical U., 1968–73. MEM.: Texas March of Dimes (chair, 1972–73); Texas Citizens Advisory Council; West Texas State U. (regent, 1972–74); Lions; Rotary Club; Texas Boys Ranch (incorporator); TX Criminal Justice Council; Junior Bar Assn. of TX (dir.); Lubbock Bar Assn.; TX Bar Assn.; ABA; C. of C.; Water, Inc.; Texas Technology Century Club. REL.: Bapt. MAILING ADDRESS: Lubbock, TX.

HANCOCK, JOHN. b. Jan 12, 1736/37, Quincy, MA; d. Oct 8, 1793, Quincy, MA; par. Rev. John and Mary (Hawke) Thaxter Hancock; m. Dorothy Quincy, Aug 28, 1775. EDUC.: grad., Harvard U., 1754. POLIT. & GOV.: member, MA General Assembly, 1766–1772; member, MA General Court, 1769; pres., Boston (MA) Town Cmte., 1770; pres., MA Provincial Congress, 1774–1775; member, Continental Congress, 1775–1780 (pres., 1775–1777), 1785–1786 (pres.); first signer, Declaration of Independence, 1776; pres., MA Constitutional Convention, 1780; elected to gov. of MA, 1780–1785, 1787–1793; pres., MA Ratification Convention, 1788; ***received 4 electoral votes for presidency of the U.S., 1789***. BUS. & PROF.: merchant; partner, Thomas Hancock and Co., 1763. MIL.: maj. gen., MA Militia, 1776. MEM.: Harvard U. (treas., 1773–1777). MISC.: threatened with bankruptcy as a result of penalties imposed due to opposition to customs duty, 1768; exempted from Gen. Thomas Gage's Amnesty Proclamation, 1775, but escaped arrest. RES.: Boston, MA.

HANCOCK, WINFIELD SCOTT. b. Feb 14, 1824, Montgomery Square, PA; d. Feb 9, 1886, Governors Island, NY; par. Benjamin Franklin and Elizabeth (Hoxworth) Hancock; m. Almira Russell, Jan 24, 1850; c. Russell; Ada Elizabeth. EDUC.: grad., U.S. Military Acad., 1844. POLIT. & GOV.: ***candidate for Democratic nomination to presidency of the U.S., 1868, 1872 (declined), 1876; Democratic candidate for presidency of the U.S., 1880***. BUS. & PROF.: soldier. MIL.: 2d lt., U.S. Army, 1846, brev. 1st lt., 1847, capt., 1855, brig. gen., 1861, maj. gen., 1862, commander, II Army Corps, 1863; commissioned brig. gen., U.S. Army, 1864, maj. gen., 1866; commander, Dept. of LA and TX, 1867; commander, Dept. of Dakota, 1870–72; commander, Div. of Atlantic and Dept. of East, 1872–86. MEM.: Loyal Legion (acting commander in chief, 1879–85; national commander in chief, 1885–86). REL.: Bapt. RES.: New York, NY.

HANFORD, BENJAMIN. b. 1861, Cleveland, OH; d. Jan 24, 1910, Brooklyn, NY; par. George Byington and Susan

Elizabeth (Martin) Hanford; m. Alice M. Burnham. EDUC.: under instruction of stepmother. POLIT. & GOV.: Socialist Labor Party candidate for gov. of NY, 1898; Social Democratic Party candidate for gov. of NY, 1900; Socialist Party candidate for gov. of NY, 1902; Social Democratic Party candidate for mayor of New York, NY, 1901; ***Socialist Party candidate for vice presidency of the U.S., 1904, 1908***; member, National Cmte., Social Democratic Party. BUS. & PROF.: printer, *The Republican*, Marshalltown, OH; printer, *New York Times*; socialist organizer; lecturer; editorial writer, *The Call*. MEM.: International Typographical Union #6. WRITINGS: *McKinley, Bryan or Debs?* (1900); *Railroading in the United States* (1901); *The Labor War in Colorado* (1904); *What Workingmen's Votes Can Do* (1904); *Shall the Mine Owners Murder Moyer and Haywood Because They Are Trade Union Officials?* (1906); *Fight for Your Life!* (1909). RES.: Brooklyn, NY.

HANISCO, CHARLES A. POLIT. & GOV.: ***independent candidate for presidency of the U.S., 1976***. MAILING ADDRESS: 3169 Richmond St., P.O. Box 12788, Philadelphia, PA 19134.

HANLEY, DAVID J. "CRASH." b. 1942. POLIT. & GOV.: candidate for Democratic nomination to gov. of MO, 1976 (withdrew); ***candidate for Democratic nomination to presidency of the U.S., 1976***. BUS. & PROF.: inventor. MISC.: noted for unsuccessful effort to stop airplane hijacking by ramming plane with automobile, Jun 24, 1972. MAILING ADDRESS: 3326 Lawn Ave., St. Louis, MO 63139.

HANLY, JAMES FRANKLIN. b. Apr 4, 1863, St. Joseph, IL; d. Aug 1, 1920, Dennison, OH; par. Elijah and Anna Eliza (Carlton) Hanly; m. Eva A. Summer, Dec 3, 1881; c. Ethel Elfrida (Mrs. Harry O. Gorman); four others. EDUC.: public schools, Champaign, IL; Eastern IL Normal School, 1879–81; studied law. POLIT. & GOV.: elected as a Republican to IN State Senate, 1889–91; elected as a Republican to U.S. House (IN), 1895–97; candidate for Republican nomination to U.S. House (IN), 1896; Republican candidate for U.S. Senate (IN), 1899; elected as a Republican to gov. of IN, 1905–09; delegate, Rep. Nat'l. Conv., 1908; ***Prohibition Party candidate for presidency of the U.S., 1916***. BUS. & PROF.: schoolteacher, 1881–89; atty.; admitted to IN Bar, 1889; law practice, Williamsport, IN, 1889–96; partner (with Will R. Wood), law firm, Lafayette, IN, 1896–1905; law practice, 1910–20; Prohibition lecturer; ed., *National Enquirer*, 1915; ed., *Indianapolis (IN) Daily Commercial;* pres., Enquirer Printing and Publishing Co. MEM.: Flying Squadron of America (pres.); Flying Squadron Foundation (pres., 1915). WRITINGS: *Occasional Addresses* (1904); *Patriotism of Peace* (1906); *Dedicatory Address: Unveiling of Morton Monument* (1907); *Indeterminate Sentence* (1907); *My Lord and Savior, Jesus Christ* (1910); *County Option in Indiana* (1910); *Battle of Gettysburg from 'The World Disarmed'* (1912); *Andersonville* (1912); *Vicksburg* (1912); *Speeches of the Flying Squadron* (ed., 1915); *A Day in the Siskiyous* (1916); *Address Accepting the Presidential Nomination* (1916); *The Conqueror of the World* (1918); *Robert G. Ingersoll, Richard W. Thompson, Abraham Lincoln*. REL.: Methodist. MISC.: died in automobile accident. RES.: Indianapolis, IN.

HANNA, MARCUS ALONZO. b. Sep 24, 1837, New Lisbon, OH; d. Feb 15, 1904, Washington, DC; par. Dr. Leonard and Samantha (Converse) Hanna; m. C. Augusta Rhodes, Sep 27, 1864. EDUC.: Western Reserve Coll. POLIT. & GOV.: chm., Rep. Nat'l. Cmte., 1896; elected as a Republican to U.S. Senate (OH), 1897–1904; ***candidate for Republican nomination to presidency of the U.S., 1904; candidate for Republican nomination to vice presidency of the U.S., 1904***. BUS. & PROF.: partner, wholesale grocery, to 1867; pres., M. A. Hanna and Co. (coal); dir., Globe Ship Manufacturing Co.; pres., Union National Bank; pres., Cleveland City Railway Co.; pres., Chapin Mining Co. HON. DEG.: LL.D., Kenyon Coll., 1900. RES.: Cleveland, OH.

HANNAH, SHANNON JOHN. b. Jan 22, 1938, Erie, PA; par. Clyde C. and Bernice Ruth (McAvoy) Hannah; m. Peggy Ann Hannah; c. Shannon, Jr.; Cindy; Renee; Rebecca; Jennie. EDUC.: East Forest H.S. POLIT. & GOV.: ***New American Majority Party candidate for presidency of the U.S., 1976***. BUS. & PROF.: painter; shopworker. REL.: interdenominational Christian. MAILING ADDRESS: Box 193, R.D. 2, Pittsfield, PA 16340.

HANSBOROUGH, M. C. POLIT. & GOV.: ***independent (Cmte. for a Constitutional Presidency) candidate for vice presidency of the U.S., 1976***. MAILING ADDRESS: Washington, DC.

HANSEN, DANIEL McGAVIN. b. Jan 10, 1942, Washoe Cty., NV; par. Oliver F. and Margaret Ruth (Holloman) Hansen; m. Sharon Reva Corner; c. Ira; Danielle; Gavin; Heidi; Sharon; Patrick; Heather. EDUC.: B.A., U. of NV, Reno, NV, 1967. POLIT. & GOV.: NV state chm., Independent American Party ; NV press sec., American Independent Party; western states vice pres., American Independent Party; Independent American Party candidate for gov. of NV, 1970; American Party candidate for U.S. House (NV), 1974; ***candidate for American Independent Party nomination to vice presidency of the U.S., 1976***; national chm., American Independent Party, 1980. BUS. & PROF.: salesman; bricklayer; general contractor; motel mgr., Sparks, NV. MEM.: John Birch Soc. (chapter leader); BSA (Eagle Scout; group leader). REL.: Church of Jesus Christ of Latter Day Saints. MAILING ADDRESS: 645 Seventh St., Sparks, NV 89431.

HANSEN, GEORGE VERNON. b. Sep 14, 1930, Tetonia, ID; par. Dean Erlease and Elmoyne Bendicta

(Brewer) Hansen; m. Constance Sue Camp, Dec 19, 1952; c. Steven George; James Vernon; Patricia Sue; William Dean; Joanne. EDUC.: A.B. (cum laude), Ricks Coll., 1956; grad., Grimms Business Coll., 1958; ID State U., 1962–63. POLIT. & GOV.: pres., Bannock Cty. (ID) Young Republicans; vice chm., Bannock Cty. Republican Central Cmte.; elected as a Republican to mayor of Alameda, ID, 1961–62 (city merged with Pocatello, 1962); candidate for Republican nomination to U.S. Senate (ID), 1962; delegate, ID Republican State Convention, 1962, 1964, 1966, 1968; member, City Comm., Pocatello, ID, 1962–65; elected as a Republican to U.S. House (ID), 1965–69, 1975–78; delegate, Rep. Nat'l. Conv., 1968; Republican candidate for U.S. Senate (ID), 1968; appointed deputy undersec. of agriculture, U.S. Dept. of Agriculture, 1969–71; ***Populist Party candidate for presidency of the U.S., 1988 (declined)***. BUS. & PROF.: grain elevator operator, 1950–51, 1954; math teacher, public schools, ID, 1956–58; lecturer; special agent, New York Life Insurance Co., 1958–. MIL.: U.S. Air Force, 1951–54; U.S.N.R., 1964–70. MEM.: Bannock Cty. Heart Assn. (chm., 1962–64); ID Municipal League (dir., 1961–63); Pocatello C. of C.; American Legion; ID Farm Bureau; Life Insurance Underwriter Assn.; Kiwanis (dir.); Pocatello 20-30 Club (pres.). AWARDS: Distinguished Service Award, Pocatello Junior C. of C., 1961; Distinguished Service Award, Young Republican National Federation, 1968; Distinguished Alumnus Award, Ricks Coll., 1969; Certificate of Merit, U.S. Dept. of Agriculture, 1971. REL.: Church of Jesus Christ of Latter Day Saints. MISC.: pleaded guilty to campaign law violations and sentenced to two months in jail, 1975; sentence reduced to $42,000 fine. MAILING ADDRESS: P.O. Box 1330, Pocatello, ID 83201.

HANSMAN, GREGORY. b. 1930. POLIT. & GOV.: candidate for Republican nomination to U.S. Senate (MO), 1974, 1976, 1982; ***candidate for Republican nomination to vice presidency of the U.S., 1976***; candidate for Republican nomination to MO state sec. of state, 1984. BUS. & PROF.: substitute teacher, University City, MO; accountant; time keeper, Cullin Steel Co., St. Louis, MO. MAILING ADDRESS: 207 Westgate, University City, MO 63130.

HANSON, ROBERT FRITCHOFF. POLIT. & GOV.: ***Democratic-Farmer Labor Party candidate for presidency of the U.S., 1992***. MAILING ADDRESS: 98 Carroll St., Trenton, NJ 08605.

HANSON, WYRETHA WILEY. POLIT. & GOV.: ***Citizens Party candidate for vice presidency of the U.S., 1980***. MAILING ADDRESS: unknown.

HAPGOOD, MARY DONOVAN. b. Feb 21, 1889, North Brookfield, MA; par. Dennis and Catherine (Rice) Donovan; m. Powers Hapgood (q.v.), Dec 28, 1927; c. Berta Donovan; Donovan. EDUC.: A.B., U. of MI. POLIT. & GOV.: Socialist Party candidate for gov. of MA, 1928; Socialist Party candidate for IN State House, 1936; ***candidate for Socialist Party nomination to vice presidency of the U.S., 1936, 1940***; member, Socialist Party National Cmte.; Socialist Party candidate for gov. of IN, 1940. BUS. & PROF.: factory inspector; textile worker; labor organizer. MEM.: various peace and civil rights organizations. REL.: atheist. MISC.: jailed in Wilkes-Barre, PA, for inciting riot; acquitted. RES.: Indianapolis, IN.

HAPGOOD, POWERS. b. Dec 28, 1899, Chicago, IL; d. Feb 4, 1949, Indianapolis, IN; par. William Powers and Eleanor (Page) Hapgood; m. Mary Donovan (q.v.), Dec 28, 1927; c. Berta Donovan; Donovan. EDUC.: grad., Shortridge H.S., Indianapolis; Phillips Acad.; A.B., Harvard U., 1920. POLIT. & GOV.: member, exec. cmte., Socialist Party, 1932–36; Socialist Party candidate for gov. of IN, 1932, 1936; ***candidate for Socialist Party nomination to vice presidency of the U.S., 1936***; appointed member, IN State Defense Council, 1941–45; appointed member, Labor Advisory Board, War Finance Cmte., 1941–45. BUS. & PROF.: ed., *Harvard Crimson*, 1919; iron miner, U.S. Steel Corp., MN, 1920; section hand, Northern Pacific, Burlington and Chicago, and Northwestern railroads; teamster, KS; employee, sugar beet factory; employee, Colorado Fuel and Iron Co.; employee, Bureau of Industrial Research, New York, NY, 1921; organizer, U.M.W. of A., 1922–23; coal miner, Europe, 1924–25; asst. mining engineer, Rocky Mountain Fuel Co., Lafayette, CO; contributor, *Labor Press*; contributor, *Nation*; contributor, *Survey Graphic*. MIL.: student, Army Training Corps, WWI. MEM.: U.M.W. of A.; CIO (New England sec., 1937; regional dir. for IN, 1941; IN chm., political action committee, 1944); League for Industrial Democracy; Sacco-Vanzetti Defense Cmte. (sec., 1927); National Religion and Labor Foundation (1933); Emergency Cmte. for Strikers' Relief (1933); U.S. Congress Against War; League Against Fascism (national exec. sec.); National Farmers' Union; Marion Cty. Farm Bureau Cooperative Assn.; A.C.L.U. (National Cmte.); United Steelworkers of America; Food, Tobacco and Agricultural Workers Union; IN Farm Bureau; Harvard Speakers Club; Inst. of 1770; Delta Kappa Epsilon; Signet Soc. (sec.); Phillips Brooks House Assn. (1919–20); Harvard Cmte. on Foreign Students (sec.); Liberal Club of Harvard (exec. cmte., 1919–20); United Shoe Workers of America (pres.); Amalgamated Clothing Workers (organizer, 1936–39); Red Cross Two Gallon Club; Cooperative Services Inc. (dir.). WRITINGS: *In Non-Union Mines* (1922). REL.: agnostic. MISC.: arrested in Boston for attempting to address Common Council on Sacco-Vanzetti case, 1927; jailed in Wilkes-Barre for inciting a riot, acquitted; fought John L. Lewis (q.v.) for control of United Mine Workers. RES.: Indianapolis, IN.

HAPKA, THOMAS EDWARD. POLIT. & GOV.: ***independent candidate for presidency of the U.S., 1988***. MAILING ADDRESS: 121 North Jefferson St., Whitewater, WI 53190.

HARBORD, JAMES GUTHRIE. b. Mar 2, 1866, Bloomington, IL; d. Aug 20, 1947, Rye, NY; par. George and Effie Critton (Gault) Harbord; m. Emma Yeatman Ovenshine, Jan 21, 1899; m. 2d, Mrs. Anne Lee Brown, Dec 31, 1938; c. none. EDUC.: B.S., KS State Agricultural Coll., 1886; grad., Infantry and Cavalry School, 1895; grad., Army War Coll., 1917. POLIT. & GOV.: appointed chief of U.S. military mission to Armenia, 1919; ***candidate for Republican nomination to vice presidency of the U.S., 1924, 1932***. BUS. & PROF.: soldier; businessman; pres., RCA, 1923–30, chm. of the board, 1930–47, hon. chm., 1947; chm. of the board, RCA Communications, Inc.; member, exec. cmte., New York Life Insurance Co.; dir., Employers Liability Assurance Corp., Ltd. (London); dir., Bankers Trust Co.; dir., NBC; member, exec. cmte., Atchison, Topeka and Santa Fe R.R.; chm. of the board, Radiomarine Corp. of America; dir., RCA Victor Co.; dir., RCA Radiotron, Inc.; dir., Marconi Telephone Cable Co.; dir., Radio Keith Orpheum Corp.; dir., Bush Terminal Co. MIL.: pvt., corp., sgt., U.S. Army, 1889–91; commissioned 2d lt., U.S.V., 1891, maj., 1898, mustered out of U.S.V., 1898; 1st lt., U.S. Army, 1898, capt., 1901, maj., 1914, lt. col., 1917, brig. gen., 1917; chief of staff, AEF in France, 1917–18; commanded U.S. Marine brigade at Chateau Thierry, 1918; maj. gen., 1918; brig. gen. (regular army), 1918, maj. gen. (regular army), 1919; deputy chief of staff, U.S. Army, 1921–22; promoted to lt. gen., U.S. Army, 1942; Army Distinguished Service Medal; Navy Distinguished Service Medal; named commander, Legion of Honor (France); knight commander, Order of St. Michael and St. George (Great Britain); grand officer, Order of the Crown (Belgium); commander, Order of St. Maurice and St. Lazarus (Italy); grand officer, Order of Polonia Restituta (Poland); Croix de Guerre with Two Palms (France); Order of Prince Danilo (Montenegro); Order of La Solidaridad, Second Class (Panama); Gold Medal of Second Division. MEM.: India House; Knickerbocker Club; National Republican Club (pres., 1931); American Red Cross (chm., 1930–45; hon. chm., NY Chapter, 1945–47); Masons (32°; Knights Templar); Army and Navy Club; Century Club of New York; Army and Navy Club of Manila; Apawamis. HON. DEG.: M.A., KS State Agricultural Coll., 1895, LL.D., 1920; LL.D., Trinity Coll., 1924; LL.D., Colgate U., 1926; LL.D., Marietta Coll., 1927; LL.D., Yale U., 1928; LL.D., Washington and Jefferson Coll., 1938. REL.: Episc. RES.: Rye, NY.

HARDIN, TY (nee ORTON WHIPPLE HUNGERFORD II). b. Jan 1, 1930, New York, NY; m. Andra Martin; m. 2d, Marlene Schmidt; m. four other times; c. twin sons; one daughter; three stepchildren. POLIT. & GOV.: member, Speakers' Bureau, Populist Party, 1984; ***candidate for Populist Party nomination to presidency of the U.S., 1984***. BUS. & PROF.: engineer, aircraft manufacturer, Los Angeles, CA, 1957; actor; appeared in *Bronco* television series, 1958–61; appeared in *Riptide* television series, 1969; evangelist; owner, laundromat chain, Spain; restaurant owner, Costa Brava, Spain; ordained minister, 1967; television preacher; publisher, *The Arizona Patriot*. MOTION PICTURE CREDITS: *The Space Children* (1958); *I Married a Monster from Outer Space* (1958); *The Chapman Report* (1962); *Merrill's Marauders* (1962); *Wall of Noise* (1963); *Palm Springs Weekend* (1963); *PT 109* (1963); *The Battle of the Bulge* (1965); *Pampa Salvaje* (1966); *Berserk* (1967); *Savage Pampas* (1967); *One Step to Hell* (1968); *Custer of the West* (1968); *The Last Rebel* (1971). REL.: Christian. MAILING ADDRESS: Prescott, AZ.

HARDING, WARREN GAMALIEL. b. Nov 2, 1865, Corsica (now Blooming Grove), OH; d. Aug 2, 1923, San Francisco, CA; par. Dr. George Tyron and Phoebe Elizabeth (Dickerson) Harding; m. Florence Kling De Wolfe, Jul 8, 1891; c. Elizabeth Ann Christian (illegitimate, by Nan Britton). EDUC.: OH Central Coll., 1879–82. POLIT. & GOV.: member, Republican Cty. Central Cmte., 1886; Republican candidate for cty. auditor, 1892; elected as a Republican, cty. auditor, Marion, OH, 1895; elected as a Republican to OH State Senate, 1899–1903; elected as a Republican to lt. gov. of OH, 1904–06; Republican candidate for gov. of OH, 1910; elected as a Republican to U.S. Senate (OH), 1915–21; temporary chm., Rep. Nat'l. Conv., 1916; ***candidate for Republican nomination to presidency of the U.S., 1916; elected as a Republican to presidency of the U.S., 1921–23***. BUS. & PROF.: schoolteacher, 1882; insurance broker, 1883; newspaper publisher; publisher, *Marion Star*, 1884; owner, Star Publishing Co., 1886. MEM.: Masons (master, Marion Lodge No. 70). REL.: Bapt. MISC.: administration noted for corruption, Teapot Dome Scandals. RES.: Marion, OH.

HARDY, JAMES ZALMER. b. Jun 5, 1928, Bowling Green, KY; par. Zalmer Benjamin and Dora Catherine (Culver) Hardy; single. EDUC.: eighth grade. POLIT. & GOV.: founder, Correction, Punishment and Remedy Party; ***Correction, Punishment and Remedy Party candidate for presidency of the U.S., 1976, 1980***. BUS. & PROF.: unskilled and semiskilled laborer. MIL.: U.S. Navy, 1945–47; World War II Victory Medal. WRITINGS: *Tornado Aftermath* (film, 1974); various articles. REL.: American/Principled Thinker. MAILING ADDRESS: 2115 Bradley Ave., Louisville, KY 40217.

HARE, WILLIAM G. POLIT. & GOV.: ***candidate for Republican nomination to vice presidency of the U.S., 1992***. BUS. & PROF.: retired teacher. MAILING ADDRESS: New Fairfield, CT.

HARKIN, THOMAS R. b. Nov 19, 1939, Cumming, IA; m. Ruth Raduenz, 1968; c. Amy; Jenny. EDUC.: B.S., IA State U., 1962; J.D., Catholic U. of America, 1972. POLIT. & GOV.: staff aide, U.S. Rep. Neal Smith (D-IA), 1969–70; Democratic candidate for U.S. House (IA), 1972; elected as a Democrat to U.S. House (IA), 1975–85; elected as a Democrat to U.S. Senate (IA), 1985–; ***candidate for Democratic nomination to presidency of the U.S., 1992***. BUS. & PROF.: atty.;

admitted to IA Bar, 1972; atty., Polk Cty. Legal Aid Soc., Des Moines, IA, 1973–74. Mil.: U.S. Navy, 1962–67; lt. commander, U.S.N.R. Mem.: American Legion. REL.: R.C. MAILING ADDRESS: P.O. Box 264, 213 Post Office Building, Ames, IA 50010.

HARLAN, JAMES. b. Aug 26, 1820, Clark Cty., IL; d. Oct 5, 1899, Mt. Pleasant, IA; par. Silas and Mary (Conley) Harlan; m. Ann Eliza Peck, Aug 20, 1845; c. Mary (Mrs. Robert Todd Lincoln, q.v.). EDUC.: grad., IN Asbury U. (now De Pauw U.), 1845. POLIT. & GOV.: elected as a Whig, IA state superintendent of public instruction, 1847; Whig Party candidate for IA state superintendent of public instruction, 1848; Whig Party candidate for IA State Senate, 1849 (declined); Whig Party candidate for gov. of IA, 1850 (declined); elected as a Whig (Free Soiler) to U.S. Senate (IA), 1855–57 (seat declared vacant), as a Republican, 1857–65, 1867–73; delegate, Peace Convention, 1861; appointed U.S. sec. of the interior, 1865–66; delegate, Loyalist Convention, 1866; ***candidate for Republican nomination to presidency of the U.S., 1868; candidate for Republican nomination to vice presidency of the U.S., 1868***; Republican candidate for U.S. Senate (IA), 1872; appointed presiding judge, Court of Commissioners of Alabama Claims, 1882–85. BUS. & PROF.: atty.; admitted to IA Bar, 1848; law practice, Iowa City, IA; principal, Iowa City Coll.; pres., IA Wesleyan U., 1853–55, 1869–70. HON. DEG.: LL.D., IN Asbury U. (now De Pauw U.), 1865. WRITINGS: *Shall the Territories Be Africanized?* (1860). REL.: Methodist (delegate, IA Annual Conference, 1872, 1896). MISC.: accused of corruption in office; exonerated. RES.: Mt. Pleasant, IA.

HARLAN, JOHN MARSHALL. b. Jun 1, 1833, Boyle Cty., KY; d. Oct 14, 1911, Washington, DC; par. James L. and Eliza Shannon (Davenport) Harlan; m. Malvina French Shanklin, Dec 23, 1856; c. James Shanklin; Edith Shanklin; Richard Davenport; John Maynard; Laura Cleveland; Ruth. EDUC.: A.B., Centre Coll., 1850; LL.B., Transylvania U., 1853; studied law under James Harlan. POLIT. & GOV.: adj. gen. of KY, 1855; elected judge, Cty. Court, Franklin Cty., KY, 1858–59; Whig Party candidate for U.S. House (KY), 1859; presidential elector, Constitutional Union Party, 1860; elected as a Unionist, atty. gen. of KY, 1863–67; Union Party candidate for atty. gen. of KY, 1867; Republican candidate for gov. of KY, 1871, 1875; ***candidate for Republican nomination to vice presidency of the U.S., 1872***; delegate, Rep. Nat'l. Conv., 1876; appointed member, LA Comm., 1877; appointed assoc. justice, Supreme Court of the U.S., 1877–1911; appointed U.S. arbitrator, Bering Sea Claims, 1892. BUS. & PROF.: atty.; admitted to KY Bar, 1853; law practice, Frankfort, KY, 1853–61; partner (with William F. Bullock), law firm, Louisville, KY, 1861, 1863–77; lecturer in constitutional law, Columbian (now George Washington) U., 1889–1910. MIL.: col., 10th KY Volunteer Infantry, 1861, brig. gen., 1863. HON. DEG.: LL.D., Centre Coll., 1884; LL.D., Bowdoin Coll., 1883; LL.D., Princeton U., 1884; LL.D., U. of PA, 1900. WRITINGS: Marriage (1907). REL.: Presb. MISC.: known as "The Great Dissenter." RES.: Louisville, KY.

HARMON, JUDSON. b. Feb 3, 1846, Newton, OH; d. Feb 22, 1927, Cincinnati, OH; par. Rev. Benjamin Franklin and Julia (Bronson) Harmon; m. Olivia Scobey, Jun 10, 1870; c. Abigail Wright; Elizabeth (Mrs. George M. Cassatt); Marjorie (Mrs. Alfred C. Cassatt). EDUC.: A.B., Denison U., 1866, LL.D., 1891; LL.B., Cincinnati Law School, 1869; read law under George Hoadly (q.v.). POLIT. & GOV.: delegate, Liberal Rep. Nat'l. Conv., 1872; elected as a Democrat to mayor of Wyoming, OH, 1875–76; elected judge, Court of Common Pleas of OH, 1876–77 (election contested; removed); elected judge, Superior Court of OH, 1878–87; appointed atty. gen. of the U.S., 1895–97; ***candidate for Democratic nomination to presidency of the U.S., 1900, 1904 (declined), 1908, 1912***; elected as a Democrat to gov. of OH, 1909–13; delegate, Dem. Nat'l. Conv., 1920, 1924 (chm., OH Delegation). BUS. & PROF.: atty.; admitted to OH Bar, 1869; school principal, Columbia, OH, 1867; partner, Hoadly, Johnson and Colston (subsequently Harmon, Colston, Goldsmith and Hoadly; law firm), Cincinnati, OH, 1887–95, 1897–1927; prof. of law, U. of Cincinnati, 1896–1927; receiver, Cincinnati, Hamilton and Dayton R.R., 1905–09; receiver, Pere Marquette R.R., 1905–09; receiver, Toledo Terminal R.R., 1905–09; dir., Federal Reserve Bank, Cincinnati, OH. MEM.: OH Bar Assn. (pres., 1897–98); Masons; Red Cross; Salvation Army. REL.: Bapt. RES.: Cincinnati, OH.

HARMON, LARRY (aka BOZO THE CLOWN). POLIT. & GOV.: ***independent candidate for presidency of the U.S., 1984***. BUS. & PROF.: clown. MAILING ADDRESS: Washington, DC?

HARPER, JESSE. b. 1823; c. 1902. POLIT. & GOV.: delegate, Rep. Nat'l. Conv., 1860; presidential elector, Greenback Party, 1876, 1880; National Greenback Party candidate for U.S. House (IL), 1878; chm., Greenback (National) Party National Cmte., 1884; ***candidate for Greenback (National) Party nomination to presidency of the U.S., 1884***; Greenback (National; Anti-Monopoly) Party candidate for gov. of IL, 1884; member, Union Labor Party, 1888; ***candidate for Union Labor Party nomination to presidency of the U.S., 1888***; People's Party candidate for U.S. House (IL), 1892. BUS. & PROF.: journalist; orator; ed., *Danville (IL) Commercial*, 1873; partner, J. & P. Harper (publishing house), Danville; publisher, *Monitor*, 1890; atty.; farmer; author. MIL.: col., U.S. Army. WRITINGS: *The Millenium Age* (1892); *Usury-Interest (These Two are One) Prohibited by Divine Law* (1895); *Land, Transportation and Money* (1896). MISC.: nominated Abraham Lincoln (q.v.) for president at Rep. Nat'l. Conv., 1864. RES.: Danville, IL.

HARPER, PAUL. POLIT. & GOV.: ***candidate for Democratic nomination to presidency of the U.S., 1992***. MAILING ADDRESS: CA?

HARPER, ROBERT GOODLOE. b. Jan 1765, Fredericksburg, VA; d. Jan 14, 1825, Baltimore, MD; par. Jesse and Diana (Goodloe) Harper; m. Catherine Carroll, May 23, 1801; c. Mary Diana; Elizabeth; son. EDUC.: grad., Princeton U., 1785. POLIT. & GOV.: elected as a Democrat to SC State House, 1790–1795; elected as a Federalist to U.S. House (SC), 1795–1801 (floor leader); elected as a Federalist to U.S. Senate (MD), 1816–22; ***Federalist candidate for vice presidency of the U.S., 1816, 1820***. BUS. & PROF.: atty.; admitted to SC Bar, 1786; surveyor; partner, Baltimore Water Co., 1804–25; mgr., Baltimore Dancing Assembly, 1810; organizer, Baltimore Exchange Co., 1816. MIL.: maj. gen., MD Militia, 1814. MEM.: American Colonization Soc. (founder); Delphian Club; Baltimore Library Co.; American Bible Soc.; American Board of Foreign Missions. HON. DEG.: LL.D., Princeton U., 1820. WRITINGS: *Select Works* (1814). RES.: Baltimore, MD.

HARRIMAN, JOB. b. Jan 15, 1861, Frankfort, IN; d. Oct 26, 1925, Sierra Madre, CA; par. Newton S. and Elizabeth (Miller) Harriman; m. M. T. Gray, 1893. EDUC.: Northwestern Christian U. (now Butler U.), 1884; CO Coll. Law School. POLIT. & GOV.: ***candidate for Socialist Labor Party nomination to presidency of the U.S., 1896 (withdrew)***; Socialistic Labor Party candidate for gov. of CA, 1898; CA state organizer, Social Democracy, 1899; ***Social Democratic Party of the U.S. candidate for presidency of the U.S., 1900 (withdrew); Social Democratic Party of America candidate for vice presidency of the U.S., 1900***; Socialist Party candidate for mayor of Los Angeles, CA, 1911, 1913; member, exec. cmte., Socialist Party National Cmte., 1913; ***candidate for Socialist Party nomination to presidency of the U.S., 1912 (withdrew)***; member, Farmer-Labor Party National Cmte., 1920. BUS. & PROF.: minister; atty.; admitted to CO Bar, admitted to IN Bar, 1885; partner, Harriman and Ryckman (law firm), Los Angeles, CA, 1886–1925; mgr., Altrurian Cooperative Store, San Francisco, CA, 1895; founder, pres., Mescal Co. (later Llano del Rio Community), 1914–18; founder, Newllano, LA, 1919–20; managing ed., contributor, *Western Comrade*, 1914–18; contributor, *The Internationalist*; contributor, *Collier's*. MEM.: Altruria Sub-Council Number Five (pres., 1895); Nationalist Club of San Francisco (1890). WRITINGS: *The Class War in Idaho* (1900); *The Socialist Trade and Labor Alliance Versus the "Pure and Simple" Trade Union . . . A Debate* (1900); "What's the Matter with L.A.?" *Collier's*, Dec 2, 1911. REL.: none. MISC.: defense counsel in McNamara case, 1910. RES.: Los Angeles, CA.

HARRIMAN, WILLIAM AVERELL. b. Nov 15, 1891, New York, NY; d. Jul 26, 1986, Washington, DC; par. Edward Henry and Mary Williamson (Averell) Harriman; m. Kitty Lanier Lawrence, Sep 21, 1915; m. 2d, Mrs. Marie Norton Whitney, Feb 21, 1930; m. 3d, Pamela Digby Churchill Hayward, Sep 27, 1971; c. Mary (Mrs. Shirley C. Fisk); Kathleen (Mrs. Stanley C. Mortimer, Jr.). EDUC.: B.A., Yale U., 1913. POLIT. & GOV.: administrator, Div. II, NRA, 1934, special asst. administrator, 1934, administrative officer, 1934–35; member, Business Advisory Council, U.S. Dept. of Commerce, 1933–39 (chm., 1937–39); ***candidate for Democratic nomination to presidency of the U.S., 1940, 1952, 1956***; chief, Materials Branch, Production Div., Office of Production Management, 1941; special representative of the president (with rank of minister) to Great Britain, 1941; chm., U.S. Mission to U.S.S.R., 1941; appointed U.S. representative to Combined Shipping Adjustment Board, 1942; appointed member, London Combined Production and Resources Board, 1942; appointed U.S. ambassador to U.S.S.R., 1943–46; appointed U.S. ambassador to Great Britain, 1946; appointed U.S. sec. of commerce, 1946–48; appointed U.S. representative in Europe for Economic Cooperative Act, with rank of ambassador, 1948–50; appointed special asst. to the president, 1950–51; appointed U.S. ambassador to North Atlantic Treaty Organization, 1951; appointed dir., Mutual Security Agency, 1951–53; elected as a Democrat to gov. of NY, 1955–59; delegate, Dem. Nat'l. Conv., 1956; *candidate for Democratic nomination to vice presidency of the U.S., 1956*; Democratic candidate for gov. of NY, 1958; appointed asst. U.S. sec. of state, 1961–63, undersec. of state, 1963–65; appointed U.S. ambassador-at-large, 1965–; chief U.S. negotiator, Vietnam Peace Talks, Paris, France, 1968–69. BUS. & PROF.: vice pres., Union Pacific R.R., 1915–17, chm. of the board, 1932–46; chm. of the board, Merchant Shipbuilding Corp., 1917–25; chm. of the board, W. A. Harriman and Co., Inc., 1920–31; partner, Brown Brothers, Harriman and Co., 1931–46, limited partner, 1946–86; chm., exec. cmte., Illinois Central R.R. Co., 1931–43, dir., 1915–46. AWARDS: Presidential Medal of Freedom, 1969. WRITINGS: *Peace With Russia?* (1959); *America and Russia in a Changing World* (1971); *Special Envoy to Churchill and Stalin* (1975). RES.: Harriman, NY.

HARRINGTON, ANTHONY STEPHEN. b. Mar 9, 1941, Taylorsville, NC. EDUC.: A.B., U. of NC, 1963; LL.B., Duke U., 1966. POLIT. & GOV.: appointed to staff of governor of NC, 1964; ***independent candidate for presidency of the U.S., 1976***. BUS. & PROF.: atty.; admitted to NC Bar, 1966; admitted to Bar of DC, 1968; editorial board, *Duke Law Journal*, 1965–66; asst. dean, Duke U. School of Law, 1966–68; assoc., Hogan and Hartson (law firm), Washington, DC. MEM.: ABA; Bar Assn. of DC; NC State Bar. MAILING ADDRESS: 815 Connecticut Ave., N.W., Washington, DC 20006.

HARRINGTON, EDWARD MICHAEL. b. Feb 24, 1928, St. Louis, MO; d. Jul 31, 1989, Larchmont, NY; par. Edward Michael and Catherine (Fitzgibbon) Harrington; m. Stephanie Gervis, May 30, 1963; c. Alexander. EDUC.: B.A., Holy Cross Coll., 1947; Yale U., 1947; M.A., U. of Chicago, 1949; D.H.L., Bard Coll., 1966. POLIT. & GOV.: delegate, International Union of Socialist Youth, 1959; member, National Exec. Cmte., Socialist Party, 1960–72 (chm., 1968–72); founder, chm., Democratic Socialist Organizing Cmte., 1973–89; delegate, Congress of Socialist International, 1963; ***candidate for***

Democratic nomination to presidency of the U.S., 1980; candidate for Democratic nomination to vice presidency of the U.S., 1980. BUS. & PROF.: social worker, St. Louis, MO, 1949–51; assoc. ed., *Catholic Worker*, New York, NY, 1951–52; staff, St. Joseph's House of Hospitality; staff, Fund for the Republic, 1954–89; contributor, *Commentary*; contributor, *Dissent*; contributor, *Commonweal*; ed., *New America*, 1961–62; prof. of political science, Queens Coll., 1972–89; ed., *Newsletter of the Democratic Left*, 1973–89. MEM.: League for Industrial Democracy (chm., 1964–89); Young Socialist League; Workers Defense League (organizational sec., 1953); A.C.L.U.; A. Philip Randolph Inst. AWARDS: George Polk Award, 1963; Sidney Hillman Award, 1963; Riordan Award, Washington (DC) Newspaper Guild, 1964; Eugene V. Debs Award, 1973. WRITINGS: *Labor in a Free Society* (co-editor, 1959); *The Other America* (1962); *The Retail Clerks* (1962); *The Accidental Century* (1965); *Toward a Democratic Left* (1968); *Why We Need Socialism in America* (1970); *Socialism* (1972); *Fragments of the Century* (1974); *The Conservative Party, 1918–70* (coauthor, 1974); *Twilight of Capitalism* (1976); *The Vast Majority: A Journey with the World's Poor* (1977). REL.: R.C. RES.: New York, NY.

HARRINGTON, JOSEPH D. POLIT. & GOV.: ***independent candidate for presidency of the U.S., 1984***. MAILING ADDRESS: P.O. Box 2731, Springfield, MA 01101.

HARRIS, CALVIN D. POLIT. & GOV.: ***candidate for Democratic nomination to presidency of the U.S., 1992***. MAILING ADDRESS: P.O. Box 1358, Chandler, AZ 85225.

HARRIS, EDDIE RAY. b. May 19, 1949, Waco, TX. POLIT. & GOV.: ***independent candidate for presidency of the U.S., 1988, 1992***. BUS. & PROF.: minister. MISC.: inmate, federal prison, Huntsville, TX (convicted of murdering his grandfather and great aunt, 1973). MAILING ADDRESS: Route 6, Ellis II FL-205 Cell, Huntsville, TX 77340.

HARRIS, ELIHU MASON. b. Aug 15, 1947, Los Angeles, CA; par. Elihu Mason and Frances (Cunningham) Harris; single. EDUC.: B.A., CA State U., Hayward, 1968; M.A., U. of CA, Berkeley, 1969; J.D., U. of CA, Davis, 1972. POLIT. & GOV.: legislative asst. to U.S. Rep. Yvonne Burke (CA), 1974–75; elected as a Democrat to CA State Assembly, 1979–; ***candidate for Democratic nomination to vice presidency of the U.S., 1980***. BUS. & PROF.: atty.; admitted to CA State Bar, 1973; exec. dir., National Bar Assn., 1976–77; senior partner, Harris, Alexander and Burris (law firm), Oakland, CA, 1979. MEM.: National Conference of Commissioners on Uniform State Laws; National Bar Assn.; ABA; NAACP; Kappa Alpha Psi; Pi Gamma Mu; National Social Honor Soc. AWARDS: Martin Luther King Research Fellow, 1969; TX Coll. Alumni Man of the Year. REL.: Methodist Episcopal Church. MAILING ADDRESS: 1305 Franklin St. 250, Oakland, CA 94612.

HARRIS, FRED ROY. b. Nov 13, 1930, Walters, OK; par. Fred Byron and Alene (Person) Harris; m. LaDonna Crawford (q.v.), Apr 8, 1949 (divorced, 1981); c. Kathryn; Byron; Laura. EDUC.: B.A., U. of OK, 1952, LL.B. (with distinction), 1954. POLIT. & GOV.: elected as a Democrat to OK State Senate, 1957–65; candidate for Democratic nomination to gov. of OK, 1962; elected as a Democrat to U.S. Senate (OK), 1965–73; member, National Advisory Comm. on Civil Disorders, 1967–68; delegate, Dem. Nat'l. Conv., 1968; chm., Dem. Nat'l. Cmte., 1969–70; ***candidate for Democratic nomination to presidency of the U.S., 1972, 1976; candidate for Democratic nomination to vice presidency of the U.S., 1972, 1976***. BUS. & PROF.: atty.; partner, Harris, Newcombe, Redman and Doolin (law firm), Lawton, OK, 1954–64; prof. of political science, U. of NM, Albuquerque, NM, 1976–. MEM.: Future Farmers of America; Southwest Center for Human Relations Studies (Advisory Board); Museum of the Great Plains (dir.); Order of the Coif; Phi Beta Kappa; Phi Alpha Delta; Masons; OK Bar Assn.; ABA. AWARDS: "Outstanding Young Man in Oklahoma," OK Junior C. of C., 1959; one of ten "Outstanding Young Men in America," National Junior C. of C., 1965. WRITINGS: *Alarms and Hopes* (1968); *Now is the Time* (1971); *The State of the Cities* (1972); *Social Science and National Policy* (1973); *The New Populism* (1973); *Potomac Fever* (1977); *America's Democracy* (1980); *America's Legislative Processes* (coauthor, 1983). REL.: Bapt. MAILING ADDRESS: Dept. of Political Science, U. of NM, Albuquerque, NM 87131.

HARRIS, LA DONNA CRAWFORD. b. Feb 15, 1931, Temple, OK; par. William and Lily (Tabbytite) Crawford; m. Fred Roy Harris (q.v.), Apr 8, 1949 (divorced, 1981); c. Kathryn; Byron; Laura. EDUC.: grad., Walters (OK) H.S., 1949. POLIT. & GOV.: appointed member, Lawton (OK) Community Human Relations Council, 1964–; appointed member, U.S. Anti-Poverty Comm., 1965; appointed member, U.S. Indian Opportunity Council, 1966–68; appointed member, Comm. on the Mental Health of Children, 1967; appointed pres., National Comm. on Mental Health, 1977–78; appointed member, Exec. Board, U.S. Comm. for UNESCO; pres., U.S. Comm. on Observance of International Women's Year, 1978; ***Citizens Party candidate for vice presidency of the U.S., 1980***. BUS. & PROF.: civic worker; exec. dir., Americans for Indian Opportunity, 1970–. MEM.: Southwest Human Relations Center, U. of OK (Exec. Board); Lawton Indian Education Project (adviser); Oklahomans for Indian Opportunity (founder; pres., 1965; hon. pres.); Museum of the Great Plains (Education Cmte.); Lawton Women's Forum (chm., Public Affairs Dept., 1960–62); Women's National Advisory Council on Poverty (chm., 1967); National Cmte. Against Discrimination in Housing; National Rural Housing Conference; National Health Forum (chm., 1970); Health Task Force, Urban Coalition (chm.); Joint Comm. on Mental Health; National Indian Opportunity Council (chm., Cmte. on Urban and Off-Reservation Indians, 1968); GSA (dir.); Antioch Coll. (trustee); U. of OK (visitor); National Assn. for Mental Health (dir.); National Health Council (dir.); National Urban League (dir.); Goodwill Industries (dir.); Oklahoma Mental Health Assn. (dir.); Common Cause (dir.); National Organization of Women (dir.); National Women's Political Caucus (dir.); Save the Children Federation (dir.). HON. DEG.: LL.D., Dartmouth Coll., 1979. MAILING ADDRESS: 1104 Waverly Way, McLean, VA 22101.

HARRIS, WILLIAM ALEXANDER. b. Oct 29, 1841, Luray, VA; d. Dec 20, 1909, Chicago, IL; par. William A. and Frances (Murray) Harris; m. Mary A. Lionberger, 1863; m. 2d, Cora M. Mackey, 1894; c. Page; Craig; Mrs. F. H. Patterson; Isabel Byrne; Mrs. Hughes F. Finley. EDUC.: grad., Columbian Coll., 1859; grad., VA Military Inst., 1861. POLIT. & GOV.: elected as a Populist to U.S. House (KS), 1893–95; Populist candidate for U.S. House (KS), 1894; elected as a Democrat to KS State Senate, 1896; elected as a Democrat to U.S. Senate (KS), 1897–1903; Democratic candidate for U.S. Senate (KS), 1902; ***candidate for Democratic nomination to vice presidency of the U.S., 1904***; Democratic candidate for gov. of KS, 1906. BUS. & PROF.: civil engineer, Union Pacific R.R. Co.; vice pres., Denver, Laramie and Northwestern R.R.; railroad land agent, 1868; farmer, 1876–1909; employee, National Livestock Assn., Chicago, IL, 1904–06; livestock breeder, 1876–1909. MIL.: asst. adj. gen., C.S.A., 1861–64. MEM.: KS State Agricultural Coll. (regent). REL.: Episc. RES.: Linwood, KS.

HARRIS, ZACHARY. POLIT. & GOV.: ***independent candidate for presidency of the U.S., 1988, 1992***. MAILING ADDRESS: 2939 Lanned, Detroit, MI 48207.

HARRISON, BENJAMIN. b. Aug 20, 1833, North Bend, OH; d. Mar 13, 1901, Indianapolis, IN; par. John Scott (q.v.) and Elizabeth Ramsey (Irwin) Harrison; m. Mrs. Caroline Lavinia Scott, Oct 20, 1853; m. 2d, Mrs. Mary Scott Lord Dimmick, Apr 6, 1896; c. Mary Scott (Mrs. James R. McKee); Russell Benjamin; Elizabeth (Mrs. James Blaine Walker, Jr.). EDUC.: Farmer's Coll.; B.A., Miami U., Oxford, OH, 1852; read law with Bellamy Storer, Cincinnati, OH, 1852; A.M., 1855. POLIT. & GOV.: elected city atty., Indianapolis, IN, 1857; Republican candidate for IN State House, 1858 (declined); sec., IN State Republican Central Cmte., 1858–60; elected reporter, Supreme Court of IN, 1860–68; candidate for Republican nomination to gov. of IN, 1872; Republican candidate for gov. of IN, 1876; Republican candidate for U.S. Senate (IN), 1879, 1887; appointed member, Mississippi River Comm., 1879–81; delegate, Rep. Nat'l. Conv., 1880, 1884; ***candidate for Republican nomination to presidency of the U.S., 1880, 1884, 1896 (declined)***; elected as a Republican to U.S. Senate (IN), 1881–87; ***elected as a Republican to presidency of the U.S., 1889–93; Republican candidate for presidency of the U.S., 1892***; counsel for Venezuela in arbitration with Great Britain, 1899; appointed to Permanent Court of Arbitration, 1900–1901. BUS. & PROF.: atty.; admitted to OH Bar, 1854; partner (with William Wallace), law firm, Indianapolis, 1855; partner, Porter, Harrison and Fishback (law firm), Indianapolis; lecturer, Stanford U., 1894. MIL.: 2d lt., IN Volunteers, 1862; capt., Company A, 70th Regt., IN Volunteer Infantry, 1862, col., 1862, brev. brig. gen., 1865. MEM.: Loyal Legion (commander, OH State Commandery). WRITINGS: *Legal Aspects of the Controversy Between the American Colonies and Great Britain* (1874); *The Speeches of President Harrison on His Recent Trip from the Atlantic to the Pacific* (1891); *Thirty Days with President Harrison* (1891); *Speeches* (1892); *Public Papers and Addresses* (1893); *No Mean City* (1897); *This Country of Ours* (1897); *Views of an Ex-president* (1901); *The Correspondence Between Benjamin Harrison and James G. Blaine* (1940). REL.: Presb. (pres., Ecumenical Conference, 1900). RES.: Indianapolis, IN.

HARRISON, BYRON PATTON "PAT." b. Aug 29, 1881, Crystal Springs, MS; d. Jun 22, 1941, Washington, DC; par. Robert and Myra Anna (Patton) Harrison; m. Mary Edwina McInnis, Jan 19, 1905; c. Catherine; Mary Ann; Byron Patton, Jr. EDUC.: MS State Coll.; LA State U., 1899–1900. POLIT. & GOV.: elected district atty., Second District of MS, 1905–10; delegate, Dem. Nat'l. Conv., 1908, 1920, 1924 (temporary chm.), 1928; elected as a Democrat to U.S. House (MS), 1911–19; chm., MS State Democratic Convention, 1916; elected as a Democrat to U.S. Senate (MS), 1919–41 (pres. pro tempore, 1941); ***candidate for Democratic nomination to presidency of the U.S., 1924, 1928***. BUS. & PROF.: atty.; admitted to MS Bar, 1902; law practice, Leakesville, MS, 1902; law practice, Gulfport, MS; semiprofessional baseball player; schoolteacher, Leakesville. MEM.: MS Bar Assn. REL.: Methodist. RES.: Gulfport, MS.

HARRISON, CALEB NOTBOHM. b. May 23, 1861, Milwaukee, WI; d. 1954; m. Lucie Pauline Herfurth, 1882; c. one. EDUC.: B.C.E., U. of WI, 1882; Ph.D., Johns Hopkins U., 1898. POLIT. & GOV.: special superintendent of public schools, Milwaukee, WI, 1883–99; Socialist Party candidate for U.S. House (PA), 1910; Industrial Party candidate for gov. of PA, 1914; ***Socialist Labor Party candidate for vice presidency of the U.S., 1916***; Socialist Labor Party delegate, Socialist Unity Convention, 1917; left (expelled from) Socialist Labor Party, 1918; national sec., member, Central Exec. Cmte., Workers Party, 1921–22. BUS. & PROF.: prof. of machine design, U. of WI, 1899–. MEM.: American Labor Alliance (national sec., 1921); Industrial Socialist League; Industrial Workers of the World—Splinter Group (gen. organizer). WRITINGS: *Arc-Spectra of Vanadium, Zirconium and Lanthanum* (with Henry A. Rowland, 1898). RES.: Pittsburgh, PA.

HARRISON, CARTER HENRY, SR. b. Feb 15, 1825, Lexington, KY; d. Oct 28, 1893, Chicago, IL; par. Carter Henry and Caroline (Russell) Harrison; m. Sophorisba Preston, 1855; m. 2d, Marguerite Stearns, 1882; c. Carter Henry (q.v.); William Preston; Caroline D. Owsley; Sophie G. EDUC.: A. B., Yale U., 1845; LL.B., Transylvania U., 1855. POLIT. & GOV.: elected as a Non-Partisan "Fire Proofer" to Board of Commissioners, Cook Cty., IL, 1871–74; Democratic candidate for U.S. House (IL), 1872; elected as a Democrat to U.S. House (IL), 1875–79; elected as a Democrat, mayor of Chicago, IL, 1879–87, 1893; delegate, Dem. Nat'l. Conv., 1880, 1884; delegate, IL State Democratic Convention, 1884; Democratic candidate for gov. of IL, 1884; ***candidate for Democratic nomination to presidency of the U.S., 1884***; independent Democratic candidate for mayor of Chicago, IL, 1891. BUS. & PROF.: atty.; admitted to IL Bar, 1855; law practice, Chicago; real estate investor; owner, *Chicago Times*, 1891–93. WRITINGS: *A Race with the Sun* (1890); *A Summer Outing and the Old Man's Story* (1891). MISC.: assassinated by disappointed office-seeker. RES.: Chicago, IL.

HARRISON, CARTER HENRY, JR. b. Apr 23, 1860, Chicago, IL; d. Dec 25, 1953, Chicago, IL; par. Carter Henry (q.v.) and Sophorisba (Preston) Harrison; m. Edith Ogden, Dec 4, 1887; c. Carter Henry; Edith Harrison Mannierre. EDUC.: A.B., St. Ignatius Coll., 1881; LL.B., Yale U., 1883. POLIT. & GOV.: elected as a Democrat to mayor of Chicago, IL, 1897–1905, 1911–15; ***candidate for Democratic nomination to vice presidency of the U.S., 1900 (declined); candidate for Democratic nomination to presidency of the U.S., 1912, 1920***; candidate for Democratic nomination to mayor of Chicago, 1915; delegate, Dem. Nat'l. Conv., 1920; appointed collector of internal revenue, Northern District of IL, 1933–44; chm., IL Advisory Board, Federal Emergency Administration of Public Works, 1933. BUS. & PROF.: atty.; admitted to IL Bar, 1883; law practice, Chicago, 1883–89; real estate business, 1889–91; publisher, ed., *Chicago Times*, 1891–94; capt., American Red Cross, Toul, France, 1918–19 (in charge of 12 hospitals). MEM.: Sons of the Revolution; SAR; Soc. of the Cincinnati; Soc. of Colonial Wars (IL gov.); Soc. of the War of 1812; Military Order of Foreign Wars; VFW; American Legion; Officer, Legion of Honor; University Club; Cliff Dwellers; Huron Mountain Club; Camp Fire Club; Masons; Knights Templar; Comm. for Encouragement of Local Art (pres., 1918–45). HON. DEG.: LL.D., St. Ignatius Coll., 1900; Litt.D., Loyola U., 1949. WRITINGS: *Stormy Years* (1935); *Growing Up With Chicago* (1944); *With the American Red Cross in France, 1918–19* (1947). RES.: Chicago, IL.

HARRISON, FRANCIS BURTON. b. Dec 18, 1873, New York, NY; d. Nov 21, 1957, Flemington, NJ; par. Burton Norvell and Constance (Cary) Harrison; m. Mary Crocker, Jun 7, 1900; m. 2d, Magel Judson Cox, Jan 16, 1907; m. 3d, Salena Elizabeth Wrentmore, May 15, 1919; m. 4th, Margaret Butten Wrentmore, Apr 8, 1927; m. 5th, Maria Teresa Lorrucea, Mar 5, 1949; c. Virginia Randolph (Mrs. Marion Dezayas); Barbara (Mrs. Lloyd Westcott); Burton; Frances Fairfax; Francis Burton; Verna (Mrs. Walter Hobson); Jeffrey. EDUC.: grad., Cutler School; A.B., Yale U., 1895; LL.B., NY School of Law, 1897. POLIT. & GOV.: elected as a Democrat to U.S. House (NY), 1903–05, 1907–13; Democratic candidate for lt. gov. of NY, 1904; ***candidate for Democratic nomination to vice presidency of the U.S., 1908***; Democratic candidate for U.S. House (NY), 1912; appointed gov. gen. of the Philippine Islands, 1913–21; ***candidate for Democratic nomination to presidency of the U.S., 1920***; adviser to the president, Philippine Commonwealth, 1935, 1942; appointed U.S. commissioner of claims, Philippine Islands, 1946–47; appointed adviser to the president, Republic of the Philippines, 1946–51. BUS. & PROF.: atty.; admitted to NY Bar, 1898; instructor, New York School of Law, 1897–99; vice pres., McVicker Realty Co. MIL.: pvt., Troop A, NY Volunteer Cavalry, 1898; capt. and adj. gen., U.S.V., 1898–99. MEM.: Knickerbocker Club; Yale Club; University Club; American Museum of Natural History (life member); New York Orthopaedic Hospital (trustee); Institution for Improved Instruction of Deaf-Mutes (trustee); Manhattan Club; City Club; City Midday Club; Union Club; Metropolitan Club; Tuxedo Club; Psi Upsilon. WRITINGS: *The Cornerstone of Philippine Independence* (1922). REL.: R.C. RES.: Califon, NJ.

HARRISON, JOHN SCOTT. b. Oct 4, 1804, Vincennes, IN; d. May 25, 1878, North Bend, IN; par. President William Henry (q.v.) and Anna (Symmes) Harrison; m. Lucretia Knapp Johnson, 1824; m. 2d, Elizabeth Ramsey Irwin, Aug 12, 1831; c. Elizabeth Short; William Henry; Sarah Lucretia; Archibald Irwin; Benjamin (q.v.); Mary Jane Irwin; Anna Symmes; John Irwin; Carter Bassett; Anna Symmes (2d); John Scott; James Friedlay; James Irwin. EDUC.: studied medicine. POLIT. & GOV.: elected as a Whig to U.S. House (IN), 1853–57; ***candidate for Whig Party nomination to presidency of the U.S., 1856 (declined)***; Whig Party candidate for U.S. House (IN), 1856. BUS. & PROF.: farmer, North Bend, IN. WRITINGS: *Speech . . . on the Nebraska and Kansas Bill* (1854); *Pioneer Life at North Bend* (1867). RES.: North Bend, IN.

HARRISON, ROBERT HANSON. b. 1745, MD; d. Apr 2, 1790, Charles Cty., MD. EDUC.: read law. POLIT. & GOV.: sec. to George Washington (q.v.), 1775–1781; chief justice, General Court of MD, 1781–1790; appointed assoc. justice, Supreme Court of the U.S., 1789 (declined); ***received 6 electoral votes for presidency of the U.S., 1789***. BUS. & PROF.: atty. MIL.: lt. col., Continental Army, 1775–1781. WRITINGS: *Letter to John Hancock* (1777); *Report of the Commissioner for Settling a Cartel for the Exchange of Prisoners* (1779). RES.: MD.

HARRISON, WILLIAM HENRY. b. Feb 9, 1773, Charles City Cty., VA; d. Apr 4, 1841, Washington, DC; par. Benjamin and Elizabeth (Bassett) Harrison; m. Anna Symmes, Nov 25, 1795; c. Elizabeth Bassett (Mrs. John Cleves

Short); John Cleves Symmes; Lucy Singleton (Mrs. David K. Este); William Henry; John Scott (q.v.); Benjamin; Mary Symmes (Mrs. John Henry Fitzhugh Thornton); Carter Bassett; Anna Tuthill (Mrs. William Henry Harrison Taylor); James Findlay. EDUC.: Hampden-Sydney Coll., 1787–1790; studied medicine under Dr. Benjamin Rush, Philadelphia, PA, 1790–1791. POLIT. & GOV.: appointed sec., Northwest Territory, 1798–1799; elected territorial delegate, U.S. House (Northwest Territory), 1799–1800; appointed gov. and Indian commissioner, Territory of Indiana, 1800–1813; appointed gov., Louisiana Territory, 1804; elected as a Whig to U.S. House (OH), 1816–19; elected as a Whig to OH State Senate, 1819–21; presidential elector, Whig Party, 1820, 1824; Whig Party candidate for U.S. House (OH), 1822; elected as a Whig to U.S. Senate (OH), 1825–28; appointed U.S. minister to Colombia, 1828–29; clerk, Cty. Court, North Bend, OH; ***Whig Party candidate for presidency of the U.S., 1836; elected as a Whig to presidency of the U.S., 1841***; died in ofice, Apr 4, 1841. BUS. & PROF.: soldier. MIL.: appointed ensign, First Infantry, U.S. Army, 1791, capt., 1797, resigned, 1798; brev. maj. gen., U.S.V., 1812; brev. brig. gen., U.S. Army, 1812; commanding gen., Army of the Northwest; maj. gen., U.S. Army, 1813, resigned, 1814. MEM.: Cty. Agricultural Soc. (pres.). REL.: Episc. MISC.: known as the "Hero of Tippecanoe" for defeat of Tecumseh and Elskwatawa, 1811; won Battle of the Thames, assuring American control of the Northwest, 1813. RES.: Vincennes, IN.

HARRITY, WILLIAM FRANCIS. b. Oct 19, 1850, Wilmington, DE; d. Apr 17, 1912, Overbrook, PA; par. Michael and Jane (McGreura) Harrity; m. Rose M. Devlin, Oct 11, 1883; c. Mary Agnes; Marguerite Marie (Mrs. Paul Monaghan); Isabelle Josephine; William Francis, Jr. EDUC.: Clarkson Taylor's Acad.; St. Mary's Coll.; A.B., La Salle Coll., 1870, A.M., 1871; studied law under Lewis C. Cassidy and Pierce Archer, Philadelphia, PA, 1872. POLIT. & GOV.: chm., Philadelphia (PA) Democratic Exec. Cmte., 1882; delegate, Dem. Nat'l. Conv., 1884, 1896 (temporary chm.); appointed postmaster, Philadelphia, 1885–89; chm., PA State Democratic Central Cmte., 1890; appointed sec. of the commonwealth of PA, 1891–95; chm., Dem. Nat'l. Cmte., 1892–96; ***candidate for Democratic nomination to vice presidency of the U.S., 1896***; member, Board of Education, Philadelphia. BUS. & PROF.: instructor in Latin and mathematics, La Salle Coll., 1870–71; atty.; admitted to PA Bar, 1873; partner (with James Gay Gordon), law firm, Philadelphia, 1880; partner, Harrity, Thompson and Haig (law firm), Philadelphia; trustee, Mutual Life Insurance Company of New York; pres., Equitable Trust Co., Philadelphia, 1881–1912; dir., Franklin National Bank; dir., Market Street National Bank; dir., Philadelphia Electric Co.; dir., American Railways Co.; dir., Distilling Company of America; dir., Kansas City Southern Railway Co.; dir., Lehigh Valley Transit Co.; dir., Midland Valley R.R. Co. MEM.: La Salle Coll. (trustee); ABA; PA State Bar Assn.; Law Assn. of Philadelphia; Pennsylvania Soc. of New York; American Catholic Hist. Soc. HON. DEG.: LL.D., St. Joseph's Coll., 1902; LL.D., Christian Brothers Coll., 1904; LL.D., Villanova Coll., 1911. REL.: R.C. RES.: Philadelphia, PA.

HARROFF, KATHLEEN G. "KAY." b. 1930. POLIT. & GOV.: founder, Cleveland Draft Goldwater Cmte., 1962; member, exec. cmte., Libertarian Party, 1973–76; founder, chairperson, Libertarian Party of OH, 1972–75; delegate, Libertarian Party National Convention, 1973 (arrangements chairperson), 1975; Libertarian Party candidate for U.S. Senate (OH), 1974; ***candidate for Libertarian Party nomination to presidency of the U.S., 1976***. BUS. & PROF.: businesswoman. MAILING ADDRESS: P.O. Box 6176, Cleveland, OH 49101.

HARROP, ROY M. b. Nov 10, 1889, Roca, NE; d. Jun 24, 1971, Omaha, NE; par. John Harrop; m. M. S. "Dess" Harrop; c. none. EDUC.: college. POLIT. & GOV.: candidate for Nebraska Railway Commissioner, 1918; Progressive Party candidate for U.S. House (NE), 1922, 1924; candidate for Omaha (NE) City Council; ***People's Progressive Party candidate for vice presidency of the U.S., 1924; National Independent (Greenback) Party candidate for vice presidency of the U.S., 1924***; Progressive Party candidate for gov. of NE, 1926; candidate for Republican nomination to gov. of NE, 1928; Farmer-Labor Party candidate for U.S. Senate (NE), 1932; national chm., Farmer-Labor Party, 1935; pres., American Prosperity Plan National Convention, 1936; ***candidate for Farmer-Labor Party nomination to presidency of the U.S., 1936***; Union Party candidate for U.S. House (NE), 1936; candidate for Democratic nomination to gov. of NE, 1942; candidate for Democratic nomination to atty. gen. of NE, 1944; candidate for Democratic nomination to lt. gov. of NE, 1946; ***candidate for Democratic nomination to presidency of the U.S., 1948***; Democratic candidate for dir., Omaha Public Power District, 1960. BUS. & PROF.: civil engineer; pres., Gold Mining Corp., Deadwood, SD, 1936; employee, Western Sales and Auction Co.; atty., Omaha, NE, 1926–71; admitted to practice before the Bar of the Supreme Court of the U.S., 1961. MEM.: Anti-Tax League of America (pres.); Nebraska Security League; American Prosperity Plan; Citizens and Taxpayers League of Omaha (sec., 1920); Better Omaha Club; Men's Club of Florence; People's Municipal Bank League (pres.); National Commercial Travelers' Economic Security Foundation, Inc. (national chm.); Western State Mining and Business Men's Assn. (exec. chm., 1965); Public Welfare Union (counsel, 1933); Omaha Citizens Council (chm., 1958); Omaha Citizens Comm. WRITINGS: *How Governments May Function Without Taxations* (ed., 1926). RES.: Omaha, NE.

HART, GARY WARREN (nee GARY WARREN HARTPENCE). b. Nov 28, 1937, Ottawa, KS; par. Carl and Nina Hartpence; m. Lee Ludwig, 1958; c. Andrea; John. EDUC.: B.A., Bethany Coll., 1958; B.D., Yale U., 1961, LL.B., 1964. POLIT. & GOV.: volunteer, John F. Kennedy for President Campaign, 1960; atty., U.S. Dept. of Justice, Washington, DC; appointed special asst. to U.S. sec. of the interior, Washington, DC; appointed dir., Denver (CO) Urban Renewal authority; volunteer, Robert F. Kennedy for President Campaign, 1968; national campaign dir., George McGovern for President Campaign, 1972; elected as a Democrat to U.S. Senate (CO), 1975–87; appointed chm., National Comm. on Air Quality, 1978–81; chm., Congressional Military Reform Caucus, 1981–82; ***candidate for Democratic nomination to presidency of the U.S., 1984, 1988 (withdrew; reentered); candidate for Democratic nomination to vice presidency of the U.S., 1984***. BUS. & PROF.: atty.; law practice, Denver, 1967–70, 1972–74, 1987–; lecturer, U. of CO Law School. MIL.: U.S.N.R., 1981–. MEM.: Park Hill Action Cmte.; U.S. Air Force Acad. (visitor, 1975–; chm., 1978–80). AWARDS: one of 50 Leaders for America's Future, *Time Magazine*; Legislator of the Year, National Wildlife Federation, 1978. WRITINGS: *Right from the Start* (1973); *A New Democracy* (1983); *America Can Win* (1986); *The Double Man* (coauthor, 1985). REL.: Protestant (nee Church of the Nazarene). MISC.: involved in sex scandal with Donna Rice, withdrew from Democratic presidential contest, May, 1987; reentered Democratic presidential race, Dec 15, 1987. MAILING ADDRESS: 1600 Downing St., Denver, CO 80218.

HART, GEORGE JOHN. b. Feb 1, 1904, Chicago, IL; par. Fred H. and Emma M. (von Selbach) Hart; m. Sarah Alla James; c. Dorothy (Mrs. Leonard Boeske); one other. EDUC.: Lane Technical H.S., Chicago, IL; U.S.A.A.F. Procurement School, Dayton, OH. POLIT. & GOV.: member, Democratic County Central Cmte. (KS); Democratic candidate for lt. gov. of KS, 1954; Democratic candidate for U.S. Senate (KS), 1956; elected as a Democrat, state treas. of KS, 1959–61; Democratic candidate for state treas. of KS, 1958, 1960; candidate for Democratic nomination to gov. of KS, 1960, 1962, 1964, 1966, 1968; write-in candidate for KS state printer, 1962; candidate for Democratic nomination to lt. gov. of KS, 1968, 1972; ***candidate for Democratic nomination to vice presidency of the U.S., 1968***; candidate for Democratic nomination to U.S. Senate (KS), 1974. BUS. & PROF.: buyer, mgr., Randy's Furniture Mart, Wichita, KS; civilian employee, Procurement Div., U.S. Air Force; buyer, mgr., Innes Department Store, 1938–41; mgr., fur store; owner, Hart Furs, 1950–. MEM.: Wichita C. of C.; Moose; Wichita Young Democratic Club; American Assn. of Retired Persons; Independent Businessmen's Assn.; NAACP; Old-Time Ball Players Assn. REL.: R.C. MAILING ADDRESS: 833 North Pinecrest, Wichita, KS 67208.

HART, PHILIP ALOYSIUS. b. Dec 10, 1912, Bryn Mawr, PA; d. Dec 26, 1976, Washington, DC; par. Philip Aloysius and Ann (Clyde) Hart; m. Jane C. Briggs, Jun 19, 1943; c. Ann Clyde; Jane Cameron; Walter Briggs; James Cox; Michael Patrick; Clyde William; Mary Catherine; Laura Elizabeth. EDUC.: A.B., Georgetown U., 1934; J.D., U. of MI, 1937. POLIT. & GOV.: appointed MI state corporations and securities commissioner, 1949–51; appointed MI state dir., Office of Price Stabilization, 1951–52; appointed U.S. atty., Eastern District of MI, 1952–53; legal counsel, office of the gov. of MI, 1953–54; elected as a Democrat to lt. gov. of MI, 1955–59; elected as a Democrat to U.S. Senate (MI), 1959–76; delegate, Dem. Nat'l. Conv., 1968; ***candidate for Democratic nomination to vice presidency of the U.S., 1976***. BUS. & PROF.: atty.; admitted to MI Bar, 1938; law practice, Detroit, MI, 1938–49. MIL.: lt. col., U.S. Army, 1941–46; Bronze Star; Purple Heart; Croix de Guerre. MEM.: Phi Delta Phi; MI Bar Foundation; Lansing World Affairs Council; American Jud. Soc.; American Soc. for Institutional Law. REL.: R.C. RES.: Mackinac Island, MI.

HART, SAMMIE HAYES. POLIT. & GOV.: ***candidate for Democratic nomination to presidency of the U.S., 1980, 1984***. MAILING ADDRESS: 10809 Forest Hills Dr., Tampa, FL 33612.

HART, WILLIAM OSBORNE. b. May 15, 1912, Chicago, IL; par. Harry Holbert and Mary Marie (Hans) Hart; m. Ruth Elizabeth Haseltine; c. Pierre Romaine; Romella Ruth; Holbert Weston. EDUC.: Chicago Training School for Missions, 1931–33; St. Olaf, 1938; U. of MO; SD State Coll., 1956; U. of ME; Bangor Theological Seminary, 1958. POLIT. & GOV.: Socialist Party candidate for clerk of the Circuit Court, Sauk Cty., WI, 1934; independent (Socialist) candidate for U.S. Senate (WI), 1962, 1976; Socialist Party candidate for gov. of WI, 1974; ***candidate for Socialist Party nomination to presidency of the U.S., 1976 (declined)***; Socialist Party candidate for WI State Supreme Court; Socialist Party candidate for state and local office, 15 additional times; Labor and Farm Party of Wisconsin candidate for U.S. Senate (WI), 1984 (withdrew). BUS. & PROF.: minister; printer; poet; missionary. MIL.: British North African Star with 8th Army Clasp. MEM.: American Jud. Soc.; Fellowship of Reconciliation; American Field Service (founder); Sauk Cty. (WI) Housing Authority (chm.). REL.: Episc. (assoc. member, Congregational Church). MAILING ADDRESS: "Harwood in the Hills," Prairie Du Sac, WI 53578.

HARTHENS, JOHN J. POLIT. & GOV.: ***candidate for Democratic nomination to vice presidency of the U.S., 1972***. MAILING ADDRESS: unknown.

HARTJE, EARL JOHN. POLIT. & GOV.: ***independent candidate for presidency of the U.S., 1992***. MAILING ADDRESS: 2750 North Mulford Rd., Box A-210, Rockford, IL 61111.

HARTKE, RUPERT VANCE. b. May 31, 1919, Stendal, IN; par. Hugo and Ida (Egbert) Hartke; m. Martha Tiernan, Jun 1943; c. Sandra; Jan; Wayne; Keith; Paul; Anita; Nadine. EDUC.: A.B., Evansville Coll., 1941; J.D. (with honors),

IN U., 1948. POLIT. & GOV.: deputy prosecuting atty., Vanderburgh Cty., IN, 1950–51; chm., Vanderburgh Cty. (IN) Democratic Central Cmte., 1952–58; elected as a Democrat to mayor of Evansville, IN, 1956–58; elected as a Democrat to U.S. Senate (IN), 1959–77; delegate, Dem. Nat'l. Conv., 1968, 1972; chm., Democratic Senatorial Campaign Cmte., 1961–62; ***candidate for Democratic nomination to presidency of the U.S., 1972***. BUS. & PROF.: ed., *Indiana Law Review*; ed., *Indiana Law Journal*; ed., *The Barker*; atty.; admitted to IN Bar, 1948; law practice, Evansville, 1948–58; dir., Evansville's Future, Inc. MIL.: lt., U.S.C.G. and U.S. Navy, 1942–46. MEM.: Lamda Chi Alpha; Phi Delta Phi; Tau Kappa Alpha; Wabash Valley Assn.; Ohio Valley Improvement Assn.; Press Exchange Club; Central Turners; Lutheran Laymen's League; National Assn. of Claimants Compensation Attorneys; Indiana Soc. of Washington; Evansville Junior C. of C.; Federal Bar Assn.; American Trial Lawyers Assn.; Authors Guild; ABA; IN Bar Assn.; National Capitol Democratic Club (vice pres., 1960–62; board member, 1963–66). HON. DEG.: LL.D., Valparaiso U., 1965; D.Pub.Ser., U. of Evansville, 1968; LL.D., U. of Vincennes, 1968; LL.D., Long Island U., 1968; LL.D., St. Joseph Coll.; LL.D., Huntington Coll. WRITINGS: *Beyond the New Frontier* (1962); *Inside the New Frontier* (1963); *The American Crisis in Vietnam* (1968); *You and Your Senator* (1970). REL.: Lutheran. MAILING ADDRESS: 6500 Kerns Court, Falls Church, VA.

HARTRANFT, JOHN FREDERICK. b. Dec 16, 1830, Fagleysville, PA; d. Oct 17, 1889, Norristown, PA; par. Samuel Engle and Lydia (Bucher) Hartranft; m. Sallie D. Sebring, Jan 26, 1854; c. one son; two daughters. EDUC.: grad., Union Coll., 1853; studied law under James Boyd, Norristown, PA. POLIT. & GOV.: elected as a Republican, deputy sheriff, Montgomery Cty., PA, 1854–61; elected as a Republican, auditor gen. of PA, 1865–72; elected as a Republican to gov. of PA, 1873–79; ***candidate for Republican nomination to presidency of the U.S., 1876, 1880***; appointed postmaster of Philadelphia, PA, 1879–81; appointed collector, Port of Philadelphia, PA, 1881–85. BUS. & PROF.: civil engineer, Mauch Chunk and Wilkes-Barre R.R.; atty.; admitted to PA Bar, 1860. MIL.: col., 51st Regt., PA Infantry, U.S. Army, 1861; brig. gen., U.S.V., 1864; brev. maj. gen., 1865; maj. gen., commander, PA National Guard, 1879–89. MEM.: GAR (commander in chief, 1875–76). REL.: Schwenkfelder Church. RES.: Philadelphia, PA.

HARVEY, JOHN CLAYTON. POLIT. & GOV.: ***independent candidate for presidency of the U.S., 1988***. MAILING ADDRESS: 17 McMoran, Croswell, MI 48422.

HARVEY, PAUL. b. Sep 4, 1918, Tulsa, OK; par. Harry Harrison and Anna Dagmar (Christiansen) Aurandt; m. Lynne Cooper, Jun 4, 1940; c. Paul, Jr. POLIT. & GOV.: ***candidate for American Independent Party nomination to vice presidency of the U.S., 1968***. BUS. & PROF.: announcer, radio station KVOO, Tulsa, OK; station mgr., Salina, KS; special events dir., radio station KXOK, St. Louis, MO; program dir., radio station WKZO, 1941–43; dir. of news and information, radio station OWI, MI and IN, 1941–43; news analyst, commentator, ABC, 1944–; syndicated columnist, General Features Corp., 1954–; television commentator, 1968. MEM.: Washington Radio and Television Correspondents Assn.; Aircraft Owners and Pilots Assn.; Chicago Press Club. WRITINGS: *Remember These Things* (1952); *Autumn of Liberty* (1954); *The Rest of the Story* (1956); *You Said It, Paul Harvey* (1969); *Our Lives, Our Fortunes, Our Sacred Honor*. Recordings: "Yesterday's Voices" (1959); "Testing Time" (1960); "Uncommon Man" (1962). AWARDS: citation, Disabled American Veterans, 1949; Freedoms Foundation Award, 1952, 1953, 1961, 1962, 1964, 1965, 1967, 1968, 1974, 1975, 1976; Radio Award, American Legion, 1952, Citation of Merit, 1955, 1957; Certificate of Merit, VFW, 1953; Bronze Christopher's Award, 1953; Award of Honor, Sumter Guards, 1955; Oklahoma Hall of Fame, 1955; National Public Welfare Services Trophy, Colorado American Legion, 1957; "Top Commentator of the Year" Award, *Radio-TV Daily*, 1962; Great American KSEL Award, 1962; Special ABC Award, 1973; Illinois Broadcaster Award, 1974; American of the Year Award, Lions International, 1975. HON. DEG.: Litt.D., Culver-Stockton Coll., 1952; Litt.D., St. Bonaventure U., 1953; LL.D., John Brown U., 1959; LL.D., MT School of Mines, 1961; LL.D., Trinity Coll., 1963; LL.D., Parsons Coll., 1968; H.H.D., Wayland Baptist Coll., 1962; LL.D., Union Coll., 1962; LL.D., Samford U., 1970. MAILING ADDRESS: 1035 Park Ave., River Forest, IL 60305.

HARVEY, WILLIAM HOPE "COIN." b. Aug 16, 1851, Buffalo, WV; d. Feb 11, 1936, Monte Ne, AR; par. Col. Robert Trigg and Anna M. (Hope) Harvey; m. Anna R. Halliday, Jun 26, 1876 (divorced, 1929); m. 2d, Mrs. May Ellston Leake, Apr 21, 1929; c. Robert H.; Thomas W.; Marie Hope Hammond; Annette. EDUC.: Buffalo (WV) Acad.; Marshall Coll.; studied law. POLIT. & GOV.: delegate, IL People's Party State Convention, 1894; ***Prosperity Party candidate for presidency of the U.S., 1932; Liberty Party candidate for presidency of the U.S., 1932***. BUS. & PROF.: schoolteacher; atty.; admitted to Cabell Cty. (WV) Bar, 1870; law practice, Barbourville, WV, 1870–74; partner (with Thomas H. Harvey), law firm, Huntington, WV, 1874–75; law practice, Cleveland, OH, 1876–79; law practice, Chicago, IL, 1879–81; legal counsel, wholesale firm, Gallipolis, OH, 1881–84; miner, CO, 1884–88; real estate investor, CO, 1888–93; owner, Coin Publishing Co., Chicago, 1893–1936; ed., *Coin's Financial Series*, Chicago; builder, Short-Line R.R., Monte Ne, AR; banker; economist; staff, St. Paul's School of Statesmanship, 1924; builder of pyramid at Monte Ne, AR. MEM.: World's Money Education League (chief exec. officer). WRITINGS: *Coin's Financial School* (1894); *Tale of Two Nations* (1894); *Coin's Financial School Up to Date* (1895); *Patriots of America* (1895); *Coin on Money, Trusts and Imperialism* (1899); *The Remedy* (1915); *Common Sense, or the Clot on the Brain of the Body Politic* (1920). RES.: Monte Ne, AR.

HASKEW, AARON LEE. POLIT. & GOV.: ***independent candidate for presidency of the U.S., 1976***. MAILING ADDRESS: 11 Westlake Dr., N.E., Albuquerque, NM 87112.

HASS, ERIC N. b. 1905, Lincoln, NE; d. Oct 2, 1980, Santa Rosa, CA; married. EDUC.: public schools, Lincoln, NE; U. of NE. POLIT. & GOV.: national organizer, Socialist Labor Party, 1932–42; ***Socialist Labor Party candidate for presidency of the U.S., 1932 (declined), 1952, 1956, 1960, 1964***; Socialist Labor Party candidate for U.S. Senate (OR), 1936; Socialist Labor Party candidate for mayor of New York, NY, 1941, 1945, 1949, 1957, 1961, 1965; Socialist Labor Party candidate for atty. gen. of NY, 1942; Industrial Government (Socialist Labor) Party candidate for U.S. Senate (NY), 1944, 1946; delegate, Socialist Labor Party National Convention, 1948 (Platform Cmte.); Socialist Labor Party candidate for gov. of NY, 1950, 1958, 1962; Socialist Labor Party candidate for president, New York City Council, 1957; expelled from Socialist Labor Party, Apr 1969. BUS. & PROF.: waiter; cook; railroad brakeman; engine wiper; newspaper reporter; ed., *Weekly People*, New York, 1938–68; lecturer; librarian, Trinity Episcopal Church, New York, 1969–77. WRITINGS: *The NRA and How Capitalists Patriotically Dodge It* (1933); *Industrial Democracy* (1934); *Radio Addresses No. 1-20* (1936); *Industrijalna demokratija* (1936); *John L. Lewis Exposed* (1937); *Socialist Industrial Unionism* (1940); *The Americanism of Socialism* (1941); *Socialist Industrial Unionism—The Workers' Power* (1941); *Konskripcija radnika* (1943); *The Labor Draft, Step to Industrial Slavery* (1943); *Socialism Answers Anti-Semitism* (1944); *Exploding Some Quibbles* (1945); *Stalinist Imperialism* (1946); *Sta je Socijalizam* (1946); *Mi a szocializmus?* (1946); *Fascism is Still a Menace* (1948); *Socialism: World Without Race Prejudice* (1949); *The Socialist Labor Party and the Internationals* (1949); *Dave Beck, Labor Merchant* (1955); *Militarism, Labor's Foe* (1955); *Militarizmus a munkassag ellensege!* (1955); *What Workers Should Know About Automation* (1956); *The Reactionary Right—Incipient Fascism* (1963); *Capitalism: Breeder of Race Prejudice* (1964); *Americanism and Socialism; What Every Puerto Rican Worker Should Know; What is Socialist Industrial Unionism?* RES.: New York, NY.

HATCHER, JESSIE. POLIT. & GOV.: ***independent candidate for presidency of the U.S., 1976***. MAILING ADDRESS: 1118 South Capitol, Indianapolis, IN 46225.

HATCHER, RICHARD GORDON. b. Jul 10, 1933, Michigan City, IN; par. Carlton and Catherine Hatcher; single. EDUC.: B.A., IN U.; LL.B., Valparaiso U. POLIT. & GOV.: Democratic candidate for justice of the peace, Valparaiso, IN, 1958; deputy prosecutor, Lake Cty., IN; elected as a Democrat to Gary (IN) City Council, 1963–66; elected as a Democrat to mayor of Gary, 1967–; member, IN Advisory Cmte., U.S. Comm. on Civil Rights; convenor, National Black Political Convention, 1972; member, steering cmte., National Black Assembly; ***candidate for Democratic nomination to vice presidency of the U.S., 1972***; chm., Gary City Democratic Cmte.; member, IN Democratic State Central Cmte., 1972–; chm., First Congressional District (IN), Democratic Party, 1972–; chm., Gary Democratic Precinct Organization, 1972–; delegate, Dem. Nat'l. Conv., 1972, 1976; pres., National Black Political Council, 1973–; member, National Democratic Comm. on delegate Selection, 1973–; delegate, Democratic National Mid-Term Conference, 1974; ***candidate for The Black Assembly nomination to presidency of the U.S., 1976***. BUS. & PROF.: atty.; admitted to IN Bar; law practice, East Chicago, IN. MEM.: U.S. Conference of Mayors; National League of Cities; Muigwithania Club (vice pres.); National Comm. of Inquiry; National Urban Coalition (member, exec. cmte.); National Black Caucus of Locally Elected Officials (founder); IN State Black Caucus (chm., 1973–); NAACP (member, Indiana Exec. Board); Greater Gary United Fund (dir.); Gary Urban League (trustee; member, Advisory Board); ABA; IN Bar Assn.; Gary Bar Assn. (exec. cmte.); Gary Junior C. of C.; Rotary Club. AWARDS: National Fellowship Award, Philadelphia (PA) Fellowship Comm.; named "Outstanding Young Man of the Year," Gary Junior C. of C., 1968; one of five "Outstanding Men in Indiana"; Loren Henry Award, IN Chapter, NAACP, 1965; Outstanding Man of the Year, National Fellowship Comm. HON. DEG.: LL.D., Duquesne U.; LL.D., Fisk U.; LL.D., Coppin State Coll. WRITINGS: *Report of the National Democratic Commission on Delegate Selection* (coauthor). REL.: Bapt. MAILING ADDRESS: City Hall, 401 Broadway, Gary, IN 46402.

HATFIELD, MARK ODOM. b. Jul 12, 1922, Dallas, OR; par. Charles Dolan and Dovil (Odom) Hatfield; m. Antoinette Kuzmanich; c. Elizabeth; Mark Odom, Jr.; Theresa; Charles Vincent. EDUC.: B.A., Willamette U., 1943; A.M., Stanford U., 1948. POLIT. & GOV.: elected as a Republican to OR State House, 1950–54; elected as a Republican to OR State Senate, 1954–56; elected as a Republican to sec. of state of OR, 1956–58; elected as a Republican to gov. of OR, 1959–67; delegate, Rep. Nat'l. Conv., 1952, 1956, 1960, 1964 (temporary chm.; keynoter), 1968; elected as a Republican to U.S. Senate (OR), 1967–; ***candidate for Republican nomination to presidency of the U.S., 1968; candidate for Republican nomination to vice presidency of the U.S., 1968***. BUS. & PROF.: assoc. prof. of political science, Willamette U., 1949–56, dean of students, 1950–56. MIL.: lt. (jg), U.S. Navy, 1943–46; Pacific Theater Ribbon. MEM.: Beta Theta Pi; Croatian Fraternal Union; Masons; Grange; American Legion; Shriners; Willamette U. (trustee); George Fox Coll. (trustee); Conservative Baptist Coll. (trustee); Dag Hammarskjold Coll. (trustee). AWARDS: hon. member, Japanese Diet, 1964; Robert A. Taft Memorial Award, 1967; Eleanor Roosevelt Humanitarian Award; Conservation Award, Izaak Walton League; War Memorial Award, New York Republican Club, 1967; Freedom Award, Order of Lafayette, 1967. HON. DEG.: LL.D., Howard U., 1980. WRITINGS: *Not Quite So Simple* (1968); *Conflict and Conscience* (1972); *Between a Rock and a Hard Place* (1976). REL.: Bapt. MAILING ADDRESS: P.O. Box 2416, Newport, OR 97365.

HAUPTLI, GARY. b. 1944. POLIT. & GOV.: ***candidate for Democratic nomination to presidency of the U.S., 1992***. BUS. & PROF.: schoolteacher, Salina (KS) Central H.S. MAILING ADDRESS: 3120 North Muir Rd., Salina, KS 67401.

HAVERKAMPF, DAVID O. MA. POLIT. & GOV.: ***candidate for Democratic nomination to presidency of the U.S., 1980***. MAILING ADDRESS: 8402 West Sunset, Apt. 236, Los Angeles, CA 90069.

HAWKINS, RAY JAMES. POLIT. & GOV.: ***independent candidate for presidency of the U.S., 1980***. MAILING ADDRESS: Marion, IL.

HAWKINSON, CARLA KATHRYN SCHRAM. par. Mr. Schram; m. Mr. Hawkinson. POLIT. & GOV.: ***candidate for Democratic nomination to presidency of the U.S., 1984, 1988, 1992***. MAILING ADDRESS: 2655 East Maple, Apt. 19, Birmingham, MI 98008.

HAWKS, TOD HOWARD. b. 1945. POLIT. & GOV.: ***candidate for Democratic nomination to presidency of the U.S., 1992***. MAILING ADDRESS: c/o Ragen Murray, 1320 S.W. 27th St., J-65, Topeka, KS 66611.

HAWLEY, JAMES HENRY. b. Jan 17, 1847, Dubuque, IA; d. Aug 3, 1929, Boise, ID; par. Thomas and Annie (Carr) Hawley; m. Mary E. Bullock, Jul 4, 1875; c. Edgar T.; Jesse B.; Emma (Mrs. Reilley Atkinson); Elizabeth (Mrs. E. W. Tucker); James H.; Harry R.; two infants. EDUC.: grad., City Coll., San Francisco, CA, 1864; studied law in offices of Sharpstein and Hastings. POLIT. & GOV.: elected as a Democrat to ID Territorial House, 1870–71; elected as a Democrat to ID Territorial Senate, 1874–75; appointed district atty., Second District of ID, 1879–83; appointed U.S. atty. for ID, 1886–90; Democratic candidate for U.S. House (ID), 1888; elected mayor of Boise, ID, 1903–05; elected as a Democrat to gov. of ID, 1911–13; Democratic candidate for gov. of ID, 1912; Democratic candidate for U.S. Senate (ID), 1914; ***candidate for Democratic nomination to vice presidency of the U.S., 1920***; delegate, Dem. Nat'l. Conv., 1924, 1928; delegate, ID State Democratic Convention, 1928. BUS. & PROF.: gold miner, CA, 1862; miner, ID, 1862–71; atty.; admitted to ID Bar, 1871; partner, Hawley and Hawley (law firm), Boise; partner, Hawley, Puckett and Hawley (law firm), Boise. WRITINGS: *History of Idaho: The Gem of the Mountains* (ed., 1920). RES.: Boise, ID.

HAWLEY, JOSEPH ROSWELL. b. Oct 31, 1826, Stewartsville, NC; d. Mar 17, 1905, Washington, DC; par. Rev. Francis and Mary (McLeod) Hawley; m. Harriet Ward Foote, 1855; m. 2d, Edith Anne Hornor, 1887; c. Marion H. Coudert; Miss Roswell. EDUC.: Oneida Conference Seminary, 1842–44; grad., Hamilton Coll., 1847. POLIT. & GOV.: delegate, CT State Republican Conventions, 1850–60; delegate, Free Soil Party National Convention, 1852; delegate, Rep. Nat'l. Conv., 1856, 1860 (alternate), 1868 (chm.), 1872, 1876, 1880; elected as a Republican to gov. of CT, 1866–67; presidential elector, Republican Party, 1868; Republican candidate for U.S. House (CT), 1868, 1875; elected as a Republican to U.S. House (CT), 1872–75; 1879–81; ***candidate for Republican nomination to vice presidency of the U.S., 1872, 1876***; appointed pres., U.S. Centennial Comm., 1873–76; Republican candidate for U.S. Senate (CT), 1879; elected as a Republican to U.S. Senate (CT), 1881–1905; ***candidate for Republican nomination to presidency of the U.S., 1884, 1888***; delegate, American Party National Convention, 1888. BUS. & PROF.: schoolteacher, Cazenovia, NY, 1847–49; atty.; admitted to CT Bar, 1850; partner, Hooker and Hawley (law firm), Hartford, CT, 1850–56; ed., *Charter Oak*, 1852; ed., *Hartford Evening Press*, 1857–67; ed., *Hartford Courant*, 1867–1905. MIL.: capt., U.S. Army, 1861, lt. col., 1861, col., 1862, brig. gen. of volunteers, 1864, brev. maj. gen. of volunteers, 1865; mustered out, 1866; appointed brig. gen., U.S. Army (on the retired list), 1905. MEM.: Wide Awakes; Hamilton Coll. (trustee, 1875); CT Hist. Soc.; GAR (junior commander in chief, 1868–69). HON. DEG.: LL.D., Hamilton Coll., 1875; LL.D., Yale U., 1886; LL.D., Trinity Coll., 1894. WRITINGS: *Address at Utica, NY* (1891); *The Credit Mobilier Investigation* (1873); *The Financial Issues* (1878); *The Military Forces of the Republic* (1879). REL.: Congregationalist. RES.: Hartford, CT.

HAYAKAWA, SAMUEL ICHIYE. b. Jul 18, 1906, Vancouver, British Columbia; d. Feb 27, 1992, Greenbrae, CA; par. Ichiro and Tora (Isono) Hayakawa; m. Margedant Peters, May 27, 1937; c. Alan Romer; Mark; Wynne. EDUC.: B.A., U. of Manitoba, 1927; M.A., McGill U., 1928; Ph.D., U. of WI, 1935. POLIT. & GOV.: candidate for Republican nomination to U.S. Senate (CA), 1974 (disqualified); elected as a Republican to U.S. Senate (CA), 1977–81; ***candidate for Republican nomination to presidency of the U.S., 1980; candidate for None of the Above Party nomination to presidency of the U.S., 1980***. BUS. & PROF.: instructor, English Extension Div., U. of WI, 1936–39; asst. prof. of English, (Armour) IL Inst. of Technology, 1940–42; columnist, *Chicago (IL) Defender*, 1942–47; ed., *ETC: A Review of General Semantics*, 1943–70; assoc. prof., IL Inst. of Technology, 1942–47; lecturer, University Coll., U. of Chicago, 1950–55; prof. of English, San Francisco State Coll., 1955–68, acting pres., 1968–69, pres., 1969–73, pres. emeritus, 1973–; certified psychologist, CA, 1959; Alfred P. Sloan Visiting Professor, Menninger School of Psychiatry, 1961; supervisory editorial board, *Funk and Wagnall's Standard Dictionary*; contributor, *Middle English Dictionary*, U. of MI, 1933–38; columnist, *Register and Tribune Syndicate*, 1970–76. MEM.: AAAS (fellow); American Psych. Assn. (fellow); American Sociological Assn. (fellow); Modern Language Assn.; International Soc. for General Semantics (pres., 1949–50); Consumers Union of the U.S. (dir., 1953–55); Inst. of Jazz Studies (dir.); San Francisco Press and Union League; Bohemian Club; Royal Soc. for the Arts; Soc. for the Psych. Study of Social Issues; Commonwealth Club. AWARDS: Claude Bernard Medal, U. of Montreal, 1959; Award for Excellence, New York Council of Churches, 1969. HON. DEG.: D.F.A., CA Coll. of Arts and Crafts, 1956; D.Litt., Grinnell Coll., 1967; L.H.D., Pepperdine U., 1972; LL.D., The Citadel, 1972. WRITINGS: *Oliver Wendell Holmes* (with Howard M. Jones, 1939); *Language in Action* (1941); *Language in Thought and Action* (1949); *Language, Meaning and Maturity* (1954); *Our Language and Our World* (1959); *Symbol, Status and Personality* (1963); *Funk and Wagnall's Modern Guide to Synonyms* (1968). RES.: Mill Valley, CA.

HAYES, EDWARD ARTHUR. b. Jan 5, 1893, Morrisonvillle, IL; d. Apr 1, 1955, Chicago, IL; par. Michael Patrick and Mary Ellen (Bray) Hayes; m. Margaret M. Muleady, Sep 10, 1918. EDUC.: grad., St. Theresa's Parochial School, 1910; LL.B., St. Louis U., 1915. POLIT. & GOV.: campaign mgr., Knox for President, 1936; ***candidate for Republican nomination to vice presidency of the U.S., 1936***. BUS. & PROF.: atty.; admitted to IL Bar, 1915; partner, Hayes and Downing (law firm), Decatur, IL, 1915–40; partner, Damon, Hayes, White and Hoban (law firm), Chicago, IL, 1945–55; gen. counsel, Bowser, Inc., 1945–55; pres., Defense Identification Service, Inc., 1951–55. MIL.: apprentice seaman, U.S. Navy, 1917; ensign, U.S.N.R., 1918–19, commissioned lt. commander, 1933. MEM.: American Legion (IL dept. commander, 1929–30; national commander, 1933–34; member, exec. cmte., 1931–55); ABA; IL Bar Assn.; Chicago Bar Assn.; Americans for America (national chm.); Knights of Columbus (4°); Chicago Athletic Assn. RES.: Chicago, IL.

HAYES, JAMES LEON. b. Nov 10, 1920, Haskell, TX; par. James Allen and Bertie Lee (Miller) Hayes; m. Mary Jean Eshbaugh, 1953; c. Pauli; Ellie; Lauri; Clayton; Merry Jessica. EDUC.: Trinity U., 2 years; U. of Denver, 2 years; U. of CO, 2 years; Metro State Coll., 1 year; audited classes, Washington and Lee Law School. POLIT. & GOV.: ***candidate for Democratic nomination to presidency of the U.S., 1992***; write-in candidate for U.S. House (CO), 1992. BUS. & PROF.: artist; master goldsmith; art history scholar. MIL.: U.S. Army, 12th F.A., 1938–41; U.S.A.A.C., 1941–45. REL.: Protestant. MISC.: active gymnast and boxer. MAILING ADDRESS: 209 East Bleeker St., Aspen, CO 81611.

HAYES, MAXIMILIAN SEBASTIAN. b. May 25, 1866, Havana, OH; d. Oct 11, 1945, Shaker Heights, OH; par. Joseph Maximilian and Elizabeth (Storer) Hoize; m. Dora Schneider, Dec 11, 1900; c. Maxine Elizabeth (Mrs. Albert Isaac Davey). EDUC.: public schools, Fremont and Cleveland, OH. POLIT. & GOV.: sec., Board of Appeals, Socialist Labor Party, 1897; ***Socialist Labor Party candidate for vice presidency of the U.S., 1900 (resigned after merger with Social Democratic Party)***; Socialist Party candidate for U.S. House (OH), 1900, 1904, 1908; Socialist Party candidate for OH state sec. of state, 1902; Socialist Party candidate for gov. of OH, 1902; member, Socialist Party National Cmte., 1914–16; chm., exec. cmte., National Labor Party, 1919; ***Farmer-Labor Party candidate for vice presidency of the U.S., 1920***; member, Farmer-Labor Party National Cmte., 1920; appointed member, Metropolitan Housing Authority, Cleveland, OH, 1933; appointed member, OH State Adjustment Board, National Recovery Administration, 1934. BUS. & PROF.: apprentice printer, Penny Press; publisher, *Cleveland Citizen*, 1891, ed., 1892–1939. MEM.: Cleveland Federation of Labor; AFL (fraternal delegate to British Trade Union Congress, 1903; candidate for union pres., 1911); Masons; Knights of Pythias; Conference for Progressive Political Action; Consumer's League of OH (founder, 1900); National Council for the Protection of Foreign Born Workers (exec. cmte., 1930); Labor Defense Council, 1923; International Workers' Aid, 1926; International Typographers Union (1884; delegate, AFL Conventions, 22 times); Workers International Relief (National Cmte., 1928); Central Labor Union; National Cmte. to Aid Victims of German Fascism, 1933; National Mooney-Billings Cmte. REL.: none (nee R.C.). RES.: Cleveland, OH.

HAYES, RUTHERFORD BIRCHARD. b. Oct 4, 1822, Delaware, OH; d. Jan 17, 1893, Fremont, OH; par. Rutherford and Sophia (Birchard) Hayes; m. Lucy Webb, Dec 30, 1852; c. Birchard Austin; Webb Cook; Rutherford Platt; Joseph T.; George C.; Frances; Scott R.; Manning F. EDUC.: Methodist Acad., Norwalk, OH; Webb Preparatory School, Middletown, CT; grad., Kenyon Coll., 1842; grad., Harvard U., 1845. POLIT. & GOV.: city solicitor, Cincinnati, OH, 1858–61; elected as a Republican to U.S. House (OH), 1865–67; elected as a Republican to gov. of OH, 1868–72, 1876–77; Republican candidate for U.S. House (OH), 1872; appointed U.S. treas., Cincinnati, (declined); ***American Alliance Party candidate for presidency of the U.S., 1876 (declined); elected as a Republican to presidency of the U.S., 1877–81; candidate for Republican nomination to presidency of the U.S., 1880***. BUS. & PROF.: atty.; admitted to OH Bar, 1845; law practice, Lower Sandusky, OH, 1845–49; law practice, Cincinnati, 1849–57. MIL.: maj., 33d Regt., OH Volunteers, 1861, brig. gen., 1864, brev. maj. gen. of volunteers, 1865. MEM.: Literary Club of Cincinnati; National Prison Assn. (pres., 1883–93); Loyal Legion (commander, OH State Commandery; national commander in chief, 1886, 1888–93); Slater Fund (trustee); Peabody Education Fund (trustee). HON. DEG.: LL.D., Kenyon Coll., 1868; LL.D., Harvard U., 1877; LL.D., Yale U., 1880; LL.D., Johns Hopkins U., 1881. REL.: Methodist. RES.: Fremont, OH.

HAYMOND, CREED. b. Apr 22, 1836, Beverly, VA (now WV); d. Jan 13, 1893, San Francisco, CA; par. W. C. Haymond; m. Cornelia Alicia Crawford, 1872; c. none. EDUC.: studied law under James A. Johnson and Judge Alexander W. Baldwin, 1859. POLIT. & GOV.: appointed member, CA Tide Land Comm., 1868 (declined); appointed chm., CA Code

Comm., 1870; elected as an independent to CA State Senate, 1875–79; delegate, Rep. Nat'l. Conv., 1880; ***candidate for Republican nomination to presidency of the U.S., 1888***. BUS. & PROF.: miner; packer; merchant; mail carrier, Wells Fargo and Co., CA, 1½ years; ditchdigger; atty., Sacramento, CA; assoc. solicitor, Central Pacific Railway Co., 1882–93. MIL.: col., First Artillery Regt., National Guard of CA; capt., Sierra Grays Militia, Sierra Cty., CA, 1860. WRITINGS: *Revised Laws of the State of California* (1871–72); *The Code of Civil Procedure of the State of California* (1872); *The California Codes* (1872); *General Statutes of the State of California* (1873); *The Penal Code of the State of California* (1874); *Chinese Immigration* (1876); *The Civil Code of the State of California* (1877); *The Taxing Power—Its Limitations* (1881); *Argument of Creed Haymond* (1881); *California Railroad Tax Cases* (1888); *The Central Pacific Railroad Company* (1888); *Pacific Railroads* (1888). RES.: Sacramento, CA.

HAYNES, LEE WAYNE. POLIT. & GOV.: ***independent candidate for presidency of the U.S., 1992***. MAILING ADDRESS: 3700 East Stewart, #347, Las Vegas, NV 89110.

HAYNES, MYRON WILBUR. b. Jan 1, 1855, Lunenburg, MA; d. Nov 28, 1932, Portland, OR; par. Elnathan and Sarah (Wheeler) Haynes; m. Florence G. Felt, Jun 20, 1879; c. Carey Dana; Mrs. Ethel Ada Arnold; Arthur Stanley. EDUC.: A.B., Colgate U., 1879; D.D., Shurtleff Coll., 1890, LL.D., 1926. POLIT. & GOV.: Prohibition Party candidate for gov. of IN, 1908; Prohibition Party candidate for U.S. Senate (IN), 1914, 1916; ***candidate for Prohibition Party nomination to presidency of the U.S., 1916***. BUS. & PROF.: ordained minister, Baptist Church, 1879; pastor, Frankfort, NY, 1879–82; pastor, Marblehead, MA, 1882–84; pastor, Kalamazoo, MI, 1884–88; pastor, Englewood Church, Chicago, IL, 1888–96; pastor, Belden Avenue Church, Chicago, 1896–1905; pres., Central Baptist Orphanage, 1895–1902; pastor, First Church, Seattle, WA, 1905–07; pastor, Delmar Avenue Church, St. Louis, MO, 1907–08; engaged in endowment movement for Central U., Pella, IA, 1908–11; engaged in endowment movement for Franklin (IN) Coll., 1911–14; engaged in endowment movement for McMinnville (OR) Coll., 1914–17; engaged in endowment movement for Keuka Coll., Cook Acad., Shurtleff Coll., North Western Bible and Missionary Training School, 1917; endowment sec., Shurtleff Coll., 1919; endowment and field sec., Keuka Coll., 1926; field sec., Western Baptist Theological Seminary, 1931. MEM.: Phi Beta Kappa; Beta Theta Pi; Shurtleff Coll. (pres., Board of Trustees, 1896–1902). WRITINGS: *Modern Evangelism* (1899). REL.: Bapt. (pres., IL State Convention, 1898–1902). RES.: McMinnville, OR.

HAYNES, ROBERT BRYANT. b. Nov 8, 1970, Norfolk, VA; par. Robert Patrick and Helen Carol (Tucker) Haynes; single. EDUC.: Perquimans H.S., Hertford, NC. POLIT. & GOV.: ***independent write-in candidate for presidency of the U.S., 1988***. BUS. & PROF.: unemployed; student. REL.: no preference. MAILING ADDRESS: Route 3, Box 359, Hertford, NC 27944.

HAYNES, SUMNER W. b. Aug 15, 1855, Portland, IN; d. Aug 11, 1936; par. Judge Jacob March and Hilina S. (Haines) Haynes; m. America E. Hays, Aug 24, 1881; c. May Beatrice; Mabel Edna. EDUC.: Earlham Coll.; LL.B., U. of MI, 1880. POLIT. & GOV.: Prohibition Party candidate for atty. gen. of IN, 1890, 1902; Prohibition Party candidate for U.S. House (IN), 1892; Prohibition Party candidate for gov. of IN, 1908; Prohibition Party candidate for judge, IN Supreme Court, 1912; ***candidate for Prohibition Party nomination to presidency of the U.S., 1916***; Prohibition Party candidate for U.S. Senate (IN), 1916; member, Prohibition Party National Cmte., 1916–24; counsel, Jay Cty. (IN) Board of Children's Guardians. BUS. & PROF.: atty.; admitted to IN Bar, 1881; partner (with Jacob March Haynes), law firm, Portland, IN, 1881–83; partner (with W. E. Cox), law firm, Portland, 1883–91; partner (with George W. Hall), law firm, Portland, 1891–99; law practice, Portland, 1899–1936. MEM.: IN State Children's Home Soc. (superintendent, 1908–10). WRITINGS: *Abraham Lincoln on Popular Sovereignty*. REL.: Presb. (delegate, General Assembly, 1892; Sunday School teacher; superintendent). RES.: Portland, IN.

HAYS, WAYNE LEVERE. b. May 13, 1911, Bannock, OH; d. Feb 10, 1989; par. Walter Lee and Bertha Mae (Taylor) Hays; m. Martha Judkins, Jun 3, 1937; c. Martha Brigitta. EDUC.: B.S., OH State U., 1933; Duke U., 1935. POLIT. & GOV.: deputy auditor, Belmont Cty., OH; elected as a Democrat to mayor of Flushing, OH, 1939–45; elected as a Democrat to OH State Senate, 1941–42; member, OH State Board of Education; elected as a Democrat, cty. commissioner, Belmont Cty., OH, 1945–49; elected as a Democrat to U.S. House (OH), 1949–76; delegate, Dem. Nat'l. Conv., 1960, 1964, 1968; ***candidate for Democratic nomination to presidency of the U.S., 1972, 1976***. BUS. & PROF.: farmer; owner, Red Gate Farms; teacher, Flushing, OH, 1934–37; teacher, Findlay, OH, 1937–38; chm. of the board, Citizens National Bank, Flushing, 1953–. MIL.: 2d lt., U.S. Army, 1941–42. MEM.: NATO Parliamentary Conference (pres., 1956; vice pres.); North Atlantic Assembly (pres., 1969–70); Rotary Club. AWARDS: Caritas Medal, Catholic Diocese of Steubenville, OH, 1969. HON. DEG.: LL.D., OH U., 1966; LL.D., Coll. of Steubenville, 1968. REL.: Presb. RES.: Flushing, OH.

HAYS, WILLIAM HARRISON "WILL." b. Nov 5, 1879, Sullivan, IN; d. Mar 7, 1954, Sullivan, IN; par. John T. and Mary (Cain) Hayes; m. Helen Louise Thomas, Nov 18, 1902; m. 2d, Jessie Herron Stutsman, Nov 27, 1930; c. Will Harrison. EDUC.: A.B., Wabash Coll., 1900, A.M., 1904. POLIT. & GOV.: Republican precinct committeeman, 1900; chm., Sullivan Cty. (IN) Republican Central Cmte., 1904–08;

elected as a Republican, city atty. of Sullivan, IN, 1910–13; Republican candidate for prosecuting atty. of Carlisle Cty., IN; member, IN Republican State Advisory Cmte., 1904–08; chm., Speakers' Bureau, Republican State Cmte. of IN, 1906–08; district chm., IN State Republican Cmte., 1910–14; chm., IN Republican State Central Cmte., 1914–18; delegate, Rep. Nat'l. Conv., 1916; chm., IN State Council of Defense, 1917–18; chm., Rep. Nat'l. Cmte., 1918–21; ***candidate for Republican nomination to presidency of the U.S., 1920***; appointed postmaster gen. of the U.S., 1921–22. BUS. & PROF.: atty.; admitted to IN Bar, 1900; partner, Hayes and Hayes (law firm), Sullivan; pres., Motion Picture Producers and Distributors of America, Inc., 1922–45, adviser, 1945–50; dir., Continental Banking Co.; dir., Chicago and Eastern Illinois R.R. Co. MEM.: Roosevelt Memorial Assn. (vice pres.); Inst. for Crippled and Disabled Men (trustee); National Council of BSA; Citizens Cmte. of the Salvation Army; ABA; IN Bar Assn.; National Inst. for Social Science; Acad. of Political Science; Phi Delta Theta (IN pres., 6 years; national pres., 1920–22); American Red Cross (chm., Coordinating Cmte. on Near East Relief, 1922); Officers' Reserve Corps (col.); Presbyterian Board of Ministerial Relief and Sustentation (chm., Laymen's Cmte., 1923); Wabash Coll. (trustee); Masons (33°; Knights Templar; Shriners); Knights of Pythias; Elks; Loyal Order of Moose; Columbia Club; Sullivan Rotary Club; Chicago Club; Indiana Soc.; Metropolitan Club; National Press Club; University Club of Washington; Chevy Chase Club; Union League; National Republican Club; Bankers Club; C. of C.; Friars Club; Advertising Club; National Geographic Soc.; Economic Club; The Cloud; Rockefeller Center Luncheon Club; The Coffee House; Lincoln Club; California Club; Bohemian Club. HON. DEG.: LL.D., Lincoln Memorial U., 1919; LL.D., Mt. Union Coll., 1926; LL.D., Wabash Coll., 1940. WRITINGS: *An Outline History* (1929); *See and Hear* (1929); *Arbitration in Business* (1930); *Memoirs* (1955). REL.: Presb. (elder). RES.: New York, NY.

HAYWOOD, WILLIAM DUDLEY "BIG BILL" (nee WILLIAM RICHARD HAYWOOD).

b. Feb 4, 1869, Salt Lake City, UT; d. May 17, 1928, Moscow, U.S.S.R.; par. William Dudley Haywood; m. Nevada Jane Minor, 1889; m. 2d, Russian wife, 1927; c. Vernie; Henrietta; infant son. EDUC.: public schools, Ophir, UT; Sisters' Acad. of the Sacred Heart, Salt Lake City, UT; St. Mark's School, Salt Lake City. POLIT. & GOV.: member, Socialist Party, 1901–12 (exec. cmte., 1912); Socialist Party candidate for gov. of CO, 1906; ***candidate for Socialist Party nomination to presidency of the U.S., 1908 (declined)***; joined Communist Party, 1919. BUS. & PROF.: indentured farmhand; errand boy; usher, Salt Lake Theater, Salt Lake City; fruit salesman, Salt Lake City, 1881; bellboy, Continental Hotel, Salt Lake City; bellboy, Walker House, Salt Lake City; miner, NV; miner, Silver City, ID, 1885–90; cowboy, Thad Hoppin Ranch, NV; homesteader; miner, boiler firer, Brooklyn Mine, UT; prospector; miner, Commonwealth Mine, Tuscarora, NV; miner, Imperial Mining Co., Kennedy, NV; labor organizer; assoc. ed., *International Socialist Review*; lecturer, International Red Aid; head, American Kuzbas Colony, Siberia, 1922. MEM.: Western Federation of Miners (National Exec. Board, 1899; sec.-treas., 1900–1908); Industrial Workers of the World (founder, 1905; pres.); International Red Aid. WRITINGS: *The General Strike* (1910); *Industrial Socialism* (with Frank Bohn, 1911); *Bill Haywood's Book* (1929). REL.: atheist (nee Episc.). MISC.: participated in Coeur d'Alenes (ID) Strike, 1899; arrested, but acquitted of murder of Gov. Steunenberg, 1905; convicted under Espionage Act, 1918; released on bail pending trial for murder; escaped to the U.S.S.R., 1920. RES.: Chicago, IL.

HEARST, GEORGE F.

b. Sep 3, 1820, Sullivan, MO; d. Feb 28, 1891, Washington, DC; par. William G. and Elizabeth (Collins) Hearst; m. Phoebe Apperson, Jun 15, 1862; c. William Randolph (q.v.). EDUC.: Franklin Mining School, MO. POLIT. & GOV.: elected as a Democrat to CA State Assembly, 1865–66; candidate for Democratic nomination to gov. of CA, 1882; Democratic candidate for U.S. Senate (CA), 1885; appointed and subsequently elected as a Democrat to U.S. Senate (CA), 1886–91; ***candidate for American Party nomination to presidency of the U.S., 1888 (declined)***. BUS. & PROF.: prospector; farmer; rancher; acquired fortune through great mineral discoveries at Ophir Mine (NV), Ontario Mine (UT), Homestake Mine (SD), Anaconda Mine (MT); owner, publisher, *San Francisco (CA) Daily Examiner*, 1880–87. RES.: San Francisco, CA.

HEARST, WILLIAM RANDOLPH.

b. Apr 29, 1863, San Francisco, CA; d. Aug 14, 1951, Beverly Hills, CA; par. Sen. George F. (q.v.) and Phoebe (Apperson) Hearst; m. Millicent Veronica Willson, Apr 28, 1903; c. William Randolph, Jr.; Randolph Apperson; David Whitmire; George. EDUC.: Harvard U., 1882–85. POLIT. & GOV.: elected as a Democrat to U.S. House (NY), 1903–09; ***candidate for Democratic nomination to presidency of the U.S., 1900, 1904, 1908, 1920, 1924***; Municipal Ownership League candidate for mayor of New York, NY, 1905; Democratic candidate for gov. of NY, 1906; founder, Independence League Party, 1908; member, National Independence League Party National Cmte., 1908; ***candidate for National Independence League Party nomination to presidency of the U.S., 1908***; Independence League (Civic Alliance) Party candidate for mayor of New York, NY, 1909; Independence League Party candidate for lt. gov. of NY, 1910; ***American Constitutional Party candidate for presidency of the U.S., 1920***. BUS. & PROF.: newspaper publisher; owner, Hearst Newspaper Chain; ed., *San Francisco (CA) Examiner*, 1886–1951; ed., *Los Angeles (CA) Examiner*; ed., *Los Angeles Herald and Express*; ed., *Chicago (IL) Herald-American*; ed., *Boston (MA) American*; ed., *Boston Sunday Advertiser*; ed., *Boston Record*; ed., *New York Journal-American*; ed., *New York Mirror*; ed., *Albany (NY) Times Union*; ed., *Baltimore (MD) Sunday American*; ed., *Baltimore News-Post*; ed., *Pittsburgh (PA) Sun-Telegraph*; ed., *Detroit (MI) Times*; ed., *Seattle (WA) Post-Intelligencer*; ed., *San Francisco Call-Bulletin*; ed., *Oakland (CA) Post-Enquirer*; ed., *San Antonio (TX)*

Light; ed., *Milwaukee (WI) Sentinel*; ed., *Hearst's Cosmopolitan*; ed., *Good Housekeeping*; ed., *Harper's and Junior Bazaars*; ed., *Motor Magazine*; ed., *Motor Boating Magazine*; ed., *American Druggist*; ed., *Town and Country*; ed., *House Beautiful*; ed., *Vanity Fair*; ed., *International Studio*. MEM.: National League of Democratic Clubs (pres.). HON. DEG.: LL.D., Oglethorpe Coll., 1927. RES.: San Simeon, CA.

HEFLIN, JAMES THOMAS. b. Apr 9, 1869, Louina, AL; d. Apr 22, 1951, Lafayette, AL; par. Dr. Wilson L. and Lavicie Catherine (Phillips) Heflin; m. Minnie Kate Schuessler, Dec 18, 1895; c. James Thomas; two infants. EDUC.: Southern U.; Agricultural and Mechanical Coll., Auburn, AL. POLIT. & GOV.: elected as a Democrat to mayor of Lafayette, AL, 1893–94; register in chancery, 1894–96; elected as a Democrat to AL State House, 1896–1900; member, AL Democratic State Exec. Cmte., 1896–1902; delegate, AL State Democratic Convention, 1900; delegate, AL State Constitutional Convention, 1901; elected as a Democrat, state sec. of state of AL, 1902–04; elected as a Democrat to U.S. House (AL), 1904–21; delegate, Dem. Nat'l. Conv., 1908, 1936; elected as a Democrat to U.S. Senate (AL), 1920–31; ***candidate for Farmer-Labor Party nomination to vice presidency of the U.S., 1928; candidate for Prohibition Party nomination to presidency of the U.S., 1928***; candidate for Democratic nomination to U.S. Senate (AL), 1930, 1938; independent candidate for U.S. Senate (AL), 1930; ***candidate for Democratic nomination to presidency of the U.S., 1932***; Democratic candidate for justice of the peace, Chilton Cty., AL, 1932; candidate for Democratic nomination to U.S. House (AL), 1934, 1938; appointed special asst. to the atty. gen. of the U.S., 1935–37; appointed special representative, Federal Housing Administration, 1935–36, 1939–42. BUS. & PROF.: atty.; admitted to AL Bar, 1893; law practice, Lafayette, AL. MISC.: noted for anti-Catholic activities and association with Ku Klux Klan; known as "Tom-Tom" or "Cotton Tom." RES.: Lafayette, AL.

HEGGER, KARL J. POLIT. & GOV.: ***candidate for Democratic nomination to presidency of the U.S., 1992***. MAILING ADDRESS: Highland, IL.

HEIN, PAUL ANTHONY, JR. b. Apr 7, 1933, St. Louis, MO; par. Paul Anthony and Rosalia (Brachtesende) Hein; m. Loretta Kohler, Jun 18, 1959; c. Ann; Paul Anthony III; Victoria; Jean. EDUC.: M.D., St. Louis U., 1958. POLIT. & GOV.: ***independent candidate for presidency of the U.S., 1976***. BUS. & PROF.: physician; special agent, Internal Revenue Service (under duress). MEM.: medical societies. REL.: R.C. MAILING ADDRESS: 339 Meadowbrook Dr., Ballwin, MO.

HEISTERKAMP, JAMES LYNN. b. Aug 1, 1930, Carroll, IA; par. Joseph W. and Elizabeth Rosa (Rettenmaier) Heisterkamp; single. EDUC.: grad., Carroll (IA) H.S., 1948; grad., Cooks and Kitchen Helpers School, Albany, NY, 1967; San Francisco City Coll., 1970–71. POLIT. & GOV.: candidate for San Francisco (CA) Board of Supervisors, 1973; candidate for mayor of San Francisco, CA, 1975; ***independent candidate for presidency of the U.S., 1976, 1980***. BUS. & PROF.: corporate consultant, asst. branch mgr., U.S. Corp. Co., Albany, NY, 1957–66; railway clerk, San Francisco, CA, 1968–; various administrative positions, city and cty. of San Francisco, CA, 1968–. MIL.: sgt., U.S. Army, to 1956. MEM.: San Francisco Street Artist Assn.; Ragtime Revisited, Inc. (pres.); Ragtime Preservation Soc., Inc. (pres.); Grassroots Projects Unlimited (founder). WRITINGS: *Talent: Songwriters and Poets of Tomorrow* (1946); *European Stars and Stripes* (1956); *New Gospel According to Saint Nasty* (1972); *Thirty Pieces of Silver* (play, 1975). REL.: Christian. MAILING ADDRESS: Box 4689, San Francisco, CA 94101.

HELLER, MILTON LOUIS. POLIT. & GOV.: ***candidate for Republican nomination to presidency of the U.S., 1988***. BUS. & PROF.: farmer; rancher, TX. MAILING ADDRESS: 335 Ocean Dr., Miami Beach, FL 33139.

HELMS, JESSE ALEXANDER, JR. b. Oct 18, 1921, Monroe, NC; par. Jesse Alexander and Ethel Mae (Helms) Helms; m. Dorothy Jane Coble, Oct 31, 1942; c. Jane (Mrs. Charles R. Knox); Nancy (Mrs. John C. Stuart); Charles. EDUC.: Wingate Junior Coll.; Wake Forest Coll. POLIT. & GOV.: administrative asst. to U.S. Sen. Willis Smith, 1951–53; administrative asst. to U.S. Sen. Alton Lennon, 1953; elected to Raleigh (NC) City Council, 1957–61; elected as a Republican to U.S. Senate (NC), 1973–; ***candidate for Republican nomination to presidency of the U.S., 1976, 1980, 1984, 1988; candidate for Republican nomination to vice presidency of the U.S., 1976, 1980; candidate for American Party nomination to presidency of the U.S., 1976; candidate for American Independent Party nomination to presidency of the U.S., 1976; candidate for None of the Above Party nomination to presidency of the U.S., 1980***. BUS. & PROF.: city ed., *Raleigh Times*, 1941–42; news and program dir., WRAL radio, Raleigh, 1948–51; exec. dir., NC Bankers Assn., 1953–60; exec. vice pres., vice chm., CBS, Raleigh, 1960–72; chm. of the board, Specialized Agricultural Publications, Inc., Raleigh, 1964–. MIL.: U.S. Navy, 1942–45. MEM.: NC Bankers Assn.; Rotary Club (pres., Raleigh Chapter, 1969–70); Masons (grand orator, Grand Lodge of Masons of NC, 1964); NC Cerebral Palsy Hospital (dir.); Camp Willow Run (dir.); United Cerebral Palsy of NC (dir.); Wake Cty. Cerebral Palsy and Rehabilitation Center (dir.); Campbell Coll. (trustee); Wingate Coll. (trustee); Meredith Coll. (trustee); John F. Kennedy Coll. (trustee); Raleigh Executives Club (pres.). AWARDS: Freedoms Foundation of Valley Forge Award for Best Television Editorial, 1962, for Best Newspaper Article, 1973; Southern Baptist National Award for Service to Mankind, 1972; Citizenship Award, NC American Legion; Citizenship Award, VFW; Citizenship Award, Raleigh

Exchange Club. REL.: Bapt. (deacon; Sunday school teacher). MAILING ADDRESS: 1513 Caswell St., Raleigh, NC 27608.

HEM, EUGENE ARTHUR. b. Feb 3, 1933, Lincoln, NE; par. Marlene Alma Gillespie; m. Roberta Lawry; c. James O'Neal; Daniel O'Neal; Kathleen O'Neal. EDUC.: B.A., North Central Coll. POLIT. & GOV.: Third Party candidate for U.S. Senate (WI), 1986; ***Third Party candidate for presidency of the U.S., 1988, 1992***. BUS. & PROF.: adjuster, Bankers Life Insurance Co.; security guard; truck loader, Gateway; teacher, public schools, Chicago, IL; teacher, public schools, Milwaukee, WI. MIL.: seaman, U.S. Navy, 1951–52. REL.: Methodist. MAILING ADDRESS: 43 West Grand, Chilton, WI 53014.

HEMENWAY, FRANCIS BENJAMIN "FRANK." b. Jun 1885, Arlington, IA; d. Jul 22, 1949, Tacoma, WA; par. Frank Benjamin and Mary (Logan) Hemenway; m. Alta McAndrew; c. Ronald Francis; Leo Dean. EDUC.: tenth grade, public schools. POLIT. & GOV.: founder, Liberty Party, 1932; chm., Tacoma (WA) Liberty Party; chm., Pierce Cty. (WA) Liberty Party; exec. sec., State Liberty Party; Liberty Party candidate for insurance commissioner of WA State, 1932; ***Liberty Party candidate for vice presidency of the U.S., 1932.*** BUS. & PROF.: farmer; owner, general store; salesman, Reynolds and King (auto accessories), Tacoma, 1929–31; partner (with Henry Johnson), H. and J. Realty Co., Tacoma. MEM.: WA State Grange. REL.: Christian Scientist. RES.: Tacoma, WA.

HEMPLE, EVYLIN (See EVELYN, EVYLIN MARTHA (HEMPLE) EICHELBERGER) (aka EVYLIN #501-14-7038).

HENDERSON, ELIZABETH B. married. POLIT. & GOV.: ***independent candidate for presidency of the U.S., 1976***; candidate for U.S. House (PA), 1976. MAILING ADDRESS: Philadelphia, PA.

HENDERSON, LEON H. b. May 26, 1895, Millville, NJ; d. Oct 19, 1986, Oceanside, CA; par. Chester Bowen and Lida C. (Beebe) Henderson; m. Myrlie Hamm, Jul 25, 1925; c. Myrlie Beebe; Lyn; Leon, Jr. EDUC.: A.B., Swarthmore Coll., 1920; U. of PA, 1920–22. POLIT. & GOV.: appointed deputy sec., Commonwealth of PA, 1924–25; economic adviser, dir. of Research and Planning Div., NRA, 1934–35; appointed member, National Industrial Recovery Board, 1934–35; economic adviser, U.S. Senate Cmte. on Manufacturers, 1935; economist, Democratic National Campaign Cmte., 1936; consulting economist, WPA, 1936–38; exec. sec., Temporary National Economic Comm., 1938–39; appointed member, Securities and Exchange Comm., 1939–41; appointed member, Advisory Cmte., Council of National Defense, 1940; appointed administrator, OPA and Civilian Supply, 1941–42; appointed member, Supply Priorities and Allocation Board, 1941–42; appointed dir., Civilian Supply Div., WPB, 1942; chm., National Independent Cmte. for Roosevelt and Truman, 1944; ***candidate for Democratic nomination to presidency of the U.S., 1952?*** BUS. & PROF.: economist; instructor, Wharton School, U. of PA, 1919–22; asst. prof. of economics, Carnegie Inst. of Technology, 1922–23; dir., Consumer Credit Research, Russell Sage Foundation, New York, NY, 1925–34; economic consultant, 1943–86; pres., American Leduc Uranium Corp., 1956–57; pres., Doeskin Products, Inc., 1957–58; author. MIL.: pvt., capt., U.S. Army, 1917–19. MEM.: National Press Club; United Nations Club; Russell Sage Foundation (dir.); American Economic Assn.; Millville Board of Trade; Delta Upsilon; Masons; Americans for Democratic Action (chm., 1947–48). RES.: New York, NY.

HENDRICKS, THOMAS ANDREWS. b. Sep 7, 1819, Zanesville, OH; d. Nov 25, 1885, Indianapolis, IN; par. John and Jane (Thomson) Hendricks; m. Eliza C. Morgan, Sep 26, 1845; c. Morgan. EDUC.: Shelby Cty. Seminary; Greenburg (IN) Acad.; grad., Hanover (IN) Coll., 1841; studied law under Judge Thomson, Chambersburg, PA, 1843. POLIT. & GOV.: elected as a Democrat to IN State House, 1848; elected as a Democrat to IN State Senate, 1849; elected delegate, IN State Constitutional Convention, 1851; elected as a Democrat to U.S. House (IN), 1851–55; Democratic candidate for U.S. House (IN), 1854; appointed commissioner of the General Land Office, 1855–59; Democratic candidate for gov. of IN, 1860, 1868; elected as a Democrat to U.S. Senate (IN), 1863–69; ***candidate for Democratic nomination to presidency of the U.S., 1868, 1876, 1880, 1884 (declined); received 42 electoral votes for presidency of the U.S., 1872***; elected as a Democrat to gov. of IN, 1873–77; chm., IN State Democratic Convention, 1874, 1878, 1880; ***Democratic candidate for vice presidency of the U.S., 1876; elected as a Democrat to vice presidency of the U.S., 1885***. BUS. & PROF.: atty.; admitted to IN Bar, 1843; law practice, Shelbyville, IN, 1843–60; law practice, Indianapolis, 1860–63, 1869–85; partner, Hendricks, Hord and Hendricks (law firm), Indianapolis, 1863–72. WRITINGS: *Reconciliation and Union* (1866); *Speech* (1866); *Reform in Earnest* (1872); *Garfield in Louisiana* (1880); *The Supreme Court* (1885). REL.: Episc. (nee Presb.; delegate, Methodist Episcopal General Convocation, 1883). RES.: Indianapolis, IN.

HENDRICKSON, FINLEY C. b. Oct 22, 1863, near Cumberland, MD, in PA; d. Nov 23, 1940, Cumberland, MD; par. Oliver P. and Sarah A. (Folck) Hendrickson; m. Edith Cora Hamilton, 1897; c. Mary Willard; Lucille (Mrs. Herbert Platt). EDUC.: studied law under Judge A. Hunter Boyd. POLIT. & GOV.: court stenographer, 1895–1908; Prohibition Party candidate for atty. gen. of MD, 1899; member, Prohibition Party National Cmte., 1904–28 (exec. cmte., 1911); state chm., MD Prohibition Party, 1906–08; Prohibition Party candidate for

U.S. House (MD), 1910; ***candidate for Prohibition Party nomination to presidency of the U.S., 1912 (withdrew), 1916; candidate for Prohibition Party nomination to vice presidency of the U.S., 1916 (withdrew)***. BUS. & PROF.: atty.; admitted to Allegany (MD) Bar, 1895; law practice, Cumberland, MD, 1895–1940; pres., Evitts Creek Water Supply Co. MEM.: Allegany Cty. Bar Assn.; Allegany Cty. Hist. Soc. (founder); Kiwanis (lt. gov., Capitol District); Duke Memorial Bible Class (pres.). WRITINGS: *A Square Deal for Prohibition* (1906); "Shall Congress Prevent Interstate Liquor Traffic?" *American Business Man*, Mar 1908; *Can They?* (1909); *The Prohibition Party's Attitude Toward Other Great Reforms* (1909); *Availability of the 1898 Prohibition Party* (1909); "The Logic of Partisanship," *Vindicator*, Feb 5, 1915; *The Constitution and Prohibition* (1918). RES.: Cumberland, MD.

HENRY, JOHN. b. Nov 1750, Dorchester Cty., MD; d. Dec 16, 1798, Dorchester Cty., MD; par. Col. John and Dorothy (Rider) Henry; m. Margaret Campbell, Mar 6, 1787; c. John Campbell; Francis Jenkins. EDUC.: West Nottingham Acad.; grad., Coll. of NJ, 1769; studied law in the Temple, London, England. POLIT. & GOV.: elected to MD House of Delegates, 1775–1777; delegate, Continental Congress, 1778–1781, 1784–1787; elected member, MD State Senate, 1781–1784; elected as a Democrat to U.S. Senate (MD), 1789–1797; ***received 2 electoral votes for presidency of the U.S., 1796***; elected as a Democrat to gov. of MD, 1797–1798. BUS. & PROF.: atty.; admitted to Middle Temple, London, England; admitted to MD Bar, 1775; law practice, Dorchester Cty., MD. MEM.: Robin Hood Club. REL.: Episc. RES.: Dorchester Cty., MD.

HENRY, JOHN ROBERT. POLIT. & GOV.: ***independent candidate for presidency of the U.S., 1988***. MAILING ADDRESS: P.O. Box 1128, B-3, Las Gaviotas, Fajardo, Puerto Rico 00648.

HENSLEY, KIRBY JAMES. b. Jul 23, 1911, Burnsville, NC; par. John and Delilah May (McPeters) Hensley; m. Lida Gouge; c. Manzanita; Anthony; Andre John. EDUC.: public schools, NC and CA; D.D., Universal Life Church. POLIT. & GOV.: founder, Universal Party, 1963; ***Universal Party candidate for presidency of the U.S., 1964, 1968***; candidate for Peace and Freedom Party nomination to gov. of CA, 1970; founder, People's Peace and Prosperity Party, 1970; People's Peace and Prosperity Party candidate for gov. of CA, 1970; ***People's Peace and Prosperity Party candidate for presidency of the U.S., 1972, 1976***. BUS. & PROF.: carpenter; student of metaphysics; Baptist preacher, NC; Christian Scientist, FL; Pentecostal preacher, OK; founder, bishop, pres., Universal Life Church, Inc., 1962–; founder, Universal Press Assn.; founder, Universal Life Law School. WRITINGS: *Highlights of Nesley's Life*; "Holy Smoke" (song). REL.: Universal Life. MAILING ADDRESS: 1766 Poland Rd., Modesto, CA 95351.

HERBERT-TROUSDALE, LEON. POLIT. & GOV.: ***independent candidate for presidency of the U.S., 1984***. MISC.: active in marijuana initiative. MAILING ADDRESS: Berkeley, CA.

HERER, JACK. POLIT. & GOV.: ***Grassroots Party candidate for presidency of the U.S., 1988, 1992***. BUS. & PROF.: activist. MEM: Help End Marijuana Prohibition (founder; nat'l director). WRITINGS: G.R.A.S.S. (1973); The Emperor Wears No Clothes (1985). MISC.: proponent of legalized marijuana. MAILING ADDRESS: 14941 Burbank Blvd., #10, Van Nuys, CA 91411.

HERMANN, BEATRICE VIVIAN. b. Jan 17, 1918, Milwaukee, WI; par. Milton and Vivian (Ryan) Erbach; m. (divorced); c. Nancy Jaeger; Guy Harmann. EDUC.: B.S., U. of WI, 1945; M.A., Howard U., 1970. POLIT. & GOV.: vice chairperson, Socialist Party, 1976–78; delegate, Socialist Party National Convention, 1976 (vice chairperson); ***candidate for Socialist Party nomination to vice presidency of the U.S., 1976 (declined)***. BUS. & PROF.: teacher, Special Education Program, Green Bay, WI; instructor, Milwaukee Area Technical Coll., Milwaukee, WI; co-editor, *Milwaukee Indian News*; ed., *Socialist Tribune*. MEM.: Native American Solidarity Cmte.; Milwaukee Area Technical Coll. Teachers' Union; American Federation of Teachers; various Native American support groups; anti–nuclear development organizations. AWARDS: Special Award, Native American Students, Milwaukee Area Technical Coll.; Community Award for Service, Milwaukee Indian Community. MAILING ADDRESS: 2642 North Frederick Ave., Milwaukee, WI 53211.

HERNDON, ROBERT VERNON. b. Jul 30, 1914, Trigg Cty., KY; par. Nick O'Demus and Maggie Lee (Dawson) Herndon; m. Mary Frances Sholar; c. Robert Hayden; Jerry Allen; Kay Carol; Donald Wayne; Sandra Faye; James Dwight; Joy Anita; Nick Anthony. EDUC.: B.A., M.A., Trinity U., San Antonio, TX; Sacramento State Coll.; Murray State U.; U. of KY; Morehead State U. POLIT. & GOV.: ***independent candidate for presidency of the U.S., 1976, 1980***. BUS. & PROF.: education counselor; ordained minister. MIL.: special investigator, U.S. Air Force, 1942–55. MEM.: TX Classroom Education Assn. (pres.). WRITINGS: *Americans the Masters of Hypocrisy* (pseud. A. H. Sog); various articles and broadsides. REL.: Bapt. MAILING ADDRESS: Route 1, Box 190, Cadiz, KY 42211.

HERSTED, CLIFFORD. POLIT. & GOV.: ***Constructionalist Party candidate for presidency of the U.S., 1976***. MAILING ADDRESS: Chicago, IL?

HERTER, CHRISTIAN ARCHIBALD. b. Mar 28, 1895, Paris, France; d. Dec 30, 1966, Washington, DC; par. Albert and Adele (McGinnis) Herter; m. Mary Caroline Pratt, Aug 25, 1917; c. Christian Archibald, Jr.; Frederic Pratt; Adele (Mrs. Joseph Seronde); Eliot Miles. EDUC.: Ecole Alsatienne, 1901–04; Browning School, 1904–11; A.B. (cum laude), Harvard U., 1915. POLIT. & GOV.: attache, U.S. Embassy, Berlin, Germany, 1916–17; special asst., U.S. Dept. of State, 1917–18; sec., U.S. Comm. to Negotiate Peace, 1918–19; asst. to U.S. sec. of commerce, 1919–24; exec. sec., European Relief Council, 1920–21; elected as a Republican to MA State House, 1931–43 (Speaker, 1939–43); elected as a Republican to U.S. House (MA), 1943–53; elected as a Republican to gov. of MA, 1953–57; ***candidate for Republican nomination to presidency of the U.S., 1956; candidate for Republican nomination to vice presidency of the U.S., 1956***; appointed U.S. undersec. of state, 1957–59; appointed U.S. sec. of state, 1959–61. BUS. & PROF.: ed., *Independent*, 1924–28; assoc. ed., *The Sportsman*, 1927–36; lecturer on international relations, Harvard U., 1929–30. MEM.: Comm. for Relief of Belgium Educational Foundation (dir.); Foreign Service Educational Foundation (chm., Board of Trustees); World Peace Foundation (trustee); Boston Library Soc. (trustee); Harvard U. (overseer, 1940–44, 1950–56); Johns Hopkins U. (trustee); Century Club; Harvard Club; Somerset Club; Tavern Club; Metropolitan Club; Alibi Club; School of Advanced International Studies (Advisory Council); YMCA (International Cmte.); Foreign Policy Assn. AWARDS: Collier's Award for Distinguished Congressional Service, 1948; Gorgas Medal; Order of the Phoenix (grand commander, Greece); Order of Merit (Italy); Order of the Crown (Belgium); Order of Polonia Restituta (Poland). HON. DEG.: LL.D., Amherst Coll., 1954; LL.D., Boston U., 1954; LL.D., Bowdoin Coll., 1954; LL.D., Clark U., 1954; LL.D., Northeastern U., 1954; LL.D., Tufts U., 1954; LL.D., Williams Coll., 1954; LL.D., Boston Coll., 1955; LL.D., Brandeis U., 1955; LL.D., Springfield Coll., 1955; LL.D., Norwich U., 1956; LL.D., Portia Law School, 1956; LL.D., Brown U., 1959; LL.D., Harvard U., 1959; LL.D., Northwestern U., 1959; LL.D., Shaw U., 1959; D.P.A. RES.: Boston, MA.

HESLOP, KATHLEEN REBECCA "KATE."

POLIT. & GOV.: ***candidate for Republican nomination to presidency of the U.S., 1988***. BUS. & PROF.: teacher; operator, food marketing business. MAILING ADDRESS: c/o Gordon Brian Heslop, P.O. Box 16465, Hattiesburg, MS 39402.

HESTER, HUGH BRYANT.

b. Aug 5, 1895, Hester, NC; d. Nov 25, 1983, Asheville, NC; par. William Alexander and Monietta (Bullock) Hester; m. Paula Hester Green; c. none. EDUC.: grad., U. of NC; George Washington U.; U. of PA; grad., Field Artillery School, 1917. POLIT. & GOV.: ***Peace Party candidate for presidency of the U.S., 1964 (declined)***. BUS. & PROF.: soldier; lecturer; author. MIL.: commissioned 2d lt., U.S. Army, 1917, promoted through ranks to brig. gen., retired, 1951; assigned to Military Government of Germany, 1945–47; U.S. Military Attache to Australia, 1947–48; Distinguished Service Medal; Silver Star. MEM.: Legion of Honor (France). WRITINGS: *On the Brink* (coauthor, 1959); "Twenty-Six Disastrous Years," *The Reporter*, Sep 1971; *The Challenge of Our Times; The USA, USSR and Peace*. REL.: Unitarian-Universalist. RES.: Asheville, NC.

HESTERMANN, BRIAN JULES.

POLIT. & GOV.: ***independent candidate for presidency of the U.S., 1980***. MAILING ADDRESS: 3529 Tall Oak Circle, #4, Memphis, TN 38118.

HEWITT, ABRAM STEVENS.

b. Jul 31, 1822, Haverstraw, NY; d. Jan 18, 1903, Ringwood, NJ; par. John and Ann (Gurnee) Hewitt; m. Sarah Amelia Cooper, 1855; c. Mrs. James O. Green; Sarah C.; Edward R.; Eleanor G.; Erskine; Peter Cooper. EDUC.: A.M. (double first), Columbia U., 1842. POLIT. & GOV.: appointed U.S. scientific commissioner, "Exposition Universelle," Paris, France, 1867; elected as a Democrat to U.S. House (NY), 1875–79, 1881–86; chm., Dem. Nat'l. Cmte., 1876–77; elected as a Democrat to mayor of New York, NY, 1887–88; Democratic candidate for mayor of New York, NY, 1888; ***candidate for American Party nomination to presidency of the U.S., 1888; candidate for Democratic nomination to presidency of the U.S., 1888***; appointed member, Palisades Inst. Park Comm., 1900. BUS. & PROF.: acting prof. of mathematics, Columbia U., 1843; atty.; admitted to NY Bar, 1845; iron manufacturer; partner, Cooper and Hewitt (controlling firm for Trenton Iron Co.; New Jersey Iron and Steel Co.; Cooper Glue Factory); pres., U.S. Smelting Co.; pres., New York and Greenwood Lake R.R. Co.; vice pres., New Jersey Iron and Steel Co.; dir., Erie R.R. Co.; dir., Lehigh Coal and Navigating Co.; dir., Alabama Coal and Iron Co.; dir., Chrysolite Silver Mining Co.; dir., Montana Smelting Co.; dir., American Electric Elevator Co.; dir., United Smelting and Refining Co.; dir., New York, Lake Erie and Western Railway Co. MEM.: Cooper Union for the Advancement of Science and Art (sec.; dir.; organizer); NY Bar Assn.; Columbia U. (trustee, 1901); Barnard Coll. (chm., Board of trustees); Carnegie Inst. (trustee, 1901); American Inst. of Mining Engineers (pres., 1876, 1890); Southside Sportsmen's Club; Church Club; Metropolitan Club; Tuxedo Club; Century Club; Players' Club; City Club; Engineers' Club; Union Club; Riding Club; Columbia U. Alumni Assn. (pres., 1883); Tammany Hall; County Democracy. HON. DEG.: LL.D., Columbia U., 1887. MISC.: introduced first American open hearth furnace; son-in-law of Peter Cooper (q.v.). RES.: New York, NY.

HEYWOOD, EZRA HERVEY.

b. Sep 29, 1829, Princeton, MA; d. May 22, 1893, Boston, MA; par. Ezra and Dorcas (Roper) Hoar; m. Angela Fiducia Tilton, Jun 6, 1865; c. Hermes; Angelo; Vesta; Psyche Ceres. EDUC.: Westminster Acad.; grad., Brown U., 1856. POLIT. & GOV.: ***candidate for Equal Rights (Cosmic; Free Love; People's) Party nomination to vice presidency of the U.S., 1872***. BUS. & PROF.: publisher; author; reformer; owner, Cooperative Publishing Co., Princeton, MA, 1871; ed., *The Word*, 1872–93. MEM.: MA Anti-Slavery Soc.; Union Reform League; Working People's International

Assn.; Mountain Home Corp. (dir.); New England Free Love League (founder, 1873); New England Labor Reform Soc. (corresponding sec.; member, exec. cmte., 1871); National Labor Union (member, exec. cmte., 1868); Worcester Labor Reform League (corresponding sec., 1868). WRITINGS: *The Labor Party* (1868); *Uncivil Liberty* (1872); *Yours or Mine* (1873); *Hard Cash* (1874); *Free Trade; The Labor Movement; The Great Strike: A Review of the Railway Troubles of 1877; The Evolutionists* (1882); *Free Speech* (1883); *Social Ethics . . . Free Rum . . . Assures Temperance* (1889); *Cupid's Yokes, or the Binding Forces of Conjugal Life.* REL.: agnostic (nee Congregationalist). MISC.: advocate of free love, peace, equal rights; changed name from "Hoar" to "Heywood" by act of MA Legislature, 1848; convicted of mailing obscene materials, 1878; imprisoned for two years, but released by presidential pardon, 1879; arrested for same offense, 1882, 1883, but acquitted both times; convicted of offense of publishing obscene articles in *The Word*, 1890, and imprisoned, 1890–92. RES.: Princeton, MA.

HICKLE, WALTER JOSEPH. b. Aug 18, 1919, Claflin, KS; par. Robert A. and Emma (Zecha) Hickle; m. Ermalee Strutz, 1945; c. Ted; Bob; Wally; Jack; Joe; Karl. EDUC.: grad., Claflin (KS) H.S., 1936. POLIT. & GOV.: member, Rep. Nat'l. Cmte., 1954–64; elected as a Republican to gov. of AK, 1967–69; delegate, Rep. Nat'l. Conv., 1968, 1972, 1976; ***candidate for Republican nomination to president of the U.S., 1968***; appointed U.S. sec. of the interior, 1969–70; elected as an independent to gov. of AK, 1991–1995. BUS. & PROF.: pres., Hickel Investment Co., chm. of the board, 1962–; dir., Western Airlines, 1972; dir., Salk Inst. of Biological Studies, 1972; author. MEM.: AAAS (member, Cmte. on Scientific Freedom and Responsibility, 1971–); Boys Clubs of Alaska (dir., 1969); Elks; Navy League of the U.S.; Knights of Columbus. AWARDS: "Alaskan of the Year," 1969; DeSmet Medal, Gonzaga U., 1969; Man of the Year, Ripon Soc., 1970; Horatio Alger Award, American Schools and Colleges Assn., 1972. HON. DEG.: D.E., Stevens Inst. of Technology, 1970; LL.D., St. Mary of the Plains Coll., 1970; LL.D., Adelphi U., 1971; LL.D., St. Martin's Coll., 1971; LL.D., U. of MD, 1971; D.P.A., Willamette U., 1971; LL.D., U. of San Diego, 1972; D.Eng., MA Technological U., 1973; LL.D., Rensselaer Polytechnic Inst., 1973; LL.D., U. of AK, 1976. WRITINGS: *Who Owns America?* (1971). REL.: R.C. MAILING ADDRESS: 1905 Loussac Dr., Anchorage, AK 99503.

HICKMAN, JOHN. b. Sep 11, 1810, West Bradford Township, PA; d. Mar 23, 1875, West Chester, PA. EDUC.: studied medicine and law. POLIT. & GOV.: delegate, Dem. Nat'l. Conv., 1844; elected as a Democrat to U.S. House (PA), 1855–61, as a Republican, 1861–63; ***candidate for Republican nomination to vice presidency of the U.S., 1860***; elected as a Republican to PA State House, 1869–71. BUS. & PROF.: atty.; admitted to PA Bar, 1833; law practice, West Chester, PA. appointed U.S. House mgr. in impeachment proceedings against Judge West H. Humphreys. RES.: West Chester, PA.

HICKMAN, WDUAN DAVID. POLIT. & GOV.: ***independent candidate for presidency of the U.S., 1988***. MAILING ADDRESS: c/o Edward Joseph Mack, 7903 Radcliffe, Detroit, MI 48210.

HIGBY, LESTER, SR. c. Lester, Jr. POLIT. & GOV.: candidate for Peace and Freedom Party nomination to gov. of CA, 1974; ***independent candidate for presidency of the U.S., 1976***. BUS. & PROF.: philosopher. MAILING ADDRESS: 1559 Hawthorne Ave., Chico, CA.

HIGGINBOTHAM, CECIL EUGENE. POLIT. & GOV.: ***independent candidate for presidency of the U.S., 1968***. MAILING ADDRESS: Bellwood, NE 68624.

HIGGINBOTHAM, RUFUS TAYLOR. b. Jun 20, 1932, Dallas, TX; par. Rufus Taylor, Sr. and Sybil (Johnson) Higginbotham; m. Lou Ann Jordan; c. Taylor; Andrew; Laura. EDUC.: B.B.A., Southern Methodist U., 1953, J.D., 1955; M.Div., Southwest Baptist Theological Seminary, 1976. POLIT. & GOV.: candidate for Dallas (TX) City Council, 1960; Democratic candidate for TX State House, 1962; candidate for U.S. House (TX), 1991; candidate for mayor of Dallas, TX, 1991; ***candidate for Democratic nomination to presidency of the U.S., 1992***. BUS. & PROF.: atty.; law practice, Dallas, 1955–73; pastoral asst., First Baptist Church, Dallas, 1976–90. MIL.: lt., U.S. Air Force, 1955–57. MEM.: National Space Soc.; Planetary Soc.; TX Bar Assocation; Idlewild Club (vice pres.). REL.: Bapt. MISC.: noted for advocacy of U.S. space program. MAILING ADDRESS: c/o Jeanette Brantley, 3511 North Hall St., Suite 301, Dallas, TX 75219.

HILDEBRANDT, FRED HERMAN. b. Aug 2, 1874, West Bend, WI; d. Jan 26, 1956, Bradenton, FL; par. Charles F. and Mary (Straub) Hildebrandt; m. Mary Berner, Jan 1, 1910. EDUC.: public schools. POLIT. & GOV.: elected as a Democrat to SD State House, 1922–23; independent candidate for U.S. House (SD), 1924; Democratic candidate for U.S. House (SD), 1926, 1928, 1930, 1942; chm., SD Game and Fish Comm., 1927–31; elected as a Democrat to U.S. House (SD), 1933–39; candidate for Democratic nomination to U.S. Senate (SD), 1938; delegate, Dem. Nat'l. Conv., 1944; ***candidate for Democratic nomination to presidency of the U.S., 1944, 1948***. BUS. & PROF.: railroad freight brakeman, Watertown, SD, 1903–06; railroad freight conductor, 1906–11; railroad passenger conductor, 1911–32. MEM.: Order of Railroad Conductors; Masons; Kiwanis. RES.: Watertown, SD.

HILDER, ANTHONY J. EDUC.: Santa Monica (CA) City Coll. POLIT. & GOV.: ***candidate for American Independent Party nomination to presidency of the U.S., 1972; candidate for American Party nomination to presidency of the U.S., 1980***. BUS. & PROF.: owner, American United Recording Co.; owner, Fact Recording Co.; owner, American Star Attractions, Hollywood, CA; public relations coordinator, Fidelis Publishing Co.; author; actor; instructor, "Basic Principles of Contemporary Illuminism," U. of CA, Santa Barbara; lecturer; radio host, station KPFK, North Hollywood, CA; television host, *Impact*, Los Angeles, CA; war correspondent, Rhodesia. MOTION PICTURE CREDITS: *Summer Love*, Universal Studios. Television Credits: M *Squad*, G.E. *Theater*. Recordings: "The Illuminati" (1967); "Communism, Big Money and You"; "The Establishment CFR"; "The Moneychangers"; "Pawns in the Game"; "A Texan Looks at Lyndon." MEM.: Screen Actors' Guild; A.F.T.R.A.; A.S.C.A.P.; American Center for Education; Families Opposing Revolutionary Donations. AWARDS: Congress of Freedom Award. WRITINGS: *The War Lords of Washington*; *The Free World* (1980). REL.: Christian. MAILING ADDRESS: 11903 West Pico Blvd., West Los Angeles, CA.

HILL, DAVID BENNETT. b. Aug 29, 1843, Havana, NY; d. Oct 20, 1910, Albany, NY; par. Caleb and Eunice (Durfey) Hill; single. EDUC.: Havana (NY) Acad.; studied law under Erastus P. Hart, Elmira, NY. POLIT. & GOV.: appointed city atty., Elmira, NY, 1865; delegate, NY State Democratic Conventions, 1868–81 (chm., 1877, 1881); elected as a Democrat to NY State Assembly, 1871–72 (Speaker, 1872); elected as a Democrat to alderman, Elmira, 1880–81; elected as a Democrat to mayor of Elmira, 1882; elected as a Democrat to lt. gov. of NY, 1882–85; delegate, Dem. Nat'l. Conv., 1884, 1896, 1900, 1904; succeeded to gov. and subsequently elected as a Democrat to gov. of NY, 1885–91; ***candidate for Democratic nomination to presidency of the U.S., 1888, 1892, 1896***; elected as a Democrat to U.S. Senate (NY), 1891–97; Democratic candidate for gov. of NY, 1894; ***candidate for Democratic nomination to vice presidency of the U.S., 1900***. BUS. & PROF.: atty.; admitted to NY Bar, 1864; law practice, Elmira, 1864–97; law practice, Albany, NY, 1897–1910; proprietor, *Elmira Gazette*. MEM.: NY State Bar Assn. (pres., 1886–87). RES.: Elmira, NY.

HILL, MICHAEL JOHN. b. Dec 28, 1954, Joliet, IL; par. Elton J. and Delores Congetta (Romano) Hill; single. EDUC.: B.S., Northern IL U., 1977. POLIT. & GOV.: ***independent candidate for presidency of the U.S., 1980 (withdrew)***. BUS. & PROF.: police reporter, *Muncie (IN) Star*, 1977–78; investigative reporter, *Oshkosh (WI) Northwestern*, 1978–. MEM.: Northern IL U. Student Assn. (adviser, 1975–76). REL.: R.C. MAILING ADDRESS: 800 A Waugoo St., Oshkosh, WI 54901.

HILL, R. C. (See ROBBINS, CROWN).

HILL, RICHARD RHORER. b. Aug 22, 1942, Fort Worth, TX; par. James Edwin and Helen Elizabeth (Rhorer) Hill; m. Margaret Josephine Corcoran, Jul 5, 1968 (divorced); c. none. EDUC.: B.A., Harvard U., 1964, J.D., 1972. POLIT. & GOV.: ***candidate for Democratic nomination to presidency of the U.S., 1980, 1984, 1988***. BUS. & PROF.: atty.; admitted to TX Bar, 1972; assoc., Baker and Botts (law firm), Houston, TX, 1972; employee, Meeker Investments, Houston, 1974–84; pres., All and Everything, Inc., Houston. MIL.: capt., U.S.M.C., 1965–67. MEM.: ABA; Houston Bar Assn.; State Bar of TX. REL.: Scientologist. MAILING ADDRESS: 3437 Overbrook Lane, Houston, TX 77027.

HILL, THOMAS HALLOWELL. b. Dec 8, 1960, Boston, MA; par. Thomas Dane and Carol (Hallowell) Hill; m. Alison Friesinger, Sep 20, 1986; c. none. EDUC.: B.A., Harvard U. POLIT. & GOV.: ***independent candidate for presidency of the U.S., 1984***. BUS. & PROF.: freelance writer. MEM.: Big Brothers of America. WRITINGS: *Salute Your Shorts: Life at Summer Camp* (1986); *Varsity Coach: Fourth and Goal* (1986). REL.: Episc. MAILING ADDRESS: 232 Elizabeth St., #5C, New York, NY 10012.

HILL, WALTER BARNARD. b. Sep 9, 1851, Talbottom, GA; d. Dec 28, 1905, Athens, GA; par. Barnard and Mary Clay (Birch) Hill; m. Sallie Parna Barker, Oct 22, 1879; c. Parna B.; Mary M.; Walter Barnard, Jr.; Roger M. EDUC.: Collingsworth Inst.; A.B. (cum laude), U. of GA, 1870, M.A., 1871, LL.B., 1871. POLIT. & GOV.: appointed member, GA State Code Comm., 1873, 1882; elected city atty., Macon, GA, 1876–82; presidential elector, Prohibition Party, 1888, 1892; ***candidate for Prohibition Party nomination to presidency of the U.S., 1892; candidate for Prohibition Party nomination to vice presidency of the U.S., 1892***. BUS. & PROF.: atty.; admitted to GA Bar, 1871; partner (with Barnard Hill), law firm, Macon, 1871–73; partner, Hill and Harris (law firm), Macon, 1873–99; prof. of law, Mercer U., 1894–99; dir., Southern Mutual Insurance Co.; contributor, *Century Magazine*; contributor, *Christian Thought*; partner, Lanier and Anderson (law firm), Macon; counsel, Covington and Macon R.R.; counsel, Empire and Dublin R.R.; counsel, Middle Georgia and Atlantic R.R.; chancellor, U. of GA, 1899–1905; member, Western and Atlantic Railroad Comm., GA. MEM.: ABA; GA Bar Assn. (pres., 1887–88); Southern GA Methodist Orphans Home (chm. of the board); Emory Coll. (trustee); GA State School for Colored Youths (trustee); Vanderbilt U. (trustee); Southern Board of Education (dir.); Southern Educational Assn. (pres.). HON. DEG.: LL.D., Emory Coll., 1899; LL.D., Southwestern Presbyterian U., 1899; LL.D., SC Coll., 1905. WRITINGS: *Code of Georgia* (1873, 1882); "Uncle Tom Without a Cabin," *Century Magazine*; "Anarchy, Socialism, and the Labor Movement," *Christian Thought* (1886); *Memoirs of the General Conference of the Methodist Episcopal Church* (1886–94). REL.: Methodist (delegate, General Conference, 1886, 1890, 1894; delegate, Ecumenical Conference, 1890; chm. of the board, Mulberry Street Methodist Church). RES.: Macon, GA.

HILLE, SACREDE LORDE CHRISTE AMERICAESE DEVILE GODE. POLIT. & GOV.: ***candidate for Democratic nomination to presidency of the U.S., 1980***. MAILING ADDRESS: 2250 Third Ave., Sacramento, CA.

HILLS, CARLA ANDERSON. b. Jan 3, 1934, Los Angeles, CA; par. Carl H. and Edith (Hume) Anderson; m. Roderick Maltman Hills, Sep 27, 1958; c. Laura Hume; Roderick Maltman, Jr.; Megan Elizabeth; Alison Macbeth. EDUC.: St. Hilda's Coll., Oxford U., 1954; A.B. (cum laude), Stanford U., 1955; LL.B., Yale U., 1958. POLIT. & GOV.: asst. U.S. atty., Civil Div., Los Angeles, CA, 1958–61; appointed member, Corrections Task Force, CA Council on Criminal Justice, 1969–71; appointed member, Standing Cmte. on Discipline, U.S. District Court for Central CA, 1970–73; member, Administrative Conference of the U.S., 1972–; appointed asst. atty. gen., Civil Div., U.S. Dept. of Justice, 1974–75; appointed U.S. sec. of housing and urban development, 1975–77; ***candidate for Republican nomination to vice presidency of the U.S., 1976***; appointed U.S. trade representative, 1989–93. BUS. & PROF.: atty.; admitted to CA Bar, 1959; admitted to the Bar of the Supreme Court of the U.S., 1965; partner, Munger, Tolles, Hills and Rickershauser (law firm), Los Angeles, CA, 1962–74; adjunct prof. of law, U. of CA at Los Angeles, 1972; dir., IBM Corp.; dir., Signal Companies, Inc.; dir., Standard Oil Co.; dir., American Airlines, Inc.; partner, Latham, Watkins and Hills (law firm), 1978–. MEM.: Yale Club of Southern CA (dir., 1972–74); State Bar of CA (member, Exec. Cmte. on Law and a Free Soc., 1973); U. of Southern CA Law Center (member, Board of Councilors, 1972–74); Pomona Coll. (trustee, 1974–); Yale Law School (member, exec. cmte., 1973–); Yale U. Council (member, Cmte. on Law School); American Bar Foundation (fellow); ABA (Council, 1974); Brookings Institution (trustee); Alliance to Save Energy (co-chm., 1977–); American Law Inst.; Federal Bar Assn. (pres., Los Angeles Chapter, 1963); Los Angeles Cty. Bar Assn. (chm., Issues and Survey Cmte., 1963–72; chm., Subcommittee on Revision of Local Rules for Federal Courts, 1966–72; member, Judicial Qualifications Cmte., 1971–72). WRITINGS: *Federal Civil Practice* (coauthor, 1961); *Antitrust Adviser* (coauthor, 1971). HON. DEG.: LL.D., Pepperdine U., 1975. MAILING ADDRESS: 3125 Chain Bridge Rd., Washington, DC 20016.

HIMMELMAN, GERARD ANDREW "JERRY." b. Jan 24, 1933, Newton, MA; c. Gerard Andrew, Jr. POLIT. & GOV.: ***candidate for Democratic nomination to presidency of the U.S., 1980, 1984***. BUS. & PROF.: inventor; composer; author; marketer, Og the Frog. MEM.: Disabled American Veterans. AWARDS: Award, Future Farmers of America, 1950. MAILING ADDRESS: 950 South Concourse, Cliffwood Beach, NJ 07735.

HINES, FRANK THOMAS. b. Apr 11, 1879, Salt Lake City, UT; d. Apr 3, 1960, Washington, DC; par. Frank L. and Martha (Hollingsworth) Hines; m. Nellie M. Vier, Oct 4, 1900; c. Mrs. Vera H. Kennedy; Frank Thomas, Jr. EDUC.: honor grad., Coast Guard Artillery School, 1904; grad., Coast Guard Artillery School, 1911. POLIT. & GOV.: delegate, Interallied Transport Council, 1918; ***candidate for Democratic nomination to presidency of the U.S., 1920***; appointed dir., U.S. Veterans' Bureau, 1923–30; ***candidate for Republican nomination to vice presidency of the U.S., 1924***; appointed administrator of Veterans' Affairs, 1930–44; appointed administrator, Re-Training and Re-Employment Administration, 1944–45; appointed U.S. ambassador to Panama, 1945. BUS. & PROF.: soldier; businessman; pres., Baltic Steamship Co.; dir., Sperry Gyroscope Corp.; dir., Continental Trust Co.; dir., Acacia Life Insurance Co. MIL.: first sgt., Battery B, UT Light Artillery, 1898–99; commissioned 2d lt., UT Light Artillery, 1899; mustered out of volunteers, 1899; commissioned 2d lt., Artillery Corps, U.S. Army, 1901; promoted through grades to brig. gen., 1918; appointed chief of Embarkation, 1918; appointed chief of transportation service, U.S. Army, 1919; resigned, 1920; appointed brig. gen., Officers' Reserve Corps, 1920; Distinguished Service Medal, U.S. Army; Distinguished Service Medal, U.S. Navy; companion, Order of the Bath (Great Britain); Grand Officer, Ordre de Leopold (Belgium); Legion of Honor (France); Order of Sacred Treasure, Second Class (Japan); War Cross (Czechoslovakia). MEM.: A.S.M.E.; Sulgrave Club; Army-Navy Club; Army and Navy Assn.; Bonneville Club; New York Stock Exchange (candidate for pres., 1941); Military Order of the World War; American Legion Reserve Corps; VFW; United Spanish War Veterans; Temple Noyes Lodge No. 32. HON. DEG.: LL.D., Agricultural Coll. of UT, 1920; LL.D., Lincoln Memorial U., 1927; LL.D., U. of AL, 1932. WRITINGS: *Service of Coast Artillery* (coauthor). REL.: Episc. (vestryman). MISC.: received 1 vote for presidential nomination on 28th ballot, Dem. Nat'l. Conv., 1920. RES.: Spring Valley, VA.

HIRSHON, RUSSELL MUNOZ BAPTISTE. b. 1962, Washington, DC. EDUC.: limited college education. POLIT. & GOV.: candidate for mayor, Washington, DC, 1991; ***candidate for Democratic nomination to presidency of the U.S., 1992***. BUS. & PROF.: bartender, Washington, DC. MAILING ADDRESS: 1630 Florida Ave., N.W., #202, Washington, DC 20009.

HISCOCK, FRANK. b. Sep 6, 1834, Pompey, NY; d. Jun 18, 1914, Syracuse, NY; par. Richard and Cynthia (Harris) Hiscock; m. Cornelia King, Nov 22, 1859; c. Albert King; Fidelio King. EDUC.: Pompey Acad.; studied law. POLIT. & GOV.: elected district atty., Onondaga Cty., NY, 1860–63; delegate, NY State Constitutional Convention, 1867; Liberal Republican Party candidate for U.S. House (NY), 1872; delegate, Rep. Nat'l. Conv., 1876; elected as a Republican to U.S. House (NY), 1877–87; elected as a Republican to U.S. Senate (NY), 1887–93; ***candidate for Republican nomination to presidency of the U.S., 1888***. BUS. & PROF.: atty.; admitted to NY Bar, 1855; law practice, Tully, NY; partner, L. H. and F. Hiscock (law firm); partner, Hiscock, Doheny and Gifford (law firm); senior partner, Hiscock, Doheny, Williams and Cowie (law firm), Syracuse, NY, 1893–1914; dir., State Bank of Syracuse; dir., Syracuse Savings Bank; dir., Trust and Deposit Company of Onondaga. RES.: Syracuse, NY.

HISGEN, THOMAS LOUIS. b. Nov 26, 1858, Petersburg, IN; d. Aug 26, 1925, Springfield, MA; par. William von and Catherine Margaret (McNally) Hisgen; m. Barbara Anne Fox, May 28, 1900; c. Thomas Louis; Catherine Elizabeth (Mrs. Edson Somerville); Henrietta Georgiana (Mrs. Courtney Warren Campbell). EDUC.: public schools, Albany, NY; public schools, IN. POLIT. & GOV.: Democratic (Independence League Party) candidate for state auditor of MA, 1906; Independence League Party candidate for gov. of MA, 1907; ***National Independence League Party candidate for presidency of the U.S., 1908***; Progressive Party candidate for U.S. House (MA), 1912. BUS. & PROF.: salesman, clothing store, Albany, 1880; manufacturer; pres., Four Brothers Axle Grease Co., 1882–98; pres., Four Brothers Independent Oil Co., 1898–1917; owner, Thomas Music Co.; pres., Farmers and Drovers Stockyards Co., Buffalo, NY. MEM.: Independent Petroleum Marketers Assn. of the U.S. (founder; pres.); Odd Fellows (noble grand master); Knights of Pythias; Loyal Order of Moose. WRITINGS: *Anti-Discrimination Unfair Trade Bill* (first antimonopoly bill passed in New England). Songs: "Language of Love" (1916); "Irish Lass of Mine" (1920). REL.: Presb. MISC.: engaged in famous antimonopoly fight with Standard Oil Co. RES.: Springfield, MA.

HITCHCOCK, GILBERT MONELL. b. Sep 18, 1859, Omaha, NE; d. Feb 3, 1934, Washington, DC; par. Phineas Warren and Annie (Monell) Hitchcock; m. Jessie Crounse, Aug 30, 1883; m. 2d, Martha Harris, Jun 1, 1927; c. Margaret (Mrs. Henry Doorly); Ruth. EDUC.: LL.B., U. of MI, 1881. POLIT. & GOV.: Democratic candidate for U.S. House (NE), 1898, 1904; elected as a Democrat to U.S. House (NE), 1903–05, 1907–11; elected as a Democrat to U.S. Senate (NE), 1911–23 (minority leader, 1919–20); ***candidate for Democratic nomination to presidency of the U.S., 1920, 1924, 1928; candidate for Democratic nomination to vice presidency of the U.S., 1920***; Democratic candidate for U.S. Senate (NE), 1922, 1930; delegate, Dem. Nat'l. Conv., 1924, 1932. BUS. & PROF.: atty.; admitted to NE Bar, 1882; law practice, Omaha, NE, 1882–85; owner, *Omaha Evening World*, 1885–89; owner, publisher, *Omaha World-Herald*, 1889–1934. RES.: Omaha, NE.

HITCHCOCK, RUFUS WILBUR. b. Jul 23, 1868, Mt. Clemens, MI; d. Feb 10, 1961, Rapid City, SD; par. Thomas Wilbur and Mary Sayer (Snook) Hitchcock; m. Mary Ann Cameron, Aug 20, 1896; c. Paul C.; John W.; Jean McRae (Mrs. Warren Morrell). EDUC.: U. of MI. POLIT. & GOV.: elected as a Republican to SD State House, 1919–34 (chm., Appropriations Cmte., 1925–31); delegate, Rep. Nat'l. Conv., 1928, 1944 (alternate); 1948 (chm., SD Delegation); publicity chm., SD State Republican Central Cmte., 1934–36; ***candidate for Republican nomination to presidency of the U.S., 1948***. BUS. & PROF.: teacher; school principal; city superintendent of schools, Crookston, MN, 1889–1901; reporter, *Daily Times*, Crookston; editorial writer, *Herald*, Duluth, MN; publisher, *Daily Pioneer*, Bimidji, MN; publisher, *Chishol (MN) Tribune;* publisher, *Buhl (MN) Advertiser;* publisher, *Hibbing (MN) Daily Tribune*, 1906–61; publisher, *Rapid City (SD) Daily Journal*, 1939–61. MEM.: Minnesota Club; Masons (Red Cross of Constantinople, 1953–59; Shriners; commandery); Elks; Rotary Club; Community Chest; Black Hills Hospital (dir.); Bennett-Clarkson Memorial Hospital (dir.). AWARDS: Meritorious Achievement in Public Affairs Award, SD School of Mines and Technology, 1954; Seventy Year Palm, Grand Lodge of Masons of South Dakota, 1957; "Boss of the Year" Award, Rapid City Junior C. of C., 1958. HON. DEG.: D.H.L., SD School of Mines and Technology, 1958. WRITINGS: various travel booklets. REL.: Presb. RES.: Rapid City, SD.

HITT, ROBERT ROBERTS. b. Jan 16, 1834, Urbana, OH; d. Sep 19, 1906, Narragansett Pier, RI; par. Thomas Smith and Emily (John) Hitt; m. Sallie Reynolds, Oct 28, 1874; c. two sons. EDUC.: Rock River Seminary (now Mount Morris Coll.); grad., De Pauw U., 1855. POLIT. & GOV.: official stenographer, IL Legislature, 1858–60; reporter, U.S. House, 1872; first sec., charge d'affaires ad interim, U.S. Legation, Paris, France, 1874–81; appointed asst. U.S. sec. of state, 1881; elected as a Republican to U.S. House (IL), 1882–1906; appointed member, Hawaiian Islands Comm., 1898; ***candidate for Republican nomination to vice presidency of the U.S., 1904***. BUS. & PROF.: reporter, Lincoln-Douglas Debates, 1858; stenographer. MEM.: Smithsonian Institution (regent, 1893–1906); World's Fair Cmte. RES.: Mount Morris, IL.

HOADLY, GEORGE. b. Jul 31, 1826, New Haven, CT; d. Aug 26, 1902, Watkins, NY; par. George and Mary Anne (Woolsey) Scarborough Hoadly; m. Mary Burnet Perry, Aug 13, 1851; m. 2d, Genevieve Groesbeck, May 5, 1894; c. Genevieve Olivia; George, Jr.; one other son. EDUC.: grad., Western Reserve Coll., 1844; Harvard U. Law School; studied law under Salmon P. Chase (q.v.). POLIT. & GOV.: elected judge, Superior Court, Cincinnati, OH, 1851–53, 1859–66; elected city solicitor, Cincinnati, 1855–58; appointed justice, Supreme Court of OH, 1856 (declined), 1862 (declined); delegate, Liberal Republican Party National Convention, 1872; elected as a Democrat to OH State Constitutional Convention, 1873–74; chm. pro tempore, Dem. Nat'l. Conv., 1880; elected as a Democrat to gov. of OH, 1883–85; ***candidate for Democratic nomination to presidency of the U.S., 1884***; Democratic candidate for gov. of OH, 1885. BUS. & PROF.: atty.; admitted to OH Bar, 1847; partner (with Salmon P. Chase), Chase and Ball (law firm), Cincinnati, 1849–51; partner, Hoadly, Jackson and Johnson (law firm), Cincinnati, 1866–87; prof., Cincinnati Law School, 1884–87; partner, Hoadly, Lauterbach and Johnson (law firm), New York, NY, 1887–1902. MEM.: U. of OH (trustee); U. of Cincinnati (trustee); Masons (Scottish Rite). REL.: Unitarian. RES.: Cincinnati, OH.

HOBART, GARRET AUGUSTUS. b. Jun 3, 1844, Long Branch, NJ; d. Nov 21, 1899, Paterson, NJ; par. Addison Willard and Sophia (Vanderveer) Hobart; m. Jennie Tuttle, Jul 21, 1869; c. Fannie Beckwith; Garret Augustus, Jr. EDUC.: grad. (with honors), Rutgers Coll., 1863; studied law under Socrates Tuttle, Paterson, NJ. POLIT. & GOV.: clerk, grand jury, Passaic Cty., NJ, 1865; elected to city counsel, Paterson, 1871–72; counsel, Board of Chosen Freeholders, Passaic Cty., 1873; elected as a Republican to NJ State House, 1873–77 (Speaker, 1874); delegate, Rep. Nat'l. Conv., 1876, 1880, 1884, 1892, 1896; elected as a Republican to NJ State Senate, 1877–82 (pres., 1881–82); chm., NJ State Republican Cmte., 1880–91; member, Rep. Nat'l. Cmte., 1884–96 (chm., 1892–96); Republican candidate for U.S. Senate (NJ), 1884; ***elected as a Republican to vice presidency of the U.S., 1897–99***. BUS. & PROF.: atty.; schoolteacher; licensed in law, 1866; admitted to NJ Bar, 1869; designated counselor at law, 1871; designated master in chancery, 1872; law practice, Paterson; partner, Tuttle and Hobart (law firm), Paterson; banker; pres., Passaic Water Co., 1885; dir., Barbour Brothers Co.; pres., Acquackanonck Water Co.; pres., People's Gas Co.; gen. mgr., East Jersey Water Co.; dir., Paterson Railway Co.; pres., Morris County R.R. Co.; dir., First National Bank of Paterson; dir., Paterson Savings Institution; dir., New York, Susquehanna and Western R.R.; dir., Edison Electric Illuminating Co.; dir., Barbour Flax Spinning Co.; dir., American Cotton Seed Oil Co.; dir., Dundee Water, Power and Light Co.; dir., Lehigh and Hudson River R.R.; dir., Liberty National Bank; dir., Pioneer Silk Co.; dir., Passaic Gas Light Co.; dir., Paterson Electric Light Co.; dir., Citizens Insurance Co.; dir., Long Branch Water Co.; dir., Highland Water Co.; treas., Cedar Lawn Cemetery Co. HON. DEG.: LL.D., Rutgers Coll., 1896. REL.: Presb. RES.: Paterson, NJ.

HOBSON, JULIUS WILSON. b. May 29, 1922, Birmingham, AL; d. Mar 23, 1977, Washington, DC; par. Julius Wilson and Irma (Gordon) Hobson; m. Carol Smith, 1947 (divorced, 1966); m. 2d, Tina Lower, 1969; c. Julius Wilson, Jr.; Jean Marie; Eric K. Lower; Conrad W. Lower. EDUC.: Industrial H.S., Birmingham, AL; Tuskegee Inst.; Columbia U.; B.S., Wayne State U., 1946; M.A., Howard U., 1949. POLIT. & GOV.: appointed member, Advisory Cmte. to Chief of Police, Washington, DC, 1964–65; elected member, DC School Board, 1968; candidate for DC School Board, 1969; chm., DC Statehood Party, 1971–77; DC Statehood Party candidate for U.S. House (DC), 1971; ***People's Party candidate for vice presidency of the U.S., 1972***; elected as a DC Statehood Party candidate to City Council, Washington, DC, 1974–77. BUS. & PROF.: educator; lecturer, American U.; dir., Washington Inst. for Quality Education; peace activist; civil rights advocate; employee, Library of Congress, Washington, DC; employee, Social Security Administration, Washington, DC. MIL.: U.S. Army, WWII; three Bronze Stars. MEM.: Slowe Elementary School PTA (pres.); Federation of Civic Associations (vice pres.); NAACP (exec. cmte.); Congress on Racial Equality (pres., DC Chapter, 1961–64); Emergency Cmte. on Transportation Crisis; Woodridge Civic Assn. (pres.); Union of Federal Employees; Associated Community Teams (founder; chm.); American Federation of State, County, and Municipal Employees; United Black Front; Advisory Cmte. on Budget, Superintendent's Cmte. on the DC Public Schools. AWARDS: "Outstanding Contribution to Civil Rights" Award, Omega Psi Phi, 1962; Humanities Award (Citizen of the Year) for Civil Rights, DC Federation of Civic Associations, 1962, 1967; "Outstanding Citizen of the Year" Award, YMCA, 1962; "Civil Rights Man of the Year" Award, Capital Press Club, 1963; Equal Opportunity Award, DC C. of C., 1963; Leadership in Human Rights Award, National Congress on Racial Equality, 1964; certificate, DC Metropolitan Police Dept.; "Outstanding Citizen in Education" Award, DC Education Assn., 1967; Liberty Bell Award for Outstanding Lay Contribution to Law in the U.S., Howard U. Law School, 1968; Liberty Bell Award, Federal Bar Assn., 1969; Award for Excellent Educational Contributions, American Federation of Teachers-Washington Teachers Union, 1970; Key to the City, Alexandria, VA, 1971. WRITINGS: *Economic Discrimination in D.C. Public Schools* (coauthor, 1957); *Civil Rights in the Nation's Capital—A Decade of Progress* (coauthor, 1959); *Democracy in the D.C. Public Schools* (contributor); *The Black Power Revolt* (contributor, 1968); "Uncle Sam is a Bigot," *Saturday Evening Post* (1968); *Center City Education Survey Methods* (1969); *Black Pride* (coauthor, 1969); *The Damned Children—A Layman's Guide to Forcing Change in Public Education* (1970); *The Damned Information*. REL.: atheist. RES.: Washington, DC.

HOBSON, RICHMOND PEARSON. b. Aug 17, 1870, Greensboro, AL; d. Mar 16, 1937, NY, NY; par. James Marcellus and Sarah Croom (Pearson) Hobson; m. Grizelda Houston Hull, May 25, 1905; c. Richmond Pearson, Jr.; Lucia Houston; George Hull. EDUC.: Southern U., 1882–85, LL.D., 1906; grad., U.S. Naval Acad., 1889; Ecole National Superieur des Mines; Ecole d'Application du Genie Maritime, 1893; M.S., Washington and Jefferson Coll., 1898. POLIT. & GOV.: presidential elector, Democratic Party, 1904; elected as a Democrat to U.S. House (AL), 1907–15; ***candidate for Democratic nomination to presidency of the U.S., 1912***; delegate, Dem. Nat'l. Conv., 1920. BUS. & PROF.: naval officer; lecturer; author; temperance advocate. MIL.: midshipman, U.S. Navy, 1889–90; on duty, U.S. Navy Dept., 1894–95; with Construction Corps, U.S. Navy, 1895–97; instructor, U.S. Naval Acad., 1897–98; prisoner-of-war, 1898; resigned, 1903; Medal of Honor, 1933; named rear adm., U.S. Navy, by act of Congress, 1934. MEM.: American Alcohol Education Assn. (organizer; gen. sec., 1921); International Narcotic Education Assn. (pres., 1923); World Conference on Narcotic Education (gen. sec., 1926); World Narcotic Defense Assn. (pres., 1927); Constitutional Democracy Assn. (pres., 1935). WRITINGS: *Alcohol and the Human Race for Truth Inoculation of Society* (1919); *Narcotic Peril* (1925); *The Modern Pirates—Exterminate Them* (1931); *Drug Addiction: A Malignant Racial Cancer* (1933). RES.: New York, NY.

HOCHMAN, LAWRENCE D. b. 1930; married; c. two. EDUC.: B.S., M.S., Wayne State U.; Ph.D., Adelphia U.,

1967. POLIT. & GOV.: ***New Politics Party candidate for vice presidency of the U.S., 1968***. BUS. & PROF.: prof. of physics, Queens Coll., New York, NY; prof. of physics, San Jose State Coll., San Jose, CA; assoc. prof. of physics, Eastern Michigan U., Ypsilanti, MI. WRITINGS: *Zionism and the Israeli State* (196?); *Calculation of the Intensity of Low Energy Secondary Cosmic Ray Nuclei in Space* (1967). MAILING ADDRESS: 1322 Brooklyn, Ann Arbor, MI.

HODGES, LUTHER HARTWELL. b. Mar 9, 1898, Pittsylvania Cty., VA; d. Oct 6, 1974, Chapel Hill, NC; par. John James and Lovicia (Gammon) Hodges; m. Martha Elizabeth Blakeney, Jun 24, 1922; m. 2d, Louise B. Finlayson, 1970; c. Betsy; Nancy; Luther. EDUC.: A.B., U. of NC, 1919. POLIT. & GOV.: appointed member, NC State Board of Education, 1929–33; member, NC State Highway Comm., c. 1933; member, NC State Public Works Comm., c. 1933; chief, Textile Div., OPA, 1944; consultant, U.S. sec. of agriculture, 1945; chief, Industry Div., Economic Cooperation Administration, West Germany, 1950; elected as a Democrat to lt. gov. of NC, 1952–54; succeeded to and subsequently elected as a Democrat to gov. of NC, 1954–61; delegate, Dem. Nat'l. Conv., 1956; ***candidate for Democratic nomination to vice presidency of the U.S., 1956***; appointed U.S. sec. of commerce, 1961–65. BUS. & PROF.: sec. to gen. mgr., Eight Mills, Spray, NC, 1919, mgr., 1933; production mgr., Marshall Field and Co., 1936–38, gen. mgr., 1938–43, vice pres. in charge of mills, 1943–50; chm. of the board, Research Triangle; NC dir., Servomation Corp.; dir., Speizman Industries; dir., Fidelity Mortgage Investors; dir., Gulf and Western Industries, Inc. MEM.: Southern Regional Education Board (dir.); Peabody Coll. (trustee); American Leprosy Cmte. (dir.); University Club; Rotary Club; Inst. of Textile Technology (dir.); Cotton Textile Inst. (dir.); Town Hall, Inc. (trustee; treas.); Merchants Club. HON. DEG.: LL.D., U. of NC, 1946. WRITINGS: *Businessman in the State House; The Business Conscience*. REL.: Methodist. RES.: Leakesville, NC.

HOEH, DAVID CHARLES. b. Dec 1, 1937, Boston, MA; par. Robert Y. and Priscilla (Smith) Hoeh; m. Sandra Unterman, Feb 9, 1963; c. Christopher; Jeffrey; Jonathan Robert. EDUC.: B.A., U. of NH, 1960; Boston Coll. Law School, 1961; A.M., Boston U., 1966; U. of MA. POLIT. & GOV.: organizer, Rockingham Cty. (NH) Democratic Cmte., 1960; treas., Strafford Cty. (NH) Democratic Cmte., 1962; campaign coordinator, King for Governor (NH), 1962; communications planning technician, state of NH, 1965–65, principal planner, 1965–67; campaign mgr., Off for Congress, 1964; chm., New Hampshire McCarthy for President, 1968; Democratic candidate for U.S. House (NH), 1968; delegate, Dem. Nat'l. Conv., 1968; ***candidate for Democratic nomination to vice presidency of the U.S., 1968***; member, NH Democratic State Central Cmte., 1968–71. BUS. & PROF.: assoc. dir., Public Affairs Center, Dartmouth Coll., 1968–71, Planners Collaborative, 1969–72; ed., *New Hampshire Freeman*, 1970–72; pres., NH Freeman Associates, Inc., 1970–72; asst. prof., U. of WI, 1972–. MEM.: Pi Gamma Mu; Pi Sigma Alpha; Tau Kappa Epsilon; American Soc. of Planning Officials; AAUP; American Inst. of Planners; APSA; A.C.L.U. WRITINGS: *Collective Bargaining in the Public Sector* (ed., 1969); "Where Do We Go From Here?" (1968). MAILING ADDRESS: 2422 East Newberry Blvd., Milwaukee, WI 53217.

HOENIG, MARIE LOUISE "PEGGY." b. Oct 19, 1928, Alexandria, LA; par. Daniel II and Marie Eve (Torres) Hurley; m. Arthur Hoenig; c. none. EDUC.: grad., St. Vincent's Inst., 1946; U. of TN, 1948–50; LA State U., 1950–51; grad., Uptown City Coll., New York, NY, 1963. POLIT. & GOV.: independent candidate for mayor of New York, NY, 1965; committee clerk, LA State Legislature; ***independent candidate for presidency of the U.S., 1976***. BUS. & PROF.: flight attendant, Pan American Air Line; administrative asst.; exec. sec.; teacher; writer; Goodwill ambassador. MEM.: National Business Women's Organization; World Wings, International; The Hudson Guild; A.C.L.U.; Police Athletic League; Animal Medical Center; Humane Soc. MAILING ADDRESS: 48 Greenwich Ave., New York, NY 10011.

HOFF, SAMUEL BOYER. b. Jun 7, 1957, Williamsport, PA; par. Samuel R. and J. Mattie (Schultz) Hoff; m. Phyllis Rose Oliveta; c. none. EDUC.: B.A., Susquehanna U., 1979; M.A., American U., 1981; M.A., State U. of NY at Stony Brook, 1983, Ph.D., 1987. POLIT. & GOV.: intern, U.S. Rep. Allen Ertel (D-PA), District Mobile Office, 1978; research asst., Subcommittee on Human Resources, Cmte. on Post Office and Civil Service, U.S. House, 1980; campus coordinator, Mondale for President, State U. of NY, Stony Brook, 1984; campus coordinator, Hochbrueckner for Congress, State U. of NY, Stony Brook, 1984; elected committeeman, Suffolk Cty. (NY) Democratic Central Cmte., 1984–86; ***candidate for Democratic nomination to presidency of the U.S., 1988; independent candidate for presidency of the U.S., 1992***. BUS. & PROF.: canvass staff, Clean Water Action Project, Washington, DC, 1980; survey staff, Smith, Berlin, and Associates, Washington, DC, 1980; political scientist; grad. teaching assistantship, State U. of NY at Stony Brook, 1981–86; instructor, Dept. of Political Science, State U. of NY at Stony Brook, 1983–85; asst. to former U.S. Sen. Jacob K. Javits, State U. of NY at Stony Brook, 1983–85; consultant, Elliott Sluhan Productions, Toledo, OH, 1985; adjunct instructor, Dept. of Social Sciences, New York Inst. of Technology, 1986; adjunct asst. prof., Dept. of Political Science, Wittenberg U., 1987; visiting asst. prof., Dept. of Government and Politics, OH Wesleyan U., 1986–87; asst. prof., Dept. of Political Science, State U. of NY, Coll. at Geneseo, 1987–88; visiting asst. prof., Dept. of Political Science, Wichita State U., 1988–89; asst. prof., Dept. of History and Political Science, DE State Coll., 1989–92, assoc. prof., 1992–; member, Board of Referees, *National Social Science Journal*; member, Board of Editors, University Press of America. MEM.: Pi Sigma Alpha; Pi Gamma Mu; Graduate Student Organization of the State U. of NY at Stony Brook (pres., 1982–83); Center for the Study of the Presidency; National Social Science Assn.; APSA; Acad. of Political

Science; Northeastern Political Science Assn.; Southern Political Science Assn.; Midwest Political Science Assn.; Western Social Science Assn.; National Capitol Area Political Science Assn.; NY State Political Science Assn.; PA Political Science Assn. AWARDS: Intercollegiate Debating Award, Susquehanna U., 1979; University Service Scholarship Award, American U., 1980; Alumni Scholarship, State U. of NY at Stony Brook, 1984; Setauket-Stony Brook Republican Club Political Science Award, 1985; NYS/UUP; Geneseo Foundation Incentive Grant, State U. of NY, Geneseo, 1988; Research Grant, Harry S. Truman Library Inst., 1988; Abilene Travel Grant, Eisenhower World Affairs Inst., 1988; Freedoms Foundation Scholarship, Valley Forge, PA, 1990; professional development grants, DE State Coll., 1990–92; named "Employee of the Year for Faculty Excellence in Research," DE State Coll., 1992. WRITINGS: articles and book reviews on political science. REL.: Lutheran. MAILING ADDRESS: 813 Maple Parkway, Dover, DE 19901.

HOFFMAN, HAROLD GILES. b. Feb 7, 1896, South Amboy, NJ; d. Jun 4, 1954, New York, NY; par. Frank and Ada Crawford (Thom) Hoffman; m. Lillie M. Ross, Sep 20, 1919; c. Ada Moss; Lillie Moss; Hope. EDUC.: high school grad., South Amboy, NJ, 1913. POLIT. & GOV.: city treas., South Amboy, NJ, 1920–25; elected as a Republican to NJ State House, 1923–24; elected mayor, South Amboy, 1924–25; sec., NJ State Senate, 1925–26; elected as a Republican to U.S. House (NJ), 1927–31; appointed NJ state commissioner of motor vehicles, 1930–35; delegate, NJ State Republican Convention, 1934, 1935, 1936, 1937; elected as a Republican to gov. of NJ, 1935–37; delegate, Rep. Nat'l. Conv., 1936; ***candidate for Republican nomination to presidency of the U.S., 1936***; appointed dir., NJ State Div. of Employment Security, 1938–42, 1946–54. BUS. & PROF.: sec.-treas., South Amboy Trust Co., South Amboy, NJ, 1919–26, exec. vice pres., 1926–42; pres., Mid-State Title Mortgage Guaranty Co., New Brunswick, NJ. MIL.: pvt., Company H, 3d NJ Infantry, 1917; promoted through grade to capt., Headquarters Co., 114th Infantry, 29th Div., 1918–19; maj., U.S.A.R., 1925; lt. col., U.S. Army, 1942–46, col., 1946; Legion of Merit; Verdun Medal. MEM.: Middlesex Cty. Bankers Assn. (pres., 1925–26); National Safety Council (vice pres.); J.O.U.A.M.; Knights of Pythias; Order of Red Men; Tall Cedars Club; Veiled Prophets; Royal Order of Jesters; Odd Fellows; Sons of the Revolution; Scottish Clan National Republican Club; Military Order of the World War; Army, Navy and Marine Club; Carteret Club; Patriotic Order of Sons of America; American Legion; VFW; Masons (Shriners; 32°; Scottish Rite); Elks; Eagles; Royal Arcanum; Lambs Club; Circus Saints and Sinners Club (pres.); New York Athletic Club. HON. DEG.: LL.D., Rutgers U., 1935. WRITINGS: *Mile a Minute Man*; *Getting Away with Murder*; *The Crime, The Case, The Challenge*. REL.: Methodist. RES.: South Amboy, NJ.

HOFFMAN, HENRY. b. Sep 6, 1851, Auburn, IN; d. c. 1945; par. Joshua Josiah and Caroline Catherine (Imhoff) Hoffman; married; c. two sons. EDUC.: D.S.T. POLIT. & GOV.: member, NE State Progressive Cmte., 1924; chm., National Progressive Party National Convention, 1928; sec.-treas., National Progressive Party, 1928–36; ***National Progressive Party candidate for presidency of the U.S., 1928, 1932***; Progressive Party candidate for U.S. House (NE), 1932, 1934. BUS. & PROF.: schoolteacher; institute lecturer; fence builder; lumberman; farmer; ditchdigger; construction worker; printer; salesman; rail-splitter; sales mgr., print shop; health practitioner; atty.; publisher, ed., *The Progressive*, 1931–32; author. MIL.: commander, Dakota National Guard. MEM.: Printers' Union. WRITINGS: *A Perfect Life and How to Live It* (1921). MISC.: known as "Doctor" Hoffman. RES.: Omaha, NE.

HOFFMAN, JOHN THOMPSON. b. Jan 10, 1828, Sing Sing, NY; d. Mar 24, 1888, Wiesbaden, Germany; par. Adrian Kassam and Jane Ann (Thompson) Hoffman; m. Ella Starkweather, Jan 1854; c. Ella (Mrs. Edward Sandford). EDUC.: grad., Union Coll., 1846; studied law under Gen. Aaron Ward and Judge Albert Lockwood, Sing Sing, NY. POLIT. & GOV.: member, NY State Democratic Central Cmte., 1848; elected as a Democrat to recorder of New York, NY, 1860–65; elected as a Democrat to mayor of New York, NY, 1865–68; Democratic candidate for gov. of NY, 1867; elected as a Democrat to gov. of NY, 1869–73; ***candidate for Democratic nomination to presidency of the U.S., 1868; candidate for Democratic nomination to vice presidency of the U.S., 1868, 1872***. BUS. & PROF.: atty.; admitted to NY Bar, 1849; partner, Woodruff, Leonard and Hoffman (law firm), New York, NY, 1849–59. MEM.: Young Men's Tammany Hall (Gen. Cmte., 1854); Tammany Soc. (1854; Central Cmte.; Grand Sachem, 1866–68); Union Coll. (trustee). HON. DEG.: LL.D., Union Coll., 1869; LL.D., Princeton U., 1870. WRITINGS: *Public Papers of Governor Hoffman* (1872); *Liberty and Order* (1876). RES.: New York, NY.

HOGAN, DANIEL. b. Oct 21, 1870, Fort Smith, AR; married; c. Freda. EDUC.: grammar school, Scott Cty., AR. POLIT. & GOV.: sec., AR Socialist Party, 4 years; Socialist Party candidate for gov. of AR, 1906, 1910, 1914; member, Socialist Party National Cmte., 1908–13; ***candidate for Socialist Party nomination to vice presidency of the U.S., 1912***; member, Farmer-Labor Party. BUS. & PROF.: journalist; ed., *Alliance Patriot*, Mansfield, OK, 1891–93; partner (with John W. Jasper), *Huntington (AR) Herald*, c. 1902, proprietor, ed., 1902–06, 1911–17; ed., *Huntington Hammer*, 1907–11; printer; atty., Huntington; lecturer; asst. mgr., publisher, *Oklahoma Leader*, Oklahoma City, OK, 1918. MEM.: International Typographers' Union; Farmer-Labor Reconstruction League (founder, 1922). RES.: Oklahoma City, OK.

HOGG, JAMES STEPHEN. b. Mar 24, 1851, Rusk, TX; d. Mar 3, 1906, Houston, TX; par. Joseph Lewis and Lucanda (McMath) Hogg; m. Sarah Ann Stinson, Apr 22, 1874; c. William; Ima; Michael; Thomas. EDUC.: studied law. POLIT. & GOV.: elected justice of the peace, Wood Cty., TX, 1873–75;

elected cty. atty., Wood Cty., TX, 1878–80; elected district atty., Seventh Judicial District of TX, 1880–84; elected as a Democrat to atty. gen. of TX, 1886–90; elected as a Democrat to gov. of TX, 1890–95; ***candidate for Democratic nomination to vice presidency of the U.S., 1900***. BUS. & PROF.: apprentice printer, Tyler, TX, 1868; printer; journalist; ed., *News*, Longview, TX, 1871, Quitman, TX, 1872–75; atty.; admitted to TX Bar, 1875; law practice, Tyler, 1884; law practice, Austin, TX; partner, Hogg, Watkins and Jones (law firm), Houston, TX, 1903–06; pres., Hogg-Swayne Syndicate (oil producers); farmer, Columbia, TX. MEM.: TX Bar. REL.: Bapt. RES.: Austin, TX.

HOGLUND, MARTHA W. POLIT. & GOV.: ***independent candidate for vice presidency of the U.S., 1980***. MAILING ADDRESS: 408 Park, Baytown, TX.

HOLCOMB, AUSTIN. b. Nov 4, 1867, Cardington, OH; d. Oct 9, 1942, Los Angeles, CA; par. Benajah Dwight and Mariah Augusta (Payne) Holcomb; m. Imogene McDuffie Mackie Sturgis, 1898; m. 2d, Mrs. Pauline Whiteman Muir, Jun 10, 1923; c. Katherine Maria; Dwight Sturgis. EDUC.: Boys H.S., Atlanta, GA, 1883. POLIT. & GOV.: ***Continental Party candidate for presidency of the U.S., 1904***. BUS. & PROF.: staff, *Jacksonville (FL) Morning News*, 1885–88; city ed., *Macon (GA) Telegraph*, 1888–90; clerk, record and pension office, U.S. War Dept., Washington, DC, 1891; partner, Holcomb Brothers (printing firm), Atlanta, GA, 1893–1900; publisher, *Atlanta Market Report*, 1899–1901; ed., Barrick Publishing Co., Kansas City, MO, 1900–1903; ed., *Kansas City Packer*, 1903–04; ed., *Brunswick Journal*; staff, *The Produce News*, New York, NY, 1910–42. MEM.: Masons (Royal Arch Mason; Shriner; Sec.-Master); Knights Templar; Red Cross Knight of the Temple; SAR. REL.: Episc. RES.: Atlanta, GA.

HOLCOMB, JOSEPH E. m. Margot Sierra Holcomb (q.v.). POLIT. & GOV.: ***candidate for Democratic nomination to presidency of the U.S., 1992***. MAILING ADDRESS: 3930 Swenson, Suite 907, Las Vegas, NV 89119.

HOLCOMB, MARGOT SIERRA. m. Joseph E. Holcomb (q.v.). POLIT. & GOV.: ***independent candidate for presidency of the U.S., 1988, 1992; candidate for Democratic nomination to presidency of the U.S., 1992***. MAILING ADDRESS: 3830 Swenson, Suite 706, Las Vegas, NV 89119.

HOLDEN, LARRY. b. 1944. POLIT. & GOV.: ***Human Party candidate for presidency of the U.S., 1984, 1988, 1992, 1996, 2000***. BUS. & PROF.: teacher. MAILING ADDRESS: Box 827, Asheville, NC 28802.

HOLDRIDGE, HERBERT CHARLES (nee HERBERT CHARLES HEITKE). b. Mar 6, 1892, Wyandotte, MI; d. Sep 29, 1974, Brecksville, OH; par. Emil and Ida (Petzke) Heitke; m. 3d, Dorothy Shaffer; c. John Herbert; Cheryl Reventlow. EDUC.: B.S., U.S. Military Acad., 1917; M.A., Columbia U., 1929; U.S. Army Command and General Staff Schools, 1941–43. POLIT. & GOV.: chm., People's Party, 1944–48; ***People's Party candidate for presidency of the U.S., 1948; candidate for Democratic nomination to presidency of the U.S., 1948, 1952, 1956, 1960; American Rally candidate for presidency of the U.S., 1952; American Vegetarian Party candidate for presidency of the U.S., 1952 (sponsored, but not nominated; withdrew)***; candidate for CA State Senate, 1956; ***candidate for Prohibition Party nomination to presidency of the U.S., 1956; Prohibition Party candidate for vice presidency of the U.S., 1956 (withdrew)***; founder, head, Constitutional Provisional Government of the U.S., 1961–. BUS. & PROF.: soldier; instructor in history, Columbia U.; ed., *Reveille* newsletter; author of various pamphlets and broadsides. MIL.: cadet, U.S. Army, 1917; advanced through grades to brig. gen., 1944; instructor in social sciences, asst. prof. of history, U.S. Military Acad., 1918–20, 1924–27; dir. of training, Army Administration Schools; commanded Army Adjutant General's School, WWII; retired, 1944. MEM.: Holdridge Foundation for the Advancement of Social Science, Inc. (pres.); Masons; General Holdridge Minute Men; Veterans of World War II (exec. sec., 1944–46); Liberal Veterans of World War II (exec. sec., 1946–48); Wolf Clan, Mohawk Nation of Iroquois Confederacy (given name of BA-HA-RE-WHE-HA-WEH). HON. DEG.: LL.D., Grinnell Coll., 1943; LL.D., American U., 1943. WRITINGS: *The Fable of Moronia* (1953); *How to Gain Freedom from Economic Slavery* (1961); *Tarnished Brass*. REL.: Mystical Buddhism. RES.: Sherman Oaks, CA.

HOLLAND, PATRICIA O'BRIEN. b. Feb 29, 1928, Boston, MA; par. Francis A. and Marie (Harrington) O'Brien; m. John Sullivan Holland; c. Maria; Christian; Martha; Anne; Anthony. EDUC.: grad., Jamaica Plain H.S., 1945; A.B., Boston U., 1949; M.Ed., Boston Teachers' Coll., 1950. POLIT. & GOV.: ***independent (Cmte. for a Constitutional Presidency) candidate for vice presidency of the U.S., 1976***. BUS. & PROF.: English teacher, Boston (MA) Public Junior High Schools; teacher, program dir., Manchester (NH) Assn. for Retarded Children; book reviewer, *The Living Light*. MEM.: NH Assn. of Mental Health; Bedford Schools Volunteer; Manchester Assn. for Retarded Children (dir.). REL.: R.C. MAILING ADDRESS: 5 Glen Rd., Bedford, NH 03102.

HOLLER, CHARLES F. POLIT. & GOV.: Prohibition Party candidate for clerk, IN State Supreme Court, 1902; ***candidate for Prohibition Party nomination to vice presidency of the U.S., 1908***. BUS. & PROF.: atty. RES.: IN.

HOLLINGS, ERNEST FREDERICK "FRITZ" HOLLINGS. b. Jan 1, 1922, Charleston,

SC; par. Adolph G. and Wilhelmine D. (Mayer) Hollings; m. (divorced); m. 2d, Rita Liddy, Aug 21, 1971; c. Michael Milhous; Helen Hayne; Patricia Salley; Ernest Frederick III. EDUC.: B.A., The Citadel, 1942; LL.B., U. of SC, 1947. POLIT. & GOV.: elected as a Democrat to SC State House, 1948–54 (Speaker pro tempore, 1951–54); member, Hoover Comm. on Intelligence Activities, 1954–55; elected as a Democrat to lt. gov. of SC, 1955–59; delegate, Dem. Nat'l. Conv., 1956, 1972; elected as a Democrat to gov. of SC, 1959–63; member, Advisory Comm. on Intergovernmental Relations, 1959–63; candidate for Democratic nomination to U.S. Senate (SC), 1962; elected as a Democrat to U.S. Senate (SC), 1967–; member, Senate Democratic Policy Cmte.; chm., Senate Democratic Campaign Cmte., 1971–73; member, Technological Assessment Board, 1973; ***candidate for Democratic nomination to vice president of the United State, 1976, 1988; candidate for Democratic nomination to presidency of the U.S., 1984, 1988***. BUS. & PROF.: atty.; admitted to SC Bar, 1947; law practice, Charleston, SC, 1963–66. MEM.: Newberry Coll. (trustee); Assn. of Citadel Men; Phi Delta Phi; Hibernian Soc.; Sertoma. AWARDS: one of ten Outstanding Young Men in American, U.S. Junior C. of C., 1954. REL.: Lutheran (member, Exec. Council, Lutheran Church of America; member, Board of Adjudication). MAILING ADDRESS: 141 East Bay St., Charleston, SC 29401.

HOLLOMON, ROY S. POLIT. & GOV.: ***candidate for Prohibition Party nomination to presidency of the U.S., 1964***. BUS. & PROF.: minister. MEM.: United Drys of KS (superintendent). MAILING ADDRESS: 218½ West Sixth, Topeka, KS.

HOLLOWAY, HUDSON EUGENE. POLIT. & GOV.: ***independent candidate for presidency of the U.S., 1980***. MAILING ADDRESS: 4115 East Busch Blvd., Tampa, FL 33617.

HOLMAN, WILLIAM STEELE. b. Sep 6, 1822, Aurora, IN; d. Apr 22, 1897, Washington, DC; par. Jesse Lynch and Elizabeth (Masterson) Holman; m. Abigail Knapp, c. 1842; c. Mrs. R. E. Fletcher; others. EDUC.: Franklin (IN) Coll., 1840–42. POLIT. & GOV.: probate judge, Dearborn Cty., IN, 1843–46; prosecuting atty., Dearborn Cty., IN, 1847–49; delegate, IN State Constitutional Convention, 1850; elected as a Democrat to IN State House, 1851–52; appointed judge, IN Court of Common Pleas, 1852–56; elected as a Democrat to U.S. House (IN), 1859–65, 1867–77, 1881–95, 1897; Democratic candidate for U.S. House (IN), 1876, 1878, 1894; ***candidate for Anti-Monopoly Party nomination to vice presidency of the U.S., 1884***. BUS. & PROF.: atty.; admitted to IN Bar; law practice, Aurora, IN. RES.: Aurora, IN.

HOLMES, GAVRIELLE. m. Larry Holmes (q.v.). POLIT. & GOV.: ***Workers World Party candidate for presidency of the U.S., 1984***. MAILING ADDRESS: 305 West 19th St., New York, NY 10011.

HOLMES, GILBERT H. POLIT. & GOV.: ***candidate for Democratic nomination to presidency of the U.S., 1992***. MAILING ADDRESS: Washington, DC.

HOLMES, LARRY. b. 1952, Roxbury, MA; m. Gavrielle Holmes (q.v.). POLIT. & GOV.: member, National Cmte., Workers World Party; delegate, Solidarity Conference for Popular Movement for the Liberation of Angola, 1976; ***Workers World Party candidate for vice presidency of the U.S., 1980, 1992; Workers World Party candidate for presidency of the U.S., 1984, 1988; Peace and Freedom Party nomination to presidency of the U.S., 1988***. BUS. & PROF.: porter; restaurant worker; mailroom clerk; community organizer; contributor, *Workers World*; antiwar activist; organizer, 1973 March on Washington; National March Against Racism, 1974; Anti-Bakke March, 1978. MIL.: U.S. Army, 1971–72; received dishonorable discharge for antiwar activities, 1972. MEM.: American Servicemen's Union (national organizer); Coalition of Black Trade Unionists; Emergency Cmte. for a National Mobilization Against Racism (organizer, 1974); Citizens Coalition to Save the Schomberg Library (founder). WRITINGS: *Weber's Wrong, The U.S. Steelworker's Union is Right; The Case for Affirmative Action* (1978). MAILING ADDRESS: 305 West 19th St., New York, NY 10011.

HOLMS, SEBASTIAN THOMAS, JR. par. Sebastian Thomas Holms, Sr. POLIT. & GOV.: ***independent candidate for presidency of the U.S., 1988***. MAILING ADDRESS: 2939 Larned, Detroit, MI 48207.

HOLT, JOSEPH. b. Jan 6, 1807, Breckenridge Cty., KY; d. Aug 1, 1894, Washington, DC; par. John and Eleanor (Stephens) Holt; m. Mary Harrison; m. 2d, Margaret Wickliffe; c. none. EDUC.: St. Joseph's Coll.; Centre Coll.; studied law under Robert Wickliffe. POLIT. & GOV.: commonwealth's atty., Fourth Louisville District, 1833–35; delegate, Dem. Nat'l. Conv., 1836; appointed U.S. commissioner of patents, 1857–59; appointed postmaster gen. of the U.S., 1859–61; appointed U.S. sec. of war, 1861; ***candidate for Republican nomination to vice presidency of the U.S., 1864***; appointed atty. gen. of the U.S., 1864 (declined). BUS. & PROF.: atty.; admitted to KY Bar, 1831; law practice, Elizabethtown, KY, 1831; asst. ed., *Louisville (KY) Advertiser*, 1832; law practice, MS, 1836–42. MIL.: appointed judge advocate gen., U.S. Army, 1862–75; brev. maj. gen., 1865. WRITINGS: *Vindication of Judge Advocate General Holt . . .* (1866). MISC.: prosecuted Clement Vallandigham, John Wilkes Booth, and co-conspirators in assassination of President Abraham Lincoln (q.v.). RES.: Washington, DC.

HOLTWICK, ENOCH ARDEN. b. Jan 3, 1881, Rhineland, MO; par. William and Aleida (Heying) Holtwick; m. Clara W. Uglow; m. 2d, Ruth E. Hamilton, Jun 27, 1946. EDUC.: A.B., Greenville (IL) Coll., 1909; A.M., U. of Southern CA, 1914; U. of WI, 1921–22; State U. of IA, 1928; U. of MI, 1934, 1941. POLIT. & GOV.: Prohibition Party candidate for IL State treas., 1936; Prohibition Party candidate for U.S. Senate (IL), 1938, 1940, 1942, 1944, 1948, 1950; ***candidate for Prohibition Party nomination to vice presidency of the U.S., 1940; candidate for Prohibition Party nomination to presidency of the U.S., 1948, 1952, 1964; Prohibition Party candidate for vice presidency of the U.S., 1952; Prohibition Party candidate for presidency of the U.S., 1956***. BUS. & PROF.: teacher, Union H.S., Englewood, CA, 1910–15; pres., Los Angeles Pacific Junior Coll., 1915–18; prof. of history and government, chm. of dept. of history, Greenville Coll., 1919–51, prof. emeritus, 1951–. MEM.: American Hist. Assn.; American Acad. of Political and Social Sciences. HON. DEG.: LL.D., Greenville Coll., 1942. WRITINGS: "Role of the Third Party in American Politics" (unpublished master's thesis). REL.: Free Methodist. RES.: Greenville, IL.

HOMER, IRVING. POLIT. & GOV.: ***America First Party candidate for vice presidency of the U.S., 1972***. BUS. & PROF.: commentator, WWDB radio, Philadelphia, PA. MAILING ADDRESS: 12138 Medford Rd., Philadelphia, PA.

HOOPES, DARLINGTON. b. Sep 11, 1896, Vale, MD; d. Sep 25, 1989, Reading, PA; par. Price and Elizabeth L. (Tucker) Hoopes; m. Hazelette Miller, Oct 16, 1925; c. Darlington, Jr.; Rae; Delite. EDUC.: U. of WI, 1914–15; correspondence course, People's Coll.; studied law in office of G. Herbert Jenkins, Norristown, PA, 1917–21. POLIT. & GOV.: member, Socialist Party Local, North Waley, PA, 1915; organizer, Montgomery Cty. (PA) Socialist Party, 1917; member, Socialist Party Local, Norristown, 1921; sec.-treas., Socialist Party of PA, 1923; member, PA Labor Party, 1924; chm., Ninth Congressional District Labor Party Campaign Cmte., 1924; appointed asst. city solicitor, Reading, PA, 1928–32; elected as a Socialist to PA State House, 1931–37; member, exec. cmte., Socialist Party, 1932–36, 1944–68 (national chm., 1946–57, 1960–68; hon. chm., 1968–89); appointed city solicitor, Reading, 1936–40; ***Socialist Party candidate for vice presidency of the U.S., 1944; candidate for Socialist Party nomination to vice presidency of the U.S., 1948***; Socialist Party candidate for U.S. House (PA), 1952; ***Socialist Party candidate for presidency of the U.S., 1952, 1956***; appointed member, PA State Council on Fair Employment Practices (exec. cmte., 1948–58; vice chm., 1954–58); member, Reading Human Relations Comm., 1968. BUS. & PROF.: farmer, 1915–21; atty.; admitted to PA Bar, 1921; law practice, Norristown, 1921–27; law practice, Reading, 1927–; dir., Eastern Cooperatives, Inc., 1947–51. MEM.: ABA; PA Bar Assn.; Berks Cty. Bar Assn. (pres., 1961–62); Montgomery Cty. Bar Assn.; A.C.L.U.; Fellowship of Reconciliation; Economic Opportunity Council; Commercial Law League; American Federation of Teachers; NAACP; YMCA; BSA; War Resisters League (National Cmte., 1931); PA Cmte. for Total Disarmament (vice chm.); League Against Fascism (National Cmte.); Eagles; Travelers Protective Agency; Harmony Grange; Inter-State Milk Producers Assn. REL.: Soc. of Friends. RES.: Reading, PA.

HOOVER, HERBERT CLARK. b. Aug 10, 1874, West Branch, IA; d. Oct 20, 1964, New York, NY; par. Jesse Clark and Hulda Randall (Minthorn) Hoover; m. Lou Henry, Feb 10, 1899; c. Herbert Clark, Jr.; Allan Henry. EDUC.: A.B., Stanford U., 1895. POLIT. & GOV.: appointed chm., American Relief Comm., 1914–15; appointed chm., Comm. for Relief in Belgium, 1915–19; appointed U.S. Food Administrator, 1917–19; member, War Trade Council; chm., U.S. Grain Corp.; chm., U.S. Sugar Equalization Board; chm., Interallied Food Council; chm., Supreme Economic Council; chm., European Coal Council; chm., American Relief Administration, 1919; vice chm., President's Second Industrial Conference, 1920; ***candidate for Republican nomination to presidency of the U.S., 1920, 1936, 1940, 1944***; appointed U.S. sec. of commerce, 1921–28; chm., President's Conference on Unemployment, 1921; member, Advisory Cmte., Limitation of Armaments Conference, 1921; ***candidate for Republican nomination to vice presidency of the U.S., 1924***; chm., War Debt Comm.; chm., Colorado River Comm.; chm., Special Mississippi Flood Relief Comm., 1927; ***candidate for Prohibition Party nomination to presidency of the U.S., 1928; elected as a Republican to presidency of the U.S., 1929–33; Republican candidate for presidency of the U.S., 1932; Prohibition Party of CA candidate for presidency of the U.S., 1932***; appointed coordinator, European Food Program, 1946; appointed chm., Comm. on Organization of the Executive Branch of Government, 1947–49, 1953–55; member, Advisory Board, World Bank for Reconstruction and Development. BUS. & PROF.: engineer; mining engineer and consultant around the world, 1895–13; representative in Europe, Panama-Pacific International Exposition, 1913–14. MEM.: Stanford U. (trustee); Mills Coll. (trustee); Carnegie Inst. (trustee); Henry E. Huntington Library and Art Gallery (trustee); C. R. B. Education Fund (chm.); American Children's Fund (chm.); Boys Clubs of America (chm.); Finnish Relief Fund, Inc. (chm.); Robert A. Taft Memorial Foundation (chm.); Woodrow Wilson Centennial Celebration Comm.; National Foundation of Medical Education (hon. chm.); Health Information Foundation; Dutch Treat Club (John O'Hara Cosgrave Medal); International Benjamin Franklin Soc. (Gold Medal, 1954); American Inst. of Mining and Metallurgical Engineers (pres., 1920); American Engineering Council (pres., 1921); American Child Health Assn. (pres., 1922). AWARDS: received 296 medals, awards, and honors, including a Gold Medal, Civic Forum; Gold Medal, National Inst. of Social Sciences; Gold Medal, National Acad. of Sciences; Gold Medal, American Inst. of Mining and Metallurgy; Gold Medal, Western Soc. of Engineers; Gold Medal, City of Lille; Gold Medal, City of Warsaw; Audiffret Prize, French Acad.; named "Freeman" in various Belgian, Polish, and Estonian cities.. HON. DEG.: received 84 honorary degrees, including degrees from Brown U.; U. of PA; Harvard U.; Yale U.; Columbia U.; Princeton U.; Johns Hopkins U.; George Washington U.; Dartmouth U.; Boston U.; Rutgers U.; U. of AL; Oberlin Coll.; Karlsruhe Tech. Coll.; U. of Liege; U. of Brussels; U. of Warsaw; U. of Cracow; Oxford U.; Rensselaer; Tufts U.; Swarthmore Coll.; Williams Coll.; U. of Manchester; U. of CA; U. of VA; U. of Lwow; U. of Prague; U. of Ghent; U. of Lemberg; Cornell Coll.; LL.D., The Citadel, 1958; LL.D., U. of the State of NY, 1958. WRITINGS: *American Individualism* (1922); *The Challenge of Liberty* (1934); *America's First Crusade* (1941); *The Problems of Lasting Peace* (1942); *Addresses on the American Road* (1938–55); *Memoirs* (1951–52); *The Ordeal of Woodrow Wilson* (1958); *Agricola de Re Metallicca* (translator, with Lou Henry Hoover); *An American Epic* (3vols., 1959–61); *Fishing for Fun and to Wash Your Soul* (1963). REL.: Soc. of Friends. RES.: New York, NY.

HOOVER, HERBERT FRANKLIN. b. Dec 18, 1923, Oskaloosa, IA; par. Benjamin Franklin and Rosina (Hinshaw) Hoover; m. Eleanor Tatum; c. Rebecca; Rachel; Rose. EDUC.: certificate in farm operations, IA State U., 1946; B.S., William Penn Coll., 1967. POLIT. & GOV.: U.S. representative, World Agricultural Fair, India, 1959; candidate for Republican nomination to U.S. Senate (IA), 1962, 1966; Iowa Party candidate for U.S. Senate (IA), 1966, 1968; ***candidate for Republican nomination to presidency of the U.S., 1964, 1968; Peace Party candidate for presidency of the U.S., 1964, 1968***; candidate for Republican nomination to U.S. House (IA), 1980. BUS. & PROF.: farmer; peace activist. MEM.: People's Party; Future Farmers of America (state pres.); Boys 4-H Clubs of Iowa (pres.). REL.: Soc. of Friends. MISC.: runner-up, National 4-H Achievement Contest, 1944; sentenced to 18 months in federal prison for refusal to serve in armed forces; paroled after 9 months; pardoned by President John F. Kennedy, Nov 1962; a fourth cousin twice removed of President Herbert C. Hoover (q.v.). MAILING ADDRESS: Rural Route 2, Oskaloosa, IA 52577.

HOOVER, JOSPHY EDGARD (See DABBS, VERNON MATTHEW).

HOPFMANN, ALWIN E. POLIT. & GOV.: candidate for Democratic nomination to U.S. House (MA), 1980; candidate for Democratic nomination to U.S. Senate (MA), 1982; ***candidate for Democratic nomination to presidency of the U.S., 1984***. BUS. & PROF.: apple farmer, Sterling, MA; high school chemistry teacher, Sterling. MEM.: John Birch Soc. MAILING ADDRESS: 29 Tuttle Rd., Sterling, MA 01564.

HOPKINS, HARRY LLOYD. b. Aug 17, 1890, Sioux City, IA; d. Jan 29, 1946, New York, NY; par. David Aldona and Anna (Pickett) Hopkins; m. Ethel Gross, 1913 (divorced, 1930); m. 2d, Barbara Duncan, 1931 (deceased, 1937); m. 3d, Mrs. Louise Macy, Jul 30, 1942; c. David; Barbara; Stephen; Robert; Diana. EDUC.: grad., Grinnell Coll., 1912. POLIT. & GOV.: exec. sec., New York (NY) Board of Civil Welfare, 1914–17; appointed exec. dir., NY Temporary Emergency Relief Administration, 1931, chm., 1932–33; appointed administrator, Federal Emergency Relief Administration, 1933–35; dir., Civil Works Administration; dir., WPA, 1935–38; appointed U.S. sec. of commerce, 1938–40; ***candidate for Democratic nomination to presidency of the U.S., 1940***; campaign mgr., Roosevelt for President, 1940; appointed dir., Lend-Lease Program, 1941; appointed special asst. to the president, 1942–45; appointed U.S. representative to Moscow to settle Polish Question, 1945; appointed impartial chm., Woman's Cloak and Suit Industry, New York, 1945; appointed chm., Munitions Assignments Board. BUS. & PROF.: social worker; dir., Christadora House (NY) Summer Boy's Camp, Bound Brook, NJ, 1912; supervisor, Assn. for Improving the Condition of the Poor, New York, 1913, 1922–24; employee, American Red Cross, 1917–22; exec. dir., NY Tuberculosis and Health Assn., 1924–31. MEM.: American Red Cross (member, Central Cmte.); Franklin Delano Roosevelt Library (trustee); Grinnell Coll. (trustee). AWARDS: Distinguished Service Medal, 1945. HON. DEG.: LL.D., Grinnell Coll., 1935; LL.D., U. of SC, 1938; LL.D., U. of AR, 1938; D.C.L., Oxford U., 1945. WRITINGS: *Spending to Save: The Complete Story of Relief* (1936). RES.: New York, NY.

HOPKINS, JOHN ORVILLE. b. Jul 19, 1876, Pleasant Grove, MN; d. May 31, 1973; par. Culver and Sara (Harris) Harris; m. Irene Cynthia Woehler; c. John W. EDUC.: LL.D., Lincoln U., 1960. POLIT. & GOV.: chm., Universal Party National Convention, 1964, 1968; chm., Universal Party National Cmte.; ***Universal Party candidate for presidency of the U.S., 1964 (declined); Universal Party candidate for vice presidency of the U.S., 1964***. BUS. & PROF.: farmer, Des Moines, IA; partner, bicycle business; pres., Hopkins Sporting Goods Co., 1902–55. MEM.: Rotary International (charter member); Williams Coll., Berkeley, CA (chm. of the board). REL.: Bapt. RES.: Des Moines, IA.

HOPKINS, R. C. POLIT. & GOV.: ***candidate for Republican nomination to vice presidency of the U.S., 1928***. RES.: Kansas City, MO?

HOPSON, ROBERT WAVERLY, III (aka HAIG, ROBERT WAVERLY). par. Robert Waverly Hopson; married. POLIT. & GOV.: ***independent candidate for presidency of the U.S., 1980***. BUS. & PROF.: self-proclaimed gen. of the armies; chief justice of the Upper Supreme Court of the U.S. MAILING ADDRESS: 460 West Hanover St., Trenton, NJ 08618.

HORBAL, KORYNE EMILY. b. Feb 11, 1937, Minneapolis, MN; par. Stanley Raymond and Emma (Jamtoos) Kaneski; m. William Orin Horbal, 1958; c. Steven Ray; Lynn

Rae. EDUC.: Gustavus Adolphus Coll.; U. of MN. POLIT. & GOV.: precinct chm., Brooklyn Center (MN) Democratic-Farmer Labor Party, 1960; chm., 20th Ward Democratic-Farmer Labor Party, Hennepin Cty., MN, 1961–; third vice chm., Hennepin Cty. Democratic-Farmer Labor Party, 1961–63, first vice chm., 1963–65; chm., Anoka Cty. (MN) Democratic-Farmer Labor Party, 1966–68; delegate, Dem. Nat'l. Conv., 1968, 1972; state chm., MN Democratic-Farmer Labor Party, 1968–72; appointed member, Mayor's Citizen Cmte. on Federal Programs, Coons Rapids, MN; member, Dem. Nat'l. Cmte., 1972–; delegate, Democratic National Charter Comm., 1974; appointed U.S. representative, U.N. Comm. on the Status of Women; ***candidate for Democratic nomination to presidency of the U.S., 1980***. BUS. & PROF.: vice pres., treas., American Contracting Corp., Minneapolis, MN, 1964–. REL.: Lutheran. MAILING ADDRESS: 1845 Innsbruck Parkway, Minneapolis, MN 55421.

HORNBERGER, DAVID LESTER. b. Jul 16, 1942, Akron, OH; single. POLIT. & GOV.: ***independent candidate for presidency of the U.S., 1980, 1988, 1992***. MISC.: sponsored convention of independent presidential candidates, Jul 1980. MAILING ADDRESS: 650 Shopper's Lane, #166, Covina, CA 91723.

HORRIGAN, WILLIAM, JR. b. 1942; par. William Horrigan, Sr. POLIT. & GOV.: ***candidate for Republican nomination to presidency of the U.S., 1988; candidate for Democratic nomination to presidency of the U.S., 1992***. BUS. & PROF.: airline pilot. MAILING ADDRESS: c/o Richard Horrigan, 660 Main St., South, Woodbury, CT 06798.

HORTON, MAURICE. POLIT. & GOV.: ***candidate for Republican nomination to presidency of the U.S., 1988, 1992***. MAILING ADDRESS: 1824 East Cedar St., Springfield, IL 62703.

HOSPERS, JOHN. b. Jun 9, 1918, Pella, ID; par. John De Gelder and Dena (Verhey) Hospers, divorced. EDUC.: B.A., Central Coll., 1939; M.A., State U. of ID, 1941; Ph.D., Columbia U., 1944. POLIT. & GOV.: ***Libertarian Party candidate for presidency of the U.S., 1972***; Libertarian Party candidate for gov. of CA, 1974; presidential elector, Libertarian Party, 1976. BUS. & PROF.: instructor, Columbia U., 1946–48; asst. prof., assoc. prof., U. of MN, 1948–56; assoc. ed., *Philosophical Studies*, 1950–; Fulbright research scholar, U. of London, 1954–55; prof., Brooklyn Coll., 1956–66; visiting prof., U. of CA, Los Angeles, 1960–61; editorial board, *Journal of Aesthetics and Art Criticism*, 1963–; consulting ed., *American Philosophical Quarterly*, 1965–; prof., CA State Coll., 1966–68; dir., school of philosophy, U. of Southern CA, 1968–; editor-in-chief, *The Personalist*, 1968–; editorial board, *Encyclopedia of Philosophy*. MEM.: American Phil. Assn.; American Soc. for Aesthetics (pres., West Coast Div.); Mind Assn.; Royal Inst. of Philosophy; Aristotelian Soc. Hon. Deg: D.Litt., Central Coll., 1962. WRITINGS: *Meaning and Truth in the Arts* (with W. Sellars, 1946); *Readings in Ethical Theory* (1952); *Introduction to Philosophical Analysis* (1953); *Human Conduct* (1962); *Readings in Introductory Philosophical Analysis* (1968); *Libertarianism: A New Turn in Political Philosophy* (1970); *Libertarianism: The Coming Political Philosophy* (1971); *Libertarianism: A Political Philosophy for Tomorrow* (1971); *Artistic Expression* (1971). MAILING ADDRESS: 8229 Lookout Mountain Ave., Los Angeles, CA 90046.

HOUGH, WILLIAM J. POLIT. & GOV.: ***American Party candidate for vice presidency of the U.S., 1920***. RES.: unknown.

HOULE, RICHARD JACQUES. POLIT. & GOV.: ***candidate for Republican nomination to presidency of the U.S., 1980***. MAILING ADDRESS: 32 Bailey Rd., Enfield, CT 06082.

HOULIHAN, JOHN JOSEPH. b. Mar 25, 1923, Chicago, IL; par. James W. and Irene (Quill) Houlihan; m. Vernal Devitt, May 25, 1946; c. James; Maureen; Michael; William; Terrence; Patricia; Denis; Brendan. EDUC.: Englewood Evening School, 1941; DePaul U., 1945–47. POLIT. & GOV.: deputy treas., Will Cty., IL, 1962–66; elected as a Democrat to IL State House, 1965–73; Democratic candidate for U.S. House (IL), 1972, 1974; ***candidate for Democratic nomination to vice presidency of the U.S., 1972***; appointed IL state dir. of veterans affairs, 1973–77; employee, U.S. VA, Washington, DC, 1978–. BUS. & PROF.: mgr., Suburban Materials Cooperative, Park Forest, IL, 1956–62; owner, insurance agency, Park Forest, to 1972. AWARDS: "Man of the Year" Award, Combined IL Veterans Associations, 1979; numerous other labor and veterans' awards. REL.: R.C. MAILING ADDRESS: 117 Balmoral Dr., East, Oxon Hill, MD 20021.

HOUSEL, CARL. b. 1938. EDUC.: seventh grade. POLIT. & GOV.: ***candidate for Democratic nomination to presidency of the U.S., 1980***. BUS. & PROF.: self-employed handyman. MAILING ADDRESS: Firehouse Lane, Box 107, Upper Black Eddy, NJ 18972.

HOUSER, FRANK. POLIT. & GOV.: ***independent candidate for presidency of the U.S., 1980***. MAILING ADDRESS: East Lakeridge Dr., Box 66, Eagle River, AR 99577.

HOUSTON, ANDREW JACKSON. b. Jun 21, 1854, Independence, TX; d. Jun 26, 1941, Baltimore, MD; par. Samuel (q.v.) and Margaret (Lea) Houston; married; c. Arladne; Marguerite. EDUC.: Baylor U.; Bastrop (TX) Military Acad.; TX Military Inst.; Old Salado (TX) Coll.; U.S. Military Acad.,

1871–73. POLIT. & GOV.: clerk, U.S. District Court, Dallas, TX, 1879–89; Reform Republican candidate for gov. of TX, 1892; Republican candidate for U.S. House (TX), 1898, 1904; appointed U.S. marshal, Eastern District of TX, 1902–10; Prohibition Party candidate for gov. of TX, 1910, 1912; ***candidate for Prohibition Party nomination to presidency of the U.S., 1912 (withdrew)***; superintendent, San Jacinto (TX) State Park, 1924–41; appointed as a Democrat to U.S. Senate (TX), 1941. BUS. & PROF.: clerk, State Dept. of Education, 1873–75; clerk, General Land Office, 1875; atty.; admitted to TX Bar, 1876; law practice, 1876–79, 1889–1902; prof. of military science, St. Mary's U., 1917–18; custodian, San Jacinto Battlefield, San Jacinto, TX. MIL.: organizer, Travis Rifles, 1874; col., TX National Guard, 1884–93; formed Cavalry Troop (but was not a member thereof), Rough Riders, 1898. WRITINGS: *Texas Independence* (1938). RES.: La Porte, TX.

HOUSTON, DAVID FRANKLIN. b. Feb 17, 1866, Monroe, NC; d. Sep 2, 1940, New York, NY; par. William H. and Cornelia Anne (Stevens) Houston; m. Helen Beall, Dec 11, 1895; c. Duval Beall; David Franklin, Jr.; Elizabeth; Helen Beall; Lawrence Reid. EDUC.: A.B., SC Coll., 1887; A.M., Harvard U., 1892. POLIT. & GOV.: appointed U.S. sec. of agriculture, 1913–20; appointed U.S. sec. of the treasury, 1920–21; appointed chm., Federal Reserve Board, 1920–21; appointed chm., Farm Loan Board, 1920–21; member, Council of National Defense, 1916–20; ***candidate for Democratic nomination to presidency of the U.S., 1924***. BUS. & PROF.: teacher; tutor in ancient languages, SC Coll., 1887–88; superintendent of schools, Spartanburg, SC, 1888–91; adjunct prof., U. of TX, 1894–97, assoc. prof., 1897–1900, dean of faculty, 1899–1902, prof. of political science, 1900–1902; pres., A&M Coll. of TX, 1902–05; pres., U. of TX, 1905–08; chancellor, Washington U., St. Louis, MO, 1908–16; pres., Bell Telephone Securities Co., 1921–40; financial vice pres., American Telephone and Telegraph Co., 1925; chm. of the board, Mutual Life Insurance Company of New York, 1927–40. MEM.: Harvard Graduate Club (pres., 1893–94); American Economic Assn.; American Acad. of Political and Social Sciences; TX State Hist. Soc. (fellow); Harvard U. (overseer); Columbia U. (trustee). HON. DEG.: LL.D., Tulane U., 1903; LL.D., U. of WI, 1906; LL.D., Yale U., 1913; LL.D., Harvard U., 1914; LL.D., U. of MO, 1914; LL.D., Brown U., 1919; LL.D., Rutgers U., 1919; LL.D., U. of NC, 1922. WRITINGS: *A Critical Study of Nullification in South Carolina* (1902); *Eight Years with Wilson's Cabinet* (1926). RES.: New York, NY.

HOUSTON, GUY V. POLIT. & GOV.: ***independent candidate for presidency of the U.S., 1976, 1980***. MAILING ADDRESS: 10 A-S.E. Sixth St., Stone Cottage in Rear, Miami, FL 33131.

HOUSTON, SAMUEL. b. Mar 2, 1793, Timber Ridge Church, VA; d. Jul 26, 1863, Huntsville, TX; par. Maj. Samuel and Elizabeth (Paxon) Houston; m. Eliza Allen, Jan 22, 1829; m. 2d, Tiana (Diana) Rogers Gentry, 1839; m. 3d, Margaret Moffette Lea, May 9, 1940; c. Samuel, Jr.; Temple Lea; Margaret (Mrs. Weston Lafayette Williams); Nancy (Mrs. Joseph Clay Stiles Morrow); Mary William; Antoinette Power; Andrew Jackson (q.v.); William Rogers. EDUC.: Maryville Acad., Maryville, TN. POLIT. & GOV.: appointed district atty., Nashville, TN, 1819; adj. gen. of TN, 1820; elected as a Democrat to U.S. House (TN), 1823–27; elected as a Democrat to gov. of TN, 1827–29; delegate, San Felipe de Austin Convention on Texas Statehood, 1833; delegate, Texas Constitutional Convention, 1835; elected pres., Republic of Texas, 1836–38, 1841–44; elected member, Congress of the Republic of Texas, 1838–40; elected as a Democrat to U.S. Senate (TX), 1846–57; ***candidate for Democratic nomination to presidency of the U.S., 1852; candidate for American (Know Nothing) Party nomination to presidency of the U.S., 1856***; Democratic candidate for gov. of TX, 1857; elected as a Democrat to gov. of TX, 1859–61 (deposed for refusal to take oath of allegiance to Confederate States of America); ***candidate for Republican nomination to vice presidency of the U.S., 1860; candidate for Constitutional Union Party nomination to presidency of the U.S., 1860***. BUS. & PROF.: atty.; admitted to TN Bar, 1818. MIL.: pvt., 39th Infantry Regt., U.S. Army, 1813, ensign, 1813; sgt., 7th Infantry Regt., Creek War, lt., 1814; maj. gen., TN Militia, 1821; commander in chief, Texas Army, 1836. MISC.: adopted by Chief Jolly of Cherokee Indians, c. 1806; moved to Cherokee Indian Territory, 1829; moved to Texas, 1833; during War for Texas Independence, routed Mexican forces and captured Gen. Santa Anna at Battle of San Jacinto, 1836; Houston, TX is named for him. REL.: Bapt. RES.: Huntsville, TX.

HOWARD, CHARLES HENRY. b. Aug 28, 1838, Leeds, ME; d. Jan 27, 1908, Glencoe, IL; par. Rowland Bailey and Eliza (Otis) Howard; m. Mary Katherine Foster, Dec 5, 1867; c. Otis McGaw; Burt Foster; Nina Foster; Arthur Day; Lawrence Riggs; Donald Charles; Katharine. EDUC.: Yarmouth Acad.; Kent's Hill Seminary; grad., Bowdoin Coll., 1859; Bangor Theological Seminary, 1860–61. POLIT. & GOV.: Indian inspector, U.S. Dept. of the Interior; appointed asst. commissioner of refugees, freedmen, and abandoned lands, 1866–68; ***Anti-Masonic Party candidate for vice presidency of the U.S., 1872 (declined); Continental Party candidate for presidency of the U.S., 1904 (declined);*** trustee, pres., New Trier Township H.S. BUS. & PROF.: teacher, high school, Holden, ME; ed.; publisher; farmer; western sec., American Missionary Soc., 1868–73; editor-in-chief, *The Advance*, Chicago, IL, 1871–82; western ed., business mgr., *National Tribune*, Washington, DC, 1884; treas., Howard Cty.; ed., *Farm, Field and Stockman*, 1885–92; ed., *Farm, Field and Fireside*, Chicago, 1892–1905; co-owner, Howard and Wilson Publishing Co., Chicago. MIL.: pvt., 3d ME Regt., 1861, 2d lt., 1862, maj., 1863, lt. col., 1864, col., brig. gen., 1865. MEM.: Military Order of the Loyal Legion of the U.S.; American Missionary Soc. WRITINGS: *Why One Veteran Left the Republican Party* (1896); *Incidents and Operations Connected with the*

Capture of Savannah; First Day at Gettysburg. REL.: Congregationalist. RES.: Chicago, IL.

HOWARD, CLINTON NORMAN. b. Jul 28, 1868, Pottsville, PA; d. Apr 25, 1955, Washington, DC; par. Rev. Squire Benjamin and Clare Schenfelder (Nagle) Howard; m. Angeline M. Kellar, May 1, 1888; c. John Gough; Neal Dow; Ella Eva; Horace Greeley; Mrs. Ruth Melody Hutchinson; Mrs. Winifred Elizabeth Snider. EDUC.: trained for ministry. POLIT. & GOV.: ***candidate for Prohibition Party nomination to presidency of the U.S., 1920***. BUS. & PROF.: ed., *Progress*; lecturer, Lyceum and Chautauqua Circuit, 1900–1955. MEM.: American Sabbath Assn.; International Lyceum Assn.; New York Civic League; National Temperance Soc. (vice pres.); American Civic Reform Union (adviser); International Reform Federation (superintendent); Prohibition Union of Christian Men (founder; pres., 1890); National United Comm. for Law Enforcement (chm., 1924–36); World Peace Comm. (pres., 1920–24). WRITINGS: *The Handwriting on the Wall* (1912); *The World on Fire* (1918); *A Joy Ride to the Grave* (1919). REL.: Bapt. RES.: Buffalo, NY.

HOWARD, GEORGE C. POLIT. & GOV.: ***candidate for Republican nomination to presidency of the U.S., 1916***; stand-in for Albert Cummins (q.v.) in OR primary. RES.: Portland, OR.

HOWARD, GUS HILL. b. Jan 31, 1878, Cusseta, GA; d. 1952, Atlanta, GA; par. Dr. Charles Nelson and Emma (Wooldridge) Howard; m. May Belle King, Jun 8, 1899; c. Eva (Mrs. T. Wesley Hill); Ross H.; Gus Hill, Jr.; Edwin; Charles; Catharine (Mrs. Bernard Johnson); May Belle (Mrs. Joe Norton); William D. EDUC.: grad., Cusseta (GA) H.S.; LL.B., Mercer U. POLIT. & GOV.: elected as a Democrat to Sandersville (GA) City Council; city atty., Sandersville; solicitor, City Court, Sandersville, 1903–07; appointed judge, Chattahoochee Circuit, GA, 1917–21; atty., GA State Highway Board, 1921–22; judge, Superior Court of GA, Atlanta Circuit, 1923–36; ***candidate for Democratic nomination to presidency of the U.S., 1932***. BUS. & PROF.: atty.; law practice, Sandersville; law practice, Columbus, GA; law practice, Atlanta, GA. MIL.: pvt., Company A, 1st GA Regt., U.S.V., 1898. MEM.: Odd Fellows; Masons; Red Men; Knights of Pythias. WRITINGS: *Codified Laws of Sandersville, Georgia*; *Codified Laws of Columbus, Georgia*. REL.: Missionary Bapt. RES.: Atlanta, GA.

HOWARD, JOHN EAGER. b. Jun 4, 1752, Baltimore, MD; d. Oct 12, 1827, Belvedere, MD; par. Cornelius and Ruth (Eager) Howard; m. Margaret "Peggy" Oswald Chew, May 18, 1787; c. Benjamin Chew; George; John Eager, Jr.; Charles; William; James; Juliana Elizabeth (Mrs. John McHenry); Sophia (Mrs. William George Reed). EDUC.: private tutors. POLIT. & GOV.: member, Cmte. of Observation, Baltimore Cty., MD, 1774; member, Cmte. to License Suits of Law, Baltimore, MD, 1775; justice, Baltimore Cty., MD, 1785–1787; justice, Orphan's Court, Baltimore, MD, 1786–1787; MD senate elector, 1786; delegate, Continental Congress, 1787–1788; elected as a Federalist to gov. of MD, 1788–1791; elected as a Federalist to MD State Senate, 1791–1796; appointed assoc. justice, Third District of MD, 1792; commissioner, Baltimore Town, MD, 1792; appointed U.S. sec. of war, 1795 (declined); elected as a Federalist to U.S. Senate (MD), 1796–1803, 1816 (declined); ***Federalist candidate for vice presidency of the U.S., 1816***. BUS. & PROF.: soldier. MIL.: commissioned capt., Col. Carvil Hall's "Flying Camp," 1776; commissioned maj., 4th MD Regt., 1777; lt. col., Fifth Maryland Regt., 1778; commissioned brig. gen., U.S. Army, 1803; led charge at Battle of Cowpens, 1781; received Gold Medal and thanks of Continental Congress. MEM.: Jockey Club; Soc. of the Cincinnati. REL.: Episc. RES.: Baltimore, MD.

HOWARD, MILDRED THERESA "MILLIE." b. Nov 18, 1937, Cincinnati, OH; par. Joseph and Marie Katherine (Kamp) Snyder; m. Donnie Gayle Sullivan, 1960–63; m. 2d, John Gilbert Howard; c. Michael Alan; Gregory Ellie; Jeffrey Todd; Julie Ann. EDUC.: grad., St. Xavier Commerician H.S., 1953; A.A., U. of Cincinnati, Clermont, OH, 2 years. POLIT. & GOV.: clerk bailiff, Clermont Cty. (OH) Court, 2 years; member, Clermont Cty. Republican Cmte., 2 years; ***independent candidate for presidency of the U.S., 1992***. BUS. & PROF.: medical sec.; real estate broker; switchboard operator; part-time employee, U.S. Nuclear Regulatory Comm., 2 years; personnel specialist; sec.; waitress. MIL.: SP/4, U.S. Army, 2 years. MEM.: Parent Teachers Organization; Scottish Rite Chorus; Forest-Aires Women's Chorus; St. Peter's Catholic Church Choir. REL.: R.C. MAILING ADDRESS: c/o Diana Darlene Shamblin, 1485 Fagin's Run Rd., New Richmond, OH 45157.

HOWARD, MILFORD WRIARSON. b. Dec 18, 1862, Rome, GA; d. Dec 28, 1937, Los Angeles, CA. EDUC.: public schools; studied law in Cedartown, GA. POLIT. & GOV.: prosecuting atty., De Kalb Cty., AL, four years; city atty., Fort Payne, AL, two terms; chm., De Kalb Cty. Democratic Exec. Cmte.; elected as a Populist to U.S. House (AL), 1895–99; chm. pro tempore, People's Party National Convention, 1900; ***candidate for People's (Middle-of-the-Road) Party nomination to presidency of the U.S., 1900***; member, National Cmte., People's Party; ***candidate for National Independence League nomination to presidency of the U.S., 1908***; Republican candidate for U.S. House (AL), 1910. BUS. & PROF.: atty.; admitted to AL Bar, 1881; law practice, Fort Payne, AL, 1881–95, 1904–18; author; founder, Master Schools (for underprivileged mountain boys and girls). MEM.: Lookout Mountain Scenic Highway Assn. (pres., 1926). WRITINGS: *If Christ Came to Congress*; *The American Plutocracy* (1896). RES.: Fort Payne, AL.

HOWARD, WILLIAM STAMPS, IV. b. Apr 1, 1964, Rome, Italy; par. William Stamps, III, and Patricia Ann (Schlegal) Howard; single. EDUC.: Woodson H.S., Fairfax, VA. POLIT. & GOV.: ***independent candidate for presidency of the U.S., 1980***. BUS. & PROF.: student. REL.: R.C. MAILING ADDRESS: 4620 Tara Dr., Fairfax, VA 22032.

HOWE, ARCHIBALD MURRAY. b. May 20, 1848, Northampton, MA; d. Jan 6, 1916; par. James Murray and Harriete Butler (Clarke) Howe; m. Arvia Sargent Dixwell, Jun 4, 1881. EDUC.: A.B., Harvard U., 1869, A.M., LL.B., 1871; studied law under George S. Hillard. POLIT. & GOV.: sec. to U.S. Rep. Henry L. Pierce, 1873–75; elected member, Common Council, Cambridge, MA, 1875–77; member, MA Exec. Cmte. of Independents, 1884; Civil Service Examiner, Cambridge; elected to the MA State House, 1891; ***National Party candidate for vice presidency of the U.S., 1900 (declined)***. BUS. & PROF.: atty.; admitted to MA Bar, 1871; law practice, Boston, MA. MEM.: MA Reform Club (vice pres.); Boston Bar Assn.; St. Botolph Club. WRITINGS: *Colonel John Brown, of Pittsfield, Massachusetts: The Brave Accuser of Benedict Arnold* (1908). REL.: Unitarian (dir., American Unitarian Assn.). RES.: Boston, MA.

HOWELL, CLARK. b. Sep 21, 1863, Erwinton, Barnwell Cty., SC; d. Nov 14, 1936, Atlanta, GA; par. Evan Park and Julia A. (Erwin) Howell; m. Harriet Glascock Barrett, Apr 9, 1887; m. 2d, Annie Comer, Jul 12, 1900; m. 3d, Margaret Cannon Carr, Apr 6, 1924; c. Clark; Susie; Hugh Comer; Albert; Julian Erwin. EDUC.: A.B., U. of GA, 1883. POLIT. & GOV.: elected as a Democrat to GA State House, 1886–91 (Speaker, 1890–91); member, Dem. Nat'l. Cmte., 1892–1924; elected as a Democrat to GA State Senate, 1900–1906 (pres., 1900–1904); ***candidate for Democratic nomination to vice presidency of the U.S., 1904, 1908***; candidate for Democratic nomination to gov. of GA, 1906; appointed member, U.S. Coal Comm., 1922; appointed member, U.S. Transportation Comm., 1932; appointed member, chm., Federal Aviation Comm., 1934. BUS. & PROF.: journalist; reporter, *New York (NY) Times*, 1883; reporter, *Philadelphia (PA) Press*, 1883; staff, night desk, *Atlanta (GA) Constitution*, 1884, night ed., 1885–89, managing ed., 1889–97, pres., editor-in-chief, 1897–1936; dir., Associated Press, 1900–1936. MEM.: U. of GA (trustee, 1896–1927). WRITINGS: *History of Georgia* (1926). MISC.: organized first Franklin Delano Roosevelt for President Clubs. RES.: Atlanta, GA.

HOWELL, TIMOTHY WILLIAM. b. May 1, 1968, Stanford, CA; par. Kenneth and Carol (Hensel) Howell; single. EDUC.: Ponderosa Elementary School. POLIT. & GOV.: ***Pondacratic Party candidate for presidency of the U.S., 1980***. BUS. & PROF.: paperboy, San Jose (CA) Mercury. Received First Place Baseball Trophy; Two Sportsmanship Awards; Second and Third Place Soccer Awards. MEM.: PAL Soccer; Sunnyvale Pioneer Little League. REL.: Christian. MAILING ADDRESS: 1036 Fernleaf Dr., Sunnyvale, CA 94086.

HOWELL, H. SCOTT. POLIT. & GOV.: ***independent candidate for presidency of the U.S., 1880***. BUS. & PROF.: atty., Keokuk, IA. RES.: Keokuk, IA.

HOWLAND, LEONARD PAUL. b. Dec 5, 1865, Jefferson, OH; d. Dec 23, 1942, Cleveland, OH; S. W. P. and Esther Elizabeth (Leonard) Howland; m. Jessie F. Pruden, Jan 18, 1905. EDUC.: A.B., Oberlin Coll., 1887, A.M., 1894; LL.B., Harvard U., 1890. POLIT. & GOV.: elected as a Republican to U.S. House (OH), 1907–13; Republican candidate for U.S. House (OH), 1912; delegate, Rep. Nat'l. Conv., 1916, 1920, 1924; ***candidate for Republican nomination to presidency of the U.S., 1916***. BUS. & PROF.: atty.; admitted to OH Bar, 1890; law practice, Jefferson, OH, 1890–94; law practice, Cleveland, OH, 1894–1942. MIL.: 2d lt., First OH Cavalry, 1898. MEM.: ABA (exec. cmte., 1918–21; chm., Cmte. on Jurisprudence and Law Reform, 1928–32); Cleveland Bar Assn. (pres.). RES.: Cleveland, OH.

HUBBARD, BARBARA MARX. b. Dec 22, 1929, Washington, DC; par. Louis and Rene (Saltzman) Marx; m. Earl Wade Hubbard (divorced); c. Suzanne Fletcher; Woodleigh; Alexandra Bryant; Earl Wade; Lloyd Frost. EDUC.: B.A. (cum laude), Bryn Mawr Coll., 1951; Sorbonne, U. of Paris, 1949–50. POLIT. & GOV.: founder, Republicans for Johnson, 1964; ***candidate for Democratic nomination to presidency of the U.S., 1972 (declined); candidate for Democratic nomination to vice presidency of the U.S., 1984***. BUS. & PROF.: author; lecturer; social activist; ed., *The Center Letter*, 1967; host, *Potentials* (television series); cofounder, pres., Futures Network, 1978–; administrator, The New Worlds Center, Washington, DC; contributor, *Futurist*. MEM.: Cmte. for the Future; Cmte. for a Positive Future; Inst. of Noetic Sciences (adviser); World Future Soc. (dir., 1968–); L-5 Soc. (dir., 1976–). WRITINGS: *The Hunger of Eve* (1976); *The Evolutionary Journey* (1978); *Theatre for the Future* (1981). REL.: Universal. MAILING ADDRESS: 2325 Porter St., N.W., Washington, DC 20008.

HUBLER, ETHEL G. single. POLIT. & GOV.: delegate, Prohibition Party National Convention, 1924, 1932, 1963; presidential elector, Prohibition Party, 1932, 1956; ***candidate for Prohibition Party nomination to vice presidency of the U.S., 1948 (declined)***. BUS. & PROF.: assoc. ed., ed., *National Voice*, Los Angeles, CA, to 1963. WRITINGS: *The Whirlwind* (1941). RES.: Los Angeles, CA.

HUCKLE, WILBUR ALLEN. POLIT. & GOV.: ***Metropolitan Party candidate for presidency of the U.S., 1964***. BUS. & PROF.: professional baseball player, Jacksonville (FL) and Norfolk (VA) minor league clubs. MISC.: campaign was promotional effort on behalf of New York Mets. MAILING ADDRESS: unknown.

HUDDLESTON THEOPPALAS, ROGER LEE. b. Jul 13, 1936, Oden, AR; par. Tom Bert and Laura Berty (Cobb) Huddleston; single. EDUC.: college, 3 years. POLIT. & GOV.: ***candidate for Republican nomination to presidency of the U.S., 1980, 1988; candidate for Republican nomination to vice presidency of the U.S., 1980; candidate for Democratic nomination to presidency of the U.S., 1980; independent candidate for presidency of the U.S., 1980, 1988***. BUS. & PROF.: inventor; author; songwriter. MIL.: petty officer, third class, U.S. Navy, 7 years. REL.: Protestant. MAILING ADDRESS: 108 Woodbine, Hot Springs, AR 71901.

HUFF, CORRINE A. m. P. Brown, Oct 1969. POLIT. & GOV.: sec. to U.S. Rep. Adam Clayton Powell, Jr. (q.v.); assigned to Cmte. on Education and Labor, U.S. House; ***1-United Nature's Organization candidate for vice presidency of the U.S., 1968, 1972***. BUS. & PROF.: sec.; pres., Huff Enterprises, Ltd. MISC.: involved in sex scandal with U.S. Rep. Adam Clayton Powell. MAILING ADDRESS: c/o Huff Enterprises, Ltd., Nassau, Bahamas.

HUFF, J. HAROLD. b. Dec 25, 1934; m. (divorced); c. two sons. EDUC.: B.S. POLIT. & GOV.: candidate for Democratic nomination to U.S. House (TN), 1980; ***candidate for Democratic nomination to presidency of the U.S., 1984***. BUS. & PROF.: journeyman machinist; tool and die maker. MAILING ADDRESS: 7036 Maynardville Pike, Knoxville, TN 37918.

HUFFMAN, DONALD LEROY. b. Oct 12, 1942, Cedarville, OH; par. Ross Lowell and Grace (Knisley) Huffman; m. Deborah Lynn; c. Sherri Lynn; Anthony Bart; Nicole Suzanne. EDUC.: eighth grade. POLIT. & GOV.: ***independent candidate for presidency of the U.S., 1980***. BUS. & PROF.: arborist, 30 years; owner, tree-cutting farm. REL.: Protestant. MISC.: proponent of "The System" (a method of conducting national referenda via television and IBM computer cards). MAILING ADDRESS: 1590 East High St., Apt. 201, Springfield, OH.

HUFFMAN, ROYCE. POLIT. & GOV.: ***United Independent Party candidate for vice presidency of the U.S., 1980***. BUS. & PROF.: policeman, Philadelphia, PA. MEM.: VFW. MAILING ADDRESS: Philadelphia, PA.

HUGHES, CHARLES EVANS. b. Apr 11, 1862, Glen Falls, NY; d. Aug 27, 1948, Washington, DC; par. Rev. David Charles and Mary Catherine (Connelly) Hughes; m. Antoinette Carter, Dec 5, 1888; c. Charles Evans, Jr.; Helen; Catherine (Mrs. Chauncey L. Waddell); Elizabeth Evans (Mrs. William T. Gossett). EDUC.: Colgate U., 1876–78; A.B., Brown U., 1881, A.M., 1884; LL.B., Columbia U., 1884. POLIT. & GOV.: Republican candidate for mayor of New York, NY, 1905 (declined); appointed special asst. U.S. atty. gen., 1906; elected as a Republican to gov. of NY, 1907–10; ***candidate for Republican nomination to presidency of the U.S., 1908, 1912, 1920, 1928***; appointed assoc. justice, Supreme Court of the U.S., 1910–16; ***Republican candidate for presidency of the U.S., 1916***; chm., Draft Appeals Board, New York, 1917–18; appointed U.S. sec. of state, 1921–25; appointed commissioner plenipotentiary, U.S. International Conference on Limitation of Armaments, 1921; appointed judge, Permanent Court of Arbitration, 1926–30; chm., U.S. Delegation, Sixth Pan-American Conference, 1928; delegate, Pan-American Conference on Arbitration and Conciliation, 1928–29; elected judge, Permanent Court of International Justice, 1928–30; appointed chief justice, Supreme Court of the U.S., 1930–41; appointed special ambassador to Brazilian Centenary Celebration, 1922; chm., NY State Reorganization Comm., 1926; pres., Guatemala-Honduras Arbitral Tribunal, 1932. BUS. & PROF.: atty.; admitted to NY Bar, 1884; clerk, Chamberlain, Carter and Hornblower (law firm), New York, 1884–86; assoc., Carter, Hornblower and Byrne (law firm), New York, 1886–88; partner, Carter, Hughes and Cravath (law firm), New York, 1888–91; prof. of law, Cornell U., 1891–93; partner, Carter, Hughes and Dwight (law firm), New York, 1893–1906; special lecturer, New York Law School, 1893–1900; partner, Hughes, Rounds, Schurman and Dwight (law firm), New York, 1917–21, 1925–30. MEM.: Smithsonian Institution (chancellor, 1930–41); Brown U. (fellow; trustee); U. of Chicago (trustee); NY State Bar Assn. (pres., 1917–18); ABA (pres., 1927–29); NY Legal Aid Soc. (pres., 1917–19); Saint David's Soc. (pres., 1917–18); Italy-America Soc. (pres., 1918–19); New York Cty. Lawyers Assn. (pres., 1919–20); Bar Assn. of the City of New York; Brown University Club; American Soc. for International Law (pres., 1925–29); American Phil. Soc.; American Acad. of Arts and Sciences (fellow); National Geographic Soc.; Middle Temple (hon. bencher); University Club; Union League (pres., 1917–19); Century Club; National Arts Club; Lawyers' Club; Delta Upsilon. AWARDS: Roosevelt Medal, 1928. HON. DEG.: LL.D., Brown U., 1906; LL.D., Columbia U., 1907; LL.D., Knox Coll., 1907; LL.D., Lafayette Coll., 1907; LL.D., Colgate U., 1908; LL.D., Union Coll., 1908; LL.D., George Washington U., 1909; LL.D., Harvard U., 1910; LL.D., U. of PA, 1910; LL.D., Williams Coll., 1910; LL.D., Yale U., 1915; LL.D., U. of MI, 1922; LL.D., Dartmouth Coll., 1923; LL.D., Amherst Coll., 1924; LL.D., Princeton U., 1924; LL.D., State U. of NY, 1924; Dr. Honoris Causa, U. of Brussels, 1924; Dr. Honoris Causa, U. of Louvain, 1924; D.C.L., NY U., 1928; LL.D., PA Military Coll., 1928. WRITINGS: *Conditions of Progress in Democratic Government* (1909); *The Pathway of Peace and Other Addresses* (1925); *The Supreme Court of the United States* (1927); *Our Relation to the Nations of the Western Hemisphere* (1928); *Pan-American Peace Plans* (1929). REL.: Bapt. (trustee, Fifth Avenue Baptist Church). RES.: Washington, DC.

HUGHES, HAROLD EVERETT. b. Feb 10, 1922, Ida Grove, IA; par. Lewis C. and Etta (Kelly) Hughes; m. Eva Mae Mercer, Aug 23, 1941; c. Connie (Mrs. Dennis Otto); Carol (Mrs. Matthew Fatino); Phyllis. EDUC.: grad., Ida Grove (IA) H.S.; U. of IA, 1940–41. POLIT. & GOV.: appointed member, Interstate Commerce Comm. Joint Boards, 1959–62; elected member, IA State Commerce Comm., 1959–63 (chm., 1959–62); Democratic candidate for gov. of IA, 1960; elected as a Democrat to gov. of IA, 1963–69; delegate, Dem. Nat'l. Conv., 1964, 1968, 1972; appointed member, Advisory Council, U.S. Office of Economic Opportunity, 1966–68; chm., Comm. on Democratic Selection of Presidential Nominees, 1968; vice chm., Special Democratic Comm. on Party Structure and Delegate Selection, 1969–; elected as a Democrat to U.S. Senate (IA), 1969–75 (asst. majority whip, 1969–75); appointed member, National Comm. on Marijuana and Drug Abuse, 1970; ***candidate for Democratic nomination to presidency of the U.S., 1972; candidate for Democratic nomination to vice presidency of the U.S., 1972***. BUS. & PROF.: employed in motor transportation industry, 1946–58; mgr., Hinrich's Truck Line, Ida Grove, 1950–53; field representative, IA Motor Truck Assn., 1953–55; founder, mgr., IA Better Trucking Bureau, 1955–58; evangelist. MIL.: pvt., U.S. Army, 1942–45. MEM.: American Legion; Knights of Pythias; Masons (Royal Arch Mason; Mizpah Commandery; Abu Bekr Shrine); National Governors' Conference (exec. cmte., 1965–67); Democratic Governors' Conference (chm., 1966–68); States Urban Action Center (trustee, 1967–68); Midwest Democratic Conference of Senators (1972–75); International Council on Alcohol and Addictions (pres.). HON. DEG.: D.Sc., Coll. of Osteopathic Medicine and Surgery, 1965; LL.D., Cornell Coll., 1966; LL.D., Buena Vista Coll., 1967; LL.D., Graceland Coll., 1967; D.H.L., Marycrest Coll., 1967; LL.D., Loras Coll., 1968; LL.D., Grinnell Coll., 1969; LL.D., Lehigh U., 1969; D.C.L., Simpson Coll., 1969. REL.: Methodist. MISC.: recovered alcoholic. MAILING ADDRESS: 2900 Grand Ave., Des Moines, IA.

HUGHES, LOUIS CAMERON. b. May 15, 1844, Philadelphia, PA; d. Nov 24, 1915, Tucson, AZ; par. Samuel and Elizabeth (Edwards) Hughes; m. E. Josephine Brawley, Jul 1868; c. John T.; Gertrude; Josephine M. EDUC.: Meadville (PA) Acad., 1866–68; PA State Normal School, 1868–69; Meadville Unitarian Theological Seminary; studied law. POLIT. & GOV.: district atty., Tucson, AZ, 2 terms; probate judge, AZ, 2 terms; atty. gen. of AZ, 1873–74; delegate, Dem. Nat'l. Conv., 1884, 1888, 1892; appointed U.S. court commissioner, 4 years (1880s); appointed territorial gov. of AZ, 1893–96; ***candidate for Prohibition Party nomination to presidency of the U.S., 1896; candidate for Prohibition Party nomination to vice presidency of the U.S., 1896***. BUS. & PROF.: atty.; law practice, Pittsburgh, PA; law practice, Tucson, 1871; publisher, *Tucson Star*, 1877–1907; chancellor, U. of AZ, 1898–1900; founder, Azurite Copper and Gold Mining Co.; managing ed., *Arizona Daily Star*. MIL.: soldier, Company A, 101st PA Volunteers, Civil War; soldier, Knapp's Pittsburgh Battery, Civil War. MEM.: Ancient Order of United Workmen (member, First Lodge in U.S.); World's Fair (member, sec., AZ Board of Commissioners, 1892–93); AZ Press Assn. (pres., 1892); U. of AZ (chm., Board of Regents, 1898–1900). REL.: Presb. MISC.: raised in Presbyterian orphanage; advocate of joint Arizona–New Mexico statehood; removed as territorial gov. in response to charge of malfeasance arising from land speculation; noted as labor reformer and advocate of 8-hour workday, women's suffrage; opponent of gambling and liquor traffic. RES.: Tucson, AZ.

HUGHES, SARAH TILGHMAN. b. Aug 2, 1896, Baltimore, MD; d. Apr 23, 1985, Dallas, TX; par. James Cooke and Elizabeth (Haughton) Tilghman; m. George E. Hughes, Mar 13, 1922. EDUC.: A.B., Goucher Coll., 1917; LL.B., George Washington U., 1922. POLIT. & GOV.: elected as a Democrat to the TX State House, 1931–35; judge, 14th District Court of TX, 1935–61; ***candidate for Democratic nomination to vice presidency of the U.S., 1952 (withdrew)***; appointed judge, U.S. District Court of North TX, 1961–1985. BUS. & PROF.: teacher, Salem Acad. and Coll., Winston-Salem, NC, 1917–19; policewoman, Washington, DC, 1919–22; atty.; admitted to TX Bar, 1922; law practice, Dallas, TX, 1922–35; instructor, Jefferson School of Law, 1923–31; instructor, YMCA Dallas, 1939–42; instructor in law, Southern Methodist U., 1942–43. MEM.: National Federation of Business and Professional Women's Clubs, 1931– (first vice pres., 1948–50; pres., 1950–52); International Federation of Business and Professional Women's Clubs (vice pres., 1953–59); Goucher Coll. (trustee); Bishop Coll. (trustee); National Comm. of UNESCO; State Bar of TX; ABA; Dallas Bar Assn.; American Jud. Soc.; National Assn. of Women Lawyers; AAUW; Phi Beta Kappa; Delta Sigma Rho; Kappa Beta Pi; Delta Gamma; Delta Kappa Gamma (hon.); ZONTA (international graternal group); League of Women Voters; Women's Club; Dallas United Nations Assn.; Inter-ABA; Council on World Affairs. AWARDS: Alumni Achievement Award, George Washington U.; Distinguished Service Award, East Texas C. of C.; ZONTA Service Award; award, Dallas Business and Professional Women's Club; named "Outstanding Woman in the Field of Law"; received Federal Bar Award; service award, TX Council of Churches; All-Time Headliner Award, Dallas Press Club; named "Texas Woman of the Year," Press Media. HON. DEG.: LL.D., Goucher Coll., 1950; LL.D., IN State U., 1967; LL.D., Southern Methodist U., 1967; LL.D., IN Wesleyan U. WRITINGS: "The Unfortunate One Per Cent Our Responsibility," *Texas Study of Secondary Education*, 1959; "Judicial Selection and Tenure," *Women Lawyers Journal*, 1964; "World Peace through World Law," *Texas Observer*, 1965. REL.: Episc. MISC.: administered oath of office to President Lyndon Baines Johnson (q.v.) aboard Air Force One, Nov 22, 1963. RES.: Dallas, TX.

HULICK, ROBERT. POLIT. & GOV.: ***independent candidate for presidency of the U.S., 1980***. MAILING ADDRESS: 1526 Mulvane, Topeka, KS 66604.

HULL, CORDELL. b. Oct 2, 1871, Overton Cty., TN; d. Jul 23, 1955, Bethesda, MD; par. William and Elizabeth (Riley) Hull; m. Rose Frances Witz Whitney, Nov 24, 1917; c. none. EDUC.: National Normal U., 1889–90; B.L., Cumberland U., 1891. POLIT. & GOV.: delegate, TN State Democratic Convention, 1890; elected as a Democrat to TN State House, 1893–97; appointed judge, Fifth Judicial Circuit of TN, 1903–07; elected as a Democrat to U.S. House (TN), 1907–21, 1923–31; Democratic candidate for U.S. House (TN), 1920; appointed chm., Dem. Nat'l. Cmte., 1921–24 (member, 1914–28); ***candidate for Democratic nomination to presidency of the U.S., 1924, 1928, 1940, 1944***; elected as a Democrat to U.S. Senate (TN), 1931–33; appointed U.S. sec. of state, 1933–44; chm., American Delegation, Monetary and Economic Conference, 1933; chm., American Delegation, International Conference of American States, 1933, 1938; chm., American Delegation, Inter-American Conference on the Maintenance of Peace, 1936; delegate, Second Consultative Meeting of Ministers of Foreign Affairs of American Republics, 1940; ***candidate for Democratic nomination to vice presidency of the U.S., 1944***; delegate, U.N. Conference, 1945. BUS. & PROF.: atty.; admitted to TN Bar, 1891; law practice, Celina, TN. MIL.: capt., Company H, Fourth TN Infantry, 1898. AWARDS: Theodore Roosevelt Distinguished Service Medal, 1945; Nobel Peace Prize, 1945. HON. DEG.: LL.D., Columbia U., 1934; LL.D., Cumberland U., 1934; LL.D., George Washington U., 1934; LL.D., U. of Notre Dame, 1934; LL.D., William and Mary Coll., 1934; LL.D., Williams Coll., 1934; LL.D., PA Military Coll., 1935; L.H.D., Rollins Coll., 1935. LL.D., U. of MI, 1935; LL.D., U. of WI, 1935. WRITINGS: *Memoirs of Cordell Hull* (2 vols., 1948). RES.: Carthage, TN.

HULST, DOROTHY JEAN VANDER STEL. POLIT. & GOV.: ***candidate for Republican nomination to presidency of the U.S., 1988***. MAILING ADDRESS: 700 Fairview, N.E., #1, Grand Rapids, MI 49503.

HUMPHREY, HUBERT HORATIO, JR. b. May 27, 1911, Wallace, SD; d. Jan 13, 1978, Waverly, MN; par. Hubert Horatio and Christine (Sannes) Humphrey; m. Muriel Fay Buck, Sep 3, 1936; c. Nancy Faye (Mrs. C. Bruce Solomonson); Hubert Horatio III; Robert Andrew; Douglas Sannes. EDUC.: Denver Coll. of Pharmacy, 1932–33; B.A. (magna cum laude), 1939, postgrad. study, 1940–41; M.A., LA State U., 1940. POLIT. & GOV.: appointed MN state dir., WPA, 1941–43; Democratic candidate for mayor of Minneapolis, MN, 1943; appointed asst. regional dir., War Manpower Comm., 1943; MN campaign mgr., Roosevelt-Truman Campaign, 1944; elected as a Democrat to mayor of Minneapolis, 1945–48; delegate, Dem. Nat'l. Conv., 1948, 1952, 1968; elected as a Democrat to U.S. Senate (MN), 1949–65 (majority whip, 1961–64), 1971–78; ***candidate for Democratic nomination to presidency of the U.S., 1952, 1960, 1964, 1972, 1976; candidate for Democratic nomination to vice presidency of the U.S., 1956***; U.S. delegate to the U.N., 1956–58; delegate, UNESCO Conference, 1958; ***elected as a Democrat to vice presidency of the U.S., 1965–69***; member, National Security Council; hon. chm., President's Council on Equal Opportunity; member, President's Cmte. on Equal Employment Opportunity; member, National Aerospace and Space Council; member, Peace Corps Advisory Council; ***Democratic candidate for presidency of the U.S., 1968***. BUS. & PROF.: pharmacist; employee, Humphrey Drug Store, Huron, SD, 1933–37; asst. instructor of political science, LA State U., 1939–40; asst. instructor of political science, U. of MN, 1940–41, prof., 1969–70; prof. of political science, Macalester Coll., 1943–44, 1969–70; chm. of the board of consultants, *Encyclopedia Britannica*; chm. of the board of consultants, Encyclopedia Britannica Educational Corp. MEM.: Smithsonian Institution (regent); Delta Sigma Rho; Phi Beta Kappa; Public Administration Soc.; APSA; American Acad. of Arts and Sciences. AWARDS: Outstanding Young Man in Minnesota, MN Junior Assn. of Commerce, 1945; Outstanding Minneapolitan, Junior Assn. of Commerce, 1945; Zionist Award; medallion, Israel Bond Organization. HON. DEG.: LL.D., Howard U., 1967; LL.D., Brandeis U.; LL.D., Hebrew Union Coll.; LL.D., National U.; LL.D., RI Coll. of Pharmacy and Allied Sciences. WRITINGS: *America and the Now Generation; The Cause is Mankind* (1964); *A Liberal Program for Modern America* (1964); *The War on Poverty* (1964); *Political Philosophy of the New Deal; Young America in the New World; School Desegregation: Documents and Commentaries* (1964). REL.: United Church of Christ. RES.: Waverly, MN.

HUMPHREYS, JAMES McADORY. POLIT. & GOV.: ***Constitutional Party candidate for presidency of the U.S., 1980; candidate for Republican nomination to presidency of the U.S., 1988***. MAILING ADDRESS: 973 Cyndi Circle, Chico, CA 95926.

HUNSCHER, WILLIAM HOMER. b. Apr 18, 1938, Lansdale, PA; par. Homer Leroy and Martha Anne (Alderman) Hunscher; m. Anne Weadon; c. Lisa Anne; William Homer, Jr.; Karen Beth. EDUC.: grad., Quakertown (PA) H.S., 1955; grad., Wyoming (PA) Seminary, 1956; B.S., Lafayette Coll., 1960; M.B.A., Babson Coll., 1970. POLIT. & GOV.: NH Republican committeeman, 1976; chm., NH Libertarian Party, 1976–79; presidential elector, Libertarian Party, 1976; Libertarian Party candidate for NH State House, 1978; ***candidate for Libertarian Party nomination to presidency of the U.S., 1980***. BUS. & PROF.: sales engineer, Union Carbide Corp.; sales mgr., Nacon Corp.; vice pres., Data Terminal Systems, Inc.; pres., Fasfax Corp.; pres., Hunscher Enterprises, Inc.; marketing dir., Functional Automation, Inc.; exec. vice pres., Sunhouse, Inc.; dir., Functional Biosystems, Inc.; management consultant, Milford, NH; tree farmer; real estate investor. MIL.: officer, U.S. Army (Airborne). MEM.: Phi Delta Theta; VFW; Alumni Assn. of Lafayette Coll. (pres.). AWARDS: Mayfield Award as Outstanding Young Alumnus, Lafayette Coll. MAILING ADDRESS: P.O. Box 37, Milford, NH 03055.

HUNT, JAMES BAXTER, JR. b. May 16, 1937, Greensboro, NC; par. James Baxter and Elsie (Brame) Hunt; m. Carolyn Joyce Leonard, Aug 20, 1958; c. Rebecca Joyce; James Baxter, III; Rachel Henderson; Elizabeth Brame. EDUC.: B.S., NC State U., 1959, M.S., 1962; J.D., U. of NC, 1964. POLIT. & GOV.: delegate, Dem. Nat'l. Conv., 1968; asst. to the chm., NC Democratic Party, 1968–70; chm., State Jefferson-Jackson Dinner, 1969; member, Dem. Nat'l. Cmte. Rules Cmte., 1969–70; chm., NC Democratic Party Study Cmte., 1969; ***candidate for Democratic nomination to vice presidency of the U.S., 1972***; elected as a Democrat to lt. gov. of NC, 1973–77; elected as a Democrat to gov. of NC, 1977–85, 1993–; Democratic candidate for U.S. Senate (NC), 1984. BUS. & PROF.: ed., *The Agriculturist*; economic adviser to government of Nepal, Ford Foundation, 1964–66; atty.; admitted to NC Bar, 1964; partner, Kirby, Webb and Hunt (law firm), 1966–72; training consultant to Peace Corps, 1966–67. MEM.: NC State U. Alumni Assn. (dir.); Coastal Plains Development Assn. (pres.); NC State U. Foundation (dir.); Farm Bureau; Good Neighbor Council; BSA; Arts Council; Educational Development Council, 1966–72; Phi Kappa Phi; Gamma Sigma Delta; Kappa Phi Kappa; Golden Chain; Blue Key; Thirty and Three; Alpha Zeta; Phi Alpha Delta; NC Young Democrats Clubs (vice pres.; pres., 1968); Sertoma Club; Junior C. of C.; Grange; NC State Bar Assn. AWARDS: Harry S Truman Award, National Young Democrats Clubs, 1975; Outstanding Young Man of the Year Award, Wilson (NC) Junior C. of C., 1969. WRITINGS: *Acreage Controls and Poundage Controls for Flue Cured Tobacco* (1962); *Rally Around the Precinct* (1968). REL.: Presb. (Elder). MAILING ADDRESS: Route 1, Box 138, Lucama, NC 27851.

HUNTER, ROBERT MERCER TALIAFERRO. b. Apr 21, 1809, Essex Cty., VA; d. Jul 18, 1887, Lloyds, VA; par. James and Maria (Garnett) Hunter; m. Mary Evelina Dandridge, Oct 4, 1836; c. Martha T.; seven others. EDUC.: grad., U. of VA, 1828. POLIT. & GOV.: elected as a Democrat to VA State House of Delegates, 1833–35; elected as a Democrat to VA State Senate, 1835–37; elected as a Democrat to U.S. House (VA), 1837–43 (Speaker, 1839–41), 1845–47; Democratic candidate for U.S. House (VA), 1843, 1847; elected as a Democrat to U.S. Senate (VA), 1847–61; ***candidate for Democratic nomination to presidency of the U.S., 1860***; delegate, Confederate Provisional Congress, 1861; appointed sec. of state, Confederate States of America, 1861–62; member, Confederate States Senate (VA), 1862–65; appointed peace commissioner, 1865; elected as a Democrat to state treas. of VA, 1877. BUS. & PROF.: atty.; admitted to VA Bar, 1830. RES.: Lloyds, VA.

HUNTINGTON, SAMUEL. b. Jul 3, 1731, Windham, CT; d. Jan 5, 1796, Norwich, CT; par. Nathaniel and Mehetable (Thurston) Huntington; m. Martha Devotion, 1761; c. Samuel (adopted); Francis (adopted). POLIT. & GOV.: member, CT General Assembly, 1765; appointed king's atty., CT, 1765; justice of the peace, New London, CT, 1765–1775; judge, Superior Court of CT, 1773–1783; appointed member, Cmte. for Defense of CT, 1775; member, Continental Congress, 1775–1784 (pres., 1779–1781); signer of Declaration of Independence, 1776; delegate, Currency Convention, 1777; chief justice, Superior Court of CT, 1784; elected to lt. gov. of CT, 1785–1786; elected as a Federalist to gov. of CT, 1786–1796; ***received 2 electoral votes for presidency of the U.S., 1789***. BUS. & PROF.: atty.; admitted to CT Bar, 1758; law practice, Norwich, CT. HON. DEG.: LL.D., Dartmouth Coll., 1785; LL.D., Yale U., 1787. REL.: Puritan. RES.: Norwich, CT.

HURLEY, PATRICK JAY. b. Jan 8, 1883, Choctaw Indian Territory; d. Jul 30, 1963, Santa Fe, NM; par. Pierce and Mary (Kelly) Hurley; m. Ruth Wilson, Dec 5, 1919; c. Patricia (Mrs. DeForest R. Lawrence); Ruth (Mrs. David Hughes); Wilson; Mary Hope (Mrs. Edwin Borden White, Jr.). EDUC.: A.B., Baptist Indian U., 1905; LL.B., National U., 1908. POLIT. & GOV.: Republican candidate for OK State Senate, 1910; delegate, Rep. Nat'l. Conv., 1924, 1952, 1956; chm., OK Republican State Convention, 1926; appointed U.S. undersec. of war, 1929; appointed U.S. sec. of war, 1929–33; chm., U.S. War Policies Comm., 1931–33; ***candidate for Republican nomination to vice presidency of the U.S., 1932; candidate for Republican nomination to presidency of the U.S., 1940***; appointed U.S. minister to New Zealand, 1942–43; appointed personal representative of the president to the U.S.S.R., 1942; appointed personal representative of the president to Egypt and the Middle East, 1943; appointed personal representative of the president to the Republic of China, 1944; appointed U.S. ambassador to the Republic of China, 1944; Republican candidate for U.S. Senate (NM), 1946, 1948, 1952. BUS. & PROF.: mule driver, Atoka (OK) Coal and Mining Co., 1894; cowpuncher, TX; atty.; admitted to OK Bar, 1908; law practice, Tulsa, OK; admitted to the Bar of the Supreme Court of the U.S., 1912; national atty., Choctaw Nation, 1912–17; law practice, Washington, DC, 1933–35; dir., First National Bank, Tulsa; pres., First Trust and Savings Bank of Tulsa; pres., Uranium Inst. of America, 1957–58. MIL.: pvt., corp., sgt., capt., Indian Territory Volunteer Cavalry, 1902–07; capt., OK National Guard, 1914–17; maj., lt. col., col., U.S. Army, 1917–19; col., U.S.A.R., brig. gen., 1942, maj. gen., 1943; Distinguished Service Medal with Oak Leaf Cluster, 1942; Silver Star; Distinguished Flying Cross, 1943; Purple Heart. MEM.: BSA (National Council); Boys Clubs of America (dir.); U.S. C. of C. (founder); ABA; OK State Bar Assn.; NM State Bar Assn.; Tulsa Bar Assn. (pres., 1910); American Legion; VFW; Disabled American Veterans; Sigma Chi; Phi Beta Kappa; Chevy Chase Club; Congressional Club. AWARDS: Aztec Eagle (Mexico, 1943); Medal of Merit, 1946; Order of Yun Hwei (Cloud Banner, 1947); Special Grand Cordon, Chinese National Government; Order of the Crown, Second Class (Iran, 1949). HON. DEG.: LL.D., George Washington U., 1913; LL.D., National U., 1934; D.H.L., U. of Dallas, 1960; LL.D., OK A&M Coll. REL.: Christian. MISC.: negotiated settlement between Luxembourg and the AEF, 1919; as chief counsel for Richfield Oil Corp., negotiated agreement between Mexico and five expropriated oil companies, 1940; wounded in Darwin, Australia, 1942; drafted Iran Declaration, Teheran Conference, 1943. RES.: Santa Fe, NM.

HURLEY, WILLIAM HENRY. b. Apr 11, 1923, Birmingham, AL; par. George and Thelma (Barnes) Hurley; m. Mavis D. Hurley, Feb 14, 1947; c. W. Bruce. EDUC.: high school grad.; business college, 2 years. POLIT. & GOV.: campaign worker, George C. Wallace (q.v.) for Governor campaigns, 1963–84; ***candidate for Democratic nomination to presidency of the U.S., 1984, 1988, 1992***. BUS. & PROF.: real estate agent; home builder; owner, insurance agency. MIL.: U.S. Air Force, 1942–45. WRITINGS: *Simple Steps to Real Estate Fortunes*. REL.: unspecified. MAILING ADDRESS: 1026-15th Place, S.W., Birmingham, AL 35211.

HURST, ELMORE W. b. Dec 6, 1851, Rock Island, IL; d. Jul 21, 1915, Rock Island, IL; m. Harriet M. Field, May, 1873. EDUC.: grad., Rock Island H.S., 1865; read law under William H. Best. POLIT. & GOV.: elected as a Democrat to IL State House, 1889–90, 1899–1900; presidential elector, Democratic Party, 1896, 1900; candidate for Democratic nomination to gov. of IL, 1908, 1912; delegate, Dem. Nat'l. Conv., 1912; ***candidate for Democratic nomination to vice presidency of the U.S., 1912***; tendered post of U.S. ambassador to Russia, 1912 (declined). BUS. & PROF.: bookkeeper, wholesale notion store, Rock Island, 1865–70; bookkeeper, cashier, Rock Island National Bank, 1870; atty.; admitted to IL Bar, 1883; partner, Jackson and Hurst (law firm), Rock Island. RES.: Rock Island, IL.

HUTCHESON, WILLIAM LEVI. b. Feb 7, 1874, Saginaw Cty., MI; d. Oct 20, 1953, Indianapolis, IN; par. Daniel O. and Elizabeth (Culver) Hutcheson; m. Bessie King, 1893; m. 2d, Jessie Tufts Sharon, 1928; m. 3d, Madaline Wilson; c. Maurice A.; Mrs. Roy G. Stephens; Mrs. J. H. Wells. EDUC.: rural schools, MI. POLIT. & GOV.: appointed member, War Labor Board, 1917–19; dir., Labor Div., National Republican Party, 1932, 1936; ***candidate for Republican nomination to vice presidency of the U.S., 1944***. BUS. & PROF.: carpenter, 1890; business representative, United Brotherhood of Carpenters and Joiners, 1906–12, second vice pres., 1912–13, first vice pres., 1913–15, gen. pres., 1915–52, pres. emeritus, 1952–53; first vice pres., AFL, 1936, 1939–40 (member, AFL Peace Cmte., 1942). MEM.: America First Cmte. (exec. cmte.); Home for Aged Carpenters (dir.); C. of C.; Shriners; Masons (Scottish Rite; York Rite; Royal Order of Scotland; 33°); Odd Fellows; Columbia Club. REL.: Methodist. RES.: Indianapolis, IN.

HYDE, ARTHUR MASTICK. b. Jul 12, 1877, Princeton, MO; d. Oct 17, 1947, New York, NY; par. Ira Barnes and Caroline Emily (Mastick) Hyde; m. Hortense Cullers, Oct 19, 1904; c. Caroline Cullers (Mrs. James Paul Kelly; Mrs. Stephen Hathaway Swift). EDUC.: Oberlin Acad.; A.B., U. of MI, 1899; LL.B., State U. of IA, 1900. POLIT. & GOV.: elected as a Republican to mayor of Princeton, MO, 1908–12; Progressive Party candidate for atty. gen. of MO, 1912; elected as a Republican to gov. of MO, 1921–25; ***candidate for Republican nomination to vice presidency of the U.S., 1924***; candidate for Republican nomination to U.S. Senate (MO), 1928; appointed U.S. sec. of agriculture, 1929–33; chm., Federal Drought Relief Cmte., 1930. BUS. & PROF.: atty.; admitted to MO Bar, 1900–1915; law practice, Princeton, 1900–1915; businessman; pres., Sentinel Life Insurance Co., Kansas City, MO, 1927–28; farmer, Trenton, MO; owner, Buick distributorship, 16 northern MO counties; law practice, Trenton, MO, 1933–47. MIL.: capt., Missouri National Guard, 1905–06. MEM.: Masons (33°; Shriner); Odd Fellows; MO Wesleyan Coll. (trustee); Conference of Methodist Laymen (founder, 1935–36); SAR; Elks; Southern Methodist U. (trustee); ABA; MO State Bar Assn.; Mercer Cty. Bar Assn.; Grundy Cty. Bar Assn.; Kansas City Club; Delta Upsilon; Kansas City C. of C.; Rotary Club; Commercial Club; National Press Club. HON. DEG.: LL.D., Park Coll., 1922; LL.D., Drury Coll., 1923; LL.D., Marshall Coll., 1923; LL.D., Westminster Coll., 1923; LL.D., U. of MI, 1929. WRITINGS: *The Hoover Policies* (coauthor, 1937). REL.: Methodist (Bible teacher). RES.: Trenton, MO.

HYDE, HENRY JOHN. b. Apr 18, 1924, Chicago, IL; par. Henry Clay and Monica (Kelly) Hyde; m. Jeanne Marie Simpson, Nov 8, 1947; c. Henry John, Jr.; Robert; Laura; Anthony. EDUC.: Georgetown U., 1942–43, B.B.S., 1947; Duke U., 1943–44; J.D., Loyola U., 1949. POLIT. & GOV.: Republican candidate for U.S. House (IL), 1962; elected as a Republican to IL State House, 1967–74 (majority leader, 1971–72); elected as a Republican to U.S. House (IL), 1975–; ***candidate for Republican nomination to vice presidency of the U.S., 1980***. BUS. & PROF.: atty.; admitted to IL Bar, 1950. MIL.: ensign, lt. (jg), U.S. Navy, 1942–46; commander, U.S.N.R., 1961–69. MEM.: Sigma Chi; Phi Alpha Delta; Trial Lawyers Club of Chicago (pres., 1962); ABA; IL State Bar Assn.; Chicago Bar Assn.; IL Defense counsel; Knights of Columbus. AWARDS: "Best Freshman Representative, 75th Illinois General Assembly," IL Political Reporters. REL.: R.C. MAILING ADDRESS: 1004 Argyle, Bensenville, IL 60106.

HYLAN, JOHN FRANCIS. b. Apr 20, 1868, Hunter, NY; d. Jan 12, 1936, Forest Hills, NY; par. Thomas H. and Juliette (Jones) Hylan; m. Marian Louise O'Hara, Sep 24, 1889; c. Virginia (Mrs. John F. Sinnott). EDUC.: LL.B., NY Law School, 1897. POLIT. & GOV.: candidate for New York (NY) municipal judge, 1905; appointed city magistrate, New York, 1906–14; appointed and subsequently elected judge, Cty. Court, Kings Cty., NY, 1914–18; elected as a Democrat to mayor of New York, 1918–25; ***candidate for Democratic nomination to presidency of the U.S., 1920; candidate for Democratic nomination to vice presidency of the U.S., 1924***; candidate for Democratic nomination to mayor of New York, 1925; appointed justice, Children's Court, New York; Recovery Party candidate for gov. of NY, 1934. BUS. & PROF.: fireman, engineer, elevated railroad, Brooklyn, NY; atty.; admitted to NY Bar, 1897; partner (with Harry C. Underhill), law firm, Brooklyn. REL.: R.C. RES.: Brooklyn, NY.

HYLTON, DONNA MARIE. b. Aug 4, 1978, Big Stone Gap, VA; par. David Wayne and Bessie (Gilliam) Hylton; single. EDUC.: Powell Valley (VA) H.S. POLIT. & GOV.: ***Youth of America Party candidate for presidency of the U.S., 1992***. BUS. & PROF.: student. REL.: Holiness Christian. MAILING ADDRESS: P.O. Box 658, Big Stone Gap, VA 21219.

IACCOCA, LIDO ANTHONY "LEE." b. Oct 15, 1924, Allentown, PA; par. Nicola and Antoinette (Perrotto) Iaccoca; m. Mary McCleary, Sep 29, 1956 (deceased, 1983); m. 2d, Peggy Johnson (divorced, 1988); m. 3d, Darrien Earle, 1990; c. Cathryn Lisa; Lia Antoinette. EDUC.: B.S., Lehigh U., 1945; M.E., Princeton U., 1946. POLIT. & GOV.: appointed member, Presidential Comm. to Restore the Statue of Liberty, 1982–86 (chm., 1986); ***candidate for Democratic nomination to presidency of the U.S., 1984, 1988; candidate for Democratic nomination to vice presidency of the U.S., 1984, 1988; candidate for Republican nomination to presidency of the U.S., 1988***. BUS. & PROF.: asst. dir., sales mgr., Ford Motor Co., Philadelphia, PA; district sales mgr., Ford Motor Co., Washington, DC, 1946–56, truck marketing mgr., 1956–57, car marketing mgr., 1957–60, vehicle marketing mgr., 1960; vice pres., gen. mgr., Ford Div., Ford Motor Co., 1960–65, vice pres. of car and truck group, 1965–67, exec. vice pres., 1967–68, pres., 1970–78; pres., Ford North American Operations, 1969–70; pres., Chrysler Corp., Highland Park, MI, 1978–79, chm. of the board, 1979–93; dir., Boston Co. MEM.: Lehigh U. (trustee); Motor Vehicle Manufacturers' Assn. (dir.); Joslin Diabetes Foundation, Inc.; Tau Beta Pi; BSA (Detroit Council); United Foundation (dir.); U. of Southern CA Graduate School of Administration (dir.); National Industrial Pollution Council; Soc. of Automotive Engineers. AWARDS: Wallace Memorial Fellow, Princeton U.; Man of the Year, City of Detroit, MI, 1982. HON. DEG.: LL.D., Muhlenberg Coll.; LL.D., Lawrence Inst. of Technology; LL.D., Babson Inst. REL.: R.C. MAILING ADDRESS: 571 Edgemere Court, Bloomfield Hills, MI 48013.

ICKES, HAROLD LeCLAIR. b. Mar 15, 1874, Blair Cty., PA; d. Feb 3, 1952, Washington, DC. EDUC.: grad., U. of Chicago, 1897; LL.B., U. of Chicago, 1907. POLIT. & GOV.: IL dir., Hiram W. Johnson (q.v.) for President Campaign, 1924; appointed U.S. sec. of the interior, 1933–46; administrator, Public Works Administration; ***candidate for Democratic nomination to vice presidency of the U.S., 1940***. BUS. & PROF.: reporter, Chicago, IL; atty.; admitted to IL Bar, 1907; newspaper columnist; author. MEM.: YMCA. WRITINGS: *The New Democracy* (1934); *Back to Work* (1935); *Autobiography of a Curmudgeon* (1943); *My Twelve Years with F. D. R.* (1948); *The Secret Diaries of Harold L. Ickes* (1953–54). MISC.: known as "Honest Harold" and "The Old Curmudgeon." RES.: MD.

IMRE, JOHN F. POLIT. & GOV.: ***independent candidate for presidency of the U.S., 1980***. MAILING ADDRESS: MO.

INGALLS, DAVID SINTON. b. Jan 28, 1899, Cleveland, OH; par. Albert Stimson and Jane (Taft) Ingalls; m. Louise Harkness, Jun 27, 1922; c. Edith; Jane; Louise; Ann; David. EDUC.: B.A., Yale U., 1920; LL.B., Harvard U., 1923. POLIT. & GOV.: elected as a Republican to OH State House, 1927–29; appointed asst. U.S. sec. of the navy for aeronautics, 1929–32; ***candidate for Republican nomination to vice presidency of the U.S., 1932***; appointed dir. for Public Health and Welfare, Cleveland, OH, 1933–35; campaign mgr., Robert A. Taft (q.v.) for President Campaign, 1952. BUS. & PROF.: atty.; admitted to OH Bar, 1923; law practice, Cleveland; partner, Squire, Sanders and Dempsey (law firm), Cleveland, 1923–29; vice pres., gen. mgr., Pan American Air Ferries, Inc., 1941–42; officer, Pan American World Airways, 1945–; vice chm., dir., Taft Broadcasting Co.; vice pres., dir., Virginia Hot Springs, Inc. MIL.: capt., lt. commander, U.S.N.R., 1917, 1942, commodore, 1945; Distinguished Flying Cross (Great Britain); Distinguished Service Cross (U.S.); Legion of Honor (France). MEM.: Union Club; Masons; American Legion; VFW; Forty and Eight; Chagrin Valley Hunt Club. REL.: Episc. RES.: Chagrin Falls, OH.

INGALLS, JOHN JAMES. b. Dec 29, 1833, Middleton, MA; d. Aug 16, 1900, East Las Vegas, NM; par. Elias Theodore and Eliza (Chase) Ingalls; m. Anna Louisa Cheseborough, Sep 27, 1865; c. Ellsworth; Ralph; Ethel (Mrs. E. G. Blair); Muriel (Mrs. A. J. Davis); Ruth; Addison; Marion; Constance; Sheffield; Faith; Louisa. EDUC.: grad., Haverhill (MA) H.S.; grad., Williams Coll.,

1855; studied law. POLIT. & GOV.: delegate, KS State Constitutional Convention, Wyandotte, KS, 1859; sec., KS Territorial Council, 1860; sec., KS State Senate, 1861; elected as a Republican to KS State Senate, 1862; candidate for Republican nomination to lt. gov. of KS, 1862; Union Party candidate for lt. gov. of KS, 1862; Republican candidate for lt. gov. of KS, 1864; elected as a Republican to U.S. Senate (KS), 1873–91 (pres. pro tempore, 1887–91); ***candidate for Republican nomination to presidency of the U.S., 1888***; Republican candidate for U.S. Senate (KS), 1890. BUS. & PROF.: atty.; admitted to MA Bar, 1857; law practice, Atchison, KS, 1860–1900; pres., Kansas Trust and Banking Co., Atchison, 1859–73; ed., *Atchison Champion*, 1863–65; founder, *Kansas Magazine*; lecturer; journalist; farmer. MIL.: maj., judge advocate, lt. col., KS Volunteers, 1863–65. HON. DEG.: LL.D., Williams Coll., 1884. WRITINGS: *Edmund Ingalls . . . and Some of His Descendants* (1881); *Cushings Manual of Parliamentary Practice*. RES.: Atchison, KS.

INGERSOLL, CHARLES ROBERTS. b. Sep 16, 1821, New Haven, CT; d. Jan 25, 1903, New Haven, CT; par. Ralph Isaacs and Margaret Catherine Eleanora (van den Heuvel) Ingersoll; m. Virginia Gregory, Dec 18, 1847; c. Francis Gregory; Justine Henrietta; Virginia (Mrs. Harry T. Gause); Charles V.; Elizabeth Shaw (Mrs. George G. Haven, Jr.); Margaret V. EDUC.: grad., Yale U., 1840, LL.B., 1844. POLIT. & GOV.: appointed clerk, CT State Assembly, 1846; elected as a Democrat to CT State House, 1856–58, 1866, 1871; elected as a Democrat to gov. of CT, 1873–77; presidential elector, Democratic Party, 1876; ***candidate for Democratic nomination to vice presidency of the U.S., 1892***. BUS. & PROF.: atty.; admitted to CT Bar, 1845; incorporator, Connecticut Savings Bank. MEM.: New Haven Hist. Soc. (adviser); CT Bar Assn. (founder; vice pres.). HON. DEG.: LL.D., Yale U., 1874. REL.: Episc. RES.: New Haven, CT.

INGERSOLL, JARED. b. Oct 27, 1749, New Haven, CT; d. Oct 31, 1822, Philadelphia, PA; par. Jared and Hannah (Whiting) Ingersoll; m. Elizabeth Pettit, Dec 6, 1781; c. Charles Jared; Joseph Reed. EDUC.: grad., Yale U., 1766. POLIT. & GOV.: member, Continental Congress, 1780; delegate, Federal Constitutional Convention, 1787; member, Philadelphia (PA) Common Council, 1789; atty. gen. of PA, 1790–1799, 1811–17; city solicitor, Philadelphia, PA, 1798–1801; appointed U.S. district atty. for PA, 1800–1801; ***Federalist candidate for vice presidency of the U.S., 1812***; presiding judge, District Court for City and Cty. of Philadelphia, PA, 1821–22. BUS. & PROF.: atty.; admitted to Philadelphia Bar, 1773; admitted to Middle Temple, London, England, 1773; admitted to practice before the Bar of the Supreme Court of the U.S., 1791; counsel in *Chisholm v. Georgia*, 1792, and *Hylton v. United States*, 1796. RES.: Philadelphia, PA.

INGERSOLL, R. J. POLIT. & GOV.: ***candidate for Democratic nomination to presidency of the U.S., 1852***. MISC.: received 1 vote for president on 48th ballot. RES.: TN?

INOUYE, DANIEL KEN. b. Sep 7, 1924, Honolulu, HI; par. Hyotaro and Kame (Imanaga) Inouye; m. Margaret Shinobu Awamura, Jun 12, 1949; c. Daniel Ken, Jr. EDUC.: B.A., U. of HI, 1950; J.D., George Washington U., 1952. POLIT. & GOV.: elected as a Democrat to HI Territorial House; elected as a Democrat to U.S. House (HI), 1959–63; elected as a Democrat to U.S. Senate (HI), 1963–; delegate, Dem. Nat'l. Conv., 1968 (temporary chm.; keynoter), 1972; ***candidate for Democratic nomination to vice presidency of the U.S., 1972***. BUS. & PROF.: atty.; admitted to HI Bar, 1953. MIL.: pvt., capt., U.S. Army, 1943–47. AWARDS: one of the ten Outstanding Young Men of the Year, U.S. Junior C. of C., 1960; one of the 100 Most Important Men and Women in the U.S., *Life Magazine*, 1962; Alumnus of the Year Award, George Washington U., 1961; Splendid American Award, Thomas A. Dooley Foundation, 1967. WRITINGS: *Journey to Washington* (1967). MISC.: co-chm., Iran-Contra scandal congressional hearings, 1987. MAILING ADDRESS: 2332 Coyne St., Honolulu, HI 96814.

IREDELL, JAMES. b. Oct 5, 1751, Lewes, England; d. Oct 20, 1799, Edenton, NC; par. Francis and Margaret (McCulloh) Iredell; m. Hannah Johnston, Jul 18, 1773. EDUC.: studied law under Samuel Johnston (q.v.). POLIT. & GOV.: appointed comptroller of customs, Edenton, NC, 1768–1774; appointed collector of customs, Port of NC, 1774–1776; judge, Superior Court of NC, 1777; elected atty. gen. of NC, 1779–1781; member, NC Council of State, 1787; delegate, NC Ratifying Convention; appointed assoc. justice, Supreme Court of the U.S., 1790–1799; ***received 3 electoral votes for presidency of the U.S., 1796***. BUS. & PROF.: atty.; licensed in law, 1771. WRITINGS: *Answer to Mr. Mason's Objections in the New Constitution, in Support of United States Constitution*. RES.: Edenton, NC.

IRELAND, ANDREW POYSELL "ANDY." b. Aug 23, 1930, Cincinnati, OH; par. Ellsworth F. and Dorothy (Poysell) Ireland; m. Diana Elmes; m. 2d, Nancy; c. Deborah; Melissa "Mimi"; Andrew P. "Drew"; Ellsworth F. "Dutch" III. EDUC.: B.S., Yale U., 1952; Columbia U. Business School; grad., LA State U. School of Banking, 1959. POLIT. & GOV.: member, City Comm., Winter Haven, FL, 1966–68; elected as a Democrat to U.S. House (FL), 1977–83, as a Republican, 1983–1993; ***candidate for Republican nomination to presidency of the U.S., 1988***. BUS. & PROF.: chm. of the board, Barnett Banks, Winter Haven, Cypress Gardens, and Auburndale, FL. MEM.: FL Bankers Assn. (treas.); American Bankers Assn. (FL vice pres.); Jax Branch, Federal Reserve Bank of Atlanta (dir.); Shriners; Moose; Kiwanis; Elks; Royal Order of the Jester. REL.: Episc. MAILING ADDRESS: 120 West Central Ave., Winter Haven, FL 33883.

ISAAC, ARTIS GAINES. b. 1921. POLIT. & GOV.: ***independent candidate for presidency of the U.S.,***

1976. BUS. & PROF.: poet. MISC.: known as "Oklahoma's Poet Lariat." MAILING ADDRESS: Parker Heights, OK.

ISAACSON, SHIRLEY RACHEL. b. Feb 13, 1931, Brooklyn, NY, 1931; par. Max and Rose (Cohn) Goodheim; m. Boris Isaacson; m. 2d, John Honigsfeld; c. Cory Michael; Dean Robert. EDUC.: B.A., Brooklyn Coll.; Ed.D., Brigham Young U. POLIT. & GOV.: member, CA State Central Cmte., Peace and Freedom Party; Peace and Freedom Party candidate for U.S. House (CA), 1986, 1988; ***candidate for Peace and Freedom Party nomination to presidency of the U.S., 1988***. BUS. & PROF.: elementary teacher, Los Angeles (CA) Unified School District, 1966–72; school psychologist, Los Angeles Unified School District, 1972–. MEM.: United Teachers of Los Angeles (representative, school psychologists). REL.: Secular Jew. MAILING ADDRESS: 350 South Fuller Ave., #2-B, Los Angeles, CA 90036.

JACKSON, ANDREW. b. Mar 15, 1767, Waxhaw, SC; d. Jun 8, 1845, Nashville, TN; par. Andrew and Elizabeth (Hutchinson) Jackson; m. Rachel Donelson Robards, Aug 1791 (remarried, Jan 17, 1794); c. Andrew, Jr. (adopted). EDUC.: studied law under Spruce Macay, Salisbury, NC, 1784; studied law under John Stokes, 1786–87. POLIT. & GOV.: appointed prosecuting atty., Western District of TN, 1788; delegate, TN Constitutional Convention, 1796; elected as a Democratic-Republican to U.S. House (TN), 1796–97; elected as a Democratic-Republican to U.S. Senate (TN), 1797–98, 1823–25; appointed judge, TN Superior Court, 1798–1804; elected as a Democrat to TN State Senate, 1807; appointed U.S. sec. of war, 1817 (declined); appointed military gov. of FL Territory, 1821; ***Democratic candidate for presidency of the U.S., 1824 (defeated in U.S. House); elected as a Democrat to presidency of the U.S., 1829–37***. BUS. & PROF.: soldier; atty.; admitted to NC Bar, 1787; law practice, Johnsonville, NC, 1787. MIL.: orderly, U.S. Army, 1780; prisoner-of-war, 1781; judge advocate, Davidson Cty. Militia Regt., 1791; maj. gen., TN Militia, 1802; maj. gen., U.S.V., 1812; defeated Creeks and Cherokee, 1814; appointed brig. gen., U.S. Army, 1814, maj. gen., 1814; won Battle of New Orleans, 1815; defeated Seminole Indians, 1818. MEM.: Masons. HON. DEG.: LL.D., Harvard U., 1833. MISC.: noted for numerous duels; known as "Old Hickory" and "Hero of New Orleans." REL.: Presb. RES.: Nashville, TN.

JACKSON, DONALD L. b. May 4, 1926, Folderville, NY; married; c. Donald L., Jr. EDUC.: AL A&M Coll.; Alcorn A&M Coll.; KY State Coll.; U. of KY; LL.B., LaSalle Extension U.; D.D., Twentieth Century Bible School. POLIT. & GOV.: candidate for Republican nomination to U.S. House (CA), 1946, 1948, 1950, 1952, 1954, 1956, 1958; chm., Negroes for Goldwater-Miller, 1964; ***Poor People's candidate for Democratic nomination to presidency of the U.S., 1976***. BUS. & PROF.: minister; author; lecturer; ed., *Wire Magazine;* real estate agent; pres., real estate corporation; producer, *The Donald Jackson Show*, (cable television program); radio commentator. MIL.: sgt., WWII and Korean War. MEM.: Jackson Educational Foundation (pres.). MAILING ADDRESS: 494 Hickery St., Buffalo, NY 14204.

JACKSON, FRANK MANTON. b. Apr 25, 1896, Indianapolis, IN; par. Frank and Martha (Large) Jackson; m. Besse Beason; m. 2d, Dorothy Mae Cook, Dec 22, 1923; c. Glint Thomas; Jo Ann Einger; Jackquline (Mrs. Wesley Scott); Martha May Cooper. EDUC.: grade school; studied machine work and equipment. POLIT. & GOV.: ***candidate for Republican nomination to presidency of the U.S., 1964***. BUS. & PROF.: farmer; millwright; machinist; employee, pump plant, Los Angeles, CA; rancher, Siskiyou Cty., CA; mechanic, Sunland Service Station, Visalia, CA, 1971–72. MIL.: pvt., 79th F.A., Sixth Army, U.S. Army, 1917–19. MEM.: American Legion. REL.: Bapt. MAILING ADDRESS: 215a, South Chinowith Rd., Visalia, CA 93272.

JACKSON, HENRY MARTIN. b. May 31, 1912, Everett, WA; d. Sep 1, 1983, Everett, WA; par. Peter and Marie (Anderson) Jackson; m. Helen Eugenia Hardin, Dec 16, 1961; c. Anna Marie; Peter Hardin. EDUC.: Stanford U.; LL.B., U. of WA, 1935. POLIT. & GOV.: elected prosecuting atty., Snohomish Cty., WA, 1938–40; elected as a Democrat to U.S. House (WA), 1941–53; elected as a Democrat to U.S. Senate (WA), 1953–83; delegate, NATO Parliamentarians' Conference, 1956–59, 1966; chm., Dem. Nat'l. Cmte., 1960–61; delegate, Dem. Nat'l. Conv., 1968; ***candidate for Democratic nomination to presidency of the U.S., 1972, 1976, 1980; candidate for Democratic nomination to vice presidency of the U.S., 1972, 1976; candidate for independent (National Unity) nomination to vice presidency of the U.S., 1980 (declined)***. BUS. & PROF.: atty.; admitted to WA Bar, 1935; law assoc., Black and Rucker (law firm), 1935–38. MIL.: U.S. Army, WWII. MEM.: International Labour Office Conference (pres., 1946); WA Bar Assn.; Phi Delta Phi; Delta Chi; Whitman Coll. (overseer); John F.

Kennedy Inst. of Politics, Harvard U. (adviser); Smithsonian Institution (regent). AWARDS: "Legislator of the Year" Award, National Wildlife Federation; Medal, American Scenic and Hist. Preservation Soc.; John Muir Award, Sierra Club; Conservation Award, Baruch Foundation. REL.: Presb. MISC.: known as "Scoop" Jackson. RES.: Everett, WA.

JACKSON, JESSE LOUIS. b. Oct 8, 1941, Greenville, NC; par. Charles Henry and Helen Jackson; m. Jacqueline Lavinia Brown, 1964; c. Santita; Jesse Louis, Jr.; Jonathan Luther; Yusef DuBois; Jacqueline Lavinia. EDUC.: U. of IL, 1959–60; B.A., Agricultural and Technical Coll. of NC, 1964; Dr.Humanities, Howard U., 1971. POLIT. & GOV.: delegate, U.S. Youth Council, 1963–64; ***candidate for Democratic nomination to presidency of the U.S., 1984, 1988; candidate for Democratic nomination to vice presidency of the U.S., 1988***; elected as a Democrat, "Shadow" U.S. senator from DC (not seated), 1989–. BUS. & PROF.: ordained minister, Baptist Church, 1968; assoc. minister, Fellowship Missionary Baptist Church; community organizer; founder, exec. dir., Operation PUSH (People United to Save Humanity), 1971–. MEM.: Black Coalition for United Community Action; Operation Breadbasket (cofounder); Southern Christian Leadership Conference; Coordinating Council of Community Organizations (national dir., 1966–77); Young Democrats; NC Intercollegiate Council on Human Rights; Congress on Racial Equality (field representative, 1965). AWARDS: Citizen of the Year Award, Greensboro, NC, 1964; International Man of the Year Award, Chicago Club Frontier, 1968; President's Award, National Medical Assn., 1969; Humanitarian Father of the Year Award, National Fathers' Day Cmte., 1971. HON. DEG.: D.D., Chicago Theological Seminary. REL.: Bapt. MAILING ADDRESS: c/o Howard Renzi, Suite 326, 733 15th St., N.W., Washington, DC 20005.

JACKSON, JOHN HOLMES. b. Mar 21, 1871, Montreal, Quebec, Canada; par. Rev. Samuel Nelson and Mary Ann (Parkyn) Jackson; m. Caroline Deming Smalley; c. Bradley Smalley. EDUC.: D.D.S., Philadelphia Dental Coll., 1890. POLIT. & GOV.: elected as a Democrat to mayor of Burlington, VT, 1917–25; delegate, Dem. Nat'l. Conv., 1920, 1924; elected as a Democrat to VT State House, 1921–23; Democratic candidate for gov. of VT, 1922; appointed member, VT State Board of Dental Examiners, two terms; ***candidate for Democratic nomination to presidency of the U.S., 1924***. BUS. & PROF.: dentist; dental practice, Barre, VT, 1890–96; dental practice, Burlington, VT, 1896–. MEM.: VT State Dental Soc. (pres.); Free and Accepted Masons; Royal Arch Masons; Knights Templar; Shriners; Elks (exalted ruler); Rotary Club; Ethan Allen Club. RES.: Burlington, VT.

JACKSON, MARIAN RUCK. b. May 5, 1922, El Dorado, KS; par. Loyd Wesley and Helen (McIntosh) Fowler; m. Eldon D. Ruck, 1941; m. 2d, George Edmund Jackson, 1970; c. Eldon Terry; Roscoe G.; Laura May. EDUC.: Butler Junior Coll., 1940–41. POLIT. & GOV.: chm., Greenwood Cty. (KS) American Party; delegate, American Party National Convention, 1976; appointed commissioner of streets and utilities, Eureka, KS, 1977–81; American Party candidate for lt. gov. of KS, 1978; ***American Party of KS candidate for vice presidency of the U.S., 1980***; chm., KS State American Party Central Cmte., 1980–82; American Party candidate for U.S. Senate (KS), 1984. BUS. & PROF.: owner, operator, Eldon Ruck Electrical and Engine Service, 1961–70. MEM.: VFW Auxiliary. REL.: Christian. MAILING ADDRESS: 102 North Mulberry, Eureka, KS 67045.

JACKSON, RICHARD ALBERT. POLIT. & GOV.: ***candidate for Republican nomination to presidency of the U.S., 1988; independent candidate for presidency of the U.S., 1992***. MAILING ADDRESS: 1852 Biltmore St., Washington, DC 20009.

JACKSON, ROBERT HOUGHWONT. b. Feb 13, 1892, Spring Creek, PA; d. Oct 9, 1954, Washington, DC; par. William Eldred and Angeline (Houghwont) Jackson; m. Irene Gerhardt, Apr 24, 1916; c. William Eldred; Mary Margaret. EDUC.: Albany Law School; B.A., Chautauqua Inst.; studied law under Frank H. Mott, Jamestown, NY. POLIT. & GOV.: appointed corporation counsel, City of Jamestown, NY, 1918; member, NY State Democratic Central Cmte.; appointed gen. counsel, Bureau of Internal Revenue, 1934–36; appointed asst. atty. gen. of the U.S., 1936–38; appointed solicitor gen. of the U.S., 1938–39; appointed atty. gen. of the U.S., 1940–41; ***candidate for Democratic nomination to presidency of the U.S., 1940***; appointed assoc. justice, Supreme Court of the U.S., 1941–54; appointed chief counsel, U.S., War Crimes Trials, 1945–46. BUS. & PROF.: atty.; admitted to NY Bar, 1913; law practice, Jamestown, NY, 1913–34; vice pres., gen. counsel, Jamestown Street Railway Co.; vice pres., gen. counsel, Jamestown Telephone Co.; vice pres., gen. counsel, Jamestown, Westfield and Northwestern R.R.; partner, Dean, Edson and Jackson (law firm), Jamestown, 1919–21; partner, Jackson, Manley and Herrick (law firm; later Jackson, Herrick, Durkin and Leet), Jamestown, 1921–33; partner, Jackson and Durkin (law firm), Jamestown, 1933–34; dir., Bank of Jamestown. MEM.: ABA (vice pres.); NY Bar Assn. (vice pres.); Federation of Bar Associations of Western (pres., 1928–32); Canadian Bar Assn. (hon. member); National Conference of Bar Associations (chm. of delegates); Erie Cty. Bar Assn.; Jamestown Bar Assn. (pres.); Assn. of the Bar of the City of New York; St. Nicholas Soc. of New York; George Washington U. (trustee); Albany Law School (trustee); Honourable Soc. of the Middle Temple (hon. bencher, 1946); Masons (33°; Knights Templar); National Press Club; University Club of Washington; Jamestown Saddle Club (pres.); American Law Inst.; Chautauqua Cty. Wilson Club (pres., 1912); Jamestown Sportsmen's Club. AWARDS: Presidential Medal of Merit, 1946. HON. DEG.: LL.D., Dartmouth Coll.; LL.D., Syracuse U.; LL.D., U. of Brussels; LL.D., U.

of Buffalo, 1946; LL.D., U. of Warsaw; LL.D., Western MD Coll., 1946. WRITINGS: *The Struggle for Judicial Supremacy* (1941); *Full Faith and Credit* (1945); *The Case Against the Nazi War Criminals* (1946); *The Nurnberg Case* (1947); *The Supreme Court in the American System of Government* (1955). REL.: Episc. RES.: Washington, DC.

JACKSON, WILLIAM PURNELL. b. Jan 11, 1868, Salisbury, MD; d. Mar 7, 1939, Salisbury, MD; par. William Humphreys and Arabella (Humphreys) Jackson; m. Sallie McCombe, 1890; m. 2d, Katherine Shelmerdine, 1900; c. William Newton; Belle; William; Elizabeth. EDUC.: Wilmington Conference Acad. POLIT. & GOV.: elected as a Non-Partisan to Salisbury (MD) City Council, 1900–1904; member, Rep. Nat'l. Cmte., 1908–32; appointed as a Republican to U.S. Senate (MD), 1912–14; elected as a Republican to MD state treas., 1918–20; ***candidate for Republican nomination to vice presidency of the U.S., 1924***. BUS. & PROF.: partner, E. E. Jackson and Co. (lumber manufacturers), Salisbury, 1887–89; partner, W. H. Jackson and Son (lumber manufacturers), Salisbury, 1893–1903; pres., Jackson Brothers Co. (lumber manufacturers), Salisbury, 1903–39; pres., Salisbury National Bank; dir., Baltimore, Chesapeake and Atlantic Railway Co.; pres., Citizens Gas Co., Salisbury; pres., Jackson-Gutman Co.; pres., Peninsular General Hospital, Salisbury. MEM.: Masons; Maryland Club of Baltimore; Union League; Manufacturers Club of Philadelphia; Elks; Knights Templar; Shriners. REL.: Methodist. RES.: Loon Lake, NY.

JACOBSON, ALVIN JOSEPH. b. Aug 8, 1919, Pittsburgh, PA; par. Esther Mollie Birnkrant; single. EDUC.: Hebrew Union Coll.; A.B., Los Angeles Valley Junior Coll., 1961; B.S., CA Polytechnical State U., 1966. POLIT. & GOV.: candidate for Republican nomination to gov. of PA, 1974, 1978, 1982; ***candidate for Republican nomination to presidency of the U.S., 1980***. BUS. & PROF.: importer; Hovercraft Products of PA. MEM.: Alpha Phi Omega; Air Force Assn.; Jewish War Veterans. REL.: Jewish. MISC.: spent 10 years in mental hospital following WWII. MAILING ADDRESS: P.O. Box 1262, Harrisburg, PA 17108.

JADA, MOTHER. b. 1940; single; children. POLIT. & GOV.: ***Preservative Party candidate for presidency of the U.S., 1980, 1984***. BUS. & PROF.: welfare recipient. MISC.: self-styled "Run-Away Grandmother." MAILING ADDRESS: Newport, OR.

JAECKEL, LOUIS ELLSWORTH. b. Sep 18, 1898, Walden, NY; d. Jun 19, 1967, Lancaster, SC; par. Charles E. and Eva (Collier) Jaeckel; m. Mary Annette Stover, Jul 18, 1924. EDUC.: A.B., Hamilton Coll. of Law, 1917, LL.B. (cum laude), 1917; M.C.Sc., Alexander Hamilton Inst., 1921. POLIT. & GOV.: administrative consultant to Gov. John G. Richards of SC, 1929–30; economic consultant to U.S. Rep. W. F. Stevenson, 1930–31; merchant marine and commerce consultant to U.S. sec. of commerce, 1933–35; co-organizational chm., American Party, 1960; ***American Party candidate for presidency of the U.S., 1964***; national chm., American Party, 1965–67. BUS. & PROF.: syndicated columnist, founder, gen. mgr., Age Herald Feature Syndicate; publisher, *Age Herald*, 1929–32; ordained minister, Baptist Church, 1938; intelligence consultant, National Roster of Scientific and Specialized Personnel, 1944–67; consultant, reconversion of port facilities on Atlantic and Gulf Coasts, 1945; lecturer in political science, current events, and international relations, 1946–67; founder, pres., exec. ed., chm. of the board, World Press Assn., 1946–67; national chaplain, administrative dir., American Foundation of Merchant Marine Missions, 1947–67; international intelligence consultant, American Vigilante Cmte. for Internal Security, 1957–67. MIL.: master mariner, U.S. Maritime Service, 1921–27; U.S. Army, 1917–19; AEF; with U.S. Army, WWII; Purple Heart; Distinguished Service Cross; Croix de Guerre. MEM.: American Acad. of Arts and Sciences; American Very Important Persons Assn. (pres., 1965–67); Automotive Safety League (pres., 1964–67); International Platform Assn.; Christian Witness Publishers (pres., 1964–67); American Legion; VFW; American Coalition of Patriotic Societies (dir.); Americans, Inc. (national pres.); SAR; Patriotic Order of Americans United (national pres.); Dixie News Service, Inc. (founder, pres., exec. ed., chm. of the board, 1934–67); Freedoms Foundation. AWARDS: George Washington Medal, Freedoms Foundation at Valley Forge, 1953, 1954, 1961, 1965. HON. DEG.: M.Sc., Maritime Acad., 1965; Ph.D. (Literature), Hamilton U., 1965. WRITINGS: *Iraq—Grave of Empires* (1936); *Pawn of Intrigue* (1938); *The Realm of Political Morality* (1959); *Moise Tshombe—A Study* (1961); *The Rise and Fall of the American Democracy* (1961); *Operation Swiftstrike* (1961); *The Grand Strategy* (1963); *The Fallacy of Bankrupt Financing* (1963); various articles. REL.: Bapt. RES.: Lancaster, SC.

JAHNKE, WILLIAM EDWARD, JR. b. Mar 6, 1918, Appleton, WI; par. William Henry and Emily Henrietta (Meyer) Jahnke; m. Evelyn Bordell McCoy (divorced, 1950); m. 2d, Francis Lyding; c. two. EDUC.: high school grad., Appleton, WI; assoc. degree in engineering, U. of WI; U. of WA. POLIT. & GOV.: American Party candidate for U.S. House (WI), 1974; campaign mgr., Stevens Point, 1976; ***candidate for Democratic nomination to presidency of the U.S., 1980, 1984***. BUS. & PROF.: investor; unemployed. MEM.: Elks; Kiwanis; American Legion. AWARDS: Medical Award; Elks Award. REL.: Methodist. MAILING ADDRESS: 15 South Charter, Madison, WI 53915.

JAMES, ARTHUR HORACE. b. Jul 14, 1883, Plymouth, PA; d. Apr 27, 1973, Plymouth, PA; par. James David and Rachel (Edwards) James; m. Ada Morris, Oct 23, 1912; m. 2d, Emily Radcliffe Case, Oct 1, 1941; c. Dorothy Rachel Sinon; Arthur Horace, Jr. EDUC.: LL.B., Dickinson School of Law,

1904. POLIT. & GOV.: elected as a Republican to district atty., Luzerne Cty., PA, 1919–26; elected as a Republican to lt. gov. of PA, 1927–31; elected judge, Superior Court of PA, 1932–39; elected as a Republican to gov. of PA, 1939–43; ***candidate for Republican nomination to presidency of the U.S., 1940***. BUS. & PROF.: breaker boy, Nottingham Breaker, Plymouth, PA, 1896; atty.; law practice, Plymouth, PA, 1905–19; law practice, Wilkes-Barre, PA, 1905–19. MEM.: PA Bar Assn.; Cumberland Cty. (PA) Bar; Luzerne Cty. (PA) Bar; Dickinson Law School (Board of Incorporators). HON. DEG.: LL.D., Susquehanna U., 1927; LL.D., Dickinson Coll., 1938; LL.D., Franklin and Marshall Coll., 1939; D.C.L., Hahnemann Medical Coll. and Hospital, 1939; LL.D., Jefferson Medical Coll., 1939; LL.D., Muhlenberg Coll., 1939; LL.D., PA Military Coll., 1939; LL.D., Temple U., 1939; LL.D., Washington and Jefferson Coll., 1939; LL.D., U. of PA, 1940; LL.D., Moravian Coll., 1944; LL.D., Lafayette Coll., 1941; LL.D., Grove City Coll., 1942; LL.D., Bucknell Coll., 1942; LL.D., Gettysburg Coll., 1942. REL.: Methodist (trustee). RES.: Plymouth, PA.

JAMES, FORREST HOOD "FOB," JR. b. Sep 15, 1934, Lanett, AL; par. Forrest Hood and Rebecca (Ellington) James; m. Bobbie Mae Mooney, Aug 20, 1955; c. Forrest Hood III; Timothy E.; Patrick F. EDUC.: B.S.C.E., Auburn U., 1957. POLIT. & GOV.: elected as a Democrat to gov. of AL, 1979–83, as a Republican, 1995–; ***candidate for Democratic nomination to presidency of the U.S., 1980***. BUS. & PROF.: professional football player, Montreal (Canada) Alouettes, 1955–58; construction superintendent, AL, 1958–62; founder, chm. of the board, Diversified Products Corp., 1962–78. MIL.: U.S. Army Corps of Engineers, 1957. MEM.: Cystic Fibrosis Foundation; BSA; AL Safety Council; Junior Achievement; Future Farmers of America Foundation; Young Presidents Organization; AL Road Builders Assn. (hon. life member); American Legion; Spade Honor Soc.; Alpha Sigma Epsilon. REL.: Episc. MAILING ADDRESS: c/o General Delivery, Magnolia Springs, AL 36555.

JAMES, OLLIE MURRAY. b. Jul 27, 1871, Marion, KY; d. Aug 28, 1918, Baltimore, MD; par. L. H. and Elizabeth J. James; m. Ruth Thomas, Dec 2, 1903. EDUC.: studied law under L. H. James. POLIT. & GOV.: page, KY Legislature, 1887; delegate, Dem. Nat'l. Conv., 1896, 1904, 1908, 1912 (chm.), 1916 (chm.); chm., KY State Democratic Convention, 1900; elected as a Democrat to U.S. House (KY), 1903–13; ***candidate for Democratic nomination to presidency of the U.S., 1912***; elected as a Democrat to U.S. Senate (KY), 1913–18. BUS. & PROF.: atty.; admitted to KY Bar, 1891; law practice, Marion, KY; counsel to Gov. William Goebel in election contest, 1899. RES.: Marion, KY.

JAMES, OLLIE MURRAY. b. Oct 16, 1908, Kuttawa, KY; par. Edgar Harrison and Mary (Campbell) James; m. Elizabeth Hazelrigg Hall, Dec 31, 1931. EDUC.: U. of Louisville; U. of KY. POLIT. & GOV.: ***independent candidate for presidency of the U.S., 1968***. BUS. & PROF.: journalist; reporter, political writer, legislative correspondent, *Lexington (KY) Herald*, 1928–34; reporter, Washington correspondent, assoc. ed., *Louisville (KY) Herald-Post*, 1934–36; editorial writer, asst. managing ed., *Cincinnati (OH) Enquirer*, 1936–44, chief editorial writer, 1944–; ed., *Union Central Advocate*; columnist, "Innocent Bystander"; lecturer. MEM.: National Conference of Editorial Writers; Sigma Nu; Sigma Delta Chi; National Press Club. WRITINGS: *Splendid Century*; various articles. MAILING ADDRESS: 1885 Dixie Highway, Fort Mitchell, Covington, KY 41011.

JANUARY, D. H. POLIT. & GOV.: ***independent candidate for presidency of the U.S., 1980***. BUS. & PROF.: evangelist. MAILING ADDRESS: Chattanooga, TN.

JARVIS, BILL. POLIT. & GOV.: ***candidate for Democratic nomination to vice presidency of the U.S., 1992***. MAILING ADDRESS: c/o William Christopher Meyer, 5428 Guide Meridian, Bellingham, WA 98226.

JAVITS, JACOB KOPPEL. b. May 18, 1904, New York, NY; d. Mar 8, 1986, West Palm Beach, FL; par. Morris and Ida (Littman) Javits; m. Marjorie Joan Ringling, Sep 12, 1933; m. 2d, Marian Ann Borris, Nov 30, 1947; c. Joy D.; Joshua M.; Carla I. EDUC.: LL.B., NY U., 1926. POLIT. & GOV.: member, Ivy Republican Club, 1932; elected as a Republican to U.S. House (NY), 1947–55; elected as a Republican to atty. gen. of NY, 1955–57; elected as a Republican to U.S. Senate (NY), 1957–80; delegate, Rep. Nat'l. Conv., 1968, 1972, 1976; ***candidate for Republican nomination to presidency of the U.S., 1968***; U.S. delegate, 25th Anniversary of U.N. General Assembly, 1970; appointed member, National Comm. on Marijuana and Drug Abuse, 1971–73; Liberal Party candidate for U.S. Senate (NY), 1980. BUS. & PROF.: atty.; admitted to NY Bar, 1927; law practice, New York, NY, 1927–86; partner, Javits and Javits (law firm), New York; partner, Javits, Trubin, Sillcocks and Edelman (law firm), New York, 1958–71; counsel, Trubin, Sillcocks, Edleman and Knapp (law firm), 1981–86; adjunct prof. of public affairs, Columbia U., 1981–86; adjunct prof., State U. of NY at Stony Brook, 1982–86. MIL.: maj., U.S. Army, 1942; asst. to chief of operations in Chemical Warfare Service, 1942–45, lt. col.; col., NY National Guard; Legion of Merit; Army Commendation Ribbon. AWARDS: Presidential Medal of Freedom, 1983. MEM.: American Legion; Phi Delta Epsilon; VFW; Amvets; Jewish War Veterans; American Veterans Cmte.; City Athletic Club; Harmonie Club of New York; Bankers Club of America; ABA; National Republican Club; Army and Navy Club; Capitol Hill Club; North Atlantic Assembly (chm., Political Cmte.; Parliamentarian's Cmte. for Less Developed Nations). HON. DEG.: received 37 honorary degrees, including LL.D., Lincoln U.; LL.D., NY U.; LL.D., Hartwick Coll.; LL.D., Yeshiva U.; D.H.L., Hebrew Union Coll.; LL.D., Long Island U.; LL.D., Ithaca Coll.; LL.D., Colgate

U.; LL.D., Niagara U.; LL.D., Jewish Theological Seminary; LL.D., Dartmouth Coll.; D.C.L., Pace Coll.; D.H.L., NY Medical Coll. WRITINGS: *A Proposal to Amend the Anti-Trust Laws* (1939); *Discrimination U.S.A.* (1960); *Order of Battle: A Republican's Call to Reason* (1964); *Who Makes War* (1973); *Javits: The Autobiography of a Public Man* (1981). REL.: Jewish. RES.: New York, NY.

JAWORSKI, LEON. b. Sep 19, 1905, Waco, TX; d. Dec 9, 1982, Houston, TX; par. Joseph and Marie (Mira) Jaworski; m. Jeannette Adam, May 23, 1931; c. Joanie; Claire; Joseph III. EDUC.: LL.B., Baylor U., 1925, LL.D., 1960; LL.M., George Washington U. POLIT. & GOV.: chm., Governor's Comm. on Public School Education; special asst. atty. gen. of the U.S., 1962–65; special counsel to the atty. gen. of TX, 1963–65, 1972–73; appointed member, President's Comm. on Law Enforcement and the Administration of Justice; U.S. member, Permanent International Court of Arbitration; appointed member, Comm. on Marine Sciences, Engineering and Resources; appointed member, President's Comm. on Causes and Prevention of Violence; appointed dir., Office of Watergate Special Prosecution Force, 1973–74; ***candidate for Democratic nomination to presidency of the U.S., 1976***. BUS. & PROF.: atty.; admitted to TX Bar, 1925; partner, Fulbright, Crooker and Jaworski (law firm), Houston, TX, 1951–82; dir., Gulf Publishing Co.; dir., Intercontinental National Bank; dir., Village National Bank; dir., Coastal States Gas Producing Co.; dir., Bank of the Southwest; dir., Southwest Bancshares, Inc.; dir., Houston, Anderson, Clayton and Co. MIL.: col., U.S. Army, 1942–46; chief, War Crimes Trial Section, JADG, U.S. Army; Legion of Merit. AWARDS: American Bar Assn. Medal, 1993. MEM.: Order of the Coif; Phi Delta Phi; Houston Club; Coronado Club; Headliners; Warwick Club; National College of District Attorneys (regent); United Fund (trustee, 1958–82); Assn. for Retarded Citizens (dir., chapter chm., 1954–55); Southwestern Legal Foundation (exec. cmte.; trustee); TX Medical Center, Baylor U. (trustee); Baylor Medical Foundation (pres.); M. D. Anderson Foundation (pres.); American College of Trial Lawyers (fellow; regent, 1958–66; pres., 1961–62); American Law Inst.; American Bar Foundation; TX Bar Assn. (pres., 1962–63); ABA (pres., 1971–72); Canadian Bar Assn. (hon. member); Houston Bar Assn. (pres., 1949); TX Civil Judicial Council (pres., 1950–52); Rotary Club; C. of C. (pres., 1960). HON. DEG.: received numerous honorary degrees, including D.H.C., Baylor U.; D.H.C., Suffolk U.; D.H.C., Wahburn U. WRITINGS: *After Fifteen Years* (1961). REL.: Presb. RES.: Houston, TX.

JAY, JOHN. b. Dec 12, 1745, New York, NY; d. May 17, 1829, Bedford, NY; par. Peter and Mary (Van Cortlandt) Jay; m. Sarah Van Brugh Livingston, Apr 28, 1774; c. Peter Augustus; William (q.v.); five others. EDUC.: grad., Kings Coll., 1764; studied law under Benjamin Kissam. POLIT. & GOV.: sec., Royal Comm. to Settle Boundary Dispute Between New York and New Jersey, 1773; delegate, Continental Congress, 1774–79 (pres., 1778–79); member, NY Provincial Congress, 1776; appointed chief justice, NY Supreme Court, 1776–78; appointed U.S. minister plenipotentiary to Spain, 1779; appointed joint U.S. peace commissioner, 1782; appointed U.S. sec. of foreign affairs, 1784–89; appointed chief justice, Supreme Court of the U.S., 1789–95, 1802 (declined); Federalist candidate for gov. of NY, 1792; appointed envoy extraordinary and minister plenipotentiary to Great Britain, 1794–95; elected as a federalist to gov. of NY, 1795–1801; ***received 1 electoral vote as a Federalist for presidency of the U.S., 1800***. BUS. & PROF.: atty.; admitted to New York City Bar, 1768. MIL.: col., NY Militia. MEM.: Westchester Bible Soc. (pres., 1818); Columbia U. (regent); American Bible Soc. (pres., 1821). HON. DEG.: LL.D., Harvard U., 1790; LL.D., U. of Edinburgh, 1792; LL.D., Brown U., 1794. WRITINGS: *Federalist Papers* (with James Madison, q.v., and Alexander Hamilton, 1787–88). REL.: Episc. MISC.: noted for decision in *Chisholm v. Georgia*, which resulted in Eleventh Amendment to the Constitution of the U.S.; formulated Jay's Treaty with Great Britain, 1794; helped draft first constitution for state of NY. RES.: Bedford, NY.

JAY, WILLIAM. b. Jun 11, 1789, New York, NY; d. Oct 14, 1858, Bedford, NY; par. John (q.v.) and Sarah Van Brugh (Livingston) Jay; m. Hannah Augusta McVickar, Sep 4, 1812; c. John. EDUC.: grad., Yale U., 1807; studied law under John B. Henry, Albany, NY. POLIT. & GOV.: appointed judge, Westchester Cty., NY, 1818–43; appointed commissioner to adjust claims of Western Indians, 1832 (declined); ***candidate for Liberty Party nomination to presidency of the U.S., 1844***. BUS. & PROF.: mgr., estate of John Jay (q.v.), Bedford, NY; abolitionist; author; pacifist; advocate of temperance, education, and Sabbath observance. MEM.: American Bible Soc. (founder, 1810); New York Anti-Slavery Soc. (founder, 1833); American Tract Soc. (dir.); American Peace Soc. (pres.). WRITINGS: *Memoirs on the Subject of a General Bible Soc. for the United States* (1815); *The Calvary Pastoral, a Tract for the Times* (1846); *The Life of John Jay, With Selections from His Correspondence and Miscellaneous Papers* (1833); *An Inquiry into the Character and Tendency of the American Colonization and American Anti-Slavery Societies* (1835); *War and Peace: The Evils of the First and a Plan for Preserving the Last* (1842); *Miscellaneous Writings on Slavery* (1853). REL.: Episc. RES.: Bedford, NY.

JEFFERIES, FRANK. b. Aug 4, 1874, Newcastle, IN; d. Jul 14, 1947, Rochester, IN; par. Jarvis and Elizabeth Jefferies; m. Glenna Pearl Hart, Nov 5, 1903. POLIT. & GOV.: ***Greenback Party candidate for vice presidency of the U.S., 1944***. BUS. & PROF.: journalist; staff, *South Bend (IN) Tribune*, 1912–19; realtor, South Bend, 1919; circulation ed., *Rochester (IN) Sentinel*; newspaperman, Delphi, IN; newspaperman, Logansport, IN; assoc. ed., field mgr., Farmers' Exchange, New Paris, IN, 1933–47. MIL.: soldier, Spanish-American War. MEM.: South Bend–Mishawaka Board of Realtors (pres.); Odd Fellows; Schuyler Rebekah Lodge; United Spanish War Veterans. REL.: Church of Christ. RES.: South Bend, IN.

JEFFERS, JAMES JOSEPH. POLIT. & GOV.: ***Pyramid Freedom Party candidate for presidency of the U.S., 1980 (withdrew)***. BUS. & PROF.: publisher, *The Kingdom Voice*; founder, dir., Kingdom of Yahweh, Jacksonville, FL; teacher; psychic; author. WRITINGS: *Yahweh—Yesterday, Today and Forever; Secrets of Health, Youth and Good Looks; Bermuda Triangle and Great Pyramid; Mars and the Mystery of Creation; Reincarnation—A Reason for Living; Dreams, Language of the Spirits; Lemuria and Atlantis; History Re-Written; Yahweh Speaks on the Beauty of Sex; The Spaceships are Coming; Miniature Folding Pyramid*. MISC.: known as "Dr. Jeffers." MAILING ADDRESS: Route 1, Box 127, St. James, MO 65559.

JEFFERSON, THOMAS. b. Apr 13, 1743 (Apr 2, 1742/43 O.S.), Shadwell, VA; d. Jul 4, 1826, Charlottesville, VA; par. Peter and Jane (Randolph) Jefferson; m. Martha Wayles Skelton, Jan 1, 1772; c. Martha Washington (Mrs. Thomas Mann Randolph); Jane Randolph; Mary ("Marie"; "Polly"; Mrs. John Wayles Eppes); Lucy Elizabeth (d. 1781); Lucy Elizabeth (d. 1785); son (d. 1777). EDUC.: Coll. of William and Mary, 1760–62; studied law under George Wythe, 1762. POLIT. & GOV.: elected delegate, VA House of Burgesses, 1769–74, 1776–79, 1781; member, Cmte. of Correspondence, 1773; deputy delegate, Continental Congress, 1775, delegate, 1776, 1783–84; elected delegate, VA Provincial Convention, 1775; drafter and signer, Declaration of Independence, 1776; elected as a Democrat to gov. of VA, 1779–81; appointed peace commissioner by Continental Congress, 1781 (declined); empowered to negotiate treaty of peace with Great Britain, 1781; drafter, constitution of VA, 1783; appointed U.S. minister plenipotentiary to France, 1782–89; on diplomatic missions in Paris, France and London, England, 1786–87; appointed U.S. sec. of state, 1789–92; ***Democratic-Republican candidate for presidency of the U.S., 1792, 1796***; appointed special U.S. envoy to Spain, 1794 (declined); ***elected as a Democratic-Republican to vice presidency of the U.S., 1797–1801; elected as a Democratic-Republican to presidency of the U.S., 1801–09***. BUS. & PROF.: landowner; farmer; atty.; admitted to VA Bar, 1767; architect; diplomat; author; rector, U. of VA, 1819–26. MEM.: Phil. Soc. (pres., 1797–1815). WRITINGS: *Notes on the State of Virgnia* (1782); *Parliamentary Manual* (1800); *Proceedings of the Government of the United States in Maintaining the Public Right to the Beach of the Mississippi* (1812). REL.: Deist. MISC.: known as the "Sage of Monticello," "Father of the Declaration of Independence," "Father of the University of Virginia." RES.: Monticello, VA.

JEFFRIES, JAMES E. b. Jun 1, 1925, Detroit, MI; par. Barbara Cray, 1947; c. James Thomas; Jeri Lee; Gregory Alan. EDUC.: MI State U., 1945–47. POLIT. & GOV.: elected as a Republican to U.S. House (KS), 1979–83; Republican candidate for U.S. House (KS), 1982; ***candidate for Populist Party nomination to presidency of the U.S., 1984***. BUS. & PROF.: livestock rancher, 1947–50; grain farmer, 1947–50; market researcher, salesman, 1950–70; investment counselor, 1970–. MIL.: master sgt., U.S.A.A.C., 1943–45. MEM.: Masons; Shriners; American Legion; YMCA; American Security Council; Agricultural Hall of Fame (gov.); Foundation for Defense Analysis. REL.: Presb. MAILING ADDRESS: 429 North Third, Atchison, KS 66002.

JENKINS, CHARLES JONES. b. Jan 6, 1805, Beaufort District, SC; d. Jun 13, 1883, Summerville, GA; par. Charles Jones Jenkins; m. Sarah Seaborn, May 24, 1832; m. 2d, Emily Gertrude Barnes, c. 1854; c. Mary McKinne; Charles; Sara Martha. EDUC.: Willington Acad.; Franklin Coll. (now the U. of GA), 1819–22; A.B., Union Coll., 1824; read law under John MacPherson Berrien. POLIT. & GOV.: elected as a Whig to GA State House, 1830–31, 1836–42, 1844–50 (Speaker, 1840, 1842, 1845, 1847); elected as a Whig to atty. gen. of GA, 1831; Whig candidate for GA State House, 1832, 1834, 1842; appointed U.S. sec. of the interior, 1851 (declined); delegate, GA State Constitutional Convention, 1850, 1865, 1877 (pres.); ***Georgia Whig Party candidate for vice presidency of the U.S., 1852***; Union Party candidate for gov. of GA, 1853; elected to GA State Senate, 1856; appointed delegate, Southern Commercial Convention, 1858; appointed assoc. justice, GA State Supreme Court, 1860–65; elected to gov. of GA, 1865–68 (removed by General Meade, q.v.); ***received 2 electoral votes for presidency of the U.S., 1872***; candidate for Democratic nomination to U.S. Senate (GA), 1877. BUS. & PROF.: atty.; admitted to GA Bar, 1826; law practice, Sandersville, GA, 1826–29; law practice (with Augustus B. Longstreet and William M. Mann), Augusta, GA, 1829–; pres., Planters' Loan and Savings Bank, Augusta; pres., Augusta Cotton Factory. MEM.: U. of GA (trustee, 1839–83; pres., 1871–83); Augusta Orphan Asylum (trustee); Phi Beta Kappa. HON. DEG.: LL.D., Union Coll., 1874. WRITINGS: *Address to Graduating Class of the Medical College of Georgia* (1842); *Eulogy on the Life and Services of Henry Clay* (1853). REL.: Episc. (vestryman). RES.: Augusta, GA.

JENKINS, FRANK. d. At age 38, OH. POLIT. & GOV.: ***Poor Man's Party candidate for vice presidency of the U.S., 1952***. BUS. & PROF.: printing press operator. RES.: Rahway, NJ.

JENKINS, JOHN H. POLIT. & GOV.: ***candidate for Democratic nomination to presidency of the U.S., 1976***. MAILING ADDRESS: c/o Honorable Joe B. Fleming, Esq., 2000 Texas Professional Tower Building, Houston 2, TX 77002.

JENKINS, WILLIAM H. POLIT. & GOV.: ***independent candidate for presidency of the U.S., 1992***. MAILING ADDRESS: P.O. Box 495, Shelby, NC 28151.

JENNER, WILLIAM EZRA. b. Jul 21, 1908, Marengo, IN; d. Mar 9, 1985, Bedford, IN; par. L. Lenwood and Jane (MacDonald) Jenner; m. Janet Cuthill, Jun 30, 1933;

c. William Edward. EDUC.: A.B., IN U., 1930, LL.B., 1932. POLIT. & GOV.: elected as a Republican to IN State Senate, 1934–42 (minority leader, 1937–39; majority leader, 1939–42; pres. pro tempore, 1939–42); elected as a Republican to U.S. Senate (IN), 1942, 1947–59; chm., IN Republican State Cmte., 1945–46; ***Texas Constitution Party candidate for vice presidency of the U.S., 1956; States Rights Party of Kentucky candidate for vice presidency of the U.S., 1956; American Party candidate for presidency of the U.S., 1960 (declined)***. BUS. & PROF.: atty.; admitted to IN Bar, 1930; law practice, Paoli and Shoals, IN, 1932–42; law practice, Bedford, IN, 1944; partner, Jenner and Brown (law firm), Indianapolis, IN. MIL.: capt., U.S.A.A.C., 1942–44. MEM.: Phi Delta Phi; IN Bar Assn.; ABA; American Legion; Elks; Masons (33°); VFW; Eagles; IN Soc. of Chicago; Indianapolis Press Club; Delta Tau Delta; Disabled American Veterans; La Societe des 40 Hommes et 8 Chevaux; IN Farm Bureau, Inc.; Bedford Rotary Club; Columbia Club. REL.: Methodist. RES.: Bedford, IN.

JENNESS, LINDA JANE OSTEEN. b. Jan 11, 1941, El Reno, OK; par. Wilson Marshal and Velma Jane (Dull) Osteen; m. Douglas Jenness. EDUC.: Antioch Coll., 1958–62. POLIT. & GOV.: Socialist Workers Party candidate for mayor of Atlanta, GA, 1969; Socialist Workers Party candidate for gov. of GA, 1970; ***Socialist Workers Party candidate for presidency of the U.S., 1972***; member, Socialist Workers Party National Cmte., 1972–. BUS. & PROF.: sec.; author; active in antiwar and women's liberation movements. WRITINGS: *Women and the Cuban Revolution* (coauthor, 1970); *Socialism and Democracy* (1972); *Feminism and Socialism* (ed., 1972). MAILING ADDRESS: 305 East 21st St., Apt. 26, New York, NY 10010.

JENSEN, ELLEN LINEA W. b. 1902; married; children. POLIT. & GOV.: ***Washington Peace Party candidate for presidency of the U.S., 1952***. BUS. & PROF.: astrologer. MISC.: self-styled "Himalayan Master" in former existence. MAILING ADDRESS: Miami, FL.

JENSEN, PAUL. POLIT. & GOV.: ***candidate for Republican nomination to presidency of the U.S., 1992***; Independent Tisch Party candidate for U.S. House (MI), 1992. MAILING ADDRESS: 1930 Woodbury, Ann Arbor, MI 48104.

JEPPSON, EARL. POLIT. & GOV.: exec. dir., American Party, 1975; national chm., American Party, 1981; ***American Party candidate for vice presidency of the U.S., 1988***. BUS. & PROF.: real estate business. MAILING ADDRESS: 3275 West, 14400 South, Bluffdale, UT 84065.

JEPSEN, BRYCE. b. Nov 17, 1929, Richfield, UT; par. Alfred and Nellie (Potter) Jepsen; m. Anita Marie Fleming; c. none. EDUC.: grad., Richfield (UT) H.S., 1949. POLIT. & GOV.: ***candidate for Democratic nomination to presidency of the U.S., 1972***. BUS. & PROF.: mason; foreman, J. & M. construction, 21 years. MEM.: Sons of Italy; British American Club; Richard III Soc.; Museum Soc. of San Francisco. REL.: none. MAILING ADDRESS: 41854 Gifford St., Fremont, CA 94538.

JEROME, WILLIAM TRAVERS. b. Apr 18, 1859, New York, NY; d. Feb 13, 1934, New York, NY; par. Lawrence Roscoe and Katherine (Hall) Jerome; m. Lavinia Taylor Howe, May 9, 1888; c. William Travers, Jr. EDUC.: Williston Seminary; LL.B., Columbia U., 1884. POLIT. & GOV.: appointed asst. district atty., New York Cty., NY, 1888–90; appointed justice of special sessions, New York, NY, 1895–1902; elected as a Democrat to district atty., New York Cty., 1901–09; ***candidate for Democratic nomination to presidency of the U.S., 1908 (declined)***. BUS. & PROF.: atty.; admitted to NY Bar, 1884; partner (with Daniel Nason), law firm, New York, 1884– 88; partner, Jerome and Rand (law firm), New York; chm. of the board, Technicolor, Inc. MEM.: ABA; Bar Assn. of the City of New York; Union Club; City Club; Manhattan Chess Club. HON. DEG.: Amherst Coll., A.M., 1892; LL.D., Colgate U., 1929. WRITINGS: *Liquor Tax Law in New York* (1905). RES.: New York, NY.

JEWELL, MARSHALL. b. Oct 20, 1825, Winchester, NH; d. Feb 10, 1883, Hartford, CT; par. Pliny and Emily (Alexander) Jewell; m. Esther E. Dickinson, Oct 6, 1852; c. Josephine M.; Florence W. POLIT. & GOV.: Republican candidate for CT State Senate, 1867; Republican candidate for gov. of CT, 1868; elected as a Republican to gov. of CT, 1869–72; appointed U.S. minister to Russia, 1873; appointed postmaster gen. of the U.S., 1873–76; ***candidate for Republican nomination to presidency of the U.S., 1876; candidate for Republican nomination to vice presidency of the U.S., 1876, 1880***; Republican candidate for U.S. Senate (CT), 1879; chm., Rep. Nat'l. Cmte., 1880–83. BUS. & PROF.: currier, Woburn, MA; partner, P. Jewell and Sons (leather belts), Hartford, CT, 1850; manufacturer; contractor, Louisville and New Orleans Telegraph Lines; superintendent, telegraph line between Boston, MA, and New York, NY; co-owner, *Hartford Evening Post*; pres., Jewell Pin Co.; pres., South New England Telephone Co.; partner, Charles Root and Co. (dry goods), Detroit, MI, 1860; dir., Phoenix Fire Insurance Co.; dir., Traveler's Insurance Co.; dir., Hartford Bank; dir., New York and New England R.R.; dir., Weed Sewing Machine Co.; dir., Landers, Frary and Clark. MEM.: U.S. Telegraph Assn. (pres.). REL.: Congregationalist. RES.: Hartford, CT.

JEWETT, HUGH JUDGE. b. Jul 1, 1817, Deer Creek, MD; d. Mar 6, 1898, Augusta, GA; par. John and Susannah (Judge) Jewett; m. Sarah Jane Ellis, 1841; m. 2d, Mrs. Sarah Elizabeth (Guthrie) Kelly, Apr 11, 1853; c. John Ellis; Mary; George Moneypenny; Charles Clarence; William Kennon; Helen Pamelia (Mrs. Thomas Hunt); Sarah Guthrie (Mrs. Julian Wainwright Robbins). EDUC.: Hopewell Acad.; Hiram Coll.; studied law under Col. John C. Groome, Elkton, MD. POLIT. &

GOV.: presidential elector, Democratic Party, 1852; elected as a Democrat to OH State Senate, 1853; appointed U.S. atty. for Southern District of OH, 1854; elected as a Democrat to OH State House, 1855, 1868–69; delegate, Dem. Nat'l. Conv., 1856, 1864; Democratic candidate for U.S. House (OH), 1860; Democratic candidate for gov. of OH, 1861; Democratic candidate for U.S. Senate (OH), 1863; elected as a Democrat to U.S. House (OH), 1873–75; ***candidate for Democratic nomination to presidency of the U.S., 1880***. BUS. & PROF.: railroad exec.; atty.; admitted to MD Bar, 1838; law practice, St. Clairsville, OH, 1838; law practice, Zanesville, OH, 1848; pres., Muskingum Cty. Branch, Ohio State Bank, 1852; pres., Central Ohio R.R. Co., 1857–69; vice pres., gen. mgr., Pittsburgh, Cincinnati and St. Louis R.R. Co., 1870; organized Pennsylvania R.R.; pres., Little Miami, Columbus and Xenia Railroads, 1869; gen. counsel, Pennsylvania Railway, 1871; pres., Cincinnati and Muskingum Valley Railroads; pres., Erie Railway Co., 1874–84; pres., New York, Lake Erie and Western R.R. Co., 1878; dir., Western Union Telegraph Co.; dir., Metropolitan Trust Co.; pres., New York Car Trust. MEM.: Masons. REL.: Soc. of Friends. RES.: Zanesville, OH.

JOHN, ANDREW. POLIT. & GOV.: ***independent candidate for presidency of the U.S., 1984***. MAILING ADDRESS: 815 Oak Tree Rd., South Plainfield, NJ 07080.

JOHNS, BOB. POLIT. & GOV.: ***Naturist (Naturalist) Party candidate for presidency of the U.S., 1968***. MEM.: Sex Anonymous. MISC.: supported by Kahoona Sam and Annie O'Brien. MAILING ADDRESS: Los Angeles, CA.

JOHNS, FRANK TEATS. b. Feb 23, 1889, Sunbury, PA; d. May 20, 1928, Bend, OR; par. Isaac Newton and Susan Agnes (Teats) Johns; m. Ruth Aurora Noble, 1911; c. Margaret Ruth; Philip Teats; Mildred Agnes. EDUC.: grad., high school, Spokane, WA. POLIT. & GOV.: organizer, Portland (OR) Socialist Labor Party, 1920; Industrial Labor Party candidate for U.S. House (OR), 1920, 1922; delegate, Socialist Labor Party National Convention, 1924 (Platform Cmte.); ***Socialist Labor Party candidate for presidency of the U.S., 1924, 1928 (replaced by Verne L. Reynolds, q.v., upon death)***. BUS. & PROF.: farmer; employee, U.S. Post Office, Spokane, WA; shipbuilder, Portland, OR, WWI; shoemaker; laborer; carpenter, Portland, OR. MEM.: AFL; Carpenters Union. REL.: Lutheran. MISC.: drowned in rescue attempt during picnic, Bend, OR, 1928. RES.: Portland, OR.

JOHNSON, ALMA J. POLIT. & GOV.: ***independent (Committee for a Constitutional Presidency) candidate for vice presidency of the U.S., 1976***. MEM.: Greater Atlanta Interfaith Network (moderator). MAILING ADDRESS: 174 Mathewson Place, S.W., Atlanta, GA 30314.

JOHNSON, ANDREW. b. Dec 29, 1808, Raleigh, NC; d. Jul 31, 1875, Carter's Station, TN; par. Jacob and Mary (McDonough) Johnson; m. Eliza McCardle, May 5, 1827; c. Martha (Mrs. David Trotter Patterson); Charles; Mary (Mrs. Daniel Stover; Mrs. William R. Brown); Robert; Andrew. EDUC.: self-taught. POLIT. & GOV.: organizer, Workingmen's Party, 1828; elected alderman, Greeneville, TN, 1828–30; elected mayor of Greeneville, TN, 1830–33; elected as a Democrat to TN State House, 1835–37, 1839–41; Democratic candidate for TN State House, 1837; presidential elector, Democratic Party, 1840; elected as a Democrat to TN State Senate, 1841; elected as a Democrat to U.S. House (TN), 1843–53; elected as a Democrat to gov. of TN, 1853–57; elected as a Democrat to U.S. Senate (TN), 1857–62, 1875; ***candidate for Democratic nomination to presidency of the U.S., 1860, 1868***; appointed military gov. of TN, 1862–65; ***elected as a Republican (National Union Party) to vice presidency of the U.S., 1865; succeeded to presidency of the U.S. on the assassination of Abraham Lincoln (q.v.), 1865–69***; Democratic candidate for U.S. Senate (TN), 1869; independent candidate for U.S. House (TN), 1872. BUS. & PROF.: apprentice tailor, Wake Cty., NC, 1822; tailor, Laurens, SC, 1824; tailor, Greeneville, TN, 1826. MIL.: brig. gen. of volunteers, U.S. Army, 1862–65. MEM.: Rhea Acad. (trustee); Masons (master, Greeneville Lodge 119). REL.: nondenominational Christian. MISC.: impeached by U.S. House while serving as president of the U.S., but acquitted in trial before U.S. Senate, 1868. RES.: Greeneville, TN.

JOHNSON, ANDREW NATHAN. b. Sep 21, 1875, London, KY; d. Aug 22, 1959, Wilmore, KY; par. William Harrison and Emma (Cogburn) Johnson; m. Augusta M. Balch, Dec 19, 1910; c. William Andrew; Marian Louise. EDUC.: Sue Bennett Memorial, London, KY; A.B., Asbury Coll., 1903; B.S., KY Normal U.; Ph.D., Milton U. POLIT. & GOV.: Prohibition Party candidate for U.S. House (KY), 1908; Prohibition Party candidate for gov. of KY, 1943; ***Prohibition Party candidate for vice presidency of the U.S., 1944***; Prohibition Party candidate for U.S. Senate (KY); Prohibition Party candidate for sec. of the commonwealth of KY. BUS. & PROF.: teacher, Perry and Clay Counties, KY; ordained minister, United Methodist Church; evangelist; lecturer; temperance advocate; author. MEM.: Asbury Coll. (dir.). AWARDS: named hon. Kentucky Colonel by Gov. Flem D. Sampson. HON. DEG.: D.D., OH Northern U., 1917. WRITINGS: *My Old Kentucky Teacher*; *Titanic* (coauthor); *The Trial of John Barleycorn*; *Twelve Striking Sermons*; *Postmillennialism and the Higher Critics* (with Leander L. Pickett, q.v., 1923); *Evolution Outlawed by Science: The Twelve "Fatal Gaps."* REL.: United Methodist Church (member, KY Annual Conference). RES.: Wilmore, KY.

JOHNSON, ARTHUR GLEASON. b. 1945. POLIT. & GOV.: ***independent candidate for presidency of the U.S., 1988, 1992***. MAILING ADDRESS: 42 Clinton St., #8, New York, NY 10002.

JOHNSON, CECIL F. b. 1913, Owen-Withee, WI. EDUC.: grad., Loyola Acad., 1929. POLIT. & GOV.: candidate for Republican nomination to U.S. House (WI), 1978; ***candidate for Republican nomination to presidency of the U.S., 1984***. BUS. & PROF.: printer; pensioner; dairy farmer. MAILING ADDRESS: Palatka, FL 32077.

JOHNSON, CHARLES MILTON. POLIT. & GOV.: ***independent candidate for presidency of the U.S., 1980***. MAILING ADDRESS: 9451 E Ave., T-12, Littlerock, CA 93543.

JOHNSON, F. DEAN. POLIT. & GOV.: ***candidate for Republican nomination to presidency of the U.S., 1992***. MAILING ADDRESS: Long Beach, CA.

JOHNSON, FRANK MINIS, JR. b. Oct 30, 1918, Haleyville, AL; par. Frank M. and Alabama (Long) Johnson; m. Ruth Jenkins, Jan 14, 1938; c. James Curtis. EDUC.: grad., Gulf Coast Military Acad., 1935; grad., Massey Business Coll., 1937; LL.B., U. of AL, 1943. POLIT. & GOV.: appointed U.S. atty. for Northern District, AL, 1953–55; appointed U.S. district judge, Middle District of AL, 1955–; ***candidate for Democratic nomination to vice presidency of the U.S., 1976, 1980***. BUS. & PROF.: atty.; admitted to AL Bar, 1943; partner, Curtis, Maddox and Johnson (law firm), 1946–53. MIL.: pvt., capt., U.S. Army, 1943–46; Purple Heart with Oak Leaf Cluster; Bronze Star. HON. DEG.: LL.D., Notre Dame U., 1973; LL.D., Princeton U., 1974. MAILING ADDRESS: 118 North Haardt Dr., Montgomery, AL 36105.

JOHNSON, HALE. b. Aug 21, 1847, Sugar Grove Township, IN; d. Nov 4, 1902, Boos, IL; par. John B. and Sarah A. (Davidson) Johnson; m. Mary E. Loofbourrow, Feb 19, 1871; c. Mrs. Jessie B. Kendall; William F.; Mabel; Fannie M.; Lotta L. EDUC.: local academy, Ladoga, IN; read law with W. Hubbard, Kinmandy, IL, 1871–74. POLIT. & GOV.: delegate, Rep. Nat'l. Conv., 1884; delegate, Prohibition Party National Convention, 1884, 1896; Prohibition Party candidate for IL state auditor, 1884; Prohibition Party candidate for IL states atty., 1884; Prohibition Party candidate for U.S. House (IL), 1892; Prohibition Party candidate for gov. of IL, 1896 (withdrew); ***Prohibition Party candidate for vice presidency of the U.S., 1896***; chm., IL Prohibition Party State Central Cmte., 1899; member, Prohibition Party National Cmte., 1900–1902; elected as a Prohibitionist to mayor of Newton, IL, c. 1900; ***candidate for Prohibition Party nomination to presidency of the U.S., 1900 (withdrew)***. BUS. & PROF.: schoolteacher; farmer; atty.; admitted to IL Bar, Jun 1875; law practice, Altamont, IL, 1875–77; partner (with James M. Honey), law firm, Newton, IL, 1877–82; partner (with James W. Gibson), law firm, Newton, 1882–1902; pres., produce dealers packing company; partner, Shup and Johnson (real estate), Newton; temperance advocate; lecturer. MIL.: pvt., Company D, 135th IN Infantry, 1864. MEM.: GAR (commander); Veteran Legion (col.). MISC.: active in prohibition amendment campaigns in MI and OH; murdered by debtor, Harry Harris, 1902. REL.: Disciples of Christ. RES.: Newton, IL.

JOHNSON, HERSCHEL VESPASIAN. b. Sep 18, 1812, Farmer's Bridge, Burke Cty., GA; d. Aug 16, 1880, Louisville, GA; par. Moses and Nancy (Palmer) Johnson; m. Ann (Polk) Walker, Dec 19, 1833; c. Emmet R.; Winder P.; Herschel Vespasian; Tomlinson F.; Tallulah; Annie; Gertrude; two other daughters. EDUC.: Monaghan Acad.; A.B., U. of GA, 1834. POLIT. & GOV.: delegate, GA State Democratic Convention, 1841; Democratic candidate for U.S. House (GA), 1841 (declined), 1843; presidential elector, Democratic Party, 1844, 1852; candidate for Democratic nomination to gov. of GA, 1845, 1847; appointed as a Democrat to U.S. Senate (GA), 1848–49; delegate, Dem. Nat'l. Conv., 1848, 1852, 1856; judge, Ocmulgee Circuit, GA, 1849–53; elected as a Democrat to gov. of GA, 1853–57; ***candidate for Democratic nomination to vice presidency of the U.S., 1856; Democratic candidate for vice presidency of the U.S., 1860***; delegate, GA Secession Convention, 1861; elected to Confederate Senate, 1862–65; pres., GA State Constitutional Convention, 1865; elected as a Democrat to U.S. Senate (GA), 1866 (not seated); appointed judge, Middle Circuit, GA Superior Court, 1873–80. BUS. & PROF.: atty.; admitted to VA Bar, 1834; law practice, Augusta, GA, 1834–39; law practice, Louisville, GA, 1839–44; law practice, Milledgeville, GA, 1844–80. REL.: Swedenborgian. RES.: Louisville, GA.

JOHNSON, HIRAM WARREN. b. Sep 2, 1866, Sacramento, CA; d. Aug 6, 1945, Bethesda, MD; par. Grove Lawrence and Annie Williams (DeMontfredy) Johnson; m. Minnie Lucretia McNeal, Jan 23, 1886; c. Hiram Warren; Archibald McNeal. EDUC.: U. of CA, 1884–87; studied law in office of Grove Lawrence Johnson. POLIT. & GOV.: appointed city atty., Sacramento, CA, 1901; appointed asst. district atty., San Francisco, CA, 1908; elected as a Republican to gov. of CA, 1911–17; founder, Progressive Party, 1912; ***Progressive Party candidate for vice presidency of the U.S., 1912***; elected as a Republican to U.S. Senate (CA), 1917–45; ***candidate for Republican nomination to vice presidency of the U.S., 1916, 1920 (declined)***; alternate delegate, Rep. Nat'l. Conv., 1920; ***candidate for Republican nomination to presidency of the U.S., 1920, 1924, 1932***. BUS. & PROF.: atty.; shorthand reporter; admitted to CA Bar, 1888; partner, Johnson, Johnson and Johnson (law firm), Sacramento, 1888–1902; law practice, San Francisco, 1902–45. MEM.: Native Sons of the Golden West; Masons; Knights Templar; Lincoln-Roosevelt Republican League; Direct Primary League. MISC.: involved in Boodling Cases prosecution of San Francisco city officials and public utilities, 1906–08. RES.: San Francisco, CA.

JOHNSON, JAMES ANDREW "GOSUNDI." b. Jun 15, 1945, Batesville, MS; par. Douglas and

Freddie Ruth (Barber) Johnson; single. EDUC.: M.S., Southern IL U.. POLIT. & GOV.: ***candidate for Democratic nomination to presidency of the U.S., 1980***. BUS. & PROF.: employee, ACTION (federal domestic volunteer program); municipal government worker; corporate and personnel mgr.; instructor; farmer; guerrilla. MAILING ADDRESS: 1139 Market St., Apt. 135, San Francisco, CA 94103.

JOHNSON, JAMES E. b. 1937. EDUC.: D.D.S., Georgetown U., 1972. POLIT. & GOV.: ***candidate for American Party nomination to vice presidency of the U.S., 1984***. BUS. & PROF.: dentist. MAILING ADDRESS: 490 L'Enfant Plaza East, S.W., Washington, DC 20034.

JOHNSON, JESSIE ALVIN. divorced. POLIT. & GOV.: ***candidate for Republican nomination to presidency of the U.S., 1988, 1992***. BUS. & PROF.: policeman; veteran. MISC.: disabled. MAILING ADDRESS: Route 1, Box 271-B, Saulsbury, TN 38067-9801.

JOHNSON, JOHN ALBERT. b. Jul 28, 1861, St. Peter, MN; d. Sep 21, 1909, Rochester, MN; par. Gustaf and Caroline Christina Hansen (Haden) Johnson; m. Elinore M. Preston, Jun 1, 1894. EDUC.: public schools, St. Peter, MN. POLIT. & GOV.: sec., Nicollet Cty. (MN) Fair; Democratic candidate for MN State Senate, 1894, 1902; elected as a Democrat to MN State Senate, 1897–1903; elected as a Democrat to gov. of MN, 1905–09; ***candidate for Democratic nomination to presidency of the U.S., 1908***. BUS. & PROF.: employee, drug store, St. Peter, MN; employee, general store, St. Peter; registered pharmacist; supply clerk, railway contractors, IA and MN; ed., *St. Peter Herald*, 1887. MIL.: capt., MN National Guard. MEM.: MN Editors and Publishers Assn. (sec., 1891; pres., 1893). HON. DEG.: LL.D., U. of PA, 1907. REL.: Presb. RES.: St. Peter, MN.

JOHNSON, LOUIS ARTHUR. b. Jan 10, 1891, Roanoke, VA; d. Apr 24, 1966, Washington, DC; par. Marcellus Alexander and Katherine Leftwich (Arthur) Johnson; m. Ruth Frances Maxwell, Feb 7, 1920; c. Lillian Maxwell; Ruth Katherine (Mrs. Arthur Cheney Clifton Hill, Jr.). EDUC.: LL.B., U. of VA, 1912. POLIT. & GOV.: elected prosecuting atty., Harrison Cty., WV, 1912; candidate for mayor of Clarksburg, WV, 1914; elected as a Democrat to WV State House, 1917–19 (majority floor leader); delegate, Dem. Nat'l. Conv., 1924, 1936; dir., Veterans Div., Dem. Nat'l. Cmte., 1932; national chm., Democratic Veterans Advisory Cmte., 1936–40; member, Federal Advisory Council, Employment Service, U.S. Dept. of Labor; appointed asst. U.S. sec. of war, 1937–40; ***candidate for Democratic nomination to vice presidency of the U.S., 1940***; appointed personal representative of the president to India, 1942; chm., National Finance Cmte., Dem. Nat'l. Cmte., 1948; appointed U.S. sec. of defense, 1949–50. BUS. & PROF.: atty.; admitted to WV Bar, 1912; partner, Rixey and Johnson (law firm), Clarksburg, 1912; partner, Steptoe and Johnson (law firm), Clarksburg and Charleston, WV, and Washington, DC, 1913–66; dir., Union National Bank, Clarksburg; dir., Community Savings and Loan Co., Clarksburg; pres., General Dyestuffs Corp., 1942; dir., Consolidated Vultee Aircraft Corp.; dir., General Analine and Film Corp. MIL.: capt., maj., U.S. Army Infantry, 1918–19; lt. col., U.S.A.R., 1919–44; Medal of Merit. MEM.: Legion of Honor (commander; France); American Legion (national commander, 1932–33); ABA; Federal Bar Assn.; WV Bar Assn.; Harrison Cty. Bar Assn.; Assn. of the Bar of the City of New York; SAR; Reserve Officers Assn.; Federation Interalliee des Anciens Combattants (vice pres. for the U.S., 1933–34); Delta Chi; Delta Sigma Rho; Tau Kappa Alpha; Raven Soc.; Masons (32°; Knights Templar; Shriners); Odd Fellows; Rotary Club; (pres.); Elks (Exalted Ruler); Metropolitan Club; Army and Navy Club; Burning Tree Club; Chevy Chase Club; 1925 F Street Club; Rotary Club; University Club; Midday Club; Drug and Chemical Club; Recess Club; Bohemian Club; National Press Club; Clarksburg C. of C.; Oral Fishing Club. AWARDS: West Virginia Distinguished Service Medal, 1961. HON. DEG.: LL.D., Salem Coll., 1938; LL.D., Kenyon Coll., 1939; LL.D., Creighton Coll., 1949; LL.D., Marietta Coll., 1949; LL.D., Villanova Coll., 1949; LL.D., WV U., 1949; LL.D., PA Military Coll., 1950. REL.: Episc. (vestryman). RES.: Clarksburg, WV.

JOHNSON, LYNDON BAINES. b. Aug 27, 1908, Stonewall, TX; d. Jan 22, 1973, San Antonio, TX; par. Sam Early, Jr., and Rebekah (Baines) Johnson; m. Claudia Alta "Lady Bird" Taylor, Nov 17, 1934; c. Lynda Bird (Mrs. Charles S. Robb); Luci (nee Lucy) Baines. EDUC.: grad., Johnson City (TX) H.S., 1924; B.S., Southwest TX State Coll., 1930; Georgetown U. Law School, 1935. POLIT. & GOV.: sec., U.S. Rep. Richard Mifflin Kleberg, 1932–35; appointed TX state dir., National Youth Administration, 1935–37; elected as a Democrat to U.S. House (TX), 1937–49; delegate, Dem. Nat'l. Conv., 1940, 1956, 1960; candidate for Democratic nomination to U.S. Senate (TX), 1941; elected as a Democrat to U.S. Senate (TX), 1949–61 (majority whip, 1951–53; minority leader, 1953–55; majority leader, 1955–61); ***candidate for Democratic nomination to presidency of the U.S., 1956, 1960, 1968 (withdrew); candidate for Democratic nomination to vice presidency of the U.S., 1956; elected as a Democrat to vice presidency of the U.S., 1961–63; succeeded to the presidency upon assassination of John F. Kennedy (q.v.) and subsequently elected as a Democrat to the presidency of the U.S., 1963–69; Theocratic Party candidate for presidency of the U.S., 1968 (declined)***. BUS. & PROF.: grade schoolteacher, Cotulla, TX, 1928–29; teacher, Sam Houston H.S., Houston, TX, 1930–31; rancher, Johnson City, TX. MIL.: special duty officer, naval intelligence, U.S.N.R., 1940; commissioned lt. commander, U.S.N.R., 1941, commander, 1948; Silver Star. MEM.: American Legion; VFW; Sovereign Military Order of Malta (1961). HON. DEG.: LL.D., Southwestern U., 1943; LL.D., Howard Payne U., 1957; LL.D., Bethany Coll., 1959; LL.D., Brown U., 1959; L.H.D., Oklahoma City U., 1960; LL.D., East KY State Coll., 1961; LL.D., Elon

Coll., 1961; LL.D., Gallaudet Coll., 1961; LL.D., U. of HI, 1961; LL.D., U. of the Philippines, 1961; LL.D., William Jewell Coll., 1961; L.H.D., Yeshiva U., 1961; D.Litt., St. Mary's Coll., 1962; LL.D., Southwest TX State Coll., 1962; LL.D., Jacksonville U., 1963; LL.D., McMurray Coll., 1963; LL.D., Tufts U., 1963; LL.D., U. of MD, 1963; LL.D., Wayne State U., 1963; L.H.D., FL Atlantic U., 1964; LL.D., Georgetown U., 1964; D.C.L., Holy Cross Coll., 1964; LL.D., Swarthmore Coll., 1964; LL.D., Syracuse U., 1964; LL.D., U. of CA, 1964; D.C.L., U. of MI, 1964; LL.D., U. of TX, 1964; LL.D., Baylor U., 1965; LL.D., Catholic U., 1965; LL.D., Howard U., 1965; LL.D., U. of KY, 1965; D.Political Science, Chulalongkorn U. (Thailand), 1966; Litt. D., Glassboro Coll., 1968. WRITINGS: *My Hope for America* (1964); *A Time for Action* (1964); *This America* (1966); *No Retreat from Tomorrow* (1967); *To Heal and to Build* (1968); *The Choices We Face* (1968); *The Vantage Point: Perspectives of the Presidency, 1963–69* (1971). REL.: Disciples of Christ. RES.: Johnson City, TX.

JOHNSON, NICHOLAS. b. Sep 23, 1934, Iowa City, IA; par. Wendell A. L. and Edna (Bockwoldt) Johnson; m. Karen Mary Chapman, 1952; c. Julie; Sherman; Gregory. EDUC.: B.A., U. of TX, 1956, LL.B., 1958. POLIT. & GOV.: appointed administrator, Maritime Administration, U.S. Dept. of Commerce, 1964–66; appointed commissioner, Federal Communications Comm., 1966–73; ***candidate for People's Party nomination to presidency of the U.S., 1972 (declined)***. BUS. & PROF.: atty.; admitted to TX Bar, 1958; admitted to DC Bar, 1963; admitted to Bar of the Supreme Court of the U.S., 1963; law clerk, U.S. Fifth Circuit Court of Appeals, 1958–59; law clerk, U.S. Supreme Court Justice Hugo L. Black, 1959–60; acting prof. of law, U. of CA (Berkeley), 1960–63; law assoc., Covington and Burling (law firm), 1963–64; adjunct prof., Georgetown U., 1971–73; chairperson, dir., National Citizens Cmte. for Broadcasting, 1974–; dir., National Citizens Communications Lobby, 1975–; commentator, National Public Radio, 1975–; visiting prof., U. of IL, 1976. MEM.: ABA; Federal Bar Assn.; State Bar of TX; International Soc. of General Semantics; Phi Beta Kappa; Order of the Coif; Phi Delta Phi; Phi Eta Sigma; Pi Sigma Alpha; National Consumers League; Public Interest Economics Center (dir.); IA Bar Assn.; DC Bar Assn.; Americans for Democratic Action (vice chairperson). AWARDS: one of ten "Outstanding Young Men in America," U.S. Junior C. of C., 1967; Public Defender Award, New Republic, 1970; De Witt Carter Reddick Award, U. of TX, 1977. HON. DEG.: L.H.D., Windham Coll., 1971. WRITINGS: *How to Talk Back to Your Television Set* (1970); *Life Before Death in the Corporate State* (1971); *Test Pattern for Living* (1972); *Broadcasting in America* (1973). REL.: Unitarian. MAILING ADDRESS: 5501 Pollard Rd., Washington, DC 20016.

JOHNSON, REVERDY. b. May 21, 1796, Annapolis, MD; d. Feb 10, 1876, Annapolis, MD; par. John and Deborah (Ghieselen) Johnson; m. Mary Mackall Bowie, Nov 16, 1819. EDUC.: grad., St. John's Coll., 1811. POLIT. & GOV.: deputy atty. gen. of MD, 1816–17; appointed chief commissioner of insolvent debtors of MD, 1817; elected as a Whig to MD State Senate, 1821–29, 1860–61 (Democrat); elected as a Whig to U.S. Senate (MD), 1845–49, 1863–68 (Democrat); appointed atty. gen. of the U.S., 1849–50; delegate, Peace Convention, 1861; ***candidate for Democratic nomination to presidency of the U.S., 1868***; appointed U.S. minister to Great Britain, 1868–69. BUS. & PROF.: atty.; admitted to MD Bar, 1816; law practice, Upper Marlboro, MD, 1816–17; law practice, Baltimore, MD, 1817. WRITINGS: *Johnson's Maryland Reports*. RES.: Baltimore, MD.

JOHNSON, RICHARD MENTOR. b. Oct 17, 1781, Beargrass, KY; d. Nov 19, 1850, Frankfort, KY; par. Robert and Jemima (Suggett) Johnson; single; c. Imogene; Adaline (both by slave, Julia Chinn). EDUC.: Transylvania U.; studied law under George Nicholas and James Brown. POLIT. & GOV.: elected as a Democrat to KY State House, 1804–07, 1819, 1841–42, 1850; elected as a Democrat to U.S. House (KY), 1807–19, 1829–37; elected as a Democrat to U.S. Senate (KY), 1819–29; Democratic candidate for U.S. Senate (KY), 1829; ***candidate for Democratic nomination to vice presidency of the U.S., 1832, 1844; candidate for Democratic nomination to presidency of the U.S., 1836, 1844; elected as a Democrat to vice presidency of the U.S., 1837–41; Democratic candidate for vice presidency of the U.S., 1840***. BUS. & PROF.: atty.; admitted to KY Bar, 1802; law practice, Great Crossings, KY, 1802. MIL.: col., KY Volunteers, 1812–13; commander of U.S. forces in Battle of the Thames; severely wounded, 1813; reputedly killed Tecumseh during battle. MEM.: Georgetown (KY) Coll. (trustee); Columbian Coll. (incorporator). MISC.: only vice president ever elected by U.S. Senate. RES.: Frankfort, KY.

JOHNSON, ROBERT L. b. Dec 14, [year unavailable], Sioux Falls, SD; par. Alexander and Gleora Matilda (Thompson) Johnson; m. Betty Orella Winterton; c. David A.; Diane L; Dawn L. EDUC.: grad., Washington (SD) H.S.; boilermaker school, U.S. Navy. POLIT. & GOV.: ***Surprise Party candidate for presidency of the U.S., 1988, 1992***. BUS. & PROF.: employee, John Morrell and Co., 43 years; employee, U.S. Post Office, Augustana Coll., Sioux Falls, SD, 6 years. MIL.: WT third class, U.S. Navy, 1942–45. MEM.: Norge Glee Club; Sons of Norway; American Legion; VFW; Soc. for the Prevention of Cruelty to Norwegians; Elks. REL.: Lutheran. MISC.: known as "Uncle Torvald." MAILING ADDRESS: 1905 South Elmwood Ave., Sioux Falls, SD 57105.

JOHNSON, SONIA ANN. b. Feb 27, 1936, Malad, ID; d. Alvin and Ida (Howell) Harris; m. Richard "Rick" Johnson, Aug 21, 1959 (divorced, Jun 1980); c. Kari; Eric; Marc; Noel Harris. EDUC.: B.A., UT State U., 1959; U. of MN, 1960–63; Ed.M., Rutgers U., 1964, Ed.D., 1965. POLIT. & GOV.: ***Peace***

and Freedom Party candidate for presidency of the U.S., 1984; Citizens Party candidate for presidency of the U.S., 1984. BUS. & PROF.: instructor, Foothill Junior Coll., Los Altos, CA, 1968; prof. of English, U. of Malawi, Zomba, Malawi, 1969–71; instructor, U. of MD, 1972–74; senior assoc., RMC Research Corp., Mountain View, CA, 1975–76; ed., Gallaudet Coll., Washington, DC, 1976–77; instructor, George Mason U., 1978–79; adjunct prof. of English, VA Polytechnic Inst. and State U., 1979; author; lecturer, 1979–. MEM.: National Organization for Women (candidate for pres., 1982); Mormons for ERA (cofounder; pres.); Feminists International for Peace (cofounder). WRITINGS: *From Housewife to Heretic* (1981); *Going Out of Our Minds: The Metaphysics of Liberation.* REL.: none (nee Church of Jesus Christ of Latter-Day Saints). MISC.: excommunicated from Church of Jesus Christ of Latter-Day Saints, Dec 1979; led fast for Equal Rights Amendment, IL; self-avowed lesbian. MAILING ADDRESS: 3318 Second St., South, Arlington, VA 22204.

JOHNSON, TILDEN WILLIAM. b. 1910. POLIT. & GOV.: candidate for Republican nomination to U.S. Senate (CA), 1956; ***Citizens Write-In Votes for Better Government candidate for presidency of the U.S., 1976.*** WRITINGS: *How Purchasers Can Secure High Wage Employment* (1950); *Prosperity is a Christian Duty* (1956). MAILING ADDRESS: 3050 West 7th St., Los Angeles, CA 90230.

JOHNSON, TOM LOFTIN. b. Jul 18, 1854, Georgetown, KY; d. Apr 10, 1911, Cleveland, OH; par. Albert L. and Helen (Loftin) Johnson; m. Margaret J. Johnson (4th cousin), 1878; c. Loftin Edwards; Elizabeth Flournoy. EDUC.: one year, Evansville, IN. POLIT. & GOV.: Democratic candidate for U.S. House (OH), 1888, 1894; appointed member, Johnstown (PA) Flood Relief Comm., 1889; elected as a Democrat to U.S. House (OH), 1891–95; elected as a Democrat to mayor of Cleveland, OH, 1901–10; Democratic candidate for gov. of OH, 1903; ***candidate for Democratic nomination to presidency of the U.S., 1908, 1912; candidate for Democratic nomination to vice presidency of the U.S., 1908***; Democratic candidate for mayor of Cleveland, 1909. BUS. & PROF.: reformer; clerk, railway office, Louisville, KY, 1869; sec., Central Passenger R.R. Co., Louisville, 1869–72, superintendent, 1872; inventor; owner, Indianapolis Street Railway, Indianapolis, IN, 1876; owner, street railway, Cleveland, 1879; consolidated with several lines as Cleveland Electric Railway Co.; owner, street railway, Detroit, MI; owner, Nassau Street Railway, Brooklyn, NY; owner, Johnson Co.; iron manufacturer, Cleveland; owner, Cambria Co., Johnstown; owner, Lorain Steel Co., Lorain, OH. WRITINGS: *My Story* (1911). MISC.: invented first fare box for streetcars; advocate of Henry George's single tax theories. RES.: Cleveland, OH.

JOHNSON, WALLACE JOHN STOCKMAN. b. Jan 29, 1931, Fort Dodge, IA; par. Edward H. and Ruth (Stockman) Johnson; m. Marion R. Vidoroni, Sep 9, 1935; c. Steven L.; Trina A. (Mrs. John C. Staten); Linda A. EDUC.: B.S., CA Inst. of Technology, 1935. POLIT. & GOV.: chm., Citizens Cmte. to Study Berkeley's School Building Needs, 1957; elected mayor of Berkeley, CA, 1963–71; dir., Bay Area Rapid Transit District, 1967–70; ***candidate for Republican nomination to vice presidency of the U.S., 1976.*** BUS. & PROF.: mechanical engineer; author; inventor; foreman, Proctor and Gamble, Long Beach, CA, 1935–38; mgr., automatic machine tool company, Berkeley, 1938–41; mgr., production engineering company, Berkeley, 1941–43; general sales mgr., Joshua Handy Iron Works, Sunnyvale, CA, 1943–45; consulting mechanical engineer, Berkeley, 1945–47; pres., principal owner, Up-Right Scaffolds Co., Berkeley, 1947–; pres., Up-Right Scaffolds, Ltd., Oshawa, Ontario, Canada; rancher, Healdsburg, CA; vintner. MEM.: Rotary Club (pres.); BSA (district chm.); Berkeley H.S. Ski Club (sponsor); Berkeley Fellows. AWARDS: Silver Anniversary All-American Award, *Sports Illustrated*, 1959; "Berkeley's Most Useful Citizen," 1967. WRITINGS: *The Uncommon Man in American Business* (1966); *Responsible Individualism* (1967); *A New Look at Patriotism.* MAILING ADDRESS: 2 Wilson Circle, Berkeley, CA 94708.

JOHNSON, WHITEFIELD S. POLIT. & GOV.: delegate, Rep. Nat'l. Conv., 1856; ***candidate for Republican nomination to vice presidency of the U.S., 1856.*** RES.: Newton, NJ.

JOHNSTON, ERIC ALLEN. b. Dec 21, 1896, Washington, DC; d. Aug 22, 1963, Washington, DC; par. Bertram Allen and Ida Fazio (Ballinger) Johnston; m. Ina Harriet Hughes, Oct 25, 1922; c. Harriet Ballinger (Mrs. William Carlin Fix); Elizabeth Hughes (Mrs. Fred Hanson; Mrs. Herbert Butler). EDUC.: LL.B., U. of WA, 1917. POLIT. & GOV.: chm., Eastern WA Welfare, 1931–33; chm., WA State Progress Comm., 1937–42; Republican candidate for U.S. Senate (WA), 1940; chm., Inter-American Economic Development Comm.; member, Economic Stabilization Board, 1943; member, Economic Development Comm.; member, War Manpower Comm.; member, Cmte. for Drafting Federal Employees, 1943; member, War Mobilization and Reconversion Cmte.; ***candidate for Republican nomination to presidency of the U.S., 1944***; member, Public Advisory Board, Economic Co-Operation Administration, 1944; member, Defense Mobilization Board, 1951; appointed administrator, Economic Stabilization Agency, 1951; chm., International Development Board, 1952; appointed special representative of the president with rank of ambassador to the Middle East, 1953. BUS. & PROF.: founder, dir., Brown-Johnston Co. (electrical retail business), Spokane, WA, 1923; founder, pres., Columbia Electric and Manufacturing Co., Spokane, 1933–40, chm. of the board, 1949–63; trustee, Washington Brick and Lime Co., 1933; pres., dir., Motion Picture Assn. of America, 1945–63; dir., Hot Shoppes, Inc.; dir., Washington McCormick and Co., Inc.; dir., Olympic Steamship Co.; dir., Seattle First National Bank; dir., Farmers New World Life; dir., Spokane and Eastern

Trust Co.; dir., United Air Lines; dir., Bank of America; dir., American Security and Trust Co.; dir., Motion Picture Export Assn.; dir., Massachusetts Mutual Life Insurance Co. MIL.: capt., U.S.M.C., 1917–22; Medal of Merit, 1947; decorations from Japan, Belgium, Italy, and Germany. MEM.: American Legion; Theta Delta Chi; Bohemian Club; California Rainier Club; Spokane Club; Kiwanis; Metropolitan Club; Alfalfa Club; Chevy Chase Club; Army-Navy Club; Spokane C. of C. (pres., 1931–32); U.S. C. of C. (dir., 1934–41; pres., 1942–46); Inland Manufacturers Assn. (pres., 1929); American Cancer Soc. (dir., 1945; chm. of the board, 1946); Whitman Coll. (trustee). HON. DEG.: LL.D., Boston U., 1943; LL.D., RI State Coll., 1943; B.A., U. of WA, 1943; LL.D., Whitman Coll., 1943; LL.D, Whitworth Coll., 1943; LL.D., Lafayette Coll., 1944; LL.D., Tufts Coll., 1945; LL.D., U. of Southern CA, 1946; LL.D., WA State U., 1947; S.C.D., NY U., 1950; LL.D., U. of MD, 1950; D.H.L., Hahnemann Medical Coll. WRITINGS: *We're All in It* (1948); *America Unlimited*. REL.: Episc. RES.: Washington, DC.

JOHNSTON, J. CHRISTOPHER. POLIT. & GOV.: ***independent candidate for presidency of the U.S., 1972***. BUS. & PROF.: minister. MAILING ADDRESS: c/o Lt. Christopher Johnston, 923 Brunswick, Cleveland, OH.

JOHNSTON, SAMUEL. b. Dec 15, 1733, Dundee, Scotland; d. Aug 18, 1816, Edenton, NC; par. Samuel and Helen (Scrymoure) Johnston; m. Frances Cathcart; c. James C. EDUC.: schools in England; studied law. Polit. & Gov: clerk, Supreme Court of Chowan Cty., NC; provincial treas., Northern Div. of NC; elected member, NC Assembly, 1760–75; member, Cmte. of Correspondence, 1773; delegate, NC Provisional Congresses, 1774 (pres., Third and Fourth Congresses); deputy naval officer, Port of Edenton, NC; moderator, Revolutionary Convention, 1775; colonial treas. of NC, 1775; member, NC Provincial Council of Safety; member, Codification Cmte.; elected member, NC State Senate, 1779, 1783–84, 1798, 1799; member, Continental Congress, 1780–82 (declined presidency, 1781); member, Massachusetts–New York Boundary Comm., 1785; elected as a Federalist to gov. of NC, 1787–89; pres., NC Ratification Convention, 1788 (convention refused ratification of federal Constitution), 1789 (convention ratified constitution); elected as a Federalist to U.S. Senate (NC), 1789–93; *received 2 electoral votes for presidency of the U.S., 1796*; appointed judge, Superior Court of NC, 1800–1803. BUS. & PROF.: paymaster of troops; atty.; admitted to NC Bar, 1767; law practice, Edenton, NC. MEM.: U. of NC (trustee, 12 years); United States Bank (dir.). RES.: Edenton, NC.

JOHNSTON, WILLIAM FREAME. b. Nov 29, 1808, Westmoreland Cty., PA; d. Oct 25, 1872, Pittsburgh, PA; par. Alexander and Elizabeth (Freame) Johnston; m. Mary Montieth, Apr 12, 1832; c. five sons; two daughters. EDUC.: studied law under Maj. J. B. Alexander. POLIT. & GOV.: appointed district atty., Armstrong Cty., PA, 1829–35; elected as a Democrat and subsequently as a Whig to PA State House, 1835–47; elected as a Whig to PA State Senate, 1847 (Speaker); succeeded to and subsequently elected as a Whig to gov. of PA, 1848–52; Whig candidate for gov. of PA, 1851; ***North American Party candidate for vice presidency of the U.S., 1856***; chm., exec. cmte. of Public Safety, Civil War; appointed collector, Port of Philadelphia, PA (not confirmed). BUS. & PROF.: atty.; admitted to PA Bar, 1829; iron manufacturer; oil developer; pres., Alleghany Valley R.R. Co. REL.: Presb. RES.: Pittsburgh, PA.

JOLLEY, WILLIAM ANDREW. b. Aug 28, 1918, Twin Falls, ID; par. Jervis Joseph and Clara (Shores) Jolley; m. Cleo Ann Briles, 1942; c. Leilani; Patricia; Ginger; Jeanne. EDUC.: high school; correspondence courses. POLIT. & GOV.: candidate for Republican nomination to U.S. Senate (CA), 1958; candidate for Republican nomination to gov. of OR, 1974, 1978; ***independent Republican candidate for presidency of the U.S., 1976***; candidate for Republican nomination to atty. gen. of OR, 1976, 1980. BUS. & PROF.: self-employed; owner, commercial industrial refrigeration and air-conditioning business, Willamina, OR. REL.: Christian. MAILING ADDRESS: Route 1, Box 48, Willamina, OR 97396.

JONES, ALFONZO. POLIT. & GOV.: ***candidate for Democratic nomination to vice presidency of the U.S., 1988, 1992***. MAILING ADDRESS: 381 Holbrook, Suite #108, Detroit, MI 48202.

JONES, ELI STANLEY. b. Jan 3, 1884, Baltimore, MD; d. 1973; par. Albin Davis and Sarah Alice (Peddicord) Jones; m. Mabel Lossing, Feb 11, 1911; c. Eunice Treffry (Mrs. J. K. Mathews). EDUC.: A.B., Asbury Coll., 1906, A.M., 1912. POLIT. & GOV.: ***candidate for Prohibition Party nomination to presidency of the U.S., 1944***. BUS. & PROF.: author; missionary; evangelist to high castes of India, 1907–; elected bishop, Methodist Episcopal Church, 1928; resigned to continue missionary work; founder, two Christian Ashrams at Sat Tal and Lucknow, India; founder, psychiatric center, Lucknow, India; contributor, *Christian Herald*; contributor, *Christian Advocate*. MEM.: Christian Ashram Movement; Assn. for United Church of America. HON. DEG.: D.D., Duke U., 1928; S.T.D., Syracuse U., 1928. WRITINGS: *The Christ of the Indian Road* (1925); *Christ at the Round Table* (1928); *The Christ of Every Road: A Study in Pentecost* (1930); *The Christ of the Mount: A Working Philosophy of Life* (1931); *Christ and Human Suffering* (1933); *Christ and Communism* (1935); *Christ's Alternative to Communism* (1935); *Victorious Living* (1936); *The Choice Before Us* (1937); *Along the Indian Road* (1939); *Is the Kingdom of God Realism?* (1940); *Abundant Living* (1942); *The Christ of the American Road* (1944); *The Way* (1946); *Mahatma Gandhi: An Interpretation* (1948); *The Way to Power and Poise* (1949); *How to Be A Transformed Person* (1951); *Growing Spiritually* (1953); *Mastery: The*

Art of Mastering Life (1955); *Christian Maturity* (1957); *Conversion* (1959); *In Christ* (1961); *The Word Became Flesh* (1963); *Victory Through Surrender* (1966); *A Song of Ascents: A Spiritual Autobiography* (1968); *The Reconstruction of the Church: On What Pattern?* (1970); *Selections from E. Stanley Jones: Christ and Human Need* (1972); *The Unshakable Kingdom and the Unchanging Persons* (1972); *The Divine Yes* (1975). REL.: Methodist Episc. RES.: New York, NY.

JONES, JESSE HOLMAN. b. Apr 5, 1874, Robertson Cty., TN; d. Jun 1, 1956, Houston, TX; par. William Hasque and Anne (Holman) Jones; m. Mary Gibbs, Dec 15, 1920. EDUC.: public schools. POLIT. & GOV.: ***candidate for Democratic nomination to presidency of the U.S., 1920, 1928, 1940***; dir. of finance, Dem. Nat'l. Cmte., 1924–28; delegate, Dem. Nat'l. Conv., 1924, 1928; chm., Advisory Finance Cmte., Dem. Nat'l. Cmte., 1928; appointed dir., RFC, 1932–39 (chm., 1933–39); member, National Emergency Council, 1933–39; chm., exec. cmte., Export-Import Bank, 1936–43; appointed administrator, Federal Loan Agency, 1939–45; ***candidate for Democratic nomination to vice presidency of the U.S., 1940***; appointed U.S. sec. of commerce, 1940–45; member, Economic Defense Board, 1941–45; member, Supply Priorities and Allocation Board, 1941–42; member, War Production Board, 1942–45; member, Economic Stabilization Board, 1942–45. BUS. & PROF.: mgr., gen. mgr., M. T. Jones Lumber Co., Dallas, TX, 1895–1905; founder, South Texas Lumber Co., 1902; dir., chm. of the board, Texas Trust Co., Houston, TX, 1909–32; vice pres., Lumberman's National Bank, 1907–15; vice pres., Union National Bank, 1910–18; chm. of the board, National Bank of Commerce, Houston; publisher, *Houston Chronicle*; real estate investor. MEM.: New York World's Fair (chm., Texas Comm., 1939); Golden Gate Exposition (chm., Texas Comm., 1937–39); San Jacinto Centennial Assn. (hon. pres.); Texas Centennial Celebration (dir.-gen., 1926–34); American Red Cross (dir.-gen., military relief, 1917; member, war council, 1918); League of Red Cross Societies of the World (founder); GSA (National Advisory Board); George Peabody Coll. for Teachers (trustee, 1929–56); Tuskeegee Inst. (trustee); Will Rogers Memorial Comm. (treas.); Woodrow Wilson Birthplace Foundation, Inc. (pres.; treas.); Soc. of Arts and Sciences (regent in finance, 1935); Newcomen Soc.; National Democratic Club; Whist Club; National Press Club; Metropolitan Club; Alfalfa Club; Jefferson Island Club; Bohemian Club. AWARDS: Grand Cordon, Order of Ching Hsin (China); commander, Royal Order of Vasa, King of Sweden, 1952; Knight of Order of San Jacinto, 1954. HON. DEG.: LL.D., Southwestern U., 1925; LL.D., Southern Methodist U., 1927; LL.D., TX A&M Coll., 1936; LL.D., NY U., 1937; LL.D., Temple U., 1937; LL.D., John Brown U., 1938; LL.D., Oglethorpe U., 1941; LL.D., Washington and Jefferson Coll., 1941; LL.D., Lafayette Coll., 1942; LL.D., St. Lawrence U., 1942; LL.D., U. of New Brunswick, 1948. WRITINGS: *Fifty Billion Dollars* (1951). REL.: Methodist. RES.: Houston, TX.

JONES, JOHN J. POLIT. & GOV.: ***Lincoln Party candidate for presidency of the U.S., 1904***. WRITINGS: *The Negroes Are an Economic Problem, Not a Race Problem: The Remedy is Modification or Nullification of the 14th and 15th Amendments* (1933). RES.: IL.

JONES, L. B. POLIT. & GOV.: ***candidate for Third World Assembly nomination to vice presidency of the U.S., 1980***. BUS. & PROF.: minister, Baptist Church; pastor, Springfield Baptist Church, Washington, DC REL.: Bapt. MAILING ADDRESS: c/o Springfield Baptist Church, 508 P St., N.W., Washington, DC.

JONES, PAUL R. POLIT. & GOV.: independent candidate for presidency of the U.S., 1980. MAILING ADDRESS: 84 West First, Corning, NY 14830.

JONES, PETER MARTIN. Polit. & Gov.: ***candidate for Democratic nomination to presidency of the U.S., 1988***. MAILING ADDRESS: 500 North Grape, Apt. 123, Escondido, CA 92025.

JONES, ROBERT O. POLIT. & GOV.: ***candidate for Democratic nomination to presidency of the U.S., 1972***. MAILING ADDRESS: c/o Packet Newspapers, 927 15th St., N.W., Room 403, Washington, DC 20005.

JONES, THOMAS E. POLIT. & GOV.: ***candidate for Republican nomination to presidency of the U.S., 1908***. RES.: unknown.

JONES, THOMAS MAUNDY JOSEPH. b. Sep 3, 1908, Cincinnati, OH; par. David Richard and Mary Elizabeth (Maundy) Jones; m. Martha Jane Barnes, 1946; m. 2d, Doretta McGowan; c. Kathleen Elizabeth Virginia; Thomas Joseph Dominic; Richard John Steven; David James John. EDUC.: grad., Westnight H.S., Cincinnati, OH; U. of Cincinnati. POLIT. & GOV.: ***independent candidate for presidency of the U.S., 1984***. BUS. & PROF.: shipping clerk; bank teller; salesman, Western and Southern Life Insurance; cost accountant, Home Owners Loan Corp., 1936–38; warehouseman, National Distiller Corp.; time study consultant, P. Goldsmith Sport Products; cost accountant, C. Schmidt (butcher supplies); U.S. ordnance inspector, 1941–43; employee, W.A.A., 1946–49; employee, U.S. Postal System, 1949–69; employee, dental laboratory; employee, optical laboratory. MIL.: pfc, U.S. Army, 1943–45; Good Conduct Medal; Service Medal. REL.: R.C. MAILING ADDRESS: 254 Brook Forest Dr., Cincinnati, OH 45238.

JONES, WALTER BURGWYN. b. Oct 16, 1888, Montgomery, AL; d. Aug 1, 1963, Montgomery, AL; par. Thomas Goode and Georgena Caroline (Bird) Jones; single. EDUC.: AL

Polytechnic Inst., 1906–07; LL.B., U. of AL, 1909. POLIT. & GOV.: sec. to U.S. judge, Middle District, AL, 1911–19; vice pres., Board of Commissioners, Montgomery, AL, 1920; elected as a Democrat to AL State House, 1919–20; member, AL State Highway Comm., 1920; elected judge, 15th Judicial Circuit of AL, 1920–63 (presiding judge, 1935–63); member, Board of Jury Supervisors, Montgomery Cty., AL, 1923–63; chm., AL War Manpower Comm., 1942–43; member, AL Judicial Council, 1944–51; special circuit judge, Phoenix City, AL, 1954; member, AL Comm. for Judicial Reform, 1957–58; pres., Montgomery Cty. Registrants Advisory Board; chm., U.S. Naval Aviation Cmte., Montgomery; ***received 1 electoral vote for presidency of the U.S., 1956***. BUS. & PROF.: atty.; admitted to AL Bar, 1909; admitted to the Bar of the Supreme Court of the U.S.; law practice, 1910–11; vice chm., Board of Directors, Union Bank and Trust Co.; ed., *Alabama Lawyer*, 1939–63; ed., *Alabama Bible Society Quarterly*; founder, pres., Jones Law School, 1928. MEM.: Montgomery Lawyers Club (pres.); Citizens Cmte. for Universal Military Training (state chm.); Montgomery Museum of Fine Arts (vice pres.; pres., 1937–45); AL State Bar Legal Inst. (dir.); Montgomery Cty. Public Library (pres.); AL Dept. of Archives and History; Scottish Rite Foundation; AL Law Library; Montgomery Law Library; National Soc. of Arts and Letters; National Sojourners; AL Assn. of Circuit Judges (pres., 1934–35, 1943–44); American Jud. Soc.; American Law Inst.; ABA; Junior Bar of AL; Newcomen Soc. of Engineering; Alabama Bible Soc. (pres.); Montgomery Boys Club (pres.); Sigma Alpha Epsilon (national pres., 1932–34); Omicron Delta Kappa; Phi Delta Phi; Masons (33°; Shriners); Elks; Knights of Pythias (grand chancellor, 1938–39, Supreme Tribunal, 1960, 1963). AWARDS: Freedoms Foundation Award, 1958; National Press Photographers Assn. Award, 1958. HON. DEG.: LL.D., Jones U., 1934; LL.D., U. of AL, 1955. WRITINGS: *Jones-Burgwin Family History* (1913); *Alabama Juror's Handbook* (1938); *Alabama Lawyers Handbook* (1944); *Alabama Practice and Forms* (1947); *Citizenship and Voting in Alabama* (1947); *Alabama Jury Instructions* (1953); *Confederate War Poems* (ed., 1959). REL.: Episc. RES.: Montgomery, AL.

JORDAN, BARBARA CHARLENE. b. Feb 21, 1936, Houston, TX; par. Benjamin M. and Arlyne Jordan; single. EDUC.: B.A. (magna cum laude), TX Southern U., 1956; J.D., Boston U., 1959. POLIT. & GOV.: administrative asst. to Harris Cty. (TX) Judge; candidate for Democratic nomination to TX State House, 1962, 1964; elected as a Democrat to TX State Senate, 1966–72 (pres. pro tempore); elected as a Democrat to U.S. House (TX), 1973–79; vice chm., TX State Democratic Central Cmte.; member, Dem. Nat'l. Cmte.; delegate, Dem. Nat'l. Conv., 1976; ***candidate for Democratic nomination to presidency of the U.S., 1976; candidate for Democratic nomination to vice presidency of the U.S., 1976, 1980; candidate for independent (National Unity) nomination to vice presidency of the U.S., 1980 (declined)***. BUS. & PROF.: atty.; admitted to MA Bar, 1959; admitted to TX Bar, 1959; law practice, Houston, TX, 1959–; faculty, Lyndon Baines Johnson School of Public Affairs, U. of TX. MEM.: House Democratic Caucus; ABA; TX Bar Assn.; MA Bar Assn.; Houston Bar Assn.; TX Trial Lawyers Assn.; NAACP; Delta Sigma Theta. AWARDS: one of ten "Most Influential Women in Texas"; one of 100 "Women in Touch with Our Time," *Harpers Bazaar*; "Democratic Woman of the Year," Women's National Democratic Club; "Woman of the Year in Politics," *Redbook*. REL.: Bapt. MAILING ADDRESS: LBJ School of Public Affairs, U. of TX, Austin, TX 78713.

JOYNER, KEVIN. POLIT. & GOV.: ***independent candidate for presidency of the U.S., 1980***. MAILING ADDRESS: unknown.

JUCUS, STANLEY. POLIT. & GOV.: ***independent candidate for presidency of the U.S., 1976***. MAILING ADDRESS: 1540 South East 12th St., Fort Lauderdale, FL 33316.

JUDD, WALTER HENRY. b. Sep 25, 1898, Rising City, NE; d. Feb 13, 1994, Mitchellville, MD; par. Horace Hunter and Mary Elizabeth (Greenslit) Judd; m. Miriam Louise Barber, Mar 13, 1932; c. Mary Louise (Mrs. Norman Carpenter); Carolyn Ruth; Eleanor Grace Quinn. EDUC.: B.A., U. of NE, 1920, M.D., 1923. POLIT. & GOV.: elected as a Republican to U.S. House (MN), 1943–63; U.S. delegate, 12th General Assembly, U.N.; ***candidate for Republican nomination to presidency of the U.S., 1960, 1964; candidate for Republican nomination to vice presidency of the U.S., 1960***; Republican candidate for U.S. House (MN), 1962. BUS. & PROF.: physician; instructor of zoology, U. of Omaha, 1920–24; intern, University Hospital, Omaha, NE, 1922–24; traveling sec., student volunteer movement, 1924–25; fellow in surgery, Mayo Foundation, 1932–34; medical missionary, American Board of Commissioners for Foreign Missions, China, 1925–31, 1934–38; lecturer; medical practice, Minneapolis, MN, 1941–42; contributing ed., *Reader's Digest*, 1963–; radio commentator, "Washington Report of the Air," American Security Council, 1964–70. MIL.: pvt., U.S. Army, 1918, 2d lt., 1919; 2d lt., F.A., ORC, 1919–24. MEM.: World Neighbors (cofounder); Aid to Refugee Chinese Intellectuals (founder); American Council for World Freedom (hon. pres.); American Emergency Cmte. for Tibetan Refugees (vice chm.); American Bureau for Medical Aid to China (vice pres.); International Coll. of Surgeons (hon. fellow); Omicron Delta Kappa; Rotary Club; Masons (33°; Shriner); Alpha Omega Alpha; Phi Rho Sigma; World Youth Crusade for Freedom (cofounder); American-Asian Educational Exchange (cofounder); Cmte. for a Free China (cofounder); Good Will Industries (dir.); Metropolitan YMCA (dir.); Republican Workshops (founder); Former Members of Congress (founder); American Medical Assn. (Judicial Council, 1963–77); MN Medical Assn.; American Acad. of Family Physicians; American Legion; China Soc.; Phi Beta Kappa. AWARDS: CARE-MEDICO Humanitarian Award, 1962; George Washington Medal, Freedoms Foundation, 1959, 1961, 1962, 1964, 1967; Great Living American Award, U.S. C. of C., 1963; Silver Buffalo Award, BSA, 1963; Outstanding Achievement Award, U. of MN, 1964; Law Churchman of the Year Award, Religious Heritage of America, 1966; Distinguished Service Award, American Medical Assn., 1961; Presidential Medal of Freedom, 1981. HON. DEG.: received 28 degrees. REL.: Congregationalist. Res: Mitchellville, MD.

JULIAN, GEORGE WASHINGTON. b. May 5, 1817, Centerville, IN; d. Jul 7, 1899, Irvington, IN; par. Isaac and Rebecca (Hoover) Julian; m. Anne Elizabeth Finch, May 13, 1845; m. 2d, Laura Giddings, Dec 31, 1863; c. Grace Giddings (Mrs. Charles B. Clarke); Paul; Edward Channing; Louis Henry; Fred. EDUC.: public schools; studied law. POLIT. & GOV.: elected as a Whig to IN State House, 1845–46; candidate for Whig Party nomination to IN State Senate, 1847; delegate, Free Soil Party National Convention, 1848; presidential elector, Free Soil Party, 1848; elected as a Free Soiler to U.S. House (IN), 1849–51; Free Soil Party candidate for U.S. House (IN), 1850; ***Free Soil Party candidate for vice presidency of the U.S., 1852***; delegate, Rep. Nat'l. Conv., 1856; candidate for Republican nomination to U.S. House (IN), 1858, 1870; elected as a Republican to U.S. House (IN), 1861–71; candidate for Republican nomination to U.S. Senate (IN), 1866; member, Cmte. to Prepare Articles of Impeachment against President Andrew Johnson (q.v.), U.S. House, 1867; candidate for Democratic nomination to U.S. House (IN), 1872; ***candidate for Labor Reform Party nomination to presidency of the U.S., 1872; candidate for Liberal Republican Party nomination to vice presidency of the U.S., 1872; candidate for Equal Rights (Cosmic, Free Love, People's) Party nomination to presidency of the U.S., 1872; received 5 electoral votes for vice presidency of the U.S., 1872***; appointed surveyor gen. of New Mexico, 1885–89. BUS. & PROF.: schoolteacher; atty.; admitted to IN Bar, 1840; law practice, Newcastle, IN, 1840; law practice, Greenfield, IN, 1840–42; law practice, Centerville, IN; author; farmer, Irvington, IN, 1873; partner, Tilford, Julian and Co. (loan and collection agency), Indianapolis, IN, 1874; contributor, *North American Review*; law practice (with William A. Meloy), Washington, DC, 1879–99. MEM.: The Dark Lyceum. WRITINGS: *Speech on the Slavery Question* (1850); *Speech* (1865); *Dangers and Duties* (1865); *Select Speeches* (1867); *Speeches on Political Questions* (1872); *The Gospel of Reform* (1876); *Political Recollections, 1840–72* (1884); *Later Speeches on Political Questions with Select Controversial Papers* (1889); *The Rank of Charles Osborn as an Anti-Slavery Pioneer* (1891); *President Harrison and Civil Service Reform* (1892); *Life of Joshua R. Giddings* (1892). REL.: Unitarian. MISC.: noted abolitionist; advocate of women's suffrage; reformer. RES.: Irvington, IN.

JULIAN, WILLIAM ALEXANDER. b. Aug 6, 1860, Franklin Cty., KY; d. May 28, 1949, Rockville, MD; par. Alexander and Elizabeth (Laughlin) Julian; m. Gertrude Means, Sep 15, 1895; c. none. EDUC.: A.B., Dodds Coll., 1887. POLIT. & GOV.: delegate, Dem. Nat'l. Conv., 1916, 1920, 1924, 1928; Democratic candidate for U.S. Senate (OH), 1920; member, Dem. Nat'l. Cmte., 1926–34; appointed treas. of the U.S., 1933–49; ***candidate for Democratic nomination to presidency of the U.S., 1948***. BUS. & PROF.: bank clerk, Cincinnati, OH; shoe manufacturer, Cincinnati, 1888; partner, Alter and Julian (shoe manufacturers), Cincinnati, 1893–1900; partner, Julian and Kokenge Co. (shoe manufacturers), Columbus, OH, 1900, pres., 1900–1917, chm. of the board, 1917–23; pres., Queen City Trust Co.; vice pres., Citizens National Bank, Cincinnati; pres., Cincinnati Shoe Co.; pres., First National Bank of Bethel; dir., Central Trust Co.; owner, Julian Assets Inc. (real estate). MEM.: Berea Coll. (chm., Investment Cmte.); Associated Charities of Cincinnati (pres.); American Red Cross (vice pres., Cincinnati Chapter); NAM; American Bankers Assn.; Metropolitan Club of Washington; Masons (33°); Burning Tree Club. REL.: Christian Church. RES.: Cincinnati, OH.

KAISER, HENRY JOHN. b. May 9, 1882, Sprout Brook, NY; d. Aug 24, 1967, Honolulu, HI; par. Francis J. and Mary (Yopps) Kaiser; m. Bessie Hannah Fosburgh, Apr 8, 1907; m. 2d, Alyce Chester, Apr 10, 1951; c. Edgar F.; Henry John, Jr. POLIT. & GOV.: ***candidate for Republican nomination to presidency of the U.S., 1944***. BUS. & PROF.: salesman; partner, owner, Brownell and Kaiser (photographic supplies), Lake Placid, NY; highway construction contractor, British Columbia, WA, CA, and Cuba, 1914–30; contractor, Mississippi levee, 1927–30; contractor, pipeline projects in southwest, 1930–33; chm., exec. cmte., Six Companies, Inc., 1931; pres., chm. of the exec. cmte., Bridge Builders, Inc., 1933; pres., Columbia Construction Co.; pres., Consolidated Builders, Inc.; chm. of the board, Kaiser Industries Corp.; chm. of the board, Kaiser Hawaii Kai Development Co.; chm. of the board, Kaiser Community Homes; chm. of the board, Kaiser Center, Inc.; founder, Kaiser Jeep Corp.; founder, Kaiser Steel Corp.; founder, Kaiser Aluminum and Chemical Corp.; founder, Kaiser Cement and Gypsum Corp.; founder, Kaiser Bauxite Co.; founder, Glacier Sand and Gravel Co.; founder, Permanente S. S. Corp.; pres., Industrias Kaiser Argentina; chm. of the board, Kaiser Foundation Health Plan; mgr., seven shipyards on Pacific coast, WWII. MEM.: Legion of Honor (chevalier); Associated General Contractors of America (national pres.); Newcomen Soc. of North America; Beavers; Beta Gamma Sigma; Elks; Automobile Old Timers; San Francisco Press Club; Commonwealth Club of CA; Saints and Sinners Club; CA Rehabilitation Center (cofounder). AWARDS: La Salle Medal, 1944; AFL-CIO Murray Green Award, 1965. HON. DEG.: LL.D., WA State U.; LL.D., MT School of Mines; LL.D., Hobart Coll.; LL.D., U. of NV; LL.D., Marshall Coll.; LL.D., St. Mary's Coll. REL.: Episc. RES.: Oakland, CA.

KAPLAN, ALAN M. POLIT. & GOV.: ***candidate for Democratic nomination to presidency of the U.S., 1992; independent candidate for presidency of the U.S., 1992***. MAILING ADDRESS: 327 Capri G, Delray Beach, FL 33484.

KARISS, ROBERT. POLIT. & GOV.: ***candidate for Democratic nomination to vice presidency of the U.S., 1972***. MAILING ADDRESS: FL.

KAROLY, BEDO ISTVAN. b. May 22, 1939, Hungary; par. (adopted); single. EDUC.: elementary school, Hungary; grad., Englewood (NJ) School for Boys; Columbia U., 1959; B.A., B.S., Ph.D., Rutgers U.; American U. Law School, 1977. POLIT. & GOV.: ***candidate for Republican nomination to presidency of the U.S., 1980, 1984***. BUS. & PROF.: pres., B. I. K. Research Foundation, Washington, DC, 1973–. REL.: Interdenominational. MAILING ADDRESS: P.O. Box 32050, Washington, DC 20007.

KASPER, FREDERICK JOHN. b. Oct 21, 1929, Camden, NJ. EDUC.: public schools, Gainesville, GA; Temple U.; Yankton (SD) Coll.; B.S., Columbia U., 1951. POLIT. & GOV.: candidate for TN State Legislature, 1962; ***National States Rights Party candidate for presidency of the U.S., 1964***. BUS. & PROF.: owner, operator, Make It New Bookstore, Greenwich Village, NY, to 1954; publisher, Square Dollar Series; owner, Cadmus Bookstore, Washington, DC, after 1954; owner, car repair business, Nashville, TN. MEM.: Seaboard White Citizens' Council, Washington, DC (founder, 1956). WRITINGS: *Segregation or Death* (1958). MISC.: associate of Ezra Pound; served three terms in Federal prisons for obstructing school integration and inciting riots in Clinton, TN; sentenced to one year in prison; released, 1958. MAILING ADDRESS: Cadmus Bookstore, 1246 Wisconsin Ave., Washington, DC.

KASSEBAUM, NANCY JOSEPHINE LANDON. b. Jul 29, 1932, Topeka, KS; par. Alfred M. (q.v.) and Theo Landon; m. Philip Kassebaum (divorced, 1979); c. John; Linda; Richard; William. EDUC.: B.A., U. of KS, 1954; M.A., U. of MI, 1956. POLIT. & GOV.: appointed member, KS State Government Ethics Comm.; appointed member, KS State Cmte. on the

Humanities; staff, U.S. Sen. James B. Pearson (KS), 1975; elected as a Republican to U.S. Senate (KS), 1979–; ***candidate for Republican nomination to vice presidency of the U.S., 1988***. BUS. & PROF.: dir., vice pres., KFH radio, Wichita, KS. MEM.: KS Press Women's Assn.; Women's Assn. of Inst. of Logopedics. REL.: Episc. MAILING ADDRESS: Wichita, KS.

KATO, FRANCK H. POLIT. & GOV.: ***candidate for Democratic nomination to presidency of the U.S., 1980***. MAILING ADDRESS: 3441½ South Arlington, Los Angeles, CA 90018.

KATZENBACH, FRANK SNOWDEN, JR. b. Nov 5, 1868, Trenton, NJ; d. Mar 13, 1929, Trenton, NJ; par. Frank Snowden and Augusta M. (Mushbach) Katzenbach; m. Natalie McNeal Brubb, Nov 10, 1904; c. Frank Snowden III; Floy McNeal. EDUC.: grad., State Model School, 1885; A.B., Princeton U., 1889; LL.B., Columbia U., 1891. POLIT. & GOV.: elected as a Democrat to Trenton (NJ) City Council, 1898–1900 (pres.); elected as a Democrat to mayor of Trenton, NJ, 1901–05; Democratic candidate for gov. of NJ, 1907; delegate, Dem. Nat'l. Conv., 1908; candidate for Democratic nomination to gov. of NJ, 1910, 1913; ***candidate for Democratic nomination to vice presidency of the U.S., 1912 (declined)***; appointed assoc. justice, Supreme Court of NJ, 1920–29; appointed judge, NJ Court of Errors and Appeals, 1920–29. BUS. & PROF.: atty.; admitted to NJ Bar, 1891; law practice, Trenton, NJ; dir., Trenton Banking Co. MEM.: Trenton School of Industrial Arts (pres., board of trustees); St. Mary's Hall (trustee); YMCA (dir.); SAR. REL.: Episc. (junior warden; Sunday school superintendent). RES.: Trenton, NJ.

KAUFFMAN, A. ROBERT. POLIT. & GOV.: ***candidate for Democratic nomination to presidency of the U.S., 1992***. BUS. & PROF.: activist, Baltimore, MD. MAILING ADDRESS: Baltimore, MD.

KAY, RICHARD BROUGHTON. b. Apr 7, 1918, Cleveland, OH; par. Joseph Stanley and Frances Anna (Broughton) Kay; single. EDUC.: A.B., Miami U., Oxford, OH, 1939; LL.B., Western Reserve U., 1948. POLIT. & GOV.: national vice chm., Willkie Youth Organization, 1940; exec. sec., Stassen for President Club of Northern OH, 1948; appointed asst. atty. gen. of OH; candidate for Republican nomination to U.S. House (OH), 1950; field organizer, Citizens for Eisenhower-Nixon, 1952; pres., Greater Cleveland Young Republican Club, 1953; candidate for Republican nomination to state treas. of OH, 1962; American Independent Party candidate for U.S. Senate (OH), 1970, 1974; American Independent Party candidate for U.S. House (OH), 1972; ***candidate for American Party nomination to presidency of the U.S., 1972, 1976; candidate for American Party nomination to vice presidency of the U.S., 1972 (withdrew)***; candidate for Democratic nomination to U.S. Senate (OH), 1976; ***candidate for Democratic nomination to presidency of the U.S., 1980, 1984, 1988***. BUS. & PROF.: atty.; admitted to OH Bar, 1948. MIL.: U.S. Navy, WWII; U.S.N.R. MEM.: United Appeal; Citizens League; Cleveland Junior C. of C.; VFW; American Legion; Cleveland Bar Assn.; Cuyahoga Cty. Bar Assn.; City Club of Cleveland; Council on World Affairs; Reserve Officers Assn. REL.: Protestant. MISC.: served as defense counsel for Lt. William Calley. MAILING ADDRESS: 1080 East Indianatown Road, Suite 202, Jupiter, FL 33477.

KAZDOY, ALAN CRAIG. POLIT. & GOV.: ***candidate for Democratic nomination to presidency of the U.S., 1992***. MAILING ADDRESS: 316 West Ashford Lane, Midlothian, TX 76065.

KEAN, THOMAS H. b. Apr 21, 1935, New York, NY; m. Deborah K. EDUC.: B.A., Princeton U., 1957; M.A., Columbia U., 1963. POLIT. & GOV.: delegate, Rep. Nat'l. Conv., 1976; elected as a Republican to NJ State Assembly, 1968–77 (Speaker, 1972–74); elected as a Republican to gov. of NJ, 1981–89; ***candidate for Republican nomination to presidency of the U.S., 1988; candidate for Republican nomination to vice presidency of the U.S., 1988***. BUS. & PROF.: television news commentator; chm., pres., Realty Transfer Co., 1977–81. REL.: Episc. MAILING ADDRESS: 123 Shrewsbury Dr., Livingston, NJ 07039.

KEENE, DAVID ARTHUR. b. May 20, 1945, Rockford, IL; par. Arthur W. and Dorothy V. (Tuenholm) Keene; m. Karlyn T. Herbolsheimer; c. none. EDUC.: B.S., U. of WI, 1967, J.D., 1970; fellow, John F. Kennedy Inst. of Politics, Harvard U., 1976–77. POLIT. & GOV.: Republican candidate for WI State Senate, 1969; appointed asst. to the vice pres. of the U.S., 1970–73; appointed asst. to U.S. Sen. James L. Buckley (q.v.), 1974–75; southern coordinator, Reagan for President, 1975–76; ***candidate for Republican nomination to vice presidency of the U.S., 1976***; deputy chm., George Bush for President, 1979–80. BUS. & PROF.: atty.; political strategist; contributor, *Human Events*; contributor, *National Review*; contributor, *The American Spectator*. MEM.: WI Bar Assn.; American Conservative Union (dir.). REL.: Protestant. MAILING ADDRESS: 814 South Lee St., Alexandria, VA 22314.

KEENER, SAMUEL FLOYD "SAM." b. May 2, 1888; d. Apr 2, 1954, West Palm Beach, FL; m.; c. John; Mrs. C. William Butler. EDUC.: 6th grade. POLIT. & GOV.: ***candidate for Republican nomination to presidency of the U.S., 1952***. BUS. & PROF.: cowboy; rancher; pres., Keener Supply Co., Wheeling, WV; pres., Suburban Trailer Sales Co., Niles, OH; oil, steel, and real estate investor; owner, Salem Engineering Co., Salem, OH, 1934–51; operator, sugar cane plantation, HI; electric furnace salesman, 1934; inspector of highways. MISC.:

built Hancock Cty. Fairgrounds, Findlay, OH; known as "The World Salesman"; invented circular soaking pit used in steel mills; wore elaborate self-designed "uniform" in travels. RES.: Salem, OH.

KEFAUVER, CAREY ESTES. b. Jul 26, 1903, Madisonville, TN; d. Aug 10, 1963, Bethesda, MD; par. Robert Cooke and Phedonia (Estes) Kefauver; m. Nancy Patterson Pigott, Aug 8, 1935; c. Eleanor Cooke; Diane Carey; Gail Estes; David Estes. EDUC.: A.B., U. of TN, 1924; LL.B., Yale U., 1927; LL.D., Western Reserve U. POLIT. & GOV.: chm., Hamilton Cty. (TN) Planning Comm., 1934; candidate for TN State Senate, 1936; TN Commissioner of Finance and Taxation, 1939; elected as a Democrat to U.S. House (TN), 1939–49; member, Dem. Nat'l. Cmte. (TN), 1940–44; elected as a Democrat to U.S. Senate (TN), 1949–63; delegate, Dem. Nat'l. Conv., 1952, 1956; ***candidate for Democratic nomination to presidency of the U.S., 1952, 1956; candidate for Democratic nomination to vice presidency of the U.S., 1952; Democratic candidate for vice presidency of the U.S., 1956***. BUS. & PROF.: atty.; admitted to TN Bar, 1926; law practice, Chattanooga, TN, 1927–63; partner, Kefauver, Duggan and Miller (law firm), Chattanooga, TN. MEM.: DC Bar Assn.; Rotary Club of Chattanooga; Mountain City Club; APSA (vice pres.); Chattanooga Bar Assn.; Kappa Sigma Pi; Pi Sigma Alpha; ABA; TN Bar Assn. (vice pres., 1934); Chattanooga Junior C. of C. (pres., 1932); National Press Club; Lions; Elks; Eagles; Phi Delta Phi. AWARDS: "Most Outstanding Young Citizen," Junior C. of C., 1937. HON. DEG.: LL.D., George Pepperdine Coll.; LL.D., Tusculum Coll.; D.C.L., Union Coll. (hon. chancellor). WRITINGS: *20th Century Congress* (co-author, 1947); *Crime in America* (1952); *In a Few Hands* (1965). REL.: Bapt. RES.: Chattanooga, TN.

KEIFER, JOSEPH WARREN. b. Jan 30, 1836, Springfield, OH; d. Apr 22, 1932, Springfield, OH; par. Joseph and Mary (Smith) Keifer; m. Eliza Stout, Mar 22, 1860; c. Joseph Warren; William White; Horace Charles; Margarette Eliza. EDUC.: Antioch Coll.; studied law in office of Anthony and Goode, Springfield, OH. POLIT. & GOV.: elected as a Republican to OH State Senate, 1868–69; delegate, Rep. Nat'l. Conv., 1876, 1908; elected as a Republican to U.S. House (OH), 1877–85 (Speaker, 1881–83), 1905–11; Republican candidate for U.S. House (OH), 1884, 1910; ***candidate for Republican nomination to presidency of the U.S., 1920***. BUS. & PROF.: atty.; admitted to OH Bar, 1858; law practice, Springfield, OH, 1858; pres., Lagonda National Bank, 1873–1927. MIL.: maj., Third OH Infantry, 1861, lt. col., 1862; col., 110th OH Infantry, 1862; brev. brig. gen. of volunteers, 1864; maj. gen. of volunteers, 1865; mustered out, Jun 27, 1865; appointed lt. col., 26th U.S. Infantry, 1866 (declined); maj. gen., U.S.V., 1898–99; wounded four times during Civil War. MEM.: GAR (junior commander in chief, OH Dept., 1871–72); United Spanish War Veterans (commander in chief, 1900–1901); OH Archaeological and Hist. Soc.; OH Soldiers' and Sailors' Orphans Home (trustee, 1870–78, 1903–04); Antioch Coll. (trustee, 1873–1932); Perry's Victory Centennial Comm.; Interparliamentary Peace Conference (life member, 1912). WRITINGS: *Slavery and Four Years of War* (1900). RES.: Springfield, OH.

KEILLOR, SCOTTIE. POLIT. & GOV.: ***independent candidate for vice presidency of the U.S., 1980***. BUS. & PROF.: doctor. MAILING ADDRESS: 219 Walnut St., Stoughton, MA 02072.

KELLEHER, ROBERT LEE "MAD MONK." b. Mar 30, 1923, Oak Park, IL; par. Leo Francis and Mary (Carlson) Kelleher; m. Geraldine DeBacker, Sep 16, 1948; m. 2d, Joan Hurdle; c. Robert Lee, Jr.; Gerrie; David P.; Mary Adele; Richard V.; Dennis M. EDUC.: Ph.B., Mt. Carmel Coll., Niagara Falls, Ontario, 1945; J. D., Catholic U. of America, 1950, M.A., 1956; George Washington U., 1951–52; Harvard U., 1953–54; Eastern MT Coll., 1960–62, 1974–75; grad., U.S. Army Command and Gen. Staff Coll., 1969. POLIT. & GOV.: atty., Criminal Div., U.S. Dept. of Justice, 1951–52; atty., U.S. Dept. of Interior, 1952–53; sec., Yellowstone Cty. (MT) Democratic Central Cmte., 1956–57; candidate for Democratic nomination to U.S. House (MT), 1964; special asst. atty. gen., State of MT; Democratic candidate for U.S. House (MT), 1968; elected delegate, MT State Constitutional Convention, 1972; ***candidate for Democratic nomination to presidency of the U.S., 1976***; candidate for Democratic nomination to gov. of MT, 1992. BUS. & PROF.: atty.; law practice, Billings, MT, 1955–. MIL.: col., U.S.A.R. (military intelligence), 1969–. MEM.: MT Bar Assn.; Yellowstone Cty. Bar Assn.; American Trial Lawyers Assn.; MT Trial Lawyers Assn.; Defense Research Inst.; Reserve Officers Assn. (pres., MT Dept.). REL.: R.C. MAILING ADDRESS: 928 North 30th St., Billings, MT 59101.

KELLEMS, VIVIEN. b. Jun 7, 1896, Des Moines, IA; d. Jan 25, 1975, Los Angeles, CA; par. Rev. David Clinton and Louisa (Flint) Kellems; single. EDUC.: A.B., U. of OR, 1918, A. M., 1920; grad. study, Columbia U., 1921–22. POLIT. & GOV.: candidate for Republican nomination to U.S. House (CT), 1942; ***Constitution Party candidate for vice presidency of the U.S., 1952***; independent Republican candidate for U.S. Senate (CT), 1952, 1956. BUS. & PROF.: Chatauqua booking agent; theatrical agent; manufacturer of cable grips; founder, pres., Kellems Co., 1928–62. MEM.: business and professional women's clubs; A.I.E.E. WRITINGS: *Toil, Taxes and Trouble*. MISC.: noted opponent of income taxes. RES.: East Haddam, CT.

KELLEY, DAVID CAMPBELL. b. Dec 25, 1833, Leeville, TN; d. May 15, 1909, Lebanon, TN; par. John and Margaret L. (Campbell) Kelley; m. Mary Owen Campbell, 1870; m. 2d, Mrs. May Elliott Knight, 1892; c. Mrs. Walter Lambuth. EDUC.: A.M., Cumberland U., 1851, D.D., 1868; M.D., U. of Nashville, 1853. POLIT. & GOV.: Prohibition Party candidate for gov. of TN, 1890; ***candidate for Prohibition Party nomination to presidency of the U.S., 1892***. BUS. & PROF.: licensed minister, Methodist Episcopal Church, 1850; Methodist Medical Missionary, China, 1853–57; pastor, Methodist Tulip Street and McKendree Station churches, Nashville, TN; sec. treas., board of missions, Methodist Episcopal Church, South, 1875–84; pastor, Methodist Episcopal Church, Gallatin, TN, 1889–90; ed., *Round Table*, 1890; presiding elder, Nashville District, Methodist Episcopal Church, South, 1898–1909; elected delegate, general conference, Methodist Episcopal Church, South, 1878, 1882, 1886, 1890, 1894, 1898, 1902; missionary sec., TN Conference, Methodist Episcopal Church, South, 1904–07. MIL.: maj., lt. col., col., C.S.A., 1860–65. MEM.: Women's Foreign Missionary Soc. (founder); Cadets of Temperance; Anti-Saloon League of America; United Confederate Veterans (lt. gen., 1900–1909); TN Soc. (pres.); National Soc. of SAR; Vanderbilt U. (trustee, 1872–85); Humane Soc. of TN (pres.); Scotch-Irish Soc. of America; American Inst. of Civics; Round Table Club of Nashville. HON. DEG.: LL.D., U. of Nashville, 1896. WRITINGS: *Short Method with Modern Doubt* (1882); *Bishop or Conference* (1893); *Life of Mrs. M. L. Kelley* (1900). REL.: Methodist Episc. Church, South. RES.: Nashville, TN.

KELLEY, DAVID MOORE. b. Aug 21, 1924, Cleveland, OH; par. Edmund and Ermine (Reick) Kelley; m. Miriam Lorene Bradley, Aug 21, 1947 (divorced, Jun 1955); c. Marilyn Sue. EDUC.: grad., Lakewood (OH) H.S., 1942; B.B.A., Fenn Coll., 1949. POLIT. & GOV.: ***candidate for Republican nomination to presidency of the U.S., 1984***. BUS. & PROF.: accountant; auditor; farmer; writer. MIL.: sgt., U.S. Army, 1943–46; known as "The Last Confederate Soldier." MEM.: American Legion. WRITINGS: *In Defense of the South* (1976). REL.: Jewish (nee R.C.). MISC.: advocate of segregation and relocation of Negroes to Africa. MAILING ADDRESS: R.D. 7, Sevierville, TN 37862.

KELLEY, VELDI ARVEL. b. 1915; m.; c. one stepdaughter; one son (adopted); one other daughter (adopted). POLIT. & GOV.: independent candidate for U.S. Senate (IL), 1980; ***candidate for Republican nomination to presidency of the U.S., 1980***; candidate for Republican nomination to gov. of IL, 1982; candidate for Republican nomination to U.S. Senate (IL), 1984. BUS. & PROF.: farmer; feed and grain supplier; carpenter; entertainer; mule skinner. MAILING ADDRESS: Oswego, IL.

KELLEY, WILLIAM DARRAH. b. Apr 12, 1814, Philadelphia, PA; d. Jan 9, 1890, Washington, DC; par. David and Hannah (Darrah) Kelley; m. Isabella Tennant; m. 2d, Caroline Bartram Bonsall; c. four. EDUC.: Congregational School, Second Presbyterian Church, Philadelphia, PA. POLIT. & GOV.: appointed deputy prosecuting atty., Philadelphia, PA, 1845–46; appointed and subsequently elected judge, Philadelphia (PA) Court of Common Pleas, 1846–56; founder, Republican Party of PA; Republican candidate for U.S. House (PA), 1856; delegate, Rep. Nat'l. Conv., 1860; elected as a Republican to U.S. House (PA), 1861–90 (chm., Ways and Means Cmte., 1881–83); ***candidate for Republican nomination to vice presidency of the U.S., 1868***. BUS. & PROF.: jeweler's apprentice, Philadelphia, PA, 1827–34; umbrella maker; copy-reader; author; atty.; admitted to PA Bar, 1841. WRITINGS: *Speeches, Addresses, and Letters on Industrial and Financial Questions* (1872); *Letters from Europe* (1880); *Lincoln and Stanton* (1885); *The Old South and the New* (1888). MISC.: noted as advocate of protectionism; known as "Pig Iron" Kelley. RES.: Philadelphia, PA.

KELLOGG, FRANK BILLINGS. b. Dec 22, 1856, Potsdam, NY; d. Dec 21, 1937, St. Paul, MN; par. Asa Fransworth and Abigail (Billings) Kellogg; m. Clara Margaret Cook, Jun 16, 1896; c. none. EDUC.: public schools; studied law under H. A. Eckholdt and R. A. Jones, Rochester, MN. POLIT. & GOV.: city atty., Rochester, MN, 1878–81; cty. atty., Olmsted Cty., MN, 1882–87; special counsel, U.S. Dept. of Justice, Standard Oil Cases; special counsel, Interstate Commerce Comm., Railroad Cases; U.S. delegate, Universal Congress of Lawyers and Jurists, 1904; delegate, Rep. Nat'l. Conv., 1904, 1908, 1912; member, Rep. Nat'l. Cmte., 1904–12; elected as a Republican to U.S. Senate (MN), 1917–23; ***candidate for Republican nomination to presidency of the U.S., 1920, 1928***; Republican candidate for U.S. Senate (MN), 1922; delegate, Fifth International Conference of American States, 1923; appointed U.S. ambassador to Great Britain, 1924; appointed U.S. sec. of state, 1925–29; elected judge, Permanent Court of International justice, 1930–35. BUS. & PROF.: atty.; admitted to MN Bar, 1877; law practice, Rochester, MN, 1877–87; prof. of equity, MN State U., 1890–93; partner, Davis, Kellogg and Severance (law firm), St. Paul, MN; partner, Davis, Kellogg, Severance and Morgan (law firm), St. Paul, MN, 1923–29; partner, Kellogg, Morgan, Chase, Carter and Headley (law firm), 1929–37; dir., First National Bank of St. Paul; chm. of the board, First Trust Co. HON. DEG.: LL.D., McGill U., 1913; LL.D., U. of PA, 1926; LL.D., George Washington U., 1927; LL.D., NY U., 1927; LL.D., Carleton Coll., 1928; LL.D., Harvard U., 1929; D.C.L., Oxford U., 1929; LL.D., St. Lawrence U., 1929; D.C.L., Trinity Coll., 1929; LL.D., Brown U., 1930; LL.D., Hamline U., 1931; LL.D., U. of MN, 1931; LL.D., Occidental U., 1931; LL.D., Princeton U., 1931; LL.D., Rollins Coll., 1934. MEM.: ABA (pres., 1912–13); Middle Temple (hon. bencher, 1929); MN Club; Minneapolis Club; Kitchi Gammi Club; Chicago Club; Chevy Chase Club; Metropolitan Club; Burning Tree Club; Smithsonian Institution (regent); Pan American Union (chm. of the board). AWARDS: Nobel Peace Prize, 1929; Order of Olive Branch (Argentina, 1930); Grand Cross of the Legion of Honor (France, 1929); Newman Award, U. of IL, 1932; Order of Jade (China, 1936). RES.: St. Paul, MN.

KELLY, JOSEPH WILBER, JR. par. Joseph Wilber Kelly. POLIT. & GOV.: ***candidate for Democratic nomina-***

tion to presidency of the U.S., 1984; independent candidate for presidency of the U.S., 1984. MAILING ADDRESS: JB Rt., Box 121-E, Cameron, LA 70631.

KELSO, JOHN GARFIELD. b. Jun 4, 1944, Fort Sill, OK; par. Elmer Garfield and Dorothy (Bradford) Kelso; m. Sally Ann Richards; c. none. EDUC.: grad., Laconia (NH) H.S., 1962; B.A., U. of MO, 1969. POLIT. & GOV.: ***candidate for Republican nomination to presidency of the U.S., 1980***. BUS. & PROF.: newspaperman, 1966–; columnist, *Austin (TX) American-Statesman*; humorist. MIL.: spec. 4th class, U.S. Army, 1971–72. WRITINGS: *Bubba (He's the One With His Tongue Hanging Out)* (1984). REL.: None So's You'd Notice. MISC.: named Trout Lake Camp Senior All-Camper. MAILING ADDRESS: 1607 Fair Oaks Dr., Austin, TX 78745.

KEMP, CARL L. POLIT. & GOV.: ***Freedom of Choice Party candidate for vice presidency of the U.S., 1992***. BUS. & PROF.: inmate, Federal prison, Lansing, KS. MAILING ADDRESS: P.O. Box 2, Lansing, KS 66043.

KEMP, JOHN FRENCH "JACK." b. Jul 13, 1935, Los Angeles, CA; par. Paul R. and Frances (Pope) Kemp; m. Joanne Main, Jul 19, 1958; c. Jeffrey; Jennifer; Judith; James. EDUC.: B.A., Occidental Coll., 1957; Long Beach State U.; CA Western U. POLIT. & GOV.: appointed special asst. to the gov. of CA, 1967; appointed special asst. to the chm., Rep. Nat'l. Cmte., 1969; elected as a Republican to U.S. House (NY), 1971–89; appointed member, President's Council on Physical Fitness and Sports; ***candidate for Republican nomination to presidency of the U.S., 1980, 1988; candidate for Republican nomination to vice presidency of the U.S., 1980, 1984, 1988; American Party of KS candidate for vice presidency of the U.S., 1980 (declined)***; candidate for Republican nomination to U.S. Senate (NY), 1982; appointed U.S. sec. of housing and urban development, 1989–93. BUS. & PROF.: professional football player; quarterback; capt., San Diego (CA) Chargers; capt., Buffalo (NY) Bills; public relations officer, Marine Midland Bank of Buffalo. MIL.: U.S. Army, 1958; U.S.A.R., 1958–62. MEM.: American Football League Players Assn. (cofounder; pres.); National Football League Players Assn. (exec. cmte.); Sierra Club; Buffalo Area C. of C.; National Assn. of Broadcasters, Engineers and Technicians; NY BSA (patron); Fellowship of Christian Athletes. AWARDS: Young Man of the Year Award, Buffalo Junior C. of C.; Distinguished Service Award, U.S. C. of C. (twice); Outstanding Citizen's Award, *Buffalo (NY) Evening News*, 1965, 1974; National Football Foundation and Hall of Fame Award; Distinguished Service Award, NY State Junior C. of C.; All-AFL Quarterback (twice); American Football League Player of the Year, 1965. REL.: Presb. MAILING ADDRESS: 5201 Leesburg Pike, Suite 1207, Falls Church, VA 22041.

KEMP, WILLIARD W. POLIT. & GOV.: ***Christian Party candidate for vice presidency of the U.S., 1936***. BUS. & PROF.: rancher, El Cajon, CA. MEM.: Silver Shirts (West Coast leader). RES.: San Diego, CA.

KEMPLIN, CYNTHIA WINGARD. POLIT. & GOV.: ***independent candidate for presidency of the U.S., 1988***. MAILING ADDRESS: c/o Shelissa A. Kemplin, 9550 Guilford Road, Columbia, MD 21046.

KENDRICK, JOHN BENJAMIN. b. Sep 6, 1857, Jacksonville, TX; d. Nov 3, 1933, Sheridan, WY; par. John Harvey and Anna (Maye) Kendrick; m. Eula Wulfjen, Jan 20, 1891; c. Rosa Maye; Manville. EDUC.: public schools. POLIT. & GOV.: elected as a Democrat to WY State Senate, 1910–14; delegate, Dem. Nat'l. Conv., 1912, 1916, 1924; Democratic candidate for U.S. Senate (WY), 1912; elected as a Democrat to gov. of WY, 1915–17; elected as a Democrat to U.S. Senate (WY), 1917–33; ***candidate for Democratic nomination to presidency of the U.S., 1924***. BUS. & PROF.: cattle rancher, WY and MT, 1885–1933. MEM.: Masons (32°); WY Stock Growers Assn. (pres., 1909). HON. DEG.: LL.D., U. of WY, 1932. REL.: Methodist. MISC.: owner of one of the largest cattle ranches in the West. RES.: Sheridan, WY.

KENDZIERSKI, JAMES JOHN. POLIT. & GOV.: ***independent candidate for presidency of the U.S., 1988***. MAILING ADDRESS: 227 Rockledge Dr., #13, Rockledge, FL 32955.

KENNA, JOSEPH JAMES. POLIT. & GOV.: ***candidate for Democratic nomination to presidency of the U.S., 1984***. MAILING ADDRESS: 191 West Annsbury St., Philadelphia, PA 19140.

KENNARTH, DAVID. b. 1942, Vicksburg, MS; m. Barbara Carter. EDUC.: college, Muskegon, MI. POLIT. & GOV.: ***Third World Assembly candidate for vice presidency of the U.S., 1980***. BUS. & PROF.: district mgr., Supreme Life Insurance Co. of America. MAILING ADDRESS: District Heights, MD.

KENNEDY, CHARLES. POLIT. & GOV.: ***independent candidate for presidency of the U.S., 1988***. MAILING ADDRESS: c/o Americans for America, P.O. Box 2017, Sequim, WA 98382-2017.

KENNEDY, EDWARD MOORE "TED." b. Feb 22, 1932, Boston, MA; par. Joseph Patrick and Rose (Fitzgerald) Kennedy; m. Virginia Joan Bennett, Nov 29, 1958 (divorced); m. 2d, Victoria Reggie, Jul 4, 1992; c. Kara Ann; Edward Moore, Jr.; Patrick Joseph. EDUC.: A.B., Harvard U., 1954; International Law School, Hague, The Netherlands, 1958; LL.B., U. of VA, 1959. POLIT. & GOV.: asst. district atty., Suffolk Cty., MA, 1961–62; elected as a Democrat to U.S. Senate (MA), 1962– (asst. majority leader, 1969–71); delegate, Dem. Nat'l. Conv., 1968; ***candidate for Democratic nomination to presidency of the U.S., 1968, 1972, 1976, 1980, 1984 (withdrew); candidate for Democratic nomination to vice presidency of the U.S., 1968, 1972, 1976, 1980***; ex-officio delegate, Democratic Mid-Term Conference, 1974. BUS. & PROF.: atty.; admitted to MA Bar, 1959. MIL.: pfc, U.S. Army, 1951–53. AWARDS: one of ten "Outstanding Young Men in America," U.S. Junior C. of C., 1967; Humanitarian Award, United Hebrew Immigrant Aid Social Service; Citation for Meritorious Service, U.S. Cmte. for Refugees; Citation for Meritorious Service, American Immigration and Citizenship Council; Order of Merit (Italy). MEM.: Joseph P. Kennedy, Jr. Foundation (pres., 1961–); Boston U. (trustee); Lahey Clinic (trustee); Childrens' Hospital Medical Center (trustee); John F. Kennedy Library (trustee); Boston Symphony (trustee); John F. Kennedy Center for Performing Arts (trustee); Robert F. Kennedy Memorial Foundation (trustee); Fletcher School (member, board of visitors); Dunbarton Oaks Research Library and Collections (member, board of advisers); Emmanuel Coll. (member, advisory board); Museum of Science, Boston, MA (trustee); MA General Hospital (dir.). HON. DEG.: LL.D., Howard U., 1979; LL.D., American International Coll.; LL.D., Assumption Coll.; LL.D., Babson Coll.; LL.D., Boston Coll.; LL.D., Gonzaga U.; LL.D., Jewish Theological Seminary of America; LL.D., Lowell Technological Inst.; LL.D., Merrimack Coll.; LL.D., Northeastern U.; LL.D., St. Per's Coll.; LL.D., Santa Clara Coll.; LL.D., Suffolk U.; LL.D., Syracuse U. MISC.: brother of John Fitzgerald Kennedy (q.v.) and Robert Francis Kennedy (q.v.). WRITINGS: *Decisions for a Decade* (1968); *In Critical Condition* (1972); *Our Day and Generation* (1979). REL.: R.C. MAILING ADDRESS: Squaw Island, Hyannis Port, MA 02647.

KENNEDY, JOHN FITZGERALD. b. May 29, 1917, Brookline, MA; d. Nov 22, 1963, Dallas, TX; par. Joseph Patrick (q.v.) and Rose (Fitzgerald) Kennedy; m. Jacqueline Lee Bouvier, Sep 12, 1953; c. Caroline Bouvier (Mrs. Edwin Schlossberg); John Fitzgerald, Jr.; Patrick Bouvier (deceased). EDUC.: Choate School, Wallingford, CT; London School of Economics, 1935; Princeton U., 1935; B.S. (cum laude), Harvard U., 1940; Stanford U. Grad. School of Business Administration, 1940. POLIT. & GOV.: sec. to U.S. Ambassador Joseph P. Kennedy (q.v.), London, England, 1939; elected as a Democrat to U.S. House (MA), 1947–53; elected as a Democrat to U.S. Senate (MA), 1953–61; delegate, Dem. Nat'l. Conv., 1956; ***candidate for Democratic nomination to vice presidency of the U.S., 1956; elected as a Democrat to presidency of the U.S., 1961–1963***. BUS. & PROF.: author; reporter, International News Service, 1945. MIL.: ensign, U.S. Navy, 1941, lt. (jg), 1943–45; commanded *PT-109* in South Pacific, sunk by Japanese destroyer *Amajiri*, 1943. MEM.: Harvard U. (overseer, 1957). AWARDS: Purple Heart; Navy Medal; Marine Medal; presidential Medal of Freedom (Posthumous); Pulitzer Prize for Biography, 1957. HON. DEG.: LL.D., U. of Notre Dame, 1950; LL.D., Tufts Coll., 1954; LL.D., Assumption Coll., 1955; LL.D., Boston U., 1955; LL.D., Harvard U., 1956; D.Sci., Lowell Inst. of Technology, 1956; LL.D., Loras Coll.; LL.D., Northeastern U.; LL.D., Rockhurst Coll. WRITINGS: *Why England Slept* (1940); *As We Remember Joe* (1945); *Profiles in Courage* (1956); *A Nation of Immigrants* (1959); *The Strategy of Peace* (1960); *To Turn the Tide* (1961); *The Burden and the Glory* (1964). REL.: R.C. MISC.: first Roman Catholic to be elected president of the U.S.; assassinated by Lee Harvey Oswald, Dallas, TX, Nov 22, 1963; brother of Edward Moore Kennedy (q.v.) and Robert Francis Kennedy (q.v.). RES.: Hyannis Port, MA.

KENNEDY, JOHN M. EDUC.: M.D. POLIT. & GOV.: ***independent candidate for presidency of the U.S., 1976***. MAILING ADDRESS: 8935 Carlyle Ave., Surfside, FL 33154.

KENNEDY, JOSEPH PATRICK. b. Sep 6, 1888, Boston, MA; d. Nov 18, 1969; par. Patrick J. and Mary (Hickey) Kennedy; m. Rose Fitzgerald, Oct 7, 1914; c. Joseph P.; John Fitzgerald (q.v.); Rosemary; Kathleen; Eunice; Patricia; Robert Francis (q.v.); Jeane; Edward Moore (q.v.). EDUC.: grad., Boston Latin School, 1908; A.B., Harvard U., 1912. POLIT. & GOV.: appointed bank examiner, State of MA, 1912–14; appointed chm., Securities Exchange Comm., 1934–35; appointed U.S. ambassador to Great Britain, 1937–40; ***candidate for Democratic nomination to presidency of the U.S., 1940 (declined)***. BUS. & PROF.: financier; pres., Columbia Trust Co., Boston, MA, 1914–17; asst. gen. mgr., Bethlehem Shipbuilding Corp., Fore River, MA, 1917–19; mgr., Hayden-Stone Co. (investment bankers), Boston, MA, 1919–24; pres., chm. of the board, Film Booking Offices of America, 1926–29; chm. of the board, Keith, Albee, Orpheum Theatres Corp., 1928–29; pres., chm. of the board, Pathe Exchange, Inc., 1929–30. MEM.: Metropolitan Club; Burning Tree Club; National Press Club; Harvard Club of NY; Oyster Harbors Club; Gulf Stream Club; Seminole Club. REL.: R.C. RES.: Hyannis Port, MA.

KENNEDY, ROBERT FRANCIS. b. Nov 20, 1925, Brookline, MA; d. Jun 6, 1968, Los Angeles, CA; par. Joseph Patrick (q.v.) and Rose (Fitzgerald) Kennedy; m. Ethel Skakel, Jun 17, 1950; c. Kathleen Hartington; Joseph Patrick; Robert Francis; David Anthony; Mary Courtney; Michael LeMoyne; Mary Kerry; Christopher George; Matthew. EDUC.: B.A., Harvard U., 1948; LL.B., VA Law School, 1951. POLIT. & GOV.: atty., Criminal Division, U.S. Dept. of Justice, 1951–52; campaign mgr., John F. Kennedy for Senate Campaign, 1952; asst. counsel, U.S. Senate Permanent Subcommittee on Investigations, 1953, chief counsel to minority, 1954, chief counsel, staff dir., 1955; asst. counsel, Hoover Comm., 1953; special asst. to campaign mgr., Stevenson for President Campaign, 1956; delegate, Dem. Nat'l. Conv., 1956; chief counsel, U.S. Senate Select Cmte. on Improper Activities of Labor on Management Field, 1957–60; campaign mgr., John F. Kennedy for President Campaign, 1960; appointed atty. gen. of the U.S., 1961–64; ***candidate for Democratic nomination to presidency of the U.S., 1964, 1968; candidate for Democratic nomination to vice presidency of the U.S., 1964***; elected as a Democrat to U.S. Senate (NY), 1965–68. BUS. & PROF.: atty.; admitted to MA Bar, 1951; admitted to the Bar of the Supreme Court of the U.S., 1955. MIL.: seaman, U.S.N.R., 1944–46. AWARDS: one of ten "Outstanding Young Men in the U.S.," U.S. Junior C. of C., 1954; "Outstanding Investigator," Soc. of Professional Investigators, Inc., 1957; Patriotism Award, U. of Notre Dame, 1958; Lantern Award, MA Council, Knights of Columbus, 1958. MEM.: U. of Notre Dame Law School (advisory council); Metropolitan Club (resigned, 1961). HON. DEG.: LL.D., Assumption Coll., 1957; LL.D., Mount St. Mary's Coll., 1958; LL.D., Tufts U., 1958; LL.D., Fordham U., 1961; LL.D., Manhattan Coll., 1962; LL.D., Nihon U., 1962; LL.D., Free U. of Berlin, 1964; LL.D., Marquette U., 1964; LL.D., U. of the Philippines, 1964. WRITINGS: *The Enemy Within* (1960); *Just Friends and Brave Enemies* (1962); *Pursuit of Justice* (1964). REL.: R.C. MISC.: brother of Edward Moore Kennedy (q.v.) and John Fitzgerald Kennedy (q.v.); assassinated by Sirhan Sirhan, Jun 6, 1968. RES.: McLean, VA.

KENNY, MARY E. JAQUES. b. 1900, Lincoln, NE; d. Nov 29, 1971, Lincoln, NE; d. Mr. Jaques; m.; c. Janet Betty. EDUC.: Lincoln (NE) H.S.; Goddard Seminary, Barre, VT. POLIT. & GOV.: pres., NE MacArthur for President Clubs, 1944–52; candidate for Republican nomination to lt. gov. of NE, 1946; NE state chm., Constitution Party; state chm., Fighters for MacArthur, NE, 1952; national co-chm., Fighters for MacArthur, 1952; candidate for Lincoln (NE) City Council; candidate for delegate, Rep. Nat'l. Conv., 1952; ***candidate for Republican nomination to presidency of the U.S., 1952***; organizer, American Party, 1952; ***Constitution Party candidate for vice presidency of the U.S., 1952 (withdrew)***; ran in 1952 NE Republican presidential primary as a stand-in for Gen. Douglas MacArthur (q.v.). BUS. & PROF.: housewife; schoolteacher. MEM.: Women of America (founder, 1944); National Emergency Cmte. (member, advisory cmte.); Grass Roots Republican Club (sec.); National Federation of Republican Women's Clubs; Lincoln Republican Women's Club (treas.). REL.: Christian Scientist. RES.: Lincoln, NE.

KENOYER, WILLA. b. 1934, Tacoma, WA; m. (divorced); c. Four. EDUC.: U. of WA; B.A., U. of CA at Berkeley, 1973; M.A. (Journalism), MI State U. POLIT. & GOV.: Left Democratic Party, 1966; active in Peace and Freedom Party, 1968; MI co-chair, Citizens Party, 1981; Midwestern Representative, Citizens Party National Exec. Cmte., 1982; national co-chair, Citizen's Party, 1983; joined Socialist Party, U.S.A., 1984; member, Socialist Party, U.S.A., national cmte., 1985–; delegate, Socialist Party National Convention, 1988; ***Socialist Party, U.S.A. candidate for presidency of the U.S., 1988; Liberty Union Party candidate for presidency of the U.S., 1988; candidate for Peace and Freedom Party nomination to presidency of the U.S., 1988***; Southern CA organizer, Socialist Party, U.S.A., 1988–. BUS. & PROF.: stringer, *Muskegon (MI) Chronicle*, 1981–87; owner, ed., publisher, *Shiawassee County (MI) Journal*, 1973; style ed., art critic, *The Dominion*, Wellington, New Zealand; co-editor, *The Socialist*, Los Angeles, CA; freelance journalist. MEM.: Happy Farmer Food Co-Op; Oceana Peace Education Network; League of Women Voters; Women Strike for Peace; Women's International League for Peace; Congress of Racial Equality; Pledge of Resistance; Young People's Socialist League (1959). MAILING ADDRESS: 1120 East Johnson Road, Shelby, MI 49455.

KENYON, WILLIAM SQUIRE. b. Jun 10, 1869, Elyria, OH; d. Sep 9, 1933, Sebasco Estates, ME; par. Fergus Lafayette and Hattie Anna (Squire) Kenyon; m. Mary J. Duncombe, May 11, 1893; c. none. EDUC.: grad., Grinnell (IA) Coll.; LL.B., IA State U., 1891. POLIT. & GOV.: prosecuting atty., Webster Cty., IA, 1892–96; district judge, 11th IA Judicial District, 1900–1902; appointed asst. to the atty. gen. of the U.S., 1910–11; appointed and subsequently elected as a Republican to U.S. Senate (IA), 1911–22; delegate, Rep. Nat'l. Conv., 1920; appointed judge, U.S. Circuit Court, Eighth Judicial Circuit, 1922–33; ***candidate for Republican nomination to vice presidency of the U.S., 1924, 1932***; appointed U.S. sec. of the navy, 1924 (declined); appointed member, National Comm. on Law Observance and Enforcement; ***candidate for Republican nomination to presidency of the U.S., 1928***. BUS. & PROF.: atty.; admitted to IA Bar, 1891; law practice, Fort Dodge, IA; counsel, Illinois Central R.R., 1904–10. AWARDS: decorated by Republic of Czechoslovakia, 1918. REL.: Congregationalist. RES.: Fort Dodge, IA.

KERN, ERIC. POLIT. & GOV.: ***Peace Party candidate for vice presidency of the U.S., 1980***. MAILING ADDRESS: Mattoon, IL.

KERN, JOHN WORTH. b. Dec 20, 1849, Alto, IN; d. Aug 17, 1917, Asheville, NC; par. Dr. Jacob Harrison and Nancy (Ligget) Kern; m. Julia Anna Hazzard, Nov 10, 1870; m. 2d, Araminta Cooper, Dec 23, 1885; c. Frederick Richmond; Julia Anna (Mrs. George Bilton Lawson); John Worth, Jr.; William Cooper. EDUC.: grad., Kokomo (IN) H.S.; LL.B., U. of MI, 1869. POLIT. & GOV.: Democratic candidate for IN State House, 1870; city atty., Kokomo, IN, 1871–84; reporter, Supreme Court of IN, 1885–89; elected as a Democrat to IN State Senate, 1893–97; appointed special asst. U.S. district atty., 1893–94; city solicitor, Indianapolis, IN, 1897–1901; Democratic candidate for gov. of IN, 1900, 1904; Democratic candidate for U.S. Senate (IN), 1905, 1916; ***Democratic candidate for vice presidency of the U.S., 1908***; elected as a Democrat to U.S. Senate (IN), 1911–17 (chm., Democratic Conference; majority leader, 1914–15); delegate, Dem. Nat'l. Conv., 1912; ***candidate for Democratic nomination to presidency of the U.S., 1912***. BUS. & PROF.: atty.; admitted to IN Bar, 1869; law practice, Kokomo, IN, 1869–85; partner (with J. F. Elliott), law firm, Kokomo, IN, 1869; law practice, Indianapolis, IN, 1885–1917. MEM.: ABA; Masons; Knights of Pythias; Elks; Commercial Club; University Club; Century Club. WRITINGS: *Indiana Reports* (ed., vols. 100–116). RES.: Indianapolis, IN.

KERN, ROBERT EDWARD. b. Oct 25, 1952, New York, NY; par. Francis and Margaret (Smith) Kern; single. POLIT. & GOV.: member, Community Board, Manhattan (Clinton) District, New York, NY, 1987; ***American Party candidate for presidency of the U.S., 1992***. BUS. & PROF.: pres., owner, Multi-Media Design Agency, 1974–86; teacher of design. MAILING ADDRESS: c/o Vivian Bernstein, 41 Perry St., #1B, New York, NY 10014.

KERR, ROBERT SAMUEL. b. Sep 11, 1896, Ada, Indian Territory; d. Jan 1, 1963, Washington, DC; par. William Samuel and Margaret Eloda (Wright) Kerr; m. Reba Shelton, Dec 5, 1919; m. 2d, Grayce Breene, Dec 26, 1925; c. Robert Samuel; Breene Mitchell; Kay Elizabeth (Mrs. Lowell D. Clark); William Graycen. EDUC.: East Central (OK) Normal School, 1909–11, 1912–15; OK Baptist U., 1911–12; U. of OK, 1915–16; studied law under J. F. McKeel, Ada, OK, 1921. POLIT. & GOV.: appointed special justice, OK State Supreme Court, 1931; pres., OK Cty. Juvenile Council, 1935–36; appointed member, Unofficial Pardon and Parole Board, 1935–38; member, Dem. Nat'l. Cmte. (OK), 1940–48; delegate, Dem. Nat'l. Conv., 1940, 1944 (keynoter), 1948, 1952, 1956, 1960; elected as a Democrat to gov. of OK, 1943–47; ***candidate for Democratic nomination to vice presidency of the U.S., 1944***; member, Interstate Oil Compact Comm., 1946; elected as a Democrat to U.S. Senate (OK), 1949–63; ***candidate for Democratic nomination to presidency of the U.S., 1952***. BUS. & PROF.: teacher, rural schools, OK; employee, law office of B. Robert Elliott, Webb City, MO, 1916–17; produce wholesaler, Ada, OK, 1919–21; atty.; admitted to OK Bar, 1922; partner, McKeel and Kee (law firm), Ada, OK; partner, Kerr, Lambert and Conn (law firm); partner, Kerr and Lambert (law firm); oil producer, 1926–63; partner, Anderson and Kerr Drilling Co., 1930; partner, An-Kerr, Inc., 1931–32; pres., A & K Petroleum Co., 1932–37; pres., Kerlyn Oil Co., 1937–44, chm. of the board, 1944–46; chm. of the board, Kerr-McGee Oil Industries, Inc., 1946–63; rancher, Poteau, OK; dir., Republic Supply Co.; chm. of the board, West Central Broadcasting Co., Peoria, IL. MIL.: 2d lt., 179th F.A., U.S. Army, 1917–19; 2d lt., Officers' Reserve Corps, 1919–21; capt., OK National Guard, 1921–25, maj., 1925–29. MEM.: National Governors' Conference (exec. cmte., 1945–46); Southern Governors' Conference (chm., 1945–46); OK Baptist Orphan's Home Cmte. (chm.); YMCA; Red Cross; BSA; Cowboy Hall of Fame (founder); Mid-Continent Oil and Gas Assn.; Masons (Shriner); American Legion (state commander, 1926); Forty and Eight; Tulsa Club; Beacon Club; Last Man's Club. MISC.: owner of world's largest herd of Black Angus cattle. REL.: Bapt. (Sunday school teacher; pres., OK Bapt. General Convention, 1944). RES.: Oklahoma City, OK.

KERREY, J. ROBERT "BOB." b. Aug 27, 1943, Lincoln, NE; par. James and Elinor Kerrey; m. (divorced); c. Benjamin; Lindsey. EDUC.: B.S. (Pharmacy), U. of NE, 1965. POLIT. & GOV.: elected as a Democrat to gov. of NE, 1983–89; elected as a Democrat to U.S. Senate (NE), 1989–; ***candidate for Democratic nomination to presidency of the U.S., 1992; candidate for Democratic nomination to vice presidency of the U.S., 1992***. BUS. & PROF.: owner, founder, developer, Grandmother's Skillet Restaurant, Omaha and Lincoln, NE, 1972–75; owner, founder, Sun Valley Bowl, Lincoln, NE; owner, founder, Wall-Bankers Racquetball Club and Fitness Center, Lincoln, NE; dir., Lincoln Center Assn. MIL.: ensign, U.S. Navy, 1967–69; Medal of Honor; Bronze Star; Purple Heart. MEM.: NE Easter Seal Soc. (dir.); American Legion; VFW; Disabled American Veterans; Lincoln C. of C.; Phi Gamma Delta; Sertoma; Lions. REL.: Congregationalist. MAILING ADDRESS: Lincoln, NE.

KERRY, JOHN FORBES. b. Dec 11, 1943, Denver, CO; par. Richard John and Rosemary (Forbes) Kerry; m. Julia Stimson Thorne, May 22, 1970 (divorced); c. Alexandra; Vanessa. EDUC.: B.A., Yale U., 1966; J.D., Boston Coll., 1976. POLIT. & GOV.: Democratic candidate for U.S. House (MA), 1972; asst. district atty., Middlesex Cty., MA, 1976–79; elected as a Democrat to lt. gov. of MA, 1983–85; elected as a Democrat to U.S. Senate (MA), 1985–; ***candidate for Democratic nomination to presidency of the U.S., 1988, 1992***. BUS. & PROF.: atty.; admitted to MA Bar, 1976; partner, Kerry and Sragow (law firm), Boston, MA, 1979–82. MIL.: lt. (jg), SUNR, 1966–69. Received Silver Star; Bronze Star with Oak Leaf Cluster; Three Purple Hearts. MEM.: Vietnam Veterans Against the War (national coordinator, 1969–71); Walsh School of Foreign Service, Georgetown U. (member, board of visitors). WRITINGS: *The New Soldier* (1971). REL.: R.C. MAILING ADDRESS: John F. Kennedy Federal Building, Room 2003F, Boston, MA 02203.

KERSEY, CHARLES THOMAS "TOMMY," JR. b. Nov 24, 1939, Henderson, GA; par. Charles Thomas and Clifford (Sullivan) Kersey; m. Joan Beddingfield, Mar 18, 1961; c. Charles Jeffry; Scott Thomas. EDUC.: grad., Perry H.S.; SC Coll., 2 years. POLIT. & GOV.: ***candidate for Democratic nomination to vice presidency of the U.S., 1980; candidate for Republican nomination to vice presidency of the U.S., 1980; candidate for Populist Party nomination to presidency of the U.S., 1984***. BUS. &

PROF.: farmer, Unadilla, GA. MIL.: U.S. Army, 1963–65. MEM.: American Agricultural Movement (pres.); Jaycees. REL.: Methodist. MAILING ADDRESS: P.O. Box 571, Unadilla, GA 31091.

KEVIN, J. RICHARD. b. 1864, La Crosse, WI; d. Jan 8, 1945, Brooklyn, NY; m. Frances Moore; c. Mrs. James J. Newman; Mrs. Gerald R. McDermott; Mrs. Edwin A. Regan. EDUC.: U. of VT; M.D., Bellevue Hospital Medical Coll., 1888; intern, St Mary's Hospital, Brooklyn, NY. POLIT. & GOV.: elected as a Democrat to alderman, Brooklyn, NY; appointed member, NY State Board of Social Welfare, 1913–45 (vice chm.); candidate for New York (NY) Health Commissioner, 1917, 1925; ***candidate for Democratic nomination to presidency of the U.S., 1924***; received 1 vote on 74th ballot for presidential nomination, Dem. Nat'l. Conv., 1924. BUS. & PROF.: physician; medical practice, Brooklyn, NY. MIL.: surgeon, 23d Regt., NY National Guard, 1909–16. MEM.: Medical Soc. of NY (pres., 1920); Kings Cty. Medical Soc. (pres.); F.A.C.S. RES.: Brooklyn, NY.

KEYES, ALAN L. b. Aug 7, 1950, New York, NY; m. Jocelyn Marcel; c. Francis; Maya. EDUC.: B.A., Harvard U., 1972, Ph.D., 1979. POLIT. & GOV.: foreign service officer, U.S. Dept. of State, 1978; consular officer, Bombay, India, 1979–80; desk officer, U.S. Dept. of State, Zimbabwe, 1980–81; policy planning staff, U.S. Dept. of State, 1981–83; appointed U.S. representative to the UNESCO, 1983–85; appointed asst. sec. of state for international organization affairs, 1985–88; Republican candidate for U.S. Senate (MD), 1988, 1992; ***candidate for Republican nomination to presidency of the U.S., 1992***. BUS. & PROF.: assn. exec. MEM.: Citizens Against Government Waste (pres.). MAILING ADDRESS: c/o Citizens Against Government Waste, 1301 Connecticut Ave., N.W., Washington, DC.

KIDDER, HARLEY WALTER. b. Jan 18, 1901, Barre, VT; par. Walter Daniel and Nellie Louise (Johnson) Kidder; m. Ruth Esther Lander, Apr 17, 1927. EDUC.: U. of VT, 1919–21, Coll. of Medicine, 1921–25; A.B., A.M., U. of IL, 1929. POLIT. & GOV.: dir. of publicity, VT Prohibition Party, 1926–; chm., exec. cmte., VT Prohibition Party, 1926–; member, VT Canvassing Board; member, Prohibition Party National Cmte., 1927– (national sec., 1932–40); delegate, Prohibition Party National Convention, 1928, 1932, 1936; ***candidate for Prohibition Party nomination to presidency of the U.S., 1932, 1936***; chief legislative draftsman, City of Barre, VT, 1936–40. BUS. & PROF.: salesman, National Map Co., Indianapolis, IN, 1920–28; dir., bureau of Political Research, Barre, VT, 1928–; minister, Baptist Church; pastor, First Universalist Church, Concord, VT, 1942–; pastor, Baptist churches, ME, VT, IL; public relations counselor. MEM.: Spaulding Alumni Assn.; Alumni Assn. of the U. of VT; Medical Alumni Assn. of U. of VT; Phi Beta Epsilon (national dir. of publicity, 1929–32; national treas., 1930–31; national custodian, 1929–); Alpha Kappa Delta; Spanish Language Club; Esperanto Club; Ministers' Monday Club (sec.-treas.); Illini Club of NY. REL.: Bapt. MAILING ADDRESS: 61 Summer St., Barre, VT.

KIEVE, HARRY. POLIT. & GOV.: ***Middle Class Party candidate for vice presidency of the U.S., 1980***. MAILING ADDRESS: NJ.

KILLEEN, CAROLINE P. b. c. 1927, Scranton, PA; single. POLIT. & GOV.: ***candidate for Democratic nomination to presidency of the U.S., 1976, 1988, 1992***; candidate for Democratic nomination to U.S. Senate (AZ), 1982. BUS. & PROF.: ecologist; nurse, Tucson, AZ; maid, Clearwater, CA. REL.: R.C. MISC.: first avowed lesbian to run for presidency of the U.S. MAILING ADDRESS: 100 Camino Miramonte, Tucson, AZ 85718.

KILPATRICK, ROBERT J. b. Jun 10, 1922, Trumbull Cty., OH; par. James B. and Hulda M. (Waggoner) Kilpatrick; m. (claims 365 wives); c. (claims 500 children). EDUC.: B.S., Youngstown Coll. POLIT. & GOV.: elected to Warren (OH) City Council, 1947–51; candidate for mayor of Warren, OH, 1951, 1953; candidate for U.S. House (OH), 1952; candidate for Warren (OH) city council, 1955, 1960; candidate for Sheriff of Trumbull Cty., OH, 1956; ***independent candidate for presidency of the U.S., 1976***. BUS. & PROF.: employee, Mullins Manufacturing Co.; employee, Warren City Manufacturing; employee, Melt Shop, Rockwell International; employee, Republic Steel Corp. REL.: Fundamentalist Mormon. MAILING ADDRESS: 139 East Main St., Cortland, OH 44410.

KILPATRICK, SHARON LEE STONE. b. Aug 5, 1939, Washington, DC; par. Walker and Donna Mae (Smith) Stone; m. M. Sean Kilpatrick, 1969; c. Heather Elaine; Douglas Stone. EDUC.: B.S., PA State U., 1961; M.Ed., U. of VA, 1967. POLIT. & GOV.: ***independent (Cmte. for a Constitutional Presidency) candidate for vice presidency of the U.S., 1976***. BUS. & PROF.: teacher; newspaper reporter. MAILING ADDRESS: Hawthorne Farm, Woodville, VA 22749.

KING, ALBERT A. POLIT. & GOV.: ***Continental Party candidate for vice presidency of the U.S., 1904***. RES.: Perry (or Percy), MO.

KING, CLENNON W. b. Jul 18, 1920; par. Clennon and Maggie (Sister) King; m. (divorced); c. Muriel; William; Lee; Earnest; Liberia Ethiopia Virginia; Tanimola Ayorinde. EDUC.: public schools, Albany, GA; Tuskegee Inst.; Oberlin School of Divinity; Western Reserve U.; U. of Chicago Oriental Inst.; FL A&M U.; Royal Islamic U., Baida, Libya. POLIT. & GOV.:

candidate for Republican nomination to presidency of the U.S., 1960; independent Afro-American Unity Party candidate for presidency of the U.S., 1960; candidate for gov. of GA, 1970; ***independent candidate for presidency of the U.S., 1972***; candidate for Democratic nomination to GA State House, 1976; candidate for Democratic nomination to Cty. Commissioner (GA), 1976; candidate for Democratic nomination to Albany (GA) City Council, 1976; candidate for U.S. House (GA), 1976; candidate for Republican nomination to U.S. House (MS), 1982. BUS. & PROF.: minister, The Divine Mission, Albany, GA; prof. of African History, Alcorn Coll.; teacher, public schools, 1940–58; teacher, Ethiopia, 1964–65. MEM.: Church of Christ. REL.: Interdenominational. MISC.: spent 4 years in CA prison for failure to provide child support; refused admission to membership in Plains (GA) Baptist Church attended by President Jimmy Carter (q.v.), 1976. MAILING ADDRESS: 600 South Jefferson St., Albany, GA.

KING, CORETTA SCOTT. b. Apr 27, 1927, Marion, AL; par. Obidiah and Bernice (McMurray) Scott; m. Martin Luther King, Jr. (q.v.), Jun 18, 1953; c. Yolanda Denise; Martin Luther III; Dexter Scott; Bernice Albertine. EDUC.: A.B., Antioch Coll., 1951; Mus.B., New England Conservatory of Music, 1954. POLIT. & GOV.: delegate, White House Conference on Children and Youth, 1960; ***Freedom and Peace Party candidate for vice presidency of the U.S., 1968 (declined)***. BUS. & PROF.: lecturer; writer; concert singer; concert debut, Springfield, OH, 1948; numerous concerts in U.S.; concert tour, India, 1959; gave performances for Freedom Concert; voice instructor, Morris Brown Coll., Atlanta, GA, 1962; commentator, Cable News Network, Atlanta, GA, 1980–. AWARDS: Annual Brotherhood Award, National Council of Negro Women, 1957; Outstanding Citizenship Award, Montgomery (AL) Improvement Assn., 1959; Merit Award, St. Louis (MO) Argus, 1960; Distinguished Achievement Award, National Organization of Colored Women's Clubs, 1962; "Woman of the Year," Utility Club of NY, 1962; Louise Waterman Wise Award, American Jewish Congress' Women's Auxiliary, 1963; citation, Women Strike for Peace, 1963; Human Dignity and Human Rights Award, Norfolk Chapter, LINKS, 1964; Myrtle Wreath Award, Cleveland (OH) Hadassah, 1965; Wateler Peace Prize, 1968; Award for Excellence in Human Relations, Soc. of the Family of Man, 1968; Universal Love Award, Premio San Valentine Cmte., 1968; "Woman of the Year," National Assn. of Radio and Television Announcers, 1968; Dag Hammarskjold Award, 1969; Pacem in Terris Award, International Overseas Service Foundation, 1969; Leadership for Freedom Award, Roosevelt U., 1971; Martin Luther King Memorial Medal, Coll. of the City of NY, 1971; International Viareggio Award, 1971. HON. DEG.: L.H.D., Boston U., 1969; H.H.D., Brandeis U., 1969; L.H.D., Marymount-Manhattan Coll., 1969; H.H.D., Bethune-Cookman Coll., 1970; L.H.D., Morehouse Coll., 1970; H.H.D., Princeton U., 1970; H.H.D., Wilberforce U., 1970; LL.D., Bates Coll., 1971; Mus.D., New England Conservatory of Music, 1971. MEM.: SANE Nuclear Policy Cmte. (sponsor); NAACP; Southern Rural Action Project, Inc.; Comm. on Economic Justice for Women (pres.); National Comm. of Inquiry (member, exec. cmte.); Clergy and Laymen Concerned About Vietnam (co-chm.); National Cmte. for Full Employment (co-chair); Martin Luther King, Jr. Center for Social Change (pres.); National Health Insurance Cmte. (co-chair); Cmte. on Responsibility (sponsor); Mobilization to End the War in Viet Nam (sponsor, 1966–67); Margaret Sanger Memorial Foundation; Martin Luther King, Jr. Foundation of Great Britain (pres.); Martin Luther King, Jr. Memorial Center (pres.); Southern Christian Leadership Conference; YWCA; Robert F. Kennedy Memorial (trustee); National Council of Negro Women; Women Strike for Peace; Women's International League for Peace and Freedom; United Church Women (member, board of managers); Alpha Kappa Alpha (hon.). WRITINGS: *My Life With Martin Luther King, Jr.* (1969). REL.: Bapt. (choir member; guild adviser). MAILING ADDRESS: 234 Sunset Ave., N.W., Atlanta, GA 30314.

KING, HENRY. POLIT. & GOV.: ***independent candidate for presidency of the U.S., 1988, 1992, received 157 write-in votes for presidency of the U.S. in OH, 1988***. MAILING ADDRESS: OH.

KING, JOHN ALSOP. b. Jan 3, 1788, New York, NY; d. Jul 7, 1867, New York, NY; par. Rufus (q.v.) and Mary (Alsop) King; m. Mary Ray, Jan 3, 1810; c. Charles Ray; John Alsop, Jr.; five others. EDUC.: Harrow School, England; Paris; studied law. POLIT. & GOV.: elected as a Whig to NY State Assembly, 1819–21, 1832, 1838, 1840; elected as a Whig to NY State Senate, 1823–25; sec., U.S. Legation, London, England, 1825, Charge d'Affaires, 1826; delegate, Whig Party National Convention, 1839, 1852; elected as a Whig to U.S. House (NY), 1849–51; pres., NY State Republican Convention, 1855; delegate, Rep. Nat'l. Conv., 1856; ***candidate for Republican nomination to vice presidency of the U.S., 1856, 1864***; elected as a Republican to gov. of NY, 1857–58; presidential elector, Republican Party, 1860; delegate, Peace Convention, 1861. BUS. & PROF.: atty.; admitted to NY Bar, 1812; farmer, Jamaica, NY. MIL.: lt., U.S. Cavalry, 1812. MEM.: Queens Cty. (NY) Agricultural Soc. (founder; pres.); NY State Agricultural Soc. (pres.). REL.: Episc. RES.: New York, NY.

KING, LEICESTER. b. May 1, 1789, Suffield, CT; d. Sep 19, 1856, North Bloomfield, OH; m. Julia Ann Huntington, Oct 12, 1814; c. Mrs. Charles Brown. POLIT. & GOV.: assoc. judge, Court of Common Pleas, Warren, OH; elected as a Whig to OH State Senate, 1835–39; Liberty Party candidate for gov. of OH, 1842, 1844; chm., Liberty Party National convention, 1843; ***Liberty (Abolitionist) Party candidate for vice presidency of the U.S., 1848 (declined)***. BUS. & PROF.: merchant, Westfield, MA, to 1817; merchant, Warren, OH, 1817–33; promoter, PA and OH Canal; pres., Pennsylvania and Ohio Canal Co. WRITINGS: *Report of the Select Committee of the Senate* (1838). MEM.:

OH Anti-Slavery Soc. (pres.). REL.: Disciples of Christ. RES.: Warren, OH.

KING, MARTIN LUTHER, JR. b. Jan 15, 1929, Atlanta, GA; d. Apr 4, 1968, Memphis, TN; par. Martin Luther, Sr. and Alberta (Williams) King; m. Coretta Scott (q.v.), Jun 17, 1953; c. Yolanda Denise; Martin Luther III; Dexter Scott; Bernise Albertine. EDUC.: A.B., Morehouse Coll., 1948; B.D., Crozer Theological Seminary, 1951; Ph.D., Boston U., 1955; D.D., Chicago Theological Seminary, 1957; D.D., Boston U., 1959. POLIT. & GOV.: ***candidate for Peace and Freedom (Freedom and Peace; independent; Peace) Party nomination to presidency of the U.S., 1968 (declined)***. BUS. & PROF.: ordained minister, Baptist Church, 1947; civil rights activist; pastor, Dexter Avenue Baptist Church, Montgomery, AL, 1955–59; copastor, Ebenezer Baptist Church, Atlanta, GA, 1959–68. MEM.: Southern Christian Leadership Conference (founder; pres., 1957–68); Alpha Phi Alpha; Sigma Pi Phi; National Sunday School and Baptist Training Union Congress, National Baptist Convention (vice pres.); Montgomery Improvement Assn. (pres.); Elks; NAACP. AWARDS: J. Louis Crozer Fellowship; Pearl Plafkner Award, Crozer Theological Seminary, 1951; one of ten "Outstanding Personalities," *Time Magazine*, 1956; Nobel Peace Prize, 1964. HON. DEG.: LL.D., Howard U., 1957; L.H.D., Morehouse Coll. 1957; L.H.D., Central State Coll., 1958; LL.D., Morgan State Coll., 1958; LL.D., U. of PA; LL.D., Harvard U. WRITINGS: *Stride Toward Freedom* (1958); *Why We Can't Wait* (1964); *Where do We Go From Here: Chaos or Community?* (1967). MISC.: led Montgomery (AL) bus boycott, 1956; assassinated by James Earl Ray, Memphis, TN, Apr 4, 1968. REL.: Bapt. RES.: Atlanta, GA.

KING, ROBERTA J. POLIT. & GOV.: ***independent candidate for presidency of the U.S., 1992***. MAILING ADDRESS: WA?

KING, RUFUS. b. Mar 24, 1755, Scarborough, ME; d. Apr 29, 1827, Jamaica, NY; par. Capt. Richard and Isabella (Bragdon) King; m. Mary Alsop, Mar 30, 1786; c. John Alsop (q.v.); Charles; James Gore. EDUC.: Dummer Acad.; B.A., Harvard U., 1777, M.A.; studied law under Theophilus Parsons. POLIT. & GOV.: elected as a Federalist to MA State House, 1782; delegate, MA General Court, 1783–85; member, Continental Congress (MA), 1784–87; delegate, U.S. Constitutional Convention, 1787 (signer of U.S. Constitution); delegate, MA Ratification Convention, 1787; elected as a Federalist to NY State Assembly, 1789–90; elected as a Federalist to U.S. Senate (NY), 1789–96, 1813–25; dir., Bank of the U.S., 1791; appointed U.S. minister to Great Britain, 1796–1803, 1825–26; ***Federalist candidate for vice presidency of the U.S., 1804, 1808***; Federalist candidate for gov. of NY, 1815; ***Federalist candidate for presidency of the U.S., 1816***; delegate, NY State Constitutional Convention, 1821. BUS. & PROF.: atty.; admitted to bar, 1780; farmer; cattle breeder. MIL.: aide to General Sullivan, RI Expedition, Revolutionary War. MEM.: Columbia U. (trustee, 1806–24); American Acad. (fellow); MA Hist. Soc. (corresponding member). HON. DEG.: LL.D., Dartmouth Coll., 1802; LL.D., Williams Coll., 1803; LL.D., 1806; LL.D., U. of PA, 1815. REL.: Protestant Episc. Church. MISC.: author of Navigation Act; opposed admission of MO as slave state and voted against MO Compromise of 1820; proposed selling public lands and using the proceeds to buy freedom for slaves. RES.: Jamaica, NY.

KING, WILLIAM E. b. Oct 7, 1945, Peoria, IL; par. Frederick Murl and Jane Hyde (McClugage) King; m. Kirstin Gisela Ekuit, Jun 1967; c. none. EDUC.: B.A., Macalester Coll., 1973; Rochdale Coll. POLIT. & GOV.: ***candidate for Democratic nomination to presidency of the U.S., 1984, 1988***. BUS. & PROF.: pres., Rochdale Coll., 1975; teacher, 1976–80, 1982–83; Carpenter, 1981–82; Employee, A. N. Palmer Co.; minister (TV sports), 1985–. Noted for grandstand appearances displaying Christian messages (e.g., "John 3:16") during professional sports events. MEM.: Full Gospel Businessmen's Fellowship International. REL.: Christian. MAILING ADDRESS: 418 Bristlecone Lane, Naples, FL 33962.

KING, WILLIAM RUFUS DEVANE. b. Apr 6, 1786, Sampson Cty., NC; d. Apr 18, 1853, Cahawba, AL; par. William and Margaret (Devane) King; single. EDUC.: grad., U. of NC, 1803. POLIT. & GOV.: elected member, NC State House of Commons, 1807–09; city solicitor, Wilmington, NC, 1810; elected as a Democrat to U.S. House (NC), 1811–16; sec., U.S. Legation, Naples, Italy, 1816; sec., U.S. Legation, St. Petersburg, Russia, 1818; delegate, AL State Constitutional Convention, 1819; elected as a Democrat to U.S. Senate (AL), 1819–44 (pres. pro tempore, 1836–41), 1848–52 (appointed and subsequently elected); appointed U.S. minister to France, 1844–46; ***candidate for Democratic nomination to vice presidency of the U.S., 1848; candidate for Democratic nomination to presidency of the U.S., 1852; elected as a Democrat to vice presidency of the U.S., 1853***. BUS. & PROF.: atty.; admitted to NC Bar, 1806; assoc., office of William Duffy (law firm), Fayetteville, NC; law practice, Clinton, NC. MISC.: took oath of office as vice pres. in Havana, Cuba, through privilege granted by special act of Congress. RES.: Fayetteville, NC.

KINGSTONE, STEPHEN ARTHUR CHAIM. b. Nov 25, 1949, New York, NY; par. Walter and Lily (Hofbauer) Kingstone; m. (divorced); c. none. EDUC.: B.A., U. of Denver; Intensive Certificate in Textiles, Leicester Polytechnic Inst.; Sonoma State U. POLIT. & GOV.: ***candidate for Republican nomination to presidency of the U.S., 1992***. BUS. & PROF.: employee, textiles/dresses/sweaters; owner, health food store; owner, clothing store; production and quality controller; designer. MAILING ADDRESS: 155 West 68th St., New York, NY 10023.

KINNEY, WILLIAM A. b. 1860, Honolulu, HI; d. Jul 28, 1930, Los Angeles, CA. EDUC.: LL.B., U. of MI. POLIT. & GOV.: member, HI Royal Legislature, 1887 (two terms); chm., HI Territorial Democratic Central Cmte.; ***candidate for Democratic nomination to vice presidency of the U.S., 1908***. BUS. & PROF.: atty.; admitted to HI Bar, 1883; partner, Smith, Thurston and Kinney (law firm), 1886–87; partner, Kinney and Ballou (law firm); partner, Kinney, McClanahan and Derby (law firm); partner, Kinney, Marx, Posser and Anderson (law firm); owner, Nova Scotia Livestock and Development Co. WRITINGS: *Report of the Commission on Advances to Homesteaders to the Governor of Hawaii* (1910); *Hawaii's Capacity for Self-Government All But Destroyed* (1927). MISC.: involved in criminal conspiracy, bribery, and harassment suit against Sen. Reed Smoot and Heber Grant, pres. of the Church of Jesus Christ of Latter-Day Saints, for destroying property and credit standing, 1928. RES.: Honolulu, HI.

KIRK, CLAUDE ROY, JR. b. Jan 7, 1926, San Bernardino, CA; par. Claude Roy and Sarah (McLure) Kirk; m. Sarah Stokes, 1947 (divorced twice); m. 2d, Erika Mattfeld, Feb 18, 1967 (divorced, 1976); c. Sarah Stokes; Katherine Gilmer; Franklin M.; William C.; Adriana; Claudia; Erik Henry. EDUC.: grad., Lanier H.S., Montgomery, AL, 1943; Emory U.; B.S., Duke U., 1945. POLIT. & GOV.: Republican candidate for U.S. Senate (FL), 1964; elected as a Republican to gov. of FL, 1967–71; delegate, Rep. Nat'l. Conv., 1968; ***candidate for Republican nomination to presidency of the U.S., 1968, 1980, 1984; candidate for Republican nomination to vice presidency of the U.S., 1968***; Republican candidate for gov. of FL, 1970, 1978; ***candidate for Democratic nomination to presidency of the U.S., 1988***; candidate for Democratic nomination to U.S. Senate (FL), 1988. BUS. & PROF.: salesman, insurance and building supplies, 1949; vice chm., American Heritage Life Insurance Co., 1954; partner, Hayden, Stone, Inc., 1960; founder, Kirk Investment Co., 1964. MIL.: 2d lt., U.S.M.C., 1943; 1st lt., 1946, released, 1946, reentered, 1950–52; Air Medal. MEM.: Sigma Alpha Epsilon; Financial Analysts Soc.; Episcopal Church Foundation (trustee); Saints and Sinners; 21 Club. HON. DEG.: LL.B., U. of AL, 1949; LL.D., Rollins Coll. REL.: Episc. MAILING ADDRESS: 720 South Ocean Dr., Palm Beach, FL 33480.

KIRKLAND, MARTHA TERRY. b. Oct 23, 1918, Gordo, AL; d. Hilliard Alexander and Sarah Loucanda (Chesser) Terry; m. Reo Kirkland, Feb 28, 1942; c. Jean (Mrs. Kyle Barrineau); Reo, Jr.; Karl. EDUC.: B.S., AL Coll., 1940. POLIT. & GOV.: appointed chief clerk, Circuit Court, Escambia Cty., AL, 1942–45; appointed chief clerk, Probate Court, Escambia Cty., AL, 1953–69; judge of probate, Escambia Cty., AL, 1969–; ***candidate for Democratic nomination to presidency of the U.S., 1984***. BUS. & PROF.: home agent, AL Extension Service, Brewton, AL, 1940–42. AWARDS: Woman of the Year, Brewton (AL) C. of C., 1972. MEM.: American Legion Auxiliary; Escambia Cty. Farm Bureau; AL Probate Judges Assn. (treas., 1972; sec., 1973; pres., 1975–76); Escambia Cattlemen's Assn. REL.: Methodist. MAILING ADDRESS: Alco Dr., Brewton, AL 36426.

KIRKPATRICK, DONALD. b. Sep 9, 1830, Salina, NY; d. Sep 19, 1889, Syracuse, NY; par. Dr. William Kirkpatrick; single. EDUC.: Chittenango Polytechnic; Homer Acad.; Mr. Tyler's School, Pittsfield, MA. POLIT. & GOV.: ***American National Party candidate for vice presidency of the U.S., 1876***. BUS. & PROF.: partner, W. & D. Kirkpatrick (Solar Salt Co.). MEM.: National Christian Assn. (convention pres., 1874); Anti-Secret Soc. Assn. REL.: Presb. RES.: Syracuse, NY.

KIRKPATRICK, FREDERICK DOUGLASS. b. Aug 12, 1933, Haynesville, LA; d. Aug 26, 1986; par. Rev. John L. and Lula Mae (Ponder) Kirkpatrick; m. Annie Pearl Thompson; c. Camilla Ann; Alfreda Denese; Brunella R. EDUC.: grad., Haynesville (LA) H.S.; grad., Grambling Coll.; TX Southern U.; LA Technical U., 1966; Ph.D. (hon.), Columbia U., 1971. POLIT. & GOV.: member, White House Conference on Children; ***independent candidate for presidency of the U.S., 1976, 1980; The Black Assembly (Freedom Party) candidate for presidency of the U.S., 1976; Farmer-Labor Party candidate for presidency of the U.S., 1980, 1984***. BUS. & PROF.: singer; composer; recording artist; teacher, LA public school system, 1959–65; coach; football player, Kansas City Chiefs, 1962; ordained minister, Fundamentalist Church, Jonesboro, LA, 1965; prof. of Anatomy and Kinesiology, Grambling Coll., 1966–68; teacher, Fordham U., 1972–. CREDITS: Recordings: "Everybody's Got a Right to Live"; "Pete Seeger Now"; "Square Dance with Soul"; "Ballads of Black America"; "The Black Struggle in Song and Story"; "Pete Seeger and 'Kirk' Visit Sesame Street"; "Clearwater"; Films: "Black Roots"; "Circle of Lights"; "Many Faces of America"; "Music That Moves Mountains"; "Down Home"; "Street Preacher"; "Patchwork of Quilt." MEM.: Southern Christian Leadership Conference (TX State dir., 1967); Deacons for Defense and Justice (founder, 1965); All-American Quarterback (Grambling Coll., 1955); Student Non-Violent Coordinating Cmte. (chm., TX Southern U., 1967); Poor People's Campaign; Resurrection City (troubador); Inst. of Black Religion (instructor, 1974–); The Many Races Cultural Foundation (pres.); People's Platform Conference; Hudson River Sloop Restoration; NY West Side Festival (dir., 1970–); Hey Brother Coffee Houses (dir., 1970–); Bookmobile Tours (dir., 1970–); Newport Jazz Festival (dir., 1969–). REL.: Holiness Church. RES.: New York, NY.

KIRKPATRICK, GEORGE ROSS. b. Feb 24, 1867, West Fayette, OH; d. Mar 17, 1937, San Gabriel, CA; par. Robert and Sarah Heslip (Williams) Kirkpatrick; m. Mrs. Marian (Pattullo) Monheimer, Jul 13, 1913; m. 2d, Florence H. Slocum; c. George Pattullo. EDUC.: OH Wesleyan U.; A.B., Albion Coll., 1893; U. of Chicago; Vanderbilt U., 1893–95. POLIT. & GOV.: joined Socialist Party, 1903; lecturer, Socialist Party; Socialist Party candidate for U.S. House (IL), 1914; ***Socialist Party candidate for vice presidency of the U.S., 1916***; chief, Literary Dept., Socialist Party, 1924–25; national sec., Socialist Party, 1925–26; Socialist Party candidate for U.S. Senate (IL), 1928; presidential elector, Socialist Party, 1932; Socialist Party candidate for U.S. Senate (CA), 1932, 1934; resigned from Socialist Party, 1936; joined Socialist Democratic Federation, 1936; member, national exec. cmte., Socialist Democratic Federation, 1936–37. BUS. & PROF.: prof. of History and Social Sciences, Southwestern Coll., 1895–98; lecturer, KS State Temperance Union, 1898–1900; prof. of History and Economics, Ripon Coll., 1901–02; instructor, Rand School of Social Science; instructor, School of International Socialism; lecturer, NY Board of Education; contributor, Appeal to Reason; contributor, American Appeal. MEM.: Intercollegiate Socialist Soc. (organizer); American Federation of Teachers. AWARDS: first honors, MI State Intercollegiate Prohibition Contest; won National Oratorical Contest, Intercollegiate Prohibition Assn., 1893. WRITINGS: *Mental Dynamite* (1906); *War—What For?* (1910); *For the Educated Proletariat* (1910); *Sota-minka thaden?* (1910); *The Socialists and the Sword; Think—Or Surrender* (1916); *Kare-ko delei?* (1917); *The Slander of the Toilers* (1919); *Silence!* (192?); *Out of Work* (1924); *Is Plenty Too Much for the Common People?* (1939). RES.: Chicago, IL.

KIRKPATRICK, JEANE DUANE JORDAN. b. Nov 19, 1926, Duncan, OK; par. Welcher F. and Leona (Kile) Jordan; m. Evron M. Kirkpatrick, Feb 20, 1955; c. Douglas Jordan; John Evron; Stuart Alan. EDUC.: A.A., Stephens Coll., 1946; A.B., Barnard Coll., 1948; M.A., Columbia U., 1950, Ph.D., 1967; postgrad. study, U. of Paris Inst. de Science Politique, 1952–53 (French Government Fellow). POLIT. & GOV.: research analyst, U.S. Dept. of State, 1951–53; consultant, U.S. Dept. of State, 1955–72; consultant, U.S. Dept. of Health, Education and Welfare, 1955–72; consultant, U.S. Dept. of Defense, 1955–72; vice chm., Cmte. on Vice Presidential Selection, Dem. Nat'l. Cmte., 1972–74; member, National Comm. on Party Structure and Presidential Nominations, Dem. Nat'l. Cmte., 1975; member, Credential Cmte., Dem. Nat'l. Conv., 1976; appointed U.S. ambassador to the U.N., 1981–85; ***candidate for Republican nomination to vice presidency of the U.S., 1984, 1988; candidate for Republican nomination to presidency of the U.S., 1988***. BUS. & PROF.: research assoc., George Washington U., 1954–56; research assoc., Fund for the Republic, 1956–58; asst. prof. of Political Science, Trinity Coll., 1962–67; assoc. prof. of Political Science, Georgetown U., Washington, DC, 1967–73, prof., 1973–; Leavey prof. in Foundations of American Freedom, 1978; resident scholar, American Enterprise Inst. for Public Policy Research, 1977–; member, International Research Council, Center for Strategic and International Studies, Georgetown U. MEM.: Helen Dwight Reid Educational Foundation (trustee, 1972–); Stephens Coll. (curator); International Political Science Assn. (member, exec. council); APSA; Southern Political Science Assn. AWARDS: Earhart Fellow, 1956–57; Distinguished Alumna Award, Stephens Coll., 1978. HON. DEG.: L.H.D., Mt. Vernon Coll., 1978; L.H.D., Georgetown U., 1981; L.H.D., U. of Pittsburgh, 1981; L.H.D., U. of West FL, 1981; L.H.D., U. of Charleston, 1982; L.H.D., Hebrew U., 1982; L.H.D., St. Anselm's Coll., 1982; L.H.D., Betheny Coll., 1983; L.H.D., CO School of Mines, 1983; L.H.D., St. John's U., 1933. WRITINGS: *Elections USA* (contributor, 1956); *Strategy of Deception* (contributor, 1963); *Foreign Students in the U.S.: A National Survey* (1966); *Mass Behavior in Battle and Captivity* (1968); *The New Class* (ed., 1968); *Leader and Vanguard in Mass Society: The Peronist Movement in Argentina* (1971); *Political Woman* (1973); *The Presidential Elite* (1976); *Dismantling the Parties: Reflections on Party Reform and Party Decomposition* (1978); *The New American Political System* (contributor, 1978); *The Reagan Phenomenon* (1982); *Dictatorships and Double-Standards* (1981). MAILING ADDRESS: 6812 Granby St., Bethesda, MD 20817.

KITMAN, MARVIN. b. Nov 24, 1929, Pittsburgh, PA; par. Myer and Rose (Kaufman) Kitman; m. Carol Sibushnick, Oct 28, 1951; c. Jamie Lincoln; Suzy; Andrea Jordana. EDUC.: B.A., City Coll. of NY, 1953. POLIT. & GOV.: ***candidate for Republican nomination to presidency of the U.S., 1964 (Satire Effort)***. BUS. & PROF.: columnist, Armstrong Daily, New York, NY, 1956–66; consultant, Al Capp Enterprises, 1961–63; lecturer, 1963–; news and managing ed., *Monocle Magazine*, 1963–; asst. to the treas., Monocle Periodicals, 1965–, dir., 1966–; staff writer, *Saturday Evening Post*, 1965–66; humorist-in-residence, Solow/Wexton, Inc., New York, NY, 1966–67; television critic, *New Leader Magazine*, 1967–; senior writer, Carl Ally, Inc., 1967–68; vice pres. for Urban Affairs, Public Relations Analysts, 1968; founder, partner, Monocle Book Division, 1968; television critic, *Newsday*, 1969–; television critic, *Los Angeles (CA) Times*, 1969–; critic-at-large, *Harper News*, WPIX-TV, New York, NY, 1973–74; co-creator, "Ball Four" (television series), 1976. MIL.: U.S. Army, 1953–55. MEM.: Spanish Civil War Roundtable of Northern NJ (exec. dir.); Leonia (NJ) Public Library, 1961–. WRITINGS: *The Number One Best Seller* (pseudonym of William Randolph Hirsch, with Richard Lingeman, 1966); *The RCAF (Red Chinese Air Force) Exercise, Diet and Sex Book* (1967); *You Can't Judge a Book by Its Covers* (1970); *George Washington's Expense Account* (1970); *The Marvin Kitman TV Show* (coauthor, 1972); *The Coward's Almanac* (1975). MAILING ADDRESS: Kitman House, Leonia, NJ.

KLAHRE, CLAYTON DALE. POLIT. & GOV.: ***independent candidate for presidency of the U.S., 1976***. MAILING ADDRESS: 204 Boise St., Johnstown, PA 15904.

KLAMMER, KENNETH ELLIS. b. Aug 18, 1948, Waukegan, IL; par. Richard Rodney and Mary Alice Grace (Pietchman) Klammer; single. EDUC.: grad., Rincon H.S., Tucson, AZ. POLIT. & GOV.: ***candidate for Democratic nomination to presidency of the U.S., 1992***. BUS. & PROF.: artist; graphic artist, New York, NY; professional racer on drag strip, sports car, and demolition derby tracks. WRITINGS: *Upon Giant Toes* (poetry). REL.: Belief in Something Greater Than Self. MAILING ADDRESS: 641 County Route 8, Germantown, NY 12526

KLAUSNER, MANUEL STUART. b. Aug 14, 1939, New York, NY; par. Isidore and Helen (Gruber) Klausner; m. Willette Jean Murphy, Feb 1, 1969. EDUC.: A.B., U. of CA at Los Angeles, 1959; LL.B., NY U., 1962, LL.M., 1963; U. of Copenhagen, 1963–64. POLIT. & GOV.: ***candidate for Libertarian Party nomination to vice presidency of the U.S., 1976***. BUS. & PROF.: assoc. managing ed., *New York University Law Review*, 1960–62; atty.; admitted to NY Bar, 1963; admitted to CA Bar, 1963; instructor, U. of Chicago Law School, 1964–65; law practice, Los Angeles, CA, 1965–; assoc., Kindel and Anderson (law firm), 1965–71, partner, 1971–; ed., *Reason Magazine*, Los Angeles, CA, 1971–; lecturer, CA State Bar Continuing Education Program, 1965, 1973, 1975. MEM.: NY U. International Law Soc. (pres., 1962–63); ABA; NY State Bar Assn.; Los Angeles Cty. Bar Assn.; Town Hall of CA; Los Angeles Junior C. of C.; NY U. Law Alumni Assn. of Southern CA (exec. board); Libertarian Law Council (chm.); Assn. of Business Trial Lawyers. AWARDS: Root-Tilden Scholar, 1962; Ford Foundation Fellow, 1963; Fulbright Scholar, 1963–64. WRITINGS: *Cavitch's Business Organizations* (coauthor, vols. 1–2, 1963). MAILING ADDRESS: 5538 Red Oak Dr., Los Angeles, CA 90068.

KLEIN, TOMMY WILLIAM. b. 1915. POLIT. & GOV.: candidate for Republican nomination to U.S. Senate (KY), 1974, 1980, 1984, 1986; ***candidate for Republican nomination to presidency of the U.S., 1976***; candidate for Republican nomination to U.S. House (KY), 1978, 1992; ***candidate for Populist Party nomination to presidency of the U.S., 1984***. BUS. & PROF.: farmer; disabled veteran. MAILING ADDRESS: 120 South Longworth Ave., Louisville, KY 40212.

KLEIN, WILLIAM DONALD. POLIT. & GOV.: ***Constitutional Party candidate for presidency of the U.S., 1988***. MAILING ADDRESS: P.O. Box 51, 320 Main St., Route 49, Scandinavia, WI 54977.

KLEMENS, BEN. b. Apr 10, 1975, Townsville, Australia; par. Gyora and Ronit (Cordova) Klemens; single. EDUC.: University H.S., Champaign, IL. POLIT. & GOV.: ***Confused Party candidate for presidency of the U.S., 1988***. BUS. & PROF.: student, University H.S., Champaign, IL. MEM.: Doctor Who Club. REL.: none. MAILING ADDRESS: 801 Breen Dr., Champaign, IL 61820.

KNAUF, RICHARD HAROLD. b. May 5, 1913, Rochester, NY; par. Fred and Ethel Louise (Whalen) Knauf; m. Edna Elizabeth Skinner; c. Richard Harold, Jr.; Edward James; Dawn Michele. EDUC.: grad., Binghamton (NY) Central H.S.; Coll. Courses. POLIT. & GOV.: appointed pres., Binghamton (NY) Recreation Comm., 1937–42; vice pres., Board of Education, Binghamton, NY, 1938–42; Republican ward worker, Binghamton, NY; delegate, Young Rep. Nat'l. Conv.; sergeant-at-arms, Rep. Nat'l. Conv.; elected as a Republican to NY State Assembly, 1943–45; candidate for NY State Assembly, 1954, 1956, 1958, 1960, 1962, 1964, 1966, 1968, 1970; elected as a Republican to supervisor, Broome Cty., NY, 1957–69; Republican candidate for supervisor, Broome Cty., NY, 1968; appointed member, Cmte. to Erect Johnson City–Vestal Bridge; ***candidate for Republican nomination to presidency of the U.S., 1972***; candidate for Republican nomination to U.S. House (NY), 1974; independent candidate for U.S. House (NY), 1974. BUS. & PROF.: dispensing optician, Binghamton, NY. MEM.: Rotary Club; Masons; Kalurah Shrine; Fraternal Order of Eagles; YMCA; Parent-Teachers Assn.; Southside Republican Club; Johnson City C. of C.; East Side Business and Professional Assn. (pres.); Grace Baptist Church (chm., board of trustees; Sunday school superintendent); Red Cross; Farm Bureau; Binghamton Civic Assn.; World's Fair Travel Assn. REL.: Methodist (ed., WY Conference United Methodist newspapers; television and radio dir., United Methodist Conference). MAILING ADDRESS: 7 Garden Ave., Binghamton, NY.

KNAUS, WILLIAM LYLE (aka CHERYL ANDREA BRUHN). b. May 6, 1935, St. Paul, MN; par. William and Mabel (Koch) Knaus; single. EDUC.: B.A. (cum laude), U. of MN, 1957, extension courses, 1973–76. POLIT. & GOV.: founder, Archonist Party; Archonist Party candidate for mayor of Mendota Heights, MN, 1971; Archonist Party candidate for U.S. Senate (MN), 1972, 1976; ***Archonist Party candidate for presidency of the U.S., 1976, 1992***. BUS. & PROF.: free-lance writer; procurement asst., Rock Island Arsenal, Rock Island, IL, 1965–66; contract specialist, Army Tank Automotive Co., Warren, MI, 1966–67; quality assurance specialist, Defense Contract Administrative Services District, St. Paul, MN, 1967–71; ed., *The Archonist Epistle* (newsletter), 1974–75. MEM.: Archonist Club. REL.: Archonist. MISC.: self-styled "lesbian-oriented transsexual without romantic interest in men." MAILING ADDRESS: 1459 Dodd Road, Mendota Heights, MN 55118.

KNIGHT, ALBION WILLIAMSON, JR. b. Jun 1, 1924, Jacksonville, FL; par. Albion Williamson and Anna Marion (Russell) Knight, Sr.; m., Lucile Stice, 1949 (deceased, 1969); m. 2d, Nancy Evans Price, 1970; c. five (one deceased). EDUC.: B.A., U.S. Military Acad., 1945; M.S., U. of IL, 1950; M.A., American U., 1977; doctoral candidate, Catholic U. of America. POLIT. & GOV.: with U.S. Dept. of Defense, Atomic Energy Comm., Energy Research and Development Administration; National Security Adviser, Joint Cmte. on Atomic Energy, U.S. Congress, 1973–76; ***U.S. Taxpayers (American Independent) Party candidate for vice presidency of the U.S., 1992***. BUS. & PROF.: soldier; ordained priest, Episcopal Church,

1954–83; visiting prof. in National Security Studies, Georgetown U.; visiting prof., Liberty U.; priest, United Episcopal Church, 1983–89, presiding bishop, 1989–92. MIL.: brig. gen., U.S. Army, 1945–73; deputy chief of staff, Logistics, U.S. Army in Vietnam, 1972; chief logistician, Central Region, North Atlantic Treaty Organization; Distinguished Service Medal; Legion of Merit with Four Oak Leaf Clusters. WRITINGS: articles on national security. REL.: Episc. (presiding bishop, United Episcopal Church). MAILING ADDRESS: 7005 Radnor Road, Bethesda, MD.

KNIGHT, GEORGE ALEXANDER. b. Jul 24, 1851, Worcester, MA; d. Jun 27, 1916; par. George H. and Elizabeth (McFalan) Knight; m. Fannie H. Wyman, Jun 1877. EDUC.: public schools, Eureka, CA; grad., Coll. of CA; studied law under Judge J. E. Wyman, Humboldt, CA. POLIT. & GOV.: elected district atty., Humboldt Cty., CA, 3 terms; Insurance Commissioner of CA; atty., CA State Board of Health, 2 terms; appointed judge advocate, col., on staff of Governor Markham; delegate, Rep. Nat'l. Conv., 1896, 1900, 1904, 1908; ***candidate for Republican nomination to vice presidency of the U.S., 1908***; member, Rep. Nat'l. Cmte. (CA), 1908–12. BUS. & PROF.: atty.; admitted to CA Bar, 1872; atty., Union Pacific R.R.; atty., Pacific Steamship Co. MEM.: Pacific Union Club; Bohemian Club. RES.: San Francisco, CA.

KNOUREK, KENYON RAYMOND. b. Feb 11, 1933, Los Angeles, CA; par. Raymond Max and Flavia Lura (Koss) Knourek; m. Naomi Ruth Scott; c. Christopher; Mark; Brent; Joseph. EDUC.: Bethany Bible Coll.; Coll. of Siskiyous. POLIT. & GOV.: ***candidate for Republican nomination to presidency of the U.S., 1976; candidate for Democratic nomination to presidency of the U.S., 1976; candidate for American Independent Party nomination to presidency of the U.S., 1976; candidate for Peace and Freedom Party nomination to presidency of the U.S., 1976***. BUS. & PROF.: carpenter; owner, Motel and Cabin Rentals, Weed, CA. REL.: Judaic-Christian (Protestant). MAILING ADDRESS: Route #1, Box 374, Weed, CA 96094.

KNOWLAND, WILLIAM FIFE. b. Jun 26, 1908, Alameda, CA; d. Feb 23, 1974, Cuerneville, CA; par. Joseph Russell and Ellie (Fife) Knowland; m. Helen Davis Herrick, Dec 31, 1926; c. Emelyn Jewett; Joseph William; Helen Estelle. EDUC.: A.B., U. of CA, 1929. POLIT. & GOV.: member, CA State Republican Central Cmte., 1930–35; elected as a Republican to CA State Assembly, 1933–35; elected as a Republican to CA State Senate, 1935–39; member, Rep. Nat'l. Cmte. (CA), 1938–42 (chm., exec. cmte., 1941–42); appointed and subsequently elected as a Republican to U.S. Senate (CA), 1945–59 (majority leader, 1953–54; Minority leader, 1955–59); U.S. delegate, General Assembly, U.N.; ***candidate for Republican nomination to presidency of the U.S., 1956, 1960, 1964***; Republican candidate for gov. of CA, 1958. BUS. & PROF.: pres., Franklin Investment Co.; asst. publisher, *Oakland (CA) Tribune*, 1933–74; pres., Tribune Publishing Co.; dir., Tribune Building Co.; dir., Gardiner Mill Co.; dir., Franklin Investment Co. MIL.: pvt., 2d lt., U.S. Army, 1942–45, maj., 1945. MEM.: Oakland Community Chest (vice chm., 1940–42); American Legion; VFW; U.S. C. of C.; CA State C. of C. (dir.); Oakland C. of C. (dir.); Zeta Psi; Sigma Delta Chi; Masons (33°; Shriner; Scottish Rite); Native Sons of the Golden West; Eagles; Moose; Elks; Bohemian Club; Anthenian-Nile Club; Red Cross (chm., Oakland Chapter, 1939–42). HON. DEG.: LL.D., U. of AK; LL.D., Mills Coll.; LL.D., U. of Southern CA. REL.: Methodist. MISC.: committed suicide. RES.: Alameda, CA.

KNOWLES, JAMES LLEWELLYN, JR. par. James Llewellyn Knowles, Sr. POLIT. & GOV.: ***independent candidate for presidency of the U.S., 1988***. MAILING ADDRESS: P.O. Box 888, Sandstone, MN 55072.

KNOX, LUTHER DEVINE (See NONE OF THE ABOVE).

KNOX, PHILANDER CHASE. b. May 6, 1853, Brownsville, PA; d. Oct 12, 1921, Washington, DC; par. David S. and Rebekah (Page) Knox; m. Lillie Smith, Feb 29, 1876; c. Rebekah P. (Mrs. James R. Tindle); Reed; Hugh S.; Philander Chase, Jr. EDUC.: U. of WV; A.B., Mount Union Coll., 1872; studied law under H. B. Swope. POLIT. & GOV.: appointed asst. U.S. district atty., Western District of PA, 1876–77; appointed atty. gen. of the U.S., 1901–04; appointed and subsequently elected as a Republican to U.S. Senate (PA), 1904–09, 1917–21; ***candidate for Republican nomination to presidency of the U.S., 1908, 1916, 1920***; appointed U.S. sec. of state, 1909–13; delegate, Rep. Nat'l. Conv., 1920. BUS. & PROF.: atty.; admitted to PA Bar, 1875; law practice, Pittsburgh, PA; partner, Knox and Reed (law firm), 1877–1921. MEM.: PA Bar Assn. (pres., 1897); Allegheny Bar Assn. (pres., 1897); Lawyers Club (NY; Philadelphia); Union League; Duquesne Club (pres.); Americus Club. HON. DEG.: LL.D., U. of PA, 1905; LL.D., Yale U., 1907; LL.D., Villanova U., 1909; LL.D., U. of Guatemala; LL.D., Mount Union Coll.; LL.D., U. of Pittsburgh; LL.D., Washington and Jefferson U. RES.: Pittsburgh, PA.

KNOX, RICK WILSON. b. Jul 30, 1949, Nashville, TN; par. Sterling Raymond and Mary Willis (Cooksey) Knox; m. Kimberly Jeanette Harris; c. Rachel Renee; Pamela Diane. EDUC.: Cumberland Coll.; B.A., U. of the State of NY; LL.B., Blackstone School of Law. POLIT. & GOV.: Republican candidate for MS State House, 1970; elected member, MS State Republican Exec. Cmte., 1974; Republican candidate for judge, Rankin Cty. (MS) Justice Court, 1979, 1983; ***candidate for Republican nomination to presidency of the U.S., 1984***. BUS.

& PROF.: political consultant; private investigator; policeman; schoolteacher; licensed insurance agent. MEM.: American Federation of Police; Conservative Republicans of America; NRA. REL.: Church of Christ. MAILING ADDRESS: P.O. Box 6281, Pearl, MS 39208.

KNOX, WILLIAM FRANKLIN. b. Jan 1, 1874, Boston, MA; d. Apr 28, 1944, Washington, DC; par. William Edwin and Sarah Collins (Barnard) Knox; m. Annie Reid, Dec 28, 1898; c. none. EDUC.: A.B., Alma Coll., 1898. POLIT. & GOV.: maj., staff of gov. of MI, 1908–10; appointed member, Board of Indian Commissioners, 1911; chm., MI Republican State Central Cmte., 1910–12; western chm., Roosevelt for President, 1912; maj., staff of gov. of NH, 1913; delegate, Rep. Nat'l. Conv., 1920; ***candidate for Republican nomination to presidency of the U.S., 1920, 1936***; chm., NH State Publicity Comm., 1922–24; candidate for Republican nomination to gov. of NH, 1924; chm., National Campaign to Combat Hoarding, 1932; ***Republican candidate for vice presidency of the U.S., 1936***; appointed U.S. sec. of the navy, 1940–44. BUS. & PROF.: newspaper publisher; reporter, city ed., circulation mgr., *Grand Rapids (MI) Herald*, 1898–1900; publisher, *Sault Ste. Marie (MI) News*, 1901–12; publisher, *Manchester (NH) Leader*, 1912–13; publisher, *Manchester (NH) Union and Leader*, 1913–14; publisher, *Boston (MA) American*, 1927–31; publisher, *Boston (MA) Daily Advertiser*, 1927–31; publisher, *Boston (MA) Sunday Advertiser*, 1927–31; gen. mgr., *Hearst Newspapers*, 1927–31; co-owner, publisher, *Chicago (IL) Daily News*, 1931–44. MIL.: Troop D, First U.S. Volunteer Cavalry (Rough Riders), 1898; capt., maj., U.S. Army, 1917–19; col., U.S.A.R. MEM.: Masons (33°); Army and Navy Club; American Legion (state commander); Rotary Club; One Hundred Club; Burning Tree Club; Chicago Club; Commercial Club; Old Elm Club; Union League; Advertising Club. HON. DEG.: LL.D., U. of NH, 1933; LL.D., Alma Coll., 1936; Litt.D., Rollins Coll., 1937; LL.D., Dartmouth Coll., 1941; LL.D., Harvard U., 1942; LL.D., Bethany Coll., 1943; LL.D., Colgate U., 1943; LL.D., Northwestern U., 1943; LL.D., Williams Coll., 1943. REL.: Congregationalist. RES.: Washington, DC.

KNUTSON, ALFRED (aka FRANK BROWN). b. Aug 28, 1880, Skaanevik, Norway; d. 1969; married. EDUC.: Concordia Coll.; A.B., U. of SD, 1912. POLIT. & GOV.: member, Socialist Party; joined Communist Party, 1919; Eastern MT, ND, and SD organizer, Workers Party, 1923; member, national exec. cmte., Farmer-Labor Party, 1924; delegate, Krestintern (Red Peasant International), Moscow, U.S.S.R., 1925; alternate member, Central Cmte., Workers Party, 1925; agricultural organizer, Workers Party, 1925–30; Farmer-Labor Party candidate for U.S. Senate (ND), 1928; independent candidate for U.S. House (ND), 1930; district organizer, Communist Party; ***independent (Communist Party) candidate for presidency of the U.S., 1940***. BUS. & PROF.: railroad track worker; farmhand; lumberjack; clerk; schoolteacher; carpenter, Williams Cty., ND; principal, public school, Leola, SD, 1912–13; ed., *United Farmer*, Bismarck, ND, 1926–29; organizer, Communist Party, southern U.S. MEM.: Western Progressive Farmers; Progressive Farmers of America (member, national educational cmte., 1926); WA Non-Partisan League (organizer; mgr., 1916–18); MN Non-Partisan League (organizer); CO Non-Partisan League (organizer); ID Non-Partisan League (mgr., 1916–18); ND Non-Partisan League (organizer, 1922); United Farmers' Education League (exec. sec., 1926–30). REL.: none (nee Lutheran). MISC.: came to U.S., 1899; organized England (AR) food riots. RES.: Moorhead, ND.

KOCH, DAVID HAMILTON. par. Fred Chase and Mary C. (Robinson) Koch. EDUC.: B.S. (Chemical Engineering), MA Inst. of Technology, 1962, M.S., 1963. POLIT. & GOV.: ***Libertarian Party candidate for vice presidency of the U.S., 1980***. BUS. & PROF.: chemical engineer; pres., Koch Engineering Co., New York, NY; pres., Abcor, Inc., MA. MAILING ADDRESS: 200 Central Park, South, #25C, New York, NY 10019.

KOCH, RACHEL DUNN. married. POLIT. & GOV.: ***candidate for Republican nomination to presidency of the U.S., 1976, 1980; independent candidate for presidency of the U.S., 1984***. MAILING ADDRESS: 12719 S.E. 24th Ave., Milwaukie, OR 97222.

KOCZAK, STEPHEN ANDREW. b. Nov 13, 1917, NJ; married. EDUC.: A.B. (cum laude), Harvard U., 1942; grad., Inst. of International Studies, Geneva, Switzerland, 1946. POLIT. & GOV.: diplomat, U.S. Dept. of State, 1946–66, stationed in Germany, Hungary, and Israel, 1946–54; intelligence research specialist, U.S. Dept. of State, 1957; ***candidate for Democratic nomination to presidency of the U.S., 1984, 1988***; candidate for Democratic nomination to U.S. House (NJ), 1986; ***candidate for Republican nomination to presidency of the U.S., 1992***. BUS. & PROF.: payroll clerk, Manufacturing Co., 1936–38; dir. of research, American Federation of Government Employees, 1966–80. MIL.: capt., U.S. Army, 1942–46. MEM.: Cleveland Park Citizens Assn. (pres.). MAILING ADDRESS: 2932 Macomb St., N.W., Washington, DC 20008.

KOEBEL, LARRY FRANCIS, JR. b. Jan 5, 1967, Columbus, OH; par. Larry Francis, Sr. and Laura Ann (DeFrancisco) Koebel; single. EDUC.: student, Westerville (OH) South H.S. POLIT. & GOV.: ***independent candidate for presidency of the U.S., 1984***. BUS. & PROF.: cashier, Gateway Supermarket, Westerville, OH, 1983–. REL.: R.C. MAILING ADDRESS: 3506 Dempsey Road, Westerville, OH 43081.

KOHLER, WALTER JODOK. b. Mar 3, 1875, Sheboygan, WI; d. Apr 21, 1940, Kohler, WI; par. John Michael and Lilly (Vollrath) Kohler; m. Charlotte H. Schroeder, Nov 3, 1900; c. John Michael; Walter Jodok, Jr.; Carl James; Robert Eugene. EDUC.: public schools, Sheboygan, WI. POLIT. & GOV.: pres., Sheboygan (WI) Board of Park Commissioners, 1915–18; presidential elector, Republican Party, 1916; member, Park Board, Kohler, WI, 1926–40; delegate, Rep. Nat'l. Conv., 1928; elected as a Republican to gov. of WI, 1929–31; candidate for Republican nomination to gov. of WI, 1930; Republican candidate for gov. of WI, 1932; ***candidate for Republican nomination to presidency of the U.S., 1936***. BUS. & PROF.: employee, Kohler Co., 1890, pres., 1905–37, chm. of the board, 1937–40; chm. of the board, Kohler Co., Ltd., London, England; chm. of the board, Vollrath Co., Sheboygan, WI; pres., Mountain States Supply Co., Salt Lake City, UT; chm. of the board, Security National Bank, Sheboygan, WI; trustee, exec. cmte., Northwestern Mutual Life Insurance Co., Milwaukee, WI; dir., Chicago and Northwestern Railway; dir., Chicago, St. Paul, Minneapolis, and Omaha Railway; pres., Kohler Improvement Co. MEM.: Milwaukee Club; U. Club of Madison; WI Manufacturers' Assn. (dir.); Sheboygan Associated Charities (vice pres.); Sheboygan Assn. of Commerce (pres., 1917–19); U. of WI (regent; pres. of Board of Regents); Lawrence Coll. (trustee); National Industrial Conference Board (vice chm.); Sheboygan Home for the Friendless (pres.); Soc. of Arts and Sciences (national service fellow, 1934); National Assn. of Manufacturers (national vice pres.; dir.); Masons; Elks; Union League; WI State Hist. Soc.; Sheboygan Cty. Hist. Soc.; Army and Navy Club; Milwaukee Press Club; Chicago Economic Club; National Arts Club; Planning Foundation of America (dir.). HON. DEG.: M.A., U. of WI, 1924; LL.D., Lake Forest U., 1929. REL.: Episc. MISC.: Noted for creation of model town of Kohler, WI; opponent of labor unions; subject of noted strike commencing in 1934. RES.: Kohler, WI.

KOPP, NORMAN F. b. Aug 28, 1924, Syracuse, NY; par. Gaylord and Mildred I. (Snogles) Kopp; m. Ruth M. Hannon, Sep 6, 1946 (divorced, Dec 16, 1975); c. Danny N.; Debra A.; Doreen M.; David A. EDUC.: high school, North Syracuse, NY (3 years). POLIT. & GOV.: ***Deprived and Discriminated Against Males candidate for presidency of the U.S., 1984***. BUS. & PROF.: delivery truck driver, 1946–80; retired. MIL.: radioman third class, U.S. Navy, 1941–45. MEM.: Teamsters Union Retirees' Assn.; Central NY Men's Rights/Divorce Reform Organization (founder; dir.); Anti-Lawyer Party (organizer). REL.: Protestant. MAILING ADDRESS: 102 South Main St., North Syracuse, NY 13212.

KORETZ, PAUL. POLIT. & GOV.: ***candidate for Democratic nomination to vice presidency of the U.S., 1980***. MAILING ADDRESS: CA.

KORNFELD, TODD HARRIS. POLIT. & GOV.: ***candidate for Democratic nomination to presidency of the U.S., 1988***. MAILING ADDRESS: 2960 Ocean Parkway, Brooklyn, NY 11235.

KOSISKY, DANIEL FRANCIS. b. Sep 11, 1930, Port Griffith, PA; par. Joseph Ambrose and Anna Marie (Slymock) Kosisky; m. Deloria Ann K., Oct 3, 1949; c. Daniel; Dennis; David; Darlene; Debra. EDUC.: grad., Greenbelt (MD) H.S.; Corcoran Art School, Washington, DC; U.S.M.C. Art School; Columbia Technical Inst. POLIT. & GOV.: ***candidate for Democratic nomination to presidency of the U.S., 1984***. BUS. & PROF.: architect, Walton and Madden, Riverdale, MD; technical illustrator, U.S. Naval Laboratory, White Oak, MD; artist. MIL.: pfc, U.S.M.C., 3 years. WRITINGS: *One Life to Live Under God* (1984). REL.: R.C. MAILING ADDRESS: 3365 Wye Mills, South, Laurel, MD 20707.

KOVIC, RON. POLIT. & GOV.: Democratic candidate for U.S. House (CA), 1990; ***candidate for Democratic nomination to presidency of the U.S., 1992***. BUS. & PROF.: author. MIL.: served in Vietnam. MISC.: inspiration for movie "Born on the Fourth of July." MAILING ADDRESS: Redondo Beach, CA.

KRAJEWSKI, HENRY B. b. 1912, Jersey City, NJ; d. Nov 8, 1966, Secaucus, NJ; m. Stephanie Pyskaty; c. Henry; Jacqueline; Victoria Gloria (Mrs. Joseph Sferiazza); Elizabeth Kemly. POLIT. & GOV.: founder, Poor Man's Party, 1949; Poor Man's Party candidate for Secaucus (NJ) Town Council, 1950; Poor Man's Party candidate for Hudson Cty. (NJ) Freeholder, 1951; ***Poor Man's Party candidate for presidency of the U.S., 1952***; NJ Veterans Bonus Party candidate for gov. of NJ, 1953; American Third Party candidate for U.S. Senate (NJ), 1954; ***American Third Party candidate for presidency of the U.S., 1956, 1960***; American Third Party candidate for gov. of NJ, 1957; Politicians Are Jokers candidate for U.S. Senate (NJ), 1958; Veterans Bonus Now candidate for gov. of NJ, 1961; independent candidate for U.S. Senate (NJ), 1966 (withdrew). BUS. & PROF.: hog farmer, Secaucus, NJ, 1940–52; owner, Tammany Hall Tavern, Secaucus, NJ; messenger boy; errand boy; newspaper salesman; wood chopper; slaughter and skin house worker. REL.: R.C. MISC.: offered to serve as President Lyndon B. Johnson's vice pres., 1964; campaigned with a pig on a leash. RES.: Secaucus, NJ.

KRAMER, H. M. POLIT. & GOV.: ***candidate for Union Labor Party nomination to vice presidency of the U.S., 1888 (declined)***. RES.: GA.

KRANZ, PETER. b. Jun 2, 1923, Buffalo, NY; par. Frederick and Lina (Longaker) Kranz; m. Nancy Thomson; c. Thomas; William. EDUC.: A.B., Harvard U., 1944. POLIT. & GOV.: candidate for Democratic nomination to U.S. House

(NY), 1954; member, Darien (CT) Building Board of Appeals, 1964; ***New Party candidate for presidency of the U.S., 1968 (declined); New Party candidate for vice presidency of the U.S., 1968 (withdrew)***. BUS. & PROF.: owner, Connecticut Research, Inc. REL.: none. MAILING ADDRESS: 145 Nearwater Lane, Darien, CT 06820.

KRATSAS, NICK C. b. between 1917 and 1921; m. Maria; c. Constantine N.; Carla Ann. POLIT. & GOV.: ***Truth and Freedom Party candidate for presidency of the U.S., 1988, 1992***. BUS. & PROF.: unknown. MIL.: armed forces, WWII. MISC.: campaigned on "Notch Baby" issue. MAILING ADDRESS: c/o Constantine N. Kratsas, 1408 East FL Ave., Youngstown, OH 44502.

KREB, CHRISTOPHER HERMANN. b. Aug 28, 1966, Chicago, IL; par. Karlheinz and Maria Regina (Wessler) Kreb; single. EDUC.: student, Chicago (IL) public schools. POLIT. & GOV.: ***Independent Party candidate for presidency of the U.S., 1984***; chm., Nuclear Disarmament Party-America, 1984–. BUS. & PROF.: mgr., shipping dept., Unicut Corp., Chicago, IL. REL.: atheist (nee R.C.). MAILING ADDRESS: 2415 West Warner Ave., Chicago, IL 60618.

KREBS, ROLAND. b. 1899. POLIT. & GOV.: ***candidate for Democratic nomination to presidency of the U.S., 1924***; received 1 vote for presidential nomination on 13th ballot, Dem. Nat'l. Conv., 1924. WRITINGS: *Making Friends Is Our Business: 100 Years of Anheuser-Busch* (1953). RES.: MI.

KREMBS, BARRY STEWART. POLIT. & GOV.: ***independent candidate for presidency of the U.S., 1980***. MAILING ADDRESS: 12727 Bingham Ave., East, Tacoma, WA 98446.

KREML, WILLIAM PARKER. b. Aug 5, 1941, Evanston, IL; par. Franklin Martin and Margaret Charlotte (Parker) Kreml; m. (divorced); m. 2d, Nancy Mace; c. Elizabeth; Suzanne. EDUC.: B.A., Northwestern U., 1962, J.D., 1965; M.A., U. of TN, 1966; Ph.D., IN U., 1972. POLIT. & GOV.: candidate for Democratic nomination to U.S. Senate (SC), 1980; ***candidate for Democratic nomination to presidency of the U.S., 1984, 1992***. BUS. & PROF.: asst. prof. of Business Law, Northern IL U., 1965–66; asst. prof. of Business Law, U. of TN, 1966–68; prof., Dept. of Government and International Studies, U. of SC, Columbia, SC, 1971–. MIL.: E-5, U.S. Army, 1959; U.S.A.R., 1959–62, inactive status, 1962–66. MEM.: International Soc. of Political Psychology. AWARDS: Education Foundation Research Award, U. of SC, 1985; "Professor of the Year," state of SC, AAUP, 1986. WRITINGS: *The Anti-authoritarian Personality* (1977); *The Middle Class Burden* (1979); *Relativism and the Natural Left* (1984); *A Model of Politics* (1984); *Psychology, Relativism and Politics* (1991); *Losing Balance: The De-Democratization of America* (1991). MAILING ADDRESS: 111 Southwood Dr., Columbia, SC 29205.

KRUEGER, MAYNARD CLARE. b. Jan 16, 1906, Alexandria, MO; d. Nov 20, 1991, Chicago, IL; par. Fred C. and Nelle Caroline (Hoewing) Krueger; m. Elsie Clara Gasperik, Aug 25, 1934; c. Karen (Mrs. Harold F. Finn); Linda (Mrs. Bruce MacLachlan); Susan (Mrs. Winston Salser). EDUC.: A.B., U. of MO, 1926, A.M., 1927; U. of Berlin, 1925–26; U. of Paris, 1926; U. of Geneva, 1927; U. of PA, 1928–32. POLIT. & GOV.: Chicago organizer, Thomas for President Campaign, 1932; delegate, Second International, Paris, France, 1933; member, National Cmte., Socialist Party, 1934–77 (national chm., 1942); ***Socialist Party candidate for vice presidency of the U.S., 1940, 1948 (declined)***; Socialist Party candidate for Sixth Ward alderman, Chicago, IL, 1943; Socialist Party candidate for U.S. House (IL), 1948; ***candidate for Socialist Party nomination to presidency of the U.S., 1948***; joined Democratic Party, 1952; candidate for nomination to various offices, Democratic Party. BUS. & PROF.: grade school teacher, Clark Cty., MO, 1922–23; instructor in History, Albion Coll., 1927–28 (fired for Socialist activities); instructor, Wharton School of Finance and Commerce, U. of PA, 1928–32; asst. prof. of Economics, U. of Chicago, 1932–47, assoc. prof., 1947–65, prof., 1965–77; instructor, Chicago School of Socialism, 1933; consultant, Far East Program, Economic Cooperation Administration, 1951; pres., Progress Development Corp., 1958–; Fulbright visiting prof., U. of Vienna, 1959–60; Fulbright visiting prof., U. of Athens, 1963–64; visiting prof., State U. of NY, 1965–66. MEM.: AAUP; Workmen's Circle; American Economic Assn.; League for Industrial Democracy (1928–32); National Religion and Labor Foundation (1933); Workers' Training School; PA Cmte. for Total Disarmament (vice chm., 1932); American Federation of Teachers (vice pres., 1934–36); Independent Voters of IL (chm., 1957–59); Northwest Hyde Park Neighborhood Redevelopment Corp. (pres., 1955); Hyde Park Community Conference; Modern Community Development Corp. WRITINGS: *Economics Question Book* (1934). REL.: none. RES.: Chicago, IL.

KRZYCKI, LEO. b. Aug 10, 1881, Milwaukee, WI; d. Jan 22, 1966, Milwaukee, WI; par. Martin and Kathryn Krzycki; m. Anna Kadau, Feb 3, 1909; c. Eugene J.; Victor L.; Leona; Knoll. EDUC.: elementary school. POLIT. & GOV.: elected as a Socialist to Milwaukee (WI) City Council, 1912–16; Socialist Party candidate for City Comptroller, Milwaukee, WI, 1916; undersheriff of Milwaukee, WI, 1918–20; chm., Milwaukee (WI) Socialist Party; Socialist Party candidate for U.S. House (WI), 1924; Socialist Party candidate for U.S. Senate (WI), 1926; state sec., WI Socialist Party, 1933; national chm., exec. cmte., Socialist Party, 1932–34; ***candidate for Socialist Party nomination to vice presidency of the U.S., 1936***; left Socialist Party, 1936. BUS. & PROF.: press tender; clothing worker; lithographer;

union organizer. MEM.: Lithographic Press Feeders' Union (vice pres., 1904–08); Amalgamated Clothing Workers of America (member, 1919–66; general exec. board, 1922–47; vice pres., 1947); CIO (political action cmte.; steel workers organizing cmte., 1936); American Slav Congress (pres., 1942); American Polish Labor Council (pres.); League Against Fascism (national cmte.); Berger National Foundation (councilor). WRITINGS: *The Union and the Socialists* (1935); *What I Saw in the Slavic Countries* (1946); *My Peace Mission to Europe* (1949). MISC.: indicted for violation of the Espionage Act, 1918; organized Needle Trades Socialists; leader, Reading (PA) Strike, 1933. RES.: Milwaukee, WI.

KUBBS, DMITRI A. "PETE." POLIT. & GOV.: ***independent candidate for presidency of the U.S., 1992***. MAILING ADDRESS: 2612 West Daniel, Champaign, IL 61821.

KUEHL, RAYMOND C., JR. b. Dec 30, 1946, WI Rapids, WI; par. Raymond C. and Des Bullion (Mavis) Kuehl; single. EDUC.: A.A. (Business Management), A.A. (Accounting), Milwaukee Area Technical Coll. POLIT. & GOV.: ***candidate for Democratic nomination to presidency of the U.S., 1988***. BUS. & PROF.: acid maker; rewinder operator; roofer; plumber's helper; construction worker; mgr., liquor store; accountant; self-employed. MIL.: infantryman, U.S. Army, 1964–67. MEM.: Phi Theta Kappa. REL.: agnostic. MAILING ADDRESS: P.O. Box 20171, Long Beach, CA 90801.

KUHARSKI, MARY ANN ELIZABETH HULL. m. Edmund Francis Kuharski; c. Philip Edmund. POLIT. & GOV.: ***candidate for Democratic nomination to vice presidency of the U.S., 1980***. MAILING ADDRESS: c/o Philip E. Kuharski, 931 Regent Court, Spokane, WA 99203.

KUHN, MARGARET ELIZA "MAGGIE." b. Aug 3, 1905, Buffalo, NY; d. Apr. 22, 1995, Philadelphia, PA; par. Samuel Frederick and Minnie L. (Kooman) Kuhn; single. EDUC.: B.A., Case-Western Reserve U., 1926; Union Theological Seminary; M.A., Temple U., 1934. POLIT. & GOV.: delegate, White House Conference on Aging, 1961 (chm., national organization section); appointed member, Governor's Task Force on Advocacy and Self-Determination (PA), 1971–72; candidate for Councilwoman-at-Large, Philadelphia, PA, 1975; ***People's Party candidate for vice presidency of the U.S., 1976 (declined; replaced by Benjamin M. Spock, q.v.)***. BUS. & PROF.: sec., YWCA, Cleveland, OH, and Germantown, PA, 1927–40; national publications ed., YWCA, New York, NY, 1940–48; assoc. sec., Office of Church and Soc., United Presbyterian Church; coordinator of programs, Division of Church and Race, United Presbyterian Church; ed., *Social Progress*; author; adviser, Hospice, Inc.; adviser, "Over Easy" (television series). MEM.: YWCA; United Presbyterian Health, Education, and Welfare Assn. (dir.); Gray Panthers (founder; convener, national steering cmte., 1970–); Memorial Soc. of Philadelphia (dir.); Philadelphia Hearing Soc.; Senior Services Law Center; People's Fund; Corporation of 65 (vice pres.); Action Alliance of Senior Citizens of Greater Philadelphia (founder); Retired Professional Action Group. AWARDS: First Annual Award for Justice and Human Development, Witherspoon Soc., 1974; Distinguished Service Award, American Speech and Hearing Assn., 1975; Freedom Award, Women's Scholarship Assn., Roosevelt U., 1976; award, Philadelphia Soc. of Clinical Psychologists, 1976; Peace-seeker Award, United Presbyterian Peace Fellowship, 1977; "Humanist of the Year" award, American Humanist Assn., 1978. WRITINGS: *Let's Get Out There and Do Something About Injustice* (1972); *Maggie Kuhn on Aging* (1977). REL.: United Presb. Church. RES.: Philadelphia, PA.

KULONGOSKI, THEODORE RALPH. b. Nov 5, 1940, Washington Cty., MO; par. Theodore Clement and Barbara Helen (Newcomer) Kulongoski; m. Lynn Ann Remsbecher, 1965; c. Theodore Edward; Kristen Marie; Justin Theodore. EDUC.: B.A., U. of MO, 1967, J.D., 1970. POLIT. & GOV.: legal counsel, OR State House, 1973; elected as a Democrat to OR State House, 1975–79; elected as a Democrat to OR State Senate, 1979–83; Democratic candidate for U.S. Senate (OR), 1980; appointed member, Lane Cty. (OR) Affirmative Action Comm.; ***candidate for Democratic nomination to vice presidency of the U.S., 1980***; Democratic candidate for gov. of OR, 1982; appointed OR State Insurance Commissioner, 1987–90. BUS. & PROF.: atty.; admitted to OR Bar, 1970; law practice, Eugene, OR, 1970–. MIL.: U.S.M.C., 1960–63. MEM.: ABA; OR Bar Assn.; MO Bar Assn.; Federal District Court Bar Assn.; Lane Cty. Bar Assn.; Lane Cty. Assn. for Retarded Citizens (dir.). REL.: R.C. MAILING ADDRESS: 30303 Maple Dr., Junction City, OR 97448.

KURLAND, NORMAN G. b. 1930. POLIT. & GOV.: chm., ownership campaign, 1980; ***candidate for Republican nomination to presidency of the U.S., 1980***. BUS. & PROF.: atty.; owner, Norman G. Kurland and Associates, Washington, DC. MISC.: advocate of employee ownership of business. MAILING ADDRESS: 4318 North 31st St., Arlington, VA 22207.

KURTZ, LOUIS A. POLIT. & GOV.: ***National Progressive Party candidate for vice presidency of the U.S., 1932***. BUS. & PROF.: soldier. MIL.: sgt., U.S. Army. MISC.: said to be able to "write poetry, prose, or a good article on anything." RES.: Chicago, IL.

KUSIC, JOHN J. POLIT. & GOV.: ***candidate for Peace and Freedom Party nomination to presidency of the U.S., 1972***. MAILING ADDRESS: 6528 Schafer, Cleveland, OH.

KUSUMI, JOHN PATRICK. POLIT. & GOV.: ***independent candidate for presidency of the U.S., 1984***. MAILING ADDRESS: 25 Eastern Ave., Waterbury, CT 06708.

KYLE, DALE HARPER. b. Mar 24, 19??, Anaheim, CA; par. Hubert John and Edith Lupveal Ivy (Stoner) Kyle (adopted); single; c. six. EDUC.: grad., Los Altos H.S., Hacienda Heights, CA; Mt. Sac Coll., Walnut, CA. POLIT. & GOV.: ***candidate for Democratic nomination to presidency of the U.S., 1984, 1988, 1992***; candidate for Democratic nomination to U.S. Senate (CA), 1986. BUS. & PROF.: activist. MIL.: G-4, U.S. Army, 1966–68. MEM.: Kyle Political Fund (chm.); Human Rights Coalition. WRITINGS: *Policeman of the World*; *Non-Communist Manifesto*; *La Pax del Mundo, I Hate You*. REL.: neo-Catholic non-Protestant. MAILING ADDRESS: P.O. Box 1612, Chino, CA 91710.

KYLE, JAMES HENDERSON. b. Feb 24, 1854, Xenia, OH; d. Jul 1, 1901, Aberdeen, SD; par. Thomas B. and Margaret J. (Henderson) Kyle; m. Anna Isabel Dugot, Apr 27, 1881; c. two. EDUC.: grad., high school, Urbana, IL; U. of IL, 1871–73; B.A., Oberlin Coll., 1878; studied law; grad., Western Theological Seminary, 1882. POLIT. & GOV.: superintendent of public schools; elected as an independent to SD State Senate, 1890; elected as an independent to U.S. Senate (SD), 1891–1901; ***candidate for People's Party nomination to presidency of the U.S., 1892***; appointed chm., U.S. Industrial Comm., 1898–1901. BUS. & PROF.: teacher of mathematics and engineering, to 1882; ordained minister, Congregational Church; pastor, Congregational Church, Echo and Salt Lake City, UT, 1882–85; pastor, Congregational Church, Ipswich, SD, 1886; pastor, Congregational Church, Aberdeen, SD; financial sec., Yankton Coll., 1890; educator. REL.: Congregationalist. RES.: Aberdeen, SD.

LADNER, ROBERT DERWOOD "BUCK."

b. May 12, 1930, Poplarville, MS; par. Robert Franklin and Mae (Rester) Ladner; m. Mary Rita LeBlanc; c. Dawn Marie; Ann Teresa; Marc Anto; Marcia Rita; Greg Damian; Cheri Susanne; Dion Michael. EDUC.: U.S. Air Force Engineering School, 1948; Pearl River Junior Coll., 1954; special studies in Tokyo, Hong Kong, Bangkok, Warsaw, Moscow, Istanbul, London, and Monterrey; D.Sc., Tulane U., 1956. POLIT. & GOV.: Democrat-Technocrat candidate for gov. of MS, 1970 (withdrew); Democrat-Technocrat candidate for U.S. House (MS), 1972; ***Democrat-Technocrat candidate for presidency of the U.S., 1980, 1988***. BUS. & PROF.: physical scientist; master architect; self-employed; vice pres., dir., Security Savings and Loan; pres., Intra-Monetary Corp. (mortgage banking). MIL.: technical sgt., U.S. Air Force, Korean War; instructor, Basic Military Science and Tactics. MEM.: A.I.A.; MS Economic Council; American Legion; VFW; U.S. Junior C. of C.; Coalition of Americans for a New Elective Majority (pres.); Gulf Regional Planning Comm. (sec.). WRITINGS: *Free-Particle Energy* (1973); *Light Energy: Solution to the Energy Crisis* (1974); *Architect of the Pyramids* (1974); *Understanding Cancer* (1975). REL.: Protestant/Catholic/Christian/Jew. MAILING ADDRESS: 158 Central Ave., Long Beach, MS 39560.

LA FOLLETTE, ROBERT MARION.

b. Jun 14, 1855, Primrose, WI; d. Jun 18, 1925, Washington, DC; par. Josiah and Mary (Furgeson) La Follette; m. Belle Case, Dec 31, 1881; c. Robert Marion, Jr. (q.v.); Philip Fox; Fola. EDUC.: B.S., U. of WI, 1879. POLIT. & GOV.: elected as a Republican, district atty., Dane Cty., WI, 1880–84; elected as a Republican to U.S. House (WI), 1885–91; Republican candidate for U.S. House (WI), 1890; delegate, Rep. Nat'l. Conv., 1896, 1904, 1912; candidate for Republican nomination to gov. of WI, 1896, 1898; elected as a Republican to gov. of WI, 1901–06; elected as a Republican to U.S. Senate (WI), 1905–25; ***candidate for Republican nomination to presidency of the U.S., 1908, 1912, 1916, 1920, 1924; candidate for Progressive Party nomination to presidency of the U.S., 1912; candidate for Farmer-Labor Party nomination to presidency of the U.S., 1920; National Service Party candidate for presidency of the U.S., 1920; Progressive (Socialist; Conference for Progressive Political Action) Party candidate for presidency of the U.S., 1924***. BUS. & PROF.: atty.; admitted to WI Bar, 1880; publisher, *La Follette's Weekly*, 1909–25. MEM.: People's Legislative Service (founder). HON. DEG.: LL.D., U. of WI, 1901. WRITINGS: *Autobiography—A Personal Narrative of Political Experience* (1913). MISC.: reform advocate; crusaded on behalf of direct election of public officials, initiative and referendum, equitable taxation of railroads and regulation of their rate structures. RES.: Madison, WI.

LA FOLLETTE, ROBERT MARION, JR.

b. Feb 6, 1895, Maldon, WI; d. Feb 24, 1953, Washington, DC; par. Robert Marion (q.v.) and Belle (Case) La Follette; m. Rachel Wilson Young, Sep 17, 1930; c. Joseph Oden; Bronson Cutting. EDUC.: grad., Western H.S., Washington, DC, 1913; U. of WI, 1913–16. POLIT. & GOV.: sec. to U.S. Senator Robert Marion La Follette (q.v.), 1919–25; chm., WI Republican State Central Cmte., 1920–24; vice chm., Progressive Party National Exec. Cmte., 1924; elected as a Republican (Progressive) to U.S. Senate (WI), 1925–47; ***candidate for Democratic nomination to vice presidency of the U.S., 1940***; candidate for Republican nomination to U.S. Senate (WI), 1946. BUS. & PROF.: author; ed., *La Follette's Magazine*, 1925–29; assoc., *The Progressive*, 1929–47; economic consultant; pres., publishing company, Madison, WI; pres., chm. of the board, WEMP Broadcasting Co., Milwaukee, WI; dir., United Fruit Co.; dir., Sears, Roebuck and Co.; dir., American-Hawaiian Steamship Co. MEM.: Cosmos Club; Metropolitan Club; Congressional Country Club; Beta Theta Pi; Sears Employees Savings and Profit Sharing Pension Fund (trustee); Public Ownership League of America (vice pres.); National Citizens Cmte. on Relations with Latin America (1927). AWARDS: one of twelve Outstanding Young Men in America, America's Young Men, 1934; received *Collier's Magazine* Award, 1946. HON. DEG.: LL.D., U. of WI, 1938. RES.: Madison, WI.

LAFONTAINE, ALBERT LEO. POLIT. & GOV.: ***candidate for Democratic nomination to presidency of the U.S., 1980***. MAILING ADDRESS: 752 Englewood Ave., St. Paul, MN 55104.

LA GUARDIA, FIORELLO HENRY. b. Dec 11, 1882, New York, NY; d. Sep 20, 1947, New York, NY; par. Achille Luigi Carlo and Irene (Coen) La Guardia; m. Thea Almerigotti, May 8, 1919; m. 2d, Marie Fisher, Feb 28, 1929; c. Fioretta; Jean (adopted); Eric (adopted). EDUC.: LL.B., NY U., 1910. POLIT. & GOV.: employee, U.S. consulate, Budapest, Hungary, 1901; employee, U.S. consulate, Trieste, Austria, 1901–04; consular agent, Fiume, Hungary, 1904–06; interpreter, Ellis Island Immigration Center, 1907–10; Republican candidate for U.S. House (NY), 1914, 1932; appointed deputy atty. gen. of NY, 1915–17; elected as a Republican (Socialist; Republican Progressive) to U.S. House (NY), 1917–19 (resigned), 1923–33; delegate, Rep. Nat'l. Conv., 1920; elected pres., Board of Aldermen, New York, NY, 1920–21; delegate, Interparliamentary Conference, 1928, 1930; Fusion Party candidate for mayor of New York, NY, 1929; elected as a Fusionist to mayor of New York, NY, 1934–45; ***candidate for Republican nomination to presidency of the U.S., 1940; candidate for Republican nomination to vice presidency of the U.S., 1940***; appointed dir., Office of Civilian Defense, 1941; appointed chm., American Section, Permanent Joint Defense Board (Canada-U.S.), 1946; appointed special U.S. ambassador to Brazil, 1946; appointed dir.-gen., UNRRA, 1946. BUS. & PROF.: truck driver; stenographer; teacher; correspondent, *Phoenix (AZ) Morning Courier*; correspondent, *St. Louis (MO) Post-Dispatch*, 1898; atty.; admitted to NY Bar, 1910; law practice, New York, NY, 1910. MIL.: 1st lt., capt., maj., U.S. Army Air Service, 1917; World War I Victory Medal; knight commander, Order of the Crown of Italy; Italian War Cross. MEM.: U.S. Conference of Mayors (pres., 1936–45); American Legion; Quiet Birdmen; Masons; Elks; Engineers Club of New York; Russian-American Industrial Corp.; Sacco-Vanzetti National League (National Cmte.); National Citizens Cmte. on Latin America (1927). AWARDS: Special War Medal of Aero Club (1919); Annual Tolerance Medal of Pi Lamda Phi (1935); American Hebrew Annual Award (1936); St. Nicholas Soc. Medal of Merit (1945); One World Award (1947); Blue Order of Jade (China); Order of the Redeemer (Greece); Order of Merit (Italy); Símon Bolvar Medal (Venezuela); Medal of Honor (Haiti); Order of Honor and Merit-Commendador (Cuba); Order of St. Olav (Norway); Delaware Award (Sweden); Order of Orange-Nassau (Netherlands); Lithuanian Air Medal; Order of the White Lion (Czechoslovakia); Polonia Restituta, First Class (Poland); Medal of Merit (U.S.); commander, Legion of Honor (France); grand commander, Order of the Phoenix (Greece). HON. DEG.: LL.D., NY U., 1938; LL.D., St. Lawrence U., 1938; LL.D., Yale U., 1940; LL.D., Washington and Jefferson Coll., 1942. REL.: Episc. (nee R.C.). RES.: New York, NY.

LAKEIN, ALAN. EDUC.: grad., Johns Hopkins U.; grad., Harvard U. POLIT. & GOV.: ***independent candidate for presidency of the U.S., 1980***. BUS. & PROF.: time-planning and life goals consultant; pres., Alan Lakein and Co. WRITINGS: "The Time of Your Life" (film); *How to Get Control of Your Time and Your Life* (1973). MAILING ADDRESS: 2918 Webster St., San Francisco, CA 94123.

LAKESTAR, LEON. b. 1907. POLIT. & GOV.: ***candidate for Democratic nomination to presidency of the U.S., 1980***. BUS. & PROF.: Blackfoot Indian Chief. MAILING ADDRESS: Dallas, TX.

LAMAGNO, CONCETTA MARIE. POLIT. & GOV.: ***Theocratic Party candidate for presidency of the U.S., 1988***. MAILING ADDRESS: New Israel with Concetta Marie, c/o James Lee Loudon, 102 North Bloomington St., Streator, IL 61364.

LAMB, BOBBIE JOE. b. 1926, Eastland Cty., TX; m. Melba Groom, 1945; c. three. EDUC.: grad., Rosebud (TX) H.S.; grad., U.S. Merchant Marine Acad. POLIT. & GOV.: ***candidate for Democratic nomination to presidency of the U.S., 1984, 1988***. BUS. & PROF.: farmer; longshoresman; stevedore; carpenter; plumber; painter; mechanic; general contractor; oilfield worker, Sunbelt Well Service, Eastland, TX. MIL.: staff sgt., U.S. Air Force, Korean War. MAILING ADDRESS: Route 1, Box 81, Carbon, TX 76435.

LAMBERT, GLEN DONALD. b. Nov 4, 1914, Parkersburg, WV; par. William C. and Bertha A. K. (Houck) Lambert; m. Mary J. Nichols; c. Carolyn; Donald; Raymond; Mary. EDUC.: B.S., WA U., 1935; U. of CO, 1960–64. POLIT. & GOV.: Republican precinct worker, Denver, CO; delegate, Republican Cty. Convention, CO; delegate, CO State Republican Convention; ***candidate for Republican nomination to presidency of the U.S., 1980***. BUS. & PROF.: senior geophysicist, Shell Oil Co., 1935–74. MIL.: lt. col., U.S. Army, 1940–45. MEM.: Mensa; Masons (32°). REL.: Presb. (elder). MAILING ADDRESS: P.O. Box 15091, Denver, CO 80215.

LAMOTTE, JOSEPH. POLIT. & GOV.: ***Living Party candidate for presidency of the U.S., 1980, 1992***. BUS. & PROF.: clerk; custodian. MAILING ADDRESS: 2255 Cropsey Ave., Brooklyn, NY.

LAND, JAMES ALBERT, JR. b. Mar 17, 1931, Kilgore, TX; par. James Albert and Oma E. (Misun) Land; m. Helga E. Leis; c. Roland R.; Bonnie J.; David A.; Belinda D.; Richard A. EDUC.: high school; G.E.D., U.S. Army. POLIT. & GOV.: ***independent candidate for presidency of the U.S., 1980***. BUS. & PROF.: owner, James Land Corp. of Texas; owner, Lloyd's of Land, Ltd. (furniture repair and upholstery firm), Fort Hood, TX; notary public; employee, furniture store, Killeen, TX. Mil: sgt. (E-6), U.S. Army. REL.: Bapt. MAILING ADDRESS: 1509 S.W. South Young Dr., Killeen, TX 76541.

LANDAR, JOSEPH. m. Sylvia Landar. POLIT. & GOV.: ***independent candidate for presidency of the U.S., 1988 (withdrew)***. MAILING ADDRESS: c/o Sylvia Landar, 49 Murdock Court, Apt. 1D, Brooklyn, NY 11223.

LANDON, ALFRED MOSSMAN. b. Sep 9, 1887, West Middlesex, PA; d. Oct 12, 1987, Topeka, KS; par. John Manuel and Anne (Mossman) Landon; m. Margaret Fleming, Jan 19, 1915; m. 2d, Theo Cobb, Jan 15, 1930; c. Margaret Anne; Nancy Josephine (q.v.; Mrs. Philip Kassebaum; divorced, 1979); John Cobb. EDUC.: Marietta Acad.; LL.B., U. of KS, 1908. POLIT. & GOV.: chm., KS State Republican Central Cmte., 1928; elected as a Republican to gov. of KS, 1933–37; ***Republican candidate for presidency of the U.S., 1936***; delegate, Pan American Conference, Lima, Peru, 1938; delegate, Rep. Nat'l. Conv., 1940, 1944, 1948, 1972 (hon.). BUS. & PROF.: bank bookkeeper, Independence, KS, to 1912; independent oil producer, 1912–; owner, radio stations, KS, 1950–87; distinguished prof., KS State U., 1968–87. MIL.: 1st lt., U.S. Army, WWI. MEM.: Phi Gamma Delta; Phi Delta Phi; Odd Fellows; Elks; American Legion; Masons; Blue Key (hon. member, 1969). AWARDS: Distinguished Citizenship Award, Washburn U., 1967; Distinguished Citizenship Award, Baker U., 1975. HON. DEG.: LL.D., Washburn Coll., 1933; LL.D., Marietta Coll., 1934; LL.D., Boston U., 1939; L.H.D., KS State U., 1968; LL.D., Coll. of Emporia, 1969. REL.: Methodist (delegate, Uniting Conference, 1939). RES.: Topeka, KS.

LANDRIEU, MOON. b. Jul 3, 1930, New Orleans, LA; par. Joseph and Lorette (Bechtel) Landrieu; m. Verna Satterlee, Sep 25, 1954; c. Mary; Mark; Melanie; Michelle; Madeline; Martin; Melinda; Maurice. EDUC.: B.B.A., Loyola U., 1952, LL.B., 1954. POLIT. & GOV.: elected as a Democrat to LA State House, 1960–66; elected councilman-at-large, City Council, New Orleans, LA, 1966–70; member, Dem. Nat'l. Cmte.; elected as a Democrat to mayor of New Orleans, LA, 1970–78; delegate, Dem. Nat'l. Conv., 1972, 1976; ***candidate for Democratic nomination to vice presidency of the U.S., 1972***; appointed U.S. sec. of housing and urban development, 1979–81. BUS. & PROF.: atty.; admitted to LA Bar, 1954; partner, Landrieu, Calogero and Kronlage (law firm), New Orleans, LA, 1958–69. MIL.: 2d lt., U.S. Army, 1954–57. MEM.: Total Community Action, Inc.; Inter-American Municipal Organization (first vice pres.); U.S. Conference of Mayors (pres., 1975–76); National League of Cities; National Urban Coalition; National Conference of Democratic Mayors; LA Municipal Assn.; Loyola U. (regent). AWARDS: "Most Influential Mayor in U.S." Award, *U.S. News and World Report*, 1977; B'nai B'rith Humanitarian Award, 1974. REL.: R.C. MAILING ADDRESS: 4301 South Prieur St., New Orleans, LA.

LANDRITH, IRA DAVID. b. Mar 23, 1865, Milford, TX; d. Oct 11, 1941, Pasadena, CA; par. Martin Luther and Mary M. (Groves) Landrith; m. Harriet Canfield Grannis, Jan 21, 1891; m. 2d, Sallie Alexander, 1935; c. Grace Grannis (Mrs. W. D. Landis); Ira DeWitt. EDUC.: B.S., Cumberland U., 1888, LL.B., 1889, theology student, 1889–90, LL.D., 1903; D.D., Trinity U., 1906. POLIT. & GOV.: ***candidate for Prohibition Party nomination to presidency of the U.S., 1916; Prohibition Party candidate for vice presidency of the U.S., 1916***. BUS. & PROF.: minister, Presbyterian Church; asst. ed., *The Cumberland Presbyterian*, 1890–95, editor-in-chief, 1896–1903; pres., Belmont Coll., 1904–12; pres., Ward Seminary, 1912–13; pres., Ward-Belmont Coll., 1913–15; ed., *Christian Endeavor World and Citizenship;* national lecturer, Anti-Saloon League of America, 1915–25; lecturer, World League Against Alcoholism, 1915–25. MEM.: Flying Squadron of America (1914–15); YMCA (TN state chm.; international president); Anti-Saloon League of America (state sec.); Cmte. of 100 (chm.); Religious Education Assn. (gen. sec., 1893–94); Presbyterian Brotherhood of America (gen. sec., 1907–09); International Soc. of Christian Endeavor (superintendent, 1915–41); Intercollegiate Prohibition Assn. (pres., 1920–27); National Temperance Council (pres., 1928–31); Allied Campaigners for Prohibition Permanency and Enforcement (1931–32); International YMCA Convention (pres., 1913). WRITINGS: *A Saloonless Nation by 1920*. REL.: Presb. (moderator, General Assembly, Cumberland Presbyterian Church, 1906). RES.: Winona Lake, IL.

LANDY, BRUCE ALLEN. POLIT. & GOV.: ***candidate for Democratic nomination to presidency of the U.S., 1988; candidate for Republican nomination to vice presidency of the U.S., 1992***. MAILING ADDRESS: 2601 Virginia Ave., N.W., Washington, DC 20037.

LANE, JOSEPH. b. Dec 14, 1801, Buncombe Cty., NC; d. Apr 19, 1881, Roseburg, OR; par. John and Elizabeth (Street) Lane; m. Polly Pierce, 1820; c. La Fayette; Nathaniel Hart; Ratcliff Boone; Joseph Samuel; Simon Robert; John; Melissa (Mrs. A. J. Barlow); Mary (Mrs. Aaron Shelby); Emily (Mrs. J. C. Floud); Winifred (Mrs. L. F. Mosher). EDUC.: public schools. POLIT. & GOV.: elected as a Democrat to IN State House, 1822–23, 1831–33, 1838–39; elected as a Democrat to IN State Senate, 1844–46; appointed gov. of OR Territory, 1849–50, 1853; elected as a Democrat to territorial delegate, U.S. House (OR), 1851–59; ***candidate for Democratic nomination to presidency of the U.S., 1852, 1860***; elected as a Democrat to U.S. Senate (OR), 1859–61; ***Southern Democratic Party candidate for vice presidency of the U.S., 1860***. BUS. & PROF.: clerk, IN, 1816; farmer; produce merchant. MIL.: col., Second IN Volunteer Regt., 1846, brig. gen., 1846; brev. maj. gen., 1847; discharged, 1848. REL.: R.C. RES.: Roseburg, OR.

LANE, MARK. b. Feb 24, 1927, New York, NY; par. Harry Arnold and Elizabeth (Brown) Lane; m. Anne-Lise Dabelsteen, Dec 23, 1966; c. Anne-Marie; Christina. EDUC.: Long Island U.; LL.B., Brooklyn Law School, 1951. POLIT. & GOV.: founder, New York Reform Democratic Movement; elected as a Democrat to NY State Assembly, 1961–63; candidate for Democratic nomination to U.S. House (NY), 1962; ***Peace and Freedom Party (New Party; New Politics Party; Freedom and Peace Party) candidate for vice presidency of the U.S., 1968***. BUS. & PROF.: atty.; admitted to NY Bar, 1951; law practice, New York, NY, 1952–62; founder, Mid-Harlem Community Parrish Narcotics Clinic, 1953; publisher, *Helping Hand,* 1971; publisher, *Citizens Quarterly,* 1975–; prof. of law, Catholic U. of America, 1975–. MIL.: U.S. Army, 1945–47. MEM.: East Harlem Reform Democratic Club (1959); Citizens Comm. of Inquiry (dir., 1975–); Wounded Knee Legal Defense–Offense Cmte. (founder, 1973); The Covered Wagon, Mountain Home, ID (founder, 1971). WRITINGS: *Rush to Judgment* (1966); *A Citizen's Dissent* (1968); *Chicago Eye-Witness* (1969); *Arcadia* (1970); *Conversations with Americans* (1970); *Executive Action* (1973); "Rush to Judgment" (film, 1967). MISC.: exposed fallout shelter corruption in NY; caused defeat of NY Assembly Speaker Joe Carlino; arrested in Mississippi Freedom Ride, 1960; investigated Kennedy assassination with James Garrison, New Orleans district atty.; atty. for Mrs. Marguerite Oswald, mother of Lee Harvey Oswald; atty. for People's Temple; present at Jonestown, Guyana, during assassination of U.S. Rep. Leo Ryan and subsequent mass suicide, 1978. MAILING ADDRESS: 105 Second St., N.E., Washington, DC 20002.

LANG, LAWRENCE JOSEPH "LARRY." b. Jun 29, 1964, Sheffield, England; par. Frank Theodore and Pauline Mary (Maher) Lang; single. EDUC.: B.S.E.E., Duke U., 1986; M.S., Stanford U., 1987. POLIT. & GOV.: ***independent candidate for presidency of the U.S., 1988***. BUS. & PROF.: systems engineer, Bell Communications Research. MEM.: Amnesty International; A.C.L.U.; Sierra Club; N.S.P.E.; I.E.E.E. AWARDS: Angier Biddle Duke Memorial Scholar. REL.: Taoist. MAILING ADDRESS: 58 Hilltop Terrace, Red Bank, NJ 07701.

LANGDON, JOHN. b. Jun 26, 1741, Portsmouth, NH; d. Sep 18, 1819, Portsmouth, NH; par. John and Mary (Hall) Langdon; m. Elizabeth Sherburne, Feb 2, 1777; c. Elizabeth; John. EDUC.: Major Hale's Latin Grammar School, Portsmouth, NH. POLIT. & GOV.: elected member, NH Legislature, 1775–81, 1784, 1786–87, 1801–05 (Speaker, 1775, 1777–81, 1786–87, 1803–05); member, Continental Congress (NH), 1775, 1783–84; appointed agent, Continental Prizes (NH), 1776; candidate for gov. of NH, 1783, 1793, 1798, 1802, 1803, 1804; elected pres., state of NH, 1785–88; delegate, U.S. Constitutional Convention, 1787; signer of Constitution of the U.S., 1787; elected as a Democrat to U.S. Senate (NH), 1789–1801 (pres. pro tempore); elected as a Democrat to gov. of NH, 1805–09, 1810–11; ***candidate for Democrat-Republican nomination to vice presidency of the U.S., 1808; received 9 electoral votes for vice presidency of the U.S., 1808***; appointed U.S. sec. of the navy, 1811 (declined); ***Democratic-Republican candidate for vice presidency of the U.S., 1812 (declined)***. BUS. & PROF.: capt., cargo vessels, 1763; merchant. MIL.: commander, Company at Saratoga, New York, and Rhode Island, Revolutionary War; aided in seizure and removal of munitions from Portsmouth Fort, 1774. MEM.: NH Bible Soc. (pres.). RES.: Portsmouth, NH.

LANGER, WILLIAM. b. Sep 30, 1886, Everest, ND; d. Nov 8, 1959, Washington, DC; par. Frank J. and Mary (Weber) Langer; m. Lyddia Cady, Feb 26, 1918; c. Emma Bulkley (Mrs. J. Peter Shaeffer); Lydia (Mrs. D. King Irwin); Mary Erskine (Mrs. Franklyn Gokey); Cornelia Lyndon (Mrs. Kenneth Noland). EDUC.: LL.B., U. of ND, 1906; A.B., Columbia U., 1910. POLIT. & GOV.: state's atty., Morton Cty., ND, 1914–16; elected as a Republican to atty. gen. of ND, 1916–20; legal adviser, Council of Defense, WWI; co-mgr., Hiram Johnson for President Campaign, 1920; Republican candidate for gov. of ND, 1920; member, ND Campaign Cmte., Sen. Robert M. La Follette for President Campaign, 1924; elected as a Republican to gov. of ND, 1933–34 (removed by Supreme Court of ND), 1937–39; candidate for Republican nomination to U.S. Senate (ND), 1938; independent candidate for U.S. Senate (ND), 1938; elected as a Republican to U.S. Senate (ND), 1941–59; ***candidate for Prohibition Party nomination to presidency of the U.S., 1956; Pioneer Party candidate for presidency of the U.S., 1956***. BUS. & PROF.: atty.; admitted to ND Bar, 1911; law practice, Mandan, ND, 1911–14; law practice, Bismarck, ND, 1916–59. MEM.: Sigma Chi. MISC.: only person ever arrested in any English-speaking country for filing an affidavit of prejudice against a judge; adopted by Sioux Indians and given name of "Mahto." RES.: Wheatland, ND.

LANGHAM, CECIL L. POLIT. & GOV.: candidate for Democratic nomination to gov. of GA, 1962; ***candidate for Democratic nomination to vice presidency of the U.S., 1972; candidate for American Independent Party nomination to presidency of the U.S., 1976***. RES.: Warrenton, GA.

LANYHOW, PAUL T. POLIT. & GOV.: ***independent candidate for presidency of the U.S., 1976***. MISC.: pseudonym for unknown candidate. MAILING ADDRESS: unknown.

LaPLANT, VIVIAN. POLIT. & GOV.: ***candidate for Republican nomination to presidency of the U.S., 1972***. MAILING ADDRESS: 1235 La Sombra Court, El Cajon, CA.

LAQUE, HENRY. POLIT. & GOV.: ***independent candidate for presidency of the U.S., 1984***. MAILING ADDRESS: Greensboro, NC.

LARDNER, RINGGOLD WILMER "RING." b. Mar 6, 1885, Niles, MI; d. Sep 25, 1933, East

Hampton, NY; par. Henry and Lena Bogardus (Phillips) Lardner; m. Ellis Abbott, Jun 28, 1911; c. John Abbott; James Phillips; Ringgold Wilmer, Jr.; David Ellis. EDUC.: Niles (MI) H.S., 1901; Armour Inst. of Technology, 1901–02. POLIT. & GOV.: ***candidate for Democratic nomination to presidency of the U.S., 1920***. BUS. & PROF.: writer; reporter, *South Bend (IN) Times*, 1905–07; sports writer, *Chicago (IL) Inter-Ocean*; sports writer, *Chicago Examiner*; sports writer, *Chicago Tribune*, 1907–10, 1913–19; ed., *Sporting News*, 1910–11; sports writer, *Boston (MA) American*, 1911; sports writer, *Chicago American*, 1911–12; sports writer, *Chicago Examiner*, 1912–13; writer, Bell Syndicate, 1919–33. WRITINGS: *Bib Ballads* (1915); *You Know Me, Al* (1915); *Gullible's Travels* (1917); *Own Your Own Home* (1917); *Treat 'Em Rough* (1918); *The Real Dope* (1918); *My Four Weeks in France* (1918); *The Young Immigrants* (1919); *Symptoms of Being 35* (1921); *The Big Town* (1921); *How To Write Short Stories* (1924); *What of It?* (1925); *The Lost Nest* (1926); *The Story of a Wonder Man* (1927); *Round Up* (1929); *June Moon* (play, with George S. Kaufman, 1929); *First and Last* (1934). MEM.: Republican Party. REL.: Episc. RES.: East Hampton, NY.

LA RIVA, GLORIA ESTELLA. b. 1955, Albuquerque, NM. EDUC.: Brandeis U. POLIT. & GOV.: Workers World Party candidate for mayor of San Francisco, CA, 1983; ***Workers World Party candidate for vice presidency of the U.S., 1984, 1988; Workers World Party candidate for presidency of the U.S., 1992***. BUS. & PROF.: typesetter, San Francisco, 1981–. MEM.: Rochester People's Energy Cmte. (organizer); People's Anti-War Mobilization (organizer); Chicano Moratorium March (organizer, 1983); Bay Area Typographical Union Local 21. MAILING ADDRESS: 3181 Mission, #29, San Francisco, CA 94110.

LAROUCHE, LYNDON HERMYLE, JR. (aka LYN MARCUS). b. Sep 8, 1922, Rochester, NH; par. Lyndon Hermyle and Jesse (Weir) Larouche; m. Janice L. (divorced); m. 2d, Helga Zepp, Dec 29, 1977; c. Daniel. EDUC.: grad., Lynn (MA) English H.S., 1940; Northeastern U., 1941–42, 1946–47. POLIT. & GOV.: member, Communist Party; member, Socialist Workers Party, 1948–60; founder, U.S. Labor Party, 1973; ***U.S. Labor Party candidate for presidency of the U.S., 1976, 1980***; chm., U.S. Labor Party, 1977–; ***candidate for Democratic nomination to presidency of the U.S., 1980, 1984, 1988, 1992; independent Democratic candidate for presidency of the U.S., 1984, 1988***; independent Democratic candidate for U.S. House (VA), 1990; ***Freedom for LaRouche (Economic Recovery; Independent; Independents for LaRouche; Justice, Industry and Agriculture; Justice, Industry and Opportunity) Party candidate for presidency of the U.S., 1992***. BUS. & PROF.: vice pres., L. H. LaRouche Research (management consultants), 1953–66; consultant, footwear manufacturing; economist; computer analyst; lecturer; chief exec., *Executive Intelligence Review*, 1974–; editor-in-chief, *Campaigner*. MIL.: pfc, U.S. Army, 1944–45. MEM.: National Caucus of Labor Cmtes. (chm.); Fusion Energy Fund; Students for a Democratic Soc.; National Democratic Policy Cmte.; New Solidarity Press Service; Club of Life (trustee); Schiller Inst. (advisory board, 1983–); NRA (life member). WRITINGS: *Dialectical Economics* (1974); *How the International Development Bank Will Work* (1975); *Case of Walter Lippman* (1977); *Theory of the European Monetary Fund* (1978); *The Power of Reason* (1978); *Will the Soviets Rule During the 1980s?* (1979); *What Every Conservative Should Know About Communism* (1980); *Operation Juarez* (1982); *Alto al genocido del Club de roma!* (1983); *A Fifty-Year Development Plan for the Indian-Pacific Oceans Basin* (1983); *Imperialism: The Final Stage of Bolshevism* (1983); *La Bomba Economics Mundial* (1983); *No Limits to Growth* (1984); *So You Wish to Learn All About Economics?* (1984); *LaRouche Warns of Economic Blowout; Leading Economist LaRouche Proposes Emergency Action Against U.S. Banking Collapse; The Power of Reason: 1988* (1987); *The Science of Christian Economy* (1991). REL.: Humanist (nee Soc. of Friends). MISC.: formerly known as Lyn Marcus; tried for credit card fraud, Boston, MA, 1987–88; convicted and imprisoned. MAILING ADDRESS: Route 1, Box 284, Round Hill, VA 22141.

LARSEN, PETER DAVID. b. Nov 15, 1943, Hilo, HI; par. David Wood and Shirley Ann (Shaw) Larsen; m. Linda Kay Larsen, 1965; m. 2d, Kathleen Hammonds, 1979; c. Kristin Wood; Paul LaForce; Megen Anne; Erin Lehua. EDUC.: The Gunnery School, Washington, CT, 1962; B.A., Dennison U., 1966. POLIT. & GOV.: Libertarian Party candidate for U.S. House (HI), 1978; ***candidate for Libertarian Party nomination to presidency of the U.S., 1980; candidate for Libertarian Party nomination to vice presidency of the U.S., 1980***. BUS. & PROF.: tin mine mgr., Malaysia, 1970–72; stockbroker, 1972–74; small business owner, real estate broker, 1974–; involved in water purification projects. MIL.: ATR 2, U.S. Navy, 1967–70. MEM.: Pacific Club. REL.: Congregationalist. MAILING ADDRESS: 4614 Kilauea Ave., Honolulu, HI 96816.

LARSEN, SCOTTY W. m. Shirley L. Larsen. POLIT. & GOV.: ***candidate for Democratic nomination to presidency of the U.S., 1980***. MAILING ADDRESS: 3010 Rose, Eau Claire, WI 54701.

LARSON, CHRISTIAN F. POLIT. & GOV.: ***American Party of New Jersey candidate for presidency of the U.S., 1976 (withdrew)***. BUS. & PROF.: fireman. MAILING ADDRESS: 464 Lawrie St., Perth Amboy, NJ 08861.

LARSON, REED EUGENE. b. Sep 27, 1922, Kensington, KS; par. George Christian and Edith Hazel (Whitney) Larson; m. Marjorie Jeanne Hess, Aug 31, 1947; c. Patricia Kay; Barbara Ann; Marcia Lynn. EDUC.: KS Wesleyan U., 1940–41; OH State U., 1943–44; B.S., KS State U., 1947. POLIT. & GOV.: ***candidate for Democratic nomination to presidency of the U.S., 1976 (declined)***. BUS. & PROF.: design engineer, Stein

Labs, Atchison, KS, 1947–48; processing engineer, Coleman Co., Wichita, KS, 1948–54; exec. vice pres., Kansans for Right to Work, Wichita, 1954–58; exec. vice pres., National Right to Work Cmte., Washington, DC, 1959–76, pres., 1976–. MIL.: U.S. Army, 1943–46. MEM.: National Right to Work Cmte.; National Right to Work Legal Defense Foundation (exec. vice pres., 1968–73, pres., 1973–); American Soc. of Assn. Executives; Farm Bureau; American National Cattlemen's Assn.; U.S. C. of C. AWARDS: Seldon Waldo Award, U.S. Junior C. of C., 1956; Silver Anvil Award, Public Relations Soc. of America, 1966. REL.: Bapt. MAILING ADDRESS: 6149 Beachway Dr., Falls Church, VA 22041.

LASITER, S. H. POLIT. & GOV.: ***independent candidate for presidency of the U.S., 1908***. RES.: CO.

LATCHFORD, VINCENT A. POLIT. & GOV.: ***candidate for Republican nomination to presidency of the U.S., 1992***. MAILING ADDRESS: Brick, NJ.

LATHAM, JOHN HUGH. b. 1896, McKinney, TX; single. EDUC.: McKinney (TX) H.S., 2½ years. POLIT. & GOV.: candidate for Democratic nomination to U.S. House (IN), 1958, 1962, 1966, 1968, 1970; ***candidate for Democratic nomination to presidency of the U.S., 1960, 1964***. BUS. & PROF.: cotton picker; carpenter; resident, Old Soldiers' Home, Leavenworth, KS, 1932–33; gas and oil pipeline fitter; farmer, Rockville, IN. MIL.: 3d Cavalry, U.S. Army, WWI. MEM.: American Legion; Fraternal Order of Eagles. REL.: Bapt. RES.: Rockville, IN.

LAUGHLIN, THOMAS ROBERT "TOM." b. 1931; m. Delores Taylor. POLIT. & GOV.: ***candidate for Democratic nomination to presidency of the U.S., 1992***. BUS. & PROF.: producer; actor; owner, Montessori School; psychology instructor, U. of CO, 1977. MOTION PICTURE CREDITS: "The Proper Time" (1958); "Born Losers" (1967); "Billy Jack" (1971); "The Trial of Billy Jack" (1974); "The Master Gunfighter"; "Billy Jack Goes to Washington" (not released); "The Return of Billy Jack" (1985; not released). WRITINGS: *The Mind and Cancer* (with James P. Moran). MAILING ADDRESS: 12953 Marlboro St., Los Angeles, CA 90049.

LAUSCHE, FRANK JOHN. b. Nov 14, 1895, Cleveland, OH; d. Apr 21, 1990, Cleveland, OH; par. Louis and Frances (Milavec) Lausche; m. Jane O. Sheal, May 17, 1928. EDUC.: Central Inst. Preparatory School, 1915–16; LL.B., John Marshall Law School, 1920. POLIT. & GOV.: Democratic candidate for OH State House, 1922, 1924; appointed and subsequently elected judge, Municipal Court, Cleveland, OH, 1932–37; elected judge, Cuyahoga Cty. (OH) Court of Common Pleas, 1937–41; elected as a Democrat to mayor of Cleveland, OH, 1941–44; elected as a Democrat to gov. of OH, 1945–46, 1949–56; Democratic candidate for gov. of OH, 1946; ***candidate for Democratic nomination to presidency of the U.S., 1956; candidate for Republican nomination to presidency of the U.S., 1956***; elected as a Democrat to U.S. Senate (OH), 1957–69; candidate for Democratic nomination to U.S. Senate (OH), 1968. BUS. & PROF.: employee, family restaurant, Cleveland, OH; street lamp lighter, Cleveland; minor league baseball third baseman, Duluth, MN, 1916; minor league baseball player, Lawrence, MA, 1917; semiprofessional baseball player, Cleveland; atty.; admitted to OH Bar, 1920; assoc., Locher, Green and Woods (law firm), Cleveland, 1920–32; law practice, Cleveland, 1947–48. MIL.: 2d lt., U.S. Army, 1917–19. MEM.: Delta Theta Phi; Phi Sigma Kappa; Omicron Delta Kappa; Cuyahoga Cty. Bar Assn.; Cleveland Bar Assn.; City Club of Cleveland. AWARDS: Centennial Award, Northwestern U.; Vet Award, Joint Veterans Cmte. of Cuyahoga Cty., 1958; Good Citizens Medal, SAR; Certificate of Merit, American Veterans of World War II. HON. DEG.: LL.M., John Marshall Law School, 1936, LL.D.; LL.D., Akron U.; LL.D., Ashland Coll.; LL.D., Defiance Coll.; LL.D., Denison U.; LL.D., Kenyon Coll.; LL.D., LeMoyne Coll.; LL.D., Marietta Coll.; LL.D., Miami U.; LL.D., Oberlin Coll.; Dr. of Humanities, OH Coll. of Chiropody; LL.D., OH Wesleyan U.; LL.D., OH U.; Dr. Public Service, Rio Grande Coll.; Dr. of Commercial Science, Tiffin Business Coll.; LL.D., Washington and Jefferson Coll.; LL.D., Western Reserve U. REL.: R.C. RES.: Gates Mills, OH.

LAUVER, DENNIS. POLIT. & GOV.: ***independent candidate for presidency of the U.S., 1980***. MAILING ADDRESS: 711 Southwest Tenth St., Willmar, MN 56201.

LAW, GEORGE. b. Oct 25, 1806, Jackson, NY; d. Nov 18, 1881, New York, NY; par. John Law; m. Miss Anderson, 1834; c. one. POLIT. & GOV.: ***candidate for American (Know-Nothing) Party nomination to presidency of the U.S., 1856***. BUS. & PROF.: construction worker, Dismal Swamp, Morris and Harlem Canals; construction worker, Delaware and Hudson Canal; construction contractor, Delaware and Hudson Canal, 1827; contractor, Croton Water Works, 1837; contractor, High Bridge on Harlem River, 1839; pres., Dry Dock Bank, 1842; owner, Harlem and Mohawk R.R.; cofounder, U.S. Mail Steamship Co., 1847 (business divided with Pacific Mail Steamship Co., 1851); pres., Eighth Avenue R.R., New York, NY, 1854–81; pres., Ninth Avenue R.R., New York, 1859; owner, Brooklyn and Staten Island Ferry Lines. RES.: New York, NY.

LAWRENCE, ABBOTT. b. Dec 16, 1792, Groton, MA; d. Aug 18, 1855, Boston, MA; par. Deacon Samuel and Susanna (Parker) Lawrence; m. Katherine Bigelow, Jun 28, 1819; c. five sons; two daughters. EDUC.: Groton Acad. POLIT. & GOV.: elected member, Common Council, Boston, MA, 1831; elected as a Whig to U.S. House (MA), 1835–37, 1839–41; boundary commissioner of MA, 1842; delegate, Whig Party National Convention, 1844; presidential elector, Whig Party, 1844; ***candidate for Whig Party nomination to presidency of the U.S., 1848; candidate for Whig Party nomination to vice presidency of the U.S., 1848***; appointed U.S. minister to Great Britain, 1849–52. BUS. & PROF.: manufacturer; philanthropist; partner, A. and A. Lawrence (imports), Boston, 1814–55; owner, cotton mills, 1830; pres., Essex Co., 1844. MEM.: Harrisburg Commercial Convention (delegate, 1827); Harvard U. (overseer, 1854). HON. DEG.: LL.D., Harvard U., 1854. REL.: Unitarian. MISC.: a founder of Lawrence, MA, 1845; promoted construction of municipal water works, Boston, 1845; donated $50,000 for establishment of Lawrence Scientific School at Harvard U. (leaving an additional $50,000 endowment upon his death). RES.: Boston, MA.

LAWRY, SAMUEL WESLEY. married. POLIT. & GOV.: ***candidate for Republican nomination to presidency of the U.S., 1944***. BUS. & PROF.: window washer. RES.: Pasadena, CA.

LAXALT, PAUL DOMINIQUE. b. Aug 2, 1922, Reno, NV; par. Dominique and Theresa (Alpetche) Laxalt; m. Jackalyn Ross, Jun 23, 1946 (divorced); m. 2d, Carol Wilson, Jan 27, 1976; c. Gail; Sheila; John; Michelle; Kevin; Kathleen. EDUC.: Santa Clara U., 1940–43; B.S., LL.B., Denver U., 1949. POLIT. & GOV.: elected as a Republican to district atty., Ormsby Cty., NV, 1951–54; elected as a Republican to city atty., Carson City, NV, 1954–55; elected as a Republican to lt. gov. of NV, 1963–67; Republican candidate for U.S. Senate (NV), 1964; elected as a Republican to gov. of NV, 1967–71; delegate, Rep. Nat'l. Conv., 1968, 1976; elected as a Republican to U.S. Senate (NV), 1975–87; campaign mgr., Reagan for President Campaign, 1976, 1980; ***candidate for Republican nomination to vice presidency of the U.S., 1976, 1980; candidate for Republican nomination to presidency of the U.S., 1980 (declined), 1988 (withdrew)***; chm., Rep. Nat'l. Cmte., 1983–87. BUS. & PROF.: atty.; admitted to NV Bar, 1949; law practice, Carson City, 1949–; partner, Laxalt, Ross and Laxalt (law firm), Carson City, 1954–62; partner, Laxalt, Berry and Allison (law firm), Carson City, 1970–; pres., gen. mgr., Ormsby House Hotel and Casino, Carson City, 1972–. MEM.: ABA; American Legion; Eagles; VFW. REL.: R.C. MAILING ADDRESS: 1600 West King St., Carson City, NV 89701.

LEA, JOYCE PADGETT. POLIT. & GOV.: ***independent candidate for presidency of the U.S., 1988***. MAILING ADDRESS: One Wornall Point, KS City, MO 64112.

LEACH, STEPHEN EUGENE. b. Mar 5, 1968, York, PA; par. William Leroy, Jr. and Dejia Jane (Myers) Leach; single. EDUC.: grad., York (PA) H.S., 1986; Franklin and Marshall Coll. POLIT. & GOV.: ***independent candidate for presidency of the U.S., 1988***. BUS. & PROF.: student; artist; publisher, *Small Press Comix*. REL.: Lutheran. MISC.: semifinalist, National Merit Scholarships. MAILING ADDRESS: 6639 Colonial Ave., York, PA 17403.

LEARN, DALE HAROLD. b. Dec 8, 1897, Cresco, PA; d. Mar 16, 1976, East Stroudsburg, PA; par. Milton S. and Nettie (Bush) Learn; m. Anna Pauline Garrison, May 19, 1923; c. Alison M. (Mrs. Waun); Glenn W.; Clyde D. EDUC.: A.B., East Stroudsburg State Teachers Coll., 1916; A. M., Dickinson Coll., 1920; LL.B., Dickinson Law School. POLIT. & GOV.: Prohibition Party candidate for gov. of PA, 1942; Prohibition Party candidate for U.S. Senate (PA), 1946; ***candidate for Prohibition Party nomination to presidency of the U.S., 1948; Prohibition Party candidate for vice presidency of the U.S., 1948***; elected to Board of Directors, Stroud Township (PA) School District; sec., Borough of East Stroudsburg, PA. BUS. & PROF.: atty.; realtor, East Stroudsburg, 1923–73; dir., Securities Bank and Trust Co. MIL.: sgt., U.S. Army, WWI. MEM.: Veterans of World War I; Pocono Mountain Real Estate Board; Pocono Mountains C. of C. (exec. dir.; dir.); Pocono Forestry Assn. (pres.); East Stroudsburg Wednesday Prayer Breakfast Group; PA Real Estate Assn. (pres.; dir.); Monroe Cty. Real Estate Board (pres.); American Legion; Gideon Soc.; Kiwanis; Patriotic Order of Sons of America; Masons (32°); Phi Kappa Sigma; Monroe Cty. Hist. Soc.; Pennsylvania Soc. of New York; East Stroudsburg Teachers Coll. (trustee); PA State C. of C. (councilor); Monroe Cty. Sunday School Assn. (pres.; treas.); East Stroudsburg State Teachers Coll. Alumni Assn. (pres.); Monroe Cty. Insurance Assn. (pres.); Lehigh Valley Laymen's Assn. (pres.); National Real Estate Assn. (Taxation Cmte.); Red Cross (dir.); Community Chest (dir.); Monroe Cty. C. of C. (exec. sec.). AWARDS: Conservation Award, Pocono Forestry Assn., 1974. REL.: United Methodist Church. RES.: East Stroudsburg, PA.

LeBRETON, S. A. c. seven sons. POLIT. & GOV.: ***New National Government candidate for vice presidency of the U.S., 1972***. MAILING ADDRESS: unknown.

LEE, ARTHUR E. POLIT. & GOV.: western states vice chm., American Independent Party, 1980; ***candidate for American Independent Party nomination to vice presidency of the U.S., 1980***. MAILING ADDRESS: 4915 Samish Way, Bellingham, WA 98225.

LEE, HENRY. b. Feb 4, 1782, Beverly, MA; d. Feb 6, 1867, Boston, MA; par. Joseph and Elizabeth (Cabot) Lee; m. Mary Jackson, Jun 16, 1809; c. Henry; Francis L.; four others. EDUC.: Phillips Andover Acad. POLIT. & GOV.: delegate, Free Trade Convention, 1831; ***Independent Party candidate for vice presidency of the U.S., 1832; received 11 electoral votes as an independent for vice presidency of the U.S., 1832***; candidate for U.S. House (MA), 1850. BUS. & PROF.: partner, trading enterprise, Boston, MA, 1800–1811; lived in Calcutta, India, 1811–14. WRITINGS: *Report of a Committee Opposed to a Further Increase of Duties on Importations* (1827); *An Exposition of Evidence* (1832). MISC.: noted as free trade advocate, 1820–67. RES.: Boston, MA.

LEE, JOSEPH BRACKEN. b. Jan 7, 1899, Price, UT; par. Arthur James and Ida May (Leiter) Lee; m. Nellie Amelia Pace, Sep 20, 1920; m. 2d, Margaret Ethel Draper, Feb 23, 1928; c. Helen Virginia (Mrs. Harold A. Nelson); James Bracken; Margaret Jon (Mrs. Taylor); Richard Lewis. EDUC.: grad., Carbon Cty. (UT) H.S., 1917. POLIT. & GOV.: elected as a Republican to mayor of Price, UT, 1936–47; candidate for Republican nomination to gov. of UT, 1939, 1956; member, Utah Bond Drive Board, WWII; candidate for Republican nomination to U.S. House (UT), 1942; Republican candidate for gov. of UT, 1944; member, UT State Cmte. for Regulation of Electric Power, 1948; elected as a Republican to gov. of UT, 1949–57; independent candidate for gov. of UT, 1956; ***Constitution Party candidate for vice presidency of the U.S., 1956***; elected as a nonpartisan to mayor of Salt Lake City, UT, 1957–72; independent candidate for U.S. Senate (UT), 1958; ***Conservative Party of New Jersey candidate for presidency of the U.S., 1960 (withdrew)***; candidate for Republican nomination to U.S. Senate (UT), 1962. BUS. & PROF.: postal clerk, 1919; insurance agent, Equitable Insurance Agency, Price, UT, 1919–30, mgr. and owner, 1930–; dir., Equitable Finance Co.; dir., Time Finance Co.; publisher, *American Statesman*, 1959–. MIL.: pvt., sgt., Company C, 21st U.S. Infantry, 1917–19; 2d lt., U.S.A.R., 1919–35. MEM.: Carbon Cty. Associated Industries (pres.); Alta Club; Western Aviation Conference (dir.); American Legion; Boys Clubs of America (state chm.; national dir., 1960–); For America (chm., 1957–); National Cmte. to Repeal the 16th Amendment (dir.); Red Cross (chm., Carbon Cty., 1944–47); Utah Municipal League (pres., 1939–40); Carbon Water Conservancy District (sec., 1942–); Elks; Masons (32°; Shriner; knight commander of Court of Honor). AWARDS: Freedom Foundation Award, 1952; Tom McCoy Award, 1967; Award of Appreciation, gov. of Utah, 1972. REL.: Protestant (nee Church of Jesus Christ of Latter-Day Saints). MAILING ADDRESS: 2031 Laird Dr., Salt Lake City, UT.

LEE, RICHARD E. b. Jul 22, 1936, Alexandria, LA; par. George W. and Alice (O'Neal) Lee; m. Betty Lou Krist, Jan 26, 1957; c. Harold L.; Richard Mark; Robert C. EDUC.: B.S., LA Coll., 1961; LL.B., LA State U., 1964. POLIT. & GOV.: appointed member, Rapids Parrish (LA) Airport Authority (chm.); elected as a Democrat to judge, city court, Prineville, LA, 1974–; ***candidate for Populist Party nomination to presidency of the U.S., 1984***. BUS. & PROF.: atty.; admitted to LA Bar, 1964; law practice, Alexandria, LA, 1964–; law practice, Prineville, 1964–. MIL.: seaman, U.S. Navy, 1954–55. MEM.: LA State Bar Assn.; Lions; Oliver Masonic Lodge; El Karubah Shriners Temple; Alexandria Shrine Club; Elks; Ward Tend Dixie Youth Baseball. REL.: Methodist (board member). MAILING ADDRESS: P.O. Box 506, Prineville, LA 71360.

LEE, RICHARD EVERETT. b. Mar 25, 1918, Washington, DC; par. Alfred Rogers and Esther Gilbert (Cristy) Lee; single. EDUC.: A.B., U. of MD, 1939; B.D., VA Theological Seminary, 1944. POLIT. & GOV.: candidate for Democratic nomination to U.S. House (MD), 1946, 1970, 1976; ***candidate for Democratic nomination to presidency of the U.S., 1968, 1980***. BUS. & PROF.: religious worker; schoolteacher; real estate salesman; home improvement salesman; office worker; employee, Library of Congress, 1940, 1945. MEM.: BSA (Eagle Scout; scoutmaster); church groups. REL.: Episc. (usher; vestryman; Sunday school teacher). MAILING ADDRESS: Box 381, College Park, MD 20740.

LEE, ROBERT KIPLEY "KIP." b. Mar 17, 1954, Culver City, CA; par. Robert and Florence Aylene (Wyly) Lee; single. EDUC.: grad., Shasta H.S., Shasta Cty., CA, 1972; A.A., Shasta Coll., 1988; CA State U., Chico, CA. POLIT. & GOV.: candidate for dir., Redding (CA) School Board, 1981, 1985; member, Legal Compliance Cmte., CA State Dept. of Education, 1981–82; candidate for sheriff, Shasta Cty., 1982; candidate for Redding City city clerk and treas., 1986, 1988; ***candidate for Democratic nomination to presidency of the U.S., 1988, 1992; candidate for Libertarian Party nomination to presidency of the U.S., 1992***; appointed member, Shasta Cty. Mental Health Advisory Board, 1992–95. BUS. & PROF.: service station attendant; busboy; sander; mover; stocker; maintenance aide; field technician; security guard. MIL.: E/3, U.S. Navy, 1972. MEM.: BSA (Life Scout). AWARDS: Gold Quill Award, BSA. WRITINGS: *Space Fleet Command: A Technical Manual #57698* (1981). REL.: New Age. MAILING ADDRESS: 1797 Kenyon Dr., Redding, CA 96001.

LEE, WILLIAM FRANCIS "SPACEMAN BILL," III. b. Dec 28, 1946, Burbank, CA. POLIT. & GOV.: ***independent candidate for presidency of the U.S., 1988***. BUS. & PROF.: major league baseball player; pitcher, Boston Red Sox, 1969–75. MISC.: lifetime earned run average, 3.40; lifetime batting average, .133. MAILING ADDRESS: General Delivery, Greensboro, VT 05841.

LEEKE, GRANVILLE BOOKER. b. Feb 23, 1889, Philadelphia, PA; d. May 29, 1955, South Bend, IN; par. William and Lucretia (Sheets) Leeke; m. Grace Mabel Matthews; c. Wallace N.; Evelyn G.; Wilma M.; Gladys M.; Laura L.; Dorothy L. Edwards. EDUC.: MD Agricultural Coll.; PA State U. POLIT. & GOV.: sec., Indiana Greenback Party; ***Greenback Party candidate for vice presidency of the U.S., 1948***. BUS. & PROF.: farmer, South Bend, IN; author; employee, maintenance dept., South Bend Lathe Works. MEM.: Direct Credits New

World Exchange (state leader). WRITINGS: poems in various magazines. REL.: Independent Fundamental Churches of America. RES.: South Bend, IN.

LEGRAND, LAURIE. POLIT. & GOV.: ***Mature Minority candidate for presidency of the U.S., 1988***. MEM.: Mature Minority (dir.). MAILING ADDRESS: c/o Mature Minority, 123 West Gwinnett St., Savannah, GA 31401.

LEHMAN, HERBERT HENRY. b. Mar 28, 1878, New York, NY; d. Dec 5, 1963, New York, NY; par. Mayer and Babette (Newgrass) Lehman; m. Edith Altschul, Apr 28, 1910; c. Peter Geraldi; John Robert; Hilda Jane Wise (Mrs. Eugene Paul). EDUC.: Sachs Collegiate Inst.; B.A., Williams Coll., 1899, M.A., 1921. POLIT. & GOV.: delegate, Dem. Nat'l. Conv., 1928, 1932, 1936, 1940, 1944, 1948, 1952, 1956; chm., Finance Cmte., Dem. Nat'l. Cmte., 1928; elected as a Democrat to lt. gov. of NY, 1929–33; elected as a Democrat to gov. of NY, 1933–42; ***candidate for Democratic nomination to presidency of the U.S., 1940***; appointed dir., Foreign Relief and Rehabilitation, U.S. Dept. of State, 1942; appointed dir. gen., UNRRA, 1943–46; Democratic candidate for U.S. Senate (NY), 1946; elected as a Democrat to U.S. Senate (NY), 1949–57. BUS. & PROF.: employee, vice pres., treas., J. Spencer Turner Co. (textile manufacturers), New York, NY, 1906; partner, Lehman Brothers (banking house), New York, 1908–29. MIL.: capt., col., U.S. Army, 1917–19; Distinguished Service Medal. MEM.: Fund for the Republic (dir.); Jewish Theological Seminary (trustee); Inst. for Advanced Study (trustee); New York Foundation (vice pres.); Hebrew Sheltering Guardian Soc. (trustee); Bureau of Jewish Social Research, New York Foundation (trustee); Joint Distribution Cmte., Palestine Economic Corp. (vice chm.); New York City Welfare Council (dir.); Henry Street Settlement (trustee); BSA (dir.; National Council); Organization for Rehabilitation Through Training Federation (dir.); American Assn. for the United Nations (dir.); Franklin Delano Roosevelt Foundation (dir., 1948); Council on Foreign Relations; National Conference of Christians and Jews; Phi Beta Kappa (hon.); Phi Gamma Delta; National Democratic Club; New York City Welfare Council (dir.); Surprise Lake Camp, NAACP (dir.); Williams Club; Bankers Club; Century Club; Harmonie Club; Fort Orange Club; Army and Navy Club. AWARDS: Presidential Medal of Freedom (1963); Sidney Hillman Foundation Award; Award, Four Freedoms Foundation. HON. DEG.: 21 honorary degrees including an LL.D., Williams Coll., 1929; LL.D., Alfred U., 1933; LL.D., NY U., 1933; LL.D., Oglethorpe U., 1933; LL.D., Yeshivah Coll., 1933; LL.D., Hamilton Coll., 1934; LL.D., St. Bonaventure Coll., 1934. REL.: Jewish. RES.: New York, NY.

LELA, WAYNE ANTHONY. b. Sep 7, 1949, Chicago, IL; par. John and Lillian (Szwed) Lela; single. EDUC.: B.A., Saint May's Coll., Winona, MN, 1971. POLIT. & GOV.: ***Open Party candidate for presidency of the U.S., 1984***. BUS. & PROF.: unemployed; writer. REL.: none (nee R.C.). MISC.: committed to IL State Mental Hospital, 1973–74; opponent of "sexual perverts." MAILING ADDRESS: 936 Warren Ave., Downers Grove, IL 60515.

LEMAY, CURTIS EMERSON. b. Nov 15, 1906, Columbus, OH; d. Oct 1, 1990, March Air Force Base, CA; par. Erving and Arizona Dove (Carpenter) LeMay; m. Helen Estelle Maitland, Jun 19, 1934; c. Patricia Jane. EDUC.: Air Corps Primary Flying School and Advanced Flying School, 1929; B.C.E., OH State U., 1932; Air Corps Tactical School, 1939; C. W. Post Coll. POLIT. & GOV.: ***candidate for Republican nomination to presidency of the U.S., 1968; American Independent (American; Courage; George Wallace; Independent) Party candidate for vice presidency of the U.S., 1968***. BUS. & PROF.: soldier; businessman; chm. of the board, Networks Electronic Corp., 1965–. MIL.: U.S. Army and U.S. Air Force, 1928–65; commissioned 2d lt., 62d F.A., U.S. Army, 1928; 2d lt., Air Reserves, 1929, 1st lt., 1935, capt., 1940, maj., 1941, lt. col., col., 1942, brig. gen., 1943, maj. gen., 1944, gen., 1951–55; commander in chief, Strategic Air Command, 1948–57; vice chief of staff, U.S. Air Force, 1957–61; chief of staff, U.S. Air Force, 1961–65; Distinguished Service Cross; Distinguished Service Medal with 3 Oak Leaf Clusters; Air Medal with 3 Clusters; Harmon Trophy; Distinguished Flying Cross with 2 Clusters; Silver Star; Presidential Unit Citation. MEM.: Sigma Tau; Tau Beta Pi; Theta Tau; Masons (33°); National Geographic Soc. (life trustee). AWARDS: Legion of Honor (commander); Mackay Trophy; Order of the Ouissam Alaouite Cherifien (Morocco); Medal for Humane Action; Croix de Guerre with Palm (Belgium); Order of the Southern Cross (Brazil); Distinguished Flying Cross (Great Britain); Order of the Patriotic War (U.S.S.R.); Gen. William Mitchell Memorial Trophy, American Legion, 1954; Order of Service Merit, First Class (Korea); Most Exalted Order of the White Elephant (Thailand); Cross of the Phoenix (Greece); Robert J. Collier Trophy. Hon Deg.: LL.D., Bradley U.; E.D., Case Inst. of Technology; LL.D., John Carroll U.; LL.D., Kenyon Coll.; D.Sc., OH State U.; D.Sc., Tufts U.; LL.D., U. of Akron; LL.D., U. of Southern CA; D.Sc., U. of WV. WRITINGS: *Mission with LeMay* (with MacKinlay Kantor, 1965); *America in Danger*. RES.: Los Angeles, CA.

LEMEN, JOHN LELAND. b. Nov 30, 1924, Dana-Newport, IN; par. John Leland and Elsie Bellwood (Wise) Lemen; m. (divorced); c. Arlan L. "Dan"; Donald R.; Marcia Kay Wade. EDUC.: Gerstmeyer Technical School; B.S., M.S., IN State U., 1961. POLIT. & GOV.: ***candidate for Democratic nomination to presidency of the U.S., 1988***. BUS. & PROF.: manufacturer; jeweler, 20 years; teacher, 20 years. MIL.: CM2/ C, 69th U.S. Navy (Seabees), WWII. MEM.: National Honor Soc.; IN State Teachers Assn.; American Federation of Teachers; Disabled American Veterans; Phi Delta Kappa; NEA; NRA; Free and Accepted Masons; Epsilon Pi Tau. AWARDS: six track letters. REL.: God (respect for all faiths). MAILING ADDRESS: Box 414, Clark Fork, IN 83811.

LEMKE, WILLIAM FREDERICK. b. Aug 13, 1878, Albany, MN; d. May 30, 1950, Fargo, ND; par. Frederick William and Julia Anna (Kleir) Lemke; m. Isabella Mary McIntyre, Apr 16, 1910; c. William Frederick, Jr.; Robert McIntyre; Mary Eleanor (Mrs. Robert Clyde Ely). EDUC.: grad., Cando H.S., 1898; B.A., U. of ND, 1902, student, 1902–03; Georgetown U., 1903–04; LL.B., Yale U., 1905. POLIT. & GOV.: chm., ND State Republican Central Cmte., 1916–20; elected as a Republican to atty. gen. of ND, 1921 (recalled); Republican candidate for gov. of ND, 1922; Farmer-Labor Party candidate for U.S. Senate (ND), 1926; elected as a Republican to U.S. House (ND), 1933–41, 1943–50; ***Union Party candidate for presidency of the U.S., 1936***; Republican candidate for U.S. House (ND), 1940 (withdrew); independent candidate for U.S. Senate (ND), 1940. BUS. & PROF.: founder, Black Earth Land and Loan Co., 1906, pres., 1906–50; founder, pres., Land Finance Co., 1907–50; atty.; admitted to ND Bar, 1905; partner, Robinson and Lemke (law firm), Fargo, ND, 1905–23; partner, Lemke and Weaver (law firm), Fargo, 1923–50. MEM.: Phi Delta Theta; Eugene Field Soc.; Equity Cooperative Exchange (counsel); National Non-Partisan League (exec. cmte., 1917–21); ND Farmers' Union (counsel); ND Bar Assn.; U. of ND Alumni Assn.; Yale Alumni Assn.; Georgetown U. Alumni Assn.; America First Cmte. WRITINGS: *Crimes Against Mexico* (1915); *You and Your Money* (1938). REL.: Lutheran. RES.: Fargo, ND.

LeMOYNE, FRANCIS JULIUS. b. Sep 4, 1798, Washington, PA; d. Oct 14, 1879, Washington, PA; par. John Julius and Nancy (McCully) LeMoyne; m. Madelaine Romaine Bureau, May 1823; c. Charlotte (Mrs. William L. Wills); Ann (Mrs. C. V. Harding); John; Romaine Wade; Jane; Madelaine; Julius; Francis. EDUC.: grad., Washington Coll., 1815; Jefferson Medical Coll., 1818–20; M.D., U. of PA, 1823. POLIT. & GOV.: ***Liberty Party candidate for vice presidency of the U.S., 1840 (declined)***; Liberty Party candidate for gov. of PA, 1841, 1844, 1847. BUS. & PROF.: physician; medical practice, Washington, PA, 1822–79; farmer, Washington; rancher, Washington; abolitionist. MEM.: Cleveland Anti-Slavery Convention (pres., 1851); Washington and Jefferson Coll. (trustee, 1830–79); Washington Anti-Slavery Soc.; Washington Female Seminary (trustee, 1836); Farmers' Club; Citizens Library Assn. (pres., Board of Trustees, 1870–79). REL.: nonsectarian (nee Presb.). MISC.: active in underground railroad; pioneer in advocating cremation, 1876–79; built first crematory in U.S., 1876; founded professorships at Washington and Jefferson Coll., 1872, 1879; endowed LeMoyne Normal Inst. for Negroes, Memphis, TN. RES.: Washington, PA.

LENNANE, JAMES PATRICK. b. MI; m. Susan Lennane; c. Jamey; three others. EDUC.: B.A., M.A., U. of Detroit; LL.D., St. Joseph's Coll., Rensselear, IN. POLIT. & GOV.: ***candidate for Republican Nomination to presidency of the U.S., 1992***. BUS. & PROF.: businessman; founder, chm. of the board, System Integrators, Inc.; international trade exec.; FAA certified jet pilot. MAILING ADDRESS: c/o Bette M. Byouk, 4820 Bayshore Dr., Suite D, Naples, FL 33962.

LENROOT, IRVINE LUTHER. b. Jan 31, 1869, Superior, WI; d. Jan 26, 1949, Washington, DC; par. Lars and Frederika Regina (Larson) Lenroot; m. Clara Pamela Clough McCoy, Jan 22, 1890; m. 2d, Elenore von Eltz, Feb 9, 1943; c. Katharine Fredrica; Dorothy Clugh (Mrs. Paul Walton Black; Mrs. Robert Blomberg). EDUC.: Parsons Business Coll. POLIT. & GOV.: official reporter, Superior Court of Douglas Cty., WI, 1893–1906; chm., Republican City Cmte.; chm., Douglas Cty. Republican Central Cmte.; delegate, WI State Republican Convention, 1900, 1902, 1904; elected as a Republican to WI State House, 1901–07 (Speaker, 1903–07); Republican candidate for U.S. Senate (WI), 1907; delegate, Rep. Nat'l. Conv., 1908; elected as a Republican to U.S. House (WI), 1909–18; elected as a Republican to U.S. Senate (WI), 1918–27; ***candidate for Republican nomination to presidency of the U.S., 1920; candidate for Republican nomination to vice presidency of the U.S., 1920***; candidate for Republican nomination to U.S. Senate (WI), 1926; appointed member, Anglo-American Conciliation Comm., 1927–35; appointed judge, U.S. Court of Customs and Patent Appeals, 1929–44. BUS. & PROF.: stenographer, law firm, 1889; court reporter, 1893; atty.; admitted to WI Bar, 1897; law practice, Superior, WI; law practice, Washington, DC, 1927–39. MEM.: ABA; Masons; Knights of Pythias; Burning Tree Country Club. HON. DEG.: LL.D., Temple U., 1918; LL.D., George Washington U., 1920; LL.D., OH Northern U., 1921. REL.: Congregationalist. RES.: Superior, WI.

LENTZ, EDWIN H. POLIT. & GOV.: ***independent candidate for presidency of the U.S., 1908***. RES.: NH.

LENTZ, JOHN JACOB. b. Jan 27, 1856, St. Clairsville, OH; d. Jul 27, 1931, Columbus, OH; par. Simon and Anna (Myer) Lentz; married; c. John Jacob, Jr. EDUC.: grad., National Normal U., 1877; U. of Wooster, 1877–78; A.B., U. of MI, 1882; LL.B., Columbia U., 1883. POLIT. & GOV.: elected as a Democrat to U.S. House (OH), 1897–1901; ***candidate for People's Party nomination to vice presidency of the U.S., 1900***; Democratic candidate for U.S. House (OH), 1900; delegate, Dem. Nat'l. Conv., 1908; pres., "Fraternal Day," Panama-Pacific Exposition, 1915; appointed member, Special Immigration Comm., U.S. Dept. of Labor, 1924. BUS. & PROF.: schoolteacher, 4 years; atty.; admitted to OH Bar, 1883; law practice, Columbus, OH, 1883–1915; partner, Nash and Lentz (law firm), Columbus, 1887–1904; insurance broker; pres., American Insurance Union, 1894–1931; built American Insurance Union citadel. MEM.: Mooseheart (gov.); Moose War Relief Comm. (1918); C. of C. of the U.S.; American Fraternal Congress (councilor); OH U. at Athens (trustee). WRITINGS: *Thomas Jefferson, The Radical* (1905). RES.: Columbus, OH.

LEONARD, ADNA BRADWAY. b. Aug 2, 1837, Berlin Township, OH; d. Apr 21, 1916, Brooklyn, NY; par. John and Nancy (Davis) Leonard; m. Caroline Amelia Kaiser, Feb 19, 1861; c. Adna Wright; Lena (Mrs. John F. Fisher); five others. EDUC.: A.B., Mount Union Coll., A.M., LL.D.; D.D., New Orleans U. POLIT. & GOV.: Prohibition Party candidate for gov. of OH, 1885; ***candidate for Prohibition Party nomination to presidency of the U.S., 1892***. BUS. & PROF.: ordained minister, Methodist Episcopal Church, 1860; pastor, Central Church, Springfield, OH, 1885; presiding elder, OH Conference, Methodist Episcopal Church; corresponding sec., Board of Foreign Missions, Methodist Episcopal Church, 1888–1912, sec. emeritus, 1912–16; missionary, Japan, China, and Korea, 1893. WRITINGS: *The Stone of Help: An Autobiography* (1915). REL.: Methodist Episc. Church. RES.: Springfield, OH.

LEONARD, JAMES F. POLIT. & GOV.: ***candidate for Democratic nomination to presidency of the U.S., 1948***. RES.: Akron, OH.

LEONARD, JONAH FITZ RANDOLPH. b. Dec 10, 1832, Waynesburg, PA; par. John and Hannah (Reinhart) Leonard; m. Margaret A. Sands, Mar 22, 1870. EDUC.: grad., Chautauqua Literary and Scientific Circle. POLIT. & GOV.: Prohibition Party candidate for gov. of VT, 1894; cty. surveyor, Chase Cty., KS; superintendent of schools, Chase Cty.; justice of the peace, Chase Cty.; founder, United Christian Party, 1898; United Christian Party candidate for lt. gov. of IA, 1899; ***United Christian (Union Reform) Party candidate for presidency of the U.S., 1900***; member, National Cmte., United Christian Party. BUS. & PROF.: farmer; abolitionist. MIL.: enlisted with Jim Lane in Kansas war for a free state; pvt., Company C, 93d Regt., IL Volunteer Infantry, 1862–65. REL.: Methodist Episc. Church. RES.: Ainsworth, IA.

LePAGE, NORMAN ARNOLD. b. Jan 23, 1924, Nashua, NH; par. Octave and Alice (Rousseau) LePage; m. Frances Keenan; c. James N.; Martha A. EDUC.: grad., Nashua (NH) H.S.; B.S., Northeastern U., 1953. POLIT. & GOV.: nonpartisan candidate for ward alderman, Nashua, 1955; elected as a Republican to selectman, Nashua, 1957–58; nonpartisan candidate for mayor of Nashua, 1957, 1959, 1961, 1963; candidate for Republican nomination to U.S. Senate (NH), 1960, 1962; ***candidate for Republican nomination to presidency of the U.S., 1964***; nonpartisan candidate for alderman-at-large, Nashua, 1965. BUS. & PROF.: self-employed accountant. REL.: Unitarian-Universalist. MAILING ADDRESS: 3 Courtland St., Nashua, NH 03060.

LE SUEUR, ARTHUR. b. Dec 7, 1867, Hastings, MN; d. Mar 19, 1950, Minneapolis, MN; par. John and Anne (Ame) Le Sueur; m. Mrs. Mayme (Marian) Lucy Wharton, c. 1916; c. Marydel Wharton (adopted); Winston Wharton (adopted); Max Wharton (adopted). EDUC.: Arvilla (ND) Classical Acad., 1889–91; U. of MI Law School, 1891–92; read law under Tracy Bangs, Fargo, ND. POLIT. & GOV.: Social-Democratic Party candidate for atty. gen. of ND, 1900; member, United Socialist Party, 1901; appointed asst. atty. gen. of ND, 1902; Socialist Party candidate for atty. gen. of ND, 1904, 1906, 1908, 1910; delegate, Socialist Party National Convention, 1905; Socialist Party candidate for U.S. House (ND), 1912; elected as a Socialist to mayor of Minot, ND, 1912; member, National Cmte., Socialist Party, 1912–16 (exec. cmte., 1915–16); ***candidate for Socialist Party nomination to presidency of the U.S., 1916***; Socialist Party candidate for U.S. Senate (ND), 1916; elected to Minneapolis (MN) School Board, c. 1922; appointed municipal judge, Minneapolis, c. 1934; candidate for municipal judge, Minneapolis, 1936. BUS. & PROF.: farmer; logger, 1880; atty.; admitted to ND Bar, 1899; law practice, Minot, 1900; ed., *Iconoclast*, Minot; partner, Le Sueur and Bradford (law firm), 1905–11; atty., Great Northern R.R., 1904–11; banker; pres., People's Coll., Fort Scott, KS, 1916–19, head, Socialist Correspondence School, 1917; atty. for Industrial Workers of the World; conducted defense of William D. Haywood (q.v.), WWI. MEM.: Non-Partisan League (legal counsel; exec. dir., St. Paul, MN, 1914); ND Bar Assn.; Modern Woodmen of America; Ancient Order of United Workmen; A.C.L.U. (National Cmte., 1920–33); Industrial Workers of the World; Farmer-Labor Party. WRITINGS: *The Right to His Day in Court* (1919). REL.: agnostic (nee Episc.). RES.: Minot, ND.

LEVERETTE, OTHA. m. Lureatha Leverette. POLIT. & GOV.: ***independent candidate for presidency of the U.S., 1976***. BUS. & PROF.: minister, Baptist Church; civil rights activist. MEM.: Southern Christian Leadership Conference (pres., Pensacola Chapter). REL.: Bapt. MAILING ADDRESS: 1541 East Leonard, Pensacola, FL.

LEVERING, JOSHUA. b. Sep 12, 1845, Baltimore, MD; d. Oct 5, 1935, Baltimore, MD; par. Eugene and Ann Sater (Walker) Levering; m. Martha W. Keyser, Nov 29, 1870; m. 2d, Margaret Ireland Keyser (sister of first wife), Mar 29, 1892; m. 3d, Helen Chase Woods, Apr 3, 1901; c. Wilson Keyser; Mary Grace (Mrs. Philip Saffrey Evans); Joshua, Jr.; Margareta (Mrs. Theodore Edmondson Brown); Martha Keyser (Mrs. Arthur Mason Sherman); Ernest Douglas; Louise Alexander (Mrs. Charles Miller Linthicum). EDUC.: private schools, Baltimore, MD. POLIT. & GOV.: pres., MD Prohibition Party State Convention, 1887, 1893; delegate, Prohibition Party National Convention, 1888, 1892; ***candidate for Prohibition Party nomination to vice presidency of the U.S., 1888 (declined), 1892 (declined)***; Prohibition Party candidate for controller of MD, 1891; Prohibition Party candidate for gov. of MD, 1895; ***Prohibition Party candidate for presidency of the U.S., 1896***; member, Prohibition Party National Cmte., 1900–1904. BUS. & PROF.: employee, partner, E. Levering and Co. (coffee imports), Baltimore, MD, 1866–1906; owner, International Trust Co., Baltimore; dir., Maryland Trust Co.; dir., National Bank of Baltimore; dir., Provident Savings Bank; financier. MEM.: Baltimore YMCA (pres., 1885; International Cmte., 1885); Southern Baptist Theological Seminary (trustee); MD Baptist Union Assn. (pres.); American Baptist Publications Soc. (vice pres.); Lord's Day Alliance (pres.); American Baptist Educational Soc. (treas., 1888); House of Refuge for Boys, Baltimore, (pres., 1887). REL.: Southern Baptist (pres., Southern Baptist Convention, 1908–10; vice pres., Foreign Missions Board; trustee, Eutaw Place Baptist Church; Sunday school superintendent, 1881–1903). RES.: Baltimore, MD.

LEVIN, JULES. b. 1922, NJ. EDUC.: grad., Vineland (NJ) H.S., 1940. POLIT. & GOV.: delegate, Socialist Labor Party National Convention, 1952, 1968, 1972, 1976; Socialist Labor Party candidate for U.S. House (NJ), 1958, 1960, 1964, 1968, 1974, 1978, 1980; Socialist Labor Party candidate for gov. of NJ, 19965, 1969, 1977; Socialist Labor Party candidate for U.S. Senate (NJ), 1966, 1970, 1972, 1982, 1984; state sec., Socialist Labor Party of NJ; Socialist Labor Party candidate for other state and local offices, NJ; ***Socialist Labor Party candidate for presidency of the U.S., 1976***. BUS. & PROF.: employee, shipyard, Camden, NJ; political organizer; owner, apartment complex; clothing store clerk; bartender. MIL.: U.S.M.C., WWII. MAILING ADDRESS: 2 Kings Highway, Haddon Heights, NJ 08035.

LEVINSON, MICHAEL STEPHEN. b. 1941. POLIT. & GOV.: candidate for Republican nomination to U.S. House (NY), 1986; ***candidate for Republican nomination to presidency of the U.S., 1980, 1988, 1992***. BUS. & PROF.: writer. WRITINGS: *The Book Ov Lev It a Kiss* (1971). MISC.: mother sold computer to aid his candidacy. MAILING ADDRESS: c/o Michael Schwartz, 978 Amherst St., Apt. #6, Buffalo, NY 14216.

LEWIN, HERBERT GEORGE. b. Jun 22, 1914, New York, NY; par. Max K. and Mary (Leshner) Lewin; m. Marie Plassman; m. 2d, Pauline Lewin; c. David; Maxine Insera. EDUC.: NY State Coll. of Forestry (now NY State Coll. of Environmental Sciences and Forestry), 1934–37. POLIT. & GOV.: founding member, Socialist Workers Party; Socialist Workers Party candidate for gov. of PA, 1954; Socialist Workers Party candidate for U.S. Senate (PA), 1956; ***International Workers Party candidate for presidency of the U.S., 1988; Peace and Freedom Party (dissident faction) candidate for presidency of the U.S., 1988; candidate for Labor Farmers Party nomination to presidency of the U.S., 1988; candidate for Liberty Union Party nomination to presidency of the U.S., 1988***. BUS. & PROF.: electrical worker, General Motors Corp., Syracuse, NY; employee, Bell Aircraft, Curtiss-Wright, Buffalo, NY; employee, Bethlehem Shipyard, Staten Island, NY; employee, Westinghouse Electric, Philadelphia, PA, 1941–75; teacher; active in civil rights, antiwar, environmental, immigrant rights, women's, and lesbian and gay rights movements. MEM.: American Federation of Teachers; U.A.W. of America (Local 1; Local 854); A.C.L.U.; Sierra Club; United Electrical Workers. MAILING ADDRESS: c/o Internationalist Workers Party, Suite 135, 3309 1/2 Mission St., San Francisco, CA 94110.

LEWIS, ARTHUR BLAIR. POLIT. & GOV.: ***independent candidate for presidency of the U.S., 1984***. MAILING ADDRESS: FL?

LEWIS, EDWARD GARDNER. b. Mar 4, 1869, Watertown, CT; d. 1950, Los Angeles, CA; par. Rev. William Henry and Catherine C. Lewis; m. Mabel G. Wellington. EDUC.: Cheshire (CT) Acad.; Trinity Coll. POLIT. & GOV.: elected mayor of University City, MO, 1906–12; police judge, University City; ***League of Women Voters candidate for presidency of the U.S., 1912***. BUS. & PROF.: patent medicine salesman; salesman, Magic Bug Chalk; pres., drug company, St. Louis, MO; pres., Diamond Candy Co.; publisher, *Winner Magazine*, 1901; owner, Tent City (World's Fair accommodations), St. Louis; publisher, ed., *Woman's Magazine*, 1900; ed., *Woman's Farm Journal*, 1902; pres., Lewis Publishing Co.; publisher, *Woman's National Daily*; publisher, *Star*, St. Louis, 1908–10; pres., dir., People's United States Bank, St. Louis, 1904–05; pres., University Heights Realty and Development Co.; pres., United States Fibre Stopper Co.; pres., American Coin Controller Co.; pres., National Installment Co.; pres., Development and Investment Co.; pres., People's Savings and Trust Co.; pres., Bachelor Pneumatic Tube Co.; pres., Atascadero Defense and Reconstruction Fund, Los Angeles, CA; pres., Atascadero Estates, Inc.; pres., Women's National Publishing Co.; pres., Atascadero Beach Lands and Improvement Co.; pres., Atascadero Mercantile Co.; pres., Atascadero Mill and Lumber Co.; pres., Atascadero Press; pres., Atascadero Copper Co.; pres., Caladero Products Co.; pres., Lewis Foundation Corp.; publisher, *California Illustrated Review*; pres., National Graphite Co.; pres., Permanent Residence Apartment Corp. MEM.: St. Louis Club; Mercantile Club; Glen Echo Club. WRITINGS: *Order Number Ten* (1911). MISC.: founder of University City, MO, 1906; founder, Atascadero, CA, 1913; involved in mail fraud in connection with People's United States Bank, St. Louis, 1905, acquitted three times; declared bankruptcy, 1925; barred from use of mails for promotion schemes in connection with Atascadero Defense and Reconstruction Fund, Los Angeles, CA, 1927; convicted of mail fraud in connection with CA land promotions, 1928; sentenced to five years in McNeil Island (WA) Federal Penitentiary and two fines of $14,000 and $15,000; paroled, 1931; returned to prison for parole violation; released, 1934. REL.: Episc. RES.: St. Louis, MO.

LEWIS, HENRY A., JR. par. Henry A. Lewis, Sr. POLIT. & GOV.: ***independent candidate for presidency of the***

U.S., 1984. MAILING ADDRESS: P.O. Box 272, Hickory, MS 39332.

LEWIS, JAMES ARTHUR. b. Apr 20, 1933, Hartford, CT; par. Charles David and Dorothy May (Kilby) Lewis; m. Judith Marr Watson (divorced); c. Stephen; Clifford; Gregg; Lauralyn. EDUC.: Guilford Coll., 1952; B.S., Babson Inst., 1958. POLIT. & GOV.: chm., Speakers' Bureau, CT Libertarian Party; Libertarian Party candidate for U.S. Senate (CT), 1982; ***Libertarian Party candidate for vice presidency of the U.S., 1984; candidate for Libertarian Party nomination to presidency of the U.S., 1988***. BUS. & PROF.: accountant, 1959–61; sales mgr., 1962–64, 1971–; family business; owner, shopping center, 1965–70; bookbinding services salesman. MIL.: sgt., 11th Airborne Div., U.S. Army, 1953–55. MEM.: CT Inst. (cofounder); Foundation for Constitutional Education (founder). WRITINGS: *Liberty Reclaimed* (1984). MAILING ADDRESS: 2 Neponset Ave., Old Saybrook, CT 06475.

LEWIS, JAMES HAMILTON. b. May 18, 1863, Danville, VA; d. Apr 9, 1939, Washington, DC; par. John Cabell Christopher and Julia Mary Cluves (Hilbern) Lewis; m. Rose Lawton Douglas, Nov 28, 1896; c. none. EDUC.: Houghton Coll.; U. of VA; read law under Gen. Alexander Robert Lawton, Savannah, GA. POLIT. & GOV.: elected as a Democrat to WA Territorial Senate, 1886; permanent chm., WA State Democratic Convention, 1889; aide, Joint High Comm. on Canada-Alaska Boundary, 1889–90; Democratic candidate for gov. of WA, 1892; elected as a Democrat to U.S. House (WA), 1896–1900; ***candidate for Democratic nomination to vice presidency of the U.S., 1896, 1900, 1920***; Fusionist candidate for U.S. House (WA), 1898; appointed U.S. commissioner to arrange customs regulations between Canada and the U.S., 1899; Democratic candidate for U.S. Senate (WA), 1899; city atty. and corporation counsel, Chicago, IL, 1905–07; Democratic candidate for gov. of IL, 1908, 1920; ***candidate for Democratic nomination to presidency of the U.S., 1912, 1920, 1932***; elected as a Democrat to U.S. Senate (IL), 1913–19, 1931–39 (whip); appointed U.S. Senate commissioner, Sea Treaty Negotiations, 1914; Democratic candidate for U.S. Senate (IL), 1918; attaché, international conferences at Genoa, Italy, 1921, Lausanne, Switzerland, 1922, Geneva, Switzerland, 1925; appointed U.S. ambassador to Belgium (declined); delegate, Dem. Nat'l. Conv., 1928. BUS. & PROF.: atty.; admitted to GA Bar, 1882; law practice, Seattle, WA, 1885–1903; law practice, Chicago, IL, 1903–09; pres., Webster Coll. of Law, 1913–14. MIL.: col., inspector gen., U.S. Army, 1898–1900. MEM.: Knights of the Round Table; Woodmen of the World; 1925 F Street Club; Union Interallie; Masons (32°); Elks; ABA; IL Bar Assn.; Chicago Bar Assn.; United Spanish War Veterans; Military Order of the World War; Geographical and Hist. Soc. of Paris; Chicago Hist. Soc.; Anti-Cruelty Soc. of Chicago; Chicago Club; Iroquois Club; Midday Club; Tavern Club; South Shore Club; Army and Navy Club; Metropolitan Club; Chevy Chase Club. AWARDS: Order of Crown (Belgium, 1919); Order of King George I (Greece, 1922). HON. DEG.: LL.D., OH Northern U., 1919; LL.D., Baylor U., 1920. WRITINGS: *Handbook on Election* (1912); *Constitutions, Statutes and Their Construction* (with A. H. Putney, 1913); *Two Great Republics—Rome and the United States; Removal of Causes from State to U.S. Courts* (1923); *Lewis and Spelling on Injunctions* (1926). REL.: Episc. MISC.: last U.S. senator chosen by a state legislature; first U.S. Senate whip. RES.: Chicago, IL.

LEWIS, JOHN FRANCIS. b. Mar 1, 1818, Lynnwood, VA; d. Sep 2, 1895, Lynnwood, VA; par. Gen. Samuel Hance and Nancy (Lewis) Lewis; m. Serena Helen Sheffey, 1842; c. Maria Hanson (Mrs. A. B. Sherwood); Daniel Sheffey; Nannie (Mrs. Ambler Smith); Helen (Mrs. Lewis David); Mary Louise (Mrs. Edward Gibbs); John; Sam. EDUC.: "Old Field" School. POLIT. & GOV.: delegate, VA Secession Convention, 1861 (refused to sign Ordinance of Secession); Union Party candidate for U.S. House (VA), 1865; elected as a True Republican to lt. gov. of VA, 1869–70; elected as a Republican to U.S. Senate (VA), 1870–75; ***candidate for Republican nomination to vice presidency of the U.S., 1872***; appointed U.S. marshal, Western District of VA, 1878–82; elected as a readjuster to lt. gov. of VA, 1881–83. BUS. & PROF.: superintendent, Mount Vernon Iron Works, Lynnwood, VA; farmer. REL.: Episc. RES.: Lynnwood, VA.

LEWIS, JOHN LLEWELLYN. b. Feb 12, 1880, Lucas, IA; d. Jun 11, 1969, Washington, DC; par. Thomas H. and Ann Louisa (Watkins) Lewis; m. Myrta Edith Bell, Jun 5, 1907; c. Margaret Mary; Florence Kathryn; John Llewellyn, Jr. EDUC.: eighth grade, Des Moines, IA. POLIT. & GOV.: appointed member, National Defense Council, 1917; appointed member, President's National Unemployment Conference, 1921; appointed member, Comm. to Investigate Government Veterans' Relief Agencies, 1921; appointed member, Advisory Comm., Limitation of Armaments Conference, 1921–22; appointed member, Labor Advisory Board; appointed member, National Labor Board, NRA; delegate, International Labor Conference, Geneva, Switzerland, 1934; ***Farmer-Labor Party candidate for presidency of the U.S., 1940 (declined)***. BUS. & PROF.: coal miner, Lucas, IA, 1897–1901, 1906–09; copper miner, MT; silver miner, UT; coal miner, CO; gold miner, AZ and Mexico, 1901–06; union leader. MEM.: U.M.W. of A. (delegate, National Convention, 1906, temporary chm., 1916; pres., Panama, IL, local, 1909; state legislative agent, District 12; vice pres., 1917–18; acting pres., 1919; pres., 1920–60; president emeritus, 1960–69; trustee, Welfare and Pension Fund, 1946–69); AFL (legislative representative, 1911–17; vice pres., to 1935); CIO (founder, 1935; pres., 1935–40); American Red Cross (dir.); National Coal Policy Conference (founder); American Acad. of Political and Social Sciences; Masons; Labor's Non-Partisan League (chm.). AWARDS: Presidential Medal of Freedom, 1964; Eugene V. Debs Foundation Award, 1965. HON. DEG.: LL.D., WV U., 1957;

L.H.D., Georgetown U., 1960. WRITINGS: *The Miners' Fight for American Standards* (1925). RES.: Washington, DC.

LEWIS, RONALD CURTIS, SR. b. Jul 30, 1929, Lake Helen, FL; par. Ellsworth Joseph and Hallie Ellen (Haywood) Lewis; m. Marilyn Clare Zimmermann, Apr 17, 1955 (divorced); c. Ronald Curtis, Jr.; Richard Eugene; Douglas Paul. EDUC.: grad., Putnam Mellon H.S., Palatka, FL, 1948. POLIT. & GOV.: candidate for Democratic nomination to gov. of FL, 1982; ***candidate for Democratic nomination to presidency of the U.S., 1984***. BUS. & PROF.: newspaper boy; delivery boy; soda jerk, Ackerman-Stewart Drug Store, Palatka, FL; district circulation mgr., *Florida Times-Union*, 1948; bookkeeper, salesman, Williams Floor Co., 1949–50; bookkeeper, salesman, Poage Concrete Co.; bookkeeper, apprentice production supervisor, Famous-Sternberg Manufacturing Clothing Co.; warehouseman, Brand Dispatching Co., 1955–58; vice pres., superintendent of warehouse operations, Rio Vista Export Co.; export shipping clerk, Dorf International; pres., Fairview Forwarding, Inc.; export shipping clerk, W. R. Zanes and Co., New Orleans, LA; inventory cardex clerk, Cool Air Corp., 1973; stock clerk, University Presses of FL, 1973–82. MIL.: pfc, corp., FL National Guard; seaman, petty officer third class, U.S. Navy, 1951–55. MEM.: FL Boys State (1947). REL.: Presb. (nee R.C.). MISC.: accident with Banana Gun resulted in numerous hospitalizations. MAILING ADDRESS: 1311 Ridgelake Dr., Metairie, LA.

LEWIS, SAMUEL. b. Mar 17, 1799, Falmouth, MA; d. Jul 28, 1854, Cincinnati, OH; par. Samuel and Abigail (Tolman) Lewis; m. Charlotte E. Goforth, 1823; c. William G. W.; Mrs. M. B. Hogans. EDUC.: public school, Falmouth, MA; public school, Scituate, MA; studied law. POLIT. & GOV.: clerk, Hamilton Cty. (OH) Court of Common Pleas, 1819; elected member, Cincinnati (OH) City Council, twice; appointed superintendent of public schools of OH, 1837–39; founder, Liberty Party; vice pres., OH Liberty Party State Convention, 1843; Liberty Party candidate for U.S. House (OH), 1843, 1848; chm., Liberty Party National Convention, 1843; Liberty Party candidate for gov. of OH, 1845; Free Soil (Free Democratic) Party candidate for gov. of OH, 1850 (declined), 1851, 1853; ***candidate for Free Soil (Free Democratic) Party nomination to vice presidency of the U.S., 1852***; pres., Union Board of High Schools, Cincinnati. BUS. & PROF.: cabin boy; farmhand; mail carrier; surveyor's helper; carpenter; atty.; admitted to OH Bar, 1822; law practice, Cincinnati, 1822–54; ordained minister, Methodist Episc. Church, 1824; founder, pres., trustee, Woodward H.S. (later Woodward Coll.), Cincinnati; publisher, *The Ohio School Director*. MEM.: Hughes Fund (trustee); Coll. of Teachers (founder, 1831); Fourth Annual Christian Anti-Slavery Convention (pres., 1853). REL.: Methodist Episc. Church (nee Congregationalist). MISC.: founded free public school system in OH; noted abolitionist. RES.: Cincinnati, OH.

LIBERATOR, AMERICUS HECTOR (aka **AMERIGO LIBERATORE).** b. Oct 3, 1910, Windber, PA; par. Antonio and Lorenzina (Sarandra) Liberatore; m. Margaret Kathryn; c. three sons. EDUC.: seventh grade. POLIT. & GOV.: candidate for sheriff, Cherry Cty., NE, 1966; ***candidate for Republican nomination to presidency of the U.S., 1968; independent candidate for presidency of the U.S., 1968, 1972, 1976, 1980, 1992; candidate for Democratic nomination to presidency of the U.S., 1976***. BUS. & PROF.: cowboy; coal miner; hobo; factory worker; farmhand; sodbuster; handmaker of saddles, harnesses, boots, shoes, and leathercrafts; traveling salesman; mason; carpenter; cabinet maker; plasterer; painter; freelance writer. MIL.: armed forces, WWII. MEM.: American Legion; Disabled American Veterans; Sod House Soc.; NRA; Tri-State Old Time Cowboy Assn. REL.: nonsectarian (nee R.C.). MAILING ADDRESS: Eva St., Valentine, NE.

LIEBENBERG, RAYMOND V(ONLY). b. Mar 18, 1920, Wrights, CA; par. Henry J. and _____ (Rosenhagen) Liebenberg; m. Celeste L., 1972; c. Ibe. EDUC.: D.C., Palmer Chiropractic Coll., 1947. POLIT. & GOV.: candidate for Santa Cruz Cty. (CA) supervisor, 1964; candidate for Democratic nomination to gov. of CA, 1978; ***candidate for Democratic nomination to presidency of the U.S., 1980, 1984; candidate for Libertarian Party nomination to presidency of the U.S., 1984; candidate for Peace and Freedom Party nomination to presidency of the U.S., 1984; candidate for American Independent Party nomination to presidency of the U.S., 1984; candidate for Republican nomination to presidency of the U.S., 1984***. BUS. & PROF.: chiropractor; tree trimmer, Paradise, CA; land developer; farmer; cosmogonist; city environmentalist. MEM.: Odd Fellows. REL.: Faithist. MAILING ADDRESS: Route 1, Box 307-F, Cherokee Rd., Oroville, CA 95965.

LIEBMAN, MONTE HARRIS. b. Jul 20, 1930, Milwaukee, WI; par. William and Ida (Zaichek) Liebman; m. (divorced); c. Lori Kay. EDUC.: B.S., U. of WI, 1953, M.D., 1957; intern, Mt. Zion Hospital, San Francisco, CA; resident, Veterans Hospital, Palo Alto, CA; fellow, Marquette U., Milwaukee, WI, 1962. POLIT. & GOV.: ***independent candidate for presidency of the U.S., 1976***. BUS. & PROF.: physician; clinical prof., Medical Coll. of WI, 1962–; lecturer; teacher, U. of Marquette Adult Non-Credit School; teacher, Free U., Milwaukee; founder, The Sayers, 1972–75; consultant, Waukesha (WI) Public Health Center, 1971–73; teacher, Central State Hospital and WI State Prison, 1974–75; psychiatrist. MEM.: American Psychiatric Assn.; American Ontoanalytic Assn.; American Group Psychotherapy Assn.; American Physician Fellowship; WI Citizens Concerned for Life; International Soc. for General Semantics; The Sayers; Milwaukee Mental Health Assn.; American Soc. of Psychoanalytic Physicians; American Soc. of Psychoanalysis; International Soc. for Psychiatric Research. WRITINGS: *The Handbook of Essential Psychotherapy; Pasticcio* (1973); "A Program for the Self," ETC. (1973); *Elements of Contemporary Counseling and Development; The Private World of a Psychiatrist; What is Love and How to Find It; Introduction to Psychotherapy; Counselors Handbook on Hysteria and Schizophrenia*. REL.: Independent Hebrew. MAILING ADDRESS: 2040 West Wisconsin Ave., Milwaukee, WI 53223.

LIGGINS, FREDDIE LEE. b. Jan 6, 1936, Milledgeville, GA; par. Arthur and Annie Mae (Johnson) Liggins; c. five. EDUC.: church schools. POLIT. & GOV.: ***independent candidate for presidency of the U.S., 1984***. BUS. & PROF.: carpenter; painter; gas station mgr. MEM.: Masons; GSA (leader). REL.: none. MAILING ADDRESS: 608 Hendricks Ave., Laredo, TX 78040.

LIGHTBURN, JOSEPH BENTON. b. Aug 29, 1899, Lightburn, WV; par. Luther C. and Florence McClung (Goodloe) Lightburn; m. Susan Adaline Davisson; c. Mary D.; Joseph Benton, Jr.; Frances M. EDUC.: high school; Army Training Corps, WV U., 1918. POLIT. & GOV.: elected as a member of the Citizens' Party to City Council, Jane Lew, WV, 1949–53; elected as a member of the Citizens' Party to mayor of Jane Lew, 1953–57; alternate delegate, Rep. Nat'l. Conv., 1952; Republican candidate for U.S. House (WV), 1954; ***Constitution Party candidate for presidency of the U.S., 1964***; Republican candidate for WV State Senate, 1968. BUS. & PROF.: operator, general store, Jane Lew, 1927–. MIL.: military service, WWII. REL.: Bapt. MAILING ADDRESS: Jane Lew, WV 26378.

LIGON, WILLIAM ORLANDO. b. Magnolia, MS; par. Robert B. Ligon; married; c. William Orlando "Buck"; Ray. POLIT. & GOV.: delegate, Rep. Nat'l. Conv., 1908; ***independent candidate for presidency of the U.S., 1928***. RES.: Gloster, MS.

LIN, GEORGE HONG-MING. b. Jun 6, 1965, New York, NY; par. H. C. and June (Ho) Lin; single. EDUC.: high school, Mattoon, IL. POLIT. & GOV.: ***Peace Party candidate for presidency of the U.S., 1980***. BUS. & PROF.: student. REL.: Presb. MAILING ADDRESS: 217 Circle Dr., Mattoon, IL 61938.

LINCOLN, ABRAHAM. b. Feb 12, 1809, Hodgenville, KY; d. Apr 15, 1865, Washington, DC; par. Thomas and Nancy (Hanks) Lincoln; m. Mary Todd, Nov 4, 1842; c. Robert Todd (q.v.); Edward Baker; William Wallace; Thomas "Tad." EDUC.: studied law under John T. Stuart. POLIT. & GOV.: Whig Party candidate for IL State House, 1832; appointed postmaster, New Salem, IL, 1833–36; deputy cty. surveyor, IL, 1833; elected as a Whig to IL State House, 1835–36, 1855; candidate for Whig Party nomination to U.S. House (IL), 1843; elected as a Whig to U.S. House (IL), 1847–49; delegate, Whig Party National Convention, 1848; appointed sec., OR Territory, 1849 (declined); appointed gov., OR Territory, 1849 (declined); Whig Party candidate for U.S. Senate (IL), 1855; ***candidate for Republican nomination to vice presidency of the U.S., 1856***; Republican candidate for U.S. Senate (IL), 1858; *elected as a Republican to presidency of the U.S., 1861–65*. BUS. & PROF.: ferry operator, Anderson River, IN, 1827; flatboat pilot, Rockport, IN, 1828; flatboat builder, Sangamon Town, IL, 1831; merchant, New Salem, IL; partner, Berry and Lincoln (saloon), Springfield, IL, 1833; atty.; admitted to IL Bar, 1837; law practice, Springfield, 1838–65; partner (with John T. Stuart), law firm, Springfield, 1838–41; partner (with Stephen T. Long), law firm, Springfield, 1841–44; partner (with William H. Herndon), law firm, Springfield, IL, 1844–65. MIL.: volunteer, Sangamon Rifle Co., Richland, IL, 1832, reenlisted as pvt. REL.: Deist. MISC.: known as the "Great Emancipator"; assassinated by John Wilkes Booth, Apr 15, 1865. RES.: Springfield, IL.

LINCOLN, BENJAMIN. b. Jan 24, 1733, Hingham, MA; d. May 9, 1810, Boston, MA; par. Benjamin and Elizabeth (Thaxter) Lincoln; m. Mary Cushing, Jan 15, 1756; c. six sons; five daughters. POLIT. & GOV.: town clerk, Hingham, MA, 1757; justice of the peace, Hingham, 1762; member, MA Legislature, 1772–73; member, MA Provincial Congress, 1774–75 (sec., Cmte. on Supplies, 1774–75; pres., 1775); appointed U.S. sec. of war, 1781–83; appointed MA commissioner to deal with Penobscot Indians on land purchases, 1784; elected as a Federalist to lt. gov. of MA, 1788; Federalist candidate for lt. gov. of MA, 1789; member, MA Ratification Convention, 1789; appointed collector, Port of Boston, MA, 1789–09; ***received 1 electoral vote as a Federalist for presidency of the U.S., 1789***; appointed negotiator with Creek Indians, 1789; appointed negotiator with Indians North of the Ohio, 1793. BUS. & PROF.: soldier; farmer, Hingham, MA. MIL.: adj., Third Regt., MA Militia, 1755, maj., 1763, lt. col., 1772, brig. gen., 1776, maj. gen., 1776; maj. gen., Continental Army, 1777; captured with his forces at Charleston by Gen. Sir Henry Clinton, 1780; led MA Militia to suppress Shay's Rebellion. MEM.: American Acad. of Arts and Sciences; MA Hist. Soc. HON. DEG.: M.A., Harvard U. WRITINGS: *Indian Tribes: The Causes of Their Decrease. . . .; Observations on the Climate, Soil and Value of the Eastern Counties in the District of Maine*. RES.: Hingham, MA.

LINCOLN, JOHN CROMWELL. b. Jul 17, 1866, Painesville, OH; d. May 24, 1959, Scottsdale, AZ; par. William Ellerby and Francis Louise (Marshall) Lincoln; m. Myrtle Virginia Humphreys, Jan 1, 1891; m. 2d, Mary Dearstyne Mackenzie, Jun 18, 1914; m. 3d, Helen Colvill, Jun 5, 1918; c. Myrtle Louise (Mrs. Peter Kerr); John Gladden; Lillia C. Howell (Mrs. Deane D. Banta); Joseph C.; David C. EDUC.: M.E., OH State U., 1888. POLIT. & GOV.: ***Commonwealth Land Party candidate for vice presidency of the U.S., 1924***. BUS. & PROF.: employee, Brush

Electric Co., Cleveland, OH; superintendent of construction, Short Electric Co., 1889–93; partner, Elliott-Lincoln Electric Co., 1893–94; founder, Lincoln Electric Co., 1895, pres., 1905–28, chm. of the board, 1928–54, hon. chm. of the board, 1954–59; founder, Lincoln Electric Manufacturing Co. (now Reliance Electric Manufacturing Co.), 1904; pres., Bagdad Copper Corp., 1944–59; pres., Camelback Inn Co., 1936–59; chm. of the board, Universal Wire Spring Co.; founder, Lincoln Bonding Co., 1914–20; pres., Henry George School of Social Science, 1947–59; inventor; real estate investor; banker; part-owner, operator, Vulture Mine; rancher; engineer, Electric Meat Curing Co., Cincinnati, OH, 1908–12; holder of over fifty patents. MEM.: Desert Mission of YMCA (dir.); Good Samaritan Hospital; John C. Lincoln Hospital (pres., 1950); Sigma Xi; Tau Beta Pi; A.S.M.E.; A.I.E.E. (fellow); American Welding Soc. AWARDS: Samuel Wylie Miller Award, American Welding Soc., 1934. HON. DEG.: D.Sc., AZ State Coll., 1958. WRITINGS: *Practical Electricity* (1898); *Christ's Object in Life* (1948); *Ground Rent, Not Taxes* (1957); *Stop Legalized Stealing* (1958). REL.: Presb. RES.: Phoenix, AZ.

LINCOLN, ROBERT TODD. b. Aug 1, 1843, Springfield, IL; d. Jul 26, 1926, Manchester, VT; par. President Abraham (q.v.) and Mary (Todd) Lincoln; m. Mary Harlan, Sep 24, 1868; c. Mary (Mrs. Charles Isham); Abraham; Jessie (Mrs. Warren Beckwith; Mrs. Frank E. Johnson). EDUC.: IL State U., 1853–59; Phillips Exeter Acad.; A.B., Harvard U., 1864, Law School, 1864–65. POLIT. & GOV.: elected supervisor, South Chicago, IL, 1876–77; delegate, IL Republican State Convention, 1880; presidential elector, Republican Party, 1880; appointed U.S. sec. of war, 1881–85; ***candidate for Republican nomination to presidency of the U.S., 1884, 1888, 1892, 1912***; appointed U.S. minister to Great Britain, 1889–93. BUS. & PROF.: atty.; admitted to IL Bar, 1867; partner, Scammon and Lincoln (law firm), Chicago, IL, 1867–72; partner (with Edward S. Isham), law firm, Chicago, 1873; partner, Isham, Lincoln and Beale (law firm), Chicago; trustee, Illinois Central R.R., 1880; special counsel, pres., The Pullman Co., 1893–1911, chm. of the board, 1911–26; dir., vice pres., Commonwealth Edison Co.; dir., Continental and Commercial National Bank; dir., Chicago Telephone Co.; dir., Pullman Trust and Savings Bank. MIL.: capt., U.S. Army, 1865. MEM.: Hasty Pudding Club (vice pres.); Chicago Bar Assn. (charter member); Ekwanok Country Club (pres.). HON. DEG.: LL.D., Harvard U., 1893. REL.: Methodist Episc. Church. RES.: Chicago, IL.

LINDBERGH, CHARLES AUGUSTUS. b. Feb 4, 1902, Detroit, MI; d. Aug 26, 1974, Maui, HI; par. Charles Augustus and Evangeline Lodge (Land) Lindbergh; m. Anne Spencer Morrow, May 27, 1929; c. Charles Augustus; Jon Morrow; Land Morrow; Anne; Reeve; Scott. EDUC.: U. of WI, 1920–22; flying school, Lincoln, NE, 1922. POLIT. & GOV.: ***candidate for Republican nomination to presidency of the U.S., 1936, 1940, 1944; candidate for Republican nomination to vice presidency of the U.S., 1936, 1940, 1944; candidate for America First Party nomination to presidency of the U.S., 1944***. BUS. & PROF.: aviator; airmail pilot, St. Louis to Chicago, 1926; technical adviser, Ford Motor Co., 1942; dir., Pan American World Airways; lecturer; soldier. MIL.: flying cadet, U.S. Air Service Reserves, 1924; 1st lt., MO National Guard, 1925; col., brig. gen., U.S. Air Force Reserves. MEM.: America First Cmte.; Pan-amin Foundation, Inc. (trustee); Carnegie Institution (trustee, 1934). AWARDS: Medal of Honor; Hubbard Medal, National Geographic Soc.; Service Cross of Order of German Eagle, 1938; Distinguished Flying Cross; Distinguished Service Cross; Woodrow Wilson Medal; Langley Medal; chevalier, Legion of Honor (France); Royal Air Cross (Great Britain); Order of Leopold (Belgium); Wright Brothers Memorial Trophy, 1949; Pulitzer Prize for Distinguished American Biography, 1954; Cross of Honor, U.S. Flag Assn.; New York Medal of Valor; one of twelve Outstanding Young Men in America, America's Young Men, 1934. HON. DEG.: M.Aero., NY U., 1928; LL.D., Northwestern U., 1928; LL.D., U. of WI, 1928; M.S., Princeton U., 1931. WRITINGS: *We* (1927); *Of Flight and Life* (1948); *The Spirit of St. Louis* (1953). MISC.: purchased "Spirit of St. Louis," 1927; winner of Orteig Prize of $25,000 for first New York to Paris nonstop flight; flew nonstop, Washington to Mexico City, 1927; known as "Lucky Lindy"; son, Charles Augustus, kidnapped and murdered in celebrated crime for which Bruno Hauptmann was convicted and executed, 1932; noted as isolationist prior to World War II. RES.: Darien, CT.

LINDSAY, JOHN VLIET. b. Nov 24, 1921, New York, NY; par. George Nelson and Florence Eleanor (Vliet) Lindsay; m. Mary Harrison, Jun 18, 1949; c. Katharine (Mrs. Richard Schaffer); Margaret (Mrs. Robert Zeeb); Anne; John Vliet. EDUC.: St. Paul's School, Concord, NH, 1940; B.A., Yale U., 1944, LL.B., 1948. POLIT. & GOV.: exec. asst. to atty. gen. of the U.S., 1955–57; elected as a Republican to U.S. House (NY), 1959–65; delegate, Rep. Nat'l. Conv., 1960, 1964, 1968; elected as a Republican to mayor of New York, NY, 1965–69, as a Liberal, 1969–73; ***candidate for Republican nomination to presidency of the U.S., 1968; candidate for Republican nomination to vice presidency of the U.S., 1968; New (New Politics) Party candidate for vice presidency of the U.S., 1968; candidate for Democratic nomination to presidency of the U.S., 1972***; candidate for Democratic nomination to U.S. Senate (NY), 1980. BUS. & PROF.: atty.; admitted to NY Bar, 1949; admitted to Federal Bar, 1950; admitted to Bar of the Supreme Court of the U.S., 1955; counsel, Webster, Sheffield, Fleischman, Hitchcock and Chrystie (law firm), New York, 1953–60, 1974–; television commentator. MIL.: lt., U.S.N.R., 1943–46; Five Battle Stars. MEM.: ABA; NY Bar Assn.; New York City Bar Assn.; Freedom House (dir.); New York Young Republican Club (pres., 1952); Council on Foreign Relations; Citizens Cmte. for Children. AWARDS: Distinguished Service Citation, U. of CA at Berkeley; Family of Man Award, National Council of Churches. HON. DEG.: LL.D., Harvard U.; LL.D., Manhattanville Coll.; LL.D., Oakland Coll.; LL.D., Pace Coll.; LL.D., Williams Coll. WRITINGS: *Journey into Politics* (1966); *The City* (1970); *The Edge*

(1976). REL.: Episc. MAILING ADDRESS: 1 Rockefeller Plaza, New York, NY 10020.

LINDSEY, BENJAMIN BARR. b. Nov 25, 1869, Jackson, TN; d. Mar 26, 1943, Los Angeles, CA; par. Landy Tunstall and Letitia Anna (Barr) Lindsey; m. Henrietta Brevoort, Dec 20, 1913; c. Benetta Brevoort. EDUC.: public schools. POLIT. & GOV.: appointed public guardian and administrator, Denver, CO, 1899; delegate, CO State Democratic Convention, 1900; member, CO State Democratic Central Cmte., 1900; appointed and subsequently elected juvenile judge, Juvenile Court of Denver, CO, 1900–1927 (removed in election contest); candidate for Democratic nomination to gov. of CO, 1906; independent candidate for gov. of CO, 1906; member, Progressive Party National Cmte., 1912; ***Prohibition Party candidate for presidency of the U.S., 1912 (declined); Prohibition Party candidate for vice presidency of the U.S., 1916 (declined)***; elected judge, Los Angeles (CA) Superior Court, 1934–43. BUS. & PROF.: reformer; atty.; admitted to CO Bar, 1894; admitted to CA Bar, 1928; author. MEM.: Kids Citizens League (founder); Juvenile Assn. for the Betterment and Protection of Children (founder); Ford Peace Expedition (1915). HON. DEG.: LL.D., Notre Dame U.; LL.D., Olivet Coll.; LL.D., Southwestern Baptist U.; LL.D., U. of Denver. WRITINGS: *Problems of the Children* (1903); *The Beast and the Jungle* (1910); *The Rule of Plutocracy in Colorado* (1908); *Children in Bondage* (1914); *The Doughboy's Religion* (1919); *Pan Germanism in America; The Revolt of Modern Youth* (1925); *Twenty-Five Years of Juvenile Court* (1925); *The House of Human Welfare*; "The Child at the Door" (play); "On Honor" (play); "A Bolt of Cloth" (motion picture synopsis); *The Companionate Marriage* (1927); *The Dangerous Life* (1931). REL.: Christian (nee R.C.). MISC.: noted as advocate of rights of children and companionate marriage. RES.: Denver, CO.

LINES, C. B. POLIT. & GOV.: ***independent candidate for presidency of the U.S., 1868***. RES.: KS.

LINGER, CLAUDE R. b. Apr 29, 1905, Flatwoods, WV; par. Nicholas Washington and Gable (Denison) Linger; m. Nelle Wynn, 1936. EDUC.: grad., Washington Irving H.S., Braxton Cty., WV; Glenville State Teachers Coll. POLIT. & GOV.: elected as a Democrat to WV State House of Delegates, 1935–39; ***candidate for Democratic nomination to presidency of the U.S., 1944***; alternate delegate, Dem. Nat'l. Conv., 1952. BUS. & PROF.: farmer, Burnsville, WV; schoolteacher, 1 year; retail grocery business, 3 years; salesman, fraternity and high school jewelry, 1925–. MEM.: Masons (32°); Shriners; Elks; Scottish Rite. MAILING ADDRESS: Burnsville, WV.

LINOVITZ, MAX. POLIT. & GOV.: ***independent candidate for presidency of the U.S., 1988***. MAILING ADDRESS: 1400 West 9 Mile Rd., Apt. 16, Ferndale, MI 48220.

LINTON, WILLIAM SEELYE. b. Feb 4, 1856, St. Clair, MI; d. Nov 22, 1927, Lansing, MI; par. Aaron and Sarah (McDonald) Linton; m. Ida M. Lowry, Apr 9, 1878; c. Raymond Aaron; Lawrence Lowry; Elsie Sarah. EDUC.: public schools. POLIT. & GOV.: elected as a Republican to Board of County Supervisors, Bay Cty., MI, 1878–79; elected member, Common Council, Saginaw, MI, 1883–87; elected as a Republican to MI State House, 1887–88; Republican candidate for lt. gov. of MI, 1890; pres., Saginaw Water Board, 1892; elected mayor of Saginaw, 1892–94; elected as a Republican to U.S. House (MI), 1893–97; ***candidate for Republican nomination to presidency of the U.S., 1896***; appointed postmaster, Saginaw, 1898–1914; candidate for Republican nomination to gov. of MI, 1913; appointed chm., MI State Tax Comm., 1919–27. BUS. & PROF.: clerk, Farwell, MI; lumber manufacturer, Saginaw, to 1892. MEM.: Northern Nut Growers Assn. (pres.); Top of MI Trail Assn.; Burns Club (pres.); Knights of the Maccabees; Masons; Foresters; MI Assn. of Postmasters (pres.); State League of Building and Loan Associations (pres.); American Protective Assn.; Tahquamenon Hunting Club (pres.); Saginaw Board of Trade (pres., 1905–11, 1913–17). RES.: Saginaw, MI.

LIPPITT, CHARLES WARREN. b. Oct 8, 1846, Providence, RI; d. Apr 4, 1924, Harmon-on-Hudson, NY; par. Gov. Henry and Mary Ann (Balch) Lippitt; m. Margaret Barbara Farnum, Feb 23, 1886; c. Charles Warren; Alex Farnum; Gordon Thayer; three infants. EDUC.: Ph.B., Brown U., 1865. POLIT. & GOV.: col., staff of Gov. Henry Lippitt of Rhode Island, 1875–76; chm., RI State Republican Convention, 1894; elected as a Republican to gov. of RI, 1895–97; ***candidate for Republican nomination to vice presidency of the U.S., 1896***. BUS. & PROF.: employee, Lippitt Woolen Co.; treas., Silver Spring Bleaching and Dyeing Co., 1871–1903; pres., Franklin Lyceum, 1875–76; pres., Social Manufacturing Co., 1891–1901; dir., Rhode Island National Bank, 1891–95, vice pres., 1895, pres., 1896–1901; vice pres., United National Bank, 1901–08. MIL.: col., Providence Marine Corps of Artillery. MEM.: Brown U. Alumni Assn. (pres., 1897); National Assn. of the Finishers of Cotton Fabrics (pres., 1898); Providence Board of Trade (vice pres., 1878–80; pres., 1881–82); National Board of Trade (vice pres., 1880); Providence Commercial Club (pres., 1883–84); Second Ward Garfield and Arthur Club (chm., 1880). WRITINGS: *Message* (1896); *Republican Principles and Progress* (1906). REL.: Congregationalist. RES.: Providence, RI.

LIPSCOMB, CALEB. POLIT. & GOV.: Socialist Labor Party candidate for gov. of KS, 1898; Socialist Democratic Party candidate for gov. of MO, 1900; Socialist Party candidate for judge, Supreme Court of MO, 1904; ***candidate for Socialist Party nomination to vice presidency of the U.S., 1908***. RES.: KS.

LIRA, WILLIAM JOSEPH. b. 1972. POLIT. & GOV.: ***independent candidate for presidency of the U.S.,***

1988. BUS. & PROF.: student. MAILING ADDRESS: Will Lira Cmte. for the Benefit of Animalism in America, c/o William Henry Powers, P.O. Box 310, Goldendale, WA 98620.

LITTLE, ARTHUR W. b. Dec 15, 1873, New York, NY; d. Jul 18, 1943; par. Joseph James and Josephine (Robinson) Little; m. Marguerite Lanier Winslow, Apr 19, 1897; m. 2d, Charlotte Houston Fairchild, Apr 27, 1927; m. 3d, Mary Alice Van Nest Barney, Jun 30, 1928; c. Winslow; Arthur W. EDUC.: private Schools, New York, NY; business college. POLIT. & GOV.: appointed member, Business Advisory and Planning Council, U.S. Dept. of Commerce, 1933–34; appointed member, Industrial Advisory Board, NRA, 1934; ***candidate for Republican nomination to vice presidency of the U.S., 1936 (declined)***; appointed chm., Mayor's Advisory Board, New York, 1939–43. BUS. & PROF.: printer; joined father's company, J. J. Little and Co. (now J. J. Little and Ives Co.), 1891, chm. of the board. MIL.: pvt., corp., Company I, 7th Regt., NY National Guard, 1891–98; capt., Company D, 171st Regt., NY National Guard, 1898; 1st lt., Company I, 71st Regt., 1899; capt., aide-de-camp to Gen. George Moore Smith, 1900–1910; maj., inspector gen., 1st Bde., 1910–12; officer, 15th Infantry (Colored), NY National Guard (later 369th U.S. Infantry), WWI; capt., Company F, regimental adj. and maj., 1st Battalion, 1917–19; col., 15th Infantry (Colored), NY National Guard, 1921; brev. brig. gen., 1922–25; wounded in action, 1918; Croix de Guerre with Two Palms, One Gold Star and One Silver Star; Order of the Purple Heart; U.S. Citation for Gallantry; chevalier, Legion of Honor; commander, Order of the Black Star (France). MEM.: Masons (life member); Elks; SAR; Sons of Vets; American Legion; VFW; National Farmers Union (life hon. member). REL.: Episc. RES.: New York, NY.

LITTLEFIELD, PAUL T. "RED FOX." b. 1949, Howell Township, NJ. POLIT. & GOV.: ***American Indian Party candidate for presidency of the U.S., 1988; Jewish Christian Action Alliance Party candidate for presidency of the U.S., 1988***. BUS. & PROF.: private investigator; owner, Paul's Tree Service, Freehold, NJ. MISC.: marathon runner. MAILING ADDRESS: RD No. 2, Box 347, Freehold, NJ 07728.

LITTLETON, MARTIN WILEY. b. Jan 12, 1872, Kingston, TN; d. Dec 19, 1934, Mineola, NY; par. Thomas Jefferson and Hannah B. (Ingram) Littleton; m. Maud Elizabeth Wilson, Dec 1, 1896; c. Martin Wiley, Jr.; Douglas. EDUC.: self-taught; studied law. POLIT. & GOV.: appointed deputy cty. clerk, Weatherford Cty., TX; appointed asst. prosecuting atty., Dallas, TX, 1893–96; appointed asst. district atty., Kings Cty., NY, 1900–1904; chm., NY State Democratic Convention, 1902; elected as a Democrat to president of the borough of Brooklyn, NY, 1904–05; delegate, Dem. Nat'l. Conv., 1904; ***candidate for Democratic nomination to vice presidency of the U.S., 1908***; elected as a Democrat to U.S. House (NY), 1911–13. BUS. & PROF.: atty.; admitted to TX Bar, 1891; law practice, Dallas, 1893–96; law practice, New York, NY, 1896–1934. RES.: Plandome, NY.

LIVENGOOD, STEVEN DEE. b. 1949. POLIT. & GOV.: ***candidate for Republican nomination to presidency of the U.S., 1984***. BUS. & PROF.: public policy research project dir., Washington, DC. MAILING ADDRESS: 320 Third St., N.E., Washington, DC 20002.

LIVINGSTONE, JAMES MEYWARD. POLIT. & GOV.: ***candidate for Democratic nomination to president of the United States, 1992***. MAILING ADDRESS: 14 Covington Rd., Decatur, GA 30032.

LLOYD, JAMES McVAY. b. Jan 4, 1886, Yankton, SD; d. Mar 10, 1969, Yankton, SD; par. David Emanuel and Dorothea (Kumpf) Lloyd; single. EDUC.: grad., Yankton (SD) H.S. POLIT. & GOV.: appointed member, SD War Finance Cmte., WWII; delegate, Rep. Nat'l. Conv., 1940, 1944; elected as a Republican to SD State Senate, 1959–65; member, Advisory Board, U.S. Savings Bonds; appointed member, Dakota Territory Centennial Comm., 1960; ***candidate for Republican nomination to presidency of the U.S., 1960***. BUS. & PROF.: clerk, First National Bank, Yankton, 1901–09; cashier, First Loan and Trust Co., 1909–11; vice pres., American State Bank, Yankton, 1911–56, pres., 1956–65; dir., treas., Yankton Building and Loan Assn., 1909–69; dir., Missouri Valley Producers, Inc. MEM.: American Cancer Soc. (chm., Yankton Unit, 1947–69); American Red Cross (chapter treas., 1917–69; state pres., 1953–55); Salvation Army (advisory board); Masons (master; treas., 1928–69; 33°; Shriners; Scottish Rite; York Rite; Oriental Consistory; commander, Court of Honor); Yankton Coll. (chm., Corp. Board; trustee); Yankton C. of C. (pres.); Odd Fellows; Moose; Elks (Yankton treas., 1928–69; exalted ruler, 1923–24); Greater SD Assn. (pres.); SD Bankers Assn. (pres., 1948–49); Yankton Old Settlers Assn. AWARDS: "Man of the Year," Yankton Junior C. of C., 1962. HON. DEG.: D.B.A., Yankton Coll., 1964. REL.: Congregationalist (trustee). RES.: Yankton, SD.

LOCK, STANLEY ONEASE, JR. b. Sep 15, 1917, Montpelier, IN; par. Stanley Onease and Eva Marie (Stone) Lock; m. Lillian Marie Turner; c. Marilyn Marie; Mary Alberta; Eva May; Lois Lorraine. EDUC.: Burnett's Corner School, seventh grade; grad., Chicago Aeronautical U., 1941; Prop and Dot Flying School; grad., Wayne H.S., Wayne, MI, 1950; MI State U., 1950–52. POLIT. & GOV.: candidate for Democratic nomination to U.S. House (MI), 1954, 1956; ***candidate for Democratic nomination to presidency of the U.S., 1988, 1992; candidate for Democratic nomination to vice presidency of the U.S., 1988***. BUS. & PROF.: truck farmer,

Mystic, CT, 1930–35; field farmer, Montpelier, IN, 1936; aircraft engine test leader, Ford Motor Co., Dearborn, MI, 1942–45; night mgr., Liright's Coffee Shop, 1945–46; technician, Ford Engineering Center, Dearborn, 1947–56; proprietor of hot dog, popcorn, and candy business, Wayne, MI, 1949; inspector, Chevrolet-Corvair, Ypsilanti, MI, 1960–62; clerk, carrier, U.S. Postal Service, Wayne, 1962; inventor; author; engine tester, Thermo Electron Engine Corp., Sterling Heights, MI, 1967–79. MIL.: U.S. Army, 1936–39; acting staff sgt., U.S.A.A.F., 1939–41. MEM.: 4-H Club (sec.). WRITINGS: "Roots of That-Zero Dim Into 6th Dimension" (unpublished, 1985). REL.: Bapt. MISC.: invented back-up lights for automobiles; philosophical definition of "That"; Onease Energy Unit; discovered sixth dimension. MAILING ADDRESS: 2967 Roosevelt, Flat 2, Hamtramck, MI 48212.

LOCKE, BOBBY. b. Jan 8, 1940, Ardmore, OK. EDUC.: U. of OK, 1959–62. POLIT. & GOV.: Republican candidate for U.S. House (TX), 1976, 1980; ***candidate for Democratic nomination to presidency of the U.S., 1984, 1988, 1992***; candidate for Democratic nomination to U.S. House (TX), 1984; candidate for Democratic nomination to gov. of TX, 1986. BUS. & PROF.: construction contractor. MIL.: U.S. Army, 2 years. AWARDS: "Outstanding Young Texan" Award. MAILING ADDRESS: 106 Riverwalk, San Antonio, TX 78205.

LOCKWOOD, BELVA ANN BENNETT McNALL. b. Oct 24, 1830, Royalton, NY; d. May 19, 1917, Washington, DC; par. Lewis Johnson and Hannah (Green) Bennett; m. Uriah H. McNall, Nov 8, 1848; m. 2d, Dr. Ezekiel Lockwood, Mar 11, 1868; c. Lura Ormes; Jessie. EDUC.: Royalton (NY) Acad.; Gasport Acad., 1853–54; B.S. (cum laude), Genessee Coll., 1857; B.L., National U., 1873. HON. DEG.: A.M., Syracuse U., 1871, LL.D., 1908. POLIT. & GOV.: ***Equal Rights Party candidate for presidency of the U.S., 1884, 1888***; chm., Industrial Reform Party National Convention, 1888; appointed U.S. representative, Geneva Congress of Charities and Corrections, 1896. BUS. & PROF.: schoolteacher, Lockport Union School, 1857–61; teacher, Gainesville Female Seminary, 1861–62; teacher, Hornellsville Seminary, 1862; proprietor, Female Seminary, Oswego, NY; teacher, Miss Harrover's Boarding and Day School, Washington, DC, 1867; atty.; admitted to DC Bar, 1873; proprietor, Union League Hall School for Young Females; admitted to practice before the Bar of the Supreme Court of the U.S., 1879; admitted to the Bar of the U.S. Court of Claims; partner, Belva Lockwood and Co. (law firm), Washington, DC; member, editorial board, *The Peacemaker*. MEM.: Universal Peace Union (corresponding sec.; vice pres.); National Arbitration Soc.; Universal Franchise Assn. (vice pres., 1867); Federation of Women's Clubs (equal property rights commissioner); Women's National Press Assn. (pres., 1901); DC Woman Suffrage Assn. (pres.); American Branch, International Peace Congress (delegate, 1889, 1906, 1908, 1911); Woman's Republic (atty. gen., 1912); Women's Convention (ambassador, 1913); World Conscience Soc., 1913; Assn. of Heads of International Societies (hon. member); Women's Literary Soc. (pres.); New York Aid Soc. (pres.). WRITINGS: *Congres Internationale de la Paix* (1891); *A Complete List of All the Treaties Entered Into by the U.S.* (1893); *Peace and the Outlook* (1899); *Arbitration and the Treaties* (n.d.); *The Central American Peace Congress* (1908). REL.: Methodist Episc. Church. MISC.: woman suffrage, temperance, and peace advocate; frequent lobbyist before U.S. Congress on behalf of equal pay for women and other reforms; first woman admitted to practice before Supreme Court of the U.S. RES.: Washington, DC.

LOCKWOOD, CHARLES E. b. Jun 14, 1867, Pittsfield, PA; par. Olvin Alonzo and Barbara (Dalrymple) Lockwood. EDUC.: LL.B., State U. of OR, 1890. POLIT. & GOV.: appointed clerk of Public Land Cmte., OR State Senate, 1889; appointed asst. U.S. atty. for OR, 1890–93; sec., OR Republican State Central Cmte.; ***candidate for Republican nomination to presidency of the U.S., 1916***; candidate for Republican nomination to presidential elector, 1920. BUS. & PROF.: atty.; admitted to OR Bar, 1889; law practice, Portland, OR, 1893. MIL.: Oregon National Guard. MEM.: OR State Bar Assn. (founder, 1891); Republican Club of Portland (sec.); Masons. RES.: Portland, OR.

LOCKWOOD, HENRY. POLIT. & GOV.: ***independent candidate for presidency of the U.S., 1988***. MAILING ADDRESS: Box 215, Amberg, WI 54102.

LODGE, GEORGE CABOT. b. Jul 7, 1927, Boston, MA; par. Henry Cabot Jr. (q.v.) and Emily (Sears) Lodge; m. Nancy Kunhardt, 1949; c. Nancy Kunhardt (Mrs. Webbe); Emily Sears; Dorothy Merserve; Henry Cabot; George Cabot; David. EDUC.: A.B. (cum laude), Harvard U., 1950. POLIT. & GOV.: dir. of information, U.S. Dept. of Labor, 1954–58; appointed asst. sec. for international affairs, U.S. Dept. of State, 1958–61; U.S. representative, International Labor Organization, 1958–61 (chm., 1960–61); Republican candidate for U.S. Senate (MA), 1962; ***candidate for Republican nomination to presidency of the U.S., 1964; National Unity Party candidate for vice presidency of the U.S., 1980 (withdrew)***. BUS. & PROF.: reporter, *Boston (MA) Herald*, 1950–54; lecturer, Harvard U. Business School, 1963–68, assoc. prof., 1968–71, prof., 1971–; vice chm., Inter-American Social Development Inst., 1970–. MIL.: seaman third class, U.S. Navy, 1945, seaman first class, 1946. MEM.: American Assn. for the United Nations; World Affairs Council of Boston; NAACP; National Council for Civic Responsibility; Inst. for American Democracy; Carnegie Endowment for International Peace (trustee); Council on Foreign Relations. WRITINGS: *Spearheads of Democracy* (1962); *Engines Change* (1970). REL.: Protestant. MAILING ADDRESS: 275 Hale St., Beverly, MA 01915.

LODGE, HENRY CABOT. b. May 12, 1850, Boston, MA; d. Nov 9, 1924, Cambridge, MA; par. John Ellerton and Anna (Cabot) Lodge; m. Anna Cabot Davis Mills, Jun 29, 1871; c. George Cabot; Constance (Mrs. Augustus Peabody Gardner; Mrs. Clarence E. Williams); John Ellerton. EDUC.: A.B., Harvard U., 1871, LL.B., 1875, Ph.D., 1876. POLIT. & GOV.: elected as a Republican to MA State House, 1880–83; delegate, Rep. Nat'l. Conv., 1880 (sec., MA delegation), 1884, 1888, 1892, 1896, 1900 (chm.), 1904, 1908 (chm.), 1912, 1916, 1920 (chm.), 1924; member, MA Republican State Central Cmte., 1881–83 (chm., 1883); Republican candidate for U.S. House (MA), 1884; elected as a Republican to U.S. House (MA), 1887–93; elected as a Republican to U.S. Senate (MA), 1893–1924 (majority floor leader, 1918–24); member, Alaskan Boundary Tribunal, 1903; member, U.S. Immigration Comm., 1907–10; commissioner plenipotentiary, International Conference on the Limitation of Armaments, 1921; ***candidate for Republican nomination to presidency of the U.S., 1916; candidate for Republican nomination to vice presidency of the U.S., 1920***. BUS. & PROF.: atty.; admitted to MA Bar, 1876; ed., *North American Review*, 1873–76; ed., *International Review*, 1879–81; lecturer on American history, Harvard U., 1876–79; lecturer, Lowell Inst., 1880. MEM.: Harvard Alumni Assn. (pres., 1914); MA Hist. Soc. (pres., 1915); Smithsonian Institution (regent); Boston Athenaeum (trustee); American Acad. of Arts and Sciences (fellow); Harvard U. (overseer, 1884–90, 1911–24); Mayflower Soc.; VA Hist. Soc.; New England Hist. and Genealogical Soc.; American Antiquarian Soc.; American Acad. of Arts and Letters; Colonial Soc. of MA; Royal Hist. Soc. HON. DEG.: LL.D., Williams Coll., 1893; LL.D., Clark U., 1902; LL.D., Yale U., 1902; LL.D., Harvard U., 1904; LL.D., Amherst Coll., 1912; LL.D., Brown U., 1918; LL.D., Dartmouth Coll., 1918; LL.D., Princeton U., 1918; LL.D., Union Coll., 1918. WRITINGS: *Ballads and Lyrics* (ed., 1881); *Complete Works of Alexander Hamilton* (ed., 1885); *Life and Letters of George Cabot* (1877); *Short History of the English Colonies in America* (1881); *Life of Alexander Hamilton* (1882); *Life of Daniel Webster* (1883); *Studies in History* (1886); *Life of Washington* (1889); *History of Boston* (1891); *Historical and Political Essays* (1892); *Speeches* (1895); *Hero Tales from American History* (with Theodore Roosevelt, q.v., 1895); *Certain Accepted Heroes and Other Essays in Literature and Politics* (1897); *Story of the Revolution* (1898); *Story of the Spanish War* (1899); *A Fighting Frigate and Other Essays; A Frontier Town and Other Essays* (1906); *Speeches and Addresses* (1910); *One Hundred Years of Peace* (1913); *Early Memories* (1913); *Democracy of the Constitution and Other Essays* (1915); *War Addresses* (1917); *Senate of the United States* (1921). RES.: Nahant, MA.

LODGE, HENRY CABOT, JR. b. Jul 5, 1902, Nahant, MA; d. Feb 27, 1985, Beverly, MA; par. George Cabot and Methilda Elizabeth Frelinghuysen (David) Lodge; m. Emily Esther Sears, Jul 1, 1926; c. George Cabot (q.v.); Henry Sears. EDUC.: grad., Middlesex (MA) School, 1920; A.B. (cum laude), Harvard U., 1924. POLIT. & GOV.: elected as a Republican to MA State House, 1933–37; elected as a Republican to U.S. Senate (MA), 1937–44 (resigned), 1947–53; ***candidate for Republican nomination to presidency of the U.S., 1940, 1964***; delegate, Rep. Nat'l. Conv., 1940, 1948 (chm., Resolutions Cmte.), 1956, 1976; ***candidate for Republican nomination to vice presidency of the U.S., 1944***; campaign mgr., Dwight D. Eisenhower (q.v.) for President Campaign, 1952; Republican candidate for U.S. Senate (MA), 1952; appointed U.S. ambassador to the U.N., 1953–60; ***Republican candidate for vice presidency of the U.S., 1960***; appointed U.S. ambassador to South Vietnam, 1963–64, 1965–67; appointed U.S. ambassador-at-large, 1967–68; appointed U.S. ambassador to Federal Republic of Germany, 1968–69; personal representative to chm., U.S. Delegation, Vietnam Peace Talks, Paris, France, 1969; appointed special envoy to the Vatican, 1970–77; appointed chm., Presidential Comm. for the Observance of the 25th Anniversary of the U.N., 1970–71. BUS. & PROF.: staff reporter, *Boston (MA) Evening Transcript*, 1923–25; staff reporter, *New York (NY) Herald Tribune*, 1924–32; dir.-gen., The Atlantic Inst., 1961–62; consultant, Time, Inc., 1961–63; dir., John Hancock Life Insurance Co., 1961–65; visiting prof., Gordon Coll., 1977, prof., 1978–85. MIL.: 1st lt., Cavalry Reserves Corps, U.S. Army; pvt., maj., U.S. Army, 1942–44, lt. col., 1944–45; maj. gen., U.S.A.R.; Bronze Star; Legion of Merit Medal; six Battle Stars; Legion of Honor; Croix de Guerre with Palm; Chevalier's Cross, Order of Polonia Restituta (Poland); Humane Order of African Redemption (Liberia); Grand Cross of Merit (Malta); National Order (Vietnam). MEM.: Somerset Club; Tavern Club; Myopia Club; Metropolitan Club; Alfalfa Club; Salvation Army (National Council, 1976); Harvard U. (overseer, 1924–32); Naval Hist. Foundation; Fletcher School of Diplomacy (overseer). AWARDS: Sylvanus Thayer Medal, U.S. Military Acad., 1960; President Eisenhower's Gold Medal, 1961; medal, Theodore Roosevelt Assn.; Marshall Medal, Assn. of the U.S. Army, 1967; Distinguished Honor Award, U.S. Dept. of State, 1967. HON. DEG.: LL.B., Northeastern U., 1938; LL.D., Clark U., 1951; LL.D., Norwich U., 1951; Docteur es Lettres, Laval U., 1952; D.C.L., Bishop's U., 1953; LL.D., Boston U., 1953; LL.D., Franklin and Marshall Coll., 1953; LL.D., Hamilton Coll., 1953; LL.D., Harvard U., 1954; LL.D., Fordham U., 1955; LL.D., NY U., 1955; LL.D., Rensselaer Polytechnic Inst., 1955; LL.D., Lehigh U., 1956; LL.D., U. of PA, 1956; LL.D., Union U., 1957; LL.D., Williams Coll., 1957; LL.D., U. of NH, 1959; LL.D., Columbia U., 1960; LL.D., Adelphia U., 1961; LL.D., Boston Coll., 1961; LL.D., Princeton U., 1961; LL.D., Notre Dame U., 1962; LL.D., U. of MA, 1962; LL.D., American U., 1967; LL.D., Salem State U., 1977. WRITINGS: *Cult of Weakness* (1932); *The Storm Has Many Eyes* (1973); *As It Was* (1976). RES.: Beverly, MA.

LOEB, SOPHIE IRENE SIMON. b. Jul 4, 1876, Rovno, Russia; d. Jan 18, 1929, New York, NY; par. Samuel and Mary (Carey) Simon; m. Anselm Loeb, Mar 10, 1896 (divorced). EDUC.: grad., McKeesport (PA) H.S. POLIT. & GOV.: appointed member, NY State Comm. for Widows' Pensions, 1914;

pres., New York (NY) Child Welfare Board; appointed New York City mediator, taxicab drivers' strike, 1917; appointed member, NY State Comm. on Child Welfare, 1920; ***candidate for Democratic nomination to vice presidency of the U.S., 1928***. BUS. & PROF.: staff writer, *New York Evening World*, 1910–29; author; social reformer. MEM.: Child Welfare Cmte. of America, Inc. (chm., 1924); National Inst. of Social Sciences; League of American Pen Women; Civic Club; Twilight Club; Authors League of America; Soc. of Arts and Sciences; Womens' City Club. AWARDS: George MacDonald Award, Big Brothers and Big Sisters, 1923. WRITINGS: *Epigrams of Eve* (1913); *Epigrams of What Eve Said* (1916); *Century Fables of Everyday Folks; Everyman's Child* (1920); *Palestine Awake* (1926). REL.: Jewish. MISC.: nominated by Irving S. Cobb (q.v.) to run on ticket with Alfred E. Smith (q.v.). RES.: New York, NY.

LOEWENHERZ, RICK. b. Aug 16, 1940, Evansville, IN; par. Stewart A. Pearce and Doris R. Sprouse; m. (divorced); c. Michael; Morgan. EDUC.: grad., Carmi Township (IL) H.S., 1958; WA U., 1958–62; LL.B., Tulsa U., 1965. POLIT. & GOV.: asst. district atty., Tulsa Cty., OK; judge, Municipal Criminal Court, Tulsa, OK; candidate for police and fire commissioner, Tulsa, 1967; ***candidate for Democratic nomination to presidency of the U.S., 1976***. BUS. & PROF.: atty.; independent oil producer. REL.: Protestant. MAILING ADDRESS: 1723 South Carson Ave., Tulsa, OK 74119.

LOGAN, JOHN ALEXANDER. b. Feb 9, 1826, Murphysboro, IL; d. Dec 26, 1886, Washington, DC; par. Dr. John and Elizabeth (Jenkins) Logan; m. Mary Simmerson Cunningham, Nov 27, 1855; c. John; Mary Elizabeth (Mrs. William F. Tucker); John Alexander. EDUC.: grad., U. of Louisville, 1851; studied law under Alexander M. Jenkins. POLIT. & GOV.: elected clerk, Jackson Cty. (IL) Court, 1849; elected as a Democrat to IL State House, 1852–53, 1856–57; elected prosecuting atty., Third Judicial District of IL, 1853–57; presidential elector, Democratic Party, 1856; elected as a Democrat to U.S. House (IL), 1859–62; elected as a Republican to U.S. House (IL), 1867–71; house mgr., impeachment trial of President Andrew Johnson (q.v.), 1868; appointed U.S. minister to Mexico, 1868 (declined); elected as a Republican to U.S. Senate (IL), 1871–77, 1879–86; Republican candidate for U.S. Senate (IL), 1877; ***candidate for Republican nomination to presidency of the U.S., 1884; Republican candidate for vice presidency of the U.S., 1884***. BUS. & PROF.: soldier; atty.; admitted to IL Bar, 1852; law practice, Chicago, IL, 1877–79; author. MIL.: lt., First IL Infantry, 1846–48; col., 21st IL Infantry, U.S. Army, 1861; brig. gen., IL Volunteers, 1862, maj. gen., 1862–65. MEM.: Soc. of the Army of the Tennessee (founder, 1865); GAR (commander in chief, 1868–70). WRITINGS: *The Great Conspiracy: Its Origins and History* (1886); *The Volunteer Soldier of America, With Memoir of the Author and Military Reminiscences from General Logan's Private Journal* (1887). MISC.: conceived idea of Memorial Day. RES.: Chicago, IL.

LOJAS, ROMAN J. POLIT. & GOV.: ***independent candidate for presidency of the U.S., 1980***. MAILING ADDRESS: P.O. Box 545, Wilmington, IL.

LOMENTO, FRANK M. b. Apr 27, 1932, Philadelphia, PA; par. Michael and Pauline (Bongavonni) Lomento; single. EDUC.: ninth grade. POLIT. & GOV.: Protester Party candidate for mayor of Philadelphia, PA, 1967, 1971; ***Protester Party candidate for presidency of the U.S., 1968, 1980***; candidate for gov. of PA, 1970; candidate for PA State House, 1972; ***candidate for Democratic nomination to presidency of the U.S., 1972, 1976, 1980***; candidate for city controller, Philadelphia, PA, 1973. BUS. & PROF.: welfare recipient; ice cream vendor; pretzel salesman. MIL.: enlisted in National Guard (dishonorable discharge because of age), 1947; enlisted in U.S. Army (general discharge for failure to "march straight"), 1949; enlisted in USMC (honorable discharge for medical reasons), 1950; enlisted in U.S. Air Force (undesirable discharge), 1951. REL.: R.C. MAILING ADDRESS: 365 Seventh St., Philadelphia, PA 19106.

LONG, ALEXANDER. b. Dec 24, 1816, Greenville, PA; d. Nov 28, 1886, Cincinnati, OH. EDUC.: academic training; studied law. POLIT. & GOV.: elected as a Democrat to OH State House, 1848–49; elected as a Democrat to U.S. House (OH), 1863–65; delegate, Dem. Nat'l. Conv., 1864, 1868, 1872, 1876; ***Independent Democratic Party candidate for presidency of the U.S., 1864 (declined)***; Democratic candidate for U.S. House (OH), 1864. BUS. & PROF.: atty.; admitted to OH Bar; law practice, Cincinnati. RES.: Cincinnati, OH.

LONG, HUEY PIERCE. b. Aug 30, 1893, Winnfield, LA; d. Sep 10, 1935, Baton Rouge, LA; par. Huey Pierce and Caledonia (Tison) Long; m. Rose McConnell, Apr 12, 1913; c. Rose Lolita (Mrs. Osmyn William McFarland); Russell Billiu; Palmer Reid. EDUC.: Shreveport (LA) H.S.; OK U.; Tulane U.. POLIT. & GOV.: elected as a Democrat to LA State Railroad Comm., 1918–21; elected as a Democrat, chm., LA State Public Service Comm., 1921–28; candidate for Democratic nomination to gov. of LA, 1924; elected as a Democrat, gov. of LA, 1928–32; member, Dem. Nat'l. Cmte., 1928–35; delegate, Dem. Nat'l. Conv., 1928, 1932; elected as a Democrat to U.S. Senate (LA), 1932–35; ***Farmer-Labor Party candidate for presidency of the U.S., 1932, 1936 (declined)***; chm., LA State Democratic Central Cmte., 1934–35; ***candidate for Democratic nomination to presidency of the U.S., 1936***. BUS. & PROF.: salesman; auctioneer; printer; sales mgr., Memphis, TN, 1912; atty.; admitted to LA Bar, 1915; law practice, Winnfield, LA, 1915–18; law practice, Shreveport, LA; publisher, *Louisiana Progress*, 1930; publisher, *American Progress*. MEM.: Home for Epileptics (founder); Share Our Wealth Soc. (founder). HON. DEG.: LL.D., Loyola Coll., 1931. WRITINGS: *Every Man a King* (1933); *My First Days in the White House* (1935). REL.: Bapt. MISC.: founded School of Medicine, LA State U.; LA state legislature twice attempted unsuccessful impeachment against him as member of the Public Service Comm., 1921, and as gov., 1929; advocate of "Share Our Wealth" plan; known as "Kingfish"; assassinated by Dr. Carl Weiss, Jr., dying two days after shooting, which occurred on Sep 8, 1935. RES.: New Orleans, LA.

LONG, HUGH WILSON, III. b. Jan 6, 1940, Columbus, OH; par. Hugh Wilson, Jr.; single. EDUC.: MA Inst. of Technology, 1957–58; B.A. (cum laude), OH State U., 1962; M.B.A., Stanford U., 1967, Ph.D., 1973. POLIT. & GOV.: ***independent (Committee for a Constitutional Presidency) candidate for presidency of the U.S., 1976***. BUS. & PROF.: instructor, OH State U., 1961–62; computer programmer, OH State Dept. of Highways, 1961–62; asst. prof. of statistics, San Jose State U., 1966–68; lecturer in quantitative methods, Stanford U., 1967–68; consultant, Ford Foundation, 1968–69; asst. prof. of finance, Tulane U., 1969–74, assoc. prof. of finance, 1974–; co-dir., Joint MBA/MPH (HSM) Degree Program, Tulane U., 1973–77; coordinator, Executive Graduate Program in Health Care Financial Management, Tulane U., 1975–77; assoc. ed., *Journal of Financial Research*, 1978–79. MIL.: lt., U.S. Army, 1962–65; Army Commendation Medal, 1963, with Oak Leaf Cluster, 1965; Distinguished Military Graduate, Army Reserve Officers Training Program, 1962. MEM.: Pi Mu Epsilon; Phi Beta Kappa; Sierra Club; A.C.L.U.; American Finance Assn.; Financial Management Assn.; Western Finance Assn.; Southwestern Finance Assn.; Hospital Financial Management Assn.; AAUP. AWARDS: Sloan Foundation Fellowship, 1965–67; Howard W. Wissner Award for Excellence in Teaching, 1975. WRITINGS: "Abandonment Value and Capital Budgeting: Comment," *Journal of Finance*, Mar 1969 (with Edward A. Dyl); "Portfolio Selection: A Three Parameter Model," *Proceedings of the Southwestern Finance Assn.* (with Edward A. Dyl, 1969); *Upton University Hospital* (1973); "Audio Tapes on Wage and Price Controls," *AUPHA Program Notes*, Nov 1973; *Financial Management of Health Care Institutions: An Outline and Annotated Bibliography* (1974); *Financial Analysis Methodology for Planning and Evaluating Capital Expenditures under Section 1122 of the Social Security Act* (with Stuart A. Capper, 1975); "Medicare Reimbursement is Federal Taxation of Tax-Exempt Providers," *Health Care Management Review*, winter, 1976; "Valuation as a Criterion in Not-for-Profit Decision Making," *Health Care Management Review*, Jul 1976; "Incorporating the Capital Asset Pricing Model into the Basic Finance Course," *Journal of Financial Education*, fall, 1976; *The Basic Theory of Corporate Finance* (with Kenneth J. Boudreaux, 1977). MAILING ADDRESS: 500 Cherokee St., New Orleans, LA 70118.

LONG, JOHN DAVIS. b. Oct 27, 1838, Buckfield, ME; d. Aug 28, 1915, Hingham, MA; par. Zadoc and Julia Temple (Davis) Long; m. Mary Woodward Glover, Sep 13, 1870; m. 2d, Agnes Pierce, May 22, 1886. EDUC.: Hebron Acad.; A.B., Harvard U., 1857; studied law, Harvard U. and private law offices, 1861. POLIT. & GOV.: elected as a Republican to MA State House, 1875–78 (Speaker, 1876–78); elected as a Republican to lt. gov. of MA, 1879; elected as a Republican to gov. of MA, 1880–83; elected as a Republican to U.S. House (MA), 1883–89; member, MA Statehouse Construction Comm.; appointed U.S. sec. of the navy, 1897–1902; ***candidate for Republican nomination to vice presidency of the U.S., 1896, 1900***. BUS. & PROF.: principal, Westford Acad., MA, 1857–59; atty.; admitted to ME Bar, 1861; law practice, Buckfield, ME, 1861–62; law practice, Boston, MA; senior partner, Long and Hemenway (law firm), Boston. MEM.: Authors Club of Boston (pres.); Harvard U. (pres., Board of Overseers); American Acad. of Arts and Sciences (fellow). HON. DEG.: LL.D., Harvard U., 1880; LL.D., Tufts U., 1902. WRITINGS: *The Republican Party: Its History, Principles and Policies* (1898, 1900); *The New American Navy* (2 vols.). RES.: Hingham, MA.

LONGLEY, JAMES BERNARD. b. Apr 22, 1924, Lewiston, ME; d. Aug 16, 1980, Lewiston, ME; par. James Bernard and Catherine (Wade) Longley; m. Helen Walsh, Sep 3, 1949; c. James Bernard; Kathryn M.; Susan Marie; Stephen J.; Nancy E. EDUC.: Bowdoin Coll., 1947; C.L.U., American Coll. of Life Underwriters, 1954; LL.B., U. of ME, 1957. POLIT. & GOV.: appointed chm., Maine Management and Cost Survey of State Government Comm., 1972–73; elected as an independent to gov. of ME, 1975–79; ***candidate for independent (Committee for a Constitutional Presidency) nomination to vice presidency of the U.S., 1976***. BUS. & PROF.: pres., Longley Associates, 1948–74; gen. agent, New England Mutual Life Insurance Co., Boston, MA; atty.; admitted to ME Bar, 1957; partner, Longley and Buckley (law firm), Lewiston, ME, 1958–74; athletic dir., Healey Home for Boys, 1958–70; dir., Casco Bank and Trust Co.; dir., First Federal Savings and Loan Assn. MEM.: Million Dollar Round Table (pres.); Androscoggin Cty. Bar Assn.; ME Bar Assn.; ABA; Andy Valley Life Underwriters Assn.; Maine Life Underwriters Assn.; Child and Family Services of Maine (dir.); Central Maine General Hospital (trustee). AWARDS: Lucien Howe Prize, Bowdoin Coll., 1947; President's Trophy Award, New England Mutual Life Insurance Co., 3 times. REL.: R.C. RES.: Lewiston, ME.

LONGWORTH, ALICE LEE ROOSEVELT. b. Feb 12, 1884, New York, NY; d. Feb 20, 1980, Washington, DC; par. Theodore (q.v.) and Alice Hathaway (Lee) Roosevelt; m. Nicholas Longworth, Feb 17, 1906; c. Pauline (Mrs. Alexander McCormick Sturm). EDUC.: private tutors. POLIT. & GOV.: member, Board of Counselors, Women's Div., Rep. Nat'l. Cmte., 1932; delegate, Rep. Nat'l. Conv., 1936; ***candidate for Republican nomination to vice presidency of the U.S., 1936***. BUS. & PROF.: columnist, *Ladies Home Journal*. MEM.: National Cmte. on Food for Five Small Democracies (1940). WRITINGS: *Crowded Hours* (1934); *The Desk Drawer Anthology; Poems for the American People* (co-editor, with Theodore Roosevelt, Jr., 1937). MISC.: known as "Princess Alice." RES.: Washington, DC.

LOOMIS, ROBERT S. POLIT. & GOV.: ***candidate for Libertarian Party nomination to presidency of the U.S.,***

1976; Libertarian Party candidate for U.S. Senate (CT), 1976; candidate for presidential elector, Libertarian Party, 1992. MAILING ADDRESS: 191 Newgate Rd., East Granby, CT 06026.

LOPEZ-ESCAPA, CESAR. POLIT. & GOV.: ***independent candidate for presidency of the U.S., 1984***. MAILING ADDRESS: P.O. Box 55-7553, Miami, FL 33155.

LORD, NANCY. b. Feb 8, 1953, New York, NY; m. Michael D. Tanner. EDUC.: B.S., U. of MD, 1973, M.D., 1978; J.D., Georgetown U., 1990. POLIT. & GOV.: Libertarian Party candidate for mayor of Washington, DC, 1990; ***Libertarian Party candidate for vice presidency of the U.S., 1992***. BUS. & PROF.: atty.; law practice, Atlanta, GA. MEM.: American Coll. of Legal Medicine; American Acad. of Clinical Toxicology; National Assn. of Criminal Defense Lawyers; DC Bar Assn.; MD Bar Assn.; VA Bar Assn.; Drug Policy Foundation; National Abortion Rights Action League; National Drug Strategy Network; National Tax Limitation Cmte.; National Taxpayers Union; NRA. REL.: Jewish. MAILING ADDRESS: 3180 Clairmont Rd., N.E., #506, Atlanta, GA 30329.

LORIMER, GEORGE HORACE. b. Oct 6, 1867, Louisville, KY; d. Oct 22, 1937, Wyncote, PA; par. Rev. Dr. George C. and Belle (Burford) Lorimer; m. Alma V. Ennis, Jun 6, 1892. EDUC.: Mosely H.S., Chicago, IL; Colby Coll.; Yale U. POLIT. & GOV.: appointed col., aide to gov. of KY, 1923; member, Comm. on Conservation and Administration of the Public Domain; ***candidate for Republican nomination to presidency of the U.S., 1936***. BUS. & PROF.: employee, Armour and Co., Chicago, IL; wholesale grocer; literary ed., *Saturday Evening Post*, 1898, editor-in-chief, 1899–1936; vice pres., Curtis Publishing Co., 1927–32, pres., 1932–34, chm. of the board, 1934–37. MEM.: Huntingdon Valley Hunt Club; Yale Club of Philadelphia. AWARDS: Chevalier de la Legion d'Honneur; commander, Order of the Crown of Italy. WRITINGS: *Letters from a Self-Made Merchant to His Son* (1902); *Old Gorgon Graham* (1904); *The False Gods* (1906); *Jack Spurlock: Prodigal* (1908). REL.: Bapt. RES.: Wyncote, PA.

LOTHROP, GEORGE VAN NESS. b. Aug 8, 1817, Easton, MA; d. Jul 12, 1897, Detroit, MI; par. Howard and Sally (Williams) Lothrop; m. Almira Strong, May 13, 1847; c. Captain Henry Brown; Cyrus Edwin; George Howard; Howard; Anne Strong (Baroness Heune); Charles Bradley; Helen Ames (Mrs. William Prall). EDUC.: Wrentham Acad., Amherst, MA, 1834; A.B., A.M., Brown U., 1838; Harvard U. Law School, 1839; studied law in offices of Joy and Porter, Detroit, MI. POLIT. & GOV.: elected as a Democrat to atty. gen. of MI, 1848–51; elected as an independent to recorder, Detroit, MI, 1851–53; Democratic candidate for U.S. House (MI), 1858, 1860; Democratic candidate for U.S. Senate (MI), 3 times; delegate, Dem. Nat'l. Conv., 1860; delegate, MI State Constitutional Convention, 1867; ***candidate for Democratic nomination to presidency of the U.S., 1880***; appointed U.S. minister to Russia, 1885–88. BUS. & PROF.: farmer, Prairie Ronde, MI, 1839–42; atty.; admitted to MI Bar, 1843; partner (with Bethune Duffield), law firm, Detroit, MI, 1843–56; mgr., Detroit Young Men's Soc., 1844; gen. counsel, Michigan Central R.R. Co., 1854–80; dir., First National Bank of Detroit; real estate investor. MEM.: Detroit Bar Assn. (pres., 1879–96). HON. DEG.: LL.D., Brown U., 1863. WRITINGS: *The People et. al., Elijah H. Drake vs. The Regents of the University of Michigan* (1856); *A Plea for Education as a Public Duty* (1878). RES.: Detroit, MI.

LOUGHLIN, JOSEPH F. POLIT. & GOV.: ***Down With Lawyers Party candidate for vice presidency of the U.S., 1980***. MAILING ADDRESS: NJ?

LOVE, ALFRED HENRY. b. Sep 7, 1830, Philadelphia, PA; d. Jun 29, 1913, Philadelphia, PA; par. William Henry and Rachel (Evans) Love; m. Susan Henry Brown, Jan 13, 1853; c. William Henry; John Brown; Elizabeth Ellis "Lillie" (Mrs. William N. Allen). EDUC.: A.B., Central H.S., Philadelphia, PA, 1847. POLIT. & GOV.: ***Equal Rights Party candidate for vice presidency of the U.S., 1888 (declined)***; official visitor to prisons, 43 years. BUS. & PROF.: merchant; senior member, A. H. Love and Co. (package woolens), Philadelphia, PA, 1853–1913; ed., *Bond of Peace*; ed., *The Voice of Peace*; ed., *The Peacemaker and Court of Arbitration*, 1866–1913; ed., *Prison Journal*; mgr., Mercantile Library and Spring Garden Inst. MEM.: Universal Peace Union (pres., 1866–1913); American Literary Union (pres., hon. pres., 1875–1913); PA Abolition Soc. (vice pres.); International Council of Women (patron); PA Prison Soc. (vice pres.); Temperance Soc. WRITINGS: *An Appeal in Vindication of Peace Principles and Against Resistance by Force of Arms* (1862); *Address Before the Peace Convention* (1866); *A Shaker Meeting* (1891); *A Brief Synopsis of Work Proposed, Aided and Accomplished by the Universal Peace Union. . . .* (1897). REL.: Soc. of Friends. RES.: Philadelphia, PA.

LOVE, JOHN ARTHUR. b. Nov 29, 1916, Gibson City, IL; par. Arthur C. and Mildred (Shaver) Love; m. Ann Daniels, Oct 23, 1942; c. Dan; Andy; Becky. EDUC.: B.A., U. of Denver, 1938, LL.B., 1941. POLIT. & GOV.: member, El Paso Cty. (CO) Republican Central Cmte.; member, CO Republican State Central Cmte., 1960–; candidate for chm., El Paso Cty. Republican Central Cmte., 1961; elected as a Republican to gov. of CO, 1963–73 (resigned); ***candidate for Republican nomination to vice presidency of the U.S., 1964***; appointed dir., U.S. Office of Energy Policy and Natural Resources, 1973; appointed asst. to the president of the U.S., 1973; delegate, Rep. Nat'l. Conv., 1976; ***candidate for Republican nomination to presidency of the U.S., 1980***. BUS. & PROF.: ed., *The Clarion*, U. of Denver, 1937–38; atty.; admitted to CO Bar, 1941; law practice, Colorado Springs, CO, 1945–; partner, Love, Cole and Murphy (law firm), Colorado Springs, 1948–62; pres., chief exec. officer, Ideal Basic Industries, Denver, CO, 1974–; dir., National Airlines; dir., Frontier Airlines; dir., National Banks of Colorado; dir., John Manville Corp.; dir., Great West Life. MIL.: lt. commander, pilot, U.S.N.R., 1942–45; two Distinguished Flying Crosses; Air Medal with Clusters. MEM.: ABA; CO Bar Assn.; El Paso Cty. Bar Assn.; Republican Governors' Conference (chm., 1966); National Governors' Conference (chm., 1969–70); Council of State Governments (exec. cmte.); Rotary Club; El Paso Cty. Young Republicans (pres., 1947–48); Colorado Springs United Fund (division chm., 1961); Colorado Springs C. of C. (pres., 1954); American Legion; Reserve Officers' Assn.; Omicron Delta Kappa; Sigma Phi Epsilon; Kiwanis; Masons. AWARDS: "Colorado Man of the Year," United Press International, 3 years. Hon. Deg: LL.D., U. of Denver, 1963; LL.D., CO Coll., 1964; LL.D., CO School of Mines. REL.: Congregationalist. MAILING ADDRESS: 400 East Eighth Ave., Denver, CO 80203.

LOVE 22 (aka LAWRENCE E. WAGNER). b. Jan 1, 1937, Providence, RI; par. Charles L. and Bess A. Wagner; m. Lynn Jacobs; c. Rand Scott; Mason Mitchell. EDUC.: grad., East Cranston (RI) H.S., 1955; B.S., U. of RI, 1960. POLIT. & GOV.: The Independent Man from Rhode Island candidate for gov. of RI, 1976, 1978, 1980; ***Independent Democratic candidate for presidency of the U.S., 1980, 1984***. BUS. & PROF.: teacher, Hope H.S., Providence, RI; teacher, North Providence H.S. MEM.: Dine Out Tonight Club (pres.; treas.); Let's Dine Out Tonight (food taster; national public relations dir.). REL.: Jewish. MISC.: noted proponent of theory that the number "22" has special significance in world affairs; self-styled "abecedarian." MAILING ADDRESS: 22 Railroad Ave., West Kingston, RI.

LOVEJOY, OWEN. b. Jan 6, 1811, Albion, ME; d. Mar 25, 1864, Brooklyn, NY; par. Rev. Daniel and Elizabeth (Pattee) Loveloy; m. Eunice (Storrs) Dunham, Jan 1843; c. seven. EDUC.: Bowdoin Coll., 1831–33; studied law. POLIT. & GOV.: ***candidate for Liberty Party nomination to vice presidency of the U.S., 1848***; elected as a Republican to IL State House, 1854–56; elected as a Republican to U.S. House (IL), 1857–64. BUS. & PROF.: ordained minister, Congregational Church, 1839; pastor, Congregational Church, Princeton, IL, 1839–56. MEM.: National Anti-Slavery Convention, 1847. WRITINGS: *Memoir of Reverend Elijah P. Lovejoy*. REL.: Congregationalist. MISC.: noted abolitionist. RES.: Princeton, IL.

LOVELAND, WILLIAM AUSTIN HAMILTON. b. May 20, 1826, Chatham, MA; d. Dec 17, 1894, Lakeside, CO; par. Rev. Leonard and Elizabeth (Eldridge) Loveland; m. Philena Shaw, May 13, 1852; m. 2d, Maranda Ann Montgomery, Aug 25, 1856; c. Francis William; William Leonard. EDUC.: McKendree Coll., 1845; Shurtleff Coll., 1846. POLIT. & GOV.: member, CO Territorial Council, 1862–70; pres., CO State Constitutional Convention, 1865; Democratic candidate for U.S. Senate (CO), 1876, 1879; Democratic candidate for gov. of CO, 1878; ***candidate for Democratic nomination to presidency of the U.S., 1880***. BUS. & PROF.: railroad exec.; wagonmaster in Mexican War, 1847; gold miner, 1849–59; merchant, Golden, CO; real estate broker; owner, *Rocky Mountain News*, 1878–86; pres., ore reduction company; dir., Union Pacific R.R. Co., 1897; promoter, pres., Colorado Central and Pacific R.R., 1876. REL.: Methodist. MISC.: Loveland, CO, is named after him. RES.: Lakeside, CO.

LOVELESS, HERSCHEL CELLEL. b. May 5, 1911, Hedrick, IA; d. May 4, 1989, Winchester, VA; par. David Helm and Ethel (Beaver) Loveless; m. Amelia Rebecca Howard, Oct 1, 1922; c. Alan Kay; Sandi Ann (Mrs. Gary Yates). EDUC.: grad., Ottumwa (IA) H.S., 1927. POLIT. & GOV.: appointed superintendent of streets, Ottumwa, IA, 1947–49; elected mayor of Ottumwa, 1949–53; delegate, Dem. Nat'l. Conv., 1952, 1956, 1960, 1964; Democratic candidate for gov. of IA, 1952; elected as a Democrat to gov. of IA, 1957–61; chm., States Cmte., Missouri Basin Inter-Agency Comm., 1959; chm., National Advisory Cmte. on Aging, Dem. Nat'l. Cmte., 1959–60; ***candidate for Democratic nomination to presidency of the U.S., 1960***; national chm., Farmers for Kennedy and Johnson, 1960; Democratic candidate for U.S. Senate (IA), 1960, 1962; appointed member, Renegotiation Board, 1961–69. BUS. & PROF.: employee, Milwaukee, St. Paul and Pacific R.R. Co., 1927–39, maintenance of way engineer, 1943–49; turbine operator, John Morrell Co., Ottumwa, 1939–43; owner, operator, Municipal Equipment Co., 1953–56; vice pres., Chromalloy American Corp., 1969–78. MEM.: Council of Former Governors (chm.); IA Engineering Soc.; BSA (National Exec. Council); dir., Southern IA Council; National Governors' Conference (exec. cmte.); Lions; Elks; Eagles; Phi Theta Pi; Red Cross; Community Club; Freedom Foundation; Wapello Cty. Polio Foundation Drive (chm.); IA League of Municipalities. AWARDS: Silver Beaver Award, BSA. REL.: Methodist. RES.: Ottumwa, IA.

LOW, SETH. b. Jan 18, 1850, Brooklyn, NY; d. Sep 17, 1916, Bedford Hills, NY; par. Abiel Abbott and Ellen Almira (Dow) Low; m. Annie Wroe Scollay Curtis, Dec 8, 1880; c. none. EDUC.: Brooklyn (NY) Juvenile H.S.; Brooklyn Collegiate and Polytechnic Inst.; A.B., Columbia U., 1870. POLIT. & GOV.: pres., Bureau of Charities, Brooklyn, NY, 1878; pres., Brooklyn Republican Campaign Club, 1880; elected as an independent to mayor of Brooklyn, NY, 1881–85; ***candidate for American (Know Nothing) Party nomination to presidency of the U.S., 1888 (declined)***; independent (Citizens' Union) candidate for mayor of Greater New York, NY, 1897; delegate, Hague Peace Conference, 1899; elected mayor of Greater New York, 1902–03; ***candidate for Republican nomination to vice presidency of the U.S., 1908***; appointed member, CO Coal Comm., 1914; delegate, NY State Constitutional Convention, 1915. BUS. & PROF.: educator; publicist; clerk, partner, A. A. Low and Brothers (tea imports), 1870–87; pres., Columbia U., 1890–1901. MEM.: Columbia U. (trustee, 1881–1914); Carnegie Institution (trustee); Cmte. of Citizens; Tuskegee Inst.

(trustee, 1905–16); Archaeological Inst. of America (pres.); Geographical Soc. of New York (pres.); New York Acad. of Political Science (pres.); New York Acad. of Sciences (vice pres.); National Civic Federation (pres., 1907); New York C. of C. (pres., 1914); Down Town Club; Century Club; University Club; Union League; Metropolitan Club; City Club; Authors Club; National Arts Club; Barnard Club; Columbia U. Club; Hamilton Club of Brooklyn. HON. DEG.: LL.D., Amherst Coll., 1889; LL.D., Harvard U., 1890; LL.D., Trinity Coll., 1890; LL.D., U. of PA, 1890; LL.D., U. of the State of NY, 1890; LL.D., Princeton U., 1896; LL.D., Yale U., 1901; LL.D., U. of Edinburgh, 1910. WRITINGS: *Addresses and Papers on Municipal Government* (1891). REL.: Episc. RES.: New York, NY.

LOWDEN, FRANK ORREN. b. Jan 26, 1861, Sunrise City, MN; d. Mar 20, 1943, Tucson, AZ; par. Lorenzo Orren and Nancy Elizabeth (Breg) Lowden; m. Florence Pullman, Apr 29, 1896; c. George Mortimer Pullman; Florence (Mrs. Charles Phillip Miller, Jr.); Harriet Elizabeth (Mrs. Albert Fridolin Madlener, Jr.); Frances (Mrs. John Burroughs Drake, Jr.; Mrs. Frederick William Wierdsma). EDUC.: ; A.B., IA State U., 1885; LL.B., Union Coll., 1887. POLIT. & GOV.: delegate, Rep. Nat'l. Conv., 1900, 1904; candidate for Republican nomination to gov. of IL, 1904; member, Rep. Nat'l. Cmte., 1904–12; elected as a Republican to U.S. House (IL), 1906–11; ***candidate for Republican nomination to presidency of the U.S., 1916, 1920, 1928***; elected as a Republican to gov. of IL, 1917–21; ***Republican candidate for vice presidency of the U.S., 1924 (declined); candidate for Republican nomination to vice presidency of the U.S., 1928 (declined); Peoples National Independent Party candidate for vice presidency of the U.S., 1936***. BUS. & PROF.: atty.; admitted to IL Bar, 1887; partner, Dexter, Herrick and Allen (law firm), Chicago, IL, 1887–90; partner, Walker and Lowden (law firm), Chicago, 1890–92; partner, Keep and Lowden (law firm), Chicago, 1893; partner, Lowden, Estabrook and Davis (law firm), Chicago, 1898–1906; prof. of law, Northwestern U., 1899; trustee, Chicago, Rock Island and Pacific Railway Co., 1933–37; dir., Foreign Bondholders Protective Council, 1933–37. MIL.: lt. col., First Infantry, IL National Guard, 1898–1903. MEM.: Masons (330); ABA; IL Bar Assn.; Phi Beta Kappa; Phi Kappa Phi; Beta Theta Pi; Phi Delta Phi; Orchestral Assn. (trustee); National Industrial Conference Board (trustee); U. of Chicago (trustee); Northwestern U. (trustee); Law Club of Chicago (pres., 1898–99); International Livestock Exposition (dir., 1919–43); Hollstein-Friesian Assn. of America (pres., 1921–30); Carnegie Endowment for International Peace (trustee); Inst. for Public Administration (trustee); Public Administration Clearing House (chm., Board of Trustees); Farm Foundation (trustee); Pullman Free School of Manual Training (pres., Board of Directors). HON. DEG.: LL.D., Knox Coll., 1918; LL.D., U. of IA, 1918; LL.D., Lincoln Memorial U., 1919; LL.D., Northwestern U., 1919; LL.D., U. of Chicago, 1921; LL.D., U. of CO, 1922; LL.D., Coll. of William and Mary, 1923; LL.D., Lafayette Coll., 1923; LL.D., Miami U., 1924; D.C.L., Syracuse U., 1924; LL.D., U. of OR, 1929; LL.D., Washington and Lee U., 1931. REL.: Protestant (trustee, Central Church, nondenominational, Chicago, IL). RES.: Oregon, IL.

LOWE, JAMES FRANKLIN. b. May 11, 1900, Jackson, MN; m. Gerda E. Sederholf. EDUC.: grad., U. of WI, 1925. POLIT. & GOV.: ***candidate for Republican nomination to presidency of the U.S., 1952***. BUS. & PROF.: newspaperman; grain dealer, Chicago, IL, 1936; employee, VA, 1946–48. MIL.: U.S. Navy, WWI, WWII; U.S.N.R. MEM.: Lamda Chi Alpha; AFL Machinists Union; Volunteer Veterans of American Armed Forces, Inc. (national commander); Chicago Board of Trade. WRITINGS: *Participating Capitalism*; one other book. MISC.: lightweight boxing champion in college, 1925. RES.: Wheaton, IL.

LOWENSTEIN, ALLARD KENNETH. b. Jan 16, 1929, Newark, NJ; d. Mar 14, 1980, New York, NY; par. Gabriel Abraham and Augusta (Goldberg) Lowenstein; m. Jennifer Lyman, Nov 25, 1966; c. Frank Graham; Thomas Kennedy; Katharine Eleanor. EDUC.: grad., Horace Mann School, 1945; B.A., U. of NC, 1949; LL.B., Yale U., 1954. POLIT. & GOV.: special asst. to U.S. Sen. Frank Graham, 1949; national chm., Students for Stevenson, 1952; foreign policy asst. to U.S. Sen. Hubert Humphrey (q.v.), 1959; alternate delegate, Dem. Nat'l. Conv., 1960, delegate, 1968, 1972, 1976; ***candidate for Democratic nomination to vice presidency of the U.S., 1968, 1972***; elected as a Democrat (Liberal) to U.S. House (NY), 1969–71; Democratic candidate for U.S. House (NY), 1970, 1974, 1976; candidate for Democratic nomination to U.S. House (NY), 1972, 1978; Liberal Party candidate for U.S. House (NY), 1972; member, Dem. Nat'l. Cmte., 1972–76; adviser, Gov. Edmund G. Brown, Jr. (q.v.), CA, 1975; appointed U.S. representative, U.N. Comm. on Human Rights, 1977; appointed U.S. representative, U.N. Trusteeship Council, 1977; campaign mgr., Edward M. Kennedy for President Campaign, 1980. BUS. & PROF.: atty.; admitted to NY Bar, 1958; faculty, Stanford U.; faculty, NC State U.; faculty, City Coll. of NY; faculty, Yale School of Urban Studies; faculty, U. of MA; faculty, New School of Social Research; visiting fellow, John F. Kennedy School of Government, Harvard U., 1971; lecturer, Yale U.. MIL.: pvt., U.S. Army, 1954–56. MEM.: Americans for Democratic Action (national chm., 1971–73); Conference of Concerned Democrats (chm., 1967). WRITINGS: *Brutal Mandate* (1962). REL.: Jewish. MISC.: assassinated by former political associate. RES.: Long Beach, NY.

LOWERY, ARTHUR J. "AJAY." b. 1926; m. Anita L. POLIT. & GOV.: ***United Sovereign Citizens Party candidate for presidency of the U.S., 1984***. BUS. & PROF.: songwriter; publisher, *Justice Times*, Clinton, AR. MIL.: U.S. Navy, WWII. MAILING ADDRESS: Clinton, AR.

LOWNDES, LLOYD. b. Feb 21, 1845, Clarksburg, WV; d. Jan 8, 1905, Cumberland, MD. EDUC.: grad., Allegheny

Coll., LL.D. POLIT. & GOV.: elected as a Republican to U.S. House (MD), 1873–75; elected as a Republican to gov. of MD, 1895–99; ***candidate for Republican nomination to presidency of the U.S., 1896; candidate for Republican nomination to vice presidency of the U.S., 1896***. BUS. & PROF.: businessman; pres., Second National Bank, Cumberland, MD; pres., Union Mining Co., Allegany Cty., MD; dir., Fidelity and Deposit Co., Baltimore, MD; dir., New York Mining Co. REL.: Episc. RES.: Cumberland, MD.

LOWNDES, WILLIAM JONES. b. Feb 11, 1782, Colleton Cty., SC; d. Oct 27, 1822, at sea; par. Rawlins and Sarah (Jones) Lowndes; m. Elizabeth Pinckney, Sep 16, 1802; c. Rawlins; Thomas Pinckney; Rebecca Motte (Mrs. Edward L. Rutledge). EDUC.: boarding school, England, 1789–92; studied law, Charleston, SC, 1800–1803. POLIT. & GOV.: elected member, SC State House, 1806–10; elected as a Democrat to U.S. House (SC), 1811–22 (Speaker, 1820); ***Democratic-Republican candidate for presidency of the U.S., 1824 (died before election)***. BUS. & PROF.: atty.; admitted to SC Bar, 1804; law practice, Charleston, SC; plantation owner. MIL.: capt., SC Militia, 1807. REL.: Episc. RES.: SC.

LOZIER, CLEMENCE SOPHIA HARNED. b. Dec 11, 1813, Plainfield, NJ; d. Apr 26, 1888, New York, NY; par. David and Hannah (Walker) Harned; m. Abraham Witton Lozier, 1830; m. 2d, John Baker, 1844 (divorced, 1861); c. Abraham Witton, Jr. EDUC.: Plainfield (NJ) Acad.; Central Coll. of NY, 1849; Rochester Eclectic Medical Coll., 1849; M.D. (summa cum laude), Syracuse Medical Coll., 1853. POLIT. & GOV.: ***Equal Rights Party candidate for vice presidency of the U.S., 1884 (declined)***. BUS. & PROF.: proprietor, school, New York, NY, 1832–43; ed., *Moral Reform Gazette*; homeopathic physician, 1853–88; lecturer on hygiene and physiology; founder, pres., clinical prof. of diseases of women and children, NY Medical Coll. and Hospital for Women, 1863–67, dean and prof. of gynecology and obstetrics, 1867–88. MEM.: Moral Reform and Female Guardian Soc. (visitor); Medical Library Assn. (founder); Moral Education Soc. (pres.); Women's American Temperance Soc.; Sorosis; American Female Guardian Soc.; Universal Peace Union (vice pres.); National Working Women's League; W.C.T.U. (pres.); New York City Suffrage League (pres., 1873–86); National Women's Suffrage Assn. (pres., 1877–78). WRITINGS: "Women in Politics," *North American Review* (1883); *Childbirth Made Easy* (1870); *Dress* (n.d.). REL.: Methodist. MISC.: noted peace advocate and women's suffrage proponent. RES.: New York, NY.

LUCAS, DONALD LAYTON. POLIT. & GOV.: ***independent (Committee for a Constitutional Presidency) candidate for vice presidency of the U.S., 1976***. MAILING ADDRESS: 30 Summit Ave., Caribou, ME 04736.

LUCAS, SCOTT WIKE. b. Feb 19, 1892, Chandlerville, IL; d. Feb 22, 1968, Rocky Mount, NC; par. William D. and Sarah Catherine (Underbrink) Lucas; m. Edith Biggs, Jan 1923; c. Scott Wike, Jr. EDUC.: grad., Virginia H.S., Virginia, IL; Normal State Teachers Coll.; LL.B., IL Wesleyan U., 1914. POLIT. & GOV.: elected states atty., Mason City, IL, 1920–26; delegate, Dem. Nat'l. Conv., 1932, 1940, 1944, 1948, 1952, 1956, 1960, 1964; appointed chm., IL State Tax Comm., 1933–35; elected as a Democrat to U.S. House (IL), 1935–39; elected as a Democrat to U.S. Senate (IL), 1939–51 (minority whip, 1947–49; majority leader, 1949–51); ***candidate for Democratic nomination to presidency of the U.S., 1940, 1948; candidate for Democratic nomination to vice presidency of the U.S., 1940, 1944, 1948***; chm., midwest regional headquarters, Campaign to Re-Elect Franklin D. Roosevelt, 1940; delegate, Refugee Conference, 1943; Democratic candidate for U.S. Senate (IL), 1950. BUS. & PROF.: professional baseball player, 3-I League, 3 years; atty.; admitted to IL Bar, 1915; law practice, Havana, IL; law practice, Springfield, IL; law practice, Washington, DC; dir., State Loan and Finance Corp.; dir., Washington Mutual Investors Funds. MIL.: pvt., U.S. Army, 1918, lt., 1918; Officers' Reserve Corps, 1918–34; col., judge advocate gen., IL National Guard, 1934–42. MEM.: Phi Alpha Delta; ABA; IL Bar Assn.; Bar Assn. of DC; Burning Tree Club; Bethesda Club (pres.); American Legion (commander, IL Dept., 1926; national judge advocate, 1927–32). HON. DEG.: LL.D., IL Wesleyan U., 1944; LL.D., John Marshall Law School; LL.D., Western MD Coll. REL.: Bapt. RES.: Springfield, IL.

LUCEY, BRIAN F. b. Jun 6, 1916, Cortland, NY; par. Cornelius Patrick and Bridget (O'Mara) Lucey; single. EDUC.: Cornell U.; State U. of NY. POLIT. & GOV.: ***candidate for Democratic nomination to presidency of the U.S., 1976***. BUS. & PROF.: businessman; employee, U.S. Post Office; employee, U.S. Dept. of the Interior; employee, U.S. Dept. of War; employee, U.S. Dept. of Agriculture. MEM.: Knights of Columbus (resigned). REL.: Christian. MAILING ADDRESS: 481 Lafayette Rd., R.D. 2, Groton, NY 13073.

LUCEY, PATRICK JOSEPH. b. Mar 21, 1918, La Crosse, WI; par. Gregory Charles and Ella Young (McNamara) Lucey; m. Jean Vlasis, Nov 14, 1951; c. Paul; Laurie; David. EDUC.: St. Thomas Coll., 1935–37; B.A., U. of WI, 1946. POLIT. & GOV.: elected as a Democrat to WI State House, 1949–51; Democratic candidate for U.S. House (WI), 1950; dir., WI Democratic Party, 1951–52, chm., 1957–63; campaign mgr., Thomas E. Fairchild for U.S. Senate Campaign, 1952; delegate, Dem. Nat'l. Conv., 1952 (alternate), 1960 (alternate), 1968 (McCarthy floor mgr.), 1972, 1976; campaign mgr., James E. Doyle for Governor Campaign, 1954; campaign mgr., William Proxmire for U.S. Senate Campaign, 1957; campaign aide, John F. Kennedy for President Campaign, 1960; member, Dem. Nat'l. Cmte. (WI), 1964; elected as a Democrat to lt. gov. of WI, 1965–67;

Democratic candidate for gov. of WI, 1966; campaign aide, Robert F. Kennedy for President Campaign, 1968; elected as a Democrat to gov. of WI, 1971–77; ***candidate for Democratic nomination to vice presidency of the U.S., 1972, 1980***; delegate, Democratic Mid-Term Conference, 1974; appointed U.S. ambassador to Mexico, 1977–80; campaign mgr., Edward M. Kennedy for President Campaign, 1980; ***independent (National Unity) candidate for vice presidency of the U.S., 1980***. BUS. & PROF.: owner, Lucey Realty Co., 1954–70; pres., Westaire, Inc.; pres., Doolittle-Barden Inc.; pres., dir., Lucey Investment Corp.; vice pres., Northern States Capital Corp.; sec., dir., LOM, Inc.; dir., Continental Mortgage Insurance Corp. MIL.: pvt., capt., U.S. Army, 1941–45. MEM.: National Governors' Conference (chm.); National Cmte. for Public Financing of Elections; Kennedy Memorial Library Fund (state chm.). HON. DEG.: LL.D., St. Norbert's Coll.; LL.D., Northland Coll. REL.: R.C. MAILING ADDRESS: 1015 Farwell Court, Madison, WI 53704.

LUELLEN, ROBERT J(ONLY). b. Jan 27, 1926, New Castle, IN; par. Robert U. and Naomi Pauline Luellen; m. (divorced); c. Robert Jeffrey. EDUC.: B.S., Purdue U., 1950; Wabash Coll. POLIT. & GOV.: candidate for Republican nomination to U.S. House (IN), 1974, 1976, 1978, 1980; ***candidate for Republican nomination to presidency of the U.S., 1976, 1980***. BUS. & PROF.: businessman; employee, IN Welfare Dept.; employee, IN Rehabilitation Dept.; employee, IN Employment Security Dept.; dir. of County Welfare, State of IN. MIL.: U.S. Air Force, 1943–49. MEM.: Phi Delta Theta (sec.); Optimist Individual; Purdue U. Alumni Assn.; Henry Cty. Hist. Soc.; Soc. of Genealogists of London, England. REL.: Presb. MAILING ADDRESS: P.O. Box 513, 1521 Castle Hills Dr., New Castle, IN 47362.

LUGAR, RICHARD GREEN. b. Apr 4, 1932, Indianapolis, IN; par. Marvin L. and Bertha (Green) Lugar; m. Charlene Smeltzer, Sep 8, 1956; c. Mark; Robert; John; David. EDUC.: grad., Shortridge H.S., Indianapolis, IN, 1950; B.A., Denison U., 1954; B.A., M.A., Pembroke Coll., Oxford U., 1956. POLIT. & GOV.: elected member, Board of School Commissioners, Indianapolis, IN, 1964–67 (vice pres., 1965–66); delegate, IN State Republican Convention, 1964, 1968 (keynoter), 1972; delegate, Rep. Nat'l. Conv., 1968, 1972 (keynoter); elected as a Republican to mayor of Indianapolis, IN, 1968–75; appointed vice chm., Advisory Comm. on Intergovernmental Relations, 1969–75; appointed member, President's Advisory Task Force on Model Cities, 1969; appointed member, Regional Export Expansion Council, U.S. Dept. of Commerce; appointed member, IN State Criminal Justice Planning Agency; appointed member, National Advisory Comm. on Criminal Justice Standards and Goals; Republican candidate for U.S. Senate (IN), 1972; elected as a Republican to U.S. Senate (IN), 1977–; ***candidate for None of the Above Party nomination to presidency of the U.S., 1980; candidate for Republican nomination to vice presidency of the U.S., 1980***. BUS. & PROF.: vice pres., treas., Thomas L. Green and Co., Inc. (manufacturers of food production equipment), Indianapolis, IN, 1960–67, sec.-treas., 1968–; treas., Lugar Stock Farm Inc., 1960–; visiting prof. of political science, IN Central U., 1976. MIL.: seaman 2/C, U.S. Navy, 1957, lt. (jg), 1960. MEM.: Phi Beta Kappa; Omicron Delta Kappa; Blue Key; Pi Delta Epsilon; Pi Sigma Alpha; Beta Theta Pi; National League of Cities (vice pres., 1969–70, pres., 1970–71, Advisory Board, 1971–73); U.S. Conference of Mayors (adviser); National Assn. of Counties (dir.); National Service to Regional Councils (dir., 1971); Urban Coalition (Steering Cmte., 1971); Westview Hospital (trustee); Hawthorne Settlement House (trustee); Denison U. (trustee); IN Central U. (trustee); Indianapolis Center for Advanced Research (dir.); American Students Assn. of Oxford (pres.); Rotary Club; Indianapolis Urban League (dir.); IN Farm Bureau; 4-H (National Council). AWARDS: one of five "Outstanding Young Men," IN Junior C. of C., 1966; Rhodes Scholar; Exceptional Service Award, Office of Economic Opportunity, 1972; hon. fellow, Seattle Pacific Coll., 1972; Fiorello La Guardia Award, 1975. HON. DEG.: numerous. REL.: Methodist. MAILING ADDRESS: Indianapolis, IN.

LUMMIS, LESLIE. b. MA. EDUC.: grad., Dartmouth Coll., 1934. POLIT. & GOV.: ***independent candidate for presidency of the U.S., 1992***. MIL.: veteran of WWII; chief A&E PX, Vietnam. MEM.: Guam Press Club. MAILING ADDRESS: P.O. Box 7661, Apt. #J-5, Tamuning, Guma Trankilidad, Guam 96911.

LUNGER, FLOYD L. POLIT. & GOV.: ***candidate for Democratic nomination to presidency of the U.S., 1976***. MAILING ADDRESS: R.D. #3, Box 167, Clinton Ave., Andersontown, Washington, NJ.

LUTHER, RON. POLIT. & GOV.: ***Tuition Cut Ticket candidate for presidency of the U.S., 1976***. MAILING ADDRESS: P.O. Box 5964, Cleveland, OH 44101.

LUX, WALTER GARHARD. POLIT. & GOV.: ***candidate for Democratic nomination to presidency of the U.S., 1980***. MAILING ADDRESS: 5931 S.W. 45th Way, Fort Lauderdale, FL 33312.

LYNEN, KURT. b. Jan 15, 1916, Proctor, VT; par. John and Anna (Pochnow) Lynen; single. EDUC.: grad., Proctor (VT) H.S., 1937; U. of VT, 1 year. POLIT. & GOV.: ***National Middle Class Party candidate for presidency of the U.S., 1980***. BUS. & PROF.: automobile parts clerk; machinist. REL.: Lutheran. MAILING ADDRESS: P.O. Box 332, Dayton, NJ 08810.

LYON, REUBEN ROBIE. b. 1856; d. Aug 5, 1916, Bath, NY. POLIT. & GOV.: Independent League Party candidate for assoc. judge, NY Court of Appeals, 1907, 1908; member, Independence League Party National Cmte., 1908; ***candidate for Independence League Party nomination to presidency of the U.S., 1908***. BUS. & PROF.: atty.; law practice, Bath, NY. RES.: Bath, NY.

LYON, ROBERT W. POLIT. & GOV.: American Independent Party candidate for CA State Assembly, 1972; ***candidate for American Party nomination to presidency of the U.S., 1976***; CA state organizing chm., Boston Tea Party. MAILING ADDRESS: 989 Concha St., Box 424, Altadena, CA 91001.

LYONS, JAMES. b. Oct 12, 1801, Hanover Town, VA; d. Dec 18, 1882, Richmond, VA; par. Dr. James and Sarah Spotswood (Waugh) Lyons; m. Henningham Carrington Watkins, 1821; m. 2d, Imogene Bradfute Penn, 1853; c. William Henry; Peter; Sally Nevison (Mrs. William Booth Taliaferro); Mrs. B. Stanard; Mrs. Robert E. Scott; Mrs. Hutter; five infant sons. EDUC.: William and Mary Coll., 1817; read law under Judge Stanard. POLIT. & GOV.: member, City Council, Richmond, VA; prosecuting atty., Richmond; delegate, VA State Constitutional Convention, 1851; elected as a Whig to VA State Senate; elected as a Whig to VA State House; elected as a representative (VA), First Congress, Confederate States of America, 1862–64; candidate for representative (VA), Second Congress, Confederate States of America, 1863; judge; chm., Straight-Out (Taproot) Democratic Party National Convention, 1872; ***candidate for Straight-Out (Taproot) Democratic Party nomination to vice presidency of the U.S., 1872; Straight-Out (Taproot) Democratic Party candidate for presidency of the U.S., 1872 (declined)***; member, exec. cmte., Straight-Out (Taproot) Democratic Party, 1872. BUS. & PROF.: atty.; admitted to VA Bar, c. 1822; partner (with Robert Craig Stanard), law firm, Richmond; partner, Lyons and August (law firm), Richmond; owner, St. Clair Hotel, Richmond. MEM.: VA Central Agricultural Soc. (pres., 1858). WRITINGS: *Four Essays on the Right and Propriety of Secession by Southern States* (1861). MISC.: defense counsel for Jefferson Davis (q.v.), 1866–67; counsel for Julia Gardiner Tyler in divorce suit, 1868; known as "Virginius." RES.: Richmond, VA.

MAAS, ELTON ROBERT. b. Feb 10, 1920, Manhattan, KS; par. Fredrick C. and Emma L. (Fix) Maas; m. Vivian Marjorie Engle; c. Nancy Louise; Robert Elton. EDUC.: high school; military schools. POLIT. & GOV.: candidate for Democratic nomination to U.S. House (CA), 1964; ***Millennium Party candidate for presidency of the U.S., 1976***. BUS. & PROF.: aircraft mechanic, Lockheed Aircraft Corp., 1951–64; Dianetic auditor; author. MIL.: A.A.C. Cadets. MEM.: Technocracy, Inc. (1942–48); peace movement; Hubbard Assn. of Scientologists, International. REL.: American Bapt. MAILING ADDRESS: 807 Gibbon Rd., Central Point, OR 97502.

MABEY, STEVEN DOUGLAS. POLIT. & GOV.: ***independent candidate for presidency of the U.S., 1984, 1992***. MAILING ADDRESS: Suite 310, 550 North Main St., Logan, UT 84321.

MACAIONE, THOMAS. POLIT. & GOV.: ***independent candidate for presidency of the U.S., 1988***. MISC.: received write-in votes in NM. MAILING ADDRESS: unknown.

MacARTHUR, DOUGLAS. b. Jan 26, 1880, Little Rock, AR; d. Apr 5, 1964, Bethesda, MD; par. Lt. Gen. Arthur and Mary P. (Hardy) MacArthur; m. Jean Marie Faircloth, Apr 30, 1937; c. Arthur. EDUC.: B.S., U.S. Military Acad., 1903; Engineering School of Application, 1908. POLIT. & GOV.: ***candidate for Republican nomination to presidency of the U.S., 1944, 1948, 1952; Christian Front candidate for presidency of the U.S., 1948; Constitution (America First, Christian Nationalist) Party candidate for presidency of the U.S., 1952; candidate for Prohibition Party nomination to presidency of the U.S., 1952***. BUS. & PROF.: soldier; author; businessman; chm. of the board, Remington Rand, Inc., 1951–55; chm. of the board, Sperry Rand Corp., 1955–64. MIL.: commissioned 2d lt., U.S. Army Engineers Corps, 1903; advanced through grades to gen., 1930, gen. of the army, 1944; chief of staff, 42d (Rainbow) Div., 1917, commanding gen., 1918; supervisor, U.S. Military Acad., 1919–22; military adviser, Commonwealth Government of the Philippines, 1935; field marshal of Philippine Army, 1936–37; commander, U.S. Forces in Far East, 1941–51; commander, occupational forces in Japan, 1945–51; commander in chief, U.N. Forces in Korea, 1950–51; Medal of Honor; Distinguished Flying Cross; Distinguished Service Cross with two Oak Leaf Clusters; Distinguished Service Medal with six Oak Leaf Clusters; Purple Heart with Oak Leaf Cluster; Silver Star with six Oak Leaf Clusters; Navy Distinguished Service Medal; Bronze Star; Air Medal; numerous others. MEM.: Military Order of the World War (commander in chief, 1927); Soc. of American Legion Founders (hon. pres.); American Olympic Cmte. (pres., 1928). HON. DEG.: D.M.Sc., PA Military Coll., 1928; LL.D., U. of MD, 1928; LL.D., U. of Western MD Coll., 1929; LL.D., U. of Pittsburgh, 1932; M.M.S., Norwich U., 1935; LL.D., U. of the Philippines, 1938; LL.D., U. of WI, 1942; LL.D., U. of Queensland, 1945; LL.D., U. of Santo Tomas, 1945; LL.D., Harvard U., 1946; D.Int.L., PA Military Coll., 1946; D.C.L., U. of HI, 1946; LL.D., U. of Seoul, 1946; LL.D., Columbia U., 1947; LL.D., MO Valley Coll., 1947; S.T.D., Midwestern Coll. WRITINGS: *Remarks at the Annual Stockholders Meeting of the Sperry Rand Corporation* (1957); *Duty, Honor, Country* (1962); *Reminiscences* (1964); *A Soldier Speaks* (1965); *Courage Was the Rule* (1965). REL.: Deist. RES.: New York, NY.

MACAULEY, ROBERT CALVIN. b. 1865, Philadelphia, PA; par. Robert Calvin Macauley; single. EDUC.: Penn Grammar School, Philadelphia, PA, 1879. POLIT. & GOV.: Republican div. committeeman, Philadelphia, PA, 1902; national chm., Single Tax Party, 1919; Single Tax Party candidate for U.S. Senate (PA), 1914, 1916; Single Tax Party candidate for gov. of PA, 1918; ***Single Tax Party candidate for presidency of the U.S., 1920***; sec., Commonwealth Land Party National Cmte., 1924; Commonwealth Land Party candidate for U.S. Senate (PA), 1926. BUS. & PROF.: clothing cutter; newspaper reporter, Philadelphia, PA, 1908–20; banker; publicity mgr., Winslow Taylor and Co. (stockbrokers); insurance salesman. MEM.: Pen and Pencil Club (pres.); Armchair Club of Philadelphia; Knights of Labor (sec., Local Assn. #1, 1884); Independent Clothing Cutters' Assn. (pres.). WRITINGS: "Knowledge" (poem, 1902). RES.: Philadelphia, PA.

MacBRIDE, ROGER LEA. b. Aug 6, 1929, New Rochelle, NY; d. March 5, 1995, Miami Beach, FL; par. William Burt and Elise (Lea) MacBride; m. Susan Ford, Sep 1961 (divorced, Jul 1972); c. Abigail Adams. EDUC.: Philips Exeter Acad., 1947; A.B., Princeton U., 1951; J.D., Harvard U., 1954. POLIT. & GOV.: elected as a Republican to town moderator, VT; elected as a Republican to VT State House, 1963–65; candidate for Republican nomination to gov. of VT, 1964; presidential elector, Republican Party, 1972; ***Libertarian Party candidate for presidency of the U.S., 1976***. BUS. & PROF.: atty.; law practice, VT; farmer, VA; television producer; owner, *Little House on the Prairie* television series; publisher, *The Mercury*, 1979–. MEM.: Mont Pelerin Soc.; Fulbright Fellow. WRITINGS: *The American Electoral College* (1952); *Treaties Versus the Constitution* (1955); *The Libertarian Challenge: A New Direction for America* (1976); *A New Dawn for America; The Lady and the Tycoon* (1972). REL.: Deist. MISC.: cast electoral vote for Libertarian Party candidates for president and vice president, even though elected as a Republican presidential elector, 1972. MAILING ADDRESS: Esmont Farm, Esmont, VA 22937.

MacDONALD, DONALD KEITH. POLIT. & GOV.: ***candidate for Republican nomination to presidency of the U.S., 1980***. MAILING ADDRESS: 20400 Brook Dr., Standard, CA 95373.

MACFADDEN, BERNARR (nee BERNARD ADOLPHUS McFADDEN). b. Aug 16, 1868, Mill Springs, MO; d. Oct 12, 1955, Jersey City, NJ; par. William R. and Mary Elizabeth (Miller) McFadden; m. Tilley Fountaine, c. 1896; m. 2d, Marguerite Kelly, 1901; m. 3d, Mary Williamson, 1913; m. 4th, Johnnie (McKinney) Lee, Apr 22, 1948; c. Byrne; Helen; Byrnece; Beulah; Braunda; Beverly; Berwyn; Brewster. EDUC.: public schools. POLIT. & GOV.: ***candidate for Republican nomination to presidency of the U.S., 1936***; candidate for Democratic nomination to U.S. Senate (FL), 1940; candidate for Republican nomination to gov. of FL, 1948; Honest Party candidate for mayor of New York, NY, 1953. BUS. & PROF.: weight lifter; inventor; wrestler; owner, Macfadden's Physical Development Gymnasium, New York, NY, 1894; physical culturist; founder, publisher, *Physical Culture Magazine*, 1899; publisher, *True Story*, 1919; publisher, *True Romances*, 1923; publisher, *Dream World*, 1924; publisher, *Love and Romance*, 1924; publisher, *True Detective Mysteries Magazine*, 1925; publisher, *Master Detective Magazine*, 1929; publisher, *Liberty Weekly*; publisher, *Photoplay*; publisher, *Movie Mirror*; publisher, *True Detective*; publisher, *Muscle Builder*; publisher, *Ghost Stories*; publisher, *True Experiences*; publisher, *The Dance*; publisher, *Fiction Lovers*; publisher, *Modern Marriage*; publisher, *New York Evening Gazette*, 1924–32; pres., chm. of the board, Macfadden Publications, Inc., 1924; author. MEM.: New York Athletic Club; Macfadden Inst. of Physical Culture (founder); American Inst. for Physical Education (founder); Bernarr Macfadden Foundation, Inc. (founder); Castle Heights Military Acad. (founder); Physical Culture Hotel, Dansville, NY (founder); Macfadden-Deauville Health Hotel, Miami Beach, FL (founder); Bernarr Macfadden Foundation for Children (founder); Italy-American Soc.; National Aeronautics Assn.; Cmte. of One Hundred; Congressional Country Club. WRITINGS: *The Athlete's Conquest* (1892); *Practical Birth Control; Physical Culture Cook Book; Strengthening the Eyes; The Truth About Tobacco; Fasting for Health and Strength; Encyclopedia of Physical Culture* (1911–12); *Hair Culture* (1921); *Foot Troubles* (1926); *Predetermine Your Baby's Sex* (1926); *How to Raise the Baby* (1926); *The Strenuous Lover; Macfadden's Physical Training; The Virile Powers of Superb Manhood; Physical Culture for Baby; Marriage a Life Long Honeymoon; Diseases of Men; Health, Beauty and Sexuality; How Success is Won; Building of Vital Power; Strength From Eating; Macfadden's New Hair Culture; Fasting, Hydropathy and Exercise; Strong Eyes; Exercise and Like It; Preparing for Motherhood; Skin Troubles; The Miracle of Milk; Stomach and Digestive Disorders; Headaches; Man's Sex Life; Woman's Sex Life; Science of Divine Healing; Keeping Fit; Power and Beauty and Superb Womanhood; Natural Cure for Rupture*. REL.: Unitarian. MISC.: founder of "Physcultopathy" (healing through physical culture); inaugurated "Cosmotarianism, the Happiness Religion," 1947. RES.: Miami Beach, FL.

MacGREGOR, HENRY FREDERICK. b. Apr 25, 1855, Londonderry, NH; d. Sep 3, 1923, Londonderry, NH; par. Lewis Aiken and Augusta Watts (Blodgett) MacGregor; m. Elizabeth Stevens, Dec 10, 1885. EDUC.: Pinkerton Acad.; grad., Bryant and Stratton Commercial Coll., 1871. POLIT. & GOV.: chm., TX Republican State Exec. Cmte., 1894–96; Republican candidate for U.S. House (TX), 1904; member, Rep. Nat'l. Cmte., 1912–23; delegate, Rep. Nat'l. Conv., 1920; ***candidate for Republican nomination to presidency of the U.S., 1920***. BUS. & PROF.: sec., Galveston (TX) R.R. Co., 1879–83; vice pres., gen. mgr., Houston (TX) Railway System, 1883–1903; real estate investor; vice pres., State Land Oil Co.; dir., Bay and Bayou Co.; dir., South Texas Commercial National Bank; dir., Houston Printing Co.; treas., dir., Glen Park Co. MEM.: Home Market Club (vice pres.); Hermann Hospital Estate (pres., Board of Trustees). REL.: Presb. RES.: Houston, TX.

MACHINSKI, JOHN JOSEPH. b. Nov 23, 1921, Detroit, MI; par. Stanley and Stella (Chinska) Machinski; single. EDUC.: G.T.A., Port Huron (MI) H.S., 1981; Alliance Technical Inst., Cambridge Springs, PA, 1957. POLIT. & GOV.: candidate for Democratic nomination to U.S. House (MI), 1976; ***candidate for Democratic nomination to presidency of the U.S., 1984***. BUS. & PROF.: tool and die maker, Chrysler Corp., 1956–86. MEM.: Polish National Alliance; Tool and Die Technical Assn.; Cmte. for Three Presidents; Holy Rosary Church. WRITINGS: *For a Better U.S.A.* (1972). REL.: R.C. MISC.:

advocate of electing 3 presidents of the U.S. to share executive authority. MAILING ADDRESS: 373 Richman Rd., Smiths Creek, MI 48074.

MACHEN, WILLIS BENSON. b. Apr 5, 1810, Caldwell Cty., KY; d. Sep 29, 1893, Hopkinsville, KY; par. Henry and Nancy (Tarrant) Machen; m. Margaret A. Lyon; m. 2d, Eliza N. Dobbins; m. 3d, Victoria Theresa Mims, 1859; c. Frank P.; Willis Benson, Jr.; Charles V.; Minnie (Mrs. Anthony Dickinson Sayers); Marjorie; two others. EDUC.: Cumberland Coll., Princeton, KY, 1830–31. POLIT. & GOV.: delegate, KY State Constitutional Convention, 1849; elected as a Democrat to KY State Senate, 1854–55; elected as a Democrat to KY State House, 1855–61; chm., KY State Provisional Government, 1861; elected to First and Second Confederate Congresses, 1862–64; candidate for Democratic nomination to gov. of KY, 1870 (declined); appointed and subsequently elected as a Democrat to U.S. Senate (KY), 1872–73; ***received 1 electoral vote for vice presidency of the U.S., 1872***; appointed member, KY State R.R. Comm., 1882. BUS. & PROF.: farmer, Eddyville, KY; iron manufacturer, Livingston Forge, KY, 1831–38; merchant, 1838–41; contractor, 1841–43; atty.; admitted to KY Bar, 1844; law practice, Lyon Cty., KY; law practice, Caldwell Cty., KY; planter. REL.: Methodist Episc. Church, South. RES.: Eddyville, KY.

MACKAY, DONALD FRANCIS, JR. b. Jun 30, 1953, Philadelphia, PA; par. Donald Francis and Elizabeth Mayfield (Miller) Mackay; single. EDUC.: grad., Roxborough H.S., Philadelphia, PA, 1972; Montgomery Cty. (PA) Community Coll.; Stockton State Coll., Pomona, NJ. POLIT. & GOV.: ***candidate for Republican nomination to presidency of the U.S., 1988***. BUS. & PROF.: employee, U.S. Civil Service, 1974–86 (PS 4–12); worked for Stratcom, Hawk Missile System. MIL.: U.S. Army. MEM.: American Legion. REL.: Episc. MAILING ADDRESS: P.O. Box 10553, State College, PA 16801.

MacKENNA, ROSCOE BERNARD. b. Sep 16, 1908, Lynn, MA; par. George B. and Edna (Gustin) MacKenna; m. Thelma Sewall; c. William B.; Edward L. EDUC.: Essex Agricultural and Technical Inst., 1926. POLIT. & GOV.: ***Universal Party candidate for vice presidency of the U.S., 1968***. BUS. & PROF.: mining engineer, Atomic Power Development, 1921; landscape architect; nurseryman; gardening business, 1926–36; city and state planner; national defense planner; electrical engineer; electronics draftsman and designer, 1936–; legal investigator, 1972–. MEM.: Horticultural Soc. (1925–29); A.I.E.E. (1949–64); Illuminating Engineering Soc. (1949–64). REL.: "I AM" Church. MISC.: self-styled "King of the Chief of the Gods of the Secret Commonwealth of Lemuria (Mt. Shasta)"; claims to be international police agent. MAILING ADDRESS: 1622 West Jonquil Terrace, Chicago, IL 60626.

MacNEIL, DONALD JAMES. b. Jul 24, 1941, Stoneham, MA; par. Thomas Henry and Jennie Williams (Perrott) MacNeil; m. Verna Valerie (divorced); c. Kenneth; Robert; Douglas; Diana; Jennie Lynn; William T. P. EDUC.: grad., American School, Chicago, IL; master's course, radio-television servicing. POLIT. & GOV.: ***candidate for Republican nomination to presidency of the U.S., 1980***. BUS. & PROF.: asst. mgr., grocery store, 2 years; artesian well driller, 2 years; microcircuit production engineer, 2½ years; mgr. and engineering assoc. REL.: Protestant. MAILING ADDRESS: L. Suncock Lake, Barnstead, NH.

MacNIDER, HANFORD. b. Oct 2, 1889, Mason City, IA; d. Feb 18, 1968, Sarasota, FL; par. Charles Henry and May Cordelia (Hanford) MacNider; m. Margaret Elizabeth McAuley, Feb 20, 1925; c. Tom; Jack; Angus. EDUC.: grad., Milton (MA) Acad., 1907; A.B., Harvard U., 1911. POLIT. & GOV.: delegate, Rep. Nat'l. Conv., 1924, 1948; appointed asst. U.S. sec. of war, 1925–28; appointed member, George Washington Bicentennial Comm., 1925–30; member, Unknown Soldier Comm.; national chm., Republican Service League; ***candidate for Republican nomination to vice presidency of the U.S., 1928, 1932***; appointed U.S. minister to Canada, 1930–32; ***candidate for Republican nomination to presidency of the U.S., 1940***. BUS. & PROF.: soldier; manufacturer; employee, First National Bank, Mason City, IA, 1911–15, dir., 1915–41, third vice pres., 1920–21, vice pres., 1921–28, chm. of the board, 1928–38; pres., First National Co., Mason City, IA, 1920–29; treas., Northwestern States Portland Cement Co., 1923–29, pres., 1929–60, chm. of the board, 1960–68; pres., Redincam Corp. (later MacNider and Co.); pres., Indianhead Farms, Inc., 1929–68. MIL.: member, 2d Infantry, IA National Guard, 1916–17; 2d lt., U.S. Army, 1917–19; advanced through grades to maj. gen., 1951, lt. gen., 1956; Distinguished Service Cross with two clusters; Distinguished Service Medal; Silver Star with two clusters; Legion of Merit (twice); Bronze Star with cluster; Air Medal; Purple Heart with cluster; Bronze Arrowhead; Distinguished Unit Citation with two clusters; Croix de Guerre (five citations); Fourragere; Croce al Merito di Guerra; commander, Legion of Honor (France); commander, Legion of Honor (Philippines). MEM.: American Legion (state commander, 1920–21; national commander, 1921–22); Grinnell Coll. (trustee, 1929–39); Harvard U. (overseer, 1946–52); Masons (33°; Shriner); Harvard Club; University Club; Racquet Club; Tavern Club; Army and Navy Club; Metropolitan Club; Euchre Club; Cycle Club; Republican Service League (chm., 1940); America First Cmte. HON. DEG.: M.M.S., Norwich Coll., 1926; LL.D., Syracuse U., 1932; LL.D., Simpson Coll., 1962. RES.: Mason City, IA.

MACON, NATHANIEL. b. Dec 17, 1758, Warrenton, NC; d. Jun 29, 1837, Macon, NC; par. Gideon and Priscilla (Jones) Macon; m. Hannah Plummer, Oct 9, 1783; c. three. EDUC.: Coll. of NJ (now Princeton U.), 1774–76; studied law, 1777. POLIT. & GOV.: elected member, NC State Senate, 1780–82, 1784–85; elected member, NC State House of Commons, 1790; elected as a Democratic-Republican to U.S. House

(NC), 1791–1815 (Speaker, 1801–07); elected as a Democratic-Republican to U.S. Senate (NC), 1815–28 (pres. pro tempore, 1826–28); ***received 24 electoral votes for vice presidency of the U.S., 1824***; pres., NC State Constitutional Convention, 1835 (refused to sign); presidential elector, Democratic Party, 1836; elected justice of the peace (NC). MIL.: member, NJ Militia, 1777; pvt., Battle of Camden, 1780. MEM.: U. of NC (trustee). MISC.: defender of slavery; supported Louisiana Purchase, War of 1812. RES.: Bucks Creek, NC.

MacPHERSON, DAVID ALLAN. POLIT. & GOV.: ***candidate for Republican nomination to presidency of the U.S., 1984***. MAILING ADDRESS: c/o Karen Pasborg, Calder Square Box 11228, State College, PA 16805.

MADDOX, LESTER GARFIELD. b. Sep 30, 1915, Atlanta, GA; par. Dean Garfield and Flonnie (Castleberry) Maddox; m. Virginia Cox, 1936; c. Linda Densmore; Lester Garfield, Jr.; Virginia Louise; Larry. EDUC.: college correspondence courses. POLIT. & GOV.: elected as a Democrat to gov. of GA, 1967–71; ***candidate for Democratic nomination to presidency of the U.S., 1968, 1972***; elected as a Democrat to lt. gov. of GA, 1971–75; ***candidate for American Party nomination to presidency of the U.S., 1972***; candidate for Democratic nomination to gov. of GA, 1974, 1990; ***American Independent Party candidate for presidency of the U.S., 1976***. BUS. & PROF.: newsboy, *Atlanta Georgian*; owner, Lester's Grill, 1944–47; owner, Pickrick Restaurant (grocery, restaurant, and furniture store), Atlanta, GA; realtor. MEM.: U.S. C. of C.; Atlanta Better Business Bureau; National Retail Assn.; Masons; Moose; J.O.U.A.M.; Travelers Protective Assn.; Buckhead 50 Club; Shriners; Georgia Sheriff's Assn.; Peace Officers' Assn.; Constables' Assn.; Westgate Merchants Assn. (pres.). WRITINGS: *Speaking Out*. REL.: Bapt. MAILING ADDRESS: 391 West Paces Ferry Rd., N.W., Atlanta, GA 30305.

MADDOX, ROBERT EARL, JR. b. Nov 15, 1918, Anderson, SC; par. Robert Earl and Marion (Breazeale) Maddox; m. Estelle Janowitz; c. Mary Lisa; Catherine Victoria; Carolyn Elizabeth; Robert Edward. EDUC.: Duke U.; McCoy (evening) Coll., Johns Hopkins U.; U. of Pittsburgh; Carnegie Inst. of Technology. POLIT. & GOV.: candidate for Democratic nomination to Board of County Commissioners, Broward Cty., FL, 1976; ***candidate for Democratic nomination to presidency of the U.S., 1980***. BUS. & PROF.: owner, Maddox Appliance Co., Hollywood, FL. WRITINGS: *The Big Jump* (drama); *The Falling Stars* (drama). REL.: Bapt. MAILING ADDRESS: P.O. Box 667, Hollywood, FL 33022.

MADISON, JAMES. b. Mar 16, 1751 (Mar 5, 1750/51 old style calendar), Port Conway, VA; d. Jun 28, 1836, Montpelier, VA; par. James and Eleanor Rose (Conway) Madison; m. Dorothea "Dolley" Dandridge Payne Todd, Sep 15, 1794; c. none. EDUC.: Donald Robertson's School, King and Queen Cty., VA, 1762–67; tutored by Rev. Thomas Martin, 1768–69; A.B., Coll. of NJ (now Princeton U.), 1771. POLIT. & GOV.: elected member, Orange Cty. (VA) Cmte. of Safety, 1774; delegate, Williamsburg Convention, 1776; member, Cmte. to Frame Constitution and Declaration of Rights of VA, 1776; elected member, VA State House of Delegates, 1776, 1783–86; candidate for VA State House of Delegates, 1777; elected member, VA State Exec. Council, 1778; elected member, Continental Congress (VA), 1780–83, 1786–88; delegate, Annapolis Convention, 1786; delegate, U.S. Constitutional Convention, 1787; delegate, VA Ratification Convention, 1788; Democratic-Republican candidate for U.S. Senate (VA), 1788; elected as a Democratic-Republican to U.S. House (VA), 1789–97; appointed U.S. minister to France, 1794 (declined); appointed U.S. sec. of state, 1794 (declined), 1801–09; presidential elector, Democratic Party, 1800; ***received 3 electoral votes for vice presidency of the U.S., 1808; elected as a Democratic-Republican to presidency of the U.S., 1809–1817***; delegate, VA State Constitutional Convention, 1829, 1834. BUS. & PROF.: atty.; admitted to VA Bar; rector, U. of VA, 1826; farmer, Montpelier, VA. MIL.: col., Orange Cty. (VA) Militia, 1775. MEM.: American Whig Soc. (founder); American Colonization Soc. (pres.); Agricultural Soc. of Albemarle (pres.); U. of VA (dir.); Coll. of William and Mary (visitor). HON. DEG.: LL.D., Coll. of NJ (now Princeton U.), 1787. WRITINGS: *Federalist Papers* (coauthor, 1788); *Vices of the Political System of the United States; Helvidius Letters* (1793); *An Examination of the British Doctrine, Which Subjects to Capture a Neutral Trade, Not Open in Time of Peace* (1806). REL.: Episc. MISC.: known as the "Masterbuilder of the Constitution." RES.: Montpelier, VA.

MAGE, JUDITH HOLLANDER. b. Feb 3, 1935, Bronx, NY; par. Irving and Helena Hollander; m. Shane Mage, 1956; c. none. EDUC.: Bronx H.S. of Science; City Coll. of New York; grad., Antioch Coll., 1957. POLIT. & GOV.: ***Peace and Freedom Party candidate for vice presidency of the U.S., 1968***. BUS. & PROF.: social worker; case worker, Dayton, OH, 1959–60; case worker, New York City Welfare Dept., 1960–; labor union organizer. MEM.: American Federation of State, County and Municipal Employees (Local 371, 1960–62); Social Service Employees Union of New York (member, 1962–; pres., 1966–68). MISC.: jailed for work slowdown and strike activity, 1965, 1967. MAILING ADDRESS: 635 Riverside Dr., New York, NY.

MAGNIFICO, GENERAL CATHERINE III TRINITY VICTORIA ALIX MEDA. b. Jul 4, 1920, Sullivan, KY; par. Nicholas Romanov and Alix (Hesse) Magnifico; m. Carl William Roof; c. none (Tom Corbin, reputed). EDUC.: grad., high school, 1932; private tutors. POLIT. & GOV.: ***candidate for Republican nomination to presidency of the U.S., 1976; candidate for Democratic nomination to presidency of the U.S., 1976; independent candidate***

for presidency of the U.S., 1976. BUS. & PROF.: claims to have been agent, U.S. Secret Service, 1938–41; claims to have been commanding gen., U.S.M.C., 1941–; claims to have been dir., OSS, 1941–45; assoc. dir., FBI, 1942, international dir., 1943; cliams to have been deputy president of the U.S. MISC.: claims four Medals of Honor; claims to be Lucy Rutherford Mercer, confidential aide to Franklin Roosevelt; claims highest I.Q. (230) in the world; claims to have turned down Republican vice presidential offer by President Gerald R. Ford, 1976. MAILING ADDRESS: 3177 Liberty Blvd., South Gate, CA 90280.

MAGNUS, ALEXANDER B., JR. POLIT. & GOV.: ***Illinois Taxpayers Party candidate for vice presidency of the U.S., 1992***. MAILING ADDRESS: 600 West Rand Rd., Arlington Heights, IL.

MAGNUSON, WARREN GRANT. b. Apr 12, 1905, Moorhead, MN; d. May 20, 1989, Seattle, WA; par. Warren Grant and Emma Carolina (Anderson) Magnuson; m. Jermaine Elliott Peralta, Oct 4, 1964; c. Juanita Peralta (Mrs. Donald Garrison). EDUC.: U. of ND, 1923–24; ND State U., 1924; J.D., U. of WA, 1929. POLIT. & GOV.: appointed special prosecutor, King Cty., WA, 1931; elected delegate, WA State Constitutional Convention, 1932; elected as a Democrat to WA State House, 1933–34; appointed asst. U.S. district atty. for WA, 1934; elected prosecuting atty., King Cty., WA, 1934–36; elected as a Democrat to U.S. House (WA), 1937–45; appointed and subsequently elected as a Democrat to U.S. Senate (WA), 1944–81; delegate, Dem. Nat'l. Conv., 1952; ***candidate for Democratic nomination to presidency of the U.S., 1956, 1980***. BUS. & PROF.: atty.; admitted to WA Bar, 1930; law practice, Seattle, WA. MIL.: lt. commander, U.S. Navy, WWII. MEM.: Elks; Eagles; Moose; Order of the Coif; American Legion; VFW; Theta Chi; University Club; Burning Tree Club; Seattle Municipal League (sec., 1930–31). AWARDS: "Maritime Man of the Year," Maritime Press Assn., 1955; "Man of the Year," National Fisheries Inst., 1964; Outstanding Service Medal, Pacific Lutheran U., 1966; Outstanding Service Medal, American Cancer Soc., 1967; Distinguished Service Award, American Coll. of Cardiology, 1972; Albert Lasker Public Service Award in Health, 1973. HON. DEG.: LL.D., Gonzaga U., 1961; LL.D., St. Martin's Coll., 1967; Dr. of Political Science, U. of the Pacific, 1970; LL.D., U. of AK, 1973. WRITINGS: *The Dark Side of the Marketplace* (with Jean Carper, 1968); *How Much for Health?* (with Elliott A. Segal, 1974). REL.: Lutheran. RES.: Seattle, WA.

MAGOON, CHARLES EDWARD. b. Dec 5, 1861, Steele Cty., MN; d. Jan 14, 1920, Washington, DC; par. Henry C. and Mehitable W. (Clement) Magoon; single. EDUC.: U. of NE; studied law in office of Mason and Wheeler, Lincoln, NE. POLIT. & GOV.: law officer, Bureau of Insular Affairs, U.S. Dept. of War, 1899–1904; gen. counsel, Isthmian Canal Comm., 1904–05; appointed member, Isthmian Canal Comm., 1905–06; appointed gov., Canal Zone, 1905–06; appointed U.S. envoy extraordinary and minister plenipotentiary to Panama, 1905–06; appointed to gov. of Cuba, 1906–09; ***candidate for Republican nomination to presidency of the U.S., 1908 (declined)***. BUS. & PROF.: atty.; admitted to NE Bar, 1882; law practice, Lincoln, NE, 1882–99. MIL.: judge advocate, maj., NE National Guard. MEM.: Metropolitan Club; Chevy Chase Club; Alibi Club; Cosmos Club. Hon. Deg: LL.D., Monmouth Coll., 1905. WRITINGS: *The Municipal Code of Lincoln* (1889); *The Law of Civil Government Under Military Occupation* (1902); *What Followed the Flag in the Philippines* (1904). REL.: Congregationalist. RES.: Lincoln, NE.

MAGUIRE, MATTHEW. b. 1850, New York, NY; d. Jan 2, 1917, Paterson, NJ; par. Christopher and Mary (Stafford) Maguire; m. Martha McCormick, 1870; c. Christopher; Mrs. John Feeney; Mrs. Charles Vreeland; Joseph; Peter. EDUC.: grad., St. John's School, Paterson, NJ. POLIT. & GOV.: elected as a Socialist-Laborite to Board of Aldermen, Paterson, NJ, 1894–98; ***candidate for Socialist Labor Party nomination to presidency of the U.S., 1896; Socialist Labor Party candidate for vice presidency of the U.S., 1896***; Socialist Labor Party candidate for Board of Aldermen, Paterson, NJ, 1898; Socialist Labor Party candidate for gov. of NJ, 1898. BUS. & PROF.: factory worker, 1864; machinist; employee, Columbia Iron Co., Brooklyn, NY, 1872; ed., proprietor, *Paterson People*, 1893–1917; trade union organizer. MEM.: Eight Hour League (shop delegate; member, National Exec. Cmte.); Machinists' and Blacksmiths' Union (sec.); Knights of Labor; Central Labor Union (sec.); Carpenters' and Joiners' Union (pres.); AFL (founder). WRITINGS: *Bericht Über die Arbeiter Bewegung in den Vereinigten Staaten* (1896). REL.: R.C. MISC.: some sources cite Maguire as the "Father of Labor Day," while others attribute the founding of Labor Day to Peter Maguire. RES.: Paterson, NJ.

MAHALCHIK, JOHN VAL JEAN "LUCKY DUSTIN." b. 1919; m. Inger M. (divorced). POLIT. & GOV.: America First Party candidate for U.S. Senate (NJ), 1964; America First Party candidate for U.S. House (NJ), 1970; ***America First Party candidate for presidency of the U.S., 1972, 1976***; Regular Democracy candidate for U.S. House (NJ), 1974, 1976, 1978; Independent Democratic candidate for U.S. House (NJ), 1974; Betsy Ross Party candidate for U.S. House (NJ), 1978. BUS. & PROF.: junk dealer; salvage materials business; antique dealer; ed., *Freedom Paper*. MISC.: involved in prolonged controversy over violation of zoning laws in NJ. MAILING ADDRESS: Route 206, Mt. Holly, NJ 08060.

MAHER, JEROME JOHN. b. Aug 8, 1934, Detroit, MI; par. James Richard and Angeline Mary (O'Malley) Maher; single. EDUC.: Mercy Coll. of Detroit; B.A., M.A., MI State U. POLIT. & GOV.: ***candidate for Democratic nomination to presidency of the U.S., 1992***. BUS. & PROF.: teacher,

30 years. MIL.: corp., U.S. Army, 2 years. MEM.: NAACP; Knights of Columbus; AmVets. REL.: R.C. MAILING ADDRESS: 532 Peachtree Place, Mason, MI 48854.

MAHONEY, PATRICK J., JR. b. 1955; par. Patrick J. Mahoney, Sr. POLIT. & GOV.: ***candidate for Democratic nomination to presidency of the U.S., 1992***. BUS. & PROF.: minister, Presbyterian Church; antiabortion activist. MEM.: Operation Rescue. REL.: Presb. MAILING ADDRESS: 1345 N.E. 4th Court, Boca Raton, FL 33432.

MAINS, RONALD RAY. POLIT. & GOV.: ***independent candidate for presidency of the U.S., 1988***. MAILING ADDRESS: RR 2, Mt. Carmel, IL 62863.

MAJOR, ELLIOTT WOOLFOLK. b. Oct 20, 1864, Lincoln Cty., MO; d. Jul 9, 1949, Eureka, MO; par. James Reed and Sarah T. (Woolfolk) Major; m. Elizabeth Myers, Jun 14, 1887; c. Micah; Elliott; Elizabeth. EDUC.: Watson Seminary, Ashley, MO; B.S., Wesleyan Coll.; studied law under Champ Clark (q.v.). POLIT. & GOV.: clerk, MO Legislature, 1889; elected as a Democrat to MO State Senate, 1897–99; Democratic candidate for atty. gen. of MO, 1904; elected as a Democrat to atty. gen. of MO, 1909–13; elected as a Democrat to gov. of MO, 1913–17; ***candidate for Democratic nomination to vice presidency of the U.S., 1916***. BUS. & PROF.: atty.; admitted to MO Bar, 1885; law practice, St. Louis, MO, 1917. MEM.: ABA; MO State Bar Assn.; Masons; Country Club. REL.: Methodist. RES.: St. Louis, MO.

MALLONEY, JOSEPH FRANCIS. b. Oct 16, 1865, Providence, RI. EDUC.: self-taught. POLIT. & GOV.: Socialist Labor Party candidate for U.S. House (MA), 1898; MA state organizer, Socialist Labor Party, 1898; delegate, Socialist Labor Party National Convention, 1900; ***Socialist Labor Party candidate for presidency of the U.S., 1900***. BUS. & PROF.: worker, cotton factory; apprentice machinist, Rhode Island Locomotive Works, 1889–92; employee, George R. Peare (q.v.), MA, 1892; machinist; lecturer; labor organizer. MEM.: International Machinists Union (delegate, National Convention, 1897; pres., Lynn, MA Lodge); Socialist Trade and Labor Alliance (organizer). RES.: Lynn, MA.

MALLOY, STEVEN P. POLIT. & GOV.: ***candidate for Democratic nomination to presidency of the U.S., 1992***. BUS. & PROF.: restaurant worker. MAILING ADDRESS: 3010 Grant St., Concord, CA 94520.

MALONE, EUGENE WAYNE "BILLY BALL MARTIN," SR. POLIT. & GOV.: ***candidate for Democratic nomination to presidency of the U.S., 1988***. MAILING ADDRESS: 1470 Mathews Way, Sacramento, CA 95822.

MALONE, DUDLEY FIELD. b. Jun 3, 1882, New York, NY; d. Oct 5, 1950, Culver City, CA; par. William C. and Rose (McKenny) Malone; m. Mary "May" P. O'Gorman, Nov 14, 1908; m. 2d, Doris Stevens, Dec 5, 1921; m. 3d, Edna Louise Johnson, Jan 29, 1930; c. Dudley Field. EDUC.: A.B., St. Francis Xavier Coll., 1903; LL.B., Fordham U., 1905. POLIT. & GOV.: appointed city atty., New York, NY, 1909–13; campaign adviser, Woodrow Wilson for President, 1912; appointed third asst. U.S. sec. of state, 1913; appointed collector, Port of New York, 1913–17 (resigned in protest of President Wilson's failure to urge passage of woman suffrage amendment); ***candidate for Farmer-Labor Party nomination to presidency of the U.S., 1920***; Farmer-Labor Party candidate for gov. of NY, 1920; delegate, Dem. Nat'l. Conv., 1932. BUS. & PROF.: atty.; admitted to NY Bar, 1905; law practice, New York, NY, 1905; assoc., Battle and Marshall (law firm), 1907–09; sports promoter; counsel, Twentieth Century Fox Corp., 1930s. MIL.: lt. (jg), U.S. Navy, 1918. MEM.: NAACP; Assn. Against the Prohibition Amendment (cofounder); A.C.L.U. REL.: R.C. MISC.: advocate of recognition of U.S.S.R.; defense assoc. counsel, Scopes Trial, 1925; campaigned for repeal of Prohibition; declared bankruptcy, 1925; appeared in "Mission to Moscow" (film) in role of Winston Churchill, 1943. RES.: New York, NY.

MALONEY, JOSEPH MICHAEL. POLIT. & GOV.: ***independent candidate for presidency of the U.S., 1980***. MAILING ADDRESS: 11 Strong St., Springfield, MA 01104.

MALONEY, WILLIAM H. POLIT. & GOV.: elected as a Democrat to mayor of Butte, MT, 1917–19; delegate, Dem. Nat'l. Conv., 1924, 1928; ***candidate for Democratic nomination to presidency of the U.S., 1924***; received 1 vote for presidential nomination on 86th ballot, Dem. Nat'l. Conv., 1924. RES.: Butte, MT.

MANDERSON, CHARLES FREDERICK. b. Feb 9, 1837, Philadelphia, PA; d. Sep 28, 1911, at sea; par. John and Katherine Manderson; m. Rebekah S. Brown, Apr 11, 1865. EDUC.: Philadelphia (PA) H.S. POLIT. & GOV.: city atty., Canton, OH, 1860–61; elected prosecuting atty., Stark Cty., OH; delegate, NE State Constitutional Convention, 1871, 1874; city atty., Omaha, NE; elected as a Republican to U.S. Senate (NE), 1883–95 (pres. pro tempore); ***candidate for Republican nomination to presidency of the U.S., 1896***. BUS. & PROF.: atty.; admitted to OH Bar, 1859; law practice, Stark Cty., OH, 1865; gen. solicitor, Burlington R.R., 1895–1911; lecturer. MIL.: pvt., brig. gen., U.S. Army, 1861–65. MEM.: ABA (pres., 1900–1901); National Geographic Soc.; Loyal Legion; GAR;

Metropolitan Club; Army and Navy Club; Omaha Commercial Club; Omaha Country Club. WRITINGS: *The Twin Seven Shooters* (1902). RES.: Omaha, NE.

MANER, PITT TYSON. d. Jun 12, 1963, Montgomery, AL; par. Olin Conner and Sally T. Maner; married; c. Pitt Tyson, Jr. EDUC.: grad., Starke U. School; grad., Gulf Coast Military Acad.; U. of AL. POLIT. & GOV.: delegate, Dem. Nat'l. Conv., 1932, 1936, 1940, 1944, 1948, 1952, 1956 (alternate); exec. sec., Gov. Bibb Graves (AL), 1937; pres., Young Democrats Clubs of America, 1937–39; asst. dir., dir., AL State Dept. of Industrial Relations, 1944; dir., AL Office of Civil Defense; floor mgr., Estes Kefauver (q.v.) for President, Dem. Nat'l. Conv., 1952; floor mgr., Albert B. Chandler (q.v.) for President, Dem. Nat'l. Conv., 1956; ***candidate for Democratic nomination to vice presidency of the U.S., 1956***. BUS. & PROF.: real estate, FL; semiprofessional baseball player; employment consultant, AL State Dept. of Industrial Relations, 1962–63. MEM.: Masons; Shriners; Elks. REL.: Methodist. RES.: Montgomery, AL.

MANGUM, WILLIE PERSON. b. May 10, 1792, Red Mountain, NC; d. Sep 7, 1861, Red Mountain, NC; par. William Person and Catharine (Davis) Mangum; m. Charity Alston Cain, Sep 30, 1819; c. Willie Person, Jr.; three daughters. EDUC.: Fayetteville (NC) Acad.; Raleigh (NC) Acad.; B.A., U. of NC, 1815, A.M.; read law under Judge Duncan Cameron. POLIT. & GOV.: elected as a Democrat to NC State House of Commons, 1818–19; elected judge, NC Superior Court, 1819 (resigned), 1826 (not confirmed by legislature), 1831 (resigned); elected as a Federalist to U.S. House (NC), 1823–26; presidential elector, Democratic Party, 1828; Democratic candidate for U.S. Senate (NC), 1828 (withdrew); elected as a Democrat to U.S. House (NC), 1831–36, as a Whig, 1840–53 (pres. pro tempore, 1842–45); ***Whig Party candidate for presidency of the U.S., 1836***; delegate, Whig Party National Convention, 1839; ***Whig Party candidate for vice presidency of the U.S., 1840 (declined)***; elected as a Whig to NC State Senate, 1840; Whig Party candidate for U.S. Senate (NC), 1852. BUS. & PROF.: atty.; admitted to NC Bar, 1817; law practice, Red Mountain, NC. HON. DEG.: LL.D., U. of NC. RES.: Walnut Hill, NC.

MANIERRE, ALFRED LEE. b. May 4, 1861, New York, NY; d. Oct 1, 1911, New York, NY; par. Benjamin F. and Caroline (Flynn) Manierre; m. Cornelia Putnam Lockwood, Nov 10, 1897; c. Ruth Lockwood; B. Franklin II; Alfred Lee, Jr. EDUC.: A.B., Columbia U., 1883. POLIT. & GOV.: member, NY State Prohibition Party Central Cmte.; chm., New York Cty. (NY) Prohibition Party Central Cmte.; Prohibition Party candidate for judge, Superior Court of New York, NY, 1893, 1894; Prohibition Party candidate for mayor of New York, 1901, 1909; Prohibition Party candidate for gov. of NY, 1902; Prohibition Party candidate for atty. gen. of NY; ***candidate for Prohibition Party nomination to presidency of the U.S., 1908***; Prohibition Party candidate for chief judge, NY Court of Appeals, 1913. BUS. & PROF.: atty.; admitted to NY Bar, 1892; partner, Manierre and Manierre (law firm), New York. MEM.: NY Red Cross Hospital (treas.; dir.); National Temperance Soc. (trustee); Prohibition Trust Fund Assn. (trustee; counsel); NY State Central Cmte. for Scientific Temperance Instruction in Public Schools (sec.; treas.); Scientific Temperance Federation (dir.); Phi Beta Kappa; Travelers' Aid Soc. (dir.; member, exec. cmte.); National League for the Protection of Colored Women (member, exec. cmte.); Cmte. for Improving the Industrial Condition of the Negro; Alpha Delta Phi; City Club; Barnard Club; New York City Bar Assn.; New York Cty. Lawyers' Assn. REL.: Presb. (elder). RES.: New York, NY.

MANN, JAMES ROBERT. b. Oct 20, 1856, Bloomington, IL; d. Nov 30, 1922, Washington, DC; par. William Henry and Elizabeth Dabney (Abraham) Mann; m. Emma Columbia, May 30, 1882. EDUC.: grad., U. of IL, 1876; LL.B., Union Coll. of Law, 1881. POLIT. & GOV.: elected member, Oakland School Board, Village of Hyde Park, IL, 1887; village atty., Village of Hyde Park, IL, 1888; elected as a Republican, alderman, Chicago, IL, 1893–96; temporary chm., IL State Republican Convention, 1894; chm., Cook Cty. (IL) Republican Convention, 1895, 1902; master in chancery, Superior Court of Cook Cty., IL, 1892–96; gen. atty., South Park Board, Chicago, IL, 1895; elected as a Republican to U.S. House (IL), 1897–1923 (minority leader, 1911–19); ***candidate for Republican nomination to presidency of the U.S., 1916***. BUS. & PROF.: atty.; admitted to IL Bar, 1881; law practice, Chicago, IL; real estate investor. MEM.: Jackson Park World's Fair Cmte. (sec.). HON. DEG.: M.L., U. of IL, 1892, LL.D., 1903. RES.: Chicago, IL.

MAR, EMMA WONG. b. Sep 7, 1926, New York, NY; par. Ying Joon and May (Gee) Wong; m. Henry March, Jul 12, 1953; c. JoAnn; Craig. EDUC.: B.A., Hunter Coll., 1948. POLIT. & GOV.: founding member, Peace and Freedom Party, 1967; Peace and Freedom Party candidate for CA State Assembly, 1982 and one other time; chairperson, Peace and Freedom Party, 1982–84; ***Peace and Freedom Party candidate for vice presidency of the U.S., 1984; Peace and Freedom Party (dissident faction) candidate for vice presidency of the U.S., 1988***. BUS. & PROF.: bacteriologist; licensed medical technologist, 1950–; laboratory technologist, New York, NY; laboratory technologist, Sutter Memorial Hospital, Sacramento, CA; medical technologist, Planned Parenthood, CA. MEM.: Women for Peace (1963–70). REL.: none. MAILING ADDRESS: 1073 Walker Ave., Oakland, CA 94610.

MARCH, CHARLES HOYT. b. Oct 20, 1870, Cedar Mills, MN; d. Aug 28, 1945, Washington, DC; par. Nelson Jonathan and Mary Jane (Morrison) March; m. Aimee Wells, Feb 28, 1899; c. Cora (Mrs. Chris L. Christensen); Wells;

Charles Hoyt, Jr. EDUC.: high school, Litchfield, MN. POLIT. & GOV.: elected mayor of Litchfield, MN; pres., Library Board, Litchfield, MN; vice chm., Safety Comm. of MN, 1918–20; delegate, Rep. Nat'l. Conv., 1920, 1924, 1928 (chm., State Delegation); campaign mgr., Calvin Coolidge (q.v.) for President, 1924; ***candidate for Republican nomination to vice presidency of the U.S., 1924***; appointed member, Federal Trade Comm., 1929–45; appointed member, Industrial Recovery Board, 1933–34; ***candidate for Republican nomination to presidency of the U.S., 1940***. BUS. & PROF.: atty.; admitted to MN Bar, 1893; admitted to practice before the Bar of the Supreme Court of the U.S.; law practice, Litchfield, MN; partner, March Brothers (law firm); counsel, Great Northern Railway Co.; vice pres., Minnesota Banks; pres., Farmers and Bankers Council of MN. MIL.: col., 4th Regt., MN Militia, 1898. MEM.: Masons (32°; Knights Templar; Shriners). REL.: Episc. RES.: Litchfield, MN.

MARCUS, EDDIE BERNARD. m. Vera Marcus. POLIT. & GOV.: ***independent candidate for presidency of the U.S., 1988***. MAILING ADDRESS: 656 Ashland, #10, St. Paul, MN 55104.

MARCUS, GILBERT LEON. b. Dec 19, 1941, Atlantic City, NJ; par. John and Gwendolyn Vivian (Cromwell) Marcus; m. Helen Lavern Farrington, Apr 23, 1959; m. 2d, Deborah Scott, Mar 10, 1978; c. none. EDUC.: U. of the State of NY, 1970; high school equivalency certificate, NJ, 1973; grad., Drake Business School, 1976. POLIT. & GOV.: ***candidate for Republican nomination to presidency of the U.S., 1984, 1988***. BUS. & PROF.: soldier. MIL.: pfc, U.S. Army, 1959–61. MEM.: ABA; Disabled American Veterans (life member); BSA. REL.: Protestant. MISC.: convicted of third degree assault, Queens Cty., NY, 1970. MAILING ADDRESS: c/o Esquire Hotel, 360 West 45th St., Apt. B-11, New York, NY 10036.

MARCUS, STEPHEN WILLIAM. b. May 7, 1967, Los Angeles, CA; par. Stephen Wassil and Sharon C. (Weatherhead) Marcus; single. EDUC.: grad., Pleasant Valley H.S., Chico, CA, 1985. POLIT. & GOV.: ***candidate for Republican nomination to presidency of the U.S., 1984***. BUS. & PROF.: student. MAILING ADDRESS: 1141 Wendy Way, Chico, CA 95926.

MARCY, WILLIAM LEARNED. b. Dec 12, 1786, Sturbridge (now Southbridge), MA; d. Jul 4, 1857, Ballston Spa, NY; par. Jedediah and Ruth (Learned) Marcy; m. Dolly Newell, Sep 27, 1812; m. 2d, Cornelia Knower, c. 1825; c. six. EDUC.: Leicester Acad.; grad., Brown U., 1808. POLIT. & GOV.: appointed recorder, Troy, NY, 1816–18; elected mayor of Troy, 1816–18, 1821–23; appointed adj. gen. of NY, 1821; elected as a Democrat to comptroller of NY, 1823–29; appointed assoc. justice, NY State Supreme Court, 1829–31; elected as a Democrat to U.S. Senate (NY), 1831–33; elected as a Democrat to gov. of NY, 1833–39; Democratic candidate for gov. of NY, 1838; appointed member, Mexican Claims Comm., 1839–42; pres., NY State Democratic Convention, 1843; ***candidate for Democratic nomination to vice presidency of the U.S., 1844***; appointed U.S. sec. of war, 1845–49; ***candidate for Democratic nomination to presidency of the U.S., 1852***; appointed U.S. sec. of state, 1853–57. BUS. & PROF.: schoolteacher, Newport, RI; atty.; admitted to NY Bar, 1811; law practice, Troy; partner, Marcy and Lane (law firm), 1818–23; ed., *Troy Budget*. MIL.: ensign, lt., capt., 155th NY Regt., 1812. MEM.: Tammany Soc. WRITINGS: *Oration on the Three Hundred and Eighteenth Anniversary of the Discovery of America* (1808); *Considerations in Favor of the Appointment of Rufus King to the Senate of the United States* (1820). MISC.: coined term *spoils system*; organized first geological survey of NY; settled NJ boundary dispute; advocated tariff of 1848; negotiated Gadsden Purchase, 1853. RES.: Albany, NY.

MARKEN, JOHN HERBERT. POLIT. & GOV.: ***independent candidate for presidency of the U.S., 1976***. MAILING ADDRESS: 1085 South Sixth, San Jose, CA.

MARKEY, EDWARD JOHN. b. Jul 11, 1946, Malden, MA; par. John E. and Christine M. (Courtney) Markey; m. Susan Blumenthal. EDUC.: B.A., Boston Coll., 1968, J.D., 1972. POLIT. & GOV.: elected as a Democrat to MA State House, 1973–77; elected as a Democrat to U.S. House (MA), 1977–; ***candidate for Democratic nomination to vice presidency of the U.S., 1980 (withdrew)***. BUS. & PROF.: atty. MIL.: U.S.A.R., 1968–73. MEM.: MA Bar Assn.; Knights of Columbus; New England Congressional Caucus; Northeast-Midwest Economic Advancement Coalition; Democratic Study Group; Environmental Study Conference. AWARDS: "Legislator of the Year," MA Bar Assn., 1975. REL.: R.C. MAILING ADDRESS: 7 Townsend St., Malden, MA 02148.

MARKHAM, EDWIN (nee CHARLES EDWARD ANSON MARKHAM). b. Apr 23, 1852, Oregon City, OR; d. Mar 7, 1940, Staten Island, NY; par. Samuel and Elizabeth (Winchell) Markham; m. Annie Cox, 1875; m. 2d, Caroline S. Bailey, 1887; m. 3d, Anna Catherine Murphy, Jun 18, 1898; c. Virgil. EDUC.: State Normal School, San Jose, CA, 1871; grad., Christian Coll., 1873; read law. POLIT. & GOV.: elected as a Republican to superintendent of schools, El Dorado Cty., CA, 1879; ***candidate for Democratic nomination to vice presidency of the U.S., 1924; candidate for Republican nomination to vice presidency of the U.S., 1924***. BUS. & PROF.: ranch hand, Suisun, CA; blacksmith; principal, teacher, Coloma, CA; poet; headmaster, Tompkins Observation School, Oakland, CA, 1889–99. Recordings: "Edwin Markham, Himself" (1938). MEM.: Poetry Soc. of America (hon. pres.); American Acad. of Arts and Letters; Town Hall

Club; MacDowell Club; Bohemian Club; International Longfellow Soc. HON. DEG.: L.H.D., Syracuse U., 1924; Litt.D., NY U., 1930; Litt.D., St. Lawrence U., 1933; Litt.D., Baylor U. WRITINGS: "A Dream of Chaos" (poem); *The Social Conscience* (1897); *The Man with the Hoe, and Other Poems* (1899); *In the Earth's Shadow; The Man with the Hoe, With Notes by the Author* (1900); *Lincoln, and Other Poems* (1901); *The Shoes of Happiness and Other Poems; The Hoe-Man in the Making* (later retitled *The Children in Bondage*, 1914); *California, the Wonderful* (1915); *Gates of Paradise* (1920); *Foundation Stones of Success* (ed., 1925); *The Ballad of the Gallows Bird* (1926); *The Book of Poetry* (ed., 1927); *California in Song and Story* (ed., 1930); *New Poems—Eighty Songs at Eighty* (1932); *Poetry of Youth* (ed., 1935); *The Star of Araby* (1937). REL.: Swedenborgian. RES.: Port Richmond, Staten Island, NY.

MARQUEZ, HECTOR. POLIT. & GOV.: ***independent candidate for presidency of the U.S., 1988***. MAILING ADDRESS: 421 South Bailey St., Palmer, AR 99645.

MARQUEZ, SAMUEL. b. Nov 16, 1948, El Paso, TX; par. Roberta and Rosa (Holquin) Marquez; single. POLIT. & GOV.: ***candidate for Democratic nomination to presidency of the U.S., 1984***. MIL.: L/CPL, U.S.M.C., 1967–71. AWARDS: Golden Key Award in Art. MISC.: noted for using candidacy to promote search for a wife. MAILING ADDRESS: 3029 Orkney Rd., El Paso, TX 79925.

MARRA, WILLIAM ANTHONY. POLIT. & GOV.: ***candidate for Democratic nomination to presidency of the U.S., 1988; Right to Life Party candidate for presidency of the U.S., 1988***. BUS. & PROF.: prof. MAILING ADDRESS: c/o William Regis Marra, Jr., 12 Indian Trail, West Milford, NJ 07480.

MARROU, ANDRE VERNE. b. Dec 4, 1938, Nixon, TX; par. Andrew Noil and Annette (Deason) Marrou; m. Eileen C. Lennon, 1979 (divorced); c. Krys; Andre; Lance. EDUC.: B.S., MA Inst. of Technology, 1962; Graduate School of Business, Columbia U., 1962; U. of Las Vegas. POLIT. & GOV.: vice chm., Alaskan Libertarian Party, 1977–78; founder, Kachemak Bay Libertarian Party, 1980–81; chm., Platform Cmte., Alaskan Libertarian Party State Convention, 1983–84; elected as a Libertarian to AK State House, 1985–87; Libertarian Party candidate for AK State House, 1986; ***Libertarian Party candidate for vice presidency of the U.S., 1988; Libertarian Party candidate for presidency of the U.S., 1992***. BUS. & PROF.: process engineer, Artisan Industries, Inc., 1963–66; project engineer, Amicon Corp., 1966–67; engineering mgr., Vacuum Industries, Inc., 1967–73; pres., Aregah Corp., 1974–76; information specialist, Trans-Alaska Pipeline, 1977–78; homesteader, Perl Island, Bear Cove, AK, 1978–80; broker, agent, Eagle Real Estate, Homer, AK, 1980–; primary sponsor, AK Initiative to Deregulate Transportation, 1983–84; commercial real estate leasing and sales, Las Vegas, NV, 1987–. MIL.: airman, U.S. Air Force R.O.T.C., 1956, first sgt., 1958; "Outstanding Cadet," U.S. Air Force R.O.T.C. MEM.: Pershing Rifles; NRA; U.S.C.G. Auxiliary; Aircraft Owners and Pilots Assn.; Experimental Aircraft Assn.; Civil Air Patrol (2d lt.); National Federal of Independent Businesses; AK Assn. of Realtors; Project 51-92 PAC (dir., 1988–91); Kachemak Board of Realtors (pres., 1984). WRITINGS: *High Vacuum Design Manual, Vacuum Industries, Inc.* (1970); "A Christmas Tree in the Alaskan Wilderness," *Alaska Magazine* (1980). MAILING ADDRESS: 5143 Blanton Dr., Las Vegas, NV 89122.

MARSH, JEFFREY FLAKE. POLIT. & GOV.: ***candidate for Democratic nomination to presidency of the U.S., 1992***. MAILING ADDRESS: 404 East Adams, Fairfield, IA 52556.

MARSHALL, CARRINGTON TANNER. b. Jun 17, 1869, Zanesville, OH; d. Jun 28, 1958; par. John Wesley and Rachel Ann (Tanner) Marshall; m. Dora Foltz, Jun 1900; c. Constance (Mrs. James T. Lowe). EDUC.: LL.B., Cincinnati Law School, 1892. POLIT. & GOV.: chief justice, Supreme Court of OH, 1921–32; chm., Cmte. of Direction of Study of Judicial Administration in OH; ***candidate for Republican nomination to presidency of the U.S., 1936***; presiding judge, U.S. Military Tribunal Number 3, Trial of War Crimes, Nuremburg, Germany. BUS. & PROF.: atty.; law practice, Zanesville, OH, 1892–1920; law practice, Columbus, OH, 1933–58. MEM.: ABA; American Law Inst. (Advisory Cmte.); OH Judicial Council (pres.); Delta Theta Phi; Civitan (international pres.). HON. DEG.: LL.D, U. of Cincinnati, 1925; LL.D., Wilmington (OH) Coll., 1926. WRITINGS: *A History of Courts and Lawyers of Ohio; New Divorce Courts for Old; Liberty Under Law in America; Law Reform and Reformers; The United Nations Charter and the Constitutional Voice* (with Roscoe C. McCulloch). REL.: Presb. RES.: Columbus, OH.

MARSHALL, GEORGE CATLETT. b. Dec 31, 1880, Uniontown, PA; d. Oct 16, 1959, Washington, DC; par. George Catlett and Laura (Bradford) Marshall; m. Elizabeth Carter Coles, Feb 11, 1902; m. 2d, Katherine Boyrce (Tupper) Brown, Oct 15, 1930; c. Molly B. Winn (stepdaughter); Clifton Stevenson (stepson); Allen Tupper (stepson). EDUC.: VA Military Inst., 1897–1901; honor grad., U.S. Infantry-Cavalry School, 1907; grad., Army Staff Coll., 1908. POLIT. & GOV.: ***candidate for Democratic nomination to presidency of the U.S., 1944***; appointed special representative of the president to China, with rank of ambassador, 1945; appointed member, American Battle Monuments Comm., 1946–59 (chm., 1949–59); appointed U.S. sec. of state, 1947–49; ***candidate for Democratic nomination to vice presidency of the U.S., 1948***; appointed U.S. sec. of defense, 1950–51; appointed chm., U.S.

Delegation to Coronation of Queen Elizabeth II, 1953. BUS. & PROF.: soldier; diplomat. MIL.: commissioned 2d lt., infantry, U.S. Army, 1901; promoted through grades to maj. gen., 1939; instructor, Army Staff Coll., 1908–10; aide-de-camp to Gen. John J. Pershing (q.v.), 1919–24; instructor, Army War Coll., 1927; asst. commandant, Infantry School, 1927–32; commander, 8th Infantry, U.S. Army, 1933; senior instructor to IL National Guard, 1933–36; commanding gen., 5th Bde., U.S. Army, 1936–38; chief, War Plans Div., General Staff, U.S. Army, 1938; gen., 1939; deputy chief of staff, 1938–39; chief of military mission to Brazil, 1939; chief of staff, U.S. Army, 1939–45; gen. of the army, 1944 (temporary), 1946 (permanent); Congressional Gold Medal; Distinguished Service Medal with Oak Leaf Cluster; Silver Star; Victory Medal with 5 bars; Croix de Guerre with Palm (France); Silver Medal of Valor (Montenegro); Grand Croix, Legion of Honor (France); officer, Order of Saints Maurice and Lazarus (Italy); officer, Order of the Crown (Italy); Order of La Soledaridad (Panama); grand commander, Order of Merit (Brazil); Star of Aldon Calderon (Ecuador); Gran Oficial del Sol del Peru (Peru); Grand Cross of Ouissam Alaouite (Morocco); Military Order of Merit, First Class (Cuba); Order del Merito (Chile); Knight of the Grand Cross, Order of the Bath (Great Britain); Order of Suvarov, First Degree (U.S.S.R.); Grand Cross, Order of Boyaca (Colombia); Grand Cross with Swords, Royal Order of George I (Greece); Knight of the Grand Cross, Order of Orange Nassau (Netherlands). MEM.: American Red Cross (pres., 1949–50); Soc. of the Cincinnati; Kappa Alpha; Army and Navy Club; Alibi Club; Army and Navy Club of San Francisco; Metropolitan Club; National Geographic Soc. (trustee); Harry S. Truman Library, Inc. (trustee); International House (hon. chm.); Franklin Delano Roosevelt Foundation, Inc. (dir.); Atlantic Union Cmte. (National Council); Masons; Union League; University Club; Rotary Club; Lions. AWARDS: Theodore Roosevelt Distinguished Service Medal, 1945; Humanitarian Award, Varities Clubs, 1947; Freedom House Award, 1947; Gold Medal, National Planning Assn., 1949; National Civic Service Award, Order of Eagles, 1949; Distinguished Service to the American Way Award, NY Board of Trade, 1949; Distinguished Public Service Award, U.S. Conference of Mayors, 1949; Citizenship Award, NY Chapter, Disabled American Veterans, 1950; Distinguished Service Medal, American Legion, 1951; Virginia Distinguished Service Medal, 1951; Four Freedoms Foundation Award, 1952; Nobel Peace Prize, 1953; Award for Distinguished Service, Woodrow Wilson Foundation, 1956; Pennsylvania Meritorious Medal, 1957; Charlemagne Prize, 1958. HON. DEG.: D.Sc., Washington and Jefferson Coll., 1939; Dr. Mil. Sci., PA Military Coll., 1940; LL.D., Trinity Coll., 1941; LL.D., William and Mary Coll., 1941; Dr.Mil.Sci., Norwich U., 1942; LL.D, Amherst Coll., 1947; LL.D., Brown U., 1947; LL.D., Columbia U., 1947; LL.D, Harvard U., 1947; LL.D., Lafayette Coll., 1947; LL.D., McGill U., 1947; Dr.Civil Law, Oxford U., 1947; LL.D., Princeton U., 1947; LL.D., U. of CA, 1948. REL.: Episc. RES.: Leesburg, VA.

MARSHALL, JOHN. b. Sep 24, 1755, Germantown, VA; d. Jul 6, 1835, Philadelphia, PA; par. Thomas and Mary Randolph (Keith) Marshall; m. Mary Willis Ambler, Jan 3, 1783; c. Thomas; Mary (Mrs. Jacquelin B. Harvis); James Keith; John; Edward Carrington; Jacqueline Ambler; four infants. EDUC.: Coll. of William and Mary, 1780. POLIT. & GOV.: elected delegate, VA State House of Burgesses, 1780, 1782–88; member, VA State Exec. Council, 1782–95; city recorder, Richmond, VA, 1783–85; delegate, VA Ratification Convention, 1788; appointed atty. gen. of the U.S., 1795 (declined); appointed U.S. minister to France, 1796 (declined); member, Special Comm. to France on Reparations, 1797–98; appointed assoc. justice of the Supreme Court of the U.S., 1798 (declined); elected as a Federalist to U.S. House (VA), 1799–1800; appointed U.S. sec. of war, 1800 (declined); appointed U.S. sec. of state, 1800–1801; appointed chief justice of the Supreme Court of the U.S., 1801–35; ***received 4 electoral votes as a Federalist for vice presidency of the U.S., 1816***; delegate, VA State Constitutional Convention, 1829. BUS. & PROF.: atty.; admitted to Fauquier Cty. (VA) Bar, 1780; law practice, Fauquier Cty.; plantation owner, Fauquier Cty. MIL.: lt., Third VA Regt., Continental Army, 1775, capt., 1777–81. MEM.: Masons; Jockey Club. WRITINGS: *The Life of George Washington* (1804–07). REL.: Unitarian. MISC.: presiding judge, trial of Aaron Burr (q.v.), 1807; noted for establishing Doctrine of Judicial Review in case of *Marbury v. Madison*; other important cases include *Fletcher v. Peck*, *Martin v. Hunter's Lessee*, *Cohens v. Virginia*, *Dartmouth College v. Woodward*, and *McCulloch v. Maryland*. RES.: Richmond, VA.

MARSHALL, SIDNEY A. POLIT. & GOV.: ***independent candidate for presidency of the U.S., 1976***. MAILING ADDRESS: P.O. Box 206, Portal, ND 58772.

MARSHALL, THOMAS RILEY. b. Mar 14, 1854, North Manchester, IN; d. Jun 1, 1925, Washington, DC; par. Daniel Miller and Martha Ann (Patterson) Marshall; m. Lois Irene Kimsey, Oct 2, 1895; c. infant son (adopted). EDUC.: A.B., Wabash Coll., 1873, A.M., 1876; read law under Judge Walter Olds, Columbia City, IN. POLIT. & GOV.: member, Columbia City (IN) School Board; Democratic candidate for prosecuting atty., Grant Cty., IN, 1880; chm., IN Democratic Congressional District Cmte., 1896–98; elected as a Democrat to gov. of IN, 1909–13; ***candidate for Democratic nomination to presidency of the U.S., 1912, 1920, 1924; elected as a Democrat to vice presidency of the U.S., 1913–1921***; delegate, Dem. Nat'l. Conv., 1920; appointed member, Federal Coal Comm., 1922–23. BUS. & PROF.: atty.; admitted to IN Bar, 1874; law practice, Columbia City, IN; partner, Marshall and McNagny (law firm), 1876–92; partner, Marshall, McNagny and Clugston (law firm), 1892–1909. MEM.: Masons (33°; Supreme Council; Scottish Rite); Phi Gamma Delta; Phi Beta Kappa; Wabash Coll. (trustee). HON. DEG.: LL.D., Wabash Coll., 1909; LL.D., Notre Dame U., 1910; LL.D., U. of PA, 1911; LL.D., U. of NC, 1913; LL.D., U. of ME, 1914; LL.D., Washington and Jefferson Coll., 1915; J.D., Villanova Coll., 1918. WRITINGS: *Recollections of Thos. R. Marshall, Vice-president and Hoosier Philospher—A Hoosier Salad* (1925). REL.: Presb. (Sunday school teacher). RES.: Indianapolis, IN.

MARTIN, DAVID HERRON. b. Mar 28, 1849, Pittsburgh, PA; d. Mar 1933; par. William and Anna (Miller) Martin; m. Angeline Starr, Oct 26, 1875; c. Park; seven others. EDUC.: public schools, Allegheny, PA. POLIT. & GOV.: Prohibition Party candidate for U.S. House (PA); elected burgess and member, Bellevue (PA) City Council, 1892–93, 1897–1900, 1903–05; ***United Christian Party candidate for vice presidency of the U.S., 1900***; member, National Exec. Cmte., United Christian Party. BUS. & PROF.: publisher of temperance papers; publisher, *The Educator*. RES.: Bellevue, PA.

MARTIN, EDWARD. b. Sep 18, 1879, Ten Mile, PA; d. Mar 19, 1967, Washington, PA; par. Joseph T. and Hannah M. (Bristor) Martin; m. Charity Scott, Dec 1, 1908; c. Edward Scott; Mary C. (Mrs. James Beall W. Murphy). EDUC.: A.B., Waynesboro Coll., 1901. POLIT. & GOV.: elected burgess of East Waynesboro, PA, 1902–05; sec., Greene Cty. (PA) Republican Central Cmte., 1905, chm., 1908; solicitor, Greene Cty., PA, 1908–10, 1916–20; member, PA State Republican Central Cmte., 1912; elected as a Republican to auditor gen. of PA, 1925–29; chm., PA State Republican Central Cmte., 1928–34; elected as a Republican to PA state treas., 1929–33; delegate, Rep. Nat'l. Conv., 1932, 1936, 1940, 1944, 1948, 1952, 1956, 1960; ***candidate for Republican nomination to vice presidency of the U.S., 1932***; appointed adj. gen. of PA, 1939–43; elected as a Republican to gov. of PA, 1943–47; elected as a Republican to U.S. Senate (PA), 1947–59; ***candidate for Republican nomination to presidency of the U.S., 1948***. BUS. & PROF.: atty.; admitted to PA Bar, 1905; law practice, Waynesboro, PA; dir., Citizens National Bank; dir., Washington County Fire Insurance Co.; pres., dir., Dunn-Mar Oil and Gas Co., Washington, PA. MIL.: member, 10th PA Volunteer Infantry, 1898–99, Mexican Border Campaign, 1916; member, 109th and 110th Infantry Regts., 1917–19, brig. gen., 1922, maj. gen., 1939; commanded 28th Div., PA National Guard, 1939; commanding gen., 28th Div., U.S. Army, 1941–42; Distinguished Service Cross with Oak Leaf; Distinguished Service Medal (National Guard); Purple Heart with Oak Leaf Cluster. MEM.: Legion of Valor; Military Order of Carabao; Spanish-American War Veterans; PA State Sabbath School Assn. (vice pres.; dir.); Masons (33°); Elks; VFW; American Legion; Waynesboro Coll. (trustee); Soc. of the 28th Div.; National Governors' Conference (chm., exec. cmte., 1945–46); Council of State Governments (pres., 1946); Washington and Jefferson Coll. (trustee); Auditors', Controllers' and Treasurers' Assn. of the United States (pres., 1932); National Guard Assn. of the United States (pres., 1940). AWARDS: Pennsylvania Reilly Medal (1937); American Legion Distinguished Service Medal; Pennsylvania Distinguished Service Medal; Distinguished Service Medal, National Guard Assn. of the United States. HON. DEG.: LL.D., Washington and Jefferson Coll., 1938; Dr.Mil.Sci., Waynesboro Coll., 1940; LL.D., U. of Pittsburgh, 1941; LL.D., Drexel Inst. of Technology, 1943; LL.D., PA Military Coll., 1943; LL.D., Temple U., 1943; LL.D., U. of PA, 1943; LL.D., Villanova Coll., 1943; LL.D., Gettysburg Coll., 1944; LL.D., Grove City Coll., 1945; L.H.D., Hahnemann Medical Coll. of the Hospital of Philadelphia, 1945; LL.D., Lafayette Coll., 1945; LL.D., Lebanon Valley Coll., 1945; LL.D., Ursinus Coll., 1945; LL.D., Westminster Coll., 1945; LL.D., Beaver Coll., 1946; D.C.L., Bucknell Coll., 1946; LL.D., St. Vincent Coll., 1946; LL.D., Geneva Coll., 1947. WRITINGS: *Always Be on Time; History of the 28th Division.* REL.: Presb. (Elder). RES.: Washington, PA.

MARTIN, FREDERICK COLLINS. b. Jun 9, 1882, Bennington, VT; d. Apr 10, 1945, Bennington, VT; par. William and Georgiana (Collins) Martin; m. Hildred Hannah Burnham, Jan 28, 1939; c. none. EDUC.: public schools, Bennington, VT. POLIT. & GOV.: elected village pres., Bennington, VT, 1909–12, 1922–25; elected as a Democrat to VT State House, 1912–15; delegate, Dem. Nat'l. Conv., 1912, 1920, 1924, 1928, 1932, 1936, 1940; Democratic candidate for gov. of VT, 1920, 1924; appointed member, VT State War Hist. Comm., 1921; appointed member, VT State Tax Comm., 1922; ***candidate for Democratic nomination to presidency of the U.S., 1924***; appointed exec. chm., VT Sesqui-Centennial Celebration, 1927 Democratic candidate for U.S. Senate (VT), 1928, 1932, 1934; appointed member, VT State Constitutional Amendment Comm., 1929; appointed member, VT Comm. to Investigate Taxation of Public Utilities, 1931; appointed collector of internal revenue (VT), 1933–45; appointed member, VT State Planning Board, 1935–39; elected trustee, Bennington (VT) Graded School District, 1939–40. BUS. & PROF.: office boy, Holden-Leonard Co., Inc., mgr., 1932; dir., County National Bank, Bennington, VT, 1926–32, exec. vice pres., 1932–42, pres., 1942–45; incorporator, mgr., dir., Bennington Cooperative Savings and Loan Assn., 1917–45; co-owner, Hotel Putnam, Inc., Bennington, VT; first vice pres., Burlington (VT) Mutual Fire Insurance Co., 1941–45. MEM.: Bennington Library Assn. (sec., 1908–45); National Foundation for Infantile Paralysis (cty. chm.; trustee, 1942–45); Green Mountain Junior Coll. (exec. cmte., 1944–45); Newcomen Soc.; Masons; Elks; Methodist Brotherhood (pres., 1914–42). REL.: Methodist (trustee, 1911–45; chm., Finance Cmte., 1922–45). RES.: Bennington, VT.

MARTIN, JOHN GOVERNOR. b. Jan 4, 1929, Aiken, SC; par. Booker T. Martin; m. Ruth E. Collins; c. De Vadia; Walter John. EDUC.: grad., Schofield H.S., Aiken, SC, 1946; B.S., SC State Coll., 1950; Howard U., 1955–56, 1969–72; Christian Theological Seminary, Indianapolis, IN. POLIT. & GOV.: Democratic candidate for Washington, DC, City Council, 1976; appointed coordinator of religious activities, DC Host Cmte., Presidential Inaugural Cmte., 1977; Democratic candidate for chm., Washington, DC, City Council, 1978; founder, Third World Political Party, 1980; ***Third World Assembly candidate for presidency of the U.S., 1980, 1984, 1988***. BUS. & PROF.: medical laboratory technician, Garfield Hospital, Washington, DC, 1954; chief chemist, Children's Hospital, Washington, DC; medical researcher, Pancreatic and Enzyme Research, Washington Hospital Center, Washington, DC, 1959–60; insurance mgr.; ordained minister, Baptist Church, 1965; founder, pastor, Holy Comforter Baptist

Church, Washington, DC, 1972. MIL.: staff sgt., U.S. Air Force, 1950–54. MEM.: Third World Assembly, Inc. (founder; exec. dir.; chm., 1979); Baptist Ministers Conference of Washington and Vicinity (statistician); Far Northeast Group Ministry; Upper Northeast Coordinating Council; D.C. Black Assembly; National Baptist Convention; Upper Northeast Group Ministry; D.C. Pastors' Conference; Alpha Theta Nu Omega Theological Fraternity (national pres.); American Baptist Convention; Southern Baptist Convention; Housing Coalition; World Inst. of Achievement (life member); American Biographical Inst. and Research Assn. (life fellow; deputy gov.); International Biographical Assn. (fellow); 14th International Congress on Arts and Communication (delegate, 1987). AWARDS: Key of Success for Achievement in Research; Statesman Award; Commemorative Medal of Honor; International Cultural Diploma of Honor. WRITINGS: *The Nature and Chemical Changes in the Human Body of Vital Importance in Health and Disease* (1960). REL.: Bapt. MAILING ADDRESS: 354 Anacostia Rd., S.E., #14, Washington, DC 20017.

MARTIN, JOSEPH WILLIAM, JR. b. Nov 3, 1884, North Attleboro, MA; d. Mar 6, 1968, Hollywood, FL; par. Joseph William and Catherine (Katon) Martin; single. EDUC.: grad., North Attleboro (MA) H.S., 1902. POLIT. & GOV.: elected as a Republican to MA State House, 1912–14; elected as a Republican to MA State Senate, 1915–17; delegate, Rep. Nat'l. Conv., 1916, 1936, 1940 (permanent chm.), 1944 (permanent chm.), 1948 (permanent chm.), 1952 (permanent chm.), 1956 (permanent chm.); appointed chm., MA Street Railway Investigation Comm., 1917; chm., MA Republican Legislative Campaign Cmte., 1917; presidential elector, Republican Party, 1920; exec. sec., MA State Republican Cmte., 1922–25; elected as a Republican to U.S. House (MA), 1925–67 (minority leader, 1939–46, 1949–53, 1955–59; Speaker, 1947–49, 1953–55); eastern mgr., Republican National Campaign, 1936; chm., Republican Congressional Cmte., 1937–38; chm., Rep. Nat'l. Cmte., 1940–42, 1948; ***candidate for Republican nomination to presidency of the U.S., 1940, 1944, 1948***; candidate for Republican nomination to U.S. House (MA), 1966. BUS. & PROF.: reporter, *Attleboro (MA) Sun* and *Providence (RI) Journal*, 1902–08; publisher, *Evening Chronicle*, North Attleboro, MA, 1908–68; publisher, *Franklin (MA) Sentinel*, 1946–68; proprietor, A. T. Parker and Co. (insurance firm), North Attleboro, 1914–68; dir., Manufacturers' National Bank, North Attleboro; trustee, Plainville Savings and Loan Assn. MEM.: Dean Acad. and Junior Coll. (trustee); Elks; Moose; Grange; MA Republican Club; Middlesex Club; Washington Press Club; North Attleboro Board of Trade (pres.); North Attleboro Fish and Game Assn. (sec.). HON. DEG.: S.M., Bryant Coll., 1939; D.C.L., Boston U., 1947; LL.D., PA Military Coll., 1947; LL.D., Tufts Coll., 1947; M.S., Bradford Durfee Technical Inst., 1955; LL.D., Dartmouth Coll., 1955; LL.D., Stonehill Coll., 1955; LL.D., Syracuse U., 1956; Dr. of Jurisprudence, Portia Law School; LL.D., New England Coll. WRITINGS: *My First Fifty Years in Politics* (1960). RES.: North Attleboro, MA.

MARTIN, PETER HARRISON. b. Apr 11, 1926, Tientsin, China; par. Rowland Harrison and Mary Elizabeth (Smith) Martin; m. Beverly Louise Brill; c. Melinda Ann Manahan; Jill Elizabeth. EDUC.: B.A., Occidental Coll., 1948. POLIT. & GOV.: ***candidate for Republican nomination to presidency of the U.S., 1980***. BUS. & PROF.: railroad yardman, 1948–50; asst. playground dir. (part-time), Los Angeles, CA, 1948–49; employee, ABC Lettering Service, 1950; employee, Union Bank, 1950–, real estate appraiser, 1965–; income tax preparer, 1957–; sec.-treas., General Ventures, Inc., Tustin, CA, 1977–79. MIL.: ensign, U.S. Navy, 1944–48. MEM.: AIREA. REL.: Presb. MAILING ADDRESS: 400 South Flower St., #167, Orange, CA 926668.

MARTIN, WARREN CHESTER. b. Oct 13, 1909, Ogden, KS; par. Lyman B. and Merle "Myrl" M. (Haney) Martin; m. Georgia Velma Proctor, Jul 27, 1936; c. Marilyn J. Dixon; Sharon R. Scoggins; W. Kenneth. EDUC.: grad., Central Coll., 1931. POLIT. & GOV.: Prohibition Party candidate for KS state printer, 1954; Prohibition Party candidate for KS state treas., 1956; Prohibition Party candidate for county commissioner (KS); Prohibition Party candidate for KS State House; Prohibition Party candidate for Junction City (KS) City Comm.; Prohibition Party candidate for gov. of KS, 1958, 1982; appointed member, KS State Board of Probation and Parole, 1959–61; delegate, Prohibition Party National Convention, 1963; Prohibition Party candidate for atty. gen. of KS, 1964; member, Prohibition Party National Cmte., 1983–; ***Prohibition Party candidate for vice presidency of the U.S., 1984***. BUS. & PROF.: asst. mgr., mgr., Scott Stores, 1935–42; farmer, rancher, co-owner, Fawley Ranch, Milford, KS, 1942–61; probation officer, state of KS, 1961–74. MEM.: KS State Farm Bureau; Geary Cty. Farm Bureau; Farmers Union Co-op Assn.; C. and W. Rural Electric Co-op Assn.; Manhattan P.O. Assn.; Young People's Missionary Soc. (superintendent, KS Conference, 1953–55); Life Line Children's Home (trustee); KS Sheriff's Assn. (assoc.). REL.: Free Methodist (Sunday school superintendent, 1946–). MAILING ADDRESS: 327 Shamrock, Junction City, KS 66441.

MARTIN-TRIGONA, ANTHONY R. b. 1945. POLIT. & GOV.: candidate for Democratic nomination to mayor of Chicago, IL, 1973, 1977; candidate for Democratic nomination to U.S. Senate (IL), 1978, 1980; ***candidate for Democratic nomination to presidency of the U.S., 1988***. BUS. & PROF.: investor. MISC.: indicted and sentenced in condominium fraud case, 1980. MAILING ADDRESS: P.O. Box 1988, Middletown, CT 06457.

MARX, ROBERT S. b. Jan 28, 1889, Cincinnati, OH; d. Sep 6, 1960, Charlevoix, MI; par. William S. and Rose (Lowenstein) Marx; single. EDUC.: LL.B., U. of Cincinnati, 1909. POLIT. & GOV.: elected as a Democrat to judge, Superior Court of Cincinnati, OH, 1920–26; ***candidate for Dem-***

ocratic nomination to vice presidency of the U.S., 1924; delegate, Dem. Nat'l. Conv., 1932, 1936. BUS. & PROF.: atty.; admitted to OH Bar, 1910; admitted to IL Bar, 1928; admitted to MI Bar, 1933; law practice, Cincinnati, OH; law practice, Chicago, IL, 1927–28; partner, Nichols, Wood, Marx and Ginter (law firm), Cincinnati, 1928–60; partner, Marx, Levi, Thrill and Wiseman (law firm), Detroit, MI; counsel for receiver, National Bank of Kentucky, 1930–45; counsel, First National Bank of Detroit, 1933–48; pres., Cincinnati Oil and Mining Co., 1945–60; prof. of law, U. of Cincinnati, 1952–56; prof., Xavier U. Law School; dir., Detroit Steel Co.; gen. counsel, dir., Schenley Industries, Inc., 1955–60; dir., Model Laundry Co.; dir., Portsmouth Steel Corp.; contributor, Journal of Legal Education. MIL.: capt., 357th Infantry, 90th Div., U.S. Army, 1917–19; maj., judge advocate gen., U.S.A.R., 1925–30; Distinguished Service Citation; Verdun Medal; Purple Heart with 3 Battle Clasps. MEM.: Dorothy and Lewis Rosenstiel Foundation (dir.); American Bar Foundation (fellow); International Acad. of Trial Lawyers; National Cmte. to Study Automobile Accident Compensation; Assn. of the Bar of NY; ABA; OH Bar Assn.; MI Bar Assn.; Detroit Bar Assn.; Cincinnati Bar Assn.; Disabled American Veterans (founder; first national commander); American Legion; Disabled Emergency Officers Assn.; YMCA; Cincinnati Club; Farmers Club; Cuvier Press Club; Clifton Meadows Club; Harbor Island Club; Robert S. Marx Charitable Foundation and Trust (founder); Legion of Valor; Wise Center (founder). HON. DEG.: L.H.D., Marietta Coll., 1954. WRITINGS: *Round the World with Stella*. REL.: Jewish. RES.: Cincinnati, OH.

MASON, JAMES GILBERT. b. Oct 31, 1842, Jonesboro, TN; d. Mar 19, 1938, Metuchen, NJ; married; c. James Gilbert, Jr.; Mrs. E. A. Harper. EDUC.: D.D., Union Theological Seminary, 1866. POLIT. & GOV.: member, U.S. Monetary Comm., Civil War; Prohibition Party candidate for gov. of NJ, 1907, 1913; ***candidate for Prohibition Party nomination to presidency of the U.S., 1916***; member, Prohibition Party National Cmte., 1920; Prohibition Party candidate for U.S. Senate (NJ), 1930. BUS. & PROF.: ordained minister, Presbyterian Church; pastor, Woodlawn Presbyterian Church, Woodlawn, NY; pastor, Metuchen Presbyterian Church, Metuchen, NJ, 1877–1925, pastor emeritus, 1925–38. REL.: Presb. MISC.: friend of Thomas Edison. RES.: Metuchen, NJ.

MASON, JOHN YOUNG. b. Apr 18, 1799, Hicksford, VA; d. Oct 3, 1859, Paris, France; par. Edmunds and Frances (Young) Mason; m. Mary Ann Fort, Aug 9, 1821; c. eight. EDUC.: A.B., U. of NC, 1816; Litchfield Law School. POLIT. & GOV.: elected as a Democrat to VA State House of Delegates, 1823–27; elected as a Democrat to VA State Senate, 1827–31; delegate, VA State Constitutional Convention, 1829–30, 1850–51 (pres.); elected as a Democrat to U.S. House (VA), 1831–37; appointed U.S. district judge for Eastern VA, 1837; appointed U.S. sec. of the navy, 1844–45, 1846–49; appointed atty. gen. of the U.S., 1845–46; ***candidate for Democratic nomination to vice presidency of the U.S., 1848***; member, VA State Democratic Central Cmte., 1852; appointed U.S. minister to France, 1854–59. BUS. & PROF.: atty.; admitted to VA Bar, 1819; law practice, Hicksford, VA; law practice, Richmond, VA, 1849–54; pres., James River and Kanawha Co., 1849. MISC.: opposed to extended suffrage, rechartering of U.S. Bank; sponsor of bill recognizing independence of Texas; opposed incorporation of Mexico into U.S. and favored treaty with Mexico signed by Nicholas Trist; signer of Ostend Manifesto, which advocated acquisition of Cuba by U.S., 1854. RES.: Richmond, VA.

MASON, MEL. b. Jan 7, 1943, Providence, KY; m. Vivian Mason, 1972; c. Melvin. EDUC.: Rosenwald H.S., Providence, KY; grad., Monterey (CA) H.S., 1960; A.A., Monterey Peninsula Coll., 1966; OR State U., 1967; U. of Santa Cruz, 1969; B.A., Golden Gate U. POLIT. & GOV.: member, Black Panther Party, 1968–69; far western regional coordinator, National Black Independent Political Party; joined Socialist Workers Party, 1976; independent candidate for Seaside (CA) School Board, 1977; independent write-in candidate for Seaside City Council, 1978; elected as a Socialist Worker to Seaside City Council, 1981–84; independent (Socialist Workers Party) candidate for gov. of CA, 1982; member, Socialist Workers Party National Cmte.; ***Socialist Workers Party candidate for presidency of the U.S., 1984***. BUS. & PROF.: employee, Western Electric, San Jose, CA, 1967–69; counselor, Monterey H.S., 1972–74; student activities coordinator, Monterey Peninsula Coll., 1974–. MIL.: radio operator, U.S. Air Force, 1961–65. MEM.: Black Workers Unity Caucus (founder, 1969); Nation of Islam (1970–71); CA State Employees Assn.; Young Socialist Alliance (adviser); Black Student Congress (adviser, 1975); CA Black Faculty/Staff Assn. (member, exec. cmte.); Community Action Coalition (cofounder, 1976); Citizens League for Progress (1979). WRITINGS: *The Making of a Revolutionary* (1982). MAILING ADDRESS: 1897 Napa St., Seaside, CA 93955.

MASTERS, ISABELL. b. Jan 9, 1914, Oklahoma City, OK; par. Walter and Cora McDaniels (Lewis) Arch; m. Alfred Masters, 1940; c. Shirley Jean Stevenson; Alfreda Dean; Cora Lavonne Wilds; Sandra Kay; Walter Ray (q.v.); Thomas A. EDUC.: B.S., Langston U., 1944; M.A., CA State U. at Los Angeles, 1970; Ph.D., U. of OK, 1981. POLIT. & GOV.: candidate for Democratic nomination to KS State Senate, 1984; ***independent candidate for presidency of the U.S., 1984***; candidate for Republican nomination to KS State House, 1986; ***candidate for Republican nomination to presidency of the U.S., 1988, 1992; Looking Back Party candidate for presidency of the U.S., 1992***. BUS. & PROF.: employee, VA; employee, police dept., Santa Monica, CA; teacher, Merrick Elementary School, Syracuse, NY; teacher, Matt Kelley Elementary School, Las Vegas, NV; teacher, Dunbar Elementary School, Oklahoma City, OK; teacher, Washington Elementary School, Pasadena, CA, 1957–71; school counselor; licensed evangelist, Church of the Living God, 1973–. AWARDS: CA Merit Mother of the Year,

1971; Most Outstanding Black Student of the Norman Campus. WRITINGS: *Brown v. Board of Education* (diss.); *A Baby Girl Was Born on Time; I Ran for President in 1984* (unpublished). REL.: Church of the Living God (evangelist). MISC.: returned to college after 25 years, earning Ph.D. while putting six children through college. MAILING ADDRESS: 2409 N.E. 24th, Oklahoma City, OK 73111.

MASTERS, JOHN PAUL, JR. par. John Paul Masters, Sr. POLIT. & GOV.: ***candidate for Democratic nomination to presidency of the U.S., 1984***. MAILING ADDRESS: Box 152, Kirkville, IA 52566.

MASTERS, WALTER RAY. par. Alfred and Isabell (Arch) Masters (q.v.). POLIT. & GOV.: ***Looking Back Party candidate for vice presidency of the U.S., 1992***. MAILING ADDRESS: 1424 Van Buren, Topeka, KS 66612.

MATALIK, EMIL. b. Jul 5, 1929, Highland, WI; par. Amelia (Matalik) Touve; single. EDUC.: public schools, Sparta, WI; John Marshall H.S., Los Angeles, CA; Harren H.S., New York, NY; Eastern NM U., Portales, NM, 1 year. POLIT. & GOV.: ***United Nations Party candidate for presidency of the U.S., 1964; 1-United Nature's Organization candidate for presidency of the U.S., 1968, 1972, 1976, 1980, 1984; #1 Party candidate for presidency of the U.S., 1976, 1988***. BUS. & PROF.: farmer. MIL.: U.S. Air Force, 1949–58. MEM.: BSA. REL.: none. MISC.: reared in orphanage; confined to St. Elizabeth's Hospital, Washington, DC, 1963; incarcerated in Spokane (WA) cty. jail, 1972; self-proclaimed candidate for president of the world, 1972, 1976; offered to donate 60 acres (later increased to 118.75 acres) of farmland to U.N.; has deeded 5-acre parcels to 177 heads of state around the world. MAILING ADDRESS: 1 Biscayne Tower, Miami, FL 33132.

MATCHETT, CHARLES HORATIO. b. May 15, 1843, Needham, MA; d. Oct 23, 1919, Allston, MA; par. Horatio and Clarissa Clifford (Batchelder) Matchett. EDUC.: Boston (MA) H.S. POLIT. & GOV.: Socialist Labor Party candidate for mayor of Brooklyn, NY; ***Socialist Labor Party candidate for vice presidency of the U.S., 1892***; Socialist Labor Party candidate for gov. of NY, 1894; ***Socialist Labor Party candidate for presidency of the U.S., 1896***; Socialist Labor Party candidate for pres. of New York City Council, 1897; Socialist Labor Party candidate for assoc. justice, NY Court of Appeals, 1903; Socialist Labor Party candidate for chief justice, NY Court of Appeals, 1904; Socialist Party candidate for U.S. House (NY), 1910, 1914. BUS. & PROF.: employee, mercantile business, Chicago, IL; employee, grocery store, Boston, MA; inventor; employee, shoe factory; carpenter; electrician, New York and New Jersey Telephone Co., 1886–1919. MIL.: seaman, U.S. Navy, 1861–62. MEM.: GAR; Knights of Labor. RES.: Brooklyn, NY.

MATHESON, SCOTT MILNE. b. Jan 8, 1929, Chicago, IL; d. Oct 7, 1990, Salt Lake City, UT; par. Scott Milne and Adele (Adams) Matheson; m. Norma Warenski, 1952; c. Scott, II; Mary Lee; James David; Thomas Douglas. EDUC.: B.S., U. of UT, 1950; J.D., Stanford U., 1952. POLIT. & GOV.: pres., U. of UT Young Democrats, 1948; city atty., Parowan, UT, 1953–54; deputy atty., Iron Cty., UT, 1953–54; law clerk, U.S. District Judge, Salt Lake City, UT, 1954–56; elected as a Democrat to gov. of UT, 1977–85; ***candidate for Democratic nomination to presidency of the U.S., 1980***; appointed chm., Democratic National Policy Council, 1985. BUS. & PROF.: atty.; asst. atty. gen., atty. gen., Union Pacific R.R. Co., 1958–69, gen. solicitor, 1972–76; asst. gen. counsel, counsel, Anaconda Co., 1969–72. MEM.: Sigma Chi; ABA (chm., Special Youth Education for Citizenship Cmte.); American Jud. Soc. (dir.); UT State Bar; Rotary Club; Alta. WRITINGS: *Out of Balance* (1986). REL.: Church of Jesus Christ of Latter-Day Saints. RES.: Salt Lake City, UT.

MATHIAS, CHARLES McCURDY, JR. b. Jul 24, 1922, Frederick, MD; par. Charles McCurdy and Theresa McElfresh (Trail) Mathias; m. Ann Hickling Bradford, Nov 8, 1958; c. Charles Bradford; Robert Fiske. EDUC.: Yale U., 1943–44; B.A., Haverford Coll., 1944; LL.B., U. of MD, 1949. POLIT. & GOV.: appointed asst. atty. gen. of MD, 1953–54; city atty., Frederick, MD, 1954–59; elected as a Republican to MD State House of Delegates, 1959–61; elected as a Republican to U.S. House (MD), 1961–69; elected as a Republican to U.S. Senate (MD), 1969–87; delegate, Rep. Nat'l. Conv., 1972; ***candidate for Republican nomination to presidency of the U.S., 1976 (declined); candidate for independent (Cmte. for a Constitutional Presidency) nomination to vice presidency of the U.S., 1976 (declined)***. BUS. & PROF.: atty.; admitted to MD Bar, 1949; admitted to practice before the Bar of the Supreme Court of the U.S., 1954; partner, Jones, Day, Reavis and Pogue (law firm), Washington, DC, 1987–. MIL.: apprentice seaman, U.S. Navy, 1942, ensign, 1944–46; capt., U.S.N.R. MEM.: Hist. Soc. of Frederick Cty.; Hood Coll. (trustee); Episcopal Free School and Orphans' Home (trustee). REL.: Episc. MAILING ADDRESS: 3808 Leland St., Chevy Chase, MD.

MATTHEWS, CLAUDE. b. Dec 14, 1845, Bethel, KY; d. Aug 28, 1898, Indianapolis, IN; par. Thomas A. and Eliza Ann (Fletcher) Matthews; m. Martha Renick Whitcomb, Jan 1, 1868; c. Mary Ewing; Helen Krekler; Renick Seymour. EDUC.: grad., Centre Coll., Danville, KY, 1867. POLIT. & GOV.: elected as a Democrat to IN State House, 1876; Democratic candidate for IN State Senate, 1882; elected as a Democrat to sec. of state of IN, 1891–93; elected as a Democrat to gov. of IN, 1893–97; ***candidate for Democratic nomination to presidency of the U.S., 1896***. BUS. & PROF.: stockbreeder; engaged in grain and stock business, Vermillion Cty., IN, 1868–98. MEM.: Farmers' Mutual Benefit Assn.; National Assn. of Breeders of

Shorthorn Cattle of the United States and Canada (founder). WRITINGS: *The Cuban Patriots' Cause is Just, the Right Shall Prevail, and in God's Own Time Cuba Shall be Free* (1895). REL.: Presb. RES.: Indianapolis, IN.

MATZAL, EDMUND OTTO. b. 1934. EDUC.: M.D., Albany Medical Coll. of Union U., 1964. POLIT. & GOV.: state chm., NJ American Party, 1974; ***American Party of New Jersey candidate for vice presidency of the U.S., 1976***. BUS. & PROF.: physician, 1964–. MISC.: indicted for income tax evasion, 1976. MAILING ADDRESS: R.D. 2, Box 278, Blairstown, NJ 07825.

MAUER, GEORGE JOSEPH. b. Aug 15, 1932, Jersey City, NJ; par. George Arthur and Julia (McCleary) Mauer; m. Clydene Ellis, Dec 23, 1984; c. Leslie; Anthony; John. EDUC.: B.A., OK State U., 1958; M.P.A., U. of KS, 1960; Ph.D., U. of OK, 1964; National Security Management course, IN Coll. Armed Forces, 1972; National Security Management course, National Defense U., 1984. POLIT. & GOV.: elected city commissioner, Norman, OK, 1963–65; exec. reserve, Federal Emergency Management, 1967–87; delegate, IA State Democratic Convention; delegate, TN State Democratic Convention; delegate, FL State Democratic Convention; senior policy analyst, Office of Exec. Management, Office of the Governor, Pierre, SD, 1974–77; ***candidate for Democratic nomination to presidency of the U.S., 1988***. BUS. & PROF.: political scientist; prof. of political science, Oklahoma City U., 1964–66; prof. of political science, OK State U., 1966–67; prof. of political science, Drake U., 1967–70; prof. of political science, U. of Akron, 1970–71; pres., City Research and Development Co., 1971–73; visiting scholar, U. of CA at Berkeley, 1973–74; management consultant, U. of TN, Knoxville, TN, 1977–82; owner, mgr., lumber company, OK; owner, mgr., Management Consultants, NM; pres., Management Co., Longwood, FL, 1982–; author. MIL.: U.S. Navy, 1951–55. MEM.: American Soc. of Public Administration (state pres.); U.S. Navy Officers' Club of Orlando, FL; FEMA (exec. pres.). WRITINGS: *Crises in Campus Management* (1976). REL.: First Christian Church. MISC.: known as "Doc" Mauer. MAILING ADDRESS: 351 Brassie Dr., Longwood, FL 32750.

MAURER, JAMES HUDSON. b. Apr 15, 1864, Reading, PA; d. Mar 16, 1944, Reading, PA; par. James R. and Sarah (Lorah) Maurer; m. Marj J. Missimer, Apr 15, 1886; c. Charles H.; Martha M. (Mrs. Ralph Dundore). EDUC.: public schools, 14 months. POLIT. & GOV.: Socialist Party candidate for Reading (PA) city controller, 1901; Socialist Party candidate for PA State House, 1902, 1912; member, exec. cmte., Socialist Party, 1904–24; Socialist Party candidate for gov. of PA, 1906, 1930; elected as a Socialist to PA State House, 1911–13, 1915–19; ***candidate for Socialist Party nomination to presidency of the U.S., 1916, 1928***; elected as a Socialist to commissioner of finance, Reading, 1927; ***Socialist Party candidate for vice presidency of the U.S., 1928, 1932***; elected as a Socialist to Reading City Council, 1928–32; Socialist Party candidate for U.S. Senate (PA), 1934; resigned from Socialist Party, 1936. BUS. & PROF.: newsboy; farmhand; factory worker; machinist's apprentice; plumber; steamfitter; ed., *Reading Kicker*, 1895; labor union official; pres., *Labor Age Monthly*. MEM.: PA Old Age Assistance Comm. (chm., 1917); American Comm. on Conditions in Ireland (1920); American Fact-Finding Comm. to Russia (1927); Brookwood Coll. (dir.); PA Federation of Labor (pres., 1912–28); Knights of Labor (worthy foreman; district master workman, 1880); Workers Educational Bureau of America (pres., 1921–29); People's Council of America for Democracy and Peace; Single-Tax Club; Plumbers and Steamfitters' Union (delegate, Central Labor Union of Reading, 1901); Building Trades Council (founder); United Workers Federation of PA (chm., 1938); League for Industrial Democracy (vice pres., 1923–44); Pioneer Youth of America; Berger National Foundation (vice pres.); Legion Against Fascism (dir.); National Cmte. for the Protection of Foreign Born Workers (dir., 1930); American Birth Control League; First American Trade Union delegate to Russia (1927); Emergency Peace Federation; A.C.L.U. (vice chm.); Cmte. on Militarism in Education; American Assn. of Old Age Security (vice pres.); National Mooney-Billings Cmte.; Fellowship of Reconciliation; Il Nuovo Mondo National Cmte.; Conference for Progressive Political Action (dir., 1922); League for Independent Political Action (vice chm.). WRITINGS: *The Far East* (1910); *Unemployment and the Mechanical Man*; *It Can Be Done* (1938). REL.: Lutheran. RES.: Reading, PA.

MAXEINER, LAWRENCE. POLIT. & GOV.: ***independent candidate for vice presidency of the U.S., 1976***. BUS. & PROF.: student. MAILING ADDRESS: 1826 Switzer Ave., St. Louis, MO 63147.

MAXEY, CARL. b. Jun 23, 1924, Tacoma, WA; par. Carl and Carolyn Maxey (adopted); m. Merrie Lou Maxey; c. William C.; Bevan J. EDUC.: U. of OR, 1946–48; LL.B., Gonzaga U., 1951. POLIT. & GOV.: appointed chm., WA State Advisory Cmte., U.S. Comm. on Civil Rights, 1963–76; candidate for Democratic nomination to U.S. Senate (WA), 1970; ***independent (Cmte. for a Constitutional Presidency) candidate for vice presidency of the U.S., 1976***; appointed member, Speedy Trial Act Cmte., U.S. District Court, Eastern District of WA, 1978–80; appointed judge pro tempore, Spokane Cty. (WA) Superior Court. BUS. & PROF.: atty.; admitted to WA Bar, 1951; partner, Fredrickson, Maxey, Bell and Allison, Inc. (law firm), Spokane, 1960–81; adjunct prof., Gonzaga U., 1972–76; partner, Maxey Law Offices, P.S., Spokane, 1981–. MIL.: U.S. Army, 1943–46. MEM.: Spokane Cty. Bar Assn. (chair, Administrative Cmte., 1983; trustee); Gonzaga President's Club; WA State Bar Assn. (pres., Criminal Law Section); ABA; National Bar Assn.; Federal Bar Assn. of the Eastern District of Washington; National Assn. of Criminal Defense Lawyers. AWARDS:

Most Excellent Lawyer of the Year, Superior Court Judge Eugene Wright, 1960; member, Inland Empire Sports Hall of Fame, 1983; William O. Douglas Bill of Rights Award, Washington Chapter, A.C.L.U., 1982. MISC.: noted civil rights activist; raised in Catholic orphanage after death of adoptive parents; won NCAA Light Heavyweight Boxing Championship, 1950. MAILING ADDRESS: South 1015 F St., Spokane, WA.

MAXEY, GEORGE WENDELL. b. Feb 14, 1878, Forest City, PA; d. Mar 20, 1950, Pittsburgh, PA; par. Benjamin and Margaret (Evans) Maxey; m. Lillian Danvers, Jan 22, 1916; c. Mary Danvers (Mrs. George John Schautz, Jr.); Dorothy (Mrs. Lesley McCreath, Jr.); Lillian Louise (Mrs. James William Swackhammer). EDUC.: Mansfield (PA) State Normal School, 1894–97; A.B., U. of MI, 1902; LL.B., U. of PA, 1906. POLIT. & GOV.: elected as a Republican to district atty., Lackawanna Cty., PA, 1914–19; delegate, Rep. Nat'l. Conv., 1920, 1924, 1948; elected as a Republican to judge, 45th District of PA, 1920–30; appointed and subsequently elected justice, Supreme Court of PA, 1930–43, chief justice, 1943–50; ***candidate for Republican nomination to vice presidency of the U.S., 1936***. BUS. & PROF.: coal miner, Forest City, PA; atty.; admitted to PA Bar, 1906; law practice (with Edwin C. Ammerman), Scranton, PA, 1906–20; owner, *Easton (PA) Free Press*, 1925; owner, anthracite coal fields. MEM.: Lotos Club; Scranton Club; Community Chest; Hahnemann Hospital of Scranton (dir.); Salvation Army (chm., Advisory Board); ABA; PA Bar Assn.; Lackawanna Cty. Bar Assn.; Assn. of Chief Justices of the United States; Masons (33°; Shriners; Knights Templar); Loyal Order of Moose; Fraternal Order of Eagles. HON. DEG.: D.C.L., Bucknell U.; LL.D., The Citadel; LL.D., Temple U.; LL.D., U. of PA. RES.: Scranton, PA.

MAXWELL, JOHN ALBERT. b. 1862, England; m. 2d, Mrs. Ethell E. A. Conrad, 1948; c. Mrs. Newton Kemp (stepdaughter). POLIT. & GOV.: ***American Vegetarian Party candidate for presidency of the U.S., 1948***. BUS. & PROF.: schoolteacher; bookkeeper; salesman; broadcaster, WCFL, Chicago, IL; columnist, *Milwaukee (WI) Leader*; naturopath; owner, operator, vegetarian restaurant and health food store, Chicago, IL. MEM.: Natural Health Foods Assn. (pres., 1938–39); Riverside Braille Club. RES.: Chicago, IL.

MAYBERRY, LUCY. b. Jan 12, 1906, Watson, OK; par. William Daniel and Elizabeth A. (Weatherbee) Mayberry; m. divorced; c. three daughters. EDUC.: high school. POLIT. & GOV.: ***independent candidate for presidency of the U.S., 1960; candidate for Republican nomination to presidency of the U.S., 1968; Eagle Party candidate for presidency of the U.S., 1968, 1972, 1976; candidate for Democratic nomination to presidency of the U.S., 1976***. BUS. & PROF.: door-to-door salesperson; photographer. REL.: none. MAILING ADDRESS: 1860 Mintwood Place, N.W., Washington, DC 20009.

MAYNARD, HORACE. b. Aug 30, 1814, Westboro, MA; d. May 3, 1882, Knoxville, TN; par. Ephraim and Diana Harriet (Cogswell) Maynard; m. Laura Ann Washburn, Aug 30, 1840; c. Washburn; Edward; James; Anne Mary (Mrs. Jerome H. Kidder); three others. EDUC.: Millbury (MA) Acad.; A.B., Amherst Coll., 1838; studied law under Ebenezer Alexander. POLIT. & GOV.: presidential elector, Whig Party, 1852; Whig Party candidate for U.S. House (TN), 1853; presidential elector, American Party, 1856; elected as an American Party candidate for U.S. House (TN), 1857–63; atty. gen. of TN, 1863–65; presidential elector, Republican Party, 1864; Union Party candidate for U.S. Senate (TN), 1865; member, TN State Constitutional Convention, 1865; delegate, Southern Loyalist Convention, 1866; elected as a Republican to U.S. House (TN), 1866–75; ***candidate for Republican nomination to vice presidency of the U.S., 1872, 1880***; Republican candidate for gov. of TN, 1874; appointed U.S. minister to Turkey, 1875–80; appointed postmaster gen. of the U.S., 1880–81; Republican candidate for U.S. Senate (TN), 1881. BUS. & PROF.: atty.; admitted to TN Bar, 1844; teacher, Millbury (MA) Acad.; instructor, prof. of mathematics, U. of East TN, 1839–44; law practice, Knoxville, TN. MEM.: East TN U. (trustee, 1865). WRITINGS: *A Discourse on Daniel Webster* (1853); *Admission of Kansas* (1860); *Retain the Tariff—Abolish the Internal Revenue* (1872); *Necessity and Effect of the Ku Klux Law* (1872). REL.: Presb. (ruling elder, Second Presbyterian Church, Knoxville, TN, 1849–82). MISC.: known as "The Little Narragansett." RES.: Knoxville, TN.

MAYNARD, RONALD EUGENE. POLIT. & GOV.: ***candidate for Democratic nomination to presidency of the U.S., 1992***. BUS. & PROF.: C.P.A. MAILING ADDRESS: 7800 S.W. Sagert, #137, Tualatin, OR 97062.

MAYO, CHARLES HORACE. b. Jul 19, 1865, Rochester, MN; d. May 26, 1939, Chicago, IL; par. William Worrall and Louise Abigail (Wright) Mayo; m. Edith Graham, Apr 5, 1893; c. Margaret; Dorothy; Charles William; Edith (Mrs. Fred Wharton Rankin); Joseph Graham; Louise (Mrs. George Treat Trenholm); Rachel; Esther (Mrs. John Berry Hartzell); Marilyn (adopted). EDUC.: M.D., Northwestern U., 1888; New York Polyclinic; New York Postgrad. Medical School. POLIT. & GOV.: appointed member, MN State Board of Health and Vital Statistics, 1900–1902; health offficer, Rochester, MN, 1912–37; elected vice pres., Rochester (MN) School Board, 1915–23; ***candidate for Democratic nomination to presidency of the U.S., 1924***. BUS. & PROF.: surgeon, Rochester, MN, 1888–1939; founder, Mayo Properties Assn., 1919; assoc. chief of staff, Mayo Clinic; surgeon, St. Mary's Hospital; surgeon, Colonial Hospital; surgeon, Warrall Hospital; prof. of surgery, medical school, U. of MN, 1919–36; prof. of surgery, grad. school, U. of MN (Mayo Foundation), 1915–36, emeritus, 1936–39; ed., *Archives of Clinical Cancer Research*, 1924–32; ed., *Gaceta Medica Espanola* (U.S. delegate, 1926–30; international patron, 1931–39); foreign collaborator, *Anales de Cirugia la Habana*; collaborating ed., *Interna-*

tional Clinics, 1907–33; contributor, *Narkose und Anaesthesie*, 1928; member, editorial board, *Nosokomien*; member, advisory board, *Encyclopedia Britannica*. MIL.: 1st lt., Medical Reserve Corps, U.S. Army, 1913, maj., col., 1917–19; chief consultant, Office of the Surgeon General, 1917–19; brig. gen., Medical Dept., U.S. Army, 1926; brig. gen., Auxiliary Army of the U.S., 1931; Distinguished Service Medal, 1920. MEM.: American Surgical Assn. (pres., 1931–32); American Medical Assn. (pres., 1916–17); American Coll. of Surgeons (regent, 1913–36; pres., 1924–25); Mayo Foundation for Medical Education and Research (founder); Carleton Coll. (trustee); Northwestern U. (trustee); Masons (32°; Shriner; Knights Templar); MN Congress of Parents and Teachers; Minneapolis Soc. of Fine Arts; Royal Coll. of Surgeons of England and Ireland; Royal Soc. of Medicine; Western Surgical Assn. (pres., 1904–05); MN State Medical Assn. (pres., 1905–06); Soc. of Clinical Surgery (pres., 1911–12); Clinical Congress of Surgeons of North America (pres., 1914–15); Chicago and North Western Railway Surgical Assn. (pres., 1927–28); Interstate Postgrad. Medical Assn. of North America (pres., 1934–35); MN Public Health Assn. (pres., 1932–36); Military Order of the World War; AAAS; American Public Health Assn.; Rochester Civic Music Foundation (hon. pres.); VFW; American Legion; Kiwanis; Rotary Club; University Club; University Club of Chicago; Minneapolis Club. AWARDS: Legion of Honor (France, 1925; certificate, Council of National Defense, 1919; officer, l'Instruction Publique et des Beaux Arts (France, 1925); Cross Commander, Royal Order of the Crown of Italy, 1932; Letter of Commendation, MN State Medical Assn., 1934; Worthy Achievement Commendation, Northwestern U. Alumni Assn., 1934; Distinguished Service Citation, American Legion; Presidential Commemorative Plaque, 1934; Certificate of Recognition, U. of MN, 1936; Bronze Medal, Interstate Postgrad. Medical Assn. of North America, 1936. HON. DEG.: M.A., Northwestern U., 1904; LL.D., U. of MD, 1909; F.A.C.S., 1913; LL.D., Kenyon Coll., 1916; D.Sc., Princeton U., 1917; Fellow, Royal Coll. of Surgeons, England, 1920; LL.D., Northwestern U., 1921; LL.D., Queen's U. (Belfast), 1925; Fellow, Royal Coll. of Surgeons, Ireland, 1921; M.Ch., U. of Dublin, 1925; LL.D., U. of Edinburgh, 1925; D.Sc., U. of PA, 1925; Fellow, Royal Soc. of Medicine, London, 1926; D.P.H., Detroit Coll. of Medicine and Surgery, 1927; D.Sc., U. of Leeds, 1929; LL.D., U. of Manchester, 1929; LL.D., Hamline U., 1930; M.D., U. of Havana, 1930; LL.D., Carleton Coll., 1932; LL.D., U. of MN, 1935; LL.D., U. of Notre Dame, 1936; LL.D., Villanova Coll., 1937; B.S., Yankton Coll., 1937. REL.: Episc. RES.: Rochester, MN.

MAZELIS, FRED. b. May 4, 1941, New York, NY; par. Irving and Gertrude K. Mazelis; single. EDUC.: B.S., City Coll. of New York, 1963. POLIT. & GOV.: leader, Trotskyist youth movement, 1958; founding member, Workers League; member, Workers League Central Cmte.; Workers League candidate for U.S. Senate (MI), 1984; Workers League candidate for mayor of New York, NY, 1989; ***Workers League candidate for vice presidency of the U.S., 1992***. BUS. & PROF.: hospital worker; medical research and clinical biochemist, 1963–74; organizer, Workers League; member, editorial board, *Workers League Bulletin*, 1974–. MEM.: International Labor Defense Cmte.; Hospital Workers Local 1199 (delegate; opposition leader). REL.: none. MAILING ADDRESS: c/o Workers League, P.O. Box 33023, Detroit, MI 48232.

McADOO, WILLIAM GIBBS. b. Oct 31, 1863, Marietta, GA; d. Feb 1, 1941, Washington, DC; par. Judge William Gibbs and Mary Faith (Floyd) McAdoo; m. Sarah Houston Fleming, Nov 18, 1885; m. 2d, Eleanor Randolph Wilson, May 7, 1914; m. 3d, Doris I. Cross, Sep 14, 1935; c. Harriet Floyd (Mrs. Clayton Platt, Jr.); Robert Hazelhurst; Francis Hugo; Nona Hazelhurst (Mrs. Nona M. Taylor); William Gibbs; Sarah "Sally" Fleming (Mrs. Brice Clagett); Ellen Wilson; Mary Faith. EDUC.: U. of TN. POLIT. & GOV.: appointed deputy clerk, U.S. Circuit Court, Southern Div., Eastern District of TN, 1882; delegate, Dem. Nat'l. Conv., 1912, 1932, 1936; vice chm., acting chm., Dem. Nat'l. Cmte., 1912; appointed U.S. sec. of the treasury, 1913–18; appointed dir.-gen. of railways, 1917–19; appointed chm., War Finance Board; appointed chm., Federal Reserve Board; chm. ex officio, Federal Farm Loan Board; appointed chm., U.S. Section, International High Comm.; ***candidate for Democratic nomination to presidency of the U.S., 1920, 1924; candidate for Democratic nomination to vice presidency of the U.S., 1932***; member, Dem. Nat'l. Cmte., 1932–40; elected as a Democrat to U.S. Senate (CA), 1933–38; candidate for Democratic nomination to U.S. Senate (CA), 1938. BUS. & PROF.: atty.; admitted to TN Bar, 1885; law practice, Chattanooga, TN, 1885–92; div. counsel, Central R.R. and Banking Co.; counsel, Richmond and Danville R.R. Co.; pres., Knoxville Street Railway Co.; founder, New York and New Jersey R.R. Co., 1902; partner (with William McAdoo), law firm, New York, NY, 1892–1902; pres., dir., Hudson and Manhattan R.R. Co., 1902–13; chm. of the board, American President Lines (steamships), 1939–41; law practice, Los Angeles, CA. MEM.: Ku Klux Klan; Metropolitan Club; Lawyers Club; Ardsley Club; Automobile Club; Southern Soc.; Metropolitan Museum of Art. HON. DEG.: A.M., Hamilton Coll., 1909; LL.D., U. of NC, 1916; LL.D., U. of Southern CA, 1923; LL.D., Mercer U., 1927; LL.D., Tusculum Coll., 1927; D.H.L., Lincoln U., 1929. WRITINGS: *The Challenge—Liquor and Lawlessnesss Versus Constitutional Government* (1928); *Crowded Years* (1931). REL.: Episc. RES.: Santa Barbara, CA.

McALPIN, EDWIN AUGUSTUS. b. Jun 9, 1848, New York, NY; par. David H. McAlpin; m. Annie Brandreth, Oct 27, 1870; c. Edwin Augustus. EDUC.: Phillips Acad. POLIT. & GOV.: postmaster, village pres., Ossining, NY; presidential elector, Republican Party; ***candidate for Republican nomination to vice presidency of the U.S., 1896***. BUS. & PROF.: pres., D. H. McAlpin Co.; pres., Consumers' Tobacco Co.; pres., John I. Cooke Co.; pres., New York Hygeia Distilled Water Co.; pres., Manhattan Hotel Co.; vice pres., Eleventh

Ward Bank; vice pres., Standard Gas Light Co.; dir., Mutual Bank of New York; dir., Morton Trust Co.; trustee, Board of Trade and Transportation Co. MIL.: pvt., National Guard of NY, 1869, 1st lt., 71st Regt., 1875, capt., 1875, maj., 1875, resigned, 1881; capt., 1881, col., 1888, adj. gen., maj. gen. MEM.: National League of Republican Clubs (pres.); League of Republican Clubs of NY (pres.); Cremorne Mission (trustee); Army and Navy Club; Union League; Lotos Club; C. of C.; St. Andrew's Soc.; Soc. of Colonial Wars. REL.: Presb. RES.: New York, NY.

McALPINE, JOHNNIE LOUIS. POLIT. & GOV.: ***candidate for Democratic nomination to presidency of the U.S., 1992***. MAILING ADDRESS: c/o Terry L. McAlpine, 127 East Maine St., Pawhuska, OK 74056.

McARTHUR, TREVOR ALAN. b. Jan 24, 1967, Lincoln, NE; par. Arthur James and Patsy Anne (Ponder) McArthur; single. EDUC.: Coll. View Acad.; U. of NE. POLIT. & GOV.: ***Superfuous (sic!) Party candidate for presidency of the U.S., 1988***; appointed member, Lincoln (NE) Parks and Recreation Advisory Board, 2 years. BUS. & PROF.: salesman; painter; maintenance man. AWARDS: Nebraska Distinguished Scholar, 1984. REL.: Seventh-Day Adventist. MISC.: active in Lincoln (NE) Community Playhouse. MAILING ADDRESS: 8031 Broadway, Lincoln, NE 68505.

McCABE, JOHN HENRY. b. Sep 27, 1913, Antwerp, OH; par. Arthur A. and Mary (Pearl) McCabe; m. Margaret Elizabeth Nyman Madden, Dec 18, 1938; c. Chica Susanna; Edward Alan. EDUC.: grad., Lincoln H.S., Ferndale, MI, 1930; grad., Jackson Junior Coll., 1934; A.B., U. of MI, 1937; International Correspondence Schools, Scranton, PA, 1946. POLIT. & GOV.: candidate for mayor of Jackson, MI; ***candidate for Republican nomination to presidency of the U.S., 1960, 1964 (withdrew), 1968***; candidate for Democratic nomination to gov. of MI, 1970; ***candidate for Democratic nomination to presidency of the U.S., 1976, 1980, 1988***. BUS. & PROF.: farmer; salesman; owner, washing machine appliance store, Battle Creek, MI; owner, Dollar Bills Restaurant, Jackson, MI; chef, Arbor Hills Country Club; chef, Devils Lake Yacht Club; chef, Gardner's Restaurant; chef, Otsego Hotel; chef, Regent Cafe; newspaper columnist, "McCabe Says." MEM.: Elks. REL.: Irish "Islander's Religion." MAILING ADDRESS: 11000 Crescent Moon, Apt. 203, Houston, TX 77064.

McCALL, SAMUEL WALKER. b. Feb 28, 1851, East Providence, PA; d. Nov 4, 1923, Winchester, MA; par. Henry and Mary Ann (Elliott) McCall; m. Ella Esther Thompson, May 23, 1881; c. Sumner Thompson; Ruth; Henry; Katherine (Mrs. Henry James Gray Rodney); Margaret (Mrs. Alfred H. Chappell). EDUC.: Mount Carroll Seminary; grad., New Hampton Acad., 1870; A.B., Dartmouth Coll., 1874. POLIT. & GOV.: delegate, Rep. Nat'l. Conv., 1888, 1900, 1916; elected as a Republican to MA State House, 1888–89, 1893; member, MA State Ballot Comm.; elected as a Republican to U.S. House (MA), 1893–1913; Republican candidate for U.S. Senate (MA), 1913; Republican candidate for gov. of MA, 1914; elected as a Republican to gov. of MA, 1916–18; ***candidate for Republican nomination to presidency of the U.S., 1916***; appointed member, President's Second Industrial Conference, 1920; appointed member, Lincoln Memorial Comm. BUS. & PROF.: ed., *Dartmouth Anvil*; atty.; admitted to MA Bar, 1875; law practice, Worchester, MA; law practice, Boston, MA; editor-in-chief, *Boston Daily Advertiser*, 1890; Phi Beta Kappa Orator, Dartmouth Coll.; Phi Beta Kappa Orator, Tufts U.; Phi Beta Kappa Orator, Harvard U.; Cole lecturer, Bowdoin Coll., 1909–10; Dodge lecturer, Yale U., 1915. MEM.: Phi Beta Kappa; American Acad. of Arts and Sciences (fellow); National Inst. of Social Sciences; World Peace Foundation (trustee); Smith Coll. (trustee); New Hampton Acad. (trustee); American Antiquarian Soc.; MA Hist. Soc.; Lynn Hist. Soc.; Saturday Club of Boston. HON. DEG.: LL.D., Dartmouth Coll., 1901; LL.D., Oberlin Coll., 1908; LL.D., Tufts U., 1914; LL.D., U. of ME, 1915; LL.D., Columbia U., 1916; LL.D., Trinity Coll., 1916; LL.D., Williams Coll., 1916; LL.D., Dalhousie Coll., 1918; LL.D., U. of Rochester, 1919. WRITINGS: *Life of Thaddeus Stevens* (1899); *The Business of Congress* (1911); *Life of Thomas R. Reed* (1914); *The Liberty of Citizenship* (1915); *The Patriotism of the American Jew* (1922). RES.: Winchester, MA.

McCANDLESS, JAMES CARVER, SR. c. James Carver. POLIT. & GOV.: ***Liberty Bell Party candidate for presidency of the U.S., 1988***. MAILING ADDRESS: P.O. Box 1316, Project City, CA 96079.

McCARL, JOHN RAYMOND. b. Nov 27, 1879, Des Moines, IA; d. Aug 2, 1940, Washington, DC; par. John Henry and Sarah (Gosslee) McCarl; m. Ethel Barnett, Nov 26, 1905; c. none. EDUC.: LL.B., U. of NE, 1903. POLIT. & GOV.: private sec., U.S. Sen. George Norris (q.v.), 1914–18; exec. sec., National Republican Congressional Cmte., 1918–21; appointed comptroller gen. of the U.S., 1921–36; ***candidate for Republican nomination to presidency of the U.S., 1936***. BUS. & PROF.: atty.; partner, Cordeal and McCarl (law firm), McCook, NE; law practice, Washington, DC, 1936–40. MEM.: Phi Delta Phi; National Press Club. REL.: Methodist. RES.: McCook, NE.

McCARLEY, JIM. POLIT. & GOV.: ***independent candidate for presidency of the U.S., 1976***. MAILING ADDRESS: Suite 4, 1093 South Main St., Salinas, CA 93901.

McCARTHY, EUGENE JOSEPH. b. Mar 29, 1916, Watkins, MN; par. Michael John and Anna (Baden) McCarthy; m. Abigail Quigley, Jun 1945; c. Ellen Anne; Mary Abigail; Michael Benet; Margaret Alice. EDUC.: A.B., St.

John's U., 1935; A.M., U. of MN, 1939. POLIT. & GOV.: elected as a Democrat to U.S. House (MN), 1949–59; delegate, Dem. Nat'l. Conv., 1952; elected as a Democrat to U.S. Senate (MN), 1959–71; ***candidate for Democratic nomination to vice presidency of the U.S., 1964, 1968, 1972; candidate for Democratic nomination to presidency of the U.S., 1968, 1972, 1992; New (New Politics) Party candidate for presidency of the U.S., 1968; candidate for People's Party nomination to presidency of the U.S., 1972 (declined); independent (Cmte. for a Constitutional Presidency) candidate for presidency of the U.S., 1976***; candidate for Democratic-Farmer Labor Party nomination to U.S. Senate (MN), 1982; ***Consumer Party candidate for presidency of the U.S., 1988***. BUS. & PROF.: high school teacher, MN and ND, 1935–40, 1945; prof. of economics and education, St. John's U., 1940–43; civilian technical asst., Military Intelligence Div., War Dept., 1944; instructor in sociology and economics, St. Thomas' Coll., 1946–49; Adlai E. Stevenson Professor of Political Science, New School for Social Research, 1973–74; ed., Simon and Schuster, 1973; syndicated columnist, 1977–. MEM.: NATO Parliamentary Conference (delegate); Knights of Columbus; Council on Religious Freedom and Public Affairs; National Conference of Christians and Jews; Coalition for Open Politics (hon. co-chm., 1977). HON. DEG.: LL.D., Coll. of St. Thomas; LL.D., St. Louis U.; LL.D., U. of Notre Dame. WRITINGS: *Frontiers in American Democracy* (1960); *Dictionary of American Politics* (1962); *A Liberal Answer to the Conservative Challenge* (1964); *Limits of Power* (1967); *Year of the People* (1969); *Other Things and the Aardvark* (1970); *The Hard Years* (1975); *Mr. Raccoon and His Friends* (1977); *America Revisited* (1978); *A Political Bestiary* (coauthor, 1978); *Ground Fog and Night* (1979). REL.: R.C. MAILING ADDRESS: Box 22, Woodville, VA 22749.

McCARTHY, JOHN MARTIN. b. Oct 13, 1943, Chicago, IL; par. John A. and Josephine McCarthy; m. Elizabeth Nesbitt, 1964 (divorced, 1972); c. Mary Jo; Jean. EDUC.: grad., Leo H.S., Chicago, IL, 1961; IN U.; Walton School of Commerce, Chicago. POLIT. & GOV.: ***candidate for Democratic nomination to presidency of the U.S., 1984, 1988; independent candidate for presidency of the U.S., 1984***. BUS. & PROF.: employee, International Harvester Co., Chicago, 1961–62; truck helper, Joyce Seven-Up Beverage Co., Chicago, 1962–64; laborer, Automatic Life Truck Co., Chicago, 1964–65; patrolman, Chicago Police Dept., 1965–72; security guard, Chicago Mercantile Exchange, 1972–73; campus policeman, U. of Chicago, 1973–83; employee, National Can Co., Chicago; employee, Universal Brush Manufacturing Co., Chicago; employee, Nestle Co., Chicago; employee, Household Finance Co., Chicago; employee, Norfolk and Western R.R. Co., Chicago; employee, Montgomery Ward, Chicago; employee, Halleran's Restaurant, Chicago; employee, U.S. Post Office, Chicago; owner, video game business, Chicago, 1983–. REL.: R.C. MAILING ADDRESS: 5476 South Archer St., Chicago, IL 60638.

McCLAREN, DAN (See RICE, DAN).

McCLELLAN, GEORGE BRINTON. b. Dec 3, 1826, Philadelphia, PA; d. Oct 29, 1885, Orange, NJ; par. Dr. George and Elizabeth (Brinton) McClellan; m. Ellen Mary Marcy, May 22, 1860; c. George Brinton, Jr. (q.v.); May Marcy (Mrs. Paul Desprez). EDUC.: U. of PA, 1840–42; grad., U.S. Military Acad., 1846. POLIT. & GOV.: ***Democratic candidate for presidency of the U.S., 1864; candidate for Democratic nomination to presidency of the U.S., 1868, 1880***; appointed comptroller, New York, NY, 1871 (declined); elected as a Democrat to gov. of NY, 1878–81. BUS. & PROF.: soldier; businessman; chief engineer, Illinois Central R.R., 1857, vice pres., 1858–60; pres., Ohio and Mississippi R.R., 1860; appointed pres., U. of CA, 1868 (declined); appointed pres., Union Coll., 1869 (declined); chief exec., Dept. of Docks, New York, 1870–72. MIL.: commissioned 2d lt., Corps of Engineers, U.S. Army, 1846; brev. 1st lt., 1847, capt., 1847; asst. instructor in practical military engineering, U.S. Military Acad., 1848–51; asst. engineer for construction of Fort Delaware, 1851; appointed capt., U.S. Cavalry, 1855, resigned, 1857; appointed maj. gen., OH Militia, 1861; appointed maj. gen., U.S. Army, 1861; commander in chief, U.S. Army, 1861–62; stopped Robert E. Lee's advance at Antietam, but did not advance and was relieved of command. WRITINGS: *McClellan's Own Story* (1887). REL.: Presb. RES.: Orange Mountain, NJ.

McCLELLAN, GEORGE BRINTON, JR. b. Nov 23, 1865, Dresden, Saxony, Germany; d. Nov 30, 1940, Washington, DC; par. Gen. George Brinton (q.v.) and Ellen Mary (Marcy) McClellan; m. Georgianna Louise Heckscher, Oct 30, 1889; c. none. EDUC.: St. John's School, Ossining, NY; A.B., Princeton U., 1886, A.M., 1889; NY Law School. POLIT. & GOV.: appointed treas., Brooklyn (NY) Bridge Board, 1889–92; delegate, Dem. Nat'l. Conv., 1892, 1896, 1900; elected as a Democrat to pres., Board of Aldermen, New York, NY, 1893–94; elected as a Democrat to U.S. House (NY), 1895–1903; ***candidate for Democratic nomination to vice presidency of the U.S., 1900***; elected as a Democrat to mayor of New York, 1903–09; ***candidate for Democratic nomination to presidency of the U.S., 1904; American Peace Party candidate for vice presidency of the U.S., 1916 (declined)***. BUS. & PROF.: reporter, *Morning Journal*, New York; reporter, *New York World*; reporter, *New York Herald*; atty.; admitted to NY Bar, 1892; partner (with Eugene Lamb Richards and Philip J. McCook), law firm, New York, 1910; Stafford Little Lecturer on Public Affairs, Princeton U., 1908–10, university lecturer, 1911–12, prof. of economic history, 1912–31, prof. emeritus, 1931–40; lecturer, Cornell U.; lecturer, Rutgers U.; lecturer, Washington and Jefferson U.; lecturer, Washington and Lee U.; lecturer, U. of NC. MIL.: maj., Ordnance Dept., U.S.A.R., 1917; lt. col., U.S. Army, 1918–19, col. (retired). MEM.: Royal Economic Soc. (life fellow); Tammany Soc.; Economic History Soc.; Military Order of the Loyal Legion; Phi Beta Kappa; Metropolitan Club; Army and Navy

Club; Chevy Chase Club; Union Club; A.I.A. (hon.); American Museum of Natural History (patron); Metropolitan Museum of Art (fellow in perpetuity); grand officer, Order of the Crown of Italy; American Acad. in Rome (trustee; vice pres.); Smithsonian Gallery of Art Comm. (chm., exec. cmte.); Automobile Club of America; Church Club; Authors Club; SAR. AWARDS: Medal of Beaux Arts Soc. of Architecture, 1909. HON. DEG.: LL.D., Fordham U., 1905; LL.D., Princeton U., 1905; LL.D., Union Coll., 1906 (hon. chancellor). WRITINGS: *The Oligarchy of Venice* (1904); *The Heel of War* (1915); *Venice and Bonaparte* (1931); *Modern Italy* (1933); *The Gentleman and the Tiger* (1956). REL.: Episc. (warden, St. John's Church, Washington, DC; trustee, Church Charities and Diocesan Church Funds, Diocese of Washington). MISC.: known as "Max" McClellan. RES.: New York, NY.

McCLERNAND, JOHN ALEXANDER. b. May 30, 1812, Breckinridge Cty., KY; d. Sep 20, 1900, Springfield, IL; m. Sarah Dunlap; c. Edward John. EDUC.: village schools, Shawneetown, IL; read law. POLIT. & GOV.: elected to IL State House, 1836–43; presidential elector, Democratic Party, 1840, 1852; elected as a Democrat to U.S. House (IL), 1843–51, 1859–61; ***candidate for Democratic nomination to vice presidency of the U.S., 1868 (declined)***; elected judge, Sangamon District, Circuit Court of IL, 1870–73; chm., Dem. Nat'l. Conv., 1876; appointed member, UT Comm. BUS. & PROF.: trader, Ohio and Mississippi rivers; soldier; farmer, Shawneetown, IL; atty.; admitted to IL Bar, 1832; ed., *Shawneetown Democrat*, 1835; law practice, Shawneetown; law practice, Springfield, IL. MIL.: fought in war against Sacs and Foxes, 1832; brig. gen., U.S.V., 1861, maj. gen., 1862–64; relieved of command of 13th Army Corps, 1863. RES.: Springfield, IL.

McCLOSKEY, BURR, JR. b. Akron, OH; par. Burr McCloskey; m. Rose McCloskey. EDUC.: grad., Central H.S., Akron, OH, 1936. POLIT. & GOV.: delegate, Central Trades and Labor Assembly; youth sec., Socialist Party; founder, Independent Labor League; founder, gen. sec., United Labor Party, 1946; member, Mahoning (OH) Organizing Cmte., United Labor Party; ***Pioneer Party candidate for vice presidency of the U.S., 1956***. BUS. & PROF.: employee, Goodyear Tire and Rubber Co., c. 1932; labor organizer; employee, Firestone Steel Co., Akron, OH. MIL.: U.S. Army, WWII. MEM.: American Rally (exec. sec., 1952); Independent Labor League; Teamsters' Union; United Mine Workers, District 50; Young People's Socialist League; Akron Rubber Union (expelled). WRITINGS: *What Attitude Toward Conscription!* (1943); *Notes in Transition* (1951). MAILING ADDRESS: Woodland Lane, Deerfield, IL 60015.

McCLOSKEY, PAUL NORTON "PETE," JR. b. Sep 29, 1927, San Bernardino, CA; par. Paul Norton and Vera (McNabb) McCloskey; m. Caroline Wadsworth, Aug 6, 1949; c. Nancy; Peter; John; Kathleen. EDUC.: Occidental Coll.; CA Inst. of Technology; B.A., Stanford U., 1950, LL.B., 1953. POLIT. & GOV.: appointed deputy district atty., Alameda Cty., CA, 1953–54; co-chm., Young Lawyers for Nixon-Lodge, 1960; Palo Alto chm., Tom Coakley for Attorney General, 1962; delegate, White House Conference on Civil Rights, 1963; chm., Spencer Williams for Attorney General, 1966; speaker, George Christopher for Governor Campaign, 1966; elected as a Republican to U.S. House (CA), 1967–83; ***candidate for Republican nomination to presidency of the U.S., 1972***; candidate for Republican nomination to U.S. Senate (CA), 1982. BUS. & PROF.: atty.; admitted to CA Bar, 1953; partner, Costello and Johnson (law firm), Palo Alto, CA, 1955–56; partner, McCloskey, Wilson, Mosher and Martin (law firm), Stanford, CA, 1956–67; lecturer, Stanford U. and Santa Clara Law School, 1964–67. MIL.: seaman 1/C, U.S. Navy, 1945–47; 2d lt., U.S.M.C., 1950–52; lt. col., U.S.M.C. Reserves; Navy Cross; Silver Star; Purple Heart. MEM.: ABA; CA State Bar; Santa Clara Cty. Bar Assn. (trustee, 1965–67); Palo Alto Area Bar Assn. (pres., 1960–61); Conference of Barristers of the State Bar of CA (pres., 1961–62); Phi Delta Phi; Phi Delta Theta; CA Republican League (pres., Portola Valley-Woodside Chapter; chm., Critical Issues Conference, 1967); Stanford Area Youth Plan (pres., 1960–66); Palo Alto Fair Play Council (1965–67); Family Service Assn. (dir., 1961–65); Cmte. for Green Foothills (1963–67); Alpine Little League (counsel); arbitrator, American Arbitration Assn. (1966–67); Planning and Conservation League for Legislative Action (1966–67); Sierra Club. AWARDS: "Outstanding Young Man of the Year," Palo Alto Junior C. of C., 1961. WRITINGS: *U.S. Constitution; Truth and Untruth* (1972). REL.: Presb. MAILING ADDRESS: 305 Grant Ave., Palo Alto, CA 94305.

McCLOUD, WALTER JAMES. m. Doris Eileen McCloud. POLIT. & GOV.: ***candidate for Republican nomination to presidency of the U.S., 1976, 1980***. MAILING ADDRESS: 8554 North 31st Ave., Phoenix, AZ 85021.

McCLURE, JAMES ALBERTUS. b. Dec 27, 1924, Payette, ID; par. William Robertson and Marie Caroline (Freehafer) McClure; m. Louise Marilyn Miller, Sep 23, 1950; c. Marilyn; Kenneth; David. EDUC.: J.D., U. of ID, 1950. POLIT. & GOV.: prosecuting atty., Payette Cty., ID, 1951–56; city atty., Payette, ID, 1953–66; elected as a Republican to ID State Senate, 1960–67 (asst. majority leader, 1965–66); member, Payette Cty. Republican Central Cmte.; sec.-treas., Little Willow Irrigation District, 1962–66; temporary chm., ID State Republican Convention, 1962; alternate delegate, Rep. Nat'l. Conv., 1964; member, ID State Constitutional Revision Comm., 1965; elected as a Republican to U.S. House (ID), 1967–73; elected as a Republican to U.S. Senate (ID), 1973–91; ***candidate for Republican nomination to vice presidency of the U.S., 1976***. BUS. & PROF.: atty.; admitted to ID Bar, 1950; employee, North ID Blister Rust Program, Potlatch Mill, ID; law practice, Payette, ID. MIL.: U.S. Naval Cadets (1942–45). MEM.: Sigma Nu.; American Jud. Soc.; American Legion; Masons; ID Reclamation Assn.

(member, Resolutions Cmte., 1954–); National Reclamation Assn. (ID representative, Study Group on Interbasin Transfer of Water); Highway 95 Assn.; Payette C. of C. (pres.); Phi Alpha Delta; Kiwanis. AWARDS: Watchdog of the Treasury Award, National Assn. of Businessmen. REL.: Methodist (trustee). MAILING ADDRESS: 634 Hughes Dr., Payette, ID 83661.

McCLURG, WILLIAM LEWIS. b. Feb 28, 1941, Milwaukee, WI; par. Ralph James and Anita Rose (Vocaact) McClurg; m. Frances Louise Maglio (divorced, 1971); c. Lisa Anne. EDUC.: B.S., U. of WI; U. of Chicago, 1964. POLIT. & GOV.: Maverick Party candidate for mayor of San Francisco, CA, 1971; ***Maverick Party candidate for presidency of the U.S., 1976, 1980***; Maverick Party candidate for mayor of Los Angeles, CA, 1977. BUS. & PROF.: substitute teacher, Milwaukee (WI) public schools; teacher's aide, Los Angeles Cty. (CA) public schools. MAILING ADDRESS: 826 South Kenmore Ave., Los Angeles, CA 90005.

McCOMBS, WILLIAM FRANK. b. Dec 26, 1875, Hamburg, AR; d. Feb 22, 1921, Greenwich, CT; par. William Faulkner and Mary Frances (Pugh) McCombs; m. Dorothy Williams, Nov 7, 1913 (divorced); c. none. EDUC.: Webb School, TN; A.B., Princeton U., 1898; LL.B., Harvard U., 1901. POLIT. & GOV.: Democratic candidate for NY State Assembly, 1904; national campaign mgr., Woodrow Wilson for President, 1912; chm., Dem. Nat'l. Cmte., 1912–16; ***candidate for Democratic nomination to vice presidency of the U.S., 1912***; appointed U.S. ambassador to France, 1913 (declined); candidate for Democratic nomination to mayor of New York, NY, 1914; Democratic candidate for U.S. Senate (NY), 1916. BUS. & PROF.: atty.; farmer; plantation owner, AR; partner (with Gilbert E. Roe), law firm, New York, 1903–10; partner (with Francis L. Wellman and Herbert C. Smythe), law firm, New York, 1916; partner, McCombs and Ryan (law firm), New York. MEM.: City Coll. of New York (trustee); Lincoln Memorial U. (trustee); ABA; NY State Bar Assn.; Assn. of the Bar of the City of New York; Metropolitan Club of New York; Metropolitan Club of Washington; University Club of New York; University Club of Washington; Bankers Club; Andiron Club; Manhattan Club; Lawyers Club; Princeton Club; Harvard Club; National Democratic Club; Oakland Club; Sleepy Hollow Club; Nassau Club. HON. DEG.: LL.D., Lincoln Memorial U.; LL.D., U. of AR. REL.: Presb. RES.: New York, NY.

McCONE, ALLEN C. POLIT. & GOV.: ***Take Back America candidate for vice presidency of the U.S., 1992***. MAILING ADDRESS: c/o John Yiamouyiannis, Box 41, Lewis Center, OH 43035.

McCORMACK, ELLEN CULLEN. b. Sep 15, 1926, New York, NY; par. William Joseph and Ellen (Bradley) Cullen; m. Francis John McCormack, 1949; c. Kathleen; Anne; Ellen; John. EDUC.: grad., All Saints H.S., New York, NY, 1944. POLIT. & GOV.: ***candidate for Democratic nomination to presidency of the U.S., 1976; candidate for American Independent Party nomination to presidency of the U.S., 1976 (declined)***; Right to Life Party candidate for lt. gov. of NY, 1978; ***Right to Life Party candidate for presidency of the U.S., 1980***. BUS. & PROF.: housewife; legal sec.; columnist, weekly newspaper. MEM.: Pro-Life Action Cmte.; Parent-Teachers Assn.; GSA; Church Women's Club (pres.). HON. DEG.: LL.D., Molloy Coll.; LL.D., Niagara U. REL.: R.C. MAILING ADDRESS: 65 Frankel Blvd., Merrick, NY 11566.

McCORMACK, JOHN WILLIAM. b. Dec 21, 1891, Boston, MA; d. Nov 22, 1980, Dedham, MA; par. Joseph H. and Mary Ellen (O'Brien) McCormack; m. M. Harriet Joyce, 1920; c. none. EDUC.: John Andrew Grammar School, Boston, MA; read law. POLIT. & GOV.: elected as a Democrat to delegate, MA State Constitutional Convention, 1917–18; delegate, MA State Democratic Conventions, 1920–80; elected as a Democrat to MA State House, 1921–23; elected as a Democrat to MA State Senate, 1923–27 (Democratic floor leader, 1925–27); candidate for Democratic nomination to U.S. House (MA), 1926; elected as a Democrat to U.S. House (MA), 1929–71 (majority leader, 1940–47, 1949–53, 1955–61; minority whip, 1947–49, 1953–55; Speaker, 1962–71); delegate, Dem. Nat'l. Conv., 1932, 1940, 1944, 1956; ***candidate for Democratic nomination to presidency of the U.S., 1956; candidate for Republican nomination to presidency of the U.S., 1956***. BUS. & PROF.: newsboy; atty.; admitted to MA Bar, 1913; law practice, Boston, MA, 1913–80; partner, McCormack and Hardy (law firm), Boston. MIL.: sgt. maj., U.S.Army, 1917–18; knight commander, Order of St. Gregory the Great, with Star; commander, Legion of Honor (Philippines). MEM.: Ancient Order of Hibernians; Elks; Moose; Catholic Order of Foresters; Knights of Columbus; Order of Malta; American Legion; South Boston Citizens Assn. AWARDS: Bellarmine Medal, 1957; Peace Medal, Third Order of St. Francis; Rosette, Knights of Malta; Cardinal Gibbons Medal, 1963. HON. DEG.: LL.D., Boston U.; LL.D., Boston Coll.; LL.D., Catholic U. of America; LL.D., Georgetown U.; LL.D., Holy Cross Coll.; LL.D., Providence Coll.; LL.D., Staley Coll.; LL.D., Stonehill Coll.; LL.D., Suffolk U.; LL.D., Tufts Coll.; LL.D., Villanova Coll. REL.: R.C. RES.: Boston, MA.

McCORMICK, ROBERT RUTHERFORD. b. Jul 30, 1880, Chicago, IL; d. Apr 1, 1955, Wheaton, IL; par. Robert Sanderson and Katherine Van Etta (Medill) McCormick; m. Amy (Irwin) Adams, Mar 10, 1915; m. 3d, Maryland (Mathison) Hooper, Dec 21, 1944; c. none. EDUC.: Ludgrove School, England, 1892–93; Groton (MA) School; B.A., Yale U., 1903; LL.B., Northwestern U., 1906. POLIT. & GOV.: elected as a Republican to Chicago (IL) City Council, 1904–06; elected pres., Chicago Sanitary District Board, 1905–10; member, Chicago Charter Comm., 1907; member, Chicago Plan Comm.; delegate, Rep. Nat'l. Conv., 1940; ***candidate for Republican nomination to presidency of the U.S., 1944 (withdrew)***. BUS. & PROF.: atty.; admitted to IL Bar, 1908; partner, Shepard,

McCormick and Thomason (law firm), Chicago, 1909–11; treas., Tribune Co., 1909–11, pres., 1911–55; co-editor, copublisher, *Chicago Tribune*, 1914–25, ed. and publisher, 1925–55; vice pres., treas., news-syndicate company, 1919–46, chm. and treas., 1946–55; publisher, *Liberty Magazine*, 1924–31; owner, Cantigny Farm, Wheaton, IL; pres., Ontario Paper Co., 1930–33; pres., WGN, Inc. (radio station), Chicago, 1924–55; chm., vice pres., treas., Chicago Tribune-News Syndicate Inc.; ed., publisher, *Washington (DC) Times-Herald*, 1949–54; war correspondent, 1915. MIL.: col., maj., IL National Guard, 1915; liaison officer, maj., lt. col., col., U.S. Army (AEF), 1917–19; commandant, Fort Sheridan, IL; Distinguished Service Medal, 1923. AWARDS: Algernon Sidney Sullivan Award, The Citadel, 1946; Distinguished Service Award, Assn. of Plaintiff Lawyers; Distinguished Service Award, Better Business Bureau of Chicago; Distinguished Service Award, Freedoms Foundation of Valley Forge; Distinguished Service Award, IL Soc. of SAR. MEM.: American Newspaper Publishers' Assn.; For America (founder, 1954); America First Cmte.; Robert R. McCormick Foundation (founder, 1953); Chicago Bar Assn.; Chicago Club. HON. DEG.: LL.D., The Citadel, 1932; LL.D., Colby Coll., 1935; LL.D., Northwestern U., 1947. WRITINGS: *With the Russian Army* (1915); *The Army of 1918* (1920); *Ulysses S. Grant: The Great Soldier of America* (1934); *Freedom of the Press* (1936); *How We Acquired Our National Territory* (1942); *The American Revolution and Its Influences on World Civilization* (1945); *The War Without Grant* (1950); *The Founding Fathers* (1951); *The American Empire* (1952); *Assaults Upon the Constitution* (1954). REL.: Presb. RES.: Chicago, IL.

McCORMICK, WILLIAM J. POLIT. & GOV.: ***independent candidate for presidency of the U.S., 1976***. MAILING ADDRESS: "Chetwynd," Chetwynd Dr., Rosemont, PA 19010.

McCOY, CHARLES GALEN. POLIT. & GOV.: ***independent candidate for presidency of the U.S., 1980***. MAILING ADDRESS: School House Rd., P.O. Box 132, Custer, WA 98240.

McCOY, TONY CHAMP. POLIT. & GOV.: ***Paint Pony Party candidate for presidency of the U.S., 1976***. MAILING ADDRESS: Veterans Administration Domiciliary, Section #4, White City, OR 97501.

McCRACKEN, JAMES D. POLIT. & GOV.: ***candidate for Democratic nomination to presidency of the U.S., 1992***. MAILING ADDRESS: 14116 Harron St., Sylmar, CA 91342.

McCRARY, THOMAS ANDREW, SR. b. Oct 4, 1909, IA; d. Dec 22, 1986, Gainesville, GA; c. Thomas Andrew, Jr. EDUC.: grad., U.S. Military Acad., 1934; U.S. Army Command and Staff Coll., 1942–43; Industrial Coll. of the Armed Forces, 1947. POLIT. & GOV.: presidential elector, American Party, 1976; chm., Platform Cmte., American Independent Party National Convention, 1980; ***candidate for American Independent Party nomination to vice presidency of the U.S., 1980***; chm., Independent Party of GA, 1980; vice chm., American Independent Party National Cmte., 1980. BUS. & PROF.: soldier; businessman; pres., McCrary-Banks Development Co. MIL.: col., 349th Infantry, 88th Div., U.S. Army, 1945; War Dept. General Staff, 1945–47; asst. chief of staff, U.S. Air Force, Korea, 1947–49; prof. of military science and tactics, Georgetown U., 1949–52; U.S. Army in Europe, 1952–53; commanding officer, 172d Infantry, 1953–54; chief of plans, CIA, 1957–61; Military Assistance Advisory Group, Vietnam, 1961–62; chief, Special Warfare Div., U.S. European Command, 1962–64; retired, 1964; Silver Star; Legion of Merit; two Bronze Stars; Combat Infantryman Badge; Army Commendation Medal. RES.: Gainesville, GA.

McCREARY, JAMES BENNETT. b. Jul 8, 1838, Richmond, KY; d. Oct 8, 1918, Richmond, KY; par. Dr. E. Robert and Sabrina (Bennett) McCreary; m. Katherine "Kate" Hughes, Jun 12, 1867; c. one son. EDUC.: A.B., Centre Coll., 1857; LL.B., Cumberland U., 1859. POLIT. & GOV.: delegate, Dem. Nat'l. Conv., 1868, 1900, 1904, 1908, 1912; presidential elector, Democratic Party, 1868 (declined); elected as a Democrat to KY State House, 1869–75 (Speaker, 1871–73); elected as a Democrat to gov. of KY, 1875–79, 1911–15; elected as a Democrat to U.S. House (KY), 1885–97; delegate, International Monetary Conference, Brussels, Belgium, 1891–92; candidate for Democratic nomination to U.S. House (KY), 1896; chm., KY State Democratic Central Cmte., 1900; elected as a Democrat to U.S. Senate (KY), 1903–09; Democratic candidate for U.S. Senate (KY), 1908, 1914; member, Pan-American Comm. of the U.S.; ***candidate for Democratic nomination to vice presidency of the U.S., 1912***. BUS. & PROF.: atty.; admitted to KY Bar, 1859; law practice, Richmond, KY. MIL.: maj., lt. col., Eleventh KY Cavalry, C.S.A., 1862–65; captured at Cheshire, OH; released in prisoner exchange, c. 1865. HON. DEG.: LL.D., Centre Coll., 1879. REL.: Presb. RES.: Richmond, KY.

McCURDY, DAVE K. b. Mar 30, 1950, Canadian, TX; par. T. L. and Aileen (Geis) McCurdy; m. Pamela McCurdy, Aug 14, 1971; c. Josh; Cydney Marie; Shannon Rose. EDUC.: B.A., U. of OK, 1971, J.D., 1975; postgrad. work, U. of Edinburgh, Scotland, 1977–78. POLIT. & GOV.: asst. atty. gen. of OK, 1975–77; elected as a Democrat to U.S. House (OK), 1981–95; ***candidate for Democratic nomination to presidency of the U.S., 1992***; Democratic candidate for U.S. Senate (OK), 1994. BUS. & PROF.: atty.; admitted to OK Bar, 1975; assoc., Luttrell, Pendarvis and Rawlinson (law firm), Norman, OK, 1978–79; law practice, Norman, 1979–80. MEM.: ABA; OK State Bar Assn. (dir.); Cleveland Cty. Bar Assn.; C. of C.; Norman Junior C. of C.; Rotary Club. AWARDS: International Rotary Graduate Fellow, 1977; one of ten "Outstanding Young Men of America," U.S. Jaycees, 1984. REL.: Lutheran. MAILING ADDRESS: Norman, OK.

McDANIEL, KYLE, JR. par. Kyle McDaniel. POLIT. & GOV.: ***independent candidate for presidency of the U.S., 1988***. MISC.: received votes in GA and MD. MAILING ADDRESS: unknown.

McDANIELS, EDISON PENROW. b. Aug 7, 1923, Wright City, OK; par. William McKinley and Ola (Warren) McDaniels; m. Florence Zadie Stowers; m. 2d, Jeanne Grant Supplee; c. Laura Ola; Vivian; Annette; Virginia Rose; Phillip David; Ronald Vaughn; Edison Penrow, Jr.; Ellys Preston; Eric Paul; Daniel G. (stepson). EDUC.: A.A., San Bernardino Valley Coll., 1952; U. of the Redlands, 1952; LL.B., Southwestern U. School of Law, 1961. POLIT. & GOV.: Democratic candidate for CA State Assembly, 1970; candidate for San Bernardino (CA) City Council; candidate for San Bernardino city atty.; candidate for San Bernardino School Board; candidate for Democratic nomination to U.S. House (CA), 1972; member, Board of Directors, Inland Counties Legal Service Corp.; member, San Bernardino Human Relations Comm.; ***candidate for Republican nomination to presidency of the U.S., 1980; independent candidate for presidency of the U.S., 1980***. BUS. & PROF.: atty.; admitted to CA Bar, 1962; law practice, San Bernardino, 1962–. MIL.: U.S. Army, 1943–45. MEM.: ABA; CA State Bar; San Bernardino Cty. Bar Assn.; American Legion; VFW. REL.: Protestant. MAILING ADDRESS: 1566 North D St., San Bernardino, CA 92405.

McDERMOTT, JAMES A. "JIM." b. Dec 28, 1936, Chicago, IL. EDUC.: B.S., Wheaton Coll., 1958; M.D., U. of IL, 1963. POLIT. & GOV.: elected as a Democrat to WA State House, 1971–73; elected as a Democrat to WA State Senate, 1975–89; ***candidate for Democratic nomination to vice presidency of the U.S., 1980***; medical officer, U.S. Foreign Service, Zaire, 1987–88; elected as a Democrat to U.S. House (WA), 1989–. BUS. & PROF.: asst. prof., U. of WA; psychiatrist, 1970–83. REL.: Episc. MAILING ADDRESS: 1650 22nd Ave., East, Seattle, WA 98105.

McDEVITT, JOHN JAY "BUTCH." b. Jun 2, 1876, Tresckow, PA; d. Feb 2, 1951, Wilkes-Barre, PA. POLIT. & GOV.: Democratic candidate for cty. treas., Luzerne Cty., PA, 1912 (withdrew); candidate for Wilkes-Barre (PA) constable; ***John Jay McDevitt Party candidate for presidency of the U.S., 1916***; candidate for Democratic nomination to U.S. Senate (FL), 1926; candidate for Democratic nomination to mayor of Wilkes-Barre, 1947; candidate for numerous other offices in Wilkes-Barre and Luzerne Cty., PA. BUS. & PROF.: slate miner, Wilkes-Barre, PA; tramp; policeman; owner, poolroom and cigar store, Wilkes-Barre; publisher, *Plain Talk*, Wilkes-Barre, 1921–25; baseball player; humorist. WRITINGS: *A Millionaire for a Day* (1914). MISC.: known as the "Millionaire for a Day" for fraudulent rental of a Pullman, 1912; financed trip in Pullman with money given to induce him to withdraw as Democratic candidate for cty. treas., 1912; suffered several business failures; took papier mâché statue of himself to Washington and offered it to U.S. Government, but was refused, 1914; once ran for 13 local offices in a single election, Wilkes-Barre, PA. RES.: Wilkes-Barre, PA.

McDEVITT, MARK ALAN. POLIT. & GOV.: ***candidate for Republican nomination to presidency of the U.S., 1988***. MISC.: used campaign to advertise for a wife. MAILING ADDRESS: c/o Mark McDevitt's First Lady Talent Search '88, 3505 Kingston Rd., York, PA 17402.

McDONALD, ANGUS WHEELER. b. Apr 21, 1927, Washington, DC; par. John Y. and Dorothy Helen (Bosworth) McDonald; m. (divorced); c. Mary Ann; Paul Yates. EDUC.: WV U., 1947–50; B.A., Columbia Union Coll., 1977. POLIT. & GOV.: ***candidate for Democratic nomination to presidency of the U.S., 1988, 1992***. BUS. & PROF.: temporary government employee, Patrick Air Force Base, Cocoa Beach, FL, 1958; self-employed, farmer, Charles Town, WV. MIL.: T/5, corp., U.S. Army, 1946–47. MEM.: Jefferson Cty. Farm Bureau; Philospa; Parents Without Partners; Audubon Soc.; Nature Conservancy; Northern WV Automobile Assn. AWARDS: 30 Year Award, Farm Bureau; 25 Year Award, Northern WV Automobile Assn. WRITINGS: *West Virginia Alumnae Association Directory* (1987). REL.: Seventh Day Adventist. MAILING ADDRESS: Rt. 3, Pleasant View Farm, Charles Town, WV 25414.

McDONALD, DUNCAN. b. Nov 25, 1873, Youngstown, OH; d. Nov 19, 1965, Springfield, IL; m. Nellie Elizabeth McDonald. EDUC.: grade school, Oglesby, IL; studied law by correspondence course. POLIT. & GOV.: ***candidate for Socialist Party nomination to presidency of the U.S., 1912 (withdrew)***; member, National Cmte., Socialist Party, 1914; Socialist Party candidate for IL State House, 1914; Labor Party candidate for gov. of IL, 1922, 1924; Farmer-Labor Party candidate for U.S. House (IL), 1922; member, National Cmte., Farmer-Labor Party, 1924; *Farmer-Labor Party candidate for presidency of the U.S., 1924 (withdrew)*; candidate for Republican nomination to U.S. House (IL), 1940. BUS. & PROF.: miner, Oglesby, IL, 1889–1903; farmer, 1889–1903; union organizer; publisher, *Illinois Industrial Review*, Springfield, IL; owner, McDonald Art and Book Store, Springfield, 1925–60. MEM.: National Progressive Union (local sec.); U.M.W. of A. (member, 1898; District Exec. Board, to 1906; National Board; sec.-treas., 1910–17; pres., IL Union, 1909); IL Federation of Labor (pres., 1919–20);

Federated Press (organizer); IL Miners Union (member, exec. board, 1904–08; International Exec. Board, 1908–09; sec.-treas., District 12, 1910–17); Central States Cooperative Soc. (sec., 1919); Cherry Relief Comm. (founder); Masons (Shriner); Odd Fellows; IA State Traveling Men's Assn. (Court of Honor). WRITINGS: *Address . . . during . . . Convention, U.M.W. of A.* (1914); *Suggestions for Starting Cooperative Stores.* RES.: Springfield, IL.

McDONALD, JOSEPH EWING. b. Aug 29, 1819, Butler Cty., OH; d. Jun 21, 1891, Indianapolis, IN; par. John and Eleanor (Piatt) McDonald; m. Nancy Ruth Buell, Dec 25, 1844; m. 2d, Mrs. Araminta W. Vance, Sep 15, 1874; m. 3d, Mrs. Josephine (Farnsworth) Bernard, Jan 12, 1880; c. Malcolm A.; Frank B.; two others. EDUC.: Wabash Coll.; grad., Asbury Coll., 1840; studied law under Zebulon Baird, Lafayette, IN, 1842–44. POLIT. & GOV.: elected as a Democrat to prosecuting atty., Lafayette (IN) Circuit, 1843–47; elected as a Democrat to U.S. House (IN), 1849–51; elected as a Democrat to atty. gen. of IN, 1856–60; Democratic candidate for gov. of IN, 1864; chm., IN Democratic State Central Cmte., 1874; elected as a Democrat to U.S. Senate (IN), 1875–81; Democratic candidate for U.S. Senate (IN), 1880; ***candidate for Democratic nomination to presidency of the U.S., 1880, 1884***; member, Special Investigating Cmte. on Election Fraud, 1877. BUS. & PROF.: saddler's apprentice; atty.; admitted to IN Bar, 1843; law practice, Crawfordsville, IN, 1847–59; partner (with Addison L. Roache), law firm, Indianapolis, 1859–69. REL.: Presb. MISC.: known as "Old Saddle-Bags." RES.: Indianapolis, IN.

McDONALD, LAWRENCE PATTON. b. Apr 1, 1935, Atlanta, GA; d. Sep 1, 1983, over Pacific Ocean; par. Harold Paul and Callie Grace (Patton) McDonald; m. (divorced); c. Tryggvi Paul; Callie Grace; Mary Elizabeth. EDUC.: Davidson Coll., 1951–53; M.D., Emory U., 1957; U. of MI, 1963–66. POLIT. & GOV.: chm., GA State Medical Education Board, 1969–74; elected as a Democrat to U.S. House (GA), 1975–1983; ***candidate for American Party nomination to presidency of the U.S., 1976***. BUS. & PROF.: physician; resident in general surgery, Grady Memorial Hospital, Atlanta, GA; resident in urology, U. of MI, Ann Arbor, MI. MIL.: lt. commander, U.S.N.R., 1957–61; Air Force Commendation Medal. MEM.: John Birch Soc. (National Council); National Movement to Restore Decency (National Board); GA Right to Life Cmte.; NRA; National Hist. Soc.; Phi Rho Sigma; Alpha Tau Omega; American Conservative Union (Advisory Board); Conservative Caucus (Advisory Board); Cmte. for the Survival of a Free Congress (Advisory Board); Rotary Club. HON. DEG.: L.H.D., Daniel Payne Coll., 1971. WRITINGS: "Correlation of Urinary Output with Serum and Spinal Fluid Mannitol Levels in Normal and Azotemic Patients," *Journal of Urology*, 1968 (coauthor); "Lobbies Control the Congress," *Review of the News*, Feb 1976; "Gun Control," *American Opinion*, May 1975. REL.: Independent Methodist. MISC.: passenger on Korean Air Lines Flight 007, shot down by U.S.S.R., 1983. RES.: Marietta, GA.

McDONALD, RICHARD HAYES. b. Jun 21, 1820, Mackville, KY; d. 1913; par. Col. James and Martha Shepard (Peter) McDonald; m. Mrs. Steinagel, Aug 5, 1851; c. Frank V.; Richard Hayes, Jr.; Martha Shepard (Mrs. John C. Spencer). EDUC.: studied medicine, Mackville and Louisville, KY; studied medicine under Thomas J. Montgomery and James R. Hughes, Springfield, 1842–44; Prather Medical Coll., 1844–46. POLIT. & GOV.: appointed cty. physician, Sacramento, CA, 1850; Prohibition Party candidate for gov. of CA, 1882; treas., CA State Prohibition Party Central Cmte.; delegate, Prohibition Party National Convention, 1884, 1888, 1892; ***candidate for Prohibition Party nomination to presidency of the U.S., 1884***; presidential elector, Prohibition Party, 1888, 1892; delegate, CA State Prohibition Party Convention, 1892 (Platform Cmte.). BUS. & PROF.: physician; employee, whiskey distillery, KY; employee, father's store, Mackville, KY; partner (with C. Gillahan), medical practice, Nauvoo, IL, 1846; physician, Prairie-du-Rocher, IL; physician, Sacramento, CA; cattle rancher; goldminer, Amador, CA; owner, Pioneer Drug Store, Sacramento; partner (with J. C. Spencer), R. H. McDonald Drug Co., Sacramento; pres., Pacific Bank of California. MIL.: orderly sgt., KY Militia, 1838; 1st lt., capt., KY Volunteers. MEM.: Masonic Relief Assn.; Masons (Royal Arch; Knights Templar); Masonic Veterans Assn. of the Pacific Coast. WRITINGS: *Catechism on the Twin Evils of Intemperance and Tobacco* (1886); *Our Ladies Book* (1891); *Silver Star Song Echo; The Nicaragua Canal* (1893). RES.: San Francisco, CA.

McDOWELL, EDDIE. b. 1942, Rocky Mount, NC. POLIT. & GOV.: ***candidate for Republican nomination to presidency of the U.S., 1980, 1984, 1988, 1992***; independent candidate for gov. of NY, 1982; candidate for Republican nomination to U.S. House (GA), 1986. BUS. & PROF.: security guard, *Washington (DC) Post*; businessman. MAILING ADDRESS: 1005 East 179th St., Bronx, NY 10460.

McGEE, BOBBY O'DELL. b. Sep 25, 1936, Hardeyville-Sencar, SC; par. Odis O'Dell and Mary R. (Gilstrap) McGee; m. Elta A. Harris; c. Rebecca; Arline; Teresa; Dell; Mary Velma; Buddy David Harris (stepson). EDUC.: eighth grade, public school, Pendleton, SC. POLIT. & GOV.: candidate for Anderson Cty. (SC) Council; Republican candidate for SC State Senate, 1976; write-in candidate for gov. of SC; candidate for Anderson Cty. Board of Education, 1984; ***independent candidate for presidency of the U.S., 1988***. BUS. & PROF.: textile worker; garbage collector; driver; carpenter; jack-of-all trades. MIL.: E-2, Company L, 10th Regt., 5th Infantry Div., U.S. Army, 1954–57. MEM.: Disabled American Veterans (life member); American Legion; Paralyzed Veterans of America. REL.: Bapt. MISC.: convicted of malicious mischief, housebreaking, and larceny, 1959; convicted of breaking and entering and petit larceny, 1967; pardoned, 1976; convicted of violating SC gun law and drawing and pointing a pistol, 1977. MAILING ADDRESS: Route 1, Box 1356, Camelot Dr., Starr, SC 29684.

McGEE, JOHN CLINTON. POLIT. & GOV.: delegate, New York Progressive Party State Convention, 1912; Progressive Party candidate for Sheriff, New York Cty., NY, 1915; appointed notary public, NY Dept. of State, Chauffeur Licensing, c. 1920; Progressive Party candidate for cty. clerk, New York Cty., 1925; ***National Progressive Party candidate for vice presidency of the U.S., 1928***. BUS. & PROF.: cowboy; policeman, New York, NY, to 1902; rider, Buffalo Bill's Wild West Show. MIL.: claimed to have been Rough Rider, 1898. MISC.: known as "Suspender Jack" McGee; dismissed from New York police force for tardiness, 1902, reinstated by act of NY Legislature, 1916; stampeded 1912 NY Progressive Party State Convention for Oscar Straus for Governor; chief marshall, Hempstead Suffrage Pageant, 1913; evicted from offices for failure to pay rent, 1913. RES.: New York, NY.

McGLYNN, EDWARD. b. Sep 27, 1837, New York, NY; d. Jan 7, 1900, New York, NY; single. EDUC.: D.D., Coll. of Propaganda, Rome, Italy, 1856–60. POLIT. & GOV.: delegate, Union Labor Party National Convention, 1888; ***candidate for Union Labor Party nomination to presidency of the U.S., 1888***. BUS. & PROF.: ordained priest, Roman Catholic Church, 1860; asst. pastor, chaplain, New York, NY, 1860–66; pastor, St. Stephen's Roman Catholic Church, New York; excommunicated, 1887; reinstated, 1892; pastor, St. Mary's Church, New York, 1895–1900. MIL.: chaplain, U.S. Army, 1862–65. MEM.: Anti-Poverty Soc. (founder, 1887). MISC.: noted advocate of single tax. RES.: New York, NY.

McGOVERN, ELEANOR FAYE STEGEBERG. b. Nov 25, 1921, Woonsocket, SD; m. George Stanley McGovern (q.v.), Oct 31, 1943; c. Ann (Mrs. Wilbur Mead); Susan (Mrs. James Rowen); Mary; Teresa; Steven. EDUC.: Dakota Wesleyan U.; George Washington U. POLIT. & GOV.: district co-chm., George McGovern for Congress Campaign, 1956; ***candidate for Democratic nomination to vice presidency of the U.S., 1972***. BUS. & PROF.: legal sec.; volunteer, parent and child care center, Washington, DC. MEM.: Women's National Democratic Club (co-chm., Program Cmte.); Democratic Congressional Wive's Forum (treas.); Suburban Women's Democratic Club; Psychiatric Inst. Foundation (Montgomery Cty., MD Board of Directors); Odyssey House (Board of Advisers); American Acad. of Medical Administrators (hon. member). MAILING ADDRESS: 1825 Connecticut Ave., N.W., #213, Washington, DC 20009.

McGOVERN, GEORGE STANLEY. b. Jul 19, 1922, Avon, SD; par. Joseph C. and Frances (McLean) McGovern; m. Eleanor Faye Stegeberg (q.v.), Oct 31, 1943; c. Ann (Mrs. William Mead); Steven; Susan (Mrs. James Rowen); Mary; Teresa. EDUC.: B.A., Dakota Wesleyan U., 1945; M.A., Northwestern U., 1949, Ph.D., 1953. POLIT. & GOV.: exec. sec., SD State Democratic Party, 1953–55; member, Advisory Cmte. on Political Organization, Dem. Nat'l. Cmte., 1954–56; elected as a Democrat to U.S. House (SD), 1957–61; Democratic candidate for U.S. Senate (SD), 1960, 1980; appointed dir., Food for Peace Program, 1961–62; appointed special asst. to the president of the U.S., 1961–62; elected as a Democrat to U.S. Senate (SD), 1963–81; ***candidate for Democratic nomination to presidency of the U.S., 1968, 1976 (declined), 1984, 1992 (withdrew); candidate for Democratic nomination to vice presidency of the U.S., 1968, 1980; Democratic candidate for presidency of the U.S., 1972***. BUS. & PROF.: prof. of history and political science, Dakota Wesleyan U., 1949–53. MIL.: 1st lt., U.S.A.A.C., 1943–45; Distinguished Flying Cross; Air Medal with three Oak Leaf Clusters. MEM.: Kiwanis; American Legion; VFW; Masons (33°; Shriners); American Hist. Assn.; Elks. HON. DEG.: LL.D., Wilmington Coll., 1962. WRITINGS: *The Colorado Coal Strike, 1913–1914* (1953); *War Against Want* (1964); *Agricultural Thought in the Twentieth Century* (1967); *A Time of War, A Time of Peace* (1968); *The Great Coalfield War* (with Leonard Guttridge, 1972); *An American Journey* (1974); *Grassroots* (1978). REL.: Methodist. MAILING ADDRESS: 1825 Connecticut Ave., N.W., #213, Washington, DC 20009.

McGROARTY, JOHN STEVEN. b. Aug 20, 1862, Wilkes-Barre, PA; d. Aug 7, 1944, Los Angeles, CA; par. Hugh and Mary M. McGroarty; m. Ida Lubrecht, Nov 19, 1890. EDUC.: Harry Hillman Acad.; studied law. POLIT. & GOV.: elected cty. treas., Luzerne Cty., PA, 1890–93; candidate for delegate, Dem. Nat'l. Conv., 1932; elected as a Democrat to U.S. House (CA), 1935–39; ***candidate for Democratic nomination to presidency of the U.S., 1936***; candidate for Democratic nomination to CA state sec. of state, 1938. BUS. & PROF.: schoolteacher, 2 years; atty.; admitted to PA Bar, 1894; law practice, Wilkes-Barre, PA; atty., legal dept., Anaconda Copper Co., Butte, MT, 1896–1901; journalist, Los Angeles, CA, 1901–44; ed., *The West Coast*, 1906–14. MEM.: Knights of St. Gregory (Vatican City, 1930); knight commander, Order of Isabella the Catholic (Spain, 1932). HON. DEG.: Litt.D., U. of CA, 1925; LL.D., U. of Santa Clara, 1927. WRITINGS: *Poets and Poetry of Wyoming Valley* (1885); *Just California* (1903); *Wander Songs* (1908); *The King's Highway* (1909); *The Mission Play* (1911); *California: Its History and Romance* (1911); *Del Mar on the South Coast; The Endless Miracle of California; Fresno County: The Geographical Hub of the State of California* (1915); *Los Angeles: A Maritime City* (1912); *Los Angeles, From the Mountains to the Sea* (1921); *Southern California; History of Los Angeles County* (1923); *La Golondrina* (drama, 1923); *The Pioneer* (1925); *Osceola* (drama, 1927); *Babylon* (drama, 1927); *Mission Memories* (1929); *The Mass* (1932); *Little Flowers of St. Francis* (translator, 1932); *California of the South* (1933–35); *The California Plutarch* (1935); *Santa Barbara, California* (1925). REL.: R.C. MISC.: advocate of Townsend Plan; known as the "Sage of Verdugo Hills"; designated poet laureate of CA by state legislature, 1933. RES.: Tujunga, CA.

McGRUE, B. J. POLIT. & GOV.: ***independent candidate for presidency of the U.S., 1908***. RES.: CO.

McINTOSH, JAMES FRANKLIN, III. par. James Franklin McIntosh. POLIT. & GOV.: ***independent candidate for presidency of the U.S., 1984***. BUS. & PROF.: minister. MAILING ADDRESS: 3228 Gun Club Rd., West, 6-C-B639, West Palm Beach, FL 33406.

McKAY, JAMES IVER. b. Jul 17, 1793, Elizabethtown, Bladen Cty., NC; d. Sep 14, 1853, Goldsboro, NC; par. John and Mary (Salter) McKay; m. Eliza Ann Harvey, Dec 3, 1818; c. one son (infant). EDUC.: Raleigh Acad.; studied law. POLIT. & GOV.: elected as a Democrat to NC State Senate, 1815–19, 1822, 1826, 1829–30; appointed U.S. district atty. for NC, 1817; elected as a Democrat to U.S. House (NC), 1831–49; ***candidate for Democratic nomination to vice presidency of the U.S., 1848***. BUS. & PROF.: atty.; admitted to NC Bar. MISC.: responsible for establishment of Fort Caswell on Cape Fear and an arsenal at Fayetteville, NC; sponsor of the Walker Tariff Bill, 1846. RES.: Goldsboro, NC.

McKEITHEN, JOHN JULIAN. b. May 28, 1918, Grayson, LA; par. Jesse Jepheth and Agnes (Eglin) McKeithen; m. Marjorie Howell Funderburk, Jun 14, 1942; c. Jay; Fox; Rebecca; Melissa; Pamela; Jenneva Maude. POLIT. & GOV.: elected as a Democrat to LA State House, 1948–52; member, LA State Public Service Comm., 1954–62; elected as a Democrat to gov. of LA, 1964–72; delegate, Dem. Nat'l. Conv., 1968; ***candidate for American Independent Party nomination to presidency of the U.S., 1972***. BUS. & PROF.: public servant. MIL.: 1st lt., U.S. Army. MEM.: VFW; American Legion; Farm Bureau; Delta Council. REL.: Methodist. MAILING ADDRESS: Columbia, LA 71418.

McKELDIN, THEODORE ROOSEVELT. b. Nov 20, 1900, Baltimore, MD; d. Aug 10, 1974, Baltimore, MD; par. James A. and Dora (Grief) McKeldin; m. Honolulu Claire Manzer, Oct 17, 1924; c. Theodore Roosevelt, Jr.; Clara Whitney (Mrs. Ziegler). EDUC.: LL.B., U. of MD, 1924; Johns Hopkins U. POLIT. & GOV.: exec. sec. to mayor of Baltimore, MD, 1927–31; elected as a Republican to mayor of Baltimore, MD, 1943–47, 1963–67; elected as a Republican to gov. of MD, 1951–59; member, Advisory Cmte. on Intergovernmental Relations; member, Indian Claims Comm.; delegate, Rep. Nat'l. Conv., 1952; member, Rep. Nat'l. Cmte., 1952–60; ***candidate for Republican nomination to vice presidency of the U.S., 1960***; appointed member, Cmte. of 22 to Visit Vietnam, 1967. BUS. & PROF.: atty.; admitted to MD Bar, 1926; law practice, Baltimore, MD, 1931–43, 1947–51, 1959–63, 1967–74; dir., Reistertown Federal Savings and Loan Assn.; faculty, U. of Baltimore Law School; faculty, Baltimore Coll. of Commerce; faculty, Baltimore Inst.; faculty, Forest Park Avenue H.S. MEM.: Omicron Delta Kappa; ABA; MD Bar Assn.; German Soc. of MD; Masons (32°; Knights Templar; Shriners); Kiwanis; Sigma Phi Epsilon; Order of the Coif; National Governors Conference; Southern Governors Conference; Brandeis U. (fellow). AWARDS: award, Sydney Hollander Foundation; 5 awards, Freedoms Foundation; International Youth Distinguished Service Citation, International Soc. for Christian Endeavor; Histadrut Award; citation, National Conference of Christians and Jews, 1953; "Man of the Year," Advertising Club of Baltimore, 1953; Annual Award, National Federation of Jewish Men's Clubs, 1954; citation, MA Cmte. of Catholics, Protestants and Jews; medal, DeMolay Legion of Honor; American-Israel Friendship Award, Mizrachi Women's Organization; grand commander, Order of the Phoenix (Greece); grand commander and grand band, Star of Africa (Liberia). HON. DEG.: Litt.D., IN Central Coll., 1952; Litt.D., Westminster Coll. (UT), 1952; LL.D., Anderson Coll., 1953; LL.D., Ithaca Coll., 1953; L.H.D., Loyola Coll., 1953; LL.D., Lincoln Coll., 1954; D.Pol.Sci., Steed Coll. of Technology, 1954; LL.D., Beaver Coll.; LL.D., Hanover Coll.; LL.D., Morgan Coll.; LL.D., Rider Coll.; LL.D., U. of MD; LL.D., Washington Coll. WRITINGS: *The Art of Eloquence* (coauthor, 1952); *Washington Bowed* (1956); *No Mean City* (1964). REL.: Episc. RES.: Baltimore, MD.

McKENNAN, THOMAS McKEAN THOMPSON. b. Mar 31, 1794, Dragon Neck (New Castle), DE; d. Jul 9, 1852, Reading, PA; par. Col. William and Elizabeth (Thompson) McKennan; m. Matilda Lowrie Bowman, Dec 6, 1815; c. William; Thomas; Isabella; Jacob Bowman; Thomas McKean Thompson, Jr.; Anne Elizabeth; John Thompson; Matilda Bowman (Mrs. George Washington Reed). EDUC.: grad., Washington Coll., 1810; studied law under Parker Campbell, Washington, PA. POLIT. & GOV.: deputy atty. gen., Washington Cty., PA, 1815–17; elected member, Washington Town Council, 1818–31; elected as a Whig to U.S. House (PA), 1831–39, 1842–43; presidential elector, Whig Party, 1840, 1848 (pres., PA Electoral College); ***candidate for Whig Party nomination to presidency of the U.S., 1848; candidate for Whig Party nomination to vice presidency of the U.S., 1848***; appointed U.S. sec. of the interior, 1850. BUS. & PROF.: tutor, Washington Coll., 1813–14; atty.; admitted to PA Bar, 1814; law practice, Washington; officer, Washington and Pittsburgh R.R. Co., 1831; pres., Hempfield R.R., 1851. MEM.: Washington Coll. (trustee, 1818–52); Washington Female Seminary (founder); Washington Cty. Agricultural Soc. REL.: Presb. RES.: Washington, PA.

McKENZIE, WILLIAM BUFORD. m. Lucille; c. Dale. POLIT. & GOV.: ***Theocratic Party candidate for vice presidency of the U.S., 1968***. BUS. & PROF.: bishop, Church of God. REL.: Church of God. MAILING ADDRESS: 312 Black Ave., Chaffee, MO 63740.

McKIM, THOMAS CAPITOLA. b. May 29, 1928, Ledbetter, KY; par. Edgar Thomas and Minnie Ola (Holloway) McKim; m. Elvera May (Bass) Waeckenley, 1951 (divorced, 1973); m. 2d, Georgianna Carol, 1976; m. 3d, Betty

Ann McFerren; c. Rebecca Kay; Patricia Louise; Judith Marie. EDUC.: high school, U.S. Navy; college, U.S. Army; college, U.S. Navy, Yuba, CA. POLIT. & GOV.: ***nonpartisan candidate for presidency of the U.S., 1988 (withdrew)***. BUS. & PROF.: heavy equipment operator; construction engineer; millwright (certified); operator, sanitary landfill; officer, McKim Enterprises (gold recovery; ore transport; mine security), Cave Junction, OR; author. MIL.: seaman apprentice, U.S. Navy, 1945–50; sgt., U.S. Army, 1950–52. MEM.: National Geographic Soc.; Rock Hounds of America; Yuba Sutter Mineral Soc.; VFW; American Legion. WRITINGS: *Book of Thoughts and Plans* (1986). REL.: Cherokee (non-Christian). MISC.: convicted of illegal cultivation of marijuana in connection with research for a book, 1976; sentenced to two years' probation and a $375 fine, and 20 weekends in jail; convicted of a felony for distributing marijuana to a minor, 1979; withdrew from presidential race because of status as ex-felon. MAILING ADDRESS: P.O. Box 404, O'Brien, OR 97534.

McKINLEY, CHARLES. b. Oct 16, 1889, Fulton, SD; d. Mar 22, 1970, Portland, OR; par. Charles Lincoln and Harriet Emma (Bull) McKinley; m. Nellie Linda Higgins, Aug 30, 1914; c. Jean (Mrs. Don N. Johnson); Donald; Hugh. EDUC.: B.A., U. of WA, 1913; M.A., U. of WI, 1916. POLIT. & GOV.: appointed member, Government Simplification Comm., Multnomah Cty., OR, 1926; appointed member, Portland (OR) City Planning Comm., 1934–64 (pres., 1935–40); consultant, National Resources Planning Board, 1935–43; staff, President's Comm. on Administrative Management, 1936; appointed member, President's AK Resources Comm., 1937; exec. sec., Administrative Council, U.S. Dept. of Agriculture, 1940–42; appointed special asst., WPB, 1942; consultant, North Pacific Planning Project, U.S. Dept. of State, 1943–44; appointed member, Regional Advisory Council, Bonneville Power Administration, 1943; consultant, U.S. Dept. of the Interior, 1947; consultant, Hoover Comm. on Reorganization of the Exec. Branch, 1948; consultant, U.S. Forest Service, 1949; consultant, President's Water Resources Policy Comm., 1950; ***New Party of Oregon candidate for presidency of the U.S., 1968***. BUS. & PROF.: chm., Ogden (UT) Senior H.S. history dept., 1917–18; instructor in political science, Reed Coll., 1918, asst. prof., 1921, prof., 1926–60; Cornelia Marvin Pierce Professor of American Institutions, Reed Coll., 1958–60; visiting prof., Maxwell School of Citizenship and Public Affairs, Syracuse U., 1925–26; visiting prof., U. of OR; visiting prof., U. of UT; visiting prof., Portland State Coll., 1960–63; visiting prof., U. of WA. MEM.: National Municipal League; American Soc. for Public Administration; Phi Beta Kappa; League of Oregon Cities (consultant, 1934–35); Social Science Research Council (Research Staff, Cmte. on Public Administration, 1935–37); Pacific Northwest Political Science Assn. (pres., 1949–50); APSA (vice pres., 1953; pres., 1954); Portland City Club (pres.); Council for a Livable World. AWARDS: Bi-Centennial Silver Medallion, Columbia U., 1954; Distinguished Service Award, U. of OR, 1964. HON. DEG.: LL.D., Reed Coll., 1960. WRITINGS: *Five Years of Planning in the Pacific Northwest* (1939); *Uncle Sam in the Pacific Northwest* (1952); *Launching Social Security* (1970); *Federal Management of Natural Resources in the Columbia River Valley*; *The Management of Land and Related Resources in Oregon*. RES.: Portland, OR.

McKINLEY, WILLIAM, JR. b. Jan 29, 1843, Niles, OH; d. Sep 14, 1901, Buffalo, NY; par. William and Nancy Campbell (Allison) McKinley; m. Ida Saxton, Jan 25, 1871; c. Katherine (infant); Ida (infant). EDUC.: Union Seminary, Poland, OH; Allegheny Coll., 1859–60; Albany Law School, 1867; studied law under Charles E. Glidden and David M. Wilson, Youngstown, OH, 1865. POLIT. & GOV.: elected prosecuting atty., Stark Cty., OH, 1869–71; candidate for prosecuting atty., Stark Cty., 1871; elected as a Republican to U.S. House (OH), 1877–84 (lost contested election and vacated seat, Mar 27, 1884), 1885–91; chm., OH State Republican Convention, 1880, 1884; delegate, Rep. Nat'l. Conv., 1880, 1884, 1888, 1892 (permanent chm.); member, Rep. Nat'l. Cmte., 1880; ***candidate for Republican nomination to presidency of the U.S., 1888, 1892***; Republican candidate for U.S. House (OH), 1890; elected as a Republican to gov. of OH, 1893–97; ***elected as a Republican to presidency of the U.S., 1897–1901***. BUS. & PROF.: schoolteacher, Poland, OH, 1860; clerk, U.S. Post Office, Poland, OH, 1861; atty.; admitted to OH Bar, 1867; law practice, Canton, OH, 1867. MIL.: pvt., Company E, 23d OH Volunteer Infantry, 1861, commissary sgt., 1862, 2d lt., 1862, 1st lt., 1863, capt., 1864; brev. maj., U.S.V., 1865. MEM.: Masons (master). WRITINGS: *The Tariff in the Days of Henry Clay and Since* (1896). REL.: Methodist. MISC.: assassinated by Leon Czolgosz, who shot him on Sep 6, 1901, with death occurring on Sep 14, 1901. RES.: Canton, OH.

McLAIN, GEORGE HENRY. b. Jun 24, 1901, Los Angeles, CA; d. Jul 12, 1965, Los Angeles, CA; par. George and Martha (Priester) McLain; m. Hannah Reardon (divorced); m. 2d, Rose Sullivan (divorced); c. George, Jr. EDUC.: Los Angeles (CA) public schools; Los Angeles City Coll. POLIT. & GOV.: member, CA Citizens' Legislative Advisory Cmte.; member, Governor's Cmte. on Aging (CA), 1943, 1960; candidate for Democratic nomination to U.S. House (CA), 1952; delegate, White House Conference on Aging, 1960; ***candidate for Democratic nomination to presidency of the U.S., 1960***; candidate for Democratic nomination to U.S. Senate (CA), 1964; delegate, Dem. Nat'l. Conv., 1964; member, Mayor's Advisory Cmte. on Aging, Los Angeles; member, Los Angeles Cty. Democratic Cmte.; member, CA State Democratic Central Cmte. BUS. & PROF.: street contractor, G. T. McLain and Son; ed., *National Welfare Advocate*; ed., *Senior Citizen Sentinel*; pres., *Senior Citizens Village*, Fresno, CA; lobbyist. MEM.: Citizens' Cmte. for Old Age Pensions (founder; dir., 1941–50); CA Inst. of Social Welfare (chm., 1950–65); National League of Senior Citizens (pres.); Old Folks Lobby; Saints and Sinners of Los Angeles; Loyal Order of Moose; Native Sons of the Golden West; Fraternal Order of Eagles; Free and Accepted Masons. REL.: Christian Scientist.

MISC.: advocate of pension reform; received 650,000 votes in the 1960 CA presidential primary. RES.: Los Angeles, CA.

McLAIN, HARLEY JAMES. b. 1951. EDUC.: grad., Jamestown (ND) Coll. POLIT. & GOV.: founder, Natural People's League; Chemical Farming Banned candidate for U.S. House (ND), 1978; ***Natural People's League candidate for presidency of the U.S., 1980***; Natural People's Party candidate for ND state commissioner of agriculture, 1980. BUS. & PROF.: organic farmer, Eckelson, ND; guitarist, Chemical Farming Banned band. MEM.: New Non-Partisan League; Natural People's League. REL.: Divine Science of Soul (Minneapolis Satsang). MISC.: involved in protracted litigation over ND election law discrimination against third parties, 1978–81; declared himself elected pres., following 1980 election. MAILING ADDRESS: 211 Wheat Ave., Hatton, ND 58240.

McLEAN, JOHN. b. Mar 11, 1785, Morris Cty., NJ; d. Apr 4, 1861, Cincinnati, OH; par. Fergus and Sophia (Blockford) McLean; m. Rebecca Edwards, 1807; m. 2d, Sarah Bella (Ludlow) Garrard, 1843; c. four daughters; three sons. EDUC.: studied law under Arthur St. Clair. POLIT. & GOV.: elected as a Whig (War Democrat) to U.S. House (OH), 1813–16; Whig Party candidate for U.S. Senate (OH), 1815 (declined); elected assoc. justice, OH State Supreme Court, 1816–22; appointed commissioner, U.S. Land Office, 1822–23; appointed postmaster gen. of the U.S., 1825–29; appointed U.S. sec. of war, 1829 (declined); appointed U.S. sec. of the navy, 1829 (declined); appointed assoc. justice, Supreme Court of the U.S., 1829–61; ***candidate for Anti-Masonic Party nomination to presidency of the U.S., 1832 (declined); candidate for Whig Party nomination to presidency of the U.S., 1836, 1844 (declined), 1848, 1852; candidate for Free Democracy (Free Soil) Party nomination to presidency of the U.S., 1848; candidate for Republican nomination to presidency of the U.S., 1856, 1860***. BUS. & PROF.: atty.; admitted to OH Bar, 1807; law practice, Lebanon, OH; publisher, *Western Star*, Lebanon, 1807. MEM.: Lebanon Debating Soc. WRITINGS: *Eulogy on James Monroe* (1831). MISC.: rendered dissenting opinion in Dred Scott case. RES.: Cincinnati, OH.

McLEAN, JOHN ROLL. b. Sep 18, 1848, Cincinnati, OH; d. Jun 9, 1916, Washington, DC; par. Washington and Mary L. McLean; m. Emily Beale, 1884; c. Edward B. EDUC.: U. of Cincinnati; Harvard U. POLIT. & GOV.: delegate, Dem. Nat'l. Conv., 1884, 1888, 1892, 1896, 1900, 1904, 1908, 1912; Democratic candidate for U.S. Senate (OH), 1885; Democratic candidate for gov. of OH, 1899; member, Dem. Nat'l. Cmte.; ***candidate for Democratic nomination to presidency of the U.S., 1896; candidate for Democratic nomination to vice presidency of the U.S., 1896***. BUS. & PROF.: member, Red Stockings Baseball Team; journalist; office boy, *Cincinnati (OH) Enquirer*, part-owner, 1873; mgr. and ed., 1877, owner and publisher, 1881–1916; owner, *New York (NY) Evening Journal*; owner, publisher, *Washington (DC) Post*, 1905–16; pres., Washington Gas Light Co.; owner, Holmead Cemetery; hotel owner; dir., Capital Traction Co. RES.: Washington, DC.

McLINN, WILLIAM. b. 1944. EDUC.: U. of San Diego Law School; Pacific School of Religion, 1972. POLIT. & GOV.: chm., Law Students for Nixon-Agnew, U. of San Diego, 1968; legislative aide, U.S. Rep. Andrew Maguire, 1975–76; ***independent candidate for presidency of the U.S., 1980 (satire effort, 1980)***. BUS. & PROF.: ordained minister, United Church of Christ; lecturer. MEM.: Federal Liaison Associates. REL.: United Church of Christ. MISC.: antiwar activist; campaigned on college campuses under guise of Mark Twain (q.v.). MAILING ADDRESS: 1 Third St., N.E., Washington, DC.

McMAHON, EUGENE JAMES. b. 1923; d. May 1984. EDUC.: B.A., Union U.; LL.B., St. John's U., 1949. POLIT. & GOV.: appointed counsel to minority leader, New York (NY) City Council, 1962; ***independent candidate for presidency of the U.S., 1976***. BUS. & PROF.: atty.; law practice, Richmond Hill, NY. RES.: Richmond Hill, NY.

McMAHON, JAMES O'BRIEN "BRIEN." b. Oct 6, 1903, Norwalk, CT; d. Jul 28, 1952, Washington, DC; par. William Henry and Eugenie Theresa J. (O'Brien) McMahon; m. Rosemary Turner, Feb 6, 1940; c. Patricia Rosemary. EDUC.: A.B., Fordham U., 1924; LL.B., Yale U., 1927. POLIT. & GOV.: appointed judge, City Court, Norwalk, CT, 1933; appointed special asst. to the atty. gen. of the U.S., 1933–35, acting asst., 1935–36, asst. atty. gen., 1936; chm., Cmte. on Survey of Release Procedures, U.S. Dept. of Justice, 1939; elected as a Democrat to U.S. Senate (CT), 1944–52; delegate, Dem. Nat'l. Conv., 1952; ***candidate for Democratic nomination to presidency of the U.S., 1952***. BUS. & PROF.: atty.; admitted to CT Bar, 1927; assoc., Keogh and Candee (law firm), Norwalk, CT; partner, McMahon, Dean and Gallagher (law firm), Washington, DC, 1939–44. MEM.: ABA; CT Bar Assn.; Yale Club of Washington; APSA; Phi Alpha Delta; Burning Tree Club; Knights of Columbus; Fordham U. Alumni Assn. (vice pres., 1945); Lions; Redmen; Norwalk C. of C.; Metropolitan Club. HON. DEG.: LL.D., Fordham U., 1946; LL.D., Wesleyan U., 1951. REL.: R.C. RES.: South Norwalk, CT.

McMILLEN, WHEELER. b. Jan 27, 1893, Ada, OH; d. Mar 4, 1992, Leesburg, VA; par. Lewis Dodd and Ella (Wheeler) McMillen; m. Dorothy Edna Doane, May 28, 1915; c. Robert Doane. EDUC.: OH Northern U., 1911–12. POLIT. & GOV.: ***candidate for Republican nomination to presidency of the U.S., 1944***; chm., NJ State Public Health Council, 1947–49; appointed U.S. delegate, International Congress on Industrial Chemistry, 1950; exec. dir., President's Comm. on Increased Industrial Use of Agricultural Products, 1956–57; appointed member, President's Council on Youth Fitness, 1957–58. BUS. & PROF.: reporter, *Cincinnati (OH) Post*, 1912; owner,

Covington (IN) Republican, 1914–18; farmer, Hardin Cty., OH, 1918–22; assoc. ed., *Farm and Fireside*, New York, NY, 1922–39; assoc. ed., *Country Home*, 1922–34, ed., 1934–37, editorial dir., 1937–39; editor-in-chief, *Farm Journal*, 1939–55, vice pres., dir., 1955–63; editor-in-chief, *Pathfinder*, Washington, DC, 1946–52; dir., New Jersey Bell Telephone Co., 1948–65; dir., Bankers National Life Insurance Co., 1955–71; vice pres., Farm Journal, Inc., 1955–63. MEM.: National Farm Chemurgic Council (pres., chm., 1937–62); American Assn. of Agricultural Editors (pres., 1934–38); BSA (National Exec. Board, 1938–63; national vice pres., 1959–63); Philadelphia Soc. for Promoting Agriculture (pres., 1960–62); Kappa Tau Alpha; Alpha Zeta; Grange; Cosmos Club; NJ State C. of C. (dir., 1943–51); Rutgers U. (trustee, 1943–52); National Audubon Soc. (dir., 1949–55). AWARDS: Silver Buffalo Award, BSA; Silver Antelope Award, BSA; Honorary American Farmer Award, Future Farmers of America; citation, National 4-H Clubs; Louis Broomfield Gold Medal, Malabar Farm Foundation, 1965; awards, Freedom Foundation. HON. DEG.: LL.D., OH Northern U., 1940; D.Litt., Parsons Coll., 1953. WRITINGS: *The Farming Fever* (1924); *The Young Collector* (1928); *Too Many Farmers* (1929); *New Riches from the Soil* (1946); *Land of Plenty* (1961); *Why the United States is Rich* (1963); *Possums, Politicians and People* (1964); *Harvest: An Anthology* (ed., 1964); *Bugs or People* (1965); *Fifty Useful Americans* (1966); *The Green Frontier* (1968); *Weekly on the Wabash* (1969); *Ohio Farmer* (1974). RES.: Lovettsville, VA.

McNAIR, ROBERT EVANDER. b. Dec 14, 1923, Cades, SC; par. Daniel Evander and Claudia (Crawford) McNair; m. Josephine Robinson, May 30, 1944; c. Robert Evander, Jr.; Robin Lee (Mrs. Jon C. Howell); Corinne Calhoun; Claudia Crawford. EDUC.: A.B., U. of SC, 1947, LL.B., 1948. POLIT. & GOV.: elected as a Democrat to SC State House, 1951–62; elected as a Democrat to lt. gov. of SC, 1962–65; elected as a Democrat to gov. of SC, 1965–71; chm., Southern Regional Education Board, 1967–68; delegate, Dem. Nat'l. Conv., 1968, 1972, 1976; chm., Education Comm. of the States, 1968–69; co-chm., Coastal Plains Regional Comm., 1967–68; co-chm., Appalachian Regional Comm., 1970; ***candidate for Democratic nomination to vice presidency of the U.S., 1968***; vice chm., Dem. Nat'l. Cmte., 1969–70; member, Dem. Nat'l. Cmte. (SC), 1970–; member, Democratic Policy Council, 1972–. BUS. & PROF.: atty.; admitted to SC Bar, 1948; law practice, Allendale, SC; senior partner, McNair, Glenn, Konduros, Corley, Singletary, Porter and Dibble (law firm), Columbia, SC, 1971–; dir., Crum and Forester; dir., Investors Heritage Life Insurance Co. of the South, 1971–; dir., Airco, Inc.; dir., Southern Railway Systems; dir., R. L. Bryan Co.; dir., Georgia-Pacific Corp.; dir., Bankers Trust Co. of South Carolina; dir., Graniteville Co.; dir., Public Broadcasting Corp. MIL.: lt. (jg), U.S.N.R., 1942–46. MEM.: Lions; Farm Bureau; Kappa Sigma Kappa; Blue Key; Masons (Shriners); American Legion; National Conference of Lieutenant Governors (chm., 1965–66); Southern Governors' Conference (chm., 1968–69); National Democratic Governors' Conference (chm., 1968–69); American Enterprise Inst. (member, Advisory Cmte.); Presbyterian Coll. of SC (member, Board of Visitors); Baptist Coll. of Charleston (trustee); SC Foundation for Independent Colleges (dir.); U. of SC Business Partnership Foundation (dir.); Columbia Coll. (member, Advisory Council). HON. DEG.: LL.D., Coll. of Charleston; LL.D., Furman U.; LL.D., Lander Coll.; LL.D., Presbyterian Coll. of SC; LL.D., U. of SC. REL.: Bapt. (deacon; Sunday school teacher). MAILING ADDRESS: 11 Sunturf Circle, Spring Valley, Columbia, SC 29206.

McNALLY, LILLIAN A. b. 1930; single. POLIT. & GOV.: ***candidate for Democratic nomination to presidency of the U.S., 1976***. BUS. & PROF.: waitress. MAILING ADDRESS: 1451 N St., N.W., Washington, DC.

McNALLY, MARTIN J. b. 1944. POLIT. & GOV.: ***Nationalist Christian Democratic Party candidate for vice presidency of the U.S., 1980***. MISC.: inmate, federal penitentiary, Marion, IL; parachuted from a hijacked plane in 1972 with $500,000 ransom, captured, convicted, and sentenced to life imprisonment. MAILING ADDRESS: Marion, IL.

McNARY, CHARLES LINZA. b. Jun 12, 1874, Salem, OR; d. Feb 25, 1944, Fort Lauderdale, FL; par. Hugh Linza and Mary Margaret (Claggett) McNary; m. Jessie Breyman, Nov 19, 1902; m. 2d, Cornelia Woodburn Morton, Dec 29, 1923; c. Charlotte (adopted). EDUC.: Leland Stanford Junior U., 1896–98; studied law under John Hugh McNary. POLIT. & GOV.: deputy cty. recorder, Marion Cty., OR, 1892–96; deputy district atty., Third Judicial District of OR, 1904–11; special counsel, OR State R.R. Comm., 1911–13; appointed assoc. justice, OR State Supreme Court, 1913–15; candidate for Republican nomination to assoc. justice, OR State Supreme Court, 1914; chm., OR State Republican Central Cmte., 1916–17; appointed as a Republican to U.S. Senate (OR), 1917–18; appointed and subsequently elected as a Republican to U.S. Senate (OR), 1918–44 (minority leader, 1933–44); ***candidate for Republican nomination to vice presidency of the U.S., 1928, 1936; candidate for Republican nomination to presidency of the U.S., 1936, 1940; Republican candidate for vice presidency of the U.S., 1940***. BUS. & PROF.: atty.; admitted to OR Bar, 1898; law practice, Salem, OR, 1898–1913; dean, law dept., Willamette U., 1908–13; filbert farmer, Marion Cty., OR. MEM.: Masons; Odd Fellows; Elks; Salem Fruit Union (pres., 1909–44); National Economic League; Burning Tree Country Club; OR Taft-Sherman Club (pres., 1912). HON. DEG.: LL.D., Linfield Coll., 1935; LL.D., Willamette U., 1935; LL.D., U. of OR, 1937. REL.: Bapt. RES.: Salem, OR.

McNEIL, ARCHIBALD, JR. b. Jul 2, 1843, Bridgeport, CT; d. Oct 13, 1941, Westport, CT; par. Abraham Archibald and Mary (Hults) McNeil; m. Jean McKenzie Ranald, 1881; c. Archibald, Jr.; two other sons. EDUC.: Hopkins Grammar School, New Haven, CT. POLIT. & GOV.: elected as a

Democrat to CT State Senate, 1903–05, 1907–09; ***candidate for Democratic nomination to vice presidency of the U.S., 1908***; Democratic candidate for U.S. House (CT), 1922; delegate, Dem. Nat'l. Conv., 1924, 1928; member, Dem. Nat'l. Cmte., 1936. BUS. & PROF.: partner (with Charles H. McNeil), fruit and produce business, 1863–76; importer; butter and cheese merchant, New York, NY, 1876; proprietor, Archibald McNeil and Sons (bituminous coal), Bridgeport, CT, 1888. MEM.: Algonquin Club (pres.); Seaside Club; Bridgeport Club. RES.: Bridgeport, CT.

McNEILL, DONALD THOMAS. b. Dec 23, 1907, Galena, IL; m. Katharine "Kay" Bennett, Sep 1931; c. Donald; Thomas; Robert. EDUC.: Ph.B., Marquette U., 1930. POLIT. & GOV.: ***Breakfast Party candidate for presidency of the U.S., 1948 (satire effort)***. BUS. & PROF.: radio broadcaster; announcer; radio ed., *Milwaukee (WI) Sentinel*, 1926; staff announcer, Louisville, KY, 1930; costar, *Don and Van, the Two Professors* (radio program) 1930; master of ceremonies, *The Pepper Pot* (radio program), NBC, 1931; originator, *Breakfast Club*, NBC, 1933. HON. DEG.: LL.D., St. Bonaventure Coll., 1942. WRITINGS: *Memory Time*. MAILING ADDRESS: c/o ABC, 222 West North Bank, Chicago, IL.

McNUTT, PAUL VORIES. b. Jul 19, 1891, Franklin, IN; d. Mar 24, 1955, New York, NY; par. John Crittenden and Ruth (Neely) McNutt; m. Kathleen Timolat, Apr 20, 1918; c. Louise. EDUC.: A.B., IN U., 1913; LL.B., Harvard U., 1916. POLIT. & GOV.: civilian aide to U.S. sec. of war for IN, 1927–28; elected as a Democrat to gov. of IN, 1933–37; ***candidate for Democratic nomination to vice presidency of the U.S., 1936, 1940, 1944***; appointed U.S. high commissioner to the Philippine Islands, 1937–39, 1945–46; appointed federal securities administrator, 1939–45; ***candidate for Democratic nomination to presidency of the U.S., 1940, 1948***; appointed dir., Office of Defense, Health and Welfare Services, 1941–43; appointed chm., War Manpower Comm., 1942–45; appointed member, Work Progress Board; appointed member, Economic Stabilization Board; appointed member, IN Corp. Survey Comm.; appointed U.S. ambassador extraordinary and plenipotentiary to the Republic of the Philippines, 1946–47. BUS. & PROF.: atty.; admitted to IN Bar, 1914; partner, McNutt and McNutt (law firm), Martensville, IN, 1914; asst. prof. of Law, IN U., 1917–19, prof., 1919, dean of law school, 1925–33; chm., Faculty Board of Editors, *Indiana Law Journal*, 1926–33; partner, McNutt and Nash (law firm), New York, NY; partner, McNutt, Dudley and Easterwood (law firm), Washington, DC; chm. of the board, Philippine-American Life Insurance Co.; dir., American International Underwriters Corp.; dir., American International Marine Agency; dir., Globe and Rutgers Fire Insurance Co.; dir., American Home Assurance Co.; dir., American Life Insurance Co.; dir., American International Assurance Co. MIL.: capt., F.A. Reserves, U.S. Army, 1917; maj., F.A., U.S. Army, 1918, lt. col., 1919, col., 1923; instructor, Officers' Training Corps, Camp Stanley; commanding officer, 6th Regt., 5th Bde. and 2d Bde., F.A. Replacement Depot; commanding officer, 326th F.A., U.S. Army, 1924–37; member, V Corps Area Advisory Board, 1927–34. MEM.: National Governors' Conference (exec. cmte., 1933–36; chm., 1934–36); Council of State Governments (pres., 1936–37); Harvard Legal Aid Bureau (pres., 1915–16); Alumni Council, IN U. (1924–30); ABA; IN Bar Assn. (chm., Cmte. on Legal Education, 1927); American Law Inst.; Assn. of American Law Schools; AAUP; Reserve Officers Assn. of the U.S.; American Peace Soc.; Order of the Coif; Phi Beta Kappa; Sigma Delta Chi; Beta Theta Pi; Phi Delta Phi; Acacia; Tau Kappa Alpha; American Legion (commander, Burton Woolery Post, 1925–26; IN state commander, 1927; member, National Exec. Cmte., 1927–28; national commander, 1928–29); American Legion Publishing Corp. (dir., 1928–31; pres., 1928–29); Masons (32°); Elks; University Club; Rotary Club; Kiwanis; Army and Navy Club; Metropolitan Club; Burning Tree Club; Chevy Chase Club; Wall Street Club. AWARDS: Medal for Merit (U.S.); Distinguished Service Star (Philippine Islands); Grand Cordon, Order of Cambodia (Indo-China); commander, Order of Polonia Restituta (Poland); commander, Legion of Honor (France); commander, Legion of Honor (Philippines). HON. DEG.: LL.D., IN U., 1933; LL.D., U. of Notre Dame, 1933; LL.D., Bethany Coll., 1936; D.H., FL Southern U., 1939; LL.D., U. of the Philippines, 1939; LL.D., American U., 1941; LL.D., U. of MD, 1941; D.C.L., Boston U., 1942. WRITINGS: *Indiana General Corporation Act Annotated* (ed.; with F. E. Schortmeier, 1929). REL.: Methodist. RES.: Indianapolis, IN.

McREYNOLDS, DAVID ERNEST. b. Oct 25, 1929, Los Angeles, CA; par. Charles Francis and Elizabeth Grace (Tallon) McReynolds; single. EDUC.: B.A., U. of CA at Los Angeles, 1953. POLIT. & GOV.: Socialist (Socialist Democratic Federation) Party candidate for U.S. House (NY), 1958; Peace and Freedom Party candidate for U.S. House (NY), 1968; ***candidate for Socialist Party nomination to presidency of the U.S., 1976 (declined); Socialist Party candidate for presidency of the U.S., 1980; candidate for Peace and Freedom Party nomination to presidency of the U.S., 1980***. BUS. & PROF.: ditch-digger; meter reader; hot dog stand server, New York, NY; typist; employee, *Liberation Magazine*, 1957–; employee, War Resisters League, 1961–; contributor, *Village Voice*; contributor, *WIN*; pacifist movement organizer; active in radical community, 1949–. MEM.: War Resisters League (organizer); Fellowship of Reconciliation (National Council); International Confederation for Disarmament and Peace (International Council); A.C.L.U.; War Resisters International (International Council); Americans for Civil Liberties. WRITINGS: *We Have Been Invaded by the 21st Century* (1969). REL.: Bessie Smith. MAILING ADDRESS: 60 East 4th St., New York, NY 10003.

McWHIRTER, FELIX TONY. b. Jul 17, 1853, Lynchburg, TN; d. Jun 5, 1915, Indianapolis, IN; par. Dr. Samuel Hogg and Nancy C. (Tyree) McWhirter; m. Luella Frances

Smith, Nov 18, 1878; c. Susan M. (Mrs. Henry E. Ostrom); Luella S. (Mrs. Frank F. Hutchins); Ethel Tyree (Mrs. Thomas B. Scoggins); Felix Marcus. EDUC.: A.B., East TN Wesleyan U., 1873, A.M., 1876; Ph.D., De Pauw U., 1885; Johns Hopkins U., 1885–86. POLIT. & GOV.: elected mayor of Athens, TN, 1877–78; presidential elector, Prohibition Party, 1892; member, Prohibition Party National Cmte., 1892–1912 (treas., 1906–12; exec. cmte., 1905–12); chm., IN State Prohibition Party Central Cmte., 1893–94, 1896–98; delegate, Prohibition Party National Convention, 1896; Prohibition Party candidate for gov. of IN, 1904; ***candidate for Prohibition Party nomination to vice presidency of the U.S., 1912 (withdrew)***. BUS. & PROF.: banker; ed., *Athens News*, 1873–76; instructor, assoc. prof. of rhetoric and English literature, De Pauw U., 1884–88; owner, ed., *Chattanooga (TN) Advocate*; real estate broker, Indianapolis, IN, 1888–1900; pres., People's State Bank, Indianapolis, 1900–1915. MEM.: IN Children's Home Finding Soc. (first vice pres., 1909–11); Indianapolis C. of C.; Delta Kappa Epsilon; Masons. WRITINGS: *Three Business Men; The Economic Phase of the Liquor Problem; A Series of Notable Debates by Men of the Hour, Dry—Wet* (contributor, 1909). REL.: Methodist Episc. Church. RES.: Indianapolis, IN.

MEAD, JAMES MICHAEL. b. Dec 27, 1885, Mount Morris, NY; d. Mar 15, 1964, Lakeland, FL; par. Thomas and Mary Jane (Kelly) Mead; m. Alice M. Dillon, Aug 25, 1915; c. James Michael, Jr. EDUC.: grammar school; evening school. POLIT. & GOV.: elected as a Democrat, member, Board of Supervisors, Erie Cty., NY, 1914; elected as a Democrat to NY State Assembly, 1915–19; elected as a Democrat to U.S. House (NY), 1919–38; elected as a Democrat to U.S. Senate (NY), 1938–47; ***candidate for Democratic nomination to vice presidency of the U.S., 1940***; candidate for Democratic nomination to gov. of NY, 1942; Democratic candidate for gov. of NY, 1946; appointed chm., commissioner, Federal Trade Comm., 1949–55; delegate, Dem. Nat'l. Cmte., 1952; dir., Washington office, NY State Dept. of Commerce, 1955–56. BUS. & PROF.: lamplighter; track walker, Erie R.R.; employee, Pullman Co.; policeman, Washington, DC, 1911–12; co-owner, Buffalo Baseball Club; orange grower, Clermont, FL. MEM.: National Assn. of Retired Civil Service Employees (vice pres., 1958–62); Postal Colony (dir.); Elks; Moose; Knights of Columbus. HON. DEG.: LL.D., Niagara U., 1937; LL.D., Adelphi Coll., 1946. WRITINGS: *Tell The Folks Back Home* (1944). REL.: R.C. MISC.: noted athlete. RES.: Buffalo, NY.

MEAD, JOHN ABNER. b. Apr 20, 1841, Fairhaven, VT; d. Jan 12, 1920, Rutland, VT; par. Roswell Rowley and Lydia Ann (Gorham) Mead; m. Mary Madelia Sherman, Oct 30, 1872; c. Mary Sherman (Mrs. Carl B. Hinsman). EDUC.: Franklin Acad.; A.B., Middlebury Coll., 1864; M.D., Coll. of Physicians and Surgeons, Columbia U., 1868. POLIT. & GOV.: member, VT State Pension Examining Board, 8 years; appointed surgeon gen. of VT, 1878–79; elected as a Republican to VT State Senate, 1892; elected as a Republican to mayor of Rutland, VT, 1893; appointed VT commissioner, Chicago Exposition, 1893; appointed VT commissioner, Mexican National Exposition, 1895; elected as a Republican to VT State House, 1906–08; elected as a Republican to lt. gov. of VT, 1908–09; elected as a Republican to gov. of VT, 1910–12; delegate, Rep. Nat'l. Conv., 1912; ***candidate for Republican nomination to vice presidency of the U.S., 1912***. BUS. & PROF.: surgeon; medical practice, Rutland, VT, 1868–88; prof. of medical school, U. of VT, 1888; treas., Rutland R.R. Co., 1880–86; pres., Vermont State Trust Co., 1881–86; treas., Addison R.R. Co., 1880–86; pres., Howe Scale Co., 1888–1920; pres., Baxter National Bank, 1904–20; dir., National Bank of Rutland; dir., Clement National Bank; pres., New England Fire Insurance Co.; pres., Chase Manufacturing Co.; pres., J. A. Mead Manufacturing Co. MIL.: pvt., 12th VT Volunteers, 1862–63. MEM.: GAR; Rutland Board of Trade (pres.); Delta Kappa Epsilon; Shriner; Middlebury Coll. (trustee). HON. DEG.: LL.D., Middlebury Coll.; LL.D., Norwich U.; LL.D., U. of VT. REL.: Congregationalist. MISC.: first mayor of Rutland, VT. RES.: Rutland, VT.

MEADOR, EDWARD KIRBY. b. Nov 6, 1885, Bedford Cty., VA; par. Jeremiah Wellington and Eliza (Lee) Meador; m. Jean Campbell Isner, 1932. POLIT. & GOV.: ***Greenback Party candidate for vice presidency of the U.S., 1952, 1956, 1960***. BUS. & PROF.: owner, Meador Publishing Co., Boston, MA; owner, Forum Publishing Co., Boston. WRITINGS: *Scrapbook of Freedom, Liberty and Democracy* (1927); *Experience of a Heart* (1931); *Literary Opportunity for Writers* (1934); *The Meadors and the Meadows* (1941); *The Meadors of Virginia* (1941); *The National Forum and University of Government and Leadership* (1962). RES.: Boston, MA.

MEADOWS, SHERRY ANN. POLIT. & GOV.: ***candidate for Democratic nomination to president of the United States, 1992***. MAILING ADDRESS: 3303 Cambridge Dr., Arlington, TX 76013.

MEADS, MORTON FREDERICK. EDUC.: M.D. POLIT. & GOV.: chm., Christian Bull Moose–Flying Tiger Party; ***Christian Bull Moose–Flying Tiger (New Frontier; Black Ink) Party candidate for presidency of the U.S., 1976***. BUS. & PROF.: physician; pres., MacArthur International Minerals Co., Inc.; pres., Pabulum Agriculture Corp.; owner and sovereign, Meads-Spratly-Humanity Nanche Islands, Republic of Songhonti-Meads, South Hon-china Sea, Southeast Asia. MAILING ADDRESS: 214 South Dr., Hale Moku, Honolulu, HI.

MEANS, RUSSELL C. b. Pine Ridge Reservation, SD. POLIT. & GOV.: ***candidate for Republican nomination to vice presidency of the U.S., 1984; candidate for Libertarian***

Party nomination to vice presidency of the U.S., 1988. BUS. & PROF.: Native American rights activist. MEM.: American Indian Movement (spokesman, 18 years). MISC.: noted for leading Native American resistance effort at Wounded Knee, SD; member of Oglala Lakota Indian Nation. MAILING ADDRESS: 444 Crazy Horse Dr., Porcupine, SD 57772.

MECHAM, EVAN. b. May 12, 1924, Duchesne, UT; m. Florence Lambert; c. seven. EDUC.: UT State U., 1942–43; AZ State U., 1947–50. POLIT. & GOV.: elected as a Republican to AZ State Senate, 1961–63; Republican candidate for U.S. Senate (AZ), 1962; Republican candidate for gov. of AZ, 1978; elected as a Republican to gov. of AZ, 1987–88; ***candidate for Populist Party nomination to presidency of the U.S., 1988***; candidate for Republican nomination to gov. of AZ, 1990. BUS. & PROF.: owner, Pontiac Automobile Agency, Ajo, AZ, 1950–54; owner, Pontiac Automobile Agency, Glendale, AZ, 1954–88. MIL.: U.S. Air Force, 1943–46; prisoner-of-war in Germany. MEM.: American Newspaper Group (pres.). WRITINGS: *Come Back America* (1982). REL.: Church of Jesus Christ of Latter-Day Saints. MAILING ADDRESS: P.O. Box 970, Glendale, AZ 85311.

MEEKINS, ISAAC MELSON. b. Feb 13, 1875, Tyrrell Cty., NC; d. Nov 21, 1946, Elizabeth City, NC; par. Jeremiah Charles and Mahalah Elizabeth (Melson) Meekins; m. Lena Allen, Jun 5, 1896; c. William Charles; Mahalah Melson (Mrs. Thomas MacMullan, Jr.); Isabella James (Mrs. Joseph John Combs); Jeremiah Charles; Mary Purefoy (Mrs. Oliver Fearing Gilbert, Jr.). EDUC.: Horner Military School; A.B., Wake Forest Coll., 1896. POLIT. & GOV.: elected as a Republican to mayor of Elizabeth City, NC, 1897; city atty., Elizabeth City, 1898; member, NC Republican State Central Cmte., 1900–1918; chm., Pasquotank Cty. (NC) Republican Central Cmte.; appointed postmaster, Elizabeth City, 1903–08; appointed asst. U.S. atty., Eastern District of NC, 1910–14; superintendent of public instruction, Pasquotank Cty.; chm., Board of Trustees of Graded Schools, Elizabeth City, 1913–17; appointed gen. counsel, Alien Property Custodian, 1921–23; appointed judge, U.S. District Court, Eastern District of NC, 1925–45; ***candidate for Republican nomination to presidency of the U.S., 1936***. BUS. & PROF.: atty.; admitted to NC Bar, 1896; partner, Griffin and Meekins (law firm), Elizabeth City, 1896; law practice, Elizabeth City, to 1916; partner, Meekins and McMullan (law firm), Elizabeth City, 1916–22; appointed gen. counsel and mgr., Enemy Insurance Companies, 1923–25; sec., treas., E. J. Johnson Co., Norfolk, VA; plantation owner. MEM.: ABA; NC State Bar Assn.; Elizabeth City Bar Assn.; Knights of Pythias; Masons (32°; Shriner). HON. DEG.: LL.D., Wake Forest Coll., 1932. REL.: Bapt. RES.: Elizabeth City, NC.

MEIER, EDWARD J. POLIT. & GOV.: ***Progressive Party candidate for presidency of the U.S., 1916***. RES.: MN.

MELFI, ROBERT VETO. POLIT. & GOV.: ***independent candidate for presidency of the U.S., 1988***. MAILING ADDRESS: 5433 N.E. Second Terrace, Fort Lauderdale, FL 33334.

MELLEN, GEORGE WASHINGTON FROST. b. 1804; d. 1875. POLIT. & GOV.: ***independent candidate for presidency of the U.S., 1856***. BUS. & PROF.: chemist; publisher, *The Gridiron*; ed., *Habeas Corpus and Scientific Journal*, 1855. MEM.: Masons. WRITINGS: *An Argument on the Unconstitutionalist of Slavery* (1841). MISC.: noted abolitionist; known as "poor, demented Mellen" and "a deranged spirit"; died in an insane asylum. RES.: Boston, MA.

MELLON, ANDREW WILLIAM. b. Mar 24, 1855, Pittsburgh, PA; d. Aug 26, 1937, Southhampton, Long Island, NY; par. Thomas and Sarah Jane (Negley) Mellon; m. Nora McMullen, Sep 12, 1900; c. Ailsa (Mrs. David Kirkpatrick Este Bruce); Paul. EDUC.: Western U. of PA. POLIT. & GOV.: appointed member, exec. cmte., PA State Council of Defense, WWI; delegate, Rep. Nat'l. Conv., 1920; appointed U.S. sec. of the treasury, 1921–32; appointed chm., World War Foreign Debt Comm., 1922; appointed chm., Federal Reserve Board; dir.-gen., U.S. Railroad Administration; appointed member, Board of Directors, RFC; appointed chm., Federal Farm Loan Board; appointed chm., U.S. Section, Inter-American High Comm.; appointed trustee, Postal Savings System; ***candidate for Republican nomination to presidency of the U.S., 1928***; delegate, International Finance Conference, 1931; appointed U.S. ambassador to England, 1932–33. BUS. & PROF.: employee, T. Mellon and Sons (banking house), 1874–87, senior partner, 1887–1902; founder, Union Trust Co., 1889; oil producer, 1890–95; founder, pres., Union Savings Bank of Pittsburgh; pres., Mellon National Bank, 1902–21; founder, Gulf Oil Corp.; founder, dir., Aluminum Co. of America; founder, Union Steel Co.; founder, Koppers Gas and Coke Co.; founder, Carborundum Co.; founder, McClintic-Marshall Construction Co.; founder, Standard Steel Car Co.; founder, New York Shipbuilding Co. MEM.: Pittsburgh Maternity Hospital (dir.); American Red Cross (War Council); YMCA (War Council); National Research Council (Advisory Cmte.); U. of PA (trustee); Mellon Inst. of Industrial Research (founder, 1931); A. W. Mellon Educational and Charitable Trust (founder, 1930); Carnegie Library (trustee); Carnegie Inst. of Technology (trustee); PA Coll. for Women (trustee). AWARDS: Chemists' Medal, American Inst. of Chemists. HON. DEG.: LL.D., U. of Pittsburgh, 1921; LL.D., Dartmouth Coll., 1922; LL.D., Columbia U., 1923; LL.D., NY U., 1923; LL.D., PA Military Acad., 1923; LL.D., Princeton U., 1923; LL.D., Rutgers U., 1923; LL.D., Kenyon Coll., 1925; LL.D., Amherst Coll., 1926; LL.D., Harvard U., 1926; LL.D., Yale U., 1926; LL.D., U. of PA, 1928; LL.D., Trinity Coll. of Hartford, 1929; LL.D., Cambridge U., 1931; LL.D., St. Lawrence U., 1931; LL.D., U. of Edinburgh, 1931. WRITINGS: *Taxation: The People's Business* (1924). REL.: Presb. MISC.: donated art collection to U.S. government to form National Gallery of Art, 1937. RES.: Pittsburgh, PA.

MENCKEN, HENRY LOUIS. b. Sep 12, 1880, Baltimore, MD; d. Jan 29, 1956, Baltimore, MD; par. August and Anna (Abhau) Mencken; single. EDUC.: grad., Baltimore Polytechnical Inst., 1896. POLIT. & GOV.: ***candidate for Democratic nomination to vice presidency of the U.S., 1912***. BUS. & PROF.: ed.; author; critic; humorist; reporter, *Baltimore (MD) Morning Herald*, 1899, city ed., 1903–05; ed., *Baltimore Evening Herald*, 1905; staff, *Baltimore Sun*, 1906–17; ed., literary critic, *The Smart Set*, 1908–23; columnist, *Baltimore Evening Sun*, 1919–; contributing ed., *Nation*, 1921; cofounder, ed., *American Mercury*, 1923–. WRITINGS: *Ventures into Verse* (1901); *George Bernard Shaw: His Plays* (1905); *The Philosophy of Friedrich Nietzsche* (1908); *Men vs. the Man* (with R. R. La Monte, 1910); *The Artist* (1912); *Europe After 8:15* (with George Jean Nathan and Willard H. Wright, 1914); *A Book of Burlesques* (1916); *A Little Book in C Major* (1916); *A Book of Prefaces* (1917); *In Defense of Women* (1917); *Damn: A Book of Calumny* (1917); *The Players Edition of Ibsen's Plays* (ed., 1909); *The American Language* (1918); *The Free Lance Books* (1919); *Prejudices: First Series* (1919); *Prejudices: Second Series* (1920); *The American Credo* (with George Jean Nathan, 1920); *Heliogabalus* (with George Jean Nathan, 1920); *Prejudices: Third Series* (1922); *Prejudices: Fourth Series* (1924); *Notes on Democracy* (1926); *Treatise of the Gods* (1930); *Making a President* (1932); *Happy Days* (1940); *Newspaper Days* (1941); *Heathen Days* (1943); *Minority Report* (1956). MISC.: known as the "Sage of Baltimore." RES.: Baltimore, MD.

MENDEZ, RAFAEL. EDUC.: Harvard U. POLIT. & GOV.: New Alliance Party candidate for lt. gov. of NY, 1986; candidate for Democratic nomination to Bronx Borough (NY) pres., 1987; New Alliance Party candidate for U.S. House (NY), 1988; ***New Alliance Party candidate for vice presidency of the U.S., 1988***. BUS. & PROF.: psychologist; soldier. MIL.: U.S. Army, Vietnam. MEM.: Bronx People's Independent Democratic Club (pres.). MAILING ADDRESS: c/o New Alliance Party, 1045 Southern Blvd., Suite 2, Bronx, NY 10459.

MERCER, DAVID HENRY. b. Jul 9, 1857, Benton Cty., IA; d. Jan 10, 1919, Omaha, NE; par. John J. and Elizabeth Mercer; m. Birdie Abbott, Jun 6, 1894. EDUC.: B.L., U. of NE, 1880; LL.B., U. of MI, 1882. POLIT. & GOV.: city clerk, police judge, Brownville, NE; sec., NE State Republican Central Cmte., 1884–85; chm., Republican City Central Cmte., Omaha, NE, 1887–90; chm., Republican Cty. Central Cmte. (NE), 1890–92; elected as a Republican to U.S. House (NE), 1893–1903; sec., Republican National Congressional Cmte., 1896; chm., NE State Republican Central Cmte., 1897–98; ***candidate for Republican nomination to vice presidency of the U.S., 1900***; special counsel, NE State Council of Defense, 1917. BUS. & PROF.: atty.; law practice, Brownville, 1882–85; law practice, Omaha, NE, 1885–1919. MEM.: Douglas Cty. Pioneer Assn. (pres., 1918). RES.: Omaha, NE.

MERCER, GARY RAYMOND. POLIT. & GOV.: ***independent candidate for presidency of the U.S., 1988***. MAILING ADDRESS: 425 Second St., N.W., Washington, DC 20001.

MERCER, RUPERT LEWIS "BOB." POLIT. & GOV.: ***independent candidate for presidency of the U.S., 1992 (withdrew)***. MISC.: antisemitic candidate. MAILING ADDRESS: Route 7, Box 439, Tifton, GA 31794.

MERE, MIRA. POLIT. & GOV.: ***Mere Party candidate for presidency of the U.S., 1980***. MAILING ADDRESS: Bayside, Humboldt Cty., CA.

MEREDITH, EDWIN THOMAS. b. Dec 23, 1876, Avoca, IA; d. Jun 17, 1928, Des Moines, IA; par. Thomas Oliver and Minnie Minerva Jane (Marsh) Meredith; m. Edna C. Elliott, Jan 8, 1896; c. Edwin Thomas, Jr.; Mildred Marie (Mrs. Frederick Owen Bohen). EDUC.: Highland Park Coll., 1893–94. POLIT. & GOV.: Democratic candidate for U.S. Senate (IA), 1914; Democratic candidate for gov. of IA, 1916; appointed member, Board of Excess Profit Advisors, 1917; appointed dir., Federal Reserve Bank, Chicago, IL, 1918–20; appointed member, Industrial Conference, 1919; appointed U.S. sec. of agriculture, 1920–21; delegate, Dem. Nat'l. Conv., 1920, 1924; ***candidate for Democratic nomination to presidency of the U.S., 1920, 1924, 1928; candidate for Democratic nomination to vice presidency of the U.S., 1920, 1924***. BUS. & PROF.: publisher, *Farmers' Tribune, 1896–1902*; ed., *Successful Farming*, 1902–28; dir., Iowa Trust and Savings Bank; publisher, *Fruit, Garden and Home*, 1922–24; publisher, *Better Homes and Gardens*, 1924–28; publisher, *Dairy Farmer*, 1922. MEM.: Masons (32°); Agricultural Publishers Assn. (vice pres.; pres.); Des Moines Club; Grant Club; Hypoerion Club; Commercial Club; Wakonda Club; Associated Advertising Clubs of the World (pres., 1919); U.S. C. of C. (dir., 1915–19, 1923–28). HON. DEG.: LL.D., Highland Park Coll., 1916; D.Ag., MD State Agricultural Coll., 1920. REL.: Methodist. MISC.: known as founder of Jefferson Highway. RES.: Des Moines, IA.

MEREPEACE, MISSISSIPPI. POLIT. & GOV.: ***independent candidate for presidency of the U.S., 1992***. MISC.: possibly Mira Mere (q.v.). MAILING ADDRESS: ID?

MERRIAM, CHARLES EDWARD. b. Nov 15, 1874, Hopkinton, IA; d. Jan 8, 1953, Rockville, MD; par. Charles Edward and Margaret Campbell (Kirkwood) Merriam;

m. Elizabeth Hilda Doyle, Aug 3, 1901; c. Charles James; John Francis; Elizabeth; Robert Edward. EDUC.: A.B., Lenox Coll., 1893; A.B., State U. of IA, 1895; A.M., Columbia U., 1897, Ph.D., 1900; studied in Berlin and Paris, 1899–1900. POLIT. & GOV.: elected as a Republican to Chicago (IL) Board of Aldermen, 1909–11, 1913–17; Republican candidate for mayor of Chicago, 1911; ***candidate for Republican nomination to vice presidency of the U.S., 1912***; appointed pres., Aviation Examining Board; appointed commissioner of America on public information, Italy, 1918; appointed member, Hoover Comm. on Recent Social Trends; appointed member, National Resources Board, 1933–43; appointed member, President's Comm. on Administrative Management, 1936; appointed member, U.S. Loyalty Review Board, 1947–48. BUS. & PROF.: docent in political science, U. of Chicago, 1900–1902, assoc., 1902–03, instructor, 1903–05, asst. prof., 1905–07, assoc. prof., 1907–11, prof., 1911–53. MIL.: capt., Signal Reserve Corps, 1917. MEM.: Social Science Research Council (pres., 1924–27); APSA (pres., 1924–25); American Phil. Soc.; American Acad. of Political and Social Science (vice pres., 1924); Quadrangle Club; City Club; University Club; Comm. on Freedom of the Press (1944–47). AWARDS: commander, Order of the Crown of Italy, 1921. HON. DEG.: LL.D., U. of CO, 1920; LL.D., U. of MI, 1935; LL.D., Princeton U., 1946; LL.D., Washington U., 1946; LL.D., Yale U., 1951. WRITINGS: *The History of the Theory of Sovereignty Since Rousseau* (1900); *A History of American Political Theories* (1903); *Municipal Revenues of Chicago* (1906); *Primary Elections* (1908); *American Political Ideas, 1865–1917* (1921); *The American Party System* (1922); *Non-voting* (with H. F. Gosnell, 1924); *New Aspects of Politics* (1925); *History of Political Theories* (ed.); *Recent Times* (1924); *Four American Party Leaders* (1926); *Chicago* (1929); *The Making of Citizens* (1931); *The Written Constitution* (1931); *Metropolitan Region of Chicago* (coauthor, 1933); *Recent Social Trends in the United States* (1933); *Civic Education in the United States* (1934); *Political Power* (1934); *Role of Politics in Social Change* (1936); *The New Democracy and the New Despotism* (1939); *Prologue to Politics* (1939); *What is Democracy?* (1941); *On the Agenda of Democracy* (1941); *Public and Private Government* (1944); *Systematic Politics* (1945); *The American Government* (with Robert E. Merriam, 1954). MISC.: known as the "Woodrow Wilson of the West" for his progressive leadership in municipal reform; one of the founders of the behavioral movement in political science. RES.: Chicago, IL.

MERRIAM, FRANK FINLEY. b. Dec 22, 1865, Hopkinton, IA; d. Apr 25, 1955, Long Beach, CA; par. Henry Clay and Ann Elizabeth (Finley) Merriam; m. Nancy Elnora Hitchcock, Jul 10, 1889; m. 2d, Mary Bronson Day, Dec 21, 1903; m. 3d, Jessie (Stewart) Lipsey, Jan 25, 1936; c. Howard. EDUC.: A.B., Lenox Coll., 1888. POLIT. & GOV.: appointed clerk, IA State House, 1892, 1894; dir., Speaker's Bureau, IA Republican State Central Cmte., 1892; elected as a Republican to IA State House, 1895–99; elected as a Republican to state auditor of IA, 1899–1903; elected as a Republican to CA State Assembly, 1917–27 (Speaker, 1923–27); chm., CA Republican State Central Cmte., 1928; elected as a Republican to CA State Senate, 1929–31; elected as a Republican to lt. gov. of CA, 1931–35; succeeded to and subsequently elected as a Republican to gov. of CA, 1934–39; ***candidate for Republican nomination to presidency of the U.S., 1936***; Republican candidate for gov. of CA, 1938; chm., CA State Advisory Pardon Board, 4 years; member, CA State Toll Bridge authority, 8 years (chm., 4 years). BUS. & PROF.: schoolteacher, Hopkinton, IA, 1888–91; school principal, Hasper, IA; superintendent of schools, Postville, IA; owner, publisher, *Hopkinton Leader*, 1893–98; owner, *Muskogee (OK) Evening Times*, 1904; employee, advertising dept., *Long Beach (CA) Telegram*, 1910–11; advertising mgr., *Long Beach Press*, 1912–24; pres., Citizens State Bank of Long Beach, 1924–26; realtor, Long Beach; peach grower; rancher. MEM.: U. of CA (regent, 12 years); BSA (chm., Long Beach Council); American Red Cross (pres., Local Chapter); Harbor District Chambers of Commerce (pres.); SAR; Sons of Veterans; Masons; CA Publishers and Press Assn.; Lincoln Club; Men's Brotherhood Sunday School Class (pres.); CA Real Estate Assn. (hon. pres.). REL.: Presb. (Sunday school superintendent). RES.: Long Beach, CA.

MERRILL, GARY FRANKLIN. b. Aug 2, 1915, Hartford, CT; d. Mar 5, 1990, Falmouth, ME; par. B. Gary and Hazel (Andrews) Merrill; m. Barbara Leeds, Nov 1941 (divorced, 1950); m. 2d, Bette Davis, Jul 1950 (divorced, 1960); c. one son; two daughters. EDUC.: grad., Loomis Preparatory School, 1933; Bowdoin Coll., 1933–34; Trinity Coll., 1934–35. POLIT. & GOV.: candidate for Republican nomination to U.S. House (ME), 1968; ***candidate for Democratic nomination to presidency of the U.S., 1976***. BUS. & PROF.: actor; television and stage performer, 1937–90. STAGE CREDITS: *The Eternal Road*; *Morning Star*; *See My Lawyer*; *Young Dr. Malone*; *Helen Hayes Theatre*; *Theatre Guild*; *Gangbusters*; *Superman*; *Born Yesterday*. Motion Picture Credits: *Winged Victory* (1944); *Slattery's Hurricane* (1949); *Twelve O'Clock High* (1949); *Where the Sidewalk Ends* (1950); *All About Eve* (1950); *Another Man's Poison* (1951); *The Frogmen* (1951); *Decision Before Dawn* (1952); *Girl in White*; *Night Without Sleep* (1952); *Phone Call From a Stranger* (1953); *Blueprint for Murder* (1954); *The Black Dakotas* (1954); *The Human Jungle* (1954); *Bermuda Affair* (1956); *Pleasure of His Company* (1961); *Clambake*; *The Incident*; *The Last Challenge*; *Farewell in Hong Kong* (1961); *At War With the Army*; *Mysterious Island* (1961); *A Girl Named Tamiko* (1962); *The Woman Who Wouldn't Die* (1965); *Around the World Under the Sea* (1966); *Destination Inner Space* (1966); *Catacombs* (1966); *The Power* (1968); *Huckleberry Finn* (1974); *Thieves* (1977). TELEVISION CREDITS: *The Mask* (1954); *Justice* (1954–55); *Reporter* (1964); Dr. Gillespie, *Young Dr. Kildare* (1973); narrator, *The Valiant Years*. MIL.: sgt., U.S. Army, 1941–45. MEM.: Screen Actors Guild; Actors' Equity Assn.; A.F.T.R.A. WRITINGS: *Bette, Rita and the Rest of My Life* (1988). RES.: Falmouth, ME.

MERWIN, JOHN DAVID. b. Sep 26, 1921, Frederiksted, St. Crois, Virgin Islands; par. Miles and Marguerite Louise (Fleming) Merwin; m. Ludmila D. Childs, Nov 8, 1958; m. 2d, (unknown). EDUC.: U. of Lausanne, 1938–39; U. of Puerto Rico, 1939–40; B.Sc., Yale U., 1943; LL.B., George Washington U., 1948. POLIT. & GOV.: elected to Virgin Islands Territorial Senate, 1955–57; appointed government sec., Virgin Islands, 1957–58; appointed to gov. of Virgin Islands, 1958–61; ***candidate for Republican nomination to presidency of the U.S., 1992***. BUS. & PROF.: atty.; admitted to CT Bar, 1949; admitted to Bar of the Virgin Islands, 1949; law practice, Virgin Islands, 1949–50; law practice, St. Croix, 1953–57; vice pres., gen. counsel, Robert L. Merwin and Co., Inc., 1953–57; banker; businessman; retired, 1984. MIL.: 2d lt., capt., U.S. Army, 1942–46, 1950–53; Bronze Star; Croix de Guerre with Silver Star (France). MEM.: American Soc. of International Law; International Bar Assn.; ABA; Phi Delta Phi; Republican Club of St. Croix (vice pres.). MAILING ADDRESS: P.O. Box 297, Mountain View Rd., Easton, NH 03580.

MESS, ROBERT BRUCE. b. Nov 24, 1937, Manistee, MI; par. Gordon B. and Betty Jane (Munson) Mess; m. Mitzi Ackerman; c. Robert Bruce, Jr.; William John; Carolyn Jo. EDUC.: Shortridge H.S., Indianapolis, IN; U. of Cincinnati. POLIT. & GOV.: ***candidate for American Party nomination to vice presidency of the U.S., 1972 (withdrew); independent candidate for vice presidency of the U.S., 1972***. BUS. & PROF.: promotional mgr., RCA; sales mgr., Ellis Trucking Co.; owner, gen. mgr., land development company; sales mgr., Office Automation of Alabama, Inc.; vice pres., Lee S. Ledgerwood and Associates (turnkey developers of college housing facilities). MEM.: Optimists; Junior C. of C.; Kiwanis; Mystic Tie Blue Lodge; Sigma Alpha Epsilon. REL.: Lutheran. MAILING ADDRESS: 3332 Valley Park Dr., Birmingham, AL 35243.

MESSENGER, JAMES ROBERT. b. Sep 4, 1948, Miami, FL; par. Robert R. and Kathryn (Trotman) Messenger; single. EDUC.: NY U., 1966–67; A.A., Middle Georgia Coll., 1967–68; A.B., U. of GA, 1972. POLIT. & GOV.: ***candidate for Democratic nomination to presidency of the U.S., 1988***. BUS. & PROF.: management consultant, John Williamson and Associates, Birmingham, AL, 1972–75; writer, producer, dir., Charlie Papa Productions, Rockville, MD, 1975–80; pres., Penguin Productions, Ltd., Silver Spring, MD, 1980–82; public relations mgr., American Telephone and Telegraph, Bedminster, NJ, 1982–. MEM.: Essex Skating Club; Public Relations Soc. of America; International Television Assn. AWARDS: Emmy Award; 2 Acad. Award nominations; Corporate Identity Award, Public Relations Soc. of America (twice). WRITINGS: *Excuse Me, Please, But I'd Like My Government Back* (1984). REL.: Southern Bapt. MAILING ADDRESS: P.O. Box 217, Piscataway, NJ 08855-0217.

MESSIAH (See SITNICK, FRED IRWIN)

MESTICE, WILLIAM R. POLIT. & GOV.: ***independent candidate for presidency of the U.S., 1980***. MAILING ADDRESS: 120 Ridge Ave., Neptune City, NJ 07753.

METCALF, HENRY BREWER. b. Apr 2, 1829, Boston, MA; d. Oct 8, 1904, Pawtucket, RI; m. Elizabeth Freeman, May 4, 1854. EDUC.: grad., English H.S., Boston, MA. POLIT. & GOV.: elected as a Republican to Pawtucket (RI) Town Council; elected as a Republican to RI State Senate, 1885–87; Republican candidate for RI State Senate, 1886; Prohibition Party candidate for gov. of RI, 1893, 1894, 1900, 1904; chm., RI State Prohibition Convention, 1896; Prohibition Party candidate for U.S. House (RI), 1896; member, Prohibition Party National Cmte., 1896–1904; ***Prohibition Party candidate for vice presidency of the U.S., 1900***. BUS. & PROF.: manufacturer; apprentice, wholesale dry goods business, to 1872; editorial staff, *New York (NY) Mail and Express*; treas., Providence County Savings Bank; treas., several manufacturing firms. MEM.: Tufts Coll. (trustee; pres., 1898–1904); National Temperance Soc.; RI Temperance Union (pres.). HON. DEG.: A.M., Tufts Coll., 1886. WRITINGS: *The Duty of the Hour* (1894). REL.: Universalist (Sunday school superintendent; pres., National Convention). RES.: Pawtucket, RI.

METCALF, JACK HOLACE. b. Nov 30, 1927, Marysville, WA; par. John Read and Eunice (Grannis) Metcalf; m. Norma Jean Grant, Oct 3, 1948; c. Marta Jean (Mrs. Rob Cahill); Gaylle Marie; Lea Lynn (Mrs. Ron Kellogg); Beverlee Ann (Mrs. Dave Bowman). EDUC.: U. of WA, 1944–46, 1965–66; B.A., B.Ed., Pacific Lutheran U., 1951. POLIT. & GOV.: elected as a Republican to WA State House, 1961–65; pres., WA State Young Republicans, 1964–65; elected as a Republican to WA State Senate, 1967–75, 1981–93; candidate for Republican nomination to U.S. Senate (WA), 1974; ***Populist Party candidate for presidency of the U.S., 1984***; elected as a Republican to U.S. House (WA), 1995–. BUS. & PROF.: teacher, Elma (WA) public schools, 1951–52; teacher, Everett (WA) public schools, 1952–81; businessman; owner, Log Castle Bed and Breakfast, 1974–. MIL.: pvt., U.S. Army, 1946–47. MEM.: Kiwanis; Whidbey Island Transportation Assn.; Elks; American Legislative Exchange Council; Honest Money for America (chm.); Council of State Governments; WA Assn. of Professional Educators (pres., 1977–79; vice pres., 1979–81); WA Education Assn. (dir., 1959–61). REL.: Christian (Unity). MAILING ADDRESS: 3273 East Saratoga Rd., Langley, WA 98260.

METZ, HERMAN AUGUST. b. Oct 19, 1867, New York, NY; d. May 17, 1934, New Rochelle, NY; par. August and Elizabeth Metz; m. Laura Alice Trant, 1891; c. Harry; Richard; Donald; Eugene. EDUC.: grad., Public School 13, New York, NY; Newark (NJ) H.S., 1 year; grad., Cooper Union Evening School. POLIT. & GOV.: Independent Democratic candidate for alderman, Brooklyn, NY; Independent Democratic candidate for U.S. House (NY); delegate, Dem. Nat'l. Conv., 1896, 1904, 1908, 1920; appointed member, Brooklyn (NY) Board of Education; appointed member, Greater New York Board of Education; elected as a Democrat, comptroller of New York, 1906–10; appointed member, New York City Charter Comm., 1907–08, 1922; appointed commissioner, NY State Board of Charities; ***candidate for Democratic nomination to vice presidency of the U.S., 1912***; elected as a Democrat to U.S. House (NY), 1913–15; Democratic candidate for U.S. House (NY), 1922. BUS. & PROF.: office boy, office of Paul Schulze-Berge, laboratory asst., clerk, salesman, agent and mgr., Boston, MA; manufacturer and importer of dyestuffs, chemicals, and pharmaceuticals; vice pres., Victor Koechl and Co., 1893–99, pres., 1899–1934; pres., H. A. Metz and Co., 1903–34; dir., Guardian Trust Co.; pres., Testileather Co.; pres., Hanseatic Corp.; pres., H. A. Metz Laboratories; pres., General Aniline Works, Inc.; dir., Bank of the United States; pres., Ettrick Realty Co.; pres., Consolidated Color and Chemical Co.; pres., General Dye-stuff Corp., 1926–34; pres., Advanced Solvents and Chemical Corp.; dir., Interborough Rapid Transit Co.; dir., Fulton Savings Bank; vice pres., treas., American I. G. Chemical Corp.; dir., Bank of the Manhattan Co. MIL.: 1st lt., capt., lt. col., brig. gen., 14th Infantry, NY National Guard; lt. col., 27th Div., U.S. Army, 1917–19; col., Ordnance Dept., ORC. MEM.: American C. of C. of Paris; Engineers Club of Boston; Army and Navy Club; Aeronautical Soc. of NY (dir.); Brooklyn Acad. of Music (dir.); German Seminary Endowment Assn. (treas.); Kings Cty. Democratic Club (pres., 1903); National Civic Club of NY (treas.; pres.); NY Reform Club (trustee); Manufacturers Assn.; Brooklyn League; NAM; Merchants Assn. of NY; NY C. of C.; NY Board of Trade and Transportation; London Soc. of Chemical Industry; Soc. of Chemical Industry of Germany; Soc. of Chemical Industry of France; Deutscher Chemiker Verein; American Chemical Soc.; Electro-Chemical Soc.; Long Island Kennel Club; Germania Club; Bushwick Club; Lincoln Club; Manhattan Club; Lotus Club; Pleiades Club; Democratic Club of NY; Salmagundi Club; Thirteen Club; Chemists Club of NY; Wool Club of NY; NY Drug Club; Masons (32°; Palestine Commandery; Mecca Temple of the Mystic Shrine of NY; Commonwealth Lodge 409; Jerusalem Chapter 8; Adelphi Council; Royal Arcanum); Adelphia Coll. (trustee); Board of Trade for German-American Commerce (pres., 1924–34). HON. DEG.: Sc.D., Union Coll., 1911; LL.D., Manhattan Coll., 1914. REL.: Protestant. RES.: New York, NY.

METZENBAUM, HOWARD MORTON. b. Jun 4, 1917, Cleveland, OH; par. Charles I. and Anna (Klafter) Metzenbaum; m. Shirley Turoff, Aug 8, 1946; c. Barbara Jo Bonner; Susan Lynn (Mrs. Joel Hyatt); Shelley Hope; Amy Beth. EDUC.: B.A., OH State U., 1939, LL.D., 1941. POLIT. & GOV.: appointed member, War Labor Board, 1942–45; elected as a Democrat to OH State House, 1943–47; elected as a Democrat to OH State Senate, 1947–50; member, OH Bureau of Code Revision, 1949–50; campaign mgr., Stephen Young for U.S. Senate Campaign, 1958, 1964; delegate, Dem. Nat'l. Conv., 1964 (alternate), 1968; member, OH State Democratic Exec. Cmte., 1966–; Gold Star member, OH State Democratic Finance Council, 1969–; member, Cleveland (OH) Metropolitan Housing Authority, 1968–70; Democratic candidate for U.S. Senate (OH), 1970; member, Lake Erie Regional Transit Authority, 1972–73; appointed as a Democrat to U.S. Senate (OH), 1974; candidate for Democratic nomination to U.S. Senate (OH), 1974; elected as a Democrat to U.S. Senate (OH), 1977–1995; ***candidate for Democratic nomination to presidency of the U.S., 1980***. BUS. & PROF.: chm. of the board, Airport Parking Company of America, 1958–66; dir., Capital National Bank, 1962–68; chm. of the board, ITT Consumer Services Corp., 1966–68; dir., Soc. National Bank and Soc. Corp., 1968; chm. of the board, ComCorp, 1969–74; owner, Little Taverns; founder, partner, Metzenbaum, Gaines, Finley and Stern Co., L.P.A. MEM.: Mt. Sinai Hospital of Cleveland (trustee, 1961–73; treas., 1966–73); Council on Human Relations (dir.); United Cerebral Palsy Assn. (dir.); National Council on Hunger and Malnutrition (dir.); Karamu House (dir.); St. Vincent Charity Hospital (dir.); St. Jude Research Hospital (dir.); National Citizens Cmte. for the Conquest of Cancer (national co-chm.); Brandeis U. (vice chm., fellows); ABA; OH State Bar Assn.; Cuyahoga Cty. Bar Assn.; Cleveland Bar Assn.; American Assn. of Trial Lawyers; Order of the Coif; Phi Eta Sigma; Tau Epsilon Rho. AWARDS: Catholic Interracial Justice Award; Town Crier Award. REL.: Jewish. MAILING ADDRESS: 18500 North Park Blvd., Shaker Heights, OH 44118.

MEYER, CULLEN. b. 1922; m. Katrina M. Meyer. EDUC.: D.V.M., OH State U., 1944. POLIT. & GOV.: ***independent candidate for presidency of the U.S., 1992***. BUS. & PROF.: veterinarian; farmer. MAILING ADDRESS: 308 East Wooster St., Box 300, Navarre, OH 44662.

MEYER, WILLIAM CHRISTOPHER. b. Jul 5, 1937, Bellingham, WA; par. Henry Fred and Jane Millicent (Haggith) Meyer; m. Peggy Annette Silves; c. Randal Eugene; Marisa Jean Ottinger. EDUC.: B.A., Western WA U., 1961, M.A., 1965. POLIT. & GOV.: candidate for WA state superintendent of public instruction, 1988; ***candidate for Democratic nomination to presidency of the U.S., 1992***. BUS. & PROF.: teacher, 1961–71; high school principal, 1971–78; insurance agent, Prudential Insurance Co., 1978–83; salesman, Viacom and R. L. Polk, 1983–. REL.: Protestant. MAILING ADDRESS: 5428 Guide Meridian, Bellingham, WA 98226.

MEYERS, FRANK S. POLIT. & GOV.: ***candidate for Democratic nomination to vice presidency of the U.S.,***

1916; delegate, Dem. Nat'l. Conv., 1924. MISC.: stand-in for Thomas R. Marshall (q.v.), in OR Democratic vice presidential primary, 1916. RES.: Portland, OR.

MEYNER, ROBERT BAUMLE. b. Jul 3, 1908, Easton, PA; d. May 27, 1990, Captiva, FL; par. Gustave Herman and Mary Sophia (Baumle) Meyner; m. Helen Day Stevenson, Jan 19, 1957. EDUC.: A.B., Lafayette Coll., 1930; LL.B., Columbia U., 1933. POLIT. & GOV.: Hatcong Township (NJ) atty., 1936–41, 1948–90; Democratic candidate for NJ State Senate, 1941, 1951; cty. counsel, Warren Cty., NJ, 1942; Democratic candidate for U.S. House (NJ), 1946; elected as a Democrat to NJ State Senate, 1948–52 (Democratic minority leader, 1950); delegate, Dem. Nat'l. Conv., 1948, 1952 (alternate), 1956, 1960, 1964, 1968, 1976; appointed member, NJ Medical Coll. Comm., 1950; chm., NJ State Democratic Convention, 1951; elected as a Democrat to gov. of NJ, 1954–62; ***candidate for Democratic nomination to vice presidency of the U.S., 1956; candidate for Democratic nomination to presidency of the U.S., 1960***; Democratic candidate for gov. of NJ, 1969. BUS. & PROF.: atty.; admitted to NJ Bar, 1934; named counsellor in law, 1937; admitted to the Bar of the Supreme Court of the U.S., 1940; law clerk, Walscheid and Rosenkranz (law firm), Union City, NJ, 1934–36; law practice, Phillipsburg, NJ, 1936–53; partner, Meyner and Wiley (law firm), 1962–90; partner, Meyner, Landis and Verdon (law firm), Newark, NJ; administrator, Cigarette Advertising Code, 1964–90; dir., Prudential Insurance Co.; dir., Engelhard Minerals and Chemicals Corp.; dir., Phillipsburg National Bank and Trust Corp.; dir., First National Bank of Newark; dir., First National State Bancorp; dir., U.S. Savings Bank of Newark; dir., Delaware and Bound Brook R.R. MIL.: lt. (jg), U.S.N.R., 1942–45, commander, 1957. MEM.: Elks; Eagles; Odd Fellows; Moose; Rotary Club; ABA; American Bar Foundation (fellow); NJ State Bar Assn. (trustee, 1941–42, 1948–90); Warren Cty. Bar Assn.; Hudson Cty. Bar Assn.; Essex Cty. Bar Assn.; Grange; Essex Club; Columbia U. Club; River Club of NY; American Legion; VFW; American Acad. of Political and Social Sciences; Acad. of Political Science; Columbia U. Law School Alumni Assn. (vice pres.); Lafayette Coll. Alumni Assn.; Alpha Chi Rho; AmVets; Pomfret Club; Greater Newark C. of C.; NJ Practicing Law Inst. (trustee, 1947); Phillipsburg C. of C. (national counselor, 1940–43); Phillipsburg Civic Assn. (pres., 1939–41); Inter-racial Council for Business Opportunities (co-chm.); United Hospitals (vice pres.). HON. DEG.: LL.D., Lafayette Coll., 1954; LL.D., Rutgers U., 1954; LL.D., Princeton U., 1956; LL.D., Long Island U., 1958; LL.D., Fairleigh Dickinson Coll., 1959; LL.D., Lincoln U., 1960; LL.D., Syracuse U., 1960; LL.D., CO Coll., 1961. REL.: Protestant. RES.: Phillipsburg, NJ.

MICHAEL, ALLEN. b. 1918. POLIT. & GOV.: ***Synthesis Party candidate for presidency of the U.S., 1980, 1984***; Synthesis Party candidate for gov. of CA, 1982. BUS. & PROF.: writer. REL.: Christian. MISC.: noted as a "contactee" with extraterrestrials. MAILING ADDRESS: Stockton, CA.

MICHAEL, STEVEN D. POLIT. & GOV.: ***candidate for Republican nomination to presidency of the U.S., 1992***. MAILING ADDRESS: WA.

MICKELLS, KATHLEEN "KATHY." b. 1951, Omaha, NE. EDUC.: A.B., U. of NE, 1972. POLIT. & GOV.: Socialist Workers Party candidate for Washington Cty. (PA) Board of Commissioners, 1983; organizer, Socialist Workers Party, Pittsburgh, PA; organizer, Socialist Workers Party, Morgantown, WV; Socialist Workers Party candidate for U.S. House (WV), 1986; ***Socialist Workers Party candidate for vice presidency of the U.S., 1988***. BUS. & PROF.: employee, deptartment store, Omaha, NE, 1966; assembler, Western Electric, Omaha; schoolteacher, Ryan H.S., Omaha, 1972; publisher, *Nebraska Dispatch*, Omaha; member, Political Theater Troupe; clerk, Burlington Northern R.R., Chicago, IL, 1978, switchperson, Cicero, IL; coal miner, U.S. Steel Corp., Cumberland Mine, Kirby, PA, 1982–87; seamstress, garment shop, Westover, WV; contributor, *Militant*; coal miner, Westover. MEM.: International Miners' Organization (delegate, London Conference, 1986; delegate, Conference on Peace and Disarmament and Against Apartheid, 1987); Revolutionary Marxist Cmte. (1975–77); U.M.W. of A. (Local 2300); Coal Employment Project (1982); United Transportation Union; Coalition of Labor Union Women (delegate, Conference for the Equal Rights Amendment); Equal Rights Amendment March on May 10, 1980 (labor outreach coordinator); African National Congress 75th Anniversary Celebration (Socialist Workers Party delegate, 1987); National Organization for Women. MISC.: advocate of unionism; peace; nonintervention in Nicaragua; mine reform (U.S. and Great Britain); Native American rights; women's liberation; active in A. T. Massey Coal Co. Strike, Oct 1984; anti–nuclear power activist; traveled to Nicaragua, 1981. MAILING ADDRESS: 68 Dunkard Ave., Westover, WV 26505.

MICKELSON, GEORGE THEODORE. b. Jul 23, 1903, Walworth Cty., SD; d. Feb 28, 1965, Sioux Falls, SD; par. George M. and Emma L. (Craig) Mickelson; m. Madge E. Turner, Apr 6, 1928; c. George Speaker; Janice Winifred (Mrs. John E. Carmody); Lavon Rae (Mrs. V. James Meyers); Patricia Ann (Mrs. Thomas C. Adam). EDUC.: LL.B., U. of SD, 1927. POLIT. & GOV.: city atty., Selby, SD, 13 years; chm., Walworth Cty. (SD) Board of Education; elected as a Republican, state's atty., Walworth Cty., 1933–37; elected as a Republican to SD State House, 1937–41 (Speaker, 1941); elected as a Republican to atty. gen. of SD, 1943–47; elected as a Republican to gov. of SD, 1947–51; ***candidate for Republican nomination to presidency of the U.S., 1952***; SD campaign mgr., Eisenhower for President Campaign, 1952; appointed U.S. district judge, District of SD, 1954–65 (chief judge). BUS. & PROF.: atty.; admitted to SD Bar, 1927; partner, Smith and Mickelson (law firm), Selby, 1927–33; law practice, Selby, 1933–45; partner, Mickelson and Homeyer (law firm), Selby, 1945–53; pres., dir., First National Bank of Selby; cattle rancher. MEM.: ABA; SD Bar

Assn.; American Jud. Soc.; Phi Delta Phi; Lamda Chi Alpha; Masons (Shriner); Red Cross of Constantine; Order of the Eastern Star (worthy grand patron); Elks; Sigma Delta Chi; Theta Alpha Phi. AWARDS: Citation for Public Service, U. of SD, 1958; Dean Marshall M. McKusick Award, U. of SD, 1961. HON. DEG.: LL.D., Dakota Wesleyan U., 1947; LL.D., U. of SD, 1955. REL.: Methodist. RES.: Sioux Falls, SD.

MIKULSKI, BARBARA ANN. b. Jul 20, 1936, Baltimore, MD; d. William and Christine Eleanor (Kutz) M.; single. EDUC.: B.A., Mount St. Agnes Coll., 1958; Loyola Coll., 1961; M.S.W., U. of MD, 1965. POLIT. & GOV.: political worker, John F. Kennedy for President Campaign, 1960; voter registration worker, Lyndon B. Johnson for President Campaign, 1964; first district coordinator, Joseph D. Tydings for Senator Campaign, 1970; elected to Baltimore (MD) City Council, 1971–76; special adviser to R. Sargent Shriver (q.v.), 1972; chairwoman, Comm. on Delegate Selection and Party Structure, Dem. Nat'l. Cmte., 1973; appointed member, Governor's Comm. on Structure and Governance of Education; elected as a Democrat to U.S. House (MD), 1977–87; delegate, Dem. Nat'l. Conv., 1980; ***candidate for Democratic nomination to vice presidency of the U.S., 1980***; elected as a Democrat to U.S. Senate (MD), 1987–. BUS. & PROF.: caseworker, Assn. of Catholic Charities, 1958–61; administrator, Dept. of Social Services, Baltimore (MD) Health and Welfare Council, 1961–63, 1966–70; teacher, VISTA Training Center, 1965–70; teacher, Mount St. Mary's Seminary, 1969; teacher, Community Coll. of Baltimore, MD, 1970–71; adjunct prof. of sociology, Loyola Coll., 1972–76; author; lecturer. MEM.: National Urban Coalition (dir.); League of Women Voters; Women's Political Caucus; Catalyst, Inc. (dir.); National Center for Urban Ethnic Affairs; Valley House (dir.); Polish Women's Alliance; Polish American Congress; National Assn. of Social Workers; American Federation of Teachers; Citizen Planning and Housing Assn.; South East Community Organization. AWARDS: "National Citizen of the Year," *Buffalo American-Political Eagle*, Buffalo, NY, 1973; "Woman of the Year," Business and Professional Women's Club Assn. of Baltimore, 1973; "Outstanding Alumnus," U. of MD School of Social Work, 1973; "Outstanding Alumnus," Loyola Coll., 1974; received National Fellowship Award, Philadelphia (PA) Fellowship Comm., 1974. HON. DEG.: LL.D., Goucher Coll., 1973; D.H.L., Pratt Inst. of Planning and Architecture, 1974. WRITINGS: "Who Speaks for Ethnic America?" *New York (NY) Times*; "Growing Up Ethnic Means Learning Who You Are," *Redbook*. REL.: R.C. MAILING ADDRESS: 309 Folcroft St., Baltimore, MD 21224.

MILBURN, ANNA THOMSEN. b. 1880, Walnut, IA; d. Nov 24, 1947, Seattle, WA; par. Moritz and Marie Thomsen; m. Henry Hanford Milburn; c. George; Moritz. EDUC.: classical education in Europe. POLIT. & GOV.: member, Seattle (WA) Park Board; member, Advisory Board, Greenback Party, 1939; ***Greenback Party candidate for presidency of the U.S., 1940 (declined)***. BUS. & PROF.: mgr., Seattle Canteen, Red Cross, 1917–19; dir., *Money Magazine*; philanthropist. MEM.: Seattle Garden Club (pres.); Sunset Club; U. of WA Arboretum (dir.); National Women's Party (WA state chm., 1924–); New Economic Group; Garden Clubs of America; English-Speaking Union (dir.); Fortnightly Study Club; Seattle Symphony Orchestra (dir.); Cornish School; Women's League for Peace and Freedom; Non-Partisan League of Women. MISC.: advocate of monetary reform and women's rights. RES.: Seattle, WA.

MILES, NELSON APPLETON. b. Aug 8, 1839, Westminster, MA; d. May 15, 1925, Washington, DC; par. Daniel and Mary (Curtis) Miles; m. Mary Hoyt Sherman, Jun 30, 1868; c. Sherman; Cecelia. POLIT. & GOV.: appointed U.S. representative to Queen Victoria's Diamond Jubilee, 1897; ***candidate for Democratic nomination to presidency of the U.S., 1904; Prohibition Party candidate for presidency of the U.S., 1904 (declined)***. BUS. & PROF.: soldier; author. MIL.: 1st lt., 22d MA Infantry, 1861; lt. col., 61st NY volunteers, 1862, col., 1862, brig. gen., 1864, maj. gen., 1865; appointed col., 40th U.S. Infantry, 1866; promoted through grades to brig. gen., 1880, maj. gen., 1890, commander in chief of U.S. Army, 1895, lt. gen., 1900, retired, 1903; commander, MA Militia, 1905; active in Indian Wars, 1875–76; commanded troops during Chicago Railroad Strike, 1894; U.S. representative at seat of Turko-Grecian War; commanded U.S. Army during Spanish-American War; Medal of Honor, 1892. MEM.: President Jefferson Memorial Assn. (pres.); Guardians of Liberty (1911); Loyal Legion (commander, CA commandery; national commander in chief, 1919–25); GAR. HON. DEG.: LL.D., Harvard U., 1896; LL.D., Brown U., 1901; LL.D., Colgate U., 1910. WRITINGS: *Personal Recollections, or From New England to the Golden Gate* (1896); *Military Europe* (1898); *Observations Abroad, or Report of Major General Nelson A. Miles, Commanding U.S. Army, of His Tour of Observation in Europe* (1899); *Serving the Republic* (1911). RES.: Washington, DC.

MILLER, BELLE K. b. Mar 19, 1905, Newport, KY; par. Saul and Minnie (Chaliff) Kondritzer; m. Noah Miller; c. Marilyn Berk; Cheryl Berk; Jessica Resnick. EDUC.: Akron U., 1923–24; R.N., Akron City School of Nursing, 1927. POLIT. & GOV.: ***candidate for Democratic nomination to presidency of the U.S., 1924; candidate for Democratic nomination to vice presidency of the U.S., 1924***; appointed member, Citizens Advisory Comm., Akron (OH) Planning Comm. BUS. & PROF.: communal worker. MEM.: Akron City Club; Council of Jewish Federations and Welfare Funds (Board of Women's Communal Service); American Joint Distribution Cmte. (Board); Jewish Family Service (Board; pres., 1959–60); Child Guidance Clinic (pres., 1953–54, 1959–60); Mental Hygiene Clinic (pres., 1955); League of Women Voters (pres., 1946–50); Jewish Welfare Fund (Board); Urban League (Board); United Community Council (vice pres.); Jewish Welfare Fund (chm., Women's Div., 1956, 1957, 1959); OH League of Women Voters (Board, 1950–52);

United Jewish Appeal (National Women's Div., 1958–60); Sagamore Hills Mental Hospital of Summit and Cuyahoga Counties, OH (Board); Sisterhood of Temple Israel (pres.). AWARDS: Brotherhood Award, 1963. REL.: Jewish. MISC.: received 1 vote from VT delegation for presidential nomination on 87th ballot, Dem. Nat'l. Conv., 1924. Identity not verified as candidate. RES.: Akron, OH.

MILLER, BRYAN M. b. Aug 23, 1900, Caldwell, ID; m. Lillian A. Dent, 1927; c. three sons. POLIT. & GOV.: ***Constitution Party candidate for vice presidency of the U.S., 1960***. BUS. & PROF.: stock rancher, ID; owner, operator, Miller Welding Supply Co., Arlington, VA. MEM.: Masons (AF & AM Lodge 324, Roanoke, VA). REL.: Protestant. MISC.: chm., McCarthy rally, Nov 11, 1954, in Washington, DC; appeared before Reese and Jenner committees investigating subversion in the U.S. RES.: Arlington, VA.

MILLER, DARLENE HARSTAD (See THOMPSON, DARLENE ANN).

MILLER, DAVE. POLIT. & GOV.: ***independent candidate for presidency of the U.S., 1980***. MAILING ADDRESS: 21145 Devonshire St., Chatsworth, CA 91311.

MILLER, ELEANOR. POLIT. & GOV.: delegate, Socialist Party National Convention, 1976 (vice chairperson); ***candidate for Socialist Party nomination to presidency of the U.S., 1976 (declined)***. MAILING ADDRESS: 1132 25th St., N.W., Washington, DC 20037.

MILLER, EMMA GUFEY. b. Jul 6, 1874, Guffey Station, PA; d. Feb 23, 1970, Grove City, PA; par. John and Barbaretta (Hough) Guffey; m. Carroll Miller, Oct 28, 1902; c. William Gardner III; John Guffey; Carroll, Jr.; Joseph F. EDUC.: Alinda Acad.; A.B., Bryn Mawr Coll., 1899. POLIT. & GOV.: Democratic precinct committeewoman, Seventh Ward, PA, 1920–30; member, Allegheny Cty. (PA) Democratic Cmte.; member, PA Democratic State Exec. Cmte.; delegate, Dem. Nat'l. Conv., 1924, 1928, 1932, 1936, 1940, 1944, 1948, 1952, 1956, 1960, 1964, 1968; ***candidate for Democratic nomination to presidency of the U.S., 1924; candidate for Democratic nomination to vice presidency of the U.S., 1924***; member, Dem. Nat'l. Cmte., 1932–70; member, Pittsburgh (PA) Mayor's Cmte. on the George Washington Bicentennial, 1932; appointed member, PA State Welfare Cmte., 1935–39; chm., Advisory Board, National Youth Administration, 1935–43; member, Hostess Cmte., Dem. Nat'l. Conv., 1936, 1948; appointed vice chm., Pennsylvania's 300th Anniversary Cmte., 1938–39; appointed member, Governor's Defense Cmte., PA, 1940; presidential elector, Democratic Party, 1940, 1944, 1960, 1964, 1968. BUS. & PROF.: writer; political analyst. MEM.: National Women's Party (life pres., 1965–70); Women's Democratic Club of Slippery Rock; Twentieth Century Club; Slippery Rock State Coll. (trustee, 1933–70); Japan International Christian Coll. Foundation; Pi Delta Phi; American Jewish Congress; Distinguished Daughters of Pennsylvania (national chm.); PA State Council of Education; Consumers' League (1910–14); Parent-Teachers Assn. (1915–18); League of Women Voters (1921–25); Women's Organization for National Prohibition Reform (adviser, 1929–33); PA Federal Constitution Cmte. (1937–38); Assn. of PA Teacher's Colleges (1937–39). AWARDS: Distinguished Daughter of Pennsylvania, 1955; citation, American Jewish Congress, 1960. WRITINGS: "The Romance of the National Pike," *Western Pennsylvania Magazine* (1927); "No Meat for a Month," *Mine Workers Journal*; "The Equal Rights Amendment," *New Times*. REL.: Episc. MISC.: suffrage advocate; received ½ vote on 21st ballot for presidential nomination and 3 votes for vice presidential nomination, Dem. Nat'l. Conv., 1924. RES.: Pittsburgh, PA.

MILLER, ERNEST L. b. 1899, Edinburg, PA. POLIT. & GOV.: ***Restoration Party candidate for presidency of the U.S., 1976***. BUS. & PROF.: ed., *The Truth Crusader*; minister; schoolteacher; principal, elementary schools and high schools, Shenandoah Cty., PA; supplier, organic food stores; owner, Better Health Store, Harrisonburg, VA; lecturer; organic farmer. REL.: Christian. MAILING ADDRESS: *The Truth Crusader*, P.O. Box 959, Harrisonburg, VA 22801.

MILLER, JOSEPH IGNAS. POLIT. & GOV.: ***Organic Growth Party candidate for presidency of the U.S., 1976***; candidate for U.S. Senate (FL), 1976. MAILING ADDRESS: 670 N.E. 120th St., Biscayne Park, FL 33161.

MILLER, JOSEPHINE ANN RUDD. POLIT. & GOV.: ***independent candidate for presidency of the U.S., 1976***. MAILING ADDRESS: R.R. #2, Kingman, IN 47952.

MILLER, JULIAN P. POLIT. & GOV.: ***independent candidate for presidency of the U.S., 1992***. MAILING ADDRESS: 356 Greenbriar Cove Rd., Union Grove, AL 35175

MILLER, AMATUL-MANNAN Q. KATHERINE BENGALEE. b. Apr 21, 1937, Chicago, IL; par. Dr. Sufi Muti-Rahman and Amatul Rahim Attiyya (Ahmad) Bengalee; m. Robert J. Miller; c. Nadim L. Ahmad; Mueen A. J. Ahmad; Amelia B.; Kent C. J. EDUC.: high school, Pakistan; U. of Punjab Junior Coll.; Truman Coll., 1984–86. POLIT. & GOV.: ***candidate for Republican nomination to presidency of the U.S., 1992***. BUS. & PROF.: artist; employee, U.S. Bureau of the Census, 1980, 1990. MEM.: National Organization for Women; National Assn. for Exec. Females; National Museum for Women in Contemporary

Art. WRITINGS: "Hands Across America" (article). REL.: Lutheran Evangelical Church. MAILING ADDRESS: 914 19th St., South, Arlington, VA 22202.

MILLER, KELSIE CARTER. POLIT. & GOV.: ***independent candidate for presidency of the U.S., 1992***. MAILING ADDRESS: Box 5199, Taos, NM 87571.

MILLER, MILTON ARMINGTON. b. Aug 23, 1862, Lebanon, OR; d. Jan 8, 1938, Portland, OR; par. Robert C. and M. J. (Irvine) Miller; m. Flora M. McCalley, Aug 1, 1888; c. Juanita. EDUC.: U. of OR, 1884–86. POLIT. & GOV.: elected mayor, Lebanon, OR, 10 years; elected member, Lebanon School Board, 20 years; elected as a Democrat to OR State House, 1890–94; delegate, Dem. Nat'l. Conv., 1896, 1900, 1908, 1912, 1932; member, Dem. Nat'l. Cmte. (OR), 1900–1904, 1908–12; elected as a Democrat to OR State Senate, 1902–13; member, OR State Textbook Board; appointed collector of internal revenue, District of OR, 1913–20; Democratic candidate for U.S. Senate (OR), 1924; ***candidate for Democratic nomination to vice presidency of the U.S., 1928, 1932***; appointed U.S. collector of customs (OR), 1933–38. BUS. & PROF.: owner, drug and book store, Lebanon, 1889. MEM.: Masons (Scottish Rite); U. of OR (trustee, 1905–38). RES.: Portland, OR.

MILLER, SAMUEL FREEMAN. b. Apr 5, 1816, Richmond, KY; d. Oct 13, 1890, Washington, DC; par. Frederick and Patsy (Freeman) Miller; m. Lucy Ballinger, c. 1839; m. 2d, Elizabeth (Winter) Reeve, 1857; c. Irvine; one other. EDUC.: M.D., Transylvania U., 1838; studied law, Barboursville, KY. POLIT. & GOV.: elected justice of the peace and member, Knox Cty. (KY) Court; chm., District Republican Cmte., Keokuk, IA; candidate for Republican nomination to gov. of IA, 1861; appointed assoc. justice, Supreme Court of the U.S., 1862–90; member, Electoral Comm., 1877; ***candidate for Republican nomination to presidency of the U.S., 1884, 1888***. BUS. & PROF.: physician; medical practice, Richmond, KY, 1838–39; medical practice, Barboursville, KY, 1839–47; atty.; admitted to Knox Cty. (KY) Bar, 1847; law practice, Barboursville, 1847–50; partner, Reeves and Miller (law firm), Keokuk, 1850–62. RES.: Barboursville, KY.

MILLER, WARNER. b. Aug 12, 1838, Hannibal, NY; d. Mar 21, 1918, New York, NY; m. Caroline Churchill, 1864. EDUC.: Charlottesville Acad.; A.B., Union Coll., 1860. POLIT. & GOV.: delegate, Rep. Nat'l. Conv., 1872, 1884, 1888, 1892, 1896; chm., Herkimer Cty. (NY) Republican Central Cmte., 10 years; elected as a Republican to NY State Assembly, 1874–76; elected as a Republican to U.S. House (NY), 1879–81; elected as a Republican to U.S. Senate (NY), 1881–87; Republican candidate for U.S. Senate (NY), 1887; Republican candidate for gov. of NY, 1888; ***candidate for Republican nomination to vice presidency of the U.S., 1896***; appointed chm., NY State Special Tax Comm., 1906. BUS. & PROF.: farmer; prof. of Greek and Latin, Ft. Edward Collegiate Inst., 1860–61; paper manufacturer, Herkimer, NY. MIL.: pvt., sgt. maj., lt. col., Fifth NY Cavalry, 1861–65. MEM.: SAR; American Pulp and Paper Assn. (pres.); Lawyers Club; Union League (vice pres.); Herkimer Cty. Hist. Soc.; Herkimer Free Library (trustee). HON. DEG.: LL.D., Syracuse U., 1891; LL.D., Union Coll. MISC.: prominent in Nicaragua Canal Project. RES.: Herkimer, NY.

MILLER, WILLIAM EDWARD. b. Mar 22, 1914, Lockport, NY; d. Jun 24, 1983, Buffalo, NY; par. Edward J. and Elizabeth (Hinch) Miller; m. Stephanie Wagner, Feb 26, 1943; c. Elizabeth Anne Fitzgerald; William Edward, Jr.; Stephanie C. Wagner; Mary Karen. EDUC.: Lockport (NY) H.S.; B.A., Notre Dame U., 1935; LL.B., Albany Law School of Union U., 1938. POLIT. & GOV.: appointed U.S. commissioner for western NY, 1940–42; appointed asst. district atty., Niagara Cty., NY, 1946–48; appointed and subsequently elected district atty., Niagara Cty., 1948–51; elected as a Republican to U.S. House (NY), 1951–65; chm., Republican Congressional Campaign Cmte., 1960–61; chm., Rep. Nat'l. Cmte., 1961–64; ***Republican candidate for vice presidency of the U.S., 1964***; delegate, Rep. Nat'l. Conv., 1968. BUS. & PROF.: atty.; admitted to NY Bar, 1938; asst. prosecutor, Nürnberg, Germany, 1945–46; partner, Holley and Miller (law firm), Lockport, NY, 1938–42, 1946–48; partner, Miller and De Lange (law firm), Lockport, 1948–53. MIL.: 1st lt., U.S. Army, 1942–46. MEM.: VFW; C. of C.; American Legion; Eagles; Young Men's Republican Club; Elks; Tuscarora Club of Lockport. AWARDS: Benjamin Cardozo Prize, 1938; REL.: R.C. MISC.: appeared in American Express television commercials. RES.: Lockport, NY.

MILLS, OGDEN LIVINGSTON. b. Aug 23, 1884, Newport, RI; d. Oct 11, 1937, New York, NY; par. Ogden and Ruth Tiny (Livingston) Mills; m. Margaret Stuyvesant Rutherford, Sep 20, 1911; m. 2d, Dorothy Randolph Fell, Sep 2, 1924; c. none. EDUC.: A.B., Harvard U., 1904, LL.B., 1907. POLIT. & GOV.: treas., NY Cty. (NY) Republican Central Cmte., 1911–26; delegate, Rep. Nat'l. Conv., 1912, 1916, 1920, 1924, 1928, 1932; Republican candidate for U.S. House (NY), 1912; elected as a Republican to NY State Senate, 1915–17 (resigned); elected as a Republican to U.S. House (NY), 1921–27; Republican candidate for gov. of NY, 1926; appointed U.S. undersec. of the treasury, 1927–32; appointed U.S. sec. of the treasury, 1932–33; ***candidate for Republican nomination to presidency of the U.S., 1936***. BUS. & PROF.: atty.; admitted to NY Bar, 1908; assoc., partner, Stetson, Jennings and Russell (law firm), New York, NY; author; lecturer; dir., Atchison, Topeka and Santa Fe R.R.; dir., Mergenthaler Linotype Co.; dir., National Biscuit Co.; dir., Shredded Wheat Co.; dir., Mexican Seaboard Oil Co.; dir., City and Suburban Homes Co.; dir., Cerro de Pasco Co.; dir., International Paper Co.; dir., Chase National Bank; dir., New York Tribune Co.; trustee, New York Trust Co. MIL.: capt., U.S. Army, 1917–19. MEM.: Provident Loan Soc. (trustee); American Museum of Natural History (trustee); Metropolitan Museum of Art (trustee); Home for Incurables (trustee); NY State Tax Assn. (pres.); Charity Organization Soc. (exec. cmte.); East Side Settlement House (member, Board of Managers); Tribune Fresh Air Fund (dir.); Acad. of Political Science; Assn. of the Bar of the City of New York; American Legion (NY state commander, 1919–20); Union Club; Harvard Club; Knickerbocker Club; Metropolitan Club of New York; Metropolitan Club of Washington. AWARDS: medal, Town Hall Club, 1933. HON. DEG.: LL.D., Harvard U., 1932; LL.D., St. Lawrence U., 1933. WRITINGS: *What of Tomorrow?* (1935); *Liberalism Fights On* (1936); *The Seventeen Million* (1937). REL.: Episc. RES.: New York, NY.

MILLS, ROGER QUARLES. b. Mar 30, 1832, Todd Cty., KY; d. Sep 2, 1911, Corsicana, TX; par. Charles Henry and Tabitha Buckner (Daniel) Mills; m. Caroline R. Jones, Jan 7, 1858; c. Sarah Lula; Nancy Buckner (Mrs. E. S. Maloney); Carrie R. (Mrs. James D. Wood); Charles H.; Fannie Halbert (Mrs. George Richards). EDUC.: public schools; studied law under Reuben A. Reeves. POLIT. & GOV.: elected as a Democrat to TX State House, 1859–60; elected as a Democrat to U.S. House (TX), 1873–92 (chm., Ways and Means Cmte.; candidate for Speaker, 1891); ***candidate for Democratic nomination to vice presidency of the U.S., 1888***; elected as a Democrat to U.S. Senate (TX), 1892–99. BUS. & PROF.: atty.; admitted to TX Bar, 1852 (by act of legislature); law practice, Corsicana, TX. MIL.: col., 10th Regt., TX Infantry, C.S.A., 1861–65. RES.: Corsicana, TX.

MILLS, WILBUR DAIGH. b. May 24, 1909, Kensett, AR; d. May 2, 1992, Searcy, AR; par. Ardra Pickens and Abbie Lois (Daigh) Mills; m. Clarine Billingsley, May 27, 1934; c. Martha Sue (Mrs. David Jack Dixon); Rebecca Ann (Mrs. Richard Yates). EDUC.: A.B., Hendrix Coll., 1930; Harvard U. Law School, 1930–33. POLIT. & GOV.: elected cty. and probate judge, White Cty., AR, 1934–38; elected as a Democrat to U.S. House (AR), 1939–77 (chm., Ways and Means Cmte.); delegate, Dem. Nat'l. Conv., 1956; ***candidate for Democratic nomination to presidency of the U.S., 1972; candidate for Democratic nomination to vice presidency of the U.S., 1972***. BUS. & PROF.: atty.; admitted to AR State Bar, 1933; cashier, Bank of Kensett, 1934–35; tax counsel, Shea, Gould, Climenko and Casey, New York, NY, 1977–. MEM.: ABA; Masons (33°). REL.: Methodist. RES.: Kensett, AR.

MILTON, JERRY ROGER. POLIT. & GOV.: ***independent candidate for presidency of the U.S., 1988***. MAILING ADDRESS: P.O. Box 339, 401 S.E. Third Ave., Alachua, FL 32615.

MILTON, JOHN. b. 1740, Halifax Cty., NC; d. Oct 19, 1817, Burke Cty., GA; par. John and Mary (Farr) Milton; m. Hannah E. Spencer; c. Homer Virgil; Anna Marie. POLIT. & GOV.: elected by legislature, sec. of state of GA, 1777–99; town commissioner, Augusta, GA, 1786–96; delegate, GA Ratification Convention, 1787–88; delegate, GA State Constitutional Convention, 1788, 1795, 1798; presidential elector, Federalist Party, 1789; ***received 2 electoral votes as a Federalist for presidency of the U.S., 1789***. BUS. & PROF.: planter, Burke Cty., GA. MIL.: ensign, 1st GA Regt., Continental Army, 1776, 1st lt., 1776, capt., 1777; aide-de-camp, Gen. Benjamin Lincoln, 1780; aide-de-camp, Col. Francis Marion, 1781; brev. maj., 1782; taken prisoner by British at Ft. Howe, GA, 1777; confined for nine months at St. Augustine, FL; ordered removal of GA public records to protect them from the British, 1778. MEM.: GA Soc. of the Cincinnati (sec., 1783–86). RES.: Burke Cty., GA.

MINETT, CYRIL W. "CY." b. Jan 23, 1930, Waynesville, NC; m. Mildred B. Liddy; c. Cyril, Jr.; Lisa; Sherie; Michael. EDUC.: grad., Waynesville Township (NC) H.S., 1947; U. of NC; B.A., East TX State Coll., 1964; AZ State U.; U. of SC, 1972. POLIT. & GOV.: ***Populist (America First) Party candidate for vice presidency of the U.S., 1992***. BUS. & PROF.: businessman; partner, Kerrisma Exotic; corporate pilot; flight instructor; ed., *Aerospace Safety Magazine*, 1970; lecturer. MIL.: lt. col., U.S. Air Force, 1953–74; Air Medal; Good Conduct Medal; Meritorious Service Medal; Vietnam Victory Medal. MEM.: Air Force Assn.; Retired Officers Assn. MAILING ADDRESS: 140 Encino Dr., Kerrville, TX 78028.

MINK, PATSY TAKEMOTO. b. Dec 6, 1927, Paia, Maui, HI; par. Suematsu and Mitama (Tateyama) Takemoto; m. John Francis Mink, Jan 27, 1951; c. Gwendolyn. EDUC.: grad., Maui (HI) H.S., 1944; Wilson Coll., 1946; U. of NE, 1947; B.A., U. of HI, 1948; J.D., U. of Chicago, 1951. POLIT. & GOV.: charter pres., Young Democratic Club of Oahu, 1954–56; atty., HI Territorial Legislature, 1955, 1960; pres., Young Democrats of HI, 1956–58; elected as a Democrat to HI Territorial House, 1956–58; delegate, National Young Democrats Convention, 1957, 1959, 1961; vice pres., National Young Democrats Clubs of America, 1957–59; elected as a Democrat to HI Territorial Senate, 1958–59; delegate, Dem. Nat'l. Conv., 1960, 1972; elected as a Democrat to HI State Senate, 1962–64; elected as a Democrat to U.S. House (HI), 1964–77, 1990–; ***candidate for Democratic nomination to presidency of the U.S., 1972***; delegate, Democratic Mid-Term Conference, 1974; appointed asst. U.S. sec. of state for oceans, 1977–81; ***candidate for Democratic nomination to vice presidency of the U.S., 1984***; candidate for Democratic nomination to U.S. House (HI), 1986. BUS. & PROF.: atty.; law practice, Honolulu, HI, 1953–65; prof. of business law, U. of HI, 1952–56, 1959–62. MEM.: Pacem in Terris II Conference (delegate); Young Political Leaders Conference (delegate, 1958); HI Assn. to Help Retarded Children (dir.); YMCA; Honolulu Symphony (dir., 1966–69); American Assn. for the U.N.; NAACP; Delta Sigma Rho; 89th Democratic Congressional Club (sec.-treas., 1965–77); Congressmen for Peace Through Law (1965–77); Democratic Study Group (vice pres., 1967–77); Dem. Nat'l. Cmte. Comm. on Rules Revision; Council of State Governments (Advisory Cmte. on State-Urban Relations); National Movement for the Student Vote (National Advisory Board, 1971); Americans for Democratic Action (vice pres., 1973–77; pres., 1978–); ABA; HI Bar Assn.; Lanakila Crafts (dir.). AWARDS: "Outstanding Woman in Politics," 1965; "Nisei of the Biennium," Japanese-American Citizen's League, 1966; "Outstanding Woman of Accomplishment" 1967; Oahu Education Assn., School Bell Award, 1967; "Distinguished American Woman Honoree," Grand Temple Daughters and Grand Lodge of Elks, 1967; Leadership for Freedom Award, 1968; Alii Award, 4-H Clubs of HI, 1969; Rehabilitation Service Medallion, 1971; Freedom Fund Recognition Award, NAACP, 1971; Distinguished Humanitarian Award, St. Louis (MO) YWCA, 1972; Human Rights Award, American Federation of Teachers, 1975; NEA Award, 1977. HON. DEG.: LL.D., Lindenwood Coll., 1965; D.H.L., Wilson Coll., 1965; LL.D., Chaminade Coll., 1975; LL.D., Syracuse U., 1976; Duff's Inst. REL.: Protestant. MAILING ADDRESS: 94-1037 Maikai St., Waipahu, Oahu, HI 96797.

MIMS, A. L. POLIT. & GOV.: People's Party candidate for gov. of TN, 1894, 1896; ***candidate for People's Party nomination to presidency of the U.S., 1896***; member, People's Party National Cmte., 1904–06. RES.: Antioch, TN.

MISKIMEN, JAMES LESLIE. POLIT. & GOV.: ***candidate for Peace and Freedom Party nomination to presidency of the U.S., 1972***. MAILING ADDRESS: Long Beach, CA.

MITCHELL, ALFRED J. POLIT. & GOV.: ***candidate for Republican nomination to presidency of the U.S., 1984***. MAILING ADDRESS: 115-A Garden Village Dr., #4, Cheektowaga, NY 14227.

MITCHELL, CHARLENE. b. Jun 8, 1930, Cincinnati, OH; par. Charles and Naomi (Taylor) Alexander; m. William Mitchell, 1950 (divorced); c. Steven. EDUC.: Waller H.S., Chicago, IL; A.A., Herzl Junior Coll., 1950. POLIT. & GOV.: campaign worker, Henry A. Wallace for President Campaign, 1948; administrative sec., Southern CA Communist Party, 1957–60; member, Communist Party, U.S.A. National Cmte., 1957–; chm., Negro Comm., Communist Party, U.S.A., 1963–67; field sec., Comm. on Black Liberation, Communist Party, U.S.A., 1968–; ***Communist Party, U.S.A. candidate for presidency of the U.S., 1968***; Independent Progressive Line candidate for U.S. Senate (NY), 1988. BUS. & PROF.: head bookkeeper, importing firm, southern CA, 1962–68. MEM.: Labor Youth League (founder; Chicago North Side organizer; member, IL State Board, 1949–55); Youth for Democracy; Congress on Racial Equality; Temporary Alliance of Local Organizations Following Watts Riot (Steering Cmte.); Chicago Conference of New Politics (Steering Cmte., Black Caucus, 1967); National Alliance Against Racist and Political Repression (exec. sec.). MAILING ADDRESS: 101 West 147th St., New York, NY 10039.

MITCHELL, GEORGE JOHN. b. Aug 20, 1933, Waterville, ME; par. George John and Mary (Saad) Mitchell; m. Sally Heath, Aug 29, 1959 (divorced); m. 2d, Heather McLaughlin, Dec 1994; c. Andrea. EDUC.: B.A., Bowdoin Coll., 1954; LL.B., Georgetown U., 1960. POLIT. & GOV.: trial atty., U.S. Dept. of Justice, Washington, DC, 1960–62; exec. asst. to U.S. Sen. Edmund Sixtus Muskie (q.v.), 1962–65; chm., ME Democratic State Cmte., 1966–68; delegate, Dem. Nat'l. Conv., 1968, 1972; member, Dem. Nat'l. Cmte. (ME), 1968–76 (exec. cmte., 1974–76); asst. atty., Cumberland Cty., ME, 1971; appointed U.S. atty. for ME, 1977–79; appointed U.S. district judge for ME, 1979–80; appointed and subsequently elected as a Democrat to U.S. Senate (ME), 1980–95 (majority leader, 1989–95); ***candidate for Democratic nomination to presidency of the U.S., 1992 (declined)***. BUS. & PROF.: admitted to ME Bar, 1960; admitted to Bar of DC, 1960; atty., Jensen and Baird, Portland, ME, 1965–77. MIL.: 2d lt., 1st lt., U.S. Army Counter Intelligence, 1954–56. MEM.: ABA; Sigma Nu. REL.: R.C. MAILING ADDRESS: 25 Channel Rd., South Portland, ME 04106.

MITCHELL, JAMES PAUL. b. Nov 12, 1900, Elizabeth, NJ; d. Oct 19, 1964, New York, NY; par. Peter J. and Anna C. (Driscoll) Mitchell; m. Isabelle Nulton, Jan 22, 1923; c. Elizabeth (Mrs. Natchez). EDUC.: grad., Batten H.S., Elizabeth, NJ, 1917. POLIT. & GOV.: appointed Union Cty. dir., NJ State Relief Administration, 1931–36; appointed dir., Labor Relations, New York City Div., WPA, 1936–40; appointed dir., Labor Relations, U.S. Army, 1940; appointed dir., Industrial Personnel, U.S. Dept. of War, 1941; appointed member, National Building Trades Stabilization Board; appointed alternate member, War Manpower Comm.; appointed member, Personnel Advisory Board, Hoover Comm. on Organization of the Exec. Branch, 1948; appointed asst. U.S. sec. of the army, 1953; appointed U.S. sec. of labor, 1953–61; ***candidate for Republican nomination to vice presidency of the U.S., 1960***; Republican candidate for gov. of NJ, 1961. BUS. & PROF.: mgr., grocery store, Elizabeth, NJ, 1918–19; owner, grocery store, Rahway, NJ, 1920–23; truck driver; salesman; expediter, Western Electric Co., Kearny, NJ, 1936; dir. of personnel and industrial relations, R. H. Macy and Co., New York, NY, 1945–47; vice pres., Bloomingdale Brothers, New York, 1947–53; dir., Crown-Zellerbach Corp., 1961–64. MEM.: Retail Labor Standards Assn. of New York (chm., exec. cmte.); National Retail Dry Goods Assn.; National Civil Service League (exec. cmte.); National Catholic Conference on Inter-Racial Justice (exec. cmte.); National Council on Agricultural Life and Labor (pres.); Fund for International Social and Economic Education (dir.); Inst. for Human Progress (dir.); National Conference of Christians and Jews (dir.); Twentieth Century Fund (trustee); American Arbitration Assn. (dir.); Stock Exchange Club; Commonwealth Club. AWARDS: Rerum Novarum Award, St. Peter's Coll., 1955; Outstanding Service Citation, Confederated Unions of America, 1956; America's Democratic Legacy Silver Medallion, Anti-Defamation League of B'nai B'rith, 1956; Stockberger Award, Soc. for Personnel Administration, 1957; Speaker of the Year Award, Tau Kappa Alpha, 1957; Equal Opportunity Day Award, National Urban league, 1957; Citation of Merit, International Assn. of Personnel in Employment Security, 1958; Vincentian Award, Coll. of St. Elizabeth, 1959; Horatio Alger Award, American Schools and Colleges Assn., 1959; Bellarmine Medal, Bellarmine Coll., 1960. HON. DEG.: LL.D., Fordham U., 1954; LL.D., MI State Coll., 1955; LL.D., Bryant Coll., 1957; LL.D., Lehigh U., 1957; LL.D., Temple U., 1957; LL.D., Fairleigh Dickinson U., 1958; LL.D., Notre Dame U., 1958; LL.D., Catholic U., 1959; LL.D., Rutgers U., 1959; LL.D., Boston U., 1960; LL.D., Seton Hall U., 1960; LL.D., Villanova U., 1960. REL.: R.C. RES.: Spring Lake, NJ.

MITCHELL, JOHN. b. Feb 4, 1870, Braidwood, IL; d. Sep 9, 1919, New York, NY; par. Robert and Martha (Halley) Mitchell; m. Katherine O'Rourke, Jun 1, 1891; c. Richard H.; James J.; Robert E.; Marie; John; Catherine. EDUC.: public schools, Braidwood, IL, 1876–80; studied law. POLIT. & GOV.: ***candidate for Democratic nomination to vice presidency of the U.S., 1908***; appointed member, NY State Workmen's Compensation Comm., 1914–15; appointed chm., NY State Industrial Comm., 1915–19; appointed chm., NY State Food Comm.; appointed chm., Federal Food Board of NY State; appointed pres., NY State Council of Farms and Markets; appointed member, Federal Milk Comm. for the Eastern States, 1917–19. BUS. & PROF.: coal miner, IL, 1882; coal miner, western states, 1885–90; union official; assoc. ed., *Boyce's Weekly*, Chicago, IL; lecturer, 1911–13. MEM.: Knights of Labor (1885); U.M.W. of A. (sec.-treas., subdistrict, 1895; organizer, 1897; national vice pres., 1898; pres., 1898–1908); National Civic Federation (member, exec. cmte.; chm., Trade Agreement Dept., 1908–11); AFL (fourth vice pres., 1898–1900; second vice pres., 1900–1914); International Mining Congress (delegate, 1904). WRITINGS: *Organized Labor* (1903); *The Wage Earner and His Problems* (1913). REL.: R.C. (nee Presb.). MISC.: involved in anthracite coal miners' strikes, 1900, 1902; sentenced to prison for strike activities; sentence overturned on appeal. RES.: Spring Valley, IL.

MITCHELL, JOHN ALLEN. b. Jul 4, 1967, Youngstown, OH; par. William Vincent and Rosemarie (Christy) Mitchell; single. EDUC.: Hubbard (OH) H.S., 1981–85. POLIT. & GOV.: ***Independence Day Party candidate for presidency of the U.S., 1984***; appointed member, Hubbard City Council Cmte. for Disaster Planning. REL.: R.C. MAILING ADDRESS: 113 Grandview Ave., Hubbard, OH 44425.

MITCHELL, JOHN LENDRUM. b. Oct 19, 1842, Milwaukee, WI; d. Jun 19, 1904, Milwaukee, WI; par. Alexander and Martha (Reed) Mitchell. EDUC.: public schools; military academy, Hampton, CT; schools in Germany and Switzerland; Grenoble U., Grenoble, France. POLIT. & GOV.: elected as a Democrat to WI State Senate, 1872–73, 1875–76; chm., Milwaukee Cty. (WI) Democratic Central Cmte.; pres., Milwaukee School Board, 1884–85; member, Dem. Nat'l. Cmte., 1888–92; elected as a Democrat to U.S. House (WI), 1891–93; chm., Democratic Congressional Campaign Cmte., 1892; ***candidate for Democratic nomination to vice presidency of the U.S., 1892***; elected as a Democrat to U.S. Senate (WI), 1893–99. BUS. & PROF.: farmer; pres., Milwaukee Gas Co., 1890–92; pres., Wisconsin Marine and Fire Insurance Co.; vice pres., Marine National Bank; vice pres., Northwestern National Insurance Co. MIL.: lt., 24th Regt., WI Volunteer Infantry, 1861–64. MEM.: Layton Art Gallery (patron); Milwaukee Coll. (trustee); City Hospital, Milwaukee, (trustee); Northwestern Trotting Horse Breeders' Assn. (pres.); WI State Agricultural Soc. (pres.); National Home for Disabled Volunteer Soldiers (Board of Managers, 1886–1904; vice pres., 1895). RES.: Milwaukee, WI.

MITCHELL, MARTHA ELIZABETH BEALL JENNINGS. b. Sep 2, 1918, Pine Bluff, AR; d. May 31, 1976, New York, NY; m. Clyde W. Jennings (divorced); m. 2d, John N. Mitchell, 1957 (separated, 1973); c. Martha "Marty"; Jay Jennings. EDUC.: Stephens Coll.; U. of AR; grad., U. of Miami. POLIT. & GOV.: ***candidate for Democratic nomination to vice presidency of the U.S., 1972***. BUS. & PROF.: schoolteacher, Mobile, AL. MISC.: noted for unrestrained participation in Watergate debate in defense of her husband, Atty. Gen. John Mitchell. RES.: New York, NY.

MITCHELL, PARREN JAMES. b. Apr 29, 1922, Baltimore, MD; par. Clarence Maurice and Elsie (Davis) Mitchell; single. EDUC.: A.B., Morgan State Coll., 1950, D.H.L.; M.A., U. of MD, 1952; Dr.Soc.Sci., Yale U., 1957; U. of CT, 1960. POLIT. & GOV.: exec. dir., MD State Comm. on Inter-Racial Problems, 1963–65; exec. dir., Community Action Agency, Baltimore, MD, 1965–68; elected as a Democrat to U.S. House (MD), 1971–87; ***candidate for Democratic nomination to vice presidency of the U.S., 1972***; delegate, Democratic Mid-Term Conference, 1974; candidate for Democratic nomination to lt. gov. of MD, 1986. BUS. & PROF.: instructor, Morgan State Coll., 1953–54, prof., 1968–70; probation officer, Supreme Court of Baltimore, MD, 1954–57, supervisor of domestic relations, 1957–63. MIL.: pvt., capt., U.S. Army, 1943–46; Purple Heart. MEM.: Alpha Kappa Phi; Congressional Black Caucus (chm.); National Assn. for Community Development; MD Cmte. for Day Care; NAACP AWARDS: Whitney M. Young, Jr., Memorial Award, Washington Urban League; Distinguished Service Award, National Bankers Assn.; Black Achievers Award, African Heritage Assn. WRITINGS: *Profile of a Domestic Relations Offender* (with R. G. Murdy, 1958); *Signal Four: Family*

Trouble (1960). REL.: Episc. MAILING ADDRESS: 951 Brooks Lane, Baltimore, MD 21217.

MITCHELL, STANLEY P. POLIT. & GOV.: ***National Liberty Party candidate for presidency of the U.S., 1904 (declined)***; pres., National Liberty Party, 1904. BUS. & PROF.: ed., Memphis, TN. MEM.: Liberty League (chm.). RES.: Memphis, TN.

MITCHELL, WILLIAM EUGENE "BILL." POLIT. & GOV.: ***independent candidate for presidency of the U.S., 1988***. MAILING ADDRESS: 1030 Stratford Ave., South Pasadena, CA 91030.

MIX, THOMAS HEZIKIAH "TOM." b. Jan 6, 1880, Mix Run, PA; d. Oct 12, 1940, Florence, AZ; par. Edward E. and Elizabeth (Smith) Mix; m. Olive Stokes; m. 2d, Kitty Jewel Perrine; m. 3d, Victoria Forde, 1917; m. 4th, Grace Allin (annulled); m. 5th, Mabel Hubbell Ward, Feb 16, 1932; c. Ruth; Thomasina. POLIT. & GOV.: sheriff, Montgomery Cty., KS; sheriff, Washington Cty., OK; appointed deputy U.S. marshall, Eastern District of OK; ***candidate for Democratic nomination to presidency of the U.S., 1924 (satire effort); candidate for Democratic nomination to vice presidency of the U.S., c. 1936 (satire effort)***. BUS. & PROF.: water boy, lumber camp; cowboy in TX, AZ, WY, and MT; livestock foreman, Miller Brothers "101" Ranch, Bliss, OK, 1906–09; motion picture actor, 1910–40; with Sells Floto Circus, 1929, 1930–31; with Tom Mix Circus and Wild West Show, 1933–40. MOTION PICTURE CREDITS: *Dick Turpin*; *The Lucky Horse-Shoe*; *Ranch Life in the Great Southwest* (1910); *Up San Juan Hill* (1910); *Briton and Boer* (1910); *The Millionaire Cowboy* (1910); *The Range Rider* (1910); *Child of the Prairie* (1913); *Cupid's Round-Up* (1918); *Tom Mix in Arabia* (1922); *Destry of Death Valley*; *Oh, Promise Me* (1922); *North of Hudson Bay* (1924); *The Last Trail* (1927); *Destry Rides Again* (1927); *Painted Post* (1928); *My Pal, the King* (1932); *The Terror Trail* (1933); *The Fourth Horseman* (1933); *The Rustler's Round-Up*; numerous others. MIL.: U.S. Army, 1898; served with British, Boer War; Texas Rangers, 3 years. MEM.: Spanish War Veterans; World War Vets; Jonathan Club; 233 Club; Masons (Scottish Rite); Los Angeles Breakfast Club; Elks (life member). MISC.: won National Riding and Roping Contest, 1909, 1911. RES.: Beverly Hills, CA.

MOANS, HARRY. POLIT. & GOV.: ***Three Horse Party candidate for presidency of the U.S., 1936***. BUS. & PROF.: self-styled "King of the Hoboes." RES.: Des Moines, IA.

MOBLEY, JAMES ARNOLD. b. Apr 8, 1928, Atlanta, GA; par. Corrie Sampson and Bertha (Martin) Mobley; m. June E. Wilkey; m. 2d, Ida Elizabeth Fisher, Jun 6, 1964; c. Rebecca Ann Gardner; Edna Faye Seal; Jamie Lynn; Larry Wayne; James Arnold, Jr.; JoAnn Coreen. EDUC.: LL.B., The Atlanta Law School, 1954. POLIT. & GOV.: ***independent candidate for presidency of the U.S., 1976***. BUS. & PROF.: ordained minister, Cumberland Presbyterian Church, 1970; chm. of the Board of Deacons, treas., Pryor Street Presbyterian Church, Atlanta, GA, 1955–58; clerk of sessions, Cumberland Presbyterian Church, Oklahoma City, OK, 1966–69; pastor, Tecumseh (OK) Cumberland Presbyterian Church, 1967–70; state clerk, OK Synod, Cumberland Presbyterian Church, 1969–70; pastor, Gum Springs Church, Dardanelle, AR, 1970–71; pastor, Bethany Cumberland Presbyterian Church, Coushatta, LA, 1971–72; pastor, Barrens Springs Cumberland Presbyterian Church, Huntingdon, TN, 1975–. MEM.: OK Council of Churches (dir.); Natchitoches (LA) Day Care Center (dir., 1973–74). REL.: Cumberland Presbyterian Church. MAILING ADDRESS: 709 Bethell Court, McKenzie, TN 38201.

MOHR, GORDON "JACK." b. Jan 1, 1916, Chicago, IL; par. Herman and Millicent (Mohr) Mansfield; m. Ruth Satterthwaite, Dec 28, 1958 (divorced); m. 2d, Doris S. Grone, Jul 7, 1972; c. Dwight Gordon. EDUC.: Moody Bible Inst., 1934–35; Minot State Coll., 1947–48. POLIT. & GOV.: ***candidate for American Independent Party nomination to presidency of the U.S., 1984***. BUS. & PROF.: lecturer on communism, 1951–; with American Opinion Speakers' Bureau, 1965–; publisher, *Christian Patriot Crusader*. MIL.: lt. col., U.S. Army, 1942–64, brig. gen.; taken prisoner by communists, 1948, Korea; Silver Star; Bronze Star with two clusters; Purple Heart with three clusters; Korean Distinguished Service Cross; three Presidential Unit Citations. MEM.: Citizens Emergency Defense System (national military coordinator); Crusade for Christ and Country; John Birch Soc. HON. DEG.: LL.D., Freelandia Inst., Cassville, MO, 1976. WRITINGS: *Hyenas in My Bedroom* (1969); *Destination Somewhere* (1971); *Formula for Survival* (1972); *Point of No Return* (1973); *Invasion from Hell* (1975); *Psychopolitics: The Communist Art of Brainwashing* (1976); *Preliminary to Chaos*; *Uncle Jack's Children's Safari*; *Memories of a Citizen Soldier*; *The Satanic Counterfeit* (1980); *Know Your Enemies* (1981); *Satan's Kids* (1982). REL.: Bapt. (Anglo-Israelite). MISC.: noted anti-Semite. MAILING ADDRESS: 113 Ballentine St., Bay St. Louis, MS 39520.

MOLLOY, POLLY. b. 1943, NJ; married. EDUC.: A.B., IN State U. POLIT. & GOV.: employee, Public Information Office, U.S. Dept. of Defense; ***independent candidate for presidency of the U.S., 1980***. BUS. & PROF.: dance teacher; choreographer; script writer; professional dancer; owner, Tampa Conservatory of Dance, Tampa, FL. MAILING ADDRESS: Tampa, FL.

MONA, LOUIS "MAD." b. 1936. POLIT. & GOV.: ***Muneco Party candidate for presidency of the U.S., 1980***. BUS. & PROF.: fortune teller; cartoonist; commercial sign painter; department store display designer; waiter, El Tropicano Hotel, San Antonio, TX. MAILING ADDRESS: San Antonio, TX.

MONDALE, WALTER FREDERICK "FRITZ." b. Jan 5, 1928, Ceylon, MN; par. Theodore Sigvaard and Claribel Hope (Cowan) Mondale; m. Joan Adams, Dec 27, 1955; c. Theodore Adams; Eleanor Jane; William Hall. EDUC.: Macalester Coll., 1946–49; B.A. (cum laude), U. of MN, 1951, LL.B., 1956. POLIT. & GOV.: campaign mgr., Freeman for Governor Campaign (MN), 1958; appointed special asst. to the atty. gen. of MN, 1958–60; appointed and subsequently elected as a Democrat-Farmer Laborite, atty. gen. of MN, 1960–64; appointed member, President's Consumer Advisory Council, 1962–64; delegate, Dem. Nat'l. Conv., 1964, 1968; appointed and subsequently elected as a Democrat-Farmer Laborite to U.S. Senate (MN), 1964–77; co-chm., United Democrats for Humphrey, 1968; ***candidate for Democratic nomination to presidency of the U.S., 1972, 1976 (withdrew)***; ex-officio delegate, Democratic Mid-Term Conference, 1974; ***elected as a Democrat to vice presidency of the U.S., 1977–1981; Democratic candidate for vice presidency of the U.S., 1980; Democratic candidate for presidency of the U.S., 1984***; appointed U.S. ambassador to Japan, 1993–. BUS. & PROF.: atty.; admitted to MN Bar, 1956; partner, Larson, Loevinger, Lindquist, Freeman and Fraser (law firm), Minneapolis, MN, 1956–60. MIL.: corp., U.S. Army, 1951–53. MEM.: U.N. Assn. of the United States; Sons of Norway; Eagles; American Legion; American Veterans Cmte.; ABA; MN Bar Assn.; Hennepin Cty. Bar Assn.; Loyal Order of Moose; Hennepin Cty. Citizens' League; MN Junior C. of C.; MN Safety Council; Smithsonian Institution (regent). AWARDS: Averell Harriman Equal Housing Opportunity Award; "Outstanding Young Man of the Year in Minnesota," 1960. WRITINGS: "Minnesota Corrupt Practices Act," *Minnesota Law Review* (1955); *The Accountability of Power—Toward a Responsible Presidency* (1976). REL.: Presb. MAILING ADDRESS: 4 Thrush Lane, St. Paul, MN 55110.

MONDRAGON, ROBERTO A. b. Jul 27, 1940, La Loma, NM; par. Severo and Lucia (Aragon) Mondragon; m. Bell Urrea, Nov 28, 1968; c. Julian Jaramillo; Geraldine Jararmillo; Robert Anthony. EDUC.: grad., Albuquerque (NM) H.S., 1958. POLIT. & GOV.: elected as a Democrat to NM State House, 1967–70; elected as a Democrat to lt. gov. of NM, 1970–75; ***candidate for Democratic nomination to vice presidency of the U.S., 1972, 1980***; dir., NM Comm. on Aging; chm., Governor's Council on Children and Youth (NM); appointed member, Governor's Council on Criminal Justice (NM); member, NM State Manpower Planning Council; member, NM Health Planning Council; member, Advisory Group, Regional Medical Programs; member, NM Advisory Comm. to U.S. Civil Rights Comm.; vice chm., Dem. Nat'l. Cmte., 1972; delegate, Dem. Nat'l. Conv., 1972; candidate for Democratic nomination to U.S. Senate (NM), 1972; Democratic candidate for U.S. House (NM), 1974; ***candidate for Democratic nomination to presidency of the U.S., 1980 (declined)***. BUS. & PROF.: Spanish-language announcer, KABQ radio, Albuquerque, NM, 1965–70. MEM.: Chicano Mobile Institutes; Albuquerque Goals Program, Amigos de las Americas (dir.); Bilingual Children's TV (dir.); Mondragon Education and Scholarship Fund (founder; dir.); Albuquerque C. of C.; American G.I. Forum; Lions; Fraternal Order of Police. REL.: R.C. MAILING ADDRESS: Route 1, Box 139-A, Santa Fe, NM 87501.

MONNETT, FRANCIS SYLVESTER. b. Mar 19, 1857, Kenton, OH; par. Thomas J. and Henrietta (Johnston) Monnett; m. Ella K. Gormly, Feb 17, 1887. EDUC.: A.B., OH Wesleyan U., 1880, M.A., 1885; LL.B., National Law School, 1882. POLIT. & GOV.: elected as a Republican, city solicitor, Crawford, OH, 1892–96; elected as a Republican, atty. gen. of OH, 1896–1900; Democratic candidate for atty. gen. of OH, 1903; Democratic candidate for U.S. House (OH), 1910; appointed special counsel, state of OK, in constitutional contest before President Theodore Roosevelt; ***candidate for Republican nomination to vice presidency of the U.S., 1916***. BUS. & PROF.: atty.; admitted to OH Bar, 1883; law practice, Bucyrus, OH, 1883; law practice, Columbus, OH, 1883. MEM.: ABA; OH State Bar Assn.; Phi Kappa Psi; OH State Assn. of City Solicitors (pres., 1894–95); National Anti-Trust League (pres.); Columbus Club. MISC.: noted for antitrust actions against oil companies. RES.: Columbus, OH.

MONROE, JAMES. b. Apr 28, 1758, Westmoreland Cty., VA; d. Jul 4, 1831, New York, NY; par. Spence and Elizabeth (Jones) Monroe; m. Eliza Kortright, Feb 16, 1786; c. Eliza Kortright (Mrs. George Hay); Maria Hester (Mrs. Samuel Lawrence Gouverneur); James Spence (infant). EDUC.: Coll. of William and Mary, 1774–76; studied law under Thomas Jefferson (q.v.), 1780–83. POLIT. & GOV.: elected member, VA State Assembly, 1780, 1782, 1786, 1810–11; member, Continental Congress (VA), 1783–86; delegate, Annapolis Convention, 1786; delegate, VA Ratification Convention, 1788; elected as a Democratic-Republican to U.S. Senate (VA), 1790–94; appointed U.S. minister plenipotentiary to France, 1794–96, 1803; elected as a Democratic-Republican to gov. of VA, 1799–1802, 1811; appointed U.S. minister to England, 1803–07; appointed U.S. envoy to Spain, 1804; ***candidate for Democratic-Republican nomination to presidency of the U.S., 1808; received 3 electoral votes as a Democratic-Republican for vice presidency of the U.S., 1808***; appointed U.S. sec. of state, 1811–17; appointed U.S. sec. of war, 1814–15; ***elected as a Democratic-Republican to presidency of the U.S., 1817–1825***; pres., VA State Constitutional Convention, 1829. BUS. & PROF.: atty.; admitted to VA Bar, 1786; author. MIL.: commissioned 2d lt., Third VA Regt., Continental Army, 1775, 1st lt., 1776, capt., 1776, maj., 1777, lt. col., military commissioner of VA, 1780. MEM.: U. of VA (Board of Visitors, 1828–31); Masons. WRITINGS: *A View of the Conduct of the Executive in the Foreign Affairs of the United States* (1797); *Calendar of the Correspondence of*

James Monroe (1891). REL.: Episc. MISC.: noted for Monroe Doctrine of supporting cessation of further European colonization of Americas. RES.: Charlottesville, VA.

MONROE, JAMES OLIVER. b. 1888; c. James Oliver, Jr. POLIT. & GOV.: elected as a Democrat to IL State Senate; Democratic candidate for U.S. House (IL), 1902, 1904; candidate for Democratic nomination to U.S. House (IL), 1914, 1922; ***Independent Democratic candidate for presidency of the U.S., 1920***; candidate for Democratic nomination to U.S. Senate (IL), 1926, 1928. BUS. & PROF.: owner, ed., *Collinsville (IL) Herald*, 1917; owner, Herald Poster Co. WRITINGS: *The End of Prohibition* (1929); *An Answer to Governor Emmerson's Message* (1931); *The Immorality of Prohibition and a Local Option Alternative* (1931); *Equalizing Educational Opportunity* (1937); *Blasting the Legislative "Last Minute" Log Jam* (1937). RES.: Chicago, IL.

MONTGOMERY, JAMES ROBERT. b. Mar 2, 1941, Lamar, MO; par. Tandy Paxton and Nellie Dorothy (Vincent) Montgomery; single. EDUC.: eighth grade, Carthage (MO) Public School. POLIT. & GOV.: ***independent candidate for presidency of the U.S., 1980***. BUS. & PROF.: employee, Rex Casket Co., Webb City, MO; pensioner. MEM.: Social Security Victims Non-Register Organization. WRITINGS: *The Social Security Fraud Scheme* (1978, under pen name of "Wally"). REL.: R.C. MAILING ADDRESS: Route 1, Box 4, Oronogo, MO 64855.

MONTGOMERY, MYRTLE CHARLOTTE. POLIT. & GOV.: ***independent candidate for presidency of the U.S., 1988***. MAILING ADDRESS: 405 Roundtree Court, Sacramento, CA 95831.

MONTOYA, JOSEPH MANUEL. b. Sep 24, 1915, Pena Blanca, NM; d. Jun 5, 1978, Washington, DC; par. Thomas and Frances (de La) Montoya; m. Della Romero, Nov 9, 1940; c. Joseph Manuel, Jr.; Patrick James; Linda Jean. EDUC.: Regis Coll., 1931, 1933–34; LL.B., Georgetown U., 1938. POLIT. & GOV.: elected as a Democrat to NM State House, 1936–40 (majority leader, 1940); elected as a Democrat to NM State Senate, 1940–46 (majority whip, 1945–46), 1953–54; elected as a Democrat to lt. gov. of NM, 1947–51, 1955–57; elected as a Democrat to U.S. House (NM), 1957–65; national co-chm., Viva Kennedy Clubs, 1960; delegate, Mexican-U.S. Interparliamentary Conference, 1961–65; elected as a Democrat to U.S. Senate (NM), 1965–77; delegate, Dem. Nat'l. Conv., 1968; ***candidate for Democratic nomination to vice presidency of the U.S., 1972***; Democratic candidate for U.S. Senate (NM), 1976. BUS. & PROF.: atty.; admitted to NM Bar, 1939; law practice, Santa Fe, NM; owner, Western Freight Lines, 1945. MEM.: Elks; Knights of Columbus; Optimists. REL.: R.C. RES.: Santa Fe, NM.

MONYEK, FANNY ROSE ZEIDWERG. b. Sep 14, 1929, Montclair, NJ; widow; c. three. EDUC.: grad., high school; college coursework. POLIT. & GOV.: member, Democratic Cty. Central Cmte. (NJ), 1978; candidate for Democratic nomination to U.S. Senate (NJ), 1979; candidate for Democratic nomination to NJ State Senate, 1982; candidate for Democratic nomination to U.S. House (NJ), 1980; candidate for Democratic nomination to gov. of NJ, 1981; Repeal Party candidate for U.S. Senate (NJ), 1982; ***candidate for Democratic nomination to presidency of the U.S., 1992***. BUS. & PROF.: office assistant; housewife. MEM.: Rahway Taxpayers Assn.; Mt. Nebo Link Club; Temple Beth Torah. REL.: Jewish. MISC.: entered presidential race after winning $1,000 in lottery. MAILING ADDRESS: 1060 West Lake Ave., Rahway, NJ 07065.

MOODY, DANIEL J. b. Jun 1, 1893, Taylor, TX; d. May 22, 1966, Austin, TX; par. Daniel J. and Nancy Elizabeth "Nannie" (Robertson) Moody; m. Mildred Paxton, Apr 20, 1926; c. Dan; Nancy Paxton (Mrs. Hubert Hudson). EDUC.: Taylor H.S., Taylor, TX; LL.B., U. of TX, 1914. POLIT. & GOV.: elected as a Democrat to cty. atty., Williamson Cty., TX, 1920–22; elected as a Democrat to district atty., 26th Judicial District of TX, 1922–25; elected as a Democrat to atty. gen. of TX, 1925–27; elected as a Democrat to gov. of TX, 1927–31; delegate, Dem. Nat'l. Conv., 1928, 1940, 1944, 1948, 1952; ***candidate for Democratic nomination to presidency of the U.S., 1928; candidate for Democratic nomination to vice presidency of the U.S., 1928***; appointed special asst. to the atty. gen. of the U.S., 1935; candidate for Democratic nomination to U.S. Senate (TX), 1942. BUS. & PROF.: atty.; admitted to TX Bar, 1914; partner (with Harris Melasky), law firm, Taylor, TX, 1914–22; law practice, Austin, TX, 1931–66; dir., Farm and Home Savings and Loan Assn. of Nevada, MO; dir., Employers Casualty Co. of Dallas; dir., E. M. Scarborough and Sons, Austin. MIL.: 2d lt., capt., TX National Guard; 2d lt., U.S. Army, WWI. MEM.: ABA; TX State Bar Assn.; American Bar Foundation; TX Law School Foundation (trustee, 1942–60); American Coll. of Trial Lawyers (fellow); American Legion; Masons (32°; Knights Templar; Shriners); Odd Fellows; Knights of Pythias; National Assn. of Railroad Trial Counsel; Order of the Coif; University Club; Kiwanis; American Jud. Soc.; Phi Delta Phi. WRITINGS: *Caesar Kleberg* (1946). REL.: Bapt. RES.: Austin, TX.

MOOMATCH, GOSGROVE. b. 1860. POLIT. & GOV.: ***Independent Fisherman's Party candidate for presidency of the U.S., 1976 (satire effort)***. BUS. & PROF.: hermit. MISC.: fictitious satire candidate. MAILING ADDRESS: Ely, MN.

MOONEY, BEATRICE ELAINE JOHNSON. b. Jul 9, 1917, Sunrise Township, MN; par. Frank August and Julia Theoline (Fallt) Johnson; m. Robert Davis Mooney, M.D. (divorced); c. Robert Davis, Jr.; Michael Frederick; James Patrick; Susan Elizabeth Rosenthal; Sarah Cole

Beckmann. EDUC.: B.S., U. of MN, 1939, adult education, 1960s; docent training, Minneapolis Inst. of Arts, 1960s; pediatric nursing research, Korolinska Inst., U. of Stockholm, Sweden, 1967–68; U. of CA at Los Angeles, 1972; Tulane U., 1973. POLIT. & GOV.: appointed member, vice chm., Health Cmte., MN Governor's Advisory Council on Children and Youth, c. 1950–60; member, Rep. Nat'l. Cmte.; candidate for Republican nomination to U.S. House (MN), 19–, 1974, 1978; candidate for Republican nomination to gov. of MN, 1974, 1978, 1982, 1986; candidate for Republican nomination to U.S. Senate (MN), 1976; ***candidate for Republican nomination to presidency of the U.S., 1980, 1984, 1988, 1992; candidate for Republican nomination to vice presidency of the U.S., 1980***; alternate, Lower St. Croix Valley Cable TV Comm., 1986–88. BUS. & PROF.: registered nurse; certified public health nurse; supervisor, newborn nursery, U. of MN Hospitals, 1939; asst. floor supervisor, floor supervisor, Minneapolis General Hospital, 1939–41; instructor, School of Nursing, U. of MN, 1942, instructor in advanced clinical pediatric nursing, 1950–52; pediatric liaison nurse, Maternal-Infant Care Project, St. Paul Ramsey Medical Center, 1968–70; health facility surveyor, MN State Dept. of Health, 1970–76; short-term nurse, 1976–78; private duty home nurse, 1979; pool staff nurse, Kelly Health Care, 1979–80; pool staff nurse, Quality Care Nursing Service, 1979–83; night nurse, Maplewood Care Center, North St. Paul, MN, 1980; charge nurse, Sholom Home, Inc., St. Paul, 1980–81; night supervisor, staff nurse, Summit Manor Health Care Center, St. Paul, 1981–83; telemarketer, C. G. Rein Co., Lilydale, MN, 1985–88; nurse, infant care, office of Sarah Mooney Beckmann, M.D., Minneapolis, MN, 1985–87. MEM.: Hi Chi Honor Soc.; U. of MN Alumni Assn. (life member); U. of MN Alumni Club; AAUW; Sigma Theta Tau (nursing honorary); American Nurses Assn.; National League for Nursing; Minneapolis Soc. of Fine Arts; Friends of Minneapolis Soc. of Fine Arts; MN Museum of Art; Women's Assn. of MN Symphony Orchestra; Federation of Republican Women; Nurses for a Peaceful Healthy World; MN Nurses Assn.; International Council of Nurses; Alpha Tau Delta; Schubert Club; MN Hist. Soc.; Camp Fire Girls; Blue Birds; BSA; Catfish Club; Parent Teacher Students' Assn.; American Swedish Inst.; Irish-American Cultural Inst.; La Leche League; Older Womens League; Order of St. Luke; MN Womens Consortium; World Federalist Assn. of MN; World Assn. of World Federalists; Miller Hospital Auxiliary; Women's Assn. of the MN Hist. Soc.; Ballet Borealis Foundation. AWARDS: Alpha Tau Delta Scholarship Award, 1939. WRITINGS: *Rooming-in Babies Cry Less Than Half as Often* (1968); *Lullabies in the Maternity Hospital* (1968); *To Be a Parent* (translator). REL.: Lutheran. MAILING ADDRESS: 1278 Quinlan Ave., Lake St. Croix Beach, MN 55043.

MOONEY, BURTON L. b. 1945, MA. EDUC.: Pasadena City Coll., 1969; B.A., U. of CA at Chico, 1973; M.A., Rollins Coll., 1982. POLIT. & GOV.: ***independent candidate for presidency of the U.S., 1992***. BUS. & PROF.: teacher, Mulberry Junior H.S., Lakeland, FL, 1974; adjunct teacher, Polk (FL) Community Coll., 1984; coach; ed., *Florida Sports and Leisure Magazine*. MIL.: U.S. Air Force, 1963. MAILING ADDRESS: P.O. Box 8172, Lakeland, FL 33802.

MOONEY, THOMAS JEREMIAH. b. Dec 8, 1882, Chicago, IL; d. Mar 6, 1942; par. Bernard and Mary (Heffernan) Mooney; m. Rena Ellen (Brink) Hermann, 1910; c. none. EDUC.: public schools, Holyoke, MA. POLIT. & GOV.: delegate, CA Socialist Party State Convention, 1908; Socialist Party candidate for judge, CA Superior Court, 1910; Socialist Party candidate for sheriff, San Francisco Cty., CA, 1911; ***Communist Party of the United States (opposition) candidate for Labor Party nomination to presidency of the U.S., 1936***. BUS. & PROF.: iron molder, Holyoke, MA, 1897, journeyman, 1901; publisher, *Revolt*. MISC.: arrested several times for violent strike activity; convicted of San Francisco Preparedness Day bombing, Jul 22, 1916; sentenced to hang, but commuted to life imprisonment by President Woodrow Wilson (q.v.); pardoned, 1939. MEM.: International Molders Union (1902; delegate, National Convention, 1912); International Socialist Congress (delegate, 1910); Industrial Workers of the World; International Workers Defense League (1910); San Francisco Labor Council (delegate, 1912). REL.: R.C. RES.: San Francisco, CA.

MOORE, ARCH ALFRED, JR. b. Apr 16, 1923, Moundsville, WV; par. Arch Alfred and Genevieve (Jones) Moore; M.S. Shelley Riley, Aug 11, 1949; c. Arch Alfred III; Shelley Wellons; Lucy St. Clair. EDUC.: Lafayette Coll., 1943; B.A., WV U., 1948, LL.B., 1951. POLIT. & GOV.: elected as a Republican to WV State House of Delegates, 1953–55; elected as a Republican to U.S. House (WV), 1957–69; member, James Madison Memorial Comm.; delegate, Rep. Nat'l. Conv., 1960, 1964, 1972, 1976; elected as a Republican to gov. of WV, 1969–77, 1985–1989; ***candidate for Republican nomination to presidency of the U.S., 1976***; Republican candidate for U.S. Senate (WV), 1978. BUS. & PROF.: atty.; admitted to WV Bar, 1951; law practice, Moundsville, WV, 1951. MIL.: sgt., 325th Infantry Regt., U.S. Army, 1943–46; Purple Heart; Combat Infantryman Badge; European Campaign Ribbon with three stars. MEM.: American Jud. Soc.; 85th Congressional Club (pres.); ABA; WV Bar Assn.; Beta Theta Pi (pres.); Council of Fraternity Presidents; Senior Men's Honorary; Men's Ranking Honorary; Phi Delta Phi; National Governors' Conference (chm., 1971–72). AWARDS: Silver Buffalo Award, BSA; Patriotic Service Medal, American Coalition of Patriotic Societies; commander, Order of Merit (Italy). HON. DEG.: LL.D., Alderson-Broaddus Coll.; Ph.D., Bethany Coll.; LL.D., Concord Coll.; LL.D., Marshall U.; LL.D., WV Inst. of Technology; LL.D., WV U.; LL.D., WV Wesleyan Coll. REL.: Methodist. MISC.: acquitted of charges of extortion while serving as governor. MAILING ADDRESS: P.O. Box 250, Moundsville, WV 26041.

MOORE, ARTHUR HARRY. b. Jul 3, 1879, Jersey City, NJ; d. Nov 18, 1952, Branchburg Township, NJ; par.

Robert White and Martha (McCoomb) Moore; m. Jennie Hastings Stevens, Mar 1911. EDUC.: Cooper Union School; LL.B., NJ Law School, 1924. POLIT. & GOV.: sec. to the mayor, Jersey City, NJ, 1908–11; city collector, Jersey City, 1911–13; elected member, Jersey City City Comm., 1913–25; elected as a Democrat to gov. of NJ, 1926–28, 1932–34, 1938–40; ***candidate for Democratic nomination to presidency of the U.S., 1932***; elected as a Democrat to U.S. Senate (NJ), 1935–38 (resigned). BUS. & PROF.: atty.; admitted to NJ Bar, 1922; law practice, Jersey City, NJ, 1922; faculty member, John Marshall Coll. of Law, 1928; prof. of legal ethics, NJ Law School, 1930–35; dir., West Side Trust Co.; dir., Bank of Lafayette; dir., Lafayette Building and Loan Assn. MEM.: American Forestry Assn.; National Anti-Pollution League; Aid Assn.; Hudson Cty. Hist. Soc.; NJ Hist. Soc.; St. Andrews Soc. of New York; Ulster Irish Soc. of New York; Ringoes Grange; Delta Theta Phi; Masons (Shriner); Elks; Loyal Order of Moose; Forester; Eagles; Scottish Clan McLeod; Carteret Club; Masonic Club; NJ Rifle Club; NJ Fish and Game Club; Circus Saints and Sinners; Washington Riding and Hunt Club. HON. DEG.: LL.D., Rutgers U., 1927; M.A., Hahnemann Medical Coll., 1928; M.Commercial Science, Rider Coll., 1928; LL.D., Seton Hall Coll., 1928; LL.D., John Marshall Coll. of Law, 1934; LL.D., NJ Law School, 1934. MISC.: noted follower of Frank Hague, political boss of Jersey City, NJ; advocate on behalf of physically handicapped children; recognized expert on playground design. RES.: Jersey City, NJ.

MOORE, CECIL FAY. b. Oct 16, 1920, Bronson, MI; par. Jesse and Mattie (Spade) Moore; m. Frances Irby, Jun 9, 1945; c. Buddy Kelly. EDUC.: Olivet Coll., 1939–40; Mercer U., 1965. POLIT. & GOV.: ***candidate for American Party nomination to presidency of the U.S., 1976***. BUS. & PROF.: barber; soldier; ordained minister, Southern Baptist Church, 1966; minister of music, Avondale, GA, 1965–66; pastor, New Providence Baptist Church, Smarr, GA, 1966–67; minister of music/assoc. pastor, Macon (GA) South Side Baptist Church, 1967–68, 1970–72; pastor, Lynmore Estates Baptist Church, Macon, 1972–74; pastor, Community Baptist Church, Centerville, GA, 1975; singing and supply pastor, various churches, GA, 1975; founding pastor, Cathedral of Christ Baptist Church, Macon, 1976–. MIL.: U.S. Army, 30 years. REL.: Southern Bapt. MAILING ADDRESS: 4092 Mikado Ave., Macon, GA 31206.

MOORE, CHARLES LEROY, JR. POLIT. & GOV.: ***candidate for Democratic nomination to presidency of the U.S., 1992; Rainbow Coalition Party candidate for presidency of the U.S., 1992***. MAILING ADDRESS: 821 North Taylor St., Wake Forest, NC 27587.

MOORE, DANIEL KILLIAN. b. Apr 2, 1906, Asheville, NC; d. Sep 8, 1986, Durham, NC; par. Fred and Lela (Enloe) Moore; m. Jeanelle Coulter, May 4, 1933; c. Edith (Mrs. Edgar B. Hamilton, Jr.); Daniel Killian, Jr. EDUC.: B.S., U. of NC, 1927, LL.B., 1928. POLIT. & GOV.: town atty., Sylvia, NC, 1931–33; cty. atty., Jackson Cty. (NC) Board of Education; elected as a Democrat to NC State House, 1941–43; Democratic precinct committeeman, NC; member, Jackson Cty. Democratic Exec. Cmte.; member, NC State Democratic Exec. Cmte.; member, Congressional Advisory Cmte.; elected solicitor, 30th Judicial District of NC, 1946–48; appointed judge, Superior Court of NC, 1948–58; member, NC State Board of Water Resources, 1959–64; elected as a Democrat to gov. of NC, 1965–69; ***candidate for Democratic nomination to presidency of the U.S., 1968***; appointed and subsequently elected assoc. justice, Supreme Court of NC, 1969–78. BUS. & PROF.: atty.; admitted to NC Bar, 1928; law practice, Sylvia, NC; counselor, asst. sec., Champion Papers, Inc., 1958–65; partner, Joyner, Moore and Howison (law firm), Raleigh, NC, 1969; partner, Ragsdal and Liggett (law firm), Raleigh; dir., Wachovia Bank and Trust Co.; dir., North Carolina R.R.; dir., radio station WWIT. MIL.: pvt. T/5, U.S. Army, 1943–45. MEM.: Phi Beta Kappa; Pi Kappa Phi; Mountain City Club; Mountain View Club; Rotary Club; Civitans; Masons; U. of NC Alumni Assn. (dir.); U. of NC Law School Foundation (dir.); High Point Coll. (trustee, 1966–); U. of NC (life trustee). HON. DEG.: LL.D., U. of NC, 1966. REL.: Methodist. RES.: Raleigh, NC.

MOORE, HAROLD. POLIT. & GOV.: ***New Alliance Party candidate for vice presidency of the U.S., 1988***. BUS. & PROF.: reporter, *Just Out*, Portland, OR. MISC.: gay activist; released from federal prison, Jan 1988. MAILING ADDRESS: 811 Burnside, Suite 114, Portland, OR 97214.

MOORE, JACK RICHARD. b. Aug 13, 1925, Zanesville, OH; par. Harold Charles and Ida Glen (Leasure) Moore; m. Betty Ruth Gibson; c. Jay Richard; John Ray; Jacqueline Ruth; Joy Rebecca; Jill Ranee. EDUC.: Grover Cleveland H.S., Zanesville, OH. POLIT. & GOV.: ***Common Man Independent Party candidate for presidency of the U.S., 1960, 1988***. BUS. & PROF.: attendant, Cambridge State Hospital, Zanesville; supervisor, Fischer Park and Shepard Park, Cocoa Beach, FL; supervisor, J. C. Penney service station; toll booth operator; lay preacher; head of housekeeping, Atlantic Beach Lodge, Cocoa Beach. MIL.: signalman first class, U.S. Navy, 1942–46. REL.: Seventh Day Church of God. MAILING ADDRESS: 1485 North Lester Court, Merritt Island, FL 32952.

MOORE, KENNETH. b. Feb 22, 1943. POLIT. & GOV.: ***Nonpartisan Party candidate for presidency of the U.S., 1984***. BUS. & PROF.: senior systems analyst; certified by U.S. Army Officer's Systems Analysis School of Data Processing. MAILING ADDRESS: George Washington Station Box 5083, Alexandria, VA 22305-5083.

MOORE, MAMIE. c. at least one. POLIT. & GOV.: ***Peace and Freedom Party candidate for vice presidency of***

the U.S., 1988; New Alliance Party candidate for vice presidency of the U.S., 1988; New Alliance Party candidate for U.S. House (NY), 1990. BUS. & PROF.: exec. dir., Somerville (NJ) Community Action Program, 1978–; political activist; trade union organizer. MEM.: New Alliance Community Services (coordinator). MAILING ADDRESS: 1 Third St., Somerville, NJ 08876.

MOORE, MICHAEL JAMES. b. Apr 17, 1960, Nashville, TN; par. James S. and Lois J. (Resent) Moore; single. EDUC.: Chandler H.S.; Gilbert H.S. POLIT. & GOV.: ***candidate for Republican nomination to presidency of the U.S., 1988; candidate for American Party nomination to presidency of the U.S., 1988***. BUS. & PROF.: soldier. MIL.: U.S. Air Force, 6 years. MISC.: known as a "working man." MAILING ADDRESS: 38 South Cholla, Gilbert, AZ 85234.

MOORE, RICHARD ARLIS. POLIT. & GOV.: ***candidate for Democratic nomination to presidency of the U.S., 1976***. MAILING ADDRESS: 8331 Southwest 13 Terrace, Miami, FL 33144.

MOORE, WILLIAM ROBERT. b. Mar 28, 1830, Huntsville, AL; d. Jun 12, 1909, Memphis, TN. EDUC.: district schools. POLIT. & GOV.: elected as a Republican to U.S. House (TN), 1881–83; ***candidate for Republican nomination to vice presidency of the U.S., 1888, 1896***; candidate for Republican nomination to gov. of TN, 1890 (declined). BUS. & PROF.: clerk, dry goods store, Beech Grove, TN; clerk, dry goods store, Nashville, TN; salesman, dry goods store, New York, NY, 1856–59; owner, wholesale dry goods store, Memphis, TN, 1859–1909. RES.: Memphis, TN.

MOORMAN, EDGAR VAUGHN. b. Jan 20, 1878, Big Springs, KY; d. Aug 8, 1942, Quincy, IL; par. Thomas R. and Lucy (McKay) Moorman; m. Jessie Seaman, May 1, 1912; c. Nelda; Bonita (Mrs. Richard K. Dowse); Melba (Mrs. William F. Campbell). EDUC.: public schools, KY. POLIT. & GOV.: appointed dir., Quincy (IL) Housing and Planning Council; ***Prohibition Party candidate for vice presidency of the U.S., 1940***. BUS. & PROF.: farmer; blacksmith; wagon maker, KY and Cincinnati, OH; manufacturer, vendor, livestock medicines, Gorin, MO; pres., Moorman Stock Medicine Co. (now Moorman Manufacturing Co.), 1900–1942; dir., Illinois National Bank, Quincy, IL. MEM.: Federal Council of Churches (Cmte. on Evangelism); American Business Men's Research Foundation; IL Wesleyan U. (trustee); Wesley Foundation of Urbana, IL (trustee); IL Manufacturers' Assn.; Laymen's Trust for Evangelism (pres.); Quincy City Farmers (pres.); AAAS; Rotary Club; Executive Club; Gideons. REL.: Methodist (member, General Cmte. on Evangelism, Promotional Literature, Missions, Budget and Audit). RES.: Quincy, IL.

MORALES, MARIO. POLIT. & GOV.: ***candidate for Democratic nomination to presidency of the U.S., 1980***. MAILING ADDRESS: 1855 Tacona St., Berkeley, CA 94707.

MORASCINI, DAVID JOHN. b. Jan 6, 1956, Morocco; par. Anthony Andrew and Jeanne Elizabeth (Hochberg) Morascini; m. Kirsten Ann Lehmann; c. Anthony; Adam; Christina. EDUC.: grad., Windham H.S.; Worchester Polytechnical Inst.; B.S., U. of London. POLIT. & GOV.: ***candidate for Democratic nomination to presidency of the U.S., 1992***. BUS. & PROF.: mechanical engineer; pres., MCM Audio-Visual, Brussels, Belgium, 1977–80; vice pres., Artsapassion Records, 1981–86; pres., Rock-It Corp., 1986–89; pres., CQBit, Inc., 1989–. REL.: R.C. MAILING ADDRESS: 26 Amidon Dr., Stafford Springs, CT 06076.

MOREHEAD, JOHN HENRY. b. Dec 3, 1861, Lucas Cty., IA; d. May 31, 1942, St. Joseph, MO; par. Andrew and Frances (Cooper) Morehead; m. Minnie Weisenreder, Feb 14, 1885; c. Dorothy L.; Edwin J. EDUC.: public schools; business college, Shenandoah, IA. POLIT. & GOV.: elected cty. treas., Richardson Cty., NE, 1896–99; elected mayor, Falls City, NE, 1900; elected as a Democrat to NE State Senate, 1910–12 (pres. pro tempore); succeeded to lt. gov. of NE upon death of incumbent, 1912–13; elected as a Democrat to gov. of NE, 1913–17; ***candidate for Democratic nomination to vice presidency of the U.S., 1916***; Democratic candidate for U.S. Senate (NE), 1918; Democratic candidate for gov. of NE, 1920; elected as a Democrat to U.S. House (NE), 1923–35; delegate, Dem. Nat'l. Conv., 1940. BUS. & PROF.: schoolteacher; farmer; stock raiser; merchant, Barada, NE; banker; real estate operator. REL.: Presb. RES.: Falls City, NE.

MORGAN, EDWIN DENISON. b. Feb 8, 1811, Washington, MA; d. Feb 14, 1883, New York, NY; par. Jasper Avery and Catherine (Copp) Morgan; m. Eliza Matilda Waterman, 1833; c. five. EDUC.: public schools; Bacon Acad., Colchester, CT. POLIT. & GOV.: elected member, Hartford (CT) City Council, 1831–36; elected alderman, New York, NY, 1849; elected as a Republican to NY State Senate, 1850–55; appointed NY Commissioner of Immigration, 1855–58; chm., NY Republican State Central Cmte.; vice chm., Rep. Nat'l. Conv., 1856; chm., Rep. Nat'l. Cmte., 1856–64, 1872–76; elected as a Republican to gov. of NY, 1859–62; delegate, Rep. Nat'l. Conv., 1860; appointed U.S. sec. of the treasury, 1861 (declined), 1881 (declined); elected as a Republican to U.S. Senate (NY), 1863–69; Republican candidate for U.S. Senate (NY), 1869, 1875; Republican candidate for gov. of NY, 1876; ***candidate for Republican nomination to presidency of the U.S., 1876***. BUS. & PROF.: partner, grocery store, Hartford, CT, 1831–36; partner (with Morris Earle), Morgan and Earle (wholesale grocers), New York, NY, 1836–37; pres., E. D. Morgan and Co., 1837–83. MIL.: maj. gen., U.S.V., 1861–63; commanded Dept. of NY,

1861–63. MEM.: Union Congressional Cmte. (chm., 1864). HON. DEG.: LL.D., Williams Coll., 1867. RES.: Hartford, CT.

MORGAN, H. d. between 1932 and 1936. POLIT. & GOV.: ***Socialist Labor Party candidate for presidency of the U.S., 1928***. BUS. & PROF.: CA field-worker, *Weekly People*. MISC.: stand-in candidate for regular Socialist Labor Party nominee. RES.: CA.

MORGAN, RUIZ JOHN REX. POLIT. & GOV.: ***candidate for Democratic nomination to presidency of the U.S., 1984***. MAILING ADDRESS: TX.

MORGAN, THOMAS ELLSWORTH. b. Oct 13, 1906, Ellsworth, PA; par. William and Mary (Lawson) Morgan; m. Winifred Strait, Aug 26, 1937; c. Mary Ann (Mrs. Gordon Youngwood). EDUC.: B.S., Waynesburg Coll., 1930; M.B., Detroit Coll. of Medicine and Surgery, 1933; M.D., Wayne State U., 1934. POLIT. & GOV.: elected as a Democrat to U.S. House (PA), 1944–77 (chm., House Foreign Affairs Cmte.); delegate, Dem. Nat'l. Conv., 1964, 1968, 1972; ***candidate for Democratic nomination to vice presidency of the U.S., 1976***. BUS. & PROF.: physician; intern, Grace Hospital, Detroit, MI, 1933–34; medical practice, Fredericktown, PA, 1934–. MEM.: Elks; Loyal Order of Moose; Owls; Waynesburg Coll. (trustee). AWARDS: Distinguished Service Award, Wayne State U. Medical School, 1964; Distinguished Alumnus Award, Waynesburg Coll., 1971; Annual Congressional Award, VFW, 1972; Patriot Award, PA American Legion, 1974. HON. DEG.: LL.D., Waynesburg Coll., 1965; LL.D., Washington and Jefferson Coll., 1975; LL.D., Wayne State U., 1976. REL.: Methodist. MAILING ADDRESS: Fredericktown, PA 15333.

MOROME, NORA. b. May 22, 1938, Brooklyn, NY; par. Abraham and Esperanza (Whiteflower) Morome; single. EDUC.: grad., Erasmus Hall H.S., 1955; St. John's U. POLIT. & GOV.: ***independent candidate for presidency of the U.S., 1976***. BUS. & PROF.: sec.; unpublished writer; cosmetic business. REL.: Keeper of the Faith. MAILING ADDRESS: 800 Bunker Hill, Los Angeles, CA.

MORON, CAPTAIN (aka WILLIAM HALTERMAN). POLIT. & GOV.: ***independent candidate for presidency of the U.S., 1976 (satire effort)***. MAILING ADDRESS: Captain Moron Campaign, Box 4374, Silver Spring, MD 20904.

MORRIS, ROBERT. b. Sep 30, 1915, Jersey City, NJ; par. John Henry and Sarah (Williams) Morris; m. Joan Russell Byles, Dec 27, 1951; c. Robert; Paul E.; Roger; Joan Byles II; William E.; John Henry II; Geoffrey. EDUC.: A.B., St. Peter's Coll., 1936; J.D., Fordham U., 1939. POLIT. & GOV.: asst. counsel, NY State Investigating Cmte., 1940–41; sec. to U.S. Rep. F. R. Coudert, Jr., 1946–50; counsel, U.S. Senate Cmte. on Foreign Relations, 1950; special counsel, U.S. Senate Internal Security Subcommittee, 1951–53, chief counsel, 1953, 1956–58; judge, NY Municipal Court, 1954–56; candidate for Republican nomination to U.S. Senate (NJ), 1958, 1960, 1984; candidate for Republican nomination to U.S. Senate (TX), 1964, 1970, 1984; ***candidate for American Independent Party nomination to presidency of the U.S., 1976***. BUS. & PROF.: newspaper reporter, 1934–36; teacher, St. Peter's Preparatory School, Jersey City, NJ, 1936–39; atty.; admitted to NY Bar, 1939; admitted to TX State Bar, 1962; admitted to the Bar of the Supreme Court of the U.S.; atty., Hines, Rearick, Door and Hammond (law firm), 1939–40; sec.-treas., Monrovia Port Management Co., 1947–49; partner, Hochwald, Morris and Richmond (law firm), 1946–52; pres., U. of Dallas, 1960–62; pres., U. of Plano, Dallas, TX, 1964–71, 1973–, chancellor, 1971–74; dir., Schick Investment Co., 1970–74; dir., Schick Electric Co. MIL.: lt. commander, U.S.N.R., 1941–46. MEM.: ABA; TX State Bar Assn.; Dallas Bar Assn.; Phi Delta Phi; City Club; University Club. HON. DEG.: LL.D., St. Francis Coll., 1954; L.H.D., Fujen U., Taipei, Taiwan, 1971. WRITINGS: *No Wonder We Are Losing* (1958); *Disarmament, Weapon of Conquest* (1963); *What is Developmental Education?* (1967). REL.: R.C. MAILING ADDRESS: 5415 Lobello Dr., Dallas, TX 75229.

MORRIS, SAMUEL N. b. 1900, Cottle Cty., TX; m. 1919. EDUC.: Wesley Coll., 3 years; grad., Hardin-Simmons Coll., 1927; M.A., Brown U., 1930. POLIT. & GOV.: Prohibition Party candidate for U.S. Senate (TX), 1941; ***candidate for Prohibition Party nomination to vice presidency of the U.S., 1940 (declined), 1944 (declined); candidate for Prohibition Party nomination to presidency of the U.S., 1944***. BUS. & PROF.: employee, saw mill; employee, Cross-Tie Camps; ordained minister, Baptist Church; pastor, First Baptist Church, Weatherford, RI; field sec., Hardin-Simmons U., Abilene, TX; pastor, First Baptist Church, Stamford, TX; radio commentator, "Voice of Temperance," radio station XEPN, Eagle Pass, TX, 1935–; pres., Preferred Risk Insurance Co. WRITINGS: *The Voice of Temperance Scrapbook* (1936); *The Glory of God's Second Call* (1936); *Blessed Assurance* (1937); *Slaves of the Bottle* (1937); *The Woe of the Wine Cup* (1937); *Mother's Bible, or Anchors of Hope* (1938); *The Booze Buster; The Ravages of Rum* (1945); *Wine, Women, and Song* (1940); *Booze and War* (1944). REL.: Bapt. MISC.: known as "The Booze Buster"; sued CBS in 1946, later withdrew suit; testified before Congress on discrimination against temperance advertising on television, 1954. MAILING ADDRESS: Eagle Pass, TX.

MORRIS, THOMAS. b. Jan 3, 1776, Berks Cty., PA; d. Dec 7, 1844, Bethel, OH; par. Isaac and Ruth (Henton) Morris; m. Rachel Davis, Nov 19, 1797; c. Isaac Newton; Jonathan David; Benjamin F.; three daughters; five other sons. EDUC.: public school, Clarksburg, VA (now WV), 3 months. POLIT. &

GOV.: elected as a Democrat to OH State House, 1806–08, 1810, 1820–21; elected as a Democrat to judge, Supreme Court of OH, 1809 (disqualified); elected as a Democrat to OH State Senate, 1813–15, 1821–23, 1825–29, 1831–33; Democratic candidate for U.S. House (OH), 1832; elected as a Democrat to U.S. Senate (OH), 1833–39; ***candidate for Liberty Party nomination to presidency of the U.S., 1844; Liberty Party candidate for vice presidency of the U.S., 1844***. BUS. & PROF.: clerk, Columbia, OH, 1795; atty.; day laborer, to 1802; admitted to OH Bar, 1804; law practice, Bethel, OH; farmer, Clermont Cty., OH; publisher, *Ohio Sun*, 1828; abolitionist. MIL.: Ranger, Indian Wars, 1793. RES.: Bethel, OH.

MORRIS, WILLIAM. b. Apr 13, 1913, Boston, MA; d. Jan 2, 1994, Columbus, OH; par. Charles Hyndman and Elizabeth Margaret (Hanna) Morris; m. Jane Frazer, Aug 7, 1939; m. 2d, Mary Elizabeth Davis, Feb 8, 1947; c. Ann Elizabeth (Mrs. Paul Downie); Susan Jane McLeod; John Boyd; William Frazer; Mary Elizabeth; Evan Nathanael. EDUC.: grad., Phillips Exeter Acad., 1930; A.B., Harvard U., 1934. POLIT. & GOV.: ***independent (Cmte. for a Constitutional Presidency) candidate for vice presidency of the U.S., 1976***. BUS. & PROF.: ed.; author; columnist; broadcaster; lexicographer; instructor in English and Latin, Newman School, 1935–37; staff, G. & C. Merriam Co., 1937–43; managing ed., Grosset and Dunlop, 1945–47, exec. ed., 1947–53, editor-in-chief, 1953–60; syndicated columnist, "William Morris on Words," The Bell-McClure Syndicate, 1954–68; consulting ed., *Funk and Wagnall's New Standard Dictionary*, 1954–58; consulting ed., *New College Standard Dictionary*, 1958–60; exec. ed., *Encyclopedia International*, 1960–62; editor-in-chief, *Grolier Universal Encyclopedia*, 1962–64; editor-in-chief, *American Heritage Dictionary*, 1964–; syndicated columnist (with Mary Morris), "Words, Wit and Wisdom," *Los Angeles Times* Syndicate, 1968–75; editor-in-chief, Xerox Intermediate and Beginning Dictionaries, 1971–; syndicated columnist, United Features Syndicate, 1975–. MIL.: lt. (jg), U.S. Maritime Service, 1943–45. MEM.: Modern Language Assn. of America; Old Greenwich Boat Club; Soc. for General Semantics; Coll. English Assn.; National Council of Teachers of English; American Library Assn.; Coffee House Club; Dutch Treat Club (pres.); Harvard Club; Overseas Press Club; Silurians; Perrot Memorial Library (dir.). WRITINGS: *Words: The New Dictionary* (ed., 1947); *Berlitz Self-Teacher Language Books* (ed., 1949–53); *Concise Biographical Dictionary* (ed., 1949); *It's Easy to Increase Your Vocabulary* (1957); *The Word Game Book* (with Mary Morris, 1959); *Dictionary of Word and Phrase Origins* (with Mary Morris, 1962–71); *William Morris Vocabulary Enrichment Program* (creator, with Mary Morris, 1964); *Your Heritage of Words* (1970); *Harper Dictionary of Contemporary Usage* (with Mary Morris, 1975). REL.: Episc. RES.: Old Greenwich, CT.

MORRIS, WINIFRED. POLIT. & GOV.: ***candidate for Democratic nomination to presidency of the U.S., 1980***. MAILING ADDRESS: P.O. Box 323, Cardiff, CA 92007.

MORRISON, FRANK BRENNER. b. May 20, 1905, Golden, CO; par. Frank and Viva Montez (Brenner) Morrison; m. Maxine Elizabeth Hepp, Jun 28, 1936; c. Frank Brenner, Jr.; David Jon; Jean Marie Galloway. EDUC.: B.S., KS State Coll., 1927; J.D., U. of NE, 1931. POLIT. & GOV.: superintendent of schools, Farwell, NE, 1928–29; research asst., Wickersham Comm. on Law Enforcement, 1931; cty. atty., Frontier Cty., NE, 1935–42; cty. atty., Red Willow Cty., NE, 1944–45; counsel, Twin Valley Project, REA, 1945–48; atty., Frenchman-Cambridge Irrigation District, 1945–57; counsel, McCook Rural Electrification Project, 1946–57; Democratic candidate for U.S. House (NE), 1948, 1954; candidate for Democratic nomination to gov. of NE, 1950; NE campaign mgr., Kefauver for President Campaign, 1952, 1956; delegate, Dem. Nat'l. Conv., 1956, 1972; Democratic candidate for lt. gov. of NE, 1956; member, Board of Directors, Consumers Public Power District, 1959–60; Democratic candidate for U.S. Senate (NE), 1960, 1966, 1970; elected as a Democrat to gov. of NE, 1961–67; ***candidate for Democratic nomination to presidency of the U.S., 1968***; appointed food consultant, Agency for International Development, 1968; appointed member, NE Comm. on Social and Industrial Reform, 1971; appointed and subsequently elected public defender, Douglas Cty., NE, 1971–; Democratic candidate for atty. gen. of NE, 1974. BUS. & PROF.: farmer; teacher, NE School of Agriculture, 1931–32; atty.; admitted to NE Bar, 1931; law practice, Maywood, NE, 1931–34; law practice, Stockville, NE, 1934–42; law practice, McCook, NE, 1942–55; partner, Morrison and Vestecka (law firm), Lincoln, NE, 1955–61; law practice, Omaha, NE, 1967–. MEM.: Tau Kappa Epsilon; Phi Alpha Delta; Delta Sigma Rho; Pi Kappa Delta; Rotary International (district gov.); Norris Memorial Foundation (pres., 1950); McCook C. of C. (dir.); Lutheran Medical Center (trustee); ABA; NE Bar Assn.; Lincoln Bar Assn.; Bar Assn. of the 14th Judicial District of KS (vice pres., 1936; sec.-treas., 1937; pres., 1955); McCook Park and Playground Assn. (pres., 1948–56); Masons (Shriner; Scottish Rite); Elks. REL.: Episc. MISC.: won KS Inter-Soc. Oratorical Contest, 1925; Pi Kappa Delta Speaking Contest, 1927. MAILING ADDRESS: 13006 Shirley, Omaha, NE 68102.

MORRISON, WILLIAM RALLS. b. Sep 14, 1825, Prairie du Long, IL; d. Sep 29, 1909, Waterloo, IL; par. John and Anne (Ralls) Morrison; m. Mary Jane Drury, 1852; m. 2d, Eleanora Horine, 1857; c. three sons (infants). EDUC.: McKendree Coll. POLIT. & GOV.: deputy sheriff, Monroe Cty., IL, 1847; clerk, Circuit Court, Monroe Cty., IL, 1852–54; elected as a Democrat to IL State House, 1854–60 (Speaker, 1859–60), 1871–72; delegate, Dem. Nat'l. Conv., 1856, 1868, 1884, 1888; elected as a Democrat to U.S. House (IL), 1863–65, 1873–87 (chm., Ways and Means Cmte., 1875–77, 1883–87); Democratic candidate for U.S. House (IL), 1864, 1866, 1886; delegate, Union National Convention, 1866; ***candidate for Democratic nomination to presidency of the U.S., 1880, 1884, 1892, 1896***; Democratic candidate for U.S. Senate (IL), 1885; appointed member, Interstate Commerce Comm., 1887–97 (chm., 1891–97). BUS. & PROF.: atty.; admitted to IL Bar, 1855; law practice, Waterloo, IL, 1855–1909. MIL.: pvt., 2d IL Regt., U.S. Army, 1848; col., 49th IL Volunteers, 1861–63. MISC.: joined CA gold rush, 1849–51. RES.: Waterloo, IL.

MORROW, CONRAD FLOURNOY. b. Jul 30, 1940, Little Rock, AR; par. Carroll and Doris Morrow; m. Betty Morrow; m. 2d, Danielle Morrow; c. Shana; Aaron; Solon. EDUC.: B.A., U. of OK, 1962; M.A., George Washington U., 1964; M.Ph., Yale U., 1970, Ph.D., 1972 (declined). POLIT. & GOV.: ***Symbiotic Union candidate for presidency of the U.S., 1976***; Symbiotic Union candidate for U.S. House (OH), 1976. BUS. & PROF.: newsboy; clerk, NEA; clerk, U.S. Dept. of Labor; prof., U. of Alberta, 1971–73; worker, natural food store and community kitchen. MIL.: capt., U.S. Army, 1965–67; soldier, Northern Corps, Symbionese Liberation Army, 1974–. MAILING ADDRESS: 22 Brown St., Dayton, OH 45402.

MORROW, DWIGHT WHITNEY. b. Jan 11, 1873, Huntington, WV; d. Oct 5, 1931, Englewood, NJ; par. James Elmore and Clara (Johnson) Morrow; m. Elizabeth Reeve Cutter, Jun 16, 1903; c. Elisabeth R. (Mrs. Aubrey N. Morgan); Anne S. (Mrs. Charles A. Lindbergh, q.v.); Dwight M.; Constance C. EDUC.: A.B. (cum laude), Amherst Coll., 1895; LL.B. (cum laude), Columbia U., 1899. POLIT. & GOV.: adviser, Allied Maritime Transport Council, 1918; appointed chm., NJ State Board of Institutions and Agencies, 1918–20; appointed chm., NJ Prison Inquiry Comm., 1919; appointed dir., War Savings Comm. of NJ, 1918; appointed member, President's Aircraft Board, 1925; appointed U.S. ambassador to Mexico, 1927–30; delegate, Sixth Pan American Conference, 1928; delegate, International Naval Conference, 1930; elected as a Republican to U.S. Senate (NJ), 1930–31; ***candidate for Republican nomination to presidency of the U.S., 1932***. BUS. & PROF.: employee, treasurer's office, Allegheny Cty., PA, 1887–91; schoolteacher; atty.; assoc., Simpson, Thacher and Bartlett (law firm), New York, NY, 1899–1905, partner, 1905–14; partner, J. P. Morgan and Co., 1914–27; dir., Bankers Trust Co.; dir., General Electric Co.; dir., Palisades Trust and Guaranty Co. MEM.: Daniel Guggenheim Fund for the Promotion of Aeronautics (dir.); Amherst Coll. (trustee); Union Theological Seminary (trustee); Russell Sage Foundation (trustee); Carnegie Endowment for International Peace (trustee); Commonwealth Fund (trustee); Smithsonian Institution (Regent); Assn. for the Improvement of the Poor of New York (trustee); Englewood Civic Assn. (pres.); American Red Cross (city campaign chm., 1923); Century Club; University Club; Metropolitan Club; India House; City Club of New York; Bankers Club; Creek Club. AWARDS: Gold Medal, National Comm. on Prisons and Prison Labor, 1919; Distinguished Service Medal, 1919; several foreign decorations. HON. DEG.: LL.D., U. of Rochester, 1920; LL.D., Princeton U., 1925; LL.D., U. of PA, 1926; LL.D., Williams Coll., 1926; LL.D., Yale U., 1927; LL.D., Brown U., 1928; LL.D., Harvard U., 1928; LL.D., Marshall U., 1928; LL.D., Bowdoin Coll., 1931; LL.D., Dartmouth Coll., 1931; LL.D., Syracuse U., 1931. WRITINGS: *The Society of Free States* (1919); *Parties and Party Leaders* (introduction, 1923). RES.: New York, NY.

MORROW, EDWIN PORCH. b. Nov 28, 1878, Somerset, KY; d. Jun 15, 1935, Frankfort, KY; par. Judge Thomas Z. and Catherine Virginia "Jennie" Crosson (Bradley) Morrow; m. Katherine Hale Waddle, Jun 18, 1905; c. Edwina Haskell (Mrs. Joseph Horgan); Charles Robert. EDUC.: St. Mary's Coll.; Cumberland Coll.; A.B., Centre Coll.; LL.B., U. of Cincinnati, 1902. POLIT. & GOV.: city atty., Somerset, KY, 1902; appointed U.S. district atty., Eastern District of KY, 1911–15; Republican candidate for U.S. Senate (KY), 1913; Republican candidate for gov. of KY, 1915; elected as a Republican to gov. of KY, 1919–23; delegate, Rep. Nat'l. Conv., 1920; ***candidate for Republican nomination to presidency of the U.S., 1920; candidate for Republican nomination to vice presidency of the U.S., 1920***; appointed member, U.S. Railroad Labor Board, 1924–26; appointed member, U.S. Board of Mediation, 1934; candidate for Republican nomination to U.S. House (KY), 1934. BUS. & PROF.: atty.; admitted to KY Bar, 1902; law practice, Lexington, KY, 1902; law practice, Somerset, KY, 1903–35. MIL.: pvt., 2d lt., 4th KY Volunteers, U.S. Army, 1898–99. MEM.: Masons; Pendennis Club; Lexington City Club; Union League. HON. DEG.: LL.D., U. of KY. REL.: Presb. RES.: Somerset, KY.

MORSA, CHUCK. b. 1936; married; c. six. POLIT. & GOV.: ***American Independent Party candidate for vice presidency of the U.S., 1988***. BUS. & PROF.: realtor, Thousand Oaks, CA. MAILING ADDRESS: c/o American Independent Party, 2069 Dacian Dr., Walnut, CA 91873.

MORSE, ALLEN BENTON. b. Jan 7, 1839, Otisco, MI; d. Jul 1, 1921, Ionna, MI; par. John L. and Susan Ann (Cowles) Morse; m. Frances Marion Van Allen, Nov 25, 1874; m. 2d, Anna Babcock, Dec 12, 1888; c. Marion (Mrs. Elvert M. Davis); Van Allen; Lucy C. (Mrs. Gilbert Lee Yates); Dan Root. EDUC.: District School, Ionia Cty., MI; MI State Agricultural Coll., 1859–61; studied law under W. B. Wells, Ionia, 1864. POLIT. & GOV.: elected as a Republican to prosecuting atty., Ionia Cty., 1867–71; elected as a Democrat to MI State Senate, 1875–76; Democratic candidate for atty. gen. of MI, 1878; delegate, Dem. Nat'l. Conv., 1880; elected as a Democrat to mayor of Ionia, MI, 1882–83; elected justice, MI State Supreme Court, 1885–92 (appointed chief justice, 1885–92); Democratic candidate for gov. of MI, 1892; ***candidate for Democratic nomination to vice presidency of the U.S., 1892, 1896***; appointed U.S. consul, Glasgow, Scotland, 1892–96. BUS. & PROF.: schoolteacher; atty.; admitted to MI Bar, 1865; partner (with W. B. Wells), law firm, Ionia, 1865–80; partner, Morse, Wilson and Trowbridge (law firm), Ionia, 1880–85. MIL.: pvt., Company B, 16th MI Infantry, 1861; commissioned 1st lt., 21st MI Infantry, asst. adj. to Col. Frank T. Sherman, mustered out, 1864; lost arm in Battle at Mission Ridge, 1863. MEM.: Free and Accepted Masons. RES.: Ionia, MI.

MORSE, WAYNE LYMAN. b. Oct 20, 1900, Madison, WI; d. Jul 22, 1974, Eugene, OR; par. Wilbur Frank and Jessie (White) Morse; m. Mildred Martha Downie, Jun 18, 1924; c. Nancy Faye (Mrs. Hugh Campbell, Jr.); Judith Mary (Mrs. Wade Eaton); Amy Ann (Mrs. John Bilich). EDUC.: Ph.B., U. of WI, 1923, M.A., 1924; LL.B., U. of MN, 1928; J.D., Columbia U., 1932. POLIT. & GOV.: member, OR Crime Comm.; member, Governor's Comm. to Consider Judicial Reform; chm., Governor's Comm. on Improvement of Sentencing, Probation and Parole; administrative dir., U.S. Attorney General's Survey of Release Procedures, 1936–39; Pacific coast arbitrator, U.S. Dept. of Labor, 1938–42; appointed chm., U.S. Railway Emergency Board, 1941; appointed alternate member, National Defense Mediation Board, 1941; appointed member, National War Labor Board, 1942–44; elected as a Republican to U.S. Senate (OR), 1945–57, as a Democrat, 1957–69; ***candidate for Republican nomination to presidency of the U.S., 1952; candidate for Democratic nomination to vice presidency of the U.S., 1956; candidate for Democratic nomination to presidency of the U.S., 1960***; appointed chm., President's Special Board for the Atlantic and Gulf Coast Maritime Industry Dispute, 1963; appointed chm., President's Emergency Board on the Airline Dispute, 1966; appointed member, President's Special Board on the Railroad Dispute, 1967; delegate, Dem. Nat'l. Conv., 1968, 1972; Democratic candidate for U.S. Senate (OR), 1968, 1974. BUS. & PROF.: farmer; lecturer; instructor, U. of WI, 1924; asst. prof., U. of MN, 1924–29; teaching fellow, Columbia U., 1928–29; asst. prof. of law, U. of OR, 1929–30, assoc. prof., 1930, prof. of law, dean, 1931–44; Distinguished Visiting Scholar, State U. of NY, 1969–70; labor arbitrator, 1969–74. MIL.: 2d lt., F.A., U.S. Army, 1923–29. MEM.: ABA; OR Bar Assn.; Lane Cty. Bar Assn.; Federal Bar Assn.; DC Bar Assn.; American Law Inst.; Order of the Coif; Delta Sigma Rho; Gamma Eta Gamma; Scabbard and Blade; Pi Kappa Alpha; Masons (Shriner); Phi Kappa Phi; Knights of Pythias; Rotary Club; Assn. of American Law Schools; Pacific Coast Inst. of Law and the Administration of Justice; Social Science Research Council of America; National Conference of Family Relations; American Council of the Inst. of Pacific Relations; American Jud. Soc.; National Electric Benefit Board (trustee); Eagles; Loyal Order of Moose; SAR; Ore-Wash Farmers Union; National Grange; Lawyers Cmte. Against the War in Vietnam (hon. chm.); Pan American Development Foundation (trustee). AWARDS: Distinguished Service Award, U. of OR, 1963. HON. DEG.: LL.D., Cornell U., 1946; LL.D., Drake U., 1947; LL.D., Coll. of South Jersey, 1947; LL.D., Centre Coll., 1952; D.Jr.Sc., Suffolk U., 1961; LL.D., American International Coll., 1962; D.C.L., Parsons Coll., 1965; Ph.D., Salem Coll., 1965; LL.D., Wilberforce U., 1966; LL.D., Pacific U., 1969. WRITINGS: *A Survey of Grand Jury Systems* (1931); *The Administration of Criminal Justice in Oregon* (with Ronald Beattie, 1932); *Attorney General's Survey of Release Procedures* (1939). REL.: Congregationalist. RES.: Eugene, OR.

MORTON, JULIUS STERLING. b. Apr 22, 1832, Adams, NY; d. Apr 27, 1902, Lake Forest, IL; par. Julius D. and Emeline (Sterling) Morton; m. Caroline Joy; c. Joy; Paul; two other sons. EDUC.: B.A., Union Coll., 1856; B.A., U. of MI, 1858. POLIT. & GOV.: elected to NE Territorial Legislature, 1855–58; appointed sec. of NE Territory, 1858–61; acting gov. of NE Territory, 1858; appointed member, pres., NE State Board of Agriculture; Democratic candidate for gov. of NE, 1866, 1880, 1884, 1892; appointed U.S. sec. of agriculture, 1893–97; ***candidate for National (Gold) Democratic Party nomination to presidency of the U.S., 1896 (declined)***. BUS. & PROF.: farmer, Nebraska City, NE; founder, owner, *Nebraska City News*; ed., *The Conservative*, 1898–1902. MEM.: NE Territorial Horticultural Soc. (pres.); American Forestry Assn. (pres.). WRITINGS: *Illustrated History of Nebraska* (ed., 1897). MISC.: founder of Arbor Day, 1872. RES.: Nebraska City, NE.

MORTON, LEVI PARSONS. b. May 16, 1824, Shoreham, VT; d. May 16, 1920, Rhinebeck, NY; par. Rev. Daniel Oliver and Lucretia (Parsons) Morton; m. Lucy Young Kimball, Oct 15, 1856; m. 2d, Ann Livingston Read Street, Feb 12, 1873; c. Edith Livingston (Mrs. William Corcoran Eustis); Lena; Laura Helen (Duchess De Valencery); Alice (Mrs. Winthrop Rutherford); Mary; two others. EDUC.: grad., Shoreham (VT) Acad. POLIT. & GOV.: Republican candidate for U.S. House (NY), 1876; appointed hon. commissioner, Paris Exposition, 1878; elected as a Republican to U.S. House (NY), 1879–81; ***candidate for Republican nomination to vice presidency of the U.S., 1880 (declined), 1896***; Republican candidate for U.S. Senate (NY), 1881, 1885, 1887; appointed U.S. sec. of the navy, 1881 (declined); appointed U.S. minister to France, 1881–85; elected as a Republican to vice presidency of the U.S., 1889–1893; elected as a Republican to gov. of NY, 1895–96; ***candidate for Republican nomination to presidency of the U.S., 1896***. BUS. & PROF.: clerk, general store, Enfield, MA, 1838–40; schoolteacher, Boscawen, NH, 1840–41; merchant, Hanover, NH, 1845–50; merchant, James M. Beebe and Co., Boston, MA, 1850–54; dry goods merchant, New York, NY, 1854–63; banker; pres., L. P. Morton and Co.; pres., Morton, Bliss and Co., New York, 1863–99; pres., Morton, Rose and Co.; pres., Morton, Chaplin and Co., London, England; pres., Morton Trust Co., New York; pres., Fifth Avenue Trust Co.; real estate investor; dir., Guaranty Trust Co.; dir., Home Insurance Co.; dir., Panama Coal Co.; dir., Washington Life Insurance Co.; dir., Equitable Life Assurance Soc. of the United States; dir., Industrial Trust Co.; dir., Newport Trust Co. MEM.: Union League; Union Club; Metropolitan Club; Century Club; Lawyers Club; Republican Club; Press Club; New England Soc.; SAR; American Geographical Soc.; Tuxedo Club; Downtown Club. HON. DEG.: LL.D., Dartmouth Coll., 1881; LL.D., Middlebury Coll., 1882. REL.: Episc. RES.: Rhinecliff-on-Hudson, NY.

MORTON, OLIVER HAZARD PERRY THROCK. b. Aug 4, 1823, Salisbury, IN; d. Nov 1, 1877,

Indianapolis, IN; par. James Throck and Sarah (Miller) Morton; m. Lucinda M. Burbank, May 15, 1845; c. five. EDUC.: private school, Springfield, OH; Wayne Cty. Seminary; grad., Miami U., Oxford, OH, 1845; studied law. POLIT. & GOV.: elected judge, Sixth Judicial Circuit of IN, 1852; People's Party candidate for gov. of IN, 1856; delegate, Rep. Nat'l. Conv., 1856, 1872, 1876; elected as a Republican to lt. gov. of IN, 1860–61; succeeded and subsequently elected as a Republican to gov. of IN, 1861–67 (dissolved legislature and ran state by dictum, 1863–65); elected as a Republican to U.S. Senate (IN), 1867–77; ***candidate for Republican nomination to presidency of the U.S., 1876; American Union Club candidate for presidency of the U.S., 1876***; appointed member, Electoral Comm., 1876. BUS. & PROF.: hatter; atty.; admitted to IN Bar, 1847; law practice, Centerville, IN, 1847–60. MISC.: known as a radical reconstructionist and supporter of Fifteenth Amendment to the Constitution of the U.S. RES.: Indianapolis, IN.

MORTON, THURSTON BALLARD. b. Aug 19, 1907, Louisville, KY; d. Aug 14, 1982, Louisville, KY; par. David Cummings and Mary Harris (Ballard) Morton; m. Belle Clay Lyons, Apr 18, 1931; c. Thurston Ballard, Jr.; Clay Lyons. EDUC.: Woodbury Forest School, 1922–25; grad., Yale U., 1929. POLIT. & GOV.: elected as a Republican to U.S. House (KY), 1947–53; delegate, Rep. Nat'l. Conv., 1948, 1952, 1956; appointed asst. U.S. sec. of state for congressional relations, 1953–56; elected as a Republican to U.S. Senate (KY), 1957–69; chm., Rep. Nat'l. Cmte., 1959–61; ***candidate for Republican nomination to vice presidency of the U.S., 1960; candidate for Republican nomination to presidency of the U.S., 1964***. BUS. & PROF.: officer, Ballard and Ballard (grain and milling business), Louisville, KY, 1929–46, pres., 1946–47, chm. of the board, 1947–51; vice chm., dir., Liberty National Bank; chm. of the board, Churchill Downs. MIL.: lt. commander, U.S.N.R., 1941–46. MEM.: Louisville Pendennis; F Street Club; Capitol Hill Club; Louisville Board of Trade (dir.); Goodwill Industries (dir.); Frontier Nursing Service (dir.); Lincoln Inst. (dir.); American Horse Council (pres.); Alpha Delta Phi; Order of the Cincinnati; Community Chest; U.S.O. (chm.). HON. DEG.: LL.D., U. of Louisville, 1948. REL.: Episc. RES.: Louisville, KY.

MOSES, GEORGE HIGGINS. b. Feb 9, 1869, Lubec, ME; d. Dec 20, 1944, Concord, NH; par. Rev. Thomas Gannett and Ruth (Smith) Moses; m. Florence Abby Gordon, Oct 3, 1893; c. Gordon. EDUC.: grad., Phillips Exeter Acad., 1887; A.B., Dartmouth Coll., 1890, A.M., 1893. POLIT. & GOV.: private sec. to governor of NH, 1889–91, 1905; sec. to the chm., NH State Republican Cmte., 1890; sec., NH State Forestry Comm., 1893–1906; member, Board of Education, Concord, NH, 1902–03, 1906–09, 1913–16; delegate, Rep. Nat'l. Conv., 1908, 1916, 1928 (chm.), 1932, 1936, 1940; appointed envoy extraordinary and minister plenipotentiary to Greece and Montenegro, 1909–12; elected as a Republican to U.S. Senate (NH), 1918–33 (pres. pro tempore, 1925–33); chm., Republican Senatorial Campaign Cmte., 1924–30; ***candidate for Republican nomination to presidency of the U.S., 1928; candidate for Republican nomination to vice presidency of the U.S., 1928***; Republican candidate for U.S. Senate (NH), 1932; candidate for Republican nomination to U.S. Senate (NH), 1936; pres., NH State Constitutional Convention, 1938. BUS. & PROF.: ed., *Concord Evening Monitor*, 1892–1918; pres., Monitor and Statesman Co., Concord, 1898–1918. MEM.: Wonalancet Club; Passaconaway Club; Athenian Club; Army and Navy Club; National Press Club; Lotos Club; Union Club. HON. DEG.: LL.D., George Washington U., 1921; LL.D., Dartmouth Coll., 1928; Litt.D., Lincoln Memorial U., 1929. REL.: Congregationalist. RES.: Concord, NH.

MOTSINGER, GRADY RAY, JR. b. Aug 22, 1933, Roseboro, NC; par. Grady Ray and Margaret (Spell) Motsinger; m. Sarah Hope Huckaby (divorced); m. 2d, Gail Anne Wachtel (divorced); c. Anna. EDUC.: grad., Pilot Mountain H.S., 1951; LL.B., Wake Forest U., 1957, J.D., 1972; NC School of the Arts, 1973–74; Middle TN State U., 1974. POLIT. & GOV.: ***candidate for American Party nomination to presidency of the U.S., 1976***. BUS. & PROF.: salesman; lifeguard; bellhop; motel mgr.; atty.; law practice, Mount Airy, NC, 1957–59; law practice, Winston-Salem, NC, 1959–; real estate developer; owner, construction company; owner, swimming pool company; involved with restaurant, nightclub, hotel, ink manufacturing firm, leasing business, investment clubs, fire alarm companies, mink ranch, entertainment consulting firm, management consulting firm. MEM.: American Red Cross (dir.); BSA (dir.); United Cerebral Palsy (dir.); Phi Delta Phi; Twin City Club; Elks; Moose; Lions; Kiwanis; Kappa Alpha. REL.: Bapt. MAILING ADDRESS: Main St., Dobson, NC 27017.

MOTTL, RONALD MILTON. b. Feb 6, 1934, Cleveland, OH; par. Milton and Anna (Hummel) Mottl; m. Debra Mary Budan, 1969; c. Ronald Milton, Jr.; Ronda Ann; Ronald Michael. EDUC.: B.S., U. of Notre Dame, 1956, LL.B., 1957. POLIT. & GOV.: asst. dir. of law, Cleveland, OH, 1958–60; elected as a Democrat to Parma City (OH) Council, 1960–61, pres., 1961–66; elected as a Democrat to OH State House, 1967–69; elected as a Democrat to OH State Senate, 1969–75; elected as a Democrat to U.S. House (OH), 1975–83; ***candidate for Democratic nomination to presidency of the U.S., 1976***; candidate for Democratic nomination to U.S. House (OH), 1982. BUS. & PROF.: atty.; admitted to OH Bar, 1957; law practice, 1957–. MIL.: pvt., U.S. Army, 1957–58. REL.: R.C. MAILING ADDRESS: 5393 Pearl Rd., Parma, OH 44129.

MOUDY, ALFRED L. b. Apr 30, 1879, DeKalb Cty., IN; par. William and Ellen Jane (Carnahan) Moudy; m. Nora May Grinder, Sep 7, 1904. EDUC.: grad., Tri-State Coll., Angola, IN, 1910; Columbia U., 1912; grad., Artillery School of Fire, Fort Sill, OK, 1917; CO State U., 1920; grad., Command

and Staff School, Fort Leavenworth, KS, 1925. POLIT. & GOV.: ***candidate for Prohibition Party nomination to vice presidency of the U.S., 1924***. BUS. & PROF.: teacher, country schools, IN, 1899–1906; teacher, superintendent of schools, Waterloo, IN, 1906–17, 1920–23; lecturer; field representative, Flying Squadron Foundation, 1923; vice pres., Deubener Shopping Bag, Inc., Indianapolis, IN. MIL.: pvt., IN National Guard, 1903–06, 2d lt., 1906–09, 1st lt., 1909–12, capt., 1912–17; maj., field artillery, U.S. Army, 1917–19; lt. col., U.S.A.R., 1920. MEM.: National Better Government Assn. (pres.); Military Order of Foreign Wars; American Legion; Masons; Shriners; Odd Fellows; Knights of Pythias; Flying Squadron Foundation. WRITINGS: *Military Courtesy* (1932). RES.: Waterloo, IN.

MOXLEY, ROBERT E. LEE. b. 1902. POLIT. & GOV.: ***Resurrected Whig Party candidate for vice presidency of the U.S., 1972***. MAILING ADDRESS: Baltimore, MD.

MOYA, ADELICIO. b. Mar 10, 1914, Chilili, NM; d. after 1985; m. Domitilia Moya; c. six daughters; Adelicio, Jr. POLIT. & GOV.: ***People's Constitutional Party candidate for vice presidency of the U.S., 1968***. MEM.: Alianza Federal de Pueblos Libres. MAILING ADDRESS: 305 Telesfor Dr., S.W., Albuquerque, NM.

MOYER, JULIE ANN. POLIT. & GOV.: ***independent candidate for presidency of the U.S., 1992***. MAILING ADDRESS: IL.

MOYNIHAN, DANIEL PATRICK. b. May 16, 1927, Tulsa, OK; par. John Henry and Margaret Ann (Phipps) Moynihan; m. Elizabeth Therese Brennan, May 29, 1955; c. Timothy Patrick; Maura Russell; John McCloskey. EDUC.: City Coll. of New York, 1943; B.A. (cum laude), Tufts U., 1948; M.A., Fletcher School of Law and Diplomacy, 1949, Ph.D., 1961; Fulbright Fellow, London School of Economics and Political Science, 1950–51 (hon. fellow, 1970). POLIT. & GOV.: dir., International Rescue Comm., 1954; asst. to the sec., asst. sec., acting sec. to governor of NY, 1955–58; sec. of Public Affairs Cmte., NY State Democratic Cmte., 1958–60; appointed member, NY State Tenure Comm., 1959–60; dir., NY State Government Research Project, Syracuse U., 1959–61; delegate, Dem. Nat'l. Conv., 1960, 1976; appointed special asst. to U.S. sec. of labor, 1961–62, exec. asst., 1962–63; appointed asst. U.S. sec. of labor, 1963–65; President's Temporary Comm. on Pennsylvania Avenue (vice chm., 1964–73); chm., Advisory Cmte., Traffic Safety Dept., U.S. Dept. of Health, Education and Welfare; appointed counsellor to the president and asst. for urban affairs, 1969–73; appointed U.S. delegate to the U.N., 1971; appointed member, President's Science Advisory Cmte., 1971–73; appointed U.S. ambassador to India, 1973–75; appointed U.S. ambassador to the U.N., 1975–76; ***candidate for Democratic nomination to presidency of the U.S., 1976, 1984***; elected as a Democrat to U.S. Senate (NY), 1977–; ***candidate for None of the Above Party nomination to presidency of the U.S., 1980; candidate for Democratic nomination to vice presidency of the U.S., 1984***. BUS. & PROF.: educator; dir., Joint Center for Urban Studies, Harvard U. and MA Inst. of Technology, 1966–73; prof. of education and urban politics, Harvard U., 1966–73, prof. of government, 1973–77. MIL.: U.S.N.R., 1944–47. MEM.: American Phil. Soc.; National Acad. of Public Administration; AAAS (vice chm., 1971; dir., 1972–73); Catholic Assn. for International Peace; American Acad. of Arts and Sciences (chm., Seminar on Poverty); Century Club; Harvard Club; Federal City Club; Woodrow Wilson International Center for Scholars (vice chm., 1971–); Joseph H. Hirshhorn Museum and Sculpture Garden (chm., Board of Trustees, 1971–); Center for Advanced Studies, Wesleyan U. (fellow, 1965–66); London School of Economics and Political Science (hon. fellow, 1970). AWARDS: Meritorious Service Award, U.S. Dept. of Labor, 1964; Arthur S. Flemming Award, 1956; Centennial Medal, Syracuse U., 1969; award, International League for Human Rights, 1975. HON. DEG.: A.M., Harvard U., 1966; LL.D., LaSalle Coll., 1966; LL.D., Seton Hall Coll., 1966; D.P.A., Providence Coll., 1967; L.H.D., U. of Akron, 1967; LL.D., Catholic U. of America, 1968; LL.D., Duquesne U., 1968; LL.D., Fletcher School of Law and Diplomacy, 1968; L.H.D., Hamilton Coll., 1968; LL.D., IL Inst. of Technology, 1968; LL.D., New School of Social Research, 1968; LL.D., St. Louis U., 1968; D.S.Sc., Villanova U., 1968; LL.D., U. of CA, 1969; LL.D., U. of Notre Dame, 1969; LL.D., Fordham U., 1970; D.H., Bridgewater State Coll., 1972; D.Sc., MI Technological U., 1972; LL.D., St. Bonaventure U., 1972; LL.D., U. of IN, 1975; LL.D., Adelphi U., 1976; LL.D., Boston Coll., 1976; LL.D., Hebrew U., 1976; LL.D., OH State U., 1976; LL.D., St. Anselm's Coll., 1976. WRITINGS: *Beyond the Melting Pot* (coauthor, 1963; Anisfield Award, 1963); *Defenses of Freedom* (ed., 1966); *On Understanding Poverty* (ed., 1969); *Maximum Feasible Misunderstanding* (1969); *Toward a National Urban Policy* (ed., 1970); *On Equality of Educational Opportunity* (co-editor, 1972); *The Politics of a Guaranteed Income* (1973); *Coping: On the Practice of Government* (1974); *Ethnicity: Theory and Experience* (co-editor, 1975); *A Dangerous Place* (1978); *Counting Our Blessings* (1980); *Loyalties* (1984); *Family and Nation* (1986). REL.: R.C. MAILING ADDRESS: Waldorf Towers, Apt. 42A, 50th St. and Park Ave., New York, NY 10022.

MUCCIGROSSO, PASQUALE PHILIP "PAT." POLIT. & GOV.: ***candidate for Republican nomination to presidency of the U.S., 1988***. MAILING ADDRESS: 457 Siwanoy Place, Pelham Manor, NY 10803.

MUDD, ROGER HARRISON. b. Feb 9, 1928, Washington, DC; par. Kostka and Irma Iris (Harrison) Mudd; m. Emma Jeanne Spears, Oct 28, 1957; c. Daniel H.; Marie M.; Jonathan; Matthew M. EDUC.: A.B., Washington and Lee U.,

1950; M.A., U. of NC, 1953. POLIT. & GOV.: ***candidate for Democratic nomination to vice presidency of the U.S., 1972***. BUS. & PROF.: teacher, Darlington School, Rome, GA, 1951–52; reporter, *Richmond (VA) News Leader*, 1953; news dir., radio station WRNL, Richmond, 1953–56; reporter, WTOP radio and television, Washington, DC, 1956–61; correspondent, CBS, 1961–. MIL.: U.S. Army, 1945–47. MEM.: Citizens Scholarship Foundation (dir.); Randolph-Macon Women's Coll. (trustee, 1971–); Robert F. Kennedy Journalism Awards Cmte. (trustee, 1971–); Radio-TV Correspondents Assn. (chm., exec. cmte., 1969–70). MAILING ADDRESS: 7167 Old Dominion Dr., McLean, VA 22101.

MUELLER, GENEVA WILMA. POLIT. & GOV.: ***independent candidate for presidency of the U.S., 1980 (declined)***. MAILING ADDRESS: 6332 Tholozan Ave., St. Louis, MO 63109.

MULHOLLAND, CAROLE. POLIT. & GOV.: ***Liberty Union candidate for vice presidency of the U.S., 1992***. MAILING ADDRESS: unknown.

MULLEN, RICK. POLIT. & GOV.: ***candidate for Democratic nomination to vice presidency of the U.S., 1980***. MAILING ADDRESS: unknown.

MUNN, EARLE HAROLD, SR. b. Nov 29, 1904, Westlake, OH; d. 1992; par. Earle O. and Ella C. (Deming) Munn; m. Luella Mae Asfahl, Sep 7, 1926; c. Earle Harold, Jr.; Lewis Edwin. EDUC.: A.B., Greenville (IL) Coll., 1925; A.M., U. of MI, 1928, postgrad. study, 1938–39; Northwestern U., 1937–38. POLIT. & GOV.: Prohibition Party candidate for mayor of Hillsdale, MI; chm., MI State Prohibition Party Cmte., 1948–54; member, Prohibition Party National Cmte., 1952– (chm., 1956–71); ***Prohibition Party candidate for vice presidency of the U.S., 1960; Prohibition Party candidate for presidency of the U.S., 1964, 1968, 1972***; Prohibition Party candidate for U.S. Senate (MI), 1966; permanent chm., Prohibition Party National Convention, 1983. BUS. & PROF.: instructor in government science and public speaking, Central Acad. and Coll., McPherson, KS, 1925–27; registrar, acting dean, and prof. of psychology and education, Greenville Coll., 1927–37; grad. asst., U. of MI, 1938–39; assoc. mgr., Munn Art Studios, 1939–77, mgr., 1977–; assoc. prof. of education, instructor in American heritage, asst. to the dean, dean, Hillsdale Coll., Hillsdale, MI, 1939–72, prof. emeritus, 1972–; pres., WTVB, Coldwater, MI, 1954–68; mgr., WBSE, Hillsdale, 1958–60; sec., WYNZ, Ypsilanti, MI, 1964–65; assoc., WSTR, Inc., Sturgis, MI. MEM.: Hillsdale Cty. School Employees Credit Union (pres., 1958–); National Prohibition Foundation (pres., 1971–). HON. DEG.: D.Ed.A., Hillsdale Coll., 1972. REL.: Free Methodist. RES.: Hillsdale, MI.

MUNOZ, MARIA ELIZABETH. b. 1958, East Los Angeles, CA. EDUC.: grad., Princeton U. POLIT. & GOV.: organizer, Peace and Freedom Party; Peace and Freedom Party candidate for gov. of CA, 1986, 1990; Peace and Freedom Party candidate for U.S. Senate (CA), 1988; Peace and Freedom Party candidate for City Council, Los Angeles, CA, 1991; ***New Alliance Party candidate for presidency of the U.S., 1992***. BUS. & PROF.: public school teacher; special education and bilingual instructor, Union Avenue Elementary School, Los Angeles, CA. MEM.: Latina Women's Caucus of Princeton U.; Aztlan East (charter member, Princeton Chapter). MAILING ADDRESS: 1917 New Jersey St., Los Angeles, CA 90033.

MUNRO, DONALD L. d. between 1932 and 1936; c. Mrs. Celia M. Purvis. POLIT. & GOV.: delegate, Socialist Labor Party National Convention, 1896, 1900; Socialist Labor Party candidate for U.S. House (PA), 1898, 1900; ***Socialist Labor Party candidate for vice presidency of the U.S., 1908***; member, exec. cmte., Socialist Labor Party, 1916. BUS. & PROF.: machinist. RES.: Blair Cty., PA.

MURCH, THOMPSON HENRY. b. Mar 29, 1838, Hampden, ME; d. Dec 15, 1886, Danvers, MA. EDUC.: public schools. POLIT. & GOV.: elected as a Greenback-Labor Reformer to U.S. House (ME), 1879–83; ***candidate for Greenback Party nomination to presidency of the U.S., 1880 (declined); candidate for Greenback Party nomination to vice presidency of the U.S., 1880 (declined)***; Greenback-Labor Reform Party candidate for U.S. House (ME), 1882. BUS. & PROF.: sailor; stonecutter; ed., publisher, *Granite Cutters' International Journal*, 1877; merchant. MEM.: Granite Cutters' International Assn. of America (sec., 1877–78). RES.: Rockland, ME.

MURDOCK, VIKKI. POLIT. & GOV.: ***Peace and Freedom Party candidate for vice presidency of the U.S., 1988***; Peace and Freedom Party candidate for U.S. House (CA), 1990. MAILING ADDRESS: 5733 Sunfield Ave., Lakewood, CA 90712.

MURPHREE, ALBERT ALEXANDER. b. Apr 29, 1870, Walnut Grove, AL; d. Dec 20, 1927, Gainesville, FL; par. Capt. Jesse Ellis and Helen (Cornelius) Murphree; m. Jennie Henderson, Jul 27, 1897; c. Alberta; Mary; Martha; John A. H.; Albert Alexander, Jr. EDUC.: Walnut Grove (AL) Coll., 1880–87; Peabody Coll., Nashville, TN, 1890–92; A.B., U. of Nashville, 1894. POLIT. & GOV.: lt. col., governor's staff, FL; ***candidate for Democratic nomination to presidency of the U.S., 1924***. BUS. & PROF.: teacher, rural schools, TN, 1887; superintendent, Cullman (AL) City Schools; principal, Summit (AL) Inst.; principal, City H.S., Cleburne, TX; prof. of mathematics, FL State Coll., 1895, pres., 1897–1905; pres., FL State Coll. for Women, 1905–09; pres., U. of FL, 1909–27; ed., *Florida School Exponent*, 1907–09. MEM.: Masons; NEA; FL Hist. Soc. (dir.); FL Education Assn.; Comm. of Higher Institutions of Learning; Kappa Alpha; National Assn. of State Universities (vice pres., 1921). HON. DEG.: A.M., U. of Nashville, 1902; LL.D., Rollins Coll., 1909; LL.D., U. of AL, 1919. REL.: Bapt. (pres., FL Baptist Convention, 1922–24; vice pres., Southern Baptist Convention, 1924–25). RES.: Gainesville, FL.

MURPHY, DANIEL J. b. May 22, 1887, MT; d. Jun 27, 1965, San Francisco, CA; m. Clover E. Grant Marymee, 1929; c. Doris Jaquith. POLIT. & GOV.: ***American Vegetarian Party candidate for presidency of the U.S., 1952***. BUS. & PROF.: switchman, towerman, Southern Pacific R.R., 1921–65; cowboy, Billings, MT; minister, Inst. of Cosmos; owner, prosthetic device shop, San Francisco, CA. MEM.: National Vegetarian Soc.; Vegetarian Brotherhood of America, Inc. (pres.). REL.: Inst. of Cosmos. RES.: San Francisco, CA.

MURPHY, EDWARD FRANKLIN. b. Jan 3, 1846, Jersey City, NJ; d. Feb 24, 1920, Palm Beach, FL; par. William Hayes and Abby Elizabeth (Hagar) Murphy; m. Janet Colwell, Jun 24, 1868; c. Franklin, Jr.; Helen M. (Mrs. William H. Kinney); John A. EDUC.: academy, Newark, NJ. POLIT. & GOV.: elected member, Newark (NJ) Common Council, 1883–86; elected as a Republican to NJ State Assembly, 1885; chm., NJ Republican State Cmte., 1892–1920; delegate, Rep. Nat'l. Conv., 1900, 1904, 1908, 1912, 1916; member, Rep. Nat'l. Cmte., 1900–1920 (exec. cmte., 1900–1908); appointed U.S. ambassador to Russia, 1900 (declined); appointed U.S. commissioner, Paris Exposition, 1900; elected as a Republican to gov. of NJ, 1902–05; ***candidate for Republican nomination to vice presidency of the U.S., 1908, 1912***; candidate for Republican nomination to U.S. Senate (NJ), 1916; member, Essex Cty. (NJ) Park Comm. BUS. & PROF.: manufacturer; founder, pres., Murphy and Co. (varnish manufacturers), 1865–91; pres., Murphy Varnish Co., 1891–1920. MIL.: 1st lt., Company A, 13th NJ Volunteer Infantry, 1862–65. MEM.: National Home for Disabled Volunteer Soldiers (member, Board of Managers, 1905–12); National Soc. of SAR (pres., 1898–1900); Reform School for Boys (trustee, 1886–89); Union League; Down Town Club; Loyal Legion; Essex Club. HON. DEG.: LL.D., Lafayette Coll., 1901; LL.D., Princeton U., 1902. REL.: Episc. RES.: Trenton, NJ.

MURPHY, FRANK. b. Apr 13, 1890, Harbor Beach, MI; d. Jul 19, 1949, Detroit, MI; par. John F. and Mary (Brennan) Murphy; single. EDUC.: A.B., U. of MI, 1912, LL.B., 1914; Lincoln's Inn, London, England; Trinity Coll., Dublin, Ireland. POLIT. & GOV.: chief asst., U.S. atty. for Eastern District of MI, 1919–20; Democratic candidate for U.S. House (MI), 1920; elected as a Non-Partisan to judge, Recorder's Court, Detroit, MI, 1923–30; elected mayor of Detroit, MI, 1930–33; appointed gov.-gen. of the Philippine Islands, 1933–35; appointed U.S. high commissioner to the Philippines, 1935–36; elected as a Democrat to gov. of MI, 1937–39; Democratic candidate for gov. of MI, 1938; appointed atty. gen. of the U.S., 1939–40; ***candidate for Democratic nomination to presidency of the U.S., 1940; candidate for Democratic nomination to vice presidency of the U.S., 1940, 1944***; appointed assoc. justice, Supreme Court of the U.S., 1940–49. BUS. & PROF.: atty.; admitted to MI Bar, 1914; law clerk, Monaghan and Monaghan (law firm), Detroit, MI, 1914–17; teacher of law, night school, Detroit, 1914–17; law practice, Detroit, 1920–23; instructor in law, U. of Detroit, 1922–27. MIL.: 1st lt., capt., U.S. Army, 1917–19. MEM.: U.S. Assn. of Mayors (pres., 1933); American Legion; Sigma Chi. HON. DEG.: LL.D., U. of Santa Tomas, 1934; LL.D., Fordham U., 1935; LL.D., Loyola U., 1936; LL.D., U. of the Philippines, 1936; LL.D., Duquesne U., 1937; LL.D., U. of Detroit, 1937; LL.D., St. John's U., 1938; LL.D., John Marshall Coll., 1939; LL.D., LA State U., 1939; LL.D., NM State Coll., 1939; LL.D., St. Bonaventure Coll., 1939; LL.D., St. Joseph's Coll., 1939; LL.D., U. of MI, 1939; LL.D., Tulane U., 1941; LL.D., Creighton U., 1942; LL.D., Wayne U., 1942. REL.: R.C. RES.: Detroit, MI.

MURRAY, JAMES EDWARD. b. May 3, 1876, St. Thomas, Ontario, Canada; d. Mar 23, 1961, Butte, MT; par. Andrew James and Anna Mary (Cooley) Murray; m. Viola Edna Horgan, Jun 28, 1905; c. James A.; William D.; Edward E.; Howard A.; Charles A.; John S. EDUC.: grad., St. Jerome's Coll., Berlin, Canada, 1895; LL.B., NY U., 1900, LL.M., 1901. POLIT. & GOV.: elected cty. atty., Silver Bow Cty., MT, 1906–08; delegate, Dem. Nat'l. Conv., 1920, 1932, 1936, 1940, 1944, 1948, 1956; appointed chm., State Advisory Board, Public Works Administration, 1933–34; elected as a Democrat to U.S. Senate (MT), 1934–61; ***candidate for Democratic nomination to presidency of the U.S., 1952***. BUS. & PROF.: atty.; admitted to MT Bar, 1901; law practice, Butte, MT, 1901–61; banker; pres., U.S. Building and Loan Assn.; vice pres., mgr., Monidah Trust Corp. MEM.: Delta Chi; Knights of Columbus; Silver Bow Club. HON. DEG.: LL.D., NY U., 1941. REL.: R.C. MISC.: became naturalized U.S. citizen, 1900. RES.: Butte, MT.

MURRAY, KEN. POLIT. & GOV.: ***candidate for Republican nomination to presidency of the U.S., 1976***. MAILING ADDRESS: Box 705, Sturgis, MI 49091.

MURRAY, LEONARD BERNARD. b. Dec 9, 1914, Cambridge, NY; par. Henry and Catherine (Welch) Murray; m. Josephine Didona; c. Harriet; John S. EDUC.: grad., Wayne (MI) H.S.; Cleary Business Coll., Ypsilanti, MI. POLIT. & GOV.: ***candidate for Democratic nomination to presidency of the U.S., 1984***. BUS. & PROF.: salesman, Crowley Milner

Department Store, Detroit, MI. MIL.: U.S. Navy, 1931; U.S. Army, 1944–45. MEM.: American Legion. REL.: R.C. MAILING ADDRESS: Apt. 10, 1440 South Second East, Salt Lake City, UT 84115.

MURRAY, WILLIAM HENRY DAVID. b. Nov 21, 1869, Collinsville, TX; d. Oct 15, 1956, Oklahoma City, OK; par. Uriah Dow Thomas and Bertha Elizabeth (Jones) Murray; m. Mary Alice Hearrell; c. Massena B.; Bancroft; Johnston; Jean; Barbara. EDUC.: B.S., College Hill Inst., 1889. POLIT. & GOV.: counsel, gov. of Chickasaw Nation, 1898–1901; member, Choctaw-Chickasaw Coal Comm., 1903; chm., OK Code Comm., 1903; vice pres., Sequoyah Constitutional Convention, 1905; pres., OK State Constitutional Convention, 1906; chm., OK State Democratic Convention, 1907; elected as a Democrat to OK State House, 1907–09 (Speaker, 1907–09); delegate, Dem. Nat'l. Conv., 1908, 1912, 1916, 1932; candidate for Democratic nomination to gov. of OK, 1910, 1918, 1938; elected as a Democrat to U.S. House (OK), 1913–17; candidate for Democratic nomination to U.S. House (OK), 1916; elected as a Democrat to gov. of OK, 1931–35; chm., OK State Code Comm., 1931–35; ***candidate for Democratic nomination to presidency of the U.S., 1932; candidate for Democratic nomination to vice presidency of the U.S., 1932***; independent candidate for U.S. Senate (OK), 1938; candidate for Democratic nomination to U.S. Senate (OK), 1942. BUS. & PROF.: cotton picker; woodchopper; employee, brickyard; farmhand; schoolteacher, Limestone and Navarro counties, TX, 1886–90; ed., *Farmer's World*, Dallas, TX, 1891; ed., *Daily News*, Corsicana, TX, 1894–95; atty.; admitted to TX Bar, 1895; law practice, Fort Worth, TX, 1896–98; moved to Tishomingo, Indian Territory, 1898; rancher, OK, 1903–56; partner, Treadwell, Murray and Lucas (law firm), Tishomingo, Indian Territory, 1898–1903; colonizer, Bolivia, 1924–29. MEM.: Masons (33°). WRITINGS: *Essays on Pocahontas and Pushmataha; Rights of Americans Under Federal Constitution; The Presidency, Supreme Court, and Seven Senators; Uncle Sam Needs a Doctor; The Finished Scholar; Memoirs of Governor Murray and True History of Oklahoma; Government from Theocracy to Foolacracy; Palestine: Should Jews or Arabs Control?; Negroes Place in the Call of Race.* REL.: Methodist. MISC.: known as "Alfalfa Bill" Murray. RES.: Broken Bow, OK.

MUSGROVE, LYCURGUS BRECKINRIDGE. b. Dec 13, 1859, Jasper, AL; par. Frances Asbury and Elizabeth (Cain) Musgrove; single. EDUC.: public schools. POLIT. & GOV.: chm., Walker Cty. (AL) Board of Education; member, AL State Board of Education; candidate for Democratic nomination to U.S. Senate (AL), 1920, 1926, and one other time; ***candidate for Democratic nomination to presidency of the U.S., 1924***. BUS. & PROF.: coal operator; banker; owner, Corona Coal Mines; pres., Jasper (AL) Bank; farmer; real estate investor. MEM.: Anti-Saloon League (dir.); U. of AL (trustee); Masons; Odd Fellows. MISC.: reputed millionaire; backed by Ku Klux Klan in AL Senate races. REL.: Methodist. RES.: Jasper, AL.

MUSKIE, EDMUND SIXTUS. b. Mar 28, 1914, Rumford, ME; d. Mar. 26, 1996, Washington, D.C., par. Stephen and Josephine (Czarnecki) Muskie; m. Jane Frances Gray, May 29, 1948; c. Stephen Oliver; Ellen (Mrs. Ernest Allen); Melinda; Martha; Edmund Sixtus, Jr. EDUC.: Rumford (ME) H.S., 1932; B.A., Bates Coll., 1936; LL.B., Cornell U., 1939. POLIT. & GOV.: elected as a Democrat to ME State House, 1947–51 (minority leader, 1948–51); Democratic candidate for mayor of Waterville, ME, 1947; member, Waterville Board of Zoning Adjustment 1948–55; chm., ME Citizens' Cmte. for Hoover Report, 1950; ME district dir., Office of Price Stabilization, 1951–52; member, Dem. Nat'l. Cmte. (ME), 1952–57; delegate, Dem. Nat'l. Conv., 1952, 1956, 1960, 1964, 1968, 1972, 1976; city solicitor, Waterville, ME, 1954; member, Roosevelt Campobello International Park Comm.; elected as a Democrat to gov. of ME, 1955–59; ***candidate for Democratic nomination to presidency of the U.S., 1956, 1972, 1976, 1980***; elected as a Democrat to U.S. Senate (ME), 1959–80 (asst. majority whip, 1966–80); ***Democratic candidate for vice presidency of the U.S., 1968;*** member, Advisory Comm. on Intergovernmental Relations; ***candidate for Democratic nomination to vice presidency of the U.S., 1972, 1976;*** appointed U.S. sec. of state, 1980–81. BUS. & PROF.: atty.; admitted to MA Bar, 1939; admitted to ME Bar, 1940; admitted to practice before the U.S. District Court, 1941; partner, Muskie and Glover (law firm), Waterville, ME, 1939–55. MIL.: lt. (jg), U.S. Navy, 1942–45; three battle stars. MEM.: Waterville Bar Assn.; Kennebec Cty. Bar Assn.; ME Bar Assn.; MA Bar Assn.; Phi Beta Kappa; Phi Alpha Delta; Lions; Commercial Law League; Elks; AmVets (national exec. dir., 1951); Bates Coll. (trustee); Cornell Law School Council; Sisters Hospital (adviser); Waterville U.S.O. (chm., 1946); Waterville BSA (chm., 1950); Eagles; Grange; Delta Sigma Rho; Waterville Veterans Council (pres., 1947); American Legion; VFW; Phi Alpha Theta. HON. DEG.: LL.D., Bates Coll.; LL.D., Bowdoin Coll.; LL.D., Colby Coll.; LL.D., Lafayette Coll.; LL.D., Nassau Coll.; LL.D., Portland U.; D.P.A., Suffolk U.; LL.D., U. of Buffalo; LL.D., U. of ME. WRITINGS: *The Mechanics of Government; The Unfinished Journey* (1972); *Journeys* (1972); *What Price Defense* (coauthor, 1974). REL.: R.C. RES.: Washington, D.C.

MUZYK, GEORGE ALEXANDER. b. Aug 4, 1943, White Plains, NY; par. Col. Alexander Frank and Evelyn Teresa (Warner) Muzyk; single. EDUC.: grad., St. John's Coll. H.S., 1961; U.S. Military Acad., 1962–64; Georgetown U., 1965–67, 1968–69. POLIT. & GOV.: Moderate Independent Party candidate for U.S. Senate (MD), 1976; ***Moderate Independent Party candidate for presidency of the U.S., 1980, 1984, 1992***. BUS. & PROF.: sales representative, Chief of Naval Operations, U.S. Navy; employee, marketing dept., Chesapeake and Potomac Telephone Co., 1965–69; chief cook, YMCA, Camp Lette, MD, 1972–75 (summers only). MIL.: U.S. Army, 1962–64; Good Conduct Medal; Marksmanship Medal. MEM.: YMCA; West Point Football Team; West Point Lacross Team. WRITINGS: *A Day on Wall Street; Framework Hall of Famers.*

REL.: R.C. MAILING ADDRESS: 8902 Glenville Rd., Silver Spring, MD 20901.

MYERS, ROBIN ELIZABETH. single. EDUC.: M.A., Columbia U. POLIT. & GOV.: national sec., Socialist Party, 1950–56; ***Socialist Party candidate for vice presidency of the U.S., 1952 (withdrew following nomination by state convention)***. BUS. & PROF.: ed., *Socialist Party Paper*; instructor in history. MEM.: A. Philip Randolph Education Fund; Workers Defense League; National Advisory Comm. on Farm Labor. WRITINGS: *Black Builders: A Job Program That Works* (with Thomas R. Brooks, 196?); *Louisiana Story: The Sugar System and the Plantation Workers* (1964); *A Dictionary of Literature in the English Language, Chaucer to 1940* (1970); *The British Book Trade* (1973). MAILING ADDRESS: 303 Fourth Ave., New York, NY 10010.

NADER, RALPH. b. Feb 27, 1934, Winsted, CT; par. Nadra and Rose (Bouziane) Nader; single. EDUC.: A.B. (magna cum laude), Princeton U., 1955; LL.B. (with distinction), Harvard U., 1958. POLIT. & GOV.: ***People's (New) Party candidate for presidency of the U.S., 1972 (declined); candidate for Democratic nomination to vice presidency of the U.S., 1972; candidate for Democratic nomination to presidency of the U.S., 1972, 1976 (declined), 1992; candidate for Citizens Party nomination to presidency of the U.S., 1980***. BUS. & PROF.: atty.; author; consumer advocate; admitted to CT Bar, 1958; admitted to MA Bar, 1959; admitted to the Bar of the Supreme Court of the U.S.; law practice, Hartford, CT, 1959–; lecturer in history and government, U. of Hartford, 1961–63; lecturer, Princeton U., 1967–68; founder, Center for Responsive Law; founder, Public Interest Research Group; founder, Center for Auto Safety; founder, Professionals for Auto Safety; founder, Project for Corporate Responsibility; founder, Public Citizens, Inc.; contributing ed., *Ladies Home Journal*, 1973–. MIL.: U.S. Army, 1959. MEM.: ABA; American Acad. of Arts and Sciences; Phi Beta Kappa. AWARDS: one of ten Outstanding Men of the Year, U.S. Junior C. of C., 1967; Woodrow Wilson Fellow; Nieman Fellow (1965–66). WRITINGS: *Unsafe at Any Speed* (1965); *Beware* (1971); *Working on the System* (1972); *What to Do with Your Bad Car* (coauthor, 1971); *Action for a Change* (coauthor, 1972); *Whistle Blowing* (ed., 1972); *You and Your Pension* (coauthor, 1973); *The Consumer and Corporate Accountability* (ed., 1973); *Corporate Power in America* (co-editor, 1973); *The Commerce Committees* (coauthor, 1975); *The Environment Committees* (coauthor, 1975); *Government Regulation: What Kind of Reform?* (coauthor, 1976); *Verdicts on Lawyers* (ed., 1976); *Taming the Giant Corporation* (coauthor, 1976); *Menace of Atomic Energy* (coauthor, 1977); *Who's Poisoning America?* (coauthor, 1981). MAILING ADDRESS: 53 Hillside Ave., Winsted, CT 06098.

NASTER, DAVID. POLIT. & GOV.: ***candidate for Republican nomination to presidency of the U.S., 1992 (withdrew)***. MAILING ADDRESS: 12100 Mastin, Overland Park, KS 66213.

NATE, JEAN JOIE DE'VIVRE. POLIT. & GOV.: ***candidate for Republican nomination to presidency of the U.S., 1992; independent candidate for presidency of the U.S., 1992***. MAILING ADDRESS: 2326 Whitman St., Clearwater, FL 34625.

NATHAN, THEODORA NATHALIA "TONIE." b. Feb 9, 1923, New York, NY; par. Bennett and Salcha (Ralska) Nathan; m. Charles Nathan, Jun 6, 1942; c. Paul Steven; Lawrence Eugene; Gregory Charles. EDUC.: Fairfax H.S., Hollywood, CA, 1940; Metropolitan Business School, Los Angeles, CA, 1940; Frank Wiggins Trade School, Los Angeles, 1941; Los Angeles City Coll., 1941; Liberty Mutual Insurance Co. Underwriting School, 1942; Los Angeles Valley Coll., 1957–64; Lane Community Coll., Eugene, OR, 1968–69; B.A., U. of OR, 1971. POLIT. & GOV.: ***Libertarian Party candidate for vice presidency of the U.S., 1972; received 1 electoral vote for vice presidency of the U.S., 1972; candidate for Libertarian Party nomination to vice presidency of the U.S., 1976***; candidate for Republican nomination to U.S. House (OR), 1976; independent (Libertarian) candidate for U.S. House (OR), 1976, 1978, 1990; community relations asst., Lane Cty., OR, 1977–78; Libertarian Party candidate for U.S. Senate (OR), 1980; state chm., Libertarian Party of OR; member, National Exec. Cmte., Libertarian Party; presidential elector, Libertarian Party (OR), 1980; Libertarian Party candidate for Lane Cty. Board of Commissioners, 1984. BUS. & PROF.: insurance agent; owner, Valley Insurance Agency, Hollywood, CA, 1947–53; professional mgr., Chase Music Co., Sun Valley, CA, 1953–60; owner, Mr. Charles Interiors, La Habra, CA, 1960–68; copy ed., *Lane Community Coll. Torch*, Eugene, OR, 1969–70; reporter, *Oregon Daily Emerald*, U. of OR, Eugene, OR, 1970–72; reporter, *Valley News*, Eugene, OR, 1971–72; correspondent, *Oregonian*, Portland, OR, 1971; producer, *Dia-*

logue, KVAL-TV, Eugene, 1972; disc jockey, KWAX-FM, U. of OR; public relations dir., Taxpayers Protective Assn.; public relations dir., U. of OR Women's Recreation Assn. MEM.: Women's Volleyball League; Theta Sigma Phi (pres.); Speak Out (National Advisory Board, 1972–73); Women in Communications (chapter pres., 1972–73); Eugene Toastmistresses; Metro Civic Club; OR Women's Political Caucus (public relations dir., 1972–73); Assn. of Libertarian Feminists (pres. pro tempore); National Women's Conference (delegate, 1977); Business and Professional Women's Club; OR Women for Timber; League of Women Voters; Guilder Soc.; Rubicon Soc. AWARDS: Commendation Award, Anchorage Libertarians for Action, 1973. MISC.: first woman to receive an electoral vote, 1972. WRITINGS: *On Libertarianism* (1981). MAILING ADDRESS: 1625 Best Lane, Eugene, OR 97401.

NATIONS, GILBERT OWEN. b. Aug 18, 1866, Farmington, MO; d. Feb 12, 1950, Chicago, IL; par. James W. and Caroline L. (Hart) Nations; m. Sallie E. McFarland, Dec 5, 1886; c. Reginald Heber; Zora Caroline (Mrs. Leonard S. Ritter; Mrs. Lescollette); Gus Orville; Myrtle Frances (Mrs. Roy Ellis); Paul Douglass; Florence Emily (Mrs. Alfred Pyatt); Karl McFarland. EDUC.: MO State Teachers' Coll.; B.S., Lebanon (OH) U., 1890; Ph.M., Hiram (OH) Coll., 1900; J.D., Oklahoma City U., 1915; Ph.D., American U., 1919; LL.D., Eugene (OR) Bible U., 1927. POLIT. & GOV.: judge, Probate Court, Farmington, MO, 1903–11; ***American Party candidate for presidency of the U.S., 1924***. BUS. & PROF.: atty.; law practice, St. Francois Cty., MO, to 1916; prof. of Roman law, canon law, and legal history, American U., 1920–35; publisher, *The Protestant*, 1921–31; ed., *The Fellowship Forum*, 1931–36. MEM.: Masons (32°; Scottish Rite). WRITINGS: *Papal Sovereignty* (1917); *Canon Law of the Papal Throne* (1926); *Political Career of Alfred E. Smith* (1928); *Roman Catholic War on Public Schools* (1931). REL.: Christian Church. RES.: Washington, DC.

NAUGLE, REGINALD B. POLIT. & GOV.: Pathfinders candidate for U.S. Senate (PA), 1938; G.I.'s Against Communism candidate for gov. of PA, 1940, 1950; ***candidate for Republican nomination to presidency of the U.S., 1952***. BUS. & PROF.: ordained minister, Lutheran Church; pastor, Resurrection Lutheran Church, Philadelphia, PA; businessman. MEM.: Independent Labor Federation of America; American Independent Unions, Inc. (pres.). MISC.: opposed CIO in Apex Hosiery Strike, 1937; sought ouster of Asst. U.S. Sec. of Labor Edward F. McGrady for activities during Apex Strike, 1937; testified before U.S. Congress in opposition to National Labor Relations Board, 1939. RES.: Conyngham, PA.

NEEDHAM, HENRY CLAY. b. 1852, Elizabethtown, KY; d. Feb 21, 1936, Los Angeles, CA; m. Lillie F. Needham; c. Nellie M. (Mrs. Miller); Pearl (Mrs. Segerstrom); Russell; Neil; Lieutenant H. P. POLIT. & GOV.: Prohibition Party candidate for U.S. House (CA), 1896, 1914, 1916; elected as a Prohibitionist to Board of Supervisors, Los Angeles Cty., CA, c. 1900; Prohibition Party candidate for U.S. Senate (CA), 1922; delegate, Prohibition Party National Convention, 1924, 1928; presidential elector, Prohibition Party, 1924; ***candidate for Prohibition Party nomination to presidency of the U.S., 1932***. BUS. & PROF.: rancher, Newall, CA, 1888–1936; oil industrialist; real estate investor. RES.: Newall, CA.

NEFF, PAT MORRIS. b. Nov 26, 1871, McGregor, TX; d. Jan 20, 1952, Waco, TX; par. Noah and Isabella (Shepherd) Neff; m. Myrtle Mainer, May 31, 1899; c. Hallie Maude (Mrs. Frank Wilcox); Pat Morris, Jr. EDUC.: A.B., Baylor U., 1894, A.M., 1898; LL.B., U. of TX, 1897. POLIT. & GOV.: elected as a Democrat to TX State House, 1901–05 (Speaker, 1903–05); elected prosecuting atty., McLennan Cty., TX, 1906–12; elected as a Democrat to gov. of TX, 1921–25; ***candidate for Democratic nomination to presidency of the U.S., 1924***; member, TX State Draft Appeal Board, 1923–25, chm., 1941–52; chm., TX Educational Survey Comm., 1925–26; member, TX Centennial Central Exposition Board; member, Centennial Comm. of Control; appointed member, U.S. Board of Mediation, 1927–29; appointed member, TX State Railroad Comm., 1929–31 (chm., 1930–31); appointed chm., TX State Parks Board, 1932–36. BUS. & PROF.: atty.; admitted to TX Bar, 1897; law practice, Waco, TX, 1897–1921; farmer; rancher; pres., Baylor U., 1932–47; dir., Texas Power and Light Co., 1935–52. MEM.: TX Bar Assn.; Baylor U. (chm., Board of Trustees, 1903– 32); Texas Watershed Assn. (pres., 1939); League to Enforce Peace (state chm.); Knights of Pythias (grand chancellor of TX, 1918–19); Anti-Saloon League of America (vice pres., 1934); Masons (32°; Shriner); Rotary Club. HON. DEG.: LL.D., Austin Coll., 1921; LL.D., Howard Payne Coll., 1921; LL.D., Baylor U., 1923; LL.D., Georgetown Coll., 1934; Litt.D., Southern U., 1936; Litt.D., Mercer U. WRITINGS: *The Battles of Peace* (1925); *Twenty-Three Addresses*. REL.: Southern Bapt. (pres., State General Convention, 1927–29; vice pres., National Convention, 1933; pres., National Convention, 1944–46). RES.: Waco, TX.

NEGLEY, JAMES SCOTT. b. Dec 22, 1826, East Liberty, PA; d. Aug 7, 1901, Plainfield, NJ; par. Jacob and Mary Ann (Scott) Negley; m. Kate De Losey, 1848; m. 2d, Grace Ashton, 1869; c. three sons; three daughters. EDUC.: grad., Western U. of PA, 1846. POLIT. & GOV.: elected as a Republican to U.S. House (PA), 1869–75, 1885–87; Republican candidate for U.S. House (PA), 1874; candidate for Republican nomination to U.S. House, 1886; ***candidate for American Party nomination to presidency of the U.S., 1888***. BUS. & PROF.: soldier; financier; railroad promoter; farmer; manufacturer; vice pres., Pittsburgh, New Castle and Lake Erie R.R., 1879; pres., New York, Pittsburgh and Chicago Railway, 1884–85; pres., Railroad Supply Co., New York, NY, 1886–1901. MIL.: enlisted in Duquesne Grays, 1843; member, 1st PA Regt., 1846–48; elected brig. gen., 18th Div., PA Militia, 1860; brev. maj. gen. of volunteers, 1862; brev. for gallantry in action during Civil War; later accused of cowardice and desertion on field of battle; cleared of charges, but resigned from U.S. Army, 1865. MEM.: National Home for Disabled Volunteer Soldiers (Board of Managers, 1874–78, 1882–88); National Union League of America (pres.); GAR; Scott's Legion; Military Order of Foreign Wars. HON. DEG.: A.M., Coll. of NJ, 1875. RES.: Plainfield, NJ.

NELSON, GAYLORD ANTON. b. Jun 4, 1916, Clear Lake, WI; par. Anton and Mary (Bradt) Hogan Nelson; m. Carrie Lee Dotson, Nov 14, 1947; c. Gaylord; Cynthia Lee; Jeffrey. EDUC.: grad., San Jose State Coll., 1939; LL.B., U. of WI, 1942. POLIT. & GOV.: chm., Madison (WI) Council on Human Rights; Republican candidate for WI State Assembly, 1946; elected as a Democrat to WI State Senate, 1949–58 (Democratic floor leader, 1949–52); Democratic candidate for U.S. House (WI), 1954; elected as a Democrat to gov. of WI, 1959–63; elected as a Democrat to U.S. Senate (WI), 1963–81; ***candidate for Democratic nomination to vice presidency of the U.S., 1980***; Democratic candidate for U.S. Senate (WI), 1980. BUS. & PROF.: atty.; admitted to WI Bar, 1942; law practice, Madison, WI, 1946–59; chm., Wilderness Soc., Washington, DC, 1981–. MIL.: 1st lt., U.S. Army, 1942–46. MEM.: American Legion; VFW; WI State Bar Assn.; Eagles. REL.: Methodist. MAILING ADDRESS: 3611 Calvend Lane, Kensington, MD 20795.

NELSON, GEORGE A. b. Nov 15, 1873, Milltown, WI; d. May 4, 1962, St. Croix Falls, WI; par. Jens Nelson; m. Anna Christine Larsen, Nov 15, 1901; c. Raymond G.; Elmer; Donald; Laura (Mrs. Harris Engelbert); Belva (Mrs. Hal Kusler); Lenore (Mrs. Joe Olivier); Bennett. EDUC.: Elkhorn (IA) Coll. POLIT. & GOV.: elected chm., Milltown Township (WI) Board; elected chm., Polk Cty. (WI) Board of Supervisors, 1915; dir., Polk Cty. (WI) Fair Board; elected school clerk, 19 years; elected as a Progressive-Republican to WI State Assembly, 1921–27; delegate, Rep. Nat'l. Conv., 1928; chm., Polk Cty. (WI) La Follette Progressive Club; Farmer–Labor Party–Progressive candidate for lt. gov. of WI; Socialist Party candidate for gov. of WI, 1934, 1944; ***Socialist Party candidate for vice presidency of the U.S., 1936***; appointed member, WI State Livestock Sanitary Board. BUS. & PROF.: sawmill employee; harvester; gold miner, AK, 1898–1901; farmer, Milltown, WI; dir., Milltown State Bank; pres., Milltown Cooperative Creamery. MEM.: National Farmers' Union (pres.); Cooperative Equity Union; U. of WI (regent); American Soc. of Equity (pres., WI Section, 1922–31); Polk Cty. Farm Holiday Assn. (sec.; pres.). WRITINGS: *Farmers: Where Are We Going?* (1934). REL.: Lutheran. RES.: Milltown, WI.

NELSON, JAMES ARTHUR, JR. par. James Arthur Nelson. POLIT. & GOV.: ***candidate for Democratic nomination to presidency of the U.S., 1980, 1984***. MAILING ADDRESS: 1501 Armerston, Sacramento, CA 95823.

NELSON, LLOYD JOHN. POLIT. & GOV.: ***candidate for Democratic nomination to presidency of the U.S., 1980***. MAILING ADDRESS: Postfach 1151/6455 Erlensee, Federal Republic of Germany ZZ.

NELSON, SCOTT MONROE. b. Dec 30, 1938, Fort Worth, TX; par. Fletcher Spencer and Mattye Lou (Scott) Nelson; m. Marie Annette Barna, May 29, 1958; c. Scotti Elizabeth; Timothy Byron. EDUC.: grad., Fair Park H.S., Shreveport, LA, 1957. POLIT. & GOV.: Texas Independent candidate for trustee, Houston (TX) School District, 1973; ***Ku Klux Klan Party candidate for vice presidency of the U.S., 1976***. BUS. & PROF.: collector, Entex, Natural Gas Distribution Co. MEM.: TX Fiery Knights of the Ku Klux Klan (imperial wizard). REL.: Bapt. MAILING ADDRESS: 3916 Arlington Square, Apt. 75, Houston, TX 77034.

NEPHEW, ALICE K. POLIT. & GOV.: ***independent candidate for presidency of the U.S., 1976***. MAILING ADDRESS: 2 Camp Ave., Walton, NY 13856.

NEUBERG, JOEL GARY. POLIT. & GOV.: ***candidate for Republican nomination to presidency of the U.S., 1992***. MAILING ADDRESS: CA?

NEVERS, ROBERT ALLISON. POLIT. & GOV.: ***independent candidate for presidency of the U.S., 1980, 1984***. MAILING ADDRESS: 99 Porter St., Stoughton, MA 02072.

NEWKIRK, JOHN D. POLIT. & GOV.: ***independent candidate for presidency of the U.S., 1980***. MAILING ADDRESS: 1537 Yucca, Medford, OR 97501.

NEWLANDS, FRANCIS GRIFFITH. b. Aug 28, 1848, Natchez, MS; d. Dec 24, 1917, Washington, DC; par. James Birney and Jessie (Barland) Newlands; m. Clara Adelaide Sharon, Nov 19, 1874; m. 2d, Edith McAllister, Sep 4, 1888; c. Sharon Frances; Edythe M. (Mrs. Charles Haven Ladd Johnston); Janet (Mrs. William Bernard Johnston); three sons (infants). EDUC.: Chicago (IL) H.S.; Yale Coll., 1863–65; Columbian Coll. Law School. POLIT. & GOV.: vice chm., National Silver Cmte.; elected as a Silver Republican-Democrat to U.S. House (NV), 1893–1903; elected as a Democrat to U.S. Senate (NV), 1903–17; ***candidate for Democratic nomination to presidency of the U.S., 1912 (withdrew)***. BUS. & PROF.: atty.; admitted to CA Bar, 1869; admitted to DC Bar, 1870; law practice, San Francisco, CA, 1870–88; trustee, estate of William Sharon, Carson City, NV; law practice, Carson City, 1888–89; law practice, Reno, NV, 1889–1917. MEM.: Metropolitan Club; Chevy Chase Club.

HON. DEG.: M.A., Yale Coll., 1901. MISC.: author of Newlands Reclamation Act. RES.: Reno, NV.

NEWMAN, JAMES WILLIAM. b. Jun 1949, Detroit, MI; par. James Newman. EDUC.: U. of Detroit; U. of MS; Wayne State U. POLIT. & GOV.: ***independent candidate for vice presidency of the U.S., 1980***. BUS. & PROF.: freelance writer; freelance photographer; songwriter; political columnist; ghostwriter; writer, Doubleday Books; editorial writer, *Detroit (MI) News*; editorial writer, *New York (NY) Times*; journalist; employee, CIA; employee, National Security Council. MEM.: National Endowment for the Arts (chm., Council for Minority Affairs). AWARDS: received awards for poetry. WRITINGS: *Made in America* (1976); *With Hellish Words* (3 vols., 1978); *Minority Lenders and Programs to Help Blacks* (1978); *What President Has Helped Blacks Move* (1978). REL.: nondenominational. MAILING ADDRESS: 3145 Heidelberg, Detroit, MI.

NEWMAN, JOSEPH WESTLEY. POLIT. & GOV.: ***Truth and Action Party candidate for presidency of the U.S., 1988***. BUS. & PROF.: inventor. MISC.: announced candidacy over New Orleans radio station. MAILING ADDRESS: c/o Annis M. Harrell, Route 1, Box 52, Lucedale, MS 39452.

NEWMAN, PAUL. b. Jan 26, 1925, Cleveland, OH; par. Arthur S. and Theresa (Fetzer) Newman; m. Jacqueline Witte, Dec 1949; m. 2d, Joanne Woodward, Jan 29, 1958; c. Scott; Susan; Stephanie; Elinor Theresa; Melissa; Clea. EDUC.: grad., Shaker Heights (OH) H.S., 1941; B.A., Kenyon Coll., 1949; Yale School of Drama, 1950–51. POLIT. & GOV.: ***New Party of Florida candidate for presidency of the U.S., 1968***. BUS. & PROF.: mgr., sporting goods business, Cleveland, OH, 1950–51; stage actor; motion picture actor; professional race car driver; food company exec. STAGE CREDITS: *Picnic* (1953–54); *Desperate Hours* (1955); *Sweet Bird of Youth* (1959); *Baby Wants a Kiss* (1964). MOTION PICTURE CREDITS: *The Silver Chalice* (1954); *Somebody Up There Likes Me* (1956); *The Rack* (1956); *Until They Sail* (1957); *The Helen Morgan Story* (1957); *The Left Handed Gun* (1958); *The Long Hot Summer* (1958); *Cat on a Hot Tin Roof* (1958); *Rally 'Round the Flag, Boys!* (1958); *The Young Philadelphians* (1959); *From the Terrace* (1960); *Exodus* (1960); *Paris Blues* (1961); *The Hustler* (1961); *Sweet Bird of Youth* (1962); *Hemingway's Adventures of a Young Man* (1962); *Hud* (1963); *A New Kind of Love* (1963); *The Outrage* (1964); *The Prize* (1964); *What a Way to Go!* (1964); *Lady L* (1965); *Torn Curtains* (1966); *Harper* (1966); *Hombre* (1967); *Cool Hand Luke* (1967); *The Secret War of Harry Frigg* (1968); *Rachel, Rachel* (dir., 1968); *Winning* (1969); *Butch Cassidy and the Sun Dance Kid* (1969); *WUSA* (1970); *Never Give an Inch* (1971; also dir.); *Sometimes a Great Notion* (1971; also dir.); *Pocket Money* (1972); *The Effect of Gamma Rays on Man-in-the-Moon Marigolds* (dir., 1972); *The Life and Times of Judge Roy Bean* (1973); *The MacIntosh Man* (1973); *The Sting* (1973); *The Towering Inferno* (1974); *The Drowning Pool* (1975); *Buffalo Bill and the Indians* (1976); *Silent Movie* (1976); *Slap Shot* (1977); *Quintet* (1979); *Fort Apache, the Bronx* (1980); *When Time Ran Out* (1980); *The Shadow Box* (dir., 1981); *Absence of Malice* (1982); *The Verdict* (1982); *Harry and Son* (1984), *The Color of Money* (1986), *Blaze* (1990), and *Nobody's Fool* (1995). MIL.: radio man, third class, U.S.N.R., 1943–46. MEM.: Actors Equity Assn.; Screen Actors Guild; A.F.T.R.A. AWARDS: nomination for Academy Award for Best Actor, 1959, 1961, 1963; Man of the Year Award, Hasty Pudding Theatrical, Harvard U., 1968; World Film Favorite Male Award, Golden Globe Awards, 1967; Producer of the Year Award, Producers Guild of America, 1968. MAILING ADDRESS: c/o Rogers and Cowan, Inc., 9665 Wilshire Blvd., Beverly Hills, CA 90210.

NICE, HARRY WHINNA. b. Dec 5, 1877, Washington, DC, d. Feb 25, 1941, Richmond, VA; par. Henry and Drucilla (Arnold) Nice; m. Edna Viola Amos, Jun 7, 1905; c. William Stone; Harry Whinna, Jr. EDUC.: Baltimore City Coll., 1889–93; Dickinson Coll., 1896–97; LL.B., U. of MD, 1899. POLIT. & GOV.: elected member, Baltimore (MD) City Council, 1903–05; sec. to the mayor, Baltimore, 1905–08; supervisor of elections, Baltimore, 1908–12; appointed asst. state's atty., state's atty., Baltimore, 1912–19; Republican candidate for gov. of MD, 1919, 1938; delegate, Rep. Nat'l. Conv., 1920; judge of Appeal Tax Court, Baltimore, 1920–24; elected as a Republican to gov. of MD, 1935–39; ***candidate for Republican nomination to presidency of the U.S., 1936; candidate for Republican nomination to vice presidency of the U.S., 1936***; Republican candidate for U.S. Senate (MD), 1940. BUS. & PROF.: atty.; admitted to MD Bar, 1899; law practice, Baltimore, MD, 1899–1941; partner, Dickerson and Nice (law firm), Baltimore, 1920–41. MEM.: ABA; MD State Bar Assn.; Baltimore City Bar Assn.; Kappa Sigma; Scimeter Club; Masons (33°; Shriners); Elks; Moose; Odd Fellows; Merchants Club; University Club; Knights of Pythias; Baltimore City Club. HON. DEG.: LL.D., Dickinson Coll., 1935; LL.D., St. John's Coll., 1935; LL.D., U. of MD, 1935; LL.D., Washington Coll., 1935. REL.: Methodist. RES.: Baltimore, MD.

NICHOLS, EMMETT A. POLIT. & GOV.: ***independent candidate for presidency of the U.S., 1980***. MAILING ADDRESS: GA.

NICHOLSON, MOLLIE DAVIS. b. Oct 17, 1879, White Post, VA, d. unknown; par. David Brown and Florence Mildred (Ramey) Davis; m. Jesse Wootten Nicholson, Oct 24, 1900; c. Davis; Jesse Frank; Dorothy Mildred (Mrs. Peter B. Stabell); David Brown. EDUC.: private schools. POLIT. & GOV.: founder, Montgomery Cty. (MD) Democratic Club, 1919; member, Dem. Nat'l. Cmte. (MD), 1923–24; founder, United Democratic Clubs of MD, 1924; vice chm., MD National Democratic Congressional Cmte., 1925; ***American Home Party candidate for vice presidency of the U.S., 1928 (declined)***. BUS. & PROF.: owner, ed., *The Woman Voter*, 1926–. MEM.: National

Women's Democratic Law Enforcement League (pres.); American Red Cross (founder, Chevy Chase Chapter, 1917); National League of American Pen Women (founder, pres., Chevy Chase Branch, 1925); National Soc. of Arts and Letters (cofounder, 1944); Montgomery Cty. Hist. Soc. (charter, life, and hon. member); DAR (regent, Chevy Chase Chapter, 1946); National Sentinels (pres., 1932–36); Washington Club; English Speaking Union; Wheel of Progress. AWARDS: citation as "Outstanding Club and Church Woman of Maryland," Hood Coll., 1948. WRITINGS: *The Woman Voter* (1936). REL.: Episc. MISC.: noted speaker against repeal of Prohibition. RES.: Chevy Chase, MD.

NICHOLSON, SAMUEL THORNE. b. Feb 2, 1852, Halifax Cty., NC, d. unknown; par. Thomas W. and Martha E. (Thorne) Nicholson; m. Jennie Conwill, Dec 26, 1899; m. 2d, Eva Spence Moore, Feb 9, 1922. EDUC.: Horner School; U. of VA; studied law. POLIT. & GOV.: ***Union Reform Party candidate for vice presidency of the U.S., 1900***. BUS. & PROF.: farmer; insurance agent; publisher, *Eclectic*; staff correspondent, National Press Bureau; assoc. ed., *National Cyclopedia of American Biography*; mgr., American Law and Credit Service. MEM.: National Christian Conference (organizer, 1895); National Good Citizenship League (gen. sec., 1897); Initiative and Referendum League (vice pres., 1908); National Economic League (National Council); Civic League of America (sec.-treas.); Commonwealth Club of New York; Bible League of America (sec.); Southern Christian Citizenship Congress (sec., 1913). REL.: Methodist. RES.: Pittsburgh, PA.

NICKEL, RON B. POLIT. & GOV.: ***Expansionist Party candidate for presidency of the U.S., 1980***. MAILING ADDRESS: P.O. Box 8213, Austin, TX 78712.

NIXON, LEWIS. b. Apr 7, 1861, Leesburg, VA; d. Sep 23, 1940, Long Beach, NJ; par. Joel Lewis and Mary Jane (Turner) Nixon; m. Sally Lewis Wood, Jan 29, 1891; m. 2d, Mary Doran Martin, Jun 28, 1938; c. Stanhope Wood. EDUC.: grad., U.S. Naval Acad., 1882; grad. (with honors), Royal Naval Coll., 1886. POLIT. & GOV.: appointed pres., East River Bridge Comm., 1898; delegate, Dem. Nat'l. Conv., 1900, 1904, 1908, 1912, 1920, 1924, 1932; leader, Tammany Hall, 1901–02; chm., Finance Cmte., Democratic Congressional Campaign Cmte., 1902; chm., NY State Democratic Convention, 1906; ***candidate for Democratic nomination to vice presidency of the U.S., 1908***; appointed delegate, Fourth Pan-American Conference, 1910; appointed member, NY Comm. to St. Louis Exposition; appointed ambassador extraordinary and minister plenipotentiary to Chilean Centenary, 1910; commissioner of public works, borough of Richmond, NY, 1914–15; appointed NY state superintendent of public works, 1919; appointed member, NY State Public Service Comm., 1919–20; ***candidate for Democratic nomination to presidency of the U.S., 1920***. BUS. & PROF.: shipbuilder; superintendent of construction, Cramp Shipyard, Philadelphia, PA, 1895; owner, Crescent Shipyard, Elizabeth, NJ, 1895–1901; founder, Standard Motor Construction Co.; pres., U.S. Shipbuilding Co.; proprietor, Lewis Nixon's Shipyard; pres., International Smokeless Powder and Dynamite Co., 1895–1904; pres., Nixon Nitration Works; pres., Raritan River Sand Co.; dir., Donald Steamship Co. MIL.: Construction Corps, U.S. Navy, 1884; naval architect, U.S. Navy, 1884–95. MEM.: Webb's Acad. and Home for Shipbuilders (pres.; trustee); U.S. Naval Acad. (visitor); Tammany Soc. (chm., Finance Cmte., 1902); New York Board of Trade; New York C. of C.; Inst. of Naval Architects and Marine Engineers (trustee); American Geographic Soc. (fellow); Union Club; Brook Club; National Democratic Club; Lawyers Club; Seneca Club; Coney Island Jockey Club; Automobile Club of America; Automobile Club of Staten Island; New York Motor Boat Club; Rittenhouse Club of Philadelphia; Metropolitan Club; Army and Navy Club. REL.: Protestant. MISC.: designed battleships *Oregon*, *Massachusetts*, and *Indiana*; built first motorboat to cross the ocean; built the first submarine torpedo boats. RES.: Tompkinsville, Staten Island, NY.

NIXON, RICHARD MILHOUS. b. Jan 9, 1913, Yorba Linda, CA; d. Apr 22 1994, New York, NY; par. Francis Anthony and Hannah (Milhous) Nixon; m. Thelma Catherine "Patricia" Ryan, Jun 21, 1940; c. Patricia "Tricia" (Mrs. Edward Finch Cox); Julie (Mrs. Dwight David Eisenhower II). EDUC.: grad. (with honors), Whittier (CA) H.S., 1930; B.A., Whittier Coll., 1934; LL.B., Duke U., 1937. POLIT. & GOV.: town atty., La Habra, CA, 1939; atty., OPA, Washington, DC, 1942; candidate for Democratic nomination to U.S. House (CA), 1946; elected as a Republican to U.S. House (CA), 1947–50; appointed and subsequently elected as a Republican to U.S. Senate (CA), 1950–53; ***elected as a Republican to vice presidency of the U.S., 1953–1961; Republican candidate for presidency of the U.S., 1960***; Republican candidate for gov. of CA, 1962; ***candidate for Republican nomination to presidency of the U.S., 1964; candidate for Republican nomination to vice presidency of the U.S., 1964; elected as a Republican to presidency of the U.S., 1969–1974 (resigned)***. BUS. & PROF.: gas station attendant, Whittier, CA; shill, Slippery Gulch Rodeo, Prescott, AZ, 1928–30; atty.; admitted to CA Bar, 1937; admitted to NY Bar, 1963; assoc., Wingert and Bewley (law firm), Whittier, 1937; partner, Wingert, Bewley and Nixon (law firm), Whittier; partner, Bewley, Knoop and Nixon (law firm), La Habra, CA; pres., Citra-Frost Co., Whittier, CA, 1940–41; counsel, Adams, Duque and Hazeltine (law firm), Los Angeles, CA, 1961–63; partner, Mudge, Stern, Baldwin and Todd (later Nixon, Mudge, Rose, Alexander, Guthrie and Stern; law firm), New York, NY, 1963–69. MIL.: lt. (jg), U.S. Navy, 1942, lt., 1943, lt. commander, 1945–46; commander, U.S.N.R., 1953. MEM.: Order of the Coif; Boys Clubs of America (hon. chm.); Whittier Coll. (trustee, 1939–68). HON. DEG.: LL.D., Bradley U., 1951; LL.D., Tehran U., 1953; Sc.D., Lowell Inst. of Technology, 1954; LL.D., Whittier Coll., 1954; Doctor Honoris Causa, National U. of

Nicaragua, 1955; D.H.L., Temple U., 1955; LL.D., U. of Santo Domingo, 1955; LL.D., Lafayette Coll., 1956; LL.D., Bethany Coll., 1957; LL.D., DePauw U., 1957; LL.D., MI State U., 1957; LL.D., U. of Liberia, 1957; H.H.D., Wilberforce U., 1957; LL.D., Yeshiva U., 1957; LL.D., Fordham U., 1959; LL.D., U. of San Diego, 1959. WRITINGS: *Six Crises* (1962); *RN, Memoirs* (1978); *The Real War* (1980); *Leaders* (1982); *Real Peace* (1984); *No More Vietnams* (1985); *1999: Victory Without War* (1988); *Seize the Moment: America's Challenge in a One-Superpower World* (1992). REL.: Soc. of Friends. MISC.: implicated in Watergate scandal; first president to resign from office (Aug 9, 1974); pardoned by President Gerald Ford (q.v.). RES.: Woodcliff Lake, NJ.

NOLAN, RICHARD MICHAEL "RICK."

b. Dec 17, 1943, Brainerd, MN; par. James Henry and Mary Jane (Aylward) Nolan; m. Marjorie C. Langer, Jun 13, 1964; c. Michael; Leah; John; Katherine. EDUC.: St. John's U., 1962; B.A., U. of MN, 1966; U. of MD, 1967. POLIT. & GOV.: staff asst. to U.S. Sen. Walter F. Mondale (q.v.), 1966–68; appointed dir., Project Headstart, MN, 1968; elected as a Democrat to MN State House, 1969–73; elected as a Democrat to U.S. House (MN), 1975–79; delegate, Dem. Nat'l. Conv., 1980; ***candidate for Democratic nomination to vice presidency of the U.S., 1980***. BUS. & PROF.: curriculum coordinator, adult basic education, Little Falls (MN) School District; teacher, Royalton, MN, 1969; project coordinator, Center for Study of Local Government, St. John's U., 1971; administrative asst. to senior vice pres., Fingerhut Corp., 1973–74. MEM.: Teamsters Union. REL.: R.C. MAILING ADDRESS: 389 Dayton Ave., St. Paul, MN 55102.

NONE OF THE ABOVE (nee LUTHER DEVINE KNOX).

b. 1929. POLIT. & GOV.: candidate for Democratic nomination to U.S. House (LA), 1978, 1980; candidate for Democratic nomination to gov. of LA, 1979; ***None of the Above Party candidate for presidency of the U.S., 1980;*** independent candidate for U.S. House (LA), 1990. BUS. & PROF.: farmer, Winnsboro, LA. MISC.: legally changed name to "None of the Above," a move that was unsuccessfully challenged by election officials. MAILING ADDRESS: Route 5, Box 190, Winnsboro, LA 71215.

NORBECK, PETER.

b. Aug 27, 1870, Vermillion, SD; d. Dec 20, 1936, Redfield, SD; par. George (nee Goran Person Kjostad) and Karen Larsdatter (Kongsvig) Larsen Norbeck; m. Lydia Anderson, Jun 7, 1900; c. Harold P.; Selma T.; Nellie (Mrs. Lester Wegner); Ruth (Mrs. Albert Jennings). EDUC.: U. of SD, 1887–89. POLIT. & GOV.: elected as a Republican to SD State Senate, 1909–15; elected as a Republican to lt. gov. of SD, 1915–17; delegate, Rep. Nat'l. Conv., 1916, 1920, 1924, 1928, 1932; elected as a Republican to gov. of SD, 1917–21; elected as a Republican to U.S. Senate (SD), 1921–36; ***candidate for Republican nomination to vice presidency of the U.S., 1936***; U.S. delegate, Icelandic Parliament Millenial Celebration, 1930. BUS. & PROF.: began drilling artesian wells, 1892; pres., Norbeck and Nickolson (well drillers), 1898–1924; pres., North Dakota Artesian Well Co., 1905–36; pres., Siva Oil Co., 1911; pres., Norbeck Co. (well drillers), 1924–36; landowner, ND. MEM.: National Conference on State Parks (dir.); American Civic Assn. (exec. board); American Planning and Civic Assn. (adviser); Norwegian-American Hist. Assn.; American-Scandinavian Foundation; Masons. AWARDS: Order of the Falcons (Denmark). REL.: Lutheran. RES.: Redfield, SD.

NORBERG, WALLACE LEE.

POLIT. & GOV.: ***Democratic-Farmer-Labor Party candidate for presidency of the U.S., 1980***. REL.: fundamentalist Christian. MAILING ADDRESS: 3304 East 24th St., Minneapolis, MN 55406.

NORCROSS, GEORGE E.

b. Oct 4, 1928, Barrington, NJ; par. George Norcross; m. Carol; c. George III; John; Donald; Philip. EDUC.: grad., Woodrow Wilson H.S., Camden, NJ; Rutgers U.; PA State U.; Cornell U. POLIT. & GOV.: member, Camden Cty. (NJ) Human Services Task Force; member, Camden City (NJ) Economic Development Authority; member, vice pres., Health Systems Agency of Southern NJ; member, Camden Cty. Industrial Pollution Control Financing authority; member, Camden City Mayor's Advisory Cmte.; ***candidate for Democratic nomination to vice presidency of the U.S., 1972***. BUS. & PROF.: union organizer. MEM.: Crescent Temple (Haines 253, Excelsior Consistory); IBEW (vice pres., Local 1448); IUE (international representative, 1950); pres., Local 106; Union Organization for Social Service, AFL-CIO Community Service Program (exec. sec., 1955–); Central Labor Union, AFL-CIO (pres., 1979–); Sports Arena Local 137; RWDSU Local 1034; NJ AFL-CIO (dir.); Cooper Medical Center (exec. cmte.; dir.); Associated United Ways of PA and NJ (dir.); Southern NJ Friendship Force; Private Industry Council, Comprehensive Education and Training Act program; Group Homes, Inc.; Senior Aides Advisory Board; Citizen's Cmte. to Rebuild Garden State Park (co-chm.); South Jersey Veterans' Administration Hospital Medical School Cmte. (chm.). MAILING ADDRESS: 211 South 6th St., Camden, NJ.

NORDSKOG, ARNE ANDREAS (aka ANDRAE B. NORDSKOG).

b. Sep 16, 1885, Story City, IA; d. Feb 12, 1962, Los Angeles, CA; par. Sivert and Bertha (Johnson) Nordskog; m. Daisy Mae Lockwood, Oct 9, 1904; m. 2d, Mrs. Gertrude McGuire Foy, Nov 18, 1949; c. Mrs. Wanda Ethylwynn Irwin; Mrs. Dona Melba Whiteside; Robert Arne; Mrs. Ruth Hingley; Gloria. EDUC.: Des Moines Coll.; studied singing with Dr. Marion Loomis Bartlett, Arthur Middleton, Dr. Edmund J. Meyer, and Louis Graveura. POLIT. & GOV.: chm., Southern CA Rate and Traffic Comm., 1924–26; ***Liberty Party candidate for vice presidency of the U.S., 1932 (withdrew); Liberty Unity Party candidate for vice presidency***

of the U.S., 1932 (withdrew); organizer, United Party movement; candidate for mayor of Los Angeles, CA; delegate, U.S. Monetary Conference, 1933; chm., National Monetary Conference, 1938, 1944. BUS. & PROF.: author; publisher; singer; tenor soloist, various U.S. churches; dir., Central IA Choral Union (Lutheran), 1909; lead tenor, Ames Opera Co., 1909; lead tenor, Standard Grand Opera Co., 1914–16; lead tenor, Knickerbocker Opera Co., 1917; toured in concert until 1921, and with wife, 1949–62; mgr., Santa Monica Bay Cities Philharmonic Courses, 1919–24; mgr., Hollywood Bowl, 1920–21; pres., Nordskog Phonograph Recording Co., Los Angeles, CA, 1921; lecturer; financial consultant; publisher, ed., *Los Angeles Gridiron*, 1926–32; publisher, ed., *New American Magazine*, 1932–34; publisher, ed., *Our Nation Magazine*, 1946; engineer, Western Electric Co.; engineer, Stromberg Carlson Switchboard Manufacturing Co.; engineer, American Electric Co.; engineer, Iowa Bell Telephone Co.; engineer, Home Telephone Co., Des Moines, IA; engineer, Corn Belt Telephone Co., Waterloo, IA; engineer, Independent Telephone Co., Council Bluffs, NE; engineer, Independent Telephone Co., Seattle, WA; engineer, Pacific Telephone and Telegraph Co.; engineer, Southern California Telephone Co., Los Angeles; engineer, United Wireless Telegraph Co., Des Moines; established two pioneer wireless telegraph stations, Ames, IA, 1909; active in exposing frauds and conspiracy in CA water distribution. MEM.: German-American Bund; America First Cmte.; Southwest Water League (pres.); Hollywood May Festival Assn. (founder; mgr., 1920); National Music Week (chm., 1921, 1924); Washington Encampment Against War (pre–WWII leader). WRITINGS: *Spiking the Gold* (1932); *Public Bond Repudiations* (1933); *We Bankers vs. Four Financial Fascists* (1936). REL.: Christian Scientist (nee Congregationalist). RES.: Los Angeles, CA.

NORRIS, GEORGE WILLIAM. b. Jul 11, 1861, Clyde, OH; d. Sep 2, 1944, McCook, NE; par. Chauncey and Mary Magdalene (Mook) Norris; m. Pluma Lashley, Jun 1, 1890; m. 2d, Ella Leonard, Jul 8, 1903; c. Hazel (Mrs. John Porteous Robertson); Marian (Mrs. Harvey Franz Nelson); Gertrude (Mrs. Gordon Brandon Rath); one infant. EDUC.: Baldwin U., 1877–78; LL.B., Northern IN Normal School (now Valparaiso U.), 1883. POLIT. & GOV.: appointed and subsequently elected cty. atty., Furnas Cty., NE, 3 terms; elected judge, 14th NE District, 1895–1903; elected as a Republican to U.S. House (NE), 1903–13; elected as a Republican to U.S. Senate (NE), 1913–43; ***candidate for Republican nomination to vice presidency of the U.S., 1924; candidate for Republican nomination to presidency of the U.S., 1928, 1936; Farmer-Labor Party candidate for presidency of the U.S., 1928 (declined); candidate for Prohibition Party nomination to presidency of the U.S., 1928; Jefferson-Lincoln League candidate for presidency of the U.S., 1928; American Home Progressive Party candidate for presidency of the U.S., 1928 (declined)***; Independent Republican candidate for U.S. Senate (NE), 1942. BUS. & PROF.: atty.; admitted to IN Bar, 1883; schoolteacher, to 1885; law practice, Beaver City, NE, 1885–99; law practice, McCook, NE, 1899–1944. MEM.: National Progressive League for Roosevelt for President (1932); Masons (Shriner; Knights Templar); Knights of Pythias; Odd Fellows; People's Legislative Service (dir.); National Popular Government League; Cmte. on Coal and Giant Power; National Citizens Cmte. on Relations with Latin America (hon. pres., 1927). MISC.: named as one of the managers to conduct impeachment proceedings against Judge Robert W. Archibald, 1921; led revolt against domination of Speaker Joseph Cannon (q.v.) over U.S. House, 1911; known as "Father of the Twentieth Amendment to the U.S. Constitution"; promoter of unicameral principle in state legislatures. REL.: Christian (nondenominational). RES.: McCook, NE.

NORRIS, W. PITT. POLIT. & GOV.: ***independent candidate for presidency of the U.S., 1880***. RES.: IA.

NORTH, OLIVER. b. Oct 7, 1943, San Antonio, TX; married. POLIT. & GOV.: staff, National Security Council, 1987; ***candidate for Republican nomination to presidency of the U.S., 1988***; Republican candidate for U.S. Senate (VA), 1994. BUS. & PROF.: col., U.S.M.C. MISC.: noted as chief architect of Iran-contra arms scandal, 1987; candidacy sponsored by Billy Joe Clegg (q.v.). WRITINGS: *Under Fire* (1991). MAILING ADDRESS: Great Falls, VA.

NORTHROP, CYRUS. b. Sep 30, 1834, Ridgefield, CT; d. Apr 3, 1922, Minneapolis, MN; par. Cyrus and Polly Bouton (Fancher) Northrop; m. Anna Elizabeth Warren, Sep 30, 1962; c. Elizabeth (Mrs. Joseph Warren Beach); Minnie Warren; Cyrus, Jr. EDUC.: Williston Seminary; A.B., Yale Coll., 1857, LL.B., 1859. POLIT. & GOV.: clerk, CT State House, 1861–63; clerk, CT State Senate, 1862; Republican candidate for U.S. House (CT), 1867; appointed collector of customs, New Haven, CT, 1869–81; appointed member, MN State High School Board; appointed member, Board of Trustees, Minneapolis (MN) Public Library; ***candidate for Republican nomination to presidency of the U.S., 1916***. BUS. & PROF.: teacher; atty.; admitted to CT Bar, 1860; editor-in-chief, *Daily Palladium*, New Haven, CT, 1862; prof. of rhetoric and English literature, Yale Coll., 1863–84; pres., U. of MN, 1884–1911, pres. emeritus, 1911–22. HON. DEG.: LL.D., Yale Coll., 1886; LL.D., IL Coll., 1904; LL.D., U. of WI, 1904; LL.D., SC Coll., 1905; LL.D., Carleton Coll., 1917. WRITINGS: *Addresses, Educational and Patriotic* (1910). REL.: Congregationalist (moderator, National Council, 1889; delegate, International Congregationalist Council, 1891). RES.: Minneapolis, MN.

NORTHRUP, HENRY H. b. Feb 27, 1839, Cheshire, MA; d. Sep 25, 1927, Portland, OR; par. Isaak W. and Maria (Brown) Northrup; m. Lydia Harkness; c. Dr. W. R.; Laura. EDUC.: Lenox Acad.; MA State Normal School. POLIT. & GOV.: elected as a Republican to OR State House, 1889–91,

1893–95; elected judge, Multnomah Cty., OR, 1895–97; ***candidate for Republican nomination to vice presidency of the U.S., 1924***. BUS. & PROF.: schoolteacher, MA; atty.; admitted to DC Bar; law practice, Portland, OR, 1871–1912. MIL.: enlisted in U.S. Army, Civil War. MEM.: Masons; GAR. RES.: Portland, OR.

NORTON, CHRISTOPHER B. "CHRIS." b. 1937, Marblehead, MA. EDUC.: B.A., Brown U., 1961; grad., U. of Geneva, 1965. POLIT. & GOV.: ***candidate for Democratic nomination to presidency of the U.S., 1992***. BUS. & PROF.: global commodities import and export business (metals and grains), 1966–86; writer; lecturer; temporary office employee. MISC.: proponent of adoption of metric system in U.S. MAILING ADDRESS: 102 West 80 St., Apt. 63, New York, NY 10024.

NORTON, MARY TERESA HOPKINS. b. Mar 7, 1875, Jersey City, NJ; d. Aug 2, 1959, Greenwich, CT; par. Thomas and Marie (Shea) Hopkins; m. Robert Francis Norton, Apr 1909; c. Robert Francis. EDUC.: grad., Packard Business Coll., 1896. POLIT. & GOV.: member, NJ State Democratic Central Cmte., 1920–44 (vice chm., 1921–32; chm., 1932–36); vice chm., Hudson Cty. (NJ) Democratic Cmte.; elected freeholder, Hudson Cty., NJ, 1923; delegate, Dem. Nat'l. Conv., 1924, 1928, 1932, 1936, 1940, 1944, 1948; elected as a Democrat to U.S. House (NJ), 1925–51; ***candidate for Democratic nomination to vice presidency of the U.S., 1932***; member, Dem. Nat'l. Cmte., 1944–52; adviser, U.S. Delegation, International Labor Organization, 1945; consultant, Women's Advisory Cmte. on Defense Manpower, Dept. of Labor, 1951–52. BUS. & PROF.: stenographer; sec., New York, NY. MEM.: Queen's Daughters Day Nursery Assn. (pres., 1916–27); Jersey City Women's Club; Business and Professional Women's Club; ZONTA; National Democratic Club; Catholic Daughters of America; NJ Housing League; American Red Cross; Friends of Lafayette. AWARDS: Achievement Award, National Women's Press Club, 1946; Sienna Medal, Phi Alpha, 1947; Outstanding Service Award, International Relations Club, St. Elizabeth's Coll., 1949. HON. DEG.: LL.D., St. Elizabeth's Coll., 1930; LL.D., Rider Coll., 1937; LL.D., St. Bonaventure U., 1950. REL.: R.C. RES.: Jersey City, NJ.

NORTON, SEYMOUR FRANCIS "FRANK." b. 1841, Starksboro, VT; d. Apr 2, 1912, Chicago, IL; par. Fanny (Collins) Norton; m. Abie Chandler; c. Fannie; Guy Francis. EDUC.: West Randolph (VT) Acad., 1859; LL.B., U. of MI, 1867. POLIT. & GOV.: Greenback Party candidate for U.S. House (IL), 1876; member, Union Labor Party National Exec. Cmte., 1888; chm. pro tempore, Union Labor Party National Convention, 1888; ***candidate for People's Party nomination to presidency of the U.S., 1892, 1896, 1900***. BUS. & PROF.: atty., 1871; pres., editor-in-chief, Chicago Telegraph Co., to 1878; publisher, ed., *Farmers' Sentinel*, Chicago, IL, 1881–91; treas., Phoenix Vernon Lead and Zinc Mining Co., Chicago, 1900; sec., Equitable Gold Mining Co., Chicago, 1910; publisher, *Chicago Express*; publisher, Seymour and Co., Chicago. MIL.: col., II Army Corps, U.S. Army, Civil War. WRITINGS: *The Soldier and the Bondholder* (1876); *Ten Men of Money Island, or, The Primer of Finance* (1892); *Zehn Männer der Geldinsel* (1892); *Still the World Goes On* (1893). MISC.: noted monetary reformer. RES.: Chicago, IL.

NORWOOD, JAMES E. POLIT. & GOV.: ***candidate for Libertarian Party nomination to presidency of the U.S., 1984***. BUS. & PROF.: soldier. MIL.: officer, U.S. Air Force. MAILING ADDRESS: Waco, TX.

NOVA, JAY LOUIS "LOU." b. Mar 16, 1913, Los Angeles, CA; d. Sep 29, 1991, Las Vegas, NV; par. Louis Jay and Wanda Belle (Parker) Nova; m. Hertha Marie Robbins (divorced); c. three sons; one daughter. EDUC.: grad., Alameda (CA) H.S., 1936; U. of CA, Davis, one year; Sacramento (CA) Junior Coll.; Ben Bard's Dramatic School. POLIT. & GOV.: ***Utopian Party candidate for presidency of the U.S., 1968***. BUS. & PROF.: prizefighter; U.S. Amateur Heavyweight Champion; Pacific Coast A.A.U. Champion, 1935; professional wrestler; Broadway actor; radio sports commentator, 1944–64; gave poetry recitals at Carnegie Hall, 1956–57; writer; owner, Lou Nova Enterprises; actor; lecturer. STAGE CREDITS: *The Happiest Millionaire*; *Blackbeard's Ghost*. MIL.: 1st lt., CA National Guard, 1941–42. MEM.: Lambs Club; Hollywood Comedy Club; Football Writers Assn.; Baseball Writers Assn.; Screen Actors Guild; A.F.T.R.A.; Actors Equity Assn.; American Guild of Variety Artists. AWARDS: Cecil B. De Mille Award, 1959. REL.: Protestant. MISC.: invented Yogi Nova health aid; aka "Ba-ba-ba Na-na-na"; challenger for World Heavyweight Boxing Title, 1941; credited with 33 knockouts; won 59 bouts, lost 9; RES.: Hollywood, CA.

NOYES, EDWARD FOLLANSBEE. b. Oct 3, 1832, East Haverhill, MA; d. Sep 4, 1890, Cincinnati, OH; par. Theodore and Hannah (Stevens) Noyes; m. Margaretta Wilson Proctor, Feb 15, 1863; c. Edward P. EDUC.: Kingston (NH) Acad.; grad., Dartmouth Coll., 1857; LL.B., Cincinnati Law School, 1858. POLIT. & GOV.: elected city solicitor, Cincinnati, OH, 1865–67; elected as a Republican, probate judge, Hamilton Cty., OH, 1867–70; elected as a Republican to gov. of OH, 1872–74; ***candidate for Republican nomination to vice presidency of the U.S., 1872***; Republican candidate for gov. of OH, 1873; Republican candidate for U.S. Senate (OH), 1873; delegate, Rep. Nat'l. Conv., 1876 (chm., OH Delegation); appointed U.S. minister to France, 1877–81; elected judge, superior court, Cincinnati, 1889–90. BUS. & PROF.: employee, *Morning Star*, Dover, NH, 1845–50; schoolteacher; atty.; law practice, Cincinnati, 1858–61; partner, Noyes and Stephenson (law firm), Cincinnati. MIL.: maj., 39th OH Infantry, U.S. Army, 1861, lt. col., 1862, col., 1862, brev. brig. gen., 1865, resigned, 1865. MEM.: GAR; Military Order of the Loyal Legion. REL.: Presb. RES.: Cincinnati, OH.

NUCKOLS, WILLIAM LESLIE. b. Dec 23, 1929, Akron, OH; par. William Alexander, Jr. and Jean (Harrison) Nuckols; m. (divorced); c. William; Collette; Thomas; Kathy; Tina; Zank Dangle. EDUC.: high school, Tuscaloosa, AL; U. of AL, 1 year. POLIT. & GOV.: ***candidate for Democratic nomination to presidency of the U.S., 1980, 1984***. BUS. & PROF.: musician; U.S. Secret Service; artist; real estate salesman, Tuscaloosa, AL. MIL.: U.S. Air Force, 16 years. AWARDS: Westchester Show Award, 1967. MEM.: Cambridge Art Assn. REL.: Presb. MISC.: owner of extensive graphic arts collection. MAILING ADDRESS: 31 Woodbine Rd., Tuscaloosa, AL 35405.

NUGENT, JOHN FROST. b. Jun 28, 1868, La Grande, OR; d. Sep 18, 1931, Silver Spring, MD; par. Edward and Agnes P. (Frost) Nugent; m. Adelma Ainslie, May 15, 1895; c. George Ainslie. EDUC.: public schools, Silver City, ID. POLIT. & GOV.: appointed official court reporter, Third Judicial Circuit of ID, 1883; elected prosecuting atty., Owyhee Cty., ID, 1899–1906; chm., Owyhee Cty. Democratic Central Cmte., 2 terms; chm., ID State Democratic Central Cmte., 1908–12; appointed and subsequently elected as a Democrat to U.S. Senate (ID), 1918–21; Democratic candidate for U.S. Senate (ID), 1920, 1926; delegate, Dem. Nat'l. Conv., 1920; ***candidate for Democratic nomination to vice presidency of the U.S., 1920***; appointed member, Federal Trade Comm., 1921–27. BUS. & PROF.: atty.; admitted to ID Bar, 1898; law practice, Silver City; senior partner, Nugent and O'Hara (law firm), Washington, DC, 1927–31. MEM.: Knights of Pythias; Elks; Woodmen of the World; National Chamber of Associated Merchants (founder, 1931). RES.: Boise, ID.

NUNN, SAMUEL AUGUSTUS "SAM." b. Sep 8, 1938, Perry, GA; par. Samuel Augustus and Elizabeth (Cannon) Nunn; m. Colleen O'Brien, Sep 25, 1965; c. Mary Michelle; Samuel Brian. EDUC.: GA Technical Coll., 1956–59; LL.B., Emory U., 1962. POLIT. & GOV.: legal counsel, Armed Services Cmte., U.S. House, 1963; elected as a Democrat to GA State House, 1969–73; elected as a Democrat to U.S. Senate (GA), 1973–; delegate, Democratic Mid-Term Conference, 1974; ***candidate for Democratic nomination to presidency of the U.S., 1988 (declined)***. BUS. & PROF.: atty.; admitted to GA Bar, 1962; partner, Nunn, Geiger and Rampey (law firm), Perry, GA, 1964–73; farmer, Perry, GA, 1964–. MIL.: seaman, U.S.C.G., 1959–68. MEM.: Perry C. of C. (pres., 1964); GA Planning Assn. (dir., 1966; pres., 1971); Bryan Honor Soc.; Phi Delta Theta; Emory U. Cmte. of 100. AWARDS: one of five Outstanding Young Men in Georgia, GA Junior C. of C., 1971; "Most Effective Legislator" Award, District Attorneys Assn., 1972. REL.: Methodist. MAILING ADDRESS: Hawkinsville Rd., Perry, GA 31069.

NYE, GERALD PRENTICE. b. Dec 19, 1892, Hortonville, WI; d. Jul 17, 1971, Washington, DC; par. Irwin R. and Phoebe Ella (Prentice) Nye; m. Anna Margaret Munch, Aug 16, 1916; m. 2d, Arda Marguerite Johnson, Dec 14, 1940; c. Marjorie Eleanor; Robert Gerald; James Prentice; Gerald Prentice; Richard Johnson; Marguerite Deborah. EDUC.: grad., Wittenberg (WI) H.S., 1911. POLIT. & GOV.: elected member, Cooperstown (ND) School Board; Republican candidate for U.S. House (ND), 1924; appointed and subsequently elected as a Republican to U.S. Senate (ND), 1925–45; ***candidate for Third Party nomination to presidency of the U.S., 1936 (declined); candidate for Republican nomination to presidency of the U.S., 1936, 1940***; Republican candidate for U.S. Senate (ND), 1944; independent candidate for U.S. Senate (ND), 1946; appointed special asst. for elderly housing, Federal Housing Administration, 1960–64; appointed staff member, U.S. Senate Cmte. on Aging, 1964–68. BUS. & PROF.: publisher, *Register*, Hortonville, WI, 1911–14; mgr., ed., *Daily Plain Dealer*, Creston, IA, 1914–15; staff, *Des Moines (IA) Register and Leader*, 1915; publisher, *Billings County Pioneer*, Fryburg, ND, 1915–19; publisher, ed., *Griggs County Sentinel-Courier*, Cooperstown, ND, 1919–71; pres., Records Engineering, Inc., Washington, DC, 1937–59; assoc., Hurley, Clark and Associates, Washington, 1964–71; housing consultant, American Baptist Service Corp., Washington, DC, 1966–71. MEM.: Masons; Knights of Pythias; Non-Partisan League; America First Cmte. AWARDS: Cardinal Newman Award, 1935. REL.: Presb. MISC.: noted isolationist. RES.: Chevy Chase, MD.

O'BRIEN, THOMAS CHARLES. b. Jun 19, 1887, Brighton, MA; d. Nov 22, 1951, Brookline, MA; par. Michael and Mary (O'Connor) O'Brien; m. Julia Madeline Hartigan, Sep 3, 1913; c. Mary Joan; Katherine Margaret; Thomas Charles, Jr.; Julia Mildred (Mrs. Jeremiah Joseph Boyle, Jr.). EDUC.: A.B., Harvard U., 1908, LL.B., 1911. POLIT. & GOV.: member, MA State Board of Parole, 1913–16; appointed deputy dir. of prisons (MA), 1916–19; appointed penal commissioner of Boston, MA, 1919–22; elected district atty., Suffolk District, MA, 1922–27; candidate for Democratic nomination to U.S. Senate (MA), 1930, 1936; candidate for Republican nomination to U.S. Senate (MA), 1936; ***Union Party candidate for vice presidency of the U.S., 1936***; appointed member, Special MA Railroad Comm., 1939–51; appointed adviser, U.S. Delegation, International Labor Conference, 1941, 1944. BUS. & PROF.: railroad brakeman; atty.; admitted to MA Bar, 1911; partner (with James P. McGinnis), law firm, Boston, MA, 1911–13; law practice, Boston, 1913–51; regional counsel, Brotherhood of Railroad Trainmen. MEM.: American Prison Assn.; MA Prison Assn.; Elks; St. Vincent de Paul Soc.; Brighton Catholic Inst.; Boston Bar Assn.; Knights of Columbus; American Inst. of Criminal Law and Criminology (pres.); MA Catholic Order of Foresters; Ancient Order of Hibernians; Boston City Club; Harvard Club of Boston. AWARDS: Boylston Orator Prize, Harvard U., 1908. REL.: R.C. RES.: Boston, MA.

O'CONNOR, LORETTA M. POLIT. & GOV.: ***candidate for Democratic nomination to presidency of the U.S., 1976***. BUS. & PROF.: employee, GSA. MAILING ADDRESS: 119-49 Sixth Ave., College Point, NY 11356.

O'CONNOR, TERRANCE. POLIT. & GOV.: ***independent candidate for presidency of the U.S., 1976***. MAILING ADDRESS: 88 Brush Hill Rd., Milton, MA 02186.

O'CONOR, CHARLES (nee CHARLES O'CONNOR). b. Jan 22, 1804, New York, NY; d. May 12, 1884, Nantucket, MA; par. Thomas and Margaret (O'Connor) O'Connor; m. Cornelia Livingston McCraken, 1854; c. none. EDUC.: studied law under Henry Stannard, Stephen P. Lemoine, and Joseph D. Fay. POLIT. & GOV.: member, NY State Constitutional Convention, 1846, 1864; Democratic candidate for lt. gov. of NY, 1848; appointed U.S. atty., Southern District of NY, 1853; ***candidate for Democratic nomination to presidency of the U.S., 1864***; special deputy atty. gen. of NY (in Tweed Ring prosecution cases), 1871–74; ***Labor Reform Party candidate for presidency of the U.S., 1872; Straight-Out (Taproot) Democratic Party candidate for presidency of the U.S., 1872***. BUS. & PROF.: apprentice, tar and lampblack manufacturing firm, 1816; atty.; admitted to NY Bar, 1824; law practice, New York, NY. MEM.: Friends of Ireland; NY Hist. Soc. (vice pres.); NY State Bar; NY Law Inst. (treas., 10 years; pres., 1869); Kent Club. HON. DEG.: LL.D., Union Coll., 1865; LL.D., Columbia Coll., 1872; LL.D., Dartmouth Coll., 1875; LL.D., Washington and Lee U., 1875; LL.D., Harvard U., 1882. WRITINGS: *Peculation Triumphant: Being the Record of a Four Years' Campaign Against Official Malversation in the City of New York, A.D. 1871 to 1875* (1875). REL.: R.C. MISC.: specialized in corporation cases; counsel for Jefferson Davis, 1866–67; counsel, Hayes-Tilden Election Contest, 1877; first Roman Catholic to run for presidency of the U.S. RES.: New York, NY.

O'CONOR, HERBERT ROMULUS. b. Nov 17, 1896, Baltimore, MD; d. Mar 4, 1960, Baltimore, MD; par. James P. A. and Mary Ann (Galvin) O'Conor; m. Mary Eugenia Byrnes, Nov 24, 1920; c. Herbert Romulus, Jr.; Mary Patricia (Mrs. John A. Farley); Eugene F.; James P.; Robert. EDUC.: A.B., Loyola Coll., 1917; LL.B., U. of MD, 1920. POLIT. & GOV.: appointed asst. state's atty., Baltimore, MD, 1921–22; elected state's atty., Baltimore, MD, 1924–34; people's counsel, MD Public Service Comm., 1923–24; elected as a Democrat to atty. gen. of MD,

1935–39; elected as a Democrat to gov. of MD, 1939–47; chm., Interstate Comm. on the Potomac River, 1943–45; chm., Interstate Cmte. on Postwar Reconstruction and Development, 1943–46; ***candidate for Democratic nomination to vice presidency of the U.S., 1944***; elected as a Democrat to U.S. Senate (MD), 1947–53; labor adviser, City of Baltimore, MD, 1953–60. BUS. & PROF.: atty.; admitted to MD Bar, 1919; law practice, Baltimore, MD; staff, *Baltimore Sun* and *Evening Sun*, 1920; counsel, American Merchant Marine Inst., 1953; dir., Fidelity-Baltimore National Bank and Trust Co.; dir., Arundel Corp.; member, Senior Advisory Council, McCormick and Co. MIL.: U.S.N.R., 1917–19. MEM.: Knights of Columbus; Phi Kappa Sigma; American Legion; VFW; Baltimore City Bar Assn.; ABA; MD State Bar Assn.; National Prosecuting Attorneys Assn. (pres.); National Governors' Conference (chm., 1942); Council of State Governments (pres., 1943); Metropolitan Club; Merchants Club; State's Attorneys Assn. of MD (pres.); Ancient Order of Hibernians; Moose; Eagles; Elks; Baltimore Athletic Club; Wednesday Club; Phi Sigma Kappa. HON. DEG.: LL.D., Loyola Coll., 1924; LL.D., Villanova Coll., 1937; LL.D., Georgetown U., 1939; LL.D., U. of MD, 1939; LL.D., Washington Coll., 1939. REL.: R.C. RES.: Baltimore, MD.

O'CUMMINGS, GRADY, III. b. Dec 16, 1932, Greenville, SC; par. Grady and Christine Murray (Lewis) O'Cummings; m. Winifred C. Boatwine Ross; c. Joseph (stepson); Patricia (stepdaughter). EDUC.: H.S. of Commerce; City Coll. of New York; Bethune Law School. POLIT. & GOV.: part-time staff, U.S. Rep. Vito Marcantonio, 1949–51; Democratic Cty. Committeeman, New York, NY, 1954–60, 1974; candidate for Democratic nomination to NY State Senate, 1957; candidate for Democratic nomination to NY State Assembly, 1958, 1961, 1964, 1974; staff, New York City Councilman Bob Low, 1959–62; candidate for Democratic nomination to New York City Council, 1962, 1969; staff, NY Assemblyman Alfred Williams; founder, national chm., National Civil Rights Party, 1963; ***National Civil Rights Party candidate for presidency of the U.S., 1964 (withdrew); candidate for Democratic nomination to presidency of the U.S., 1964 (withdrew), 1968, 1972, 1976, 1980, 1984, 1988, 1992***; National Civil Rights Party candidate for U.S. House (NY), 1964; candidate for Democratic nomination to U.S. House (NY), 1966; candidate for Democratic nomination to mayor of New York, 1973. BUS. & PROF.: radio commentator; freelance newsman; employee, Western Union; public relations specialist; publisher, *New York Speakout*; publisher, *East New York Looking News*, New York; restaurant owner; lobbyist. MEM.: Pioneer Reform Democratic Club (pres.); Welfare Policemen's Benevolent Assn. (community relations representative); NAACP (pres., Manhattan Youth Council, 1955–56); Adam Clayton Powell Democratic Club; American Legion; Urban League; League for Teenager Service; YMCA; Cypress Tenants Assn.; Fort Green Youth Services; National Black Investors Club. AWARDS: Community Service Award; Volunteer Patrol Award. REL.: Bapt. (nee R.C.). MISC.: death erroneously reported in *New York Times*, Nov 5, 1969. MAILING ADDRESS: 198 McDougal St., Apt. 3A, Brooklyn, NY 11233.

O'DANIEL, WILBERT LEE. b. Mar 11, 1890, Malta, OH; d. May 11, 1969, Dallas, TX; par. William Barnes and Alice Ann (Thompson) Earich O'Daniel; m. Merle Estella Butcher, Jun 30, 1917; c. Pat; Mike; Molly (Mrs. Wrather White). EDUC.: grad., Arlinton (KS) H.S., 1906; grad., Salt City Business Coll., Hutchinson, KS, 1908. POLIT. & GOV.: elected as a Democrat to gov. of TX, 1938–41; elected as a Democrat to U.S. Senate (TX), 1941–49; ***American Democratic National Committee candidate for presidency of the U.S., 1944 (declined); candidate for Democratic nomination to presidency of the U.S., 1948, 1952***; candidate for Democratic nomination to gov. of TX, 1956, 1958; independent (write-in) candidate for gov. of TX, 1956. BUS. & PROF.: stenographer, sales mgr., Kramer Milling Co., Anthony, KS, 1908–12; sales mgr., Kingman Milling Co., Kingman, KS, 1912–16; co-owner, Independent Milling Co., Kingman, KS, 1916–20; employee, U.S. Flour Milling Co., Kansas City, MO, and New Orleans, LA, 1921–25; sales mgr., pres., Burrus Mill and Elevator Co., Fort Worth, TX, 1925–35; promoter, Light Crust Doughboys (band), 1930; owner, W. Lee O'Daniel Flour Co., Fort Worth, TX, 1935–38; radio announcer; promoter, Hillbilly Boys (band), 1935; owner, operator, life insurance companies; composer; real estate mgr.; bandleader. MEM.: Masons (Shriner); Fort Worth C. of C. (pres., 1937). Writings (songs): "Beautiful Texas"; "The Boy Who Never Gets Too Big to Comb His Mother's Hair"; "Your Own Sweet Darling Wife"; "Wrecks Along Life's Highway." REL.: Christian Church (elder). MISC.: known as "Pass the Biscuits Pappy" O'Daniel. RES.: Dallas, TX.

O'DAY, SHEILA DOYLE COYNE-CARNAC. b. Jul 4, 1926, San Francisco, CA; par. Richard E. and Gladys (Sullivan) Doyle; m. John Cook O'Day, Sep 16, 1977; c. W. James Coyne; Colum Patrick Coyne; John Sullivan Carnac. EDUC.: Convent of the Sacred Heart; Dominican Convent; B.A., Dominican Coll., San Rafael, CA, 1948. POLIT. & GOV.: ***independent (Committee for a Constitutional Presidency) candidate for vice presidency of the U.S., 1976***. BUS. & PROF.: children's aide; volunteer worker. MEM.: Catholic Social Service Auxiliary; Stanford Children's Hospital Auxiliary; Symphony Foundation; De Young Museum Soc.; Soc. of CA Pioneers Women's Auxiliary. REL.: R.C. MAILING ADDRESS: 2662 Union St., San Francisco, CA 94123.

ODELL, BENJAMIN BARKER, JR. b. Jan 14, 1854, Newburgh, NY; d. May 9, 1926, Newburgh, NY; par. Benjamin Barker and Ophelia (Bookstaver) Odell; m. Estell Cristee, Apr 25, 1977; m. 2d, Mrs. Linda Crist Traphagen, 1891; c. two sons; one daughter. EDUC.: Bethany Coll., 1873; Columbia U., 1873–75. POLIT. & GOV.: Republican candidate for NY State Senate; member, NY State Republican Central

Cmte., 1884–96, chm., 1898–1900; elected as a Republican to U.S. House (NY), 1895–99; ***candidate for Republican nomination to vice presidency of the U.S., 1900***; elected as a Republican to gov. of NY, 1901–05. BUS. & PROF.: employee, ice delivery company, Newburgh, NY; pres., Orange Cty. Traction Co.; pres., Newburgh Electric Light Co.; sec.-treas., Muchattoes Lake Ice Co.; organizer, Haverstraw Electric Light, Heat and Power Co.; treas., pres., Central Hudson Steamboat Co. MIL.: NY National Guard. MEM.: Odd Fellows; Masons (Master Mason); Royal Arch Masons; Newburgh C. of C. (pres.); Newburgh City Club; Knights of Pythias; Patriarchs Militant; Orange Lake Club. HON. DEG.: LL.D., Columbia U., 1903. RES.: Newburgh, NY.

ODELL, TRACY AUSTIN, SR. POLIT. & GOV.: candidate for U.S. House (CA), 1966?; ***candidate for Republican nomination to presidency of the U.S., 1980***. MAILING ADDRESS: 218 Grand Ave., Long Beach, CA 90803.

O'DONNELL, EDWARD THOMAS, JR. b. Jan 15, 1948, Wilmington, DE; par. Edward Thomas and Kathryn (Brooks) O'Donnell; single. EDUC.: B.A., Colgate U., 1970; Harvard U. Divinity School, 1970–71; Rockefeller Fellow. POLIT. & GOV.: appointed member, Governor's Advisory Council on Mental Health (DE), 1978–82; ***candidate for Democratic nomination to presidency of the U.S., 1984, 1992***. BUS. & PROF.: pres., Winthrop Foundation, 1975–. MEM.: United Negro Coll. Fund of DE (state chm., 1978); U.N. Assn. of DE (state pres., 1979); Foreign Policy Assn. Great Decisions Program of DE (state chm., 1980); United Way Allocations Cmte. of DE (1978). REL.: R.C. MAILING ADDRESS: 203 Dakota Ave., Wilmington, DE 19803.

ODORIZE, MILDRED CATHERINE. b. WY. EDUC.: Moody Bible Course. POLIT. & GOV.: ***candidate for Republican nomination to presidency of the U.S., 1972, 1976***. BUS. & PROF.: inventor. MISC.: claims to be "God-Mother Nature." MAILING ADDRESS: 4118 North Ken More Mansion, Home Number 202, Chicago 13, IL.

O'DWYER, PETER PAUL. b. Jun 29, 1907, Bohola, Cty. Mayo, Ireland; par. Patrick and Bridget (McNicholas) O'Dwyer; m. Kathleen Rohan, Aug 19, 1935; c. William; Eileen (Mrs. Thomas J. Hughes, Jr.); Brian; Rory. EDUC.: National U. of Ireland, 1924; Fordham U., 1925–26; B.L., St. John's Law School, Brooklyn, NY, 1929. POLIT. & GOV.: Democratic (American Labor Party) candidate for U.S. House (NY), 1948; founder, Cmte. for Democratic Voters, 1958; co-chm., NY Citizens Cmte. for Kennedy-Johnson, 1960; candidate for Democratic nomination to U.S. House (NY), 1960; budget dir., Citizens Cmte. for the Re-Election of Mayor Wagner, 1961; candidate for Democratic nomination to U.S. Senate (NY), 1962, 1970, 1976; appointed chm., NY Medicare Campaign, 1962; chm., NY City Voter Registration Drive, 1962; campaign mgr., Edward R. Dudley for Attorney General Campaign, 1962; elected as a Democrat to councilman-at-large, New York City Council, 1963–65; delegate, Dem. Nat'l. Conv., 1964, 1968; candidate for Democratic nomination to mayor of New York, 1965; campaign mgr., Percy Sutton for Manhattan Borough President Campaign, 1966; Democratic candidate for U.S. Senate (NY), 1968; ***candidate for Democratic nomination to vice presidency of the U.S., 1968; New (New Reform) Party candidate for vice presidency of the U.S., 1968***; campaign chm., Goldberg-Paterson Campaign, 1970; elected as a Democrat to pres., New York City Council, 1973–77. BUS. & PROF.: garment worker; deckhand, *S.S. Colbrook*, 1931; atty.; admitted to NY Bar, 1931; assoc., Holmes and Bernstien (law firm), New York; counsel, Transit Workers Union; partner, O'Dwyer and Bernstien (law firm), New York, 1935–. MEM.: National Lawyers Guild (pres.); American League for Free Israel (dir., 1946–49); National Trial Lawyers Assn.; International Longshoremen's Union; Lawyers Cmte. for Justice in Palestine (chm., 19466–47); American Cmte. for Ulster Justice (founder, 1971); Irish Inst. (pres.; chm., Gifts Cmte.); United Jewish Appeal (chm., Trial Lawyers Div.); Mayor Foundation for the Handicapped (pres.); Democratic Reform Movement (founder); Mayomen's Patriotic and Benevolent Assn. (pres.); American League for an Undivided Ireland. WRITINGS: *Counsel for the Defense* (1979). REL.: R.C. MAILING ADDRESS: 350 Central Park West, New York, NY 10025.

OERTEL, JOHN JOSEPH. POLIT. & GOV.: ***candidate for Democratic nomination to presidency of the U.S., 1988***. MAILING ADDRESS: c/o Lets Have a Pizza Jam Presidential Cmte., 1351 Chestnut St., Redding, CA 96001.

OGILVIE, RICHARD BUELL. b. Feb 22, 1923, Kansas City, MO; par. Kenneth S. and Edna Mae (Buell) Ogilvie; m. Dorothy Louise Shriver, Feb 11, 1950; c. Elizabeth. EDUC.: B.A., Yale U., 1947; J.D., Chicago Kent Coll. of Law, 1949. POLIT. & GOV.: chm., Cook Cty. (IL) Young Republicans, 1953–54; appointed asst. U.S. atty., Chicago, IL, 1954–55; appointed special asst., atty. gen. of the U.S., 1958–60; elected as a Republican to sheriff, Cook Cty., 1962–66; elected as a Republican to pres., Board of Commissioners, Cook Cty., 1966–69; delegate, Rep. Nat'l. Conv., 1968, 1972, 1976; elected as a Republican to gov. of IL, 1969–73; Republican candidate for gov. of IL, 1972; ***candidate for Republican nomination to presidency of the U.S., 1976***; candidate for Republican nomination to mayor of Chicago, IL, 1986. BUS. & PROF.: atty.; admitted to IL Bar, 1950; law practice, Chicago, 1950–54, 1955–58, 1961–62, 1973–; partner, Lord, Bissell and Brook (law firm), Chicago, 1950–58; partner, Stevenson, Conaghan, Hackbert, Rooks and Pitts (law firm), Chicago, 1960–62; partner, Isham, Lincoln and Beale (law firm), Chicago, 1973–; trustee, Chicago, Milwaukee and St. Paul R.R.; dir., jewel companies; dir., CNA Finance Corp.; dir., Fansteel Corp.; dir., La Salle Street Fund; dir., Chicago Board of Options Exchange. MIL.: sgt., U.S. Army, 1942–45; Purple Heart; ETO ribbon. MEM.: ABA; Federal Bar Assn.;

IL Bar Assn.; Chicago Bar Assn.; Soc. of Trial Lawyers; Phi Alpha Delta; Beta Theta Pi; Masons; Chicago Club; Glen View Club; Free and Accepted Masons; Tavern Club; Casino Club; Sangamo Club; Old Elm Club; Young Republican Organization of Cook Cty. (chm., 1953–54). HON. DEG.: LL.D., Chicago Kent Coll. of Law; LL.D., Greenville Coll.LL.D., IL Wesleyan U.; LL.D., Lake Forest Coll.; LL.D., Lincoln Coll.; LL.D., MacMurray Coll.; LL.D., Millikin U. REL.: Presb. MAILING ADDRESS: 1500 Lake Shore Dr., Chicago, IL 60610.

OGIN, FREDERICK EUGENE. b. Apr 26, 1946, Minneapolis, MN; par. Robert Earl and Barbara (Leeback) Ogin; single. EDUC.: grad., Kailua H.S., Oahu, HI; Foothill Coll., 1964–66; Chabot Junior Coll., Hayward, CA, 1968–82; CA State U., Hayward, CA, 1975–77. POLIT. & GOV.: ***candidate for Republican nomination to presidency of the U.S., 1984; candidate for Republican nomination to vice presidency of the U.S., 1992***. BUS. & PROF.: pensioner. MIL.: Spec. 4th class, U.S. Army, 1966–68. MEM.: VFW. REL.: R.C. MAILING ADDRESS: 18668 Lamson Rd., Castro Valley, CA 94546.

OGLESBY, CARL PRESTON, JR. b. Jul 30, 1935, Akron, OH; par. Carl Preston Oglesby; married; c. three. EDUC.: Kent State U.; U. of MI. POLIT. & GOV.: ***Peace and Freedom Party candidate for vice presidency of the U.S., 1968***; Libertarian Party candidate for U.S. House (MA), 1992. BUS. & PROF.: technical writer, Bendix Systems Div., Ann Arbor, MI; author; playwright; investigative reporter; contributor, *Liberation Magazine*; artist; instructor, Antioch Coll. MEM.: Students for a Democratic Soc. (pres., 1965–66); Radical Education Project (founder); International War Crimes Tribunal, Stockholm, Sweden, 1967. WRITINGS: *Containment and Change* (coauthor); *That Bright Necessary Day of Peace* (1965); *Trapped in a System* (1965); *The Vietnam War: World Revolution and American Containment* (1965); *Let Us Shape the Future* (1966); *Democracy is Nothing If It is Not Dangerous* (196–); *U.S. Imperialism and South Africa* (1969); *Notes on a Decade Ready for the Dustbin* (1969). MAILING ADDRESS: Red Clover Collective, P.O. Box 272, Putney, VT 05346.

OGLESBY, RICHARD JAMES. b. Jul 25, 1824, Floydsburg, Oldham Cty., KY; d. Apr 24, 1899, Elkart, IL; par. Jacob and Isabella (Watson) Oglesby; m. Anna E. White, 1859; m. 2d, Emma (Gillett) Keyes, Nov 1873; c. Felicite; John Gillett; James; Olive Snyder; Robert; Dickey; Richard James, Jr.; Jasper. EDUC.: studied law under Silas W. Robbins, Springfield, IL; grad., Louisville (KY) Law School, 1848. POLIT. & GOV.: presidential elector, Whig Party, 1852; Republican candidate for U.S. House (IL), 1858; elected as a Republican to IL State Senate, 1860–61; elected as a Republican to gov. of IL, 1865–69, 1873, 1885–89; elected as a Republican to U.S. Senate (IL), 1873–79; ***candidate for American Party nomination to presidency of the U.S., 1888 (declined)***; Republican candidate for U.S. Senate (IL), 1891. BUS. & PROF.: atty.; admitted to IL Bar, 1845; law practice, Sullivan, IL, 1845–46; law practice, Decatur, IL, 1847–49, 1851; gold prospector, CA, 1849–51. MIL.: 1st lt., Company C, 4th IL Volunteers, 1846; col., 8th IL Volunteers, U.S. Army, 1861–62, brig. gen., 1862, maj. gen., 1862–64. REL.: Episc. MISC.: known as "Uncle Dick" Oglesby. RES.: Elkart, IL.

O'GORMAN, JAMES ALOYSIUS. b. May 5, 1860, New York, NY; d. May 17, 1943, New York, NY; par. Thomas and Ellen (Callan) O'Gorman; m. Anne Miriam Leslie, Jan 2, 1884; c. Mary (Mrs. Dudley Field Malone, q.v.); Ellen (Mrs. William Leo Duffy); Edith (Mrs. James Edward McDonald); Dolorita (Mrs. John Anthony Maher); Alice; Ann (Mrs. Paul March White); Agnes (Mrs. Joseph Sanford Shanley); James Aloysius, Jr.; Richard; Robert Emmet. EDUC.: City Coll. of New York; LL.B., NY U., 1882. POLIT. & GOV.: United Labor Party candidate for New York (NY) civil judge, 1887; elected justice, NY District Court, 1893–1900; elected justice, NY State Supreme Court, 1900–1911; elected as a Democrat to U.S. Senate (NY), 1911–17; delegate, Dem. Nat'l. Conv., 1912; ***candidate for Democratic nomination to vice presidency of the U.S., 1912***; appointed referee, NY State Supreme Court, 1934–43. BUS. & PROF.: employee, D. Appleton and Co. (publishing house), New York, NY; atty.; admitted to NY Bar, 1882; law practice, New York, 1882–93; partner, O'Gorman, Battle and Marshall (law firm), New York, 1911–13; partner, O'Gorman, Battle, Vandiver and Levy (law firm), New York, 1913–22; law practice, New York, 1922–34; dir., New York Title and Mortgage Co.; dir., Bank of Manhattan Co. MEM.: NY U. (trustee, 1920–27); Coll. of New Rochelle (trustee); Anti-Monopoly League; Tammany Soc. (chm., 17th Assembly District; grand sachem, 1903–05); ABA; NY State Bar Assn.; Assn. of the Bar of the City of New York; American Law Inst.; New York Law Inst.; New York Cty. Lawyers Assn. (pres., 1923–24); Lawyers Club (pres., 1932–33); National Democratic Club; Catholic Club; Manhattan Club. HON. DEG.: LL.D., Villanova Coll., 1904; LL.D., Fordham U., 1908; LL.D., NY U., 1909; LL.D., Georgetown U., 1911. REL.: R.C. RES.: New York, NY.

O'HARA, LOUIS DONA GINGRAS (nee **LOUIS DONA O'HARA GINGRAS).** b. Mar 15, 1922, New York, NY; par. Dona Joseph Gingras and Elizabeth O'Hara; m. Carol Gilmore Doyle; m. 2d, Louise Angers; m. 3d, Nora Edelgard Dieberg; m. 4th, Saeta Maharaj; m. 5th, Aline Delphine Brunet; c. David Alan; Donna Louise; John Richard. EDUC.: Boston U., 1940–42; B.A., U.S. Military Acad., 1945; NY U., 1947–49; U. of PA. POLIT. & GOV.: candidate for U.S. House (PA), 1956, 1958; independent candidate for U.S. House (RI), 1960, 1962, 1968; candidate for Republican nomination to U.S. House (RI), 1962, 1980; candidate for Republican nomination to U.S. Senate (RI), 1976; ***candidate for Republican nomination to vice presidency of the U.S., 1976; candidate for Republican nomination to presidency of the U.S., 1980***. BUS. & PROF.: civil engineer; registered professional engineer,

1953; owner, Continental Engineering Service, 1957–; political scientist; civil engineer, Philadelphia, PA; city engineer, Providence, RI; town engineer, Holliston, MA. MIL.: capt., U.S.A.R. MEM.: VFW; Disabled American Veterans; AmVets; American Legion; Moose; Taxpayers League; Fleet Reserve; Reserve Officers Assn.; National Guard Assn.; Assn. of U.S. Military Acad. Graduates; AUS Assn.; A.S.N.E.I.; Engineers Club; University Club; L'Avant Garde; L'Alliance Francais d'Amerique; Parti Quebecois; LeFoyer; Debate Club Canadien; Cercle Laurier; Club Mongenais; Blue Noses; Irish Club. WRITINGS: *Workable Taxation by Representation by Revenue Sharing* (1958); *Parti Quebecois-Canada* (1974); *Alternative 200th Birthday Constitutional Convention II for North America* (1976). REL.: Ecumenist Catholic/Episcopal Protestant. MAILING ADDRESS: 771 Lonsdale Ave., Central Falls, RI 02863.

O'HARE, KATE RICHARDS (See CUNNINGHAM, KATHLEEN "KATE" RICHARDS O'HARE).

OLDENBURG, MARK ARTHUR. b. Jul 14, 1953, Streator, IL; par. Arthur Henry and Rosemary Lou Oldenburg; single. EDUC.: U. of IL; Eureka Coll.; IL State U.; IL Valley Community Coll. POLIT. & GOV.: ***candidate for Republican nomination to presidency of the U.S., 1988***. BUS. & PROF.: farmer; employee, Washington National Insurance Co.; employee, Country Companies; employee, Eureka Co.; employee, Behlen Manufacturing Co.; employee, Kent Lumber Co. MIL.: Sp/4, U.S. Army, 1979–84; 1st lt., U.S. Air Force Reserve, 1984–. MEM.: Junior C. of C.; Rep. Nat'l. Cmte. (1981–). AWARDS: James Scholar. REL.: United Church of Christ (Sunday school teacher). MAILING ADDRESS: 284 East Seventh Rd., Rutland, IL 61358-0177.

OLDS, DARYL MARTIN. b. Oct 8, 1952, Gillette, WY; par. Charles Clyde and Vera (Hollas) Olds; single. EDUC.: A.A., Sheridan Coll., 1975. POLIT. & GOV.: member, Campbell Cty. (WY) Democratic Central Cmte., 1974– (treas., 1975–); delegate, WY State Democratic Convention, 1976, 1978, 1980, 1982; Democratic candidate for coroner, Campbell Cty., WY, 1976; Democratic candidate for cty. treas., Campbell Cty., 1978; member, Canvass and Election Board, Campbell Cty., 1976–; ***NAP Party candidate for vice presidency of the U.S., 1984***. BUS. & PROF.: service mgr., Gillette Cycle Shop, Gillette, WY, 1975–. MEM.: Odd Fellows (noble grand, 1981–83); Lions (dir., 1980–81); Campbell Hist. Soc. (vice pres., 1983–); Campbell Cty. Rockpile Museum (treas., 1975–). REL.: Presb. MAILING ADDRESS: 900 East Fifth St., Gillette, WY 82716.

OLIVER, ETHEL I. POLIT. & GOV.: ***independent candidate for presidency of the U.S., 1976***. MAILING ADDRESS: 2844 West Holt Rd., Mason, MI 48854.

OLMSTED, FREDERICK LAW. b. Apr 26, 1822, Hartford, CT; d. Aug 28, 1903, Waverly, MA; par. John and Charlotte Law (Hull) Olmsted; m. Mary Cleveland Perkins, Jun 13, 1859; c. John Theodore; Frederick Law, Jr.; Marion; John Charles (stepson); Charlotte (stepdaughter); Owen (stepson). EDUC.: Ellington H.S.; studied engineering under Frederick A. Barton, Andover, MA, and Collinsville, CT, 1837–40; Yale U., 1842–43. POLIT. & GOV.: appointed landscape architect and superintendent, Central Park, New York, NY, 1857–58; appointed sec., U.S. Sanitary Comm., 1861–63; appointed street commissioner, New York, 1862; appointed commissioner of Yosemite and Mariposa Big Tree Grove, 1864; appointed member, Cmte. for CA State Agricultural Fair, 1865; appointed commissioner of NY Dept. of Public Works (pres.; treas.), 1872; ***Independent Liberal Republican (Revenue Reform) Party candidate for vice presidency of the U.S., 1872***. BUS. & PROF.: employee, Benkard and Hutton (French dry goods importers), New York, 1840–42; farmer, Guilford, CT, 1847–57; farmer, Staten Island, NY, 1848–54; ed., *Putnam's Magazine*, 1855–56; partner, publishing business, 1855–56; landscape architect; superintendent, Fremont Mariposa Mining Estates, CA, 1863; partner, Olmsted, Vaux and Co.; partner, F. L. and J. C. Olmsted, 1884–89; partner, F. L. Olmsted and Co., 1889–93; partner, Olmsted, Olmsted and Eliot, 1893–97. MEM.: Richmond Cty. Agricultural Soc. (corresponding sec., 1850); American Freedman's Union (gen. sec., refused, 1865); Union League Club; A.I.A. (hon.); Boston Soc. of Architects (hon.). HON. DEG.: A.M., Harvard U., 1864, LL.D., 1893; A.M., Amherst Coll., 1867; LL.D., Yale U., 1893. WRITINGS: *Walks and Talks of an American Farmer in England* (1852); *A Journey in the Seaboard Slave States* (1856); *A Journey Through Texas* (1857); *A Journey to the Back Country* (1860); *The Cotton Kingdom* (1861); *Public Parks and the Enlargement of Towns* (1871); *A Consideration of the Justifying Value of a Public Park* (1881); *The Spoils of the Park* (1882). REL.: Unitarian. MISC.: designed public parks in Boston, Bridgeport, Brooklyn, Buffalo, Chicago, Louisville, Milwaukee, Montreal, New York, Trenton, U.S. Capitol grounds, and Chicago World's Fair. RES.: Brookline, MA.

OLNEY, RICHARD. b. Sep 15, 1835, Oxford, MA; d. Apr 9, 1917, Boston, MA; par. Wilson and Eliza L. (Butler) Olney; m. Agnes Park Thomas, Mar 6, 1861; c. Agnes (Mrs. George R. Minot); Mary (Mrs. C. H. Abbot). EDUC.: A.M. (with high honors), Brown U., 1856; LL.B., Harvard U., 1858. POLIT. & GOV.: elected as a Democrat to MA State House, 1873–74; Democratic candidate for MA State House, 1874; Democratic candidate for MA State Senate, 1875; Democratic candidate for atty. gen. of MA, 1876; appointed atty. gen. of the U.S., 1893–95; appointed U.S. sec. of state, 1895–97; ***candidate for Democratic nomination to presidency of the U.S., 1896, 1904***; Democratic candidate for U.S. Senate (MA), 1901; appointed U.S. ambassador to England, 1913 (declined); appointed member, Federal Reserve Board, 1914 (declined); Democratic candidate for U.S. House (MA), 1914, 1916; appointed U.S. representative, International Comm. Between U.S. and France,

1915–17. BUS. & PROF.: atty.; admitted to MA Bar, 1859; partner (with Judge Benjamin F. Thomas), law firm, Boston, MA, 1859–79. MEM.: Brown U. (fellow, 1894–97); Smithsonian Institution (regent, 1900–1908); MA Hist. Soc.; American Phil. Soc.; American Soc. of International Law (vice pres.); Franklin Union (mgr.). HON. DEG.: LL.D., Brown U., 1893; LL.D., Harvard U., 1893; LL.D., Yale U., 1901. RES.: Boston, MA.

OLSON, ANDY. POLIT. & GOV.: ***candidate for Democratic nomination to presidency of the U.S., 1992***. MAILING ADDRESS: CA?

O'MAHONEY, JOSEPH CHRISTOPHER. b. Nov 5, 1884, Chelsea, MA; d. Dec 1, 1962, Bethesda, MD; par. Denis and Elizabeth (Sheehan) O'Mahoney; m. Agnes Veronica O'Leary, Jun 11, 1913; c. none. EDUC.: Columbia U., 1905–07; LL.B., Georgetown U., 1920. POLIT. & GOV.: exec. sec. to U.S. Sen. John B. Kendrick (q.v.), 1917–20; vice chm., WY State Democratic Cmte., 1922–30; delegate, WY State Democratic Convention, 1924, 1926, 1928, 1930, 1932; delegate, Dem. Nat'l. Conv., 1924, 1928, 1932, 1936, 1940, 1944, 1948, 1956; member, Dem. Nat'l. Cmte., 1929–34 (vice chm., 1932); city atty., Cheyenne, WY, 1929–31; appointed first asst. postmaster gen. of the U.S., 1933; appointed and subsequently elected as a Democrat to U.S. Senate (WY), 1934–53, 1954–61; ***candidate for Democratic nomination to vice presidency of the U.S., 1940, 1944***; Democratic candidate for U.S. Senate (WY), 1952. BUS. & PROF.: city ed., *Boulder (CO) Herald*, 1908–16; city ed., *Cheyenne (WY) State Leader*, 1916; atty.; admitted to WY Bar, 1920; law practice, Cheyenne, 1920–32; law practice, Washington, DC, 1920–32. MEM.: ABA; WY State Bar Assn.; Knights of Columbus (4°); Sigma Alpha; Phi Kappa Sigma; National Conference of Commissioners on Uniform State Laws (commissioner, 1925–26). HON. DEG.: LL.D., Columbia U., 1938; LL.D., Georgetown U., 1941; Litt.D., De Paul U., 1946; LL.D., U. of WY, 1947; D.Sc. (Bus. Admin.) Hill Coll., 1948; D.C.L., St. Joseph's Coll. REL.: R.C. RES.: Cheyenne, WY.

O'MALLEY, SHAWN P. POLIT. & GOV.: ***independent candidate for presidency of the U.S., 1972***. MAILING ADDRESS: Euclid, WA.

O'MALLEY, WALTER JOSEPH, JR. par. Walter Joseph O'Malley. POLIT. & GOV.: ***candidate for Democratic nomination to presidency of the U.S., 1976, 1980***. MEM.: Pro-Life Action Cmte. MAILING ADDRESS: 15201 Kingsbury St., Mission Hills, CA 91345.

OMEGA, ELIJAH ANDERSON. POLIT. & GOV.: ***independent non-partisan candidate for presidency of the U.S., 1992***. MEM.: Elijah and the People for a Better World Organization. MAILING ADDRESS: P.O. Box 1449, Palmdale, CA 93550.

ONTIVERAS, RITA SUE. b. Apr 26, 1950, Starke, FL; par. George Edward and Emma Louvania (Allen) Grover; m. Alejandro Ontiveras (divorced); c. Jonathan Adam; Alejandro (Alex), Jr.; Crispen Edward. EDUC.: grad., Bradford (FL) H.S., 1968; Liberty U., 1989–91; Santa Fe Junior Coll., 1991–92. POLIT. & GOV.: ***candidate for Libertarian Party nomination to presidency of the U.S., 1992***. BUS. & PROF.: job search counselor; day care counselor; clerk typist specialist; social worker; notary public, 1981–94. MEM.: Parent-Teachers Assn.; Future Homemakers of America; Phi Beta Lamda. REL.: Christian. MAILING ADDRESS: P.O. Box 337, Lulu, FL 32061.

ORANGE, AARON M. b. Jul 11, 1905, New York, NY; par. Adolph and Tina (Kemp) Orange; m. Ruth Keefner; c. none. EDUC.: B.S., City Coll. of New York, 1926; M.A., Columbia U., 1928. POLIT. & GOV.: Socialist Labor Party candidate for gov. of NY, 1932, 1934, 1936, 1938 (Industrial Government), 1942, 1946 (Industrial Government); Socialist Labor Party candidate for mayor of New York, NY, 1933; Labor Party candidate for justice, Supreme Court, New York, 1935; ***Socialist Labor Party candidate for vice presidency of the U.S., 1940***; organizer, Manhattan Subdivision, Socialist labor Party, 1941; delegate, recording sec., Socialist Labor Party National Convention, 1948, 1952, 1956, 1960, 1964 (Platform Cmte.), 1968. BUS. & PROF.: teacher, public schools, New York, 1926–70. WRITINGS: *The Economic Basis of Education* (1932). REL.: none. MAILING ADDRESS: 63 Adrian Ave., New York, NY.

ORMSBY, GEORGE. m. Miriam. POLIT. & GOV.: chief plumbing and building inspector, Aston Township, PA; chief plumbing and building inspector, Chester Township, PA; delegate, International Congress for the Prevention of Alcoholism, Nice, France; member, exec. cmte., Prohibition Party National Cmte., 1987–; ***Prohibition Party candidate for vice presidency of the U.S., 1988, 1992***. BUS. & PROF.: partner, air conditioning business, 1950–80. MIL.: Seabees, U.S. Navy, WWII. MEM.: International Order of Good Templars (national pres.); National Temperance and Prohibition Council; trade associations. REL.: Presb. (treas.; pres., Board of Trustees; elder, 1952–). MAILING ADDRESS: Aston, PA.

ORNSTEIN, RAPHAEL. EDUC.: M.D. POLIT. & GOV.: ***candidate for Democratic nomination to presidency of the U.S., 1984***. BUS. & PROF.: physician. MAILING ADDRESS: 803 Fourth St., #9, San Rafael, CA 94901.

ORR, LEONARD DIETRICH. b. 1937; c. Spirit. POLIT. & GOV.: ***candidate for Democratic nomination to***

presidency of the U.S., 1988. MAILING ADDRESS: 1 Campbell Hot Springs Rd., Sierraville, CA 96126.

O'RYAN, JOHN FRANCIS. b. Aug 21, 1874, New York, NY; d. Jan 29, 1961, South Salem, NY; par. Francis and Anna (Barry) O'Ryan; m. Janet Holmes, Apr 9, 1902; c. Mrs. Donald Bowman; Mrs. Richard Woolworth; Holmes. EDUC.: City Coll. of New York; LL.B., NY U., 1898; grad., Army War Coll., 1914. POLIT. & GOV.: appointed NY state transit commissioner, 1921–26; Reform candidate for mayor of New York, NY, 1933 (withdrew); appointed police commissioner, New York, 1934; ***Independent Citizens League candidate for Republican nomination to presidency of the U.S., 1940; Independent Citizens League candidate for Democratic nomination to presidency of the U.S., 1940***; appointed chm., U.S. Economic Comm. to Japan, Manchuria, and North China, 1940; appointed NY state dir. of civilian defense, 1941. BUS. & PROF.: atty.; admitted to NY Bar, 1898; partner, Loucks, O'Ryan and Cullen (law firm), New York; pres., Colonial Airways, Inc., 1919. MIL.: pvt., Company G, 7th Infantry, NY National Guard, 1897, capt., 1907, maj., 1911, maj. gen., NY Div., 1916; maj. gen., 27th Div., U.S. Army, 1917; Distinguished Service Medal; knight commander, Order of St. Michael and St. George; commander, Victorian Order; Legion of Honor; Croix de Guerre with Palm (France); Order of Leopold; Croix de Guerre with Palm (Belgium); Order of Saints Maurice and Lazarus (Italy). MEM.: Delta Upsilon; Fighting Funds for Finland (chm., 1940); Lawyers Club; Metropolitan Club. HON. DEG.: LL.D., NY U., 1919. WRITINGS: *The Modern Army in Action* (1914); *General Plan and Syllabus for Physical Training* (1917); *The Story of the 27th Division* (1921); *The Maintenance of World Peace* (1923); *Business Needs World Security* (1931); *Report of the New York State World War Memorial Comm.* (1931). REL.: R.C. RES.: Westchester Cty., NY.

OSBORN, CHASE SALMON. b. Jan 22, 1860, Huntington Cty., IN; d. Apr 11, 1949, Poulan, GA; par. George Augustus and Margaret Ann (Fannon) Osborn; m. Lillian Gertrude Jones, May 7, 1881; m. 2d, Stellanova Brunt, Apr 9, 1949; c. Ethel Louise (Mrs. Adam Ernest Ferguson); George Augustus; Chase Salmon; Lillian Margaret; Oren Chandler; Miriam Gertrude; Emily Fisher (Mrs. Richard Sanderson); Stellanova Brunt (adopted; adoption annulled). EDUC.: Purdue U., 1874–77. POLIT. & GOV.: appointed postmaster, Sault Ste. Marie, MI, 1889–93; appointed MI state fish and game warden, 1895–99; candidate for Republican nomination to U.S. House (MI), 1896; candidate for Republican nomination to gov. of MI, 1900; appointed member, MI State Railroad Comm., 1899–1903; elected as a Republican to gov. of MI, 1911–13; Republican candidate for gov. of MI, 1914; candidate for Republican nomination to U.S. Senate (MI), 1918, 1930; organizer, Leonard Wood for President Campaign, 1920; ***candidate for Republican nomination to vice presidency of the U.S., 1928 (declined)***; appointed member, MI Unemployment Compensation Comm., 1932; hon. chm., MI State Republican Central Cmte., 1934; member, Cmte. of 1912 Progressives for Landon, 1936; presidential elector, Republican Party, 1936; appointed chm., MI State Mackinac Straits Bridge Cmte., 1938; vice chm., National Cmte. of Independent Voters for Franklin D. Roosevelt, 1940; appointed member, MI Advisory Board, WPA, 1941. BUS. & PROF.: reporter, *Chicago (IL) Tribune*, 1879; reporter, *Home Journal*, Lafayette, IN, 1880; reporter, *Evening Wisconsin*, Milwaukee, WI, 1880–83; owner, *Mining News*, Florence, WI, 1883–87; prospector, 1883–87; city ed., *Milwaukee Sentinel*, 1887; founder, *Miner and Manufacturer*; publisher, ed., *Sault Ste. Marie News*, 1887–1901; co-owner, owner, *Saginaw (MI) Courier-Herald*, 1902–12; owner of substantial timber and mining interests; philanthropist. MIL.: Company B, 107th Engineers, MI National Guard. MEM.: National Progressive Republican League (1911); MI Republican Newspaper Assn. (pres., 1894); MI Press Assn. (pres., 1895); U. of MI (regent, 1908–11); Sault Koorhaan Fly Club; Pi Gamma Mu; Red Arrow Div., AEF (hon.); Three Score and Ten Club; Heart O' Nature Club; Espanore Club; National Arts Club; The Players; Le Sault Club; Lions; Kiwanis; Albany Club; Sylvester Club; Waycross Club; MI Good Roads Federation; Masons (33°); Elks; Future Farmers of America; Spanish War Veterans; Odd Fellows; Grange; Knights of Pythias; Sigma Chi (national grand orator, 1933, 1935, 1937; grand trustee, 1937–39); Sigma Rho; Sigma Delta Chi (hon. pres., 1912–19); Detroit Club; University Club of Detroit; University Club of Chicago; Gristmill Club; Prismatic Club; Algonquin Club; Purdue Club; Camp Fire Club; Cliff Dwellers; Burns Club; Herty Forest Inst. (patron); Georgia Bicentennial Comm. (hon. patron, 1933); Detroit Exposition (adviser, 1935); Gabriel Richard Day Cmte. (1937); Mackinac Straits Bridge Assn.; American Red Cross; BSA; MI C. of C. (vice chm.); C. of C. of the U.S. (national councillor); Alexander Blain Hospital (trustee); Detroit Phil. Soc. (trustee); AAAS (fellow); Madagascar Acad. of Science; Archaeological Inst. of America; American Bison Soc.; American Forestry Assn.; American Geographical Soc.; American Soc. of Mammalogists; American Inst. of Mining and Metallurgical Engineers; American Museum of Natural History; American Ornithologists Union; Seismological Soc. of America; National Audubon Soc.; National Economic League; National Parks Assn.; American Pioneer Trails Assn.; William T. Hornaday Foundation; Sulgrave Inst.; Wilson Ornithological Club; Geographical Soc. of Chicago; Lake Superior Mining Inst.; Cranbrook Inst. of Science; GA Mineralogy Soc.; MI Acad. of Science, Arts and Letters; Great Lakes Hist. Soc.; Mississippi Valley Hist. Assn.; Roosevelt Memorial Assn.; Oregon Trail Memorial Assn.; IN Hist. Soc.; State Hist. Soc. of MI; IN Soc. of Chicago; Northern MI Sportsmen's Assn.; MI Authors Assn.; NRA; Bibb Cty. Fish and Game Club; Worth Cty. Sportsmen's Club; GA Press Assn.; American Huguenot Soc.; SAR; Leif Eriksen Memorial Assn.; Norse Civic Assn.; Macon Hist. Soc.; Authors League of America; Outdoor Writers Assn. of America; Atlanta Hist. Soc.; Chippewa Cty. Hist. Soc.; Detroit Hist. Soc.; Izaak Walton League; Essex Cty. Humane Soc.; Mark Twain Soc. of America; MI Amateur Press Assn.; Societe Historique du Ontario Nouvelle; Tippecanoe Cty.

Hist. Assn. HON. DEG.: M.D., Detroit Coll. of Medicine, 1909; LL.D., Olivet Coll., 1911; LL.D., U. of MI, 1911; LL.D., Alma Coll., 1912; LL.D., Northwestern U., 1922; B.S., Purdue U., 1926; LL.D., Atlanta Law School, 1935; Sc.D., Wayne U., 1944. WRITINGS: *The Andean Land* (1909); *The Iron Hunter* (1919); *Law of Divine Concord* (1921); *Madagascar: The Land of the Man-Eating Tree* (1924); *Short History of Michigan* (1926); *The Earth Upsets* (1927); *Following the Ancient Gold Trail of Hiram of Tyre* (1932); *North Woods Sketches* (1934); *The Conquest of a Continent* (coauthor, 1939); *Schoolcraft-Longfellow-Hiawatha* (coauthor, 1942); *Hiawatha, With Its Original Indian Legends* (coauthor, 1944); *Errors in Official U.S. Area Figures* (coauthor, 1945); *Official Encyclopedia of Michigan* (contributing ed.). REL.: Presb. (nee Methodist). RES.: Sault Ste. Marie, MI.

OSBORNE, JOHN EUGENE. b. Jun 19, 1858, Westport, NY; d. Apr 24, 1943, Rawlins, WY; par. John C. and Mary E. (Reil) Osborne; m. Selina Smith, Nov 3, 1907; c. Jean Curtis. EDUC.: Westport (NY) H.S.; M.D., U. of VT, 1880. POLIT. & GOV.: member, WY Territorial Legislature, 1883–85; chm., WY Territorial Penitentiary Comm., 1888; elected as a Democrat to mayor of Rawlins, WY, 1888; delegate, Dem. Nat'l. Conv., 1892 (alternate), 1896; elected as a Democrat to gov. of WY, 1893–95; Democratic candidate for gov. of WY, 1894 (declined), 1904; member, WY Bimetallic Democratic State Cmte., 1895; elected as a Democrat to U.S. House (WY), 1897–99; vice chm., Democratic National Congressional Cmte., 1898; Democratic candidate for U.S. Senate (WY), 1899, 1918; member, Dem. Nat'l. Cmte., 1900–1920; ***candidate for Democratic nomination to vice presidency of the U.S., 1912***; appointed asst. U.S. sec. of state, 1913–17. BUS. & PROF.: apprentice, drugstore, VT; asst. surgeon, Union Pacific R.R.; wholesaler and druggist, 1886; rancher, 1887–1943; banker; pres., Rawlins Drug Co.; pres., Rawlins Electric Light Co.; pres., Rawlins Hotel Co.; owner, Rawlins Opera House; founder, Osborne Block Realty Co.; founder, Rawlins National Bank. MEM.: Masons; Knights Templar (eminent commander); Royal Arch Masons (high priest). REL.: Episc. RES.: Rawlins, WY.

OTIS, HARRISON GRAY. b. Feb 10, 1837, Marietta, OH; d. Jul 10, 1917, Los Angeles, CA; par. Stephen and Sarah (Dyer) Otis; m. Eliza A. Wetherby, Sep 11, 1859; c. Harrison Gray; Lillian; Marian (Mrs. Harry Chandler); Mabel (Mrs. Franklin Booth); Esther. EDUC.: Wetherby's Acad.; Western Liberal Inst.; grad., Granger's Commercial Coll., 1861. POLIT. & GOV.: delegate, Rep. Nat'l. Conv., 1860; appointed official reporter, OH State House, 1866–67; appointed chief of div., U.S. Patent Office, 1870–76; special agent, U.S. Dept. of the Treasury, 1879–81; ***candidate for Republican nomination to vice presidency of the U.S., 1896***; appointed U.S. commissioner to the Centennial of Mexican Independence, 1910. BUS. & PROF.: soldier; journalist; foreman, U.S. Government Printing Office, 1868–69; ed., *Santa Barbara (CA) Press*, 1876; ed., gen. mgr., *Los Angeles (CA) Times*, 1882–86, pres., 1886–1917; dir., Times-Mirror Printing Co.; dir., California-Mexico Land and Cattle Co.; pres., Los Angeles Sururban Homes Co.; pres., Colorado River Land Co. MIL.: pvt., 12th OH Infantry, U.S. Army, 1861, 2d lt., 1862, 1st lt., 1863, capt., 23d OH Infantry, U.S. Army, 1864; brev. maj., lt. col. of volunteers, 1865, mustered out, 1865; brig. gen., U.S.V., 1898, maj. gen., 1893. MEM.: American Acad. of Sciences; Associated Press; American Newspaper Publishers Assn.; GAR; Military Order of the Loyal Legion; Soc. of the Army of the Potomac; Military Order of Foreign Wars; United Spanish War Veterans; National Soc. of the Army of the Philippines; SAR; Archaeological Soc. of the Southwest. WRITINGS: *Plan to End War* (1915). RES.: Los Angeles, CA.

OTT, CHARLES J. POLIT. & GOV.: ***independent candidate for presidency of the U.S., 1988***. MAILING ADDRESS: c/o Chuck Ott's Believe It or Not Serious Presidential Campaign, 35-28 80th St., Jackson Heights, NY 11372.

OUTHOUSE, ROB. POLIT. & GOV.: ***independent candidate for presidency of the U.S., 1992***. MAILING ADDRESS: NY.

OVERMAN, JAY RANDALL. POLIT. & GOV.: ***candidate for Democratic nomination to presidency of the U.S., 1984; independent candidate for vice presidency of the U.S., 1984***. MAILING ADDRESS: c/o Hugh Bagley, P.O. Box 167, Poughkeepsie, NY 12602.

OVERSTREET, HOWARD M. b. TX. POLIT. & GOV.: ***candidate for Democratic nomination to presidency of the U.S., 1932, 1936***. BUS. & PROF.: policeman, Washington, DC, 1931–36. RES.: Washington, DC.

OVERTURF, JACK. POLIT. & GOV.: ***independent candidate for presidency of the U.S., 1980***. MAILING ADDRESS: 2347 North Guyer, Hobart, IN 46342.

OWEN, ROBERT DALE. b. Nov 9, 1801, Glasgow, Scotland; d. Jun 24, 1877, Lake George, NY; par. Robert and Ann Caroline (Dale) Owen; m. Mary Jane Robinson, Apr 12, 1832; m. 2d, Littie Walton Kellogg, Jun 23, 1876; c. Ernest Dale; Florence Dale (d. 1834); Florence Dale; Julian Dale; Rosamond Dale. EDUC.: New Lanark School; Fellenberg Acad., 1818–22. POLIT. & GOV.: elected as a Democrat to IN State House, 1836–38, 1851; Democratic candidate for U.S. House (IN), 1839, 1840, 1847; elected as a Democrat to U.S. House (IN), 1843–47; delegate, IN State Constitutional Convention, 1850; appointed chargé d'affaires, Italy, 1853–54; appointed U.S. minister to Italy, 1854–58; appointed Commissioner to Purchase Arms for Indiana Militia, 1861–63; appointed chm., Cmte. on Freedmen, 1863; ***candidate for Equal Rights (Cosmic, Free***

Love, People's) Party nomination to vice presidency of the U.S., 1872. BUS. & PROF.: teacher, New Harmony, IN; ed., *New Harmony Gazette*, 1826–29; ed., *Free Enquirer*, New York, NY, 1828–32; ed., *New York Daily Sentinel*, 1830–31; co-editor, *The Crisis*, England, 1832–33; reformer. MEM.: Smithsonian Institution (regent); Assn. for the Protection of Industry and for the Promotion of National Education. HON. DEG.: LL.D., U. of IN, 1872. WRITINGS: *An Outline of the System of Education at New Lanark* (1824); *Moral Physiology* (1831); *Popular Tracts* (1831); *Personality of God and Authority of the Bible* (1832); *Address on the Hopes and Destinies of the Human Species* (1836); *Pocahontas: A Historical Drama* (1837); *A Lecture on Consistency* (1842); *Free Inquiry* (1843); *Hints on Public Architecture* (1849); *Treatise on Construction of Plank Roads* (1856); *Divorce: Being a Correspondence Between Horace Greeley and Robert Dale Owen* (1860); *Footfalls on the Boundary of Another World* (1860); *The Future of the Northwest* (1863); *The Policy of Emancipation* (1863); *Emancipation is Peace* (1863); *The Conditions of Reconstruction* (1863); *The Wrong of Slavery* (1864); *Beyond the Breakers* (1870); *The Debatable Land Between This World and the Next* (1872); *Threading My Way* (1874); *Address on the Influence of the Clerical Profession*. REL.: Spiritualist. RES.: Lake George, NY.

OWEN, ROBERT LATHAM. b. Feb 3, 1856, Lynchburg, VA; d. Jul 19, 1947, Washington, DC; par. Robert Latham and Narcissa (Chisholm) Owen; m. Daisey Deane Hester, Dec 31, 1889; c. Dorothea; Robert Latham (adopted). EDUC.: A.M., Washington and Lee U., 1877. POLIT. & GOV.: U.S. Indian Agent for Five Civilized Tribes, 1885–89; member, Dem. Nat'l. Cmte., 1892–96; delegate, Dem. Nat'l. Conv., 1892, 1896, 1924; vice chm., OK Democratic State Campaign Cmte., 1906; elected as a Democrat to U.S. Senate (OK), 1907–25; ***candidate for Democratic nomination to presidency of the U.S., 1916, 1920, 1924***. BUS. & PROF.: principal teacher, Cherokee Orphan Asylum, 1879–80; sec., Cherokee National Board of Education, 1881–84; atty.; admitted to OK Bar, 1880; law practice, Tahlequah, Territory of OK, 1880; ed., publisher, *Indian Chieftain*, 1884; pres., First National Bank, Muskogee, OK, 1890–1900; real estate investor; rancher; farmer; law practice, Washington, DC, 1925–47. MEM.: Sound Money League (pres.); National Monetary Conference (pres.); World Language Foundation (pres.); Alpha Omega; National Popular Government League (pres., 1913–47); Elks (life member); Masons (32°). HON. DEG.: LL.D., 1908. REL.: Episc. RES.: Washington, DC.

OWENS, WARREN RAY. m. Gloria P. POLIT. & GOV.: ***independent candidate for presidency of the U.S., 1972; Independent Husband's Liberation Party candidate for vice presidency of the U.S., 1972***; independent candidate for gov. of MD, 1972. MAILING ADDRESS: 11117 Dewey Rd., Kensington, MD.

OWENS, WILLIAM. b. Jul 6, 1937, Demopolis, AL; par. Jonathan and Mary A. (Clemons) Owens; m. Cora E. Hilliard c. Laurel; Curtis; William; Adam. EDUC.: Boston U., 1970; M.Ed., Harvard U., 1971; U. of MA. POLIT. & GOV.: dir., Career Opportunities Program, MA State Dept. of Education, 1970; elected as a Democrat to MA State House, 1973–75; elected as a Democrat to MA State Senate, 1975–83; ***candidate for The Black Assembly nomination to presidency of the U.S., 1976***. BUS. & PROF.: owner, mgr., Sunrise 1-Hour Cleaners, Boston, MA, 1960–68; project coordinator, Urban League of Greater Boston, 1968–70; dir., Project Jesi-Jobs and Education for Self-Improvement, U. of MA, 1971–72. MEM.: MA Legislature Black Caucus; Urban League of Greater Boston (vice pres.; education dir.); Boston Black United Front (dir.); National Assn. of School Administrators; NAACP; National Educators Assn.; Big Black Brother Alliance (award of merit); MA Black Political Assembly; National Black Political Assembly; Council of State Governments; Ad Hoc Cmte. on Prison Reform; Roxbury Defenders (dir.); Resthaven Corp. (dir.); South End Neighborhood Action Program (dir.); Harvard Club of Boston; Carribean-American Carnival Day Assn.; Boston Black Repertory Co. (dir.); Roxbury Multi-Service Center (dir.). AWARDS: Man of the Year Award, New Hope Baptist Church; Black Big Brother Award of Excellence; Houston Urban League Plaque; Fort Devens Black Historical Plaque. WRITINGS: "Corporal Punishment and Physical Abuse of Children," *Survival Magazine*, 1969. REL.: Protestant. MAILING ADDRESS: 115 Hazelton St., Boston, MA 02126.

OWENS, ZELMA FAYE. POLIT. & GOV.: ***candidate for Democratic nomination to presidency of the U.S., 1984***. MAILING ADDRESS: 12214 Duncan Ave., Lynwood, CA 90262.

OWSLEY, ALVIN MANSFIELD. b. Jun 11, 1888, Denton, TX; d. Apr 3, 1967, Dallas, TX; par. Alvin Clark and Sallie (Blount) Owsley; m. Lucina Ball, May 16, 1925; c. Alvin Mansfield, Jr.; Constance (Mrs. Joseph L. Garrett); David Thomas. EDUC.: grad., VA Military Inst., 1909; studied law, U. of TX, 1911–12; law courts, London, England. POLIT. & GOV.: elected as a Democrat to TX State House, 1912–14; elected district atty., Denton, TX, 1915–17; appointed asst. atty. gen. of TX, 1919–20; ***candidate for Democratic nomination to vice presidency of the U.S., 1924***; candidate for Democratic nomination to U.S. Senate (TX), 1928; appointed U.S. minister to Romania, 1933–35; appointed U.S. minister to Irish Free State, 1935–37; appointed U.S. minister to Denmark, 1937–39; TX state chm., Citizens' Cmte. for the Hoover Report. BUS. & PROF.: atty.; admitted to TX Bar, 1912; partner, Owsley, Sullivan and Owsley (law firm), Denton, TX, 1912–17; partner, Burgess, Owsley, Story and Stewart (law firm), Dallas, TX, 1919–33; assoc., Will Thompson Law Firm, Indianapolis, IN, 1939–41; dir., Ball Brothers Co., Muncie, IN, 1941–67; dir., All State Life Insurance Co., Dallas, TX; radio and television narrator. MIL.: student, Officer Training Corps, Leon Springs, TX, 1917; senior instructor, Officer Training Corps, Camp Bowie, Fort Worth,

TX; commissioned maj. and advanced through grades to lt. col., U.S. Army Infantry, 1919; adj., 36th Div., AEF, WWI; Order of Polonia Restituta (Poland, 1924); Confederate Service Cross (1927); Legion of Honor (France, 1923). MEM.: American Red Cross (dir., War Finance Comm.); Savings Bond Drive (co-chm.); Dallas Symphony Orchestra (sponsor); Dallas Grand Opera Assn. (underwriter); American Legion (national commander, 1922–23); Americanism Endowment Fund (chm.); Military Order of the World Wars; ABA; TX State Bar Assn.; Beta Theta Phi; Delta Sigma Rho; Boy Scouts of TX (hon. member); Boy Scouts of NY (hon. member); Lions; Reserve Officers Club; Elks; Army and Navy Club; Rotary Club (hon.); Dallas Business Executives Club; Newcomen Soc.; Assn. of U.S. Army; Air Force Assn.; Knights of Pythias; Kiwanis; University Club; Dallas Hist. Soc.; Lancers Club; Southwestern Legal Foundation (trustee); Citizens Cmte. of 1000. HON. DEG.: L.H.D., Lincoln Memorial U., 1941; LL.D., Hillsdale Coll., 1948. WRITINGS: *The Peace-Time Program of the American Legion* (1922); *The Drafting of Industry in War Time* (1923); *What Constitutes American Citizenship* (1923). REL.: Christian Church. MISC.: named Chief of Chippewa Tribe, 1923. RES.: Dallas, TX.

PACKER, ASA. b. Dec 29, 1805, Groton, CT; d. May 18, 1879, Philadelphia, PA; par. Elisha Packer, Jr.; m. Sarah Minerva Blakeslee, Jan 23, 1828; c. Lucy (Mrs. Linderman); Mary (Mrs. Cummings); Harry E.; Robert; Marion (Mrs. Skeer); three infants. EDUC.: district schools. POLIT. & GOV.: elected as a Democrat to PA State House, 1842–43; elected assoc. judge, Carbon Cty., PA, 1843–44; elected as a Democrat to U.S. House (PA), 1853–57; delegate, Dem. Nat'l. Conv., 1868; ***candidate for Democratic nomination to presidency of the U.S., 1868***; Democratic candidate for gov. of PA, 1869; appointed member, U.S. Centennial Exhibition Comm., 1876. BUS. & PROF.: tanner's apprentice; carpenter's apprentice, Springfield, PA, 1822; farmer; owner and master, canal boat, Philadelphia, PA, 1823; operator (with R. W. Packer), store and boatyard, 1831–37; merchant, Mauch Chunk, PA, 1833; builder, pres., Lehigh Valley R.R., 1852–79; contractor, Lehigh Coal and Navigation Co.; owner, mines, Hazelton, PA. MEM.: Lehigh U. (founder, 1866); Ancient York Masons. REL.: Episc. (warden; vestryman). RES.: Mauch Chunk, PA.

PACKWOOD, AUBURN LEE. b. Dec 1, 1928, Cape Fair, MO; par. Luther Henry and Sarah Addaline (Hardin) Packwood; m. Betty Jane Musso; c. Auburn Lee, Jr.; Luther Raymond; David Paul; Sandra Marie; Jonathon Eli; Sarah Victory. EDUC.: B.S., CA Baptist Coll.; U. of NM; CA Polytechnic; Stanaslavce Teachers Coll.; San Jose State U.; Eureka State Teachers Coll. POLIT. & GOV.: ***candidate for Democratic nomination to vice presidency of the U.S., 1976; Loyal American Party candidate for vice presidency of the U.S., 1976; independent candidate for presidency of the U.S., 1988***. BUS. & PROF.: minister; preacher, 1955–; administrator, Heaven of Rest Christian School, MO. MAILING ADDRESS: 2658 South Golden Ave., Springfield, MO.

PAGE, IGNATIUS, JR. par. Ignatius Page, Sr. POLIT. & GOV.: ***independent candidate for presidency of the U.S., 1988***. MAILING ADDRESS: 5747 Goodfellow Blvd., St. Louis, MO 63136.

PAGE, MANN. b. Apr 21, 1835, Shelby, VA; c. May 28, 1904, Richmond, VA; par. Thomas Nelson and Julia (Randolph) Page; m. Kate Crane. POLIT. & GOV.: elected as a Conservative Democrat to VA State House of Delegates, 1875–77; Democratic candidate for VA State Senate, 1883; Democratic candidate for U.S. House (VA), 1886, 1890 (declined); delegate, Dem. Nat'l. Conv., 1892 (declined); delegate, People's Party National Convention, 1892, 1896; member, People's Party National Cmte., 1892–94; ***candidate for People's Party nomination to presidency of the U.S., 1892***; People's Party candidate for gov. of VA, 1893 (declined); ***candidate for People's Party nomination to vice presidency of the U.S., 1896***. BUS. & PROF.: clerk, Richmond, VA, c. 1860; businessman, Richmond, to 1865; partner, Randolph and Page (Commission House), Richmond; farmer, Upper Brandon, VA, 1865. MIL.: pvt., Company F, 21st VA Regt., C.S.A., 1861; commissioned adj., 1862; maj., brigade division, II Army Corps, Staff of Jubal Early, Army of Northern VA, C.S.A., to 1865. MEM.: VA Farmers Assembly (delegate, 1888–89); Free and Accepted Masons (state grand master); Grange (Petersburgh district master); VA State Farmers' Alliance (vice pres., 1880; delegate, St. Louis Convention, 1889); National Farmers Alliance and Industrial Union (founder, 1889; VA state pres., 1890–93; delegate, Supreme Council, 1890; member, exec. cmte.; pres., 1896). REL.: Episc. (vestryman; parish treas.). RES.: Prince George Cty., VA.

PAIGE, DAVID BREWSTER. b. Dec 30, 1963, Houlton, ME; par. Paul and Alice (McDowell) Paige; single. EDUC.: Camelback H.S., Phoenix, AZ, 1978–80. POLIT. & GOV.: ***candidate for Republican nomination to presidency of the U.S., 1980***. BUS. & PROF.: student; part-time employee, Good Samaritan Hospital, Phoenix, AZ, 1978–79; part-time employee, St. Joseph's Hospital, Phoenix, 1980. MEM.: L-5 Soc.

REL.: Evangelical Covenant Church of America. MAILING ADDRESS: 2513 East Devonshire, Phoenix, AZ 85016.

PAINE, PHYLLIS J. married. POLIT. & GOV.: ***independent (Committee for a Constitutional Presidency) candidate for vice presidency of the U.S., 1976***. MAILING ADDRESS: 3266 South 104th Ave., Omaha, NE 68124.

PALEVEDA, CARL AUGUST. POLIT. & GOV.: ***candidate for Republican nomination to presidency of the U.S., 1988, 1992***. MAILING ADDRESS: 4014 San Nicholas, Tampa, FL 33629.

PALM, NANCY DALE. b. Apr 14, 1921, Nashville, TN; d. Dillard Young and Mary (Bishop) Dale; m. William Morrison Palm, Jul 4, 1942. EDUC.: B.A., Vanderbilt U., 1942. POLIT. & GOV.: Republican precinct committeewoman, Harris Cty., TX, 1964–68; vice chm., Harris Cty. Republican Party, 1968, chm., 1968–; presidential elector, Republican Party, 1968; delegate, Rep. Nat'l. Conv., 1972; ***candidate for Republican nomination to vice presidency of the U.S., 1976***. BUS. & PROF.: public relations sec., Harris Cty. Medical Soc., 1951–57. MEM.: Mortar Board; Gamma Phi Beta; Athenians; Lotus Eaters; International Relations Club; Pro America Houston Chapter, Freedoms Foundation. REL.: Presb. MAILING ADDRESS: 612 East Friar Tuck Lane, Houston, TX 77024.

PALMER, ALEXANDER MITCHELL. b. May 4, 1872, Moosehead, PA; d. May 11, 1936, Washington, DC; par. Samuel Bernard and Caroline (Albert) Palmer; m. Roberta Bartlett Dixon, Nov 23, 1898; m. 2d, Margaret Fallon Burrall, Aug 29, 1923; c. Mary Dixon (Mrs. David Lichtenberg). EDUC.: Moravian Parochial School; A.B. (highest honors), Swarthmore Coll., 1891. POLIT. & GOV.: official stenographer, Forty-Third Judicial District of PA, 1892; member, PA State Democratic Exec. Cmte.; elected as a Democrat to U.S. House (PA), 1909–15; delegate, Dem. Nat'l. Conv., 1912, 1916, 1932; member, exec. cmte., Dem. Nat'l. Cmte., 1912–20; appointed U.S. sec. of war, 1913 (declined); Democratic candidate for U.S. Senate (PA), 1914; appointed judge, U.S. Court of Claims, 1915–17; appointed alien property custodian, 1917–19; appointed atty. gen. of the U.S., 1919–21; ***candidate for Democratic nomination to presidency of the U.S., 1920***. BUS. & PROF.: atty.; admitted to PA Bar, 1893; law practice (with John B. Storm), Stroudsburg, PA, 1893–1901; dir., Stroudsburg National Bank; dir., Stroudsburg Water Co.; dir., Scranton (PA) Trust Co.; dir., International Boiler Co.; dir., Potomac Joint Stock Land Bank; dir., Citizens Gas Co.; partner, Palmer, Davis and Scott (law firm), Washington, DC. MEM.: ABA; PA Bar Assn.; Phi Beta Kappa; Phi Kappa Psi. HON. DEG.: LL.D., Lafayette Coll., 1919; LL.D., Swarthmore Coll., 1919; LL.D., George Washington U., 1920. REL.: Soc. of Friends. RES.: Stroudsburg, PA.

PALMER, JOHN McAULEY. b. Sep 13, 1817, Eagle Creek, KY; d. Sep 25, 1900, Springfield, IL; par. Louis D. and Ann Hansford (Tutt) Palmer; m. Malinda Ann Neely, Dec 20, 1842; m. 2d, Mrs. Hannah Lamb Kimball, Apr 4, 1888; c. Elizabeth (Mrs. John P. Matthews); Thomas; Lucy; Margaret; Mary; Louis J.; Susie; Mrs. Harriet Crabbe; John Mayo; Jessie Lyon (Mrs. N.W. Weber). EDUC.: public schools, KY and IL; Alton (later Shurtleff) Coll., 1834; studied law under John S. Greathouse, Carlinville, IL, 1835–38. POLIT. & GOV.: Democratic candidate for cty. clerk, Macoupin Cty., IL, c. 1836; elected probate judge, Macoupin Cty., IL, 1843–47; elected delegate, IL State Constitutional Convention, 1847; elected cty. judge, Macoupin Cty., 1849–52; elected as a Democrat to IL State Senate, 1852–56 (resigned); delegate, IL State Republican Convention, 1856; Democratic candidate for U.S. House (IL), 1856 (declined); delegate, Rep. Nat'l. Conv., 1856, 1860; Republican candidate for U.S. House (IL), 1859; presidential elector, Republican Party (IL), 1860; delegate, Peace Convention, 1861; candidate for gov. of TN, 1863 (declined); elected as a Republican to gov. of IL, 1869–73; ***candidate for Liberal Republican Party nomination to presidency of the U.S., 1872; candidate for Liberal Republican Party nomination to vice presidency of the U.S., 1872; candidate for Labor Reform Party nomination to presidency of the U.S., 1872***; Liberal Republican Party candidate for gov. of IL, 1872 (declined); ***received 3 electoral votes for vice presidency of the U.S., 1872***; Democratic candidate for U.S. Senate (IL), 1877; ***candidate for Democratic nomination to presidency of the U.S., 1880, 1892***; delegate, Dem. Nat'l. Conv., 1884; Democratic candidate for gov. of IL, 1888; ***candidate for American Party nomination to presidency of the U.S., 1888***; elected as a Democrat to U.S. Senate (IL), 1891–97; ***National (Gold Democratic) Party candidate for presidency of the U.S., 1896***; National (Gold Democratic) Party candidate for U.S. House (IL), 1896. BUS. & PROF.: atty.; admitted to IL Bar, 1839; schoolteacher, 1835–39; partner, Palmer and Pittman (law firm), Carlinville, IL, 1839–67; owner, *Free Democrat*, Carlinville, 1856; owner, *Illinois State Register*, 1879; partner (with Milton Hays), law firm, Springfield, IL, 1867–68; partner, Palmer, Robinson and Shutt (law firm), 1873–1900. MIL.: col., 14th Regt., IL Volunteer Infantry, 1861, brig. gen., 1861, maj. gen., 1862–66; military commander, Dept. of KY, 1865–66. MEM.: Free Masons; GAR (IL dept. commander; commander in chief, 1891). WRITINGS: *The Bench and Bar of Illinois* (ed., 1899); *Personal Recollections of John M. Palmer: The Story of an Ernest Life* (1901). REL.: Bapt. RES.: Springfield, IL.

PALMER, SAMUEL. POLIT. & GOV.: ***independent candidate for presidency of the U.S., 1988***. MAILING ADDRESS: c/o Servant of Servants-7-SOS-7-Star, 2924 Bailey Ave., Jackson, MS 39213.

PALMER, THOMAS WITHERELL (nee THOMAS JAMES PALMER). b. Jan 25, 1830,

Detroit, MI; d. Jun 1, 1913, Detroit, MI; par. Thomas and Mary Amy (Witherell) Palmer; m. Elizabeth "Lizzie" Pitts Merrill, Oct 16, 1855; c. Grace Palmer Rice (adopted); Harold (adopted); one other (adopted). EDUC.: Thompson's Acad., St. Clair, MI; U. of MI, 1845–48, A.B., 1876; LL.D., Albion Coll., 1904. POLIT. & GOV.: elected delegate, Whig Party Cty. Convention, Green Bay, WI, 1850; candidate for Republican nomination to alderman, Detroit, MI, 1860; elected member, Detroit (MI) Board of Estimates, 1873; candidate for Republican nomination to U.S. House (MI), 1876; elected as a Republican to MI State Senate, 1879–80; candidate for Republican nomination to gov. of MI, 1880; elected as a Republican to U.S. Senate (MI), 1883–89; pres., Waterways Convention, Sault Ste. Marie, MI, 1887; ***candidate for American Party nomination to presidency of the U.S., 1888 (declined)***; appointed envoy extraordinary and minister plenipotentiary to Spain, 1889–90. BUS. & PROF.: made walking tour of Spain and South America; merchant, Appleton, WI, to 1853; partner, Thomas Palmer and Son (real estate investments), 1853–55; partner, Charles Merrill and Co. (real estate), Detroit, MI, 1855–1903; lumber merchant; farmer; mill owner; dir., American Exchange National Bank; dir., Wayne Cty. Savings Bank; dir., Security and Safe Deposit Co. of Detroit; dir., Detroit Steam Navigation Co.; dir., Michigan Lake Navigation Co.; dir., Frontier Iron Works; dir., Michigan Mutual Life Insurance Co.; pres., Preston National Bank; pres., Percheron Navigation Co. MEM.: World's Columbian Comm. (pres., 1892–93); Soc. for the Prevention of Cruelty to Animals (pres.); Chi Psi; GAR; YMCA; Detroit Art Museum (founder); Vingt Club (founder); Detroit Humane Soc. (founder); MI Soldiers' Monument Assn. (sec., 1861–65); Equal Suffrage Club; National American Women's Suffrage Assn.; Light Guards (hon. member); Zion Lodge Number 1. WRITINGS: *Detroit Sixty Years Ago* (1897); *Mr. Thompson's School at St. Clair in 1842* (1907). REL.: Unitarian. RES.: Detroit, MI.

PALMER, WILLIAM JACKSON. b. Sep 18, 1836, Kent Cty., DE; d. Mar 13, 1909, Colorado Springs, CO; par. John and Matilda (Jackson) Palmer; m. Mary Lincoln "Queen" Mellen, Nov 8, 1870; c. Elsie (Mrs. Leo H. Myers); Dorothy; Marjorie (Mrs. Henry C. Watt). EDUC.: public and private schools. POLIT. & GOV.: ***independent candidate for presidency of the U.S., 1872, 1900***. BUS. & PROF.: railroad official; rodman, Hempfield R.R., 1853; sec., treas., Westmoreland Coal Co., 1856–58; private sec. to the president, Pennsylvania R.R., 1857–61; treas., dir. of surveys, mgr. of construction, Kansas Pacific Railway, 1861–70; pres., Denver and Rio Grande Railway, 1870–83; pres., Rio Grande Western Railway, 1883–1901; pres., Mexican National Railway, 7 years; pres., Colorado Coal and Iron Co. MIL.: commissioned capt., 15th PA Cavalry, 1861, col., 1862, brev. brig. gen. of volunteers, 1864, mustered out, 1865; captured behind enemy lines during Civil War, exchanged, 1863; awarded Medal of Honor for attacking and defeating superior force in Battle at Red Hill in 1865, 1894. MEM.: CO Coll. (trustee, 1873–1909); American Civic Improvement League (third vice pres.). WRITINGS: *Report of Surveys Across the Continent, in 1867–68* (1869). REL.: Soc. of Friends. RES.: Colorado Springs, CO.

PALMORE, WILLIAM BEVERLY. b. Feb 24, 1844, Fayette Cty., TN; d. Jul 5, 1914, Richmond, VA; par. William Pledge and Elizabeth Ann (Hobson) Palmore; single. EDUC.: private schools, Vanderbilt U.; D.D., Central Coll. POLIT. & GOV.: chaplain, MO State Senate; chaplain, MO State Penitentiary; ***candidate for Prohibition Party nomination to presidency of the U.S., 1908; candidate for Prohibition Party nomination to vice presidency of the U.S., 1908 (declined)***. BUS. & PROF.: ordained minister, Methodist Episc. Church, 1877; pastor, Methodist Episc. Church, Kansas City, MO; pastor, Methodist Episc. Church, Springfield, MO; pastor, Methodist Episc. Church, Independence, MO; pastor, Methodist Episc. Church, Marshall, MO; pastor, Methodist Episc. Church, Jefferson City, MO; pastor, Methodist Episc. Church, Booneville District, MO; ed., publisher, *St. Louis (MO) Christian Advocate*, 1890–94; founder, Collegio Palmore (Mexico); founder, Palmore Inst. (Japan). MIL.: member, C.S.A., 1861–65. MEM.: Order of the New Century Knighthood (founder); Central Coll. for Women (curator; pres.). REL.: Methodist Episc. Church (member, Ecumenical Methodist Conference, 1891, 1901; member, four general conferences). RES.: St. Louis, MO.

PAPE, G. W. POLIT. & GOV.: ***independent candidate for presidency of the U.S., 1900***. RES.: VT.

PAPOON, GEORGE C. b. 1913, Poonton, KS; par. George and Mamie (Cox) Papoon; married; c. son. EDUC.: Columbia U. POLIT. & GOV.: ***National Surrealist Party candidate for presidency of the U.S., 1972, 1976***. BUS. & PROF.: pilot, U.S. Air Mail Service, 1935; barnstormer; member, Ace Cochran's Air Aces; employee, CIA; librarian, U.S. Information Agency; goonrat, Sumatra, 1951; owner, Poon's Farm Restaurant, Wentzville, MO. MIL.: U.S. Naval Intelligence, 1938. MEM.: Young Arachnids for Freedom. MAILING ADDRESS: Poon's Farm, Wentzville, MO.

PAPPAS, GAS K. POLIT. & GOV.: ***independent candidate for presidency of the U.S., 1940***. MAILING ADDRESS: CA.

PARIS, DANIEL GARY. b. Nov 25, 1949, San Gabriel, CA; par. Charles R. and Alberta L. (Petty) Paris; m. (divorced); c. four. EDUC.: self-educated. POLIT. & GOV.: ***candidate for Democratic nomination to presidency of the U.S., 1988***. BUS. & PROF.: professional analyst; photoengraver; marketing developer; inventor. REL.: Full Gospel Church. MAILING ADDRESS: 12610 Central Ave., #184, Chino, CA 91710.

PARKER, AARON M. POLIT. & GOV.: ***independent candidate for vice presidency of the U.S., 1988***. MAILING ADDRESS: 218 North Franklin St., Whitewater, WI 53190.

PARKER, ALTON BROOKS. b. May 14, 1852, Cortland, NY; d. May 10, 1926, New York, NY; par. John Brooks and Harriet F. (Stratton) Parker; m. Mary Louise Schoonmaker, Oct 16, 1873; m. 2d, Amelia Day Campbell, Jan 16, 1923; c. John; Bertha (Mrs. Charles Mercer Hall). EDUC.: Cortland Acad.; Cortland Normal School; studied law in offices of Schoonmaker and Hardenburgh, Kingston, NY, 1871; LL.B., Albany Law School, 1873. POLIT. & GOV.: clerk, Board of Supervisors, Ulster Cty., NY, 1873–76; elected as a Democrat to surrogate, Ulster Cty., 1877–85; delegate, NY State Democratic Convention, 1882; delegate, Dem. Nat'l. Conv., 1884, 1908, 1912 (temporary chm.); appointed asst. postmaster gen. of the U.S., 1885 (declined); chm., NY State Democratic Cmte., 1885; appointed and subsequently elected justice, NY State Supreme Court, 1885–89; appointed judge, NY State Court of Appeals, Second Div., 1889–92, general term, 1893–96, Appellate Div., 1896–97, chief justice, 1898–1904; ***Democratic candidate for presidency of the U.S., 1904***; chm., NY State Democratic Convention, 1908, 1910 (temporary), 1912; counsel, managers of impeachment trial of Gov. William Sulzer (q.v.), 1913. BUS. & PROF.: atty.; admitted to NY Bar, 1873; partner (with William S. Kenyon, q.v.), law practice, Kingston, NY; partner, Parker, Hatch and Sheehan (law firm), New York, NY, 1904–12; partner, Marshall, Miller and Auchincloss (law firm), New York, NY, 1912–26; trustee, Ulster Cty. Savings Institution (pres., 1896–1904). MEM.: ABA (pres., 1906–07); New York Cty. Lawyers Assn. (pres., 1909–11); NY Bar Assn. (pres., 1913–14); National Civic Federation (pres., 1919–26); Japan Soc.; American Acad. of Jurisprudence (vice pres.); Sulgrave Institution (American pres.); Thomas Jefferson Memorial Assn. (founder); Town Hall; International Garden Club; Century Club; Church Club; National Democratic Lawyers' Club; Metropolitan Club; League to Enforce Peace (vice pres.); Manhattan Club. HON. DEG.: LL.D., Union Coll., 1902; LL.D., McGill U., 1913; LL.D., U. of Toronto, 1915; LL.D., Coll. of William and Mary, 1921. REL.: Episc. RES.: Esopus, NY.

PARKER, BENJAMIN FRANKLIN. b. Jul 27, 1839, Conneaughtville, PA; d. Jan 24, 1912; par. Ledyard and Hannah (Thompson) Parker; m. Lucille W. Penniman, Feb 3, 1868. EDUC.: Meadville (PA) public schools and academies. POLIT. & GOV.: ***Prohibition Party nomination to vice presidency of the U.S., 1904***. BUS. & PROF.: soldier. MIL.: pvt., 1st lt., U.S.V., 1861–65; advanced through grades from lt. to lt. col., WI National Guard, 28 years; lt. col., 3d WI Infantry, Spanish-American War. MEM.: Ancient Order of United Workmen of Wisconsin (grand master); International Order of Good Templars (grand sec. of WI, 1873–1900, 1909–12; international sec., 1885–1908). RES.: Milwaukee, WI.

PARKER, FLOYD COTTNER, JR. b. Jun 10, 1933, Raton, NM; par. Floyd Cottner and Roxie Joyce Parker; m. Naomi Eileen Welch; c. Susan; Joyce; Annalyn; Melanie; Rita; Tina. EDUC.: grad., Tucumcari (NM) H.S., 1953; B.S., Baylor U., 1955; M.D., U. of CO, 1959. POLIT. & GOV.: member, Populist Party, 1984–88; ***Populist Party candidate for vice presidency of the U.S., 1988***. BUS. & PROF.: physician, 1959–; founder, agent, San Juan National Bank, Farmington, NM; pres., Parko Oil and Gas Co., Farmington; owner, Farmington Clinic. MIL.: capt., U.S. Air Force, 1960–62; capt., U.S. Air Force Reserves, 1962–72. MEM.: American Medical Assn.; NM Medical Soc.; San Juan Cty. Medical Soc.; Rotary International (1963–67); Demolay (1948–52). REL.: Southern Bapt. MAILING ADDRESS: 3110 Crescent, Farmington, NM 87401.

PARKER, HARRISON MAGMAN. b. Jul 9, 1877, San Francisco, CA; par. Thomas G. and Mary (Owings) Parker; m. Edith Stubbs, Oct 23, 1901; c. Harrison Magman, Jr.; Mary Stubbs. EDUC.: grad., high school, San Francisco, CA; U. of CA; Coll. of Divines of the Puritan Church. POLIT. & GOV.: candidate for Cook Cty. (IL) assessor; Co-op candidate for gov. of IL, 1920; ***Anti-New Deal candidate for presidency of the U.S., c. 1936***. BUS. & PROF.: advertising agent; employee, business dept., *The Wave*, San Francisco, CA, 1895; employee, business dept., *Chicago (IL) Times Herald*; employee, business dept., *Chicago Daily News*; employee, business dept., *Collier's Weekly*; business mgr., *Philadelphia North American*; advertising mgr., *Chicago Tribune*; vice pres., Stack-Parker Co., 1909; pastor, Puritan Church, La Grange, IL, 1940–48; chancellor, The Puritan Church—The Church of America, 1945; pastor, Puritan Church, Washington, DC, 1948–; operator, Protestant Embassy, Washington, DC; publisher, *Warning Letters*; publisher, *Liberty Bell*, 1950; owner, investment company; owner, life insurance company; owner, dairy farms; owner, grocery store chain; publisher, *Chicago American*; promoter, North American Trust Co.; promoter, Iroquois Trust Co.; promoter, Illinois Valley Trust Co. MEM.: Cooperative Soc. of America (trustee, 1918); United Woodmen; Union League; Mid-Day Club. REL.: Puritan Church (nee Methodist). MISC.: fined $7,272 for promotional schemes, 1932; indicted for income tax evasion, c. 1948; noted anti-Catholic activist. RES.: Chicago, IL.

PARKER, JO A. b. Jul 28, 1869, Cambridge City, IN; par. William Franklin and Mary F. (Callender) Parker; single. EDUC.: Forestville Acad., NY. POLIT. & GOV.: People's Party candidate for clerk, KY Court of Appeals, 1897; member, exec. cmte., People's Party National Cmte., 1896–1905 (chm., 1900–1904); delegate, People's Party National Convention, 1900; chm., KY State People's Party Central Cmte., 1895; founder, Jeffersonian Democratic Party, 1904; ***National (Greenback) Party candidate for vice presidency of the U.S., 1932 (declined)***. BUS. & PROF.: newspaperman; manufacturer of timber products; land and timber broker; author; lecturer. MEM.: National Reform Press Assn. (sec., 5 years). RES.: Louisville, KY.

PARKER, JOEL. b. Nov 24, 1816, Freehold, NJ; d. Jan 2, 1888, Philadelphia, PA; par. Charles and Sarah S. (Coward) Parker; m. Maria M. Gummere, 1843; c. Frederick; Charles; Bessie. EDUC.: Trenton (NJ) H.S.; Lawrenceville H.S.; A.B., Coll. of NJ (now Princeton U.), 1839, A.M., 1842; studied law under Henry Woodhull Green. POLIT. & GOV.: elected as a Democrat to NJ State House, 1847–51; appointed prosecuting atty., Monmouth Cty., NJ, 1852–57; candidate for Democratic nomination to U.S. House (NJ), 1854 (declined), 1858 (declined); candidate for Democratic nomination to gov. of NJ, 1856 (declined), 1859 (declined); presidential elector, Democratic Party (NJ), 1860, 1876; elected as a Democrat to gov. of NJ, 1863–66, 1872–75; ***candidate for Democratic nomination to presidency of the U.S., 1868, 1876, 1880, 1884; candidate for Labor Reform Party nomination to presidency of the U.S., 1872; Labor Reform Party candidate for vice presidency of the U.S., 1872 (withdrew)***; appointed atty. gen. of NJ, 1875; appointed justice, NJ State Supreme Court, 1880–88. BUS. & PROF.: atty.; admitted to NJ Bar, 1842; law practice, Freehold, NJ; publisher, *The Spirit of Democracy*, 1860; member, Union Fire Co., Trenton, NJ; member, Freehold Fire Dept. MIL.: brig. gen., NJ Militia, 1857, maj. gen., 1861. MEM.: Odd Fellows; Masons; Military Order of the Loyal Legion; Tammany Soc.; Soc. of the Cincinnati (hon.); Monmouth Cty. Agricultural Soc.; NJ Hist. Soc. (exec. cmte.). HON. DEG.: LL.D., Rutgers Coll., 1872. WRITINGS: *Our National Troubles* (1864); *Monmouth County During the Provincial Era* (1872); *Oration to the Memory of John Hart* (1896). REL.: Presb. MISC.: aided in recruitment of supply troops, Civil War. RES.: Freehold, NJ.

PARKER, JOHN MILLIKEN. b. Mar 16, 1863, Bethel Church, MS; d. May 20, 1939, Pass Christian, MS; par. John Milliken and Roberta (Buckner) Parker; m. Cecile Airey, Jan 11, 1888; c. John Milliken, Jr.; Thomas Airey; Virginia (Mrs. Walker Saussy); Saidie. EDUC.: grad., Mt. Pleasant Acad., Sing Sing, NY, 1881. POLIT. & GOV.: dir., LA State Flood Relief, 1912, 1922, 1927; Progressive Democratic candidate for gov. of LA, 1916; ***Progressive Party candidate for vice presidency of the U.S., 1916; Prohibition Party candidate for vice presidency of the U.S., 1916 (declined); American Party candidate for vice presidency of the U.S., 1916 (declined)***; delegate, Dem. Nat'l. Conv., 1920; elected as a Democrat to gov. of LA, 1920–24; ***candidate for Democratic nomination to presidency of the U.S., 1924***. BUS. & PROF.: cotton grower, New Orleans, LA, 1880–1939; pres., John M. Parker Co., 1893–1939. MEM.: Mississippi Valley Assn. (pres., 1919); New Orleans Board of Trade (pres., 1893); New Orleans Cotton Exchange (pres., 1897–98); Southern Commercial Congress (pres., 1908–12); Constitutional League of LA (pres., 1929); Press Club; Boston Club of New Orleans; Masons; Good Government League. REL.: Presb. RES.: New Orleans, LA.

PARKER, LUCY. POLIT. & GOV.: ***independent candidate for presidency of the U.S., 1976***. MAILING ADDRESS: P.O. Box 191, Gaston, IN 47342.

PARKER, WILLIAM EDWARD. b. Feb 7, 1924, Rich Square, NC; par. Eulas Henry and Beulah May (Elliott) Parker; m. Mary Elsie Spiers; c. Donna; Barbara; Joann. EDUC.: B.I.E., NC State U., 1951; U.S. Navy Flight School. POLIT. & GOV.: American Party candidate for Jefferson Cty. (KY) Board of Commissioners, 1969; American Party candidate for U.S. Senate (KY), 1974; vice chm., American Party of KY, 1974; ***candidate for American Party nomination to vice presidency of the U.S., 1976***; American Party candidate for U.S. House (KY), 1986. BUS. & PROF.: industrial engineer, long-range planning div., General Electric Co., 1951–. MIL.: lt., U.S. Navy, WWII; Distinguished Flying Cross. MEM.: Tau Beta Pi; Alpha Pi Mu; Jefferson Cty. Citizens' Cmte. to Stop Tyranny and Busing. AWARDS: General Electric Managerial Award; Silver Beaver Award, BSA. REL.: Episc. MAILING ADDRESS: 9800 Tiverton Way, Louisville, KY 40222.

PARKS, EUGENE HOWARD. POLIT. & GOV.: ***candidate for Democratic nomination to presidency of the U.S., 1980; independent candidate for presidency of the U.S., 1980***. MAILING ADDRESS: 12914 Aste Lane, Houston, TX 77065.

PARRY, R. W. POLIT. & GOV.: ***independent candidate for vice presidency of the U.S., 1900***; delegate, Rep. Nat'l. Conv., 1908. RES.: Reno, NV.

PARTRIDGE, SAMUEL G. POLIT. & GOV.: ***candidate for Universal Party nomination to presidency of the U.S., 1992***. MAILING ADDRESS: Grass Valley, CA.

PATRICK, ABRAM W. POLIT. & GOV.: elected as a Democrat to OH State House, 1872–73; ***candidate for Democratic nomination to vice presidency of the U.S., 1900***. RES.: OH.

PATRICK, WILLIAM PENN. b. Mar 31, 1930, Roper, NC; d. Jun 9, 1973, Clear Lake Oaks, CA; m. Marie M. Oliva (separated); c. two. EDUC.: U. of IL; grad., CA State Coll., Sacramento, CA. Polit. & gov.: candidate for Republican nomination to gov. of CA, 1966; candidate for Republican nomination to U.S. Senate (CA), 1968; *Patriotic Party candidate for vice presidency of the U.S., 1968 (withdrew)*; repudiated by Patriotic Party. BUS. & PROF.: farmer; theater usher; busboy; gas station attendant; cooking utensil salesman; elementary school teacher, West Sacramento, CA, 3 years; owner, wig business; owner, jewelry business; distributor, Nutri-Bio Products; chm., U.S. Universal, Inc., Las Vegas, NV; founder, chm. of the board, Holiday Magic Cosmetics, Inc., 1964–73; founder, Leadership Dynamics Inst., Inc., 1970–73; owner, Spectrum Air, Inc.; owner, Albert Taylor, Inc.; owner, Mind Dynamics, Inc. MIL.: staff sgt., U.S. Air Force, 1947–53. Recording: "Happiness and Success

Through Principle." MISC.: accused of pyramid promotional sales activities. RES.: Tiburon, CA.

PATTERSON, ELLIS ELLWOOD. b. Nov 28, 1898, Yuba City, CA; d. Aug 25, 1985, Los Angeles, CA; par. William R. and Anna Marie (Botler) Patterson; m. Helen Hjelti, Jun 1928; c. Ellis Ellwood, Jr.; Helen Jane; Robert Edward. EDUC.: A.B., U. of CA, 1921, law student, 1931–36; Stanford U. POLIT. & GOV.: elected as a Republican to CA State Assembly, 1933–39; elected as a Democrat to lt. gov. of CA, 1939–43; ***candidate for Democratic nomination to presidency of the U.S., 1940***; elected as a Democrat to U.S. House (CA), 1945–47; candidate for Democratic nomination to U.S. Senate (CA), 1946; Democratic candidate for U.S. House (CA), 1946, 1948. BUS. & PROF.: atty.; admitted to CA Bar, 1937; schoolteacher, Colusa Cty., CA, 1922–24; district superintendent of schools, South Monterey Cty., CA, 1923–32; law practice, Sacramento, CA; law practice, Los Angeles, CA, 1937–. MIL.: seaman first class, U.S. Navy, 1917–18. MEM.: Masons (Scottish Rite); Forty and Eight; Elks; American Legion. REL.: Protestant. MISC.: wrestling champion, 175-lb. and unlimited weight classes, Pacific Coast American A.A.U., 1918–21. RES.: King City, CA.

PATTISON, ROBERT EMORY. b. Dec 8, 1850, Quantico, MD; d. Aug 1, 1904, Philadelphia, PA; par. Rev. Robert Henry and Catherine P. (Woollford) Pattison; m. Anna Barney Smith, Dec 28, 1872; c. three. EDUC.: A.B., Central H.S., 1870; studied law under Lewis C. Cassidy, Philadelphia, PA, 1869. POLIT. & GOV.: candidate for Democratic nomination to auditor gen. of PA, 1877; elected as a Democrat to comptroller, Philadelphia, PA, 1878–82; elected as a Democrat to gov. of PA, 1882–86, 1891–95; appointed auditor, U.S. Treasury, 1887 (declined); appointed member, U.S. Pacific Railroad Comm., 1887–90; ***candidate for Democratic nomination to presidency of the U.S., 1892, 1896, 1904; candidate for Democratic nomination to vice presidency of the U.S., 1896, 1900***; Democratic candidate for U.S. House (PA), 1900; Democratic candidate for gov. of PA, 1902; delegate, Dem. Nat'l. Conv., 1904. BUS. & PROF.: atty.; admitted to PA Bar, 1872; law practice, Philadelphia; pres., Chestnut Street National Bank, 1886; pres., Security Trust and Life Insurance Co. MEM.: American U. (trustee); Dickinson Coll. (trustee). HON. DEG.: LL.D., Dickinson Coll., 1884. WRITINGS: *Discrimination by Railroads* (1886). REL.: Methodist Episc. Church (delegate, General Conference, 1884, 1888; fraternal delegate, Methodist Episc. Church, South, General Conference, 1890; delegate, Ecumenical Conference, 1891). RES.: Philadelphia, PA.

PATTON, ANCEL ELVIN "PAT." b. Oct 25, 1930, Elgin, IL; par. Ancel Elvin and Jean (Peterson) Patton; single. EDUC.: self-taught. POLIT. & GOV.: candidate for Republican (Democratic; Peace and Freedom Party; American Independent Party) nomination to U.S. House (CA), 1972; ***candidate for Republican nomination to presidency of the U.S., 1972***; candidate for Democratic nomination to U.S. House (CA), 1974; ***candidate for Democratic nomination to presidency of the U.S., 1976; independent candidate for presidency of the U.S., 1976***; independent candidate for U.S. House (CA), 1976. BUS. & PROF.: farm laborer in southern CA, OR, and IL; employee, General Motors Corp.; employee, aircraft industry; employee, U.S. Postal Service. MEM.: YMCA; BSA. REL.: Theist. MAILING ADDRESS: P.O. Box 7174, Los Angeles, CA 90022.

PATTON, ROBERT HOWARD. b. Jan 18, 1860, Auburn, IL; d. Mar 12, 1939, Springfield, IL; par. Mathew and Margaret J. Patton; m. Mary Etta Gordon, Sep 23, 1886. EDUC.: B.S., IL Wesleyan U., 1883, M.S., 1886; studied law at IL Wesleyan Law School and offices of Patton and Hamilton. POLIT. & GOV.: delegate, Prohibition Party National Convention, 1892, 1896, 1900, 1904, 1908 (temporary chm.), 1916, 1920, 1924; ***Prohibition Party candidate for vice presidency of the U.S., 1896 (declined)***; Prohibition Party candidate for atty. gen. of IL, 1896; Prohibition Party candidate for U.S. House (IL), 1900; delegate, Continental Party National Convention, 1904; Prohibition Party candidate for gov. of IL, 1904; elected national chm., Prohibition Party National Cmte., 1904 (declined); ***Prohibition Party candidate for presidency of the U.S., 1908 (declined)***; member, exec. cmte., IL State Prohibition Party Central Cmte. (vice chm.; chm., 1912–24); member, Prohibition Party National Cmte., 1912–24; appointed special asst. U.S. district atty., 1920. BUS. & PROF.: atty.; admitted to IL Bar, 1885; law practice, Springfield, IL. MEM.: Phi Gamma Delta; Knights of Pythias. WRITINGS: *The Liquor Traffic and Inalienable Rights* (1904); "Reply to Anti-Saloon League Attack Upon the Prohibition Party," *National Prohibitionist*, Sep 24, 1908; *The Real Progressive Party* (1912). RES.: Springfield, IL.

PATTY, HUBERT DAVID. b. Apr 1, 1927, Sevier Cty., TN; par. David Washington and Martha Elizabeth (Grooms) Patty; single. EDUC.: grad., Walland (TN) H.S., 1947; B.S., U. of TN at Knoxville, 1950, LL.B., 1954, J.D.; Infantry School; Judge Advocate General's School; Civil Affairs/Military Government School; Command and General Staff Coll.; Industrial War Coll. POLIT. & GOV.: delegate, TN State Constitutional Convention, 1959; chm., Republican Primary Board, Maryville, TN; Republican candidate for gov. of TN, 1962; candidate for Republican nomination to U.S. Senate (TN), 1964, 1972, 1978; appointed special general sessions judge, TN; candidate for Republican nomination to gov. of TN, 1970, 1978; independent candidate for gov. of TN, 1974, 1978; ***candidate for Republican nomination to presidency of the U.S., 1976, 1988, 1992***; candidate for Republican nomination to U.S. House (TN), 1976; ***candidate for Populist Party nomination to presidency of the U.S., 1988; Populist Party candidate for vice presidency of the U.S., 1988 (withdrew)***. BUS. & PROF.: atty.; admitted to TN Bar, 1954; law practice, Maryville,

TN, 1954–; admitted to practice before the Bar of the Supreme Court of the U.S.; admitted to practice before the U.S. Court of Military Appeals. MIL.: capt., col., U.S. Army, WWII, Korean War; Judge Advocate General's Corps, U.S.A.R. MEM.: ABA; TN Bar Assn.; Blount Cty. Bar Assn.; Junior C. of C.; Optimists; Reserve Officers Assn.; Young Republican Club (pres.); American Legion (judge advocate). REL.: Bapt. (deacon; adult teacher; chm., Finance Cmte., Miller's Cove Baptist Church). MAILING ADDRESS: 515-517 Blount National Bank Building, Maryville, TN 37801.

PAUL, RONALD E. "RON." b. Aug 20, 1935, Pittsburgh, PA; m. Carol Wells, 1957; c. Ronald; Lori; Randal; Robert; Joy Lynette. EDUC.: grad., Dormant H.S., Pittsburgh, PA, 1953; B.A., Gettysburg Coll., 1957; M.D., Duke U., 1961. POLIT. & GOV.: Republican candidate for U.S. House (TX), 1974, 1976; elected as a Republican to U.S. House (TX), 1976–77, 1979–85; candidate for Republican nomination to U.S. Senate (TX), 1984; ***Libertarian Party candidate for presidency of the U.S., 1988; candidate for Republican nomination to presidency of the U.S., 1992***. BUS. & PROF.: physician; obstetrician; gynecologist; publisher, ed., *The Ron Paul Investment Letter*, Houston, TX. MIL.: capt., flight surgeon, U.S. Air Force, 1963–65. MEM.: Brazoria Cty. Medical Soc.; Council for Monetary Reform (founder); Foundation for Rational Economics and Education, Inc. (founder, 1976); Cmte. to Abolish the Fed (chm.); Ludwig von Mises Inst. (counsellor); TX Medical Soc.; Kiwanis; Brazosport C. of C.; American Coll. of Obstetrics/Gynecology (fellow); Elks; 94th Club. AWARDS: "Taxpayer's Best Friend in Congress," National Taxpayers Union; Liberty Award, American Economic Council. WRITINGS: *Gold, Peace and Prosperity: The Birth of a New Currency; The Case for Gold; Ten Myths About Paper Money; Abortion and Liberty*. REL.: Episc. MAILING ADDRESS: 101 Blossom Lake, Jackson, TX 77566.

PAULING, LINUS CARL. b. Feb 28, 1901, Portland, OR; d. Aug 19, 1994, Big Sur, CA; par. Herman Henry William and Lucy Isabelle (Darling) Pauling; m. Ava Helen Miller, Jun 17, 1923; c. Linus Carl, Jr.; Peter Jeffress; Linda Helen Lamb; Edward Crellin. EDUC.: B.S., OR State Coll., 1922, Sc.D., 1933; Ph.D. (summa cum laude), CA Inst. of Technology, 1925; postgrad. courses, U. of Munich, U. of Copenhagen, U. of Zurich, 1926–27. POLIT. & GOV.: ***Peace candidate for presidency of the U.S., 1960***; independent (write-in) candidate for gov. of CA, 1962. BUS. & PROF.: chemist; Crellin Teaching Fellow, CA Inst. of Technology, 1922–25, research fellow, 1925–27, asst. prof., 1927–29, assoc. prof., 1929–31, prof. of chemistry, 1931–64, chm., Div. of Chemistry and Chemical Engineering and dir., Gates and Crellin Laboratories of Chemistry, 1936–58, member, Exec. Cmte. and Board of Trustees, 1945–48; fellow, National Research Council, 1925–26; fellow, John S. Guggenheim Memorial Foundation, 1926–27; assoc. ed., *Journal of American Chemical Soc.*, 1930–40; assoc. ed., *Journal of Chemical Physics*, 1932–37; George Eastman Professor, Oxford U., 1948; fellow, Falliol Coll., 1948; research prof., Center for the Study of Democratic Institutions, 1963–67; prof. of chemistry, Stanford U., 1969–74; lecturer; consultant to governmental agencies and research groups; pres., Linus Pauling Inst. of Science and Medicine, 1973–75, research prof., 1973–. MEM.: Delta Upsilon; Sigma Xi; Alpha Chi Sigma; Tau Beta Pi; Sigma Tau; Phi Lamda Upsilon; American Chemical Soc. (pres., 1948); American Phil. Soc.; AAAS (pres., Pacific Div., 1942–45); National Acad. of Sciences. AWARDS: Nobel Prize in Chemistry, 1954; Nobel Peace Prize, 1962; Fermat Medal; Paul Sabatier Medal; Pasteur Medal; Medal with Laurel Wreath, International Grotius Foundation, 1957; U.S. Presidential Medal of Merit, 1948; International Lenin Peace Prize, 1972; U.S. National Medal of Science, 1974. HON. DEG.: Sc.D., U. of Chicago, 1941; Sc.D., Princeton U., 1946; D.Sc., Cambridge U., 1947; D.Sc., U. of London, 1947; D.Sc., Yale U., 1947; D.Sc., Oxford U., 1948; Dr. Honoris Causa, U. of Paris, 1948; Dr. Honoris Causa, U. of Toulouse, 1949; L.H.D., Tampa U., 1950; U.J.D., U. of New Brunswick, 1950; D.Sc., Brooklyn Polytechnical Inst., 1955; Dr. Honoris Causa, U. of Liege, 1955; D.F.A., Chouinard Art Inst., 1958; Dr. Honoris Causa, U. of Montpellier, 1958; D.Sc., Humboldt U., 1959; LL.D., Reed Coll., 1959; Dr. Honoris Causa, Jagiellonian U., 1964; D.Sc., U. of Melbourne, 1964; Sc.D., Adelphi U., 1967; Sc.D., U. of Delhi, 1967; Sc.D., Marquette School of Medicine, 1969; L.H.D., Tampa U., 1980. WRITINGS: *Introduction to Quantum Mechanics* (coauthor, 1935); *General Chemistry* (1935); *The Structure of Line Spectra* (coauthor, 1939); *The Nature of the Chemical Bond and the Structure of Molecules and Crystals* (1939); *Coll. Chemistry* (1950); *No More War!* (1958); *The Architecture of Molecules* (coauthor, 1965); *The Chemical Bond* (1967); *Vitamin C and the Common Cold* (1970); *Vitamin C, The Common Cold and the Flu* (1976); *Cancer and Vitamin C* (coauthor, 1979). MISC.: developed theory of chemical bond, 1939; noted exponent of vitamin C therapy. RES.: Pasadena, CA.

PAULOS, LEON C. POLIT. & GOV.: ***candidate for Peace and Freedom Party nomination to presidency of the U.S., 1992***. MAILING ADDRESS: CA?

PAULSEN, PATRICK LAYTON. b. North Cove, South Bend, WA; m. (three times), including Jane Paulsen; c. Terry; Monty; Justin. EDUC.: San Francisco City Coll. POLIT. & GOV.: ***Straight Talking American Government (STAG) Party candidate for presidency of the U.S., 1968; candidate for Republican nomination to presidency of the U.S., 1972, 1980, 1988, 1992; independent candidate for presidency of the U.S., 1980***; candidate for mayor, Longboat Key, FL, 1990; ***candidate for Democratic nomination to presidency of the U.S., 1992***. BUS. & PROF.: comedian; actor; editorial vice pres., *Smothers Brothers Comedy Hour*, CBS-TV; nightclub comic; photostat operator; television commercial actor; member, Musical Comedy Trio; owner, winery, CA. MOTION PICTURE CREDITS: *Night Must Fall; Where Were You When the Lights Went Out*. AWARDS: Emmy Award, 1967–68.

MAILING ADDRESS: 8170 Beverly Blvd., #104, Los Angeles, CA 90048.

PAULUS, NORMA JEAN PETERSEN. b. Mar 13, 1933, Belgrade, NE; par. Paul Emil and Ella Marie (Hellbusch) Paulus; m. William G. Paulus, Aug 16, 1958; c. Elizabeth; William Frederick. EDUC.: LL.B., Willamette U., 1962. POLIT. & GOV.: sec. to Harney Cty. (OR) district atty., 1950–53; sec. to chief justice, OR State Supreme Court, 1955–61; appointed member, Salem (OR) Human Rights Comm., 1967–70; appointed member, Marion-Polk Boundary Comm., 1970–71; elected as a Republican to OR State House, 1971–77; elected as a Republican, OR state sec. of state, 1977–85; ***candidate for Republican nomination to vice presidency of the U.S., 1980***; Republican candidate for gov. of OR, 1986; elected as a Republican, OR superintendent of public instruction, 1989–. BUS. & PROF.: atty.; admitted to OR Bar, 1962; legal sec., Salem, OR, 1953–55; counsel, Paulus and Callaghan (law firm), Salem, 1971–76. AWARDS: Distinguished Service Award, Salem, 1971; Golden Torch Award, Business and Professional Women's Organization, 1971; fellow, Eagleton Inst. of Politics, 1971; "Woman of the Year" award, OR Women Lawyers, 1982; "Woman of the Future," *Ladies Home Journal*, 1979, 1980. MAILING ADDRESS: 3090 Pigeon Hollow Rd., South, Salem, OR 97302.

PAWLEY, WILLIAM DOUGLAS, JR. b. Jun 21, 1920; par. Ambassador William Douglas and Annie-Haha (Dobbs) Pawley, Sr.; m. Catherine Hundley; Catherine Wilmot (stepdaughter); Charles Wilmot (stepson). EDUC.: Riverside Military Acad.; Long Beach (CA) Junior Coll.; U. of Miami; FL Bible Coll. POLIT. & GOV.: ***candidate for Democratic nomination to presidency of the U.S., 1992***. BUS. & PROF.: founder, pres., Zenith Petroleum Co.; pres., Pawley Oil and Gas Co. MIL.: pilot, U.S.A.A.F., 1942–46; Distinguished Flying Cross; Air Medal with Oak Leaf Cluster; Chinese War Medal; Presidential Unit Citation. REL.: Presb. (lay preacher). MAILING ADDRESS: 9830 S.W. 158th St., Miami, FL 33157.

PAYNE, BILLIE DELLE. POLIT. & GOV.: ***candidate for Democratic nomination to presidency of the U.S., 1992***. MAILING ADDRESS: CA?

PAYNE, HENRY B. b. Nov 30, 1810, Hamilton, NY; d. Sep 9, 1896, Cleveland, OH; par. Elisha and Esther (Douglass) Payne; m. Mary Perry, Aug 16, 1836; c. Nathan Perry; Oliver Hazard; Flora (Mrs. William Collins Whitney, q.v.); Henry Wilson; Howard Elisha; Mary Perry (Mrs. Charles William Bingham). EDUC.: A.B., Hamilton Coll., 1832, A.M., 1836; studied law under John C. Spencer. POLIT. & GOV.: city clerk, Cleveland, OH, 1836; elected member, Cleveland City Council, 1846–48; presidential elector, Democratic Party, 1848; elected as a Democrat to OH State Senate, 1849–51; Democratic candidate for U.S. Senate (OH), 1851; member, Cleveland Water Works Comm., 1854; delegate, Dem. Nat'l. Conv., 1856, 1860, 1872 (delegation chm.); Democratic candidate for gov. of OH, 1857; pres., Board of Sinking Fund Commissioners, Cleveland, 1862– 96; elected as a Democrat to U.S. House (OH), 1875–77; Democratic candidate for U.S. House (OH), 1876; appointed member, Electoral Comm., 1876–77; ***candidate for Democratic nomination to presidency of the U.S., 1876, 1880, 1884; candidate for Democratic nomination to vice presidency of the U.S., 1880***; elected as a Democrat to U.S. Senate (OH), 1885–91. BUS. & PROF.: atty.; admitted to Cleveland Bar, 1833; partner (with Hiram V. Willson), law firm, Cleveland, 1834–46; founder, Cleveland and Columbus R.R., 1849, pres., 1851–54; dir., Cleveland, Painesville and Ashtabula R.R. Co., 1855; stockholder, dir., 18 corporations. MEM.: Case School of Applied Science (incorporator); Union Club of Cleveland. REL.: Presb. RES.: Cleveland, OH.

PAYNE, HENRY CLAY. b. Nov 23, 1843, Ashfield, MA; d. Oct 4, 1904, Washington, DC; par. Orrin Pierre and Eliza Etta (Ames) Payne; m. Lydia Wood Van Dyke, Oct 15, 1867; c. none. EDUC.: grad., Shelburne Falls (MA) Acad., 1859. POLIT. & GOV.: sec., chm., Young Men's Republican Club, 1872; appointed postmaster, Milwaukee, WI, 1876–86; sec., chm., Milwaukee Cty. (WI) Republican Central Cmte.; sec., chm., WI State Republican Central Cmte., to 1892; member, Rep. Nat'l. Cmte., 1880–1904; ***candidate for Republican nomination to vice presidency of the U.S., 1900***; appointed postmaster gen. of the U.S., 1902–04; temporary chm., Rep. Nat'l. Conv., 1904. BUS. & PROF.: cashier, Nowell and Pratt (dry goods), Milwaukee, WI, 1863–67; insurance agent; pres., Wisconsin Telephone Co., 1886–1904; receiver, Northern Pacific R.R., 1893–94; pres., Chicago and Calument Terminal Railway, 1893–94; founder, Milwaukee Light, Heat and Traction Co.; pres., Fox River Electric Co.; vice pres., Milwaukee Electric Railway and Light Co., 1886, pres., 1889–1904. MEM.: American Street Railway Assn. (pres., 1893–94). REL.: Methodist. RES.: Milwaukee, WI.

PAYNE, JOHN BARTON. b. Jan 26, 1855, Pruntytown, VA (now WV); d. Jan 24, 1935, Washington, DC; par. Dr. Amos and Elizabeth Barton (Smith) Payne; m. Kate Bunker, Oct 17, 1878; m. 2d, Jennie Byrd Bryan, May 1, 1913. EDUC.: private schools, Orleans, VA, 1860–70. POLIT. & GOV.: appointed asst. clerk, Circuit Court, Taylor Cty., VA; chm., Preston Cty. (WV) Democratic Cmte., 1877–82; appointed special judge, Circuit Court, Tucker Cty., WV, 1880; elected as a Democrat to mayor of Kingwood, WV, 1882; elected as a Democrat to judge, Superior Court, Cook Cty., IL, 1893–98; appointed solicitor gen. of the U.S., 1913 (declined); appointed gen. counsel, U.S. Shipping Board, 1917–18, chm., 1919–20; appointed gen. counsel, U.S. Railroad Administration, 1917–19; appointed U.S. sec. of the interior, 1920–21; appointed U.S. dir. of railroads, 1920–21; appointed U.S. commissioner to Mexico, 1923; appointed pres., Board of South Park Commissioners, Chicago, IL, 1911–24; ***candidate for Democratic nomination to presidency of the U.S.,***

1924. BUS. & PROF.: clerk, general store, Warrenton, VA; publisher, *West Virginia Argus*; atty.; admitted to VA Bar, 1876; law practice, Kingwood, WV, 1877–82; law practice, Chicago, 1883–93; partner, Winston, Payne, Strawn and Shaw (law firm), Chicago, to 1918. MEM.: American Red Cross (chm., 1921); League of Red Cross Societies (chm., Board of Governors); Chicago Law Inst. (pres., 1889); Union League; Knights Templar. AWARDS: Legion of Honor (France); Medaille du Cinquantenaire (French Red Cross); Grand Order of Leopold II (Belgium); Order of King George I (Greece); Order of the Rising Sun with Grand Cordon (Japan); First Class Chiabo with Grand Cordon (China); Costa Rican Red Cross Medal of Merit; Grand Cross of Honor, Chilean Red Cross; Swedish Red Cross Medal; Commander's Cross with Star, Order of Polonia Restituta (Poland); Medal of First Class, Belgian Red Cross; First Class Medal of Honor, Austrian Red Cross. HON. DEG.: LL.D., George Washington U., 1919; LL.D., U. of Cincinnati, 1920; LL.D., Coll. of William and Mary, 1926; LL.D., Washington and Lee U., 1926. REL.: Episc. RES.: Washington, DC.

PAYNE, WILLIAM C. b. 1867, Warrenton, VA. EDUC.: Wayland Seminary, Washington, DC. POLIT. & GOV.: ***National Liberal Party candidate for vice presidency of the U.S., 1904***. BUS. & PROF.: sailor; teacher; founder, industrial school, Ponce, Puerto Rico. MIL.: cabin steward, U.S. Navy, Spanish-American War; served on USS *Dixie*. MEM.: Republican Party. WRITINGS: *The Cruise of the U.S.S. Dixie, or, On Board with Maryland Boys in the Spanish-American War* (1899). RES.: Warrenton, VA.

PEABODY, ENDICOTT. b. Feb 15, 1920, Lawrence, MA; par. Malcolm E. and Mary (Parkman) Peabody; m. Barbara Welch Gibbons, Jun 24, 1944; c. Barbara; Endicott, Jr.; Robert Lee. EDUC.: B.A., Harvard U., 1942, LL.B., 1948. POLIT. & GOV.: appointed asst. regional counsel, Office of Price Stabilization, 1951; appointed deputy regional administrator, Small Defense Plants Administration, 1952; governor's councillor, MA, 1955–56; Democratic candidate for atty. gen. of MA, 1956, 1958; Democratic candidate for gov. of MA, 1960, 1964; delegate, Dem. Nat'l. Conv., 1960, 1964, 1968; elected as a Democrat to gov. of MA, 1963–64; Democratic candidate for U.S. Senate (MA), 1966; appointed asst. dir., Office of Emergency Preparedness, 1967–68; appointed chm., Sports Cmte., President's Comm. on U.S.-Mexico Border Development and Friendship, 1967–69; ***candidate for Democratic nomination to vice presidency of the U.S., 1972, 1992***; delegate, Democratic Mid-Term Conference, 1974; Democratic candidate for U.S. Senate (NH), 1986. BUS. & PROF.: atty.; admitted to MA Bar, 1948; partner, Peabody, Koufman and Brewer (law firm), Boston, MA, 1952–62; counsel, Roche and Leen, Boston, 1965–67; partner, Peabody, Rivlin, Gore, Cladouhos and Lambert (law firm), Washington, DC, 1969–; counsel, Roche, Carens and DeGiacomo (law firm), Boston, 1969–. MIL.: U.S. Navy, WWII; Silver Star. MEM.: ABA; Federal Bar Assn.; MA Bar Assn.; Boston Bar Assn.; Harvard Club of Washington; Harvard Varsity Club; Cambridge Tennis Club; Harvard Law School Assn. of DC; MA Mental Health Campaign (chm., 1957); Heart Fund (chm., 1960); Federal City Club; Middletown Valley Hunt Club. AWARDS: "Outstanding Young Man," Boston Junior C. of C., 1954; All-American left guard, Harvard U., 1941; Knute Rockne Memorial Trophy; "Outstanding Lineman," 1941; "Outstanding Football Player in New England," 1941; Bulger-Lowe Trophy winner; National Football Hall of Fame, 1973. REL.: Episc. MISC.: known as "Chub" Peabody. MAILING ADDRESS: 33 Main St., Hollis, NH 03049.

PEACE, MR. POLIT. & GOV.: ***independent candidate for presidency of the U.S., 1980***. MAILING ADDRESS: 18034 Poplar St., Boyes Hot Springs, CA 95416.

PEACE, MRS. POLIT. & GOV.: ***independent candidate for vice presidency of the U.S., 1980***. MAILING ADDRESS: 18034 Poplar St., Boyes Hot Springs, CA 95416.

PEARCE, JAMES ALFRED. b. Dec 14, 1805, Alexandria, VA; d. Dec 21, 1862, Chestertown, MD; par. Gideon and Julia (Dick) Pearce; m. Martha J. Laird, Oct 6, 1829; m. 2d, Mathilda Cox Ringgold, Mar 22, 1847; c. James Alfred, Jr.; three daughters. EDUC.: B.A., Coll. of NJ (now Princeton U.), 1821, M.A.; studied law under Judge John Glenn, Baltimore, MD. POLIT. & GOV.: elected as a Whig to MD State House of Delegates, 1831–35; elected as a Whig to U.S. House (MD), 1835–39, 1841–43; Whig Party candidate for U.S. House (MD), 1838; elected as a Whig to U.S. Senate (MD), 1843–61, 1861–62 (Democrat); appointed U.S. sec. of the interior, 1850 (declined); ***candidate for Democratic nomination to presidency of the U.S., 1860***. BUS. & PROF.: atty.; admitted to MD Bar, 1824; law practice, Cambridge, MD, 1824; farmer, LA, 1825–28; law practice, Chestertown, MD, 1828–62; lecturer in law, Washington Coll., 1850–62. MEM.: Smithsonian Institution (regent); Cliosophic Soc.; Washington Coll. (visitor, 1832). HON. DEG.: LL.D., Coll. of NJ (now Princeton U.); LL.D., Coll. of St. James. RES.: Chestertown, MD.

PEARE, GEORGE R. b. May 13, 1847; d. Jul 15, 1912, Lynn, MA; m. Sarah Slade; c. William Henry; Ora G.; Leo. POLIT. & GOV.: Socialist Labor Party candidate for U.S. House (MA), 1894; Socialist Labor Party candidate for mayor of Lynn, MA; delegate, Socialist Labor Party National Convention, 1896; ***candidate for Socialist Labor Party nomination to presidency of the U.S., 1896***; Socialist Labor Party candidate for gov. of MA, 1898, 1899. BUS. & PROF.: mechanical inventor. RES.: Lynn, MA.

PECKHAM, RUFUS WHEELER. b. Nov 8, 1838, Albany, NY; d. Oct 24, 1909, Altamont, NY; par. Rufus

Wheeler and Isabella A. (Lacey) Peckham; m. Harriette M. Arnold, Nov 14, 1866; c. two sons. EDUC.: Albany (NY) Acad.; studied law under Rufus W. Peckham and Lyman Tremain, Albany, NY, 1857. POLIT. & GOV.: elected district atty., Albany Cty., NY, 1869–72; delegate, Dem. Nat'l. Conv., 1876, 1880; appointed corporation counsel, City of Albany, 1881–83; elected justice, Supreme Court of NY, 1883–86; elected assoc. justice, NY Court of Appeals, 1886–95; appointed assoc. justice, Supreme Court of the U.S., 1895–1909; ***candidate for Democratic nomination to presidency of the U.S., 1908***. BUS. & PROF.: atty.; admitted to NY Bar, 1859; partner (with Lyman Tremain), law firm, Albany, 1860–78. HON. DEG.: LL.D., Union Coll., 1894; LL.D., Yale U., 1896; LL.D., Columbia U., 1901. REL.: Episc. RES.: Washington, DC.

PEEK, GEORGE NELSON. b. Nov 19, 1873, Polo, IL; d. Dec 17, 1943, San Diego, CA; par. Henry Clay and Adeline (Chase) Peek; m. Georgia Lindsey, Dec 22, 1903; c. none. EDUC.: grad., Oregon (IL) H.S., 1891; Northwestern U., 1891–92. POLIT. & GOV.: appointed commissioner of finished products, War Industries Board, 1918; appointed chm., Industrial Board, U.S. Dept. of Commerce, 1919; chm., Alfred E. Smith Independent Organizations Cmte., 1928; appointed administrator, A.A.A., 1933; appointed special counsel to the president on Foreign Trade, 1934–35; appointed pres., Export-Import Bank, 1934–35; ***candidate for Republican nomination to vice presidency of the U.S., 1936***. BUS. & PROF.: employee, Deere and Webber Co., Minneapolis, MN, 1893–1901; vice pres., mgr., John Deere Plow Co., Omaha, NE, 1901–11; vice pres., Deere and Co., Moline, IL, 1911–19; pres., gen. mgr., Moline Plow Co., Moline, IL, 1919–23; dir., Maizewood Insulation Co.; dir., Merchants National Bank. MEM.: American Council of Agriculture (pres.; chm., North Central States Agricultural Conference, 1925–28); Omaha Club; Chicago University Club; National Press Club; Elks; America First Cmte. (1940); Metropolitan Club; Chevy Chase Club. AWARDS: Distinguished Service Medal; chevalier, Legion of Honor (France); commander, Order of the Crown (Belgium); Knight of the Crown of Italy. WRITINGS: *Equality for Agriculture* (coauthor); *Why Quit Our Own?* (coauthor, 1936). REL.: none. RES.: Moline, IL.

PELL, CLAIBORNE de BORDA. b. Nov 22, 1918, New York, NY; par. Herbert Claiborne and Matilda (Bigelow) Pell; m. Nuala O'Donnell, Dec 16, 1944; c. Herbert Claiborne II; Christopher T. Hartford; Nuala Dallas; Julia Lorillard Wampage. EDUC.: A.B. (cum laude), Princeton U., 1940; A.M., Columbia U., 1946. POLIT. & GOV.: special asst., U.N. Conference, San Francisco, CA, 1945; exec. asst., RI State Democratic chm., 1952, 1954; consultant, Dem. Nat'l. Cmte., 1953–60; delegate, RI State Constitutional Convention, 1955; U.S. delegate, Intergovernmental Maritime Consultative Organization, 1955, 1959; Democratic National Registration chm., 1956; chief delegate tally clerk, Dem. Nat'l. Conv., 1956, 1960, 1964, 1968; elected as a Democrat to U.S. Senate (RI), 1961–; delegate, Dem. Nat'l. Conv., 1968, 1972, 1976; ***candidate for Democratic nomination to vice presidency of the U.S., 1972***; delegate, Democratic Mid-Term Conference, 1974. BUS. & PROF.: diplomat, U.S. Dept. of State, 1945–52; business exec.; limited partner, Auchincloss, Parker, and Redpath (investments), New York, NY, 1958–; dir., International Investors, Inc., 1955–60. MIL.: lt., U.S.C.G., 1941–45; capt., U.S.C.G. Reserves. MEM.: American Immigration Conference (treas., 1957–60); International Rescue Cmte. (vice pres., 1957–60); National Council of Refugees; Franklin Delano Roosevelt Foundation (dir., 1952–); World Affairs Council of RI (dir., 1954); North American Newspaper Alliance (dir.); Soc. of the Cincinnati; Reading Room of Newport; Hope Club; St. George's School; Brown U. (trustee); White's Club of London; Travellers Club of Paris; St. James Club of London; U.S. Flag Foundation (hon. co-chm.); Knickerbocker Club; Brook Club; Metropolitan Club of Washington. AWARDS: Red Cross of Merit (Portugal, 1941); Crown of Italy (Italy, 1946); Caritas Elizabeth Medal, 1957; Legion of Honor (France, 1958); Order of the Knights of Malta, First Class, with Crown (Malta, 1960); Grand Cross of Merit (Liechtenstein). HON. DEG.: 19. WRITINGS: *Rochambeau and Rhode Island*; *Megalopolis Unbound* (1966); *Challenge of the Seven Seas* (coauthor, 1966); *Power and Policy* (1972). REL.: Episc. MAILING ADDRESS: Ledge Rd., Newport, RI 02840.

PELLETTIERE, MICHAEL. POLIT. & GOV.: ***New Alliance Party candidate for vice presidency of the U.S., 1988***. MAILING ADDRESS: unknown.

PELLEY, WILLIAM DUDLEY. b. Mar 12, 1890, Lynn, MA; d. Jun 30, 1965, Noblesville, IN; par. William George A. and Grace (Goodale) Pelley; m. Marion Harriet Stone, Dec 16, 1911 (divorced); m. 2d, Wilhelmina Hannsmann, Jul 4, 1936; m. 3d, A. Marion Henderson, 1956; c. William; Adelaide Pearson; Harriet. EDUC.: public schools. POLIT. & GOV.: founder, Christian Party, 1935; ***Christian Party candidate for presidency of the U.S., 1936***. BUS. & PROF.: journalist; author; ed., publisher, *Philosopher Magazine*, 1909; treas., mgr., Pelley Tissue Corp., 1909–12; feature writer, *Springfield (MA) Homestead*; night writer, *Boston (MA) Globe*; ed., publisher, *Chicopee (MA) Journal*, 1913; ed., publisher, *Wilmington (VT) Times*, 1914; ed., *Deerfield Valley Times*, Wilmington; staff, *Bennington (VT) Banner*; staff writer, *The American*, 1917; toured Orient under sponsorship of Methodist Centenary Movement; with YMCA (Red Triangle) in Siberia, 1917–18; ed., *St. Johnsbury Caledonian*, 1917–20; owner, Brief Meal Corp. (restaurant chain), 1927–29; ed., publisher, *Liberation*, 1930; founder, Galahad Coll., Asheville, NC, 1931; ed., publisher, *Pelley's Weekly*; ed., publisher, *Roll Call*; ed., publisher, *Silver Shirt Weekly*, 1934; ed., publisher, *The Galilean*, 1941–42; ed., publisher, *Valor*; ed., publisher, *Little Visits Magazine*; owner, publisher, *Soulcraft Fellowship, Inc.*; founder, Galahad Press; founder, Skyland Press; founder, Pelley Publishers; founder, Fellowship Press; ed., *Reality*; owner, *Western Film Magazine*; owner, real estate firm; owner, advertising agency. MEM.: Silver Legion of America (founder, 1933–40); Christian American Patriots (founder); Silver Shirts (founder); Foundation for Christian Economics (chm.); Republican Party. WRITINGS: *The Greater Glory* (1919); *One-Thing-at-a-Time O'Day* (1919); *The Fog* (1921); *Mother's Madness* (1923); *Entrance in Rear* (1923); *Thrown Away* (1923); *Drag* (1924); *Seven Minutes in Eternity* (1929); *Golden Rubbish* (1929); *The Trend is Upward* (1930); *The Blue Lamp* (1931); *No More Hunger* (1933); *What Manner of Government is the Christ to Set Up?* (1933); *Nations-in-Law* (1935); *Door to Revelation* (1936); *editorials by Pelley* (1936); *Behold Life* (1937); *Thinking Alive* (1937); *What Every Congressman Should Know* (1937); *Bright Trails* (1938); *Little Visits With Great Americans* (1938); *Little Lectures on Life's Great Mysteries; Benjamin Franklin* (1939); *Dupes of Judah* (1939); *The Key to Crisis* (1939); *The 45 Questions Most Frequently Asked About Jews* (1939); *Jews Say So!* (1939); *The Bolt on North Carolina; Cabin Smoke* (1939); *Indians Aren't Red* (1940); *Duress and Persuasion; Earth Comes* (1941); *The Soulcraft Scripts* (12 vols.); *The Golden Scripts* (1941); *Why I Believe the Dead Are Alive* (1942); *Weekly Studies in Soulcraft* (1942); *All About Soulcraft; Star Guests* (1950); *Road Into Sunrise* (1950); *Twilight Clear* (1951); *Thresholds of Tomorrow* (1951); *Something Better* (1952); *Figure Yourself Out* (1953); *New Quatrains of Nostradamus; Adam Awakes* (1953); *Getting Born* (1954); *Beyond Grandeur* (1954); *Know Your Karma* (1954); *Soul Eternal* (1955); *Undying Mind* (1955); *As Thou Lovest* (1955); *Elucidata; Out of the Tumult; Stairs to Greatness* (1956). REL.: spiritualist (nee Methodist). MISC.: given 5-year suspended sentence in 1935 for violation of NC securities laws; convicted of sedition in WWII and sentenced to federal penitentiary, Terre Haute, IN, 1942–50 (on a 15-year sentence). RES.: Noblesville, IN.

PENDLETON, GEORGE HUNT. b. Jul 19, 1825, Cincinnati, OH; d. Nov 24, 1889, Brussels, Belgium; par. Nathaniel Greene and Jane Frances (Hunt) Pendleton; m. Alice Kay, 1846; c. Francis Kay; Mary Lloyd (Mrs. John Rutledge Abney); Jane Frances (Mrs. Arthur T. Brice). EDUC.: Cincinnati Coll., to 1841; U. of Heidelberg, c. 1845; studied law in office of Stephen Fales, Cincinnati, OH. POLIT. & GOV.: elected as a Democrat to OH State Senate, 1853–56; Democratic candidate for U.S. House (OH), 1854, 1864, 1866; elected as a Democrat to U.S. House (OH), 1857–65; ***Democratic candidate for vice presidency of the U.S., 1864***; delegate, Union Convention, 1866; ***candidate for Democratic nomination to presidency of the U.S., 1868, 1884***; Democratic candidate for gov. of OH, 1869; ***candidate for Straight-Out (Taproot) Democratic Party nomination to presidency of the U.S., 1872***; elected as a Democrat to U.S. Senate (OH), 1879–85; chm., U.S. Comm. on Civil Service, 1883; candidate for Democratic nomination to U.S. Senate (OH), 1884; appointed envoy extraordinary and minister plenipotentiary to Germany, 1885–89. BUS. & PROF.: atty.; admitted to OH Bar, 1847; partner (with George E. Pugh), law firm, 1847–52; pres., Kentucky Central R.R., 1869–79. WRITINGS: *Power of the President to Suspend the Privilege of Habeas Corpus* (1861); *But, Sir, Armies, Money, Blood Cannot Maintain This Union . . . Justice, Reason, Peace May* (1861); *The Resolution to Expel Mr. Long of Ohio* (1864); *Hear Hon. Geo. H. Pendleton* (1864); *Payment of the Public Debt in Legal Tender Notes* (1867). MISC.: known as "Gentleman George." RES.: Cincinnati, OH.

PENDLETON, LATON. POLIT. & GOV.: ***candidate for Democratic nomination to presidency of the U.S., 1992***. MAILING ADDRESS: P.O. Box 11099, Lansing, MI 48901.

PENN, E. P. POLIT. & GOV.: ***Lincoln Party candidate for presidency of the U.S., 1904***. RES.: WV.

PENNINGTON, AARON S. b. Jan 17, 1800, Newark, NJ; d. Aug 25, 1869, Paterson, NJ; par. William Sanford and Phoebe (Wheeler) Pennington. POLIT. & GOV.: prosecutor in pleas, Passaic Cty., NJ; elected as a Whig to NJ State Senate; delegate, Rep. Nat'l. Conv., 1856; ***candidate for Republican nomination to vice presidency of the U.S., 1856***. BUS. & PROF.: atty.; lawyer in chancery. MEM.: Soc. for Establishing Useful Manufactures (acting gov.). RES.: Paterson, NJ.

PENNOYER, SYLVESTER. b. Jul 6, 1831, Groton, NY; d. May 31, 1902, Portland, OR; par. Justus Powers and Elizabeth (Howland) Pennoyer; m. Mrs. Mary A. (Peters) Allen, 1856; c. Robert William; Grace; Horace Nathaniel; Agnes; Gertrude Elizabeth (Mrs. George Fish Russell). EDUC.: Homer Acad.; grad., Harvard U., 1854. POLIT. & GOV.: superintendent of schools, Multnomah Cty., OR, 1860–62; candidate for mayor of Portland, OR, 1885; elected as a Democrat to gov. of OR, 1886–94; elected as a Democrat (People's Party) to mayor of Portland, OR, 1896–98; ***candidate for Democratic nomination to presidency of the U.S., 1896***. BUS. & PROF.: atty.; law practice, Puget Sound, WA; teacher, Portland, OR; partner, Portland Lumbering and Manufacturing Co., 1862; real estate investor; owner, ed., *Oregon Herald*, 1868–71. WRITINGS: "The Paramount Questions of the Campaign," *North American Review*, Oct 1892. RES.: Portland, OR.

PEPIN, JOHN RAYMOND. POLIT. & GOV.: Socialist Labor Party candidate for IL state sec. of state, 1896; financial sec., IL Socialist Labor Party, 1897; ***candidate for Socialist Labor Party nomination to presidency of the U.S., 1900; candidate for Socialist Labor Party nomination to vice presidency of the U.S., 1900, 1904***; Socialist Labor Party candidate for mayor of Chicago, IL, 1901. BUS. & PROF.: engineer. RES.: Chicago, IL.

PEPPER, CLAUDE DENSON. b. Sep 8, 1900, Dudleyville, AL; d. May 30, 1989, Washington, DC; par. Joseph

Wheeler and Lena C. (Talbot) Pepper; m. Mildred Irene Webster, Dec 29, 1936. EDUC.: A.B., U. of AL, 1921, LL.B., Harvard U., 1924. POLIT. & GOV.: member, FL State Democratic Central Cmte., 1928–29; elected as a Democrat to FL State House, 1929–30; member, FL State Board of Public Welfare, 1931–32; member, FL Board of Law Examiners, 1933–34; candidate for Democratic nomination to U.S. Senate (FL), 1934, 1950, 1958; elected as a Democrat to U.S. Senate (FL), 1937–51; delegate, Interparliamentary Union, 1938, 1950; delegate, Dem. Nat'l. Conv., 1940 (chm.), 1944 (chm.), 1948, 1952, 1956, 1960, 1964, 1968; ***candidate for Democratic nomination to vice presidency of the U.S., 1944, 1948, 1972; candidate for Democratic nomination to presidency of the U.S., 1948, 1984***; elected as a Democrat to U.S. House (FL), 1963–1989. BUS. & PROF.: teacher, public schools, Dothan, AL, 1917–18; employee, steel mill, Ensley, AL; atty.; admitted to AL Bar, 1924; admitted to FL Bar, 1925; instructor in law, U. of AR, 1924–25; law practice, Perry, FL, 1925–30; law practice, Tallahassee, 1930–37; Marfleet Lecturer, U. of Toronto, 1942; dir., Washington Federal Savings and Loan Assn., Miami Beach, FL; dir., Washington Security Insurance Co., Miami Beach; law practice, Miami Beach. MIL.: pvt., Students Army Training Corps, Company A, U. of AL, 1918. MEM.: Kappa Alpha; Blue Key; Phi Beta Kappa; Omicron Delta Kappa; Sigma Upsilon; Phi Alpha Delta; ABA; Dade Cty. Bar Assn.; Tallahassee Bar Assn.; Miami Beach Bar Assn.; Coral Gables Bar Assn.; Inter-ABA; International Bar Assn.; FL State Bar Assn. (exec. council, 1934); Assn. of the Bar of the City of New York; Kiwanis International (lt. gov., Western Div. of FL); C. of C. of the Americas (dir.); American Legion; Forty and Eight; Masons; Shriners; Elks; Moose; Jefferson Island Club; Harvard Club of Washington; Harvard Club of Miami; Army and Navy Club; Woodmen of the World; Burning Tree Club; Muscular Dystrophy Fund Drive; World War I Vets. AWARDS: Albert Lasker Public Service Award, 1967; Eleanor Roosevelt–Israel Humanities Award, 1968; "Outstanding Alumnus," Phi Alpha Delta, 1975. HON. DEG.: LL.D., McMaster U., 1941; LL.D., U. of AL, 1942; LL.D., U. of Toronto, 1942; LL.D., Rollins Coll., 1944; D.Sc., U. of Miami, 1974. WRITINGS: *Pepper: Eyewitness to a Century* (1987). REL.: Bapt. RES.: Miami Beach, FL.

PERCY, CHARLES HARTING. b. Sep 27, 1919, Pensacola, FL; par. Edward H. and Elisabeth (Harting) Percy; m. Jeanne Valerie Dickerson, Jun 12, 1943 (deceased); m. 2d, Loraine Diane Guyer, Aug 27, 1950; c. Valerie Jeanne; Sharon Lee (Mrs. John D. Rockefeller IV); Roger; Gail; Mark. EDUC.: A.B., U. of Chicago, 1941. POLIT. & GOV.: appointed special ambassador and personal representative of the president to presidential inauguration ceremonies, Peru and Bolivia, 1956; vice chm., Republican National Finance Cmte., 1957–59; delegate, Rep. Nat'l. Conv., 1960 (chm., Platform Cmte.), 1964, 1968, 1972, 1976; Republican candidate for gov. of IL, 1964; elected as a Republican to U.S. Senate (IL), 1967–85; ***candidate for Republican nomination to presidency of the U.S., 1968, 1972, 1976; candidate for Republican nomination to vice presidency of the U.S., 1968, 1972, 1976, 1980***; appointed U.S. delegate, U.N. General Assembly, 1974; Republican candidate for U.S. Senate (IL), 1984. BUS. & PROF.: sales trainee, Bell and Howell Corp., 1938, mgr., War Coordinating Dept., 1941–43, asst. sec., 1943–46, corporation sec., 1946–49, pres., 1949–61, chief exec. officer, 1951–63, chm. of the board, 1961–66; sales promoter, Crowell-Collier Publishing Co., 1939; dir., Harris Trust and Savings Bank, 1967; dir., Outboard Marine Corp. MIL.: lt., U.S.N.R., 1943–45. MEM.: National Conference of Christians and Jews (chm., Chicago Branch); U. of Chicago Alumni Foundation (trustee); IL Inst. of Technology (trustee, 1950–54); Ford Foundation Fund for Adult Education (chm., 1958–61); CA Inst. of Technology (trustee); New IL Comm. (chm., 1965–69); Chicago Assn. of Commerce; American Management Assn. (dir.); National Photographic Manufacturers Assn.; United Republican Fund of IL (pres., 1955); Photographic Soc. of America; Phi Delta Phi; Alpha Delta Phi (national sec.); Chicago Club; Economic Club (dir.); Executives Club (dir.); Commercial Club; Commonwealth Club. AWARDS: one of ten "Outstanding Young Men in America," U.S. Junior C. of C., 1949; World Trade Award, World Trade Award Comm., 1955; National Sales Executives Management Award, 1956; Legion of Honor, 1961; "Businessman of the Year," *Saturday Review*, 1962; Statesmanship Award, Harvard Business School Assn., 1962; Humanitarian Service Award, Abraham Lincoln Center, 1962; Top Hat Award, National Federation of Business and Professional Women's Clubs, 1965; Business Administration Award, Drexel Inst. of Technology, 1965. HON. DEG.: LL.D., IL Coll., 1961; LL.D., Roosevelt U., 1961; LL.D., Lake Forest Coll., 1962; H.H.D., Willamette U., 1962; LL.D., Bradley U., 1963; D.H.L., National Coll. of Education, 1964; LL.D., Defiance Coll., 1965; D.H.L., Knox Coll., 1973. WRITINGS: *Growing Old in the Country of the Young* (1974); *I Want to Know About the U.S. Senate* (1976). REL.: Christian Scientist. MAILING ADDRESS: Wilmette, IL 60091.

PERKINS, DOROTHY L. m. Marvin E. Perkins (q.v.). POLIT. & GOV.: ***independent candidate for vice presidency of the U.S., 1980***. MAILING ADDRESS: TX.

PERKINS, GEORGE CLEMENT. b. Aug 23, 1839, Kennebunkport, ME; d. Feb 26, 1923, Oakland, CA; par. Clement and Lucinda (Fairchild) Perkins; m. Ruth A. Parker, 1864; c. three sons; four daughters. POLIT. & GOV.: elected as a Republican to CA State Senate, 1869–76; elected as a Republican to gov. of CA, 1879–83; appointed and subsequently elected as a Republican to U.S. Senate (CA), 1893–1915; ***candidate for Republican nomination to vice presidency of the U.S., 1896 (declined)***. BUS. & PROF.: farmer; sailor; cabin boy, 1852–55; merchant, San Francisco, CA; banker; miller; miner; owner, Pacific Steamship Co.; member, Goodall, Perkins and Co.; dir., First National Bank of San Francisco. MEM.: San Francisco Merchants' Exchange; San Francisco C. of C. (pres.); San Francisco Art Assn. (pres.); CA Acad. of Sciences (dir.); Boys' and Girls' Aid Soc. (pres.); Pacific Union Club; Bohemian Club;

Athenian Club; Acad. of Sciences (trustee); CA Mining Bureau (trustee); CA Inst. for the Deaf, Dumb and Blind (trustee); Masons; Loyal Legion. RES.: Oakland, CA.

PERKINS, MARVIN E. m. Dorothy L. Perkins (q.v.). POLIT. & GOV.: ***independent candidate for presidency of the U.S., 1980***. MAILING ADDRESS: TX.

PERON, DENNIS. POLIT. & GOV.: candidate for Democratic nomination to supervisor, San Francisco City-County, CA, 1980; ***candidate for Democratic nomination to vice presidency of the U.S., 1980***. BUS. & PROF.: marijuana dealer, San Francisco, CA; owner, Island Restaurant, San Francisco, CA; gay activist. MEM.: Democratic Club. MISC.: prominent political ally of Harvey Milk. MAILING ADDRESS: San Francisco, CA.

PEROT, HENRY ROSS. b. Jun 27, 1930, Texarkana, TX; par. Gabriel Ross and Lulu Ray Perot; m. Margot Birmingham, 1954; c. Ross, Jr.; Nancy; Suzanne; Carolyn; Catherine. EDUC.: Texarkana Junior Coll.; grad., U.S. Naval Acad., 1953. POLIT. & GOV.: appointed chm., TX War on Drugs Cmte., 1979; ***independent candidate for presidency of the U.S., 1992 (withdrew before declaring; reentered)***. BUS. & PROF.: salesman, data processing, IBM Corp., 1957–62; founder, Electronic Data Systems Corp., Dallas, TX, 1962–, chm. of the board, chief exec. officer; founder, Perot Systems Corp. Motors Corp.; dir., General Motors Corp. MIL.: lt. (jg), U.S. Navy, 1953–57. MEM.: Perot Foundation (dir.); United We Stand, America (founder). AWARDS: Winston Churchill Award; Raoul Wallenberg Award; Jefferson Award for Public Service; Patrick Henry Award; Sarnoff Award; Eisenhower Award; Smithsonian Computerworld Award; Horatio Alger Award; National Business Hall of Fame Award. MISC.: reportedly one of the richest men in the world; attempted rescue of hostages held by Iran, 1979, 1986. MAILING ADDRESS: 1700 Lakeside Square, Dallas, TX 75251.

PERRIN, E. W. POLIT. & GOV.: ***independent candidate for presidency of the U.S., 1900***. BUS. & PROF.: blacksmith. WRITINGS: *Labor's Prayer* (1900). MISC.: noted Socialist orator; possibly same person as E. W. Perry (q.v.). RES.: Little Rock, AR.

PERRY, CHARLES E. POLIT. & GOV.: ***candidate for Populist Party nomination to vice presidency of the U.S., 1984***; candidate for U.S. Senate (ND), 1986. MAILING ADDRESS: P.O. Box 332, Valley City, ND 58072.

PERRY, E. W. POLIT. & GOV.: ***independent candidate for presidency of the U.S., 1888***. MISC.: possibly same person as E. W. Perrin (q.v.). RES.: IA.

PERSHING, JOHN JOSEPH. b. Sep 13, 1860, Laclede, MO; d. Jul 15, 1948, Washington, DC; par. John Frederick and Ann E. (Thompson) Pershing; m. Helen Frances Warren, Jan 26, 1905; c. Helen Elizabeth; Anne; Francis Warren; Mary Margaret. EDUC.: Kirksville Normal School, 1880; grad., U.S. Military Acad., 1886; LL.B., U. of NE, 1893. POLIT. & GOV.: chief, Bureau of Insular Affairs, 1899; appointed gov., Moro Province, Philippine Islands, 1906–14; ***candidate for Democratic nomination to presidency of the U.S., 1916, 1920, 1928; candidate for Republican nomination to presidency of the U.S., 1916, 1920, 1928***. BUS. & PROF.: soldier. MIL.: 2d lt., Sixth U.S. Cavalry, 1886; served in Apache campaign, 1886, Sioux campaign, 1890–91; 1st lt., 1892; military instructor, U. of NE, 1891–95; instructor in tactics, U.S. Military Acad., 1897–98; maj., 1899; capt., 1901; military attache, Tokyo, Japan, 1905–06; brig. gen., 1906; commander, Dept. of Mindanao, Philippine Islands, 1906–14; maj. gen., 1916; commander, U.S. campaign against Poncho Villa, 1916; gen., 1917; commander in chief, AEF, 1917–19; gen. of the armies of the U.S., 1919; appointed chief of staff, U.S. Army, 1921; retired, 1924; Distinguished Service Medal; Grand Cross of the Order of the Bath; Grand Cross of the Legion of Honor; Croix de Guerre; Medaille Militaire; Grand Cordon of the Order of the Paulawnia; Grand Cordon of the Order of Leopold; Belgian Croix de Guerre; Great Cross, Order of the White Lion (Czechoslovakia); Croix de Guerre (Czechoslovakia); Order of Saint Savior (Greece); Grand Cross of the Order of Saints Maurizio e Lazzaro (Italy); Military Order of Savoy (Italy); Grand Cordon of Prince Danilo I (Montenegro); Obilitch Medal (Montenegro); Medal of La Solaridad (Panama); Virtuti Militari and Polonia Restituta (Poland); Grand Cordon of the Order of the Precious Light of Chia Ho (China); Order of the Star of Kara-Georges (Serbia); Order of Mihai Bravul (Rumania). MEM.: American Battle Monuments Comm. (chm.); Goethals Memorial Comm. (chm.); Masons (32°); Metropolitan Club; Army and Navy Club. HON. DEG.: LL.D., U. of NE, 1917; LL.D., U. of Cambridge, 1919; D.C.L., U. of Oxford, 1919; LL.D., U. of St. Andrews (Scotland), 1919; LL.D., Yale U., 1920; Dr. Mil. Sci., PA Military Acad., 1921. WRITINGS: *My Experiences in the World War* (1931). RES.: Washington, DC.

PERSONS, ROBERT LEO. b. Sep 25, 1931, Chester, OH; par. Elchard Leo and Stella Lucill (Smith) Persons; m. Bronis Lucill Young; c. Margerett Ann; Betty Jean; Janet Lucill; Coleen Christeen; Barbara Sue; Donna Mae. EDUC.: grad., Cheshire (OH) H.S., 1950; D.D., Life Science Church Coll. POLIT. & GOV.: ***candidate for Republican nomination to presidency of the U.S., 1976***. BUS. & PROF.: owner, operator, auto body repair shop, Middleport, OH; minister, Life Science Church. MEM.: Meigs Ministerial Assn. REL.: nondenominational Protestant. MAILING ADDRESS: Route 1, Cheshire, OH 45620.

PETERSEN, VERNON LEROY. b. Nov 3, 1926, Mason, NV; par. Vernon and Lenora E. (Dickson) Petersen; m. 2d, Thelma P.; c. Anne C.; Ruth M. EDUC.: Naval Architecture Certificate, U. of CA, 1944; Personnel Management Certificate, Armed Forces Inst., 1949; Plant Engineering, Supervision and Management Certificate, U. of CA, Los Angeles, 1976; Real Estate Exchanging Certificate, Orange Coast Coll., 1978. POLIT. & GOV.: hon. mayor of Mason, NV; civil defense dir., Lyon Cty., NV; candidate for Republican nomination to U.S. House (NV), 1956; applicant for appointment to gov. of American Samoa, 1975; ***candidate for Republican nomination to presidency of the U.S., 1980***. BUS. & PROF.: chief, real estate office in the Philippines, U.S. Army Corps of Engineers, 1950–55; pres., chief exec. officer, Mason Mercantile Co., Mason, NV, 1956–62; pres., chief exec. officer, Mason Water Co., 1956–62; pres., chief exec. officer, Petersen Enterprises (facilities engineering), 1962–79; installation mgr., Pacific Architects and Engineers, Inc., Los Angeles, CA, and South Vietnam, 1969–71, Saudi Arabia, 1979–; building engineer, Purex Co., Inc., Lakewood, CA, 1975–79; pres., chief exec. officer, Vernon L. Petersen, Inc., Downey, CA, 1980–. MIL.: sgt., U.S. Army, 1944–47. MEM.: S.A.M.E. (life member; fellow); American Inst. of Plant Engineers; Orange Cty. Engineering Council (pres., 1978–79); American Legion (pres., China Post #1 in Exile). AWARDS: "Engineer of the Year," *Orange County (CA) Post*, S.A.M.E., 1977; Engineer Merit Award, Chapter 38, American Inst. of Plant Engineers, 1977–78. REL.: Church of Jesus Christ of Latter-Day Saints. MAILING ADDRESS: 10506 Western, Downey, CA 90241.

PETERSON, KIM. POLIT. & GOV.: ***independent candidate for presidency of the U.S., 1992***. MISC.: write-in candidate in GA. MAILING ADDRESS: unknown.

PETERSON, LOIS. POLIT. & GOV.: ***candidate for Populist Party nomination to vice presidency of the U.S., 1984***. BUS. & PROF.: activist. MEM.: Liberty Lobby (dir.). MAILING ADDRESS: c/o Liberty Lobby, 300 Independence Ave., S.E., Washington, DC 20003.

PETRONELLA, BOB. POLIT. & GOV.: ***independent candidate for vice presidency of the U.S., 1972***. MAILING ADDRESS: unknown.

PEYTON, DAVID WESLEY. POLIT. & GOV.: ***independent candidate for presidency of the U.S., 1984***. MAILING ADDRESS: 208 Elm Wood Court, Los Gatos, CA 95030.

PHELPS, JOHN SMITH. b. Dec 22, 1814, Simsbury, CT; d. Nov 20, 1886, St. Louis, MO; par. Elisha and Lucy (Smith) Phelps; m. Mary Whitney, Apr 30, 1837; c. five. EDUC.: grad., Trinity Coll., 1832; A.B., Washington Coll., 1859 (as member of class of 1832); studied law under Elisha Phelps. POLIT. & GOV.: elected as a Democrat to MO State House, 1840; elected as a Democrat to U.S. House (MO), 1845–63; delegate, Dem. Nat'l. Conv., 1856; appointed military gov. of AR, 1862–65; ***candidate for Democratic nomination to vice presidency of the U.S., 1864***; delegate, National Union Convention, 1866; Democratic candidate for gov. of MO, 1868; elected as a Democrat to gov. of MO, 1877–81. BUS. & PROF.: atty.; admitted to CT Bar, 1835; law practice, Simsbury, CT, 1835–37; law practice, Springfield, MO, 1837; law practice, St. Louis, MO. MIL.: brigade inspector, MO Militia, 1841; organizer, Phelps Regt., MO Volunteers, 1861; pvt., capt., Coleman's MO Infantry; lt. col., U.S.V., 1861, col., 1861, brig. gen., 1862. RES.: Springfield, MO.

PHELPS, JOHN WOLCOTT. b. Nov 13, 1813, Guilford, VT; d. Feb 2, 1885, Guilford, VT; par. Judge John and Lucy (Lovell) Phelps; m. Mrs. Anna B. Davis, 1883; c. John. EDUC.: grad., U.S. Military Acad., 1836. POLIT. & GOV.: delegate, American National Party National Convention, 1876; ***American Party candidate for presidency of the U.S., 1880***. BUS. & PROF.: soldier; author; journalist, Brattleboro, VT, 1859–61. MIL.: 2d lt., Fourth Artillery, 1836, 1st lt., 1838, brev. capt., 1847 (declined), capt., 1850, resigned, 1859; appointed col., First VT Volunteers, 1861, brig. gen. of Volunteers, May 17, 1861, resigned Aug 21, 1862; offered appointment as maj. gen., U.S. Army (declined); engaged in Florida Indian Wars, 1836–39; organized first Negro troops at camp near New Orleans, for which Confederate government declared him an outlaw, 1862. MEM.: National Christian Assn.; VT Hist. Soc. (vice pres., 1863–85); VT Teachers' Assn. (vice pres., 1865–85). WRITINGS: *History of Secret Societies and of the Republican Party of France From 1830–1848* (1856); *Sibylline Leaves* (1858); *Cradle of Rebellions* (translator, 1864); *Secret Societies, Ancient and Modern* (1873); *Good Behavior* (1880); *First Class Reader for District Schools; The Island of Madagascar* (1883); *History of Madagascar* (1884); *The Local History of Guilford, Vermont, 1754–1888* (1888); *The Fables of Florian* (translator, 1888). RES.: Brattleboro, VT.

PHELPS, WILLIAM WALTER. b. Aug 24, 1839, New York, NY; d. Jun 17, 1894, Englewood, NJ; par. John Jay and Rachel Badgerly (Phinney) Phelps; m. Ellen Maria Sheffield, Jun 26, 1860; c. John J.; Sheffield; Marion (Mrs. Franz von Rottenburg). EDUC.: Mount Washington Inst.; grad., Yale U., 1860; LL.B. (valedictorian), Columbia U., 1863. POLIT. & GOV.: appointed judge, Sixth District Court of NY, c. 1870 (declined); elected as a Republican to U.S. House (NJ), 1873–75, 1883–89; Republican candidate for U.S. House (NJ), 1874; candidate for Republican nomination to gov. of NJ, 1877; delegate, Rep. Nat'l. Conv., 1880, 1884; appointed U.S. minister to Austria-Hungary, 1881–82; ***candidate for Republican nomination to presidency of the U.S., 1888; candidate for Republican nomination to vice presidency of the U.S., 1888***; appointed U.S. commissioner, International Conference on the Samoan

Question, 1889; appointed U.S. minister to Germany, 1889–93; appointed judge, NJ Court of Error and Appeals, 1893–94; delegate, NJ State Constitutional Convention, 1894. BUS. & PROF.: atty.; admitted to NY Bar, 1863; law practice, New York, 1863–68; banker, New York; dir., National City Bank; dir., The Second National Bank; dir., U.S. Trust Co.; dir., Farmers Loan and Trust Co.; dir., Delaware, Lackawanna and Western R.R.; dir., Oswego and Syracuse R.R.; dir., Syracuse and Binghamton R.R.; dir., Cayuga and Susquehanna R.R.; dir., Texas International; dir., Houston and Great Northern R.R.; dir., New Haven and Northampton R.R.; dir., Morris and Essex R.R.; corporate counsel. MEM.: Yale U. (trustee, 1872–92); New York C. of C. (hon.); Smithsonian Institution (regent); Union League; University Club; Columbia Law School Alumni Assn. (pres.); Century Club; Downtown Club; American Museum of Natural History; New England Soc.; Yale Alumni Assn. (vice pres.). HON. DEG.: LL.D., Rutgers U., 1889; LL.D., Yale U., 1890. RES.: Teaneck, NJ.

PHEROMONE, JIMMY. POLIT. & GOV.: ***independent candidate for presidency of the U.S., 1988***. MAILING ADDRESS: 3750 University Blvd., #101, Kensington, MD 20895.

PHILIPP, EMANUEL LORENZ. b. Mar 25, 1861, Sauk Cty., WI; d. Jun 15, 1925, Milwaukee, WI; par. Luzi and Sabina (Ludwig) Philipp; m. Bertha Schweke, Oct 27, 1887; c. Florence I.; Cyrus L.; Josephine. EDUC.: grad., Sauk Cty. (WI) H.S. POLIT. & GOV.: chm., Milwaukee Cty. (WI) Republican Convention, 1900; member, Rep. Nat'l. Cmte., 1908; police commissioner, Milwaukee, WI, 1909–14; elected as a Republican to gov. of WI, 1915–21; ***candidate for Republican nomination to presidency of the U.S., 1920***. BUS. & PROF.: schoolteacher; railroad telegrapher, Baraboo, WI, 1880; exec., Gould System Lines, 1889–1902; exec., Schlitz Brewing Co.; mgr., lumber company, MS, 1894–1902; founder, Union Refrigerator Transit Co. of Wisconsin, 1903; dir., Chicago, Milwaukee and St. Paul R.R. MEM.: Marquette U. (trustee); WI Humane Soc.; Masons; Milwaukee Commerce Assn. (pres., 1923); Milwaukee Club; Wisconsin Club. WRITINGS: *The Truth About Wisconsin Freight Rates* (1904); *Political Reform in Wisconsin* (1910). REL.: Lutheran. RES.: Milwaukee, WI.

PHILLIPS, BRUCE V. "U. UTAH." b. 1935, Cleveland, OH; m. Sheila Collins. POLIT. & GOV.: Peace and Freedom Party candidate for U.S. Senate (UT), 1968; ***Sloth and Indolence Party candidate for presidency of the U.S., 1976, 1980***. BUS. & PROF.: employee, road gang, Yellowstone National Park, 1950; dishwasher; printer; warehouseman; archivist; operator, Joe Hill House, Salt Lake City, UT; composer; singer; union organizer; guitarist; poet; truck farmer, Spokane, WA, 1974–. MIL.: U.S. Army, Korea, 1956–59. MEM.: Poor People's Party; International Workers of the World. WRITINGS: *Starlight on the Rails and Other Songs* (1973); *Good Though!* (record); *Welcome to Coffee Lena* (record); *El Capitan* (record). MISC.: known as "The Golden Voice of the Southwest." MAILING ADDRESS: 1720 West 14th, Spokane, WA 99204.

PHILLIPS, CALVIN E., SR. POLIT. & GOV.: ***independent candidate for presidency of the U.S., 1992***. MAILING ADDRESS: 471 Noah Ave., Akron, OH 44320.

PHILLIPS, CHANNING EMERY. b. Mar 23, 1928, Brooklyn, NY; d. Nov 11, 1987, New York, NY; par. Porter W. and Dorothy A. (Fletcher) Phillips; m. Jane Celeste Nabors, Dec 22, 1956; c. Channing Durward; Sheilah Nahketah; Tracy Jane; Jill Celeste; John Emery. EDUC.: U. of UT, 1945–46; A.B. (magna cum laude), VA Union U., 1950; M.Div., Colgate Rochester Divinity School, 1953; Drew U., 1953–56. POLIT. & GOV.: delegate, Dem. Nat'l. Conv., 1968, 1972; ***candidate for Democratic nomination to presidency of the U.S., 1968***; member, Dem. Nat'l. Cmte., 1968–72; candidate for Democratic nomination to delegate, U.S. House (DC), 1970; Congressional Liaison Officer, National Endowment for the Humanities, 1978–82. BUS. & PROF.: ordained minister, United Church of Christ, 1952; instructor, Howard U., 1956–58; minister, Grace Congregational Church, Harlem, NY, 1958–59; minister, Haynes Congregational Church, South Ozone Park, Long Island, NY, 1959–61; senior minister, Lincoln Temple, Washington, DC, 1961–70; pres., Housing Development Corp., 1967–74; vice pres., VA Union U., 1974–75; lecturer; minister of planning and coordination, Riverside Church, New York, NY, 1982–87. MIL.: pvt., sgt., U.S.A.A.F., 1946–47. MEM.: A.C.L.U. (adviser); Southern Election Fund (dir.); International City Management Assn.; Alpha Phi Alpha; Alpha Kappa Mu; Center for Community Change (dir.). AWARDS: Man of the Year, Potomac Chapter, National Assn. of Housing and Redevelopment Officials; Top Hat Award, *Pittsburgh (PA) Courier*, 1968. HON. DEG.: D.D., Pacific School of Religion; D.D., Mary Holmes Coll.; L.H.D., Elmhurst Coll. WRITINGS: "Urban Crisis: The Challenge of Black Power," in *Black Politician: His Struggle for Power*; *Church Related Colleges and the Black Student* (1970); "Unity," in *Earth Day—The Beginning* (1970). REL.: United Church of Christ. RES.: Washington, DC.

PHILLIPS, HOWARD. b. Feb 3, 1941; m. Peggy Phillips; c. Doug; Amanda; Brad; Jenny; Alexandra; Sam. EDUC.: grad., Boston Latin School, 1958; grad., Harvard U., 1962. POLIT. & GOV.: chm., Boston (MA) Republican Party, 1964; asst. to the chm., Rep. Nat'l. Cmte., 1966–68; appointed chm., President's Council on Youth Opportunity; chm., "Opportunities Unlimited Program," Rep. Nat'l. Cmte.; appointed dir., U.S. Office of Economic Opportunity, Washington, DC, to 1973; ***candidate for Republican nomination to presidency of the U.S., 1992; U.S. Taxpayers (American Independent; Illinois Taxpayers; Tisch Independent Citizens) Party candidate for presi-***

dency of the U.S., 1992. BUS. & PROF.: assn. exec.; ed., *Issues and Strategy Bulletin*; owner, Policy Analysis, Inc.; consultant. MEM.: Harvard Student Council (pres.); U.S. Taxpayers Alliance (chm.); Council for National Policy (exec. cmte.); National Constitutional Center (dir.); Tax Policy Inst. (pres.); The Conservative Caucus (chm., 1974–). WRITINGS: *The Next Four Years: A Vision of Victory*. MAILING ADDRESS: 9520 Bent Creek Lane, Vienna, VA 32182.

PHILLIPS, JOHN. POLIT. & GOV.: ***candidate for Democratic nomination to presidency of the U.S., 1992***. MAILING ADDRESS: 604 East Capitol St., N.E., Washington, DC 20003.

PHILLIPS, WENDELL. b. Nov 29, 1811, Boston, MA; d. Feb 2, 1884, Boston, MA; par. John and Sarah (Walley) Phillips; m. Ann Terry Greene, Oct 12, 1837; c. Phoebe Garnaut (adopted). EDUC.: Boston Latin School; grad., Harvard U., 1831, LL.B., 1833; studied law under Thomas Hopkinson, Lowell, MA. POLIT. & GOV.: candidate for gov. of MA, 1841; Labor Reform–Prohibition Party candidate for gov. of MA, 1870; chm., Labor Reform Party National Convention, 1871; ***candidate for Labor Reform Party nomination to presidency of the U.S., 1872; candidate for Equal Rights (Cosmic, Free Love, People's) Party nomination to vice presidency of the U.S., 1872***; Labor Reform Party candidate for gov. of MA, 1875; Labor Reform–Greenback–Workingmen's Party candidate for gov. of MA, 1877; candidate for U.S. House (MA), 1882. BUS. & PROF.: atty.; admitted to Suffolk Cty. (MA) Bar, 1834; law practice, Boston, MA, 1834–39; contributor, *Anti-Slavery Standard*; contributor, *Liberator*; abolitionist; reformer; author. MEM.: MA Anti-Slavery Soc., 1837; World's Anti-Slavery Convention (delegate, 1840); American Anti-Slavery Soc. (pres., 1865–70); Vigilance Cmte.; Hasty Pudding Club; Porcellian Club (pres.); Gentlemen's Club; Harvard Washington Corps; Owls. WRITINGS: *Can Abolitionists Vote or Take Office Under the Constitution?* (1845); *Review of Lysander Spooner's Essays on the Constitutionality of Slavery* (1847); *Review of Webster's 7th of March Speech* (1850); *Vindication of the Course Pursued by the American Abolitionists* (1853); *The Constitution: A Pro-Slavery Compact* (1856); *Argument Against Repeal of the Personal Liberty Law* (1861); *The Immediate Issue* (1865); *Remarks at a Mass Meeting of Workingmen at Faneuil Hall* (1865); *The People Coming to Power* (1871); *Who Shall Rule Us? Money or the People?* (1878); *Speeches, Lectures and Letters* (1894). REL.: Calvinist. RES.: Boston, MA.

PICKETT, CARL LEON. b. Oct 28, 1926, Houston, TX; m. Theresa E. Pickett; c. one. EDUC.: U. of Houston, 1968. POLIT. & GOV.: candidate for Republican nomination to gov. of TX, 1972; ***independent Republican candidate for presidency of the U.S., 1980***; Republican candidate for U.S. House (TX), 1982. BUS. & PROF.: publisher, ed., *The Pickett Line*; field salesman; investment broker; real estate broker. MIL.: U.S. Army, 3 years. MEM.: Citizens Against National Nuclear Overkill Technology (dir.); Houston Solar Energy Soc. (founder). MAILING ADDRESS: 221-223 Aurora, Houston, TX 77008.

PICKETT, LEANDER LYCURGUS. b. 1859; d. May 9, 1928, Middleboro, KY; m. Millie Dorough; m. 2d, Ludie Day; c. Elbert Deets. POLIT. & GOV.: Prohibition Party candidate for gov. of KY, 1907, 1915; state chm., KY Prohibition Party, 1908; delegate, Prohibition Party National Convention, 1916; delegate, American Party National Convention, 1916; ***American Party candidate for vice presidency of the U.S., 1924***; member, Prohibition Party National Cmte., 1924–28. BUS. & PROF.: minister, Southern Methodist Church; evangelist; hymn writer; owner, Pickett Publishing Co., Louisville, KY; author. MEM.: International Purity Congress (1907); American Federation of Patriotic Societies (first vice pres., 1916). WRITINGS: *St. Paul on Holiness* (1888); *Why I Do Not Immerse* (1887); *The Holy Day* (1888); *The Book and Its Theme* (1890); *The Danger Signal* (1890); *Leaves From the Tree of Life* (1891); *Our King Cometh* (1896); *A Plea for the Present Holiness Movement* (1896); *The Pickett-Smith Debate* (1897); *Gems* (1900); *Careful Cullings for Children* (1903); *The Blessed Hope of His Glorious Returning* (1901); *The Renewed Earth* (1903); *Gems #2* (1904); *My Gatling Gun* (1907); *Cheerful Songs: Songs and Sayings for You* (1911); *Tears and Triumphs; The Booze Devil and How to Kill Him* (1914); *Victorious Sons* (1915); *Uncle Sam, or the Pope—Which?* (1916); *Who Is the Beast?* (1919); *Irish Home Rule* (1920); *Postmillennialism and the Higher Critics* (with Andrew Johnson, q.v., 1923); *Die "Rum" Frage* (19–); *The "Catholic Church" and the Ku Klux Klan* (1924); *Why I am a Premillennialist* (1927); *The Sabbath Day; A Shot at the Foe; The Anti-Christ and some Mistakes Concerning Him* (1928); *Blessed Fruit; The Millennium and Related Events*. REL.: Southern Methodist. MISC.: noted anti-evolutionist. RES.: Wilmore, KY.

PIERCE, FRANKLIN. b. Nov 23, 1804, Hillsborough, NH; d. Oct 8, 1869, Concord, NH; par. Benjamin and Anna (Kendrick) Pierce; m. Jane Means Appleton, Nov 18, 1834; c. Franklin; Frank Robert; Benjamin. EDUC.: Hancock Acad., 1818; Francetown Acad., 1819; B.A., Bowdoin Coll., 1824; studied law under John Burnham, 1824; studied law under Levi Woodbury, 1825; studied law under Edmund Parker. POLIT. & GOV.: appointed justice of the peace, Hillsborough, NH, 1829; elected as a Democrat to NH State House, 1829–33 (Speaker, 1832–33); elected as a Democrat to U.S. House (NH), 1833–37; elected as a Democrat to U.S. Senate (NH), 1837–42; leader, NH Democratic Party, 1842–47; appointed as a Democrat to U.S. Senate (NH), 1845 (declined); Democratic candidate for gov. of NH, 1845 (declined), 1848 (declined); appointed atty. gen. of the U.S., 1845 (declined); appointed member, U.S. Armistice Comm., 1847; pres., NH State Constitutional Convention, 1850; ***elected as a Democrat to presidency of the U.S.,***

1853–1857; candidate for Democratic nomination to presidency of the U.S., 1856, 1860. BUS. & PROF.: atty.; admitted to Hillsborough Cty. (NH) Bar, 1827; law practice, Hillsborough, NH, 1827–42; law practice, Concord, NH, 1842–46. MIL.: pvt., commissioned col., 9th Regt., NH Infantry, 1847; appointed brig. gen., U.S.V., 1847, resigned, 1848; served in Battle of Contreras and Battle of Churubusco. MEM.: Phi Beta Kappa. REL.: Episc. MISC.: toured Europe, 1857–60; noted for Gadsden Purchase, 1853; attempted to purchase Cuba, 1854. RES.: Concord, NH.

PIERCE, GRACE WAGNER. b. May 9, 1926, Coatesville, PA; par. Jacob Heinly and Grace Anne Thompson (Wallace) Wagner; m. Willard Lemar Pierce, Dec 15, 1945; c. Linda Dolan; Barry Wallace Clark; Susan Butler Gottfried. EDUC.: Goldey Coll., 1944; Wesley Junior Coll., 1970, 1973; studied art under Howard Schroder, Loren Kohut and Lon Fluman. POLIT. & GOV.: Republican committeewoman, 29th District, Kent Cty., DE, 1966–69; chm. of volunteers, Kent Cty. Republican Central Cmte., 1968; delegate, Rep. Nat'l. Conv., 1968; program chm., DE Federation of Republican Women, 1969–72; vice chm., Kent Cty. Republican Central Cmte., 1969–72, vice chm. of Education Cmte., 1973–; pres., DE Federation of Republican Women, 1970–72; chm., Kent Cty. Campaign for R. W. Peterson for Governor, 1972; Republican committeewomen, 31st District, Kent Cty., 1973–; Republican candidate for DE State House, 1974; appointed member, DE Water Quality Awareness Cmte., 1975–80; national environmental dir., National Unity Party Campaign, 1980; treas., City Council of Slaughter Beach, DE, 1981–; ***National Unity Party of KY candidate for vice presidency of the U.S., 1984***. BUS. & PROF.: owner, Pierce's Pharmacy, Inc., Dover, DE, 1962–; national issues specialist, Wilderness Soc., Washington, DC, 1975–78. MEM.: DE Audubon Soc. (dir., 1981–; vice pres., 1983; pres., 1984); Cmte. to Study Hazardous Waste Dump Sites in DE; Rehoboth Art League; Kent General Hospital (pres., Junior Board, 1960–62); Watch Our Waterways (chm., 1978– 80); East Coast Environmental Leadership Conference (chm., 1974); DE Technical and Community Coll. Board of Directors (Women's Study Cmte.); Delawareans for Orderly Development. REL.: Presb. MAILING ADDRESS: 535 American Ave., Dover, DE 19901.

PIERCE, PAULINE ELIZABETH. POLIT. & GOV.: ***candidate for Democratic nomination to presidency of the U.S., 1980***. MAILING ADDRESS: 760 Triton Rd., Atlantic Beach, FL 32233.

PIERRE, JEAN. POLIT. & GOV.: ***independent candidate for presidency of the U.S., 1964***. BUS. & PROF.: artist. MAILING ADDRESS: 2132 Oakes, Everett, WA 98201.

PIG, PIGASUS J. b. 1963 or 1964, MT; m. Piggy Wiggy. EDUC.: studied law for 3 years (by candlelight). POLIT. & GOV.: ***Youth International Party candidate for presidency of the U.S., 1968 (satire effort)***. MISC.: described as a "20-pound pig," "squirming, squealing." REL.: R.C./Protestant/Jew. MAILING ADDRESS: Youth International Party, 32 Union Square East, New York, NY.

PILES, SAMUEL HENRY. b. Dec 28, 1858, Smithland, KY; d. Mar 11, 1940, Los Angeles, CA; par. Samuel Henry and Gabrielle (Lillard) Piles; m. Mary E. Barnard, Sep 15, 1891; c. Ross Barnard; Ruth Lillard (Mrs. William McCausland, Jr.); Samuel Henry, Jr. EDUC.: private schools; studied law. POLIT. & GOV.: asst. prosecuting atty., Third Judicial District, Territory of WA, 1887–89; city atty., Seattle, WA, 1888–89; delegate, WA State Republican Convention, 1888–1940; elected as a Republican to U.S. Senate (WA), 1905–11; ***candidate for Republican nomination to vice presidency of the U.S., 1908***; appointed envoy extraordinary and minister plenipotentiary to Colombia, 1922–28. BUS. & PROF.: atty.; admitted to WA Bar; law practice, Snohomish, WA, 1883–86; law practice, Spokane, WA, 1886; law practice, Seattle, WA, 1886; partner, Piles, Donworth, Howe and Farrell (law firm), Seattle; gen. counsel, Pacific Coast Co., 1895–1905. MEM.: Rainier Club. RES.: Seattle, WA.

PILLOW, GIDEON JOHNSON. b. Jun 8, 1806, Williamson Cty., TN; d. Oct 8, 1878, Helena, AR; par. Gideon and Anne (Payne) Pillow; m. Mary Martin; c. Mrs. Thomas J. Brown; Mrs. John D. Mitchell; Mrs. Wilbur F. Johnson; Mrs. F. Wade; Mrs. Melville Williams; Mrs. Landon C. Haynes; Mrs. D. G. Fargason; Robert G.; George; Gideon. EDUC.: grad., U. of Nashville, 1827; studied law under Judge W. E. Kennedy and William L. Brown. POLIT. & GOV.: delegate, Dem. Nat'l. Conv., 1844; member, Southern Convention, 1850; ***candidate for Democratic nomination to vice presidency of the U.S., 1852, 1856***. BUS. & PROF.: atty.; admitted to TN Bar; partner (with James Knox Polk, q.v.), law firm, Columbia, TN; farmer, TN; partner (with Isham G. Harris, q.v.), law firm, Memphis, TN, 1865–78. MIL.: appointed brig. gen., U.S.V., 1846, maj. gen., 1846; appointed senior maj. gen., Provisional Army of TN, 1861; brig. gen., C.S.A., 1861. RES.: Memphis, TN.

PINCHBACK, PINCKNEY BENTON. b. May 10, 1837, Macon, GA; d. Dec 21, 1921, Washington, DC; par. William Pinchback and Eliza Stewart; m. (unknown); m. 2d, Nina Emily Hawthorne, 1860; c. Pinckney Napoleon; Walter A.; Nina; two other sons; two other daughters. EDUC.: public schools, Cincinnati, OH; grad., Straight Coll., 1887. POLIT. & GOV.: delegate, LA Reconstruction Convention, 1868; delegate, Rep. Nat'l. Conv., 1868, 1872, 1876, 1880, 1884, 1888, 1892, 1896, 1900, 1904, 1908, 1912, 1916, 1920; elected as a Republican to LA State Senate, 1868–71; appointed dir., New Orleans (LA) Board of Education, 1871–77; elected as a Republican to lt. gov. of LA, 1871–72 (acting gov., 1872); Republican candidate for gov. of LA, 1872 (withdrew); elected as a Republican to

U.S. House (LA), 1872; elected as a Republican to U.S. Senate (LA), 1873 (election contested and Pinchback was not seated); delegate, LA State Constitutional Convention, 1879; appointed surveyor of customs, New Orleans, LA, 1882; ***Colored Party candidate for presidency of the U.S., 1892; candidate for National Liberty Party nomination to presidency of the U.S., 1904***. BUS. & PROF.: cabin boy; steward, river boats. MIL.: capt., Company A, Second LA Native Guards, Union Army, 1862–63. BUS. & PROF.: atty.; admitted to LA Bar, 1887. RES.: New Orleans, LA.

PINCHOT, GIFFORD. b. Aug 11, 1865, Simsbury, CT; d. Oct 4, 1946, New York, NY; par. James and Mary (Eno) Pinchot; m. Cornelia Elizabeth Bryce, Aug 15, 1914; c. Gifford Bryce. EDUC.: Phillips Exeter Acad.; B.A., Yale U., 1889; Ecole Nationale Forestiere. POLIT. & GOV.: appointed member, National Forest Comm., 1896; sec., Public Lands Comm., 1903; appointed member, Inland Waterways Comm.; appointed member, Country Life Comm.; appointed member, National Conservation Comm.; Republican candidate for U.S. Senate (PA), 1914; appointed member, U.S. Food Administration, 1917–19; appointed PA state forester, 1920; ***candidate for Republican nomination to presidency of the U.S., 1920, 1932, 1936***; elected as a Republican to gov. of PA, 1923–27, 1931–35; *candidate for American Party nomination to presidency of the U.S., 1924; candidate for Farmer-Labor Party nomination to presidency of the U.S., 1928 (declined); Coalition Party candidate for presidency of the U.S., 1928 (declined)*. BUS. & PROF.: forester; consulting forester, New York, NY, 1892; consulting forester, state of NJ, 1895–96; chief, forestry div., U.S. Dept. of Agriculture; chief forester, U.S. Forest Service; lecturer, Yale U., 1900–1903, nonresident prof. of forestry, 1903–36, prof. emeritus, 1936–46. MEM.: University Club of Philadelphia; City Club of Philadelphia; University Club of New York; Explorers Club; Century Club; Yale Club; Cosmos Club (pres., 1908); Yale-in-China (Council, 1926–30); Federal Council of Churches of Christ; Comm. for Relief in Belgium (1914–15); American Red Cross (incorporator); Soc. of American Foresters (pres., 1900–1908, 1910–11); National Conservation Assn. (chm., 1908–10, pres., 1910–25); Graduates Club of New Haven; AAAS (fellow); American Acad. of Political and Social Sciences (fellow); National Soc. of Sons and Daughters of the Pilgrims; American Forestry Assn.; Royal English Arboricultural Soc.; American Museum of Natural History; PA Acad. of Science; Washington (DC) Acad. of Science; Theodore Roosevelt Memorial Assn. AWARDS: Welfare Medal, National Acad. of Sciences, 1916; Roosevelt Medal, 1925; Sir William Schlick Forestry Medal, Soc. of American Foresters, 1940. HON. DEG.: M.A., Yale U., 1901, LL.D., 1925; M.A., Princeton U., 1904; Sc.D., MI Agricultural Coll., 1907; LL.D., McGill U., 1909; LL.D., PA Military Coll., 1923; LL.D., Temple U., 1931. WRITINGS: *Biltmore Forest* (1893); *The White Pine* (coauthor, 1896); *Timber Trees and Forests of North Carolina* (coauthor, 1897); *Adirondack Spruce* (1898); *Study of Forest Fires and Wood Production in Southern New Jersey* (1899); *A Primer of Forestry* (1899–1905); *Recommendations on Policy, Organization and Procedure for the Bureau of Forestry of the Philippine Islands* (1903); *Conservation of Natural Resources* (1908); *The Fight for Conservation* (1910); *Training of a Forester* (1914); *Six Thousand Country Churches* (coauthor, 1919); *The Forest: A Basic Resource* (1922); *Talks on Forestry* (1923); *The Power Monopoly: Its Make-Up and Its Menace* (1928); *To the South Seas* (1930); *Let's Go Fishing* (1931); *Just Fishing Talk* (1936); *Breaking New Ground* (1948). REL.: Episc. MISC.: noted as Progressive; negotiated settlement of anthracite coal strike, 1923. RES.: Milford, PA.

PINCKNEY, CHARLES COTESWORTH. b. Feb 25, 1746, Charleston, SC; d. Aug 16, 1825, Charleston, SC; par. Charles and Elizabeth "Eliza" (Lucas) Pinckney; m. Sarah "Sally" Middleton, Sep 28, 1773; m. 2d, Mary Stead, Jul 23, 1786; c. Charles Cotesworth; Eliza; Harriett; Maria Henrietta. EDUC.: Christ Church Coll., 1764. POLIT. & GOV.: member, SC Provincial Assembly, 1769, 1775; acting atty. gen., Camden, Georgetown, and the Cherows, SC, 1773; member, SC State House of Commons, 1778, 1782; pres., SC State Senate, 1779; delegate, U.S. Constitutional Convention, 1787; delegate, SC Ratification Convention, 1788; delegate, SC State Constitutional Convention, 1790; appointed U.S. minister to France, 1796–98 (French directory refused recognition of appointment); ***received 1 electoral vote for presidency of the U.S., 1796; Federalist candidate for presidency of the U.S., 1800, 1804, 1808; Federalist candidate for vice presidency of the U.S., 1800***. BUS. & PROF.: atty.; admitted to Middle Temple, 1764; admitted to English Bar, 1769; admitted to SC Bar, 1770. MIL.: capt., First Regt., SC Militia, 1775, col., 1776; prisoner of war, 1782; appointed brig. gen., Continental Army, 1783; appointed commander of U.S. Forces and Posts, South of MD, 1798. MEM.: Charleston Bible Soc. (pres., 1810); Soc. of the Cincinnati (pres.-gen., 1805–25); Charleston Library Soc. (vice pres., 1786–96; pres., 1796–1807); Charleston Jockey Club; Charleston Museum; SC Coll. (trustee). REL.: Episc. MISC.: precipitated "XYZ Affair" as negotiator in France. RES.: Charleston, SC.

PINCKNEY, THOMAS. b. Oct 23, 1750, Charleston, SC; d. Nov 2, 1828, Charleston, SC; par. Charles and Elizabeth (Lucas) Pinckney; m. Elizabeth Motte, Jul 22, 1779; m. 2d, Frances (Motte) Middleton, Oct 19, 1797; c. Thomas; Elizabeth (Mrs. William Lowndes); Harriet Lucas (Mrs. Francis K. Huger); Charles Cotesworth. EDUC.: grad., Oxford U.; French Military Coll.; studied at Middle Temple, London, England, 1768. POLIT. & GOV.: elected as a Federalist to gov. of SC, 1787–88; pres., SC Ratification Convention, 1788; elected as a Federalist to SC State House of Commons, 1791; appointed U.S. minister to England, 1791–95; appointed special U.S. commissioner to Spain, 1794–95; ***Federalist candidate for vice presidency of the U.S., 1796***; elected as a Federalist to U.S. House (SC), 1797–1801. BUS. & PROF.: atty.; admitted to English Bar, 1774; admitted to SC Bar, 1774; law practice, Charleston, SC. MIL.: capt., First Regt., SC Militia, 1775, maj., 1778; military aide to Count d'Estaing and Marquis de Lafayette; maj. gen., U.S.V., 1812. MEM.: Soc. of the Cincinnati (pres.-gen., 1825–28). MISC.: negotiated Treaty of San Lorenzo el Real (Pinckney Treaty), to determine southern boundary of the U.S. and navigational rights on the Mississippi River, 1795; negotiated Treaty of Fort Jackson with Creek Indian Nation, 1814. RES.: Charleston, SC.

PIRMAN, ANTON. POLIT. & GOV.: ***Commonwealth Party of the U.S. candidate for presidency of the U.S., 1976***. MAILING ADDRESS: 5465 West Division, Chicago, IL 60651.

PIRTLE, PHILIP ANDREW. POLIT. & GOV.: ***independent candidate for presidency of the U.S., 1992***. MAILING ADDRESS: c/o Dmitri Kubbs (q.v.), 741 South Mattis, Champaign, IL 61821.

PITTMAN, KEY H. b. Sep 19, 1872, Vicksburg, MS; d. Nov 10, 1940, Reno, NV; par. William Buckner and Catherine (Key) Pittman; m. Mimosa Nigella June Gates, Jul 8, 1900; c. none. EDUC.: Southwestern Presbyterian U., 1890; studied law under James Hamilton Lewis (q.v.) POLIT. & GOV.: organizer, "Consent" Government, Nome, AK, 1899; district atty., Nome, AK, 1899; appointed NV commissioner, St. Louis Exposition, 1904; appointed NV commissioner, Lewis and Clark Exposition, 1905; appointed NV commissioner, National Irrigation Congress, 1907; Democratic candidate for U.S. Senate (NV), 1910; elected as a Democrat to U.S. Senate (NV), 1913–40 (pres. pro tempore, 1933–40); sec., Democratic Senate Caucus, 1913–17; member, Dem. Nat'l. Cmte. (NV); delegate, chm., Platform Cmte., Dem. Nat'l. Conv., 1924, 1928; ***candidate for Democratic nomination to vice presidency of the U.S., 1924***; U.S. delegate, World Economic Conference, 1933. BUS. & PROF.: atty.; admitted to bar, 1892; law practice, Seattle, WA, 1892–97; gold miner, Klondike, AK, 1897–99; law practice, Nome, AK; law practice, Tonapah, NV, 1902–40; counsel, Anti-Corruption Agitators, Dawson, AK; counsel, Alaskan Gold Miners, 1901. MEM.: Masons (32°); Sigma Alpha Epsilon; Elks; Chevy Chase Club; University Club; Army and Navy Club (hon.); National Press Club; Jefferson Island Club. HON. DEG.: LL.D., Southwestern Presbyterian U., 1919; LL.D., George Washington U., 1921; LL.D., U. of NV, 1937. REL.: Episc. RES.: Tonapah, NV.

PIZZO, CECILIA M. POLIT. & GOV.: candidate for Democratic nomination to gov. of LA, 1975; candidate for mayor of New Orleans, LA, 19??; ***American People's Party candidate for presidency of the U.S., 1976, 1980***. MISC.: filed suit in federal court challenging Louisiana Purchase and claiming LA still belongs to Spain, 1976; waged campaign against pigeons on public buildings in New Orleans, LA, 1979. MAILING ADDRESS: 3720 Baudin, New Orleans, LA.

PLUNKETT, MICHAEL OLIVER. b. May 27, 1940, Providence, RI; par. Thomas Oliver and Margaret Agnes (Dolan) Plunkett; single. EDUC.: B.S., Auburn U., 1963; J.D., FL Law School, 1966. POLIT. & GOV.: staff atty., FL State Senate, 1967; appointed asst. atty. gen. of FL, 1967–69; public defender, 1969; Democratic candidate for U.S. House (FL), 1972, 1983, 1984; ***candidate for Democratic nomination to presidency of the U.S., 1984***. BUS. & PROF.: atty. MEM.: FL Bar Assn. REL.: none (nee R.C.). MAILING ADDRESS: 2127 Essex, Berkeley, CA 94705.

POFF, RICHARD HARDING. b. Oct 19, 1923, Radford, VA; par. Beecher David and Irene Louise (Nunley) Poff; m. Jo Ann R. Topper, Jun 24, 1945; c. Rebecca Topper; Thomas Randolph; Richard Harding, Jr. EDUC.: Roanoke Coll.; LL.B., U. of VA, 1948. POLIT. & GOV.: elected as a Republican to U.S. House (VA), 1953–72; ***candidate for Republican nomination to vice presidency of the U.S., 1960***; delegate, Rep. Nat'l. Conv., 1968; vice chm., National Comm. on Reform of Federal Crime Laws; chm., Republican Task Force on Crime; sec., Republican Conference; elected justice, Supreme Court of VA, 1972–. BUS. & PROF.: atty.; admitted to VA Bar, 1947; law practice, Radford, VA, 1948; partner, Dalton, Poff, Turk and Stone (law firm), Radford, 1949–70. MIL.: pilot, U.S.A.A.C., 1943–45; Distinguished Flying Cross; Special Presidential Unit Citation. MEM.: ABA; VA Bar Assn.; American Jud. Soc.; VFW; American Legion; Pi Kappa Phi; Sigma Nu Phi; Masons; Moose; Lions. AWARDS: VA, "Outstanding Young Man of the Year," Junior C. of C., 1954; National Collegiate Athletic Assn. Award, 1966; Roanoke Coll. Medal, 1967; Legislative Citation, Assn. of Federal Investigators, 1969; Thomas Jefferson Public Sesquicentennial Award, U. of VA, 1969; Distinguished Virginian Award, VA District Exchange Clubs, 1970; Presidential Certificate of Appreciation, 1971; Japanese American Citizens League Award, 1972. HON. DEG.: LL.D., Roanoke Coll., 1969. REL.: Presb. MAILING ADDRESS: 2910 West Brigstock Rd., Midlothian, VA 23113.

POINDEXTER, MILES. b. Apr 22, 1868, Memphis, TN; d. Sep 21, 1946, Greenlee, VA; par. William Bowyer and Josephine Alexander (Anderson) Poindexter; m. Elizabeth Gale Page, Jun 16, 1892; m. 2d, Mrs. Elinor Jackson (Junkin) Latane, Aug 27, 1926; c. Gale Aylett. EDUC.: Fancy Hill Acad.; LL.B., Washington and Lee U., 1891. POLIT. & GOV.: elected prosecuting atty., Walla Walla Cty., WA, 1892; asst. prosecuting atty., Spokane Cty., WA, 1898–1904; judge, Superior Court of WA, 1904–08; elected as a Republican to U.S. House (WA), 1909–11; elected as a Republican to U.S. Senate (WA), 1911–23; ***candidate for Republican nomination to presidency of the U.S., 1920***; chm., Republican Senatorial Campaign Cmte., 1920–21; Republican candidate for U.S. Senate (WA), 1922, 1928; appointed U.S. ambassador to Peru, 1923–28. BUS. & PROF.: atty.; admitted to WA Bar, 1891; law practice, Walla Walla, WA, 1891–97; law practice, Spokane, WA, 1897–1923; law practice,

Washington, DC, 1929–46. MEM.: Geographical Soc. of Lima, Peru (hon.); American Ethnological Soc.; AAAS; American Geographical Soc. (fellow); Royal Geographical Soc. (fellow); Phi Beta Kappa; Order of El Sol de'el Peru. AWARDS: Gold Medal, Lima, Peru, 1923, 1924. HON. DEG.: LL.D., George Washington U., 1919. WRITINGS: *Ayar-Incas* (1930); *Peruvian Pharoahs* (1938). REL.: Presb. RES.: Spokane, WA.

POINTER, ROBERT R. b. 1862, Eaton Cty., MI; d. Feb 11, 1937, West Branch, MI; m. Anna Pointer; c. Etta (Mrs. A. R. Babcock); Russell; Robert S.; John. POLIT. & GOV.: deputy sheriff, Wayne Cty., MI; deputy sheriff, Ogemaw Cty., MI; pres., Ford for President Clubs, Dearborn, MI, 1924; ***People's Progressive Party candidate for presidency of the U.S., 1924***; candidate for Republican nomination to gov. of MI, 1928 (withdrew); People's Progressive Party candidate for gov. of MI, 1932, 1934. BUS. & PROF.: insurance broker; real estate broker; farmer, West Branch, MI; lumberman, 1900–1905. MEM.: West Branch (MI) C. of C. (pres.). RES.: West Branch, MI.

POKINES, JAY KEVIN. b. Dec 19, 1953, Bennington, VT; par. Walter Anthony and Meryle Hazel (Minor) Pokines; single. EDUC.: grad., Hoosick Falls (NY) H.S., 1972; Hudson Valley Community Coll. POLIT. & GOV.: ***independent candidate for presidency of the U.S., 1988***. BUS. & PROF.: retail worker, Old Faithful Lodge, Yellowstone National Park, 1986–89. MEM.: Hoosick Township Hist. Soc. (dir.). REL.: no preference. MAILING ADDRESS: 48 Abbott St., Hoosick Falls, NY 12090.

POLAND, HAROLD LAWRENCE. b. Jan 15, 1955, Washington, DC; par. Harold Davis and Leatha Ruth (Case) Poland; single. EDUC.: G.E.D., 1973; Business Management Diploma, La Salle Extension U., 1976; D.D., CA Church of the Gospel Ministry, 1977; D.D., Church of the God Within; Doctor of Metaphysics, Universal Life Church; Doctor of Universal Life, Universal Life Church; D.D.; D.Litt and Phil. POLIT. & GOV.: ***Independent Democratic candidate for presidency of the U.S., 1980***; candidate for Democratic nomination to U.S. House (VA), 1982; ***Christian Charity Federalist Independent Democratic Party candidate for presidency of the U.S., 1980, 1984, 1988, 1992***; candidate for Democratic nomination to U.S. Senate (VA), 1986; ***candidate for Democratic nomination to presidency of the U.S., 1992***. BUS. & PROF.: unemployed; minister, archbishop, cardinal, saint, Universal Life Church, Modesto, CA, 1981; minister, Church of the God Within, Miami, FL; minister, Church of Gospel Ministry, Chula Vista, CA, 1977; minister, Fonthill Abbey, Church of the Gospel Ministry; bishop, Church of the Holy Light, 1980–. MEM.: Moral Majority; Mt. Vernon Social Center; National Right-to-Life Cmte.; People for the American Way; Bronze Medal Club; Special Olympics. WRITINGS: *Rorkes Drift 1879* (1977); *Wellington's Victories; Clive at Plessey*. REL.: Protestant (Disciples of Christ; Church of Jesus Christ of Latter-Day Saints; United Methodist; Baptist; Universal Life Church). MAILING ADDRESS: 108 East Linden St., Alexandria, VA 22301.

POLING, DANIEL ALFRED. b. Nov 30, 1884, Portland, OR; d. Feb 7, 1968, Philadelphia, PA; par. Charles C. and Savilla (Kring) Poling; m. Susan Jane Vandersall, Sep 25, 1906; m. 2d, Lillian Diebold Heingartner, Aug 11, 1919; c. Clark Vandersall; Elizabeth Jane; Daniel Kring; Mary Savilla (Mrs. Lyman Philip Wood); Treva Mabel (Mrs. Philip Howard Roy); Joan Brommage (adopted; Mrs. Reid Malcolm); Rachel (adopted; Mrs. William Gardner Van Note); Ann Louise (adopted). EDUC.: A.B., Dallas (OR) Coll., 1904, A.M., 1906; Lafayette Seminary; OH State U., 1907–09. POLIT. & GOV.: delegate, Prohibition Party National Convention, 1904, 1908, 1912, 1916 (temporary chm.); Prohibition Party candidate for U.S. House (OH), 1908; Prohibition Party candidate for gov. of OH, 1912; member, Prohibition Party National Cmte., 1916–20; ***candidate for Prohibition Party nomination to presidency of the U.S., 1920, 1928; candidate for Democratic nomination to presidency of the U.S., 1928***. BUS. & PROF.: minister; ordained minister, Reformed Church in America, 1908; pastor, Marble Collegiate Reformed Church, New York, NY, 1922–30; contributing ed., *Christian Endeavor World*, 1926–66; ed., *Christian Herald*, 1926–66; pastor, Baptist Temple, Philadelphia, PA, 1936–48; chaplain, Chapel of Four Chaplains, 1948; incorporator, Presbyterian Ministers Life Insurance Fund. MIL.: maj., Chaplain Officers, Reserves. MEM.: World's Christian Endeavor Union (hon. life pres.); Bucknell U. (trustee); General War-Time Comm. of the Churches; American Legion; Military Order of Foreign Wars; Newcomen Soc.; Masons (32°); National Press Club; Overseas Press Club; Union League; Greater New York Federation of Churches (pres., 1926–27); Federal Council of Churches of Christ (member, Temperance Cmte.); Bowery Mission (dir.); Penney Foundation (dir.); Intercollegiate Prohibition Assn. (vice pres., 1920–21); United Soc. of Christian Endeavor (pres., 1924); National Temperance Council of America (pres., 1912); Flying Squadron of America (sec., 1914–15); Anti-Saloon League of America (vice pres., 1914–18); MA Anti-Saloon League (1915–20). AWARDS: Silver Buffalo Award, BSA; Humanitarian Award, Welcome Chapter, Eastern Star, 1940; War Dept. Award, 1946; Medal of Merit, 1947; Benjamin Franklin Award, 1961; Order of Lafayette, 1961; Clergyman of the Year Award, Religious Heritage Assn., 1963; Ten Commandments Award, Order of Eagles, 1964; Israeli Citation, 1965. HON. DEG.: LL.D., Albright Coll., 1916; Litt.D., Defiance Coll., 1921; Litt.D., Norwich U., 1925; D.D., Hope Coll., 1925; S.T.D., Syracuse U., 1927; LL.D., Temple U., 1937; D.D., U. of VT, 1934; D.D., Phillips U., 1939; L.H.D., Bucknell U., 1946; L.H.D., Bates Coll., 1952; D.D., William Jewell Coll., 1960; L.H.D., Clarkson Coll.; H.H.D., Huntington Coll. WRITINGS: *Mothers of Men* (1914); *Save America and Save the World* (1916); *Huts in Hell* (1918); *Learn to Live* (1923); *What Men Need Most* (1923); *An Adventure in Evangelism* (1925); *The Furnace* (1925); *John of Oregon* (1926); *Radio Talks to Young People* (1926); *Dr. Poling's Radio Talks* (1927); *The Heretic* (1928); *Youth and Life* (1929); *Between Two*

Worlds (1930); *John Barleycorn—His Life and Letters* (1933); *Youth Marches* (1937); *Fifty-Two Story Sermons for Children* (1940); *Opportunity is Yours* (1940); *A Treasury of Best-Loved Hymns* (1942); *A Preacher Looks at War* (1943); *Your Daddy Did Not Die* (1944); *A Treasury of Great Sermons* (1944); *Faith is Power for You* (1950); *Prayers for the Armed Forces* (1950); *The Glory and Wonder of the Bible* (with H. Thomas); *Your Questions Answered with Comforting Counsel; Mine Eyes Have Seen* (1959); *Jesus Says to You* (1961); *He Came from Galilee* (1965). REL.: Dutch Reformed (pres., General Synod, Reformed Church of America, 1929–30). RES.: Philadelphia, PA.

POLK, JAMES KNOX. b. Nov 2, 1795, Pineville, NC; d. Jun 15, 1849, Nashville, TN; par. Samuel and Jane (Knox) Polk; m. Sarah Childress, Jan 1, 1824; c. none. EDUC.: B.A., U. of NC, 1818; read law under Felix Grundy, Nashville, TN, 1819. POLIT. & GOV.: chief clerk, TN State Senate, 1819–23; elected as a Democrat to TN State House, 1823–25; elected as a Democrat to U.S. House (TN), 1825–39 (Speaker, 1835–39); elected as a Democrat to gov. of TN, 1839–41; ***received 1 electoral vote as a Democrat for vice presidency of the U.S., 1840***; Democratic candidate for gov. of TN, 1841, 1843; ***elected as a Democrat to presidency of the U.S., 1845–1849***. BUS. & PROF.: atty.; admitted to TN Bar, 1820. MEM.: Masons (Master). REL.: Methodist. MISC.: reduced tariff with Walker Tariff Law, 1846; signed Independent Treasury Bill of 1846; compromised on annexation of OR in treaty with Great Britain, 1846; attempted to purchase CA from Mexico, then declared war on Mexico, 1846; received CA and NM in treaty with Mexico, 1848; opposed Wilmot Proviso, 1848. RES.: Nashville, TN.

POLK, LEONIDAS LAFAYETTE. b. Apr 24, 1837, Anson Cty., NC; d. Jun 11, 1892, Washington, DC; par. Andrew and Serena (Autry) Polk; m. Sarah Pamela Gaddy, Sep 23, 1857; c. Lula (Mrs. J. W. Denman); Juanita; four other daughters; one son (infant). EDUC.: public schools. POLIT. & GOV.: elected as a Unionist to NC State Legislature, 1860, 1864–65 (as the soldiers' candidate); delegate, NC State Constitutional Convention, 1865–66; first commissioner, NC State Dept. of Agriculture, 1877–80; chm., Reformers, National Convention, St. Louis, MO, 1892; ***candidate for People's Party nomination to presidency of the U.S., 1892; candidate for People's Party nomination to vice presidency of the U.S., 1892***. BUS. & PROF.: farmer; ed., *Polkton Ansonian*, 1872; merchant; partner, Dodd, Polk and Co.; owner, L. L. Polk and Co., Raleigh, NC, to 1883; patent medicine salesman, "Polk's Diphtheria Cure," 1879–; ed., *Raleigh News*, 1880–81; publisher, *Progressive Farmer*, 1886–92. MIL.: pvt., sgt., maj., lt., NC Regt., C.S.A., Civil War. MEM.: Grange; NC State Coll. of Agriculture and Mechanic Arts (founder); Southern Alliance (vice pres., 1887; pres., 1889); National Farmers Alliance and Industrial Union (vice pres., 1887–89; pres., 1889–92); Industrial Conference (chm., 1892). WRITINGS: *Address* (1887); *Agricultural Depression: Its Causes, The Remedy* (1890); *Address* (1891); *The Protest of Farmers* (1891). REL.: Bapt. RES.: Raleigh, NC.

POLK, ROBERT H. b. Boston, MA. POLIT. & GOV.: ***independent candidate for presidency of the U.S., 1988***. BUS. & PROF.: stock and commodity broker; business administrator; personnel mgr.; wage and salary specialist; employment counselor; ex-offender counselor; rehabilitation counselor; private investigator; legal asst.; congressional liaison to Speaker John W. McCormack (q.v.); market analyst; advertising exec. MIL.: U.S. Army, 20 years. MAILING ADDRESS: 80 Greenwood St., Dorchester, MA 02124.

POLK, TRUSTEN. b. May 29, 1811, Bridgeville, DE; d. Apr 16, 1876, St. Louis, MO; par. William Nutter and Lavenia (Causey) Polk; m. Elizabeth Newberry Skinner, Dec 26, 1837; c. Anne; Mary; Cornelia; Elizabeth; one son (infant). EDUC.: grad. (with honors), Yale U., 1831, law school, 1832–34; studied law under John Rogers. POLIT. & GOV.: appointed city counselor, St. Louis, MO, 1843; delegate, MO State Constitutional Convention, 1845; presidential elector, Democratic Party, 1848; ***candidate for Democratic nomination to vice presidency of the U.S., 1856***; elected as a Democrat to gov. of MO, 1856–57; elected as a Democrat to U.S. Senate (MO), 1857–62 (expelled for disloyalty). BUS. & PROF.: atty.; admitted to MO Bar, 1835; law practice, St. Louis, MO. MIL.: col., judge advocate gen., C.S.A., 1864–65; presiding judge, Military Dept. of MS, 1864–65. REL.: Methodist Episc. Church, South. RES.: St. Louis, MO.

POLLAND, MILTON R. POLIT. & GOV.: ***independent candidate for vice presidency of the U.S., 1984***. MAILING ADDRESS: c/o Larry Harmon, 650 North Burnside, Los Angeles, CA 90004.

POLLARD, I. G. POLIT. & GOV.: Prohibition Party candidate for judge, IN Court of Appeals, 2 times prior to 1916; candidate for Prohibition Party nomination to lt. gov. of IN, 1915; delegate, Prohibition Party National Convention, 1916; delegate, American Party National Convention, 1916; ***American Party candidate for vice presidency of the U.S., 1916 (declined)***. RES.: IN.

POLLASKY, MARCUS. POLIT. & GOV.: candidate for Republican nomination to gov. of MI; candidate for Republican nomination to lt. gov. of MI; ***candidate for Republican nomination to vice presidency of the U.S., 1920***. RES.: Alma, MI.

POMERENE, ATLEE. b. Dec 6, 1863, Berlin, OH; d. Nov 12, 1937, Cleveland, OH; par. Dr. Peter Piersol and Elizabeth (Wise) Pomerene; m. Mary Helen Bockius, Jun 29, 1892; c. none. EDUC.: Vermillion Inst.; A.B. (with honors), Princeton U., 1884, A.M., 1887; LL.B., Cincinnati Law School, 1886. POLIT. & GOV.: city solicitor, Canton, OH, 1887–91; prosecuting atty., Stark Cty., OH, 1897–1900; appointed member, Honorary Tax Comm. of OH, 1906; candidate for Democratic nomination to gov. of OH, 1908; chm., OH State Democratic Convention, 1910, 1918; elected as a Democrat to lt. gov. of OH, 1911; elected as a Democrat to U.S. Senate (OH), 1911–23; delegate, Dem. Nat'l. Conv., 1920, 1924; ***candidate for Democratic nomination to presidency of the U.S., 1920, 1924, 1928***; Democratic candidate for U.S. Senate (OH), 1922, 1926; appointed U.S. delegate, Fifth Pan American Congress, 1923; appointed prosecutor, Naval Petroleum Reserve Oil Cases, 1924; ***candidate for Democratic nomination to vice presidency of the U.S., 1928***; appointed chm. of the board, RFC, 1932–33; chm., OH Ratification Convention, 1933. BUS. & PROF.: atty.; admitted to OH Bar, 1886; partner (with Charles Russell Miller), law firm, Canton, OH, 1886; partner, Squire, Sanders and Dempsey (law firm), Cleveland, OH, 1923–37; founder, Commercial and Savings Bank, Canton, 1909. MEM.: Cleveland Public Library (trustee); Cleveland City Hospital (trustee); American Law Inst.; International Law Assn.; ABA; OH State Bar Assn.; Cleveland Bar Assn.; Canton Bar Assn.; National Economic League; American Acad. of Political and Social Sciences; Ohio Soc. of New York; Elks; Union Club; National Press Club. HON. DEG.: LL.D., Mount Union-Scio Coll., 1913; LL.D., Coll. of Wooster, 1919; LL.D., Miami U., 1921; LL.D., Kenyon Coll., 1924. REL.: Presb. RES.: Cleveland, OH.

POMEROY, SAMUEL CLARKE. b. Jan 3, 1816, Southhampton, MA; d. Aug 27, 1891, Whitinsville, MA; par. Samuel and Dorcas (Burt) Pomeroy; m. Annie Pomeroy; m. 2d, Lucy Ann Gaylord, Apr 23, 1846; m. 3d, Mrs. Martha Whitin; c. infant. EDUC.: Amherst Coll., 1836–38. POLIT. & GOV.: temporary chm., Wayne Cty. (NY) Liberty Party Convention, 1840; Liberty Party candidate for MA State House, 1844; elected as a Liberty Party candidate to MA State House, 1852–53; delegate, Rep. Nat'l. Conv., 1856, 1860; ***candidate for Republican nomination to vice presidency of the U.S., 1856, 1868***; elected as a Republican to mayor of Atchison, KS, 1858–59; delegate, KS "Free State" Constitutional Convention, Lawrence, KS, 1859; elected as a Republican to U.S. Senate (KS), 1861–73; Republican candidate for U.S. Senate (KS), 1872, 1879; ***American Party candidate for vice presidency of the U.S., 1880; American Party candidate for presidency of the U.S., 1884 (withdrew); American Prohibition Party candidate for presidency of the U.S., 1884***. BUS. & PROF.: schoolteacher, Onondaga Cty., NY; partner (with Mr. Bissell), mercantile business, Onondaga Cty., NY; proprietor, ed., *Squatter Sovereign*, Atchison, KS; financial agent, New England Emigrant Aid Co., 1854. MEM.: Cmte. for KS Drought and Famine Relief (chm., 1860–61); KS Cmte. of Public Safety. HON. DEG.: LL.D., Howard U., 1872. MISC.: known as "Seed Corn" Pomeroy. RES.: Atchison, KS.

POOLE, JAMES THOMAS. m. Patsy A.; c. Tommy; Danny; Markie. POLIT. & GOV.: ***candidate for Republican nomination to presidency of the U.S., 1984***. BUS. & PROF.: unemployed. MISC.: involved in dispute with Posey Cty. (IN) Welfare Office over custody of son Markie. MAILING ADDRESS: 246 South Elm, Mount Vernon, IN 47620.

POPE, HAROLD. POLIT. & GOV.: ***independent candidate for vice presidency of the U.S., 1992***. BUS. & PROF.: pastor. MAILING ADDRESS: Route 2, Box 69H, Mt. Gilead, NC 27306.

POREMSKI, DONALD JAMES BUTLER. POLIT. & GOV.: ***candidate for Republican nomination to presidency of the U.S., 1976***. MAILING ADDRESS: Route 24, Chester, NJ 07930.

PORSTER, BARRY. b. 1947, Philadelphia, PA; m. Ann P. EDUC.: college. POLIT. & GOV.: member, Central Cmte., Workers League; ***Workers League candidate for vice presidency of the U.S., 1988***. BUS. & PROF.: staff writer, *Bulletin* (Workers League weekly), Detroit, MI, 1976–, labor ed., 1978–. MAILING ADDRESS: 2704 Yemans, Hamtramck, MI 48212.

PORTER, ALBERT S. b. Nov 29, 1904, Lakewood, OH; par. Albert S. and Lena May Porter; m. Genevieve S. Porter; c. Lee A.; Alan C.; Carol S. EDUC.: high school, Lakewood, OH, 1922; B.C.E., OH State U., 1928. POLIT. & GOV.: appointed member, OH State Beach Erosion Board, 1947–48; appointed member, City Beach Erosion Board (OH), 1947–48; member, OH Freeway Exec. Cmte., 1946–51; appointed Cuyahoga Cty. (OH) Engineer, 1947–76; appointed member, Highway Study Cmte., 1949–51; appointed member, President's Highway Safety Conference, 1949, 1951; appointed dir., Regional Geodetic Survey; appointed member, OH Regional Planning Comm. (exec. cmte.); member, Freeway Board, 1951–; appointed Civil Defense dir. of supply, 1951; appointed member, Highway Investigating Cmte. (Steering Cmte.), 1952; appointed dir., County-Wide Traffic Survey, 1952–55; delegate, Dem. Nat'l. Conv., 1952, 1960, 1964, 1968, 1972; candidate for mayor of Cleveland, OH, 1953; chm., OH State Democratic Convention, 1958; candidate for Democratic nomination to gov. of OH, 1958; chm., Cuyahoga Cty. Airport Building Comm., 1958; appointed member, Traffic Advisory Cmte., Cleveland Safety Council, 1959 (vice pres., 1960); chm., Cuyahoga Cty. Charter Comm., 1959; ***candidate for Democratic nomination to presidency of the U.S., 1960, 1964***; chm., Cuyahoga Cty. Democratic Exec. Cmte., 1963–69; chm., Cuyahoga Cty. Democratic Central Cmte., 1964–70; chm., OH State Democratic Exec. Cmte., 1964; member, Dem. Nat'l. Cmte. (OH), 1964–72. BUS. & PROF.: asst. engineer, draftsman, Columbus (OH) City Plan Comm., 1925–

29; engineer, Cleveland (OH) Highway Research Bureau, 1929–32; asst. to div. engineer, OH State Highway Dept., 1932–33; chief deputy cty. engineer, Cuyahoga Cty., OH, 1933–41, 1946–47. MIL.: Civil Engineers Corps, U.S. Navy, 1941–46. MEM.: Tau Beta Pi; Sigma Xi; Pi Mu Epsilon; Texnikoi; Chi Sigma Chi (pres.); Sigma Phi Epsilon (controller); N.S.P.E.; County Engineers Assn. of OH (pres., 1948–49); A.S.C.E.; Free and Accepted Masons; Al Sirat Grotto; Masons (32°); Heroes of '76; SAR; National Sojourners; Cleveland Auto Club; City Club of Cleveland; American Roadbuilders Assn.; Cleveland Aviation Club (dir.); Aircraft Owners and Pilots Assn.; Small Business Assn.; Metro (exec. cmte.); National Assn. of County Officials; National Assn. of County Engineers; Cleveland Open Golf Tournament (exec. board, 1964–); Reserve Officers Assn.; Reserve Officers of the Naval Service; American Legion; VFW; Military Order of the World Wars; Koran Club; Acacia Country Club (dir., 1963–64); Eagles; Western Reserve Hist. Soc.; Phyllis Wheatley Assn.; Shrine Luncheon Club. AWARDS: "Engineer of the Year," Cleveland Soc. of Professional Engineers and Cleveland Engineering Soc., 1964; Civic Award for Community Service, Knights of Columbus, 1964. REL.: Episc. MAILING ADDRESS: 31179 South Woodland Road, Cleveland, OH 44115.

PORTER, ANDREW JEFFREY. POLIT. & GOV.: ***candidate for Democratic nomination to presidency of the U.S., 1984***. MAILING ADDRESS: Route 4, Box MH-344, Tuttle, OK 73089.

PORTER, HORACE. b. Apr 15, 1837, Huntingdon, PA; d. May 29, 1921, New York, NY; par. David Rittenhouse and Josephine (McDermett) Porter; m. Sophie King McHarg, Dec 23, 1963; c. Elsie (Mrs. Edwin Mende); Horace M.; Clarence; William. EDUC.: Lawrence Scientific School; B.A., U.S. Military Acad., 1860. POLIT. & GOV.: appointed asst. U.S. sec. of war, 1866; appointed exec. sec. to President U. S. Grant (q.v.), 1869–73; ***candidate for Republican nomination to vice presidency of the U.S., 1896***; appointed U.S. ambassador to France, 1897–1905. BUS. & PROF.: soldier; financier; vice pres., Pullman Palace Car Co., 1873; pres., New York West Shore and Buffalo R.R.; pres., St. Louis and San Francisco Railway Co.; orator. MIL.: commissioned 2d lt., U.S. Army, 1861, 1st lt., 1861, capt., 1863; lt. col., aide-de-camp to Gen. U.S. Grant (q.v.), 1864; maj., 1864, lt. col., 1864; col., U.S.V., 1865; col., U.S. Army, 1865; brig. gen.; Medal of Honor, 1863; Grand Cross of the Legion of Honor (France, 1904); Gold Medal for Patriotism (Turkey, 1901). MEM.: SAR (pres.-gen., 1892–97); Assn. of West Point Graduates (pres., 1906–07, 1909–10); Great Monument Assn. (pres., 1891–1919); Navy League of the U.S. (pres., 1909); International Law Assn.; American Geographical Soc.; Military Order of the Loyal Legion; Metropolitan Museum of Art; American Museum of Natural History; Military Order of the French Alliance; Metropolitan Club; Century Club; University Club; National Arts Club; Down Town Club; Lawyers Club; Lotos Club; Republican Club of New York; Cercle de l'Union; Union League Club of New York (pres., 1893–97). HON. DEG.: LL.D., Union Coll., 1894; LL.D., Princeton U., 1906; LL.D., Williams Coll., 1907; LL.D., Harvard U., 1910. WRITINGS: *West Point Life* (1860); *Campaigning with Grant* (1897). REL.: Presb. RES.: New York, NY.

POST, LOUIS FREELAND. b. Nov 15, 1849, Vienna, NJ; d. Jan 10, 1928, Washington, DC; par. Eugene Jerome and Elizabeth Lyon (Freeland) Post; m. Anna Johnson, Jul 6, 1871; m. 2d, Alice Thacher, Dec 2, 1893; c. Edna; Charles Johnson. EDUC.: public schools; studied law, New York, NY, 1867–70. POLIT. & GOV.: appointed asst. U.S. atty., NY, 1874–75; Labor Party candidate for U.S. House (NY), 1882; Greenback Party candidate for atty. gen. of NY, 1883; chm., NY United Labor Party Convention, 1887; United Labor Party candidate for district atty., New York, 1887; appointed member, Chicago (IL) Board of Education, 1906–09; member, Chicago Charter Convention, 1906–08; appointed asst. U.S. sec. of labor, 1913–21; ***candidate for Farmer-Labor Party nomination to presidency of the U.S., 1920***. BUS. & PROF.: apprentice printer, *Hackettstown (NJ) Gazette*, 1864–65; law clerk, office of David T. Corbin, SC, 1871–72; atty.; admitted to NY Bar, 1870; admitted to practice before the Bar of the Supreme Court of the U.S., 1878; admitted to DC Bar, 1921; partner, Lockwood and Post (law firm), New York, 1875–80; editorial writer, *New York Daily Truth*, 1879–82; law practice, 1883–90; ed., *Daily Leader*, 1886; ed., *The Standard*, 1891–92; ed., *Cleveland (OH) Recorder*, 1896–97; founder, ed., *The Public*, 1898–13. MEM.: Single Tax National Conference (chm., 1890, 1893); National Popular Government League; International Free Trade Conference (delegate, 1908); Manhattan Single Tax Club; Literary Club of Chicago; Chicago City Club; Cosmos Club; Henry George Assn.; Press Club. WRITINGS: *The George-Hewitt Campaign* (1887); *Outlines of Louis F. Post's Lectures* (1894); *The Single Tax* (1899); *The Chinese Exclusion Act* (1901); *Success in Life* (1902); *Subsidies the Climax of the Protective Superstition* (1902); *Ethics of Democracy* (1905); *The Prophet of San Francisco* (1905); *Our Advancing Postal Censorship* (1905); *The Traction Issue in the Municipal Election in Chicago* (1905); *Our Despotic Postal Censorship* (1906); *Ethical Principles of Marriage and Divorce* (1906); *Social Service* (1909); *The Open and the Closed Shop* (1912); *Origin and Progress of the Single Tax* (1913); *Land Value Taxation* (1915); *Outline of Lectures on the Taxation of Land Values* (1915); *Trusts, A Single-Tax View; A Syllabus of Progress and Poverty by Henry George; Documentary Outline of the Philippine Case; Henry George on Congress; The Deportations Delirium of 1920* (1923); *What is the Single Tax?* (1926); *The Basic Facts of Economics* (1927). REL.: Swedenborgian. RES.: Chicago, IL.

POTGETTER, GEORGE. POLIT. & GOV.: ***Three Horse Party candidate for vice presidency of the U.S., 1936***. MAILING ADDRESS: Steamboat Rock, IA.

POUSQUET, NORMAN JOSEPH. POLIT. & GOV.: ***independent candidate for presidency of the U.S., 1984***. MAILING ADDRESS: P.O. Box 2251, Worcester, MA 01613.

POWELL, ADAM CLAYTON, JR. b. Nov 29, 1908, New Haven, CT; d. Apr 4, 1972, Miami, FL; par. Adam Clayton and Mattie Fletcher (Schafer) Powell; m. Isabel Geraldine Washington, Mar 8, 1933 (divorced, 1943); m. 2d, Hazel Scott, Aug 1945 (divorced, 1960); m. 3d, Yvette Marjorie Flores Diago (separated, 1965); c. Adam Clayton III; Adam Diago; Preston (adopted). EDUC.: A.B., Colgate U., 1930; M.A., Columbia U., 1932; D.D., Shaw U., 1935. POLIT. & GOV.: elected as a Democrat to New York (NY) City Council, 1941; employee, Consumer Div., NY Office, OPA, 1942–44; appointed member, Manhattan Council on Civil Defense, 1942–45; elected as a Democrat to U.S. House (NY), 1945–67, 1967 (did not serve); 1969–71; appointed delegate, Parliamentary World Government Conference, London, 1951–52; delegate, Dem. Nat'l. Conv., 1952; delegate, International Labor Organization Conference, Geneva, Switzerland, 1961, 1963, 1964; ***candidate for Democratic nomination to vice presidency of the U.S., 1968***; candidate for Democratic nomination to U.S. House (NY), 1970. BUS. & PROF.: instructor, Columbia U. Extension School, 1932–40; editorial writer, *Daily Newspaper*, New York, 1932; ordained minister, Abyssinian Baptist Church, New York, 1937–60; founder, copublisher, editor-in-chief, *People's Voice*, 1942; author; civil rights activist. MEM.: NAACP (life member); World Assn. of Parliamentarians on World Government (vice pres.); National Negro Congress (cofounder); Coordinating Cmte. for Employment (chm.). AWARDS: Order of the Golden Cross (Ethiopia, 1954); "Outstanding Man of the Year," VFW, 1956; "Pastor of the Year," New England Baptist Missionary Convention, 1961; "Educator of the Year," International Protective and Benevolent Order of Elks, 1961; honored by National Assn. of Colored Women's Clubs; Tau Gamma Delta; Prince Hall Grand Masons; Royal Order of Ethiopian Jews; Alpha Phi Alpha; American Jewish Congress; National Medical Assn. HON. DEG.: LL.D., VA Union U., 1947. WRITINGS: *Is This a White Man's War* (1942); *Stage Door Canteen* (1944); *Marching Blacks* (1945); *Adam Clayton Powell* (1960); *Keep the Faith, Baby* (1967); *Adam by Adam* (1971). REL.: Bapt. MISC.: excluded from U.S. House, 1967; elected to U.S. House in special election, 1967, but did not take seat. RES.: New York, NY.

POWELL, A. W. POLIT. & GOV.: ***candidate for Democratic nomination to presidency of the U.S., 1944***. RES.: unknown.

POWELL, COLIN LUTHER. b. Apr 5, 1937, New York, NY; m. Alma Vivian Johnson, 1962; c. Michael; Linda; Annamarie. EDUC.: City Coll. of New York; M.B.A., George Washington U., 1971. POLIT. & GOV.: appointed asst. to the deputy dir., Office of Management and Budget, 1972; appointed deputy national security adviser, 1987; appointed national security adviser to the president, 1987–89; ***candidate for Republican nomination to vice presidency of the U.S., 1988, 1992***. BUS. & PROF.: soldier. MIL.: commissioned 2d lt., U.S. Army, 1958; Army Airborne School; Ranger School; advanced through ranks to lt. gen.; commander, 2d Bde., 101st Airborne Div., U.S. Army; asst. chief of staff, 23d Infantry Div., U.S. Army; commanding gen., V Corps, U.S. Army, Germany; appointed chm., JCS, 1989–1993; Bronze Star; Soldiers Medal. MEM.: Pershing Rifles. AWARDS: White House Fellow, 1972. WRITINGS: *An American Journey* (1995). MAILING ADDRESS: Pentagon, Washington, DC.

POWELL, LAZARUS WHITEHEAD. b. Oct 6, 1812, Henderson Cty., KY; d. Jul 3, 1867, Henderson, KY; par. Lazarus and Ann (McMahon) Powell; m. Harriet Ann Jennings, Nov 8, 1837; c. Henry; James H.; Charles J.; Richard P. EDUC.: grad., St. Joseph's Coll., 1833; Transylvania U.; studied law under John Rowan. POLIT. & GOV.: elected as a Democrat to KY State House, 1836; Democratic candidate for KY State House, 1838; presidential elector, Democratic Party, 1844; Democratic candidate for gov. of KY, 1848; elected as a Democrat to gov. of KY, 1851–55; appointed U.S. peace commissioner to UT, 1858; elected as a Democrat to U.S. Senate (KY), 1859–65; ***candidate for Democratic nomination to vice presidency of the U.S., 1864***; Democratic candidate for U.S. Senate (KY), 1864, 1867; delegate, National Union Convention, 1866. BUS. & PROF.: atty.; admitted to KY Bar, 1835; partner (with Archibald Dixon), law firm, Henderson, KY, 1835–39; law practice, Henderson, 1839–67; plantation owner, KY. RES.: Henderson, KY.

POWELL, SAMUEL WESLEY. b. Oct 13, 1915, Portsmouth, NH; d. Jan 6, 1981, Hampton Falls, NH; par. Samuel Wesley and Mary (Gosse) Powell; m. Beverly Swain, Sep 2, 1942; c. Samuel Wesley; Peter Wendell; Nancy. EDUC.: U. of NH; LL.B., Southern Methodist U., 1940. POLIT. & GOV.: chief of staff to U.S. Sen. Styles Bridges (q.v.), 1940–43, 1945–49; candidate for Republican nomination to U.S. Senate (NH), 1950; independent candidate for U.S. Senate (NH), 1950; candidate for Republican nomination to gov. of NH, 1956, 1962; elected as a Republican to gov. of NH, 1959–63; appointed member, President's Cmte. on Safety, 1961; ***candidate for Republican nomination to presidency of the U.S., 1964 (withdrew)***. BUS. & PROF.: atty.; admitted to NH Bar, 1941; law practice, Hampton Falls, NH, 1949–59, 1963–81; owner, *Hampton (NH) Union*; owner, *Rockingham County (NH) Gazette*. MIL.: U.S.A.A.F., 1943–45. MEM.: New England Governors' Conference (chm., 1961); U.S. Governors' Conference (chm., 1961); Council of State Governments (pres., 1962). HON. DEG.: M.A., Dartmouth Coll.; D.C.L., New England Coll.; LL.D., U. of NH. REL.: Congregationalist. RES.: Hampton Falls, NH.

POWERS, JAMES P. POLIT. & GOV.: ***Berkeley Self-Defense Group candidate for vice presidency of the U.S., 1968***. MAILING ADDRESS: CA.

PRATT, DANIEL. b. Apr 11, 1809, Prattville, MA; d. Jun 20, 1887, Boston, MA; par. Daniel and Mary (Hall) Pratt; single. POLIT. & GOV.: ***independent candidate for presidency of the U.S., 1872***. BUS. & PROF.: carpenter's apprentice; vagrant; lecturer. HON. DEG.: C.O.D., Dartmouth Coll. WRITINGS: *The Four Kingdoms* (lecture); *The Harmony of the Human Mind* (lecture); *The Solar System* (lecture); *The Vocabulaboratory of the World's History* (lecture). MISC.: self-styled "General" and "Great American Traveler." RES.: Boston, MA.

PREDGEN, JOHN L. POLIT. & GOV.: ***Your Bull Party candidate for presidency of the U.S., 1976, 1980***. BUS. & PROF.: capt. MAILING ADDRESS: 1028 Inverness Way, Sunnyvale, CA 94087.

PRESSLER, LARRY. b. Mar 29, 1942, Humboldt, SD; par. Antone Lewis and Loretta Genevive (Claussen) Pressler; m. Harriet Dent, 1982. EDUC.: B.A., U. of SD, 1964; diplomat, Rhodes Scholar, Oxford U., 1966; M.A., Harvard U., 1971, J.D., 1971. POLIT. & GOV.: student aide, U.S. Sen. Francis Case; aide, SD Republican State Central Cmte., 1962; elected as a Republican to U.S. House (SD), 1975–79; elected as a Republican to U.S. Senate (SD), 1979–; ***candidate for Republican nomination to presidency of the U.S., 1980 (withdrew)***. BUS. & PROF.: soldier; employee, Office of Legal Advice, U.S. Dept. of State, 1971–74. MIL.: 2d lt., U.S. Army, Vietnam, 1966, 1st lt., 1968. MEM.: Phi Beta Kappa; American Assn. of Rhodes Scholars; VFW; American Legion; Harvard Alumni Exec. Council; Lions; American Audubon Soc.; ABA; SD Hist. Soc.; Congressional Vietnam Veterans Caucus; Environmental Study Conference. AWARDS: National 4-H Citizenship Award, 1962; Report to the President 4-H Award, 1962. WRITINGS: *U.S. Senators from the Prairie* (1982). MISC.: 1 of 4 All-American 4-H Delegates to Agricultural Fair, Cairo, Egypt, 1961. MAILING ADDRESS: Humboldt, SD.

PRESTON, JAMES HARRY. b. Mar 1860, Harford Cty., MD; d. Jul 14, 1938; par. James Bond and Mary Amelia (Wilks) Preston; m. Helen Fiske Jackson, Nov 14, 1893; c. Alice Wilks (Mrs. Edward C. Carrington); James Harry, Jr.; Mary Bond (Mrs. Harry P. Galligher); Wilbur Jackson; Helen Jackson. EDUC.: St. John's Coll.; LL.B., U. of MD, 1881. POLIT. & GOV.: elected as a Democrat to MD State House of Delegates, 1890–94 (Speaker, 1894); col., staff of Governor Brown (MD), 1892–96; member, MD State Board of Police Commissioners, 1904–08; Democratic candidate for U.S. House (MD), 1910; elected as a Democrat to mayor of Baltimore, MD, 1911–19; ***candidate for Democratic nomination to vice presidency of the U.S., 1912***; chm., Baltimore Port Development Comm.; pres., Star-Spangled Banner Centennial Comm., 1914; candidate for Democratic nomination to mayor of Baltimore, 1919; independent candidate for mayor of Baltimore, 1923; chm., Baltimore George Washington Bicentennial Comm.; vice chm., MD State George Washington Bicentennial Comm. BUS. & PROF.: atty.; admitted to MD Bar, 1880; law practice, Baltimore, MD; vice pres., Calvert Bank; dir., Miller Fertilizer Co.; dir., Development and Securities Corp.; dir., Lorraine Electric Railway Co.; dir., Baltimore Steamship Co.; dir., Union Acid Works. MEM.: SAR (MD state pres.; national pres.); MD State Bar Assn.; Baltimore Bar Assn.; MD Hist. Soc.; MD Club; Baltimore Club; Hillendale Golf Club (pres.). REL.: Episc. RES.: Baltimore, MD.

PRESTON, MARTIN R. b. 1883, TN; d. May 9, 1924, Los Angeles, CA; married. POLIT. & GOV.: ***Socialist Labor Party candidate for presidency of the U.S., 1908***. BUS. & PROF.: miner; employee, restaurant, Goldfield, NV; lineman; electrician. MEM.: Industrial Workers of the World. MISC.: convicted of murdering John Silva (his employer); sentenced to 10–25 years in NV state prison, Carson City, NV, 1907; was serving sentence at time of nomination; replaced as presidential candidate of the Socialist Labor Party by August Gillhaus (q.v.) as proxy, 1908; released from prison, Apr 28, 1914; electrocuted while working on lines, Los Angeles, CA, 1924. RES.: Los Angeles, CA.

PRICE, ERIC LINDSAY, SR. married; c. Eric Lindsay, Jr. POLIT. & GOV.: ***independent candidate for presidency of the U.S., 1984, 1988; candidate for Democratic nomination to presidency of the U.S., 1988***. MAILING ADDRESS: 1002 East Seventh St., Los Angeles, CA 90021.

PRICE, RALPH "SHORTY." b. Oct 3, 1921, Louisville, AL; par. J. P. and Rosa (Pickett) Price; m. Delores Bigham; c. Ralph, Jr.; Donny Ray; Vicki. EDUC.: grad., Louisville (AL) H.S., 1940; U. of AL; law school. POLIT. & GOV.: candidate for Democratic nomination to AL State House, 1950; alternate delegate, Dem. Nat'l. Conv., 1952; candidate for Democratic nomination to lt. gov. of AL, 1954; candidate for Democratic nomination to gov. of AL, 1958, 1970, 1974; candidate for Democratic nomination to U.S. House (AL), 1968; independent candidate for U.S. House (AL), 1968; ***candidate for Democratic nomination to presidency of the U.S., 1976***. BUS. & PROF.: owner, Shorty Price Insurance Agency; author. MIL.: U.S. Army; Purple Heart, 1944. MEM.: VFW; Disabled American Veterans; American Legion. WRITINGS: *Alabama Politics—Tell It Like It Is* (1973). REL.: Bapt. MAILING ADDRESS: P.O. Box 127, Louisville, AL 36048.

PRINCEVAC, SINISA M. EDUC.: M.D. POLIT. & GOV.: ***independent candidate for presidency of the U.S.,***

1988. BUS. & PROF.: physician. MAILING ADDRESS: 2475 West Gunnison St., Chicago, IL 60625.

PRINE, CHARLES, SR. POLIT. & GOV.: ***candidate for Democratic nomination to vice presidency of the U.S., 1980***. MAILING ADDRESS: TX.

PRITCHARD, JETER CONNELLY. b. Jul 12, 1857, Jonesboro, TN; d. Apr 10, 1921, Asheville, NC; par. William H. and Leizabeth L. (Brown) Pritchard; m. Augusta Ray, 1877; m. 2d, Melissa Bowman, Oct 18, 1892; m. 3d, Lillian E. Saum, Nov 14, 1903; c. William; George Moore; Arthur; Ida (Mrs. Thomas Rollins); McKinley. EDUC.: Odd Fellows Inst.; Martins Greek Acad.; studied law. POLIT. & GOV.: presidential elector, Republican Party, 1880; elected as a Republican to NC State House, 1884–88, 1890–92; Republican candidate for lt. gov. of NC, 1888; Republican candidate for U.S. Senate (NC), 1891; delegate, Rep. Nat'l. Conv., 1892; Republican candidate for U.S. House (NC), 1892; state chm., NC Republican Party, c. 1894; member, Rep. Nat'l. Cmte., c. 1894; elected as a Republican to U.S. Senate (NC), 1894–1903; ***candidate for Republican nomination to vice presidency of the U.S., 1900, 1920***; Republican candidate for U.S. Senate (NC), 1903; appointed assoc. justice, Supreme Court of DC, 1903; appointed judge, U.S. Circuit Court, Fourth Judicial Circuit, 1904–11; appointed judge, U.S. Circuit Court of Appeals, 1912–21; pres., Wage Arbitration Board, 1914; ***candidate for Republican nomination to presidency of the U.S., 1920***. BUS. & PROF.: printer's apprentice, *Jonesboro (NC) Tribune-Herald*; owner, coeditor, *Roan Mountain Republican*, 1875–87; atty.; admitted to NC Bar, 1887; law practice, Marshall, NC. MEM.: NC Protective Tariff League (pres., 1891). RES.: Asheville, NC.

PROCELL, ALBERTA. POLIT. & GOV.: American Independent Party candidate for lt. gov. of CA, 1974; ***candidate for American Independent Party nomination to presidency of the U.S., 1976***. MAILING ADDRESS: Bakersfield, CA.

PROCTOR, REDFIELD. b. Jun 1, 1831, Proctorsville, VT; d. Mar 4, 1908, Washington, DC; par. Jabez and Betsy (Parker) Proctor; m. Emily J. Dutton, May 26, 1858; c. Fletcher D.; four others. EDUC.: A.B., Dartmouth Coll., 1851, A.M., 1854; LL.B., Albany Law School, 1860. POLIT. & GOV.: elected as a Republican to VT State House, 1867–68, 1888; elected as a Republican to VT State Senate, 1874–75 (pres. pro tempore, 1888); elected as a Republican to lt. gov. of VT, 1876–78; elected as a Republican to gov. of VT, 1878–80; delegate, Rep. Nat'l. Conv., 1884, 1888, 1896; appointed U.S. sec. of war, 1889–91; appointed and subsequently elected as a Republican to U.S. Senate (VT), 1891–1911; ***candidate for Republican nomination to vice presidency of the U.S., 1896***. BUS. & PROF.: atty.; law practice, Boston, MA, 1860–61, 1863; pres., Marble Manufacturing Co., 1880–1908. MIL.: quartermaster, Third VT Regt., U.S. Army, 1861; maj., Fifth VT Regt., 1861; col., 15th VT Volunteers, 1862; mustered out, 1863. WRITINGS: *Records of Conventions in the New Hampshire Grants for the Independence of Vermont, 1776–1777*. RES.: Proctor, VT.

PROEHL, FREDERICK C. b. 1880, Otter Tail Cty., MN; d. after 1968; married; c. two daughters; one son. POLIT. & GOV.: appointed special deputy MN state bank examiner, 1936; vice chm., Greenback Party; WA organizer, Greenback Party; ***Greenback Party candidate for presidency of the U.S., 1952, 1956***; national chm., Greenback Party, 1961–. BUS. & PROF.: asst. bank cashier, Parker's Prairie, MN; bank cashier, Golva, ND; founder, bank, Lincoln, MN; personnel clerk, timekeeper, Boeing Airplane Co., Seattle, WA, 1942–51; grocer; owner, operator, Sav-Tyme Grocery, Perrinville, WA; owner, grocery store, Seattle, WA. WRITINGS: *Service Manual for Lutheran Chaplains* (1942); *Marching Side by Side* (1945); *Lightning Over the U.S. Halls of Congress; The Truth Shall Make Us Free; The Banker's Interest Atom Bomb*. RES.: Edmonds, WA.

PROPHET OF THE INCARNATION (aka DAVID CORNELIUS ELEY). b. Dec 22, 1937, Detroit, MI; par. Edward Cornelius and Martha Emma (Merritt) Eley; m. Shirley Ann Moore; m. 2d, Donna Weber Kinsey; c. Kim Janetz, Kent Julian; Kevin Merritt; Adrian Giebler. EDUC.: Inkster H.S., Detroit, MI; Detroit Inst. of Technology, 1959–61. POLIT. & GOV.: campaign worker, Democratic Party, 1968; campaign mgr., God for President (experimental campaign), 1972; ***National American Bicentennial Party candidate for presidency of the U.S., 1976 (withdrew to enter Democratic primary); candidate for Democratic nomination to presidency of the U.S., 1976***. BUS. & PROF.: minister; prophet; dir., God's Workshop, Washington, DC; philosopher. WRITINGS: *A Voice in the Wilderness* (1968); *Because I Love You* (1974). REL.: Deist. MISC.: declared mentally ill and hospitalized 58 days, 1965; engaged in criminal activity until conversion, 1965; claims campaign was a religious campaign under direction of God, carried on under His order. MAILING ADDRESS: 9231 Quincy, Detroit, MI 48204.

PROXMIRE, EDWARD WILLIAM. b. Nov 11, 1915, Lake Forest, IL; par. Theodore Stanley and Adele (Flanigan) Proxmire; m. Elsie Rockefeller, Sep 15, 1946 (divorced, 1955); m. 2d, Ellen Hodges Sawall, Dec 1, 1956; c. Elsie Stillman; Theodore Stanley; Douglas Clark. EDUC.: grad., Hill School, Pottstown, PA; B.A., Yale U., 1938; M.B.A. (cum laude), Harvard U., 1940, M.P.A., 1948. POLIT. & GOV.: elected as a Democrat to WI State Assembly, 1951–53; Democratic candidate for gov. of WI, 1952, 1954, 1956; delegate, Dem. Nat'l. Conv., 1956, 1960; elected as a Democrat to U.S. Senate (WI), 1957–89; ***candidate for Democratic nomination to presi-***

dency of the U.S., 1972, 1980. BUS. & PROF.: employee, J. P. Morgan and Co., New York, NY, 1940–41; political and labor reporter, *Capital Times*, Madison, WI, 1949; reporter, *Madison Union Labor News*, 1950; vice pres., Brooke Implement Co., Sun Prairie, WI, 1952–53; pres., Artcraft Press, Waterloo, WI, 1954–57. MIL.: pvt., 1st lt., U.S. Army, 1941–46. WRITINGS: *Report from Wasteland: America's Military-Industrial Complex* (1970); *The Fleecing of America; Uncle Sam: Last of the Big Time Spenders* (1972); *You Can Do It* (1973). REL.: Episc. MAILING ADDRESS: 3025 Ordway St., N.W., Washington, DC.

PRUIT, HENRY ARCHIE. b. Mar 12, 1938, Atoka, OK; par. Columbus McKinley and Mary Ellen (Rains) Pruit; m. Winstina Carol Marcy; c. Carl; Gary; Carol; Karla; Kathy. EDUC.: A.A., Modesto (CA) Junior Coll., 1959; Th.D., CA Missionary Baptist Seminary, 1964. POLIT. & GOV.: ***Pruit Fundamentalist Party candidate for presidency of the U.S., 1980 (withdrew)***. BUS. & PROF.: minister, Baptist Church; pastor, Baptist Church, Fresno, CA; pastor, Baptist Church, Easton, CA; pastor, Baptist Church, Ridgecrest, CA; pastor, Baptist Church, Empire, CA; pastor, Baptist Church, San Pablo, CA; pastor, Brookside Missionary Baptist Church, San Pablo, CA. MEM.: Contra Cost County Assn. for the Mentally Retarded; American Assn. of Christian Counselors; National Assn. for Retarded Citizens; NRA; Masons; American Bapt. Assn. REL.: Bapt. MAILING ADDRESS: 2060 Brookside Dr., San Pablo, CA 94806.

PRYOR, THEODORE MARCUS. m. Sophonia M. Pryor. POLIT. & GOV.: ***Crispus Attucks Party candidate for presidency of the U.S., 1976***; Crispus Attucks Party candidate for U.S. Senate (CT), 1976. MAILING ADDRESS: 105 Ridgefield St., Hartford, CT 06112.

PULLEVERDOWN, I. POLIT. & GOV.: ***independent candidate for presidency of the U.S., 1992***. MISC.: advocate of following Jesus as the "True Leader." MAILING ADDRESS: 1055 North Recker Residence 1276, Mesa, AZ 85205.

PULLEY, CLEVE ANDREW. b. May 5, 1951, Sidon, MS; m. Jeanne Pulley; c. Aislinn. EDUC.: John Adams H.S., Cleveland, OH, to 1968. POLIT. & GOV.: Socialist Workers Party candidate for U.S. House (CA), 1971; ***Socialist Workers Party candidate for vice presidency of the U.S., 1972***; Socialist Workers Party candidate for U.S. House (IL), 1976; Socialist Workers Party candidate for mayor of Chicago, IL, 1979; ***Socialist Workers Party candidate for presidency of the U.S., 1980***; Socialist Workers Party candidate for U.S. House (MI), 1984, 1986, 1990; Socialist Workers Party candidate for gov. of WV, 1988. BUS. & PROF.: railroad switchman; cotton picker; sharecropper; steelworker; child preacher, Bapt. Church, 1964–66; porter; part-time cook, Rhoton's Restaurant; employee, Young Socialist Alliance, 1973–74. MIL.: pvt., Company B, 14th Battalion, 4th Bde., U.S. Army, 1968–69; court martialed for inciting to riot, disobedience, and disrespect; one of Fort Jackson Eight, 1969; charges dropped; dishonorably discharged. MEM.: G.I.'s United Against the War; United Steelworkers Local 1066 (Gary, IN); Black and Brown Task Force to End the War in Vietnam (Fort Jackson, SC, coordinator); National Student Coalition Against Racism. WRITINGS: *How I Became a Socialist* (1980). REL.: none (nee Bapt.). MAILING ADDRESS: 4700 South Lake Park, Chicago, IL.

PUTNAM, HAROLD L. POLIT. & GOV.: candidate for Republican nomination to U.S. House (MA), 1956, 1958; ***United Party candidate for vice presidency of the U.S., 1964***. MAILING ADDRESS: MA.

PUTNAM, ROGER LOWELL. b. Dec 19, 1893, Boston, MA; d. Nov 24, 1972, Springfield, MA; par. William Lowell and Elizabeth (Lowell) Putnam; m. Caroline Piatt Jenkins, Oct 19, 1919; c. Caroline Canfield; Roger Lowell, Jr.; William Lowell; Anna Lowell (Mrs. James Joseph Finnerty); Mary Compton (Mrs. Michael Q. Post; Mrs. Charles Chatfield); Michael Courtney Jenkins. EDUC.: A.B., (magna cum laude), Harvard U., 1915; MA Inst. of Technology, 1915–16. POLIT. & GOV.: appointed member, MA Unemployment Compensation Study Comm., 1934; appointed member, MA State Advisory Comm. on Education, 1936; elected as a Democrat to mayor of Springfield, MA, 1937–43; delegate, Dem. Nat'l. Conv., 1940; ***candidate for Democratic nomination to vice presidency of the U.S., 1940***; Democratic candidate for gov. of MA, 1942; appointed deputy dir., Office of Contract Settlement, 1944–46, dir., 1946; appointed member, Advisory Board, RFC; appointed member, Springfield (MA) Cmte. on the Museum of Fine Arts; appointed member, Springfield Housing Authority; appointed administrator, Economic Stabilization Agency, 1951–53; chm., New England Interstate Water Pollution Control Comm., 1954; member, MA State Board of Regional Community Colleges (vice chm., 1958–72); member, Springfield (MA) Park Comm. BUS. & PROF.: manufacturer; diesel worker, New London Engine and Ship Co., 1916; asst. plant superintendent, Multibestos Co., Walpole, MA, 1917; salesman, package machinery company, East Longmeadow, MA, 1919–21, vice pres., 1921–27, pres., 1927–42, 1948–52, chm. of the board, 1942–48, 1952–72; dir., Van Norman Machine Tool Co.; chm. of the board, Springfield Television Broadcasting Corp., 1957–72; dir., Perkins Machine and Gear Co.; dir., American Bosch Corp.; dir., Third National Bank and Trust Co.; dir., Gorton Pew Fisheries Co.; dir., Springfield National Bank; dir., Future Springfield, Inc. MIL.: ensign, U.S. Navy, 1917–19, lt. commander, 1943–44. MEM.: United World Federalists (dir., MA branch; dir., New England Council); American Management Assn. (dir.); Lowell Observatory (trustee, 1927–67); Petersham Memorial Library (trustee); Harvard Memorial Soc.; Nobles Club; Fly Club; Springfield Centennial

Cmte. (chm., 1952); Soldiers' Home (chm., Board of Trustees); American Red Cross (chapter pres.); Springfield Library Assn. (dir.); AAAS (fellow); Elks; Kiwanis; American Astronomical Soc.; Astronomical Soc. of the Pacific; Army and Navy Club; Delta Psi; Harvard Club; Colony Club; Knights of Columbus; Harvard Observatory (visitor); Newton Coll. of the Sacred Heart (trustee); New England Council (dir.); Inst. of 1770; Hasty Pudding Club; Iroquois Club. AWARDS: Master Knight of the Sovereign Military Order of Malta. HON. DEG.: LL.D., Boston Coll., 1949; LL.D., St. Anselm's Coll.; LL.D., U. of MA. REL.: R.C. RES.: Springfield, MA.

QUAY, MATTHEW STANLEY. b. Sep 30, 1833, Dillsburg, PA; d. May 28, 1904, Beaver, PA; par. Anderson Beaton and Catherine (McCain) Quay; m. Agnes Barclay, Oct 10, 1855; c. Richard Roberts; Major Andrew Gregg Curtin; Mary Agnew Davidson; Susan Willard; Coral. EDUC.: Beaver Acad.; Indian Acad.; grad., Jefferson Coll., 1850; studied law in offices of Penney and Sterrett, Pittsburgh, PA. POLIT. & GOV.: elected prothonotary, Beaver Cty., PA, 1856–60; military sec. to governor of PA, 1861–65; private sec. to governor of PA, 1865–67; elected as a Republican to PA State House, 1865–67; delegate, Rep. Nat'l. Conv., 1872, 1876, 1880, 1888, 1892, 1896, 1900; appointed sec. of the commonwealth of PA, 1872–78, 1879–82; elected as a Republican to recorder, Philadelphia, PA, 1878–79; chm., PA Republican State Cmte., 1878–79; elected as a Republican to state treas. of PA, 1885–87; member, Rep. Nat'l. Cmte., 1885–1904 (chm., 1888; exec. cmte., 1896); elected as a Republican to U.S. Senate (PA), 1887–99, 1901–04; ***candidate for Republican nomination to presidency of the U.S., 1896; candidate for Republican nomination to vice presidency of the U.S., 1896***; Republican candidate for U.S. Senate (PA), 1899; appointed as a Republican to U.S. Senate (PA), 1899 (not seated). BUS. & PROF.: atty.; admitted to PA Bar, 1854; law practice, Beaver, PA, 1854–61, 1865–1904; owner, ed., *Beaver Radical*, 1867–72; ed., *Recorder*, Philadelphia, PA. MIL.: lt., 10th Regt., PA Reserves, 1861–65; lt. col., asst. commissary gen., PA Military Agent, Washington, DC; col., 134th Regt., PA Volunteer Infantry; Medal of Honor. MEM.: GAR. REL.: Presb. MISC.: tried for misappropriation of funds and acquitted, Apr 21, 1899; appointed on same day to U.S. Senate (PA), but not seated by resolution of U.S. Senate of Apr 24, 1900. RES.: Beaver, PA.

QUAYLE, JAMES DANFORTH "DAN." b. Feb 4, 1947, Indianapolis, IN; par. James C. and Corinne (Pulliam) Quayle; m. Marilyn Tucker, Nov 18, 1972; c. Tucker Danforth; Benjamin Eugene; Mary Corrine. EDUC.: B.A., DePauw U., 1969; J.D., IN U., 1974. POLIT. & GOV.: staff, Consumer Protection Div., Office of Attorney General, state of IN, 1970–71; administrative asst. to gov. of IN, 1971–73; appointed dir., IN State Inheritance Tax Div., 1973–74; elected as a Republican to U.S. House (IN), 1977–81; elected as a Republican to U.S. Senate (IN), 1981–89; ***elected as a Republican to vice presidency of the U.S., 1989–1993; Republican candidate for vice presidency of the U.S., 1992***. BUS. & PROF.: atty.; admitted to IN Bar, 1974; pressman, reporter, *Huntington (IN) Herald-Press*, 1965–69, assoc. publisher, gen. mgr., 1974–76; instructor in business law, Huntington Coll., 1975. MIL.: IN National Guard, 1969–75. MEM.: IN Bar Assn.; Huntington Bar Assn.; Hoosier State Press Assn.; Fort Wayne Press Club; Huntington Cty. Retarded Citizens; Huntington Newspapers, Inc.; Rotary Club; Elks; C. of C. WRITINGS: *Standing Firm* (1994). REL.: Protestant. MAILING ADDRESS: North Jefferson St., Huntington, IN 46750.

QUITMAN, JOHN ANTHONY. b. Sep 1, 1798, Rhinebeck, NY; d. Jul 17, 1858, Natchez, MS; par. Rev. Frederick Henry and Anna Elizabeth (Hueck) Quitman; m. Eliza Turner, Dec 24, 1824; c. Edward; John; two daughters. EDUC.: grad., Hartwick Seminary, 1816. POLIT. & GOV.: elected as a Democrat to MS State House, 1826–27; chancellor, Superior Court of MS, 1828–35; delegate, MS State Constitutional Convention, 1832; elected as a Democrat to MS State Senate, 1835–36 (pres., 1835); elected acting gov. of MS, 1835–36; Democratic candidate for U.S. House (MS), 1836, 1847; appointed judge, High Court of Errors and Appeals, MS, 1838; presidential elector, Democratic Party, 1848; ***candidate for Democratic nomination to vice presidency of the U.S., 1848, 1856***; elected as a Democrat to gov. of MS, 1850–51; Democratic candidate for gov. of MS, 1851 (withdrew); ***Southern Rights Democratic Party candidate for vice presidency of the U.S., 1852***; elected as a Democrat to U.S. House (MS), 1855–58. BUS. & PROF.: adjunct prof. of English, Mount Airy Coll., PA, 1818; atty.; admitted to OH Bar, 1821; law practice, Natchez, MS, 1821; dir., Planters' Bank; superintendent, cotton and sugar plantation, MS. MIL.: brig. gen., MS Militia; brig. gen., U.S.V., 1846; maj. gen.,

U.S. Army, 1847–48; appointed military gov. of Mexico City, Mexico, 1847. MEM.: Masons (grand master of MS, 1826–38, 1840, 1845; Grand Council, Scottish Rite); Jefferson Coll. (pres., Board of Trustees); Natchez Acad. (trustee); Soc. for the Suppression of Duelling (pres.); MS State Hospital (dir.); MS State U. (trustee); MS Lyceum (trustee). HON. DEG.: A.M., Coll. of NJ (now Princeton U.); LL.D., Coll. of La Grange, KY. REL.: Lutheran. MISC.: noted as supporter of Nullification Doctrine; indicted for violation of neutrality laws as result of support for Cuban Independence, 1851; resigned gov.; acquitted. RES.: *Monmouth*, Natchez, MS.

QUINN, JOHN. b. c. 1924. POLIT. & GOV.: ***independent candidate for presidency of the U.S., 1972***. BUS. & PROF.: atty. MAILING ADDRESS: Key West, FL.

RAAFLAUB, DAVID. POLIT. & GOV.: Libertarian Party candidate for mayor of Ann Arbor, MI; ***candidate for Libertarian Party nomination to presidency of the U.S., 1992***. MISC.: known as the "Golden Mouth of Libertarianism." MAILING ADDRESS: Ann Arbor, MI.

RACHNER, MARY JANE. b. 1922. POLIT. & GOV.: candidate for Republican nomination to U.S. House (MN), 1992 and one other time; candidate for U.S. Senate (MN); ***candidate for Republican nomination to presidency of the U.S., 1988, 1992***. BUS. & PROF.: teacher. MISC.: noted for opposition to homosexuality. MAILING ADDRESS: 1917 Pinehurst Ave., St. Paul, MN 55116.

RAFETERY, THOMAS. b. 1870, NY. POLIT. & GOV.: campaign worker, Benjamin Harrison for President, 1892; ***candidate for Republican nomination to presidency of the U.S., 1932***. MAILING ADDRESS: 133 Lincoln Place, Brooklyn, NY.

RAINEY, HENRY THOMAS. b. Aug 20, 1860, Carrollton, IL; d. Aug 19, 1934, St. Louis, MO; par. John and Kate (Thomas) Rainey; m. Ella McBride, Jun 27, 1889; c. none. EDUC.: Knox Acad.; A.B., Amherst Coll., 1883, A.M., 1886; LL.B., Union Coll. of Law, 1885. POLIT. & GOV.: master in chancery, Greene Cty., IL, 1887–95; elected as a Democrat to U.S. House (IL), 1903–21, 1923–34 (Democratic leader, 1931–33; Speaker, 1933–34); Democratic candidate for U.S. House (IL), 1920; delegate, Dem. Nat'l. Conv., 1920, 1924; ***candidate for Democratic nomination to presidency of the U.S., 1928***. BUS. & PROF.: atty.; admitted to IL Bar, 1885; law practice, Carrollton, IL, 1885–1902; farmer. HON. DEG.: LL.D., U. of IL, 1930; LL.D., Amherst Coll., 1931; LL.D., Grove City Coll., 1933. RES.: Carrollton, IL.

RALPH, MYRON. POLIT. & GOV.: ***independent candidate for presidency of the U.S., 1988***. MAILING ADDRESS: c/o Cmte. to Elect Myron Ralph for a Highly Principled Government, P.O. Box 121, Woodgate, NY 13494.

RALSTON, SAMUEL MOFFETT. b. Dec 1, 1857, New Cumberland, OH; d. Oct 14, 1925, Indianapolis, IN; par. John and Sarah (Scott) Ralston; m. Mary Josephine Backous, Dec 26, 1881; m. 2d, Jennie Craven, Dec 30, 1889; c. Emmet Grattan; Julian Cravens; Ruth Ralston. EDUC.: Valparaiso (IN) Normal School; grad., Central IN Normal Coll., 1884. POLIT. & GOV.: Democratic candidate for IN State Senate, 1888; presidential elector, Democratic Party, 1888, 1892; Democratic candidate for IN state sec. of state, 1896, 1898; candidate for Democratic nomination to gov. of IN, 1908; elected pres., Lebanon (IN) School Board, 1908–11; elected as a Democrat to gov. of IN, 1913–17; delegate, Dem. Nat'l. Conv., 1920; elected as a Democrat to U.S. Senate (IN), 1923–29; ***candidate for Democratic nomination to presidency of the U.S., 1924***. BUS. & PROF.: schoolteacher, Fontanet, IN; atty.; admitted to IN Bar, 1886; law practice, Lebanon, IN, 1886; partner, Ralston, Gates, Lairy, Van Nuys and Barnard (law firm), Indianapolis, 1917. MEM.: Masons; Knights of Pythias. WRITINGS: *League of Nations* (1919); *Mellon Tax Plan* (1924). REL.: Presb. RES.: Indianapolis, IN.

RAMPTON, CALVIN LEWELLYN. b. Nov 6, 1913, Bountiful, UT; par. Lewellyn Smith and Janet (Campbell) Rampton; m. Lucybeth Cardon, Mar 10, 1940; c. Margaret R. Munk; Janet R. Warburton; Anthony L; Vincent C. EDUC.: B.S., U. of UT, 1936, J.D., 1940; George Washington U., 1937–40. POLIT. & GOV.: administrative asst. to U.S. Rep. J. W. Robinson, 1936–38; elected cty. atty., Davis Cty., UT, 1939–41; asst. atty. gen. of UT, 1941–42, 1946–48; elected as a Democrat to gov. of UT, 1965–77; chm., Education Comm. of the States, 1967–68; delegate, Dem. Nat'l. Conv., 1968, 1972;

candidate for Democratic nomination to presidency of the U.S., 1976. BUS. & PROF.: automobile business, Bountiful, UT, 1931–33; atty.; admitted to UT Bar, 1940; admitted to practice before the Bar of the Supreme Court of the U.S.; partner, Pugsley, Hayes, Rampton and Watkiss (law firm), Salt Lake City, UT, 1948–64. MIL.: member, UT National Guard, 1932–37; U.S.A.R. Field Judiciary Service (1932–43, 1946–64; col.); 2d lt., U.S. Army, 1937, maj., 1945; member, U.S. Army Claims Comm.; Bronze Star; Army Commendation Ribbon with Rhineland and West Germany Battle Stars. MEM.: Bar and Gavel Law Soc.; National Governors' Conference (chm., 1974–75); Council of State Governments (pres., 1974–75); International Acad. of Trial Lawyers; The New Coalition (chm., 1974–75); Western Governors' Conference (chm., 1969–70); Federation of Rocky Mountain States (chm., 1966–67, 1970–71, 1975–76). AWARDS: Distinguished Service Award, Environmental Planning Guide; "Outstanding Public Administrator of the Year," Inst. of Government Service, 1971; Presidential Citation, 1973; citation, U.S. Dept. of Justice; Brotherhood Award, UT Chapter, National Conference of Christians and Jews, 1973. HON. DEG.: LL.D., U. of Utah, 1970. REL.: Church of Jesus Christ of Latter-Day Saints. MAILING ADDRESS: 1270 Fairfax Rd., Salt Lake City, UT 84103.

RAMSEY, DAVID SHERMAN. POLIT. & GOV.: ***candidate for Republican nomination to presidency of the U.S., 1992***. MAILING ADDRESS: P.O. Box 1002, Mesa, AZ 85211.

RANDALL, CHARLES HIRAM. b. Jul 23, 1865, Auburn, NE; d. Feb 18, 1951, Los Angeles, CA; par. Rev. Elia J. and Sarah Frances (Schooley) Randall; m. May Ethel Stanley, Nov 15, 1885; m. 2d, Mrs. Edith B. Leake, Nov 24, 1932; m. 3d, Eva C. Wheeler; c. Violet V. Cassels. EDUC.: public schools. POLIT. & GOV.: member, Los Angeles (CA) Municipal Park Comm., 1909–10; elected as a Republican to CA State Assembly, 1911–12; elected as a Republican (Democrat-Prohibitionist-Progressive) to U.S. House (CA), 1915–21; Prohibition Party candidate for U.S. House (CA), 1920, 1922, 1924 (Prohibition-Democratic-Socialist), 1926, 1934, 1940; temporary chm., Prohibition Party National Convention, 1924; ***candidate for Prohibition Party nomination to presidency of the U.S., 1924; candidate for Prohibition Party nomination to vice presidency of the U.S., 1924; American Party candidate for vice presidency of the U.S., 1924 (declined)***; elected member, pres., Los Angeles City Council, 1925–33; Prohibition Party candidate for U.S. Senate (CA), 1928; Republican candidate for U.S. House (CA), 1932. BUS. & PROF.: ed., publisher, *The Observer*, Kimball, NE, 1885–92; railway mail clerk, 1892–1904; ed., *Herald*, Highland Park, CA, 1906–15. WRITINGS: "Telegraphic Demands for War-Time Prohibition," *Congressional Record*, Jun 20, 1917. REL.: Methodist (vice pres., National Board of Temperance, Prohibition and Public Morals). MISC.: first candidate of Prohibition Party elected to Congress; coauthor of Eighteenth Amendment to Constitution of the U.S. RES.: Los Angeles, CA.

RANDALL, SAMUEL JACKSON. b. Oct 10, 1828, Philadelphia, PA; d. Apr 13, 1890, Washington, DC; par. Josiah and Ann (Worrell) Randall; m. Fannie Agnes Ward, Jun 24, 1851; c. Mrs. Lancaster; one other daughter; one son. EDUC.: University Acad., Philadelphia, PA. POLIT. & GOV.: elected as an American Whig to Philadelphia (PA) Common Council, 1852–55; elected as a Democrat to PA State Senate, 1858–59; elected as a Democrat to U.S. House (PA), 1863–90 (Speaker, 1876–81); ***candidate for Democratic nomination to presidency of the U.S., 1880, 1884***; delegate, Dem. Nat'l. Conv., 1884. BUS. & PROF.: merchant; soldier. MIL.: member, First Troop, Philadelphia City Cavalry, 1861; sgt., Second U.S. Cavalry, 1861; cornet, provost marshall; capt., U.S. Army, 1861–63. RES.: Philadelphia, PA.

RANDOLPH, ASA PHILIP. b. Apr 15, 1889, Crescent City, FL; d. May 16, 1979, New York, NY; par. James William and Elizabeth Randolph (Robinson) Randolph; m. Lucille E. Campbell Green, 1914. EDUC.: Cookman Inst.; City Coll. of NY. POLIT. & GOV.: appointed member, New York (NY) Comm. on Race, 1935; ***candidate for Socialist Party nomination to presidency of the U.S., 1948***; hon. chm., White House Conference on Civil Rights, 1966; hon. chm., Socialist Party; *candidate for Democratic nomination to presidency of the U.S., 1976*. BUS. & PROF.: porter, Consolidated Edison Co.; waiter, restaurant, Jersey City, NJ; elevator operator; co-editor, *The Messenger*; labor organizer; lecturer, Rand School of Social Science; contributor, *Opportunities*; contributor, *Survey Graphic*. MEM.: Brotherhood of Sleeping Car Porters (pres., 1925–68; pres. emeritus, 1968–79); AFL-CIO (vice pres.; member, exec. council); League for Industrial Democracy; National Religion and Labor Foundation; Teachers' Union; A. Philip Randolph Inst. (pres., 1964–79); National Council for Permanent Fair Employment Practices Cmte. (co-chm.); March on Washington Movement (national dir.); Urban Coalition (co-chm., 1968); American Cmte. on Africa; Masons; Elks; Continental Congress for Economic Reconstruction. AWARDS: Presidential Medal of Freedom, 1964. HON. DEG.: LL.D., Howard U., 1940. WRITINGS: *Terms of Peace and the Darker Races; Truth About Lynching*. REL.: Methodist. MISC.: organizer, first union of elevator operators; led march on Washington, resulting in creation of Cmte. on Fair Employment Practices, 1941. RES.: New York, NY.

RANDOLPH, JENNINGS FITZ. b. Mar 8, 1902, Salem, WV; d. 1989, Washington, DC; par. Ernest and Idell (Bingman) Randolph; m. Mary Katherine Babb, Feb 18, 1933; c. Jennings, Jr.; Frank Babb. EDUC.: A.B. (magna cum laude), Salem Coll., 1924. POLIT. & GOV.: Democratic candidate for U.S. House (WV), 1930; elected as a Democrat to U.S. House (WV), 1933–47; appointed member, Governor's Cmte. on Employment of the Handicapped; appointed chm., WV Planning Board, Aviation Comm., 1940–45; chm., WA Aviation Planning Comm., 1947–49; delegate, Dem. Nat'l. Conv., 1948, 1952, 1956, 1964, 1968, 1976; chm., Airport Panel, Transportation Council, U.S. Dept. of Commerce, 1953; elected as a Democrat to U.S. Senate (WV), 1959–85; appointed member, President's Cmte. on Employment of the Handicapped; appointed U.S. delegate, Interparliamentary Union, 1962; appointed U.S. delegate, NATO Parliamentarians Conference, 1963; appointed U.S. delegate, Mexico-U.S. Interparliamentary Conference, 1970, 1973, 1975; appointed U.S. delegate, North Atlantic Assembly Plenary Session, 1973; appointed member, National Comm. on Water Quality; appointed member, Highway Beautification Comm.; ***candidate for Democratic nomination to presidency of the U.S., 1976, 1980***. BUS. & PROF.: ed., *Green and White*, 1922–23; ed., *The Message*, Salem, WV, 1922–25; editorial staff, *Clarksburg (WV) Daily Telegram*, 1924–25; assoc. ed., *West Virginia Review*, 1925–26; chm., Dept. of Public Speaking and Journalism, athletic dir., Davis and Elkins Coll., 1926–32; prof. of Public Speaking, Southeastern U., 1935–53, dean, Coll. of Business Administration, 1952–58; instructor, Leadership Training Inst., 1948–58; asst., dir. of Public Relations, Capital Airlines, 1947–58; assoc. ed., co-owner, *Randolph Enterprize-Review*. MEM.: Elkins C. of C. (dir.); WV C. of C. (dir.); WV Hist. Soc.; Randolph Cty. Hist. Soc.; WV Press Assn.; National Aeronautical Assn. (vice pres.); National Assn. of Physically Handicapped; People to People; U.S. Capitol Hist. Soc.; WV Acad. of Science; Lions Club (district gov., 1931–32; international counsellor); Tau Kappa Alpha; National Press Club; University Club; American Rd. Builders Assn. (pres., Airport Division, 1948–50; treas.); WA Board of Trade (dir.); World Trade Comm. (chm., 1947–50); Elkins Industrial Development Corp.; Baptist World Alliance (vice chm., North American Fellowship); Council for the Advancement of Small Colleges (national board); Salem Coll. (trustee); Claude Worthington Benedum Foundation (dir.); National Blinded Veterans Assn. (adviser); United Business Schools Assn. (adviser); National U.S.O. (gov.); Southeastern U. (trustee); Davis and Elkins Coll. (hon. trustee); James Madison Memorial Comm.; Youth Governors Conference (national sponsoring cmte., 1962–); Moose; Cabell Cty. Assn. for Mentally Retarded Children; U. of Washington Club. AWARDS: B'nai B'rith Award, 1961; West Virginian of the Year Award, *Gazette-Mail*, 1964; West Virginia Speaker of the Year Award, Delta Sigma Rho, 1968; Gold Medal of Merit, VFW, 1969; award, Cabell Cty. Assn. for Mentally Retarded Children, 1971; City of Hope Award, 1971; Man of the Year Award, National Federation of Independent Businessmen, 1971; President's Award, National Rehabilitation Assn., 1971; Migel Medal, American Foundation for the Blind, 1972; National Service Recognition Award, Izaac Walton League, 1972; Elder Statesman of Aviation Award, National Aeronautics Assn., 1972; Leadership Award, President's Cmte. on Employment of the Handicapped, 1972; Neil J. Curry Memorial Award, Highway Users Federation, 1974; Man of the Year Award, National Cmte. for Resource Recovery, 1976; Legislative Award, American Legion, 1978; Wright Brothers Memorial Trophy, National Aeronautics Assn., 1978. HON. DEG.: LL.D., Davis and Elkins Coll., 1930; Litt.D., Southeastern U., 1940; D.Aero.Sci., Salem Coll., 1943; H.H.D., WV State Coll., 1964; LL.D., U. of Pittsburgh, 1965; LL.D., Alderson Broaddus Coll., 1966; L.H.D., Maryville Coll., 1966; LL.D., Milton Coll., 1967; LL.D., Waynesburg Coll., 1967; LL.D., WV U., 1967; LL.D., WV Wesleyan U., 1967; D.Pub.Service, Bethany Coll., 1970; LL.D., Oral Roberts U., 1972; LL.D., Morris Harvey Coll., 1973; LL.D., Pikeville Coll., 1973; LL.D., Gallaudet Coll., 1974; LL.D., Marshall U., 1977. WRITINGS: *Mr. Chairman, Ladies and Gentlemen* (coauthor, 1939); *Going to Make a Speech?* (1948). REL.: Seventh-Day Bapt. RES.: Elkins, WV.

RANGE, MARGARET S. POLIT. & GOV.: ***candidate for Republican nomination to presidency of the U.S., 1992***. MAILING ADDRESS: 1120 Southwood Dr., Birmingham, AL 35217.

RANSOM, STEPHEN BILLINGS. b. Oct 12, 1814, Salem, CT; d. Dec 3, 1893, Jersey City, NJ; par. Amasa and Betsy Ransom; m. Maria C. Apgar, May 14, 1845; m. 2d, Eliza W. Hunt, Jul 1856; c. Stephen B., Jr.; four other sons; two daughters. EDUC.: Bacon Acad., Colchester, CT, to 1835; studied law under Phineas B. Kennedy, Belvidere, NJ; studied law under William Thompson, Somerville, NJ, 1841–44. POLIT. & GOV.: delegate, Rep. Nat'l. Conv., 1856; founder, NJ Temperance Party, 1869; member, Prohibition Party National Cmte., 1869–82; ***candidate for Prohibition Party nomination to vice presidency of the U.S., 1872***; Temperance Party candidate for gov. of NJ, 1880; Temperance Party candidate for NJ State Senate; presidential elector, Prohibition Party. BUS. & PROF.: teacher, Colchester, CT, 1835; teacher, Mendham, NJ; teacher, Belvidere, NJ; teacher, Hope, NJ; teacher, New Germantown, NJ; teacher, Chester, NJ; atty.; admitted to NJ Bar, 1844; law practice, New Germantown, NJ, 1844–47; law practice, Somerville, NJ, 1848–56; law practice, Jersey City, NJ, 1854–93; ed., *Ledger*, Jersey City, NJ; ed., *Mirror*, Jersey City. MIL.: commander, militia, New Germantown, NJ, 1845–46. MEM.: Sons of Temperance (most worthy patriarch, 1870–72). REL.: Methodist Episcopal Church. RES.: Jersey City, NJ.

RAPER, RALPH MILTON. b. Jan 27, 1917, Dalton, GA; par. John Robert and Evelyn Rebecca (Fraker) Raper; m. Cora Bernice Sosebee; c. Frank; Raymond; Zita; Kathy; Kristie. EDUC.: ninth grade, Rock Spring (GA) Junior H.S. POLIT. & GOV.: candidate for GA State Senate,, 1954; ***Rocking Chair Party candidate for vice presidency of the U.S., 1960***. BUS. & PROF.: country musician; songwriter; owner, Ralph's Music-Record Shop, Demorest, GA; radio-television technician; recording artist; publisher. MEM.: Masons; Odd Fellows. AWARDS: award, Broadcast Music, Inc., 1960. WRITINGS: *Country Music on Parade* (1959, 1960, 1961). REL.: Bapt.

MAILING ADDRESS: c/o Ralph's Music-Record Shop, Demorest, GA 30535.

RARICK, JOHN RICHARD. b. Jan 29, 1924, Waterford, IN; m. Marguerite Gertrude Pierce; c. John Richard, Jr.; Carolyn Cheri; Laurie Lee. EDUC.: Ball State Teachers Coll., 1942, 1944–45; LA State U., 1943–44; J.D., Tulane U., 1949. POLIT. & GOV.: elected district judge, 20th Judicial District of LA, 1961–66; elected as a Democrat to U.S. House (LA), 1967–75; candidate for Democratic nomination to gov. of LA, 1967; candidate for Democratic nomination to U.S. House (LA), 1974; ***candidate for American Party nomination to presidency of the U.S., 1976; candidate for American Independent Party nomination to presidency of the U.S., 1976, 1984***; independent candidate for U.S. House (LA), 1976; ***American Independent Party candidate for presidency of the U.S., 1980***. BUS. & PROF.: atty.; admitted to LA Bar, 1949; publisher, *You've A Right to Know*. MIL.: U.S. Army, WWII; captured in the Battle of the Bulge and spent four months in German prison camp; escaped and returned to U.S. lines; Bronze Star; Purple Heart; Two Battle Stars. MEM.: Lions; Toastmasters' Club; Masons (32°; Knight Commander, Court of Honor; Shriners; Knights Templar); American Legion; Order of the Eastern Star; Moose; Disabled American Veterans; VFW; NRA (life member); Farm Bureau; American Patriots Hall of Fame. AWARDS: George Washington Medal, Freedom Foundation of Valley Forge; Liberty Award, Congress of Freedom; Distinguished Service Award, Americans for Constitutional Action; Statesman of the Year Award, We, The People; J. Edgar Hoover Memorial Award, SCV; Number One Representative Award, National Economic Council; Man of the Year Award, Continental Congress of American Patriots; Honor Award, National Soc. of Magna Charta Dames; Queen Otha Medal, Women's Assn. for Defense of the Four Freedoms for Ukraine; Appreciation Award, LA Sugar Cane Industry Assn.; Citation, IL Gun Collectors Assn.; Environmental Ecology Award, LA Pine Tree Festival; Outstanding Service Award, SAR; American Citizen Award, Federation of American Citizens of German Descent; Southern Dames Award; Freedom Award for Christian Education, LA Farm Bureau; Patrick Henry Award, VA Conservative Party; Americanism Award, Catholic War Veterans; John Hampden Chalice, National SCV; Watchdog of the Treasury Award, National Assn. of Businessmen, 4 times; Appreciation Award, Americans of Italian Descent; medal, German American National Congress, Inc.; Eisenhower Proclamation Medal, Captive Nations Cmte.; Man of the Year Award, Women for Constitutional Government; Cardinal Mindzenty Medal. REL.: Bapt. MAILING ADDRESS: Box 236, St. Francisville, LA 70775.

RAVENAL, EARL CEDRIC. b. Mar 29, 1931, New York, NY; par. Alan M. and Mildred Phyllis (Sherman) Ravenal; m. Carol Myers, May 26, 1956; c. Cornelia Jane; John Brodhead; Rebecca Eliza. EDUC.: B.A. (summa cum laude), Harvard U., 1952, grad. study, 1958; Henry Fellow, Cambridge U., 1952–53; M.A., Johns Hopkins U., 1971, Ph.D., 1975. POLIT. & GOV.: dir., Asian Division, Systems Analysis, U.S. Dept. of Defense, 1967–69; member, Advisory Panel on Foreign Affairs, Democratic Presidential Campaign, 1972; adviser on foreign and national security policy, Gov. Edmund G. Brown, Jr., for President Campaign, 1976; adviser on foreign and national security policy, Edward E. Clark Presidential Campaign, 1980; ***candidate for Libertarian Party nomination to presidency of the U.S., 1984***. BUS. & PROF.: treas., vice pres., Elbe File and Binder Co., Inc., Fall River, MA, 1955–65, pres., 1965–67; assoc. fellow, Inst. for Policy Studies, Washington, DC, 1970–73; prof. of American Foreign Policy, School of Advanced International Studies, Johns Hopkins U., 1973–78; contributing ed., *Inquiry*; member, editorial board, *Cato Journal*; member, editorial board, *Journal of Libertarian Studies*; adjunct prof. of International Relations, School of Foreign Service, Georgetown U., 1974–. MIL.: corp., U.S. Army, 1953–55. MEM.: Council on Foreign Relations; APSA; Phi Beta Kappa; New Democratic Coalition (policy advisory council, 1977–79); RI Chamber Concerts (exec. cmte., 1957–67); Federation of American Scientists; Center for Defense Information (adviser); International Inst. for Strategic Studies; International Studies Assn.; Inter-University Seminar on Armed Forces and Soc.; Policy Studies Organization; Center for the Study of Ethics and International Affairs (overseer); Center for Libertarian Studies (adviser); National Capital Area Political Science Assn.; American Cmte. on East-West Accord; Cato Inst. (dir.); Inst. for the Study of Diplomacy; Cosmos Club; Federal City Club; Signet Soc.; Harvard Club of NY. WRITINGS: *Peace with China* (1971); *Atlantis Lost* (1976); *Foreign Policy in an Uncontrollable World* (1977); *Toward World Security* (1978); *NATO's Unremarked Demise* (1979); *Strategic Disengagement and World Peace* (1979); *Never Again* (1980); *Beyond the Balance of Power*. REL.: Unitarian. MAILING ADDRESS: 4439 Cathedral Ave., N.W., Washington, DC 20016.

RAY, ROBERT D. b. Sep 26, 1928, Des Moines, IA; par. Clark A. and Mildred (Dolph) Ray; m. Billie Lee Hornberger, Dec 21, 1951; c. Randi Sue; Lu Ann; Vicki Jo. EDUC.: B.A., Drake U., 1952, J.D., 1954. POLIT. & GOV.: chm., IA State Republican Central Cmte., 1963–67; elected as a Republican to gov. of IA, 1969–83; member, IA Geologic member, IA Exec. Council; member, Advisory Comm. on Intergovernmental Relations; member, President's National Reading Council; delegate, Rep. Nat'l. Conv., 1964, 1972, 1976; ***candidate for Republican nomination to vice presidency of the U.S., 1976***. BUS. & PROF.: atty.; admitted to IA Bar, 1954; assoc., Lawyer, Lawyer and Ray (law firm), Des Moines, IA, 1954–69. MIL.: U.S. Army, 1946–48. MEM.: Omicron Delta Kappa; Sigma Alpha Epsilon; Alpha Kappa Psi; Polk Cty. Bar Assn.; IA Bar Assn.; ABA; IA Trial Lawyers Assn.; Family Services of Des Moines; Practicing Law Inst. (dir.); BSA; March of Dimes (IA chm., 1960–62); Order of the Coif; Alpha Zeta; Midwest Assn. of Republican State Chairmen (chm., 1965); National Republican State Chairmen Assn. (chm., 1967–72); National Governors' Conference; Council of State Governments (vice pres.); Midwest Governors' Conference (chm., 1972); Republican Governors' Assn.; Delta Theta Phi; Make Today Count (hon. board member); Future Farmers of America. AWARDS: National Distinguished Service Award, Future Farmers of America, 1970; Distinguished Alumnus Award, Drake U. HON. DEG.: Central Coll.; Cornell Coll.; Grinell Coll.; IA Wesleyan Coll.; Luther Coll.; St. Ambrose's Coll.; Still Osteopathic Coll.; Upper IA Coll; Westmar Coll. REL.: Disciples of Christ. MAILING ADDRESS: 2900 Grand Ave., Des Moines, IA 50312.

RAYBURN, SAMUEL TALIAFERRO. b. Jan 6, 1882, Roane Cty., TX; d. Nov 16, 1961, Bonham, TX; par. William Marion and Martha (Waller) Rayburn; single. EDUC.: B.S., East TX Coll., 1903; studied law, U. of TX. POLIT. & GOV.: elected as a Democrat to TX State House, 1907–13 (Speaker, 1911–13); elected as a Democrat to U.S. House (TX), 1913–61 (majority leader, 1937–40; Speaker, 1940–47, 1949–53, 1955–61; minority leader, 1947–49, 1953–55); ***candidate for Democratic nomination to vice presidency of the U.S., 1940, 1944***; permanent chm., Dem. Nat'l. Conv., 1948, 1952, 1956. BUS. & PROF.: atty.; admitted to TX Bar, 1908; law practice, Bonham, TX; farmer, Bonham, TX. MEM.: National Press Club. RES.: Bonham, TX.

RAYMOND, PATRICK. b. 1949. POLIT. & GOV.: ***candidate for Democratic nomination to presidency of the U.S., 1984***. BUS. & PROF.: roofer; job estimator. MAILING ADDRESS: Sterling, MA.

RAYNER, KENNETH. b. Jun 20, 1808, Bertie Cty., NC; d. Mar 4, 1884, Washington, DC; par. Amos and _____ (Williams) Rayner; m. Susan Spratt Polk. EDUC.: Tarborough Acad.; studied law under Chief Justice Thomas Ruffin. POLIT. & GOV.: elected delegate, NC State Constitutional Convention, 1835; elected as a Whig to NC State House of Commons, 1836–39, 1846–52; elected as a Whig to U.S. House (NC), 1839–45; presidential elector, Whig Party, 1848; ***candidate for Whig Party nomination to vice presidency of the U.S., 1848***; elected as an American (Know Nothing) to NC State Senate, 1854; member, Grand Council, American (Know Nothing) Party; ***candidate for American (Know Nothing) Party nomination to presidency of the U.S., 1856; American (Know Nothing) Party candidate for vice presidency of the U.S., 1856 (declined)***; delegate, NC Secession Convention, 1861; Republican candidate for justice, Supreme Court of MS, 1873; appointed Court Commissioner of AL Claims, 1874–77; appointed solicitor, U.S. Dept. of the Treasury, 1877–84. BUS. & PROF.: atty.; admitted to NC Bar, 1829; law practice, Hertford Cty., NC; plantation owner, NC, AR, and MS; owner, sawmill, TN, 1869. WRITINGS: *To the People of North Carolina* (coauthor, 1840); *Speech . . . July 6, 1841* (1841); *Speech . . . June 15, 1841* (1841); *Address . . . Before Graduating Class of the U.S. Military Academy* (1853); *Reply* (1855); *Life and Times of Andrew Johnson* (1866). MISC.: secretly joined Peace Movement in NC during Civil War. RES.: Hertford Cty., NC.

READ, JOHN MEREDITH. b. Jul 21, 1797, Philadelphia, PA; d. Nov 29, 1874, Philadelphia, PA; par. John and Martha (Meredith) Read; m. Priscilla Marshall, Mar 20, 1828; m. 2d, Amelia Thompson, Jul 26, 1855; c. John Meredith, Jr.; four daughters. EDUC.: grad., U. of PA, 1812; LL.D., Brown U., 1860. POLIT. & GOV.: elected to PA State House, 1823–25; elected member, select council, Philadelphia, PA, 1827–28; city solicitor, Philadelphia, PA, 1830–31; appointed U.S. district atty. for Eastern PA, 1837–44; appointed assoc. justice, Supreme Court of the U.S., c. 1846 (not confirmed); appointed atty. gen. of PA, 1846; organizer, Free Soil Party; delegate, PA Free Soil Party State Convention, 1849; organizer, Republican Party; elected as a Republican, judge, PA State Supreme Court, 1858–73 (chief justice, 1872–73); ***candidate for Republican nomination to presidency of the U.S., 1860; candidate for Republican nomination to vice presidency of the U.S., 1860***. BUS. & PROF.: atty.; admitted to PA Bar, 1818; law practice, Philadelphia, PA, 1846–58. WRITINGS: *Speech . . . on the Power of Congress . . .* (1856); *Views, Sustained by Facts, on the Suspension of the Privilege of the Writ of Habeas Corpus* (1863). RES.: Philadelphia, PA.

REAGAN, RONALD WILSON. b. Feb 6, 1911, Tampico, IL; par. John Edward and Nelle (Wilson) Reagan; m. Jane Wyman, Jan 25, 1940 (divorced); m. 2d, Nancy Davis, Mar 4, 1952; c. Maureen Elizabeth; Michael Edward; Patricia Ann; Ronald Prescott. EDUC.: B.A., Eureka Coll., 1932. POLIT. & GOV.: member, CA Republican State Central Cmte., 1964–66; elected as a Republican to gov. of CA, 1967–75; appointed member, Presidential Comm. on CIA Activities Within the U.S., 1976; ***Conservative Party of VA candidate for vice presidency of the U.S., 1968***; delegate, Rep. Nat'l. Conv., 1968, 1972; ***candidate for Republican nomination to presidency of the U.S., 1968, 1976; candidate for Republican nomination to vice presidency of the U.S., 1976; candidate for American Party nomination to presidency of the U.S., 1976; candidate for American Independent Party nomination to presidency of the U.S., 1976; NM American Independent Party candidate for presidency of the U.S., 1976 (declined); received 1 electoral vote for presidency of the U.S., 1976; American Party of KS candidate for presidency of the U.S., 1980 (declined); elected as a Republican, presidency of the U.S., 1981–1989***. BUS. & PROF.: rancher; businessman; actor; commentator; sports announcer, radio station WHO, Des Moines, IA, 1932–37; actor, Warner Brothers, Universal Studios, 1937–54; actor, production supervisor, "General Electric Theatre" (television series), 1954–62; actor, host, "Death Valley Days" (television series), 1962–66. MOTION PICTURE CREDITS: "Love is on the Air" (1937); "Submarine D-1"; "Hollywood Hotel" (1938); "Swing Your Lady" (1938); "Sergeant Murphy" (1938); "Accidents Will Happen" (1938); "Cowboy from Brooklyn" (1938);

"Boy Meets Girl" (1938); "Girls on Probation" (1938); "Brother Rat" (1938); "Going Places" (1939); "Secret Service of the Air" (1939); "Dark Victory" (1939); "Code of the Secret Service" (1939); "Naughty But Nice" (1939); "Hell's Kitchen" (1939); "Angels Wash Their Faces" (1939); "Smashing the Money Ring" (1939); "Brother Rat and a Baby" (1940); "An Angel From Texas" (1940); "Murder in the Air" (1940); "Knute Rockne—All American" (1940); "Tugboat Annie Sails Again" (1940); "Santa Fe Trail" (1940); "The Bad Man" (1941); "Million Dollar Baby" (1941); "International Squadron" (1941); "Nine Lives Are Not Enough" (1941); "King's Row" (1941); "Juke Girl" (1942); "Desperate Journey" (1942); "This Is the Army" (1943); "Stallion Road" (1947); "That Hagen Girl" (1947); "The Voice of the Turtle" (1947); "Night Unto Night" (1948); "John Loves Mary" (1949); "The Girl From Jones Beach" (1949); "It's a Great Feeling" (1949); "The Hasty Heart" (1950); "Louisa" (1950); "Storm Warning" (1951); "Bedtime for Bonzo" (1951); "The Last Outpost" (1951); "Hong Kong" (1952); "She's Working Her Way Through College" (1952); "The Winning Team" (1952); "Tropic Zone" (1953); "Law and Order" (1953); "Prisoner of War" (1954); "Cattle Queen of Montana" (1954); "Tennessee's Partner" (1955); "Hellcats of the Navy" (1957); "The Killers" (1964). MIL.: capt., U.S. Army, 1942–46. MEM.: Tau Kappa Epsilon; Republican Governors' Assn. (chm., 1968–73); A.F.T.R.A.; Screen Actors Guild (pres., 1947–52, 1959); Cmte. on Present Danger (dir.); Citizens for the Republic (founder); Motion Picture Industry Council (pres.); Lions; Friars Club. AWARDS: "Great American of the Decade" Award, Virginia Young Americans for Freedom, 1960, 1970; "Man of the Year" Free Enterprise Award, San Fernando Valley Business and Professional Assn., 1964; award, American Legion, 1965; Horatio Alger Award, 1969; George Washington Honor Medal, Freedom Foundation of Valley Forge, 1971; National Humanitarian Award, National Conference of Christians and Jews; Torch of Life Award for Humanitarian Service, City of Hope; award, American Newspaper Guild; Distinguished American Award, National Football Foundation Hall of Fame; named to American Patriots Hall of Fame; Medal of Valor, State of Israel. WRITINGS: *Where's the Rest of Me?* (1965); *An American Life* (1990). REL.: Christian Church (attends Presb. Church). MAILING ADDRESS: 668 St. Cloud Rd., Bel Air, CA 90077.

REAMS, PRETTY BOB S. b. Nov 30, 1943, Flint, MI; par. Cleavon and Alpha Reams; single. EDUC.: elementary school. POLIT. & GOV.: independent candidate for mayor of Flint, MI; ***independent candidate for presidency of the U.S., 1988***; candidate for gov. of MI; ***candidate for Republican nomination to presidency of the U.S., 1992***. MAILING ADDRESS: 2113 Howard St., Flint, MI 48503.

REAUX, DON. POLIT. & GOV.: ***candidate for Democratic nomination to presidency of the U.S., 1980***. MAILING ADDRESS: Freeport, TX.

REBER, RICHARD FREDERICK, JR. par. Richard Frederick Reber, Sr. POLIT. & GOV.: ***candidate for Republican nomination to presidency of the U.S., 1992***. MAILING ADDRESS: 685 Winding Creek Trail, Dacula, GA 30211.

REDFIELD, WILLIAM COX. b. Jun 18, 1858, Albany, NY; d. Jun 13, 1932, New York, NY; par. Charles Bailey and Mary (Wallace) Redfield; m. Elsie Mercein Fuller, Apr 8, 1885; c. Elsie M. (Mrs. Charles K. Drury); Humphrey F. EDUC.: high school, Pittsfield, MA. POLIT. & GOV.: Gold Democratic Party candidate for U.S. House (NY), 1896; delegate, Gold Democratic Party National Convention, 1896; appointed commissioner of public works, Brooklyn, NY, 1902–03; elected as a Democrat to U.S. House (NY), 1911–13; ***candidate for Democratic nomination to vice presidency of the U.S., 1912***; appointed U.S. sec. of commerce, 1913–19; member, Federal Board of Vocational Education; member, National Council of Defense; member, War Trade Council; chm., American-Canadian Fisheries Conference. BUS. & PROF.: employee, Pittsfield (MA) Post Office; employee, R. Hoe and Co. (stationary and printing), New York, NY, 1879–83; treas., J. H. Williams and Co. (drop forgings), Brooklyn, NY, 1887–1901, pres., 1905; vice pres., Warp Twisting-in Machine Co., 1904; pres., Sirocco Engineering Co., 1907–11; vice pres., American Blower Co., 1909–13; dir., Equitable Life Assurance Soc., 1905–13; lecturer. MEM.: National Inst. of Social Sciences (pres.); American Manufacturers' Export Assn. (pres.); National Soc. for the Promotion of Industrial Education; American-Russian C. of C.; The Netherlands C. of C. in NY. WRITINGS: *The New Industrial Day* (1912); *With Congress and Cabinet* (1924); *Glimpses of Our Government* (1924–25); *Dependent America* (1926); *We and the World* (1927). REL.: Episc. RES.: New York, NY.

REDMOND, WILLIAM ALOYSIUS. b. Nov 25, 1908, Chicago, IL; par. William P. and Gertrude (Crowe) Redmond; m. Rita Riordan, Mar 6, 1943; c. Mary; William Patrick; Colleen. EDUC.: B.S., Marquette U., 1931; J.D., Northwestern U., 1934. POLIT. & GOV.: village atty., Bensenville, IL; school board atty.; elected as a Democrat to IL State House, 1959–81 (Speaker, sessions 79–81); chm., Du Page Cty. (IL) Democratic Central Cmte., 1973–; ***candidate for Democratic nomination to vice presidency of the U.S., 1980***; appointed member, IL Prison Review Board, 1982–. BUS. & PROF.: atty.; admitted to IL Bar; law practice, Chicago, IL, 1934–42. MIL.: lt. commander, U.S.N.R., 1941–45. MEM.: ABA; IL Bar Assn.; Du Page Cty. Bar Assn.; American Legion; Lions; Knights of Columbus. REL.: R.C. MAILING ADDRESS: 250 Tioga, Bensenville, IL 60106.

REDSTONE, ALFRED E. POLIT. & GOV.: delegate, Independent Party National Convention, 1876; member, Independent Party National Exec. Cmte., 1876; delegate, Union

Labor Party National Convention, 1888; temporary chm., Industrial Reform Party National Convention, 1888; ***Industrial Reform Party candidate for presidency of the U.S., 1888***. BUS. & PROF.: patent atty., Washington, DC; publisher, *Reform Journal*. MIL.: col. MEM.: Commonweal; Coxey's Army; National Labor Council (pres.). WRITINGS: *Handbook of Ready Reference for the Reform Forces of America* (1898). RES.: CA.

REECE, BRAZILLA CARROLL. b. Dec 22, 1889, Butler, TN; d. Mar 19, 1961, Bethesda, MD; par. John Isaac and Sarah E. (Maples) Reece; m. Louise Despard Goff, Oct 30, 1923; m. 2d, Shirley R.; c. Louise Goff (Mrs. George W. Marthens). EDUC.: Watuauga Acad.; Carson and Newman Coll., 1910–14; NY U., 1915–16; U. of London, 1919. POLIT. & GOV.: elected as a Republican to U.S. House (TN), 1921–31, 1933–47, 1951–61; Republican candidate for U.S. House (TN), 1930; delegate, Rep. Nat'l. Conv., 1932, 1936, 1940, 1944, 1948; chm., Rep. Nat'l. Cmte., 1946–48; Republican candidate for U.S. Senate (TN), 1948; ***candidate for Republican nomination to presidency of the U.S., 1948***. BUS. & PROF.: asst. sec. and instructor in Economics, NY U., 1916–17, dir., School of Commerce, Accounts and Finance, 1919–20; partner, Reece Brothers (merchants and lumbermen); atty.; pres., Carter Cty. Bank; pres., First National Bank of Jonesboro; pres., First People's Bank; pres., Kingsport National Bank; pres., Farmers Bank, Blountville, TN; publisher, *Bristol (VA) Herald Courier*; pres., Sullivan Cty. Bank. MIL.: lt., 3d Battalion, 102d Infantry, U.S. Army, 1917–19; Distinguished Service Cross; Distinguished Service Medal; Purple Heart; Croix de Guerre with Palm (France). MEM.: Smithsonian Institution (regent); American Economic Assn.; American Statistical Assn.; American Acad. of Political Science; ABA; TN Bar Assn.; Bar Assn. of DC; Delta Sigma Pi; Elks; J.O.U.A.M.; Masons (32°; Shriners); Metropolitan Club; Chevy Chase Club; Lotos Club; Metropolitan Club of NY; Newcomen Soc.; Robert A. Taft Memorial Foundation, Inc. (pres.). HON. DEG.: LL.D., Cumberland U., 1928; Dr.Humanities, Lincoln Memorial U., 1946; LL.D., Tusculum Coll. WRITINGS: *Addresses and Articles on the Life of Andrew Johnson*. REL.: Bapt. RES.: Johnson City, TN.

REED EVELYN NOVACK. b. Oct 31, 1905, Haledon, NJ; d. Mar 22, 1979, New York, NY; d. David and Ruth (Kramer) Horwitt; m. George Novack; c. none. EDUC.: Parsons School of Design and Art Students League; studied painting with John Sloan, George Luks, Grant Wood; U. of IA, 1933–34. POLIT. & GOV.: ***Socialist Workers Party candidate for presidency of the U.S., 1972 (proxy for Linda Jenness, q.v.)***. BUS. & PROF.: asst. in household of Leon Trotsky, Mexico, 1939–40; exec. dir., Civil Rights Defense Cmte., 1940–45; staff writer, *Militant*, 1945–79; contributor, *Fourth International*; contributor, *International Socialist Review*; anthropologist; lecturer; author; political activist. MEM.: Socialist Scholars Conference (1970); Southern Female Rights Union Conference (1970); Women's National Abortion Action Council; Civil Rights Defense Cmte. WRITINGS: *Problems of Women's Liberation* (1969); *Is Biology Woman's Destiny?: An Answer to the Naked Ape*; *Writings of Leon Trotsky* (1969); *Writings of Leon Trotsky, 1937–38* (1970); *In Defense of the Women's Movement* (coauthor, 1970); *The Origin of the Family, Private Property, and the State* (introduction, 1972); *Women's Evolution from Matriarchal Clan to Patriarchal Family* (1975); *Sexism and Science* (1978); *Abortion and the Catholic Church* (coauthor); *Abortion Is a Woman's Right* (coauthor); *Cosmetics, Fashions, and the Exploitation of Women* (1986). REL.: none. RES.: New York, NY.

REED, JAMES ALEXANDER. b. Nov 9, 1861, Mansfield, OH; d. Sep 8, 1944, Fairview, MI; par. John A. and Nancy (Crawford) Reed; m. Lura Mansfield Olmsted, Aug 1, 1887; m. 2d, Mrs. Nell Quinlan Donnelly, Dec 13, 1933; c. none. EDUC.: Coe Coll.; studied law in offices of Hubbard, Clark and Dawley, Cedar Rapids, IA, 1882–85. POLIT. & GOV.: chm., Cty. Democratic Central Cmte., IA, 1879; elected counselor, Kansas City, MO, 1897–98; elected prosecuting atty., Jackson Cty., MO, 1898–1900; elected as a Democrat, mayor of Kansas City, MO, 1900–1904; candidate for Democratic nomination to gov. of MO, 1904; delegate, Dem. Nat'l. Conv., 1908, 1912, 1916, 1920, 1924; elected as a Democrat to U.S. Senate (MO), 1911–29; member, exec. cmte., Dem. Nat'l. Cmte., 1912–14; ***candidate for Democratic nomination to presidency of the U.S., 1924, 1928, 1932; Farmer-Labor Party candidate for vice presidency of the U.S., 1928 (declined)***; appointed member, Comm. on Construction of U.S. Supreme Court Building. BUS. & PROF.: atty.; admitted to IA Bar, 1885; law practice, Cedar Rapids, IA, 1885–87; law practice, Kansas City, MO, 1887; partner, Reed and Harvey (subsequently Reed, Yates, Mastin and Harvey; Reed, Holmes, Higgins and Harvey; law firm), Kansas City, MO, 1904–29. MEM.: MO Bar Assn.; Kansas City Club; National Jeffersonian Democrats Club (founder, 1936). WRITINGS: *The Rape of Temperance* (1931). RES.: Kansas City, MO.

REED, PAUL. POLIT. & GOV.: ***independent candidate for presidency of the U.S., 1980***. MAILING ADDRESS: 1226-B West 168th, Gardena, CA 90247.

REED, PAUL TERRY. b. Jul 22, 1947, Waterbury, CT; par. John Paul and Alice E. (Schell) Reed; m. Claudia Brainerd; c. Shane David; Jason Paul. EDUC.: grad., Rockville H.S., Vernon, CT; Holyoke Community Coll. POLIT. & GOV.: ***independent candidate for presidency of the U.S., 1980***. BUS. & PROF.: correctional officer, Somers Prison. REL.: R.C. MAILING ADDRESS: 44 Beech Rd., Enfield, CT 06082.

REED, RALPH RANDOLPH. b. 1944, Hampton, VA. POLIT. & GOV.: independent candidate for U.S. House (VA), 1974; independent candidate for U.S. Senate (VA), 1976, 1978; ***U.S. People's Party candidate for vice presi-***

dency of the U.S., 1976; Thedeonalm independent candidate for presidency of the U.S., 1976. BUS. & PROF.: employee, paint shop, Eastern State Hospital, VA; employee, Hospitality House, Williamsburg, VA, 1974; kitchen helper, Williamsburg Inn, Williamsburg, VA, 1976; employee, Fass Brothers, Phoebus, VA, 1977; employee, city of Newport News, VA, 1978. MIL.: U.S.M.C., 1 year. REL.: Presb. MAILING ADDRESS: 5500 Orcutt Ave., Newport News, VA.

REED, THOMAS BRACKETT. b. Oct 18, 1839, Portland, ME; d. Dec 7, 1902, Washington, DC; par. Thomas Brackett and Mathilda P. (Mitchell) Reed; m. Mrs. Susan Prentice (Marrill) Jones, Feb 5, 1870; c. Katharine (Mrs. Arthur T. Balentine). EDUC.: grad., Bowdoin Coll., 1860; studied law. POLIT. & GOV.: elected as a Republican to ME State House, 1868–69; elected as a Republican to ME State Senate, 1870; elected as a Republican, atty. gen. of ME, 1870–72; candidate for Republican nomination to atty. gen. of ME, 1873; city solicitor, Portland, ME, 1874–77; elected as a Republican to U.S. House (ME), 1877–99 (Speaker, 1889–91, 1895–99); ***candidate for Republican nomination to presidency of the U.S., 1892, 1896; candidate for Republican nomination to vice presidency of the U.S., 1892, 1896***. BUS. & PROF.: teacher, Portland (ME) H.S.; atty.; admitted to CA Bar, 1863; admitted to ME Bar, 1865; law practice, Portland, ME; partner, Reed, Simpson, Thatcher and Barnum (law firm), New York, NY, 1899–1902. MIL.: acting asst. paymaster, U.S. Navy, 1864–65. WRITINGS: *Modern Eloquence* (ed., 10 vols., 1901); *Reed's Rules* (1894). REL.: Free Thinker. RES.: Portland, ME.

REEDER, ANDREW HORATIO. b. Jul 12, 1807, Easton, PA; d. Jul 5, 1864, Easton, PA; par. Absalom and Christiana (Smith) Reeder; m. Amelia Hutter, 1831; c. eight. EDUC.: Rev. Mr. Bishop's School, Easton, PA; studied law under Peter Ihrie, 1825. POLIT. & GOV.: appointed as a Democrat, territorial gov. of KS, 1854–55 (removed at request of legislature); delegate, Big Springs Convention, 1855; Republican candidate for U.S. House (KS), 1854; elected as a Republican to U.S. Senate (KS), 1856 (not seated); pres., Cleveland Convention for KS Aid, 1856; delegate, Rep. Nat'l. Conv., 1860, 1864; ***candidate for Republican nomination to vice presidency of the U.S., 1860***. BUS. & PROF.: atty.; admitted to NJ Bar, 1828. MIL.: brig. gen., U.S. Army, 1861 (declined); indicted for treason, but escaped by way of Missouri River disguised as an Irish laborer, 1855. RES.: Easton, PA.

REEDY, WINDI APRIL. b. Apr 11, 1975, Cody, WY. POLIT. & GOV.: ***independent candidate for presidency of the U.S., 1984 (satire effort)***. BUS. & PROF.: Labrador Retriever owned by Rose Reedy; sponsored as a satire effort by Gil Campbell (q.v.). MAILING ADDRESS: 4150 Riverside, Boulder, CO 80303.

REGAN, FRANK STEWART. b. Oct 2, 1862, Rockford, IL; d. Jul 25, 1944, Canton, IL; par. Marshall H. and Adelaide Regan; m. Helen M. Crumb, Jun 11, 1895; c. Adelaide; Frances L.; Leland S. EDUC.: grad., Rockford (IL) H.S., 1881. POLIT. & GOV.: elected as a Prohibitionist, alderman, Rockford, IL; elected as a Prohibitionist to IL State House, 1899–1901; Prohibition Party candidate for atty. gen. of IL, 1900, 1908; Prohibition Party candidate for U.S. House (IL), 1902; member, Prohibition Party National Cmte., 1904–08; ***Prohibition Party candidate for vice presidency of the U.S., 1932***; Prohibition Party candidate for IL state treas., 1934. BUS. & PROF.: atty.; lecturer; cartoonist; admitted to IL Bar, 1895; law practice, Rockford, IL, 1895; sec.-treas., Rockford Abstract Co. (now Holland-Ferguson Title Co.), 1894; pres., Regan Oil and Service Co. (distributors of Dixie Products Co.); ed., *The Taxpayer*; completed abstract of books of Winnebago, IL, 1888. MEM.: Masons; Young People's No License League (pres.); Citizens Assn. (chm.). WRITINGS: *The Fool Taxpayer*; *What is Wrong with Prohibition?*; *One Percent Tax Limit for Illinois*; *Things That Are Wrong Don't Pay*; *Taxes: Who Pays and Who Escapes*. REL.: Congregationalist. RES.: Rockford, IL.

REHFIELD, DAVID MICHAEL. b. Aug 19, 1942, Mason City, IA; par. William Rehfield. EDUC.: grad., Marquette H.S., Yakima, WA, 1960; B.S., Seattle U., 1964; M.S., U. of AZ, 1967; Ph.D., McGill U., 1977. POLIT. & GOV.: ***Peace and Freedom Party candidate for vice presidency of the U.S., 1968***. BUS. & PROF.: physicist; teaching asst., U. of AZ, 1964–67; fellow, II Physikalishes Institut Justus Liebzig U., Germany, 1977–79; research assoc., Foster Radiation Laboratory, McGill U., 1979–81; instructor, Vanier Coll., Montreal, Canada, 1981–82; asst. prof., Swarthmore Coll., 1981–82; visiting scientist, Brookhaven National Laboratory, 1980–; research collaborator, National Research Council of Canada, 1981–; asst. prof. of Physics, Lafayette Coll., 1982–. MEM.: Cmte. to Resist the Draft; Sigma Xi; American Assn. of Physics teachers. MISC.: convicted of draft card burning and sentenced to indeterminate sentence in Federal Youth Correction Camp, 1968. MAILING ADDRESS: 1710 Broadway, Yakima, WA.

REID, WHITELAW. b. Oct 27, 1837, Xenia, OH; d. Dec 15, 1912, London, England; par. Robert Charlton and Marian Whitelaw (Ronalds) Reid; m. Elizabeth Mills, Apr 26, 1881; c. Ogden Mills; Jean Templeton (Mrs. John Hubert Ward). EDUC.: A.B., Miami U., Oxford, OH, 1856. POLIT. & GOV.: sec., Republican Cty. Central Cmte., Xenia, OH, 1860; clerk, Military Cmte., U.S. House, 1862–63; librarian, U.S. House, 1863–66; appointed U.S. minister to Germany, 1877 (declined), 1881 (declined); elected to NY U. Board of Regents, 1878; appointed U.S. minister to France, 1889–92; ***Republican candidate for vice presidency of the U.S., 1892; candidate for Republican nomination to vice presidency of the U.S., 1896***; appointed special ambassador to Queen Victoria's Jubilee, 1897;

appointed U.S. delegate, Paris Peace Comm., 1898; appointed special U.S. ambassador to Coronation of King Edward VII, 1902; appointed U.S. ambassador to England, 1905–12. BUS. & PROF.: journalist; ed., *Xenia (OH) News*, 1858–59; city ed., legislative correspondent, *Cincinnati (OH) Gazette*, 1860–61, war correspondent, 1861–62, Washington (DC) correspondent, 1862–68; cotton planter, Concordia Parish, LA, 1866–67; editorial staff, *New York (NY) Tribune*, 1868–69, managing ed., 1869–72, editor-in-chief, proprietor, 1872–1905; vice chancellor, NY U., 1902–04, chancellor, 1904; founder, linotype company. MIL.: capt., U.S. Army, 1861. MEM.: U. of NY (regent; vice chancellor, 1902; chancellor, 1904); Stanford U. (trustee). HON. DEG.: A.M., U. of the City of New York, 1872; A.M., Dartmouth Coll., 1873; LL.D., Miami U., Oxford, OH, 1890; LL.D., Princeton U., 1899; LL.D., Yale U., 1901; LL.D., Cambridge U., 1902; LL.D., St. Andrew's Coll., 1905; D.C.L., Oxford U., 1907; LL.D., Manchester U., 1909. WRITINGS: *After the War: A Southern Tour* (1867); *Ohio in the War* (1868); *Schools of Journalism* (1870); *Newspaper Tendencies* (1874); *Town Hall Suggestions* (1881); *Two Speeches at the Queen's Jubilee* (1897); *Some Consequences of the Last Treaty of Paris* (1899); *Our New Duties* (1899); *Later Aspects of Our New Duties* (1899); *A Continental Union* (1900); *Our New Interests* (1900); *Problems of Expansion* (1900); *Carnegie Institute Address* (1902); *Monroe Doctrine* (1903); *Greatest Fact in Modern History* (1906); *How American Faced Its Educational Problem* (1906); *American and English Studies* (2 vols., 1913); *Tallyrand's Memoirs* (introduction, 1891); *Thackeray's Vanity Fair* (introduction, 1908). RES.: New York, NY.

REID, WILLIE MAE. b. Mar 27, 1939, Memphis, TN; d. Willie and Arvella (Moore) R.; single. EDUC.: grad., Manassas H.S., Memphis, TN, 1957; Knoxville Coll., 1957–58; Loop Junior Coll., Chicago, IL, 1966–68; U. of IL, Chicago, IL, 1968–69; IL Inst. of Technology, 1970–72. POLIT. & GOV.: Socialist Workers Party candidate for U.S. House (IL), 1971, 1974; Socialist Workers Party candidate for mayor of Chicago, IL, 1975; chair, Socialist Workers Party Campaign Cmte., Chicago, IL, 1975; ***Socialist Workers Party candidate for vice presidency of the U.S., 1976, 1992***; chair, Socialist Workers Party National Campaign Cmte., 1977. BUS. & PROF.: hospital kitchen worker, Memphis, TN; hotel worker, Memphis, TN; cotton picker; garment worker, Memphis, TN, and Chicago, IL; clerk, Prudential Insurance Co., Chicago, IL, 1958–68, computer programmer, 1970–74; staff writer, *Militant*, 1976–79; oil refinery worker, Exxon-Bayway, 1979–. MEM.: Loop Afro-American Soc.; Together One Community (publicity dir., 1969–71); Women's Abortion Action Coalition; National Black Feminist Organization; National Organization for Women; NAACP; Resident Development Corp. (sec., 1970–72). AWARDS: Community Service Award, Prudential Insurance Co., 1972. WRITINGS: *The Racist Offensive Against Busing* (coauthor); *Black Women's Struggle for Equality* (coauthor). REL.: none. MAILING ADDRESS: 8435 South Dorchester, Chicago, IL 60619.

REIMER, ARTHUR ELMER. b. Jan 15, 1882, South Boston, MA; d. Jan 1, 1933, West Roxbury, MA; m. Ann Ross. EDUC.: LL.B., YMCA Law School (now Northeastern U. Law School), 1912. POLIT. & GOV.: joined Socialist Labor Party, 1898; Socialist Labor Party candidate for MA State sec. of state, 1907; delegate, Socialist Labor Party National Convention, 1908; member, Socialist Labor Party National Cmte., 1911–14 (representative, International Socialist Bureau); ***Socialist Labor Party candidate for presidency of the U.S., 1912, 1916***; Socialist Labor Party candidate for gov. of MA, 1913, 1914; Socialist Labor Party delegate, Unity Convention, 1917; left Socialist Labor Party, 1918. BUS. & PROF.: tailor; atty. MEM.: Workingmen's Sick and Death Benefit Fund; Elks; Masons; Industrial Workers of the World (1905–08). MISC.: participated in NJ Silk Strike, 1912. RES.: West Roxbury, MA.

REINERT, CHARLES NORTON. POLIT. & GOV.: ***independent candidate for presidency of the U.S., 1980***. MAILING ADDRESS: 556 Saratoga Ave., Grover City, CA 93433.

REITER, JULIUS JOHN. b. Jul 4, 1869, Elgin, MN; d. Nov 29, 1940, Rochester, MN; par. Julius John Reiter; m. Bertha Kruger, Aug 5, 1891; c. Oscar A.; Clarence; Mrs. Merle R. Jewell; Mrs. Bess Gordy. POLIT. & GOV.: elected as a Democrat, alderman, Rochester, MN, 1899–1903; appointed deputy State Oil Inspector, Olmsted Cty., MN, 1905; chm., Rochester (MN) Street Cmte.; chm., Democratic Cty. Central Cmte., Rochester, MN; elected as a Democrat, mayor of Rochester, MN, 1907–09, 1917–19, 1923–25, 1931–35; member, MN State Democratic Central Cmte., 1904; appointed member, Rochester (MN) Utility Board (pres., 1911); candidate for Democratic nomination to gov. of MN, 1908; Democratic candidate for lt. gov. of MN, 1908; Democratic candidate for MN State Railroad and Warehouse Commissioner, 1912; founder, MN Farmer-Labor Party; Farmer-Labor Party candidate for U.S. House (MN), 1920, 1924, 1928, 1930; ***Farmer-Labor Party candidate for vice presidency of the U.S., 1932***. BUS. & PROF.: grocer; partner, Reiter Brothers Grocery, 1892–1916; partner, restaurant, 1894–95; owner, Reiter Grocery, 1916–40; owner, Reiter Apartments, 1918–40. MEM.: National Retail Grocerymen's Assn.; Southern MN Fair Assn. (dir.); MN Commercial Federation (dir., 1909); Federation of Commercial Clubs (exec. dir., 1909). REL.: Lutheran. RES.: Rochester, MN.

REITSMA, JEROME DONALD. b. Apr 22, 1958, Minneapolis, MN; par. Donald William and Mildred Beatrice (O'Konek) Reitsma; single. EDUC.: Brown Inst.; U. of MN. POLIT. & GOV.: ***independent candidate for presidency of the U.S., 1984***. BUS. & PROF.: student, U. of MN; announcer-reporter, KVFC Radio, Cortez, CO; poet. REL.: R.C. MAILING ADDRESS: 727 15th Ave., S.E., Minneapolis, MN 55414.

RELANTE, MORRIS. POLIT. & GOV.: ***Commonwealth Party candidate for vice presidency of the U.S., 1976.*** MAILING ADDRESS: c/o National Maritime Union, 7602 Navigation Boulevard, Houston, TX 77012.

REMMEL, VALENTINE. b. Mar 10, 1853, Pittsburgh, PA; par. Conrad Remmel; m. Jennie Harlan, Jun 3, 1889. EDUC.: public schools. POLIT. & GOV.: entered socialist movement, 1895; Socialist Labor Party candidate for mayor of Pittsburgh, PA; sec., PA State Socialist Labor Party Central Cmte., 1898; Socialist Labor Party candidate for U.S. House (PA), 1898, 1910; Socialist Labor Party candidate for judge, Superior Court of PA, 1899; ***candidate for Socialist Labor Party nomination to presidency of the U.S., 1900; Socialist labor Party candidate for vice presidency of the U.S., 1900.*** BUS. & PROF.: labor advocate; carry-in boy, Atterbury's Glass Factory, 1864; glass blower, 1871–; trade union organizer. MEM.: AFL; Glass Workers Union; Socialist Trade and Labor Alliance (1898); Knights of Labor (organizer, 1876); American Federation of Glass Workers Unions (organizer; founder, 1879); American Federation of Trades (delegate, 1881). RES.: Pittsburgh, PA.

RENDELL, EDWARD GENE. b. Jan 5, 1944, New York, NY; par. Jesse T. and Emma (Sloat) Rendell; m. Marjorie Osterlund, Jul 10, 1971; c. Jesse Thompson. EDUC.: B.A., U. of PA, 1965; J.D., Villanova U., 1968. POLIT. & GOV.: appointed asst. district atty., Philadelphia, PA, 1968–74; appointed special prosecutor, Philadelphia, PA, 1977; elected as a Democrat, district atty. of Philadelphia, PA, 1977–?; ***candidate for Democratic nomination to vice presidency of the U.S., 1980***; candidate for Democratic nomination to gov. of PA, 1986; elected as a Democrat, mayor of Philadelphia, PA, 1991–. BUS. & PROF.: atty.; admitted to PA Bar, 1968; admitted to the Bar of the Supreme Court of the U.S., 1981. MIL.: 2d lt., U.S.A.R., 1968–74. MEM.: ABA; United Jewish Organizations; Jewish War Veterans; B'nai B'rith. REL.: Jewish. AWARDS: "Man of the Year," VFW, 1980; "Man of the Year," American Cancer League, 1981; Distinguished Public Service Award, PA Cty. Detectives Assn., 1981. MAILING ADDRESS: 3425 Warden Dr., Philadelphia, PA 19129.

RENSHAW, MAIDEE B. MILNOR. m. Clarence Renshaw; c. Josephine Elizabeth. POLIT. & GOV.: delegate, Dem. Nat'l. Conv., 1924; ***candidate for Democratic nomination to vice presidency of the U.S., 1924***; received 3 votes from PA delegation for Democratic vice presidential nomination, 1924. RES.: Edgewood, PA.

REPLOGLE, JACOB LEONARD. b. May 6, 1876, Bedford Cty., PA; d. Nov 25, 1948, New York, NY; par. Rhinehart Z. and Mary Ann (Furry) Replogle; m. Blanche Kenly McMillen, Jan 10, 1905. EDUC.: public schools, Johnstown, PA. POLIT. & GOV.: appointed dir., Steel Supply, War Industries Board, Council of National Defense, WWI; ***candidate for Republican nomination to vice presidency of the U.S., 1932, 1936***; member, Rep. Nat'l. Cmte. (FL). BUS. & PROF.: office boy, Cambria Steel Co., 1889, vice pres., gen. mgr. of sales, 1912–15; vice pres., gen. mgr. of sales, American Vanadium Co., 1915–17, pres., 1917–19; pres., Vanadium Corp. of America, 1919–23; chm. of the board, Replogle Steel Co., 1919–24; pres., Wharton and Northern R.R. Co., 1919–29; chm. of the board, Wharton Steel Co.; partner, Harris, Upham and Co. (stockbrokers), 1928–32; chm. of the board, Warren Foundry and Pipe Co.; dir., Wickwire-Spencer Steel Co.; dir., Wabash R.R. Co.; dir., John Wanamaker Estate. MEM.: American Iron and Steel Inst.; Army Ordnance Assn.; PA Soc. (pres.); Gulf Stream Club; Piping Rock Club; Recess Club; C. of C.; Duquesne Club; Western Railway Club; Everglades Club; Bankers Club; Automobile Club; Army and Navy Club; Bankers Club; Travellers Club of Paris; India House; Railroad Club. AWARDS: Distinguished Service Award; chevalier, Legion of Honor; Order of the Crown of Italy (commander); Order of the Crown of Belgium. RES.: New York, NY.

REUSCH, DALE RICHARD. b. May 24, 1939, Valley City, OH; par. Earl and Helen (Indorf) Reusch; m. Valerie Pesta; c. Mark; Ricky. EDUC.: grad., high school, OH. POLIT. & GOV.: candidate for Democratic nomination to sheriff, Medina Cty., OH, 1972; candidate for Democratic nomination to gov. of OH, 1974, 1978; ***Ku Klux Klan Party candidate for presidency of the U.S., 1976; candidate for Democratic nomination to vice presidency of the U.S., 1976.*** BUS. & PROF.: engine tester, Ford Motor Co., Cleveland, OH, 1957–. MEM.: U.A.W. (Local 1250); Knights of the Ku Klux Klan, 1964– (grand dragon, OH, 1969–). REL.: Christian. MAILING ADDRESS: 220 Gaylord St., Lodi, OH 44254.

REUSS, HENRY SCHOELLKOPF. b. Feb 22, 1912, Milwaukee, WI; par. Gustav A. and Paula (Schoellkopf) Reuss; m. Margaret Magrath, Oct 24, 1942; c. Christopher; Michael; Jacqueline; Anne. EDUC.: A.B., Cornell U., 1933; LL.B., Harvard U., 1936. POLIT. & GOV.: asst. corp. counsel, Milwaukee Cty., WI, 1939–40; appointed asst. gen. counsel, OPA, Washington, DC, 1941–42; Non-Partisan candidate for mayor of Milwaukee, WI, 1948, 1960; appointed member, advisory cmte., Natural Resources Board, 1948–52; appointed deputy gen. counsel, Marshall Plan, Paris, France, 1949; appointed special prosecutor, Milwaukee Cty. (WI) Grand Jury, 1950; alternate delegate, Dem. Nat'l. Conv., 1952; candidate for Democratic nomination to U.S. Senate (WI), 1952; elected member, Milwaukee (WI) School Board, 1953–54; elected as a Democrat to U.S. House (WI), 1955–83; ***candidate for Democratic nomination to vice presidency of the U.S., 1968.*** BUS. & PROF.: atty.; admitted to WI Bar, 1936; law practice, Milwaukee, WI, 1936–55; dir., White Elm Nursery Co., Hartland, WI; dir., Marshall and Ilsley Bank, Milwaukee, WI; dir., Niagara Share Corp.,

Buffalo, NY; lecturer, WI State Coll., 1950–51. MIL.: 2d lt., capt., 663d and 75th Infantry divisions, U.S. Army, 1943–45; chief, Price Control, Branch Office, Military Government of Germany, 1945; Bronze Star. MEM.: Milwaukee March of Dimes (chm., 1953); Cornell U. (council member); American Youth Hostels (dir.); Children's Service Soc. (dir.); Youth Bar Assn. of Milwaukee (vice chm.); Milwaukee Cty. Bar Assn.; Milwaukee Bar Assn.; Chi Psi Alumni Assn. (vice pres.); Milwaukee City Club; Harvard Law Review (overseer, 1956–60); Foreign Policy Assn.; Cornell U. Alumni Assn.; Harvard Law School (visitor, 1957–60). WRITINGS: *The Critical Decade: An Economic Policy for America and the Free World* (1964); *Revenue Sharing: Crutch or Catalyst for State and Local Governments?* (1970); *On the Trail of the Ice Age* (1976); *To Save Our Cities: What Needs to Be Done?* (1977). MAILING ADDRESS: 517 East Wisconsin, Milwaukee, WI 53202.

REYNOLDS, JAMES B. POLIT. & GOV.: Republican candidate for U.S. House (MA); ***candidate for Republican nomination to vice presidency of the U.S., 1904***; appointed asst. U.S. sec. of the treasury, 1905–09; member, Rep. Nat'l. Cmte. (MA). RES.: MA.

REYNOLDS, JAMES BRONSON. b. Mar 17, 1861, Kiantone, NY; d. Jan 1, 1924, North Haven, CT; par. William T. and Sarah M. (Painter) Reynolds; m. Florence Blanchard Dike, Jul 16, 1898. EDUC.: A.B., Yale U., 1884, B.D., 1888; Columbia U.; NY Law School. POLIT. & GOV.: appointed member, NY State Tenement House Comm., 1900; appointed sec. to Mayor Seth Low, New York, NY, 1902–03; appointed special adviser to presidency of the U.S. on Municipal Affairs of DC; appointed member, Special Presidential Comm. to Investigate Chicago Stock Yards, 1906; appointed chm., Presidential Comm. to Investigate Industrial Conditions at Panama; appointed asst. district atty., New York Cty., NY, 1910–13; ***candidate for Republican nomination to vice presidency of the U.S., c. 1916***. BUS. & PROF.: reformer; official representative, Coll. YMCA of America, 1889–93; headworker, University Settlement, New York, NY, 1894; atty.; admitted to NY Bar, 1900. MEM.: Cmte. of 70 (1893); Cmte. of City Club (1897); Citizen's Union (chm., exec. cmte., 1897); American Social Hygiene Assn. (counsel, 1913–16); National Arts Club; City Midday Club; NY Republican Club; Century Assn.; Social Reform Club; NY City Club; National Municipal Reform League; Underwriters' Club. RES.: New York, NY.

REYNOLDS, JOHN W. b. Apr 4, 1921, Green Bay, WI; par. John W. and Madge (Flatley) Reynolds; m. Patricia Ann Brody, May 26, 1947; m. 2d, Jane Conway, Jul 31, 1971; c. Kate M.; Molly; James; Tom; Jacob; Frances. EDUC.: grad., East H.S., Green Bay, WI, 1938; B. S., U. of WI, 1942, LL.B., 1949. POLIT. & GOV.: Democratic candidate for U.S. House (WI), 1950; chm., Brown Cty. (WI) Democratic Party, 1952–56; district dir., Office of Price Stabilization, 1951–52; appointed U.S. Commissioner for Eastern Judicial District of WI, 1955–58; appointed member, WI State Administrative Comm., 1955–58; elected as a Democrat, atty. gen. of WI, 1959–63; delegate, Dem. Nat'l. Conv., 1960, 1964; elected as a Democrat to gov. of WI, 1963–65; Democratic candidate for gov. of WI, 1964; ***candidate for Democratic nomination to presidency of the U.S., 1964***; appointed U.S. district judge, Eastern District of WI, 1965– (chief judge). BUS. & PROF.: atty.; admitted to WI Bar, 1949; law practice, Green Bay, WI. MIL.: pvt., master sgt., U.S. Army, 1942–44, 2d lt., 1st lt., 1944–46. MEM.: ABA; WI Bar Assn.; Brown Cty. Bar Assn.; Kiwanis; Young Democrats; Knights of Columbus. REL.: R.C. MAILING ADDRESS: 4654 North Woodburn, Milwaukee, WI 53211.

REYNOLDS, ROBERT RICE. b. Jun 18, 1884, Weaverville, NC; d. Feb 13, 1963, Asheville, NC; par. William Taswell and Mamie (Spears) Reynolds; m. Frances Jackson, 1909; m. 2d, Mary Bland; m. 3d, Denise d'Arcy, 1920; m. 4th, Eva Brady, Feb 1930; m. 5th, Evalyn W. McLean, Oct 9, 1941; c. Frances Jackson; Robert Rice; Mary Bland; Mamie Spears (Mrs. Luigi Joseph Anthony Chinette). EDUC.: Weaver Coll.; LL.B., U. of NC, 1907. POLIT. & GOV.: elected as a Democrat, prosecuting atty., 15th Judicial District of NC, 1901–14; candidate for Democratic nomination to U.S. House (NC), 1914; candidate for Democratic nomination to lt. gov. of NC, 1924; candidate for Democratic nomination to U.S. Senate (NC), 1926, 1950; presidential elector, Democratic Party, 1928; elected as a Democrat to U.S. Senate (NC), 1933–45; founder, American Nationalist Party, 1938; ***America First Party candidate for presidency of the U.S., 1944 (declined)***. BUS. & PROF.: atty.; admitted to NC Bar, 1907; law practice, Asheville, NC, 1907; law practice, Washington, DC, 1945–63; pres., Caribbean Ferry System; cattle rancher, Asheville, NC. MEM.: Moose (national grand commander, 1937–38); American Automobile Assn. (vice pres.); Beta Theta Pi; Elks; J.O.U.A.M.; Biltmore Forest Club; National Press Club; Explorers Club; Vindicators (founder); NC Bar Assn.; Roosevelt Motor Club of America; NY City Club. WRITINGS: *Wanderlust* (1914); *Gypsy Trails* (1925). REL.: Episc. RES.: Asheville, NC.

REYNOLDS, VERNE L. b. Mar 7, 1884, Parsons, KS; d. Sep 16, 1959, Phoenix, AZ; m. Pauline Reynolds; c. William; Roy; Dallas; Vivian (Mrs. O'Gara). POLIT. & GOV.: Labor Party candidate for U.S. House (MD), 1922; ***Socialist Labor Party candidate for vice presidency of the U.S., 1924; Socialist Labor Party candidate for presidency of the U.S., 1928, 1932***. BUS. & PROF.: farmer, CA; traveling salesman; oil worker, TX and OK; newspaper advertising salesman; steamfitter, Baltimore, MD, 1918; insurance agent. MEM.: Steamfitters' Union (expelled for radical views); Socialist Unions. WRITINGS: *The Party's Work* (1925); *A 30-oras Munkaido-Torveny* (1933); *The Thirty-Hour Bill* (1933); *Tridesetocasovni rad—mogu li se ekonomski zakoni kapitalizma opozvati politickim zakonima?* (1934). REL.: atheist. RES.: Baltimore, MD.

RHODES, JAMES ALLEN. b. Sep 13, 1909, Coalton, OH; par. James Llewellyn and Susan (Howe) Rhodes; m. Helen Rawlins, Dec 18, 1941; c. Suzanne (Mrs. Richard Moore); Saundra (Mrs. John Jacob); Sharon. EDUC.: grad., Springfield (OH) H.S., 1930; OH State U. POLIT. & GOV.: clerk, OH State House; elected Republican Precinct Committeeman, 1933; elected member, Columbus (OH) Board of Education, 1937–40; elected Columbus (OH) City Auditor, 1941–44; elected as a Republican, mayor of Columbus, OH, 1944–53; elected as a Republican, OH State Auditor, 1953–63; Republican candidate for gov. of OH, 1954, 1986; elected as a Republican to gov. of OH, 1963–71, 1975–83; ***candidate for Republican nomination to presidency of the U.S., 1964, 1968; candidate for Republican nomination to vice presidency of the U.S., 1968***; candidate for Republican nomination to U.S. Senate (OH), 1970; delegate, Rep. Nat'l. Conv., 1972, 1976. BUS. & PROF.: school janitor; newspaper boy; clerk, haberdashery; clothing salesman, Hills' Tailor Shop; auditor; founder, James A. Rhodes and Associates. MEM.: National Amateur Athletic Union (pres.); Pan-American Sports Congress (delegate); International Sports Federation; National Caddie Assn., Inc. (founder); All-American Newspaper Boys Scholarships, Inc.; Columbus Boys' Club; Professional Golfer's Assn.; advisory cmte., U.S. Olympic Cmte.; Masons (32°); Kiwanis; University City (founder); Knot Hole Gang. WRITINGS: *Johnny Shiloh* (1959); *The Trial of Mary Todd Lincoln* (1959); *Teen-Age Hall of Fame* (1960); *The Court Martial of Commodore Perry* (1961). AWARDS: Helms Foundation Award; Silver Keystone Award, Boys Clubs of America. REL.: Presb. MISC.: noted for role in National Guard shootings of antiwar demonstrators, Kent State U., May 4, 1970. MAILING ADDRESS: 2375 Tremont Rd., Columbus, OH 43221.

RIBICOFF, ABRAHAM ALEXANDER. b. Apr 9, 1910, New Britain, CT; par. Samuel and Rose (Sable) Ribicoff; m. Ruth Siegel, Jun 28, 1931; m. 2d, Lois Mathes, 1972; c. Peter; Jane. EDUC.: LL.B. (cum laude), U. of Chicago, 1933. POLIT. & GOV.: elected as a Democrat to CT State House, 1938–42; Municipal judge, Hartford, CT, 1941–43, 1945–47; chm., CT Assembly of Municipal Court judges, 1941–42; member, Hartford (CT) Charter Revision Comm., 1945–46; Hearing Examiner, CT Fair Employment Practices Act, 1947–49; elected as a Democrat to U.S. House (CT), 1949–53; Democratic candidate for U.S. Senate (CT), 1952; delegate, Dem. Nat'l. Conv., 1952, 1956, 1960, 1968; elected as a Democrat, gov. of CT, 1955–61; appointed U.S. sec. of health, education, and welfare, 1961–62; elected as a Democrat to U.S. Senate (Connecticut), 1963–81; ***candidate for Democratic nomination to vice president of the U.S., 1968, 1972***. BUS. & PROF.: atty.; admitted to CT Bar, 1933; law practice, Kensington, CT; counsel, Ribicoff and Kotkin (law firm), Hartford, CT; special counsel, Kaye, Scholer, Fierman, Hays and Handler (law firm), New York, NY, 1981–; dir., Hartford Insurance Group. MEM.: Order of the Coif; American Arbitration Assn. (motion picture panel, 1941); ABA; Hartford Cty. Bar Assn. HON. DEG.: LL.D., American International Coll.; LL.D., Amherst Coll.; LL.D., Bard Coll.; LL.D., Boston Coll.; LL.D., U. of Bridgeport; LL.D., Bryant Coll.; LL.D., U. of CA; LL.D., Coe Coll.; LL.D., De Paul U.; LL.D., Dropsie Coll.; LL.D., Fairfield U.; LL.D., Hebrew Union Coll.; LL.D., Hillver Coll.; LL.D., Jewish Theological Seminary; LL.D., Kenyon Coll.; LL.D., NY U.; LL.D., Trinity Coll.; LL.D., Wesleyan U.; LL.D., Yeshiva U. WRITINGS: *Politics: The American Way* (with Jon O. Newman, 1967); *America Can Make It: A Senator Rejects Safe Politics* (1972); *The American Medical Machine* (1972). REL.: Jewish. MAILING ADDRESS: 30 Woodland St., Hartford, CT.

RICE, DAN (nee DANIEL McCLAREN). b. Jan 25, 1823, New York, NY; d. Feb 22, 1900, Long Branch, NJ; par. Daniel and Elizabeth (Crum) McClaren; m. three times. POLIT. & GOV.: ***candidate for Republican nomination to presidency of the U.S., 1868***. BUS. & PROF.: clown; part-owner, trained pig; singer; circus strong man; press agent, Prophet Joseph Smith (q.v.), 1841–44; appeared as clown in various circuses, 1844–85; with Seth B. Howe's Circus, Philadelphia, PA, 1845–47; with Spaulding's Circus, New Orleans, LA, 1847, partner, to 1850; with Adam Forepaugh's Circus, 1864; with O'Brien's Circus, 1866; owner, Riverboat Circuses; temperance lecturer. MIL.: brev. col., U.S. Army, c. 1848. MISC.: had trained horse act with horses Excelsior and Excelsior, Junior; forced to retire due to chronic alcoholism. RES.: Long Branch, NJ.

RICE, FLORENCE M. POLIT. & GOV.: ***Consumer Party candidate for vice presidency of the U.S., 1988***. MEM.: Harlem Consumer Education Council (founder). MAILING ADDRESS: 540 West 158th St., New York, NY 10032.

RICE, JAMES A. POLIT. & GOV.: ***candidate for Democratic nomination to presidency of the U.S., 1924***. RES.: OH.

RICHARDS, FRANK. POLIT. & GOV.: ***independent candidate for presidency of the U.S., 1980***. MAILING ADDRESS: unknown.

RICHARDS, ROBERT EUGENE "BOB." b. Feb 20, 1926, Champaign, IL; par. Leslie Haines and Margaret Harriet (Palfrey) Richards; m. Mary Leah Cline, Feb 17, 1946; m. 2d, Joan Richards; c. Robert Eugene, Jr.; Paul David; Carol Ann Jackson; Brandon Robert; Thomas Wayne; Tammy Joan. EDUC.: Bridgewater Coll., 1944–46; A.B., U. of IL, 1947, M.A., 1948; Bethany Biblical Seminary, 1948–49. POLIT. & GOV.: appointed U.S. Goodwill ambassador to Asia, 1954; appointed member, President's Council on Youth Fitness; ***Populist Party candidate for presidency of the U.S., 1984***. BUS. & PROF.: lecturer; ordained minister, Church of the Brethren, 1946; asst. prof. of Sociology, U. of IL, 1949; pastor, Church of the Brethren, Long Beach, CA; asst. prof. of Philosophy, La Verne Coll.,, La

Verne, CA, 1951–; businessman; oil and land developer, TX; spokesman, "Wheaties" Breakfast Cereal; television actor. MEM.: IL Athletic Club; Los Angeles Athletic Club; Heart of America Corp. (founder, 1979). AWARDS: won Bronze Medal in pole vault, Olympics, 1948; Gold Medal in pole vault, Olympics, 1952, 1956; winner of 26 national indoor and outdoor track championships; elected to Helms Hall of Fame, 1955; IL Hall of Fame; Madison Square Garden Hall of Fame; U.S. Track and Field Hall of Fame; National Track and Field Hall of Fame; U.S. Olympic Hall of Fame; Helms Trophy, 1951; James E. Sullivan Memorial Trophy, Amateur Athletic Union, 1951; one of five "Outstanding Young Men in CA," 1956; one of ten "Outstanding Young Men in America," U.S. Junior C. of C., 1957. WRITINGS: *The Heart of a Champion* (1957); *To Save Our Nation*. REL.: Protestant (nee Church of the Brethren). MAILING ADDRESS: 1616 Estates Dr., Waco, TX 76710.

RICHARDSON, DARCY G.

POLIT. & GOV.: ***independent Party candidate for presidency of the U.S., 1992***. MAILING ADDRESS: 1103 Prospect Ave., Melrose Park, PA 19126.

RICHARDSON, ELLIOT LEE.

b. Jul 20, 1920, Boston, MA; par. Edward P. and Clara (Shattuck) Richardson; m. Anne Francis Hazard, Aug 2, 1952; c. Henry Shattuck; Anne Hazard; Michael Elliot. EDUC.: A.B. (cum laude), Harvard U., 1941, LL.B. (cum laude). POLIT. & GOV.: law clerk, Judge Learned Hand, 1947–48; law clerk, Assoc. Justice Felix Frankfurter, 1948–49; administrative asst. to U.S. Sen. Leverett Saltonstall (q.v.), 1953–54; administrative asst. to Gov. Christian A. Herter (q.v.), MA, 1955–56; appointed asst. sec. for Legislation, U.S. Dept. of Health, Education, and Welfare, 1957–59; appointed U.S. atty. for MA, 1959–61; appointed special asst. to the atty. gen. of the U.S., 1961; elected as a Republican to lt. gov. of MA, 1965–67; elected as a Republican, atty. gen. of MA, 1967–69; appointed undersec. of state, U.S. Dept. of State, 1969–70; appointed U.S. sec. of health, education, and welfare, 1970–73; appointed U.S. sec. of defense, 1973; appointed atty. gen. of the U.S., 1973; appointed U.S. ambassador to Great Britain, 1975–76; delegate, Rep. Nat'l. Conv., 1976; appointed U.S. sec. of commerce, 1976–77; ***candidate for Republican nomination to presidency of the U.S., 1976; candidate for Republican nomination to vice presidency of the U.S., 1976, 1980***; appointed U.S. ambassador-at-large, special representative of the pres. for Law of the Sea Conference, 1977–; candidate for Republican nomination to U.S. Senate (MA), 1984. BUS. & PROF.: atty.; admitted to MA Bar, 1949; assoc., Ropes, Gray, Best, Coolidge and Rugg (law firm), Boston, MA, 1949–53, 1954–56; lecturer in Law, Harvard U., 1952; partner, Ropes and Gray (law firm), Boston, MA, 1961–64; law practice, Washington, DC, 1974–75. MIL.: 1st lt., U.S. Army, 1942–45; Bronze Star; Purple Heart with Oak Leaf Cluster; Combat Medal; ETO Medal with Five Battle Stars. MEM.: Harvard Alumni Assn. (dir.); ABA; MA Bar Assn.; Boston Bar Assn.; Council on Foreign Relations (gov.); Disabled American Veterans; VFW; American Legion; Federal Bar Assn.; American Acad. of Arts and Sciences (Fellow); American Bar Foundation; Woodrow Wilson International Center for Scholars (Fellow); MA Bar United Fund (vice pres.; dir.); Trustees of Reservations (advisory council); American Red Cross (gov.); World Affairs Council of Boston (pres.; dir.); Salzburg Seminar in American Studies (dir.); United Community Services of Metropolitan Boston (dir.); Greater Boston United Fund Campaign (chm.); MA General Hospital (trustee); Radcliffe Coll. (trustee); Cambridge Drama Festival (trustee); Brookline Public Library (trustee); Harvard Coll. (board of overseers; Cmte. to Visit John F. Kennedy School of Government). HON. DEG.: L.H.D., Brandeis U.; LL.D., Gallaudet Coll.; LL.D., Emerson Coll.; LL.D., Harvard U., 1947; LL.D., Lincoln U.; LL.D., Lowell Technological Inst.; L.H.D., MA Coll. of Optometry; LL.D., MI State U.; LL.D., U. of NH; LL.D., OH State U.; LL.D., U. of Pittsburgh; LL.D., Springfield Coll.; LL.D., Temple U.; L.H.D., Whittier Coll.; LL.D., Yeshiva U. WRITINGS: "Poisoned Politics," *Atlantic Monthly*, 1961; "Judicial Intervention in the Civil Rights Movement," *Boston University Law Review*, 1966; *Responsibility and Responsiveness* (1972); *The Creative Balance: Government, Politics and the Individual in America's Third Century* (1976). REL.: Unitarian. MAILING ADDRESS: 1100 Crest Lane, McLean, VA 22101.

RICHARDSON, RICHARD GARFIELD.

POLIT. & GOV.: ***independent candidate for presidency of the U.S., 1980***. MAILING ADDRESS: 501 East 20th St., Baltimore, MD 21218.

RICKENBACKER, EDWARD VERNON "EDDIE."

b. Oct 8, 1890, Columbus, OH; d. Jul 23, 1973, Zurich, Switzerland; par. William and Elizabeth (Barcler) Rickenbacker; m. Mrs. Adelaide Frost Durant, Sep 16, 1922; c. David E.; William F. EDUC.: grad., International Correspondence School. POLIT. & GOV.: special envoy, U.S. sec. of war, WWII; ***candidate for Republican nomination to presidency of the U.S., 1944 (declined)***. BUS. & PROF.: aviator; autoracer; vice pres., Rickenbacker Motor Car Co.; asst. sales mgr., Cadillac Motor Car Co.; vice pres., Fokker Aircraft Corp. of America; vice pres., American Airways, 1932–33; asst. to the pres., Aviation Corp., 1932–33; vice pres., North American Aviation, Inc., 1933–34; gen. mgr., Eastern Air Lines, Inc., 1935–38, pres., gen. mgr., dir., 1938–53, chm. of the board, 1954–63; dir., Wackenhut Corp. MIL.: officer, Motor Car Staff, U.S. Army, 1917; assigned to Air Service, 1917; commanding officer, 94th Aero Pursuit Squadron, capt., 1919; Distinguished Service Cross with 9 Oak Leaves; Medal of Honor, 1931; Medal of Merit, 1947; Legion of Honor; Croix de Guerre with 4 Palms (France); Air Ace credited with 26 victories in WWI; forced down in flight over Pacific Ocean, 1942, rescued after 24 days at sea on a raft. MEM.: FL Press Club (dir.); Air Force Aid Soc. (dir.); BSA (exec. board); Boys Clubs of America (dir.). AWARDS: Silver Buffalo Award, BSA, 1944; Big Brother of the Year Award, 1953. HON. DEG.:

Dr.Aero.Sci., PA Military Coll., 1938; Dr.Aero.Sci., Brown U., 1940; Dr.Aero.Sci., U. of Miami, 1941; D.Sc., U. of Tampa, 1942; L.H.D., University Foundations and American Theological Seminary, 1943; LL.D., Oklahoma City U., 1944; Sc.D., Westminster Coll., 1944; LL.D., Capital U., 1945; Dr.Eng., Lehigh U., 1948; LL.D., Coll. of South Jersey, 1948; Sc.D., Lafayette Coll., 1952; Sc.D., The Citadel, 1954; LL.D., Hamilton Coll., 1956; Sc.D., OH State U., 1957; LL.D., William Jewell Coll., 1962. WRITINGS: *Fighting the Flying Cross* (1919); *Seven Came Through: Rickenbacker's Full Story* (1943); *Rickenbacker: An Autobiography* (1967); *From Father to Son: The Letters of Captain Eddie Rickenbacker to His Son William, From Boyhood to Manhood* (1970). RES.: New York, NY.

RICKETTS, JAMES H., SR. married; c. James H. R., Jr. POLIT. & GOV.: ***independent candidate for presidency of the U.S., 1988***. MEM.: Army of the Reconvention. MAILING ADDRESS: c/o Army of the Reconvention, P.O. Box 2768, 1613 East Nowland Ave., Indianapolis, IN 46206.

RIDDICK, MERRILL KEITH. b. Mar 7, 1895, Madison, WI; d. Mar 9, 1988, Annapolis, MD; par. Carl Wood and Grace (Keith) Riddick; m. Helen May Williams; c. Merrill Keith, Jr.; Barbara (Mrs. Ornbaun); Mary Ruth (Mrs. Kittrell). EDUC.: Valparaiso U.; Columbia U.; School of Military Administration. POLIT. & GOV.: ***candidate for Union Party nomination to presidency of the U.S., 1936***; candidate for Democratic nomination to gov. of MT, 1968; candidate for Republican nomination to U.S. Senate (MT), 1972; ***Puritan Epic, Prohibition and Magnetohydrodynamics Party candidate for presidency of the U.S., 1976, 1980, 1984***. BUS. & PROF.: prospector; barnstormer; performer, Harry Perkins Air Circus; instructor, National Air U., 1928–38; asst. superintendent, U.S. Post Office, Chicago, IL; technical adviser, Boeing Aircraft Co., Seattle, WA; inventor; ed., *Journal of Applied Human Ecology*. MIL.: lt., U.S.A.A.C., 1917–18, capt.; maj., U.S. Air Force, WWII. MEM.: Air Pioneers; Missleman (hon.); OX5 Club of America; Silver Wings Fraternity; hon. adm., Flagship Fleet, American Airlines; U.S. Air Mail Pioneers; Aviation Pathfinders. REL.: Bapt. RES.: Philipsburg, MT.

RIFKIN, JEREMY "JERRY." b. 1945, Chicago, IL; m. Jo Nina R. EDUC.: U. of PA; M.A., Tufts U. POLIT. & GOV.: delegate, Socialist Party National Convention, 1976; ***candidate for Socialist Party nomination to vice presidency of the U.S., 1976 (declined)***. BUS. & PROF.: VISTA Volunteer, Harlem, NY; economist; philosopher; teacher; organizer; author. MEM.: National Mobilization Against the War (cosponsor, 1967); People's Bicentennial Comm. (exec. dir.); People's Business Comm.; Foundation for Economic Trends. WRITINGS: *The Emerging Order*; *Entropy*; *Algeny*; *Who Should Play God*; *Declaration of a Heretic*. MISC.: noted for opposition to technological innovations without ethical content. REL.: Jewish. MAILING ADDRESS: 74 Crestline Dr., San Francisco, CA 94131.

RIGAZIO, JOHN DONALD. POLIT. & GOV.: ***candidate for Democratic nomination to presidency of the U.S., 1992***. MAILING ADDRESS: Rochester, NH.

RIGDON, SIDNEY. b. Feb 19, 1793, Piny Fork, PA; d. Jul 14, 1876, Friendship, NY; par. William and Nancy (Gallaher) Rigdon; m. Phoebe Brooks, Jun 12, 1820; c. Nancy. EDUC.: district schools. POLIT. & GOV.: Democratic candidate for U.S. House (OH), 1832; appointed postmaster, Nauvoo, IL; member, city council, Nauvoo, IL; trustee, city atty., Nauvoo, IL; ***independent candidate for vice presidency of the U.S., 1844***. BUS. & PROF.: printer; worked on father's farm to 1817; licensed preacher, Baptist Church, 1819; pastor, Baptist Church, Pittsburgh, PA, 1820; tanner, OH, 1824–26; pastor, Cambellite Church, Mentor, OH, 1828; joined Church of Jesus Christ of Latter-Day Saints, 1830; land speculator (with Joseph Smith, Jr., q.v.), Kirtland, OH; prof. of Church History, U. of the City of Nauvoo; counsellor, First Presidency, Church of Jesus Christ of Latter-Day Saints, 1833; expelled from Church of Jesus Christ of Latter-Day Saints following unsuccessful leadership fight against Brigham Young, 1844; elected First President, Prophet, Seer, Revelator, Translator, and Trustee, New Church of Christ, 1845–76; ed., *Messenger and Advocate of the Church of Christ*; lecturer on Geology, Friendship, NY. MEM.: Kirtland Safety Soc. Anti-Banking Co. WRITINGS: *Lectures on Faith*; *A Collection of Sacred Hymns*; *Oration* (1838). REL.: New Church of Christ (founder; formerly counsellor, First Presidency, Church of Jesus Christ of Latter-Day Saints; nee Bapt.). MISC.: reputed to be author of *The Book of Mormon*; imprisoned with Joseph Smith, Jr. (q.v.), Liberty, MO; fled MO to escape mob violence and judicial action over illegal bank notes; carried Cambellite ideas to Mormonism; supported communistic order. RES.: Nauvoo, IL.

RIGGS, GUY W. POLIT. & GOV.: Libertarian Party candidate for NY State Assembly, 1972, 1974; ***candidate for Libertarian Party nomination to presidency of the U.S., 1976***. BUS. & PROF.: employee, IBM, New York, NY, 1952–; columnist, *Poughkeepsie (NY) Journal*. MEM.: Mid-Hudson Libertarian Club (founder). MAILING ADDRESS: 32 Saddle Rock Dr., Poughkeepsie, NY.

RILEY, JOHNNIE MAE. POLIT. & GOV.: ***candidate for Democratic nomination to presidency of the U.S., 1988, 1992***. MAILING ADDRESS: 1702 Prism, Houston, TX 77043.

RITCHIE, ALBERT CABELL. b. Aug 29, 1876, Richmond, VA; d. Feb 24, 1936, Baltimore, MD; par. Judge Albert and Elizabeth Caskie (Cabell) Ritchie; m. Elizabeth Catherine Baker, May 18, 1907 (divorced); c. none. EDUC.: A.B., Johns Hopkins U., 1896; LL.B., U. of MD, 1898. POLIT. & GOV.: appointed asst. city solicitor, Baltimore, MD, 1903–10; appointed asst. gen. counsel, MD Public Service Comm., 1910–13; elected as a Democrat, atty. gen. of MD, 1916–20; delegate, Dem. Nat'l. Conv., 1916, 1920, 1924, 1928, 1932; gen. counsel, War Industries Board, 1918; elected as a Democrat to gov. of MD, 1920–35; ***candidate for Democratic nomination to presidency of the U.S., 1924, 1928, 1932; candidate for Democratic nomination to vice presidency of the U.S., 1924, 1936***; Democratic candidate for gov. of MD, 1934. BUS. & PROF.: atty.; admitted to MD Bar, 1898; partner, Steele, Semmes, Carey and Bond (law firm), Baltimore, MD, 1898–1903; partner, Ritchie and Janney (law firm; subsequently Ritchie, Janney and Griswold; Ritchie, Janney and Steuart), Baltimore, MD, 1903–20; prof. of Law, U. of MD, 1907–20. MEM.: ABA; MD Bar Assn.; Baltimore City Bar Assn.; American Acad. of Political and Social Sciences; Delta Phi; University Club; Johns Hopkins Club; MD Club; Merchants Club; Baltimore Club. HON. DEG.: St. John's Coll., 1920; LL.D., WA Coll., 1923; LL.D., Loyola Coll., 1929. WRITINGS: *Law of Municipal Condemnation in Maryland* (1904). REL.: Episc. RES.: Baltimore, MD.

RITTER, ELI FOSTER. b. Jun 18, 1838, Morgan Cty., IN; d. Dec 11, 1913, Indianapolis, IN; par. James and Rachel (Jessup) Ritter; m. Narcissa "Narcie" Lockwood, Jul 18, 1865; c. Hermann; Roscoe H.; Raymond; Dwight Schuyler; Mary (Mrs. Charles Austin Beard); Ruth (Mrs. Edgar O'Daniel); Halstead Lockwood. EDUC.: Northwestern Christian U.; De Pauw U., 1859; grad., Indianapolis Law Coll., 1866. POLIT. & GOV.: permanent chm., Prohibition Party National Convention, 1892; ***candidate for Prohibition Party nomination to presidency of the U.S., 1892***. BUS. & PROF.: atty.; admitted to IN Bar, 1866; partner, Levi and Eli Ritter (law firm), Indianapolis, IN, 1866–94; partner, Ritter, Walker and Ritter, Indianapolis, IN, 1873–80; law practice, Indianapolis, IN, 1894–1913; contributor, *Voice*; contributor, *Western Christian Advocate*. MIL.: pvt., adj., capt., U.S. Army, 1861–65, maj., 1865; col., First Regt., IN State Militia, 1878–81. MEM.: IN Anti-Saloon League; IN Soldiers' Home (trustee, 1903–09); Indianapolis Commercial Club (charter member); Masons; Phi Beta Kappa; Phi Gamma Delta. WRITINGS: *Is License Constitutional?* (1891); *Moral Law and Civil Law: Parts of the Same thing* (1896). REL.: Methodist Episcopal Church (delegate, general conference). RES.: Indianapolis, IN.

RITTER, GRANT ADOLPH. b. Sep 30, 1891, Chicago, IL; d. May 22, 1967, Monroe, WI; par. Adolph and Marie (Guttered) Ritter; m. Sophie Ecklon; m. 2d, Elsie Rekett, 1920; c. Grant L.; Robert; Lucille (Mrs. Wright); Dorothea (Mrs. Paulson). POLIT. & GOV.: elected member, Rock Cty. (WI) Board of Supervisors; chm., Newark Township,, WI; delegate, Rep. Nat'l. Conv., 1944; Emergency Food Production asst., Rock Cty. (WI) Agent, 1944; ***candidate for Republican nomination to presidency of the U.S., 1952***; ran in 1952 WI presidential primary as a stand-in for Gen. Douglas MacArthur (q.v.). BUS. & PROF.: farmer, Beloit, WI, 1934–67; farm dir., WCLO radio; commentator, "Country Caller," WCLO; mgr., WEKZ radio, Monroe, WI; wire-chief, Bell Telephone Co., Chicago, IL. RES.: Beloit, WI.

RIVES, WILLIAM CABELL. b. May 4, 1792, Nelson Cty., VA; d. Apr 26, 1868, Albemarle Cty., VA; par. Robert and Margaret (Cabell) Rives; m. Judith Page Walker, Mar 24, 1819; c. Amelie; Alfred Landon. EDUC.: Hampden-Sydney Coll.; grad., Coll. of William and Mary, 1809. POLIT. & GOV.: delegate, VA State Constitutional Convention, 1816; elected as a Democrat to VA State House of Delegates, 1817–19, 1822–23; elected as a Democrat to U.S. House (VA), 1823–29; appointed U.S. minister to France, 1829–32, 1849–53; elected as a Democrat to U.S. Senate (VA), 1832–34, 1836–39, as a Whig, 1841–45; ***candidate for Democratic nomination to vice presidency of the U.S., 1836; candidate for Constitutional Union Party nomination to presidency of the U.S., 1860***; delegate, Peace Convention, 1861; delegate, VA Secession Convention, 1861; member, Confederate Provisional Congress, 1861; elected member, House (VA), Second Confederate Congress, 1861–62. BUS. & PROF.: atty.; admitted to VA Bar, 1814; law practice, Charlottesville, VA; author. MIL.: aide to Gen. John H. Cocke, 1814. WRITINGS: *On Agriculture* (1842, 1853); *Discourses on the Uses and Importance of History* (1847); *Discourses . . . on the Ethics of Christianity* (1845); *Discourse on the Character and Services of John Hampden* (1855); *History of the Life and Times of James Madison* (1859–68). RES.: Albemarle Cty., VA.

ROARK, JAMES HAROLD. b. Dec 29, 1933, Scottsville, KY; par. Harlin S. and Lois I. (Moore) Roark; m.; c. Cynthia Diane; Victoria Jean; Kimberly Jo; James Michael. EDUC.: grad., Plant City (FL) H.S. POLIT. & GOV.: ***candidate for Democratic nomination to presidency of the U.S., 1976***. BUS. & PROF.: newsboy; mattress maker; farm laborer; carpenter; clerk, grocery store; truck driver; factory worker; welder; mechanic; steel fabricator; owner, operator, heavy equipment and pipeline construction business; life insurance salesman. MEM.: Junior C. of C.; Elks. REL.: Methodist. MAILING ADDRESS: P.O. Box 8066, Lakeland, FL 33802.

ROBB, CHARLES SPITTAL. b. Jun 26, 1939, Phoenix, AZ; par. James Spittal and Francis Howard (Woolley) Robb; m. Lynda Bird Johnson, Dec 9, 1967; c. Lucinda Desha; Catherine Lewis; Jennifer Wickliffe. EDUC.: Cornell U., 1957–58; B.B.A., U. of WI, 1961; J.D., U. of VA, 1973. POLIT. & GOV.: law clerk, John D. Butzner, Jr., U.S. Court of Appeals, 1973–74; member, Fairfax Cty. (VA) Democratic Central Cmte.,

1975–; member, VA State Democratic Central Cmte., 1976–; chm., VA Forum on Education, 1978–82; elected as a Democrat to lt. gov. of VA, 1978–82; vice chm., Local Government Advisory Comm., 1978–82; elected as a Democrat to gov. of VA, 1982–86; ***candidate for Democratic nomination to presidency of the U.S., 1988 (declined)***; elected as a Democrat to U.S. Senate (VA), 1988–. BUS. & PROF.: atty.; admitted to VA Bar, 1973; admitted to practice before the Bar of the Supreme Court of the U.S., 1976; atty., Williams, Connolly and Califano (law firm), Washington, DC, 1974–77; partner, Hunton and Williams (law firm), Fairfax, VA; vice pres., dir., LBJ Co., 1971–81; vice pres., dir., Northern Virginia Radio Co., 1978–81; dir., United Virginia Bankshares, Inc. MIL.: company commander, aide to commanding gen., U.S.M.C., 1961–70; infantry company commander, U.S.M.C., Vietnam; Bronze Star; Vietnam Service Medal with Four Stars; Vietnamese Cross of Gallantry with Silver Star. MEM.: Democratic Leadership Council (founder; dir.); Concerned Citizens of the Commonwealth (vice chm., 1978–82); National Conference of Lieutenant Governors (exec. cmte.); American Council of Young Political Leaders (chm., Delegation to People's Republic of China, 1979); Education Comm. of the States (chm., 1985); Southern Growth Policies Board (exec. cmte.); Southern Regional Education Board; U. of VA (board member, 1974–); U. of Richmond (board member, 1974–); Hampton Inst. of Technology (board member, 1977–82); BSA (exec. board, National Capital Area, 1976–; chm., Northern VA Scout Exposition, 1976, 1977); American Cancer Soc. (exec. board, Fairfax Cty., VA); Carnegie Foundation; Enterprise Foundation; United Way of Fairfax Cty.; ABA; VA Bar Assn.; DC Bar Assn.; VA Trial Lawyers Assn.; National Governors' Assn.; Southern Governors Assn. (chm.); Democratic Governors Assn. (chm.); Coalition for a Democratic Majority; Reserve Officers Assn.; U.S.M.C. Reserve Officers Assn.; American Legion; Raven Soc.; Omicron Delta Kappa. AWARDS: Raven Award, 1973; Seven Societies Award, U. of VA. REL.: Episc. MAILING ADDRESS: 612 Chain Bridge Rd., McLean, VA 22101.

ROBBINS, CROWN (aka R. C. HILL). POLIT. & GOV.: ***United Citizens Party candidate for presidency of the U.S., 1976***. MAILING ADDRESS: P.O. Box 184, Winnetka, IL.

ROBERTS, EARL A., JR. b. 1947; par. Earl A. Roberts, Sr.; m. (unknown); m. 2d, Grace Taylor; c. two. EDUC.: Eastern CT U. POLIT. & GOV.: ***Statesman Party candidate for presidency of the U.S., 1992***. BUS. & PROF.: farmer, Autumn Acres Farm; nurseryman; environmental activist. MIL.: Aviation Ordnance, U.S. Navy. MEM.: Future Alternatives, Unlimited. MISC.: advocate of organic gardening. MAILING ADDRESS: c/o Grace Taylor Roberts, 609 Sterling Rd., Sterling, CT 06377.

ROBERTS, JOSEPH CLAUDE "JAY." b. Jan 23, 1936, Jacksonville, FL; par. Leroy Claude and ____ (Geoghagan) Roberts; m. Thelma Faye Craft (divorced); c. Jay Claude (deceased). EDUC.: grad., Paxon H.S., 1957; U. of Judaism. POLIT. & GOV.: ***candidate for Democratic nomination to presidency of the U.S., 1976***. BUS. & PROF.: master carpenter; worker; foreman; superintendent; inventor. MEM.: United Inventors and Scientists of America; United Brotherhood of Carpenters and Joiners of America; NRA MISC.: claims responsibility for Federal law requiring yielding of party line in an emergency. REL.: Jewish. MAILING ADDRESS: 6820 Laurel Canyon Boulevard, North Hollywood, CA.

ROBERTS, OWEN JOSEPHUS. b. May 2, 1875, Philadelphia, PA; d. May 17, 1955, Chester Springs, PA; par. Josephus R. and Emma Elizabeth (Lafferty) Roberts; m. Elizabeth Caldwell Rogers, Jun 15, 1904; c. Elizabeth (Mrs. Roger Hamilton). EDUC.: grad., Germantown (PA) Acad., 1891; A.B., U. of PA, 1895, LL.B., 1898. POLIT. & GOV.: appointed first asst. district atty., Philadelphia Cty., PA, 1901–04; appointed special prosecutor for Eastern PA, 1918; member, Board of City Trusts, Philadelphia, PA, 1920–24; appointed special atty. to investigate Teapot Dome, 1924; appointed assoc. justice, Supreme Court of the U.S., 1930–45; ***candidate for Republican nomination to presidency of the U.S., 1940***; appointed chm., Advisory Board on Clemency, U.S. Dept. of War, 1945–47; chm., Board of Award of Medals of Merit; chm., American Comm. for Monuments in War Areas, 1943–46; chm., President's Amnesty Board, 1946–47. BUS. & PROF.: atty.; instructor, asst. prof., prof. of Law, U. of PA, 1898–1918; assoc., White and White (law firm), Philadelphia, PA, 1903–12; partner (with William W. Montgomery and Charles L. McKeehan), law firm, Philadelphia, PA, 1912–23; partner, Roberts and Montgomery (law firm), Philadelphia, PA, 1923; dir., Land Title and Trust Co., 1920–27; dir., Bell Telephone Co. of PA, 1920–29; dir., Franklin Fire Insurance Co., 1923–29; dir., American Telephone and Telegraph, 1927–29; Bacon lecturer, Boston U., 1947; Holmes lecturer, Harvard U., 1951; contributing ed., *Freedom and Union*, 1945–55; dean, U. of PA Law School, 1948–51. MEM.: Fund for the Advancement of Education (chm.); PA Cmte. for the Selection of Rhodes Scholars (chm.); PA Bar Assn. (pres., 1947); Psi Upsilon; Phi Beta Kappa; American Phil. Soc. (pres., 1952); Atlantic Union (pres.); U. of PA (trustee, 1943–55); Girard Coll. (trustee); Lincoln U. (trustee); Jefferson Medical Coll. (trustee, 1921–24); Chester Cty. BSA (trustee, 1930–55; national exec. board). HON. DEG.: LL.D., Beaver Coll., 1925; LL.D., Ursinus Coll., 1926; LL.D., U. of PA, 1929; LL.D., Lafayette Coll., 1930; LL.D., Dickinson Coll., 1931; LL.D., PA Military Coll., 1931; LL.D., Trinity Coll., 1931; LL.D., Williams Coll., 1933; LL.D., Princeton U., 1934; LL.D., Temple U., 1946; D.C. L., Oxford U., 1951. WRITINGS: *Some Observations on the Case of Private Wadsworth* (1903). REL.: Episc. (pres., House of Deputies, 1946). RES.: Philadelphia, PA.

ROBERTSON, CHARLES FRANKLIN. b. May 15, 1915, Follansbee, WV; par. Chauncy Bertrand and Britta

Nora (Butler) Robertson; m. Gunda C. Simonsen, Dec 25, 1935; c. Charles Bertrand; Darlene Smith; Kay Peterson; Brittarose Morgan. EDUC.: Life Bible Coll. POLIT. & GOV.: ***Christian Nationalist Party candidate for vice presidency of the U.S., 1956***. BUS. & PROF.: minister; ed., *The Cross and the Flag*; coordinator, Elna M. Smith Foundation. MEM.: C. of C. (dir.). REL.: Full Gospel Church. RES.: Eureka Springs, AR.

ROBERTSON, MARION GORDON "PAT." b. Mar 22, 1930, Lexington, VA; par. A. Willis and Gladys (Churchill) Robertson; m. Adelia "Dede" Elmer; c. Timothy; Elizabeth; Gordon; Ann. EDUC.: B.A., Washington and Lee U., 1950; J.D., Yale U., 1955; M.Div., NY Theological Seminary, 1959. POLIT. & GOV.: appointed member, Presidential Task Force on Victims of Crime, 1982–83; ***candidate for Republican nomination to presidency of the U.S., 1988***. BUS. & PROF.: clergyman; broadcast exec.; writer; educator; ordained minister, Southern Baptist Church; exec. asst., W. R. Grace Co., 1954–55; partner, Curry Sound Corp., New York, NY, 1955–56; founder, pres., Christian Broadcasting Network, Inc., Virginia Beach, VA, 1960–; founder, chancellor, Christian Broadcasting Network U., Virginia Beach, VA, 1977–; founder, pres., Christian Network Continental Broadcasting Network, 1978–; Host, "The 700 Club," CBN television, 1968–; dir., United Virginian Bank; dir., National Religious Broadcasting. MIL.: 1st lt., U.S.M.C., 1950–62. MEM.: Phi Beta Kappa. AWARDS: Knesset Medallion, Israel Pilgrimage; International Clergyman of the Year, Religion in Media, 1981; Bronze Halo, Southern CA Motion Picture Council, 1982; George Washington Medal of Honor, Freedoms Foundation at Valley Forge, 1982. HON. DEG.: D.Theology, Oral Roberts U., 1983. WRITINGS: *Shout It From the Housetops* (1972); *My Prayer for You* (1977); *The Secret Kingdom* (1982). REL.: Southern Bapt. MAILING ADDRESS: Christian Broadcasting Network, Inc., 1000 Centerville Turnpike, Virginia Beach, VA 23463.

ROBERTSON, TOM HOWARD. b. Sep 29, 1894, Hillsdale, MI; d. Nov 6, 1954, Detroit, MI; par. Hartley Dayton and Nellie Gertrude (Barnes) Robertson; m. Gertrude Mildner, Jul 28, 1937; c. none. EDUC.: M.D., U. of MI, 1918; intern, Harper's Hospital, Detroit, MI. POLIT. & GOV.: ***independent candidate for presidency of the U.S., 1944***. BUS. & PROF.: surgeon; medical practice, Detroit, MI, 1920–50; emergency surgeon, MI Mutual Industrial Hospital, Detroit, MI; medical examiner, John Hancock Life Insurance Co.; medical examiner, Clan Stewart; medical examiner, Modern Woodmen of the World; medical examiner, Daughters of Scotia. MEM.: American Medical Assn.; MI State Medical Soc.; Wayne Cty. Medical Soc.; SAR; Modern Woodmen of the World; Odd Fellows; Masons (32°; Shriner); Sigma Phi Epsilon; Phi Beta Pi; U. of MI Round Up Club. REL.: Presb. RES.: Detroit, MI.

ROBICHAUX, KENNETH GEORGE. b. Nov 10, 1953, New Orleans, LA. EDUC.: grad., Jesuit H.S., New Orleans, LA, 1971; B.A., (Economics), LA State U., 1976; B.S. (Electrical Engineering), Tulane U., 1982. POLIT. & GOV.: law clerk, office of the district atty., New Orleans, LA, 1977–78; ***Prix Party candidate for presidency of the U.S., 1988***. BUS. & PROF.: inventor; employee, Instrumentation Dept., Waldemar S. Nelson, New Orleans, LA, 1978–82; employee, Middle South Utilities, New Orleans, LA, 1982–85; project engineer, Engineering Planning Group, Orleans Parish, New Orleans, LA, 1985–; pres., Robichaux Research Laboratory, New Orleans, LA. MEM.: I.E.E.E. (pres., 1981–82). MISC.: inventor of laser test for diamonds; champion, karate expert. MAILING ADDRESS: 3505 Chestnut St., New Orleans, LA 70115.

ROBINO, JOSEPH THOMAS, JR. par. Joseph Thomas Robino, Sr. POLIT. & GOV.: ***Peace Party candidate for presidency of the U.S., 1976, 1980, 1984***; Peace Party candidate for U.S. Senate (AL), 1978. MAILING ADDRESS: 704 Merriam St., Plaquemine, LA 70764.

ROBINSON, ARTHUR RAYMOND. b. Mar 12, 1881, Pickerington, OH; d. Mar 17, 1961, Indianapolis, IN; par. John F. and Catherine (Beard) Robinson; m. Freda A. Elfers, Dec 27, 1901; c. Arthur Raymond, Jr.; Willard E.; Kathryn C. (Mrs. Lynn Petross). EDUC.: grad., OH Northern U., 1901; LL.B., IN Law School, 1910; Ph.B., U. of Chicago, 1913. POLIT. & GOV.: elected as a Republican to IN State Senate, 1915–18 (floor leader, 1915–16; pres. pro tempore, 1917–18); appointed judge, Marion Cty. (IN) Superior Court, 1921–22; delegate, Rep. Nat'l. Conv., 1924, 1932; appointed and subsequently elected as a Republican to U.S. Senate (IN), 1925–35; Republican candidate for U.S. Senate (IN), 1934; ***candidate for Republican nomination to presidency of the U.S., 1936***. BUS. & PROF.: atty.; admitted to IN Bar, 1910; partner, Robinson, Symmes and Melson (law firm), Indianapolis, IN, 1910–25. MIL.: pvt., U.S. Army, 1917; commissioned 1st lt., 1917, capt., maj., 1919. MEM.: ABA; IN Bar Assn.; Indianapolis Bar Assn.; Phi Delta Theta; Delta Theta Phi; Masons (33°); Columbia Club; Service Club. HON. DEG.: LL.D., OH Northern U., 1901; LL.D., Marietta Coll. WRITINGS: *Memory and the Executive Mind* (1912). REL.: Methodist. RES.: Indianapolis, IN.

ROBINSON, CARL RAY, JR. par. Carl Ray Robinson, Sr. EDUC.: M.D., U. of AL School of Medicine, 1953; J.D. POLIT. & GOV.: ***independent candidate for presidency of the U.S., 1992***. BUS. & PROF.: physician; atty. MAILING ADDRESS: 1702 Sixth Ave., North, Bessemer, AL 35020.

ROBINSON, HENRY A. POLIT. & GOV.: ***candidate for Union Labor Party nomination to presidency of the U.S., 1888 (withdrew)***. RES.: MI.

ROBINSON, JOSEPH TAYLOR. b. Aug 26, 1872, Lonoke, AR; d. Jul 14, 1937, Washington, DC; par. James and Matilda (Swaim) Robinson; m. Ewilda Gertrude Miller, Dec 15, 1896; c. none. EDUC.: U. of AR; studied law under Judge Thomas C. Trimble, 1892; U. of VA, 1895. POLIT. & GOV.: elected as a Democrat to AR State House, 1895–97; presidential elector, Democratic Party, 1900; elected as a Democrat to U.S. House (AR), 1903–13 (resigned); elected as a Democrat to gov. of AR, 1913; elected as a Democrat to U.S. Senate (AR), 1913–37 (minority leader, 1923–33; majority leader, 1933–37); delegate, Dem. Nat'l. Conv., 1920 (permanent chm.), 1924, 1928 (permanent chm.), 1932 (permanent chm.), 1936; ***candidate for Democratic nomination to presidency of the U.S., 1920, 1924***; appointed U.S. delegate, World Trade Conference, 1927; ***Democratic candidate for vice presidency of the U.S., 1928***; appointed member, Samoan Government Comm., 1929; delegate, London Naval Conference, 1930; U.S. delegate, inauguration of the president of the Philippine Commonwealth, 1935. BUS. & PROF.: atty.; admitted to AR Bar, 1895; law practice, Lonoke, AR, 1895; partner, Coleman, Robinson and House (law firm), Little Rock, AR. MEM.: ABA; AR Bar Assn.; Woodmen of the World; Masons (Scottish Rite); Knights of Pythias; Jefferson Island Club; Alfalfa Club; Smithsonian Institution (regent). HON. DEG.: LL.D., U. of AR, 1922. REL.: Methodist. RES.: Little Rock, AR.

ROCKEFELLER, HER ROYAL HIGHNESS FIFI (see CARPENTER-SWAIN, FAY T.).

ROCKEFELLER, GUY W. (See TAFT, GUY W. ROCKEFELLER).

ROCKEFELLER, JOHN DAVID "JAY," IV.

b. Jun 18, 1937, New York, NY; par. John Davison, III and Blanchette (Hooker) Rockefeller; m. Sharon Percy, 1967; c. Jamie; Valerie; Charles; Justin. EDUC.: International Christian U., Tokyo, Japan, 1957–60; B.A., Harvard U., 1961. POLIT. & GOV.: appointed member, national advisory council, Peace Corps, 1961; asst. to Peace Corps dir., R. Sargent Shriver, 1962; Indonesian Operations Officer, U.S. Dept. of State, 1963–64; staff, Community Development, Office of Economic Opportunity, Charleston, WV, 1964–66; staff member, Presidential Comm. on Juvenile Delinquency and Youth Crime, 1964–66; elected as a Democrat to WV House of Delegates, 1967–69; elected as a Democrat, sec. of state of WV, 1979–73; alternate delegate, Dem. Nat'l. Conv., 1972, delegate, 1980; elected as a Democrat to gov. of WV, 1977–85; elected as a Democrat to U.S. Senate (WV), 1985–; ***candidate for Democratic nomination to presidency of the U.S., 1992; candidate for Democratic nomination to vice presidency of the U.S., 1992***. BUS. & PROF.: pres., WV Wesleyan Coll., 1972–76. MEM.: U. of Notre Dame (trustee); U. of Chicago (trustee); Charleston Rotary Club; Rockefeller Foundation (trustee). AWARDS: one of ten "Outstanding Young Men in America," U.S. Jaycees, 1975; One of 200 Leaders in America, *Time Magazine*, 1975. HON. DEG.: LL.D., U. of AL; LL.D., U. of Cincinnati; LL.D., Davis and Elkins Coll.; LL.D., Dickinson Coll.; LL.D., Yale U. REL.: Bapt. MAILING ADDRESS: 1515 Barberry Lane, Charleston, WV 25314.

ROCKEFELLER, NELSON ALDRICH.

b. Jul 8, 1908, Bar Harbor, ME; d. Jan 26, 1979, New York, NY; par. John Davison, Jr. and Abby Greene (Aldrich) Rockefeller; m. Mary Todhunter Clark, Jun 23, 1930 (divorced, 1962); m. 2d, Margaretta Fitler "Happy" Murphy, May, 1963; c. Rodman; Ann (Mrs. Robert Laughlin Pierson; Mrs. Ann R. Coste); Steven C. (deceased); Michael C. (deceased); Mary (Mrs. Thomas B. Morgan); Nelson Aldrich; Mark Fitler. EDUC.: Lincoln School of Teachers' Coll., New York, NY, 1917–26; B.A., Dartmouth Coll., 1930. POLIT. & GOV.: appointed coordinator, Office of Inter-American Affairs, 1940–44; appointed asst. U.S. sec. of state for American republics, 1944–45; chm., International Development Advisory Board, 1950–51; appointed undersec. of health, education and welfare, 1953–54; appointed chm., President's Advisory Comm. on Governmental Organization, 1953–58; appointed chm., Special Cmte. on Reorganization of the Defense Dept., 1953; appointed special asst. to the presidency of the U.S., 1954–55; chm., NY State Constitution Study Cmte., 1956–59; elected as a Republican to gov. of NY, 1959–73; ***candidate for Republican nomination to presidency of the U.S., 1960, 1964, 1968, 1976 (declined); candidate for Republican nomination to vice presidency of the U.S., 1960, 1976 (declined); independent candidate for presidency of the U.S., 1968***; member, Advisory Comm. on Intergovernmental Relations, 1965–69; appointed personal representative of the president to Latin America, 1969; appointed member, Foreign Intelligence Advisory Board, 1969–74; appointed chm., Comm. on Water Quality, 1973–77; ***appointed as a Republican to vice presidency of the U.S., 1974–1977***; vice chm., Domestic Council, Exec. Office of the President, 1975–77; ***independent Nuclear Navy candidate for vice presidency of the U.S., 1976***. BUS. & PROF.: dir., Rockefeller Center, Inc., 1931–38, pres., 1938–45, 1948–51, chm., 1945–53, 1956–58; dir., Creole Petroleum Corp., 1934; organizer, Compania de Fomento Venezolana, 1940; pres., dir., International Basic Economy Corp., 1947–53, 1956–58, chm. of the board, 1958. MEM.: Phi Beta Kappa; Psi Upsilon; Century Assn.; Dartmouth Club of NY; Cosmos Club; Museum of Primitive Art (founder); Museum of Modern Art (treas., 1935–39; pres., 1939–41, 1946–53; chm., 1957–58); Comm. on Critical Choices for America (chm., 1973–75); 4-H Clubs; Rockefeller Brothers Fund (pres., 1956–58); Inst. for International Social Research (trustee); National Conference of Christians and Jews (dir., 1949–52); Government Affairs Foundation (chm., 1953–58); Metropolitan Club of WA; NY Herald-Tribune Fresh Air Fund (dir., 1951–58); University Club; Knickerbocker Club; Coffee House Club; River Club. AWARDS: Order of Merit of Chile, 1945; National Order of the Southern Cross (Brazil), 1946; Order of the Aztec Eagle (Mexico), 1949; Gold Medal Award, National Inst. of Social Sciences, 1967; Conservation and Water Management Award, Great Lakes Comm., 1970.

WRITINGS: *The Future of Federalism* (1962); *Unity, Freedom and Peace* (1968); *Our Environment Can Be Saved* (1970). REL.: Bapt. MISC.: brother of Winthrop Rockefeller (q.v.). RES.: North Tarrytown, NY.

ROCKEFELLER, WINTHROP. b. May 1, 1912, New York, NY; d. Feb 22, 1973, Palm Springs, CA; par. John Davison, Jr. and Abby Greene (Aldrich) Rockefeller; m. Barbara Paul "Bobo" Sears, Feb 14, 1948; m. 2d, Jeannette Edris, Jun 11, 1956; c. Winthrop Paul. EDUC.: Lincoln School; Loomis School, Windsor, CT, 1928–31; Yale U., 1931–34. POLIT. & GOV.: appointed chm., AR Industrial Development Comm., 1955–64; member, Rep. Nat'l. Cmte., 1961–71; Republican candidate for gov. of AR, 1964, 1970; elected as a Republican to gov. of AR, 1967–71; appointed pres., Jamestown-Williamsburg-Yorktown Celebration Comm.; ***candidate for Republican nomination to presidency of the U.S., 1968***. BUS. & PROF.: employee, Humble Oil and Refining Co., 1934–37; employee, Chase National Bank, 1937–38; exec. vice pres., Greater NY Fund, 1938; employee, Foreign Dept., Socony-Vacuum Oil Co., 1939–51; dir., Rockefeller Brothers, Inc.; dir., Rockefeller Center, Inc.; trustee, industrial relations counselors; chm., Ibee Housing Corp., 1951; dir., Union National Bank of Little Rock; chm. of the board, Colonial Williamsburg, Inc.; chm. of the board, Williamsburg Restoration, Inc.; chm., Winrock Enterprises, Inc.; rancher; cattle breeder. MIL.: pvt., lt. col., U.S. Army, 1941–46; Bronze Star with Oak Leaf Cluster; Purple Heart. MEM.: National Urban League (trustee, 1940–64); Rockefeller Brothers Fund (trustee); Loomis School (trustee); Vanderbilt U. (trustee); South West Center for Advanced Studies (trustee); Santa Gertrudis Breeders International Assn. (pres.; dir.); Delta Kappa Epsilon; Yale Club; AR Livestock Show Assn. (dir.); Red Cross (pres., Pulaski Cty. Chapter); U. of AR Coll. of Medicine (chm., Advisory Cmte.). HON. DEG.: LL.D., U. of AR; LL.D., Hendrix Coll.; L.H.D., U. of San Francis Xavier, Sucre, Bolivia; D.C.L., Southwestern U.LL.D., Coll. of William and Mary; REL.: Bapt. MISC.: brother of Nelson Aldrich Rockefeller (q.v.). RES.: Little Rock, AR.

ROCKHILL, HAROLD KING. b. Mar 12, 1869, OH; d. Mar 1, 1941, Tacoma, WA; m. Ruth R.; c. Randall; Robert; Walter; Mrs. H. E. Wade. POLIT. & GOV.: Prohibition Party candidate for sec. of state of OH, 1904; sec. to the mayor, Tacoma, WA, 1914; ***candidate for Prohibition Party nomination to vice presidency of the U.S., 1916***; member, Prohibition Party National Cmte., c. 1937. BUS. & PROF.: journalist; reporter, Columbus, OH; ed., newspaper, Lorain, OH; sports staff, interocean, Chicago, IL; editorial staff, *Tacoma (WA) Times*, 1906–14; editorial staff, *News Tribune*, Tacoma, WA. RES.: Tacoma, WA.

ROCKWELL, GEORGE LINCOLN. b. Mar 9, 1918, Bloomington, IL; d. Aug 25, 1967, Arlington, VA; par. George Lovejoy "Doc" Rockwell; m. (divorced); m. 2d (divorced); c. seven. EDUC.: Hebron Acad.; Brown U., 1938; Pratt Inst. POLIT. & GOV.: founder, Union of Free Enterprise National Socialists, 1959; founder, leader, American Nazi Party, 1960–66; world leader, World Union of National Socialists, 1962–67; ***candidate for Republican nomination to presidency of the U.S., 1964***; independent candidate for gov. of VA, 1965; founder, National Socialist White People's Party, 1966–67; ***American Nazi (National Socialist White People's) Party candidate for presidency of the U.S., 1972 (deceased)***. BUS. & PROF.: political organizer; lecturer; author; sign painter; photographer; owner, *U.S. Lady Magazine*, 1954; employee, Campaign for the 48 States; staff writer, *American Mercury*; employee, advertising agency; writer, *The Virginian*; cartoonist; ed., *Rockwell Report*; ed., *The Storm-Trooper*. MIL.: pilot, U.S. Navy, 1941–45. MEM.: National Cmte. to Free America From Jewish Domination (founder). AWARDS: Art Prize, National Soc. of Illustrators, 1948. WRITINGS: *This Time the World*; *White Power*. MISC.: assassinated by John Patler, a disgruntled follower, Aug 25, 1967. RES.: Arlington, VA.

RODE, SHARON LEE. b. Jul 29, 1937, Grand Rapids, MI; d. John and Anna E. (Shafer) Tracy; m. ____ Knuth; m. 2d, Jim Marlin Rode; c. Edward L. Knuth; Loren R. Knuth; Ruth Van Houten; Barbara Helzer; Betsy McIntyre; Mary Carpenter; Carol Sue Rode (stepdaughter). EDUC.: grad., high school; Grand Rapids (MI) Junior Coll. POLIT. & GOV.: ***candidate for Republican nomination to presidency of the U.S., 1980***. BUS. & PROF.: operator, ice cream store, Comstock Park, MI. MEM.: Moose; Toastmasters; Foresters; Northwest Federation of Republican Women. AWARDS: for aviation; judo; bowling. REL.: Bapt. MAILING ADDRESS: 3950½ West River Rd., Comstock Park, MI 49321.

RODEN, GEORGE BUCHANAN. b. Jan 17, 1938, Gladewater, TX; par. Ben L. and Lois I. (Scott) Roden; m. Wallen R.; c. Jonathan; Judy; Sharon; Ben; Joshua. EDUC.: grad., high school; D. D., Davidic-Levitical Inst., c. 1954; studied accounting, business management, aviation, communications; Palo Verde Coll., Blythe, CA, 1972–73. POLIT. & GOV.: ***candidate for Democratic nomination to presidency of the U.S., 1976, 1984, 1988***; candidate for Democratic nomination to gov. of CA, 1978. BUS. & PROF.: minister, Branch Davidian Seventh-Day Adventist Church, 1961–; vice pres., Davidic-Levitical Inst.; truck driver; house mover; oil field worker, 1944–57. MEM.: Americans United (pres., Loma Linda, CA, Chapter); Branch Organic Agricultural Assn. of Israel (vice pres.); Branch Davidian Seventh-Day Adventist Assn. REL.: Branch Davidian Seventh-Day Adventist. MAILING ADDRESS: Route 7, Box 471-B, Waco, TX 76705.

RODINO, PETER WALLACE, JR. b. Jun 7, 1909, Newark, NJ; par. Peter and Margaret (Gerard) Rodino; m. Mariana Stango, Dec 27, 1941; c. Margaret Ann (Mrs. Charles

Stanziale, Jr.); Peter Wallace III. EDUC.: grad., U. of Newark; LL.B., NJ Law School, 1937. POLIT. & GOV.: Democratic candidate for U.S. House (NJ), 1946; elected as a Democrat to U.S. House (NJ), 1949–89; ***candidate for Democratic nomination to vice presidency of the U.S., 1972, 1976; candidate for Democratic nomination to presidency of the U.S., 1976***. BUS. & PROF.: atty.; admitted to NJ Bar, 1938; teacher, YMCA, 1930–32; teacher, Federation of Clubs, 1930–32; managing ed., *Jersey Review*, 1934; law practice, Newark, NJ, 1938–; partner, Metro and Rodino (law firm), Newark, NJ. MIL.: capt., U.S. Army, 1941–46; Bronze Star; War Cross; Knight of the Order of the Crown (Italy); Knight of Saints Maurizio e Lazzaro; Knight of Sovereign Military Order of Malta; Cavaliere di Gran Croce (Italy); Order of Merit (Italy); Star of Solidarity; Equestrian Order of St. Agata (San Marino); Friend of Lithuania Medal. AWARDS: award for Distinguished Government Service, American Bill of Rights Day Assn., 1964; Congressional Silver Helmet Award, AmVets, 1965; Silver Star of Merit, VFW; Distinguished Service Award, Catholic War Veterans; Distinguished Service Award, Jewish War Veterans; International Award, Pious Soc. of St. Charles, 1966; Guglielmo Marconi Award, Sons of Italy, 1967; Upward Bound Certificate of Appreciation, Bloomfield Coll., 1969; Martin Luther King, Jr. Award, Southern Christian Leadership Conference, 1975; Bicentennial Americanism Award, UNICO Nat., 1976; Hubert H. Humphrey Civil Rights Award, Leadership Conference on Civil Rights, 1978. HON. DEG.: LL.D., LeMoyne Coll., 1974; LL.D., St. John's U., 1974; LL.D., Lehigh U., 1975; LL.D., NY Law School, 1975; LL.D., Princeton U., 1975; LL.D., Rutgers U., 1975; LL.D., Brooklyn Law School, 1976; LL.D., Seton Hall U., 1976. REL.: R.C. MAILING ADDRESS: 205 Grafton Ave., Newark, NJ 07104.

RODNEY, DANIEL. b. Sep 10, 1764, Lewes, DE; d. Sep 2, 1846, Lewes, DE; par. John and Ruth (Hunn) Rodney; m. Sarah Fisher, Mar 5, 1788; c. five sons; two daughters. EDUC.: public schools. POLIT. & GOV.: appointed assoc. judge, Court of Common Pleas, 1793–1806; presidential elector, Federalist Party, 1808; elected as a Federalist to gov. of DE, 1814–17; ***received 4 electoral votes for vice presidency of the U.S., 1820***; elected as a Federalist to U.S. House (DE), 1822–23; appointed as a Federalist to U.S. Senate (DE), 1826–27. BUS. & PROF.: merchant; master of a coaster, 1812. REL.: Episc. MISC.: twice captured by British cruisers, 1812. RES.: Lewes, DE.

ROE, JAMES ALOYSIUS. b. Jul 9, 1896, Flushing, NY; d. Apr 22, 1967, Hollywood, FL; par. James Aloysius and Elizabeth (McDonnell) Roe; m. Margaret Farrell, Jul 16, 1921; c. James Aloysius, Jr.; Patricia E.; Frances C.; John E. EDUC.: Flushing (NY) H.S. POLIT. & GOV.: chm., Queens Cty. (NY) Democratic Central Cmte.; member, NY State Democratic Central Cmte.; elected as a Democrat to U.S. House (NY), 1945–47; ***candidate for Democratic nomination to presidency of the U.S., 1948***; delegate, Dem. Nat'l. Conv., 1952, 1956. BUS. & PROF.: soldier. MIL.: lt., U.S.A.A.C., WWI; lt. col., Corps of Engineers, U.S. Army, 1943. MEM.: National Democratic Club of NY (gov.); Holy Family Hospital (gov.); North Shore Civic Assn.; YMCA; C. of C.; American Legion; Reserve Officers Assn.; Flushing Memorial Assn.; A.S.M.E.; NRA; Order of Daedalians; Holy Name Soc.; St. Vincent DePaul Soc.; American Red Cross; Knights of Columbus; Elks. REL.: R.C. RES.: Flushing, NY.

ROGERS, GEORGE PRICE. b. Jan 14, 1821; d. Nov 24, 1893, New London, CT; par. Seabury and Elizabeth "Betsy" (Daniels) Rogers; m. Susan E. Renouf, Oct 10, 1854; c. none. POLIT. & GOV.: elected member, Court of Common Council, New London, CT, one term; Prohibition Party candidate for lt. gov. of CT, 2 times; Prohibition Party candidate for gov. of CT, 1880, 1882; member, Prohibition Party National Cmte., 1882–92; ***candidate for Prohibition Party nomination to vice presidency of the U.S., 1884 (declined)***. BUS. & PROF.: partner, confectionary business, New London, CT; partner, ice business, 1843–93; correspondent, *The Morning Telegraph*, New London, CT. REL.: Congregationalist. RES.: New London, CT.

ROGERS, MICHAEL WADE. POLIT. & GOV.: ***candidate for Republican nomination to presidency of the U.S., 1988***. MAILING ADDRESS: 3115 Ninth Ave., Arcadia, CA 91006.

ROGERS, TENNIE BEATRICE. b. Aug 1, 1927, Russell, AR; m., 1952; c. two. EDUC.: B.A., 1967, M.A., 1972; attended Harding U.; Pasadena City Coll.; CA State U., Los Angeles. POLIT. & GOV.: ***candidate for Republican nomination to presidency of the U.S., 1992***. BUS. & PROF.: teacher; registered nurse, 1990–. MAILING ADDRESS: 421 North Baldwin Ave., Sierra Madre, CA 91024.

ROGERS, WILLIAM HENRY "LUCKY BUCK" (aka MAGNUS CIRCARA). b. St. Paul, MN; par. Mason Henry and Elsmore Rogers; m. Ruth R.; c. Monica; Lucile. EDUC.: none. POLIT. & GOV.: sec., Revived American Mugwump Party of 1884, 1976; ***Revived American Mugwump Party of 1884 candidate for presidency of the U.S., 1976, 1980***. BUS. & PROF.: ed.; proprietor, print shop, Sacramento, CA. MIL.: safety engineer, Spokane Air Technical Service Command, Galena, WA, WWII. WRITINGS: *There Shall Be No Peace* (1956); *Much Ado About the Black Man's Hue* (1966); *The President's Guest* (1974). REL.: polydenominational. MAILING ADDRESS: 1512 19th St., Sacramento, CA 95814.

ROGERS, WILLIAM PENN ADAIR "WILL." b. Nov 4, 1879, Oologah, Indian Territory; d. Aug 15, 1935, Point Barrow, AK; par. Clem Vann and Mary (Schrimpsher) Rogers; m. Betty Blake, Nov 25, 1908; c. Will Vann, Jr.; Mary Elizabeth; Jim Blake; infant. EDUC.: Willie

Hassell School; Kemper Military Acad. POLIT. & GOV.: ***candidate for Democratic nomination to presidency of the U.S., 1924, 1932;*** ; received 1 vote on 68th ballot for presidential nomination, Dem. Nat'l. Conv., 1924; ***Bunkless Party candidate for presidency of the U.S., 1928; Aden Sheriff Party candidate for presidency of the U.S., 1936***. BUS. & PROF.: humorist; "The Cherokee Kid" (rope artist), Cummings Wild West Show, 1904; vaudeville, Hammerstein's Roof Garden, New York, NY, 1905; with Ziegfield Follies and Night Frolics, 1914–35; columnist, McNaught Syndicate, 1922–35; motion picture actor; author. CREDITS: Plays: "Wall Street Girl" (1912); "Merry-Go-Round" (1914); "Hands Up" (1915). MOTION PICTURE CREDITS: "Laughing Bill Hyde" (1918); "Almost a Husband" (1919); "Water, Water, Everywhere" (1919); "Jubilo" (1919); "Jes' Call Me Jim" (1920); "The Strange Boarder" (1920); "Scratch My Back" (1920); "A Poor Relation" (1920); "Cupid the Cowpuncher" (1920); "Honest Hutch" (1920); "Guile of Women" (1921); "Boys Will Be Boys" (1921); "An Unwilling Hero" (1921); "Doubling for Romeo" (1921); "One Glorious Day" (1921); "Follies, Midnight Frolics" (plays, 1921–24); "The Headless Horseman" (1922); "The Ropin' Fool" (1922); "One Day in 365" (1922); "Hustling Hank" (1922); "Uncensored Movies" (1922); "Fruits of Faith" (1922); "Just Passing Through" (1923); "Gee Whiz Genevieve" (1923); "Highbrow Stuff" (1923); "Family Fits" (1923); "The Cake Eater" (1924); "Big Moments from Little Pictures" (1924); "Don't Park There" 1924); "The Cowboy Sheik" (1924); "Going to Congress" (1924); "Our Congressman" (1924); "A Truthful Liar" (1924); "Two Wagons" (1924); "Cochran's Review of 1926" (play, 1926); "Three Cheers" (play); "A Texas Steer" (1927); "Tiptoes" (1927); "They Had to See Paris" (1929); "Happy Days" (1930); "So This Is London" (1930); "Lightnin'" (1930); "Down to Earth" (film); "A Connecticut Yankee in King Arthur's Court" (1931); "Young as You Feel" (1931); "Ambassador Bill" (1931); "Too Busy to Work" (1931–32); "Business and Pleasure" (1932); "State Fair" (1933); "Doctor Bull" (1933); "Mr. Skitch" (1933); "Ah, Wilderness" (play, 1933); "David Harum" (1934); "Handy Andy" (1934); "Judge Priest" (1934); "The County Chairman" (1935); "Life Begins at Forty" (1935); "Doubting Thomas: (1935); "In Old Kentucky" (1935); "Steamboat Round the Bend" (1935). MEM.: Masons; Elks. WRITINGS: *Rogerisms—The Cowboy Philosopher on Prohibition* (1919); *Rogerisms—The Cowboy Philosopher on the Peace Conference* (1919); *Rogerisms—What We Laugh At* (1920); *Illiterate Digest* (1924); *Letters of a Self-Made Diplomat to His President; There's Not a Bathing Suit in Russia* (1927). REL.: Methodist. MISC.: died in plane crash with Wiley Post, Point Barrow, AK, Aug 15, 1935. RES.: Beverly Hills, CA.

ROGERS, WILLIAM RICHARD. b. May 1, 1923, Rougemont, NC; par. William R., Sr., and Julia A. (Lunsford) Rogers; m. Clara R. Burch; c. William Richard III; Sheila; Vicky. EDUC.: high school, Helena, NC. POLIT. & GOV.: ***Theocratic Party candidate for vice presidency of the U.S., 1964; candidate for Theocratic Party nomination to presidency of the U.S., 1968 (withdrew)***; chm., Theocratic Party. BUS. & PROF.: baseball umpire, Kitty League and Mountain State League, 1946–48; bishop, Church of God, 1956–; served pastorates in seven states; lecturer. MIL.: U.S. Navy, WWII. REL.: Church of God. MAILING ADDRESS: 311 West Second St., Fulton, MO 65251.

ROGERS, Z. A. POLIT. & GOV.: ***independent candidate for presidency of the U.S., 1928***. RES.: MS.

ROGGE, OETJE JOHN. b. Oct 12, 1903, Cass Cty., IL; d. Mar 22, 1981, New York, NY; par. Hermann and Lydia Anne (Satorius) Rogge; m. Nellie Alma Luther, Jan 1, 1926; m. 2d, Wanda Lucille Johnston, Dec 15, 1940; c. Genevieve Oetjeanne; Hermann. EDUC.: A.B., U. of IL, 1922; LL.B., Harvard U., 1925, S.J.D., 1931. POLIT. & GOV.: appointed counsel, RFC, 1934–37; appointed special counsel, S.E.C., 1937–38, asst. gen. counsel, 1938–39; appointed asst. atty. gen. of the U.S., 1939–40; ***candidate for Democratic nomination to presidency of the U.S., 1940***; appointed special asst. to the atty. gen. of the U.S., 1943–46; ***candidate for Progressive Party nomination to vice presidency of the U.S., 1948***. BUS. & PROF.: atty.; admitted to IL Bar, 1925; law practice, Chicago, IL, 1925–30; partner, Weisman, Celler, Spett, Modlin and Wertheimer (law firm), New York, NY; ed., *Harvard Law Review*. MEM.: Egypt Exploration Soc.; ABA; New York Cty. Lawyers Assn.; Assn. of the Bar of the City of New York; Phi Beta Kappa. WRITINGS: *Our Vanishing Civil Liberties* (1949); *Why Men Confess* (1959); *The First and the Fifth* (1960); *The Official German Report* (1961); *Obscenity Litigation in 10 American Jurisprudence Trials* (1965); *The Rights of the Accused* (contributing author). MISC.: noted as prosecutor in Nuremberg War Crimes Trials, 1945–46. RES.: New York, NY.

ROLLAND, JOANNE. POLIT. & GOV.: ***Third Party candidate for vice presidency of the U.S., 1992***. MAILING ADDRESS: WI.

ROLLINSON, RAYMOND ALLEN PETER. b. Dec 29, 1921, Yonkers, NY; par. Thomas Samuel and Alice May Cecile (Toburn) Rollinson; m. Jeanette Dorothy Therese Travis, Jun 16, 1943; c. Janet Marie Doll (Mrs. Gary Kreger); Brian Gerard George; Lynn Marie Doll; Jill Marie Doll. EDUC.: B.B.A., Manhattan Coll., 1952; M.S., Columbia U., 1956. POLIT. & GOV.: candidate for Democratic nomination to U.S. House (NJ), 1976, 1984; ***candidate for Democratic nomination to vice presidency of the U.S., 1976, 1980***; candidate for Democratic nomination to U.S. Senate (NJ), 1978; ***Honest Man's candidate for Democratic nomination to presidency of the U.S., 1980, 1984, 1988, 1992.*** BUS. & PROF.: partner, Rollinson Brothers Movers; pot and pan salesman; waiter; bartender; businessman; poet. MIL.: pfc, U.S. Army, 1940–42, aviation cadet, 1942–44. MEM.: Waiters and Bartenders, Hotel Employees International Union, AFL-CIO (Local 178; charter member). WRITINGS: "Floating as Waste, Back and Forth with the Tide" (poem); "Shalom to You, Israel" (trilogy); "Progression Seven Trilogy" (poem). REL.: R.C. MISC.: known as "The great poet from Yonkers"; "Tu-Te-The-Lion"; claims to be grandson of Chief Crazy Horse and great-grandson of Chief Mic Mec; nominated by U.S. Sen. Connie Mack (R-FL) and U.S. Rep. Earl Hutto (R-FL) for appointment as poet laureate of the U.S., Jan 1990; endorsements withdrawn because of Rollinson's racist views and writings; used slogan "Keep White Hope Alive in America." MAILING ADDRESS: R.D. # 1, Box 32, Columbia, NJ 07832.

ROMER, HENRY A. "HARRY." b. Dec 9, 1898; d. Mar 24, 1953, St. Henry, OH; par. J. J. Romer; m. Margaret Severt, Oct 22, 1919; c. Verna (Mrs. Buschar); Lowell; Harry, Jr.; Myra (Mrs. Delzeith); Julia (Mrs. Stahl); Madonna (Mrs. Welch); Ann Kay; one other daughter. POLIT. & GOV.: ***America First Party candidate for vice presidency of the U.S., 1944; Christian Nationalist Party candidate for vice presidency of the U.S., 1948***. BUS. & PROF.: merchant; funeral dir.; owner, Romer Funeral Home, St. Henry, OH. MEM.: American Legion; Holy Name Soc.; Loyal Order of Moose; Knights of Columbus; Knights of St. John; Eagles; National Funeral Directors Assn. REL.: R.C. RES.: St. Henry, OH.

ROMIEH, HASSAN M. M. (aka GEORGE WASHINGTON AMERICA, q.v.). b. Aug 29, 1942, Washington, DC; par. Betty Naulty (adopted); m. Cathy Elizabeth Reynolds, May 10, 1980 (divorced, 1984); m. 2d, Sherry Guinn; c. Melissa (adopted). EDUC.: high school, 1955–58; B.A., Journalism Coll., Cologne, West Germany, 1958–64; M.E., Engineering Coll., Cologne, West Germany. POLIT. & GOV.: member, Republican Party, 1979–; ***independent candidate for presidency of the U.S., 1988, 1992***. BUS. & PROF.: publisher; freelance writer, reporter, publisher, 1957–75; publisher, owner, International Freedom Organization, 1975–; informer, FBI, 1979–; owner, Americana Publishing and Media Co., New York, NY. WRITINGS: *Strength For Peace* (1980). REL.: Presb. MAILING ADDRESS: 142 West 112th St., Suite B-45, New York, NY 10026-3703.

ROMNEY, GEORGE WILCKEN. b. Jul 8, 1907, Chihauhua, Mexico; d. July 26, 1995, Bloomfield Hills, MI; par. Gaskell and Anna Amelia (Pratt) Romney; m. Lenore LaFount, Jul 2, 1931; c. Lynn (Mrs. Loren G. Keenan); Jane (Mrs. Bruce H. Robinson); Scott; Willard Mitt. EDUC.: Latter-Day Saints University H.S. and Junior Coll.; U. of UT, 1928–29; George Washington U., 1929–30. POLIT. & GOV.: tariff specialist, office of U.S. Sen. David I. Walsh (q.v.), 1929–30; appointed managing dir., Automotive Council on War Production, 1942–45; appointed management member, War Manpower Comm.; appointed management member, Labor Management Council; elected as a Republican to gov. of MI, 1963–69; delegate, Rep. Nat'l. Conv., 1964, 1968; ***candidate for Republican nomination to presidency of the U.S., 1964, 1968; candidate for Republican nomination to vice presidency of the U.S., 1968***; appointed U.S. sec. of housing and urban development, 1969–73. BUS. & PROF.: apprentice, Aluminum Co. of America, 1930, salesman, Los Angeles Office, 1931; Washington (DC) rep., Aluminum Co. of America and Aluminum Wares Assn., 1932–38; Detroit mgr., Automobile Manufacturers Assn., 1939–41, gen. mgr., 1942–48; asst. to the pres., Nash-Kelvinator Corp., 1948–50, vice pres., 1950–53, exec. vice pres., 1953–54, dir., 1953–54; pres., chm. of the board, gen. mgr., American Motors Corp., 1954–62; dir., Douglas Aircraft Corp., 1960–62; chief exec. officer, National Center for Volunteer Action, 1973–. MEM.: Citizens for MI (chm., 1959– 62); Metal Trades Industry Conference (delegate, 1946–49); WA Trade Assn. Executives (pres., 1937–38); Detroit Victory Council (vice pres.; dir.); Citizens' Advisory Cmte. on School Needs (chm., 1958); Detroit Tomorrow (Inter-Community Relations Cmte.); Detroit Trade Assn. (pres., 1941); American Trade Assn. Executives (dir., 1944–47); National Automobile Golden Jubilee Comm. (managing dir., 19466); National Conference of Christians and Jews (dir.); United Foundation (dir.); Cranbrook School (dir.); Detroit Club; Burning Tree Club; National Press Club. AWARDS: Cranbrook School A. P. Industry Man of the Year, 1958–61. REL.: Church of Jesus Christ of Latter-Day Saints (missionary to Scotland and England, 1927–28; pres., Detroit Stake, 1952–62). MAILING ADDRESS: 1830 Valley Rd., Bloomfield Hills, MI 48013.

ROOSEVELT, ANNA ELEANOR. b. Oct 11, 1884, New York, NY; d. Nov 7, 1962, New York, NY; d. Elliott and Anna (Hall) Roosevelt; m. Franklin Delano Roosevelt (q.v.), Mar 17, 1905; c. infant; Anna Eleanor (Mrs. James Halsted); James (q.v.); Elliott Franklin Delano, Jr.; John Aspinwall. EDUC.: private schools; L.H.D., Russell Sage Coll., 1929. POLIT. & GOV.: finance chm., Women's Division, NY State Democratic Central Cmte., 1924–28; member, Women's Advisory Cmte., Democratic National Campaign Cmte., 1928; ***candidate for Democratic nomination to presidency of the U.S., 1940; candidate for Democratic nomination to vice presidency of the U.S., 1940, 1948 (declined)***; appointed asst. dir., Office of Civilian Defense, 1941–42; appointed U.S. rep. to U.N. General Assembly, 1945, 1949–52, 1961; appointed chm., Comm. on Human Rights, U.N. Economic and Social Council, 1946. BUS. & PROF.: teacher, Todhunter School for Girls, New York, NY, 1928–33; columnist, "My Day," 1936–62; humanitarian. MEM.: American Assn. for the U.N.; NY League of Women Voters (vice pres.); Altrusa Club; NY Women's Club; Cosmopolitan Club; 100,000 Mile Club. AWARDS: Churchman's Award, 1936; Humanitarian Award, 1939; Nation Award, 1940; First Annual Franklin Delano Roosevelt Brotherhood Award, 1946; First American Award in Human Relations, 1949; Four Freedoms Award, 1950; Prince Carl Medal of Sweden, 1950; Irving Geist Foundation Award, 1950; Highest Award, National Soc. for Crippled Children and Adults, 1950. WRITINGS: *When You*

Grow Up to Vote (1932); *Hunting Big Game in the Eighties* (ed., 1932); *It's Up to the Women* (1933); *A Trip to Washington with Bobby and Betty*; *This Is My Story* (1937); *My Days* (1938); *Christmas: A Story* (ed., 1940); *The Moral Basis of Democracy* (ed., 1940); *If You Ask Me* (1946); *This I Remember* (1949); *India: The Awakening East* (1952); *On My Own* (1955); *You Learn by Living* (1960); *The Autobiography of Eleanor Roosevelt* (1961). REL.: Episc. RES.: Hyde Park, NY.

ROOSEVELT, FRANKLIN DELANO. b. Jan 30, 1882, Hyde Park, NY; d. Apr 12, 1945, Warm Springs, GA; par. James and Sara (Delano) Roosevelt; m. Anna Eleanor Roosevelt (q.v.), Mar 17, 1905; c. infant; Anna Eleanor (Mrs. John Boettiger; Mrs. James H. Halsted); James (q.v.); Elliott Franklin Delano, Jr.; John Aspinwall. EDUC.: Groton School, 1896–1900; A.B., Harvard U., 1904; Columbia U. Law School, 1904–07. POLIT. & GOV.: appointed member, Hudson-Fulton Celebration Comm., 1909; elected as a Democrat to NY State Senate, 1910–13; appointed member, Plattsburgh (NY) Centennial Comm., 1913; appointed asst. U.S. sec. of the navy, 1913–20; candidate for Democratic nomination to U.S. Senate (NY), 1914; appointed member, National Comm. for Panama-Pacific International Exposition, 1915; ***Democratic candidate for vice presidency of the U.S., 1920***; delegate, Dem. Nat'l. Conv., 1920, 1924, 1928; ***candidate for Democratic nomination to presidency of the U.S., 1924***; elected as a Democrat to gov. of NY, 1929–33; ***elected as a Democrat, presidency of the U.S., 1933–1945***. BUS. & PROF.: atty.; admitted to NY Bar, 1907; assoc., Carter, Ledyard and Milburn (law firm), New York, NY, 1907–10; partner, Roosevelt and O'Connor (law firm), New York, NY, 1924–33; vice pres., Fidelity and Deposit Co., 1920–28. MEM.: Harvard U. (overseer, 1918–24); American National Red Cross (pres.); GA Warm Springs Foundation; Naval History Soc.; NY Hist. Soc.; Holland Soc.; Alpha Delta Phi; Phi Beta Kappa; Masons. HON. DEG.: LL.D., Rutgers U., 1933; LL.D., WA Coll., 1933; LL.D., William and Mary Coll., 1934; LL.D., Yale U., 1934; LL.D., U. of Notre Dame, 1935; Litt.D., Rollins Coll., 1936; D.C.L., Oxford U., 1941. WRITINGS: *Whither Bound* (1926); *The Happy Warrior: Alfred E. Smith* (1928); *Government—Not Politics* (1932); *Looking Forward* (1933); *On Our Way* (1934). REL.: Episc. (senior warden, St. James' Church, Hyde Park, NY). MISC.: in charge of demobilization efforts at conclusion of World War I, 1919. RES.: Hyde Park, NY.

ROOSEVELT, JAMES. b. Dec 23, 1907, New York, NY; d. Aug 13, 1991, Newport Beach, CA; par. Franklin Delano (q.v.) and Anna Eleanor (Roosevelt, q.v.) Roosevelt; m. Betsey Cushing, Jun 1930 (divorced, 1940); m. 2d, Romelle Schneider (divorced, 1955); m. 3d, Gladys Irene Owens, Jul 9, 1956 (divorced, 1969); m. 4th, Mary Lena Winskill, Oct 3, 1969; c. Sara Delano Wilford; Kate Roosevelt Whitney; James; Michael; Anne Johnston; Hall Delano; Rebecca Mary. EDUC.: Harvard U., 1930. POLIT. & GOV.: member, Dem. Nat'l. Cmte. (CA), 1948–52; Democratic candidate for gov. of CA, 1950; elected as a Democrat to U.S. House (CA), 1955–67; appointed U.S. Rep. to ECOSOC, 1965–66; appointed member, Orange Cty. (CA) Transportation Comm., 1979– (chm., 1985–86); ***candidate for Democratic nomination to vice presidency of the U.S., 1988***. BUS. & PROF.: business consultant; insurance broker, Obrion, Russell and Co., Boston, MA, 1930; pres., Roosevelt and Sargent, Inc. (insurance), Boston, MA, 1930–37, exec. vice pres. for West Coast, 1946; motion picture industry, 1938–40; pres., James Roosevelt and Co.; with IOS Management Co., 1966–70, pres., 1970–71, business consultant, 1970–91; pres., IOS Development Co., Ltd.; exec. dir., Enterprise Inst., Chapman Coll.; lecturer in Social Ecology, U. of CA at Irvine Chancellors Club; lecturer in Political Science, Woodbury U.; lecturer in Political Science, Chapman Coll. MIL.: capt., col., U.S.M.C. Reserves, 1940–45, brig. gen. (retired); Navy Cross; Silver Star. MEM.: Eleanor Roosevelt Cancer Foundation (vice pres.); National Foundation for the March of Dimes (dir.); Metropolitan Club; Chapman Coll. (trustee); Arm and Hammer Peace and Human Rights Conferences, 1979, 1980, 1981; Elks; National Cmte. to Preserve Social Security (chm.). AWARDS: Humanitarian Award, National Conference of Christians and Jews, 1981; National Americanism Award, Anti-Defamation League of B'nai B'rith. HON. DEG.: LL.D., Woodbury U., 1977; Ph.D., CA Western U.; B.S., Chapman Coll., 1985. WRITINGS: *Affectionately, F. D. R.* (1959); *My Parents* (1976); *A Family Matter* (1979). REL.: Episc. MISC.: unofficial running mate of Walter R. Buchanan (q.v.), 1988. RES.: Santa Ana, CA.

ROOSEVELT, ROBERT JOHN (nee ROBERT GRANT). b. Apr 20, 1910, Fresno, CA. POLIT. & GOV.: candidate for Democratic nomination to U.S. Senate (MD), 1974, 1982; ***candidate for Democratic nomination to presidency of the U.S., 1976, 1980, 1984***; candidate for Democratic nomination to U.S. House (MD), 1976, 1978, 1986. BUS. & PROF.: construction worker. MAILING ADDRESS: 7904 Flower Ave., Takoma Park, MD 20912.

ROOSEVELT, THEODORE. b. Oct 27, 1858, New York, NY; d. Jan 6, 1919, Oyster Bay, NY; par. Theodore and Martha (Bulloch) Roosevelt; m. Alice Hathaway Lee, Oct 27, 1880; m. 2d, Edith Kermit Carow, Dec 2, 1886; c. Alice Lee; Theodore, Jr. (q.v.); Kermit; Ethel Carow; Archibald Bulloch; Quentin. EDUC.: A.B., Harvard U., 1880. POLIT. & GOV.: elected as a Republican to NY State Assembly, 1882–84 (minority leader, 1882); delegate, Rep. Nat'l. Conv., 1884; Republican candidate for mayor of New York, NY, 1886; appointed U.S. Civil Service Commissioner, 1889–95; appointed pres., NY (NY) Police Board, 1895–97; appointed asst. U.S. sec. of the navy, 1897–98; elected as a Republican to gov. of NY, 1899–1900; ***elected as a Republican, vice presidency of the U.S., 1901; succeeded to the office of presidency of the U.S. on death of William McKinley (q.v.) and subsequently elected as a Republican to presidency of the U.S., 1901–1909; candidate for Republican nomination to presidency of the U.S., 1908, 1912,***

1916, 1920; Progressive Party candidate for presidency of the U.S., 1912, 1916 (declined). BUS. & PROF.: rancher, ND, 1884–86; lecturer; author; reformer; explorer; contributing ed., *The Outlook*, 1909–10. MIL.: organizer, lt. col., col., First U.S. Cavalry (Rough Riders), 1898. MEM.: American Museum of Natural History (trustee; hon. fellow); NY State Charities Aid Assn. (dir.); London Alpine Club; Boone-Crockett Club (pres.); Union League; Century Club; Harvard U. (overseer, 1895); Naval Club; Military Order of the Spanish-American War. AWARDS: Nobel Peace Prize, 1906 HON. DEG.: LL.D., Northwestern U., 1893; LL.D., Columbia U., 1899; LL.D., Hope Coll., 1901; LL.D., Yale U., 1901; LL.D., Harvard U., 1902; LL.D., U. of CA, 1903; LL.D., U. of Chicago, 1903; LL.D., Clark U., 1905; LL.D., U. of PA, 1905; LL.D., George Washington U., 1909; Ph.D., U. of Berlin, 1910; LL.D., Cambridge U., 1910; D.C.L., Oxford U., 1910. WRITINGS: *History of the Naval War of 1812* (1882); *Hunting Trips of a Ranchman* (1885); *Life of Thomas Hart Benton* (1886); *Life of Gouverneur Morris* (1887); *Ranch Life and Hunting Trail* (1888); *Winning of the West* (1889–96); *History of New York* (1890); *The Wilderness Hunter* (1893); *American Ideals and Other Essays* (1897); *The Rough Riders* (1899); *Life of Oliver Cromwell* (1900); *The Strenuous Life* (1900); *Works* (1902); *The Deer Family* (1902); *Outdoor Pastimes of an American Hunter* (1906); *Good Hunting* (1907); *True Americanism; African and European Addresses* (1910); *African Game Trails* (1910); *The New Nationalism* (1910); *Realizable Ideals* (1912); *Conservation of Womanhood and Childhood* (1912); *History as Literature, and Other Essays* (1913); *Autobiography* (1913); *Life Histories of African Game Animals* (1914); *Through the Brazilian Wilderness* (1914); *America and the World War* (1915); *A Booklover's Holidays in the Open* (1916); *Fear God, and Take Your Own Part* (1916); *Foes of Our Own Household* (1917); *National Strength and International Duty* (1917). REL.: Dutch Reformed Church. MISC.: appointed special ambassador to funeral of King Edward VII, 1910; survived assassination attempt, 1912; discovered "Rio Teodoro" in Brazil, 1914. RES.: Oyster Bay, Long Island, NY.

ROOSEVELT, THEODORE, JR. b. Sep 13, 1887, Oyster Bay, NY; d. Jul 12, 1944, Meautis, Normandy, France; par. Theodore (q.v.) and Edith Kermit (Carow) Roosevelt; m. Eleanor Butler, Jun 20, 1910; c. Grace Green (Mrs. William McMillan); Theodore; Cornelius Van Schaak; Quentin. EDUC.: Groton School; A.B., Harvard U., 1908. POLIT. & GOV.: elected as a Republican to NY State Assembly, 1919–21; ***candidate for Republican nomination to vice presidency of the U.S., 1920, 1924, 1936***; appointed asst. U.S. sec. of the navy, 1921–24; Republican candidate for gov. of NY, 1924; temporary chm., NY State Republican Convention, 1927; appointed civil gov. of Puerto Rico, 1929–32; appointed gov. gen. of the Philippines, 1932–33; candidate for Republican nomination to gov. of NY, 1936. BUS. & PROF.: wool sorter, Hartford Carpet Co., Thompsonville, CT, mgr., San Francisco (CA) Branch, 1910–12; bond salesman, Berton, Griscom and Jenks, New York, NY, 1912–14; partner, Montgomery, Clothier and Tyler (brokerage house), Philadelphia, PA, 1914; dir., Sinclair Oil and Refining Co.; dir., J. G. White Manufacturing Corp.; dir., Broadway Improvement Co.; dir., White Motor Co.; chm. of the board, American Express, 1934–35; vice pres., Doubleday Co., 1934–44. MIL.: maj., U.S.A.R. Corps, 1917, lt. col., 1918, col., 1919; brig. gen., 26th Infantry, 1st Div., U.S. Army, 1941–44; conducted scientific expeditions to Central Asia, 1925–26, Indochina, 1928–29; Distinguished Service Medal; Distinguished Service Cross; U.S. Legion of Merit; Croix de Guerre (Belgium); Croix de Guerre with Three Palms (France); Grand Cordon of Prince Danilo I; Medal for Valor (Montenegro); Legion of Honor (France); Medal of Honor (posthumous). MEM.: National Conference on Outdoor Recreation (chm., 1924); National Health Council (pres., 1934); American Bureau for Medical Aid to China (chm., 1940); BSA (vice pres.); Field Museum of Natural History (trustee); Howard U. (trustee); American Legion (founder); Royal Geographical Soc.; American Geographical Soc.; Izaak Walton League; Knickerbocker Club; Harvard Club; River Club; Explorers Club; Racquet Club. HON. DEG.: M.A., Harvard U., 1919. WRITINGS: *Average Americans* (1919); *East of the Sun and West of the Moon* (1926); *Rank and File* (1928); *All in the Family* (1929); *Trailing the Giant Panda* (1929); *Taps* (1932); *Three Kingdoms of Indo-China* (1933); *Colonial Policies of the United States* (1937); *The Desk-Drawer Analogy* (1937). REL.: Episc. RES.: New York, NY.

ROOT, ELIHU. b. Feb 15, 1845, Clinton, NY; d. Feb 7, 1937, New York, NY; par. Oren and Nancy Whitney (Buttrick) Root; m. Clara Wales, Jan 8, 1878; c. Edith (Mrs. U.S. Grant III); Elihu; Edward Wales. EDUC.: A.B., Hamilton Coll., 1864, A.M., 1867. POLIT. & GOV.: appointed U.S. district atty., Southern District of NY, 1883–85; delegate, NY State Constitutional Convention, 1894, 1915 (pres.); appointed U.S. sec. of war, 1899–1904; appointed member, Alaskan Boundary Tribunal, 1903; chm., Rep. Nat'l. Conv., 1904, 1912; appointed U.S. sec. of state, 1905–09; chm., NY State Republican Convention, 1908, 1910, 1913, 1914, 1916, 1920, 1922; elected as a Republican to U.S. Senate (NY), 1909–15; member, Permanent Court of Arbitration, 1910–37; U.S. counsel, North Atlantic Fisheries Arbitration, 1910; pres., Hague Tribunal of Arbitration between Great Britain, France, Spain, and Portugal, 1913; ***candidate for Republican nomination to presidency of the U.S., 1916***; appointed U.S. ambassador extraordinary to Russia, 1917; member, Comm. of International Jurists on New Permanent Court of International justice, 1921; appointed U.S. Commissioner Plenipotentiary, International Conference on Limitations of Armaments, 1921; presidential elector, Republican Party, 1925; hon. pres., NY State Repeal Convention, 1933. BUS. & PROF.: teacher, Rome Acad., 1865; atty.; admitted to NY Bar, 1867; law practice, New York, NY; author; instructor in Political and Administrative Sciences, U. of San Marcos, Lima, Peru, 1906. MEM.: A.I.A.; Carnegie Endowment for International Peace (pres., 1910–25); Carnegie Institution (chm., board of trustees, 1913–37); Hamilton Coll. (trustee, 1912–37); NY Public Library (trustee); Metropolitan Museum of Art (trustee); American Federation of Arts (trustee); NY State Charities Aid Assn. (trustee);

New England Soc. in NY (pres., 1893–95); Union League Club (pres., 1898–99, 1915–16); Assn. of the Bar of the City of New York (pres., 1904–05); American Soc. of International Law (pres., 1906–37); NY State Bar Assn. (pres., 1910); ABA (pres., 1915); NY Law Inst. (pres.); Mexican Acad. of Legislation and Jurisprudence; Brazilian Inst. of Advocates (hon.); Pan-American Conference (hon. pres., 1906); American Inst. of International Law (hon. pres.); National Security League (hon. pres.); NY Assn. for the Blind; National Soc. for the Prevention of Blindness; Century Club (pres.); British Acad. (corresponding fellow); Institut de Droit International; NY C. of C.; Soc. of the Cincinnati; American Phil. Soc.; American Acad. of Arts and Letters; MA Hist. Soc. (corresponding fellow); American Acad. of Arts and Sciences (fellow); U.S. Government War Savings Investments Soc. (chm., 1918); American Law Inst. (hon. pres.). AWARDS: Nobel Peace Prize, 1912; Roosevelt Medal, 1924; Woodrow Wilson Foundation Medal, 1926; Dodge Lectureship, Yale U., 1907; Stafford Little Lectureship, Princeton U., 1913; Grand Cordon de l'Ordre de la Couronne (Belgium, 1919); Royal Order of George I (Greece). HON. DEG.: LL.B., NY U., 1867; LL.D., Hamilton Coll., 1894; LL.D., Yale U., 1900; LL.D., Columbia U., 1904; LL.D., NY U., 1904; LL.D., Williams Coll., 1905; LL.D., U. of Buenos Aires, 1906; LL.D., Princeton U., 1906; LL.D., Harvard U., 1907; LL.D., Wesleyan Coll., 1909; Dr.Polit.Sci., U. of Leyden, 1913; LL.D., McGill U., 1913; D.C.L., Oxford U., 1913; LL.D., Union U., 1914; LL.D., U. of the State of NY, 1915; LL.D., U. of Toronto, 1918; LL.D., Colgate U., 1919; Dr. Honoris Causa, U. of Paris, 1921; LL.D., U. of CA, 1923; D.C.L., NY U., 1929. WRITINGS: *The Citizen's Part in Government* (1907); *Experiment in Government and the Essentials of the Constitution* (1913); *Addresses on International Subjects* (1916); *Addresses on Government and Citizenship* (1916); *Military and Colonial Policy of the United States* (1916); *Latin America and the United States* (1917); *Russia and the United States* (1917); *Miscellaneous Addresses* (1917); *Men and Policies* (1924). REL.: Presb. RES.: New York, NY.

ROSECRANS, WILLIAM STARKE. b. Sep 6, 1819, Kingston, OH; d. Mar 11, 1898, Redondo, CA; par. Crandall and Jemima (Hopkins) Rosecrans; m. Ann Eliza Hegeman, Aug 24, 1843; c. eight. EDUC.: grad., U.S. Military Acad., 1842. POLIT. & GOV.: ***candidate for Republican nomination to vice presidency of the U.S., 1864 (declined)***;Union Party candidate for gov. of OH, 1865 (declined); appointed dir. of the U.S. Mint, San Francisco, CA, 1867 (declined); Democratic candidate for gov. of CA, 1867 (declined); Conservative Republican candidate for gov. of CA, 1867 (declined); appointed U.S. minister to Mexico, 1868–69; Workingmen's Party candidate for mayor of San Francisco, CA, (declined); Democratic candidate for gov. of OH, 1869 (declined); elected as a Democrat to U.S. House (CA), 1881–85; ***candidate for Democratic nomination to vice presidency of the U.S., 1884 (withdrew)***; elected regent, U. of CA, 1884–85; appointed register, U.S. Treasury, 1885–93. BUS. & PROF.: clerk, Utica, OH; architect, civil engineer, Cincinnati, OH; pres., Coal River Navigation Co., 1856; pres., Preston Oil Co., 1857–61; engaged in mining business, Mexico and CA; pres., Safety Powder Co., Los Angeles, CA, 1875; soldier. MIL.: brev. 2d lt., U.S. Army Corps of Engineers, 1842; asst. prof., U.S. Military Acad., 1843–47; superintendent of repairs, Fort Adams, MA, 1847–53; 1st lt., 1953, resigned, 1854; col., 1861, brig. gen., 1861, commanding gen., Dept. of OH, 1861; maj. gen., U.S.V., 1862, commanding gen., Army of the Cumberland, 1863, commanding gen., Dept. of MO, 1864; brev. maj. gen., 1865, resigned, 1867; commissioned brig. gen. (retired), 1889. REL.: R.C. (convert). RES.: Los Angeles, CA.

ROSELLINI, ALBERT DEAN. b. Jan 21, 1910, Tacoma, WA; par. John and Annunziata (Pagni) Rosellini; m. Ethel K. McNeil, Jun 1, 1938; c. John Michael; Janey (Mrs. Campbell); Lynn; Sue; Albert Dean. EDUC.: Coll. of Puget Sound; B.A., LL.B., U. of WA, 1933. POLIT. & GOV.: appointed asst. deputy prosecutor, King Cty., WA, 1935–41; elected as a Democrat to WA State Senate, 1939–57 (Democratic floor leader); appointed special asst. atty. gen. of WA, 1941–43; elected as a Democrat to gov. of WA, 1957–65; ***candidate for Democratic nomination to presidency of the U.S., 1960***; Democratic candidate for gov. of WA, 1964, 1972; delegate, Dem. Nat'l. Conv., 1968. BUS. & PROF.: atty.; admitted to WA Bar, 1933; partner (with Lloyd Shorett), law firm, Seattle, WA, 1933–57; partner (with M. E. Casey, Bruce Bartley, Raymond C. Brumbach and William Hennessey), law firm, Seattle, WA, 1957–; pres., Premium Olympia Beer Distributors. MEM.: U.S. Olympic Cmte. (pres.); National Governors' Conference (pres., 1962–63); Council of State Governments (pres., 1962–63); St. Martin's Coll. (regent); Elks; Eagles; Moose; Knights of Columbus; Kiwanis; Tau Kappa Epsilon; Phi Alpha Delta; Scandinavian Fraternity; Rainier Businessmen's Club of Seattle. REL.: R.C. MAILING ADDRESS: 6320 North East 57th St., Seattle, WA 98105.

ROSENBAUM, ARY DOV. b. May 3, 1972, Brooklyn, NY; par. Mordachai and Edith (Berta) Rosenbaum; single. EDUC.: student, Kingsway Acad.; student, Rabbi Harry Halpern Day School, 1986. POLIT. & GOV.: ***candidate for Democratic nomination to presidency of the U.S., 1988***. BUS. & PROF.: student. MEM.: Soc. of Friends of Tovro Synagogue. REL.: Jewish. MAILING ADDRESS: 1448 East 96th St., Brooklyn, NY 11236.

ROSENBLUM, ARTHUR "ART." b. Nov 14, 1927, New York, NY; par. Joseph and Sadie (Skoletsky) Rosenblum. EDUC.: Hiram Coll., 1946–47. POLIT. & GOV.: ***candidate for Universal Party nomination to presidency of the U.S., 1972***. BUS. & PROF.: mechanic; electronics technician; farmer; translator; inventor; customs agent, communal group, Paraguay; dir., Aquarian Research Foundation, Philadelphia, PA, 1969–; ed., *Aquarian Research Foundation Newsletter*; ed., *Green Revolution Magazine*. MEM.: Aquarian Research Foundation; International Platform Assn. WRITINGS: *Natural Birth Control* (1973); *The Natural Birth Control Book* (with Leah Jackson, 1974); *Unpopular Science* (1974). REL.: Jewish-Christian nondenominational. MAILING ADDRESS: 5620 Morton St., Philadelphia, PA 19144.

ROSENHAFT, ANN WILLIAMS. b. Dec 26, 1926, Chicago, IL; par. Robert Trafton and Trean V. (Benfer) Williams; m. Seymour Rosenhaft; c. Eve. EDUC.: grad., Hunter Coll. H.S.; B.S., NY U., 1955, grad. school; City U. of NY. POLIT. & GOV.: delegate, Socialist Party, U.S.A. National Convention, 1976, 1987; ***candidate for Socialist Party, U.S.A. nomination to presidency of the U.S., 1976 (declined); candidate for Socialist Party, U.S.A. nomination to vice presidency of the U.S., 1976 (declined), 1980 (declined)***; office mgr., McReynolds/Drufenbrock Campaign Cmte., 1980. BUS. & PROF.: social investigator, New York (NY) Dept. of Social Services, 1963–73, dir., 1973–78. MEM.: Parent-Teachers Assn.; S.A.N.E.; American Federation of State, County, and Municipal Employees (Local 371); A.C.L.U.; National Organization for Women; National Assn. for Reform of Abortion Laws; The Abortion Fund; The American Museum. REL.: atheist. MAILING ADDRESS: 356 East 8th St., New York, NY 10009.

ROSENTHAL, ABRAHAM MICHAEL "ABE." b. May 2, 1922, Sault Ste. Marie, Ontario, Canada; par. Harry and Sarah (Dickstein) Rosenthal; m. Ann Marie Burke, Mar 12, 1949; m. 2d, Shirley Lord, Jun 10, 1987; c. Jonathan Harry; Daniel Michael; Andrew Mark. EDUC.: B.S., City Coll. of New York, 1944. POLIT. & GOV.: ***independent candidate for presidency of the U.S., 1984***. BUS. & PROF.: staff, *New York (NY) Times*, 1944–; U.N. correspondent, 1946–54, assigned to India, 1954–58, Warsaw, Poland, 1958–59, Geneva, Switzerland, 1960–61, Tokyo, Japan, 1961–63, metropolitan ed., 1963–66, asst. managing ed., 1967–68, assoc. managing ed., 1968–69, managing ed., 1969–77; exec. ed., 1977–. MEM.: Foreign Correspondent Assn. of India (pres., 1957). AWARDS: citation, Overseas Press Club, 1956, 1959, 1960 (Number One Award), 1965; Pulitzer Prize for International Reporting, 1960; George Polk Memorial Award, 1960, 1965; Page One Award, Newspaper Guild, New York, NY, 1960; hon. award, Assn. of Indians in America, 1974; award, New York Cty. Bar Assn., 1978. HON. DEG.: LL.D., City Coll. of New York, 1974; LL.D., State U. of NY, 1984. WRITINGS: *38 Witnesses*; *One More Victim* (coauthor); *The Night the Lights Went Out* (co-editor); *The Pope's Journey to the United States* (co-editor). REL.: Jewish. MISC.: came to U.S., 1926, naturalized, 1951. MAILING ADDRESS: c/o *New York Times*, 229 West 43rd St., New York, NY 10036.

ROSER, HENRY HARVOLEAU. b. Oct 27, 1863, St. Louis, MO; par. Henry and Mary Theresa Roser; m. Ida Lillian Smith, Oct 8, 1899. EDUC.: grad., WI State Normal School, 1882; B. L., U. of WI, 1886. POLIT. & GOV.: joined Prohibition Party; joined Liberty Party, 1896; presidential elector, Liberty Party, 1896; sec., national exec. cmte., Liberty Party; ***National Liberty Party candidate for vice presidency of the U.S., 1900; American Commonwealth Party candidate for presidency of the U.S., 1936***. BUS. & PROF.: schoolteacher; ed.; Prohibition lecturer; character actor, Hollywood, CA; atty.; law practice, KS. MIL.: capt., Company F, National Guard of CO, 1899–1902, col. MEM.: Independent Order of Good Templars (Grand Chief Templar, 1899–1901); Direct Legislation League of CO (sec., 1899–1904); U.S. Monetary League (gen. sec., 1899–1904). WRITINGS: *The Dragon in Politics* (1889); *The Spirit of Reform and Other Poems* (1895); *Indian Legends of the Southwest* (1905). RES.: Wellington, KS.

ROSS, JAMES. b. Jul 12, 1762, Essex, NY; d. Nov 27, 1847, Allegheny City, PA; par. Joseph and Jane (Graham) Ross; m. Ann Woods, Jan 13, 1791; c. at least one son. EDUC.: Robert Smith's Acad.; Rev. John McMillan's Acad. POLIT. & GOV.: elected as a Federalist to PA Constitutional Convention, 1789–90; appointed Federal Commissioner to Treat with Insurgents During Whiskey Rebellion, 1794; elected as a Federalist to U.S. Senate (PA), 1794–1803 (pres. pro tempore, 1799); Federalist candidate for gov. of PA, 1799, 1802, 1808; ***received 5 electoral votes for vice presidency of the U.S., 1816***; elected as a Federalist, pres., select council, Pittsburgh, PA, 1816–33. BUS. & PROF.: teacher of Latin and Greek, McMillan's Acad., Washington, PA, 1780–82; atty.; admitted to PA Bar, 1784; atty. for President George Washington's (q.v.) western PA estates; law practice, Washington, PA, 1784–95. WRITINGS: *Free Navigation of the Mississippi* (1803). RES.: Pittsburgh, PA.

ROSS, JOHN. b. 1946, TX; single. EDUC.: Portland State U. POLIT. & GOV.: candidate for Democratic nomination to U.S. Senate (OR), 1980; ***candidate for Democratic nomination to presidency of the U.S., 1980***. BUS. & PROF.: branch mgr., Benjamin Franklin Savings and Loan Assn.; steamship agent, Portland, OR, 1973–. MAILING ADDRESS: 7129 Northeast Broadway, Portland, OR 97213.

ROSS, NANCY JANE. b. Apr 17, 1943, Boston, MA; d. Albert and Bess (Pransky) Ross; single; c. one. EDUC.: B.A., NY U., 1965. POLIT. & GOV.: elected member, Community School Board, New York, NY, 1977–80; candidate for NY (NY) City Council, 1981; candidate for gov. of NY, 1982; coordinator, New Alliance Party; ***New Alliance Party candidate for vice presidency of the U.S., 1984***. BUS. & PROF.: community activist; coordinator, New Alliance Party; exec. dir., Rainbow Lobby, Washington, DC. MEM.: Women Against Reaction; Parent-Teachers Assn.; Rainbow Lobby (exec. dir.); National Caucus of Labor Committees (1974; resigned). AWARDS: award for Progressive Leadership, National Federation of Independent Unions. WRITINGS: "Jews Without Conscience," *Practice*;

"Building Unity from the Bottom Up," *Practice*. REL.: Jewish. MAILING ADDRESS: c/o Rainbow Lobby, 236 Massachusetts Ave., N.E., Suite 409, Washington, DC 20002.

ROSS, NELLIE TAYLOE. b. Nov 29, 1876, St. Joseph, MO; d. Dec 20, 1977, Washington, DC; par. James Wynns and Elizabeth Blair (Green) Tayloe; m. Gov. William Bradford Ross, Sep 11, 1902; c. George Tayloe; James Ambrose; Alfred Duff; William Bradford, Jr. EDUC.: public and private schools. POLIT. & GOV.: elected as a Democrat to gov. of WY, 1925–27; Democratic candidate for gov. of WY, 1926; vice chm., Dem. Nat'l. Cmte., 1928–32; delegate, Dem. Nat'l. Conv., 1928; ***candidate for Democratic nomination to vice presidency of the U.S., 1928***; appointed dir., U.S. Mint, 1933–53. BUS. & PROF.: lecturer; magazine writer. MEM.: Women's Club. REL.: Episc. RES.: Cheyenne, WY.

ROSS, OLIN JONES. b. Apr, 1858, Fayette Cty., PA; d. Jan 16, 1941, Columbus, OH; single. EDUC.: public schools, Hillsboro, OH; studied law. POLIT. & GOV.: Prohibition Party candidate for atty. gen. of OH, 1897; ***candidate for Prohibition Party nomination to presidency of the U.S., c. 1924 (and before); candidate for Republican nomination to presidency of the U.S., 1928, 1932, 1936, 1940***. BUS. & PROF.: carpenter; atty.; admitted to OH Bar, 1882; law practice, Hillsboro, OH, 1900; law practice, Columbus, OH, 1903–41; Temperance Advocate. MEM.: Columbus Rationalist Soc. (founder, 1914; sec.-treas., 1914–41); 600 Club. WRITINGS: *The Sky Blue: A Tale of the Iron Horse and of the Coming Civilization* (1904); *Four Speeches*; *Superstitious Beliefs and the Toleration of Opinion*. REL.: atheist. MISC.: known as the "Demosthenes of the American Bar." RES.: Columbus, OH.

ROSS, ROBERT G. b. Feb 20, 1867, Ripley, OH; d. 1951; m. Della Salisburg (divorced); c. Nettie. EDUC.: 8th grade; studied medicine. POLIT. & GOV.: elected road overseer, Gillan Precinct, Dawson Cty., NE, 1893–95; Prohibition Party candidate for U.S. House (NE), 1910; ***candidate for Republican nomination to presidency of the U.S., 1916, 1920, 1928; candidate for Democratic nomination to presidency of the U.S., 1920***; candidate for Republican nomination to gov. of NE, 1926, 1928. BUS. & PROF.: laborer, alfalfa mill, Lexington, NE; engineer; steamboat cook; grocery and drug clerk; cowboy; farmer, Lexington, NE. MEM.: Epworth League. REL.: Presb./Methodist. RES.: Lexington, NE.

ROSS, WALTER. POLIT. & GOV.: ***independent candidate for presidency of the U.S., 1868***. RES.: KS.

ROTHBARD, GERALD MARTIN. b. May 19, 1931, Brooklyn, NY; par. Louis and Anna (Dinces) Rothbard; single. EDUC.: Tilden H.S., Brooklyn, NY, 3 years. POLIT. & GOV.: candidate for Miami (FL) City Commissioner, 1957, 1967; candidate for mayor of Miami, FL; candidate for Democratic nomination to FL State House; candidate for Dade Cty. (FL) Commissioner, 1972; candidate for Democratic nomination to gov. of FL; ***candidate for Democratic nomination to presidency of the U.S., 1980***. BUS. & PROF.: storekeeper, news stand, 8 years; employee, juice stand, 2 years; employee, RCA Records Distributors; employee, Sea Coast Appliances, 2 years; employee, Alfred A. Knopf Publishing Co., 1½ years. MEM.: Jewish Community Center of Miami (Young Adult League pres., 1955); Zionist Organization of America (life member, 1972); Brotherhood of Show Troupers of Miami (founder, 1956–57); W.J.V.J. (Watch Citizen of the Week). WRITINGS: poetry in *New Voices in American Poetry* (1977); "Great Democracy" (song). REL.: Jewish. MAILING ADDRESS: 6448 Wiley St., Hollywood, FL 33023.

ROTHBARD, MURRAY NEWTON. b. Mar 2, 1926, New York, NY; par. David and Ray (Babushkin) Rothbard; m. JoAnn Beatrice Schumacher, Jan 16, 1953. EDUC.: A.B., Columbia U., 1945, M.A., 1946, Ph.D., 1956. POLIT. & GOV.: ***candidate for Libertarian Party nomination to presidency of the U.S., 1976 (declined)***. BUS. & PROF.: instructor, Coll. of the City of New York, 1948–49; research grantee, Inst. of Public Service, New York, NY, 1952; Washington (DC) columnist, Faith and Freedom, 1954–56; research grantee, William Volker Fund, 1953–56; research grantee, Earhart Foundation, 1956–57; consulting economist, Princeton Panel, 1957–61; research grantee, Foundation for Foreign Affairs, Chicago, IL, 1963–66; assoc. prof. of Economics, Polytechnical Inst. of Brooklyn, 1966–70, prof. of Economics, 1970–; assoc., University Seminar on History of Legal and Political Thought, Columbia U., 1964–; ed., *Libertarian Forum*, 1969–; prof., U. of NV, Las Vegas, NV; author. MEM.: Birch Walthen Alumni Assn. (pres.); National Taxpayers Union; Mont Pelerin Soc.; American Economic Assn.; Assn. of Evolutionary Economics; American Hist. Assn.; Organization of American Historians; Medieval Club; Inst. for Humane Studies (member, Council of Advisers); Mises Inst. (vice pres. for Academic Affairs). WRITINGS: *Man, Economy and State* (1962); *Panic of 1819* (1962); *America's Great Depression* (1963, 1972); *Left and Right* (ed., 1965–68); *Power and Market* (1970); *Egalitarianism as a Revolt Against Nature and Other Essays* (1973); *For a New Liberty* (1973); *The Ethics of Liberty; Conceived in Liberty; Toward a Reconstruction of Utility and Welfare Economics* (1977); *Individualism and the Philosophy of Social Sciences* (1979); *Freedom, Inequality and Primitivism*. MAILING ADDRESS: 333 Jay St., Brooklyn, NY 11201.

ROUNDS, WILLARD ALBERT. b. Mar 23, 1880, Lockport, NY; d. Jan 5, 1952, Great Falls, MT; m. Henrietta R.; c. Master Sgt. Willard H.; Harold (stepson); Wayne (stepson). POLIT. & GOV.: ***Farmer-Labor Party candidate for presidency of the U.S., 1936***. BUS. & PROF.: hod carrier, Spokane, WA; hod carrier, Green Bluff, WA; hod carrier, Denver, CO; hod carrier, Great Falls, MT, 1909, 1922–52. MEM.: Hod Carrier's Union; Emergency Relief Assn. (mgr., 1931). MISC.: convicted of bootlegging, 3 times. RES.: Great Falls, MT.

ROUSE, DONALD EDWARD "BIGFOOT." POLIT. & GOV.: ***candidate for Republican nomination to presidency of the U.S., 1988***. BUS. & PROF.: missionary. MAILING ADDRESS: P.O. Box 7041, Tahoe City, CA 95730.

ROUSE, GUY H. b. Jones Cty., NC. POLIT. & GOV.: candidate for sheriff, Jones Cty., NC; ***independent Republican candidate for presidency of the U.S., 1968***. BUS. & PROF.: construction worker. RES.: Ochopee, FL.

ROUSSEAU, LOVELL HARRISON. b. Aug 4, 1818, Stanford, KY; d. Jan 7, 1869, New Orleans, LA. EDUC.: public schools; studied law. POLIT. & GOV.: elected as a Whig to IN State House, 1844–45; elected as a Whig to IN State Senate, 1847–49; elected as a Republican to KY State Senate, 1860–61; ***candidate for Republican nomination to vice presidency of the U.S., 1864***; Radical candidate for U.S. Senate (KY), 1865; elected as a Republican to U.S. House (KY), 1865–67; resigned seat in Congress after he attacked Rep. Josiah Crinnell in Capitol building, 1866; reelected to fill vacancy created by his resignation. BUS. & PROF.: atty.; admitted to Bloomfield, IN Bar, 1841; law practice, Bloomfield, IN; law practice, Louisville, KY, 1849. MIL.: Commissioned capt., Second IN Infantry, 1846; organized Fifth Regt., KY Militia, 1861; col., Third KY Infantry, 1861; brig. gen., U.S.V., 1861, maj. gen., 1862; brig. gen. with brevet rank of maj. gen., U.S. Army, 1867; dispatched to AK to receive territory from Russia, 1867; appointed commander, Dept. of LA, 1868–69. MISC.: credited with preventing secession of KY during Civil War. RES.: Louisville, KY.

ROY, CONRAD W. b. 1932. POLIT. & GOV.: ***candidate for Democratic nomination to presidency of the U.S., 1988***. BUS. & PROF.: clerk, grocery store. MAILING ADDRESS: Nashua, NH.

RUBIN, BLANCHE. POLIT. & GOV.: ***candidate for Democratic nomination to presidency of the U.S., 1992***. MAILING ADDRESS: 3710 East Bellevue, #410, Tucson, AZ 85716.

RUBIN, JERRY CLYDE. b. Jul 14, 1938, Cincinnati, OH; d. Nov 28, 1994, Los Angeles, CA; par. Robert and Esther (Katz) Rubin; single. EDUC.: grad., Walnut Hills H.S., Cincinnati, OH, 1956; Oberlin Coll.; B.A., U. of Cincinnati, 1961; Hebrew U., 1962; U. of CA, Berkeley, CA. POLIT. & GOV.: candidate for mayor of Berkeley, CA, 1966; founder, Youth International Party, 1967; ***candidate for Peace and Freedom Party nomination to vice presidency of the U.S., 1968; candidate for Democratic nomination to vice presidency of the U.S., 1972***; Peace and Freedom Party candidate for U.S. House (CA), 1974. BUS. & PROF.: reporter, city desk writer, youth ed., *Cincinnati (OH) Post* and *Times-Star*, 1956–61; lecturer; writer, 1968–; group leader, Esalen Workshops, 1973–74; therapist, Eischer-Hoffman Psychic Therapy Process, 1974; guest on television and radio shows; author; securities analyst, John Muir and Co., New York, NY. MEM.: Youth International Party (founder); Vietnam Day Cmte.; New Mobilization Cmte. (Project dir., 1967); Congress on Racial Equality; Free Speech Movement; Filthy Speech Movement. WRITINGS: *Do It!* (1969); *We Are Everywhere* (1970); *Vote* (1972); *Growing Up at 37* (1976). REL.: Jewish. MISC.: antiwar organizer, 1965–67; defendant in Chicago Seven Trial, 1969. RES.: Los Angeles, CA.

RUCKELSHAUS, WILLIAM DOYLE. b. Jul 24, 1932, Indianapolis, IN; par. John K. and Marion (Doyle) Ruckelshaus; m. Jill Elizabeth Strickland, May 12, 1962; c. Catherine Kiley; Mary Hughes; Jennifer Lea; William justice; Robin Elizabeth. EDUC.: B.A. (cum laude), Princeton U., 1957; LL.B., Harvard U., 1960. POLIT. & GOV.: appointed deputy atty. gen. of IN, 1960–65 (chief counsel, 1963–65); candidate for Republican nomination to U.S. House (IN), 1964; minority atty., IN State Senate, 1965–67; elected as a Republican to IN State House, 1967–69 (majority leader, 1967–69); Republican candidate for U.S. Senate (IN), 1968; appointed asst. atty. gen. of the U.S., 1969–70; appointed administrator, Environmental Protection Agency, 1970–73, 1983–84; appointed acting dir., FBI, 1973; appointed deputy atty. gen. of the U.S., 1973–74 (resigned); ***candidate for Republican nomination to vice presidency of the U.S., 1976***. BUS. & PROF.: atty.; admitted to IN Bar, 1960; partner, Ruckelshaus, Bobbitt and O'Connor (law firm), Indianapolis, IN, 1960–68; partner, Ruckelshaus, Beveridge, Fairbanks and Diamond (law firm), Washington, DC, 1973–76; senior vice pres., Weyerhauser Co., 1976–; chm. of the board, Geothermal Kinetics, Inc.; dir., Nordstrom, Inc.; dir., American Paper Inst.; dir., Pacific Gas Transmission Co.; dir., Cummins Engine Co.; dir., Peabody-Galion Corp.; dir., Twentieth Century Fund; dir., Church and Dwight Co., Inc. MIL.: sgt., U.S. Army, 1953–55. MEM.: ABA; Federal Bar Assn.; IN Bar Assn.; Indianapolis Bar Assn.; APSA; Indianapolis Council on Foreign Relations; Audubon Soc.; Urban Inst.; Inst. for Congress; Columbia Club; Federal City Club; Congressional Club; Conservation Fund (dir.); Woodrow Wilson School, Princeton U. (advisory board); Navajo Bicentennial Comm. (chm., advisory council); Council for Public Interest Law (co-chm.); IN Privacy Comm. (chm.); Cottage Club; Pacific Science Center Foundation (trustee); Seattle Art Museum (dir.); John F. Kennedy School of Government, Harvard U. (overseer); Seattle U. (regent). AWARDS: "Outstanding Republican Legislator, IN House," Working Press, 1967; "Outstanding First Year Legislator in IN House," IN Broadcasters Assn., 1967; "Man of the Year,"

Indianapolis Junior C. of C., 1967. WRITINGS: *Reapportionment: A Continuing Problem* (1963). REL.: R.C. MAILING ADDRESS: 1015 Evergreen Point Rd., Medina, WA 98039.

RUCKER, HORTON B. POLIT. & GOV.: ***independent candidate for vice presidency of the U.S., 1980***. MAILING ADDRESS: GA.

RUDNICKI, CHESTER M. POLIT. & GOV.: ***candidate for Democratic nomination to presidency of the U.S., 1972, 1976, 1984***. MAILING ADDRESS: 5 Shelby St., East Boston, MA 02128.

RUFFING, JOHN L., JR. par. John L. Ruffing, Sr. POLIT. & GOV.: ***independent candidate for presidency of the U.S., 1972***. MAILING ADDRESS: Cleveland Heights, OH.

RUGGIERRIO, STANLEY RANDOLPH. POLIT. & GOV.: ***candidate for Republican nomination to presidency of the U.S., 1980***. BUS. & PROF.: doctor. MAILING ADDRESS: 89 North Ohio Ave., Columbus, OH 43203.

RUMS, JOHN B. POLIT. & GOV.: ***American Tradition Party candidate for vice presidency of the U.S., 1984***. MAILING ADDRESS: c/o A. Lancham, gen. mgr., Blue Eagle Services, Box 246, Seattle, WA 98111.

RUMSFELD, DONALD HENRY. b. Jul 9, 1932, Chicago, IL; par. George Donald and Jeannette (Husted) Rumsfeld; m. Joyce Pierson, Dec 27, 1954; c. Valeria Jeanne; Marcy Kay; Donald Nicholas. EDUC.: A.B., Princeton U., 1954. POLIT. & GOV.: administrative asst. to U.S. Rep. Dennis Denison, 1958; administrative asst. to U.S. Rep. Robert Griffin, 1959; elected as a Republican to U.S. House (IL), 1963–69; appointed dir., Office of Economic Opportunity, 1969–70; appointed asst. to the pres., 1969–70, 1974–75; appointed dir., Cost of Living Council, 1971–73; appointed U.S. ambassador to North Atlantic Treaty Organization, 1973–74; appointed U.S. sec. of defense, 1975–77; ***candidate for Republican nomination to vice presidency of the U.S., 1976, 1980; candidate for Republican nomination to presidency of the U.S., 1988 (withdrew)***. BUS. & PROF.: registered representative, A. G. Becker and Co. (investment brokers), Chicago, IL, 1960–62; dir., Sears, Roebuck and Co.; dir., Bendix Corp.; dir., Eastern Air Lines, Inc.; dir., Peoples Gas Co.; dir., Rand Corp.; chief exec. officer, G. D. Searle and Co., 1977–. MIL.: lt. (jg), U.S. Navy, 1954– 57; U.S. Navy Wrestling Champion, 1956. MEM.: American Health Foundation (dir.); International Inst. for Strategic Affairs (London, England). AWARDS: Distinguished Eagle Scout Award, 1976; Medal of Freedom, 1977. HON. DEG.: LL.D., IL Coll.; LL.D., Lake Forest Coll.; LL.D., Park Coll. REL.: Protestant. MAILING ADDRESS: 1373 Ashland Lane, Wilmette, IL 60091.

RUSH, RICHARD. b. Aug 29, 1780, Philadelphia, PA; d. Jul 30, 1859, Philadelphia, PA; par. Dr. Benjamin and Julia (Stockton) Rush; m. Catherine Eliza Murray, Aug 29, 1809; c. ten. EDUC.: grad., Coll. of NJ, 1797; studied law under William Lewis. POLIT. & GOV.: appointed atty. gen. of PA, 1811; appointed comptroller of U.S. Treasury, 1811; appointed atty. gen. of the U.S., 1814–17; appointed U.S. sec. of state, 1817; appointed U.S. minister to Great Britain, 1817–24; ***received 1 electoral vote for vice presidency of the U.S., 1820***; appointed U.S. sec. of the treasury, 1825–28; ***National Republican Party candidate for vice presidency of the U.S., 1828; Anti-Masonic Party candidate for presidency of the U.S., 1832 (declined)***; appointed commissioner on OH-MI boundary dispute, 1835; appointed U.S. Agent to Secure Smithson Bequest, 1836–38; appointed U.S. minister to France, 1847–49. BUS. & PROF.: atty.; admitted to PA Bar, 1800. MEM.: Smithsonian Institution (regent); American Phil. Soc. WRITINGS: *The Laws of the United States* (ed., 1815); *John Randolph at Home and Abroad* (1828); *Memoranda of a Residence at the Court of London* (1833); *Washington in Domestic Life*; *Occasional Productions, Political, Diplomatic and Miscellaneous* (1860). RES.: Philadelphia, PA.

RUSHTON, PETER E. POLIT. & GOV.: ***Maniac Party candidate for presidency of the U.S., 1988***. MAILING ADDRESS: P.O. Box 477, Oakland, ME 04963.

RUSK, JEREMIAH McLAIN. b. Jun 17, 1830, Malta, OH; d. Nov 21, 1893, Viroqua, WI; par. Daniel and Jane (Faulkner) Rusk; m. Mary Martin, Apr 5, 1849; m. 2d, Elizabeth M. Johnson, Dec 1856; c. Mary E.; Lycurgus J.; Charity; Ida; Blaine Daniel; Alonzo. EDUC.: public schools, Deerfield, OH. POLIT. & GOV.: elected sheriff, Viroqua, WI, 1855–57; elected coroner, Viroqua, WI, 1857; elected as a Republican to WI State House, 1861–62; elected as a Republican, WI State Bank Controller, 1865, 1867–69; elected as a Republican to U.S. House (WI), 1871–77; appointed U.S. minister to Uruguay and Paraguay, 1881 (declined); appointed U.S. minister to Denmark, 1881 (declined); appointed chief, U.S. Bureau of Engraving and Printing, 1881 (declined); elected as a Republican to gov. of WI, 1882–89; ***candidate for Republican nomination to presidency of the U.S., 1888; candidate for American Party nomination to presidency of the U.S., 1888 (declined)***; appointed U.S. sec. of agriculture, 1889–93. BUS. & PROF.: farmer; construction foreman; tavern keeper, Viroqua, WI, 1853; owner, stageline; owner, hotel, Viroqua, WI. MIL.: maj., 25th WI Infantry, 1862; lt. col., U.S.V., 1863, brev. col. and brig. gen., 1865. REL.: Methodist. RES.: Viroqua, WI.

RUSK, THOMAS JEFFERSON. b. Dec 5, 1803, Pendleton District, SC; d. Jul 29, 1857, Nacogdoches, TX; par.

John and Mary (Sterritt) Rusk; m. Mary F. Cleveland, 1827; c. seven. EDUC.: studied law under John C. Calhoun (q.v.). POLIT. & GOV.: delegate, TX Constitutional Convention, 1836; signer, TX Declaration of Independence; Framer, Constitution of the Republic of TX; elected sec. of war, Provisional Government, Republic of TX, 1836; appointed sec. of war, Republic of TX, 1837; member, House of Republic of TX, 1838; elected chief justice, Supreme Court of Republic of TX, 1838–42; pres., TX State Constitutional Convention, 1845; elected as a Democrat to U.S. Senate (TX), 1846–57 (pres. pro tempore, 1857); ***candidate for Democratic nomination to vice presidency of the U.S., 1852, 1856; candidate for Democratic nomination to presidency of the U.S., 1856 (declined)***. BUS. & PROF.: atty.; admitted to GA Bar; law practice, Clarksville, GA, 1825; partner (with John Cleveland), mercantile business, 1828. MIL.: elected capt., TX Rangers, 1835; col.; commander, Army of the Republic of TX, 1836; maj. gen., Militia of the Republic of TX, 1838, brig. gen., maj. gen., 1843; favored annexation of TX to the U.S.; cleared East TX of hostile Indian tribes. MISC.: committed suicide. RES.: Nacogdoches, TX.

RUSS, NORMAN A. POLIT. & GOV.: ***candidate for Republican nomination to presidency of the U.S., 1992***. MAILING ADDRESS: P.O. Box 508, Route 12, Norwich, CT 06360.

RUSSEL, JAMES. EDUC.: M.D. POLIT. & GOV.: ***independent candidate for vice presidency of the U.S., 1984***. BUS. & PROF.: physician. MAILING ADDRESS: c/o Dr. Isabell Masters, P.O. Box 2155, Topeka, KS 66601.

RUSSELL, CHARLES EDWARD. b. Sep 25, 1860, Davenport, IA; d. Apr 23, 1941, Washington, DC; par. Edward and Lydia (Rutledge) Russell; m. Abby Osborn Rust, 1884; m. 2d, Theresa Hirschl, Jul 5, 1909; c. John Edward. EDUC.: grad., St. Johnsbury (VT) Acad., 1881. POLIT. & GOV.: Socialist Party candidate for gov. of NY, 1910, 1912; ***candidate for Socialist Party nomination to presidency of the U.S., 1912***; Socialist Party candidate for mayor of New York, NY, 1913; Socialist Party candidate for U.S. Senate (NY), 1914; ***Socialist Party candidate for presidency of the U.S., 1916 (declined)***; expelled from Socialist Party, 1917; appointed member, Special U.S. Diplomatic Mission to Russia, 1917; appointed commissioner to Great Britain, U.S. Cmte. on Public Information, 1918; appointed member, President's Industrial Comm., 1919. BUS. & PROF.: journalist; author; city ed., *New York (NY) World*, 1894–97; managing ed., *New York (NY) American*, 1897–99; publisher, *Chicago (IL) American*, 1900–1902; magazine contributor; lecturer on Sociology and Literature, 1904–41; ed., *Non-Partisan League Leader*, 1915. MEM.: U.S. Civil Legion (pres., 1932–33); League for Industrial Democracy (dir., 1931); Berger National Foundation (dir.); Public Ownership League of America (vice pres.); American Assn. for Recognition of the Irish Republic (hon. pres.); Authors Club; Arts Club; IA Free Trade League (founder, 1881); Non-Partisan League; NAACP (founder, 1909). HON. DEG.: LL.D., Howard U., 1923. AWARDS: Pulitzer Prize for Biography, 1928. WRITINGS: *Such Stuff as Dreams* (1902); *The Twin Immortalities* (1904); *The Greatest Trust in the World* (1905); *That Blessed Word "Regulation"* (1906); *The Uprising of the Many* (1907); *Lawless Wealth* (1908); *Thomas Chatterton, the Marvelous Boy* (1908); *Songs of Democracy* (1909); *Why I Am a Socialist* (1910); *Business, the Heart of the Nation* (1911); *Stories of the Great Railroads* (1912); *These Shifting Scenes* (1914); *The Story of Wendell Phillips* (1915); *Unchained Russia* (1918); *After the Whirlwind* (1919); *Bolshevism and the United States* (1919); *The Outlook for the Philippines* (1922); *Railroad Melons, Rates and Wages* (1922); *The Hero of the Filipinos: Jose Rizal* (1923); *Julia Marlowe: Her Life and Art* (1926); *The American Orchestra and Theodore Thomas* (1927); *A'Rafting on the Mississippi* (1928); *An Hour of American Poetry* (1929); *From Sandy Hook to 62°* (1929); *Haym Salomon and the Revolution* (1930); *Blaine of Maine* (1931); *Bare Hands and Stone Walls* (1933). RES.: New York, NY.

RUSSELL, JOHN. b. Sep 20, 1822, Geneseo, NY; d. Nov 3, 1912, Detroit, MI; par. Jesse and Catherine (Barber) Russell; m. Catherine Pulver, Sep 19, 1841; m. 2d, Mary Jane Herriman, Jan 21, 1852; c. Charles P.; John, Jr.; Edward T.; William A.; George F.; Mary (Mrs. E. Ross Parrish); Jennie T. (Mrs. Charles M. Stafford); Edith (Mrs. Frank A. Luttenbacker). EDUC.: district school, Adrian, MI, to 1842. POLIT. & GOV.: delegate, National Temperance Convention, 1866; member, Prohibition Party National Cmte., 1867–76, 1880–92 (chm., 1867–72); temporary chm., chm., Prohibition Party National Convention, 1869, 1872; Prohibition Party candidate for U.S. House (MI), 1870, 1882, and several other times; ***candidate for Prohibition Party nomination to presidency of the U.S., 1872 (declined); Prohibition Party candidate for vice presidency of the U.S., 1872; candidate for Prohibition Party nomination to vice presidency of the U.S., 1884***; Prohibition Party candidate for Regent, U. of MI, 1889; State chm., MI Prohibition Party, 1890–92; Prohibition Party candidate for gov. of MI, 1892. BUS. & PROF.: farmer; cooper; licensed as Methodist Episcopal Exhorter, 1841, local preacher, 1842, ordained minister, 1845; pastor, Methodist Episcopal churches, Port Huron, MI, 1843–47; pastor, Methodist Episcopal churches, Pontiac, Marquette, Lake Superior District, Ypsilanti and Mount Clemens, MI, 1847; pastor, Methodist Episcopal churches, Utica and New Haven, MI; pastor, Methodist Episcopal Church, Romeo, MI, 1845, 1861–65; pastor, First Methodist Episcopal Church, Flint, MI, 1857–59; pastor, Old Congress Street Methodist Church, Detroit, MI; publisher, *Peninsular Herald*, Romeo (later Detroit), MI, 1863–64; publisher, *Romeo (MI) Observer*, 1866; co-editor, *Michigan Advocate*; ed., *The Better Age*, 1873. MEM.: Waians; Sons of Temperance; Independent Order of Good Templars (Grand Worthy Chief Templar of MI; pres., World Lodge, 1871–72; Right Worthy Good Templar). WRITINGS: *Is a Prohibition Party a Feasible and Reliable Agency for Securing Enactment and Execution of Prohibitory Laws?*; *An Adequate Remedy for a National Evil; The Liquor*

Traffic Versus Political Economy. REL.: Methodist Episc. Church (presiding elder, 8 years; chm., Temperance Cmte. General Conference, 1860, 1880; delegate, General Conference, 1860, 1880, 1891). MISC.: known as the "Father of the Prohibition Party." RES.: Romeo, MI.

RUSSELL, RICHARD BREVARD. b. Nov 2, 1897, Winder, GA; d. Jan 21, 1971, Washington, DC; par. Richard Brevard and Ina (Dillard) Russell; single. EDUC.: grad., Seventh District A&M School, 1914; grad., Gordon Inst., 1915; B.L., U. of GA, 1918. POLIT. & GOV.: elected cty. atty., Barrow Cty., GA; elected as a Democrat to GA State House, 1921–31 (Speaker, 1927–31); candidate for Democratic nomination to U.S. Senate (GA), 1926; elected as a Democrat to gov. of GA, 1931–33; delegate, Dem. Nat'l. Conv., 1932, 1952; elected as a Democrat to U.S. Senate (GA), 1933–71 (pres. pro tempore, 1969–71); ***candidate for Democratic nomination to presidency of the U.S., 1948, 1952, 1964***; member, Presidential Comm. to Investigate the Assassination of President John F. Kennedy. BUS. & PROF.: atty.; law practice, Winder, GA. MEM.: ABA; GA State Bar Assn.; American Legion; Forty and Eight; Sphinx; Sigma Alpha Epsilon; Odd Fellows; Masons; Elks; Burns Club. AWARDS: Distinguished Service Award, U.S. Junior C. of C., 1931; "Minute Man of the Year in National Defense," Reserve Officers' Assn., 1959. HON. DEG.: LL.D., Mercer U., 1957; LL.D., The Citadel. REL.: Methodist. RES.: Winder, GA.

RUSSELL, THELMA ANN. POLIT. & GOV.: ***Polly Party candidate for presidency of the U.S., 1980***. MAILING ADDRESS: 312 South Broad St., Lititz, PA 17543.

RUSSELL, WILLIAM EUSTIS. b. Jan 6, 1857, Cambridge, MA; d. Jul 16, 1896, St. Adelaide, Quebec, Canada; par. Charles Theodore and Sarah Elizabeth (Ballister) Russell; m. Margaret Manning Swan, Jun 3, 1885; c. William Eustis, Jr.; Richard Manning; Margaret. EDUC.: A.B., Harvard U., 1877; LL.B. (summa cum laude), Boston U. Law School, 1879. POLIT. & GOV.: elected as a Democrat to Cambridge (MA) Common Council, 1882; elected as a Democrat, alderman, Cambridge, MA, 1883–84; elected as a Democrat, mayor of Cambridge, MA, 1884–88; Democratic candidate for U.S. House (MA), 1886 (declined); Democratic candidate for gov. of MA, 1888, 1889; elected as a Democrat to gov. of MA, 1891–93; ***candidate for Democratic nomination to presidency of the U.S., 1892, 1896***; delegate, Dem. Nat'l. Conv., 1896. BUS. & PROF.: atty.; admitted to Suffolk, MA Bar, 1880; assoc., C. T. and T. H. Russell (law firm), Boston, MA, 1880. MEM.: Boston U. Law School Alumni Assn. (pres., 1884). HON. DEG.: LL.D., Williams Coll., 1891. RES.: Cambridge, MA.

RUTHERFORD, KRISTOPHER PAUL. POLIT. & GOV.: ***candidate for Democratic nomination to presidency of the U.S., 1988***. MAILING ADDRESS: 15 Lawn Ave., Gorham, ME 04038.

RUTLEDGE, CHRISTOPHER JOHN. b. May 11, 1967, Far Rockaway, Queens, NY; par. Leo Ray and Janet (LaRue) Rutledge; single. EDUC.: grad., high school, 1985; Georgetown U., 1985–89. POLIT. & GOV.: ***candidate for Democratic nomination to presidency of the U.S., 1988***. BUS. & PROF.: office mgr., Georgetown U.; writer, WGTB radio. MEM.: Alpha Phi Omega (pres., Pledge Class, 1987); CARE-DC. REL.: none. MAILING ADDRESS: Box 2275, Hoya Station, Washington, DC 20057.

RUTLEDGE, JOHN. b. Sep 1739, Charlestown, SC; d. Jul 23, 1800, Charleston, SC; par. Dr. John and Sarah (Hext) Rutledge; m. Elizabeth Grimke, May 1, 1763; c. John, Jr.; Martha; Sarah; Edward; Frederick; Charles; William; Thomas; Elizabeth; States. EDUC.: Middle Temple, London, England; studied law, Charleston, SC. POLIT. & GOV.: elected member, SC House of Commons, 1761–76; atty. gen. pro tempore of SC, 1764–65; member, Stamp Act Congress, 1765; elected member, Continental Congress (SC), 1774–76, 1782–83; elected member, SC Council of Safety, 1776; drafter, SC Constitution, 1776; elected pres., SC General Assembly, 1776–78; elected as a Federalist to gov. of SC, 1779–82; elected as a Federalist to SC State House, 1781–82, 1784–90; appointed U.S. minister to Holland, 1783 (declined); elected judge, SC Chancery Court, 1784; delegate, U.S. Constitutional Convention, 1787 (chm., Cmte. on Detail); elected member, SC Ratification Convention, 1788; ***received 6 electoral votes for vice presidency of the U.S., 1789***; appointed assoc. justice, Supreme Court of the U.S., 1789–91; elected chief justice, SC Supreme Court, 1791–95; appointed chief justice, Supreme Court of the U.S., 1795 (served Aug term; not confirmed by Senate). BUS. & PROF.: atty.; called to English Bar, 1760; law practice, Charleston, SC, 1761. REL.: Anglican. RES.: Charleston, SC.

RUWART, MARY JEAN. b. Oct 16, 1949, Detroit, MI; par. William and Jean (Choinere) Ruwart; m. (divorced); c. none. EDUC.: B.S. (magna cum laude), MI State U., 1970, Ph.D., 1974. POLIT. & GOV.: candidate for Kalamazoo (MI) City Comm., 1982; candidate for MI State House, 1982; ***candidate for Libertarian Party nomination to presidency of the U.S., 1984; candidate for Libertarian Party nomination to vice presidency of the U.S., 1984, 1992***; candidate for Kalamazoo (MI) Cty. Comm., 1985; appointed member, Public Safety Task Force, 1985. BUS. & PROF.: biophysicist; NIH trainee in Biophysics, MI State U., 1970–73; research assoc. in Surgery, Medical School, St. Louis U., 1974–75, instructor to asst. prof., 1975–76; research scientist, Gastroenteral, Upjohn Co., Kalamazoo, MI, 1976–; contributor, various professional journals. MEM.: American Gastroenteral Assn.; American Federation for Clinical Research; Soc. for Experimental Biology and Medicine;

AAAS; American Women in Science; Phi Beta Kappa; Soc. for Cryobiology; Biophysics Soc. AWARDS: Detroit Metropolitan Science Fair College Scholarship, 1967; National Assn. of Teachers Scholarship, 1967–68; MI Higher Education Tuition Scholarship, 1969–70; NSF Summer Student Program Award, 1969; NIH Trainee Award, 1970–74. WRITINGS: *Healing Our World: The Other Piece of the Puzzle* (1992). REL.: Unitarian. MISC.: holder of patents for methods of treating gastrointestinal inflammation; liver protection using PGE's; methods of inhibition bacterial toxin released by PG's. MAILING ADDRESS: 1901 Hawk Dr., Kalamazoo, MI 49008.

RYALS, OPHELIA CANDYCE (aka OPHELIA CANDYCE RYALS THIGPEN WOMAN). b. May 7, 1929, Walthall Cty., MS; par. Wendy Hardy Alton Magee and Alma Japonica (Thigpen) Ryals; m. Jacob Freimuth; c. Pamela (adopted); Tina (adopted); Timothy (adopted). EDUC.: public school. POLIT. & GOV.: ***independent candidate for presidency of the U.S., 1992***. BUS. & PROF.: waitress, coffee shop; licensed day-care provider, CA; singer. MEM.: Gideon Soc. Rel: Theist. MISC.: claims to be Prophetess of God. MAILING ADDRESS: 5361 Linda Lane, Santa Rosa, CA 95404.

RYAN, JOSEPH A. b. Nov 20, 1931, Canaan Township, PA; par. daughter of James W. Nolan; m. Helen R. EDUC.: Foymoy Elementary School, Honesdale, PA; Niagara U.; LL.B., U. of St. John, 1954. POLIT. & GOV.: elected municipal judge, New York, NY; elected district atty., Onondaga Cty., NY, 1961–63; candidate for Democratic nomination to atty. gen. of NY, 1962; ***candidate for Democratic nomination to presidency of the U.S., 1976***. BUS. & PROF.: newsboy; clerk; railroad worker; coal miner; prize fighter; head waiter; salesman; foundry worker; airway traffic controller; songwriter; author; soldier; small businessman; atty.; admitted to NY Bar, 1954; admitted to HI Bar; admitted to practice before the Bar of the Supreme Court of the U.S.; law practice, New York, NY, 1954–64; partner, Ryan and Ryan (law firm), Honolulu, HI, 1964–. WRITINGS: *Coin of Justice*. REL.: Abraham Lincoln American Christian of the Tribe Americana. MAILING ADDRESS: Ryan and Ryan, 1136 Union Mall, Honolulu, HI.

RYAN, WILLIAM FITTS. b. Jun 28, 1922, Albion, NY; d. Sep 17, 1972, New York, NY; par. Bernard and Harriet (Earle) Ryan; m. Priscilla Marbury, 1949; c. William Fitts, Jr.; Priscilla; Virginia; Catherine. EDUC.: B.A., Princeton U., 1944; LL.B., Columbia U., 1949. POLIT. & GOV.: asst. district atty., New York Cty., NY, 1950–61; chm., Morningside-Columbia Cmte. for Adlai E. Stevenson, 1956; Democratic leader, Seventh Assembly District, NY, 1957–61; elected as a Democrat to U.S. House (NY), 1961–72; candidate for Democratic nomination to mayor of New York, NY, 1965; delegate, Dem. Nat'l. Conv., 1968; ***candidate for Democratic nomination to vice presidency of the U.S., 1968***. BUS. & PROF.: atty.; admitted to NY Bar, 1949; assoc., Hatch, Wolfe, Nash and Ten Eyck (law firm), New York, NY, 1949–50. MIL.: 1st lt., 32d Infantry Div., U.S. Army, 1943–46. MEM.: NY Young Democratic Club (pres., 1955–56); Riverside Democrats, Inc. (founder, 1957). REL.: R.C. RES.: New York, NY.

RYDEN, CONRAD A. POLIT. & GOV.: ***candidate for Republican nomination to presidency of the U.S., 1992***. MAILING ADDRESS: Goldsboro, NC.

RYDER, RED. POLIT. & GOV.: ***candidate for Democratic nomination to presidency of the U.S., 1992***. MAILING ADDRESS: CA?

RYNDER, THEODORE P. c. Theodore Lee R. POLIT. & GOV.: Greenback Party candidate for auditor gen. of PA, 1884; delegate, Industrial Reform Party National Convention, 1888; member, national exec. cmte., Union Labor Party, 1888; Republican candidate for U.S. House (PA), 1888; ***candidate for Union Labor Party nomination to vice presidency of the U.S., 1888***; Labor Party candidate for gov. of PA, 1890; People's Party candidate for PA State sec. of internal affairs, 1898; ***candidate for People's Party nomination to vice presidency of the U.S., 1900, 1904***; member, People's Party National Cmte., 1905–06. BUS. & PROF.: printer; insurance agent. RES.: Erie, PA.

RYNG, EDWARD WILLIAM. POLIT. & GOV.: ***candidate for Republican nomination to presidency of the U.S., 1992***. MAILING ADDRESS: c/o American Justice Cmte., 1329 Oliver Ave., San Diego, CA 92109.

SABITINI, VINCENT J. b. 1920; m. Willa; c. Robert; Michael. POLIT. & GOV.: ***candidate for Democratic nomination to presidency of the U.S., 1976, 1984***. BUS. & PROF.: employee, Big Three Construction Co., Houston, TX. MAILING ADDRESS: 8202 Bendell Dr., Houston, TX 77017.

SACK, ROGER A. POLIT. & GOV.: ***candidate for Democratic nomination to presidency of the U.S., 1992***. MAILING ADDRESS: 7908 Cabrini Dr., S.E., Port Orchard, WA 98366.

SAGAN, CYRIL EMIL. b. Sep 8, 1927, Springdale, PA; par. Cyril Thomas and Bertha (Kosa) Sagan; m. 1960 (divorced, 1976); c. Rosalind; Monica; Cyril; Agnes; Clement. EDUC.: grad., Springdale (PA) H.S., 1945; B.S., U. of Pittsburgh, 1950; M.S., Wayne State U., 1969; Ph.D., Cornell U., 1974. POLIT. & GOV.: independent candidate for U.S. House (PA), 1978; independent candidate for U.S. Senate (PA), 1980, 1982; candidate for Democratic nomination to U.S. Senate (PA), 1982, 1986; ***candidate for Democratic nomination to presidency of the U.S., 1984, 1988, 1992***. BUS. & PROF.: teacher, Elizabeth Forward H.S., 1960–61; teacher, Beaver Falls H.S., 1961–64; prof. of chemistry, Slippery Rock State Coll., Slippery Rock, PA, 1964– (dept. chm., 1977–79). MIL.: U.S. Army Medical Corps, 1946–47. MAILING ADDRESS: R.D. 2, Volant, PA 16156.

ST. JAMES, MARGARET JEAN "MARGO." b. Sep 12, 1937, Bellingham, WA; d. George Lawrence and Dorothy Evelyn (Wellman) St. James; m. Don F. Sobjack (divorced, 1959); c. one son. EDUC.: grad., Mount Baker H.S., Deming, WA, 1955; City Coll. of San Francisco; Lincoln U., 1963–64; Art Inst., San Francisco, CA, 1964; studied dance under Ruth Beckford, San Francisco, CA. POLIT. & GOV.: ***COYOTE candidate for Republican nomination to presidency of the U.S., 1980***. BUS. & PROF.: self-employed, 1962–; process server; carpenter's asst.; dance instructor; owner, Margo's Miracle Maids (domestic service); private investigator (CA License A 6510); lecturer, 1967–; author; minister, Universal Life Church; expert witness in prostitution cases, 1974–; ed., *COYOTE HOWLS*; contributor, *City Magazine*, 1976; contributor, *The Realist*; civil rights advocate; reformer. MOTION PICTURE CREDITS: "Hookers" (film, 1974); "Hard Work" (film, 1976). MEM.: COYOTE (Cast Off Your Old Tired Ethics; founder, 1973); League of Women Voters; San Diego State Students of Criminal Justice Assn. (life member); National Organization for Women; Dolphin-Southend Runners; Women's Olympics (third overall, 1974); UNESCO Abolitionists Federation; U.N. International Women's Year Conference, 1975; Victoria Woodhull Foundation (dir.; founder); Judicial Advocates for Women (dir.); National Task Force on Prostitution. AWARDS: one of 10 Low-Power Humanitarian Awards, Marin Cty., CA, 1972; American Film Festival Award, 1978, Golden Eagle CINE Award, 1978. WRITINGS: *Spit in the Ocean*; *Majority Report*; *Politics of Prostitution*. REL.: none. MISC.: ascended Pike's Peak, 1975, 1976; participated in Honolulu Marathon, 1978; noted for annual masqueradeballs, 1974–. MAILING ADDRESS: P.O. Box 26354, San Francisco, CA 94126.

ST. JOHN, JOHN PIERCE. b. Feb 25, 1833, Brookville, IN; d. Aug 31, 1916, Olathe, KS; par. Samuel and Sophia (Snell) St. John; m. Mary Jane Brewer, 1852; m. 2d, Susan J. Parker, Mar 28, 1860; c. Henry; Lutie; John Pierce, Jr. EDUC.: public schools, IN; studied law in offices of Starkweather and McLain, Charlton, IL, 1860. POLIT. & GOV.: elected as a Republican to KS State Senate, 1873–74; Republican candidate for gov. of KS, 1876 (declined), 1882; elected as a Republican to gov. of KS, 1879–83; ***Prohibition Party candidate for presidency of the U.S., 1884; candidate for American Prohibition Party nomination to presidency of the U.S., 1884 (declined)***; chm., Prohibition Party National Convention, 1888 (permanent), 1892 (temporary); member, Prohibition Party National Cmte., 1892–96 (vice chm.); vice chm., National Party

National Cmte., 1896. BUS. & PROF.: store clerk; wood chopper; miner; steamboat employee, 1856; atty.; admitted to IL Bar, 1861; law practice, Independence, MO, 1861; law practice, Olathe, KS, 1869–1916; lecturer, National Prohibition Lecture Bureau, 1884–97. MIL.: capt., Company C, 68th IL Infantry; lt. col., 143d IL Infantry, Civil War; fought in Modoc War, 1852–53; twice wounded in battle. REL.: Christian Scientist (nee Universalist; Congregationalist). RES.: Olathe, KS.

SALAMAN, MAUREEN KENNEDY. b. Apr 4, 1936, Glendale, CA; par. Jim and Matilda (Peters) McFarlin; m. Jay Franklin Salaman; c. Sean David; Coleen Ruth. EDUC.: San Mateo Coll.; U. of NV. POLIT. & GOV.: ***candidate for Populist Party nomination to presidency of the U.S., 1984; Populist Party candidate for vice presidency of the U.S., 1984; candidate for Populist Party nomination to vice presidency of the U.S., 1984 (declined)***. BUS. & PROF.: first ed., *Choice Magazine*; asst. ed., *Public Scrutiny*; assoc. ed., *Health Freedom News*; contributing ed., *Let Live*; author; West Coast reporter, WMCA radio, New York, NY; talk-show host, "Totally Yours," KEST radio. AWARDS: Patrick Henry Liberty Award. MEM.: National Health Federation (pres.); Project Freedom (vice pres.). WRITINGS: *Nutrition: The Cancer Answer* (1983). REL.: Christian. MAILING ADDRESS: 1177 CA, #1608, San Francisco, CA 94108.

SALAY, TIM. POLIT. & GOV.: ***candidate for American Independent Party nomination to presidency of the U.S., 1972***. MAILING ADDRESS: Euclid, OH.

SALTONSTALL, LEVERETT. b. Sep 1, 1892, Chestnut Hill, MA; d. Jun 17, 1979, Dover, MA; par. Richard Middlecott and Eleanor (Brooks) Saltonstall; m. Alice Wesselhoeft, Jun 27, 1916; c. Leverett, Jr.; Rosalie; Emily B. (Mrs. Byrd); Peter Brooks; William Lawrence; Susan. EDUC.: grad., Nobel and Greenough School, 1910; A.B., Harvard U., 1914, LL.B., 1917. POLIT. & GOV.: elected as a Republican, Board of Aldermen, Newton, MA, 1920–22; appointed asst. district atty., Middlesex Cty., MA, 1921–22; elected as a Republican to MA State House, 1923–36 (Speaker, 1929–36); elected as a Republican to gov. of MA, 1939–44; elected as a Republican to U.S. Senate (MA), 1945–67; ***candidate for Republican nomination to presidency of the U.S., 1948***; delegate, Rep. Nat'l. Conv., 1956, 1968, 1972. BUS. & PROF.: atty.; admitted to MA Bar, 1919; partner, Gaston, Snow, Saltonstall and Hunt (law firm), Boston, MA, 1919–28; dir., Ivest Fund, Inc.; dir., Shawmut Bank of Boston; dir., Boston Safe Deposit and Trust Co.; mgr., Farm and Trade School. MIL.: 1st lt., 301st F.A., U.S. Army, 1917–18. MEM.: Harvard U. (board of overseers, 1928–41, 1943–49; pres., 1943–49); Masons; Elks; Harvard Club; Boston Club; Somerset Club; Norfolk Hunting Club; Grange; American Legion; VFW; Ancient and Honorable Artillery Co.; Tavern Club; Alfalfa Club; Greater Boston Community Fund (dir., 1938); New England Governors' Conference (chm., 1939–44); National Governors' Conference (chm., 1944); Phi Beta Kappa; Hasty Pudding Club; Porcellian Club; Delta Kappa Epsilon; Sigma Kappa. HON. DEG.: LL.D., Northeastern U., 1936; LL.D., Bates Coll., 1939; LL.D., Boston U., 1940; LL.D., Bowdoin Coll., 1940; LL.D., Amherst Coll., 1941; LL.D., Williams Coll., 1941; LL.D., Colby Coll., 1942; LL.D., Harvard U., 1942; LL.D., Holy Cross Coll., 1942; LL.D., Tufts Coll., 1942; LL.D., De Pauw U., 1943; LL.D., Clark U., 1944; LL.D., Franklin and Marshall U., 1947; LL.D., Trinity Coll., 1947; LL.D., William and Mary Coll., 1948; LL.D., Northwestern U., 1949; LL.D., Worcester Polytechnic Inst., 1950; LL.D., Kenyon Coll., 1953; LL.D., Toledo U., 1954; M.S., New Bedford Inst. of Textile and Technology, 1955; LL.D., Norwich U., 1955; J.D., Portia Law School, 1957; D.P.A., Suffolk U., 1957; LL.D., Brandeis U., 1958; Dr.Bus.Admin., Babson Inst., 1961; M.S., U. of MA, 1963; LL.D., Merrimack Coll., 1967; Sc.D., Lowell Inst. of Technology, 1968; D.S. (Oratory), Curry Coll., 1969. REL.: Unitarian. RES.: Chestnut Hill, MA.

SALZGEBER, ROBERT GARFIELD. POLIT. & GOV.: ***independent candidate for presidency of the U.S., 1984***. MAILING ADDRESS: P.O. Box 58, Langenthal, ZZ.

SAMPSON, AMOS A. POLIT. & GOV.: ***candidate for National Liberty Party nomination to presidency of the U.S., 1848***. RES.: unknown.

SANBORN, PHILIP V. POLIT. & GOV.: ***independent candidate for presidency of the U.S., 1980***. MAILING ADDRESS: 239 West Division St., Wautoma, WI 54982.

SANCHEZ, ARTHUR P. m. Pauline S. POLIT. & GOV.: ***independent candidate for presidency of the U.S., 1980***. MAILING ADDRESS: 14843 Bluebriar St., Sunnymead, CA 92388.

SANDERS, CARL EDWARD. b. May 15, 1925, Augusta, GA; par. Carl Thomas and Roberta J. (Alley) Sanders; m. Betty Bird Foy, Sep 6, 1947; c. Betty Foy; Carl Edward, Jr. EDUC.: LL.B., U. of GA, 1947. POLIT. & GOV.: elected as a Democrat to GA State House, 1954–56; elected as a Democrat to GA State Senate, 1956–62 (floor leader, 1959; pres. pro tempore, 1960–62); elected as a Democrat to gov. of GA, 1963–67; appointed member, President's Advisory Comm. on Federal-State Relations, 1963–65; delegate, Dem. Nat'l. Conv., 1964 (chm., Rules Cmte.); ***candidate for Democratic nomination to vice presidency of the U.S., 1964 (declined)***; appointed member, National Comm. on Urban Affairs, 1967; appointed member, advisory council, Office of Economic Opportunity, 1967; candidate for Democratic nomination to gov. of GA, 1970; chm., Finance Council, Dem. Nat'l. Cmte., 1979–. BUS. & PROF.: atty.; admitted to GA Bar, 1947; partner, Hammond, Kennedy and

Sanders (law firm), Augusta, GA, 1948–52; senior partner, Sanders, Thurmond, Hester and Jolles (law firm), Augusta, GA, 1952–62; senior partner, Sanders, Hester, Holley, Ashmore and Boozer (law firm), Atlanta, GA; partner, Troutman, Sanders, Lockerman, and Ashmore (law firm), Atlanta, GA; dir., Natco Corp.; dir., First Georgia Bankshares; dir., Fuqua Industries; dir., First Railroad and Banking Co.; dir., Cousins Mortgage and Equity Investors; dir., Public Broadcasting Corp., 1968–70; dir., First GA Bank. MEM.: Centennial of GA Railroad (advisory cmte.); U. of GA Alumni Soc. (pres., 1969–70); Lawyers Club; Chi Phi; GA Conservancy; Southern Governors' Conference (vice chm., 1965–66; counsel, 1966–); National Citizens Cmte. for Public Television; Exchange Club; ABA; Augusta Bar Assn.; American Legion; Phi Delta Phi; Moose; Masons; Elks; YMCA (dir.; vice pres.); American Red Cross (dir., Augusta Chapter); BSA (member, exec. cmte., Georgia-Carolina Council); John F. Kennedy Memorial Library Foundation (trustee); Conference of Appalachian Governors (chm., 1964–65); National Governors' Conference (exec. cmte., 1964–65). AWARDS: "Young Man of the Year," Augusta (GA) Junior C. of C., 1955; one of five "Outstanding Young Men," GA Junior C. of C., 1959; Golden Key Award, NEA, 1965; named to Athletic Hall of Fame, 1968. REL.: Bapt. (Deacon). MAILING ADDRESS: 1500 Candler Building, Atlanta, GA 30303.

SANDERS, EVERETT. b. Mar 8, 1882, Coalmont, IN; d. May 12, 1950, Washington, DC; par. James and Melissa Everal (Stark) Sanders; m. Ella Neal, Dec 13, 1903; m. 2d, Hilda Ann Sims, Jul 11, 1936; c. none. EDUC.: IN State Normal School, 1900–1902; LL.B., IN U., 1907. POLIT. & GOV.: elected as a Republican to U.S. House (IN), 1917–25; ***candidate for Republican nomination to vice presidency of the U.S., 1924***; dir., Speakers' Bureau, Rep. Nat'l. Cmte., 1924; appointed sec. to President Calvin Coolidge (q.v.), 1925–29; sergeant-at-arms, Rep. Nat'l. Conv., 1932; chm., Rep. Nat'l. Cmte., 1932–34. BUS. & PROF.: schoolteacher, 3 years; atty.; admitted to IN Bar, 1907; partner, McNutt, Wallace, Sanders and Randel (law firm), Terre Haute, IN, 1907–17; partner, Sanders, Gravelle, Whitlock and Howrey (law firm), Washington, DC, 1929–50. MEM.: Gamma Eta Gamma (hon.); Order of the Coif; ABA; DC Bar Assn.; Elks; Knights of Pythias; Alfalfa Club; Congressional Country Club. WRITINGS: *Coolidge Character*. REL.: missionary Bapt. RES.: Washington, DC.

SANDERSON, DANIEL ERNEST. b. San Francisco, CA; par. Charles E. and Flora Effae (Balenger) Sanderson; m. (divorced); c. one daughter. EDUC.: Winfield Scott School; Lincoln Law U., San Francisco, CA; Foothill Coll. of Psychology. POLIT. & GOV.: ***candidate for Democratic nomination to presidency of the U.S., 1980, 1984***. BUS. & PROF.: musician; construction worker; carpenter; blacksmith; dying and cleaning business, San Francisco, CA; car salesman; public relations man, International Teamsters' Union; real estate salesman; inventor; psychiatrist's asst.; owner, operator, Sanderson Construction and Development Corp. MIL.: carpenter's mate (first class), U.S.N.R., 1944. AWARDS: 100 Hours Certificate of Appreciation, Foothill Coll. MEM.: Musicians' Local Union #6; Carpenters' Union, Local 35. REL.: Full Gospel Protestant. MAILING ADDRESS: 465 South Elm, Apt. No. 81, Arroyo Grande, CA 93420.

SANDERSON, SANDER O. b. 1868, Rock Dell, MN. EDUC.: grad., Darling's Business Coll., Rochester, MN. POLIT. & GOV.: town treas., Rock Dell, MN; elected town auditor, Rock Dell, MN; ***Farmer-Labor Party candidate for vice presidency of the U.S., 1936***. BUS. & PROF.: farmer; blacksmith; clerk, Nels Magneson Store, Rock Dell, MN, 1885; bookkeeper, salesman, Boston Clothing House, Rochester, MN; partner (later sole proprietor), Nels Magneson Store, Rock Dell, MN; treas., Zumbro Creamery Co.; treas., Rock Dell Butter and Cheese Co.; treas., Northwestern School Supply Co., Minneapolis, MN. RES.: Rochester, MN.

SANFORD, JAMES TERRY. b. Aug 20, 1917, Laurinburg, NC; par. Cecil LeRoy and Elizabeth Terry (Martin) Sanford; m. Margaret Rose Knight, Jul 4, 1942; c. Elizabeth Knight; James Terry. EDUC.: Presbyterian Junior Coll., 1935; A.B., U. of NC, 1939, LL.B., 1946. POLIT. & GOV.: appointed sec.-treas., NC Ports Authority, 1950–53; elected as a Democrat to NC State Senate, 1953–54; delegate, Dem. Nat'l. Conv., 1956, 1960, 1964, 1968, 1972; elected as a Democrat to gov. of NC, 1961–65; National chm., Citizens for Humphrey-Muskie, 1968; ***candidate for Democratic nomination to vice presidency of the U.S., 1968, 1972; candidate for Democratic nomination to presidency of the U.S., 1972, 1976***; chm., Democratic Charter Comm., 1972–74; delegate, Democratic Mid-Term Conference, 1974; elected as a Democrat to U.S. Senate (NC), 1987–93; Democratic candidate for U.S. Senate (NC), 1992. BUS. & PROF.: asst. dir., Inst. of Government, U. of NC, 1940–41, 1946–48; special agent, FBI, 1941–42; atty.; admitted to NC Bar, 1946; partner, Sanford, Phillips, McCoy and Weaver (law firm), Fayetteville, NC, 1948–65; partner, Sanford, Cannon, Adams and McCullough (law firm), 1965–; dir., Security Life and Trust Co.; dir., Equire, Inc.; dir., North Carolina Natural Gas Corp.; dir., First National Life Insurance Co.; dir., Study of American States, Duke U., 1965–67; pres., Urban America, Inc., 1968–69; pres., Duke U., 1969–86. MIL.: 1st lt., 501st Parachute Infantry Regt., U.S. Army, 1942–45; commander, Fayetteville Unit, NC National Guard, 1948–55; Bronze Star; Purple Heart. MEM.: NC Young Democratic Clubs (pres., 1949–50); Children's Home Soc. of NC, Inc. (dir.); Arts Council of America (dir.); Methodist Coll. (trustee); Citizens' Conference on State Legislatures (trustee); Shaw U. (trustee); U. of NC (trustee); Southern Regional Education Board (chm., 1961–63); ABA; American Acad. of Political and Social Sciences; American Jud. Soc.; Cordell Hull Foundation; Children's TV Workshop (dir., 1967–71); American Legion; VFW; Masons (Shriner); Fayetteville Junior C. of C.; Rotary Club; Howard U. (trustee); American

Arbitration Assn. (dir.); National Municipal League (vice pres.); Good Neighbor Council (founder); American Red Cross (chm., Fayetteville Chapter); United Services Fund (pres.); Fayetteville Area Industrial Development Corp. (charter member). HON. DEG.: LL.D., U. of NC, 1965. WRITINGS: *But What About the People* (1966); *Storm Over the States* (1967). REL.: Methodist (district lay reader). MAILING ADDRESS: 307 Sylvan Rd., Fayetteville, NC 28305.

SANFORD, NATHAN. b. Nov 5, 1777, Bridgehampton, NY; d. Oct 17, 1838, Flushing, NY; par. Thomas and Phebe (Baker) Sanford; m. Eliza Van Horne, May 9, 1801; m. 2d, Mary Isaacs, Apr 14, 1813; m. 3d, Mary Buchanan; c. at least 3. EDUC.: Clinton Acad.; Yale U.; studied law under Samuel Jones, New York, NY. POLIT. & GOV.: appointed U.S. Commissioner of Bankruptcy, 1802; appointed U.S. district atty. for NY, 1803–16; elected as a Democrat to NY State Assembly, 1808–09, 1811 (Speaker); elected as a Democrat to NY State Senate, 1813–15; Democratic candidate for NY State Senate, 1814; elected as a Democrat to U.S. Senate (NY), 1815–21, 1826–31; elected delegate, NY State Constitutional Convention, 1821; ***received 30 electoral votes for vice presidency of the U.S., 1824***; chancellor, state of NY, 1823–26; ***Democratic candidate for vice presidency of the U.S., 1824***. BUS. & PROF.: atty.; admitted to NY Bar, 1799; law practice, New York, NY, 1799; law practice, Flushing, NY, 1831–38. MEM.: Tammany Soc. RES.: Flushing, NY.

SANGER, PAUL EMANUEL. b. Jul 15, 1910, Nez Pierce, ID; par. Rev. Perry Henderson and Lydia (Lehman) Sanger; m. Ruth Knier Daugherty, 1934; c. Rachel; Paul Emanuel, Jr.; Ray; Grace Arnold; Lydia; Mary Gettle; John D.; one other son. EDUC.: grad., high school; Bible Study Course, Elizabethtown Coll.; Peppert Auction School. POLIT. & GOV.: elected as a Republican, Township Auditor, Jackson Township, Lebanon Cty., PA, 1940's; elected as a Republican to Lebanon Cty. (PA) Board of Commissioners, 1952–55 (chm.); candidate for Republican nomination to U.S. Senate (PA), 1956; candidate for Republican nomination to U.S. House (PA), 1950s; candidate for Republican nomination to PA State Senate, 1966; ***candidate for American Party nomination to presidency of the U.S., 1976***. BUS. & PROF.: farmer; owner, Land and Cattle Auction Co., Myerstown, PA; health and agricultural research specialist; dairyman; gen. mgr., P. E. Sanger Dairy Farm; founder, first commercial airport, Lebanon Cty., PA; owner, Sangerdale Farms, Myerstown, PA; owner, Hickory Hill Farm, Fredericksburg, PA; auctioneer; pres., Orgomineral Research, Cottonwood, AL. AWARDS: Natural Foods and Farm Award, National Health Federation. MEM.: C. of C.; Lebanon Valley Farm Bureau (charter member); State Farmers Assn.; Polled Ayrshire Clubs (national sec.); Holstein Registry Assn. (vice pres.); Full Gospel Businessmen's Assn. (vice pres.); Kiwanis; Future Farmers of America; Optimists; New Testament Missionary Fellowship. WRITINGS: *Sanger's Orgomineral Method of Farming and Gardening*; *Daniel's 10 Day Feast* (1970); *How to Farm Without Poison Chemicals*; *How I Live Past 75 Years of Age, No Aches and Pains* (1986). REL.: Church of the Brethren (treas.; lay minister; choir member; Sunday school teacher). MAILING ADDRESS: 935 East Maple St., Lebanon, PA 17042.

SANO, CHARLES. POLIT. & GOV.: ***candidate for Democratic nomination to presidency of the U.S., 1992***. MAILING ADDRESS: CA?

SANTIAGO, GEORGE. b. 1929, San Sebastian, Puerto Rico. EDUC.: Cornell U.; Fordham U.; B.A. (Labor Management), Thomas A. Edison State Coll. of NJ; M.A., Queens Coll., City Coll. of NY; Ph.D., U. of the City of NY. POLIT. & GOV.: appointed member, Mayor's Cmte. Against the Exploitation of Workers, New York, NY, 1961; appointed member, Community District Planning Boards of Brooklyn, NY, 1963; appointed U.S. rep., North Atlantic Regional Manpower Advisory Cmte.; appointed member, Special Advisory Cmte. on Public Opinion, U.S. Dept. of State; ***candidate for Democratic nomination to presidency of the U.S., 1988***. BUS. & PROF.: assembler and wirer, lamp and fixture shop, New York, NY, 1946; international rep., IBEW, AFL-CIO, 1966–. MIL.: U.S. Army; Medal of Occupation of Germany. MEM.: Local 3, IBEW (steward; international rep., 1966–); NY Puerto Rican Parade (organizer; member, exec. board; chm., banquet, 1963); Brooklyn Tuberculosis and Health Assn., Inc. (dir., 1965–67); NY Police Athletic League; Puerto Rican Community Development Project (dir., 1964); National Assn. for Puerto Rican Civil Rights (charter member); Eleanor Roosevelt Job Orientation in Neighborhoods Center (advisory board); Santiago Iglesias Educational Soc. (founder); Sons of San Sebastian (pres.). AWARDS: citation, City of NY, 1965; certificate of appreciation, Eleanor Roosevelt JOIN Center. WRITINGS: *Power and Affiliation Within a Local Trade Union: Local 3 of the International Brotherhood of Electrical Workers* (diss.); *The History of Local 3 of the I.B.E.W.*; *Commitment to Social Equality of Ethnic and Racial Minorities*; *A Brief Examination of the History and Effectiveness of Pilgrim State Mental Hospital*; *The Federal and the NY State Food Stamp Program*; *The Communication of Class and States on Television*; *How Coordinated Bargaining Has Developed: Advantages and Disadvantages*. MAILING ADDRESS: 69-10 164th St., Flushing, NY 11365.

SARGEANT, LARRY BRANT. POLIT. & GOV.: American Freedom Party candidate for U.S. House (NV), 1976; ***American Freedom Party candidate for presidency of the U.S., 1976, 1988***. MAILING ADDRESS: Route 2, Box 89, Yerington, NV 89447.

SARTAIN, AARON WAYNE. POLIT. & GOV.: ***candidate for Republican nomination to presidency of the U.S., 1992***. MAILING ADDRESS: Oasey Apartments, Blue Ridge Circle, Grandview, MO 64030.

SATTERLY, WILLIAM WILSON. b. Apr 11, 1837, La Porte, IN; d. May 27, 1893, Minneapolis, MN; m. Sarah Stout, 1856; c. five. EDUC.: studied medicine. POLIT. & GOV.: member, Prohibition Party National Cmte., 1876–80, 1882–88; Prohibition Party candidate for gov. of MN, 1879, 1882; state chm., MN Prohibition Party, to 1887 (sec., 1893); ***candidate for Prohibition Party nomination to vice presidency of the U.S., 1888, 1892***. BUS. & PROF.: physician; ordained minister, Methodist Church, 1860; pastor, Methodist churches in WI and MN; agent, MN Temperance Union, 1873–80; prof. of Political Economy and Scientific Temperance, Grant Memorial U., 1887–93; ed., *Liberty Blade*; publisher, *Minnesota Radical*. MEM.: Independent Order of Good Templars; Sons of Temperance; Red Ribbon Movement; MN Reform Club. HON. DEG.: LL.D., Grant Memorial U. WRITINGS: *The Political Prohibitionist Textbook* (1883); *What I Saw*. REL.: Methodist Episc. Church (delegate, general conference, 1888). RES.: Minneapolis, MN.

SAUCKE, ORLAN ARDELL. b. Rockwell City, IA. POLIT. & GOV.: ***independent candidate for presidency of the U.S., 1976, 1980***. MAILING ADDRESS: P.O. Box 21163, Chickamauga Station, Chattanooga, TN 37421.

SAULSBURY, ELI. b. Dec 29, 1817, Mispillion Hundred, DE; d. Mar 22, 1893, Dover, DE; par. William and Margaret (Smith) Saulsbury; single. EDUC.: Dickinson Coll., Carlisle, PA; studied law under Willard Saulsbury, Georgetown, DE. POLIT. & GOV.: elected as a Democrat to DE State House, 1853–54; delegate, Dem. Nat'l. Conv., 1864; elected as a Democrat to U.S. Senate (DE), 1871–89; ***Labor Reform Party candidate for vice presidency of the U.S., 1872 (declined)***; Democratic candidate for U.S. Senate (DE), 1888. BUS. & PROF.: atty.; admitted to DE Bar, 1857; law practice, Dover, DE. REL.: Methodist Episc. Church. MISC.: advocate of temperance and white supremacy. RES.: Dover, DE.

SAULSBURY, WILLARD. b. Apr 17, 1861, Georgetown, DE; d. Feb 20, 1927, Wilmington, DE; par. Willard and Annie Milby (Ponder) Saulsbury; m. May du Pont, Dec 5, 1893; c. none. EDUC.: U. of VA, 1877–79; studied law under Willard Saulsbury. POLIT. & GOV.: appointed chm., Board of Censors, New Castle, DE; member, Sussex Cty. (DE) Democratic Central Cmte., 1892–1900; member, DE State Democratic Central Cmte., 1892–1919 (chm., 1900–1906); delegate, Dem. Nat'l. Conv., 1896, 1904, 1912, 1916, 1920; Democratic candidate for U.S. Senate (DE), 1899, 1901, 1903, 1905, 1907, 1911, 1918; member, Dem. Nat'l. Cmte., 1908–20; elected as a Democrat to U.S. Senate (DE), 1913–19 (pres. pro tempore, 1916–19); appointed member, advisory cmte., Limitation of Armaments Conference, 1921–22; appointed U.S. delegate, Pan-American Conference, 1923; ***candidate for Democratic nomination to presidency of the U.S., 1924***. BUS. & PROF.: atty.; admitted to DE Bar, 1882; partner (with Victor du Pont), law firm, Wilmington, DE, 1882–88; partner (with James W. Ponder and Charles M. Curtis), law firm, Wilmington, DE, 1888; senior partner, Saulsbury, Morris and Rodney (law firm), Wilmington, DE; dir., Equitable Trust Co.; dir., Union National Bank. MEM.: New Castle (DE) Bar Assn. (pres.); ABA; Wilmington (DE) Bar Assn.; DE Hist. Soc.; SAR; Soc. of Colonial Wars; Delta Psi; St. Anthony Club; Manhattan Club; National Democratic Club; Southern Soc.; Metropolitan Club; Chevy Chase Club; Wilmington Club (pres., 1910–13); Wilmington Country Club (vice pres., 1909; pres., 1910–13); U. of VA Alumni Club (DE pres.); Hope Farm Anti-Tuberculosis Soc. (vice pres.). REL.: Episc. RES.: Wilmington, DE.

SAUNDERS, ROBERT LEE "BOBBY." b. Nov 2, 1951, Calhoun Falls, SC; single. EDUC.: electronic and electrical schools, U.S. Navy. POLIT. & GOV.: Independence Party candidate for MD State Senate, 1983; ***Independence Party candidate for presidency of the U.S., 1984, 1988, 1992***; Independence Party candidate for gov. of MD, 1986. BUS. & PROF.: E.E., Seal and Co., Washington, DC; electrical contractor, Washington (DC) Metro System; instructor, Wider Opportunities for Women; electrician, WG-10, G.S.A.; composer; mortgage banker broker. MIL.: electrician, U.S. Navy; National Defense Medal and Ribbon. MEM.: BSA; Brotherhood of Electrical Workers, Local 26. REL.: deist. MAILING ADDRESS: 3108 Church St., N.W., Lanham, MD 20706.

SAWYER, CHARLES. b. Feb 10, 1887, Cincinnati, OH; d. Apr 7, 1979, Palm Beach, FL; par. Edward Milton and Caroline (Butler) Sawyer; m. Margaret Sterret Johnston, Jul 15, 1918; m. 2d, Countess Elizabeth Lippelman de Veyrac, Jun 10, 1942; c. Anne (Mrs. John Pattison Williams; Mrs. John Bradley); Jean Johnston (Mrs. John J. Weaver); John; Charles, Jr.; Edward. EDUC.: B.A., Oberlin Coll., 1908; LL.B., U. of Cincinnati, 1911. POLIT. & GOV.: elected as a Democrat to Cincinnati (OH) City Council, 1911–15; Democratic candidate for U.S. House (OH), 1930; elected as a Democrat to lt. gov. of OH, 1933–34; member, Dem. Nat'l. Cmte., 1934–44; Democratic candidate for gov. of OH, 1938; ***candidate for Democratic nomination to presidency of the U.S., 1940***; appointed U.S. ambassador to Belgium and U.S. minister to Luxembourg, 1944–45; appointed U.S. sec. of commerce, 1948–53. BUS. & PROF.: atty.; admitted to OH Bar, 1911; law practice, Cincinnati, OH, 1911; partner, Taft, Stettinius and Hollister (law firm), Cincinnati, OH; partner, Dinsmore, Sawyer and Dinsmore (law firm), Cincinnati, OH, 1921; owner, *Lancaster (OH) Eagle-Gazette*, 17 others; owner, radio station WING, OH; owner, radio station WIZE, OH. MEM.: ABA; Federal Bar Assn.; OH State Bar Assn.; Queen City Club; Oberlin Coll. (trustee); Masons; Chevy Chase Club; Community Chest (Cincinnati chm., 1954); United Fund (chm., 1955–60); Citizens Development Comm. of Cincinnati (chm.); Comm. on Money and Credit (1959–60); Commercial Club; Commonwealth Club; National Press Club; Everglades Club. HON. DEG.: LL.D., U. of Cincinnati, 1950. REL.: Episc. RES.: Cincinnati, OH.

SCANLAN, CHARLES. b. Oct 5, 1869, Three Churches, WV; d. Mar 21, 1927, Pittsburgh, PA; par. Michael and Mary Eliza (Garrett) Scanlan; m. Mary A. E. Walker, Apr 2, 1894; c. Michael W.; Mary B.; Pauline R.; Helen Ruth; Alice Walker; Ella Hill. EDUC.: B.S., Valparaiso U., 1895, A.M., 1899; U. of MN, 1901. POLIT. & GOV.: national lecturer, Prohibition Party, 1902; Prohibition Party candidate for gov. of MN, 1902; Permanent chm., Prohibition Party National Convention, 1908; ***candidate for Prohibition Party nomination to presidency of the U.S., 1908***; presidential elector, Prohibition Party, 1912; appointed U.S. rep., International Congress Against Alcoholism (12th, 13th, 14th, 15th, and 16th Congresses). BUS. & PROF.: teacher, public schools, WV; teacher, Normal School, VA, 1890–94; ordained minister, Presbyterian Church; pastor, Presbyterian Church, MN, 1895–99; pastor, House of Faith Presbyterian Church, Minneapolis, MN, 1899–1903; prof., Macalester Coll., 1899–1901; gen. sec., Temperance Board, Presbyterian Church of the U.S.A., 1904–27; ed., *Moral Welfare*; ed., *National Advocate*. MEM.: National Temperance Soc. (sec., 1919–22; pres., 1922); World Prohibition Federation (hon. treas.; pres., American Section); National Inter-Church Temperance Federation (sec.); National Prohibition Trust Fund (trustee); Federal Motion Picture Council of America, Inc. (founder, 1922; pres.); Scientific Temperance Federation. HON. DEG.: LL.D., Coll. of Wooster (OH), 1916. REL.: Presb. RES.: Pittsburgh, PA.

SCANLIN, JOHN JOSEPH "JACK." b. Dec 27, 1925, Llanarch, PA; par. James L. and Sarah C. (O'Connor) Scanlin; m. Helen M. Schrotz; c. Dennis; Susan; John Joseph, Jr.; Marie; Patricia; Timothy; Kathleen. EDUC.: B.S., U. of NM, 1951; M.A., Trenton State Teachers Coll., 1977. POLIT. & GOV.: ***New Directions Party candidate for presidency of the U.S., 1980***. BUS. & PROF.: owner, J. J. Scanlin Associates, Inc. (sales and consulting engineers), 1954–70; teacher, high school, 1971–. REL.: unaffiliated (nee R.C.). MAILING ADDRESS: 1528 Makefield Rd., Yardley, PA 19067.

SCHAEFER, VIRGINIA JUSTINE. POLIT. & GOV.: ***candidate for Democratic nomination to presidency of the U.S., 1992***. MAILING ADDRESS: 1511 East Flossmoor Ave., Mesa, AZ 85204.

SCHECHTER, BERNARD B. b. c. 1918. POLIT. & GOV.: ***candidate for Democratic nomination to presidency of the U.S., 1976***. BUS. & PROF.: soldier; retired. MIL.: col., U.S. Air Force. MAILING ADDRESS: P.O. Box 1987, Oceanside, CA 92054.

SCHILLACI, CHRISTOPHER. POLIT. & GOV.: ***independent candidate for presidency of the U.S., 1976***. MAILING ADDRESS: Hicksville, NY 11801.

SCHLAFLY, PHYLLIS STEWART. b. Aug 15, 1924, St. Louis, MO; d. John Bruce and Odile (Dodge) Stewart; m. Fred Schlafly, Oct 20, 1949; c. John F.; Bruce S.; Roger S.; Phyllis Liza; Andrew L.; Anne V. EDUC.: B.A., WA U., 1944, 1974–; M.A., Radcliffe Coll., 1945. POLIT. & GOV.: Republican candidate for U.S. House (IL), 1952, 1960, 1970; delegate, Rep. Nat'l. Conv.,, 1956, 1960 (alternate), 1964, 1968; appointed member, IL State Comm. on the Status of Women, 1975–; ***candidate for American Party nomination to presidency of the U.S., 1976***. BUS. & PROF.: author; publisher, Phyllis Schlafly Report, 1967–; broadcaster, "Spectrum," CBS radio network, 1973–; commentator, "Matter of Opinion," radio WBBM, Chicago, IL, 1973–75; syndicated columnist, Copley News Service, 1979–. MEM.: IL Federation of Republican Women (pres., 1960–64); National Federation of Republican Women (first vice pres., 1964–67); Stop ERA (national chm., 1972–); DAR (national chm., American History, 1965–68; national chm., Bicentennial Cmte., 1967–70); Phi Beta Kappa; Pi Sigma Alpha; Eagle Forum (pres., 1975–); National Defense Club (chm., 1977–); Junior League of St. Louis. AWARDS: Honor Medal, Freedom Foundation, 9 times; Brotherhood Award, National Conference of Christians and Jews, 1975; "Woman of Achievement in Public Affairs," *St. Louis Globe-Democrat*, 1963. HON. DEG.: LL.D., Niagara U., 1976. WRITINGS: *A Choice, Not an Echo* (1964); *The Gravediggers* (1964); *Strike from Space* (1965); *Safe Not Sorry* (1967); *The Betrayers* (1968); *Mindzenty the Man* (1972); *Kissinger on the Couch* (1975); *Ambush at Vladivostok* (1976); *The Power of the Positive Woman* (1977). MAILING ADDRESS: 68 Fairmount, Alton, IL 62002.

SCHLEY, WINFIELD SCOTT. b. Oct 9, 1839, Frederick City, MD; d. Oct 2, 1909, New York, NY; par. John Thomas and Georgiana Virginia (McClare) Schley; m. Annie R. Franklin, Sep 10, 1863. EDUC.: grad., U.S. Naval Acad., 1860. POLIT. & GOV.: ***candidate for Democratic nomination to presidency of the U.S., 1900; candidate for Democratic nomination to vice presidency of the U.S., 1900***. BUS. & PROF.: sailor. MIL.: midshipman, U.S. Navy, 1860, master, 1861, lt., 1862, lt. commander, 1866, commander, 1874, capt., 1888, commodore, 1898, rear adm., 1899; served on *Niagara*, 1860–61; *Keystone State*, 1861; *Potomac*, 1861–62; *Winona*, 1862–63; *Wateree*, 1864–66; on duty, U.S. Naval Acad., 1866–69, 1872–76; served on *Benicia*, 1869–72; commander, *Essex*, 1876–79; light house inspector, Second District, 1880–83; commander, Thetis and Greely Expeditions, 1884; chief, Bureau of Equipment and Repair, 1884–89; commander, Baltimore, 1889–92; member, Board of Inspection and Survey, 1896–97; chm., Lighthouse Board, 1897–98; commander, Flying Squadron, 1898; destroyed Spanish fleet at Battle of Santiago, Jul 3, 1898; commander in chief, South Atlantic Squadron, 1899–1901; requested board of inquiry to investigate charges against his leadership during Spanish-American War, 1901; majority reported against him and report was upheld by President Theodore Roosevelt, 1902; retired, 1901. AWARDS: Gold Watch and Vote of Thanks, MD Legislature; Gold Medal,

MA Humane Soc.; Gold Sword, People of PA; Silver Sword, Royal Arcanum WRITINGS: *The Rescue of Greely* (1885); *Forty-Five Years Under the Flag* (1904). RES.: Washington, DC.

SCHLIEDER, LYLE MORRIS. POLIT. & GOV.: ***independent candidate for presidency of the U.S., 1988***. MAILING ADDRESS: 5436 Pepperwood Ave., Lakewood, CA 90712.

SCHMIDT, JOHN RAYMOND. b. Oct 6, 1886, Mt. Vernon, IN; d. Apr 23, 1964, Washington, DC; par. Edward and Henrietta (Fellemende) Schmidt; m. Ruth Andrew, Sep 12, 1923. EDUC.: A.B., De Pauw U., 1910. POLIT. & GOV.: asst. chm., IN State Prohibition Cmte., 1911; chm., OH State Prohibition Cmte., 1911–13; delegate, Prohibition Party National Convention, 1912, 1916, 1920, 1924, 1928, 1932, 1940, 1944, 1948, 1952; chm., IN State Prohibition Cmte., 1914–18; field rep., Prohibition Party, 1919–24; member, Prohibition Party National Cmte., 1914–; ***candidate for Prohibition Party nomination to vice presidency of the U.S., 1944 (declined)***. BUS. & PROF.: lecturer; prohibition advocate; business mgr., American Advance, 1913; sec., YMCA (army service), 1918–19; field sec., Intercollegiate Prohibition Assn., 1919–20; lecturer, Prohibition Foundation, 1921–23; ed., *World Dry*, 1921–23; lecturer, International Reform Federation, 1923–35; ed., *Twentieth Century Progress*, 1923–35; sec., gen. superintendent, National Civic League, 1935–64; ed., *Civic Forum*, 1935–64; assoc. ed., *National Voice*, 1936–64. MEM.: Anti-Cigarette Alliance of DC (vice pres.); International Federation of Narcotic Education (vice pres.); Flying Squadron of America; Allied Organizations of DC (pres.); United Dry Forces of DC; Independent Order of Rechabites; Independent Order of Good Templars (national superintendent of Legislative Work, 1936–64); Intercollegiate Prohibition Assn.; YMCA; International Reform Federation; Prohibition Foundation; National Civic League. HON. DEG.: LL.D., Pasadena (CA) Coll., 1942. REL.: Methodist. RES.: Washington, DC.

SCHMIDT, O. B. A. POLIT. & GOV.: ***independent candidate for presidency of the U.S., 1976***. BUS. & PROF.: author; producer, political recordings. MAILING ADDRESS: Box 278, Woodland, TX 77373.

SCHMIDT, SUSANNE EDITH. m. Charles C. S. POLIT. & GOV.: ***independent candidate for presidency of the U.S., 1984***. MAILING ADDRESS: 4977 Battery Lane, #907, Bethesda, MD 20814.

SCHMIDT, WILLIAM SMITH. POLIT. & GOV.: ***candidate for Republican nomination to presidency of the U.S., 1964***. MAILING ADDRESS: Astoria, Long Island, NY.

SCHMITZ, JOHN GEORGE. b. Aug 12, 1930, Milwaukee, WI; par. Jacob J. and Wilhelmina (Frueh) Schmitz; m. Mary Ethel Suehr, Jul 10, 1954; c. John; Joseph; Jerome; Mary Kay; Theresa Ann; Elizabeth Louise; Philip J. EDUC.: Marquette U. H.S., 1948; B.S., Marquette U., 1952; M.A., CA State Coll., Long Beach, CA, 1960; Claremont Graduate School, 1961–66. POLIT. & GOV.: elected as a Republican to CA State Senate, 1965–71, 1979–; elected as a Republican to U.S. House (CA), 1971–73; candidate for Republican nomination to U.S. House (CA), 1972, 1984; ***American Party candidate for presidency of the U.S., 1972***; candidate for Republican nomination to CA state sec. of state, 1974; candidate for Republican nomination to U.S. Senate (CA), 1976, 1980, 1982; Republican candidate for U.S. House (CA), 1976. BUS. & PROF.: instructor in Philosophy, History, and Political Science, Santa Ana Coll., 1960–79; instructor in Philosophy, History, and Political Science, Saddleback Coll., 1976–79. MIL.: aviator, U.S.M.C., 1952–60; lt. col., col., U.S.M.C. Reserves, 1960–. MEM.: Military Order of the World Wars; American Legion; John Birch Soc.; Knights of Columbus; Order of the Alhambra; Phi Alpha Theta; NRA; CA Rifle and Pistol Assn.; Marine Corps Reserve Officers Assn.; Marine Corps League; National Soc. of State Legislators (charter member); CA State Soc. of Washington, DC (vice pres.); Orange Cty. Conservative Coordinating Council (dir.); CA Young Republicans; United Republicans of CA; Boys Club of Tustin (advisory board); Orange Cty. Coordinating Republican Assembly (chm.); Santa Ana Coll. Young Republicans (faculty adviser); CA Republican Assembly. AWARDS: award, Police Officers Research Assn. of CA, 1968; “Citation of Appreciation,” American Legion, 6th District, Dept. of CA, 1969; award, United Organization of Taxpayers, Inc., 1969; award, CA Republican Assembly, 1969; Distinguished Service Award, Americans for Constitutional Action, 1970; “Bulldog of the Year” Award, National Associated Businessmen, 1970; “Statesman of the Year” Award, We, the People, 1970; Champion of the People Award, Southern CA Chapter, Pro America, 1970; National Legislative Award, National SAR, 1971; Outstanding Citizen Award, Federation of American Citizens of German Descent in the U.S.A., Inc., 1972; “Man of the Year” Award, Congress of Freedom, 1972; “Number One Congressman in the U.S.” Award, National Economic Council, Inc., 1972; Award, Freedoms Foundation, 1973, 1974. REL.: R.C. MAILING ADDRESS: 18002 Irvine Blvd., Tustin, CA 92680.

SCHMUCKER, VERNON MICHAEL. POLIT. & GOV.: ***independent candidate for presidency of the U.S., 1988***. MAILING ADDRESS: Bakersfield, CA.

SCHNEIDER, WILLIAM RICHARD. b. Dec 22, 1888, Pilger, NE; par. Frederick L. and Augusta (Kant) Schneider; m. (divorced, 1930); m. 2d, Irma D. Beckley, 1933; c. none. EDUC.: B.S., Wayne Coll., Wayne, NE; LL.B., U. of MI, 1911. POLIT. & GOV.: candidate for St. Louis (MO) Board of

Aldermen, 1917; elected as a Republican to MO State House, 1925–29, 1931–33; candidate for Republican nomination to gov. of MO, 1928; ***candidate for Republican nomination to presidency of the U.S., 1952***. BUS. & PROF.: schoolteacher; principal, high school; post card and encyclopedia salesman; clerk, law firm; atty.; admitted to MO Bar, 1912; law practice, St. Louis, MO, 1912–70; part-time instructor, law school, St. Louis, MO; counsel, Union Electric Co.; counsel, Associated Industries of MO, 1919–25; counsel, St. Louis Streetcar Men's Union; beekeeper; lecturer; expert on workmen's compensation laws. MEM.: ABA; MO Bar Assn.; St. Louis Bar Assn.; St. Louis Public Questions Club. WRITINGS: *Workmen's Compensation Law*; *Life's Happy Accidents*. REL.: Protestant. RES.: St. Louis, MO.

SCHOENFELD, BENJAMIN FRANKLIN. b. Sep 6, 1942, Corvallis, OR; par. Benjamin Franklin and Gertrude Evelyn (Wardrip) Schoenfeld; m. Maria Aydee Cuesta-Torres, Apr 28, 1979 (d. 1982); c. Bill (twin); Roy Cheyne (twin). EDUC.: G.E.D., State of AZ, 1962. POLIT. & GOV.: ***candidate for Republican nomination to presidency of the U.S., 1984, 1988; candidate for Democratic nomination to presidency of the U.S., 1988; candidate for Communist Party nomination to presidency of the U.S., 1992***. BUS. & PROF.: engineer, electronic defense plants. MIL.: E-4 (T), U.S. Army, 1959–62. REL.: Monotheistic Christian. MAILING ADDRESS: 12028 Venice Blvd., Suite 4-115, Los Angeles, CA 90066.

SCHOONMAKER, L. CRAIG. b. 1945. EDUC.: B.A., City U. of NY. POLIT. & GOV.: ***Expansionist Party candidate for presidency of the U.S., 1992***. BUS. & PROF.: writer; activist; word processor. Self-avowed homosexual. MAILING ADDRESS: New York, NY.

SCHORR, DANIEL LOUIS. b. Aug 31, 1916, New York, NY; par. Louis and Tillie (Godiner) Schorr; m. Lisbeth Bamberger, 1967; c. Jonathan; Lisa. EDUC.: B.S., Coll. of the City of NY, 1939. POLIT. & GOV.: ***candidate for Democratic nomination to vice presidency of the U.S., 1976***. BUS. & PROF.: radio-television commentator; asst. ed., Jewish Telegraphic Agency, 1934–41; news ed., ANETA (Netherlands) News Agency, New York, NY, 1941–48; freelance correspondent, 1948–53; Washington (DC) correspondent, CBS News, 1953–55, chief, Moscow Bureau, 1955, roving assignments in U.S. and Europe, 1958–60; chief, CBS News Bureau in Germany and Central Europe, 1960–66, Washington (DC) correspondent, CBS News, 1966–76; regents prof., U. of CA, Berkeley, CA, 1977; columnist, *Des Moines (IA) Register*, Tribune Syndicate; commentator, National Public Radio and independent television, 1979; senior Washington (DC) correspondent, Cable News Network, 1980–. MEM.: A.F.T.R.A.; Council on Foreign Relations. AWARDS: Grand Cross of Merit (Germany); Orange Nassau Decoration (Netherlands, 1955); award, Overseas Press Club, 1956; Award for Best Television Interpretation of Foreign News, 1963; Emmy Award for Coverage of Watergate Scandal, 1972, 1973, 1974. WRITINGS: *Don't Get Sick in America!* (1971); *Clearing the Air* (1977). REL.: Jewish. MAILING ADDRESS: 3113 Woodley Rd., N.W., Washington, DC 20008.

SCHREINER, JOHN C. "INVENTOR JOHN." POLIT. & GOV.: ***candidate for Democratic nomination to presidency of the U.S., 1984***; CA write-in. MAILING ADDRESS: unknown.

SCHROCK, FRANKLIN. POLIT. & GOV.: ***candidate for Republican nomination to presidency of the U.S., 1980***. MAILING ADDRESS: 1815 West Norfolk Ave., Tampa, FL 33604.

SCHROEDER, EUGENE. POLIT. & GOV.: ***candidate for Republican nomination to vice presidency of the U.S., 1980***. MAILING ADDRESS: unknown.

SCHROEDER, HANS. POLIT. & GOV.: Libertarian Party candidate for Bucks Cty. (PA) Comm.; Libertarian Party candidate for U.S. House (PA); chm., Libertarian Party of PA, 1978–80; ***candidate for Libertarian Party nomination to presidency of the U.S., 1992***. BUS. & PROF.: publisher, *The Pragmatist*. MAILING ADDRESS: PA.

SCHROEDER, PATRICIA SCOTT. b. Jul 10, 1940, Portland, OR; d. Lee Combs and Bernice Lemoin (Scott) Scott); m. James White Schroeder, Aug 18, 1962; c. Scott William; Jamie Christine. EDUC.: B.A. (magna cum laude), U. of MN, 1961; J.D., Harvard U., 1964. POLIT. & GOV.: field atty., National labor Relations Board, Denver, CO, 1964–66; member, Denver Democratic Central Cmte., 1968–69; Hearings Officer, CO Dept. of Personnel, 1971–72; elected as a Democrat to U.S. House (CO), 1973–; co-chairperson, Congressional Women's Caucus, 1977–; ***candidate for Democratic nomination to vice presidency of the U.S., 1984; candidate for Democratic nomination to presidency of the U.S., 1988 (declined), 1992***. BUS. & PROF.: atty.; admitted to CO Bar, 1964; law practice, Denver, CO, 1966–72; faculty, U. of CO, 1969–72; faculty, Community Coll. of Denver, 1969–70; faculty, Regis Coll., Denver, CO, 1970–72; dir., Century Casualty Co. MEM.: National Organization for Women; International House; Fair Housing Center; Denver Young Democrats (dir.); Denver Bar Assn.; Mortar Board; Members of Congress for Peace Through Law; Democratic Advisory Council; Democratic Study Group; National Women's Political Caucus; Jefferson Cty. Human Relations Council (dir.); Planned Parenthood of CO (dir.); ABA; Congressional Clearinghouse on the Future; League of Women Voters (unit leader, 1967–68); Chi Omega; Phi Beta Kappa; Sigma Epsilon Sigma.

REL.: Congregationalist. MAILING ADDRESS: 836 Dexter St., Denver, CO 80220.

SCHUMACHER, JAMES D. POLIT. & GOV.: ***candidate for American Independent Party nomination to presidency of the U.S., 1980***. MAILING ADDRESS: AZ.

SCHWAB, CHARLES MICHAEL. b. Feb 18, 1862, Williamsburg, PA; d. Sep 18, 1939, New York, NY; par. John A. and Pauline (Farabaugh) Schwab; m. Emma Eurana Dinkey, 1883; c. none. EDUC.: grad., St. Francis Xavier's Catholic Coll., 1880. POLIT. & GOV.: appointed dir. gen. for Shipbuilding, U.S. Shipping Board, Emergency Fleet Corp., 1918; ***candidate for Republican nomination to presidency of the U.S., 1920, 1940***. BUS. & PROF.: grocery clerk, Braddock, PA; stage driver; employee, Edgar Tomson Steel Works, asst. superintendent, chief engineer, 1881, asst. mgr., 1881, gen. superintendent, 1889–97; superintendent, Carnegie Steel Co. (Homestead Plant), 1887–89, gen. superintendent, 1892–97, pres., 1897–1901; pres., U.S. Steel Corp., 1901–03; chm. of the board, Bethlehem Steel Corp., 1904–39; dir., Metropolitan Life Insurance Co.; dir., Chicago Pneumatic Tool Co.; dir., Clyde Steamship Co.; dir., Elgin, Joliet and Eastern Railway Co.; dir., Empire Trust Co.; dir., Greenwater Copper Mines and Smelter Co.; dir., H. C. Fricke Coke Co.; dir., MN Iron Co.; dir., Montgomery-Shoshone Consolidated Mining Co.; dir., National Bank of North America; dir., National Tube Co.; dir., National Tube Works Co.; dir., U.S. Realty and Improvement Co. MEM.: American Iron and Steel Inst. (pres., 1926–32; chm. of the board, 1933–34). AWARDS: Melchett Medal (Great Britain), 1932; Legion of Honor; Gary Medal; Bessemer Medal. HON. DEG.: Dr.Eng., Lehigh U., 1914; D.C.S., NY U., 1918; LL.D., Lincoln Memorial U., 1917; Dr.Eng., Stevens Inst. of Technology, 1921; LL.D., St. Francis Xavier's Catholic Coll., 1923; LL.D., Franklin and Marshall Coll., 1924; LL.D., Juniata Coll., 1926; Sc.D., U. of PA, 1927. REL.: R.C. RES.: New York, NY.

SCHWARTZ, DANIEL X. B. "DIXBIE." b. Sep 8, 1920, Brooklyn, NY; par. Louis and Isabella (Rosen) Schwartz; m. Cyndy Betty Brown; c. Barbara Joy. EDUC.: grad., Samuel J. Tilden H.S., Brooklyn, NY, 1938; B.B.A., St. John's U., 1947; Cornell U., 1947; Brooklyn Coll.; George Washington U. POLIT. & GOV.: founder, chm. of the board, National Tax Savers Party; ***National Tax Savers Party candidate for presidency of the U.S., 1964, 1968***; National Tax Savers Party candidate for gov. of NY, 1966; hon. deputy mayor, New York, NY. BUS. & PROF.: reporter, Office of Government Reports, Washington, DC; public accountant; tax consultant; management consultant; chm. of the board, National Beef Corp. of America; chm. of the board, Dixbie Management Co.; partner, Black Angus Cattle Management Co.; writer; publisher, Mardi-Gras Books; performer. MIL.: col., U.S. Army Special Services, 1948–50. MEM.: Rosicrucian Order, A.M.O.R.C.; Mayans. WRITINGS: *Daniel's Tax Savers*; popular songs. REL.: Universalist. MAILING ADDRESS: 888 Seventh Ave., Apt. 400, New York, NY 10019; 200 West 57th St., New York, NY 10019.

SCHWARTZ, STEPHEN H. POLIT. & GOV.: ***candidate for Democratic nomination to presidency of the U.S., 1991***. MAILING ADDRESS: East Hampton, NY.

SCHWEHR, DAVID WILLIAM. POLIT. & GOV.: ***candidate for Republican nomination to presidency of the U.S., 1988***. MAILING ADDRESS: 111 South Bassett, Apt. 101, Madison, WI 53703.

SCHWEIKER, RICHARD SCHULTZ. b. Jun 1, 1926, Norristown, PA; par. Malcolm Allderfer and Blanche (Schultz) Schweiker; m. Claire Joan Coleman, Sep 10, 1955; c. Malcolm C.; Llani L.; Kyle C.; Richard Schultz, Jr.; Lara Kristi. EDUC.: B.A., PA State U., 1950. POLIT. & GOV.: delegate, Rep. Nat'l. Conv., 1952 (alternate), 1956 (alternate), 1972, 1980; member, PA State Republican exec. cmte.; elected as a Republican to U.S. House (PA), 1961–69; elected as a Republican to U.S. Senate (PA), 1969–81; member, Technological Assessment Board; ***candidate for Republican nomination to vice presidency of the U.S., 1976***; appointed U.S. sec. of health and human services, 1981–83; vice presidential choice of Ronald Reagan (q.v.) at 1976 Rep. Nat'l. Conv. (prior to balloting for presidential nomination). BUS. & PROF.: business exec., 1950–60; pres., American Council on Life Insurance, 1983–; dir., National Medical Enterprises, Inc. MIL.: electronics technician, second class, U.S. Navy, 1944–46. MEM.: Navy League; VFW (life member); Rotary Club; AmVets; Anthracosilicosis League of PA; Schwenkfelder Library (dir.); BSA (hon. member, national council); SAR; Phi Beta Kappa; Lions; Kiwanis; Slumbering Groundhog Lodge; American Legion; PA Soc. AWARDS: "Outstanding Young Man in PA," PA Junior C. of C., 1960; Liberty Bell Award, PA Junior Bar Assn., 1965; Appreciation Award, JFK Council, Knights of Columbus, 1966; "Bringer of Light" Award, Jewish National Fund, 1971; Daroff Humanitarian Award, Anti-Defamation League of B'nai B'rith, 1971; Distinguished Alumnus Award, PA State U., 1970; award, National Soc. for the Prevention of Blindness, 1974; Dr. Charles H. Best Award, American Diabetes Assn., 1974; Humanitarian Award, Juvenile Diabetes Foundation, 1974; award, National Assn. for Mental Health, 1974; SER Award, 1974; award, Opportunities Industrialization Centers, 1974; Israel Prime Minister's Medal, 1974; "Outstanding Alumnus for the Year" Award, Phi Kappa Sigma, 1982; Gold Medal, PA Assn. of Broadcasters, 1982; National Outstanding Service Award, Headstart, 1983. HON. DEG.: LL.D., Ursinus Coll., 1963; D.P.S., Temple U., 1970; LL.D., Dickinson Coll., 1972; LL.D., PA Medical Coll., 1972;

LL.D., Albright Coll., 1973; LL.D., LaSalle Coll., 1973; L.H.D., PA Coll. of Podiatric Medicine, 1973; D.C.L., Widener Coll., 1973; D.Sc., Georgetown U., 1981. REL.: Schwenkfelder Church. MAILING ADDRESS: American Council on Life Insurance, 1850 K St., N.W., Washington, DC 20006.

SCOTT-DAVENPORT, BARBARA S. POLIT. & GOV.: ***candidate for Peace and Freedom Party nomination to presidency of the U.S., 1992; candidate for Libertarian Party nomination to presidency of the U.S., 1992; candidate for Democratic nomination to presidency of the U.S., 1992; candidate for Republican Party nomination to presidency of the U.S., 1992; candidate for American Independent Party nomination to presidency of the U.S., 1992; independent candidate for presidency of the U.S., 1992***. MAILING ADDRESS: CA?

SCOTT, IRVING MURRAY. b. Dec 25, 1837, Hebron Mills, MD; d. 1903. EDUC.: Milton Acad.; Baltimore Mechanics' Inst. POLIT. & GOV.: ***candidate for Republican nomination to vice presidency of the U.S., 1900***. BUS. & PROF.: employee, factory of Obed Hussey (reaping machinery), Baltimore, MD; draftsman; mechanical engineer; inventor; vice pres., gen. mgr., Union Iron Works, San Francisco, CA. MEM.: Mechanics Inst. (pres.); San Francisco Art Inst. (pres.); U. of CA (regent); Leland Stanford, Jr., U. (trustee). MISC.: built Battleship *Oregon*; designed machinery for working Comstock mines; invented improved cut-off engines. RES.: San Francisco, CA.

SCOTT, JOHN G. b. 1880, Greenwood, IN; d. Nov 2, 1953, East Taghkanic, NY; m. Jo Ann Scott; c. John; Mack E.; Mrs. Ozalea Dyer; Mrs. Neva Helpman; Mrs. Shelley Frisch. EDUC.: U. of MO; Columbia U. POLIT. & GOV.: organizer, Nationalist Party; ***Greenback Party candidate for presidency of the U.S., 1948***; joined Republican Party. BUS. & PROF.: farmer; publisher, *Socialist Magazine*, MO; ed., *Mother Earth: A Libertarian Farm Paper*, Craryville, NY, 1933–34; ed., proprietor, *Money*, 1936–53; teacher, Pittsburgh (KS) State Normal School. MEM.: Phi Beta Kappa; Farm Holiday Assn. of NY (pres., 1930's); National Farm Holiday Assn.; Social Credit Movement; Congress of Monetary Organizations. MISC.: *Money* magazine banned from U.S. mails, 1942; self-styled "Thoreauvian Anarchist." RES.: Craryville, NY.

SCOTT, LLOYD OSBORNE "ALAMO." b. Aug 26, 1930, Anson, TX; par. William Allen and Ada Mae (McCammant) Scott; m. Barbara Sue McCoy; c. none. EDUC.: B.A., Hardin Simmons U., 1957; Master of Divinity, Southwestern Seminary, 1963. POLIT. & GOV.: ***U.S. Fellowship Party candidate for presidency of the U.S., 1976, 1992; candidate for Democratic nomination to presidency of the U.S., 1980***. BUS. & PROF.: teacher of history and english, public schools, Lubbock, TX. MIL.: sgt., U.S. Army, 1952–54. WRITINGS: *Hope: Unifying Link of Christian Doctrines*. MAILING ADDRESS: 5102 46th, Lubbock, TX 79414.

SCOTT, ROCHELLE M. POLIT. & GOV.: ***independent candidate for presidency of the U.S., 1976***. MAILING ADDRESS: 111 North 49th St., Center Building, 3rd Floor, Room 2, Philadelphia, PA 19139.

SCOTT, TERRANCE R. POLIT. & GOV.: ***independent candidate for presidency of the U.S., 1992***. MAILING ADDRESS: 932 Portland Place, Boulder, CO 80304.

SCOTT, THOMAS ALEXANDER. b. Dec 28, 1824, Fort Loudon, PA; d. May 21, 1881, Darby, PA; par. Thomas and Rebecca (Douglas) Scott; m. Anna Margaret Mullison, 1847; m. 2d, Anna Dike Riddle, 1865; c. James P.; Miriam D. (Mrs. Howard D. Bickley); Mary; Edgar Thomson; one other son; one other daughter. EDUC.: country schools. POLIT. & GOV.: clerk, Office of PA Collector of Tolls, 1840–45; chief clerk, Office of Philadelphia (PA) Collector of Tolls, 1847–49; appointed asst. U.S. sec. of war, 1861–62; ***candidate for Republican nomination to vice presidency of the U.S., 1872***. BUS. & PROF.: handyman, Stewart's General Store, Waynesboro, PA, 1835–37; clerk, Metcalfe and Ritchie, Mercersburg, PA; clerk, Diller and Baker, Huntingdon Cty., PA; co-owner, sawmill, Columbia, PA, 1843; shipper, Leech and Co., 1849; station agent, Pennsylvania R.R. Co., Duncansville, PA, 1850, third asst. superintendent (Pittsburgh, PA), 1852, gen. superintendent, 1858, first vice pres., 1860, pres., 1874–80; mgr., Northern Central R.R., 1861; pres., The Pennsylvania Co., 1870; pres., Pittsburgh, Cincinnati and St. Louis Railway, 1871; pres., Union Pacific R.R. Co., 1871–72; dir., Southern Railway Security Co.; dir., Kansas Pacific; dir., Denver and Rio Grande R.R.; pres., Texas and Pacific Railway Co., 1872–80; pres., Atlantic and Pacific Railway, 1873. MIL.: col., U.S.V., 1861–62. WRITINGS: *Texas and Pacific Railway* (1876). RES.: Darby, PA.

SCOTT, WILLIAM T. b. 1844, Newark, OH. EDUC.: public schools. POLIT. & GOV.: ***National Liberty Party candidate for presidency of the U.S., 1904 (replaced by George Edwin Taylor, q.v.)***. BUS. & PROF.: barber; owner, hotel, Cairo, IL, 1863; ed., *Cairo (IL) Daily Gazette*, to 1902; ed., *East St. Louis (IL) Leader*, 1902–. MIL.: wardroom steward, U.S. Navy, 1862; on board USS *Victoria*. MEM.: Black secret societies (officer); National Democratic League (vice pres.); National Anti-Expansion, Anti-Imperialist, Anti-Trust and Anti-Lynching League (pres., 1900). MISC.: known as "colonel Scott"; first Negro candidate for presidency of the U.S.; convicted of keeping a disorderly house; sentenced to 20 days in Belleville (IL) jail, 1904. RES.: Belleville, IL.

SCOTT, WINFIELD. b. Jun 13, 1786, Laurel Branch, VA; d. May 29, 1866, West Point, NY; par. William and Ann

(Mason) Scott; m. Maria D. Mayo, Mar 11, 1817; c. two sons; five daughters. EDUC.: Coll. of William and Mary, 1805–06; studied law under David Robertson. POLIT. & GOV.: ***candidate for Whig Party nomination to presidency of the U.S., 1840, 1844, 1848; Whig Party candidate for presidency of the U.S., 1852***. BUS. & PROF.: atty.; admitted to VA Bar, 1806; temperance advocate; soldier. MIL.: lance corp., Petersburg (VA) Cavalry, 1807; capt., Light Artillery, U.S. Army, 1808; court marshalled, 1809, and suspended from army for 1 year; staff, Brig. Gen. Wade Hampton, 1811–12; lt. col., 1812; captured by British at Battle of Queenstown (NY), 1812, paroled, 1812; col., 1813; brig. gen., 1814; chm., Military Discharge Board, 1814; pres., Board of Tactics, U.S. Army, 1815, 1821, 1824, 1826; commander, U.S. Army, Black Hawk War, 1832; commander, U.S. Army, Creek and Seminole Wars, 1835; commander, Eastern Div., U.S. Army, 1837; gen. in chief, U.S. Army, 1841–61; captured Vera Cruz, 1847; occupied Mexico City, 1847; lt. gen., 1855; retired, 1861. HON. DEG.: M.A., Princeton Coll. WRITINGS: *Infantry Tactics*; *General Regulations for the Army*. RES.: Elizabethtown, NJ.

SCOVEL, JAMES MATLACK. b. Jan 16, 1833, Harrison, OH; d. Dec 2, 1904, Cape May, NJ; par. Silvester Fithian and Hannah Cook (Matlack) Scovel; m. Mary Mulford, May 21, 1859; m. 2d, Mrs. Morehead; c. Henry Sydney; Annie (Mrs. Charles Brooke); Mamie. EDUC.: grad., Hanover Coll., 1850; read law under Abraham Browning. POLIT. & GOV.: delegate, NJ State Democratic Convention, 1860; elected as a Republican to NJ State House, 1863; elected as a Republican to NJ State Senate, 1864–66 (pres., 1866); appointed commissioner of the Draft, First Congressional District (NJ), Civil War; delegate, Rep. Nat'l. Conv., 1864; appointed U.S. commissioner to England, Civil War; candidate for Republican nomination to U.S. Senate (NJ), 1866; candidate for Republican nomination to gov. of NJ, 1871; state chm., NJ Liberal Republican Party, 1872; ***candidate for Liberal Republican Party nomination to vice presidency of the U.S., 1872***; Liberal Republican Party candidate for U.S. House (NJ), 1872; appointed special agent, U.S. Dept. of the Treasury, 1881–84. BUS. & PROF.: schoolteacher, Memphis, TN, 1850–52; atty.; admitted to NJ Bar, 1856; law practice, Camden, NJ; minister, Baptist Church, 1893–1904. MIL.: col., Sixth Regt., NJ Volunteers, Civil War. WRITINGS: *Speech Before the Anti-Monopoly Convention* (1865); *Speech in the NJ Senate . . . on the Airline Railroad Bill; Our Relations with the Rebellious States* (1866); *Three Speeches* (1870). REL.: Bapt. RES.: Camden, NJ.

SCRANTON, WILLIAM WARREN. b. Jul 19, 1917, Madison, CT; par. Worthington and Marion Margery (Warren) Scranton; m. Mary Lowe Chamberlin, Jul 6, 1942; c. Susan (Mrs. Richard Wolf); William Worthington; Joseph Curtis; Peter Kip. EDUC.: Hotchkiss School; B.A., Yale U., 1939, LL.B., 1946. POLIT. & GOV.: appointed special asst. to U.S. sec. of state, 1959–60; elected as a Republican to U.S. House (PA), 1961–63; elected as a Republican to gov. of PA, 1963–67; ***candidate for Republican nomination to presidency of the U.S., 1964***; delegate, PA State Constitutional Convention, 1967–68; appointed vice chm., President's Comm. on Insurance for Riot-torn Areas, 1967; appointed U.S. ambassador to INTELSAT, 1969; appointed member, President's Advisory Comm. on Arms Limitation and Disarmament, 1969–76; appointed chm., President's Comm. on Campus Unrest, 1970; appointed member, President's Price Comm., 1971–72; appointed consultant to the presidency of the U.S., 1974–76; delegate, Rep. Nat'l. Conv., 1976; appointed U.S. ambassador to the U.N., 1976–77. BUS. & PROF.: atty.; admitted to PA Bar, 1946; assoc., O'Malley, Harris, Harris, and Warren (law firm), Scranton, PA, 1947; vice pres., International Textbook Co., 1947–52; vice pres., Haddon Craftsman, Inc., 1947–52; pres., Scranton-Lackawanna Trust Co., 1954–56; chm. of the board, Northeastern Pennsylvania Broadcasting Co., Inc., 1953–59; chm. of the board, National Liberty Life Insurance Co., 1969–71; dir., International Business Machines Corp.; dir., *New York (NY) Times*; dir., Scott Paper Co.; dir., Bethlehem Steel Corp.; dir., Cummins Engine Corp.; dir., American Express; chm. of the board, Northeastern National Bank of PA, 1973–76; dir., Lackawanna R.R.; dir., International Salt Co.; dir., International Correspondence Schools World, Ltd. MIL.: capt., U.S.A.A.C., 1941–45, lt. col.; maj., U.S. Air Force Reserves. MEM.: Lackawanna Industrial Fund Enterprises; Scranton-Lackawanna Industrial Building Co.; Industrial Development Cmte.; Scranton C. of C. (New Industries Cmte.); Tri-Lateral Comm. (exec. cmte., 1971); Yale Political Union; National Conference of Governors (chm., 1974–76); Urban Inst. (chm., 1974–76). HON. DEG.: 32. REL.: Presb. MAILING ADDRESS: P.O. Box 116, Marworth, Dalton, PA 18414.

SEAMAN, FRED. POLIT. & GOV.: ***candidate for Democratic nomination to vice presidency of the U.S., 1972***. MAILING ADDRESS: TX?

SEAMAN, K. CORE. married. POLIT. & GOV.: founder, God and Country Party; ***God and Country Party candidate for presidency of the U.S., 1976, 1980, 1984***. MEM.: The American Patriots. MAILING ADDRESS: 1160 Sherman St., Denver, CO 80203.

SEARS, JOHN PATRICK. b. Jul 3, 1940, Syracuse, NY; par. James Louis and Helen Mary (Fitzgerald) Sears; m. Carol Jean Osborne, Aug 25, 1962; c. James Louis; Ellen Margaret; Amy Elizabeth. EDUC.: B.S., U. of Notre Dame, 1960; J.D., Georgetown U., 1963. POLIT. & GOV.: clerk, NY Court of Appeals, 1962–65; exec. dir., Nixon for President Cmte., 1967; appointed deputy counsel to the pres., 1969–70; campaign dir., Reagan for President Cmte., 1976, 1980 (resigned); ***candidate for Republican nomination to vice presidency of the U.S., 1976***. BUS. & PROF.: atty.; admitted to NY Bar, 1963; assoc., Nixon, Mudge, Rose, Guthrie, Alexander and Mitchell (law firm), New York, NY, 1965–66; personal staff, Richard M. Nixon (q.v.), 1966–69; partner, Gadsby and Hannah (law firm), Washington, DC, 1970–75; fellow, Kennedy Inst. of Politics, Harvard U., 1970; partner, Baskin and Sears (law firm), Washington, DC, 1977–. REL.: R.C. MAILING ADDRESS: 7718 Falstaff Court, McLean, VA 22101.

SEAT, MARVIN. POLIT. & GOV.: ***candidate for Populist Party nomination to presidency of the U.S., 1988***. BUS. & PROF.: businessman. MAILING ADDRESS: KY.

SEATON, FREDERICK ANDREW. b. Dec 11, 1909, Washington, DC; d. Jan 16, 1974, Minneapolis, MN; par. Fay Noble and Dorothea Elizabeth (Schmidt) Seaton; m. Gladys Hope Dowd, Jan 23, 1931; c. Donald Richard (adopted); Johanna Christine Epp (adopted); Monica Margaret Hansen (adopted); Alfred Noble (adopted). EDUC.: KS State Coll., 1927–31. POLIT. & GOV.: vice chm., KS State Republican Central Cmte., 1934–37; member, Young Rep. Nat'l. Cmte., 1935; delegate, Rep. Nat'l. Conv., 1936, 1968; sec. to Gov. Alfred M. Landon (q.v.), 1936; elected as a Republican to NE State Senate, 1945–49; appointed as a Republican to U.S. Senate (NE), 1951–52; appointed asst. U.S. sec. of defense, 1953–55; appointed administrative asst. to the presidency of the U.S., 1955; appointed deputy asst. to the presidency of the U.S., 1955–56; appointed U.S. sec. of the interior, 1956–61; appointed member, Presidential Comm. on the Celebration of the Bicentennial of the American Revolution; ***candidate for Republican nomination to vice presidency of the U.S., 1960***; Republican candidate for gov. of NE, 1962. BUS. & PROF.: dir., sports publicity, KS State Coll., 1927–31, asst., Dept. of Public Speaking, 1929–30; sports announcer, KSAC and WIBW, Manhattan, KS, 1929–37; news ed., *Manhattan (KS) Morning Chronicle*, 1932; city ed., *Manhattan (KS) Evening Mercury*, 1933; asst. ed., Seaton Publications, 1933–37; pres., Sheridan (WY) Newspapers, Inc., 1937; pres., Seaton Publishing Co., Hastings, NE, 1937; publisher, *Hastings (NE) Daily Tribune*, 1937–74; pres., KHAS-TV, Hastings, NE; pres., Nebraska Television Corp.; pres., Seaton Publishing Co., Lead, SD; pres., Winfield Publishing Co.; pres., Manhattan Broadcasting Co.; pres., Alliance Publishing Co.; pres., Nebraska Broadcasting Co.; pres., Western Farm Life Publishing Co.; vice pres., Seaton Publishing Co., Manhattan, KS; vice pres., Midwest Broadcasting Co.; vice pres., Coffeyville Publishing Co.; dir., Investors Life Insurance Co. MEM.: Rotary Club; Masons (Shriner); Elks; Beta Theta Pi; Sigma Delta Chi; Pi Kappa Delta; Newcomen Soc.; Lincoln University Club; Radio Free Europe Fund (state chm.); BSA (hon. member, national council); Associated Press Newspapers of NE (pres.); National Trust for Historic Preservation (dir.); Young Republican Clubs of KS (vice chm., 1932–34; chm., 1934–37); Inland Daily Press Assn. (chm., board of directors); Innocents, U. of NE (hon.); Hastings Coll. (trustee); U. of NE Foundation (trustee); National Rivers and Harbors Congress (vice pres., 1951); NE State Reclamation Assn. (dir.); NE State Grain Improvement Assn. (dir.); National Editorial Assn.; American Acad. of Political and Social Sciences; NE Press Assn. AWARDS: U.S. Medal of Freedom, 1955. HON. DEG.: LL.D., KS State Coll., 1955; L.H.D., Maryville Coll., 1955; LL.D., U. of AK, 1958; LL.D., Gettysburg Coll., 1959; LL.D., U. of HI, 1959; LL.D., Miami U., 1959; LL.D., U. of the Redlands, 1959; D.Eng., CO School of Mines, 1960; LL.D., John Carroll U., 1960; LL.D., U. of MD, 1960; LL.D., Rose Polytechnical Inst., 1960. REL.: Episc. RES.: Hastings, NE.

SEAWELL, JERROLD LAUDERDALE. b. Sep 2, 1897, Clusa, CA; d. Oct 20, 1952,, Los Angeles, CA; par. Josiah Lauderdale and Sarah Elizabeth (Gillaspy) Seawell; m. Mildred Alberta Brown, Aug 13, 1922; c. Robert Niles; Jerry Jean (Mrs. Gerald Nichols Winter). EDUC.: grad., high school, Oakland, CA. POLIT. & GOV.: elected trustee, Roseville (CA) Board of Education, 1927–28; elected as a Republican to CA State Assembly, 1929–33; elected as a Republican to CA State Senate, 1933–37, 1939–46 (pres. pro tempore, 1939–41, 1943–46); ***candidate for Republican nomination to presidency of the U.S., 1940***; elected as a Republican-Democrat, member, CA State Board of Equalization, 1946–52 (chm., 1952). BUS. & PROF.: grocery clerk, Marysville, CA; blacksmith; construction worker; locomotive engineer, Southern Pacific R.R., Roseville, CA, 1917–27; real estate broker, Seawell and Minard, Inc., Roseville, CA; insurance salesman. MEM.: Brotherhood of Locomotive Firemen and Enginemen (hon. member); Order of the Eastern Star (Potentate); Free and Accepted Masons; Shriners; Elks; Eagles; Knights Templar; Redmen; Lions. RES.: Roseville, CA.

SEBASTIAN, ERIC ALEXANDER. b. Nov 2, 1924, New York, NY; par. Clinton P. and Elizabeth (Spellman) Sebastian; m. Diana Barrett (deceased); c. none. EDUC.: B.A., Harvard U., 1945; M.A., Oxford U. (Queens Coll.), 1949. POLIT. & GOV.: chm., National Youth for Dewey Clubs, 1947–48; active in Eisenhower presidential campaign, 1952; East Coast Campaign mgr., Knowland for President, 1956; campaign strategist, Rockefeller for Governor, NY, 1958; active in Draft Lodge movement, 1960; left Republican Party, 1960; founder, National Hamiltonian Party; ***National Hamiltonian Party candidate for presidency of the U.S., 1968, 1972, 1976 (satire effort)***. BUS. & PROF.: investor. MEM.: Alexander Hamilton Assn. (pres., 1961); National Hamiltonian Study Group (founder). REL.: R.C. MISC.: allegedly fictitious candidate created by Mike Kelly and others, 1966. MAILING ADDRESS: Suite 307, 2734 Parkside Dr., Flint, MI 48503.

SEDDON, JAMES ALEXANDER. b. Jul 13, 1815, Fredericksburg, VA; d. Aug 19, 1880, Goochland Cty., VA; par. Thomas and Susan Pearson (Alexander) Seddon; m. Sarah Bruce, 1845; c. James Alexander, Jr. EDUC.: B.L., U. of VA, 1835. POLIT. & GOV.: elected as a Democrat to U.S. House (VA), 1845–47, 1849–51; delegate, Dem. Nat'l. Conv., 1856; ***candidate for Democratic nomination to vice presidency of the***

U.S., 1856 (withdrew); appointed delegate, Peace Convention, 1861; elected to First Congress, Confederate States of America, 1861; appointed sec. of war, Confederate States of America, 1862–65. BUS. & PROF.: atty.; admitted to VA Bar, 1838; law practice, Richmond, VA. RES.: Goochland Cty., VA.

SEELYE, JULIUS HAWLEY. b. Sep 14, 1824, Bethel, CT; d. May 12, 1895, Amherst, MA; par. Seth and Abigail (Taylor) Seelye; m. Elizabeth Tillman James, Oct 23, 1854; c. four. EDUC.: grad., Amherst Coll., 1849; grad., Auburn Theological Seminary, 1852; U. of Halle (Germany), 1 year. POLIT. & GOV.: appointed member, MA Comm. for Revision of State Tax Laws; elected as an independent to U.S. House (MA), 1875–77; ***candidate for American Prohibition Party nomination to presidency of the U.S., 1884***. BUS. & PROF.: ordained minister, Reformed Protestant Dutch Church, 1833; pastor, First Dutch Reformed Church, Schenectady, NY, 1853–58; prof. of Philosophy, Amherst Coll., 1858–76, pres., 1876–90; lecturer in India, 1872. MEM.: Andover Theological Seminary (member, board of visitors, 1887). WRITINGS: *History of Philosophy* (translator, 1856); *System of Moral Science* (ed., 1880); *Empirical Psychology* (ed., 1882). RES.: Amherst, MA.

SEGAL, MARY ANN TOMKINS. EDUC.: M.D. POLIT. & GOV.: ***candidate for Democratic nomination to presidency of the U.S., 1992***. BUS. & PROF.: physician. MAILING ADDRESS: 1451 Belmont St., Washington, DC.

SEIBERLING, JOHN FREDERICK. b. Sep 8, 1918, Akron, OH; par. J. Frederick and Henrietta (Buckler) Seiberling; m. Elizabeth Pope Behr, Jun 4, 1949; c. John Buckler; David Pope; Stephen Maddox. EDUC.: Staunton Military Acad., 1933–37; A.B., Harvard U., 1941; LL.B., Columbia U., 1949. POLIT. & GOV.: member, Tri-County Regional Planning Comm., Akron, OH, 1964–70 (pres., 1966–69); member, Summit Cty. (OH) Democratic Central Cmte., 1966–75 (vice chm., 1970–71); elected as a Democrat to U.S. House (OH), 1971–87; ***candidate for Democratic nomination to presidency of the U.S., 1976***. BUS. & PROF.: atty.; admitted to NY Bar, 1950; admitted to OH Bar, 1955; assoc., Donovan, Leisure, Newton and Irvine (law firm), New York, NY, 1949–54; Anti-Trust Specialist, Goodyear Tire and Rubber Co., 1954–71. MIL.: pvt., maj., U.S. Army, 1942–46; Legion of Merit; Bronze Star with Three Battle Stars; Medaille de la Reconnaissance Francaise; Ordre de Leopold III. MEM.: ABA; Akron Bar Assn.; Summit Cty. Cmte. for Peace in Viet Nam (founder); United World Federalists of Akron (pres.); World Peace Through Law Cmte., Akron Bar Assn. (pres.); Stan Hywet Hall Foundation (vice pres.); Sierra Club; Cuyahoga Valley Assn. (trustee); Northeast OH Congressional Council (co-chm.); Environmental Study Conference; Democratic Study Group; Members of Congress for Peace Through Law (chm.). REL.: United Church of Christ. MAILING ADDRESS: 913 Canyon Trail, Akron, OH 44303.

SEIDEL, EMIL. b. Dec 13, 1864, Ashland, PA; d. Jun 24, 1947, Milwaukee, WI; par. Otto F. T. and Henriette Seidel; m. Lucy Geissel, May 8, 1894; c. Viola (Mrs. Verhein). EDUC.: public schools, to 1877; learned woodcarving in Germany, 1885–93. POLIT. & GOV.: founder, Socialist Party, 1898; Socialist Party candidate for gov. of WI, 1902, 1918; elected as a Socialist, alderman, Milwaukee, WI, 1905–10, 1916–21, 1932–36; Socialist Party candidate for mayor of Milwaukee, WI, 1908, 1912, 1914; elected as a Socialist, mayor of Milwaukee, WI, 1910–12; ***candidate for Socialist Party nomination to presidency of the U.S., 1912; Socialist Party candidate for vice presidency of the U.S., 1912***; national lecturer, Socialist Party, 1912–16; Socialist Party candidate for U.S. Senate (WI), 1914, 1932; member, Socialist Party National Cmte., 1916; sec., WI Socialist Party, 1920–24; Socialist Party candidate for treas. of Milwaukee, WI, 1920. BUS. & PROF.: asst., German Exhibit, Chicago Exposition, 1893; wood carver; farmer, 1924. MEM.: Wood Carvers' Union (founder, 1884; sec., 1884–85). RES.: Florence, WI.

SEILER, JOHN. b. 1933. POLIT. & GOV.: campaign worker, Eugene McCarthy for President Campaign, MA, 1968; ***New Party candidate for presidency of the U.S., 1968***. BUS. & PROF.: prof., New Haven Coll. MAILING ADDRESS: 149 Old Sachems Head Rd., Guilford, CT 06437.

SEITZ, JOHN. b. Mar 12, 1829, Bloom Township, Seneca Cty., OH; par. Lewis and Barbara (Kagy) Seitz; m. Celia Hite, Apr 9, 1851; c. Milford K.; Omar B.; Marshall; May (Mrs. R. W. Thornburg); Nettie; Orin; Jay. EDUC.: public schools; Seneca Cty. Acad. POLIT. & GOV.: elected justice of the peace, Bloom Township, OH, 1863–65; elected to OH State House, 1869–73; elected as a Greenbacker to OH State Senate, 1873–75, 1877–81; Greenback Party candidate for U.S. House (OH), 1880, 1882; Greenback Party candidate for gov. of OH, 1881; Greenback Party candidate for OH State treas., 1883; ***candidate for Greenback Party nomination to presidency of the U.S., 1884***; presidential elector, Greenback Party, 1884; Union Labor Party candidate for gov. of OH, 1887; Permanent chm., Union Labor Party National Convention, 1888; ***candidate for Union Labor Party nomination to presidency of the U.S., 1888 (declined)***; People's Party candidate for gov. of OH, 1891. BUS. & PROF.: farmer, Eden Township, OH. MISC.: known as the "Watchdog of the OH State Treasury." RES.: Tiffin, OH.

SELL, DANNY PAGE. b. Jan 25, 1946, Dayton, OH; par. Simon K. and Martha Emily Sell; m. Margarette Reed; c. Gary (adopted); Wilma (adopted); Wanda (adopted); Diana (adopted); Rick (adopted); Darrell (adopted); Paul (adopted). EDUC.: high school. POLIT. & GOV.: ***Common American Party candidate for presidency of the U.S., 1976***. BUS. & PROF.: pres., Lakeside Village, Inc. REL.: Bapt. MAILING ADDRESS: Box 69-140844, London, OH 43140.

SELWA, ROBERT ALLEN MARK. b. Sep 30, 1957; par. Frank and Carmeline (Pitruzzello) Selwa; single. EDUC.: B.A., U. of MI; Rudolf Steiner Inst. of Anthroposophy, 10 years. POLIT. & GOV.: ***Federalist Party candidate for presidency of the U.S., 1992***. BUS. & PROF.: self-employed, 1986–; founder, Selwa Corp., Inc., 1991–. MEM.: General Anthroposophical Soc.; Detroit Zoological Soc.; Detroit Inst. of Arts. WRITINGS: *The Purpose of Religion*; *Democracy and the Republic*; *A Treatise on the Development of a World Economy*. REL.: R.C. MAILING ADDRESS: 20919 Ardmore Park Dr., St. Clair Shores, MI 48081.

SEMENSI, JOHN JOSEPH. POLIT. & GOV.: ***candidate for Democratic nomination to presidency of the U.S., 1980***. MAILING ADDRESS: 664 North St., Randolph, MA 02368.

SENKO, GEORGE MICHAEL. POLIT. & GOV.: ***independent candidate for presidency of the U.S., 1988***. MAILING ADDRESS: 5625 North Buffwood Place, Agoura Hills, CA 91301.

SERGEANT, JOHN. b. Dec 5, 1779, Philadelphia, PA; d. Nov 23, 1852, Philadelphia, PA; par. Jonathan Dickinson and Margaret (Spencer) Sergeant; m. Margaretta Watmough, Jun 23, 1813; c. ten. EDUC.: U. of PA; grad., Princeton Coll., 1795; studied law under Jared Ingersoll (q.v.). POLIT. & GOV.: appointed deputy atty. gen. of PA, 1800; appointed PA Commissioner of Bankruptcy, 1801; elected as a Federalist to PA State House, 1808–10; elected as a Federalist to U.S. House (PA), 1815–23, 1827–29, 1837–41; appointed pres., PA State Board of Canal Commissioners, 1825; appointed U.S. Envoy to Panama Congress, 1826; Federalist candidate for U.S. House (PA), 1828; ***National Republican Party candidate for vice presidency of the U.S., 1832***; National Republican Party candidate for U.S. House (PA), 1833; pres., PA State Constitutional Convention, 1838; ***candidate for Whig Party nomination to presidency of the U.S., 1840, 1848***; appointed U.S. minister to England, 1841 (declined); ***candidate for Whig Party nomination to vice presidency of the U.S., 1844; Whig Party candidate for presidency of the U.S., 1852***. BUS. & PROF.: atty.; admitted to PA Bar, 1799; law practice, Philadelphia, PA, 1799–1849. MEM.: Apprentice's Library (pres.); House of Refuge (pres.). HON. DEG.: LL.D., Dickinson Coll., 1826; LL.D., Harvard U., 1844. WRITINGS: *Select Speeches of John Sergeant of PA* (1832). RES.: Philadelphia, PA.

SERRETTE, DENNIS L. b. 1940. POLIT. & GOV.: delegate, National Black Political Assembly, 1972; joined independent Alliance, 1982; ***independent Alliance Party candidate for presidency of the U.S., 1984***; resigned from New Alliance Party, 1985; campaign mgr., Ron Daniels (q.v.) for President, 1992. BUS. & PROF.: phone technician; union organizer. MEM.: Communications Workers of America; Rainbow Coalition. WRITINGS: "The Making of a Revolutionary," *Practice*, spring, 1984; "Inside the New Alliance Party aka Rainbow alliance aka Rainbow Lobby aka the Organization aka," *Radical America*, Mar 1989. MAILING ADDRESS: Washington, DC.

SETTLE, THOMAS. b. Jan 23, 1831, Rockingham, NC; d. Dec 1, 1888; par. Thomas and Mary Henrietta (Graves) Settle; m. Mary Glenn, c. 1854; c. Thomas; two other sons; six daughters. EDUC.: grad., U. of NC, 1850; studied law under Judge Richmond M. Pearson. POLIT. & GOV.: pvt. sec. to Gov. David S. Reid of NC; elected as a Democrat to NC State House of Commons, 1854–59 (Speaker, 1858–59); presidential elector, Democratic Party, 1856; elected solicitor, Fourth Judicial District, NC, 1861–62; delegate, NC State Constitutional Convention, 1865; delegate, Johnson Convention, 1865; elected as a Republican to NC State Senate, 1865 (Speaker); elected assoc. justice, NC State Supreme Court, 1868–71, 1873–76; appointed U.S. minister to Peru, 1871–72; chm., Rep. Nat'l. Conv., 1872; Republican candidate for U.S. House (NC), 1872; Republican candidate for gov. of NC, 1876; appointed U.S. District judge for FL, 1877–88; ***candidate for Republican nomination to vice presidency of the U.S., 1880***. BUS. & PROF.: atty.; admitted to NC Bar, 1854. MIL.: capt., Third NC Regt., C.S.A., 1861. RES.: Wilmington, NC.

SEWALL, ARTHUR. b. Nov 25, 1835, Bath, ME; d. Sep 5, 1900, Small Point, ME; par. William Dunning and Rachel Allyn (Trufant) Sewall; m. Emma Duncan Crooker, Mar 29, 1859; c. William D.; Demmer; Harold Marsh. EDUC.: public schools, Bath, ME. POLIT. & GOV.: elected member, Board of Aldermen, Bath, ME, 1876–77; delegate, Dem. Nat'l. Conv., 1880, 1896; member, Dem. Nat'l. Cmte., 1888–96; Democratic candidate for U.S. Senate (ME), 1893; ***Democratic candidate for vice presidency of the U.S., 1896; Silver Party candidate for vice presidency of the U.S., 1896; candidate for People's Party nomination to vice presidency of the U.S., 1896***. BUS. & PROF.: shipbuilder; industrialist; apprentice, shipyards; partner, E. and A. Sewall (shipbuilders), 1854–1900, pres., 1879–1900; owner, Arthur Sewall and Co.; dir., Maine Central R.R., 1875–84, pres., 1884–93; pres., Bath National Bank; dir., Mexican Central and Sonora Railway; pres., Fourth National Bank of Maine; pres., Portland, Mount Desert and Machias Steamboat Co.; pres., Eastern R.R.; dir., Boston and Maine R.R.; dir., New York and New England R.R.; dir., Portland and Rochester R.R.; dir., Atchison, Topeka and Santa Fe R.R.; pres., Poland Paper Co., to 1893. MEM.: Sagadahock Club; Masons (Dunlap commandery; Knights Templar). REL.: Swedenborgian. RES.: Bath, ME.

SEWARD, WILLIAM HENRY. b. May 16, 1801, FL, NY; d. Oct 10, 1872, Auburn, NY; par. Dr. Samuel S. and Mary (Jennings) Seward; m. Frances Miller, Oct 10, 1824; c. Augustus Henry; Frederick William; Cornelia; William Henry,

Jr.; Fanny; Olive Risley (adopted). EDUC.: grad., Union Coll., 1820; studied law. POLIT. & GOV.: elected as an Anti-Mason to NY State Senate, 1830–34; Anti-Masonic Party candidate for NY State Senate, 1833; Whig Party candidate for gov. of NY, 1834; elected as a Whig to gov. of NY, 1838–42; elected as a Whig to U.S. Senate (NY), 1849–55, as a Republican, 1855–61; ***candidate for Republican nomination to presidency of the U.S., 1856, 1860***; appointed U.S. sec. of state, 1861–69. BUS. & PROF.: teacher, 1819–20; atty.; admitted to NY Bar, 1822; law practice, Auburn, NY; Agent, Holland Co. HON. DEG.: LL.D., Yale U., 1854. WRITINGS: *Travels Around the World* (1873); *Autobiography of William H. Seward, from 1801 to 1834, with a Memoir of His Life and Selections from His Letters, from 1831 to 1846* (1877). REL.: Episc. MISC.: noted for negotiating purchase of AK ("Seward's Folly") from Russia, 1867; target of assassination plot, 1865. RES.: Auburn, NY.

SEYMOUR, HORATIO. b. May 31, 1810, Pompey Hill, NY; d. Feb 12, 1886, Deerfield Hills, NY; par. Henry and Mary Ledyard (Forman) Seymour; m. Mary Bleecker, May 31, 1835; c. none. EDUC.: Oxford Acad.; Geneva Acad.; Patridge's Military School; studied law under Green C. Bronson and Samuel Beardsley. POLIT. & GOV.: appointed military sec. to Gov. William L. Marcy (NY), 1833–39; elected as a Democrat to NY State Assembly, 1841–42, 1844–45 (Speaker, 1845); elected as a Democrat, mayor of Utica, NY, 1842; Democratic candidate for mayor of Utica, NY, 1843; Democratic candidate for gov. of NY, 1850, 1854, 1864, 1876 (declined); elected as a Democrat to gov. of NY, 1852–54, 1862–64; ***candidate for Democratic nomination to presidency of the U.S., 1860, 1864, 1880***; chm., NY State Democratic Convention, 1867, 1868; chm., Dem. Nat'l. Conv., 1864, 1868; ***Democratic candidate for presidency of the U.S., 1868***; candidate for Democratic nomination to U.S. Senate (NY), 1875 (declined); presidential elector, Democratic Party, 1876; candidate for Democratic nomination to gov. of NY, 1879. BUS. & PROF.: atty.; admitted to NY Bar, 1832; businessman. MEM.: National Dairymen's Assn. (pres., 1875); Prison Assn. of the U.S. (pres.). HON. DEG.: LL.D., Hamilton Coll., 1858. WRITINGS: *A Lecture on the Topography and History of New York* (1856). REL.: Episc. MISC.: associated with Hunker faction in NY Democratic Party; instrumental in expulsion of William March Tweed from NY Democratic Party organization; opponent of prohibition and abolition. RES.: Utica, NY.

SEYMOUR, THOMAS HART. b. Sep 29, 1807, Hartford, CT; d. Sep 3, 1868, Hartford, CT; par. Henry and Jane (Ellery) Seymour; single. EDUC.: grad., Partridge's Military Acad., 1829; studied law. POLIT. & GOV.: elected as a Democrat to probate judge, Hartford (CT) Judicial District, 1836–38; Democratic candidate for U.S. House (CT), 1841, 1844 (declined); clerk, Superior Court of CT, 1842; elected as a Democrat to U.S. House (CT), 1843–45; Democratic candidate for gov. of CT, 1849, 1863; elected as a Democrat to gov. of CT, 1850–53; presidential elector, Democratic Party, 1852; appointed U.S. minister to Russia, 1853–58; ***candidate for Democratic nomination to presidency of the U.S., 1864, 1868***. BUS. & PROF.: atty.; admitted to CT Bar, 1833; ed., *The Jeffersonian*, 1837–38. MIL.: commander, Hartford (CT) Light Guard, 1837–41; commissioned maj., CT Volunteers, 1847; commissioned maj., 9th Infantry, U.S. Army, 1847; lt. col., 12th Infantry, 1847, brev. col., 1847. MEM.: Masons (Washington commandery; eminent commander). RES.: Hartford, CT.

SHACKELFORD, RUFUS E. m. Norma B. S.; c. five. POLIT. & GOV.: member, National Cmte., American Party (chm., 1979); ***American Party candidate for vice presidency of the U.S., 1976***; national chm., Constitution Party, 1979–. BUS. & PROF.: tomato farmer, FL, TX, and CA; rancher. MIL.: U.S. Army, WWII. MEM.: American Education League (dir.); Young Americans for Freedom (vice pres.). AWARDS: award, Congress of Freedom, 5 times. REL.: Christian. MAILING ADDRESS: 104 Inglis Way, Wauchula, FL 33873.

SHAFER, RAYMOND PHILIP. b. Mar 5, 1917, New Castle, PA; par. David Philip and Mina Belle (Miller) Shafer; m. Jane Harris Davies, Jul 5, 1941; c. Diana Elizabeth (Mrs. Ian C. Strachan); Raymond Philip, Jr.; Jane Ellen. EDUC.: A.B. (cum laude), Allegheny Coll., 1938; LL.B., Yale U., 1941. POLIT. & GOV.: elected as a Republican, district atty., Crawford Cty., PA, 1948–56; elected as a Republican to PA State Senate, 1959–63 (pres.); elected as a Republican to lt. gov. of PA, 1963–67; delegate, Rep. Nat'l. Conv., 1964, 1968, 1972, 1976; elected as a Republican to gov. of PA, 1967–71; ***candidate for Republican nomination to presidency of the U.S., 1968***; appointed member, Advisory Comm. on Intergovernmental Relations, 1968; appointed chm., National Comm. on Marijuana and Drug Use, 1971; appointed counselor to the vice presidency of the U.S., 1975–77. BUS. & PROF.: atty.; admitted to NY Bar; admitted to PA Bar; assoc., Winthrop, Stimson, Putnam and Roberts (law firm), New York, NY; law practice, Meadville, PA, 1945–63; counsel, Walker, Shafer, Dornhaffer, Swick and Bailey (law firm); visiting prof., U. of PA, 1973–; chm., TelePrompter Corp., New York, NY. MIL.: commander, U.S. Navy, 1942–45; Bronze Star; Purple Heart; Philippine Liberation Medal. MEM.: Grange; Rotary Club; American Legion; VFW; Allegheny Coll. (chm., board of trustees); ABA; PA Bar Assn.; Crawford Cty. Bar Assn. (pres., 1961–63); Phi Beta Kappa; Phi Kappa Psi; Masons (33°); PA United Fund (trustee); PA Heart Fund (chm.); Cancer Crusade (chm.); BSA (trustee); PA Hospital Assn. (trustee); Republican Governors' Assn. (vice chm., 1969; chm., 1970); Yale Moot Court; Yale Barristers' Union. AWARDS: Gold Medal Award, Soc. of the Family of Man, 1972. HON. DEG.: LL.D., Allegheny Coll., 1963. REL.: Presb. MAILING ADDRESS: 485 Chestnut St., Meadville, PA 16335.

SHAKER, MITCHELL FRANCIS. b. Jan 3, 1922, Niles, OH; par. Isaac and Sophia (Joseph) Shaker; m. Mary

K. Christopher, 1945; c. Mary Alice Weiss; Margaret Ann; Mitchell Francis, Jr.; Kathryn T. Earnhart; Thomas J.; Patricia L.; Christopher J.; Robert I. EDUC.: B.A. (magna cum laude), John Carroll U., 1945; J.D., Western Reserve U., 1948. POLIT. & GOV.: law dir., Niles, OH, 1950–55, 1962–63, 1966–79; exec. sec., Trumbull Cty. (OH) Democratic Central Cmte., 1963–; member, Board of Elections, Trumbull Cty., OH, 1966–67; ***candidate for Democratic nomination to presidency of the U.S., 1976***. BUS. & PROF.: atty.; admitted to OH Bar, 1948; law practice, Niles, OH, 1948–. MIL.: midshipman, lt. (jg), U.S. Navy, 1943–45. MEM.: Alpha Sigma Nu; Order of the Coif; Delta Theta Phi; American Legion; Knights of Columbus; Elks. REL.: R.C. MAILING ADDRESS: 403 Hogarth Ave., Niles, OH 44446.

SHANNON, DONALD JOSEPH. POLIT. & GOV.: ***independent candidate for presidency of the U.S., 1976***. MAILING ADDRESS: 2646 Park St., Camelot Hotel, Detroit, MI.

SHANNON, HOWARD ALAN. b. Aug 31, 1949, Arcata, CA; par. Grant Arthur and Katherine Mary (Bugenig) Ramey; m. Debi (divorced); c. Jamon Christopher; Dawn Marie. EDUC.: Elementary Schools, McKinleyville, CA; grad., McKinleyville (CA) H.S., 1967; A.A., Coll. of the Redwoods, 1974. POLIT. & GOV.: ***candidate for American Independent Party nomination to presidency of the U.S., 1972***. BUS. & PROF.: mill worker, Ramey Lath, Arcata, CA. MIL.: s/sgt., U.S. Air Force. MEM.: Dows Prairie Grange; 4-H Club; VFW (chaplain, Thomas De Vore Post #2481, Blue Lake, CA). REL.: R.C. MAILING ADDRESS: 208-A Hamilton St., Fairfield, CA.

SHAPIRO, HENRY A. POLIT. & GOV.: ***independent candidate for presidency of the U.S., 1988***; "Reform" candidate. MAILING ADDRESS: 265 Quentin Rd., Brooklyn, NY 11223.

SHAPP, MILTON JERROLD. b. Jun 25, 1912, Cleveland, OH; d. Nov 24, 1994, Wynnewood, PA; par. Aaron Shapiro and Eva (Smelsey) Shapp; m. Muriel Matzkin, May 19, 1947; c. Dolores (Mrs. Gary Graham); Richard; Joanne. EDUC.: B.S., Case Inst. of Technology, 1933. POLIT. & GOV.: consultant, Peace Corps, 1961–63; consultant, U.S. Dept., 1961–63; appointed vice chm., National Public Advisory Cmte. on Area Redevelopment, 1961–64; chm., Philadelphia Peace Corps Service Organization; chm., Manpower Utilization Comm., Philadelphia, PA; appointed member, Governor's Cmte. of 100 for Better Education; Democratic candidate for gov. of PA, 1966; delegate, Dem. Nat'l. Conv., 1968, 1972, 1976; elected as a Democrat to gov. of PA, 1971–79; ***candidate for Democratic nomination to presidency of the U.S., 1976***. BUS. & PROF.: pres., Jerrold Corp., Philadelphia, PA, 1947–66; pres., Shapp Corp., 1967–. MIL.: capt., U.S. Army, 1942–46. MEM.: Jewish Community Relations Council; American Jewish Council; United World Federalists; Jewish War Veterans; B'nai B'rith; PA Democratic Study Cmte. (chm., 1971–); Tau Beta Pi; Sigma Alpha Mu. AWARDS: Humanitarian Award, National Business League, 1962; Good Citizenship Award, PA AFL-CIO, 1963; Alumni Award, Case Inst. of Technology, 1963; William Penn Lodge Youth Award, 1964; Reuben J. Miller Youth Award, B'nai B'rith, 1964; B'nai B'rith Youth Service Award, 1965; Humanitarian Award, PA State Baptist Convention, 1966; Humanitarian Award, Anti-Defamation League of B'nai B'rith, 1973; Distinguished Service Award, Centurion Junior C. of C., 1973; "Man of the Year" Award, PA Assn. of Broadcasters, 1975. WRITINGS: *The Shapp Report* (1965); *New Growth, New Jobs for Pennsylvania*. REL.: Jewish. RES: Wynnewood, PA.

SHARGAL, SUSAN K. Y. EDUC.: Ph.D. POLIT. & GOV.: ***Bridge Party candidate for presidency of the U.S., 1988; candidate for Democratic nomination to vice presidency of the U.S., 1992***. BUS. & PROF.: clinical psychologist. MAILING ADDRESS: 306 Chester Rd., Auburn, NH 03032.

SHARKEY, WILLIAM LEWIS. b. Jul 12, 1798, Mussel Shoals, TN; d. Apr 29, 1873, Washington, DC; par. Patrick and Mrs. (Rhodes) Sharkey; m. Minerva (Hyland) Wren. EDUC.: public schools, Greenville, TN; studied law. POLIT. & GOV.: elected to MS State House, 1828–29; National Republican Party candidate for U.S. House (MS), 1831; elected chief justice, MS High Court of Errors and Appeals, 1832–50; pres., Southern States Convention, 1850; appointed U.S. consul to Cuba, 1851 (declined); appointed U.S. sec. of war, 1851 (declined); appointed Commissioner of MS Code Revision, 1857; ***candidate for Constitutional Union Party nomination to presidency of the U.S., 1860***; appointed MS Peace Commissioner, 1865; appointed provisional gov. of MS, 1865; elected to U.S. Senate (MS), but not seated, 1866. BUS. & PROF.: atty.; admitted to MS Bar, 1822; law practice, Jackson, MS, 1850. MEM.: U. of MS (trustee, 1844–65); Masons. RES.: MS.

SHAW, CARROLL S. POLIT. & GOV.: ***candidate for Democratic nomination to presidency of the U.S., 1952***. BUS. & PROF.: electrician; ed., *Free Press*, Hollywood, FL. MAILING ADDRESS: Hollywood, FL.

SHAW, EDWARD WALTER. b. Jul 13, 1923, Lake Cty., IL; m. Rita Roth, Mar 2, 1949; c. two. EDUC.: grad., high school, 1941; Armour Coll. of Engineering; IL Inst. of Technology. POLIT. & GOV.: Socialist Workers Party candidate for U.S. Senate (MI), 1954; national organizer, Socialist Workers Party, 1964–; ***Socialist Workers Party candidate for vice presidency of the U.S., 1964***. BUS. & PROF.: auto worker; printer; stationary engineer (steam power plants); political activist.

MIL.: Merchant Marine, 1942–48. MEM.: International Typographers Union; other labor unions. REL.: none. MAILING ADDRESS: 215 Audubon Ave., New York, NY.

SHAW, LESLIE MORTIMER. b. Nov 2, 1848, Morristown, VT; d. Mar 28, 1932, Washington, DC; par. Boardman Osias and Lovisa Warren (Spaulding) Shaw; m. Alice Crawshaw, Dec 6, 1877; c. Enid Nell (Mrs. John Milton McMillin); Earl Boardman; Erma Lovisa. EDUC.: B.S., Cornell Coll., 1874, M.S.; LL.B., IA Coll. of Law, 1876. POLIT. & GOV.: elected pres., School board, Denison, IA; elected as a Republican to gov. of IA, 1898–1902; Permanent chm., International Monetary Convention, 1898; appointed U.S. sec. of the treasury, 1902–07; ***candidate for Republican nomination to presidency of the U.S., 1908***. BUS. & PROF.: schoolteacher; atty.; partner, Shaw and Kuehnle (law firm), Denison, IA, 1876–97; pres., Banks in Denison, Manilla, and Charter Oak, IA, 1880; lecturer; author; pres., Carnegie Trust Co., New York, NY, 1907–08; pres., First Mortgage Guarantee and Trust Co., Philadelphia, PA, 1909–13; dir., Cities Service Co., 1908. HON. DEG.: LL.D., Simpson Coll., 1898; LL.D., Cornell Coll., 1899; LL.D., Wesleyan U., 1904; LL.D., Dickinson Coll., 1908. WRITINGS: *Current Issues* (1908); *Vanishing Landmarks, The Trend Toward Bolshevism* (1919). REL.: Methodist Episc. Church (delegate, gen. conference, 1888, 1892, 1896, 1900). RES.: New York, NY.

SHAW, MARK REVELL SADLER. b. Jan 22, 1889, Grand Rapids, MI; par. Solomon Benjamin and Etta Ellen (Sadler) Shaw; m. Alma Bowyer Cox Dodds, Jun 17, 1920; c. Mark Dodds. EDUC.: grad., Jefferson H.S., Chicago, IL, 1907; Taylor U.; B.A., OH Wesleyan U., 1913, M.A., 1916; S.T.B., Boston U. School of Theology, 1920. POLIT. & GOV.: member, MA State Prohibition Cmte., 1916–20; Prohibition Party candidate for U.S. Senate (MA), 1946, 1952, 1958, 1960, 1962, 1966, 1970; Prohibition Party candidate for gov. of MA, 1948, 1950, 1956; state chm., MA Prohibition Party, 1954–73; member, exec. cmte., Prohibition Party National Cmte., 1946–73 (vice chm.); ***candidate for Prohibition Party nomination to presidency of the U.S., 1964, 1968, 1972; Prohibition Party candidate for vice presidency of the U.S., 1964; candidate for Prohibition Party nomination to vice presidency of the U.S., 1968***. BUS. & PROF.: field adviser, Intercollegiate Prohibition Assn., 1914–16, sec., Eastern District, 1917–20, assoc. gen. sec., 1920–22, adviser to Japan Temperance League and Japan Intercollegiate Prohibition League; ordained minister, Methodist Episcopal Church, 1919; ed., *Intercollegiate Statesman*, 1920–22; methodist missionary to Japan, 1922–27; assoc. sec., Cmte. on Temperance and Social Welfare, Japan Methodist Church, 1924; pastor, Methodist Church, Holliston, MA, 1927–31; pastor, First Congregational Church, Holliston, MA, 1931–37; New England sec., National Council for Prevention of War, 1937–58; assoc. minister, Cliftondale Methodist Church, Saugus, MA, 1958–73; ed., *Peace Action* (monthly), 1955–63. MEM.: Phi Beta Kappa; Delta Sigma Rho; MA Temperance League (dir.); Foundation for Alcohol Education; Japan National Christian Council; Japan Intercollegiate Prohibition League; OH Intercollegiate Prohibition Assn. (pres., 1912); U.S. War Prohibition Conservation Cmte. (1917–18); United Cmte. on War Temperance Activities in the Army and Navy (1917–18); National Temperance Council (1916; exec. cmte., 1920–22); World League Against Alcoholism (permanent international cmte.; gen. Council, 1920–21; delegate, International Congress, 1927); National Temperance League of Japan (counselor, 1922); Fellowship of Reconciliation (national council, 1917–73); Inst. of Pacific Relations; America-Japan Soc.; Japan National Council of Churches; Foreign Policy Assn.; U.N. Assn.; American Council; Asiatic Soc.; Pan Pacific Club; Churchmen's League for Civic Welfare; Consultative Peace Council; Church and World Order Conference (delegate, 1940, 1942, 1945, 1949). REL.: United Methodist Church (Board of Temperance, Prohibition and Public Morals). RES.: Melrose, MA.

SHAW, STACIE DIANE. b. Jan 17, 1962, Portland, OR; d. Howard A. and Shirley M. (Young) S.; single. EDUC.: Hillcrest Elementary School; Horace Mann Elementary School; Mount Fort Junior H.S.; Ben Lomond H.S. POLIT. & GOV.: ***candidate for Democratic nomination to presidency of the U.S., 1980***. BUS. & PROF.: student; employee, Lorin Farr Amusement Park, 1979. MEM.: Key Club. AWARDS: Sterling Scholar for Social Studies. REL.: Protestant. MAILING ADDRESS: 990 Taylor Ave., Ogden, UT 84404.

SHEA, GEORGE J. POLIT. & GOV.: presidential elector, American Independent Party, 1972; CA state chm., American Independent Party, 1976; ***candidate for American Independent Party nomination to presidency of the U.S., 1976***; won CA American Independent Party presidential primary, 1976. MAILING ADDRESS: 27286 Crest Dr., Highland, CA 92346.

SHEARER, EILEEN M. KNOWLAND. b. 1921, Detroit, MI; d. D. F. and Violet Knowland; m. William K. Shearer; c. Nancy; three others. EDUC.: public schools, Minneapolis, MN; McPhail School of Music. POLIT. & GOV.: staff, CA Legislative Assembly, 1963–65; founder, American Independent Party, 1967; member, exec. cmte., CA American Independent Party; member, San Diego Cty. (CA) American Independent Party Central Cmte.; presidential elector, American Independent Party, 1972; member, American Independent Party National Cmte., 1973–; ***candidate for American Independent Party nomination to vice presidency of the U.S., 1976 (declined); American Independent Party candidate for vice presidency of the U.S., 1980***; national campaign consultant, Populist Party, 1984. BUS. & PROF.: realtor, Tarbell Realtors; partner, Banner Advertising (political consultants), 1963–; columnist;

copublisher, advertising mgr., Weekly Newspapers, San Diego, CA. MEM.: American Independent Women's Organization (pres.); National Assn. of Realtors; CA Assn. of Realtors; San Diego Bar Assn. Auxiliary. MAILING ADDRESS: 8158 Palm St., Lemon Grove, CA 92045.

SHECHAN, MARY ANN ELIZABETH. POLIT. & GOV.: ***independent candidate for presidency of the U.S., 1992***. MAILING ADDRESS: 414 East Pearl Ave., Stockton, CA 95207.

SHEEN, DANIEL ROBINSON. b. Nov 29, 1852, Radnor, IL; d. Apr 23, 1926, Peoria, IL; par. Peter and Melissa (Robinson) Sheen; m. Sarah A. Stiehl, Jun 28, 1876; c. Robert. EDUC.: IL Normal School, Peoria, IL; Brown's Business Coll.; studied law in offices of Ingersoll, Puterbaugh Brothers, and McCune, Peoria, IL, 1872–73. POLIT. & GOV.: Left Democratic Party and joined Prohibition Party, 1876; Prohibition Party candidate for U.S. House (IL), 1896; member, IL State Prohibition Party Cmte.; delegate, Prohibition Party National Convention, various times; elected as a Prohibitionist to IL State House, 1905–07; independent (Prohibition) candidate for mayor of Peoria, IL, 1907; Prohibition Party candidate for U.S. Senate (IL), 1907; Prohibition Party candidate for gov. of IL, 1908; ***candidate for Prohibition Party nomination to presidency of the U.S., 1908***. BUS. & PROF.: atty.; admitted to IL Bar, 1874; law practice, Peoria, IL, 1874–1926; partner (with Thomas Black), law firm, Peoria, IL; partner (with M. C. Quinn), law firm, Peoria, IL, to 1885; partner (with R. H. Lovett), law firm, Peoria, IL, 1885–93; partner (with Frank T. Miller), law firm, Peoria, IL; partner, Sheen and David (law firm), Peoria, IL, to 1912; partner, Sheen and Galbraith (law firm), Peoria, IL, 1912–26. MEM.: Peoria Bar Assn.; IL Bar Assn.; Independent Order of Good Templars. WRITINGS: *Location of Fort Creve Couer* (1919). REL.: Christian. RES.: Peoria, IL.

SHELDON, CHARLES MONROE. b. Feb 26, 1857, Wellsville, NY; d. Feb 24, 1946, Topeka, KS; par. Stewart and Sarah (Ward) Sheldon; m. Marry Abby Merriam, May 20, 1891; c. Merriam Ward. EDUC.: grad., Phillips Acad., 1879; A.B., Brown U., 1883, D.D., 1923; B.D., Andover Theological Seminary, 1886; D.D., Temple Coll., 1898; D.D., Washburn Coll., 1900. POLIT. & GOV.: ***candidate for United Christian Party nomination to presidency of the U.S., 1900; United Christian Party candidate for vice presidency of the U.S., 1900 (declined)***; United Christian Party candidate for U.S. Senate (IA), 1900. BUS. & PROF.: minister; ordained, Congregational Church, 1886; pastor, Waterbury, VT, 1886–88; pastor, Central Congregational Church, Topeka, KS, 1889–1911, 1916–19; prohibition advocate, 1912–15; editor-in-chief, *Christian Herald*, 1920–25, contributing ed., 1925–46; ed., *Topeka (KS) Capital*, 1900; author. MEM.: KS State Temperance Union (exec. cmte.); Flying Squadron of American (1915–16). WRITINGS: *Richard Bruce* (1891); *Robert Hardy's Seven Days* (1892); *The Twentieth Door* (1893); *The Crucifixion of Philip Strong* (1893); *John King's Question Class* (1894); *His Brother's Keeper* (1895); *One Hundred and One Poems of the Day* (ed., 1896); *In His Steps* (1896); *Malcolm Kirk* (1897); *Lend a Hand* (1897); *The Redemption of Freetown* (1898); *The Miracle at Markham* (1898); *One of the Two* (1898); *For Christ and the Church* (1899); *Edward Blake* (1899); *Born to Serve* (1900); *Who Killed Joe's Baby* (1901); *The Wheels of the Machine* (1901); *The Reformer* (1902); *The Narrow Gate* (1902); *The Heart of the World* (1905); *Paul Douglas; The Good Fight; A Sheldon Year Book* (1909); *The High Calling* (ed., 1911); *The War Ship Builders* (ed., 1912); *Jesus Is Here* (ed., 1913); *Howard Chase* (1917); *A Little Book for Every Day* (1917); *All the World* (1918); *Heart Stories* (1920); *In His Steps Today* (1921); *The Richest Man in Kansas* (1921); *Dramatic Version of In His Steps* (1923); *The Everyday Bible* (ed., 1924); *The Happiest Day of My Life* (1925); *Two Old Friends* (1925); *Charles M. Sheldon: His Life and Story* (1925); *The Thirteenth Resolution* (ed., 1928); *Let's Talk It Over* (ed., 1929); *The Treasure Book* (ed., 1930); *He Is Here* (ed., 1931); *The Marks of a Christian* (ed., 1935); *A Vote on War* (ed., 1935); *All Over Forty* (ed., 1935); *The Ministers' Strike* (ed., 1941); *The Scrap Book* (ed., 1942). REL.: Congregationalist. RES.: Topeka, KS.

SHELDON, GEORGE LAWSON. b. May 31, 1870, Nehawka, NE; d. Apr 5, 1960, Jackson, MS; par. Lawson and Julia Ann (Pollard) Sheldon; m. Rose Higgins, Sep 4, 1895; c. George Lawson, Jr.; Mary Ellen Higgins; (Mrs. Gordon Lester House); Anson Hoisington; Julia Ann Pollard (Mrs. George Urquart Griffin). EDUC.: B.L., U. of NE, 1892; A.B., Harvard U., 1893. POLIT. & GOV.: elected treas., Nehawka (NE) School Board, 1894–1904; elected as a Republican to NE State Senate, 1903–07; elected as a Republican to gov. of NE, 1907–09; delegate, Rep. Nat'l. Conv., 1908; ***candidate for Republican nomination to vice presidency of the U.S., 1908***; Republican candidate for gov. of NE, 1908; chm., MS Republican Party; elected sec.-treas., Consolidated School, Avon, MS, 1919–22; elected as a Republican to MS State House, 1920–24; Republican candidate for U.S. Senate (MS), 19??; appointed Collector of Internal Revenue, MS, 1930–35; Republican candidate for gov. of MS, 1947. BUS. & PROF.: farmer; cattle rancher, Nehawka, NE, to 1909; pres., Nehawka (NE) Bank; plantation owner, Washington Cty., MS. MIL.: capt., Company B, Third NE Infantry, 1898. MEM.: Masons (Shriners; Knights Templar); Woodmen of the World; Odd Fellows; Federal Farm Loan Assn. of WA Cty., MS (sec.-treas., 1920–26). HON. DEG.: LL.D., Hastings Coll., 1908. REL.: Episc. RES.: Nehawka, NE.

SHELLEY, MARGARET REBECCA. b. 1887, Sugar Valley, PA; d. Jan 21, 1984, Battle Creek, MI; m. Felix Rathmer, 1922; c. none. EDUC.: grad., U. of MI, 1910. POLIT. & GOV.: ***Peace Party candidate for vice presidency of the U.S., 1964***. BUS. & PROF.: teacher of German, high school, Freeport, IL; teacher, WA and WI; ed., *Agricultural Journal*, Battle Creek, MI, c. 1919; ed., *Modern Poultry Breeder's Magazine*, Battle Creek, MI, 1920–27; farmer, "Peaceways," Battle Creek, MI; ed., Fellowship of Reconciliation Newsletter, MI, 1958; peace activist. MEM.: Ford Peace Ship Expedition (1915); International Congress of Women (delegate, 1915); American Neutral Conference Cmte. (1916); Emergency Peace Federation; People's Council of America; Fellowship of Reconciliation; Women's International League for Peace and Freedom (founder); Phi Beta Kappa; Women's Strike for Peace; World Conference on Vietnam (1967); Peaceways Foundation (founder); First American Conference for Democracy and Terms of Peace (founder); Greenwood Non-Violent Community. AWARDS: International Women's Year Citation, U. of MI, 1967; MI International Citizen Award, 1979; George Award, *Battle Creek (MI) Enquirer*, 1981. WRITINGS: "Bicentennial Prayer for Peace" (poem); "Many Voices" (poem); A Widow's Mite; Je M'Accuse; In Mourning for the War Dead; others. REL.: Mennonite. MISC.: known as the "Voice of America's Conscience"; lost American citizenship in 1922 due to marriage to German national; citizenship restored after protracted legal battle, 1944. RES.: Battle Creek, MI.

SHELLHOUSE, EDWIN JAMES, JR. par. Edwin James Shellhouse, Sr. POLIT. & GOV.: ***candidate for Democratic nomination to presidency of the U.S., 1980***. MAILING ADDRESS: 353 South Wells Ave., Reno, NV 89502.

SHELTON, FRANK WINFRED. b. Feb 2, 1907, Independence, KS; d. Nov 28, 1983, Cherryvale, KS; par. Dr. Frank Winfred and Dr. Violetta (Gilman) Shelton; m. Jean Crain, 1929; m. 2d, Katherine Jasko, 1960; m. 3d, Gayleen Truman; c. Frank Winfred III; Kersten Knox; Gretl Gilman. EDUC.: grad., Independence (KS) H.S., 1924; A.B., U. of Cincinnati, 1928; LL.B., Franklin U., 1941; J.D., Capital U., 1966. POLIT. & GOV.: appointed member, OH State Highway Recodification Comm.; vice chm., OH State Housing Board; chm., OH Rural Zoning Comm., 1947–51; chm., Hanover Township (NJ) Sewerage authority, 1961–66; delegate, KS State Republican Convention, 1976; area finance chm., Citizens for Reagan, 1976; American Party of KS candidate for gov. of KS, 1978, 1982; ***American Party of KS candidate for presidency of the U.S., 1980***; national chm. pro tempore, Constitution Party, 1980–. BUS. & PROF.: farmer, MA; farmer, Cleveland, OH; instructor in Embryology and Comparative Anatomy, U. of Cincinnati; owner, Shelton Flying Service, Cincinnati, OH, 1932; engineer, OH State Dept. of Highways, 1933–41; Registered Professional Engineer (OH), 1937; publisher, ed., *The State Employee*, Cincinnati, OH, 1937–38; atty.; asst. div. atty., labor lawyer, asst. to the gen. mgr., information mgr., American Telephone and Telegraph Co., to 1967; staff, Bell System Exec. Conference, 1954–55; engineer of consultant contracts, OH State Dir. of Highways, 1967–70; exec. dir., OH Transportation Research Center, 1970–71, dir. emeritus, 1971–84; rancher, Mound Valley, KS; orchardist; rancher, Cherryvale, KS. MEM.: Delta Tau Delta; Pi Delta Epsilon; Order of the Curia; OH State Bar Assn.; Federal District Bar Assn.; Bar of the Supreme Court of the U.S.; SAR; KS Livestock Assn. (Taxation and Legislative Committees); American Assn. of Retired Persons (pres., Chapter 1999); OH Civil Service Employees Assn. (charter member, 1937); Young Patriots for Freedom (chm. of the board); OH Highway Employees Credit Union (dir.; atty.); Bowling Green State U. (advisory cmte. on technology); U. of Cincinnati (exec. cmte., board of consultants, The Herman Schneider Laboratory of Basic and Applied Science Research); OH Soc. of Professional Engineers (counsel). REL.: Presb. MISC.: holder of world flying record (soloing first day in plane). RES.: Cherryvale, KS.

SHELTON, HERBERT MacGOLPHIN. b. Oct 6, 1895, Wylie, TX; par. Thomas Mitchell and Mary Francis (Guthrie) Shelton; m. Ida Julia Pape, Jun 4, 1921; c. Bernarr; Walden; Willowdeen. EDUC.: Doctor of Physiological Therapeutics, International Coll. of Drugless Physicians, 1920; Doctor of Naturopathy, American School of Naturopathy, 1922. POLIT. & GOV.: ***American Vegetarian Party candidate for presidency of the U.S., 1956***. BUS. & PROF.: naturopathic physician; staff writer, MacFadden Publications, 1925–28; owner, operator, Dr. Herbert M. Shelton's Health School, San Antonio, TX, 1928–; ed., publisher, *Dr. Shelton's Hygienic Review*, 1939–. MEM.: American Hygiene Soc. WRITINGS: *Human Life: It's Philosophy and Laws*; *Hygienic System* (7 vols.); *Basic Principles of Natural Hygiene*; *Natural Hygiene: Man's Pristine Way of Life*; *Rubies in the Sand*; *Syphilis*; *Werewolf of Medicine*; *Human Beauty: It's Culture and Hygiene (1958)*; *Hygienic Care of Children*; *Fasting Can Save Your Life*; *Health for the Millions*; *Food Combining Made Easy*; *Living Life to Live It Longer*; *Superior Nutrition*; *Health for All*; *Getting Well*; *Introduction to Natural Hygiene*; *Joys of Getting Well*; various other pamphlets and health books. REL.: none. MISC.: arrested for illegal practice of medicine, New York, NY, 1936. RES.: San Antonio, TX.

SHEPHERD, DAVID W. POLIT. & GOV.: ***candidate for Democratic nomination to presidency of the U.S., 1988***. MAILING ADDRESS: c/o Margaret C. Cyrus, Box 67, Lewiston, ID 83501.

SHEPHERD, GEORGE S. b. May 5, 1866, Scotland; d. Nov 11, 1941, Portland, OR. EDUC.: Willamette U.; LL.B., U. of OR, 1895. POLIT. & GOV.: elected pres., Portland (OR) City Council, 1906–07; Republican candidate for U.S. House (OR), several times; ***candidate for Republican nomination to vice presidency of the U.S., 1924***. BUS. & PROF.: atty.; admitted to OR Bar, 1895; partner (with George B. Cellars), law firm, Portland, OR, 1895; seaman, sailing ship, 1904; ed., *Island Wappato*. MIL.: OR Naval Militia (capt., 1910–19). MEM.: ABA; OR Bar Assn.; Multnomah Cty. Bar Assn. (pres.); Multnomah Amateur Athletic Club (life member); Scottish Clan MacCleay. REL.: Protestant. RES.: Portland, OR.

SHEPPARD, ALICE FEGGINS. POLIT. & GOV.: ***candidate for Republican nomination to presidency of the U.S., 1988.*** MAILING ADDRESS: 174 West Lena Ave., Freeport, NY 11520.

SHEPPARD, JOHN MORRIS. b. May 28, 1875, Wheatville, TX; d. Apr 9, 1941, Washington, DC; par. John Levi and Alice (Eddins) Sheppard; m. Lucille Sanderson, Dec 1, 1909; c. Janet (Mrs. Richard L. Arnold); Susan (Mrs. Cornelius McGillicuddy, Jr.); Lucile (Mrs. Arthur Hawkins Keyes, Jr.). EDUC.: A.B., U. of TX, 1895, LL.B., 1897; LL.M., Yale U., 1898. POLIT. & GOV.: elected as a Democrat to U.S. House (TX), 1902–13; elected as a Democrat to U.S. Senate (TX), 1913–41; ***Prohibition National Cmte. candidate for Democratic nomination to presidency of the U.S., 1920.*** BUS. & PROF.: atty.; admitted to TX Bar, 1897; partner, Sheppard, Jones and Sheppard (law firm), Pittsburg, TX, 1898–99; law practice, Texarkana, TX, 1899–1941. MEM.: Modern Woodmen of the World; Woodmen of the World Life Insurance Soc. (Sovereign Banker); TX Fraternal Congress (pres., 1901); Phi Beta Kappa; Elks; Knights of Pythias; Odd Fellows; Red Men; Masons (32°); Kappa Alpha; SAR. HON. DEG.: LL.D., Southern Methodist U., 1918. WRITINGS: *Fraternal and Other Addresses* (1910). REL.: Methodist. RES.: Texarkana, TX.

SHERIDAN, PHILIP HENRY. b. Mar 6, 1831, Albany, NY; d. Aug 5, 1888, Nonquitt, MA; par. John and Mary (Meenagh) Sheridan; m. Irene Rucker, Jun 3, 1875; c. Irene; Louise; Philip, Jr.; Mary. EDUC.: grad., U.S. Military Acad., 1853. POLIT. & GOV.: ***candidate for Republican nomination to presidency of the U.S., 1880 (declined).*** BUS. & PROF.: soldier. MIL.: served in Rio Grande and Northwest, 1853–60; commissioned capt., U.S. Army, 1861; col., Second MI Cavalry, 1862; brig. gen., U.S.V., 1862, maj. gen., 1862; commanded Cavalry of the Army of the Potomac, 1864; commanded Army of the Shenandoah, 1864; maj. gen., U.S. Army, 1864; commander, Div. of the Gulf, 1865–67; appointed military gov., Fifth Military District (LA and TX), 1867; lt. gen., 1869; commanding gen., 1884, gen., 1888. MEM.: Loyal Legion (commander, IL State commandery; national commander in chief, 1886–88). WRITINGS: *Personal Memoirs* (2 vols., 1888). REL.: R.C. MISC.: known as "Little Phil." RES.: Nonquitt, MA.

SHERMAN, JAMES SCHOOLCRAFT. b. Oct 24, 1855, Utica, NY; d. Oct 30, 1912, Utica, NY; par. Gen. Richard Updike and Mary Frances (Sherman) Sherman; m. Carrie Babcock, Jan 26, 1881; c. Sherrill; Richard Updike; Thomas M. EDUC.: Utica Acad.; grad., Whitestown (NY) Seminary, 1874; A.B., Hamilton Coll., 1878, LL.B., 1880; studied law in offices of Beardsley, Cookinham and Burdick. POLIT. & GOV.: elected as a Republican, mayor of Utica, NY, 1884–85; elected as a Republican to U.S. House (NY), 1887–91, 1893–1909; Republican candidate for U.S. House (NY), 1890; delegate, Rep. Nat'l. Conv., 1892; chm., NY State Republican Convention, 1895, 1900, 1908; ***candidate for Republican nomination to vice presidency of the U.S., 1900***; chm., Republican National Congressional Cmte., 1906; ***elected as a Republican, vice presidency of the U.S., 1909–1912; Republican candidate for vice presidency of the U.S., 1912 (deceased).*** BUS. & PROF.: atty.; admitted to NY Bar, 1880; law practice, Utica, NY; partner, Cookinham, Gibson and Sherman (law firm), Utica, NY, 1880–1907; pres., New Hartford Canning Co., 1895; pres., Utica Trust and Deposit Co., 1899. Known as "Sunny Jim" and "Father Wau-be-ka-chunk." MEM.: Elks; Royal Arcanum; Hamilton Coll. (trustee, 1905–12); Hamilton Coll. Alumni Assn. (pres., WA Chapter); Fort Schuyler Club; Utica C. of C.; Oneida Hist. Soc.; Union League; NY Republican Club; NY Transportation Club; Metropolitan Club. HON. DEG.: LL.D., Hamilton Coll., 1903. REL.: Dutch Reformed Church. RES.: Utica, NY.

SHERMAN, JOHN. b. May 10, 1823, Lancaster, OH; d. Oct 22, 1900, Washington, DC; par. Charles Robert and Mary (Hoyt) Sherman; m. Margaret Sarah Cecilia Stewart, Aug 30, 1848; c. Mary Stewart (adopted; Mrs. James Iver McCallum). EDUC.: Howe's Acad., 1835–37; Homer Acad.; studied law under Judge Jacob Parker and Charles Taylor Sherman. POLIT. & GOV.: delegate, Whig Party National Convention, 1848 (sec.),, 1852; chm., OH Republican State Convention, 1855; elected as a Whig and subsequently as a Republican to U.S. House (OH), 1855–61; elected as a Republican to U.S. Senate (OH), 1861–77, 1881–97 (minority leader, 1893–95; majority leader, 1895–97); appointed U.S. sec. of the treasury, 1877–81; ***candidate for Republican nomination to presidency of the U.S., 1880, 1884, 1888***; appointed U.S. sec. of state, 1897–98. BUS. & PROF.: junior rodman, Army Corps of Engineers, Muskingum, OH, 1839; atty.; admitted to OH Bar, 1844; law practice, Mansfield, OH, 1844–1900. MEM.: Odd Fellows. WRITINGS: *Selected Speeches and Reports on Taxation* (1879); *Recollections of Forty Years in the House, Senate and Cabinet* (1895). MISC.: brother of William Tecumseh Sherman (q.v.). RES.: Mansfield, OH.

SHERMAN, LAWRENCE YATES. b. Nov 8, 1858, Piqua, OH; d. Sep 15, 1939, Daytona Beach, FL; par. Nelson and Maria (Yates) Sherman; m. Ella M. Crews, May 27, 1891; m. 2d, Estelle Spitler, Mar 4, 1908; c. Virginia. EDUC.: Lee's Acad.; LL.B., McKendree Coll., 1882. POLIT. & GOV.: city atty., Macomb, IL, 1885–87; elected county judge, McDonough Cty., IL, 1886–90; elected as a Republican to IL State House, 1897–1905 (Speaker, 1899–1903); Republican candidate for gov. of IL, 1904; elected as a Republican to lt. gov. of IL, 1905–09; appointed member, Spanish Treaty Claims Comm., 1907 (declined); Republican candidate for mayor of Springfield, IL, 1908; ***candidate for Republican nomination to vice presidency of the U.S., 1908***; pres., IL State Board of Administration, 1909–13; delegate, Rep. Nat'l. Conv., 1912, 1920, 1924, 1928; elected as a Republican to U.S. Senate (IL), 1913–21; member, Rep. Nat'l. Cmte. (IL), 1916–24; ***candidate for Repub-***

lican nomination to presidency of the U.S., 1916. BUS. & PROF.: schoolteacher, 6 years; atty.; admitted to IL bar, 1882; law practice, Macomb, IL, 1882; law practice, Springfield,, IL; law practice, Daytona Beach, FL, 1924–33; pres., First Atlantic National Bank, Daytona Beach, FL, 1925, chm. of the board, 1925–27; dir., Atlantic National Bank, Jacksonville, FL, 1930–33. MEM.: Masons (Knights Templar; Shriners; Consistory); Knights of Pythias. RES.: Macomb, IL.

SHERMAN, WILLIAM TECUMSEH. b. Feb 8, 1820, Lancaster, OH; d. Feb 14, 1891, New York, NY; par. Charles Robert and Mary (Hoyt) Sherman; m. Eleanor Boyle "Ellen" Ewing, May 1, 1850; c. Thomas Ewing; Mary Elizabeth "Lizzie"; Eleanor Mary "Ellie" (Mrs. A. M. Thackara); Maria "Minnie" (Mrs. Thomas W. Fitch); Philemon Tecumseh; Rachel (Mrs. Thorndike); William Ewing; Charles Celestine. EDUC.: grad., U.S. Military Acad., 1840. POLIT. & GOV.: appointed envoy, U.S. Mission to Mexico, 1866; appointed U.S. sec. of war, 1869; ***candidate for Republican nomination to presidency of the U.S., 1884***. BUS. & PROF.: soldier; banker, San Francisco, CA, 1853–59; atty.; partner (with Thomas Ewing and Hugh Boyle Ewing), law firm, Leavenworth, KS; pres., St. Louis (MO) Street Railway Co., 1861. MIL.: 1st lt., U.S. Army, 1841, resigned, 1853; superintendent, Military Acad., Alexandria, LA, 1859–61; col., 13th Infantry, 1861; brig. gen., U.S.V., 1861, maj. gen., 1862; brig. gen., U.S. Army, 1863, maj. gen., 1864, supreme commander in the West, 1864, lt. gen., 1866; commanding gen., 1869–83; noted for his "March to the Sea," 1865. MEM.: Loyal Legion (commander, IL commandery). WRITINGS: *Memoirs* (1875). REL.: R.C. MISC.: instrumental in construction of transcontinental railroad; established military school, Fort Leavenworth, KS, 1881; brother of John Sherman (q.v.). RES.: New York, NY.

SHERWOOD, ISAAC RUTH. b. Aug 13, 1835, Stanford, NY; d. Oct 15, 1925, Toledo, OH; par. Aaron and Maria (Yeomans) Sherwood; m. Katharine Margaret Brownlee, Sep 1, 1859; c. James Brownlee; Lenore. EDUC.: Hudson River Inst., 1852–54; Antioch Coll., 1854–56; grad., OH Law Coll.; studied law under Judge Hogeboom, Hudson, NY. POLIT. & GOV.: elected mayor of Bryan, OH, c. 1860; elected probate judge, Williams Cty., OH, 1860–61 (resigned); elected as a Republican to sec. of state of OH, 1869–73; elected as a Republican to U.S. House (OH), 1873–75; elected as a Greenbacker, Probate judge, Lucas Cty., OH, 1878–81; Democratic candidate for U.S. House (OH), 1896; elected as a Democrat to U.S. House (OH), 1907–21, 1923–25; ***candidate for Democratic nomination to vice presidency of the U.S., 1912***; Democratic candidate for U.S. House (OH), 1924. BUS. & PROF.: ed., *Williams County (OH) Gazette*, Bryan, OH, 1857; ed., *Toledo (OH) Daily Commercial*, 1865; political ed., *Cleveland (OH) Leader*, 1865–66; owner, *Toledo (OH) Journal*, 1875–84; ed., *Canton (OH) News-Democrat*, 1885–93; author. MIL.: pvt., 14th Regt., OH Volunteer Infantry, 1861; 1st lt., adj., 111th OH Volunteer Infantry, 1862, maj., 1863, lt. col., 1864, brev. brig. gen., 1865, mustered out, 1865. MEM.: Elks; GAR; Loyal Legion. WRITINGS: *Sherwood Dollar-a-Day Bill; Medal of Honor Bill; The Army Grayback* (1889); *Memories of the War* (1923). REL.: Presb. MISC.: organized OH Bureau of Statistics, 1869; voted against American declaration of war against Germany, 1917. RES.: Toledo, OH.

SHEWALTER, CHESTER A. POLIT. & GOV.: ***All-American Nationalist Party candidate for presidency of the U.S., 1936***. BUS. & PROF.: chicken farmer, Belle Plaine, KS; mechanic, General Motors Corp., Flint, MI. RES.: Belle Plaine, KS.

SHIBLEY, GEORGE HENRY. b. Sep 4, 1861, Randall, WI; par. Jacob B. and Harriet (McClellan) Shibley; m. Alice Smith Patterson, 1906. EDUC.: Union Coll. of Law, Chicago, IL, 1885–86; U. of Chicago, 1893–94; George Washington U., 1907–09; Ph.D. POLIT. & GOV.: member, People's (Fusion) Party National Cmte., 1901; ***Continental Party candidate for vice presidency of the U.S., 1904 (declined)***. BUS. & PROF.: sociologist; atty.; admitted to IL Bar, 1888; admitted to practice before the Bar of the Supreme Court of the U.S., 1911; founder, Bureau of Economic Research, New York, NY, 1899; dir., research inst., Washington, DC, 1900–; author. MEM.: National Federation for People's Rule (founder, 1902); League for World Federation (pres., 1914–); Prosperity Federation of U.S.A. (exec. sec., 1928–); School Republic Federation (national sec.); League for World Peace (pres.). WRITINGS: *Elements of Law; The Iowa Plan for Character Education; The University and Social Problems; The Trust Problem Solved; Guarded Representative Government; The Money Question* (1896); *Outline of Social Evolution* (1898); *The Monopoly Question* (1900); *The People's Rule in Place of Machine Rule* (4th ed., 1906); *Preparedness Plus* (1916); *The Road to Victory* (1918); *The League of Nations* (1919); *The Road to Prosperity* (1921). MISC.: won $20,000 Prize for *The Iowa Plan for Character Education*. RES.: Mount Vernon, NY.

SHIEKMAN, TOM. EDUC.: J.D., U. of Miami Law School; M.A., Claremont Grad. School. POLIT. & GOV.: ***candidate for Democratic nomination to presidency of the U.S., 1992***. BUS. & PROF.: comedian; atty.; real estate marketing exec. MEM.: DC Bar Assn. MAILING ADDRESS: 740 North Kings Rd., #118, West Hollywood, CA 90069.

SHIGETA, RONALD TAKEO. b. Feb 1, 1939, Paia, HI; par. James Yutaka and Jessie Tomoe (Matsuoka) Shigeta; m. Elizabeth Jane Fujii, Jun 1963 (divorced, 1976); c. Ronald Takeo II; Anne Christine; Scott Y. EDUC.: B.S., OR State U., 1961; M.B.A., Harvard Business School, 1968. POLIT. & GOV.: ***independent candidate for presidency of the U.S., 1984, 1988***. BUS. & PROF.: management consultant, Battelle Memorial Inst., Columbus, OH, 1968–74; management consultant, 1974–. MIL.: U.S. Navy, 1961–65; U.S.N.R., 1965–79. MEM.: Kiwanis;

U.N. Assn. of the U.S.A. (Washington, DC, Council, 1981–82). AWARDS: NROTC scholarship; Blue Key Senior Men's Honorary. REL.: United Church of Christ in the U.S.A. MAILING ADDRESS: 1555 Wilhelmina Rise, Honolulu, HI 96816.

SHIVELY, BENJAMIN FRANKLIN. b. Mar 20, 1857, St. Joseph Cty., IN; d. Mar 14, 1916, Washington, DC; par. Joe and Elizabeth Shively; m. Laura Jenks, Jun 19, 1889. EDUC.: Northern IN Normal School; LL.B., U. of MI, 1886. POLIT. & GOV.: elected as a National Anti-Monopolist to U.S. House (IN), 1884–85, as a Democrat, 1887–93; Democratic candidate for gov. of IN, 1896; ***candidate for People's Party nomination to vice presidency of the U.S., 1900; candidate for Democratic nomination to vice presidency of the U.S., 1900***; Democratic candidate for U.S. Senate (IN), 1903; Democratic candidate for U.S. House (IN), 1906; elected as a Democrat to U.S. Senate (IN), 1909–16. BUS. & PROF.: teacher, 1874–80; journalist, 1880–84; atty.; admitted to IN Bar, 1886; law practice, South Bend, IN, 1886. MEM.: IN U. (pres., board of trustees); National Anti-Monopoly Assn. (sec., 1883). RES.: South Bend, IN.

SHOFNER, BOBBIE WELDON. POLIT. & GOV.: ***candidate for Democratic nomination to vice presidency of the U.S., 1980; candidate for Democratic nomination to presidency of the U.S., 1984, 1988***. MAILING ADDRESS: 764 Twain, Apt. 5 F, Las Vegas, NV 89109.

SHORT, DEWEY JACKSON. b. Apr 7, 1898, Galena, MO; d. Nov 19, 1979, Washington, DC; par. Jackson Grant and Permelia Cordelia (Long) Short; m. Helen Gladys Hughes, Apr 20, 1937. EDUC.: grad., Marionville (MO) Coll., 1917; A.B., Baker U., 1919; S.T.B., Boston U., 1922; Oxford U., 1922–25. POLIT. & GOV.: elected as a Republican to U.S. House (MO), 1929–31, 1935–57; Republican candidate for U.S. House (MO), 1930, 1956; candidate for Republican nomination to U.S. Senate (MO), 1932; delegate, Rep. Nat'l. Conv., 1932; delegate, International Parliamentary Union, 1939, 1947; ***candidate for Republican nomination to vice presidency of the U.S., 1940***; appointed alternate delegate, U.S.-Japanese Peace Treaty Signing, 1951; appointed asst. sec. of the army, 1957–61. BUS. & PROF.: prof. of Philosophy and Psychology, Southwestern Coll., Winfield, KS, 1923–24, 1926–28; minister, Methodist Church; pastor, Grace Methodist Episcopal Church, Springfield, MO, 1927; lecturer. MIL.: acting lt., infantry, U.S. Army, WWI. MEM.: National Rivers and Harbors Congress (pres., 1938–44); American Legion; Delta Tau Delta; Pi Gamma Mu; Masons; MO Soc.; Young Republicans Assn. of MO; Frank D. Howard Fellowship; Lions. HON. DEG.: LL.D., Drury Coll., 1930; LL.D., Boston U., 1941; Harvard U.; U. of Berlin; Heidelberg U. REL.: Methodist. RES.: Galena, MO.

SHOUP, OLIVER HENRY NELSON. b. Dec 13, 1869, Champaign, IL; d. Sep 30, 1940, Santa Monica, CA; par. William R. and Delia Janette (Ferris) Shoup; m. Unetta Small, Sep 18, 1891; m. 2d, Mary Alice Hackett, Mar 3, 1930; c. Reba (Mrs. John Leeming), Oliver Henry, Merrill Edgar, Verner Reed. EDUC.: public schools, Colorado Springs, CO; CO Coll. POLIT. & GOV.: elected member, school board, Colorado Springs, CO, 1917–18; elected as a Republican to gov. of CO, 1919–23; ***candidate for Republican nomination to vice presidency of the U.S., 1924***; Republican candidate for gov. of CO, 1926. BUS. & PROF.: employee, Colorado Springs Co.; founder, pres., Midwest Oil Co., 1911–16; pres., Midwest Refining Co., 1914–16; pres., Westland Securities Co., 1920–35; pres., Valley Guaranty Co., 1932–39; vice pres., Colorado Savings Bank, Colorado Springs, CO, 1920–30; vice pres., Capital Prize Mining Co., Georgetown, CO, 1933–39; dir., Exchange National Bank, Colorado Springs, CO; dir., Grand Valley National Bank; dir., Denver National Bank; real estate investor. MEM.: CO Coll. (trustee, 1917–31); Presbyterian Hospital of Denver (pres.); Knights of Pythias; Elks; El Paso Club; Rocky Mountain Club. REL.: Presb. RES.: Colorado Springs, CO.

SHOWELL, MILTON WINFIELD. b. 1936. POLIT. & GOV.: ***independent candidate for presidency of the U.S., 1980***. BUS. & PROF.: lay minister. MAILING ADDRESS: 7224 Easy St., Camp Springs, Westchester, MD 20031.

SHREVE, JONATHAN LEO. b. Apr 8, 1961, Osceola, IA; par. Warren Eugene and Roberta Gail (Orthel) Shreve; single. EDUC.: grad., Fargo (ND) H.S., 1978; Carleton Coll., 1978–. POLIT. & GOV.: ***candidate for Democratic nomination to presidency of the U.S., 1980***. BUS. & PROF.: head cook, Paradiso; taco bender, Taco John's; ticket salesman; math grader; tutor, Carleton Coll.; ed., *Postal Chess Fiesta News*, 1979–. MEM.: Joe Fabeetz Memorial DBC (mgr.); U.S. Chess Federation; National Forensic League (special distinction); Mathematical Assn. of America. REL.: Deism. MAILING ADDRESS: Carleton Coll., Northfield,, MN 55057.

SHRIVER, EUNICE MARY KENNEDY. b. Jul 10, 1921, Brookline,, MA; d. Joseph Patrick (q.v.) and Rose Elizabeth (Fitzgerald) Kennedy; m. Robert Sargent Shriver, Jr. (q.v.), May 23, 1953; c. Robert Sargent III, Maria Owings (Mrs. Arnold Alois Schwarzenegger), Timothy Perry, Mark Kennedy, Anthony Paul Kennedy. EDUC.: B.S., Stanford U., 1943. POLIT. & GOV.: employee, Special War Problems Div., U.S. Dept. of State, 1943–46; adviser on Prevention and Control of Juvenile Delinquency, U.S. Dept. of Justice, 1947–48; campaign worker, John F. Kennedy congressional and presidential campaigns; co-chm., Women's Cmte., Dem. Nat'l. Conv., 1956; appointed member, Chicago (IL) Comm. on Youth Welfare, 1959–62; appointed consultant, President's Panel on Mental Retardation, 1961; ***candidate for Democratic nomination to vice presidency of the U.S., 1980***. BUS. & PROF.: social worker, Federal Penitentiary for Women, Alderson, WV, 1950; social worker, House of Good Shepherd, Chicago, IL, 1951–54; exec. vice pres., Joseph P. Kennedy, Jr. Foundation, 1956–. MEM.: Special Olympics (pres., 1968–); Flame of Hope Inc. (founder); Community Fund–Red Cross Joint Appeal (regional chm., Women's Div., Chicago, IL, 1958). AWARDS: Philip Murray-William Green Award, 1966; Albert Lasker Public Service Award, 1966; Order of the Legion of Honor (France, 1974); Humanitarian Award, A.A.M.D., 1973; National Volunteer Service Award, 1973; Philadelphia Civic Ballet Award, 1973; Prix de la Couronne Francaise, 1974; Presidential Medal of Freedom, 1984. HON. DEG.: Litt.D., U. of Santa Clara, 1962; L.H.D., D'Youville Coll., 1962; L.H.D., Manhattanville Coll. of the Sacred Heart, 1963; LL.D., Regis Coll., 1963; L.H.D., Newton Coll., 1973; L.H.D., Brescia Coll., 1974. REL.: R.C. MAILING ADDRESS: Timberlawn, Edson Lane, Rockville, MD 20852.

SHRIVER, ROBERT SARGENT, JR. b. Nov 9, 1915, Westminster, MD; par. Robert Sargent and Hilda (Shriver) Shriver; m. Eunice Mary Kennedy (q.v.), May 23, 1953; c. Robert Sargent III, Maria Owings (Mrs. Arnold Alois Schwarzenegger), Timothy Perry, Mary Kennedy, Anthony Paul Kennedy. EDUC.: Canterbury School; B.A. (cum laude), Yale U., 1938, LL.B., 1941. POLIT. & GOV.: elected member, Chicago (IL) Board of Education, 1955–60 (pres.); appointed dir., Peace Corps, 1961–66; appointed dir., U.S. Office of Economic Opportunity, 1964–66; appointed special asst. to the presidency of the U.S., 1965–68; appointed U.S. ambassador to France, 1965–68; ***candidate for Democratic nomination to vice presidency of the U.S., 1968, 1976***; candidate for Democratic nomination to gov. of MD, 1970 (withdrew); ***candidate for Democratic nomination to presidency of the U.S., 1972, 1976; Democratic candidate for vice presidency of the U.S., 1972***. BUS. & PROF.: atty.; admitted to NY Bar, 1941; admitted to IL Bar, 1959; admitted to the Bar of the Supreme Court of the U.S., 1969; admitted to DC Bar, 1971; staff, Winthrop, Stimson, Putnam and Roberts, 1940–41; asst. ed., *Newsweek*, 1945–46; assoc., Joseph P. Kennedy Enterprises, 1947–48; asst. gen. mgr., Merchandise Mart, Chicago, IL, 1948–61; senior partner, Fried, Frank, Harris, Shriver and Jacobson (law firm), New York, NY, 1971–. MIL.: lt. commander, U.S.N.R., 1940–45. MEM.: Yale Law School Assn. (exec. cmte.); Navy League (life member); Chicago Council on Foreign Relations (dir.); Delta Kappa Epsilon; Catholic Inter-Racial Council, Chicago, IL (pres., 1955–60); BSA (national council); Joseph P. Kennedy Jr. Foundation (exec. dir.); Congressional Leadership for the Future (chm., 1970); Sierra Club; Economic Club; Racquet Club; Yale Club of NY City; Chevy Chase Club; Onwentsia Club; Executives Club. AWARDS: Yale Medal, 1957; Chicago Medal of Merit, 1957; James J. Hoey Award, Catholic Interracial Council of NY, 1958; "Lay Churchman of the Year," Religious Heritage of America, 1963; Golden Heart Presidential Award, Government of the Philippines, 1964; Laetare Medal, U. of Notre Dame, 1968; Presidential Medal of Freedom, 1994. HON. DEG.: LL.D., St. Procopius Coll., 1959; LL.D., DePaul U., 1961; LL.D., Notre Dame U., 1961; LL.D., Seton Hall Coll., 1961; LL.D., Brandeis U., 1962; LL.D., KS State U., 1962; LL.D., St. Louis U., 1962; LL.D., Boston Coll., 1963; H.H.D., Bowling Green State U., 1963; LL.D., Duquesne U., 1963; LL.D., Fordham U., 1963; D.C.L., U. of Liberia, 1963; LL.D., NY U., 1963; LL.D., St. Michael's Coll., 1963; H.H.D., Salem Coll., 1963; L.H.D., Springfield Coll., 1963; LL.D., Wesleyan U., 1963; LL.D., Yale U., 1963; L.H.D., U. of Scranton; L.H.D., Providence Coll.; Dr.Polit.Sci., Chulalongkorn U. WRITINGS: *Point of the Lance* (1964). REL.: R.C. MAILING ADDRESS: Timberlawn, Edson Lane, Rockville, MD 20852.

SHUBERT, JIMMY RAY. POLIT. & GOV.: ***independent candidate for presidency of the U.S., 1980***. MEM.: Council of Contraestablishment Conservationists. MAILING ADDRESS: c/o Mary Ann Shubert, P.O. Box 153, Manvel, TX 77578.

SHULER, GEORGE KENT. b. Dec 15, 1884, Lyons, NY; d. Oct 16, 1942, New York, NY; m. Blanche Stewart; c. Blanche, Mrs. Jean Cosgrove. EDUC.: Dawd's Army and Navy Acad. POLIT. & GOV.: Democratic candidate for NY State Senate; Democratic candidate for U.S. House (NY), 1920; elected as a Democrat to state treas. of NY, 1923–24; ***candidate for Democratic nomination to vice presidency of the U.S., 1924***; candidate for Democratic nomination to state comptroller of NY, 1926; employee, Internal Revenue Service, New York, NY, 1933–42. BUS. & PROF.: reporter, *Washington (DC) Post*; publisher, *Motion Picture Magazine*; publisher, *Motion Picture Classic*; dir., Commercial and Security Corp. MIL.: 2d lt., maj., 3d Battalion, 6th Regt., U.S.M.C., 1910–22; Army Distinguished Service Medal; Navy Distinguished Service Medal; Legion of Honor; Croix de Guerre (3 Palms); Distinguished Service Cross (3 times). RES.: New York, NY.

SHULTZ, ARTHUR C. m. Catherine S. POLIT. & GOV.: ***independent candidate for presidency of the U.S., 1976***. BUS. & PROF.: retired. MAILING ADDRESS: 1703 North Kaley St., South Bend, IN 46628.

SHULTZ, GEORGE PRATT. b. Dec 13, 1920, New York, NY; par. Birl E. and Margaret Lennox (Pratt) Shultz; m. Helena M. O'Brien, Feb 16, 1946; c. Margaret Ann, Kathleen Pratt (Mrs. Jorgensen), Peter Milton, Barbara Lennox, Alexander George. EDUC.: B.A., Princeton U., 1942; Ph.D., MA Inst. of Technology, 1949. POLIT. & GOV.: appointed U.S. sec. of labor, 1969–70; appointed dir., Office of Management and Budget, exec. office of the pres., 1970–72; appointed U.S. sec. of the treasury, 1972–74; appointed asst. to the presidency of the U.S., 1972–74; U.S. sec. of state, 1982–89; ***candidate for Republican nomination to presidency of the U.S., 1988 (declined)***. BUS. & PROF.: faculty, MA Inst. of Technology, 1946–57, assoc. prof. of Industrial Relations, 1955–57; prof. of Industrial Relations, grad. school of business, U. of Chicago, 1957–68, dean,

1962–68; fellow, Center for Advanced Studies in Behavioral Sciences, 1968–69; prof. of management and public policy, Stanford U., 1974–82; exec. vice pres., Bechtel Corp., San Francisco, CA, 1974–75, pres., 1975–80; dir., pres., Bechtel Group, Inc., 1981–82; dir., General Motors Corp.; dir., Dillon, Read and Co., Inc. MIL.: capt., U.S.M.C. Reserves, 1942–45. MEM.: American Economic Assn.; Industrial Relations Research Assn. (pres., 1968); National Acad. of Arbitrators. AWARDS: Presidential Medal of Freedom, 1989. WRITINGS: *Management Organization and the Computer* (coauthor, 1960); *Strategies for the Displaced Worker* (coauthor, 1966); *Workers and Wages in the Urban Labor Market* (coauthor, 1970); *Economic Policy Beyond the Headlines* (coauthor, 1978); *Turmoil and Triumph: My Years as Secretary of State* (1993). MAILING ADDRESS: 776 Dolores St., Stanford, CA 94305.

SHULZE, JOHN ANDREW. b. Jul 19, 1775, Tulpehocken, PA; d. Nov 18, 1852, Lancaster, PA; par. Christopher and Ava (Muhlenberg) Shulze; m. Susan Kimmell; c. two. POLIT. & GOV.: elected as a National Republican, member, PA State House, 1806–09, 1821; register and clerk, Sessions Court of Lebanon Cty., PA, 1813; elected as a National Republican, member, PA State Senate, 1822; elected as a National Republican to gov. of PA, 1823–29; ***candidate for National Republican nomination to vice presidency of the U.S., 1828***; delegate, PA State Constitutional Convention, 1839; presidential elector, Whig Party, 1840, 1852. BUS. & PROF.: ordained minister, German Lutheran Synod, eastern PA, 1796. REL.: Lutheran. RES.: Lancaster, PA.

SIANO, DICK. POLIT. & GOV.: elected as a Libertarian, Township Committeeman, Kingwood Township, NJ, 1981–; organizer, Tax Protest Day, 1982; ***candidate for Libertarian Party nomination to presidency of the U.S., 1984***. BUS. & PROF.: pilot, Trans-World Airlines. MAILING ADDRESS: R.D. 1, Box 287, Frenchtown, NJ 08825.

SIBLEY, JOSEPH CROCKER. b. Feb 18, 1850, Friendship, NY; d. May 19, 1926, Franklin, PA; par. Joseph Crocker and Lucy Elvira (Babcock) Sibley; m. Metta Evaline Babcock, Mar 17, 1870; m. 2d, Ida Lorena Rew, Dec 6, 1913; c. Josephine (Mrs. William Emerson Heathcote), Celia (Mrs. William McCalmont Wilson). EDUC.: Springville Acad.; Friendship Acad.; studied medicine. POLIT. & GOV.: elected as a Republican, mayor of Franklin, PA, 1879; member, PA State Board of Agriculture; elected as a Democrat-Populist-Prohibitionist to U.S. House (PA), 1893–95; Democratic-Populist candidate for U.S. House (PA), 1894, 1896; ***candidate for Silver Party nomination to presidency of the U.S., 1896; candidate for Democratic nomination to vice presidency of the U.S., 1896; National Reform Party candidate for presidency of the U.S., 1896***; elected as a Democrat to U.S. House (PA), 1899–1901, as a Republican, 1901–07; chm., PA Republican State Convention, 1902; Republican candidate for U.S. House (PA), 1910 (declined). BUS. & PROF.: clerk, Miller's General Store, Franklin, PA, 1866; schoolteacher; owner, oil refining business, Franklin, PA; employee, Miller and Coon (dry goods), Franklin, PA, 1869; inventor; pres., Signal Oil Works, 1873–1901; chm. of the board, Galena Signal Oil Co., 1902–12; partner, Sibley and Miller Stock Farm; breeder of horses and cattle. MEM.: PA State Dairymen's Assn. (pres.); Bucknell U. (trustee); American Trotting Register Assn. (founder); National Trotting Assn. (board of review); Venango Cty. (PA) Bar Assn.; American Jersey Cattle Assn. (dir.); Allegheny River Improvement Assn. (dir.); Union League; Chevy Chase Club; Nursery Club. REL.: Bapt. MISC.: developed superior signal oil and other lubricants. RES.: Franklin, PA.

SIEGER, H. J. "JIM." POLIT. & GOV.: ***independent candidate for presidency of the U.S., 1976***. MAILING ADDRESS: P.O. Box 4403 G.S., Springfield, MO 65804.

SIITONEN, HARRY. POLIT. & GOV.: delegate, Socialist Party National Convention, 1976 (chairperson); ***candidate for Socialist Party nomination to presidency of the U.S., 1976 (declined); candidate for Socialist Party nomination to vice presidency of the U.S., 1976 (declined)***. MAILING ADDRESS: 106 Sanchez St., #17, San Francisco, CA 94114.

SIKORSKI, GERRY. b. Apr 26, 1948, Breckenridge, MN; par. Elroy and Helen (Voit) Sikorski; m. Susan Jane Erkel, Aug 24, 1974; c. Anne. EDUC.: B.A. (summa cum laude), U. of MN, 1970, J.D. (magna cum laude), 1973. POLIT. & GOV.: chm., MN Young Democrats, 1968–69; chm., Governor's Citizens' Council on Aging, MN, 1975–76; elected as a Democratic-Farmer Laborite to MN State Senate, 1977–83 (majority whip, 1981–83); ***candidate for Democratic nomination to vice presidency of the U.S., 1980***; elected as a Democratic-Farmer Laborite to U.S. House (MN), 1983–. BUS. & PROF.: atty. MEM.: Phi Beta Kappa; Rivertown Restoration, Inc. (pres.); Washington Cty. Bar Assn. (pres.); Washington Cty. Legal Aid Assistance (pres.); Legal Assistance of MN (treas.); Bayport Jaycees; Stillwater Jaycees; Assn. of Retarded Citizens. REL.: R.C. MAILING ADDRESS: 9367 Otchipwe, Stillwater, MN 55082.

SILBIGER, STEVEN ALAN. b. 1962. POLIT. & GOV.: ***independent candidate for presidency of the U.S., 1980***. BUS. & PROF.: high school student. MAILING ADDRESS: 5721 Lockton Lane, Fairway, KS 66205.

SILER, EUGENE EDWARD. b. Jun 26, 1900, Williamsburg, KY; d. Dec 5, 1987, Louisville, KY; par. Adam and Minnie (Chandler) Siler; m. Lowell Jones, Oct 17, 1925; c. Dorothy, Annette, Carolyn, Eugene Edward, Jr. EDUC.: A.A., Cumberland Coll., 1920; A.B., U. of KY, 1922, student,

1923–24; Columbia U., 1922. POLIT. & GOV.: elected judge, Seventh KY Court of Appeals, 1945–49; Republican candidate for gov. of KY, 1951; elected as a Republican to U.S. House (KY), 1955–65; ***Splinter Party candidate for presidency of the U.S., 1964 (satire effort)***; alternate delegate, Rep. Nat'l. Conv., 1968; candidate for Republican nomination to U.S. Senate (KY), 1968. BUS. & PROF.: atty.; admitted to KY Bar, 1923; partner, Tye, Siler, Gillis and Siler (law firm), 1925–38; partner, Tye and Siler (law firm), 1938–42; law practice, Williamsburg, KY, 1945–; dir., Bank of Williamsburg; dir., Kentucky Mine Supply Co.; dir., Kingsport Grocery Co. MIL.: seaman, U.S. Navy, WWI; capt., U.S. Army, 1942–45. MEM.: American Legion (district commander, KY); J.O.U.A.M.; KY Bar Assn.; Sigma Alpha Epsilon; Phi Alpha Delta; Masons; Odd Fellows; Cumberland Coll. (trustee). REL.: Bapt. (KY moderator, 1952–53). RES. : Louisville, KY.

SILEVEN, EVERETT. POLIT. & GOV.: ***candidate for Populist Party nomination to vice presidency of the U.S., 1988 (declined).*** BUS. & PROF.: pastor. REL.: Christian. MAILING ADDRESS: NE.

SILFIN, IRA ELIJAH. b. Feb 29, 1964, Bethpage, NY; par. Howard and Irene (Katz) Silfin; single. EDUC.: grades K–4, Hebrew Acad. of Nassau Cty.; grades 5–6, Central Boulevard School; grades 7–8, JFK Junior H.S.; grades 9–11, Bethpage H.S. POLIT. & GOV.: ***independent candidate for presidency of the U.S., 1980***. BUS. & PROF.: student. MEM.: Bethpage H.S. Chess Club (treas.); Bethpage Mathletes. AWARDS: 2d place, Nassau Cty. (NY) Junior Mathletes, 1977–78; Silver Pin, Nassau Cty. (NY) Mathletes, 1979–80; 1st place, 9th grade, Bethpage H.S., National High School Mathematics Test, 1978. REL.: Jewish. MAILING ADDRESS: 15 Audley Circle, Plainview, NY 11803.

SILVERMAN, EDWARD JOSEPH. b. Aug 2, 1913, Nashville, TN; d. Aug 12, 1980, Kenbridge, VA; par. Benjamin Harrison and Willie (McWright) Silverman; m. Hedren Estelle Roberts; c. Sidney Ronald, Atwell Nathaniel, Thelbert Raye. EDUC.: U. of the South. POLIT. & GOV.: ***Conservative Party of Virginia candidate for vice presidency of the U.S. (as stand-in for Thomas J. Anderson, q.v.), 1960***; Conservative Party of Virginia candidate for U.S. House (VA), 1966. BUS. & PROF.: advertising mgr., Nottoway Publishing Co., Blackstone, VA; gen. mgr., WKLV radio, Blackstone, VA; reporter, *Courier-Record*, Blackstone, VA. MEM.: Lions; 4-H Club; C. of C.; Masons; Ruritan Club; Volunteer Fire Dept. (emergency squad); VA Folk Music Assn.; VA State Guard; VA Cmte. for Constitutional Government (vice chm.). AWARDS: 4-H All Star; Truly a Lion; Outstanding Citizen, Kenbridge (VA) C. of C.; Friend of Country Music, VA Folk Music Assn.; Outstanding Citizen, Lunenberg Modern Woodmen of the World; Outstanding Citizen, Blackstone VFW. REL.: Disciples of Christ. RES.: Blackstone, VA.

SILVERMAN, FRED. b. Sep 13, 1937, New York, NY; m. Catherine Ann Kihn; c. Melissa Anne, William Laurence. EDUC.: B.A., Syracuse U., 1958; M.A. (Television and Theatre), OH State U., 1959. POLIT. & GOV.: ***independent candidate for presidency of the U.S., 1980***. BUS. & PROF.: staff producer, dir. of Program Development, WGN-TV, Chicago, IL, 1959–63; exec., WPIX-TV, New York, NY, 1963; dir. of Daytime Programs, CBS-TV, New York, NY, 1963–66, vice pres. of Daytime Programming, 1966–70, vice pres. of Programs, 1970–75; pres., ABC Entertainment, 1975–78; pres., NBC-TV, 1978–81; independent film producer, 1981–. MAILING ADDRESS: c/o Metro-Goldwyn Mayer Film Co., 10202 West Washington Blvd., Culver City, CA 90230.

SILVERSTEIN, SAM KITSEL. b. Aug 2, 1920, Conshohocken, PA; par. Marvin and Esther (Lavin) Silverstein; m. Shirley; c. Harry Boris. EDUC.: high school grad. POLIT. & GOV.: ***independent candidate for presidency of the U.S., 1976***. BUS. & PROF.: sheet metal worker. MEM.: Lions; American Legion; Eagles; International Order of Odd Fellows. REL.: Jewish. MAILING ADDRESS: 507 Fifth Ave., New York, NY 10017.

SILZER, GEORGE SEBASTIAN. b. Apr 14, 1870, New Brunswick, NJ; d. Oct 16, 1940, Newark, NJ; par. Theodore C. and Christina (Zimmerman) Silzer; m. Henrietta T. Waite, Apr 18, 1898; c. Parker Waite. EDUC.: public schools. POLIT. & GOV.: elected member, Board of Aldermen, Brunswick, NJ, 1892–96; chm., Middlesex Cty. (NJ) Democratic Central Cmte., 10 years; elected as a Democrat to NJ State Senate, 1907–12; appointed prosecutor of Pleas, Middlesex Cty., NJ, 1912–14; appointed circuit judge, NJ, 1914–22; elected as a Democrat to gov. of NJ, 1923–26; delegate, Dem. Nat'l. Conv., 1924; ***candidate for Democratic nomination to presidency of the U.S., 1924; candidate for Democratic nomination to vice presidency of the U.S., 1924***; appointed chm., Port of NY Authority, 1926–28. BUS. & PROF.: atty.; admitted to NJ Bar, 1892; law practice, Newark, NJ; chm. of the board, New Brunswick Trust Co.; chm. of the board, dir., Interstate Trust Co., New York, NY, 1929–30; trustee, Central Savings Bank, New York, NY; chm. of the board, Broad and Market National Bank of Newark. MEM.: Elks; Masons; NJ Bar Assn.; NY C. of C.; National Democratic Club of NY; Princeton Club; Bankers Club. HON. DEG.: LL.D., Rutgers U., 1923. REL.: Episc. RES.: Metuchen, NJ.

SIMMONS, FURNIFOLD McLENDEL. b. Jan 20, 1854, Polloksville, NC; d. Apr 30, 1940, New Bern, NC; par. Furnifold Green and Mary (McLendel) Jerman Simmons; m. Eliza (Humphrey) Hill, Nov 26, 1874; m. 2d, Belle Gibbs, Jun 29, 1886; c. Mary Rebecca (Mrs. Louis August Mahler), James Humphrey, Eliza Humphrey (Mrs. Graham Harris Andrews), Ella McLendel (Mrs. Wade Meadows), Isabelle (Mrs. Joseph Flanner Patterson). EDUC.: Wake Forest Coll., 1868–70; A.B., A.M.,

Trinity Coll., 1873; studied law. POLIT. & GOV.: Democratic candidate for NC State House, twice; elected as a Democrat to U.S. House (NC), 1887–89; Democratic candidate for U.S. House (NC), 1888; chm., NC State Democratic Exec. Cmte., 1892, 1898–1907; appointed Collector of Internal Revenue, Fourth District (NC), 1893–97; elected as a Democrat to U.S. Senate (NC), 1901–31; ***candidate for Democratic nomination to presidency of the U.S., 1920***; member, Dem. Nat'l. Cmte., 1924–28; candidate for Democratic nomination to U.S. Senate (NC), 1930. BUS. & PROF.: atty.; admitted to NC Bar, 1875; partner, Manly, Simmons and Manly (law firm), New Bern, NC, 1875–87; law practice, New Bern, NC, 1887–98; partner, Simmons, Pou and Ward (law firm), New Bern, Smithfield, and Raleigh, NC, 1898–1901. MEM.: Duke U. (trustee, 1892–1940). HON. DEG.: LL.D., Duke U., 1901; LL.D., U. of NC, 1915. REL.: Episc. RES.: New Bern, NC.

SIMMONS, RICKEY D. POLIT. & GOV.: ***independent candidate for presidency of the U.S., 1992***. MAILING ADDRESS: P.O. Box 301, Sterling, AK.

SIMON, PATRICIA A. STONE. b. 1927; m.; c. David, daughters. POLIT. & GOV.: delegate, Dem. Nat'l. Conv., 1976; ***candidate for Democratic nomination to vice presidency of the U.S., 1980***. BUS. & PROF.: housewife; coordinator, Democrats Against the Draft. MEM.: Democrats Against the Draft. MISC.: mother of draftee killed in Vietnam War, 1968. MAILING ADDRESS: 41 Oxford Rd., Newton Centre, MA.

SIMON, PAUL. b. Nov 29, 1928, Eugene, OR; par. Rev. Martin Paul and Ruth (Troemel) Simon; m. Jeanne Hurley, Apr 21, 1960; c. Sheila, Martin. EDUC.: U. of OR, 1945–46; Dana Coll., 1946–48. POLIT. & GOV.: elected as a Democrat to IL State House, 1955–63; elected as a Democrat to IL State Senate, 1963–69; delegate, Dem. Nat'l. Conv., 1968, 1972 (alternate), 1976; elected as a Democrat to lt. gov. of IL, 1969–72; candidate for Democratic nomination to gov. of IL, 1972; elected as a Democrat to U.S. House (IL), 1975–85; ***candidate for Democratic nomination to presidency of the U.S., 1980, 1988***; elected as a Democrat to U.S. Senate (IL), 1985–. BUS. & PROF.: publisher, *Troy (IL) Tribune*, 1948–66; fellow, JFK Inst. of Politics, Harvard U., 1973; prof. of Public Affairs, Sangamon State U., 1973–74. MIL.: pvt., counterintelligence corps, U.S. Army, 1951–53. MEM.: Wheatridge Foundation (dir.); Lutheran Human Relations Assn.; American Legion; Urban League; VFW; NAACP; Sigma Delta Chi; Lions Club. AWARDS: award, APSA, 1957; "Best Legislator," 7 times. HON. DEG.: LL.D., Dana Coll., 1965; D.Litt., McKendree Coll., 1965; LL.D., Concordia Coll., 1968; D.C.L., Greenville Coll., 1968; LL.D., Lincoln Coll., 1969; LL.D., Loyola U., 1969; LL.D., Valparaiso U., 1976. WRITINGS: *Lovejoy: Martyr to Freedom* (1964); *Lincoln's Preparation for Greatness* (1966); *A Hungry World* (coauthor, 1966); *Protestant-Catholic Marriages Can Succeed* (1967); *You Want to Change the World? So Change It!* (1971); *The Politics of World Hunger* (coauthor, 1973). REL.: Lutheran. MAILING ADDRESS: Route 1, Makanda, IL 62958.

SIMON, WILLIAM EDWARD. b. Nov 27, 1927, Paterson, NJ; par. Charles and Eleanor (Kearns) Simon; m. Carol Girard, 1950; c. two sons, five daughters. EDUC.: Newark Acad.; B.A., Lafayette Coll., 1952. POLIT. & GOV.: appointed deputy U.S. sec. of the treasury, 1973–74; appointed U.S. sec. of the treasury, 1974–77; chm., Economic Policy Board, 1974–77; chm., East-West Foreign Trade Board, 1975–77; administrator, Federal Energy Office, 1973–74; chm., President's Energy Resources Council; chm., National Advisory Council on International Monetary and Financial Policies; chm., Council on International Economic Policy; chm., Joint U.S.-Saudi Arabian Comm. on Economic Cooperation; chm., U.S.-Israel Joint Comm. on Investment and Trade; chm., Federal Financing Bank; chm., National Comm. on Supplies and Shortages; chm., Environmental Financing Authority; U.S. gov., International Monetary Fund; U.S. gov., International Bank for Reconstruction and Development; U.S. gov., Inter-American Development Bank; U.S. gov., Asian Development Bank; chm., Emergency Loan Guarantee Board; member, Domestic Council; member, Cmte. on Interest and Dividends; member, U.S.-Egyptian Comm. on Economic Development; member, U.S. Railway Assn.; ***candidate for Republican nomination to vice presidency of the U.S., 1976, 1980; candidate for Republican nomination to presidency of the U.S., 1980***. BUS. & PROF.: employee, Union Securities Co., New York, NY, 1952–57; asst. vice pres., mgr., Municipal Trading Dept., 1955–57; vice pres., Weeden and Co., New York, NY, 1957–64; senior partner, Salomon Brothers, New York, NY, 1964–72; consultant, Blythe, Eastman, Dillon and Co., Inc. (investment councilors), New York, NY, 1977–; dir., Citibank; dir., Citicorp; dir., INA Corp.; dir., Xerox Corp.; dir., Dart Industries, Inc.; chm. of the board, The Trib, New York, NY, 1977–; dir., Olin Corp.; senior adviser, Booz, Allen and Hamilton. MIL.: lt., U.S. Army, 1946–48; Order of the Nile (Egypt). MEM.: Lafayette Coll. (trustee); Mannes Coll. of Music (trustee); Newark Acad. (trustee); U.S. Olympic Cmte. (chm., fund raising cmte.); NY Debt Management Cmte. (chm.); Investment Bankers' Assn. of America (gov., to 1972); Securities Industry Assn. (dir.); Public Finance Council; Assn. of Primary Dealers in U.S. Government Securities (pres.); John M. Olin Foundation (pres.); Council on Foreign Relations; Commonwealth Club of CA; Order of Malta; Burning Tree Club; Chevy Chase Club; River Club; Maidstone Club; Alfalfa Club; Balboa Bay Club; Mont Pelerin Soc.; Pilgrims of the U.S.; Friendly Sons of St. Patrick; Wolf Trap Center for the Performing Arts (trustee); Smithsonian Institution (regent); National Gallery of Art (trustee). AWARDS: "Man of the Year" Award, ASME; Dean's Citation, American U.; Distinguished Service Award, Fairleigh Dickinson U.; American Eagle Award, Invest in America Council; Government Service Award, Public Relations Soc. of America; President's Cup Award, National Defense Transportation Assn.; Gold Medal Award, National Inst. for Social

Science; Executive Government Award, OIC Government Relations Service; Distinguished Service Award, The Tax Foundation; Bicentennial Award, U.S. Citizens' Congress; "Outstanding Citizen of the Year" Award, Advertising Club of NJ; Jefferson Award, 1978. HON. DEG.: LL.D., Lafayette Coll., 1973; LL.D., Pepperdine U., 1975; D.C.L., Jacksonville U., 1976; Doctor Philosophiae Honoris Causa, Tel Aviv U., 1976; Hon. Scriptural Degree, Israel Torah Research Inst. WRITINGS: *A Time for Truth* (1978). REL.: R.C. MAILING ADDRESS: 1404 Langley Place, McLean, VA 22101.

SIMONETTI, JOSEPH. POLIT. & GOV.: ***candidate for Democratic nomination to presidency of the U.S., 1992***. MAILING ADDRESS: PA.

SIMONS, ALGIE MARTIN. b. Oct 9, 1870, North Freedom, WI; d. Mar 11, 1950, Martinsville, WV; par. Horace Buttoph and Linda (Blackman) Simons; m. Eleanor May Wood (q.v.), Jun 1897; c. Lawrence Wood, Miriam Eleanor. EDUC.: grad., Baraboo (WI) H.S., 1891; B.L., U. of WI, 1895 (special honors in Economics). POLIT. & GOV.: joined Socialist Labor Party, 1897; Social Democratic Party candidate for U.S. House (IL), 1900; member, National Exec. Cmte., Socialist Party, 1905; Socialist Party candidate for board of trustees, U. of IL, 1906; Socialist Party candidate for U.S. House (IL), 1908; ***candidate for Socialist Party nomination to presidency of the U.S., 1908***; member, Cook Cty. (IL) Socialist Party Central Cmte., 1911; delegate, Socialist Party National Convention, 1917; expelled from Socialist Party, 1917. BUS. & PROF.: author; personnel management expert; medical economist; reporter, *Madison (WI) Democrat*; correspondent, Chicago (IL) Record; social worker, U. of Cincinnati Settlement, 1895; social worker, Stockyards District, United Charities of Chicago, 1896–99; ed., *Worker's Call* (later *Chicago Socialist*), 1899–1900; ed., *International Socialist Review*, 1900–1906; ed., *Chicago (IL) Daily Socialist*, 1906–10; ed., *The Coming Nation*, Girard, KS, 1910–13; ed., *Milwaukee (WI) Leader*, 1913–16; teacher, U. of WI Extension Service, 1920; employee, Leffingwell-Ream (management engineers), 1920–21; sec., American School, Chicago, IL, 1921–30; researcher, American Coll. of Dentists, 1930–31; staff member, Bureau of Medical Economics, American Medical Assn., 1932–44. MEM.: WI Defense League (1917); WI Loyalty Legion (literary bureau, 1917–18); Cmte. on Public Information; Alliance for Labor and Democracy (delegate, national convention, 1917, charter member); Socialist and Labor Mission to England, France, and Italy, 1918; Social Democratic League (charter member); American Economics Assn.; Phi Beta Kappa. WRITINGS: *Compensation* (1900); *Socialism* (1900); *Labor Politics* (1900); *What Is a Scab?* (1900); *A Tale of a Churn* (1902); *The American Farmer* (1902); *What Party Should Workingmen Support?* (1904); *Class Struggles in America* (1907); *Packingtown* (1909); *The Man Under the Machine*; *Social Forces in American History* (1911); *Wasting Human Life*; *The Vision for Which We Fought* (1919); *Personnel Relations in Industry* (1921); *Production Management* (1922); *Success Through Vocational Guidance* (with James McKinney, 1922); *The Way to Health Insurance* (with Nathan Sinai, 1932). REL.: Bapt. RES.: Evanston, IL.

SIMONS, ELEANOR MAY WOOD. b. Baraboo, WI; d. Dec 3, 1948; d. Philip Aurey and Anna (Crook) Wood; m. Algie Martin Simons (q.v.), Jun 1897; c. Lawrence Wood, Miriam Eleanor. EDUC.: Ph.B. (cum laude), U. of Chicago, 1905; A.M., Northwestern U., 1909, Ph.D., 1930; studied in France and Belgium. POLIT. & GOV.: lecturer, Lyceum Bureau, Socialist Party; Socialist Party candidate for board of trustees, U. of IL, 1904, 1908; Socialist Party candidate for IL State Superintendent of Public Instruction, 1906; delegate, Socialist Party National Convention, 1908, 1910, 1912; ***candidate for Socialist Party nomination to vice presidency of the U.S., 1908***; member, national cmte., Socialist Party, 1908–11; delegate, International Socialist Congress, 1910; chm., National Education Cmte., Socialist Party; member, National Woman's Cmte., Socialist Party, 1913–14; chm., Americanization Cmte., Milwaukee Cty. (WI) Council of Defense, c. 1917. BUS. & PROF.: economist; author; asst. ed., *Chicago (IL) Daily World*, 4 years; high school teacher; instructor in Economics, Ruskin Coll., 1906–07; ed., *International Socialist Review*; assoc. ed., *Chicago (IL) Daily Socialist*, 1907–10; instructor, Dept. of Economics, Northwestern U.; assoc. ed., *The Coming Nation*, Girard, KS, 1910–13. MEM.: Intercollegiate Socialist Soc. (lecturer); IL League of Women Voters (chm., Citizenship Training Cmte., 1922–30); APSA; AAUP; AAUW; Royal Economical Soc.; American Economics Assn.; Pi Beta Phi; Alpha Pi Zeta; American Acad. of Arts and Sciences (fellow); Evanston Woman's Club; American Assn. for Labor Legislation; White Rats. WRITINGS: *Woman and the Social Problem* (1899); *Industrial Education in Chicago*; *Education in the South*; *Why the Professional Woman Should Be a Socialist* (1913); *Wisconsin Citizens' Handbook* (1920); *Outline of Civics*; *Everyday Problems in Economics* (1945). AWARDS: Harris Prize in Economics, Northwestern U., 1909. REL.: Episc. RES.: Evanston, IL.

SIMPSON, H. A. POLIT. & GOV.: ***candidate for United Christian Party nomination to vice presidency of the U.S., 1908***. RES.: Pana, IL.

SIMPSON, WILLIAM GERALD. POLIT. & GOV.: ***candidate for Republican nomination to presidency of the U.S., 1916***; candidate for Republican nomination to U.S. Senate (MI), 1918. RES.: Detroit, MI.

SINCLAIR, UPTON BEALL. b. Sep 20, 1878, Baltimore, MD; d. Nov 25, 1968, Bound Brook, NJ; par. Upton Beall and Priscilla (Harden) Sinclair; m. Meta H. Buller, 1900; m. 2d, Mary Craig Kimbrough, Apr 21, 1913; m. 3d, Mary Elizabeth Willis, Oct 14, 1961; c. David. EDUC.: A.B., Coll. of the City of NY, 1897; Columbia U. POLIT. & GOV.: Socialist

Party candidate for U.S. House (NJ), 1906; Socialist Party candidate for U.S. House (CA), 1920; Socialist Party candidate for U.S. Senate (CA), 1922; Socialist Party candidate for gov. of CA, 1926, 1930; ***candidate for Socialist Party nomination to presidency of the U.S., 1928***; Democratic candidate for gov. of CA, 1934; ***candidate for Democratic nomination to presidency of the U.S., 1936***. BUS. & PROF.: author; founder, Helicon Home Colony, Englewood, NJ, 1906; contributor, *New Masses*; publisher, Upton Sinclair's Magazine, 1918–19. MEM.: Intercollegiate Socialist Soc. (founder); A.C.L.U. (founder); League for Industrial Democracy (founder); American Newspaper Guild; John Reed Club; American Cmte. for Struggle Against War; U.S. Congress Against War; International Union of Revolutionary Writers; International Labor Defense (dir., 1928); Sacco-Vanzetti National League; Peace Patriots; International Workers Aid (dir.); End Poverty In California (EPIC); Workers International Relief (dir., 1928); Berger National Foundation; Workers Cultural Federation; Conference for Progressive Political Action (1933); International Cmte. for Political Prisoners; Commonwealth Coll.; Freethinkers Ingersoll Cmte.; World Congress Against War; National Cmte. for the Defense of Political Prisoners; Emergency Cmte. on Political Prisoners; A.S.M.F.S. AWARDS: Pulitzer Prize for Fiction, 1943; award, American Newspaper Guild, 1962. WRITINGS: *Springtime and Harvest* (1901); *King Midas* (1901); *The Journal of Arthur Stirling* (1903); *Prince Hagen: A Phantasy* (1903); *Manassas: A Novel of the Civil War* (1904); *The Jungle* (1906); *Markets and Misery* (1907); *The Industrial Republic* (1907); *The Overman* (1907); *The Metropolis* (1908); *The Money-Changers* (1908); *Samuel, The Seeker* (1909); *The Fasting Cure* (1911); *Love's Pilgrimage* (1911); *Plays of Protest* (1911); *Sylvia* (1913); *Damaged Goods* (1913); *Sylvia's Marriage* (1914); *The Cry for Justice* (1915); *King Coal: A Novel of the Colorado Strike* (1917); *The Profits of Religion* (1918); *Jimmie Higgins* (1919); *The Brass Check* (1919); *100%: The Story of a Patriot* (1920); *They Call Me Carpenter* (1922); *The Book of Life* (1922); *The Goose Step—A Study of American Education* (1923); *Hell* (1923); *The Goslings: A Study of the American Schools* (1924); *Singing Jailbirds* (1924); *Mammonart* (1925); *Bill Porter* (1925); *Letters to Judd* (1926); *Spokesman's Secretary* (1926); *Oil!* (1927); *Money Writes!* (1927); *Boston* (1928); *Mountain City* (1930); *Mental Radio* (1930); *Roman Holiday* (1931); *The Wet Parade* (1931); *American Outpost* (1932); *Upton Sinclair Presents William Fox* (1933); *The Way Out* (1933); *I, Governor of California—And How I Ended Poverty* (1933); *I, candidate for Governor—And How I Got Licked* (1935); *We People of America—And How We Ended Poverty* (1935); *Depression Island* (1936); *What God Means to Men* (1936); *The Gnomobile* (1936); *Co-Op* (1936); *Wally for Queen* (1936); *No Pasaran: Story of the Battle of Madrid* (1937); *The Flivver King: A Story of Ford-America* (1937); *Our Lady* (1938); *Little Steel* (1938); *Your Million Dollars* (1939); *Marie Antoinette* (1939); *Expect No Peace* (1939); *World's End* (1940); *Between Two Worlds* (1941); *Peace or War in America: Debate Between Upton Sinclair and Philip F. LaFollette* (1941); *Dragon's Teeth* (1942); *Wide is the Gate* (1943); *Presidential Agent* (1944); *Dragon Harvest* (1945); *A World to Win* (1946); *Presidential Mission* (1947); *A Giant's Strength* (1948); *One Clear Call* (1948); *O Shepherd, Speak* (1949); *Another Pamela* (1950); *The Enemy Had It Too* (1950); *A Personal Jesus: A Biography* (1952); *The Return of Lanny Budd* (1953); *A Cup of Fury* (1956); *The Deeds of Didymus* (1958); *Theirs Be the Guilt* (1959); *My Lifetime in Letters* (1960); *Cicero* (1960); *Affectionately, Eve* (1961); *The Autobiography of Upton Sinclair* (1963); *The Cry for Justice* (1963). RES.: Monrovia, CA.

SINGLETON, JAMES WASHINGTON. b. Nov 23, 1811, Paxton, VA; d. Apr 4, 1892, Baltimore, MD; par. Gen. James and Judith Throckmorton (Ball) Singleton; m. Catherine McDaniel; m. 2d, Ann Craig; m. 3d, Parthenia McDonald, 1844; c. Lily Thomas Osburn, six others. EDUC.: Winchester Acad.; studied law and medicine. POLIT. & GOV.: elected as a Democrat, delegate, IL State Constitutional Convention, 1847, 1861; elected as a Democrat to IL State House, 1850–54, 1860–62; delegate, Dem. Nat'l. Conv., 1856; appointed IL Commissioner, U.S.-Canadian Water Communications Comm., 1862; Democratic candidate for U.S. House (IL), 1868, 1882; ***candidate for National independent (Greenback) Party nomination to presidency of the U.S., 1876 (withdrew)***; elected as a Democrat to U.S. House (IL), 1879–83; ***candidate for Democratic nomination to presidency of the U.S., 1884***. BUS. & PROF.: atty.; admitted to IL Bar, 1838; law practice, Mt. Sterling, IL; farmer, Quincy, IL; pres., Quincy and Toledo R.R.; pres., Quincy, Alton and St. Louis R.R. MIL.: brig. gen., IL State Militia, 1844. MEM.: Peace Convention (delegate, 1864). MISC.: noted as Peace Democrat; engaged in "Mormon War," 1844. RES.: Quincy, IL.

SINKOLA, GARY LEE. POLIT. & GOV.: ***candidate for Republican nomination to presidency of the U.S., 1992***. MAILING ADDRESS: 106 Front St., Fairbanks, AK 99701.

SIRICA, JOHN JOSEPH. b. Mar 19, 1904, Waterbury, CT; d. Aug 14, 1992, Washington, DC; par. Fred Ferdinand and Rose (Zinno) Sirica; m. Lucile M. Camalier, Feb 26, 1952; c. John Joseph, Jr., Patricia Anne, Eileen Marie. EDUC.: LL.B., Georgetown U., 1926. POLIT. & GOV.: appointed U.S. atty. for DC, 1930–34; appointed gen. counsel, U.S. House Select Cmte. to Investigate the Federal Communications Comm., 1944; appointed judge, U.S. District Court for DC, 1957–86 (chief judge, 1971–74, senior judge, 1977–86); ***candidate for Democratic nomination to presidency of the U.S., 1976***. BUS. & PROF.: automobile mechanic; professional boxer; atty.; admitted to the Bar of the District Court of DC, 1926; admitted to the Bar of the U.S. Court of Appeals for DC; admitted to practice before the Bar of the Supreme Court of the U.S.; law practice, Washington, DC, 1926–30, 1934–44; assoc., partner, Hogan and Hartson (law firm), Washington, DC, 1949–57; adj. prof. of Law, Georgetown U. Law Center. MEM.: ABA (State chm., Junior Bar Conference, 1938–39); Bar Assn. of DC (hon.); John Carroll Soc.; Phi Alpha Delta; Congressional Country Club; National

Lawyers Club; Lido Civic Club; Georgetown U. (regent). AWARDS: Award of Merit, American Judges Assn., 1973; "Man of the Year," *Time Magazine*, 1973; "Timmie" Award, Touchdown Club of WA, 1974; John Carroll Award, Georgetown U. Alumni Assn., 1974; Good Government Award, Key West Junior C. of C., 1974; Certificate of Achievement, Italian Hist. Soc. of America, 1974; award, Phi Alpha Delta, 1974; Brien McMahon Memorial Award, Fordham University Club of WA, 1975; "Outstanding Trial Judge of 1975," Assn. of Trial Lawyers of America, 1975; Award of Merit, Federal Administrative Law Judges Conference, 1975; James Cardinal Gibbons Medal, Catholic U. of America Alumni Assn., 1975; Award of Merit, U.S. Dept. of Justice, 1975; Award of Merit, American Justinian Soc. of Jurists, 1975; Outstanding Achievement Award, National Assn. of Secondary School Principals, 1976; Award of Merit, Italian American Bicentennial Tribute, 1976; Judiciary Award, Assn. of Federal Investigators, 1976; Award of Merit, American Acad. of Achievement, 1977; Humanitarian Award, Kappa Alpha Psi, 1977; "Jurisprudence Father of the Year," National Father's Day Cmte., 1978; Award of Merit, Jewish National Fund, 1978; award, DC Bar, 1978; Centennial Medal, Vanderbilt U., 1978. HON. DEG.: LL.D., Boston U.; LL.D., Brown U.; LL.D., City Coll. of NY; LL.D., Duke U.; LL.D., Fairfield U.; LL.D., Georgetown U.; LL.D., Gettysburg Coll.; LL.D., Mount St. Mary's Coll.; LL.D., New England School of Law; LL.D., Coll. of New Rochelle; WRITINGS: *To Set the Record Straight* (1979). REL.: R.C. MISC.: noted for presiding at Watergate trials. RES.: Washington, DC.

SITNICK, FRED IRVIN "MESSIAH" (aka MESSIAH). POLIT. & GOV.: ***candidate for Democratic nomination to presidency of the U.S., 1988, 1992.*** MAILING ADDRESS: c/o Haven Michael Sitnick, 6 Painters Place, Owings Mills, MD 21117.

SITNICK, HAVEN MICHAEL. POLIT. & GOV.: ***candidate for Democratic nomination to vice presidency of the U.S., 1988.*** MAILING ADDRESS: 6 Painters Place, Owings Mills, MD 21117.

SIZEMORE, BARBARA ANN. b. Dec 17, 1927, Chicago, IL; m. (divorced); m. 2d, Jake Milliones, Jr.; c. Kymara Chase; Furman G.; Beatena Milliones; DuBois Milliones; Momar Milliones; Marimba Milliones. EDUC.: B.A., Northwestern U., 1947, M.A., 1954; Ph.D., U. of Chicago, 1965. POLIT. & GOV.: ***candidate for The Black Assembly nomination to presidency of the U.S., 1976***; appointed member, U.S. National Comm. for UNESCO. BUS. & PROF.: teacher, Shoop Public School, Chicago, IL, 1947–54; teacher, Gillespie Public School, 1954–57; teacher, Drew Elementary School, 1957–63; principal, Anton Dvorak Elementary School, 1963–65; principal, Forrestville H.S., 1965–67; instructor, Center for Inner City Studies, Northeast IL State Coll., 1965–71; staff assoc., Midwest Administrative Center, U. of Chicago, 1967–69; dir., Woodlawn Experimental Schools Project, 1969–71; Coordinator of Proposal Development, Chicago (IL) Public Schools, 1971–73; assoc. sec., American Assn. of School Administrators, 1973; appointed Superintendent of Schools, DC Public Schools, 1973–75; self-employed consultant, 1975–; assoc. prof., Dept. of Black Studies, U. of Pittsburgh, 1977–80; author. MEM.: Black Sisters Conference (consultant); Danforth Fellows; Chicago Board Fellows (1965–67); Student Cmte. on Undergrad. Education (consultant); National Urban Coalition; Assn. of Afro-American Educators; National Alliance of Black Educators; American Assn. of School Administrators; African Heritage Study Assn. (dir.); National Council of Administrative Women in Education; National Council of Negro Women; Inst. of the Black World (dir.); Delta Sigma Theta. AWARDS: Northwestern U. Alumni Award, 1974. WRITINGS: "Separatism: A Reality Approach to Inclusion?" *Racial Crisis in American Education* (1969); "Social Science and Education for the Black Identity," *Black Self-Concept* (1971); "Is There a Case for Separate Schools?" *Phi Delta Kappan* (1972); "Making the Schools a Vehicle for Cultural Pluralism," *Cultural Pluralism in Education* (1973); "Shattering the Melting Pot Myth," *Teaching Ethnic Studies* (1973); "Education for Liberation," *School Review* (May, 1973); "Sexism and the Black Male," *Black Scholar* (1973); "Community Power and Education," *Yearbook of the Association of Supervision and Curriculum Development*; "Is Accommodation Enough?" *Journal of Negro Education* (1975). MAILING ADDRESS: c/o U. of Pittsburgh, 230 South Bouquet St., Forbes Triangle, Pittsburgh, PA 15260.

SKINNER, HARRY. b. May 25, 1855, Hertford, NC; d. May 19, 1929, Greenville, NC; par. James C. and Elmyra (Ward) Skinner; m. Lottie Monteiro, Jun 5, 1878; m. 2d, Ella Monteiro, Oct 26, 1895; c. four. EDUC.: Hertford (NC) Acad.; LL.B., U. of KY, 1875. POLIT. & GOV.: elected as a Democrat to Greenville (NC) Town Council, 1878; member, staff of gov. of NC, 1879–86; chm., Democratic Exec. Cmte., First Congressional District of NC, 1880–90; chm., Pitt Cty. Democratic exec. cmte., 1880–92; elected as a Democrat to NC State House, 1891–93; candidate for Democratic nomination to lt. gov. of NC, 1890; chm., People's Party Central Cmte., Pitt Cty., NC, 1892–96; member, NC State People's Party Central Cmte., 1892–96; delegate, People's Party National Convention, 1892 (declined); People's Party candidate for gov. of NC, 1892 (declined); People's Party candidate for U.S. House (NC), 1892 (declined); permanent chm., NC People's Party State Convention, 1894; elected as a Populist (People's Party) to U.S. House (NC), 1895–99; ***candidate for People's Party nomination to vice presidency of the U.S., 1896***; Fusion Party candidate for U.S. House (NC), 1898; joined Republican Party, 1901; appointed U.S. district atty. for Eastern District of NC, 1902–10; delegate, Rep. Nat'l. Conv., 1908; candidate for judge, Eastern District of NC, 1909. BUS. & PROF.: atty.; admitted to NC Bar, 1876; partner, Latham and Skinner (law firm), Greenville, NC, 1876–95; partner, Skinner and Whedbee (law firm), Greenville, NC, 1895–

1910; law practice, Greenville, NC, 1910–29. MEM.: NC Bar Assn. (pres., 1915); ABA (state vice pres.); Masons; Farmers' Alliance; U. of NC (trustee, 1890–96). WRITINGS: "The Hope of the South," *Frank Leslie's Illustrated Newspaper*, Nov 30, 1889. REL.: Episc. RES.: Greenville, NC.

SKOW, PHILIP P. b. 1954. POLIT. & GOV.: ***candidate for Republican nomination to presidency of the U.S., 1992***. MAILING ADDRESS: 213 North St., Carbondale, KS 66414.

SLACKER, HUGH A. POLIT. & GOV.: ***Apathy Party candidate for presidency of the U.S., 1992***. MAILING ADDRESS: P.O. Box 292, Old Town, ME 04468.

SLATE, JEROLD S. POLIT. & GOV.: ***independent candidate for presidency of the U.S., 1976***. MAILING ADDRESS: 225 Broadway, New York, NY 10007.

SLAYTON, JOHN M. POLIT. & GOV.: Greenback Party candidate for U.S. House (PA), 1878; Socialist Party candidate for U.S. House (PA), 1900, 1906, 1908, 1910, 1912, 1914, 1916, 1918, 1924, 1934; Socialist Party candidate for gov. of PA, 1902, 1910, 1926; delegate, Socialist Party National Convention, 1908; ***candidate for Socialist Party nomination to vice presidency of the U.S., 1908, 1912***; member, Socialist Party National Cmte., 1911–14. BUS. & PROF.: carpenter. MEM.: Carpenters' Union. WRITINGS: *The Old Red Flag of Peace, Industry and Universal Brotherhood* (1919). RES.: McKeesport, PA.

SLEMP, CAMPBELL BASCOM. b. Sep 4, 1870, Turkey Cove, VA; d. Aug 7, 1943, Knoxville, TN; par. Campbell and Nannie B. (Cawood) Slemp; single. EDUC.: grad., VA Military Inst., 1891; U. of VA Law School. POLIT. & GOV.: page, VA State House, 1881–82; chm., VA State Republican Central Cmte., 1905–18; elected as a Republican to U.S. House (VA), 1907–23; member, Rep. Nat'l. Cmte., 1918; appointed sec. to President Calvin Coolidge (q.v.), 1923–25; appointed commissioner gen., French Colonial Exposition, Paris, France; ***candidate for Republican nomination to vice presidency of the U.S., 1928***. BUS. & PROF.: atty.; adjunct prof. of Mathematics, VA Military Inst., 1900–1901; admitted to VA Bar, 1901; law practice, Big Stone Gap, VA, 1901–32; pres., Hamilton Realty Co.; pres., Slemp Coal Co. MIL.: commandant of cadets, Marion Military Inst., 1 year. MEM.: U. of VA Inst. of Public Affairs (founder); American Soc. of the French Legion of Honor; National Republican Club; U.S. Naval Acad. (visitor); NY Southern Soc.; Army and Navy Club; Lonesome Pine Club; Burning Tree Club; Metropolitan Club; Press Club. AWARDS: Legion of Honor (France). WRITINGS: *The Mind of the President*; *Selected Addresses*; *Addresses of Famous Southwest Virginians*. RES.: Big Stone Gap, VA.

SLETTEDAHL, EDWARD C. b. Sep 6, 1900, Dawson, MN; m.; c. Harvey A.; one other son. EDUC.: Mankota Teachers' Coll.; Columbia U.; U. of MN. POLIT. & GOV.: elected justice of the peace, Wilkin Cty., MN; ***candidate for Republican nomination to presidency of the U.S., 1952***; Republican candidate for U.S. House (MN), 1956; candidate for Republican nomination to U.S. Senate (MN), 1958. BUS. & PROF.: teacher, St. Paul, MN; building contractor, AK; accountant, AK; building con-tractor, MN. MEM.: MN Fighters for MacArthur (chm., 1952). MAILING ADDRESS: 309 West Arlington, St. Paul, MN.

SLIGH, HENRY MICHAEL. POLIT. & GOV.: ***candidate for Democratic nomination to president of the U.S., 1992***. MAILING ADDRESS: P.O. Box 706, Myrtle Beach, SC 29578.

SLINKER, KEITH HAROLD. POLIT. & GOV.: ***independent candidate for presidency of the U.S., 1992***. MAILING ADDRESS: c/o Richard Courtney Nicol, 412 Ridge Ave., Butler, PA 16001.

SLOAN, TOM. POLIT. & GOV.: ***candidate for American Independent Party nomination to vice presidency of the U.S., 1976***. BUS. & PROF.: prof., Dept. of Communications, Gloucester Cty. Coll., Sewell, NJ. MAILING ADDRESS: c/o Dept. of Communications, Gloucester Cty. Coll., Tanyard Rd., Sewell, NJ 08080.

SLOCOMB, WHITNEY HART. b. Jan 2, 1895, Marietta, OH; d. Sep 25, 1961, Los Angeles, CA; m. Jewel S. POLIT. & GOV.: ***Greenback Party candidate for presidency of the U.S., 1960***. BUS. & PROF.: author. HON. DEG.: LL.D. WRITINGS: *A New Philosophy* (1931); *How to Put Technocracy Into Practice* (1933); *The Causes and Cure of Depressions* (1933); *The Causes and Cure of This Depression* (1933); *The Sovereign Individual vs. Communism and Fascism* (1951); *Do You Want to Be a Slave of the State, or Should the State Be Your Servant?* (1953); *Mass Production and Money*; *Communist Constitution vs. The U.S. Constitution* (1955). RES.: Los Angeles, CA.

SLOCUM, GEORGE W. POLIT. & GOV.: ***independent candidate for presidency of the U.S., 1872***. RES.: IA.

SLOCUM, WILL ROGER. b. Dec 29, 1922, Alhambra, CA; par. Paul Jay and Stella Elva (Redfield) Slocum; m. Pearl Alice Cox; c. Roger William; Linda Alice. EDUC.: high school, Spokane, WA. POLIT. & GOV.: independent candidate for U.S. House (CA), 1967; Peace and Freedom Party candidate for CA State Assembly, 1968, 1972; ***candidate for Peace and Freedom Party nomination to presidency of the U.S., 1972; candidate for Republican nomination to presidency of the U.S., 1972***. BUS. & PROF.: apprentice and journeyman jockey, 15 years; salesman; janitor; taxi driver; sign painter; artist; writer; publisher. MEM.: San Mateo Cty. Human Relations Task Force; Common Cause; Little People of America; CA Assn. of Physically Handicapped. REL.: self-actualization. MAILING ADDRESS: 310 Cuardo Ave., Millbrae, CA 94030.

SMABY, ALPHA. POLIT. & GOV.: ***independent (MN Progressives) candidate for vice presidency of the U.S., 1988***. MAILING ADDRESS: c/o Jim Richardson, 226 North Lexington Parkway, St. Paul, MN 55104.

SMALL, SAMUEL WHITE. b. Jul 3, 1851, Knoxville, TN; d. Nov 21, 1931; par. Alexander Benson and Elizabeth Jane (White) Small; m. Annie I. Arnold, 1873; c. Samuel White, Jr.; Robert Toombs. EDUC.: A.B., Emory and Henry Coll., 1871, A.M., 1887; Ph.D., Taylor U., 1894; D.D., OH Northern U., 1894. POLIT. & GOV.: sec. to President Andrew Johnson (q.v.); court reporter, Atlanta (GA) Circuit Court; official reporter, GA State Constitutional Convention, 1877; sec., American Comm. to Paris Exposition, 1878; cmte. reporter, U.S. Senate, 1879–81; Prohibition Party candidate for GA State Senate, 1888; delegate, Prohibition Party National Convention, 1888, 1892; ***candidate for Prohibition Party nomination to vice presidency of the U.S., 1888***; member, Prohibition Party National Cmte., 1888–96; Prohibition Party candidate for U.S. House (GA), 1892; appointed staff, Governor Terrell of GA, 1902. BUS. & PROF.: atty.; admitted to TN Bar; journalist; evangelist; stenographer; newspaper reporter; editorial staff, *Atlanta (GA) Constitution*, 1875–1931; founder, *Norfolk (VA) Daily Pilot*, 1894; founder, *Daily Oklahoman*, Oklahoma City, OK; Evangelist (with Sam Jones), Atlanta, GA, 1885; reform lecturer; employee, Anti-Saloon League. MIL.: reserve soldier, C.S.A., 1865; lt. col., aide-de-camp, GA National Guard; capt., chaplain, Third U.S. Volunteer Engineers, 1898–99. MEM.: National Reform Assn.; Sons of the Revolution; Military Order of Foreign Wars; United Spanish War Veterans; United Con-federate Veterans (aide-de-camp); Army and Navy Club; National Press Club; Naval and Military Order of the Spanish-American War (chaplain-in-chief); Masons; Odd Fellows; Knights of Pythias; Order of Red Men; Anti-Saloon League. WRITINGS: *Old Si's Savings* (1886); *Pleas for Prohibition* (1889); *The White Angel of the World* (1891). REL.: Methodist. RES.: Rosslyn, VA.

SMALLRIDGE, RODGER D. b. Nov 17, 1920, Iowa Falls, IA; par. Leland E. and Bernice C. (Boyington) Smallridge; m. (divorced); m. 2d, Caroljean Shaffer; c. ten. EDUC.: high school grad.; correspondence courses; pilot training school. POLIT. & GOV.: ***Christian Conservative Coalition Party candidate for presidency of the U.S., 1988***. BUS. & PROF.: railroad fireman; railroad engineer; diesel engineer, riverboat; master electrician; mgr., contracting firm; self-employed; ordained Melchizedec priest, Oct 1954; pastor, independent churches, 30 years. MIL.: sgt., U.S.A.A.C., 1940–45. REL.: Christian. WRITINGS: *The Revelations of Jesus* (Melchizedec translation, 1980). MAILING ADDRESS: 120 Vista, #6, Madisonville, LA 70447-9613.

SMALLWOOD, FRANKLIN. b. Jun 24, 1927, Ridgewood, NJ; par. J. William and Carolyn (Linkroum) Smallwood; m. Ann Logie, Sep 8, 1951; c. Susan; Sandra; David; Donald. EDUC.: A.B., Dartmouth Coll., 1951; M.P.A., Harvard U., 1953, Ph.D., 1958. POLIT. & GOV.: elected as a Republican to VT State Senate, 1973–75; appointed chm., VT Comm. on Higher Education, 1973–80; ***National Unity Party candidate for vice presidency of the U.S., 1980***. BUS. & PROF.: employee, Atomic Energy Comm., 1953–57; asst. to the pres., Dartmouth Coll., 1957–59, faculty, 1959–67, prof. of Government, 1967–84, Nelson A. Rockefeller prof. of Government, 1984– (chm., City Planning and Urban Studies Program, 1965–72; chm., Social Sciences Div., 1968–72; assoc. dean of faculty, 1968–72; acting dean, 1972; vice pres., Student Affairs, 1975–77; chm., Policy Studies Program, 1977–83; dir., Nelson A. Rockefeller Center for Social Science, 1983–). MIL.: U.S. Army, 1945–47. MEM.: VT State Colleges (trustee, 1967–73); APSA; American Soc. for Public Administration; National Municipal League. AWARDS: Superior Achievement Award, Atomic Energy Comm., 1957; fellow, Inst. of Public Administration, 1960; Dartmouth Coll. faculty fellow, 1962–63; Nuffield Coll. visiting fellow, 1981. WRITINGS: *Metro Toronto: A Decade Later* (1963); *Greater London: The Politics of Metropolitan Reform* (1965); *Free and Independent* (1976); *The Politics of Policy Implementation* (1980); *The Other Candidates* (1983). MAILING ADDRESS: Willey Hill, Norwich, VT 05055.

SMATHERS, GEORGE ARMISTEAD. b. Nov 14, 1913, Atlantic City, NJ; par. Frank and Lura Frances (Jones) Smathers; m. Rosemary Townley, Mar 19, 1939; m. 2d, Carolyn Hyder, Jan 1972; c. John Townley; Bruce Armistead. EDUC.: B.A., U. of FL, 1937, LL.B., 1938. POLIT. & GOV.: appointed asst. U.S. district atty. for FL, 1940–42; appointed asst. to the atty. gen. of the U.S., 1945–46; elected as a Democrat to U.S. House (FL), 1947–51; elected as a Democrat to U.S. Senate (FL), 1951–69; delegate, Dem. Nat'l. Conv., 1952, 1956, 1968; ***candidate for Democratic nomination to presidency of the U.S., 1960, 1968***; appointed delegate, International Tariff Conference, 1966; appointed delegate, Organization of American States, 1967. BUS. & PROF.: atty.; admitted to FL Bar, 1938; law practice (with Walter Dunigan), Miami, FL, 1938–40; partner, Smathers, Thompson, Maxwell and Dyer (law firm), Miami, FL, 1940; senior partner, Smathers and Thompson (law firm), Miami, FL, 1969–; partner, Smathers, Merrigan and Herlong (law firm), Washington, DC, 1969–. MIL.: 1st lt., maj., U.S.M.C., 1942–45; U.S.M.C. Reserves (col.). MEM.: ABA; FL Bar Assn.; Dade Cty. Bar Assn.; FL Junior C. of C. (dir.; pres., 1940); Kiwanis; Phi Delta Phi; Tau Kappa Alpha; Blue Key; Sigma Alpha Epsilon; American Legion; VFW; American Veterans of World War II; Military Order of the World Wars; Masons; Elks; Odd Fellows. AWARDS: "Outstanding Young Man," Miami Junior C. of C., 1940; "Outstanding Young Man in FL," FL Junior C. of C., 1945; "Outstanding Young Man in Government," U.S. Junior C. of C., 1948; "Man of the Year," Alianza Inter-Americana, 1955; Grand Cross (Cuba), 1956. REL.: Methodist. MAILING ADDRESS: 1410 West 24th St., Sunset Island 3, Miami Beach, FL.

SMIT, CHARLES THOMAS. b. Mar 7, 1944, Sheboygan, WI; par. Charles Rudolph and Sarah Catherine (Fox) Smit; m. Anne Miriam Doyle, Sep 17, 1983; c. Charles Matthew Isaiah; Teresa Elizabeth; Thomas James Noah. EDUC.: grad., Wabasha (MN) H.S., 1962; B.A., U. of MN, 1967; Religious Studies, Ecumenical Inst., Chicago, IL, 1966–67. POLIT. & GOV.: candidate for Republican nomination to U.S. House (MN), 1984, 1986, 1990; ***candidate for Republican nomination to presidency of the U.S., 1992***. BUS. & PROF.: freelance writer, 1967–; poet; temporary assignments, Delta Plus, Apple Valley, MN, 1987; delivery driver, Group Health, Inc., Eden Prairie, MN, 1985–86; schoolbus driver, KAL Lines, Burnsville, MN, 1986–87; yardman, Lamperts Building Materials, Apple Valley, MN, 1989–90; coder, Quorum Systems, Control Data Corp., Minneapolis, MN, 1989–90; schoolbus driver, Septran, Inc., Minneapolis, MN, 1991; schoolbus driver, Medicine Lake Bus Co., 1991; contributor of articles in the *Minnesota Daily*, Minneapolis, MN; *Eagan (MN) Chronicle*; *Saint Paul (MN) Pioneer Press*; *Moody Street Irregulars*; *National Catholic Reporter*; *MPIRG Statewatch*; *The United Methodist Reporter*; *Friends Journal*; *Park Penworks* (poetry collection of St. Anthony Park Writer's Workshop, 1983); *Fellowship Magazine*; *The College Reporter* (Mankato State Coll.); *Moorhead State College Zone*. WRITINGS: *Who Needs More Turkey?* (1978); *Conscription: A Civil War Inheritance*, *A Constitutional Question*, *A Personal Conviction*, *A Presidential Campaign Issue* (1979); *Essays Interpreting Christian Non-Violence for a New Age* (1980); *Dress Rehearsals for Armageddon* (1982); *Was It Worth the Wait?* (1985). REL.: nondenominational Christian. MAILING ADDRESS: 3395 Yankee Doodle Rd., Apt. 102, Eagan, MN 55121.

SMITH, ALFRED EMANUEL. b. Dec 30, 1873, New York, NY; d. Oct 4, 1944, New York, NY; par. Alfred Emanuel and Catherine (Mulvihill) Smith; m. Catherine A. Dunn, May 6, 1900; c. Alfred Emanuel III; Emily (Mrs. John Adams Warner); Catherine (Mrs. Francis J. Quillinan); Arthur; Walter. EDUC.: St. James Parochial School, New York, NY. POLIT. & GOV.: clerk, Office of Commissioner of Jurors, New York, NY, 1895–1903; elected as a Democrat to NY State Assembly, 1903–15 (Speaker, 1913); Democratic candidate for U.S. House (NY), 1912, 1914; delegate, NY State Constitutional Convention, 1915, 1938 (hon. pres.); elected as a Democrat, sheriff, New York Cty., NY, 1915–17; elected as a Democrat, pres., Board of Aldermen, Greater New York, NY, 1917; elected as a Democrat to gov. of NY, 1919–21, 1923–29; delegate, Dem. Nat'l. Conv., 1920; ***candidate for Democratic nomination to presidency of the U.S., 1920, 1924, 1932, 1936***; Democratic candidate for gov. of NY, 1920; appointed member, Port of NY Authority, 1921; appointed member, U.S. Board of Indian Commissioners, 1921; ***candidate for Prohibition Party nomination to presidency of the U.S., 1928 (satire effort); Democratic candidate for presidency of the U.S., 1928***. BUS. & PROF.: asst. bookkeeper; checker, Fulton Fish Market, New York, NY; asst. bookkeeper, Davison Steam Pump Works, Brooklyn, NY; chm., U.S. Trucking Corp., 1921; pres., Empire State, Inc.; chm. of the board, Lawyers Trust Co., 1928; dir., New York Life Insurance Co.; dir., National Surety Corp.; trustee, Hubert Charitable and Educational Trust Fund, 1929; ed., *The New Outlook*, 1932–34; dir., Knott Hotels Corp.; trustee, Postal Telegraph and Cable Co., 1937. MEM.: Soc. of Tammany (Sachem); Catholic U. of America (trustee, 1933–44); American Liberty League; National Democratic Club; NY Press Club; Fort Orange Club; National Legion of Decency (advisory chm., 1934); Fordham U. (trustee); Soc. of Friendly Sons of St. Patrick (hon. member); Manhattan Democratic Club. AWARDS: Laetare Medal, U. of Notre Dame, 1929; Catholic Action Medal, St. Bonaventure's Coll., 1933; Knight of Malta, 1939; Papal Chamberlain, 1939; Bronze Medal, NY Acad. of Public Education, 1940. HON. DEG.: LL.D., Fordham U., 1919; LL.D., Manhattan Coll., 1919; LL.D., Columbia U., 1926; LL.D., Dublin U., 1930; LL.D., Harvard U., 1933; LL.D., State U. of NY, 1933; D.Litt., Catholic U. of America. WRITINGS: *Up to Now* (1929). REL.: R.C. MISC.: builder of Empire State Building. RES.: New York, NY.

SMITH, BRIAN C. POLIT. & GOV.: ***candidate for Republican nomination to presidency of the U.S., 1992***. MAILING ADDRESS: 596 Willett Ave., Riverside, RI 02915.

SMITH, CHARLES EMORY. b. Feb 18, 1842, Mansfield, CT; d. Jan 19, 1908, Philadelphia, PA; par. Emory Boutelle and Arvilla Topliff (Royce) Smith; m. Ella Huntley, Jun 30, 1863; m. 2d, Nettie Nichols, Oct 3, 1907. EDUC.: grad., Union Coll., 1861. POLIT. & GOV.: chm., Cmte. on Resolutions, NY State Republican Conventions, 1874–80; appointed U.S. minister to Russia, 1890–92; appointed postmaster gen. of the U.S., 1898–1902; ***candidate for Republican nomination to vice presidency of the U.S., 1900***. BUS. & PROF.: journalist; ed., *Albany (NY) Express*, 1865–70; ed., *Albany (NY) Journal*, 1870–80; ed., *Philadelphia (PA) Press*, 1880. MIL.: organized Union volunteer regiment, Civil War. MEM.: NY State Press Assn. (pres., 1874); U. of the State of NY (regent, 1879–80); Union Coll. (trustee, 1881). HON. DEG.: LL.D., Union Coll., 1889; LL.D., Knox Coll., 1900; LL.D., Lafayette Coll., 1900; LL.D., Wesleyan U., 1901. RES.: Philadelphia, PA.

SMITH, CRAWFORD. POLIT. & GOV.: ***candidate for Republican nomination to presidency of the U.S., 1992***. MAILING ADDRESS: Route 8, Box 401, Lancaster, SC 29720.

SMITH, DONALD GENE. b. Dec 8, 1923, Parke Cty., IN; par. Harold C. and Mildred F. (Waldridge) Smith; m. Margaret Fultz; m. 2d, Elnora L. Rossi; c. Randall L.; William R. Toth (stepson). EDUC.: grad., Montezuma (IN) H.S.; Purdue U.; grad., Brown Business Coll., Terre Haute, IN. POLIT. & GOV.: elected to Rockeville (IN) School Board, 1957–60 (pres.); ***candidate for Democratic nomination to presidency of the U.S., 1984***. BUS. & PROF.: mgr., Bosby's Implement Store, Rockeville, IN, 1947–55; self-employed, 1955–61; new car mgr., 1961–66; maintenance foreman, J. L. Case, Terre Haute, IN, 1967–68; maintenance foreman, Quality Inns, Fort Lauderdale, FL, 1970–76; maintenance foreman, Pompano Beach, FL, 1977–78; maintenance man, IN State U., Terre Haute, IN, 1979–. MIL.: staff sgt., U.S. Army, 1942–45. MEM.: Masons. REL.: Protestant. MAILING ADDRESS: Box 61, Rural Route 3, Rosedale, IN 47874.

SMITH, EUGENE R. "GENE." b. Feb 6, 1929, Keene, NH; m. Lane Neihardt, 1968; c. three. EDUC.: Boston U.; studied for Metropolitan Opera. POLIT. & GOV.: member, local school board (resigned after 1 month); ***candidate for Democratic nomination to presidency of the U.S., 1992***. BUS. & PROF.: actor, broadway and television; columnist, "Social Addictions"; licensed real estate agent (CA); business consultant; psychologist. MIL.: U.S. Navy, WWII. Tried out for Boston Red Sox professional baseball team. MEM.: student council (Boston U.); Actors' Equity (shop steward); International Olive Branch Foundation (pres.; founder). WRITINGS: *Mid Matter Motion*. REL.: Protestant. MAILING ADDRESS: P.O. Box 5538, South Lake Tahoe, CA 95729.

SMITH, GERALD LYMAN KENNETH. b. Feb 27, 1898, Pardeeville, WI; d. Apr 15, 1976, Glendale, CA; par. Lyman Z. and Sarah (Henthorn) Smith; m. Eleanor Marion "Elna" Sorenson, Jun 21, 1922; c. Gerry (adopted). EDUC.: grad., high school, Viroqua, WI; Valparaiso U.; grad., Butler Coll., Indianapolis, IN. POLIT. & GOV.: ***candidate for Democratic nomination to presidency of the U.S., 1932, 1936***; spokesman, Union Party, 1936; independent Republican candidate for U.S. Senate (MI), 1942; founder, America First Party; ***America First Party candidate for presidency of the U.S., 1944***; founder, national dir., Christian Nationalist Party, 1947; ***Christian Nationalist Party candidate for presidency of the U.S., 1948, 1956***. BUS. & PROF.: propagandist; minister, Disciples of Christ Church, 1917; lecturer; chaplain, Butler Coll.; pastor, Deep River, IN; pastor, Seventh Christian Church, Indianapolis, IN, 1922–28; pastor, Butler University Church; pastor, King's Highway Church, Shreveport, LA, 1928–34; publisher, The Cross and the Flag, 1942–76; pamphleteer. MEM.: Share-the-Wealth Club (organizer); Silver Shirts (1933); Cmte. of One Million (founder, 1937); Christian Nationalist Crusade (founder, 1946); Western Hemisphere Cmte. Against Communism; Political Tract Soc.; Inner Circle; Mid-Western Political Survey Inst.; Citizens Congressional Cmte. (founder); "Christ of the Ozarks" Memorial (founder; Magnetic Mountain, Eureka Springs, AR). WRITINGS: *The Hoop of Steel* (1942). REL.: Disciples of Christ. MISC.: delivered Sen. Huey Long's (q.v.) funeral oration; worked with Dr. Francis E. Townsend (q.v.) and Rev. Charles E. Coughlin (q.v.). RES.: Eureka Springs, AR.

SMITH, GERRIT. b. Mar 6, 1797, Utica, NY; d. Dec 28, 1874, New York, NY; par. Peter and Elizabeth (Livingston) Smith; m. Wealthy Ann Backus, Jan 11, 1819; m. 2d, Ann Carroll Fitzhugh, Jan 3, 1822; c. Greene; Elizabeth S. (Mrs. C. D. Miller); two others. EDUC.: Clinton Acad., Clinton, NY; grad., Hamilton Coll., 1818; studied law. POLIT. & GOV.: delegate, NY State Anti-Masonic Party Convention, 1824, 1828; Anti-Masonic Party candidate for NY State Senate, 1826, 1831; founder, Liberty Party, 1840; Liberty Party candidate for gov. of NY, 1840; founder, Anti-Dramshop Party, 1842, revived, 1871; ***candidate for Liberty Party nomination to presidency of the U.S., 1844; candidate for Liberty Party nomination to vice presidency of the U.S., 1844; Liberty Party candidate for presidency of the U.S., 1848 (declined), 1852; Liberty League candidate for presidency of the U.S., 1848; Industrial Congress candidate for presidency of the U.S., 1848***; elected as an Ultra-Abolitionist to U.S. House (NY), 1853–54 (resigned); ***Land Reform (Abolition) Party candidate for presidency of the U.S., 1856***; People's State Ticket candidate for gov. of NY, 1858; ***candidate for Republican (Union) nomination to presidency of the U.S., 1860; Union Party candidate for presidency of the U.S., 1860***; joined Republican Party, 1864; delegate, Rep. Nat'l. Conv., 1872; ***candidate for Prohibition Party nomination to presidency of the U.S., 1872***. BUS. & PROF.: land speculator; atty.; admitted to NY Bar, 1853; law practice, Peterboro, NY, 1853; philanthropist; reformer; abolitionist; temperance advocate; vegetarian. MEM.: American Peace Soc. (vice pres.); KS Aid Soc.; New England Emigrant Aid Co.; American Colonization Soc. WRITINGS: *Speeches of Gerrit Smith in Congress* (1856); *Religion of Reason* (1864); *Speeches and Letters of Gerrit Smith on the Rebellion* (1864–65); *The Theologies* (1866); *Nature's Theology* (1867); *A Letter From Gerrit Smith to Albert Barnes* (1868). REL.: Presb. MISC.: advocate of Sunday Observance, women's suffrage, women's dress reform, and reform of the prison system; implicated in John Brown's raid on Harper's Ferry, 1859. RES.: Peterboro, NY.

SMITH, GREEN CLAY. b. Jul 2, 1832, Richmond, KY; d. Jun 29, 1895, Washington, DC; par. John Speed and Eliza Lewis (Clay) Smith; m. Lena Duke, 1856; c. Mrs. J. L. Whitehead; Mamie; Green Clay, Jr.; Duke; Mrs. James B. Hawkins. EDUC.: Center Coll., Danville, KY; grad., Transylvania U.,

1849; LL.B., Lexington Law School, 1853. POLIT. & GOV.: school commissioner (KY), 1853–57; elected as a Democrat to KY State House, 1861–63; elected as a Unionist to U.S. House (KY), 1863–66; delegate, Rep. Nat'l. Conv., 1864; ***candidate for Republican nomination to vice presidency of the U.S., 1864*** (came within one-half vote of Republican vice presidential nomination; appointed gov. of MT Territory, 1866–69; temporary chm., Prohibition Party National Convention, 1876; *National Prohibition Reform Party candidate for presidency of the U.S., 1876; candidate for Prohibition Party nomination to presidency of the U.S., 1888 (declined)*. BUS. & PROF.: atty.; admitted to KY Bar, 1852; law practice, Covington, KY, 1853; ordained minister, Baptist Church, 1870; evangelist; pastor, Metropolitan Baptist Church, Washington, DC, 1890–95. MIL.: 2d lt., First Regt., KY Volunteer Infantry, 1846–47; col., Fourth Regt., KY Volunteer Infantry, 1862, brig. gen., 1862, resigned, 1863; brev. maj. gen. of Volunteers, 1865. MEM.: Order of Good Templars (KY pres.); Sons of Temperance (KY pres.); GAR; Union Veterans Union (commander); Masons; Knights Templar; Union Veterans Legion; Baptist Coll. (founder). REL.: Bapt. (pres., General Assn. of Baptist Churches in KY). RES.: Washington, DC.

SMITH, HENRY. b. Jul 22, 1838, Baltimore, MD; d. Sep 16, 1916, Milwaukee, WI. EDUC.: public schools. POLIT. & GOV.: elected member, Common Council, Milwaukee, WI, 1868–72, 1880–82, 1884–87; elected to WI State Assembly, 1878; city comptroller, Milwaukee, WI, 1882–84; elected as a Populist (People's Party) to U.S. House (WI), 1887–89; ***candidate for Union Labor Party nomination to presidency of the U.S., 1888 (declined)***; People's Party candidate for U.S. House (WI), 1888; elected member, Board of Aldermen, Milwaukee, WI, 1898–1916. BUS. & PROF.: millwright; architect; builder. RES.: Milwaukee, WI.

SMITH, HOKE. b. Sep 2, 1855, Newton, NC; d. Nov 27, 1931, Atlanta, GA; par. Dr. Hosea Hilldreth and Mary Brent (Hoke) Smith; m. Marion "Birdie" Cobb, Dec 19, 1883; m. 2d, Mazie Crawford, Aug 27, 1924; c. Marion; Hildreth; Mary Brent Ransom; Lucy Hoke Grant; Callie Hoke May. EDUC.: private tutors; studied law in offices of Collier, Mynatt and Collier, Atlanta, GA. POLIT. & GOV.: chm., Fulton Cty. (GA) Democratic Central Cmte., 1876; delegate, GA State Democratic Convention, 1882; delegate, Dem. Nat'l. Conv., 1892; appointed U.S. sec. of the interior, 1893–96; pres., Atlanta (GA) Board of Education, 1896–1907; elected as a Democrat to gov. of GA, 1907–09, 1911; candidate for Democratic nomination to gov. of GA, 1908; elected as a Democrat to U.S. Senate (GA), 1911–21; candidate for Democratic nomination to U.S. Senate (GA), 1920; ***candidate for Democratic nomination to presidency of the U.S., 1920***. BUS. & PROF.: atty.; admitted to GA Bar, 1873; law practice, Atlanta, GA, 1873–93, 1896–1907; owner, *Atlanta (GA) Evening Journal*, 1887, ed., 1887–1900; founder, Piedmont Hotel; founder, Fulton (GA) National Bank. MEM.: Young Men's Library of Atlanta (pres., 1881–83). REL.: Presb. (Elder). RES.: Atlanta, GA.

SMITH, INGRID. b. 1945, New Orleans, LA; m. Robert J. Smith; c. seven. EDUC.: U. of MI. POLIT. & GOV.: ***candidate for Democratic nomination to presidency of the U.S., 1980***. BUS. & PROF.: housewife. MEM.: Democrats Against the Draft; Women's International League for Peace and Freedom (Anti-Militarism Task Force). MAILING ADDRESS: 714 Mount Pleasant, Ann Arbor, MI.

SMITH, JOE. POLIT. & GOV.: ***candidate for Republican nomination to vice presidency of the U.S., 1956 (satire effort); candidate for Democratic nomination to vice presidency of the U.S., 1972***; fictitious candidate nominated by delegate Terry Carpenter (NE) at Rep. Nat'l. Conv., 1956. MAILING ADDRESS: South Bluff, NE.

SMITH, JOHN KENNEDY ROCKEFELLER. POLIT. & GOV.: ***candidate for Republican nomination to presidency of the U.S., 1980***. MAILING ADDRESS: 4580 Eisenhower Ave., Alexandria, VA.

SMITH, JOHN WALTER. b. Feb 5, 1845, Snow Hill, MD; d. Apr 19, 1925, Baltimore, MD; par. John Walter and Charlotte (Whittington) Smith; m. Mary Frances Richardson, Jun 2, 1869; c. two daughters. EDUC.: Union Acad. POLIT. & GOV.: elected as a Democrat to MD State Senate, 1889–99 (pres., 1894); chm., MD Democratic State Cmte., 1895; Democratic candidate for U.S. Senate (MD), 1896, 1920; elected as a Democrat to U.S. House (MD), 1899–1900; delegate, Dem. Nat'l. Conv., 1900, 1904, 1912, 1916, 1920; ***candidate for Democratic nomination to vice presidency of the U.S., 1900***; elected as a Democrat to gov. of MD, 1900–1904; elected as a Democrat to U.S. Senate (MD), 1908–21. BUS. & PROF.: clerk, George S. Richardson and Brothers (merchants); partner, Richardson, Smith, Moore and Co. (merchants; subsequently Smith, Moore and Co.); lumberman in MD, VA, and NC, 1865–1925; pres., First National Bank of Snow Hill, 1887; pres., Equitable Fire Insurance Co.; partner, Surrey Lumber Co. REL.: Presb. RES.: Snow Hill, MD.

SMITH, JOSEPH, JR. b. Dec 23, 1805, Sharon, VT; d. Jun 27, 1844, Carthage, IL; par. Joseph and Lucy (Mack) Smith; Polygamous Marriages: m. Emma Hale, Jan 18, 1827; m. 2d, Fannie Alger; m. 3rd, Lucinda Pendleton Morgan Harris, 1838; m. 4th, Prescinda Huntington Buell; m. 5th, Nancy Marinda Johnson Hyde; m. 6th, Clarissa Reed Hancock; m. 7th Louisa Beaman, 1841; m. 8th, Zina Diantha Huntington Jacobs; m. 9th, Mary Elizabeth Rollins Lightner; m. 10th, Patty Bartlett Sessions; m. 11th, Delcena Johnson Sherman; m. 12th, Mrs. Durfee; m. 13th, Sally Ann Fuller Gulley; m. 15th, Mrs. A. S.; m. 16th, Miss B.; m. 17th, Eliza Roxey Snow; m. 18th, Sarah Ann Whitney; m. 19th, Sarah M. Kinsley Cleveland; m. 20th, Elvira A. Cowles; m. 21st, Martha McBride; m. 22nd, Ruth D. Vose Sazers; m. 23rd, Deademona Wadsworth Fullmer; m. 24th, Emily Dow Partridge, 1843; m. 25th, Elza M. Patridge, 1843; m. 26th, Almera Woodward Johnson; m. 27th, Lucy Walker; m. 28th, Helen Mar Kimball; m. 29th, Maria Lawrence; m. 30th, Sarah Lawrence; m. 31st, Flora Ann Woodworth; m. 32nd, Rhoda Richards; m. 33rd, Hannah Ells; m. 34th, Melissa Lott; m. 35th, Fanny Young Murray; m. 36th, Olive Grey Frost; m. 37th, Mary Ann Frost; m. 38th, Olive Andrews; m. 39th, Mrs. Edward Blossom; m. 40th, Elizabeth Davis; m. 41st, Mary Huston; m. 42nd, Vienna Jacques; m. 43rd, Cordelia Calista Morley; m. 44th, Sarah Scott; m. 45th, Sylvia Sessions; m. 46th, Nancy Maria Smith; m. 47th, Jane Tibbets; m. 48th, Phebe Watrous; m. 49th, Nancy Mariah Winchester; m. 50th, Sophia Woodman; c. Joseph III; Alexander Hale; David Hyrum; Don Carlos; Frederick; six others. POLIT. & GOV.: mayor, Nauvoo, IL; ***independent candidate for presidency of the U.S., 1844***. BUS. & PROF.: prophet; received visions, 1820–27; discovered plates of gold, Manchester, NY; founder, prophet, Church of Jesus Christ of Latter-Day Saints (Mormons), 1830; removed community to Kirtland, OH, 1831; removed to Jackson Cty., MO, 1838; removed to Nauvoo, IL, 1839; lt. gen., Nauvoo Legion; involved in bank failures, Nauvoo, IL; arrested Jun 10, 1844; shot by mob, Jun 27, 1844. WRITINGS: *The Book of Mormon* (1830); *A Book of Commandments* (1833); *Doctrine and Covenants* (1835). REL.: Church of Jesus Christ of Latter-Day Saints (founder; prophet). RES.: Nauvoo, IL.

SMITH, JOSEPHINE "E.R.A."

POLIT. & GOV.: ***candidate for Democratic nomination to vice presidency of the U.S., 1976 (satire effort)***; fictitious candidate.

SMITH, LAURENCE CORTELYOU.

b. 1905, Yonkers, NY; par. Edward Anderson and Isabel (Waack) Smith; m. Feroll Moore; c. Laurence Cortelyou, Jr.; Peter Cropsey; Kerby Chambless; Karen Chandler. EDUC.: B.S., Dartmouth Coll., 1926. POLIT. & GOV.: candidate for Republican nomination to U.S. House (KS), 1964; ***candidate for Republican nomination to vice presidency of the U.S., 1968; candidate for Republican nomination to presidency of the U.S., 1972***. BUS. & PROF.: exec. sec., CT Merit System Assn.; asst. personnel dir., state of CT, c. 1940s; dealer, rep., General Motors Corp.; organic farmer; beekeeper; writer; lecturer; worked in various capacities in federal government. MEM.: U.S. Constitutional Council (charter member; chm.); National Republican Constitution Cmte. (charter member); Organization for the Survival of Small Business (founder); Liberty Amendment Cmte. of NY (organizer); Stop All Withholding Taxes (S.W.A.T.; founder); Citizens for Constitutional vs. Administrative Law (chm.). WRITINGS: *Does the White Race Deserve to Die?* (1968); *Genocide (Destruction) of the White and Black Races in America* (1970); *How Much Longer Can The White Race Survive in These United States* (1971). REL.: Psychiana. MAILING ADDRESS: Squires, MO 65755.

SMITH, LINDA L.

POLIT. & GOV.: ***American Political Party candidate for vice presidency of the U.S., 1992***. MAILING ADDRESS: c/o George L. Berish, 60 North Beretania St., #3502, Honolulu, HI 96817.

SMITH, MARGARET.

POLIT. & GOV.: ***independent candidate for presidency of the U.S., 1980***. MAILING ADDRESS: 1073 Walker Ave., Oakland, CA 94610.

SMITH, MARGARET MADELINE CHASE.

b. Dec 14, 1897, Skowhegan, ME; d. May 29, 1995, Skowhegan, ME; d. George Emery and Carrie Matilda (Murray) Chase; m. Clyde Harold Smith, May 14, 1930; c. none. EDUC.: grad., Skowhegan (ME) H.S., 1916. POLIT. & GOV.: member, ME Republican State Central Cmte., 1930–36; sec. to U.S. Rep. Clyde H. Smith, 1937–40; elected as a Republican to U.S. House (ME), 1940–49; chm., ME Republican State Convention, 1944; elected as a Republican to U.S. Senate (ME), 1949–73; ***candidate for Republican nomination to vice presidency of the U.S., 1952; candidate for Republican nomination to presidency of the U.S., 1964***; Republican candidate for U.S. Senate (ME), 1972. BUS. & PROF.: teacher, Skowhegan, ME, 1916; clerk, Maine Telephone and Telegraph Co.; circulation mgr., independent reporter, 1919–28; office mgr., Daniel E. Cummings Co. (woolen mills), Skowhegan, ME, 1928–30; treas., New England Waste Process Co., Fairfield, ME, 1928–30; visiting prof., Woodrow Wilson National Fellowship Foundation, 1973–76; lecturer, U. of Notre Dame; lecturer, U. of AL; lecturer, U. of the South; lecturer, OK Baptist U.; lecturer, DePauw U.; lecturer, Pacific Lutheran U.; columnist, *McCall's Magazine*; columnist, United Feature Syndicate. MIL.: lt. col., U.S. Air Force Reserves. MEM.: Freedom House (chm., 1970–77); Lilly Endowment (dir., 1976–); Northwood National Women's Board (chm., 1978–); American Acad. of Arts and Sciences; Theta Sigma Phi; Pi Sigma Alpha; Sigma Kappa; Delta Kappa Gamma; Beta Sigma Phi; Showhegan Business and Professional Club (pres., 1923); Skowhegan Sorosis (pres., 1923–24); ME Federation of Business and Professional Women's Clubs (pres., 1926; ed., *The Pine Cone*, 1924–25). AWARDS: Year's Outstanding Woman Award, Radio Editors' Poll, 1949; Woman of the Year in Politics Award, Associated Press, 1949, 1954, 1957; Freedom Foundation Award, 1951; Pi Gamma Mu Key, Catholic U. of America, 1951; Voice of Democracy Award, 1953; National Achievement Award, Chi Omega, 1954; Medal for Americanism, VFW, 1954; Distinguished Service Award, National Federation of Business and Professional Women's Clubs, 1955; Distinguished Service Award, Reserve Officers Assn., 1955; Woman of Achievement Award,

Soroptimist International, 1956; one of ten "Most Influential Women," Press Poll, 1956; multiple awards for National Health Leadership, 1960; Gold Medal Award for Humanitarianism, Inst. of Social Science, 1964; Women's Twentieth Century Hall of Fame, 1965; NEA Award, 1968; American Education Award, 1973. HON. DEG.: A.M., Colby Coll., 1943; LL.D., Wilson Coll., 1945; LL.D., AL Coll., 1949; LL.D., Coe Coll., 1949; LL.D., U. of ME, 1949; LL.D., Smith Coll., 1949; L.H.D., Hood Coll., 1951; LL.D., Bowdoin Coll., 1952; LL.D., Syracuse U., 1952; LL.D., Columbia U., 1955; LL.D., Drexel Inst. of Technology, 1955; L.H.D., Hamilton Coll., 1955; LL.D., Lafayette Coll., 1955; LL.D., U. of New Brunswick, 1955; LL.D., U. of NC, 1955; Litt.D., Temple U., 1955; LL.D., Tufts Coll., 1955; LL.D., Wesleyan U., 1955; D.C.L., Pace Coll., 1956; LL.D., U. of RI, 1956; L.H.D., Rollins Coll., 1956; LL.D., Russell Sage Coll., 1956; LL.D., Western Coll. for Women, 1956; L.H.D., Keuka Coll., 1957; LL.D., Mills Coll., 1957; J.S.D., Portia Law School, 1957; LL.D., WA Coll., 1957; LL.D., George Washington U., 1958; LL.D., Gettysburg Coll., 1958; numerous others. WRITINGS: *Gallant Women* (1968); *Declaration of Conscience* (1972). REL.: Methodist. RES.: Skowhegan, ME.

SMITH, MARGUERITE "MAUREEN." b. 1939; married; c. three. POLIT. & GOV.: chairperson, Peace and Freedom Party, 1980–88; ***Peace and Freedom Party candidate for presidency of the U.S., 1980***; Northern CA State Chair, Sonia Johnson for President Campaign, 1984; ***Consumer Party candidate for vice presidency of the U.S., 1988***. BUS. & PROF.: clerical worker, Santa Cruz Cty. Government, Santa Cruz Cty., CA. MAILING ADDRESS: 564 Santa Marguerita Dr., Aptos, CA 95003.

SMITH, OSCAR, JR. par. Oscar Smith, Sr. POLIT. & GOV.: ***candidate for Democratic nomination to presidency of the U.S., 1992***. BUS. & PROF.: store production mgr.; high school teacher. MAILING ADDRESS: 300 Skillman Ave., Brooklyn, NY 11211.

SMITH, ROBERT JUNIOR "PRINCE." POLIT. & GOV.: candidate for U.S. House (IL), 1986; ***candidate for Republican nomination to presidency of the U.S., 1988; candidate for Democratic nomination to presidency of the U.S., 1988***; candidate for U.S. House (UT); ***American Party candidate for presidency of the U.S., 1992***. BUS. & PROF.: businessman, Salt Lake City, UT; professional staff, Computer and Electronics Co.; retired. MISC.: known as "Prince Robert." MAILING ADDRESS: 1205 West 110th Place, Chicago, IL 60643; UT.

SMITH, TUCKER POWELL. b. Jan 29, 1898, Perry, MO; d. Jun 25, 1970, Ojai, CA; m. Myra E. Blaker; c. Alice Ellen Eskow. EDUC.: A.B., U. of MO, 1921, M.A., 1922; Columbia U., 1928–29; NY U. POLIT. & GOV.: member, Exec. Cmte., Socialist Party, 1948–; national chm., Socialist Party, 1948; ***Socialist Party candidate for vice presidency of the U.S., 1948; Socialist Party candidate for presidency of the U.S., 1952 (withdrew)***. BUS. & PROF.: teacher, Perry, MO, 1914; student YMCA dir., Springfield Coll., Springfield, MA; faculty, NY U., New York, NY; pres., dir., Brookwood Labor Coll., Katonah, NY, 1933–36; regional dir., U.A.W., Pontiac, MI, 1936–40; chm., Dept. of Economics, Olivet Coll., Olivet, MI; prof. of economics, Olivet Coll., Olivet, MI; farmer, Perry, MO. MEM.: American Economic Assn.; Cmte. on Militarism in Education (sec., 1930–33); Intercollegiate Socialist Soc.; United Retail, Wholesale and Department Store Employees (regional dir.; member, exec. board, 1940); American Friends Service Cmte. (rep., 1945–46); Fellowship of Reconciliation (asst. treas.); YMCA (gen. sec.); League for Industrial Democracy (dir.); World Peaceways; National Religion and Life Foundation (1933); U.S. Congress Against War Cmte.; War Resisters League (dir.). RES.: Perry, MO.

SMITH, WILLIAM. b. 1762, NC; d. Jun 26, 1840, Huntsville, AL; m. Margaret Duff, 1781; c. one daughter. EDUC.: grad., Mount Zion Collegiate Inst., 1780. POLIT. & GOV.: elected as a Democrat to U.S. House (SC), 1797–99; elected as a Democrat to SC State Senate, 1802–08 (pres., 1806–08), 1831; elected judge, SC Circuit Court, 1808–16; elected as a Democrat to U.S. Senate (SC), 1816–23, 1826–31 (pres. pro tempore); Democratic candidate for U.S. Senate (SC), 1823, 1830; elected as a Democrat to SC State House, 1824–26; ***received 7 electoral votes for vice presidency of the U.S., 1828***; appointed assoc. justice, Supreme Court of the U.S., 1829 (declined), 1836 (declined); elected as a Democrat to AL State House, 1836–40; presidential elector, Democratic Party, 1836; ***received 30 electoral votes for vice presidency of the U.S., 1836***. BUS. & PROF.: atty.; admitted to SC Bar, 1784; law practice, Pinckneyville, SC; law practice, Yorkville, SC; planter. MEM.: Alexandria Coll. (trustee, 1797); Bethel Acad. (trustee, 1818); SC Coll. (trustee, 1805–16). RES.: Yorkville, SC.

SMITH, WILLIAM ALDEN. b. May 12, 1859, Dowagiac, MI; d. Oct 11, 1932, Grand Rapids, MI; par. George Richard and Leah Margaret (Allen) Smith; m. Nana A. Osterhout, Oct 21, 1886; c. William Allen. EDUC.: public schools; studied law in offices of Burch and Montgomery, Grand Rapids, MI. POLIT. & GOV.: page, MI State House, 1879; asst. sec., MI State Senate, 1883; MI state game warden, 1887–91; member, MI Republican State Central Cmte., 1888–92; elected as a Republican to U.S. House (MI), 1895–1907; elected as a Republican to U.S. Senate (MI), 1907–19; ***candidate for Republican nomination to presidency of the U.S., 1916***. BUS. & PROF.: newsboy; messenger, Western Union Telegraph Co.; atty.; admitted to MI Bar, 1883; law practice, Grand Rapids, MI; partner, Smiley, Smith and Steven (law firm), 1899–1932; gen. counsel,

Chicago and West Michigan Railway; gen. counsel, Detroit, Lansing and Northern Railway; owner, Lowell and Hastings R.R., 1900–1932; chm. of the board, Steamboat Transit Co.; pres., *Grand Rapids (MI) Herald*, 1906–32. HON. DEG.: A.M., Dartmouth Coll., 1901. RES.: Grand Rapids, MI.

SMITH, WILLIAM LLOYD. b. 1924. EDUC.: M.S., UT State Agricultural Coll., 1956. POLIT. & GOV.: ***Beat Consensus candidate for presidency of the U.S., 1960***. BUS. & PROF.: book seller. WRITINGS: *Non-Return Conception Rate of Artificially Inseminated Cows, as Affected by Dilution Rate, Grade, Bull Source, and Age of Semen Shipped by Utah Artificial Breeding Association* (1956). MISC.: beatnik philosopher; self-styled "Pacific Anarchist." MAILING ADDRESS: 834 West Wolfram, Chicago, IL.

SMOTHERS, CLAIBORNE W. "CLAY." b. Apr 1, 1935, Malakoff, TX; par. J. W. and Alice (Winfield) Smothers; m. Barbara Dixon, 1957; c. Donna; Clay W. II. EDUC.: B.S., Prairie View A&M Coll., 1959, grad. study, 1961–66; Chicago Teachers' Coll. POLIT. & GOV.: delegate, Dem. Nat'l. Conv., 1972; ***candidate for Democratic nomination to vice presidency of the U.S., 1972; candidate for American Party nomination to vice presidency of the U.S., 1972 (withdrew)***; elected as a Democrat to TX State House, 1977–; Republican candidate for U.S. House (TX), 1980. BUS. & PROF.: administrator, St. Paul Industrial Training School for Disadvantaged Children; founder, Alice O. Smothers Acad. for Disadvantaged Children; columnist, "Observations of a Black Conservative," *Oak Cliff (TX) Tribune* and *Houston (TX) Tribune*, 1971–; author; police officer; radio talkshow moderator. MIL.: corp., U.S. Army, 1953–56. MEM.: Oak Cliff C. of C.; Defense Orientation Conference; Dallas War on Poverty (dir., 1971); Conservative Caucus (Citizens' Cabinet). AWARDS: 1st place, TX Press Assn., 1971; 3d place, Dallas Press Club, 1976; "Freshman of the Year," TX State Legislature, 1977; American Patriots Medal, Freedoms Foundation at Valley Forge, 1978. REL.: Bapt. MAILING ADDRESS: 3411 Holliday Rd., Dallas, TX 75224.

SMURR, JOHN WELLING. b. May 6, 1922, Sacramento, CA; par. Hylen and Mary (Napton) Smurr; m. Margaret Clapp; c. Hylen; Daniel; Matthew; Katherine. EDUC.: B.A., U. of MT, 1950, M.A., 1951; Ph.D., IN U., 1960. POLIT. & GOV.: ***independent candidate for presidency of the U.S., 1980***. BUS. & PROF.: prof. of History, U. of MT, 1955–60; prof. of History, Moorhead State Coll., 1961–66; prof. of History, CA State Coll., Stanislaus, CA, 1967–. MEM.: Sigma Nu; E Clampus Vitus. WRITINGS: *Historical Essays on Montana and the Northwest in Honor of Paul Chrisler Phillips* (co-editor, 1957); *The Fur Trade* (coauthor, 1960); *Territorial Jurisprudence* (1970); *Catholicon, or The New Common Sense* (1980). REL.: Seeker. MAILING ADDRESS: 1033 Sierra Dr., Turlock, CA 95380.

SNELL, BERTRAND HOLLIS. b. Dec 9, 1870, Colton, NY; d. Feb 2, 1958, Potsdam, NY; par. Hollis and Flora E. (Kimball) Snell; m. Sara Louise Merrick, Jun 3, 1903; c. Helen L. (Mrs. Harold William Cheel); Sara Louise (Mrs. William E. Peterson). EDUC.: grad., State Teachers Coll., Potsdam, NY, 1889; A.B., Amherst Coll., 1894. POLIT. & GOV.: delegate, Rep. Nat'l. Conv., 1912, 1916, 1920, 1924, 1928, 1932 (permanent chm.), 1936 (permanent chm.), 1940; member, NY State Republican Central Cmte., 1914–48 (chm., exec. cmte., 4 years); elected as a Republican to U.S. House (NY), 1915–39 (minority leader, 1931–39); ***candidate for Republican nomination to vice presidency of the U.S., 1932; candidate for Republican nomination to presidency of the U.S., 1936***. BUS. & PROF.: owner, Canton Lumber Co., Potsdam, NY, 1904; mgr., Raquette River Paper Co.; owner, lumber and timber lands; owner, Snell Power Co.; pres., Phenix Cheese Co.; pres., New York State Oil Co., 1941; publisher, *Potsdam (NY) Courier-Freeman*, 1934–49; pres., Northern Wall Paper Co.; pres., F. H. Watkins Lumber Co.; dir., New York Trust Co.; dir., Agricultural Insurance Co.; dir., Gould Pumps, Inc.; dir., People's Bank; dir., Citizen's Bank; dir., Potsdam Milling Co.; pres., Higley Falls Power Co., 1911–25; pres., York State Oil Co., 1918–48; owner, Chazy Orchards; pres., Potsdam Clothing Co.; trustee, Building and Loan Assn. of Potsdam; dir., St. Lawrence Cty. National Bank. MEM.: National Republican Club of NY; Chevy Chase Club; Metropolitan Club; Beta Theta Pi; Union League Club; Black River Valley Club; Potsdam Club; Clarkson Memorial Coll. (trustee, 1920–45); Potsdam Public Library (trustee); A. B. Hepburn Memorial Hospital (trustee); Potsdam Normal School (dir.); Masons (Knights Templar; Shriners); Northern NY Development League (vice pres., 1908–10); Potsdam State Teachers Coll. (trustee, 1910–48); Burning Tree Club; Amherst Club. HON. DEG.: LL.D., George Washington U., 1920; LL.D., Amherst Coll., 1929; Sc.D., Clarkson Coll. of Technology, 1943. REL.: Episc. RES.: Potsdam, NY.

SNOW, WALLACE, JR. b. Jul 19, 1936, Henry, SC; par. Wallace and Isabella (Wilson) Snow; m. Mary Spurill; c. none. POLIT. & GOV.: ***Federalist Preserver Party candidate for presidency of the U.S., 1972, 1976, 1980***. BUS. & PROF.: student; farmer; laborer; carpenter's asst.; sewage inspector; cement finisher's asst.; landscaper; boxer; junior electrical engineer. MIL.: noncommissioned officer, U.S. Air Force. REL.: Christian. MAILING ADDRESS: P.O. Box 748, Trenton, NJ 08604.

SNYDER, BERT PHILLIP. POLIT. & GOV.: ***candidate for Democratic nomination to presidency of the U.S., 1984***. MAILING ADDRESS: 340 West 72nd St., New York, NY 10023.

SNYDER, SIMON. b. Nov 5, 1759, Lancaster, PA; d. Nov 9, 1819, Selinsgrove, PA; par. Anthony and Maria Knippenburg (Kraemer) Snyder; m. Elizabeth Michael; m. 2d, Catherine

Antes, Jun 12, 1796; m. 3d, Mrs. Mary Slough Scott, Oct 16, 1824. POLIT. & GOV.: justice of the peace, Selinsgrove, PA, c. 1786; later judge, Court of Common Pleas, Northumberland Cty., PA; delegate, PA State Constitutional Convention, 1789–90; elected member, PA Legislature, 1797–1807 (Speaker, 3 terms); elected as a Republican (Democratic-Republican) to gov. of PA, 1808–17; ***candidate for Republican (Democratic-Republican) nomination to vice presidency of the U.S., 1816***; elected as a Democrat to PA State Senate, 1817. BUS. & PROF.: farmer, Selinsgrove, PA. MISC.: noted for States' Rights views. RES.: Selinsgrove, PA.

SOBIN, DENNIS. b. 1945; m. Paulette B. Powell (divorced); m. 2d, Eleanor Pohorylo; c. Darrin; Teague; Karen Pohorylo; Jesse; Lynn. POLIT. & GOV.: independent candidate for mayor of Washington, DC, 1982, 1986; independent candidate for school board, Washington, DC, 1983; ***independent candidate for presidency of the U.S., 1988***; Libertarian Party candidate for Washington, DC, City Council, 1988. BUS. & PROF.: owner, Sex Store, Washington, DC; author; tenant, Skivvy Works, Washington, DC; performer, ragtime and blues guitar; music teacher; radio and television producer; owner, telephone sex hotline; publisher; prostitute. MEM.: First Amendment Consumer and Trade Soc. (pres.); A.C.L.U. MISC.: noted for handing out packets of condoms as campaign advertising; known as the "Sultan of Sleaze"; convicted of concealing assets during bankruptcy proceedings, 1993. MAILING ADDRESS: 1718 Connecticut Ave., N.W., Washington, DC.

SOETERS, KENT M. b. 1946; m. Rachel; c. Bevin. EDUC.: U. of CA, Los Angeles, CA. POLIT. & GOV.: ***independent candidate for presidency of the U.S., 1964; Berkeley Self-Defense Group candidate for presidency of the U.S., 1968***. MAILING ADDRESS: 40 Frances Way, Walnut Creek, CA.

SOLDO, JOHN JOSEPH DANIEL (aka JOHN JOSEPH DANIEL DAVI FERRARI-SOLDO). b. May 16, 1945, Brooklyn, NY; par. Victor and Mildred Carmela (Farrari) Soldo; m. Martha Schwink, Aug 22, 1968 (divorced, Apr 1971). EDUC.: grad., Xavier H.S., New York, NY; B.A. (magna cum laude), Fordham U., 1966 (class pres.); Thomas More Coll.; Ladies' Coll.; M.A., Harvard U., 1968, Ph.D., 1972; King's Coll., 1969. POLIT. & GOV.: ***Pearl Party candidate for presidency of the U.S., 1976 (withdrew); candidate for Democratic nomination to presidency of the U.S., 1988***. BUS. & PROF.: taxi driver; asst. prof., Wells Coll., 1971–72; asst. prof., City U. of NY, 1972–73; asst. prof., Bronx Community Coll., 1972–73; asst. prof., Kingsborough Community Coll., 1972–73; asst. prof., Columbia U., 1973–77; freelance writer, 1977–78, 1984–; assoc. prof., Eastern NM University, Portales, NM, 1978–84 (chm., Dept. of Languages and Literature, 1978–82); author; poet; playwright; producer; dir. of Advanced Projects in Creative Writing, Columbia U.; owner, The Pearl Press; publisher, *Considered Embrace*. MIL.: capt., U.S. Army. MEM.: Fordham Club; Phi Beta Kappa; Thanksgiving Fast for Freedom (organizer); Liberal Club (cofounder); Fordham Booster Club; Fordham German Club; Fordham Glee Club; Harvard English Graduate Student Organization (chm.); Modern Language Assn. of America; American Studies Association; Soc. for Values in Higher Education; Poets and Writers; NY Poetry Forum; NM State Poetry Soc. AWARDS: Hughes Award in Philosophy; First Honors Gold Medal, Fordham U.; Award of Acad. des Beaux Arts, 1976; Dean's List Pin; Honorable Mention Award, German Essay Contest, Carl Schurz Foundation; Award, Mayor's Cmte. on Scholastic Achievement. WRITINGS: "Advent of Friendly Love" (poem); *Delano's Destiny* (1970); *Delano in America and Other Early Poems* (1974); *The Tempering of T. S. Eliot* (1983); *Odes and Cycles* (1984); *Sonnets for Our Risorgimento*; *Mirrors for the Harmony of Sex*; *Passage to Philia*; *Making Your Life Into a Poem*; *The Mind of T. S. Eliot*; *In an Arid Clime* (1984); *Studies* (1984); *Now Old with My Youth* (1984). REL.: R.C. MISC.: noted scholar of works of T. S. Eliot. MAILING ADDRESS: 7 East 81st St., New York, NY 10028.

SOMMERS, SALLY J. POLIT. & GOV.: ***independent (Cmte. for a Constitutional Presidency) candidate for presidency of the U.S., 1976***. MAILING ADDRESS: 1031 Cherry St., Missoula, MT 59801.

SONNIER, PAUL ELMORE, JR. par. Paul Elmore Sonnier. POLIT. & GOV.: ***independent candidate for presidency of the U.S., 1980***. MAILING ADDRESS: 4301 Bit and Spur Rd., Mobile, AL 36608.

SOUTHERLAND, MILTON J. POLIT. & GOV.: ***candidate for Republican nomination to presidency of the U.S., 1992***. MAILING ADDRESS: CA?

SOUTHGATE, JAMES HAYWOOD. b. Jul 12, 1859, Norfolk, VA; d. Sep 29, 1916, Durham, NC; par. James and Delia Haywood (Wynne) Southgate; m. Kate Shepard Fuller, Dec 5, 1882; c. Thomas Fuller; one daughter; two infants. EDUC.: Horner and Graves Military Acad., Hillsboro, NC; U. of NC, 1876–79. POLIT. & GOV.: pres., Durham Cty. (NC) Fair; delegate, Prohibition Party National Convention, 1892 (Platform Cmte.), 1896 (Platform Cmte.); chm., NC Prohibition State Cmte., 1894–96; ***National (Liberty, Free Silver Prohibition) Party candidate for vice presidency of the U.S., 1896***. BUS. & PROF.: banker, Moorehead Banking Co.; insurance agent, J. Southgate and Son, 1882–1917; dir., Citizens National Bank; pres., Durham Land and Security Co.; gen. agent, American Union Life Insurance Co. of NY, c. 1896. MEM.: NC YMCA (pres.); Trinity Coll. (trustee; pres., 1897); National Assn. of Insurance Writers (pres., 1913–14); NC Assn. of Underwriters (pres.); NC Peace Soc. (pres.); Durham C. of C. (pres.);

Durham Public Library (dir.); Southern Conservatory of Music (trustee); Durham Business School (adviser); NC Sunday school Assn.; Knights of Pythias. REL.: Methodist Episc. Church (steward; delegate, gen. conference, 1902). RES.: Durham, NC.

SPAHR, MARTIN, SR. b. Jan 15, 1895, San Antonio, TX; d. 1982, South Norwalk, CT; m. Barbara Behrle; c. Martin, Jr. EDUC.: high school. POLIT. & GOV.: delegate, Socialist Labor Party National Convention, 1964; ***Socialist Labor Party candidate for presidency of the U.S., 1976***. BUS. & PROF.: plumber; owner, Spahr and Son (plumbers), Norwalk, CT. MIL.: U.S. Army, WWI. RES.: South Norwalk, CT 06854.

SPANGLER, RONALD W. POLIT. & GOV.: ***independent candidate for presidency of the U.S., 1984***. MAILING ADDRESS: 8660 Ferndale St., Philadelphia, PA 19115.

SPANNAUS, WARREN RICHARD. b. Dec 5, 1930, St. Paul, MN; par. Albert Carl and Anna (Korner) Spannaus; m. Marjorie Louise Clarkson, Dec 19, 1964; c. Christine Ann; David Clarkson; Laura Zo. EDUC.: B.B.A., U. of MN, 1958, J.D., 1963. POLIT. & GOV.: appointed special asst. atty. gen. of MN, 1963–65; staff, U.S. Sen. Walter Mondale (q.v.), 1965–66; campaign dir., Mondale for U.S. Senate, 1966; chm., MN Democratic-Farmer Labor Party, 1967–69; elected as a Democrat to atty. gen. of MN, 1971; delegate, Dem. Nat'l. Conv., 1980; ***candidate for Democratic nomination to presidency of the U.S., 1980***. BUS. & PROF.: atty.; admitted to MN Bar, 1963; law practice, Minneapolis, MN, 1969–70. MIL.: petty officer 3, U.S.N.R., 1951–54; Good Conduct Medal. MEM.: MN State Bar Assn.; Ramsey Cty. Bar Assn.; Hennepin Cty. Bar Assn.; National Assn. of Attorneys General; School for Social Development of Minneapolis (dir.); United Cerebral Palsy of Greater St. Paul (dir.); Midwest Assn. of Attorneys General (chm., 1972–73); American Jud. Soc. REL.: Methodist. MAILING ADDRESS: 2619 Robbins St., Minneapolis, MN 55410.

SPARKMAN, JOHN JACKSON. b. Dec 20, 1899, Hartselle, AL; d. Nov 16, 1985, Huntsville, AL; par. Whitten J. and Julia Mitchell (Kent) Sparkman; m. Ivo Hall, Jun 2, 1923; c. Julia Ann "Jan" (Mrs. Tazewell Shepard, Jr.). EDUC.: B.A., U. of AL, 1921, LL.B., 1923, A.M., 1924. POLIT. & GOV.: U.S. commissioner, Huntsville, AL, 1930–31; elected as a Democrat to U.S. House (AL), 1937–46 (majority whip, 1946); elected as a Democrat to U.S. Senate (AL), 1946–79; ***Democratic candidate for vice presidency of the U.S., 1952***; delegate, Dem. Nat'l. Conv., 1956; ***candidate for Democratic nomination to presidency of the U.S., 1956***. BUS. & PROF.: atty.; admitted to AL Bar, 1925; law practice, Huntsville, AL, 1925–37; instructor, Huntsville Coll., 1925–28; partner, Taylor, Richardson and Sparkman (law firm), Huntsville, AL, 1930–36; partner, Sparkman and Shepard (law firm), Huntsville, AL, 1979–85. MIL.: Students Army Training Corps, U.S. Army, WWI; organized reserves, 1921–85 (lt. col.). MEM.: Phi Beta Kappa; American U. (trustee); Huntsville C. of C.; American Legion (commander); Pi Kappa Alpha; Phi Alpha Delta; Eagles; Masons; Eastern Star; Woodmen of the World; Kiwanis; Athens Coll. (trustee, 1936). HON. DEG.: LL.D., Spring Hill Coll., 1956; LL.D., U. of AL, 1958; LL.D., Auburn U., 1960; LL.D., National U. of Seoul, 1969. REL.: Methodist. RES.: Huntsville, AL.

SPARROW, CLEVELAND B., SR. c. Cleveland S., Jr. POLIT. & GOV.: ***Third World Assembly candidate for vice presidency of the U.S., 1988***. BUS. & PROF.: minister. MAILING ADDRESS: 5801 16th St., N.W., Washington, DC.

SPEED, JAMES. b. Mar 11, 1812, Louisville, KY; d. Jun 25, 1887, Louisville, KY; par. John and Lucy Gilmer (Fry) Speed; m. Jane Cochran, 1841; c. John; Henry Pirtle; Charles; Breckenridge; James; Joshua; one other son. EDUC.: grad., St. Joseph's Coll., 1828; studied law, Transylvania U. POLIT. & GOV.: elected to KY State Legislature, 1841; emancipation candidate for delegate, KY State Constitutional Convention, 1849; member, Union Party Central Cmte.; elected as a Unionist to KY State Senate, 1861–63; appointed atty. gen. of the U.S., 1864–66; chm., Southern Radical Convention, 1866; Republican candidate for U.S. Senate (KY), 1867; ***candidate for Republican nomination to vice presidency of the U.S., 1868***; Republican candidate for U.S. House (KY), 1870; delegate, Rep. Nat'l. Conv., 1872, 1876. BUS. & PROF.: employee, cty. clerk's office, Louisville, KY, 1828–30; atty.; admitted to KY Bar, 1833; law practice, Louisville, KY, 1833; prof. of Law, Louisville U., 1856–58, 1872–79. MISC.: known as a Radical Reconstructionist; supported Grover Cleveland (q.v.) for pres., 1884. RES.: Louisville, KY.

SPELBRING, RALPH EUGENE. b. May 9, 1945, Brazil, IN; par. Harold Eugene and Virginia (Craft) Spelbring; single. EDUC.: B.A., DePauw U., 1967; IN U., 1967–68; IN State U., 1970–71. POLIT. & GOV.: Democratic candidate for IN State House, 1982; candidate for Elkhart (IN) City Council, 1983; Democratic candidate for IN State Senate, 1984; candidate for Democratic nomination to U.S. House (IN), 1986, 1988; ***candidate for Democratic nomination to presidency of the U.S., 1992***. BUS. & PROF.: teacher; science teacher, Corydon (IN) Central H.S., 1968–69; chemistry teacher, LaSalle H.S., South Bend, IN, 1971; chemist, Whitehall Laboratories, Elkhart, IN, 1972–91. MEM.: American Chemical Soc.; American Inst. of Chemists; IN C. of C.; Greater Elkhart C. of C.; OCAW Local 7-838; Sigma Xi; Elkhart Jaycees. REL.: Protestant. MAILING ADDRESS: 236 Bank St., Elkhart, IN 46516.

SPELLACY, THOMAS JOSEPH. b. Mar 6, 1880, Hartford, CT; d. Dec 5, 1957, New York, NY; par. James and Catherine (Bourke) Spellacy; m. 2d, Elizabeth B. Gill, Aug

23, 1934; c. Bourke. EDUC.: A.B., Holy Cross Coll., 1899; LL.B., Georgetown U., 1901. POLIT. & GOV.: elected as a Democrat to CT State Senate, 1907–11; delegate, Dem. Nat'l. Conv., 1912, 1920, 1924, 1928, 1936, 1940; appointed U.S. district atty. for CT, 1915–19; Democratic candidate for gov. of CT, 1918; appointed asst. atty. gen. of the U.S., 1919–21; Democratic candidate for U.S. Senate (CT), 1922; appointed member, Comm. to Demobilize U.S. Navy in Europe; legal adviser, U.S. sec. of the navy, WWI; ***candidate for Democratic nomination to presidency of the U.S., 1924***; eastern mgr., Democratic presidential campaign, 1924; member, Dem. Nat'l. Cmte., 1925–29; elected as a Democrat, mayor of Hartford, CT, 1935–43 (resigned); appointed CT State Insurance Commissioner, 1955–57. BUS. & PROF.: atty.; admitted to CT Bar, 1903; law practice, Hartford, CT, 1903–57; partner, Spellacy and Aron (law firm), Hartford, CT; owner, *Hartford (CT) Evening Post*; co-owner, *Hartford (CT) Sunday Globe*. MEM.: ABA; CT Bar Assn.; Hartford Cty. Bar Assn.; Park River Flood Comm.; Metropolitan District Comm. for Hartford Cty. REL.: R.C. RES.: Hartford, CT.

SPENCER, JULIUS A. b. 1828, New York, NY; d. Jun 13, 1881, Cleveland, OH; m. Hannah E. Van Natter; c. Ray (d. 1854). POLIT. & GOV.: sec., Prohibition National Convention, 1869; ***candidate for Prohibition Party nomination to vice presidency of the U.S., 1872***; pres., OH Prohibition Party, 1872. BUS. & PROF.: journalist; printer, Spencer and Allardt, Cleveland, OH, 1859; ed., prohibition era, Cleveland, OH, 1870; ed., *Sunday Post*, Cleveland, OH, 1875; temperance advocate. MEM.: Independent Order of Good Templars (Worthy Degree Templar, North Star Degree Temple, 1869; Right Worthy Grand Secretary, OH Grand Lodge); World Temperance Convention (delegate, 1873); Benjamin Franklin Soc. (chm., 1855); Forest City Lyceum; Cuyahoga Cty. Temperance Soc. (sec., 1860); National Typographers Union (pres., Cleveland Local #53; second vice pres., national convention, 1863). WRITINGS: *History of the United States* (1856); *A Digest of the Laws, Decisions and Usages of the R. W. C. Lodge of North America and the Grand Lodge of Ohio, Independent Order of Good Templars* (1868). RES.: Cleveland, OH.

SPENCER, TERENCE J. b. 1927. POLIT. & GOV.: Democratic candidate for U.S. House (NY), 1972; candidate for Democratic nomination to U.S. House (NY), 1974; ***independent (Cmte. for a Constitutional Presidency) candidate for vice presidency of the U.S., 1976***. MAILING ADDRESS: Green Rd., R.D. 1, Holcomb, NY 14469.

SPOCK, BENJAMIN McLANE. b. May 2, 1903, New Haven, CT; par. Benjamin Ives and Milldred Louise (Stoughton) Spock; m. Jane Davenport Cheney, Jun 25, 1927 (divorced); m. 2d, Mary Morgan Councille, Oct 24, 1976; c. Michael; John Cheney. EDUC.: B.A., Yale U., 1925; Yale Medical School, 1925–27; M.D., Coll. of Physicians and Surgeons, Columbia U., 1927. POLIT. & GOV.: ***Independent Political Action Against the War candidate for vice presidency of the U.S., 1968 (withdrew); Freedom and Peace Party candidate for presidency of the U.S., 1968 (declined); Peace and Freedom Party candidate for vice presidency of the U.S., 1968***; co-chm., New Party; ***People's (Peace and Freedom) Party candidate for presidency of the U.S., 1972; Liberty Union Party candidate for presidency of the U.S., 1972; candidate for Democratic nomination to vice presidency of the U.S., 1972; candidate for People's Party nomination to presidency of the U.S., 1976 (declined); People's Party candidate for vice presidency of the U.S., 1976; candidate for Peace and Freedom Party nomination to presidency of the U.S., 1980***. BUS. & PROF.: intern, Presbyterian Hospital, New York, NY, 1929–31; intern in Pediatrics, NY Nursery and Child's Hospital, 1931–32; intern in Psychiatry, NY Hospital, 1932–33; asst. attending pediatrician, NY Hospital, 1933–47; staff, Inst. on Personality Development, 1938–47; consultant in Pediatric Psychiatry, NY City (NY) Health Dept., 1942–47; consultant in Psychiatry, Mayo Clinic; assoc. prof. of Psychiatry, Mayo Foundation, U. of MN, 1947–51; prof. of Child Development, U. of Pittsburgh, 1951–55; prof. of Child Development, Western Reserve U., 1955–67. MIL.: lt. commander, U.S. Navy (Medical Corps), 1944–46. MEM.: National Cmte. for a Sane Nuclear Policy (cochm., 1967); Scroll and Key; New Mobilization to End the War in Viet Nam. AWARDS: Family Life Book Award, 1963. WRITINGS: *Common Sense Book of Baby and Child Care* (1946); *A Baby's First Year* (with J. Reinhart and W. Miller, 1954); *Feeding Your Baby and Child* (with M. Lowenberg, 1955); *Dr. Spock Talks with Mothers* (1961); *Problems of Parents* (1962); *Caring for Your Disabled Child* (with M. Lerrigo, 1965); *Dr. Spock on Viet Nam* (with Mitchell Zimmerman, 1968); *Decent and Indecent* (1970); *Teenager's Guide on Life and Love* (1971); *Raising Children in a Difficult Time* (1974); *Spock on Spock* (coauthor, 1989). MAILING ADDRESS: Lagoon Marina, Red Hook, St. Thomas, Virgin Islands.

SPOONER, JOHN COIT. b. Jan 6, 1843, Lawrenceburg, IN; d. Jun 11, 1919, New York, NY; par. Judge Philip L. and Lydia (Coit) Spooner; m. Annie E. Main, Sep 10, 1868. EDUC.: A.B., U. of WI, 1864, A.M., 1969. POLIT. & GOV.: pvt. and military sec. to Gov. Lucius Fairchild (q.v.; WI), 1866–67; appointed asst. atty. gen. of WI, 1868–70; elected as a Republican to WI State Assembly, 1872–73; elected as a Republican to U.S. Senate (WI), 1885–91, 1897–1907; delegate, Rep. Nat'l. Conv., 1888, 1892, 1896, 1904; Republican candidate for gov. of WI, 1892; appointed U.S. sec. of the interior, 1898 (declined); appointed member, British-American Joint High Comm., 1898; ***candidate for Republican nomination to vice presidency of the U.S., 1900***; appointed atty. gen. of the U.S., 1901 (declined). BUS. & PROF.: atty.; admitted to WI Bar, 1867; law practice, Madison, WI, 1867–70; law practice, Hudson, WI, 1870–84; counsel, Chicago and North Western Railway; law practice, New York, NY, 1907–19. MIL.: pvt., Company A, 40th WI Infantry; capt., brev. maj., 50th WI Infantry, U.S. Army, Civil War. MEM.: U. of WI (regent, 1882–85). HON. DEG.: Ph.B., U. of

WI, LL.D., 1895; LL.D., Yale U., 1908; LL.D., Columbia U., 1909. WRITINGS: *Affairs in Cuba* (1898); *Government for Puerto Rico* (1900). RES.: Madison, WI.

SPOTTED TAIL (aka SINTEGALESKA). b. winter of 1823/24, White River, WY; d. Aug 5, 1881, Rosebud, WY; par. Cunka Chomineeshee (aka Jumping Buffalo) and Walks-with-the-Pipe; m. Minniscurrin and four others; c. Ah-ho-ap-pa (aka Wheat Flour, Monica, or Hinzinwin); Chau-hu-luta (aka Red Road); Mrs. Charles Tackett; Stays-at-Home (aka William); Talks-with-Bear (aka Oliver); Bugler (aka Max); Little Scout (aka Pollock); Little Spotted Tail (aka Sintegaleska Chika); Young Spotted Tail; between 25 and 27 others (13 by first wife; 1–2 each by second and third wives; 9 sons by Minniscurrin; 9 daughters by fifth wife). POLIT. & GOV.: ***candidate for Equal Rights (Cosmic; Free Love; People's) Party nomination to vice presidency of the U.S., 1872***. BUS. & PROF.: chief of Lower Brule Sioux; head chief, Oglalas and Sioux, 1880; captured in fight near Fort Laramie and interned, 1854–56; signatory, peace treaty establishing SD Indian Reservation, 1868; joined Red Cloud in effort to sell mineral rights to federal government, 1874; assisted in obtaining surrender of Chief Crazy Horse, 1877. MISC.: murdered in WY, Aug 5, 1881. RES.: Fort Sheridan, WY.

SPRAGUE, MONTY DALE. b. Aug 23, 1934, Buchanan, MI; par. Victor Dale and Ora Edna (Babock) Sprague; m. Norma Dean Keel; c. David Eric; Melonie Ann; Matt Eric; Amy Louise. EDUC.: G.E.D., 1956; Los Angeles (CA) City Coll.; CA Polytechnical Coll. POLIT. & GOV.: ***independent candidate for presidency of the U.S., 1988***. BUS. & PROF.: design engineer; cost accountant; retail and contracting, commercial and residential. MIL.: Third Army, 11th Airborne, 82d Airborne, U.S. Army. MEM.: C. of C., 1960–63. REL.: "God is All." MAILING ADDRESS: c/o God's Children, Norma Dean Sprague, Route 1, Box 309K, Cunningham, TN 37052.

SPRINGER, JOHN WALLACE. b. Jul 16, 1859, Jacksonville, IL; par. John Thomas and Sarah (Henderson) Springer; m. Eliza Clifton Hughes, Jun 17, 1891; m. 2d, Jannette Muir Lotave, Aug 26, 1915. EDUC.: A.B., Asbury (now De Pauw) U., 1878. POLIT. & GOV.: elected as a Republican to IL State House, 1891–93; elected as a Republican, mayor of Denver, CO, 1904 (Counted Out); ***candidate for Republican nomination to vice presidency of the U.S., 1904***. BUS. & PROF.: atty.; admitted to IL Bar, 1880; law practice, Dallas, TX, 1891–96; banker, Dallas, TX, 1891–96; moved to Denver, CO, 1896; vice pres., Capitol National Bank, Denver, CO, 1902; pres., Continental Trust Building; pres., Continental Trust Co.; pres., Continental Safe Deposit and Securities Co.; pres., Queen of the West Silver Mines Co.; pres., Sunland Farms Co., Pueblo, CO; vice pres., Continental Divide Co. MEM.: National Live Stock Assn. of the U.S. (pres., 1898–1905). RES.: Littleton, CO.

SPRINGS, LENA JONES. b. 1883, Pulaski, TN; d. May 18, 1942, New York, NY; d. Thomas Meriwether and Lena May (Buford) Jones; m. Col. Leroy Springs, Nov 29, 1913. EDUC.: Martin Coll.; B.A., Sullins Coll.; VA Coll. POLIT. & GOV.: appointed member, SC State Comm. on World War Memorial, 1919; member, Dem. Nat'l. Cmte., 1922–28; delegate, Dem. Nat'l. Conv., 1924, 1928; ***candidate for Democratic nomination to vice presidency of the U.S., 1924***. BUS. & PROF.: chm., English Dept., Queen's Coll., Charlotte, NC, 1911–13; lecturer. MEM.: Charlotte Women's Club; DAR; International Council of Women (life member); Lancaster Women's Club; SC Equal Suffrage League (treas., 1916; vice pres., 1917; district dir., 1917–20); National Democratic Women's Club; Lancaster Equal Suffrage League (pres., 1916–18); Lancaster Red Cross (chm., 1917–18); SC Federation of Women's Clubs (district vice pres., 1917–18; pres., 1918–19); SC Liberty Loan (District chm.; chm., women's organizations, 1917–18); SC Federated Endowment Fund (chm., 1920–25); SC League of Women Voters (district dir., 1920–25); SC Cmte. for Law Enforcement (chm., 1924–25); Women's Citizen Club (board member, 1924–25); Regency Club; Congressional Country Club. HON. DEG.: D.Litt., Presbyterian Coll. of SC, 1924. REL.: Presb. RES.: Lancaster, SC.

SPROUL, WILLIAM CAMERON. b. Sep 16, 1870, Octoraro, PA; d. Mar 21, 1928, Chester, PA; par. William Hall and Deborah Dickinson (Slokom) Sproul; m. Emeline Wallace Roach, Jan 21, 1892; c. Dorothy Wallace (Mrs. Laurence P. Sharples); John Roach. EDUC.: B.S. (honors), Swarthmore Coll., 1891. POLIT. & GOV.: elected as a Republican to PA State Senate, 1896–1918 (pres. pro tempore, 1903–05); chm., PA State Hist. Comm., 1913–19; delegate, Rep. Nat'l. Conv., 1916, 1924; elected as a Republican to gov. of PA, 1919–23; ***candidate for Republican nomination to presidency of the U.S., 1920***. BUS. & PROF.: farmer; journalist; manufacturer; pres., *Chester (PA) Daily Times*, 1891–1928; pres., *Chester (PA) Morning Republican*; owner, Roach Shipyards, Chester, PA, 1898; pres., Seaboard Steel Casting Co., 1900; chm. of the board, General Refractories Co., 1910; chm. of the board, Lebanon Iron Co.; chm. of the board, Lackawanna and Wyoming Valley R.R.; orchard grower; pres., Kanawha Valley Traction Co.; owner, Camden (NJ) Interstate Railway; pres., Coal River Railway; pres., Charleston and Southside Bridge Co.; pres., Spruce River Coal and Land Co.; treas., Kanawha Bridge and Terminal Co.; dir., Commercial Trust Co.; dir., Delaware County Trust Co.; dir., First National Bank of Chester; dir., Delaware County National Bank. MEM.: Swarthmore Coll. (trustee, 1902–28); Mercersburg Acad. (trustee); Masons; Elks; PA Hist. Soc.; DE Cty. Hist. Soc.; Phi Beta Kappa; Franklin Inst.; Scotch-Irish Soc.; Swedish Colonial Soc.; Phi Kappa Psi; Union League Club (pres., 1917–18, 1925–26). AWARDS: Order of the Crown of Italy (commander); Order of the Crown of Belgium (commander). HON. DEG.: LL.D., Franklin and Marshall Coll., 1912; LL.D., Gettysburg Coll., 1918; LL.D., Lafayette Coll., 1919; LL.D., PA Military Coll., 1919; LL.D., U. of PA, 1919; LL.D., U. of Pittsburgh, 1919; LL.D., Swarthmore Coll., 1919; LL.D., Allegheny Coll., 1920; LL.D., Grove City Coll., 1920. REL.: Soc. of Friends. MISC.: known as the "Father of Good Roads in Pennsylvania." RES.: Chester, PA.

SPURGEON, OTIS LEE. b. 1880. POLIT. & GOV.: independent candidate for U.S. Senate (IA), 1914; Prohibition Party candidate for gov. of IA, 1916; national sec., Liberal Party; ***Liberty Party candidate for vice presidency of the U.S., 1932***. BUS. & PROF.: ordained minister, Baptist Church, IA; pastor, Baptist Church, Kansas City, MO. MIL.: chaplain, WWI; capt., 384th F.A. Officers Reserves. MEM.: American Federation of Patriotic Societies and Voters. WRITINGS: *10,132* (1920). REL.: Bapt. MISC.: anti-Catholic; mobbed in Denver, CO, c. 1914; speaker at American Federation of Patriotic Societies and Voters Conference, Chicago, IL, Jun 13–25, 1914. RES.: Kansas City, MO.

STALLARD, DAVID LEE. b. Mar 31, 1931, Lawrence, KS; par. Hobart M. and Lottie G. (Schenck) Stallard; m. Carolyn J. Meek; c. Diane; Scott; Linda. EDUC.: B.S., Washburn U., 1959. POLIT. & GOV.: American Party candidate for Derby (KS) City Council, 1972; State chm., KS American Party; ***candidate for American Party nomination to presidency of the U.S., 1976***. BUS. & PROF.: computer systems analyst. MEM.: John Birch Soc. (life member); Sigma Phi Epsilon. REL.: Bapt. MAILING ADDRESS: 528 South Derby, Derby, KS 67037.

STALLINGS, RICHARD H. b. Oct 7, 1940, Ogden, UT; par. Howard J. and Elizaveth (Austin) Stallings; m. Ranae Garner, Sep 5, 1963; c. Richard H., Sallianne, Daniel. EDUC.: B.S., Weber State Coll., 1965; M.S., UT State U., 1968; CO Coll., 1968. POLIT. & GOV.: Democratic candidate for U.S. House (ID), 1982; elected as a Democrat to U.S. House (ID), 1985–93; ***candidate for Democratic nomination to presidency of the U.S., 1988***; Democratic candidate for U.S. Senate (ID), 1992. BUS. & PROF.: teacher, Bonneville H.S., Ogden, UT, 1964–69; prof., Ricks Coll., Rexburg, ID, 1969–79, chm., History Dept., 1979–84. MAILING ADDRESS: ID.

STANCILL, WILLIS JOHNSTON. POLIT. & GOV.: ***Clean Government Party candidate for presidency of the U.S., 1980, 1984, 1988***. MAILING ADDRESS: 1807 South Elm St., Greenville, NC 27834.

STANDARD, MITCH. POLIT. & GOV.: ***American Partiers Party candidate for vice presidency of the U.S., 1988***. MAILING ADDRESS: 232 South College St., Macomb, IL 61455.

STANFORD, AMASA LELAND. b. Mar 9, 1824, Watervliet, NY; d. Jun 21, 1893, Palo Alto, CA; par. Josiah and Elizabeth (Phillips) Stanford; m. Jane Elizabeth Lathrop, Sep 30, 1850; c. Leland, Jr. EDUC.: Clinton Liberal Inst.; Cazenovia Seminary; studied law in offices of Wheaton, Doolittle and Hadley, Albany, NY, 1845. POLIT. & GOV.: elected justice of the peace, Michigan Bluffs, CA; Republican candidate for CA state treas., 1857; Republican candidate for gov. of CA, 1859; delegate, Rep. Nat'l. Conv., 1860; elected as a Republican to gov. of CA, 1861–63; elected as a Republican to U.S. Senate (CA), 1885–93; ***candidate for American Party nomination to presidency of the U.S., 1888 (declined); candidate for People's Party nomination to presidency of the U.S., 1892***. BUS. & PROF.: atty.; admitted to WI Bar, 1847; law practice, Port Washington, WI, 1848–52; storekeeper, Michigan Bluffs, CA, 1853; pres., Central Pacific R.R., 1861–93; pres., Southern Pacific R.R., 1885–90. MISC.: noted as promoter of transcontinental railroad; opponent of railroad regulation; founder, Leland Stanford Junior U. (now Stanford U.), 1885. RES.: Palo Alto, CA.

STANTON, ELIZABETH CADY. b. Nov 12, 1815, Johnstown, NY; d. Oct 26, 1902, New York, NY; d. Daniel and Margaret (Livingston) Cady; m. Henry Brewster Stanton, May 10, 1840; c. Daniel Cady; Henry; Gerrit Smith; Theodore; Margaret (Mrs. Frank E. Lawrence); Harriet Eaton (Mrs. Henry Blatch); Robert. EDUC.: Johnstown Acad.; grad., Troy Female Seminary, 1832. POLIT. & GOV.: independent candidate for U.S. House (NY), 1866; ***candidate for Equal Rights (Cosmic; Free Love; People's) Party nomination to vice presidency of the U.S., 1872***. BUS. & PROF.: contributor, *Lily*; contributor, *Una*, 1853; ed., *Revolution*, 1868–69; lecturer, NY Lyceum Bureau, 1869–81. MEM.: Presbyterian Girls' Club; Conversation Club; New England Labor Reform Soc. (vice pres., 1871); Woman's Legal League (pres., 1861); National Women's Suffrage Assn. (pres., 1865–93; hon. pres., 1894–1902); Woman's State Temperance Soc. of NY (pres., 1853); Women's Loyal National League; International Council of Women; Anti-Slavery Soc.; Working Woman's Assn.; National Labor Union (delegate, national convention); People's League (vice pres., declined, 1853). WRITINGS: *The History of Woman Suffrage* (with Susan B. Anthony and Matilda Joslyn Gage, 1881); *Report of the International Council of Women* (with Susan B. Anthony and Rachel Avery, 1888); *The Degradation of Disfranchisement* (1891); *The Solitude of Self* (1892); *The Woman's Bible* (1895); *Eighty Years and More* (1895). REL.: Agnostic (nee Presb.). RES.: Seneca Falls, NY.

STAR-MARTINEZ, R. ALISON. POLIT. & GOV.: ***candidate for Peace and Freedom Party nomination to presidency of the U.S., 1992***. MAILING ADDRESS: P.O. Box 611, Claremont, CA 91711.

STARADUMSKY, JOHN JOSEPH. POLIT. & GOV.: ***candidate for Democratic nomination to presidency of the U.S., 1992***. BUS. & PROF.: retailer; officer mgr.; truck driver. MIL.: U.S.C.G. MEM.: International Brotherhood of Teamsters (22 years). MAILING ADDRESS: 44 Oak Terrace, P.O. Box 316, Mapleville, RI 02839.

STARK, LLOYD CROW. b. Nov 23, 1886, Louisiana, MO; d. Sep 17, 1972, Louisiana, MO; par. Clarence McDowell and Lilly (Crow) Stark; m. Margaret Pearson Stickney, Nov 11, 1908; m. 2d, Katherine Lemoine Perkins, Nov 23, 1931; c. Lloyd Stickney; John Wingate; Mary (Mrs. Richard Strassner); Katherine (Mrs. Richard Clark Bull). EDUC.: B.S., U.S. Naval Acad., 1908. POLIT. & GOV.: elected as a Democrat to gov. of MO, 1937–41; ***candidate for Democratic nomination to vice presidency of the U.S., 1940***. BUS. & PROF.: nurseryman; vice pres., gen. mgr., Stark Brothers Nurseries, 1912–17, 1919–35, chm. of the board, 1935–37, 1941–71, emeritus chm. of the board, 1971–72. MIL.: naval officer, 1904–12; maj., battalion commander, acting asst. Divisional Chief of Staff, 80th Div., and commander, 315th F.A., U.S. Army, 1917–19; Victory Medal with Two Clasps. MEM.: National Governors' Conference (chm., 1939); Council of State Governments (pres., 1939; member, board of mgrs., 1941–47); U.S. Naval Acad. Alumni Assn. (trustee); BSA (exec. board, MO Council, 1941; member, national council); National Arboretum (member, advisory council, 1946–70); MO State C. of C. (vice pres.; dir., 1925–29); American Assn. of Nurserymen (life member; pres., 1917, 1920); Federation of Garden Clubs of MO; MO Soc. of WA; Naval Inst.; MO Hist. Soc. (dir.); Garden Clubs of America; Sons of the Revolution; American Saddle Horse Breeders Assn. (pres.); Naval Acad. Graduates Assn.; Navy Athletic Assn.; Navy League of the U.S. (vice pres.; dir., 1941–46); Pan-American Soc. (St. Louis commissioner, 1941); University Club of St. Louis; Army and Navy Club; Rotary Club. AWARDS: Hall of Fame Award, American Assn. of Nurserymen, 1967; Patriots Award, Sons of the Revolution, 1969. HON. DEG.: LL.D., Westminster Coll., U. of MO, 1937; LL.D., Central Coll., 1939; LL.D., Beloit Coll., 1941; LL.D., Washington U., 1941. REL.: Episc. MISC.: discovered Stark Golden Delicious Apple, 1913. RES.: Louisiana, MO.

STARKY, STUART MARC. POLIT. & GOV.: ***candidate for Democratic nomination to presidency of the U.S., 1992***. MAILING ADDRESS: 1750 West Belmont Ave., Chicago, IL 60657.

STARR, FRANK (nee FRANKLIN DELANO GULLEDGE). m. Stella Montgomery. POLIT. & GOV.: ***Non-Partisan Third World Perpetual candidate for presidency of the U.S., 1980; Non-Partisan Third World Perpetual candidate for president of the World, 1980***. BUS. & PROF.: recording artist, Nashville, TN; guitarist, "The Gene Travis Band," Starr Records; founder, minister, The Mainstream Faith Movement. MEM.: International Assn. of Educators for World Peace; NAACP; U.N. Assn.; International Platform Association; American Security Council; Friends of the World Council of Churches; Signal World Amity Soc.; World Encounter for God; Local 3-10, AFL-CIO; Amnesty International; International Woodworkers of America. REL.: The Mainstream Faith. MISC.: known as "Patriot-Prophet, World Rectifier, Chief of the Common People, Religionist-Revolutionist, Abolitionist-Creationist." MAILING ADDRESS: Star Route, Box 117, Kingston, ID 83839.

STARR, JEREMIAH J. CHRISTOPHER, II. POLIT. & GOV.: ***U.S. Party candidate for presidency of the U.S., 1980***. BUS. & PROF.: minister. MAILING ADDRESS: 4021 Evanston Ave., North, Seattle, WA 98103.

STARR, RICHARD PIERCE. POLIT. & GOV.: ***candidate for Democratic nomination to presidency of the U.S., 1988***. MAILING ADDRESS: 332 Ponce De Leon Ave., #21, Atlanta, GA 30308.

STASSEN, HAROLD EDWARD. b. Apr 13, 1907, West St. Paul, MN; par. William and Elsie (Mueller) Stassen; m. Esther G. Glewwe, Nov 14, 1929; c. Glen Harold; Kathleen Esther. EDUC.: B.A., U. of MN, 1927, LL.B., 1929; LL.D. POLIT. & GOV.: elected as a Republican, cty. atty., Dakota Cty., MN, 1930–38; delegate, Rep. Nat'l. Conv., 1936, 1950 (temporary chm.; keynoter); elected as a Republican to gov. of MN, 1939–45; ***candidate for Republican nomination to presidency of the U.S., 1944, 1948, 1952, 1960, 1964, 1968, 1972, 1976, 1980, 1984, 1988, 1992***; appointed U.S. delegate, International Conference on the U.N., 1945; appointed U.S. Mutual Security Administrator, 1953; appointed dir., Foreign Operations Administration, 1953–55; appointed deputy rep. of the U.S., U.N. Disarmament Conference, 1955; appointed special asst. to the presidency of the U.S., 1955–58; ***candidate for Republican nomination to vice presidency of the U.S., 1956***; candidate for Republican nomination to gov. of PA, 1958; candidate for Republican nomination to U.S. Senate (MN), 1978; Republican candidate for U.S. House (MN), 1986. BUS. & PROF.: atty.; admitted to MN Bar, 1929; law practice, South St. Paul, MN, 1929; Godkin lecturer, Harvard U., 1946; pres., U. of PA, 1948–53; partner, Stassen, Kostos and Mason (law firm), 1958–; partner, Stassen, Kephart, Sarkis and Scullin (law firm), 1958–; trustee, Penn Mutual Life Insurance Co. MIL.: lt. commander, U.S. Navy, 1943–45 (asst. chief of staff); Legion of Merit; Bronze Star; Presidential Citation Ribbon with Two Battle Stars. MEM.: MN Young Republicans (pres., 1936); National Governors' Conference (chm., 1940–42); Council of State Governments (chm., 1940–41); Sigma Alpha Epsilon; Delta Sigma Rho; Gamma Eta Gamma; International Council for Religious Education (pres., 1942–50); National Council of Churches (vice pres., 1950–52; pres., Div. of Christian Education, 1952–); Masons (Shriners); Grey Friars; National Conference of Christians and Jews (national chm., Brotherhood Week, 1946); World Law

Days (chm., 1965–67); American Heart Assn. (chm., 1948); American Phil. Soc.; AAAS; ABA; Phi Beta Kappa; Rotary Club; Kiwanis; Elks. AWARDS: "Outstanding Young Man," National Junior C. of C., 1939. HON. DEG.: Hamline U., 1939; LL.D., U. of PA, 1948; L.H.D., Temple U., 1949; LL.D., Princeton U., 1950; LL.D., U. of AL; LL.D., Bates Coll.; LL.D., Dartmouth Coll.; LL.D., Drexel Inst. of Technology; LL.D., MacMurray Coll.; LL.D., Washington and Jefferson U. WRITINGS: *Where I Stand* (1947); *Man Was Meant to Be Free* (coauthor, 1955); *Eisenhower: Turning the World Toward Peace* (1990). REL.: Bapt. (pres., American Baptist Convention, 1963–64). MAILING ADDRESS: 310 Salem Church Rd., Sunfish Lake, MN 55118.

STAUBACH, ROGER THOMAS. b. Feb 5, 1942, Cincinnati, OH; par. Robert and Betty Staubach; m. Marianna Hoobler, Sep 4, 1965; c. three daughters. EDUC.: St. John's Parochial School, Deer Park, OH; grad., Purcell H.S., Cincinnati, OH; NM Military Acad.; B.S., U.S. Naval Acad., 1965. POLIT. & GOV.: ***candidate for Republican nomination to vice presidency of the U.S., 1976***. BUS. & PROF.: professional football player; quarterback, Dallas Cowboys, 1969–; owner, real estate company, Dallas, TX. MIL.: U.S. Navy, 1961–69. AWARDS: Thompson Trophy, U.S. Naval Acad., 1962, 1963, 1964; Heisman Trophy, 1963; Sword Award, Naval Acad. Athletic Assn., 1965; Bert Bell Award, 1971; Outstanding Player in Super Bowl Award, 1971; "Player of the Year," National Football Conference, 1971. REL.: R.C. MISC.: holder of NCAA passing record. MAILING ADDRESS: c/o Staubach Co., 6750 LBJ Freeway, #1100, Dallas, TX 75240.

STEARNS, PERRY JAY. b. Nov 25, 1890, Grand Island, NE; d. Jun 21, 1966, Milwaukee, WI; par. George Orlo and Lacy (Dings) Stearns; m. Mae Belle Brook, Sep 14, 1915; m. 2d, Agena Kreimann; c. Forest Walden; David Brook; Perry Orlo; Rhodora Adaline (Mrs. Carl Leyse). EDUC.: grad., East Side H.S., Milwaukee, WI; B.A., Harvard U., 1913, B.L., 1916; U. of WI, 1915. POLIT. & GOV.: member, Milwaukee Cty. (WI) Council of Defense; chm., Shorewood (WI) Republican Club, 1942–44; Republican Committeeman, Shorewood, WI, 1942–44; candidate for Republican nomination to U.S. Senate (WI), 1944; ***candidate for Republican nomination to presidency of the U.S., 1952***. BUS. & PROF.: field organizer, extension div., U. of WI, 1916; atty.; admitted to WI Bar, 1916; assoc., partner, Upham, Black, Russell and Richardson (law firm; later, Richardson, Reeder, Stearns and Weidner), Milwaukee, WI, 1916–44. MEM.: Bryce Law Club; Delta Upsilon; Phi Delta Phi; League of Nations Assn. (State pres.); YWCA (trustee); Milwaukee Cty. Council of Churches (exec. cmte.); A.C.L.U.; Milwaukee Refugee's Cmte.; Masons (Free and Accepted Masons; Scottish Rite; Royal Arch Masons; A.A.O.N.M.S.); Community War Chest (chm., Downtown District, 1944); Milwaukee Legal Advisory Board (1917–19); Stair Soc. of Scotland; Selden Soc. of England; ABA; WI Bar Assn.; Milwaukee Cty. Bar Assn.; WI Hist. Soc. (life member); New England Historic Genealogical Soc.; Professional Men's Club of Milwaukee (sec.); Milwaukee Legal Aid Soc. REL.: Unitarian (pres.; Sunday school superintendent). RES.: Milwaukee, WI.

STEBBINGS, JEHIEL. POLIT. & GOV.: ***Sovereign People's candidate for presidency of the U.S., 1852 (satire effort)***, fictitious candidate sponsored by The Green Bag. BUS. & PROF.: sailor. MIL.: ensign, U.S. Navy. MEM.: Spunkville Sewing Circle. MAILING ADDRESS: Spunkville, NY.

STEDMAN, SEYMOUR. b. 1871; d. Jul 9, 1948, Chicago, IL; m. Irene S. POLIT. & GOV.: founder, Social Democratic Party, 1898; member, national exec. cmte., Social Democratic Party; Socialist Party candidate for IL State's atty., 1904, 1908; ***candidate for Socialist Party nomination to vice presidency of the U.S., 1908***; elected as a Socialist to IL State House, 1913–15; member, Socialist Party National Cmte., 1911; Socialist Party candidate for IL State House, 1914; Socialist Party candidate for mayor of Chicago, IL, 1915; Socialist Party candidate for gov. of IL, 1916; ***Socialist Party candidate for vice presidency of the U.S., 1920***; Socialist Party candidate for U.S. House (IL), 1923. BUS. & PROF.: atty.; partner, Stedman and Soelke (law firm), Chicago, IL; vice pres., City State Bank of Chicago, to 1929. MEM.: Cooperative Soc. of America (trustee, to 1921). WRITINGS: *Socialism and Peace* (1917); *Brief in Stokes v. United States* (1918); *Brief in the U.S. Circuit Court of Appeals for the Seventh Circuit* (1918); *The Case of the Chicago Socialists* (1918); *Brief in Debs v. United States* (1919). MISC.: indicted and convicted of receiving deposits while City State Bank was insolvent, 1931; charge dropped on appeal, 1935. RES.: Chicago, IL.

STEED, THOMAS JEFFERSON "TOM." b. Mar 2, 1904, Rising Star, TX; d. Jun 8, 1983, Shawnee, OK; par. Walter H. and Sallie (Johnson) Steed; m. Hazel Bennett, Feb 26, 1923; c. Richard N.; Roger. EDUC.: public schools, Konawa, OK. POLIT. & GOV.: employee, OWI, 1944–45; administrative asst. to U.S. Reps. P. L. Gassaway, R. L. Hill, and Gomer Smith; elected as a Democrat to U.S. House (OK), 1949–81; delegate, Dem. Nat'l. Conv., 1968; ***candidate for Democratic nomination to presidency of the U.S., 1980***. BUS. & PROF.: automobile dealer, OK, 1945–48; reporter, *Bartlesville (OK) Examiner*; reporter, *McAlester (OK) News Capitol*; reporter, *Daily Oklahoman*; managing ed., *Shawnee (OK) News and Star*, 4 years. MIL.: pvt., 2d lt., U.S. Army, 1942–45. MEM.: Masons. AWARDS: elected to Minute Man Hall of Fame, 1970; OK Hall of Fame, 1971. REL.: Methodist. RES.: Shawnee, OK.

STEELE, ADAM. b. 1946; single. POLIT. & GOV.: candidate for U.S. Senate (CA), 19??; ***independent candidate for presidency of the U.S., 1980***. BUS. & PROF.: delinquent bill investigator, Associated Bureaus. MAILING ADDRESS: 1821 University Ave., Suite N 178, St. Paul, MN 55104.

STEELMAN, ALAN WATSON. b. Mar 15, 1942, Little Rock, AR; par. Ples C. and Flossie (Watson) Steelman; m. Carolyn Findley, Aug 29, 1962; c. Robin; Kimble; Alan Watson, Jr.; Allison. EDUC.: B.A., Baylor U., 1964; M.L.A., Southern Methodist U., 1971; fellow, John F. Kennedy Inst. of Politics, Harvard U., 1972. POLIT. & GOV.: exec. dir., Republican Party, Dallas Cty., TX, 1966–69; appointed exec. dir., President's Advisory Council on Minority Business Enterprise, 1969–71; appointed member, Special White House Speakers' Task Force on Phases I and II, 1969–72; elected as a Republican to U.S. House (TX), 1973–77; Republican candidate for U.S. Senate (TX), 1976; ***candidate for Republican nomination to vice presidency of the U.S., 1976***. BUS. & PROF.: exec. dir., Dallas Federal Savings and Loan Assn., Dallas, TX, 1965–66; dir., KERA-TTV, 1969–72; management consultant, Alexander Proudfoot Co., Chicago, IL. MEM.: Sam Wyly Foundation (exec. dir., 1969); Bishop Coll. (board of development); Lyndon B. Johnson Library (friend); Tryon Coterie Social Club; Pi Sigma Alpha; Sigma Phi Epsilon (hon.); Common Cause (dir.); Dallas Civic Opera; L. Q. C. Lamar Soc. (dir.); Carnegie-Mellon Inst. of Research (dir.). AWARDS: "Future Leader," *Time Magazine*, 1974; "Watch Dog of the Treasury," 1974, 1976; "Guardian of Small Business," 1974; Golden Age Hall of Fame, 1975; Woodrow Wilson Fellow. REL.: Bapt. MAILING ADDRESS: 6938 Wabash Circle, Dallas, TX 75214.

STEFFEY, JOHN WESLEY. b. May 29, 1925, Baltimore, MD; par. Charles Henry and Louetta (Plitt) Steffey; m. Judith Ridgely; c. Linda; John Wesley, Jr.; William C. EDUC.: B.S., U.S.C.G. Acad., 1946; MA Inst. of Technology; Johns Hopkins U. POLIT. & GOV.: member, Anne Arundel Cty. (MD) Republican Central Cmte.; member, MD Republican State Central Cmte.; member, Baltimore (MD) Charter Comm.; appointed member, Governor's Advisory Cmte. on Patuxent River Watershed, MD; ***candidate for Republican nomination to presidency of the U.S., 1964***; elected as a Republican to MD State Senate, 1965–7?; candidate for Anne Arundel (MD) Cty. exec., 1970. BUS. & PROF.: real estate broker; builder. MIL.: U.S.C.G., 1943–49. MEM.: MD Real Estate Assn. (pres.); MD Home Builders Assn. (dir.); Greater Baltimore and Anne Arundel Cty. Real Estate Board; Greater Baltimore Cmte.; Citizens Planning and Housing Assn.; Elks; Anne Arundel Cty. Trade Council; Historic Annapolis, Inc.; Greater Annapolis C. of C.; MD Republican Founders Club; Navy League; Advertising Club of Baltimore; U.S. Power Squadron; YMCA; Center Club. MAILING ADDRESS: 18 East Lexington St., Baltimore, MD 21202.

STEIN, DUANE FRANCIS. POLIT. & GOV.: ***independent (Cmte. for a Constitutional Presidency) candidate for vice presidency of the U.S., 1976***. MAILING ADDRESS: RR 1, Barnum, IA 50518.

STEINER, WILHELM FRIEDRICH. b. Mar 26, 1941, New Castle, PA; single (two annulments); c. two given up for adoption, 1973; three given up for adoption, 1987. EDUC.: grad., Redlands (CA) Union H.S., 1959; college grad., 1964 (returned degree in 1974). POLIT. & GOV.: candidate for various positions in German Democratic Republic, 1989–90; candidate for appointment to U.S. Senate (PA, VA, and CA), 1990; ***candidate for Democratic nomination to presidency of the U.S., 1992; candidate for Republican nomination to presidency of the U.S., 1992; candidate for Republican nomination to vice presidency of the U.S., 1992; candidate for independent nomination to vice presidency of the U.S., 1992***. BUS. & PROF.: mathematics instructor, college, 1961–64; employee, IBM Corp., 1964–71; unemployed, 1971–75, 1986–; self-employed, 1971–75; philosopher, 1988–. MIL.: volunteered for U.S.M.C., 1959, denied enlistment due to deafness. MEM.: Alpha Sigma Pi; Mid Hudson Valley Silent Club (pres.); various Deaf Clubs in Dallas, TX, San Francisco, CA, Cincinnati, OH, and Allentown, PA. WRITINGS: claims more than 75 publications on philosophical topics. REL.: Spinozan Pantheist. MAILING ADDRESS: P.O. Box 53, Alhambra, CA 91802.

STEIWER, FREDERICK W. b. Oct 13, 1883, Jefferson, OR; d. Feb 3, 1939, Washington, DC; par. John Frederick and Ada Eugenia (May) Steiwer; m. Frieda Roesch, Dec 11, 1911; c. Elisabeth (Mrs. Ralph Talbot McElvenny); Frederick Herbert. EDUC.: B.S., OR State Agricultural Coll., 1902; B.A., U. of OR, 1906; studied law. POLIT. & GOV.: appointed deputy district atty., Umatilla and Morrow counties, OR, 1909–10; elected district atty., Umatilla and Morrow counties, OR, 1912–16; elected as a Republican to OR State Senate, 1916–17; elected as a Republican to U.S. Senate (OR), 1927–38; delegate, keynoter, Rep. Nat'l. Conv., 1936; ***candidate for Republican nomination to presidency of the U.S., 1936; candidate for Republican nomination to vice presidency of the U.S., 1936***. BUS. & PROF.: clerk, First National Bank, Eugene, OR, 1906–07; atty.; admitted to OR Bar, 1908; law practice, Pendleton, OR, 1909–26; partner, Raley, Raley and Steiwer (law firm), Pendleton, OR, 1919; partner, Maguire, Shields and Morrison (law firm), Portland, OR; law practice, Washington, DC, 1938–39; wheat grower. MIL.: 1st lt., 65th Artillery, Battery F, U.S. Army, 1917–19. MEM.: Masons; Elks; Rotary Club; OR Cooperative Hay Growers Assn. (founder; counsel); Umatilla Rapids Assn.; Sigma Nu; Phi Delta Phi; American Legion; VFW. REL.: Episc. RES.: Portland, OR.

STELMAN, CARL F. b. 1931. EDUC.: D.D.S., NY U., 1956. POLIT. & GOV.: ***independent candidate for presidency of the U.S., 1976***. BUS. & PROF.: dentist. MEM.: American Dental Assn. MAILING ADDRESS: 54 North Broadway, Red Hook, NY 12571.

STEPHENS, ALEXANDER HAMILTON. b. Feb 11, 1812, Wilkes Cty. (later Taliaferro Cty.), GA; d. Mar 4, 1883, Atlanta, GA; par. Andrew and Margaret (Grier)

Stephens. EDUC.: grad., U. of GA, 1832. POLIT. & GOV.: elected as a Whig to GA State House, 1836–41; elected as a Whig to GA State Senate, 1842; elected as a Whig (and subsequently as a Democrat) to U.S. House (GA), 1843–59, 1873–82; joined Democratic Party, 1852; presidential elector, Democratic Party, 1860; delegate, Confederate Constitutional Convention, 1861; ***elected by Confederate Provisional Congress, vice president of the Confederate States of America, 1861–1865***; elected as a Democrat to U.S. Senate (GA), 1865 (not seated); elected as a Democrat to gov. of GA, 1882–83. BUS. & PROF.: schoolteacher, 18 months; atty.; admitted to GA Bar, 1834; law practice, Crawfordville, GA; owner, *The Southern Sun*, 1871. WRITINGS: *A Constitutional View of the Late War Between the States* (1870); *The Reviewers Reviewed* (1872); *A Compendium of the History of the United States* (1875). MISC.: imprisoned at Fort Warren, Boston, MA, 1865. RES.: Crawfordville, GA.

STERN, MICHAEL ALAN. b. Jan 21, 1945, New York, NY; par. Hillel and Estelle Beatrice (Laxer) Stern; m. Helen Jackow Bowitz; m. 2d, Lisa Ruth Kolins; c. none. EDUC.: grad., William Howard Taft H.S., New York, NY, 1962; Sullivan Cty. (NY) Community Coll., 1972–73. POLIT. & GOV.: elected as a Conservative to Community School Board #28, Ferndale, NY, 1975–77; appointed member, North Country Scenic Trail Advisory Council, U.S. Dept. of the Interior, 1983–85; Heritage Party candidate for U.S. House (NY), 1984, 1986; ***candidate for Republican nomination to presidency of the U.S., 1988; Heritage Party candidate for presidency of the U.S., 1988***. BUS. & PROF.: security officer, clerk, acting mgr., Internal Revenue Service, 10 years; owner, tax preparation and self-defense businesses; founder, pres., Pleasureway Clubs and Resorts Corp. MEM.: Sullivan Cty. C. of C.; Young Americans for Freedom (Sullivan Cty. chm., 1971–73; NY State dir., 1978–82); American Conservatives for Freedom (founder; national chm.). WRITINGS: The Conservative Party of the United States (unpublished). REL.: Jewish. MAILING ADDRESS: R.F.D. #1, Box 91, Old Route 17, Ferndale, NY 12734.

STETTINIUS, EDWARD REILLY, JR. b. Oct 22, 1900, Chicago, IL; d. Oct 31, 1949, Greenwich, CT; par. Edward Reilly and Judith (Carrington) Stettinius; m. Virginia Gordon Wallace, May 15, 1926; c. Edward R.; Wallace; Joseph. EDUC.: Pomfret (CT) School; U. of VA, 1919–24. POLIT. & GOV.: liaison officer, National Industrial Recovery Administration/Industrial Advisory Board, 1933; chm., War Resources Board; member, advisory board, Petroleum Administration for War; appointed member, advisory comm., Council on National Defense, 1940; chm., Priorities Board, and dir., Priorities Div., Office of Production Management, 1941; appointed Lend-Lease Administrator, special asst. to the pres., 1941–43; appointed undersec. of state, U.S. Dept. of State, 1943–44; appointed U.S. sec. of state, 1944–45; ***candidate for Democratic nomination to vice presidency of the U.S., 1944***; appointed personal rep. of the pres., 1945; appointed U.S. rep. to the U.N., 1945–46; chm., American Delegation, Inter-American Conference on Problems of War and Peace, Mexico City, Mexico, 1945. BUS. & PROF.: employee, Hyatt Roller Bearing Works, Harrison, NJ, employment mgr., 1924; asst. to John L. Pratt, vice pres., General Motors Corp., 1926–30; asst. to Alfred P. Sloan, Jr., pres., General Motors Corp., 1930; dir., Metropolitan Life Insurance Co., 1930–34; dir., General Electric Co.; dir., International General Electric Co.; dir., Federal Reserve Bank of Richmond; dir., member, exec. cmte., North American Aviation, Inc.; dir., Transcontinental and Western Air, Inc., 1930–34; chm. of the board, Liberia Co.; dir., World Commerce Corp.; vice pres., General Motors Corp., 1931; dir., vice pres., General Aviation Corp., 1934; dir., Western Air Express Corp.; dir., Eastern Air Lines, Inc.; dir., chm. of Finance Cmte., U.S. Steel Corp., 1936–38, chm. of the board, 1938–40. MEM.: National Share the Work Movement (1932); American Red Cross (chm., 1939 Roll Call, NY Chapter); Dumbarton Oaks Conversations on International Security (chm., 1944); Thomas Jefferson Memorial Foundation (dir.); U. of VA (Rector, 1946–47); English Speaking Union (chm., board of directors, 1947); Judson Health Center (dir.); NY Museum of Science and Industry (trustee); Pomfret School (trustee); Roosevelt Hospital (trustee); VA Episcopal Theological Seminary (trustee); American Foreign Service Assn. (hon. member); The Pilgrims (London); India House; Union Club; Piping Rock Club; St. Anthony Club; The Riding Club; Century Club of NY; Delta Psi. AWARDS: one of twelve of "America's Outstanding Young Men," 1934–35; Medal for Merit, 1946; Gold Medal, National Acad. of Social Science; Hero of Peace Award, National Conference of Christians and Jews; Commander, Legion of Honor (France). HON. DEG.: LL.D., American U.; LL.D., U. of CA; LL.D., U. of Chattanooga; LL.D., Colgate U.; LL.D., Columbia U.; LL.D., Elmira Coll.; LL.D., Lafayette Coll.; LL.D., NY U.; D.C.L., Oxford U.; L.H.D., Roanoke Coll.; LL.D., Rutgers U.; Dr.Engineering, Stevens Inst. of Technology; LL.D., Union Coll. WRITINGS: *Roosevelt and the Russians: The Yalta Conference* (1949). REL.: Episc. RES.: New York, NY.

STEVENS, EARL VERN "BLACKJACK." m. Linda S. POLIT. & GOV.: ***independent candidate for presidency of the U.S., 1980***. BUS. & PROF.: publisher, *National C.B. Truckers' News*; publisher, *American Truck Trader*. MAILING ADDRESS: P.O. Box 1192, 911 Springfield Rd., Lebanon, MO 65535.

STEVENS, HERMAN EUGENE. POLIT. & GOV.: ***candidate for Republican nomination to presidency of the U.S., 1984***. MAILING ADDRESS: 5 Pinto Circle, Downingtown, PA 19335.

STEVENS, STELLA. b. Oct 1, 1938, Yazoo City, MS; d. Thomas Ellett and Divey Estelle (Caro) Eggleston; m. Noble H. Stephens, Sep 1, 1954; c. Andrew. EDUC.: Memphis State U.

Polit. & Gov.: ***One Party candidate for presidency of the U.S., 1976***. Bus. & Prof.: actress; author; artist; songwriter; motion picture dir.; model; appeared on "Ben Casey" (television series), 1965; "Flamingo Road" (television series), 1980–81. Motion Picture Credits: "Say One for Me" (1958); "Lil Abner" (1959); "Too Late Blues" (1961); "The Courtship of Eddy's Father" (1963); "The Nutty Professor" (1963); "Synanon" (1965); "The Secret of My Success" (1965); "The Silencers" (1966); "How to Save a Marriage" (1967); "The Mad Room" (1969); "The Ballad of Cable Hogue" (1970); "A Town Called Bastard" (1971); "Stand Up and Be Counted" (1971); "Poseidon Adventure" (1972); "Arnold" (1974); "Cleopatra Jones and the Casino of Gold" (1974); "Las Vegas Lady" (1974); "Nickelodeon" (1976); "The Manitou" (1978); "The Night They Took Miss Beautiful" (television, 1977); "Cruise into Terror" (television, 1978); "Rage." Mailing Address: 2180 Coldwater Canyon, Beverly Hills, CA 90210.

STEVENSON, ADLAI EWING. b. Oct 23, 1835, Christian Cty., KY; d. Jun 15, 1914, Chicago, IL; par. John Turner and Eliza (Ewing) Stevenson; m. Letitia Green, Dec 20, 1866; c. Lewis Green (q.v.); Mary; Julia; Letitia. Educ.: IL Wesleyan U.; studied law. Polit. & Gov.: master-in-chancery, IL, 1860–64; presidential elector, Democratic Party, 1864; district atty., IL, 1865–69; elected as a Democrat to U.S. House (IL), 1875–77, 1879–81; Democratic (Greenback) candidate for U.S. House (IL), 1876, 1880, 1882; delegate, Dem. Nat'l. Conv., 1884, 1888, 1892; appointed first asst. postmaster gen. of the U.S., 1885–89; ***candidate for Democratic nomination to presidency of the U.S., 1892, 1896; elected as a Democrat, vice presidency of the U.S., 1893–1897; Democratic candidate for vice presidency of the U.S., 1900; Silver Republican Party candidate for vice presidency of the U.S., 1900; People's Party candidate for vice presidency of the U.S., 1900***; appointed member, U.S. Bimetallic Comm. to Europe, 1897; Democratic candidate for gov. of IL, 1908. Bus. & Prof.: atty.; admitted to IL Bar, 1858; law practice, Metamora, IL; partner (with J. S. Ewing), law firm, Bloomington, IL, 1869. Mem.: U.S. Military Acad. (visitor). Hon. Deg.: LL.D., Centre Coll., Danville, KY. Writings: *Something of Men I Have Known* (1909). Rel.: Presb. Misc.: grandfather of Adlai Ewing Stevenson II (q.v.) and great-grandfather of Adlai Ewing Stevenson III (q.v.). Res.: Bloomington, IL.

STEVENSON, ADLAI EWING, II. b. Feb 5, 1900, Los Angeles, CA; d. Jul 14, 1965, London, England; par. Lewis Green (q.v.) and Helen Louise (Davis) Stevenson; m. Ellen Borden, Dec 1, 1928 (divorced); c. Adlai Ewing III (q.v.); Borden; John Fell. Educ.: A.B., Princeton U., 1922; J.D., Northwestern U., 1926. Polit. & Gov.: appointed special counsel, A.A.A., 1933–34; appointed asst. to U.S. sec. of the navy, 1941–44; chief, Economic Mission to Italy, 1943; delegate, U.S. War Dept. Mission to Europe, 1944; appointed asst. to U.S. sec. of state, 1945, 1957; adviser, U.S. Delegation to U.N. Conference, 1945; U.S. minister, chief, U.S. Delegation to U.N. Preparatory Comm., 1945; appointed U.S. delegate, U.N. General Assembly, 1946–47; elected as a Democrat to gov. of IL, 1949–53; ***Democratic candidate for presidency of the U.S., 1952, 1956***; delegate, Dem. Nat'l. Conv., 1956; ***candidate for Democratic nomination to presidency of the U.S., 1960***; appointed U.S. ambassador to the U.N., 1961–65. Bus. & Prof.: reporter, ed., *Daily Pantagraph*, Bloomington, IL; atty.; admitted to IL Bar, 1926; assoc., Cutting, Moore and Sidley (law firm), Chicago, IL, 1927–33; partner, Sidley, Austin, Burgess and Smith (law firm), Chicago, IL, 1935–41; law practice, 1955–60; senior partner, Stevenson, Rifkind and Wirtz (law firm), Chicago, IL; partner, Paul, Weiss, Stevenson, Wharton and Garrison (law firm), New York, NY. Mil.: apprentice seaman, U.S.N.R., 1918; Distinguished Service Award, U.S. Navy, 1945. Mem.: U. of IL (trustee); Eleanor Roosevelt Memorial Foundation (chm.); Worcester Coll. (fellow); Oxford U. (fellow); Morse Coll. (fellow); Yale U. (fellow); ABA; IL Bar Assn.; Chicago Bar Assn.; NY Bar Assn.; American Acad. of Arts and Sciences; American Soc. of International Law; Decalogue Soc. of Lawyers; APSA; Phi Beta Kappa; Chicago Club; Attic Club; Onwentsia Club; Metropolitan Club of WA; Century Club; River Club; Knickerbocker Club; Woodrow Wilson Foundation (dir.); Chicago Council of Foreign Relations (dir.); International House, U. of Chicago (dir.); IL Childrens' Home and Aid Soc. (dir.); Immigrants Protective League (dir.); Hull House (dir.). Awards: Merit Award, Decalogue Soc. of Lawyers, 1952; Ben Franklin Magazine Award, 1953; Patriotism Award, Notre Dame U., 1963; George Foster Peabody Award, 1963; Woodrow Wilson Award, Princeton U., 1963. Hon. Deg.: LL.D., Northwestern U., 1946; LL.D., Princeton U., 1954; LL.D., Columbia U.; LL.D., Harvard U.; LL.D., Oxford U.; LL.D., IL Wesleyan U.; others. Writings: *Call to Greatness* (1954); *What I Think* (1956); *The New America* (1957); *Friends and Enemies* (1958); *Putting First Things First* (1960); *Looking Outward* (1963). Rel.: Unitarian. Res.: Libertyville, IL.

STEVENSON, ADLAI EWING, III. b. Oct 10, 1930, Chicago, IL; par. Adlai Ewing (q.v.) and Ellen (Borden) Stevenson; m. Nancy L. Anderson, Jun 25, 1955; c. Adlai Ewing IV; Lucy Wallace; Katherine Randolph; Warwick Lewis. Educ.: grad., Milton Acad., 1948; A.B., Harvard U., 1952, LL.B., 1957. Polit. & Gov.: law clerk, IL Supreme Court, 1957–58; elected as a Democrat to IL State House, 1965–67; elected as a Democrat, state treas. of IL, 1967–70; elected as a Democrat to U.S. Senate (IL), 1971–81; ***candidate for Democratic nomination to vice presidency of the U.S., 1972, 1976; candidate for Democratic nomination to presidency of the U.S., 1976, 1980; independent candidate for presidency of the U.S., 1980 (withdrew)***; Democratic candidate for gov. of IL, 1982, 1986 (resigned); Solidarity Party candidate for gov. of IL, 1986. Bus. & Prof.: atty.; admitted to IL Bar, 1957; assoc., Mayer, Friedlich, Spiess, Tierney, Brown and Platt (law firm), Chicago, IL, 1958–66, partner, 1966–67. Mil.: 1st lt., capt., U.S.M.C., 1952–54. Mem.: U.S.M.C. Reserves (capt., 1961); ABA; IL Bar

Assn.; Chicago Bar Assn.; American Political Items Collectors. REL.: Unitarian. MAILING ADDRESS: Hanover, IL 61041.

STEVENSON, JOHN WHITE. b. May 4, 1812, Richmond, VA; d. Aug 10, 1886, Covington, KY; par. Andrew and Mary Page (White) Stevenson; m. Sibella Winston, Jun 15, 1843; c. John White, Jr.; Samuel Winston; Sally Coles (Mrs. Edward Colston); Mary White (Mrs. Edward Colston); Judith White (Mrs. John F. Winslow). EDUC.: Hampden-Sydney Coll., 1828–29; grad., U. of VA, 1832; read law under Willoughby Newton. POLIT. & GOV.: elected member, city council, Covington, KY; cty. atty., Kenton Cty., KY; elected as a Democrat to KY State House, 1845–49; delegate, Dem. Nat'l. Conv., 1848, 1852, 1856, 1880 (chm.); delegate, KY State Constitutional Convention, 1849; appointed Commissioner to Revise the Laws of KY, 1850–51; presidential elector, Democratic Party, 1852, 1856; elected as a Democrat to U.S. House (KY), 1857–61; delegate, Union Convention, 1865; elected as a Democrat to lt. gov. of KY, 1867; succeeded to office of gov. upon death of John L. Helm and subsequently elected as a Democrat to gov. of KY, 1867–71; elected as a Democrat to U.S. Senate (KY), 1871–77; ***candidate for Democratic nomination to vice presidency of the U.S., 1872***. BUS. & PROF.: atty.; admitted to MS Bar, 1833; law practice, Vicksburg, MS; partner (with Jefferson Phelps), law firm, Covington, KY, 1841–43; partner (with James T. Morehead), law firm, Covington, KY, 1843–86; gen. counsel, Kentucky Central R.R.; prof. of Criminal Law and Contracts, Cincinnati Law School, 1878–86. MEM.: ABA (pres., 1884). WRITINGS: *Code of Practise in Civil and Criminal Cases* (1854); *Speech of Honorable J. W. Stevenson, of Kentucky, on the State of the Union* (1875); *Tax and Tariff* (1875); *River and Harbor Appropriations* (1876); *The Electoral Vote* (1876). REL.: Episc. RES.: Covington, KY.

STEVENSON, LEWIS GREEN. b. Aug 15, 1868, Chenoa, IL; d. Apr 5, 1929, Bloomington, IL; par. Adlai Ewing (q.v.) and Letitia (Green) Stevenson; m. Helen Louise Davis, Nov 23, 1892; c. Adlai Ewing II (q.v.); Mrs. Elizabeth Ives. EDUC.: Washington and Jefferson Coll., 1895–97. POLIT. & GOV.: appointed private sec. to Vice President Adlai Ewing Stevenson (q.v.), 1894–97; appointed chm., IL State Board of Pardons, 1913–14; appointed and subsequently elected as a Democrat, sec. of state of IL, 1914–17; delegate, Dem. Nat'l. Conv., 1920, 1928; ***candidate for Democratic nomination to vice presidency of the U.S., 1928***. BUS. & PROF.: newspaper correspondent, Japan and China, 1893–94; mgr., Hearst Mines, AZ and NM, 1897–1903; farmer; mgr., 49 farms in IL, IA, and IN, comprising 10,500 acres. MIL.: special investigator, U.S. Navy, 1917–18. MEM.: Iroquois Club; Press Club of Chicago; University Club. RES.: Bloomington, IL.

STEWARD, ALPHONSO DEWITT. b. Sep 20, 1929, Baltimore, MD; par. Milton Sheridan and Grace Hayes (Page) Steward; m. Bernice Lawrence; m. 2d, Ernestine Dudley; c. none. EDUC.: U. of WI, 1948; U. of NC, 1956; Medical Aidman Basic, U.S. Acad. of Medical Science, 1957; Queens Coll., 1960–62; Community Coll. of Baltimore; VA Commonwealth U. POLIT. & GOV.: ***candidate for Democratic nomination to presidency of the U.S., 1984; candidate for Republican nomination to presidency of the U.S., 1992; independent candidate for presidency of the U.S., 1992***. BUS. & PROF.: writer; worker, volunteer coordinator, New Hope, Inc.; project dir., Project Love; ordained minister, Universal Life Church; founder, steward, Our Church of the Living God, Sharing Our Unconditional Love in Christ; law apprentice, Eber and Thompson (law firm), Columbus, GA; process server, H. Edward Longer, atty., New York, NY; postal clerk/carrier, U.S. Post Office, New York, NY; sales rep., Stuart-McGuire, Salem, VA; desk clerk, The Union Mission, Roanoke Rapids, NC. MIL.: administrative noncommissioned officer, sgt., U.S. Army, 10 years; Combat Infantryman's Badge; Army Service Medal; "Outstanding Graduate," 82d Airborne Div. Basic Aidman's Course, 1956. MEM.: International Black Writer's Conference (NC Circle); National Writer's Union; Thomas Wynn P.A.L. Youth Center; Les Petite Ronards Social Club; NAACP (1952–53, 1982–83); Writer's Workshop; Universal Writer's Club (founder); Social Science Assoc., Halifax Community Coll.; LaSalle Extension U. (life member); Bible Inst. (Baltimore, MD), 1972–73. WRITINGS: "You Touched Me" (song). REL.: Bapt. MAILING ADDRESS: 1104-06 West 13th St., Winston-Salem, NC 27105.

STEWART, ALVAN. POLIT. & GOV.: ***candidate for Liberty Party nomination to vice presidency of the U.S., 1844***. BUS. & PROF.: abolitionist; lecturer. RES.: Utica, NY.

STEWART, ANDREW. b. Jun 11, 1791, Fayette Cty., PA; d. Jul 16, 1872, Uniontown, PA; par. Abraham and Mary (Oliphant) Stewart; m. Elizabeth Shriver; c. Andrew; five others. EDUC.: grad., WA Coll.; studied law, Uniontown, PA. POLIT. & GOV.: elected as a Democrat to PA State House, 1815–18; appointed U.S. district atty. for Western PA, 1818–20; elected as a Democrat to U.S. House (PA), 1821–29, 1831–35, as a Whig, 1843–49; Whig Party candidate for U.S. House (PA), 1834, 1841; ***candidate for Whig Party nomination to presidency of the U.S., 1848***; appointed U.S. sec. of the treasury (declined); joined Republican Party; Republican candidate for U.S. House (PA), 1870. BUS. & PROF.: schoolteacher; atty.; admitted to PA Bar, 1815; law practice, Uniontown, PA, 1815; builder; real estate speculator, PA; dir., Chesapeake and Ohio Canal Co. MISC.: supporter of protective tariff; known as "Tariff Andy." RES.: PA.

STEWART, ANDREW JOHN. POLIT. & GOV.: ***New World Council candidate for presidency of the U.S., 1988***. BUS. & PROF.: writer, Stewart Communications, Washington, DC. MEM.: New World Council. MAILING ADDRESS: 922 24th St., N.W., #814, Washington, DC 20037.

STEWART, CALVIN. b. Feb 22, 1868, Du Plain, MI; d. Nov 19, 1945, Kenosha, WI; par. Joel and Mary (Overholt) Stewart; m. Emma W. Werve, Jul 14, 1900; c. Donald W. EDUC.: public schools, Ionia, MI; I. M. Pouchers' Business Coll.; M.A. Grayes' Literary Inst.; studied law under Judge Jesse Higbie, La Crosse, WI; studied law in offices of Ritchie and Heck, Racine, WI. POLIT. & GOV.: member, WI State Democratic Central Cmte.; Democratic candidate for U.S. House (WI), 1904, 1910, 1912, 1914, 1924, 1938; city atty., Kenosha, WI, 1910–12; ***candidate for Democratic nomination to presidency of the U.S., 1924***; delegate, Dem. Nat'l. Conv., 1924, 1928; judge, Municipal Court, Kenosha, WI, 1930–38. BUS. & PROF.: farmer; foundryman; employee, automobile repair shop; traveling salesman; atty.; admitted to WI Bar, 1896; law practice, Kenosha, WI, 1899–1945. MEM.: WI Bar Assn.; Kenosha Bar Assn.; Elks; Eagles. RES.: Kenosha, WI.

STEWART, CHARLES. b. May 28, 1778, Philadelphia, PA; d. Nov 6, 1869, Bordentown, NJ; par. Charles and Sarah (Ford) Stewart; m. Delia Tudor, Nov 25, 1813; c. Delia Tudor (Mrs. John Henry Parnell); Charles Tudor. POLIT. & GOV.: ***candidate for Democratic nomination to presidency of the U.S., 1844; candidate for Democratic nomination to vice presidency of the U.S., 1844***. BUS. & PROF.: sailor. MIL.: cabin boy, Merchant Marine, 1792; naval officer; commissioned lt., U.S. Navy, 1798; commanded Schooner *Experiment*, 1800; commanded Brig *Siren*, 1802; served in war with Tripoli and Tunis; commissioned capt., 1806; appointed Superintendent of Construction of Gunboats, 1806–07; commander, USS *Constitution*, 1813; commander, USS *Franklin*, 1816; promoted to commodore, 1824; court martialed for irregularities in connection with South American internal controversies, 1824, acquitted; naval commander, 1830–32; pres., U.S. Navy Examining Board, 1829; chief, Philadelphia (PA) Navy Yard, 1838–41, 1846, 1854–61; promoted to senior commodore, U.S. Navy, 1856, flag officer, 1860, rear adm. (retired), 1862. AWARDS: Gold Medal and Sword of Thanks from U.S. Congress, 1816. RES.: Philadelphia, PA.

STEWART, CORA WILSON. b. Jan 17, 1875, farmers, KY; d. Dec 9, 1958, Tryon, NC; d. Jeremiah and Annie Eliza (Halley) Wilson; m. Ulysses Grant Carey; m. 2d, Alexander T. Stewart, Sep 23, 1904; c. William Halley. EDUC.: Morehead Normal School; State U. of KY; National Normal U., 1892–93; Commercial Coll., 1898. POLIT. & GOV.: elected superintendent, Rowan Cty. (KY) Schools, 1910–14; appointed member, KY Illiteracy Comm., 1914–20 (chm.); delegate, Dem. Nat'l. Conv., 1920; ***candidate for Democratic nomination to presidency of the U.S., 1920***; received 1 vote for presidential nomination on 36th ballot, Dem. Nat'l. Conv., 1924; appointed chm., U.S. Comm. on Illiteracy, 1929–33. BUS. & PROF.: educator; author; instructor, Commercial Coll., 1899; principal, Morehead Public School, 1906–07; principal, Model School, Morehead Normal School, 1908; founder, Moonlight Schools, 1911; ed., *Rowan County (KY) Messenger*. MEM.: KY Education Assn. (pres., 1911–12); NEA (Illiteracy Comm., 1918–25; exec. cmte., 1923–24); National Council of Education (Illiteracy Comm., 1920); General Federation of Women's Clubs (Illiteracy Div., 1921); World Federation of Education Associations (Illiteracy Comm., 1923); National Arts Club; Morehead Women's Club (pres.); National Illiteracy Crusade (dir., 1926); Rowan Cty. Schools Assn.; 16th District Christian Women's Board of Missions (pres.). AWARDS: Pictorial Review Achievement Award, 1925; Ella Flagg Young Medal, 1930; Clara Barton Award, 1930; award, KY Education Assn.; award, General Federation of Women's Clubs, 1941. WRITINGS: *Country Life Readers*; *Soldiers First Book* (1917); *Moonlight Schools* (1922); *The Women of Feudland*; *The Mountain Girl*; *The Breathitt County Vendetta*; *Mother's First Book* (1930); *Indian First Book*. REL.: Christian Church. RES.: Morehead, KY.

STEWART, GIDEON TABOR. b. Aug 7, 1824, Johnstown, NY; d. Jun 9, 1909, Pasadena, CA; par. Rev. Nicholas Hill; m. Abby N. Simmons, 1857; c. three sons. EDUC.: Oberlin Coll.; studied law under N. H. Swayne, Norwalk, OH. POLIT. & GOV.: elected as a Whig, auditor, Huron Cty., OH, 1850–56; Prohibition Party candidate for U.S. House (OH), 1854; chm., OH Temperance Convention, 1857; Prohibition Party candidate for judge, circuit court (3 times); Prohibition Party candidate for justice, OH State Supreme Court, 1869, 1870, 1874, 1881, 1886, 1887, 1889, 1896, 1899, and 1 other time; member, Prohibition Party National Cmte., 1869, 1882–84; delegate, Prohibition Party National Convention, 1869, 1872, 1876 (chm., platform cmte.); Prohibition Party candidate for gov. of OH, 1871, 1873, 1879; ***candidate for Prohibition Party nomination to vice presidency of the U.S., 1872; candidate for Prohibition Party nomination to presidency of the U.S., 1876, 1880, 1884, 1892; Prohibition Party candidate for vice presidency of the U.S., 1876***; chm., Prohibition Reform Party, 1880–82; chm., Prohibition Home Protection Party, 1882–85; ***candidate for American Prohibition Party nomination to presidency of the U.S., 1884***. BUS. & PROF.: atty.; admitted to OH Bar, 1846; admitted to the Bar of the Supreme Court of the U.S., 1866; ed., *Norwalk (OH) Reflector*, 1847; ed., *Dubuque (IA) Times*, 1861–65; ed., *Toledo (OH) Blade*; ed., *Toledo (OH) Commercial*; law practice, Norwalk, OH, 1846–61, 1876–1901. MEM.: Sons of Temperance (Grand Worthy Patriarch); Independent Order of Good Templars of OH (Grand Worthy Chief Templar, 3 times); Bible Soc. (life member); Huron Cty. Law Library Assn. (pres.); Fireland Hist. Soc. (pres.); Whittlesey Acad. of Arts and Sciences (pres.); OH State Woman's Suffrage Assn. (pres.); Anti-Saloon League; SAR; American Scotch-Irish Assn.; National Temperance Soc.; Washingtonians. WRITINGS: *Early Poems*; *Life of John Quincy Adams*; *The Prohibition Party Against the Rum Power* (1904); *Famed in American History: The Lives of John Adams and John Quincy Adams* (1906). RES.: Norwalk, OH.

STEWART, JAMES DONALD "DULL." b. Feb 5, 1934, Patten, ME; par. Andrew Avon and Elaine Catherine (Gerow) Stewart; m. Lorraine G. Dube, 1954; c. Karen; Glenn; Pamela; Laurie; Jon. EDUC.: B.A., U. of ME. POLIT. & GOV.: Common Folks Party candidate for supervisor, Henrietta, NY; ***Common Folks Party candidate for presidency of the U.S., 1988***. BUS. & PROF.: senior statistical analyst, senior pricing analyst, Eastman Kodak Co., Rochester, NY; publisher, *The Snooze News*; *WHIMSY* (contributor, 1987). MIL.: U.S. Air Force, 1953–57; top secret cryptographic security clearance. MEM.: Phi Beta Kappa; Phi Kappa Phi; Junior C. of C.; United Way (capt.); International Dull Folks, Unlimited (chm. of the bored). AWARDS: Southwestern ME Scholarship, Elks Club; honor student, U.S. Air Force Acad., Cheyenne, WY. REL.: R.C. MAILING ADDRESS: 129 Gate House Trail, Henrietta, NY 14467.

STEWART, MARGARET TURNER (aka MRS. FRANK STEWART). b. Sycamore, AL; m. Frank Ross Stewart, Jul 31, 1934; c. Frank Ross, Jr. EDUC.: Jacksonville State U.; Auburn U.; grad. school, U. of AL; Birmingham School of Law; OH State U.; Peabody Coll. for Teachers. POLIT. & GOV.: candidate for Democratic nomination to U.S. Senate (AL), 1966, 1984, 1986, 1992; ***candidate for Democratic nomination to presidency of the U.S., 1984, 1988, 1992***. BUS. & PROF.: history teacher, Spring Garden H.S., Cherokee Cty., AL, 10 years; pres., Steward U. System, 1971–. MIL.: officer, U.S.M.C. and WAVES, WWII. MEM.: Eastern Star; Pen Women; Birmingham Civic Club; Business and Professional Women's Club; National Assn. of Parliamentarians; DAR; American Legion; International Platform Assn.; U.D.C.; National Genealogical Soc.; Southern Soc. of Genealogists; TN Valley Genealogical Soc.; TN Valley Hist. Soc.; Natchez Trace Genealogical Soc.; American Assn. of Retired Persons. REL.: Southern Bapt. MAILING ADDRESS: R.F.D. 5, Box 109, Piedmont, AL 36272.

STEWART, OLIVER WAYNE. b. May 22, 1867, Mercer Cty., IL; d. Feb 15, 1937, Bloomington, IL; par. Charles and Eliza J. Stewart; m. Elvira "Ella" J. Seass, Aug 20, 1890. EDUC.: A.B., Eureka Coll., 1890. POLIT. & GOV.: Prohibition Party candidate for U.S. House (IL), 1890; member,, IL State Prohibition Cmte., 1894–1908 (chm., 1896–1900); chm., IL Prohibition Party State Convention, 1896, 1908, 1916; member, Prohibition Party National Cmte., 1896–1912 (exec. cmte.; national chm., 1900–1905); chm., Prohibition Party National Convention, 1896; elected as a Prohibitionist to IL State House, 1902–03; Prohibition Party candidate for mayor of Chicago, IL, 1905; ***candidate for Prohibition Party nomination to presidency of the U.S., 1904, 1908, 1912, 1920***; chm., National Prohibition Party Campaign Cmte., 1916. BUS. & PROF.: ordained minister, Church of Christ, 1887–1937; lecturer; temperance advocate; ed., *National Enquirer*, Indianapolis, IN, 1915; asst. ed., *Daily Commercial*, Indianapolis, IN, 1918–20; ed., *Allied News*. MEM.: Independent Order of Good Templars (sec., district lodge, 1887); IL Christian Endeavor Union (sec., 1893–95; pres., 1895–97); Prohibition Trust Fund Assn. of NY (pres., 1900–1912); National Prohibitionist Extension Cmte. (chm., 1907–11); National Temperance Soc. of NY (field sec., 1910–12); Flying Squadron of America (vice pres., 1915–20; pres., 1920); United Cmte. for Prohibition Enforcement (vice pres., 1924–25); National Organizations for Dry Planks (exec. cmte., 1928); National Conference of Prohibition Organizations Supporting the 18th Amendment (1928); Cooperative Cmte. for Prohibition Enforcement (exec. cmte.; founder, 1929); National Temperance Council (1913–17); National Legislative Conference; Flying Squadron Foundation; Allied Forces for Prohibition (founder; vice chm., 1931); National Board of Strategy (1932); Flying Squadron Campaigners (1934–35). HON. DEG.: LL.D., Eureka Coll., 1916. WRITINGS: *Party Fidelity* (1903); "Wine Making in the Home Unfairly Charged to the Volstead Law," *National Enquirer*, Jun 4, 1925. REL.: Church of Christ. RES.: Chicago, IL.

STEWART, SAMUEL VERNON. b. Aug 2, 1872, Monroe Cty., OH; d. Sep 15, 1939, Helena, MT; par. John Wilson and Maria Adele (Carle) Stewart; m. Stella Dyer Baker, Apr 27, 1905; c. Emily (Mrs. Philip H. Stephen); Marjorie (Mrs. Roland G. Keeton); Leah (Mrs. James E. Brickett). EDUC.: KS Normal School; State Normal School; LL.B., U. of KS, 1898. POLIT. & GOV.: elected city atty., Virginia City, MT, 5 years; elected cty. atty., Madison Cty., MT, 1904–08; Democratic candidate for MT State Senate, 1902; chm., MT Democratic State Central Cmte., 1910–12; elected as a Democrat to gov. of MT, 1913–21; ***candidate for Democratic nomination to presidency of the U.S., 1916, 1920***; delegate, Dem. Nat'l. Conv., 1920, 1924; city atty., Helena, MT, 1922–27; candidate for Democratic nomination to U.S. Senate (MT), 1928, 1936; elected as a Democrat to MT State House, 1931–33; elected assoc. justice, Supreme Court of MT, 1933–39. BUS. & PROF.: atty.; admitted to MT Bar, 1898; law practice, Virginia City, MT, 1898; partner, Stewart and Brown (law firm), Helena, MT, 1921–33; dir., Madison State Bank, Virginia City, MT; dir., Conrad Bank, Helena, MT. MEM.: ABA; MT Bar Assn.; Lewis and Clark Cty. Bar Assn.; MT Club; Masons; Elks; Eagles; Modern Woodmen of America. REL.: Bapt. RES.: Helena, MT.

STOCKDALE, JAMES BOND. b. Dec 23, 1923, Abingdon, IL; par. Vernon Beard and Mabel Edith (Bond) Stockdale; m. Sybil Elizabeth Bailey, Jun 28, 1947; c. James Bond; Sidney Bailey; Stanford Baker; Taylor Burr. EDUC.: B.S., U.S. Naval Acad., 1946; M.A., Stanford U., 1962. POLIT. & GOV.: ***independent candidate for vice presidency of the U.S., 1992***. BUS. & PROF.: naval pilot; senior research fellow, Hoover Institution, Stanford, CA. MIL.: naval aviator, 1950; advanced through grades to vice adm., U.S. Navy, 1977; commander, Fighter Squadron 51, USS *Ticonderoga*, 1963–64; commander, Air Wing 16, USS *Oriskany*, 1964–65; senior naval service prisoner of war, Hanoi, North Vietnam, 1965–73; commander, Anti-Submarine Warfare Wing, U.S. Pacific Fleet,

1974–76; dir. of Strategy, Plans and Policy Div., Office of the Chief of Naval Operations,1976–77; pres., Naval War Coll., 1977–79; pres., The Citadel, The Military Coll. of SC, 1979. Prisoner-of-War, Hoa Lo Prison, Hanoi, Vietnam, 1965–69; Medal of Honor; Distinguished Flying Cross with Oak Leaf Cluster; Distinguished Service Medal with Two Oak Leaf Clusters; Silver Medal with Three Oak Leaf Clusters; Bronze Star with Oak Leaf Cluster; Legion of Merit with Combat V; Purple Heart with Oak Leaf Cluster. MEM.: U.S. Naval Acad. Foundation (trustee); SAR; American Acad. of Achievement; Ends of Earth Soc.; Explorers Club of NY; American Mensa Soc.; Medal of Honor Soc.; Tavern Club of Boston; Metropolitan Club of WA. AWARDS: John Paul Jones Award for Inspirational Leadership, Navy League of the U.S., 1973; Medal of Honor, National Soc. of DAR, 1975. HON. DEG.: Brown U.; The Citadel; U. of MA; Norwich U.; Salve Regina Coll. MAILING ADDRESS: 547 A Ave., Coronado, CA 92118.

STOCKTON, DUKE ESTEN. b. May 27, 1929, Oklahoma City, OK; par. Milburn and Mildred (Coe) Stockton; m. Rosetta Smith; c. Romae. EDUC.: B.A., Western WA U., 1956. POLIT. & GOV.: candidate for Democratic nomination to gov. of WA, 1976; ***candidate for Democratic nomination to presidency of the U.S., 1980, 1984, 1988 (withdrew from presidential race after learning he had cancer, July 18, 1987)***; candidate for Democratic nomination to U.S. Senate (WA), 1983. BUS. & PROF.: schoolteacher, 17 years. AWARDS: letter and sweater for boxing. MEM.: NEA; WA Education Assn. REL.: Protestant. MAILING ADDRESS: 7820 Whittaker Rd., N.W., Olympia, WA 98502.

STOCKTON, RICHARD. b. Apr 17, 1764, Princeton, NJ; d. Mar 7, 1828, Princeton, NJ; par. Richard and Annis (Boudinot) Stockton; m. Mary Field; c. Robert Field (q.v.); eight others. EDUC.: grad., Coll. of NJ, 1779, M.A., 1783; studied law under Elisha Boudinot. POLIT. & GOV.: presidential elector, Federalist Party, 1792, 1800; elected as a Federalist to U.S. Senate (NJ), 1796–99; appointed judge, U.S. District Court, 1801 (declined); Federalist candidate for gov. of NJ, 1801, 1802 (tie vote), 1803, 1804; elected as a Federalist to NJ State House, 1813–15; elected as a Federalist to U.S. House (NJ), 1813–15; ***received 8 electoral votes for vice presidency of the U.S., 1820***; appointed member, NJ Comm. on Eastern Boundary, 1827. BUS. & PROF.: atty.; admitted to NJ Bar, 1784; law practice, Princeton, NJ; landowner, NC and Oneida, NY. MEM.: Coll. of NJ (treas., 1788; trustee, 1791–1828). MISC.: promoted development of steamboat and improvement of canals. RES.: Princeton, NJ.

STOCKTON, ROBERT FIELD. b. Aug 20, 1795, Princeton, NJ; d. Oct 7, 1866, Princeton, NJ; par. Richard (q.v.) and Mary (Field) Stockton; m. Harriet Marie Potter, 1825; c. John Potter; Robert Field, Jr.; one other son; six daughters. EDUC.: Princeton Coll. POLIT. & GOV.: appointed aide to U.S. sec. of the navy; appointed U.S. sec. of the navy, 1841 (declined); appointed military gov. of CA, 1846–47; elected as a Democrat to U.S. Senate (NJ), 1851–53; ***Conservative North American Party candidate for presidency of the U.S., 1856***; delegate, Peace Convention, 1861. BUS. & PROF.: pres., Delaware and Raritan Canal, 1853–66; investor, Camden and Amboy R.R.; race horse breeder; sailor. MIL.: midshipman, U.S. Navy, 1811, lt., 1814, capt., 1838; advanced through grade to commodore; resigned commission, 1850; captured Mexican Capital (Los Angeles) in CA, 1845, and organized civil government; served as commander in chief of CA Militia, 1846–47. MEM.: NJ Colonization Soc. (pres.). MISC.: aided American Colonization Soc. in obtaining tract that became Republic of Liberia. RES.: Princeton, NJ.

STOCKWELL, GEORGE E. b. 1842, VT; par. George L. and Mary W. Stockwell; m. Sarah S.; c. Albert; Charles; George. POLIT. & GOV.: Prohibition Party candidate for gov. of NY, 1908; member, Prohibition Party National Cmte., 1908–11; ***candidate for Prohibition Party nomination to vice presidency of the U.S., 1912 (withdrew)***. BUS. & PROF.: farmer; minister, Methodist Church. REL.: Methodist. RES.: Fort Plain, NY.

STOKES, LOUIS. b. Feb 23, 1925, Cleveland, OH; par. Charles and Louise Stokes; m. Jeanette "Jay" Francis, Aug 21, 1960; c. Shelley; Angela; Louis C.; Lorene. EDUC.: Western Reserve U.; J.D., Marshall Law School, 1953. POLIT. & GOV.: appointed member, vice chm., exec. board, Cleveland Subcmte., U.S. Comm. on Civil Rights, 1966; elected as a Democrat to U.S. House (OH), 1969–; ***candidate for Democratic nomination to presidency of the U.S., 1976***; delegate, Dem. Nat'l. Conv., 1976; member, exec. cmte., Cuyahoga Cty. (OH) Democratic Central Cmte.; member, exec. cmte., OH State Democratic Central Cmte. BUS. & PROF.: atty.; admitted to OH Bar, 1953; law practice, Cleveland, OH, 1954–; partner, Stokes, Character, Terry and Perry (law firm), Cleveland, OH; admitted to practice before the Bar of the Supreme Court of the U.S.; lecturer; author. MIL.: U.S. Army, 1943–46. MEM.: NAACP (vice chm., Cleveland branch, 1965–66); Cleveland Bar Assn. (dir.); Cuyahoga Cty. Bar Assn. (dir.); Congressional Black Caucus (chm.); OH State Bar Assn. (chm., Criminal Justice Cmte.); BSA (district chm.); YMCA (district chm.); Rainey Inst.; United Appeal (section chm., 1959–61); The Welfare Federation; Martin Luther King, Jr. Center for Social Change (trustee); Forest City Hospital (trustee); Karamu House (dir.); Cleveland State U. (trustee); Masons; Urban League; Citizens League; ABA; John Harlan Law Club; Kappa Alpha Psi (life member); A.C.L.U.; The Plus Club; American Legion; African-American Inst. (international advisory council). AWARDS: Civic Award, Cleveland Branch, NAACP; Civic Award, Cleveland Section, U.S. Comm. on Civil Rights. HON. DEG.: LL.D., Shaw U.; LL.D., Wilberforce U. WRITINGS: "Criminal Law," *Cuyahoga County Bar Association Law and Fact*, Apr 1966. REL.: Methodist (trustee, St. Paul A.M.E. Zion Church). MAILING ADDRESS: 4361 Clarkwood Parkway, Warrensville Heights, OH 44128.

STOLIKER, JOAN. b. OR. POLIT. & GOV.: ***independent candidate for presidency of the U.S., 1976***. MAILING ADDRESS: St. Francis Hotel, 5533 Hollywood Blvd., Hollywood, CA 90028.

STONE, KEITH KNOWLES. b. Jan 20, 1922, Maitland, FL; par. Forrest Brewer and Louise Marion (Knowles) Stone; m. Anna Jane Eberhart; c. Linda A.; Carl A. EDUC.: grad., Guilford (CT) H.S., 1940. POLIT. & GOV.: ***independent Republicrat candidate for presidency of the U.S., 1976, 1980***. BUS. & PROF.: taxi owner and operator, 1947–53; chauffeur; dental laboratory worker, 1957–76; owner, dental laboratory; certified dental technician. MIL.: U.S. Army, WWII. MEM.: Civil Air Patrol; Half Century Club; FL Dental Laboratory Assn.; Central FL Dental Technicians' Soc. (vice pres.; treas.); Over 18 Club (treas.); Virginia Heights Assn. (sec.-treas.; board member); Cub Scouts of America. REL.: Congregationalist (deacon). MAILING ADDRESS: 511 Melrose Ave., Apt. 512, Winter Park, FL 32789.

STONE, WARREN SANFORD. b. Feb 1, 1860, Ainsworth, IA; d. Jun 12, 1925, Cleveland, OH; par. John and Sarah (Stewart) Stone; m. Carrie E. Newell, Oct 15, 1885; c. none. EDUC.: WA (IA) Acad.; Western Coll.; M.A. (hon.), Oberlin Coll., 1925. POLIT. & GOV.: treas., National Conference for Progressive Political Action; ***candidate for Progressive Party nomination to vice presidency of the U.S., 1924***. BUS. & PROF.: fireman, Chicago, Rock Island and Pacific R.R., 1879, engineer, 1884; founder, Brotherhood of Locomotive Engineers Cooperative Bank of Cleveland, 1920; dir., Empire Trust Co. of NY, 1923; founder, Brotherhood Holding Co.; founder, Brotherhood Investment Co.; labor union exec. MEM.: Brotherhood of Locomotive Engineers (member, 1885; local sec.-treas.; Grand Chief Engineer, 1903–24; pres., 1925); Cooperative League (dir.); Industrial Peace Cmte. MISC.: custodian of Nobel Peace Prize. RES.: Cleveland, OH.

STONE, WILLIAM JOEL. b. May 7, 1848, Madison Cty., KY; d. Apr 14, 1918, Washington, DC; m. Sarah Louise Winston, Apr 2, 1874. EDUC.: grad., U. of MO, 1867. POLIT. & GOV.: city atty., Bedford, IN, 1870; cty. Prosecutor, Vernon Cty., MO, 1873–74; presidential elector, Democratic Party, 1876; elected as a Democrat to U.S. House (MO), 1885–91; elected as a Democrat to gov. of MO, 1893–97; member, Dem. Nat'l. Cmte., 1896–1904 (vice chm., 1900–1904); ***candidate for Democratic nomination to presidency of the U.S., 1900***; elected as a Democrat to U.S. Senate (MO), 1903–18. BUS. & PROF.: atty.; admitted to IN Bar, 1869; law practice, Bedford, IN; law practice, NV, MO, 1870; law practice, St. Louis, MO, 1897. HON. DEG.: LL.D., U. of MO. RES.: St. Louis, MO.

STONE, WILLIS EMERSON. b. Jul 20, 1899, Denver, CO; par. Harry Burlingame and Lea (Emerson) Stone; m. Marion Travis (deceased, Jun 25, 1971). EDUC.: public schools, Denver, CO; Denver U. POLIT. & GOV.: ***candidate for Republican nomination to presidency of the U.S., 1968***; member, Speakers' Bureau, Populist Party, 1984. BUS. & PROF.: industrial engineer; newspaper columnist, American Way Features; publisher, *Freedom Magazine*. MEM.: American Legion; Lions (District Gov.); Liberty Amendment Cmte. (national chm.). AWARDS: George Washington Medal, Freedom Foundation; Patriots' Award, American Coalition of Patriotic Societies. WRITINGS: *Where the Money Went*. REL.: Presb. MISC.: author of the Liberty Amendment. MAILING ADDRESS: 6413 Franklin Ave., Los Angeles, CA 90028.

STONER, JESSE BENJAMIN. b. Apr 13, 1924, Lookout Mountain, GA; single. EDUC.: McCallie School; Chattanooga (TN) H.S.; LL.B., Atlanta Law School. POLIT. & GOV.: founder, Stoner Anti-Jewish Party, 1946; Stoner Anti-Jewish Party candidate for U.S. House (GA), 1948; cofounder, Christian Anti-Jewish Party, 1952; campaign mgr., Adm. John G. Crommelin (q.v.) for Governor of AL Campaign, 1958; vice chm., gen. counsel, National States Rights Party, 1964, chm.; ***National States Rights Party candidate for vice presidency of the U.S., 1964***; candidate for Democratic nomination to gov. of GA, 1970, 1978; candidate for Democratic nomination to U.S. Senate (GA), 1972, 1980. BUS. & PROF.: atty.; admitted to GA Bar, 1952; law practice, 1952. MEM.: Knights of the Ku Klux Klan (Kleagle, 1942); Associated Klans of America (organizer, Chattanooga Klavern 317; expelled for antisemitic activities, 1950); Columbians; Christian Knights of the Ku Klux Klan (Imperial Wizard, 1959). WRITINGS: *The Gospel of Jesus Christ Versus the Jews*; *The Stoner Anti-Jewish Party*. REL.: Lutheran. MISC.: indicted for conspiring to interfere with Federal Court desegregation order; indicted and convicted for fatal bombing of Baptist Church, Birmingham, AL in 1958, Jan 1980; escaped, surrendered to Federal authorities, 1983. MAILING ADDRESS: 591 Cherokee St., Marietta, GA.

STOUFFER, JOHN HARTZELL. b. Aug 26, 1927, Santa Ana, CA; par. Robert H. and Dorothy Louise (Brokaw) Stouffer; m. Caroline Jane Apfel; c. Mallary Anne; Douglas Stewart. EDUC.: A.B., Cornell Coll., 1951; M.A., Columbia U., 1955. POLIT. & GOV.: ***independent (Cmte. for a Constitutional Presidency) candidate for vice presidency of the U.S., 1976***. BUS. & PROF.: teacher, Monticello (IA) H.S.; teacher, Milton (MA) H.S.; receiving mgr., Gilchrist Co., Boston, MA; teacher, Hingham (MA) H.S. MEM.: NEA; MA Teachers Assn.; MA Marine Educators Assn. REL.: Protestant. MAILING ADDRESS: 7 Howard Rd., Hingham, MA 02043.

STOUT, ROBERT GARY. b. May 26, 1950, Detroit, MI; par. Robert S. and Colleen (Johnson) Stout; m. (divorced);

c. Jeffrey; Mike. EDUC.: grad., Dondero H.S.; A.A., Macomb Cty. (MI) Community Coll. POLIT. & GOV.: candidate for Democratic nomination to U.S. House (MI), 1984; candidate for Democratic nomination to U.S. Senate (MI), 1984; ***candidate for Democratic nomination to presidency of the U.S., 1984, 1988***. BUS. & PROF.: employee, Chrysler Corp., 1973–79; security guard, Wackenhut Corp., 1982. MIL.: ensign fourth class, U.S. Navy. MEM.: Young Democrats; United Automobile and Aerospace Workers Union. REL.: Deist. MAILING ADDRESS: 906 Greenleaf, Royal Oak, MI 48067.

STOVER, FRED WILLIAM. b. Aug 6, 1898, Franklin Cty., IA; par. John and Annie M. (Rachel) Stover; m. Dorothy par. Niehouse; c. Ruth; Leon; Glen; Dale; Joan. EDUC.: Hamilton U., 1921. POLIT. & GOV.: field representative, A.A.A., 1933–39; liaison officer between U.S. sec. of agriculture and U.S. Dept. of Agriculture War Boards, 1942–43; chm., IA Progressive Party, 1948; nominated Henry A. Wallace (q.v.) for pres., 1948; delegate, fourth vice chm., Progressive Party National Convention, 1948; ***candidate for Democratic nomination to presidency of the U.S., 1976***. BUS. & PROF.: farmer; mgr., Hemp Plant Industries, Hampton, IA, 1943–44; dir., Ever Normal Granary for Central Region, to 1942; ed., *Iowa Union Farmer*; ed., *U.S. Farm News*. MEM.: IA Farmers Union (pres., 1945); U.S. Farmers Assn. (pres.). REL.: Bapt. MAILING ADDRESS: 416 Central Ave., East, Hampton, IA.

STOW, MARIETTA LOIS "LUCY" BEERS. b. 1830; d. 1902; d. Mr. and Mrs. Beers; m. Joseph W. Stow. POLIT. & GOV.: independent candidate for gov. of CA, 1882; chm., Equal Rights Party National Convention, 1884; ***Equal Rights Party candidate for vice presidency of the U.S., 1884; independent candidate for vice presidency of the U.S., 1892***. BUS. & PROF.: ed., *Woman's Herald of Industry and Social Science Cooperator*, San Francisco, CA, 1881–84; therapeutic "Electrician." MEM.: Woman's Republic (founder); Cold Food Order (founder). WRITINGS: *Probate Confiscation* (1876); *The Unjust Laws Which Govern Women* (1877); *An Act for the Protection of Widows* (1878); *Probate Chaff* (1879); *An Equal Rights Marriage Property Act and Comparative Law* (1879). MISC.: invented "Tripple S" costume. RES.: San Francisco, CA.

STRANGE, ROBERT. b. Sep 20, 1796, Manchester, VA; d. Feb 19, 1854, Fayetteville, NC. EDUC.: WA Coll.; grad., Hampden-Sydney Coll., 1815; studied law. POLIT. & GOV.: elected as a Democrat to NC State House of Commons, 1821–23, 1826; elected judge, Superior Court of NC, 1827–36; elected as a Democrat to U.S. Senate (NC), 1836–40; Solicitor, Fifth Judicial District of NC; ***candidate for Democratic nomination to vice presidency of the U.S., 1852***. BUS. & PROF.: atty.; admitted to NC Bar; law practice, Fayetteville, NC; author. HON. DEG.: LL.D., Rutgers U., 1840. RES.: Fayetteville, NC.

STRAUSS, MICHAEL ROSS TUNICK. b. Nov 5, 1957, Portchester, NY; par. Harry and Bertty Tunick; single. EDUC.: S.B., M.A., MA Inst. of Technology, 1979; Ph.D., 1985. POLIT. & GOV.: ***Need a Job Party candidate for presidency of the U.S., 1992***. BUS. & PROF.: consultant in computer modeling; dir. of Lignin Research, IOGEN Corp., 1985–88; consultant, Ventana Systems, 1988–90; self-employed, 1990–. AWARDS: Rotary Club Award; Hitachi Fellowship for Grad. Work. WRITINGS: *Coagulation in Processing of Ceramic Suspensions: Powder Size Distribution Effects* (1985); *The Effect of Particle Size Distributions on the Coagulation of Ceramic Suspensions* (1985); *Osmotic Pressure for Concentrated Suspensions of Polydisperse Particles with Thick Double Layers* (1987). REL.: none. MAILING ADDRESS: 67 Gilbert Rd., Belmont, MA 02178.

STRAUSS, ROBERT SCHWARZ. b. Oct 9, 1918, Lockhart, TX; par. Charles H. and Edith V. (Schwarz) Strauss; m. Helen Jacobs, May 27, 1941; c. Robert A.; Richard C.; Susan (Mrs. Philip Robertson). EDUC.: LL.B., U. of TX, 1941. POLIT. & GOV.: appointed member, TX State Bank Board, 1963–76; member, Dem. Nat'l. Cmte. (TX), 1968–72, exec. cmte., 1969–76, treas., 1970–72, chm., 1972–76; chm., National Cmte. to Re-Elect a Democratic Congress, 1972; delegate, Democratic Mid-Term Conference, 1974; appointed U.S. Trade Negotiator, 1977–79; appointed presidential personal rep. for Middle East Negotiations, 1979–80; chm., Carter for President Campaign, 1980; ***candidate for Democratic nomination to presidency of the U.S., 1984***; appointed U.S. ambassador to the Union of Soviet Socialist Republics, 1991, to Russia, 1991–93. BUS. & PROF.: special agent, FBI, 1941–45; atty.; admitted to TX Bar, 1941; admitted to the Bar of DC, 1971; partner, Akin, Gump, Strauss, Hauer and Feld (law firm), Dallas, TX, 1945–77; pres., Strauss Broadcasting Co., 1964–; chm., Valley View State Bank, Dallas, TX. MEM.: TX State Bar Assn.; ABA; Dallas Bar Assn.; Temple Emanuel (pres., board of trustees). REL.: Jewish. MAILING ADDRESS: 6223 De Loache, Dallas, TX 75225.

STREETER, ALSON JESSUP. b. Jan 18, 1823, Rensselaer Cty., NY; d. Nov 24, 1901, Galesburg, IL; par. Roswell and Eleanor (Kenyon) Streeter; m. Deborah Boon, Aug 1847; m. 2d, Susan Menold, Jan 10, 1861; c. Frank W.; George A.; Fanny R.; Nellie May; Minnie G.; Charles D. EDUC.: Inlet Grove School; Knox Coll., 1846–49. POLIT. & GOV.: elected to Cty. Board of Supervisors, New Windsor, IL; elected as a Democrat to IL State House, 1873–75; founder, Labor Party, 1873; delegate, vice pres., independent National (Greenback) Party National Convention, 1876; presidential elector, Greenback Party, 1876; National (Greenback) Party candidate for U.S. House (IL), 1878; National (Greenback) Party candidate for gov. of IL, 1880; treas., Greenback Party National Cmte., 1884; temporary chm., Anti-Monopoly Party National Convention, 1884; elected as a Democrat to IL State Senate, 1885–89; chm., Union Labor Party National Convention, 1887; ***Union Labor Party candidate for presidency of the U.S., 1888***; Farmers' Mutual Benefit Assn.

candidate for U.S. Senate (IL), 1891. BUS. & PROF.: trapper; hunter; ox-driver; shingle maker; gold miner, CA, 1849–51; drover; cattle rancher, New Windsor, IL, 1854; farmer, Galesburg, IL. MEM.: Northwestern Alliance (pres., 1886); National Farmers' Alliance (pres., 1886–87); Farmers' Mutual Benefit Assn.; Grange; Masons (Royal Arch Mason). RES.: Galesburg, IL.

STREETER, GRAHAM G. POLIT. & GOV.: ***independent candidate for presidency of the U.S., 1984***. MAILING ADDRESS: 3745 Chelsea Rd., Shingle Springs, CA 95682.

STROOM, LOWELL MILTON. POLIT. & GOV.: ***candidate for Republican nomination to presidency of the U.S., 1980***. MAILING ADDRESS: 4030 Spruce St., Philadelphia, PA 19104.

STROUD, J. O. POLIT. & GOV.: ***independent candidate for presidency of the U.S., 1984, 1988 (withdrew)***; suffered heart attack in Jul 1987 and withdrew from presidential race. MAILING ADDRESS: 324 South Park St., Sapulpa, OK 74067.

STRUBLE, WALLACE R. POLIT. & GOV.: United Christian Party candidate for IL State Auditor, 1900; ***candidate for United Christian Party nomination to presidency of the U.S., 1900***; presidential elector, United Christian Party, 1900; sec., Christian Union Party. BUS. & PROF.: minister. WRITINGS: *A Jab at the Devil* (1895). RES.: Chicago, IL.

STUART, ARTHUR LINCOLN, III (aka GABRIEL THE ARCHANGEL; ARTHUR LINCOLN SWARTZ, III). POLIT. & GOV.: ***candidate for Democratic nomination to presidency of the U.S., 1984***. MAILING ADDRESS: P.O. Box 467, Mira Loma, CA 91752.

STUART, GEORGE RUTLEDGE. b. Dec 14, 1857, Talbott's Station, TN; d. May 11, 1926, Birmingham, AL; par. Caswell Cobb and Mariah (Worley) Stuart; m. Zollie Sullins, Sep 6, 1882; c. David Sullins; Mary; Margaret; Elizabeth; George Rutledge, Jr. EDUC.: A.B., Emory and Henry Coll., 1882, A.M., 1884, D.D. POLIT. & GOV.: ***candidate for Prohibition Party nomination to presidency of the U.S., 1908***. BUS. & PROF.: ordained minister, Methodist Episcopal Church, 1883; pastor, Methodist Episcopal Church, Cleveland, TN, 1883–84; prof. of English, Centenary Coll., 1885–90; pastor, Centenary Methodist Episcopal Church, Chattanooga, TN, 1890–91; evangelist, Methodist Episcopal Church, 1892–1907; Chautauqua lecturer, 1907–12; pastor, Methodist Episcopal Church, Knoxville, TN, 1912–16; pastor, First Methodist Episcopal Church, Birmingham, AL, 1916–26. MEM.: Anti-Saloon League; Independent Order of Good Templars; Blue Ribbon Movement; Southern Assembly (dir.). HON. DEG.: LL.D., Birmingham Southern Coll., 1923. WRITINGS: *Sermons and Lectures, Stories, and Parables* (1907); *Sam Jones' Famous Sayings* (1908); *The Saloon Under the Searchlight* (1908); *What Every Methodist Should Know* (1923); *Lectures on Evangelism*; *Song Books*. REL.: Methodist Episcopal Church. RES.: Birmingham, AL.

STUCK, PAUL LESLIE. POLIT. & GOV.: ***Readers of The New American (ROTNA) candidate for presidency of the U.S., 1992***. (The *New American* is a magazine published in Appleton, WI.) MAILING ADDRESS: 701 Ash St., Copperas Cove, TX 76522.

STULL, DANIEL. b. 1943. POLIT. & GOV.: ambassador to Hutt River Kingdom; ambassador in Exile to Republic of Minerva; ambassador to principality of Sealand; ***independent candidate for presidency of the U.S., 1984***. BUS. & PROF.: minister. MAILING ADDRESS: 1308 N.E. Second Ave., #1, Fort Lauderdale, FL 33304.

SUITER, LEO FRANK. b. Sep 18, 1925, Fairfield, MO; par. Noah M. and Myrtle Lee (Simpson) Suiter; m. Polly Mozingo; m. 2d, Alice Greene; c. three sons. EDUC.: U. of MO; U. of MD; Troy State Coll. POLIT. & GOV.: ***independent candidate for vice presidency of the U.S., 1980***; Conservative Party candidate for gov. of AL, 1982. BUS. & PROF.: U.S. Civil Service, 10 years; self-employed entertainer; country music singer. MIL.: U.S. Army, 20 years. MEM.: Lions Club; Masons. REL.: Bapt. MAILING ADDRESS: 27 Andrews Dr., Daleville, AL 36322.

SUITS, GARVICE RANDALL, JR. par. Garvice Randall Suits, Sr. POLIT. & GOV.: ***candidate for Republican nomination to presidency of the U.S., 1980***. MAILING ADDRESS: 1115 Mohawk Dr., Elgin, IL 60120.

SULLIVAN, CHARLES LOTEN. b. Aug 20, 1924, New Orleans, LA; par. O. U. and Jennie (Lewis) Sullivan; m. Mary Lester Rayner, Sep 4, 1939; c. Charles Lester; David Hewitt; Mary Loten; John Marshall. EDUC.: Knox Coll.; Tulane U.; LL.B., U. of MS, 1950. POLIT. & GOV.: municipal judge, Clarksdale, MS, 1953–55; elected as a Democrat, district atty., 11th District, MS, 1956–59; candidate for Democratic nomination to gov. of MS, 1959, 1963, 1971, 1978; ***Constitution Party candidate for presidency of the U.S., 1960***; elected as a Democrat to lt. gov. of MS, 1968–72; candidate for Democratic nomination to U.S. Senate (MS), 1978. BUS. & PROF.: atty.; admitted to MS Bar, 1950; senior partner, Sullivan, Dunbar and Smith (law firm), Clarksdale, MS; pres., Northern Mississippi Savings and Loan Assn. MIL.: U.S.A.A.C., WWII, Korean War; MS Air National Guard (maj.). MEM.: Phi Alpha Delta;

MS State Bar; ABA; Masons (Shriner); Lions; Elks. AWARDS: "Outstanding Man of the Year," MS Junior C. of C., 1959; "Outstanding Man of the Year," MS Newspaper Editors, 1959; Distinguished Service Award, MS C. of C., 1960; Distinguished Civilian Service Award, 1969. REL.: Bapt. MAILING ADDRESS: 426 West Second St., Clarksdale, MS 38614.

SULLIVAN, DONALD JEROME. POLIT. & GOV.: ***independent candidate for presidency of the U.S., 1980, 1984***. MAILING ADDRESS: 24 Crosby St., Arlington, MA 02174.

SULLIVAN, JERRY BARTHOLOMEW. b. Jan 1, 1859, Mt. Pleasant, IA; d. Apr 17, 1948; par. Stephen and Mary (Bresnahan) Sullivan; m. Martha Groves, Dec 1886. EDUC.: public and private schools. POLIT. & GOV.: city atty., Creston, IA, 1887–89; member, Creston (IA) Board of Education, 6 years; Democratic candidate for gov. of IA, 1903; member, Des Moines (IA) Board of Education, 1907–12 (pres., 1 year); ***candidate for Democratic nomination to vice presidency of the U.S., 1908***; appointed U.S. gen. appraiser, 1913; appointed pres., board of general appraisers, 1914–25; appointed member, U.S. Customs Court, 1925–39. BUS. & PROF.: atty.; admitted to IA Bar, 1881; law practice, Creston, IA, 1882–1904; law practice, Des Moines, IA, 1904–13; partner, Sullivan and Sullivan (law firm). MEM.: ABA; IA State Bar Assn. REL.: R.C. RES.: Des Moines, IA.

SULLIVAN, JEREMIAH C. "JERRY." m. Marian D. S. POLIT. & GOV.: ***independent Husband Liberation Party candidate for vice presidency of the U.S., 1972***. BUS. & PROF.: bricklayer, William F. Nelson Construction, Washington, DC. MAILING ADDRESS: 1308 Adams St., N.E., Apt. 2, Washington, DC.

SULLIVAN, JOHN LAWRENCE. b. Jun 16, 1899, Manchester, NH; d. Aug 8, 1982, Exeter, NH; par. Patrick Henry and Ellen J. (Harrington) Sullivan; m. Priscilla Manning, Dec 28, 1932; c. Patricia; Charles Manning; Deborah. EDUC.: A.B., Dartmouth Coll., 1921; LL.B., Harvard U., 1924. POLIT. & GOV.: elected as a Democrat, Cty. Solicitor, Hillsborough Cty., NH, 1929–33; Democratic candidate for gov. of NH, 1934, 1938; appointed asst. to U.S. Commissioner of Internal Revenue, 1939; appointed asst. U.S. sec. of the treasury, 1940–44; appointed asst. U.S. sec. of the navy for Air, 1945; appointed undersec. of the navy, 1946–47; appointed U.S. sec. of the navy, 1947–49; ***candidate for Democratic nomination to vice presidency of the U.S., 1948***. BUS. & PROF.: atty.; admitted to NH Bar, 1923; law practice, Manchester, NH, 1924; partner, Sullivan and White (law firm); partner, Sullivan and Sullivan (law firm), 1930–31; senior partner, Sullivan and Wynot (law firm), Manchester, NH; partner, Sullivan, Beauregard, Clarkson, Moss and Brown (law firm), Washington, DC; dir., National Savings and Trust Co.; dir., Life Insurance Securities Corp.; dir., Alcan, Ltd.; dir., MGM Studios; dir., Martin Marietta Corp.; dir., Brown Corp. MIL.: apprentice seaman, U.S. Navy, 1918; Distinguished Service Award. MEM.: BSA (trustee, Daniel Webster Council; hon. member, national council); Naval History Foundation (trustee); DC Bar Assn.; NH Bar Assn.; Order of the Coif; Navy League of the U.S. (dir.); American Legion (commander, NH Dept., 1937); Chi Phi; Delta Sigma Rho; Knights of Columbus; Brook Club; Clover Club; Burning Tree Club; Chevy Chase Club; NH Children's Aid and Protective Soc. (dir.); Camp Carpenter (trustee); ABA; Friendly Sons of Saint Patrick; Metropolitan Club; Inst. for Contemporary Russian Studies (advisory board); Foundation for Religious Action in Social and Civil Order (advisory council); Federal Bar Assn.; American Jud. Soc.; Abenaqui Club. AWARDS: Silver Medal, U.S. Dept. of the Treasury, 1947. HON. DEG.: LL.D., Duquesne U., 1948; LL.D., Dartmouth Coll., 1949; LL.D., Loyola U., 1949; LL.D., U. of NH, 1949; LL.D., U. of Portland. REL.: R.C. RES.: Manchester, NH.

SULLIVAN, ROGER CHARLES. b. Feb 2, 1861, Belvidere, IL; d. Apr 14, 1920, Chicago, IL; par. Eugene and Mary (O'Sullivan) Sullivan; m. Helen M. Quinlan, Feb 11, 1885; c. Boetius Henry; Mary (Mrs. Robert Nicholas Wolf); Helen (Mrs. William Paul McEvoy); Frances (Mrs. Leo Patrick Cummings); Virginia (Mrs. Thomas V. Brennan). EDUC.: Bryant and Stratton Public School. POLIT. & GOV.: elected as a Democrat, probate clerk, Cook Cty., IL, 1890–94; member, Cook Cty. (IL) Democratic Central Cmte., 1890–1920; delegate, Dem. Nat'l. Conv., 1892, 1896, 1900, 1904, 1908, 1912, 1916; member, Dem. Nat'l. Cmte., 1904–20; Democratic candidate for U.S. Senate (IL), 1914; ***candidate for Democratic nomination to vice presidency of the U.S., 1916***; appointed member, IL State Council of Defense, WWI. BUS. & PROF.: pres., Ogden Gas Co., Chicago, IL; chm. of the board, Sawyer Biscuit Co., 1901; pres., Chicago and Great Lakes Dredge and Dock Co., 1912–20; dir., Union Carbide and Carbon Corp.; dir., Cosmopolitan Electric Co. MEM.: Union League; Iroquois Club; Mid-Day Club. REL.: R.C. MISC.: noted as Boss of Cook Cty. (IL) Democratic Party. RES.: Chicago, IL.

SULZER, WILLIAM. b. Mar 18, 1863, Elizabeth, NJ; d. Nov 16, 1941, New York, NY; par. Thomas and Lydia (Jelleme) Sulzer; m. Clara Rodelheim, Jan 7, 1908; c. none. EDUC.: public schools; Columbia Coll. Law School. POLIT. & GOV.: elected as a Democrat to NY State Assembly, 1889–94 (Speaker, 1893), 1913–14 (Independent-Progressive); delegate, Dem. Nat'l. Conv., 1892, 1896, 1900, 1904, 1908, 1912; elected as a Democrat to U.S. House (NY), 1895–1912; ***candidate for Democratic nomination to vice presidency of the U.S., 1900, 1912***; elected as a Democrat to gov. of NY, 1912–13 (impeached and removed from office, Oct 18, 1913); ***candidate for Democratic nomination to presidency of the U.S., 1912***; candidate for Progressive Party nomination to gov. of NY, 1914; independent (Prohibition; American) candidate for gov. of NY, 1914; *candidate for Prohibition Party nomination to presidency of the U.S., 1916; American Party candidate for presidency of the U.S., 1916 (declined), 1920 (declined).* BUS. & PROF.: atty.; admitted to NY Bar, 1884; law practice, New York, NY, 1884–1941. MEM.: American Federation of Patriotic Societies; Masons; Tammany Hall Soc. REL.: Presb. RES.: New York, NY.

SUMNER, CHARLES. b. Jan 6, 1811, Boston, MA; d. Mar 11, 1874, Washington, DC; par. Charles Pinckney and Relief (Jacob) Sumner; m. Mrs. Alice (Mason) Hooper, Oct 17, 1866 (divorced, 1873). EDUC.: Boston (MA) Latin School, 1821–26; grad., Harvard U., 1830, Harvard Law School, 1833. POLIT. & GOV.: appointed commissioner, U.S. Circuit Court (MA), 1835; delegate, MA Free Soil Party State Convention, 1848; Free Soil Party candidate for U.S. House (MA), 1848, 1850; elected as a Free Soil-Democrat to U.S. Senate (MA) and subsequently reelected as a Republican, 1850–74; ***candidate for Republican nomination to presidency of the U.S., 1856, 1960, 1868, 1872; candidate for Republican nomination to vice presidency of the U.S., 1856; candidate for Liberal Republican Party nomination to presidency of the U.S., 1872; candidate for Democratic nomination to presidency of the U.S., 1872***; Liberal Republican-Democratic candidate for gov. of MA, 1872 (declined). BUS. & PROF.: atty.; admitted to MA Bar, 1834; law practice, Boston, MA, 1834; lecturer, Harvard U. Law School, 1834–37; contributor, *American Jurist*. MEM.: Harvard Temperance Soc. (pres.); Phi Beta Kappa (Harvard vice pres.); MA Hist. Soc.; American Peace Soc. AWARDS: Franklin Medal, Boston Latin School. HON. DEG.: LL.D., Amherst Coll., 1856; LL.D., Yale U., 1856; LL.D., Harvard U., 1859. WRITINGS: *Dunlap's Treatise on the Practice of the Courts of Admiralty . . .* (ed., 1833); *Reports of Cases . . . in the High Court of Chancery* (1844–45, annotations only); *The Works of Charles Sumner* (1870–83). REL.: Unitarian (nee Episc.). RES.: Washington, DC.

SUNDAY, WILLIAM ASHLEY "BILLY." b. Nov 18, 1862, Ames, IA; d. Nov 6, 1935, Chicago,, IL; par. William and Mary Jane (Cory) Sunday; m. Helen A. Thompson, Sep 5, 1888; c. Helen Edith (Mrs. M. P. Haines); George Marquis; William Ashley; Paul Thompson. EDUC.: high school, Nevada, IA; Northwestern U.; D.D., Westminster Coll., 1912. POLIT. & GOV.: ***candidate for Republican nomination to presidency of the U.S., 1920; candidate for Prohibition Party nomination to presidency of the U.S., 1920; independent candidate for presidency of the U.S., 1928***. BUS. & PROF.: hotel employee, Nevada, IA; farmhand for Col. John Scott, NV, IA; janitor; employee, furniture store, Marshalltown, IA; baseball player; outfielder, Chicago White Sox, National League, 1883–91; outfielder, Pittsburgh Pirates, National League, 1888–90; outfielder, Philadelphia Phillies, National League, 1890; evangelist; asst. sec., YMCA, Chicago, IL, 1891–95; preacher, 1896–1935; ordained minister, Presbyterian Church, 1903; temperance advocate. WRITINGS: *Life and Labors of Reverend William A. (Billy) Sunday* (1908); *Billy Sunday, the Man and His Message* (1914); *The Three Groups* (1914); *Burning Truths from Billy's Bat* (1914); *Seventy-Four Complete Sermons of the Omaha Campaign* (1915); *Great Love Stories of the Bible and Their Lessons for Today* (1917). REL.: Presb. (delegate, general assembly, 1918). MISC.: lifetime batting average, .248. RES.: Winona Lake, IN.

SUNDBERG, ANDREW PETER. b. Jan 6, 1941, Hackensack, NJ; par. Edward Bernard and Ruth (Wildebush) Sundberg; m. Chastal Messan; c. Nancy; Stephanie. EDUC.: B.S., U.S. Naval Acad., 1962; M.A., Oxford U., 1966. POLIT. & GOV.: chm., Democrats Abroad in Switzerland, 1977–79, 1980–81; ***candidate for Democratic nomination to vice presidency of the U.S., 1980***; chm., Democrats Abroad (worldwide), 1981–85; ***candidate for Democratic nomination to presidency of the U.S., 1988***. BUS. & PROF.: consultant, Geneva, Switzerland, 1968–. MIL.: midshipman, U.S. Navy, 1958–62, lt., 1962–68. MEM.: American Childrens Citizenship Rights League (dir., 1977–79); American Citizens Abroad (dir., 1978–). AWARDS: Rhodes Scholar, 1963. WRITINGS: publications on international business and economics. REL.: Protestant. MAILING ADDRESS: 157 Route du Grand-Lancy, 1213 ONEX, Geneva, Switzerland.

SURGES, MARY ANN. b. Jan 9, 1936, Chicago, IL; d. Frank Joseph and Marie (Lillig) Silovsky; m. (divorced); c. John Philip; James Lloyd; Catherine Marie; Ann Marie; Edward Joseph; Marie Terese. EDUC.: B.S.N., Loyola U., 1957; M.A. (Theology), Duquesne U., 1973. POLIT. & GOV.: ***independent (Cmte. for a Constitutional Presidency) candidate for vice presidency of the U.S., 1976***. BUS. & PROF.: head nurse, Lewis Memorial Maternity Hospital, Chicago, IL, 1957–59; instructor, Municipal Contagious Disease Hospital, 1959–60; instructor, Religious Studies and Humanities, Loretto Heights Coll., Denver, CO, 1976–. MEM.: A.C.L.U.; Park Hill Improvement Assn., Inc.; U.N. Assn. of the U.S.; American Teilhard Assn. on the Future of Man; CO Education Assn.; United Teaching Professors (advisory board). WRITINGS: *Personal Christogenesis: The Significance of the Individual in the Paradigm of Teilhard de Chardin* (1973). REL.: Catholic Judaeo-Christian. MAILING ADDRESS: 1960 Fairfax St., Denver, CO 80220.

SUSSINA, JOHN J. POLIT. & GOV.: ***candidate for Democratic nomination to presidency of the U.S., 1976***. MAILING ADDRESS: 37 Poplar St., North Haven, CT 06473.

SUTHERLAND, HOWARD. b. Sep 8, 1865, Kirkwood, MO; d. Mar 12, 1950, Washington, DC; par. John Webster and Julia P. (Reavis) Sutherland; m. Effie Harris, May 28, 1889; c. Howard (deceased); Howard; Natalie (Mrs. John Sidney Walker, Jr.); Richard Kerens; Virginia Berkeley (Mrs. George Marshall Lyon); Katherine Reairs (Mrs. Paul Mayo); Margaret Lindsay (Mrs. Wallace B. Dunckel); Lucy Howard; Elizabeth (Mrs. Stanley Raymond Harris); Sarah Howard. EDUC.: A.B., Westminster Coll., 1889. POLIT. & GOV.: appointed Chief of Population, U.S. Bureau of the Census, 1890–93; chm., Randolph Cty. (WV) Republican exec. cmte., 1904–08; elected as a Republican to WV State Senate, 1908–12; elected as a Republican to U.S. House (WV), 1913–17; elected as a Republican to U.S. Senate (WV), 1917–23; ***candidate for Republican nomination to presidency of the U.S., 1920***; Republican candidate for U.S. Senate (WV), 1922; delegate, Rep. Nat'l. Conv., 1924, 1928, 1932, 1936; appointed Alien Property Custodian, 1925–33; chm., WV Good Roads Comm. BUS. & PROF.: ed., *Republican*, Fulton, MO, 1889–90; general land agent, Davis-Elkins Coal and R.R. Co., 1893–1903; pres., Greenbriar Land Co.; pres., Valley Co.; pres., Middle Fork Coal and Land Co.; dir., Davis Trust Co.; dir., Baldwin Supply Co.; vice pres., Hambleton and Co. (Stock Brokers), Washington, DC, 1925; pres., Fidelity Investment Assn.; lumberman. MEM.: Beta Theta Pi; Masons (32°; Knights Templar); WV Board of Trade (vice pres.); Davis and Elkins Presbyterian Coll. (trustee); Burning Tree Club; Metropolitan Club; Chevy Chase Club. HON. DEG.: LL.D., Columbian U. REL.: Presb. RES.: Elkins, WV.

SUZZALO, ANTHONY HENRY. b. Aug 22, 1875, San Jose, CA; d. Sep 25, 1933, Seattle, WA; par. Peter and Anne (Zucalo) Suzzalo; m. Edith Moore, Feb 8, 1912; c. none. EDUC.: San Jose State Normal School; A.B., Stanford U., 1899; M.A., Columbia U., 1902, Ph.D., 1905. POLIT. & GOV.: deputy superintendent of public schools, San Francisco, CA; Reform candidate for mayor of San Francisco, CA, 1906 (declined); member, WA State Board of Education; chm., WA State Council of Defense, 1917–19; chm., National Metal Trades Board; Northwest Representative, U.S. Shipping Board; adviser, War Labor Policy Board; Wage Umpire, National War Labor Board, 1918; member, National Passport and Postal Reform Comm., 1920; member, Rep. Nat'l. Cmte.; ***candidate for Democratic nomination to presidency of the U.S., 1928***; dir., National Advisory Cmte. on Education, 1929. BUS. & PROF.: teacher, Alviso, CA, 1897; school principal, Alameda, CA, 1899; ed., *Riverside Education Monographs*, 1900; asst. prof. of education, Stanford U., 1902–07; adjunct prof. of education, Columbia U., 1907–09, prof. of educational sociology, 1909–15, acting dean of Teachers' Coll.; pres., U. of WA, 1915–26; ed., Houghton-Mifflin Educational Classics; editor-in-chief, *Collier's National Encyclopedia*; prof., Teachers' Coll., Columbia U., 1926–33; visiting prof., Carnegie Endowment for International Peace, 1927; trustee, Carnegie Corp., 1930–33; ed., *Journal of Educational Sociology*. MEM.: Carnegie Foundation for the Advancement of Teaching (trustee, 1919–33; chm. of the board of trustees, 1926–27; pres., 1930–33); NEA; American Council on Education; National Assn. of State Universities (pres., 1921–22); Inst. of International Education; Liberal League (select council; editorial board, Independent Inter-Weekly); American Assn. for Adult Education; Commonwealth Fund (educational research cmte., 1925–27); American Economic Assn.; Rainier Club; University Club; Coll. Club; Rhodes Scholarship Trust (chm., Cmte. of Selection, 1915–26); BSA (educational cmte., National council); American Federation of Arts (dir.); Stevens Inst. of Technology (trustee, 1927); National Research Council (Div. of State Relations, 1919–23); U. of Denver (policy adviser); U. of WY (policy adviser); CO Coll. (policy adviser); U.S. Naval Acad. (visitor, 1924); AAAS (fellow); National Inst. of Social Sciences; American Acad. of Political and Social Sciences; American Sociological Soc.; National Soc. for the Scientific Study of Education; Royal Soc. of Literature; Zeta Psi; Phi Delta Kappa; Phi Beta Kappa; Royal Inst. of Public Health (vice pres., Congress, 1921); National Dante Cmte. (1921); English Speaking Union (adviser, 1920); Hall of Fame (elector, 1920). AWARDS: Order of the Crown of Italy (knight commander). HON. DEG.: LL.D., U. of CA, 1918; LL.D., U. of British Columbia, 1925; LL.D., U. of AL, 1929; Sc.D., U. of Southern CA, 1930; LL.D., U. of CO, 1930. WRITINGS: *Our Faith in Education* (1924). REL.: Episc. (nee R.C.). RES.: Seattle, WA.

SWALLOW, SILAS COMFORT. b. Mar 5, 1839, Wilkes Barre, PA; d. Aug 13, 1930, Harrisburg, PA; par. George and Sarah (Thompson) Swallow; m. Rebecca Louise Robins, Jan 30, 1866; c. Addison Marr Robins (adopted); Bessie Robins (Mrs. Charles Bailey Bingaman; adopted); Harold Swallow Bingaman (adopted). EDUC.: Wyoming Seminary, Kingston, PA; Susquehanna Seminary, 1860; D.D., Taylor U., Fort Wayne, IN, 1889; studied law under Volney B. Maxwell. POLIT. & GOV.: delegate, Prohibition Party National Convention, 1896, 1908; Prohibition Party candidate for PA state treas., 1897; Prohibition Party candidate for U.S. House (PA), 1898; Prohibition (People's; Liberty; Honest Government) Party candidate for gov. of PA, 1898, 1902 (Prohibition); ***candidate for Prohibition Party nomination to presidency of the U.S., 1900 (declined); United Christian (Union Reform) Party candidate for presidency of the U.S., 1900 (declined); Prohibition Party candidate for presidency of the U.S., 1904***; presidential elector, Prohibition Party, 1912. BUS. & PROF.: teacher, WY (PA) Seminary; teacher, Drums, PA; minister, Methodist Church, 1862–86 (presiding elder and bishop, Altoona District, 1880–81); financial solicitor, Dickinson Coll., 1886; pastor, Ridge Avenue Methodist Church, Harrisburg, PA, 1887–92; ed., *Pennsylvania Methodist*, 1892–1905; superintendent, Methodist Book Rooms, Harrisburg, PA, 1892–1905; ed., *The Church Forum*, 1908–10. MIL.: 1st lt., Company E, 18th Regt, PA Militia Emergency Volunteers, 1862. MEM.: Masons (York Rite, 1862); Mt. Gretna Chautauqua (member, board of managers). WRITINGS: *Camp Meetings and the Sabbath* (1879); *III Score and X, or Selections, Collections, and Recollections of Seventy Busy Years* (1909). REL.: Methodist (delegate, gen. conference, 1880, 1896). MISC.: known as "The Fighting Parson"; noted for expose of PA politicians, 1897; tried and acquitted for charges made in expose. RES.: Harrisburg, PA.

SWAN, HENRY. POLIT. & GOV.: ***United American Party candidate for vice presidency of the U.S., 1976***. MAILING ADDRESS: P.O. Box CZ, Bisbee, AZ 85603.

SWANSON, THEODORE SHELBY. b. Jun 22, 1929, Chicago, IL; par. Elmer Theodore and Edna (Shelby) Swanson; m. Roberta Jenelle Hadley, 1961; m. 2d, Josefa Artiles, 1972; c. Theodore, Jr.; Richard Hadley; Rebecca Diane. EDUC.: U. of NC, 1948–49; Berea Coll., 1949–51; B.A., MI State U., 1955, M.A., 1958. POLIT. & GOV.: ***Protest Party candidate for presidency of the U.S., 1984***. BUS. & PROF.: psychologist, Glenwood State School, Glenwood, IA, 1959; psychologist, Lincoln (NE) State Hospital, 1960; psychologist, Chicago (IL) Municipal Courts, 1961–63; psychologist, Adult and Child Guidance Center, MI City, IN, 1963–67; psychologist, Beatty Hospital, 1967–71; psychologist, Worthington, Hurst, Chicago, IL, 1972–73; psychologist, IN State Prison, 1975; psychologist, private practice, 1975–80; psychologist, Gary (IN) Mental Health Center, 1978–. MIL.: corp., U.S. Army, 1952–84. MEM.: People-in-Politics (vice pres., 1968–72); American Federation of Musicians (Local 421, 1961–). WRITINGS: "When Jazz was Zut," *Escapade*, Oct 1956; *The Open and Closed Mind* (contributor, 1960). REL.: agnostic. MAILING ADDRESS: 101 Kenwood Place, MI City, IN 46360.

SWEENEY, WILLIAM EDWARD FRANCIS. POLIT. & GOV.: ***candidate for Democratic nomination to presidency of the U.S., 1976***. MAILING ADDRESS: 49 Johnson Ave., Medford, MA 02156.

SWEET, THADDEUS C. b. Nov 16, 1872, Phoenix, NY; d. May 1, 1928, Whitney Point, NY; par. Anthony Wayne and Sarah Elizabeth (Campbell) Sweet; m. Lena May McCarthy, Dec 5, 1894; c. Richard Wilmot; Vera Mae (Mrs. Harold L. Schultz); Ruth Eleanor; Berton Wayne. EDUC.: grad., Phoenix (NY) Acad. and H.S. POLIT. & GOV.: elected town clerk, Phoenix, NY, 1896–99; delegate, Rep. Nat'l. Conv., 1908, 1912, 1916, 1920, 1924; elected as a Republican to NY State Assembly, 1909–20 (Speaker, 1914–20); member, Republican Cty. Central Cmte.; member, exec. cmte., NY State Republican Central Cmte.; ***candidate for Republican nomination to vice presidency of the U.S., 1920***; elected as a Republican to U.S. House (NY), 1923–28. BUS. & PROF.: clerk; traveling salesman, Syracuse, NY; founder, Sweet Brothers Paper Manufacturing Co., 1893, pres., 1919–28; pres., Hydro-Asphalt Products Co.; chm. of the board, Oswego Cty. Trust Co. MEM.: Masons (Knights Templar; Shriners); Odd Fellows; Elks; Potsdam Citizens Club; Granshue Sporting Club; Masonic Club. REL.: Bapt. MISC.: noted for successful efforts to deny socialists seats in the NY legislature, 1920. RES.: Phoenix, NY.

SWEET, WILLIAM ELLERY. b. Jan 27, 1869, Chicago, IL; d. May 9, 1942, Denver, CO; par. Channing and Emeroy Levonia (Stevens) Sweet; m. Joyeuse Lennig Fullerton, Oct 19, 1892; c. Lennig; Channing Fullerton; Joyeuse Elise (Mrs. Munroe Raymond); William Ellery. EDUC.: A.B., Swarthmore Coll., 1890. POLIT. & GOV.: elected as a Democrat to gov. of CO, 1923–25; delegate, Dem. Nat'l. Conv., 1924; ***candidate for Democratic nomination to presidency of the U.S., 1924; farmer Labor Party candidate for vice presidency of the U.S., 1924***; Democratic candidate for gov. of CO, 1924; Democratic candidate for U.S. Senate (CO), 1926; ***candidate for farmer Labor Party nomination to presidency of the U.S., 1928 (declined); Coalition Party candidate for vice presidency of the U.S., 1928 (declined)***; appointed Education dir., NRA, 1932–33. BUS. & PROF.: owner, William E. Sweet and Co. (investment bankers), Denver, CO, 1894–1920 (subsequently known as Sweet, Causey, Foster and Co.). MEM.: Phi Beta Kappa; YMCA (Denver pres., 1902–35; div. sec. in France, 1917; pres., International Convention, 1920; member, national council); Sons of the Revolution (pres.); Phi Kappa Psi; Denver Club; National Institution of Public Affairs (trustee, 1935); Denver U. (dir.); Denver U. Club. HON. DEG.: LL.D., Swarthmore Coll., 1936. REL.: Congregationalist (moderator, gen. council, 1940–42). RES.: Denver, CO.

SWIDER, PETER PAUL SEBASTIAN. b. 1948. POLIT. & GOV.: ***candidate for Democratic nomination to presidency of the U.S., 1984, 1992***. BUS. & PROF.: office mgr., Hamtramck, MI. MAILING ADDRESS: 2319 Norwalk, Hamtramck, MI 48212.

SWINNEY, RICKEY LYNN. b. Mar 15, 1953, Fort Worth, TX; par. Bobby Joe and Nancy Lue (McDonald) Swinney; m. Stella May Gilbert; c. Rickey Lynn, Jr. EDUC.: Parker H.S., Fort Worth, TX. POLIT. & GOV.: ***independent candidate for presidency of the U.S., 1988***. BUS. & PROF.: salesman, Riverside Tire Co., Fort Worth, TX; evangelist. REL.: Pentecostalist. MAILING ADDRESS: 6612 South Freeway, Apt. 38, Fort Worth, TX 76140.

SWINTON, JOHN. b. Dec 12, 1829, Salton, Edinburgh, Scotland; d. Dec 15, 1901, Brooklyn, NY; par. William and Jane (Currie) Swinton; m. Orsena Fowles Smith, 1877; c. none. EDUC.: Easthampton (MA) Seminary; NY Medical Coll., 1859. POLIT. & GOV.: Industrial Party candidate for mayor of New York, NY, 1874; Union Labor Party candidate for NY State Senate, 1887; ***candidate for Union Labor Party nomination to vice presidency of the U.S., 1888***. BUS. & PROF.: apprentice printer, witness, Montreal, Canada, 1843; moved to New York, NY; mgr., *Lawrence (KS) Republican*, 1856; chief, editorial staff, *New York (NY) Times*, 1860–70; chief of staff, editorial writer, *New York (NY) Sun*, 1875–83, 1888–97; publisher, ed., *John Swinton's Paper*, 1883–87; labor reformer; abolitionist. WRITINGS: *New Issue: The Chinese-American Question* (1870); *Eulogy of Henry J. Raymond* (1870); *John Swinton's Travels* (1880); *Storm and Stress* (1881); *Oration on John Brown* (1881); *Striking for Life* (1894); *On the Way to Nazareth*; *Model Factory in a Model City*. REL.: Presb. RES.: Brooklyn, NY.

SYMINGTON, WILLIAM STUART. b. Jun 26, 1901, Amherst, MA; d. Dec 14, 1988, New Canaan, CT. William Stuart and Emily Haxall (Harrison) S.; m. Evelyn Wadsworth, Mar 1, 1924; m. 2d, Ann Hemingway Watson, 1978; c. William Stuart; James Wadsworth. EDUC.: A.B., Yale U., 1923; international correspondence schools; D.S.B.A., Bryant Coll., 1948. POLIT. & GOV.: chm., Surplus Property Board, 1945; appointed asst. sec. of war for air, 1946–47; appointed U.S. sec. of the air force, 1947–50; appointed chm., National Security Resources Board, 1950–51; appointed administrator, RFC, 1951–52; elected as a Democrat to U.S. Senate (MO), 1953–77; delegate, Dem. Nat'l. Conv., 1956, 1972; ***candidate for Democratic nomination to presidency of the U.S., 1956, 1960; candidate for Democratic nomination to vice presidency of the U.S., 1956, 1960; independent candidate for presidency of the U.S., 1960***; appointed member, U.S. Territorial Expansion Memorial Comm. BUS. & PROF.: assoc. ed., *Yale Daily News*; office boy; machinist apprentice; reporter, Baltimore, MD; iron moulder, lathe operator, Symington Co., Rochester, NY, 1923–26, exec. vice pres., 1927–37; pres., Eastern Clay Products, 1925–27; pres., Gould Car Light Co.; pres., Valley Appliances, 1927–30; officer, Gould Storage Battery Co.; pres., Colonial Radio Co., 1930–35; pres., Rustless Iron and Steel Co., 1935–38; pres., Emerson Electrical Manufacturing Co., 1938–45; dir., Mercantile Trust Co., St. Louis, MO; vice chm., First American Bankshares, 1980–88. MIL.: pvt., 2d lt., U.S. Army, 1917–19; Medal for Merit, 1947; Distinguished Service Medal, 1952. MEM.: American Legion; Masons (32°; Shriner); Yale Club of NY; Delta Kappa Epsilon; National Cathedral Assn. (pres., 1974–77). General H. H. Arnold Award, Air Force Association, 1948, 1956; Aviation Man of the Year Award, VFW, 1957; Wright Brothers Memorial Trophy, National Aeronautic Assn., 1957. HON. DEG.: LL.D., Baylor U., 1950; LL.D., William Jewell Coll., 1953; LL.D., Park Coll., 1957; D.Lett., Coll. of Osteopathy and Surgery, 1958; LL.D., U. of MA, 1959; LL.D., Rockhurst Coll., 1959; LL.D., Avila Coll., 1963; D.H.L., MO Valley Coll., 1963; LL.D., U. of MO at Columbia, 1965; LL.D., WA U., 1966; LL.D., William Woods Coll., 1969; LL.D., Drury Coll., 1972. REL.: Episc. RES.: Creve Coeur, MO.

SYMMS, STEVEN DOUGLAS. b. Apr 23, 1938, Nampa, ID; par. George Darwin and Mary Irene (Knowlton) Symms; m. Frances E. Stockdale, 1959; c. Dan; Susan; Amy; Katy. EDUC.: B.S., U. of ID, 1960. POLIT. & GOV.: elected as a Republican to U.S. House (ID), 1973–81; ***candidate for American Independent Party nomination to presidency of the U.S., 1976 (declined); candidate for Republican nomination to vice presidency of the U.S., 1976***; elected as a Republican to U.S. Senate (ID), 1981–93. BUS. & PROF.: personnel mgr., Symms Fruit Ranch, Inc., Caldwell, ID, 1963–72, production mgr., 1963–72, vice pres., 1966–72, dir., 1967–; franchisee, Elaine Powers Figure Salons, Nampa, ID, 1969–72. MIL.: 1st lt., U.S.M.C. Reserves, 1959–63. MEM.: Sigma Nu; Rotary Club; C. of C.; ID Horticultural Soc.; ID Fresh Fruit and Vegetable Organization; Canyon Cty. Republican Boosters' Club (pres., 1966–67); U. of ID Alumni Assn. (pres., 1967–68); National Cmte. to Stop Aid to North Viet Nam (chm., 1973). REL.: Protestant. MAILING ADDRESS: R.R. 6, Caldwell, ID.

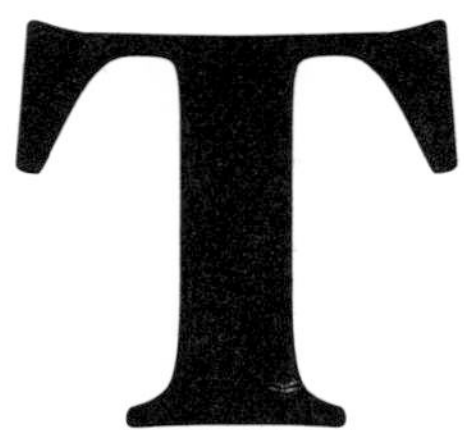

TAFT, GUY W. ROCKEFELLER (aka GUY W. ROCKEFELLER).

b. Sep 1, 1914; m. H.R.H. Princess Running Waters C. T. Red Legs Saint Swanee (aka Fay Turner Carpenter-Swain, q.v.); c. daughter. EDUC.: U. of IL; U. of Louisville; Oxford U.; U. of CA. POLIT. & GOV.: ***candidate for Democratic nomination to vice presidency of the U.S., 1976; candidate for Democratic nomination to presidency of the U.S., 1976, 1980***. BUS. & PROF.: retired R.R., VA, CCC. MEM.: Parent-Teachers' Assn.; A.A.A. WRITINGS: *From Here to Eternity*; *Carpenter Magic Book*; *First Magic Set with Book*. REL.: Bapt. MAILING ADDRESS: 1421-23 Republic St., Cincinnati, OH 45210.

TAFT, ROBERT ALPHONSO.

b. Sep 8, 1889, Cincinnati, OH; d. Jul 31, 1953, New York, NY; par. William Howard (q.v.) and Helen (Herron) Taft; m. Martha Wheaton Bowers, Oct 17, 1914; c. William Howard III; Robert Alphonso, Jr.; Lloyd Bowers; Horace Dwight. EDUC.: Taft School; B.A., Yale U., 1910, M.A., 1936; LL.B., Harvard U., 1913. POLIT. & GOV.: appointed asst. counsel, U.S. Food Administration, 1917–19; counsel, American Relief Administration, 1919; chm., Columbia Township (OH) Republican Cmte.; chm., Hamilton Cty. (OH) Republican Exec. Cmte.; elected as a Republican to OH State House, 1921–26 (Speaker, 1926); elected as a Republican to OH State Senate, 1931–32; delegate, Rep. Nat'l. Conv., 1932, 1940, 1944; ***candidate for Republican nomination to presidency of the U.S., 1936, 1940, 1948, 1952; candidate for Republican nomination to vice presidency of the U.S., 1936***; elected as a Republican to U.S. Senate (OH), 1939–53 (majority leader, 1953); ***candidate for Democratic nomination to presidency of the U.S., 1952***. BUS. & PROF.: atty.; admitted to OH Bar, 1913; assoc., Maxwell and Ramsey (law firm), Cincinnati, OH, 1913–17; partner, Taft and Taft (law firm), Cincinnati, OH, 1922–23; partner, Taft, Stettinius and Hollister (law firm), Cincinnati, OH, 1923–39, counsel, 1939–53; dir., Central Trust Co.; dir., Covington and Cincinnati Bridge Co.; dir., Gruen Watch Co.; dir., Cincinnati Times-Star Co. MEM.: Queen City Club; Cincinnati Club; Camargo Club; Yale Corporation (Fellow); Psi Upsilon; Cincinnati Union Bethel (trustee); Cincinnati Inst. of Fine Arts (trustee); Cincinnati Conservatory of Music (trustee); Thomas J. Emery Memorial (trustee); Cincinnati Symphony Orchestra (trustee); ABA; OH State Bar Assn.; Cincinnati Bar Assn.; Burning Tree Club. WRITINGS: *A Foreign Policy for Americans* (1951). HON. DEG.: LL.D., Miami U., 1939; LL.D., Wittenberg Coll., 1939; LL.D., Grove City Coll., 1943; LL.D., Bethany Coll., 1944; LL.D., U. of Cincinnati, 1949; LL.D., Kenyon Coll., 1949; D.C.L., Marietta Coll., 1949; LL.D., OH Wesleyan U., 1949; D.I.L., PA Military Coll., 1951; D.C.L., Ripon Coll., 1951; LL.D., Western Reserve U., 1951; LL.D., William Jewell Coll., 1951. REL.: Episc. MISC.: known as "Mr. Republican." RES.: Cincinnati, OH.

TAFT, WILLIAM HOWARD.

b. Sep 15, 1857, Cincinnati, OH; d. Mar 8, 1930, Washington, DC; par. Alphonso and Louisa Maria (Torrey) Taft; m. Helen Herron, Jun 19, 1886; c. Helen Herron (Mrs. Frederick Johnson Manning); Robert Alphonso (q.v.); Charles Phelps. EDUC.: grad., Woodward H.S., Cincinnati, OH, 1874; B.A., Yale U., 1878; LL.B., Cincinnati Law School, 1880. POLIT. & GOV.: appointed asst. prosecuting atty., Hamilton Cty., OH, 1881–83; appointed asst. cty. solicitor, Hamilton Cty., OH, 1885–87; judge, Superior Court of Cincinnati, OH, 1887–90; appointed solicitor gen. of the U.S., 1890–92; appointed judge, U.S. Circuit Court, Sixth Judicial Circuit, 1892–1900; appointed pres., U.S. Philippine Comm., 1900–1901; appointed gov. of the Philippine Islands, 1901–04; appointed assoc. justice, Supreme Court of the U.S., 1903 (declined twice); appointed U.S. sec. of war, 1904–08; appointed provisional gov. of Cuba, 1907; ***elected as a Republican, presidency of the U.S., 1909–13; Republican candidate for presidency of the U.S., 1912; candidate for Republican nomination to presidency of the U.S., 1916, 1920***; appointed member, National War Labor Conference, 1918–19 (co-chm.); ***candidate for Democratic nomina-***

tion to presidency of the U.S., 1920; appointed chief justice, Supreme Court of the U.S., 1921–30. BUS. & PROF.: atty.; admitted to OH Bar, 1880; law reporter, *Cincinnati (OH) Times* (later *Commercial*), 1880; law practice, Cincinnati, OH, 1883–87; prof., dean of law, U. of Cincinnati, 1896–1900; Kent prof. of Law, Yale U., 1913–21; author. MEM.: American National Red Cross (pres., 1906–13); ABA (pres., 1913); American Acad. of Jurisprudence (pres., 1914); League to Enforce Peace (pres.); Hon. Bencher, Middle Temple, 1922; Smithsonian Institution (chancellor, 1923). HON. DEG.: LL.D., Yale U., 1893; LL.D., U. of PA, 1902; LL.D., Harvard U., 1905; LL.D., Miami U., Oxford, OH, 1905; LL.D., State U. of IA, 1907; LL.D., Wesleyan U., 1909; LL.D., Princeton U., 1912; D.C.L., Hamilton Coll., 1913; LL.D., McGill U., 1913; LL.D., Aberdeen U., 1922; LL.D., Cambridge U., 1922; D.C.L., Oxford U., 1922; LL.D., U. of Cincinnati, 1925. WRITINGS: *Four Aspects of Civic Duty* (1906); *The Anti-Trust Act and the Supreme Court* (1914); *The United States and Peace* (1914); *Our Chief Magistrate and His Powers* (1916); *Taft Papers on the League of Nations* (1920). REL.: Unitarian. RES.: Cincinnati, OH.

TAKEI, MILTON SHIRO. b. Oct 31, 1948, Honolulu, HI; par. Shiro and Florence (Yamachi) Takei; single. EDUC.: B.A., U. of CA at Santa Barbara, 1970. POLIT. & GOV.: member, Los Angeles Cty. (CA) Peace and Freedom Party; Peace and Freedom Party candidate for CA State Assembly, 1972; member, CA State Peace and Freedom Party Central Cmte., 1972–78 (chm., 1976–78); Peace and Freedom Party candidate for U.S. House (CA), 1978; ***candidate for Peace and Freedom Party nomination to presidency of the U.S., 1980***. BUS. & PROF.: factory worker; political organizer; dishwasher; mgr., Westside Environmental Center, Los Angeles, CA, 1973–74. MEM.: Milpas Natural Food Cooperative; Santa Barbara People Against Nuclear Power; New American Movement; Community Environmental Council; Santa Barbara Coalition for Human Rights; Santa Barbara Rent Control Alliance. MAILING ADDRESS: 533 State St., #302, Santa Barbara, CA 93101.

TALBOW, FLORENCE JOY. POLIT. & GOV.: ***independent candidate for presidency of the U.S., 1976***. MAILING ADDRESS: P.O. Box 4201, Phoenix, AZ 85030.

TALBOW, LEONARD DENNIS. POLIT. & GOV.: ***candidate for Democratic nomination to presidency of the U.S., 1984, 1992***. MAILING ADDRESS: 411 West Bijou St., Colorado Springs, CO 80905.

TALMADGE, EUGENE. b. Sep 23, 1884, Forsyth, GA; d. Dec 21, 1946, Atlanta, GA; par. Thomas Romalgus and Carrie (Roberts) Talmadge; m. Mattie (Thurmond) Peterson, Sep 12, 1909; c. Herman Eugene; Margaret (Mrs. William H. Kimbrough; Mrs. Scott Shepherd); Vera (Mrs. Charles St. Lair Smyley); John A. Peterson (stepson). EDUC.: LL.B., U. of GA, 1907. POLIT. & GOV.: solicitor, McRae (GA) City Court, 1918–20; Telfair Cty. (GA) atty., 1920–23; elected as a Democrat, GA State Commissioner of Agriculture, 1927–33; elected as a Democrat to gov. of GA, 1933–37, 1941–43, 1946; ***candidate for Democratic nomination to presidency of the U.S., 1936; Constitutional Jeffersonian Democratic Party candidate for presidency of the U.S., 1936***; candidate for Democratic nomination to U.S. Senate (GA), 1936, 1938; candidate for Democratic nomination to gov. of GA, 1942. BUS. & PROF.: farmer, Monroe Cty., GA; farmer, Sugar Creek, GA; atty.; admitted to GA Bar, 1908; law practice, McRae, GA, 1908; assoc., Dorsey, Brewster and Howell (law firm), Atlanta, GA; ed., *The Statesman*, 1932–46; partner, Talmadge, Fraser and Camp (law firm), 1937–46. MEM.: Masons; Sigma Nu; Phi Kappa Phi; Odd Fellows; Woodmen of the World. REL.: Bapt. MISC.: known as "The Wild Man from Sugar Creek"; noted as opponent of integration and equal rights for Negroes. RES.: McRae, GA.

TANNER, JOHN THOMAS. b. Aug 25, 1820, Madison Cty., AL; d. Jun 15, 1899, Athens, AL; par. Samuel and Margaret Tanner; m. Susan Owen Wilson, Nov 26, 1846; c. Margaret Elizabeth (Mrs. R. McWilliams); Jason; John Blackwood. POLIT. & GOV.: elected mayor of Athens, AL; temporary chm., AL State Temperance Convention, 1882; member, Prohibition Party National Cmte., 1882–84; chm., AL Prohibition Party State Convention, 1886; Prohibition Party candidate for gov. of AL, 1886; state chm., AL Prohibition Party, 1887; ***candidate for Prohibition Party nomination to vice presidency of the U.S., 1888***. BUS. & PROF.: owner, Land Development Co., AL; pres., Athens (AL) Female Inst.; contributor, *Athens (AL) Post*, 1876; sec., treas., Alabama and Tennessee Central R.R. MEM.: AL State Temperance Assn. (sec., 1884); Athens Coll. (trustee); AL Temperance Alliance (pres., 1884). REL.: Methodist. RES.: Athens, AL.

TARVIN, JAMES PRYOR. b. 1860; d. Aug 20, 1907, Cleveland, OH; m. Miss Strothes; c. none. POLIT. & GOV.: elected as a Democrat, judge, Covington (KY) Circuit Court, 6 years; Democratic candidate for judge, Covington (KY) Circuit Court; ***candidate for Democratic nomination to vice presidency of the U.S., 1900***. BUS. & PROF.: atty., Covington, KY; partner, Tarvin and Huggins (law firm), Louisville, KY. MISC.: noted as supporter of William Jennings Bryan (q.v.). RES.: Covington, KY.

TATE, JAMES ALEXANDER. b. Feb 26, 1860, Maness, VA; d. Jan 25, 1951, Shelbyville, TN; par. John M. and Martha Rose (Maness) Tate; m. Laetitia La Rue Cornforth, May 17, 1887; c. Rose Eleanor (Mrs. A. B. Stewart); James Alexander, Jr. EDUC.: public schools, Sneedville, TN, 1870–74; A.B., Milligan Coll., 1882, A.M., 1885. POLIT. & GOV.: chm., TN Prohibition Party State Convention, 2 times; delegate, Prohibition Party National Convention, 1888, 1892; presidential elector, Prohibition Party, 1888; chm., TN State Prohibition Party Central Cmte., 1890–1907; member, Prohibition Party National Cmte., 1888–1908 (sec., 1894–1905; national organizer, 1902–03; vice chm., exec. cmte.); ***candidate for Prohibition Party nomination to vice presidency of the U.S., 1900 (withdrew)***; appointed asst. to the dir. of education for TN, National Youth Administration, 1935–37. BUS. & PROF.: clerk, mercantile store, Scott Cty., VA, 1874–77; teacher; instructor, Milligan Coll., 1882–84; atty.; law practice, Nashville, TN, 1893; ed., *The Pilot*, 1894; pres., West TN Coll., Dyer, TN, 1898–1900; lecturer; temperance advocate, 1884–1951; chancellor, American U., Harriman, TN, 1903–08; headmaster, Tate School, Shelbyville, TN, 1908–33. MEM.: Flying Squadron Foundation (dir.; sec.); TN Anti-Saloon League (superintendent, 1928–30); Prohibition Democratic Cmte. of TN; United Prohibition Forces of TN (dir., 1933–36); United Dry Forces of TN, Inc. (pres., 1937–51). REL.: Christian Church. RES.: Harriman, TN.

TATE, JAMES HUGH JOSEPH. b. Apr 10, 1910, Philadelphia, PA; d. May 27, 1983, Somers Point, NJ; par. James E. Tate; m. Anne M. Daly, 1942; c. Frank X.; Anne Marie. EDUC.: Strayer's Business Coll.; Tucker Inst.; Labor School; LL.B., Temple U., 1938. POLIT. & GOV.: elected as a Democrat to PA State House, 1940–46; elected as a Democrat to Philadelphia (PA) City Council, 1951–62 (pres., 1955–62); vice chm., Philadelphia (PA) Democratic City Cmte., 1952; appointed member, Delaware River Port Authority, 1956–63 (chm., 1962–63); delegate, Dem. Nat'l. Conv., 1960, 1964, 1968, 1972; elected as a Democrat, mayor of Philadelphia, PA, 1962–72; ***candidate for Democratic nomination to vice presidency of the U.S., 1968***; member, PA State Democratic Central Cmte., 1972–75; appointed member, Southeastern PA Transportation authority, 1972–75; appointed member, PA State Tax Equalization Board, 1975–. BUS. & PROF.: atty.; dir., WHYY-TV, Philadelphia, PA. MEM.: Philadelphia Citizens' Crime Comm.; Knights of Columbus (Grand Knight); Downtown Club; Temple University Club; Midday Club; National League of Cities (pres., 1967–68); U.S. Conference of Mayors (pres., 1970–71); National Urban Coalition (exec. cmte., 1967–74); International Eucharistic Congress (gov., 1975–76); Immaculata Coll. (trustee); Villanova Economic Development Council (trustee); Old Philadelphia Development Corp. (dir.); Einstein Medical Center (trustee, 1968–); St. Joseph's Hospital (adviser); Temple U. Alumni (dir.); Serra International (Philadelphia pres., 1974–75); Temple U. Law Alumni Assn.; World Affairs Council of Philadelphia; American Acad. of Political and Social Sciences; Federal Bar Assn. HON. DEG.: LL.D., Drexel Inst.; LL.D., La Salle Coll.; LL.D., St. Joseph's Coll.; LL.D., Villanova U. REL.: R.C. RES.: Philadelphia, PA.

TAVOLACCI, ANN. POLIT. & GOV.: alternate delegate, Dem. Nat'l. Conv., 1972; ***candidate for Democratic nomination to vice presidency of the U.S., 1972***. MAILING ADDRESS: 31705 Haldane, Livonia, MI 48152.

TAYLOR, BARBARA R. POLIT. & GOV.: ***New Alliance Party candidate for vice presidency of the U.S., 1988***. MAILING ADDRESS: NJ?

TAYLOR, CARL W. POLIT. & GOV.: ***independent candidate for presidency of the U.S., 1992***. MAILING ADDRESS: WA?

TAYLOR, DONALD H. POLIT. & GOV.: ***independent (Cmte. for a Constitutional Presidency) candidate for vice presidency of the U.S., 1976***. BUS. & PROF.: soldier. MIL.: col., U.S. Air Force, to 1975. MAILING ADDRESS: Route 1, Box 711 P, Accokeek, MD 20607.

TAYLOR, FRANK, JR. b. Sep 28, 1937, Westwood, CA; par. Frank and Grace Ann (Rueck) Taylor; m. Charlotte Elizabeth Swan, Jun 30, 1961; c. Elizabeth Ann; Suzanne Natasha; Victoria Alexandria; Sabra Vanessa; Frank III; John Moroni; Daniel II; America Ann Grovenberg. EDUC.: Stockton Junior Coll.; Monica City Coll.; Los Angeles Trade and Technical Junior Coll. POLIT. & GOV.: founder, United American Party, 1975; ***United American Party candidate for presidency of the U.S., 1976***. BUS. & PROF.: journalist; photographer; employee, Spreckles Sugar Co., Stockton, CA, 1957; employee, Singer Sewing Machine Co., Stockton, CA; salesman, Triangle Sewing Machine Co., San Francisco, CA; employee, Harold W. Thompson Co., Stockton, CA, 1959; employee, Commercial Credit Corp., Stockton, CA, 1961; employee, Camera/Photography Studio, Stockton, CA; employee, May Co., Los Angeles, CA; employee, *Los Angeles (CA) Herald-Examiner*; employee, Life-Time Baby Studio; employee, 20th Century-Fox Studios; reporter, sports ed., *North American Mail*, Granada Hills, CA; asst. dir. of public relations, Palm Springs, Aerial Tramway; dir., special projects, Universal City Studios; ed., *San Fernando Valley*; ed., *Que Magazine*; ed., *Hollywood Studio Magazine*; ed., *Car Classics*; ed., *Western Treasures*; employee, Milton Jones Agency; writer, *Four Wheeler*; writer, *Sports Buggies*; writer, *Off-Road Racing News*; employee, Western Trails Publishing Co.; freelance writer; film maker; unit publicist, "Ryan's Daughter" (film), Metro-Goldwyn-Mayer Studio; partner, ed., *Western Treasures*, Bisbee, AZ, 1971; owner, editor-in-chief, *Car Classics*, 1973–75; promoter, Texas Treasure Show; promoter, Palm Springs Gold Mining and Treasure Show; promoter, Pacific Treasure Show, 1975–; pres., Sunshine Publishing House, Bisbee, AZ; editor-in-chief, *Thunderbird Illustrated*, Orange, CA. MEM.: San Quentin Prison Film Workshop (hon.); Soc. of Automobile Historians; Pierce Arrow Soc.; American Horseless Carriage Club; American Hollywood Publicist Guild. WRITINGS: *Western Treasures Ghost Town Guide* (1973); *Hitler and the Automobile*; *Trucks That*

Built America. REL.: Church of Jesus Christ of Latter-Day Saints (dir., mission publications, South Africa, 1959–61). MAILING ADDRESS: P.O. Box 824, Bisbee, AZ 85603.

TAYLOR, GEORGE EDWIN. b. Aug 4, 1857, Little Rock, AR; d. Jan 16, 1925, Jacksonville, FL; orphan; m. Marie. POLIT. & GOV.: elected justice of the peace, Hilton, IA; delegate, Union Labor Party National Convention, 1888; joined Republican Party, 1889–92; delegate, Dem. Nat'l. Conv., 1896; ***National Liberty Party candidate for presidency of the U.S., 1904***; member, exec. cmte., National Liberty Party, 1904. BUS. & PROF.: journalist; ed., *Knights of Labor Paper*, 1880s; ed., *The Negro Solicitor*, Oskaloosa, IA, 1893–1900; lecturer. MEM.: Civil and Personal Liberty League; Negro National Democratic League (pres., 1904; chm., advisory board, 1904); Knights of Labor. WRITINGS: "The National Liberty Party's Appeal," *Independent*, Oct 13, 1904; *The American Negro*. RES.: Oskaloosa, IA.

TAYLOR, GEORGE SAM. b. Feb 4, 1915, Mahanoy City, PA; m. Frances M. Taylor; c. two sons; two daughters. EDUC.: Mahanoy City H.S.; Wagner Inst. of Science, Philadelphia, PA; William Penn Evening H.S.; Northeast Evening H.S., Philadelphia, PA; Temple U., 1 year. POLIT. & GOV.: organizer, Socialist Labor Party, 30 years; member, national exec. cmte., Socialist Labor Party; Socialist Labor Party candidate for mayor of Philadelphia, PA; Socialist Labor Party candidate for PA state auditor gen., 1940; Socialist Labor Party candidate for gov. of PA, 1946, 1950, 1962, 1966, 1970; Socialist Labor Party candidate for U.S. Senate (PA), 1956, 1958, 1964; delegate, Socialist Labor Party National Convention, 1960, 1964, 1968; ***Socialist Labor Party candidate for vice presidency of the U.S., 1968***; Socialist Labor Party candidate for various offices, 17 times. BUS. & PROF.: electronics technician. MAILING ADDRESS: 7467 Rhoads St., Philadelphia, PA 19151.

TAYLOR, GLEN HEARST. b. Apr 12, 1904, Portland, OR; d. Apr 28, 1984, Burlingame, CA; par. Rev. Pleasant John and Olive Oatman (Higgins) Taylor; m. 1922 (divorced, 1929); m. 2d, Dora Marie Pike, Mar 31, 1931; c. Glen Arod; Paul Jon; Gregory Alan; Olive. EDUC.: 8th grade, public schools, Kooskia, ID. POLIT. & GOV.: Democratic candidate for U.S. House (ID), 1938; Democratic candidate for U.S. Senate (ID), 1940, 1942, 1954; elected as a Democrat to U.S. Senate (ID), 1945–51; ***candidate for Democratic nomination to vice presidency of the U.S., 1948; Progressive Party candidate for vice presidency of the U.S., 1948***; candidate for Democratic nomination to U.S. Senate (ID), 1950, 1956. BUS. & PROF.: sheepherder, Bitterroot Mountains, ID; mgr., Silent Motion Picture Theaters; sheet metal worker's apprentice; actor, 1919–28; partner, Taylor Players, 1919–22; partner, Glendora Players (theatrical company), 1928–38; country and western singer; sheet metal mechanic, ordnance plant, San Francisco, CA, 1942–44; pres., Coryell Construction Co., 1950–52; founder, pres., Taylor Topper, Inc. (wigs and hairpieces), Millbrae, CA, 1957–84. WRITINGS: *The Way It Was With Me* (1979). REL.: Christian Church. RES.: Pocatello, ID.

TAYLOR, HOWARD SINGLETON "HARRY." b. Jan 19, 1846, Staunton, VA. EDUC.: studied law. POLIT. & GOV.: joined Prohibition Party, 1884; chm., Cook Cty. (IL) Prohibition Party Central Cmte., 1892–1905; delegate, IL State People's Party Convention, 1892 (chm.); People's Party candidate for U.S. House (IL), 1894; appointed city prosecutor, Chicago, IL, 1897; ***candidate for People's Party nomination to vice presidency of the U.S., 1900***; member, Independent Party National Cmte. BUS. & PROF.: poet; composer; schoolteacher; lecturer; temperance advocate; minister, Baptist Church, to 1890; atty.; admitted to IL Bar, 1884; law practice, Chicago, IL; real estate salesman, Chicago, IL. MIL.: private, U.S. Army, 1863–65. WRITINGS: *Creed of the Flag*; *The Battle of 1900* (coauthor); *Temperance Battle Hymns*; "The Man With the Musket" (poem); "The Liberty Bell" (poem). Songs: "The Brewers' Big Horses"; "The Sunday School Man"; "The Walls of Jericho"; "Get Aboard the Ark"; "Lillibulero"; "Clear the Track"; "Molly and the Baby"; "Roll Along, Children"; "Get There"; "The Battle Cry." REL.: Bapt. RES.: Chicago, IL.

TAYLOR, HOYT PATRICK, JR. b. Apr 1, 1924, Wadesboro, NC; par. H. P. and Inez (Wooten) Taylor; m. Elizabeth Lockhart, Mar 17, 1951; c. Elizabeth Ann; Hoyt Patrick III; Adam Lockhart. EDUC.: B.S., U. of NC, 1945, LL.B., 1948. POLIT. & GOV.: member, Young Democrats; delegate, Dem. Nat'l. Conv., 1952; elected as a Democrat to NC State House, 1955–66 (Speaker, 1965–66); elected as a Democrat to lt. gov. of NC, 1969–73; candidate for Democratic nomination to gov. of NC, 1972; ***candidate for Democratic nomination to vice presidency of the U.S., 1972***. BUS. & PROF.: atty.; admitted to NC Bar, 1948. MIL.: 1st lt., U.S.M.C., 1945–46, 1951–52. MEM.: Phi Gamma Delta; Delta Sigma Pi; Phi Delta Phi. REL.: Methodist. MAILING ADDRESS: Wadesboro, NC 28170.

TAYLOR, JAMES WILLIS. b. Aug 28, 1880, Lead Mine Bend, TN; d. Nov 14, 1939, La Follette, TN; par. James Willis and Sarah Elizabeth (Rogers) Taylor; m. Mossie Kincaid, Oct 4, 1905; c. Elizabeth Kincaid; Katharine Lafayette. EDUC.: Holbrook Normal Coll.; American Temperance U.; Cumberland U.; LL.B., Lebanon Law School, 1902. POLIT. & GOV.: appointed postmaster, La Follette, TN, 1904–09; elected as a Republican, mayor of La Follette, TN, 1910–13, 1918–19; appointed as a Republican, insurance commissioner of TN, 1913–14; delegate, Rep. Nat'l. Conv., 1916, 1920, 1924, 1928, 1932, 1936; chm., TN Republican State Exec. Cmte., 1917–18; elected as a Republican to U.S. House (TN), 1919–39; member, Rep. Nat'l. Cmte., 1922–39; ***candidate for Republican nomination to vice presidency of the U.S., 1924***. BUS. & PROF.: teacher, Norton

Knobs School; atty.; admitted to TN Bar, 1902; law practice, La Follette, TN, 1902–39. MEM.: Masons; Odd Fellows; Knights of Pythias. REL.: Methodist. MISC.: known as "J. Will Taylor." RES.: La Follette, TN.

TAYLOR, JOHN H. POLIT. & GOV.: ***candidate for Democratic nomination to vice presidency of the U.S., 1928***. WRITINGS: *The Great Campaign Song: Shout Down Free Silver Revolution* (1896). RES.: Newark, NJ.

TAYLOR, JOHN ROWNALD. POLIT. & GOV.: ***candidate for Republican nomination to presidency of the U.S., 1988; candidate for Republican nomination to presidency of the U.S., 1992***. MAILING ADDRESS: 1809 Percival, Rockport, TX 78382.

TAYLOR, ROGER H. POLIT. & GOV.: ***independent candidate for presidency of the U.S., 1976***. MAILING ADDRESS: 2811 William St., Champaign, IL 61820.

TAYLOR, ROY ARTHUR. b. Jan 31, 1910, Vader, WA; par. Arthur A. and Lola (Morgan) Taylor; m. Evelyn Reeves, May 8, 1932; c. Alan F.; Toni T. Robinson. EDUC.: grad., Asheville-Biltmore Coll., 1929; A.B., Maryville Coll., 1931; LL.B., Asheville U., 1936. POLIT. & GOV.: elected as a Democrat to NC State House, 1947–49, 1951–53; Democratic candidate for NC State House, 1949; cty. atty., Buncombe Cty., NC, 1949–60; elected as a Democrat to U.S. House (NC), 1961–77; ***candidate for Democratic nomination to vice presidency of the U.S., 1972***. BUS. & PROF.: atty.; admitted to NC Bar, 1936; law practice, Asheville, NC, 1936; partner, Finch and Taylor (law firm), Asheville, NC, 1946–. MIL.: lt. (senior grade), U.S. Navy, 1943–46. MEM.: Asheville-Biltmore Coll. (trustee, 1949–); Lions (district gov., 1951–52); J.O.U.A.M. REL.: Bapt. (deacon). MAILING ADDRESS: 110 Connally St., Black Mountain, NC 28711.

TAYLOR, ZACHARY. b. Nov 24, 1784, Montebello, VA; d. Jul 9, 1850, Washington, DC; par. Richard and Sarah Dabney (Strother) Taylor; m. Margaret Mackall Smith, Jun 18, 1810; c. Ann Margaret Mackall (Mrs. Robert Crooke Wood); Sarah Knox (Mrs. Jefferson Davis, q.v.); Mary Elizabeth (Mrs. William Wallace Smith Bliss; Mrs. Philip Pendleton Dandridge); Richard; Octavia Pannel; Margaret Smith. POLIT. & GOV.: ***elected as a Whig to presidency of the U.S., 1849–1850***. BUS. & PROF.: soldier; plantation owner, Feliciana Parish, LA. MIL.: commissioned 1st lt., 7th Infantry, U.S. Army, 1808, capt., 1810, brev. maj., 1812; commander, Fort Knox, KY, 1814–15; commissioned lt. col., 4th Infantry, 1819; Indian Superintendent, Fort Snelling, 1829–32; col., 1st Regt., 1832; brev. brig. gen., 1837; led troops in Black Hawk War, 1838; commander, U.S. Army in TX, 1845; brev. maj. gen., 1846; captured Monterey, Mexico, 1846; defeated Mexican forces at Battle of Buena Vista, 1847. REL.: Episc. MISC.: known as "Old Rough and Ready." RES.: Jefferson Cty., LA.

TAZEWELL, LITTLETON WALLER. b. Dec 17, 1774, Williamsburg, VA; d. May 6, 1860, Norfolk, VA; par. Henry and Dorothy Elizabeth (Waller) Taylor; m. Anne Stratton Nivison, 1802; c. several. EDUC.: A.B., William and Mary Coll., 1792; studied law under John Wickham, Richmond, VA. POLIT. & GOV.: elected as a Democrat to VA State House of delegates, 1796–1800, 1806, 1816–17; elected as a Democrat to U.S. House (VA), 1800–1801; appointed U.S. Commissioner of claims in FL, 1820; appointed U.S. sec. of war, (declined); appointed U.S. minister to Great Britain, (declined); elected as a Democrat to U.S. Senate (VA), 1824–32 (pres. pro tempore, 1832); delegate, VA State Constitutional Convention, 1829; elected as a Democrat to gov. of VA, 1834–36; ***candidate for Democratic nomination to vice presidency of the U.S., 1840***. BUS. & PROF.: atty.; admitted to VA Bar, 1796; law practice, James City Cty., VA; law practice, Norfolk, VA, 1802–60. WRITINGS: *A Review of Negotiations between the United States of America and Great Britain . . .* (1829). RES.: Richmond, VA.

TEAGUE, NETTIE. POLIT. & GOV.: ***candidate for Democratic nomination to vice presidency of the U.S., 1980***. MAILING ADDRESS: c/o Gerald M. Rothbard, 6448 Wiley St., Hollywood, FL 33023.

TEAGUE, RAYMOND L. m. Bessie M. Teague; c. Carol. POLIT. & GOV.: ***Theocratic Party candidate for vice presidency of the U.S., 1960***. BUS. & PROF.: ordained minister, Church of God; bishop, Church of God; gen. overseer, Church of God, Detroit, MI, 1963–64; gen. overseer, Church of God, Anchorage, AK, 1963–67; gen. overseer, Church of God, Prescott, AZ, 1963–67; gen. overseer, Church of God, Los Angeles, CA, 1963–67; ambassador to other churches, Church of God, 1968; left Church of God, c. 1972. MIL.: U.S. Army, WWII; wounded in battle during WWII; hospitalized in veteran's hospital, Detroit, MI, 1963. MAILING ADDRESS: Church of God, 675 South Crenshaw Blvd., Los Angeles, CA.

TEICHERT, EDWARD A. b. 1904, Greensburg, PA; d. Aug 16, 1981, Morristown, NJ; par. Ernest R. Teichert; m.; c. Edward A., Jr.; Gail Johns; Shirley Murphy. EDUC.: public schools, to 1918. POLIT. & GOV.: joined Socialist Labor Party, 1930; state sec., PA Socialist Labor Party, 1933–45; delegate, Socialist Labor Party National Convention, 1936, 1940, 1944, 1948, 1952, 1956; ***Socialist Labor Party candidate for presidency of the U.S., 1944, 1948***; member, exec. cmte., Socialist Labor Party, 1945; left Socialist Labor Party, 1976. BUS. & PROF.: steelworker, Railroad Industrial Engineering Co., Greensburg, PA, 30 years; Good Humor salesman, Long Island, NY, 1965–79. MISC.: brother of Emil F. Teichert (q.v). RES.: Greensburg, PA.

TEICHERT, EMIL F. b. Dec 17, 1897, West Newton, PA; d. Jan 9, 1972, Lake Hill, NY; par. Ernest R. Teichert; m. Silveria Mauser; c. Mrs. Joanna Borrero. EDUC.: night school. POLIT. & GOV.: joined Socialist Labor Party, 1921; staff member, Socialist Labor Party, 1931; Socialist Labor Party candidate for lt. gov. of NY, 1932, 1934; state sec., NY Socialist Labor Party, 1933–46; Socialist Labor Party candidate for various municipal offices, New York, NY; ***Socialist Labor Party candidate for vice presidency of the U.S., 1936***; delegate, Socialist Labor Party National Convention, 1964. BUS. & PROF.: factory worker; employee, Transportation and Expense Dept., Pennsylvania R.R. Co.; mechanical engineer; writer, "World News" feature, *The Weekly People*, acting ed., 1938; ed., *Das Bulletin*. WRITINGS: *Sozialistische Marksteine* (ed.). MISC.: brother of Edward A. Teichert (q.v.). RES.: New York, NY.

TEIGEN, TORFIN AUSTIN. b. Aug 20, 1901, Chippewa Cty., MN; par. Hon. Austin F. and Inga (Amundson) Teigen; m. Victoria Teigen; c. Ferdinand; Danny; Marjorie. EDUC.: Waldorf Coll.; B.A., Concordia Coll., 1925; U. of MN; Chicago Law School, 1931; Chicago School of Divinity. POLIT. & GOV.: cty. judge, MN; candidate for Democratic nomination to U.S. House (MN); candidate for Democratic nomination to U.S. House (ND), 1970, 1972, 1976; candidate for justice, ND Supreme Court, 1972; ***candidate for Democratic nomination to presidency of the U.S., 1976***; independent candidate for U.S. House (ND), 1980. BUS. & PROF.: farmer; businessman; inventor; author; ed., *Prairie News*, Fargo, ND; poet. MEM.: Rough Riders Assn. of America. WRITINGS: *Goldbook* (1937); *Major Problems in America*; *The Farm Crisis* (1970). REL.: Lutheran. MAILING ADDRESS: 346 21st St., North, Fargo, ND 58102.

TELFAIR, EDWARD. b. 1735, Town Head, Scotland; d. Sep 17, 1807, Savannah, GA; m. Sally Gibbons, May 18, 1774; c. Thomas; two other sons; three daughters. EDUC.: grad., Kircudbright Grammar School. POLIT. & GOV.: elected member, GA Commons House of Assembly, 1768; member, GA Provincial Congresses; member, GA Council of Safety, 1775–76; delegate, GA Provincial Congress, Savannah, GA, 1776; member, Continental Congress, 1778–82, 1784–85, 1788–89; asst. justice, justice, Burke Cty., GA, 1781–84; signer, Articles of Confederation, 1785; appointed U.S. commissioner to the Creeks and Cherokees, 1783; elected to GA State Legislature, 1785, 1789; elected gov. of GA, 1786, 1789–93; member, GA Ratification Convention, 1788; ***received 1 electoral vote for presidency of the U.S., 1789***. BUS. & PROF.: owner, sawmill; farmer; merchant; owner, Comm. House, Savannah, GA, 1766. MIL.: asst. commander, Up-Country Militia. REL.: Protestant. MISC.: came to VA, c. 1758; joined "Liberty Boys," 1774–76; organized donations for Boston sufferers, 1774. RES.: Savannah, GA.

TELLER, HENRY MOORE. b. May 23, 1830, Granger, NY; d. Feb 23, 1914, Denver, CO; par. John and Charlotte (Moore) Teller; m. Harriett M. Bruce, Jun 7, 1862; c. Emma A. (Mrs. George Edward Tyler); Harrison John; Henry Bruce. EDUC.: Rushford Acad. studied law under Judge Martin Grover. POLIT. & GOV.: elected as a Republican to U.S. Senate (CO), 1876–82, 1885–1909 (Independent Silver Republican, 1897–1903; Democrat, 1903–09); appointed U.S. sec. of the interior, 1882–85; ***candidate for Democratic nomination to presidency of the U.S., 1896; candidate for Democratic nomination to vice presidency of the U.S., 1896; candidate for People's Party nomination to presidency of the U.S., 1896***; appointed member, U.S. Monetary Comm., 1908–12. BUS. & PROF.: schoolteacher; atty.; admitted to NY Bar, 1858; law practice, Morrison, IL, 1858–61; partner, H. M. and W. Teller (law firm), Central City, CO, 1861–1905; pres., Colorado Central Railway, 1872–76; law practice, Denver, CO, 1909–14. MIL.: maj. gen., CO Militia, 1862–64. MEM.: Masons; Knights Templar (CO grand master; grand commander of CO, 1876; grand prior of supreme council, 1913). HON. DEG.: LL.D., Alfred U., 1886; LL.D., U. of CO, 1903; LL.D., U. of Denver, 1909. REL.: Methodist Episc. RES.: Central City, CO.

TEMPLE, SHIRLEY (See BLACK, SHIRLEY JANE TEMPLE).

TEMPLETON, RALPH DEAN. b. Jan 18, 1931, Flint, MI; d. Jan 25, 1975, Ellensburg, WA; par. Ralph and Myrtle Irene (Grosbeck) Templeton; m. (divorced); c. Mark. POLIT. & GOV.: ***independent candidate for presidency of the U.S., 1976***. BUS. & PROF.: ed., *Templeton's Round Up*. REL.: Nature's God. MISC.: murdered in Ellensburg, WA, 1975. RES.: Ellensburg, WA.

TENNEY, JACK BRECKINRIDGE. b. Apr 1, 1898, St. Louis, MO; d. Nov 4, 1970, Glendale, CA; par. John Henry and Helen (Burch) Tenney; m. Florence Gruber; m. 2d, Linnie Wymore, Aug 23, 1946; c. Virginia Woodward; Leila Donegan. EDUC.: B.A., Los Angeles Coll. of Law, 1935; Doctor of Humanities, Sequoia U., 1953. POLIT. & GOV.: elected as a Democrat to CA State Assembly, 1937–43 (Democrat-Progressive, 1939); elected as a Democrat-Republican to CA State Senate, 1943–54 (Republican, 1945–54); ***Constitution Party candidate for presidency of the U.S., 1952; Christian Nationalist Party candidate for vice presidency of the U.S., 1952***; candidate for Republican nomination to U.S. House (CA), 1952, 1962. BUS. & PROF.: pipe organist, to 1921; architectural draftsman, Warner Brothers Motion Picture Studios, Hollywood, CA, 1925; architectural draftsman, MGM Studios, Hollywood, CA, 1926–27; ed., *Hollywood Reflector*; columnist, "Inside Facts," to 1930; orchestra leader, 14 years; West Coast correspondent, Metrone, 1930–40; composer; atty.; admitted to CA Bar, 1935; admitted to practice before Federal courts, 1936; admitted to practice before the Bar of the Supreme Court of the U.S., 1945; law practice, Los Angeles, CA,

1935–70; chm., CA State Senate Cmte. on Un-American Activities, 1941–49. MIL.: U.S. Army, 1918–19. MEM.: American Legion; VFW; Eagles; Elks; American Federation of Musicians (life member; pres., Local 369, Las Vegas, NV, 1930; vice pres., Local 47, 1937, pres., 1938–39; organized CA-AZ conference, 1937, pres., 1937–40); Ancient Egyptian Order of Sciots (Pharoah, Inglewood Pyramid); Masons; A.S.C.A.P. WRITINGS: *The Tenney Committee . . . The American Record* (1952). Songs: "Mexacali Rose"; "Drowsy Moon"; "Some Day I'll Learn to Forget You"; "Song of the Legionnaire"; "On the Banks of the Old Merced"; "A Thousand Years from Now"; "Little One"; "Blue Sierra Hills"; "I Want to Wake Up in Hawaii." REL.: Protestant. RES.: Los Angeles, CA.

TERRELL, BEN STOCKTON. b. Jul 10, 1842, Colorado Cty., TX; d. Mar 28, 1928, Seguin, TX; par. Henry Terrell; m. Katie Heaner, Feb 23, 1876; c. Mamie Eloise (Mrs. Ed Harpel; adopted). POLIT. & GOV.: city atty., Seguin, TX; cty. atty., Guadalupe Cty., TX; People's Party candidate for U.S. House (TX), 1892, 1894 (withdrew); delegate, Founding Convention, People's Party, 1892; temporary chm., People's Party National Convention, 1892; ***candidate for People's Party nomination to vice presidency of the U.S., 1892***. BUS. & PROF.: farmer, Seguin, TX; farmer, Guadeloupe Cty., TX, 1865–86; trader, Mexico; atty.; ed., *National Economist*. MIL.: enlisted, Company A, 4th Regt., TX Infantry, C.S.A., 1861; member, 8th TX Cavalry, C.S.A., 1865. MEM.: Delaney Farmers' Alliance (lecturer, 1886); State Alliance of TX (member, exec. cmte.); National Farmers' Alliance and Industrial Union (national lecturer, 1887; chm., Cmte. on Confederation, 1890; pres.); Confederated Industrial Organizations (chm., 1892); Odd Fellows; TX Alliance Exchange (treas., 1886); Confederation of Industrial Organizations (pres., 1891). WRITINGS: "The Growth of the Alliance," in Dunning, N. A., *The Farmers' Alliance and Agricultural Digest* (1891). REL.: Methodist. RES.: Seguin, TX.

TERRY, PEGGY. b. 1923, Haileyville, OK; d. Mary Ousley; m. Twice (divorced); c. Doug Youngblood; two others. POLIT. & GOV.: ***Peace and Freedom Party candidate for vice presidency of the U.S., 1968***. BUS. & PROF.: switchboard operator; waitress; welfare recipient; fieldworker, citrus and cotton farms; ed., *JOIN Community Union Firing Line*. MEM.: JOIN. MAILING ADDRESS: c/o Mary Ousley, Route 1, Box 104 H, West Paducah, KY 42086.

THACKER, MARLIN DALE. b. Oct 6, 1933, Fyffe, AL; par. Clarence Lee and Blanche Drucilla (Upton) Thacker; m. Class Mae Weaver, Aug 10, 1968; c. Elizabeth Dean; Don Alton; Peggy Mae. EDUC.: Fort Payne School of Business; David Roberts Veterinary School, Waukesha, WI. POLIT. & GOV.: candidate for Democratic nomination to sheriff, Crossville, AL, 1978, 1982; ***candidate for Democratic nomination to presidency of the U.S., 1980, 1984, 1992; independent candidate for vice presidency of the U.S., 1988, 1992***. BUS. & PROF.: veterinary employee, McElrath Farms, Albertville, AL; employee, egg processing plant, Crossville, AL. MIL.: airman second class, U.S. Air Force, 1954–55. REL.: Free Holiness Church. MAILING ADDRESS: Route 3, Box 273, Crossville, AL 35962.

THAYER, MERLE MELVIN. b. Mar 31, 1922, Belmond, IA; par. John and Lida (Mason) Thayer; m. Gwen Wave; c. Jenilea; Laura; Roger; Scott. EDUC.: Belmond (IA) H.S.; B.S., Oak Park U., Ames, IA. POLIT. & GOV.: American Independent Party candidate for U.S. House (IA), 1966; ***Christian Constitutional Party candidate for vice presidency of the U.S., 1968***. BUS. & PROF.: owner, Merle Thayer and Associates (materials and packaging equipment), Davenport, IA; sales engineer, dock specialists. REL.: Lutheran. MAILING ADDRESS: Merle Thayer and Associates, 2811 Kelling St., P.O. Box 2053, Davenport, IA 52804.

THEINERT, EDWARD W. POLIT. & GOV.: ***candidate for Socialist Labor Party nomination to vice presidency of the U.S., 1900***. RES.: RI.

THOMAS, ELBERT DUNCAN. b. Jun 17, 1883, Salt Lake City, UT; d. Feb 11, 1953, Honolulu, HI; par. Richard Kendall and Caroline (Stockdale) Thomas; m. Edna Harker, Jun 25, 1907; m. 2d, Ethel Evans, Nov 6, 1946; c. Chiyo (Mrs. Horton Rockwood Telford); Esther (Mrs. Wayne Clayton Grover); Edna Louise (Mrs. Lawrence Lee Hansen). EDUC.: A.B., U. of UT, 1906; Ph.D., U. of CA, 1924. POLIT. & GOV.: sec., U. of UT Board of Regents, 1917–22; Democratic candidate for sec. of state of UT, 1920; elected as a Democrat to U.S. Senate (UT), 1933–51; member, Thomas Jefferson Memorial Comm., 1933–53 (chm., 1944–53); delegate, Interparliamentary Union, 1936, 1937; delegate, International Labor Organization Conference, 1944, 1945, 1946, 1948; ***candidate for Democratic nomination to vice presidency of the U.S., 1944***; delegate, Dem. Nat'l. Conv., 1948; Democratic candidate for U.S. Senate (UT), 1950; appointed U.S. High Commissioner, Trust Territories of the Pacific, 1951–53. BUS. & PROF.: instructor in Latin and Greek, U. of UT, 1914–16, prof. of Political Science, 1924–33; author. MIL.: 2d lt., maj., UT National Guard and U.S.A.R., 1917–26. MEM.: Council of American Learned Societies; Honolulu Social Science Assn.; Carnegie International Conference of American Professors, 1926; Columbia Institution for the Deaf (dir., 1939–47); Honolulu C. of C. (hon. member); APSA (vice pres., 1940–41); AAUP; American Soc. for International Law (vice pres.); American Oriental Soc.; Chinese Political and Social Science Assn.; Phi Kappa Phi; Phi Delta Theta; Alpha Pi Zeta; Pi Gamma Mu; Timpanagos Club; New Orient Soc.; U.S. Princeton Bicentennial Comm.; UT Alumni Assn. (pres., 1913–14). AWARDS: Political Science Fellowship, U. of CA, 1922–24; Oberlaender Award for Study in Germany, 1934. HON. DEG.: Litt.D., National U., 1935; LL.D., U.

of Southern CA, 1935; LL.D., U. of HI, 1951. WRITINGS: *Sukui No Michi* (1911); *Chinese Political Thought* (1927); *World Unity Through Study of History* (1929); *Thomas Jefferson—World Citizen* (1942); *The Four Fears* (1944); *This Nation Under God* (1950). REL.: Church of Jesus Christ of Latter-Day Saints (missionary in Japan, 1907–12; gen. board, Deseret Sunday School Union, 1927–38). RES.: Salt Lake City, UT.

THOMAS, FRANK L. POLIT. & GOV.: ***candidate for Democratic nomination to presidency of the U.S., 1988***. MAILING ADDRESS: Thousand Oaks, CA.

THOMAS, JIM. POLIT. & GOV.: ***candidate for Democratic nomination to vice presidency of the U.S., 1980***. ADDRESS: OK.

THOMAS, JOHN JOSEPH. b. Aug 21, 1932, New York, NY; m. (divorced); c. one son. EDUC.: B.M.E., Rensselaer Polytechnic Inst., 1958. POLIT. & GOV.: ***Moderate Democratic candidate for presidency of the U.S., 1980 (withdrew)***. BUS. & PROF.: nuclear engineer. MEM.: N.S.P.E.; Fulbright Alumni Assn.; Rensselaer Alumni Assn. AWARDS: Fulbright Scholarship, England, 1958–59. REL.: Christian. MAILING ADDRESS: 1420 Rhode Island Ave., N.W., Washington, DC 20005.

THOMAS, MIKE. b. 1963; par. Robert and Phyllis Thomas; single. EDUC.: high school, Williamston, MI. POLIT. & GOV.: ***independent candidate for presidency of the U.S., 1980***. BUS. & PROF.: student. MAILING ADDRESS: 3085 Williamston Rd., Williamston, MI 48895.

THOMAS, NORMAN MATTOON. b. Nov 20, 1884, Marion, OH; d. Dec 19, 1968, Huntington, NY; par. Welling Evan and Emma (Mattoon) Thomas; m. Frances Violet Stewart, Sep 1, 1910; c. Norman Mattoon, Jr.; William Stewart; Mary Cecil (Mrs. Herbert Miller); Frances Beatrice (Mrs. John Friebely); Rebekah Lovett; Evan Welling, II. EDUC.: A.B., Princeton U., 1905, Litt.D., 1932; B.D., Union Theological Seminary, 1911. POLIT. & GOV.: joined Socialist Party, 1918; Socialist Party candidate for gov. of NY, 1924, 1938; Socialist Party candidate for mayor of New York, NY, 1925, 1929; Socialist Party candidate for NY State Senate, 1926; Socialist Party candidate for NY (NY) Board of Aldermen, 1927; ***Socialist Party candidate for presidency of the U.S., 1928, 1932, 1936, 1940, 1944, 1948***; member, Socialist Party National Cmte., 1932–68 (hon. chm.); ***candidate for Farmer-Labor Party nomination to presidency of the U.S., 1928***; Socialist Party candidate for U.S. Senate (NY), 1934. BUS. & PROF.: social worker, Spring Street Presbyterian Church and Settlement House, New York, NY; asst. to the pastor, Christ Church, New York, NY; ordained minister, Presbyterian Church, 1911; assoc. minister, Brick Presbyterian Church, New York, NY, 1910–11; pastor, East Harlem Church, New York, NY, 1911–18; chm., American Parish, New York, NY, 1911–18; sec., Fellowship of Reconciliation, 1917; resigned church responsibilities, 1918; demitted ministry, 1931; ed., *The World Tomorrow*, 1918–21; lecturer, Rand School; assoc. ed., *Nation*, 1921–22; ed., *Leader*, 1923; contributor, *New Leader*, 1924–35; contributor, *Socialist Call*, 1935–60; contributor, *New America*, 1960–68; columnist, *Denver (CO) Post*; author. MEM.: League for Industrial Democracy (co-dir., 1922–37); A.C.L.U. (founder; member, exec. cmte.); American Fund for Public Service; Press Writers Union; American Union Against Militarism; Fellowship of Reconciliation; Phi Beta Kappa; Southern Tenant Farmers Union (organizer; subsequently became Agricultural Workers Union); Keep America Out of War Cmte.; Workers Defense League; National Religion and Life Foundation (exec. cmte., 1933); National Citizens Cmte. on Relations with Latin America; Sacco-Vanzetti National League (adviser); National Council for Prevention of War; Garland Fund (founder); Labor Defense Council (dir., 1923); Cmte. on Militarism in Education (dir.); League for Independent Political Action; Emergency Cmte. for Strike Relief; League Against Fascism (national cmte., 1933); U.S. Congress Against War; People's Freedom Union (1920); National Advisory Council on Radio in Education (1933–34); Non-Intervention Citizens Cmte. (exec. cmte., 1927); National World Court Cmte.; Berger National Foundation (1931); Pioneer Youth of America (adviser); Il Nuovo Mondo National Cmte.; World Peaceways; Joint Cmte. on Unemployment (vice chm.); Cmte. on Coal and Giant Power; Conference for Progressive Political Action; Russian Reconstruction Farms (1925); Post-War World Council (chm.); Inst. for International Labor Research; National Cmte. for a Sane Nuclear Policy; American Cmte. for Cultural Freedom; American Cmte. on Africa; Spanish Refugee Aid, Inc.; American Newspaper Guild; Order of the Condor of the Andes (Bolivia); Order of Solidarity (Italy). HON. DEG.: LL.D., Johnson C. Smith U.; Bucknell U. WRITINGS: *The Conscientious Objector in America* (1923); *The Challenge of War* (1925); *New Tactics in Social Conflict* (with Harry Laidler, 1926); *Is Conscience a Crime?* (1927); *What is Industrial Democracy* (1927); *The Socialism of Our Times* (with Harry W. Laidler, 1929); *America's Way Out—Program for Democracy* (1930); *As I See It* (1932); *What Socialism Is and Is Not* (1932); *What's the Matter with New York: A National Problem* (with Paul Blanshard, 1932); *A Socialist Looks at the New Deal* (1933); *The Choice Before Us: Mankind at the Crossroads* (1934); *Human Exploitation in the United States* (1934); *War: No Glory, No Profit, No Need* (1935); *You Can't Cure Tuberculosis with Cough Drops* (1936); *Emancipate Youth from Toil, Old Age from Fear* (1936); *Shall Labor Support Roosevelt?* (1936); *Which Road for American Workers—Socialist or Communist?* (1936); *After the New Deal, What?* (1936); *Socialism on the Defensive* (1938); *Keep America Out of War: A Program* (with Bertram D. Wolfe, 1939); *We Have a Future* (1941); *What is Our Destiny?* (1944); *Appeal to the Nations* (1947); *How Can the Socialist Party Best Serve Socialism?* (1949); *A Socialist's Faith* (1951); *The Test of Freedom* (1954); *Mr. Chairman, Ladies and Gentlemen—Reflections on Public Speaking* (1955); *The Prerequisites for Peace* (1959); *Great Dissenters* (1961); *Socialism Re-Examined* (1963). REL.: Presb.

MISC.: arrested during Paterson (NJ) strike, 1932. RES.: New York, NY.

THOMAS, SCOTT STEWART. b. Jul 15, 1971, Great Barrington, MA; par. John Boyne and Alma Louise (Stewart) Thomas; single. EDUC.: Cholla Junior H.S., Glendale, AZ. POLIT. & GOV.: ***independent candidate for presidency of the U.S., 1984***. BUS. & PROF.: student, Cholla Junior H.S., Glendale, AZ. MEM.: BSA. REL.: R.C. MAILING ADDRESS: 11834 North 49th Dr., Glendale, AZ 85304.

THOMAS, WALTER S. POLIT. & GOV.: ***candidate for Republican nomination to vice presidency of the U.S., 1888***. RES.: TX.

THOMAS, WILLIAM AUBREY. b. Jun 7, 1866, Y Bynea, Wales; d. Sep 8, 1951, Talladega, AL; par. John R. and Margaret (Morgan) Thomas; single. EDUC.: Mount Union Coll., 1883–85; Rensselaer Polytechnic Inst., 1886–88. POLIT. & GOV.: elected member, city council, OH, 1892–96; elected as a Republican to U.S. House (OH), 1904–11; Republican candidate for U.S. House (OH), 1910; ***candidate for Democratic nomination to presidency of the U.S., 1924***. BUS. & PROF.: chemist, 1888–90; mgr., Thomas Furnace Co., 1890–98, vice pres., 1900; pres., Minerva Pig Iron Co., 1898–1900; vice pres., Niles Fire Brick Co.; pres., Mahoning Steel Co.; pres., Jenifer Iron Co. RES.: Talladega, AL.

THOMPSON, CARL DEAN. b. Mar 24, 1870, Berlin (now Marne), MI; d. Jul 3, 1949, Lincoln, NE; par. Abram and Rachel (Eddy) Thompson; m. Kate Mygatt, Aug 3, 1898; c. Harold Dean; Stanley Wendell. EDUC.: A.B., Gates Coll., 1895; B.D., Chicago Theological Seminary, 1898; M.A., U. of Chicago, 1900. POLIT. & GOV.: elected as a Socialist to WI State House, 1907–09; ***candidate for Socialist Party nomination to presidency of the U.S., 1908***; member, Socialist Party National Cmte., 1908–11 (exec. cmte.; candidate for chm., 1916); elected as a Socialist, city clerk, Milwaukee, WI, 1910–11; Socialist Party candidate for gov. of WI, 1912; dir. of Information and Research, Socialist Party, 1912–16; Socialist Party candidate for U.S. House (IL), 1914, 1916; consultant, Bonneville Power Administration, U.S. Dept. of the Interior, 1938–47. BUS. & PROF.: author; public power expert; minister, Congregational Church, to 1901; economist; ed., *Public Ownership*. MEM.: American National Cmte., Third World Power Conference; Public Ownership League of America (dir.); American Acad. of Political and Social Science; APSA; Pi Gamma Mu; League for Industrial Democracy (lecturer, 1934); People's Coll. (trustee); Emergency Peace Fund (1917); Ford Peace Ship Party; Office Employees Union; AFL. HON. DEG.: LL.D., Doane Coll., 1930. WRITINGS: *The Principles and Program of Socialism* (1900); *The Rising Tide of Socialism* (1911); *Municipal Ownership* (1917); *Public Ownership of Railways* (1918); *Municipal Electric Light and Power Plants in the United States and Canada* (1922); *Public Ownership* (1924); *Public Superpower* (1925); *Confessions of the Power Trust—A Review of the Finds of the Federal Trade Commission* (1932); *Studies in Public Power*; *The Biggest Dam on Earth (Grand Coulee)*; *Municipal Railways in the United States and Canada*; *Public Ownership of Public Utilities* (ed.). REL.: Congregationalist. RES.: Chicago, IL.

THOMPSON, DARLENE ANN (aka DARLENE HARSTAD MILLER). POLIT. & GOV.: ***candidate for Republican nomination to presidency of the U.S., 1984; candidate for Democratic nomination to presidency of the U.S., 1984; candidate for American Independent Party nomination to presidency of the U.S., 1984***. MAILING ADDRESS: CA?

THOMPSON, ERIK McBRIDE. b. Jul 21, 1957, Northfield, MN; single. EDUC.: A.B., Stanford U., 1979, M.A., 1982, M.B.A., 1984; certificate in Public Management. POLIT. & GOV.: member, Peace Corps, Micronesia, 1979–81; ***Peace and Justice Party candidate for presidency of the U.S., 1992***. BUS. & PROF.: political scientist; food researcher; activist. REL.: Christian. MISC.: served three months in a Federal Prison Camp and fined $8,600 for a misdemeanor trespassing conviction at the NV Nuclear Test Site, 1990. MAILING ADDRESS: Route 1, Box 276, Richville, MN 56576.

THOMPSON, FLOYD EUGENE. b. Dec 25, 1887, Roodhouse, IL; d. Oct 18, 1960, Evanston, IL; par. Albert Alonzo and Sarah Josephine (Edwards) Thompson; m. Irene Condit Worcester, Jul 2, 1918; c. Mary Ellen (Mrs. Pierre Goff Beach, Jr.). EDUC.: grad., Roodhouse (IL) H.S.; self-educated in law. POLIT. & GOV.: elected state's atty., Rock Island Cty., IL, 1912–19; elected justice, Supreme Court of IL, 1919–28 (chief justice, 1922–23); ***candidate for Democratic nomination to presidency of the U.S., 1924***; Democratic candidate for gov. of IL, 1928; delegate, U.S. Attorney General's Crime Conference, 1934; appointed chm., Advisory Cmte. on Revision of the Federal Judicial and Criminal Code, 1944–46; appointed member, Advisory Comm. on Military justice, 1946. BUS. & PROF.: teacher, IL, 1907–09; principal, Manchester (IL) H.S., 1909–10; ed., publisher, *East Moline (IL) Herald*, 1911–12; atty.; admitted to TN Bar, 1911; admitted to IL Bar, 1911; partner, Poppenhusen, Johnston, Thompson and Cole (law firm), Chicago, IL, 1928; partner, Thompson, Raymond, Mayer, Jenner and Bloomstein (law firm), Chicago, IL. MEM.: ABA; IL State Atty. Assn. (pres., 1916–17); IL State Bar Assn. (pres., 1933–34); Chicago Bar Assn. (pres., 1943–44); American Law Inst. (life member; councilman, 1944–60); Assn. of the Bar of NY; American Jud. Soc.; Coll. of Trial Lawyers; SAR (IL pres., 1936–37); Chicago Assn. of Commerce; Order of the Coif; Elks (Grand Forum, 1927–32; Exalted Ruler, 1932–33; trustee; sec., 1937); Law Club;

Union League; Chicago Farmers' Club (pres., 1947–48); American Inst. of Criminal Law and Criminology; International Assn. of Insurance Counsel. HON. DEG.: LL.D., Knox Coll. REL.: Presb. RES.: Rock Island, IL.

THOMPSON, HENRY ADAMS. b. Mar 23, 1837, Stormstown, PA; d. Jul 8, 1920, Dayton, OH; par. John and Lydia (Blake) Thompson; m. Harriet E. Copeland, Aug 7, 1862; c. one son; two daughters. EDUC.: A.B., Jefferson Coll., Canonsburg, PA, 1858, D.D., 1873; Western Theological Seminary. POLIT. & GOV.: joined Prohibition Party, 1874; Prohibition Party candidate for U.S. House (OH), 1874, 1910; Prohibition Party candidate for lt. gov. of OH, 1875; Prohibition Party candidate for gov. of OH, 1877, 1887, 1911; chm., Prohibition Party National Convention, 1876; member, Prohibition Party National Cmte., 1876–80; ***candidate for American National Party nomination to vice presidency of the U.S., 1876 (withdrew)***; chm., OH State Prohibition Cmte.; temporary chm., Prohibition Party National Convention, 1880; ***Prohibition Party candidate for vice presidency of the U.S., 1880***; appointed Commissioner of Dept. of Science and Education, OH Centennial Exposition, 1889; Prohibition Party candidate for U.S. House (NY), 1900. BUS. & PROF.: schoolteacher, Marion and Noblesville, IN, 1861; prof. of Mathematics, Western Coll., 1861–62; prof. of Mathematics, Otterbein U., 1862–67, pres., 1872–86; superintendent of public schools, Troy, OH, 1867–71; prof. of Mathematics, Westfield Coll., 1871–72; assoc. ed., Sunday School literature, 1893–97; editor-in-chief, Sunday School literature, United Brethren Church, 1897–1901; ed., *United Brethren Quarterly Review*, 1901–09; contributor, *Telescope (Journal of the United Brethren Church)*; clergyman. MEM.: National Prohibition Alliance (pres., 1877); OH Sabbath Assn. (field sec.); Methodist Ecumenical Conference, London, England, 1881. HON. DEG.: LL.D., Westfield Coll., 1886. WRITINGS: *Schools of the Prophets*; *Power of the Invisible* (1882); *Our Bishops* (1889); *Biography of Bishop Jonathan Weaver, D.D.* (1901); *Bible Study and Devotion* (1905); *Women of the Bible* (1914). REL.: United Brethren Church. RES.: Dayton, OH.

THOMPSON, HUNTER STOCKTON. b. Jul 18, 1939, Louisville, KY; par. Jack R. and Virginia (Ray) Thompson; m. Sandra Dawn, May 19, 1963; c. Juan. POLIT. & GOV.: ***candidate for Democratic nomination to vice presidency of the U.S., 1976***; appointed member, Sheriff's Advisory Cmte., Pitkin Cty., CO, 1976–81. BUS. & PROF.: Caribbean correspondent, *Time*, 1959; Caribbean correspondent, *NY (NY) Herald-Tribune*, 1959–60; South American correspondent, *National Observer*, 1961–63; West Coast correspondent, *Nation*, 1964–66; columnist, *Ramparts*, 1967–68; columnist, *Scanlan's*, 1969–70; national affairs dir., *Rolling Stone*, 1970–75; global affairs correspondent, *High Times*, 1977–. MIL.: U.S. Air Force, 1956–58. MEM.: National Book Awards (judge, 1975); National Organization to Repeal Marijuana Laws (advisory board, 1976–); Woody Creek Rod and Gun Club (exec. dir.); Press Club; Key West Club; Overseas Press Club; U.S. Naval Inst.; Air Force Assn.; Kona Coast Marlin Fishermen's Assn.; Hong Kong Foreign Correspondents' Assn. WRITINGS: *Hell's Angels* (1966); *Rum Diary* (1976); *Fear and Loathing in Las Vegas* (1972); *Fear and Loathing on the Campaign Trail '72* (1973); *The Great Shark Hunt* (1977); *The Curse of Lono* (1982); *The Silk Road* (1984). MISC.: creator of Gonzo School of Journalism. MAILING ADDRESS: Woody Creek, CO 81656.

THOMPSON, HUSTON (See THOMPSON, SAMUEL HUSTON).

THOMPSON, JAMES ROBERT. b. May 8, 1936, Chicago, IL; par. Dr. James Robert and Agnes Josephine (Swanson) Thompson; m. Jayne A. Carr, 1976; c. Samantha Jane. EDUC.: U. of IL, 1953–55; WA U., 1955–56; J.D., Northwestern U., 1959. POLIT. & GOV.: asst. prosecutor, state's atty., Cook Cty., IL, 1959–64; appointed member, Mayor's Cmte. to Combat Organized Crime, Chicago, IL, 1964–67; adviser, President's Comm. on Law Enforcement and the Administration of Justice, 1967; appointed member, President's Task Force on Crime, 1967; appointed asst. atty. gen. of IL, 1969–70; appointed asst. to U.S. atty., Northern District of IL, 1970; dir., Chicago Crime Comm.; appointed U.S. atty., Northern District of IL, 1971–75; elected as a Republican to gov. of IL, 1977–91; ***candidate for Republican nomination to presidency of the U.S., 1980 (declined); candidate for Republican nomination to vice presidency of the U.S., 1980, 1988***. BUS. & PROF.: atty.; admitted to IL Bar, 1959; codir., criminal law course, Chicago Police and Industrial Security Personnel, 1962–64; assoc. prof., Northwestern U., 1964–69; admitted to practice before the Bar of the Supreme Court of the U.S., 1964; editorial board, *Criminal Law Bulletin*; asst. to the editor-in-chief, *Journal of Criminal Law, Criminology, and Police Science*, 1965–69; counsel, Winston and Strawn (law firm), Chicago, IL, 1975–77. MEM.: ABA; IL Bar Assn.; Americans for Effective Law Enforcement (vice pres., 1967–69). WRITINGS: *Cases and Comments on Criminal justice* (1968; 1974); *Criminal Law and Its Administration* (1970). REL.: Presb. MAILING ADDRESS: 554 West Fullerton Parkway, Chicago, IL 60610.

THOMPSON, SAMUEL HUSTON. b. Nov 1, 1875, Lewisburg, PA; d. Feb 17, 1966, Washington, DC; par. Samuel Huston and Martha Jane (McIlwain) Thompson; m. Caroline Margaret Cordes, Sep 16, 1909; c. Caroline (Mrs. John Farr Simmons). EDUC.: grad., Lawrenceville Preparatory School, 1893; A.B., Princeton U., 1897; LL.B., NY Law School, 1900. POLIT. & GOV.: appointed asst. atty. gen. of CO, 1907–09; appointed asst. atty. gen. of the U.S., 1913–18; adviser, National Park Service, 1916–30; appointed member, Federal Trade Comm., 1918–24 (chm., 1920–21, 1923–24); ***candidate for Democratic nomination to presidency of the U.S., 1924, 1928; candidate for Democratic nomination to vice presidency of the U.S., 1924; candidate for Progressive Party nomination to vice presidency of the U.S., 1924***; appointed member, Emergency

Board on Railroad Disputes, 1941; pres., National Democratic Council; delegate, First Inter-American Conference on Indian Life. BUS. & PROF.: atty.; admitted to CO Bar, 1900; law practice, Denver, CO, 1900; assoc., office of John Ewing (law firm), Denver, CO, 1900–1913; lecturer on Law, U. of Denver Law School, 1903–06; partner, Bright, Thompson, Hinrichs and Warren (law firm), Washington, DC, 1927–29; partner, Bright, Thompson and Mast (law firm), Washington, DC, 1929–55. MEM.: BSA (pres., DC council; chm., Regional council); Town Hall (pres., board of directors, 1936); ABA; DC Bar Assn.; CO Bar Assn.; Phi Alpha Delta; Order of the Coif; Chevy Chase Club; Cosmos Club; Alfalfa Club; Cactus Club; Mile High Club; Princeton Club of WA; National Parks Assn. (trustee, 1916–66); Assn. of Friends of the Land (hon. vice pres.); WA YMCA (dir.); American Peace Soc. (vice pres.); American Economic Assn.; Lawyers Club. HON. DEG.: LL.D., George Washington U., 1922. REL.: Presb. RES.: Washington, DC

THOMPSON, WILLIAM HALE. b. May 14, 1869, Boston, MA; d. Mar 18, 1944, Chicago, IL; par. William Hale and Medora (Gale) Thompson; m. Mary Walker Wyse, Dec 5, 1901; c. none. EDUC.: Charles Fessenden Preparatory School, Chicago, IL; Metropolitan Business Coll., Chicago, IL. POLIT. & GOV.: elected as a Republican to board of aldermen, Chicago, IL, 1900–1902; elected as a Republican to Cook Cty. (IL) Comm., 1902–04; elected as a Republican, mayor of Chicago, IL, 1915–23, 1927–31; member, Rep. Nat'l. Cmte., 1916–20; candidate for Republican nomination to U.S. Senate (IL), 1918; delegate, Rep. Nat'l. Conv., 1920; ***candidate for Republican nomination to presidency of the U.S., 1920; candidate for Republican nomination to vice presidency of the U.S., 1928***; Republican candidate for mayor of Chicago, IL, 1931; Union Party candidate for gov. of IL, 1936; candidate for Republican nomination to mayor of Chicago, IL, 1939. BUS. & PROF.: cowboy, rancher, Standard Cattle Co. holdings in CO, MT, and WY; mgr., cattle ranch, Ewing, NE, 1888–91; real estate mgr., 1891. MEM.: Sportsman's Club of America (pres.); Chicago Real Estate Board; America First Foundation (founder); Chicago Yacht Club (commodore); Hamilton Club; Marquette Club; IL Athletic Club (pres.). HON. DEG.: LL.D., Wilberforce U., 1927. REL.: Methodist. MISC.: won Chicago to Mackinac Regatta, 3 times, on board yacht *Valmore*; known as "Big Bill" Thompson; leading isolationist; charged with sedition, 1919. RES.: Chicago, IL.

THOMPSON, WILLIAM RAY, JR. par. William Ray Thompson, Sr. POLIT. & GOV.: ***independent candidate for presidency of the U.S., 1992***. MAILING ADDRESS: 38B Madrone Trail, Austin, TX 78737.

THOMSON, MELDRIM, JR. b. Mar 8, 1912, Pittsburgh, PA; par. Meldrim, Sr. and Beaulah (Booth) Thomson; m. Anne Gale Kelly, Oct 29, 1938; c. Peter; David; Thomas; Marion Gale; Janet; Robb. EDUC.: grad., Miami (FL) H.S., 1930; U. of Miami; Mercer U.; LL.B., U. of GA. POLIT. & GOV.: elected chm., school board, Stony Brook, Long Island, NY, c. 1950; elected chm., school board, Orford, NH, 1959–62; candidate for Republican nomination to NH State House, 1962; elected delegate, NH State Constitutional Convention, 1964; candidate for Republican nomination to gov. of NH, 1968, 1970, 1980; American Party candidate for gov. of NH, 1970; elected as a Republican to gov. of NH, 1973–79; ***candidate for American Party nomination to presidency of the U.S., 1976; candidate for American Independent Party nomination to presidency of the U.S., 1976, 1980***; Republican candidate for gov. of NH, 1978, 1980; ***Constitution Party candidate for presidency of the U.S., 1980***; independent candidate for gov. of NH, 1982. BUS. & PROF.: instructor in Political Science, U. of GA; atty.; law practice, FL; admitted to practice before the Bar of the Supreme Court of the U.S.; editor-in-chief, Law Book Publishing Co., Brooklyn, NY; owner, publishing company, Long Island, NY; owner, Mt. Cube Maple Sugar Co.; pres., Equity Publishing Co., Orford, NH, 1954–. MEM.: BSA; Conservative Caucus (founder; chm.); Public School Assn. (cofounder); Bar of GA; FL Bar Assn.; Taxfighters, Inc. (cofounder). WRITINGS: *Federal Control of Schools: Myth or Fact* (1966). REL.: Bapt. MAILING ADDRESS: Mount Cube Farm, Orford, NH.

THON, ELMER EUGENE. b. Dec 31, 1922, Belleville, IL; par. William Henry and Ida (Leibundgut) Thon; single. EDUC.: Columbia U., 1½ years; Boston U., ½ year; Santa Monica City Coll., ½ year; AR Technical Coll., ½ year; Victoria (TX) Coll., 1 year. POLIT. & GOV.: claims to have been policy adviser to Dwight D. Eisenhower (q.v.), Richard M. Nixon (q.v.), John V. Lindsay (q.v.), Nelson A. Rockefeller (q.v.), Ronald Reagan (q.v.), and Jack Williams; ***candidate for Republican nomination to presidency of the U.S., 1976***. BUS. & PROF.: motion picture script writer; author; inventor; chef; operator, Baldwin Gleaner; farmer; businessman. MIL.: U.S. Army, 1943–46. MEM.: Piper Cub Airplane Pilots Assn. REL.: Christian Scientist. MAILING ADDRESS: 249 North Third Ave., c/o General Delivery, Patagonia, AZ 85624.

THORN, BILL. POLIT. & GOV.: ***Consumer Party candidate for vice presidency of the U.S., 1984***. BUS. & PROF.: consumer advocate; community activist. MAILING ADDRESS: Philadelphia, PA.

THORNTON, CURLY. b. May 20, 1948, Butte, MT; m. Debbie; c. six. EDUC.: B.A., Carroll Coll.; M.A., Eastern MT Coll.; doctoral studies, MT State U. POLIT. & GOV.: candidate for Democratic nomination to gov. of MT, 1988, 1992; candidate for Democratic nomination to U.S. Senate (MT), 1990; ***candidate for Democratic nomination to presidency of the U.S., 1992***. BUS. & PROF.: miner, warehouseman, Anaconda Co., MT; construction worker, Kraling/Nelson Construction, MT;

teacher; principal; coach; employee, cty. clerk and recorder's office, MT; pres., MT Foundation for the Prevention of Alcohol/ Drug Abuse; pres., The House of David Foundation, Billings, MT; Drug and Alcohol counselor. MIL.: U.S. Navy. MEM.: Disabled American Veterans; MT Council on Alcoholism (exec. dir.); NEA; MT Education Assn.; International Brotherhood of Teamsters; AFL-CIO; U.M.W. of A. MISC.: recovered alcoholic/drug addict. MAILING ADDRESS: 208 North 29th St., Suite 208, Billings, MT 59101.

THORNTON, DANIEL ISAAC J. b. Jan 31, 1911, Hall Cty., TX; d. Jan 18, 1976, Carmel Valley, CA; par. Clay C. and Ida (Fife) Thornton; m. Jessie Willock, Apr 4, 1934. EDUC.: TX Technical Inst., 1930–31; U. of CA at Los Angeles, 1932. POLIT. & GOV.: elected as a Republican to CO State Senate, 1949–51; elected as a Republican to gov. of CO, 1951– 54; ***candidate for Republican nomination to vice presidency of the U.S., 1952, 1956***; appointed member, President's Economic Comm. to Korea and the Far East, 1954; appointed member, Advisory Comm. on Intergovernmental Relations, 1954–55; Republican candidate for U.S. Senate (CO), 1956. BUS. & PROF.: bit player, Warner Brothers Studios; gas station operator; roughneck; rancher, AZ, 1936–41; owner, Thornton Hereford Ranch, Gunnison, CO; dir., Financial Industrial Fund, Inc.; dir., Cycle Manufacturing Co.; dir., National Western Stock Show. MEM.: C. of C.; Community Chest; Elks; Rotary Club; 4-H Club (pres., TX Congress, 1927). RES.: Carmel Valley, CA.

THORPE, OSIE. par. G. W. Thorpe. POLIT. & GOV.: ***candidate for Democratic nomination to presidency of the U.S., 1988***; candidate for Democratic nomination to mayor of Washington, DC, 1990. BUS. & PROF.: bishop. MAILING ADDRESS: c/o Tama E. Gillis, 2900 Central Ave., N.E., Washington, DC 20018.

THRONEBERRY, MARVIN EUGENE. b. Sep 2, 1933, Collierville, TN; par. Walter Hugh and Mary (Callicutt) Throneberry; m. Dixie Lee Morton; c. Gail T. Brewer; Sandra T. Clement; Gil C.; Lorie L.; Jody K. EDUC.: South Side H.S., 3 years; Christian Brothers Coll. POLIT. & GOV.: ***Metropolitan Party candidate for vice presidency of the U.S., 1964***. BUS. & PROF.: professional baseball player; New York Yankees, 1955–60; Kansas City Athletics, 1960–61; Baltimore Orioles, 1961–62; New York Mets, 1962–63; actor; appeared in television commercial, Miller "Lite" Beer, 1979. REL.: Bapt. MISC.: lifetime professional league batting average: 0.237; known as "Marvelous Marv" Throneberry. MAILING ADDRESS: 12102 Macon Rd., Collierville, TN 38017.

THUNDERBERG, RUFUS. POLIT. & GOV.: ***independent candidate for presidency of the U.S., 1984***. BUS. & PROF.: Indian chief. MAILING ADDRESS: CT.

THURMAN, ALLEN GRANBERRY. b. Nov 13, 1813, Lynchburg, VA; d. Dec 12, 1895, Columbus, OH; par. Pleasant and Mary Granberry (Allen) Thurman; m. Mrs. Mary Dun Tompkins, Nov 14, 1844; c. Mrs. Richard C. McCormick; several others. EDUC.: Chillicothe Acad.; studied law under William Allen (q.v.). POLIT. & GOV.: private sec., Gov. Robert Lucas (OH), 1834; elected as a Democrat to U.S. House (OH), 1845–47; elected assoc. justice, OH Supreme Court, 1851–56 (chief justice, 1854–56); Democratic candidate for gov. of OH, 1867; elected as a Democrat to U.S. Senate (OH), 1869–81; delegate, Dem. Nat'l. Conv., 1876, 1880, 1884; ***candidate for Democratic nomination to presidency of the U.S., 1876, 1880, 1884***; member, Electoral Comm., 1877; Democratic candidate for U.S. Senate (OH), 1881, 1886; U.S. rep., International Monetary Conference, 1881; ***candidate for Anti-Monopoly Party nomination to presidency of the U.S., 1884 (declined)***; candidate for Democratic nomination to gov. of OH, 1887 (declined); appointed member, Interstate Commerce Comm., 1887 (declined); ***Democratic candidate for vice presidency of the U.S., 1888***. BUS. & PROF.: atty.; admitted to OH Bar, 1835; law practice, Ross Cty., OH, 1835–81; law practice, Columbus, OH, 1881–95. RES.: Columbus, OH.

THURMAN, JEROME HAMLIN (See HAMLIN, JEROME THURMAN).

THURMOND, JAMES STROM. b. Dec 5, 1902, Edgefield, SC; par. John William and Eleanor Gertrude (Strom) Thurmond; m. Jean Crouch, Nov 7, 1947; m. 2d, Nancy Moore, Dec 22, 1968; c. Nancy Moore; James Strom, Jr.; Juliana Gertrude; Paul Reynolds. EDUC.: B.S., Clemson Coll., 1923; Doctor of Military Science, The Citadel, 1961; Doctor of Humanities, Trinity Coll., 1965; Litt.D., CA Grad. School of Theology, 1970. POLIT. & GOV.: city and cty. atty., Edgefield, SC; elected member, Edgefield Cty. (SC) Board of Education, 1924–25; Edgefield Cty. (SC) superintendent of education, 1929–33; member, SC Comm. on Literacy; appointed member, National Advisory Comm. on Illiteracy; delegate, Dem. Nat'l. Conv., 1932, 1936, 1948, 1952, 1956, 1960; elected as a Democrat to SC State Senate, 1933–38; circuit judge, SC, 1938–42, 1946; elected as a Democrat to gov. of SC, 1947–51; member, Dem. Nat'l. Cmte., 1948; ***States Rights Party candidate for presidency of the U.S., 1948***; candidate for Democratic nomination to U.S. Senate (SC), 1950; appointed and subsequently elected as a Democrat to U.S. Senate (SC), 1955–67, as a Republican, 1967–; joined Republican Party, 1964; ***American Party candidate for presidency of the U.S., 1964***; delegate, Rep. Nat'l. Conv., 1968, 1972, 1976; ***1976 Cmte. candidate for vice presidency of the U.S., 1968; candidate for Democratic nomination to presidency of the U.S., 1984***. BUS. & PROF.: teacher, Edgefield, McCormick, and Ridge Spring high schools, SC, 1923–29; atty.; admitted to SC Bar, 1930; farmer; partner, Thurmond and Thurmond (law firm), Aiken, SC, 1930; partner, Thurmond, Lybrand and Simons (law firm), Aiken, SC, 1951–55; pres., Aiken Federal Savings and Loan Assn., 1951–55; dir., The Security Bank;

dir., Edgefield Hospital; dir., Franklin National Life Insurance Co. MIL.: member, ORC, 1924–37; lt. col., U.S. Army, 1942–46; maj. gen., U.S.A.R.; Legion of Merit; Bronze Star with V; Army Commendation Ribbon; Bronze Arrowhead; Purple Heart; Presidential Distinguished Unit Citation; Five Battle Stars; Croix de Guerre; Cross of the Order of the Crown (Belgium); Medal of Honor; Dept. of the Army Certificate of Appreciation; OCAMG Certificate of Achievement; European Theater Medal; Pacific Theater Medal; American Theater Medal; Victory Medal. MEM.: Reserve Officers Assn. (pres.); The Military Government Assn. (pres.); Republican Policy Cmte.; ABA; BSA (dir., GA-Carolina Council); Winthrop Coll. (trustee, 1936–38); SC Bar Assn. (vice pres., 1933, 1935); Clemson Coll. Alumni Assn. (pres.); Grange; Military Order of World Wars; National Governors' Conference (exec. cmte., 1947–48); Southern Governors' Conference (pres., 1950); American Red Cross; Assn. of the U.S. Army; SCV; American Legion; VFW; SAR; SC Farm Bureau; Blue Key; Phi Alpha Delta; Masons; Knights of Pythias; Moose; Modern Woodmen of the World; J.O.U.A.M. (state councillor, 1935); Lions (pres.); Clariosophic Literary Soc.; Tiger Brotherhood; Strawberry Leaf Club; C. of C.; Grange; Columbia Social Club; SC Hist. Soc.; Veterans of Global Wars. AWARDS: Selective Service Medal; Freedom Award, Order of Lafayette; Government Award, Young Americans for Freedom; Distinguished Service Award, Military Order of World Wars; Award for Outstanding Services, National Soc. of SAR; Award for Notable Patriotic Service, DAR; Distinguished Service Award, Americans for Constitutional Action; Distinguished Public Service Award, SC American Legion; Service to Mankind Award, Sertoma International; Distinguished Service Award, Clemson Coll. Alumni; Minuteman of the Year Award, Reserve Officers Assn., 1971; award, Soc. of National Patriots, 1974. HON. DEG.: LL.D., Bob Jones U., 1948; LL.D., Presbyterian Coll., 1960. WRITINGS: *The Faith We Have Not Kept* (1968). REL.: Bapt. MAILING ADDRESS: Box 951, Aiken, SC 29801.

THURSTON, JOHN MELLEN. b. Aug 21, 1847, Montpelier, VT; d. Aug 9, 1916, Omaha, NE; par. Daniel Sylvester and Ruth (Mellen) Thurston; m. Martha Poland, Dec 25, 1872; m. 2d, Lola Purman, Nov 1899. EDUC.: grad., Wayland U., Beaver Dam, WI, 1868; studied law. POLIT. & GOV.: appointed justice of the peace, Omaha, NE, 1871–74; elected as a Republican to Omaha (NE) City Council, 1872–74; city atty., Omaha, NE, 1874–77; elected as a Republican to NE State House, 1875–77; presidential elector, Republican Party, 1880; delegate, Rep. Nat'l. Conv., 1884, 1888 (temporary chm.), 1896 (chm.), 1900; Republican candidate for U.S. Senate (NE), 1887, 1893; elected as a Republican to U.S. Senate (NE), 1895–1901; ***candidate for Republican nomination to vice presidency of the U.S., 1896***; appointed U.S. commissioner to St. Louis Exposition, 1901. BUS. & PROF.: farmer; manual laborer; atty.; admitted to WI Bar, 1869; asst. atty., Union Pacific R.R. Co., 1877–88, gen. counsel, 1888–1916; partner, Thurston, Crow and Morrison (law firm), Omaha, NE. MEM.: Republican League of the U.S. (pres., 1889–91). RES.: Omaha, NE.

TIBBLES, THOMAS HENRY. b. May 22, 1838, Washington Cty., OH; d. May 14, 1928, Omaha, NE; par. William and Martha (Cooley) Tibbles; m. Amelie Owen, 1861; m. 2d, Susette "In-stha-the-um-ba" LaFlesche (known as "Bright Eyes"), 1881; m. 3d, Ida Belle Riddle, Feb 24, 1907; c. Edda (Mrs. Herbert Bates); May (Mrs. J. Allen Barris). EDUC.: studied law, Council Bluffs, IA; Mt. Union Coll., Alliance, OH. POLIT. & GOV.: member, People's Party National Cmte., 1892; ***People's Party candidate for vice presidency of the U.S., 1904***. BUS. & PROF.: member, John Brown's Co., KS, 1856–59; scout and plains guide; atty.; law practice, Winterset, IA; secret service agent, Civil War; ordained minister, Methodist Church; minister, Presbyterian Church; staff writer, *Omaha (NE) Bee*, 1873–74; staff writer, *Omaha (NE) Herald* and *World-Herald*, 1876–89; Washington (DC) correspondent, *Nonconformist*, 1893–94; founder, *The Independent*, 1895; ed., *The Investigator*, 1905–10; ed., feature writer, *Omaha (NE) World-Herald*, 1910–28; lecturer. MEM.: Soldier's Lodge (IA Indian Lodge); National Farmers' Alliance. WRITINGS: *Hidden Power* (1880); *Ponca Chiefs* (1881); *The American Peasant* (1890). REL.: Unitarian (nee Methodist; Presb.). MISC.: advocate of reform in treatment of Indians. RES.: Bancroft, NE.

TILDEN, SAMUEL JONES. b. Feb 9, 1814, New Lebanon, NY; d. Aug 4, 1886, Greystone, NY; par. Elam and Polly Younglove (Jones) Tilden; single. EDUC.: Yale U., 1834; grad., U. of the City of NY, 1841. POLIT. & GOV.: leader, Barnburners, 1845; elected as a Democrat to NY State Assembly, 1846, 1872; delegate, NY State Constitutional Convention, 1846, 1867; "Soft Shell" candidate for atty. gen. of NY, 1855; chm., NY State Democratic Central Cmte., 1866–74; elected as a Democrat to gov. of NY, 1875–76; ***Democratic candidate for presidency of the U.S., 1876; candidate for Democratic nomination to presidency of the U.S., 1880, 1884***; lost presidential election to Rutherford B. Hayes (q.v.) by vote of Electoral Comm. along party lines, receiving 184 electoral votes to 185 for Hayes. BUS. & PROF.: atty.; admitted to NY Bar, 1841; corporation counsel, New York, NY, 1843; publisher, *New York (NY) Morning News*, 1844. MEM.: Bar Assn. of the City of New York (founder); Tilden Trust. HON. DEG.: LL.D., Yale U., 1875. WRITINGS: *Writings and Speeches* (1885). MISC.: exposed Tweed Ring, 1868–72; reformed NY judiciary; exposed Canal Ring. RES.: New York, NY.

TILLMAN, BENJAMIN RYAN. b. Aug 11, 1847, Trenton, SC; d. Jul 3, 1918, Washington, DC; par. Benjamin Ryan and Sophia (Hancock) Tillman; m. Sallie Starke, Jan 8, 1868; c. Adeline "Addie"; Benjamin Ryan III; Henry Cummings; Margaret Malona (Mrs. Charles S. Moore); Sophia Oliver (Mrs. Henry W. Hughes); Sallie Mae (Mrs. John W. Schuler); Samuel Starke. EDUC.: Bethany Acad. POLIT. & GOV.: chm., Edgefield Cty. (SC) Democratic Central Cmte.; delegate, SC State Democratic Convention, 1890, 1892, 1894, 1896,

1898, 1900, 1902, 1904, 1906, 1908, 1910, 1912, 1914, 1916, 1918; elected as a Democrat to gov. of SC, 1890–94; delegate, Dem. Nat'l. Conv., 1892, 1896, 1900, 1904, 1908, 1912, 1916; elected as a Democrat to U.S. Senate (SC), 1895–1918; delegate, SC State Constitutional Convention, 1895; ***candidate for Democratic nomination to presidency of the U.S., 1896***; member, Dem. Nat'l. Cmte., 1912–18. BUS. & PROF.: farmer, SC, 1866–86; reformer. MIL.: joined C.S.A., 1864; capt., Edgefield Hussars, 1884–90. MEM.: Farmers' Alliance (founder); Clemson A&M Coll. (founder, 1893); Winthrop Normal and Industrial Coll. (founder, 1895). MISC.: advocate of industrial and technical education; known as "Pitchfork Ben" Tillman; lost left eye as result of early illness. RES.: Trenton, SC.

TILLMAN, LEROY R. b. Jul 4, 1889, Tattnall Cty., GA; par. James and Nona (Anderson) Tillman; m. Vida Padgett; c. Benjamin C.; James Harold; Edgar Paschal. EDUC.: studied law. POLIT. & GOV.: ***Farmer-Labor Party candidate for vice presidency of the U.S., 1928***. BUS. & PROF.: atty.; laborer. RES.: Glennville, GA.

TILSON, JOHN QUILLIN. b. Apr 5, 1866, Clearbranch, TN; d. Aug 14, 1958, New London, NH; par. William Erwin and Katharine (Sams) Tilson; m. Marguerite North, Nov 10, 1910; c. John Quillin, Jr.; Margaret Field (Mrs. Brice Shafer); Katharine Sams (Mrs. John Gregg Murray). EDUC.: private schools, Flag Pond, TN, and Mars Hills, NC; B.A., Carson-Newman Coll., 1888; A.B., Yale U., 1891, LL.B., 1893, M.L., 1894. POLIT. & GOV.: elected as a Republican to CT State House, 1905–09 (Speaker, 1907–09); elected as a Republican to U.S. House (CT), 1909–13, 1915–32 (minority leader); Republican candidate for U.S. House (CT), 1912; ***candidate for Republican nomination to vice presidency of the U.S., 1928 (declined)***; delegate, Rep. Nat'l. Conv., 1932. BUS. & PROF.: atty.; admitted to TN Bar, 1894; law practice, TN, 1894–95; ed., *Yale Banner*; ed., *Yale Shingle*; admitted to CT Bar, 1898; assoc., White and Daggett (law firm; subsequently White, Daggett and Tilson), New Haven, CT, 1898–1909; law practice, New Haven, CT, 1909–58; law practice, Washington, DC, 1933–40; lecturer, Yale U.; partner, Wiggin and Dana (law firm), New Haven, CT, 1939–58. MIL.: member, New Haven Grays, CT National Guard, 1897, advanced through grades to brig. gen.; 2d lt., 6th Regt., U.S. Volunteer Infantry, 1898; lt. col., Second Infantry, CT National Guard, 1916; Medal of King George (Great Britain); Order of the Crown of Italy (Grand Officer); Citation (France). MEM.: Save the Children Federation (treas., 1941; chm. of the board of directors); New Haven Taxpayers Research Council (pres.); ABA; DC Bar Assn.; CT Bar Assn.; New Haven Bar Assn.; Lake Sunapee Yacht Club; Psi Upsilon; Phi Delta Phi; Masons (33°); Chevy Chase Club; Graduate Club of New Haven. WRITINGS: *Yale '91 Class Book* (ed., 1891); *Speeches* (1912–20); *Prepare by Providing Those Things Without Which All Else Will Be Ineffective* (1916); *Senior Service Corps* (1917); *Arms, Ammunition, Airplanes, and Gas Masks* (1918); *The War Time Control of Industry* (1923); *Anniversary of the Birth of George Washington* (1925); *The Protective Tariff* (1928); *Parliamentary Law and Procedure* (1935); *The Embargo on Spain* (1939); *A Manual of Parliamentary Procedure* (1948); *How to Conduct a Meeting* (1950). REL.: Bapt. RES.: New Haven, CT.

TILT, ADRIAN. POLIT. & GOV.: member, National Hamiltonian Party National Cmte.; National Hamiltonian Party candidate for U.S. Senate (MD), 1966; ***National Hamiltonian Party candidate for vice presidency of the U.S., 1968, 1972, 1976 (satire effort)***. MISC.: reportedly a fictitious character created by Mike Kelly, 1966. MAILING ADDRESS: Suite 307, 2734 Parkside Dr., Flint, MI 48503.

TILTON, THEODORE. b. Oct 2, 1835, New York, NY; d. May 25, 1907, Paris, France; par. Silas and Eusebia (Tilton) Tilton; m. Elizabeth Richards, Oct 2, 1855 (divorced); c. Carroll; Florence; Alice; Paul; Ralph. EDUC.: Public School No. 1, New York, NY; grad., City Coll. of NY, 1855. POLIT. & GOV.: delegate, Liberal Republican Party National Convention, 1872; ***candidate for Equal Rights (Cosmic, Free Love, People's) Party nomination to vice presidency of the U.S., 1872***. BUS. & PROF.: reporter, *New York (NY) Tribune*; reporter, *The Churchman*; reporter, *New York (NY) Observer*; journalist; author; ed., *The Independent*, New York, NY, 1856–70; Lyceum lecturer, 1865–84; ed., *The Golden Age*, 1871–74; ed., *Brooklyn (NY) Union*, 1874–76. MEM.: New England Soc. of NY; American Equal Rights Assn.; Union Woman Suffrage Assn. (pres., 1870); Equal Rights Assn. WRITINGS: *The American Board and American Slavery* (1860); *The Fly* (1865); *The Two Hungry Kittens* (1865); *Golden Haired Gertrude* (1865); *The King's Ring* (1866); *The True Church* (1867); *The Sexton's Tale and Other Poems* (1867); *Sancta Sanctorum, or Proof-Sheets from an Editor's Table* (1869); *The Golden Age Tracts No. 3: Victoria C. Woodhull, A Biographical Sketch . . .* (1871); *Tempest Tossed* (1875); *Thou and I, and Other Poems* (1893); *Swabian Stories* (1882); *The Chameleon's Dish, and Other Poems* (1893); *Great Tom, the Curfew Bell at Oxford* (1894); *Heart's Ease, and Other Poems* (1895); *A Career Unique, a Memorial to Frederick Douglass* (1895); *Complete Poetical Works* (1897); *Our American Don Quixote* (1898); *Confessions of a Pyramid, and Other Poems* (1905); *The Fading of the Mayflower* (1906). REL.: Bapt. MISC.: advocate of equal rights for women; abolitionist; involved in famous trial charging Henry Ward Beecher with adultery with his wife. RES.: New York, NY.

TIMINSKI, ALFRED. POLIT. & GOV.: ***candidate for Democratic nomination to presidency of the U.S., 1984***. MAILING ADDRESS: 576 Forest St., First Floor, Orange, NJ 07050.

TIMMERMAN, GEORGE BELL, JR. b. Aug 11, 1912, Anderson, SC; par. George Bell and Mary Vandiver

(Sullivan) Timmerman; m. Helen M. DuPre, Feb 16, 1935. EDUC.: The Citadel, 1930–34; LL.B., U. of SC, 1937, J.D., 1970. POLIT. & GOV.: elected as a Democrat to lt. gov. of SC, 1947–55; pres., SC State Democratic Convention, 1948; delegate, Dem. Nat'l. Conv., 1948, 1956; pres., Lexington Cty. (SC) Democratic Convention, 1950, 1952; member, SC State Democratic Exec. cmte., 1952–54; elected as a Democrat to gov. of SC, 1955–59; ***candidate for Democratic nomination to presidency of the U.S., 1956***; presidential elector, Democratic Party, 1964; appointed judge, 11th Judicial Circuit of SC, 1967–. BUS. & PROF.: atty.; admitted to SC Bar, 1937; partner, Timmerman and Timmerman (law firm), Lexington, SC, 1937–41; trial atty., SC Public Service Authority, 1941–42; law practice, Lexington, SC, 1942, 1946–55, 1959–67. MIL.: ensign, lt., U.S.N.R., 1942–46. MEM.: BSA (national council, 1947–48); American Cancer Soc. (campaign chm., SC Div., 1947); ABA; SC Bar Assn.; American Jud. Soc.; U.S. Judicial Conference (permanent member, 4th Circuit); American Legion; Forty and Eight; VFW; Reserve Officers Assn.; SC Hist. Soc.; Blue Key; Phi Delta Phi; Wig and Robe; Pi Kappa Phi; National Governors' Conference (exec. cmte., 1957–58); Lions; Batesburg-Leesville C. of C.; Lexington C. of C.; Modern Woodmen of the World. HON. DEG.: LL.D., The Citadel, 1955. REL.: Bapt. (deacon). MAILING ADDRESS: 207 Main St., Lexington, SC 29072.

TIMMONS, BASCOM NOLLEY. b. Mar 31, 1890, Collin Cty., TX; d. Jun 7, 1987, Washington, DC; par. Commodore Amplias and Martha Ann (Crenshaw) Timmons; m. Ethel Boardman, Aug 8, 1925; c. none. EDUC.: public schools; military acad. POLIT. & GOV.: ***candidate for Democratic nomination to vice presidency of the U.S., 1940, 1944***. BUS. & PROF.: journalist; reporter, *Fort Worth (TX) Record*, 1906; reporter, *Dallas (TX) Times-Herald*, 1907; managing ed., *Amarillo (TX) News*, 1910; staff, *Milwaukee (WI) Sentinel*, 1911; staff, *Washington (DC) Post*, 1912–13; owner, ed., *Daily Panhandle*, Amarillo, TX, 1914–16; DC correspondent, *Houston (TX) Chronicle*, 1917–73; DC correspondent, *Fort Worth (TX) Star-Telegram*; DC correspondent, *Wilmington (DE) Morning News*; DC correspondent, *Wilmington (DE) Evening Journal*; DC correspondent, *Baton Rouge (LA) State Times*; DC correspondent, *New Orleans (LA) States-Item*; DC correspondent, *Shreveport (LA) Times*; DC correspondent, *Arkansas Democrat*; DC correspondent, *Nashville (TN) Tennessean*; DC correspondent, *Chattanooga (TN) News-Free Press*; DC correspondent, *Raleigh (NC) News and Observer*; DC correspondent, *Youngstown (OH) Vindicator*; DC correspondent, *Jackson (MS) Clarion-Ledger*; DC correspondent, *Wichita (KS) Eagle and Beacon*; DC correspondent, *Dayton (OH) Herald Journal*. MIL.: pvt., U.S. Army, WWI. MEM.: Phil. Soc. of TX; Elks; National Press Club (pres., 1932); Sigma Delta Chi (member, Hall of Fame, 1971); Gridiron Club. AWARDS: Biography Award, TX Heritage Foundation, 1958. WRITINGS: *Garner of Texas*; *Portrait of an American: A Biography of Charles Gates Dawes*; *Jesse H. Jones, the Man and the Statesman*. REL.: Methodist. RES.: Amarillo, TX.

TINLEY, MATHEW ADRIAN. b. Mar 5, 1876, Council Bluffs, IA; d. Mar 11, 1956, Council Bluffs, IA; par. Mathew Hugh and Rose (Dolan) Tinley; m. Lucy Shaw Williams, Oct 8, 1902; c. Winifred M.; Robert E. EDUC.: M.D., U. of NE, 1902; NY postgrad. school of Medicine, 1902. POLIT. & GOV.: ***candidate for Democratic nomination to vice presidency of the U.S., 1932***. BUS. & PROF.: industrial surgeon; staff surgeon, Janie Edmundson Hospital, 1903; surgeon, Union Pacific R.R. Co., 1905–20; surgeon, Wabash R.R. Co., 1920–36; surgeon, C. & N.W. R.R., 1936; examiner for Aetna Connecticut Mutual Insurance Co., and Iowa Employers Mutual Insurance Co. MIL.: U.S. Army, Philippine Islands, 1898–99; col., 168th Infantry, 42d Div., WWI; maj. gen., U.S. National Guard, 1940; lt. gen., IA State Guard; Distinguished Service Medal; Philippines Congressional Medal (U.S.); Legion of Honor (France); Croix de Guerre (France). MEM.: Elks; Phi Rho Sigma; Knights of Columbus; Council Bluffs Club; Order of Carribao; Newcomen Soc. (Great Britain); American Legion (first deputy commander of IA); VFW; F.A.C.S.; American Medical Assn.; IA State Medical Assn. (vice pres., 1920); Wabash Surgeons Assn. (pres., 1934); American Assn. of Railroad Surgeons (pres., 1939); National Rainbow Veterans Soc. (pres.); National Guard Assn. of America (pres., 1934). AWARDS: Gold Medal, U.S. Flag Assn., 1934. REL.: R.C. RES.: Council Bluffs, IA.

TIPTON, THOMAS WESTON. b. Aug 5, 1817, Cadis, OH; d. Nov 26, 1899, Washington, DC; par. Rev. William and _______ (Weston) Tipton; m. Rachel Irwin Moore; c. Thomas Corwin; William M.; D. Perry; Kate (Mrs. H. M. Atkinson). EDUC.: Alleghany Coll., 1836–38; grad., Madison Coll., 1840; studied law. POLIT. & GOV.: elected as a Whig to OH State House, 1845; appointed to position, U.S. Land Office, 1849–52; member, NE State Constitutional Convention, 1859, 1867; member, NE Territorial Council, 1860; appointed Assessor of Internal Revenue for NE, 1865; elected as a Republican to U.S. Senate (NE), 1867–75; ***candidate for Liberal Republican Party nomination to vice presidency of the U.S., 1872***; Democratic candidate for gov. of NE, 1880; appointed Receiver, U.S. Land Office, Bloomington, NE, 1885. BUS. & PROF.: atty.; admitted to Bar, 1844; law practice, 1844–99; law practice, McConnelsville, OH, 1853; minister, Methodist Episcopal Church, 1856; pres., Brownville Coll., Brownville, NE, 1858. MIL.: chaplain, 1st Regt., NE Volunteer Infantry, 1861–65. WRITINGS: *Forty Years of Nebraska* (1902). REL.: Congregationalist (nee Methodist Episc.). RES.: Brownville, NE.

TIREBITER, GEORGE L. POLIT. & GOV.: ***National Surrealist Party candidate for vice presidency of the U.S., 1972, 1976***. MISC.: reportedly a pseudonym for for Randy Ossman, a member of the Firesign Theater, Santa Barbara, CA. MAILING ADDRESS: Santa Barbara, CA.

TISCH, ROBERT EMMANUEL "BOB." b. Mar 28, 1920, Jackson, MI; par. Emmanuel A. and Clara

(Schlenker) Tisch; m. Bethel J. York; c. Susan; Cathy; Betsy; Robert C.; Heidi. EDUC.: MI State U.; U. of MI; Lansing Community Coll.; U.S. Armed Forces Inst.; U. of FL. POLIT. & GOV.: elected pres., Shiawassee Cty. (MI) Board of Education, 1956; member, Shiawassee Cty. (MI) Drain Commission, 1977–; city judge; city assessor; police chief; constable; member, elections board; Tisch Independent Citizens Party candidate for gov. of MI, 1982, 1990; founder, chm., Tisch Independent Citizens Party; ***Tisch Independent Citizens Party candidate for vice presidency of the U.S., 1992***. BUS. & PROF.: co-owner, outdoor advertising firm; cabinet and furniture maker; printer; cattle rancher. MIL.: chemical-biological-bacteriological warfare officer, 85th Infantry, U.S. Army, WWII; commanding officer, mortar unit, 13th Airborne Div., Korean War; Presidential Unit Citation. REL.: Lutheran. MISC.: leader of property tax limitation movement. MAILING ADDRESS: 113 North Woodhull St., Laingsburg, MI 48848-0381.

TISDAL, VICTOR CLIFFORD. b. Jan 3, 1886, Fannin Cty., TX; d. May, 1948, Oklahoma City, OK; m. Inez St. John Smith; m. 2d, Ina Garnett; c. Victor Clifford, Jr.; Edwina Joy Ferguson; Jack Edwin. EDUC.: certificate, Cordell Acad.; U. of OK; M.D., Fort Worth (TX) Medical School, 1910. POLIT. & GOV.: ***Jobless Party candidate for vice presidency of the U.S., 1932***; elected mayor of Elk City, OK, 1939–43; appointed member, National Emergency Medical Service Cmte., WWII. BUS. & PROF.: physician; medical practice, Hammon, OK, 1908–13; medical practice, Elk City, OK, 1913–48; founder, partner, Francis Hospital, Elk City, OK, 1913–18; founder, chief of staff, Tisdal Hospital, Elk City, OK, 1924–48; founder, Nurses School, Tisdal Hospital, Elk City, OK, 1924–32; owner, chief of staff, Sayre Hospital, 1930–48. MIL.: surgeon, U.S. Army, 1918; National Guard (maj.). MEM.: Elk City C. of C. (pres., 1936); Rotary International (Elk City pres.); OK State Medical Assn. (delegate, 1929–41, pres., 1941). REL.: Methodist. RES.: Elk City, OK.

TITTL, PETER FREDERICK. b. Manitowac, WI; par. Frederick Karl and Rita Marie (Daley) Tittl; m. Suzette Marie Kosner. EDUC.: B.A., U. of WI, 1977. POLIT. & GOV.: ***independent candidate for presidency of the U.S., 1980***. BUS. & PROF.: freelance writer; novelist; journalist. REL.: R.C. MAILING ADDRESS: 417 Oakland Ave., Apt. 1, South Beloit, IL 61080.

TITUS, CHARLES EDWARD. b. Jul 1, 1941, Riverview, MI; par. Charles R. Titus; m. Danielle R. T.; c. one. EDUC.: high school. POLIT. & GOV.: ***American Reform Cmte. candidate for presidency of the U.S., 1980***. REL.: yes. MAILING ADDRESS: P.O. Box 109, Johannesberg, MI 49751.

TOAL, ROBERT AUGUSTINE. b. Nov 22, 1928; deceased. EDUC.: B.S., St. Joseph's Coll., 1950; M.S., Richmond Professional Inst., 1956. POLIT. & GOV.: ***independent (Cmte. for a Constitutional Presidency) candidate for vice presidency of the U.S., 1976***. BUS. & PROF.: psychologist, Central State Hospital, Petersburg, VA, 1956; asst. in psychology, Medical Coll. of VA, 1956–57; asst. psychologist, Eastern State Hospital of TN, 1957–58; junior psychologist, Oak Ridge Mental Health Center, Oak Ridge, TN, 1958–; prof. of Psychology, Purdue U. MIL.: psychiatric asst., U.S. Air Force, 1950–54. MEM.: American Psych. Assn. RES.: KNOXVILLE, TN.

TOBIN, ROBERT L. POLIT. & GOV.: ***independent candidate for presidency of the U.S., 1992***. MISC.: known as "Fugly." MAILING ADDRESS: 1107 Madison St., Suite 3, Syracuse, NY 13210.

TOD, DAVID. b. Feb 21, 1805, Youngstown, OH; d. Nov 13, 1868, OH; par. George and Sarah (Isaacs) Tod; m. Maria Smith, Jun 4, 1832; c. seven. EDUC.: Burton Acad.; read law under Powell Stone. POLIT. & GOV.: appointed postmaster, Warren, OH, 1830–38; elected as a Democrat to OH State Senate, 1838–40; Democratic candidate for gov. of OH, 1844, 1846; appointed U.S. minister to Brazil, 1847–51; delegate, Dem. Nat'l. Conv., 1860; elected as a Unionist to gov. of OH, 1861–63; candidate for Union Party nomination to gov. of OH, 1863; appointed U.S. sec. of the treasury, 1864 (declined); ***candidate for Republican nomination to vice presidency of the U.S., 1864***; presidential elector, Republican Party, 1868. BUS. & PROF.: atty.; admitted to OH Bar, 1827; founder, Youngstown Iron Industry; pres., Cleveland and Mahoning Valley R.R., 1858–68. RES.: Youngstown, OH.

TODD, ALBERT MAY. b. Jun 3, 1850, Nottawa, MI; d. Oct 6, 1931, Kalamazoo, MI; par. Alfred and Mary Ann (Hovey) Todd; m. Augusta Margaret Allman, Jan 23, 1878; c. William Alfred; Albert John; Ethel May (Mrs. Edwin LeGrand Woodhams); Paul Harold; Allman. EDUC.: grad., Sturgis (MI) H.S.; Northwestern U., 1867–68. POLIT. & GOV.: Prohibition Party candidate for gov. of MI, 1894; ***National Reform Party candidate for vice presidency of the U.S., 1896***; elected as a Fusionist to U.S. House (MI), 1897–99; Democratic candidate for U.S. House (MI), 1898. BUS. & PROF.: chemist; pres., A. M. Todd and Co., Kalamazoo, MI, 1889–1929, chm. of the board, 1929–31; philanthropist; advocate of public ownership; peppermint farmer. MEM.: Todd Foundation (pres.); Public Ownership League of America (founder; pres., 1916–22; hon. pres., 1922–31); American Acad. of Political and Social Science; American Proportional Representation League; MI Acad. of Science, Arts and Letters; National Direct Legislation League (vice pres.); Cooperative League of America; A.C.L.U.; League for Industrial Democracy; National Child Labor Cmte.; Soc. of Chemical Industry; AAAS; American Pharmaceutical Assn.; American Chemical Soc.; American Peace Soc.; Archaeological Inst. of America; Bibliographical

Soc.; Oxford Bibliographical Soc.; Fabian Soc.; St. Andrew's Soc.; Union Internationale des Villes; National Arts Club; Civic Club; Grolier Club; Cosmos Club; Gaxton Club; CA Book Club. HON. DEG.: A.M., U. of MI, 1922. WRITINGS: *Municipal Ownership in Europe and America* (1918); *The Relation of Public Ownership to Social justice and Democracy* (1920). RES.: Kalamazoo, MI.

TOMLINSON, HOMER AUBREY. b. Oct 25, 1892, Westfield, IN; d. Dec 6, 1968, New York, NY; par. Ambrose Jessup and Mary Jane (Taylor) Tomlinson; m. Marie Wunch, Nov 22, 1919; c. Halcy; Ambrose Jess; Homer E. EDUC.: U. of TN, 1911–13. POLIT. & GOV.: ***Church of God Party candidate for presidency of the U.S., 1952***; founder, Theocratic Party; ***Theocratic Party candidate for presidency of the U.S., 1960, 1964, 1968***. BUS. & PROF.: staff, Church of God Publishing House, Cleveland, TN, 1900–1923; principal, high school, TN, 1913–14; sec., Culver Military Acad. Summer School, 1914–17; employee, various advertising firms, schools, colleges, and publishing houses, New York, NY, 1916–28; ordained minister, Church of God, 1923–68; NY State overseer, Church of God, 1923–43; pastor, Jamaica Tabernacle (Church of God), 1923–43; co-founder, Lee Coll.; gen. overseer, Church of God, 1943–68; ed., *The Church of God*. MIL.: tank corps, U.S. Army, WWI. MEM.: World Wars Tank Corps Assn. (national chaplain); American Legion. WRITINGS: *Home Study Bible Lessons* (20 vols., 1919); *The Church of God* (1919); *The Great Vision of the Church of God* (1939); *Diary of A. J. Tomlinson, 1901–43* (3 vols., 1949); *Amazing Fulfillment of Prophecy* (1935); *The Kingdom of God* (1960); *Theocracy* (1962); *The Shout of a King* (1968). REL.: Church of God. MISC.: self-proclaimed "King of All the Nations of Men." RES.: Queens Village, NY.

TOMOSOVICH, GLENDA JEAN. POLIT. & GOV.: ***independent candidate for presidency of the U.S., 1988***. MAILING ADDRESS: Route 6, Box 151, Rocky Mount, VA 24151.

TOMPKINS, DANIEL D. b. Jun 21, 1774, Scarsdale, NY; d. Jun 11, 1825, Staten Island, NY; par. Jonathan G. and Sarah (Hyatt) Tompkins; m. Hannah Minthorne, Feb 20, 1798; c. Arietta; Griffin; Hannah Ellsworth; Sarah Ann; Minthorne; Daniel Hyatt; Susan McLaren; Ray. EDUC.: grad., Columbia U., 1795. POLIT. & GOV.: delegate, NY State Constitutional Convention, 1801, 1821 (pres.); elected as a Democrat to NY State Assembly, 1803; elected as a Democrat to U.S. House (NY), 1804; appointed assoc. justice, NY State Supreme Court, 1804–07; elected as a Democrat to gov. of NY, 1807–17; appointed U.S. sec. of state, 1814 (declined); ***elected as a Democrat to vice presidency of the U.S., 1817–1825***; Democratic candidate for gov. of NY, 1820. BUS. & PROF.: atty.; admitted to NY Bar, 1797; law practice, New York, NY. MIL.: commander in chief, NY Militia, 1812–14. MEM.: NY State Hist. Soc. (founder). REL.: Presb. MISC.: middle initial added to name to distinguish Tompkins from a classmate of the same name. RES.: New York, NY.

TOMPKINS, VINTON MICHAEL "MIKE." b. Nov 29, 1948, Boston, MA. EDUC.: grad. (with honors), Harvard U., 1970; doctorate in the Science of Creative Intelligence, Maharishi European Research U. (Switzerland), 1984. POLIT. & GOV.: ***Natural Law Party candidate for vice presidency of the U.S., 1992***. BUS. & PROF.: author; lecturer. REL.: follower of Maharishi Mahesh Yogi. AWARDS: National Merit Scholar, 1966; Presidential Scholar, 1966. MAILING ADDRESS: 403 Silver Lakes Dr., Fairfield, IA 52556.

TOOLE, JOHN KENNEDY. b. Apr 28, 1944, South Orange, NJ; par. John Crawford, Sr. and Helen (Storvinger) McDonald; m. Mary Ellen Early, 1963; m. 2d, Alice Ann Anderson, 1972; c. John; Patrick; Andrea; Ashley. EDUC.: Bayley-Ellard, 1962. POLIT. & GOV.: NY state dir., Kennedy for President Campaign, 1980; candidate for Democratic nomination to U.S. House (NY), 1980, 1982; ***candidate for Democratic nomination to presidency of the U.S., 1984***. BUS. & PROF.: pres., Sales and Bargains; vice pres., Warnaco (Hathaway-Patch Div.). MEM.: Junior C. of C.; John Kennedy Toole Federal Club; United Democratic Service Corp. (pres.); Toole's Plan. AWARDS: "Jaycee of the Month," 1963. WRITINGS: *Silent Tears* (1969). REL.: R.C. MAILING ADDRESS: 211 East 81st St., Room 105, New York, NY 10028.

TOOMBS, ROBERT AUGUSTUS. b. Jul 2, 1810, Wilkes Cty., GA; d. Dec 15, 1885, Washington, DC; par. Robert and Catherine (Huling) Toombs; m. Julia Ann DuBois, Nov 18, 1830; c. Sallie; Mary Louisa; Lawrence Catlett. EDUC.: U. of GA, 1824–28; A.B., Union Coll., 1828; U. of VA, 1828–29. POLIT. & GOV.: elected as a Whig to GA State House, 1837–40, 1841–44; delegate, Dem. Nat'l. Conv., 1844; elected as a State's Rights Democrat to U.S. House (GA), 1845–53; elected as a Constitutional Unionist-Democrat to U.S. Senate (GA), 1853–61 (withdrew); delegate, GA Secession Convention, 1861; delegate, Montgomery Convention, 1861; member, Provisional Congress, Confederate States of America, 1861; appointed sec. of state, Confederate States of America, 1861; ***independent candidate for president of the Confederacy, 1861***; candidate for Senate, Confederate States of America, 1863; delegate, GA State Constitutional Convention, 1877; ***candidate for Democratic nomination to presidency of the U.S., 1884***. BUS. & PROF.: atty.; admitted to GA Bar, 1830; law practice, Washington, GA, 1828; upon conclusion of Civil War, returned to GA and resumed law practice. MIL.: commanded company, Creek War, 1836; brig. gen., C.S.A., 1861–62; inspector gen., GA Militia, 1864. REL.: Methodist. MISC.: strong proponent of slavery; fled to London following end of Civil War, 1865–67. RES.: Washington, GA.

TOPHAM, LAWRENCE REY. b. Aug 11, 1936, Salt Lake City, UT; par. Merlin June and Dorothy (Giles) Topham; m. Cathleen Jaquier; c. Michael; Lane; Cory; April; Heidi. EDUC.: L.D.S. Business Coll., U. of UT. POLIT. & GOV.: candidate for mayor of Salt Lake City, UT, 1967; ***candidate for American Party nomination to presidency of the U.S., 1976***; American Party candidate for U.S. House (UT), 1978; candidate for American Party nomination to U.S. Senate (UT), 1980; American Party candidate for gov. of UT, 1980; Independent Party of UT candidate for U.S. House (UT), 1990. BUS. & PROF.: life insurance agent; securities agent; private investigator, UT Special Patrol; purchasing agent, Primary Children's Hospital; gold and silver broker. MEM.: BSA. REL.: Church of Jesus Christ of Latter-Day Saints. MAILING ADDRESS: 3991 Las Flores St., Salt Lake City, UT 84119.

TORRES, JOSE ANTONIO, II. b. Sep 29, 1957, Santurce, Puerto Rico; par. Joe and Carmen Delia (Rosario) Torres; single. EDUC.: B.A., U. of TX; art schools. POLIT. & GOV.: ***Protectionist-Democrat, Conservative-Republican candidate for presidency of the U.S., 1976***. BUS. & PROF.: employee, Amway Corp.; college student. MEM.: college organizations. REL.: R.C.-Tarchanic. MAILING ADDRESS: 2923 Harrison Ave., El Paso, TX 79930.

TORRES, JUSTIN ALAN. POLIT. & GOV.: ***independent candidate for presidency of the U.S., 1988***. MAILING ADDRESS: 4329 Lawrence St., Alexandria, VA 22309.

TORREY, JAY LINN. b. Oct 16, 1852; d. Dec 4, 1920; par. Amos Root and Minerva Lucretia (Norton) Torrey. POLIT. & GOV.: elected as a Republican to WY State House (Speaker, 1895–97); ***candidate for Republican nomination to vice presidency of the U.S., 1900***. BUS. & PROF.: ed., *Bankruptcy Magazine*, 1897; pres., Embar Cattle Co.; rancher; atty. MIL.: col., Rough Riders, 1898; Torrey's unit did not leave the U.S. during the Spanish-American War. WRITINGS: *Bankruptcy* (1889); *Report of the Committee on Bills*; *The Torrey Bankrupt Bill*; *Military Record and an Appreciation of Robert Augustus Torrey, by His Brother Linn* (1917). RES.: Embar, WY.

TORVALD, UNCLE (See JOHNSON, ROBERT L.).

TOTTEN, GLEN ELDON. b. Nov 26, 1939, Mt. Erie, IL; par. Chester O. and Margie Elva (Marks) Totten; m. Barbara Statler (divorced); m. 2d, Dorothy Conley (divorced); c. Keith Eric. EDUC.: Cisne (IL) Community H.S.; Fairfield (IL) H.S.; Calvary Bible Inst., Lakeland, FL. POLIT. & GOV.: ***independent candidate for presidency of the U.S., 1980***. BUS. & PROF.: sign painter; silk screen artist; office mgr., Johnson Park, Inc., Springfield, IL; author. MEM.: Junior C. of C. AWARDS: Jaycee of the Year; Outstanding Jaycee; John H. Armbruster Award. REL.: Episc. MISC.: inmate in correctional institutions, 22 years; incarcerated at Federal Correctional Institution, Oxford, WI (for bank robbery), 1973–. MAILING ADDRESS: Post Office Box 1000, Oxford, WI 53952.

TOUCEY, ISAAC. b. Nov 5, 1796, Newton, CT; d. Jul 30, 1869, Hartford, CT; par. Zalmon and Phebe (Booth) Toucey; m. Catherine Nichols, Oct 28, 1827; c. none. EDUC.: studied law under Asa Chapman. POLIT. & GOV.: state's atty., Hartford Cty., CT, 1822–35, 1842–44; elected as a Democrat to U.S. House (CT), 1835–39; Democratic candidate for U.S. House (CT), 1838; Democratic candidate for gov. of CT, 1845, 1847; elected as a Democrat to gov. of CT, 1846 (election by legislature); appointed atty. gen. of the U.S., 1848–49; acting U.S. sec. of state; elected as a Democrat to CT State Senate, 1850–52; elected as a Democrat to CT State House, 1852; elected as a Democrat to U.S. Senate (CT), 1852–57; appointed U.S. sec. of the navy, 1857–61; ***candidate for Democratic nomination to presidency of the U.S., 1860***. BUS. & PROF.: atty.; admitted to CT Bar, 1818; law practice, Hartford, CT. RES.: Hartford, CT.

TOVAR, ERIC. m. Irene Tovar. POLIT. & GOV.: ***candidate for Democratic nomination to vice presidency of the U.S., 1980***. MAILING ADDRESS: c/o Irene Tovar, 14801 Wolfskill St., Mission Hills, CA 91345.

TOWER, JOHN GOODWIN. b. Sep 29, 1925, Houston, TX; d. Apr 5, 1991, Brunswick, GA; par. Joe Z. and Beryl (Goodwin) Tower; m. Joza Lou Bullington, Mar 21, 1952 (divorced); c. Penelope; Marian; Jeanne. EDUC.: B.A., Southwestern U., 1948, Litt.D., 1964; M.A., Southern Methodist U., 1953; London School of Economics and Political Science, 1952–53. POLIT. & GOV.: elected as a Republican to U.S. Senate (TX), 1961–85; delegate, Rep. Nat'l. Conv., 1956, 1960, 1964, 1968, 1972; ***candidate for Republican nomination to presidency of the U.S., 1968; candidate for Republican nomination to vice presidency of the U.S., 1968***; appointed U.S. sec. of defense, 1989 (not confirmed). BUS. & PROF.: asst. prof. of Political Science, Midwestern U., 1951–60. MIL.: seaman first class, U.S. Navy, 1943–46; CPO, U.S.N.R. MEM.: Southern Methodist U. (trustee); Southwestern U. (trustee); AAUP; APSA; International Political Science Assn.; Shriners; Kiwanis; Masons (32°); American Legion; U.S. Naval Inst.; TX Hist. Soc.; C. of C.; Wichita Falls Symphony; Kappa Sigma (Worthy Grand Procurator). AWARDS: "Man of the Year," Kappa Sigma, 1961. HON. DEG.: LL.D., Howard Payne Coll., 1963. WRITINGS: *Consequences* (1991). REL.: Methodist. RES.: Wichita Falls, TX.

TOWERS, REGINALD SULLIVAN VOYLE. POLIT. & GOV.: ***candidate for Democratic nomination to presidency of the U.S., 1976, 1988, 1992; independent Mammon Party candidate for presidency of the U.S.,***

1976. BUS. & PROF.: desk clerk, Brentmar, Inc., Santa Monica, CA. MAILING ADDRESS: 1801 Darby Rd., Sebastopol, CA 95472.

TOWNE, CHARLES ARNETTE. b. Nov 21, 1858, Pontiac, MI; d. Oct 22, 1928, Tucson, AZ; par. Charles Judson and Laura Ann (Fargo) Towne; m. Maude Irene Wiley, Apr 20, 1887; m. 2d, Alice Reinhart Elkin, Mar 3, 1917; c. none. EDUC.: Owosso (MI) H.S.; Ph.B., U. of MI, 1881; studied law. POLIT. & GOV.: chief clerk, MI State Dept. of Public Instruction, 1881; clerk, MI State Treasury Dept.; Republican candidate for U.S. House (MN), 1888 (declined); judge advocate gen. of MN, 1893–95; elected as a Republican to U.S. House (MN), 1895–97; delegate, Rep. Nat'l. Conv., 1896; Democratic (Fusion) candidate for U.S. House (MN), 1896, 1898; ***candidate for People's Party nomination to presidency of the U.S., 1896; candidate for Democratic nomination to presidency of the U.S., 1896, 1900, 1904, 1908, 1912***; chm., National Silver Republican Party, 1897–1901; Democratic (Fusion) candidate for U.S. Senate (MN), 1899; ***candidate for Democratic nomination to vice presidency of the U.S., 1900, 1908***; chm., Silver Republican Party National Convention, 1900; ***Silver Republican Party candidate for vice presidency of the U.S., 1900 (declined); People's Party candidate for vice presidency of the U.S., 1900 (declined)***; appointed as a Democrat to U.S. Senate (MN), 1900–1901; delegate, Dem. Nat'l. Conv., 1904; elected as a Democrat to U.S. House (NY), 1905–07. BUS. & PROF.: atty.; admitted to MI Bar, 1886; law practice, Marquette, MI, 1886–89; law practice, Chicago, IL, 1889–90; partner (with Samuel H. Moer and Luther C. Harris), law firm, Duluth, MN, 1890–93; partner, Phelps, Towne and Harris (law firm), Duluth, MN, 1895; law practice, New York, NY, 1901–28; partner, Towne and Spellman (law firm), New York, NY; pres., Central Asphalt and Refining Co.; pres., Export Oil and Pipe Line Co.; pres., Charles A. Towne and Co., Inc., New York, NY; dir., California King Gold Mines Co.; dir., Rio Del Monte Mining Co. WRITINGS: *The Restoration of Silver the Duty of the Republican Party* (1896). MISC.: advocate of bimetallism. RES.: New York, NY.

TOWNSEND, FRANCES EVERETT. b. Jan 13, 1867, Fairbury, IL; d. Sep 1, 1960, Los Angeles, CA; par. George Warren and Sarah Jane (Harper) Townsend; m. Mrs. Wilhelmina Mollie "Minnie" Bogue, Oct 30, 1906; c. Robert Craig; Marlyn (Mrs. Lester Pennock); two others. EDUC.: grad., Franklin Acad., 1893; M.D., U. of NE, 1903. POLIT. & GOV.: appointed asst. Health Officer, Long Beach, CA; ***candidate for Republican nomination to presidency of the U.S., 1936***; founder, Union Party, 1936. BUS. & PROF.: farmer, KS, 1893–98; laborer, CO; stove salesman, KS; physician; medical practice, Belle Fourche, SD, 1903–19; medical practice, Long Beach, CA, 1919–31; pres., Townsend Plan, Inc.; pres., Townsend National Weekly; pres., United Publishing Co. MIL.: 1st lt., medical corps, U.S. Army, 1917–18. MEM.: Townsend Plan, Inc. (pres.); Townsend Foundation (pres.; trustee). AWARDS: Wilson Service Medal; winner, "Life Begins at Eighty" Contest, Mutual Broadcasting System, 1949. HON. DEG.: LL.D., Metropolitan U. of Los Angeles, 1950. WRITINGS: *The Townsend National Recovery Plan* (1934); *Old Age Revolving Pensions* (1934); *New Horizons* (1943). MISC.: physician to indigent; originator of Townsend Old Age Revolving Pension Plan; sentenced to jail for contempt of Congress; received presidential commutation, 1937. RES.: Los Angeles, CA.

TOWNSEND, RALPH PRESTON. b. Mar 11, 1915, Texarkana, TX; par. Eli Larry and Pearl Beatrice (Rodgers) Townsend; m. Evelyn Lorraine James; c. five. EDUC.: grad., Texarkana (TX) H.S.; Texarkana Business Coll.; Dallas (TX) Aviation School. POLIT. & GOV.: candidate for Dallas (TX) City Council, 1981; ***independent Democratic candidate for presidency of the U.S., 1988***. BUS. & PROF.: employee, Bell Helicopter Co., Fort Worth, TX; employee, Braniff Airways; employee, Dallas Aero Service; instructor, Dallas Aviation School. MEM.: Masons (Royal Arch; Knights Templar; Scottish Rite; Eastern Star; Shriners). AWARDS: Order of High Priesthood; Order of Silver Trowel; Order of Malta. REL.: Presb. (elder). MAILING ADDRESS: 3326 June Dr., Dallas, TX 75211.

TRACY, BENJAMIN FRANKLIN. b. Apr 26, 1830, Owego, NY; d. Aug 6, 1915, Brooklyn, NY; par. Benjamin Franklin and Bathseba Woodin (Jewett) Tracy; m. Delinda E. Catlin, 1851; c. Emma Louise; Mary Farrington; Frank Broadhead. EDUC.: Owego Acad.; studied law under N. W. Davis, Owego, NY. POLIT. & GOV.: elected as a Whig, district atty., Tioga Cty., NY, 1853–59; founder, Republican Party of NY, 1854; elected as a Republican to NY State Assembly, 1862; appointed U.S. district atty., Eastern District of NY, 1866–73; appointed judge, NY Court of Appeals, 1881–82; appointed U.S. sec. of the navy, 1889–93; pres., Greater NY Charter Comm., 1896; ***candidate for Republican nomination to presidency of the U.S., 1896; candidate for Republican nomination to vice presidency of the U.S., 1896***; Republican candidate for mayor, Greater New York, NY, 1897. BUS. & PROF.: atty.; admitted to NY Bar, 1851; partner, Benedict, Burr and Benedict (law firm), New York, NY, 1865–66; law practice, Brooklyn, NY, 1873–81; partner (with William C. DeWitt and F. B. Tracy), law firm, Brooklyn, NY, 1883–89; partner, Tracy, MacFarland, Boardman and Platt (law firm), New York, NY, 1885–1915; horse breeder, Tioga Cty., NY. MIL.: col., 109th NY Volunteers, 1862–64; col., 127th U.S. Colored Troops, 1864; commander, military post, Elmira, NY, 1864–65; brev. brig. gen., U.S.V., 1865; Medal of Honor, 1895. MEM.: GAR. REL.: Congregationalist. RES.: Brooklyn, NY.

TRACY, JOSEPH PLATT. b. Feb 28, 1866, Monmouth, IL; par. Alexander H. and Harriet (Sherwin) Tracy; m. Ada M. Heuston, Sep 17, 1899. EDUC.: Monmouth (IL) Coll. POLIT. & GOV.: Prohibition Party candidate for Sheriff, Cook

Cty., IL, 1902; ***candidate for Prohibition Party nomination to presidency of the U.S., 1908***. BUS. & PROF.: gen. mgr., Transportation Lines, Chicago, IL. MEM.: Minnehaha Club (pres.); Union League. RES.: Chicago, IL.

TRAFICANT, JAMES A., JR. b. May 8, 1941, Youngstown, OH; par. James A. and Agnes (Faras) Traficant; m. Patricia Choppa; c. Robin; Elizabeth. EDUC.: B.S., U. of Pittsburgh, 1963, M.S., 1973; M.S., Youngstown State U., 1976. POLIT. & GOV.: sheriff, Mahoning Cty., OH, 1981–85; elected as a Democrat to U.S. House (OH), 1985–; ***candidate for Democratic nomination to presidency of the U.S., 1988; candidate for Populist Party nomination to presidency of the U.S., 1988***. BUS. & PROF.: dir., Mahoning Cty. Drug Program, 1971–81; consumer finance dir., Youngstown (OH) Community Action Program; state mgr., Girard Life Insurance. AWARDS: Outstanding Citizen Award, Youngstown (OH) Fraternal Order of Police, 1980; Outstanding Service Award, Inner City Helping Hand, Inc., 1984. REL.: R.C. MAILING ADDRESS: 11 Overhill Dr., Youngstown, OH 44512.

TRAIN, GEORGE FRANCIS. b. Mar 24, 1829, Boston, MA; d. Jan 19, 1904, New York, NY; par. Oliver and Maria (Pickering) Train; m. Wilhelmina Wilkinson Davis, Oct 5, 1851; c. Lily; Susan (Mrs. P. D. Gulager); George; Elsey McHenry. EDUC.: public schools. POLIT. & GOV.: delegate, Peace Convention, 1863; ***candidate for Democratic nomination to presidency of the U.S., 1864, 1868, 1872; Citizens Party candidate for pres., 1864, 1872***; candidate for Republican nomination to U.S. House (NY), 1868; ***candidate for Liberal Republican Party nomination to presidency of the U.S., 1872; candidate for Labor Reform Party nomination to presidency of the U.S., 1872***; delegate, Straight-Out (Taproot) Democratic Party National Convention, 1872; ***candidate for Straight-Out (Taproot) Democratic Party nomination to presidency of the U.S., 1872; independent candidate for presidency of the U.S., 1900 (declined)***. BUS. & PROF.: farmer; grocery clerk; shipping clerk, Enoch Train Shipping Co. (mgr., Liverpool office, 1850); author; founder, Train and Co. (shipping agents), Melbourne, Australia, 1853; partner, Caldwell, Train and Co.; financier; initiated clipper service to CA, 1849; railroad promoter (Atlantic and Great Western R.R., 1858; European Lines, 1860–62; Union Pacific R.R., 1864–69); founder, Credit Mobilier of America, 1862; landowner, NE; investor, restaurants and turkish baths; ed., *The Train Ligne*; publisher, *London American*; publisher, *Train's Penny Magazine*. WRITINGS: *An American Merchant in Europe, Asia and Australia* (1857); *Young America Abroad* (1857); *Young America on Slavery* (1857); *Young America in Wall Street* (1858); *Spread Eagleism* (1859); *Every Man His Own Autocrat* (1859); *Observations on Horse Railways* (1860); *The Facts: or, at Whose Door Does the Sin (?) Lie?* (1860); *Street Railways* (1860); *Young America After Old Ireland* (1862); *Downfall of England* (1862); *Train's Speeches in England on Slavery and Emancipation* (1862); *G. F. T., Unionist, on T. Colley Grattan, Secessionist* (1862); *Train's Union Speeches Delivered in England During the Present War* (1862); *George Francis Train and the Pennsylvanians* (1864); *Irish Independence* (1861); *G. F. T.'s Great Speech on the Withdrawal of McClellan and the Impeachment of Lincoln* (1864); *Letter from George F. Train* (1864); *G. F. T. In Cleaning Out the Copperheads Follows Up George B. McClellan With a Sharp Stick* (1864); *A Voice from the Pit* (1864); *Speech of G. F. T. on Irish Independence and English Neutrality* (1865); *G. F. T. Showing Up the Monroe Doctrine* (1866); *Championship of Women* (1867); *G. F. T. in a British Jail* (1868); *An American Eagle in a British Cage, or Four Days in a Felon's Cell* (1868); *My Life in Many States and in Foreign Lands* (1902). REL.: atheist (nee Methodist). MISC.: organized French commune at Marseilles, Oct 1870; made four trips around the world (holding world record for same), inspiring Jules Verne's novel *Around the World in Eighty Days*; advocate of Irish Republic; arrested for printing "obscene material" (Biblical passages defending Victoria Woodhull, q.v.); offered presidency of proposed Australian Five Star Republic, 1854 (declined); campaigned for "Dictator of the U.S.," 1873; known as "The Great American Crank." RES.: New York, NY.

TRAMUTOLO, ROBERT J. "BOB TRAM." POLIT. & GOV.: ***independent candidate for presidency of the U.S., 1988***. MAILING ADDRESS: P.O. Box 10945, Midwest City, OK 73140.

TRAPNELL, GARRETT BROCK. b. Jan 31, 1938, Waltham, MA; par. Commander Walter Scott Kennedy and Elizabeth (Brock) Zang Trapnell; m. twice (possibly 6 times); c. two. EDUC.: high school dropout. POLIT. & GOV.: ***Nationalist Christian Democratic Party candidate for presidency of the U.S., 1980, 1984***. BUS. & PROF.: gun runner for Fidel Castro; forger; prisoner; inmate #72021-158-H, U.S. Penitentiary, Marion, IL; prisoner, federal penitentiary, Atlanta, GA; jewel thief; bank robber; hijacker; mental patient. MIL.: U.S. Army, 1955–58. MISC.: twice escaped from mental institutions, including Montreal, 1971; stole airplane in Santa Ana, CA, 1970, and flew to Freeport, Bahamas, where he robbed a jewelry store; returned to Atlanta, GA, and disappeared; wanted in Canada for six bank robberies (including Nova Scotia, 1970; Toronto, 1969, 1970); shot during hijack attempt aboard TWA 707 en route from Los Angeles to NY, Jan 29, 1972; sentenced to two simultaneous life terms, 1972; attempted two escapes, 1978; has used at least 25 aliases, including Gary Trapnell. MAILING ADDRESS: Box 1000, Marion, IL 62959.

TRAPP, DONALD J. b. 1954. POLIT. & GOV.: ***independent candidate for presidency of the U.S., 1984***. MAILING ADDRESS: 50 Spencer Place, A-2, Garfield, NJ 07026.

TRAYLOR, MELVIN ALVAH. b. Oct 21, 1878, Breeding, KY; d. Feb 14, 1934, Chicago, IL; par. James Milton and Kitty Frances (Harvey) Traylor; m. Dorothy Arnold Yerby, Jun 6,

1906; c. Nancy Frances; Melvin Alvah, Jr. EDUC.: studied law. POLIT. & GOV.: elected city clerk, Hillsboro, TX, 1901–04; appointed asst. cty. atty., Hill Cty., TX, 1904–05; appointed dir. of sales, Seventh Federal Reserve District; delegate, Dem. Nat'l. Conv., 1928; ***candidate for Democratic nomination to presidency of the U.S., 1932***. BUS. & PROF.: schoolteacher, Leatherwood Creek, KY; atty.; admitted to TX Bar, 1901; cashier, bank, Maloney, TX, 1905; cashier, Citizens National Bank, Ballinger, TX, 1907, vice pres., 1908; pres., First National Bank, 1909; vice pres., Stockyards National Bank, East St. Louis, IL, 1911; vice pres., Live Stock Exchange National Bank, Chicago, IL, 1914–15, pres., 1916; pres., Chicago Cattle Loan Co., 1914–19; pres., First Trust and Savings Bank, Chicago, IL, 1919; vice pres., First National Bank of Chicago, 1919–25, pres., 1925; organizer, Bank for International Settlements, 1929; dir., Standard Oil of Indiana; dir., General Electric Corp.; dir., U.S. Gypsum Co.; dir., Fairbanks, Morse and Co.; dir., Pan American Petroleum and Transport Co.; dir., NBC. MEM.: IL Bankers Assn. (pres., 1923–24); American Bankers Assn. (pres., 1926– 27); Berea Coll. (trustee); Newberry Library (trustee); Shedd Aquarium Soc. (pres., 1924–34); American Economic Assn.; Chicago Real Estate Board; Art Inst. of Chicago; Masons; U.S. Golf Assn. (pres., 1928); Northwestern U. (trustee); Southern Soc. of Chicago; Chicago Club; Bankers Club; Mid-Day Club; Bond Men's Club; University Club; Industrial Club; Press Club; Iroquois Club; Commercial Club; Saddle and Cycle Club; Old Elm Club; Racquet Club of Chicago; Recess Club of NY; Saddle and Sirloin Club; Glenview Club. HON. DEG.: M.A., IL Coll., 1922. RES.: Chicago, IL.

TREE, LAMBERT. b. Nov 29, 1832, Washington, DC; d. Oct 9, 1910, New York, NY; par. Lambert and Laura Matilda (Burrows) Tree; m. Anna Josephine Magie, Nov 24, 1859; c. Arthur; one other son. EDUC.: LL.B. (cum laude), U. of VA, 1855; studied law under James Mandeville Carlisle. POLIT. & GOV.: Democratic candidate for IL State Senate, 1864; elected as a Democrat, circuit judge, Chicago, IL, 1870–74; Democratic candidate for U.S. House (IL), 1878, 1880, 1882; delegate, Dem. Nat'l. Conv., 1884; Democratic candidate for U.S. Senate (IL), 1885; appointed U.S. minister to Belgium, 1885–88; appointed U.S. minister to Russia, 1888–89; appointed delegate, International Monetary Conference, 1891; ***candidate for Democratic nomination to vice presidency of the U.S., 1892***. BUS. & PROF.: atty.; admitted to DC Bar, 1855; partner, Clarkson and Tree (law firm), Chicago, IL, 1856; trustee, Mercantile Loan and Trust Co.; dir., Edison Electric Co.; publicist. MEM.: Chicago Law Inst. (pres., 1864); Newberry Library (life trustee); IL State Hist. Library Board (pres., 1892–96); Chicago Hist. Soc. (second vice pres.); American Red Cross (national incorporator; IL vice pres.); SAR; Chicago Art Inst. (dir.); Chicago Club; Iroquois Club; Union Club of Chicago; Union Club of NY; Metropole Club; Century Club. AWARDS: Legion of Honor (France); Grand Officer, Order of Leopold (Belgium). RES.: Chicago, IL.

TREEN, DAVID CONNER. b. Jul 16, 1928, Baton Rouge, LA; par. Joseph Paul and Elizabeth (Speir) Treen; m. Dolores Yvonne Brisbi, May 26, 1951; c. Jennifer Anne (Mrs. Jack Neville); David Conner, Jr.; Cynthia Lynn. EDUC.: B.A., Tulane U., 1948, LL.B., 1950. POLIT. & GOV.: member, Jefferson Parish (LA) Republican Exec. Cmte., 1962–67 (chm., 1963–67); member, LA State Republican Central Cmte., 1962–; chm., LA Young Republican Federation, 1962–64 (exec. cmte., 1964–66; gen. counsel, 1966); Republican candidate for U.S. House (LA), 1962, 1964, 1968; permanent chm., Second Congressional District Republican Convention, 1964; delegate, Rep. Nat'l. Conv., 1964, 1968, 1972, 1976; Republican candidate for gov. of LA, 1973, 1983; member, Rep. Nat'l. Cmte., 1972–74; elected as a Republican to U.S. House (LA), 1973–80; ***candidate for Republican nomination to vice presidency of the U.S., 1976***; elected as a Republican to gov. of LA, 1980–84. BUS. & PROF.: atty.; admitted to LA Bar, 1950; assoc., Deutsch, Kerrigan and Stiles (law firm), New Orleans, LA, 1950–51; vice pres., Simplex Manufacturing Corp., New Orleans, LA, 1952–57; partner, Beard, Blue, Schmitt and Treen (law firm), New Orleans, LA, 1957–74. MIL.: 1st lt., U.S. Air Force, 1951–52. MEM.: LA Bar Assn.; Order of the Coif; Phi Delta Phi; Kappa Sigma; Omicron Delta Kappa; Metropolitan District Political Action Council (dir., 1966–67). AWARDS: Distinguished Service Award, National Young Republican Federation, 1968. REL.: Methodist. MAILING ADDRESS: 430 Dorrington Dr., Metairie, LA 70005.

TREEP, LOUIS WILLIAM. POLIT. & GOV.: ***candidate for Democratic nomination to presidency of the U.S., 1988***. MAILING ADDRESS: c/o Mary Davis/Pauline Thornhill, 530 49th St., South, St. Petersburg, FL 33707.

TREGENZA, MICHAEL DEREK. b. Feb 20, 1940, Devon, England; par. Henry and Versey Tregenza; single. EDUC.: private Schools. POLIT. & GOV.: ***independent candidate for presidency of the U.S., 1976***. BUS. & PROF.: self-employed. REL.: nonconformist Christian. MAILING ADDRESS: Ranchi, Longdown, near Exeter, Devon, England.

TREGILLIS, HARRY ROBERT. b. May 21, 1940, Grand Rapids, MN; par. Sidney Quentin and Genevieve Celestin (Wehman) Tregillis; m. Janice Lee Skogen (divorced); c. Antingua Michelle. EDUC.: grad., Greenway H.S., Coleraine, MN; U. of MN; Northern Technical Business Inst. POLIT. & GOV.: candidate for Democratic-Farmer-Labor Party nomination to sheriff of Itasca Cty., MN, 1970; candidate for Democratic-Farmer-Labor Party nomination to mayor of Minneapolis, MN, 1971, 1973; candidate for Democratic-Farmer-Labor Party nomination to sheriff of Hennepin Cty., MN, 1974; ***candidate for Democratic nomination to presidency of the U.S., 1980***. BUS. & PROF.: stenographer; interior designer; mixologist; machinist; owner, Townservant Escort Agency; salesman, divorce forms; social scientist. MEM.: Odd Fellows (Degree of Honor); Toastmasters; Ducks Unlimited; BSA. REL.: nonsectarian Methodist. MAILING ADDRESS: 1206 Adams, N.E., Minneapolis, MN 55413.

TRENT, PAUL EDWARD. b. 1929; m. Lon Altus Dana. EDUC.: grad., OK State U. POLIT. & GOV.: independent candidate for U.S. Senate (OK), 1972, 1974, 1978, 1980; ***independent candidate for presidency of the U.S., 1972, 1976, 1980, 1984, 1992***; independent candidate for U.S. House (OK), 1976, 1980, 1982. BUS. & PROF.: farmer, Altus, OK; oil worker; artist. MISC.: developed Paul's Panic Plot and Paul's Profit Principle; noted as photographer of UFO in McMinnville, OR, May 11, 1950. MAILING ADDRESS: Route 2, Box 15, Altus, OK 73521.

TREVELLICK, RICHARD F. b. May 2, 1830, St. Mary's, Scilly Islands, England; d. Feb 14, 1895, Detroit, MI; par. Nancy (Johns) Trevellick; m. Victoria A. Atwell; c. Ford Atwell; Richard F., Jr.; Alfred E.; Samuel Mumford; Winifred. EDUC.: informal. POLIT. & GOV.: delegate, Labor Reform Party National Convention, 1872; ***candidate for Labor Reform Party nomination to presidency of the U.S., 1872 (declined)***; member, national exec. cmte., Equal Rights Party, 1872; founding member, Greenback Party; pres., MI Greenback Party, 1875; delegate, Greenback Party National Convention, 1876; temporary chm., Greenback Labor Party National Convention, 1878; chm., Greenback Party National Convention, 1880; ***candidate for Union Labor Party nomination to vice presidency of the U.S., 1888***. BUS. & PROF.: union organizer; ship's carpenter; employee, shipyard, Southampton, England; employee, Pacific Mail Steamship Co., 1855; foreman, Marine Railway, Brooklyn, NY; ship carpenter, New Orleans, LA, 1857–60; employee, Campbell and Owen's Ship Yard, Detroit, MI; employee, Dry Dock Co., Detroit, MI; organizer, lecturer, Knights of Labor. MIL.: seaman, first class petty officer, Peruvian navy. MEM.: Vegetarian Soc.; New Zealand Eight-Hour League (pres., Auckland Chapter, 1854); Australian Eight-Hour League; MI state labor Union; Detroit Harness Makers' Union; NY Ship Carpenters' Union (1850); Melbourne (Australia) Ship Carpenters' Union (pres., 1852); New Orleans Ship Carpenters' Union (pres., 1857); Detroit Ship Carpenters' Union (pres., 1863); Temperance Soc.; Detroit Trades' Assembly (pres., 1864); International Industrial Assembly of North America (delegate, national convention, 1864); International Union of Ship Carpenters and Caulkers (pres., 1865); National Labor Union (delegate, National Convention, 1867; pres., 1868, 1871–73); Grand Eight-Hour League; International Workingmen's Assn. (delegate, 1867); Knights of Labor. WRITINGS: *Money and Panics*; *Decisions of the U.S. Supreme Court and the High Court of Great Britain on the Financial Question* (1893). REL.: Methodist. MISC.: advocate of temperance and the 8-hour day. RES.: Detroit, MI.

TRINSEY, JACK. POLIT. & GOV.: ***candidate for Republican nomination to presidency of the U.S., 1992***. MAILING ADDRESS: Royersford, PA.

TRIPP, ALICE. POLIT. & GOV.: candidate for Democratic nomination to gov. of MN, 1978; ***candidate for Democratic nomination to presidency of the U.S., 1980***. MISC.: power line protestor. MAILING ADDRESS: RFD, Belgrade, MN 56312.

TRIPP, BARTLETT. b. Jul 15, 1842, Harmony, ME; d. Dec 9, 1911, Yankton, SD; par. William and Naamah (Bartlett) Tripp; m. Ellen M. Jennings, Sep 1863; m. 2d, Mrs. Maria Janet (Davis) Washburn, Nov 6, 1887; c. Maude Bartlett (Mrs. C. H. Dillon). EDUC.: grad., Waterville Coll., 1861; LL.B., Albany Law School, 1867. POLIT. & GOV.: delegate, Dem. Nat'l. Conv., 1872, 1876, 1880, 1884, 1888, 1892; elected pres., Yankton (SD) School Board, 1875–85; appointed member, Dakota Territorial Code Revision Comm., 1877; Democratic candidate for delegate, U.S. House (Dakota Territory), 1878; pres., Dakota State Constitutional Convention, 1883; appointed chief justice, Supreme Court of the Dakota Territory, 1885–89; appointed U.S. minister to Austria, 1893–97; appointed member, chm., U.S. Samoan Comm., 1899; ***candidate for Republican nomination to vice presidency of the U.S., 1900***; appointed member, SD State Code Revision Comm., 1902. BUS. & PROF.: schoolteacher; atty.; admitted to Dakota Territorial Bar; law practice, Augusta, ME, 1867–69; law practice, Yankton, SD, 1869–1911; lecturer, prof. of Constitutional Law, U. of SD, 1902–11. MEM.: Yankton Coll. (incorporator, 1881); U. of SD (regent); Dakota Territorial Bar Assn. (pres.); SD Bar Assn. (pres.). HON. DEG.: LL.D., U. of SD, 1893; LL.D., Colby U., 1898; LL.D., Yankton Coll., 1906. WRITINGS: *My Trip to Samoa* (1901). RES.: Yankton, SD.

TROTTER, JIM. b. 1947. POLIT. & GOV.: member, Peace and Freedom Party; member, Santa Barbara (CA) Libertarian Party; ***candidate for Libertarian Party nomination to vice presidency of the U.S., 1976***; Libertarian Party candidate for U.S. House (CA), 1980. BUS. & PROF.: coin dealer; instructor in monetary investments. MIL.: U.S.M.C. MEM.: students for a Democratic Society; NRA; antiwar movement. MAILING ADDRESS: 1376 Vallecito, Carpenteria, CA 93013.

TROUP, GEORGE McINTOSH. b. Sep 8, 1780, McIntosh Bluff, GA (now AL); d. Apr 26, 1856, Montgomery Cty., AL; par. George and Catharine (McIntosh) Troup; m. Ann St. Clare McCormick, Oct 30, 1803; m. 2d, Anne Carter, Nov 8, 1809; c. George McIntosh, Jr.; Oralie; four other daughters. EDUC.: private tutors; Erasmus Hall, Flatbush, NY; A.B., Coll. of NJ (now Princeton U.), 1797; studied law under John Y. Noel. POLIT. & GOV.: elected as a Democratic-Republican to GA State House, 1803–05; Democratic candidate for U.S. House (GA), 1806; elected as a Democrat to U.S. House (GA), 1807–15; elected as a States Rights Democrat to U.S. Senate (GA), 1816–18, 1829–33; States Rights Democratic candidate for gov. of GA, 1819, 1821; elected as a States Rights Democrat to gov. of GA, 1823–27; delegate, States Rights Convention, 1832; ***States Rights Party candidate for presidency of the U.S., 1832***; delegate, Nashville (TN) Convention, 1850; ***Southern Rights Party of AL candidate for presidency of the U.S., 1852 (declined)***. BUS. & PROF.: atty.; admitted to GA Bar, 1799; law practice,

Savannah, GA, 1799; plantation owner, Laurens Cty., GA, and Montgomery Cty., AL. RES.: Montgomery Cty., AL.

TROXELL, RICHARD KIMBALL. b. Sep 9, 1928, Tulsa, OK; par. John Nill and Janice Meredith (Kimball) Troxell; m. Betty Lynn Riedel, Dec 28, 1949; c. Mildred Ann; Laura Lynn; Richard Kimball, Jr.; David Riedel. EDUC.: B.A., Southern Methodist U., 1950. POLIT. & GOV.: Constitution Party candidate for U.S. House (TX), 1966; chm., exec. cmte., TX State Constitution Party, 1966–70; ***Christian Constitution Party candidate for presidency of the U.S., 1968***. BUS. & PROF.: owner, Troxell and Associates (advertising firm), 1950–. MEM.: Delta Tau Delta; Kiwanis; Southern Methodist U. Alumni Assn.; Assn. of Industrial Advertisers; Racquet Club; Republican Party. REL.: Methodist. MAILING ADDRESS: 12134 Broken Bough, Houston, TX 77024.

TRUMAN, HARRY S b. May 8, 1884, Lamar, MO; d. Dec 26, 1972, Kansas City, MO; par. John Anderson and Martha Ellen (Young) Truman; m. Elizabeth Virginia "Bess" Wallace, Jun 28, 1919; c. Mary Margaret (Mrs. Clifton Daniel). EDUC.: grad., Independence (MO) H.S., 1901; Kansas City School of Law, 1923–25; D.C.L., Oxford U., 1956. POLIT. & GOV.: page, Dem. Nat'l. Conv., 1900; election clerk, Grandview, MO, 1906; appointed postmaster, Grandview, MO, 1915; elected cty. judge, Jackson Cty., MO, 1923–25; candidate for cty. judge, Jackson Cty., MO, 1924; elected presiding judge, Jackson Cty., MO, 1926–33; appointed reemployment director of MO, 1933; elected as a Democrat to U.S. Senate (MO), 1934–45; appointed member, Interstate Commerce Comm., 1940 (declined); appointed chm., Dem. Nat'l. Cmte., 1943 (declined); ***elected as a Democrat, vice presidency of the U.S., 1945; succeeded to the office of president and subsequently elected as a Democrat to presidency of the U.S., 1945–1953; candidate for Republican nomination to presidency of the U.S., 1948, 1952***; delegate, Dem. Nat'l. Conv., 1952; ***candidate for Democratic nomination to presidency of the U.S., 1952***. BUS. & PROF.: clerk, Clinton (MO) Drug Store, 1895; timekeeper, railroad construction contractor, 1901; mail room clerk, *Kansas City (MO) Star*, 1902; clerk, National Bank of Commerce, Kansas City, MO, 1903; bookkeeper, Union National Bank, Kansas City, MO, 1904; farm mgr., Grandview, MO, 1906–16; partner, Truman and Jacobson Haberdashery, Independence, MO, 1919–22; salesman, Kansas City Automobile Club, 1925. MIL.: pvt., Battery B, 129th F.A., MO National Guard, 1905; 1st lt., Battery F, 2d MO F.A., 1917, capt., 1918, maj., 1919; col., F.A., U.S.A.R. Corps, 1927–45. MEM.: Masons (33°; Grand Master of MO); MO National Guard; American Legion; Officers Reserve Corps No. 1 (founder). WRITINGS: *Years of Decision* (1955); *Years of Trial and Hope* (1956); *Mr. Citizen*. REL.: Bapt. RES.: Independence, MO.

TRUMBULL, LYMAN. b. Oct 12, 1813, Colchester, CT; d. Jun 25, 1896, Chicago, IL; par. Benjamin and Elizabeth (Mather) Trumbull; m. Julia Maria Jayne, Jun 21, 1843; m. 2d, Mary J. Ingraham, Nov 3, 1877; c. Lyman, Jr.; Walter; Perry; Lyman III; Henry; Mae; Allma; one other son. EDUC.: Bacon Acad.; read law under Hiram Warner. POLIT. & GOV.: elected as a Democrat to IL State House, 1840–41; appointed state sec. of state of IL, 1841–43; candidate for Democratic nomination to gov. of IL, 1846; Democratic candidate for U.S. House (IL), 1846; elected justice, IL State Supreme Court, 1848–54; elected as a Democrat to U.S. House (IL), 1854; elected as a Republican to U.S. Senate (IL), 1855–73; delegate, Rep. Nat'l. Conv., 1856; ***candidate for Republican nomination to presidency of the U.S., 1856***; offered post as U.S. minister to England, 1870 (declined); ***candidate for Liberal Republican Party nomination to presidency of the U.S., 1872; candidate for Liberal Republican Party nomination to vice presidency of the U.S., 1872***; Democratic candidate for gov. of IL, 1880; drafted platform, Chicago People's Party, 1894; ***candidate for People's Party nomination to presidency of the U.S., 1896***. BUS. & PROF.: schoolteacher, Portland, CT, 1829–33; schoolteacher, Greenville, GA, 1833– 36; atty.; admitted to GA Bar, 1836; law practice, Greenville, GA; partner, Tyman and George Trumbull (law firm), Belleville, IL, 1837–49; law practice, Chicago, IL; counsel for Samuel J. Tilden (q.v.) in election contest, 1876. MEM.: Chicago Bar Assn.; IL Bar Assn. (pres.). HON. DEG.: LL.D., McKendree Coll.; LL.D., Yale U. WRITINGS: *Admission of Kansas* (1856); *Great Speech* (1858); *Remarks on Seizure of Arsenals at Harper's Ferry* (1859); *Speech on Confiscation* (1861); *The Constitutionality and Expediency of Confiscating Vindicated* (1862); *Speech on Amending the Constitution to Prohibit Slavery* (1864); *Freedmen's Bureau* (1866); *Power of Congress Over Pacific Railroads* (1876); *The Duties of the Hour* (1880); *Presidential Inability* (1881). REL.: Presb. MISC.: sponsor of Thirteenth Amendment to U.S. Constitution; voted against impeachment and removal of President Andrew Johnson (q.v.). RES.: Chicago, IL.

TRUMP, DONALD JOHN. b. 1946, New York, NY; par. Fred C. and Mary Trump; m. Ivana Winkelmayr, divorced; m. 2d, Marla Maples; c. Donald; Ivanka; one other. EDUC.: NY Military Acad.; Fordham U.; B.A., U. of PA, 1968. POLIT. & GOV.: appointed co-chm., Vietnam Veterans Memorial Comm.; ***candidate for Democratic nomination to presidency of the U.S., 1988***. BUS. & PROF.: real estate exec.; pres., Trump Organization, New York, NY; owner, New Jersey Generals, U.S. Football League; owner, Trump Enterprises, Inc.; owner, The Trump Corp.; owner, Trump Development Co.; owner, Wembley Realty, Inc.; owner, Park South Co.; owner, Land Corp. of California; owner, Gold Co.; partner, Trump-Equitable Fifth Avenue Co.; partner, Regency-Lexington partners; partner, Seashore Corp. of Atlantic City; partner, Trump Plaza; partner, Trump Equities, Inc.; partner, Trump Management, Inc.; partner, Trump Construction Co. WRITINGS: *The Art of the Deal* (1987); *Surviving at the Top* (1990). MAILING ADDRESS: c/o The Trump Organization, 730 Fifth Ave., New York, NY 10020.

TRUNNELL, HEBER J. POLIT. & GOV.: ***independent candidate for presidency of the U.S., 1980, 1984***. MAILING ADDRESS: Box 26214, Salt Lake City, UT 84126.

TSONGAS, PAUL EFTHEMIOS. b. Feb 14, 1941, Lowell, MA; par. Efthemios S. and Katina Tsongas; m. Nicola Sauvage, Dec 21, 1969; c. Ashley; Katina. EDUC.: B.A., Dartmouth Coll., 1962; LL.B., Yale U., 1967; M.P.A., Harvard U., 1973. POLIT. & GOV.: appointed member, Governor's Comm. on Law Enforcement (MA), 1968–69; appointed deputy atty. gen. of MA, 1969–71; city councillor, Lowell, MA, 1973–74; elected cty. commissioner, Middlesex Cty., MA, 1973–74; elected as a Democrat to U.S. House (MA), 1975–79; elected as a Democrat to U.S. Senate (MA), 1979–85; ***candidate for Democratic nomination to presidency of the U.S., 1980, 1992***. BUS. & PROF.: Peace Corps volunteer, Ethiopia, 1962–64, training coordinator, West Indies, 1967–68; atty.; admitted to MA Bar, 1967; law practice, MA, 1971–74; founder, Concord Coalition, 1993–. REL.: Greek Orthodox Church. MAILING ADDRESS: 80 Mansur St., Lowell, MA 01853.

TUCK, WHITFIELD LEON. b. Jun 13, 1855, Georgeville, Quebec, Canada; d. Sep 1, 1937, Winchester, MA; par. John C. and Susan (Channell) Tuck; m. Susan Parker; c. Leon P.; Beatrice. EDUC.: public schools. POLIT. & GOV.: sec., Winchester (MA) Democratic Club; sec., Winchester (MA) Town Cmte.; Democratic candidate for MA State Senate, 1900, 1930, 2 other times; ***candidate for Democratic nomination to presidency of the U.S., 1920***; delegate, Dem. Nat'l. Conv., 1924 (alternate), 1928 (alternate); candidate for Democratic nomination to gov. of MA, 1930 (withdrew); candidate for Democratic nomination to U.S. House (MA); candidate for Democratic nomination to sheriff, Middlesex Cty., MA; appointed member, MA State Ballot Comm., 1934–37. BUS. & PROF.: owner, dry goods store, Derby Line, VT, 1876–81; owner, dry goods store, Boston, MA, 1881–1930 (?). MEM.: Knights Templar; Masons (32°); Odd Fellows; SAR; Thomas Jefferson League of MA (pres.); Bryan Club of MA. REL.: Episc. MISC.: naturalized U.S. citizen; known as the "original Wilson man" in MA; advocate of prohibition. RES.: Winchester, MA.

TUCKER, JOSEPH HOWARD. b. May 22, 1933, Atlanta, GA; par. Haywood James and Emma Lois (Higgins) Tucker; single. EDUC.: grad., Ashby Street Elementary School, Atlanta, GA; Booker T. Washington H.S., Atlanta, GA; Atlanta U. POLIT. & GOV.: candidate for Republican nomination to U.S. Senate (GA), 1972; independent candidate for mayor of Atlanta, GA, 1972; independent candidate for gov. of GA, 1974; ***independent Democratic-Republican candidate for presidency of the U.S., 1976***. BUS. & PROF.: real estate salesman, 30 years; ordained minister, Universal Holiness Church, 1965. MIL.: corp., U.S. Army, 1952–54. MEM.: Universal Holiness Crusade (founder); NAACP. AWARDS: Outstanding Service Award, Fulton Cty. (GA) Republican Club, 1971. WRITINGS: Stop Profanity (unpublished). REL.: Universal Holiness Church (founder; minister, 1965–; Evangelist). MAILING ADDRESS: 280 Ashby St., N.W., Atlanta, GA 30314.

TUCKER, SOPHIE (nee SOPHIE KALISH ABUZA). b. 1884, Russia; d. Feb 9, 1966, New York, NY; d. Charles Abuza; m. Louis Tuck, 1900; m. 2d, Frank Westphal; m. 3d, Al Lackey; c. Bert. EDUC.: grad., high school, Boston, MA. POLIT. & GOV.: ***independent candidate for presidency of the U.S., c. 1936 (satire effort)***. BUS. & PROF.: singer, entertainer, German Village Cafe, New York, NY, 1906; singer, vaudeville; appeared at Music Hall, 1906; appeared at Tony Pastor's Theatre, New York, NY; burlesque player; singer, Ziegfield Follies; on tour with Town Topics, 1916; organized "The Five Kings of Syncopation" jazz band; "Queen of Jazz"; concert singer, Winter Garden Theater, 1919; appeared in "Hello Alexander," 1919; toured British music halls, 1922; appeared in "Round in Fifty," England; traveled Orpheum Circuit; appeared at Kit-Kat Klub, London, 1925, 1928; appeared in Charlot's Revue; billed as "Last of the Red-Hot Mamas"; appeared in comedy "Follow a Star," London, 1930; gave command performance for King and Queen of England, 1934; actress; appeared in musical comedy "Leave It to Me," 1938. MEM.: American Federation of Actors (pres., 1938). WRITINGS: *Some of These Days* (1945). MOTION PICTURE CREDITS: "Honky Tonk" (1929); "Gay Love" (1934); "Gay Time" (1934); "Broadway Melody of 1937" (1937); "Thoroughbreds Don't Cry" (1937); "Atlantic City" (1944); "Follow the Boys" (1944); "Sensations of 1945" (1944). MISC.: political campaign was promotional effort. RES.: New York, NY.

TUCKER, STERLING WOODWARD, III. b. Dec 21, 1923, Akron, OH; par. John Clifford and Una Mave (Vinson) Tucker; m. Edna Alloyce Robinson, Aug 14, 1948; c. Michele Alloyce; Lauren Alloyce. EDUC.: B.A., U. of Akron, 1946, M.A., 1950. POLIT. & GOV.: chm., Washington (DC) Metropolitan Area Transit authority; appointed as a Democrat, vice chm., city council, Washington, DC, 1969–74, chm., 1974–78; ***candidate for Republican nomination to presidency of the U.S., 1972***; candidate for Democratic nomination to mayor, Washington, DC, 1978; appointed asst. sec. for Fair housing and equal opportunity, U.S. Dept. of Housing and Urban Development, 1979; candidate for Democratic nomination to chair, city council of DC, 1982; appointed member, Washington (DC) Mayor's Cmte. on Economic Development; appointed co-chm., Poverty Task Force, White House Conference on Youth; appointed member, Advisory Council on Vocational Rehabilitation; appointed antidrug czar, DC, 1989–90. BUS. & PROF.: asst. exec. dir., Urban League, Akron, OH, 1949–53; exec. dir., Urban League, Canton, OH, 1953–56; exec. dir., Urban League, Washington, DC, 1956–74; dir. of Field Services, National Urban League, 1968–70; consultant; visiting lecturer, Foreign Service Inst.; lecturer, U.S. Information Agency. MEM.: American U. (member, advisory council, Washington (DC) Urban Semester); Self-Determination for DC (pres.); APSA (board); National Assn. of Social Workers (metropolitan exec. cmte.); Acad. of Certified Social Workers; Urban Coalition (metropolitan area vice pres.); Interreligious Cmte. on Race Relations; Metropolitan Washington (DC) Council of Churches (dir.); National League of Cities; Alpha Phi Alpha; debate team; student council, U. of Akron. AWARDS: "Outstanding Young Man of the Year," Washington (DC) Junior C. of C., 1964; citation, Republic of Liberia, 1966; Whitney M. Young Award, Washington (DC) Urban League; Distinguished Public Service Award, NAACP; citation, Foreign Service Inst. HON. DEG.: A.A., Marion Webster Coll. WRITINGS: *Beyond the Burning: Life and Death of the Ghetto* (1968); *Black Reflections on White Power* (1969); *For Blacks Only* (1971). REL.: Episc. MAILING ADDRESS: 14th and E St., N.W., Washington, DC 20004.

TUCKER, WILLIAM F. POLIT. & GOV.: ***independent candidate for presidency of the U.S., 1976***; candidate for U.S. Senate (RI), 1976. MAILING ADDRESS: Mt. Hygeia Rd., Gloucester, RI.

TULLY, ARTHUR. POLIT. & GOV.: ***independent candidate for presidency of the U.S., 1976***. MAILING ADDRESS: Los Angeles, CA.

TUMULTY, JOSEPH PATRICK. b. May 5, 1879, Jersey City, NJ; d. Apr 8, 1954, Baltimore, MD; par. Philip and Alicia (Feehan) Tumulty; m. Mary Catherine Byrne, Jun 1, 1903; c. Joseph Patrick, Jr.; four others. EDUC.: B.A., St. Peter's Coll., 1899; studied law in office of Bedle, McGree and Bedle; studied law under Gilbert Collins. POLIT. & GOV.: elected as a Democrat to NJ State Assembly, 1907–10; appointed private sec. to Gov. Woodrow Wilson (q.v.), NJ, 1910–13; appointed clerk, Supreme Court of NJ, 1912; appointed sec. to the presidency of the U.S., 1913–21; ***candidate for Democratic nomination to vice presidency of the U.S., 1928***; appointed member, Thomas Jefferson Memorial Comm., 1935. BUS. & PROF.: atty.; admitted to NJ Bar, 1902; law practice, NJ, 1902–08; law practice, Washington, DC, 1921–54. WRITINGS: *Woodrow Wilson as I Know Him* (1921). REL.: R.C. RES.: Olney, MD.

TUNNEY, JOHN VARICK. b. Jun 26, 1934, New York, NY; par. James Joseph "Gene" and Mary Josephine (Lauder) Tunney; m. Mieke Sprengers, Feb 5, 1959; m. 2d, Kathinka Osborne, Apr 1977; c. Edward Eugene; Mark Andrew; Arianne Sprengers; Tara Theodora. EDUC.: grad., Westminster H.S., Simsbury, CT, 1952; B.A., Yale U., 1956; Acad. of International Law, The Hague, Netherlands, 1957; J.D., U. of VA, 1959. POLIT. & GOV.: appointed special adviser, President's Comm. on Juvenile Delinquency and Youth Crime, 1963–68; elected as a Democrat to U.S. House (CA), 1965–71; elected as a Democrat to U.S. Senate (CA), 1971–77; delegate, Dem. Nat'l. Conv., 1972; ***candidate for Democratic nomination to presidency of the U.S., 1972***; Democratic candidate for U.S. Senate (CA), 1976. BUS. & PROF.: atty.; admitted to NY Bar, 1959; admitted to VA Bar, 1963; admitted to CA Bar, 1963; assoc., Cahill, Gordon, Reindel and Ohl (law firm), New York, NY, 1959–60; instructor in Business Law, U. of CA at Riverside, 1961–62; admitted to CA Bar, 1963; law practice, Riverside, CA, 1963–; partner, Manatt, Phelps, Rothenberg, Manley and Tunney (law firm), Los Angeles, CA, 1977–; chm. of the board, Cloverleaf, Inc. MIL.: capt., judge advocate, U.S. Air Force, 1961–63. MEM.: CA Indian Legal Services (trustee); Riverside Junior C. of C.; Lions; Center for Urban Affairs, U. of Southern CA (councilor); Center for Policy Study on Urban Environments, U. of Chicago (dir.); Delta Psi; ABA; CA Bar Assn.; Academia Internationalis—Lex et Scientia; Westminster School (trustee); Loyola Law School (member, board of visitors); Multiple Sclerosis Soc. (member, national advisory council); Citizens Research Foundation (adviser); Comm. on Soviet Jewry (adviser); Constitutional Rights Foundation (member, Lawyers Advisory Council); Riverside Aiding Leukemia Stricken American Children. AWARDS: Chubb Fellow, Yale U., 1967. REL.: R.C. MAILING ADDRESS: 4080 Lemon St., Riverside, CA 92501.

TUPAHACHE, ASIBA. POLIT. & GOV.: ***independent candidate for vice presidency of the U.S., 1992***. BUS. & PROF.: founder, publisher, *The Spirit of January Monthly*. MISC.: Native American. MAILING ADDRESS: Great Neck, NY.

TURNER, GEORGE. b. Feb 25, 1850, Edina, MO; d. Jan 26, 1932, Spokane, WA; par. Granville Davenport and Maria (Taylor) Turner; m. Bertha C. Dreher, Jun 4, 1878. EDUC.: public schools. POLIT. & GOV.: appointed U.S. marshal, Southern and Middle Districts of AL, 1876–80; delegate, Rep. Nat'l. Conv., 1876, 1880, 1884; appointed assoc. justice, Supreme Court of the Territory of WA, 1884–88; delegate, WA State Constitutional Convention, 1889; Republican candidate for U.S. Senate (WA), 1889, 1893; elected as a Fusionist (Silver Republican-Populist-Democrat) to U.S. Senate (WA), 1897–1903; appointed member, AK Boundary Tribunal, 1903; Democratic candidate for gov. of WA, 1904; ***candidate for Democratic nomination to vice presidency of the U.S., 1904***; U.S. counsel, North Eastern Fisheries Arbitration, 1910; appointed member, International Joint Comm. between the U.S. and Canada, 1913–14, counsel, 1918–24. BUS. & PROF.: atty.; admitted to AL Bar, 1870; law practice, Mobile, AL, 1870–76; law practice, Spokane, WA, 1888–1932; pres., mgr., Le Roi Mine, Rossland, British Columbia; pres., Constitution Mine; pres., Sullivan Group (mining interests), Cranbrook, British Columbia; owner, *Seattle (WA) Post-Intelligencer*, 1897–99. MIL.: U.S. military telegraph operator, 1861–65. RES.: Spokane, WA.

TURNER, JAMES MILTON. b. May 16, 1840, St. Louis, MO; d. Nov 1, 1915, Ardmore, OK; par. John "Colburn" and Hannah Turner; m. Ella De Burton; c. none. EDUC.: Oberlin Coll., 1854. POLIT. & GOV.: appointed U.S. minister resident and consul gen. to Liberia, 1871–78; ***candidate for National Liberty Party nomination to presidency of the U.S., 1904***; member, exec. cmte., National Liberty Party. BUS. & PROF.: teacher, Kansas City, MO, 1866–68; civil rights leader. MIL.: officer's valet, U.S. Army, Civil War. MEM.: Masons; Lincoln U. (founder, 1866; trustee). MISC.: slave; purchased and freed by father for $50 at age of four; advocate of equity claims by freed slaves of OK Indian tribes. RES.: St. Louis, MO.

TURNER, LAWRENCE DOUGLAS. POLIT. & GOV.: ***independent candidate for presidency of the U.S., 1984***. MAILING ADDRESS: 2101 Fifth, P.O. Box 2057, Bay City, MI 48707.

TURNEY, DANIEL BRAXTON. b. Apr 17, 1848, Shawneetown, IL; d. Jan 17, 1926; par. L. Jay S. and Elizabeth (Parrish) Turney; m. Emma Virginia Oglesby, Apr 14, 1875. EDUC.: public schools; Willamette U.; A.M.; D.D. POLIT. & GOV.: Prohibition Party candidate for justice, Supreme Court of IA, 1890; Prohibition Party candidate for U.S. House (IL), 1900; ***United Christian Party candidate for presidency of the U.S., 1908, 1912***. BUS. & PROF.: ordained minister, Methodist Protestant Church, 1873; pastor, Methodist Protestant Church, 1873–1926. MEM.: Union of American Pacificators (pres.). HON. DEG.: LL.D., Willamette U. WRITINGS: *The Mythifying Theory* (1871); *Darwinism Dissected* (1871); *Campaigning for Christ* (1872); *Three Discourses on Baptism* (1873); *Office and Work of the Holy Spirit* (1873); *Bible Discrepancies, Reply to Ingersoll* (1874); *Will the Coming of Christ Be Pre-Millennial and After a Great War?* (1874); *The Mode of Baptism According to the Scriptures* (1887); *Discussion of the Sabbath Question*. REL.: Methodist Protestant Church (delegate, gen. conferences; delegate, annual conferences). RES.: Decatur, IL.

TURNEY, EDGAR WILLIAM. POLIT. & GOV.: ***independent candidate for presidency of the U.S., 1976***. BUS. & PROF.: news reporter, WMAL-TV, Washington, DC. MAILING ADDRESS: 1611 Sanford Rd., Silver Spring, MD 20902.

TURPIE, DAVID. b. Jul 8, 1829, Hamilton Cty., OH; d. Apr 21, 1909, Indianapolis, IN. EDUC.: grad., Kenyon Coll., 1848; studied law. POLIT. & GOV.: elected as a Democrat to IN State House, 1853, 1858, 1872–75 (Speaker, 1874–75); appointed judge, Court of Common Pleas (IN), 1854–56; appointed judge, Circuit Court of IN, 1856; Democratic candidate for lt. gov. of IN, 1860; elected as a Democrat to U.S. Senate (IN), 1863, 1887–99; appointed Commissioner to Revise the Laws of IN, 1878–81; appointed U.S. district atty. for IN, 1886–87; delegate, Dem. Nat'l. Conv., 1888; ***candidate for Democratic nomination to presidency of the U.S., 1896***; Democratic candidate for U.S. Senate (IN), 1898. BUS. & PROF.: atty.; admitted to Logansport (IN) Bar, 1849; law practice, Logansport, IN, 1849–65, 1868–72; law practice, Monticello, IN, 1865–68; law practice, Indianapolis, IN, 1872–1900. WRITINGS: *Address Upon the Life and Public Service of Honorable Thomas A. Hendricks* (1890); *Sketches of My Own Times* (1903); *Speculative Evidence*. RES.: Indianapolis, IN.

TURPIN, BERNARD "BEN." b. Sep 17, 1869, New Orleans, LA; d. Jul 1, 1940, Santa Monica, CA; par. Ernest and Sarah (Buckley) Turpin; m. Carrie Lemieux, 1907; m. 2d, Babette E. Dietz. POLIT. & GOV.: ***candidate for Democratic nomination to presidency of the U.S., 1924 (satire effort)***. BUS. & PROF.: comedian; hobo, 1886–91; vaudeville comedian, Chicago, IL, 1891; portrayed Happy Hooligan, vaudeville, 1897–1914; comedian, Essanay Studio, Chicago, IL, 1907–16; comedian, Keystone Studio, Edendale, CA, 1916–25; worked under Mack Sennett; movie star; actor. MOTION PICTURE CREDITS: "Ben Gets a Duck and Is Ducked" (1907); "Midnight Disturbance" (1909); "Sweedie and the Lord" (1914); "Sweedie and the Double Exposure" (1914); "Sweedie's Skate" (1914); "Sweedie Springs a Surprise" (1914); "The Fickleness of Sweedie" (1914); "She Landed a Big One" (1914); "Sweedie and the Trouble Maker" (1914); "Sweedie at the Fair" (1914); "Madame Double X" (1914); "Sweedie Learns to Swim" (1914); "Hogan's Romance Upset" (1915); "Hogan Out West" (1915); "Social Splash" (1915); "A Hash House Fraud" (1915); "A Christmas Revenge" (1915); "His New Job" (1915); "A Night Out" (1915); "Sweedie and Her Dog" (1915); "Sweedie's Suicide" (1915); "Two Hearts That Beat as Ten" (1915); "Sweedie's Hopeless Love" (1915); "Love and Trouble" (1915); "Sweedie Learns to Ride" (1915); "Sweedie Goes to College" (1915); "Sweedie's Hero" (1915); "Curiosity" (1915); "The Clubman's Wager" (1915); "A Coat Tale" (1915); "Others Started But Sophie Finished" (1915); "A Quiet Little Game" (1915); "Sophie and the Fakir" (1915); "The Merry Models" (1915); "Snakeville's Hen Medic" (1915); "Snakeville's Champion" (1915); "Snakeville's Debutantes" (1915); "Snakeville's Twins" (1915); "How Slippery Slim Saw the Show" (1915); "Two Bold, Bad Men" (1915); "The Undertaker's Wife" (1915); "A Bunch of Matches" (1915); "The Bell Hop" (1915); "Versus Sledge Hammers" (1915); "Too Much Turkey" (1915); "By the Sea" (1915); "A Night Out" (1915); "The Delinquent Bridegroom" (1916); "Carmen" (1916); "When Papa Died" (1916); "His Blowout" (1916); "The Iron Mitt" (1916); "Hired and Fired" (1916); "A Deep Sea Liar" (1916); "For Ten Thousand Bucks" (1916); "Some Liars" (1916); "The Stolen Booking" (1916); "Doctoring a Lead" (1916); "Poultry a la Mode" (1916); "Ducking a Discord" (1916); "He Did and He Didn't" (1916); "Picture Pirates" (1916); "Shot in the Fracas" (1916); "Jealous Jolts" (1916); "The Wicked City" (1916); "A Safe Proposition" (1916); "Some Bravery" (1916); "A Waiting Game" (1916); "Taking the Count" (1916); "National Nuts" (1916); "Nailing on the Lid" (1916); "Just for a Kid" (1916); "Lost and Found" (1916); "Bungling Bill's Dress" (1916); "Roping Her Romeo" (1917); "Are Waitresses Safe?" (1917); "Taming Target Center" (1917);

"A Circus Cyclone" (1917); "The Musical Marvels" (1917); "The Butcher's Nightmare" (1917); "His Bogus Boast" (1917); "A Studio Stampede" (1917); "Frightened Flirts" (1917); "Sole Mates" (1917); "Why Ben Bolted" (1917); "Masked Mirth" (1917); "Bucking the Riger" (1917); "Caught in the End" (1917); "A Clever Dummy" (1917); "Lost—A Cook" (1917); "The Pawnbroker's Heart" (1917); "She Loved Him Plenty" (1918); "Sheriff Nell's Tussle" (1918); "Saucy Madeline" (1918); "The Battle Royal" (1918); "Two Tough Tenderfeet" (1918); "Hide and Seek" (1918); "Detectives" (1918); "Yankee Doodle in Berlin" (1919); "East Lynne with Variations" (1919); "Uncle Tom Without a Cabin" (1919); "Salome vs. Shenendoah" (1919); "Cupid's Day Off" (1919); "When Love Is Blind" (1919); "No Mother to Guide Him" (1919); "Sleuths" (1919); "Whose Little Wife Are You?" (1919); "You Wouldn't Believe It" (1920); "The Daredevil" (1920); "Down on the Farm" (1920); "Married Life" (1920); "The Star Boarder" (1920); "A Small Town Idol" (1921); "Home Talent" (1921); "Love's Outcast" (1921); "Love and Doughnuts" (1921); "Foolish Wives" (1922); "Bright Eyes" (1922); "Step Forward" (1922); "Home-Made Movies" (1922); "The Shriek of Araby" (1923); "Hollywood" (1923); "Where's My Wandering Boy Tonight?" (1923); "Pitfalls of a Big City" (1923); "Asleep at the Switch" (1923); "Romeo and Juliet" (1924); "Yukon Jake" (1924); "Ten Dollars or Ten Days" (1924); "The Hollywood Kid" (1924); "Three Foolish Weeks" (1924); "The Reel Virginian" (1924); "Hogan's Alley" (1925); "Wild Goose Chaser" (1925); "Rasberry Romance" (1925); "The Marriage Circus" (1925); "Steele Preferred" (1926); "A Harem Knight" (1926); "A Blonde's Revenge" (1926); "When a Man's a Prince" (1926); "A Prodigal Bridegroom" (1926); "The College Hero" (1927); "A Woman's Way" (1927); "The Pride of Pickeville" (1927); "Broke in China" (1927); "A Hollywood Hero" (1927); "The Jolly Jilter" (1927); "Love's Languid Lure" (1927); "Daddy Boy" (1927); "The Wife's Relations" (1928); "Show of Shows" (1929); "The Love Parade" (1929); "Swing High" (1930); "Cracked Nuts" (1931); "Our Wife" (1931); "Make Me a Star" (1932); "Million Dollar Legs" (1932); "Hypnotized" (1932); "Law of the Wild" (1934); "Keystone Hotel" (1935); "Bring 'Em Back a Lie" (1935); "Hollywood Cavalcade" (1939); "Saps at Sea" (1940). MISC.: noted for cross-eyes. RES.: Hollywood, CA.

TWAIN, MARK (See CLEMENS, SAMUEL LANGHORNE).

TYDINGS, MILLARD EVELYN. b. Apr 6, 1890, Havre de Grace, MD; d. Feb 9, 1961, Havre de Grace, MD; par. Millard F. and Mary B. (O'Neill) Tydings; m. Eleanor Davies Cheseborough, 1935; c. Eleanor (Mrs. J. Shapiro); Joseph Davies (stepson). EDUC.: B.S.M.E., MD Agricultural Coll., 1910; LL.B., U. of MD, 1913. POLIT. & GOV.: elected as a Democrat to MD State House of delegates, 1915–21 (Speaker, 1919–21); elected as a Democrat to MD State Senate, 1921–23; elected as a Democrat to U.S. House (MD), 1923–27; elected as a Democrat to U.S. Senate (MD), 1927–51; ***candidate for Democratic nomination to presidency of the U.S., 1940***; Democratic candidate for U.S. Senate (MD), 1950, 1956 (withdrew); appointed member, MD Comm. on State War Memorial Building. BUS. & PROF.: civil engineer, Baltimore and Ohio R.R., 1911; atty.; admitted to MD Bar, 1913; law practice, Havre de Grace, MD; partner, Tydings, Sauerwein, Levy and Archer (law firm), Baltimore, MD; partner, Davies, Richberg, Tydings, Beebe and Landa (law firm), Washington, DC; partner, Tydings and Rosenburg (law firm), Baltimore, MD. MIL.: pvt., U.S. Army, 1916, 2d lt., lt., 1917, capt., maj., 1918; lt. col., 29th Div., 1918–19; grad., Army Center of Artillery Studies; grad., Second Corps Machine Gun School; honor grad., School of Musketry; Distinguished Service Medal; Distinguished Service Cross (3 citations); Distinguished Service Star of the Commonwealth of the Philippines. MEM.: Masons; Elks; American Legion; VFW; MD Club; Chevy Chase Club; Metropolitan Club; University Club; Burning Tree Club; Sulgrave Club; Havre de Grace Yacht Club. HON. DEG.: LL.D., WA Coll., 1927; LL.D., St. John's Coll., 1935. WRITINGS: *Machine Gunners of the Blue and Gray*; *Philippine Independence Bill*; *Before and After Prohibition* (1930); *Counter-Attack—A Battle Plan to Defeat the Depression* (1933). REL.: Episc. MISC.: opponent of the New Deal. RES.: Havre de Grace, MD.

TYDLASKA, JOSEPH JOHN, JR. b. Sep 20, 1939; par. Joseph John Tydlaska. EDUC.: A.A., NM Military Inst., 1960; Eastern NM U.; B.S., Coll. of the Southwest, 1969. POLIT. & GOV.: ***candidate for Republican nomination to presidency of the U.S., 1976 (withdrew)***. BUS. & PROF.: banker; social studies teacher. MIL.: U.S.M.C.; spec. 4th class, U.S. Army, Germany. MEM.: student council (vice pres.); bowling team; Inter-Dorm Council; Young Republicans (vice pres.); Dorm Government (vice chm.); German Club. MAILING ADDRESS: 1001 West Roxana, Hobbs, NM.

TYLER, JOHN. b. Mar 29, 1790, Charles City Cty., VA; d. Jan 18, 1862, Richmond, VA; par. John and Mary Marot (Armistead) Tyler; m. Letitia Christian, Mar 29, 1813; m. 2d, Julia Gardiner, Jun 26, 1844; c. Mary (Mrs. Henry Lightfoot Jones); Robert; John; Letitia (Mrs. James A. Semple); Elizabeth (Mrs. William Nevison Waller); Anne Contesse; Alice (Mrs. Henry Mandeville Denison); Tazewell; David Gardiner; John Alexander; Julia (Mrs. William H. Spencer); Lachlan; Lyon Gardiner; Robert FitzWalter; Pearl (Mrs. William Mumford Ellis). EDUC.: grad., Coll. of William and Mary, 1807. POLIT. & GOV.: elected as a Democratic-Republican to VA State House of Delegates, 1811–16, 1823–25, 1839 (Speaker); elected member, VA Council of State, 1816; elected as a Democratic-Republican to U.S. House (VA), 1817–21; elected as a Democratic-Republican to gov. of VA, 1825–27; elected as a Democratic-Republican to U.S. Senate (VA), 1827–36 (pres. pro tempore, 1835–36); delegate, VA State Constitutional Convention, 1829–30; ***Whig Party candidate for vice presidency of the U.S., 1836; elected as a Whig, vice presidency of the U.S., 1841; succeeded to the Office of presidency of the U.S., 1841–1845; National Demo-***

cratic Party candidate for presidency of the U.S., 1844; delegate, Peace Convention, 1861 (pres.); delegate, VA Secession Convention, 1861; delegate, Provisional Congress, Confederate States of America, 1861; elected to Confederate House, 1862 (died before taking seat). BUS. & PROF.: atty.; admitted to Charles City Cty. (VA) Bar, 1809; law practice, Charles City Cty., VA; rector and chancellor, Coll. of William and Mary, 1859. MIL.: capt., VA Military Company, 1813. MEM.: VA African Colonization Soc. (pres., 1838); American Colonization Soc. (pres.). REL.: Episc. RES.: Greenway, VA.

TYLER, SHERMAN LEE, JR. b. Aug 22, 1949, Oak Ridge, LA; par. Sherman Lee and Ella (Harden) Tyler; m. Phyllis Barne Parker; c. Adran J.; Charlene Denise; Yon Darwin. EDUC.: grad., Morehouse H.S., Bastrop, LA, 1967; B.S.B., Southern U., 1971. POLIT. & GOV.: ***Third People's Choice Party candidate for presidency of the U.S., 1984, 1988***. BUS. & PROF.: sales and service engineer, Hughes Drilling Fluids; oil field engineering consultant. MEM.: Development Opportunity Group of America (pres.); Minority Purchase Council of America; American Petroleum Inst.; Knights of the Golden Lion. AWARDS: Sales and Marketing Executive Award, New Orleans, LA. REL.: Bapt. MAILING ADDRESS: 4822 Ligonberry St., Houston, TX 77033.

TYNER, JARVIS. b. Jul 11, 1941, Philadelphia, PA; Separated; c. Keith; Colby DuBois. EDUC.: grad., high school, 1959. POLIT. & GOV.: ***Communist Party, U.S.A. candidate for vice presidency of the U.S., 1972, 1976***; member, Political Cmte., Communist Party, U.S.A.; chm., Communist Party of NY; Communist Party candidate for gov. of NY, 1978. BUS. & PROF.: messenger; printer; lithographer, 1961–; furniture craftsman, 1965; community organizer. MEM.: International Brotherhood of Teamsters (shop steward); Amalgamated Lithographers Union; Young Workers Liberation League (national chm., 1970–75); W. E. B. DuBois Clubs of America (national chm., 1967–); People's Coalition for Peace and justice (coordinating cmte.); World Federation of Democratic Youth (exec. cmte.). REL.: none (nee Bapt.). MAILING ADDRESS: 2130-4 First Ave., New York, NY.

TYREE, ROY WAYNE. POLIT. & GOV.: ***independent candidate for presidency of the U.S., 1992***. MAILING ADDRESS: IL.

TYSON, LAWRENCE DAVIS. b. Jul 4, 1861, Greenville, NC; d. Aug 24, 1929, Strafford, PA; pa. Richard Lawrence and Margaret Louise (Turnage) Tyson; m. Bettie Humes McGhee, Feb 10, 1886; c. Charles McGhee; Isabella McGhee (Mrs. Kenneth Newcomber Gilpin). EDUC.: Greenville Acad.; grad., U.S. Military Acad., 1883; LL.B., U. of TN, 1894. POLIT. & GOV.: appointed military gov. of Northern Puerto Rico, 1899; elected as a Democrat to TN State House, 1903–05 (Speaker); delegate, Dem. Nat'l. Conv., 1908; Democratic candidate for U.S. Senate (TN), 1913; ***candidate for Democratic nomination to vice presidency of the U.S., 1920 (withdrew), 1928***; elected as a Democrat to U.S. Senate (TN), 1925–29; delegate, Interparliamentary Union Conference, 1927. BUS. & PROF.: soldier; atty.; admitted to TN Bar, 1894; law practice, Knoxville, TN; partner, Lucky, Sanford and Tyson (law firm), Knoxville, TN, 1895; manufacturer; pres., Knoxville Sentinel Co., Knoxville, TN; pres., Knoxville Cotton Mills; pres., Tennessee Mills; pres., Knoxville Spinning Co.; pres., Southern Valve Gear Co.; vice pres., Roane Iron Co.; vice pres., Cambria Mining and Manufacturing Co.; pres., Nashville Street Railway Co.; pres., Poplar Creek Coal and Iron Co.; pres., Lenoir City Land Co.; pres., East TN Coal and Iron Co.; vice pres., Coal Creek Mining and Manufacturing Co. MIL.: 2d lt., 9th U.S. Infantry, 1883, 1st lt., 1889; prof. of Military Science, U. of TN, 1891–95; col., 6th Regt., U.S. Volunteer Infantry, 1898–99; brig. gen., inspector gen., TN National Guard; brig. gen., 59th Bde., 30th Div., U.S. Army, 1917–19; Distinguished Service Medal. MEM.: American Assn. of Cotton Manufacturers (pres., 1923); TN Bar Assn.; Sons of the Revolution; Masons. REL.: Episc. RES.: Knoxville, TN.

UDALL, MORRIS KING. b. Jun 15, 1922, St. Johns, AZ; par. Levi S. and Louise (Lee) Udall; m. 2d, Ella Royston, 1968; m. 3d, Norma Gilbert, Aug 1976; c. Mark; Judith; Randolph; Anne; Bradley; Katherine. EDUC.: LL.B. (cum laude), U. of AZ, 1949. POLIT. & GOV.: appointed chief deputy cty. atty., Pima Cty., AZ, 1951–52; cty. atty., Pima Cty., AZ, 1953–54; delegate, Dem. Nat'l. Conv., 1956, 1972, 1980 (keynoter); chm., AZ Volunteers for Stevenson, 1956; elected as a Democrat to U.S. House (AZ), 1961–91; ***candidate for Democratic nomination to presidency of the U.S., 1976, 1980, 1984; candidate for Democratic nomination to vice presidency of the U.S., 1976, 1984***. BUS. & PROF.: atty.; admitted to AZ Bar, 1949; partner, Udall and Udall (law firm), Tucson, AZ, 1949–61; cofounder, Bank of Tucson; cofounder, Catalina Savings and Loan Assn.; legal counsel, Better Business Bureau, Tucson, AZ; lecturer, U. of AZ, 1955–56. MIL.: capt., U.S. Air Force, 1942–46. MEM.: AZ Cmte. for Modern Courts (chm., 1960); Metropolitan YMCA (dir.); Arizona-Sonora Desert Museum (trustee); Tucson Boys Band (pres.); ABA; AZ Bar Assn. (gov.); Pima Cty. Bar Assn. (exec. cmte.); American Jud. Soc.; American Legion; Phi Kappa Phi; Phi Delta Phi. WRITINGS: *Arizona Law of Evidence* (1960); *The Job of the Congressman* (with Donald G. Tacheron, 1966); *Education of a Congressman* (1972); *Too Funny to Be President* (1988). REL.: Church of Jesus Christ of Latter-Day Saints. MAILING ADDRESS: 142 South Calle Chaparita, Tucson, AZ 85716.

UHLER, CHARLOTTE. POLIT. & GOV.: ***independent candidate for presidency of the U.S., 1992 (withdrew)***. BUS. & PROF.: sec.; artist. MAILING ADDRESS: 3912 Dorchester Rd., Baltimore, MD 21207.

UNCAPHER, MARSHALL EUGENE. b. Jul 23, 1929, Madison, KS; par. Daniel Milton and Willia Ellen (Patteson) Uncapher; m. Virginia Chambers; c. Marshall Eugene, Jr. EDUC.: public schools, Madison, KS; public schools, Connersville, IN; B.A., God's Bible Coll., Cincinnati, OH, 1959; Frankfort Pilgrim Coll.; Emporia State teachers Coll.; Washburn U.; B.S., McPherson Coll., 1963. POLIT. & GOV.: Prohibition Party candidate for KS State Insurance Comm., 1964, 1966; Prohibition Party candidate for gov. of KS, 1968, 1970, 1974; ***candidate for Prohibition Party nomination to presidency of the U.S., 1972; Prohibition Party candidate for vice presidency of the U.S., 1972***; state chm., KS Prohibition Party, 1968–; member, exec. cmte., Prohibition Party. BUS. & PROF.: teacher, Culver, KS, 1964–66; principal, Netawaka, KS, 1966–67; pastor, Peabody Church of the Nazarene, Peabody, KS, 1964–; chm., Board of Stewards, Peniel Church of the Nazarene; sales rep., purchasing agent, M. W. Hartman Manufacturing Co. MEM.: KS State Teachers Assn.; NEA; Culver Development Council; Peabody Ministerial Assn. REL.: Church of the Nazarene. MAILING ADDRESS: 728 West Sherman, Hutchinson, KS 67501.

UNDERWOOD, OSCAR WILDER. b. May 6, 1862, Louisville, KY; d. Jan 25, 1929, Accotink, VA; par. Eugene and Frederica VA (Smith) Underwood; m. Eugenia Massie, Oct 8, 1884; m. 2d, Bertha Woodward, Sep 10, 1904; c. John Lewis; Oscar Wilder, Jr. EDUC.: rugby school; U. of VA. POLIT. & GOV.: chm., 9th District, Democratic Campaign Cmte. of AL, 1892; elected as a Democrat to U.S. House (AL), 1895–96 (lost seat in contested election), 1897–1915 (Democratic floor leader, 1911–15); ***candidate for Democratic nomination to presidency of the U.S., 1912, 1920, 1924***; elected as a Democrat to U.S. Senate (AL), 1915–27 (Democratic floor leader, 1921–23); appointed Commissioner Plenipotentiary, U.S. International Conference on the Limitation of Armaments, 1921; appointed member, International Peace Comm. Between U.S. and France, 1927; delegate, Sixth International Conference of American States, 1928. BUS. & PROF.: atty.; admitted to AL Bar, 1884; law practice, St. Paul, MN; law practice, Birmingham, AL, 1884–1928; partner (with J. J. Garrett), law firm, Birmingham, AL. MEM.: Jeffersonian Soc. (pres., 1884). WRITINGS: *Drifting Sands of Party Politics* (1928). REL.: Episc. RES.: Birmingham, AL.

UNRUH, JESSE MARVIN. b. Sep 30, 1922, Newton, KS; d. Aug 4, 1987, Marina del Rey, CA; par. Isaac P. and Nettie Laura (Kessler) Unruh; m. Virginia June Lemon, Nov 2, 1943; c. Bruce; Bradley; Robert; Randall; Linda Lu. EDUC.: B.A., U. of Southern CA, 1948, postgrad., 1949. POLIT. & GOV.: district staff dir., U.S. Bureau of the Census, 1950; member, CA State Democratic Central Cmte., 1954–87; elected as a Democrat to CA State Assembly, 1954–70 (Speaker, 1961–68; Democratic leader, 1968–70); Southern CA Campaign mgr., John F. Kennedy for President Campaign, 1960; member, Advisory Cmte. on Intergovernmental Relations, 1967–70; state chm., Robert F. Kennedy for President Campaign, 1968; delegate, Dem. Nat'l. Conv., 1968 (state delegation chair); ***candidate for Democratic nomination to presidency of the U.S., 1968***; Democratic candidate for gov. of CA, 1970; ***candidate for Democratic nomination to vice presidency of the U.S., 1972***; elected as a Democrat, state treas. of CA, 1985–87. BUS. & PROF.: employee, Pacific Car DeMurrage Bureau, 1950–54; visiting prof. of Political Science, San Fernando Valley State Coll., 1970; visiting prof., U. of Southern CA Law School, 1971–72; consultant, prof. of Political Science, Eagleton Inst. of Politics, Rutgers U., 1965–87. MIL.: U.S.N.R., 1942–45. MEM.: Seminar of Young Legislators, Carnegie Corp. (co-chm.); National Conference of State Legislative Leaders (pres., 1966); U. of CA (regent, 1961–68); CA State Coll. System (trustee, 1961–68); Citizens Conference on State Legislatures; Inst. for American Universities. AWARDS: Chubb Fellow, Yale U., 1962. HON. DEG.: LL.D., U. of Southern CA, 1967. RES.: Los Angeles, CA.

UPSHAW, WILLIAM DAVID. b. Oct 15, 1866, Newnan, GA; d. Nov 21, 1952, Glendale, CA; par. Isaac David and Adeline "Addie" (Stamps) Upshaw; m. Margaret Beverly, May 5, 1909; m. 2d, Lily Swinnea Galloway, Oct 8, 1946; c. Margaret Adeline (Mrs. Charles Whitworth); Charlotte Beverly (Mrs. Singleton Wolfe). EDUC.: Mercer U., 1895–97. POLIT. & GOV.: elected as a Democrat to U.S. House (GA), 1919–27; ***candidate for Democratic nomination to vice presidency of the U.S., 1924; candidate for American Party nomination to vice presidency of the U.S., 1924***; candidate for Democratic nomination to U.S. House (GA), 1926; ***Prohibition Party candidate for presidency of the U.S., 1932***; candidate for Democratic nomination to U.S. Senate (GA), 1942. BUS. & PROF.: engaged in agricultural and mercantile pursuits, until physically incapacitated by accident in youth (confined to bed for seven years); founder, ed., *The Golden Age Magazine*, 1906–19; lecturer, Anti-Saloon League; lecturer, W.C.T.U.; evangelist; author; ordained minister, Baptist Church, 1938; vice pres., faculty member, Linda Vista Baptist Bible Coll. and Seminary, San Diego, CA, 1949–50. MEM.: Bessie Tift Coll. for Women (trustee); Anti-Saloon League of America (vice pres.); National Christian Citizenship Foundation (pres., 1933–52); Scandinavian Commercial Comm. (vice chm.); GA Anti-Saloon League (vice pres.); Southern Rebellion in Defense of the Union (founder, 1928); McBeath Literary Circle; Laymen's Speech Inst. of America (vice pres., 1946–48); Kiwanis. HON. DEG.: Dr. Humanities, Lanier-Milton U., 1949. WRITINGS: *Earnest Willie, or Echoes from a Recluse* (1893); *The Clarion Calls from Capitol Hill* (1923); *Scattering Sunshine* (1928); *Baptist Water and Methodist Fire; Bombshells for Wets and Reds* (1936); *Fighting for the Right* (1938); *The Colossal Failure of Prohibition Repeal* (1944); *Upshaw's Startling Challenge* (1944); *Sunshine, Salvation and Healing* (1951). REL.: Bapt. (vice pres., Southern Baptist Convention, twice). MISC.: worked way through college selling book he authored; temperance advocate and supporter of Ku Klux Klan. RES.: Atlanta, GA.

URY, STEVEN KENNETH. b. May 9, 1970, Walnut Creek, CA; par. Frank Alan and Karen Eileen (Davis) Ury; single. EDUC.: Sonoma Valley (CA) H.S. POLIT. & GOV.: ***Legion of Dynamic Discord candidate for presidency of the U.S., 1984***. BUS. & PROF.: student. MEM.: Legion of Dynamic Discord. REL.: no preference. MAILING ADDRESS: 4480 Grove St., Sonoma, CA 95476.

UTT, JAMES BOYD. b. Mar 11, 1899, Tustin, CA; d. Mar 1, 1970, Bethesda, MD; par. Charles Edward and Mary M. (Sheldon) Utt; m. Charlena Elizabeth Dripps, May 7, 1921; c. James Sheldon. EDUC.: Santa Ana Junior Coll., 1942–43; LL.B., U. of Southern CA, 1946. POLIT. & GOV.: elected as a Republican to CA State Assembly, 1933–37; appointed inheritance tax appraiser, office of the CA State Controller, 1937–52; elected as a Republican to U.S. House (CA), 1953–70; ***American Party candidate for vice presidency of the U.S., 1964***. BUS. & PROF.: atty.; admitted to CA Bar, 1947; partner, Utt and Hubbard (law firm), Santa Ana, CA, 1947–70. MEM.: Santa Ana C. of C. (dir.); Knights of Pythias; Elks; Masons (Shriner). HON. DEG.: LL.D., Bob Jones U., 1965. REL.: Presb. RES.: Tustin, CA.

VALENCIA, DAVID JOSEPH McCOY. BUS. & PROF.: *candidate for Democratic nomination to presidency of the U.S., 1984.* MAILING ADDRESS: unknown.

VALENTI, GIACOMO. POLIT. & GOV.: ***independent candidate for presidency of the U.S., 1980, 1984.*** MAILING ADDRESS: 1145 Grandview, Boulder, CO.

VALERIO, JUDITH HICKS. m. Thomas Valerio; c. Brian. POLIT. & GOV.: ***Truth and Freedom Party candidate for vice presidency of the U.S., 1988, 1992.*** BUS. & PROF.: community volunteer. MAILING ADDRESS: Youngstown, OH.

VAN BUREN, JOHN. b. Feb 18, 1810, Hudson, NY; d. Oct 13, 1866, on board ship *Scotia*, at sea; par. President Martin (q.v.) and Hannah (Hoes) Van Buren; m. Elizabeth Van der Poel, Jun 22, 1841; c. Anna. EDUC.: Albany Acad.; grad., Yale U., 1828; studied law under Benjamin F. Butler (q.v.); studied law under Aaron Van de Poel. POLIT. & GOV.: appointed sec., U.S. Legation, London, England, 1831–32; delegate, NY State Democratic Conventions, 1836–48; organizer, Barnburners, 1843–48; elected as a Democrat, atty. gen. of NY, 1845; ***candidate for Free Soil Party nomination to presidency of the U.S., 1848 (declined)***; candidate for atty. gen. of NY, 1865. BUS. & PROF.: atty.; admitted to NY Bar, 1830; law examiner, Albany, NY; partner (with James McKnown), law firm, 1837–45; lobbyist, NY Legislature. WRITINGS: *The Syracuse Convention* (1847). MISC.: known as "Prince John" and "The Young Fox"; counsel in Edwin Forrest divorce case; member of Albany Regency, 1834. RES.: Albany, NY.

VAN BUREN, MARTIN. b. Dec 5, 1782, Kinderhook, NY; d. Jul 24, 1862, Kinderhook, NY; par. Abraham and Maria Hoes (Van Alen) Van Buren; m. Hanna Hoes, Feb 21, 1807; c. Martin, Jr.; John (q.v.); Abraham; Smith Thompson. EDUC.: Kinderhook Acad.; studied law under William Van Ness, New York, NY, 1801. POLIT. & GOV.: delegate, Troy (NY) Democratic Convention, 1800; surrogate, Columbia Cty., NY, 1808–13; elected as a Democrat to NY State Senate, 1813–20; appointed atty. gen. of NY, 1815–19; delegate, NY State Constitutional Convention, 1821; elected as a Democrat to U.S. Senate (NY), 1821–28; elected as a Democrat to gov. of NY, 1829; appointed U.S. sec. of state, 1829–31; appointed U.S. minister to Great Britain, 1832 (nomination rejected by Senate); ***elected as a Democrat to vice presidency of the U.S., 1833–1837; elected as a Democrat to presidency of the U.S., 1837–1841; Democratic candidate for presidency of the U.S., 1840; candidate for Democratic nomination to presidency of the U.S., 1844, 1848; Free Soil Party candidate for presidency of the U.S., 1848.*** BUS. & PROF.: atty.; admitted to NY Bar, 1803; law practice, Kinderhook, NY, 1803–09; partner (with Benjamin F. Butler, q.v.), law firm, Albany, NY, 1816. MEM.: NY U. (Regent); Phi Beta Kappa. WRITINGS: *Inquiry Into the Origin and Causes of Political Parties* (1867); *Autobiography* (1920). REL.: Dutch Reformed Church. MISC.: known as "The Fox" and "The Little Magician"; member of the Albany Regency. RES.: Kinderhook, NY.

VANDENBERG, ARTHUR HENDRICK. b. Mar 22, 1884, Grand Rapids, MI; d. Apr 18, 1951, Grand Rapids, MI; par. Aaron and Alpha (Hendrick) Vandenberg; m. Elizabeth Watson, 1905; m. 2d, Hazel H. Whittaker, Jun 14, 1918; c. Arthur Hendrick, Jr.; Barbara Elizabeth. EDUC.: U. of MI, 1901–02. POLIT. & GOV.: member, Grand Rapids (MI) Charter Comm., 1912; chm., MI Comm. to Place Statue of Zachariah Chandler in U.S. Capitol, 1913; chm., MI State Republican Convention, 1916, 1928; member, MI State Republican Central Cmte., 1912–18; appointed and subsequently elected as a Republican to U.S. Senate (MI), 1928–51 (pres. pro tempore, 1947–49); ***candidate for Republican nomination to vice presidency of the U.S., 1936, 1940; candidate for Republican nomination to presidency of the U.S., 1940, 1948; George Washington Party candidate for pres-***

idency of the U.S., 1940; delegate, U.N. Conference, San Francisco, CA, 1945; delegate, U.N. General Assembly, 1946; U.S. adviser, Council of Foreign Ministers, 1946; delegate, Pan American Conference, 1947. BUS. & PROF.: journalist; writer, *Collier's Weekly*; ed., publisher, *Grand Rapids (MI) Herald*, 1906–28; author. MEM.: SAR; Loyal Legion; Delta Upsilon; Masons (33°; Shriner); Elks; Modern Woodmen of the World; Peninsular Club; Authors' Club. AWARDS: Collier Award for Distinguished Congressional Service, 1946, 1949; Freedom Award, Freedom House, 1948; Roosevelt Medal of Honor, 1948. HON. DEG.: M.A., U. of MI, 1925; LL.D., Hope Coll., 1926; LL.D., Alma Coll., 1937; D.C.L., Union Coll., 1938; LL.D., Syracuse U., 1939; D.H.L., Albion Coll., 1941; LL.D., Columbia U., 1948; LL.D., Dartmouth Coll. WRITINGS: *Alexander Hamilton, The Greatest American* (1921); *If Hamilton Were Here Today* (1923); *The Trail of a Tradition* (1925). REL.: Congregationalist. RES.: Grand Rapids, MI.

VANDER JAGT, GUY ADRIAN. b. Aug 26, 1931, Cadillac, MI; par. Harry and Marie (Copier) Vander Jagt; m. Carol Doorn, Apr 4, 1964; c. Virginia Marie. EDUC.: B.A., Hope Coll., 1953; B.D., Yale U., 1955; Rotary Fellow, Bonn U., 1956; LL.B., U. of MI, 1960. POLIT. & GOV.: elected as a Republican to MI State Senate, 1965–66; elected as a Republican to U.S. House (MI), 1969–93; chm., Republican Congressional Campaign Cmte.; delegate, Rep. Nat'l. Conv., 1980 (keynoter); ***candidate for Republican nomination to vice presidency of the U.S., 1980***; candidate for Republican nomination to U.S. House (MI), 1992. BUS. & PROF.: news dir., WWTV, 1956; atty.; admitted to MI Bar, 1960; assoc., Warner, Norcross and Judd (law firm), Grand Rapids, MI, 1965–66. MEM.: Masons; Rotary Club; MI Bar Assn.; DC Bar Assn.; Hope Coll. Alumni Assn. (pres.). AWARDS: one of five "Outstanding Young Men in MI," MI Junior C. of C., 1956. WRITINGS: *A Country Worth Saving* (1984). REL.: Presb. MAILING ADDRESS: Luther, MI 49656.

VANDER PYL, ELLIS CUTLER. b. Jan 9, 1899, Holliston, MA; par. Nicholas and Ada Alice (Forbes) Vander Pyl; m. Marie Sherrer, Jun 30, 1925; Marie Ada; Ellis Cutler, Jr.; Robert. EDUC.: elected as a Republican to South Euclid (OH) City Council, 1935–42; co-chm., Veterans Div., Thomas J. Herbert for Governor Campaign, 1946; candidate for delegate (pledged to Harold Stassen), Rep. Nat'l. Conv., 1948; *candidate for Republican nomination to presidency of the U.S., 1948*. BUS. & PROF.: sportscaster, WHK radio; merchandising mgr., announcer, and sportscaster, WGAR radio, 1932–41; newscaster, commentator, WTAM radio, 1942–; advertising exec. MIL.: member, Lost Battalion, 26th Yankee Div., U.S. Army, WWI; U.S.A.A.C., 1942–45, lt. col., 1948–; chief of interrogation, Nurenberg Trials; U.S.A.R. (maj.); Croix de Guerre with Palm. MEM.: American Legion. MAILING ADDRESS: 2040 Stearns Rd., Cleveland, OH.

VAN DER VOORT, PAUL. b. Jul 12, 1846, Harveysburg, OH; d. 1902. EDUC.: public schools. POLIT. & GOV.: appointed deputy cty. treas., McLean Cty., IL; postal clerk, Chief of Railway Mail Service, Omaha, NE; Superintendent of Mails; left Republican Party, 1891; delegate, People's Party National Convention, 1892; delegate, Bimetallic Conventions, 1893; ***candidate for People's Party nomination to presidency of the U.S., 1896***. BUS. & PROF.: newspaperman. MIL.: pvt., U.S. Army, 1862–65; imprisoned at Andersonville, Millen, Bell Island, and Savannah prisons during Civil War. MEM.: GAR (post commander; aide-de-camp on dept. and national staff; dept. commander of NE; asst. adj. gen. of IL; senior vice commander in chief; senior commander in chief, 1878; commander in chief, 1882); National Women's Relief Corps (hon. life member); National Industrial Legion of the U.S. (commander in chief, 1892). WRITINGS: *Address of the Commander-in-Chief* (1883); *History of the Grand Army of the Republic* (1885); *Case for Bi-Metallism* (1894). RES.: Omaha, NE.

VANIK, CHARLES ALBERT. b. Apr 7, 1913, Cleveland, OH; par. Charles Anton and Stella (Kvasnicka) Vanik; m. Beatrice Marian Best, Feb 2, 1945; c. Phyllis Jean; John Charles. EDUC.: A.B., Western Reserve U., 1933, LL.B., 1936. POLIT. & GOV.: referee, OH State Industrial Comm., 1936; examiner, OH State Dept. of Highways, 1937; elected as a Democrat to Cleveland (OH) City Council, 1938–40; elected as a Democrat to OH State Senate, 1940–41; elected to Cleveland (OH) Board of Education, 1941–42; appointed member, Cleveland (OH) Library Board, 1946–47; elected judge, Cleveland (OH) Municipal Court, 1947–54; elected as a Democrat to U.S. House (OH), 1955–1981; ***candidate for Democratic nomination to presidency of the U.S., 1976***. BUS. & PROF.: atty.; admitted to OH Bar, 1936; partner, Vanik, Monroe, Zucco and Klein (law firm), Cleveland, OH, 1936–. MIL.: ensign, U.S.N.R., 1942, lt. (active duty), 1945. MEM.: Cleveland Bar Assn.; Cuyahoga Cty. Bar Assn. MAILING ADDRESS: Arlington, VA.

VANN, JOHN W. (aka JOHN BILAL, q.v.).

VAN PETTEN, ALBERT ARCHER. POLIT. & GOV.: ***candidate for Democratic nomination to presidency of the U.S., 1988 (withdrew)***. MAILING ADDRESS: 2005 Fantero Ave., Escondido, CA 92025.

VAN RONK, DAVE. POLIT. & GOV.: ***candidate for independent nomination to vice presidency of the U.S. (with Jim Ronald Glover, q.v), 1992 (declined)***. MAILING ADDRESS: unknown.

VAN SKIVER, RAYMOND JOHN. b. May 14, 1923, Chicago, IL; par. John and Lucy Mabel (Sack) Van Skiver; m. Alma V.; c. Janet (Mrs. Gale Cacannouer); Nancy;

Sandra; Jack. EDUC.: B.S., NE Wesleyan U., 1948; M.S., OK State U., 1953. POLIT. & GOV.: candidate for Republican nomination to gov. of KS, 1968, 1970; candidate for Republican nomination to atty. gen. of KS, 1972, 1974; candidate for Republican nomination to cty. commissioner, KS, 1980; ***candidate for Democratic nomination to presidency of the U.S., 1992***. BUS. & PROF.: teacher, 30 years; teacher, NE, IA; teacher, South Haven, KS; teacher, John Marsall Junior H.S., Wichita, KS, 1953; self-employed home builder and developer, 1955–. MIL.: combat engineer, U.S. Army, 24th Infantry Div., WWII, 3 years; U.S.N.R., 3 years. WRITINGS: *The Way Out* (1971). REL.: opposed to "Government Churches." MAILING ADDRESS: c/o 2220 North Cedar Crest, Wichita, KS 67223

VAN TILBORG, GRANT VAN. POLIT. & GOV.: ***United Party candidate for presidency of the U.S., 1964***. MAILING ADDRESS: unknown.

VAN VLIET, STEPHANIE DIANA. POLIT. & GOV.: ***candidate for Republican nomination to presidency of the U.S., 1988***. MAILING ADDRESS: 15615 Meadowgate Rd., Encino, CA 91436.

VAN WYCK, AUGUSTUS. b. Oct 14, 1850, New York, NY; d. Jun 8, 1922, New York, NY; par. William and Lydia A. (Maverick) Van Wyck; m. Leila G. Wilkins; c. William; Leila Gray (Mrs. James W. Osborne). EDUC.: Phillips Exeter Acad.; A.B., U. of NC, 1964, A.M. POLIT. & GOV.: pres., Kings Cty. (NY) General Cmte., 1882; member, NY State Democratic Central Cmte.; elected judge, Superior Court of Brooklyn, NY, 1884–96; elected justice, Supreme Court of NY, 1896–98; delegate, Dem. Nat'l. Conv.; Democratic candidate for gov. of NY, 1898; ***candidate for Democratic nomination to presidency of the U.S., 1900***. BUS. & PROF.: atty.; law practice, Richmond, VA; law practice, Brooklyn, NY, 1871. MEM.: Zeta Psi (grand master, 1882; pres., NY Assn., 1913); Holland Soc. of New York (pres., 1892, 1919–20); U. of NC Alumni Assn. of NY (pres., 1900–1913); New England Soc. (trustee; pres.); Commercial Travelers and Hotel Men's Anti-Trust League. REL.: Episc. RES.: Brooklyn, NY.

VARNEY, WILLIAM FREDERICK. b. Oct 1, 1884, Paterson, NJ; d. Dec 13, 1960, East Rockway, NY; par. Frederick William and Lizzie Jane (Leith) Varney; m. Leonia Beatrice Abrams, Aug 31, 1905; c. Beatrice Leonia (Mrs. Austen Schupp); Laura; William Frederick, Jr.; Evelyn Marion (Mrs. Warren Everett Mott). EDUC.: public schools; commercial school. POLIT. & GOV.: field sec., NJ Prohibition Party, 1912–19; dir., Prohibition Party Cty. Campaigns, 1913–19; member, Prohibition Party National Cmte., 1924–60 (vice chm., 1942); sec., Prohibition Party National Convention, 1924; ***candidate for Prohibition Party nomination to presidency of the U.S., 1924; Prohibition Party candidate for presidency of the U.S., 1928***; chm., NY State Prohibition Party, 1932–60; Law Preservation Party candidate for U.S. House (NY), 1932; Home Protection Party candidate for mayor of Rockville Centre, NY, 1934; Law Preservation Party candidate for gov. of NY, 1934. BUS. & PROF.: messenger, *Paterson (NJ) Daily Press*, 1897–1902; mgr., Wright, Veith and Newman (pillow shams and scarfs), 1902–05; mgr., Stahli, Reitmann and Co. (curtains and novelties), 1905–11; insurance specialist, Rockville Centre, NY, 1919–57. MEM.: Nassau Cty. Assn. of Local Agents, Inc. (pres.); Patriotic Order of the Sons of America; National Assn. of Insurance Agents; NY State Assn. of Insurance Agents; Suburban NY Assn. of Insurance Agents. REL.: Methodist. RES.: Rockville Centre, Long Island, NY.

VARNUM, FRANK L. b. CA. POLIT. & GOV.: ***American Party candidate for vice presidency of the U.S., 1980***. BUS. & PROF.: orchardist; agricultural investment realtor; pilot, capt., American Airlines; aircraft maintenance technician; parachute rigging and packing salesman; air freight pilot. MIL.: flight training instructor, U.S. Army. MAILING ADDRESS: Route 2, Box 1073, Roseburg, OR 97470.

VAUCLAIN, SAMUEL MATTHEWS. b. May 18, 1856, Philadelphia, PA; d. Feb 4, 1940, Philadelphia, PA; par. Andrew Constant and Mary Ann (Campbell) Vauclain; m. Annie Kearney, Apr 17, 1879; c. Samuel Matthews; Mary (Mrs. Franklin Abbott); Jacques Leonard; Anne; Charles Parry; Constance Marshall (Mrs. William H. Hamilton). EDUC.: public schools, Altoona, PA. POLIT. & GOV.: chm., Locomotive and Car Comm., Council on National Defense; chm., Special Advisory Cmte. on Plants and Munitions, War Industries Board; chm., Municipal Gas Comm., Philadelphia, PA; delegate, Rep. Nat'l. Conv., 1920; ***candidate for Republican nomination to presidency of the U.S., 1920***. BUS. & PROF.: employee, Pennsylvania R.R. Co., 1872–83; foreman, Burnham, Parry, Williams and Co. (locomotive works), 1883–86, plant superintendent, 1886–96, partner, 1896–1909; gen. superintendent, Baldwin Locomotive Works, 1909–11, vice pres., 1911–17, senior vice pres., 1917–19, pres., 1919–29, chm. of the board, 1929–40; chm. of the board, Standard Steel Works Co.; chm. of the board, Baldwin-Southwark Corp.; chm. of the board, Whitcomb Locomotive Co.; chm. of the board, Federal Steel Foundry Co.; chm. of the board, I. P. Morris and De La Vergne, Inc.; chm. of the board, De La Vergne Engine Co.; chm. of the board, Manufacturers Mutual Fire Insurance Co.; mgr., Northern Liberties Hospital. MEM.: Legion of Honor (chevalier, France, 1919); Order of Polonia Restituta (Poland, 1923); Order of the Crown of Italy (Il Cancelliere, 1920); Bryn Mawr Hospital (pres.; trustee); John Scott Medal Fund Cmte.; Misericordia Hospital (trustee); Catholic Hospital of West Philadelphia (trustee). AWARDS: Distinguished Service Medal, 1919; John Scott Medal, 1891, 1931. HON. DEG.: Sc.D., U. of PA, 1906; LL.D., Villanova Coll., 1926; LL.D., Worcester Polytechnic Inst., 1931. REL.: Episc. MISC.: invented wrought iron center for locomotive truck and driving wheels, 1889; designed first compound locomotive, 1889 RES.: Rosemont, PA.

VAUGHN, WILLIAM T. b. Apr 12, 1861, Osage, IL; par. William and Elizabeth (Price) Vaughn; m. Viola Deason, Aug 15, 1888. EDUC.: Benton (OR) H.S., 1879; Ewing Coll., 1880–82; law school, Bloomington, IL. POLIT. & GOV.: ***candidate for Democratic nomination to vice presidency of the U.S., 1920 (withdrew)***. BUS. & PROF.: atty.; admitted to IL Bar, 1892; admitted to OR Bar, 1900; law practice, El Paso, IL, 1892–94; law practice, Pinckneyville, IL, 1894–99; law practice, Portland, OR, 1899–. RES.: Portland, OR.

VEATCH, RON. POLIT. & GOV.: ***Freedom Party candidate for presidency of the U.S., 1976***. MAILING ADDRESS: 4408 Lawrence Rd., Fort Worth, TX 76114.

VELOZ, ALFONSO A. "AL." POLIT. & GOV.: candidate for Democratic nomination to gov. of TX, 1968; candidate for Democratic nomination to U.S. Senate (TX), 1972; ***candidate for Democratic nomination to presidency of the U.S., 1980, 1988***. MAILING ADDRESS: 12306 Fourth St., Apt. A, Yucaipa, CA 92399.

VERA, MILTON. POLIT. & GOV.: ***Workers World Party candidate for vice presidency of the U.S., 1984***. MAILING ADDRESS: 482 Fort Washington Ave., New York, NY 10033.

VEREEN, WILLIAM JEROME "WILL." b. Jun 11, 1885, Wheeler Cty., GA; d. Oct 1, 1952, Moultrie, GA; par. William Coachman and Mary (McNeill) Vereen; m. Lottie Thompson, Dec 29, 1908; c. Mary Ellen (Mrs. Thomas A. Huguenin); Rosalind Eugenia (Mrs. George H. Lanier, Jr.); William Coachman; Thompson Jerome. EDUC.: grad., GA Military Acad., 1902. POLIT. & GOV.: elected as a Democrat, mayor of Moultrie, GA, 1916–17; chm., GA State Democratic Exec. Cmte., 1920–21; ***Farmer-Labor Party candidate for vice presidency of the U.S., 1928 (declined)***; appointed member, Industrial Advisory Board, NRA, 1933–34; appointed member, Business Advisory Council, U.S. Dept. of Commerce, 1933–36; member, Board of Regents, University System of GA, 1933–35. BUS. & PROF.: employee, Moultrie Cotton Mills, 1903–17, vice pres., 1917–43, pres., 1943–52; pres., Riverside Manufacturing Co., Moultrie, GA, 1937–52; vice pres., dir., Moultrie Banking Co.; dir., First National Bank of Atlanta. MEM.: Cotton Manufacturers Assn. of GA (pres., 1919); American Cotton Manufacturers Assn. (pres., 1925–26); Southern Garment Manufacturers Assn. (pres., 1937–43, chm. of the board, 1943–52); Rotary Club; Capital City Club of Atlanta; C. of C.; YMCA; BSA. REL.: Presb. (chm., board of deacons, 25 years). RES.: Moultrie, GA.

VERNON, JOHN RICHARD. b. Mar 18, 1940, Cushing, OK; par. Richard Buckley and Mary Louise (Raedeker) Vernon; single. EDUC.: grad., high school, Oklahoma City, OK; private tutors in languages; Kansas City Bible Coll. POLIT. & GOV.: candidate for city council, Oklahoma City, OK, 1975; ***candidate for Libertarian Party nomination to vice presidency of the U.S., 1976***; member, exec. cmte., Libertarian Party, 1976–; Libertarian Party candidate for U.S. House (CA), 1988. BUS. & PROF.: chef; owner, Chez Vernon Restaurant, Oklahoma City, OK, 1971–; newspaper columnist. MEM.: OK Restaurant Assn.; Vice Conseiller Culinier, Confrerie de la Chaine des Rotisseurs; Libertarians for Gay Rights (pres.); Oklahoma City C. of C.; Christian Childrens Fund; OK League for the Blind; Civic Music Assn.; Oklahoma City Symphony (contributor). REL.: none. MAILING ADDRESS: 1206 N.E. 40th St., Oklahoma City, OK.

VEST, GEORGE GRAHAM. b. Dec 6, 1830, Frankfort, KY; d. Aug 9, 1904, Sweet Springs, MO; par. John Jay and Harriet (Graham) Vest; m. Sallie E. Sneed, 1854; c. three. EDUC.: grad., Center Coll., 1848; LL.B., Transylvania U., 1853. POLIT. & GOV.: presidential elector, Democratic Party, 1860; elected as a Democrat to MO State House, 1860–61; elected to Confederate House (MO), 1862–65; appointed to Confederate Senate (MO), 1865; delegate, Dem. Nat'l. Conv., 1872; elected as a Democrat to U.S. Senate (MO), 1879–1903; ***candidate for Democratic nomination to presidency of the U.S., 1896; candidate for People's Party nomination to presidency of the U.S., 1896***. BUS. & PROF.: atty.; admitted to MO Bar, 1853; law practice, Georgetown, MO, 1853–56; law practice, Boonville, MO, 1856; law practice, Sedalia, MO, 1865–77; law practice, Kansas City, MO, 1877–1903. MIL.: judge advocate, C.S.A., 1862. WRITINGS: *Missouri: Its History and Resources*. REL.: Presb. RES.: Sweet Springs, MO.

VICK, CHARLES GORDON. b. 1917; m.; c. two. EDUC.: J.D.; D.D.; Ph.D. POLIT. & GOV.: elected notary public, state of TN, 11 terms; candidate for Democratic nomination to U.S. Senate (TN), 1964, 1978; independent candidate for gov. of TN, 1966; independent candidate for U.S. House (TN), 1966, 1968; candidate for Democratic nomination to U.S. House (TN), 1968, 1972; candidate for Democratic nomination to gov. of TN, 1974, 1978; ***candidate for Democratic nomination to presidency of the U.S., 1976, 1980, 1988, 1992***; candidate for Republican nomination to U.S. Senate (TN), 1986; independent candidate for U.S. Senate (TN), 1990. REL.: Christian. MAILING ADDRESS: 1481 Robin Hood Lane, Memphis, TN 38111.

VIDEEN, GORDON WAYNE. POLIT. & GOV.: ***Minor Party candidate for presidency of the U.S., 1980***. MAILING ADDRESS: 2515 Indian Ridge Rd., Tucson, AZ 85715.

VIGUERIE, RICHARD ART. b. Sep 23, 1933, Houston, TX; par. Arthur C. and Elizabeth (Stoufflet) Viguerie;

m. Elaine Adele O'Leary, 1962; c. Renee; Michelle; Richard Ryan. EDUC.: B.A., U. of Houston, 1956. POLIT. & GOV.: chm., Harris Cty. (TX) Young Republicans, 1959; ***candidate for American Independent Party nomination to presidency of the U.S., 1976; candidate for American Independent Party nomination to vice presidency of the U.S., 1976***; candidate for U.S. Senate (VA), 1976; candidate for Republican nomination to lt. gov. of VA, 1985. BUS. & PROF.: mail order consultant; pres., publisher, *Conservative Digest*, 1975–; chm. of the board, Jefferson Communications; publisher, *New Right Report*; pres., Prospect House, Inc.; pres., American Mailing List Corp.; chm. of the board, Diversified Mail Marketing, Inc.; founder, pres., Richard A. Viguerie Co., 1965–. MIL.: U.S. Army. MEM.: Young Americans for Freedom (exec. sec., 1961); Freedom of Choice; Cmte. for a New Majority (founder, 1975); Conservative Caucus. WRITINGS: *The New Right: We're Ready to Lead* (1980); *The Establishment vs. the People* (1983). REL.: R.C. MAILING ADDRESS: 7777 Leesburg Pike, Falls Church, VA; McLean, VA.

VINCENT, EDWARD JESSE. POLIT. & GOV.: ***candidate for Democratic nomination to presidency of the U.S., 1984***. MAILING ADDRESS: P.O. Box 1001, Colfax, CA 95713.

VINICKI, JON JAY. b. Feb 28, 1970, Creve Coeur, MO; par. John and Betty Jo (Tillery) Vinicki; single. EDUC.: Starkville (MS) H.S. POLIT. & GOV.: ***independent candidate for presidency of the U.S., 1984***. BUS. & PROF.: student, Starkville (MS) H.S., 1983–. AWARDS: Honorable Mention, MS Regional Science Fair. REL.: Church of Christ. MAILING ADDRESS: Route 5, Box 65, Starkville, MS 39759.

VOELKER, CALVIN J. POLIT. & GOV.: ***candidate for Democratic nomination to presidency of the U.S., 1976***. MAILING ADDRESS: Rt. 1, Box 142, Peterson, MN 55962.

VOGEL, ALLAN. POLIT. & GOV.: ***independent candidate for presidency of the U.S., 1980 (declined)***. MAILING ADDRESS: P.O. Box 25043, Houston, TX 77005.

VOGEL, ROGER E. "CATFISH." POLIT. & GOV.: ***candidate for Republican nomination to presidency of the U.S., 1988***. MAILING ADDRESS: 1997 Riverview Dr., Defiance, OH 43512.

VOIGT, SHARON GAY TRACY. b. Dec 19, 1938, Lemmon, SD; d. Walter James and Ada Hannah (Voigt) Tracy. EDUC.: public library. POLIT. & GOV.: ***candidate for Republican nomination to presidency of the U.S., 1980; independent candidate for presidency of the U.S., 1980***. BUS. & PROF.: sec.; freelance writer. REL.: Christian. MISC.: assumed name of maternal grandparents for professional purposes. MAILING ADDRESS: P.O. Box 1180, Las Vegas, NV 89101.

VOLPE, JOHN ANTHONY. b. Dec 8, 1908, Wakefield, MA; d. Nov 11, 1994, Nahant, MA; par. Vito and Filomena (Benedetto) Volpe; m. Jennie Benedetto, Jun 18, 1934; c. John Anthony, Jr.; Loretta Jean (Mrs. Roger Rotondi). EDUC.: Wentworth Inst., 1928–30. POLIT. & GOV.: deputy chm., MA State Republican Cmte., 1950–53; appointed member, MA State Public Works Comm., 1953–56; appointed first Federal Highway Administrator, 1956–57; delegate, Rep. Nat'l. Conv., 1960, 1964, 1968, 1972; candidate for Republican nomination to gov. of MA, 1958; elected as a Republican to gov. of MA, 1961–63, 1965–69; Republican candidate for gov. of MA, 1962; ***candidate for Republican nomination to presidency of the U.S., 1968***; appointed U.S. sec. of transportation, 1969–73; appointed U.S. ambassador to Italy, 1973–77. BUS. & PROF.: pres., John A. Volpe Construction Co., Malden, MA, 1933–60, chm. of the board, 1960– 69; publisher, *Malden (MA) News*; publisher, *Medford (MA) Daily Mercury*. MIL.: lt. (jg), lt. commander, U.S. Navy, 1943–46. MEM.: Don Orione Home for the Aged (treas., advisory board, 1950–53); Capitol Hill Club; Knights of Malta; Knights of Columbus; Sons of Italy in America; American Legion; Order of Merit (Knight of the Grand Cross, Italy); Equestrian Order of the Holy Sepulchre of Jerusalem (knight commander with star); S.A.M.E. (pres.); Associated General Contractors of America (pres.); Ancient and Honorable Artillery Company; Wentworth Inst. (trustee); Army and Navy Club; Elks; MA C. of C. (pres.); Greater Boston C. of C.; Rotary Club. AWARDS: People to People Town Affiliation Award, 1966; Construction Man of the Year Award, 1970. HON. DEG.: L.H.D., St. Michael's Coll., 1955; D.Eng., Northeastern U., 1956; D.H.L., Merrimack Coll., 1961; D.H.L., Stonehill Coll., 1961; D.P.A., Suffolk U., 1961; D.Sc., Lowell Technological Inst., 1963; D.H.L., American International Coll., 1965; D.P.A., Southwestern MA Technological Inst., 1966; LL.D., Boston U., 1966; D.H.L., Brandeis U., 1967; LL.D., Anna Maria Coll., 1967; LL.D., Long Island U., 1967; LL.D., U. of MA, 1967; LL.D., Butler U.; LL.D., Calvin Coolidge Coll.; LL.D., Catholic U. of America; LL.D., U. of Chicago; LL.D., Lesley Coll.; LL.D., Loyola U.; LL.D., Niagara U.; LL.D., Oblate Coll.; LL.D., OH State U.; LL.D., Salem State Coll.; LL.D., Southern U.; LL.D., U. of Southern CA. REL.: R.C. RES.: Nahant, MA.

VON RASE, DONALD JAMES. b. 1931, Chicago, IL; m. Doris Von R. POLIT. & GOV.: ***candidate for Democratic nomination to presidency of the U.S., 1976***. BUS. & PROF.: press agent; public affairs counsel. MAILING ADDRESS: 4229 Beverly Rd., Madison, WI 53711.

VOORHEES, DANIEL WOLSEY. b. Sep 26, 1827, Liberty, OH; d. Apr 10, 1897, Washington, DC; par.

Stephen and Rachel (Elliott) Voorhees; m. Anna Hardesty, Jul 18, 1850; c. Charles Stewart; Harriet Cecilia; James Paxton; Daniel W. EDUC.: A.B., IN Asbury (now De Pauw) U., 1849, A.M., 1852; studied law in offices of Lane and Wilson, Crawfordsville, IN. POLIT. & GOV.: appointed prosecuting atty., IN Circuit Court, 1853; Democratic candidate for U.S. House (IN), 1856, 1872; appointed U.S. district atty. (IN), 1858–61; elected as a Democrat to U.S. House (IN), 1861–66, 1869–73; ***candidate for Democratic nomination to vice presidency of the U.S., 1864, 1872***; appointed and subsequently elected as a Democrat to U.S. Senate (IN), 1877–97; Democratic candidate for U.S. Senate (IN), 1897. BUS. & PROF.: atty.; admitted to IN Bar, 1851; law practice, Covington, IN, 1851–57; law practice, Terre Haute, IN, 1957–. HON. DEG.: LL.D., IN Asbury, 1884; WRITINGS: *Speech Delivered in Fountain Circuit Court, July, 1857* (1857); *The American Citizen* (1860); *Address on the Trial of John E. Cook* (1861); *The Rights of Citizens* (1863); *Speech* (1862); *Greeley as the Democratic Candidate for President*; *Speeches* (1875); *Boudinot Tobacco Case* (1880); *The Library of Congress* (1880); *Address . . . to the Jury in the Case of Kilbourn vs. Thompson* (1882); *Address Favoring Joseph E. McDonald for President* (1884); *Speech in Defense of Captain Edward T. Johnson* (1885); *Forty Years of Oratory* (1898). REL.: Episc. MISC.: known as the "Tall Sycamore of the Wabash." RES.: Terre Haute, IN.

VOSS, MICHAEL. b. 1953. EDUC.: Miami-Dade Community Coll. POLIT. & GOV.: ***Christian Party candidate for vice presidency of the U.S., 1976***. BUS. & PROF.: music student, Miami-Dade Community Coll., Miami, FL. MAILING ADDRESS: c/o Dr. Ruth Greenfield, Miami-Dade Community Coll., Music Dept., 4th St., N.E., Miami, FL 33101.

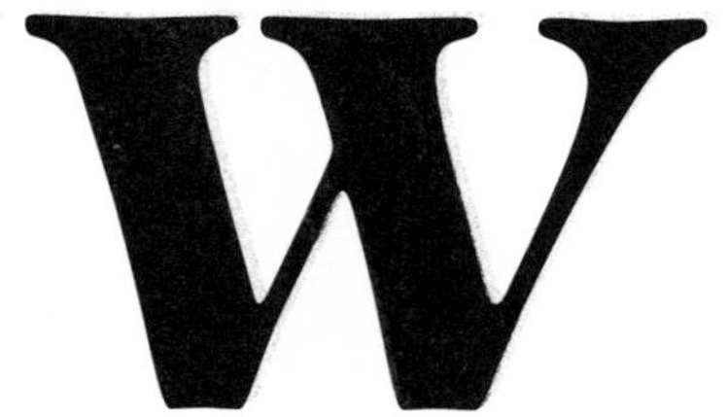

WADE, BENJAMIN FRANKLIN. b. Oct 27, 1800, Feeding Hills, MA; d. Mar 2, 1878, Jefferson, OH; par. James and Mary (Upham) Wade; m. Caroline M. Rosecrans, May 19, 1841; c. James F.; Henry P. EDUC.: studied medicine, Albany, NY, 1823–25; studied law in office of Whittlesey and Newton, Canfield, OH, 1826–27. POLIT. & GOV.: elected as a Whig, prosecuting atty., Ashtabula Cty., OH, 1835–37; elected as a Whig to OH State Senate, 1837–39, 1841–43; Whig candidate for OH State Senate, 1839; elected by legislature, presiding judge, Third Judicial District of OH, 1847–51; elected as a Whig to U.S. Senate (OH), 1851–57; elected as a Republican to U.S. Senate (OH), 1857–69 (pres. pro tempore, 1867–69); ***candidate for Republican nomination to presidency of the U.S., 1860, 1868***; delegate, Southern Loyalist Convention, 1866; ***candidate for Republican nomination to vice presidency of the U.S., 1868***; candidate for Republican nomination to U.S. Senate (OH), 1868; appointed member, Santo Domingo Comm., 1871; ***candidate for Equal Rights (Cosmic, Free Love, People's) Party nomination to vice presidency of the U.S., 1872***; delegate, Rep. Nat'l. Conv., 1876. BUS. & PROF.: laborer, Erie Canal, 1825–26; schoolteacher; atty.; admitted to OH Bar, 1827; law practice, Jefferson, OH, 1827; partner (with Joshua R. Giddings, q.v.), law firm, 1831–38; partner (with Rufus P. Ranney), law firm, 1838–47; counsel, Northern Pacific Railway. WRITINGS: *Speech on the Nebraska and Kansas Bills* (1854); *Plain Truths for the People* (1858); *Invasion of Harper's Ferry* (1859); *Facts for the People* (1864); *Speech . . . on the State of the Union* (1860); *Properties in the Territories* (1860); *Speech . . . on the Confiscation Bill* (1862); *Traitors and Their Sympathizers* (1862); *Against the Immediate Restoration of the Seceded States* (1866). REL.: Deist. RES.: Jefferson, OH.

WADE, DAVID VINCENT. POLIT. & GOV.: ***candidate for Democratic nomination to presidency of the U.S., 1980***. MAILING ADDRESS: c/o Harry Jewett, P.O. Box 320, Prudential Center, Boston, MA.

WADE, MARTIN JOSEPH. b. Oct 20, 1861, Burlington, VT; d. Apr 16, 1931, Los Angeles, CA; par. Michael and Mary (Breen) Wade; m. Mary Gertrude McGovern, Apr 4, 1888; c. Julia R.; Eleanor M. EDUC.: St. Joseph's Coll.; LL.B., U. of IA, 1886. POLIT. & GOV.: elected judge, 8th Judicial District of IA, 1893–1902; elected as a Democrat to U.S. House (IA), 1903–05; Democratic candidate for U.S. House (IA), 1904; delegate, Dem. Nat'l. Conv., 1904, 1912; member, Dem. Nat'l. Cmte., 1907–14; ***candidate for Democratic nomination to vice presidency of the U.S., 1912***; appointed judge, U.S. District Court, Southern District of IA, 1915–31. BUS. & PROF.: atty.; admitted to IA Bar, 1886; law practice, Iowa City, IA, 1886–93; partner (with C. S. Ranck), law firm, Iowa City, IA, 1886; partner, Wade, Dutcher and Davis (law firm), Iowa City, IA, 1905–15; lecturer on Law, U. of IA, 1891–1903; prof. of Medical Jurisprudence, 1895–1905. MEM.: IA State Bar Assn. (pres., 1897–98). WRITINGS: *A Selection of Cases on Malpractice of Physicians, Surgeons and Dentists* (1909); *Lessons in Americanism* (1920); *The Short Constitution* (with W. F. Russell, 1921); *The Constitution Through Problems* (1931); *Lessons in Citizenship*; *The Constitution and You*; *Down With the Constitution*. RES.: Iowa City, IA.

WADSWORTH, JAMES WOLCOTT. b. Oct 12, 1846, Philadelphia, PA; d. Dec 24, 1926, Washington, DC; par. Gen. James Samuel and Mary Craig (Wharton) Wadsworth; m. Louisa Travers, Sep 14, 1876; c. James Wolcott, Jr. (q.v.); Harriet Travers (Mrs. Fletcher Harper). EDUC.: Hopkins Grammar School; Yale U., 1865–67. POLIT. & GOV.: elected as a Republican, supervisor of Geneseo, NY, 1873–78; elected as a Republican to NY State Assembly, 1878–79; elected as a Republican, NY state controller, 1880–81; elected as a Republican to U.S. House (NY), 1881–85, 1891–1907; Republican candidate for U.S. House (NY), 1906; ***candidate for Republican nomination to vice presidency of the U.S., 1908***; delegate, NY State Constitutional Convention, 1914; appointed chm., NY State Racing Comm.

BUS. & PROF.: farmer, Geneseo, NY, 1865–1926; pres., Genesee Valley National Bank, to 1924; horse breeder. MIL.: capt., U.S. Army, 1864, brev. maj., 1865. MEM.: National Home for Disabled Volunteer Soldiers (pres., board of managers). HON. DEG.: M.A., Yale U., 1898. REL.: Episc. RES.: Geneseo, NY.

WADSWORTH, JAMES WOLCOTT, JR.

b. Aug 12, 1877, Geneseo, NY; d. Jun 21, 1952, Washington, DC; par. James Wolcott (q.v.) and Louisa (Travers) Wadsworth; m. Alice Hay, Sep 30, 1902; c. Evelyn (Mrs. William Stuart Symington, q.v.); James Jeremiah; Reverdy. EDUC.: St. Mark's School; B.A., Yale U., 1898. POLIT. & GOV.: elected as a Republican to NY State Assembly, 1905–10 (Speaker, 1906–10); delegate, Rep. Nat'l. Conv., 1908, 1912, 1916, 1920, 1924, 1928, 1936, 1940; Republican candidate for lt. gov. of NY, 1912; elected as a Republican to U.S. Senate (NY), 1915–27; Republican candidate for U.S. Senate (NY), 1926; ***candidate for Republican nomination to presidency of the U.S., 1932, 1936***; elected as a Republican to U.S. House (NY), 1933–51; ***candidate for Republican nomination to vice presidency of the U.S., 1936***; appointed chm., National Security Training Comm., 1951–52. BUS. & PROF.: livestock farmer, Geneseo, NY, 1899–1952; ranch mgr., Paloduro, TX, 1911–15; dir., Genesee Valley Bank and Trust Co. MIL.: enlisted, Battery A, PA F.A., U.S. Army, 1898–99. MEM.: Soc. of the Cincinnati; SAR; American Liberty League (founder); Loyal Legion; Delta Kappa Epsilon; Spanish War Veterans; Grange; Carnegie Institution (trustee); University Club; Yale Club; Metropolitan Club; Fort Orange Club; Cornell U. (trustee). AWARDS: named to Walter Camp's All-American Baseball Team while at Yale U. REL.: Episc. RES.: Geneseo, NY.

WAGGONER, IRA R.

POLIT. & GOV.: ***independent candidate for presidency of the U.S., 1976***. MAILING ADDRESS: Box 1145, Champaign, IL 61820.

WAGNER, LAWRENCE PAUL.

POLIT. & GOV.: ***independent candidate for presidency of the U.S., 1984***. MAILING ADDRESS: 124 Capistrano Place, Los Gatos, CA 95030.

WAGNER, ROBERT FERDINAND, JR.

b. Apr 20, 1910, New York, NY; d. Feb 13, 1991, New York, NY; par. Robert Ferdinand and Margaret (McTeague) Wagner; m. Susan Edwards, Feb 14, 1942; m. 2d, Barbara Joan Cavanaugh, Jul 1965 (annulled); m. 3d, Phyllis Fraser Cerf, Jan 1975; c. Robert Ferdinand III; Duncan Weaver. EDUC.: A.B., Yale U., 1933, LL.B., 1937; Harvard U., 1934. POLIT. & GOV.: elected as a Democrat to NY State Assembly, 1938–41; appointed New York (NY) City Tax Commissioner, 1946; appointed Commissioner of Housing and Buildings, New York, NY, 1947; appointed chm., New York (NY) Planning Comm., 1948; delegate, Dem. Nat'l. Conv., 1948, 1952, 1956, 1960, 1964, 1968, 1972 (alternate), 1976; elected as a Democrat-Liberal, pres., Borough of Manhattan, NY, 1949–53; candidate for Democratic nomination to U.S. Senate (NY), 1952; elected as a Democrat, mayor of New York, NY, 1954–66; Democratic candidate for U.S. Senate (NY), 1956; ***candidate for Democratic nomination to vice presidency of the U.S., 1956***; appointed member, President's Comm. on Crime, 1965–66; appointed chm., Democratic Nationalities Council; first vice pres., NY State Constitutional Convention, 1967; appointed U.S. ambassador to Spain, 1968–69; delegate, Democratic Mid-Term Conference, 1974; appointed personal envoy of the president to the Vatican, 1978–80; member, New York (NY) Temporary Comm. on City Finances; member, NY State Law Revision Comm.; vice chm., Port of NY Authority; candidate for Democratic nomination to mayor of New York, NY, 1969. BUS. & PROF.: atty.; admitted to NY Bar, 1937; partner, Finley, Kumble, Wagner, Heine and Underberg (law firm), 1972–91. MIL.: lt. col., U.S. Air Force, 1942–45, col.; 6 Battle Stars; Croix de Guerre. MEM.: United Neighborhood Houses (pres.); NY Landmarks Conservancy (dir.); Elks; American Legion; Grand Street Boys; Knights of Columbus; National Conference of Christians and Jews. HON. DEG.: LL.D., Brooklyn Law School; LL.D., Fordham U.; LL.D., Long Island U.; LL.D., St. John's Law School. REL.: R.C. RES.: New York, NY.

WAINWRIGHT, JONATHAN MAYHEW.

b. Aug 23, 1883, Fort Walla Walla, WA; d. Sep 2, 1953, San Antonio, TX; par. Robert Powell Page and Josephine (Serrell) Wainwright; m. Adele Howard Holley, Feb 18, 1911; c. Jonathan Mayhew. EDUC.: grad., U.S. Military Acad., 1906; grad., Army War Coll. POLIT. & GOV.: ***candidate for Republican nomination to presidency of the U.S., 1952 (declined)***. BUS. & PROF.: soldier; businessman; pres., Armed Forces Mutual Life Insurance Co.; chm. of the board, Time Life Insurance Co., San Antonio, TX; chm. of the board, Hom-Ond Food Stores; mgr., Alamo Stock Farm; vice pres., Acme Sash Window Balance Co. MIL.: commissioned 2d lt., First Cavalry, U.S. Army, 1906; lt. col., asst. chief of staff, 82d Div., 1917–19; asst. chief of staff, American Army of Occupation of Germany, 1919–20; maj., 1920; dir. of instruction, asst. commandant, Cavalry School, Fort Riley, KS; lt. col., 1929, col., 1935, brig. gen., 1938; commander, maj. gen., Philippine Div., 1940, lt. gen., 1941, gen., 1945–47; surrendered U.S. forces to Japanese at Corregidor, 1942; prisoner of war, 1942–45; Distinguished Service Medal with Oak Leaf Cluster, 1920; Distinguished Service Cross, 1942; Medal of Honor, 1945; Croix de Guerre (Belgium); Legion of Honor (France); Medal of Valor (Philippines). MEM.: VFW; Military Order of the Carabao; SAR; Alpha Phi Gamma; Elks; Rotary Club; Army and Navy Club; Fort Worth Club; Masons (33°); Disabled American Veterans (life member; national commander, 1949); American Legion (life member); Military Order of the World Wars; Third U.S. Cavalry Veterans Assn.; Loyal Legion (hon. commander in chief); Military Order of Foreign Wars of the U.S. (companion); American Flag Day Assn. (hon. life member); Yakima Tribe (adopted member); Soldiers and Sailors Club of NY (hon. vice pres.). HON. DEG.: Dr.Mil.Sci., PA Military Coll., 1942; LL.D., NM Coll. of A&M Arts, 1945; LL.D., Coll. of Puget Sound, 1945; LL.D., Syracuse U., 1945; LL.D., Whitman Coll., 1945; L.H.D., Rollins Coll., 1946. WRITINGS: *General Wainwright's Story* (1945). RES.: San Antonio, TX.

WAITT, WILLIAM S. POLIT. & GOV.: ***Industrial Congress Party candidate for vice presidency of the U.S., 1848***. RES.: IL.

WAKEFIELD, WILLIAM HARRISON THOMPSON. b. Dec 13, 1834, Vandalia, IL; par. John Allen and Eliza (Thompson) Wakefield; m. Emma Wakefield (cousin), Dec 22, 1869; c. Harry Louis; Lulu May; Charles Henry; John Allen. EDUC.: public schools; Plattville (WI) Acad.; studied law under John Allen Wakefield. POLIT. & GOV.: sec., KS Republican Territorial Convention, 1856; United Labor Party candidate for State Auditor of KS, 1886; ***United Labor Party candidate for vice presidency of the U.S., 1888 (withdrew)***. BUS. & PROF.: farmer, Douglas Cty., KS, 1854; atty.; journalist; ed., *Kansas Daily Tribune*; ed., *Topeka (KS) Daily Journal*; ed., *The Anti-Monopolist*, 1883; ed., *The Jeffersonian*. MIL.: scout, First KS Infantry, 1861; clerk, Company B, 12th KS Volunteers, 1862; commanded Company E, 11th U.S. Colored Troops; judge advocate gen., provost marshall, VII Army Corps, brev. lt. col.; discharged, 1866; prisoner of war, Civil War. REL.: agnostic. RES.: Mound City, KS.

WALDEN, JIM. POLIT. & GOV.: ***candidate for Democratic nomination to presidency of the U.S., 1988***. BUS. & PROF.: doctor. MAILING ADDRESS: 162 Flat Rock Rd., Stockbridge, GA 30281.

WALKER, CHARLS EDWARD. b. Dec 24, 1923, Graham, TX; par. Pinkney Clay and Sammye D. (McCombs) Walker; m. Harmolyn Hart, Jun 24, 1949; c. Carolyn; Charls Edward. EDUC.: B.B.A., U. of TX, 1947, M.B.A., 1948; Ph.D., U. of PA, 1955. POLIT. & GOV.: financial economist, Federal Reserve Bank, Philadelphia, PA, 1953; financial economist, Federal Reserve Bank, Dallas, TX, 1954–61 (vice pres., 1958–61); appointed asst. to the U.S. sec. of the treasury, 1959–61; appointed U.S. undersec. of the treasury, 1969–72; appointed U.S. deputy sec. of the treasury, 1972–73; ***candidate for Democratic nomination to presidency of the U.S., 1976***. BUS. & PROF.: economist; instructor in Finance, U. of TX, 1947–48, asst. prof., assoc. prof., 1950–54; instructor in Finance, Wharton School, U. of PA, 1948–50; economist, Republic National Bank, Dallas, TX, 1955–56; pres., Charls E. Walker Associates, Inc., Washington, DC, 1973–. MIL.: 2d lt., U.S.A.A.F., 1943–45. MEM.: Union Club; American Bankers Assn. (exec. vice pres., 1961–69); American Council for Capital Formation (chm.); Cmte. on the Present Danger (chm.); Burning Tree Club; Congressional Club; Federal City Club; Council on Foreign Relations; Joint Council on Economic Education (vice chm.). AWARDS: Alexander Hamilton Award, U.S. Dept. of the Treasury; award, Urban League. WRITINGS: *The Banker's Handbook* (co-editor). MISC.: served as co-chm., presidential debates, 1976. MAILING ADDRESS: 10120 Chapel Rd., Potomac, MD 20854.

WALKER, DANIEL. b. Aug 6, 1922, Washington, DC; par. Lewis W. and Virginia (Lynch) Walker; m. Roberta Dowse, Apr 12, 1947; c. Kathleen; Daniel; Julie Ann; Roberta Sue; Charles; Margaret Ann; William. EDUC.: B.S., U.S. Naval Acad., 1945; J.D., Northwestern U., 1950. POLIT. & GOV.: law clerk, U.S. Supreme Court, 1950–51; Commissioner, U.S. Court of Military Appeals, 1951–52; administrative asst. to Gov. Adlai E. Stevenson (q.v.), 1952; candidate for Democratic nomination to atty. gen. of IL, 1960; sec., acting chm., IL Public Aid Comm., 1962–63; pres., Chicago (IL) Crime Comm., 1967–69; dir., Chicago Study Team, National Comm. on Violence, 1968; appointed member, Chicago (IL) Riot Study Comm., 1968; elected as a Democrat to gov. of IL, 1973–77; ***candidate for Democratic nomination to presidency of the U.S., 1976***; candidate for Democratic nomination to gov. of IL, 1976. BUS. & PROF.: atty.; admitted to IL Bar, 1950; law practice, Chicago, IL, 1953–72; assoc., Ross, McGowan and O'Keefe (law firm), Chicago, IL, 1953–54; assoc., Hopkins, Sutter, Owen, Mulroy, Wentz and Davis (law firm), Chicago, IL, 1954–66; vice pres., sec., gen. counsel, Montgomery Ward, Chicago, IL, 1966–71; dir., vice pres., gen. counsel, MARCOR, Inc., 1968–71; dir., Pioneer Trust and Savings Bank, 1967–71; partner, Walker, Gende, Hatcher, Berz and Giamanco (law firm), Chicago, IL, 1977–. MIL.: U.S. Navy, 1939–47, 1951. MEM.: ABA; IL Bar Assn.; Chicago Bar Assn.; Law Club; Legal Club (exec. cmte., 1969); Bar Assn. of the 7th Federal Circuit; American Soc. for International Law; Northwestern U. Alumni Assn. (pres., 1969); Order of the Coif; Mid-America Club; Executives Club; Economic Club; Leadership Council for Metropolitan Open Communities (dir., 1966–71). AWARDS: Alumni Merit Award, Northwestern U., 1969; Roger Baldwin Award, 1969; Civic Award, Chicago Newspaper Guild, 1969. HON. DEG.: L.H.D., Carroll Coll., 1969. WRITINGS: *Military Law* (1955); *Rights in Conflict* (1968). MISC.: convicted and imprisoned for bribery following term as governor. MAILING ADDRESS: 1152 Norman Lane, Deerfield, IL 60015.

WALKER, EDWIN ANDERSON. b. Nov 10, 1909, Center Point, TX; par. George Pinckney and Charlotte (Thornton) Walker; single. EDUC.: Schreiner Inst.; NM Military Inst., 1927; B.S., U.S. Military Acad., 1931; grad., F.A. School, 1937; grad., Command and Gen. Staff Coll., 1946; grad., Air War Coll., 1948. POLIT. & GOV.: candidate for Democratic nomination to gov. of TX, 1962; ***candidate for Democratic nomination to presidency of the U.S., 1964***. BUS. & PROF.: soldier; businessman; vice pres., Eagle Publishing Co., 1962–68, pres., 1969–; author; lecturer. MIL.: U.S. Army, 1931–61; advanced through grades to maj. gen., 1957; Silver Star; Bronze Star with Cluster; Legion of Merit with Cluster; Korean Unit Citation; Croix de Guerre; Order of St. Olav (Norway); Order of the British Empire; Ulchi Medal with Gold and Silver Stars (Korea). MISC.: commanded U.S. troops during integration controversy, Little Rock, AR, 1959. MAILING ADDRESS: 4011 Turtle Creek Blvd., Dallas, TX 75219.

WALKER, GEORGE HERBERT. b. Jun 11, 1874, St. Louis, MO; par. David D. and Martha A. (Beakey) Walker; m. Loulie Wear, Jan 17, 1899; c. George Herbert, Jr. EDUC.: LL.B., WA U., 1897. POLIT. & GOV.: ***candidate for Republican nomination to presidency of the U.S., 1920***. BUS. & PROF.: organizer, senior partner, George H. Walker and Co., St. Louis, MO; chm. of the board, International Great Northern Railway Co.; pres., W. A. Harriman and Co.; dir., American Ship and Commerce Corp.; dir., Belgian-American Coke Ovens Corp.; dir., The Cuba Co.; dir., Pennsylvania Coal and Coke Corp.; dir., Certain-Teed Products Corp.; chm. of the board, Habirshaw Cable and Wire Corp. RES.: New York, NY.

WALKER, GILBERT CARLTON. b. Aug 1, 1832, Cuba, NY; d. May 11, 1885, New York, NY; par. Sabinus and Matilda (Gallowy) Walker; m. Olive E. Evans, Apr 14, 1857; c. none. EDUC.: DE Acad.; Binghampton Acad.; Williams Coll., 1851–52; A.B., Hamilton Coll., 1854, A.M., 1857; read law under Judge Horace S. Griswold. POLIT. & GOV.: Democratic candidate for district atty., Tioga Cty., NY, 1856; sec., NY State Democratic Convention, 1858; Democratic candidate for Chicago (IL) Corporation Counsel; candidate for delegate, VA State Constitutional Convention, 1867; appointed provisional gov. of VA, 1869–70; elected as a Democrat to gov. of VA, 1870–74; ***candidate for Liberal Republican Party nomination to vice presidency of the U.S., 1872***; elected as a Conservative to U.S. House (VA), 1875–77, 1877–79 (as a Democrat). BUS. & PROF.: atty.; admitted to NY Bar, 1855; law practice, Owego, NY, 1955–59; law practice, Chicago, IL, 1859–64; law practice, Norfolk, VA, 1864–69; banker; pres., Exchange National Bank, 1864; pres., American Fire Insurance Co.; pres., Atlantic Iron Works and Dock Co., 1866–70; law practice, Binghamton, NY, 1879–81; law practice, New York, NY, 1881–85; pres., New York Underground R.R. Co. WRITINGS: *Address at Commencement of the Virginia Agricultural and Mechanical College* (1873); *The President's Veto of the Silver Bill* (1878). RES.: Binghamton, NY.

WALKER, ISAAC PIGEON. b. Nov 2, 1815, Wheeling, VA (now WV); d. Mar 29, 1872, Milwaukee, WI. EDUC.: public schools, IL; studied law. POLIT. & GOV.: elected as a Democrat to IL State House, 1839–41; presidential elector, Democratic Party, 1840; elected as a Democrat to WI Territorial House, 1847–48; elected as a Democrat to U.S. Senate (WI), 1848–55; ***Industrial Congress Party candidate for presidency of the U.S., 1852***. BUS. & PROF.: clerk, store; atty.; admitted to IL Bar, 1834; law practice, Springfield, IL; law practice, Milwaukee, WI; farmer, Eagle, WI. WRITINGS: *Speech . . . on the Bill to Cede the Public Lands* (1850); *Speech of Mr. Walker of Wisconsin* (1850); *Speech* (1851). RES.: Eagle, WI.

WALKER, JAMES ALEXANDER. b. Aug 27, 1832, Mount Meridian, VA; d. Oct 21, 1901, Wytheville, VA; par. Alexander and Hannah (Hinton) Walker; m. Sarah A. Pouge, 1858; c. four sons; two daughters. EDUC.: grad., VA Military Inst., 1852; U. of VA, 1854–55. POLIT. & GOV.: elected commonwealth's atty., Pulaski Cty., VA, 1860; Conservative Party candidate for lt. gov. of VA, 1869 (withdrew); elected as a Democrat to VA State House of Delegates, 1871–72; elected as a Democrat to lt. gov. of VA, 1877; joined Republican Party, 1893; elected as a Republican to U.S. House (VA), 1895–99; ***candidate for Republican nomination to vice presidency of the U.S., 1896***; Republican candidate for U.S. House (VA), 1898. BUS. & PROF.: civil engineer, Covington R.R., 1852–54; atty.; admitted to VA Bar, 1856; law practice, New Bern, VA, 1856. MIL.: capt., Pulaski Guards (later Company C, 4th VA Infantry), C.S.A., 1861; lt. col., 13th VA Infantry, 1861, col., 1862, brig. gen., 1863–65; severely wounded at Spotsylvania, 1864. RES.: Wytheville, VA.

WALKER, JAMES BARR. b. Jul 29, 1805, Philadelphia, PA; d. Mar 6, 1887, Wheaton, IL; par. James and Margaret (Barr) Walker; m. Rebecca Randall, Jun 6, 1833; m. 2d, Mary (Myrtle) Weamer, Apr 3, 1876; c. thirteen (adopted). EDUC.: grad., Western Reserve Coll., 1831. POLIT. & GOV.: elected to MI State Senate, 1865; ***American National Party candidate for presidency of the U.S., 1876***. BUS. & PROF.: errand boy; printer's apprentice; schoolmaster; co-owner, *Western Courier*, Ravenna, OH; atty.; agent, American Bible Soc.; ed., religious paper, Hudson, OH, 1833–35; ordained minister, Presbyterian Church, 1837; pastor, Presbyterian Church, Akron, OH, 1837–39; ed., *The Watchman of the Valley*, Cincinnati, OH, 1840–42; ed., *The Herald of the Prairies*, Chicago, IL, 1846–50; pastor, Congregational Church, Mansfield, OH, 1842–46, 1850–57; pastor, Congregational Church, Sandusky, OH, 1857–63; lecturer, Chicago Theological Seminary, 1859–65; prof., Lawrenceberg, OH; pres., Benzonia Coll., MI; ed., *Advance*; prof. of Intellectual and Moral Philosophy and Belles-Lettres, Wheaton (IL) Coll., 1870–87; pastor, Coll. Church, Wheaton, IL, 1871–87. MIL.: capt., AAG, U.S. Army, 1863–65. HON. DEG.: D.D., Western Reserve Coll. WRITINGS: *The Philosophy of the Plan of Salvation* (1841); *God Revealed in the Process of Creation* (1855); *Philosophy of Skepticism and Ultraism* (1857); *The Philosophy of the Divine Operation in the Redemption of Man* (1862); *The Doctrine of the Holy Spirit* (1869); *The Living Questions of the Age* (1869); *Poetry of Reason and Conscience* (1871); *Experience of Pioneer Life in the Early Settlements and Cities of the West* (1881). REL.: Congregationalist. RES.: Wheaton, IL.

WALKER, JAMES JOHN JOSEPH. b. Jun 19, 1881, New York, NY; d. Nov 18, 1946, New York, NY; par. William Henry and Ellen Ida (Roon) Walker; m. Janet Frances Allen, Apr 11, 1912; m. 2d, Violet Holling Compton, Apr 18, 1933; c. Mary Ann (adopted); James John Joseph (adopted). EDUC.: St. Francis Xavier School; La Salle School; St. Francis Xavier Coll.; LL.B., NY Law School, 1912. POLIT. & GOV.: elected as a Democrat to NY State Assembly, 1909–14; elected as a Democrat to NY State Senate, 1915–25 (minority leader, 1921); elected as a Democrat, mayor of New York, NY, 1925–32; ***candidate for Democratic nomination to presidency of the U.S., 1928***; appointed asst. counsel, NY State Transit Comm., 1937; appointed chm., National Cloak and Suit Industry Arbitration Board, 1940–45. BUS. & PROF.: atty.; admitted to NY Bar, 1912; law practice, New York, NY, 1912–46; sec., asst. treas., New York and Brooklyn R.R.; songwriter; lumberman; pres., Majestic Records, Inc., 1945–46. MEM.: Grand Street Boys' Assn.; Elks. WRITINGS: "Will You Love Me in December as You Do in May" (song). REL.: R.C. MISC.: resigned as mayor, 1932, after charges of corruption had been filed against him; known as "Gentleman Jimmy" Walker. RES.: New York, NY.

WALKER, PERCY. b. Dec 1812, Huntsville, AL; d. Dec 31, 1880, Mobile, AL; par. John Williams Walker. EDUC.: M.D., U. of PA, 1835. POLIT. & GOV.: State's atty., 6th Judicial District of AL; elected to AL State House, 1839, 1847, 1853; elected as an American (Know Nothing) Party candidate to U.S. House (AL), 1855–57; ***candidate for American (Know Nothing) Party nomination to vice presidency of the U.S., 1856***. BUS. & PROF.: physician; medical practice, Mobile, AL; atty.; admitted to AL Bar; law practice, Mobile, AL. MIL.: served in campaign against Creek Indians. RES.: Mobile, AL.

WALL, EDWARD CLARENCE. b. Aug 11, 1843, Milwaukee, WI; d. Apr 25, 1915, Milwaukee, WI; par. Caleb and Julia Maria Wall; m. Anna J. Hearding, 1878; m. 2d, Martha D. Ahrendt, 1906; c. Alexander. EDUC.: Racine Coll.; Beloit Coll. POLIT. & GOV.: elected as a Democrat, alderman, Milwaukee, WI, 1874–76; Democratic candidate for WI State Assembly, 1876; pres., Milwaukee (WI) Board of Health, 1876; pres., Young Men's Tilden and Hendricks Club, 1876; elected as a Democrat to WI State Assembly, 1878–79; member, WI State Democratic Cmte., 1878–85, 1890–95 (chm.); appointed Collector of Internal Revenue, 1885–89; member, Dem. Nat'l. Cmte., 1892–1900; ***candidate for Democratic nomination to presidency of the U.S., 1904***. BUS. & PROF.: employee, Caleb Wall's Store, 1861–67, pres., 1868; founder, Wall and Bigelow (Grain Brokers), Milwaukee, WI, 1868. MEM.: Milwaukee C. of C. (pres., 1901–02, 1909); U.S. Military Acad. (visitor, 1894). REL.: Episc. RES.: Milwaukee, WI.

WALLACE, EDWARD ARTHUR. b. May 18, 1928, Portsmouth, OH; par. Harrison L. and Hazel M. (Samonis) Wallace; m. Barbara Ann Goodman; c. Priscilla Marguerite; Tracey Lee; Robin Lynn; Aaron Arthur. EDUC.: Portsmouth (OH) H.S., 1944; Portsmouth (OH) Business Coll., 1949. POLIT. & GOV.: candidate for clerk of Courts, Montgomery Cty., OH, 1968; ***independent candidate for presidency of the U.S., 1972***. BUS. & PROF.: employee, Demurrage and Industry Car Control System (IBM), Pennsylvania Central R.R.; friden and teletype operator, Pennsylvania Central R.R. MEM.: VFW; Family and Children's Service Assn.; Foster Parents. REL.: Protestant. MAILING ADDRESS: 1205 Nunnery Dr., Miamisburg, OH 45342.

WALLACE, GEORGE CORLEY. b. Aug 25, 1919, Clio, AL; par. George Corley and Mozell (Smith) Wallace; m. Lurleen Burns, May 22, 1943; m. 2d, Cornelia Ellis Snively, Jan 5, 1971; m. 3d, Lisa Taylor, Sep 1981; c. Bobbie Jo; Peggy Sue; George Corley; Janie Lee. EDUC.: LL.B., U. of AL, 1942. POLIT. & GOV.: appointed asst. atty. gen. of AL, 1946–47; elected as a Democrat to AL State House, 1947–53; elected circuit judge, Third Judicial District of AL, 1953–59; delegate, Dem. Nat'l. Conv., 1956; candidate for Democratic nomination to gov. of AL, 1958; elected as a Democrat to gov. of AL, 1963–67, 1971–79, 1983–87; ***candidate for Democratic nomination to presidency of the U.S., 1964, 1968, 1972, 1976; Patriotic Party candidate for presidency of the U.S., 1968; Conservative Party of VA candidate for presidency of the U.S., 1968; American (American Independent; Courage; George Wallace; Conservative; Constitution) Party candidate for presidency of the U.S., 1968; candidate for Democratic nomination to vice presidency of the U.S., 1972, 1976; American Party of KY candidate for presidency of the U.S., 1972; candidate for American Independent Party nomination to presidency of the U.S., 1976; candidate for American Party nomination to presidency of the U.S., 1976***. BUS. & PROF.: atty.; admitted to AL Bar, 1942; law practice, Clayton, AL, 1958–62. MIL.: flight sgt., U.S.A.A.C., 1942–45. MEM.: AL Tuberculosis Assn. (dir.); American Legion; VFW; Disabled American Veterans; Masons; Parent-teachers Organization; Shriners; Moose; Elks; Order of the Eastern Star; Modern Woodmen of the World; Civitan International. REL.: Methodist (Sunday School teacher; superintendent). MISC.: husband of Gov. Lurleen Wallace of AL; victim of assassination attempt by Arthur Bremer during presidential campaign, 1972. MAILING ADDRESS: 3465 Norman Bride Rd., Montgomery, AL.

WALLACE, GREGORY AUTRY. b. Dec 20, 1957, Bakersfield, CA; par. Manuel Lewis and Linda (Sheer) Wallace; single. EDUC.: degree in Commercial Art, Platt Coll., 1985; Mesa Coll.; San Diego (CA) City Coll.; Southwestern Coll., 1986–. POLIT. & GOV.: ***Birthday Party candidate for presidency of the U.S., 1988 (satire effort)***. BUS. & PROF.: secret agent, U.N.C.L.E., 1966–86; poet; psychonaut. MEM.: Cub Scouts of America (Weblow, 1966–71). AWARDS: Science Award, Chula Vista City School District, 1966; Safety Award, 1967. WRITINGS: poems in "Athena Incognito," San Francisco, CA, 1981–88; "The

Pumpkin Papers" (1987). REL.: Zen Buddhist. MAILING ADDRESS: 322 Kimbull Terrace, Chula Vista, CA 92010.

WALLACE, HENRY AGARD. b. Oct 7, 1888, Orient, IA; d. Nov 18, 1965, Danbury, CT; par. Henry Cantwell and May (Brodhead) Wallace; m. Ilo Browne, May 20, 1914; c. Henry Browne; Robert Browne; Jean Browne (Mrs. Wallace Leslie Douglas). EDUC.: B.S., IA State Coll., 1910. POLIT. & GOV.: delegate, International Conference on Agricultural Economics, 1929; appointed U.S. sec. of agriculture, 1933–40; delegate, Dem. Nat'l. Conv., 1940, 1944; ***candidate for Democratic nomination to presidency of the U.S., 1940, 1948; elected as a Democrat to vice presidency of the U.S., 1941–1945; candidate for Democratic nomination to vice presidency of the U.S., 1944***; appointed U.S. sec. of commerce, 1945–46; ***candidate for Republican nomination to presidency of the U.S., 1948; Progressive Party candidate for presidency of the U.S., 1948***. BUS. & PROF.: farmer; plant breeder; assoc. ed., *Wallace's Farmer*, 1910–24, ed., 1924–29; ed., *Wallace's Farmer and Iowa Homestead*, 1929–33; ed., *The New Republic*; author. MEM.: Agricultural Round Table (chm., 1927); Phi Beta Kappa; Sigma Delta Chi; IA State U. Alumni Assn.; Delta Tau Delta; Alpha Zeta. AWARDS: Distinguished Service Citation, IA State U. Alumni Assn. HON. DEG.: M.S., IA State Coll., 1920; D.Sc., IA State Coll., 1934; LL.D., U. of AZ; LL.D., Columbia U.; LL.D., Drake U.; LL.D., Harvard U.; LL.D., LA State U.; LL.D., Washington and Jefferson Coll. WRITINGS: *Agricultural Prices* (1920); *Corn and Corn Growing* (1923); *Correlation and Machine Calculation* (1924); *America Must Choose* (1934); *Statesmanship and Religion* (1934); *New Frontiers* (1934); *Whose Constitution?* (1936); *Technology, Corporations and the General Welfare* (1937); *Paths to Plenty* (1938); *Price of Freedom* (1940); *The American Choice* (1940); *The Century of the Common Man* (1943); *Democracy Reborn* (1944); *Sixty Million Jobs* (1945); *Toward World Peace* (1948); *Corn and the Midwestern Farmer* (1956); *Corn and Its Early Fathers* (with Dr. Brown, 1956); *The Long Look Ahead* (1960). REL.: Episc. MISC.: experimented with breeding high-yield strains of corn, 1913–33. RES.: South Salem, NY.

WALLACE, SAM. POLIT. & GOV.: ***independent candidate for presidency of the U.S., 1976, 1988***. MAILING ADDRESS: 4416 Clairmount Ave., Birmingham, AL.

WALLACE, WILLIAM JAMES. POLIT. & GOV.: ***Single Tax Party candidate for presidency of the U.S., 1916***; pres., Commonwealth Land Party National Convention, 1924; ***Commonwealth Land Party candidate for presidency of the U.S., 1924***. BUS. & PROF.: pres., Eck Dynamo and Motor Co., Belleville, NJ. RES.: Newark, NJ.

WALLER, THOMAS McDONALD (nee THOMAS McDONALD ARMSTRONG). b. 1840, New York, NY; d. Jan 25, 1924; par. Thomas Christopher and Mary Armstrong; adopted by Robert K. Waller; m. Charlotte Bishop; c. five sons; one daughter. EDUC.: grad., Bartlett Grammar School. POLIT. & GOV.: elected as a Democrat to CT State House, 1867–68, 1872, 1876 (Speaker, 1876); elected as a Democrat, sec. of state of CT, 1870; elected mayor of New London, CT, 1873–79; appointed state's atty., New London, CT, 1876–83; elected as a Democrat to gov. of CT, 1882–84; reelected gov. by popular vote without constitutional majority, but lost election in legislature to Henry B. Harrison; ***candidate for Democratic nomination to vice presidency of the U.S., 1884***; appointed U.S. consul-gen., London, England, 1885–89; appointed commissioner, Chicago (IL) Exposition, 1893; pres., CT State Democratic Convention, 1906. BUS. & PROF.: atty.; admitted to CT Bar, 1861; partner (with Samuel H. Davis), law practice, New London, CT; partner, Waller, Cook and Wagner (law firm), New York, NY, 1889; investor, Ocean Beach Developments; incorporator, New London Street Railway; incorporator, Mechanics Savings Bank. MIL.: enlisted, Second CT Regt., U.S.V., 1861, 4th sgt., Company E. HON. DEG.: A.M., Yale U., 1883. RES.: New London, CT.

WALLGREN, MONRAD CHARLES. b. Apr 17, 1891, Des Moines, IA; d. Sep 18, 1961, Olympia, WA; par. Oscar Swan and Carrie (Helgeson) Wallgren; m. Mabel C. Liberty, Sep 8, 1910. EDUC.: grad., high school, 1909; Everett Business Coll.; grad., WA State School of Optometry, 1914; Coast Artillery School. POLIT. & GOV.: elected as a Democrat to U.S. House (WA), 1933–40; elected as a Democrat to U.S. Senate (WA), 1940–45; elected as a Democrat to gov. of WA, 1945–49; ***candidate for Democratic nomination to vice presidency of the U.S., 1948***; appointed member, Federal Power Comm., 1949–51. BUS. & PROF.: nightclerk, Grayport Hotel, Grays Harbor Cty., WA; optometrist; jeweler, 1915–22; citrus farmer, Coachella Valley, CA; uranium claims developer, Twenty-Nine Palms, CA. MIL.: pvt., Coast Guard Artillery Corps, WA National Guard, 1917; 2d lt., 63d Regt., Coast Artillery Corps; instructor in Heavy Artillery, Puget Sound, WA, 1918–19; adj., 3d Battalion, WA National Guard, 1921–22. MEM.: WA State Retail Jewelers Assn. (pres., 1921–22); American Legion; Forty and Eight; Masons; Knights Templar; Elks; Eagles; Rotary Club; VFW. REL.: Lutheran. MISC.: won National Amateur Balk-Line Billiards Championship, 1929. RES.: Palm Desert, CA.

WALSH, DAVID IGNATIUS. b. Nov 11, 1872, Leominster, MA; d. Jun 11, 1947, Brighton, MA; par. James and Bridget (Donnelly) Walsh; single. EDUC.: A.B., Holy Cross Coll., 1893; LL.B., Boston U., 1897. POLIT. & GOV.: chm., Democratic Town Cmte., Clinton, MA, 1898–1900; moderator, town meetings, Clinton, MA, 1898–1900; elected as a Democrat to MA State House, 1900–1901; Democratic candidate for lt. gov. of MA, 1911; delegate, Dem. Nat'l. Conv., 1912, 1916, 1920, 1924, 1932, 1936, 1940, 1944; elected as a Democrat to lt.

gov. of MA, 1913; elected as a Democrat to gov. of MA, 1914–15; Democratic candidate for gov. of MA, 1915; delegate, MA State Constitutional Convention, 1917; elected as a Democrat to U.S. Senate (MA), 1919–25, 1926–47; Democratic candidate for U.S. Senate (MA), 1924, 1946; ***candidate for Democratic nomination to presidency of the U.S., 1924; candidate for Democratic nomination to vice presidency of the U.S., 1940***. BUS. & PROF.: atty.; admitted to MA Bar, 1897; law practice, Fitchberg, MA, 1897–1947; partner, Walsh and Walsh (law firm), Boston, MA, 1915–47. HON. DEG.: LL.D., Boston U.; LL.D., Fordham U.; LL.D., Georgetown U.; LL.D., Holy Cross Coll.; LL.D., Notre Dame U. REL.: R.C. RES.: Clinton, MA.

WALSH, FRANK E. POLIT. & GOV.: ***candidate for Farmer-Labor Party nomination to presidency of the U.S., 1920; candidate for Farmer-Labor Party nomination to vice presidency of the U.S., 1920***. RES.: unknown.

WALSH, K. J. POLIT. & GOV.: ***candidate for Democratic nomination to vice presidency of the U.S., 1908***. RES.: CT.

WALSH, ROY E. b. 1939; m. Frances W. POLIT. & GOV.: ***independent candidate for presidency of the U.S., 1980***. BUS. & PROF.: construction worker. MAILING ADDRESS: 324 Ninth St., South East, Watertown, SD 57201.

WALSH, THOMAS JOSEPH. b. Jun 12, 1859, Two Rivers, WI; d. Mar 2, 1933, Wilson, NC; par. Felix and Bridget (Comer) Walsh; m. Elinor Cameron McClements, Aug 15, 1889; m. 2d, Maria Nieves Perez Chaumont de Truffin, Feb 25, 1933; c. Genevieve Arlisle (Mrs. Emmet Carlyle Gudger). EDUC.: LL.B., U. of WI, 1884; studied law under James Anderson, Manitowoc, WI. POLIT. & GOV.: Democratic candidate for U.S. House (MT), 1906; delegate, Dem. Nat'l. Conv., 1908, 1912, 1916, 1920, 1924 (permanent chm.), 1928, 1932 (permanent chm.); Democratic candidate for U.S. Senate (MT), 1910; elected as a Democrat to U.S. Senate (MT), 1913–33; ***candidate for Democratic nomination to presidency of the U.S., 1924, 1928; candidate for Democratic nomination to vice presidency of the U.S., 1924, 1932***; appointed atty. gen. of the U.S., 1933 (died before assuming post). BUS. & PROF.: schoolteacher; principal, high school, Sturgeon Bay, WI; atty.; admitted to SD Bar, 1884; partner (with Henry Comer Walsh), law practice, Redfield, SD, 1884–90; law practice, Helena, MT, 1890–1933; partner, Walsh, Nolan and Scallon (law firm), Helena, MT, 1907–25; partner, Walsh, Scallon and Wine (law firm), Helena, MT, 1925–29; partner, Walsh and Scallon (law firm), Helena, MT, 1929–33. MEM.: ABA. HON. DEG.: LL.D., Loyola U., 1928; LL.D., U. of WI, 1931. REL.: R.C. RES.: Helena, MT.

WALTERS, GUY-TAFT CLAY **(See TAFT, GUY W. ROCKEFELLER).**

WALTHALL, EDWARD CARY. b. Apr 4, 1831, Richmond, VA; d. Apr 21, 1898, Washington, DC; par. Barrett White and Sally (Wilkinson) Walthall; m. Sophie Bridges, 1856; m. 2d, Mary Lecky Jones, 1859; c. Mrs. John B. Ross (adopted). EDUC.: St. Thomas Hall; studied law. POLIT. & GOV.: deputy clerk, Circuit Court of MS; elected district atty., Tenth Judicial District of MS, 1856–61; delegate, Dem. Nat'l. Conv., 1868 (vice pres.), 1876, 1880, 1884, 1896; appointed and subsequently elected as a Democrat to U.S. Senate (MS), 1885–94, 1895–98; ***candidate for Democratic nomination to vice presidency of the U.S., 1896***. BUS. & PROF.: atty.; admitted to MS Bar, 1852; law practice, Coffeeville, MS, 1852–61, 1865–71; law practice, Grenada, MS, 1871–85. MIL.: lt., 15th MS Regt., C.S.A., 1861, lt. col., 1861–62; col., 29th MS Regt., C.S.A., 1862, brig. gen., 1862, maj. gen., 1864–65. RES.: Holly Springs, MS.

WALTON, RICHARD JOHN. b. May 24, 1928, Saratoga Springs, NY; par. Richard James and Gertrude Frances Helena (Boyle) Walton; m. Margaret Anne Hilton, Jun 8, 1957 (divorced); m. 2d, Mary Una Jones, Dec 11, 1975 (divorced); c. Richard Mackay; Catherine Anne. EDUC.: A.B., Brown U., 1951; Sc.M., Columbia U., 1954. POLIT. & GOV.: delegate, Citizens Party National Convention, 1980; member, New York City (NY) Citizens Party Central Cmte., 1980–81; member, NY State Citizens Party Central Cmte., 1980–81; member, Citizens Party National Cmte., 1980–; co-chair, RI State Citizens Party Central Cmte., 1981–; ***Citizens Party candidate for vice presidency of the U.S., 1984***. BUS. & PROF.: announcer, news ed., *WICE*, Providence, RI, 1952–53; reporter, *Providence (RI) Journal*, 1954–55; reporter, *New York (NY) World-Telegram* and *The Sun*, 1955–59; producer, host, "Report to Africa," Voice of America, Washington, DC, 1959–62; principal U.N. correspondent, Voice of America, 1962–67; author. MIL.: journalist's mate, third class, U.S. Navy, 1946–48; lt. (jg), U.S.N.R. MEM.: Caucus of CT Democrats (member, steering cmte., 1970); P.E.N. American Center; National Book Critics Circle. WRITINGS: *The Siege of Brooklyn Bridge* (1962); *The Remnants of Power: The Tragic Last Years of Adlai Stevenson* (1968); *America and the Cold War* (1969); *Beyond Diplomacy* (1970); *Congress and American Foreign Policy* (1972); *Cold War and Counter-Revolution* (1972); *Canada and the United States of America* (1972); *The United States and Latin America* (1972); *The United States and the Far East* (1974); *Henry Wallace, Harry Truman, and the Cold War* (1976); *The Power of Oil* (1977). REL.: none (nee R.C.). MAILING ADDRESS: 5 Grenore St., Warwick, RI 02888.

WANAMAKER, JOHN. b. Jul 11, 1838, Philadelphia, PA; d. Dec 12, 1922, Philadelphia, PA; par. John Nelson and Elizabeth D. (Kockersperger) Wanamaker; m. Mary B. Brown; c. Lewis Rodman; Thomas B.; two daughters. EDUC.: public schools. POLIT. & GOV.: Republican candidate for U.S. House (PA), 1882 (declined); independent candidate for mayor of Philadelphia, PA, 1886 (declined); presidential elector, Republican Party, 1888; member, Republican Nat'l. Exec. Cmte.,

1889–93; appointed postmaster gen. of the U.S., 1889–93; candidate for Republican nomination to U.S. Senate (PA), 1896; candidate for Republican nomination to gov. of PA, 1898; ***candidate for Republican nomination to presidency of the U.S., 1916***. BUS. & PROF.: errand boy, bookstore, 1852; retail clothing salesman, 1856–58; founder, Wanamaker and Brown Clothing House, Philadelphia, PA, 1861–68; founder, John Wanamaker and Co. (department store), Philadelphia, PA, 1876; founder, department store, New York, NY, 1896; dir., Merchants Bank; pres., First Penny Savings Bank; founder, Wanamaker Inst. of Industries; founder, Bethany Dispensary. MEM.: Bethany Sunday School (superintendent, 1858–1922); YMCA (sec., 1858–61); Christian Comm. (founder, during Civil War); Philadelphia YMCA (pres., 1870–83); Centennial Exposition (member, board of finance, 1876); Presbyterian Hospital (founder; trustee); University Hospital (mgr.); Union League. AWARDS: Order of the Legion of Honor, 1912. HON. DEG.: LL.D., Howard U., 1897; LL.D., U. of PA; LL.D., Ursinus Coll. REL.: Presb. MISC.: sent two relief ships to Belgium, 1914. RES.: Philadelphia, PA.

WARBURTON, NATHANIEL CALVIN, JR. b. May 28, 1910, Lynn, MA; par. Nathaniel Calvin and Susan (Dillihunt) Warburton; m. Janice Orens Fitch, 1935; c. David; Natalie Sable; Mary Ward; Ellen Levesque; Edward. EDUC.: B.S., Boston U., 1932, S.T.B., 1935; U. of NH, 1946–48; Th.M., Burton School of Theology, 1961. POLIT. & GOV.: member, school board, Great Bend, NY, 1952–53; chm., Ethics Cmte., Raymond, NH, 1976–79; elected as a Republican to NH State House, 1979–; joined Libertarian Party, Jul 16, 1991; ***candidate for Libertarian Party nomination to vice presidency of the U.S., 1992***. BUS. & PROF.: pastor, Methodist churches, NH, 1935–42, 1945–48, 1965–71, KS, 1957–65, MA, 1971–75. MIL.: 1st lt., U.S. Army, 1942, promoted to lt. col. MEM.: Masons; American Legion; Heroes of '76; Kiwanis. REL.: Methodist. MAILING ADDRESS: P.O. Box 365 Main St., Raymond, NH 03077.

WARD, WILLIAM LUKENS. b. Sep 2, 1856, Pemberwick, CT; d. Jul 16, 1933, New York, NY. EDUC.: Friends Seminary; Columbia Coll. POLIT. & GOV.: presidential elector, Republican Party, 1896; delegate, Rep. Nat'l. Conv., 1896, 1900, 1904, 1908, 1912, 1916, 1920, 1924, 1928, 1932; chm., NY State Republican Cmte.; elected as a Republican to U.S. House (NY), 1897–99; member, Rep. Nat'l. Cmte., 1904–12; ***candidate for Republican nomination to presidency of the U.S., 1920***. BUS. & PROF.: manufacturer of bolts, nuts, and rivets, Port Chester, NY. RES.: New York, NY.

WARDWELL, WILLIAM THOMAS. b. Feb 1, 1827, Bristol, RI; d. Jan 3, 1911, New York, NY; par. William Taylor and Mary (Hawes) Wardwell; m. Eliza Wilber Lanterman, Oct 14, 1852; m. 2d, Martha Wallace Ruff, Dec 18, 1889; c. William Lanterman; Samuel Hawes; Charles Hunt; Mary; George Wyckoff; Clara Cutler (Mrs. Frank Herbert Jones); Eliza; Allen. EDUC.: public schools, Niles, MI. POLIT. & GOV.: joined Prohibition Party, 1880; Prohibition Party candidate for mayor of New York, NY, 1886, 1888; member, Prohibition Party National Cmte., 1888–1908 (exec. cmte.; sec., 1892); Prohibition Party candidate for comptroller of New York, NY, 1890; ***candidate for Prohibition Party nomination to presidency of the U.S., 1892***; Prohibition Party candidate for gov. of NY, 1900. BUS. & PROF.: clerk, office of Samuel W. Hawes, Buffalo, NY; partner, Wardwell, Webster and Co. (oil dealers), 1848; partner, Joy, Cowing and Co. (oil refinery), 1864; pres., Long Island Oil Co., 1866; vice pres., Davoe Manufacturing Co.; treas., Standard Oil Co. of NJ, 1891–99; treas., Standard Oil Co. of NY, 1894–98; trustee, Colonial Trust Co.; trustee, Greenwich Savings Bank. MEM.: NY Red Cross Hospital (pres.; treas.); National Prohibition Bureau (vice pres.); NY Polyclinic Hospital (dir.); NY C. of C.; Soc. of Mayflower Descendants; National Temperance Soc. (dir.); SAR; American Temperance Union (treas.); Masons; NY Red Cross (pres.); Red Cross Relief Assn. (treas.); National Red Cross Soc. (trustee, 1905); St. John's Guild (treas.). REL.: Unitarian. RES.: New York, NY.

WARNER, ADONIRAM JUDSON. b. Jan 13, 1834, Wales, NY; d. Aug 12, 1910, Marietta, OH; par. Levi and Hepsibah (Dickinson) Warner; m. Susan Elizabeth Butts, Apr 5, 1856; c. Arthur J.; eight others. EDUC.: Beloit Coll.; NY Central Coll., 1853; studied law. POLIT. & GOV.: superintendent of schools, Mifflin Cty., PA; elected as a Democrat to U.S. House (OH), 1879–81, 1883–87; Democratic candidate for U.S. House (OH), 1880; chm., First National Silver Convention, 1889; chm., Second National Silver Convention, 1892; delegate, Dem. Nat'l. Conv., 1896; ***candidate for Democratic nomination to presidency of the U.S., 1896***. BUS. & PROF.: principal, Lewiston (PA) Acad.; principal, Mercer Union School, PA, 1856–61; atty.; admitted to IN Bar, 1865; builder, Marietta and Cleveland R.R.; builder, Walhonding R.R.; builder, U Street Railway, Washington, DC; partner, Gates, Skinner and Co. (oil developers); founder, Gainesville Railway Co.; founder, Georgia Power Co. MIL.: capt., 10th PA Reserves, 1861, lt. col., 1862, col., 1863; col., Veteran Reserve Corps, 1863; brev. brig. gen., 1865. MEM.: American Bimetallic League (pres., 1892); American Bimetallic Union (pres., 1895); American Economic Assn.; American Social Economic Assn. WRITINGS: *The Appreciation of Money* (1877); *Source of Value in Money* (1882); *Silver in the 51st Congress* (1890); *Facts About Silver* (1891). MISC.: advocate of bimetallism. RES.: Marietta, OH.

WARNER, JOHN WILLIAM. b. Feb 18, 1927, Washington, DC; par. John William and Martha Stuart (Budd) Warner; m. Catherine C. Mellon, Aug 7, 1957; m. 2d, Elizabeth Taylor, Dec 4, 1976 (divorced); c. Mary Conover; Virginia Stuart; John William IV. EDUC.: B.S., Washington and Lee U., 1949; LL.B., U. of VA, 1953. POLIT. & GOV.: law clerk, U.S. Circuit Judge E. Barrett Prettyman, 1953–54; appointed special asst. to U.S. atty., 1956–57; appointed asst. U.S. atty., U.S. Dept. of Justice, 1957–60; national dir., United Citizens for Nixon-Agnew, 1968; appointed undersec. of the navy, 1969–72; appointed U.S. sec. of the navy, 1972–74; appointed administrator, U.S. Bicentennial Administration, 1974–76; elected as a Republican to U.S. Senate (VA), 1979–; ***candidate for Republican nomination to presidency of the U.S., 1980; candidate for Republican nomination to vice presidency of the U.S., 1980***. BUS. & PROF.: atty.; admitted to VA Bar, 1953; partner, Hogan and Hartson (law firm), 1960–68. MIL.: U.S.N.R., 1944–46; capt., U.S.M.C. Reserves, 1949–52. MEM.: Washington and Lee U. (trustee); ABA; Bar Assn. of DC; WA Inst. on Foreign Affairs; Beta Theta Pi; Phi Alpha Delta; Metropolitan Club; Burning Tree Club; Chevy Chase Club; Alfalfa Club; Alibi Club. REL.: Episc. MAILING ADDRESS: Atoka Farm, P.O. Box 1320, Middleburg, VA 22117.

WARNER, SIDNEY SARDUS. b. Apr 17, 1829, Suffield, CT; d. Jul 6, 1908, Wellington, OH; par. Chauncey and Eliza (Kent) Warner; m. Margaret Anna Bradner, 1851; c. Orrie Louisa (Mrs. W. R. Wean); Sidney Kent; Albert Rollin; George Bradner. EDUC.: Oberlin Coll. POLIT. & GOV.: elected as a Unionist to OH State House, 1862–64; elected as a Republican, state treas. of OH, 1866–72; appointed trustee, Cleveland (OH) Hospital for the Insane, 1871–80, 1881– (pres., 1874–); ***Cheese Party candidate for presidency of the U.S., 1872***; candidate for Republican nomination to gov. of OH, 1873; candidate for Republican nomination to U.S. House (OH), 1876; presidential elector, Republican Party, 1880. BUS. & PROF.: banker; farmer; manufacturer; pres., First National Bank of Wellington, OH, 1864–1908; pres., Horr, Warner and Co. (cheese manufacturers), 1869–; pres., Clarksfield Stone Co., 1881–; pres., Cleveland National Bank, 1883–1903; partner, Wean, Horr, Warner and Co. (agricultural firm); horse breeder. MEM.: Citizens Mutual Relief Assn. (pres.). REL.: Christian (nee Bapt.). RES.: Wellington, OH.

WARREN, CHARLES BEECHER. b. Apr 10, 1870, Bay City, MI; d. Feb 3, 1936, Grosse Pointe Farms, MI; par. Robert Lincoln and Caroline (Beecher) Warren; m. Helen Hunt Wetmore, Dec 2, 1902; c. Wetmore; Charles Beecher, Jr.; Robert; John Buel. EDUC.: Ph.B., U. of MI, 1891; LL.B., Detroit Law School, 1893; studied law under Don M. Dickinson. POLIT. & GOV.: assoc. counsel for U.S., Bering Sea Case, 1896; counsel for U.S., North Atlantic Fisheries Case, 1909–10; delegate, Rep. Nat'l. Conv., 1908, 1912, 1916, 1920, 1924; member, Rep. Nat'l. Cmte., 1912–20; ***candidate for Republican nomination to presidency of the U.S., 1920***; appointed U.S. ambassador to Japan, 1921–23; appointed special commissioner, U.S.-Mexico diplomatic negotiations, 1923; ***candidate for Republican nomination to vice presidency of the U.S., 1924***; appointed U.S. ambassador to Mexico, 1924; appointed atty. gen. of the U.S., 1925 (not confirmed by Senate). BUS. & PROF.: editor-in-chief, *The Islander*, Ann Arbor, MI; atty.; admitted to MI Bar, 1893; assoc., Don M. Dickinson Law Firm, 1893–97; partner, Dickinson, Warren and Warren (law firm), Detroit, MI, 1897–1900; partner, Shaw, Warren and Cady (law firm), 1900–1911; partner, Warren, Cady, Hill and Hamblen (law firm), 1911–25; partner, Warren, Hill and Hamblen (law firm; subsequently known as Warren, Hill, Hamblen, Essery and Lewis), 1925–36; dir., National Bank of Commerce; dir., Union Trust Co.; dir., Union Commerce Investment Co. MIL.: maj., U.S. Army, 1917, lt. col., 1918, col., 1918; Distinguished Service Medal, 1918. MEM.: American Soc. of International Law; MI Bar Assn.; Detroit Bar Assn.; Phi Beta Kappa; University Club of NY; University Club of Detroit; Metropolitan Club; Detroit Club; Detroit Board of Commerce (pres.); ABA; Masons (33°); Albion Coll. (trustee); University School of Detroit (pres., board of trustees); National Cathedral Assn. (exec. cmte.); Chevy Chase Club; Huron Mountain Club. HON. DEG.: M.A., U. of MI, 1916; LL.D., Albion Coll., 1924. REL.: Episc. (delegate, gen. convention, 1928). RES.: Grosse Pointe Farms, MI.

WARREN, EARL. b. Mar 19, 1891, Los Angeles, CA; d. Jul 9, 1974, Washington, DC; par. Methias H. and Chrystal (Hernland) Warren; m. Nina Palmquist Meyers, Oct 14, 1925; c. James C. (adopted); Virginia (Mrs. John Charles Daly); Earl, Jr.; Dorothy (Mrs. Harry Van Knight); Nina Elizabeth (Mrs. Stuart Brien); Robert. EDUC.: B.L., U. of CA, 1912, J.D., 1914. POLIT. & GOV.: appointed clerk, Judiciary Cmte., CA State Assembly, 1919; appointed deputy city atty., Oakland, CA, 1919–20; appointed deputy district atty., Alameda Cty., CA 1920–23; elected district atty., Alameda Cty., CA, 1925–38; appointed chm., board of managers, CA Bureau of Criminal Identification and Investigation, 1929–39; chm., CA State Republican Central Cmte., 1934–36; member, Rep. Nat'l. Cmte., 1936–38; delegate, Rep. Nat'l. Conv., 1928 (alternate), 1932, 1944 (temporary chm.; keynoter); ***candidate for Republican nomination to presidency of the U.S., 1936, 1944, 1948, 1952***; elected as a Republican (Democrat, Progressive) to atty. gen. of CA, 1939–43; elected as a Republican to gov. of CA, 1943–53; ***candidate for Republican nomination to vice presidency of the U.S., 1944, 1952, 1956; Republican candidate for vice presidency of the U.S., 1948***; appointed special U.S. ambassador to coronation of Queen Elizabeth II of Great Britain, 1953; appointed chief justice, Supreme Court of the U.S., 1953–69; chm., Special Comm. to Investigate the Assassination of President John F. Kennedy, 1963–64. BUS. & PROF.: atty.; admitted to CA Bar, 1914; counsel, Associated Oil Co., San Francisco, CA, 1914; reporter, *Bakersfield (CA) Californian*; law clerk, Robinson and Robinson (law firm), Oakland, CA; research assoc., Bureau of Public Administration, U. of CA, 1932–40. MIL.: pvt., Company I, 363d Infantry, 91st Div., U.S. Army, 1917, 2d lt., 1918, 1st lt., 1918; capt., Officers Reserve Corps, 1919–36. MEM.: CA Bar Assn.; Alameda Cty. Bar Assn.; Sacramento Cty. Bar Assn.; District Attorneys' Assn. of CA (pres., 1931–32); National Assn. of Attorneys General (vice pres., 1940–41); Council of State Governments (mgr.); National Governors' Conference (exec. cmte., 1943); Olympic Club; Commonwealth Club; Bohemian Club; Exchange Club; Jonathon Club; Sutter Club; Masons (33°; Shriners; Knight Commander of the Court of Honor; Grand

Master of CA, 1935–36); Elks; Native Sons of the Golden West; Odd Fellows; Moose; Phi Delta Phi; Peace Officers Assn. of CA; Smithsonian Institution (chancellor, 1953–69); Western Governors' Conference (chm., 1950); Interstate Comm. on Crime (treas., 1940–42); CA Technical Inst. for Police Training (adviser, 1934–42); Sigma Phi; International Assn. of Chiefs of Police (vice chm.); ABA; National Art Gallery (chm., board of trustees, 1953–69); American Acad. of Arts and Sciences; National Geographic Soc. (trustee); American Philosophical Soc.; Selden Soc.; CA Club. AWARDS: U.S. Flag Assn. Medal, 1934; British Coronation Medal; Grand Cross of the Royal Order of the North Star (Sweden); Legion of Honor (commander); Star of Solidarity (Italy); Order of Orange Nassau (Netherlands); Crown of Oak (Luxembourg). HON. DEG.: LL.D., Coll. of the Pacific, 1943; LL.D., U. of the Redlands, 1943; LL.D., U. of Santa Clara, 1947; LL.D., U. of Southern CA, 1947; D.C.L., Union Coll., 1947; LL.D., U. of WY, 1947; Dr.Pol.Sci., U. of AK; LL.D., Amherst Coll.; LL.D., Boston U.; LL.D., Brandeis U.; D.C.L., Bucknell U.; LL.D., U. of Cincinnati; LL.D., Columbia U.; LL.D., Cornell Coll.; LL.D., Delhi U.; LL.D., Hamilton Coll.; LL.D., U. of IL; LL.D., U. of IN; LL.D., U. of Ireland; LL.D., Jewish Theological Seminary; LL.D., Lafayette U.; H.H.D., MacMurray Coll.; LL.D., U. of MI; LL.D., Mills Coll.; LL.D., Mount Holyoke Coll.; D.C.L., U. of NY; LL.D., Niagara U.; LL.D., U. of Notre Dame; LL.D., Occidental Coll.; LL.D., U. of PA; LL.D., U. of Pittsburgh; LL.D., U. of Puerto Rico; LL.D., Roosevelt U.; LL.D., Temple U.; LL.D., Tufts U.; LL.D., U. of VT; LL.D., Villanova U.; LL.D., WA U.; LL.D., Wesleyan U.; LL.D., Coll. of William and Mary; D.H.L., Wilmington Coll. REL.: Bapt. RES.: Washington, DC.

WARREN, JAMES MAC. b. 1952, Memphis, TN. EDUC.: grad., Hamilton H.S., Memphis, TN, 1970. POLIT. & GOV.: joined Socialist Workers Party, 1972; delegate, National Black Political Assembly, 1972, 1974, 1976; Socialist Workers Party candidate for U.S. House (MA), 1976; member, National Cmte., Socialist Workers Party, 1976–; founding member, National Black Independent Political Party, 1980; IA district organizer, Socialist Workers Party, 1986–87; ***Socialist Workers Party candidate for presidency of the U.S., 1988, 1992***; Socialist Workers Party candidate for mayor of Chicago, IL, 1991. BUS. & PROF.: field laborer, cotton, corn, and soybean farms, AR; reporter, *The Root*, Grand Rapids, MI, 1970; employee, Ford Motor Co., River Rouge, MI; reporter, *The Militant*, 1980; steelworker, AM Castlemetals, Chicago, IL. MEM.: Young Socialist Alliance (national chairperson, 1982–83); Anti–Viet Nam War Movement; Civil Rights Movement; National Student Coalition Against Racism (organizer, 1975); Coordinated Social Services Council; U.A.W. Local 600; NAACP (Boston Chapter); United Steelworkers of America (Local 3247). WRITINGS: *Independent Black Political Action, 1954–1978* (ed.); *The National Black independent Political Party* (co-editor). MISC.: organized African Liberation Day Demonstration, Washington, DC, 1972; visited Grenada, New Zealand, Cuba, and Jamaica in support of radical political movements. MAILING ADDRESS: 28 Duncan Ave., #309, Jersey City, NJ 07304.

WARREN, TALMADGE MARTIN. b. prior to 1941, Big Stone Gap, VA; par. Thomas and Grace (Martin) Warren; m. EDUC.: B.S., B.A., Xavier U.; M.A., U. of Cincinnati, postgrad. study. POLIT. & GOV.: ***Constitutional Party candidate for presidency of the U.S., 1972, 1976, 1980, 1984, 1988, 1992***. BUS. & PROF.: educator; 8th grade teacher, Powell Valley Middle School, Big Stone Gap, VA; instructor, Cultural Geography, Clinch Valley Coll.; counselor; admissions officer; financial aid officer. MIL.: U.S. armed forces. MAILING ADDRESS: 520 East Fifth St., South, Big Stone Gap, VA 24219.

WASHBURN, WILLIAM DREW. b. Jan 14, 1831, Livermore, ME; d. Jul 29, 1912, Minneapolis, MN; par. Israel and Martha (Benjamin) Washburn; m. Elizabeth M. Muzzy, Apr 19, 1859; c. William Drew, Jr.; Cadwallader; Mary C.; Edwin S.; Elizabeth; Stanley. EDUC.: public schools; A.B., Bowdoin Coll., 1854; studied law under Israel Washburn and John A. Peters, Bangor, ME. POLIT. & GOV.: elected as a Republican to MN State House, 1861–65, 1871, 1874, 1880, 1882; appointed U.S. surveyor gen. of MN, 1861–65; Republican candidate for U.S. House (MN), 1864; candidate for Republican nomination to gov. of MN, 1873; elected as a Republican to U.S. House (MN), 1879–85; ***candidate for Republican nomination to presidency of the U.S., 1888***; elected as a Republican to U.S. Senate (MN), 1889–95; Republican candidate for U.S. Senate (MN), 1895; ***candidate for Republican nomination to vice presidency of the U.S., 1900***. BUS. & PROF.: atty.; admitted to ME Bar, 1857; law practice, Minneapolis, MN, 1857; agent, dir., Minneapolis Mill Co., 1857–67; owner, Lincoln Saw Mill; manufacturer; dir., owner, managing agent, Minneapolis Water Power Co.; projector, vice pres., Minneapolis and St. Louis Railway, 1870–75, pres., 1875; lumberman; dir., Sioux City R.R.; founder, *Minneapolis (MN) Tribune*, 1867; pres., Minneapolis, St. Paul and Sault Ste. Marie R.R., to 1889; dir., Sault Ste. Marie R.R., 1888; dir., Pillsbury-Washburn Mills; owner, Minneapolis Harvester Works; owner, Washburn-Crosby Flouring Mills; owner, W. D. Washburn and Co., 1878. MEM.: Commercial Club; Minneapolis Club; Union League Club; First Universalist Soc. of Minneapolis. HON. DEG.: LL.D., Bowdoin Coll., 1901. REL.: Universalist (pres., national convention). MISC.: brother of Elihu Benjamin Washburne (q.v.). RES.: Fair Oaks, MN.

WASHBURNE, ELIHU BENJAMIN. b. Sep 23, 1816, Livermore, ME; d. Oct 22, 1887, Chicago, IL; par. Israel and Marth (Benjamin) Washburne; m. Adele Gratiot, Jul 31, 1845; c. seven. EDUC.: Kent's Hill Seminary, 1836; Harvard U., 1839–40; studied law under John Otis, 1838–39. POLIT. & GOV.: delegate, Whig Party National Convention, 1844, 1852; Whig Party candidate for U.S. House (IL), 1848; elected as a Whig (subsequently as a Republican) to U.S. House (IL), 1853–69; Republican candidate for U.S. House (IL), 1868; appointed U.S. sec. of state, 1869; appointed U.S. minister to France, 1869–77; ***candidate for Republican nomination to presidency of***

the U.S., 1876, 1880; Republican candidate for U.S. Senate (IL), 1877; ***candidate for Republican nomination to vice presidency of the U.S., 1880***. BUS. & PROF.: printer's apprentice; employee, asst. ed., *Kennebec Journal*, Augusta, ME; atty.; admitted to MA Bar, 1840; law practice, Galena, IL, 1840. MEM.: Chicago Hist. Soc. (pres., 1884–87). WRITINGS: *History of the English Settlements in Edwards County, Illinois* (1882); *The Papers of Governor Ninian Edwards* (ed., 1884); *Recollections of a Minister to France, 1869–77* (1887). MISC.: nominated Henry Clay (q.v.) for president at Whig Party National Convention, 1844; brother of William Drew Washburn (q.v.). RES.: Chicago, IL.

WASHINGTON, BOOKER TALIAFERRO.

b. 1859, Hale's Ford, VA; d. Nov 14, 1915, Tuskegee, AL; par. Jane Ferguson; m. Fannie N. Smith, 1882; m. 2d, Olivia A. Davidson, 1885; m. 3d, Margaret James "Maggie" Murray, Oct 12, 1893; c. two sons; one daughter. EDUC.: grad., Hampton Inst., 1875; Wayland Seminary, 1878–79. POLIT. & GOV.: ***candidate for United Christian Party nomination to vice presidency of the U.S., 1900; candidate for Republican nomination to vice presidency of the U.S., 1908***. BUS. & PROF.: waiter; brick mason; educator; teacher, Hampton Inst.; principal, Tuskegee Inst., 1884–1915; author; lecturer. HON. DEG.: A.M., Harvard U., 1896; LL.D., Dartmouth Coll., 1901. WRITINGS: *Sowing and Reaping* (1900); *Up From Slavery* (1901); *Future of the American Negro* (1899); *Character Building* (1902); *Story of My Life and Work* (1903); *Working With Hands* (1904); *Tuskegee and Its People* (ed., 1905); *Putting the Most Into Life* (1906); *Life of Frederick Douglass* (1907); *The Negro in Business* (1907); *The Story of the Negro* (1909); *My Larger Education* (1911); *The Man Farthest Down* (1912). MISC.: born a slave owned by Mr. Burrows. RES.: Tuskegee, AL.

WASHINGTON, ELWOOD.

POLIT. & GOV.: ***candidate for Republican nomination to vice presidency of the U.S., 1920, 1924***. RES.: Hammond, IN.

WASHINGTON, GEORGE.

b. Feb 22, 1732 (Feb 11, 1731/32 O.S.), Pope's Creek, VA; d. Dec 14, 1799, Mount Vernon, VA; par. Augustine and Mary (Ball) Washington; m. Mrs. Martha (Dandridge) Custis, Jan 6, 1759; c. Martha Parke Custis (stepdaughter); John Parke Custis (stepson). EDUC.: Old Field School; Mr. William's School. POLIT. & GOV.: official surveyor, Culpepper Cty., VA, 1749; elected to VA House of Burgesses, 1758–74; justice of the peace, Fairfax Cty., VA, 1770; delegate, Williamsburg Convention, 1773; member, VA Provincial Convention, 1774; elected delegate, Continental Congress, 1774–75; delegate, U.S. Constitutional Convention, 1787 (pres.); ***elected as a Federalist to presidency of the U.S., 1789–1797; Federalist candidate for presidency of the U.S., 1796 (declined); received 2 electoral votes for presidency of the U.S., 1796; Procrastinators of America candidate for presidency of the U.S., 1968 (after elections; satire effort)***. BUS. & PROF.: licensed surveyor, 1749; ferry operator, Potomac River, VA, 1769–90; plantation owner, Mount Vernon, VA; pres., Potomac Co., 1785; chancellor, Coll. of William and Mary, 1788; soldier. MIL.: appointed adj. gen. of VA, maj., 1752, lt. col., 1754, col., 1754; aide-de-camp to Gen. Braddock, French and Indian War, 1755; appointed commander in chief, VA Militia, 1755–58; elected by Congress, commander in chief, gen., Army of the United Colonies, 1775–83; appointed lt. gen., commander in chief, Armies of the U.S., 1798–99; Congressional Medal, 1776. MEM.: Soc. of the Cincinnati (pres.-gen., 1783); Free and Accepted Masons (master). HON. DEG.: LL.D., Harvard U., 1776; LL.D., Yale U., 1781; LL.D., U. of PA, 1783; LL.D., WA Coll., 1789; LL.D., Brown U., 1790. WRITINGS: *The Journal of Major George Washington* (1754). REL.: Episc. RES.: Mount Vernon, VA.

WASHINGTON, GEORGE.

b. Belgium. POLIT. & GOV.: ***candidate for American Party nomination to presidency of the U.S., 1920***. BUS. & PROF.: merchant, Brooklyn, NY. MISC.: became U.S. citizen, May 1918; apparently name entered in SD presidential primary as a "joke." RES.: Brooklyn, NY.

WASHINGTON, GEORGE.

POLIT. & GOV.: ***candidate for Democratic nomination to presidency of the U.S., 1976***. MEM.: American Federation of State, County, and Municipal Employees; People United to Save Humanity; NAACP; AFL-CIO. MAILING ADDRESS: 910 South Michael Ave., Chicago, IL 60605.

WASHINGTON, GEORGE CORBIN.

b. Aug 20, 1789, Oak Grove, VA; d. Jul 17, 1854, Georgetown, DC. EDUC.: Harvard U.; studied law. POLIT. & GOV.: elected as a Whig to U.S. House (MD), 1827–33, 1835–37; appointed U.S. Commissioner on Indian Claims, 1844; ***Native American Party candidate for vice presidency of the U.S., 1852 (declined)***. BUS. & PROF.: plantation owner, MD; pres., Chesapeake and Ohio Canal Co. RES.: Dumbarton Heights, Georgetown, DC.

WASHINGTON, ROBERT LEE, JR.

par. Robert Lee Washington, Sr. POLIT. & GOV.: ***candidate for Democratic nomination to presidency of the U.S., 1976; independent Democratic candidate for presidency of the U.S., 1976***. MAILING ADDRESS: 2808 North 15th St., Milwaukee, WI 53206.

WASHINGTON, WILLIAM.

POLIT. & GOV.: ***Imperialist Party candidate for Emperor of the U.S., 1876***. RES.: Nashville, TN.

WAT, GORDON E.

POLIT. & GOV.: ***independent candidate for presidency of the U.S., 1968***; ran in NH primary,

1968. Bus. & Prof.: minister. Mailing Address: Springfield, MA.

WATERMAN, CHARLES H. Polit. & Gov.: ***American Political Alliance candidate for vice presidency of the U.S., 1880***. Res.: New York, NY.

WATERMAN, JOHN MALLON. b. Sep 17, 1952, Washington, DC; par. Guy Van Voorst and Emily Louise (Morrison) Waterman; single. Educ.: Western WA State Coll., 1971–72; U. of AK, 1974–75. Polit. & Gov.: candidate for Fairbanks (AK) School Board, 1979; ***Feed the Starving Party candidate for presidency of the U.S., 1980***. Bus. & Prof.: laborer, Fairbanks, AK. Writings: "Mount Hunter Climbed Solo," *American Alpine Journal*, 1979. Rel.: atheist. Mailing Address: P.O. Box 81513, Fairbanks, AK 99708.

WATERS, AGNES. b. 1893, New York, NY; m.; c. Marie Cecilia; one other. Polit. & Gov.: ***candidate for Democratic nomination to presidency of the U.S., 1944; candidate for Republican nomination to presidency of the U.S., 1944; independent candidate for presidency of the U.S., 1944, 1948, 1952, 1960***. Bus. & Prof.: real estate salesman; contributor, *Women's Voice*. Mem.: We, The Mothers, Mobilize for America; National Blue Star Mothers of America; Mothers of America; Mothers of the USA. Writings: *The White Papers* (1940); *Save America from the Horror of War* (1949); *Statement of Mrs. Agnes Waters Against the Nomination of Dean Acheson for Secretary of State* (1949); *The Hour for United Action Has Struck*; *Warning! International Plots in Making!* (1949); *To the Congress of the United States—Petition for Redress of Wrongs* (1951); *Secret Jewish World Government* (1958). Rel.: Church of Jesus Christ of Latter-Day Saints. Misc.: frequent witness before congressional hearings; claims descent from King James II of England. Res.: Washington, D.C.

WATERS, LEVI ANTHONY. Polit. & Gov.: ***Disco Fever Party candidate for presidency of the U.S., 1980***. Mailing Address: 1245 Vine, Room #324, Hollywood, CA 90038.

WATKINS, AARON SHERMAN. b. Nov 29, 1863, Rushsylvania, OH; d. Feb 10, 1941, Lima, OH; par. William White and Rebecca J. (Elliott) Watkins; m. Emma Laura Davis, Nov 8, 1890; c. Willard Merrill. Educ.: B.S., OH Northern U., 1886, M.S., 1907; studied law, 1886–90. Polit. & Gov.: chm., Prohibition Party, Williams and Hardin counties, OH; Prohibition Party candidate for U.S. House (OH), 1904; Prohibition Party candidate for gov. of OH, 1905, 1908, 1932, 1936; ***Prohibition Party candidate for vice presidency of the U.S., 1908, 1912***; member, Prohibition Party National Cmte., 1911–20; ***candidate for Prohibition Party nomination to presidency of the U.S., 1912 (withdrew)***; Prohibition Party candidate for U.S. Senate (OH), 1916; temporary chm., Prohibition Party National Convention, 1920; ***Prohibition Party candidate for presidency of the U.S., 1920***. Bus. & Prof.: teacher, public schools, OH, 1880–83, 1890–93; atty.; admitted to OH Bar, 1889; entered Methodist Episcopal ministry, 1893, ordained, 1895; pastor, Methodist Episcopal churches, Continental, Ottawa, Edgerton, Delta, North Baltimore, OH, 1893–1905; prof. of Literature and Philosophy, OH Northern U., 1905–09, vice pres., 1907–09, trustee, 1914–19; pres., Asbury Coll., 1909–10, lecturer, 1910–15; pastor, Methodist Episcopal Church, Van Wert, OH, 1915–16; pastor, Methodist Episcopal Church, Columbus Grove, OH, 1916–18; pastor, Methodist Episcopal Church, Germantown, OH, 1918–20; prof. of English, Miami Military Inst., 1918–20; pastor, Methodist Episcopal Church, Linwood, Cincinnati, OH, 1920–23; pastor, Winston Place Church, Cincinnati, OH, 1923–27; pastor, Methodist Episcopal Church, Waynesville, OH, 1927–28; pastor, Wesley Church, Lima, OH, 1928–32; pastor, Methodist Episcopal Church, Cairo, OH, 1932–35. Mem.: Putnam Cty. Dry Federation. Hon. Deg.: LL.D., Taylor U., 1902; L.H.D., OH Northern U., 1923; D.D., Asbury Coll., 1930. Writings: *Principles of English Grammar*; "The Present Crisis in Non-Partisanship," *American Advance*, May 20, 1911; *Why I Am a Prohibitionist* (1912). Rel.: Methodist Episc. (delegate, gen. conference, 1924). Res.: Cincinnati, OH.

WATKINS, WILLIAM. Polit. & Gov.: Socialist Labor Party candidate for gov. of OH, 1895, 1897; delegate, Socialist Labor Party National Convention, 1896; ***candidate for Socialist Labor Party nomination to presidency of the U.S., 1896***. Bus. & Prof.: agent, *Weekly People*, 1900; chm., American Rank and File Delegation to Soviet Russia. Mem.: Switchmen's Union of North America No. 206. Writings: *Socialism*; *The Evolution of Industry* (1897). Res.: Dayton, OH.

WATSON, ANDREW J. b. 1913. Polit. & Gov.: chm., Constitutional Party of PA; Constitutional Party candidate for U.S. House (PA), 1968, 1972; Constitutional Party candidate for gov. of PA, 1970; ***candidate for American Independent Party nomination to presidency of the U.S., 1976***; Constitutional Party candidate for U.S. Senate (PA), 1976; candidate for Republican nomination to gov. of PA, 1978; candidate for Democratic nomination to gov. of PA, 1978; candidate for Republican nomination to U.S. Senate (PA), 1980. Bus. & Prof.: businessman. Mailing Address: R.D. #3, Box 730, Harrisburg, PA 17112.

WATSON, CLAUDE ALONZO. b. Jun 26, 1884, Manton, MI; par. Joseph A. and Emma Jane (Dove) Watson; m. Maude L. Hager; c. Ralph Bradley; Claudia Jean Cutler; Robert Kendall. Educ.: grad., Alma (MI) H.S.; Alma Coll.; J.D., Blackstone Coll.; LL.B., La Salle Extension U. Polit. &

GOV.: Prohibition Party candidate for city atty.; ***Prohibition Party candidate for vice presidency of the U.S., 1936***; Prohibition Party candidate for atty. gen. of CA, 1938, 1942, 1946, 1950; ***Prohibition Party candidate for presidency of the U.S., 1944, 1948***; Prohibition Party candidate for district atty., Los Angeles Cty., CA, 1952; ***candidate for Prohibition Party nomination to presidency of the U.S., 1964***; joined Republican Party. BUS. & PROF.: accountant, auditor, U.S. Steel Corp.; gen. mgr., Four Drive Tractor Co., Inc.; minister, Free Methodist Church, 1911–; atty.; law practice, 1928–. MEM.: Highland Park (CA) Kiwanis Club (pres.); Christian Businessmen's Breakfast Club of Highland Park; CA Bar Assn.; Northeast Bar Assn. (pres.); U.S. Air Force Auxiliary Civil Air Patrol (maj.). HON. DEG.: LL.D., Greenville Coll. WRITINGS: *Traitors to America* (1944); *God's Plan for Civil Government*; *Repeal Has Succeeded* (1946); *Fifth Columnists in America*; *Bloody Hands*. REL.: Free Methodist (gen. counsel; sec., exec. comm.). RES.: Los Angeles, CA.

WATSON, FRANK RAMEY, JR. par. Frank Ramey Watson, Sr. POLIT. & GOV.: ***independent candidate for presidency of the U.S., 1988***. MAILING ADDRESS: 43632 Parsons Rd., Oberlin, OH 44074.

WATSON, JAMES ELI. b. Nov 2, 1863, Winchester, IN; d. Jul 29, 1948, Washington, DC; par. Enos Lindsey and Margaret (Judd) Watson; m. Flora Miller, Dec 12, 1893; c. Edwin Gowdy; James Eli; Florine; Kathryn (Mrs. Ernest Arnold Gross); Joseph C. EDUC.: grad., Winchester (IN) H.S., 1881; A.B., DePauw U., 1886. POLIT. & GOV.: presidential elector, Republican Party, 1892; Republican candidate for state sec. of state of IN, c. 1892; elected as a Republican to U.S. House (IN), 1895–97, 1899–1909; candidate for Republican nomination to U.S. House (IN), 1896; chm., IN State Republican Convention, 1904, 1906, 1912, 1918, 1920, 1924, 1926; Republican candidate for gov. of IN, 1908; delegate, Rep. Nat'l. Conv., 1912, 1920, 1924, 1932, 1936, and 4 other times; elected as a Republican to U.S. Senate (IN), 1916–33 (majority leader, 1929–33); ***candidate for Republican nomination to presidency of the U.S., 1920, 1928; candidate for Republican nomination to vice presidency of the U.S., 1924***; Republican candidate for U.S. Senate (IN), 1932. BUS. & PROF.: atty.; admitted to IN Bar, 1887; partner, Watson and Cheney (law firm), Winchester, IN, 1887–93; partner, Watson, Martin and Magee (law firm), Rushville, IN, 1893–1933; partner, Watson and MacNeil (law firm), Washington, DC, 1933–48. MEM.: Knights of Pythias (Grand Chancellor, 1891–93); Lincoln League; ABA; IN Bar Assn.; Epworth League (state pres., 1892–94); DC Bar Assn.; Columbia Club; Masons; Odd Fellows; Elks; Modern Woodmen of the World; Improved Order of Red Men; Phi Kappa Psi. HON. DEG.: A.M., DePauw U., 1906; LL.D., Notre Dame U., 1910; LL.D., Lincoln Memorial U., 1916. WRITINGS: *As I Knew Them* (1936). REL.: Methodist. RES.: Rushville, IN.

WATSON, THOMAS EDWARD. b. Sep 5, 1856, Thomson, GA; d. Sep 26, 1922, Washington, DC; par. John Smith and Ann Eliza (Maddox) Watson; m. Georgia Durham, Oct 9, 1878; c. John Durham; two daughters. EDUC.: Mercer Coll., Macon, GA. POLIT. & GOV.: delegate, GA State Democratic Convention, 1880; elected as a Democrat to GA State House, 1882–83; presidential elector, Democratic Party, 1888; elected as a Populist to U.S. House (GA), 1891–93; People's Party candidate for U.S. House (GA), 1892, 1894, 1895; ***People's Party candidate for vice presidency of the U.S., 1896***; People's Party candidate for gov. of GA, 1898; ***People's Party candidate for presidency of the U.S., 1904, 1908***; delegate, Dem. Nat'l. Conv., 1912; candidate for Democratic nomination to U.S. House (GA), 1918; ***candidate for Democratic nomination to presidency of the U.S., 1920***; elected as a Democrat to U.S. Senate (GA), 1921–22. BUS. & PROF.: teacher, Central Warrior Acad., Macon, GA, 1874; atty.; admitted to GA Bar, 1875; law practice, Thomson, GA, 1876–91; farmer; ed., *People's Party Paper*, Atlanta, GA, 1891–98; ed., *Daily Press*, 1894; publisher, *Tom Watson's Magazine*, 1905; publisher, *Watson's Jeffersonian Magazine*, 1906–17; publisher, *The Weekly Jeffersonian* 1906–17; founder, Jefferson Publishing Co., 1911; ed., *The Guard*, 1917; author; pres., McDuffie Bank; publisher, *The Sentinel*, 1919–22. MEM.: Phi Delta Soc. (asst. librarian); Guardians of Liberty (1911). WRITINGS: *People's Party Campaign Book* (1892); *The Railroad Question* (1894); *The Story of France* (1898); *Thomas Jefferson* (1900); *Napoleon: A Sketch of His Life, Character, Struggles and Achievements* (1902); *Life and Times of Thomas Jefferson* (1903); *Bethany: A Study and Story of the Old South* (1904); *Life and Times of Andrew Jackson* (1907); *Handbook of Politics and Economics* (1908); *Sketches from Roman History* (1908); *Life and Speeches of Thomas E. Watson* (1908); *The Methods of Foreign Missions Exposed* (1909); *History of Southern Oratory* (ed., 1909); *The Roman Catholic Hierarchy* (1910); *Waterloo* (1910); *Socialists and Socialism* (1909); *A Tariff Primer* (1911); *Sketches: Biographical, Historical, Literary* (1912); *Prose Miscellanies* (1912); *Speech Against the Conscription Act* (1917); *Mr. Watson's Editorials on the War Issues* (1917); *What Are Your Constitutional Rights* (1917); *Is Your Brain for Sale?* REL.: Deist. MISC.: tried several times for publishing anti-Catholic articles, but acquitted each time, 1914–17; opposed conscription during WWI, with result that mails were closed to his publications. RES.: Thomson, GA.

WATTERSON, HENRY. b. Feb 16, 1840, Washington, DC; d. Dec 22, 1921, Jacksonville, FL; par. Harvey Magee and Talitha (Black) Watterson; m. Rebecca Ewing, Dec 20, 1865. EDUC.: Acad. of the Episcopal Diocese of PA; D.C.L., U. of the South, 1891. POLIT. & GOV.: elected as a Democrat to U.S. House (KY), 1876–77; delegate, Dem. Nat'l. Conv., 1876 (temporary chm.), 1880 (chm., platform cmte.), 1884, 1888 (chm., platform cmte.), 1892; ***candidate for Democratic nomination to vice presidency of the U.S., 1892***; member, Dem. Nat'l. Cmte.; appointed vice pres., Interstate Perry Memorial Comm., 1910.

BUS. & PROF.: journalist; orator; author; reporter, *Washington States*, 1858–61; ed., *Democratic Review*, 1860–61; ed., *Chattanooga (TN) Rebel*, 1862–63; ed., *Republican Banner*, Nashville, TN, 1865–68; ed., *Louisville (KY) Courier-Journal*, 1868–1919. MIL.: staff officer, C.S.A., 1861–65. MEM.: Hall of Fame, U. of NY (juror, 1914). HON. DEG.: LL.D., Brown U., 1906; LL.D., U. of KY, 1915. WRITINGS: *History of the Spanish-American War* (1899); *History of the Manhattan Club*; *The Compromises of Life: Lectures and Addresses* (1902); *Marse Henry, Looking Backward Sketches* (1919); *Oddities of Southern Life and Character* (ed., 1882). REL.: Episc. RES.: Jeffersontown, KY.

WATTS, CONNIE N. b. 1889. POLIT. & GOV.: ***Rocking Chair Party candidate for presidency of the U.S., 1960***. BUS. & PROF.: farmer, Banks Cty., GA. MEM.: Dixie Martin-Bluebird Cooperative Club (pres.). RES.: Baldwin, GA.

WATTS, HOWARD O. POLIT. & GOV.: ***candidate for Republican nomination to presidency of the U.S., 1984***. MAILING ADDRESS: CA?

WATTS, RICHARD CANNON. b. Mar 15, 1853, Laurens, SC; d. Oct 13, 1930, Laurens, SC; par. John and Elizabeth C. (Cannon) Watts; m. Alleine Ellerbe Cash, Nov 2, 1881; m. 2d, Lottie Harrington McIver, Apr 16, 1896; c. Cash; Gus (Mrs. Jared David Sullivan); Courtnay (Mrs. Frank Fuller Stokes); Bessie (Mrs. Robert Venning Royall, Jr.); John. EDUC.: U. of VA, 1871–72; studied law with Col. Beaufort W. Ball. POLIT. & GOV.: appointed lt. col., aide-de-camp to Gov. Wade Hampton, SC, 1877–79; appointed chief of staff to Gov. W. D. Simpson, SC, 1879–80; elected as a Democrat to SC State House, 1890–94; judge, Fourth Judicial Circuit, SC, 1894–1912; elected assoc. justice, Supreme Court of SC, 1912–30 (chief justice, 1927–29); ***candidate for Democratic nomination to presidency of the U.S., 1928***. BUS. & PROF.: atty.; admitted to SC Bar, 1873 (by special act of the legislature); partner, Young J. Pope (law firm), Newberry, SC, 1874–80; partner, Ball and Watts (law firm), 1880–92. MEM.: Masons (Knight Templar); SC Bar; SC Club (pres.). REL.: Episc. MISC.: served as Red Shirt Rider for Wade Hampton (q.v.), 1876. RES.: Cheraw, SC.

WATTS, VERA. POLIT. & GOV.: ***candidate for Democratic nomination to presidency of the U.S., 1992***. MAILING ADDRESS: 919.5 West Washtenaw, Lansing, MI 48901.

WATUMULL, DAVID. b. Oct 24, 1927, Honolulu, HI; par. G. J. and Ellen (Jensen) Watumull; m. Sheila Hessian, Feb 22, 1968; c. David; Rann; Teren; Denton; Melanie. EDUC.: B.S., U. of CA at Los Angeles, 1947. POLIT. & GOV.: ***candidate for Republican nomination to presidency of the U.S., 1968***; candidate for Republican nomination to gov. of HI, 1970. BUS. & PROF.: land developer; partner, Watumull Investment Co., Honolulu, HI, 1957–; pres., Hawaiian Paradise Park Corp., 1959–. MEM.: Watumull Foundation (trustee; sec.). MAILING ADDRESS: 2207 Kalakaua Ave., Honolulu, HI 96715.

WEATTER, NAN C. POLIT. & GOV.: ***independent candidate for presidency of the U.S., 1992***. MAILING ADDRESS: P.O. Box 1292, Muskegon, MI 49441.

WEAVER, JAMES BAIRD. b. Jun 12, 1833, Dayton, OH; d. Feb 6, 1912, Des Moines, IA; par. Abram and Susan (Imley) Weaver; m. Clara Vinson, Jul 13, 1858; c. James Bellamy; Maud (Mrs. Charles E. Sullenberger); Susan (Mrs. H. C. Evans); Abram C.; Ruth (Mrs. Harvey Denny); Laura (Mrs. A. R. Ketcham); Esther (Mrs. Edward Cohrt). EDUC.: public schools; LL.B., Cincinnati Law School, 1856. POLIT. & GOV.: candidate for Republican nomination to lt. gov. of IA, 1865; elected as a Republican, district atty., Second Judicial District, IA, 1866–70; appointed assessor of internal revenue, First District of IA, 1867–73; ***independent candidate for presidency of the U.S., 1872***; candidate for Republican nomination to U.S. House (IA), 1873; candidate for Republican nomination to gov. of IA, 1875; organizer, IA Greenback Party, 1876; ***candidate for Greenback Party nomination to presidency of the U.S., 1876***; member, IA State Greenback Party Central Cmte.; elected as a Greenbacker to U.S. House (IA), 1879–81; ***National Greenback Party candidate for presidency of the U.S., 1880***; Greenback Party candidate for U.S. House (IA), 1882; Greenback (Industrial Alliance) Party candidate for gov. of IA, 1883; ***candidate for Anti-Monopoly Party nomination to presidency of the U.S., 1884 (declined)***; elected as a Democrat-Greenback-Laborite to U.S. House (IA), 1885–89; ***candidate for Union Labor Party nomination to presidency of the U.S., 1888***; Democrat-Greenback-Laborite candidate for U.S. House (IA), 1888; ***People's Party candidate for presidency of the U.S., 1892; received 22 electoral votes for presidency of the U.S., 1892***; Democrat-People's Party candidate for U.S. House (IA), 1894; Democratic (Fusion) candidate for U.S. House (IA), 1898; elected mayor of Colfax, IA, 1901–06; member, People's (Fusion) Party National Cmte., 1901; delegate, Dem. Nat'l. Conv., 1904. BUS. & PROF.: atty.; admitted to IA Bar, 1856; law practice, Bloomfield, IA; ed., *Iowa Tribune*, Des Moines, IA. MIL.: pvt., Second IA Volunteers, 1861, 1st lt., 1861, maj., 1862, col., 1862, brev. brig. gen., 1864, mustered out, May 27, 1864. WRITINGS: *A Call to Reason* (1892). RES.: Colfax, IA.

WEAVER, JAMES HOWARD. b. Aug 8, 1927, Brookings, SD; par. Leo C. and Alice (Flittie) Weaver; m. Sally Cummins, Jun 11, 1955; c. Regan; Allison; Sarah. EDUC.: B.S., U. of OR, 1952. POLIT. & GOV.: staff dir., OR State Legislative Interim Cmte. on Agriculture, 1959–60; delegate, Dem.

Nat'l. Conv., 1960, 1964; delegate, Democratic Mid-Term Conference, 1974; elected as a Democrat to U.S. House (OR), 1975–87; ***candidate for Democratic nomination to vice presidency of the U.S., 1980***; Democratic candidate for U.S. Senate (OR), 1986 (resigned). BUS. & PROF.: publisher's rep., Prentice-Hall, 1954–58; builder; developer, 1960–74. MIL.: U.S.N.R., 1945–46. MEM.: Eugene-Springfield Metro-Civic Club. MAILING ADDRESS: 2301 Spring Blvd., Eugene, OR 97403.

WEBB, FRANK ELBRIDGE. b. Sep 1, 1869, Calaveras, CA; d. Jun 15, 1949, Washington, DC; par. Elbridge and Annie E. (Settle) Webb; m. Elsa White Reid, Apr 1928. EDUC.: grad., Lincoln H.S., San Francisco, CA; studied law under John H. Dickinson, San Francisco, CA. POLIT. & GOV.: appointed confidential representative of presidency of the U.S., Spanish-American War; ***Farmer-Labor Party candidate for presidency of the U.S., 1928, 1932 (declined; replaced by Jacob S. Coxey, q.v.); Liberty Party candidate for presidency of the U.S., 1932 (replaced by William Hope Harvey, q.v.)***. BUS. & PROF.: farmer; businessman; industrial engineer; engineer with John A. Bensel, 1906–16; supervisor of San Francisco Bridge Project, 1922. MIL.: joined National Guard, 1884; sgt., U.S. Army, 1898–99; quarter master, Dept. of the Army; col. MEM.: SAR; Knight Commander of the Holy Sepulchre; Knight Commander of the Crown of Charlemagne. REL.: Presb. RES.: San Francisco, CA.

WEBB, ROBERT GENE. POLIT. & GOV.: ***candidate for Democratic nomination to presidency of the U.S., 1992***. MAILING ADDRESS: c/o Alexandria Hotel, 501 Spring, Los Angeles, CA 90053.

WEBSTER, DANIEL. b. Jan 18, 1782, Salisbury, NH; d. Oct 24, 1852, Marshfield, MA; par. Ebenezer and Abigail (Eastman) Webster; m. Grace Fletcher, May 29, 1808; m. 2d, Caroline LeRoy, Dec 12, 1829; c. Fletcher; Edward; Julia Appleton. EDUC.: Phillips Exeter Acad.; grad., Dartmouth Coll., 1801; studied law under Christopher Gore. POLIT. & GOV.: elected as a Federalist to U.S. House (NH), 1813–17; Federalist candidate for U.S. House (NH), 1816; presidential elector, Democratic-Republican Party, 1820; delegate, MA State Constitutional Convention, 1820; elected as a Whig to MA State House, 1822; elected as a Whig to U.S. House (MA), 1823–27; elected as a Whig to U.S. Senate (MA), 1827–41, 1845–50; ***Whig Party candidate for presidency of the U.S., 1836, 1852***; appointed U.S. sec. of state, 1841–43, 1850–52; *candidate for Whig Party nomination to presidency of the U.S., 1848; Native American Party candidate for presidency of the U.S., 1852*. BUS. & PROF.: principal, acad., Fryeburg, ME, 1802; atty.; admitted to Boston (MA) Bar, 1805; law practice, Boscawen, NH, 1805–07; law practice, Portsmouth, NH, 1807–16; law practice, Boston, MA, 1816–52. MEM.: Harvard U. (overseer, 1822–52); American Acad. (fellow); MA Hist. Soc. HON. DEG.: M.A., Harvard U., 1804; LL.D., Princeton U., 1818; LL.D., Dartmouth Coll., 1823; LL.D., Columbia U., 1824; LL.D., Harvard U., 1824; LL.D., Allegheny Coll., 1840. RES.: Marshfield, MA.

WEBSTER, WILLIAM GRANT. b. Feb 24, 1866, Kingston, IL; par. Rev. Calvary Morris and Ann Catherine (Parker) Webster; single. EDUC.: A.B., Harvard U., 1886; LL.M., Columbian U. (now George Washington U.), 1888. POLIT. & GOV.: employee, U.S. Civil Service, 1883–85, 1887–93; Republican candidate for U.S. Senate (IL), 1906, 1908; candidate for Republican nomination to U.S. Senate (IL), 1912; candidate for Republican nomination to U.S. House (IL), 1912, 1914; ***candidate for Republican nomination to vice presidency of the U.S., 1916, 1920, 1924, 1928***. BUS. & PROF.: atty.; admitted to DC Bar, 1888; admitted to practice before the Bar of the Supreme Court of the U.S., 1893; law practice, Chicago, IL, 1893; dean, Cleveland Law School, 1897; dean, RI Law School, 1898–1901; dean, John Marshall Law School, 1899. MEM.: Delta Kappa Epsilon. RES.: Chicago, IL.

WEDEMEYER, ALBERT COADY. b. Jul 9, 1897, Omaha, NE; d. Dec 17, 1989, Fort Belvoir, VA; par. Albert Anthony and Margaret E. (Coady) Wedemeyer; m. Elizabeth Dade Embick, Feb 5, 1925; c. Albert Dunbar; Robert Dade. EDUC.: B.S., U.S. Military Acad., 1919; grad., General Staff School, Fort Leavenworth, KS, 1936; grad., German War Coll., 1938. POLIT. & GOV.: appointed ambassador to represent presidency of the U.S. in China and Korea, 1947; ***candidate for Republican nomination to presidency of the U.S., 1952 (declined)***. BUS. & PROF.: industrialist; soldier; author; vice pres., dir., Avco Manufacturing Co., 1951–54; vice pres., dir., Rheem Manufacturing Co., 1954–56; dir., National Airlines, Inc. MIL.: commissioned 2d lt., U.S. Army, 1919, advanced through grades to gen., 1954; gen. staff, War Dept., 1941–43; commanding gen., China Theater, 1944–46; chief of staff to Generalissimo Chiang Kai-shek; Distinguished Service Medal (Two Clusters); Distinguished Flying Cross; Order of the Commander of the Bath (Great Britain); Order of the White Sun and Blue Sky (China); Grand Cross, Order of the Phoenix (Greece); Commander's Cross, Order of Polania Restituta (Poland); Order of Military Merit (Brazil). MEM.: Army and Navy Club; Chevy Chase Club; Bohemian Club; Metropolitan Club; Dutch Treat Club. HON. DEG.: Ph.D., China Acad.; LL.D., Creighton U.; LL.D., DePauw U.; LL.D., U. of PA; LL.D., Rollins Coll.; LL.D., U. of San Francisco; LL.D., U. of Southern CA; L.H.D., Temple U. WRITINGS: *Wedemeyer Reports* (1958). RES.: Boyds, MD.

WEEKS, JOHN WINGATE. b. Apr 11, 1860, Lancaster, NH; d. Jul 12, 1926, Mount Prospect, NH; par. William Dennis and Mary Helen (Fowler) Weeks; m. Martha A. Sinclair, Oct 7, 1885; c. Katherine S. (Mrs. John W. Davidge); Charles Sinclair. EDUC.: grad., U.S. Naval Acad., 1881. POLIT. & GOV.: member, Military Advisory Board of MA,

1894–1900; member, Military Board of Examiners, 1894–1900; chm., MA State Republican Convention, 1895, 1905; elected alderman, Newton, MA, 1900–1903; elected mayor of Newton, MA, 1903–04; elected as a Republican to U.S. House (MA), 1905–13; elected as a Republican to U.S. Senate (MA), 1913–19; ***candidate for Republican nomination to presidency of the U.S., 1916***; Republican candidate for U.S. Senate (MA), 1918; delegate, Rep. Nat'l. Conv., 1920; member, Rep. Nat'l. Cmte., 1920; appointed U.S. sec. of war, 1921–25. BUS. & PROF.: civil engineer; surveyor; asst. land commissioner, Florida Southern R.R., 1886–88; assoc., Hornblower and Weeks (banking and brokerage firm), Boston, MA, 1888–1912; pres., Newtonville Trust Co.; pres., MA National Bank; vice pres., First National Bank of Boston. MIL.: midshipman, U.S. Navy, 1881–83; capt., MA Naval Bde., 1890–98; lt., Second Div. Auxiliary, U.S. Navy, 1898–99; rear adm., U.S.N.R., 1900. MEM.: U.S. Naval Acad. (visitor, 1896); Soc. of the Cincinnati; SAR; Soc. of the War of 1812; Military Order of Foreign Wars; Military Order of the Spanish-American War; American Forestry Assn. (vice pres.); University Club; Middlesex Club; Newton Club; Metropolitan Club; Chevy Chase Club; Army and Navy Club; Wardroom Club. RES.: West Newton, MA.

WEICKER, LOWELL PALMER, JR. b. May 16, 1931, Paris, France; par. Lowell Palmer and Mary (Bickford) Hastings Weicker; m. Marie Louise Godfrey, Jun 13, 1953; m. 2d, Camille DiLorenzo Butler, Nov 5, 1977; c. Scot Bickford; Gray Godfrey; Brian Kennedy. EDUC.: grad., Lawrenceville School, 1949; B.A., Yale U., 1953; LL.B., U. of VA, 1958; Sc.D., Bridgeport Engineering Inst. POLIT. & GOV.: elected as a Republican to CT State House, 1963–69; elected as a Republican, First Selectman, Greenwich, CT, 1964–68; legislative consultant, CT Transportation Authority, 1965; sec., CT State Tax Study Comm., 1966–67; elected as a Republican to U.S. House (CT), 1969–71; elected as a Republican to U.S. Senate (CT), 1971–89; delegate, Rep. Nat'l. Conv., 1972; ***candidate for Republican nomination to presidency of the U.S., 1976, 1980; candidate for Republican nomination to vice presidency of the U.S., 1976***; Republican candidate for U.S. Senate (CT), 1989; elected as an independent to gov. of CT, 1991–1995. BUS. & PROF.: atty.; admitted to CT Bar, 1960. MIL.: 1st lt., U.S. Army, 1953–55; capt., U.S.A.R., 1959–64. MEM.: Yale Political Union. HON. DEG.: LL.D., U. of Bridgeport, 1974; LL.D., John Carroll U., 1974; LL.D., Fairleigh Dickenson U., 1975; LL.D., U. of ME, 1975; LL.D., Franklin Pierce Coll., 1978. REL.: Episc. MAILING ADDRESS: 445 Round Hill Rd., Greenwich, CT 06830.

WEILAND, FRED, III. b. 1919, WV; par. Fred Weiland, II. EDUC.: B.S.; grad., U.S. Army Command and Gen. Staff Coll.; grad., Industrial Coll. of the Armed Forces. POLIT. & GOV.: American Party candidate for U.S. Senate (MD), 1972; left American Party, 1972; independent candidate for U.S. Senate (WV), 1976; ***independent candidate for presidency of the U.S., 1980***; candidate for Republican nomination to U.S. Senate (WV), 1984. BUS. & PROF.: electronics engineer; management engineer; administrative engineer; investor; radio repairman; electrician; mechanic; office clerk; laborer; contract specialist; cost control mgr.; dir. of training. MIL.: officer, U.S. Army. MEM.: VFW; American Legion; American Economic Assn.; AAAS; Inst. of Radio and Electronics; American Management Assn. MISC.: advocate of national referenda via telephone. MAILING ADDRESS: 1340 Cherry Lane, Morgantown, WV 26505.

WEISS, MYRA TANNER. b. May 17, 1917, Salt Lake City, UT; d. Myron Clark and Marie (Boshard) T.; m. Morris Paul Weiss; c. none. EDUC.: B.A., Brooklyn Coll., 1969; M.A., NY U., 1972. POLIT. & GOV.: joined Socialist movement, 1935; Los Angeles organizer, Socialist Workers Party, 1942–52; Socialist Workers Party candidate for mayor of Los Angeles, CA, 1945, 1947, 1949; Socialist Workers Party candidate for U.S. House (CA), 1948, 1950; ***Socialist Workers Party candidate for vice presidency of the U.S., 1952, 1956, 1960***. BUS. & PROF.: migratory worker; political organizer; typographer; staff writer, *The Militant*, 1953–62; staff writer, *International Socialist Review*, 1953–62. MEM.: Mexican Agricultural Workers Union (hon.); Brooklyn Alumni Assn.; APSA WRITINGS: *Vigilante Terror in Fontana* (1946). REL.: none. MAILING ADDRESS: 80½ Jane, New York, NY 10014.

WELBORN, JOHN ALVA "JACK." b. Kalamazoo, MI; par. Harry Sterling and Elizabeth (Dougherty) Welborn; m. Dorothy Beatrice Yeomans, 1952; c. Kayle Jane; Kami Ellen; John Robert. EDUC.: Richland H.S. POLIT. & GOV.: member, Cooper Township (MI) Republican Cmte., 1951–66; precinct committeeman, Republican Party; delegate, MI State Republican Convention, 16 times; member, Gull Lake (MI) School Board, 1965–67; elected as a Republican, supervisor, Cooper Township, MI, 1967–73; elected as a Republican to MI State House, 1973–75; elected as a Republican to MI State Senate, 1975–83; delegate, Rep. Nat'l. Conv., 1976, 1980; ***candidate for Republican nomination to vice presidency of the U.S., 1976***; candidate for Republican nomination to gov. of MI, 1982. BUS. & PROF.: fireman, Cooper Township, MI, 1950–83; dairy farmer, Cooper Township, MI, 1951–70; insurance agent, Sumney Agency, Kalamazoo, MI. MIL.: U.S. Navy, 1949–51. MISC.: known as "Mr. Free Spirit." MAILING ADDRESS: 6304 North Riverview Dr., Kalamazoo, MI 49001.

WELDON, WILD BILL. POLIT. & GOV.: ***Apathy Party candidate for vice presidency of the U.S., 1992***. MAILING ADDRESS: One Plaza South, Suite 129, Tahlequah, OK 74464.

WELK, LAWRENCE. b. Mar 11, 1903, Strasburg, ND; d. May 17, 1992, Santa Monica, CA; par. Ludwig and Christine (Schwab) Welk; m. Fern Renner, Apr 18, 1931; c. Shirley J. (Mrs. Robert Fredericks); Donna (Mrs. Jim Mack); Larry. EDUC.: public schools. POLIT. & GOV.: ***candidate for Democratic nomination to presidency of the U.S., 1976***. BUS. & PROF.: orchestra leader; accordionist, 1920; appeared on radio station WNAX, Yankton, SD; bandleader, 1927–; host, "The Lawrence Welk Show," ABC-TV, 1955–71; host, "The Lawrence Welk Show," Syndicated Network, 1971–; recording artist. AWARDS: Top Dance Band of America Award, National Ballroom Operators of America, 1955; Number One TV Musical Program Award, 1955; TV Radio Mirror Award, 1956–57; American Legion Award, 1957; Horatio Alger Award, 1967; Freedom Award, Freedoms Foundation of Valley Forge, 1968, 1969; Brotherhood Award, National Conference of Christians and Jews, 1969. HON. DEG.: Mus.D., ND State U., 1965. WRITINGS: *Ah-One, Ah-Two: Life With My Musical Family* (with Bernice McGeehan, 1975); *Wunnerful, Wunnerful* (1973). REL.: R.C. RES.: Santa Monica, CA.

WELLER, JOHN B. b. Feb 22, 1812, Montgomery, OH; d. Aug 17, 1875, New Orleans, LA; m. Miss Ryan; m. 2d, Miss Bryan; m. 3d, Susan McDowell Taylor; m. 4th, Lizzie Brocklebank Stanton. EDUC.: Miami U., 1825–29; studied law under Jesse Corwin. POLIT. & GOV.: prosecuting atty., Butler Cty., OH, 1833–36; elected as a Democrat to U.S. House (OH), 1839–45; Democratic candidate for gov. of OH, 1848; appointed member, U.S. Comm. on California-Mexico Boundary, 1849–50; elected as a Union Democrat to U.S. Senate (CA), 1851–57; ***candidate for Democratic nomination to presidency of the U.S., 1852; candidate for Democratic nomination to vice presidency of the U.S., 1852***; Union Democratic candidate for U.S. Senate (CA), 1857; elected as a Democrat to gov. of CA, 1858–60; appointed U.S. minister to Mexico, 1860–61; Democratic candidate for U.S. House (CA), 1863; delegate, Dem. Nat'l. Conv., 1864. BUS. & PROF.: atty.; admitted to OH Bar, 1832; law practice, Hamilton, OH; law practice, San Francisco, CA, 1850; law practice, New Orleans, LA, 1867–75. MIL.: lt. col., col., U.S.V., 1846–47. RES.: New Orleans, LA.

WELLER, LUMAN HAMLIN. b. Aug 24, 1833, Bridgewater, CT; d. Mar 2, 1914, Minneapolis, MN. EDUC.: CT State Normal School; Suffield Literary Inst.; read law. POLIT. & GOV.: justice of the peace, IA, 1865; independent candidate for IA State House, 1867; elected as a National Greenback-Democrat to U.S. House (IA), 1883–85; National Greenback-Democratic candidate for U.S. House (IA), 1884; member, People's Party National Cmte., 1890–1914; candidate for judge, Supreme Court of IA, twice; People's Party candidate for gov. of IA, 1901; ***candidate for Allied People's Party nomination to vice presidency of the U.S., 1904***. BUS. & PROF.: farmer, Chickasaw Cty., IA, 1859; atty.; admitted to IA Bar, 1869; law practice, Bradford, IA; farmer, Nashua, IA; owner, ed., *Farmer's Advocate*, Independence, IA. MEM.: Chosen Farmers of America (pres.). RES.: IA.

WELLES, CHARLES STUART. b. Feb 2, 1848, London, Ontario, Canada; d. Feb 5, 1927, Bletchley, England; par. Henry Spalding and Amelia (Beardsley) Welles; m. Ella Celeste (Miles) O'Halloran, Aug 11, 1881; c. Charles Stuart, Jr.; Francis Channing Miles; Utica (Mrs. Thomas Beecham). EDUC.: Bellevue Hospital Medical Coll.; M.D., Dartmouth Coll., 1884. POLIT. & GOV.: appointed sec. to Gov. Morgan, NY; first sec., U.S. embassy, London, England; ***Equal Rights Party candidate for vice presidency of the U.S., 1888***; Socialist Party candidate for NY State Senate, 1908. BUS. & PROF.: employee, H. S. Wells and Co. (contractors), 1869; physician; surgeon; head physician, Polyclinic Hospital, New York, NY; physician, NY Board of Health; painter; author; lecturer on Women's Rights; ed., *The Humanitarian*, 1892–95. MEM.: Union League; Royal Automobile Club of London; SAR; Masons (32°). WRITINGS: *The Constitution of the United States of the World*; *The New Marriage and Other Uniform Laws*; *Lillian*; *The Ellwoods*; *Boheme*; *The Lute and Lays*. RES.: New York, NY.

WELSH, MATTHEW EMPSON. b. Sep 15, 1912, Detroit, MI; par. Matthew William and Inez (Empson) Welsh; m. Virginia Homann, Sep 25, 1937; c. Kathryn Louise; Janet Marie. EDUC.: B.S., Wharton School of Commerce, U. of PA, 1934; IN U. School of Law, 1935–36; J.D., U. of Chicago, 1937. POLIT. & GOV.: elected as a Democrat to IN State House, 1941–43; Democratic candidate for judge, IN State Court of Appeals, 1946; chm., Seventh District Democratic Cmte., 1948; appointed U.S. atty., Southern District of IN, 1950–52; elected as a Democrat to IN State Senate, 1955–61 (Democratic floor leader, 1957–61); candidate for Democratic nomination to gov. of IN, 1956; elected as a Democrat to gov. of IN, 1961–65; member, Dem. Nat'l. Cmte., 1964–68; ***candidate for Democratic nomination to presidency of the U.S., 1964***; appointed chm., U.S. Section, U.S.-Canadian International Joint Comm., 1966–70; co-chm., IN State Constitutional Revision Comm., 1967–71; Democratic candidate for gov. of IN, 1972. BUS. & PROF.: sec.-treas., M. W. Welsh and Co., Vincennes, IN; sec., dir., Universal Scientific Co., Vincennes, IN; dir., Security Bank and Trust Co., Vincennes, IN; atty.; admitted to IN Bar, 1937; law practice, Vincennes, IN, 1937–61; dir., Morgan County Bank and Trust Co.; dir., Lincoln National Co. Variable Annuity Funds, Fort Wayne, IN; partner, Bingham, Summers, Welsh and Spilman (law firm), 1965–. MIL.: lt. (jg), U.S. Navy, 1943–46. MEM.: Friars Club; Delta Kappa Epsilon; Phi Delta Phi; ABA; IN Bar Assn.; Knox Cty. Bar Assn.; Indianapolis Bar Assn.; Vincennes U. (trustee); American Legion; Vincennes YMCA (trustee); Elks; Kiwanis; Kennedy Memorial Christian Home (dir.); Christian Theological Seminary (trustee); National Lawyers Club; Christian Church Foundation (trustee); John A. Hartford Foundation (trustee). HON. DEG.: LL.D., Franklin Coll.; LL.D., IN U.; LL.D., IN State U.; LL.D., St. Joseph's Coll.; LL.D., Tri-State Coll.; LL.D., Vincennes U. REL.: Disciples of Christ (trustee; elder). MAILING ADDRESS: 719 Busseron St., Vincennes, IN.

WENDELKIN, MARTIN E. POLIT. & GOV.: independent candidate for U.S. House (NJ), 1972, 1980; candidate for Republican nomination to U.S. House (NJ), 1974; candidate for Republican nomination to U.S. Senate (NJ), 1976; ***independent candidate for presidency of the U.S., 1980***; independent candidate for U.S. Senate (NJ), 1982. BUS. & PROF.: owner, Martin E. Wendelkin Associates; owner, Jacketmaster Products Co. MAILING ADDRESS: 36 Jerome Ave., Glen Rock, NJ 07452.

WENDT, RICK. POLIT. & GOV.: ***independent candidate for vice presidency of the U.S., 1992***. BUS. & PROF.: farmer, Ricketts, IA. MAILING ADDRESS: Ricketts, IA.

WENTWORTH, BYRON CHESTER. POLIT. & GOV.: ***candidate for Democratic nomination to presidency of the U.S., 1976, 1980***. MAILING ADDRESS: 15 Lovell St., Worcester, MA 01603.

WERDEL, THOMAS HAROLD. b. Sep 13, 1905, Emery, SD; d. Sep 30, 1966, Bakersfield, CA; par. Bernard and Mary Laura (Burke) Werdel; m. Rosemary Cutter; c. Thomas Harold, Jr.; Charles Cutter; Terrance John. EDUC.: A.B., U. of CA (Berkeley), 1930, LL.B., 1936. POLIT. & GOV.: elected as a Republican to CA State Assembly, 1943–47; elected as a Republican to U.S. House (CA), 1949–53; ***candidate for Republican nomination to presidency of the U.S., 1952***; Republican candidate for U.S. House (CA), 1952; ***States Rights (Constitution, American Constitution, Conservative, American, Independent) Party candidate for vice presidency of the U.S., 1956***. BUS. & PROF.: atty.; admitted to CA Bar, 1936; law practice, Bakersfield, CA, 1936–66. MEM.: ABA; State Bar Assn. of CA; Kern Cty. Bar Assn.; University Club of WA. RES.: Bakersfield, CA.

WEST, ABSALOM MADDEN "AMOS." b. 1818, Marion, AL; d. Sep 30, 1894, Holly Springs, MS; par. Anderson and Olivia (Tubb) West; m. Caroline O. "Carrie" Glover, 1845; c. infant; Olivia (Mrs. W. T. McCarty); Absalom Madden, Jr.; Edgar; Benjamin G.; Carrie W. (Mrs. Lemuel Augustus Smith); Charles; Sidney Y. EDUC.: district and subscription schools, to 1833. POLIT. & GOV.: elected as a Union Whig to MS State House, 1848–54, 1890; elected as a Union Whig to MS State Senate, 1854–61, 1878–82; Whig candidate for gov. of MS, 1863; elected as an Anti-Secessionist to U.S. House (MS), but not seated, 1865; ***candidate for Labor Reform Party nomination to vice presidency of the U.S., 1872***; member, exec. cmte., Labor Reform Party, 1872; appointed pres., MS State Board of Centennial Commissioners, 1876; presidential elector, Democratic Party, 1876; joined National Labor Party, 1876; National Greenback Labor Party candidate for U.S. Senate (MS), 1880; ***candidate for National (Greenback) Party nomination to vice presidency of the U.S., 1880; candidate for Greenback Party nomination to presidency of the U.S., 1884; Greenback (Anti-Monopoly) Party candidate for vice presidency of the U.S., 1884***. BUS. & PROF.: planter, Holmes Cty., MS, 1837–61; railway mgr.; pres., Mississippi Central R.R., 1864–78; farmer, Holly Springs, MS, 1870–94; pres., Mississippi Valley Co. MIL.: brig. gen., quartermaster gen., paymaster gen., commissary gen., MS Troops, C.S.A., 1861–65. REL.: Methodist Episc. Church. MISC.: founder, McComb City, MS. RES.: Holly Springs, MS.

WESTERBEEK, MRS. L. D. b. 1903, ID; married. POLIT. & GOV.: ***Patriotic Protestants of America United candidate for presidency of the U.S., 1964***. BUS. & PROF.: evangelistic minister; seer; prophet. MAILING ADDRESS: Clarkdale, AZ 86324.

WETHERELL, WESTON B. b. 1957. POLIT. & GOV.: ***candidate for Republican nomination to presidency of the U.S., 1980; candidate for Democratic nomination to presidency of the U.S., 1980***. BUS. & PROF.: singer, rock band; salesman, evangelical literature. MAILING ADDRESS: 1323 Hill Ave., Wheaton, IL 60137.

WEYMOUTH, PATRICIA PERKINS. b. Dec 31, 1918, Birmingham, MI; m. (divorced); c. three. EDUC.: A.B., Russell Sage Coll., 1940; Ph.D., U. of Cincinnati, 1944. POLIT. & GOV.: employee, Atomic Energy Comm., 1946; ***independent (Cmte. for a Constitutional Presidency) candidate for vice presidency of the U.S., 1976***. BUS. & PROF.: biochemist; asst. biochemist, Armored Medical Research Laboratory, Fort Knox, KY, 1944–46; research assoc. in Medical Physics, CA, 1946–49; radio, Stanford-Lane Hospital, San Francisco, CA, 1949–52; faculty, Vassar Coll., 1952–54; faculty, Clarkson Technological Inst., 1954–58; biochemist and nutritionist, NE, 1958–67; faculty, Natural Science Dept., MI State U., 1967–69, assoc. prof., 1969–. MEM.: AAAS (fellow); American Assn. for Cancer Research; American Chemical Soc.; NY Acad. of Science. MAILING ADDRESS: 4544 Van Atta Rd., Okemos, MI 48864.

WHARTON, GORDON HELD. b. Aug 22, 1921, San Antonio, TX; par. Sidney F. and Effie Mae (Held) Wharton; m. Margaret L. Anderson; c. Thomas A.; Charles E.; Sylvia A. EDUC.: grad., Missoula (MT) H.S., 1939; Kansas City Art Inst., 1939–40; Coll. of Puget Sound, 1940; Sacramento (CA) Junior Coll., 1941–42; U.S. Air Force Navigation School, 1943; B.S., U. of Southern CA, 1947. POLIT. & GOV.: delegate, Democratic Convention, El Paso Cty., TX, c. 1956; Republican precinct committeeman, Tacoma, WA, 1972–74; ***independent candidate for presidency of the U.S., 1976; candidate for Republican nomination to presidency of the U.S., 1988***. BUS. & PROF.: employee, Chicago and Southern (now Delta) Airlines, 1947–49; employee, Southern Pacific R.R.,

1950; employee, El Paso Natural Gas Co., 1952–56; accounting clerk, American Smelting and Refining Co., El Paso, TX, 1959–68, Tacoma, WA, 1968–. MIL.: U.S. Air Force, 1942–45, lt. navigator, 1950–52, capt. MEM.: VFW; Masons; U.S. Chess Federation. REL.: Bapt. MAILING ADDRESS: 212 Koberlin, Apt. #41, San Angelo, TX 76903.

WHEATON, SALLY LOUISE. POLIT. & GOV.: ***independent (Cmte. for a Constitutional Presidency) candidate for vice presidency of the U.S., 1976***. MAILING ADDRESS: 413 University Ave., Selinsgrove, PA.

WHEELER, BURTON KENDALL. b. Feb 27, 1882, Hudson, MA; d. Jan 7, 1975, Washington, DC; par. Asa Leonard and Mary Elizabeth (Tyler) Wheeler; m. Lulu M. White, Sep 7, 1907; c. John Leonard; Elizabeth Hale (Mrs. Edwin W. Coleman); Edward Kendall; Richard Burton; Frances Lulu; Marion MT (Mrs. Robert Scott). EDUC.: grad., Hudson (MA) H.S., 1900; LL.B., U. of MI, 1905. POLIT. & GOV.: elected as a Democrat to MT State House, 1911–13; candidate for Democratic nomination to mayor of Butte, MT, 1911; appointed U.S. district atty. for MT, 1913–18; Democratic candidate for gov. of MT, 1920; elected as a Democrat to U.S. Senate (MT), 1923–47; ***candidate for Democratic nomination to presidency of the U.S., 1924, 1940; Progressive Party candidate for vice presidency of the U.S., 1924; Conference for Progressive Political Action candidate for vice presidency of the U.S., 1924; candidate for Democratic nomination to vice presidency of the U.S., 1940, 1944***; Democratic candidate for U.S. Senate (MT), 1946. BUS. & PROF.: stenographer, Boston, MA; waiter; book salesman; atty.; admitted to MT Bar, 1905; law practice, Butte, MT; partner, Wheeler and Wheeler (law firm), Washington, DC. MEM.: MT Bar Assn.; Masons (Shriner); Elks. WRITINGS: *Yankee From the West* (coauthor with Paul F. Healy, 1962). REL.: Methodist. RES.: Washington, DC.

WHEELER, CHARLES BERTAN. b. Aug 10, 1926, Kansas City, MO; par. Charles Bertan and Florence (Martin) Wheeler; m. Marjorie Martin, Aug 21, 1948; c. Gordon; Mark; Marian (Mrs. Lavole); Graham; Nina. EDUC.: A.B., U. of Louisville, 1946; M.D., U. of KS, 1950; J.D., U. of MO, 1959; diplomate, American Board of Pathology. POLIT. & GOV.: coroner, Jackson Cty., MO, 1965–67; elected as a Democrat, western judge, Board of County Commissioners, Jackson Cty., MO, 1967–71; elected as a Democrat, mayor of Kansas City, MO, 1971–79; ***candidate for Democratic nomination to vice presidency of the U.S., 1976***. BUS. & PROF.: pathologist, dir. of Laboratories, Kansas City (MO) General Hospital and Medical Center, 1957–63; assoc. pathologist, Research Hospital and Medical Center, Kansas City, MO, 1963–65; dir., Wheeler Medical Laboratories, Kansas City, MO, 1965–; assoc. pathologist, North Kansas City (MO) Memorial Hospital, 1966–68; assoc. pathologist, Independence (MO) Sanitarium and Hospital, 1968–; asst. clinical prof., U. of KS Medical School. MIL.: seaman, U.S.N.R., 1944–56; capt., U.S. Air Force, 1950–53. MEM.: American Coll. of Legal Medicine (fellow); MO Soc. of Pathologists (pres.); MO Medical Assn. (delegate); Vanguard Club; Rotary Club; Jackson Cty. Medical Soc. (exec. council); Coll. of American Pathologists; American Soc. of Clinical Pathologists; U. of KS Medical Alumni Assn. (pres., 1969); Sigma Nu; Nu Sigma Nu; Zeitgeist Club; National League of Cities; MO Municipal League (pres.); U.S. Conference of Mayors. AWARDS: "Man of the Year," MO Retail Liquor Assn.; "Man of the Year," U. of MO, 1975. WRITINGS: *Doctor in Politics* (1974). REL.: Episc. MAILING ADDRESS: 830 West 53rd St., Kansas City, MO 64112.

WHEELER, FREDERICK FREEMAN. b. Feb 25, 1859, Oshkosh, WI; d. Feb 8, 1917, Los Angeles, CA; par. John Collister and Adaline (Freeman) Wheeler; m. Alice M. Amsden, Dec 25, 1879; m. 2d, Hattie L. Hall, Jun 6, 1893; m. 3d, Allie E. Simmons, Jul 3, 1914; c. Alice W. (Mrs. Ray Allen); Effie (Mrs. Will Boggess); Herbert A.; one other. EDUC.: grad., H.S., Vineland, NJ. POLIT. & GOV.: state chm., NY Prohibition Party, 1884–89; member, Prohibition Party National Cmte., 1896–1900, 1904–08; Prohibition Party candidate for U.S. House (CA), 1902; ***candidate for Prohibition Party nomination to presidency of the U.S., 1908, 1916***; Prohibition Party candidate for U.S. Senate (CA), 1914; pres., Board of Public Utilities, Los Angeles, CA. BUS. & PROF.: owner, furniture business, Albany, NY, 1882–98; vice pres., South End Bank of Albany; vice pres., West End Savings and Loan Assn.; mgr., Albany Terminal Warehouse Co.; assoc. dir., National Life Assn. of Hartford; Real Estate Investor, Los Angeles, CA. MEM.: Albany C. of C. (sec.); Citizens Cmte. of Fifty; Independent Order of Good Templars (marshall; chief templar; cty. sec.); Los Angeles C. of C.; Los Angeles City Club; Los Angeles Federation Club. REL.: Unitarian. MISC.: led citizens' movement to make "California Dry in 1914." RES.: Los Angeles, CA.

WHEELER, JIM. POLIT. & GOV.: ***candidate for Democratic nomination to vice presidency of the U.S., 1980***. MISC.: possibly James Howard Weaver (q.v.). MAILING ADDRESS: unknown.

WHEELER, JOSEPH. b. Sep 10, 1836, Augusta, GA; d. Jan 25, 1906, Brooklyn, NY; par. Joseph and Julia Knox (Hull) Wheeler; m. Daniella Jones, Feb 8, 1866; c. Joseph; Thomas H.; Lucy Louise; Annie Early; Julia Hull; Carrie Peyton. EDUC.: Cheshire (CT) Episcopal Acad.; B.A., U.S. Military Acad., 1859; studied law, Wheeler, AL, 1868. POLIT. & GOV.: elected as a Democrat to U.S. House (AL), 1881–82, 1883, 1885–1900; ***candidate for Democratic nomination to vice presidency of the U.S., 1900 (declined)***. BUS. & PROF.: planter; atty.; admitted to AL Bar, 1868; law practice, Wheeler, AL; law practice, Courtland, AL; soldier. MIL.: commissioned 2d lt.,

U.S. Cavalry, 1859–61; commissioned 1st lt., C.S.A., 1861; col., 19th AL Infantry, 1861, brig. gen., 1862, maj. gen., 1863–65, lt. gen., 1865; maj. gen. of Volunteers, U.S. Army, 1898–1900, brig. gen., 1900. MEM.: Soc. of the Army of Santiago (pres.; vice pres.); U.S. Military Acad. (board of visitors, 1887–95; pres., 1895); Smithsonian Institution (regent, 1886–1900). HON. DEG.: LL.D., Georgetown U., 1899. WRITINGS: *Account of the Kentucky Campaign* (1862); *Cavalry Tactics* (1863); *Military History of Alabama*; *The Santiago Campaign* (1898); *History of Cuba, 1496 to 1899* (1899); *History of the Effect Upon Civilization of the Wars of the Nineteenth Century*. MISC.: known as "Fighting Joe." RES.: Wheeler, AL.

WHEELER, WILLIAM ALMAN. b. Jun 30, 1819, Malone, NY; d. Jun 4, 1887, Malone, NY; par. Alman and Eliza (Woodworth) Wheeler; m. Mary King, Sep 17, 1845; c. none. EDUC.: Franklin Acad.; U. of VT, 1838–40; studied law under Asa Hascell, Malone, NY. POLIT. & GOV.: elected town clerk, Malone, NY; school commissioner; school inspector; elected as a Unionist, district atty., Franklin Cty., NY, 1846–49; elected as a Whig to NY State Assembly, 1850–51; elected as a Republican to NY State Senate, 1858–60 (pres. pro tempore); elected as a Republican to U.S. House (NY), 1861–63, 1869–77; pres., NY State Constitutional Convention, 1867–68; ***candidate for Republican nomination to presidency of the U.S., 1876; elected as a Republican to vice presidency of the U.S., 1877–81***; pres., NY State Republican Convention, 1879; Republican candidate for U.S. Senate (NY), 1881. BUS. & PROF.: atty.; admitted to NY Bar, 1845; law practice, Malone, NY; trustee, Mortgage Holders of Northern Railway, 1853–66. REL.: Presb. RES.: Malone, NY.

WHETSTONE, JAMES DEYERLE. b. 1918, MS; m. Leena W. EDUC.: Ph.D. (external), Wayne State Coll. (IN). POLIT. & GOV.: candidate for Raleigh (NC) City Council, 1967; ***candidate for Republican nomination to presidency of the U.S., 1980***. BUS. & PROF.: customer service mgr., automobile dealership, Raleigh, NC, 1958–69; announcer, radio station, Smithfield, NC; pres., Whetstone Creations; public relations consultant; writer; lecturer; producer; dir. MIL.: officer, U.S. Air Force, to 1958. MEM.: Parent-Teachers Assn. REL.: Presb. (deacon). MISC.: known as "Bing." MAILING ADDRESS: 713 Winterlochen Rd., Raleigh, NC 27603.

WHITE, ANDREW DICKSON. b. Nov 7, 1832, Homer, NY; d. Nov 4, 1918, Ithaca, NY; par. Horace and Clara (Dickson) White; m. Mary A. Outwater, Sep 24, 1857; m. 2d, Helen Magill, Sep 10, 1890; c. two daughters. EDUC.: A.B. (cum laude), Yale U., 1853, A.M., 1856; U. of Berlin, 1853–54. POLIT. & GOV.: attache, U.S. Legation, St. Petersburg, Russia, 1854–55; elected as a Republican to NY State Senate, 1863–67; pres., NY State Republican Convention, 1871; appointed U.S. Commissioner to Santo Domingo, 1871; delegate, Rep. Nat'l. Conv., 1872; presidential elector, Republican Party, 1872; chm., Jury of Public Instructors, Centennial Exposition, Philadelphia, PA, 1876; appointed hon. U.S. commissioner to Paris Exposition, 1878; appointed U.S. minister to Germany, 1879–81; ***candidate for Republican nomination to presidency of the U.S., 1884***; appointed U.S. minister to Russia, 1892–94; appointed member, Venezuela Comm., 1896–97; appointed U.S. ambassador to Germany, 1897–1902; appointed member, U.S. delegate, Peace Comm., The Hague, Netherlands, 1899. BUS. & PROF.: historian; prof. of History and English Literature, U. of MI, 1857–63, lecturer, 1863–67; lecturer, U. of PA; lecturer, Stanford U.; lecturer, Tulane U.; pres., Cornell U., 1867–85. MEM.: Hobart Coll. (trustee, 1866–77); Cornell U. (trustee, 1866–1918); Carnegie Institution for Research (trustee); Carnegie Peace Endowment (trustee); Smithsonian (regent); Legion of Honor (France); Phi Beta Kappa; Royal Acad. of Sciences of Berlin (hon. member); American Hist. Assn. (pres., 1884–85); New England Hist. and Genealogical Soc. (hon. member); American Social Science Assn. (pres.); American Phil. Soc.; American Acad. of Arts and Letters. AWARDS: Yale Literary Gold Medal; De Forest Gold Medal; First Clark Prize; Royal Gold Medal of Prussia for Arts and Sciences, 1902. HON. DEG.: LL.D., U. of MI, 1867; LL.D., Cornell U., 1886; L.H.D., Columbia U., 1887; LL.D., Yale U., 1887; Ph.D., U. of Jeno, 1889; LL.D., Johns Hopkins U., 1902; D.C.L., Oxford U., 1902; LL.D., St. Andrew's Coll., 1902; LL.D., Dartmouth Coll., 1906; LL.D., Robert Coll., 1911; Sorbonne; Coll. de France. WRITINGS: *Outline of Lectures on History* (1860); *A Word from the Northwest* (1862); *A Plan of Organization for Cornell University* (1865); *Paper Money Inflation in France . . .* (1876); *On Studies in General History* (1885); *A History of the Warfare of Science with Theology in Christendom* (1895); *The Warfare of Humanity with Unreason* (1903); *Seven Great Statesmen in the Warfare of Humanity with Unreason* (1911); *The New Germany*; *History of the Doctrine of Comets*; *Paper Money Inflation in France*; *Autobiography of Andrew Dickson White* (1905); *The Work of Benjamin Hale* (1911). REL.: Episc. RES.: Ithaca, NY.

WHITE, DAVID. POLIT. & GOV.: ***candidate for Republican nomination to presidency of the U.S., 1984***. MAILING ADDRESS: unknown.

WHITE, GEORGE. b. Aug 21, 1872, Elmira, NY; d. Dec 15, 1953, West Palm Beach, FL; par. Charles Watkins and Mary Sophia (Bach) White; m. Charlotte McKelvy, Sep 25, 1900; m. 2d, Mrs. Agnes Hofman Baldwin, Apr 15, 1936; c. David McKelvy; Mary Louise; Charlotte (Mrs. Frank E. Hamilton); Robert McKelvy; Charles Zane. EDUC.: public schools; A.B., Princeton U., 1895. POLIT. & GOV.: elected as a Democrat to OH State House, 1905–08; Democratic candidate for U.S. House (OH), 1908, 1914, 1918; elected as a Democrat to U.S. House (OH), 1911–15, 1917–19; chm., Dem. Nat'l. Cmte., 1920–21; delegate, Dem. Nat'l. Conv., 1924; ***candidate for Democratic nomination to vice presidency of the U.S., 1928, 1932***; elected as a Democrat to gov. of OH, 1931–35; ***candidate for***

Democratic nomination to presidency of the U.S., 1932; appointed chm., Northwest Territory Comm., 1938. BUS. & PROF.: schoolteacher, Titusville, PA; yard man, Devonian Oil Co., Pittsburgh, PA, 1898; gold miner, Klondike, AK, 1898–1901; partner, White and McKelvy (oil producers), Marietta, OH; vice pres., dir., People's Banking and Trust Co., Marietta, OH; sec., Melrose Oil and Gas Co., 1906; sec.-treas., Permian Oil and Gas Co., 1926–53; dir., Tidewater Associated Oil Co. MEM.: Marietta Coll. (vice chm., board of trustees, 1934–53); Masons (33°); Moose; Elks; Columbus Club; Princeton Club of NY; Rocky Fort Hunt Club. HON. DEG.: LL.B., Marietta Coll., 1919; LL.D., Dennison U., 1933; LL.D., OH State U., 1951. REL.: Presb. RES.: Marietta, OH.

WHITE, HUGH LAWSON. b. Oct 30, 1773, Iredell Cty., NC; d. Apr 10, 1840, Knoxville, TN; par. James and Mary (Lawson) White; m. Elizabeth Moore Carrick, 1798; m. 3d, Mrs. Ann E. Peyton, Nov 30, 1832; c. twelve. EDUC.: classical studies, Philadelphia, PA; studied law under James Hopkins, Lancaster, PA, 1795. POLIT. & GOV.: private sec. to Governor Blount, 1793–94; judge, TN Superior Court, 1801–07; elected as a Whig to TN State Senate, 1807–09, 1817–25; appointed U.S. district atty. for Eastern TN, 1808–09; justice, TN Supreme Court, 1809–15; elected as a Whig to U.S. Senate (TN), 1825–40 (pres. pro tempore, 1832); ***Whig Party candidate for presidency of the U.S., 1836***. BUS. & PROF.: atty.; admitted to TN Bar, 1796; law practice, Knoxville, TN; pres., TN State Bank, 1812–27. MIL.: soldier, Cherokee War; killed Chief Kingfisher in Cherokee War. REL.: Presb. RES.: Knoxville, TN.

WHITE, MARK WELLS, JR. b. Mar 17, 1940, Henderson, TX; par. Mark Wells and Sarah Elizabeth White; m. Linda Gale Thompson, Oct 1, 1966; c. Mark Wells III; Andrew; Elizabeth Marie. EDUC.: B.B.A., Baylor U., 1962, J.D., 1965. POLIT. & GOV.: appointed asst. atty. gen., TX State Insurance, Banking and Securities Div., 1966–69; appointed sec. of state of TX, 1973–79; appointed atty. gen. of TX, 1979–83; delegate, Dem. Nat'l. Conv., 1980; appointed adviser, Federal Election Comm.; elected as a Democrat to gov. of TX, 1983–87; ***candidate for Democratic nomination to vice presidency of the U.S., 1984***; Democratic candidate for gov. of TX, 1986. BUS. & PROF.: atty.; admitted to TX Bar, 1965; partner, Reynolds, White, Allen and Cook (law firm), Houston, TX, 1969–73. MIL.: member, TX National Guard, 1966–69. MEM.: St. David's Hospital (dir.); South Western Baptist Theological Seminary (adviser); Christian Education Coordinating Board; National Assn. of Secretaries of State (treas.; pres., 1977). AWARDS: Lawyer of the Year, Baylor U. Chapter, Phi Alpha Delta, 1975. REL.: Bapt. MAILING ADDRESS: 2403 Trail of Madrones, Austin, TX 78745.

WHITE, MELVIN "SLAPPY." b. 1921, Baltimore, MD; d. Nov 7, 1995, Brigantine, NJ; m. Pearl Mae Bailey (q.v.; divorced). EDUC.: Morgan State U.; U. of MS. POLIT. & GOV.: ***candidate for Democratic nomination to vice presidency of the U.S., 1972, 1976 (satire effort)***. BUS. & PROF.: comedian; member, "Zephyrs" Comedy Team; teamed with Redd Foxx, 1950s; played with Club Alabam; Great Gorge Resort Hotel, McAfee, NJ; Playboy Club, New Orleans, LA; Apollo Theatre; entertainer, Hotel Sahara, Las Vegas, NV; actor. MOTION PICTURE CREDITS: "The Man from O.R.G.Y." (1970); "Amazing Grace" (1974). TELEVISION CREDITS: "Comedy World"; "Sanford and Son"; "O. J. Simpson is Alive and Well and Getting Roasted Tonight" (1974); "Salute to Redd Foxx" (1974); "That's My Mama" (1974); "Merv Griffin Show" (1975); "Celebrity Review" (1976). Recordings: "Elect Slappy White for Vice President" (1976); "The First Slappy White Astronaut." RES.: Brigantine, NJ.

WHITE, OTHO RAYMOND. b. 1906. POLIT. & GOV.: ***independent candidate for presidency of the U.S., 1976***. MAILING ADDRESS: 1703 Simpson Place, St. Louis, MO 63104.

WHITE, RICHARD HAROLD. POLIT. & GOV.: ***independent candidate for presidency of the U.S., 1988***. MAILING ADDRESS: 711 Queen Valley Dr., Queen Valley, AZ 85219.

WHITE, STEPHEN MALLORY. b. Jan 19, 1853, San Francisco, CA; d. Feb 21, 1901, Los Angeles, CA; par. William and Fannie J. (Russell) White; m. Hortense Secriste, Jun 5, 1883; c. two sons; two daughters. EDUC.: St. Ignatius Coll.; grad., Santa Clara Coll., 1871; studied law. POLIT. & GOV.: joined Independent Party, 1870s; elected as a Democrat, district atty., Los Angeles Cty., CA, 1882–86; chm., CA State Democratic Cmte., 1884–86; elected as a Democrat to CA State Senate, 1886–90 (pres. pro tempore; acting lt. gov., 1888–90); member, Board of Regents, U. of CA; delegate, Dem. Nat'l. Conv., 1888 (temporary chm.), 1892, 1896 (chm.), 1900; Democratic candidate for U.S. Senate (CA), 1890; elected as a Democrat to U.S. Senate (CA), 1893–99; ***candidate for Democratic nomination to vice presidency of the U.S., 1896***. BUS. & PROF.: farmer, Santa Cruz, CA; atty.; admitted to CA Bar, 1874; law practice, Los Angeles Cty., CA, 1874. RES.: Los Angeles, CA.

WHITFORD, ERNEST WAYNE "UTOPIA IN '76." b. Feb 8, 1915, Albion, WI; par. Elmer W. and Hazel Maude (Drake) Whitford; m. (divorced); m. 2d, Tess Johnson; c. Jimmie; Paul; Mary Sue. EDUC.: Lincoln Union H.S., Lincoln, CA. POLIT. & GOV.: ***candidate for Republican nomination to presidency of the U.S., 1976***. BUS. & PROF.: auditor, U.S. Army, 1946; pipefitter, U.S. government, to 1973. REL.: Deist. MAILING ADDRESS: 957½ West 12th St., San Pedro, CA 90731.

WHITLOCK, BRAND. b. Mar 4, 1869, Urbana, OH; d. May 24, 1934, Cannes, France; par. Rev. Elias D. and Mallie (Brand) Whitlock; m. 1893; m. 2d, Ella Brainerd, Jun 8, 1895. EDUC.: public schools; studied law under John M. Palmer (q.v.). POLIT. & GOV.: clerk, IL state sec. of state's office, 1893–97; elected as an independent, mayor of Toledo, OH, 1905–13; appointed U.S. minister to Belgium, 1913–19; appointed U.S. ambassador extraordinary and plenipotentiary to Belgium, 1919–22; ***candidate for Democratic nomination to vice presidency of the U.S., 1924***. BUS. & PROF.: diplomat; newspaper reporter, Toledo, OH, 1887–90; political correspondent, *Chicago (IL) Herald*, 1890–93; atty.; admitted to OH Bar, 1894; law practice, Toledo, OH, 1894–1905; partner, Cole, Whitlock and Milroy (law firm), Toledo, OH; partner, Whitlock, Milroy and Mellows (law firm), Toledo, OH; contributor, *Encyclopedia Britannica*. MEM.: American Acad. of Arts and Letters; Poetry Soc. of America; Authors' League of America; Comm. for Relief in Belgium (patron); Grand Cordon de l'Ordre de Leopold (1917); Royal Acad. of Belgium (assoc. member, 1919); Royal Belgian Acad. of French Languages and Literature (1922); Grand Serment Royal St. George (hon. member); The Players Club; Century Club; Toledo Club; Inverness Club; Cliff Dwellers Club; Authors Club; Royal Golf Club (Belgium); Royal Knocke Golf Club de Zoute; Cannes Country Club (France). AWARDS: Gold Medal, National Inst. of Social Sciences; Civic Cross of Belgium, First Class; Commemorative Medal, Comite National (Belgium, 1919); Grand Cross of St. Sava (Serbia, 1920); Grand Cross, Order of the Rising Sun (Japan, 1922); Burgher of Brussels (1918); Burgher of Liege (1919); Honorary Citizen of Antwerp (1919); Burgher of Ghent (1920); Grand Officer, Legion of Honor (France, 1929). HON. DEG.: LL.D., Brown U., 1916; LL.D., OH Wesleyan U., 1917; Docteur en droit, Brussels U., 1919; LL.D., Western Reserve U., 1919; Docteur en droit, U. of Louvain, 1927. WRITINGS: *The 13th District* (1902); *Her Infinite Variety* (1904); *The Happy Average* (1904); *The Turn of the Balance* (1907); *Abraham Lincoln* (1908); *The Gold Brick* (1910); *On the Enforcement of Law in Cities* (1910); *The Fall Guy* (1912); *Forty Years of It* (1914); *Belgium Under the German Occupation* (1918); *Belgium: A Personal Record* (1919); *J. Hardin & Son* (1923); *Uprooted* (1926); *Transplanted* (1927); *Big Matt* (1928); *La Fayette* (1929); *The Little Green Shutter* (1931); *Narcissus* (1931); *Stranger on the Island* (1933). REL.: Episc. RES.: Toledo, OH.

WHITMAN, CHARLES SEYMOUR. b. Aug 28, 1868, Hanover, CT; d. Mar 29, 1947, New York, NY; par. Rev. John Seymour and Lillie (Arne) Whitman; m. Olive Hitchcock, Dec 22, 1908; m. 2d, Thelma Somerville (Cudlipp) Grosvenor, Apr 6, 1933; c. Charles Seymour, Jr.; Olive (Mrs. John Jennings Parsons). EDUC.: Adelbert Coll., 1886–87; A.B., Amherst Coll., 1890; LL.B., NY U., 1894. POLIT. & GOV.: asst. corporation counsel, New York, NY, 1901–03; appointed member, pres., Board of City Magistrates, New York, NY, 1904–07; appointed judge, Court of General Sessions of NY, 1907; district atty., New York Cty., NY, 1910–14; elected as a Republican and subsequently reelected as a Republican-American-Progressive-Independence League candidate to gov. of NY, 1915–19; ***candidate for Republican nomination to presidency of the U.S., 1916; candidate for Republican nomination to vice presidency of the U.S., 1916***; Republican candidate for gov. of NY, 1918; delegate, Rep. Nat'l. Conv., 1920; appointed commissioner, Port Authority of NY, 1935–47. BUS. & PROF.: teacher, Adelphi Acad.; atty.; admitted to NY Bar, 1894; law practice, New York, NY, 1894–1901, 1907–09; partner, Whitman, Ottinger and Ransom (law firm), New York, NY; partner, Whitman, Ransom, Coulson and Goetz (law firm), New York, NY, 1919–47. MEM.: Cornell U. (trustee); Union U. (trustee); Adelphi Coll. (trustee); NY Probation Assn.; Masons (33°); Soc. of the Cincinnati; Soc. of Colonial Wars; SAR; St. Nicholas Soc.; ABA (pres., 1926–27); NY Bar Assn.; Bar Assn. of the City of New York; OH Soc.; Anti-Policy Soc. of NY (pres.); New England Soc.; NY C. of C.; Down Town Assn.; Alpha Delta Phi; Union League; University Club; Metropolitan Club; Century Club; NY Skin and Cancer Hospital (trustee); Army and Navy Club; Lying-In Hospital (trustee); NY U. Law School Alumni Assn. (pres., 1933–34); NY Soc. of Military and Naval Officers. HON. DEG.: M.A., Williams Coll., 1904; LL.D., Amherst Coll., 1913; LL.D., NY U., 1913; LL.D., Williams Coll., 1914; LL.D., Hamilton Coll., 1918; LL.D., Syracuse U., 1918; LL.D., Whitman Coll., 1936. REL.: Presb. RES.: New York, NY.

WHITMAN, DUDLEY A. POLIT. & GOV.: ***candidate for Democratic nomination to vice presidency of the U.S., 1992***. BUS. & PROF.: businessman. MIL.: Pilot, U.S. Air Force, WWII. MAILING ADDRESS: 167 Bal Bay Dr., Bal Harbour, FL 33154.

WHITNEY, HENRY MELVILLE. b. Oct 22, 1839, Conway, MA; d. Jan 25, 1923; par. James Scollay and Laurinda (Collins) Whitney; m. Margaret F. Green, Oct 3, 1878; c. four daughters; one son. EDUC.: Williston Seminary. POLIT. & GOV.: Democratic candidate for gov. of MA, 1907; ***candidate for Democratic nomination to presidency of the U.S., 1912***. BUS. & PROF.: capitalist; bank clerk, Conway, MA; clerk, Bank of Mutual Redemption, Boston, MA; clerk, navy agent, 1860; shipper, New York, NY, 1860–65; agent, Metropolitan Steamship Co., Boston, MA, 1866–78, pres., 1878–1923; pres., West End Railway Co.; founder, Dominion Coal Co.; founder, Massachusetts Pipe Line Gas Co.; founder, New England Gas and Coke Co.; founder, Dominion Iron and Steel Co. MISC.: brother of William Collins Whitney (q.v.). RES.: Brookline, MA.

WHITNEY, WILLIAM COLLINS. b. Jul 15, 1841, Conway, MA; d. Feb 2, 1904; par. Gen. James Scollary and Laurinda (Collins) Whitney; m. Flora Payne, Oct 13, 1869; m. 2d, Mrs. Edith Sibyl (May) Randolph, Sep 29, 1896; c. Pauline (Mrs. Almeric Hugh Paget); William Payne; Dorothy (Mrs. Elmhirst); Henry "Harry" Payne; Leonora; Olive. EDUC.:

Williston Seminary; grad., Yale U., 1863; Harvard U., 1863–64. POLIT. & GOV.: inspector of schools, New York, NY, 1872; Democratic candidate for district atty., New York Cty., NY, 1872; appointed U.S. sec. of the navy, 1885–89; delegate, Dem. Nat'l. Conv., 1892; ***candidate for Democratic nomination to presidency of the U.S., 1892, 1896***. BUS. & PROF.: atty.; admitted to NY Bar, 1865; law practice, New York, NY; partner, Dimmock and Whitney (law firm), New York, NY, 1867–70; partner (with F. H. Betts), law firm, New York, NY, 1870; corporation counsel, New York, NY, 1875–82; dir., real estate company; financier; horse breeder; owner, racing stable and stud farm. MEM.: Young Men's Democratic Club of NY (organizer, 1871); Driving Club; Suburban Riding Club; Metropolitan Club; Union Club; Knickerbocker Club; Manhattan Club; Yale Club; University Club; Century Club; Jockey Club; Soc. of the Mayflower; Peabody Museum (trustee); American Museum of Natural History (trustee); Metropolitan Museum of Art (trustee); Metropolitan Opera (dir.); Yale Alumni Assn. HON. DEG.: LL.D., Yale U., 1888. WRITINGS: *The Whitney Stud* (1902). REL.: Episc. MISC.: prominent in NY street railway system development, 1883–1902; active in movement against Tweed Ring; brother of Henry Melville Whitney (q.v.). RES.: New York, NY.

WIEDMAN, BILL. POLIT. & GOV.: ***Apathy Party candidate for vice presidency of the U.S., 1992***. MAILING ADDRESS: unknown.

WIGGINTON, PETER DINWIDDIE. b. Sep 6, 1839, Springfield, IL; d. Jul 7, 1890, Oakland, CA. EDUC.: U. of WI; studied law. POLIT. & GOV.: elected district atty., Merced Cty., CA, 1864–68; elected as a Democrat to U.S. House (CA), 1875–79; ***American Party candidate for presidency of the U.S., 1884***; American Party candidate for gov. of CA, 1886; chm., American Party National Convention, 1888; ***American Party candidate for vice presidency of the U.S., 1888***. BUS. & PROF.: atty.; admitted to WI Bar, 1859; ed., *Dodgeville (WI) Advocate*; law practice, WI, 1859–62; law practice, Snelling, CA, 1862–80; law practice, San Francisco, CA, 1880–90. RES.: San Francisco, CA.

WIHLBORG, JAMES HERBERT. POLIT. & GOV.: ***independent candidate for presidency of the U.S., 1980***. MAILING ADDRESS: P.O. Box 142, Tok, AK 99780.

WILDER, LAWRENCE DOUGLAS. b. Jan 31, 1931, Richmond, VA; c. Lynn; Larry; Loren. EDUC.: B.S., VA Union U., 1951; J.D., Howard U., 1959. POLIT. & GOV.: elected as a Democrat to VA State Senate, 1968–86; elected as a Democrat to lt. gov. of VA, 1986–90; delegate, Dem. Nat'l. Conv., 1980; elected as a Democrat to gov. of VA, 1990–94; ***candidate for Democratic nomination to presidency of the U.S., 1992 (withdrew)***. BUS. & PROF.: atty.; public servant. MIL.: pvt., sgt., U.S. Army, 1952–53; Bronze Star. MEM.: C. of C.; Masons; Shriners; ABA; VA Bar Assn.; National Bar Assn.; American Jud. Soc.; Omega Psi Phi; NAACP Legal Defense Fund (lobbyist); United Givers Fund (dir.); Richmond Urban League (dir.). MAILING ADDRESS: 3215 Hawthorne Ave., Richmond, VA 23222.

WILDER, VICTOR A. b. 1846, Cuther, ME. EDUC.: public schools, Boston, MA. POLIT. & GOV.: member, NY United Labor Party State Central Cmte. (exec. cmte.); United Labor Party candidate for NY state controller, 1887; ***candidate for United Labor Party nomination to presidency of the U.S., 1888***; Democratic (Independence League) candidate for U.S. House (NY), 1906. BUS. & PROF.: employee, lumber firm, Brooklyn, NY, 1865–75; miner, prospector, CO, 1875–82; employee, treas., NY Railway Supply Co., Brooklyn, NY, 1885–; rep., King Syndicate, New York, NY, c. 1903. MIL.: pvt., 44th MA Volunteer Infantry, 4 months, Civil War; sharpshooter with General Burnside, NC campaign; col. MISC.: indicted in Huntington, WV, for conspiracy and bribery as representative of King Syndicate, 1903. RES.: Brooklyn, NY.

WILEY, HARVEY WASHINGTON. b. Oct 18, 1844, Kent, IN; d. Jun 30, 1930, Washington, DC; par. Preston Pritchard and Lucinda Weir (Maxwell) Wiley; m. Anna Campbell Kelton, Feb 27, 1911; c. Harvey Washington, Jr.; John Preston. EDUC.: A.B., Hanover Coll., 1867, A.M., 1870; M.D., IN U., 1871; B.S., Harvard U., 1873. POLIT. & GOV.: appointed IN State Chemist, 1874–83; appointed chief, Bureau of Chemistry, U.S. Dept. of Agriculture, 1883–1912; appointed chm., U.S. Board of Food and Drug Inspection, 1907–12; jury member, Chicago Exposition, 1893; jury member, Paris Exposition, 1900; U.S. delegate, International Congress on Applied Chemistry, 1898, 1900, 1903, 1906, 1909; jury member, Jamestown Exposition, 1907; hon. pres., First International Congress on Repression of Adulteration of Alimentary and Pharmacological Products, 1908; ***candidate for Democratic nomination to vice presidency of the U.S., 1912***. BUS. & PROF.: prof. of Latin and Greek, Butler U., 1868–70, prof. of Chemistry, 1873; science teacher, Indianapolis (IN) H.S., 1871–73; prof. of Chemistry, Purdue U., 1874–83; contributor, *Science Monthly*; prof. of Agricultural Chemistry, George Washington U., 1899–1910; consulting prof., Polytechnic Inst. of Brooklyn, 1905; Pure Food Advocate; ed., *Good Housekeeping*, 1912–29. MIL.: enlisted, 137th IN Regt., U.S. Army, 1863; Order of Chevalier, Merite Agricole (France, 1900); Legion of Honor (France, 1909); Elliott Cresson Medal, Franklin Inst., 1910; Medal (First Class), Physico-Chemical Acad. (Italy). MEM.: Assn. of Official Agricultural Chemists (sec., 1899–1909; hon. life pres., 1912–30); U.S. Pharmacopeial Convention (pres., 1910–20); Premier Congres International pour la Repression des Fraudes Alimentaires et Pharmaceutiques (hon. pres., 1908); AAAS (vice pres., 1886; gen. sec., 1891); American Chemical Soc. (pres., 1893–94); American Medical Assn.; American Pharmaceutical Assn.;

American Public Health Assn.; American Soc. of Biological Chemists; American Therapeutic Soc. (pres., 1911); IN Acad. of Science (pres., 1902); Soc. of Medical Jurisprudence; WA Acad. of Sciences (vice pres., 1909); Franklin Inst.; Soc. of the Chemical Industry; Soc. of Biological Chemistry; American Brewing Inst. (hon. member); Franklin Inst.; Philadelphia Coll. of Pharmacy; British Federated Inst. of Brewers; Soc. of Public Analysis; School of Chemical Science, Museo de La Plata (hon. member, Argentina); Societe Scientifique d'Hygene Alimentaire; Cosmos Club (pres., 1910–11); Chevy Chase Club; National Press Club; Harvard Union Club; Arts Club of WA; Chemists Club of NY. HON. DEG.: Ph.D., Hanover U., 1876, LL.D., 1898; LL.D., U. of VT, 1911; Sc.D., Lafayette Coll., 1912; A.M., Hahnemann Medical Coll., 1923. WRITINGS: *Songs of Agricultural Chemists* (1892); *Principles and Practice of Agricultural Analysis* (1894–97); *Foods and Their Adulteration* (1907); *Beverages and Their Adulteration* (1914); *Lure of the Land* (1915); *1001 Tests* (1916); *Not By Bread Alone* (1919); *Health Reader for Schools* (1919); *History of Crime Against the Food Law* (1929); *Autobiography* (1930). REL.: Church of the Disciples (Cambellite). RES.: Washington, DC.

WILKINS, WILLIAM. b. Dec 10, 1779, Carlisle, PA; d. Jun 23, 1865, Homewood, PA; par. John and Catherine (Rowan) Wilkins; m. Catherine Holmes, 1815; m. 2d, Mathilda Dallas, Oct 1, 1818; c. three sons; four daughters. EDUC.: grad., Dickinson Coll., 1802. POLIT. & GOV.: elected pres., Pittsburgh (PA) Common Council, 1816–19; elected as a Federalist to PA State House, 1819–20; appointed presiding judge, Fifth Judicial District of PA, 1821–24; appointed judge, U.S. District Court for Western PA, 1824–31; Democratic candidate for U.S. House (PA), 1826, 1840; elected as a Democrat-Anti-Mason to U.S. Senate (PA), 1828, 1831–34; ***received 30 electoral votes for vice presidency of the U.S., 1832***; appointed U.S. minister to Russia, 1834–35; elected as a Democrat to U.S. House (PA), 1843–44; appointed U.S. sec. of war, 1844–45; elected as a Democrat to PA State Senate, 1855–57. BUS. & PROF.: atty.; admitted to Allegheny Cty. (PA) Bar, 1801; founder, Pittsburgh Manufacturing Co., 1810; pres., Bank of Pittsburgh, 1814–19; pres., Monongahela Bridge Co.; pres., Greensburg and Pittsburgh Turnpike Co. MIL.: maj. gen., PA Home Guard, 1862. RES.: Homewood, PA.

WILLIAMS, BETTY JEAN. b. Mar 1, 1933, Birmingham, AL; d. Chusler and Alice Bell (Stephens) Heard; m. Jethro E. Williams, Feb 14, 1954; c. none. EDUC.: degree in Education; state certificates. POLIT. & GOV.: candidate for Democratic nomination to mayor of Chicago, IL; ***candidate for Democratic nomination to presidency of the U.S., 1984***; candidate for Democratic nomination to U.S. Senate (IL), 1986. BUS. & PROF.: employee, state of IL; employee, city of Chicago, IL; civic activist. MEM.: GSA; BSA. REL.: Lutheran (Sunday school teacher). MAILING ADDRESS: 9600 Eggleston Ave., Chicago, IL 60628.

WILLIAMS, FRANK W. POLIT. & GOV.: ***candidate for Allied People's Party nomination to presidency of the U.S., 1904***. RES.: IN.

WILLIAMS, GEORGE FRED. b. Jul 10, 1852, Dedham, MA; d. Jul 11, 1932, Brookline, MA; par. George William and Henrietta Whitney (Rice) Williams; m. Frances Ames Barrett Hopkins, Jun 13, 1913; c. Barrett. EDUC.: grad., Dedham (MA) H.S., 1868; A.B., Dartmouth Coll., 1872; U. of Heidelberg, 1870–71; Berlin U., 1870–71; Boston U. POLIT. & GOV.: member, Dedham (MA) School Cmte.; elected as a Democrat to MA State House, 1889–90; elected as a Democrat to U.S. House (MA), 1891–93; Democratic candidate for U.S. House (MA), 1892; Democratic candidate for gov. of MA, 1895, 1896, 1897; member, Dem. Nat'l. Cmte.; delegate, Dem. Nat'l. Conv., 1896, 1900, 1904, 1908; ***candidate for Democratic nomination to vice presidency of the U.S., 1896***; appointed envoy extraordinary and minister plenipotentiary to Greece and Montenegro, 1913–14. BUS. & PROF.: schoolteacher, West Brewster, MA, 1872–73; reporter, *Boston (MA) Globe*; atty.; admitted to MA Bar, 1875; law practice, Boston, MA, 1875–1930; partner, Farmer and Williams (law firm), Boston, MA, 1875–85; partner, Williams and Anderson (law firm), Boston, MA, 1891–97; partner (with Judge James A. Halloran), law firm, Boston, MA, to 1930. MEM.: Union Club; Botolph Club; University Club. WRITINGS: *Williams' Citations of Massachusetts Cases* (ed., 1878); *Annual Digest of the United States* (ed., vols. 10–17, 1880–87). RES.: Brookline, MA.

WILLIAMS, GERHARD MENNEN. b. Feb 23, 1911, Detroit, MI; d. Feb 2, 1988, Detroit, MI; par. Henry Phillips and Elma Christina (Mennen) Williams; m. Nancy Lace Quirk, Jun 26, 1937; c. Gerhard Mennen; Nancy Quirk (Mrs. Theodore Ketterer); Wendy Stock (Mrs. Michael R. Burns). EDUC.: Detroit U. School, 1919–25; Salisbury School, 1925–29; A.B. (cum laude), Princeton U., 1933; J.D. (cum laude), U. of MI, 1935. POLIT. & GOV.: atty., Social Security Board, 1936–38; appointed asst. atty. gen. of MI, 1938–39; appointed exec. asst. to the atty. gen. of the U.S., 1939–40; counsel, U.S. Dept. of Justice, 1940–41; appointed deputy dir., OPA, MI Div., 1946–47; appointed Liquor Control Commissioner, state of MI, 1948; elected as a Democrat to gov. of MI, 1949–61; delegate, Dem. Nat'l. Conv., 1952, 1956; vice chm., Dem. Nat'l. Cmte., 1950s; ***candidate for Democratic nomination to vice presidency of the U.S., 1956, 1960; candidate for Democratic nomination to presidency of the U.S., 1960***; appointed asst. U.S. sec. of state for African Affairs, 1961–66; Democratic candidate for U.S. Senate (MI), 1966; appointed U.S. ambassador to the Philippines, 1968–69; elected as a Democrat, justice, State Supreme Court of MI, 1971–86 (chief justice, 1983–86). BUS. & PROF.: atty.; admitted to MI Bar, 1936; partner, Griffiths, Williams, and Griffiths (law firm), Detroit, MI, 1947–48; faculty, U. of Detroit Law School, 1986–88. MIL.: lt. commander, U.S.N.R., 1942–46; Legion of Merit with Combat V; Presidential Unit Citation (3 Stars); Order of Orange Nassau (Netherlands); Royal Order of the Phoenix (Greece); Humane Band of African Redemption (Liberia); Order of Niger (Grand Officer); Order of Ivory Coast; Pro Merito (Latvia); Polonia Restituta (Poland); Order of Sikatuna (Philippines). MEM.: Federal Bar Assn.; MI State Bar Assn.; Detroit Bar Assn.; Grange; AmVets; American Legion; Princeton Young Republican (pres.); VFW; Reserve Officers Assn.; SAR; Ahepa; Steuben Soc.; Edelweiss Club; Order of the Coif; Phi Beta Kappa; Phi Gamma Delta; Phi Delta Phi; Masons (33°); Eagles; Moose; Quadrangle Club; Library Club; American Veterans Cmte.; University Club; Omicron Beta Kappa; Phi Tau Delta. HON. DEG.: LL.D., Wilberforce U., 1951; H.H.D., Lawrence Inst. of Technology, 1952; LL.D., MI State U., 1955; LL.D., U. of Liberia, 1958; LL.D., Aquinas Coll., 1961; LL.D., Ferris Inst., 1961; LL.D., U. of MI, 1961; LL.D., St. Augustine's Coll., 1961; LL.D., Western MI U., 1963; D.C.L., Lincoln U., 1964; LL.D., Morris Brown Coll.; LL.D., World U. WRITINGS: *A Governor's Notes* (1961); *Africa for the Africans* (1969). REL.: Episc. MISC.: known as "Soapy" Williams, as heir of Mennen soap industry fortune. RES.: Grosse Pointe Farms, MI.

WILLIAMS, HERMAN B. (BARNES B.). POLIT. & GOV.: The Lord's candidate for FL State Commissioner of Education, 1978; ***candidate for Republican nomination to presidency of the U.S., 1980; The Lord's candidate for presidency of the U.S., 1980***. MAILING ADDRESS: 1102 N.E. 20th Ave., Gainesville, FL 32601.

WILLIAMS, JAMES ROBERT. b. Dec 27, 1850, Carmi, IL; d. Nov 8, 1923, Loma Linda, CA; par. Thomas and Susan (Ralls) Williams; m. Minnie Shannon, Nov 26, 1884. EDUC.: A.B., IN State U., 1875; LL.B., Union Coll. of Law, 1876. POLIT. & GOV.: master in chancery, White Cty., IL, 1880–82; cty. judge, White Cty., IL, 1882–86; presidential elector, Democratic Party, 1888; elected as a Democrat to U.S. House (IL), 1889–95, 1899–1905; ***candidate for Democratic nomination to vice presidency of the U.S., 1896, 1904***; chm., IL delegation, Dem. Nat'l. Conv., 1900; Democratic candidate for U.S. Senate (IL), 1903. BUS. & PROF.: atty.; admitted to IL Bar, 1876; law practice, Carmi, IL, 1876–1923. RES.: Carmi, IL.

WILLIAMS, JOHN SHARP. b. Jul 30, 1854, Memphis, TN; d. Sep 27, 1932, Yazoo City, MS; par. Col. Christopher Harris and Annie Louise (Sharp) Williams; m. Elizabeth Dial Webb, Oct 2, 1877; c. Mary Sharp (Mrs. Edwin Ruthven Holmes); Robert Webb; Annie Louise; John Sharp, Jr.; Julia Fulton (Mrs. Thomas Reeves Boykin); Allison Ridley; Sally Shelby (Mrs. Joel William Bunkley); Christopher Harris. EDUC.: KY Military Inst.; U. of the South; U. of VA; U. of Heidelberg. POLIT. & GOV.: delegate, Dem. Nat'l. Conv., 1892, 1904 (temporary chm.), 1912, 1920; elected as a Democrat to U.S. House (MS), 1893–1909 (minority leader, 1903–09); ***candidate for Democratic nomination to presidency of the U.S., 1904, 1920; candidate for Democratic nomination to vice presidency of the U.S., 1904***; elected as a Democrat to U.S. Senate (MS), 1911–23. BUS. & PROF.: atty.; admitted to TN Bar, 1877; law practice, Yazoo City, MS, 1878–1932; partner, Barnett and Williams (law firm), Yazoo City, MS, 1878; partner, Williams, Thornton and Williams (law firm), Yazoo City, MS; cotton planter, MS. MEM.: Soc. of the Cincinnati; Elks; Masons; Knights of Pythias; Phi Beta Kappa. WRITINGS: *Permanent Influence of Thomas Jefferson on American Institutions* (1913). REL.: Episc. RES.: Yazoo City, MS.

WILLIAMS, MARY E. HUMPHREY. b. Freeport, MI; m.; c. daughter. POLIT. & GOV.: ***candidate for Republican nomination to presidency of the U.S., 1976***. BUS. & PROF.: R.N.; poet. MEM.: Ave Maria Inst. WRITINGS: "Irish" (poem); "Today She is 89 Years Old" (essay). REL.: R.C. MAILING ADDRESS: c/o House of Williams, 837 East Clinton St., Hastings, MI 49058.

WILLIAMS, ROBERT. POLIT. & GOV.: ***candidate for Democratic nomination to vice presidency of the U.S., 1904***. RES.: unknown.

WILLIAMS, ROBERT ORMAND. b. Feb 25, 1954, Fort Worth, TX; par. Wade Ormand Williams; m. Sandra Kay Williams; c. Darla R.; Echo S.; Connie Ann. EDUC.: technical associate's degree, computer electronics. POLIT. & GOV.: ***candidate for Democratic nomination to presidency of the U.S., 1992***. BUS. & PROF.: electronics technician. MIL.: pvt., U.S.M.C., 1971–73. REL.: Methodist. MAILING ADDRESS: 18014 North Michelle Dr., Phoenix, AZ 85032.

WILLIAMS, ROGER IRVING. b. Jul 5, 1933, Eastbrookfield, MA; par. Guy S. and Lillian E. (Olson) Williams; m. (divorced); c. none. EDUC.: A.A., Worcester (MA) Junior Coll., 1954; B.B.A., Clark U., 1956. POLIT. & GOV.: Prohibition Party candidate for MA State Auditor, 1966, 1970; ***candidate for Prohibition Party nomination to vice presidency of the U.S., 1972***. BUS. & PROF.: mortgage consultant; dispatcher; computer operator; Amway distributor. MIL.: U.S. Army. MEM.: League of American Wheelmen; BSA; John B. Gough Soc. REL.: Bapt. MAILING ADDRESS: 151 Uncatina Ave., Worcester, MA 01606.

WILLIAMS, SAMUEL WARDELL. b. Feb 7, 1851, Mount Carmel, IL; d. Aug 5, 1913, Vincennes, IN; par. Fleming and Ella (Wardell) Williams; m. Mary Winn, Aug 26, 1887. EDUC.: Presb. Acad., Friendsville, IL; studied ministry and law. POLIT. & GOV.: appointed deputy cty. clerk, Wabash Cty., IL, 1871; appointed prosecuting atty., Knox Cty., IN, 1877; elected as a Democrat to IN State House, 1882–86; appointed deputy atty. gen. of IN, 1884 (declined); left Democratic Party,

1884; organizer, People's Party, 1890; ***candidate for Allied People's Party nomination to vice presidency of the U.S., 1904***; member, People's Party National Cmte., 1905–12 (chm., 1912); ***People's Party candidate for vice presidency of the U.S., 1908***; chm., People's Party National Convention, 1912. BUS. & PROF.: ed., *Democrat*, Mount Carmel, IL; traveling grocery salesman; assoc., Cauthorn and Boyle (law firm), Vincennes, IN, 1873; atty.; admitted to IN Bar, 1874; law practice, Vincennes, IN; publisher, *Vincennes (IN) Index*. MEM.: Vincennes' Foresters (chief ranger); Knox Cty. Bar Assn.; National Ben Hur Defense League (mgr.); IN Single Tax League; Industrial Legion; Knights of Labor; Order of 38. REL.: Presb. RES.: Vincennes, IN.

WILLIAMS, THOMAS OWEN. b. Mar 6, 1935, Huntington, WV; par. Owen Morgan and Ruth Eleanor (Tilton) Williams; m. Minnie Florence Allison; c. Kathryn "Kitty" Louise Kelly; David Owen; Susan Grance; Linda Eleanor. EDUC.: grad., St. Albans H.S., St. Albans, WV, 1953; B.E.S., Marshall Coll., 1960. POLIT. & GOV.: ***candidate for Republican nomination to presidency of the U.S., 1976; independent Republican candidate for presidency of the U.S., 1976***. BUS. & PROF.: licensed professional engineer; engineer, U.S. Forest Service; private consultant; sales engineer and mgr., Armco Steel; employee, IL State Div. of Highways; employee, Keystone Steel; employee, Wallace Steel Co.; author; poet. MEM.: National Honor Soc.; Civil War Round Table; Sangamon Cty. Hist. Soc.; Springfield (IL) Music Reviewer. AWARDS: Golden Horseshoe Award for WV History. WRITINGS: "Immortal Beloved"; "Letters from Ole Tom." REL.: Protestant. MAILING ADDRESS: 410 East Yates St., Ithaca, NY 14850.

WILLIAMS, WALTER DAKIN. b. Feb 21, 1919, St. Louis, MO; par. Cornelius Coffin and Edwina (Dakin) Williams; m. Joyce Coffin; c. Francesco M.; Anne Lanier. EDUC.: A.B., WA U., 1942; Harvard Grad. School of Business Administration, 1942; CO U. POLIT. & GOV.: appointed first asst. U.S. atty. for Eastern District of IL, 1960–65; candidate for Democratic nomination to U.S. Senate (IL), 1972, 1974, 1980; candidate for Democratic nomination to gov. of IL, 1976, 1978; ***candidate for Democratic nomination to presidency of the U.S., 1984 (withdrew)***. BUS. & PROF.: atty.; admitted to IL Bar, 1942; prof. of Law, St. Louis U.; partner, Massa and Williams (law firm), Collinsville, IL. MIL.: maj., U.S. Air Force, WWII and Korean War. MEM.: Knights of Columbus; Tau Kappa Epsilon. HON. DEG.: LL.D., U. of WA. AWARDS: Jefferson Davis Award, U.D.C. WRITINGS: *Nails of Protest* (1955); *The Bar Bizarre* (1980); *Tennessee Williams: An Intimate Biography* (1983). REL.: R.C. MISC.: brother of playwright Tennessee Williams. MAILING ADDRESS: 97 Dewey Dr., Collinsville, IL 62234.

WILLIAMS, WALTER HENRY, JR. m. Diana Marie Williams. POLIT. & GOV.: ***Couch Potato Coalition candidate for presidency of the U.S., 1992***. MAILING ADDRESS: c/o Laid Back Cmte., 7413 Whitewood Dr., Fort Worth, TX 76137.

WILLIS, FRANK BARTLETT. b. Dec 28, 1871, Lewis Center, OH; d. Mar 30, 1928, Delaware, OH; par. Jay B. and Lavinia A. (Buell) Willis; m. Allie Dustin, Jul 19, 1894; c. Helen Dustin. EDUC.: Galena (OH) H.S.; A.B., OH Northern U., 1894, A.M., 1904; LL.B., OH Wesleyan U., 1906. POLIT. & GOV.: elected as a Republican to OH State House, 1900–1904; elected as a Republican to U.S. House (OH), 1911–15; elected as a Republican to gov. of OH, 1915–17; delegate, Rep. Nat'l. Conv., 1916, 1920, 1924; ***candidate for Republican nomination to presidency of the U.S., 1916, 1928***; Republican candidate for gov. of OH, 1916, 1918; elected as a Republican to U.S. Senate (OH), 1921–28. BUS. & PROF.: atty.; prof. of history and economics, OH Northern U., 1894–1906, prof. of Law, 1906–10; admitted to OH Bar, 1906. RES.: Delaware, OH.

WILLIS, LYLE LEONARD. b. 1904. EDUC.: Lincoln Memorial U. POLIT. & GOV.: candidate for Democratic nomination to U.S. House (KY), 1956, 1976, 1978, 1982; Democratic candidate for U.S. House (KY), 1970, 1972, 1974; ***candidate for Democratic nomination to presidency of the U.S., 1976***. BUS. & PROF.: merchant; realtor. MEM.: Masons; Shriners. AWARDS: Hon. Kentucky Colonel. REL.: Bapt. MAILING ADDRESS: 25 East Barbourville Highway, Corbin, KY 40701.

WILLIS, NOAH GERALD. b. Jan 6, 1940, Piedmont, AL; par. Rev. Sanford Willis; m. Frances Keener, 1959; c. Keith; Kim; Lee Breeska. EDUC.: grad., White Plains (AL) H.S., 1959. POLIT. & GOV.: elected member, Calhoun Cty. (AL) Democratic Exec. Cmte., 1966; elected member, White Plains (AL) School Board of Trustees, 1967; elected as a Democrat to Calhoun Cty. (AL) Board of Commissioners, 1971; elected as a Democrat to AL State House, 1979–83; ***candidate for Democratic nomination to presidency of the U.S., 1984; candidate for Democratic nomination to vice presidency of the U.S., 1984; candidate for Populist Party nomination to presidency of the U.S., 1984; candidate for American Party nomination to presidency of the U.S., 1984; Conservative Party candidate for presidency of the U.S., 1984***. BUS. & PROF.: cement finisher; electrician; farmer, Piedmont, AL; owner, Gerald Willis Lumber Co., Piedmont, AL. MEM.: White Plains PTA (pres.); White Plains Civitan Club (pres., 1968); Calhoun Cty. (AL) Farm Bureau (pres., 1974); Piedmont Lions Club (dir., 1973); Piedmont C. of C. (dir., 1975); Calhoun Cty. Forestry Assn. (founder, 1975); Piedmont UGF Drive (chm., 1977–78). AWARDS: Civitan International Merit Club Award, 1969; T. G. Parker Award, Piedmont C. of C., 1976; Piedmont (AL) Citizen of the Year, 1982–83. REL.: Protestant (nee Congregational Holiness Church). MAILING ADDRESS: Route 2, Box 286, Piedmont, AL 36272.

WILLIS, SIMEON S. b. Dec 1, 1879, Lawrence Cty., OH; d. Apr 5, 1965; par. John H. and Abigail (Slavens) Willis; m. Idah Lee Millis, Apr 14, 1920; c. Sara Leslie (Mrs. Henry Meigs II). EDUC.: public schools. POLIT. & GOV.: elected as a Republican, city solicitor, Ashland, KY, 1918–22; appointed member, KY State Board of Bar Examiners, 1922–28; elected assoc. justice, KY State Court of Appeals, 1927–33; candidate for assoc. justice, KY State Court of Appeals, 1932, 1951; elected as a Republican to gov. of KY, 1943–47; ***candidate for Republican nomination to presidency of the U.S., 1944***; appeal agent, Boyd Cty., KY, WWI, WWII; appointed member, Public Service Comm. of KY, 1956–60; appointed member, KY State Board of Parole, 1961–65. BUS. & PROF.: principal, Springville, KY; reporter; atty.; admitted to KY Bar, 1901; law practice, Ashland, KY; dir., Park City Land Co. MEM.: ABA; KY Bar Assn.; Civil Legion (life member); Elks; Masons. HON. DEG.: LL.D., U. of KY, 1944; LL.D., KY Wesleyan Coll., 1944; LL.D., Centre Coll., 1947. WRITINGS: *Thornton's Law of Oil and Gas* (ed., 1931). REL.: Methodist. RES.: Ashland, KY.

WILLKIE, WENDELL LEWIS. b. Feb 18, 1892, Elwood, IN; d. Oct 8, 1944, New York, NY; par. Herman Francis and Henrietta (Trisch) Willkie; m. Edith Wilk, Jan 14, 1918; c. Philip Herman. EDUC.: A.B., IN U., 1913, LL.B., 1916. POLIT. & GOV.: delegate, Dem. Nat'l. Conv., 1924; ***Republican candidate for presidency of the U.S., 1940; candidate for Republican nomination to presidency of the U.S., 1944***. BUS. & PROF.: schoolteacher, Coffeyville (KS) H.S., 1913; atty.; admitted to IN Bar, 1919; admitted to NY Bar, 1930; partner, Willkie and Willkie (law firm), Elwood, IN, 1916–19; assoc., law dept., Firestone Tire and Rubber Co., Akron, OH, 1919; partner, Mather, Nesbitt and Willkie (law firm), Akron, OH, 1919–29; partner, Weadock and Willkie (law firm), New York, NY, 1929–32; pres., Commonwealth and Southern Corp., 1933–40; dir., Northern Ohio Power and Light Co., 1928; dir., First National Bank of NY; dir., Lehman Brothers; partner, Willkie, Owen, Otis, Farr and Gallagher (law firm), New York, NY, 1941–44; chm. of the board, 20th Century Fox Corp., 1942. MIL.: capt., U.S. Army, 1917–18. MEM.: Century Assn.; Lawyers Club; Downtown Assn.; Assn. of the Bar of the City of New York; NY Hospital (trustee); Beekman Street Hospital (trustee); Hampton Inst. (trustee); Akron Bar Assn. (pres., 1926); Union Coll. (hon. chancellor); IN U. Foundation (trustee); United China Relief (hon. chm.); Phi Beta Kappa (hon. member); National Republican Club; Freedom House (founder; dir.); Recess Club; University Club; Metropolitan Club. AWARDS: Gold Medal, National Inst. of Social Science, 1940; award, The Churchman, 1941. HON. DEG.: LL.D., IN U., 1938; LL.D., Bowdoin Coll., 1941; LL.D., Dartmouth Coll., 1941; LL.D., Rutgers U., 1941; Sc.D., Stevens Inst. of Technology, 1941; LL.D., Yale U., 1941; LL.D., Union Coll., 1942; LL.D., Boston U., 1943; LL.D., Oberlin Coll., 1943. WRITINGS: *Free Enterprise* (1940); *Loyal Opposition* (1940); *Occasional Addresses* (1940); *Quotations* (1940); *This is Wendell Willkie* (1940); *One World* (1943); *The American Program* (1944). REL.: Episc. (vestryman). RES.: New York, NY.

WILLOUGHBY, JOYCE HOOVER. POLIT. & GOV.: ***independent candidate for vice presidency of the U.S., 1972***. MAILING ADDRESS: 4014 Byrd Rd., Kensington, MD.

WILMINGTON, VERNON LEROY. b. Jul 19, 1940, Boulder, CO; par. Wilbur Ernest and Ruth Francis (Christian) Wilmington; m. Marion Joy Harris; c. David Christopher; Julie Nicole; Tiffany Michelle; Lisa Marie. EDUC.: high school; technical drafting school. POLIT. & GOV.: ***independent candidate for presidency of the U.S., 1992***. BUS. & PROF.: draftsman, 1962–. REL.: none. MISC.: campaigned through use of chain letter. MAILING ADDRESS: 712 Camellia Dr., North Fort Myers, FL 33903.

WILMOT, DAVID. b. Jan 20, 1814, Bethany, PA; d. Mar 16, 1868, Towanda, PA; par. Randall and Mary (Grant) Wilmot; m. Ann Morgan, Nov 28, 1836; c. three. EDUC.: Aurora (NY) Acad.; read law under George W. Woodward, Wilkes Barre, PA, 1832. POLIT. & GOV.: delegate, PA State Democratic Convention, 1844; elected as a Democrat to U.S. House (PA), 1845–51; delegate, PA State Free Soil Party Convention, 1847; delegate, PA State Democratic Convention, 1848; delegate, Free Soil Party National Convention, 1848; pres.-judge, 13th PA Judicial District, 1851–61; founding member, Republican Party, 1854; member, Rep. Nat'l. Cmte., 1854; delegate, Rep. Nat'l. Conv., 1856, 1860 (temporary chm.); ***candidate for Republican nomination to vice presidency of the U.S., 1856***; delegate, PA State Republican Convention, 1856; Republican candidate for gov. of PA, 1857; elected as a Republican to U.S. Senate (PA), 1861–63; appointed judge, U.S. Court of Claims, 1863–68. BUS. & PROF.: atty.; admitted to PA Bar, 1834; law practice, Towanda, PA, 1834–44. MISC.: author of Wilmot Proviso. RES.: Towanda, PA.

WILSON, EDITH BOLLING GALT. b. Oct 15, 1872, Wytheville, VA; d. Dec 28, 1961, Washington, DC; d. William Holcombe and Sallie (White) Bolling; m. Norman Galt, Apr 30, 1896; m. 2d, Thomas Woodrow Wilson (q.v.), Dec 18, 1915; c. none. POLIT. & GOV.: ***candidate for Democratic nomination to presidency of the U.S., 1928***. BUS. & PROF.: first lady. MISC.: reportedly ran federal government in name of her ill husband, President Woodrow Wilson, during his final days as president. RES.: Princeton, NJ.

WILSON, GEORGE IRVING. b. 1855, Bridgeport, CT; d. Aug 19, 1935, Vineland, NJ; m. Caroline Agusta Barnes; c. Mildred Geissinger; Margaret A.; Jean Bell. POLIT. &

GOV.: member, People's Party, 1890; ***National (Greenback) Party candidate for presidency of the U.S., 1932 (withdrew)***. BUS. & PROF.: teacher, Quaker school; employee, Wood's Drug Store, West Haven, CT; owner, Health Food Store, Philadelphia, PA, 1890–1908; operator, Wooley's Drug Store, Ocean Grove, NJ; proprietor, General Drug Store and News Stand, Vineland, NJ, 1908–35. WRITINGS: *A Catechism of Finance* (1893); *A Monstrous Money System* (1897). REL.: Soc. of Friends. MISC.: one of first licensed druggists in NJ, 1877; organizer, Coxey's Army, 1894; committed suicide. RES.: Vineland, NJ.

WILSON, HENRY (nee JEREMIAH JONES COLBATH). b. Feb 16, 1812, Farmington, NH; d. Nov 22, 1875, Washington, DC; par. Winthrop and Abigail (Witham) Colbath; m. Harriet Malvina Howe, Oct 28, 1840; c. Henry Hamilton. EDUC.: Stratford (NH) Acad.; Wolfsboro (NH) Acad., 1836–37; Concord (NH) Acad., 1837. POLIT. & GOV.: Temperance Party candidate for MA State House, 1839; elected as a Whig to MA State House, 1841–42; Whig Party candidate for MA State House, 1842; elected as a Whig to MA State Senate, 1844–46, 1850–52 (pres., 1851–52); delegate, Whig Party National Convention, 1848; candidate for Whig Party nomination to U.S. House (MA), 1848; chm., MA Free Soil Party, 1849–52; Free Soil Party candidate for MA State Senate, 1851; candidate for Free Soil Party nomination to gov. of MA, 1851, 1852; chm., Free Soil Party National Convention, 1852; Free Soil Party candidate for U.S. House (MA), 1852; delegate, MA Constitutional Convention, 1853; Free Soil Party candidate for gov. of MA, 1853; Republican candidate for gov. of MA, 1854; elected as a Free Soil-American-Democrat and subsequently reelected as a Republican to U.S. Senate (MA), 1855–73; ***candidate for Republican nomination to vice presidency of the U.S., 1856, 1868; National Workingmen's Party candidate for vice presidency of the U.S., 1872; elected as a Republican to vice presidency of the U.S., 1873–1875***. BUS. & PROF.: farmer; shoemaker; shoe manufacturer, Natick, MA; schoolteacher, Natick, MA; owner, ed., *Boston (MA) Republican*, 1848–51. MIL.: brig. gen., MA Militia; col., 22d Regt., MA Volunteer Infantry, 1861–62. MEM.: Natick (MA) Debating Soc.; Concord Abolition Soc. (delegate, MA Anti-Slavery Convention, 1837); Congressional Temperance Soc.; American National Council (1855). WRITINGS: *Address to Constituents* (1853); *How Ought Working Men to Vote in the Coming Election?* (1860); *Letter . . . to Caleb Cushing* (1860); *Position of John Bell and His Supporters* (1860); *Democratic Leaders for Disunion* (1860); *Aggressions of the Slave Power* (1860); *The Draft* (1863); *The Death of Slavery in the Life of the Nation* (1864); *History of the Anti-Slavery Measures of the Thirty-Seventh and Thirty-Eighth U.S. Congresses* (1864); *Military Measures of the U.S. Congress, 1861–65* (1866); *Executive Patronage* (1866); *History of the Reconstruction Measures of the Thirty-Ninth and Fortieth Congresses* (1868); *The Relations of Churches and Ministers to the Temperance Cause* (1870); *The New Departure* (1871); *A Contribution to History* (1871); *History of the Rise and Fall of the Slave Power in America* (3 vols., 1872–77); *Stand by the Republican Colors* (1873); *Father Mathew: The Temperance Apostle* (1873). REL.: Congregationalist. RES.: Natick, MA.

WILSON, JOHN JOHNSTON. b. Jul 25, 1901, Washington, DC; d. May 18, 1986, Washington, DC; par. John Henry and Mattie Belle (Coursey) Wilson; m. Alice Adelaide Grant, Sep 25, 1923; m. 2d, Betty M. Rawlings, Aug 18, 1979; c. Mary Craddock (stepdaughter). EDUC.: LL.B., George Washington U., 1921. POLIT. & GOV.: appointed asst. U.S. atty. for DC, 1931–40, chief asst., 1938–40; appointed member, Comm. on Admissions and Grievances, U.S. District Court for DC, 1945–58; member, chm., Personnel Security Board, Atomic Energy Comm., 1957–71; appointed vice chm., Comm. on Judicial Disabilities and Tenure, 1971–73; campaign mgr., U.S. Rep. Walter E. Fauntroy (q.v.; DC), 1971; ***candidate for Democratic nomination to presidency of the U.S., 1972***. BUS. & PROF.: atty.; admitted to DC Bar, 1922; atty., Tucker, Kenyon and MacFarland (law firm), Washington, DC, 1922–31; senior partner, Whiteford, Hart, Carmody and Wilson (law firm), Washington, DC, 1940–76, counsel, 1977–86. MEM.: George Washington U. (hon. trustee; charter trustee, 1962–77); American Coll. of Trial Lawyers (fellow); ABA; DC Bar Assn.; Kappa Alpha; Phi Delta Phi; Barristers Club (pres.); Lawyers Club (pres.); Metropolitan Club; Federal Bar Assn. AWARDS: Alumni Achievement Award, George Washington U., 1965; Lawyer of the Year Award, DC Bar Assn., 1962. HON. DEG.: LL.D., George Washington U., 1978. REL.: Bapt. MISC.: noted for Watergate defense of H. R. Haldeman and John D. Ehrlichman. RES.: Washington, DC.

WILSON, LUTHER JAMES (aka LUTHER I-666). b. Jun 29, 1935, Waugh City, AL; par. Edward Moore and Mary Louise (Davis) Wilson; m. Clara Bell White (divorced); c. Edward Luther III; James Luther II; Carolyn Marie; Marcus Luther II; Barbara Ann. EDUC.: U. of Louisville; B.A., B.M., Bellarmine Coll., 1976. POLIT. & GOV.: candidate for Republican nomination to U.S. House (KY), 1970, 1974; independent candidate for U.S. House (KY), 1974; ***candidate for Republican nomination to presidency of the U.S., 1980, 1984; Union Party candidate for presidency of the U.S., 1984, 1988***. BUS. & PROF.: pres., Luther J. Wilson Realty Co., 1968–77; sec., Cosby-Wilson Corp., 1969–72; pres., Wilson Trust Co., 1972–. MIL.: U.S. Army, 1958–61. MISC.: known as "Luther I-666, The King"; seeks coronation as King of the U.S. MEM.: YMCA; NAACP. WRITINGS: *View from Below* (in print). REL.: Bapt. MAILING ADDRESS: 664 South Fourth St., Louisville, KY 42101.

WILSON, THOMAS WOODROW. b. Dec 28, 1856, Staunton, VA; d. Feb 3, 1924, Washington, DC; par. Rev. Joseph Ruggles and Jessie Janet (Woodrow) Wilson; m.

Ellen Louise Axson, Jun 24, 1885; m. 2d, Edith Bolling Galt (q.v.), Dec 18, 1915; c. Jessie Woodrow (Mrs. Francis Bowes Sayre); Eleanor Randolph (Mrs. William Gibbs McAdoo); Margaret Woodrow. EDUC.: Davidson Coll., 1874–75; A.B., Princeton U., 1879, A.M., 1882; LL.B., U. of VA, 1881; Johns Hopkins U., 1883–85, Ph.D., 1886. POLIT. & GOV.: Democratic candidate for U.S. Senate (NJ), 1907; elected as a Democrat to gov. of NJ, 1911–13; ***elected as a Democrat to presidency of the U.S., 1913–1921***; chief, American Comm. to Negotiate Peace, 1918–19; ***candidate for Democratic nomination to presidency of the U.S., 1920***. BUS. & PROF.: atty.; admitted to GA Bar, 1882; law practice, Atlanta, GA, 1882–83; assoc. prof. of History and Political Economy, Bryn Mawr Coll., 1885–88; prof., Wesleyan U., 1888–90; prof. of Jurisprudence, Princeton U., 1890–1910, pres., 1902–10; law practice, Washington, DC, 1921–24. MEM.: American Hist. Assn.; Southern History Assn.; American Economic Assn.; American Phil. Soc.; American Acad. of Hist. and Political Science; ABA; MA Hist. Soc. (corresponding member); Hist. Soc. of AL. AWARDS: Nobel Peace Prize, 1920. HON. DEG.: LL.D., Wake Forest Coll., 1887; LL.D., Tulane U., 1898; Litt.D., Yale U., 1901; LL.D., Johns Hopkins U., 1902; LL.D., Rutgers U., 1902; LL.D., Brown U., 1903; LL.D., U. of PA, 1903; LL.D., Harvard U., 1907; LL.D., Williams Coll., 1908; LL.D., Dartmouth Coll., 1909. WRITINGS: *Congressional Government: A Study in American Politics* (1885); *The State: Elements of Historical and Practical Politics* (1889, 1911); *Division and Reunion, 1829–89* (1893); *An Old Master and Other Political Essays* (1893); *Mere Literature and Other Essays* (1893); *George Washington* (1896); *A History of the American People* (1902); *Constitutional Government in the United States* (1908); *Free Life* (1913); *The New Freedom* (1913); *When a Man Comes to Himself* (1915); *On Being Human* (1916). REL.: Presb. RES.: Princeton, NJ.

WILSON, WILLIAM LYNE. b. May 3, 1843, Middleway, VA (now WV); d. Oct 17, 1900, Lexington, VA; par. Benjamin and Mary Whiting (Lyne) Wilson; m. Nannine Huntington, Aug 6, 1868; c. William Huntington; Arthur; Mary; Bettie; two others. EDUC.: Charles Town (VA) Acad.; grad., Columbian Coll., 1860, LL.B., 1867; U. of VA, 1860–61. POLIT. & GOV.: delegate, Dem. Nat'l. Conv., 1880; presidential elector, Democratic Party, 1880; elected as a Democrat to U.S. House (WV), 1883–95; permanent chm., Dem. Nat'l. Conv., 1892; Democratic candidate for U.S. House (WV), 1894; appointed postmaster gen. of the U.S., 1895–97; ***candidate for National (Gold) Democratic Party nomination to presidency of the U.S., 1896***. BUS. & PROF.: asst. prof. of ancient languages, Columbian Coll., 1865–71; atty.; admitted to VA Bar, 1869; partner, Baylor and Wilson (law firm), Charles Town, VA, 1871–82; pres., WV U., 1882–83; pres., Washington and Lee U., 1896–1900. MIL.: pvt., 12th VA Cavalry, 1861. MEM.: National Assn. of Democratic Clubs (pres.). HON. DEG.: LL.D., Central Coll. of MO.; LL.D., Columbian Coll.; LL.D., Hampden-Sidney Coll.; LL.D., U. of MS; LL.D., Tulane U.; LL.D., WV U. RES.: Charles Town, WV.

WINANT, JOHN GILBERT. b. Feb 23, 1889, New York, NY; d. Nov 3, 1947, Concord, NH; par. Frederick and Jeanette L. (Gilbert) Winant; m. Constance Rivington Russell, Dec 20, 1919; c. Constance Russell (Mrs. Carlos Velando); John Gilbert, Jr.; Rivington Russell. EDUC.: St. Paul's School. POLIT. & GOV.: elected as a Republican to NH State House, 1917–19, 1923–25; elected as a Republican to NH State Senate, 1921–23; elected as a Republican to gov. of NH, 1925–27, 1931–35; candidate for Republican nomination to gov. of NH, 1927; appointed chm., Textile Inquiry Board, 1934; appointed asst. dir., International Labor Office, Geneva, Switzerland, 1935, 1937–39; appointed chm., Social Security Board, 1935; ***candidate for Democratic nomination to presidency of the U.S., 1936***; appointed U.S. ambassador to Great Britain, 1941–46; appointed U.S. rep., European Advisory Comm., 1943; ***candidate for Democratic nomination to vice presidency of the U.S., 1944***; appointed U.S. delegate, Economic and Social Council, U.N., 1946. BUS. & PROF.: teacher, asst. principal, St. Paul's School, Concord, NH; owner, *Concord (NH) Monitor*; owner, *New Hampshire Patriot*; owner, Concord Oil Co. MIL.: pvt., First Aero Squadron, U.S. Army, 1917, capt., 1919; Honorary Order of Merit (Great Britain, 1946). MEM.: New England Council; National Recreation Assn. (vice pres.); NH Tuberculosis Assn. (pres.); National Consumers League (pres.); American Assn. for Labor Legislation (vice pres.); International YMCA (trustee); Wonolancet Club; Odd Volumes Club; Century Club; Holderness School (trustee); American Legion; American Youth Hostels (pres., 1946); National Municipal League (pres., 1941); NH Hist. Soc.; Soc. for the Preservation of NH Forests; American Brotherhood Week (chm., 1947). HON. DEG.: M.A., Dartmouth Coll., 1925; M.A., Princeton U., 1925, LL.D.; LL.D., U. of NH, 1926; LL.D., Bristol U., 1941; LL.D., U. of Edinburgh, 1941; LL.D., Aberdeen U., 1943; LL.D., Birmingham U., 1943; LL.D., U. of Cambridge, 1945; LL.D., Oxford U., 1945; LL.D., Hobart Coll. WRITINGS: *Letter from Grosvenor Square* (1947). REL.: Episc. MISC.: committed suicide. RES.: Concord, NH.

WINDOM, WILLIAM. b. May 10, 1827, Belmont Cty., OH; d. Jan 29, 1891, New York, NY; par. Hezekiah and Mercy (Spencer) Windon; m. Ellen P. (Towne) Hatch, Aug 20, 1856; c. Ellen H.; Florence B.; William D. EDUC.: Martinsburg (OH) Acad.; studied law. POLIT. & GOV.: elected as a Whig, prosecuting atty., Knox Cty., OH, 1852; elected as a Republican to U.S. House (MN), 1859–69; Republican candidate for U.S. Senate (MN), 1865; appointed and subsequently elected as a Republican to U.S. Senate (MN), 1870–81, 1881–83; ***candidate for Republican nomination to presidency of the U.S., 1880, 1884, 1888***; appointed U.S. sec. of the treasury, 1881, 1889–91; Republican candidate for U.S. Senate (MN), 1882. BUS. & PROF.: tailor's apprentice, Fredericktown, OH; atty.; admitted to OH Bar, 1850; law practice, Mount Vernon, OH, 1850–55; partner, Sargent, Wilson and Windom (law firm), Winona, MN; law practice, New York, NY, 1883–89. REL.: Soc. of Friends (Hicksite). RES.: Winona, MN.

WING, SIMON. b. Aug 29, 1826, St. Albans, ME; d. Feb 1, 1911, Charlestown, MA; par. Joshua and Anna (Osborn) Wing; m. Mary Merrill; c. Harvey T.; Anna Towne; Mary B. POLIT. & GOV.: delegate, Socialist Labor Party National Convention, 1892; ***Socialist Labor Party candidate for presidency of the U.S., 1892***; left Socialist Labor Party, c. 1896. BUS. & PROF.: tailor; daguerreotype maker, Waterville, ME, 1846–61; owner, S. Wing and Co. (photographers), Boston and Charlestown, MA, 1861–1903. REL.: Spiritualist. MISC.: inventor of process for making multiple photographs, tintype albums, brass mats, and preservers; fought for his patent rights in several cases reaching the U.S. Supreme Court. RES.: Charlestown, MA.

WINGATE, ROBERT F. POLIT. & GOV.: Republican candidate for U.S. House (MO), 1874; ***candidate for National Independent (Greenback) Party nomination to presidency of the U.S., 1876; candidate for National Independent (Greenback) Party nomination to vice presidency of the U.S., 1876***. WRITINGS: *Speeches* (1864); *Address On American Finance: Its Evils and Remedies* (1873). MISC.: known as "General" Wingate. RES.: MO.

WINGLER, ORAN RICHARD. b. Oct 10, 1943, Washburn Cty., WI; par. Elmo Hilary and Florence Rose Carpenter (Longley) Wingler; m. Marcia J. Haymond, Jan 20, 1968 (divorced, 1986); m. 2d, Marcia J. Haymond, Jun 11, 1988 (remarriage); c. Jennifer; Todd; Alison. EDUC.: grad., West Waterloo (IA) H.S., 1962; State Coll. of IA; U. of Northern IA. POLIT. & GOV.: independent candidate for Waterloo (IA) City Council, 1971; ***independent candidate for presidency of the U.S., 1988***. BUS. & PROF.: real estate agent; business owner; farmer; deliveryman, Pizza Hut, Phoenix, AZ, 1987–. MIL.: ground observer corps, 1957; specialist fifth class, U.S.A.R., 1966–72. MEM.: Exchange Club (1979); Farm Bureau (1973–80); National Assn. of Home Builders (1979); National Assn. of Realtors (1979–80). AWARDS: "Employee of the Month," Pizza Hut, Phoenix, AZ, Aug 1988. REL.: non-denominational Christian. MISC.: known as "He Who Is and Yet is Not and Yet Is"; announced candidacy for president anonymously, and revealed identity later in campaign. MAILING ADDRESS: 14832 North 35th Place, Phoenix, AZ 85032.

WINN, EDWARD "ED." b. 1936, Wilmington, NC. POLIT. & GOV.: joined Workers League, 1976; member, Central Cmte., Workers League; ***Workers League candidate for presidency of the U.S., 1984, 1988***. BUS. & PROF.: mechanic, New York City (NY) Transit Authority, 1966–88. MEM.: Transport Workers Union (shop steward; member, exec. board, Local 100, New York, NY, 1977–81). MISC.: civil rights activist; participated in March on Washington (DC), 1963. MAILING ADDRESS: 61 Somers St., Brooklyn, NY 11233.

WINN, ROBERT BRYANT (aka ROBERT BRYANT WYNN). b. Aug 14, 1947, Oxnard, CA; par. David J. and Jean (Bryant) Winn; single. EDUC.: grad., Troy (MT) H.S., 1965; MT State U., 1965–66. POLIT. & GOV.: ***independent candidate for presidency of the U.S., 1984, 1988***. BUS. & PROF.: copper miner; sawmill laborer; electrician; construction worker; citrus fruit harvester. MIL.: ETR-3, U.S. Navy, 4 years. REL.: Church of Jesus Christ of Latter-Day Saints. MAILING ADDRESS: 1954 East McKellips, Mesa, AZ 85203.

WINPISINGER, WILLLIAM WAYNE. b. Dec 10, 1924, Cleveland, OH; m. Pearl W.; c. five. EDUC.: public schools. POLIT. & GOV.: appointed member, Federal Comm. on Apprenticeships; co-chm., Machinists Non-Partisan Political League; candidate for ***Democratic nomination to vice presidency of the U.S., 1980***; member, Democratic Socialist Organizing Cmte. BUS. & PROF.: automotive mechanic, 1947–51; union official. MIL.: U.S. Navy, 1942–45. MEM.: AFL-CIO (exec. council); International Assn. of Machinists and Aerospace Workers (1947–; Grand Lodge representative, 1951–58; Air Transportation Dept., 1958–64; automotive coordinator, 1965–67; gen. vice pres., 1967; pres., 1967–); International Assn. of Machinists and Aerospace Workers Pension Fund (trustee); NY State School of Industrial and Labor Relations, Cornell U. (dir.); National Planning Assn. (adviser); Citizen/Labor Energy Coalition (founder); Americans for Democratic Action (vice pres.); Collective Bargaining and Group Relations Inst. (pres.). AWARDS: Peace Award, NJ SANE; Eugene V. Debs/Norman Thomas Award, Democratic Socialist Organizing Cmte. HON. DEG.: LL.D., Lincoln U. MAILING ADDRESS: Machinists' Building, 1300 Connecticut Ave., Washington, DC 20036.

WINSLOW, CALVIN. m. Barbara Winslow. EDUC.: B.A., Antioch Coll.; U. of Leeds (England); M.A., U. of WA. POLIT. & GOV.: ***Peace and Freedom Party candidate for vice presidency of the U.S., 1968***. BUS. & PROF.: grad. student (History), U. of WA; teaching asst. in History, U. of WA. MEM.: U. of WA Vietnam Cmte. (chm.); Students for a Democratic Soc. MAILING ADDRESS: 1508 35th Ave., Seattle, WA 98122.

WIRT, WILLIAM. b. Nov 8, 1772, Bladensburg, MD; d. Feb 18, 1834, Washington, DC; par. Jacob and Henrietta Wirt; m. Mildred Gilmer, May 28, 1795; m. 2d, Elizabeth (Gamble) Washington, Sep 7, 1802; c. twelve. EDUC.: studied law under William P. Hunt. POLIT. & GOV.: clerk, VA State House of Delegates, 1800; elected presiding judge, VA Chancery District, 1802; appointed prosecutor, Aaron Burr (q.v.) trial, 1806; elected to VA State House of Delegates, 1808; appointed U.S. atty. for Richmond District of VA, 1816–17; appointed atty. gen. of the U.S., 1817–1829; ***Anti-Masonic Party candidate for presidency of the U.S., 1832***. BUS. & PROF.: atty.; admitted to VA Bar,

1792; law practice, Culpepper Court House, VA. MEM.: Masons; MD Bible Soc. (pres.). HON. DEG.: LL.D., Harvard U., 1824. WRITINGS: *The Letters of the British Spy* (1802); *The Rainbow* (1808); *The Old Bachelor* (1810–13); *The Life and Character of Patrick Henry* (1817); *Life of J. P. Kennedy* (1849). REL.: Presb. RES.: Richmond, VA.

WIRTZ, WILLIAM WILLARD. b. Mar 14, 1912, DeKalb, IL; par. William Wilbur and Alpha Belle (White) Wirtz; m. Mary Jane Quisenberry, Sep 8, 1936; c. Richard; Philip. EDUC.: Northern IL State Coll., 1928–30; U. of CA, Berkeley, 1930–31; A.B., Beloit Coll., 1933; LL.B., Harvard U., 1937. POLIT. & GOV.: appointed asst. gen. counsel, Board of Economic Warfare, 1942–43; with War Labor Board, 1943–45, gen. counsel, 1945; appointed chm., National WSB, 1946; appointed member, IL State Liquor Control Comm., 1950–56; appointed member, Winnetka (IL) Library Board, 1950–56; appointed U.S. undersec. of labor, 1961; appointed U.S. sec. of labor, 1962–69; ***candidate for Democratic nomination to vice presidency of the U.S., 1964***. BUS. & PROF.: instructor, Kewanee (IL) H.S., 1933–34; instructor, U. of IA, 1937–39; asst. prof. of Law, Northwestern U., 1939–42, prof., 1946–54; atty.; partner, Stevenson, Rifkind and Wirtz (law firm), Chicago, IL, 1956–60; partner, Wirtz and Gentry (law firm), Washington, DC, 1970–78; partner, Wirtz and Lapointe (law firm), Washington, DC, 1979–. MEM.: ABA; IL Bar Assn.; National Acad. of Arbitrators; Phi Beta Kappa; Beta Theta Pi; Delta Sigma Phi. MAILING ADDRESS: 5009 39th St., N.W., Washington, DC.

WISE, BEVERLY KATHLEEN. b. May 21, 1943, Detroit, MI; d. Walter and Catherine (Kopas) Zabowski; m. ____ Wise (divorced); c. one. EDUC.: grad., Saints Cyril and Methodius H.S.; Detroit Business Inst., 1 year; Wayne State U. POLIT. & GOV.: ***Independent Party candidate for presidency of the U.S., 1988; candidate for Socialist Workers Party nomination to presidency of the U.S., 1992***. BUS. & PROF.: sec., National Bank of Detroit, Detroit, MI; sec., General Motors Technical Center; sec., Detroit Dental Soc., Detroit, MI; sec., Kelly Girls. MEM.: A.C.L.U. REL.: R.C. MAILING ADDRESS: 8141 Denwood, Sterling Heights, MI 48077.

WISE, HENRY ALEXANDER. b. Dec 3, 1806, Drummondtown, VA; d. Sep 12, 1876, Richmond, VA; par. Maj. John and Sarah Corbin (Cropper) Wise; m. Ann Jennings, Oct 8, 1828; m. 2d, Sarah Sergeant, Nov 1840; m. 3d, Mary Lyons, Nov 1, 1853; c. John Sergeant; Richard Alsop; Mary (Mrs. A. Y. P. Garnett); Henry Alexander, Jr.; Obadiah Jennings; Ann Jennings (Mrs. Frederick Plumer Hobson); Margaretta Ellen (Mrs. William C. Mayo). EDUC.: grad., WA Coll., 1825; law school, Winchester, VA. POLIT. & GOV.: elected as a Democrat to U.S. House (VA), 1833–44; appointed U.S. sec. of the navy, 1841 (declined); appointed U.S. minister to France, 1843 (rejected by U.S. Senate); appointed U.S. minister to Brazil, 1844–47; presidential elector, Democratic Party, 1848, 1852; delegate, VA State Constitutional Convention, 1850–51; delegate, Dem. Nat'l. Conv., 1852; elected as a Democrat to gov. of VA, 1856–60; ***candidate for Democratic nomination to presidency of the U.S., 1860***; delegate, VA Secession Convention, 1861; appointed member, VA and MD Boundary Comm. BUS. & PROF.: atty.; admitted to TN Bar, 1828; law practice, Nashville, TN, 1828–30; law practice, Accomac Cty., VA, 1830–76. MIL.: brig. gen., C.S.A., 1861. WRITINGS: *Seven Decades of the Union* (1872). MISC.: quelled John Brown's Raid, 1859; opposed secession, but supported Confederacy after formation. RES.: Richmond, VA.

WOBSER, DAVID. POLIT. & GOV.: ***independent candidate for presidency of the U.S., 1988***; received write-in votes in OH. MAILING ADDRESS: unknown.

WOERTENDYKE, JAMES H. b. Nov 24, 1869, Monmouth, IL; par. Frederick and Mary Elizabeth (Romans) Woertendyke. EDUC.: self-taught; Ph.D.; LL.B. POLIT. & GOV.: chm., CA State Prohibition Party, 1909–13; Prohibition Party candidate for gov. of IL, 1920; ***candidate for Prohibition Party nomination to vice presidency of the U.S., 1920***. BUS. & PROF.: atty.; admitted to CA Bar, 1904; law practice, CA, 1904–11; law practice, IL, 1911–; lecturer, Flying Squadron, 1921–23. MEM.: Flying Squadron; National League to Enforce Laws (pres.); World League of Christian Faith (gen. mgr.); Independent Order of Good Templars. REL.: Methodist. RES.: Kansas City, MO.

WOFFORD, HARRIS LLEWELLYN. b. Apr 9, 1926, New York, NY; par. Harris Llewellyn and Estelle (Gardner) Wofford; m. Emmy Lou Clare Lindgren, Aug 14, 1948; c. Susanne; Daniel; David. EDUC.: B.A., U. of Chicago, 1948; LL.B., Yale U., 1954; studied in India, 1949; studied in Israel, 1950. POLIT. & GOV.: asst. to Chester Bowles (q.v.), 1953–54; appointed legal asst., U.S. Comm. on Civil Rights, 1958–59; asst. to Sen. John F. Kennedy (q.v.), 1960; appointed special asst. to the pres., 1961–62; appointed special rep. for Africa, dir., Ethiopian Program, U.S. Peace Corps, 1962–64; assoc. dir., U.S. Peace Corps, 1964–66; co-chm., Cranston for President Cmte., 1983–84; chm., PA State Democratic Central Cmte., 1986; appointed PA sec. of labor and industry, 1987–91; appointed and subsequently elected as a Democrat to U.S. Senate (PA), 1991–95; ***candidate for Democratic nomination to vice presidency of the U.S., 1992***; Democratic candidate for U.S. Senate (PA), 1994. BUS. & PROF.: atty.; admitted to DC Bar, 1954; admitted to the Bar of the Supreme Court of the U.S., 1958; admitted to the PA Bar, 1978; assoc., Covington and Burling (law firm), Washington, DC, 1954–58; visiting prof., Howard Law School, 1956; assoc. prof., Notre Dame Law School, 1959–60; pres., Coll. at Old Westbury, State U. of NY, 1966–70; pres., Bryn Wawr Coll., 1970–78; counsel, Schnader, Harrison, Segal and Lewis (law firm), Philadelphia, PA, 1978–86; author. MEM.: Comm. to Study the Organization of Peace; The American Coll. Bryn Mawr (trustee, 1975–83); U.S.-South Africa Leader Exchange Program (council member, 1971–); International League for Human Rights (dir., 1979–; pres.); Public Interest Law Center (dir.); Martin Luther King Center for Nonviolent Social Change (dir.); Wilderness Soc. (gov.); ABA; Century Assn.; U.S.-Zululand Educational Foundation (trustee). HON. DEG.: LL.D., Howard U., 1954. WRITINGS: *It's Up to Us* (1946); *India Afire* (with Clare Wofford, 1951); *Report of the U.S. Commission on Civil Rights* (co-editor, 1959); *Embers of the World* (ed., 1970); *Of Kennedy's and Kings* (1980). REL.: R.C. MAILING ADDRESS: Suite 3600, 1600 Market St., Philadelphia, PA 19103.

WOLCOTT, EDWARD OLIVER. b. Mar 26, 1848, Long Meadow, MA; d. Mar 1, 1905, Monte Carlo, Monaco; par. Samuel and Harriet Amanda (Pope) Wolcott; m. Frances (Metcalfe) Bass, May 14, 1891 (divorced, 1900). EDUC.: Norwich Acad.; Central H.S., Cleveland, OH; Yale Coll., 1866; LL.B., Harvard Law School, 1875. POLIT. & GOV.: elected as a Republican, district atty. and town atty., Georgetown, CO, 1876–79; elected as a Republican to CO State Senate, 1879–82; elected as a Republican to U.S. Senate (CO), 1889–1901; delegate, Rep. Nat'l. Conv., 1892, 1900; ***candidate for Republican nomination to vice presidency of the U.S., 1900***; Republican candidate for U.S. Senate (CO), 1901, 1902, 1903. BUS. & PROF.: schoolteacher, Blackhawk, CO, 1871; ed., *Georgetown (CO) Miner*; atty.; admitted to CO Bar, 1871; law practice, Georgetown, CO, 1871–79; atty., Denver and Rio Grande R.R., Denver, CO, 1879, gen. counsel, 1884. MIL.: pvt., 150th Regt., OH Volunteer Infantry, 1865. HON. DEG.: LL.D., Yale Coll., 1896. REL.: Congregationalist. MISC.: advocate of free silver. RES.: Denver, CO.

WOLFENBARGER, ANDREW GIVENS. b. Mar 24, 1856, Greenbank, VA; d. Oct 8, 1923, Lincoln, NE; par. William Wolfenbarger; m.; c. Ethel Goodrich (adopted; Mrs. Arthur Stevenson); Edward S. (adopted). EDUC.: Montrose (IA) H.S.; LL.B., U. of NE. POLIT. & GOV.: sec., NE State Prohibition Convention; sec., field mgr., NE State Prohibition Cmte.; member, Prohibition Party National Cmte., 1887–92, 1900–1912 (vice chm., 1911–12); delegate, Prohibition Party National Convention, 1888, 1892 (temporary sec.), 1904 (permanent chm.); ***candidate for Prohibition Party nomination to presidency of the U.S., 1892***; Prohibition Party candidate for justice, NE State Supreme Court, 1895; Prohibition Party candidate for atty. gen. of NE, 1898; chm., NE State Prohibition Party, 1904. BUS. & PROF.: atty.; admitted to NE Bar, 1890; law practice, Lincoln, NE; lecturer; schoolteacher, York Cty., NE, 1877; journalist; ed., *David City (NE) Republican*, 1880–85; founder, managing ed., *New Republic*, Lincoln, NE, 1885–90. MEM.: NE Irrigation Assn. (pres.); Independent Order of Good Templars (Deputy Right Worthy Grand Templar of Western Hemisphere; International Supreme Lodge); Masons (Knights Templar; Ancient Free and Accepted Masons; Scottish Rite; Mystic Shrine). WRITINGS: "Stupendous Failure of High License," in *The Prohibition Leaders of America*; *Nebraska Legislative Year Book of 1897* (1897). REL.: Methodist Episc. Church. RES.: Lincoln, NE.

WOLFSON, ABRAHAM (nee WOLFE, ABRAHAM). b. Nov 24, 1881, Narevke, Russia; par. Osher and Esther (Nitzberg) Wolfe; m. Helen Gross, Jun 2, 1912; c. Dr. Oliver W. Wolfson; Evelyn (Mrs. Edwin H. Niman). EDUC.: D.D.S., NY U., 1907. POLIT. & GOV.: ***American Vegetarian Party candidate for vice presidency of the U.S., 1964***. BUS. & PROF.: dental surgeon, Roosevelt Hospital, New York, NY; founder, Spinoza Inst. of America; founder, Spinoza Center of NY; founder, pres., Spinoza Forum for Adult Education, Miami Beach, FL, 1935–; philosopher; lecturer. MEM.: B'nai B'rith Lodge of Miami; Alumni Assn. of NY U. WRITINGS: *Spinoza: A Life of Reason* (1964); *The Wisdom of Spinoza* (1963); *The Road to Health and Happier Living*; *Live a Hundred Years Happily*. REL.: Jewish. RES.: Miami Beach, FL.

WOMACK, DAVID WESLEY. b. Jan 28, 1966, Belville, IL; par. George Wesley and Wanda Lucille (Bartimus) Womack; single. EDUC.: grad., Macomb (IL) Senior H.S., 1984; Tarkio (MO) Coll. POLIT. & GOV.: American Partiers Party candidate for Bardolph Village (IL) president; ***American Partiers Party candidate for presidency of the U.S., 1988***. BUS. & PROF.: student; staff, Macomb (IL) H.S. Sentinel, 1983–84; feature ed., *Tarkio College Torch*, 1985. MEM.: International Thespian Soc. (pres., Troupe 465, 1983–85). AWARDS: Honor Thespian; "Best Partier," 1985. REL.: Salvation Army. MAILING ADDRESS: P.O. Box 55, Bardolph, IL 61416.

WOMBLES, TERRY HOWARD (aka HICKERSON). POLIT. & GOV.: ***independent Democratic candidate for presidency of the U.S., 1980; Prime Time of Life Party candidate for presidency of the U.S., 1980.*** MAILING ADDRESS: 515 Grant Dr., Quincy, IL 62301.

WOOD, ALFRED M. POLIT. & GOV.: Republican candidate for U.S. House (NY), 1868; ***candidate for Democratic nomination to presidency of the U.S., 1920***. RES.: NY.

WOOD, EDWARD RANDOLPH. b. Jun 21, 1840, Philadelphia, PA; d. Feb 14, 1932, Philadelphia, PA; par. Richard Davis and Juliana (Fitz-Randolph) Wood; m. Mary Honeyman, Jul 24, 1866; m. 2d, Erma Evelyn, Dec 24, 1919; c. Richard Davis; Anna Kneass; Charles Randolph; Juliana; Mariane Honeyman (Mrs. Marcellino Diaz); Edward Randolph, Jr.; Roger Davis. EDUC.: A.B., Haverford Coll., 1856, A.M., 1859; LL.B., U. of PA, 1861. POLIT. & GOV.: member, platform cmte., Rep. Nat'l. Conv., 1880, 1900; cmte. chm., National

Board of Trade, 1900; ***candidate for Republican nomination to presidency of the U.S., 1920***; won 1920 PA presidential primary. BUS. & PROF.: industrialist; atty.; employee, R. D. Wood and Sons (cotton manufacturers); treas., Millville Manufacturing Co., 1865; pres., Millville Improvement Co.; financier. MEM.: Municipal Reform Assn. (sec.); Cmte. of 100; Union Benevolent Soc. (pres.); Philadelphia Board of Trade (first vice pres.); Philadelphia Art Club. WRITINGS: "Comedy of the Twentieth Century" (poem). REL.: Soc. of Friends. RES.: Philadelphia, PA.

WOOD, LEONARD. b. Oct 9, 1860, Winchester, NH; d. Aug 7, 1927, Boston, MA; par. Charles Jewett and Caroline F. (Hager) Wood; m. Louisa A. Condit Smith, Nov 18, 1890; c. Leonard, Jr.; Osborne Cutler; Louise Barbara. EDUC.: Pierce Acad.; M.D., Harvard U., 1884; Dr.Mil.Sc., PA Military Coll., 1913; Dr.Mil.Sc., Norwich U., 1915; D.Sc., Rensselaer Polytechnic Inst., 1920. POLIT. & GOV.: appointed military gov. of Cuba, 1899–1902; ***candidate for Republican nomination to vice presidency of the U.S., 1900***; appointed gov. of Moro Province, Philippine Islands, 1903–06; appointed special U.S. ambassador to Argentina, 1910; ***candidate for Republican nomination to presidency of the U.S., 1916, 1920; candidate for Democratic nomination to presidency of the U.S., 1920; candidate for Prohibition Party nomination to presidency of the U.S., 1920***; appointed gov. gen. of the Philippine Islands, 1921–27. BUS. & PROF.: soldier; provost, U. of PA, 1921. MIL.: asst. surgeon, U.S. Army, 1886, capt., 1891; col., First U.S. Volunteer Cavalry (Rough Riders), 1898, brig. gen., 1898, maj. gen., 1898; brig. gen., 1901, maj. gen., 1903, retired, 1921; chief of staff, 1910–14; Medal of Honor, 1898; Distinguished Service Medal, 1919; Legion of Honor (France, 1909). MEM.: Soc. of Mayflower Descendants (gov. gen., 1915–19); Royal Geographical Soc. (fellow); University Club; Metropolitan Club; Harvard Club; Chicago Club; Tavern Club. AWARDS: Order of Saints Mauritius and Lazarus (Italy, 1920); Roosevelt Medal of Honor (1923); Order of the Rising Sun (Japan, 1931); Order of the Golden Grain (China, 1931); Medal of Peace, Roman Catholic Church; award, Japanese Red Cross. HON. DEG.: LL.D., Harvard U., 1899; LL.D., Williams Coll., 1902; LL.D., U. of PA, 1903; LL.D., Princeton U., 1916; LL.D., U. of GA, 1917; LL.D., U. of the South, 1917; LL.D., George Washington U., 1918; LL.D., U. of MI, 1918; LL.D., Union Coll., 1918; LL.D., Wesleyan Coll., 1918; LL.D., Abraham Lincoln U., 1919; LL.D., U. of the Philippines, 1922. WRITINGS: *Our Military History: Its Facts and Fallacies* (1916); *A Report of the Special Mission to the Philippines* (coauthor, 1921). REL.: Episc. RES.: Manila, Philippine Islands.

WOOD, NANCY TATE. POLIT. & GOV.: ***independent (Cmte. for a Constitutional Presidency) candidate for vice presidency of the U.S., 1976***. MAILING ADDRESS: NJ.

WOOD, ROBERT A. b. 1929; m. 1952; c. one son. POLIT. & GOV.: ***candidate for Democratic nomination to presidency of the U.S., 1980***. BUS. & PROF.: realtor; independent fee appraiser; real estate broker, Wood Realty. MIL.: Korean War. MEM.: Disabled American Veterans (life member; commander, Wyandotte Chapter 62); Detroit City Rescue Mission (dir.); American Assn. of Certified Appraisers; Downriver Board of Realtors (pres.; dir.); National Board of Realtors; MI State Board of Realtors. MAILING ADDRESS: P.O. Box 1142, Southgate, MI 48195.

WOODBEY, GEORGE WASHINGTON. b. Oct 5, 1854, Johnson Cty., TN; d. After 1916; par. Charles and Rachel (Wagner) Woodbey; m. Mary W. EDUC.: public schools. POLIT. & GOV.: member, Republican Party, MO and KS; member, Prohibition Party, NE; Prohibition Party candidate for lt. gov. of NE, 1890, 1896; Prohibition Party candidate for U.S. House (NE), 1896; joined People's Party, 1900; member, exec. cmte., CA Socialist Party; delegate, Socialist Party National Convention, 1904, 1908, 1912; ***candidate for Socialist Party nomination to vice presidency of the U.S., 1908***; Socialist Party candidate for CA state treas., 1914. BUS. & PROF.: slave; miner; factory worker; ordained minister, Baptist Church, Emporia, KS, 1874; pastor, African Church, Omaha, NE; minister, Mount Zion Baptist Church, San Diego, CA, 1902–16; correspondent, *Chicago (IL) Daily Socialist*; Christian Socialist orator. MEM.: Free Speech League; Industrial Workers of the World. WRITINGS: *Testimonial* (1901); *What to Do and How to Do It, or Socialism versus Capitalism* (1903); *The Bible and Socialism: A Conversation Between Two Preachers* (1904); *The Distribution of Wealth* (1910); *Why the Negro Should Vote the Socialist Ticket* (1908); *Method of Procedure in Baptist Church Trials* (1916). REL.: Bapt. MISC.: known as "the Great Negro Socialist Orator." RES.: San Diego, CA.

WOODBURY, LEVI. b. Dec 22, 1789, Francestown, NH; d. Sep 4, 1851, Portsmouth, NH; par. Peter and Mary (Woodbury) Woodbury; m. Elizabeth Williams Clapp, Jun 1819; c. Charles Levi; Mrs. Montgomery Blair; three other daughters. EDUC.: grad., Dartmouth Coll., 1809; Litchfield Law School. POLIT. & GOV.: clerk, NH State Senate, 1816; assoc. justice, NH Superior Court, 1817–23; elected as a Democrat to gov. of NH, 1823–24; elected as a Democrat to NH State House, 1825 (Speaker); elected as a Democrat to U.S. Senate (NH), 1825–31, 1841–45; appointed U.S. sec. of the navy, 1831–34; appointed U.S. sec. of the treasury, 1834–41; ***candidate for Democratic nomination to presidency of the U.S., 1844, 1848, 1852; candidate for Democratic nomination to vice presidency of the U.S., 1844***; appointed chief justice, NH Superior Court, 1841 (declined); appointed U.S. ambassador to Great Britain, 1845 (declined); appointed assoc. justice, Supreme Court of the U.S., 1845–51. BUS. & PROF.: atty.; admitted to NH Bar, 1812; law practice, Francestown, NH, 1813–16. HON. DEG.: LL.D., Dartmouth Coll., 1823; LL.D., Wesleyan U., 1843. RES.: Portsmouth, NH.

WOODCOCK, LEONARD FREEL. b. Feb 15, 1911, Providence, RI; par. Ernest and Margaret (Freel) Woodcock; m. Loula Martin, May 28, 1941; m. 2d, Sharon Lee Tuohy, Apr 14, 1978; c. Leslie (Mrs. Tentler); Janet; John. EDUC.: St. Wilfred's Coll., 1920–23; Northhampton Town and Country School, 1923–26; Wayne State U., 1928–30; Walsh Inst. of Accountancy, 1928–30. POLIT. & GOV.: delegate, Dem. Nat'l. Conv., 1952, 1956; ***candidate for Democratic nomination to vice presidency of the U.S., 1972***; presidential elector, Democratic Party, 1976; appointed chief of mission, U.S. Liaison Office, People's Republic of China, 1977–79; appointed U.S. ambassador to People's Republic of China, 1979–81. BUS. & PROF.: machine assembler, Detroit Gear and Machine Co., Detroit, MI, 1933; staff rep., U.A.W., 1940–46, administrative asst. to the pres., 1946–47, regional dir., 1947–55, vice pres., 1955–70, pres., 1970–77, pres. emeritus, 1977–; dynomometer operator, Continental Aviation and Engineering Co., Muskegon, MI, 1947; assoc., Labor Studies, Charles Stewart Mott Community Coll., Flint, MI, 1977; adjunct prof., U. of MI, 1981–. MEM.: NAACP (life member); Wayne State U. (gov., 1970); U.A.W.; National Citizens Cmte. for Public Television; Urban League; A.C.L.U.; Metropolitan Fund (dir.); Joint Comm. on Mental Health of Children (dir.); Detroit Educational Television Foundation (trustee); United Foundation (trustee); American Acad. of Transportation (trustee). AWARDS: Sesquicentennial Award, U. of MI, 1967, Presidential Medal of Freedom, 1994. HON. DEG.: D.H.L., Grand Valley State Coll., 1973; D.H.L., U. of Toledo, 1973; A.A.S., Schoolcraft Coll., 1976; D.P.S., Northeastern U., 1977; D.P.S., U. of RI, 1977. REL.: Christian (nee R.C.). MAILING ADDRESS: 2404 Vinewood Ave., Ann Arbor, MI 48104.

WOODFORD, STEWART LYNDON. b. Sep 3, 1835, New York, NY; d. Feb 14, 1913, New York, NY; par. Josiah Curtis and Susan (Terry) Woodford; m. Julia Evelyn Capen, Oct 15, 1857; m. 2d, Isabel Hanson, Sep 26, 1900; c. Susan Curtis; three others. EDUC.: A.B., Columbia U., 1854, A.M., 1866. POLIT. & GOV.: delegate, Rep. Nat'l. Conv., 1860, 1872, 1876, 1880, 1908 (nominated Charles Evans Hughes, q.v., for president); messenger, Electoral Coll., 1860; appointed asst. U.S. district atty., Southern District of NY, 1861–62; elected as a Republican to lt. gov. of NY, 1866–68; Republican candidate for U.S. House (NY), 1868 (declined); Republican candidate for gov. of NY, 1870; presidential elector, Republican Party, 1872; elected as a Republican to U.S. House (NY), 1873–74; ***candidate for Republican nomination to vice presidency of the U.S., 1876, 1880***; appointed U.S. district atty., Southern District of NY, 1877–83; member, Greater NY Charter Comm., 1896; appointed envoy extraordinary and minister plenipotentiary to Spain, 1897–98; pres., Hudson-Fulton Comm., 1907. BUS. & PROF.: atty.; admitted to NY Bar, 1857; law practice, New York, NY, 1857–1913; partner, Ritch, Woodford, Bovee and Wallace (law firm), New York, NY; dir., counsel, Metropolitan Life Insurance Co.; trustee, Franklin Trust Co.; trustee, City Savings Bank. MIL.: lt. col., 127th NY Infantry, 1862; col., 103d U.S. Colored Troops, 1865; brev. brig. gen. of Volunteers, 1865; Union commander of Charleston, SC, and Savannah, GA; Order of the Rising Sun, Second Class (Japan, 1908); Crown Order of First Class (Germany, 1910). MEM.: Phi Beta Kappa; Columbia Alumni Assn.; Delta Psi; NY Bar Assn.; Century Assn.; Army of the Potomac; Loyal Legion; University Club; Lawyers Club; Lotos Club; Cornell U. (trustee, 1867–1913); St. Anthony's Club; Hamilton Club; Montauk Club; Union League; New England Soc. (pres.); GAR; SAR; Military Order of Foreign Wars. HON. DEG.: A.M., Yale U., 1866; A.M., Trinity Coll., 1869; LL.D., Dickinson Coll., 1889; D.C.L., Syracuse U., 1894; LL.D., Marietta Coll., 1908. REL.: Presb. (trustee, First Presbyterian Church, New York, NY). RES.: New York, NY.

WOODHULL, VICTORIA CLAFLIN. b. Sep 23, 1838, Homer, OH; d. Jun 10, 1927, Bredon's Norton, Worchestershire, England; d. Reuben Buckman and Roxanna (Hummel) Claflin; m. Dr. Canning Woodhull, 1853; m. 2d, James H. Blood (q.v.), 1866 (divorced, 1868), 1869 (divorced, 1876); m. 3d, John Biddulph Martin, Oct 31, 1883; c. Byron; Zulu Maud. POLIT. & GOV.: ***Equal Rights (Cosmic, Free Love, People's) Party candidate for presidency of the U.S., 1872; independent candidate for presidency of the U.S., 1880, 1884, 1888, 1984 (satire effort); Humanitarian Party candidate for presidency of the U.S., 1892***. BUS. & PROF.: medium and seer, 1841–68; patent medicine saleswoman; actress; reformer; partner, Woodhull, Claflin and Co. (Stock Brokers), New York, NY, 1870; founder, publisher, *Woodhull and Claflin's Weekly*, 1870–72; publisher, *The Humanitarian*, 1892. MEM.: Section Twelve, Communist International Workingman's Assn.; Psychical Research Soc.; Woman's International Agricultural Assn. (founder); Ladies Automobile Club; Manor House Club. WRITINGS: *Origin, Tendencies and Principles of Government* (1871); *The Elixir of Life, or, Why Do We Die* (1873); *Breaking the Seals* (1875); *The Argument for Women's Electoral Rights Under Amendments XIV and XV* (1887); *A Fragmentary Record of Public Work Done in America, 1871–77* (1887); *Stirpiculture, or the Scientific Propagation of the Human Race* (1888); *Social Freedom*; *Rapid Multiplication of the Unfit*; *Argument for Woman's Electoral Rights*; *Garden of Eden*; *The Alchemy of Maternity* (1889); *The Human Body: The Temple of God* (1890); *Pharmacy of the Soul*; *Aristocracy of Blood*; *Humanitarian Government*; *Humanitarian Money* (1892); *Brief Sketches of the Life of Victoria Woodhull* (1893); *And the Truth Shall Make You Free* (1894). REL.: Spiritualist. MISC.: advocate of free love and equal rights; arrested for publishing expose of Henry Ward Beecher's private life; first woman stockbroker under sponsorship of Cornelius Vanderbilt, 1870; first woman candidate for presidency of the U.S., 1872. RES.: New York, NY.

WOODRUFF, KENNETH RAYMOND. b. 1921. POLIT. & GOV.: ***candidate for Democratic nomination to presidency of the U.S., 1976***. BUS. & PROF.: unemployed. MAILING ADDRESS: c/o The Ken Woodruff Working Peoples Cmte., Box 344, Arnold, MO 63010.

WOODRUFF, TIMOTHY LESTER. b. Aug 4, 1858, New Haven, CT; d. Oct 12, 1913, New York, NY; par. John and Harriet Jane (Lester) Woodruff; m. Cora Eastman, Apr 13, 1880; m. 2d, Isabel Morrison, Apr 24, 1905; c. John Eastman. EDUC.: Phillips Exeter Acad.; A.B., Yale U., 1879, A.M., 1889; Eastman's National Business Coll. POLIT. & GOV.: delegate, NY State Republican Convention, 1885–1913; delegate, Rep. Nat'l. Conv., 1888, 1908; appointed park commissioner, Brooklyn, NY, 1895; elected as a Republican to lt. gov. of NY, 1897–1903; ***candidate for Republican nomination to vice presidency of the U.S., 1900, 1908***; candidate for Republican nomination to gov. of NY, 1904; chm., NY State Republican Central Cmte., 1906–10; joined Progressive Party, 1912. BUS. & PROF.: clerk, partner, Nash, Whiton and Co. (salt and provision merchants), Brooklyn, NY, 1881; pres., Maltine Manufacturing Co., 1888; pres., Pneum-electric Machine Co., Syracuse, NY; treas., Worcester Salt Co.; pres., Smith-Premier Typewriting Co.; pres., Provident Life Assurance Co., 1906; dir., Paper Mills, Hudson, NY; dir., Empire Warehouse Co., 1888; sec., Brooklyn Grain Warehouse Co., 1889; dir., Hamilton Trust Co.; dir., Kings Cty. Trust Co.; dir., Manufacturers Trust Co.; dir., Merchants Exchange National Bank. MEM.: Adelphi Coll. (trustee); Brooklyn Republican Club; NY C. of C.; Masons (32°); SAR; Union League; Yale U. Club; Lotos Club; Hamilton Club; Brooklyn Club; Montauk Club. REL.: Presb. RES.: Brooklyn, NY.

WOODS, CHARLES (nee CHARLES ARTHUR MORRIS). b. Aug 31, 1921, Birmingham, AL; par. P. A. Woods (adopted); m. (divorced); m. 2d, Nayereh; c. David; eight others (by first wife); Scarlet. EDUC.: grad., high school, Headland, CA, 1939. POLIT. & GOV.: appointed chm., AL State Prison Board, 1959–63; candidate for Democratic nomination to gov. of AL, 3 times; ***candidate for Democratic nomination to presidency of the U.S., 1992***; candidate for Democratic nomination to U.S. Senate (NV), 1992; candidate for Republican nomination to U.S. Senate (NV), 1994. BUS. & PROF.: owner, Homebuilding Construction Co., 1950; owner, WTVY-TV, Dothan, AL, 1955–; owner, Downtown Buildings, San Diego, CA, 1977–83; owner, KARD-TV, West Monroe, LA; owner, KDEB-TV, Springfield, MO; owner, KLBK-TV, Lubbock, TX; owner, WTVW-TV, Evansville, IN; owner, WO8BY (low-power television station), Milwaukee, WI; owner, WO4BN (low-power television station), Orlando, FL; owner, WO4BR (low-power television station), Atlanta, GA; owner, WO7BP (low-power television station), Ocala, FL; owner, W13BE (low-power television station), Chicago, IL; owner, WACV-AM (radio), Montgomery, AL; owner, WTVY-FM (radio), Dothan, AL; owner, KESE-FM (radio), Amarillo, TX; owner, cattle ranch, NV. MIL.: fighter pilot, Royal Canadian Air Force, 1939–41; pilot, Royal Air Force (Britain), 1941; maj., pilot, U.S.A.A.C., 1942–50; plane went down over Himalayas, 1944, and Woods was sole survivor, albeit with third-degree burns covering his face and hands; he spent the next five years in military hospitals undergoing plastic surgery. AWARDS: "American of the Year," American Super Bowl Game, Tampa, FL, 1969; "Lifetime Achievement Award," AL Broadcasters Assn., 1991. MAILING ADDRESS: c/o Linda Lou Prescott, 687 Cristina Dr., Incline Village, NV 89451.

WOODS, JAMES MORRIS. POLIT. & GOV.: ***Freedom Party candidate for presidency of the U.S., 1980***. MAILING ADDRESS: 4300 Coleman Dr., Stone Mountain, GA 30083.

WOODS, THOMAS L. POLIT. & GOV.: ***candidate for Democratic nomination to presidency of the U.S., 1988***. BUS. & PROF.: doctor. MAILING ADDRESS: 2103 East Sixth St., #5, Long Beach, CA 90814.

WOODSON, ROBERT BERNARD. POLIT. & GOV.: ***independent candidate for presidency of the U.S., 1988***. MAILING ADDRESS: 2946 Greenville St., Oroville, CA 95966.

WOOLEVER, HARRY EARL. b. Mar 19, 1881, Van Etten, NY; d. May 30, 1941; par. Charles P. and Frances Belle (boardman) Woolever; m. Marien Eloise Andrews, Sep 8, 1909. EDUC.: grad., Cazenovia (NY) Seminary, 1903; A.B., Syracuse U., 1907, D.D., 1916; Drew Theological Seminary, 1909–10; Columbia U., 1917–18; American U., 1927–28. POLIT. & GOV.: ***candidate for Prohibition Party nomination to presidency of the U.S., 1936 (withdrew)***. BUS. & PROF.: ed., *Syracuse (NY) University Daily*, 1905–07; sec., YMCA, 1908–10; ordained minister, Methodist Episcopal Church, 1910; ed., *Northern Christian Advocate*, 1910–15; asst. ed., *Christian Advocate*, 1915–23; pastor, NY Methodist Episcopal churches, 1919–22; acting pastor, Washington Square Church, New York, NY, 1919; assoc. pastor, St. Paul's Church, New York, NY, 1922; ed., dir., National Methodist Press, 1923–36; dir., American Christian Foundation, 1937–39; ed., *These Times*, 1937–39; dir. of adult education, American U. Grad. School, 1932–35; ed., International Religious Press, 1930–33; pastor, Methodist Episcopal Church, Mansfield, PA. MEM.: Cazenovia Seminary (trustee); Sibley Hospital (trustee); Lucy Webb Hayes School (trustee); American U. (trustee); Phi Kappa Psi; Masons (Knights Templar; 32°); Odd Fellows; Clergy Club; Torch Club; National Press Club; Cosmos Club; Authors Club of London; Christian Crusade (founder; dir.); Federation of Churches (member, exec. cmte., 1930–33). REL.: Methodist (delegate, gen. conference, 1924, 1928, 1932, 1936; delegate, Ecumenical Methodist Conference, 1921, 1931; sec., General Conference Comm. on Interdenominational Relations, 1928–41; exec. sec., Joint Comm. on Methodist Union, 1938–41; delegate, Uniting Conference, Methodist Church). RES.: Mansfield, PA.

WOOLF, BENJAMIN EDWARD. b. Feb 16, 1836, London, England; par. Edward Woolf. POLIT. & GOV.:

candidate for Greenback Party nomination to presidency of the U.S., 1880. BUS. & PROF.: musician; composer; conductor; musical and drama critic. WRITINGS: *Mighty Dollar*. RES.: Boston, MA.

WOOLLEN, EVANS. b. Nov 28, 1864, Indianapolis, IN; d. May 20, 1942, Indianapolis, IN; par. William Watson and Mary Allen (Evans) Woollen; m. Nancy Baker, Jun 9, 1896; c. Evans, Jr. EDUC.: B.A., Yale U., 1886, M.A., 1889. POLIT. & GOV.: Democratic candidate for U.S. Senate (IN), 1926; ***candidate for Democratic nomination to presidency of the U.S., 1928; candidate for Democratic nomination to vice presidency of the U.S., 1928***. BUS. & PROF.: atty.; law practice, Indianapolis, IN, 1888; counsel, vice pres., credit officer, Fletcher American National Bank; pres., Fletcher Trust Co., 1912–34, chm. of the board, 1934–42. MEM.: Indianapolis Foundation (organizer, 1916); Psi Upsilon; Art Assn. of Indianapolis (pres.); Century Club. HON. DEG.: LL.D., Wabash U., 1928; LL.D., Butler U., 1929; LL.D., IN U., 1929. WRITINGS: *Benjamin Franklin* (1906); *After the War* (1917); *The Federal Reserve Act*. REL.: Presb. RES.: Indianapolis, IN.

WOOLLEY, JOHN GRANVILLE. b. Feb 15, 1850, Collinsville, OH; d. Aug 13, 1922, Granada, Spain; par. Edwin Corlis and Elizabeth Kyle (Hunter) Woolley; m. Mary Veronica Gerhardt, Jun 26, 1873; c. Paul Gerhardt; Edwin Campbell; John Rea. EDUC.: DePauw U., 1867–68; A.B., OH Wesleyan U., 1871, A.M., 1874; B.L., U. of MI, 1873. POLIT. & GOV.: city atty., Paris, IL, 1876–77; elected prosecuting atty., Minneapolis, MN, 1881; states atty., Minneapolis, MN, 1884–86; joined Prohibition Party, 1888; ***candidate for Prohibition Party nomination to presidency of the U.S., 1896 (declined); United Christian (Union Reform) Party candidate for vice presidency of the U.S., 1900 (declined); Prohibition Party candidate for presidency of the U.S., 1900***; Prohibition Party candidate for U.S. Senate (IL), 1902. BUS. & PROF.: atty.; admitted to Bar of the Supreme Court of IL, 1873; admitted to Bar of the Supreme Court of MN, 1878; law practice, Paris, IL, 1873–78; law practice, Minneapolis, MN, 1878–86; admitted to the Bar of the Supreme Court of the U.S., 1886; law practice, New York, NY, 1886; lecturer, 1888; lecturer, Young People's Soc. of Christian Endeavor, 1893; ed., *Chicago (IL) Lever*, 1898; publisher, ed., *New Voice*, Chicago, IL, 1899–1906; superintendent, HI Anti-Saloon League, 1907; co-superintendent, WI Anti-Saloon League, 1911–12. MEM.: Phi Kappa Psi; Phi Beta Kappa. HON. DEG.: LL.D., OH Wesleyan U., 1906. WRITINGS: *Seed, Number One Hard* (1893); *Church Resolutions* (1896); *The Christian Citizen* (1897); *Civilization by Faith* (1899); *The Sower* (1900); *The Lion Hunter* (1900); *Christian Endeavor Speeches* (1902); *Temperance Progress in the 19th Century* (with William E. Johnson, 1903); *South Sea Letters* (1905); *Civic Sermons* (1913); *The Call of an Epoch* (1914); *The Spirit of the Road*; *The Prohibition Party*. REL.: Protestant (Church of the Strangers, New York, NY). MISC.: recovered alcoholic. RES.: Chicago, IL.

WORKMAN, ALONZO F. POLIT. & GOV.: ***candidate for Democratic nomination to presidency of the U.S., 1928***. RES.: Joplin, MO.

WORSWICK, WINTON DANLEY. b. La Jolla, CA. EDUC.: grad., Pasadena (CA) H.S. POLIT. & GOV.: ***independent candidate for presidency of the U.S., 1992***. BUS. & PROF.: retired; soldier. MIL.: sgt., 25th Infantry, U.S. Army, to 1971; wounded in action, Vietnam. MAILING ADDRESS: P.O. Box 0129, Silver City, NV 89428.

WORTH, WILLIAM JENKINS. b. Mar 1, 1794, Hudson, NY; d. May 7, 1849, San Antonio, TX; par. Thomas and ____ (Jenkins) Worth; m. Margaret Stafford, Sep 18, 1818; c. William Scott; three daughters. EDUC.: public schools. POLIT. & GOV.: ***candidate for Democratic nomination to presidency of the U.S., 1848***. BUS. & PROF.: merchant, Hudson, NY; merchant, Albany, NY, to 1812; soldier. MIL.: appointed 1st lt., 23d Infantry, U.S. Army, 1813; aide-de-camp to Gen. Winfield Scott (q.v.), 1818; brev. capt., maj.; appointed commandant, U.S. Military Acad., 1820–28; brev. lt. col., 1824; col., 8th Infantry, U.S. Army, 1838; brev. brig. gen., 1845; brev. maj. gen., 1846; appointed commander, Dept. of TX, 1848–49; engaged in Seminole War, 1830; Mexican War, 1846; first person to plant American flag on the Rio Grande; presented with sword by resolution of the Congress of the U.S., 1847. REL.: Soc. of Friends. RES.: NY.

WORTHY, HOWARD. b. 1937, Detroit, MI. EDUC.: U. of Detroit; grad., Detroit Police Acad., 1968; Parker Inst. POLIT. & GOV.: elected precinct delegate, Detroit, MI, 1984; member, Permanent Cmte. on Rules and Organization, MI State Convention, 1984; independent candidate for MI State rep., 1984, 1986, 1988, 1992; independent candidate for Detroit (MI) City Council, 1985; ***independent candidate for presidency of the U.S., 1992***. BUS. & PROF.: bodyguard; guard, Chrysler Corp.; police officer, Detroit, MI; chief of microbiology and autopsy technician; advertising project dir., East Coast Chambers of Commerce; private detective; pres., Investigation Confidential. MIL.: Company B, 4th Platoon, 3d Training Regt., U.S. Army, 1959. MEM.: union (steward); MI Black Private Detectives Assn. (pres.); Match Point Civic Assn. (pres.); NAACP; Boys Clubs of Detroit; YMCA (basketball coach); Detroit C. of C.; Kiwanis of Cosmopolitan Detroit; Detroit Public Schools (volunteer); Most Worshipful Prince Hall Grand Lodge, Unity-28; Eighth Precinct Community Relations. AWARDS: named to Detroit (MI) Free Press Annual Prep H.S. All City Basketball Team. REL.: Bapt. MAILING ADDRESS: 16560 Patton, Detroit, MI 48219.

WOYTOWICH, MICHAEL. POLIT. & GOV.: ***independent candidate for presidency of the U.S., 1976***. BUS.

& PROF.: steel worker. MAILING ADDRESS: 606 Beaver Rd., Cambridge, PA 15003.

WRIGHT, DONALD ROSE. POLIT. & GOV.: ***candidate for Republican nomination to presidency of the U.S., 1988***. MAILING ADDRESS: 1314 Heldiver Way, Fairbanks, AK 99706.

WRIGHT, DORRICE. POLIT. & GOV.: ***Unity Party candidate for vice presidency of the U.S., 1976***. BUS. & PROF.: welder. MAILING ADDRESS: 1103 North Grant Dr., Sherman, TX.

WRIGHT, FIELDING LEWIS. b. May 16, 1895, Rolling Fork, MS; d. May 4, 1956, Rolling Fork, MS; par. Henry James and Fannie (Clements) Wright; m. Nan Kelly, Jul 16, 1917; c. Fielding Lewis, Jr.; Elaine. EDUC.: Webb School, Belbuckle, TN; LL.B., U. of AL. POLIT. & GOV.: elected as a Democrat to MS State Senate, 1928–32; elected as a Democrat to MS State House, 1932–40 (Speaker, 1936–40); elected as a Democrat to lt. gov. of MS, 1944–46; succeeded to office of gov. of MS and subsequently elected as a Democrat to gov. of MS, 1946–52; ***States Rights Party candidate for vice presidency of the U.S., 1948; independent candidate for presidency of the U.S., 1948***; delegate, Dem. Nat'l. Conv., 1952; candidate for Democratic nomination to gov. of MS, 1955. BUS. & PROF.: atty.; admitted to MS Bar; law practice, Vicksburg, MS; semiprofessional baseball player; law practice, Jackson, MS; law practice, Rolling Fork, MS. MIL.: pvt., U.S. Army, 1918–19; capt., Company B, 106th Engineers, MS National Guard, 1919–28. REL.: Methodist. RES.: Rolling Fork, MS.

WRIGHT, HENDRICK BRADLEY. b. Apr 24, 1808, Plymouth, PA; d. Sep 2, 1881, Wilkes-Barre, PA; par. Joseph and Ellen (Hendrick) Wadhams Wright; m. Mary Ann Bradley Robinson, Aug 21, 1835; c. ten. EDUC.: Dickinson Coll., 1829; studied law. POLIT. & GOV.: appointed district atty., Luzerne Cty., PA, 1834; elected as a Democrat to PA State House, 1841–43 (Speaker, 1843); ***candidate for Democratic nomination to vice presidency of the U.S., 1844***; delegate, Dem. Nat'l. Conv., 1844 (temporary chm.; permanent chm.), 1848, 1852, 1856, 1860, 1868, 1876; Democratic candidate for U.S. House (PA), 1850, 1854, 1880; elected as a Democrat to U.S. House (PA), 1853–55, 1861–63, 1877–81; ***candidate for Greenback Party nomination to presidency of the U.S., 1880***. BUS. & PROF.: atty.; admitted to PA Bar, 1831; law practice, Wilkes-Barre, PA, 1831–81; assoc., office of John N. Conyngham (law firm), Wilkes-Barre, PA, 1831; publisher, *Anthracite Monitor*. MIL.: col., PA Militia. WRITINGS: *A Practical Treatise on Labor* (1871). RES.: Wilkes-Barre, PA.

WRIGHT, JAMES W. "JIM." POLIT. & GOV.: ***independent candidate for presidency of the U.S., 1992***. MAILING ADDRESS: OR?

WRIGHT, MARGARET NUSOM. b. Dec 15, 1922, Tulsa, OK; m. 1937; m. 2d, Alfred R. Wright, 1954; c. Carole Sweeney; two others. EDUC.: Pontiac (MI) H.S.; grad., high school, Los Angeles, CA; college, 2 years. POLIT. & GOV.: appointed member, Black Education Comm., Los Angeles (CA) Board of Education; candidate for Los Angeles (CA) Board of Education, 1971; designated nonmember "Minister of Education," Black Panther Party; ***candidate for People's Party nomination to vice presidency of the U.S., 1972***; Peace and Freedom Party candidate for Los Angeles (CA) City Council, 1975; ***People's (Peace and Freedom) Party candidate for presidency of the U.S., 1976***; presidential elector, Peace and Freedom Party, 1976. BUS. & PROF.: riveter, Lockheed Aircraft, Los Angeles, CA, 1944–47; housekeeper; day laborer; operator, nursery school, Los Angeles, CA; instructor in Urban Education, U. of Southern CA, 1968; vice pres., KVST-TV, Los Angeles, CA; commentator, "Education with Margaret Wright," KPFK, Los Angeles, CA; education consultant; feminist; civil rights and peace activist. MEM.: United Parents Council (founder, 1964; chairperson); NAACP; Black Congress (member, exec. board, 1967); Women Against Repression (founder, 1966). MAILING ADDRESS: 10041 La Salle Ave., Los Angeles, CA 90047.

WRIGHT, SEABORN J. b. Nov 30, 1857, Rome, GA; d. Dec 14, 1933, Rome, GA; par. Judge August R. and Adeline R. (Allman) Wright; m. Anna E. Moore, Feb 23, 1883; c. Barry; Louis; Graham; Robert; Max. EDUC.: A.B. (cum laude), Mercer U., 1878. POLIT. & GOV.: elected as an independent to GA State House, 1880–84, as a Prohibitionist, 1900–1901, 1905–08, as a Democrat, 1917–19, 1927–29; People's Party candidate for gov. of GA, 1896; Prohibition Party candidate for gov. of GA, 1896; ***candidate for Prohibition Party nomination to presidency of the U.S., 1908***; candidate for Democratic nomination to U.S. Senate (GA), 1922; elected as a Democrat to GA State Senate, 1929. BUS. & PROF.: atty.; admitted to GA Bar, 1879. MEM.: Anti-Saloon League. REL.: Presb. RES.: GA.

WRIGHT, SILAS, JR. b. May 24, 1795, Amherst, MA; d. Aug 27, 1847, Canton, NY; par. Silas and Eleanor (Goodale) Wright; m. Clarissa Moody, Sep 11, 1833; c. none. EDUC.: grad., Middlebury (VT) Coll., 1815; studied law under Roger Skinner, Sandy Hill, NY. POLIT. & GOV.: surrogate, St. Lawrence Cty., NY, 1821–24; elected as a Democrat to NY State Senate, 1823–27; elected as a Democrat to U.S. House (NY), 1827–29; appointed comptroller of NY, 1829–33; delegate, NY State Democratic Convention, 1830, 1832; delegate, Dem. Nat'l. Conv., 1832; elected as a Democrat to U.S. Senate (NY), 1833–44; appointed assoc. justice, Supreme Court of the U.S., 1844 (declined); ***Democratic candidate for vice presidency of the U.S., 1844 (declined)***; elected as a Democrat to gov. of NY, 1845–47; Democratic candidate for gov. of NY, 1846. BUS. & PROF.: atty.; admitted to NY Bar, 1819; law practice, Canton, NY; brig. gen., NY Militia, 1827. REL.: Presb. MISC.: known as a member of the "Albany Regency." RES.: Canton, NY.

WRIGLEY, WILLIAM, JR. b. Sep 30, 1861, Philadelphia, PA; d. Jan 26, 1932, Phoenix, AZ; par. William and Mary A. (Ladley) Wrigley; m. Ada E. Foote, Sep 17, 1885; c. Philip K.; Dorothy W. (Mrs. James R. Offield). EDUC.: public schools. POLIT. & GOV.: delegate, Rep. Nat'l. Conv., 1920; ***candidate for Republican nomination to vice presidency of the U.S., 1924***. BUS. & PROF.: manufacturer; employee, William Wrigley's Co., Philadelphia, PA, 1882–91; founder, William Wrigley, Jr., and Co., Chicago, IL, 1891; pres., William Wrigley, Jr., Co., 1911–25, chm. of the board, 1925–32; manufacturer of chewing gum; dir., First National Bank; dir., First Trust and Savings Bank; dir., Boulevard Bridge Bank; dir., Consumers Co.; chm. of the board, Bon Air Coal and Iron Corp.; chm. of the board, Wilmington Transportation Co.; chm. of the board, Santa Catalina Island Co.; chm. of the board, Chicago Cubs National League Baseball Club; chm. of the board, Angel City Baseball Club; dir., Erie R.R.; owner, Arizona Biltmore Properties; owner, Catalina Island, 1919–32. MEM.: Loyal Legion; Chicago Club; CA Club; Field Museum of Natural History (trustee); American Red Cross (exec. cmte., Chicago Chapter). RES.: Chicago, IL.

WULFORST, WILLIAM JOSEPH. POLIT. & GOV.: ***candidate for Democratic nomination to presidency of the U.S., 1984***. MAILING ADDRESS: Interstate Highway Circle off I-95, Portsmouth, NH 03801.

YAGER, JAMES BELL. b. 1933. POLIT. & GOV.: ***independent Party candidate for presidency of the U.S., 1980, 1984, 1988***. BUS. & PROF.: inmate, IN Youth Center, Plainfield, IN. MEM.: National Prisoners' Rights Union (founder, 1972; exec. dir.). MAILING ADDRESS: 902 Renfroe Rd., Talladega, AL 35160.

YATES, JAMES ELMER. POLIT. & GOV.: ***Greenback Party candidate for vice presidency of the U.S., 1940***. MAILING ADDRESS: 1827 East Monterey Ave., Phoenix, AZ.

YEAGER, R. W. b. Sep 28, 1932, Ashland, KS; S. W. R. and Margaret (Piatt) Y.; m. Doris L. Schwab; c. Nancy; R. W., Jr.; Susan; Guy. EDUC.: Blessed Sacrament Grade School, Wichita, KS; St. Joseph Military Acad., Hays, KS; B.S., KS State U. POLIT. & GOV.: ***candidate for Republican nomination to presidency of the U.S., 1976, 1980***. BUS. & PROF.: self-employed contractor. MEM.: Metal Building Dealers Assn.; ABC Contractors Assn.; National C. of C.; Norton C. of C. REL.: no preference. MAILING ADDRESS: 505 Pool Dr., Norton, KS 67654.

YEZO, ANNE MARIE DOPYERA. b. 1919, Hoboken, NJ; m. Louis Yezo; c. Louis, Jr.; Rhonda. EDUC.: grad., Joseph of Merit H.S. POLIT. & GOV.: ***American Third Party candidate for vice presidency of the U.S., 1956, 1960, 1964***. BUS. & PROF.: employee, North Bergen, NJ Board of Elections; employee, Tammany Hall (tavern), Secaucus, NJ; housewife. REL.: Lutheran. MAILING ADDRESS: 8617 Durham Ave., North Bergen, NJ 07047.

YIAMOUYIANNIS, JOHN ANDREW. b. Sep 25, 1942, Hartford, CT; par. Andrew and Caroline (Hofstetter) Yiamouyiannis; m. Natalie Y.; m. 2d, Darla Bolon; c. six. EDUC.: grad., Hartford (CT) H.S., 1960; B.S. (Biochemistry), U. of Chicago, 1963; Ph.D. (Biochemistry), U. of RI, 1967. POLIT. & GOV.: independent candidate for OH State Senate, 1974; ***Take Back America Party candidate for presidency of the U.S., 1992***. BUS. & PROF.: science dir., Natural Health Federation; exec. dir., Health Action; consumer advocate; lecturer; author; environmentalist. MEM.: Safe Water Foundation (pres.). WRITINGS: *High Performance Health* (1987); *Fluoride: The Aging Factor* (1983, 1986). MISC.: managed campaign to stop dam in San Antonio, TX, 1991. MAILING ADDRESS: Box 41, Lewis Center, OH 43035.

YORK, ALVIN CULLUM. b. Dec 13, 1887, Pall Mall, TN; d. Sep 2, 1964, Nashville, TN; par. William and Mary (Brooks) York; m. Grace Williams, Jun 7, 1919; c. Rev. George Edward Buxton; Alvin Cullum, Jr.; Woodrow Wilson; Thomas Jefferson; Andrew Jackson; Betsy Ross Lowrey; Mary Alice (Mrs. Franklin). EDUC.: 3d grade, public schools, Pall Mall, TN. POLIT. & GOV.: ***Prohibition Party candidate for vice presidency of the U.S., 1936 (declined)***. BUS. & PROF.: farmer; worker, road gang. MIL.: enlisted, U.S. Army, 1917; sgt., Company C, 328th Infantry, 82d Div., 1917–19; maj.; killed 25 Germans, captured Hill 223, and compelled surrender of 132 enemy soldiers and 35 machine guns while armed with a Springfield rifle and revolver, Argonne, France, Oct 8, 1918; Medal of Honor; Croix de Guerre; Distinguished Service Cross; Medaille Militaire; Croce di Guerra; Legion of Honor; War Medal of Montenegro. MEM.: TN National Guard (col.); York Foundation (founder); York Agricultural Inst. (founder); American Legion. REL.: Church of Christ and Christian Union. RES.: Pall Mall, TN.

YORTY, SAMUEL WILLIAM. b. Oct 1, 1909, Lincoln, NE; par. Frank Patrick and Johanna (Egan) Yority; m. Elizabeth Hensel, Dec 1, 1938; c. William Egan. EDUC.: Southwestern U.; LaSalle Extension U.; U. of Southern CA, 1946–50;

U. of CA, 1948. POLIT. & GOV.: elected as a Democrat to CA State Assembly, 1936–40, 1949–50; candidate for Democratic nomination to U.S. Senate (CA), 1940, 1956; candidate for Democratic nomination to gov. of CA, 1942 (withdrew), 1970; candidate for Democratic nomination to mayor of Los Angeles, CA, 1945; elected as a Democrat to U.S. House (CA), 1951–55; Democratic candidate for U.S. Senate (CA), 1954; elected as a Democrat, mayor of Los Angeles, CA, 1961–73; ***candidate for Democratic nomination to presidency of the U.S., 1964, 1972***; candidate for Republican nomination to U.S. Senate (CA), 1980. BUS. & PROF.: atty.; admitted to CA Bar, 1939; law practice, Los Angeles, CA, 1940–42, 1945–50, 1954–61. MIL.: capt., U.S.A.A.C., 1942–45; Encomineda Medal (Spain); Order of the Lion (Finland); National Order of the Southern Cross (Brazil); Order of Merit (Commander's Cross, Germany); Great Silver Insignia of Honor with Star (Austria); Order of Civil Merit (Korea); Legion of Honor (Knight, France); Order Homayoun Medal (Iran); Order of the Sun (Peru). WRITINGS: *Report to the People* (1964). MAILING ADDRESS: 320 North Vermont, Los Angeles, CA 90006.

YOUNG, GAYLORD BRYAN. POLIT. & GOV.: ***candidate for Democratic nomination to presidency of the U.S., 1980***. MAILING ADDRESS: Jarnyan's Trailer Park, Mountcastle St., Jefferson City, TN 37760.

YOUNG, OWEN D. b. Oct 27, 1874, Van Hornesville, NY; d. Jul 11, 1962; par. Jacob Smith and Ida (Brandow) Young; m. Josephine Sheldon Edmonds, Jun 30, 1898; m. 2d, Mrs. Louise Powis Clark, Feb 1937; c. Charles Jacob; John; Josephine; Philip; Richard. EDUC.: A.B., St. Lawrence U., 1894; LL.B. (cum laude), Boston U., 1896. POLIT. & GOV.: appointed alternate delegate, National Industrial Conference, 1918, member, 1919; appointed member, President's Conference on Unemployment, 1921; appointed chm., Comm. on Unemployment and Business Cycles, 1922; Class B dir., Federal Reserve Bank of NY, 1923–27, Class C dir., 1927–40 (deputy chm., 1927–28; chm., 1938–40); appointed chm., National Distribution Conference, 1924; adviser, Reparations Comm., 1924; adviser, London Conference of Prime Ministers, 1924; general agent, Reparations Comm., 1924; appointed member, Comm. on Recent Economic Changes, 1928; adviser, Nationalist Government of China, 1928; ***candidate for Democratic nomination to presidency of the U.S., 1928, 1932***; appointed chm., Comm. on Mobilization of Relief Resources, 1931; appointed member, Comm. on Re-Organization of the Executive Branch of Government; appointed member, national advisory council, National Youth Administration, 1940; appointed member, National Patent Planning Comm., 1941; appointed chm., National Comm. on Transportation Problems, 1940; appointed member, NY Regional Cmte., War Manpower Council, 1942; member, NY State Board of Regents, 1945. BUS. & PROF.: atty.; admitted to MA Bar, 1896; law practice, Boston, MA, 1896; instructor in Common Pleadings, Boston U., 1896–1903; partner, Tyler and Young (law firm), Boston, MA, 1907–13; vice pres., gen. counsel, General Electric Co., 1913–22, chm. of the board, 1922–39, 1942–44; chm. of the board, RCA, to 1929, chm., exec. cmte., to 1933; dir., ABC, 1948–62. MEM.: Pierpont Morgan Library (fellow); ABA; Masons; Odd Fellows; National Grange; Harvard Club; Manhattan Club; University Club; Engineers Club (hon.); Tavern Club; American Youth Comm. (chm., 1936–42); St. Lawrence U. (trustee, 1912–34); General Education Board; International Education Board (1925–40); Conference on Children in a Democracy (1939); Holstein-Friesian Assn. of America (pres., 1948). AWARDS: Gold Medal, National Inst. of Social Sciences, 1923; award, Roosevelt Memorial Assn., 1929; Order of the Rising Sun (Japan, 1921); Legion of Honor (commander, 1924); Order of Leopold of Belgium, 1925; First Order of the German Red Cross, 1925; Grand Cross of the Crown of Belgium, 1930. HON. DEG.: LL.D., Union Coll., 1922; D.H.L., St. Lawrence U., 1923; LL.D., Dartmouth Coll., 1924; LL.D., Harvard U., 1924; LL.D., Tufts U., 1924; LL.D., Colgate U., 1925; LL.D., Columbia U., 1925; LL.D., Johns Hopkins U., 1925; LL.D., Yale U., 1925; LL.D., Lehigh U., 1926; LL.D., Princeton U., 1926; LL.D., Rutgers U., 1926; D.C.S., NY U., 1927; LL.D., Brown U., 1928; LL.D., U. of the State of NY, 1928; LL.D., Hamilton Coll., 1929; LL.D., U. of CA, 1930; LL.D., Wesleyan U., 1931; LL.D., U. of Notre Dame, 1932; LL.D., Queen's U., 1933; LL.D., U. of NE, 1934; LL.D., Marietta Coll., 1935; Litt.D., Rollins Coll., 1936; LL.D., Syracuse U., 1940; LL.D., Boston U., 1945; Litt.D., U. of Buffalo, 1946; LL.D., U. of FL, 1948; LL.D., Middlebury Coll., 1948. RES.: Van Hornersville, NY.

YOUNG, STEPHEN MARVIN. b. May 4, 1889, Norwalk, OH; d. Dec 1, 1984, Washington, DC; par. Stephen Marvin and Isabelle (Wagner) Young; m. Ruby Louise Dawley, Jan 18, 1911; m. 2d, Rachel Louise Bell, Mar 28, 1957; c. Stephen Marvin; Richard Dawley; Marjorie Louise (Mrs. Robert R. Richardson). EDUC.: Adelbert Coll.; LL.B., Western Reserve U., 1911; D.PublicService, Rio Grande Coll. POLIT. & GOV.: elected as a Democrat to OH State House, 1913–17; appointed chief asst. prosecutor, Cuyahoga Cty., OH, 1919–20; Democratic candidate for atty. gen. of OH, 1922, 1956; candidate for Democratic nomination to gov. of OH, 1930, 1936; member, OH Comm. on Unemployment Insurance, 1931–32; elected as a Democrat to U.S. House (OH), 1933–37, 1941–43, 1949–51; Democratic candidate for U.S. House (OH), 1942, 1950; elected as a Democrat to U.S. Senate (OH), 1959–71; ***candidate for Democratic nomination to presidency of the U.S., 1968***. BUS. & PROF.: atty.; admitted to OH Bar, 1911; law practice, Norwalk, OH; law practice, Cleveland, OH; partner, Young, Meyers and Young (law firm), Cleveland, OH. MIL.: pvt., 3d OH Infantry, Mexican border, 1916; U.S. Army F.A., WWI; maj. to lt. col., 1942–46; appointed military gov. of Reggio Emilia, Italy; lt. col., U.S.A.R.; First World War Victory Medal; Second World War Victory Medal; Order of the Crown (Italy); Chubb Fellowship; Bronze Star; Purple Heart; Army Commendation Ribbon; European-African-Middle Eastern Theater Campaign Medal with Four Stars. MEM.: ABA; OH State Bar Assn.; Cuyahoga Cty. Bar Assn. (pres.); War Veterans Bar Assn. (pres.); American Legion; Army and Navy Country Club; Delta Kappa Epsilon; Phi Delta Phi; DC Bar Assn.; Cleveland Bar Assn. HON. DEG.: M.C.L., Kenyon Coll., 1933; LL.D., Central State Coll. REL.: Methodist. RES.: Cleveland, OH.

YOUNGKEIT, LOUIE GENE. b. Anaheim, CA; par. Cecil "Coy" Youngkeit. POLIT. & GOV.: ***independent candidate for presidency of the U.S., 1988***. MISC.: claims CIA tortured and tried to kill him when he was 12 years old; claims to be heir to Howard Hughes's fortune. MAILING ADDRESS: c/o Cecil "Coy" Youngkeit, 164 West 960 North, Provo, UT 84604.

Z

ZAEHRINGER, GEORGE WASHINGTON DE PAUL. POLIT. & GOV.: ***candidate for Democratic nomination to presidency of the U.S., 1988***. MAILING ADDRESS: 120 East St. Lawrence, #336, Janesville, WI 53545.

ZAGARELL, MICHAEL. b. 1944, Bronx, NY. EDUC.: grad., H.S. of Music and Art (NY); Hunter Coll. (evening classes for 2 years). POLIT. & GOV.: member, Communist Party, 1962–; national sec. for Youth Affairs, Communist Party, 1964–; member, national cmte. (Secretariat), Communist Party; ***Communist Party candidate for vice presidency of the U.S., 1968***; independent Progressive Line candidate for U.S. House (NY), 1988. BUS. & PROF.: ed., *Daily Worker*. MEM.: Advance (pres., 1958); Youth Against Air Raid Drills (NY organizer); W. E. B. DuBois Clubs of America (founder); Lower East Side (NY) DuBois Club; Stop the Draft Week (steering cmte., Oct 1967); Student Mobilization Cmte. (founder); International Student Strike Against the War, Racism, and the Draft (organizer, Apr 1968). MISC.: arrested in 1964 World's Fair demonstration against discrimination. MAILING ADDRESS: 2918 Holland Ave., Bronx, NY 10467.

ZAHND, JOHN. b. 1878, Doolittle's Mill, WV; d. Feb 2, 1961, Indianapolis, IN; m. Erma J. Zahnd; c. Henry J. POLIT. & GOV.: Socialist Party candidate for U.S. House (IN), 1912; ***National Independent (Greenback) Party candidate for presidency of the U.S., 1924 (withdrew), 1928, 1932, 1936, 1940***; National Party candidate for U.S. Senate (IN), 1928; national chm., National Independent (Greenback) Party, 1940–61. BUS. & PROF.: real estate agent. WRITINGS: *The Long Trail . . . Written for the Benefit of Those Who Seek Good Government* (1945). REL.: Church of Jesus Christ of Latter-Day Saints. RES.: Beech Grove, IN.

ZAMMUTO, STEPHEN THOMAS. d. Sep 30, 1992, St. Petersburg, FL. POLIT. & GOV.: ***independent candidate for presidency of the U.S., 1992***. RES.: St. Petersburg, FL.

ZAR, CURTIS. POLIT. & GOV.: ***independent candidate for presidency of the U.S., 1992***. MAILING ADDRESS: P.O. Box 49-1703, Fort Lauderdale, FL 33349.

ZARNOWSKI, JOSEPH PETER. POLIT. & GOV.: ***independent candidate for presidency of the U.S., 1976***. MAILING ADDRESS: 18 Jackson Terrace, Freehold, NJ 07728.

ZEIDLER, FRANK PAUL. b. Sep 20, 1912, Milwaukee, WI; par. Michael W. and Clara A. E. (Nitschke) Zeidler; m. Agnes Reinke; c. Clara; Dorothy; Michael; Anita; Mary; Jeannette. EDUC.: Marquette U., 1930; U. of WI Extension, 1930–70. POLIT. & GOV.: elected Milwaukee Cty. (WI) Surveyor, 1938–40; Progressive Party candidate for Milwaukee (WI) Board of Supervisors, 1940; Progressive Party candidate for WI State treas., 1940; Socialist Party candidate for gov. of WI, 1942; elected member, Milwaukee (WI) Board of School Directors, 1941–48; Socialist Party candidate for mayor of Milwaukee, WI, 1944; Socialist Party candidate for U.S. House (WI), 1946; elected as a Socialist, mayor of Milwaukee, WI, 1948–60; appointed member, U.S. National Comm. on UNESCO, 1953, 1956; appointed dir., WI State Dept. of Resource Development, 1963–64; national chairperson, Socialist Party, U.S.A., 1974–; ***candidate for Peace and Freedom Party nomination to presidency of the U.S., 1976; Socialist Party candidate for presidency of the U.S., 1976***. BUS. & PROF.: surveyor; consultant in public administration; arbitrator; lecturer, U. of WI, Milwaukee, WI; lecturer, U. of WI Fox Valley Center, Menasha, WI; instructor, Alverno Coll. MEM.: Martin Luther King Advisory Comm.; Greater Milwaukee Conference on Religion and Urban Affairs; U.N. Assn. (pres., Milwaukee Chapter; sec., Wisconsin Div.); Central North Community Council (pres.); Milwaukee

Turners; Public Enterprise Cmte. (sec.); Alverno Coll. (trustee); Commonwealth Mutual Savings Bank (trustee); Knights of Pythias; Technical Engineers Assn.; United World Federalists. AWARDS: one of ten "Outstanding Young Men," National Junior C. of C., 1949; Good Government Award, Milwaukee (WI) Junior C. of C., 1956. HON. DEG.: LL.D., U. of WI, 1958; LL.D., St. Olaf Coll., 1988. WRITINGS: *Shakespeare's Plays in Modern Verse*. REL.: Lutheran (member, management cmte., North American Mission Div., Lutheran Church of America). MAILING ADDRESS: 2921 North Second St., Milwaukee, WI 53212.

ZIEHLKE, MARION KNITTER. POLIT. & GOV.: ***candidate for Republican nomination to presidency of the U.S., 1992***. MAILING ADDRESS: 711 Broadview, S.E., Grand Rapids, MI 49507.

ZILLY, MARGARET BERNICE. b. Jul 18, 1907, Peoria, IL; d. Thomas and Mary Magdalene (Rossman) McWhinney; m. George Samuel Zilly, Nov 29, 1930; c. Thomas Samuel; Barbara (Mrs. Henry Jude Heck). EDUC.: Bradley U., 1923–25; B.S., U. of IL, 1927; M.Ed., Wayne State U., 1938. POLIT. & GOV.: member, MI Republican State Central Cmte., 1965–71; member, MI Republican Congressional District Cmte., 1966–71; ***candidate for Republican nomination to presidency of the U.S., 1972***. BUS. & PROF.: teacher, high school, Peoria, IL, 1927–29; teacher, high school, Detroit, MI, 1930–34, 1936–43. MEM.: Keep Detroit Beautiful, Inc. (pres., 1955–58); Bernice Zilly Day (1958); College Women's Volunteer Service (pres., 1957–59); Beautification Council of Southeastern MI (pres., 1958–60); Keep MI Beautiful, Inc. (vice pres., 1960–62); American Red Cross (dir., 1969–75; 1977–; member, exec. cmte., 1973–75); White House Fellows Selection Cmte. (1976); MI Federation of Republican Women (vice pres., 1958–60); Women's Republican Club of Grosse Pointe (pres., 1956–58); Catholic Youth Organization (dir., 1960–75); AAUW (pres., Detroit Branch, 1951–53); U. of IL Alumni Assn. (Detroit pres., 1935–40); Women's City Club of Detroit (dir., 1968–70); National Council of Catholic Women (pres.); Catholic Council of Women of Archdiocese of Detroit (pres.); Alpha Delta Pi. AWARDS: Keep American Beautiful Award, 1962; "Keys to the City," Detroit (MI), Indianapolis (IN), Galveston (TX), and Southfield (MI); "Honorary Citizen," Galveston, TX, 1975. REL.: R.C. (member, pastoral council, archdiocese of Detroit, 1975–). MAILING ADDRESS: 380 Merriweather Rd., Grosse Pointe Farms, MI 48236.

ZIMMERMAN, HARRY C. POLIT. & GOV.: ***independent candidate for presidency of the U.S., 1964***. MAILING ADDRESS: Berkley, MO.

ZIMMERMAN, MATILDE. b. 1943. EDUC.: U. of WI. POLIT. & GOV.: ***Socialist Workers Party candidate for vice presidency of the U.S., 1980***. BUS. & PROF.: staff writer, *The Militant*, 1975–. MEM.: Young Socialist Alliance (1967–); G.I. Civil Liberties Defense Cmte. (national sec.); Women's National Abortion Action Coalition (national coordinator, 1970–71); National Organization for Women. MAILING ADDRESS: 139 West 19th St., New York, NY.

ZIMMERMANN, GEORGE A. b. 1926. POLIT. & GOV.: ***candidate for Republican nomination to presidency of the U.S., 1992***. BUS. & PROF.: business consultant. MAILING ADDRESS: 11218 Candlelight Lane, Dallas, TX 75229.

ZUBER, PAUL BURGESS. b. Dec 20, 1926, Williamsport, PA; par. Paul Alexander and Jennie (Baer) Zuber; m. Barbara Johnson, Jun 6, 1953; c. Paul; Patricia. EDUC.: A.B., Brown U., 1947; LL.B., Brooklyn Law School, 1956, J.D. POLIT. & GOV.: Republican candidate for NY State Senate, 1958; ***candidate for Republican nomination to presidency of the U.S., 1964***. BUS. & PROF.: atty.; admitted to NY Bar, 1957; law practice, New York, NY, 1957–; adjunct prof., Rensselaer Polytechnic Inst., 1969–70, visiting assoc. prof., 1970–71, assoc. prof. of Law and Urban Affairs, 1971–, dir., Graduate Center for Urban and Environmental Studies, 1971–. MIL.: armed services, 1944–46, 1950–52. REL.: Episc. MISC.: civil rights advocate; trial counsel, school segregation cases, New Rochelle, NY (1960–61), Englewood, NJ (1961–63), Newark, NJ (1961–62), Chicago, IL (1961), Mount Vernon and Poughkeepsie, NY (1966). MAILING ADDRESS: Briggs Lane, Box 256, Croton-on-Hudson, NY 10520.

ZUCKER, IRWIN. b. 1932. POLIT. & GOV.: ***candidate for Democratic nomination to presidency of the U.S., 1988***. MAILING ADDRESS: Eatontown, NJ.

ZUCKERMAN, ETHAN R. POLIT. & GOV.: ***independent candidate for presidency of the U.S., 1988***. MAILING ADDRESS: P.O. Box 460, Pound Ridge, NY 10576.

ZWILLINGER, DANIEL IAN. POLIT. & GOV.: ***independent candidate for presidency of the U.S., 1992***. MAILING ADDRESS: 61 Highland Ave., Arlington, MA 02104.